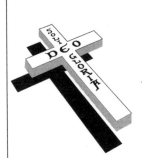

The
Episcopal
Church
Annual

2016

The Episcopal Church Annual

General Convention Edition

2016

NEW YORK

ISBN: 978-0-8192-3275-5
90000

9 780819 232755

THE EPISCOPAL CHURCH ANNUAL

Published by

 Morehouse Publishing
NEW YORK

Morehouse Publishing
An imprint of Church Publishing Incorporated
19 East 34th Street
New York, NY 10016
Fax (212) 779-3392
www.churchpublishing.org
www.theredbook.org

Information and statistics have been compiled from material supplied by the bishops and secretaries of the dioceses, the Executive Office of the General Convention, The Church Pension Fund, the national, provincial, diocesan, and parochial institutions and organizations of The Episcopal Church and the Anglican Consultative Council. This Annual includes information as of January 1, 2013, which is subject to change.

Although extensive effort was made to assure the accuracy and completeness of the information included in this Annual, Church Publishing Incorporated and its affiliates do not guarantee the accuracy of such information and disclaim any liability associated with this Annual. Please use our website www.theredbook.org or write to the Editor, Episcopal Church Annual, 19 East 34th Street, New York, NY 10016 to report any errors and/or omissions.

Any discrepancy between the clerical status of an individual in this Annual and the official records of The Episcopal Church shall be resolved by reference to such official records. All benefits provided to clergy of The Episcopal Church are governed by the terms of the official plan documents and policies.

Cataloging-in-Publication data is available from the Library of Congress.

ISBN 978-0-8192-3275-5

Printed in the United States of America

Contents

SERVING THE EPISCOPAL CHURCH THROUGH THE CENTURIES
TIMELINE OF THE EPISCOPAL CHURCH ANNUAL

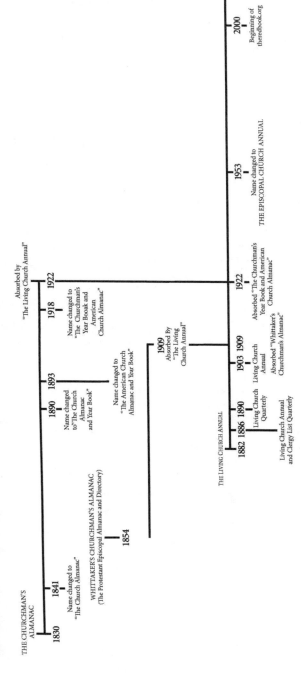

THE CHURCHMAN'S ALMANAC

1830

1841
Name changed to "The Church Almanac"

WHITTAKER'S CHURCHMAN'S ALMANAC (The Protestant Episcopal Almanac and Directory)

1854

1890
Name changed to "The Church Almanac and Year Book"

1893
Name changed to "The American Church Almanac and Year Book"

1918
Name changed to "The Churchman's Year Boook and American Church Almanac"

1922
Absorbed by "The Living Church Annual"

1922
Absorbed "The Churchman's Year Book and American Church Almanac"

1953
Name changed to THE EPISCOPAL CHURCH ANNUAL

2000
Beginning of theredbook.org

THE LIVING CHURCH ANNUAL

1882
Living Church Annual and Clergy List Quarterly

1886

1890
Living Church Quarterly

1903
Living Church Annual

1909
Absorbed "Whittaker's Churchman's Almanac"

1909
Absorbed By "The Living Church Annual"

DIOCESES WITHIN EACH PROVINCE

Province I
Diocese of Connecticut
Diocese of Maine
Diocese of Massachusetts
Diocese of New Hampshire
Diocese of Rhode Island
Diocese of Vermont
Diocese of Western
  Massachusetts

Province II
Diocese of Albany
Diocese of Central New York
Diocese of Haiti
Diocese of Long Island
Diocese of New Jersey
Diocese of New York
Diocese of Newark
Diocese of Rochester
Diocese of Virgin Islands
Diocese of Western New York
Convocation of American
  Churches in Europe

Province III
Diocese of Bethlehem
Diocese of Central
  Pennsylvania
Diocese of Delaware
Diocese of Easton
Diocese of Maryland
Diocese of Northwestern
  Pennsylvania
Diocese of Pennsylvania
Diocese of Pittsburgh
Diocese of Southern Virginia
Diocese of Southwestern
  Virginia
Diocese of Virginia
Diocese of Washington
Diocese of West Virginia

Province IV
Diocese of Alabama
Diocese of Atlanta
Diocese of Central Florida
Diocese of Central Gulf
  Coast

Diocese of East Carolina
Diocese of East Tennessee
Diocese of Florida
Diocese of Georgia
Diocese of Kentucky
Diocese of Lexington
Diocese of Louisiana
Diocese of Mississippi
Diocese of North Carolina
The Episcopal Church in
  South Carolina
Diocese of Southeast Florida
Diocese of Southwest Florida
Diocese of Tennessee
Diocese of Upper South
  Carolina
Diocese of West Tennessee
Diocese of Western North
  Carolina

Province V
Diocese of Chicago
Diocese of Eastern Michigan
Diocese of Eau Claire
Diocese of Fond du Lac
Diocese of Indianapolis
Diocese of Michigan
Diocese of Milwaukee
Diocese of Missouri
Diocese of Northern Indiana
Diocese of Northern
  Michigan
Diocese of Ohio
Diocese of Southern Ohio
Diocese of Springfield
Diocese of Western Michigan

Province VI
Diocese of Colorado
Diocese of Iowa
Diocese of Minnesota
Diocese of Montana
Diocese of Nebraska
Diocese of North Dakota
Diocese of South Dakota
Diocese of Wyoming
Province VII

Diocese of Arkansas
Diocese of Dallas
Diocese of Fort Worth
Diocese of Kansas
Diocese of Northwest Texas
Diocese of Oklahoma
Diocese of Rio Grande
Diocese of Texas
Diocese of West Missouri
Diocese of West Texas
Diocese of Western Kansas
Diocese of Western Louisiana

Province VIII
Diocese of Alaska
Diocese of Arizona
Diocese of California
Diocese of Eastern Oregon
Diocese of El Camino Real
Diocese of Hawaii
Diocese of Idaho
Diocese of Los Angeles
Diocese of Navajoland
Diocese of Nevada
Diocese of Northern
  California
Diocese of Olympia
Diocese of Oregon
Diocese of San Diego
Diocese of San Joaquin
Diocese of Spokane
Diocese of Taiwan
Diocese of Utah

Province IX
Diocese of Colombia
Diocese of Dominican
  Republic
Diocese of Ecuador Central
Diocese of Ecuador Litoral
Diocese of Honduras
Diocese of Puerto Rico
Diocese of Venezuela

Abbreviations of Dioceses and States

Obvious variants are sometimes used.

A	Albany	NAM	Navajoland Area Mission
AK	Alaska	NB	Nebraska
AL	Alabama	NC	North Carolina
AR	Arkansas	NCA	Northern California
At	Atlanta	ND	North Dakota
AZ	Arizona	NH	New Hampshire
BE	Bethlehem	NI	Northern Indiana
C	Chicago	NJ	New Jersey
CA	California	Nk	Newark
CEcu	Central Ecuador	NM	New Mexico (state)
CF	Central Florida	NMI	Northern Michigan
CGC	Central Gulf Coast	NT	NW Texas
CNY	Central New York	NV	Nevada
CO	Colorado	NWPA	Northwestern Pennsylvania
Colom	Colombia	NY	New York
CPA	Central Pennsylvania	OH	Ohio
CT	Connecticut	OK	Oklahoma
Dal	Dallas	OL	Olympia
DC	District of Columbia	OR	Oregon
DE	Delaware	PA	Pennsylvania
DomR	Dominican Republic	Pgh	Pittsburgh
E	Easton	PR	Puerto Rico
EauC	Eau Claire	quniRG	Rio Grande
EC	East Carolina	RI	Rhode Island
ECR	El Camino Real	Roch	Rochester
EcuL	Ecuador Litoral	SanD	San Diego
EMI	Eastern Michigan	SanJ	San Joaquin
EO	Eastern Oregon	SC	South Carolina
Er	Erie	SD	South Dakota
ETN	East Tennessee	SeF	Southeast Florida
Eur	Europe	SO	Southern Ohio
FdL	Fond du Lac	Sp	Springfield
FL	Florida	Spok	Spokane
FtW	Fort Worth	SV	Southern Virginia
GA	Georgia	SwF	Southwest Florida
GU	Guam	SwV	Southwestern Virginia
Hai	Haiti	Tai	Taiwan
HI	Hawaii	TN	Tennessee
Hond	Honduras	TX	Texas
IA	Iowa	USC	Upper South Carolina
ID	Idaho	UT	Utah
IL	Illinois	VA	Virginia
IN	Indiana	VEN	Venezuela
Ind	Indianapolis	VI	Virgin Islands
KS	Kansas	VT	Vermont
KY	Kentucky	W	Washington (dio)
LA	Louisiana	WA	Washington (state)
Lex	Lexington	WI	Wisconsin
LI	Long Island	WKS	Western Kansas
LosA	Los Angeles	WLA	Western Louisiana
MA	Massachusetts	WMI	Western Michigan
MD	Maryland	WMA	Western Massachusetts
ME	Maine	WMO	West Missouri
MI	Michigan	WNC	Western North Carolina
Mil	Milwaukee	WNY	Western New York
MN	Minnesota	WT	West Texas
MO	Missouri	WTN	West Tennessee
MS	Mississippi	WV	West Virginia
MT	Montana	WY	Wyoming

Abbreviations Used In The Clergy List
Which Differ From The Abbreviations of Dioceses and States List

Ala	Alabama	**NI**	Northern Indiana
Alb	Albany	**NMich**	Northern Michigan
Ark	Arkansas	**Nwk**	Newark
CFla	Central Florida	**NwT**	Northwest Texas
Chi	Chicago	**O**	Ohio
Colo	Colorado	**Okla**	Oklahoma
CP	Central Pennsylvania	**Oly**	Olympia
Del	Delaware	**Ore**	Oregon
DR	Dominican Republic	**SeFla**	Southeast Florida
Eas	Easton	**SJ**	San Joaquin
Eau	Eau Claire	**Spr**	Springfield
Fla	Florida	**SVa**	Southern Virginia
Haw	Hawaii	**SwFla**	Southwest Florida
Ida	Idaho	**SwVa**	Southwestern Virginia
Kan	Kansas	**Tenn**	Tennesseeaa
Los	Los Angeles	**Tex**	Texas
Mass	Massachusetts	**WDC**	Washington
Mich	Michigan	**WK**	Western Kansas
Minn	Minnesota	**WMass**	Western Massachusetts
Miss	Mississippi	**WMich**	Western Michigan
Mont	Montana	**WTenn**	West Tennessee
NCal	Northern California	**WTex**	West Texas
Neb	Nebraska	**WVa**	West Virginia
Nev	Nevada	**Wyo**	Wyoming

Acronyms

AandD	Alcohol and Drugs	FODC	Franciscan Order of the Divine Compassion
AIDS	Acquired Immune Deficiency Syndrome (see also HIV)	GTS	General Theological Seminary
BCP	Book of Common Prayer 1979	HIV	Human Immunodeficiency Virus
BSG	Brotherhood of St. Gregory	LAND	Leadership Academy for New Directions
CA	Church Army Community of the Ascension	NCC	National Council of Churches
CDO	Clergy Deployment Office(r)	NECAD	National Episcopal Coalition on Alcohol and Drugs
CDSP	Church Divinity School of the Pacific	OCP	Order of the Community of the Paraclete
CHC	Church Hymnal Corporation	OHC	Order of the Holy Cross
CPF	Church Pension Fund	OSA	Order of St. Augustine Order of St. Anne
COM	Commission on Ministry		
CHS	Community of the Holy Spirit	OSB	Order of St. Benedict
CSJB	Community of St. John the Baptist	OSH	Order of St. Helena
CSM	Community of St. Mary	OSL	Order of St. Luke the Physician
CSSS	Congregation of the Companions of the Holy Savior	RACA	Recovered Alcoholic Clergy Association
DCE	Director/Department of Christian Education	RC	Roman Catholic
EC	Executive Council	SSC	Society of the Holy Cross
ECL	Executive Council Liaison	SSF	Society of St. Francis
ECC	Episcopal Church Center	SSJE	Society of St. John the Evangelist
EDS	Episcopal Divinity School	SSM	Society of St. Margaret
ECW	Episcopal Church Women	SSP	Society of St. Paul
ECS	Episcopal Community Services	USAF	United States Air Force
ESMA	Episcopal Society for Ministry on Aging	USA	United States Army
		USN	United States Navy
ETSW	Episcopal Theological Seminary of the Southwest	WCC	World Council of Churches

Partial List of Abbreviations
NAMES

Adv	Advent	M	Martyr
Alb	Alban	Magd	Magdalene
All SS	All Saints	Mer	Merciful
Amb	Ambrose	Med	Mediator
Ancn	Annunciation	Mem	Memorial
Ang	Angels	Mes	Messiah
Ant(h)	Ant(h)ony	Miss	Mission
Apos	Apostle(s), Apostól	Mt	Mount
Arim	Arimathaea	Mths	Matthias
Ben	Benedict	Mthw	Matthew
Beth	Bethany	O	Our
Ble	Bless, Blessed	Pr	Prince
Cbury	Canterbury	Par	Parish
Chap	Chapel	Raph	Raphael
Chrys	Chrysostom	Rdmn	Redemption,
Comf	Comforter		Redemción
Comm	Communion	Rdmr	Redeemer
Cong	Congregation	Recon	Reconciliation
Crux	Crucifixion	Resr	Resurrection,
Cyp	Cyprian		Resurrección
Dun	Dunstan	S	Saint, San
Edm	Edmund		(in parish name)
Edw	Edward	SS	Saints
Emm	Emmanuel	Sac	Sacrament
Evan	Evangelist	Sav	Savior
Faith	Faithful	Shpd	Shepherd
Fell	Fellowship	Sim	Simon, Simeon
Gab	Gabriel	Seb	Sebastian
Gd	Good	Smtn	Samaritan
Geo	George	St	Saint
Geth	Gethsemane		(in other names)
Gr	Grace	Sta	Santa
H	Holy	Ste	Sainte
Heav	Heavenly		(in other names)
Ign	Ignatius	Thad	Thaddeus
Incsn	Intercession	Theo	Theodore
K	King	Trsfg	Transfiguration,
Law(u)	Law(u)rence		Transfiguracción
Lk	Luke	V	Virgin, Virgen

Other Abbreviations

accom	accommodations Admin		Lit	Liturgy, Liturgics
	Administrative		lm	lay missioner
Amb	Ambassador		lr	lay reader
Angl	Anglican		lt	loc ten
Archdcn	Archdeacon			(locum tenens)
Bdwy	Broadway		lv	lay vicar
Bp	Bishop		Min	Ministry, Minister
c	curate		Miss	Missioner,
cap	capacity			Missionary
cath	cathedral		Mtn	Mountain
chap	chaplain		N	North
ch	church		NT	New Testament
Cn	Canon		NYC	New York City,
Coadj	Coadjutor			New York
Coll	College		Ord	Ordinary
Chanc	Chancellor		OT	Old Testament
Comm	Communion		par	parish
	Committee		Past	Pastoral
	Commission		Pk	Park
	Community		Pkwy	Parkway
Commun	Communication		p-in-c	priest-in-charge
Conf	Conference		prog	program
cont ed	continuing		prov	province, provincial
	education		Pt	part time
Cont	Controller,		Pt	Port, Point
	Comptroller		ptnshp	partnership
convoc	convocation		r	rector
coord	coordinator		res	residence
ctr	center		ret	retirement
dio	diocese, diocesan		retr	retreat
dir	director		Rt	Route
dcn	deacon		sch	school
Dn	Dean		sem	seminary
d-in-c	deacon-in-charge		So	South
E	East		Spg(s)	Spring(s)
ecum	ecumenical		spir	spiritual/spirituality
em	emeritus		spon	sponsor
Episc	Episcopal		sr	sister
fac	facility		Ste	Suite
fam	family		SR	State Rd/Star
grp	group			Route
Hd	Head		svc	service
	(master, mistress)		Theol	Theol,
Hisp	Hispanic			Theologian
Hon	Honorable		trng	training
Hse	House		Twp	Township
indiv	individual		urb	urban
inst	institute		V	Very
int	interim		v	vicar
Inter	Interpretation		W	West
Is	Island		yr-rnd	year-round
Lib	Library, Librarian		yth	youth

CALENDAR FOR 2016

Major Holy Days from *The Book of Common Prayer*

JANUARY

1-Fr The Holy Name
2-Sa [Vedanayagam Samuel
        Azariah]
4-Mo [Elizabeth Seton]
6-We The Epiphany
8-Fr Harriet Bedell
9-Sa Julia Chester Emery
12-Tu Aelred of Rievaulx
13-We Hilary of Poitiers
15-Fr Martin Luther King, Jr.
        (alt. to April 4)
16-Sa [Richard Meux Benson
        and Charles Gore]
18-Mo The Confession of St. Peter
19-Tu Wulfstan of Worcester
20-We Fabian of Rome
21-Th Agnes of Rome
22-Fr Vincent of Saragossa
23-Sa Phillips Brooks
25-Mo The Conversion of St. Paul
26-Tu Timothy and Titus
        [and Silas]
27-We [Lydia, Dorcas, and
        Phoebe]
28-Th Thomas Aquinas
29-Fr [Andrei Rublev]

FEBRUARY

1-Mo Brigid (Bride)
2-Tu The Presentation of
        Our Lord Jesus Christ
3-We [The Dorchester
        Chaplains]
4-Th Anskar of Scandinavia
5-Fr [Roger Williams and
        Anne Hutchinson]
6-Sa [The Martyrs of Japan]
10-We Ash Wednesday
11-Th [Frances Jane (Fanny)
        Van Alstyne Crosby]
12-Fr [Charles Freer Andrews]
13-Sa Absalom Jones
15-Mo Thomas Bray
16-Tu [Charles Todd Quintard]
17-We Ember Wednesday,
        Janani Luwum
18-Th Martin Luther
19-Fr Ember Friday
20-Sa Ember Saturday,
        [Frederick Douglass]
22-Mo [Eric Liddell]
23-Tu Polycarp of Smyrna
24-We St. Matthias
25-Th [John Roberts]
26-Fr [Emily Malbone Morgan]
27-Sa George Herbert
29-Mo [John Cassian]

MARCH

1-Tu David of Wales
2-We Chad of Litchfield
3-Th John and Charles Wesley
4-Fr [Paul Cuffee]
7-Mo Perpetua and her
        Companions
8-Tu [Geoffrey Anketell
        Studdert Kennedy]
9-We Gregory of Nyassa
12-Sa Gregory the Great
17-Th Patrick of Ireland
18-Fr Cyril of Jerusalem
19-Sa St. Joseph
20-Su Palm Sunday
24-Th Maundy Thursday
25-Fr Good Friday
26-Sa Holy Saturday
27-Su Easter

APRIL

4-Mo The Annunciation (tr)
5-Tu [Pandita Mary Ramabai]
6-We [Daniel G. C. Wu]
7-Th Tikhon
8-Fr William Augustus
        Muhlenberg [and
        Anne Ayers]
9-Sa Dietrich Bonhoeffer
11-Mo George Augustus Selwyn
12-Tu [Adoniram Judson]
14-Th [Edward Thomas Demby
        and Henry Beard Delany]
15-Fr [Damian and Marianne
        of Molokai]
16-Sa [Mary (Molly) Brant
        (Konwatsijayenni)]
19-Tu Alphege of Canterbury
21-Th Anselm of Canterbury
22-Fr [John Muir and
        Hudson Stuck]
23-Sa [George], [Toyohiko
        Kagawa]
25-Mo St. Mark
26-Tu [Robert Hunt]
27-We [Christina Rosetti]
29-Fr Catherine of Siena
30-Sa [Saarah Josepha Buel Hale]

MAY

2-Mo St. Philip and St. James
        (tr), Rogation Day
3-Tu Rogation Day
4-We Rogation Day, Monnica
5-Th Ascension Day
7-Sa [Harriet Starr Cannon]
9-Mo Gregory of Nazianzus
10-Tu [Nicolaus Ludwig von
        Zinzendorf]
13-Fr [Frances Perkins]
15-Su The Day of Pentecost:
        Whitsunday
16-Mo [The Martyrs of the Sudan]
17-Tu [William Hobart Hare],
        [Thurgood Marshall]

MAY (cont.)

18-We Ember Wednesday,
        The First Book of
        Common Prayer
19-Th Dunstan of Canterbury
20-Fr Ember Friday, Alcuin
        of Tours
21-Sa Ember Saturday,
        [John Eliot]
23-Mo [Nicolaus Copernicus
        and Johannes Kepler]
24-Tu Jackson Kemper
25-We The Venerable Bede
26-Th Augustine of Canterbury
27-Fr [Bertha and Ethelbert]
28-Sa [John Calvin]
30-Mo [Jeanne d'Arc (Joan of
        Arc)]
31-Tu The Visitation of the
        Blessed Virgin Mary

JUNE

1-We Justin
2-Th Blandina and Her
        Companions, the Martyrs
        of Lyons
3-Fr The Martyrs of Uganda
4-Sa [John XXIII (Angelo
        Giuseppe Roncalli)]
6-Mo [Ini Kopuria]
7-Tu [Pioneers of the
        Episcopal Anglican
        Church of Brazil]
8-We [Roland Allen]
9-Th Columba of Iona
10-Fr Ephrem of Edessa
11-Sa St. Barnabas
13-Mo [Gilbert Keith Chesterton]
14-Tu Basil the Great
15-We Evelyn Underhill
16-Th [George Berkeley and]
        Joseph Butler
18-Sa Bernard Mizeki
22-We Alban of Britain
24-Fr Nativity of St. John
        the Baptist
25-Sa [James Weldon Johnson]
27-Mo [Cornelius Hill]
28-Tu Irenaeus of Lyons
29-We St. Peter and St. Paul

JULY

1-Fr [Harriet Beecher Stowe],
        [Pauli Murray]
2-Sa [Walter Rauschenbusch,
        Washington Gladden,
        and Jacob Riis]
4-Mo Independence Day
6-We [John Hus]
11-Mo Benedict of Nursia
12-Tu [Nathan Söderblom]
13-We [Conrad Weiser]
14-Th [Samson Occum]

16-Sa ["The Righteous Gentiles"]
18-Mo [Bartolomé de las Casas]
19-Tu Macrina, [Adelaide Teague Case]
20-We Elizabeth Cady Stanton, Amelia Bloomer, Sojourner Truth, Harriet Ross Tubman
21-Th [Albert John Luthuli]
22-Fr St. Mary Magdalene
25-Mo St. James
26-Tu Joachim and Anne, Parents of the Blessed Virgin Mary
27-We William Reed Hutington
28-Th [Johann Sebastian Back, George Frederick Handel, and Henry Purcell]
29-Fr Mary, Martha, [and Lazarus] of Bethany, [First Ordination of Women to the Priesthood in The Episcopal Church]
30-Sa William Wilberforce [and Anthony Ashley-Cooper, Lord Shaftsbury]

AUGUST

1-Mo Joseph of Arimathaea
2-Tu [Samuel Ferguson]
3-We [George Freeman Bragg, Jr.], [William Edward Burghardt DuBois]
5-Fr [Albrecht Dürer, Matthias Grünewald, and Lucas Cranach the Elder]
6-Sa The Transfiguration of our Lord
8-Mo Dominic
9-Tu [Herman of Alaska]
10-We Laurence of Rome
11-Th Clare of Assisi
12-Fr Florence Nightingale
13-Sa Jeremy Taylor
15-Mo St. Mary the Virgin
17-We [Samuel Johnson, Timothy Cutler, and Thomas Bradbury Chandler], [The Baptisms of Manteo and Virginia Dare]
18-Th William Porcher DuBose
20-Sa Bernard of Clairvaux
23-Tu [Martin de Porres, Rosa de Lima, and Toribio de Mogrovejo]
24-We St. Bartholomew
25-Th Louis of France
27-Fr Thomas Gallaudet with Henry Winter Syle
29-Mo [John Bunyan]
30-Tu [Charles Chapman Grafton]
31-We Aidan and Cuthbert of Lindisfarne

SEPTEMBER

1-Th David Pendleton Oakerhater
2-Fr The Martyrs of New Guinea
3-Sa [Prudence Crandall]
5-Mo [Gregorio Aglipay]
7-We [Elie Naud]
8-Th [Nikolai Grundtvig], [Søren Kierkegaard]
9-Fr Constance and Her Companions
10-Sa Alexander Crummell
12-Mo John Henry Hobart
13-Tu John Chrysostom
14-We Holy Cross Day
15-Th Cyprian of Carthage, [James Chisholm]
16-Fr Ninian of Galloway
17-Sa Hildegard of Bingen
19-Mo Theodore of Tarsus
20-Tu John Coleridge Patterson and his Companions
21-We St. Matthew
22-Th Philander Chase
23-Fr Ember Friday, [Thecla]
24-Sa Ember Saturday
26-Mo Lancelot Andrewes, [Wilson Carlile]
27-Tu [Vincent de Paul], [Thomas Traherne]
28-We [Richard Rolle, Walter Hilton, and Margery Kempe]
29-Th St. Michael and All Angels
30-Fr Jerome of Bethlehem

OCTOBER

1-Sa Remigius of Rheims
3-Mo [George Kennedy Allen Bell], [John Ralegh Mott]
4-Tu Francis of Assisi
6-Th William Tyndale [and Miles Coverdale]
7-Fr [Henry Melchior Muhlenberg]
8-Sa [William Dwight Porter Bliss and Richard Theodore Ely]
10-Mo Vida Dutton Scudder
11-Tu Philip
14-Fr Samuel Isaac Joseph Schereschewsky
15-Sa Teresa of Avila
17-Mo Ignatius of Antioch
18-Tu St. Luke
19-We Henry Martyn, [William Carey]
24-Mo St. James of Jerusalem (tr)
26-We Alfred the Great
28-Fr St. Simon and St. Jude
29-Sa James Hannington and his Companions
31-Mo [Paul Shinji Sasaki and Philip Lindel Tsen]

NOVEMBER

1-Tu All Saints' Day

2-We All Faithful Departed
3-Th Richard Hooker
7-Mo Willibrord of Utrecht
8-Tu James Theodore Holly (alt to March 13)
10-Th Leo the Great
11-Fr Martin of Tours
12-Sa Charles Simeon
14-Mo Samuel Seabury
15-Tu [Francis Asbury and George Whitefield]
16-We Margaret of Scotland
17-Th Hugh, and Robert Grosseteste
18-Fr Hilda of Whitby
19-Sa Elizabeth of Hungary
21-Mo [William Byrd, John Merbecke, and Thomas Tallis]
22-Tu [Cecelia], Clive Staples Lewis
23-We Clement of Rome
24-Th Thanksgiving Day
24-Fr James Otis Sargent Huntington
25-Sa [Isaac Watts]
28-Mo Kamehameha and Emma
30-We St. Andrew

DECEMBER

1-Th Nicholas Ferrar, [Charles de Foucauld]
2-Fr Channing Moore Williams
3-Sa [Francis Xavier]
5-Mo Clement of Alexandria
6-Tu Nicholas of Myra
7-We Ambrose of Milan
8-Th [Richard Baxter]
10-Sa [Karl Barth], [Thomas Merton]
13-Tu [Lucy(Lucia)]
14-We Ember Wednesday, [Juan de la Cruz (John of the Cross)]
15-Th [John Horden], [Robert McDonald]
16-Fr Ember Friday, [Ralph Adams Cram and Richard Upjohn, and John LaFrage]
17-Sa Ember Saturday, [William Lloyd Garrison and Maria Stewart]
19-Mo [Lillian Trasher]
21-We St. Thomas
22-Th [Charlotte Diggs (Lottie) Moon], [Henry Budd]
24-Sa Christmas Eve
25-Su The Nativity of Our Lord Jesus Christ
26-Mo St. Stephen
27-Tu St. John
28-We The Holy Innocents
29-Th Thomas Becket
30-Fr Frances Joseph Gaudet
31-Sa [Samuel Ajayi Crowther]

Provinces of the Episcopal Church
2016-2018 Triennium

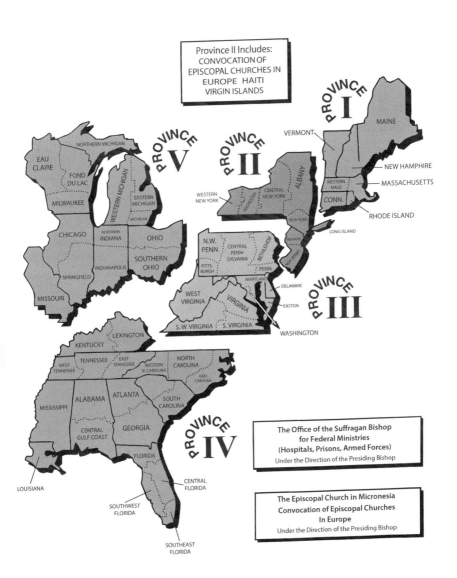

Province II Includes:
CONVOCATION OF
EPISCOPAL CHURCHES IN
EUROPE HAITI
VIRGIN ISLANDS

PROVINCE I

MAINE

VERMONT

NEW HAMPHIRE

MASSACHUSETTS

WESTERN
MASS

CONN.

RHODE ISLAND

PROVINCE V

NORTHERN MICHIGAN

EAU
CLAIRE

FOND
DU LAC

MILWAUKEE

WESTERN
MICHIGAN

EASTERN
MICHIGAN

MICHIGAN

CHICAGO

NORTHERN
INDIANA

OHIO

SOUTHERN
OHIO

INDIANAPOLIS

SPRINGFIELD

MISSOURI

PROVINCE II

WESTERN
NEW YORK

ROCHESTER

CENTRAL
NEW YORK

ALBANY

NEW YORK

NEWARK

LONG ISLAND

NEW JERSEY

N.W.
PENN

CENTRAL
PENN-
SYLVANIA

BETHLEHEM

PITTS-
BURGH

PENN.

MARYLAND

DELAWARE

WEST
VIRGINIA

VIRGINIA

EASTON

S. W. VIRGINIA

S. VIRGINIA

WASHINGTON

PROVINCE III

LEXINGTON

KENTUCKY

TENNESSEE

EAST
TENNESSEE

WEST
TENNESSEE

WESTERN
N. CAROLINA

NORTH
CAROLINA

EAST
CAROLINA

ALABAMA

ATLANTA

SOUTH
CAROLINA

MISSISSIPPI

CENTRAL
GULF COAST

GEORGIA

PROVINCE IV

FLORIDA

LOUISIANA

CENTRAL
FLORIDA

SOUTHWEST
FLORIDA

SOUTHEAST
FLORIDA

The Office of the Suffragan Bishop
for Federal Ministries
(Hospitals, Prisons, Armed Forces)
Under the Direction of the Presiding Bishop

The Episcopal Church in Micronesia
Convocation of Episcopal Churches
In Europe
Under the Direction of the Presiding Bishop

SUMMARY OF STATISTICS
as of January 2016

	Reported for 2014	Reported for 2013	Net Change	Percent Change
Parishes and Missions....................................	6,553	6,622	-69	-1.04%
Active Baptized Members............................	1,817,004	1,866,758	-49,754	-2.67%
Communicants in Good Standing.............	1,450,472	1,491,423	-40,951	-2.75%
Others Active in Congregation...................	179,638	184,035	-4,397	-2.39%
Average Sunday Attendance........................	600,411	623,691	-23,280	-3.73%
Church School Pupils..................................	173,682	184,859	-11,177	-6.05%
Baptisms..	28,124	29,497	-1,373	-4.65%
Confirmations..	19,142	20,077	-935	-4.66%
Received..	6,201	6,263	-62	-0.99%
Marriages..	10,337	9,933	404	4.07%
Burials..	29,011	28,960	51	0.18%
Clergy (incl. non-parochial)......................	18,198	18,170	28	0.15%

Notes:

1. These figures, except for clergy, are based on 2014 Parochial Reports compiled for the Domestic Dioceses of Provinces I through VIII. Non-domestic figures are not included in the above statistics. For Province IX and other non-domestic Dioceses see the *Table of Statistics of the Episcopal Church.*

2. Average Sunday Attendance is a 52-Sunday Average of Sunday worship attendance (which includes attendance on Saturday when Saturday services are considered to be Sunday worship).

3. Clergy totals include all clergy listed in the clergy list in the *Episcopal Church Annual* including clergy reported as ordained but not yet entered in the clergy list. Source: The Church Pension Group.

Table of Statistics of the Episcopal Church
From 2014 Parochial Reports. Source: The Office of the General Convention as of January 2016

Province	Diocese	Open Parishes & Missions	Active Baptized Members	Commun. in Good Standing	Others Active in Cong.	Average Sunday Attendance	Church School Pupils	BAPTISMS Children	BAPTISMS Adults	CONFIRMATIONS Children	CONFIRMATIONS Adults	Received	Marriages	Burials
Province 1	Connecticut	165	52,175	40,045	3,334	15,101	4,938	671	56	334	151	123	250	922
	Maine	64	11,890	10,012	981	4,053	994	130	20	25	40	37	102	248
	Massachusetts	163	60,130	45,229	4,692	16,024	6,128	875	56	333	146	62	313	1001
	New Hampshire	49	13,161	10,400	1167	4,675	1,435	154	19	23	76	39	92	290
	Rhode Island	51	18,349	12,941	1,645	4,988	1,354	283	23	27	99	46	122	350
	Vermont	46	6,549	5,187	609	2,193	493	57	8	15	18	14	49	127
	Western Massachusetts	59	15,729	11,660	767	4,593	1,223	225	41	29	58	53	63	299
	Total	597	177,983	135,474	13,195	51,627	16,565	2,395	223	786	588	374	991	3,237
Province 2	Albany	112	15,232	12,139	901	6,143	1,159	229	60	30	78	33	104	352
	Central New York	81	13,281	9,743	796	4,129	913	146	32	22	50	22	91	330
	Churches in Europe	16	3,548	2,879	152	1,095	251	31	18	24	12	6	24	21
	Haiti	111	85,499	24,177	2665	15,635	7,546	1,317	653	545	515	114	136	190
	Long Island	135	44,694	32,462	3,309	13,685	2,970	840	135	223	274	83	255	721
	New Jersey	149	43,021	31,125	3,325	12,556	3,566	651	51	321	163	166	280	697
	New York	198	59,035	45,921	3,619	18,009	4,154	811	116	362	217	200	327	710
	Newark	102	27,120	21,514	1,368	8,260	2,954	408	47	205	126	60	175	454
	Rochester	46	7,800	6,744	648	3,063	801	108	11	50	29	37	63	171
	Virgin Islands	14	3,894	3,092	77	1,814	341	54	11	36	4	9	22	94
	Western New York	58	9,984	6,662	599	3,350	748	138	21	36	36	35	94	276
	Total	1,022	313,108	196,458	17,459	87,739	25,403	4,733	1,148	1,854	1,504	765	1,571	4,016
Province 3	Bethlehem	59	10,652	8,292	739	3,518	1066	132	17	31	23	22	82	232
	Central Pennsylvania	66	12,570	10,268	1,046	4,435	922	158	29	63	53	43	79	221
	Delaware	33	9,645	7,883	658	3,422	839	122	19	62	39	50	100	194
	Easton	38	7,974	5,992	799	2,595	562	84	18	41	41	21	72	174
	Maryland	106	39,982	28,917	2,385	10,256	3,463	470	70	162	207	124	191	629
	Northwestern Pennsylvania	31	3,445	2,733	182	1,385	275	66	16	9	29	25	27	105
	Pennsylvania	136	43,451	35,997	5,168	13,188	3,767	595	53	244	137	138	359	767
	Pittsburgh	37	8,709	6,965	540	2,375	634	98	7	39	35	15	75	127
	Southern Virginia	106	27,194	21,780	3,630	9,632	2,522	303	58	82	196	90	135	460
	Southwestern Virginia	56	10,593	9,103	1,532	4,166	1,047	105	19	62	56	58	56	190
	Virginia	182	77,377	62,595	10,339	23,669	7,759	991	106	413	378	270	415	844
	Washington	88	40,342	31,137	6,639	13,330	4,120	508	43	124	185	92	228	466
	West Virginia	63	8,106	6,482	385	2,759	664	85	22	11	35	19	40	170
	Total	1,001	300,040	238,144	34,042	94,730	27,640	3,717	477	1,343	1,414	967	1,859	4,579
Province 4	Alabama	89	31,516	26,986	3,433	9,646	4,523	362	36	227	325	57	164	350
	Atlanta	95	50,420	40,577	6,419	15,324	5,597	798	71	273	353	252	182	558
	Central Florida	87	28,386	24,120	4,626	13,085	2,363	366	71	136	261	232	136	613
	Central Gulf Coast	62	18,473	15,044	1,420	5,903	1,739	171	27	106	166	52	89	241
	East Carolina	68	17,496	15,026	2,084	6,360	1,405	200	31	88	101	77	89	252
	East Tennessee	48	15,339	11,969	1,647	5,056	1,483	149	25	115	149	137	80	242
	Florida	61	25,822	21,890	3,063	8,457	2,551	247	71	102	172	63	117	356
	Georgia	67	16,186	12,418	1,467	5,744	1,702	168	22	115	113	81	91	279
	Kentucky	36	8,380	7,230	533	3,147	1,014	103	15	45	53	25	51	131
	Lexington	34	6,806	5,696	706	2,768	772	102	29	27	45	40	43	104
	Louisiana	48	17,461	13,757	1,548	4,670	1,416	278	19	81	87	43	108	223
	Mississippi	83	18,677	15,163	1,866	6,117	2,076	199	32	120	185	61	111	266
	North Carolina	112	50,218	40,404	7,061	14,617	9,749	688	56	414	301	140	219	566

Province	Diocese	Open Parishes & Missions	Active Baptized Members	Commun. in Good Standing	Others Active in Cong.	Average Sunday Attendance	Church School Pupils	BAPTISMS Children	BAPTISMS Adults	CONFIRMATIONS Children	CONFIRMATIONS Adults	Received	Marriages	Burials
	South Carolina	30	6,387	4,684	1,068	2,812	1,113	120	7	50	75	46	41	94
	Southeast Florida	77	33,404	27,203	2,853	12,478	2,318	701	66	165	175	164	230	498
	Southwest Florida	77	30,421	24,603	5,716	12,718	1,881	320	68	111	120	106	138	576
	Tennessee	45	16,795	13,711	3,571	5,680	2,112	231	25	73	168	37	109	140
	Upper South Carolina	59	23,617	19,118	1,732	7,492	3,583	301	32	28	192	104	99	247
	West Tennessee	31	8,258	7,089	1,069	3,205	908	96	10	30	134	12	44	117
	Western North Carolina	62	15,268	13,370	2,172	6,327	1,386	138	18	97	184	132	92	300
	Total	1,271	439,330	360,058	54,054	151,606	49,691	5,738	731	2,403	3,359	1,861	2,233	6,153
Province 5	Chicago	125	35,967	29,289	2,757	12,186	3,849	553	36	279	138	104	223	507
	Eastern Michigan	47	6,237	4,922	239	2,096	399	72	18	18	15	20	55	212
	Eau Claire	20	1,850	1,421	109	789	156	22	6	16	11	6	10	50
	Fond Du Lac	34	5,440	4,234	618	2,026	361	71	6	10	8	27	43	98
	Indianapolis	48	9,475	7,836	715	3,694	992	104	22	7	116	42	72	148
	Michigan	78	18,730	15,105	1,525	6,478	1,636	200	40	21	80	50	130	428
	Milwaukee	53	9,182	7,860	561	3,543	849	122	12	20	66	55	85	182
	Missouri	43	11,402	9,654	762	3,778	993	127	18	59	37	20	57	163
	Northern Indiana	36	4,256	3,833	330	2,115	335	50	13	15	72	16	27	121
	Northern Michigan	22	1,432	1,067	106	509	79	13	0	2	1	2	15	35
	Ohio	86	19,615	15,537	2,079	6,381	1,518	221	44	82	80	59	111	375
	Southern Ohio	75	19,925	16,497	1,402	6,863	1,944	249	29	70	111	39	138	312
	Springfield	33	4,242	3,261	179	1,574	302	49	12	12	38	14	28	80
	Western Michigan	57	9,663	7,270	856	3,770	962	127	41	3	52	34	71	230
	Total	757	157,416	127,786	12,238	55,802	14,375	1,980	297	614	825	488	1,065	2,941
Province 6	Colorado	101	25,675	21,952	4,811	9,804	2,460	387	41	37	119	60	141	493
	Iowa	61	8,350	6,765	495	2,674	768	97	14	30	37	32	50	164
	Minnesota	104	20,874	16,803	1,581	6,749	2,432	348	29	78	102	75	161	340
	Montana	35	4,478	3,834	394	1,497	304	54	4	15	8	4	32	79
	Nebraska	53	7,495	6,143	282	2,612	582	104	9	29	20	19	48	134
	North Dakota	19	2,535	1,857	125	679	258	72	2	17	7	29	9	55
	South Dakota	78	9,663	5,400	397	1,943	512	282	6	32	17	38	26	249
	Wyoming	46	7,073	5,085	887	1,787	534	108	25	23	25	62	60	137
	Total	497	86,143	67,839	8,972	27,745	7,850	1,452	130	261	335	321	527	1,651
Province 7	Arkansas	56	13,877	11,260	934	4,775	1,343	156	50	46	181	53	74	216
	Dallas	67	32,222	27,377	3,252	11,465	4,324	522	68	309	199	107	117	392
	Fort Worth	15	4,617	3,805	292	1,429	350	60	19	9	35	15	9	55
	Kansas	46	10,823	9,319	1,126	3,647	946	124	21	42	80	41	67	195
	Northwest Texas	32	6,739	5,028	383	1,734	719	97	30	28	90	19	29	122
	Oklahoma	69	16,642	14,053	748	5,371	1,359	194	72	62	187	32	83	298
	Rio Grande	55	10,960	9,084	1,149	3,657	615	99	21	29	67	47	71	195
	Texas	151	75,431	61,218	7,716	25,286	7,734	1,219	150	490	595	294	308	889
	West Missouri	49	10,099	8,289	1,803	3,340	877	105	32	16	67	22	62	171
	West Texas	88	23,126	18,659	3,036	8,865	2,636	359	56	156	188	120	132	398
	Western Kansas	29	1,498	1,272	67	602	143	23	6	2	8	15	11	43
	Western Louisiana	45	9,095	7,250	653	3,122	607	112	16	61	68	27	54	164
	Total	702	215,129	176,614	21,159	73,293	21,653	3,070	541	1,250	1,765	792	1,017	3,138
Province 8	Alaska	49	7,146	5,260	696	1,463	468	152	26	27	37	7	39	153
	Arizona	59	21,483	19,305	2,810	8,448	1,781	364	80	92	142	89	109	433
	California	80	25,066	20,876	1,944	7,635	2,697	326	49	103	83	22	161	348
	Eastern Oregon	22	1,999	1,491	530	935	112	17	6	3	8	7	16	66

Province	Diocese	Open Parishes & Missions	Active Baptized Members	Commun. in Good Standing	Others Active in Cong.	Average Sunday Attendance	Church School Pupils	BAPTISMS Children	BAPTISMS Adults	CONFIRMATIONS Children	CONFIRMATIONS Adults	Received	Marriages	Burials
	El Camino Real	43	11,914	9,107	956	3,925	841	135	27	55	35	68	68	169
	Hawaii	33	6,518	5,405	579	3,003	480	127	37	27	73	30	69	140
	Idaho	30	4,781	4,136	414	1,498	458	45	23	3	6	5	18	86
	Los Angeles	134	52,647	39,620	3,821	16,078	3,964	666	123	169	329	128	299	654
	Micronesia	2	222	196	12	100	26	7	0	4	4	1	0	1
	Navajo Missions	9	754	515	37	187	86	5	7	0	0	0	8	32
	Nevada	30	5,444	4,889	1,382	2,517	412	102	26	38	46	39	44	110
	Northern California	67	13,659	12,143	718	5,414	1,157	176	48	56	96	76	82	231
	Olympia	92	25,490	19,783	1,974	9,093	2,300	242	62	62	132	95	122	445
	Oregon	72	16,183	12,947	1,422	6,092	1,529	169	46	12	101	76	101	279
	San Diego	46	14,622	12,140	3,237	5,695	1,318	217	38	34	70	75	65	237
	San Joaquin	20	2,131	1,799	103	925	208	35	15	9	42	16	14	43
	Spokane	37	5,539	4,528	435	1,853	342	67	18	17	22	15	28	113
	Taiwan	13	1,221	894	95	735	247	20	44	11	30	17	6	17
	Utah	24	5,420	4,303	355	1,652	490	66	27	9	39	14	13	62
	Total	862	222,239	179,337	21,520	77,248	18,916	2,938	702	731	1,295	780	1,262	3,619
Province 9	Colombia	29	2,829	1,142	107	977	179	110	18	26	26	67	108	18
	Dominican Republic	60	6,059	3,411	677	3,214	1,440	184	104	31	131	57	8	117
	Ecuador, Central	22	2,332	1,365	288	1,117	640	242	11	15	24	107	19	47
	Ecuador, Litoral	26	9,911	1,466	341	1,053	322	144	61	361	115	29	57	18
	Honduras	124	17,270	10,574	2,766	5,174	2,854	190	46	32	53	12	50	62
	Puerto Rico	50	5,374	4,134	706	2,581	749	132	17	61	93	155	50	94
	Venezuela	24	879	471	49	442	141	75	27	0	22	11	7	20
	Total	335	44,654	22,563	4,934	14,558	6,325	1,077	284	526	464	438	299	376
	Domestic Dioceses	6,553	1,817,004	1,450,472	179,638	600,411	173,682	24,594	3,530	8,622	10,520	6,201	10,337	29,011
	Non-Domestic Dioceses	491	139,038	53,801	7,935	33,937	14,736	2,506	1,003	1,146	1,029	585	487	699
	The Episcopal Church	7,044	1,956,042	1,504,273	187,573	634,348	188,418	27,100	4,533	9,768	11,549	6,786	10,824	29,710

Note: These figures are compiled from 2014 Parochial Reports submitted to the Office of the General Convention, 815 Second Avenue, New York, NY 10017-4564. For further information about the Parochial Report, contact the research office, DFMS, pr@gdfms.org, or phone (800) 334-7626. Figures for Venezuela are from 2013. Figures for individual non-reporting congregations are carried over from the previous year.

Comparative Statistics of the Episcopal Church, U.S.A.

Year Reported	Parishes and Missions	Clergy	Baptized Members	Communicants Domestic	Communicants Overseas	Communicants Total	Church School Pupils*	Day School Staff†	Day School Pupils*	Cand's for Orders	Ordinations Deacons	Ordinations Priests	Baptisms Infant	Baptisms Adult	Baptisms Total	Confirmations (Including Received)	Marriages	Burials	Total Receipts (Gross Receipts) $
1850		1,595				89,359	44,148			175			18,232	2,727	20,959	7,554	2,987	6,226	342,936.49
1855	1,821	1,821				107,560	82,731			236		83	18,812	3,618	22,430	10,584	6,777	12,542	727,477.00
1860	2,128	2,156				146,588	135,925			292	102		26,518	5,247	31,765	14,781	7,356	12,989	1,870,914.98
1865	2,322	2,467				154,118	150,400			220	94	91	24,689	5,297	29,986	15,360	7,487	15,650	2,700,004.08
1870	2,605	2,838				207,762	213,862			361	102	91				21,622	9,261	15,802	4,907,872.57
1875		3,187				261,003	235,943			298	110	122				22,095	9,690	18,969	6,899,305.94
1880	4,151	3,432		345,433	408	345,841	299,070			431	136	96	40,557	8,188	48,745	25,903	12,163	22,518	7,013,762.86
1885	4,565	3,787		397,084	108	397,192	326,203			321	134	108	46,962	11,227	58,189	34,069	14,040	27,893	9,017,155.16
1890	5,330	4,180		504,898	3,394	508,292	393,795			299			49,777	11,645	61,422	40,911	15,819	30,136	12,754,767.53
1895	6,269	4,610		614,136	5,297	619,433	418,674			529			48,118	10,418	58,536	44,627	17,242	34,761	13,449,925.95
1900	6,774	5,011		712,997	6,543	719,540	429,830			506			50,119	12,899	63,018	43,788	19,039	34,138	16,069,580.49
1905	7,480	5,302		817,845	10,548	828,393	450,212			459			49,981	14,086	64,067	51,341	22,527	37,628	16,296,693.95
1910	7,987	5,543		928,780	17,472	946,252	456,275			438			53,289	14,537	67,826	55,020	24,044	45,566	18,382,609.85
1915	8,506	5,800		1,040,896	17,908	1,058,804	483,936			430			50,315	10,025	60,340	61,284	26,231	50,080	20,972,589.78
1920	8,365	5,987		1,075,820	21,075	1,096,895	417,695			310			54,879	12,181	67,060	50,779	28,485	47,788	24,392,091.64
1925	8,397	6,140		1,164,911	28,410	1,193,321	498,814			454	177	157	52,200	11,559	63,759	65,064	29,420	50,336	41,746,055.91
1930	8,253	6,304	1,939,453	1,254,227	33,204	1,287,431	483,413			485	192	193	50,499	12,200	62,699	64,668	30,576	56,163	45,944,896.82
1935	8,098	6,410	2,038,477	1,351,999	37,593	1,389,592	506,400			426	193	162	56,288	13,130	69,418	67,096	25,639	52,611	30,425,500.75
1940	7,995	6,335	2,171,562	1,449,327	40,057	1,489,384	492,554			301	181	209	72,377	14,033	86,410	74,318	28,799	53,446	34,618,420.82
1945	7,818	6,449	2,269,962	1,527,762	40,390	1,568,152	394,456			229	152	149	87,487	16,550	104,037	68,868	31,597	54,650	46,170,035.30
1950	7,784	6,654	2,540,548	1,651,426	37,185	1,688,611	514,754			486	255	240	98,595	20,388	118,983	85,989	28,695	55,354	73,844,880.41
1955	8,053	7,573	3,013,570	1,781,262	84,653	1,865,915	696,028			677	415	354	98,312	18,415	116,727	113,443	24,789	53,114	131,354,945.37
1960	7,657	9,079	3,444,265	2,027,671	95,439	2,123,110	874,550	3,187	44,075	800	424	427				127,861	24,111	57,574	173,013,803.63

18

Year Reported	Parishes and Missions	Clergy	Baptized Members	Communicants Domestic	Communicants Overseas	Communicants Total	Others Active in Congregations	Church School Staff	Church School Pupils*	Day School Staff	Day School Pupils*	Cand's for Orders	Ordinations Deacons	Ordinations Priests	Baptisms Children	Baptisms Adult	Baptisms Total	Confirmations (Including Received)	Marriages	Burials	Total Receipts (Gross Receipts) ‡
1965	7,539	10,309	3,615,643	2,202,607	69,534	2,272,141	—	105,221	880,912	4,590	58,712	710	442	426	91,695	13,627	105,322	128,066	27,728	60,190	223,016,214.03
1970	7,464	11,772	3,475,164	2,238,538	56,017	2,294,555	—	89,611	711,791	6,088	79,962	510	379	311	74,577	8,359	82,936	102,059	37,836	59,504	‡299,426,994.00
1975	7,382	12,035	3,039,136	2,051,914	77,337	2,129,251	—	74,574	559,648	8,897	100,465	702	316	271	63,503	5,965	69,468	77,038	36,535	53,473	411,418,722.00
1980	7,591	13,089	3,037,420	1,933,080	85,790	2,018,870	—	69,459	507,448	—	104,839	425	321	314	64,367	8,611	72,978	64,912	39,862	50,070	648,937,788.00
1985	7,858	14,482	2,972,607	1,881,250	82,375	1,963,625	—	70,383	496,930	—	120,259	563	475	330	65,152	7,142	72,294	59,718	36,073	48,277	1,028,818,309.00
1990	7,354	14,878	2,446,050	1,698,240	—	—	—	72,668	495,537	—	100,589	407	379	296	56,862	7,844	64,706	47,270	31,795	43,568	1,379,782,885.00
1991	7,367	14,879	2,474,625	1,615,505	—	—	—	74,350	336,251	—	95,903	405	380	296	55,869	7,714	63,583	46,068	30,557	43,538	1,433,467,803.00
1992	7,391	15,076	2,491,996	1,614,081	—	—	—	72,153	335,297	—	99,366	407	378	290	53,095	7,071	60,166	46,820	28,844	42,226	1,582,457,015.00
1993	7,403	15,004	2,506,047	1,579,444	—	—	—	75,959	327,157	—	101,752	423	378	290	51,643	8,044	59,687	44,509	28,291	43,010	1,613,697,551.00
1994	7,413	14,645	2,517,520	1,577,951	—	—	142,900	72,988	328,512	13,674	102,145	352	399	317	51,049	6,545	57,594	43,234	27,631	42,259	1,311,990,815.00
1995	7,417	15,138	2,411,841	1,584,760	—	—	150,417	71,773	333,645	—	107,203	372	347	265	50,784	7,250	58,034	43,474	27,324	44,239	1,398,179,032.00
1996	7,395	14,295	2,366,054	1,592,693	—	—	159,199	72,874	325,156	20,416	102,042	329	341	296	49,525	6,688	56,213	42,378	25,931	42,244	1,470,455,496.00
1997	7,379	14,428	2,339,113	1,716,977	—	—	168,595	73,940	319,393	†	103,748	326	332	284	49,545	7,433	56,978	42,486	25,989	41,030	1,577,769,316.00
1998	7,384	14,428	2,318,238	1,763,650	—	—	180,253	75,027	309,713	†	†	326	332	284	48,563	7,191	55,754	41,478	23,974	39,735	1,685,701,827.00
1999	7,368	16,891◆	2,296,936	1,812,434	—	—	196,574	†	275,382	†	†	◊	◊	◊	47,519	7,665	55,184	42,579	23,042	45,587	1,864,447,191.00
2000	7,347	16,783◆	2,319,844	1,857,843	—	—	187,927	†	300,010	†	†	◊	◊	◊	46,403	7,231	53,634	44,892	22,341	44,762	2,019,266,027.00
2001	7,344	17,336	2,317,515	1,868,960	—	—	199,446	—	297,635	—	—	—	—	—	45,566	6,969	52,535	42,268	19,354	44,199	1,939,281,740.00
2002	7,305	17,443	2,320,221	1,902,525	—	—	209,416	—	303,061	—	—	—	—	—	44,995	6,299	51,294	40,482	18,798	38,154	1,994,893,155.00
2003	7,220	17,174	2,284,233	1,866,157	—	—	208,094	—	287,998	—	—	—	—	—	43,068	6,248	49,316	39,557	18,260	35,840	2,044,377,792.00
2004	7,200	17,209	2,247,819	1,834,530	—	—	200,917	—	275,087	—	—	—	—	—	41,376	5,754	47,130	36,244	17,149	34,744	2,083,916,019.00
2005	7,155	17,817	2,205,376	1,796,017	—	—	203,390	—	266,080	—	—	—	—	—	38,680	5,620	44,300	32,412	16,190	34,372	2,199,993,228.00
2006	7,095	17,922	2,154,572	1,749,073	71,820	1,820,893	191,460	—	253,304	—	—	—	—	—	36,387	4,501	40,888	—	14,805	32,564	2,223,317,477.00
2007	7,055	18,019	2,116,749	1,720,477	75,306	1,795,783	189,671	—	242,557	—	—	—	—	—	34,194	4,020	38,214	23,556	13,438	31,457	2,269,075,042.00
2008	6,964	18,002	2,057,292	1,666,202	68,320	1,734,522	181,367	—	227,619	—	—	—	—	—	32,731	3,816	36,547	23,359	12,816	31,212	2,233,075,961.00
2009	6,895	17,868	2,006,343	1,624,025	69,060	1,693,085	183,674	—	216,953	—	—	—	—	—	30,682	3,978	34,660	22,762	11,647	30,853	2,128,331,169.00
2010	6,794	17,975	1,951,907	1,576,721	75,525	1,652,525	180,360	—	203,774	—	—	—	—	—	28,990	3,746	32,736	22,265	10,990	30,109	2,088,030,689.00
2011	6,736	18,112	1,923,046	1,542,072	70,755	1,612,827	179,256	—	197,734	—	—	—	—	—	28,201	3,939	32,140	20,942	10,950	29,813	2,127,489,576.00
2012	6,667	18,040	1,894,181	1,516,117	71,940	1,588,057	179,000	—	190,606	—	—	—	—	—	27,140	3,836	30,976	20,474	10,366	29,442	2,170,806,058.00
2013	6,622	18,170	1,866,758	1,491,423	57,585	1,549,008	184,035	—	184,859	—	—	—	—	—	25,822	3,675	29,497	20,077	9,933	28,960	2,215,042,224.00
2014	6,553	18,198	1,817,004	1,450,472	53,801	1,504,273	179,638	—	173,682	—	—	—	—	—	24,594	3,530	28,124	19,142	10,337	29,011	2,248,977,732.00

*New category or revised in 1992.

◆ See notes on clergy on page 15

†Statistics on Day Schools and church school staff are no longer maintained.

‡From 1970 on, excludes all non-income items; includes "other parish funds" (not previously reported.)

◊ Not available

A Table of the General Conventions

No.	Opened — Closed	Place of Meeting	Presiding Bishop	Pres. House of Deputies	Preacher
1	Sept. 27—Oct. 7, 1785	Philadelphia.	....	Rev. Wm. White, D.D.	Rev. Wm. Smith, D.D.
2	June 20—June 26, 1786	Philadelphia.	....	Rev. David Griffith.	Rev. Wm. White, D.D.
	Oct. 10—Oct. 11, 1786	Wilmington, Del.	....	Rev. Samuel Provoost, D.D.	Rev. Samuel Megaw, D.D.
3	July 28—Aug. 8, 1789	Philadelphia.	....	Bishop William White,[1]	Rev. Wm. Smith, D.D.
	Sept. 29—Oct. 16, 1789	Philadelphia.	....	Rev. Wm. Smith, D.D.	....
4	Sept. 11—Sept.19, 1792	New York.	Bp. William White.	Rev. Wm. Smith, D.D.	Bishop Samuel Seabury.
5	Sept. 8—Sept.18, 1795	Philadelphia.	Bp. Samuel Seabury.	Rev. Wm. Smith, D.D.	Bishop Samuel Provoost.
6	June 11—June 19, 1799	Philadelphia.	Bp. Samuel Provoost.	Rev. Wm. Smith, D.D.	....
7	Sept. 8—Sept.12, 1801	Trenton, N.J.	Bp. William White.	Rev. Abraham Beach, D.D.	Bishop William White.
8	Sept. 11—Sept.18, 1804	New York.	Bp. William White.	Rev. Abraham Beach, D.D.	Bishop Benjamin Moore.
9	May 17—May 26, 1808	Baltimore.	Bp. William White.	Rev. Abraham Beach, D.D.	Bishop William White.
10	May 21—May 24, 1811	New Haven.	Bp. William White.	Rev. Isaac Wilkins.	Bishop William White.
11	May 17—May 24, 1814	Philadelphia.	Bp. William White.	Rev. John Croes, D.D.	Bishop John Henry Hobart.
12	May 20—May 27, 1817	New York.	Bp. William White.	Rev. Isaac Wilkins, D.D.	Bishop Alex. V. Griswold.
13	May 16—May 24, 1820	Philadelphia.	Bp. William White.	Rev. Wm. H. Wilmer, D.D.	Bishop Richard C. Moore.
1	Oct. 30—Nov. 3, 1821	Philadelphia.	Bp. William White.	Rev. Wm. H. Wilmer, D.D.	Bishop James Kemp.
14	May 20—May 26, 1823	Philadelphia.	Bp. William White.	Rev. Wm. H. Wilmer, D.D.	Bishop John Cross.
15	Nov. 7—Nov. 15, 1826	Philadelphia.	Bp. William White.	Rev. Wm. H. Wilmer, D.D.	Bishop Nathaniel Bowen.
16	Aug. 12—Aug. 20, 1829	Philadelphia.	Bp. William White.	Rev. Wm. E. Wyatt, D.D.	Bishop Thomas C. Brownell.
17	Oct. 17—Oct. 31, 1832	New York.	Bp. William White.	Rev. Wm. E. Wyatt, D.D.	Bishop Henry U. Onderdonk.
18	Aug. 19—Sept. 1, 1835	Philadelphia.	Bp. William White.	Rev. Wm. E. Wyatt, D.D.	Bishop Wm. Murray Stone.
19	Sept. 5—Sept.17, 1838	Philadelphia.	Bp. Alexander Viets Griswold.	Rev. Wm. E. Wyatt, D.D.	Bishop Wm. Meade.
20	Oct. 6—Oct. 19, 1841	New York.	Bp. Alexander Viets Griswold.	Rev. Wm. E. Wyatt, D.D.	Bishop Benj. T. Onderdonk.
21	Oct. 2—Oct. 22, 1844	Philadelphia.	Bp. Philander Chase.	Rev. Wm. E. Wyatt, D.D.	Bishop Levi S. Ives.
22	Oct. 6—Oct. 28, 1847	New York.	Bp. Philander Chase.	Rev. Wm. E. Wyatt, D.D.	Bishop John Henry Hopkins.
23	Oct. 2—Oct. 16, 1850	Cincinnati.	Bp. Philander Chase.	Rev. Wm. E. Wyatt, D.D.	Bishop Benj. B. Smith.
24	Oct. 5—Oct. 26, 1853	New York.	Bp. Thomas Church Brownell.	Rev. Wm. Creighton, D.D.	Bishop Charles P. McIlvaine.
25	Oct. 1—Oct. 21, 1856	Philadelphia.	Bp. Thomas Church Brownell.	Rev. Wm. Creighton, D.D.	Bishop Geo. W. Doane.
26	Oct. 5—Oct. 22, 1859	Richmond, Va.	Bp. Thomas Church Brownell.[2]	Rev. Wm. Creighton, D.D.	Bishop James H. Otey.
A1	July 3—July 6, 1861[3]	Montgomery, Ala.	Bp. Stephen Elliott.	Met as a single house.	None mentioned.
A2	Oct. 16—Oct. 24, 1861[3]	Columbia, S.C.	Bp. William Meade.	Met as a single house.	Bishop William Meade.
27	Oct. 1—Oct. 17, 1862	New York.	Bp. Thomas Church Brownell.[4]	Rev. James Craik, D.D.	Bishop Sam. A. McCoskry.
A3	Nov. 12—Nov. 22, 1862[5]	Augusta, Ga.	Bp. Stephen Elliott.	Rev. Christian Hanckel, D.D.	Bishop Henry C. Lay.
28	Oct. 4—Oct. 24, 1865	Philadelphia.	Bp. John Henry Hopkins.	Rev. James Craik, D.D.	Bishop Fulford of Montreal.
A4	Nov. 8—Nov. 10, 1865[6]	Augusta, Ga.	Bp. Stephen Elliott.	Rev. C. C. Pinckney, D.D.	None mentioned.
29	Oct. 7—Oct. 29, 1868	New York.	Bp. Benjamin Bosworth Smith.	Rev. James Craik, D.D.	Bishop Henry W. Lee.
30	Oct. 4—Oct. 26, 1871	Baltimore.	Bp. Benjamin Bosworth Smith.	Rev. James Craik, D.D.	Bishop John Johns.
31	Oct. 7—Nov. 3, 1874	New York.	Bp. Benjamin Bosworth Smith.	Rev. James Craik, D.D.	Bishop Selwyn of Lichfield.
32	Oct. 3—Oct. 25, 1877	Boston.	Bp. Benjamin Bosworth Smith.	Rev. Alex. Burgess, D.D.	Bishop John Williams.
33	Oct. 6—Oct. 27, 1880	New York.	Bp. Benjamin Bosworth Smith.	Rev. E. E. Beardsley, D.D.	Bishop Wm. I. Kip.
34	Oct. 6—Oct. 28, 1883	New York.	Bp. Benjamin Bosworth Smith.[7]	Rev. E. E. Beardsley, D.D.	Bishop Thomas M. Clark.
35	Oct. 6—Oct. 28, 1886	Chicago.	Bp. Alfred Lee.	Rev. Morgan Dix, D.D.	Bishop Gregory T. Bedell.
36	Oct. 2—Oct. 24, 1889	New York.	Bp. John Williams.	Rev. Morgan Dix, D.D.	Bishop Henry B. Whipple.
37	Oct. 5—Oct. 25, 1892	Baltimore.	Bp. John Williams.	Rev. Morgan Dix, D.D.	Bishop Richard H. Wilmer.

38	Oct. 2—Oct. 22, 1895	Minneapolis.	Bp. John Williams,[8]	Rev. Morgan Dix, D.D.	Bishop Arthur C. Coxe.
39	Oct. 5—Oct. 25, 1898	Washington.	Bp. John Williams,[8]	Rev. Morgan Dix, D.D.	Bishop Daniel S. Tuttle.
40	Oct. 2—Oct. 17, 1901	San Francisco.	Bp. Thomas March Clark.[9]	Rev. J. S. Lindsay, D.D.	Bishop Benj. W. Morris.
41	Oct. 2—Oct. 25, 1904	Boston.	Bp. Daniel Sylvester Tuttle.	Rev. R. H. McKim, D.D.	Bishop Wm. C. Doane.
42	Oct. 2—Oct. 19, 1907	Richmond, Va.	Bp. Daniel Sylvester Tuttle.	Rev. R. H. McKim, D.D.	Bishop Ingram of London.
43	Oct. 5—Oct. 21, 1910	Cincinnati.	Bp. Daniel Sylvester Tuttle.	Rev. R. H. McKim, D.D.	Bp. Wordsworth of Salisbury.
44	Oct. 8—Oct. 25, 1913	New York.	Bp. Daniel Sylvester Tuttle.	Rev. Alex. Mann, D.D.	Bishop William Lawrence.
45	Oct. 11—Oct. 27, 1916	St. Louis.	Bp. Daniel Sylvester Tuttle.	Rev. Alex. Mann, D.D.	Bishop Daniel S. Tuttle.
46	Oct. 8—Oct. 24, 1919	Detroit.	Bp. Daniel Sylvester Tuttle.	Rev. Alex. Mann, D.D.	Bishop Charles H. Brent.
47	Sept. 6—Sept. 23, 1922	Portland, Oreg.	Bp. Daniel Sylvester Tuttle.	Rev. Alex. Mann, D.D.	Bishop Edwin S. Lines.
48	Oct. 7—Oct. 24, 1925	New Orleans, La.	Bp. Ethelbert Talbot.	Rev. Ernest M. Stires, D.D.	Bishop Theo. DuB. Bratton.[10]
49	Oct. 10—Oct. 25, 1928	Washington, D.C.	Bp. John Gardner Murray.	Rev. ZeB. Phillips, D.D.	Bishop Charles P. Anderson.
50	Sept. 16—Sept. 30, 1931	Denver, Colo.	Bp. James DeWolf Perry.	Rev. ZeB. Phillips, D.D.	Bishop Purse of St. Albans.
51	Oct. 10—Oct. 23, 1934	Atlantic City, N.J.	Bp. James DeWolf Perry.	Rev. ZeB. Phillips, D.D.	Bishop James DeWolf Perry.
52	Oct. 6—Oct. 19, 1937	Cincinnati.	Bp. James DeWolf Perry.	Rev. ZeB. Phillips, D.D.	Bishop Edward L. Parsons.
53	Oct. 9—Oct. 19, 1940	Kansas City, Mo.	Bp. Henry St. George Tucker.	Rev. ZeB. Phillips, D.D.	Bishop H. St. George Tucker.
54	Oct. 2—Oct. 11, 1943	Cleveland.	Bp. Henry St. George Tucker.	Rev. Phillips E. Osgood, D.D.	Bishop H. St. George Tucker.
55	Sept. 10—Sept. 20, 1946	Philadelphia.	Bp. Henry St. George Tucker.	Hon. Owen J. Roberts.	Bishop Henry Knox Sherrill.
56	Sept. 26—Oct. 7, 1949	San Francisco.	Bp. Henry Knox Sherrill.	V.Rev. Claude W. Sprouse, D.D.	Bishop Henry Knox Sherrill.
57	Sept. 8—Sept. 19, 1952	Boston.	Bp. Henry Knox Sherrill.	V.Rev. C. W. Sprouse, D.D.[11]	Bishop Henry Knox Sherrill.
				Rev. T. O. Wedel, Ph.D.	
58	Sept. 4—Sept. 15, 1955	Honolulu, T.H.	Bp. Henry Knox Sherrill.	Rev. Theodore O. Wedel, Ph.D.	Bishop Henry Knox Sherrill.
59	Oct. 5—Oct. 17, 1958	Miami Beach, Fla.	Bp. Henry Knox Sherrill.	Rev. Theodore O. Wedel, Ph.D.	Bishop Henry Knox Sherrill.
60	Sept. 17—Sept. 29, 1961	Detroit, Mich.	Bp. Arthur Lichtenberger.	Clifford P. Morehouse, LL.D.	Bishop Arthur Lichtenberger.[12]
61	Oct. 11—Oct. 23, 1964	St. Louis, Mo.	Bp. Arthur Lichtenberger.	Clifford P. Morehouse, LL.D.	Bishop John Elbridge Hines.
62	Sept. 17—Sept. 27, 1967	Seattle, Wash.	Bp. John Elbridge Hines.	Clifford P. Morehouse, LL.D.	Bishop John Elbridge Hines.
11	Aug. 31—Sept. 5, 1969	South Bend, In.	Bp. John Elbridge Hines.	V. Rev. John B. Coburn.	Bishop John Elbridge Hines.
63	Oct. 11—Oct. 22, 1970	Houston, Tx.	Bp. John Elbridge Hines.	V. Rev. John B. Coburn.	Bishop John Elbridge Hines.
64	Sept. 26—Oct. 22, 1973	Louisville, Ky.	Bp. John Maury Allin.	V. Rev. John B. Coburn.	Bishop John Maury Allin.
65	Sept. 11—Sept. 22, 1976	Minneapolis, Mn.	Bp. John Maury Allin.	V. Rev. John B. Coburn.	Bishop John Maury Allin.
66	Sept. 8—Sept. 20, 1979	Denver, Co.	Bp. John Maury Allin.	Charles R. Lawrence, Ph.D.	Bishop John Maury Allin.
67	Sept. 5—Sept. 15, 1982	New Orleans, LA	Bp. John Maury Allin.	Charles R. Lawrence, Ph.D.	Bishop John Maury Allin.
68	Sept. 7—Sept. 14, 1985	Anaheim, CA	Bp. Edmond Lee Browning.	Charles R. Lawrence, Ph.D.	Archbishop Robert A. K. Runcie.
69	July 2—July 11, 1988	Detroit, MI	Bp. Edmond Lee Browning.	V. Rev. David B. Collins.	Bishop Edmond Lee Browning.
70	July 11—July 20, 1991	Phoenix, AZ	Bp. Edmond Lee Browning.	V. Rev. David B. Collins.	Bishop Edmond Lee Browning.
71	Aug. 24—Sept. 2, 1994	Indianapolis, IN	Bp. Edmond Lee Browning.	Pamela P. Chinnis.	Pamela P. Chinnis.
72	July 16—July 25, 1997	Philadelphia, PA	Bp. Frank T Griswold	Pamela P. Chinnis.	Archbishop George Leonard Carey.
73	July 5—July 14, 2000	Denver, CO	Bp. Frank T Griswold	Pamela P. Chinnis.	Bishop Simon Elija Chiwanga.
74	July 30—Aug. 8, 2003	Minneapolis, MN	Bp. Frank T Griswold	V. Rev. George L. W. Werner.	Archbishop Josiah Idowu-Fearon.
75	June 13—June 21, 2006	Columbus, OH	Bp. Katharine Jefferts Schori.	V. Rev. George L. W. Werner.	Dr. Jenny Te Paa.
76	July 8—July 17, 2009	Anaheim, CA	Bp. Katharine Jefferts Schori.	Bonnie Anderson.	Bishop Katharine Jefferts Schori.
77	July 5—July 12, 2012	Indianapolis, IN	Bp. Katharine Jefferts Schori.	Bonnie Anderson.	Bishop Katharine Jefferts Schori.
78	June 25—July 13, 2015	Salt Lake City, Utah	Bp. Katharine Jefferts Schori.	Rev. Gay Clark Jennings.	Bishop Katharine Jefferts Schori.
79	July 2018	Austin, Texas	Bp. Michael B. Curry.	Rev. Gay Clark Jennings.	

1) From 1785 through the first session of 1789 the General Convention was a single house and Bishop White was president of the Convention at its first session. 2) Absent because of advanced years; Bishop William Meade presided. 3) The First Preliminary meeting of dioceses of the Confederate States was called unofficially. For the Second Preliminary meeting, all dioceses in the Confederate States were officially called by the members of the withdrawn First Preliminary meeting. In those two meetings there was no official Presiding Bishop, but the oldest bishop in point of consecration, who was present, presided. The dioceses involved had not at that time officially withdrawn from The Protestant Episcopal Church in the United States of America, although in practice they had done so. There was no officially appointed Presiding Bishop until the first meeting of the General Council of The Protestant Episcopal Church in the Confederate States of America. 4) Absent because of advanced years; Bishop John Henry Hopkins presided. 5) First General Council of The Protestant Episcopal Church in the Confederate States of America. 6) Second General Council of The Protestant Episcopal Church in the Confederate States of America. 7) Because of Bishop Smith's advanced years, Bishop Alfred Lee presided and signed the minutes. 8) Absent because of illness; Bishop Wm. C. Doane was Chairman of the House of Bishops and signed the minutes. 9) Absent because of illness; Bishop Thomas U. Dudley of Kentucky was Chairman of the House of Bishops and signed the minutes. 10) Read by Bishop T. F. Gailor because of Bishop Bratton's illness. 11) Died during first day's session. 12) Read by Bishop Ned Cole, at the request of Bishop Lichtenberger.

THE CANONICAL STRUCTURE OF THE CHURCH

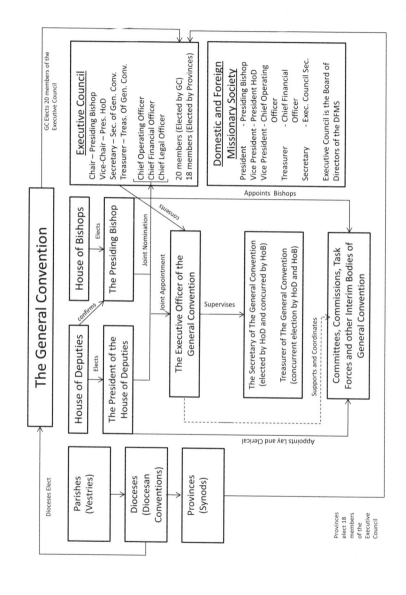

The information listed in this section was generously provided by the Office of the General Convention of The Episcopal Church.

The General Convention of The Episcopal Church
ELECTED OFFICERS OF THE GENERAL CONVENTION

The Most Rev. Michael Curry, *Presiding Bishop and Primate*; The Rev. Gay Clark Jennings, *President of the House of Deputies*; The Rev. Canon Dr. Michael Barlowe, *Secretary of the General Convention*; Mr. N. Kurt Barnes, *Treasurer*.

The Most Rev. Michael Curry
Presiding Bishop and Primate

The Rev. Gay Clark Jennings
President of the House of Deputies

THE EPISCOPAL CHURCH CENTER

815 Second Ave, New York, NY 10017 (800) 334-7626 *Web:* www.episcopalchurch.org Staff members may be reached via e-mail using their first initial with their last name (Ex: jdoe@episcopalchurch.org).

EXECUTIVE OFFICE OF THE GENERAL CONVENTION

(800) 334-7626 *Fax:* (212) 972-9322 *Web:* www.generalconvention.org

Rev Cn Dr Michael Barlowe, *Executive Officer of the General Convention*; Rev Cn Dr Michael Barlowe, *Secretary of the General Convention*; Ms Lori M Ionnitiu, *General Convention Manager*; The Rt. Rev. Mary Gray-Reeves, *Vice-Chair, House of Bishops*; Rt Rev Dean Elliot Wolfe, *Vice-Chair, House of Bishops*; Hon Byron Rushing, *Vice President, House of Deputies*; Mr N Kurt Barnes, *Treasurer*; Rev Cn Charles K Robertson, PhD, *Registrar*; Rev Cn Gregory Howe, *Custodian, Standard Book of Common Prayer*; Mark J Duffy, *Canonical Archivist and Director of Archives, Board of the Archives of The Episcopal Church, PO Box 2247, Austin, Texas 78768 (800) 525-9329*; The Church Pension Fund, *Recorder of Ordinations, 445 Fifth Ave, New York, New York 10016 (800) 223-6602 x884*; Dr Robert Bruce Mullin, *Historiographer*; Ms Betsey Bell, *Assistant to the President of the House of Deputies*; Ms Marian Conboy, *Executive Assistant and Deputy for Legislation*; Ms Cheryl J Dawkins, *Staff Assistant for Administration*; Mr Brian Murray, *Staff Assistant for Meetings*; Mr Patrick J Haizel, *Manager for Finance and Meetings*; Dr Kirk Hadaway, *Officer, Congregational Research*; Ms Iris J Martinez, *Administrative Assistant*.

THE GENERAL CONVENTION

The 79th General Convention will be held July 2018 in Austin, TX.

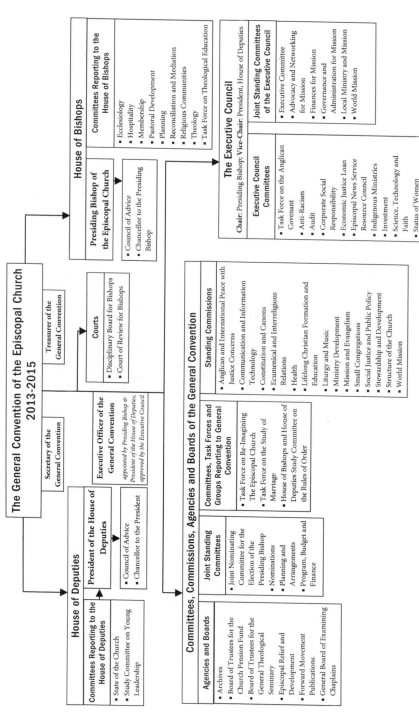

The General Convention of the Episcopal Church 2013-2015

Secretary of the General Convention

Treasurer of the General Convention

Executive Officer of the General Convention
appointed by Presiding Bishop & President of the House of Deputies, approved by the Executive Council

House of Deputies

President of the House of Deputies
- Council of Advice
- Chancellor to the President

Committees Reporting to the House of Deputies
- State of the Church
- Study Committee on Young Leadership

Courts
- Disciplinary Board for Bishops
- Court of Review for Bishops

House of Bishops

Presiding Bishop of the Episcopal Church
- Council of Advice
- Chancellor to the Presiding Bishop

Committees Reporting to the House of Bishops
- Ecclesiology
- Hospitality
- Membership
- Pastoral Development
- Planning
- Reconciliation and Mediation
- Religious Communities
- Theology
- Task Force on Theological Education

The Executive Council
Chair: Presiding Bishop; Vice-Chair: President, House of Deputies

Executive Council Committees
- Task Force on the Anglican Covenant
- Anti-Racism
- Audit
- Corporate Social Responsibility
- Economic Justice Loan
- Episcopal News Service Resource Council
- Indigenous Ministries
- Investment
- Science, Technology and Faith
- Status of Women

Joint Standing Committees of the Executive Council
- Executive Committee
- Advocacy and Networking for Mission
- Finances for Mission
- Governance and Administration for Mission
- Local Ministry and Mission
- World Mission

Committees, Commissions, Agencies and Boards of the General Convention

Agencies and Boards
- Archives
- Board of Trustees for the Church Pension Fund
- Board of Trustees for the General Theological Seminary
- Episcopal Relief and Development
- Forward Movement Publications
- General Board of Examining Chaplains

Joint Standing Committees
- Joint Nominating Committee for the Election of the Presiding Bishop
- Nominations
- Planning and Arrangements
- Program, Budget and Finance

Committees, Task Forces and Groups Reporting to General Convention
- Task Force on Re-Imagining The Episcopal Church
- Task Force on the Study of Marriage
- House of Bishops and House of Deputies Study Committee on the Rules of Order

Standing Commissions
- Anglican and International Peace with Justice Concerns
- Communication and Information Technology
- Constitution and Canons
- Ecumenical and Interreligious Relations
- Health
- Lifelong Christian Formation and Education
- Liturgy and Music
- Ministry Development
- Mission and Evangelism
- Small Congregations
- Social Justice and Public Policy
- Stewardship and Development
- Structure of the Church
- World Mission

THE HOUSE OF BISHOPS

Chair: **Curry,** Most Rev Michael; *Vice- Chair:* **Gray-Reeves,** Rt Rev Mary; *Vice-Chair:* **Wolfe,** Rt Rev Dean; *Secretary:* **Bruce,** Rt Rev Diane M. Jardine; *Chancellor to the PB:* **Vacant**

Committees of the House of Bishops

Advisory Council to the Presiding Bishop

(All terms 2018) **Curry,** Most Rev Michael *Chair); Province I:* **Lane,** Rt Rev Stephen; *Province II:* **Provenzano,** Rt Rev Lawrence; *Province III:* **Klusmeyer,** Rt Rev William; *Province IV:* **Johnson,** Rt Rev Don; *Province V:* **Breidenthal,** Rt Rev Thomas; *Province VI:* **Prior,** Brian; *Province VII:* **Konieczny,** Rt Rev Edward; *Province VIII:* **Mathes,** Rt Rev James; *Province IX:* **Holguin,** Rt Rev Julio; *Staff:* **Baerga,** Ms Ednice 815 2nd Ave New York New York 10017-4594.

House of Bishops Committee on Ecclesiology

(All terms 2015) **Buchanan,** Rt Rev John C; **Gregg,** Rt Rev William O; **Whalon,** Rt Rev Pierre Welte.

House of Bishops Committee on Hospitality

(All terms 2015) **Benhase,** Rt Rev Scott; **Guerrero,** Rt Rev Orlando; **Hollingsworth** Jr, Rt Rev Mark.

House of Bishops Committee on Membership

(All terms 2015) **Ahrens,** Rt Rev Laura J; **Little,** Rt Rev Edward S; **Rivera,** Rt Rev Bavi E; **Smith,** Rt Rev Dabney T; **Waldo,** Rt Rev W Andrew.

House of Bishops Committee on Pastoral Development

To be named

House of Bishops Planning Committee

To be named

House of Bishops Committee on Reconciliation and Mediation

(All terms 2015) **Gray-Reeves,** Rt Rev Mary; **Little** II, Rt Rev Edward S; **Milliken,** Rt Rev Michael P.

House of Bishops Committee on Religious Communities

(All terms 2015) **Jacobus,** Rt Rev Russell E *(Chair);* **Garrison,** Rt Rev J Michael; **Lee,** Rt Rev Jeffrey D; **Love,** Rt Rev William H; **Rivera,** Rt Rev Bavi E; **Williams** Jr, Rt Rev Arthur B; *Ex-Officio:* **Jefferts Schori;** Most Rev Katharine.

House of Bishops Theology Committee

(All terms 2016) **Burnett,** Rt Rev Joe *(Chair);*

Bauerschmidt, Rt Rev John C; **Benfield,** Rt Rev Larry R; **Breidenthal,** Rt Rev Thomas E; **Fisher,** Rt Rev Douglas; **Smith,** Rt Rev George Wayne; **Taylor,** Rt Rev G Porter; **Vono,** Rt Rev Michael L; **Whalon,** Rt Rev Pierre Welte

House of Bishops Task Force on Theological Education

(All terms 2015) **Alexander,** Rt Rev Neil J; **Doyle,** Rt Rev C Andrew; **Shand,** Rt Rev James J; **Smith,** Rt Rev Michael G.

THE HOUSE OF DEPUTIES

President: **Jennings,** Rev Gay Clark; *Vice-President:* **Rushing,** Hon Byron; *Secretary:* **Barlowe,** Rev Cn Dr Michael

Committees of the House of Deputies

Advisory Council to the President of the House of Deputies

Jennings, Rev Gay Clark *(Chair);* **Barlowe,** Rev Cn Dr Michael; **Glass,** Esq, Michael; **Johnson,** Esq, Sally A; **Krislock,** Esq, Bryan; **Little,** Esq, Thomas A; **O'Brien III,** Thomas G; **Rowe,** Rt Rev Sean W; **Rushing,** Hon Byron; **Smith,** Mr Steve; **Varghese,** Rev Winnie S; *Staff:* **Bell,** Ms Betsey; **Joseph,** Mr Bill; **Naughton,** Mr Jim; **Wilson,** Ms Rebecca.

House of Deputies Committee on the State of the Church

(All Terms 2018) **Varghese,** Rev Winnie *(Chair);* **Medina,** Rev Ernesto *(Vice Chair);* **Lawton,** Ms Sarah *(Secretary);* **Commins,** Rev Gary; **Fonder,** Rev Kim; **Garner,** Rev Evan; **Gould,** Rev Jane; **Graham,** Mr Roger; **Linares,** Rev Ivette; **Metoyer,** Rev Eric; **Moore,** Mr Gary; **O'Sullivan-Hale,** Mr Brendan; **Packard,** Mr Daniel; **Russell,** Ms. Laura; **Strohl,** Rev Patrick; **Weaver,** Ms. Bonnie; *Staff* **Hadaway,** Dr Kirk; *Ex Officio:* **Jennings,** Rev Gay Clark

JOINT COMMITTEE

House of Bishops and House of Deputies Study Committee on Rules of Order

(All Terms 2015) **Barlowe,** Rev Cn Dr Michael *(Chair);* **Krislock,** Esq, Bryan *(Vice Chair);* **Rowe,** Rt Rev Sean *(Vice Chair);* **Beers,** Esq, David Booth; **Bruce,** Rt Rev Diane M Jardine; **Daniel;** Rt Rev Clifton; **Johnson,** Esq, Sally A; **Little,** Esq, Thomas A; **Rushing,** Hon Byron; **Simons,** Rev Dr James; **Wolfe,** Rt Rev Dean E; **Wright,** Rt Rev Wayne; *Ex-Officio:* **Jefferts Schori,** Most Rev Katharine; **Jennings,** Rev Gay C; *Staff:* **Bell,** Ms Betsy.

THE COURTS

Court of Review for Bishops

Barker, Rt Rev J Scott *(2021)*; **Brookhart,** Rt Rev C Franklin *(2018)*; **Glasspool,** Rt Rev Mary *(2021)*; **Gray-Reeves,** Rt Rev Mary *(2018)*; **Howard,** Rt Rev S Johnson *(2018)*; **Milliken,** Rt Rev Michael *(2021)*.

Disciplinary Board for Bishops

Waynick, Rt Rev Catherine *(2021, Chair)*; **Alarid,** Mr Joseph; **Douglas,** Rt Rev Ian; **Fleener, Jr,** Mr William; **Harrison,** Rt Rev Dena; **Henderson, Jr,** Rt Rev Dorsey; **Holding,** Rev Cn Suzann; **Hollerith,** Rt Rev Herman; **Knisely,** Rt Rev W Nicholas; **Larsen,** Rev Erik; **Mayer,** Rt Rev J Scott; **O'Neill,** Rt Rev Robert; **Shepherd,** Rev Dr Angela; **Singh,** Rt Rev Prince; **Smith,** Mr Marcellus; **Stokes,** Ms Deborah; **Tuttle,** Rev Peggy.

EXECUTIVE COUNCIL

Curry, Most Rev Michael *(PB & Primate, Chair)*; **Jennings,** Rev Gay Clark *(Vice-Chair)*; *Elected until GC 2018: VIII:* **Bailey,** Rt Rev David E; *III:* **Daniel** III, DD, Rt Rev Clift on; *IV:* **Ferrell,** Mr Joseph S; **George,** Dr Anita P; *III:* **Johnson** IV, Mr John B; *VIII:* **Koonce,** Ms Nancy; *VII:* **Longenecker,** Ms Karen Ann; *III:* **Simons,** Rev Dr James B; **Snook,** Rev Susan B; *I:* **Thompsett,** Dr Fredrica Harris; *Elected by Province until 2018: I:* **Wallace,** Rev Cn Tanya A; *II:* **Gandell,** Rev Dahn; *III:* **Pierce,** Rev Nathaniel; *IV:* **Judge,** Ms Tess; *V:* **Luckey,** Rev Marion; *VI:* **Floberg,** Rev Cn John F; *VII:* **Runnels,** Rev Dr R Stan; *VIII:* **Baker,** Very Rev Brian; *IX:* **Jimenez de Salazar,** Mrs Pragedes Coromoto; *Elected until GC 2021: IV:* **Ballentine,** Rev Jabriel Simmonds; *VII:* **Butler,** Ms. Diane; *VII:* **Harris,** Ms Julia Ayala; *VIII:* **Glosson,** Mr Louis; *IX:* **Gonzales Polanco,** Ms Mayra Liseth; *VII:* **Konieczny,** Rt Rev Edward; *I:* **Lloyd,** Rev Mally Ewing; *VIII:* **Nishibayashi,** Cn Dr Steven; *IV:* **Powell,** Ms Holli; *IV:* **Smith,** Rt Rev Dabney; *Elected by Province until 2021: I:* **Link,** Ms. Alexizendria; *II:* **Duncan,** Ms. Noreen; *III:* **Randle,** Mr Russell; *IV:* **Logue,** Rev Frank; *V:* **Cisluycis,** Ms Jane; *VI:* **Wing,** Mr George; *VII:* **Alexander,** Mr Thomas; *VIII:* **Wong,** Mr. Warren; *IX:* **Allen,** Rt Rev Lloyd; *Seat and Voice:* **Barlowe,** Rev Cn Dr Michael *(Secretary)*; **Barnes,** Mr N Kurt *(Treasurer)*; **Rushing,** Hon Byron (VP, HOD); **Sauls,** Rt Rev Stacy F *(COO & VP, DFMS)*; *Chancellors:* **Beers,** Esq, David Booth *(to PB)*; **Johnson,** Esq, Sally A *(to PHOD)*; *Liaisons:* **Wall,** Very Rev Peter *(ACC)*; **Herr,** Rev Stephen *(ELCA)*; *Staff:* **Conboy,** Ms Marian.

STANDING COMMITTEES OF THE EXECUTIVE COUNCIL

Executive Council Executive Committee

(All terms 2018) **Curry,** Most Rev Michael *(Chair)*;

Jennings, Rev Gay Clark *(Vice- Chair)*; **Brown Snool,** Rev Susan; **George,** Dr Anita; **Judge,** Ms Tess; **Konieczny,** Rt Rev Edward; **Longnecker,** Ms Karen; **Thompsett,** Dr Fredrica; **Wong,** Hon Warren; *Ex-Officio:* **Barlowe,** Rev Cn Dr Michael; **Barnes,** Mr N Kurt; *Staff:* **Conboy,** Ms Marian.

Joint Standing Committee on Advocacy and Networking for Mission

(All terms 2018) **George,** Dr Anita *(Chair)*; **Harris,** Ms Julia Ayala *(Vice-Chair)*; **Runnels,** Rev Dr R Stan *(Secretary)*; **Baily,** Rt Rev David; **Ballentine,** Rev Jabriel; **Gonzales Polanco,** Ms Mayra Liseth; **Johnson IV,** Mr John; **Nishibayashi,** Cn Dr Steven; *Ex Officio:* **Curry,** Most Rev Michael; **Jennings,** Rev Gay C.

Joint Standing Committee on Finances for Mission

(All terms 2018) **Judge,** Ms Tess *(Chair)*; **Koonce,** Ms Nancy *(Vice-Chair)*; **Powell,** Ms. Holli *(Secretary)*; **Daniel,** Rt Rev Clifton; **Floberg,** Rev Cn John; **Link,** Ms Alexizendria; **Lloyd,** Rev Mally Ewing; *Ex Officio:* **Curry,** Most Rev Michael; **Jennings,** Rev Gay C; *Staff:* **Barlowe,** Rev Cn Dr Michael; **Barnes,** Mr N Kurt; **Brockway,** Ms JoAnn; **Caparulo,** Ms Nancy; **Crosnier de Bellaistre,** Ms Margareth; **Haizel,** Mr Patrick; **Nix,** Mr Paul; **Sauls,** Rt Rev Stacy F.

Joint Standing Committee on Governance and Administration for Mission

(All terms 2018) **Thompsett,** Dr Fredrica *(Chair)*; **Randle,** Mr Russell *(Vice-Chair)*; **Ferrell,** Mr Joseph *(Secretary)*; **Butler,** Ms. Diane; **Cisluycis,** Ms Jane; **Glosson,** Mr Louis; **Konieczny,** Rt Rev Edward; *Ex Officio:* **Curry,** Most Rev Michael; **Jennings,** Rev Gay C.

Joint Standing Committee on Local Ministry and Mission

(All terms 2018) **Brown Snook,** Rev Susan *(Chair)*; **Logue,** Rev Cn Frank *(Vice-Chair)*; **Wing,** Mr George *(Secretary)*; **Alexander,** Mr Thomas; **Baker,** Vy Rev Dr Brian; **Gandell,** Rev Dahn; **Smith,** Rt Rev Dabney; **Wallace,** Rev Cn Tanya; *Ex Officio:* **Curry,** Most Rev Michael; **Jennings,** Rev Gay C; *Staff:* **Skov,** Mrs Bronwyn; *ELCA Liaison:* **Herr,** Rev Stephen.

Joint Standing Committee on World Mission

(All terms 2018) **Longenecker,** Ms. Karen *(Chair)*; **Jimenez de Salazar,** Sra Pragedes Coromoto *(Vice-Chair)*; **Duncan,** Cn Noreen *(Secretary)*; **Allen,** Rt Rev Lloyd; **Luckey,** Rev Marion; **Pierce,** Rev Nathaniel; **Simons,** Rev Dr James; *Ex Officio:* **Curry,** Most Rev Michael; **Jennings,** Rev Gay C; *Staff:* **Copley,** Rev David; *Liaison from Anglican Church of Canada:* **Wall,** Vy Rev Peter.

COMMITTEES OF COUNCIL

Joint Audit Committee of the Executive Council and the DFMS

(All terms 2018) **Krislock**, Mr Bryan *(Chair)*; **Fisher**, Rt Rev Jeff; **Glover**, Dr Delbert; **Haas**, Mr G William; **Koonce**, Ms Nancy; **Racusin**, Rev Michele; *Ex Officio:* **Curry**, Most Rev; **Jennings**, Rev Gay C.

Investment Committee of the Executive Council

(All terms 2018) **Kerr**, Mr Michael *(Chair)*; **Alvarez-Roldan**, Mr David Lorenzo; **Barnes**, Mr N Kurt; **Frith Moore**, Ms Dena; **Michel**, Rt Rev Rodney; **Partridge**, Mr Benjamin Waring; **Porter**, Ms Maibeth; **Radcliff**, Mr Ronald; **Thomas**, Mr Owen.

Executive Council Committee on Anti-Racism

(All terms 2018) **James**, Dr Navita *(Chair)*; **Nawrocki**, Rev Cindy *(Vice-Chair)*; **Steagall**, Rev Patricia *(Secretary)*; **Burns**, Ms. Carla; **Lee**, Ms Lelanda; **Martin Fumero**, The Rev Emilio; **McKim**, Mr James; **Mutope-Johnson**, Ms Ayesha; **Shepherd**, Rev Dr Angela; **Singh**, Rt Rev Prince; *Ex Officio:* **Curry**, Most Rev Michael; **Jennings**, Rev Gay C; **Ballentine**, *Liaison of Executive Council:* Rev Jabriel; *Staff:* **Kim**, Ms Heidi

Executive Council Committee on Corporate Social Responsibility

(All terms 2015) **Byham**, Mr Edgar K *(Chair)*; **Cullinane**, Rev Cn Kathleen J; **Danford**, Rev N Chase; **McKeown**, Mr William B; **Sanborn**, Ms Anita; **Webb**, Rev Benjamin; **Williams**, Rev Dr Monrelle; **Wright**, Rt Rev Robert C; *Ex-Officio:* **Jefferts Schori**, Most Rev Katharine; **Jennings**, Rev Gay Clark; *EC Liaison:* **Quiñones**, Mr Francisco; *Staff:* **Barnes**, Mr N Kurt; **Baumgarten**, Mr Alexander D; **Caparulo**, Mrs Nancy; **Crosnier de Bellaistre**, Ms Margareth; *Consultants:* **Neuhauser**, Mr Paul M; **van Buren**, Dr Ariane; *Other:* **Kerr**, Mr Michael John; **Lamb**, Mr William; **Sanborn**, Ms Nancy; **Yoon**, Ms Lisa.

Executive Council Economic Justice Loan Committee

(All terms 2015) **Parker**, Ms Lindsey W *(Chair)*; **Gould**, Rev Jane S; **Jacobs**, Rev Cn Gregory A; **McKeown**, Mr William B; **Sutton**, Rt Rev Eugene T; **Wong**, Mr Warren J; *Ex-Officio:* **Jefferts Schori**, Most Rev Katharine; **Jennings**, Rev Gay Clark; *Staff:* **Barnes**, Mr N Kurt; **Baumgarten**, Mr Alexander D; **Caparulo**, Mrs Nancy; **Crosnier de Bellaistre**, Ms Margareth; **Gonzalez**, Mr Jose; *ELCA Liaison:* **Johnson** IV, Mr John B; *Other:* **Lipson**, Ms Beth; **Odland**, Mr Robin; **Sullivan**, Mr T Dennis.

Episcopal News Service Resource Council

(All terms 2015) **Richardson**, Rev James *(Convener)*; **Dagher**, Ms Veronica; **Giraldo**, Rev

Edgar; **Ross**, Ms Nan; **Sears**, Mr Mitch; **Skipper**, Cn Jere; **Stokes**, Ms Beckett; **Wirth**, Mr Craig; *Ex Officio:* **Jefferts Schori**, Most Rev Katharine; **Jennings**, Rev Gay Clark; *Staff:* **Davies**, Mr Matthew; **Rudig**, Ms Anne; **Schjonberg**, Rev Mary Frances; **Wilson**, Ms Lynette.

Executive Council Committee on Indigenous Ministries

(All terms 2015) **Bostock**, Ms Jasmine *(Chair)*; **Smith**, Rt Rev Michael G *(Vice-Chair)*; **Crist**, Rev Dr Mary *(Secretary)*; **Ackley**, Mr Richard; **Bailey**, Rt Rev David E; **Frank**, Rev Cn Anna; **Goodhouse**, Ms Carmine C; **Hardy-Constant**, Mrs LaCinda; **Lattime**, Rt Rev Mark; **Oberly**, Mr Frank L; **Quito**, Rev Eulogio; **Standing Bear**, Ms Wilma; **Tarrant**, Rt Rev John; *Ex-Officio:* **Jefferts Schori**, Most Rev Katharine; **Jennings**, Rev Gay Clark; *EC Liaison:* **Floberg**, Rev Cn John F; *Staff:* **Eagle Heart**, Ms Sarah.

Executive Council Committee on Science, Technology and Faith

(All terms 2015) **So**, Rev Alistair *(Chair)*; **Day**, Mr H Talmage; **Evelyn**, Mr Shawn; **Fortuna**, Rev Dr Lisa R; **Johnson**, Rev Stephanie; **Knisely**, Rt Rev W Nicholas; **Manzella**, Rev Evelyn; **Rawls**, Rev Meredith; **Sisk**, Rt Rev Mark S; **Sisson**, Dr Edward B; **Trainor**, Rev Dr R James; **Wolyniak**, Mr Joseph; *Ex-Officio:* **Jefferts Schori**, Most Rev Katharine; **Jennings**, Rev Gay Clark; *EC Liaison:* **Sherrod**, Ms Katie; *Staff:* **Serota**, Mr Richard.

Executive Council Committee on the Status of Women

(All terms 2015) **Nesbit**, Rev Dr Paula *(Chair)*; **Person**, Rev K Jeanne *(Vice-Chair)*; **Goff**, Rt Rev Susan; **Gray-Reeves**, Rt Rev Mary; **Mann**, Ms Barbara G; **Murray**, Mr Alan; **Peters**, Rev Yejide; **Phelan**, Rev Dr Shane; **Rosero-Nordalm**, Rev Dcn Ema; **Shimpfky**, Ms Jamel; *Ex-Officio:* **Jefferts Schori**, Most Rev Katharine; **Jennings**, Rev Gay Clark; *EC Liaison:* **Gandell**, Rev Dahn; *Staff:* **Main**, Ms Lynnaia.

JOINT STANDING COMMITTEES

Joint Nominating Committee for the Election of the Presiding Bishop

(All terms 2018) *I:* **Ahrens**, Rt Rev Laura; **Ambrogi**, Ms Sarah; **Sanborn**, Rev Calvin; *II:* **Franklin**, Rt Rev R William; **Sconiers**, Hon Rose H; **Wilson**, Rev Cn Sandye A; *III:* **Budde**, Rt Rev Mariann; **Kitch**, Rev Cn Anne; **Klip**, Mr David; *IV:* **Johnson**, Rev Cn David; **Kistler**, Ms Matilda O; **White**, Rt Rev Terry; *V:* **Byrd, Sr**, Rev Ronald C; **Chapman**, Ms Pam; **Lee**, Rt Rev Jeffrey; *VI:* **Johnson**, Rev Christopher A; **Scarfe**, Rt Rev Alan; **Two Bulls**, Ms. Twilla; *VII:* **Bailey**, Ms Catherine; **George**, Rev Dr Mitzi

Milliken, Rt Rev Michael; *VIII*: **Brannon**, Rev Kenneth; **Diehl**, Mr Jeff; **Thom**, Rt Rev Brian; *IX:* **Christian Reynoso**, Sra Grecia; **Leon Lozano**, Rev Cn Cristobal; **Ramos-Orench**, Rt Rev Wilfrido.

Joint Standing Committee on Nominations

(*All terms 2018*) **Hart**, Mr Christopher (*Chair*); **Glasspool**, Rt Rev Mary (*Vice-Chair*); **Two Bulls**, Ms Twilla *(Secretary)*; **Bartol**, Ms Cynthia; **Berger**, Rev Martha; **Cato**, Rev Brooks; **Dunlap**, Ms Janice L; **Harrison**, Rt Rev Dena; **Hayashi**, Rt Rev Scott; **Kusumoto**, Mr Ryan; **Marquez**, Rev Juan; **Miller**, Canon Richard; *Ex-Officio:* **Curry**, Most Rev Michael; **Jennings**, Rev Gay Clark.

Joint Standing Committee on Planning and Arrangements

(*All terms 2018*) **Barlowe**, Rev Cn Dr Michael; **Barnes**, Mr N Kurt; **Bruce**, Rt Rev Diane M Jardine; **Fisher**, Rt Rev Jeff; **Gray-Reeves**, Rt Rev Mary; **Guest**, Ms Linda; **Ionnitiu**, Ms Lori M; **Johnson**, Esq, Sally A; **Ortiz**, Ms. Halley; **Rushing**, Mr Byron; **Simons**, Rev Dr James B; **Simpson**, Vy Rev Ward; **Towle**, Ms Lisa; **Wolfe**, Rt Rev Dean E; **Wright**, Rt Rev Wayne P; *Ex-Officio:* **Curry**, Most Rev Michael; **Jennings**, Rev Gay Clark.

Joint Standing Committee on Program, Budget and Finance

(*All terms 2015*) **Lloyd**, Rev Cn Mally Ewing (*Chair*): **Lane**, Rt Rev Stephen T (*Vice-Chair*); **Sparks**, Rev Dr Douglas E (*Secretary*); **Adams** III, Rt Rev Gladstone Bailey; **Alvarez**, Rt Rev David; **Ballentine**, Cn Rosalie Simmonds; **Barker**, Rt Rev J Scott; **Cisluycis**, Ms Jane; **Downing**, Rev Patty; **Eaton**, Rev Cn Cornelia; **Ehmer**, Rev Cn J Michael; **Floberg**, Rev Cn John F; **Gould**, Mr Samuel J; **Heard**, Rev Cn Victoria R T; **Konieczny**, Rt Rev Dr Edward J; **Logue**, Rev Cn Frank S; **Mathes**, Rt Rev James R; **Miles**, Ms Barbara L; **Perfater**, Cn Charles H; **Quiñones**, Mr Francisco; **Quittmeyer**, Mr David R; **Racusin**, Rev Michele Ann; **Ray**, Rt Rev Rayford; **Salazar**, Rev Cn Jose Francisco; **Shand**, Rt Rev James J; **Spencer**, Mr Michael P; **White**, Rt Rev Terry A; *Secretary of GC:* **Barlowe**, Cn Dr Michael; *Ex-Officio:* **Jefferts Schori**, Most Rev Katharine; **Jennings**, Rev Gay Clark; *Rep, PHOD:* **Smith**, Mr Steve; *Treasurer:* **Barnes**, N Kurt; *Staff:* **Brockway**, Ms JoAnne; **Caparulo**, Ms Nancy; **Crosnier de Bellaistre**, Ms Margareth; **Haizel**, Mr Patrick; *Other:* **Snook**, Rev Susan B; **Hollingsworth** Jr, Rt Rev Mark.

STANDING COMMISSIONS

Standing Commission on Anglican and International Peace with Justice Concerns

Hamilton, LCSW, Ms Brenda (*2015 Chair*); **Magness**, Rt Rev James B (*2018 Vice-Chair*); **Anderson**, Rev Devon (*2015*); **Duque**, Rt Rev

Francisco (*2015*); **Frade**, Rt Rev Leopold (*2015*); **Geiger** II, Mr T J (*2015*); **Ihiasota**, Rev Cn Dr Isaac I (*2015*); Kitagawa, Rev John E; **Mbuwayesango**, Dr Dora (*2018*); **Snow**, Ms D Rebecca (*2018*); **Vesely-Flad**, Mr Ethan (*2015*); **Wilson**, Ms Rebecca (*2018*); *Ex-Officio:* **Jefferts Schori**, Most Rev Katharine (*2015*); **Jennings**, Rey Gay Clark (*2015*); *Rep, PHOD:* **Richardson**, Rev Jon M (*2015*); *EC Liaison:* **Longenecker**, Ms Karen (*2015*); *Staff:* **Baumgarten**, Mr Alexander D.

Standing Commission on Communication and Information Technology

Woerman, Ms Melodie (*2015 Chair*); **Mauldin**, Ms Robyn (*2018 Vice-Chair*); **Behre**, Ms Holly (*2015 Secretary*); **Escobar**, Mr Miguel (*2018*); **Giraldo**, Rev Edgar (*2018*); **Joseph**, Mr Bill (*2018*); **Lightcap**, Rev Torey (*2015*); **Mackenzie**, Rev Lester V (*2015*); **Marray**, Rt Rev Santosh (*2018*); **Shott**, Cn Heidi (*2015*); **Smith**, Rt Rev Kirk Stevan (*2015*); *Ex-Officio:* **Jefferts Schori**, Most Rev Katharine (*2015*); **Jennings**, Rev Gay Clark (*2015*); *EC Liaison:* **Anderson**, Ms Elizabeth L (*2015*); *Staff:* **Rudig**, Mrs Anne.

Standing Commission on Constitution and Canons

Cathcart, Esq, William R (*2015 Chair*); **Simon**, Mr James S (*2018 Vice-Chair*); **Smith** Jr, Mr Marcellus L (*2015 Secretary*); **Ahrens**, Rt Rev Laura J (*2018*); **Brownridge**, Very Rev Walter B A (*2015*); **Castellan**, Rev Megan (*2018*); **Getz**, Esq, Pauline (*2018*); **Henderson** Jr, Rt Rev Dorsey F (*2015*); **Hollerith** IV, Rt Rev Herman (*2018*); **Wells**, Ms Kathleen (*2015*); **Wirth**, Rev Cn Bradley S (*2018*); *Ex-Officio:* **Jefferts Schori**, Most Rev Katharine (*2015*); **Jennings**, Rev Gay Clark (*2015*); *Rep, PHOD:* **Porpeglia**, Ms Dorothy-Jane (*2015*); *EC Liaison:* **Runnels**, Rev Dr R Stanley (*2015*); *Staff:* **Kostel**, Ms Mary.

Standing Commission on Ecumenical and Interreligious Relations

Duncan II, Rt Rev Philip M (*2015 Chair*); **Ring**, Elizabeth (*2018 Vice-Chair*); **Hall**, Mr Matthew J (*2015 Secretary*); ; **Brookhart** Jr, Rt Rev C Franklin (*2015*); **Diaz-Littauer**, Ms Carrie (*2015*); **Eaton**, Very Rev Peter (*2015*); **Freeman**, Mr T J (*2018*); **Hayashi**, Rt Rev Scott B (*2018*); **O'Donnell**, Hon Joanne (*2015*); **Smith**, Rev Steve (*2015*); **Vance** III, Mr Charles Edward (*2015*); **Zacharia**, Rev Manoj Mathew (*2018*); *Ex-Officio:* **Jefferts Schori**, Most Rev Katharine (*2015*); **Jennings**, Rev Gay Clark (*2015*); *Rep, PHOD:* **Medina**, Rev Ernesto R (*2015*); *EC Liaison:* **Cole**, Rev Brian L (*2015*); *EDEIO Liaison:* **Biegler**, Rev James; *Staff:* *Mammana, Mr Richard;* **Rose**, Rev Margaret R.

Standing Commission on Health

Andrus, Rt Rev Marc Handley (*2018 Chair*); **Scott**, Rev Marshall S (*2018 Vice-Chair*); **Baker**, Rev

Stannard (*2018 Secretary*); **Alvarez**, Rt Rev David (*2015*); **Brokenleg**, Mr Isaiah (*2015*); **Cardenas-Torres**, Rev Dcn Adrian (*2018*); **Davis**, Ms Mary Margaret (*2018*); **Embler**, Ms Elizabeth (*2018*); **Grant**, Ms Mimi (*2018*); **Kollin**, Rev Harriet (*2015*); **O'Dell**, Dr Molly L (*2018*); **Saloom**, Dr Salem G (*2018*); *Ex-Officio:* **Jefferts Schori**, Most Rev Katharine (*2015*); **Jennings**, Rev Gay Clark (*2015*); *Rep, PHOD:* **Hanen**, Rev Dr. Patricia (*2015*); *EC Liaison:* **Cheney**, Ms Stephanie T (*2015*); *Staff:* **Hafner**, Ms Jayce.

Standing Commission on Lifelong Christian Formation and Education

O'Brien III, Cn Thomas G (*2018 Vice-Chair*); **Hino**, Rev Moki (*2015 Secretary*); **Bailey**, Ms Laurie (*2015*); **Franklin**, Rt Rev R William (*2018*); **Garner**, Rev Evan D (*2018*); **McKellar**, Ms Andrea (*2015*); **Nishibayashi**, Ms Kathryn (*2018*); **Rabb**, Rt Rev John L (*2015*); **Rowe**, Mrs Carly (*2018*); **Svoboda-Barber**, Rev Helen C (*2015*); **Thompson** Jr, Rt Rev Morris K (*2018*); *Ex-Officio:* **Jefferts Schori**, Most Rev Katharine (*2015*); **Jennings**, Rev Gay Clark (*2015*); *Rep, PHOD:* **Frey**, Ms Ruth (*2015*); *EC Liaison:* **Stokes**, Ms Deborah (*2015*); *Staff:* **Skov**, Mrs Bronwyn.

Standing Commission on Liturgy and Music

Anderson, Rev Devon (*2021 Chair*); **Fluellen**, Dr Jay (*2021 Vice-Chair*); **Anderson**, Ms Liza (*2018 Secretary*); **Breidenthal**, Rt Rev Thomas (*2018*); **Burford**, Ms Martha (*2021*); **Carmona**, Rev Dr. Paul (*2018*); **Decatur**, Mr Christopher (*2018*); **Fromberg**, Rev Paul (*2021*); **Hernandez**, Ms Ana M (*2018*); **Johnston**, Rt Rev Shannon (*2021*); **Keane**, Mr Drew Nathaniel (*2018*); **Lee**, Rt Rev Jeffrey (*2021*); **McConnell**, Rt Rev Dorsey (*2018*); **Morrill**, Ms Beck (*2021*); **Nelson**, Ms Jessica (*2021*); **Olsen**, Dr Derek (*2018*); **Plank**, Dr Steven (*2021*); **Smith**, Rt Rev George Wayne (*2018*); **Turrell**, Rev Cn James (2021); **Wilson**, Rev Cn Sandye (*2018*); *Ex-Officio:* **Curry**, Most Rev Michael (*2018*); **Jennings**, Rev Gay Clark (*2018*); *Rep, PHOD:* **Burrows**, Rev Paul (*2018*); *Liaisons: EC:* **Alexander**, Mr Thomas (*2018*); *Custodian, BCP:* **Oliver**, Rev Dr Juan M C (*2018*).

Standing Commission on Ministry Development

Akao, Mr Keane JK (*2018 Chair*); **Thom**, Rt Rev Brian (*2015 Vice-Chair*); **Vanatta**, Ms Natalie (*2018 Secretary*); **Bautista Betances**, Rev Cn Simón (*2018*); **Glasspool**, Rt Rev Mary D (*2018*); **Hall**, Very Rev Gary R (*2015*); **Lytle**, Dr Julie (*2015*); **Mathis**, Cn Jill (*2015*); **Melnyk**, Ms Debby (*2018*); **Phillippi**, Mr Jay (*2015*); **Pompa**, Very Rev Anthony (*2018*); **Ray**, Rt Rev Rayford (*2015*); *Ex-Officio:* **Jefferts Schori**, Most Rev Katharine (*2015*); **Jennings**, Rev Gay Clark (*2015*); *Rep, PHOD:* **James**, PhD, Rev Molly F (*2015*); *EC Liaison:*

Thompsett, Dr Fredrica Harris (*2015*); *Staff:* **Collins**, Ms Ruth-Ann (*2015*); **Kelly**, Ms Shannon (*2015*).

Standing Commission on the Mission and Evangelism of The Episcopal Church

Royals, Rev Deborah (*2015 Chair*); **Stevenson**, Mrs Mary B (*2015 Vice-Chair*); **Alston**, Ms Kaileen (*2018 Secretary*); **Blauser**, Rev Dennis A (*2018*); **Doctor**, Rev Cn Virginia (*2015*); **Elfring-Roberts**, Ms Rebecca (*2018*); **Holguin**, Rt Rev Julio Cesar (*2015*); **Lee**, Rt Rev Jeffrey D (*2015*); **Smith**, Rt Rev Dabney T (*2018*); *Ex-Officio:* **Jefferts Schori**, Most Rev Katharine (*2015*); **Jennings**, Rev Gay Clark (*2015*); *Rep, PHOD:* **Velez-Rivera**, Rev Daniel (*2015*); *EC Liaison:* **Snook**, Rev Susan B (*2015*); *Staff:* **Brackett**, Rev Thomas.

Standing Commission for Small Congregations

Wing, Mr George (*2015 Chair*); **Harrigan**, Rev Cn Katherine GL (*2015 Vice-Chair*); **Moreland-Moyer**, Mrs Diana (*2015 Secretary*); **Cisluycis**, Ms Jane (*2018 Co-Secretary*); **D'Anieri**, Rev Margaret (*2015*); **Edwards**, Rt Rev Dan T (*2015*); **McGrath Green**, Rev Nancy Sargent (*2015*); **Owensby**, Rt Rev Jacob W (*2018*); **Smith**, Ms Cindy J (*2018*); **Smith**, Mr Jamal (*2018*); **Steadman**, Mr James R (*2018*); **Tarrant**, Rt Rev John (*2015*); *Ex-Officio:* **Jefferts Schori**, Most Rev Katharine (*2015*); **Jennings**, Rev Gay Clark (*2015*); *EC Liaison:* **Romero** Jr, Rev Silvestre E (*2015*); *Staff:* **Hadaway**, Dr C Kirk.

Standing Commission on Social Justice and Public Policy

Lawton, Ms Sarah E (*2015 Chair*); **Russell**, Ms Laura (*2015 Vice-Chair*); **Hahn**, Ms Athena (*2018 Secretary*); **Charles**, Rev Randolph C (*2015*); **Frazier**, Ms Caitlin (*2018*); **Gutierrez**, Rev Cn Daniel (*2018*); **Hanley**, Rt Rev Michael J (*2018*); **Scarfe**, Rt Rev Alan (*2015*); **Singh**, Rt Rev Prince G (*2015*); **Smith** III, Mr Newland F (*2015*); **Titus**, Rev Bessie (*2015*); **Weaver**, Ms Bonnie (*2018*); *Ex-Officio:* **Jefferts Schori**, Most Rev Katharine (*2015*); **Jennings**, Rev Gay Clark (*2015*); *EC Liaison:* **Johnson** IV, Mr John B (*2015*); *Staff:* **Baumgarten**, Mr Alex; **Hafner**, Ms Jayce.

Standing Commission on Stewardship and Development

McMahon, CFRE, Mr James R (*2015 Chair*); **Bellows**, CFRE, Ms Holly A (*2018 Vice-Chair*); **Wiseman**, Rev Grant B (*2015 Secretary*); **Cole Flanagan**, Rev Cn Carol (*2018*); **Collins**, Rev Cn Dr Lynn A (*2018*); **Huber**, Mr James R (*2018*); **Huey**, Ms Jeanette (*2015*); **Lillibridge**, Rt Rev Gary (*2018*); **Mance**, Ms Diane (*2018*); **Mance**, Ms Diane (*2018*); **Moosbrugger**, Ms Elizabeth M (*2015*); **Provenzano**, Rt Rev Lawrence (*2015*); **Rickel**, Rt Rev Gregory H (*2015*); *Ex- Officio:* **Jefferts Schori**,

Most Rev Katharine (*2015*); **Jennings**, Rev Gay Clark (*2015*); *Rep, PHOD:* **Van Brunt**, Mr Paul (*2015*); *EC Liaison:* **Simons**, Rev Dr James B (*2015*); *Staff:* **Lowell**, Ms Elizabeth.

Standing Commission on Structure, Governance, Constitution and Canons

Getz, Ms Pauline (*2018 Chair*); **Gibbs**, Rt Rev Wendell (*2021 Vice-Chair*); **James**, Rev Dr Molly (*2021 Secretary*); **Ahrens**, Rt Rev Laura J (*2018*); **Alexander**, Rev Sharon (*2021*); **Bonillas**, Dr Luisa (*2021*); **Buchanan**, Cn Annette (*2021*); **Castellan**, Rev Megan (*2018*); **Duque**, Rt Rev Francisco (*2018*); **Feliberty-Ruberte**, Dr Victor (*2018*); **Glass**, Mr Michael (*2021*); **Johnson**, Ms Sally (*2021*); **Klusmeyer**, Rt Rev William (*2021*); **McKellaston**, Ms Louisa (*2018*); **Owensby**, Rt Rev Jake (*2021*); **Simon**, Mr James S (*2018*); **Smith**, Mr Jamal (*2021*); **Sullivan**, Rev Cn Rosemari (*2018*); **Wirth**, Rev Cn Bradley S (*2018*); *Ex-Officio:* **Curry**, Most Rev Michael (*2018*); **Jennings**, Rev Gay Clark (*2018*); *EC Liaison:* **Cisluycis**, Ms Jane (*2018*); *Staff:* **Kostel**, Ms Mary.

Standing Commission on World Mission

McPhee, Ms Sandra F (*2015 Chair*); **Rawlins**, Very Rev P Allister (*2018 Vice-Chair*); **Morck**, Ms Trish (*2018 Secretary*); **Appleyard**, Rev Daniel S (*2018*); **Brewer**, Rt Rev Gregory (*2018*); **Conley**, Cn Judith G (*2018*); **Daniel**, Mrs Angela M (*2015*); **Fitzpatrick**, Rt Rev Robert (*2018*); **Jaramillo**, Ms Tania (*2015*); **Smylie**, Rt Rev John S (*2018*); **Stewart**, Dr Charles N (*2018*); **Tanabe**, Rev Irene (*2015*); **Turner**, Ms Charlene (*2015*); *Ex-Officio:* **Jefferts Schori**, Most Rev Katharine (*2015*); **Jennings**, Rev Gay Clark (*2015*); *Rep, PHOD:* **Cox**, Rev R David (*2015*); *EC Liaison:* **Pierce**, Rev Nathaniel (*2015*); *Staff:* **Copley**, Rev David (*2015*).

OTHER GROUPS

Episcopal Relief & Development

President Robert W **Radtke;** *Deputy to the President* Mary **Carr;** *Chief Operating Officer* Esther **Cohen;** *Senior Vice President for Programs* Abagail **Nelson;** *Senior Director, International Programs* Kirsten Laursen **Muth;** *Senior Director, Marketing and Communications* Malaika **Kamunanwire;** *Senior Director, Advancement* Joy **Shigaki;** *Director, Engagement* Sean **McConnell**

Task Force on Re-Imagining The Episcopal Church

(*All terms 2015*) **George**, Dr Catherine (*Convener*); **Loya**, Rev Cn Craig (*Convener*); **Adams**, Rev Jennifer L; **Harris**, Ms Julia Ayala; **Chambers**, Rev Joseph M C; **Clarke**, ThD, Rev Sathianathan; **Conley**, Cn Judith G; **Curry**, Rt Rev Michael Bruce;

Doyle, Rt Rev C Andrew; **Ell**, Rev Cn Marianne S; **Elliott**, Very Rev Peter G; **Feliberty-Ruberte**, Victor; **Franken**, Ven Robert Anton; **Gray- Reeves**, Rt Rev Mary; **Hauff**, Rev Dr Bradley S; **Howell**, Rev Miguelina; **Lim**, Rev Leng Leroy; **Little**, Esq, Thomas A; **Miller**, Ms Sarah; **Nichols**, Rev Cn Kevin; **Rowe**, Rt Rev Sean W; **Shannon**, Ms Margaret B; **Sullivan**, Mr T Dennis; **York**, Mr Jonathan McKenzie; **Zscheile**, Rev Dr Dwight; *Ex-Officio:* **Barlowe**, Rev Cn Dr Michael; **Jefferts Schori**, Most Rev Katharine; **Jennings**, Rev Gay Clark.

Task Force on the Study of Marriage

(*All terms 2018*) **Taylor**, Rev Brian C (*Chair*); **Geiszler-Ludlum**, Ms Joan (*Vice-Chair*); **Dinwiddie**, Rev Philip (*Secretary*); **Baker**, Rev Stannard; **Ellis**, Mr James; **Ely**, Rt Rev Thomas; **Hayes-Martin**, Rev Gia; **Hylden**, Rev Jordan; **Meyers**, Rev Dr Ruth; **Miller**, Rt Rev Stephen; **Paulino**, Rev Canon Humphrey; **Russell**, Rev Cn Susan; **Stokes**, Ms Deborah; **Thom**, Rt Rev Brian; **Woerman**, Ms. Melodie; *Ex-Officio:* **Curry**, Most Rev Michael; **Jennings**, Rev Gay Clark.

AGENCIES AND BOARDS

Board of the Archives of the Episcopal Church

Adams-McCaslin, Ms Pan (*2021*); **Bardol**, Ms Anne (*2021*); **Baskerville-Burrows**, Rev Jennifer L (*2021*); **Bishop**, Ms Kay (*2018*); **Franklin**, Rt Rev R William (*2021*); **Gebracht**, Dr Frederick (*2021*); **Hitt II**, Esq, Lawrence (*2018*); **Lillibridge**, Rt Rev Gary R (*2018*); **Rushing**, Hon Byron (*2018*); **Sessum**, Rev Robert (*2018*); **Taylor**, Rt Rev G Porter (*2021*); **Wilbert**, Rev Dr Brian Kurt (*2021*); *Ex-Officio:* Duffy, Mr Mark J (*2018*); **Curry**, Most Rev Michael (*2018*); Jennings, Rev Gay Clark (*2018*).

Episcopal Church Building Fund

Abdow, Mr Steve; **Bruttell**, Ven Thomas; **Cabe**, PhD Walt; **Cooney**, Mr Paul; **Ivey**, Ms Mary Lou H; **Nutt-Powell**, PhD Thomas E; **Schleicher**, Dr Heidi; **Wagner**, Ms Anne; **Yeo**, Ms Bobbi; *Staff:* **Woodliff-Stanley**, Rev Ruth (*ECBF Interim President*).

Board of Trustees for the Church Pension Fund

Creed, Esq, Barbara B (*2018, Chair*); **Mitchell**, Rev Dr Timothy J (*2021, Vice-Chair*); **Swan**, Ms Sandra (*2021, Vice-Chair*); **Alexander**, Hon Martha B (*2021*); **Brown**, Rev Thomas J (*2021*); **Bruce**, Rt Rev Diane M Jardine (*2018*); **Currie** Jr, Mr Vincent C (*2018*); **Daniel**, Rt Rev Clifton (*2018*); **Fowler**, Mr Gordon (*2018*); **Glover**, Dr Delbert C (*2018*); **Kusumoto**, Mr Ryan K (*2018*); **Lind**, Very Rev Tracey (*2021*); **Lindahl**, Mr Kevin (*2021*); **McCormick**, Cn Kathryn Weathersby

(*2018*); **McPhee**, Ms Sandra (*2021*); **Niles**, Esq, Margaret A (*2021*); **Owayda**, Mr Sleiman (*2018*); **Pollard**, Ms Diane B (*2018*); **Prior**, Rt Rev Bran N (*2021*); **Rickel**, Rt Rev Gregory (*2021*); **Simmonds Ballentine**, Cn Rosalie (*2018*); **Vickers**, Ms Anne (*2021*); **Wilson**, Rev Cn Sandye (*2021*); **Wold**, Ms Mary Kate; **Wray**, Esq, Cecil (*2018*).

Board for Transition Ministry

Stark, Ms Judith A (*2018 Chair*); **Wright**, Rev Cn Stuart (*2018 Secretary*); **Clark**, Rev Paul (*2021*); **Easton**, Rev Cn Elizabeth (*2021*); **Fisher**, Rt Rev Douglas (*2021*); **Hodges-Copple**, Anne (*2018*); **Mathis**, Cn Jull (*2021*); **Obando**, Ms Denise (*2021*); **Pritchett** Jr, Rev Cn James H (*2018*); **Shin**, Rt Rev Allen (*2021*); **Smith**, Rt Rev Kirk Stevan (*2018*); **Spencer**, Mr Michael (*2018*); *Ex-Officio*: **Curry**, Most Rev Michael (*2018*); **Jennings**, Rev Gay Clark (*2018*).

Episcopal Relief and Development Board of Directors

Lane Jr, Esq, Daniel McNeel (*Chair*); **Brown**; Dr Meredith A (*Secretary*); **Berger**, Mr. Franklin M; **Chin**, Dr Pearl; **Coats**, Ms Lindsey; **Hicks**, Ms Josephine H; **Hilpert**, Ms Sharon; **Lee**, Rt Rev Jeffrey D; **McAfee**, Ms Flo; **Moodey**, Mr Tucker; **Morrison**, Ms Judith; **Perry**, Ms Constance R; **Razim**, Rev Canon Genevieve; **Singh**, Rt Rev Prince G; **Stevenson**, Rev Canon E Mark; **Stoever** Jr, Mr Thomas W; *Ex-Officio*: **Barnes**, Mr N Curt; **Curry**, Most Rev Michael; **Radtke**, Dr Robert.

Forward Movement Board of Directors

Jones, The Rev Gary (*Chair*); **Phillips**, Mr Mike (*Treasurer*); **Escobar**, Mr Michael; **Gomez**, Ms Pamela Wesley; **Harlan**, Rev James; **de Jesus**, Mr Carlos; **Martins**, Rt Rev Daniel; **Murley**, Mimi; **Peters**, Rev Yejide; **Schmidt**, Ms Anne Rudacille; **Breidenthal**, The Rt Rev Thomas (*Ex Officio*); **Curry**, The Most Rev Michael (*President*).

General Board of Examining Chaplains

Benfield, Rt Rev Larry R (*2018 Chair*); **Ahrens**, Rt Rev Laura (*2021*); **Anderson**, Ms. Liza (*2021*); **Bamberger**, Vy Rev Cn Michael (*2021*); **Black**, Rev Dr Cn Katharine (*2021*); **Franklin**, Rt Rev William (*2018*); **Gerbracht**, Dr Frederick (*2018*); **Givens**, Dr Norma (*2021*); **Holmgren**, Rev Cn Dr Stephen (*2018*); **Kirkpatrick**, Rev Dr Frank (*2018*); **Kradel**, Rev Adam (*2021*); **LeVeque**, Ms Anne (*2021*); **Malloy**, Rev Patrick (*2018*); **Michael**, Dr Sandra D (*2018*) 288 Loretta Ln Vestal New York 13850; **Nesbitt**, Rev Dr Paula (*2018*); **Powers Roth**, Ms Janet (*2018*); **Smith**, Rev Dr Duane (*2021*); **Tumminio**, Rev Danielle (*2018*); **Vanderveen**, Rev Peter (*2018*); *Ex-Officio*: **Curry**, Most Rev Michael (*2018*); **Jennings**, Gay Clark (*2018*).

Domestic and Foreign Missionary Society of the Protestant Episcopal Church USA (DFMS)

The corporate and legal entity of The Episcopal Church Board of Directors (*Executive Council*): *Pres* Most Rev Michael Curry; *Vice-Pres* Rev Gay Clark Jennings; *Vice-Pres & COO* Rt Rev Stacy F Sauls; *Sec* Rev Cn Dr Michael Barlowe; *Treas* Mr N Kurt Barnes.

DFMS STAFF
Office of the Presiding Bishop

The Presiding Bishop & Primate The Most Rev Michael B **Curry** *Canon to the Presiding Bishop for Ministry Within the Episcopal Church* The Rev Canon Michael B **Hunn** *Canon to the Presiding Bishop for Ministry Beyond the Episcopal Church* The Rev Canon Charles K **Robertson** *Canon to the Presiding Bishop for Evangelism and Reconciliation* The Rev Canon Stephanie **Spellers** *Executive Assistant to the Presiding Bishop* Sharon **Jones** *Administrative Assistant to the Canons* Ednice **Baerga** *Chief Operating Officer* The Rt Rev Stacy F **Sauls** *Executive Assistant to the COO & Operations Manager* Su **Hadden** *Executive Director of Pastoral Development* The Rt Rev F Clayton **Matthews** *Executive Director General Board of Examining Chaplains* Duncan C **Ely** *Bishop for Convocation of American Churches in Europe* The Rt Rev Pierre **Whalon** *Bishop for Armed Services & Federal Ministries* The Rt Rev Dr James **Magness**

> 3504 Woodley Road NW,
> Washington, DC 20016
> Tel: 202-459-9998
> www.basfm.org

Administration

Legal Counsel Paul B. **Nix** Esq *Director, Human Resources* John E **Colón** *Senior Human Resources Officer* Patricia E **Holley** *Human Resources Officer* Michael H **Walsh** *Director, Information Technology* Richard **Serota**

Development Office

Director Tara Elgin **Holley**

Finance

Treasurer and Chief Financial Officer N Kurt **Barnes** *Assistant to the Treasurer* June A **Victor** *Director of Investment Management and Banking* Margareth **Crosnier de Bellaistre** *Controller* JoAnne **Brockway** *Assistant Controller* Arlissa **Dean** *Assistant Controller* Tanie **Oconer** *Grants Auditor* Jose **Gonzalez** *Payroll Manager* Jacqueline **Franco**

Mission Department

Deputy COO & Director of Mission Samuel A **McDonald**

Global Partnerships

Mission Personnel Officer & Team Leader The Rev David **Copley** *Deputy for Ecumenical and Interreligious Collaboration* The Rev Margaret R **Rose** *Global Networking Officer* Elizabeth **Boe** *Global Relations Officer* Lynnaia **Main** *Middle East Partnerships Officer* The Rev Robert D **Edmunds** *Global Networking and Africa* The Rev Ranjit **Mathews** *Officer for Asia and the Pacific* Canon Peter **Ng** *Officer for Latin America/Caribbean & Province IX* The Rev Glenda **McQueen** *Missioner, United Thank Offering* The Rev Heather **Melton** *Officer for Africa Relation* The Rev Canon Dr Isaac **Kawuki Mukasa**

Formation and Congregational Development

Lifelong Christian Formation & Youth Officer & Team Leader Bronwyn Clark **Skov** *Adult Formation & Lifelong Learning Officer* Vacant *Missioner for Young Adult &Campus Ministries* The Rev. Shannon **Kelly** *Missioner for Transition Ministry* The Rev Meghan F **Froehlich** *Missioner, New Church Starts & Missional Initiatives* The Rev Tom **Brackett** *Officer for Congregational Research* Kirk **Hadaway**

Diversity and Ethnic Ministries

Missioner, Latino/Hispanic Ministries & Team Leader The Rev Anthony **Guillen** *Native American &Indigenous Ministries* Vacant *Missioner, Asian American Ministries* The Rev Dr Winfred B **Vergara** *Missioner, Black Ministries* The Rev Angela S **Ifill**

Episcopal Migration Ministries

Director & Team Leader Deborah **Stein** *Deputy Director* Demetrio **Alvero** *Program Manager, Church Outreach & Engagement* Allison **Duvall** *Program Manager, Communications & Media Development* Wendy **Johnson**

Public Engagement and Mission Communication

Director Alexander D **Baumgarten** *Communication Director* Vacant *Operations Manager* Bernice **David** *Public Affairs Officer* Neva Rae **Fox** *Associate Public Affairs Officer & InfoLine* Lisa **Webb** *Mission Communication Officer* Mary **Brennan** *Manager, Multimedia Services* Michael F **Collins** *Manager, Digital Marketing and Advertising Sales* The Rev Jake **Dell** *Manager, Web & Social Media Service* Barry **Merer** *Editor/Writer, Episcopal News Service* Lynette **Wilson** *Editor/Writer, Episcopal News Service* The Rev Mary Frances **Schjonberg** *Editor/Writer, Episcopal News Service* Matthew **Davies**

Justice & Advocacy Ministries

Domestic Poverty Missioner & Team Leader The Rev Mark **Stevenson** *Missioner, Social Justice and Advocacy Engagement* Charles A **Wynder** Jr *Missioner, Racial Reconciliation* Heidi **Kim**

Office of Government Relations (OGR)

Immigration and Refugee Policy Analyst Vacant *Domestic Policy Analyst* Jayce **Hafner** *Legislative Representative for International Issues* Patricia **Kisare** *Manager, Grassroots and Advocacy Communication* Lacy **Broemel**

110 Maryland Ave NE Suite 309
Washington DC 20002
Tel: (800) 228 0515 or (202) 547 7300
Fax: (202) 547 4457
e-mail: eppn@episcopalchurch.org

Armed Services & Federal Ministries (BASFM) (DC)

Bishop for Armed Services & Federal Ministries The Rt Rev Dr James **Magness;** *Executive Assistant & Deputy Endorser* The Rev Wally **Jensen**

DFMS Regional Offices:

(LA)	**Los Angeles, California** The Cathedral Center of St Paul 840 Echo Park Avenue Los Angeles, California 90026 Tel: (213) 482 2040 Tel: (206) 323-1126; (206) 323-1137
(DC) (OGR)	**Washington DC** **Office of Government Relations** 110 Maryland Ave NE Suite 309 Washington DC 20002 Tel: (800) 228 0515 or (202) 547 7300 Fax: (202) 547 4457 E-mail: eppn@episcopalchurch.org
(BASFM)	**Office of the Bishop for Armed Services and Federal Ministries** 3504 Woodley Road NW Washington, DC 20016 Tel: 202-459-9998 www.basfm.org

MISSION COMPANIONS OF THE EPISCOPAL CHURCH

Sending agency key: DFMS—Domestic and Foreign Missionary Society.

Brazil

Ms. Rachel McDaniel, Diocese of South Western Brazil, Av. Rio Branco 880, Santa Maria, RS 97010-422, BRAZIL – (DFMS)

Ms. Ellen Sandin, c/o Mission Personnel, Episcopal Church Center, 815 Second Avenue, New York, NY 10017 – (DFMS)

Ms. Rachel Schnabel, c/o Mission Personnel, Episcopal Church Center, 815 Second Avenue, New York, NY 10017 – (DFMS)

Ms. Heidi Schmidt, Centro Cultural Missionario, SGAN 905 Conjunto "C", 70790-050 Brasilia DF, Brasil – (DFMS)

Ms. Monica Vega, Centro Cultural Missionario, SGAN 905 Conjunto "C", 70790-050 Brasilia DF, Brasil – (DFMS)

Mr. Bryan Velez Garcia, c/o Mission Personnel, Episcopal Church Center, 815 Second Avenue, New York, NY 10017 – (DFMS)

China
Ms. Mary Grace Benhase , Mariners' Club, 11 Middle Road, Tsim Sha Tsui, Kowloon, Hong Kong, SAR China – (DFMS)

Mr. Andrew Cameron, Mariners' Club, 11 Middle Road, Tsim Sha Tsui, Kowloon, Hong Kong, SAR China – (DFMS)

Costa Rica
Ms. Alejandra Garcia Gonzalez, Diocese of Costa Rica, De CEMACO 75 metros norte sobre calle paralela contigua al taller Land Rover, Zapote, San José, Costa Rica (DFMS)

Ms. Katherine Snow, Diocese of Costa Rica, De CEMACO 75 metros norte sobre calle paralela contigua al taller Land Rover, Zapote, San José Costa Rica (DFMS)

Cyprus/Gulf
The Rev. William Schwartz, PO Box 3210, Doha, Qatar - (DFMS)

Dominican Republic
Ms. Karen Carroll, DMG 16664, 100 Airport Avenue, Venice, FL 34285 - (DFMS)

The Rev. Emilio M Fumero, Episcopal Diocese, Calle Santiago 253, Gascue Santo Domingo, Dominican Republic – (DFMS)

Mr. Charles Nakash, Episcopal Diocese, Calle Santiago 253, Gascue Santo Domingo, Dominican Republic - (DFMS)

Egypt
The Rev. Paul-Gordon Chandler & Mrs. Lynne Chandler, c/o PO Box 360, Winfield, IL 60190 – (DFMS)

El Salvador
Mr. James Guandique, Colonia Miralvalle, Calle Hamburgo #414, San Salvador, El Salvador, C.A. – (DFMS)

England
Ms. Annie Marie Jacob, c/o Mission Personnel, Episcopal Church Center, 815 Second Avenue, New York, NY 10017 – (DFMS)

France
Ms. Naomi Cunningham, c/o The American Cathedral, 23 Avenue George V, Paris 75008 France – (DFMS)

Canon Jere Skipper, c/o The American Cathedral, 23 Avenue George V, Paris 75008, France – (DFMS)

Ghana
Dr. Jenny Coley, Ph, MPH, MSc. CLS, Anglican Health Ministry, Anglican University College of Technology, College of Agriculture and Life Sciences Campus, PO Box 78, Nkronza, Brong Ahafo, Ghana – (DFMS)

Haiti
Ms. Elizabeth Brinkley, 63 Rue 16E, Cap-Haitien, Haiti

Ms. Kyle Evans, 5628 Quail Drive, Doylestown, PA 18902 – (DFMS)

The Rev. Donnel & Janet O'Flynn, Episcopal University of Haiti, c/o Mission Personnel, Episcopal Church Center, 815 Second Avenue, New York, NY 10017 – (DFMS)

Mr. Dan Tootle, 108 Askewton Road, Severna Park, MD 21146 – (DFMS)

Mr. Perry Alan Yarborough, 7 Sail Maker Court Salem, SC 29676 – (DFMS)

Honduras
The Rev. Matthew Engleby, El Hogar Projects, Apartado Postal 764, Tegucigalpa DC, Honduras – (DFMS)

The Rev. Stephen Robinson, IMC SAP, Dept. 215 – PO Box 52-3900 - Miami, FL 33152-3900

Ms. Emilie Street, IMC SAP, Dept 225, PO Box 52-3900, Miami, FL 33252-3900 - (DFMS)

Italy
Mr. Charles Graves, 58 Via Napoli, Roma, Italia 00184 – (DFMS)

Ms. Paola Sanchez Figueroa, 58 Via Napoli, Roma, Italia 00184 – (DFMS)

Japan
Mr. James Rose, Kobe Mariners' Centre, Motomachi-dori 3-1-16, Chuo-ku. Kobe 650-0022 Japan – (DFMS)

Jerusalem
The Rev. Honey Becker, PO Box 1248, Jerusalem 91000, Via Israel – (DFMS)

Kenya
The Rev. Dr. Ndungu Ikenye, Ph.D., & Mrs. Rose Ikenye, Maki Estate, PO Box 1899, Thika, Kenya – (DFMS)

Mozambique
Mr. Roger LeCompte, 29 Fenwood Road, Old Saybrook, CT 06475 - (DFMS)

Panama
Mr. James Fitzpatrick, Casa Cural de la Iglesia Episcopal, Changuinola, El Empalme, Finca 13, Calle Principal, Frente a la Estacion de Bombero – (DFMS)

Mr. Vernon Wilson & Mrs. Francis Wilson, c/o Iglesia Episcopal de Panama, Box 0843-01258, Panama, Rep of Panama - (DFMS)

Ms. Eleanor Withers, Panamá república de Panamá, Ancón, calle culebra, edificio 332, 0843-01258 – (DFMS)

Philippines
Catherine Belous, c/o Mission Personnel, Episcopal Church Center, 815 Second Avenue, New York, NY 10017 – (DFMS)

Eric Canter, c/o Mission Personnel, Episcopal Church Center, 815 Second Avenue, New York, NY 10017 – (DFMS)

Tristan Holmberg, c/o Mission Personnel, Episcopal Church Center, 815 Second Avenue, New York, NY 10017 – (DFMS)

Romania
The Rev. Dorothee Hahn, c/o Episcopia Huşilor - Str. Kogalniceanu, Nr. 19 - Municipiul Huşi - 6575, jud. – Vaslui - Romania – (DFMS)

South Africa
Mr. Thomas Balch, c/o Mission Personnel, Episcopal Church Center, 815 Second Avenue, New York, NY 10017 – (DFMS)

Mr. Timothy Hamlin, c/o Mission Personnel, Episcopal Church Center, 815 Second Avenue, New York, NY 10017 – (DFMS)

Mr. Jacob Nastruz, c/o Mission Personnel, Episcopal Church Center, 815 Second Avenue, New York, NY 10017 – (DFMS)

Ms. Lacey Oliver, c/o Mission Personnel, Episcopal Church Center, 815 Second Avenue, New York, NY 10017 – (DFMS)

Mrs. Jennifer McConnachie, RN, Mariya uMama weThemba Monastery, PO Box 6013, Grahamstown, South Africa 6141 - (DFMS)

Tanzania
Mr. Andrew Russell, DCT CAMS Lower Compound, 27 Biringi Ave, Kilimani, Dodoma, Tanzania - (DFMS)

Uruguay
Ms Kirsten Lowell, Anglican Diocese of Uruguay, Reconquista #522, Casilla de Correos 6108, Montevideo 1100, Uruguay – (DFMS)

USA
The Rev. Paul-Gordon Chandler & Mrs. Lynne Chandler, CARAVAN Project-c/o The Robinsons, PO Box 360, Winfield, IL 60190–(DFMS)

PROVINCIAL CONTACTS

Province I New England
Comprises the dioceses of ME NH VT MA WMA RI CT *Pres* The Rt Rev Stephen Lane 143 State St Portland ME 04101 (207) 772-6923 *E-mail:* slane@episcopalmaine.org; *VPres* The Rev. Kit Wang 121 Mill Ln York ME 03909 (207) 475-7198 *E-mail:* kiturgy@yahoo.com; *Treas* Terry Reimer 143 State Street Portland ME 04101 (207) 772-1953 x134 *E-mail:* treasurer@province1.org; *Exec Dir* Julie Lytle PhD 81 Blueberry Hill Rd Hyannis MA 02601 (617) 669-8411 *E-mail:* executive.director@province1.org *Web:* www.Province1.org; *Reps Exec Council* Alexizendria Link 734 Pleasant Street, Unit 2, Worcester, MA 0160 (617) 447-8039 *Email:* atl029@mail.harvard.edu; The Rev Tanya Wallace (MA) (Rector) All Saints Episcopal Church 7 Woodbridge St South Hadley MA 01075 (413) 532-8917 *E-mail:* trwallace72@gmail.com; *Cultural Competency and Anti-Racism* James McKim *E-mail:* jtmckim@gmail.com; *Campus Min* vacant; *Deacons* The Rev Kyle Pedersen Diocese of CT *E-mail:* kyle_pedersen@yahoo.com; *Altar Guild* Nancy Feid 6 Reservoir St North Attleborough MA 02760 (508) 695-9798; *Daughters of the King* Donna Abramov (Trinity-Rutland/VT) *E-mail:* donnaabramov@yahoo.com; *ECW Pres* Delores Alleyne (CT) *E-mail:* delores-alleyne@aol.com; *VP* Rev Ema Rosero-Nordalm *E-mail:* erosero@bu.edu; *Sec* Roberta Stockdale *E-mail:* rls55@cox.net; *Treas* Priscilla D McFarland *E-mail:* pdmcfarland1@gmail.com; *VP Prog Nat ECW* Linda Guest *E-mail:* lindaeguest@verizon.net; *Prov I Rep to Nat ECW* Gloria Rogers *E-mail:* grogers878@yahoo.com; *Prov I UTO Rep* Sherri Dietrich *E-mail:* ssdietrich@gmail.com; *Province I Rep to CPC* Marilyn Mason.

Province II New York New Jersey Haiti Virgin Islands & Convocation of American Churches in Europe
Comprises the dioceses of NY LI A CNY Roch WNY Nk NJ Haiti VI and Convoc of Amer Chs in Europe *Web:* www.province2.org *Pres:* Rt Rev Lawrence Provenzano, 36 Cathedral Ave Garden City NY 11530 *E-mail:* lprovenzano@dioceseli.org; *VP* Rosalie S Ballentine PO Box 309396 St Thomas VI 00803 (340) 774-3378 *E-mail:* roselaw@viaccess.net *Exec Coord* Cn Charles Perfater 8 Aquetong Ln W Trenton NJ 08628 (609) 538-1200 *E-mail:* chperfater@comcast.net; *Sec* Cn Paul Ambos, Esq (NJ) 418 Magnolia St Highland Park NJ 08904 732-572-8795 *E-Mail* pambos@amboslaw.com Representatives to Provincial *Council* Rt Rev R William Franklin (WNY) 1064 Brighton Rd Tonawanda NY 14150 *E-Mail* rwfranklin@

episcopalwny.org Rev Gloria Payne-Carter 15 Fernhill Ave Buffalo, NY 14215 716-833-0442 *E-Mail* geepcar@hotmail.com Bert Jones (NWK) 75 Lafayette Ave East Orange NJ 973-634-3095 *E-Mail* bjones9234@verizon.net *Exec Coun Lay* Cn Noreen Duncan One Kensington Ave Trenton NJ 08618 646-932-9515 *E-Mail* noreen.duncan@att.net *Exec Coun Clergy* Rev Dahn Gandell 2 Riverside St Rochester NY 14613 *E-mail:* motherdahn@hotmail. com; *Min Dev* Connie White (215) 321-0722 *E-mail:* connielouwhite@msn.com; *Yth Min* Myra Garnes Shuler Director of Youth and Young Adult Ministries (516) 248-4800 x118 *E-Mail:* youth@ dioceseli.org; *Ecum and Interfaith Min* Rev Denise Yarbrough 935 East Ave Rochester NY 14607 (585) 340-9540 *E-mail:* dyarbrough@crcds.edu; *Anti-Racism* Carla Burns (212) 864-2400 x213 *E-mail:* biblio999@gmail.com; *Bro of St Andrew* Allan Inniss (917) 930-0440 *E-mail:* arinniss@msn.com; *UTO* Birdie Blake-Reid *E-mail:* birdieblakereid#verizon. net; ECW Jennifer Kenna (315) 646-2022 *E-mail:* jenken@nnyonline.net & Margaret Cash (877) 628- 5329 *E-mail:* province2@ecwnational.org; *Comp Dio Coord* Rev PA Rawlins (516) 483-2771 *E-mail:* par54nev@aol.com; *Newsletter* InProv2: Jan Paxton 11 Fine Rd High Bridge NJ 08829 (201) 851-1428 *E-mail:* jpaxton46@gmail.com or inprov2@ episcopalwny.org; Immigration Laura Russell (646) 340-1949 *E-mail:* larussell46@legal-aid.org; *Haiti* Doris Crocker (732) 542-3009 *E-mail:* dhcrocker@ comcast.net; *Stewardship* contact Chuck Perfater *E-mail:* chperfater@comcast.net;

Province III Mid-Atlantic

Comprises the dioceses of PA Pgh Be CPA DE E MD NWPA VA SV W WV SwV *Pres* Rev Melanie McCarley (WV) 221 E Washington St Charles Town WV 25414 (304) 725-5312 *E-mail:* rector@ zionepiscopal.org; *V Pres* The Rt. Rev. William "Mike" Klusmeyer (WV) 1608 Virginia St East Charleston WV 25361 (304) 344-3597 *E-mail:* mklusmeyer@wvdiocese.org; *Sec* Rose Longmire (WASH) 540 Plainview Drive Huntingtown MD 20639 (410) 414-5258 *E-mail:* roselongmire@ hotmail.com; *Treas* Karen Kinnamont Stewart (MD) 4 E University Pkwy Baltimore MD 21218 (410) 467-1399 *E-mail:* kstweart@episcopalmaryland. org; *Coord* Rev Barbara J Seras (MD) 67 River Bend Pk Lancaster PA 17602 (717) 385-2667 *E-mail:* p3coordinator@gmail.com; *Exec Coun* Russell Randle (VA) 2445 M Street NW Washington DC 20037 (202) 457-5282 *E-mail:* rrandle@ pattonboggs.com; The Rev Nathaniel W Pierce (Easton) 3864 Rumsey Dr Trappe MD 21673 (410 476-4556 *E-mail:* nwpierce@verizon.net; *Coun Members* Bonnie Chambers (CPA) 242 W Walnut St Palmyra PA 17078 (717) 838-4416 *E-mail:* bchambers242@comcast.net; Rev Sheila B Sharpe (DE) AF 65 E Stephen Dr Newark DE 19713 (302) 738-5681 *E-mail:* sgsharpe@comcast.net; Eddie Vance (Easton) 10 Central Ave Ridgely MD 21660

(410) 634-2707 *E-mail:* cevance@verizon.net; Rev Mary Norton (NWPA) 218 Center St Ridgway PA 15853 (724) 654-8761 *E-mail:* mnorton7@alltel.net; Christoper S Hart (PA) 145 Montrose Ave Rosemont PA 19010 (610) 527-8276 (610) 293-7122 *E-mail:* cervus@veritasliberat.net; Rev Scott T Quinn (PGH) 33 Alice St Pittsburgh PA 15205 (412) 921-4103 *E-mail:* stquinn537@comcast.net; Rev Marian Windel (VA) 1782 Yanceyville Rd Louisa VA 23093 (540) 223- 2769 *E-mail:* marian_1782@cvalink.com; Cleo Shield (SVA) 1745 Rice Creek Rd Meherrin VA 23954 (434) 223-7743 *E-mail:* cleoagain@gmail.com; K Scott Norris (SVA) 6355 Pine Dr Chincoteague VA 23336 (757) 336-1595 *Cell:* (201) 895-4536 *E-mail:* k.norris@att.net; Leticia "Leti" Marques (Wash) 4201 31st St South Apt 837Arlington VA 22206 (571) 643-5192 *E-mail:* marqlet@gmail.com; The Rev Julie N Harris (WVA) Trinity Episcopal Church 200 W King St Martinsburg WV 25403 (304) 263- 0994 *E-mail:* revjulie2@comcast.net; *Altar Guild* Sharon Stewart Nachman (VA) 866 Vine Street Herndon VA 20170 (703) 598-6478 *E-mail:* sharonsnachman@ gmail.com; *Anti Racism* Nancy Travis Bolden 1253 Murdoch Rd Pittsburgh PA 15217 (412) 683-8888 *E-mail:* nltbolden@yahoo.com; *Chr Ed* Kellee Wattenbarger DCF (VA) St Christopher's Church 6320 Hanover Ave Springfield VA 22150 (703) 451-1088 *E-mail:* dce@saintchristophers. net; *Church Periodical Club* Debbie Ventura (WV) 201 Shady Cares Ln Daniels WV 25932 (304) 712-6901 *E-mail:* dventura1021@gmail.com; *COM* Rev James Rinehart 200 Centre St Pottsville PA 17901 (570) 622-8720 *E-mail:* jmsrnhrt@aol.com; *ECW* Rose Longmire (MD) 540 Plainview Dr Huntingtion MD 20639 (410) 414-5258 *E-mail:* roselongmire@ hotmail.com; *Epis Campus Min* Ms Ashley Scruggs (SVA) 600 Talbot Hall Rd Norfolk VA 23505 (757) 213-3393 *E-mail:* ascruggs@diosova.org; *Justice and Peace* vacant; *UTO* Dena Lee (SVA) 295 Ridge Rd Amherst VA 24521 (434) 946-9611 *Cell:* (434) 258-6102 *E-mail:* dglee7880@gmail.com; *Yth Min* Teri Valente 35143 Homestead Way Lewes DE 19958 (302) 945-0610 x5 *E-mail:* terivalente@ gmail.com; *Comm* Sharon Tillman 4 E University Pkwy Baltimore MD 21218 (410) 467-1399 *E-mail:* stillman@episcopalmaryland.org; *Sm Church Min* Rev Judy Parish 989 Pigeon Hill Rd Roseland VA 22967 *E-mail:* revgr8hugger@aol.com; *Health Min* Sharon Logsdon (MD) 24 Parkside Blvd Cumberland MD 21502 (301) 729-6044 *E-mail:* sll@atlantic.net; *Cong Dev* The Rev Mary Norton (NWPA) 218 Center St Ridgeway PA 15853 (814) 335-7789 *E-mail:* mnorton7@alltel.net.

Province IV Southeast

Comprises the dioceses of AL NC EC SC CGC GA AT FL LA MS TN WTN ETN KY LEX CF SEF SWF WNC USC *Pres* Angela Daniel 1 Rice Court Columbia SC 29206 (803) 799-5041 *Cell:* (803) 422-8518 *E-mail:* amdaniel@sc.rr.com; *VP* The Rt Rev Don Johnson, Bishop Diocese of West Tennessee

692 Poplar Ave Memphis TN 38105 (901) 526-0023 *E-mail:* bishopjohnson@episwtn.org; Treas. Cn Kathryn W McCormick 1833 St. Ann St Jackson 39202 (601) 948-5954 *Fax:* (601) 354-3401 *E-mail:* kwmccormick@dioms.org; Sec Athena Hahn, 6424 Mailbu Dr Raleigh NC 28603 (757) 735-3263 *E-mail:* athenahahn@hotmail.com; Adm H Eugene (Gene) Willard PO Box 2878 Morganton NC 28680-2878 (828) 413-0040 *E-mail:* p4admin@icloud.com; *Reps to Exec Coun;* Cler Rev Cn Frank Logue Episcopal Diocese of Georgia 611 E Bay St Savannah GA 31401 (912) 236-4279 *E-mail:* flogue@gaepiscopal. org; Lay Tess Judge 4016 Ivy Ln Kitty Hawk NC 27949 (252) 261-8003 *E-mail:* tessjudgeobx@gmail. com; *UTO* Marci Cherau 382 Balboa Dr Poinciana FL 34759 (912) 398-8052 *E-mail:* mssrsav3@ bellsouth.net; *ECW Pres* Dr Patricia Rutenberg Diocese of East Tennessee (865) 604-5479 *E-mail:* pbrutenberg@gmail.com; *COM* vacant; *HIV/AIDS* Lola Thomas PO Box 2225 Cartersville GA 30120 (770) 655-1532 *E-mail:* l lola.thomas5252@gmail. com; *Altar Guild* Lynn Hendricks 1590 Panorama Dr Birmingham AL 35216 (205) 822-6202 *E-mail:* lyhend@mindspring.com; *Campus Min Michael Wood-Miles Episcopal Campus Minister Georgia Southern University Statesboro GA* (912) 507-4883 *E-mail:* michaelwoodmiles@gmail.com; *Christian Form* Jenny Beaumont 427 South Sharon Amity Rd Suite A Charlotte NC 28211 (704) 442-1718 *E-mail:* jennyatswan@netscape.net; *Ch Periodical Club* Rebecca Markert 805 Bishopgate Rd Antioch TN 37013 *Home:* (615) 366-1887 *Cell:* (615) 430-0535 *E-mail:* sewfun100@bellsouth.net; *Yth* Cookie Cantwell St James Episcopal Church 25 S Third St Wilmington NC 28401 (910) 763- 1628 *Fax:* (910) 762-5115 *E-mail:* cookie@stjames.org; *Latino/Hisp Min* vacant; *Envir Min* The Rev Dr Jerry Cappel 5719 Prince William St Louisville KY 40207 (502) 541-8278 *E-mail:* jjcappel@hotmail.com; *Anti-Racism* vacant; *Companion Dios* Martha B Alexander 1096 Hollyheath Ln Charlotte NC 28209 (704) 558-4670 *E-mail:* marthaebalexander@hotmail.com; *Bishops Chap to the Ret and Surv Spouses* The Rt Rev David B Reed 5226 Moccasin Trail Louisville KY 40207 *Home:* (502) 897-9282 *Cell:* (502) 235-8289 *E-mail:* david.reed@ecunet.org; *ER&D* Eugene Johnston 4 Elizabeth Place Mobile AL 36606 (251) 478-5354 *E-mail:* ejohnston14@comcast.net; *Cong Dev and Evan* vacant; *Young Adult Min* vacant.

Province V Midwest

Comprises the dioceses of OH SO NI Ind C Sp MI WMI NMI EMI FdL Mil EauC MO *Pres* Genevieve L Callard *E-mail:* gcallard@edwm.org; *VP* Rt Rev Mark Hollingsworth *E-mail:* MH@dohio.org; *Sec* Edie Wakevainen *E-mail:* wakevainene@macomb. edu; *Treas* Courtney Reid *E-mail:* creid@episcopal-chicago.org; *Coord* Jo Gantzer *E-mail:* jogantzer@ gmail.com; *Episcopal Church Exec Coun* Rev Marion Luckey *E-mail:* mluckey@chartermi.net; Jane Cis-luycis *E-mail:* jane@upepiscopal.org; The Rev Fran

Holliday (C) *E-mail:* Fran@stmaryepiscopal.org; Katie Forsyth (EMI) *E-mail:* kforsyth@eastmich. org; The Rev Robert Hoekstra (EauC) *E-mail:* rbh. dmin@gmail.com; Nancy Kuhn (FdL) *E-mail:* nck-uhn@charter.net; Ind: Joan Amati *E-mail:* jomati81@ hotmail.com; MI: Jo Ann Hardy *E-mail:* jhardy@ edomi.org; Mil: The Rev Anna Doherty *E-mail:* pastoranna@staidanshartford.org; MO: TBD; NI: The Rev Matthew Cowden *E-mail:* frmatthew-cowden@gmail.com; NMI: Jane Cisluycis *E-mail:* jane@UPepiscopal.org; OH: The Rev Aaron Gerlach *E-mail:* RevGerlach@gmail.com; S: Jan Goossens *E-mail:* utospil@sbcglobal.net; SO: The Rev Jack Koepke *E-mail:* jkoepke@diosohio.org; WMI: Judy Fleener *E-mail:* fleenerj@gmail.com; *Church Periodical Club* Karen Powers *E-mail:* kpowers1@new. rr.com; *ECW* Karen Birr *E-mail:* ksbirr@charter. net; *ER&D* Dr Melanie R Stewart *E-mail:* drmel@ wi.rr.com; *Health Min* Maryfran Crist *E-mail:* mjcrist@crtelco.com; *JPIC* The Rev Cindy Nawrocki *E-mail:* rocki@att.net; *UTO* Peg Cooper *E-mail:* coopermh@slu.edu; *Yth Min* Chad Sentua *E-mail:* fuller@csentua@episcopalchicago.org.

Province VI Land of Mountains Lakes and Plains

Comprises the dioceses of MN IA NE CO MT SD ND WY *Pres* Rt Rev Brian N Prior Episcopal Church in Minnesota 1730 Clifton Place Ste 201 Minneapolis MN 55403 (612) 871-5311 *E-mail:* brian.p@ episcopalmn.org; *VP* Lelanda Lee 8591 Bridle Court Longmont CO 80503 (303) 994-5140 *E-mail:* lelandalee@gmail.com; *Sec* Rev William Graham 607 Toluca Ave Alliance NE 69301-3274 (308) 762-7010 *E-mail:* wjgraham@bbc.net; *Treas* Mr. Charles Plantz 605 S Chestnut St Kimball NE 69145 (308) 360-2025 *E-mail:* jawa175@aolcom; *Chanc* Thomas W Carpenter 405 37th St #302 Des Moines IA 50312 (515) 245-4300 *E-mail:* tcarpenter@grefesidney. com; *Prov Coord* Ellen Bruckner 260 Brentwood Cir NE Cedar Rapids IA 52402 *E-mail:* ellenwb@mchsi. com; *Lay Reps Clergy Reps;* Shelby Benitz 1109 First Ave S Clear Lake IA 50428; (641) 357-8636 *E-mail:* hawkeyenp2012@gmail.com; The Rev Michael Pipkin 1730 Clifton Place Ste 201 Minneapolis MN 55403 (612) 214-7097 *E-mail:* Michael.p@ecmn.org; The Rev Joan Grant (MT) Christ Church Episcopal Kalispell MT 59901 *E-mail:* Joangrant33@hotmail. com; The Rev Chris Plantz (NE) 605 S Chestnut Kimball NE 69145 *Cell:* (308) 230-2071 *E-mail:* PastorPlantz@gmail.com; Cindy King 2000 West 41st Street Casper WY 82604 (307) 266-4134 *E-mail:* cindylking@junco.com *Min High Ed* Steve Mullaney University of Minnesota Episcopal Community (763) 226-3965 *E-mail:* stevenmichaelmullaney@ gmail.com; *UTO* Robin Summers 4055 Becket Drive Colorado Springs CO 80908 *E-mail:* rwe@prismnet. com; *ECW* Mary Whisler 645 S 43rd St Boulder CO 80305 (303) 499-5551 *E-mail:* wwhis52649@aol. com; *Ecum* The Rev Warren Murphy 50 Diamond View Rd Cody WY 82414 (307) 587-9775 *E-mail:*

warrencmurphy@gmail.com; *ECW* Sandra Squires 681 S 85th St Omaha NE 68144 (402) 397-4059 *E-mail:* sksquires@cox.net; *Anti-Racism* Lelanda Lee 8591 Bridle Ct Longmont CO 80503 (303) 994-5140 *E-mail:* lelandalee@gmail.com; *ERD* Barb Hagen 515 N Park Ave Helena MT 59601 (406) 442- 2230 *E-mail:* mtbizmgr@qwest.net; *Daughters of the King* Nancy Sevrin 428 Prospect St Ft Morgan CO 80701 (303) 867-6826 *E-mail:* nssfhs@bresnan.net; *Ex Council Reps* George Wing PO Box 757 Colorado Springs CO 80901 (719) 635-4716 E-mail gwing@ winglaw.com; The Rev John Floberg 820 W Central Ave Bismarck ND 58501 (701) 222-0041 (701) 891-2911 *E-mail:* jffloberg@gmail.com.

Province VII Southwest
Comprises the diocese of WMO WLA AR TX DAL KS RG NWTX WT OK WKS FtW *Pres* Sherry Denton 2524 Bret Salina KS 67401 (785) 827-4354 *Cell:* (785) 342-6476 *E-mail:* sherry@bkrx.com; *VP* The Rt Rev Ed Koniecny 924 N Robnson Oklahoma City OK 73102 (405) 232-4820 *E-mail:* BishopEd@episcopalokahoma.org; *Sec* Kate Huston 1513 Camrose Ct Oklahoma City OK 73159 *Cell:* (405) 514-7735 *Office:* (405) 235-3436 *E-mail:* katehuston@stpaulsokc. org; *Treas* Rev Nancy Igo 1802 Broadway Lubbock TX 79401 *Cell:* (806) 252-0192 *Office:* (806) 763-1370 X5 *E-mail:* nigo@nwtdiocese.org; *Members at Large* evc John Bedingfield, Vy Rev Mark Goodman, Lee Spence; *Exec Council* The Rev Stan Runnels 11 E 40th Kansas City MO 64111 (816) 931-2850 *E-mail:* srunnels@stpaulskcmo.org; Thomas Alexander 291 Pleasant Valley Dr Little Rock AR 72212 (501) 940-7941 *E-mail:* AlexanderTM@hendrix.edu; *ECW* JoAnn Rachele PO Box 62711 San Angelo TX 76906 *Cell:* (406) 249-6135 *E-mail:* joannrachele@ msn.com; *Commun/Web Page* Susan Hanson; *Prog Coord* Sally Russell 2 Hyde Park Dr Hutchinson KS 67502 (620) 662-8024 *Cell:* (620) 694-9145 *E-mail:* sallyruss@sbcglobal.net; *Youth* The Rev Karen Schlabach, 10003 W 70th Tr Merriam KS 66203 (913) 708-5927 *E-mail:* KSchlabach@episcopal-ks. org; *Higher Ed* The Rev Matthew Wise 3908 Faimes Ct College Station TX 77845 (210) 363-9259 *E-mail:* canterburytamu@gmail.com; *Christian Formation* Sabrina Evans 924 N Robinson Oklahoma City OK 73102 (405) 232-4820 *E-mail:* SEvans@epiok. org; *ER&D* The Rev Virginia Holleman 5518 Merrimac Dr Dallas TX 75206 (214) 450-9652 *E-mail:* vfholleman@sbcglobal.net; *Multi-Cultural; Restorative Justice/Prison* Dr Ed Davis 2003 Ave P Huntsville TX 77340 (936) 662-3842 *E-mail:* edsalpc@ yahoo.com; *Min to Senior Min:* Janet Nocher 4408 Foxfire Way Ft Worth TX (817) 975-4863 *E-mail:* janet.nocher@sbcglobal.net; Helen Appelberg *E-mail:* helenappelberg@gmail.com.

Province VIII West and Pacific Rim
Comprises the dioceses of AK AZ CA ECR EO HI ID LosA Navajoland NCA NV OL OR SanD SanJ Spok Tai UT *Pres* The Rt Rev James R Mathes

2083 Sunset Cliff s Blvd San Diego CA 92106 (619) 481-5450 *E-mail:* bishopmathes@edsd.org; *VP* D. Rebecca Snow, PO Box 337, Ashland, OR 97520 (541)708-5155*E-mail:* snowak71@gmail.com; *Treas* Nancy Koonce 864 Filer Ave PO Box 1292 Twin Falls ID 83303 (208) 733- 4730 *E-mail:* nkoonce@ idahocpa.com; *Sec* The Rev. Rachel Taber-Hamilton, 2301 Hoyt Ave, Everett, WA 98201, (425)252-4129, E-mail: chaplain@whidbey.com *Chanc* Miller Adams Esq 601 W Mercer Pl #501 Seattle WA 98119 (206) 300-997 *E-mail:* rma99977@gmail.com; *Reps Exec Coun* Warren J Wong 4620 California St San Francisco CA 94118-1225 (415) 823-3222 *E-mail:* wjwstjames@gmail.com; The Very Rev Brian Baker Trinity Episcopal Cathedral 2620 Capitol Ave Sacramento CA 95816 (916) 446-2513 *E mail:* tvrbaker@ trinitycathedral.org; *Cluster One (Christian Formation) Convener* The Rev Cn. Julia McCray-Goldsmith *Canon for Discipleship Ministries, Episcopal Diocese of California* 1055 Taylor St San Francisco CA 94108 (415) 869-7826 *E-mail:* juliam@diocal.org; *Altar Guild* Albe Larsen 409 Greenbrier Rd Half Moon Bay CA 94019 (650) 726-3236 *E-mail:* amlarsen@ coastside.net; *Hlth Min* Mary Margaret Davis 1359 Great View Ln Fairbanks AK 99712 (907) 457-2865 *E-mail:* mmdavis@acsalaska.net; *Coord of COM* The Rev Holladay Sanderson (208) 954-1555 *E-mail:* hsanderson@q.com; *Campus Min/ High Ed* The Rev Andy Shamel, Campus Minister, Stanford University (858) 774 0264 *E-mail:* revandy@stanford.edu *Lifelong Chr* Dr. Jennifer Snow, Church Divinity School of the Pacific, 2451 Ridge Road, Berkeley, CA 94709 (773) 383-3876 *E-mail:* jsnow@cdsp.edu; *Yth* Anne Clarke, Missioner, Episcopal Diocese of Northern California, 350 University Avenue, Suite 280 Sacramento, CA 95825 (219) 476-5014, *E-mail: Cluster Two (Peace & Justice Ministries) Convener* Warren J Wong 4620 California St San Francisco CA 94118-1225 (415) 823-3222 *E-mail:* wjwstjames@ gmail.com; *Anti-Racism:* The Rev. Patricia Steagall Millard St Catherine of Alexandria Church 36335 N Hwy 101, Nehalem OR 97131 (503) 368-7890 E-mail: pvmillard@gmail.com; *Asian Min* The Rev Jay Watan St. Ambrose Church 900 Edgewater Blvd Foster City CA 94404 *Work:* (650) 574-1369 *Cell:* (415) 309-8968 *E-mail:* igorothighlander@hotmail. com and the Rev. Robert "Moki" Hino Holy Apostles Church 1407 Kapiolani St Hilo HI 96720 (808) 935-5545 E-mail: mokionthego@gmail.com; *Black/ African American/Caribbean* Judy Conley 3004 N 190 Dr Litchfield Park AZ 85340 (623) 393-0342 *E-mail:* judyjudithconley@q.com; *Indigenous Native American/Alaskan/Hawaiian* Paul Nahoa Lucas PO Box 80 Ka'a'awa, HI 96730 (808) 561-7417 *E-mail:* palucas@ksbe.edu; *Latino* The Rev Martir Vasquez St Andrews Church 6300 West Camelback Rd Glendale AZ 85301-7305 Work: (623) 846-8046 Cell: (623) 889-4061 *E-mail:* revmartir@gmail.com or standrewrector1@qwestoffice.net; *Cluster Three (Women's Ministries) Convener* Barbara Schafer 10098 Gold Thorn St Las Vegas NV 89183 (702) 469-3554 *E-mail:* bschafer12@cox.net; *CPC* Mary

Kay Ferrell 2311 W 16th Ave Lot 259 Spokane WA 99224 (509) 474-1387 *E-mail:* quilt12golf@q.com; *UTO* Barbara Schafer 10098 Gold Thorn St Las Vegas NV 89183 (702) 469-3554 *E-mail:* bschafer12@cox.net; *DOK* Cynthia Carson 91-1096 Kai Weke St, Ewa Beach HI 96706 (808) 237-9362 *E-mail:* raksha.the.wolf@googlemail.com *ECW* Louise L Aloy 1005 Laelae St Wailulu HI 96793 (808) 264-9830 *Email* louisealoy63@gmail.com *Deacons of Prov VIII* The Rev Tina Campbell 1617 32nd Ave Sacramento CA 95822-3013 (916) 805-8040 *Email* tinarcampbell@comcast.net *Bro St Andrew* Jack Hanstein 10109 W Manzanita Dr Sun City AZ 85373 (623) 251-2752 *Email* jackhanstein@gmail.com

Province IX Caribbean/Latin America/ Northern South America
Comprises the dioceses of Colom DomR CEcu EcuL Hond PR Ven *Pres* The Rt Rev Julio Cesar Holguin Khoury Calle Santiago No 114 Apartado Postal 764 Santo Domingo DN República Dominicana 809-688-6014 *Cel.* 809-223-7116; 809-540-6631 *E-mail:* bishopholguin@hotmail.com; *VP* The Rt Rev Victor A Scantlebury PO Box 6167 Westwind Rd Jackson MS 39206 (Estados Unidos) Sarmiento N39-54 y Portete Quito Ecuador (El Batan) - (Ecuador) 098-569-1454; (593-2) 245-6948 *E-mail:* bpvictor864@aol.com; *Canciller* Rev. D. John Infante Apartado Aereo 52- 964 Carrera 6 N 49-85 Bogota 2 Colombia 011 (57-1) 288-3167 011 (57-1) 288-3227 Aereo 52-964 Carrera 6 N 49-85 *E-mail:* johnedwin168@hotmail.com; *Sec* Gina Angulo Zamora Amarilis Fuentes 603 y Jose Vicent Trujillo Barrio Centenario Sur Guayaquil Ecuador 011 (593-4) 244-6699 011 (593-9) 374-8478 *E-mail:* gina197919@hotmailcom; *Treas* Mrs Darling Martinez Carretera 848 km Bo Saint Just Trujillo Alto PR (787) 761-9800 (787) 675-3962 *E-mail:* dmartinez@episcopalpr.org ; *Vocal RP* Roberto Aaron Martinez Amengual, Redidencial Girasoles II Etapa; B - S 2; C- 1805; Tegucigalpa Honduras C.A Redidencial Girasoles II Etapa; B-S 2; C-1805; Tegucigalpa, Honduras, C.A ; (504) 9996 8092; (504) 2221 7833; *E-mail* romamartin54@yahoo.com; *Vocal RC* Rafael L. Morales Calle Pino 339 Urbanización Montecasino Toa Alta, Puerto Rico 00953 *E-mail:* padrerafaelpr@gmail.com; 787-604-3135 *E-mail Vocal* Sr Marco Antonio Ramos Califano Caracas, Venezuela, 0058 414 2224052; 0058 212 7533622 *E-mail:* califanomarco@hotmail.com; *Sra* Lorraine Candelario Carretera 848 km Bo Saint Just Trujillo Alto PR (787) 761-9800 (787) 675-3962 *E-mail:* lcandelario704@gmail.com; *Coord* The Rev Canon Consuelo Sanchez (aka Connie) Lomas de Mirafl ores Sur Bloque D casa 4318 frente apartamentos Venecia Tegucigalpa MDC Honduras (504)-2221 7843; (504)-9992 7744 *E-mail:* csanchezhn@gmail.com; *Lay Representative to the Executive Council* Sra Coromoto de Salazar Apartado 49-143 Caracas 1042 Venezuela (011) (58) 212-753-0723 *E-mail:* pragcjimenez04@hotmail.com; *Clergy Representative to the EC* The Rt Rev Lloyd Emmanuel

Allen 23 Avenida Calle 21 Colonia Trejo San Pedro Sula Cortes Honduras 021104; (504)2556 5783; 9990 3638 H *E-mail:* bishopallen43@yahoo.com; Ecu Rel Rdmo Orlando Guerrero Apartado 49-143 Caracas 1042-A Venezuela (011) (58) 212-753-0723 or 751-3046 or *Fax:* (011) (58) 212-751-3180 or 753-1122 *E-mail:* obispoguerrero@iglesianglicanavzla.org; *ECW* Sra Judita Ellis; Veneto Holiday Beach & Casino Curazao; (+599)(9)6904016 *E-mail* jellis@holiday-beach.com *UTO* Sra Reyna de Madrid 23 Avenida Calle 21 Colonia Trejo San Pedro Sula Cortes Honduras 021104; (504)2556 5783 *E-mail:* rilopez1957@gmail.com.

PROGRAM SUPPORT SERVICES
United Thank Offering Board
Staff: *UTO Missioner* The Rev Heather L Melton Episcopal Church Center 815 Second Ave New York NY 10017 (1-800) 334-7626 *E-mail:* hmelton@episcopalchurch.org; *UTO Grant Associate* Michelle Jobson Episcopal Church Center 815 Second Ave New York NY 10017 (800) 334-7626 x6022 *E-mail:* mjobson@episcopalchurch.org; *Province Representatives: Prov I* Sherri Dietrich; *Prov II* Vernese Smith *Prov III* Joyce Douglas; *Prov IV* Joyce Landers; *Prov V* Margaret H Cooper; *Prov VI* Elizabeth Campbell; *Prov VII* Valinda Jackson; *Prov VIII* Barbara Schafer; *Prov IX* Reina Isabel Lopez; *Pres* Sandra Squires *VPres* Marcie Cherau *Sec* Birdie Blake-Reid *Appointed Members* The Rev Sarah Carver *Young Adult* Caitlyn Darnell

Episcopal Diocesan Ecumenical and Interreligious Officers (EDEIO)
Pres The Very Rev Daniell Hamby 47 W Aft on Ave Yardley PA 19067-1619 *E-mail:* daniell@standrewsyardley.org; *V Pres* The Rev Christopher M Agnew 12433 Richards Ride King George VA 22485-5466 *E-mail:* drcma@crosslink.net; *Fin Off* The Rev James Biegler 400 E Ohio Ste #3003 Chicago IL 60611 *E-mail:* edeioexchequer@comcast.net; *Sec & Comm Off* The Rev D Simmons PO Box 824 Waukesha WI 53187 *E-mail:* dsimmons@mac.com; *Prov Coords I* Rev Dr William Bergmann 209 Union St Clinton MA 01510-2903 *E-mail:* rector@goodshepherdclinton.org; *II* Rev Richard Townley 50 York St Lambertville NJ 08530 *E-mail:* standrews@snip.net; *III* Rev Canon Joe Seville 1104 Wedgewood Way Mechanicsburg PA 17040 *E-mail:* jseville03@gmail.com; *IV* Rev Joshua Caler 900 Broadway Nashville TN 37203 *E-mail:* jcaler@christcathedral.org; *V* Rev David Simmons St Matthias Episcopal Church PO Box 824 Waukesha WI 53187 *E-mail:* dsimmons@mac.com; *VI* Rev Warren Murphy 50 Diamond View Rd Cody WY 82414 *E-mail:* warrencmurphy@gmail.com; *VII* Rev Ross Stuckey; *VIII* Rev Dr Carolyn Fairweather 4061 Hayes Ste #28 Newberg OR 97132 *E-mail:* revcmf1@comcast.net; *At large:* Rev Timothy Anderson 705 Iron Horse Dr Ashland NE 68003-6225 *E-mail:* tanderson@episcopaltrifaith.org.

OFFICIAL AGENCIES OF THE EPISCOPAL CHURCH

Archives of the Episcopal Church, The
PO Box 2247 Austin TX 78768-2247 (512) 472-6816 *Fax:* (512) 480-0437 *Website:* http://episcopalarchives.org *E-mail:* research@episcopalarchives.org *Facebook:* facebook.com/episcopalarchives. *Dir and Can Archivist* Mark J Duffy *Archives:* 606 Rathervue Pl Austin TX 78705. Research center for The Episcopal Church, including the Domestic and Foreign Missionary Society, the General Convention, and related church-wide organizations, also individual Episcopalians of note. The Archives collects, preserves, and makes available original source data to Church leaders, members, and the public. Maintains online digital archives, digital repository holdings, and provides consulting services to dioceses and parishes. *Records Administration:* 815 Second Ave New York NY 10017-4594. Administers corporate records. *Rights and Permissions Office:* PO Box 2247 Austin TX 78768-2247. Administers rights and permissions for non-current DFMS/General Convention publications.

The Church Pension Fund
19 East 34th St New York NY 10016 (212) 592-1800 or (800) 223-6602. www.cpg.org. The principal mission of The Church Pension Fund and its affiliates (the "Church Pension Group") is to provide comprehensive, cost-effective retirement, health and life insurance benefits to the Episcopal Church, its clergy and lay employees. The Church Pension Group also provides property and casualty insurance and risk management services and resources for Episcopal church institutions; and worship materials, curriculum and Christian education materials, books, and music for the Episcopal Church. Over its history, The Church Pension Fund has paid more than $5.3 billion in benefits. The Church Pension Group consists of the following core companies: *The Church Pension Fund* (founded in 1914), *Church Life Insurance Corporation* (founded 1922), *The Episcopal Church Medical Trust* (founded 2002), *The Church Insurance Company* (founded 1929), *The Church Insurance Agency Corporation* (founded 1930), *The Church Insurance Company of New York* (founded 2007), *The Church Insurance Company of Vermont* (founded 1999), and *Church Publishing Incorporated* (founded 1918). The CEO and President of The Church Pension Fund is Mary Kate Wold.

Episcopal Church Building Fund
Established in 1880, the ECBF, an autonomous, self-funding and self-governing agency, provides non-mortgage loans up to $1 million (larger mortgage loans also available) for the purchase, construction, repair, improvement, or refinancing of properties, churches, rectories, schools, and other parochial buildings. Provides consultations on the creative use of church buildings and properties to support a congregations' financial sustainability and increase their connection and relevance to the community. Partners with ecumenical groups to achieve a common mission. Provides guidance on the building planning process. Web resources on accessibility, greening, liturgical design, and full video presentations from national symposiums. *Interim Pres* The Rev Ruth Woodliff-Stanley; *VP* Sally O'Brien 563 Southlake Blvd, Richmond VA 23236 (804) 893-3436 *E-mail:* buildchurch@ecbf.org *Web:* www.ecbf.org.

Forward Movement
The mission of Forward Movement is inspiring disciples and empowering evangelists. Primary publications include the devotionals *Forward Day by Day* and *Adelante Día a Día* as well as pamphlets, books, and digital resources for study, devotional, pastoral, and congregational development use. Executive Director is the Rev Canon Scott Gunn 412 Sycamore St Cincinnati OH 45202 (513) 721-6659 *E-Mail:* orders@forwardmovement.org *Web:* www.forwardmovement.org.

Institutions and Organizations

EDUCATIONAL
THEOLOGICAL SEMINARIES
Berkeley Divinity School at Yale

Founded in 1854, since 1971 the Berkeley Divinity School has functioned as an affiliate of Yale University. Berkeley has its own dean, board of trustees, and bylaws. Berkeley and Yale Divinity School share a single admissions process, a united curriculum and faculty, and Yale degrees are granted to all students, with Berkeley diplomas and certificates in Anglican Studies to those undertaking the Berkeley program. Berkeley Center 363 St Ronan St New Haven CT 06511 *Administrative Offices:* 409 Prospect St New Haven CT 06511 (203) 432-9285 *Fax:* (203) 432-9353 *Web:* berkeleydivinity.yale.edu

Dean and Pres—V Rev Andrew B McGowan BA BD MA PhD

Assoc Dean and Dir Form—Rev Cathy George MDiv

Dir of Ed Ldrship and Min Prog—Rev F Washington (Tony) Jarvis

Berkeley-affiliated faculty at Yale are:

Bp Percy Goddard Prof of Lit Studies and Pastoral Theol—Rev B Spinks MTh PhD

Prof Hebrew Scriptures—Rev Carolyn Sharp MAR PhD

Walter H Gray Assoc Prof of Anglican Studies and Patristics—Rev Christopher Beeley MDiv PhD

Noah Porter Prof of Philosophical Theol—John Hare BA PhD

Henry B Wright Prof of Systematic Theol—Miroslav Volf MA DTh

Prof of Religion and Lit—Peter S Hawkins BA MDiv PhD

Assoc Prof of Asian Theol—Chloe Starr MA DPhil

Frederick Marquand Prof Systematic Theol—Kathryn Tanner MA PhD

Dean of Marquand Chapel—Maggi Dawn BA PhD

Gilbert L Stark Prof of Christian Ethics and Assoc Dean for Acad Affairs, YDS—Jennifer A Herdt BA MA PhD

Bexley Hall Seabury Western Theological Seminary Federation

www.bexleyseabury.edu

Bexley Hall and Seabury Western have inaugurated a new seminary Federation, bringing the two historic institutions together with a single Board, faculty, and mission. There are two locations: in Columbus, Ohio, on the campus of Trinity Lutheran Seminary; and in Chicago, housed at the ELCA Churchwide headquarters. Bexley Seabury is committed to educating lay and ordained leaders for the church in an ecumenical setting. We offer a residential MDiv program primarily in Columbus, and the DMin with specialization in Congregational Development and preaching. A Diploma in Anglican Studies (for students enrolled at non-Episcopal seminaries) and programs in leadership education are offered at both sites, including courses in non-profit management in partnership with the Kellogg School of Non-Profit Management at Northwestern University and in asset-based community development.

Columbus: 583 Sheridan Ave Columbus, OH 43209-2324 (614) 231-3095

Chicago: 8765 Higgins Road Chicago IL (773) 380-6780 www.bexleyseabury.edu

Pres and Prof Biblical Interpretation and Practice of Ministry—Rev Roger A Ferlo PhD

Academic Dean and Assoc Prof Church Hist—Rev Thomas Ferguson PhD

Prof Theol and Culture—Rev John A Dally, PhD

Assoc Prof of Theol—Rev Jason Fout PhD

Director DMin and Lecturer Practical Theo—Rev Suzann Holding

Director Field Ed and Formation—Rev KyungJa Oh

Lecturer Sacred Music—M Milner Seifert MM

Research Prof Theol and Ethics—Rev Ellen K Wondra PhD

Church Divinity School of the Pacific

2451 Ridge Rd Berkeley CA 94709 (510) 204-0700 *Fax:* (510) 644-0712 *E-mail:* info@cdsp.edu *Web:* www.cdsp.edu.

Pres and Dean—Rev WM Richardson PhD

Dean Acad Aff—Rev R Meyers PhD

Hodges/Hayes Prof Litur—Rev R Meyers PhD

Assist Prof Theol—S MacDougall PhD

Visiting Prof Ch Hist—Rev W Stafford PhD

Assoc Prof Min Dev—Rev S Singer

Prof Christian Ethics—C Moe-Lobeda PhD

Assist Prof OT—J Gonzalez PhD

DMin Dir—Rev S Singer PhD

Faculty Emer—Rev JL Kater PhD, Rev AG Holder PhD, Rev L Weil PhD, Rev LL Clader PhD

Asst Prof Ch Mus/Dir Chapel Mus—G Emblom MM

Dir Operations and Personal Management—Rev B Rybicki

Dean Stud/ Dn of Chapel—Rev LA Hallisey

Dir of Ext Learning / Prof Practical Theo—J Snow PhD

Reg—E Rhee

Dir Recruit—A Hybl

Episcopal Divinity School

Continuing Episcopal Theological School and Philadelphia Divinity School 99 Brattle Cambridge MA 02138-3494. Affiliated with Boston Theological Institute (617) 868-3450 *Fax:* (617) 864-5385 *Web:* www.eds.edu.

Interim President and Dean—The Very Rev Francis Fornaro

Academic Dean and Harvey H Guthrie Jr Professor of Bible, Culture, and Interpretation—Dr Angela Bauer-Levesque

Interim Dean of Student & Community Life—The Very Rev Thomas Eoyang Jr DMin

Chief Financial & Business Development Officer—William F Judge

Vice President of Institutional Advancement—Christopher Hartley

Director of Communications & Marketing—Brendan Hughes

Director of Technology Services—Chris Carr

Director of the Annual Fund—Kathleen Hart

Otis Charles Visiting Professor in Applied Theology & Faculty Emeritus—The Rev Dr Christopher Duraisingh

Ethelbert Talbot Professor of Biblical Studies—Lawrence Wills

William F Cole Professor of Christian Theology and Spirituality—Dr Kwok Pui Lan

William W Rankin Associate Professor of Christian Social Ethics at Episcopal Divinity School—The Rev Dr Joan M Martin

Nancy W King Professor of Biblical Studies—Dr Gale A Yee

Director of Human Resources—Samaria A Stallings

Controller—Joanne Manning

Manager of Student Records/ Registrar—Cecelia M Cull MS

Manager of Recruitment & Admissions —Hillary Kody

Sr. Assistant Director, Library Services—Aura A Fluet

Director of Alumni/ae and Constituent Engagement—Christianne Humphrey

Director of The Mission Institute—Diane D'Souza

Program Coordinator, Faith-based Leadership—Liz Magill

Financial Aid Manager and Financial Analyst—Valerie Paterson

Director of Liturgy, Music, and the Arts—Ellen Oak

Artist-in-Residence, and Faculty in Voice, Body, and Culture—Suzanne Ehly

Director of Alumni/ae and Constituent Engagement—Christianne Humphrey

General Theological Seminary of the Protestant Episcopal Church in the United States

Established by the General Convention, May 27, General Theological Seminary of the Protestant Episcopal Church in the United States Established by the General Convention, May 27, 1817. Constitution adopted by General Convention, 1822. Incorporated April 5 1822. 440 West 21st St NY NY 10011-2981 (212) 243-5150 *Fax:* (212) 727- 3907 *Web:* www.gts. edu.

Pres and Dean – The Very Rev. Kurt H. Dunkle

Prof Ch Mus and Organist—David J Hurd MusD

Prof of NT—Deirdre J Good ThD

Prof of Preaching—Rev Mitties M DeChamplain PhD

Prof of OT—Rev Robert J Owens PhD

Assoc Prof in H Boone Porter Chair of Liturgics—Rev Patrick Malloy PhD

Asst Prof of Pastoral Theology—Rev Amy Lamborn PhD

Assoc Prof of Ascetical Theology—Rev Clair McPherson PhD

Asst Prof of New Testament—Andrew Irving ThD

Controller—Robert Elliot

VP of Advancement—Donna Ashley

VP of Operations—Anthony Khani

Dir of HR and Financial Aid—Trecia O'Sullivan

Dir of Keller Library—Rev Andrew G Kadel MLS

Registrar—Emily Beekman

Exec Dir Preschool and Daycare—Susan Stein

Exec Asst to Dean—Kim Robey

Dir of Commun—Chad Rancourt

Herbert Thompson Prof of Church and Soc, Dir of the Desmond Tutu Center—The Rev Dr Michael Battle

Asst Prof of NT—The Rev Dr Todd HW Brewer

Adj Prof of Church and Soc and Dir of Mission and Reconciliation—The Rev Canon Stephanie Spellers

Affiliate Prof of Sys Theo—Dr Alina N Feld

Affiliate Prof of Liturgics—The Rev Dr Kevin Moroney

Affiliate Prof of Church Music and Chapel Organist—The Rev Dr Shane Scott-Hamblen

Nashotah House

2777 Mission Rd Nashotah WI 53058-9793 (262) 646-6500 *Fax:* (262) 646-6504 *E-mail:* rhartley@ nashotah.edu *Web:* www.nashotah.edu

Dean and Pres and Prof Homiletics and Church History—Rev SA Peay PhD

Assoc Dean for Academic Affairs and Prof Philosophical and Systematic Theol—Rev AT Grosso PhD

Prof NT and Greek—GP Anderson PhD

Prof Ch Mus and Dir Chap Mus—Cn JA Kucharski DMus

Prof Ethics and Moral Theol—Rev DA Westberg DPhil (Oxon)

Prof Hist and Syst Theol—Rev TL Holtzen PhD

Dir Library and Assoc Prof of Ascetical Theology—DG Sherwood DMin

Assoc Prof Church History—TN Buchan PhD

Assoc Prof Practical Theology—Rev JS Gabig PhD

Asst Prof OT and Hebrew—T Bott, PhD

Assoc Dean of Students and Affil Prof Ascetical and Pastoral Theol—Rev RS Hartley DMin, STM

Assoc Dean for Admin—Rev PJ Cunningham MBA MDiv

Dir Devel—Rev NS Lawson MDiv

Dir of Field Education—Rev S Leannah MDiv

Protestant Episcopal Theological Seminary In Virginia, The

Seminary Post Office 3737 Seminary Rd Alexandria VA 22304 (703) 370-6600 *Fax:* (703) 370-6234 *Web:* www.vts.edu.

Dean and Pres—V Rev Ian Markham PhD

Assoc Dean for Acad Affrs—TF Sedgwick MA PhD

Assoc Dean of Students—A Dyer PhD

Exec Dir Ctr for Ang Comm Studies/Prof Pastoral Theo—Rev JB Hawkins IV MDiv PhD

Dir Field Ed—Rev Allison St Louis MDiv PhD

Doc of Min Prog and Prof of Evan and Cong Ldrshp—Rev David Gortner MA MDiv PhD

Prof NT—Rev LA Lewis MDiv MA MPhil PhD

Prof NT—Rev K Grieb MDiv JD PhD

Prof NT—J Yieh MA MDiv PhD

Prof Ch Hist—Rev RW Prichard MDiv PhD

Asst Prof Ch Hist—Jonathan Gray MA PhD

Prof Theol—Rev K Sonderegger MDiv STM PhD

Asst Prof Hom—Rev R Hooke MAR MA MPhil PhD

Assoc Prof OT—Rev Judy Fentress-Williams MDiv PhD

Prof OT Language and Lit—Stephen L Cook MA MDiv MPhil PhD

Prof of Practical Theol—Rev J Mercer MDiv DMin PhD

Prof of Ch Music—William B Robert MCM DMA

V Pres Admin and Fin—H Zdancewicz MBA

V Pres Inst Advancement—Rev JB Hawkins IV MDiv PhD

Librarian/Prof—M Jarrett-Budde MA MLib DMin

Dir of CMT and Chrs Form and Cong Ldrshp Elizabeth M Kimball MEd PhD

Assoc Prof of Theo and Liturgy—The Rev James W Farwell, PhD

The School of Theology, University of the South, Sewanee, Tenn.

335 Tennessee Ave Sewanee TN 37383-0001 (800) 722-1974 *Fax:* (931) 598-1852 *E-mail:* theology@sewanee.edu *Web:* http://theology.sewanee.edu.

Dean—The Rt Rev J Neil Alexander, Th.D.

Admin Asst to the Dean—Nickie Peardon

Asst Dir for Training, Education for Ministry—Elsa Swift Bakkum

CK Benedict Prof of New Testament Emer/Ed of Sewanee Theological Review—The Rev Dr Christopher Bryan

Assoc Dir for Alumni/ae and Advancement—Sukey Byerly

Assoc Dean and Dir of The School of Theol's Beecken Center—Dr Courtney Cowart

Assoc Dir of The Beecken Center—James M Goodmann

Assoc Dean for Community Life—The Rev Deborah Jackson

Executive Dir, Education for Ministry—Karen M Meridith

Assoc Dean for Recruitment and Admissions—The Rev Annwn Hawkins Myers

Dir of Publications, Marketing and Communications, The School of Theology—Mary Ann Patterson

Dir of Marketing and Communications, The Beecken Center—Paul Schutz

Dir of Contextual Education and Lect in Contextual Theol—The Rev Kathryn Mary (Kammy) Young

Prof of Liturgy, Charles Todd Quintard Prof of Dogmatic Theol—The Rt Rev J Neil Alexander

Prof of Homiletics—The Rev Dr William F Brosend II,

Prof of Christian Ethics and Theology—Dr Cynthia S W Crysdale,

School of Theol Librarian Lect in New Testament—Dr James Warren Dunkly

Prof of Pastoral Theol—The Rev Dr Julia Gatta

Prof of New Testament—Dr Paul A Holloway

Assoc Prof of Church History and Dir of the Advanced Degrees Prog—The Rev Dr Benjamin John King

Assoc Prof of Theol—The Rev Dr Robert Carroll MacSwain

Dist Visiting Prof of Global Anglicanism—The Rt Rev James Tengatenga, Ph.D.

Postdoctoral Fellow in Env Ethics—Dr Andrew R H Thompson

Assoc Prof of Liturgy/Norma & Olan Mills Prof of Divinity/Assoc Dean of Academic Affairs/Sub-Dean of the Chapel of the Apostles—The Rev Canon James F Turrell, Ph.D.

CK Benedict Prof of Old Testament—The Rev Dr Rebecca Abts Wright

Visiting Assistant Professor of Preaching—The Rev Dr Benjamin Anthony

Visiting Lect of World Religions—The Rev Dr Donna S Mote *Visiting Instructor for Christian Ed*—Mary Hunter Rouse

Instructor in Music—Susan Kay Rupert

Visiting Instructor in Pastoral Spanish—John C Solomon

Visiting Asst. Professor of Church History—Dr. Edward Bond

Major Gifts Officer—Anne Chenoweth

Seminary of the Southwest (Episcopal Theological Seminary of the Southwest)

501 E 32nd St Austin TX 78705 (Box 2247 Austin TX 78768) (512) 472-4133 *Fax:* (512) 472-3098 *E-mail:* info@ssw.edu *Web:* www.ssw.edu.

Dean & Pres—Very Rev Cynthia Briggs Kittredge ThD

Exec VPres—Frederick Clement

Acad Dean and Prof Christian Ethics & Moral Theology—Scott Bader-Saye PhD

Associate Prof Theol—Anthony Baker PhD

Dir Library—Alison Poage MLS

Assistant Prof of NT—Rev Jane Patterson PhD

Assistant Prof of Counselor Education—Gena Minnix PhD

Assistant Prof of Counselor Education—Stephanie Ramirez PhD

Assoc Prof Church History—Daniel Joslyn-Siemiatkoski PhD

Associate Prof Lit and Ang Studies—Rev Nathan Jennings PhD

Director of Comprehensive Wellness & Associate Prof Preaching—Rev Micah Jackson PhD

Associate Prof OT—Steven Bishop PhD

Interim Dir Hisp Ch Stu—Rev Al Rodriguez MDiv

VPres Inst Adv—Tara Elgin Holley MM

Dir Loise Henderson Wessendorff Ctr for Chr Min and Voc—Rev Dave Scheider DMin

Dir Cert Prog Chr Form—Rev Jean McGraw MDiv

Assoc Prof Pastoral Theology—Rev Kathleen Russell DMin

Registrar—Madelyn Snodgrass

Dir Information Tech – Erik Morrow

VP Enrollment Management—search underway

VP Commun—Nancy Springer-Baldwin MAR

Trinity Episcopal School for Ministry

311 Eleventh St Ambridge PA 15003 (724) 266-3838 *Fax:* (724) 266-4617 *E-mail:* info@tsm.edu *Web:* www.tsm.edu. Trinity offers the Master of Divinity, Master of Arts in Religion (now available entirely online), Master of Sacred Theology, and the Doctor of Ministry degrees. Also offered are three diploma programs (Diploma in Anglican Studies, Diploma in Christian Ministry, and the Spanish Language Post-Graduate Diploma in Anglican Studies) and the Certificate in Diaconal Studies. In addition to our regular on-campus courses, Trinity offers week-long Intensive courses in January and June as well as various online courses.

Dean and Pres/Prof Systematic Theol—Very Rev Justyn Terry PhD

Prof Biblical Studies—Rev Peter Walker PhD

Assoc Prof Biblical Studies—Don Collett PhD

Asst Prof Biblical Studies—Wesley Hill PhD

Dir of Library—Susanah Hanson MLS

Assoc Prof Ch Hist—Philip Harrold PhD

Dean of Students—Geoffrey Mackey

Assoc Prof Mission and Evang/Dir Stanway Institute—Rev Cn John Macdonald DMiss

Prof Biblical Studies—Erika Moore PhD

Registrar/Dir Acad Support Services—Stacey Williard

Acad Dean/Asst Prof Homiletics/Dir Extension Ministries—The Ven Mark Stevenson PhD

Dean DMin Studies/Assoc Prof Liturgy—Rev H Lawrence Thompson DMin

Asst Prof Systematic Theol—William Witt PhD

Asst Prof Historical Theol/Dir Robert E Webber Center—Rev Joel Scandrett PhD

Assoc Prof Liturgy and Homiletics/Pres North American Lutheran Seminary (NALS)—Rev Amy Schifrin STS PhD

Prof Systematic Theology and Ethics—David Yeago PhD

SCHOOLS OF THEOLOGY

Bloy House, the Episcopal Theological School at Claremont

1325 N College Ave Claremont CA 91711-3199 (909) 621-2419 *Fax:* (909) 625-2224 *E-mail:* bloyhouse@cst.edu *Web:*www.bloyhouse.org. A weekend commuter seminary on the campus of Claremont School of Theology offering lay, diaconal, and priestly ministry formation programs including accredited M. Div. coursework that can be taken through the joint Bloy House/CST program or the Bloy House partnership with other Episcopal Seminaries in the country. Certificates for Anglican Studies, Diaconal Studies, and Lay Leadership are also offered.

Dean and Pres—Very Rev Sylvia Sweeney PhD

Prof OT—Canon James A Sanders PhD

Prof Greek—Jonathan Burke, PhD

Prof Liturgics—Very Rev Sylvia Sweeney PhD

Prof Ang Studies—Rev Sheryl Kujawa-Holbrook PhD

Prof Theo and Ethics—Michael J McGrath PhD

Prof Past Counsel—Rev Ron David PhD

Prof Church Leadership—Rev Robert Honeychurch DMin

Prof Church History— Rev Pat Ash, PhD

Prof Spiritual Care and Counseling—Rev Karri Backer

George Mercer Jr Memorial School of Theology

65 Fourth St Garden City NY 11530 (516) 248-4800 x140 *Fax:* (516) 248-4883 *E-mail:* merceroffice@dioceseli.org *Web:* www.mercerschool.org.

Canon for Formation & Dean—The Very Rev John P McGinty PhD

Lib—Charles Egleston

Admin & Reg—Diane Muscarella

DIOCESAN TRAINING PROGRAMS

ALABAMA—Diaconate School Rev B King PO Box 2121 Clanton AL 35046 (205) 755-3339 *E-mail:* bp3king@bellsouth.net.

ARKANSAS—Iona Initiative Arkansas, a three-year program to train clergy locally; *Dean* The Rev Sandra Curtis.

ATLANTA—Beloved Community: Dismantling Racism Dr. Catherine Meeks, 2744 Peachtree Rd NW, Atlanta, GA 30305

ATLANTA—Education for Ministry (EfM) Mentor Training Ruth Elizabeth Conine 2744 Peachtree Rd NW Atlanta, GA 30305.

ATLANTA—Institute for Ministry & Theological Education Nancy Armstrong, 2744 Peachtree Rd NW Atlanta GA 30305. Diocesan sponsorship of a variety of lifelong learning events for Clergy and Lay persons.

ATLANTA—Foundations for Christian Education Certification Course, Education & Formation for Congregational Growth, Nancy Armstrong 2744 Peachtree Rd NW Atlanta GA 30305. In-depth two-year certification course specifically for those in positions of church leadership and formation.

ATLANTA—Learning to Lead, Alicia Schuster Weltner, 2744 Peachtree Rd. NW, Atlanta, GA 30305, Training for Episcopal Clergy in navigating during the critical period of transition

ATLANTA—Safeguarding God's Children and Safeguarding God's People. Rev Dr. Deborah Silver Trainings based on the Model Policies developed by the Church Pension Group and Praesidium partnership. They include information and guidelines on screening, interacting, monitoring, training, and reporting with regard to adult supervision of and interaction with children and youth.

BETHLEHEM—Basic training for diaconate 333 Wyandotte Bethlehem PA 18015 (610) 691-5655. Education for Ministry, for Laity, Clergy Training Days and Annual Clergy Retreat

BETHLEHEM—Ecumenical Committee for Continuing Education *Priest* Judith Snyder 333 Wyandotte Bethlehem PA 18015 (610) 691-5655.

BETHLEHEM—Bishop's School (Basic training for diaconate—open to all) Rotating Leadership 333 Wyandotte Bethlehem PA 18015 (610) 691-5655.

CALIFORNIA—Episcopal School for Deacons *Dn* RB Dugliss 2451 Ridge Rd #114 Berkeley CA 94709-1217 (510) 848-1723 *Fax:* (510) 666-9118 *Web:* www.sfd.edu.

CALIFORNIA—Veriditas: The Labyrinth Project *Fdr & Crea Dir* Rev Cn L Artress 101 San Antonio Rd Petaluma CA 94952 (707) 283-0373 *Fax:* (707) 283-0372 *Web:* www.veriditas.org. Conferences, courses, spiritual direction.

CENTRAL FLORIDA—Institute for Christian Studies *Dn* Ven Kristen N Alday 1017 E Robinson St Orlando FL 32801 (407) 423-3567 *Fax:* (407) 872-0006 *E-mail:* kalday@cfdiocese.org. Lay and diaconal training.

CENTRAL PENNSYLVANIA—Stephenson School for Ministry *Dn* Very Rev Robyn Szoke-Coolidge

101 Pine St Harrisburg PA 17101. Lay, diaconal, and priest local trng, mutual ministry program.

CHICAGO—Bishop Anderson House Rev Thomas S Rogers, III *Exec Dir* 1653 W Congress Expressway Chicago IL 60612-3833 (312) 563-4824 *Fax:* (312) 942-5279 *E-mail:* trogers@bishopandersonhouse.org *Web:* www.bishopandersonhouse.org. Chaplains trng.

COLOMBIA—Project Development Training for Sustainability.

COLORADO—Church Development Institute Office of the Bishop 1300 Washington Ave Denver CO 80203 (303) 837-1173 *Contact* The Rev Lou Blanchard *E-mail:* Lblanchard@coloradodiocese.org.

CONNECTICUT—Education for Ministry (EFM) 1335 Asylum Ave Hartford CT 06105 (860) 283-4481 *Fax:* (860) 523-1410 Prog of Theology education-at-a-distance of the School of Theology of the Universityof the South. Students sign up one year at a time for 4-yr prog. Covers basics OT, NT, ch history, liturgy, theology. Students meet regularly in seminars. Prog grants certificate at the end of 4 yrs.

CONVOCATION OF EPISCOPAL CHURCHES IN EUROPE—European Institute of Christian Studies American Cathedral 23 Ave George V Paris France 75008 +33 1 53 23 84 06 *Fax:* +33 1 49 52 96 85 *E-mail:* office@tec-europe.org.

DALLAS—Renewal Center *Dir* Rev Bob Corley 516 S O'Connor Irving TX 75060 (972) 253-7124 *Fax:* (972) 253-6448.

DALLAS—Evangelism 101 *Dir* Carrie Headington 1630 N Garrett Ave Dallas TX 75206 (214) 826-8310 *Fax:* (214) 826-5968.

DALLAS—Parish Mission Vision *Dir* Carrie Headington 1630 N Garrett Ave Dallas TX 75206 (214) 826-8310 *Fax:* (214) 826-5968.

DALLAS—Harvest Unlimited *Dir* Carrie Headington 1630 N Garrett Ave Dallas TX 75206 (214) 826-8310 *Fax:* (214) 826-5968.

DALLAS—Apologetics 101 *Dir* Carrie Headington 1630 N Garrett Ave Dallas TX 75206 (214) 826-8310 *Fax:* (214) 826-5968.

DALLAS—Congregational Development Workshops *Dir* Victoria Heard 1630 N Garrett Ave Dallas TX 75206 (214) 826-8310 *Fax:* (214) 826-5968

DALLAS—Communications and Marketing Consulting *Dir* K Durnan 1630 N Garrett Ave Dallas TX 75206 (214) 826-8310 *Fax:* (214) 826-5968.

DALLAS—Bishop Stanton Center for Ministry Formation *Dir* Janet Page 5100 Ross Ave Dallas TX 75206 (214) 823-8134 *Fax:* (214) 823-1048.

EAST TENNESSEE—Anti-Racism

EAST TENNESSEE—Fresh Start

EAST TENNESSEE—Safeguarding God's Children

EAST TENNESSEE—Safeguarding God's People

EL CAMINO REAL—Audit Training Dio Admin *Trainer* Rev Brian Nordwick 154 Central Ave Salinas CA 93901 *E-mail:* brian@realepiscopal.org.

EL CAMINO REAL—Seeing the Face of God in Each Other *Dio Admin* Rev Brian Nordwick.

EL CAMINO REAL—Anti-racism training *Trainer* Diane Lovelace.

EL CAMINO REAL—Safeguarding God's Children and Safeguarding God's People *Dio Admin* Rev Brian Nordwick 154 Central Ave Salinas CA 93901 *E-mail:* brian@realepiscopal.org Ethical sexual behavior training. *Trainer:* The Rev Kathleen Crowe.

EL CAMINO REAL—Stewardship Workshops *Chair, Rector,* SCV Rev Channing Smith 227 Loma Alta Los Gatos CA 95030 (650) 924-8107 *E-mail:* channing@st-andrews-saratoga.org.

EL CAMINO REAL—Eucharistic Ministers and Eucharistic Visitors *Admin and Trainer.*

FOND DU LAC—Deacons School *Dean* Rev Mary Trainor E942 Whispering Pines Rd Waupaca WI 54981 *E-mail:* pastormaryt@gmail.com.

FOND DU LAC—Education for Ministry (EFM) Rev R Patience 130 Cherry Ct Appleton WI 54915 *E-mail:* dcnpatience@gmail.com.

HAITI—Theological Seminary Cn Ogé Beauvoir Port-au-Prince Haiti Lay Leaders Training Montrouis.

HONDURAS—Programa Diocesano de Educación Teológica V Rev Pascual Torres 23 Ave 21 Calle "C" Col Trejo Apdo postal 586 San Pedro Sual 011-504-556-6155 *Fax:* 011-504-556-6467 Trng for clergy and lay min devel.

IOWA—EfM Anne Williams *E-mail:* annewill@ netins.net.

IOWA—eSeminary Alice Haugen (319) 351-7302 *E-mail:* alice.haugen@gmail.com.

IOWA—Summer Ministries School & Retreat Judith Crossett (319) 337-7943 *E-mail:* judith-crossett@uiowa.edu.

KANSAS—Bishop Kemper School for Ministry The Rev Andrew Grosso *Dean* 300 S Fifth St Atchison KS 66002 (913) 367-3171. The diocese, along with West Missouri, Western Kansas, and Nebraska, are the partner dioceses that operate and oversee the school. It provides education for those seeking ordination as deacons and priests, as well as for lay ministers and lay leaders. Faculty members come from all four dioceses. Classes meet at Upton Hall and Grace Cathedral in Topeka.

KENTUCKY—School of Ministry *Dir* Rose Bogal-Allbritten 1504 Kirkwood Dr Murray KY 42071 (270) 293-9490 *E-mail:* rosebogal@gmail.com.

LEXINGTON—DOCC Training E Conrad.

LEXINGTON—EFM Training Dale Chapman Lexington KY.

LONG ISLAND—The George Mercer Jr Memorial School of Theology 65 Fourth St Garden City NY 11530 (516)248-4800 x140 *Fax:* (576) 248-4883 *E-mail:* merceroffice@dioceseli.org.

LOS ANGELES—Education for Ministry (EFM) *Dio Coord* Jan Jones *E-mail:* JLJ72541@aol.com.

LOS ANGELES—Kaleidoscope Institute *Dir* Rev Canon Eric Law Box 512164 Los Angeles CA 90051-0164 (213) 482-2040

LOS ANGELES—Safeguarding God's Children, Child Abuse and Sexual Misconduct Prevention Training as a matter of diocesan policy, all clergy and lay people working with children and teens, as well as church musicians, custodial staff, lay Eucharistic ministers, and others in local congregations must receive sexual misconduct prevention and child abuse prevention training every five years. Training includes "Safeguarding God's Children" and Sexual Misconduct Prevention units. Open to clergy and laity in the diocese. *Contact:* Human Resources (213) 482-2040 x250.

MAINE—Deacon Formation Program Bishop's Office 143 State St Portland ME 04101 (207) 772-1953 x125 *E-mail:* bmartin@episcopalmaine.org.

MARYLAND—Exploring Baptismal Ministry K Boyer 9684 Norfolk Ave Laurel MD 20723.

MARYLAND—Discerning Ordained Vocation K Boyer 9684 Norfolk Ave Laurel MD 20723.

MARYLAND—Deacon Formation—Ven MS Doran *dcn* 1641 Fairhill Dr Edgewater MD 21037 & Ven CW Wright *priest* 7859 Tick Neck Rd Pasadena MD 21122.

MASSACHUSETTS—Anti-RacismTraining Program Rev Karen Montagno 138 Tremont St Boston MA 02111 (617) 482-5800 *E-mail:* kmontagno@diomass.org.

MASSACHUSETTS—Clergy Continuing Education Committee Marsha Searle 138 Tremont St Boston MA 02111 (617) 482-5800 *E-mail:* msearle@ diomass.org.

MASSACHUSETTS—Diaconate Training Program The Ven Pat Zifcak 138 Tremont St Boston MA 02111 (617) 482-5800 pzifcak@diomass.org

MASSACHUSETTS—Education for Ministry *Coords* Rev Lyn Brakeman & Rev Richard Simeone 203 Pemberton St Unit 3 Cambridge MA 02140

(617) 354-1481 *E-mail:* lgb3888@earthlink.net or rjs4166@earthlink.net.

MASSACHUSETTS—**Lay Eucharistic Ministry Training** Constance Melahoures 15 Fremont St Plymouth MA 02360-3323 (508) 746-3805 *E-mail:* conmel@aol.com.

MASSACHUSETTS—**Safe Church Training Program** Rev Karen Montagno 138 Tremont St Boston MA 02111 (617) 482-5800 *E-mail:* kmontagno@diomass.org.

MICHIGAN—**Whitaker Institute** 4800 Woodward Ave Detroit MI 48201 (313) 833-4423 *E-mail:* ewilliams@edomi.org; *Ex Dir* The Rev Eric Williams: As the formation/education arm of the Diocese of Michigan, Whitaker Institute seeks to provide lifelong Christian formation for all baptized members, equipping people for a life in ministry as the Body of Christ, broken for the world.

MILWAUKEE—**DeKoven Center** Max Dershem *Dir* 600 21st St Racine WI 53403 (262) 633-6401 Cont ed for clergy and retreats.

MILWAUKEE—**Church Development Institute**— Margaret Bean *Bp Assist for Cong Dev* 804 E Juneau Ave Milwaukee WI 53202 (414) 272-3028.

MISSISSIPPI—**Cooperative College for Congregational Development** Rev Cn David Johnson PO Box 23107 Jackson MS 39225-3107 (601) 948-5954.

MISSISSIPPI—**Post Ordination Consultation (POC)** 2 year training. Rev Marian Fortner PO Box 1483 Hattiesburg MS 39403 (601) 544-5551.

MISSISSIPPI—**Fresh Start** 2 year training. Rev Betsy Baumgarten 310 N Cleveland Ave Long Beach MS 39560.

MISSISSIPPI—**Education for Ministry (EfM)** Barbara Jones 845 On the Green Dr Biloxi MS 39532 (228) 697-0014.

MISSISSIPPI—**Safeguarding God's Children: Safe Church Training** Rev Annie Elliott 370 Old Agency Rd Ridgeland MS 39157 (601) 853-6016.

MISSISSIPPI—**Deacon's School** Rev Charles Hawkins 705 Rayburn Ocean Springs MS 39564 (228) 875-4454.

MISSISSIPPI—**Racial Reconciliation (Anti-Racism) Training** Dr Anita George 301 Briarwick Dr Starkville MS 39759 (662) 324-0586.

MISSISSIPPI—**Wardens' and Treasurers' Training** Rev Brian Ponder PO Box 23107 Jackson MS 39225-3107 (601) 948-5954.

MISSISSIPPI—**New Vestry Members Training** Cn Kathryn McCormick PO Box 23107 Jackson MS 39225-3107 (601) 948-5954.

MISSISSIPPI—**Adults Working With Children (AWWY) Training** Whitney Robinson 124 Price Street Oxford MS 38655 (601) 810-5133.

MISSISSIPPI—**Camp Musician Training** Rev Annie Elliot St Andrew's Episcopal Day School 370 Old Agency Rd Ridgeland MS 39157 (601) 853-6016.

MISSISSIPPI—**Counselors in Training (CIT)** Duncan Gray IV 515 Wedgewood Oxford MS 38655 (601) 956-8256.

MISSISSIPPI—**Stewardship Training** Rev Kyle Seage 5400 Old Canton Rd Jackson MS 39211 (601) 956-5788.

MISSISSIPPI—**Lay Worship Leader Training** Danny Meadors 5287 Espy Ave Long Beach MS 39560 (228) 452-7325.

MISSOURI—**Camp Phoenix** *Director* B. Butler (314) 231-1220 *E-mail:* camp-phoenix@diocesemo. org.

MISSOURI—**Commission on Dismantling Racism** *Chair* The Rev. Chester Hines (314) 231-1220 *E-mail:* info@diocesemo.org. The commission leads the 14-hour mandatory training for clergy and lay leadership as mandated by the 73rd General Convention.

MISSOURI—**Commission on Ministry** The Rev. Pat Glenn, chair, Dr. Michael Booker, The Rev. Renee Fenner, Ms. Kathy Alexander, Ms. Lisann Backsmeyer, The Rev. Mark Kozielec, The Rev. Dr. Paula Hartsfield, The Rev. Harry Leip III, Ms. Celeste Smith, The Rev. Michael Angell, Dr. Carter Whitson

MISSOURI—**Community of Hope** Trains and supports lay people for pastoral ministry within and beyond their congregations. Church of St. Michael and St. George, Nancy Ferriss, Coordinator naferriss@gmail.com; Debbie Caby, Grace Circle of Care 1, debbiecaby@yahoo.com

MISSOURI—**Deaconess Anne House** 1210 Locust St Louis MO 63103 *Dir* The Rev. Rebecca Ragland (314) 231-1220 x1381. Intentional community, Episcopal Service Corps.

MISSOURI—**Episcopal School for Ministry** *Dn* The Rev. Dr Daniel J Handschy 1210 Locust St St Louis MO 63103 (314) 231-1220 *Fax:* (314) 231-3373 *E-mail:* ESMdean@diocesemo.org *Web:* www.diocesemo.org. Training for lay and diaconal ministry and congregational development.

NAVAJOLAND AREA MISSION—**Hooghan Learning Circle** Anna Fowler Box 720 Farmington NM 87499 (505) 327-7549 *Fax:* (505) 327-6904 *E-mail:* bikerjack_anna@msn.com.

NAVAJOLAND AREA MISSION—**Steven Plummer Leadership School** *E-mail:* ceaton@ec-n.org.

NEVADA—**Wes Frensdorff School of Christian Formation** *Web:* www.frensdorffschool.webs.com *Canon for Adult-Formation* Chuck McCray *E-mail:* chuck@episcopalnevada.org.

NEW HAMPSHIRE—**Leadership Institute** Judith Esmay *Cn for Lay Ldrshp (Dean)* (603) 643-9085

E-mail: judithesmay@gmail.com 63 Green St Concord NH 03301.

NEW HAMPSHIRE—Evangelism Institute The Rev Jason A Wells 63 Green St Concord NH 03301 (603) 643-9085 *E-mail:* Fr.jawells@gmail.com.

NEW HAMPSHIRE—Safe Church Training Lynn Eaton 63 Green St Concord NH 03301 (603) 224-1914 *E-mail:* leaton@nhepiscopal.org.

NEW HAMPSHIRE—Stewardship Institute **Steward-ship** Kathryn Buttrick *Cn for Mission Res* 63 Green St Concord NH 03301(603) 224-1914 *E-mail:* kbuttrick@nhepiscopal.org.

NEW JERSEY—Anti-Racism Training *Co-Chairs:* The Rev Theodore E Moore, Dcn *E-mail:* tmoore@syncom.net; The Rev Mark Van Sant *E-mail:* mvansant56@verizon.net

NEW JERSEY—Sexual Misconduct Awareness Training The Rev Charles N Lochner; The Rev Dr Paul S Rimassa; The Rev Dr Carolyn A Bradley, Dcn; The Rev Carol Ann Pepe, Dcn

NORTH CAROLINA—School of Ministry Ayliffe Mumford *Dir* 301 N Elm St Ste 308C St Greensboro NC 27401 (336) 273-5770 *E-mail:* ayliffe.mumford@episdionc.org.

NORTH DAKOTA—Deacon Formation 3600 S 25th St Fargo ND 58104 (701) 235-6688.

NORTHERN MICHIGAN—LifeCycles On-going formation for congregations, covenant groups and ministry support teams.

NORTHWEST TEXAS—School of Ordained Ministry 1802 Broadway Lubbock TX 79401 (806) 763-1370 x1 *Dean* Dcn Melissa Wafer-Cross *E-mail:* ethames@nwtdiocese.org. Formation program for the diaconate and bi-vocational priesthood.

NORTHWESTERN PENNSYLVANIA—Institute for Ministry 145 W 6th St Erie PA 16501 (814) 456-4203. Training for deacons and local priests; lay ministry.

OREGON—The Academy Rev M Hagen, Director 1800 SE Military Ln, Portland OR 97219 *E-mail:* maureenhagen@gmail.com

PENNSYLVANIA—Continuing Education Jill Mathis Church House 3717 Chestnut St Suite 300 Philadelphia PA 19104 (215) 627-6434 *Fax:* (267) 900-2928 *E-mail:* jillm@diopa.org.

PENNSYLVANIA—Education for Ministry Coordination *Coord* Alan Lindsay Church House 3717 Chestnut St Suite 300 Philadelphia PA 19104 (215) 627-6434 x127 *E-mail:* alanadiopa.org. Four-year education course for adults, based on core curriculum of School of Theology of the University of the South Sewanee TN. Study takes place in small groups. Trained mentors lead in locations around the Diocese.

PENNSYLVANIA—Leadership Institute and Ministry Resource Center (LI & MRC) Henry Carnes Church House 3717 Chestnut St Suite 300 Philadelphia PA 19104 (215) 627-6434 *Fax:* (267) 900-2928 *E-mail:* henryc@diopa.org. MRC houses collection of curric and provides materials for loan, research, and program/resource recommendations. Consultations provided in Christian Educ, stewardship, vestry, evang, leadership development, multi-media technology.

PENNSYLVANIA—Philadelphia Theology Institute Rev JL Shannon PO Box 96 Lansdowne PA 19050 *E-mail:* james@philadelphiatheologicalinstitute.org. Offers workshops, conferences and consultations on Theology issues and challenges facing the church in the 5-county Philadelphia area.

PENNSYLVANIA—Training and Formation of Deacons c/o The Rev Dr Pamela Nesbit 3717 Chestnut St Suite 300 Philadelphia PA 19104 (215) 598-0948 *E-mail:* pamelanesbit@gmail.com.

PITTSBURGH—Deacon Formation Program

PITTSBURGH—Education for Ministry *Coord* Vanessa Sterling 155 W Hutchinson Ave Pittsburgh PA 15218 (412) 551-2042 *E-mail:* vmsterling@gmail.com.

PITTSBURGH—Lay Ministry Initiative *Coord* Jessie Hipolit 36 Swallow Hill Rd Carnegie PA 15106 (412) 429-9287 *E-mail:* jessiehipolit@comcast.net.

PUERTO RICO—Escuela para Ministerios Laicos, Escuela para el Diaconado Vocacional, Seminario San Pedro y San Pablo.

SAN DIEGO—Diocesan School for Ministry Rev Cn Allisyn Thomas 2083 Sunset Cliffs Blvd San Diego CA 92107 (619) 481-5451 *Fax:* (619) 481-3091 *E-mail:* athomas@edsd.org *Web:* www.sfmedsd.org.

SAN DIEGO—The School for Ministry 2083 Sunset Cliff s Blvd San Diego CA 92107 (619) 481-5466 *Website:* http://www.sfmedsd.org/#/home/home. The vision for the School for Ministry is to excite and engage the people of the diocese and those who are not yet our members as lifelong inquirers into the life of the Christian faith. The School for Ministry seeks to realize this vision by partnering with adult learners as they navigate various paths for learning both in the preparation for ordained ministry and in the advancement of ongoing lay and ordained ministry within the life of the Church.

SAN JOAQUIN—Celebration of Ministry Workshops.

SAN JOAQUIN—Eucharistic Minister and Visitor Training.

SAN JOAQUIN—Leadership Workshops.

SAN JOAQUIN—Safeguarding God's Children.

SAN JOAQUIN—Treasurer's Workshops.

SAN JOAQUIN—Deacon School within Diocese working with School for Deacons, Berkeley, CA.

SOUTH DAKOTA—**Niobrara School for Ministry** Rev P Sneve 500 S Main Ave Sioux Falls SD 57104-6814 (605) 338-9751 *Fax:* (605) 336-6243

SOUTHEAST FLORIDA—**School for Christian Studies** The Ven Tom Bruttell

SOUTHERN OHIO—**Formation Programs** Rev Cn Anne Reed 412 Sycamore St Cincinnati OH 45202 (800) 582-1712. School for Ministry, New Clergy Residency Program.

SOUTHERN VIRGINIA—**Education for Ministry** *Coord* Anne Meyer 1333 Jamestown Rd Williamsburg VA 23185 (757) 229-1111 *E-mail:* ann@stmartinswmbg.org.

SOUTHWEST FLORIDA—**Anti-Racism** The Rev Cn Michael Durning **8005 25th St East Parrish FL 34219** (941) 556-0315 *Fax:* (941) 556-0321 *E-mail:* mdurning@episcopalswfl.org.

SOUTHWEST FLORIDA—**Safeguarding** The Rev Cn Michael Durning 8005 25th St East Parrish FL 34219 (941) 556-0315 *Fax:* (941) 556-0321 *E-mail:* mdurning@episcopalswfl.org.

SOUTHWEST FLORIDA—**School for Ministry** The Ven Dennis McManis 8005 25th St East Parrish FL 34219 (941) 556-0314 *Fax:* (941) 556-0321 *Web:* www.episcopalswfl.org. Christian education for various ministries.

SOUTHWESTERN VIRGINIA—**Bishop Marmion Resource Center** *Coord* Kate Garcia Box 2279 Roanoke VA 24009 (540) 342-6797 *Fax:* (540) 343-9114 *E-mail:* bmrc@dioswva.org *Web:* www.bmrc-online.org. Christian formation and other materials useful to parishes.

SOUTHWESTERN VIRGINIA—**Grace House Learning/Training Center** *Dir* Anita Boyd 5100 Pewter Dr St Paul VA 24283 (276) 395-6588 *Fax:* (276) 395-6588 *E-mail:* aboydgrchse@yahoo.com *Web:* www.gracehouse.dioswva.org. Weekend retreats, day-long planning sessions, summer labor/ learning exchange progs.

TAIWAN—**St John's University** Rev LYR Chang 499 Sec 4 Tam-King Rd Hsinpu Tamshui TAIWAN 251 2-2801-3131 x6330, 6331 *Fax:* 2-2801-3424.

TAIWAN—**Trinity Hall Episcopal Center for Theological Studies** Rev WB Tzeng 7 Ln 105 Hang-chow S Rd Sec 1 Taipei TAIWAN 10060 2-2341-1265 *Fax:* 2-2396-2014 *E-mail:* skhtpe@ms12.hinet.net.

UTAH—**Utah Ministry Formation Program (UMFP)** The Rev Cn Mary June Nestler 75 S 200 E Salt Lake City UT 84111-2147 (801) 322-4131 *Web:* www.episcopal-ut.org. Provides educational preparation for those seeking ordination as well as continuing education for lay and clergy.

VERMONT—**Safe Church Training** *Coord* L Bates.

WASHINGTON—**Shalem Institute for Spiritual Formation** 3025 Fourth St NE Washington DC 20017.

WEST TENNESSEE—**Anti-Racism**

WEST TENNESSEE—**Safeguarding God's Children** information: www.episwtn.org/ governance—administration/ *Contact* Lauren Stone (901) 526-0023 *E-mail:* lstone@episwtn.org.

WEST TENNESSEE—**Safeguarding God's People** information: www.episwtn.org/governance—admin-istration/ *Contact* Chip Davis (901) 937-4782 *E-mail:* cdavis@episwtn.org.

WEST VIRGINIA—**ConneXions** Cn Faith C Perrizo PO Box 5400 Charleston WV 25361 (304) 344-3597 *E-mail:* fperrizo@wvdiocese.org.

WESTERN LOUISIANA—**Diocesan School of Theology** Rev Dr Frank Hughes 103 Chandler St Minden LA 71055 (318) 377-1259 *E-mail:* fwhughes54@hotmail.com.

WESTERN NEW YORK—**Canterbury Institute** M Gingell, *Director*

Prepared to Serve licensing program P Dempesy-Sims

Discover Sundays M Gingell

Pathways Adult Education B Price

POST-ORDINATION AND TRAINING INSTITUTIONS

Ecumenical Theological Seminary

DMin MDiv MA in Pas Min and Urban Min Diploma progs. Only ecum Theology sem in SE Mich; accredited by ATS. *Pres* Dr Marsha Foster Boyd 2930 Woodward Ave Detroit MI 48201. (313) 831-5200. *Fax:* (313) 831-1353. *E-mail:* ETS@ etseminary.edu. *Web:* www.etseminary.edu.

New Directions Ministries Inc

Provides developmental trng prog for laity and clergy in small congs with emphasis on mins of all persons, regional and cluster ministries. Leadership Academy for New Directions (LAND) is available for national, regional, dio levels (urban as well as rural). Ecumenical. *Pres* LaDonna Wind 4434 Buttonbush Glen Dr Louisville KY 40241-4189 (502) 412-0196 *E-mail:* vanzoelen05@gmail.com; *VPres* The Rev John T Harris PO Box 1291 Gridley CA 95948 (530) 846-4257 *E-mail:* +john1@sbcglobal.net; The Rev Warren Frelund 1029 West State St Mason City IA 50401 (641) 423-1138 *E-mail:* wfrelund@q.com.

School of Theology University South DMin and STM Program

3-week summer session at Sewanee. Write to Advanced Degrees Program 335 Tennessee Ave School of Theology Sewanee TN 37383-0001 (931) 598-1478 *Fax:* (931) 598-1852. *E-mail:* advdeg@ sewanee.edu *Web:* http://theology.sewanee.edu.

Trinity Institute

Trinity Institute equips clergy and lay persons in the Episcopal Church for imaginative and catalytic leadership. Outreach of Trinity Parish in NYC. 120 Broadway, New York, NY, 10271 (212) 602-0800 *Fax:* (212) 602-0722 *Web:* http://www.trinitywallstreet.org/education/trinity-institute.

CHURCH COLLEGES AND UNIVERSITIES

Colleges and Universities of the Anglican Communion/Assoc of Episcopal Colleges

815 Second Ave NY 10017 (212) 716-6148 *Fax:* (212) 986-5039 *E-mail*: office@cuac.org *Web:* www.cuac.org. *General Secretary:* Rev Cn James G. Callaway, DD, *Chair* The Rev Dr Robert Derrenbacker Thorneloe University Sudbury Ontario CANADA. Includes ten accredited undergrad colleges listed below. AEC develops programs to support Christian values on and off campus; provides liaison, public relations, and fund raising support for the colleges; and provides the means for distributing gifts or bequests equitably among some or all members. Offers volunteer opportunities for students and recent graduates, some including formal study for academic credit, and most based at church-related service agencies. AEC was instrumental in the 1993 founding of Colleges and Universities of the Anglican Communion (CUAC), a worldwide association of 130 academic institutions of Anglican foundation on five continents, and continues as the American chapter to serve as its headquarters and staff support. CUAC is a "network" of the Anglican Communion. CUAC also maintains an informal network for Anglican theological colleges and programs worldwide.

Bard College

PO Box 5000 Annandale-on-Hudson NY 12504-5000 (845) 758-6822. Coed 1860. Liberal arts, sciences, and fine arts offering a four-year B.A. and a five-year B.S./B.A. degree in economics and finance. M.A. in curatorial studies, and M.S. in environmental policy and climate science and policy at the Annandale campus; M.F.A. and M.A.T. at multiple campuses; and M.A., M.Phil., and Ph.D. in the decorative arts at the Bard Graduate Center in Manhattan. Internationally, Bard confers dual B.A. degrees at the Faculty of Liberal Arts and Sciences, St Petersburg State University, Russia (Smolny College), and American University of Central Asia in Kyrgyzstan; and dual B.A. and M.A.T. degrees at Al-Quds University in East Jerusalem. *Pres* Leon Botstein PhD, *Chap* Rev Bruce D Chilton, PhD. *E-mail:* admission@bard.edu *Web:* www.bard.edu

Cuttington University

Box 10-0277 1000 Monrovia 10 Liberia West Africa 011-231-227-413. 1889. Reopened in fall 1998. Emphasis on trad liberal arts, research, and community partnerships in the context of Christian service. *Interim Pres* Dr Evelyn Kandakai, *Chap* Rev James Tamba. Inquiries may also be addressed to CUAC. *E-mail:* cuttingtonuniversity@yahoo.com *Web*: www.cuttington.org.

Hobart and William Smith Colleges

Geneva NY 14456 (315) 789-5500. 1822. Oldest Coll continuously associated with Epis Church in US. William Smith College (for women) and Hobart share faculty, library, and labs. *Pres* Dr Mark D Gearan *Chap* Rev D. Maurice Charles *E-mail:* admissions@hws.edu *Web:* www.hws.edu.

Kenyon College

Gambier OH 43022 (740) 427-5000. Coed 1824. Fine Arts, Humanities, Natural Sciences, and Social Sciences. Publisher of *Kenyon Review* and *Psychological Record.* New Olin Library. *Pres* Sean M Decatur PhD *E-mail:* admissions@kenyon.edu *Web:* www.kenyon.edu.

St Augustine College

1333-1345 W Argyle St Chicago IL 60640-3594 (773) 878-8756. 1980. Coed bilingual: Spanish/English. 2-yr technological and vocational prog; fully accredited. Main campus, plus four satellite facilities in areas of high concentration of Hispanic residents. *Pres* Dr Everett B. Ward *Web:* www.staugustine.edu.

Saint Augustine's University

1315 Oakwood Ave Raleigh NC 27610 (919) 516-4000. Coed 1867. Historically Black. Liberal Arts differential curriculum with an academic focus in STEM, Mass Communication and Journalism, Public Health and Criminal Justice. *Pres* Dr Everett B Ward, *Chap* Rev. Nita Johnson Byrd *E-mail:* admissions@st-aug.edu *Web:* www.st-aug.edu.

The University of the South

735 University Ave Sewanee TN 37383 (931) 598-1000. Coed 1857. Coll of Arts and Sciences and School of Theology. Publ *Sewanee Review,* oldest lit-crit quarterly in US and *Sewanee Theological Review. Chanc* Rt Rev Samuel Johnson Howard, DD, *Vice-Chanc and Pres* JohnM.McCardell Jr PhD, *Chap* Rev Thomas E Macfie Jr *E-mail:* admiss@ sewanee.edu *Web:* www.sewanee.edu.

Trinity University of Asia

Cathedral Heights 275 E Rodriguez Sr Ave Quezon City Philippines 1100 011-63-2-702-2882. Coed. Episc Cathedral complex includes pre-school through college with 3,600 students at coll and grad level. Lib Arts, Bus Adm, Ed, Nursing, Med Tech. MA in Educ. *Pres* Josefina S Sumaya PhD, *Chap* Chap Rev Edwin J. Ayabo *Web:* www.tua.edu.ph.

Université Episcopale d'Haiti

14 rue Légitime, Champ de Mars, B.P. Box 2730, Port-au-Prince, Haiti. 509 22 27 7963. Coed 1994. Francophone. Programs in agronomy, education, theology, accounting, management. Affiliated with FSIL Nursing School (Léogâne), Bishop Tharp Business & Technology Institute (Les Cayes), St. Barnabas Agricultural School (Terrier Rouge), Episcopal Theology Seminary (Port-au-Prince). *Pres* Dr Lucien Jean Bernard *E-mail* unephhaiti@hotmail.com *Web* www.uneph.org.

Voorhees College
Denmark SC 29042 (803) 708-1234. Coed 1897. Historically Black. 4-yr Liberal Arts Coll with 4 acad divisions: Business and Economics, Education and Humanities, Natural Sciences and Mathematics, Social Sciences. Offers 2-yr degree in Secretarial Science and Criminal Justice. Collaborative arrangement with Denmark Technical School and SC State Coll. *Pres* Dr Cleveland L Sellers Jr, *Chap* Rev Dr James T Yarsiah *E-mail:* admissions@ voorhees.edu *Web:* www.voorhees.edu.

MINISTRY IN HIGHER EDUCATION

Office for Young Adult and Higher Education Ministries
815 Second Ave New York NY 10017 (800) 334-7626. Rev G Douglas Fenton *Staff Off* (x6323)

Annual New Campus Ministers' Orientation and Chaplains' Gathering
The Office of Young Adult and Higher Education Ministries offers an annual seminar for new chaplains and a conference/retreat for professional development for all campus chaplains.

Chaplains Serving in Colleges and Universities
For complete information, access an online ecumenical directory at www.higheredmin.org.

PROVINCE I
Episcopal BU: Episcopal Campus Ministry at Boston University The Rev. Cameron Partridge *E-mail:* cepart@bu.edu
Episcopal Center at University of Rhode Island The Rev. David W. Dobbins *E-mail:* staugustineschurch@ necoxmail.com
Episcopal Chaplaincy at Harvard The Rev. Luther Zeigler *E-mail:* chaplain@harvardepiscopalians. org
Episcopal Church at Yale The Rev. Nihal C. de Lanerolle *E-mail:* episcopal@yale.edu
Lutheran Episcopal Ministry at Massachusetts Institute of Technology The Rev. Thea Keith-Lucas *E-mail:* theakl@mit.edu
Lutheran-Episcopal Campus Ministry at Northeastern University The Rev. Judith Stuart *E-mail:* j.stuart@ neu.edu
Plymouth State University Campus Ministry The Rev. Grace Burson *E-mail:* gburson@mail.plymouth. edu
St. Mark's Episcopal Chapel at UConn The Rev. Hilary Greer *E-mail:* admin@stmarkschapel.org
Trinity College Office of Spiritual and Religious Life The Rev. Allison Read *E-mail:* allison.read@ trincoll.edu

PROVINCE II
Canterbury Club at Columbia University and Barnard College Richard Sloan *E-mail:* rs3046@ columbia.edu
Canterbury Club at West Point The Rev. Judith Ferguson *E-mail:* holyinnocents@verizon.net
Canterbury Downtown serving New York University, The New School, Cooper Union, Pace University The Rev. Mary Cat Young *E-mail:* chaplain@ canterburynyc.org
Canterbury House: The Episcopal Church at The College of New Jersey The Rev. Lisa Caton *E-mail:* caton@tcnj.edu
Diocese of New York Young Adult Network The Rev. Mary Cat Young *E-mail:* ednyyanetwork@gmail. com
Episcopal campus presence Colgate University The Rev Donnel O'Flynn *E-mail:* stchurch@cnymail. com
Episcopal Church at Cornell University The Rev. Clark R. West *E-mail:* crw86@cornell.edu
Protestant Campus Ministry at Stony Brook University Brenda Denise Ford *E-mail:* revbrenda.ford@ stonybrook.edu
Religious Life Office of Hobart and William Smith Colleges The Rev. Lesley M. Adams *E-mail:* ladams@hws.edu
Rutgers Canterbury House The Rev. Gregory Bezilla *E-mail:* episcmin@rci.rutgers.edu
St. Jamesians Young Adult Group Bowie Snodgrass *E-mail:* bsnodgrass@stjames.org
The Episcopal Church at Princeton University The Reverend Peter French *E-mail:* pfrench@ princeton.edu

PROVINCE III
20's/30's Group at St. Columba's Episcopal Church, Washington DC The Rev. Jason Cox *E-mail:* jcox@ columba.org
All Saints Episcopal Church Christian College & Young Adults Group Gary Weider *E-mail:* gary. wieder@allsaintschurch.net
ARISE (a ministry of United College Ministries in Northern Virginia) The Rev. Mark Montgomery *E-mail:* arisegmu@gmail.com
Canterbury - Episcopal Campus Ministry at Washington & Lee University and Virginia Military Institute James Keane *E-mail:* chaplain@relee-church.org
Canterbury Club Episcopal Campus Ministry to Christopher Newport University Lauren McDonald *E-mail:* revlauren4@gmail.com
Canterbury Episcopal & Lutheran Campus Ministry at the University of Mary Washington The Rev. Anne A. Jones *E-mail:* anne@christ-lutheran-church.org
Canterbury Episcopal Campus Ministry at Lynchburg College Nina Vest Salmon *E-mail:* salmon@ lynchburg.edu
Canterbury Episcopal Campus Ministry at Radford University Robert Morris *E-mail:* sarahcarper@ hotmail.com
Canterbury Episcopal Campus Ministry of Harrisonburg The Rev. Laura Minnich Lockey *E-mail:* hburg.canterbury@gmail.com
Canterbury Episcopal Center at Old Dominion

University The Rev. Wendy Wilkinson *E-mail:* chaplain@oducanterbury.org

Canterbury Episcopal Student Ministry at the University of Virginia Elaine Ellis Thomas *E-mail:* canterbury@stpaulsmemorialchurch.org

Canterbury Fellowship/Episcopal Campus Ministry at Virginia Tech The Rev. Scott A. West *E-mail:* saw764@yahoo.com

Carpe Deum Young Adults Group at St. Paul's Parish, Washington DC Steven Chlapecka *E-mail:* carpedeum@stpauls-kst.com

Church of the Epiphany 20's-30's Group The Rev. Randolph Charles *E-mail:* mdail@epiphanydc.org

College of William & Mary Canterbury Association The Rev. John Maxwell Kerr *E-mail:* canterbury@email.wm.edu

Episcopal (Anglican) Campus Ministry at Penn State E-mail: ccd2@psu.edu

Episcopal Campus Ministry at Haverford and Bryn Mawr College Melissa Wilcox *E-mail:* mwilcox@theredeemer.org

Episcopal Church of the Ascension at the University of Pittsburgh The Rev. Stacey Fussell *E-mail:* mail@ascensionbradford.org

Episcopal Diocese of Virginia Young Adults and Campus Ministry programs Paris Ball *E-mail:* pball@thediocese.net

Episcopal Service Corps-Maryland Jan Hamill *E-mail:* escmaryland@gmail.com

Episcopal-Anglican Presence at American University Carolyn Seaton *E-mail:* cseaton1@starpower.net

Episcopal-Lutheran Campus Ministry for Longwood University and Hampden-Sydney College Bob Zupanek *E-mail:* bob@johnsmemorial.org

George Washington University Canterbury Club JoAnne Beard *E-mail:* stmaryschurch728@gmail.com

Georgetown Episcopal Ministry David Bujard *E-mail:* bujardd@georgetown.edu

Grace Church, Georgetown: 20s/30s/40s Group Jane Mosbacher *E-mail:* Jane.Mosbacher@gmail.com

Hood College Chapel The Rev. Beth O'Malley *E-mail:* omalley@hood.edu

Howard University's Episcopal/Anglican Ministry The Rev. Robyn Franklin-Vaughn *E-mail:* robyn116@msn.com

Latrobe Fellowship, Young Adults at St. John's Episcopal Church in Lafayette Square The Rev. Mike Angell *E-mail:* mike.angell@stjohns-dc.org

St. Albans Episcopal Church Young Adult Ministry The Rev. Matthew Hanisian *E-mail:* matthewh@stalbansdc.org

St. Mark's Episcopal Church, Capitol Hill: Young Adults Group Laurel Kennedy *E-mail:* angela.nedd@stmarks.net

St. Mary's College Episcopal Campus Ministry The Rev. John Ball *E-mail:* Trinitysmcmd@olg.com

Trinity Episcopal Church Volunteer Corps, Washington DC The Rev. Canon John Harmon *E-mail:* TVC@Trinitychurchdc.org

UMBC Episcopal Campus Ministry The Rev. Dr.

Katrina Grusell *E-mail:* kgrusell@umbc.edu

University of Delaware Christian Fellowship with Episcopal Campus Ministry Deacon Cecily Sawyer Harmon *E-mail:* udel.episcopalians@gmail.com

University of Maryland Episcopal/Anglican Campus Ministry The Rev. Otis Gaddis, III *E-mail:* eaterps@umd.edu

Virginia Commonwealth University Episcopal Campus Ministry The Rev. Kimberly (Kim) Reinholz *E-mail:* kreinholz@ghtc.org

Washington National Cathedral: 20's and 30's Group Jeff Stitz *E-mail:* 20sand30s@cathedralcongregation.org

Young Adults Group at St. John's Episcopal Church, Georgetown Jaimie Hoop *E-mail:* info@stjohnsgeorgetown.com

PROVINCE IV

20s30s Group at The Cathedral of St. Philip Toby Reed *E-mail:* tobias@linny.net

Absalom Jones Episcopal Center serving AUC communities The Rev. Kimberly Jackson *E-mail:* chaplain@absalomjonesauc.org

All Saints Atlanta Young Adults' Ministry Tim Black *E-mail:* tblack@allsaintsatlanta.org

All Saints' Chapel at Sewanee: The University of the South Tom Macfie, University Chaplain *E-mail:* coutten@sewanee.edu

Athens Episcopal Young Adults The Rev. Edwin Beckham *E-mail:*

Barth House Episcopal Center, University of Memphis The Rev. John B. Burruss *E-mail:* john@episcopalcordova.org

Birmingham Episcopal Campus Ministries The Rev. Bill Blackerby *E-mail:* bill@trinitycommons.org

Campus Ministry in Charleston Caleb Lee *E-mail:* CLee@gracesc.org

Canterbury at Davidson College The Rev. Elizabeth Marie Melchionna *E-mail:* chaplain@canterburyatdavidson.org

Canterbury at Presbyterian College Jessica Taylor / Rachel Parsons-Wells *E-mail:* jntaylor@presby.edu

Canterbury Chapel Episcopal Church and Student Center at the University of Alabama The Rev. Marc Burnette *E-mail:* canterburychapel@gmail.com

Canterbury Club at All Saints Episcopal Church Cynthia C. Selby *E-mail:* landerson@allsaintsmorristown.org

Canterbury Club of Northwest Georgia The Rev. Janice Bracken Wright *E-mail:* janicewright001@bellsouth.net

Canterbury Episcopal Campus Ministry at Jacksonville State University The Rev. Michael Rich *E-mail:* office@stlukesal.org

Canterbury Fellowship at Morehead State University The Rev. Keila Carpenter Thomas *E-mail:* stalbansmorehead@gmail.com

Canterbury of Columbia at University of South Carolina Joe Setzer / Thomas Duncan *E-mail:* jsetzer270@gmail.com

Canterbury of Furman Hannah Wheeler *E-mail:* hannah.wheeler@furman.edu

Canterbury of Spartanburg Helen Strickland / Matthew Yochum *E-mail:* stricklandhm1@email.wofford.edu

Church of the Servant Adam Pierce *E-mail:* apierce1987@gmail.com

Columba House Young Adult Ministry Center Rudy Reyes *E-mail:* info@columbahouse.org

Cooperative Christian Ministry of Charlotte The. Rev. Steve Cheyney *E-mail:* steve@campus-ministry.org

CrossTies 20s and 30s Group at Chapel of the Cross in Chapel Hill The Reverend Tambria E. Lee *E-mail:* tlee@thechapelofthecross.org

Diocese of Atlanta Young Adults The Rev. M. Edwin Beckham *E-mail:* edwin.beckham@gmail.com

Elon University Chaplaincy The Rev. Jan Fuller *E-mail:* jfuller3@elon.edu

Emory University Episcopal Center The Rev. Mandy Brady *E-mail:* mo.mandy.brady@emory.edu

Episcopal Campus Ministry at Georgia Southern University Michael Wood *E-mail:* Michaelwoodmiles@gmail.com

Episcopal Campus Ministry at University of Louisville Erendira Jimenez-Pike *E-mail:* episcopalcampusministryuofl@gmail.com

Episcopal Campus Ministry at Western Kentucky University The Rev. Michael Blewett *E-mail:* ben@cecbg.com

Episcopal Campus Ministry of Armstrong Atlantic State University The Rev. Michael Chaney *E-mail:* ECM.AASU@Gmail.com

Episcopal Center at Duke University The Rev. Nils Chittenden *E-mail:* nils.chittenden@duke.edu

Episcopal Chapel of the Incarnation at the University of Florida The Rev. Rich Clark *E-mail:* chaplain@ufchapelhouse.com

Episcopal Church at Ole Miss, Oxford, MS The Rev. Dr. Taylor Moore *E-mail:* administrator@stpetersoxford.org

Episcopal Church at University of Southern Mississippi Elizabeth Lentz-Hill *E-mail:* elizabeth.lentz@usm.edu

Episcopal Church Center at the University of Miami The Rev. Frank J. Corbishley *E-mail:* fcorbishley@miami.edu

Episcopal Church of the Resurrection & The Canterbury Fellowship of MSU, Starkville, MS The Rev. Carol Mead *E-mail:* MSUchaplain@gmail.com

Episcopal Lutheran Campus Ministry *E-mail:* egowdycanady@diocese-eastcarolina.org

Kennesaw State University Canterbury Club Ellen Mintzmyer *E-mail:* canterburyksu@gmail.com

Middle Tennessee State University Campus and Young Adult Ministry (YAMS) Steven Lefebvre *E-mail:* slefebvre@stpaulsmboro.org

Murray State University Canterbury Club The Rev. Matthew Bradley *E-mail:* msu.canterburyclub@murraystate.edu

Osprey Episcopalians...Birds of Pray The Rev. Amy Austin Slater *E-mail:* revamyslater@gmail.com

Project Canterbury at University of Tennessee, Chattanooga Noel Reagan *E-mail:* noel@projectcanterbury.org

Raleigh-Area Episcopal Campus Ministry The Rev. Deborah Fox *E-mail:* deborah.fox@ecm-raleigh.org

SEEK{ers} Community & Sanctuary Teresa B Pasquale *E-mail:* teresa@stpaulsdelray.org

St. Anselem's Episcopal University Chapel Center at the University of South Florida The Rev. Alisa Carmichael *E-mail:* usfchapelcenter@gmail.com

St. Dunstan's Episcopal Church at Auburn University The Rev. Dr. John Wells Warren *E-mail:* wells@saintdunstans.net

St. Francis Young Adult Gathering The Rev. Ben R Wells *E-mail:* ben@stfrancismacon.org

St. Mary's Chapel at UGA The Rev. Gregory Tipton *E-mail:* btipton13@gmail.com

St. Mary's Chapel at UGA The Rev. Gregory Tipton *E-mail:* chaplain@episcopalcenter.org

St. Mary's House at University of North Carolina The Rev. Kevin B. Matthews *E-mail:* smh@stmaryshouse.org

St. Philip's Chapel - Voorhees College, Denmark, SC Father James Yarsiah *E-mail:* jyarsiah@voorhees.edu

The Chapel of the Holy Spirit: Episcopal & ELCA Campus Ministry to Tulane & Loyola The Rev. Minka Shura Sprague, Th.D *E-mail:* msprague@tulane.edu

The Episcopal University Center at Ruge Hall: Serving FSU, TCC and FAMU The Rev. Kyle Stillings *E-mail:* office@rugehall.org

The WELL - Episcopal Lutheran Campus Ministry Rev. Donna Kraus *E-mail:* puglovingpastor@gmail.com

Tyson House Episcopal/Lutheran Campus Ministry at University of Tennessee, Knoxville The Rev. John Tirro *E-mail:* johntirro@mac.com

Vocare Young Adult Ministry in Georgia Julie Shipp *E-mail:* laydirector@vocareingeorgia.org

Winthrop Episcopal Lutheran Campus Ministry Rebecca Lord *E-mail:* pastorlord@comporium.net

Young Adults of St. Bartholomew's Episcopal Church The Rev. Sharon Hiers *E-mail:* sharon@stbartsatlanta.org

PROVINCE V

20s and 30s Group at Christ Church Cathedral The Very Rev. Mike Kinman *E-mail:* lspargo@gmail.com

Brent House: Episcopal Campus Ministry at the University of Chicago The Rev. Stacy Alan *E-mail:* office@brenthouse.org

Calvary Episcopal Church, Cincinnati, Young Adult Group (YAG) Devin Rodgers / Edy Dreith *E-mail:* calvary.episcopal.yag@gmail.com

Campus Ministry at Ferris State University The Rev. Dr. Gary D. Hamp *E-mail:* andrewsrector@gmail.com

Campus Ministry at Indiana University The Rev. Dr. Linda C. Johnson *E-mail:* lijohnso@indiana.edu

Campus Ministry for Midtown Detroit Kit Ilardi *E-mail:* kilardi@detroitcathedral.org

Canterbury at Baldwin-Wallace College The Rev. Gayle Catinella *E-mail:* revgaylecatinella@sbcglobal.net

Canterbury at Kenyon College The Rev. Helen Svoboda-Barber *E-mail:* svobodabarberh@kenyon.edu

Canterbury Club of Truman State University Johnnette Shane *E-mail:* trinity.kirksville@gmail.com

Canterbury House at University of Michigan The Rev. Reid Hamilton *E-mail:* rhhamilt@umich.edu

Canterbury House for Michigan Technological University Rick Buis *E-mail:* chouse@mtu.edu

Canterbury Northwestern The Rev. Michael Kitt *E-mail:* mkittskitt@cs.com

Chapel of the Good Shepherd at Purdue University The Rev. Peter Bunder *E-mail:* sheep@goodshep.org

Church of Our Saviour/Iglesia de Nuestro Salvador Young Adult Ministry The Rev. Paula M Jackson *E-mail:* Mother.Paula@ChurchofOurSaviourCincinnati.org

DePaul Christian Ministries The Rev. Diane Dardon *E-mail:* ddardon@depaul.edu

Episcopal Campus Ministry at Eastern Michigan University The Rev. Dr. JoAnn Kennedy Slater *E-mail:* info@stlukesypsi.org

Episcopal Campus Ministry at the University of Illinois and Parkland College The Reverend Sean Ferrell *E-mail:* stjohns@chapelsjd.org

Episcopal Campus Ministry at University of Wisconsin, Eau Claire The Very Rev. Michael Greene *E-mail:* ccceauclaire@gmail.com

Episcopal Campus Ministry in Columbia, Missouri The Rev. Christina Cobb *E-mail:* Ecmmizzou@gmail.cm

Episcopal Church of the Good Shepherd/Good Earth Farm serving Ohio University The Rev. Katharin Foster *E-mail:* chogs@chogs.org

Grace Place Campus Ministry at Northern Illinois University The Rev. Amy Fallon *E-mail:* info@graceplaceniu.com

Grace Unlimited: Indianapolis Lutheran-Episcopal Campus Ministry The Rev. Dr. Charles W. Allen *E-mail:* charlesallen5@yahoo.com

Hope and Grace Christian Baron *E-mail:* christianjohnbaron@gmail.com

Lutheran Episcopal Campus Ministry (LECM) Whitewater The Rev. Oscar A. Rozo *E-mail:* lecmww@gmail.com

Miami Episcopal Student Ministry Tobie Dahlman *E-mail:* htrector@gmail.com

One Community Lutheran/Episcopal Campus Ministry at Michigan State University *E-mail:* emmsu@msu.edu

Rockwell House Episcopal Campus Ministry at Washington University The Rev. Joseph Chambers *E-mail:* therevjoe@rockwellhouse.org

South Loop Campus Ministry, Episcopal/Lutheran The Rev. Thomas R. Gaulke *E-mail:* slcmpastor@gmail.com

St Francis House Episcopal Student Center at University of Wisconsin The Rev. Jonathan Melton *E-mail:* chaplain@stfrancisuw.org

St. Stephen's Episcopal Campus Ministry at The Ohio State University The Rev. Karl Stevens *E-mail:* campusministry@diosohio.org

The Edge House: Lutheran Campus Ministry at University of Cincinnati The Rev. Alice Connor *E-mail:* pastor@edge-uc.org

The Episcopal Commons at Kent State University Lorenzo Thomas *E-mail:* lthomas9@kent.edu

Trinity Cathedral on Campus at Cleveland State University The Rev. Sahra Harding *E-mail:* sharding@dohio.org

United Campus Ministries of ISU, Saint Mary-of-the-Woods College, Rose-Hulman Institute of Technology The Rev. Dr. Joni Clark *E-mail:* mail@unitedcampusministries.org

PROVINCE VI

All Saints Campus Ministry Mark Heiman *E-mail:* canterbury@allsaintsnorthfield.org

Bozeman Episcopal Young Adult Ministry (BEYAM) Fr. Clark *E-mail:* sj5westolive@msn.com

Campus & Young Adult Ministry at St Paul's on the Hill The Rev. Diana M. Rogers *E-mail:* dianarogers@stpaulsonthehillmn.org

Canterbury Colorado: The Episcopal Ministry to Colorado University, Boulder The Rev. Mary Kate Rejouis *E-mail:* ProgramCoordinator@canterburycolorado.org

Emmaus Campus Ministry at the University of Montana The Rev. John Lund *E-mail:* Johnlund66@gmail.com

Episcopal Campus Ministry at the University of Iowa The Rev. Raisin Horn *E-mail:* rhorn@trinityic.org

Episcopal Campus Ministry in the Duluth area The Rev. Sally Maxwell *E-mail:* smaxwell@d.umn.edu

Episcopal Chaplaincy at Iowa State University Jim Tener *E-mail:* jamestener60@gmail.com

Episcopal Diocese of Iowa Summer Camps Lydia Kelsey Bucklin *E-mail:* lbucklin@iowaepiscopal.org

St Matthews Campus Ministry Lisa Wiens Heinsohn *E-mail:* office@stmatthewsmn.org

United Campus Ministry at Montana State University, Billings The Rev. Rob Kirby *E-mail:* rkirby@msubillings.edu

University Episcopal Community at University of Minnesota Steve Mullaney *E-mail:* info@uec-mn.org

Young Adult Intentional Community on Rosebud The Rev. Lauren Stanley *E-mail:* merelaurens@gmail.com

PROVINCE VII

Autry House: The Episcopal Mission to Rice University The Rev. Patrick M. Hall *E-mail:* phall@

autryhouse.org

Baylor University Spiritual Life Dr. Burt Burleson *E-mail:* Spiritual_Life@baylor.edu

Campus Ministries of the Episcopal Diocese of Kansas E-mail:

Canterbury Association at the University of Central Oklahoma The Rev. Mark Story *E-mail:* fathermark@stmarysedmond.org

Canterbury Campus Ministry at University of New Mexico and Central New Mexico College Vicki Kelsey *E-mail:* campusministry@ccmabq.org

Canterbury Club at Pitt State E-mail: psucanterburyclub@gmail.com

Canterbury Episcopal Campus Ministries at Texas Tech The Rev. Dr. Jennifer Holder *E-mail:* chaplain@texastechcanterbury.org

Canterbury House at The Episcopal Student Center, Texas A&M University The Rev. Matthew Wise *E-mail:* canterburytamu@gmail.com

Christ Chapel at Texas State University Pastor James C. Bouzard *E-mail:* christchapel@txstate.edu

Christ Church Cathedral 20s and 30s Group, Houston Jeremy Bradley *E-mail:* jbradley@christchurchcathedral.org

Church of the Incarnation Young Adults Ministry, Dallas Ryan Waller *E-mail:* rwaller@incarnation.org

Diocese of West Missouri Campus Ministry Coordinator Beth Marshall *E-mail:* campusministry.ediowemo@gmail.com

Episcopal Campus Ministry at Allen County Community College The Reverend Janet A. Chubb *E-mail:* janchubb@sbcglobal.net

Episcopal Campus Ministry at Emporia State The Rev. Chris Arnold *E-mail:*

Episcopal Campus Ministry at Kansas State University E-mail: internKSU@episcopal-ks.org

Episcopal Campus Ministry at Labette Community College The Rev. Sharon Billman *E-mail:* vicar@stjohnsparsons.org

Episcopal Campus Ministry at Neosho County Community College E-mail:

Episcopal Campus Ministry at Tarlton State University The Rev. Curt Norman *E-mail:* curt.norman@gmail.com

Episcopal Campus Ministry at University of Kansas E-mail: internKU@episcopal-ks.org

Episcopal Campus Ministry at University of Texas in Arlington Darryl Green *E-mail:* priority7@gmail.com

Episcopal Campus Ministry of Wichita E-mail:

Episcopal College Community at Lamar University Paul Howell *E-mail:* phowell@stmarksbeaumont.org

Episcopal College Ministry (Canterbury) at Prairie View A & M The Rev. Everett Fredholm *E-mail:*

Episcopal Student Center at Sam Houston State University The Rev. Nan Doerr *E-mail:* ndoerr@sbcglobal.net

Episcopal Student Center at Sam Houston State

University The Rev. Mary E. Robbins *E-mail:*

neXtgen Ministry for Young Adults, Dallas Ted Clarkson *E-mail:* http://nextgenfig.org/contact/

St. Adrian of Canterbury Episcopal Student Association at the University of Tulsa J.C. Diaz *E-mail:* diaz@utulsa.edu

St. Anselm of Canterbury at the University of Oklahoma The Rev. Hal Greenwood *E-mail:* oucanterbury@yahoo.com

St. Augustine Canterbury Center at Oklahoma State University Fr. Jeff Huston *E-mail:* osucanterbury@gmail.com

St. David's Young Adult Community Amy Moehnke *E-mail:* amy.m@stdave.org

St. Martin's Episcopal University Center at the University of Arkansas, Fayetteville Joshua Daniel *E-mail:* uastmartins@gmail.com

Texas Lutheran University Canterbury E-mail:

The Canterbury Association at Southeastern Oklahoma State University The Rev. Jim Blagg *E-mail:* Canterbury@student.se.edu

The Episcopal Student Center at University of Texas The Rev. Beth Magill *E-mail:* bmagill@utepiscopal.org

Trinity Episcopal Church Young Adults, Baytown The Rev. Nick Novak *E-mail:* Nick@trinitybaytown.org

United Campus Ministries Serving Angelo State University and Howard College The Rev. Gary Sanford *E-mail:* ucm4asu@verizon.net

William Temple Episcopal Center, Galveston, TX Larissa W. Botik *E-mail:* wtecgalveston@gmail.com

Women Gathered in Faith at Central Methodist University Elizabeth Marshall-Belcher *E-mail:* ebelcher17@att.net

Young Saints Young Adult Ministry at All Saints Episcopal Church, Fort Worth The Rev. Jordan H. Ware *E-mail:* mthware@asecfw.org

PROVINCE VIII

Agape House: Episcopal-Lutheran Campus Ministry Center at SDSU The Rev. Darin Johnson *E-mail:* Agapehousesdsu@gmail.com

All Saints' Episcopal Church Young Adults (20+/40-), Phoenix The Rev. Licia Affer *E-mail:* laffer@allsaints.org

All Saints Young Adult Ministry The Rev. Holladay Sanderson *E-mail:* priest@allsaintsboise.org

Canterbury Bridge Episcopal Ministries at SJSU The Rev. Dcn. Kathleen A. Crowe *E-mail:* chaplain@sjspirit.org

Canterbury Episcopal Campus Ministry in Flagstaff Brad Eubanks *E-mail:* naucanterburychap@gmail.com

Canterbury Irvine: Episcopal Campus Ministry at UC Irvine The Rev. Dr. Fennie Hsin-Fen Chang *E-mail:* canterburyirvine@gmail.com

Canterbury Ministry of San Luis Obispo Berkeley Johnson *E-mail:* canterburyslo@gmail.com

Canterbury Outreach at University of Idaho The Rev. Robin Biffle *E-mail:* rector@moscow.com
Canterbury Outreach at University of Idaho The Rev. Robin Biffle *E-mail:* rector@moscow.com
Canterbury USC The Rev. Dr. Glenn M. Libby *E-mail:* ecusa@usc.edu
Diocese of Olympia Young Adults The Rev. Rebecca Kirkpatrick *E-mail:* youngadults@ecww.org
Ecumenical House (EcHouse) Campus Ministry at San Francisco State University Pastor Matthew Pearson *E-mail:* outreach@echouse.org
EpiC (Episcopal Campus Ministry) The Rev. Josh Hosler *E-mail:* fatherjosh@stpaulsbellingham.org
Episcopal Campus Ministry at Arizona State University, Tempe The Rev. Dr. Gil Stafford *E-mail:* asuecm@gmail.com
Episcopal Campus Ministry at the University of Arizona E-mail: ECMTucson@Gmail.com
Episcopal Campus Ministry at UCLA (Canterbury Westwood) The Reverend Paul Elder *E-mail:* paulelder1@gmail.com
Episcopal Campus Ministry at UofA, Tucson, AZ The Rev. Benjamin Garren *E-mail:* ECMTucson@Gmail.com
Episcopal Lutheran Campus Ministry at Stanford University The Rev. Greg Schaefer *E-mail:* PrGreg@stanford.edu
Holy Ground of Long Beach The Rev. Sean Lanigan *E-mail:* holygroundlb@gmail.com
Incarnation Campus Ministry at Arizona State University| Polytechnic Fr. Robert Berra *E-mail:* rberra@asu.edu
St. George's Campus Ministry The Rev. Khushnud Azariah *E-mail:* stgeorgesepiscopal.riv@gmail.com
St. Michael & All Angels Church and the Episcopal Campus Ministry at UCSB The Rev. Nicole Janelle *E-mail:* saintmikesucsb@gmail.com
The Belfry: Lutheran Episcopal Campus Ministry at UC Davis Pastor Jocelynn Jurkovich-Hughes *E-mail:* pastor@thebelfry.org
University of Oregon Episcopal Campus Ministry The Rev. Peter A. Fones *E-mail:* uochaplain@comcast.net
UW Episcopal Campus Ministry The Rev. Rebecca Kirkpatrick *E-mail:* Campus@ecww.org
Whitman College, Walla Walla University E-mail: stpauls@stpaulsww.org
Feast United Campus Christian Ministry at UCSC E-mail: uccm@ucsc.edu
Georgia Tech / Georgia State University Center The Rev. Chris Hannum *E-mail:*
The Abundant Table of California State University Sarah Nolan *E-mail:* info@theabundanttable.org
University Chapel at UC Berkeley Tom Poynor *E-mail:* calcanterbury@gmail.com
University of Iowa Chaplaincy, Iowa City, IA The Rev. Julia Easley - Chaplain *E-mail:* jkeasley@inav.net
University of North Texas Canterbury Episcopal Ministry Fr. Clint Wilson *E-mail:* fatherwilson@stdavidsdenton.org

PROVINCE IX
Episcopal Campus Ministry of Puerto Rico Rvdo. P Angel Davila Colon *E-mail:* ecm.puertorico@gmail.com

EPISCOPAL SCHOOLS
National Assoc of Episcopal Schools, Inc. (NAES)
Gov Bd Pres Doreen S Oleson EdD, Altadena CA. *Office* 815 Second Ave Third Floor NY NY 10017. (212) 716-6134, (800) 334-7626 x6134. *Fax* (212) 286-9366. *E-mail:* info@episcopalschools.org. *Web* http://www.episcopalschools.org/. *Ex Dir* Rev Daniel R Heischman DD *Assoc Dir* Ann Mellow *Dir Oper* Linda A Glad *Commun & Events Manager* David J Schnabel *Advancement Manager* Sarah E Badgerow *Adm Asst* Stephanie M Koch.

NAES is an independently incorporated, voluntary membership organization that supports, serves, and advocates for the vital work and ministry of those who serve nearly 1,200 Episcopal schools, early childhood education (ECE) programs, and school establishment efforts throughout The Episcopal Church. Chartered in 1965, with historic roots dating to the 1930s, NAES is the only pre-collegiate educational association that is both national in scope and Episcopal in character. The Association advances Episcopal education and strengthens Episcopal schools through essential services, resources, conferences, and networking opportunities on Episcopal school identity, leadership, and governance, and on the spiritual and professional development of school leaders.

Church and Church-Related Schools
Episcopal schools and ECE programs vary in size, scope and educational philosophy. They are parish, cathedral, diocesan, seminary, religious order and independent schools; Montessori and military schools; day and boarding schools; co-educational and single-sex schools.
Parishes and cathedrals with schools and ECE programs are identified in the Diocesan Lists with the symbol §. These programs may or may not be NAES members. The following list comprises diocesan, seminary, religious order and church-related independent schools listed in the NAES database. 2014-2015 NAES members, as of December 12, 2014, are identified with the symbol •. The schools are listed alphabetically by diocese and then name. The first individual listed is the head of school or director; those following are the school's chaplains.
For a searchable database of current NAES member schools, ECE programs and school establishment efforts, visit http://www.episcopalschools.org/forms/CompanyFormPublic/search.
Alabama *Holy Cross Episcopal School* • 4400 Bell Rd Montgomery AL 36116 *Grades:* P–6 *Contact:* Ms. Melissa Coumanis *Chaplain(s):* Rev David H Peeples (334) 395-8222

Albany *Doane Stuart School* • 199 Washington Ave Rensselaer NY 12144 *Grades:* P–12 *Contact:* Ms Pamela J Clarke *Chaplain(s):* Mrs Patricia Hodgkinson Ms Sandi Miller (518) 465-5222

Albany *Hoosac School* • PO Box 9 Hoosick NY 12089 *Grades:* 8–PG *Contact:* Mr Dean S Foster *Chaplain(s):* Rev Canon Clinton Dugger (518) 686-7331

Arizona *Imago Dei Middle School* • PO Box 3056 Tucson AZ 85702 *Grades:* 5–8 *Contact:* Rev Anne Sawyer *Chaplain(s):* Rev Susan Anderson-Smith (520) 882-4008

Atlanta *Saint George's Episcopal School* • 103 Birch St Milner GA 30257 *Grades:* P–8 *Contact:* Mr Larry Collins *Chaplain(s):* Ms Diana Pearson (770) 358-9432

Central Florida *All Saints' Academy* • 5001 State Rd 540 West Winter Haven FL 33880 *Grades:* P–12 *Contact:* Mrs Carolyn Baldwin *Chaplain(s):* Rev Richard H Gomer Jr (863) 293-5980

Central Florida *Holy Trinity Episcopal Academy* • 5625 Holy Trinity Dr Melbourne FL 32940 *Grades:* P–12 *Contact:* Mr Christopher Hayes *Chaplain(s):* Rev Joy Willard-Williford Ms Garcia Barnswell-Schmidt (321) 723-8323

Central Florida *Saint Edward's School* • 1895 Saint Edward's Dr Vero Beach FL 32963 *Grades:* P–12 *Contact:* Mr Michael Mersky *Chaplain(s):* Rev Jason Murbarger (772) 231-4136

Central Florida *Trinity Preparatory School of Florida* • 5700 Trinity Prep Ln Winter Park FL 32792 *Grades:* 6–12 *Contact:* Mr Craig S Maughan *Chaplain(s):* Rev Kenneth N Vinal (407) 671-4140

Central Gulf Coast *Holy Nativity Episcopal School* • 205 Hamilton Ave Panama City FL 32401 *Grades:* P–8 *Contact:* Mrs Judy Hughes *Chaplain(s):* Rev Steven B Bates (850) 747-0060

Central Gulf Coast *St Paul's Episcopal School* • 161 Dogwood Ln Mobile AL 36608 *Grades:* P–12 *Contact:* Mr Marty Lester *Chaplain(s):* (251) 342-6700

Chicago *Rose Hall Montessori Preschool* 1140 Wilmette Ave Wilmette IL 60091 *Grades:* P *Contact:* Ms Elizabeth Friedman *Chaplain(s):* (847) 256-2002

Colorado *St Anne's Episcopal School* • 2701 S York St Denver CO 80210-6098 *Grades:* P–8 *Contact:* Mr Alan Smiley *Chaplain(s):* Rev Merrie D Need (303) 756-9481

Colorado *St Elizabeth's School* • 2350 Gaylord St Denver CO 80205 *Grades:* K–4 *Contact:* Mrs Sally Thomas *Chaplain(s):* Rev Susan A Greenwood (303) 322-4209

Connecticut *Kent School* • PO Box 2006 Kent CT 06757-0640 *Grades:* 9–12 *Contact:* Rev Richardson W Schell *Chaplain(s):* Rev Kate E Kelderman (860) 927-3501

Connecticut *Pomfret School* 398 Pomfret St Pomfret CT 06258 *Grades:* 9–12 *Contact:* Mr J Timothy Richards *Chaplain(s):* Rev Bradley Davis (860) 963-6100

Connecticut *Salisbury School* 251 Canaan Rd Salisbury CT 06068 *Grades:* 9–PG *Contact:* Mr Chisholm S Chandler *Chaplain(s):* (860) 435-5700

Connecticut *South Kent School* • 40 Bull's Bridge Rd South Kent CT 06785-9747 *Grades:* 9–PG *Contact:* Mr Andrew J Vadnais *Chaplain(s):* Rev Stephen B Klots Rev William H Low (860) 927-3539

Connecticut *The Rectory School* PO Box 68 Pomfret CT 06258 *Grades:* K–9 *Contact:* Mr Frederick W Williams *Chaplain(s):* Rev Ronald Glaude (860) 928-7759

Connecticut *Wooster School* • 91 Miry Brook Rd Danbury CT 06810 *Grades:* P–12 *Contact:* Matthew Byrnes *Chaplain(s):* Rev Garrett M Mettler (203) 830-3900

Dallas *Episcopal School of Dallas* • 4100 Merrell Rd Dallas TX 75229 *Grades:* P–12 *Contact:* Ms Meredyth M Cole *Chaplain(s):* Rev Amy G Heller Rev K Cn Michael Harmuth (214) 358-4368

Dallas *Holy Family School* PO Box 1039 McKinney TX 75070 *Grades:* P *Contact:* Ms Kristen Hendrix *Chaplain(s):* Rev Michael W Michie (972) 562-5476

Dallas *St Philip's School and Community Center* 1600 Pennsylvania Ave Dallas TX 75215 *Grades:* P–6 *Contact:* Terry J Flowers PhD *Chaplain(s):* (214) 421-5221

Dallas *The Canterbury Episcopal School* 1708 N Westmoreland Rd DeSoto TX 75115 *Grades:* K–12 *Contact:* Mr Sandy Doerge *Chaplain(s):* Rev Michael G Wallens (972) 572-7200

Delaware *St Andrew's School* • 350 Noxontown Rd Middletown DE 19709-1605 *Grades:* 9–12 *Contact:* Mr Daniel T Roach Jr *Chaplain(s):* Rev John F Hutchinson Jr Rev David P Desalvo (302) 378-9511

Delaware *St Anne's Episcopal School* • 211 Silver Lake Rd Middletown DE 19709 *Grades:* P–8 *Contact:* Mr Peter C Thayer *Chaplain(s):* Ms Kathy Hanna (302) 378-3179

Delaware *St Michael's School and Nursery Inc* 305 E 7th St Wilmington DE 19801 *Grades:* P–K *Contact:* Ms Helen C Riley *Chaplain(s):* Ms Estella DeRamus (302) 656-3389

East Tennessee *All Saints' Episcopal School* • 3275 Maple Valley Rd Morristown TN 37813 *Grades:* P-8 *Contact:* Mr Henry G Selby *Chaplain(s):* Rev Scherry Vickery Fouke (423) 586-3280

East Tennessee *St Nicholas School* • 7525 Min-Tom Drive Chattanooga TN 37421-1835 *Grades:* P–5 *Contact:* Mr Mark J Fallo *Chaplain(s):* Rev Janice Robbins (423) 899-1999

East Tennessee *The Episcopal School of Knoxville* • 950 Episcopal School Way Knoxville TN 37932 *Grades:* K–8 *Contact:* Mr James J Secor III *Chaplain(s):* Rev Joshua Hill (865) 777-9032

Ecuador Central *Canterbury School* Box 17-11-6165 Quito Ecuador

Ecuador Central *Escuela Episcopal Chimbacalle* Box 17-11-6165 Quito Ecuador *Grades: Contact:* Sra Ana Armijos

El Camino Real *York School* 9501 York Rd Monterey CA 93940 *Grades:* 8–12 *Contact:* Mr Chuck Harmon *Chaplain(s):* Mr Murray Walker (831) 372-7338

Florida *Episcopal Children's Services Inc* • 8443 Baymeadows Road #1 Jacksonville FL 32256 Grades:

P *Contact:* Ms Connie Stophel *Chaplain(s):* (904) 726-1500

Haiti *Holy Trinity School* c/o LINXS AIR PO Box 407139 Fort Lauderdale FL 33340 *Grades:* K–12 *Contact:* Rev David Cesar

Hawaii *Iolani School* • 563 Kamoku St Honolulu HI 96826 *Grades:* K–12 *Contact:* Timothy R Cottrell PhD *Chaplain(s):* Rev Daniel L Leatherman Rev Nicole M Simopoulos (808) 949-5355

Hawaii *Seabury Hall* • 480 Olinda Rd Makawao HI 96768 *Grades:* 6–PG *Contact:* Mr Joseph J Schmidt *Chaplain(s):* Rev David Jackson (808) 572-7235

Hawaii *The St. Andrew's Schools* 224 Queen Emma Square Honolulu HI 96813 *Grades:* K–12 *Contact:* Ms Sandra J Theunick *Chaplain(s):* Rev Anna Joo (808) 536-6102

Kansas *Bishop Seabury Academy* • 4120 Clinton Parkway Lawrence KS 66047 *Grades:* 6–12 *Contact:* Donald Schawang PhD *Chaplain(s):* (785) 832-1717

Kentucky *St Francis School* 11000 W Highway 42 Goshen KY 40026 *Grades:* P–8 *Contact:* Mr John Delautre *Chaplain(s):* (502) 228-1197

Los Angeles *Campbell Hall (Episcopal)* • PO Box 4036 North Hollywood CA 91617 *Grades:* K–12 *Contact:* Rev Canon Julian P Bull *Chaplain(s):* Rev Stefanie G Wilson Rev Cn Norman S Hull (818) 980-7280

Los Angeles *Harvard-Westlake School* PO Box 1037 North Hollywood CA 91604-0037 *Grades:* 7–12 *Contact:* Mr Richard B Commons *Chaplain(s):* Rev James J Young Rabbi Emily Feigenson (818) 980-6692

Los Angeles *St Margaret's Episcopal School* • 31641 La Novia Ave San Juan Capistrano CA 92675 *Grades:* P–12 *Contact:* Mr William N Moseley *Chaplain(s):* Rev Heather B Erickson Rev Earl Gibson Rev James Livingston (949) 661-0108

Los Angeles *The Episcopal School of Los Angeles* • PO Box 691404 Los Angeles CA 90069 *Grades:* 6-8 *Contact:* Rev Maryetta M Anschutz *Chaplain(s):* Rev Megan Hollaway (203) 747-4200

Los Angeles *The Gooden School* • 192 N Baldwin Ave Sierra Madre CA 91024 *Grades:* K–8 *Contact:* Ms Patricia Patano *Chaplain(s):* Rev Michael E Cooper (626) 355-2410

Louisiana *Episcopal High School of Baton Rouge* 3200 Woodland Ridge Boulevard Baton Rouge LA 70816 *Grades:* P–12 *Contact:* Mr Hugh McIntosh *Chaplain(s):* Rev Kirkland W Knight Rev Charles deGravelles (225) 753-3180

Louisiana *St Martin's Episcopal School* • 225 Green Acres Rd Metairie LA 70003-2484 *Grades:* P–12 *Contact:* Mrs Merry Sorrells *Chaplain(s):* Rev Ford Jefferson Millican Jr Rev Michael C Kuhn DMin (504) 733-0353

Maryland *Saint James School* • 17641 College Rd Saint James MD 21740 *Grades:* 8–12 *Contact:* D Stuart Dunnan DPhil *Chaplain(s):* Rev William O Daniel (301) 733-9330

Maryland *St Anne's School of Annapolis* • 3112 Arundel-on-the-Bay Rd Annapolis MD 21403-4605

Grades: P–8 *Contact:* Ms Lisa Nagel *Chaplain(s):* Rev Diana E Carroll (410) 263-8650

Maryland *St Paul's School* • PO Box 8100 Brooklandville MD 21022-8100 *Grades:* P–12 *Contact:* Mr David C Faus *Chaplain(s):* Rev Daniel S Meck III (410) 825-4400

Maryland *St Paul's School for Girls* • 11232 Falls Rd Brooklandville MD 21022 *Grades:* 5–12 *Contact:* Ms Penny B Evins *Chaplain(s):* (410) 823-6323

Maryland *St Timothy's School* • 8400 Greenspring Ave Stevenson MD 21153 *Grades:* 9–PG *Contact:* Mr Randy S Stevens *Chaplain(s):* Rev Kirk A Kubicek (410) 486-7400

Maryland *The Wilkes School* 707 Park Ave Baltimore MD 21201 *Grades:* P-5 *Contact:* Mrs Sandra G Shull *Chaplain(s):* Rev Frederick S Thomas (410) 539-1395

Maryland *Trinity School of Frederick* 6040 New Design Rd Frederick MD 21703 *Grades:* K–6 *Contact:* Ms Barbara Cartwright *Chaplain(s):* (301) 228-2333

Massachusetts *Brooks School* • 1160 Great Pond Rd North Andover MA 01845-1298 *Grades:* 9–12 *Contact:* Mr John R Packard *Chaplain(s):* Rev Alden B Flanders (978) 686-6101

Massachusetts *Epiphany School* • 154 Centre St Dorchester MA 02124 *Grades:* 5–8 *Contact:* Rev John H Finley IV *Chaplain(s):* (617) 326-0425

Massachusetts *Esperanza Academy* • 198 Garden St Lawrence MA 01840 *Grades:* 5–8 *Contact:* Mr Christopher H Wilson *Chaplain(s):* (978) 686-4673

Massachusetts *Groton School* • Farmers Row, PO Box 991 Groton MA 01450-0991 *Grades:* 8–12 *Contact:* Mr Temba T Maqubela *Chaplain(s):* Rev Mary Beth Humphrey PhD (978) 448-3363

Massachusetts *St Mark's School* • PO Box 9105 Southborough MA 01772-9105 *Grades:* 9–12 *Contact:* Mr John Warren *Chaplain(s):* Rev Barbara Talcott Mr Stephen Hebert (508) 786-6000

Milwaukee *St John's Northwestern Military Academy* • 1101 Genesee St Delafield WI 53018 *Grades:* 7–PG *Contact:* Mr Jack H Albert Jr *Chaplain(s):* Rev H Pickett Wall (262) 646-7191

Minnesota *Breck School* • 123 Ottawa Ave North Minneapolis MN 55422 *Grades:* P–12 *Contact:* Mr Edward Kim *Chaplain(s):* Rev John E Bellaimey Ms Alexis Kent Ms Nan Zosel (763) 381-8100

Minnesota *Shattuck-St Mary's School* • PO Box 218 Faribault MN 55021-0218 *Grades:* 6–PG *Contact:* Mr Nicholas J B Stoneman *Chaplain(s):* Rev Eva M K Cavaleri (507) 333-1500

Mississippi *Coast Episcopal School* • 5065 Espy Ave Long Beach MS 39560 *Grades:* P–6 *Contact:* Ms Betsy Grant *Chaplain(s):* Ms Kirby Barkley (228) 452-9442

Mississippi *Trinity Episcopal Day School* • 1 Mallan G Morgan Drive Natchez MS 39120 *Grades:* P–12 *Contact:* Mr Les Hegwood *Chaplain(s):* Rev Calvin J Meaders (601) 442-5424

New Hampshire *Heronfield Academy* • 356 Exeter Rd Hampton Falls NH 03844 *Grades:* 6–8 *Contact:* Ms Martha Shepardson-Killam *Chaplain(s):* (603) 772-9093

New Hampshire *Holderness School* • PO Box 1879 Plymouth NH 03264-1879 *Grades:* 9-PG *Contact:* Mr R Phillip Peck *Chaplain(s):* Rev Richard C Weymouth (603) 536-1257

New Hampshire *St Paul's School* • 325 Pleasant St Concord NH 03301-2591 *Grades:* 9–12 *Contact:* Mr Michael G Hirschfeld *Chaplain(s):* Rev Michael E Spencer Rev Richard E Greenleaf Rev Alice H Courtright (603) 229-4600

New Hampshire *The White Mountain School* • 371 West Farm Rd Bethlehem NH 03574 *Grades:* 9–PG *Contact:* Tim Breen PhD *Chaplain(s):* Rev Paul H Higginson (603) 444-2928

New Jersey *Doane Academy* • 350 Riverbank Burlington NJ 08016 *Grades:* P-12 *Contact:* Mr John F McGee *Chaplain(s):* Rev J Connor Haynes (609) 386-3500

New York *Children's Garden at The General Theological Seminary* • 440 West 21st St New York NY 10011 *Grades:* P *Contact:* Ms Susan Stein *Chaplain(s):* (212) 243-5150

New York *St Hilda's & St Hugh's School* • 619 W 114th St New York NY 10025 *Grades:* P–8 *Contact:* Ms Virginia Connor *Chaplain(s):* Rev Elizabeth H Garnsey (212) 932-1980

New York *The Episcopal School in the City of New York* • 35 E 69th St New York NY 10021 *Grades:* P *Contact:* Ms Judith R Blanton *Chaplain(s):* (212) 879-9764

New York *Trinity School* • 139 W 91st St New York NY 10024 *Grades:* K–12 *Contact:* Mr John C Allman *Chaplain(s):* Rev Timothy L Morehouse Rev Michael S Bárbaro (212) 873-1650

New York *Trinity-Pawling School* • 700 Route 22 Pawling NY 12564 *Grades:* 7–PG *Contact:* Mr Archibald A Smith III *Chaplain(s):* Mr John Gedrick (845) 855-3100

North Carolina *Canterbury School* • 5400 Old Lake Jeanette Rd Greensboro NC 27455-1322 *Grades:* K–8 *Contact:* Mr A Burns Jones *Chaplain(s):* Rev Nathan M Finnan (336) 288-2007

North Carolina *Palisades Episcopal School* • 13120 Grand Palisades Parkway Charlotte NC 28278 *Grades:* K–6 *Contact:* Ms Kerin S Hughes *Chaplain(s):* (704) 583-1825

North Carolina *Saint Mary's School* • 900 Hillsborough St Raleigh NC 27603 *Grades:* 9–12 *Contact:* Monica M Gillespie PhD *Chaplain(s):* Rev Anne P Bonner-Stewart (919) 424-4100

North Carolina *St David's School* • 3400 White Oak Rd Raleigh NC 27609 *Grades:* K–12 *Contact:* Mr Kevin J Lockerbie *Chaplain(s):* (919) 782-3331

North Carolina *Trinity Episcopal School* • 750 E 9th St Charlotte NC 28202-3102 *Grades:* K–8 *Contact:* Mr Thomas J Franz *Chaplain(s):* Rev Loris N Adams Ms Emily Philips Rev W Burley Salmon (704) 358-8101

Northern Indiana *The Howe School* PO Box 240 Howe IN 46746-0240 *Grades:* 9–12 *Contact:* Mr David Watson *Chaplain(s):* Rev David D Yaw (260) 562-2131

Northwest Texas *All Saints Episcopal School* 3222 103rd St Lubbock TX 79423 *Grades:* P–9 *Contact:* Michael Bennett Ed.D *Chaplain(s):* Mrs Paige McKay (806) 745-7701

Northwest Texas *Trinity School of Midland* • 3500 W Wadley Ave Midland TX 79707 *Grades:* P–12 *Contact:* Rev Walter L Prehn III PhD *Chaplain(s):* Rev John H Barrett (432) 697-3281

Oklahoma *Casady School* • 9500 N Pennsylvania Ave Oklahoma City OK 73120 *Grades:* P–12 *Contact:* Mr Nathan Sheldon *Chaplain(s):* Rev Charles F Blizzard Rev TimSean Youmans (405) 749-3100

Oklahoma *Holland Hall School* • 5666 E 81st St Tulsa OK 74137-2099 *Grades:* P–12 *Contact:* Mr Jared P Culley *Chaplain(s):* Rev Robert L Bibens Rev Arthur P Scrutchins (918) 481-1111

Oklahoma *Oak Hall Episcopal School* • PO Box 1807 Ardmore OK 73401 *Grades:* P–8 *Contact:* Mr Kenneth R Willy *Chaplain(s):* Rev Stephen R Bilsbury

Olympia *Annie Wright Schools* 827 N Tacoma Ave Tacoma WA 98403 *Grades:* P–12 *Contact:* Mr Christian Sullivan *Chaplain(s):* Rev Rebecca B Kirkpatrick (253) 272-2216

Olympia *Charles Wright Academy* 7723 Chambers Creek Rd West University Place WA 98467-2099 *Grades:* P–12 *Contact:* Mr Robert A Camner *Chaplain(s):* Mr Michael Moffitt (253) 620-8300

Oregon *Oregon Episcopal School* • 6300 SW Nicol Rd Portland OR 97223 *Grades:* P–12 *Contact:* Ms Mo Copeland *Chaplain(s):* Rev C Phillip Craig Jr Rev Jennifer B Cleveland Rev Heather W Wenrick (503) 246-7771

Pennsylvania *The Church Farm School* • 1001 E Lincoln Highway Exton PA 19341 *Grades:* 7–12 *Contact:* Rev Edmund K Sherrill II *Chaplain(s):* Rev John D Daniels (610) 363-7500

Pennsylvania *The Episcopal Academy* • 1785 Bishop White Drive Newtown Square PA 19073 *Grades:* P–12 *Contact:* Thomas J Locke EdD *Chaplain(s):* Rev James R Squire Rev Albert E R Zug Sr Rev Timothy P Gavin III (484) 424-1400

Rhode Island *St Andrew's School* 63 Federal Rd Barrington RI 02806-2407 *Grades:* 6–12 *Contact:* Mr John D Martin *Chaplain(s):* (401) 246-1230

Rhode Island *St George's School* • PO Box 1910 Newport RI 02840-0190 *Grades:* 9–12 *Contact:* Mr Eric F Peterson *Chaplain(s):* Rev Jeffrey C Lewis (401) 847-7565

San Diego *The Bishop's School* • 7607 La Jolla Boulevard La Jolla CA 92037 *Grades:* 6–12 *Contact:* Ms Aimeclaire Roche *Chaplain(s):* Rev Brian E Fidler (858) 459-4021

South Carolina *Porter-Gaud School* • 300 Albemarle Rd Charleston SC 29407 *Grades:* 1–12 *Contact:* Mr D DuBose Egleston Jr *Chaplain(s):* Rev Brian McGreevy Rev Jennie C Olbrych Mr Hutson Dodds (843) 556-3620

South Carolina *Trinity-Byrnes Collegiate School* 5001 Hoffmeyer Rd Darlington SC 29532 *Grades:* 7–12 *Contact:* Mr Ed Hoffman *Chaplain(s):* Rev Charles D Cooper (843) 395-9124

Southeast Florida *Palmer Trinity School* • 7900 SW 176 St Palmetto Bay FL 33157 *Grades:* 6–12 *Contact:* Mr Patrick H F Roberts *Chaplain(s):* Rev Mary Ellen Cassini DMin (305) 251-2230

Southeast Florida *Saint Andrew's School* • 3900 Jog Rd Boca Raton FL 33434-4498 *Grades:* P–12 *Contact:* Mr Peter B Benedict II *Chaplain(s):* Rev David Taylor Rev Faye Somers Rev Charles A Browning II (561) 210-2000

Southern Ohio *Bethany School* • 555 Albion Ave Cincinnati OH 45246 *Grades:* K–8 *Contact:* Ms Cheryl L Pez *Chaplain(s):* Rev Kimberly A Knight (513) 771-7462

Southern Virginia *Chatham Hall* • 800 Chatham Hall Circle Chatham VA 24531 *Grades:* 9–12 *Contact:* Mrs. Suzanne W Buck *Chaplain(s):* Rev Ned W Edwards Jr DMin (434) 432-2941

Southern Virginia *Trinity Episcopal School* 3850 Pittaway Drive Richmond VA 23235 *Grades:* 8–12 *Contact:* Thomas G Aycock PhD *Chaplain(s):* Mr Brian Griffen (804) 272-5864

Southwest Florida *Berkeley Preparatory School* • 4811 Kelly Rd Tampa FL 33615-0009 *Grades:* P–12 *Contact:* Mr Joseph W Seivold *Chaplain(s):* Rev Peter M Carey (813) 885-1673

Southwest Florida *Saint Paul's School* • 1600 St Paul's Drive Clearwater FL 33764 *Grades:* P–8 *Contact:* Mrs Samantha L Kemmish *Chaplain(s):* (727) 536-2756

Southwest Florida *Saint Stephen's Episcopal School* • 315 41st St West Bradenton FL 34209 *Grades:* P–7 *Contact:* Janet S Pullen EdD *Chaplain(s):* Rev Nathan S Speck-Ewer (941) 746-2121

Southwest Florida *The Canterbury School of Florida* 990 62nd Ave NE St Petersburg FL 33702 *Grades:* P–12 *Contact:* Mr Mac H Hall *Chaplain(s):* Rev John C Suhar (727) 525-1419

Southwestern Virginia *Boys' Home, Inc* • 306 Boys' Home Rd Covington VA 24426 *Grades:* 6–12 *Contact:* Mr Donnie E Wheatley *Chaplain(s):* Rev Connie W Jackson (540) 965-7700

Southwestern Virginia *Stuart Hall* • PO Box 210 Staunton VA 24402-0210 *Grades:* P–12 *Contact:* Mr Mark H Eastham *Chaplain(s):* (540) 885-0356

Southwestern Virginia *Virginia Episcopal School* PO Box 408 Lynchburg VA 24505 *Grades:* 9–12 *Contact:* Mr G Thomas Battle Jr *Chaplain(s):* Mrs Aimee K Bostwick Mr Chad Hanning (434) 385-3600

Tennessee *St Andrew's-Sewanee School* • 290 Quintard Rd Sewanee TN 37375-3000 *Grades:* 6–12 *Contact:* Rev John T Thomas *Chaplain(s):* Rev M Andrew Bunting (931) 598-5651

Texas *All Saints Episcopal School* • 4108 Delaware Beaumont TX 77706 *Grades:* P–8 *Contact:* Ms Catherine Clark *Chaplain(s):* (409) 892-1755

Texas *All Saints Episcopal School* • 2695 South Southwest Loop 323 Tyler TX 75701 *Grades:* P–PG *Contact:* Mr Randal E Brown *Chaplain(s):* (903) 579-6000

Texas *Archway Academy* 6221 Main St Houston TX 77030 *Grades:* 9-12 *Contact:* Ms Sasha McLean *Chaplain(s):* (713) 328-0780

Texas *Episcopal High School* • 4650 Bissonnet Bellaire TX 77401 *Grades:* 9–12 *Contact:* Mr C Edward Smith *Chaplain(s):* Rev Adam Greene Rev Beth Holden (713) 512-3400

Texas *Holy Trinity Episcopal School* 11810 Lockwood Houston TX 77044-5392 *Grades:* P–8 *Contact:* Nicola Esch EdD *Chaplain(s):* (281) 459-4323

Texas *St Andrew's Episcopal School* • 1112 W 31st St Austin TX 78705 *Grades:* 1–12 *Contact:* Mr Sean Murphy *Chaplain(s):* Rev Robert J Leacock Ms Ashley Brandon (512) 299-9800

Texas *St Stephen's Episcopal School* • 6500 St Stephen's Drive Austin TX 78746-1727 *Grades:* 6–12 *Contact:* Mr Robert E Kirkpatrick *Chaplain(s):* Rev Todd R FitzGerald Mr Jim Crosby Ms Morgan Stokes (512) 327-1213

Texas *Trinity Episcopal School of Austin* • 3901 Bee Cave Rd Austin TX 78746-6403 *Grades:* K–8 *Contact:* Ms Marie H Kidd *Chaplain(s):* Rev Brin Bon (512) 472-9525

Upper South Carolina *Christ Church Episcopal School* • 245 Cavalier Drive Greenville SC 29607 *Grades:* K–12 *Contact:* Leonard R Kupersmith PhD *Chaplain(s):* Mr Joseph E Britt Ms Valerie M Riddle (864) 299-1522

Upper South Carolina *Heathwood Hall Episcopal School* • 3000 South Beltline Boulevard Columbia SC 29201-5199 *Grades:* P–12 *Contact:* D Michael Heath PhD *Chaplain(s):* Mrs Raven G Tarpley (803) 765-2309

Utah *Rowland Hall-St Mark's School* 720 Guardsman Way Salt Lake City UT 84108 *Grades:* P–12 *Contact:* Mr Alan Sparrow *Chaplain(s):* Rev Trace M Browning (801) 355-7485

Vermont *Rock Point School* 1 Rock Point Rd Burlington VT 05401 *Grades:* 9–12 *Contact:* Mr C J Spirito *Chaplain(s):* (802) 863-1104

Virginia *Anna Julia Cooper Episcopal School* • 2124 N 29th St Richmond VA 23223 *Grades:* 6-8 *Contact:* Mr Michael J Maruca *Chaplain(s):* (804) 822-6610

Virginia *Blue Ridge School* 273 Mayo Drive St George VA 22935 *Grades:* 9–12 *Contact:* Mr William Darrin III *Chaplain(s):* Rev David B McIlhiney PhD (434) 985-2811

Virginia *Christchurch School* • 49 Seahorse Lane Christchurch VA 23031-9999 *Grades:* 9–PG *Contact:* Mr John E Byers *Chaplain(s):* (804) 758-2306

Virginia *Episcopal High School* • 1200 N Quaker Lane Alexandria VA 22302 *Grades:* 9–12 *Contact:* Mr F Robertson Hershey *Chaplain(s):* Rev Gideon L K Pollach Rev Thomas C Hummel PhD Rev Elizabeth C Gonzalez (703) 933-3000

Virginia *St Anne's-Belfield School* 2132 Ivy Rd Charlottesville VA 22903 *Grades:* P–12 *Contact:* Mr David S Lourie *Chaplain(s):* Mr Robert Clark (434) 296-5106

Virginia *St Catherine's School* • 6001 Grove Ave Richmond VA 23226 *Grades:* P–12 *Contact:* Terrie Hale Scheckelhoff PhD *Chaplain(s):* Rev Dorothy A White DMin Ms C Rives Priddy (804) 288-2804

Virginia *St Christopher's School* • 711 St Christopher's Rd Richmond VA 23226 *Grades:* P–12 *Contact:* Mr Charles M Stillwell *Chaplain(s):* Rev

Melissa K Hollerith Rev Durwood R Steed Ms Mary Via (804) 282-3185

Virginia *St Margaret's School* • PO Box 158 Tappahannock VA 22560 *Grades:* 8–12 *Contact:* Mrs Ms Lindy Williams *Chaplain(s):* Rev Anita L Braden (804) 443-3357

Virginia *St Stephen's and St Agnes School* • 1000 St Stephen's Rd Alexandria VA 22304 *Grades:* P–12 *Contact:* Mrs Kirsten P Adams *Chaplain(s):* Rev Sean H Cavanaugh Rev Rosemary Beales (703) 751-2700

Virginia *The Butterfly House* • Virginia Theological Seminary 3737 Seminary Rd Alexandria VA 22304 *Grades:* P *Contact:* Mrs Kerry Hual *Chaplain(s):* (703) 461-1786

Washington *Rosemount Center* 2000 Rosemount Ave Washington DC 20010 *Grades:* P *Contact:* Marsha Boveja EdD *Chaplain(s):* (202) 265-9885

Washington *St Andrew's Episcopal School* • 8804 Postoak Rd Potomac MD 20854-3553 *Grades:* P–12 *Contact:* Mr Robert F Kosasky *Chaplain(s):* Rev Patricia Alexander Rev Cn Sarah Slater (301) 983-5200

Washington *The Bishop John T Walker School for Boys* • 3640 Martin Luther King Jr Ave SE Washington DC 20032 *Grades:* P–2 *Contact:* Mr James R Woody *Chaplain(s):* Rev Rondesia Jarrett (202) 678-1515

Washington *Washington Episcopal School* • 5600 Little Falls Pkwy Bethesda MD 20816 *Grades:* P–8 *Contact:* Ms. Nancy Wright *Chaplain(s):* Mr. Tim Kennedy (301) 652-7878

West Tennessee *St Mary's Episcopal School* • 60 Perkins Extended Memphis TN 38117 *Grades:* P–12 *Contact:* Mr Albert Throckmorton *Chaplain(s):* Rev Katherine M Bush Ms Susan Whitten(901) 537-1440

West Texas *Good Samaritan Center* • 1600 Saltillo San Antonio TX 78207-6842 *Grades:* P *Contact:* Ms Jill Oettinger *Chaplain(s):* (210) 434-5531

West Texas *St Mary's Hall* PO Box 33430 San Antonio TX 78265-3430 *Grades:* K–12 *Contact:* Mr John Thomas *Chaplain(s):* Rev April Coldsmith (210) 483-9100

West Texas *TMI—The Episcopal School of Texas* • 20955 West Tejas Trail San Antonio TX 78257-9708 *Grades:* 6–12 *Contact:* John W Cooper PhD *Chaplain(s):* Rev Nathan L Bostian (210) 698-7171

West Virginia *Greenbrier Episcopal School* 3100 Houfnaggle Rd Lewisburg WV 24901 *Grades:* P–8 *Contact:* Ms Gretchen Graves *Chaplain(s):* Rev C Christopher Thompson (304) 793-2420

Western Kansas *St John's Military School* • Box 5020 Salina KS 67402-5020 *Grades:* 7–12 *Contact:* Mr Andy England *Chaplain(s):* Mr Matthew Lewis (785) 823-7231

Western Louisiana *Episcopal School of Acadiana, Inc* • PO Box 380 Cade LA 70519 *Grades:* P–12 *Contact:* Paul Baker PhD *Chaplain(s):* Rev Anne B Etheredge (337) 365-1416

Western North Carolina *Christ School* • 500 Christ School Rd Arden NC 28704-9914 *Grades:* 8–12 *Contact:* Mr Paul Krieger *Chaplain(s):* Rev David C Brown (828) 684-6232

CAMP, CONFERENCE, AND RETREAT CENTERS

EPISCOPAL CAMPS AND CONFERENCE CENTERS INC (ECCC)

Organization with advocacy role, providing support and educational opportunities; newsletters; annual conference; consultation services. Membership open to Episcopal Church camps, conference and retreat centers. *Exec Dir* Peter Bergstrom PO Box 2320 Julian CA 92036 (760) 550-0028 *E-mail:* peter@episcopalccc.org; *Assoc Dir* Bill Slocumb (760) 445-6774 *E-mail:* staff@episcopalccc.org *Web:* www.episcopalccc.org.

ALABAMA

Camp McDowell 105 DeLong Rd Nauvoo AL 35578 (205) 387-1806 *Fax:* (205) 221-3454 *E-mail:* mark@campmcdowell.com *Web:* www.campmcdowell.com *Contact: Exec Dir* The Rev Mark Johnston. Total Beds: 400.

ARIZONA

Chapel Rock 1131 Country Club Dr Prescott AZ 86303 (928) 445-3499 *Fax:* (928) 445-0370 *E-mail:* info@chapelrock.net *Web:* www.chapelrock.net *Contact: Exec Dir* Kelly Wood. Total Beds: 270.

ARKANSAS

Camp Mitchell 10 Camp Mitchell Rd Morrilton, AR 72110 (501) 727-5451 *Fax:* (501) 727-5761 *E-mail:* director@campmitchell.org *Web:* www.campmitchell.org *Contact: Exec Dirs* Richard & Helen Hargreaves. Total Beds: 165

ATLANTA

Georgia Episcopal Conference Center at Honey Creek 299 Episcopal Conference Center Rd Waverly GA 31565 (912) 265-9218 *Fax:* (912) 267-6907 *E-mail:* office@honeycreek.org *Web:* www.honeycreek.org *Contact: Dir* Dade Brantley. Total Beds: 150.

CALIFORNIA

St Columba Church 12835 Sir Francis Drake Blvd (PO Box 430) Inverness CA 04937 (415) 669-1039. 32 person capacity.

St Dorothy's Rest PO Box B Camp Meeker CA 95419 (707) 874-3319 *Fax:* (707) 874-3349 *E-mail:* sdr@monitor.net *Web:* www.stdorothysrest.org *Contact: Exec Dir* Katie Evenbeck. Total Beds: 120.

The Bishop's Ranch 5297 Westside Rd Healdsburg, CA 95448 (707) 433-2440 *Fax:* (707) 433-3431 *E-mail:* info@bishopsranch.org *Web:* www.bisopsranch.org *Contact: Exec Dir* Sean Swift. Total Beds: 100.

Easton Hall Conference Center—CDSP 2451 Ridge Rd Berkeley CA 94709 (510) 204-0732 *E-mail:* eastonhall@cdsp.edu *Web:* www.cdsp.edu/conference.php. Total Beds: 22.

CENTRAL GULF COAST
Beckwith Camp and Retreat Center (Diocese of Central Gulf Coast) 10400 Beckwith Ln Fairhope AL 36532 (251) 928-7844 *Fax*: (251) 928-7811 *E-mail*: Eleanor@BeckwithAL.com *Web*: www.beckwithal.com. Total Beds: 200.

COLORADO
Cathedral Ridge Retreat & Conference Center, 1364 County Road 75, Woodland Park CO 80863, (719) 687-9038. office@cathedralridge.org.

CONNECTICUT
Incarnation Center PO Box 577 Ivoryton CT 06442 (860) 767-0848 *Fax*: (860) 767-8432 *E-mail*: info@incarnationcenter.org *Web*: www.incarnationcenter.com *Contact: Dir* Nancy Pilon. Total Beds: 217.

Camp Washington Camp and Retreat Ctr 190 Kenyon Rd Lakeside CT 06758 (860) 567-9623 *Fax*: (860) 567-3037 *E-mail*: camp@campwashington.org *Web*: wwwcampwashington.org *Contact: Dir* Bart Geissinger. Total Beds: 160.

DELAWARE
Camp Arrowhead 913 Wilson Road Wilmington DE 19803 (302) 256-0374 *Fax*: (302) 543-8084 *E-mail*: kathymoore@dioceseofdelaware.net *Web*: www.camparrowhead.net *Contact: Dir* Walt Lafontaine. Total Beds: 325.

Memorial House For Contact Information see Camp Arrowhead above. Total Beds: 31.

EASTERN MICHIGAN
Camp Chickagami 111 West Graham Lansing MI 48901 (888) 440-2267 *Fax*: (517) 699-0846 *E-mail*: mbade@eastmich.org *Web*: www.campchickagami.org *Contact:* McKenzie Bade. Total Beds: 130.

FLORIDA
Camp Weed and Cerveny Conference Center 11057 Camp Weed Place Live Oak FL 32060 386-364-5250 *Fax*: 386-362-7557 *E-mail*: drcw@campweed.org *Web*: www.campweed.org *Contact: Exec Dir* Charles Wallace. Total Beds: 278.

Camp Wingmann 3404 Wingmann Rd Avon Park FL 33825 866-526-3380 *E-mail*: wingmann@strato.net *Web*: www.campwingmann.org *Contact:* Rev Deke Miller. Total Beds: 147.

Day Spring Conference Center PO Box 661 Ellenton FL 34222 (941) 776-1018 *Fax*: (941) 776-2678 *E-mail*: execdirctor@dayspringfla.org *Web*: www.dayspringfla.org *Contact: Exec Dir* Carla Odell. Total Beds: 315.

Duncan Conference Center 15820 South Military Trail Delray Beach FL 33484 (561) 496-4130 *Fax*: (561) 496-1726 *E-mail*: jbush@duncancenter.org *Web*: www.duncancenter.org *Contact: Exec Dir* Jesse Bush. Total Beds: 79.

Canterbury Retreat and Conference Center 1601 Alafaya Trail (SR 434) Oviedo FL 32765 (407) 365-5571 *Fax*: (407) 365-9758 *E-mail*: jon@canterburyretreat.org *Web*: www.canterburyretreat.org *Contact: Exec Dir* The Rev Jon Davis. Total Beds: 92.

GEORGIA
Mikell Camp and Conference Center Rt 3 Box 3495 Toccoa GA 30577 (706) 886-7515 *Fax*: (706) 886-7580 *E-mail*: mikell@alltel.net *Web*: www.campmikell.com *Contact: Dir* The Rev Kenneth Struble. Total Beds: 236.

HAWAII
Camp Mokuleia 68-729 Farrington Hwy Waialua HI 96791 (808) 637-6241 *Fax*: (808) 637-5505 *E-mail*: reservations@campmokuleia.com *Web*: www.campmokuleia.com *Contact:* David Turner. Total Beds: 212.

IDAHO
Paradise Point Camp PO Box 936 Boise ID 83701 (208) 345-4522 *Fax*: (208) 345-9735 *E-mail*: mbeck@idahodiocese.org *Web*: www.paradisepointcamp.org *Contact: Dir* Marty Beck. Total Beds: 100.

ILLINOIS
Toddhall Retreat and Conference Center 350 Todd Center Dr Columbia IL 62236 (618) 281-8180 *Fax*: (618) 281-8187 *E-mail*: toddhall@htc.net *Web*: www.toddhallrc.org *Contact: Exec Dir* Jim Moeller. Total Beds: 92.

INDIANA
Waycross Episcopal Camp and Conference Center 7363 Bear Creek Rd Morgantown IN 46160 (812) 597-4241 *Fax*: (812) 597-4291 *E-mail*: info@waycrosscenter.org *Web*: www.waycrosscenter.org *Contact: Exec Dir* Van Beers. Total Beds: 226.

Wawasee Episcopal Center 7830 E Vawter Park Rd Syracuse IN 46567 (574) 233-6489 *Fax*: (574) 287-7914 *E-mail*: treasurer@edin.org *Web*: www.ednin.org *Contact: Dir* Sharon Katona. Total Beds: 26.

KENTUCKY
All Saints Episcopal Center 833 Hickory Grove Rd Leitchfield KY 42754 (270) 259-3514 *Fax*: (270) 259-0526 *E-mail*: crystal@allsaintscenter.org *Web*: www.allsaintscenter.org *Contact: Mgr* Crystal Holman. Total Beds: 114.

The Cathedral Domain 800 Highway 1746 Irvine KY 40336-8701 (606) 464-8254 *Fax*: (606) 464-0759 *E-mail*: asigmon@diolex.org *Web*: www.cathedraldomain.org *Contact: Fac Dir* Andy Sigmon. Total Beds: 315.

LOUISIANA
The Solomon Episcopal Conference Center 54296 Highway 445 Loranger LA 70446 (985) 748-6634 *Fax*: (985) 748-2843 *E-mail*: info@solomoncenter.org *Web*: www.solomoncenter.org *Contact: Dir* Frank Hall Total Beds: 88.

MAINE
Camp Bishopswood 143 State St (Winter) Portland ME 04101 (207) 772-1953 x127 *Fax*: (207) 773-

0095 *E-mail*: info@bishopwood.org *Web*: www. bishopwood.org *Contact: Dir* Michael Douglas *E-mail:* mike@bishopswood.org. Total Beds: 100.

MARYLAND

Bishop Clagget Center PO Box 40 Buckeystown MD 21717 (301) 874-5147 *Fax*: (301) 874-0834 *E-mail:* info@bishopclagget.org *Web*: www.bishopclaggett. org *Contact: Dir* Tom Robertson. Total Beds: 173.

MASSACHUSETTS

Barbara C Harris Camp and Conference Center PO Box 204 Greenfield NH 03047 (603) 547-3400 *Fax*: (603) 547-3038 *E-mail*: info@bchcenter.org *Web*: www.bchcenter.org. Total Beds: 198.

MICHIGAN

Emrich Retreat Center at Parishfield 7380 Teahen Rd Brighton MI (810) 231-1060 *Web*: www. discoveremrich.org. Overnight accommodations for 90 on 26 beatutiful, well kept acres.

MISSISSIPPI

Duncan M Gray Episcopal Camp and Conference Center 1530 Way Rd Canton 39046 (601) 859-1556 *Fax*: (601) 859-1495 *E-mail*: lindac@graycenter.org *Web*: www.graycenter.com *Contact: Exec Dir* Grae Dickson. Total Beds: 220.

MONTANA

Camp Marshall 41524 Melita Island Rd Polson MT 59860 (406) 849-5718 *E-mail*: christianformation@ diomontana.com *Web*: www.diomontana.com *Contact: Exec Dir.* Rev. Wren Blessing. Total Beds: 150.

NEVADA

Camp Galilee 1776 Highway 50 South PO Box 236 Glenbrook NV 89413 (775) 749-5546 *E-mail*: executivedirector@galileetahoe.org *Web*: www. galileetahoe.org *Contact: Exec Dir* Stuart Campbell. Total Beds: 68.

NEW JERSEY

Crossroads Outdoor Ministries 29 Pleasant Grove Rd Port Murray NJ 07865 (908) 832-7264 *Fax*: (908) 832-6593 *E-mail*: www.crossroadsretreat.com *Web*: www.crossroadsretreat.com *Contact: Dir* Anthony Briggs. Total Beds: 300.

NEW MEXICO

Bishop Stoney Camp and Conferance Center 7855 Old Santa Fe Trail Santa Fe NM 87505 (505) 983-5610 *Fax*: (505) 983-9150 *E-mail*: info@campstoney. org *Web*: www.campstoney.org. Total Beds: 100.

NEW YORK

Camp DeWolfe PO Box 487 Wading River NY 11792 (631) 929-4325 *Fax*: (631) 929-6553 *E-mail*: office@campdewolfe.org *Web*: www.campdewolfe. org *Contact: Dir* Matt Tees. Total Beds: 150.

Christ the King Spiritual Life Center 575 Burton Rd Greenwich NY 12834 (518) 692-9550 *E-mail*: mbaker@ ctkcenter.org *Web*: www.Christ-the-King-Center.org *Contact:* Cn Mathew Baker. Total Beds: 160.

NORTH CAROLINA

Kanuga Confererences PO Box 250 Hendersonville NC 28793-0250 (828) 692-9136 *Fax*: (828) 696-3589 *E-mail*: info@kanuga.org *Web*: www.kanuga.org *Contact: Pres* Stanley B Hubbard Jr. Total Beds: 750.

Lake Logan Conference Center 154 Suncrest Mill Rd Canton NC 28716 (828) 646-0095 *Fax*: (828) 648-8937 *E-mail*: info@lakelogan.org *Web*: www. lakelogan.org *Contact: Exec Dir* Susan Merrill. Total Beds: 196.

Trinity Center PO Box 380 Salter Path NC 28575 (888) 874-6287 *Fax*: (252) 247-3290 *E-mail*: penn@ trinityctr.com *Web*: www.trinityctr.com *Contact: Exec Dir* Penn Perry. Total Beds: 180.

Valle Crucis Conference Center PO Box 654 Valle Crucis NC 28691 (828) 963-4453 *Fax*: (828) 963-8806 *E-mail*: vccc@highsouth.com *Web*: www. highsouth.com/vallecrusis *Contact: Exec Dir* Margaret Lumpkin Love. Total Beds: 156.

OHIO

Procter Conference Center 11235 State Rd 38 London OH 43130 (740) 874-3355 *Fax*: (740) 874-3356 *E-mail*: rkimbler@diosohio.org *Web*: www. proctercenter.org *Contact: Dir* Total Beds: 124.

Cedar Hills Camp and Conference Center— CLOSED

Sheldon Calvary Camp 4410 Lake Rd Conneaut OH 44030 (440) 593-4381 *Fax*: (440) 593-6250 *E-mail*: executivedirector@calvarycamp.org *Web*: www.calvarycamp.org *Contact: Dir* Timothy Green. Total Beds: 250.

Transfiguration Spirituality Center 495 Albion Ave Cincinnati OH 45246 (513) 771-5291 *E-mail*: ctretreats@gmail.com *Contact: Exec Dir* Toni Thomas-Feren. Total Beds: 50.

OKLAHOMA

St Crispin's Conference Center Rt 2 Box 381 Wewoka OK 74884 (405) 382-1619 *Fax*: (405) 382-1631 *E-mail*: stcrispins@yahoo.com *Web*: www. episcopaloklahoma.org *Contact: Dirs* Joanne & Mike Roberts. Total Beds: 180.

OREGON

Ascension School PO Box 278 Cove OR 97824 (541) 568-4514 *E-mail*: patty@coveascensionschool.com *Web*: www.episdioeo.org *Contact: Exec Dir* Patty Olson Lindsey. Total Beds: 130.

PITTSBURGH

Sheldon Calvary Camp 4411 Lake Rd Conneaut, OH 44030 (440) 593-4381 *Exec Dir* Tim Green *E-mail*: executivedirector@calvarycamp.org *Web*: www.calvarycamp.org.

RHODE ISLAND

Episcopal Conference Center 872 Reservoir Rd Pascoag RI 02859 (401) 568-4055 *Fax*: (401) 568-7805 *E-mail*: director@eccri.org *Web*: www.eccri.org *Contact: Dir* Rev Meaghan Kelly Brower. Total Beds: 225.

RIO GRANDE

Bishop Stoney Camp and Conference Center 7855 Old Santa Fe Trail Santa Fe NM 87505 (505) 983-5610 *Fax:* (505) 983-9150 *E-mail:* info@campstoney.org *Web:* www.campstoney.org. Total Beds: 100.

Bosque Center, The 6400 Coors Boulevard NW Albuquerque NM 87120 (505) 881-0636 *Fax:* (505) 883-9048 *E-mail:* psoukup@dioceserg.org *Web:* www.bosquecenter.org; Total Beds: 39.

SOUTH DAKOTA

Thunderhead Episcopal Center PO Box 890 Lead SD 57754 605-584-2233 (summer) *Fax:* 605-582-2242 *E-mail:* camp.diocese@midconetwork.com *Contact:* Camp Dir. Portia Corbin Total Beds: 106.

TENNESSEE

DuBose Conference Center PO Box 339 Monteagle TN 37356 (931) 924-2353 *Fax:* (931) 924-2291 *E-mail:* David@DuboseConferenceCenter.org *Web:* www.duboseconf.org *Contact:* David Ramsey. Total Beds: 240.

Grace Point Camp and Retreat Center 300 Chamberlain Cove Rd Kingston TN 37763 (865) 567-1159 *E-mail:* gracepoint@etdiocese.net *Web:* www.etdiocese.net. Total Beds: 46.

St Columba Episcopal Conference Center 4577 Billy Maher Rd Memphis TN 38135 (901) 377-9284 *Fax:* (901) 371-0700 *Web:* www.saintcolumbamemphis.org. *Dir* Brad Thompson. Total Beds: 77.

St Mary's Sewanee PO Box 188 Sewanee TN 37375 (931) 598-5342 *Fax:* (931) 598-5884 *E-mail:* reservations@stmaryssewanee.org *Web:* www.stmaryssewanee.org *Contact:* Exec Dir Rev John Runkle. Total Beds: 100.

TEXAS

All Saints Camp and Conference Center 418 Stanton Way Pottsboro TX 75076 (903) 786-3148 *Fax:* (903) 786-7535 *E-mail:* info@allsaintstexoma.org *Web:* www.allsaintstexoma.org *Contact:* Exec Dir David Campbell. Total Beds: 176.

Camp Allen 18800 FM 362 Navasota TX 77868 (936) 825-7175 *Fax:* (936) 825-8495 *E-mail:* frontdesk@campallen.org *Web:* www.campallen.org *Contact:* Pres George Dehan. Total Beds: 600.

Camp Capers PO Box 9 Waring TX 78074 (830) 995-3966 *Fax:* (830) 995-2393 *E-mail:* capers@hctc.net *Web:* www.campcapers.org *Contact:* Rob Watson. Total Beds: 220.

Camp Crucis 2875 Camp Crucis Court Granbury TX 76048 (817) 573-3343 *Fax:* (817) 279-7974 *E-mail:* info@campcrucis.org *Web:* www.campcrucis.org *Contact:* Dir Jason Bontke. Total Beds: 340.

Mustang Island Conference Center PO Box 130 Port Arkansas TX 78373 (361) 749-1800 *Fax:* (361) 749-1802 *E-mail:* lynn.corby@dwtx.org *Web:* www.mustangisland.org *Contact:* Oper Mgr Lynn Corby. *Dir* Kevin Spaeth. Total Beds: 55.

UTAH

Camp Tuttle 80 South 300 East Salt Lake City UT 84110 (801) 322-4131 *Fax:* (801) 322-5096 *E-mail:* mlees@episcopal-ut.org *Web:* www.camptuttle.org *Contact:* Melanie Lees. Total Beds: 165.

VERMONT

Bishop Booth Conference Center 20 Rock Point Circle Burlington VT 05401 (802) 658-6233 *Fax:* (802) 658-8836 *E-mail:* bishopbooth@dioceseofvermont.org *Web:* www.dioceseofvermont.org *Contact:* Tony Drapelick. Total Beds: 110.

VIRGINIA

Virginia Diocesan Center at Roslyn 8727 River Rd Richmond VA 23229 (804)288-6045 *Fax:* (804) 285-3430 *E-mail:* info@roslyncenter.org *Web:* www.roslyncenter.org *Contact:* Katherine Lawrence. Total Beds: 96.

Shrine Mont 221 Shrine Mont Circle Orkney Springs VA 22845 (540) 856-2141 *Fax:* (540) 856-8520 *E-mail:* shrine@shentel.net *Web:* www.shrinemont.com *Contact:* Exec Dir Kevin Moomaw. Total Beds: 550.

WASHINGTON

Camp Cross 245 E 13th Ave Spokane WA 99202 (509) 624-3191 *Fax:* (509) 747-0049 *E-mail:* campcross@spokanediocese.org *Web:* www.campcross.org *Contact:* Colin Haffner. Total Beds: 110.

Huston Camp and Conference Center PO Box 140 Gold Bar WA 98251 (360) 793-0441 *Fax:* (360) 793-3822 *E-mail:* info@huston.org *Web:* www.huston.org *Contact:* Dir Bill Tubbs. Total Beds: 237.

WEST VIRGINIA

Peterkin Camp and Conference Center 286 Clubhouse Rd Romney WV 26757-7521 (304) 822-4519 Fax: (304) 822-7771 *E-mail:* daisymcb1@hotmail.com *Web:* www.peterkin.org *Contact:* Daisy McBride. Total Beds: 150.

Sandcrest Conference and Retreat Center 143 Sandcrest Dr Wheeling WV 26003 (304) 277-3022 *Fax:* (304) 277-3840 *E-mail:* sandcrest@1stnet *Web:* www.sandscrest.com *Contact:* Exec Dir Sarah Lydick. Total Beds: 35.

WESTERN MICHIGAN

Saugatuck Retreat House WMI Diocese PO Box 189 Saugatuck MI 49453 (269) 857-5201. Total 14 rooms. Five bedroom house for overnight and longer retreats run by All Saints Episcopal Church.

WISCONSIN

DeKoven Center 600 21st St Rancine WI 53403 (262) 633-6401 *E-mail:* info@dekovencenter.org *Web:* www.dekovencenter.pair.com *Contact:* Dir Max Dershem. Total Beds: 60.

WYOMING

Wyoming Wilderness Camp 123 S Durbin Casper WY 82601 (307) 265-5200 *Fax:* (307) 577-9939 *E-mail:* jessica@wyomingdiocese.org *Web:* www.wyomingdiocese.org. Total Beds: 30.

SOCIAL AGENCIES AND INSTITUTIONS/ GENERAL SERVICE ORGANIZATIONS

Assembly of Episc Healthcare Chaplains

Professional organization of Epis chaplains and health care institutions. Fosters and promotes advocacy, communication and education for chaplaincy. An affiliate of the COMISS Commission on the Accreditation of Healthcare Organizations (CCAHO) and the Coalition on Ministry in Specialized Settings (COMISS). *Pres* E Nefstead *Pres Elect* S Roberts *Comm Off* Rev R Waff 2443 Lawson Blvd Gurnee IL 60031 *E-mail:* RazzW@aol.com *Web:* www. episcopalchaplain.org. For information on ecclesiastical endorsement for AAPC, ACPE, or APC call Terry Foster, (800) 334-7626, x6068 *E-mail:* tfoster@ episcopalchurch.org.

Episcopal Health Ministries

Episcopal Health Ministries (EHM) is a network that promotes health ministry (including parish nursing) in Episcopal congregations. EHM provides health ministry resources to local congs, dioceses and provinces; collaborates with other faith communities institutions and health orgs; offers education for Episcopal health ministry and parish nursing; and supports those engaged in cong health min. For information see www. EpiscopalHealthMinistries.org 6050 N Meridian St Indianapolis IN 46208 (317) 253-1277 x34 *E-mail:* NEHM@episcopalhealthministries.org.

HEALTH AND WELFARE AGENCIES RELATED TO DIOCESES OR PARISHES OF THE EPISCOPAL CHURCH

FOREWORD

In most communities throughout the country, there are resources available to clergy and lay people interested in helping people in need. Larger communities may have agencies offering a variety of services, usually coordinated through community planning councils; other, smaller localities may have a few organized social services. In most instances, the State Department of Public Welfare in the state capital or local public welfare agencies will prove to be the best sources of information about local resources for use and for referral.

This directory is based on material submitted by the dioceses and covers facilities in the United States. Those interested in church-related facilities overseas are advised to contact the appropriate Anglican or Episcopal authority as listed in *The Episcopal Church Annual.* It should also be noted that in addition to the agencies listed most parishes sponsor a wide variety of community services, many located in parish houses.

This listing is supplied only as information and does not constitute endorsement by the *Executive Council of Agency Policy.* For details on program, policy, or any other information, we recommend that the agency be contacted directly.

HOW TO USE THIS DIRECTORY

Dioceses of the Episcopal Church are listed in alphabetical order.

Agencies in each diocese are also listed in alphabetical order. The specific category is indicated in parenthesis by the following abbreviations:

(CYF) Children, Youth, and Families.

(CHAP) Chaplaincy Services: Counseling.

(FSO) Facilities and Services for Older Persons.

(HCC) Hospitals, Convalescent Homes, and Clinics.

(NCS) Neighborhood and Community Services.

(R) Residences, Rest Homes, and Retreat Centers.

(SpM) Specialized Ministries.

To find an appropriate service in your area, it is recommended that you review more than one category, as there is some overlapping in categories and some agencies offer multiple services.

AGENCIES LISTED ACCORDING TO DIOCESE

DIOCESE OF ALABAMA

AIDS Alabama (SpM) PO Box 55703 Birmingham AL 35255 (800) 592-2437 or (205) 324-9822 *E-mail:* aidsalabama@aidsalabama.org. Sponsors housing programs for people living with HIV/AIDS.

Bridge Ministries (NCS) PO Box 55216 Birmingham AL 35255 (205) 930-0309 *Fax:* (205) 930-3175 *Exec Dir* Lisa Isay. Interdenominational outreach ministry to the poor in the greater Birmingham area.

Community Kitchens (NCS) 1024 S 12th St Birmingham AL 35205 (205) 251-3569 *E-mail:* ablackert@thecommunitykitchens.org *Exec Dir* Andrea Blackert. Feeding the hungry, the homeless and the working poor in two Episcopal parishes.

Counseling Ministry Professionals Inc (CHAP) 1788 McFarland Blvd N Ste A Tuscaloosa AL 35406 (205) 345-5885 *Fax:* (205) 345-5884 *E-mail:* cmp3155@bellsouth.net *Exec Dir* Rev Margaret Scalise MD.

Diocesan Pastoral Counseling Center (CHAP) 1024 S 12th St Birmingham AL 35205 (205) 251-7887 *Pastoral Counselor* The Rev Dr Felix Joffrion.

Episcopal Place I & II (FSO) 1100 & 1112 26th St S Birmingham AL 35205 (205) 939-0085 *Fax:* (205) 939-0101 *E-mail:* epdir@bham.rr.com *Web:* www.episcopalplace.org *Exec Dir* Tim Blanton. A subsidized apartment community for elderly and young disabled with limited income. *Exec Dir* Tim Blanton.

Good Samaritan Health Clinic (HCC) 401 Arnold St NE Ste A Cullman AL 35055 (256) 775-1389.

Holy Comforter House Inc (FSO) 745 Walnut St Gadsden AL 35901 (256) 547-3430 *Fax:* (256) 547-9168 *E-mail:* hchouse@bellsouth.net *Mgr*

Dawn Aldridge. A non-denominational high-rise retirement community.

Integrity/Alabama (SpM) PO Box 530002, Birmingham AL 35253) (205) 595-3159 *Web:* www.integrityusa.org *Convenor* David Gary. A ministry to gay, lesbian, bisexual and transgender Episcopalians, family and friends.

Interfaith Mission Service (SpM) 701 Andrew Jackson Way NE Huntsville AL 35801 (256) 536-2401 *E-mail:* ims@knology.net. *Web:* www.interfaithmissionservice.org

Kairos Alabama (SpM) Ecumenical ministry to prison inmates. *Web:* www.kairos-al.org

PAC T/Parents and Children Together (CYF) PO Box 1247 Decatur AL 35602 (256) 355-7252 *Web:* www.pactfamily.org *Exec Dir* Susan Roberts. Family resource center serving Morgan County.

Pond House Retreat Center (SpM) Located on Logan Martin Lake in Pell City; sponsored by St Peters Church Talladega AL (256) 362-2505. A place for solitude with God and for personal healing; suitable for day retreats and small group overnights.

St Martins-in-the-Pines (FSO) 4941 Montevallo Rd Birmingham AL 35210 (205) 956-1831 *Pres/CEO* Terence E Rogers *Dir Pastoral Care* Rev Jennifer Riddle. Retirement community.

St Martin's At Home (FSO) 4941 Montevallo Rd Birmingham AL 35210 (205) 956-1831 *Pres/CEO* Terence Rogers. Home care service.

St Michaels Community Services Center (HCC) 1005 W 18th St PO Box 1884 Anniston AL 36202 *Clinic:* (256) 236-6060 *St Michaels Church:* (256) 237-4011. Free medical clinic for those who have no insurance, Medicare or Medicaid, and are unable to afford medical care.

The Hermitage (SpM) PO Box 4 Trussville AL 35173 (205) 655-7667 *Dirs* Rev Dr Ron DelBene & Dr Eleanor McKenzie DelBene. Opportunities in spiritual growth and direction.

Third Order Society of St Francis (SpM) 1919 South Hull St Montgomery AL 36104 *E-mail:* ywillie@juno.com. *Contact:* Lucy Blount. For a deeper, richer, more disciplined spiritual journey.

DIOCESE OF ALASKA

St Jude Jubilee Ctr Box 55458 North Pole AK *Exec Dir* Rev J Hunter II.

DIOCESE OF ARIZONA

Episcopal Community Services 114 W Roosevelt St Phoenix AZ 85003 (602) 544-5879.

St Andrew's Children's Clinic (HCC) 969 W Country Club Nogales AZ 85621 (520) 648-3242 *E-mail:* office@standrewsclinic.org. Serve children from Mexico with special health needs.

St Luke's in the Desert (R FSO) 615 E Adams Tucson AZ 85705 (520) 628-1512. Res fac for elderly of limited means.

St Mary Manor (R, FSO) 6515 N 39 Ave Phoenix AZ 85019 (602) 973-3139. Low-cost housing for elderly and disabled.

DIOCESE OF ARKANSAS

Good Shepherd Ecum Ret Home (FSO) 2701 Aldersgate Rd Little Rock AR 72205 (501) 224-7200 *Fax:* (501) 224-0910 *CEO* Mark Davis. Retirement residence. Independent living (200 units) for men and women. Cafeteria fac spon by Meth, Presby, RC and Episcopal judicatories.

St Francis House, Episc Urban Ctr (NCS) Box 4490 Little Rock AR 72214 (501) 664-5036 *Fax:* (501) 663-8908 *Dir* Darlene Bourgeois *E-mail:* stfrancis72204@att.net. Neighborhood and comm svcs; counseling and referral svcs; cultural implementation.

St Francis' House Northwest (NCS) 614 E Emma Ste 300 Springdale AR 72764 (479) 751-7417 *Dir* Kathy Grisham. Provides primarily dental care and some medical assistance to clients in NW AR.

DIOCESE OF ATLANTA

Appleton Episcopal Ministries Macon, GA, 2744 Peachtree Rd NW Atlanta GA 30305 *Missioner* J Groce (478) 731-5901. A century-old ministry that exists to support vulnerable children in the communities of the Macon Convocation.

Canterbury Ct (FSO) 3750 Peachtree Rd NE Atlanta GA 30319-1322 (404) 261-6611 *Admin* Andrea Price *Web:* www.canterburycourt.org. Ret home.

Cathedral Counseling Center (CHAP) 2744 Peachtree Rd NW Atlanta GA 30308 (404) 636-1457 x577 Kim Woodard.

Cathedral Towers Inc (FSO) 2820 Peachtree Rd NW Atlanta GA 30305-2935 (404) 231-3020 *Admin* KR Gottlieb. High-rise fac for the elderly 195 units, no vacancies, for persons living on limited incomes. Sponsored by the Cathedral of St Phil.

Chattahoochee Valley Episc Ministry Inc (NCS) Box 5811 Columbus GA 31906-0811 (706) 327-0400 *Lay* Vicky B Partin. Outreach arm of convoc which provides direct emergency services to people in need; enables ecumenical projects such as food centers, jobs counseling, interagency groups, housing, prison work church networking; training and service opportunities for parishioners in 6 parishes.

Church of the Common Ground (SpM) Downtown Atlanta 2744 Peachtree Rd NW Atlanta GA 30305 *Vicar* Rev M Wetzel *E-mail:* marywetz@gmail.com. Worshiping community that provides support for the spiritual, social, emothional and physical needs of Atlanta's unhoused men and women.

Emmaus House (SpM) 1017 Hank Aaron Dr Atlanta GA 30315 (404) 525-5948 *Dir Lay* J Mole *E-mail:* josephmole@emmaushouse.org *Web:* www.emmaushouse.org. Episcopal Community Center serving the Peoplestown and Summerhill neighborhoods of Atlanta, providing a poverty rights office, summer program for children and community for all.

Hartsfield-Jackson Atlanta International Airport 2744 Peachtree Rd NW Atlanta GA 30305 *Vicar* Rev D Mote *E-mail:* dsmote@mac.com. Mission is to be an active, visible and positive Episcopal presence at the world's busiest airport—drawing the circle of inclusion wider, welcoming more people home to the Episcopal Church and representing the church and Christ in the world.

Holy Comforter (SpM) 737 Woodland Ave SE Atlanta GA 30316-2454 (404) 627-6510 Rev A Chase *Web:* www.holycomforter.atlanta.org. Church and fellowship center reaching out to the intellectually impaired

St Anne's Terr (FSO) 3100 Northside Pkwy NW Atlanta GA 30327-1563 (404) 238-9200 *Admin* Burl Gault *Web:* www.saintannesterrace.org. 100 apts for persons 65 and older.

St George's Ct (FSO) 110 N 10th Griffin GA 30223-2854 (404) 229-5405 *Admin* Martha McDaniel. New complex of 125 multiple apartmens. Sponsored by St George's Church.

St George's Woods (FSO) 1401 Old Macon Rd Griffin GA 30223 (770) 412-6005 *Admin* R Thomas. Seniors community w/personal care. Sponsored by St George's Church.

St Paul's Apts (FSO) 1330 Forsyth Macon GA 31201-1448 (478) 745-0829 *Admin* Stuart Davis *Web:* www. homestore.com. High-rise facility for the elderly.

DIOCESE OF BETHLEHEM

Episc Apts of the Slate Belt (FSO) 684 American-Bangor Rd Bangor PA 18013 (610) 863-7626 *Mgr* Gwendolyn A Gonzalez. Residence for middle income elderly. Non-denominational.

Episc House (FSO) 1440 Walnut Allentown PA 18102 (610) 821-0311 *Mgr* Christine Bauder *E-mail:* cbauder@episcopalhouse.com. Residence for middle income elderly. Non-denominational.

Episc House (FSO) 50 N Ninth St Reading PA 19601 (610) 376-6535 *Dir* Nevin Hollinger. Residence for middle income elderly. Under auspices of Christ Church, 5th & Court Sts Reading.

New Bethany Ministries Bldg 333 W 4th Bethlehem PA 18015 (610) 691-5602 *Fax:* (610) 866-3427 *Dir* Diane Elliott *E-mail:* newbethany@ newbethanyministries.org. Shelter for homeless, meal center, daytime drop-in center, transitional housing, single room occupancy. Nondenominational.

DIOCESE OF CALIFORNIA

The Seamen's Church Institute (SpM) International Maritime Center 4001 7th St Oakland CA 94607 (510) 839-2226 *Fax:* (510) 839-8193 *Web:* www. seamenschurch.org. *Dir* Adrienne Yee; See Mission to Seafarers section of Annual.

Canon Kip Community House (NCS, FSO) 705 Natoma St San Francisco CA 94103 (415) 487-3800 x6211 *Dir* Lolita Kintanar (Episcopal Community Services). Community education and recreation programs for elderly. Senior feeding program. Work

and life skills training for homeless. Housing units for formerly homeless.

Canterbury Woods (FSO) 651 Sinex Ave Pacific Grove CA 93950 (831) 373-3111 *Exec Dir* (Episc Senior Communities). Life care for men and women over 65.

Clausen House (SpM) 88 Vernon St Oakland CA 94610 (510) 839-0050 *Exec Dir* Martin Harris *E-mail:* martin@clausenhouse.org *Web:* www.clausenhouse. org. Residence facility for adults with developmental disabilities. Education, recreation, drama programs, volunteer placement w/community agencies, vocational job placement.

Sojourn: Chaplaincy at San Francisco General Hosp (CHAP) 1001 Potrero Ave Rm 2F4 San Francisco CA 94110 (415) 206-8918 *Exec Dir* Karen Tomcala. Provides Episcopal presence within a county hospital and trains lay chap to work w/ in hospital. *Web:* sojournchaplaincy.org.

Episc Charities (SpM) 1055 Taylor St San Francisco CA 94108 (415) 869-7813 *Exec Dir* Kathleen Piraino *Web:* www.episcopalcharities.org. Provides technical, financial and human resources for nonprofit organizations serving needy in Bay Area.

Episc Community Services of San Francisco (NCS) 165 8th St 3rd Flr San Francisco CA 94103 Ken Reggio (415) 487-3300 *Fax:* (415) 252-1743 *Web:* www.ecs-sf.org.

Episc Ministry to Convalescent Hospitals (CHAP) 1700 Santa Clara Ave Alameda CA 94501 (510) 521-3041 *Web:* www.aemch.org *Chap Coord* Rev Nancy Eswein. Coordinates work, through parishes, to bring church presence to people living in convalescent hospitals.

Episc Senior Communities (FSO) 2185 N California Blvd Ste 575 Walnut Creek CA 94596 (925) 956-7400 *Pres & CEO* Kevin Gerber *Web:* www.jtm-esc.org.

Good Samaritan Family Resource Ctr (NCS, CYF) 1294 Potrero Ave San Francisco CA 94110 (415) 401-4253 *Fax:* (415) 824-9527 *Exec Dir* Mario Paz *Web:* www.goodsamfrc.org. Training and support system for new immigrants and refugees. Provides senior food programs, ESL training.

Los Gatos Meadows (FSO) 110 Wood Rd Los Gatos CA 95030 (408) 354-0211 *Fax:* (408) 354-4193 *Exec Dir* Ira Kurtz (Episc Senior Communities). Life care for men and women over 65.

Oasis/California (SpM) 1055 Taylor St San Francisco CA 94108 *Pres* Thomas Jackson *E-mail:* communications@oasiscalifornia.org *Web:* www. oasiscalifornia.org. Min to gay and lesbian comm.

Oak Center Towers (FSO) 1515 Market St Oakland CA 94607 (510) 465-1166 *Mgr* Vincent Cheung (Episc Senior Communities). 195 low-income apartments. Over 62, income restrictions.

Ohlhoff Recovery Programs (SpM) 601 Steiner St San Francisco CA 94117 (877) 677-4543 *Exec Dir* Arlene Stanich-Prince. Residence and programs for recovering male alcoholics. Outpatient substance abuse and eating disorders programs. Programs for friends and families of substance abusers. *Web:* ohlhoff.org

Presidio Gate Apts (FSO) 2770 Lombard St San Francisco CA 94123 (415) 567-1050 *Admin* Pamela Higgins (Episc Senior Communities). 55 low-income apartment rentals for persons over 62. Income restrictions.

San Francisco Towers (FSO) 1661 Pine St San Francisco CA 94109 (415) 776-0500 *Exec Dir* John W Milford (Episc Senior Communities). Life care retirement residence for men and women over 65.

The Sanctuary (NCS) 201 8th St San Francisco CA 94103 (415) 487-3740 *Dir* Viviana Martinez (Episc Comm Srv). 24-hour shelter, meals, job counseling and referrals, health care, support groups, counseling and rehab for homeless persons.

Spring Lake Village (FSO) 5555 Montgomery Dr Santa Rosa CA 95409 (800) 795-1267 *Fax:* (707) 579-6997 *Exec Dir* Sharon Eldridge (Episc Senior Communities). Life care for men and women over 65.

St Paul's Towers (FSO)100 Bay Place Oakland CA 94610 (510) 835-4700 *Fax:* (510) 891-8110 *Exec Dir* Cherese Holland (Episc Senior Communities). Life care retirement residence for men and women over 65.

DIOCESE OF CENTRAL FLORIDA

Episc-Cath Apts Inc (FSO) 500 Ave L NW Winter Haven FL 33880 (863) 299-4481. Apartments for senior citizens. Rentals.

Orlando Cloisters, The (FSO) 757 S Orange Ave Orlando FL 32801 (407) 423-1928. Senior citizen/handicap residence. Rentals.

DIOCESE OF THE CENTRAL GULF COAST

Murray House (R)1257 Government Mobile AL 36604 (251) 432-2272 *Fax:* (251) 432-1935 *E-mail:* connieanderson1257@yahoo.com *Ex Dir* Connie Anderson. Indiv living apts for elderly.

Wilmer Hall (CYF) 3811 Old Shell Rd Mobile AL 36608 (251) 342-4931 *Fax:* (251) 342-1782 *E-mail:* development@wilmerhall.org *Exec Dir* Sally Greene. Intake policy: neglected or dependent, abused children of the states of AL and north FL.

Beckwith Camp and Retreat Center 10400 Beckwith Ln Fairhope AL 36532 (251) 928-7844 *E-mail:* eleanor@beckwithal.com *Exec Dir* Eleanor Reeves

DIOCESE OF CENTRAL NEW YORK

Good Shepherd-Fairview Home (FSO) 80 Fairview Ave Birmington NY 13904 (607) 724-2477 *Admin* D Governanti. 2 homes at 3 levels of care. Adult home for women, health related facility and skilled nursing for men and women. Licensed under NYS Health Department. Age 65 and over. Multi-discipline, full range of services. 140 res. *Svc area:* Diocese of CNY and Susquehanna Valley Presbytery.

House of the Good Shepherd, The (CYF) 1550 Champlin Ave Utica NY 13502 (315) 733-0436 *Exec Dir* William Holicky. Provides progressive residence, therapeutic, ed, and community service programs to help emotionally disturbed youth and their families realize fullest potential. *Svc area:* NY state. Coed.

St Margaret's House & Ecumenical Center (R) Jordan Rd New Hartford NY 13413-2385 (315) 724-2324 *Fax:* (315) 724-0174 Linda Balutis *E-mail:* smhec47@aol.org. Chap services to institutions; rest and retr; urban parish; mission work.

DIOCESE OF CENTRAL PENNSYLVANIA

Episc Commons (FSO) 502 S 4th Newport PA 17074 (717) 567-3626 *Mgr* Ron Zellers. 30 units for low income elderly and/or disabled men, women and couples (USDA RECDS).

Episc Home for the Aged, The (FSO) 206 E Burd Shippensburg PA 17257 *Dir* Cn Mary Grace Shearer. *Reqs:* age 65; male and female.

Episc Square (FSO) 101 N Prince Shippensburg PA 17257 (717) 530-1277 *Mgr* Marcia Poe (Stevenson Hse and Heistand Hse). A project of Episcopal Towers/Shippensburg. 95 units for men, women and couples (HUD 202).

Honaman House (FSO) 55 E Main Thompsontown PA 17094 (717) 535-5531 *Mgr* Ron Zellers. Project of Episcopal Gardens/Thompsontown. Includes 50 units for men, women and couples. (HUD 202).

DIOCESE OF CHICAGO

Bishop Anderson House Rev Thomas S Rogers, III *Exec Dir* 1653 W Congress Expressway Chicago IL 60612-3833 (312) 563-4824 *Fax:* (312) 942-5279 *E-mail:* trogers@bishopandersonhouse.org *Web:* www.bishopandersonhouse.org. Chaplains trng. Hospital pastoral patient and fam care lay trng, deaf and hearing impaired svcs (incl HIV/AIDS support grps); Operation Bear Hug—a special min for children.

Cathedral Counseling Ctr (SpM) 50 E Washington Ste 301 Chicago IL 60602 (312) 252-9500 *Fax:* (312) 337-9243 *Exec Dir* Maureen Kelly *E-mail:* mkellyccc@aol.com *Web:* www.cathedralcounseling.org. Sliding scale outpatient mental health svcs w/ sensitivity to both spir and psychological concerns.

ReVive Center for Housing and Healing (SpM) 1668 W Ogden Ave Chicago IL 60612 (312) 997-2222 *Fax:* (312) 997-3160 *Dir Dev* Rev J Seymour *E-mail:* jseymour@cathedralshelter.org *Web:* www.cathedralshelter.org. Res and outpatient addiction treatment; food distribution; emergency social svcs; supportive housing prog for formerly homeless persons and fam recovering from addiction.

Church Home/Montgomery Place, The (FSO) 5550 S Shore Dr Chicago IL 60637 (773) 753-4100 *Fax:* (773) 752-0056 *Exec Dir* Rev J Buenting *E-mail:* jbuenting@montgomeryplace.org *Web:* www.montgomeryplace.org. Senior citizen ret housing, nursing and special care facility for 250 res.

Episc Charities and Community Services 65 E Huron Chicago IL 60611 (312) 751-6720 *Exec Dir* Georgianna Gleason *E-mail:* gleason@eccsonline.net. Agencies and centers.

Lawrence Hall Youth Services (CYF) 4833 N Francisco Ave Chicago IL 60625 (773) 769-3500 *Fax:* (773) 769-6467 Kara Teeple *CEO E-mail:* kteeple@lawrencehall.org. Res, special and alt ed programs; employment training and job placement; independent living; relative, specialized, and regular foster care; early childhood intervention.

Primo Center for Women and Children (NCS) 4241 W Washington Blvd Chicago IL 60624 (773) 722-0544 Christine Achre *Exec Dir E-mail:* cachre@primocenter.org *Web:* www.primocenter.org. Comprehensive neighborhood-based services for low income families and individuals, day shelter for homeless, medical care, ed, employment assistance, food distribution.

Ravenswood Community Services (NCS) 4550 N Hermitage Ave Chicago IL 60640 (773) 769-0282 *Fax:* (773) 277-4445 *Exec Dir* Lori Gee *E-mail:* lori@ravenswoodcommunityservices.org *Web:* www.ravenswoodcommunityservices.org. Neighborhood services, food pantry, Community Kitchen.

Shelter Care Ministries (SpM) 412 N Church Rockford IL 61103 (815) 964-5520 *Fax:* (815) 964-9812 *Exec Dir* Sarah Parker-Scanlon *E-mail* sparker@shelter-care.org *Web:* www.shelter-care.org Emergency/transitional housing, drop-in-ctr for mentally ill/homeless persons, comm soup kitchen.

St Leonard's Ministries (SpM) 2100 W Warren Blvd Chicago IL 60612 (312) 738-1414 *Fax:* (312) 738-1417 *Exec Dir* Walter Boyd *E-mail:* slmexecdir@slministries.org *Web:* www.slministries.org. Rehab svcs for men (St Leonard's Hse) and women (Grace Hse) recently released from prison, counseling, transitional housing, employment assistance.

St Mary's Services (CYF) 300 Northwest Hwy Arlington Heights IL 60004 (847) 870-8181 *Fax:* (847) 870-8325 *Exec Dir* Joanne Bratta *E-mail:* jbratta@stmaryservices.com *Web:* www.stmaryservices.com. Dom and international adoption services; placement; counseling for adoptive parents and birth mothers; birth parent support group.

Youth Guidance (CYF) 1 N LaSalle St Ste 900 Chicago IL 60602 (312) 253-4900 *Fax:* (312) 253-3917 *Exec Dir* Michelle Adler Morrison *E-mail:* mmorrison@youth-guidance.org *Web:* www.youthguidance.org. School-based svcs for yth, indiv, grp and fam counseling; crisis intervention; creative arts; employment development; vocational ed; Comer School Development Prog.

DIOCESE OF COLOMBIA

Hogar Geriatrico Divino Salvador Clle 58 Sur N 14F-78 Este 571-3672824 Rev J Romero *E-mail:* joseromero_747@hotmail.com.

Hogar Geriatrico San Marcos Rev Dcn J Aldana *E-mail:* aldaajar@hotmail.com.

Jardin Infantil Ingles Carrera 79 A No 53 A–75 Medellin Colombia 2343940 E Boss *E-mail:* eboss616@yahoo.com.

DIOCESE OF COLORADO

St Clair's Ministries 126 W 2nd Ave Denver CO 80223 *Contact* The Rev Melanie Christopher. Weekly dinner and clothes to the needy.

St Francis Center (CHAP) 2323 Curtis S Denver CO 80205 (303) 297-1576 *Exec Dir* Tom Luehrs. Emergency community services provides drug and alcohol counseling, emergency assistance, referral; provides for homeless and people in transition, showers, locked storage, telephone and mail facilities, clothing, medical clinic, day safe house, payee program, job placement. Advocacy program provides advocacy w/Department of Social Services.

DIOCESE OF CONNECTICUT

Armsmear (FSO) 80 Wethersfield Ave Hartford CT 06114 (860) 246-4025 M Sullivan *Exec Sec* Apts. Clergy widows and gentlewomen.

Episcopal Migration Ministries Integrated Refugee and Immigration Services 235 Nicoll St 2nd fl New Haven CT 06511 (203) 562-2095 Christopher George *Dir* Refugee resettlement min.

George Beach Home (FSO) 70 Allen Pl Hartford CT 06106 (860) 247-2318 Imagineers LLC *Agt* Apts. Ladies or gentlemen.

Seabury Retirement Comm (FSO) 200 Seabury Dr Bloomfield CT 06002 (860) 286-0243 R Heath *Exec Dir.*

DIOCESE OF DELAWARE

TRIAD (SpM) 1108 N Adams St Wilmington DE 19801 (302) 652-8605 (302) 652-8611. Trinity Alcohol and Drug Prog Trinity Parish.

The Way Home (SpM) Georgetown DE 19947 (302) 856-9870. A program for ex-offenders.

DIOCESE OF DOMINICAN REPUBLIC

Centro Buen Pastor Barrio las Flores, Miramar Apdo 128 San Pedro de Macoris (809) 526-7004 Rdo P Rul Guaillas, *Rector E-mail:* ven.groc@gmail.com. Proveen alimentacion y medicina a los estudiantes y a las madres, incluyedo vacunancion.

Clinica Esperanza y Caridad Calle Sanchez #2 Miramar San Pedro de Macoris (809) 529-0330 Esther Baez *Admin E-mail:* ccaridad@hotmail.com Ofrece servicios de laboratorio, odontologia, consultas de medicina general y ha inciado un programa de control y ayuda enfermos con VIH/SIDA.

Jesus Perigrino Children's Shelter and Nutrition Ctr Barahona (829) 383-6236 Fr Carlos Santana *E-mail:* iglepidom@verizon.net.do Internatl Board of people from Baraho support the program.

Programa Solidaridad en el Evangelio con la Prevencion del SIDA (ProSolidaridad) Av Bolivar #20, 2do, Piso, Gazue Libertador #18, San Carlos Santo Domingo (809) 221-6787 Loyda Perez

Hematologa E-mail: prosolidaridad@yahoo.es loidap@hotmail.com Trabaja con pastores, lideres y jovenes de las iglesias en capacitacion para la prevencion y atencio de VIH/SIDA.

DIOCESE OF EAST CAROLINA

Episcopal Farmworker Ministry (CYF) PO Box 160 Newton Grove NC 28366 (910) 567-6917 *Interim Dir* Juan Carabana *E-mail:* efmdirector@intrstar.net. Sponsored by Diocese of EC and NC, program to meet physical and spiritual needs of migrant farmworkers/ families, immigration, translation and tax services, ESL classes, food, clothing, pastoral counseling, religious services, transportation and advocacy.

Interfaith Refugee Ministry (SpM) 1913 Trent Blvd New Bern NC 28560 (252) 633-9009 *Coord* Susan Husson *E-mail:* shusson@helpingrefugees.org, Develop and coordinate resettlement opportunities in EC. Affiliate of Episcopal Migration Ministries, NY.

Thompson Children's Home See Diocese of NC.

DIOCESE OF EAST TENNESSEE

Metropolitan Mercy Ministries (NCS) 1112 McCallie Ave Chattanooga TN 37404 (423) 624-9650 *Exec Dir* Rebecca Whelchel.

St Barnabas' Senior Living Services (FSO) 950 Siskin Dr Chattanooga TN 37403 (423) 267-3764 *Chap* The Rev Buckley Robbins. Provides full nursing care, including intensive care, physiotherapy.

DIOCESE OF EASTON

Children's Home Foundation of the Eastern Shore of MD (CYF) 314 North St Easton MD 21601 (410) 822-1919. Functions as a foundation granting vocational and technical school scholarships, summer camperships and emerg aid to needy children.

Camp Agape (CYF) 314 North St Easton MD 21601 *Camp Dir* N Hastings, K Breithut. Week-long summer camp for children of an incarcerated parent.

Camp Wright 400 Camp Wright Ln Stevensville MD 21666 (410) 643-4171 *Fax:* (410) 643-8421 *E-mail:* director@campwright.com *Web:* www.campwright. com *Contact:* Stu Tripler. Total Beds: 185.

Retreat House at Hillsboro, Retreat Center F Thayer francie@retreathousehillsboro.org

DIOCESE OF EL CAMINO REAL

Canterbury Woods (FSO) 651 Sinex Ave Pacific Grove CA 93950 (831) 373-3111 *Fax:* (831) 373-2140 *Admin* Norma Brambilla (Episc Homes Foundation). Life care for men and women over 65.

Los Gatos Meadows (FSO) 110 Wood Rd Los Gatos CA 95030 (408) 354-0211 *Fax:* (408) 354-4193 *Admin* Ira Kurtz *Web:* www.ehf.org. (Episc Homes Foundation). Life care for men and women over 65.

Santa Maria Urban Ministry 778 S Almaden Ave San José CA 95110 (408) 292-3314 *Fax:* (408) 292-0728 *Exec Dir* LA Robles *E-mail:* smum83@gmail.com. Multi-ethnic outreach ministry to needy families, children, seniors, handicapped in San José inner city.

EUROPE, CONVOCATION OF EPISCOPAL CHURCHES IN

Joel Nafuma Refugee Center Rome

DIOCESE OF FLORIDA

Advent Day School (CYF) 815 Piedmont Dr Tallahassee FL 32312 (850) 386-5100 *Dir* Cristene York.

Aging True—Community Senior Services (FSO) 4250 Lakeside Dr Ste 300 Jacksonville FL 32210 (904) 807-1300 *Fax:* (904) 807-1351 *Exec Dir* Teresa Barton *E-mail:* tbarton@cathedralfoundationjax. com. Urban retirement community, health care and low/moderate income housing and health services. Sponsored by St John's Cath, Jacksonville FL.

All Saints' Early Learning Day Care Ctr (CYF) 4171 Hendricks Ave Jacksonville FL 32207 (904) 737-7800 *Exec Dir* Marian Wilcher *E-mail:* mwilcher@allsaintsjax.org.

All Saints' Episc Day Care for the Elderly (FSO) 4171 Hendricks Ave Jacksonville FL 32207 (904) 737-7800 *Exec Dir* Marian Wilcher *E-mail:* mwilcher@allsaintsjax.org.

Cathedral Gerontology Ctr (FSO) 333 E Ashley Jacksonville FL 32202 (904) 798-5300 *Fax:* (904) 354-4436 *Admin* Sharon Brown. Nursing home extended care and skilled nursing care. A division of the Cath Found of Jacksonville Inc.

Cathedral Residences (FSO) 601 N Newnan Jacksonville FL 32202 (904) 798-5353 *Fax:* (904) 798-9470. Retirement community for men, women and couples over 62. Non-profit, non-denom. Program of health maintenance, recreation and creative activity; supportive services. Cath Ct, 16 units; Cath Town Hse, 186 units; Cath Terr, 247 units; Cath Towers, 227 units. Division of the Cath Found of Jacksonville Inc. *Sr Community Manager* Marie Williams.

Episc Children's Services (CYF) 8443 Baymeadows Rd Ste 1 Jacksonville FL 32256 (904) 726-1500 *Fax:* (904) 726-1520 *CEO* Connie Stophel *Web:* www. ECS4kids.org.

Baker County Early Head Start 522 S 6th St Macclenny FL 32063 (904) 259-8982 Almeda Wallace.

Baker County Head Start 418 8th St MacClenny FL 32063 (904) 259-1177 Wendy Brunette.

Starke Head Start 1080 N Pine St Starke FL 32091 (904) 964-8280 Madelina Conlon.

Callahan Head Start 45089 3rd Ave Callahan FL 32011 (904) 879-2811 Mary Lockwood.

The Cathedral School 330 N Market St Jacksonville FL 32202 (904) 353-4050 Kristina Rodman.

Christ Episcopal Church PreSchool 400 San Juan Dr Ponte Vedra Beach FL 32082 (904) 285-6371 Janet Blacker.

ECS Learning Ctr @ Belmont 15 Belmont Blvd Orange Park FL 32073 (904) 213-3071 Lisa Gordon.

ECS Learning Ctr @ Belmont 2648 W 5th St

Jacksonville FL 32254 (904) 693-5042 Karreesha Newby.

ECS Learning Ctr @ Green Cove Springs Head Start 1107 Martin Luther King Blvd Green Cove Springs FL 32043 (904) 529-1150 Marisol Butrago.

Middleburg Head Start & Early Head Start 2506 Blanding Blvd Middleburg FL 32068 (904) 291-5472 Krishna Lopez.

Northside Early Head Start 1070 W 18th St Jacksonville FL 32209 (904) 359-2612 Debbie Hicks

ECS Earling Learning Ctr@Good Shepherd Episcopal Church 1100 Stockton St Jacksonville FL 32209 (904)387-5691

Peck Head Start 516 S 10th St Fernandina Beach FL 32034 (904) 491-3630 Delisa Turner.

Holy Trinity Child Caring Center (CYF) 100 NE 1st St Gainesville FL 32601 (352) 377-2290 & 1503 NW 16th Ave Gainesville FL 32605 (352) 373-1481 *Exec Dir* Rebekah Reneke *E-mail:* htcc@holytrinitygnv.org.

St Catherine's Preschool (CYF) 4758 Shelby Ave Jacksonville FL 32210 (904) 381-0935 *Exec Dir* Kimberly Murray *E-mail:* stcatherines@bellsouth.net.

St Michael's Day School (CYF) 4315 NW 23rd Ave Gainesville FL 32606 (352) 376-1771 *Dir* Mary Holmes.

Trinity Learning Center 215 St George St St Augustine FL 32084 (904) 824-2876 *Dir* Tammie Walthall.

Urban Jacksonville Inc (Part of Aging True) (FSO) 4250 Lakeside Dr Jacksonville FL 32210 (904) 807-1200 *Fax:* (904) 807-1220 *Exec Dir* Teresa Barton *E-mail:* tbarton@cathedralfoundationjax.com. Serves elders and their families by providing support so elders can remain independent and stay in their home.

DIOCESE OF FOND DU LAC

Broken Bread (NCS) 51 W Division St Fond du Lac WI 54935 Terry Hansen-Beno. A Jubilee Ministry/food distribution program.

Double Portion (NCS) 226 Washington St Menasha WI 54952 Bill Steinhilber, Gayle Varner. Community feeding program.

Love IN the Name of Christ Sheboygan (NCS) PO Box 1241 Sheboygan WI 53081 Ecumenical outreach ministry.

Our Lady's Pantry (NCS) 1011 N 7th St Sheboygan WI 53081 Rev Karl Schaffenburg. Jubilee Ministry/Community food bank.

Personal Essentials Pantry (NCS) 320 Oak St Wisconsin Rapids WI 54491 Kyle Ruud. Essential Personal Products Program.

St John's Thrift Store (NCS) 107 N Water St New London WI 54691 Wendy Nelson. Community thrift shop.

St John's Food Pantry (NCS) 209 S Pearl St New London WI 54691 Wendy Nelson. Community food pantry.

St Matthias Thrift Shop (NCS) 439 Front St Minocqua WI Jan Denger. Community thrift shop.

The Bread Basket (NCS) 415 S Main St (Main at Randall) Waupaca WI 54981 Rev Nigel Bousfield. Ecumenical feeding program.

The Neighborhood Table (NCS) 320 Oak St Wisconsin Rapids WI 54494 Ginny Steen. Community feeding program.

The Sharing Closet (NCS) 320 E Main St Plymouth WI 53073 Lisa Dicker. Lends personal Medical Equipment.

The Table (NCS) 39 S Pelham St Rhinelander WI 54501 Jubilee Ministry/community feeding program.

The Table (NCS) 320 E Main St Plymouth WI 53073 Rev Marie Gray. Ecumenical feeding program.

DIOCESE OF GEORGIA

Emmaus House of Savannah Inc (SpM) 18 Abercorn Savannah GA 31401. Ecumenical soup kitchen. Operates Monday-Friday, 11:30 am-12:15 pm.

Episc Youth and Children Services (CYF) 611 E Bay Savannah GA 31401 (912) 236-2007 *Web:* www.eycs.org Non-res; fin asst; Dio GA. Episc, 22 or under, in fields of health, education and welfare.

Habitat for Humanity, Inc (NCS) 419 W Church Americus GA 31709 (229) 924-6935 *Fax:* (229) 928-2697 *Web:* www.habitat.org. Ecumenical community sponsored self-help program. Non-profit. Helps needy construction and repair housing.

Oak Street Episcopal Mission 519 Oak Street, Thomasville, GA 31799 An Episcopal Community Development Agency committed to the revitalization of the Stevens Street historic district.

St Mark Towers (FSO) 1 Towers Plaza Brunswick GA 31520 (912) 267-7125. Residence community for elderly.

DIOCESE OF HAITI

Clinique St Paul c/o Lynx Air PO Box 407139 Ft Lauderdale FL 33340-7139 (011-509) 527-1565 Rev P Kerwin Delicat *E-mail:* KerwinDelicat@yahoo.fr. Cooperative proj of Episc Dio of Haiti, USAID/MSH.

Covenant Hospital de Mombin Crochu (HCC) c/o Lynx Air PO Box 407139 Ft Lauderdale FL 33340-7139 (011) 404-1496 Rev P Noe Bernier *E-mail:* noelybernier@hotmail.com. Cooperative proj of Episc Dio of Haiti, Presbyterian Church (USA), and Medical Benevolence Foundation.

Hôpital Sainte Croix de Leogane (HCC) c/o Lynx Air Rue Lacroix Leogane PO Box 407139 Ft Lauderdale FL 33340-7139 Ft Lauderdale FL 33340-7139 [011-509] 87-0746 or 87-0749 (509) 235-1895 *Dir* Rev Jean Jacques Deraril *Web:* www.hospitalstecroix.org 130-bed full-service hospital, joint proj of Episc and Presbyterian Churches and other sources.

Hospital and Clinic Bon Saveur de Cange (HCC) 643 Huntington Ave 4th Fl Boston MA 02115 Partners

in Health *E-mail*: info@pih.org Hospital for care of infectious diseases. Hlth worker teams and outpatient clinics, TB clinic, expanded care to Central Plateau.
St Vincent's Center for Handicapped Children in Port-au-Prince c/o Agape Flights 7990 15th St E Sarasota FL 34243 [011-509] 22-0120; (11509) 406-3392 *Dir* Rev P Fritz Desire *E-mail:* desous12@hotmail.com School and med care for 400+ children, physical therapy dept.

DIOCESE OF HONDURAS
Clínica Médica Colonia Episcopal (HCC) Colonia Episcopal Apdo 16 Puerto Cortés, Cortés Rural medical clinic.
Clínica Médica Colonia Suyapa (HCC) Colonia Suyapa Apdo 16 Puerto Cortés, Cortés Rural medical clinic.
Clínica Médica Conversión de San Pablo (HCC) Corinto Oma, Cortés Apdo 586 San Pedro Sula, Cortés Rural medical clinic.
Clínica Médica Dr. Gene Lee (HCC) San Joaquín Petoa, SB Apdo 586 San Pedro Sula, CortésRural medical clinic.
Clínica Médica Episcopal (HCC) Santa Ana de Chasniqua Villanueva, Cortés Apdo 586 San Pedro Sula, Cortés Rural medical clinic.
Clínica Médica Emanuel (HCC) El Cruce Santa Ana, F.M. Apdo 15023, Col. Kennedy Tegucigalpa, M.D.C. Rev Flvia María Galindo MD *Dir* Rural medical clinic.
Clínica Médica San Juan Apóstol (HCC) Carretera al Batallón Bº San Juan Apdo 30 Siguatepeque, Comayagua 011-504-773-5660 011-504-773-5660 Dr Jaime Luis Abascal *Dir* Medical clinic for urban poor.
Clínica Médica San Pedro Apóstol (HCC) Col 15 de Enero Petoa, S.B. Apdo 586 San Pedro Sula, Cortés Dr W Javier Madrid *Dir* Rural medical clinic.
Clínica Médica Santa Lucía (HCC) Protección Conceptión del Norte, S.B. Apdo 586 San Pedro Sula, Cortés Dr W Javier Madrid *Dir* Rural medical clinic.
Clínica Médica Santísima Trinidad (HCC)Bº Suyapa Apdo 28 La Ceiba, Atlántida
Dr Carole Dennison *Dir* Medical clinic for urban poor.
Clínica Médica Wyoming (HCC) Chalmeca Nueva Arcadia, Copán Apdo 586 San Pedro Sula, Cortés Rural medical clinic.
Cooperativa de Servicios Múltiples Santa María (COMISMAL) (NCS) Col Florencia Norte Apdo 15023, Col Kennedy Tegucigalpa MDC Sr Luis Arevalo *Dir* Gereuten *E-mail:* efesios4013@david-interterl.hn Development agency.
El Hogar Ministries (CYF) Col Florencia Norte Apdo 764 Tegucigalpa, MDC 011-504-235-9214 011-504-235-9214 Rev Barry and Kay Wyckham *Exec Dirs Web:* www.episcopalian.org/elhogar Orphanages and trng schs.
Home of Love and Hope (El Hogar de Amor y Esperanza)(CYF) San José de la Vega Comayagüela

Apdo 764 Tegucigalpa, MDC 011-504-246-4787 011-504-235-9214 Sr Richard Kunz *Exec Dir Lic.* Lazaro Juarez *Sub-Dir Web:* www.episcopalian.org/elhogar Home and sch for abandoned and orphaned boys.
Proyecto De Vivienda Aldea Episcopal Aldea Episcopal, La Ceiba Apartado Postal 28 La Ceiba Atlantida (011-504)-443-2641 E. Albert Brooks *Dir* Proyecto de Vivienda Colonia Episc (SpM) Col. Episcopal Apdo 16 Puerto Cortés, Cortés 011-504-665-5859 V Rev Antonio Cárcel *Dir* Home construction project for hurricane victims in conjunction w/the Dio of W.
Proyecto de Vivienda Colonia Suyapa (SpM) Col Suyapal Apdo 16 Puerto Cortés, Cortés 011-504-665-5859 V Rev Antonio Cárcel *Dir* Home construction project for hurricane victims in conjunction w/the South American Miss Soc (SAMS).
Proyecto de Vivienda Fe, Alegría y Esperanza (SpM) Ave "C" y 21 Calle Col Trejo Apdo 586 San Pedro Sula Cortés 011-504-556-6155 011-504-556-6467 *E-mail:* honduras@anglicano.hn Colonia Episcopal, El Ocotillo, San Pedro Sula.
Proyecto de Vivienda Nueva Esperanza (SpM) Col. Kenney Apdo 15023 Col Kennedy Tegucigalpa, M.D.C. 011-504-239-6978 011-504-239-6865 Lloyd E Allen *Dir E-mail:* efesios4-13@david.intertel. hn Col Nueva Esperanza, Amarateca. Home construction project for hurricane victims.

DIOCESE OF INDIANAPOLIS
Alternatives Incorporated PO Box 1302 Anderson IN 46015 (765) 643-0218 *Fax:* (765) 643-0291 *Exec Dir* Mary Jo Lee *E-mail:* mjlee@alternativesdv.org. 24-hr shelter for battered women and their children.
Damien Center (CHAP) 26 N Arsenal St Indianapolis IN 46201 (317) 632-0123 *Fax:* (317) 632-4362 *Exec Dir* Tom Bartenbach *E-mail:* tbartenbach@damien.org. Provides counseling and chap services for persons with AIDS.
Dayspring (Metro Shelter) (SpM) 1537 Central Ave PO Box 44105 Indianapolis IN 46244 (317) 635-6780 *Fax:* (317) 632-6788 *Exec Dir* Lori Casson *E-mail:* lori@dayspring.org. Shelter for the homeless.
Exodus-Refugee Immigration (SpM) 1125 Brookside Ave Ste C Indianapolis IN 46202 (317) 921-0836 *Fax:* (317) 921-1992 *Exec Dir* Carleen Miller *E-mail:* cmiller@exodusrefugee.org. Coordinates resettlement of refugees statewide.
John P Craine House (SpM) 6130 N Michigan Ave Indianapolis IN 46205 (317) 925-2834 *Fax:* (317) 925-2833 *Exec Dir* Suzy Pierce *E-mail:* suzy@crainehouse.org. Residence facility providing alternative to incarceration for women offenders.
Julian Center (CHAP) 2011 N Meridian Indianapolis IN 46202 (317) 941-2200 *Fax:* (317) 941-2209 *Dir* Jessica White *E-mail:* jwhite @juliancenter.org. 24-hour shelter for battered women and their children.
St. Richard's School 33 East 33rd Street Indianapolis IN 46205 (317) 926-0425 *Fax:* (317) 921-3367

HdMaster David Amstutz *E-mail:* damstutz@ strichadsschool.org. Independent Episcopal day school educating children from pre-school to the eighth grade.

DIOCESE OF IOWA

Chaplaincy at Universityof Iowa Hospitals (CHAP) Iowa City IA 52245. State-owned hospital. Episc Ch has min team serving within the fac.

St Paul's Urban Indian Health Services, Inc. (SpM) 1000 W 6th (Box 895) Sioux City IA 51102. Health needs assessment, basic health ed and health referral. (Replacement Pending).

Sioux City Indian Community Program (SpM) St Paul's Indian Miss 524 Center St (Box 895) Sioux City IA 51102. Outreach to Indian comm for housing, elderly, yth, and health.

DIOCESE OF KANSAS

Episc Community Services of Kansas City (NCS) 11 E 40th (207) Kansas City MO 64111 (816) 561-8920 (816) 561-4939 *Pres/CEO* Beau Heyen *E-mailbheyen@episcopalcommunity.orgWeb:* www.episcopalcommunity.org. Offers volunteer opportunities in serving the poor and ill, youth, families and aged. Aids pars w/outreach planning/ community problem solving. Administers urban service programs, including food, Meals on Wheels, Kansas City Community Kitchen. Partners with parish-based ministries, including Breakfast at St Paul's.

Episc Social Services (NCS) 1005 E 2nd St N Wichita KS 67214 (316) 269-4160 (316) 269-3550 *Exec Dir* Dr Barbara Andres *E-mail:* barbara@ esswichita.org *Web:* www.esswichita.org Creates opportunities for positive changes in people's lives. Educates and strengthens families, nurtures youth, helps unemployed find work, provides money mgmt for those with disabilities and offers professional counseling to anyone in need of a helping hand.

St Paul's Church (SpM) 1300 N 18th Kansas City KS 66102 (913) 321-3535 *E-mail:* office@ stpaulskck.org. Food pantry, breakfast at St Pauls and emergency food assistance (913) 321-3535. Sat Hot Meal Program (913) 321-3535.

DIOCESE OF KENTUCKY

Episc Church Home (FSO) 7504 Westport Rd Louisville KY 40222-4398 (502) 425-8840 or (502) 736-7800 *Fax:* (502) 425-5277. Buckwalter chap *E-mail:* stlukchpl@aol.com. Requirements: either sex, self care.

St George's Community Ctr (NCS) 1205 S 26th Louisville KY 40210 (502) 775-6232 *Fax:* (502) 776-2087 *Admin/Dir* Arthur Cox. Neighborhood youth and welfare work.

Aaron McNeil Community Center PO Box 137 Hopkinsville KY 42240 (270) 886-9734.

DIOCESE OF LEXINGTON

Cardinal Meadow (FSO) Harrodsburg KY (859) 276-5388 Ret home for elderly and disabled. Under mgmt of Winterwood Inc 342 Waller Ave Lexington KY 40504.

Christ Church Apts (FSO) 137 Rose Lexington KY 40507 (859) 254-7762 Donna Radtke *Mgr* A "self-care" ret res for people 62 or older. Rent is 30% of adjusted monthly income.

McKee Manor (FSO) E McKee McKee KY 40447 (859) 225-3334 60 one-bedroom units, 6 designed for the handicapped. Under mgmt of SMC Group 125-C Trade Lexington KY 40511.

Shepherds House (SpM) 154 Bonnie Brae Lexington KY 40508 (859) 252-1939 (Also 347 Linden Walk Lexington KY 40502 (859) 233-9891). Half-way house for adult male alcoholics.

St Agnes' House (HCC) 635 Maxwelton Ct Lexington KY 40508 (859) 254-1241 *Dir E-mail:* stagneshouse@diolex.org. Hospice for patients rcvg treatment for cancer at the University of KY Med Ctr.

Trinity Apts (FSO) 400 Trinity Dr Georgetown KY 40324 (502) 868-0226. 28 apartment units available to low-income elderly and/or handicapped people.

DIOCESE OF LONG ISLAND

Bishop Chas W MacLean Nursing Home (FSO, R) 17-11 Brookhaven Ave Far Rockaway NY 11691 (718) 869-8000 *Fax:* (718) 869-8065 *Admin* Ceceile Carroll-Byfield *E-mail:* ccarroll@ehs.org *Web:* www. ehs.org. Physically linked to St Johns Hospital. Nursing care, subacute and rehab services. Alzheimer program, hospice care.

Bishop Henry B Hucles Episc Nursing Home (FSO, R) 835 Herkimer Brooklyn NY 11233 (718) 221-2600 *Fax:* (718) 221-2691 *Admin* Barry T Dukes *E-mail:* bdukes@ehs.org *Web:* www.ehs.org. Special service including Alzheimer's and subacute care. Physical, occupational and speech therapy. Long and short term care. Adult day health program.

Episc Charities of LI (SpM) 36 Cathedral Ave Garden City NY 11530 (516) 248-4800 x119 *Fax:* (516) 248-8625 *Web:* www.dioceselongisland.org/ episcopalcharities *E-mail:* development@dioceseli. org. Resource development and grantmaking for institutions, agencies and programs in the Dio of LI.

Episc Community Services (CYF, CHAP) 36 Cathedral Ave Garden City NY 11530 (516) 248-4800 x115 (Nass & Suff), (718) 776-2333 (Queens), (718) 708-7733 (Brklyn) *Fax:* (718) 479-0205 *Exec Dir* Rev Can Charles F McCarron *E-mail:* cmccarron@ ecslongisland.net. Family preservation services, parish health ministry, immigration services, emergency assistance, pre-marital preparation, counseling. A benefiting agency of Episcopal Charities of LI.

St John's Episc Hospital (HCC) 327 Beach 19 Far Rockaway NY 11691 (718) 869-7320 *Fax:* (718) 869-7089 *Int CEO* Richard Brown *E-mail:* ntoebbe@ehs. org *Web:* www.ehs.org. Auspices of Episcopal Health Services. Teaching hospital w/diagnostic services and general hospital.

DIOCESE OF LOS ANGELES

1736 Project (CYF) 1736 Monterey Blvd Hermosa Beach CA 90254 (213) 379-3620/372-5843 *Dir* Carol Adelkoff Fam crisis center. Shelter for runaways and homeless youth, age 10-17. Shelter for homeless women, children, battered wives. 24-hour hotline. Outpatient counseling. Referrals.

Bishop Gooden Home, The e (SpM) 191 N El Molino Pasadena CA 91106 (626) 356-0078 *Dir* Rev EF Williams Jr. Res alcohol and drug recovery program for men.

Canterbury, The (FSO) 5801 W Crestridge Rd Rancho Palos Verdes CA 90274 (310) 541-2410 *Admin* Consuelo Haire. 127 units, 28-bed nursing facility. *Reqs:* 62 years and over. Ambulatory and able to meet accom and monthly financial fees. No waiting list.

Casa de los Amigos (FSO) 123 Catalena Ave Redondo Beach CA 90277 *Pres* vacant. Moderate rental apartments for self-sufficient seniors and disabled. Age and income limitations only. No geographical, religious, racial restrictions. Provides various community services.

Community Management Housing Services (R) 12881 W 166th St Ste 150 Cerritos CA 90703 (562) 802-0740 *Exec Dir* George Mercer *E-mail:* george@chmshousing.org *Web:* www.chmshousing. org. Encourages and assists in the development, operation and preservation of low-income housing for families, senior citizens and the mentally and physically disabled. With more than 20 properties, CHMS has a social contract to provide more than quality property management for residents, and provides a wide range of social services.

Covington, The (FSO) 3 Pursuit Aliso Viejo CA 92656 (949) 362-9662 *E-mail:* info@thecovington. org. An Episcopal Home Community that opened in 2004, this state-of-the-art community features cottages and apartments on 12 acres, offering residential living, assisted living, skilled nursing and dementia care.

Episc Housing Alliance PO Box 512164 Los Angeles CA 90051-0164 (213) 482-9300 *Exec Dir* Dr Joe Colletti.

Good Shepherd Hospice 3303 W Vernon Ave Los Angeles CA 90008 (310) 295-4131 *Dir* Amy Howell. Volunteer services to families w/terminally ill members in their homes. No fee. Area served-SC Los Angeles and Inglewood.

Good Shepherd Housing for Handicapped 510 Centinella Inglewood CA 90301 (310) 628-1036. Barker Mgmt.

Good Shepherd Manor (FSO) 4411 11th Ave Los Angeles CA 90043 *Admin* Jesse Gant. 143 units, senior citizens, age 62 and over, who can care for themselves. No stairs.

Hands in Healing Institute (SpM) Box 512164 Los Angeles CA 90051, Th is anti-violence institution provides informative booklets and a basic curriculum of the Hands in Healing teach-ins conducted on the national itinerary and in Southern California. Each section provides 10 points of information and action addressing the areas of domestic violence, child abuse, sexual assault, gang activity, hate crimes, elder abuse, gun safety and terrorism.

Hillsides: The Episc Home for Children (CYF) 940 Ave 64 Pasadena CA 91105 (323) 254-2274 *Dir* John M Hitchcock. Boys and girls, age 4-14. Res treatment incl casework, grp therapy and psychiatric consultation. No geographic, religious or racial restrictions.

Holy Family Adoption Services Agency PO Box 512164 Los Angeles CA 90051-0164 (213) 202-9000 *Exec Dir* Debra Richardson.

Holy Spirit 2601 Hyperion Ave Los Angeles CA 90027 (213) 413-0452 *E-mail:* info@holyspirit-la.org *Web:* www.holyspirit-la.org.

Hospital of the Good Samaritan (HCC) 616 S Witmer Los Angeles CA 90017 John H Westerman *Exec Dir* George G Lindesmith MD *Chief of Staff* General hospital, res, intern and nurses' trng.

Interfaith Refugee and Immigration Service (IRIS) (SpM) 3621 Brunswick Ave Los Angeles CA 90039-1727 (323) 667-0489 x105 *Com Res Dev* Debbie Decker. For over 25 years, IRIS staff have served clients fleeing religious persecution in Russia, Iran, Iraq and Cuba; war and poverty in Ethiopia, Eritrea, Somalia, Sierra Leon, Congo, Vietnam, the Philippines and Liberia; and other intolerable situations in countries around the globe. IRIS provides a gracious welcome and tangible tools for self-sufficiency to refugees newly relocated to the United States.

Neighborhood Youth Assoc (CYF) 3877 Grandview Blvd Los Angeles CA 90066 (323) 390-6641 *Exec Dir* Frances Cuciti (West area office). Delinq prevention and treatmt, working within the comm on drug abuse, st violence, etc. Prog in Venice, Wilmington, Harbor City, Carson.

Our Saviour Center/Cleaver Family Wellness Clinic (SpM) 4368 Sata Anita Ave El Monte CA 91731 *Center:* (626) 579-2190 *Clinic:* (626) 579-0290 *E-mail:* rbotengan@churchofoursaviour.org. Provides a variety of services including food, emergency shelter, job assistance, parenting instruction, computer training, youth after-school programs, preschool and scouting programs and clinical health services.

Parsonage LA/La Morada de los Amigos 4222 Santa Monica Blvd Los Angeles CA 90029. Multifaceted min and resource fac within local gay and lesbian comm and among multi-ethnic populations. AIDS support grps in English/Spanish and volunteer trng progs.

Project New Hope (SpM) 1004 Echo Park Ave Los Angeles CA 90026 (213) 977-4909 *Pres* Jack Plimpton. Svc-enriched perm housing for low income persons w/HIV; spec voc trng and job placemt assist.

Scripps Kensington, Alhambra (FSO) 1428 S Marengo Ave Alhambra CA 91803 (626) 576-1031 *E-mail:* info@scrippskensington.org Founded in 1923, the original Episcopal Home Community features a broad variety of apartment accommodations on 12 acres, with residential living, assisted living and skilled nursing.

Stillpoint: Center for Christian Spirituality PO Box 34535 Pasadena CA 91109 *E-mail:* erechterstillpointca@icloud.com *Exec Dir* The Reverend Elizabeth Rechter

St Barnabas Senior Ctr of Los Angeles (CHAP) 675 Carondelet Los Angeles CA 90057 *Chief Exec Dir* Martha Spinks PhD. Comprehensive social svcs to senior citizens.

St Francis' Ministry Outreach Center PO Box 3057, 2855 Sterling Avenue San Bernardino CA 92413 (909) 3862-3104

St John's Well-Child Ctr (HCC) 514 W Adams Blvd Los Angeles CA 90007 *Exec Dir* Katherine G Lawrence. Free clinic providing immun, dental care for children (birth-10 yrs) of needy fams-volunteer med and lay staff.

St Luke's Ministry Outreach Center PO Box 3333 16577 Upland Ave Fontana CA 9233 (909) 822-2012 *Dir* The Reverend James A. Maronde

St Michael's Ministry Outreach Center 4070 Jackson St Riverside CA 92503 (909) 689-0642

St Timothy's Manor and Tower (FSO) 415 S Oleander Compton CA 90220. Low rental apts for self-sufficient seniors and disabled. Age and income limitations only. No geo, rel, racial restrictions. Provides various comm svcs.

Thad's 1316 3rd St Ste 109 Santa Monica CA 90401 (310) 892-0395 *E-mail:* jbartz@thads.org.

Thom's *E-mail:* zinchy@gmail.com *Web:* www.thomsoc.org

Young and Healthy, Pasadena (CYF) 37 N Holliston Ave Pasadena CA 91106 (626) 695-5166 *Exec Dir* Mary Donnelley-Crocker *E-mail:* younghealth@mindspring.com *Web:* www.youngandhealthy-pas.org. A volunteer program by All Saints' Episcopal Church in Pasadena, *Young and Healthy* connects needy children with doctors, dentists, therapists and other health care professionals who donate their services. The program also provides follow-up support and help for families navigating that often perplexing health care system.

DIOCESE OF LOUISIANA

Episc Community Services (CYF) 1623 Seventh St New Orleans LA 70115-4411 *Web:* www.ecsla.org. Info and referral resource svc. Scholarship aid for minority students in Episc schs in Dio of LA.

DIOCESE OF MAINE

St Elizabeth's Essentials Pantry (NCS) 143 State St Portland ME 04101 *Exec Dir* R Rasner *E-mail:* rrasner@maine.rr.com. Providing essentials not covered by government services to families in Portland.

Seeds of Hope Jubilee Ctr (NCS) 35 South St Biddeford ME 04005 (207) 571-9601 *Exec Dir* Shirley Bowen *E-mail:* rev.shirley@seedsofhope4me.org. Offers hope to those who are struggling, care for those in need, companionship for those who are alone and compassionate love for all.

Trinity Jubilee Ctr (NCS) 247 Bates St Lewiston ME 04240 *E-mail:* trinitylewiston@gmail.com. Offers extensive feeding prog, maternal and child care, prison min, drop-in ctr, and crisis intervention svcs.

DIOCESE OF MARYLAND

Integrace: Buckingham's Choice (FSO) 3200 Baker Circle Adamstown MD 21710 (301) 874-5630. Sponsored by Epis Min to the Aging Inc. A continuing care ret comm.

Chase Home for Women (FSO) 22 Maryland Ave Annapolis MD 21401 (410) 263-2723 *Pres* Mollie Smith. *Reqs:* female, not incapacitated.

Integrace: Copper Ridge (SpM) 710 Obrecht Rd Sykesville MD 21784 (410) 795-8800. Sponsored by Episcopal Ministry to Aging Inc. State of art care and treatment for dementia, including Alzheimer's.

Episc Community Services of Maryland 1014 W 36th St Baltimore MD 21211 (410) 467-1264 *Exec Dir Vacant* (Formerly Church Miss of Help). Cares for children at risk, strengthens families and works to end behaviors such as addiction that put children and families at risk.

Integrace: Fairhaven (FSO) 7200 3rd Ave Sykesville MD 21784 (410) 795-8800. Sponsored by Episcopal Ministry to the Aging Inc. A res retirement community. Providing life care in 274 cottage and apartment units w/109-bed health center. One-time entrance fee payment, with monthly charges thereafter.

Joseph Richey Hospice: Residential Hospice for terminally ill persons, affiliated with Gilchrist Hospice. (410-523-2150) Catherine Hamel, *Ex. Dir.*

DIOCESE OF MASSACHUSETTS

Chinese Ministry (SpM) 138 Tremont St Boston MA 02111 (617) 482-5800 *Cn for Asia-American Min* Rev Can Connie Ng Lam *E-mail:* connienglam@diomass.org *Web:* ebcmonline.org (Boston Chinese Min). Holy Eucharist weekly, ed and social activities program for youth and adults. Leadership training; after-school program.

Church Home Society, The (CYF) 138 Tremont St Boston MA 02111 (617) 482-5328 *Exec Dir* Roberta A Tripp *E-mail:* rat@diomass.org. Grants to church and secular organizations to benefit young people.

Episc City Mission (NCS) 138 Tremont Boston MA 02111 (617) 482-5800 *Acting Exec Dir* Rt Rev Bud Cederholm *E-mail:* ecm@diomass.org *Web:* www.diomass.org/ecm. Specialized work in urban miss, community-based organizations and public policy.

Operates Pelham Fund (loans) and Burgess Fund (grants). Runs network of public policy advocates. Owns Morville Hse, housing for low-income elderly.

Hispanic Ministry (SpM) Grace Box 467 Lawrence MA 01840 (978) 682-6003 Rev Ennis Duffis. Bilingual worship services, education and social activities for youth and adults.

Hispanic Ministry (SpM) St Peters 24 St Peter St Salem MA 01970 (978) 745-2291 *Priest* Rev Silvestre E Romerio

Hispanic Ministry (SpM) Iglesia de St Lucas 201 Washington Chelsea MA 02150 (617) 884-4278 *Priest-in-Charge* Rev Edgar Gutierrez-Duarte. Holy Eucharist weekly; soup kitchen, pantry and thrift store.

Hispanic Ministry (SpM) Iglesia de San Juan, c/o Christ Church Box 366202 Hyde Park MA 02136 (617) 361-3081 *Priest* Rev Lisa Fortuna. Holy Eucharist weekly, educational and social services for youth and adults.

Hispanic Ministry (SpM) 138 Tremont St Boston MA 02111 (617) 482-5800 Rev Ema Rosero-Nordalm erosero@diomass.org

Hospital Ministry Program (CHAP) 138 Tremont Boston MA 02111 (617) 482-5800 V Rev JP Streit. Chap svcs to hospital patients in major Boston-area hospitals; also trng of volunteers.

Sherrill House (HCC) 135 S Huntington Ave Boston MA 02130 (617) 731-2400 *Chief Exec Officer* Patrick Stapleton *Web:* www.sherrillhouse.org. Skilled nursing care.

DIOCESE OF MICHIGAN

Canterbury on the Lake (FSO) 5601 Hatchery Rd Waterford MI 48329 (248) 674-9292 *Fax:* (248) 674-5344 *Dir* Susan Dembiec *Chap* W Hale *Web:* www.canterburyonthelake.com. Canterbury is a retirement community, offering Independent Senior Living Apartments, Assisted Living Apartments and a health center, which offers short-term rehabilitation and long-term care nursing.

Chaplaincy to the Medical Ctr (CHAP) E 8102 University Hospital 1405 E Ann Ann Arbor MI 48104.

Crossroads (NCS) 2424 W Grand Blvd Detroit MI 48208 (313) 831-2000 *Fax:* (313) 821-0261 *Dir* Mary Honsel. Crossroads is a not-for-profit agency that supports the community at large by providing emergency assistance, advocacy, and counseling to anyone in need.

Emmanuel Community House Inc (NCS) 18313 John Rd Detroit MI 48203 (313) 869-7107 *Exec Dir* K Washington. Neighborhood prog serving children and fams.

Mariners' Inn (SpM) 445 Ledyard Detroit MI 48201 (313) 962-6395 *Exec Dir* David Sampson *E-mail:* marinersinn@aol.com *Web:* www.marinersinn.org. The Mariners' Inn is a nonprofit agency that has been providing shelter, substance abuse treatment,

and transitional housing for Detroit's homeless men since 1934.

Opportunity Resource Fund (SpM) 2727 2nd St 301 Detroit MI 48201 (313) 964-7300 *Fax:* (313) 964-7313 *Exec Dir* C Coady Narayanan *Web:* www.interfaithtrust.org. a not-for-profit community development financial institution serving the entire State of Michigan. Provides funding for affordable housing and mortgages, job creation, supports small businesses and funds the development of commercial spaces.

St Anne's Mead Retirement Home (FSO) 16106 W 12 Mile Southfield MI 48076 (248) 557-3142. a senior residence community offering health care and supportive services in a safe, secure, and loving home. *Ex. Director* J Collins Web: www.stannesmead.org

Williams Pavilion (FSO) 99 E Forest Detroit MI 48201 *Admin* B Wright. Provides independent living for seniors and persons with disabilities.

DIOCESE OF MILWAUKEE

Gathering, The (NCS) 804 E Juneau Ave Milwaukee WI 53202 *Exec Dir* Ginny Schrag. Multiple site ecum vol meal prog. Jubilee Ctr.

Neighborhood House (NCS) 941 N 28 Milwaukee WI 53208 *Dir* Clarence Johnson. Settlement svcs to neighborhood. Nursery sch, social grp work, svcs to children and adults, specialized svcs for aged.

Our Next Generation Inc (NCS) 804 E Juneau Ave Milwaukee WI 53202 *Exec Dir* LaToya Sykes Ed and rec progs serving children and fams in central city of Milwaukee.

St John's Home on the Lake (FSO) 1840 N Prospect Ave Milwaukee WI 53202 *Dir* Kathie Eilers. Indep liv hlth svcs.

St Luke's Hospitality Center Lief Peterson 614 Main St Racine WI 53403 (262) 853-2886.

DIOCESE OF MINNESOTA

Breck School 123 Ottawa Ave N Golden Valley MN 55422 (763) 381-8205 *Head of School* Edward Kim.

Chaplains Mayo Clinic (CHAP) Rochester MN 55901.

Episc Homes of Minnesota 490 E Lynhurst Ave St Paul MN 55104 (651) 632-8855 *Exec Dir* Marvin J Plakut.

House of Prayer PO Box 5888 Collegeville MN 56321 (320) 363-3293 *Dir* Rev Ward Bauman.

Shattuck St Mary's 1000 Shumway Ave Faribault MN 55021 (507) 333-1500 *Head of School* Nick Stoneman.

Sheltering Arms Foundation 1730 Clifton Place #100 Minneapolis MN 54403 *Fax:* (612) 871-9210 *Exec Dir* Denise Mayotte.

DIOCESE OF MISSISSIPPI

All Saints' House (FSO) 480 S Main Grenada 38901 *Mgr* Jan Willis. Ret home for elderly. Spon by All Sts Grenada.

Episc Prison Ministries Mississippi State Penitentiary Box 40 Parchman 38738.

St Mark's Villa (FSO) 903 W Pearl Jackson 39203. A 24-unit non-profit home for aged and handicapped.

DIOCESE OF MISSOURI

Deaconess Anne House 1210 Locust St Louis MO 63103 *Dir* Jonathan Stratton (314) 231-1220 x1381. Intentional community, Episcopal Service Corps.

Episcopal City Mission (CHAP) 1210 Locust St Louis MO 63103 (314) 436-3545 *ECM Exec Dir* Beth Goad *E-mail:* info@ecitymission.org *Web:* www.ecitymission.org. Chap svcs to juvenile detention ctrs. Juvenile Courts, Lakeside. Yth counseling svc. Teenagers.

Episcopal Presbyterian Health Trust 1210 Locust St Louis MO 63103 (314) 231-1220. Trustees: The Rt Rev Wayne Smith, The Rev Dr Marc Smith, The Rev Dr Deborah Goldfeder

Affinia Health Care (HCC) 100 N Tucker St Louis MO 63101 (314) 241-2200 (314) 241-8938 *Pres & CEO* Alan Freeman *Web:* affiniahealthcare.org. Comprehensive Primary Care in addition to an array of Health Support Services and Community Health Programs.

Grace Hill Neighborhood Health Ctr (HCC) 100 N Tucker St Louis MO 63101 (314) 241-2200 (314) 241-8938 *Dir* Alan Freeman *Web:* www.gracehill.org. 6 ctrs providing med svcs, outpatient clinic, postnatal and prenatal care.

Grace Hill Settlement House (NCS) 2600 Hadley St Louis MO 63106 (314)-584-6900 info@gracehillsettlement.org *Pres/CEO* Roderick Jones *Web:* gracehillsettlement.org. 13 neighborhood ctrs providing comm org, neighborhood svc and fam svc. Grp and indiv help. Professional social workers. Recreation and med clinic. Emergency aid and referral svcs.

St Andrew's Resources for Seniors System (FSO) 6633 Delmar Blvd St Louis MO 63017 (314) 726-0111 *Dir* Mary Alice Ryan *E-mail:* info@standrews1.com *Web:* www.standrews1.com. Housing and in-home services for persons 65 and over. Partial med, hospitalization, emergency nursing care.

St Luke's Hosp 232 S Woods Mill Rd Chesterfield MO 63017 *E-mail:* www.stlukesstl.com. Premiere regional healthcare provider 493 not for profit hospital.

DIOCESE OF NEBRASKA

Clarkson College 101 S 42nd St Omaha NE 68131 (402) 552-3100 *Pres* Louis W Burgher MD PhD *Web:* www.clarksoncollege.edu.

DIOCESE OF NEVADA

St. Hugh of Lincoln Episcopal Outreach Center *Dcn* Michael Slater (775) 443-8871 *Admin* Norma Kennemer (775) 577-9606 4280 US Highway 50 Silver Springs NV 89429-8359 (775) 577-9606 *Web:* www.strempke.wix.com/st-hugh-of-lincoln *E-mail:* EpiscopalSlvrStg@aol.com

St. John the Apostle Episcopal Outreach Center *Dcn* Michael Slater (775) 443-8871 140 Pike St Dayton, NV 89403-6758 (775) 246-2587 *Web:* www.strempke.wix.com/st-john-the-apostle *E-mail:* EpiscopalDayton@aol.com

St Jude's Ranch for Children (CYF) Natl Headquarters 100 St Jude's (Box 60100) Boulder City NV 89006-0100 (702) 294-7100 M Whitley *CEO* A non-profit, res care ctr for neglected and troubled children of all ages. Boys and girls of any race or relig background. Child Care Dept children ages 6-18. Not a dio institute; separate Bd of Trustees, indep elected. (800) 492-3562.

DIOCESE OF NEW JERSEY

Evergreens Continuing Care Facility (FSO) 309 Bridgeboro Rd Moorestown NJ 08057 (856) 439-2000 *Fax:* (856) 439-2106 *Pres /CEO* Rev DC Halvorsen *E-mail:* dhalvorsen@evergreens.org *Web:* www.evergreens.org. Facility and services for older persons.

Trinity Counseling Service (SpM) 22 Stockton Princeton NJ 08540 (609) 924-0060 *Fax:* (609) 924-7436 *Dir* WhitneyRoss *E-mail:* wbrnyc@gmail.com *Web:* www.trinitycounseling.org. Clergy and laity, indiv, couples and fams. Crisis and supportive help. Local and regional workshops/seminars for grps.

DIOCESE OF NEW YORK

Amsterdam House (FSO) Amsterdam Nursing Home Corp 1060 Amsterdam Ave New York NY 10025.

Episc Social Services (SpM) 305 7th Ave 4th Fl New York NY 10011-6008 (212) 675-1000 (212) 989-1132 *Exec Dir* Elizabeth McCarthy *E-mail:* mccarthye@es-s.org *Web:* www.essnyc.org. Grp homes for boys and girls, comm res for handicapped adults, foster homes. East Midtown Svcs to Older People (home care), 11 E 29 NY 10016. Comm-bldg progs in NY city schs, w/parolees and probationers and in housing projects. Provides chap to public institutions.

Psychotherapy and Spirituality Institute (CHAP) 120 Broadway 38th Fl New York NY 10271. (212) 285-0043 *Exec Dir* Kathleen Kelley MDiv LMFT; *Man Dir* Kelly Murphy Mason PsyD MDiv LCSW. Indiv, fam, couple and grp pastoral psychotherapy. Consultation and referrals. Ed prog and resources for pars. Centers in 10 NY chs.

Episcopal Charities 1047 Amsterdam Ave New York NY 10025 (212) 316-7403. *Exec Dir* Mary Beth Sasso, *E-mail:* episcopalcharities@dioceseny.org *Web:* http://www.episcopalcharities-newyork.org. As the outreach arm of the Episcopal Diocese of New York, Episcopal Charities equips parish-affiliated outreach programs to transform the lives of people in need in their diverse communities. Through grants and technical support, nearly 100 programs are supported that transform lives and strengthen communities.

Holy Apostles Soup Kitchen 296 Ninth Ave New York NY 10001-5703 (212) 924-0167 *Web:* www.

holyapostlessoupkitchen.org. *Exec Dir* The Rev Glen Chalmers. As New York's largest emergency food program, the Soup Kitchen serves a hearty and nutritious meal to more than 1,000 homeless and hungry New Yorkers every day. In addition to the food program, committed staff and volunteers work with guests to ensure they are receiving full benefits, connect them to additional supportive services, help with job applications and even reunite them with family members.

Adults & Children in Trust (ACT) 1047 Amsterdam Ave New York NY 10025 (212) 316-7530 *Exec Dir and Day Camp Dir* José Torres *E-mail:* act@stjohndivine.org. The program provides a safe haven where toddlers to teens from many faiths, cultures and economic backgrounds gather to learn, play and grow, as they participate in a broad range of programs among highly-trained and caring adults.

Cathedral Community Cares (CCC) 1047 Amsterdam Ave New York NY 10025 (212) 316-7581 *E-mail:* ccc@stjohndivine.org. *Prog Dir* Lauren Phillips.The mission of Cathedral Community Cares is to combat and alleviate poverty through preventive poverty services, education and advocacy—specifically targeting the issues of health and hunger. CCC tackles these problems on multiple fronts by addressing the immediate and beyond-emergency needs of the underserved, while seeking long-term policy solutions that will benefit both clients and the greater community.

DIOCESE OF NEWARK

Apostles' House 18 Grant St Newark NJ 07104 (973) 482-0625 *Exec Dir* Sandra Accomando Transitional housing, emergency aid.

Canterbury Village (FSO) 33 Mt Pleasant Ave West Orange NJ 07052 (973) 736-1194 *Dir* Art Dunsmore Men, women and couples 62 and over. Personal care facility.

Christ Hospital (HCC) 176 Palisade Ave Jersey City NJ 07306 (201) 795-8200 *Fax:* (201) 795-8796. Gen hospital. Office of Pastoral Care.

Crossroads Outdoor Ministries (R) 29 Pleasant Grove Rd Port Murray NJ 07865 (908) 832-7264 *Fax:* (908) 832-6593 *E-mail:* www.crossroadsretreat. com *Web:* www.crossroadsretreat.com Retreat ctr.

Episcopal Community Development 620 Clinton Ave NJ 07108 (973) 710-1501 *Exec Dir* Gerard Haizel Home buyer training, housing.

Heath Village (FSO) Schooley's Mtn Rd Hackettstown NJ 07840 (908) 852-4801 *Dir* Patrick E Brady. Ret comm and nursing home (Medicare).

House of the Good Shepherd (FSO) Willow Grove St Hackettstown NJ 07840 (908) 852-1430 *Dir* Fred Heleine Men, women and couples 65 and over. Rates according to ability to pay. Infirmary. Medicaid.

Jersey City Community Development Corp 118 Summit Ave Jersey City NJ 07304 (201) 209-9301 *Fax:* (201) 209-0284. Training, housing.

NAMASTE (SpM) 31 Mulberry St Newark NJ 07102 (973) 430-9902 The commission works to engage the diocese at every level—individuals, congregations, diocesan organizations and staff—in the work of dismantling racism in hearts, churches, our communities and the decision-making and institutional life of the church.

Oasis, The (SpM) 31 Mulberry St Newark NJ 07102 (973) 430-9902 *Web:* www.theoasis@ dioceseofnewark.org Min of the dio w/gay and lesbian people, their fams, and friends.

Prison Ministry Committee (SpM) Grace Church 200 Highfield Ln Nutley NJ 07110 (973) 235-1177 *Fax:* (973) 235-0677 Rev Pamela Bakal *E-mail:* fthrpam@aol.com.

Seamen's Church Institute NY/NJ 118 Export St Port Newark NJ 07114 (973) 589-5828 (973) 589-7463 *Dir* Andy Moore See Mission to Seafarers section of *Annual.*

Senior Ministries (FSO) 31 Mulberry St Newark NJ 07102 (973) 622-4306 (973) 678-2342. Hope Lampe *E-mail:* hopelampehhiam@aol.com.

Youth Consultation Service (CYF) 284 Broadway Newark NJ 07104 (973) 482-8411 (973) 482-4530 *CEO/Pres* Richard Mingoia *E-mail:* info@ycs.org *Web:* www.ycs.org. Also at 179 Palisade Ave Jersey City 07307.

Youth Ministry (CYF) 31 Mulberry St Newark NJ 07102 (973) 430-9991 *Fax:* (973) 622-3503 *Dir of Yth & YA Min* Kaileen Alston Esq *E-mail:* kalston@ dioceseofnewark.org *Web:* www.dioceseofnewark. org/youth.

DIOCESE OF NORTH CAROLINA

Bishop Edwin A Penick Village (FSO) E Rhode Island Ave Southern Pines NC 28387 (910) 692-0300 (910) 692-8287 *Exec Dir* Jeff Hutchins. Ret skilled nursing facs, aged 65 plus, mon rates, private rms w/full bath, central dining, maid svc, activities, creative living for older people.

Galilee Ministries of East Charlotte 3601 Central Ave, Charlotte, NC 28205 (704) 523-4333 *Missioner* Toni Hagerman. Center housing multiple agencies and ministries serving refugee and immigrant population, including ESL classes, resettlement services, food pantry and community garden.

Thompson Child and Family Focus 6800 St Peter's Ln Matthews NC 28105 (704) 536-0375 (704) 531-9266 (Formerly Episc Child Care Svcs of NC). Res ctr for emotionally disturbed children 6-12. Also weekend respite care prog for mentally handicapped yth, after-school prog, summer day camp prog. Goldsboro Group Home, boys 8-18. Fletcher Group Home, boys 8-18. Spon by the Dios of NC, EC and WNC.

DIOCESE OF NORTHERN CALIFORNIA

Noel Porter Camp & Conference Center *Mailing:* PO Box 50, Tahoe City, CA 96145; *Physical:* 855 West Lake Blvd., Highway 89, Tahoe City, CA

96145; *Tel:* (530) 583-3014; *Fax:* (530) 583-4362; *Email:* campnoelporter@sbcglobal.net; *Web:* http://campnoelportertc.com. Total Beds: 52.

Diocesan Health Ministries *Coordinator* Rev. Susan Wahlstrom RN *E-mail:* Wahlstrom@volcano.net.

Episcopal Community Services of NOCA (ECS) 350 University Avenue, Ste. 280, Sacramento CA 95825.

Episcopal Foundation of NOCA (EFNC) 350 University Avenue, Ste. 280, Sacramento CA 95825.

The Living Room (NCS) Incarnation Church, Santa Rosa, CA 95401; *Executive Director* Cheryl Parkinson.

River City Community Services 1800 28th St Sacramento CA 95816 (916) 446-2627 *Exec Dir* Eileen Thomas *Web:* www.rivercitycommunityservices.org. Emergency food and shelter.

Wallace House 126 N. Main St., Cloverdale, CA 95425. Drop-in for homeless women and children, hot meals, referrals; *Executive Director* Colleen Halbohm

DIOCESE OF NORTHWEST TEXAS

Seabury Ctr (HCC) St John's Episc Retirement Corp 2443 16th Odessa TX 79763 (915) 333-2904 *Dir* Colleen Smith *E-mail:* seabury@cableone.net. 96-bed intermed care nursing home for men and women. Adult day care unit for elderly and handicapped. Min proj St John's Par.

DIOCESE OF NORTHWESTERN PENNSYLVANIA

Ball Pavilion (HCC) 5416 E Lake Rd Erie PA 16511 (814) 899-8600. Spon by the Cath of St Paul Erie. Skilled nursing and intermediate care for long and short term patients 65 and over. Address inq to Dir of Adm at Brevillier Village.

Barnabas Court (FSO) 5416 E Lake Rd Erie PA 16511 (814) 899-8600. Spon by the Cath of St Paul Erie. Asst living/licensed personal care fac. *Reqs:* men and women, 62 and over. Address inq to Dir of Adm at Brevillier Village.

Conrad House (FSO) 5436 E Lake Rd Harborcreek PA 16511 (814) 899-4238. Spon by the Cath of St Paul Erie. Reqs: men and women, 62 and over. Ind living (HUD 236); reasonably priced. Address inq to Dir of Adm at Brevillier Village (814) 899-8600.

DIOCESE OF OHIO

Episc Community Services (ECS) 2230 Euclid Ave Cleveland OH 44115 *Admin Asst* Betty Kondrich bkondrich@dohio.org. Funding 95 human svc agencies in dio.

DIOCESE OF OLYMPIA

Earth Ministry (SpM) 6512 23rd Ave NW Ste 317 Seattle WA 98117 (206) 632-2426 *Exec Dir* LeeAnne Beres *Web:* www.earthministry.org Enviro concerns.

Episc Retirement Communities (FSO) 703 Callahan Dr Bremerton WA 98310 (360) 377-0113 *Exec Dir* Beverly Maine *E-mail:* bevmaine@donobi.net.

Holy Family of Jesus Community Services (SpM)

Box 11839 Tacoma WA 98411 (253) 473-6705 *Onsite Dir* Sue Bernstein. Cambodian min.

Mission to Seafarers (SpM) 3568 West Marginal Way SW Seattle WA 98106 (206) 935-3439 *Exec Dir* Ken Hawkins *E-Mail:* director@mts-Seattle.org.

Refugee Resettlement Min (SpM) 1610 S King Seattle WA 98144 (206) 323-3152 *Fax:* (206) 322-7632 *Dir* Greg Hope; Assoc. Dir Sumonnat Puttavon *E-mail:* hotel2@mindspring.com.

St James Family Center (CYF) 1134 Columbia St Cathlamet WA 98612 (360) 795-8612 *Fax:* (360) 795-6027 *Exec Dir* Beth Hansen *E-mail:* bhansen@stjamesfamilycenter.org.

DIOCESE OF PENNSYLVANIA

Cathedral Village (FSO) 600 E Cathedral Rd Philadelphia PA 19128 (215) 487-1300 *Pres* Dennis Koza. Continuing care ret. CCAC and JCAHO accred. Hlth club and indoor pool. Skilled nursing and Alzheimer's care. Medicare, Aetna-US Healthcare and Keystone Medicare.

Dolphins of Delaware Valley (FSO) St Chris 226 Righters Mill Rd Gladwyne PA 19035 (610) 649-5594 (610) 649-5643 *Admin* Jo Parker *Coord* Judy Steck. Trng vols for 1-to-1 visits to res of nursing and ret homes.

Episc Community Services (CYF, NCS, CHAP) 225 S 3rd St Philadelphia PA 19106 (215) 351-1400 *Fax:* (215) 351-1497 *Exec Dir* David Griffith *E-mail:* griffithd@ecs1870.org *Web:* www.els1870.org. Human svc agency of Dio. Direct svc, referrals, info, advocacy, counseling to all faiths. Shelter for homeless women and children, home-care and delivered meals for elderly, comfort to children in fams affected by AIDS. Chaplaincy in nursing homes, hospitals and prisons. ECS volunteer svcs offer consultations w/ parishes on outreach mins.

Kearsley (FSO) 2100 N 49 St Philadelphia PA 19131 (215) 877-1565 TTD: (215) 870-4608. Ret comm for adults w/modest incomes: apts, personal care studio apts and nursing home.

St Anna's (NCS) 115 N Van Pelt St Philadelphia PA 19103 (215) 665-8889 (All Sts Sisters). Sisters have a small mission house in Center City for spreading the Gospel through teaching.

St Barnabas Mission of ECS 6006 W Girard Ave Philadelphia PA 19151 (215) 528-5419 *Fax:* (215) 528-5409 *Dir* Victoria Bennett *E-mail:* victoriab@els1870.org. Serves homeless women and children by providing emerg shelters, counseling, day care, job readiness trng. Serves homebound elderly and disabled through case mgmt, counseling, home health aid svcs and frozen meals. Chap svcs to people in prisons, nursing homes and hospitals. Provides legislative advocacy and comm bldg on grass-roots level. (Info and referral svcs.)

DIOCESE OF PITTSBURGH

Chemical Dependency Ministry 272 Caryl Dr Pittsburgh PA 15236 (412) 653-4585 *Dir* Rev JD Else *E-mail:* cfs12step@aol.com. Consultant of Coalition for Addictive Diseases, offering intervention, eval, ed, and counseling referrals.

Sheldon Calvary Camp 4411 Lake Rd. Conneaut, OH 44030 (440) 593-4381 *Web:* www.calvarycamp. org *Exec Dir* Tim Green *E-mail:* executivedirector@calvarycamp.org

Shepherd Wellness Community Scott Peterman *Exec Dir* 4800 Sciota St Pittsburgh PA 15224 (412) 683-4477 *E-Mail:* shepherdwellness@aol.com *Web:* www.swconline.org. A safe, supportive community empowering people affected by HIV/AIDS to live with dignity.

DIOCESE OF PUERTO RICO

Servicios de Salud Episcopales Hospital San Lucas Ponce, Hospital San Lucas Guayama, Servicios de Salud en el Hogar y Hospicio San Lucas

Servicios Sociales Episcopales/VIDAS

Servicio Episcopal de Vivienda (Home for the Elderly)

DIOCESE OF RHODE ISLAND

Episc Charities (NCS) 275 N Main Providence RI 02903 (401) 274-4500 x234 *Fax:* (401) 331-9430 Peggy Amatore *Dir E-mail:* charities@episcopalri. org *Web:* www.episcopalri.org Raises and distributes money to agencies to provide direct service to those in need in RI.

Hallworth House (HCC) 66 Benefit Providence RI 02904 (401) 274-4505 *Fax:* (401) 521-3947 Kathleen Lavallee *Admin* Skilled nursing care fac.

Seamen's Church Institute 18 Market Sq Newport RI 02840 (401) 847-4260 *Fax:* (401) 847-4284 John Feld *Supt E-mail:* jpfeld@gmail.com *Web:* www. seamensnewport.org See Mission to Seafarers section of *Annual*.

Shepherd Program, The 420 Fruit Hill Ave N Providence RI 02911 (401) 784-3530 Carlene McCann *Dir* Provides in-home support for fams and children in need.

St Elizabeth Community (HCC) 1 St Elizabeth Way Greenwich RI 02818 (401) 471-6060 Steven J Horowitz *Pres & CEO Web:* www. stelizabethcommunity.com A grp care fac offering casework, res fac, daycare, diagnostic svcs, adoptive home svc, and foster boarding home care.

St Mary's Home for Children (CYF) St Martha's Hse 420 Fruit Hill Ave N Providence RI 02911 (401) 353-3900 *Fax:* (401) 354-7986 Bernard Smith *Dir* ACSW *Web:* www.smhfc.org A grp care fac offering casework, res fac, day care, diagnostic svcs, adoptive home svc and foster boarding home care.

DIOCESE OF SAN DIEGO

Camp Stevens Camp and Conference Center PO Box 2320 Julian CA 92036 (760) 765-0028 *Fax:* (760) 765-0153 *E-mail:* info@campstevens.org *Web:* www. campstevens.org *Contact: Exec Dir* Beth Bojarski. Total Beds: 124.

Episc Community Services 401 Mile of Cars Way Suite 350 National City CA 91950 (619) 228-2800

Fax: (619) 228-2801 *Exec Dir* Lesslie Keller *E-mail:* contact@ecscalifornia.org *Web:* www.ecscalifornia. org. Comprehensive social services agency focusing on the needs of the greater San Diego County and Coachella Valley communities. Programs and services provide an effective, successful continuum of care for thousands of children and adults each year in areas of homelessness, mental illness, domestic violence, hunger, poverty, child development and education, and substance abuse.

Episc Refugee Network (RefugeeNet) 4265 Fairmount Ave Ste 130 San Diego CA 92105 (619) 283-1337 *Exec Dir* Jake Young *E-mail:* jake@ernsd.org *Web:* www.refugee-net.org. Serving refugee families who have settled in San Diego. Primary service areas are City Heights and El Cajon. Programs and services include orientation to life in the US; casework with families needing transportation and translation services at immigration, education, medical appointments; tutoring services for school age children; distribution of fresh fruit and produce; and provision of clothing and household items. Over 200 families are served.

Vida Joven de Mexico: 2728 Sixth Ave San Diego CA 92103 (619) 786-4387 *E-mail:* Beth Beall bbeall@vidajovendemexico.org or Elizabeth Carey ehcarey@vidajovendemexico.org *Web:* www. VidaJovenDeMexico.org. We love, protect and educate 35 children in Tijuana, Mexico, who have no place else to go. The children have parents in prison or have been abandoned. We provide the childrenwith a safe homee, and see to their needs for love, food, education, and medical care.

THE EPISCOPAL CHURCH IN SOUTH CAROLINA

Bishop Gadsden Episc Community (FSO) 1 Gadsden Way Charleston SC 29412 (843) 762-3300 William Trawick *Dir.* Res care fac for older adults. Indep living cottages and apts, 70 units w/private baths. Svcs incl 3 meals daily, housekeeping, activities, transportation and med asst 44-bed skilled and intermed health care ctr.

Canterbury House Episc Dio Housing Inc (FSO) 175 Market Charleston SC 29401 (843) 577-5553 Sally Lorbach *Dir.* Non-denom, non-profit ret comm for persons 62 and over of limited income. 204 apts, efficiency and one-bedrm. Canterbury East: 46 apts. Recreational facs.

SC Episc Retirement Comm at Still Hopes (FSO) PO Box 2959 W Columbia SC 29171 (803) 796-6490. Spon by dios of SC and USC. Located in Dio of USC. Res care facility for the elderly; skilled nursing care.

Thompson Child and Family Focus (CYF) 234 Kings Mtn St York SC 29745 (803) 684-4011 Spon by Dios of SC and USC and Dio of NC. Located in Dio of NC. Res treatment for emotionally disturbed children. Casework svcs for families.

DIOCESE OF SOUTHEAST FLORIDA

Casa del Marino 1207 SW 21st Ct Ft Lauderdale

FL 33315 (954) 467-7330 (Seafarers House) Seaport min.

Episc Mental Health Ministries Inc (CYF) 1700 Blount Rd Pompano Beach FL 33060 (954) 972-2958 x23 *Exec Dir* Lorry Hurdeen *E-mail:* st_laurencechapel@hotmail.com (St Laurence Chap). Refuge and rehab ctr for homeless indivs and fams.

Holy Comforter Jubilee Ministry (R) 150 SW 13th Ave Miami FL 33135 (305) 643-2711 Rev Rafael Garcia.

Holy Cross Jubilee Ministry 3635 NE 1st Ave (Box 370748) Miami FL 33137 (305) 576-0852 Rev L Ortez.

Jubilee Center of South Broward PO Box 221340 Hollywood FL 33004 (954) 920-0106 LeAnna Vasquez.

New Life Family Ctr (CYF) 3620 NW 1st Ave Miami FL 33127 (305) 573-3333 *Dir* Tessa Painson.

St George's Jubilee Ctr 21 W 22nd Riviera Beach FL 33404 (561) 844-7713 *Dir* Cinthia Becton.

Tri-Parish Council 1003 Allendale Rd W Palm Beach FL 33405 (561) 833-7605 *Dir* Cindy Rybovich.

DIOCESE OF SOUTHERN OHIO

Canterbury Court 450 N Elm W Carrollton OH 45449 (937) 859-1106 *Fax:* (937) 859-4174 *Dir* Denise A Bowell; *Chap* Rev J Talk *E-mail:* dbowell@erhinc.com. Indep living ret res, 150 apts. HUD-subsidized rents.

Caracole Inc 1821 Summit Rd #001 Cincinnati OH 45237 (513) 761-1480 *Fax:* (513) 761-3377 *Dir* Linda Seiter *E-mail:* oracle@caracole.org. Res and housing asst for indivs and fams living w/AIDS.

Caring Place, The 6312 Kennedy Ave Cincinnati OH 45213 (513) 841-1499 *Fax:* (513) 841-1498 *Dir* Ceal Bellman *E-mail:* ceal@zoomtown.com. Ecum and social svc agency providing food, counseling. Helping fams achieve self-suffiency thru support, ed, trng and employment. Parents as teachers, an early-learning prog for parents with children birth to age 3.

Cincinnati Children's Hospital Med Ctr (HCC) 3333 Burnet Ave Cincinnati OH 45229-3039 (513) 636-4200 *Chm Ex Officio* Rt Rev Thomas E Breidenthal; *Pres/CEO* James M Anderson; *Dir Past Care* Rev WE Scrivener; *Assoc Dir* Judith Ragsdale. Affiliation of 7 child-care orgs. Full range of inpatient or ambulatory hlth svcs to children w/ varying degrees and kinds of disorders.

Co-Operative Society, The 3333 Burnet Ave Cincinnati OH 45229; (513) 984-1064 *Pres* Nancy Sorg, Development Dept. Children's Hospital Med Ctr auxiliary program.

Deupree House The 3939 Erie Ave Cincinnati OH 45208 (513) 561-6363 *Chap* Angela Puopolo. Also Deupree Cottages at 3999 Erie Ave Cincinnati OH 45208 Houses 24 nursing care private apartments.

Episcopal Community Services Foundation 412 Sycamore St Cincinnati OH 45202 (513) 421-

0311 *Min Ldr* The Rev Terri Thornton *Web:* www.ecsfsouthernohio.org. Supports food, clothing and education ministries in the Diocese of Southern by providing funding to outreach programs.

Episc Retirement Homes Inc Corp Office 3870 Virginia Ave Cincinnati OH 45227 (513) 271-9610 *Fax:* (513) 271-9648 *CEO* R Douglas Spitler; *Chair* William Knodel *Web:* www.episcopalretirement.com. Non-profit org which provides hlth care svcs and living options to meet needs of older adults, in the Dio of SO.

Her Place 1003 W Town Columbus OH 43222 (614) 221-9328 *Coord* Rev Lee Anne Reat. Monthly women's per and spir dev grps build self-esteem and allow women living in poverty to explore spir issues in a safe enviro.

His Place 1003 W Town Columbus OH 43222 (614) 221-9328 *Coord* Gay Roberts. Urban outreach min; meals, worship, emerg asst, referral provided to res of W and SW Columbus.

Interparish Ministry Inc (SpM) 3509 Debolt Rd Cincinnati OH 45244 (513) 561-3932 *Fax:* (513) 272-5704 *Exec Dir* Lindsey Ein *E-mail:* info@interparish.com *Web:* www.interparish.org. Wide variety of counseling, programs, and educ assistance.

Marjorie P Lee Retirement Community 3550 Shaw Ave Cincinnati OH 45208 (513) 871-2090 *Fax:* (513) 533-5096 *Hlth Svcs Admin* Ginny Uehlin; *Dir of Spir Svcs* CD Cottrill *E-mail:* G/Uehlin@erhinc.com. Full-svc ret comm.

Neighborhood House, Inc. 1000 Atcheson St Columbus OH 43203 (614) 252-4941 *Dir of Comm Rel* Lela Boykin *E-mail:* lboykin@neighborhoodhouseinc.org *Web:* www.nhicolumbus.org; Assist children, families and single adults in their efforts to become self sufficient.

Open Door Ch Adv 2366 Kemper Ln Cincinnati OH 45206 (513) 961-2259 *Exec Dir* Evie Foulkes *E-mail:* eviefoulkes@zoomtown.com. Rep payee min managing disability incomes for mentally ill; feed asst to fams in zip codes 45206, -07, -19, -20; food pantry; drop-in area; neighborhood progs.

Prospect House Inc Box 5117 Cincinnati OH 45205 (513) 921-1613 (513) 921-4244 *Exec Dir* David F Logan. Long-term res alcoholism and substance abuse treatment fac.

DIOCESE OF SOUTHERN VIRGINIA

Ballentine, The (FSO) 7211 Granby St Norfolk VA 23505 (757) 440-7400 *Fax:* (757) 489-8233 *Admin* Christina Driscoll *E-mail:* Admin@TheBallentine.com *Web:* www.TheBallentine.com. 40-unit ret home.

Boys Home, The (CYF) 306 Boys Home Rd Covington VA 24426 (540) 965-7700 *Fax:* (540) 965-7702 *Exec Dir* Donnie Wheatley *E-mail:* DEWheatley@Boyshomeinc.com *Web:* www.boyshomeinc.com. Co-spon by Dio of SV. Boys 6-18.

Full Circle (SpM) 344 W Bute St Norfolk VA 23510

(757) 622-2989 *Fax:* (757) 622-2990 *Exec Dir* Staci Walls-Beegle *Web:* www.fullcircleaids.com. AIDS hospice prog provides med case mgmt, meals, respite care, and vol trng for Hampton Rds area.

Jackson-Feild Episc Homes for Girls Inc (CYF) 546 Walnut Grove Dr Jarrett VA 23867 (434) 634-3217 *Fax:* (434) 634-6467 *Exec Dir* Tricia Delano *E-mail:* tdelano@jacksonfeild.org *Web:* www.jfhomes.org Girls 4-14.

Magnolia Gardens (FSO) 219 Prospect Rd Suffolk VA 23434 (757) 923-4260 *Fax:* (757) 923-4264 *Mgr* Nancy Vick *E-mail:* MagnoliaGardens@earthlink. net *Web:* www.nuom.org. 67-unit apt for low-income elderly and handicapped.

Norfolk Urban Outreach Ministry (SpM) 972 Norfolk Sq Norfolk VA 23502 (757) 461-4213 *Fax:* (757) 461-4507 *Dir* Rev RO Bridgford *E-mail:* Info@ Nuom.com *Web:* www.nuom.org. Ch social min resource ctr.

Trinity Woods (FSO) 200 2nd St Emporia VA 23847 (434) 348-9354 *Fax:* (434) 634-8674 *Mgr* William Bobbitt *E-mail:* twoods@nuom.com *Web:* www. nuom.org. 71-unit apt for low-income elderly and handicapped.

Tucker House (FSO) 7700 Armfield Ave Norfolk VA 23505 (757) 489-7770 *Fax:* (757) 489-7787 Janet Truesdale *Mgr E-mail:* thouse@nuom.com *Web:* www.nuom.org. 129-unit apt for low-income elderly and handicapped.

Westminster-Canterbury of Hampton Rds (FSO) 3100 Shore Dr Virginia Beach VA 23451 (757) 496-1100 *Fax:* (757) 496-1122 *Dir* Benjamin Unkle Jr *Web:* www.wcbay.com. Spon by Dio of SV and Norfolk Presbytery. Toll-free (800) 349-1722.

DIOCESE OF SOUTHWEST FLORIDA

Bishop Gray Retirement Foundation PO Box 233 Winter Park FL 32790 (407) 644-9866 *Fax:* (267) 295-8679

Peterborough Apts R 440 4th Ave N St Petersburg FL 33701 (727) 823-5145. 152-unit adult comm in heart of St Petersburg. Res over 62 or handicapped. Housing subsidy avail.

St Giles Manor R 5041 82nd Ave N Pinellas Park FL 33781 (727) 541-5741. 106-unit ret res apts for low-to-middle income grp over 62, w/federal rent subsidy. Males, females or couples.

Suncoast Manor R 6090 9th St S St Petersburg FL 33705 (727) 867-1131.

DIOCESE OF SOUTHWESTERN VIRGINIA

Boys Home of Virginia (CYF) 414 Boys' Home Rd Covington VA 24426 (540) 965-7700 (540) 965-7702 *Dir* DE Wheatley *E-mail:* dewheatley@ boyshomeinc.org *Web:* www.boyshomeofva.org. Co-spon by the dios of VA, SV and SwV. Boys, 6-18 yrs. Financial and med reqs.

Westminster-Canterbury of Lynchburg (FSO) 501 VES Rd Lynchburg VA 24503 (434) 386-3500 (434) 386-3535 *Chap* Rev Kristie Miles *Web:* www.

wclynchburg.org. 246-apt, 80-nursing bed ret fac, spon by the Dio of SwV and the Presbyterian Synod of the Virginias.

DIOCESE OF TENNESSEE

Mid-Cumberland Mountain Ministry (NCS) 282 N Bluff Circle Monteagle TN 37356 *Mailing:* PO Box 706 Monteagle TN 37356 (931) 924-3380 *Pres* Cathy Kirkland. Counseling, housing, past care in rural mtn areas.

St Luke''s Community House (NCS) 5601 New York Ave Nashville TN 37209 (615) 350-7893 *Fax:* (615) 350-6622 *Dir* Brian Dillar. Recreation, counseling, day care for ages 6 wks-12 yrs, health svcs, toy store, mobile meals, social svcs, Second Harvest emergency food.

DIOCESE OF TEXAS

El Buen Samaritano Episc Mission (NCS) 7000 Woodhue Dr Austin TX 78745-5454 *Fax:* (512) 441-7977 (512) 439-0742 *E-mail:* info@elbuen.org *Web:* www.elbuen.org.

St James House (FSO) 5800 W Baker Rd Baytown TX 77520 (281) 424-4541 *Fax:* (281) 424-1922 *Web:* www.stjameshouse.org. Men and women, interdenom.

St Vincent's House (NCS) 2817 Post Office St Galveston TX 77550 (409) 763-8521 *Fax:* (409) 763-0572 *Dir* Rev F M Brown *E-mail:* stvhope@stvhope. org *Web:* www.stvhope.org.

William Temple Episcopal Center c/o Trinity Episcopal Church 2216 Ball St Galveston TX 77550 (409) 765-6317 Email: wtecgalveston@gmail.com Web: www.williamtempleepiscopalcenter.org

Episcopal Health Foundation (NCS) 500 Fannin, Ste. 300 Houston, TX 77002 (713) 225-0900 Fax: (713) 225-0901 Pres. E Marks E-mail: emarks@ episcopalhealth.org Web: www.episcopalhealth.org

DIOCESE OF UPPER SOUTH CAROLINA

Finlay House (FSO) 2100 Blossom Columbia SC 29205 (803) 799-6524 *Web:* www.Finlayhouse. com. Unique 19 story building in the Heart of Columbia, South Carolina, provides high quality, supportive independent living in 203 apartments. Recreational facs.

South Carolina Episc Home at Still Hopes (CYF) Knox Abbott Dr at 7th W Columbia SC 29169 (803) 796-6490 Rev Johnnie Davis *Chap Web:* www.sceh. org, Ret fac spon by Episcopal Church in South Carolina and USC. Large wooded acreage. 24-hr nurse on duty. Private rms and bath.

York Place, A Division of Thompson Child and Family Focus (CYF) 6800 Saint Peter's Lane Matthews NC 28105 (704) 644-4366 Mary Jo Powers *Pres /CEO* Res treatment for emotionally disturbed children; casework svcs for fams Spon by Episcopal Church in SC and USC.

DIOCESE OF UTAH

Community Soup Kitchen with Grace 1072 E 900

S St. George UT 84790 *Dir* Jim Roberts *E-mail:* gmsfool@earthlink.net. Provides food days a week

St Mark's Gardens (FSO) 514 N 300 W Kaysville UT 84037 (801) 544-4231. 72 units. Apts for low-income elderly and handicapped. Owned by the Epis Mgt Corp and spon by the Dio of UT. Progs for elderly.

St Mark's Hospital, Pastoral Care Dept (CHAP) 1200 E 3900 S Salt Lake City UT 84124 (801) 268-7870 *Dir* Rev Lincoln Ure. ACPE certified supervisor and chap.

St Mark's Millcreek (FSO) 418 E Front Ave Salt Lake City UT 84115 (801) 486-3431. 24-unit apts for the low-income elderly and handicapped. Owned by the Episc Mgmt Corp and spon by the Dio of UT. Progs for elderly.

St Mark's Tower (FSO) 50 N 500 W Brigham City UT 84302 (435) 734-2169. 32-unit apt for low-income elderly and handicapped. Owned by the Episc Mgmt Corp and spon by the Dio of UT. Progs for elderly.

St Mark's Terrace (FSO) 50 N 500 W Brigham City UT 84302 (435) 734-2169. 32-unit apt for low-income elderly and handicapped. Owned by the Episc Mgmt Corp and spon by the Dio of UT. Progs for elderly.

Union Gardens (FSO) 468 3rd St Ogden UT 84404 (801) 392-7230. 50-unit apts for the low-income elderly and handicapped. Owned by the Episc Mgmt Corp and spon by the Dio of UT. Progs for elderly.

Youth Impact (CYF) 2305 Grant Ave Ogden UT 84401 (801) 612-3001 *Dir* Robb Hall *E-mail:* robb.hall@youthimpactogden.org. Provides a fam enviro 5-6 hrs a day for 200 children, ages 10-18, who are at risk for sch failure, drug/alcohol abuse, gang involvement, and failure to thrive.

DIOCESE OF VERMONT

Brookhaven Treatment and Learning Center (CYF) Box 127 Chelsea VT 05038 (802) 685-4458 *Dir* Dr Anthony Iazzo. Res treatment fac for boys, providing grp care, on-campus schooling, tutoring, recreation and counseling.

Rock Point School (CYF) 1 Rock Point Rd Burlington VT 05408 (802) 863-1104 *Hdmstr* CJ Spirito. Provides an alt living and ed opportunity for high sch age young people in grp setting.

DIOCESE OF VIRGINIA

Bloomfield Inc (SpM) Box 2 Ivy VA 22945 (540) 687-6316 *Fax:* (540) 687-6368 *Pres* Courtney G Kohler. Charitable foundation for children and young adults w/physical disabilities. Bloomfield's mission is to provide grants to indiv to enable them to achieve their highest level of indep living.

Goodwin House (FSO) 4800 Fillmore Ave Alexandria VA 22311 (703) 578-1000 *Pres* and *CEO* Kathleen Anderson *Dir Marketing* David Taylor Lifecare ret comm w/278 apts, 90 nursing beds. Cert as ext-care fac by Medicare and licensed by State Dept of Health. Founder's fee and mon maintenance

fee; fellowships avail for communicants of Dio of VA.

Goodwin House West (FSO) 3440 S Jefferson Bailey's Crossroads Falls Church VA 22041 (703) 578-7201 *Pres & CEO* Kathleen Anderson *Dir Marketing* Kathie Miller Life-care ret comm of 320 apts, 60 personal care units, 73 nursing beds. Cert as extcare fac by Medicare and licensed by State Dept of Health. Founder's fee and mon maintenance fee; fellowships avail for communicants of Dio of VA.

Rappahannock Westminster-Canterbury Inc (FSO) 132 Lancaster Dr Irvington VA 22480 (804) 438-4000 *Pres* & CEO Stuart Bunting. *Marketing Assoc* Andrea Hathaway. A continuing care ret comm with apts, cottages, asst living suites and skilled nursing, beds. Cert by Medicare, licensed by State Dept of Health and Social Svcs. Entrance fee and mon svc fee; fellowships avail to qualified applicants.

Westminster-Canterbury Richmond (FSO) 1600 Westbrook Ave Richmond VA 23227 (804) 264-6000 *Pres & CEO* John D Burns. Ret res spon by Dio of VA and the Presb Synod of the Virginias and 352 independent living apts, 130 personal care units and 158 nursing beds, ext care fac. Cert by Medicare and licensed by the State Dept of Health. Hospice and Home Health svcs are avail. Founder's fee and mon maintenance fee; fellowships avail for communicants of Dio of VA and Presby Synod of VA.

Westminster-Canterbury of the Blue Ridge 250 Pantops Mtn Rd Charlottesville VA 22911 (434) 972-2622 *Pres & CEO* Gary Selmeczi. Life-care ret comm. Apt and cottage living, licensed nursing care on site. Founder's fee and mon maintenance fees; fellowship avail to qualified applicants.

Shenandoa Valley Westminster-Canterbury (FSO) 300 Westminster-Canterbury Dr Winchester VA 22603 (540) 665-0156. A continuing ret comm w/ apts, cottages, asst living apts and skilled nursing, beds. Licensed by the State Dept of Health and Soc Svcs. Cert by Medicare. Founder's fee and mon maintenance fee; fellowships.

DIOCESE OF WASHINGTON

Collington Episc Life Care Community Inc (FSO) 10450 Lottsford Rd Mitchellville MD 20721 (301) 925-9610 *Web*: www.collington.com *Exec Dir* Marvell Adams. Cont care ret comm in Prince George's County MD. Cottages and apts, health ctr, asst living and full nursing care. Meals and supportive svcs and activities incl fitness/wellness prog.

Friendship Terrace Episc Church Home, Friendship Inc 4201 Butterworth Pl NW Washington DC 20016 (202) 244-7400 *Fax:* (202) 362-2587 *Exec Dir* Deborah Royster *Admin* Ronnie Tobin. Rental ret comm for people 62 yrs and over. Entertainment, wellness progs, rel svcs, transportation and vol opportunities avail. Fees incl apt, utilities and evening meals begin at less than $1000 a month. Lunch is opt. No max income or asset limits and a long wait list for subsidies. Svcs provided by nurse consultant and care mngrs are avail on a sliding-fee scale. Asst w/housekeeping and personal care can be arranged through Homecare Partners on a special fee basis.

House of Mercy (CYF) 2000 Rosemount Ave NW Washington DC 20010 (202) 265-9888. Formerly provided care for unwed mothers and babies. For files research, call. Presently supports progs related to single mother, no on-site services.

Rosemount Ctr, The (CYF) 2000 Rosemount Ave NW Washington DC 20010 *Dir* Jacques Rondeau. (Sponsored by House of Mercy.) Spanish-English day home prog, presch. Subsidized care avail. Parent ed, fam counseling, comm liaison.

Seabury Resources for Aging 4201 Butterworth Pl NW Washington DC 20016 (202) 414-6315 *Fax:* (202) 289-5693 *Web:* www.seaburyresources.org. A non-profit corp serving seniors and fam members in the Dio of W. Svcs incl transportation, geriatric care mgmt, info and in-home care. ESM coord min w/ cong and other orgs and ed progs. It also provides asst living grp homes for seniors in Silver Spring MD, Bowie MD and Wash DC and an Age-in-Place prog for the Northeast Wash comm.

St Mary's Court (FSO) 725 24th St NW Washington DC 20037 (202) 223-5712 *Web:* www.stmaryscourt.org *Exec Dir* Margaret Pully. 140-unit apt hse for low-to-moderate income elderly and qualified handicapped persons. HUD rent supplements. Evening meals req. On the premises are: progs for recreation, ed, exercise and art; DC office on Aging Elderly Nutrition Program site serving daytime noon meal; progs for health, legal and support svcs; reg worship svcs and spir forum hours.

DIOCESE OF WEST MISSOURI

Bishop Spencer Place Inc (R, CHAP, FSO) 4301 Madison Kansas City MO 64111 (816) 931-4277 *Fax:* (816) 931-4717. Rental ret comm for elderly mod-income res.

Episcopal Community Services (NCS) 11 E 40th Kansas City MO 64111 (816) 561-8920 *Fax:* (816) 561-4939 *Exec Dir* John Hornbeck Facilitates Episc min to needy in Kansas City area.

St Luke's Hospital and Mid-America Heart Institute of Kansas City (HCC, CHAP) 4401 Wornall Rd PO Box 119000 Kansas City MO 64171 (816) 932-2180 *Chaps* Revs M Scott, E Anderson. Fully accred 686-bed tertiary care, teaching hospital and trauma ctr.

St Luke's Nursing Ctr (HCC) 1220 E Fairview Carthage MO 64836 (417) 358-9084 *Admin* Sue Joslen. 120-bed skilled nursing fac.

DIOCESE OF WEST TEXAS

Good Samaritan Community Services (NCS) 1600 Saltillo St San Antonio TX 78207 (210) 434-5531 Jill Oettinger *Exec Dir E-mail:* oettinger_j@goodsamcenter.com *Web:* www.good-samaritancommunity services.org Human svc agency of Dio. Nationally accredited childcare; after school and summer enrichment programs, education and employment readiness for youth at high risk; family case management and support, senior activity center. Provides youth development services to 15 counties of Central and South Texas.

DIOCESE OF WEST VIRGINIA

Highland Educational Project: Premier Learning Center (CYF) Box 204 Welch WV 24801 750 Stone Coal Branch Rd Premier WV 24878 (304) 436-2641 *Fax:* (304) 436-2699 *Director* Lori Osborne.

DIOCESE OF WESTERN KANSAS

St Francis Community Services (CYF) Nat'l Office 509 E Elm (Box 1340) Salina KS 67402-1340 (800) 423-1342 *Fax:* (785) 825-2502 *Dean* The Rev Robert N Smith *E-mail:* Robert.Smith@st-francis.org. (Accred by JCAHO. Approved by Ch Life.) Facs in Dio of WK, KS.

DIOCESE OF WESTERN LOUISIANA

Holy Cross Villas (Bossier City) 2140 Airline Dr Bossier City LA 71111 *Contact:* Sharon Edwards. A ministry of H Cross Ch Shreveport. 78-unit apt complex for men, women and couples (HUD 202).

Holy Cross Villas (West Shreveport) 9333 Normandie Dr Shreveport LA 71118 *Contact:* Sharon Edwards. A ministry of H Cross Ch Shreveport. 48-unit apt complex for men, women and couples (HUD 202).

Day Shelter for Homeless People (Hope House) 762 Austin Pl Shreveport LA 71101 *Manager:* Donna Earnest. Telephone and voice-mail, mailboxes, shower facilities, laundry, referral services, clothing. Owned by H Cross Ch Shreveport.

DIOCESE OF WESTERN NEW YORK

The Episcopal Partnership for Mission and Outreach *Chair* S van Pletzen-Rands

DIOCESE OF WESTERN NORTH CAROLINA

Deerfield Episc Retirement Comm (FSO) 1617 Hendersonville Rd Asheville NC 28803 (828) 274-1531 Robert F Wernet Jr/Lin Walton, *Dir* Chaplain Hses, condos, rms Health ctr and comm ctr, Alzheimer's prog. St Giles Chapel at Deerfield.

Thompson Child and Family Focus 6800 Saint Peter's Ln Matthews NC 28105 (704) 531-9266 Mary Jo Powers *Exec Dir* See Dio of NC.

DIOCESE OF WYOMING

Cathedral Home for Children, The (CYF) Box 520 Laramie WY 82073 (307) 745-8997 *Web:* www.cathedralhome.org. Residential treatment and fully accredited school for children and adolescents with emotional and behavioral problems, including deaf and hard of hearing troubled youth ages 10-18; JCAHO accredited serving Wyoming and the western region as well as the rest of the US.

SPECIAL MINISTRIES

Armed Forces and Federal Ministries

OFFICE OF THE BISHOP SUFFRAGAN FOR ARMED FORCES AND FEDERAL M'NISTRIES
3504 Woodley Rd NW Washington, DC 20016
(202) 459-9998 Web: www.basfm.org

Bishop Suffragan—Rt Rev James B Magness

Canon to the Bishop—Rev Dr Wollom (Wally) Jensen

Assistant to the Bishop Suffragan—Maggie Mount

The primary charge of this episcopacy is to ensure the rights to the free exercise of religion for Episcopalians who serve in the military, the Bureau of Prisons, and the Veterans Administration system. The means of serving these populations includes the recruitment, formation, ecclesiastical endorsement, and support of clergy for service as chaplains. All chaplains are endorsed by the Bishop for Armed Forces and Federal Ministries with the concurrence of their diocesan bishops. Though diverse in makeup and location, there is unity in the missional nature of these various ministries within the federal ministry spectrum.

NAVY CHAPLAINS (ACTIVE DUTY)
Bezy, BA CDR (Lex)
Carter, H LT (USC)
Castro, R LT (CFla)
Delaney, T LT (WA)
Duprey, DL LCDR (WY)
Fish, CH CPT (CNY)
Fornea, SW CPT (EC)
Hinson, JA CPT (WMO)
Hoffman, RE CDR (SV)
McInnis, VE LCDR (MS)
Munoz, FP LCDR (Sp)
Orsburn, KR, ENS (OK)
Perdue, TH LCDR (Pgh)
Pike, SP CAPT (KY)
Pumphrey, CM CDR (IA)
Rodgers, PB LT (FL)
Sheldon, II, JV CPT (Springfield)
Thames, DB CDR (TX)
Thornton, CT LCDR (HI)
Tiff, RO LT (LosA)
Winward, MS CDR (Sp)

NAVAL RESERVE CHAPLAINS
Cox, SA CDR (TX)
Cravens, JO, CPT (Sp)
Dell, J LTJG (Albany)
Johnston, PN ENS (CT)
Marta, DL CDR (MN)
Towers, RA LT (Chi)

ARMY CHAPLAINS (ACTIVE DUTY)
Andrews, L CPT (GA)

Bernardez, TK Jr CPT (NV)
Brisson, JL COL (AZ)
Budez, JH CPT (WNY)
Clark, RO MAJ (EC)
Demmon, MDS CPT (CO)
Echols, BM LTC (WA)
Gustafson EM, CPT (Chi)
Houck, II, IC LTC (BE)
Kochenburger, PA MAJ (CFla)
Masillem, B CPT (AK)
Oliver, A CPT (NV)

ARMY RESERVE CHAPLAINS
Baker, AA CPT (CA)
Illas, A, CPT (PR)
Knaup, DJ LTCOL (OH)
Newland, BJ CPT (Oly)
Peters DW, Maj (Sp)
Valcourt, TP CPT (CGC)
Watan JS, 1Lt. (CA)

ARMY NATIONAL GUARD CHAPLAINS
Clark, APCOL (CFla)
Jenkins, W COL (KS)
Kester, MR MAJ (IA)
Minor, PL COL (MA)

AIR FORCE CHAPLAINS (ACTIVE DUTY)
Juchter, MR Capt. (NWPA)
Karanja, Daniel LtCol (SP)
Nyberg, KY Maj. (WMO)
Rivera, AC Capt (CA)

AIR FORCE RESERVE CHAPLAINS
Algernon, M LtCol (SWFla)
Blizzard, C CPT (OK)
Johnson, AB Capt. (WLA)
Milian, M 1Lt (AZ)
Schnack, P 2LT (Oly)

AIR NATIONAL GUARD CHAPLAINS
Adelia, LA Lt. Col. (AZ)
Boeve, PD Lt. Col. (Mil)
Cunningham, PJ CPT (WTx)
Leatherman, DL LtCol (HI)
McIntosh, KL Capt. (Nwk)
Shirley, SA Lt. Col. (WA)

DEPT. OF VETERANS AFFAIRS CHAPLAINS
Adelia, L (AZ)
Farrar, CT (AL)
Garfield, LA
Hekel, UD (Mil)
McElwain, D (WY)
Thompson, RW (WV)
Thullbery, MF (NC)
Wilburn, JM (TX)
Wooliver, TS (MD)

FEDERAL BUREAU OF PRISONS CHAPLAINS
Walker, EA (WV)
Waweru, C (LI)

CIVIL AIR PATROL CHAPLAINS
(AIR FORCE AUXILIARY)
Albert, EE Capt. (SO)
Alford, WT Maj. (CPA)
Arlin, CN Lt. Col. (Nwk)
Beaumont, JF Lt. Col. (CFla)
Cooter, E MAJ (SwFla)
Harrigan, K (PA)
Kirby, HS Capt. (EauC)
McKeown, S 1Lt. (Scottish Episc Church)
Polk, PW Maj. (NCA)
Smalley, NT Lt. Col. (Dal)
Sumners, CA Jr Capt. (CO)
Tattersall, EA Lt. Col. (NV)
Taylor, R MAJ (WNC)
Wood, CL Lt. Col. (MI)

DISTINCTIVE FAITH GROUP LEADERS
Baguyos, A (KS)
Durham, D (MD)
Hart, A (EU)
Humphreys, W (EU)
Lane, E (KY)
McKay, J (WA)
Wass, J (OK)
Wollitz, JL
Zeilfelder, EW (NJ)

CONTRACT PRIESTS
Baguyos, AT (KS)
Bauer, TW (MD)

EVANGELISM
Church Army USA
Church Army USA is part of a worldwide cadre of evangelists within the Anglican Communion. Captains are trained in a two-year program and are commissioned evangelists to serve the least, the last and the lost to the glory of God. Church Army USA partners with local churches and agencies to build communities of recovery. We provide affordable housing, spiritual growth and recovery instruction.

NATIONAL HEADQUARTERS: *Natl Dir* Rev Greg Miller *Bd Chr* James S Moore (412) 780-2457.
Church Army USA
Uncommon Grounds Cafe
PO Box 413
Aliquippa, PA 15001
Phone: (724) 375-5659
Fax: (724) 375-6145
Web: www.churcharmyusa.org.

CHURCH ARMY OFFICERS
Active Officers
Adams, Brett 1201Hambrooks Blvd Cambridge MD 21613
Bowers, Donald 918 Lewis St Brownsville PA 15417
Branderhorst, Scott 1209 Davidson St Aliquippa PA 15001

Brightwell, Steven PO Box 995 Port St Joe FL 32457
Bruno, Rev Roland 7530 Reche Canyon Rd, Colton CA 92324
Bywater, Rev Byran 108 Whitman Ave West Hartford CT 06107
Chellis, Rev Shane 437 W Fleming Ave Fort Wayne IN 46807
Colburn, Scott 813 Franklin Ave Aliquippa PA 15001
Dudley, Robert 4316 Sabana Loop SE #C Rio Rancho NM 87124
Fairweather, Rose 6438 W Hatcher Rd Glendale AZ 85302
Giles, Rev James 2929 Northwest 56th St Ocala FL 34475
Giles, Mary 2929 Northwest 56th St Ocala FL 34475
Holewinski, Brad 421 Th orn St Sewickley PA 15143
Hedrick, Mark PO Box 755 Park Hills MO 63601
Malcom, Ern 6711 Autumn Wood Dr Spotsylvania VA 22553
O'Leary, Nancy 1817 McMinn St Aliquippa PA 15011
Parr, Anna 607 Reed St Aliquippa PA 15001
Parr, Dudley 607 Reed St Aliquippa PA 15001
Pierce, Rev Dr George Global Teams 212 21st St Ste 2 Bakersfield CA 93301
Stanley, John Sr Associate Minister 17 Forster St New Town Tasmania 7008 Australia
Thompson, Mary Edna 859 South Main St Apt 5 Hillsville VA 24343
Wyatt, Robert 711 Shetland St Rockville MD 20851

Retired Officers
Andrew, Rev Robert 3800 W 33rd St Cleveland OH 44109
Brown, Lloyd 206 Madrona Way Bainbridge Island WA 98110-1879 Dec'd
Clarke, Bertha 319 Wellness Way Apt 223 Washington PA 15301 Dec'd
Horn, Henry 209 Wherry St New Boston TX 75570 Dec'd
Jones, Janice 1581 SE Flintlock Rd Port St Lucie FL 34952
Kastorff, Jeannette 431 McKelvey Ave Bakersfield CA 93308
Larson, Rev Wayne 15 East Bishops Rd Baltimore MD 21218
Leavitt, Florence 7500 N Calle Sin Envidia Apt 117 Tucson AZ 85718 Dec'd
Thomas, The Rev John 4418 Helena St NE St Petersburg FL 33703 Dec'd

MINISTRIES TO PERSONS WITH SPECIAL NEEDS
MINISTERING TO THE ALCOHOLIC
The Recovered Alcoholic Clergy Assn (RACA) is a working network of Episc clergy who are recovering from the disease of alcoholism. Its purpose is threefold: mutual self-help, fellowship and pastoral concern for clergy with a drinking problem. Strict anonymity is observed outside

the ranks of RACA. RACA's special ministry is supported by voluntary contributions. *Pres/Dir* Richard Vinson 96 Cherry Lane, Doylestown, PA 18901 808 343-2008 E-Mail rlvinson@icloud. com *Treas* S Winsett *E-mail:* stevewinsett@gamil.com *Web:* www.racapecusa.org.

MINISTRIES TO THOSE SUFFERING FROM ADDICTION

Recovery Ministries of the Episcopal Church is an independent, nationwide network of Episcopal laity and clergy, dioceses and parishes, schools, agencies, and other institutions—all with a common commitment to address the effects of addiction, in all its forms, in relation to the church's mission. Recovery Ministries responds through education, training, and advocacy within the Church. *Contact:* Shannon Tucker *Pres* PO Box 40764 Memphis TN 38174 *Toll Free:* (866) 306-1542 *E-mail:* shannon.tucker@gmail.com *VPres* The Rev Deacon Lisa Kirby *E-mail:* lisakirby@suddenlink.net *Treas* The Rev Deacon Steve Lane *E-mail:* rev.lane@outlook.com *Sec* The Rev Angie Cipolla *E-mail:* rev.angie.cipolla@gmail.com; *E-mail:* info@episcopalrecovery.org *Web:* www.episcopalrecovery.org.

MINISTERING TO THE BLIND

American Bible Society Bible engagement tools and print Scriptures. 1865 Broad way New York NY 10023 (212) 408-1200. *Customer Service:* (800) 32-BIBLE. *E-mail:* info@americanbible.org *Web:* www.americanbible.org.

Forward Movement Braille, Cassette, and Large Print editions of *Forward Day by Day*. The entire 1979 Book of Common Prayer in Braille (13 volumes)—individual sections also available). Online prayer resources, including the Daily Office, *Forward Day by Day*, the lectionary, and more are available in an accessible website, http://prayer.forwardmovement.org. 412 Sycamore St Cincinnati OH 45202 (800) 543-1813 *Fax:* (513) 721-0729 *E-Mail:* orders@forwardmovement.org *Web:* www.forwardmovement.org.

MINISTERING TO THE DEAF

The Episcopal Conference of the Deaf Nat'l organization of clergy and lay people ministering in the deaf community. *Pres* Rev Marianne D Stuart; *1st VP* The Rev Erich Krengle; *Treas* Steve Holst; *Sec* Cass Martensen; *Mbrs at Large* Laurie J Anderson, Greg Randall.

Official Contact: 3794 Crosshaven Dr Birmingham AL 35223 *E-mail:* mariannedstuart@gmail.com *Web:* www.ecdeaf.org. Maintains, promotes, and expands the Church's min among deaf people provides trng for clergy and leaders to increase their effectiveness and competency. Short term grants for new dio ministries, sponsors workshops and conferences for clergy and lay leaders. Convention in summer of year B. *Newsletter Ed* The Rev Preston Colangelo *E-mail:* deacon_bench@bellsouth.net.

Clergy Ministering in Deaf Communities (partial list not including ret.)

Krengel, The Rev Erich St Paul's Church for the Deaf W Hartford 191Margarite Rd Middletown CT 06457 *E-mail:* DeafEpiscopalCT@aol.com. Campbell, The Rev Randy St Alfreds Epis Church Interpreted 1601 Curlew Rd Palm Harbor FL 34683 Deats, The Rev C 61 High Glen Ridge NJ 07028 *E-mail:* revcathy@viconet.com. Hillquist Davis, The Rev Dr Emily St Thomas Epis Church for the Deaf 514 E Argonne Dr Kirkwood MO 63122. Johnston, The Rev Dcn Suzanne Dcn for Min Ephphatha Deaf Mission Church of the Epiphany 3285 Buff alo Rd Rochester NY 14624. Price, The Rev Barbara Ephphatha Epis Church of the Deaf 205 Longmeadow Rd Eggertsville NY14226. Stuart, The Rev Marianne St John's Church for the Deaf 3794 Crosshaven Dr Birmingham AL 35223 *E-mail:*mariannedstuart@gmail.com. Williams, The Rev Peter 121 St Louis Ave Syracuse NY 13207 Vicar of Ephphatha Parish of the Deaf CNY.

Lay Missioners/Leaders

David Early St Thomas Episcopal Church for the Deaf 800 Mullaphy Dr Florissant MO 63031 *E-mail:* DAVEARL@aol.com. Cass Martensen 2089 Golden Circle Escondido CA 92026 *E-mail:* cassmart@aol.com. Suzanne Onderdonk, St Mark's Episcopal Church for the Deaf Mobile, AL suzy1bythebay@aol.com. Thomas Hattaway, St Barnabas Episcopal Church for the Deaf Chevy Chase, Maryland. thomashattaway@gmail.com.

Voluntary Agencies

American Speech-Language-Hearing Assn 10801 Rockville Pike Rockville MD 20852.

Gallaudet University Higher education for deaf people 800 Florida Ave NE Washington DC 20002.

John Tracy Clinic Correspondence courses in ed of deaf and deaf-blind preschool children. Free to parents. England Spanish 806 W Adams Blvd Los Angeles 90007 (800) 522-4582.

National Assn of the Deaf 814 Thayer Ave Silver Spring MD 20910-4500. Deafness-related consumer advocacy. Info clearinghouse. Bookstore of products and books on the subject of deafness.

NTID 52 Lomb Memorial Dr, LBJ Bldg, Rochester NY 14623-5604 *Web:* www.rit.edu/RIT/NTID. Provides informational materials on issues related to deaf people and deaf culture.

MINISTERING TO PEOPLE WITH AIDS

National Episcopal AIDS Coalition (NEAC) Non-profit, grass-roots membership org, works for AIDS/HIV ministry on all levels of Episc Church. NEAC works to expand and serve growing network of Episc AIDS ministries; provides references to ministry models in education, pastoral care, direct service. Maintains Nat'l Episc AIDS Database, produces newsltr. *Exec Dir* Matthew Ellis 6050 N Meridian St Indianapolis IN 46208 (800) 588-6628, (317) 534-0480 *Fax:* (317) 726-0569 *E-mail:* neac@neac.org

Web: www.neac.org.

National AIDS Hotline (800) CDC–INFO (232-4636) English and Spanish.

National Aids Treatment Information Service (800) 448-0440 English and Spanish.

MINISTERING TO SEAFARERS
The Seamen's Church Institute

Seamen's Ch Inst of NY & NJ 50 Broadway, Floor 26 New York, NY 10004 (212) 349-9090, *Fax:* (212) 349-8342. *Pres & Exec Dir* The Rev David M. Rider. Founded in 1834 and affiliated with the Episcopal Church, though nondenominational in terms of its trustees, staff and service to mariners, the Seamen's Church Institute of New York & New Jersey (SCI) is the largest, most comprehensive mariners' service agency in North America. Annually, its chaplains visit thousands of vessels in the Port of New York and New Jersey, the Port of Oakland, and along 2,200 miles of America's inland waterways extending into the Gulf of Mexico. SCI's maritime education facilities provide navigational training to nearly 1,600 mariners each year through simulator-based facilities located in Houston, TX and Paducah, KY. The Institute and its maritime attorneys are recognized as leading advocates for merchant mariners by the United States Government, including the US Congress, the US Coast Guard, and the Department of Homeland Security, as well as the United Nations, the International Maritime Organization, the International Labour Organization and maritime trade associations. Newsletters and publications upon request. *E-mail* sci@seamenschurch.org *Web:* seamenschurch.org

The Mission to Seafarers in North America and the Caribbean

The Mission to Seafarers in North America and the Caribbean is the Society's regional cooperative arm for the USA, Canada, the Caribbean, and Central America.

Episc Promoter and Liais Bp for Canada Rt Rev TE Finlay. *Liais Bp for Caribbean* Rt Rev CW Bess Bp of Trinidad and Tobago Hayes Ct 21 Maraval Rd Port of Spain Trinidad WEST INDIES (868) 622-7387 *Fax:* (868) 628-1319 *E-mail:* diocese@tstt.net. tt. *Anchorage* AK Ven NHV Elliott 2401 Galewood Anchorage AK 99508-4036 (907) 277-4804 *Cell:* (907) 240-8714 *E-mail:* nelliott@gci.net.

Baltimore MD Rev M Davisson Int'l Seafarers Center 1430 Wallace St Baltimore MD 21230 (410) 685-1240 *Fax:* (410) 685-1241 *E-mail:* baltseafarers@aol.com.

Barbours Cut Rev L Largent; Lou Lawler Seafarer's Ctr PO Box 1434 La Porte TX 77571 (281) 470-2411 *Fax:* (281) 470-0263.

Bermuda–Sandys Ven Dr A Hollis S Jas Rectory Box MA74 Sandys MABX Bermuda (1441) 234- 2025 *Fax:* (1441) 234-2723 *E-mail:* athol@logic.bm.

Charleston SC Rev L Williams Charleston Maritime Ministry Box 5293 126 Coming St Charleston SC

29403 (843) 722-7345.

Chicago IL Rev EL Van Baldwin Jr 9711 S Peoria St Chicago IL 60643 (773) 239-2296.

Corpus Christi TX QE Williams ISC 1501 N Mesquite St Corpus Christi TX 78401-1117 (361) 883-8405. *Fax:* (361) 883-4529 *E-mail:* seamanscenter@yahoo.com.

Ft Lauderdale FL Seafarers House Box 13034 Ft Lauderdale FL 33316 (954) 467-7330 *Fax:* (954) 766-2699 *E-mail:* info@seafarershouse.org.

Green Bay WI Rev JA Cell Seafarer's Min of Green Bay 825 N Webster Ave Green Bay WI 54302-1436 (920) 432-4688 *Fax:* (920) 432-4688.

Honduras–Atlantida Rev JD Batiz SantissimaTrin Apdo 28 Ave Morazan 1175 La Ceiba Atlantida HONDURAS (504)-42-2641.

Honduras–Puerto Cortes Rev P Torres S Jn Sch Apdo 16 Puerto Cortes HONDURAS (504)-55-0200.

Houston TX Rev L Largent ISC City Dock 23, Upper Level Box 9506 Houston TX 77261 (713) 672-0511 *Fax:* (713) 672-2444 *E-mail:* houstonchaplains@yahoo.com.

Jamaica–Montego Bay WI VRev HP Lynch Holy Trin Box 98 Montego Bay 1 JAMAICA *Tel/Fax:* (876) 952-1270.

Jamaica–St Anns WI Rev G Prince The Rectory PO Box 35 Mamee Bay St Anns Bay St Anns JAMAICA (876) 972-2305 *Fax:* (876) 972-2305 *E-mail:* glen@princeworks.com.

Los Angeles CA Rev K Crawford SCI of Los Angeles World Cruise Ctr Berth 93A, CML 101 San Pedro CA 90733-1620 (310) 548-3200 *Fax:* (310) 832-0239 *E-mail:* chaplain@seaLns.org.

Mayaguez PR Rev M Munoz Box 59 Maya guez PR 00708 (809) 832-1116.

New Haven CT C Marshall Davidson Woman's Seamen's Friend Society 291 Whitney Ave New Haven CT 06511 (203) 777-2165.

Newport SCI of New port 18 Market Sq Newport RI 02840-3035 (401) 847-4260 *Fax:* (401) 847-4284.

Norfolk VA Rev CJ Turner Inter'l Sea man's Hse 1222 W Olney Rd Norfolk VA 23507(757) 623-4222 *Fax:* (757) 627-7872 *E-mail:* STELMARI@aol.com.

Philadelphia PA Rev Canon J VonDreele SCI of Phila 475 N 5th St Phila PA 19123 (215) 940- 9900 *Fax:* (215) 922-0737 *E-mail:* seamens@sciphiladelphia.org.

Port-au-Prince Haiti V Rev Y Francois Cathedrale Episcopale Bp 1309 Port-au-Prince HAITI (509) 238-2737.

San Pedro CA *Dir* Rev K Crawford SCI Worldport Cruise Ctr Berth 93A CML 101 San Pedro CA 90731-1620 PO Box 1620 (310) 548-3200 *Fax:* (310) 832-0239 *E-mail:* chaplain@seaLns.org*Santurce* PR Rev Cn W Ramos Box 9262 Santurce PR 00908 (809) 721-3395.

Seattle WA Capt C Hubbard Seattle Seafarers Ctr 101 Alaskan Way S Pier 48 Seattle WA 98194 (206) 748-0347 *Fax:* (206) 292-5786 *E-mail:* seafarersmission@aol.com.

Stockton CA Rev W Gubuan S Jn Evang Epis Ch 316 N El Dorado St Stockton CA 95202 (209) 466-6916 *Fax:* (209) 466-9701 *E-mail:* stjohn316N@aol.com.

Trinidad WI Mariners' Club Wrightson Rd (Box 561) Port of Spain Trinidad WI (868) 625-4826.

Wilmington DE Rev G Karney S Barn 2800 Duncan Rd Wilmington DE 19808 (302) 994-6607.

Voluntary Agencies

Seamen's Ch Inst of NY and NJ 50 Broadway, Floor 26 New York NY 10004 (212)-349-9090 *Fax* (212) 349- 8342. *Pres & Exec Dir* The Rev David M. Rider. Founded in 1834 and affiliated with the Episcopal Church, though nondenominational in terms of its trustees, staff and service to mariners, the Seamen's Church Institute of New York & New Jersey (SCI) is the largest, most comprehensive mariners' service agency in North America. Annually, its chaplains visit thousands of vessels in the Port of New York and New Jersey, the Port of Oakland, and along 2,200 miles of America's inland waterways extending into the Gulf of Mexico. SCI's maritime education facilities provide navigational training to nearly 1,600 mariners each year through simulator-based facilities located in Houston, TX and Paducah, KY. The Institute and its maritime attorneys are recognized as leading advocates for merchant mariners by the United States Government, including the US Congress, the US Coast Guard, and the Department of Homeland Security, as well as the United Nations, the International Maritime Organization, the International Labour Organization and maritime trade associations. Newsletters and publications upon request. *E-mail* sci@seamenschurch.org *Web:* seamenschurch.org.

Seamen's Ch Inst of Philadelphia and South Jersey 475 N 5th St Phila PA 19123 (215) 940-9900 *Fax* (215) 922-0737. *Exec Dir* The Rev Canon Dr Peter B Stube Founded in 1843, an indep cross-cultural agency historically and closely assoc with Episc Ch. Fully ecum miss to meet needs of US and intl mer chant and cruise ship seafarers in Port of Phila and Camden on 125-mile stretch of Delaware River. Annually serves 40,000 from 100+ nations and all world religs with mins of hospitality and justice. In operation 7 days/ nights. *E-mail:* seamens@sciphiladelphia.org *Web:* www.sciphiladelphia.org.

MINISTERING TO PERSONS WITH DISABILITIES

Episcopal Disability Network

Provides resources, assistance, and advocacy for persons with disabilities. Networks with other denoms and sec orgs about disab concerns. Educational programs, assistance with archit access, help with new and expanding min. Taped books, multi-media mat, books and pamphlets avail on free loan. *Contact* Rev B Ramnaraine Episcopal Disability Network 3024 E Minnehaha Pkwy Minneapolis MN 55406 (612) 729-4322 *Toll Free:* (855) 249-3480 *E-mail:* disability99@earthlink.net. *Web:* www.episcability.org.

CHURCH PERIODICALS

(4)—number of issues published yearly.

General Periodicals

Abbey Letter S Gregory's Abbey 56500 Abbey Rd Three Rivers MI 49093-9595 (4) *Web:* saintgregorysthreerivers.org.

Adelante Día a Día The Spanish version of *Forward Day by Day*, a daily devotional centering on one of the day's lectionary readings. Forward Movement. Ms Richelle Thompson Ed 412 Sycamore St Cincinnati OH 45202 (513) 721-6659 *E-mail:* orders@forwardmovement.org *Web:* www.forwardmovement.org.

Anglican and Episcopal History Edward L Bond *Ed-in-Chief* 902 State St Natchez 39120 (256) 372-5343 *E-mail:* edward.bond@aamu.edu; aeheditor@earthlink.net *Book Review Ed* Sheryl Kujawa-Holbrook *E-mail:* sherylkujawa1e@msn.com *Ch Review Ed* Barrie Bates *E-mail:* churchrevieweditor@gmail.com *Bus & Subsc Mgr* Matthew C Payne 82 Cherry Ct Appleton WI 54915 (844) 819-2900 *Office* (920) 574-2168 *Cell* (920) 279-6267 *E-mail:* administration@hsec.us *Web:* www.hsec.us. (4).

Anglican The The Rev William Loring *Ed E-mail:* Fr.Bill@comcast.net; Linda Bridges. *Sub and Treas* 305 E 72nd St NY NY 10021 *E-mail:* lbridges2@mindspring.com (212) 849-2811. The Anglican Society (4).

Anglican Digest The Rev John D Burton *Ed E-mail:* editor@anglicandigest.org; Tom Walker *Adv Bus Circ* 805 CR 102 Eureka Springs AR 72632-9705 (479) 253-9701 (4).

Anglican Theological Review *Pres* Newland F Smith 3rd *Exec Dir and Mng Ed* Jacqueline Winter 8765 W Higgins Rd Ste 650 Chicago IL 60631 (773) 380-7046 *Fax:* (773) 380-6788 *E-mail:* atr@seabury.edu. *Web:* www.anglicantheologicalreview.org. *Ed in Chief* Rev Dr Richard G Leggett Saint Faith's Anglican Church 7284 Cypress St Vancouver BC V6P 5M3 Canada (604) 266-8011 *E-mail:* liturgypacific@me.com (4).

"Brother, Give Us a Word" A Brother's word of help and hope—arrives daily electronically: www.SSJE.org/word.

Cathedral Age Communications Department *Ed* Washington National Cathedral 3101 Wisconsin Ave NW Washington DC 20016-5098 (202) 537-5681 *E-mail:* communications@cathedral.org *Web:* www.nationalcathedral.org (4).

Church Militant of NY The Shandra Velez 335 W 51 NY NY 10019. Protestant Episc Evangelists (212) 265-5433 (4).

Communiqué Quarterly publication of the National Board of the Episcopal Church Women. Virginia Lief *Ed* 310 Riverside Dr #822 New York NY 10025 *E-mail:* vpinformationcommunication@ecwnational.org (4).

Congregational Libraries Today 10157 SW Barbur Blvd #102C Portland OR 97219. Judith Janzen *Admin* (503) 244-6919 (800) LIB-CSLA *Fax:* (503) 977-3734 *E-mail:* csla@worldaccessnet.com *Web:* www.cslainfo.org (4).

Cowley, a magazine of the Society of St John the Evangelist 980 Memorial Dr Cambridge MA 02138 (617) 876-3037. Can be downloaded from website *E-mail:* monastery@ssje.org *Web:* www.ssje.org (3).

CPC Quarterly Newsletter of the Church Periodical Club 47 West Shore Dr Otisfield ME 04270 Linda Vaill Ed *E-mail:* lindavaill@myfairpoint.net *Web:* www.churchperiodical.com.

Deaf Episcopalian The Episcopal Conference of the Deaf. Ed Kathryne M Sheldon 2311 Minnesota St Louis MO 63104 *E-mail:* kathyart@sbcglobal.net (4).

Episcopal News Service 815 Second Ave NY NY 10017 (800) 334-7626 *Ed/Reporter* Matthew Davies *E-mail:* mdavies@episcopalchurch.org *Ed/Reporter* The Rev. Mary Frances Schjonberg *E-mail:* mfschjonberg@episcopalchurch.org *Ed/Reporter* Lynette Wilson *E-mail:* lwilson@episcopalchurch.org.

Episcopal Teacher Dorothy Linthicum *Ed* Free quarterly newspaper from the Center for the Ministry of Teaching, Virginia Theology Sem; can be downloaded from website. (703) 461-1885 *Web:* http://www.vts.edu/cmt/published/et.

Epistle Deborah Bradley *Manag Ed* 1166 E Oak St LaGrange TX 78945 (979) 702-1933 *E-mail:* DeborahBradleyEvents@gmail.com Official publ of the Natl Altar Guild Assn (4).

Forward Day by Day A daily devotional centering on one of the day's lectionary readings. Forward Movement. Ms Richelle Thompson *Ed* 412 Sycamore St Cincinnati OH 45202 (800) 543-1813 *E-mail:* orders@forwardmovement.org *Web:* www.forwardmovement.org.

Historiographer The Pub of National Episcopal Historians and Archivists and Historical Society of the Episcopal Church 82 Cherry Ct Appleton WI 54915 (920) 543-6342 TheHistoriographer@gmail.com (4).

Homiletic John McClure *Gen Ed* A Rev of Publns in Rel Comm c/o Vanderbilt Divinity School 411 21st Ave S Nashville TN 37240-1121 *E-Mail:* homiletic@vanderbilt.edu.

Living Church The Christopher Wells *Ex Dir* 816 E Juneau Ave Milwaukee WI 53202 (MAIL: Box 510705 Milwaukee WI 53203-0121) *E-mail:* tlc@livingchurch.org *Web:* www.livingchurch.org. LC Foundation (52).

Mandate Journal of the Prayer Book Soc PO Box 913 Brookhaven PA 19105-0913 (800) PBS-1928 *Ed* Dr Roberta Bayer. News, informa tion, and opinion in the Episcopal Church *Web:* www.pbusa.org.

Mission Link, Rock the World Youth Mission Alliance Box 43 Ambridge PA 15003. Stories of changed lives and annual report. Published electronically. *Web:* www.rocktheworld.org *E-mail:* info@rocktheworld.org (1).

Mundi Medicina Holy Cross Monastery Box 99 West Park NY 12394-0099 (845) 384-6660 x3027 *Fax:* (845) 384-6031 *E-mail:* holycross@hcmnet.org *Web:* holycrossmonastery.com (3).

News from the Hill Newsletter of Virginia Theological Seminary. Contact: Curtis Prather *E-mail:* cprather@vts.edu.

OPEN Online Journal of the Associated Parishes for Liturgy and Mission, publishing articles on the renewal of the liturgy and mission of the Church, reviews and resources, with electronic response and conversation. For additional info and archived copies, visit www.associatedparishes.org.

Royal Cross The Order of the Daughters of the King, The *Ed* Katherine Marshall-Polite *E-mail:* royalcrosseditor@doknational.org 208 Sandpiper Ct Yorktown Hts NY 10598 *Assoc Ed* Susan Towson *E-mail:* royalcrossnews@doknational.org 1211 Mundy Dr Jacksonville FL 32207 *Web:* www.doknational.org. $15 Subscriptions are handled by National Office 101 Weatherstone Dr Ste 870 Woodstock GA 30188 (4).

St Andrew's Cross Publication of the Brotherhood of St Andrew Inc Box 632 Ambridge PA 15003 (724) 266-5810. *Fax:* (724) 266-9577. *E-mail:* brotherhoodofstandrew@verizon.net *Web:* www.brothersandrew.net. *Attn: Ed* Jim Goodson *E-mail:* jimgoodson@aol.com (4).

saint helena 414 Savannah Barony Dr North Augusta SC 29841. Order of St Helena. Stories and news from sisters whose mission is to show forth Christ through a life of monastic prayer, hospitality and service. *E-mail:* sisters@osh.org *Web:* www.osh.org (4).

Servant The 305 W Lafayette Av Baltimore MD 21217. Brotherhood of St Gregory *E-mail:*servant@gregorians.org *Web:* www.gregorians.org (4).

Sewanee Theological Review "An Anglican Journal of Theology Reflection." Ed Christopher Bryan *Man Ed* James David Jones Sch of Theology University of the South Sewanee TN 37383 (931) 598-1475. $24 annual (4).

Sharing–A Journal of Christian Healing Office pub of Intl Order of S Lk the Phys (OSL). Articles on healing, teach, theol, and OSL activities. $25/ year. OSL Ofc PO Box 780909 San Antonio TX 78278-0909 (877) 992-5222 *E-mail:* OSL@satx.rr.com *Web:* www.orderofstluke.org (10).

Timelines, the online newsletter/blog of EWHP, the Episcopal Women's History Project. Regular meetings every other month by conference calls. Annual Meeting once a year. Participate in the Tri-History

conference as well as our own conferences. *Pres*
The Rev Dr Matilda EG Dunn c/o Christoph Keller
Jr Library General Theological Seminary 440 W
21st St New York NY 10011 (212) 243-5150 *E-mail:*
episcopalwomenshistory@gmail.com. (4)

Transfiguration Quarterly The 495 Albion Ave
Cincinnati OH 45246 Community of Transfig
E-mail: CTSISTERS@aol.com. (4).

Virginia Seminary Journal The Virginia Theological
Seminary in Virginia 3737 Seminary Rd Alexandria
VA 22304 (703) 461-1764 Contact: Curtis Prather
E-mail: cprather@vts.edu.

DIOCESAN PERIODICALS

Alabama *The Alabama Episcopalian* Rev D Drachlis
521 N 20th St Birmingham AL 35203 (205) 715-2060
E-mail: ddrachlis@dioala.org.

Albany *The Albany Episcopalian* George Marshall
580 Burton Rd Greenwich NY 12834 (518) 692-3350
x519 *E-mail:* taeeditor@albanydiocese.org.

Arizona *Az Episcopalian* Nicole Krug 114 West
Roosevelt Phoenix AZ 85003 (602) 254-0976.

Arkansas *The Arkansas Episcopalian* Jaman
Matthews PO Box 164668 Little Rock AR
72216-4668 (501) 372-2168 *E-mail:* jmatthews@
episcopalarkansas.org.

Atlanta *Pathways* Nan Ross Diocese of Atlanta
2744 Peachtree St Atlanta GA 30305 (800) 537-6743
E-mail: news@episcopalatlanta.org *E-Newsletter:*
"Connecting".

California *Pacific Church News* 1055 Taylor St San
Francisco CA 94108 (415) 869-7820 Web: diocal.
org/pcn/welcome.

Central Florida *Central Florida Episcopalian* Joe
Thoma 1017 E Robinson St Orlando FL 32801 (407)
423-3567 *E-mail:* jthoma@cfdiocese.org.

Central Gulf Coast *The Coastline E-mail:*
communications@diocgc.org.

Central New York *The E-Messenger Editor* Meredith
K Sanderson 1020 7th North St Liverpool NY 13088
(315) 474-6596 *E-mail:* messenger@cnyepiscopal.
org Published Thursday of each month.

Central Pennsylvania *Diocesan Digest* Linda
Arguedas PO Box 11937 Harrisburg PA 17108 (717)
236-5959 *E-mail:* larguedas@diocesecpa.org.

Chicago *Thrive Magazine.*

Colombia Boletín Anglicano de Colombia Diócesis
de Colombia Apartado Aereo 52964 Bogotá 2
CO(571) 288-3187 (571) 288-3167 *E-mail:* iec@
iglesiaepiscopal.org.co.

Colorado *Colorado Episcopalian* Rebecca Jones
1300 Washington St Denver CO 80203-2008 (303)
837-1173 *E-mail:* cenews@coloradodiocese.org.

Connecticut *Crux* Karin Hamilton 1335 Asylum
Ave Hartford CT 06105 (860) 233-4481 *E-mail:*
editor@ctdiocese.org.

Dallas *Esprit* 1630 N Garrett Ave. Dallas TX 75206-
7702 (214) 826-8310 *E-mail:* kdurnan@edod.org.

Delaware *Delaware Communion* Jen Mason 913
Wilson Road Wilmington DE 19803 (302) 256-0374
E-mail: communion@comcast.net.

Dominican Republic *Episcopax* Apartado Postal
764 Santo Domingo Dominican Republic (809) 686-
7493 *E-mail:* iglepidom@codetel.net.do.

East Tennessee *The East Tennessee Episcopalian*
Vikki Myers 814 Episcopal School Way Knoxville TN
37932 (865) 966-2110 *E-mail:* editor@etdiocese.net.

Eastern Oregon *Oregon Trail Evangelist* Angela
Gorham 1104 Church St PO Box 236 Cove OR
97824 (541) 568-4514 *E-mail:* communication@
episdioeo.org.

Easton *The Eastern Shore Episcopalian* Maggie
Michand 314 North St Easton MD 21601 (410) 822-
1919 *E-mail:* maggie@dioceseofeaston.org.

Ecuador Central *Camino Episcopal* Editor Box 17-
11-6165 Quito EQ Ecuador (011) 593-2522 *E-mail:*
ecuacen@uio.satnet.net.

El Camino Real *The Good News Along the King's
Highway* Elrond G Lawrence PO Box 689 Salinas
CA 93902 (831) 394-4465 *E-mail:* Elrond@
realepiscopal.org

Europe *The Convocation Newsletter* Raymond
Hodgkinson *E-mail:* raymond.hodgkinson@
messer-cw.de.

Florida **Connect** *(bi-montly e-news),* **Engage**
(quarterly e-news), **The Diocesan Magazine** (printed
twice a year) Mary Hamilton 325 N Market St
Jacksonville FL 32204 (904) 356-1328. *E-mail:*
mhamilton@diocesefl.org

Fond du Lac *The Clarion* Beth Jacobson 1051 N
Lyndale Dr Ste 1B Appleton WI 54914 *E-mail:*
editor@diofdl.org.

Fort Worth *Common Purpose* (newsletter) *Beauty &
Bravery* (blog)

Georgia *From the Field* newsandevents@
gaepiscopal.org, weekly electronic newsletter.

Haiti *Ecclesia* Rev Jean-Elie Charles Boite Postale
1309 Port-au-Prince HT Haiti (509) 257-1624
epihaiti@hotmail.com.

Hawaii *e-Chronicle* (digital newspaper), published
bi-monthly.

Honduras *La Voz Anglicana* The Rev Vaike Marika
Madisson PO Box 586 San Pedro Sula Honduras
(504) 556-6155 vaikemm@yahoo.com.mx.

Honduras *Episconotas* The Rev Vaike Marika
Madisson PO Box 586 San Pedro Sula Honduras tel
(504) 556-6155 *E-mail:* vaikemm@yahoo.com.mx.

Idaho *The Idaho Episcopalian* Jes Benson 1858 W
Judith Ln Boise ID 83705 (208) 345-4440.

Indianapolis *Go Forth* Kathy Copas 1100 W 42nd St Indianapolis IN 46208 (317) 926-5454 *E-mail:* kathycopas@aol.com.

Iowa *Iowa Connections* Dave Mable 225 37th St Des Moines IA 50312-4305 (515) 277-6165 *E-mail:* dmable@iowaepiscopal.org

Kansas *The Harvest* Melodie Woerman 835 SW Polk St Topeka KS 66612 (785) 235-9255 *E-mail:* mwoerman@episcopal-ks.org.

Kentucky *Kentucky ENews* (online) Brian Kinnaman 425 S 2nd St Louisville KY 40202 (502) 584-7148 *E-mail:* bkinnaman@episcopalky.org.

Long Island *Soundings* 36 Cathedral Ave Garden City NY 11530 (516) 248-4800 x150 *Editor* The Rev Can Shawn P Duncan *E-mail:* sduncan@dioceseli.org.

Los Angeles *The Episcopal News* Janet Kawamoto Box 512164 Los Angeles CA 90051-0164 (213) 482-2040 *E-mail:* editor@ladiocese.org.

Los Angeles *The Angelus* the Clergy Newsletter Rev Pat McCaughan Box 512164 Los Angeles CA 90051-0164 (213) 482-2040 *E-mail:* revpat@stgeorgeparish.org.

Louisiana *Churchwork* 1623 Seventh St New Orleans LA 70115 (504) 895-6634.

Maine Diocesan Communications *Twitter:* www.twitter.com/episcopalmaine; www.twitter.com/bishop_maine; *Facebook:* www.facebook.com/episcopalmaine; *Blog:* "Round Maine with Bishop Lane" www.roundmaine.org; *Young People:* www.bishopswood.org, maineyouth.org, facebook.com/maineepiscopalchristianed; *Deacons:* deaconsbench.wordpress.com Susie Blanchard; sblanchard@stgeorgesyorkharbor.org.

Maine *The New Northeast (NNE)* www.www.newnortheast.me Heidi Shott (207) 772-1953 x126; hshott@episcopalmaine.org.

Maryland *Maryland Church News* Sharon Tillman 4 E University Pkwy Baltimore MD 21218 (410) 467-1399 *E-mail:* MCN@episcopalmaryland.org.

Maryland *Maryland Episcopalian* Sharon Tillman 4 E University Pkwy Baltimore MD 21218 (410) 467-1399 *E-mail:* MCN@episcopalmaryland.org.

Massachusetts *E-news* Tracy Sukraw 138 Tremont Street Boston MA 02111 (617) 482-5800 *E-mail:* news@diomass.org

Michigan *The Record Editor* Rick Schulte 4800 Woodward Ave Detroit MI 48201 (313) 833-4425 *E-mail:* rschulte@edomi.org. The Record is a quarterly magazine of the diocese.

Mississippi *The Mississippi Episcopalian* The Rev Scott Lenoir PO Box 23107 Jackson 39225 (601) 948-5954 *E-mail:* slenoir1@gmail.com.

Missouri *Seek News* Beth Felice 1210 Locust St St Louis MO 63103 (314) 231-1220 *E-mail:* bfelice@diocesemo.org.

Missouri *iSeek Newsletter* via email or online Beth Felice 1210 Locust St St Louis MO 63103 (314) 231-1220 *E-mail:* bfelice@diocesemo.org.

Missouri *The Bishop's Column Monthly News* Beth Felice 1210 Locust St St Louis MO 63103 (314) 231-1220 *E-mail:* bfelice@diocesemo.org.

Missouri *"Seeking Our Past, Creating Our Future: For Congregations Exploring Their History with Racism"* Beth Felice 1210 Locust St St Louis MO 63103 (314) 231-1220 *E-mail:* bfelice@diocesemo.org. A resource from the Dismantling Racism Commission of the Episcopal Diocese of Missouri.

Navajoland *Navajoland News* Editor PO Box 720 Farmington NM 87499 (505) 327-7549 *E-mail:* rhsnyder@ec-n.org.

Nevada *Nevada Diocesan Journal* 9480 S Eastern Ave Ste 236 Las Vegas NV 89123 (702) 737-9190 *E-mail:* michelle@episcopalnevada.org.

New Hampshire *News from the Vine* Laura Simoes 63 Green St Concord NH 03301-4243 *E-mail:* lsimoes@nhepiscopal.org

New Hampshire *E-News* Laura Simoes 63 Green St Concord NH 03301-4243 (603) 224-1914 *E-mail:* enews@nhepiscopal.org.

New York *Episcopal New Yorker* Nicholas Richardson 1047 Amsterdam Ave NY NY 10025 (212) 932-7352 *E-mail:* eny@dioceseny.org.

Newark *The Voice* 31 Mulberry Newark NJ 07102 (973) 430-9907 *E-mail:* nnicholson@dioceseofnewark.org.

North Carolina *The North Carolina Disciple* 200 W Morgan St Ste 300 Raleigh NC 27601 (919) 834-7474.

North Dakota *The Sheaf* 3600 S 25th St Fargo ND 58104 (701) 235-6688 *E-mail:* dioceseND@cableone.net.

Northern Indiana *Around Our Diocese* Editor 117 N Lafayette Blvd South Bend IN 46601 (574) 233-6489 *E-mail:* info@ednin.org.

Northern Michigan *The Church in Hiawathaland* 131 East Ridge St Marquette MI 49855 (906) 228-7160 *E-mail:* diocese@upepiscopal.org.

Northwestern Pennsylvania *The Forward* Julien Goulet 6 W Sixth St Erie PA 16501 (814) 456-4203 *E-mail:* jgoulet@dionwpa.org.

Ohio *ChurchLife!* 2230 Euclid Ave Cleveland OH 44115 (216) 771-4815 *E-mail:* churchlife@dohio.org.

Oregon *In Conversation* JT Quanbeck 11800 SW Military Ln Portland OR 97219 (503) 636-5613 *E-mail:* jtq@diocese-oregon.org.

Pennsylvania *Episcopal News Weekly* A weekly e-mail publication of the Diocese of Pennsylvania's Communication Network. Submit articles to Henry Carnes *E-mail:* henryc@diopa.org.

Pittsburgh *Grace Happens* e-newsletter, Andy Muhl c/o Episcopal Diocese of Pittsburgh 325 Oliver Avenue, Suite 300, Pittsburgh, PA 15222 *E-mail:* asmuhl@episcopalpgh.org.

Puerto Rico CREDO ONLINE: www.episcopalpr.org.

Rhode Island *Risen Ben* Sibielski 275 N Main Providence RI 02903 (401) 274-4500 *E-mail:* risen@episcopalri.org.

Rio Grande *Together* 6400 Coors Blvd NW Albuquerque NM 87120 (505) 881-0636 *E-mail:* together@dioceserg.org.

Rochester *E-Newsletter*

San Diego *The Messenger* Hannah Wilder 2083 Sunset Cliffs Blvd San Diego CA 92107 (619) 481-5456 *E-mail:* hwilder@edsd.org.

South Dakota *South Dakota Church News* Mary Armin 500 S Main Ave Sioux Falls SD 57104-6814 (605) 338-9751 *E-mail:* office.diocese@midconetwork.com.

Southeast Florida *The Net; Grapevine* Altoria White 525 NE 15 St Miami FL 33132 (305) 373-0881 *E-mail* altoria@diosef.org.

Southern Ohio *Connections* Julie Murray 412 Sycamore St Cincinnati OH 45202 (800) 582-1712 x150 *E-mail:* jmurray@diosohio.org.

Southwest Florida *Bridges* eNewsletter Garland Pollard 8005 25th St E Parrish FL 34219 (941) 556-0315 *E-mail:* gpollard@episcopalswfl.org.

Southwest Florida *Southern Cross* magazine of the Diocese of Southwest Florida Garland Pollard 8005 25th St E Parrish FL 34219 (941) 556-0315 *E-mail:* gpollard@episcopalswfl.org.

Southwestern Virginia *One in Mission* PO Box 2279 Roanoke VA 24009-2279 (540) 342-6797 *E-mail:* kgarcia@dioswva.org

Spokane www.spokanediocese.org Cate Wetherald catew@spokanediocese.org

Springfield *Springfield Current* Jason Cerezo 821 S Second St Springfield IL 62704 (217) 525-1876 *E-mail:* editor@episcopalspringfield.org.

Taiwan *Taiwan Episc Ch News (Chinese) and Friendship (Eng)* Editor Ln 105 Hangchow S Rd Sec 1 Taipei Taiwan 10060 2-2341-1265 *E-mail:* skhtpe@ms12.hinet.net.

Tennessee *Connections* Editor 3700 Woodmont Blvd Nashville TN 37215 (615) 251-3322 *E-mail:* chendrix@edtn.org.

Texas *Diolog Magazine* (quarterly) Carol Barnwell 1225 Texas Ave Houston TX 77002 (713) 520-6444 *E-mail:* cbarnwell@epicenter.org.

Upper South Carolina *E~DUSC* 1115 Marion St Columbia SC 29201 (803) 771-7800.

Utah *Connections* enewsletter Craig Wirth 75 S 200 E Salt Lake City UT 84111-2147 (800) 343-4756

E-mail: cwirth@episcopal-ut.org.

Vermont *E-Mountain News* 5 Rock Point Rd Burlington VT 05408 (802) 863-3431 *E-mail:* adminasst@dioceseofvermont.org.

Virginia *Virginia Episcopalian* Editor A Michel. 110 W Franklin St Richmond VA 23220 (804) 643-8451 *Web:* www.thediocese.net.

West Missouri *Spirit* magazine *Comm Dir* Mr. Gary Allman 420 W 14th St Kansas City MO 64105 (816) 471-6161 *E-mail:* communications@diowestmo.org

West Tennessee *The Diocesan Communicator* enewsletter 692 Poplar Ave Memphis TN 38105 (901) 526-0023 *E-mail:* lstone@episwtn.org. Published every other Monday and posted to website.

West Texas *The Church News* Laura Shaver Box 6885 San Antonio TX 78209 (210) 824-5387 *E-mail:* laura.shaver@dwtx.org.

West Texas *Reflections* Marjorie George Box 6885 San Antonio TX 78209 (210) 824-5387 *E-mail:* marjorie.george@dwtx.org.

West Virginia *Dayspring* Linda Comins 28 Springhaven Rd Wheeling WV 26003 (304) 243-1329 *E-mail:* lcomins@frontier.com.

Western Kansas *Prairie Spirit* Toni Cottrell 1 North Main Ste 502 Hutchinson KS 67501 (620) 669-0006 *E-mail:* tec.wks2011@gmail.com.

Western Louisiana *Alive!* Robert Harwell 4321 Youree Drive Ste 400 Shreveport LA 71105 (318) 868-2303 *E-mail:* robertharwell@centurytel.net.

Western Massachusetts *Abundant Times* Victoria Ix 37 Chestnut St Springfield MA 01103-1787 (413) 737-4786 x124 *Fax:* (413) 746-9873 *E-Mail:* communications@diocesewma.org.

Western New York *Postings* e-newsletter A Brown 1064 Brighton Rd Tonawanda NY 14150 (716) 881-0660 alicebrown@episcopalwny.org.

Western North Carolina *The Highland Episcopalian* H Eugene Willard PO Box 2878 Morganton NC 28680-2878 (828) 432-5665 *E-mail:* thewillardgroup@earthlink.net.

Wyoming *The Spirit of Wyoming* 123 S Durbin St Casper WY 82601 (307) 265-5200 *E-mail:* Kate@wyomingdiocese.org.

CHURCH VIDEO AND FILM

Cathedral Films and Video Rev JL Friedrich 4685 Taylor Ave NE Bainbridge Island WA 98110 *E-mail:* frjimfr@earthlink.net.

The Episcopal Church, Office of Communication Anne Rudig *Dir of Communication* 815 Second Ave New York NY 10017 (212) 922-5385 *E-mail:* arudig@episcopalchurch.org *Web:* www.episcopalchurch.org.

Episcopal Media Center Peter Wallace *Pres & Exec Prod* Thomas Keuneke *CFO* 2715 Peachtree

Rd NE Atlanta GA 30305 (800) 229-3788 *Fax:* (404) 815-0495 *E-mail:* thk@episcopalmedia.org *Web:* www.episcopalonline.org.

Trinity Television/New Media 74 Trinity Pl 4th flr New York NY 10006 (212) 602-0767 *Fax:* (212) 602-0770 *E-mail:* info@trinitywallstreet.org *Web:* www.trinitywallstreet.org.

EPISCOPAL PUBLISHERS

Church Publishing Incorporated *(Morehouse Publishing, Church Publishing)* Davis Perkins, Publisher, 19 East 34th St New York NY 10016 (800) 223-6602 *Fax:* (212) 779-3392 *E-mail:* churchpublishing@cpg.org *Web:* www.churchpublishing.org.

Forward Movement The Rev Canon Scott Gunn *Exec Dir* 412 Sycamore St Cincinnati OH 45202 (800) 543-1813 *E-Mail:* orders@forwardmovement.org *Web:* www.forwardmovement.org.

LeaderResources Delbert Glover PO Box 302 Leeds MA 01053-0302 (800) 941-2218 (413) 320-4773 *E-mail:* Del@LeaderResources.org *Web:* www.leaderresources.org.

St Mark's Press 8021 W 21 St Wichita KS 67205 (800) 365-0439 *E-mail:* stmarkspress@gmail.com *Web:* www.stmarkspress.net.

NATIONAL ALTAR GUILD ASSOCIATION

Formed in 1921. www.nationalaltarguildassociation.org *Pres* Lynn V Hendricks *E-mail:* Lvhend@mindspring.com *1st VP* Dianne Walters *E-Mail:* dirdh68@gmail.com David Hawley-Lowry *E-mail:* Davidh@stmarksgr.org; *Sec* Donna Anderson *E-mail:* Anglican312@msn.com; *Treas* Frances Elmore *E-mail:* djmfle@aol.com. Meets every 3 years at Gen Conv with program and election of officers. Natl Assn mbrshp is $35/year for parishes and individuals; $65/year for diocese. Member incl quarterly issues of newsletter, *Epistle.*

Provincial Presidents
Province I:
Province II: Jane Mercer *E-mail:* jpmercer@comcast.net
Province III: Sharon Nachman *E-mail:* sharon-snachman@gmail.com
Province IV: Sarah Hill *E-mail:* sarahhill.fl@gmail.com
Province V: David Hawley-Lowry *E-mail:* Davidh@stmarksgr.org
Province VI: Marcia Himes: *E-mail:* rthimes@wyoming.com
Province VII: Jacqueline Frahm *E-mail:* Rafpc@grandecom.net
Province VIII: Albe Larsen *E-mail:* Amlarsen@coastside.net

Altar Guild Diocesan Presidents
AL Martha Noble 2905 Clydebank Cir Birmingham AL 35242

AT Diocesan Altar Guild 2744 Peachtree Rd Atlanta GA 30305

AZ Constance Castillo 10106 West Signal Butte Circle Sun City AZ 85373

CA Jane Phillips 2211 Latham St #302 Mountain View, CA 94040

CFL Judy Henderson 1978 Red Bud Circle NW, Palm Bay FL 32907

CGC Ceil Lacey 403 Holmes Blvd NW Ft Walton Beach FL 32548-4001

CT Jean Kelsey 21 Fairview St Manchester CT 06040

E Barry Passano PO Box 27 Oxford MD 21654

ECR Jane Pomeroy 1496 Jupiter Court Milpitas CA 95035

ETN Joyce Collom 393 Deep Draw Dr Crossville TN 38555

FL Janet Robinson 2150 Spencer Rd Orange Park FL 32073

FTW Susan Yarger 2617 Tillman Dr Arlington TX 76006

HI Rosella Newell 229 Queen Emma Sq Honolulu HI 96813

IA Dioc of Iowa 225 37th St. Des Moines, IA 50312

LA Carolyn Douglas Box 991 St Francisville LA 70775

LI Margaret Ripton 242-315 1st Ave Douglaston NY 11362

LOSA Bea Floyd Box 512164 Los Angeles CA 90051-0164 (213) 482-2040

MA Diane Grondin 18 Hilldale Rd South Weymouth MA 02190

ME Vicki Wiederkehr 143 State St Portland ME 04101

MI Novie Duffy PO Box 430357 Pontiac MI 48343

MIL Jane Henning 2006 Chadbourne Madison WI 53726

MS Anne Heidelberg 607 Parkwood Dr. Long Beach, MS 39560

NC Dioc of NC 200 W. Morgan St. Suite 300 Raleigh, NC 27601

NE Diocesan Altar Guild 109 18th St Omaha NE 68102

NH Sue Ingram PO Box 185 North Hampton NH 03862

NJ Sarah Page 80 W State St Trenton NJ 08618

NK Sr Suzanne Elizabeth CSJB Box 240 Mendham NJ 07945

NWPA Mary Blaine Prince 522 W Corydon St Bradford PA 16701

NWTX Paula Howbert 3803 Stanolind Dr Midland TX 79707

OK Mary Lu Jarvis 3820 S Hiwassee St Choctaw OK 73020

OL Sherry Garman PO Box 12126 Seattle WA 98102

OR Donna Anderson PO Box 1576 Roseburg, OR 97470

PA Dioc of PA 5421 Germantown Ave Philadelphia PA 19144

PGH Priscilla Castner 165 Summerlawn Dr Sewickley PA 15143

PI Dioc of Pittsburg/ Shelley Snyder 602 Danbury St. Pittsburg, PA 15214

Q Linda K Wells 218 Warrior Way Metamora IL 61548 Jean Quigg 13723 N Ivy Lake Rd Chillicothe IL 61523

RG Diocesan Altar Guild 4304 Carlisle Blvd NE Albuquerque NM 87107

RI Liz Crawley 275 N Main St. Providence, RI 02903

SAND Diocesan Altar Guild 840 Echo Park Ave Los Angeles CA 90026

SANJ Susan Ohanneson 41 Cedarwood Lane, Bakersfield, CA 93308

SWF/NORTH Sara Hill 1906 Carolina Ave NE St Petersburg FL 33703

SWF/SOUTH Carol Ann Brumbach 7086 Cedarhurst Dr Ft Myers FL 33901

TN Sue Hays 408 N Cameron Ct Hermitage TN 37076

TX Ellen Cook 2235 Broadlawn Dr. Houston, TX

USC Valerie Riley 81 Cannonade Court Irmo, SC 29063

VT Sarah Maynard 79 Green St St Johnsbury VT 05819

WLA Ginger Norvell 120 Harolyn Park Dr. Lafayette, LA 70503

WMA MA Worton 7 Leland Hill Rd South Graft on MA 01560

WMI David Hawley-Lowry 10312 Riley St. Zeeland, MI 49464

WMO The Rt Rev Barry Howe PO Box 413227 Kansas City MO 64141

WNC Lois Lynn 468 Vision Rd Canton NC 28716

WNY Janice Beam 134 Bridle Path Williamsville NY 14221

WTN Ann McCormick 3071 Dumbarton Rd Memphis TN 38128

WTX Frances Schrader 4615 Duquesne Dr. San Antonio, TX 78229

WVA Holly Mitchell 5119 Brookside Dr Cross Lakes W VA 25313

EPISCOPAL CHURCH WOMEN

Board Officers
Website for national ECW: www.ecwnational. org; *Pres* Lisa H Towle 110 Dutchess Dr Cary NC 27513-4209 *Tel:* (919) 228-8329 *E-mail:* president@

ecwnational.org; *1st VP* Linda Guest 29 Hazelwood St Cranston RI 02910 *Tel:* (401) 781-3538 *E-mail:* firstvp@ecwnational.org; *2nd VP* Virginia (Ginger) Lief 310 Riverside Dr Apt 822 New York NY 10025-4123 *Tel:* (212) 662-3257 *E-mail:* secondvp@ ecwnational.org; *Sec* Patricia (Pat) Wellnitz PO Box 96 Rushville NE 69360 *Tel:* (308) 360-3234 *E-mail:* secretary@ecwnational.org; *Treas* Karen O Patterson PO Box 1866 Dade City, FL 33526 *Tel:* (352) 567-6254 *E-mail:* treasurer@ecwnational.org.

Board Members-at-Large
Multimedia Mayra Brown Calle Santiago No 114 Gazcue Apartado 764 Santo Domingo Dominican Republic *Tel:* (829) 542-3970 *E-Mail:* multimedia@ ecwnational.org. *Social Justice* Beblon G Parks 8210 Trabue Rd Richmond, VA 23235 *Tel:* (804) 683-2802 *E-mail:* socialjustice@ecwnational.org.

Board Provincial Representatives
I–Gloria Rogers 1375 Paradise Ave Hamden CT 06514 *Tel:* (203) 868-1151 *E-mail:* province1@ ecwnational.org; *II*–The Rev Jennifer Kenna PO Box 354 Cape Vincent NY 13618 *Tel:* (315) 767-1971 *E-mail:* province2@ecwnational.org; *III*–Margaret H Gordon 602 Sonata Way Silver Spring MD 20901 *Tel:* (301) 681-5262 E-*mail:* province3@ecwnational.org; *IV*–Mary Beth Welch 86 Huckleberry Rd Ellisville, MS 39437 *Tel:* (601) 763-5200 *E-mail:* province4@ ecwnational.org; *V*–Connie Ott 7995 Shagbark Cir Cross Plains WI 53528 *Tel:* (608) 798-3688 *E-mail:* province5@ecwnational.org; *VI*– Vacant; *VII*–Jackie Meeks 3816 Walton Ave Ft Worth TX 76133 *Tel:* (817) 939-6693 *E-mail:* province7@ ecwnational.org; *VIII*–Evita Krislock 14711 E 15th Ave Spokane Valley WA 99037 *Tel:* (509) 922-0180 *E-mail:* province8@ecwnational.org; *IX*–Juditta Ellis Steenenkoraal 102-B Willemstad Curacao (part of Diocese of Venezuela) *Tel:* +5999-690-4016 *E-mail:* province9@ecwnational.org.

Provincial Presidents
I–Delores M Alleyne *E-Mail:* deloresalleyne@aol. com; *II*–Pamela Stewart *E-Mail:* pamelastewart733@ gmail.com; *III*–Rose M. Longmire *E-Mail:* roselongmire@hotmail.com; *IV*–Dr Pat Rutenberg *E-Mail:* pbrutenberg@gmail.com; *V*–Karen Birr *E-Mail:* ksbirr@charter.net; *VI*–Sandra Squires *E-Mail:* sksquires@cox.net; *VII*–Joann Rachele *E-Mail:* joannrachele@msn.com; *VIII*–Louise Aloy *E-Mail:* louisealoy63@gmail.com; *IX*–Juditta Ellis *E-Mail:* jellis@holiday-beach.com.

Diocesan Presidents/Contacts: Province I
Connecticut (CT)–Valzie Peterkin *Pres* 518 Scenic Rd Orange CT 06477 *Tel:* (203) 877-4701 *E-mail:* valziep@gmail.com.

Maine (ME)–Barbi Tinder *Contact* 149 Butters Hill Rd Stoneham ME 04231 *Tel:* (207) 928-3603 *E-mail:* B5tinder@gmail.com.

Massachusetts (MA)–Elizabeth Murray *Pres* 102 Cabot St Newton MA 02458 *Tel:* (617) 332-5939 *E-mail:* eg.murray@verizon.net.

New Hampshire (NH)–Marjorie Burke *Contact* 47 Merrill Rd Weare NH 03281 *Tel:* (603) 529-7792 *E-mail:* mmburke2@comcast.net.

Rhode Island (RI)–Margaret E Noel *Pres* 617 Forbes St Riverside RI 02915-1220 *Tel:* (401) 935-7936 *E-mail:* Margaret_e_noel@hotmail.com.

Vermont (VT)–Winifred Grace *Contact* PO Box 1132 Middletown Springs VT 05757 *Tel:* (802) 235-2221 *E-mail:* wingrace@vermontel.net.

Western Massachusetts (WMA)–Susan Howland *Pres* 132 Osgood Rd Charlton MA 01507 *Tel:* (508) 248-6112 *E-mail:* howlands@charter.net.

Diocesan Presidents/Contacts: Province II
Albany (A)–Mary Young *Contact* 14640 Rte 22 New Lebanon NY 12125 *Tel:* (518) 794-7538 *E-mail:* mar049@yahoo.com.

Central New York (CNY)–Jennifer Kenna *Contact* PO Box 354 Cape Vincent NY 13618 *Tel:* (315) 767-1971 *E-mail:* jenken372@gmail.com.

Europe (EUR)–Kristi Strzyzewski *Contact* c/o Emmanuel Church 3 Rue de Monthoux CH 12-1 Geneva Switzerland *E-mail:* mstrzyzewski@bluewin.ch.

Haiti (Hai)–Gloria Orelien *Pres* Bureau Diocesan PO Box 1309 Port-au-Prince Haiti WI 26165 *Tel:* 011-340-770-2235 *E-mail:* gloriaorelien@hotmail.com.

Long Island (LI)–June S Gerbracht *Pres* 3155 Hickory St Wantagh NY 11793 *Tel:* (516) 785-5807 *E-mail:* junegerbracht@gmail.com.

New Jersey (NJ)–Carol Council *Pres* 7 Kim Court Piscataway NJ 08854 *Tel:* (732) 752-5734 *E-mail;* council@chubb.com.

New York (NY)–Dianne Roberts *Pres* 5700 Arlington Ave Apt 15X Riverdale NY 10471 *Tel:* (718) 601-0872 *E-mail:* drobertslaw@gmail.com.

Newark (Nk)–Doris Mardirosian *Contact* 7113 Cenrose Cir Westwood NJ 07675 *Tel:* (201) 664-4548.

Rochester (Roch)– No Contact.

Virgin Islands (VI)–Ura Gosha *Pres* PO Box 6093 St Thomas VI 00804 *Tel:* 011-340-776-2235 *E-mail:* gosha_ura@yahoo.com.

Western New York (WNY)– No Contact.

Diocesan Presidents/Contacts: Province III
Bethlehem–Dorothy Shaw *Pres* 46 Ole Coach Rd Tunkhannock PA 18657 *Tel:* (570) 240-1049 *E-mail:* flamingo10@frontier.com.

Central Pennsylvania (CPA)–Shirley Wagner *Pres* 2052 Weeping Willow Ln Mount Joy PA 17552 *Tel:* (717) 653-6783 *E-mail:* srw2052@centurylink.net.

Delaware (DE)–Beth Fitzpatrick *Pres* 1900 Fairfield Dr Wilmington DE 19810 *Tel:* (302) 529-1766 *E-mail:* gr8tart@aol.com.

Easton (E)–Ramona Eller *Pres* 2749 Old Country Rd Newark DE 19702 *Tel:* (302) 834-3074 *E-mail:* eller1214@netzero.net.

Maryland (MD)–Dorothy (Dottie) Arthur *Pres* 2001 Parsonage Rd Parkton MD 21120 *Tel:* (410) 357-8857 *E-mail:* reparthur@gmail.com.

Northwestern Pennsylvania (NWPA)–Enid Bishop *Pres* 4210 Davison Ave Apt 306 Erie PA 16504 *E-mail:* tgreene@psu.edu.

Pennsylvania (PA)–Shirley Smith *Presider* 2237 Charles St Glenside PA 19038 *Tel:* (215) 887-9448 *E-mail:* granny7sm@gmail.com.

Pittsburgh (Pgh)–Betty Duckstein *Pres* 834 Washington Ave Carnegie PA 15106 *Tel:* (412) 498-5277 *E-mail:* Bette520@msn.com.

Southern Virginia (SV)–Nancy Sands *Pres* 610 Mountain Cross Rd Apt C1 Danville VA 24540 *Tel:* (434) 836-1466 *E-mail:* beachpeach7@hotmail.com.

Southwestern Virginia (SwV)–Jackallen (Jackie) Arthur *Pres* 1758 Timberlake Dr Lynchburg VA 24502 *Tel:* (434) 444-1102 *E-mail:* jackallena@aol.com.

Virginia (VA)–Jodie Pully *Pres* 7661 Yarmouth Dr Richmond VA 23225 *Tel:* (804) 320-1033 *E-mail:* jodiepully@veizon.net.

Washington (W)–Deanne R Samuels *Pres* 122 College Station Dr Upper Marlboro MD 20774 *Tel:* (301) 792-2019 *E-mail:* deanne005@yahoo.com.

West Virginia (WV)–Becki Krzywdik PO Box 526 Wellsburg WV 26070 *Tel:* (304) 737-2886 *E-mail:* bkrzywdik@msn.com.

Diocesan Presidents/Contacts: Province IV
Alabama (AL)–Andrea Peacock *Pres* 1892 Cathy Cir Alexander City AL 35010 *Tel:* (256) 329-0667 *E-mail:* andreapeacock60@gmail.com.

Atlanta (At)–Dr Phyllis E Smith *Pres* 1111 Strawberry Ln Ellenwood GA 30294 *Tel:* (404) 988-6154 *E-mail:* teachbio65@gmail.com.

Central Florida (CF)–Winsome Stern *Pres* 2880 SW 162nd Ln Ocala FL 34473 *Tel:* (352) 454-9090 *E-mail:* winsomestern@yahoo.com.

Central Gulf Coast (CGC)–Becky Taylor-Scott *Pres* 222 Prestwick Dr Dothan AL 36305 *Tel:* (903) 571-0652 *E-mail:* bekatay@me.com.

East Carolina (EC)–Ginger Jacocks *Pres* 304 Shoreline Dr Cedar Point NC 28584 *Tel:* (252) 393-8083 *E-mail:* jacocks@ec.rr.com.

East Tennessee (ETN)–Lynn Spires *Pres* 124 Clower Rd Kingston TN 37763 *Tel:* (865) 376-1462 *E-mail:* lspires49@aol.com.

Florida (FL)–Linda Wilcox *Pres* 4125 NW 67th Ter Gainesville, FL 32606 *Tel:* (352) 213-1151 *E-mail:* joyfullyurs@earthlink.net.

Georgia (GA)–Beth Mithen *Pres* 248 Mills Rd Bainbridge GA 39817 *Tel:* (229) 416-5025 *E-mail:* bethmithen@gmail.com.

Kentucky (KY)– No Contact.

Lexington (Lex)–Lisa Edwards *Pres* 22 Greenbriar Ave Ft Mitchell KY 41017 *Tel:* (859) 391-5452 *E-mail:* lisaedwards102@gmail.com.

Louisiana (LA)–Laurel McCartney *Pres* 1000 Buckingham Dr Slidell LA 70460 *Tel:* (985) 390-9041 *E-mail:* lmcartney@bellsouth.net.

Mississippi (MS)–Lindsey Richard *Pres* 984 Kaimuki Ct Diamondhead MS 39525 *Tel:* (228) 342-8764 *E-mail:* Lindsey.L.Lind@aol.com.

North Carolina (NC)–Mary B Gordon *Interim Pres* 1211 Watermark Ct High Point NC 27265 *Tel:* (336) 869-7642 *E-mail:* interimpresident@ecw-nc.org.

Episcopal Church in South Carolina–Jackie Robe *Contact* 4649 Fringetree Dr Murrell's Inlet SC 29576 *Tel:* (727) 992-2336 *E-mail:* jrobe18413@aol.com.

Southeast Florida (SeF)–Gloria H Clausell *Pres* 3520 NW 205th St Miami Gardens FL 33056 *Tel:* (305) 318-9657 *E-mail:* gnurse43@bellsouth.net.

Southwest Florida (SwF)–Lana J Fitzgerald *Pres* 300 S Collier Blvd Apt 602 Marco Island FL 34145 *Tel:* (239) 281-4963 *E-mail:* lfitzgerald@marcocable.com.

Tennessee (TN)–Jenny Ladefoged *Pres* 6268 Palomar Ct Nashville TN 37211 *Tel:* (310) 490-5505 *E-mail:* momladefoged@gmail.com.

Upper South Carolina (USC)–Whitney Evans *Pres* 2411Preston St Columbia SC 29205 *Tel:* (803) 576-0020 *E-mail:* upperscecwpresident@gmail.com.

West Tennessee (WTN)–Jean Arehart *Pres* 378 Fleets Hill Dr Cordova TN 38018 *Tel:* (901) 299-6061 *E-mail:* jeanarehart@gmail.com.

Western North Carolina (WNC)–Mary Ann Ransom *Pres* 170 Ransom Rd Lake Lure NC 28746 *Tel:* (828) 625-8338 *E-mail:* mransom1@bellsouth.net.

Diocesan Presidents/Contacts: Province V
Chicago (C)–Beth C Pett *Pres* 503 Cloverleaf Ct Naperville IL 60565 Naperville IL 60565 *E-mail:* president@ecwchicago.org.

Eastern Michigan (EMI)–Barb Meikle *Bishop's Office Contact* 924 N Niagara St Saginaw MI 48602 *Tel:* (989) 752-6020 *E-mail:* bmeikle@eastmich.org.

Eau Claire (EauC)–Debra Lorenze 2304 Country Club Ln Eau Claire WI 54701 *Tel:* (715) 839-7912 *E-mail:* lorenzes@charter.net.

Fond du Lac (FdL)– No Contact.

Indianapolis (Ind)–Janet Higbie *Co-Pres* 7851 Admirals Ct Indianapolis IN 46236 *Tel:* (317) 847-0657 *E-mail:* jlhigbie@gmail.com; Bev Ruebeck *Co-Pres* 10954 Windjammer Dr N Indianapolis IN 46256 *Tel:* (317) 490-3212 *E-mail:* beverlyruebeck@gmail.com.

Michigan (MI)–Darlene Williams *Chair* 15851 Hayden St Detroit MI 48223 *Tel:* (313) 515-0883 *E-mail:* darwills1@aol.com.

Milwaukee (Mil)–Connie Ott *Pres* 7995 Shagbark Cir Cross Plains WI 53528 *Tel:* (608) 798-3688 *E-mail:* cott@chorus.net.

Missouri (MO)–Cheryl Ward *Pres* 107 Watercrest Ct Wildwood MO 63040 *Tel:* (314) 753-6142 *E-mail:* forbeslit@sbcglobal.net.

Northern Indiana (NI)–Charlotte Strowhorn *Pres* 1033 Williams St Gary IN 46404 *Tel:* (219) 944-0620 *E-mail:* charlotte1033@sbcglobal.net.

Northern Michigan (NMI)–Teena Maki *Co-Contact* 470 US Hwy 141 Crystal Falls MI 49920 *Tel:* (906) 875-4020 *E-mail:* makifarm@up.net; Coralie Hambleton *Co-Contact* 603 High St Marquette MI 49855 *Tel:* (906) 869-2046 *E-mail:* cvhamblet@hotmail.com.

Ohio (OH)–Hilary Nerby *Pres* 10219 Andover Dr Twinsburg OH 44087 *Tel:* (330) 487-5633 *E-mail:* hilarynerby@gmail.com.

Southern Ohio (SO)–Kathy Mank *Pres* 9559 Kelly Dr Loveland OH 45140 *Tel:* (513) 560-2126 *E-mail:* kathymank@gmail.com.

Springfield (Sp)–Jan Goosens *Pres* 2400 Little Round Top Dr Edwardsville IL 62025 *Tel:* (618)-655-0326 *E-mail:* utospil@sbcglobal.net.

Western Michigan (WMI)–Janine S Dekker *Pres* 208 N Division St Spring Lake MI 49456 *Tel:* (616) 403-2750 *E-mail:* janine-dekker@yahoo.com.

Diocesan Presidents/Contacts: Province VI
Colorado–The Rev Twyla Zittle *Pres* 2902 Airport Rd Apt 123 Colorado Springs CO 80910 *Tel:* (719) 475-8627 *E-mail:* tjzittle@comcast.net.

Iowa– No Contact.

Minnesota–Susan Triebenbach *Contact* 185 Skillman Ave W Roseville MN 55113 *Tel:* (651) 788-9343 *E-mail:* sue9966@gmail.com.

Montana– No Contact.

Nebraska–Deacon Christine Grosh *Convener* 7921 N Hazelwood Dr Lincoln NE 68510-4335 *Tel:* (402) 468-3259 *E-mail:* cgrosh@windstream.net.

North Dakota– No Contact.

South Dakota–Diana Regan *Pres* 708 Sawyer St Lead SD 57754-2117 *Tel:* (605) 722-2718 *E-mail:* gmaregan@gmail.com.

Wyoming–Melissa Hyde *Pres* 720 W 47th St Casper WY 82601 *Tel:* (307) 267-8065 *E-mail:* mhyde1973@ gmail.com.

Diocesan Presidents/Contacts: Province VII

Arkansas–Wanda Dunwoody *Pres* 3803 North Hills Blvd AR 72116 *Tel:* (501) 412-3998 *E-mail:* ladywandadunwoody@hotmail.com.

Dallas– No Contact.

Fort Worth–Sandy Shockley *Pres* 830 Country Road 109 Hamilton TX 76531 *Tel:* (254) 386-4412 *E-mail:* dshock9510@aol.com.

Kansas–Daria Condon *Pres* 16105 Ness Rd Altamont KS 67330 *Tel:* (620) 784-2316 *E-mail:* daria_condon@hotmail.com.

Northwest Texas–Joann Rachele *Pres* PO Box 62711 San Angelo TX 76906 *Tel:* (325) 949-5601 *E-mail:* joannrachele@msn.com.

Oklahoma–Bebe Dotter *Pres* 8837 NW 119th St Oklahoma City OK 73162 *Tel:* (405) 760-4304 *E-mail:* labluv@cox.net.

Rio Grande–Cynthia Davis *Pres* 1122 Mariano Trail SW Albuquerque NM 87121 *Tel:* (505) 379-7327 *E-mail:* cdavis@CynthiaDavisAuthor.com.

Texas–Lisa Martin *Pres* 3312 Silk Oak Dr Austin TX 78748 *Tel:* (512) 431-7716 *E-mail:* dmartin12@ austin.rr.com.

West Missouri–Judy Turner *Pres* 1333 Sheridan Dr Joplin MO 64801 *Tel:* (417) 623-1464 *E-mail:* jannet@cableone.net.

West Texas–Jane Ahuero *Pres* 15027 Spring Mist San Antonio TX 78247 *Tel:* (210) 452-7713 *E-mail:* jmahuero@gmail.com.

Western Kansas–Lana Mederos *Pres* 2205 Dover Dr Hutchinson KS 67502 *Tel:* (620) 960-3254 *E-mail:* ecw.wks@gmail.com.

Western Louisiana–Suzanne Corley *Pres* 111 Circle Dr Pineville LA 71360 *Tel:* (318) 623-1331 *E-mail:* lovehimmore@peoplepc.com.

Diocesan Presidents/Contacts: Province VIII

Alaska–Pearl Chanar *Contact* 3137 W 35th Ave Anchorage AK 99517 *Tel:* (907) 306-3276 *E-mail:* pdchanar@gci.net.

Arizona–Kerry Jo Hanstein *Pres* 10109 W Manzanita Dr Sun City AZ 85373 *Tel:* (623) 262-2230 *E-mail:* kjhanstein@gmail.com

California–Stephanie McLead *Pres* 21 Turnberry Rd Half Moon Bay CA 94019-2604 *E-mail:* mordred1919@yahoo.com.

Eastern Oregon–c/o Episcopal Diocese of Eastern Oregon *Contact* PO Box 236 Cove OR 97824 *E-mail:* diocese@episdioeo.org.

El Camino Real–Wanda Bryan *Pres* 378 El Portal Way San Jose CA 95123 *Tel:* (408) 226-5593 *E-mail:*wandadon@earthink.net.

Hawaii–Louise Aloy *Pres* 1005 Laelae St Wailuku HI 96793-8403 *Tel:* (808) 264-9830 *E-mail:* louisealoy63@gmail.com.

Idaho–Stephanie Ledwich *Contact* 1858 W Judith Ln Boise ID 83705 *Tel:* (208) 345-4440 *E-mail:* sledwich@idahodiocese.org.

Los Angeles–Martha Estes *Pres* 874 Decatur Cir Claremont CA 91711 *Tel:* (909) 482-0936 *E-mail:* marthakestes@aol.com.

Navajoland–Madeline Sampson *Contact* PO Box 322 Bluff UT 84512 *Tel:* (435) 672-2206 *E-mail:* madelinesampson15@gmail.com.

Nevada–Margaret Bouzek *Pres* 22 Cygnus Way Sparks NV 89441 *Tel:* (775) 424-3767 *E-mail:* dbouzek@nybell.net.

Northern California–c/o Bishop's Staff Episcopal Diocese of Northern California *Contact* 350 University Ave Suite 280 Sacramento CA 95825 *Tel:* (916) 442-6918 *E-mail:* infor@norcalepiscopal.org.

Olympia– No Contact.

Oregon–Katherine Hunt *Pres* 130 Hansen Ln Eugene OR 97404 *Tel:* (541) 607-0106 *E-mail:* keehhunt@ gmail.com.

San Diego–Sally Nichols *Pres* 4315 Mount Hukee Ave San Diego CA 92117-4743 *Tel:* (858) 277-1872 *E-mail:* sanfhs@aol.com.

San Joaquin–Clara Disinger *Pres* 1245 B N Linden Ave Fresno CA 93728-2308 *Tel:* (559) 623-1178 *E-mail:* clara.disinger@sbcglobal.net.

Spokane–Evita Krislock *Convener* 14711 E 15th St Ave Spokane Valley WA 99037 *Tel:* (509) 922-0180 *E-mail:* evita@krislock.com.

Taiwan–Pai-Hui Hsu *Contact* *E-mail:* hph100@ yahoo.com.tw.

Utah–Linda Garner *Contact* 1614 34th St Ogden UT 84403 *Tel:* (801) 399-0428 *E-mail:* mydietcoke@ comcast.net.

Diocesan Presidents/Contacts: Province IX
Diocesis en la Nueva Provincia

Diocesis de Colombia– No Contact

Diocesis de Ecuador Central– No Contact

Diocesis de Ecuador Litoral–Elizabeth Calderón *Pres* Amarilis Fuentes 603 entre José Vicente Trujillo y la "D". Guayaquil *Tel:* 590-424-3050 *E-mail:* elicalsa_24@hotmail.com.

Diocesis de Honduras– No Contact

Diocesis de Puerto Rico–Zoraida Maldonado *Pres* Trujillo Alto 00976 Puerto Rico *Tel:* 787-969-6010 *E-mail:* zmaldonado@episcopalchurchpr.org.

Diocesis de la Republica Dominicana–Maritza Camacho *Pres* Calle Santiago, #114 Gazcue DN Santo Domingo Republica Dominicana *Tel:* 829-542-3970 *E-mail:* maritzacamacho05@yahoo.com.

Diocesis de Venezuela–Coromoto Jimenez *Pres* Avenida Caroni #100 Colinas de Bello Monte Municipio Baruta Estado Miranda Caracas Venezuela Apartado Postal 1050 *Tel:* 58 416- 623-1328 *Skype:* corosalazar *E-mail:* pragcjimenez04@gmail.com.

CLERGY INCREASE

Church Scholarship Society, The
Aids candidates for Holy Orders who are accountable to Bp of CT. *Pres* Rt Rev Ian T Douglas The Episcopal Church in CT 290 Pratt Street Box 52 Meriden CT 06450.

Episcopal Leadership Institute for Young Adults (ELIYA)
The leadership institute provides opportunities for young adults (18-30 years old) from all walks of life to explore and expand their own understandings and call to ministry both within and beyond the Episcopal Church. Through short term immersion experiences, small groups of young adults gain access to cutting age conversations around the church on topics most concerning them. Mentors assist them in discerning their own vocations and developing their leadership capacities. To learn about upcoming ELIYA events and existing resources please contact coordinator Jason Sierra, Officer for Young Adult Leadership and Vocations at the Episcopal Church Center at 646-316-0783 or jsierra@episcopalchurch. org. (*mailing address:* c/o Diocese of Olympia, 1551 10th Ave E Seattle, WA 98102)

Society for the Increase of the Ministry (SIM)
A national organization which has, since 1857, provided financial aid to Postulants and Candidates for Holy Orders. Inquiries to: Trinity Church 120 Sigourney Street Hartford CT 06105 (860) 233-1732. *Exec Dir* Thomas Moore III *E-mail:* info@simministry.org *Web:* www.simministry.org.

SUPPORT SYSTEMS FOR DEACONS

Association for Episcopal Deacons
Provides resources and advocacy for the diakonia of all believers; promotes and supports the Episcopal diaconate. For information: Dn Lorraine (Lori) Mills-Curran AED Executive Office PO Box 1516 Westborough MA 01581-6516 (508) 873-1881 *E-mail:* lori@episcopaldeacons.org *Web:* www.episcopaldeacons.org.

Fund for the Diaconate, The
The financial allowance for deacons who qualify. *Donations:* Rev. RA Franken, PO Box 2073, Frisco, CO 80443 *E-mail:* rfranken@stratraventure. com. *Grant Appl:* Rev Wm Jones 2208 Waters Mill Circle, Bon Air VA 23235 *E-mail:* deaconbill1989@verizon.net. *Other Fund Information:* Rev E Ross 113 N 18th St Omaha NE 68102 *E-mail:* ereimerross@hotmail.com. The Independent Auditor's Report ending July 31, 2014, may be accessed on our website at www.fundforddiaconate.org.

DEVOTIONAL ORGANIZATIONS

Anglican Fellowship of Prayer
International prayer ministry founded in 1958. Our mission: To serve the church by encouraging, facilitating, and promoting the understanding and discipline of prayer in the Anglican Communion. We especially emphasize the value of small group prayer and the parish as a center of prayer. See our website www.afp.org. *Pres* The Rev Dr John R Throop 39 East Church St Adams NY 13605 *E-mail:* drthroop123@gmail.com.

Brotherhood of St Andrew, Inc
A 132-yr-old min to men in the Episc/Angl Comm. Preparing men for Christian lay min through the establishment of Parish Chapters, providing Chapter training and calling for acceptance of the disciplines of prayer study and service. Organizational material and St Andrew's Cross pub. *Natl Pres* Robert J Dennis. *Inquiries to Central Office* Box 632 Ambridge PA 15003 (724) 266-5810 *Fax:* (724) 266-9577 *E-mail:* brotherhoodofstandrew@verizon.net *Web:* www.brothersandrew.net.

Confraternity of Blessed Sacrament of Body and Blood of Christ
Founded 1862 to honor Presence of our Lord in the Sacrament and to promote preparation and devotion to the Holy Eucharist as well as mutual and special intercession. *Sup* Rt Rev D Henderson *Sec* Very Rev W Willoughby III 224 E 34th St Savannah GA 31401-8104 *E-mail:* frwwiii@aol.com *Web:* www. sandiego.edu/~baber/CBS.

Contemplative Outreach, Ltd
An ecumenical spiritual network committed to renewing the contemplative dimension of the Gospel through the practice of Centering Prayer. *Exec Dir* Gail Fitzpatrick-Hopler 10 Park Place 2nd Fl Ste B Butler NJ 07405 (973) 838-3384 *Fax:* (973) 492-5795 *E-mail:* office@coutreach.org *Web:* www. contemplativeoutreach.org.

The Episcopal Community
We are a community of Episcopal women committed to living out our Baptismal Covenant as we nurture and support each other's spiritual journeys. Using the Rule of Benedict as our guide, we develop and follow a personal Rule of Life. While supporting our clergy, our parishes, and The Episcopal Church with our prayers and service, we also provide instruction

and mentoring in spiritual disciplines that foster spiritual growth and transformation. *National Pres* Nancy Young *National Office* Box 242, Sewanee TN 37375 *E-mail:* covenant@theepiscopalcomminity.org *Web:* www.theepiscopalcommunity.org.

Evelyn Underhill Association, Ltd

Established in the US in 1990 to honor, recognize, and carry on the legacy of this outstanding English woman whose "most valuable contribution to spiritual literature must surely be her conviction that the mystical life is not only open to a saintly few, but to anyone who cares to nurture it and weave it into everyday experience" (*LFF*). Events include Annual Quiet Day in June at Washington National Cathedral. Annual newsletter. *Contact:* Kathleen Henderson Staudt 9407 Spruce Tree Circle Bethesda MD 20814 (301) 588-9116 *E-mail:* evelynunderhill@gmail.com *Web:* www.evelynunderhill.org.

Fellowship of Contemplative Prayer

Founded in 1949 in England. Members follow a simple Rule stressing daily contemplation of the Word of God and an annual retreat. Clergy and laity. Milo G Coerper 7315 Brookville Rd Chevy Chase MD 20815 (301) 652-8635 *E-mail:* wmcoerp@verizon.net.

Fellowship of the Way of the Cross

A society of clergy who seek to live a holy integration of prayer and action in life and ministry. Share rule of life and prayer. Annual retreat and days of reflection. *Sup* Rev Michael DeVine, 47 Ruskin St Springfield MA 01108 *E-mail:* ap735@earthlink.net *VSup* Rev Dcn Christine Burton 15 Holmes St Westerly RI 02891 *E-mail:* chris5882@verizon.net *Sec/Treas* Rev William Loring 15 Pleasant Dr Danbury CT 06811 *E-mail:* fr.bill@comcast.net.

Guild of All Souls

Prayer guild founded in 1873. Seeks to promote the Church's teaching in regard to the Faithful Departed, to pray for the sick and the dead, to encourage Christian customs in the burial of the dead, and to urge celebration of the Mass at the time of burial according to the Propers appointed in the Book of Common Prayer. *Sup Gen* Rev Cn BEB Swain SSC *E-mail:* rector@resurrectionnyc.org *Sec Gen* Rev JA Lancaster SSC PO Box 721172 Berkley MI 48072 *E-mail:* jalssc1@gmail.com.

Guild of the Living Rosary

Guild of intercessors who use the traditional rosary. The Rev Cn David M Baumann SSC PO Box 303 Salem IL 62881 *E-mail:* guildlivingrosary@gmail.com *Web:* www.guildlivingrosary.com. *Facebook:* facebook.com/guildlivingrosary.

The Order of the Daughters of the King

An Order for lay or ordained women who commit to a lifelong program of prayer, svc, and evangelism, dedicated to strengthening the spiritual life of her parish and spreading Christ's Kingdom. *Pres* Susan O'Brien email: susanobrien@doknational.org *Natl*

Off Admin Mary Fletcher (x25) *Natl Off:* 101 Weatherstone Dr #870 Woodstock GA 30188-7007 (770) 517-8552 *E-mail:* DOK1885@doknational.org *mag: Royal Cross, Cross+Links Web:* www.doknational.org.

Order of the Thousandfold

Develops Christian spiritual resources by encouraging daily use of The Thousandfold Prayer. Prayer and tracts in 22 languages. *Dir* Rev DA Puckett PO Box 276 Graniteville SC 29829 *E-mail:* dap@gforcecable.com.

Society of King Charles the Martyr (SKCM) American Region

Founded 1894; American Region incorporated 2008. Promotes devotion to King Charles I and his martyrdom in defense of the Catholic faith in the Church of England and encourages commemorations of the anniversary of his martyrdom. Open to all Christians. Publishes semiannual *SKCM News* magazine and monthly e-mail *Communique.* Annual Mass at 11 am on the last Sat in January 2016, Church of the Holy Communion Charleston SC; same day and time in January 2017 at St Clement's Church Philadelphia PA.. Details, future events, and membership information at www. skcm-usa.org. *Pres* Cn William H Swatos Jr PhD *E-mail:* skcm@skcm-usa.org *Sec-Treas* David Lewis 1001 Wilson Blvd #405 Arlington VA 22209 *E-mail:* membership@skcm-usa.org.

Society of Mary

A devotional society within the Anglican Communion promoting the honor due the Blessed Virgin Mary. *Sup* The Rev John D Alexander *Sec* Dr Paul Cooper 415 Pennington-Titusville Rd Titusville, NJ 08560-2012 *Membership Adm* Lynne V Walker PO Box 930 Lorton VA 22079 *Web:* www.somamerica.org.

Society of the Companions of the Holy Cross, The

The Women of Episcopal Church devoted to intercession, thanksgiving, and simplicity. Summer conferences and retreats at Adelynrood with overnight accommodations for under 75 persons, and fall, winter, and spring day conference facilities for 30 or fewer persons. 46 Elm St Byfield MA 01922 (978) 462-6721 *Web:* www.Adelynrood.org. *Contact: Companion-in-Charge* Susan Butler.

PRAYER BOOK SOCIETIES

Bible and Common PB Soc of Episc Ch

Society for donation of Bibles, PB's, and Hymnals on request with bishop's endorsement. *Pres* Rt Rev Rodney R Michel *Sec* Rev Warren E Haynes *Mgr* Rev Dr David G Henritzy 815 Second Ave NY NY 10017 (212) 716-6131 *E-mail:* biblesandprayerbooks@episcopalchurch.org.

Bishop White PB Society

Donates Prayer Books and Hymnals on Bishop's endorsement. *Sec* Rev Mark J Ainsworth c/o All

Hallows Church 262 Bent Rd Wyncote PA 19095 (215) 885-1641 *E-mail:* rector@allhallowswyncote. org.

Margaret Coffin PB Society

Provides free Prayer Books and Hymnals on request with Bishop's endorsement. Given to parishes, missions, and institutions at home and abroad, unable to purchase them. Rev Marshall W Hunt PO Box 1205 E Harwich MA 02645 (508) 432-2612.

GENERAL ORGANIZATIONS

Alcuin Club

Promotes study of liturgy and worship of the Christian Church by publishing works of scholarship. Members receive two "Liturgical Studies" and a major book *Collection* annually for their dues (US $44 with optional air mail surcharge of US $10)— with occasional disc on other books. For information and membership contact John Collins 5 Saffron St Royston Herts SG8 9TR UK +44 (0) 1763-248676 *E-mail:* alcuinclub@gmail.com *Web:* www.alcuinclub.org.uk.

American Anglican Council

The American Anglican Council is a network of individuals (laity, deacons, priests and bishops), parishes and specialized ministries who affirm Biblical authority and Christian orthodoxy within the Anglican Communion and who are working to build up and defend Great Commission Anglican churches in North America and worldwide. *President/Chairman of the Board* The Rt Rev David C Anderson; *CEO* The Rev Cn Phil Ashey; *Dir of Human Res* Mary Orr; *Dir of Comm* Robert Lundy; *Admin Asst* Nina Brown-Perry 2296 Henderson Mill Rd NE Ste 406 Atlanta GA 30345 (800) 914-2000 *Fax:* (770) 414-1518 *E-mail:* info@americananglican. org *Web:* www.americananglican.org.

American Bible Society

American Bible Society Distributes the Holy Scriptures without doctrinal note or comment. For catalog of Am Bible Soc or publication *The Record* write to Autumn Black 1865 Broadway NY NY 10023 (212) 408-1215 *Web:* www.americanbible.org.

American Friends of the Episcopal Diocese of Jerusalem, The

An independent, tax-exempt non-political corp operating in partnership with the Episcopal Diocese of Jerusalem. AFEDJ raises funds to support hospitals, schools, institutes for the disabled and programs, and educates people in the US about the humanitarian work of the Diocese in Palestine, Israel, Lebanon, Jordan and Syria. 25 Old King's Highway No Ste 13 Darien CT 06820 *Board Chair* The Rt Rev Barry R Howe 10133 Gulf Blvd Treasure Island FL 33706 *E-mail:* barryrhowe@gmail.com; *Pres* Anne K Lynn 25 Old King's Highway No Ste 13 Darien CT 06820 (203) 655-3575 *E-mail:* aklynn@ afedj.org *Web:* www.afedj.org.

Anglican Frontier Missions

Mission agency dedicated to planting churches in the 25 largest and least evangelized peoples of the world. Agency uses full resources of worldwide Body of Christ, full ecumenical and international cooperation and relies on most recent technology and thorough research for networking and strategy. *Dir* The Rev Christopher Royer PhD PO Box 18038 Richmond VA 23226 (804) 355-8468 *Fax:* (804) 355-8260 *E-mail:* info@afm-us.org *Web:* www. anglicanfrontiers.com.

Anglican Musicians, Association of

For church musicians serving Episcopal and Anglican churches. Seeks to promote excellence in church music, working with clergy, commissions on liturgy and music, composers and other artists, and seminaries. Maintains a mentoring program for young and student church musicians. Encourages equitable compensation and benefits for professional church musicians and all lay employees. Annual conference. Monthly professional journal. *Pres* James G Garvey. PO Box 7530 Little Rock AR 72217 *Voice/Fax:* (501) 661-9925 *E-mail:* office@anglicanmusicians.org *Web:* www.anglicanmusicians.org.

Anglican Society

To promote and maintain Catholic faith and practice in accordance with the principles of the BCP, to explore and affirm Anglican identity and self-understanding. Rev JR Wright 177 9th Ave Apt 2-H NY NY 10011-4977 *E-mail:* wright@gts.edu *Web:* www.anglicansociety.org.

Anglican Women's Empowerment (AWE)

AWE seeks to be an effective and empowered voice for Anglican Women at the United Nations and throughout the Anglican Communion, with particular focus on the UN Commission on the Status of Women committed to worldwide reconciliation, right relationships and shared work for peace and justice through empowerment and education around global issues through the Beijing Platform for Action, the Millennium Development Goals, and working as appropriate for equal representation of women in the Anglican Consultative Council. *Web:* anglicanwomensempowerment.org.

Anglicans for Life

AFL is the global Anglican/Episcopal ministry that educates, equips, and engages the Church in fulfilling Scripture's mandate to protect the vulnerable, defend the fatherless and plead for the widow. AFL encourages and supports ministry, advocacy and education through local Life Chapters and published resources for ministry including adult education DVD curriculums; Project Life & Embrace the Journey. *Chairman of the Board* Greg Plizga *Pres* The Rev Georgette Forney 405 Frederick Ave Sewickley PA 15143-1522 (800) 707-6635 *E-mail:* info@anglicansforlife.org *Web:* www. anglicansforlife.org.

Associated Parishes for Liturgy and Mission (APLM)

Network of Anglicans in North America who promote renewal of liturgy and mission in Episcopal Church and Anglican Church of Canada through education and formation, advocacy, development of resources and cooperation with renewal efforts in other churches. Members support this work, and participate in online and list-serve discussions. *Mail* 3405 Alman Dr Durham NC 27705 *E-mail*: info@associatedparishes.org *Web*: www. associatedparishes.org.

Bible Reading Fellowship

Produces and distributes daily Bible reading materials and various other resources for church growth. *Exec Dir* David Laird, *Pres* Trip Tucker Box 380 Winter Park FL 32790-0380 (407) 628- 4330 (800) 749-4331 *Fax*: (407) 647-2406 *E-mail*: brf@ biblereading.org *Web*: www.biblereading.org.

Bishops' Executive Secretaries Together— BEST

Provides communication and support among bishops' secretaries for a "common ministry." Meets annually. *For info*: Beth Matthews Dio of AR Box 164668 Little Rock AR 72216 (501) 372-2168 *Fax*: (501) 372-2147 *E-mail*: Bethily@aol.com.

Church Missions Publishing Co

Granting agency for miss-related publication projs of the Church. *Pres* Rt Rev Ian T Douglas The Commons of The Episcopal Church in Connecticut 290 Pratt St Box 52 Meriden CT 06450 (203) 639-3501 *Fax*: (203) 235-1008 *E-mail*: ahollo@ episcopalct.org.

Church Periodical Club

Gives grants for books, periodicals, audio and videotapes, and computer software throughout the Anglican Community. Grants for materials enable ministries with limited resources. Founded in 1888, it operates at all levels of the church. *Pres* Cai Armstrong 103 West Ashford Way Irmo SC 29063-8325 (803) 261-6861 *E-mail*: churchperiodicalpresident@ gmail.com *Admin* Pamela Stewart 815 Second Ave NY NY 10017 (800) 334-7626 x6130 *E-mail*: cpc@ episcopalchurch.org *Web*: www.churchperiodical. com.

CODE

The Conference of Diocesan Executives was founded in 1963. Membership is open to lay and ordained people who report to Diocesan Bishops while serving on a Bishop's staff. Key is building relationships and sharing experiences. Facilitates collegiality, confidence, and support. Helps members to find healthy solutions to challenges and to build up the body of Christ. Holds annual conference offering best in speakers, seminars and workshops on a wide ranging variety of topics. Fun is an integral part of CODE Conference experience. *Pres* Rev Cn

Eric Cooter *E-mail*: ecooter@episcopalswfl.org *VP* Re. Cn Lucy Amerman *E-mail*: lucya@diopa.org *Treas* David Ramkey *E-mail*: dramkey@wvdiocese. org *Co-Sec* Melinda Showalter *E-mail*: mshowalter@ diocesefl.org *Co-Sec* Rev Cn Kate Cullinane *E-mail*: kcullinane@diosanjoaquin.org *Comm/Registrar* Tammy Mazure *E-mail*: tmazure@edwm.org *Web Worker*: Rev Cn Bruce Gray *E-mail*: gray@indydio. org. *Web*: http://codeepiscopal.org/ *Facebook*: https:// www.facebook.com/groups/625497357532880/.

Conference of Anglican Religious Orders in the Americas

Association of officially recognized religious orders who live in community under vows. Coordinates interest and experience of members, provides opportunities for mutual support, and presents a coherent understanding of religious life to the Church. *Gen Sec* The Rev Dr Donald Anderson PO Box 99 Little Britain Ontario K0M 2C0 Canada (705) 786-3330 *E-mail*: dwa1319@gmail.com *Web*: www.caroa.net.

Consortium of Endowed Episcopal Parishes, The

CEEP links members for networking and information exchange on subjects like ministry, stewardship, endowments, leadership, and more. Publishes monthly e-newsletter, and maintains a resource library for members. National, regional conferences *Exec Dir* Cynthia Cannon McWhirter 301 E 8th St Austin TX 78701 (855) 663-2337 *E-mail*: ccannon@endowed-parishes.org *Web*: www.endowedparishes.org.

Council of Episcopal Women's Organizations, The (CEWO)

This Council includes women's organizations of the Episcopal Church. Organizational Presidents or their representatives meet annually for networking and organizing in order to increase the effectiveness of women's ministries, to support their different gifts, and to advance the roles of women in God's mission as expressed through the Episcopal Church. *Contact*: The Rev Cynthia Black.

Cursillo

Cursillo is a movement of the Episcopal Church, under the authority of the Presiding and Diocesan Bishops. The goal of Cursillo is to bring the world to Christ by empowering adult Christian leaders through the use of a specific method that is taught as part of a three-day weekend. The method, a tool for evangelism, equips and encourages Christians to live out their Baptismal covenant to serve Christ. Episcopal Cursillo Ministry (formerly known as the National Episcopal Cursillo) PO Box 460506 Aurora CO 80046 (303) 905-6053. *E-mail*: necoffice@nationalepiscopalcursillo.org *Web*: http:// nationalepiscopalcursillo.org.

Educational Center, The

A spiritual resource center for seekers, learners and religious educators. Publishers of BibleWorkbench and TeenText; lectionary based studies, discussion guides and sermon preparation. PO Box 11892 Charlotte NC 28220 (704) 375-1161 *E-mail:* info@educationalcenter.org *Web:* www.educationalcenter.org.

Episcopal Appalachian Ministries (EAM)

(Formerly APSO—Appalachian People's Service Organization) A network of ministries serving people within the Appalachian region; currently there are 11 supporting dioceses. EAM coordinates resources and acts as a clearing house for those seeking or providing ministry in Appalachia. EAM sponsors work camps, provides small grants for ministry in Appalachia, co-sponsors an annual conference (Mountain Grace Conference), provides ministry resources through its website and social networking sites (Facebook), a quarterly newsletter, education materials, advocacy guidance with social justice issues and small church resources. *Exec Coord* The Rev L Gordon Brewer Jr 5337 Heritage Lane, Kingsport TN 37664 (423) 408-2771 *Fax:* (888) 395- 1262 *E-mail:* episcopalappministries@gmail.com *Web:* www.visit-EAM.org.

Episcopal Booksellers Association Inc.

Independent and church-owned book and gift stores serving the church and general public. Organized in 1998 to support education, outreach, and a positive presence for stores serving the Episcopal market by means of information and resource sharing, advertising, and liaison among retail store managers and publishers. *Exec Dir* Kathleen Abrams PO Box 170112 Spartanburg SC *Toll Free* (888) 589-8020 *E-mail:* info@episcopalbooksellers.org. For listing of nationwide member stores and vendors see www.episcopalbooksellers.org.

Episcopal Camps and Conference Centers, Inc

A national network within the Episcopal Church, ECCC links diocesan-related camp and conference center facilities together providing educational services, newsletters and professional support. ECCC sponsors an Annual Conference for executive directors, senior staff and board members. Consultative services focusing on executive search, strategic planning, business plans and board development etc. are also available. For information contact *Director* Bill Slocumb (760) 445- 6774 *E-mail:* staff@episcopalccc.org *Web:* www.episcopalccc.org.

Episcopal Church and Visual Arts (ECVA)

Episcopal Church and Visual Arts (ECVA) is a virtual organization at www.ecva.org. ECVA curates visual arts exhibitions on-line; sponsors diocesan chapters; and networks artists and organizations around the country. ECVA assists dioceses and churches in integrating the visual arts into congregational ministry, liturgy, and mission programs. *Acting Pres* Bob Tate 815 Second Ave NY NY 10017 *E-mail:* info@ecva.org *Web:* www.ecva.org.

Episcopal Church Foundation (ECF), The

Partners with congregations, dioceses, and other faith communities to help them discern what God is calling them to do and to empower them for the work of ministry by developing the leadership and financial resources they need. ECF's programs, products, and services help congregations respond to the changing needs of the Episcopal Church in the 21st century. Some of these programs include: Vital Teams—training and practical resources for building effective lay+clergy leadership teams; Strategic Solutions—facilitation and assistance to envision and implement future ministries; Fellowship Partners Program—Support for emerging leaders and scholars to transform the Church; Vital Practices (www.ecfvp.org)—innovative ideas for and from Episcopalians who are leading healthy, vital, and vibrant faith communities; Educational Events—workshops and webinars that equip clergy and laity with knowledge, skills, and best practices; Planned Giving & Endowment Management Solutions—tools and training to raise and manage resources to fund ministries today and for future generations; Capital Campaigns—partnerships with dioceses, congregations and other organizations to achieve financial goals, strengthen relationships and enhance communication. Through ECF's programs lay+clergy leadership teams are equipped to bring about transformation, renewal, and positive change in their communities, live out Christian stewardship, and develop new approaches to mission and ministry. ECF is a lay-led and independent organization, serving the Episcopal Church for the past 65 years. *Chair* Richard L Clements *Pres* Donald V Romanik 815 Second Ave New York NY 10017 (800) 697-2858 *E-mail:* all@EpiscoaplFoundation.org *Web:* www.EpiscopalFoundation.org.

Episcopal Communicators

A self-supporting organization of persons with communications responsibilities in the Episcopal Church. *Pres* Sarah Bartenstein (2013- 2016) St Stephen's Church 6000 Grove Ave Richmond VA 23226 (804) 288-2867 *E-mail:* sbartenstein@saintstephensrichmond.net, episcopalcommunicators@gmail.com *Web:* www.episcopalcommunicators.org.

Episcopal Community Services in America

Episcopal Community Services in America (ECSA) is an umbrella 501(c)3 non-profit organization. ECSA, like Lutheran Social services and Catholic Charities, seeks to provide a network to build resources, foster relationships, and encourage advocacy to the approximately 550 health and human service agencies associated with the Episcopal Church. Serving Episcopal Community Services, Episcopal Social Services, Episcopal Charities, Senior Services to include Continuing Care Facilities, Assisted Living, Nursing Homes, Retirement Centers. Also, neighborhood settlement house services, child and adolescent centers, juvenile justice, restorative justice, alcohol and drug treatment programs, homeless shelters, housing and health clinics. *Web:* ecsamerica.org.

Episcopal Health Ministries

Episcopal Health Ministries (EHM) is a network that promotes health ministry (including parish nursing) in Episcopal congregations. EHM provides health ministry resources to local congs, dioceses and provinces; collaborates with other faith communities, institutions and health orgs; offers education for Episcopal health ministry and parish nursing; and supports those engaged in cong health min. For information see www. EpiscopalHealthMinistries.org 6050 N Meridian St Indianapolis IN 46208 (317) 253-1277 x34 *E-mail:* NEHM@episcopalhealthministries.org.

Episcopal Marriage Encounter

Conducts weekend sessions nationwide, teaching a positive communication technique for married couples within God's plan for sacramental marriages. Contact: *Natl Exec Clergy Couple* Fr John & Janet Duncan 110 San Benito Ave Aptos CA 95003-4415 (831) 688-1383 *E-mail:* jnjduncan@yahoo.com *Natl Exec Lay Couple* Bill & Lee Gill 6 Eames Drive Oxford CT 06478-1183 (203) 888-2043 *E-mail:* bgill96178@aol.com.

Episcopal Media Center, Inc

A division of the Alliance for Christian Media, the Episcopal Media Center is part of an interdenominational, international, multimedia ministry that offers a full range of communications programs and services to enhance the mission of the church. Among its programs is "Day 1," (formerly the Protestant Hour), the nation's longest running ecumenical radio program. In addition to its online store offering media programs for education and inspiration, the Center offers Episcopal branded merchandise and distribution/ fulfillment services to church agencies and nonprofit organizations. *CFO* Thomas Keuneke *Pres* Rev Peter Wallace 2715 Peachtree Rd NE Atlanta GA 30305 (800) 229-3788 *Fax:* (404) 815-0495 *E-mail:* thk@episcopalmedia.org *Web:* www. episcopalmedia.org.

Episcopal Peace Fellowship

A national membership organization assisting Episcopalians and others to realize and live out Christ's call for peace, justice and reconciliation. Promotes prayer, study, education and action; organizes chapters and action groups around the country, and provides nonviolence retreats and training. Publishes peace and justice resources including a biannual journal called *Episcopal Peace Witness.* PO Box 15 Claysburg PA 16625 *Exec Dir* Rev Allison Liles *Chair* Rev Will Wauters *Vice Chair* Rev Bill Exner (312) 922-8628 *E-mail:* epf@epfnational.com *Web:* www.epfnational.org.

Episcopal Preaching Foundation, Inc

The mission and ministry of the Episcopal Preaching Foundation is to support and enhance preaching in the Episcopal Church, currently providing conferences, seminars and programs throughout the United States and in Canada. Educational programs include an annual national conference for seminarians (Preaching Excellence Program [PEP/PEPII]), and clergy and diocesan preaching events. *Chair* Dr A Gary Shilling (973) 467-0070 *E-mail:* gary@agaryshilling.com; *Exec Dir* Rev. Diane Pike 500 Morris Ave Springfield NJ 07081 (973) 367-6014 *E-mail:* dpike@preachingfoundation.org *Web:* www.preachingfoundation.org.

Episcopal Public Policy Network

A nationwide grassroots network of Episcopalians who call, write or e-mail members of Congress and the administration to advocate positions of the church on public policy and who are committed to the ministry of justice and peace. *Public Policy Network Mgr* Mary Getz 110 Maryland Ave NE Ste 309 Washington DC 20002 (800) 228-0515 (202) 547-7300 *Fax:* (202) 547-4457 *E-mail:* eppn@episcopalchurch.org *Web:* www.episcopalchurch.org/eppn.

Episcopal Women's Caucus

The Episcopal Women's Caucus is a justice organization of women and men dedicated to the Gospel values of equality and liberation for all, and committed to the incarnation of God's unconditional love. Founded in 1971 to work for the ordination of women, the Caucus continues to advocate for and support women in leadership and challenge all forms of discrimination with particular attention to matters affecting women. Quarterly journal, local chapters and participation in partnership and coalitions. *Contact:* Christine Mackey-Mason 1103 Magnolia St South Pasadena CA 91030 (626) 201-2363 *E-mail:* mackeychristine@att.net *Web:* www. episcopalwomenscaucus.org.

Episcopal Women's History Project

National organization to make the church aware of the roles taken by women in the past, pointing up their valuable contributions to the church and society. Funds support research, grants for scholarly work, use of archives, education for parish historians, oral history training, and communication encouraging interest in women's history. *Timelines* online and snail newsletter published quarterly. One meeting per year with speakers and workshops. *Pres* The Rev Dr Matilda EG Dunn 7013 Rocky Tr Chattanooga TN 37421 (423) 400-7760 *E-mail:* megd613@gmail.com *Web:* www.ewhp.org.

Episcopalians on Baptismal Mission (EBM)

A partnership of individuals and groups dedicated to the ministry of all the baptized in daily life. Formed in 2006, participation is open to all who share our vision and purpose—and a willingness to help move the church forward. OUR PURPOSE: (1) To be a voice of advocacy and an educational resource within The Episcopal Church for recognizing and furthering faithful ministry in the daily lives of baptized persons by initiating and supporting efforts to enhance the centrality of baptismal living; exploring common ground and natural alliances with other Episcopal and Anglican groups; assisting congregations, dioceses, and provinces in planning and implementing educational events focused on the calling of all the baptized in daily life; and developing resources for faithfulness in daily life. (2) To provide a communications link among partners to share programs, ideas, concerns, needs, etc. EBM is led by a steering committee composed of laypersons, priests, and bishops. *Web:* http://livinggodsmission. org/ *Contact:* J Fletcher Lowe Jr 1600 Westbrook Ave Apt G27 Richmond VA 23227 *E-mail:* jflowe@aol. com.

Episcopalians for Traditional Faith, Inc.

An all-volunteer, nonprofit organization dedicated to preserving and promoting the faith, order, and doctrine of the Episcopal Church through the classic *1928 Book of Common Prayer. Pres* Douglas A Hard *Exec VP* Jan Mahood PO Box 361 Mill Neck NY 11765 (585) 500-8936 *E-mail:* tcranmer@etf1928. org *Web:* www.etf1928.org.

Evangelical Education Society of the Episcopal Church (EES)

Founded 1862. Awards Evangelism for the 21st Century grants to Episcopalians at all ATS-accredited seminaries: faculty, students, staff, spouses and partners. Supports innovative ministry projects that take the gospel to the unchurched, empower lay and ordained ministers to bring new evangelical vigor to parish churches, and help believers to understand and articulate the Christian faith. *Publication:* The Lantern. *Chair* Rev Jimmy Bartz *Exec Dir* Day Smith Pritchartt PO Box 7297 Arlington VA 22207 (703) 807-1862 *E-mail:* office@ees1862.org *Web:* www.ees1862.org.

Evangelicals in the Episcopal Church

Encouragement for Evangelicals who are committed to the Episcopal Church, and working for its reformation and renewal. We promote biblical teaching, preaching, and worship, and sponsor conferences and workshops for Episcopalian Evangelicals, lay and ordained, in these ministries. For more information contact the Rev Philip Wainwright at pw35@kentforlife.net, or visit our website at www. barnabasproject.wordpress.com. The website is updated regularly.

Faith Encouragement Ministries

Faith Encouragement Ministries delivers church renewal programs for the entire parish family—adults, teens, and children—that take place at the church. An experienced Faith Encouragement Ministries leader works with the clergy and church lay leaders to determine and plan the most effective program for the church. The programs include the unchanged standard *Faith Alive* weekend program, and the flexible program, *Faith Journey*, which is customized to meet the needs of the congregation. Both programs emphasize prayer and the baptismal vows. The Faith Encouragement Ministries programs include visitor team members sharing faith stories, small groups meeting in homes, men's and women's lunches, and the children and teen programs. The team members serve as facilitators and listeners as the members of the congregation focus on the presence of Christ in their lives and their own faith journey. National Office: PO Box 51776 Albuquerque NM 87181 (505) 255-3233 *Fax:* (505) 255-2282 *Program Office:* 6579 SE 82nd Ave Newberry FL 32669 (352) 472-1992 *Program Director E-mail:* info@faithencourage. org *Web:* www.faithencourage.org

Forward in Faith, North America (FIFNA)

Formerly Episcopal Synod of America. Association of Episcopal and Anglican congregations, chapters, institutions, laity, religious and clergy who embrace the Gospel of Jesus Christ and uphold the Evangelical faith and Catholic order of the Church. Publication: *Forward in Christ.* Membership open to those who subscribe to the FIFNA Declaration and Agreed Statement on Communion. Inquiries: FIFNA PO Box 210248 Bedford TX 76095-7248 (800) 225-3661 *E-mail:* office@fifna.org *Web:* www.fifna.org.

Friends of Canterbury Cathedral in the US (FOCCUS)

A charitable, not-for-profit corporation whose mission is to provide scholarship funds for seminarians from Third World Countries to attend International Study at Canterbury Cathedral; build relationships between Episcopalians and the Cathedral; encourage involvement with Cathedral's mission; strengthen capacity of the Cathedral as retreat center, support the Cathedral's programs, preservation, and restoration. *Chair* Rt Rev Peter J Lee *V Chairs* Eugene Johnston & Barbara Q Harper 888 17th St NW Ste 220 Washington DC 20006 (202) 822-8994.

Gather the Family Institute for Evangelism and Congregational Development

Provides consultants, training workshops to help congregations and dioceses learn the concepts and skills necessary to develop individualized programs for evangelism and incorporation (assimilation) min. *DMin* Rev GK Sturni PO Box 38447 Germantown TN 38183-0447 (901) 754-7282 *E-mail:* gsturni@ copper.net.

Gathering the Next Generations (GTNG) Network

An online network sustained by lay and ordained Episcopalians of Generation X and following generations (born in or after 1961) to connect and support leadership of the "next generations" in the church and further the mission of Christ. *E-mail:* gtng-owner@yahoogroups.com *Web:* www.gtng.org.

Guild of St Ives

Association of Episcopal lawyers and judges who live, work or worship in the Diocese of NY. Annually observes Law Day with Choral Evensong between Law Day (May 1) and the Feast of St Ives to recognize public service by members of the legal profession on behalf of the community. Presents the Servant of Justice Award in recognition of commitment to the legal profession, public service, and mission of the Church. *Coord* Rev RD Sloan 1047 Amsterdam Ave NY NY 10025 *E-mail:* rsloan@dioceseny.org.

"Happening—A Christian ExperienceSM"

A diocesan renewal and evangelism program for HS youth to "Share God's Love Through Community." During a 2-day weekend, participants experience the wonder and love of God's love as shown through their peers, lay adults and clergy. A Happening National Leadership Conference occurs in the summer of even-numbered years. *Exec Dir* Randy Winton *E-mail:* wintons@gmail. com *E-mail:* happeninginfo@gmail.com *Web:* www. happeningnational.org.

Historical Society of the Episcopal Church

Organization for preservation of Episcopal heritage within the Anglican Communion, fostering research, publishing *Anglican & Episcopal History* (*Ed* Edward L Bond) *Dir of Oper* Matthew P Payne 82 Cherry Ct Appleton WI 54915 (920) 383-1910 *Pres* Dr Robert Prichard *VP* Dr Pamela Cochran *Sec* Dr J Michael Utzinger *Treas* Rober Panfil *E-mail:* administration@ hsec.us *Web:* hsec.us. African American Episcopal Historical Collection (AAEHC), a joint project of Virginia Theological Seminary and the Historical Society of the Episcopal Church *Web:* www.vts. edu/aaehc *AAEHC Archivist* Dr Joseph Downing Thompson *E-mail:* jthompson@vts.edu.

Integrity USA

A lesbian, gay, bisexual, and transgender justice ministry in and to the Episcopal Church. There are 62 chapters in 8 provinces. Annual dues start at $25. *Pres* Rev Dr Caro Hall *Exec Dir* Vivian Taylor 770 Massachusetts Ave #390170 Cambridge MA 02139 (800) 462-9498 *E-mail:* info@integrityusa.org *Web:* www.integrityusa.org.

International Order of
St Luke the Physican (OSL)

Interdenom Christian fellowship of faith, prayer and service. Members lay and clergy who believe healing to be essential part of teaching and practice of Our Lord and who believe that healing ministry of Christ belongs in the church today. *Contact:* North American OSL Ofc PO Box 780909 San Antonio TX 78278 (877) 992-5222 *E-mail:* OSL2@satx.rr.com *Web:* www.orderofstluke.org.

International Order of St Vincent is a worldwide fellowship of lay sanctuary ministers of all ages serving the One, Holy, Catholic, and Apostolic Church. We promote liturgical knowledge, understanding of ritualistic detail and meaning, and encourage intercessory prayer and holy living among our members. The Order is open to all acolytes, lay readers, lectors, lay eucharistic ministers, sacristans, ushers, greeters, vergers, and choristers (men and women, girls and boys). Believing that we are also called to serve, we strive to instill reverence, cooperation, responsibility, discipline, mentorship, leadership, humility, quest for excellence, and joy of servanthood by emphasizing a stairway of lay ministry that leads to active adult churchmanship. The OSV is sacramentally centered and encourages living a rule of life (we pray, worship, read, and give). The OSV also publishes a wide range of illustrated liturgical manuals, teaching materials and historical tracts. *Dir Gen* Philip G Dixon PO Box 1245 Summerville SC 29484 (843) 442-1288 *E-mail:* Director-General@orderstvincent.org *Web:* www.orderstvincent.org.

KEEP (Kiyosato Educational Experiment Project) American Committee for KEEP (ACK)

Japanese lay organization established 1938, Am partner established 1950, to provide Christian witness through people to people outreach and education, focusing on rural comm devel and sustainable ag in SE Asia and environmental advocacy in Japan. *Founder:* the late Dr Paul Rusch *Pres ACK* Rt Rev Stacy Sauls 825 Green Bay Rd Ste 122 Wilmette IL 60091 (847) 853-2500 or (800) 368-KEEP *Fax:* (847) 853-8901 *E-mail:* ack@ackeep.org *Web:* www.ackeep.org.

Living Church Foundation, Inc

Dedicated to providing quality publications for the Episcopal Church and the Anglican Communion. Publishes *The Living Church, Illuminations & Epis Musician's Handbook. Pres* Rt Rev D Bruce MacPherson *Exec Dir* Dr Christopher Wells *Office/ Business Mgr* Ruth Schimmel PO Box 510705 Milwaukee WI 53203-0121.

National Association for the Self-Supporting Active Ministry

NASSAM is an organization of ordained Episcopal clergy who are not employed full time by the parish church; rather, they are bi-vocational, tentmaking clergy who represent various models of ministry in concert with the parish institution. *Info:* Davis Fisher (847) 733-9977 *E-mail:* davisfishr@aol.com or Marc Strong (847) 217-4027 *E-mail:* fr.marc_coi@hotmail. com *Web:* www.nassam.org.

National Association of
Episcopal Christian Communities, The

NAECC is a coalition of Christian Communities recognized under the canons of the Episcopal Church working with communities-in-formation, dedicated to sharing and communicating the fruits of the Gospel—realized in many forms of community—with the church and the world. *Web:* www.naecc.us.

National Episcopal Historians and Archivists

Organization of congregational and diocesan historians and archivists to encourage collection, preservation and organization of church records and sharing of church history. *Pub* The Historiographer. *Pres* Susan Stoensifer *V Pres* Amy Cunningham *Sec* Kurt Cook *Treas* Matthew Payne *Office Manager* Kurt Cook 231 E 100 S Salt Lake City UT 84111 *Tel/Fax:* 920-543-NEHA (6342) *E-mail:* nehahqs@aol.com *Web:* episcopalhistorians.org.

Network of Episcopal Clergy Associations (NECA)

Mission: Through NECA, we seek, serve, and proclaim Christ by leading clergy in the Episcopal Church into collegial relationships for education, self-care, advocacy, and spiritual growth. *Past Pres:* The Rev Ed Shiley *Pres:* The Rev Jeffrey Ross *VPres:* The Rev Leslie Hague *Treas:* The Rev Peter Powell *Sec:* The Rev Ann Tillman *Web:* www.episcopalclergy.org *Facebook:* NECA: Network of Episcopal Clergy Associations *E-mail:* NNECABoard@gmail.com.

North American Regional Committee of St George's College, Jerusalem

St George's College is an international center for fieldwork, study, reflection and pilgrimage in the Holy Land. It is located in the compound of St George's Cathedral, the seat of the Anglican Diocese of Jerusalem. The North American Committee links together individuals who have made pilgrimage to Saint George's and works to support the ministry of the College through scholarships, public relations, education and fundraising. *Pres* The Rev J Barney Hawkins IV *Exec Dir* Lesley Markham *Exec Sec* The Rev James Bimbi PO Box 12073 (3737 Seminary Rd) Alexandria VA 22304 (703) 461-1877 *E-mail:* nacstgeorges@outlook.com.

Operation Pass Along

Accepts contributions of new and used books about the church, vestments, clericals and altar fittings and passes them along, without charge, to seminarians, newly ordained priests, and deacons, newly formed parish and mission libraries and others. 805 CR 102 Eureka Springs AR 72632-9705 (800) 572-7929 *E-mail:* OperationPassAlong@anglicandigest.org.

Prayer Book Society of the USA, The

Maintaining the order of doctrine, discipline and worship in the Episcopal Church as provided by the *1928 Book of Common Prayer. Pres* Rev Gavin Dunbar *VP* Rev Edward Rix PO Box 137 Jenkintown PA 19046-0137 (800) PBS-1928 *Web:* www.pbsusa.org.

Protestant Episcopal Evangelists

Emphasizes inner-city ministries. St Paul's House trains for evangelism. *Pres* Rev T Jones *Dir* Shandra Velez 335 W 51st NY NY 10019 (212) 265-5433 *Fax:* (212) 265-5435 *E-mail:* admin@stpaulshouse.org *Web:* saintpaulshouse.org.

Rock the World Youth Mission Alliance

Offers internships, conferences, and training for youth and adults to multiply young Christian leaders and advance parish student ministries. *Contact Rock the World* PO Box 43 Ambridge PA 15003 (724) 266-8876 *E-mail:* info@rocktheworld.org *Web:* www.rocktheworld.org.

Rural Ministries Network (formerly Rural Workers Fellowship)

Supports and fosters community among small congregations, urban and rural, acting as advocate for their communities and concerns with the Church and public policy. For clergy and lay leaders in small congregation min within the Episc Church, USA, the Anglican Church of Canada, and others. The approach is ecumenical and other denominations are welcome. Founded 1924 as Rural Workers Fellowship; renamed in 2005. Open to all persons concerned with this ministry of encouragement, education, and advocacy within changing social structures. Information, prayer cycle published on-line, *Crossroads* quarterly. *Pres* Rev Warren Frelund 1029 West State St Mason City IA 50401 *E-mail:* wfrelund@q.com *Web:* www.ruralministriesnetwork.org.

SAMS—Society of Anglican Missionaries and Senders

Formerly known as the South American Missionary Society, SAMS is a society of missionaries serving in partnership with the Anglican Church globally. We are also, vitally, a society of senders of these missionaries through giving, praying, and supporting. Our central identity is a community in Christ. SAMS' purpose is to raise up, send, and support Episcopal and other Anglican missionaries to be witnesses and make disciples for Jesus Christ in fellowship with the Anglican Church globally. SAMS serves Episcopalians and Episcopal parishes, guiding those who are discerning calls to serve as missionaries and assisting the church to send. SAMS also creates mentored cross-cultural internships and helps in the equipping and connecting of short-term mission teams with missionaries around the world. SAMS missionaries evangelize, disciple, establish churches, train leaders, and minister through health clinics, microenterprise development, Christian schools, and outreach by integrating word and deed. *Brd Ch* Jeff Rawn *Pres & Dir* Stewart Wicker *Assoc Dir* Denise Cox (724) 266-0669 *E-mail:* info@sams-usa.org *Web:* www.sams-usa.org.

Seedlings Inc

Non-profit corp provides Episcopal curriculum for small churches and other unique educational materials. Sunday School lessons over 4-yr cycle, "Every Member Uncanvass, Adult Inquirers," and youth confirmation curricula. *Pres* Rev Betty W Fuller PO Box 1638 Corpus Christi TX 78401 (361) 739-7009 *E-mail:* seedlings@aol.com *Web:* www. seedlingsinc.com.

Society for Promoting Christian Knowledge (SPCK)
Provides resources for Christian discipleship around the world. Works for the creation, preparation, and distribution of Christian knowledge by utilizing print and other media. Recycles theological books to seminaries around the world. SPCK/USA is the American arm of the world's oldest mission agency founded in London 300 years ago. *Chair* Richard Hall *Exec Dir* Patti J Posan Box 879 Sewanee TN 37375-0879 (931) 598-1103 *E-mail:* spck@sewanee. edu. *Web:* www.spckusa.org.

Solo Flight: Catch the Vision
A national ministry for single adults in the Episcopal Church providing leadership training, programs, retreats, and specially designed on-site workshops. *Pres* Kay Collier McLaughlin PhD (859) 252-6527 *Fax:* (859) 231-9077 *E-mail:* kcollierm@diolex.org.

SOMA—Sharing of Ministries Abroad
SOMA USA prepares and sends short-term mission teams across national and cultural boundaries. Teams equip and train leaders to minister in the power of the Holy Spirit who renews individuals, empowers the Church, and transforms society. *Natl Dir* Dr Glen Petta SOMA 2501 Ridgmar Plaza #99 Fort Worth TX 76116 (817) 737-SOMA (7662) *E-mail:* office@somausa.org *Web:* www.somausa.org.

SPEAK
Society for Promoting and Encouraging Arts and Knowledge [of the Church]. *Chr Bd* Rt Rev EL Salmon Jr Hillspeak 805 CR 102 Eureka Springs AR 72632.

TENS (The Episcopal Network for Stewardship)
An association of church leaders who understand, practice, and proclaim God's call to generosity. Our Purpose: Inspiring Generosity and Faithful Discipleship. Our Vision: TENS' vision is to provide training and resources for stewardship leaders across The Episcopal Church and beyond, around the following core competencies: Training clergy and lay leaders in the spirituality of money, and the skills required to address questions of money in the congregation; providing targeted stewardship leadership training for clergy and seminarians, at seminaries and at the diocesan level, including both the theology and the practice of stewardship; mentoring a new generation of stewardship leaders, with special attention to youth, young adults, Generation Xers, newly ordained clergy; and developing and utilizing methods of providing resources using web-based and other electronic techniques. TENS 840 Echo Park Avenue Los Angeles, CA 90026 (626) 399-0332 (USA & Canada) *E-mail:* tens@tens.org *Web:* www.tens.org.

Union of Black Episcopalians
Organized in 1968 as the Union of Black Clergy and Laity, the Union of Black Episcopalians stands in the continuing tradition of more than 200 years of Black leadership fighting racism in the Episcopal Church. It is the proud inheritor of the work of those people in earlier organizations—the Convocation of Colored Clergy, the Conference of Church Workers Among Colored People—all dedicated to justice and ministry and the inclusion of persons of African descent (Blacks) in the life and leadership of the church. *Natl Pres* Annette L Buchanan; *Immediate Past Pres* John Harris *Natl Off* 701 Oglethorpe St NW Washington DC 20011 (202) 248-3941 *E-mail:* leadership@theube.org *Web:* www.ube.org.

The Vergers Guild of the Episcopal Church (VGEC)
VGEC is an all-volunteer service organization supporting liturgical volunteers and liturgical leaders in the ministry of the verger. A verger is a member of the laity who works under the direction of the parish priest, in any size congregation, assisting with the organization and operation of religious services in the Episcopal Church in the US, The Anglican Church of Canada, the Church of England, and the Anglican Communion worldwide. Through our education programs, diocesan chapters, 2015 revised training course, online resources at vergers. org, and opportunities for fellowship, the VGEC has over one thousand active members in the US and abroad. Anyone can become a member of the VGEC. The only requirement for membership is interest in the ministry of the verger. Free 6-month trial membership available at try.vergers.org. When the trial membership expires you will be prompted to renew as a paid member: $40 annual membership, $20 students/retired, $500 lifetime membership. All include our weekly blog, Facebook page, Vergers Guild Shop, updated training course at additional fee, and annual 4-day conferences (additional fee) in different locales every fall. Prefer email inquires at info@vergers.org. PO Box 280, Round Rock, TX 78680-0280

Vocare International
A Vocare weekend allows young adults to look at God's call and what it means in all areas of life. Primarily in the 19-30 age range, participants share ideas and ways to incorporate Christianity today. Annual Conference in Spring. *Coord* Liz Williams 2007 Belmont Ave Tifton GA 31794 (404) 202-7284 *E-mail:* admin@vocare.org *Web:* www.vocare.org.

Washington National Cathedral
Washington National Cathedral is a church for national purposes called to embody God's love and to welcome people of all faiths and perspectives. A unique blend of the spiritual and the civic, this Episcopal Cathedral is a voice for generous spirited Christianity and a catalyst for reconciliation and interfaith dialogue to promote respect and

understanding. We invite all people to share in our commitment to create a more hopeful and just world. Washington National Cathedral 3101 Wisconsin Ave NW (Massachusetts & Wisconsin Aves NW) Washington DC 20016-5098 (202) 537-6200 *Web:* www.nationalcathedral.org.

GENERAL YOUTH ORGANIZATIONS

The Junior Daughters of the King

Baptized young women and girls ages 7-21 who make a promise of daily Prayer and Service which provides a special opportunity to grow in their Christian faith and commitment. *Chair* Anna Stevenson (210) 912-5505 *E-mail:* astevenson@doknational.org *Natl Off Admin* Mary Fletcher *Natl Off* 101 Weatherstone Dr #870 Woodstock GA 30188-7003 (770) 517-8552 X25 *Fax:* (770) 517-8066 *E-mail:* dok1885@doknational.org *Web:* www.doknational.org.

GFS/USA—Girls' Friendly Society, USA

International, not-for-profit, faith-based organization affiliated with the Episcopal Church for girls and young women 5-21. Our purpose is to provide girls and women with a support system aimed at developing the whole person. GFS parish-based programs focus on worship, outreach, study and recreation. The mission of GFS is to establish a positive Christian environment just for girls that fosters an outward expression of our motto, *Bear One Another's Burdens*, and encourages sisterhood in a complicated world. The Girls Friendly Society is a place where girls can grow spiritually through service to each other and their community. We help our members develop their talents and skills, empowering them with faith, self-esteem and confidence to cope in the world today. *E-mail:* deloresalleyne@aol.com or gfspresident@gmail.com *Facebook:* https://www.facebook.com/gfsusa/info *Web:* www.gfsus.org.

RELIGIOUS ORDERS AND COMMUNITIES

Editor's Note: Beginning with the 2002 Edition of *The Episcopal Church Annual,* only those religious orders and communities officially recognized by the Standing Committee on Religious Communities of the House of Bishops are listed in *The Annual.* For information about applying for official status, please contact The Rt Rev Russell E Jacobus *Chair,* House of Bishops Committee on Religious Communities PO Box 155 Townsend WI 54715 (920)585-7481.

Traditional Orders

FOR MEN

Brothers of Saint John the Evangelist (OSB)

Contemplative semi-monastic religious community within the Order of St Benedict, clergy and lay, living a life of prayer, personal growth, and service to the Church. Emphasis as a monastic community is on the traditional worship, music and arts of the Church

Our Fellowship includes Oblates and Associates, with some residing at the Monastery and others as Externs. *Superior* Br Richard Tussey EFSJ *Prior & Oblate Director* Br David McClellan EFSJ Tanglewood Hill Monastery PO Box 782 Freeland WA 98249 *E-mail:* efsj@whidbey.com *Web:* www.brothersofsaintjohn.org.

Order of St Benedict, The

Comm of monks in Episcopal Church living Benedictine rule. *Abbot* Rt Rev A Marr OSB St Gregory's Abbey 56500 Abbey Rd Three Rivers MI 49093-9595 (269) 244-5893 *E-mail:* abbot@saintgregorysthreerivers.org *Web:* www.saintgregorysthreerivers.org.

Order of the Holy Cross, The

A Benedictine monastic community for clergy and laymen. *Superior* Br Robert Sevensky OHC H Cross Monastery Box 99 West Park NY 12493 (845) 384-6660 x3006 *Fax:* (845) 384-6031 *E-mail:* ohcsuperior@gmail.com Mt Calvary Monastery Box 1296 Santa Barbara CA 93102 (805) 682-4117 H Cross Priory 204 High Park Ave Toronto M6P 2S6 Ontario CANADA (416) 767-9081 Mariya uMama weThemba Monastery Box 6013 Grahamstown 6141 S AFRICA (011) 27-46-622-6465.

Society of St Francis

Community of men (lay and ordained) living under the vows of poverty, chastity, and obedience. After the example of Francis of Assisi, the brothers engage in urban ministry, retreats, prayer, and study. *Min Prov* Br Jude SSF Prov Headquarters, S Damiano Friary 573 Dolores San Francisco CA 94110 (415) 861-1372 *E-mail:* judehillssf@aol.com. *Web:* www.societyofstfrancis.org.

Society of St John the Evangelist

A community of ordained and lay brothers who take vows of poverty, celibacy, and obedience. Oldest Anglican religious order for men, founded by Richard Meux Benson at Oxford, England in 1866. *Sup* Br Geoffrey Tristram SSJE Monastery of St Mary and St John and the Guesthouse 980 Memorial Dr Cambridge MA 02138-5717 (617) 876-3037 *Web:* www.ssje.org *Brs E-mail:* monastery@ssje.org *Guesthouse E-Mail:* guesthouse@ssje.org *Vocational Info:* Br David Vryhof *E-mail:* vocations@ssje.org. Emery Hse 21 Emery Ln W Newbury MA 01985 (617) 876-3037 *Web:* www.ssje.org.

Society of St Paul

Celebrating a life of prayer, personal growth, and service to others. *Rector* Cn Barnabas Hunt SSP The Society of St Paul 2567 Second Ave Unit 504 San Diego CA 92103 (619) 794-2095.

FOR MEN AND WOMEN

Order of Julian of Norwich, The

Monastic, enclosed, contemplative community for men and women following the spirituality of Dame

Julian. Associate and Oblate affiliations for laity and clergy. *Guardian* Mthr Hilary OJN Our Lady of the Northwoods Monastery W704 Alft Road White Lake WI 54491-9715, (262) 349-3283 *E-mail:* ojn@orderofjulian.org *Web:* www.orderofjulian.org.

FOR WOMEN

Community of the Holy Spirit

Monastic observance of the Divine Offices, biodynamic farming, spiritual direction and social justice ministries underscore the creative charism of the Community of the Holy Spirit — a community of life professed sisters, resident companions and associates. Limited guest facilities. *Leadership: Community Council.* St Hilda's House 454 Convent Ave New York NY 10031 212-666-8249 ext 205. Bluestone Farm and Living Arts Center at Melrose Convent 118 Federal Hill Rd Brewster NY 10509 *E-mail:* chssisters@chssisters.org *Web:* www.chssisters.org.

Community of St Francis, The

Franciscan Sisters living a life of prayer, study, and work with special concern for poor and deprived. *Min Prov* Sr Sister Pamela Clare St Francis House 3743 Cesar Chavez St San Francisco CA 94110 (415) 824-0288 *E-mail:* csfsfo@aol.com *Web:* www.communitystfrancis.org.

Community of St John Baptist

A Community of prayer and service, reaching out to God's people. Retreats, conferences, lay and ordained ministry, outreach to the needy, spiritual direction and other ministries Assoc, Oblate and Alongsider affiliations for lay and clergy. Outreach to addicted youth at residential center on property. Mission to orphans in Cameroon. St Marguerite's Retreat House open to groups. Convent of St John Baptist Box 240 82 W Main St Mendham NJ 07945 (973) 543-4641 *Fax:* (973) 543-0327 *E-mail:* csjb@csjb.org *Web:* www.csjb.org *Branch House* St Mary's Mission House Church of St Mary the Virgin 145 W 46th St NY NY 10036 (646) 329-6313.

Community of St Mary

A Benedictine Community for women with special dedication to St. Mary offering retreats, conferences, private guest accommodations, a summer Monastic Intern Program at the Greenwich house and an Organic Prayer Internship Program at Sewanee house. *Eastern Prov* Mother Miriam CSM St Marys Convent 242 Cloister Way Greenwich NY 12834-7922 (518) 692-3028 *Fax:* (518) 692-3029 *E-mail:* Compunun@stmaryseast.org Branch House: St Marys Convent PO Box 20280 Luwinga Mzuzu2 Malawi. *Web:* www.stmaryseast.org *Western Prov* Sr Letitia CSM 1840 N Prospect Ave #504 Milwaukee, WI 53202 *E-mail:* srletitia@earthlink.net *Southern Prov* Sr Madeleine Mary CSM St Mary's Convent 1100 S Mary's Ln Sewanee TN 37375-2614 (931) 598-0046; fax (931)598-9519, *Web:* stmary-conventsewanee.org; *Facebook page:* Community of St. Mary, South-

ern Province. St. Mary's Convent Sagada Mtn Province PHILIPPINES.

Community of the Teachers of the Children of God, The

Originally founded in 1934 as a traditionally monastic order for women, now a Community of both women and men, whose mission is to continue to support educational organizations to educate children of all abilities. Consisting of two professed nuns, who continue to the live the religious life, and lay members, the Community is dedicated to the education work of the Episcopal Church and offers through the *Rule of the Associates* the opportunity for religious instruction and spiritual development. *Contact:* Nannette Akins Associate CTCG 5790 E. 14th Street Tucson, AZ 85711 (520) 591-4178. *E-mail:* nannetteak@aol.com.

Community of the Transfiguration

Prayer, worship, hospitality and retreats, educational and recreational ministry with children. Sup Sr Teresa M Martin CT Convent of the Transfiguration 495 Albion Ave Cincinnati OH 45246 *E-mail:* ctsisters@aol.com *Web:* www.ctsisters.org (513) 771-5291 *Fax:* (513) 771-0839 Local Ministries: Transfiguration Spirituality Ctr *Web:* www.ctretreats.org *E-mail:* ctretreats@gmail.com; Bethany Sch: (513) 771-7462 *Web:* www.bethanyschool.org; S Monica's Rec Ctr *E-mail:* mpearl121@gmail.com; Branch Ministries, hospitality and retreats: Trsfg House Eureka CA 95501; *E-mail:* srdianact@gmail.com; Tabor Ministry Butler OH 44822 *E-mail:* hilaritas@aol.com

Episcopal Carmel of Saint Teresa

Semi-enclosed, monastic, contemplative, Carmelite community for women in the tradition of Teresa of Avila and John of the Cross. The community also includes vowed Oblates. Associates are Christian men and women. Life of prayer, silence and solitude lived within community, 123 Little New York Road, Rising Sun, MD. 410-658-6736, STIPerk@gmail.com. http://www.ecst.ang-md.com

Order of St Anne—Bethany

A religious community for women and a ministry of hospitality and community service within the Bethany Convent and Bethany House of Prayer. Sr CA Ana Clara OSA *Superior* 25 Hillside Ave Arlington MA 02476 (781) 643-0921 *E-mail:* bethanyconvent@aol.com

Order of St Anne—Chicago

The Order of St Anne's Chicago is a traditional order of Anglican nuns in the Episcopal Church. Since 1921, we have been an active presence in the heart of the city of Chicago. Currently we are called to parish work at the Episcopal Church of the Ascension, and active ministry to the local community. Sr Judith Marie OSA *Superior* 1125 N LaSalle Blvd Chicago IL 60610 (312) 642-3638 *E-mail:* stannechicago@hotmail.com.

Order of St Helena

A religious community for women dedicated to prayer, community and service. *Leadership Council* The Rev Sr Carol Andrew OSH, Sr Mary Lois OSH, The Rev Sr Ellen Francis OSH. Convent of St Helena 414 Savannah Barony Drive, North Augusta, SC 29841 *E-mail:* sisters@osh.org *Web:* www.osh.org.

Sisterhood of the Holy Nativity

Special dedication to the Incarnation. Religious Order with strong emphasis on life of prayer in community. External ministries are evangelistic in nature and take many forms. Mother House W14164 Plante Dr Ripon WI 54971 (920) 748-5332 *Mother Sup* Sr Abigail *E-mail:* abizac50@hotmail.com *Web:* caroa.net/sites/sisterhoodhn/.

Society of St Margaret

Mission focused Sisters living an ancient tradition with a modern outlook. We were founded in 1855 in East Grinstead, England, by The Rev John Mason Neale. The American House was established in Boston in 1873. Sr Adele Marie SSM *Superior*; St Margaret's Convent PO Box C (50 Harden Hill Rd) Duxbury MA 02331 (781) 934-9477 *E-mail:* sisters@ssmbos.org *Web:* www.ssmbos.org. *Dependencies:* Boston House for Urban Ministry, Dorchester MA; St Margaret's Convent Port-au-Prince HAITI; Sisters of St Margaret Neale House 50 Fulton New York NY 10038.

OTHER CHRISTIAN COMMUNITIES

Anamchara Fellowship

Founded in 2003, Anamchara Fellowship is a dispersed community, open to men and women: single, married and partnered. Dedicated to the Holy Trinity, members use "Celtic Daily Prayer" as part of their daily round of prayer. Members take vows of Simplicity, Fidelity and Obedience and must be approved by their ecclesial authority where they live in order to become part of the Fellowship. Our focus of ministry is pastoral care, catechesis and spiritual direction, and we seek to provide these to our parishes and dioceses from which we come. We seek to be guided by our charisms of generosity, hospitality, compassion and love; and the inspiration of the Celtic saints. As a form of the "New Monasticism," Anamchara Fellowship seeks to bridge the gap between the traditional spirit of monastic community and the spirit of the emerging church. For further information view our website fwww.anamcharafellowship.org or contact: Sister Barbara Clare at bconroy2207@gmail.com.

Anglican Order of Preachers

A dispersed community open to women, men, lay and ordained, married or single. Dedicated to the mission of preaching the Gospel of Jesus Christ with passion appropriate to the subject we proclaim and teaching others the art of preaching with the self-same passion and skill. An apostolic community following the practice and spirituality founded by Saint Dominic de Guzman. For further information view our website http://anglicandominicans.org/ or e-mail us at anglicanorderofpreachers@ymail.com

Brotherhood of St Gregory

Open to Anglican men, clergy and lay, without regard to marital status, living under a common Rule and serving the Church on parochial, diocesan and national levels. The brothers live individually, in small groups, or with their families, and support the Community's activities from their secular or church-related employment. Inquiries? Please visit our website: www.gregorians.org.

Community of Celebration

Residential community of men/women, lay/clergy, married/single shares common life undergirded by Daily Prayer Book Offices, weekly Eucharist, monthly Taize worship. Members take Benedictine vows of stability, obedience, and conversion of life. Ministry is to be a Christian presence among the poor, to offer hospitality, retreats, sabbaticals, and conferences. Internships and Companion relationships welcome. Bill Farra *Primary Guardian* Box 309 Aliquippa PA 15001 (724) 375-1510. *E-mail:* mail@communityofcelebration.com *Web:* www.communityofcelebration.com.

Community of the Gospel

We are a non-residential community, open to men and women, single, married and partnered. Dedicated to living the Gospel message through the vows of Daily Prayer, Reflective Study, and Personal Service, these common roots lead to unique responses to God's love in our lives. Each member develops his or her Personal Rule of Life based on these vows, and has a personal spiritual direction team. For more information visit our website at www.communityoft hegospel.org or contact Br Daniel-Joseph, Guardian, at N1582 Midway Road, Hortonville, WI 54944 or *E-mail:* dschroeder003@new.rr.com. *Bishop Visitor*: Chilton Knudsen.

Order of the Community of the Paraclete

Serving since 1971. The Paracletians are men and women, single or married, leading a life of prayer and ministry under a rule and vows. Our work is to bring wholeness to those who need healing in spirit, mind, and body, through the power of the Holy Spirit. Our work is done in three states: AZ, FL, and WA. *Contact:* Min Br John Ryan St Dunstan's Church 722 N 145th St Shoreline WA 98133 *Web:* www.theparacletians.org. *Bishop Visitor*: Bavi Rivera.

Companions of St Luke, OSB

Companions of St Luke OSB is a community founded on the Rule of St Benedict. The Community honors the richness of its tradition, yet knows that each age needs to bring innovation to its history and practice. CSL-OSB is a dispersed community with each member living the Benedictine experience within the context of our parishes and the world.

The members of the community live into the Rule of St. Benedict with daily prayer, Lectio Divina, contemplation, study of scripture and the Rule. The Companions of St. Luke, OSB is open to single and partnered persons, lay or ordained. Vocations include Vowed life and Oblation with respective vows and promises made of obedience, conversion of life and stability. For more information visit our website at http://www.csl-osb.org/ or contact us at csl91.membership@gmail.com. *Superior:* Br. Basil Edwards, OSB. *Bishop Visitor:* The Right Reverend R. William Franklin.

Congregation of the Companions of the Holy Saviour

Celibate male bishops, priests, deacons, and cand for H Orders. Founded 1891. Common Rule, but not in community. All attend annual Chapter and retreat. Rule for Priests' Assoc and Lay men and women, monthly area conferences. *Contact:* Fr Justin A Falciani Christ Episcopal Church Box 97 157 Shore Rd Somers Point NJ 08244 (609) 927-6262. *E-mail:* ccsprector@Verizon.net.

The Little Sisters of St. Clare, A Franciscan Women's Community

The Little Sisters of St. Clare is a Community of women who seek to live a contemplative life of prayer, study, and service, in the tradition of St. Clare and St. Francis. As a Community, our beliefs are seen in our actions, in worship, and in our commitment to a common life. We gather monthly, most typically in small chapters located throughout the greater Puget Sound area of Western Washington. We serve a variety of local and global ministries – guiding children and youth, serving the poor, the ill, and the marginalized; nurturing the environment; and healing the other. We have been recognized by The Episcopal Church's House of Bishops since 2002. As individuals, our faith is rooted in our baptismal covenant; we express our response to God's call in a lifestyle which interprets monastic traditions in a contemporary way. We guide our lives by the simple vows of simplicity, fidelity, and purity. We live independently, valuing our proximity to each other, and are single, married and in committed relationships. *Mother Guardian:* DedraAnn "D." Bracher 400 NW Gilman Blvd. #2511 Issaquah, WA 98027. *Tel:* (253)-569-4759 *Email:* lsscmotherguardian@gmail.com *Web:* http://stclarelittlesisters.org

Order of Saint Anthony the Great

The intent of the Order is to foster a contemplative spiritual life within the laity and clergy of the Church. We do so through intentional community and weekly classes open to all. We are a community open to men and women, celibate and coupled, in residence and dispersed that live under the vows of stability, constancy, simplicity, and obedience. We currently hold meetings each week in our two Chapter Houses in Atlanta, GA and Houston, TX. We are under the supervision of The Rt. Rev Dorsey Henderson, retired Bishop of Upper South Carolina, Bishop Visitor to the Order. *Abbot* Br. Kenneth Hosley, O.P.C. currently leads our community. You can find out more about the order at www.ordersaintanthony.org, or reach out to Br. Hosley at br.kenneth@gmail.com.

Rivendell Community, The

Rivendell is a Eucharistic community working and praying to renew the vision of the Church as a holy priesthood, in and on behalf of the world. The Community's goals include: creating and serving houses of prayer and hospitality; participating in ministries of parish leadership, religious education, and social justice; and providing well educated and holy priestly ministry for smaller, less affluent churches. Members include men, women, celibate, married, lay, ordained, residential and nonresidential. All follow a common Rule which sustains and nourishes us to live contemplative and active lives "at right angles to the world" in our diverse ministries. The Rivendell Community PO Box 43 Bolivar MO 65613 (316) 323-3961 *E-mail:* rivendellcommunity.inc@gmail.com *Guardian Rev* Virginia Dabney Brown.

Sisters of Saint Gregory

A religious community of women in the Episcopal Church who have discerned a call to the religious life. Founded in 1987 as a companion order by the Brotherhood of St Gregory, we became autonomous in 1999. We are clergy and lay, without regard to marital status, living dispersed in the world under a common rule as women of prayer and serving the Church on parochial, diocesan, and national levels. The sisters support the community's activities by their secular or church-related employment. All women eighteen years of age and older who are discerning a vocation to the religious life and who are in good standing with the Episcopal or a sister church are welcome to inquire. *Inquiries:* Sr Susanna Bede Caroselli SSG 505 Allenview Dr Mechanicsburg PA 17055-6187 *Web:* www.sistersofsaintgregory.org.

Society of St Anna the Prophet, The (SSAP)

The SSAP is a dispersed vowed community of women, both lay and ordained, called to Godly aging and to ministry with elders and with children. The vows are simplicity, creativity and balance. The SSAP is open to any woman over 50 years old, confirmed in the Episcopal Church, whose vocation to this prophetic life and ministry is discerned. Vows are taken after a minimum of one provisional year and one novice year. Life vows may be taken after five years. The SSAP includes elders living in care, as well as working and retired elders living independently. Annas are single, married, widowed, and partnered. Founded in the Diocese of Atlanta, the Society is beginning to expand into other areas. Those interested may visit the website at annasisters.org or write the Director of Provisionals and Novices, the Rev. Mary Moore SSAP, Chapter House 1655 Rainier Falls Drive NE Atlanta GA 30329-4107.

Worker Brothers of the Holy Spirit, The

International Covenant Community for Lay Brothers, Lay Workers and Clergy regardless of marital status. Life commitment to common Rule, Benedictine in orientation but not lived in Community. From a Contemplative model of prayer, meditation, worship, the Eucharist and a focus on the Theology concept of being and the Fruit of the Spirit, come the action of miss and ministry in the local parish, church, and world. For contacts, see Worker Sisters of the Holy Spirit, below *Web:* www.workerbrothers.org.

Worker Sisters of the Holy Spirit, The

International Covenant Community for Lay Sisters, Lay Workers, and Clergy regardless of marital status. Life Commitment to common Rule, Benedictine in orientation but not lived in Community. From a Contemplative model of prayer, meditation, worship, the Eucharist, and a focus on the Theology concept of being and the Fruit of Spirit, come the action of miss and ministry in the local parish, church, and world. *Co-Directors* Sr Christine WSHS & Sr Deborah WSHS *US Dir* Sr Christine WSHS 528 First St Windsor CO 80550 *E-mail:* casturges@msn.com *Canada Dir* Sr Deborah WSHS 711 McMurtry Rd Midland Ontario L4R 0B9 CANA DA *E-mail:* strdeborah@hotmail.com *Web:* www.workersisters.org.

PREVIOUS BISHOPS OF THE DIOCESES, DISTRICTS, AND JURISDICTIONS

coadj: coadjutor, const: constituted, dio: diocesan, m: missionary, org: organized, suffr: suffragan

Anking (1910) Daniel T. Huntington 1912-40, Lloyd R Craighill 1940-49. Became Dio of Wan-Gan, H Catholic Church in China 1949.

Asheville Became Dio of WNC 1907.

Boise Became Idaho in 1907.

Central America and Panama Canal Zone (const 1919) Separated into Panama and the Canal Zone, and Central America 1956. See Panama and the Canal Zone.

Central America (const 1956) David E Richards 1957-67. Divided 1967 into 5 districts: CR, ES, Guat, Hond, Nic.

Central Brazil (const 1950) Louis C Melcher 1950-58, Edmund K Sherrill 1959-65. Now part of the Igreja Episcopal do Brasil.

Central Pennsylvania see Bethlehem and Harrisburg.

Central Philippines (const 1901) Chas H Brent 1901-18, Gouveneur F Mosher 1920-40, Robt F Wilner suffr 1936-56, Norman S Binsted 1942-57, Lyman C Ogilby suffr 1953 Bp 1956-67, Ed G Longid suffr 1963-71, CB Manguramas suffr 1969-71, Benito C Cabanban suffr 1957 Bp 1967-78, Manuel C Lumpias coad 1977 Bp 1978-90. Became part of the Province of the Philippines in 1990.

Costa Rica (const 1967) David E Richards 1967-68, Jose Antonio Ramos 1969-76. Became extra-provincial in 1976. Became part of the Province of Central America 1998.

Cuba (const 1901) Albion W Knight 1904-13, Hiram R Hulse 1915-38, Alexander H Blankingship 1939-61, Romualdo Gonzalez 1961-66. Became autonomous dio under metropolitan council in 1966.

Cuernavaca (const 1989) Jose Saucedo 1989-. Became part of the Church of the Province of Mexico 1994.

Dakota Separated into ND and SD in 1883.

Duluth (const 1895) James D Morrison 1897-1922, Granville G Bennett coadj 1920 Bp 1922-23, Benj T Kemerer coadj 1930 Bp 1933-43. Reunited with Minnesota 1944.

Eastern Diocese (org 1810) Alexander V Griswold 1811-43. Incl all of New England except CT. VT separated 1832, NH 1832, RI ME and MA 1843.

Eastern Oklahoma (const 1910) Theodore P Thurston 1911-19. Reunited with Oklahoma 1919.

El Salvador (const w/Bps in charge 1967-1992) Martin Barahona 1992-. Became part of the Province of Central America 1998.

Erie see Northwestern Pennsylvania.

Guatemala (const w/Bps in charge 1967-1981) Armando Guerra 1982-. Became part of the Province of Central America 1998.

Hankow (const 1910) James A Ingle 1902-03, Logan H Roots 1904-37, Alfred A Gilman suffr 1925 Bp 1937-48. Became part of H Catholic Church in China 1948.

Harrisburg (org 1904) James H Darlington 1905-30, Hunter Wyatt-Brown 1931-43, John T Heistand 1943-66, Earl M Honaman suffr 1956-69. *Renamed Central Pennsylvania in 1971.*

Honolulu see Hawaii.

Illinois see Chicago.

Kansas City see West Missouri.

Kearney see Platte.

Kyoto (const 1898) Sidney C Partridge 1900-11, Henry St G Tucker 1912-23, Shirley N Nichols 1926-40. Trans to H Catholic Church in Japan 1941.

Laramie see Platte.

Liberia (const 1851) John Payne 1851-71, John G Auer 1873-74, Chas C Pennick 1877-83, Samuel D Ferguson 1885-1916, Walter H Overs 1919-25, Theophilus M Gardiner suffr 1921-41, Robt E Campbell OHC 1925-36, Leopold Kroll 1936-45, Bravid W Harris 1945-64, Dillard H Brown Jr 1964-69, Geo D Browne 1970-82. Now part of the Province of West Africa.

Marquette see Northern Michigan.

Mexico (est 1879) Sergio Carranza-Gomez 1989. Became part of the Church of the Province of Mexico 1994.

Michigan City see Northern Indiana.

New Mexico and Southwest Texas see Rio Grande.

Nicaragua (const w/Bps in charge 1969-1985) Sturdie Downs 1985-. Became part of the Province of Central America 1998.

Niobrara (1871-83) see South Dakota.

North Central Philippines (const 1989) Artemio M Zabala 1989-90. Became part of the Province of the Philippines in 1990.

North Kwanto (org 1893 as No Tokyo, 1938 as No Kwanto) John McKim 1893-1935, Chas S Reifsnyder suff 1924 Bp 1935-41. Became part of the H Catholic Church of Japan.

North Texas Became Dio of Northwest Texas in 1958.

North Tokyo see North Kwanto.

Northern Mexico (const 1973) German Martinez-Marquez 1987-. Became part of the Church of the Province of Mexico 1994.

Northern New Jersey see Newark.

Northern Luzon (const 1986) Richard A Abellon 1986-90. Became part of the Province of the Philippines in 1990.

Northern Philippines (const 1972) Ed G Longid 1972-75, Richard A Abellon 1975-86, Robt LO Longid 1986-90. Became part of the Province of the Philippines in 1990.

Northern Texas see Dallas.

Northwest Diocese Jos C Talbot 1860-65.

Okinawa Edmond L Browning 1968-71. *Transferred to the Nippon Sei Ko Kai 1972.*

Oregon and Washington see Oregon. Washington separated 1880.

Panama (const 1919) James C Morris 1920-30, Harry Beal 1937-44, Reginald H Gooden 1945-72, Lemuel Barnett Shirley 1972-83, Victor Scantlebury suff 1991-94, James H Ottley 1984-95, Clarence Wallace Hayes Dewar 1995-. Became part of the Province of Central America 1998.

Platte, The (const 1889. Name changed to Laramie 1898, Kearney 1908, Western Nebraska 1913) Anson R Graves 1890-1910, Geo A Beecher 1910-43. Reunited with Nebraska 1946.

Puerto Rico (const 1902) James H Van Buren 1902-12, Manuel Ferrando suff 1923-34, Chas B Colmore 1913-47, Chas F Boynton coadj 1944 Bp 1947-51, A Ervine Swift 1951-65, Francisco Reus-Froylan 1965-79. Became extra-provincial in 1980.

Sacramento see Northern California.

Salina see Western Kansas.

Salt Lake see Utah.

Shanghai Wm J Boone 1844-64, Channing M Williams 1866-74, Samuel IJ Schereschewsky 1877-83, Wm J Boone 1884-91, Fredk R Graves 1893-1937, John W Nichols suffr 1934-38, Wm P Roberts

1937-49. Became Dio of Kiangsu, H Catholic Church in China 1949.

South Florida (const 1892 as Southern Florida, 1922 as South Florida) Wm C Gray 1892-1913, Cameran Mann m 1913 dio 1922-32, John D Wing coadj 1925 Bp 1932-50, Martin J Bramm suffr 1951-56, Wm F Moses suffr 1956-61 Henry I Louttit suffr 1945 coadj 1948 dio 1951-69, James L Duncan suffr 1961-69, Wm L Hargrave suffr 1961-69. *South Florida divided into Central Fla., Southeast Fla. and Southwest Fla. 1969.*

Southern Brazil (est 1890 rec'd into American Church 1907) Lucien L Kinsolving 1907-28, Wm MM Thomas suffr 1925 Bp 1928-49, Louis C Melcher coadj 1948 Bp 1949-50, Athalicio T Pithan suffr 1940 Bp 1950-55, Egmont M Krischke 1955-65. Now part of Igreja Episcopal do Brasil.

Southern Philippines (const 1972) CB Manguramas 1972-84. Narcisco V Ticobay 1986-90. Became part of the Province of the Philippines in 1990.

Southwest Temporary mission jurisdiction 1859-65.

Southwest Texas Included in New Mexico and Southwest Texas since 1895.

Southwestern Brazil Egmont M Krischke 1950-55, Plinio L Simoes 1956-65. Now part of Igreja Episcopal do Brasil.

Southwestern Mexico (const 1989) Claro Huerto-Ramos 1989-. Became part of the Church of the Province of Mexico 1994.

Tohoku (const 1920) Norman S Binsted 1928-41. Transferred to the Holy Catholic Church in Japan 1941.

Washington Territory see Olympia.

Western Colorado (const 1892) Wm M Baker 1894-94, admin by Abiel Leonard 1894-1903, part of Salt Lake 1904-07, recreated 1907, Edward J Knight 1907-08, Benj Brewster 1909-16, Frank H Touret 1917-19. Reunited with Colorado 1919.

Western Mexico (const 1973) Samuel Espinoza 1983-. Became part of the Church of the Province of Mexico 1994.

Western Nebraska see Platte.

Western Texas see West Texas.

Wisconsin see Milwaukee.

Diocesan and Parochial Lists

FOR QUICK REFERENCE, some words have been abbreviated. Please see lists of abbreviations on pages 7, 8, and 9 and at the beginning of some sections.

ADDRESSES OF THE CLERGY may be found in the alphabetical Clergy List in the last section of the *Annual.* Please send Clergy List changes to The Editor of Directories, Church Publishing, 445 Fifth Ave, New York, NY 10016.

CHURCH LISTINGS follow this order:

1 *Official postal name of city*
2 *Name of church*
3 *Type of church (capital letter in bold face):*
   P = parish
   M= mission
   PS = preaching station
   CC = college chapel
   SC = summer chapel
   HC = historical church
   NH = nursing home
   PM = prison ministry
   I = Inactive
   O = Other
4 *Number of communicants in good standing* Actual numbers shown reflect information from the 2008 Parochial Report provided by Congregational Research and the Office of the General Convention, Episcopal Church Center. Information from the 2009 Report will be uploaded to www.theredbook.org in Fall 2010.
5 " § " designates a *Parish Day School.*
6 *St Address*
7 *Zip Code*
8 *Alternate mailing address* if applicable
9 *City* (if applicable) and *church,* if city has more than one, of which the church is a mission, or whose clergy serve the mission.
10 *Members of the Clergy.*
11 *Parish Telephone Number*

EXAMPLES

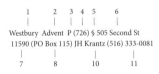

Church of the Advent is a parish in the city of Westbury, has 726 communicants and a Parish Day School. It is located at 505 Second St with a mailing address of PO Box 115 11590. Its clergy is the Rev J.H. Krantz, and the phone number is (516) 333-0081.

St. Paul's Church is a mission in the city of Irvington, has 54 communicants, and is located at 264 E. Main St. which is also its mailing address. It is either a mission of St. Luke's Church in Mobile, which has more than one church, or is a diocesan mission served by the clergy of St. Luke's.

✠ at beginning of an entry indicates Cathedral or Pro-Cathedral.

PARISH DAY SCHOOLS. Parishes with day schools (above nursery or kindergarten level) are identified by the symbol § . For more information, write directly to the parish or to The National Association of Episcopal Schools, 815 2nd Ave New York NY 10017 (800) 334-7626 x6134 for the *Directory of Episcopal Church Schools.*

NON-PAROCHIAL CLERGY. The list includes retired clergy as well as clergy engaged in a variety of ministries. Abbreviations include: ret (retired) dcn (deacon) chap (chaplain) ret Bp (retired Bishop) Dn (Dean) prof (professor) tchr (teacher) dio staff (diocesan staff).

To Make Additions or Corrections

Listings for congregations may be updated using CPG's Employee Roster.

Other corrections to diocesan information, information concerning organizations and the governing structures of the Church come from the dioceses, organizations themselves or from The Executive Council.

Please send Clergy List changes to the Recorder of Ordinations, 19 East 34th St, New York, NY 10016.

STATE OF ALABAMA
Dioceses of Alabama and Central Gulf Coast

DIOCESE OF ALABAMA
(PROVINCE IV)
Comprises northern and central counties in the state of Alabama
DIOCESAN OFFICE 521 N 20th St Birmingham AL 35203
TEL (205) 715-2060   FAX (205) 715-2066
E-MAIL diooffice@dioala.org   WEB www.dioala.org

Previous Bishops—
Nicholas H Cobbs 1844-61, Richard H Wilmer 1862-1900, Henry M Jackson asst 1891-1900, Robt W Barnwell 1900-02, Chas M Beckwith 1902-28, Wm G McDowell coadj 1922 Bp 1928-38, Chas CJ Carpenter 1938-68, Randolph R Claiborne Jr suffr 1949-53, Geo M Murray suffr 1953 coadj 1959 Bp 1969-70, Wm A Dimmick asst 1984, Furman C Stough 1971-88, Robt O Miller suffr 1986-88 Bp 1988-98, Henry Nutt Parsley Jr Bp Coad 1996-1998 Bp 1999-2011, Onell A Soto asst 1999-01, Mark H Andrus suffr 2002-06, J McKee Sloan suffr 2008-12

Bishop—John McKee Sloan (1024) (Dio 7 Jan 12)

Assistant Bishop—Santosh Kumar Marray (1072) (Dio 27 Nov 12)

Staff Off Fin and Admin Rev RP Morpeth; *Staff Off Cler Trans & Min Dev* S Sartain; *Bookkeeper* J Cook; *Admin Asst to Bp Sloan* J Hall; *Admin Asst to Asst Bp Marray/Receptionist* D Servant; *Coord Employee Ben & Data* C Jones; *Lifelong Form Coord* K Graham; *Spec Events Coord* G Perrine; *Sawyerville Proj Dir* L Manning; *Yth Min Coord* S Oakes; *Comm Coord* Rev Dcn D Drachlis; *Archdcn* L Thibodaux

Officers: Sec D Thornton; *Treas* H Hargrove; *Asst Sec-Treas* R Morpeth; *Chanc* M Porter Esq

Stand Comm—Cler: J Alvey S Sloan E Garner J Gibbes; *Lay: Pres* J McLemore D Clark R Holliday H Hill

Council—Cler: J Rengers D Meginniss L Shafer R McCown C Frazer A Pearson; *Lay:* B Garrett P Hall B Meyer S Hudson B Sandidge J Thornton

Disciplinary Board—Cler: S Arnold K Jacob G Evans R Webster; *Lay:* R Hamner Esq S Herring G Weaver

*Trustees of the University of the South—*J Bradford C Mayer Rev A Anderson

Depts: Com on Min Rev R Kendrick; *Stew* Rev R McCown; *Task Force for Stew of Creation* R Byrd; *AL Epis Found Brd Dirs* R Thurber; *Christian Form* Rev M Scalise; *Rec Min* K Hollifield; *Sawyerville* L Manning; *Happening* C Jones; *Spirit* L Howell; *Yth*

S Oakes; *Mission & Outreach* R Rothrock; *Comp Dio* Rev C Van Slyke; *Race Relations* Rev C Foster; *Hisp Min* Rev J Comer; *Parish Dev* Rev L Shafer; *Architecture* D Cosper; *Lit* Rev C Youngston; *Altar Guild* M Noble; *Ecum* Rev J Evans; *Higher Ed* Rev M Rich; *Camp McDowell* Rev M Johnston; *Fin* H Hargrove; *ECW* B Mayhall; *Cursillo* N Bromberg

Dio Conv: TBD

PARISHES, MISSIONS, AND CLERGY

Alabaster Church of the Holy Spirit **P** (234) 858 **Alabaster** Church of the Holy Spirit **P** (124) 858 Kent Dairy Road 35007-2027 (Mail to: PO Box 2365 35007-2027) Mary Sullivan Elton Wright (205) 621-3418

Albertville Christ Episcopal Church **P** (194) 607 E Main St 35950-2447 (Mail to: PO Box 493 35950-0008) (256) 878-3243

Alexander City St James Episcopal Church **P** (263) 347 S Central Ave 35010-2579 (Mail to: 347 S Central Ave 35010-2579) Robert St Germain-Iler (256) 234-4752

Alpine Trinity Church **P** (26) 6898 Grist Mill Road 35014-0095 (Mail to: PO Box 75 35014-0075)

Anniston Church of St Michael & All Angels **P** (212) 1000 West 18th St 36201 (Mail to: PO Box 1884 36202-1884) Chris Hartley Hugh Jones

Anniston Grace Episcopal Church **HC** (352) 1000 Leighton Ave 36207-5702 (Mail to: PO Box 1791 36202-1791) Lee Shafer (256) 236-4457

Athens St Timothys Episcopal Church **P** (97) 207 E Washington St 35611-2651 (Mail to: 207 E Washington St 35611-2651) Jeffrey Evans (256) 232-3541

Auburn Holy Trinity Episcopal Church **P** (740) § 100 Church Dr 36830-5903 (Mail to: 100 Church Dr 36830-5903) Geoffrey Evans Jonathan Chesney (334) 887-9506

Auburn St Dunstan Episcopal Church **Campus Ministry** (198) 136 E Magnolia Ave 36830-4722 (Mail to: 136 E Magnolia Ave 36830-4722) John Warren Norbert Wilson

Bessemer Trinity Episcopal Church **P** (61) 2014 Berkley Ave 35020-4236 (Mail to: 2014 Berkley

Avenue 35020-4236) (205) 966-3938

Birmingham All Saints Episcopal Church **P** (1683) 110 West Hawthorne Road 35209-3999 (Mail to: 110 West Hawthorne Road 35209-3999) Glenda Curry Anna Russell Friedman Charles Youngson (205) 879-8651

Birmingham Birmingham Episcopal Campus Ministry **CC** Mrs Ruth Ramsey 2709 Ensley 5 Point 35218-2852 (Mail to: 1024 12th St S 35205-5234) Thomas Joyner (205) 320-1500

✠ **Birmingham** Cathedral Church of the Advent **O** (3690) Attn Bryan Helm 2017 6th Ave N 35203-2701 (Mail to: 2017 6th Ave N 35203-2701) Joseph Gibbes Deborah Leighton Stephen McCarthy Andrew Pearson Matthew Schneider Richard Smalley (205) 251-2324

Birmingham Church of the Ascension **P** (520) 1912 Canyon Rd 35216-1753 (Mail to: 1912 Canyon Rd 35216-1753) Stephen Hood David Hall (205) 822-3480

Birmingham Grace Episcopal Church **P** (196) 5712 1st Ave N 35212-1604 (Mail to: 5712 1st Ave N 35212-1604) Robyn Arnold John Cruse Martha Holmes Roberts Johnson Joseph Knott Jonathan Waddell (205) 595-4636

Birmingham St Andrews Parish **P** (255) 1024 12th St S 35205-5234 (Mail to: 1024 S 12th St 35205-5234) Maurice Goldsmith Michael Rich (205) 251-7898

Birmingham St Johns For the Deaf Church **P** (59) 3794 Crosshaven Dr 35223-2833 (Mail to: 3794 Crosshaven Dr 35223-2833) Marianne Stuart

Birmingham St Lukes Episcopal Church **P** (2878) 3736 Montrose Rd 35213-3832 (Mail to: 3736 Montrose Rd 35213-3800) Rebecca Debow John Mark Ford Maurice Goldsmith Katherine Nakamura Rengers Richmond Webster (205) 871-3583

Birmingham St Marks Episcopal Church **P** (58) 228 Dennison Ave SW 35211-3803 (Mail to: 228 Dennison Ave SW 35211-3803) Jayne Pool (205) 322-8449

Birmingham St Marys on The Highlands Church **P** (1744) 1910 12th Ave S 35205-3804 (Mail to: 1910 12th Ave S 35205-3804) Harry Gardner William Manning Danielle Thompson (205) 933-1140

Birmingham St Stephens Episcopal Church **P** (1582) 3775 Crosshaven Dr 35223-2832 (Mail to: 3775 Crosshaven Dr 35223-2832) Donna Gerold Maurice Goldsmith Virginia Monroe Joy Phipps Daniel Strandlund (205) 967-8786

Birmingham St Thomas Episcopal Parish **P** (355) 2870 Acton Rd 35243-2502 (Mail to: 2870 Acton Rd 35243-2502) Josiah Rengers Louise Thibodaux

Boligee St Mark Episcopal Church (Boligee) **P** (5) Rr 1 Box 10 35443-9798 (Mail to: PO Box 839 35462-0839) (205) 372-4071

Carlowville St Pauls Church Carlowville **P** (24) 310 County Rd 4 36761-3626 (Mail to: PO Box

27 36761-0027) (334) 872-3674

Chelsea St Catherines Episcopal Church **P** (99) 4163 County Rd 39 35043-6713 (Mail to: PO Box 577 35043-0614) William Blackerby (205) 618-8367

Childersburg St Mary Episcopal Church **P** (34) 5th Ave & 5th St 35044 (Mail to: PO Box 303 35044-0303) Frank Young (256) 378-8020

Clanton Trinity Episcopal Church **P** (80) 503 Second Avenue South 35046-2121 (Mail to: PO Box 2121 35046-2121) (205) 755-3339

Cullman Grace Episcopal Church **P** (298) 305 Arnold St NE 35055-2910 (Mail to: 305 Arnold St NE 35055-2910) James McAdams (256) 734-6212

Decatur Church of the Good Shepherd **P** (98) 3809 Spring Ave SW 35603-3203 (Mail to: 3809 Spring Ave SW 35603-3203) David Dill (256) 351-9955

Decatur St Johns Episcopal Church **P** (606) No 202 Gordon Dr SE 35601-2528 (Mail to: 202 Gordon Dr SE 35601-2528) Evan Garner John Olson (256) 353-9615

Demopolis Trinity Episcopal Church **HC** (166) No 401 N Main Ave 36732-2019 (Mail to: PO Box 560 36732-0560) John Barnes (334) 289-3363

Eutaw St Stephens Church **P** (93) 403 Norht Eutaw Ave 35462-0839 (Mail to: PO Box 839 35462-0839) Josiah Rengers James Vaughn (205) 301-0483

Fairfield Christ Episcopal Church **P** (92) 4912 Richard M Scrushy Pkwy 35064-1456 (Mail to: PO Box 424 35064-1456) (205) 787-2053

Faunsdale St Michael/Holy Cross Episcopal Chur **P** (27) 45 Watkins St 36738 (Mail to: 516 County Road 54 36738) (334) 289-3363

Fayette St Michaels Episcopal Church **P** (87) 431 10th St NW 35555-1834 (Mail to: 431 Tenth St NW 35555-1834) Mary Dunlap (205) 932-6929

Florence St Bartholomew's Episcopal Church **P** (86) 1900 Darby Dr 35630-2625 (Mail to: 1900 Darby Dr 35630-2625) Anna Brawley Wilbur Eich (256) 764-2000

Florence Trinity Episcopal Church **P** (660) 410 North Pine Street 35630-4655 (Mail to: PO Box M 35631-1912) Andrew Keyse Callie Plunket-Brewton (256) 764-6149

Forkland St Johns in the Prairie Episcopal Ch **P** (12) A L Issac Rd 36740-4216 (Mail to: PO Box 839 35462-0839) James Vaughn (205) 289-0399

Fort Payne St Philip's Episcopal Church **P** (78) 2813 Godfrey Ave NE 35967-3746 (Mail to: 2813 Godfrey Ave NE 35967-3746) Forrest Ethridge (256) 845-1192

Gadsden Church of the Holy Comforter **P** (417) 156 S 9th St 35901-3646 (Mail to: 156 S 9th St 35901-3646) Edward Hunt David Barfield (256) 547-5361

Gainesville St Alban's Church **P** (4) 290 Chestnut St 35459 (Mail to: C O PO Box 1422 35470-1422) Richard Losch (205) 652-4210

Greensboro St Pauls Episcopal Church **HC** (81) 905 Church St 36744-1520

Guntersville Church of the Epiphany **P** (427) 1101 Sunset Dr 35976-1003 (Mail to: PO Box 116 35976-0116) Aaron Raulerson (256) 582-4897

Hartselle St Barnabas Episcopal Church **P** (43) 1450 Sparkman St NW 35640-4534 (Mail to: PO Box 614 35640-0614) Elvin Basinger (256) 773-4206

Heflin Church of the Messiah **P** (62) Corner Of Lake View & Vaughn 36264 (Mail to: PO Box 596 36264-0596) John Bagby (256) 463-2928

Hoover Church of the Holy Apostles **P** (350) 424 Emery Dr 35244-4548 (Mail to: 424 Emery Dr 35244-4548) Blake Hutson (205) 988-8000

Hoover St Albans Episcopal Church **P** (169) 429 Cloudland Dr 35226-1100 (Mail to: 429 Cloudland Dr 35226-1100) Margaret Doyle (205) 822-2330

Huntsville Church of the Nativity **P** (1763) 208 Eustis Ave SE 35801-4233 (Mail to: 208 Eustis Ave SE 35801-4293) Elenor Anderson William McCown Bonnie McCrickard (256) 533-2455

Huntsville Holy Cross - St Christopher **P** (27) 3740 Meridian St N 35811-1116 (Mail to: 3740 Meridian St N 35811-1116) Charleen Hill (256) 534-7750

Huntsville St Stephens Episcopal Church **P** (365) 8020 Whitesburg Dr SE 35802-3002 (Mail to: 8020 Whitesburg Dr SW 35802-3002) Susan Sloan

Huntsville St Thomas Episcopal Church **P** (693) 12200 Bailey Cove Rd SE 35803-2641 (Mail to: 12200 Bailey Cove Rd SE 35803-2641) Mary Catherine Akamatsu David Drachlis Paul Pradat David Stricker

Jacksonville St Lukes Church **P** (145) 400 Chinabee Ave SE 36265-2810 (Mail to: PO Box 55 36265-0055) (256) 435-9271

Jasper St Marys Church **P** (135) 801 The Trce W 35504-7454 (Mail to: 801 the Trce W 35504-7454) Timothy Murphy (205) 387-7746

Leeds Church of the Epiphany **P** (237) 1338 Montevallo Road 35094-2472 (Mail to: 1338 Montevallo Rd 35094-2472) Monica Carlson (205) 699-2404

Leeds St Matthias Episcopal Church **P** (150) No 1338 Montevallo Rd 35094-2472 (Mail to: 1338 Montevallo Rd 35094-2472) David Hall (205) 553-7282

Livingston St James Church **P** (25) C/O T Raiford Noland 109 Spring 35470 (Mail to: PO Box 446 35470-0446) (205) 652-7462

Lowndesboro St Pauls Episcopal Church **P** (59) 164 Broad St 36752 (Mail to: PO Box 216 36752-0216) Joseph Knight

Madison St Matthews Episcopal Church **P** (682)

786 Hughes Rd 35758-8972 (Mail to: 786 Hughes Rd 35758-8972) Stephen Gruman (250) 864-0788

Marion St Wilfrids Episcopal Church **P** (93) 104 Clements St 36756-1806 (Mail to: PO Box 43 36756-0043) (334) 683-9628

Mentone St Josephs on the Mountain Church **P** (78) 21145 Scenic Hwy 35984 (Mail to: PO Box 161 35984-0161)

Millbrook St Michael and All Angels Church **P** (172) 5941 Robinson Sprin 36054 (Mail to: PO Box 586 36054-0012) Mark Waldo (334) 285-3905

Montevallo St Andrews Episcopal Church **P** (40) 925 Plowman St 35115-3809 (Mail to: 925 Plowman St 35115-3809) Judy Quick Stephen Shanks (205) 665-1667

Montgomery All Saints Episcopal Church **P** (258) 645 Coliseum Blvd 36109 (Mail to: PO Box 3073 36109-0073) (334) 272-2591

Montgomery Church of the Ascension **P** (699) 315 Clanton Ave 36104-5541 (Mail to: 315 Clanton Ave 36104-5598) Andrew Thayer Rosa Lindahl Mark Waldo (334) 263-5529

Montgomery Church of the Good Shepherd **P** (27) 493 S Jackson St 36104-4749 (Mail to: 493 S Jackson St 36104-4749) Elizabeth Powell (334) 834-9280

Montgomery Church of the Holy Comforter **P** (251) 2911 Woodley Rd 36111-2842 (Mail to: 2911 Woodley Rd 36111-2898) Robert Hennagin Jay Croft (334) 281-1337

Montgomery St Johns Episcopal Church **P** (1399) 113 Madison Ave 36104-3623 (Mail to: 113 Madison Ave 36104-3699) Robert Wisnewski Candice Frazer Daniel Strandlund

✠ **Nauvoo** Chapel of the Ascension **Other** 105 Delong Rd 35578 (Mail to: Camp McDowell 35578) Mark Johnston (205) 387-1806

Oneonta Calvary Church **P** (38) 1002 Park Ave 35121-0010 (Mail to: PO Box 821 35121-0010) Joan Henrick (205) 274-9444

Opelika Emmanuel Episcopal Church **P** (24) 800 1st AVE 36801-4346 (Mail to: PO Box 2332 36803-2332) (334) 745-2054

Pelham St Francis of Assisi Church **P** (216) 3545 Cahaba Valley Rd 35124-3527 (Mail to: 3545 Cahaba Valley Road 35124-3527) Donald Owen (205) 988-4371

Pell City St Simon Peter Church **P** (146) 3702 Mays Bend Rd 35128 (Mail to: PO Box 432 35125-0432) Mollie Roberts (205) 884-0877

Pike Road Grace Episcopal Church **P** (150) 906 Pike Road 36064 (Mail to: 906 Pike Road PO Box 640096 36064-0096) David Peeples

Prattville St Marks Episcopal Church **P** (255) 178 E 4th St 36067-3110 (Mail to: 178 E 4th St 36067-3110) Scott Arnold (334) 365-5289

Rainbow City Church of the Resurrection **P** (208) 113 Brown Ave 35906-3122 (Mail to: 113 Brown Ave 35906-3122) Thomas Goldsmith

(256) 442-6862

Roanoke St Barnabas Episcopal Church **P** (53) 809 Rock Mills Rd 36274-5347 (Mail to: 809 Rock Mills Rd 36274-5347) (334) 863-6021

Scottsboro St Lukes Church **P** (275) 402 S Scott St 35768-1935 (Mail to: 404 S Scott St 35768-1935) (256) 574-6216

Seale St Matthews in the Pines **P** (24) 38 Longview Ct 36875-3716 (Mail to: PO Box 221 36875-0221) Donna Gafford (706) 366-6568

Selma St Pauls Episcopal Church **P** (407) 210 Lauderdale St 36701-4521 (Mail to: PO Box 1306 36702-1306) John Alvey Joseph Knight (334) 874-8421

Sheffield Grace Episcopal Church **P** (293) 103 Darby Ave 35660-1505 (Mail to: PO Box 838 35660-0838) (256) 383-2014

Smiths Station St Stephens Episcopal Church **P** (68) 45 Lee County Road 567 36877-3285 (Mail to: 45 Lee County Road 567 36877-3285)

Sylacauga St Andrews Episcopal Church **P** (53) 10 W Walnut St 35150-3312 (Mail to: 10 W Walnut St 35150-3312) Frank Young (256) 249-2411

Talladega St Peters Episcopal Church **P** (189) 208 North St E 35160-2110 (Mail to: PO Box 206 35161-0206) (256) 362-2505

Tallassee Church of the Epiphany **P** (54) 2602 Gilmer Ave 36078-7212 (Mail to: Attn: Betty Eldon 2602 Gilmer Ave 36078-7212) John Warren (334) 252-8618

Trussville Church of the Holy Cross **P** (224) 90 Parkway Dr 35173-1318 (Mail to: 90 Parkway Dr 35173-1318) (205) 655-7668

Tuscaloosa Canterbury Chapel and College Center **P** (447) 812 5th Ave 35401-1206 (Mail to: 812 5th Ave 35401-1206) William Burnette (205) 345-9590

Tuscaloosa Christ Church **P** (1334) 605 Lurleen B Wallace Blvd N 35401 (Mail to: 605 Lurleen B Wallace Blvd N 35401) David Meginniss Catherine Collier (205) 758-4252

Tuskegee Institute St Andrews Episcopal Church **P** (75) 701 W Montgomery Rd 36088-1913 (Mail to: PO Box 1213 36087-1213) (334) 727-3210

Uniontown St Michaels/Holy Cross **P** Franklin Street 36786

Wetumpka Trinity Episcopal Church **P** (272) 5371 US Highway 231 36092-3168 (Mail to: 5375 US Highway 231 36092-3168) Robert Henderson

NON-PAROCHIAL CLERGY

Afanador-Kafuri H *ret* Remlap AL
Akin MA *ret* Birmingham AL
Alford HB *ret* Beaumont TX
Aston GP *dcn* Homewood AL
Barbour GFW *ret* Pleasant Grove AL
Beckett KY *dcn* Rainbow City AL
Bender WD *ret* Scottsboro AL

Blackwell RH *ret* Cullman AL
Branscomb WM *ret* Foley AL
Brown JT *ret* Birmingham AL
Bullard LH *dcn* Huntsville AL
Bunch WH Birmingham AL
Caradine BC *ret* Asotin WA
Carmody AC *ret* Vestavia AL
Carpenter DM *ret* Birmingham AL
Cherbonneau AR Mentone AL
Cleckler MH Birmingham AL
Colangelo PH *dcn* Bessemer AL
Comer JF *ret* Prattville AL
Comer JW *ret* Fort Payne AL
Creasy JA *ret* Opelika AL
Cunningham WW *dcn*
DeBuys JF Birmingham AL
Degweck SW *ret* Birmingham AL
Del Bene RN *ret* Trussville AL
Drube BJ *dcn* Jacksonville AL
Easton SE *dcn* Jacksonville AL
Elliott JE *ret* Gadsden AL
Foreman HV *ret* Owens Cross Roads AL
Fowler RF Carrollton GA
Franklin DN *ret* Birmingham AL
Gaede SH Florence AL
Garfield LA *ret* Auburn AL
Gossett EF Birmingham AL
Groff JW *ret* Mequon WI
Groff ME *dcn* Guntersville AL
Grunfeld MT Montgomery AL
Hammonds J *dcn* Selma AL
Harper JH *ret* Birmingham AL
Hinkle RH Hoover AL
Hoff TJ *ret* Tuscaloosa AL
Holder-Joffrion KE Huntsville AL
Holland-Shuey MB Huntsville AL
Horn PM *ret*
Hudlow AK *dcn* Fayette AL
Jackson TL Tyler TX
Jacob JE *dcn* Cullman AL
Jenkins JWA Augusta GA
Joffrion FH *ret* Birmingham AL
Kearley DA *ret* Sewanee TN
Keith JM *ret* Cary NC
Keyes SN
King WM *ret* Birmingham AL
Landers DT *ret* Tuscaloosa AL
Lanphere L *ret* Leeds AL
Lee JH *dcn*
Lewallen JP *ret* Sewanee TN
Lewis KR *dcn* Fairfield AL
Liles AS Crozet VA
Limehouse FF *ret* Birmingham AL
Marler ML
Marshall RG *ret* St Augustine FL
Miller SL Omaha NE
Morpeth RP Birmingham AL
Motes BE Decatur AL
Murray RL *ret* Nashville TN
Oberheide RD *ret* Montgomery AL
Obregon EM Trussville AL

O'Flinn NC *dcn* Birmingham AL
Pearce CW *dcn* Wilsonville AL
Perkins AD *ret* Montgomery AL
Powell DB *ret* Selma AL
Pradat RW *ret* Tuscaloosa AL
Putman RB *ret* Birmingham AL
Quiggle GW *ret* Dadeville AL
Richardson GW *ret* Gadsden AL
Riddle JL Odenville AL
Robinson LGHH Buford GA
Robison J *dcn* Huntsville AL
Roff LL *dcn* Tuscaloosa AL
Ross RL *ret* Vestavia AL
Roth FA *ret* Tuscaloosa AL
Rowell EE Richmond VA
Scalise MM Tuscaloosa AL
Schiesz CM *dcn* Florence AL
Scott JC *ret* Eutaw AL
Seales HS Auburn AL
Sharpton L *ret* Montgomery AL
Shaw SG *ret* Birmingham AL
Skipper JLD *ret* Montgomery AL

Smith KB *dcn* Vestavia AL
Taylor MH *ret* Birmingham AL
Thornton DI *ret* Marion AL
Tuohy JF *ret* Birmingham AL
Turnage BW *ret* Birmingham AL
Van Dyke RH *ret* Sewanee TN
Van Slyke CS *dcn*
Vandagriff MC *dcn* Homewood AL
Walter FX *ret* Sewanee TN
Warren JP *ret* Birmingham AL
Wells RD Birmingham AL
Wendel DD *ret* New Braunfels TX
Wesley JW *ret* Montevallo AL
Whetstone RD *dcn* Anniston AL
Wilkinson MC *ret* Washington DC
Williams JW *ret* Atlanta GA
Wilson WH *ret* Birmingham AL
Winslett H *ret* Tuscaloosa AL
Winters WM *ret*
Woodson JP *ret* Tuscaloosa AL
Yon WA *ret* Chelsea AL

DIOCESE OF ALASKA
(PROVINCE VIII)
Comprises the State of Alaska
DIOCESAN OFFICE 1205 Denali Way Fairbanks AK 99701-4178
TEL (907) 452-3040   FAX (907) 456-6552
WEB www.episcopalak.org

Previous Bishops—
Peter T Rowe 1895-1942, John B
Bentley suffr 1931 Bp 1943-48, Wm J
Gordon Jr 1948-74, David R Cochran
1974-81, George C Harris 1981-91,
Steven Charleston 1991-1996, Mark
L McDonald 1997-2008, Rustin
Kimsey asst

Bishop—Rt Rev Mark Lattime (1050) (Dio 4
Sept 2010)

Bps Exec Asst G Love; *Cn for Fin and Adm* S Krull; *Asst Fin and Admin* L Winfrey; *Treas* M Duggar; *Chanc* E Wohlforth; *V Chanc* T Middleton; *Hunger* Rev J Hunter; *UTO* W Nowak; *Safe Church* Rev K Hunt

Stand Comm—Cler: Pres A Whitney A Frank C Malseed C Oktollik; *Lay: VPres* H Davis P Fisher D Hall A Swan M Thomas

Dio Conv: October 2016 Sitka AK

PARISHES, MISSIONS, AND CLERGY

Allakaket St Johns in the Wilderness Episcopal **M**
(131) General Delivery 99720-9999 (Mail to:
General Delivery 99720-9999) (907) 968-2240
Anchorage All Saints Episcopal Church **P** (252)
545 W 8th Ave 99501-3517 (Mail to: PO Box

100686 99510-0686) Norman Elliott (907) 279-
3924
Anchorage Christ Church Episcopal **P** (89) 5101
O'Malley Rd 99507-6850 (Mail to: PO Box
111963 99511-1963) Katherine Hunt Gail
Loken (907) 345-7914
Anchorage St Christophers Church **P** (66) 7208
Duben Ave 99504-1321 (Mail to: 7208 Duben
Ave 99504-1321) Gayle Nauska (907) 333-5010
Anchorage St Marys Episcopal Church **P** (1016)
2222 E Tudor Rd 99507-1072 (Mail to: 2222
E Tudor Rd 99507-1072) Michael Burke Cecil
Cole Sara Gavit Sara Gavit Judith Lethin Gayle
Nauska Robert Thwing (907) 563-3341
Anvik Christ Episcopal Church **M** (89) PO Box
138 99558-0138 (Mail to: PO Box 103 99558-
0103) (907) 663-6343
Arctic Vlg Bishop Rowe Chapel **M** (141) General
Delivery 99722-9999 (Mail to: General
Delivery 99722-9999) (907) 587-5320
Beaver St Matthews Episcopal Church **M** (92) C
St 99724 (Mail to: PO Box 24009 99724-0009)
(907) 628-6114
Chalkyitsik St Timothys Episcopal Church **M**
(79) PO Box 54 99788-0054 (Mail to: PO Box
54 99788-0054) (907) 848-8211
Circle Holy Trinity Episcopal Church **M** (82) No
Street Identified 99733 (Mail to: PO Box 16

99733-0016) (907) 457-8823

Cordova St Georges Episcopal Church **P** (52) 100 Lake Ave 99574 (Mail to: PO Box 849 99574-0849) Margaret Mickelson (907) 424-5143

Eagle St Johns Episcopal Church **M** (21) PO Box 17 99738-0017 (Mail to: PO Box 17 99738-0017) (907) 547-2226

Eagle River Holy Spirit Episcopal Church **P** (167) 17545 N Eagle River Loop Rd 99577 (Mail to: PO Box 773223 99577-3223) Betty Lou Elmer-Anthony (907) 694-8201

Fairbanks Chapel of Alaska Saints **Chapel** 1205 Denali Way 99701-4137 (Mail to: 1205 Denali Way 99701-4137) (907) 452-3040

Fairbanks St Matthews Church **P** (1235) 1029 First Ave 99701 (Mail to: 1030 2nd Ave 99701-4355) John David Charles Davis John Holz Shirley Lee Bella Savino Montie Slusher (907) 456-5235

Fort Yukon St Peters Episcopal Church **M** (24) PO Box KBC 99740 (Mail to: C/O Birch Creek Tribal Council PO Box Kbc 99740-8999) (907) 662-2383

Fort Yukon St Stephens Episcopal Church **M** (291) (Mail to: PO Box 289 99740-0289) Teresa Thomas (907) 662-7556

Grayling St Pauls Episcopal Church **M** (259) General Delivery 99590-9999 (Mail to: General Delivery 99590-9999) (907) 453-5128

Haines St Michael & All Angels **P** (73) 1.5 Mile Haines Hwy 99827-1236 (Mail to: PO Box 1236 99827-1236) Janice Hotze (907) 766-3041

Homer St Augustines Episcopal Church **M** (16) 770 E End Rd 99603 (Mail to: PO Box 4274 99603-4274) (907) 235-1225

Hughes St Pauls Episcopal Church **M** (49) Front St 99745 (Mail to: PO Box 45035 99745-0035) (907) 889-2255

Huslia Good Shepherd Mission **M** (127) PO Box 78 99746-0078 (Mail to: PO Box 78 99746-0078) (907) 829-2233

Juneau Church of the Holy Trinity **P** (187) 415 4th St 99801-1126 (Mail to: 415 4th St 99801) Gordon Blue (907) 586-3532

Juneau St Brendans Episcopal Church **P** (113) 4207 Mendenhall Loop Rd 99801-9176 (Mail to: 4207 Mendenhall Loop Rd 99801-9176) Caroline Malseed (907) 789-5152

Kenai St Francis by the Sea Church **P** (12) 110 S Spruce St 99611-7937 (Mail to: 110 S Spruce St 99611-7937) Marian Nickelson (907) 283-6040

Ketchikan St Johns Episcopal Church **P** (142) 503 Mission St 99901-6423 (Mail to: 503 Mission St 99901) David Yaw Ronald Kotrc Earle Palmer (907) 225-3680

Kivalina Kivalina Epiphany Church **M** (374) General Delivery 99750-9999 (Mail to: General Delivery 99750-9999) Jerry Norton (907) 645-2164

Kodiak St James the Fisherman Church **P** (103) 421 Thorsheim St 99615 (Mail to: PO Box 1668

99615-1668) Elizabeth Simmons (907) 486-5276

Kotzebue St Georges in the Arctic **M** (46) 215 3rd Ave 99752-0269 Kris Lethin (907) 442-2360

Minto St Barnabas Episcopal Church **M** (53) PO Box 58064 99758 (Mail to: PO Box 58064 99758-0064) (907) 798-7414

Nenana St Marks Church **M** (129) Front & Market Sts 99760 (Mail to: PO Box 469 99760-0469) (907) 347-4115

Noatak Episcopal Congregation **PS** (10) General Delivery 99761

North Pole St Judes Episcopal Church **PS** (50) 3408 Laurance Rd 99705 (Mail to: PO Box 55458 99705-0458) (907) 488-9329

Palmer St Bartholomews Episcopal Church **P** (61) 323 N Alaska St 99645-6233 (Mail to: 323 N Alaska St 99645-6233) (907) 745-3526

Petersburg St Andrews Episcopal Church **P** (23) PO Box 1815 99833-1815 (Mail to: PO Box 1815 99833-1815) Dawn Allen-Herron (907) 254-0526

Point Hope St Thomas Episcopal Church **M** (270) Natchiq Street 99766 (Mail to: PO Box 29 99766-0029) Carrie Oktollik (907) 368-6200

Point Lay St Albans in the Arctic **M** (60) (Mail to: PO Box 59022 99759-0022) (907) 833-2623

Rampart Episcopal Congregation **PS** (53) General Delivery 99761 (Mail to: General Delivery 99767-9999) (907) 485-2144

Seward St Peters Episcopal Church **P** (37) 239 2nd Ave 99664 (Mail to: PO Box 676 99664-0676) Arthur Thomas Gail Loken (907) 224-3975

Shageluk St Lukes Episcopal Church **M** (131) General Delivery 99665-9999 (Mail to: PO Box 50 99665-0050) (907) 473-8292

Sitka St Peters by the Sea **P** (226) 611 Lincoln St 99835-7647 (Mail to: PO Box 1130 99835-1130) Julie Platson

Skagway St Saviors Congregation **M** (3) (Mail to: PO Box 617 99840-0617) (907) 983-3868

Stevens Vlg St Andrews Episcopal Church **M** (48) General Delivery 99774-9999 (Mail to: General Delivery 99774-9999) (907) 478-7127

Talkeetna Denali Episcopal Church **M** (9) Talkeetna Spur Rd 99676-0038 (Mail to: PO Box 38 99676-0038) (907) 373-0625

Tanacross St Timothys Episcopal Church **M** (93) General Delivery 99776-9999 (Mail to: c/o Betty Thomas-Denny PO Box 284 99780-0284) (907) 883-5576

Tanana St James Episcopal Church **M** (152) 1 Front St 99777 (Mail to: PO Box 207 99777) (907) 366-7251

Valdez Epiphany Lutheran/Episcopal Church **HC** (80) 309 Pioneer Dr 99686-0829 (Mail to: PO Box 829 99686-0829) (907) 835-4541

Venetie Church of the Good Shepherd **M** (208) General Delivery 99781-9999 (Mail to: General Delivery 99781-9999) (907) 849-8129

Wasilla St David's Epsicopal Church **P** (97) 2301

N Wasilla Fishhook Rd 99654 (Mail to: 2301 N Wasilla Fishhook Rd 99654) Ann Whitney (907) 373-0625

Wrangell St Philips Episcopal Church **P** (59) 444 Church St 99929 (Mail to: PO Box 409 99929-0409) A Wilson Valentine (907) 874-3047

NON-PAROCHIAL CLERGY

Adams PW Salem OR
Boesser MA *ret* Juneau AK
Britnell OW *ret* Eagle River AK
Curran MJ Juneau AK
DeHart EA *dcn* Kodiak AK
Doctor VC Tanana AK
Dufour MJ Eagle River AK
Duggar ME Nenana AK
Eddy CH *ret* Willow AK
Elsensohn DD *ret* Sitka AK
Fisher SO Fairbanks AK
Frank A *ret* Fairbanks AK
Gilbert T Arctic Village AK
Hanscom JD Anchorage AK
Hawley OR
Hillman HR Wasilla AK
Hunter JN *ret* North Pole AK
Knapick VH *ret* Palmer AK
Lawton JK *ret* Palmer AK
Mandrell HD
Masillem BB

Massenburg BJ Ketchikan AK
McMurtry HC *ret* Mount Vernon WA
Moore TM Palos Verdes Estates CA
Nathaniel M Chalkyitsik AK
Neakok WP Point Lay AK
Nelson RW *ret* Kihei HI
Norton MJ
Orrin DV *ret* Fredericksburg TX
Parsons AR *dcn* Sitka AK
Peters HS *dcn* Fairbanks AK
Price BD *dcn*
Reed SK Longmont CO
Rice GA *dcn* Sitka AK
Richmond AP Anchorage AK
Rockwood DA *dcn* Ketchikan AK
Sampson PK Terrace
Simmonds RF *ret* Minto AK
Smith CL Odessa TX
Smith PB *ret* Eagle River AK
Snelling KS *dcn* Sitka AK
Steele GR Anchorage AK
Stipe NM *dcn* Avondale Estates GA
Swan CE Kivalina AK
Swope RL *ret* La Veta CO
Titus BC
Titus L *ret* Minto AK
Wagner RF *ret* Palmer AK
Wilcox GM *ret*
Zimmerman BA *dcn* Kodiak AK

DIOCESE OF ALBANY
(PROVINCE II)
Comprises 19 counties in Northeast NY
DIOCESAN OFFICE 580 Burton Rd Greenwich NY 12834
TEL (518) 692-3350   FAX (518) 692-3352
E-MAIL diocese@albanydiocese.org   WEB www.albanyepiscopaldiocese.org

Previous Bishops—
Wm C Doane 1869-1913, Richd H Nelson coadj 1904 Bp 1913-29, Geo A Oldham coadj 1922 Bp 1929-49, Fredk L Barry coadj 1945 Bp 1949-60, David E Richards suffr 1951-57, Allen W Brown suffr 1959 Bp 1961-74, Charles B Per sell Jr suffr 1963-76, Wilbur E Hogg 1974-84, David S Ball coadj 1984 Bp 1984-98, Daniel W Herzog coadj 1997-98, Bp 1998-2007, David J Bena suffr 2000-2007

Bishop—Rt Rev William H Love (1007) (Dio 1 Feb 2007)

Sec Ven H Huth; *Treas* C Curtis; *Asst Treas* Rev W Tatem; *Lay Cn for Admin* RJ Carroll; *Chanc* Rev W Strickland; *COM* Rev S Waldron; *Deploy* E Strickland; *Cn to Ord* Rev RF Haskell; *Acct Mgr* S

Stanley; *Comm* Rev J Stellman; *Diaconal Form* Ven H Huth

Stand Comm—Cler: S Garno C Vance H Huth M Neufeld E Papazoglakis D Roy *Lay: Pres* SE Reutsch *Sec* J B Beaulac J Dean L Gibbs S Gladstone M Haskell

Deans: Metro N McMillan; *N Adirondack* D Ousley; *S Adirondack* D Beaulac; *St Lawrence* C Brown; *U Hudson* D Roy; *Hudson* J Thompson; *Susquehanna* K Hunter; *W Mohawk* N Longe

Dio Conv: 10-12 June 2016 Speculator NY

PARISHES, MISSIONS, AND CLERGY

✠ **Albany** Cathedral of All Saints **O** (393) 62 S Swan St 12210-2301 (Mail to: 62 S Swan St 12210-2301) David Collum Paul Hunter Robert Limpert Paul Pierson Steven Scherck Susan

Waldron Hugh Wilkes (518) 465-1342

Albany Grace & Holy Innocents Church **P** 498 Clinton Ave 12206-2705 (Mail to: 498 Clinton Ave 12206-2705) (518) 465-1112

Albany St Andrews Episcopal Church **P** (376) 10 N Main Ave 12203-1403 (Mail to: 10 N Main Ave 12203-1488) Mary White Keith Scott (518) 489-4747

Albany St Michaels Episcopal Church **P** (177) 49 Killean Park 12205-4035 (Mail to: 49 Killean Park 12205-4087) Stephen Hart (518) 869-6417

Albany St Pauls Episcopal Church **P** (153) 21 Hackett Blvd 12208-3407 (Mail to: 21 Hackett Blvd 12208-3407) Edward Dougherty John McMillan Nancy Rosenblum (518) 463-2257

Albany St Peters Episcopal Church **P** (423) 107 State St 12207-1622 (Mail to: 107 State St 12207-1683) Paul Hartt Susan Waldron

Amsterdam St Anns Episcopal Church **P** (186) 37 Division St 12010-4324 (Mail to: 37 Division St 12010-4398) Neal Longe Alan Hart Mary Hart (518) 842-2362

Au Sable Forks St James Episcopal Church **P** (39) 14216 State Rte 9N 12912 (Mail to: PO Box 98 12912-0098) David Ousley (518) 647-5312

Ballston Spa Christ Episcopal Church **P** (577) 15 W High St 12020-1912 (Mail to: 15 W High St 12020-1912) Derik Roy Albert Moser William Pearson (518) 885-1031

Bloomville St Pauls Church **P** (7) 464 River St 13739-1173 (Mail to: PO Box 742 13739-0742) (607) 434 5501

Blue Mountain Lake Church of the Transfiguration **SC** (27) 1 Cedar Ln 12812 (Mail to: C/O The Rev Dr Chip Lee PO Box 2188 21550-0588) (240) 442-2152

Bolton Landing Church of St Sacrement **P** (68) 4879 Lake Shore Dr PO Box 1185 12814 (Mail to: PO Box 1185 12814-1185) Colin Belton (518) 644-9613

Bovina St James Church **P** (56) 55 Lake Delaware Dr 13753 (Mail to: 55 Lake Delaware Dr 13753-7440) James Krueger (607) 832-4401

Brant Lake Church of the Good Shepherd **PS** NY State Route 9 12815 (Mail to: PO Box 119 12815-0119) Dennis Pressley Michael Webber (518) 494-3314

Brant Lake St Hubert of the Lakes Church **P** (7) Route 8 12108 (Mail to: PO Box 158 12108-0158) (518) 494-3314

Brant Lake St Pauls Church **PS** 6596 State Rte 8 12815 (Mail to: PO Box 119 12815-0119) Dennis Pressley Michael Webber (518) 494-3314

Burnt Hills Calvary Episcopal Church **P** (284) 85 Lake Hill Rd 12027-9597 (Mail to: PO Box 41 12027-0041) John Scott Marian Sive Oscar Sodergren Peter Sweeney (518) 399-7230

Cairo Calvary Episcopal Church **P** (18) 1 Jerome Ave 12413-3047 (Mail to: PO Box 561 12413-0561) John Miller (518) 622-9172

Cambridge St Lukes Church **P** (68) 4 St Lukes Pl 12816-1111 (Mail to: 4 St Lukes Pl 12816-1111) Ian Montgomery (518) 677-2632

Canajoharie The Church of The Good Shepherd **P** (41) 26 Moyer St 13317-0118 (Mail to: PO Box 118 13317-0118) Virginia Ogden (518) 673-3440

Canton Grace Episcopal Church **P** (149) 9 E Main St 13617-1416 (Mail to: 9 E Main St 13617-1416) (315) 386-3714

Castleton St Davids Episcopal Church **P** (215) 2647 Brookview Rd 12033-3709 (Mail to: C/O Gail Neal PO Box 475 12061-0475) James Brisbin (518) 477-4536

Catskill St Lukes Church **P** (151) 50 William St 12414-1419 (Mail to: PO Box 643 12414-0643) Leander Harding David Sutcliffe Henry Verdaasdonk (518) 943-4180

Champlain Christ & St Johns Parish **P** (55) 8 Butternut St 12919-5121 (Mail to: PO Box 240 12919-0240) (518) 298-8543

Chatham St Luke Episcopal Church **P** (25) 12 Woodbridge Ave 12037-1314 (Mail to: 12 Woodbridge Ave 12037) (518) 392-2278

Cherry Valley Grace Church **P** (39) 32 Montgomery St 13320-3562 (Mail to: PO Box 382 13320-0382) Thomas Grennen (607) 264-8303

Clifton Park St Georges Episcopal Church **P** (1023) 912 Route 146 12065-3702 (Mail to: 912 Route 146 12065-3702) Katharine Foster Elizabeth Papazoglakis Thomas Papazoglakis Robert Roach Scott Underhill

Cobleskill St Christopher's Episcopal Church **P** (33) 121 St Christopher Pl 12043 (Mail to: St Christopher's Church PO Box 386 12043-0386) Nina George-Hacker (518) 234-3912

Cohoes St Johns Church **P** (95) 405 Vliet Blvd 12047-2019 (Mail to: 405 Vliet Blvd 12047-2019) (518) 237-6013

Colton Zion Episcopal Church **P** (77) 91 Main St 13625 (Mail to: PO Box 9 13625-0009) (315) 262-3106

Cooperstown Christ Church Episcopal **P** (424) 69 Fair St 13326-1309 (Mail to: 69 Fair St 13326-1309) Matthew Stromberg (607) 547-9555

Copake Falls St John in the Wilderness **P** (127) 261 State Route 344 12517-5337 (Mail to: PO Box 180 12517-0180) John Thompson

Coxsackie Christ Episcopal Church **P** (95) 70 Mansion St 12051-1214 (Mail to: 70 Mansion St 12051-1214) Anne Curtin (518) 731-9883

Delhi St Johns Church **P** (82) 134 1/2 Main St 13753 (Mail to: PO Box 121 13753-0121) Darius Mojallali Nancy Truscott (607) 746-3437

Delmar St Stephens Episcopal Church **P** (326) 16 Elsmere Ave 12054-2118 (Mail to: 16 Elsmere

Ave 12054-2100) Adam Egan Justine Guernsey Harvey Huth (518) 439-3265

Deposit Christ Episcopal Church **P** (86) 14 Monument St 13754-1216 (Mail to: 14 Monument St 13754-1216) Daniel Jones Linda Servetas (607) 467-3031

Downsville St Marys Episcopal Church **P** (59) 15121 Main St 13755 (Mail to: PO Box 334 13755-0334) Michael Shank (607) 363-2565

Duanesburg Christ Episcopal Church **P** (102) 132 Duanesburg Churches Road 12056 (Mail to: PO Box 92 12056-0092) Deborah Beach (518) 895-2383

Elizabethtown Church of the Good Shepherd **P** (113) 10 William St 12932 (Mail to: PO Box 146 12932-0146) (518) 873-2509

Essex St Johns Episcopal Church **P** (73) Church St 12936 (Mail to: PO Box 262 12936-0262)

Fort Edward Parish of St James **P** (22) 112 Broadway 12828-1722 (Mail to: 112 Broadway 12828-1722) (518) 963-7775

Franklin St Pauls Episcopal Church **P** (43) Main and Institute Sts 13775 (Mail to: PO Box 72 13775-0072) Scott Garno (607) 829-6404

Gilbertsville Christ Episcopal Church **P** (107) 36 Marion Ave 13776 (Mail to: PO Box 345 13776-0345) Donna Steckline (607) 783-2267

Glens Falls Church of the Messiah **P** (477) 296 Glen St 12801-3501 (Mail to: 296 Glen St 12801-3553) Nancy Goff Karl Griswold-Kuhn (518) 792-1560

Gouverneur Trinity Episcopal Church **P** (44) 30 Park St 13642 (Mail to: PO Box 341 13642-0341) Gregory Bailey

Granville Trinity Episcopal Church **P** (41) 35 E Main St 12832-1331 (Mail to: 35 E Main St 12832-1331) Arthur Peters (518) 642-2883

Greenville Christ Episcopal Church **P** (125) 11226 State Route 32 12083-3600 (Mail to: PO Box 278 12083-0278) Mark Diebel (518) 966-5713

Greenwich St Pauls Episcopal Church **P** (50) 145 Main St 12834-1214 (Mail to: PO Box 183 12834-0183) Margaret Quackenbush William Strickland (518) 692-7492

Guilderland St Boniface Episcopal Church **P** (223) 5148 Western Tpke 12084 (Mail to: PO Box 397 12084-0397) Steven Scherck (518) 355-0134

Herkimer Christ Episcopal Church **P** (78) 300 N Main St 13350-1949 (Mail to: 300 N Main St 13350-1949) Barbara Stellman (315) 866-0551

Hoosick Falls All Saints Church **P** (81) 4935 Rt 7 12090 (Mail to: PO Box 211 12089-0211) Gary Strubel (518) 686-9037

Hoosick Falls Church of the Holy Name **P** (46) 33 Simmons Rd 12090-5000 (Mail to: 33 Simmons Rd 12090-5000) (518) 465-3129

Hoosick Falls St Marks Episcopal Church **P** (50) 70 Main St 12090-2004 (Mail to: PO Box 272 12090-0272) (518) 686-4982

Hudson Christ Episcopal Church **P** (320) 431 Union St 12534-2426 (Mail to: PO Box 411 12534-0411) Eileen Weglarz (518) 828-1329

Hudson Falls Zion Episcopal Church **P** (186) 224 Main St 12839-1705 Richard Chandler (518) 747-6514

Ilion St Augustines Church **P** (146) 78 2nd St 13357-2118 (Mail to: PO Box 118 13357-2118) (315) 894-3775

Johnstown St Johns Episcopal Church **P** (407) 1 N Market St 12095-2139 (Mail to: PO Box 395 12095-0395) Laurie Garramone (518) 762-9210

Keeseville St Pauls Church **P** (31) 107 Clinton St 12944-0143 (Mail to: PO Box 1029 12901-0108) Blair Biddle (518) 563-6836

Kinderhook St Pauls Episcopal Church **P** (114) 10 Silvester St 12106-2013 (Mail to: PO Box 637 12106-0637) Thomas Malionek Jan Volkmann (518) 758-6271

Lake George St James Episcopal Church **P** (129) 172 Ottawa St 12845-1414 (Mail to: 172 Ottawa St 12845-1414) Jean Devaty (518) 668-2001

Lake Luzerne St Marys Episcopal Church **P** (103) 220 Lake Ave PO Box 211 12846 (Mail to: PO Box 211 12846-0211) David Beaulac (518) 696-3030

Lake Placid St Eustace Church **P** (133) 2450 Main Street 12946-3300 (Mail to: 2450 Main St 12946-3300) (518) 523-2564

Latham St Matthews Episcopal Church **P** (275) 129 Old Loudon Rd 12110 (Mail to: 129 Old Loudon Road 12110) (518) 785-6029

Little Falls Emmanuel Episcopal Church **P** (339) 588 Albany St 13365-1543 (Mail to: PO Box 592 13365-0592) Steven Scarcia (315) 823-1323

Malone St Marks Episcopal Church **P** (62) 34 Elm St 12953-1507 (Mail to: PO Box 331 12953-1507) Elizabeth Papazoglakis (518) 521-3303

Margaretville St Margarets Church **M** (40) 63 Orchard St 12455 (Mail to: 87 East Main St 13838) Michael Shank (607) 563-9414

Massena St Johns Church **P** (138) 139 Main St 13662-1908 (Mail to: PO Box 15 13662-0015) Thomas Papazoglakis

Mechanicville St Lukes Episcopal Church **P** (253) 40 McBride Road 12118-2325 (Mail to: 40 McBride Rd 12118-0648) Fredric Leach David Haig (518) 664-4834

Mohawk Grace Church **P** (66) 7-9 East Main St 13407 (Mail to: 7 East Main St 13407-0056) William Wheeler (315) 866-4782

Morris All Saints Chapel of Zion Church **Chapel** 1854 State Highway 51 13808 (Mail to: PO Box 156 13808-0156) Robert Witt (607) 263-5783

Morris Zion Episcopal Church **P** (105) 158 Main Street 13808-0156 (Mail to: PO Box 156 13808-0156) Robert Witt Joseph Norman (607) 263-5927

Morristown Christ Church **P** (45) Main St 13664

(Mail to: PO Box 16 13664-0016) Edgar LaCombe (315) 375-4497

N Creek St Christophers Church **PS** Ridge St 12853 (Mail to: PO Box 119 12815-0119) Dennis Pressley Michael Webber (518) 494-3314

N Granville All Saints Chapel **SC** State Route 22 12854 (Mail to: PO Box 166 12854-0166) Jere Berger (518) 743-1740

New Lebanon Church of Our Saviour **P** (90) 14660 Route 22 12125 (Mail to: PO Box 827 12125-0827) Clinton Dugger Randolph Lukas (518) 794-8702

Newcomb St Barbaras Church **PS** 65 Sanford Ln 12852-1709 (Mail to: PO Box 119 12815-0119) Dennis Pressley Michael Webber (518) 494-3314

Norwood St Philips Church **P** (57) PO Box 225 13668-0225 (Mail to: PO Box 225 13668-0225) Kathryn Boswell (315) 353-8833

Ogdensburg St Johns Episcopal Church **P** (217) 500 Caroline St 13669-2604 (Mail to: PO Box 658 13669-0658) Michael O'Donnell Arthur Garno (315) 393-5470

Old Forge St Peters Church By-the-Lake **SC** 4800 State Route 28 13420-0111 (Mail to: PO Box 111 13331-0111) (315) 360-6879

Oneonta St James Episcopal Church **P** (290) 305 Main St 13820-2520 (Mail to: 305 Main St 13820-2596) Kenneth Hunter (607) 432-1458

Palenville Gloria Dei Episcopal Church **P** (14) 3393 Route 23a 12463-2318 (Mail to: 3393 Route 23a 12463-2318) John Miller (518) 329-4562

Paul Smiths St Johns in the Wilderness **SC** 350 White Pine Rd 12970 (Mail to: A W Cooper 1365 County Route 60 12989-2101) Allen Cooper (518) 891-6746

Philmont St Marks Episcopal Church **P** (27) Main St & Maple Ave 12565 (Mail to: PO Box 628 12565-0628) Mark Mc Darby (518) 672-4062

Plattsburgh Trinity Episcopal Church **P** (149) 18 Trinity Pl 12901-2933 (Mail to: 18 Trinity Pl 12901-2933) Glen Michaels David Ousley (518) 561-2244

Potsdam Trinity Episcopal Church **P** (216) 8 Maple St Fall Island 13676-1149 (Mail to: 8 Maple St Fall Island 13676-1149) Christopher Brown Lora Smith Margaret Theodore (315) 265-5754

Pottersville Adirondack Mission **Cluster** (122) 316 Valentine Pond Rd 12860 (Mail to: PO Box 119 12815-0119) John Cairns (518) 494-3314

Pottersville Christ Church **P** (16) Nys Route 9 12860 (Mail to: PO Box 119 12815-0119) Dennis Pressley Michael Webber (518) 494-3314

Rensselaer Church of the Redeemer **P** (55) 1249 3rd St 12144-1821 (Mail to: 1 Hazel Ter 12144-1309) Nancy Kin (518) 326-6722

Rensselaerville Trinity Church Rensselaerville **P**

(38) 10 Trinity Ln 12147 (Mail to: PO Box 86 12147-0086) (518) 797-5295

Richfld Spgs St Johns Episcopal Church **P** (40) 98 Main St 13439-2535 (Mail to: PO Box E 13439-1901) John Bartle (315) 858-1121

Round Lake All Saints Church **P** (70) Simpson Ave 12151 (Mail to: PO Box 35 12151-0035) Scott Evans (518) 899-5510

Salem St Paul's Church **P** (29) E Broadway 12865 (Mail to: E Broadway 12865) Gary Kriss (518) 854-7294

Saranac Lake St Luke the Beloved Physician **P** (306) 102 Main St 12983 (Mail to: 136 Main St 12983-1734) Julianna Caguiat Ann Gaillard (518) 891-3605

Saratoga Spg Church of Bethesda **P** (454) 41 Washington St 12866-4116 (Mail to: 41 Washington St 12866-4116) Paul Evans Marshall Vang (518) 584-5980

Schenectady Christ Church **P** (308) 970 State St 12307-1520 (Mail to: 970 State St 12307-1520) Nelson Jones Lawrence Hubert Howard Smith (518) 374-3064

Schenectady St Andrews Church **P** (189) 50 Sacandaga Rd 12302-1828 (Mail to: 50 Sacandaga Rd 12302) Michael Neufeld Richard Lehmann (518) 374-8391

Schenectady St Georges Episcopal Church **P** (243) 30 N Ferry St 12305-1609 (Mail to: 30 N Ferry St 12305-1697) (518) 374-3163

Schenectady St Pauls Episcopal Church **P** (243) 1911 Fairview Ave 12306-4129 (Mail to: 1911 Fairview Ave 12306-4129) Harold Reed (518) 393-5118

Schenectady St Stephens Church **P** (150) 1229 Baker Ave 12309-5711 (Mail to: 1229 Baker Ave 12309-5711) James Mcdonald Patricia Jones (518) 346-6241

Schenevus Church of the Holy Spirit **P** (25) Arch St 12155 (Mail to: PO Box 354 12155-0354) Richard Knudson (607) 432-6835

Schroon Lake St Andrews Church **P** St Rte 9 12870 (Mail to: PO Box 119 12815-0119) Dennis Pressley Michael Webber (518) 494-3314

Schuylerville St Stephens Episcopal Church **P** (89) 1 Grove St 12871-1403 (Mail to: 1 Grove St 12871-1479) (518) 695-3918

Sidney St Pauls Church **P** (110) 25 River St 13838-1132 (Mail to: 25 River St 13838-1132) James Shevlin (607) 563-3391

Springfield Ctr St Marys Church **P** (40) 7690 State Hwy 80 13468 (Mail to: PO Box 376 13468-0376) Thomas Grennen (315) 858-4016

Stamford St Peters Church **P** (18) 16155 County Highway 18 12167-1801 (Mail to: 16155 County Highway 18 12167-1801) Darius Mojallali (607) 538-9503

Star Lake Church of the Nativity **SC** (2) No 4051 State Highway 3 13690 (Mail to: PO Box 50 13690-0050)

Stockport St John the Evangelist **P** (20) 107 County Route 25 12171 (Mail to: 580 Burton Rd 12834-7913) (518) 692-3350

Tannersville St Johns Church **SC** Philadelphia Hill 12485 (Mail to: PO Box 224 12485-0224) (518) 589-5412

Ticonderoga The Episcopal Church of the Cross **P** (35) 129 Champlain Ave 12883-1313 (Mail to: 129 Champlain Ave 12883-1313) Marjorie Floor (518) 585-4032

Troy St Johns Episcopal Church **P** (376) 146 1st St 12180-4431 (Mail to: 146 1st St 12180-4413) Stephen Schlossberg Paul Carney Sandra Tatem (518) 274-5884

Troy St Pauls Church **P** (157) 58 3rd St 12180-3906 (Mail to: 58 3rd St 12180-3962) Michael Gorchov (518) 273-7351

Troy Trinity Episcopal Church **P** (270) 545 4th Ave 12182-2616 (Mail to: PO Box 212 12182-0212) (518) 235-3873

Tupper Lake Church of St Thomas **P** (51) 8 Brentwood Ave 12986-1513 (Mail to: 8 Brentwood Ave 12986-1513) Allen Cooper (518) 359-8786

Twilight Park Memorial Church of All Angels **SC** 69 Balsam Rd 12485 (Mail to: Twilight Park 12436)

Unadilla St Matthews Church **P** (94) 240 Main St 13849-2245 (Mail to: 240 Main St 13849-2245) Scott Garno (607) 369-3081

Waddington St Pauls Church **P** (60) 129 Lincoln Ave 13694-3183 (315) 388-5680

Walton Christ Church **P** (65) 41 Gardiner Pl 13856-1320 (Mail to: 41 Gardiner Pl 13856-1320) (607) 865-4698

Warrensburg Church of the Holy Cross **P** (163) 3764 Main St 12885-1836 (Mail to: 3764 Main St 12885-1836) Thomas Pettigrew (518) 623-3066

Waterford Grace Church **P** (139) 34 3rd St 12188 (Mail to: 34 3rd St 12188-2538) Katherine Alonge-Coons Herbert Sanderson William Strickland (518) 237-7370

Watervliet Trinity Episcopal Church **P** (107) 1336 1st Ave 12189-3317 (Mail to: 1336 1st Ave 12189-3317) Nicolas Hernandez William Tatem (518) 272-0644

West Middleburgh St Paul's Episcopal Church **P** (16) 100 Church Street 12122 (Mail to: C/O Carolyn Snyder 214 Bridge St 12157-1723) (518) 702-5005

Westford St Timothys Episcopal Church **P** (17) 1776 Co Rte 34 13488 (Mail to: PO Box 74 13488-0074) (607) 369-9214

Whitehall Trinity Church **P** (29) 58 Broadway 12887-1201 (Mail to: 58 Broadway 12887-1201) James Kenyon (518) 480-5833

NON-PAROCHIAL CLERGY

Abbott SB *ret* Cooperstown NY
Acanfora JG South New Berlin NY
Adams JT *ret* Lyndeborough NH

Arnold DJ *ret* Gansevoort NY
Austin EE Canton NY
Ayers B *dcn*
Bailey CL *dcn* Oneonta NY
Bailey PR *dcn* Oneonta NY
Baker B Lake Placid NY
Baker MS Greenwich NY
Baker PE *ret* Cambridge NY
Baker-Borjeson SCW *ret* Daytona Beach Shores FL
Ballert IF *ret* Sidney NY
Bartlett LL *dcn* Burnt Hills NY
Beauharnois PA *dcn* Champlain NY
Bissell-Thompson GV *ret* Lebanon VA
Blakelock DP *dcn* Unadilla NY
Bowers AW *ret* Sewaren NJ
Bowman SB *ret* Delmar NY
Caldwell EF *ret* Camillus NY
Calvo GA
Caron JA *ret* Greenwich NY
Carpenter AD *ret dcn* Albany NY
Chapman M Brentwood NY
Chesnut MD Johnstown NY
Chilton MH *ret* West Sand Lake NY
Clark WW *dcn* Medusa NY
Clarke JM *ret* Downsville NY
Clemmons GD *ret* Troy NY
Crimi LB *dcn* Stillwater NY
Curtis FL *ret* Southbury CT
Curtis LMP *dcn* Clifton Park NY
Delaney RR
DeLaura GF *dcn* Glens Falls NY
Demler MA *dcn* Clifton Park NY
Dennis FH *ret* Saranac Lake NY
Donahue RL *ret* Downsville NY
Erickson RP *dcn* Castleton-On-Hudson NY
Evans JJ Round Lake NY
Famulare JA Little Falls NY
Felty RA Columbiaville NY
Ferguson FM *ret* Harwich MA
Fiebke EJ *ret* Bradenton FL
Francis DC *ret* Bloomington IL
Garceau JE *dcn* Palm Springs CA
Gerber RD *ret* Milford DE
Gormley SP
Graham RL *ret* Ottawa ON
Greene GB *ret* Whitesboro NY
Grigg JT Massena NY
Groneman LJ *dcn*
Guile FC *ret* Granville NY
Gwinn TW *ret* North Stratford NH
Handy DA Chester VA
Hanson-Foss PJ *dcn* Au Sable Forks NY
Hanstine BA *dcn* Hancock NY
Harding SM Queensbury NY
Harrison RE *ret* Latham NY
Haskell RF *ret* Burnt Hills NY
Henry JW *ret* Clifton Park NY
Hinrichs WR *ret* Cohoes NY
Hopkins JL *ret* Burnt Hills NY
Hunter MV *dcn* Oneonta NY
Jenkins DP *ret* Pompano Beach FL
Jones BJ *ret dcn* Hobe Sound FL

Jones JS Johnstown NY
Jones MS *ret* Youngstown OH
Kettlewell JM *ret* Schuylerville NY
King CB *ret* Colonie NY
LaVine PI *dcn* Norwood NY
Lewis CR *ret* Sarasota FL
Littlejohn NR *dcn*
Lockwood FR Coxsackie NY
Logan MD *dcn* Malone NY
Lundberg NJ *ret* Rensselaer NY
Lyons LM Niskayuna NY
MacCollam JA Oceanside CA
Malcolm KG *dcn*
Mason BE Lake Luzerne NY
McCabe CP Denver CO
McCaulley ED Chatan Japan
McConkey DB *ret* Northampton
McConnell TA *ret*
McGowan SM *dcn* Castleton NY
McPartlin JH *ret* Hague NY
Michael MA Herndon VA
Miller LJ *dcn* Walton NY
Moore DM *dcn* Waterford NY
Morgan BJ *ret* Great Barrington MA
Morris AG *ret* Melrose NY
Mudge HE Troy NY
Mudge JH Wynantskill NY
Mudge S Manchester CT
Neufeld EC Columbus GA
Nickles BJ Chatham NY
North JJ
Peay SA Nashotah WI
Peyton AT Atlanta GA
Plaske SA *dcn* Albany NY
Quinby CH *ret* Burlington VT

Radzik DR Milwaukee WI
Reddie GT Coxsackie NY
Rivera-Georgescu AM Au Sable Forks NY
Rockwell RE *dcn* Scotia NY
Rogers GM New York NY
Scarff SD Guilford CT
Schofield P Niskayuna NY
Serra-Lima F *ret* Old Chatham NY
Servetas N *ret* Deposit NY
Shaw ME *ret* Plymouth IN
Skramstad DM *dcn* Lake Luzerne NY
Small WD *ret* Paul Smiths NY
Smith AE
Smith CS Potsdam NY
Smith CA *ret* Hagaman NY
Sowan MG *ret* Bolton Landing NY
Springer DR *ret* West Sand Lake NY
Steuer LW *dcn* Gansevoort NY
Sullivan DA *dcn* Elizabethtown NY
Tatlock AR *dcn* Ballston Spa NY
Teetz MLS *dcn* Schenectady NY
Thomas MA *dcn* Greenwich NY
Thompson HD *dcn* North Lawrence VA
Todaro AB *dcn* Troy NY
Vance CM Troy NY
Vandermark RJ *dcn* Unadilla NY
Vitet K Brooklyn NY
Wallner LJ *dcn* Hudson FL
Wampler DD *ret* Schenectady NY
Wendell MP *ret* Valley Falls NY
Williams M *dcn* Lampasas TX
Williams PP *ret* Blue HIll ME
Wilson LL South Kortright NY
Wright WJ *dcn* Deposit NY
Zimmerman JP *ret* Altamont NY

DIOCESE OF ARIZONA
(PROVINCE VIII)
Comprises the State of Arizona, except for Navajoland,
the Cities of Page and Bullhead City, and Yuma County
DIOCESAN OFFICE 114 W Roosevelt St Phoenix AZ 85003-1406
TEL (602) 254-0976   FAX (602) 495-6603
E-MAIL cathy@azdiocese.org   WEB www.azdiocese.org

Previous Bishops—
Ozi W Whitaker (NV and AZ) 1869-74, Wm-F Adams (NMex and AZ) 1875-76, Geo K Dunlap (NMex and AZ) 1880-88, John M Kendrick (NMex and AZ) 1889-1911, Julius W Atwood 1911-25, Walter Mitchell 1926-45, Arthur B Kinsolving II 1959-62, Joseph M Harte 1962-79, Joseph T Heistand coad 1976-79, Bp 1979-92, Wesley Frensdorff asst 1985-88, Robert R Shahan 1992-2004

Bishop—Rt Rev Kirk Stevan Smith, PhD (996)
(Dio 15 Oct 2004)

Assisting Bishop—Rt Rev William G Burrill DD (784)

Cn for Admin and Asst to Bp CC Black; *Cn to Ord Trans and Cong Dev* M Traquair; *Cn for Finance* VG Hohnbaum; *Cn for Hispanic Ministry* IM Vasquez; *Dir for Yth and Young Adults* J Villegas; *Dir for Children's Min* NB Shumaker; *Cn of Comm/Media* N Krug; *Chanc* CH Gregor; *Treas* J Colaric;*Sec to Conv* L Crosland; *Dn of Cathedral* T Mendez; *Archdcn* VM Ritson

Stand Comm—Cler: Pres B White R Aguilar
J Christopher; *Lay:* R Dewey R Clingenpeel I
Chamberlain

Dio Conv: TBD

PARISHES, MISSIONS, AND CLERGY

Benson St Raphael in the Valley Episcopal-
Lutheran Church **M** (53) 730 S Hwy 80 85602
(Mail to: PO Box 1224 85602) (520) 586-4335

Bisbee St Johns Sweet Memorial Church **M** (73)
19 Sowle Ave 85603 (Mail to: PO Box 368
85603-0368) Richard Aguilar (520) 432-7006

Casa Grande St Peters Church **P** (197) 704 E
McMurray Blvd 85122 (Mail to: PO Box
10606 85130-0606) Kenneth Katona Jeanne
Rasmussen

Cave Creek Good Shepherd of the Hills **P** (238)
6502 E Cave Creek Rd 85331 (Mail to: PO Box
110 85327-0110) Nordon Winger Joseph Harte
Susan Harte Glenn Jenks (480) 488-3283

Chandler Saint Matthew's Church **P** (620) 901
W Erie St 85225-4477 (Mail to: PO Box 1959
85244-1959) Debora Adinolfi William Forrest
Dominic Moore David Pettengill Susan
Youngblood (480) 899-7386

Clarkdale St Thomas of the Valley **M** (79) 889 1st
South St 86324 (Mail to: PO Box 1175 86324-
1175) Julie Williams (928) 634-8593

Coolidge St Michaels Church **M** (87) 800 W Vah
Ki Inn Rd 85228-9312 (Mail to: PO Box 547
85128-0010) Carol Hosler (520) 723-3845

Douglas St Stephens Episcopal Church **M** (22) No
749 E 11th St 85607-2240 (Mail to: PO Box 1291
85608-1291) Richard Aguilar (520) 364-7971

Flagstaff Church of the Epiphany **P** (630) 423 N
Beaver St 86001-4511 (Mail to: 423 N Beaver St
86001-4511) Bess Driver (928) 774-2911

Gila Bend Epiphany on the Desert **M** (31) 401 E
Papago St 85337 (Mail to: PO Box 889 85337)
John Christopher (602) 757-9282

Glendale St Andrews Church **P** (218) No 6300
W Camelback Rd 85301-7305 (Mail to: 6300
W Camelback Rd 85301-7305) Irineo Vasquez
Janice Watts (623) 846-8046

Glendale St John the Baptist Church **P** (367) No
4102 W Union Hills Dr 85308-1702 (Mail to:
4102 W Union Hills Dr 85308-1702) Bruce
Jackson Charles Milhoan (623) 582-5449

Globe St Johns Church **M** (140) No 185 E Oak
St 85501-2115 (Mail to: PO Box 1051 85501-
1051) Byron Mills (928) 425-9300

Green Valley St Francis-in-the-Valley **P** (366)
600 S La Canada Dr 85614-1902 (Mail to: 600
S La Canada Dr 85614-1902) Daniel Messier
Patricia Kirk (520) 625-1370

Holbrook St Georges Church **M** (22) 168 W
Arizona St 86025-2824 (Mail to: 168 W
Arizona St 86025-2824) Deborah Royals (928)
524-2361

Kingman Trinity Church **M** (75) 425 E Spring
St 86402 (Mail to: PO Box 3277 86402-0590)

Philip Shaw (928) 754 5658

Lakeside Church of Our Saviour **P** (135) 5147
Show Low Lake Rd 85929-5218 (Mail to:
5147 Show Low Lake Rd 85929-5218) Kerry
Neuhardt (928) 537-7830

Litchfield Park St Peters Episcopal Church **P**
(707) 400 S Old Litchfield Rd 85340-4721
(Mail to: 400 S Old Litchfield Rd 85340-4721)
Gae Chalker (623) 935-3279

Lk Havasu City Grace Church **P** (198) 111
Bunker Dr 86403-6856 (Mail to: 111 Bunker
Dr 86403-6856) Lisa Goforth (928) 855-2525

Mesa Church of the Transfiguration **P** (206) 514
S Mountain Rd 85208-5412 (Mail to: 514 S
Mountain Rd 85208-5412) Michael Bauschard
Robert Saik

Mesa St Marks Church **P** (206) No 322 N Horne
85203-7933 (Mail to: 322 N Horne St 85203-
7933) Gerardo Brambila (480) 964-5820

Morenci Saints Philip and James **M** (19) No 784
Mountain Ave 85540 (Mail to: PO Box Ee
85540-0109) Sandra Chilese (928) 439-4015

Nogales St Andrew's Episcopal Church **P** (239) No
969 W Country Club Dr 85621-3985 (Mail to:
969 W Country Club Dr 85621-3985) Ernest
Galaz James Fitzsimmons Derwent Suthers

Oro Valley Episcopal Church of the Apostles **M**
(290) 12111 N La Cholla Blvd 85755-9725
(Mail to: PO Box 68435 85737-8435) Debra
Asis (520) 544-9660

Paradise Valley Christ Church of the Ascension
P (698) § 4015 E Lincoln Dr 85253-3946 (Mail
to: 4015 E Lincoln Dr 85253-3946) Elizabeth
Blunt Daniel Richards William Young (602)
840-8210

Parker St Philips Church **PS** 1209 S Eagle Ave
85344-5847 (Mail to: 1209 S Eagle Ave 85344)
(928) 770-4589

Payson St Pauls Church **M** (231) 1000 N Easy St
85541-3811 (Mail to: 1000 N Easy St 85541-
3811) Daniel Tantimonaco (928) 474-3834

Phoenix All Saints Church & Day School **P** (1685)
§ 6300 N Central Ave 85012-1109 (Mail to:
6300 N Central Ave 85012-1109) Poulson Reed
James Bade William Burrill Holly Davis Anne
Ellsworth Vergie Ferguson (602) 279-5539

Phoenix Iglesia Episcopal de San Pablo **M** (532)
2801 N 31st St 85008-1126 (Mail to: 2801 N
31st St 85008-1126) Enrique Cadena Sally
Durand (602) 255-0602

Phoenix Santa Maria Episcopal Church **M** No
6501 N 39th Ave 85019-1303 (Mail to: 6522
N 39th Ave 85019-1304) Carmen Guerrero-
Stamp (602) 374-4855

Phoenix St Judes Episcopal Church **M** (78) 6531
N 39th Ave 85019-1303 (Mail to: 6531 N 39th
Ave 85019-1303) John Christopher (602) 492-
1772

Phoenix St Lukes at the Mountain Church **M**
(389) 848 E Dobbins Rd 85042 (Mail to: PO
Box 8667 85066-8667) Angelito Cubillas (602)
276-7318

Phoenix St Marys Church **P** (151) 6501 N 39th Ave 85019-1303 (Mail to: 6533 N 39th Ave 85019-1304) Robert Bustrin (602) 354-7540

Phoenix St Paul the Apostle Sudanese Mission **M** (220) 527 W Pima St 85003-2754 (Mail to: 527 W Pima St 85003-2754) Anderia Lual (602) 253-4094

Phoenix St Stephens Church **P** (200) No 2310 N 56th St 85008-2611 (Mail to: 2310 N 56th St 85008-2611) Julie O'Brien (602) 840-0437

✣ **Phoenix** Trinity Cathedral **O** (683) 100 W Roosevelt St 85003-1406 (Mail to: 100 W Roosevelt St 85003-1406) Myra Kingsley Whitney Kirby Troy Mendez (602) 254-7126

Prescott St Lukes Episcopal Church **P** (396) No 2000 Shepard Ln 86301-6143 (Mail to: 2000 Shepherds Ln 86301-6143) Kimball Arnold Pierre-Henry Buisson (928) 778-4499

Safford All Saints Episcopal Church **M** (55) 210 W Main St 85546-2349 (Mail to: 210 W Main St 85546-2349) Gail Carlsen (928) 348-9430

Scottsdale Episcopal Church of the Nativity **P** (380) No 22405 N Miller Rd 85255-4939 (Mail to: 22405 N Miller Rd 85255) Susan Snook Wayne Whitney (480) 307-9216

Scottsdale St Anthony on the Desert **P** (445) No 12990 E Shea Blvd 85259-5305 (Mail to: 12990 E Shea Blvd 85259-5305) Dorian Mulvey Susan Cihak Gordon Gilfeather (480) 451-0860

Scottsdale St Barnabas on the Desert **P** (1541) 6715 N Mockingbird Ln 85253-4344 (Mail to: 6715 N Mockingbird Lane 85253-4344) James Clark Elizabeth Blunt Elizabeth Roles Nicholas Roosevelt Erika Von Haaren (480) 948-5560

Sedona St Andrews Episcopal Church **P** (200) 100 Arroyo Pinon Dr 86336-5004 (Mail to: 100 Arroyo Pinon Dr 86336-5004) Mary Piotrowski (928) 282-4457

Sierra Vista St Stephen's Church **P** (203) 2750 E Cardinal Dr 85635 (Mail to: 2750 Cardinal Dr 85635-5447) Victor Sarrazin (520) 458-4432

Sun City All Saints of the Desert Church **P** (222) 9502 W Hutton Dr 85351-1462 (Mail to: 9502 W Hutton Dr 85351-1462) Robert Burton (623) 974-8404

Sun City St Christophers Church **P** (209) 10233 W Peoria Ave 85351-4248 (Mail to: 10233 W Peoria Ave 85351-4248) John Fabre (623) 972-1109

Sun City West Church of the Advent **P** (525) No 13150 W Spanish Garden Dr 85375-5052 (Mail to: 13150 W Spanish Garden Dr 85375-5052) Janet Gooltz (623) 584-0350

Tempe Church of the Epiphany **P** (866) § 2222 S Price Rd 85282-3013 (Mail to: 2222 S Price Rd 85282-3013) Ronald Poston Lynn Adwell (480) 968-4111

Tempe St Augustines Church **M** (273) § 1735 S College Ave 85281-6695 (Mail to: 1735 S College Ave 85281-6695) Chad Sundin Rebecca Williamson Vivian Winter Chaser (480) 967-3295

Tempe St James the Apostle Church **M** (202) No 975 E Warner Rd 85284-3232 (Mail to: 975 E Warner Rd 85284-3232) Frederick Huls Susan Wilmot (480) 345-2686

Tombstone St Pauls Church **M** (39) No PO Box 1489 85638-1489 (Mail to: PO Box 1489 85638-1489) John Smart (520) 553-3290

Tucson Christ the King Church **P** (275) 2800 W Ina Rd 85741-2502 (Mail to: 2800 W Ina Rd 85741-2502) Jeffrey Bullock Joseph King (520) 297-2551

Tucson Grace St Pauls Episcopal Church **P** (1172) 2331 E Adams St 85719-4308 (Mail to: 2331 E Adams St 85719-4308) Stephen Kelsey (520) 327-6857

Tucson St Albans Episcopal Church **P** (912) § Sabino Canyon At Old Sabino Canyon Rd 85750 (Mail to: Sabino Canyon At Old Sabino Canyon Rd 85750-2102) Bruce White Doyle Dietz-Allen Katlin McCallister (520) 296-0791

Tucson St Andrews Church Epis Church **M** (95) 545 S 5th Ave 85701 (Mail to: PO Box 1165 85702-1165) Kathryn Bradsen Jefferson Bailey (520) 622-8318

Tucson St Michael and All Angels Episcopal Church **P** (530) 602 N Wilmot Rd 85711-2702 (Mail to: 602 N Wilmot Rd 85711-2702) Thomas Kinman Clare Yarborough (520) 886-7292

Tucson St Philips in the Hills **P** (1765) 4440 N Campbell Ave 85718-6504 (Mail to: PO Box 65840 85728-5840) Clifford Blinman Frank Clark Beverley Edminster David Gillespie William Holt Thomas Lindell Norma Rogers Rosa Sandwell-Weiss (520) 299-6421

Tucson The Episcopal Church of St Matthew **P** (382) 9071 E Old Spanish Trl 85710-6265 (Mail to: PO Box 17116 85731-7116) Richard Wilson Franklyn Bergen Ruth Brown Mary Martin Michael Smith (520) 298-9782

Wickenburg St Albans Church **P** (147) 357 W Yavapai St 85390-3211 (Mail to: 357 W Yavapai St 85390-3211) Pamela Mulac (928) 684-2133

Williams St Johns Episcopal-Lutheran Church **M** (58) 202 W Grant Ave 86046-2535 (Mail to: PO Box 307 86046-0307) Marc McDonald (928) 635-2781

Winslow St Pauls Church **M** (53) 600 Henderson St 86047-2427 (Mail to: PO Box 1018 86047-1018) Norman Burke (928) 289-3851

NON-PAROCHIAL CLERGY

Abraham JL *ret* Tucson AZ
Adelia LA Phoenix AZ
Anderson-Smith S Tucson AZ
Archer MG Lincoln City OR
Atwell JJ *ret* Mesa AZ
Baird KJA Tucson AZ
Beaumont KJ *dcn*
Berra RM Tempe AZ
Bladon DG *dcn* Monticello AR
Booker J Deland FL
Breckenridge WA *ret* Tucson AZ

Brisson JL Fayetteville NC
Buckwalter PW *ret* Tucson AZ
Carlozzi CG *ret* Scottsdale AZ
Carlson PL *ret* Scottsdale AZ
Chatham CE *ret* Wickenburg AZ
Cheney PG *ret* Tucson AZ
Cohee WP *dcn* Phoenix AZ
Conner M *ret* Sun City AZ
Conrad JW *ret* Woodland Hills CA
Crowell PL *ret* Jamestown NC
Dalrymple SG *dcn* Lakeside AZ
Davidson TW *ret* Goodyear AZ
De Rijk CJ *ret* Phoenix AZ
De Silva SS *ret* Tucson AZ
Deasy JS *dcn* Flagstaff AZ
Delaney MJ Tucson AZ
Dombek TM Glendale AZ
Donnelly JK *ret* Bisbee AZ
Douglas MJ *dcn* Litchfield Park AZ
Douglas RO *ret* Palm Desert CA
Dugan RP *ret* Phoenix AZ
Durham EM *ret* Safford AZ
England MJ *ret dcn* San Diego CA
Finn EA Sun City West AZ
Fitzgerald JM Tucson AZ
Fitzsimmons J *dcn*
Foraker GA Tucson AZ
Ford SR Phoenix AZ
Garren BN Tucson AZ
Getts SJ *dcn*
Gibson ED San Juan Capistrano CA
Gillespie HS *dcn* Green Valley AZ
Goodwin JC *dcn*
Guida AG Berkeley CA
Gustafson KE *ret* North Las Vegas NV
Hackler WKD *dcn*
Halle MA *dcn* Chandler AZ
Hankins SS *ret* Santa Fe NM
Haring C *dcn* Tucson AZ
Harvey RW *ret* Bloomington MN
Haugh WW *ret* Vail AZ
Herron DP *dcn* Mesa AZ
Hesse VK Tucson AZ
Hill GC *dcn* Phoenix AZ
Hollis RAB *dcn* Tempe AZ
Hooper RI *dcn* Tucson AZ
Hosler SO *ret* Kearny AZ
Huls PT *dcn* Phoenix AZ
Hutson LD *dcn* Oro Valley AZ
Hyde PW Westport CT
James CJ *ret* Flagstaff AZ
Johnson AR *ret* Flagstaff AZ
Johnson AES *dcn* Fort Thomas AZ
Johnson MMV *dcn* Phoenix AZ
Johnson WG *ret* Tucson AZ
Jones SD Mesa AZ
Kapp JD *dcn* Tucson AZ
Keplinger SJ Tucson AZ
Kitagawa JE *ret* Tucson AZ
Knight HS *ret* Mesa AZ
Ledyard CM *dcn* Tucson AZ
Leonard TE *ret* Tubac AZ

Long LH *ret* Phoenix AZ
Marino MA Phoenix AZ
Martin WJ *dcn* Tucson AZ
McLaughlin MJ *dcn* Sun City AZ
Meister Book ND *dcn*
Meyer AK Portland OR
Meyers MW *dcn* Tucson AZ
Millar JD *ret* Scottsdale AZ
Mix LJ Cambridge MA
Moline ME *ret* Prescott AZ
Morrison HTN Ketchum ID
Morrison RN Gilbert AZ
Moulinier DW *dcn* Sedona AZ
Noonan DA Tucson AZ
Oluloro EB *dcn* Phoenix AZ
Pella DM Hartsdale NY
Perdue L *dcn* Phoenix AZ
Perry MR *dcn* Green Valley AZ
Polley SA Bisbee AZ
Porter JR *ret* Albuquerque NM
Porteus JM *ret* Helston
Puckle DE *ret* Sierra Vista AZ
Reed JB *ret* Tucson AZ
Rich EA *ret* Sun City AZ
Richardson DA *ret* Lake Havasu City AZ
Ritson VM *dcn* Phoenix AZ
Robertson CK New York NY
Rodenbeck BD *dcn* Kingman AZ
Romack GH *dcn* Litchfield Park AZ
Ryan FIS *dcn* Flagstaff AZ
Sawyer AM
Schuyler PW *ret* San Marcos CA
Scott RT *ret* Tucson AZ
Seaman ML *dcn* Scottsdale AZ
Seaton AC Holbrook AZ
Sinisi GA *ret* Surprise AZ
Skaug J *dcn*
Smith CH *ret* Chandler AZ
Smith JA *dcn*
Smith JR *ret* Tucson AZ
Somerville BL *ret* Sierra Vista AZ
Sotelo GS *ret* Oro Valley AZ
Souder DJ *ret* Winter Park FL
Sowinski CP *dcn* Phoenix AZ
Stafford GW
Stevens-Taylor SH *dcn* Tucson AZ
Strong AL *dcn* Tucson AZ
Taylor RD *dcn* Tucson AZ
Thom DL *ret* Wickenburg AZ
Traquair MM Laveen AZ
Turberg JE *ret* Casa Grande AZ
Valadez-Jaime A Phoenix AZ
Vellom LS *dcn* Nogales AZ
Vidal GV Phoenix AZ
Wagaman SW *dcn* Green Valley AZ
Waszczak MB *dcn* Tucson AZ
Way HL *ret* Glendale AZ
Williams RB *ret* Tucson AZ
Wilson WJ *ret* Pueblo CO
Woodlief VA *dcn* Green Valley AZ
Wyes GW *ret* Tucson AZ

DIOCESE OF ARKANSAS
(PROVINCE VII)
Comprises the State of Arkansas
DIOCESAN OFFICE 310 W 17th St Little Rock AR 72206
(MAIL: Box 164668 Little Rock AR 72216-4688)
TEL (501) 372-2168   FAX (501) 372-2147
E-MAIL dioark@episcopalarkansas.org   WEB www.episcopalarkansas.org

Previous Bishops—
Leonidas Polk 1838-41, Geo W Freeman 1844-58, Henry C Lay 1859-69, Henry N Pierce m 1870 dio 1871-99, Wm M Brown coadj 1898 Bp 1899-1912, James R Winchester coadj 1911 Bp 1912-31, Edwin W Saphore suffr 1917 Bp 1935-37, Edward T Demby suffr 1918-39, Richard B Mitchell 1938-56, Robt R Brown coadj 1955 Bp 56-70, Christoph Keller Jr coadj 1967 Bp 1970-81, Herbert A Donovan Jr coadj 1980 Bp 1981-93, Larry E Maze dio 1994-2006

Bishop—Rt Rev Larry R Benfield (1011)
(Dio 6 Jan 07)

Sec of Conv J Drymon *Treas and Fin* M Rudisill 705 Quapaw Hot Springs 71901; *Chanc* J Tisdale 305 Crystal Ct Little Rock 72205; *Reg* B Matthews; *Fin Coord* MJ Hodges; *Deploy* J Alexander; *Cath Affairs* C Keller; *Com* M Vano; *Hist* M McNeely; *ECW* W Dunwoody; *UTO* P Cromwell; *Yth and YA Coord* R Curtis; *Bp Adm Asst* B Matthews; *Comm* J Matthews; *Archdcn* S Loudenslager

Stand Comm—Cler: Pres D Stayton J Perkins P Morgan; *Lay:* J Ring J McCabe E Gray

Dio Conv: 19-20 Feb 2016 Little Rock AR

PARISHES, MISSIONS, AND CLERGY

Batesville St Pauls Episcopal Church **P** (267) 482 E Main St 72501-5628 (Mail to: PO Box 2255 72503-2255) John Drymon (870) 793-2203

Bella Vista St Theodores Episcopal Church **P** (355) 1001 Kingsland Rd 72714-5105 (Mail to: 1001 Kingsland Rd 72714-5105) (479) 855-2715

Benton St Matthews Episcopal Church **M** (137) 1112 Alcoa Rd 72015-3502 (Mail to: 1112 Alcoa Rd 72015-3502) Lorraine Slaymaker (501) 766-4176

Bentonville All Saints Church **P** (461) No 406 West Central Ave 72712 (Mail to: 406 W Central Ave 72712-2057) Roger Joslin Guillermo Castillo (479) 426-1561

Blytheville St Stephens Episcopal Church **M** (30) 1512 Willow St 72315-2361 (Mail to: PO Box 597 72316-0597) John Trotter (870) 763-8646

Camden St Johns Episcopal Church **M** (30) Corner of Harrison & Vanburen 71701 (Mail to: PO Box 694 71711-0694) (870) 836-2658

Cherokee Village St Andrews Episcopal Church **M** (13) #2 Wyott 72525-0471 (Mail to: PO Box 471 72525-0471) (870) 257-3224

Conway St Peters Episcopal Church **P** (385) 925 Mitchell St 72034-5147 (Mail to: 925 Mitchell St 72034-5147) Teresa Daily Nelda McDermott (501) 329-8174

Crossett St Marks Episcopal Church **M** (45) 909 Hickory St 71635-3513 (Mail to: PO Box 795 71635-0795) Robert Allen Amber Carswell (870) 364-2664

Devalls Bluff St Peters Episcopal Church **M** (194) Rr 1 Box 110a 72041-9748 (Mail to: 1002 Highway 86 E 72041-9635) (870) 255-3190

El Dorado St Marys Episcopal Church **P** (305) 512 Champagnolle Rd 71730-4732 (Mail to: 512 Champagnolle Rd 71730-4732) Charles Chapman Charles Chapman (870) 863-7064

Eureka Spgs St James Episcopal Church **M** (150) 28 Prospect Ave 72632-3039 (Mail to: 28 Prospect Ave 72632-3039) Dennis Campbell Elizabeth Porter (479) 253-8610

Fayetteville St Martins University Center **Campus Ministry** 814 W Maple St 72701-3233 (Mail to: 814 W Maple St 72701-3233) (479) 443-4791

Fayetteville St Pauls Episcopal Church **P** (1994) 224 N East Ave 72701-5225 (Mail to: PO Box 1190 72702-1190) Emily Bost Lowell Grisham Suzanne Stoner Charles Walling Lora Walsh (479) 442-7373

Foreman St Barnabas Episcopal Church **M** (43) Bell St & 2nd Ave 71836 (Mail to: PO Box 9 71836-0009) (870) 542-6880

Forrest City Christ Episcopal Church **M** (44) 1120 Ophelia St 72335-4624 (Mail to: PO Box 1077 72336-1077) Belinda Snyder (870) 633-6118

Forrest City Church of the Good Shepherd **P** (42) 400 Hill Ave 72335-3218 (Mail to: 400 Hill Ave 72335-3218) (870) 633-3093

Fort Smith St Augustines Episcopal Church **M** (11) 1400 N 9th St 72901-1341 (Mail to: PO Box 8283 72902-8283) (479) 785-1140

Fort Smith St Bartholomews Episcopal Church **P** (304) 2701 Old Greenwood Rd 72903-3317 (Mail to: 2701 Old Greenwood Rd 72903-3399) Jeffrey Champlin (479) 783-2101

Fort Smith St Johns Episcopal Church **P** (583) 215 N 6th St 72901-2105 (Mail to: 214 N 6th St 72901-2106) Michael Lager (479) 782-9912

Harrison St Johns Episcopal Church **P** (167) 707 West Central Ave 72601-4901 (Mail to: 707 W Central Ave 72601-4901) Gregory Hoover (870) 741-5638

Heber Springs St Francis in the Pines Episcopal

Ch **M** (97) 20 Woodland Cove Dr 72543-7688 (Mail to: 20 Woodland Cove Dr 72543-7688) Mary Dalby (501) 362-3311

Helena St Johns Episcopal Church **P** (117) 625 Pecan 72342-3201 (Mail to: PO Box 770 72342-0770) (870) 338-8115

Hope St Marks Episcopal Church **M** (26) 301 S Elm St 71801-5219 (Mail to: PO Box 285 71802-0285) (870) 777-3297

Horseshoe Bnd St Stephens Episcopal Church **M** (12) 1005 Third St 72512-3724 (Mail to: 1005 S Third St 72512) (870) 670-5214

Hot Springs Holy Trinity Episcopal Church **P** (203) 199 Barcelona Rd 71909-3801 (Mail to: 199 Barcelona Rd 71909-3801) Neil Kaminski (501) 922-0299

Hot Springs St Lukes Episcopal Church **P** (696) 228 Spring St 71901-4151 (Mail to: PO Box 1117 71902-1117) Clarence Baker Sara Milford (501) 623-1653

Jacksonville St Stephens Episcopal Church **M** (81) 2413 Northeastern Ave 72076-2969 (Mail to: 2413 Northeastern Ave 72076-2969) James Dalton Bruce Limozaine (501) 982-8701

Jonesboro St Marks Episcopal Church **P** (318) § 531 W College Ave 72401-4984 (Mail to: 531 W College Ave 72401-4984) Jesse Perkins Amber Carswell (870) 932-2124

Lake Village Emmanuel Episcopal Church **M** (35) 422 North Lakeshore Dr 71653 (Mail to: PO Box 389 71653-0389) (870) 265-2230

Little Rock Christ Episcopal Church **P** (475) 509 Scott St 72201-3807 (Mail to: 509 Scott St 72201-3891) James Walters Kathryn Alexander Brooks Cato (501) 375-2342

Little Rock Church of the Good Shepherd **M** (60) 2701 S Elm St 72204-6339 (Mail to: PO Box 23668 72221-3668) Michael Courtney (501) 663-8908

Little Rock St Francis House **Chapel** 2701 E Elm St 72204 (Mail to: 2701 E Elm St 72204)

Little Rock St Margarets Episcopal Church **P** (308) 20900 Chenal Pkwy 72223-9556 (Mail to: 20900 Chenal Pkwy 72223-9556) Mary Vano (501) 821-1311

Little Rock St Marks Episcopal Church **P** (1305) 1000 N Mississippi St 72207-5982 (Mail to: 1000 N Mississippi St 72207-5982) Daniel Schieffler Lisa Fry William Griffin Phillip Plunkett (501) 225-4203

Little Rock St Michaels Episcopal Church **P** (343) 12415 Cantrell Rd 72223-1727 (Mail to: 12415 Cantrell Rd 72223-1727) Claudia Heath Lisa Hlass Edwin Wills (501) 224-1442

✠ **Little Rock** Trinity Episcopal Cathedral **O** (1475) 310 W 17th St 72206-1461 (Mail to: 310 W 17th St 72206-1461) Christoph Keller Paul McLain (501) 372-0294

Magnolia St James Episcopal Church **M** (29) 901 Highland Cir 71753-2540 (Mail to: PO Box 846 71754-0846) Bruce Heyvaert (870) 234-6944

Marianna St Andrews Episcopal Church **P** (33) 49 S Carolina St 72360-2228 (Mail to: PO Box 241 72360-0241) Marion Miller (870) 295-2534

Maumelle St Nicholas Church **M** (52) 4002 Club Manor Dr 72113 (Mail to: PO Box 13677 72113-0677) Walter Brown (501) 291-6262

McGehee St Pauls Episcopal Church **M** (6) 100 N 3rd St 71654-2218 (Mail to: PO Box 246 71654-0246) (870) 222-6519

Mena Christ Episcopal Church **M** (26) 311 8th St 71953-3023 (Mail to: 803 Church Ave 71953-3250) (479) 216-2645

Monticello St Marys Episcopal Church **M** (26) 836 N Hyatt St 71655-4036 (Mail to: PO Box 193 71657-0193) (870) 536-5493

✠ **Morrilton** Camp Mitchell Episcopal Church **Other** 10 Camp Mitchell Rd 72110 (Mail to: 10 Camp Mitchell Rd 72110-9348) (501) 727-5451

Mountain Home St Andrews Episcopal Church **M** (123) 1050 S Church St 72653-4734 (Mail to: 511 Coley Dr 72653-2503) James McDonald (870) 425-3560

N Little Rock St Lukes Episcopal Church **P** (301) 4106 John F Kennedy Blvd 72116-8250 (Mail to: 4106 John F Kennedy Blvd 72116-8250) Carey Stone (501) 753-4281

Newport St Pauls Church **P** (121) 301 Hazel St 72112-3825 (Mail to: PO Box 367 72112-0367)

Osceola Calvary Episcopal Church **M** (29) 101 N Ash St 72370-2648 (Mail to: PO Box 292 72370-0292) John Trotter (870) 563-2416

Paragould All Saints Episcopal Church **M** (30) No 10th & Main Sts 72450 (Mail to: PO Box 212 72451-0212) (870) 236-2367

Pine Bluff Grace Episcopal Church **P** (77) No 4101 S Hazel St 71603-6832 (Mail to: 4101 S Hazel St 71603-6832) Curtis Jones Lorraine Slaymaker (870) 535-3852

Pine Bluff Trinity Episcopal Church **P** (390) 703 W 3rd Ave 71601-4009 (Mail to: PO Box 8069 71611-8069) Walter Windsor (870) 534-3832

Rogers St Andrews Episcopal Church **P** (94) Corner of 9th & Oak Sts 72757 (Mail to: PO Box 339 72757-0339) David Benham Craig Gavin (479) 636-4042

Russellville All Saints Episcopal Church **P** (382) 501 S Phoenix Ave 72801-7607 (Mail to: 501 S Phoenix Ave 72801-7607) Jos Tharakan (479) 968-3622

Searcy Trinity Episcopal Church **P** (142) 200 N Elm St 72143-5271 (Mail to: 200 N Elm St 72143-5271) Patrick Barker (501) 268-5270

Siloam Springs Grace Episcopal Church **P** (180) 617 N Mt Olive St 72761 (Mail to: PO Box 767 72761-0767) Stanley McKinnon Lora Walsh (479) 524-8782

Springdale St Thomas Episcopal Church **P** (329) 2898 S 48th St 72762-5844 (Mail to: 2898 S 48th St 72762-5844) Pamela Morgan (479) 751-9184

Stuttgart St Albans Episcopal Church **P** (99) 1201 S Main St 72160-5307 (Mail to: PO Box 726 72160-0726) Darrell Stayton (870) 673-2848

Van Buren Trinity Episcopal Church **M** (155) 918 N 9th St 72956-2720 (Mail to: PO Box 382 72957-0382) Michael Robinson

West Memphis Church of the Holy Cross **P** (53) 209 Park Dr 72301-3055 (Mail to: 209 Park Drive 72301-3055) Andrew Macbeth (870) 735-4517

NON-PAROCHIAL CLERGY

Alexander JL Little Rock AR
Baird GC *dcn* Siloan Springs AR
Barry PS Forrest City AR
Barton JC *ret* Albuquerque NM
Bates AL *ret* Rogers AR
Bauman DR Tunas MO
Baustian DE *ret* Ames IA
Briggs ME Granby CO
Burton J Eureka Springs AR
Burton LA
Carriere AS *ret* Mountain Home AR
Caruthers MC *ret*
Childress JR Little Rock AR
Clark CL *ret* Pine Bluff AR
Cook NB *dcn* Hot Springs AR
Curtis SO Little Rock AR
Dalton JF *dcn* Jacksonville AR
Doyle SP *ret* Harrison AR
Duncan-O'Neal WMK *ret* Overland Park KS
Frank TR Bella Vista AR
Fribourgh CK *dcn* Little Rock AR
Fry GJ Little Rock AR
Gitau SN *ret* Memphis TN
Hardy PJ *ret dcn* Little Rock AR
Hargreaves HJ *dcn* Morrilton AR
Hart GB *ret* Crossett AR
Hays MB *ret* Conway AR
Hearn AW *ret* Marianna AR
Hedges MH *dcn* Roland AR

Helmer BE *ret* Eureka Springs AR
Hoffman EHH *ret* Little Rock AR
Hybl AD Conway AR
Jackson RE *ret* Roland AR
Kettlewell CG *ret* Gainesville VA
Klee GM *ret* Blytheville AR
Loudenslager SC *dcn* Bigelow AR
Lund JA Bentonville AR
Lupton JH *ret* Belhaven NC
Lyon SL *dcn* Little Rock AR
Maroney GE Smackover AR
Mckee DD *ret* Madison MS
McLean JR *ret* Leland MI
Morgan MK *dcn* Conway AR
Murray NP *ret* Little Rock AR
Parks KT *ret* Bella Vista AR
Payne HW *ret* Little Rock AR
Payne SS *ret* Little Rock AR
Powell FH *ret* Hot Springs AR
Proffitt JR *ret* Chatsworth GA
Pugh JW *ret* Salisbury
Reese JV *dcn* Bentonville AR
Robertson CR Jacksonville AR
Scheel WP *ret* Wimberley TX
Schmidt AW *dcn* Saint Louis MO
Seibert JJ *dcn* Little Rock AR
Serdahl DL *ret* Mountain Home AR
Sifford TA *ret* Hot Springs Village AR
Sisk EK *ret* Overland Park KS
Smith SS *ret* Little Rock AR
Smith VM
Snapp JR
Spellman ALM Fayetteville AR
Staggs KA *dcn* Russellville AR
Strickland HS *ret* Bentonville AR
Tharakan AH Russellville AR
Toberman HF *dcn* Bloomingdale IL
West ID *dcn* Little Rock AR
Wootten JAH *dcn* Wake Forest NC
Wootten ML *ret* Wake Forest NC

DIOCESE OF ATLANTA
(PROVINCE IV)
Comprises middle and north GA
DIOCESAN OFFICE 2744 Peachtree Rd Atlanta GA 30305
TEL (404) 601-5320 FAX (404) 601-5330 WATS 800-537-6743
E-MAIL news@episcopalatlanta.org WEB www.episcopalatlanta.org

Previous Bishops—
Cleland K Nelson 1907-17, Henry J Mikell 1917-42, John M Walker 1942-51, John B Walthour 1952-52, Randolph R Claiborne Jr 1953-72, Milton L Wood suffr 1967-74, Bennett J Sims 1972-83, C Judson

Child Jr 1983-88, Frank Kellogg Allan 1989-2000 J Neil Alexander (2001-2012)

Bishop—Rt Rev Robert C Wright (1069) (Dio 13 Oct 12)

Assistant Bishop—Rt Rev Keith Whitmore (946) (Dio 10 Apr 99)

Assisting Bishop—Rt Rev Don Wimberly (789) (dio 1984)

Cn to Ord A Shuster Weltner *Treas* B King 2744 Peachtree Rd 30305; *Chanc* R Perry 2744 Peachtree Rd 30305; *V Chanc* T Christopher; *Sec of Council* HR Atkinson; *Min* J Thompson-Quartey; *COM Co-Chair* R Allen ; *Comm* Rev C Vaughn; *Educ* K Maxwell; *Stew* T Pallot; *Church Archtr & Constr* T Norris; *Mikell Conf Center* Rev K Struble; *Liturg* M Brady; *Annual Council* J Patterson; *Dir ECF* L Lowry; *Dir Fin* B Burgess; *Youth* Miss E Davis; *Hispanic Miss* Rev IA Rodriguez

Stand Comm—Cler: J Jackson S Kidd J Strizak *Lay:* R Schreidber A Canipe J Hendricks

Deans of Convoc—NE GA M Demmler; *Chatta-hoochee Valley* A Pruitt; *Mid-Atlanta* C Fischer; *Marietta* R Wood; *N Atlanta* A Chase; *NE Metro:* K Branstetter; *SW Atlanta* H Glover *E Atlanta* C Vaughn; *Macon* J Shippen; *NW GA* J Brackenwright

Dio Conv: 18-19 Nov 2016 GA International Convention Center, College Park

PARISHES, MISSIONS, AND CLERGY

Acworth St Teresas Episcopal Church **P** (529) 5725 Fords Rd NW 30101-4674 (Mail to: 5725 Fords Rd NW 30101-4674) Sandra Brice (770) 590-9040

Athens Emmanuel Episcopal Church **P** (1040) 498 Prince Ave 30601-2449 (Mail to: 498 Prince Ave 30601-2449) Robert Salamone Christopher Cole (706) 543-1294

Athens Episcopal Center at UGA **CC** 980 S Lumpkin St 30605-5119 (Mail to: 980 S Lumpkin St 30605-5119) (706) 353-2330

Athens St Gregory the Great Epis Church **P** (386) 3195 Barnett Shoals Rd 30605-4327 (Mail to: Attn: Kendall Kookogey 3195 Barnett Shoals Rd 30605-4327) Beth Long (706) 546-7553

Atlanta Absalom Jones Student Center **CC** C/O The Rev Frank M Ross 634 W Peachtree St SW 30308-1925 (Mail to: 807 Atlanta Student Movement Blvd 30314-3758) (404) 521-1602

Atlanta All Saints Episcopal Church **P** (3051) 634 W Peachtree St NW 30308-1925 (Mail to: 634 W Peachtree St NW 30308-1925) Geoffrey Hoare Timothy Black William Clarkson Margaret Crammer James Donald Charles May Judson Mull Walter Smith Noelle York-Simmons (404) 881-0835

✠ **Atlanta** Cathedral of St Philip **O** (6284) 2744 Peachtree Rd NW 30305-2937 (Mail to: 2744 Peachtree Rd NW 30305-2920) Samuel Candler John Sanders George Maxwell J William Harkins Charles Marsh Louis Schueddig Todd Smelser Theophus Smith Carolynne Williams Cathy Zappa (404) 365-1000

Atlanta Church of Our Saviour **P** (144) 1068 N Highland Ave NE 30306-3551 (Mail to: 1068 N Highland Ave NE 30306-3551) Carole Maddux

Zachary Thompson (404) 872-4169

Atlanta Church of the Epiphany **P** (620) 2089 Ponce De Leon Ave NE 30307 (Mail to: 2089 Ponce De Leon Ave NE 30307-1345) Sharon Hiers Benno Pattison Barbara Ryder (404) 373-8338

Atlanta Church of the Holy Comforter **P** (87) 737 Woodland Ave SE 30316-2454 (Mail to: 737 Woodland Ave SE 30316-2454) Michael Tanner Katharine Hilliard-Yntema Bert Smith

Atlanta Church of the Incarnation **P** (143) 2407 Cascade Rd SW 30311-3225 (Mail to: 2407 Cascade Rd SW 30311-3225) (404) 755-6654

Atlanta Emmaus House **P** (119) 1017 Hank Aaron Dr SW 30315-1705 (Mail to: 1017 Hank Aaron Dr SW 30315-1705) (404) 525-5948

Atlanta Georgia Tech/Georgia State Epis Ctr **CC** 2744 Peachtree Rd NW 30305 (Mail to: 2744 Peachtree Rd NW 30305) (404) 881-0835

Atlanta Holy Innocents Episcopal Church **P** (2188) 805 Mount Vernon Hwy NW 30327-4321 (Mail to: 805 Mount Vernon Hwy NW 30327-4321) Michael Sullivan Lisa Zaina Timothy Black James Case Grady Crawford William Stanley (404) 255-4023

Atlanta Iglesia Episcopal de Santa Maria **P** (233) 845 Glenway Dr 30344-6703 (Mail to: 845 Glenway Dr 30344-6703) (404) 707-1217

Atlanta Saint Anne's Episcopal Church **P** (1268) 3098 Saint Annes Ln 30327-1638 (Mail to: 3098 Saint Anne's Ln NW 30327-1638) Licia Affer Ruth Pattison (404) 237-5589

Atlanta St Bartholomews Episcopal Church **P** (890) 1790 Lavista Rd NE 30329-3604 (Mail to: 1790 Lavista Rd NE 30329-3604) William Thigpen Beverley Elliott Andrew McGehee (404) 634-3336

Atlanta St Bedes Episcopal Church **P** (1191) 2601 Henderson Mill Rd NE 30345-2134 (Mail to: 2601 Henderson Mill Rd NE 30345-2134) Steven Vaughn Caroline Branch Lynnsay Buehler Fabio Sotelo (770) 938-9797

Atlanta St Dunstan's Episcopal Church **P** (116) 4393 Garmon Rd NW 30327-3831 (Mail to: 4393 Garmon Rd NW 30327-3831) Patricia Templeton Margaret Harney (404) 266-1018

Atlanta St Johns Episcopal Church **P** (164) 3480 Main St 30337-2064 (Mail to: 3480 E Main St 30337-2064)

Atlanta St Luke's Episcopal Church **P** (2008) 435 Peachtree St NE 30308-3228 (Mail to: 435 Peachtree St NE 30308-3228) Daniel Matthews Lauren Holder Dennis Patterson Elizabeth Shows Caffey David Wagner (404) 873-7600

Atlanta St Martin in the Fields Episcopal Ch **P** (1458) 3110 Ashford Dunwoody Rd NE 30319-2751 (Mail to: 3110 Ashford Dunwoody Rd NE 30319-2751) John McCard Lauren Kuratko (404) 261-4292

Atlanta St Patricks Episcopal Church **P** (404) 4755 N Peachtree Rd 30338-5812 (Mail to:

4755 N Peachtree Rd 30338-5812) Paul Game Sarah Fisher Julia Rusling (770) 455-6523

Atlanta St Pauls Episcopal Church **P** (973) 294 Peyton Rd SW 30311-2152 (Mail to: 294 Peyton Rd SW 30311-2152) Charles Fischer Arlette Benoit Caroline Peacock (404) 696-3620

Atlanta The Episcopal Church at Emory **Chaplaincy** 1660 N Decatur Rd NE Rm 211 Emory University 30307-1010 (404) 377-0680

Austell Church of the Good Shepherd **P** (154) 6216 Love St 30168-4714 (Mail to: PO Box 682 30168-1050) (678) 851-2006

Blairsville St Clares Episcopal Church **P** (116) 1272 Ledford Rd 30512-3107 (Mail to: 777 Ledford Rd 30512-3110) Elizabeth Schellingerhoudt

Buford St Mary & St Martha of Bethany **P** (580) 4346 Ridge Road 30519-4210 (Mail to: 4346 Ridge Road 30519-4210) Timothy Watts George Mustard (770) 271-4067

Calhoun St Timothys Episcopal Church **P** (175) PO Box 701 30703-0701 (Mail to: 224 Trammell St 30701-2218) (706) 629-1056

Canton St Clements Episcopal Church **P** (315) 2795 Ridge Rd 30114-9501 (Mail to: PO Box 4156 30114-0010) James Stutler (770) 345-6722

Carrollton St Margarets Episcopal Church **P** (648) 606 Newnan St 30117-3429 (Mail to: 606 Newnan St 30117-3429) Hazel Glover Robert Fowler (770) 832-3931

Cartersville Church of the Ascension **P** (239) 205 W Cherokee Ave 30120-3003 (Mail to: 205 W Cherokee Ave 30120-3003) Mary Erickson (770) 382-2626

Cedartown St James Episcopal Church **P** (53) 302 West Ave.30125-3422 (Mail to: PO Box 85 30125-0085) Paul Anderson (770) 748-2894

Clarkesville Grace Calvary Church **P** (314) 260 E Green St 30523 (Mail to: PO Box 490 30523-0009) Samuel Buice (706) 754-2451

Clayton St James Episcopal Church **P** (179) 206 Warwoman Rd 30525-5100 (Mail to: PO Box 69 30525-0002) Stephen Hall Anthony Sgro (706) 782-6179

Columbus Church of St Thomas **P** (466) 2100 Hilton Ave 31906-1500 (Mail to: 2100 Hilton Ave 31906-1500) Lydia Burton-Edwards (706) 324-4264

Columbus St Mary Magdalene Episcopal Church **P** (45) 4244 Saint Marys Rd 31907-6243 (Mail to: 4244 Saint Marys Rd 31907-6243) (706) 689-2790

Columbus Trinity Episcopal Church **HC** (575) PO Box 1146 31902-1146 (Mail to: PO Box 1146 31902-1146) Timothy Graham Nicholas Hull (706) 322-5569

Conyers St Simons Episcopal Church **P** (196) 1522 Highway 138 NE 30013-1266 (Mail to: PO Box 102 30012-0102) Jane Weston

Covington Church of the Good Shepherd **P** (320) 4140 Clark St SW 30014-2713 (Mail to: 4140 Clark St SW 30014-2713) Maurice Beckham Ruth Healy (770) 786-3278

Cumming Church of the Holy Spirit **P** (385) PO Box 1010 30028-1010 (Mail to: PO Box 1010 30028-1010) Keith Oglesby Bonnie Underwood (770) 887-8190

Dahlonega St Elizabeths Episcopal Church **P** (143) 1188 Hamp Mill Rd 30533-4872 (Mail to: 1188 Hamp Mill Rd 30533-4872) Paul Roberts

Dalton St Marks Episcopal Church **P** (359) 901 W Emory St 30720-2330 (Mail to: 901 W Emory St 30720-2330) Virginia Royalty (706) 278-8857

Decatur Church of the Holy Cross **P** (705) 2005 S Columbia Pl 30032-5945 (Mail to: 2005 S Columbia Pl 30032-5945) Brian Jemmott (404) 284-1211

Decatur Holy Trinity Parish **P** (555) 515 E Ponce De Leon Ave 30030-1941 (Mail to: 515 E Ponce De Leon Ave 30030-1941) Jimmy Tallant Joseph Pearson Ellen Purdum Jenna Strizak (404) 377-2622

Decatur St Timothys Episcopal Church **P** (95) 2833 Flat Shoals Rd 30034-1040 (Mail to: 2833 Flat Shoals Rd 30034-1040) Daniel Dice (404) 241-7711

Douglasville St Julians Episcopal Church **P** (118) 5400 Stewart Mill Rd 30135-2545 (Mail to: 5400 Stewart Mill Rd 30135-2545) James Duke (770) 949-9949

Eatonton All Angels Episcopal Church **P** (27) PO Box 4695 31024-4695 (Mail to: PO Box 4695 31024-4695) (478) 718-9189

Elberton St Albans Episcopal Church **P** (28) 109 Brookside Dr 30635-2503 (Mail to: 109 Brookside Dr 30635-2503) John Keeler (706) 376-1489

Fayetteville Church of the Nativity **P** (185) 130 Antioch Rd 30215-5701 (Mail to: 130 Antioch Rd 30215-5701) Rita Henault (770) 460-6390

Fort Valley St Andrews Episcopal Church **P** (42) PO Box 308 31030-0308 (Mail to: 309 Central Ave 31030-3740) (478) 987-8291

Fort Valley St Lukes Episcopal Church **P** (113) PO Box 770 31030-0770 (Mail to: PO Box 770 31030-0770) Brian Davy (706) 975-3264

Gainesville Grace Episcopal Church **P** (731) 431 Washington St SE 30501-3612 (Mail to: 422 Brenau Ave 30501-3612) Stuart Higginbotham Alan Cowart Michael McCann Cynthia Park (770) 536-0126

Greensboro Episcopal Church of the Redeemer **P** (183) 303 North Main St 30642-0093 (Mail to: PO Box 93 30642-0093) (706) 453-7171

Griffin St George's Episcopal Church **P** (469) 132 N 10th St 30223-2841 (Mail to: 132 N 10th St 30223-2841) Nancy Shepherd

Hamilton St Nicholas Episcopal Church **P** (207) 69 Mobley Rd 31811 (Mail to: PO Box 752

31811) Jeffery Jackson (706) 628-7272

Hartwell St Andrews Episcopal Church **P** (103) 579 Fairview Ave 30643-2166 (Mail to: 579 Fairview Ave 30643-2166) Susan Hardaway (706) 376-4986

Jasper Church of the Holy Family **P** (293) 100 Griffith Rd 30143-4422 (Mail to: 202 Griffith Rd 30143-4422) George Yandell Charles Hackett Byron Tindall (770) 893-4525

Kennesaw Christ Episcopal Church **P** (363) 1210 Wooten Lake Rd NW 30144-1347 (Mail to: 1210 Wooten Lake Rd NW 30144-1347) (770) 422-9114

LaGrange St Marks Episcopal Church **P** (396) 207 N Greenwood St 30240-2603 (Mail to: 207 N Greenwood St 30240-2603) Robert Pruitt (706) 884-8911

Lawrenceville St Edwards Episcopal Church **P** (557) 737 Moon Rd 30045-6109 (Mail to: 737 Moon Rd 30046-6109) Kent Branstetter (770) 963-6128

Lilburn Christ the King Episcopal Church **P** (92) 4805 Lawrenceville Hwy NW Suite 403 30047-3845 (Mail to: 4805 Lawrenceville Hwy NW 30047-3845) John Ray (770) 309-8589

Macon Christ Episcopal Church **P** (739) 538 Walnut St 31201-2709 (Mail to: 582 Walnut St 31201-2762) Bryan Hinson Joseph Shippen Arthur Villarreal (478) 745-0427

Macon St Francis Episcopal Church **P** (447) 432 Forest Hill Rd 31210-4824 (Mail to: 432 Forest Hill Rd 31210-4824) Richmond Jones (478) 477-4616

Macon St James Episcopal Church **P** (51) 1080 Courtland Ave 31204-3930 (Mail to: 1080 Courtland Ave 31204-3930) Shirley Porter

Macon St Pauls Episcopal Church **P** (314) 753 College St 31201-1720 (Mail to: 753 College St 31201-1720) Pamela Lightsey (478) 743-4623

Madison Church of the Advent **P** (195) 338 Academy St 30650-1545 (Mail to: 338 Academy St 30650-1545) Charles Baldwin Daniel Brown (706) 342-4787

Marietta Church of St Peter & St Paul **P** (1314) 1795 Johnson Ferry Rd 30062-6400 (Mail to: 1795 Johnson Ferry Rd 30062-6400) Louis Faucette Elisa Harres Ashley Lytle Thomas Pumphrey (770) 977-7473

Marietta Church of the Annunciation **P** (333) 1673 Jamerson Rd 30066-1213 (Mail to: 1673 Jamerson Rd 30066-1213) Hugo Jackson Paul McCabe (770) 928-7916

Marietta St Catherines Episcopal Church **P** (982) 571 Holt Rd NE 30068-3039 (Mail to: 571 Holt Rd NE 30068-3039) Susan Johnson Charles Taylor (770) 971-2839

Marietta St James Episcopal Church **P** (1327) 161 Church St NE 30060-1629 (Mail to: 161 Church St NE 30060-1629) Roger Allen Daron Vroon (770) 428-5841

Marietta St Judes Episcopal Church **P** (162)

220 Windy Hill Rd SW 30060-5547 (Mail to: 220 Windy Hill Rd SW 30060-5547) William Austin Charles Fulton (770) 435-0936

Mcdonough St Josephs Episcopal Church **P** (325) 1865 Highway 20 W 30253-7316 (Mail to: 1865 Highway 20 E 30252-2264) Scott Harding (770) 957-7517

Milledgeville St Stephens Episcopal Church **P** (259) 220 W Wayne St 31061-3442 (Mail to: PO Box 309 31059-0309) David Probst (478) 452-2710

Milton St Aidans Episcopal Church **P** (498) 13560 Cogburn Rd 30004-3648 (Mail to: 13560 Cogburn Road 30004-3648) Robert Wood (770) 521-0207

Monroe St Albans Episcopal Church **P** (69) 210 N Broad St 30655-1844 (Mail to: PO Box 655 30655-0655) Alan Hansen (855) 398-4597

Montezuma St Marys Episcopal Church **P** (11) 608 Rawls St 31063-1332 (Mail to: 901 Drayton Rd 31063-7201) Donald Tate Ruth Tate (478) 472-8758

Morrow St Augustine of Canterbury **P** (334) 1221 Morrow Rd 30260-1624 (Mail to: PO Box 169 30260-0169) Barry Griffin (770) 961-9353

Newnan St Pauls Episcopal Church **P** (733) 576 Roscoe Rd 30263-4782 (Mail to: 576 Roscoe Rd 30263-4782) Joseph Sandlin Peter Wallace (770) 253-4264

Norcross Christ Episcopal Church **P** (628) 400 Holcomb Bridge Rd 30071-2040 (Mail to: 400 Holcomb Bridge Rd 30071-2040) Cecilia Duke Paul Coil Jody Greenwood (770) 447-1166

Oakwood St Gabriels Episcopal Church **P** (225) 2920 Landrum Education Dr 30566-3405 (Mail to: 2920 Landrum Education Dr 30566-3405) Richard Sanders (770) 503-7555

Peachtree City St Andrews in the Pines Epis Church **P** (514) 316 N Peachtree Pkwy 30269-1360 (Mail to: 316 N Peachtree Pkwy 30269-1360) Paul Elliott (770) 487-8415

Perry St Christophers at the Crossroads **P** (117) 1207 Macon Rd 31069-2612 (Mail to: 1207 Macon Rd 31069-2612) Lorna Erixson (478) 987-2190

Rome Church of the Transfiguration **P** (69) 304 Coker Dr SW 30165-3416 (Mail to: 304 Coker Dr SW 30165-3416) Linda Pineo (706) 234-0197

Rome St Peters Episcopal Church **P** (942) 101 E 4th Ave 30161-3119 (Mail to: 101 E 4th Ave 30161-3119) John Herring Thelma Mathis Janice Wright (706) 291-9111

Roswell St Davids Episcopal Church **P** (1902) 1015 Old Roswell Rd 30076-1607 (Mail to: 1015 Old Roswell Rd 30076-1607) Kenneth Swanson Antonio Brito Michelle Ortiz Anne Swiedler (770) 993-6084

Sandy Springs Church of the Atonement **P** (447) 4945 High Point Rd NE 30342 (Mail to: 4945 High Point Road NE 30342) (404) 252-3324

Sautee Nacoochee Episcopal Church of the Resurrection (236) 1755 Duncan Bridge Rd 30571-3611 Scott Kidd (706) 865-9680

Smyrna St Benedicts Episcopal Church **P** (1014) 2160 Cooper Lake Rd SE 30080-6328 (Mail to: 2160 Cooper Lake Rd SE 30080-6328) Brian Sullivan Rebekah Hatch (678) 279-4300

Snellville The Church of St Matthew **P** (660) 1520 Oak Rd 30078-2230 (Mail to: 1520 Oak Rd 30078-2230) Elizabeth Hendrick (770) 979-4210

Stone Mountain St Michael & All Angels Episcopal Ch **P** (506) 6780 James B Rivers Dr 30083-2249 (Mail to: 6780 James B Rivers Dr 30083-2235) (770) 469-8551

Suwanee St Columbas Episcopal Church **P** (1249) 5400 Laurel Springs Pkwy Ste 1 30024-6056 (Mail to: 939 James Burgess Rd 30024-1128) Paul Norris Robert Millott (770) 888-4464

Thomaston St Thomas of Canterbury Epis Church **M** (14) 400 Georgia Ave 30286-3518 (Mail to: PO Box 807 610 Avalon Rd 30286-0011) Brian Davy (706) 646-3364

Toccoa St Matthias Episcopal Church **P** (208) 995 E Tugalo St 30577-1930 (Mail to: 995 E Tugalo St 30577-1938) Mary Demmler (706) 886-4413

Trion St Barnabas Episcopal Church **P** (74) 100 Central Ave 30753-1125 (Mail to: PO Box 685 30753-0685) (706) 734-3098

Warner Robins All Saints Episcopal Church **P** (240) 1708 Watson Blvd 31093-3632 (Mail to: 1708 Watson Blvd 31093-3632) Scott Petersen

Washington Church of the Mediator **P** (80) PO Box 716 30673 (Mail to: PO Box 93 30642-0093) Loreen Reed (706) 678-7226

West Point St Johns Episcopal Church **P** (59) 501 Avenue C 31833-2037 (Mail to: 304 E 6th St 31833-2026) (706) 645-2156

Winder St Anthonys Episcopal Church **P** (59) 174 Saint Anthonys Dr 30680-1587 (Mail to: 174 Saint Anthonys Dr 30680-1587) Harold Harrison (770) 867-5633

NON-PAROCHIAL CLERGY

Ader TE *dcn* Marietta GA
Alexander GW *ret* Marietta GA
Anderson CN *ret* College Park GA
Anderson WA *ret dcn* Charleston SC
Anthony BJ
Anthony JD *ret* Lilburn GA
Ard EJ *ret* Smyrna GA
Ard RH *ret* Rome GA
Arledge TL *ret* Perry GA
Armentrout KJ *dcn* Jasper GA
Atkinson HR *ret* Elberton GA
Bagay MJ *ret*
Bailey RZ Atlanta GA
Baker MJ *ret* cleveland GA
Baltz FB *ret* Marietta GA
Bancroft JG *ret* Mcdonough GA
Bartlett H *ret* Clarkston GA

Baxter NJ *ret* Atlanta GA
Betances RA Marietta GA
Black GD *ret* Rome GA
Bolton JD *ret* Milton GA
Book RTM Atlanta GA
Bott HR *ret* Atlanta GA
Bowron JD Charlotte NC
Boyd WO *ret* Washington GA
Brady AB
Brewster JP *ret* Sewanee TN
Brigham RD *ret* Peachtree City GA
Britt SES *dcn* Marietta GA
Brown DH *ret* Gaithersburg MD
Brown DL *ret* Toccoa GA
Buice BC *ret* Milledgeville GA
Burdett AB Atlanta GA
Burtenshaw NC *ret* Alpharetta GA
Burton WA
Callaway RH *ret*
Carlson WD *ret dcn* Ashville NC
Cave JP *ret* Kansas City MO
Cekuta NA Charlotte NC
Certain RG *ret* Roswell GA
Chase AM Decatur GA
Chrisner MR *ret* Ocala FL
Collins DB *ret* Woodstock GA
Combs WL Oakwood GA
Conley TH *ret* Atlanta GA
Cooper-White PC New York NY
Coulter SL Marietta GA
Courtney P *ret* Athens GA
Cruz-Diaz N *dcn* Norcross GA
Curtis JD *ret* Atlanta GA
Curtis WL Atlanta GA
Dailey DG Gainesville GA
Daviou AG *ret* Dahlonega GA
Day MB Atlanta GA
Dendtler RB *ret* Greensboro GA
Deneke WT *ret* Decatur GA
Dondero CD *dcn* Atlanta GA
Drake LA *dcn* Smyrna GA
Dukes JE Signal Mountain TN
Eckardt RR *dcn* Atlanta GA
Elberfeld KAF *ret* Marietta GA
Elliott PA *ret* Stone Mountain GA
Evans KP *ret* Marietta GA
Farr BA
Farwell JW Alexandria VA
Ford AM *ret* Atlanta GA
Frearson AR Doraville GA
Freeman SM *ret* Gainesville GA
Fulghum CB *ret* Atlanta GA
Fuller EB *dcn* Atlanta GA
Galloway DA Atlanta GA
Gearing CE *dcn* Stone Mountain GA
Gedrick J Pawling NY
Gibson RB *ret* Blairsville GA
Girardeau CM *ret* Tucker GA
Gotko RM *ret* Mont Eagle TN
Grant HM Eastsound WA
Hackett AR *dcn* Morrow GA

Hall J *ret* Exeter RI
Hally JE *ret* Atlanta GA
Hamner JE Atlanta GA
Hanahan GH Atlanta GA
Hannum CCL Marietta GA
Hare DE *ret* Fletcher NC
Harris GS *ret* Atlanta GA
Hartley MM Sewanee TN
Hays JS *ret* Griffin GA
Hegg CS *ret* Macon GA
Herring JD *ret* Johns Creek GA
Hilton EG *dcn* Morrow GA
Hizer CA Covington GA
Holman KD *dcn* Marietta GA
Howell TR *dcn* Atlanta GA
Hudson JP *ret* Roswell GA
Huff SE *dcn* Lawrenceville GA
Hungate CV *dcn* Douglasville GA
Huston JW *ret* Atlanta GA
Jackson KS
Johnson RD *ret* Conyers GA
Jones EC *ret* Stone Mountain GA
Jones FL *ret* Kent OH
Jones TG *ret* Columbus GA
Kalom JCL *dcn*
Kennedy NN Mableton GA
Kidd PD *ret* Hawthorne FL
Lanier SL Waycross GA
Lee KA Atlanta GA
Lema JM Norcross GA
Lemley KC *dcn* Atlanta GA
Lockett HJ *ret*
Lowe WJ *dcn* Atlanta GA
Lowrey PL Atlanta GA
Martin WT *ret* Williamsburg VA
Martinez LAR *ret dcn* Kennesaw GA
McCann SB
McGraw SE *ret* Charleston SC
Merchant JE *ret* Asheville NC
Merchant PL *ret* Cincinnati OH
Meroney AE *ret* Macon GA
Monroe Loes BF West Point GA
Moss DM Atlanta GA
Moss DS *ret*
Mote DS Decatur GA
Mulligan EB Atlanta GA
Newman GA *dcn* Milledgeville GA
Nixon JT *ret* Marietta GA
Northup FB *ret* Asheville NC
Ogier DE *ret* Clarkesville GA
Okunsanya AG *ret*
Owens GW *dcn* Atlanta GA
Owens RM *ret* Sewanee TN
Padgett JMP *dcn* Kennesaw GA
Palmgren CL Stone Mountain GA
Pappas JC Sewanee TN
Patterson BAB Decatur GA
Peyton RL Hartwell GA
Pippin T *dcn* Atlanta GA
Pope NK *dcn* Cumming GA
Porter JJ *ret* Atlanta GA

Porter Cade WM Wilmington DE
Pritcher JJ Atlanta GA
Rees EF *dcn* Braselton GA
Reichmann JH *ret* Jacksonville Beach FL
Rein LA *dcn* Decatur GA
Rickard RB *ret* Marietta GA
Roberts KA Avondale Estates GA
Rodriguez IA *ret* Atlanta GA
Roles EA New York NY
Roper CM *ret* Roswell GA
Rosser JB Smyrna GA
Ruyle EE *ret* Roswell GA
Sabom WS Decatur GA
Salmon WB
Sandoval J *dcn* Marietta GA
Saunders CG Sandy Springs GA
Saussy H *ret* Dania FL
Schultz AM Atlanta GA
Schuster Weltner AD Atlanta GA
Shepherd WH Griffin GA
Shew DAM Atlanta GA
Shortell BM *ret* Flowery Branch GA
Silver DL Grovetown GA
Simmons HJ *ret* Augusta GA
Simrill SD *ret* Minneapolis MN
Smart JD *ret* Atlanta GA
Smith DG *ret* Kennesaw GA
Smith JL *ret* Wadley GA
Smith JW *ret* Sewanee TN
Soper LD *ret* Southern Pines NC
Stanton JR *ret* Richmond VA
Starr CC Sandy Springs GA
Sterne MP *ret* Atlanta GA
Stevens PD *ret* Johnston SC
Struble KC Toccoa GA
Suthers DA *ret* Rio Rico AZ
Szarke CJ Ithaca NY
Taylor BB Clarkesville GA
Taylor SE Atlanta GA
Temple G *ret* Duluth GA
Temple PC *ret* Atlanta GA
Templeton JH *ret* Clayton GA
Thim PR *ret* Decatur GA
Thompson HP *dcn* McDonough GA
Tidwell JR *dcn* Macon GA
Tipton GB Athens GA
Titus JC *dcn* Stone Mountain GA
Tonsmeire LE *ret* Calhoun GA
Uitti AL *ret* East Palatka FL
Via JA *ret* Port Republic VA
Warner CS Sullivans Island SC
Warner KR *ret* Christiansted VI
Watt JT *dcn* Atlanta GA
Weidman HJ Macon GA
Wells BR Macon GA
Wells LF *ret* Athens GA
Westerhoff JH *ret* Atlanta GA
Willcox HL Atlanta GA
Williams LC *ret* Hot Springs AR
Wilson FF *ret* Monroe GA
Windom BS *dcn* Macon GA

Wires JW *ret* Annandale VA
Woodall PJ *ret* Stuart FL
Woodling EW *dcn* Atlanta GA
Wright JAF *dcn* Kennesaw GA
Wright RL *dcn*

Yancey NR *dcn* Norcross GA
Wright RL *dcn*
Wright JAF *dcn* Kennesaw GA
Yancey NR *dcn* Norcross GA

AUSTRIA; BELGIUM
See Europe

DIOCESE OF BETHLEHEM
(PROVINCE III)
Comprises 14 counties of Northeastern PA
DIOCESAN OFFICE 333 Wyandotte St Bethlehem PA 18015
TEL (610) 691-5655 FAX (610) 691-1682
E-MAIL office@diobeth.org WEB www.diobeth.org

Previous Bishops—
Mark AD Howe 1871-95, Nelson
S Rulison coadj 1884 Bp 1895-97,
Ethelbert Talbot 1898-1928, Frank
W Sterrett coadj 1923 Bp 1928-
54, Fred J Warnecke coadj 1953
Bp 1954-71, Lloyd E Gressle coadj
1970 Bp 1971-83, Mark Dyer coadj
1982 Bp 1983-95, Paul V Marshall
Bp, 1996-2013

**Bishop Provisional—Rt Rev Sean Rowe
(1019)** (March 1, 2014)

Archd Ven RI Cluett; *Sec* Rev K Kern; *Treas* Rev C
Barebo 4550 S 5th St Emmaus PA 18049; *Chanc* L
Henry 621 Fifteenth St Bethlehem PA 18018; *Pres
Trustees* D Feick; *Cn for Min Form & Trans* Rev AE
Kitch; *Cn for Admin & Comm* J Trepagnier

Stand Comm—Cler: Pres A Gerns TS Allen J Rinehart
E Trygar J Bender; *Lay:* EH House R Arcario L
Holzinger K Smith K Fanning, C McMullen

Dio Conv: 7-8 Oct 2016 Christ Church, Reading PA

PARISHES, MISSIONS, AND CLERGY

Allentown Church of the Mediator **P** (233) 1620
W Turner St 18102-3637 (Mail to: 1620 W
Turner St 18102-3637) Maria Tjeltveit Twila
Smith (610) 434-0155

Allentown Grace Episcopal Church **P** (68) 108
N 5th St 18102-4108 (Mail to: 108 N 5th St
18102-4108) Rodney Conn

Allentown St Andrews Church **P** (176) 1901
Pennsylvania Ave 18109-3111 (Mail to: 1900
Pennsylvania Ave 18109-3187) Thomas Allen
(610) 865-3603

Archbald St James-St George Epis Church **P**
(182) C/O Carol Propst Treasurer 900 Pike

St 18403-2202 (Mail to: 398 Washington Ave
18433-1342) Frank Cliff Francis Pearson (570)
876-4896

✠ **Ashland** Memorial Church of St John **Other** 106
N 12th St 17921 (Mail to: PO Box 487 17931-
0487) (570) 874-4532

Athens Trinity Episcopal Church **P** (86) 701 S
Main St 18810-1009 (Mail to: 701 S Main St
18810-0009) Benjamin Lentz (570) 888-5715

✠ **Bethlehem** Cathedral Church of the Nativity **O**
(981) 321 Wyandotte St 18015-1527 (Mail
to: 321 Wyandotte St 18015-1527) Anthony
Pompa John Board Michael Moyer Michelle
Moyer (610) 865-0727

Bethlehem Trinity Church **P** (520) 44 E Market
St 18018-5926 (Mail to: 44 E Market St 18018-
5926) Laura Howell Elizabeth Miller (610)
867-4741

Carbondale Trinity Episcopal Church **P** (121)
58 River St 18407-2306 (Mail to: 58 River St
18407-2306) Donald Schaible (570) 282-3620

Clarks Summit The Church of the Epiphany **P**
(567) 25 Church HL Dalton 18414-7739 (Mail
to: PO Box 189 18411-0189) (570) 563-1564

Dallas Church of the Prince of Peace **P** (164)
420 Main St 18612-1807 (Mail to: 420 Main St
18612-1807) Joseph Rafferty (570) 675-1723

Douglassville St Gabriels Episcopal Church **P**
(304) 1188 Ben Franklin Hwy E 19518-1803
(Mail to: PO Box 396 19518-0396) David
Green Sarah Bosler (610) 385-3144

Drifton St James Church **P** (51) Rt 940, Main St
18221 (Mail to: PO Box 217 18221-0217) (570)
636-3967

Easton Trinity Episcopal Church **P** (511) 234
Spring Garden St 18042-3657 (Mail to: 234
Spring Garden St 18042-3657) Andrew Gerns
Ellen Barrett (610) 253-0792

Emmaus St Margarets Church **P** (139) 150 Elm St 18049-2622 (Mail to: 150 Elm St 18049-2622) Elizabeth Diely (610) 967-1450

Forest City Christ Church **P** (73) 700 Delaware St 18421-1002 (Mail to: 700 Delaware St PO Box 118 18421-1002) (570) 282-3620

✢ **Frackville** Christ Episcopal Church **Other** 140 West Frack Street 17931 (Mail to: PO Box 487 17931-0487) (570) 874-4532

Hamlin St Johns Episcopal Church **P** (169) 564 Easton Turnpike 18427 (Mail to: PO Box 118 18427-0118)

Hazleton St Peters Episcopal Church **P** (140) 46 S Laurel St 18201-6311 (Mail to: 46 S Laurel St 18201-6399) (570) 454-6543

Hellertown St Georges Episcopal Church **P** (133) 735 Delaware Ave 18055-1819 (Mail to: 735 Delaware Ave 18055-1899) Harold Mayo (610) 838-9355

Honesdale Christ Church **P** (35) 432 W Park St 18431 (Mail to: 210 9th St 18431-1913) (570) 253-3144

Honesdale Grace Episcopal Church **P** (117) 827 Church St 18431-1824 (Mail to: 827 Church St 18431-1824) Edward Erb (570) 253-2760

Jim Thorpe St Marks and St Johns Episcopal Church **P** (223) 21 Race St 18229-2003 (Mail to: 21 Race St 18229-2003) John Wagner Rebeca Parsons-Cancelliere (570) 325-2241

Kingston Grace Episcopal Church **P** (158) 30 Butler St 18704 (Mail to: 30 Butler Street 18704-5012) John Hartman (570) 287-8440

Kutztown St Barnabas Episcopal Church **P** (34) 234 E Main St 19530 (Mail to: PO Box 236 19530-0236) (610) 683-7787

Lansford Trinity St Philips Church **P** (13) 5 E Ridge St 18232-1409 (Mail to: 333 Wyandotte St 18015-1527) (610) 691-5655

Lebanon St Lukes Church Episcopal **P** (477) No 22 S 6th St 17042-5338 (Mail to: 22 S 6th St 17042-5338) David Zwifka (717) 272-8251

Lehighton All Saints Episcopal Church **P** (230) 301 N 2nd St 18235-1418 (Mail to: PO Box 147 18235-0147) Jane Bender (610) 377-2675

Milford Good Shepherd & St Johns Church **P** (127) 110 W Catherine St 18337-1418 (Mail to: 110 W Catherine St 18337-1418) Van Bankston (570) 296-8123

Montrose St Pauls Church **P** (78) 276 Church St 18801-1271 (Mail to: PO Box 314 18801-1231) Paul Towers (570) 278-2954

Morgantown St Thomas Church **P** (78) 6251 Morgantown Rd (Rr 10) 19543 (Mail to: PO Box 97 19543-0097) Megan Dembi Donald Howells (610) 286-9547

Moscow St Marks Episcopal Church **P** (118) 1109 Church St 18444-0678 (Mail to: PO Box 678 18444-0678) Earl Trygar (570) 842-7231

Mount Pocono Trinity Episcopal Church **P** (115) Hcr # Box 1 18344 (Mail to: 137 Trinity Hill Rd 18344) Robert Criste-Troutman (570) 839-9376

Mountain Top St Martins Church **P** (103) 3085 Church Rd 18707-9035 (Mail to: 3085 Church Rd 18707-9035) Daniel Fitzsimmons (570) 868-5358

Nanticoke St Andrews Church **P** (38) 14 E Kirmar Ave 18634-3608 (Mail to: 127 West Union Street c/o Susan Maza, Sr Warden 18634) Charles Warwick (570) 825-0547

Nazareth St Brigids Church **P** (149) 310 Madison Ave 18064-2613 (Mail to: 310 Madison Ave 18064-2613) William Martin (610) 746-3910

New Milford St Marks Episcopal Church **P** (26) 1148 Main St 18834-2011 (Mail to: PO Box 406 18834-0406) (570) 465-3896

Palmerton St Johns Episcopal Church **P** (105) 365 Lafayette Ave 18071-1617 (Mail to: 365 Lafayette Ave 18071-1617) Abraham Valiath (610) 826-2611

Pen Argyl St Josephs Church **P** (28) 1440 Verona Ave 18072-1350 (Mail to: 806 Alpha Rd 18091-1109) (610) 759-0973

Pittston Trinity Episcopal Church **P** (154) 200 Montgomery Ave 18643-2137 (Mail to: 220 Montgomery Ave 18643-2137) John Major (570) 654-3261

Pottsville Trinity Episcopal Church **P** (246) 200 S 2nd St 17901-3520 (Mail to: 200 S 2nd St 17901-3520) (570) 622-8720

Reading Christ Church **P** (624) 5th & Court St 19603 (Mail to: PO Box 1094 19603-1094) John Francis (610) 374-8269

Reading St Albans Episcopal Church **P** (363) 2848 Saint Albans Dr 19608-1028 (Mail to: 2848 Saint Albans Dr 19608-1028) Karl Kern Charles Beem Jeffrey Funk Walter Krieger Nancy Packard (610) 678-7001

Reading St Marys Church **P** (37) 100 W Windsor St 19601-2033 (Mail to: PO Box 13685 19612-3685) Bruce Baker (610) 374-7914

Sayre Church of the Redeemer **P** (180) 201 S Wilbur Ave 18840-1605 (Mail to: 201 S Wilbur Ave 18840-1605) (570) 888-2270

Scranton Church of the Good Shepherd **P** (50) 2425 N Washington Ave 18509-1422 (Mail to: 1780 N Washington Ave 18509) Howard Stringfellow (570) 347-1760

Scranton St Lukes Episcopal Church **P** (171) 232 Wyoming Ave 18503-1437 (Mail to: 232 Wyoming Ave 18503-1464) Brian Pavlac (570) 342-7654

Schuylkill Haven St James Episcopal Church **P** (64) 100 Dock St 17972-1208 (Mail to: PO Box 603 17972-1208) (570) 385-0737

✢ **St Clair** Holy Apostles Episcopal Church **Other** Nicholas and Hancock Sts 17970 (Mail to: PO Box 487 17931-0487) James Smith (570) 429-2771

St Clair North Parish Episcopal Church **P** (176) 307 E Hancock St 17970 (Mail to: PO Box 487 17931-0487) Timothy Albright James Smith (570) 429-7107

Stroudsburg Christ Episcopal Church **P** (222)

205 N 7th St 18360-2113 (Mail to: 205 N 7th St 18360-2113) James Moyer (570) 421-7481

Susquehanna Christ Episcopal Church **P** (17) 302 W Main St 18847 (Mail to: PO Box 222 18847-0222) (570) 853-9003

Tamaqua Calvary Episcopal Church **P** (33) 300 W Broad St 18252-1821 (Mail to: 309 W Broad St 18252-1820) Robert Gildersleeve (610) 377-0874

Towanda Christ Episcopal Church **P** (161) One Main St 18848-1900 (Mail to: One Main St 18848-1900) Maureen Hipple Joseph Holman (570) 265-5035

Trexlertown St Anne's Episcopal Church **P** (453) 6667 Lower Macungie Rd 18087 (Mail to: PO Box 368 18087-0368) Bernice Reichard (610) 398-3321

Troy St Pauls Episcopal Church **P** (67) 195 Elmira St 16947-1201 (Mail to: 130 Elmira St 16947-1201) Arie Van den Blink (570) 297-4864

Tunkhannock St Peters Episcopal Church **P** (84) PO Box 459 18657-0459 (Mail to: PO Box 459 18657-0459) Mary Lou Divis (570) 836-2233

Whitehall St Stephens Episcopal Church **P** (135) 3900 Mechanicsville Rd 18052-3324 (Mail to: 3900 Mechanicsville Rd 18052-3347) Harold Mayo

Wilkes Barre Holy Cross Episcopal Church **P** (160) 373 N Main St 18702-4409 (Mail to: 373 N Main St 18702-4409) Timothy Alleman John Leo (570) 823-2600

Wilkes Barre St Clement and St Peters Church **P** (105) 70 Lockhart St 18702-3604 (Mail to: 70 Lockhart St 18702-3604) John Major Brian Pavlac

✠ **Wilkes Barre** St Stephens Pro-Cathedral **O** (420) 35 S Franklin St 18701-1202 (Mail to: 35 S Franklin St 18701-1202) William Marshall Brian Pavlac (570) 825-6653

Wind Gap St Marys Episcopal Church **P** (105) 340 S Lehigh Ave, 18091-0365 (Mail to: PO Box 365 18091-0365) (610) 863-8007

NON-PAROCHIAL CLERGY

Atkinson JW *ret* Bethlehem PA
Bader-Saye DL Clarks Summit PA
Baldyga AP Sayre PA
Barebo CJ *dcn*
Barnes RA New York NY
Bartlett LS *ret* Sinking Spring PA
Berk DBA
Blumer GR *ret* Portland PA
Bray DS Palmerton PA
Carlyon RD *ret* Orwigsburg PA
Carr CB *ret* Bethlehem PA
Cembalisty Innes SE *ret* Clarks Summit PA
Cluett RI *ret* Allentown PA
Coble JR *ret* Bethlehem PA
Cochran PC *ret*
Davis JW *dcn* Scranton PA
Day CV *ret* Tobyhanna PA
Day VR *ret* Tobyhanna PA
De Acetis JL Flanders NJ

Dover SH *ret* Macungie PA
D'Urbano FJ *ret* Lancaster PA
Dwyer PM
Evans DE Conestoga PA
Fill M *ret* Philadelphia PA
Francis EW *ret* Adamstown MD
Gill JL *ret* East Winthrop ME
Gunn DC Wilkes Barre PA
Harbort RL *ret* Bethlehem PA
Hart Garner EE *ret* Mount Joy PA
Haynes ES *ret* Cresco PA
Hazen SM *ret* Bandon OR
Heffner JH *ret* Bryn Mawr PA
Hinkle DW Atglen PA
Hlavacek F *dcn* Milford PA
Hollywood TL Athens PA
Houck IC Columbia SC
Howe RJ *ret* Cary NC
Hunt HB *dcn* Towanda PA
Jones DG Dunmore PA
Kaighn RS *ret* Lake Ariel PA
Kitch AE Bethlehem PA
Knapp DH *ret* Allentown PA
Lefevre AR *dcn* Palm Bay FL
Lewellis VE *ret* Whitehall PA
Loeffler GC *dcn* Kempton PA
Magnus RF *ret* Mars Hill NC
Mahaffey GG *ret* Sayre PA
Male HA *ret* Norway ME
Malloy PL New York NY
Matylewicz SJ Jermyn PA
McGinty WJ *ret* Matamoras PA
Meiss M *dcn* Hazleton PA
Meneeley BA *dcn*
Miller LH *ret* Millsboro DE
Miller VA Doral FL
Morris CH *ret* Harwich MA
Moulton EJ *ret* Montrose PA
Myers EW *ret* Hackettstown NJ
Peterson IE Danbury CT
Piovane MF *ret* Trexlertown PA
Reed EH Allentown PA
Reinholz AC
Reinholz KA Stroudsburg PA
Richards GW *ret* Lebanon PA
Rinehart JA *ret* Pottsville PA
Romeril GJ *ret* Bethlehem PA
Roth RC *ret* Wernersville PA
Schenkel RD *ret* Bethlehem PA
Sefchick FS Weatherly PA
Shallcross LH *ret* Emmaus PA
Sherrer WC Emmaus PA
Snyder AE *ret* Farmingdale NY
Snyder JU Bethlehem PA
Sweeney CC *ret* Clarks Summit PA
Teter JE *ret* Bethlehem PA
Turrell JF Sewanee TN
West-Doohan S *ret* Strange Creek WV
Williams RJ Bethlehem PA
Yale ES
Zabriskie AC *ret* Burlington VT
Zanetti DP Reading PA

STATE OF CALIFORNIA

Dioceses of California (CA), El Camino Real (ECR), Los Angeles (LA), Northern California (NCA), San Diego (SD) and San Joaquin (SanJ).

Alameda—CA
Albany—CA
Alhambra—LA
Alpine—SD
Altadena—LA
Alturas—NCA
Anaheim—LA
Anderson—NCA
Antelope—NCA
Antioch—CA
Apple Valley—LA
Aptos—ECR
Arcadia—LA
Arcata—NCA
Arroyo Grande—ECR
Atascadero—ECR
Atwater—SanJ
Auburn—NCA
Avery—SanJ
Bakersfield—SanJ
Barstow—LA
Beaumont—LA
Belmont—CA
Belvedere Tiburon—CA
Benicia—NCA
Ben Lomond—ECR
Berkeley—CA
Beverly Hills—LA
Big Bear Lake—LA
Bolinas—CA
Bonita—SD
Borrego Spgs—SD
Brawley—SD
Brentwood—CA
Buena Pk—LA
Burbank—LA
Burlingame—CA
Calistoga—NCA
Camarillo—LA
Cambria—ECR
Cameron Pk—NCA
Carlsbad—SD
Carmel by the Sea—ECR
Carmel Valley—ECR
Carmichael—NCA
Castro Valley—CA
Chico—NCA
Chula Vista—SD
Claremont—LA
Clayton—CA
Cloverdale—NCA
Colusa—NCA
Compton—LA

Concord—CA
Corning—NCA
Corona—LA
Corona Del Mar—LA
Coronado—SD
Corte Madera—CA
Costa Mesa—LA
Covina—LA
Crescent City—NCA
Crockett—CA
Cupertino—ECR
Daly City—CA
Danville—CA
Davis—NCA
Del Mar—SD
Desert Hot Spgs—SD
Desert Shores—SD
Downey—LA
El Cajon—SD
El Centro—SD
El Monte—LA
El Segundo—LA
Encinitas—SD
Encino—LA
Escondido—SD
Eureka—NCA
Fair Oaks—NCA
Fairfield—NCA
Fallbrook—SD
Ferndale—NCA
Fillmore—LA
Folsom—NCA
Ft Bragg—NCA
Fortuna—NCA
Foster City—CA
Fremont—CA
Fresno—SanJ
Fullerton—LA
Galt—NCA
Garden Grove—LA
Gardena—LA
Gilroy—ECR
Glendale—LA
Glendora—LA
Goleta—LA
Granada Hills—LA
Grass Valley—NCA
Gridley—NCA
Gualala—NCA
Hacienda Hts—LA
Half Moon Bay—CA
Hanford—SanJ
Hawthorne—LA
Healdsburg—NCA
Hemet—SD

Hermosa Bch—LA
Hesperia—LA
Hollister—ECR
Huntington Bch—LA
Huntington Pk—LA
Idyllwild—SD
Indio—SD
Inglewood—LA
Inverness—CA
Irvine—LA
Isla Vista—LA
Jolon—ECR
Kenwood—NCA
Kernville—SanJ
King City—ECR
La Canada—LA
La Crescenta—LA
LaFayette—CA
La Jolla—SD
La Mesa—SD
La Verne—LA
Laguna Bch—LA
Laguna Hills—LA
Laguna Niguel—LA
Lake Almanor—NCA
Lake Elsinore—SD
Lakeport—NCA
Lancaster—LA
Lemon Grove—SD
Lincoln—NCA
Livermore—CA
Lodi—SanJ
Lompoc—LA
Long Bch—LA
Los Altos—CA
Los Angeles—LA
Los Gatos—ECR
Los Olivos—LA
Los Osos—ECR
Madera—SanJ
Malibu—LA
Marina—ECR
Martinez—CA
Marysville—NCA
Menifee—SD
Menlo Pk—CA
Mill Valley—CA
Milpitas—ECR
Modesto—SanJ
Monrovia—LA
Monterey—ECR
Monterey Pk—LA
Monte Rio—NCA
Moraga—CA
Moreno Valley—LA

Morgan Hill—ECR
Morro Bay—ECR
Mt Shasta—NCA
Mtn View—ECR
Napa—NCA
National City—SD
Needles—LA
Nevada City—NCA
Norwalk—LA
Novato—CA
Oakland—CA
Oakhurst—SanJ
Oak Park—LA
Oceanside—SD
Ojai—LA
Ontario—LA
Orange—LA
Orinda—CA
Oroville—NCA
Oxnard—LA
Pacific Grove—ECR
Pacific Palisades—LA
Pacifica—CA
Palm Desert—SD
Palm Spgs—SD
Palo Alto—CA & ECR
Palos Verdes Est—LA
Paradise—NCA
Pasadena—LA
Paso Robles—ECR
Pauma Valley—SD
Petaluma—NCA
Pico Rivera—LA
Pinole—CA
Placentia—LA
Placerville—NCA
Pleasant Hill—CA
Pleasanton—CA
Pomona—LA
Portola Valley—CA
Poway—SD
Quincy—NCA
Ramona—SD
Rancho Cordova—NCA
Rancho Sta Marg—LA
Red Bluff—NCA
Redding—NCA
Redlands—LA
Redondo Bch—LA
Redwood City—CA
Rialto—LA
Richmond—CA
Ridgecrest—SanJ
Rio Vista—NCA

Riverbank—SanJ
Riverside—LA
Rocklin—NCA
Roseville—NCA
Ross—CA
Sacramento—NCA
St Helena—NCA
Salinas—ECR
San Andreas—SanJ
San Ardo—ECR
San Bernardino—LA
San Bruno—CA
San Carlos—CA
San Clemente—LA
San Diego—SD
San Fernando—LA
San Francisco—CA
San Gabriel—LA
San Jose—ECR
San Juan Capistrano—LA
San Leandro—CA

San Luis Obispo—ECR
San Marino—LA
San Marcos—SD
San Mateo—CA
San Pedro—LA
San Rafael—CA
Santa Ana—LA
Santa Barbara—LA
Santa Clara—ECR
Santa Cruz—ECR
Santa Maria—LA
Santa Monica—LA
Santa Paula—LA
Santa Rosa—NCA
Santee—SD
Saratoga—ECR
Sausalito—CA
Scotts Valley—ECR
Seal Bch—LA
Seaside—ECR
Sebastopol—NCA
Sierra Madre—LA

Simi Valley—LA
Skyforest—LA
Sonoma—NCA
Sonora—SanJ
So Gate—LA
So Pasadena—LA
So San Francisco—CA
Stockton—SanJ
Studio City—LA
Susanville—NCA
Sutter Creek—NCA
Taft—SanJ
Tahoe City—NCA
Temecula—SD
Thousand Oaks—LA
Torrance—LA
Tulare—SanJ
Turlock—SanJ
Tustin—LA
Twentynine Palms—LA
Ukiah—NCA
Upland—LA

Vacaville—NCA
Valencia—LA
Vallejo—NCA
Van Nuys—LA
Ventura—LA
Visalia—SanJ
Vista—SD
Walnut Creek—CA
Watsonville—ECR
Wheatland—NCA
Whittier—LA
Willits—NCA
Willows—NCA
Wilmington—LA
Winnetka—LA
Woodland Hills—LA
Woodland—NCA
Yuba City—NCA
Yucaipa—LA
Yucca Valley—LA
Yuma—SD

DIOCESE OF CALIFORNIA
(PROVINCE VIII)
Comprises 5 counties in west-central CA
DIOCESAN OFFICE 1055 Taylor St San Francisco CA 94108
TEL (415) 673-5015   FAX (415) 673-1510
E-MAIL bishopmarc@diocal.org   WEB www.diocal.org

Previous Bishops—
Wm I Kip m 1853 dio 1857-93, Wm F Nichols coadj 1890 Bp 1893-1924, Edward L Parsons coadj 1919 Bp 1924-40, Karl M Block coadj 1938 Bp 1941-58, Henry H Shires suffr 1950-58, James A Pike coadj 1958 Bp 1958-66, G Richard Millard suffr 1960-1978, C Kilmer Myers 1966-79, William E Swing 1979-2006

Bishop—Rt Rev Marc Handley Andrus (974) (Dio 22 Jul 2006)

CFO T Ferguson; *Chanc* C Hayes; *V Chanc* PS B oone Jr Esq 44 Montgomery St Ste 3585 SF 94104 (415) 274-2507; *Can to Ord* Rev Cn S Schatz (415) 869-7825; *Comm Off* S Rev J Peters-Mathews (415) 869- 7820; *Faith Form Coord* J McCray-Goldsmith (415) 869-7826; *Camps & Conf* J Dowling (707) 433-2440; *Gift Planning* A Kiernan; *Com* M Ridlon; *Treas* R McCaskill; *Conv Sec* D Frangquist;

Stand Comm—Cler: A Rankin *Pres* L Walton M Spaulding S Vasquez; *Lay:* R Hermanson B Paulin J DeMersman A Lee

Exec Coun—Cler: M Dutton-Gillett S Larrimore K Trapani M Wilson; *Lay* W Cullen S Sims J Jennings J McConnell K Fuller J Brown K Quick-Pawala R Johnson J Wiant M Chambers A Larsen R Patenaude D Roberts B Barber D Gilmour

Dio Conv: October 14 & 15, 2016 Grace Cathedral San Francisco

PARISHES, MISSIONS, AND CLERGY

Alameda Christ Episcopal Church **P** (386) 1700 Santa Clara Ave 94501-2515 (Mail to: 1700 Santa Clara Ave 94501-2515) Stephen McHale Laureen Moyer (510) 523-7200

Albany St Albans Episcopal Church **P** (191) 1501 Washington Ave 94706 (Mail to: 1501 Washington Ave 94706) Julia Wakelee-Lynch Beth Foote Duane Sisson Kathleen Van Sickle (510) 525-1716

Antioch St Georges Episcopal Church **M** (168) 301 E 13th St 94509-1997 (Mail to: 301 E 13th St 94509-1997) (925) 757-4934

Belvedere Tiburon St Stephens Episcopal Church **P** (675) 3 Bayview Ave 94920-2302 (Mail to: PO Box 97 94920-0097) Wendy Cliff Shari Young Sherry Young

Belmont Good Shepherd Episcopal Church **M** (31) 1300 Fifth Ave 94002-3831 (Mail to: 1300 5th Ave 94002-3831) Michael Arase-Barham (650) 593-4844

Berkeley All Souls Parish **P** (527) 2220 Cedar St 94709-1519 (Mail to: 2220 Cedar St 94709-1519) Philip Brochard Donald Brown Joseph Delgado Horace Griffin Michael Lemaire Ruth Meyers Paula Nesbitt Daniel Prechtel David Stone Elizabeth Tichenor (510) 848-1755

Berkeley Good Shepherd Episcopal Church **M** (79) 1823 9th St 94710-2102 (Mail to: 1823 9th St 94710-2102) Este Cantor Louis Countryman Ellen Ekstrom Jay Johnson (510) 549-1433

Berkeley St Clements Episcopal Church **P** (734) 2837 Claremont Blvd 94705-1446 (Mail to: 2837 Claremont Blvd 94705-1446) Bruce O'Neill Deborah White (510) 843-2678

Berkeley St Marks Episcopal Church **P** (459) 2300 Bancroft Way 94704-1604 (Mail to: 2300 Bancroft Way 94704-1604) Lizette Larson-Miller Coryl Lassen Thomas Murdock Stephen Trever Patricia Walker-Sprague (510) 848-5107

Bolinas St Aidans Episcopal Church **M** (37) 30 Brighton Ave 94924 (Mail to: PO Box 629 94924-0629) (415) 868-1852

Brentwood St Albans Episcopal Church **M** (120) 508 2nd St 94513-1349 (Mail to: PO Box 101 94513-0101) Kathleen Bradford Max Nye (925) 634-1893

Burlingame St Pauls Episcopal Church **P** (468) 415 El Camino Real 94010-5122 (Mail to: 415 El Camino Real 94010-5197) Thomas Skillings Julie Graham Martha Korienek (650) 348-4811

Castro Valley Holy Cross Episcopal Church **P** (452) No 19179 Center St 94546-3616 (Mail to: 19179 Center St 94546-3616) Mark Spaulding Martha Kuhlmann Patricia Pearson (510) 889-7233

Clayton St Johns Episcopal Church **M** (189) 5555 Clayton Rd 94517-1013 (Mail to: 5555 Clayton Rd 94517-1013) Francine Gardner-Smith Amanda May Nancy Eswein John McDermott Jane Stratford (925) 672-8855

Concord St Michael and All Angels Episcopal **M** (191) 2925 Bonifacio St 94519-2511 (Mail to: 2925 Bonifacio St 94519-2511) Laina Casillas (925) 685-8859

Corte Madera Holy Innocents Episcopal Church **P** (113) 2 Tamalpais Dr 94925 (Mail to: PO Box 5 94976-0005) Lynn Oldham Robinett Palmer Wilkins (415) 924-4393

Crockett St Marks Episcopal Church **P** (90) 800 Pomona St 94525-1400 (Mail to: PO Box 515 94525-0515) Christian Lehrer (510) 787-2989

Daly City Holy Child and St Martins Episcopal Church **M** (220) 777 Southgate Ave 94015-3665 (Mail to: 777 Southgate Ave 94015-3665) Leonard Oakes Lynn Bowdish (650) 991-1560

Danville St Timothys Episcopal Church **P** (1413) 1550 Diablo Rd 94526-1952 (Mail to: 1550 Diablo Rd 94526-1952) Stacey Grossman (925) 837-4993

Foster City St Ambrose Episcopal Church **P** (246) 900 Edgewater Blvd 94404-3709 (Mail to: 900 Edgewater Blvd 94404-3709) David Ota Jay Watan (650) 574-1369

Fremont St Annes Episcopal Church **P** (141) 2791 Driscoll Rd 94539-4449 (Mail to: 2791 Driscoll Rd 94539-4449) Beth Foote Robert Partanen (510) 490-0553

Fremont St James Episcopal Church **P** (368) 37051 Cabrillo Dr 94537-0457 (Mail to: PO Box 457 94537-0457) Lori Walton Kenneth Parris John Trubina (510) 797-1492

Half Moon Bay Holy Family Episcopal Church **M** (88) 1590 Cabrillo Hwy S 94019-2245 (Mail to: PO Box 27591 93729-7591) Michael Arase-Barham (650) 726-0506

Inverness St Columbas Episcopal Church **P** (54) 12835 Sir Francis Drake Blvd 94937 (Mail to: PO Box 430 94937-0430) Robert Weldy (415) 669-1039

Lafayette St Anselms Episcopal Church **P** (335) 682 Michael Ln 94549-5360 (Mail to: 682 Michael Ln 94549-5360) John Sutton Naomi Chamberlain-Harris Ting Yao (925) 284-7420

Livermore St Bartholomews Episcopal Church **P** (175) 678 Enos Way 94551-5917 (Mail to: 678 Enos Way 94551-5917) Joyce Parry-Moore (925) 447-3289

Los Altos Christ Episcopal Church **P** (370) 1040 Border Rd 94024-4724 (Mail to: 1040 Border Rd 94024-4724) John Buenz David Starr (650) 948-2151

Martinez Grace Episcopal Church **P** (219) 130 Muir Station Rd 94553-4420 (Mail to: PO Box 2338 94553-0233) Jeffrey Frost (925) 228-6574

Menlo Park Holy Trinity Church **P** (874) 330 Ravenswood Ave 94025-3420 (Mail to: 330 Ravenswood Ave 94025-3420) Matthew Dutton-Gillett Mary Greene Elizabeth Riley (650) 326-2083

Menlo Park St Bedes Episcopal Church **P** (340) 2650 Sand Hill Rd 94025-7018 (Mail to: 2650 Sand Hill Rd 94025-7018) Gianetta Hayes-Martin John Oda-Burns (650) 854-6555

Mill Valley The Episcopal Church of Our Saviour **HC** (366) 10 Old Mill St 94941-1813 (Mail to: 10 Old Mill St 94941-1813) Richard Helmer Annette Rankin

Moraga St Giles Episcopal Church **Chapel** (87) Saint Marys College Chapel 1928 Saint Marys Rd 94556-2744 (Mail to: PO Box 187 94556-0187) Justin Cannon

Novato St Francis of Assisi Epis Church **P** (199) 967 5th St 94945-3105 (Mail to: 967 5th St 94945-3105) Vanessa Glass Kathleen Crary (415) 892-1609

Oakland Episcopal Church of Our Saviour **P** (146) 1011 Harrison St 94607-4426 (Mail to: 1013 Harrison St Ste 202 94607-4457) (510)

834-6447

Oakland St Augustines Episcopal Church **P** (105) 525 29th St 94609-3512 (Mail to: 525 29th St 94609-3512) Tyrone Fowlkes (510) 832-6462

Oakland St Cuthberts Episcopal Church **M** (56) 7932 Mountain Blvd 94605-3708 (Mail to: 7932 Mountain Blvd 94605-3799) Pamela Cranston Laurie Willis (510) 635-4949

Oakland St James the Apostle Church **P** (70) 1540 12th Ave 94606-3803 (Mail to: 1540 12th Ave 94606-3803) Dessordi Leite (510) 533-2136

Oakland St Johns Episcopal Church **P** (490) 1707 Gouldin Rd 94611-2120 (Mail to: 1707 Gouldin Rd 94611-2120) Scott Denman Krista Fregoso Franklin Sterling Fran Toy

Oakland St Pauls Episcopal Church **P** (204) 114 Montecito Ave 94610-4556 (Mail to: 114 Montecito Ave 94610-4556) Mauricio Wilson Carolyn Bolton (510) 834-4314

Orinda St Stephens Episcopal Church **P** (1237) 66 Saint Stephens Dr 94563-1949 (Mail to: 66 Saint Stephens Dr 94563-1949) Stephen Hassett (925) 254-3770

Pacifica St Edmunds Episcopal Church **M** (105) 1500 Perez Drive 94044 (Mail to: PO Box 688 94044-0688) (650) 359-3364

Palo Alto St Marks Episcopal Church **P** (637) 600 Colorado Ave 94306-2510 (Mail to: 600 Colorado Ave 94306-2510) Matthew McDermott Ricardo Avila (650) 326-3800

Pinole Episcopal Church of Christ the Lord **M** (90) 592 Tennent Ave 94564-1629 (Mail to: 592A Tennent Ave 94564) Susan Champion (510) 724-9141

Pleasant Hill Episcopal Church of the Resurrection **P** (513) 399 Gregory Ln 94523-2837 (Mail to: 399 Gregory Ln 94523-2837) Bruce Smith Barbara Dawson Kathleen Trapani (925) 685-2288

Pleasanton St Clares Episcopal Church **P** (414) 3350 Hopyard Rd 94588-5105 (Mail to: 3350 Hopyard Rd 94588-5105) Ronald Culmer John Trubina (925) 462-4802

Portola Valley Christ Episcopal Church **P** (318) 815 Portola Rd 94028-7206 (Mail to: 815 Portola Rd 94028-7206) Dorothy Jamison Joseph Peters-Mathews Elizabeth Phillips David Sheetz (650) 851-0224

Redwood City El Buen Pastor Iglesia Episcopal **M** (127) 1835 Valota Rd 94061 (Mail to: Pastor El Buen 1835 Valota Rd 94061-2626) (650) 245-7759

Redwood City St Peters Episcopal Church **P** (255) 178 Clinton St 94062-1552 (Mail to: 178 Clinton St 94062-1583) Grant Bushee Susan Parsons (650) 367-0777

Richmond Holy Trinity Episcopal Church **M** (163) 555 37th St 94805-2205 (Mail to: 555 37th St 94805-2272) Jose Torres Bayas Mary Hinse Katherine Salinaro (510) 232-7896

Ross St Johns Episcopal Church **P** (1303) 14

Lagunitas Rd 94957 (Mail to: PO Box 217 94957-0217) Chris Rankin-Williams Charlton Fotch William Rankin Virginia Strickland Jan West (415) 456-1102

S San Fran St Elizabeths Episcopal Church **M** (103) 280 Country Club Dr 94080-5743 (Mail to: 280 Country Club Dr 94080-5743) Deborah Hawkins (650) 583-3720

San Bruno St Andrews Episcopal Church **M** (79) 1600 Santa Lucia Ave 94066-4736 (Mail to: 1600 Santa Lucia Ave 94066-4798) Deborah Hawkins (650) 583-6678

San Carlos Episcopal Church of the Epiphany **P** (526) 1839 Arroyo Ave 94070-3810 (Mail to: 1839 Arroyo Ave 94070-3899) Melanie Donahoe Hailey Delmas Alan Gates (650) 591-0328

San Francisco All Saints Episcopal Church **P** (168) 1350 Waller St 94117-2986 (Mail to: 1350 Waller St 94117-2921) Kenneth Schmidt Thomas Traylor (415) 621-1862

San Francisco Christ Episcopal Church Sei Ko Kai **M** (59) 2140 Pierce St 94115-2214 (Mail to: 2140 Pierce St 94115-2214) Merry Ong (415) 921-6395

San Francisco Church of St Mary the Virgin **P** (1200) 2325 Union St 94123-3905 (Mail to: 2325 Union St 94123-3905) Nancy Bryan Mary Jizmagian Claire Ranna (415) 921-3665

San Francisco Episcopal Church of the Incarnation **P** (103) 1750 29th Ave 94122-4223 (Mail to: 1750 29th Ave 94122-4223) David Lui Joseph Holt Darren Miner Christopher Webber

✠ **San Francisco** Grace Cathedral **O** (1690) 1100 California St 94108-2206 (Mail to: 1100 California St 94108) Randal Gardner Elizabeth Grundy Jude Harmon Andrew Lobban Nina Pickerrell Mark Stanger Malcolm Young (415) 749-6300

San Francisco Holy Innocents Episcopal Church **M** (187) 455 Fair Oaks St 94110-3618 (Mail to: 455 Fair Oaks St 94110-3618) John Ayers Jane Mcdougle Kathleen Sylvester (415) 824-5142

San Francisco Iglesia Del Buen Samaritano **M** (70) 1661 15th St 94103-3511 (Mail to: Episcopal Diocese of California 1055 Taylor Street 94108) Thomas Murdock (415) 869-7810

San Francisco St Aidans Episcopal Church **P** (193) 101 Gold Mine Dr 94131-2538 (Mail to: 101 Gold Mine Dr 94131-2538) Donald Fox Angela Guida Mark Henderson Audrey Miskelley Gary Ost David Stickley (415) 285-9540

San Francisco St Cyprians Episcopal Church **M** (94) 2097 Turk Blvd 94115-4326 (Mail to: 2097 Turk Blvd 94115-4326) William Scott Thomas Jackson Eric Metoyer Michael Reddig (415) 567-1855

San Francisco St Francis Episcopal Church **P** (417) 399 San Fernando Way 94127-1913

(Mail to: 399 San Fernando Way 94127-1913) Elizabeth Sherman Clarence Davis George Flora Keshgegian Robert Kossler (415) 334-1590

San Francisco St Gregory of Nyssa Episcopal Church **P** (391) 500 De Haro St 94107-2306 (Mail to: 500 De Haro St 94107-2306) Paul Fromberg (415) 255-8100

San Francisco St James Episcopal Church **P** (250) 4620 California St 94118-1225 (Mail to: 4620 California St 94118-1225) John Kirkley Gwen Buehrens Teduan Jang Ronnie Willis (415) 751-1198

San Francisco St John the Evangelist Epis Church **P** (96) 1661 15th St 94103 (Mail to: 1661 15th St 94103-3511) Jacqueline Cherry Albert Pearson Richard Smith (415) 861-1436

San Francisco St Lukes Episcopal Church **P** (260) 1755 Clay St 94109-3612 (Mail to: 1755 Clay St 94109-3612) Dana Corsello Jeffrey Dodge (415) 673-7327

San Francisco St Peters Episcopal Church **P** (48) 420 29th Ave 94121-1726 (Mail to: 1668 Bush St 94109) Ronald Mcbride (415) 751-4942

San Francisco The Advent of Christ the King **P** (68) 261 Fell St 94102-5147 (Mail to: 162 Hickory St 94102-5908) Graham Hill Gregory Martin Roderick Thompson (415) 431-0454

San Francisco Trinity Episcopal Church **M** (83) 1668 Bush St 94109-5308 (Mail to: 1668 Bush St 94109-5388) Patricia Cunningham (415) 775-1117

San Francisco True Sunshine Episcopal Church **P** (183) 1430 Mason St 94133-4222 (Mail to: 1430 Mason St 94133-4222) Franco Kwan Thomas Chesterman

San Leandro All Saints Episcopal Church **P** (192) 911 Dowling Blvd 94577-2125 (Mail to: 911 Dowling Blvd 94577-2190) Jose Bernal Justin Cannon Karen Swanson (510) 569-7020

San Mateo Episcopal Church of St Matthew **P** (592) 1 S El Camino Real 94401-3800 (Mail to: PO Box 648 94401-0648) Eric Hinds Robert Caughey Amber Evans Lindsay Hills (650) 342-1481

San Mateo Transfiguration Episcopal Church **P** (323) 3900 Alameda De Las Pulgas 94403-4110 (Mail to: 3900 Alameda De Las Pulgas 94403-4110) Matthew Woodward Monica Whitaker (650) 341-8206

San Rafael Episcopal Church of the Nativity **P** (183) 333 Ellen Dr 94903-1666 (Mail to: 333 Ellen Dr 94903-1666) David Hammond Rebecca Morehouse Kirsten Spalding

San Rafael Episcopal Church of the Redeemer **M** (71) 123 Knight Dr 94901-1427 (Mail to: 123 Knight Dr 94901-1427) Molly Haws (415) 456-0508

San Rafael St Pauls Episcopal Church **P** (232) 1123 Court St 94901-2909 (Mail to: 1123 Court St 94901-2909) Christopher Martin Harold

Weicker (415) 456-4842

Sausalito Christ Episcopal Church **P** (203) 70 Santa Rosa Ave 94965-2041 (Mail to: 70 Santa Rosa Ave 94965-2041) Sloane Larrimore Catherine Costas Daniel London (415) 332-1539

Walnut Creek St Lukes Episcopal Church **P** (69) 1944 Tice Valley Blvd 94595 (Mail to: PO Box 2088 94595-0088) Anne Bailey (925) 937-4820

Walnut Creek St Paul's Episcopal Church **P** (489) 1924 Trinity Ave 94596-4037 (Mail to: 1924 Trinity Ave 94596-4099) Martha Vasquez Donald Adolphson Laina Casillas Jeffrey Dodge (925) 934-2324

NON-PAROCHIAL CLERGY

Abernethy-Deppe DE Castro Valley CA
Abernethy-Deppe JR Palm Springs CA
Abidari M San Francisco CA
Andersen FI *ret* Donvale Victoria VI
Archer JR *ret* Hamden CT
Artress L *ret* San Francisco CA
Bachmann DP *ret* Martinez CA
Backlund MA Angels Camp CA
Baird CM *ret* Ambler PA
Baker JT *ret* Bellingham WA
Barlowe ML New York NY
Barnett BF San Francisco CA
Barton LW *ret* Vancouver WA
Bayne BGC *ret* Reno NV
Bender-Breck B *ret* Oakland CA
Benjamin JE *ret dcn* Ojai CA
Bergmans SE Berkeley CA
Bess W Fairfax CA
Bettinger RL *ret* San Diego CA
Bidwell-Waite D *dcn* San Francisco CA
Billington JH San Mateo CA
Bingham PM Treasure Island FL
Bingham SG San Francisco CA
Blair A *ret* Berkeley CA
Blasdell ML Lansing KS
Bliss JDC *ret* Westport CT
Boelter S *ret* Belleville MI
Bowen CS *dcn*
Bright JA *ret* Portland OR
Brindley T *ret* Novato CA
Britton JH Albuquerque NM
Brogan MC *ret* Alameda CA
Brown JT *ret* Sebastopol CA
Burrows P *ret* Long Island City NY
Butler TE *ret* Sparks NV
Carey PH *dcn* Oakland CA
Carter B *ret* San Francisco CA
Cazden JS *ret dcn* Arlington TX
Champion PO *ret* Rodeo CA
Chase C San Diego CA
Christoffersen TR Walnut Creek CA
Clark CR *ret* Hucclecote Gloucester AE
Cleland CE *ret* Palo Alto CA
Coats JR *ret* Spring TX
Conger JP

Cook CL *ret* Livermore CA
Coolidge RT *dcn* Westmount QC
Cosby AW *ret dcn* Newark CA
Crim MJ *dcn* San Francisco CA
Cromey RW *ret* San Francisco CA
Cummings PL Los Gatos CA
Curry DR *ret* San Diego CA
Darling LT Vallejo CA
De Ruff EA Ross CA
Debenham WW *ret* Berkeley CA
DeCoss DA *dcn* Oakland CA
Deeths ME *dcn* San Rafael CA
Del Castillo GR *ret* El Sobrante CA
Dobbin RA *dcn* Danville CA
Donnelly JJ
Duckworth PT *ret* San Jose CA
Dumke EJ San Mateo CA
Dyer-Chamberlain ME *dcn*
Eastwood JH *ret* San Francisco CA
Edwards R San Diego CA
Ellington WF *ret* McAlester OK
Elmiger-Jones MK *dcn* Danville CA
Erhard MEC *dcn* San Francisco CA
Erickson S San Francisco CA
Eunson LK Banchory
Evans PF *ret* Saratoga Springs NY
Fabian RG *ret* San Francisco CA
Fenton FA *ret* Concord CA
Fineanganofo SA Tracy CA
Forbes DR *ret* San Francisco CA
Ford RB *ret* Healdsburg CA
Fox MT Oakland CA
Fredricks JR *ret* San Mateo CA
Gaines MMT *ret* San Francisco CA
Gallagher JM *ret* Larkspur CA
Gardner J San Francisco CA
Geisler WF *ret* San Anselmo CA
George ST *dcn* Melrose MA
Gibbs CP *ret* Kensington MD
Goldberg RL Daly City CA
Golenski J San Francisco CA
Gompertz CB *ret* Nicasio CA
Gordon DW *ret* Sonoma CA
Goss JP *dcn* San Rafael CA
Gray VS *dcn*
Green DE *ret* Oakland CA
Green TM *dcn* Huntington Beach CA
Greene TP San Francisco CA
Gregg RC *ret* Stanford CA
Griffin PJ Portland OR
Hansen JV Burlingame CA
Hansen M *ret* San Francisco CA
Harden RL Asheville NC
Harrigfeld CL *dcn* Granite Bay CA
Hay LJH San Francisco CA
Heglund JN *dcn* Fairfax CA
Herth DE *ret* Ripon North Yorkshire
Hess RW *ret* Puerto Vallarta
Hewetson RW *ret*
Higgins P *ret* Benicia CA
Hiller M San Francisco CA

Hintz ML *dcn* Richmond CA
Hobbs EC *ret* Wellesley MA
Hoche-Mong R *ret* Montara CA
Hocker W Oakland CA
Holder AG *ret* Berkeley CA
Holland J *ret* Ashland OR
Honodel J Napa CA
Horton ER *dcn* Woodridge IL
Hoy GL *ret* Orinda CA
Humber MR Denver CO
Hunter LS *ret* Ashland OR
Hur WJ Boston MA
Jensen AH *ret* Oakland CA
Jester PJ San Leandro CA
Johnson IL *ret* San Leandro CA
Jones A *ret* San Francisco CA
Jones DL *dcn* Danville CA
Jones DK *dcn* Tiburon CA
Jones VE *ret* Redwood City CA
Kater JL *ret* Walnut Creek CA
Kerr RS *ret* San Francisco CA
Kieschnick FM *ret* Mill Valley CA
Kinney EW *ret* San Francisco CA
Kinsey TH El Cerrito CA
Kirchhoffer JH *ret* Vallejo CA
Knight TLJ *dcn* Berkeley CA
Lane JA *ret* Altadena CA
Lange-Soto A Campbell CA
Larson LJ *ret* Corvallis OR
Lau GK *ret* Alameda CA
Lawrence A Sacramento CA
Lawson PR *ret* Petaluma CA
Lehman KM *ret* Kerrville TX
Licari L *dcn* Toronto ON
Lindeman MJ *ret* Cranston RI
Linn DN Moraga CA
Longacre TE *dcn* Oakland CA
Low-Skinner DL Campbell CA
Luther C *ret* Oakland CA
Lyman JR Woodside CA
MacKenzie VV *dcn* Belvedere CA
Maitrejean JP *ret* Rio Rico AZ
Manley WT Berlin VT
Manoogian P *dcn* Berkeley CA
Manson M San Francisco CA
Mapplebeckpalmer RW *ret* Martinez CA
Maxwell KB Belmont CA
McBride DP *ret* Los Alamitos CA
McCann RE *ret* Lafayette CA
McCombs L *dcn* Los Altos CA
McCray-Goldsmith JM Danville CA
McIlroy ELF Santa Rosa CA
McInerney JL
McKeon JMK Half Moon Bay CA
McKnight JF *ret* Chicago IL
McManus MC *dcn* San Francisco CA
McSpadden CT
Merrell RN *ret* San Jose CA
Mertz A Alexandria VA
Miller DS *ret* Stevenson WA
Moon CJ Liverpool AL

148 *Diocese of California*

Moore R *ret* Cincinnati OH
Morris CL *ret* Brooklyn NY
Nefstead E San Francisco CA
Nelson LL *dcn* San Francisco CA
Nern WB *ret*
Newnam EA *ret* San Francisco CA
Nipps L Oakland CA
Oakes SEH
Olmedo-Jaquenod N *ret* Alameda CA
Osgood TM *ret* Klamath Falls OR
Owens JM *dcn* Daly City CA
Pennekamp N *dcn*
Peterson RT *ret dcn* Sunnyvale CA
Phelps WE *ret* Vacaville CA
Phillips JB *ret* Camarillo CA
Pifke L *ret* Fremont CA
Pizzuto VA Fairfax CA
Pope K *ret* Port Angeles WA
Porter JH San Francisco CA
Powell E *dcn* San Francisco CA
Powell JL *ret* Folsom CA
Powell KJ *dcn*
Pummill JH *ret* Berkeley CA
Putnam KT Foster City CA
Ramsden CL *ret* San Leandro CA
Ramsey WA *dcn* San Francisco CA
Rawlinson JE San Leandro CA
Ray HH *ret* Palm Springs CA
Redding PJ *ret* Concord CA
Reichert ES *ret* San Rafael CA
Reynolds RE *ret* Cincinnati OH
Rhodes EF *ret* Greenwich CT
Richardson MM *ret* San Diego CA
Richardson SE *ret* San Francisco CA
Richardson WM Berkeley CA
Rickey D *ret* San Francisco CA
Riedell WG *dcn* Englewood CO
Ring B Moss Beach CA
Rivera AC Brentwood CA
Rosen EP *dcn* Ross CA
Ross DJ *dcn* Pinole CA
Ross GCL *ret* Woodbridge CA
Ross N
Ross PL *dcn* San Francisco CA
Rosso PA *dcn* San Bruno CA
Roundtree P *ret* Novato CA
Ruyak M Mill Valley CA
Rybicki R San Francisco CA
Sanders JM Stanford CA
Schaper RL *ret* Mill Valley CA
Schatz SS Reno NV
Schell DJ *ret* San Francisco CA
Schoenbrun ZC Belvedere CA
Schooler WT *dcn* Atherton CA
Schreiber MN *dcn* San Francisco CA

Schultz TH Santa Barbara CA
Shamel A Indianapolis IN
Shaon GE *ret dcn* Kansas City MO
Shaw JA San Francisco CA
Shippen SE *ret* Edmonds WA
Silbaugh MC *ret* Ashland OR
Sims EE *dcn* Alameda CA
Sims GK *ret* Boonville CA
Sinclair SG Kensington CA
Singer SJ San Francisco CA
Smith AL *ret* Aptos CA
Smith SE *ret* Eugene OR
Smith TC *dcn* San Francisco CA
Smith WH Washington DC
Sox HD *ret* Surrey
Sparrow KH Cambridge MA
Staller MB *dcn* Concord CA
Stewart B *dcn* Castro Valley CA
Stickney J *ret* El Cerrito CA
Strid PE *ret* Albuquerque NM
Sturgess AD Richmond CA
Swanson RA *ret* Oxnard CA
Sweet FM *dcn* Alameda CA
Switz RW *ret* Mount Pleasant SC
Taylor CW *ret*
Thompson E Alameda CA
Thompson SM *ret* Pacifica CA
Thornell KA *ret* Silver Spring MD
Tirrell JA
Tolley JC *ret* Chula Vista CA
Tornquist FC *ret* Belmont CA
Towers AR *ret* El Cerrito CA
Trafton CW *ret* Palm Springs CA
Trezevant MA *dcn* San Francisco CA
Trutner TK *ret* Orinda CA
Turner ME *ret* Pleasanton CA
Vaggione RP Berkeley CA
Vettel-Becker RA Billings MT
Wagner SL *dcn* Oakley CA
Waldron TJ Sacramento CA
Walters RS *dcn* Walnut Creek CA
Walters SFD *ret* Walnut Creek CA
Ward J *ret* San Rafael CA
Ward KL *ret* Oakland CA
Weil L *ret* Berkeley CA
Welch EJ San Francisco CA
Wheeler DR *dcn* San Francisco CA
Wilemon ZH San Jose CA
Williams LVW San Francisco
Wilmington RN *ret* Rancho Mirage CA
Wong S
Wood LA *ret* Oakland CA
Yates DG *dcn*
Yeoman EB Stockton CA

DIOCESE OF CENTRAL FLORIDA
(PROVINCE IV)
Comprises Central Florida
DIOCESAN OFFICE 1017 E Robinson St Orlando FL 32801
Tel (407) 423-3567   FAX (407) 872-0006
WEB www.cfdiocese.org

Previous Bishops —
Wm C Gray 1892-1913, Cameron Mann m 1913 dio 1922-32, John D Wing coadj 1925 Bp 1932-50, Martin J Bram suffr 1951-56, Wm F Moses suffr 1956-61, Henry I Louttit suffr 1945 coadj 1948 Bp 1951-69, James L Duncan suffr 1961-69, Wm L Hargrave suffr 1961-69, Wm H Folwell 1970-89, John W Howe 1989-2012

Bishop—Rt Rev Gregory O Brewer (1063) (Dio 24 March 2012)

Cn to Ord T Nunez; *Sec* S Caprani; *Treas* B Bauder 1417 E Concord St Orlando 32803; *Chanc* C Wooten Jr 236 S Lucerne Ave Orlando 32801-4490; *COM* O Kimbrough; *Ecum* Rt Rev H Pina-Lopez

Stand Comm—Cler: J Davis A Petiprin E Turner W Garrison; Lay: P Tew S Shannon S Glynn

Dio Conv: 23-23 Jan 2016 Melbourne FL

PARISHES, MISSIONS, AND CLERGY

Apopka Church Of The Holy Spirit **P** (402) 601 S Highland Ave 32703-5343 (Mail to: 601 S Highland Ave 32703-5343) John Pallard (407) 886-1740

Auburndale St Alban's Episcopal Church **P** (52) 202 Pontotoc Plaza 33823-3408 (Mail to: PO Box 1125 33823-1125) John Gullett Timothy Shaw

Avon Park Church of the Redeemer **M** (49) 910 W Martin Road 33825 (Mail to: 910 W Martin Rd 33825) (863) 453-5664 William Yates

Bartow Holy Trinity Episcopal Church **P** (185) 500 West Stuart Street 33830 (Mail to: PO Box 197 33831-0197) Gary Jackson Patrice Behnstedt (863) 533-3581 Patricia Spencer

Belleview St Marys Episcopal Church **P** (325) 5750 SE 115th Street 34420 (Mail to: PO Box 2373 34421-2373) Lisa Hinkle Carolyn Quinnell Robert Quinnell (352) 347-6422

Bushnell St Francis of Assisi Church **M** (89) 313 N Grace St 33513 (Mail to: PO Box 566 33513-0566) Karen House (352) 793-3187 Lawrence Recla

Clermont St Matthias Episcopal Church **P** (286) 574 W Montrose St 34711-2261 (Mail to: 574 West Montrose Street 34711-2285) James Dorn (352) 394-3855

Cocoa St Marks Episcopal Church **P** (470) 4 Church St 32922-7912 (Mail to: 4 Church St 32922-7999) (321) 636-3781 John Bender

Cocoa Beach St Davids by the Sea Episcopal Church **P** (264) 600 S 4th St 32931-2612 (Mail to: PO Box 320026 32932-0026) Scott Holcombe (321) 783-2554 Carla Rhodes

Crystal River St Annes Episcopal Church **P** (378) 9870 W Fort Island Trl 34429-5383 (Mail to: 9870 W Fort Island Trl 34429-5383) Cheryl Bakker Henry Brown Gilbert Larsen

Daytona Beach St Marys Episcopal Church **P** (309) 216 Orange Ave 32114-4312 (Mail to: 216 Orange Ave 32114-4312) (386) 255-3669 Robert Anderson

Daytona Beach St Timothys Episcopal Church **M** (111) C/O Ms Gertrude Sheppard PO Box 10176 32120-0176 (Mail to: 381 N Lincoln St 32114-3077) Neville Crichlow (386) 255-2077 Willamarie Smith Edmonson Asgill

Deland St Barnabas Episcopal Church **P** (457) 319 W Wisconsin Ave 32720-4132 (Mail to: 319 W Wisconsin Ave 32720) William Garrison Nancy Kline (386) 734-1814 Catherine Stater

Deland The Church of the Holy Presence **M** (29) 355 N Kepler Rd 32724-4713 (Mail to: 355 N Kepler Road 32724-4713) Carol McDonald (386) 734-5228

Deltona All Saints Episcopal Church **P** (326) 155 Clark St 32725-8188 (Mail to: 155 Clark Street 32725-8188) Philip Dunbar Linda Kromhout Robin Morical Gerald Raschke Linda Coulter

Dunnellon Church of the Advent **P** (151) 11251 SW Highway 484 34432-6415 (Mail to: 11251 SW Hwy 484 34432-6415) (352) 465-7272 William Barrett

Dunnellon Holy Faith Church **P** (108) 19924 W Blue Cove Dr 34432-5811 (Mail to: 19924 W Blue Cove Dr 34432-5811) John Gerhart (352) 489-2685

Eustis Church of St Thomas **P** (396) 317 S Mary St 32726-4201 (Mail to: 317 S Mary St 32726-4201) Janet Clarke Richard Labud John Lipscomb (352) 357-4358

Fort Meade Christ Episcopal Church **M** (15) 1 N Cleveland Ave 33841-3017 (Mail to: 1 N Cleveland Ave 33841-3017) (863) 368-1465

Fort Pierce Church of St Simon the Cyrenian **P** (60) 1700 Avenue E 34950-7953 (Mail to: 1700 Ave E 34950) (772) 461-2519

Fort Pierce St Andrews Episcopal Church **P** (490) 210 S Indian River Dr 34950-4337 (Mail to: 210 S Indian River Dr 34950-4337) John Liebler Frank Sawyer

Fruitland Pk Holy Trinity Episcopal Church **P** (172) 2201 Spring Lake Rd 34731-5256

(Mail to: 2201 Spring Lake Rd 34731-5256) Theodore Koelln Gerald Steidl (352) 787-1500 Janice Gordon-Barnes

Haines City St Marks Episcopal Church **P** (260) 102 N 9th St 33844-4314 (Mail to: 102 N 9th St 33844-4314) Christopher Brathwaite (863) 422-1416

Inverness St Margarets Episcopal Church **P** (226) 114 N Osceola Ave 34450-4121 (Mail to: 114 N Osceola Ave 34450-4121) Eugene Reuman Barbara Pemberton Kathleen Pennybacker John Thompson (352) 726-3153

Kissimmee St Johns Episcopal Church **P** (585) 1709 N John Young Pkwy 34741-3218 (Mail to: 1709 N John Young Pkwy 34741-3218) Cecil Radcliff Luis De la Cruz (407) 847-2009

Lake Mary St Peters Episcopal Church **P** (756) 700 Rinehart Rd 32746-4875 (Mail to: 700 Rinehart Rd 32746-4875) Charles Holt Wesley Sharp Dane Wren (407) 444-5673

Lake Placid St Francis of Assisi Epis Church **P** (212) 43 Lake June Rd 33852 (Mail to: 43 Lake June Rd 33852-8910) Elizabeth Nelson (863) 465-0051 William Going 863-840-0608

Lake Wales The Church of the Good Shepherd **P** (536) No 221 S 4th St 33853-3856 (Mail to: 221 S 4th St 33853-3856) Thomas Seitz Joan Brawley John Motis Suzanne Mulkin (863) 676-8578

Lakeland All Saints Episcopal Church **P** (1103) 202 S Massachusetts Ave 33801-5012 (Mail to: 209 S Iowa Ave 33801-5018) John Birtch Larry Hensarling (863) 688-4502

Lakeland Christ the King Episcopal Church **P** (99) 6400 N Socrum Loop Rd 33809-4141 (Mail to: 6400 N Socrum Loop Rd 33809-4141) Carolyn Biggs Robert Dinnerville (863) 858-1948 Edward Tatlian

Lakeland St Davids Episcopal Church **P** (561) 145 E Edgewood Dr 33803-4014 (Mail to: 145 E Edgewood Dr 33803-4014) Robert Moses Raymond Perica Joan Verret (863) 686-4143

Lakeland St Stephens Church **P** (458) 1820 E County Road 540a 33813-3737 (Mail to: 1820 E County Road 540A 33813-3737) David Peoples Douglas Jump (863) 646-6115

Lecanto Shepherd of the Hills Church **P** (450) No 2540 W Norvell Bryant Hwy 34461-9422 (Mail to: PO Box 1375 34460-1375) Joan Clark George Conger Michael Hall Linda Liebert-Hall (352) 527-0052

Leesburg St James Episcopal Church **P** (660) 204 N Lee St 34748-4915 (Mail to: 204 N Lee St 34748-4915) Thomas Ryan Thomas Trees (352) 787-1981 Donald Gross

Longwood Christ Episcopal Church **P** (60) 151 W Church Ave 32750-4105 (Mail to: 151 W Church Ave 32750-4105) Noy Sparks (407) 339-6812

Longwood Church of the Resurrection **P** (739) 251 E Lake Brantley Dr 32779-4808 (Mail

to: 251 E Lake Brantley Dr 32779-4808) Paul Mcqueen Stephen Clifton (407) 788-3704 Aileen Walther

Maitland Church of the Good Shepherd **P** (225) 331 Lake Ave 32751 (Mail to: 331 Lake Ave 32751) Sarah Bronos Richard Costin

Melbourne Holy Trinity Episcopal Church **P** (638) 50 W Strawbridge Ave 32901-4438 (Mail to: 1830 S Babcock St 32901) Pamela Easterday Stephen Easterday Stacey Westphal (321) 723-5272 Meghan Farr

Melbourne Hope Episcopal Church **P** (191) 190 Interlachen Rd 32940-1979 (Mail to: 190 Interlachen Rd 32940-1979) Deborah Vann (321) 259-5810 Pamela Garton

Melbourne St Johns Episcopal Church **P** (167) 610 Young St 32935-7059 (Mail to: 610 Young St 32935-7059) Eric Turner Elizabeth Murray

Melbourne Bch St Sebastians by the Sea **P** (187) 2010 Oak St 32951-2713 (Mail to: 2010 Oak St 32951-2713) Norman Desrosiers George Smodell (321) 723-3015

Merritt Island St Lukes Episcopal Church **P** (293) 5555 N Tropical Trl 32953-7202 (Mail to: PO Box 541025 32954-1025) Peter Roberts (321) 452-5260

Mount Dora St Edward the Confessor **P** (251) 460 N Grandview St 32757-5676 (Mail to: 460 N Grandview St 32757-5676) John Crandall (352) 383-2832 Mickey Maxwell

Mulberry St Luke the Evangelist Church **M** (29) 505 NE 1st Ave 33860-2434 (Mail to: 505 NE 1st Ave 33860-2434) (863) 425-2472 Katherine Yotter

New Smyrna St Peter the Fisherman Church **P** (271) 4220 Saxon Dr 32169-3923 (Mail to: 4220 Saxon Dr 32169-3923) James Spencer (386) 428-7383 Dinesh Bissoondial

New Smyrna Beach St Pauls Episcopal Church **P** (330) 1650 Live Oak St 32168-7771 (Mail to: 1650 Live Oak St 32168-7771) Rodney Roehner David Hoag (386) 428-8733

Ocala Grace Episcopal Church **P** (395) 503 SE Broadway St 34471-2250 (Mail to: 510 SE Broadway St 34471-2256) Jonathan French Mary Delancey Chester Trow (352) 622-7881

Ocala St Patricks Episcopal Church **P** (129) 3803 NE 7th St 34470-1041 (Mail to: 3803 NE 7th St 34470-1041) James Giles (352) 694-3414

Ocala St Stephens Episcopal Church **M** (65) 55 Palm Rd 34472-2418 (Mail to: PO Box 831933 34483-1933) Margaret Silk-Wright (352) 687-2400

Okahumpka Corpus Christi Episcopal Church **M** (95) 3430 Country Road 470 34762 (Mail to: PO Box 68 34762-0068) Amanda Bordenkircher (352) 787-8430 Jacqueline Guernsey

Okeechobee Church of Our Saviour **P** (239) 200 NW 3rd St 34972-4125 (Mail to: 200 NW 3rd St 34972-4125) James Shevlin (863) 763-4843

Robert Brandt Deche Hamill

Orange City St Judes Episcopal Church **P** (193) 815 E Graves Ave 32763-5307 (Mail to: 815 E Graves Ave 32763-5307) Phyllis Bartle Pauline Butler Wanda Sherrouse

✠ **Orlando** Cathedral Church of St Luke **O** (1163) Attn Anne Clarke PO Box 2328 32802-2328 (Mail to: 130 N Magnolia Ave 32801-2300) Anthony Clark Joshua Bales Justin Holcomb Reggie Kidd Michael Matheny Nancy Oliver Carolyn Petersen (407) 849-0680 Danielle Morris

Orlando Christ the King Episcopal Church **P** (221) 26 Willow Dr 32807-3220 (Mail to: 26 Willow Dr 32807-3220) (407) 277-1151 Edward Weiss

Orlando Church of the Ascension **P** (532) 4950 S Apopka Vineland Rd 32819-3104 (Mail to: 4950 S Apopka Vineland Rd 32819-3104) James Sorvillo Matthew Ainsley Beth Wagner (407) 876-3480 Elizabeth Bellner Deborah Buechner

Orlando Emmanuel Episcopal Church **P** (491) 1603 E Winter Park Rd 32803-2228 (Mail to: 1603 E Winter Park Rd 32803-2296) David Bumsted (407) 894-1641 Janice Honea

Orlando Holy Family Episcopal Church **P** (493) 1010 N Hiawassee Rd 32818-6711 (Mail to: 1010 N Hiawassee Rd 32818-6711) Peter Magill (407) 293-2236

Orlando Iglesia Episcopal Jesus de Nazaret **M** (169) 26 Willow Dr 32807-3220 (Mail to: 26 Willow Dr 32807-3220) Raul Rubiano-Alvarado (407) 222-7995

Orlando Iglesia Episcopal San Cristobal **M** (149) 7500 Forest City Rd 32810-3710 Carlos Marin Aquilino Vinas-Plasencia (407) 293-5653

Orlando St John the Baptist Church **P** (199) 1000 Bethune Dr 32805-3404 (Mail to: 1000 Bethune Dr 32805-3404) Jabriel Ballentine (407) 295-1923 Patricia Roberts

Orlando St Mary of the Angels Epis Church **P** (247) 6316 Matchett Rd 32809-5150 (Mail to: 6316 Matchett Rd 32809-5196) Andrew Petiprin Gerardo De Jesus James Whitten

Orlando St Matthews Episcopal Church **P** (428) 5873 N Dean Rd 32817-3201 (Mail to: 5873 N Dean Rd 32817-3201) Sonia Sullivan-Clifton David Somers Kenneth Vinal (407) 657-9199

Orlando St Michaels Church **P** (647) 2499 N Westmoreland Dr 32804-4934 (Mail to: 2499 N Westmoreland Dr 32804-4994) Richard Luoni Carter Smith (407) 843-8448 Happy Gafford

Ormond Beach Church of the Holy Child **P** (109) 1225 W Granada Blvd 32174-5914 (Mail to: 1225 W Granada Blvd 32174-5914) (386) 672-4470 Stephen Pessah Madelyn Martin

Ormond Beach St James Episcopal Church **P** (716) 38 S Halifax Dr 32176-6597 (Mail to: 38 S Halifax Dr 32176-6597) (386) 677-1811

Ernest Bennett Terri Malia Judith Mathis

Oviedo Church of the Incarnation **M** (193) 1601 Alafaya Trl 32765-9485 (Mail to: 1601 Alafaya Trl 32765) Rory Harris Jose Rodriguez Dave Aycock

Palm Bay Church of Our Savior **P** (227) 1000 Jersey Ln NE 32905-5519 (Mail to: 1000 Jersey Ln NE 32905-5519) Loren Fox Thomas Williams (321) 723-8032

Palm Bay Epis Ch of the Blessed Redeemer **M** (125) 1225 Degroodt Rd SW 32908-7102 (Mail to: PO Box 111565 32911-1565) (321) 725-6881

Port Orange Grace Episcopal Church **P** (305) 4110 S Ridgewood Ave 32127-4519 (Mail to: PO Box 290245 32129-0245) Charles Burhans Susan McCaffrey (386) 767-3583 Patricia Longacre

Port St Lucie Church of the Nativity **P** (364) 1151 SW Del Rio Blvd 34953-1520 (Mail to: 1151 SW Del Rio Blvd 34953-1520) Mary Rosendahl John Jasper (772) 343-0401

Port St Lucie Holy Faith Episcopal Church **P** (393) 6990 S Us Highway 1 34952-1424 (Mail to: 6990 S US Highway 1 34952-1499) Orlando Addison (772) 446-9619 Burnet Cherisol (772) 672-1309

Saint Cloud Church of St Luke & St Peter **P** (244) 2745 Canoe Creek Rd 34772-6502 (Mail to: 2745 Canoe Creek Rd 34772-6502) Robert Longbottom (407) 892-3227

Sanford Holy Cross Episcopal Church **P** (237) 410 S Magnolia Ave 32771-1918 (Mail to: 410 S Magnolia Ave 32771-1918) Jim Booker Ann Kruger (407) 322-4611

Satellite Bch Church of the Holy Apostles **P** (215) 505 Grant Ave 32937-2921 (Mail to: 505 Grant Ave 32937-2921) Todd Schmidtetter (321) 777-0024

Sebastian St Elizabeths Episcopal Church **P** (263) 901 Clearmont St 32958-4978 (Mail to: 901 Clearmont St 32958-4978) David Newhart (772) 589-2770 Lori Hoey

Sebring St Agnes Episcopal Church **P** (309) 3840 Lakeview Dr 33870-2066 (Mail to: 3840 Lakeview Dr 33870-2066) Scott Walker Eugene Fernsler

The Villages St George Episcopal Church **P** (643) 1250 Paige Place 32159-9315 (Mail to: 1250 Paige Pl 32159-9315) Nancy Bryson (352) 750-1010 John Kelly Tom Bankowski Edward Bartle

Titusville St Gabriels Episcopal Church **P** (310) PO Box 6584 32782-6584 (Mail to: 414 Pine St 32796-3542) Robert Goodridge Mark Lafler (321) 267-2545 Daniel Mannen

Vero Beach St Augustine of Canterbury **P** (743) 475 43rd Ave 32968-1836 (Mail to: 475 43rd Ave 32968-1836) Michael Goldberg Berek Smith (772) 770-3494

Vero Beach Trinity Episcopal Church **P** (282)

2365 Pine Ave 32960-0528 (Mail to: 2365 Pine Ave 32960-0528) Christopher Rodriguez Jason Murbarger

Wauchula St Anns Episcopal Church **M** (25) 204 N 9th Ave 33873-2616 (Mail to: PO Box 1874 33873-1874) James McConnell (863) 773-6418

Winter Garden Church of the Messiah **P** (330) 241 N Main Street 34787 (Mail to: 241 N Main St 34787) Thomas Rutherford Julie Altenbach (407) 656-3218 Tim Wetherington

Winter Haven Holy Cross Church **P** (149) 201 Kipling Ln 33884-2316 (Mail to: 201 Kipling Lane 33884-2316) Richard Bordin Elizabeth Harrison (863) 324-4021

Winter Haven St Pauls Church **P** (314) 656 Avenue L NW 33881-4058 (Mail to: 656 Avenue L NW 33881-4030) Paul Head Susan Hansell (863) 294-8888

Winter Park All Saints Episcopal Church **P** (1748) 338 E Lyman Ave 32789-4415 (Mail to: 338 E Lyman Ave 32789-4494) Robert Lord Christopher Nations Elizabeth Tucker Russell Wohlever (407) 647-3413

Winter Park St Richards Episcopal Church **P** (437) 5151 Lake Howell Rd 32792-1027 (Mail to: 5151 Lake Howell Rd 32792-1027) Alison Harrity (407) 671-4211

NON-PAROCHIAL CLERGY

Adams HK *dcn* Ormond Beach FL
Alday KN *dcn* Orlando FL
Appleton ME *dcn* Winter Park FL
Arrunategui H *ret* Clermont FL
Asgill EO *dcn* Daytona Beach FL
Austin WB *ret* Smyrna GA
Ball E *dcn* Bradenton FL
Beaumont JF Chelsea MI
Beikirch PM *dcn* Lakeland FL
Blake SL Mount Dora FL
Boland GA *ret* Haines City FL
Bosscher M Longwood FL
Boyer W Howey In The Hills FL
Brady WD *dcn* Crystal River FL
Britcher SA *dcn* Fort Pierce FL
Brokaw RG *ret* St Petersburg FL
Bromiley HP *ret* The Villages FL
Bruckart RM *ret* Melbourne FL
Buechner DA *dcn* Ocoee FL
Cameron RS *dcn*
Casto RR *ret* St Mary's FL
Castro R Escondido CA
Chadwick LW *ret* Ocala FL
Chambers RGM *ret* Seymour CT
Cilley NH *dcn* Auburndale FL
Cole CA *ret* Sanford FL
Coleman JP *ret* Orlando FL
Collins VL *dcn* Melbourne FL
Connelly AP *ret* Weaverville NC
Cooper MO *ret* Aiken SC
Dass S Ocala FL
Davis MC *dcn* Dunnellon FL

Davis RJ Oviedo FL
Dear AT *ret* New Smyrna FL
Deegan VE *dcn* Deland FL
Downs TA *ret* Chuluota FL
Duer D *ret* Micanopy FL
Dugger TM Miramar FL
Egerton KC *ret* Winter Park FL
Eldridge BA *dcn* Titusville FL
Evans RE *ret* Fort Lauderdale FL
Fritch CO *ret* Casselberry FL
Gabel MF *dcn* Orlando FL
Galbreath JL *dcn* Fruitland Park FL
Garvin GB *ret* Coconut Creek FL
Gibson TW *ret* Cocoa Beach FL
Gilkey SB *dcn* St Cloud FL
Goglia BM *dcn* Fredericksburg VA
Gomer RH Lakeland FL
Greatwood RN *ret* Orlando FL
Gross DW *ret* Leesburg FL
Gwyn L *dcn* Vero Beach FL
Hagood M Vero Beach FL
Hahne RO *dcn* Boca Raton FL
Hamilton RJ *ret* Orlando FL
Harper AK *dcn* Belleview FL
Hartling DC *ret* Deltona FL
Hayes ML *dcn*
Hazelett WH *ret* Kissimmee FL
Hoover RA *ret dcn* Lakeland FL
Howe KE *dcn* Locust Grove VA
Howze L Lakeland FL
Hudson MB *dcn* Cocoa FL
Jackson PP *dcn* Winter Park FL
Jacobs JR Pinehurst NC
Jenkins AW *ret* Lakeland FL
Jensen PA *dcn* Tampa FL
Kearns JD Oviedo FL
Keen GC *ret* Ormond Beach FL
Knox DP Longwood FL
Kochenburger PA APO, AE
Ann Kruger Sanford FL
Krumbhaar AR *ret* San Antonio Tlaycapan
Kundinger HD *ret* Melbourne FL
Kurtz JE *ret* Apopka FL
Lamb TV *dcn* Daytona Beach FL
Leahy JJ *ret* New Bern NC
Lewis WG *ret* Indialantic FL
L'Hommedieu JG *ret* Orlando FL
John Liebler *ret*
Linebaugh JA Fort Lauderdale FL
Lobs DB *dcn* Advance NC
Lobs GR *ret* Advance NC
Longacre PS Port Orange FL
Madson PG *ret* Altamonte Springs FL
Maher JA *ret* Port Orange FL
Manning RF *ret* Palm Coast FL
Matthews WT Orlando FL
Maurais RI *ret* Mount Dora FL
McBryde GK *ret* Webster FL
McDowell JL *ret* Cocoa Beach FL
McGlashon H *ret* Haines City FL
McLeod RB *ret* Tucson AZ

Meheux SA *dcn* Holly Hill FL
Mercer RC *ret* Winter Haven FL
Merola CR *dcn* Hendersonville NC
Messina MF *ret* Ocala FL
Miller RE *ret* Windermere FL
Miller WD Avon Park FL
Minshew N *dcn ret* Davenport FL
Mountford RT *ret* Lake Mary FL
Norman T *dcn*
Nunez TC Casselberry FL
Olsen LL *ret* Orlando FL
Pasay MC *dcn* Dunnellon FL
Patterson-Urbaniak PE *ret* Banner Elk NC
Pessah EJ
Phillips RW *ret* Winter Park FL
Pinder NW *ret* Orlando FL
Pobjecky JR *ret* Titusville FL
Raby EG *dcn* Smithfield VA
Rambo B Deland FL
Raehn JS Dyer TN
Ravndal E *ret* Orlando FL
Reynolds WA *ret* Bartow FL
Rider JF *ret*
Roberts JBG *ret* Babson Park FL
Rodgers BW *ret* Summerfield FL
Rose JA *ret* Daytona Beach FL
Rowe SJ *dcn* Breckenridge CO
Rule AR *ret* Daytona Beach FL
Schilling WB *ret* Melbourne FL
Seals WF *dcn* Hendersonville NC
Seay DR *ret* Dousman WI

Sholander ME Auburndale FL
Sitts CJ *ret* Longwood FL
Smith RK *ret* Lakeland FL
Sorvillo AL *ret* Ormond Beach FL
Squire WS *ret* The Villages FL
Stebbins GG *dcn* The Villages-Lady Lake FL
Stevens RE *ret* Evanston IL
Stichweh MT *ret* Indianapolis IN
Taylor JD *ret* Ormond Beach FL
Thompson W ret Winter Haven FL
Toalster RD Lakeland FL
Toney MA *dcn* Belleview FL
Towson LA *ret* Satellite Beach FL
Travis RC *ret* Cocoa FL
Vance W ret dcn Orlando FL
Vani BS *ret* Palm Bay FL
Vaughan J Orlando FL
Venezia DL Kissimmee FL
Wait BW Atlantic Beach FL
Walmsley JW *ret*
Wanstall D dcn ret Ormond Beach FL
Warren-Brown JA
Wilcoxson FD *dcn* Benton TN
Wilcoxson JAV *dcn* Benton TN
Willard-Williford JA Melbourne FL
Williams HE *ret* Lakeland FL
Wilson HD *ret* Franklin TN
Wood HP *dcn* Lake Wales FL
Woolard LP *dcn* Merritt Island FL
Wyld KA

DIOCESE OF THE CENTRAL GULF COAST
(PROVINCE IV)
Comprises Southern AL and Northwest FL
DIOCESAN OFFICE 201 N Baylen St Pensacola FL 32502 (MAIL: Box 13330 Pensacola FL 32591-3330)
TEL (850) 434-7337   FAX (850) 434-8577
E-MAIL (staff name)@diocgc.org   WEB www.diocgc.org

Previous Bishops—
George Mosley Murray 1971-81,
Charles Farmer Duvall DD 1981-
2001, Philip Menzie Duncan II
2001-15

**Bishop—Rt Rev James Russell
Kendrick** (Dio July 25 2015)

Dio Admin D Babcock; *Chanc (AL)* K Miller Box 290
Mobile AL 36601; *Chanc (FL)* S Remmington Box
13010 Pensacola FL 32591; *Reg & Hist* K Caffey 119
Laurel Pl Daphne AL 36526; *Treas* M Nicrosi

Stand Comm—Cler: G Riggall T Dyson R
McCormick R Crow M Shephard; *Lay: Pres* M Foote
W Hamilton B Jones M Nicrosi A Stevens G Wilson
V Currie A Richey L Ferren

Dio Conv: 18-20 Feb 2016 St Paul's Episcopal
Church, Daphne, AL

PARISHES, MISSIONS, AND CLERGY
Alabama
Andalusia St Marys Episcopal Church **P** (119)
1307 E Three Notch St 36420-3403 (Mail to:
1307 E Three Notch St 36420-3403) Cynthia
Howard (334) 222-2487
Atmore St Annas Episcopal Church **M** (143) 100
Lynn McGhee Dr 36502-5057 (Mail to: 100
Lynn McGhee Dr 36502-5057) Teresa Leifur
(251) 368-8606
Atmore Trinity Episcopal Church **P** (39) 203 S
Carney St 36502-2404 (Mail to: 203 S Carney
St 36502-2404) Mark McDonald (251) 368-
5933
Bay Minette Immanuel Episcopal Church **M** (50)
700 McMillan Ave 36507-4425 (Mail to: 700
McMillan Ave 36507-4425) Mark Mcdonald
(251) 937-7900

Bon Secour St Peters Episcopal Church **P** (168) 6270 Bon Secour Hwy 36511 (Mail to: PO Box 29 36511-0029) Bryan Gentry Susan McKee (251) 949-6254

Brewton St Stephens Episcopal Church **P** (167) 1510 Escambia Ave 36426-1124 (Mail to: PO Box 1261 36427-1261) (251) 867-4545

Citronelle St Thomas Episcopal Church **M** (4) 19030 S Center St 36522-2546 (Mail to: PO Box 813 36522-0813) Dennis Brown (251) 866-7003

Coden St Marys by the Sea Episcopal Church **M** (52) 4875 Highway 188 36523-3703 (Mail to: 4875 Highway 188 36523-3703) (251) 873-5602

Daphne St Pauls Episcopal Church **P** (926) 28788 N Main St 36526-7258 (Mail to: 28788 N Main St 36526-7258) Thack Dyson Spergeon Kennington Mary Alice Mathison (251) 626-2421

Dauphin Islnd St Francis Episcopal Church **M** (53) 401 Key St 36528 (Mail to: PO Box 407 36528-0407) (251) 861-2300

Dothan Episcopal Church of the Nativity **P** (549) 205 Holly Ln 36301-1438 (Mail to: 205 Holly Ln 36301-1438) Peter Wong Linda Suzanne Borgen (334) 793-7616

Enterprise Episcopal Church of the Epiphany **M** (67) 302 East Grubbs St 36330-2613 (Mail to: 302 East Grubbs St 36330-2613) (334) 347-8210

Eufaula St James Episcopal Church **P** (202) 100 Saint James Pl 36027-1551 (Mail to: 100 Saint James Pl 36027-1551) Eleanor Whitelaw (334) 687-3619

Fairhope St James Episcopal Church **P** (1271) 860 N Section St 36532-6376 (Mail to: 860 N Section St 36532-6376) Donald Smith (251) 928-2912

Foley St Pauls Episcopal Church **P** (519) 506 N Pine St 36535-2039 (Mail to: PO Box 1745 36536-1745) Thomas Talbert Steven Pankey

Greenville St Thomas Episcopal Church **P** (156) 210 Church St 36037-2606 (Mail to: 210 Church St 36037-2606) Reid McCormick (334) 382-8914

Gulf Shores Holy Spirit Episcopal Church **P** (371) 616 W Fort Morgan Rd 36542-4300 (Mail to: PO Box 2346 36547-2346) Jeffery Garner Allen Ruth

Jackson St Peters Episcopal Church **M** (35) 100 Hospital Dr 36545-2424 (Mail to: PO Box 146 36545-0146) Patrick Dunn (251) 246-8092

Lillian Church of the Advent **M** (79) 12099 County Road 99 36549-5128 (Mail to: 12099 County Rd 99 36549-5128) Mark Mcdonald (251) 961-2505

Magnolia Sprgs St Pauls Episcopal Church **P** (140) 14755 Oak Ave 36555 (Mail to: PO Box 2 36555-0002) Dennis Day Susan McKee Aaron Smith (251) 965-7452

Mobile All Saints Episcopal Church **P** (418) 151 S Ann St 36604-2302 (Mail to: 151 S Ann St 36604-2302) James Flowers Mary Robert

Mobile Christ Church Cathedral **P** (593) 115 S Conception St 36602-2606 (Mail to: 115 S Conception St 36602-2606) Beverly Gibson Daniel Wagner (251) 438-1822

Mobile Church of the Good Shepherd **P** (206) 605 Donald St 36617-3401 (Mail to: 605 Donald St 36617-3401) (251) 452-9596

Mobile Episcopal Church of the Redeemer **P** (261) 1100 Cody Rd S 36695-4400 (Mail to: 7125 Hitt Rd 36695-4431) (251) 639-1948

Mobile St Andrews Episcopal Church **M** (48) 1854 Staples Rd 36605-4560 (Mail to: 1854 Staples Rd 36605-4560) (251) 479-0336

Mobile St Johns Episcopal Church **P** (148) No 1707 Government St 36604-1103 (Mail to: 1707 Government St 36604-1103) Thomas Heard (251) 479-5474

Mobile St Lukes Episcopal Church **P** (648) 1050 Azalea Rd 36693-2804 (Mail to: 1050 Azalea Rd 36693-2804) Walter Cumbie (251) 666-2990

Mobile St Marks For the Deaf **M** (7) 6109 Howells Ferry The Willmer Hall 36618-3147 (Mail to: PO Box 180068 36618-0068) (251) 281-2148

Mobile St Matthews Episcopal Church **P** (64) 5901 Overlook Rd 36618-2803 (Mail to: 5901 Overlook Rd 36618-2899) (251) 342-1178

Mobile St Michaels Episcopal Church **M** (65) 300 Grant St 36611-2132 (Mail to: PO Box 11484 36671-0484) (251) 300-0278

Mobile St Pauls Episcopal Church **P** (2365) 4051 Old Shell Rd 36608-1337 (Mail to: 4051 Old Shell Rd 36608-1337) Marshall Craver John Riggin Reuben Rockwell

Mobile Trinity Episcopal Church **P** (453) 1900 Dauphin St 36606-1414 (Mail to: PO Box 6176 36660-0176) Lynn Norman

Monroeville St Johns Episcopal Church **P** (81) 200 Whetstone St 36460-2698 (Mail to: PO Box 853 36461-0853) (251) 743-4549

Ozark St Michaels Episcopal Church **M** (74) 427 Camilla Ave 36320-2281 (Mail to: PO Box 955 36361-0955) (334) 774-2617

Robertsdale St John the Evangelist Epis Church **M** (110) 22764 Us Highway 90 36567-2805 (Mail to: PO Box 1137 36567) George Gilbert (251) 914-6011

Troy St Mark's Episcopal Church **P** (193) 401 W College St 36081-2108 (Mail to: 401 W College St 36081-2108) Jeffrey Byrd (334) 566-2619

Florida

Apalachicola Trinity Episcopal Church **P** (158) 79 6th St 32329 (Mail to: PO Box 667 32329-0667) Martha Harris (850) 653-9550

Cantonment St Monicas Episcopal Church **P** (118) 699 S Highway 95a 32533-6485 (Mail to: 699 S Highway 95A 32533-6485) Anthony

Macwhinnie (850) 937-0001

Chipley St Matthews Episcopal Church **M** (67) 736 West Blvd 32428-1629 (Mail to: PO Box 63 32428-0345) (850) 638-7837

Crestview Episcopal Church of the Epiphany **M** (107) PO Box 612 32536-0612 (Mail to: 424 Garden St 32536-1704) Glenn Rohrer (850) 689-1410

Defuniak Spgs St Agathas Episcopal Church **M** (70) 144 Circle Dr 32435-2545 (Mail to: 150 Circle Dr 32435) Sandra Mcleod (850) 892-7254

Destin St Andrew's By-the-Sea Epis Church **P** (92) 307 Harbor Blvd 32541-2383 (Mail to: PO Box 1658 32540-1658) Robert Crow (850) 650-2737

Ft Walton Bch St Simons on-the-Sound Epis Church **P** (586) 28 Miracle Strip Pkwy SW 32548-6613 (Mail to: 28 Miracle Strip Pkwy SW 32548-6613) Eric Zubler (850) 244-8621

Gulf Breeze St Francis of Assisi Epis Church **P** (287) 1 Saint Francis Dr 32561-4825 (Mail to: 1 Saint Francis Dr 32561-4825) Timothy Backus (850) 932-2861

Marianna St Lukes Episcopal Church **P** (142) 4362 Lafayette St 32446-2916 (Mail to: 4362 Lafayette St 32446-2916) John Coleman David Green (850) 482-2431

Milton St Marys Episcopal Church **P** (161) 6841 Oak St 32570-6791 (Mail to: 6849 Oak St 32570) Matthew Dollhausen (850) 623-2905

Navarre St Augustine of Canterbury **P** (133) 7810 Navarre Pkwy 32566-7585 (Mail to: 7810 Navarre Pkwy 32566-7585) (850) 939-2261

Niceville St Judes Episcopal Church **P** (278) 200 N Partin Dr 32578 (Mail to: 200 N Partin Dr 32578) Denis Baum Charles Hein (850) 678-7013

Panama City Holy Nativity Episcopal Church **P** (703) 222 N Bonita Ave 32401-3853 (Mail to: 222 N Bonita Ave 32401) Steven Bates

Panama City St Andrews Episcopal Church **P** (251) 1608 Baker Ct 32401-1900 (Mail to: 1608 Baker Ct 32401-1900) (850) 763-7636

Panama City St Patricks Episcopal Church **M** (76) 4025 East Fifteenth Street 32404-5862 (Mail to: PO Box 36943 32412-6943) Julia Phillips (850) 763-7847

Panama City Beach Grace Episcopal Church **P** (124) 9101 Panama City Beach Pkwy 32407-4021 (Mail to: PO Box 9087 32417-9087) Joseph Hagberg (850) 235-4136

Panama City Beach St Thomas by-the-Sea Epis Church **M** (95) 20408 First Ave 32413-8902 (Mail to: PO Box 7359 32413-8902) (850) 234-2919

Pensacola Christ Episcopal Church **P** (2123) § 18 W Wright St 32501 (Mail to: PO Box 12683 32591-2683) Jessica Babcock Betty Brenemen Christine Hord James Knight James Lord John Phillips (850) 432-5115

Pensacola Holy Cross Episcopal Church **P** (388) 7979 N 9th Ave 32514-6460 (Mail to: 7979 N 9th Ave 32514-6460) Glenn Rohrer (850) 477-8596

Pensacola Holy Trinity Episcopal Church **P** (115) 850 N Blue Angel Pkwy 32506-6304 (Mail to: PO Box 3068 32516-3068)

Pensacola St Christophers Episcopal Church **P** (1118) 3200 N 12th Ave 32503-4007 (Mail to: 3200 N 12th Ave 32503-4007) Walter Kindergan Susan Sowers (850) 433-0074

Pensacola St Cyprians Episcopal Church **M** (47) 500 N Reus St 32501 (Mail to: PO Box 17165 32522) Hayden Hill (850) 438-1958

Pensacola St Johns Episcopal Church **P** (108) 401 Live Oak Ave 32507-3431 (Mail to: 401 Live Oak Ave 32507-3431) Anna Butterbaugh (850) 453-9076

Port St Joe St James Episcopal Church **P** (119) 800 22nd St 32456-2298 (Mail to: 800 22nd St 32456-2298) Thomas Dwyer (850) 227-1845

Santa Rosa Bch Christ the King Episcopal Church **P** (298) 480 N Hwy 393 32459 (Mail to: PO Box 1677 32459-1677) Richard Proctor (850) 267-3332

Wewahitchka St John the Baptist Episcopal Church **M** (52) 4060 N Highway 71 PO Box 595 32465-0595 (Mail to: PO Box 595 235 E. Chipola Av 32465-0595) (850) 639-2280

NON-PAROCHIAL CLERGY

Baker ML Cantonment FL
Baldwin GL *ret* Brewton AL
Barker KL Tulsa OK
Betenbaugh HR *ret*
Bogan LE *ret* Gulf Breeze FL
Brewer JL *dcn* Navarre FL
Bright CC *ret* Muscle Shoals AL
Bush AA *ret* Birmingham AL
Carson RJ *dcn* Mobile AL
Coats CV *ret* Orange Beach AL
Cook JW *ret* Fairhope AL
Cooper FM *ret* Santa Rosa Beach FL
Dean BW *dcn* Santa Rosa Beach FL
Dixon RP Brewton AL
Douglas DR *ret* Mobile AL
Durst LE *ret* Valrico FL
Elam WL *ret* Fairhope AL
Floyd CR *ret* Panama City Beach FL
Ford RW Gulf Shores AL
Goff TL *dcn* Mobile AL
Goldsborough CN *ret* Pensacola FL
Graham WN *ret* Lawrenceville GA
Graves LR *ret* Pensacola FL
Hewis CM *dcn* Pensacola FL
Hickenlooper AM *ret* Panama City FL
Hicks JW *ret* Mobile AL
Hual JC Washington DC
Huft JR *ret* Wewahitchka FL
Hyer DS Fort Walton Beach FL
James CS *ret* Bon Secour AL

James WE *ret* Atlanta GA
Jencks JA *ret* Pensacola FL
Kelson LJ *dcn* Gulf Breeze FL
Klopfenstein TD *ret* Bonaire GA
Knight JS *ret* Selma AL
Kreamer MH *ret* Lillian AL
Lakeman TE *ret* Fairhope AL
Lindstrom DF *ret* Franklin NC
Lockett DA Troy AL
Mayer SC *ret* Mobile AL
Mcdowell-Fleming DH *ret* Pensacola FL
McLuen RE *ret* Kent WA
McMahan LW *ret* Bloomington IN
Murray JW *ret* Jacksonville FL
Nixon TE *ret* Ozark AL
Plovanich EM
Porter RC *ret* Mobile AL
Powers DA *ret* Mobile AL
Pruitt AW *ret* Decatur GA

Richards ET *dcn* Panama City Beach FL
Richardson JD Birmingham AL
Riggall GG *ret* Mobile AL
Schmidt RH *ret* Fairhope AL
Schroeter GH *ret* Spanish Fort AL
Shepard MS *ret* Panama City FL
Starr ML *ret* Port Townsend WA
Tipton HS *ret* Crestview FL
Totman GP *ret* Enterprise AL
Valcourt TPF Pensacola FL
Watkins JH *ret* Pensacola FL
Wave JE *ret* Panama City FL
Weller TC *ret* Panama City FL
Wheeler KB *dcn* Albany GA
Wilkins AE *ret* Mobile AL
Wishart RD *dcn* Lynn Haven FL
Withrock JW Troy AL
Womelsdorf CS *ret* Tallassee AL

DIOCESE OF CENTRAL NEW YORK
(PROVINCE II)
Comprises 14 counties in Central NY
DIOCESAN OFFICE 1020 7th North St Ste 200 Liverpool NY 13088
Tel (315) 474-6596 FAX (315) 478-1632
E-mail office@cnyepiscopal.org   WEB www.cnyepiscopal.org

Previous Bishops—
Frederic D Huntington 1869-1904, Chas T Olmstead coadj 1902 Bp 1904-21, Chas Fiske coadj 1915 Bp 1921-36, Edward H Coley suffr 1924 Bp 1936-42, Malcolm E Peabody coadj 1938 Bp 1942-60, Walter M Higley suffr 1948 coadj 1959 Bp 1960-69, Ned Cole coadj 1964 Bp 1969-83, O'Kelley Whitaker coadj 1981 Bp 1983-92, David B Joslin coadj 1991 Bp 1992-99 David Bowman asst Bp 2000-01

Bishop — Rt Rev Gladstone B Adams III (972)
(Dio 27 Oct 01)

Comm M K Sanderson; *Exec Asst* KD McDaniel; *Conv Sec* J Fried; *Chanc* PJ Curtin Jr 42 Albany St Cazenovia NY 13035; *COM* Rev D Cleaver-Bartholomew; *Cursillo* T Weir; *Ecum Off* Rev Dr W Lutz; *ER&D* Rev P Mouncey G Lipp; *Lit* Rev Dr R Tembeckjian; *Stew* Rev Dr L Mozeliak; *UTO* M Dawson; *Yth Rev* L Busby; *Safe Church* TBA; *Comp Dio* Dr C Stewart; *Deploy* J Fried; *Global* Miss Rev Dcn D Pierce

Stand Comm: Cler: Pres C Day G Hegney J Szachara J Kenna; *Lay:* F Hallanan S Balduf M Dawson B Hallinan

Dio Bd—Cler: Ch Bp GB Adams; Rev J Martinichio Very Rev C Schofield-Broadbent Rev W Copeland Rev Dr L Mozeliak; *Lay:* Ch PJ Curtin; *Treas* D Smith T Weir E Patterson P Currier

Dio Conv: 11-12 Nov 2016 Holiday Inn Convention Center Liverpool NY

PARISHES, MISSIONS, AND CLERGY

Adams Emmanuel Episcopal Church **P** (133) 40 E Church St 13605 (Mail to: PO Box 29 13605) John Throop (315) 232-2916

Afton St Anns Church **P** (65) 125 Main St 13730 (Mail to: PO Box 22 13730-0022) (607) 639-2330

Alexandria Bay Church of St Lawrence **SC** 7 Fuller St 13607 (Mail to: 7 Fuller St 13607-1811) John Andersen

Auburn Epis Church of SS Peter and John **P** (268) 169 Genesee St 13021-3403 (Mail to: 169 Genesee St 13021-3403) Kathlyn Schofield (315) 252-5721

Aurora United Ministry of Aurora **P** (17) Main St 13026 (Mail to: PO Box 91 13026-0091) (315) 364-8543

Bainbridge St Peters Episcopal Church **P** (173) 1 Church St 13733-1237 (Mail to: 1 Church St 13733-1237) Thomas Margrave (607) 967-3441

Baldwinsville Grace Episcopal Church **P** (338) 110 Oswego St 13027-1129 (Mail to: PO Box 6 13027-0006) Catherine Carpenter (315) 635-3214

Barneveld St Davids Episcopal Church **P** (79) 140 Mappa Ave 13304-2422 (Mail to: PO Box 344 13304-0344) Sarah Lewis (315) 896-2595

Berkshire St Johns Episcopal Church **P** (33) 1504

Seventy 6 Rd 13736 Richard Schaal (607) 687-1425

Binghamton Christ Church Episcopal **P** (255) 187 Washington St 13901-2713 (Mail to: 10 Henry St 13901-2720) Elizabeth Ewing Charles Jones (607) 722-2308

Binghamton St Marks Episcopal Church **P** (306) No 728 River Rd 13901-1263 (Mail to: PO Box 458 13745-0458) Mark Giroux

Binghamton Trinity Memorial Church **P** (245) 44 Main St 13905-3108 (Mail to: 44 Main St 13905-3181) Rebecca Drebert Kay Drebert (607) 723-3593

Black River St Johns Episcopal Church **P** (63) 145 W Remington St 13612-3124 (Mail to: PO Box 247 13612-0247) Ninon Hutchinson (315) 788-3738

Brownville St Pauls Episcopal Church **P** (68) 210 Washington St 13615 (Mail to: PO Box 146 13615-0146) (315) 788-3730

Camden Trinity Episcopal Church **P** (53) 98 Main St 13316-1303 (Mail to: PO Box 102 13316-0102) (315) 245-1987

Camillus St Lukes Episcopal Church **P** (284) 5402 W Genesee St 13031-2138 (Mail to: PO Box 91 13031-0091) Kathryn Corley (315) 487-1771

Canastota Trinity Episcopal Church **P** (67) 400 S Peterboro St 13032-1416 (Mail to: 400 S Peterboro St 13032) James Heidt

Candor St Marks Episcopal Church **P** (76) 17 Main St 13743-1617 (Mail to: PO Box 14 13743-0014) (607) 659-7479

Cape Vincent St Johns Church **P** (52) 352 S Market St 13618 (Mail to: PO Box 561 13618) John Crosswaite (315) 654-3833

Carthage Grace Episcopal Church **P** (71) 421 State St 13619-1413 (Mail to: 421 State St 13619-1413) (315) 493-0382

Cazenovia St Peters Episcopal Church **P** (160) No 10 Mill St 13035-1406 (Mail to: PO Box 419 13035-0419) Jeanne Hansknecht (315) 655-9063

Chadwicks St Georges Episcopal Church **P** (110) 9389 Elm St PO Box P 13319 (Mail to: PO Box P 13319) Terry Sheldon (315) 737-8124

Chittenango St Pauls Church **P** (218) 204 Genesee St 13037-1705 (Mail to: 204 Genesee St 13037-1705) (315) 687-6304

Clark Mills St Marks Episcopal Church **P** (110) 19 White St 13321 (Mail to: PO Box 363 13321-0363) Terry Sheldon (315) 853-8124

Clayton Christ Episcopal Church **P** (180) 235 John St 13624-1014 (Mail to: 235 John St 13624-1014) John Crosswaite (315) 686-3703

Clinton St James Episcopal Church **P** (362) 9 Williams St 13323-1705 (Mail to: 9 Williams St 13323-1705) (315) 853-5359

Constableville St Pauls Episcopal Church **P** (10) 27 Church St 13325 (Mail to: Gilda Krywosa 6546 Bailey Rd 13309-1901) (315) 942-4726

Constantia Trinity Episcopal Church **P** (24) 1492

George Street 13044-0124 (Mail to: PO Box 124 13044-0124) (315) 623-7431

Copenhagen Grace Church **P** (34) 21 Cataract St 13626 (Mail to: PO Box 6 13626-0006) Holly Evans (315) 688-2867

Cortland Grace and Holy Spirit Church **P** (247) 13 Court St 13045-2603 (Mail to: PO Box 170 13045-0170) Thomas Margrave Peter Williams

East Syracus Emmanuel Episcopal Church **P** (120) 400 W Yates St 13057-2140 (Mail to: 400 W Yates St 13057-2140) Gerard Beritela (315) 463-4310

Elmira Emmanuel Church **P** (70) 380 Pennsylvania Ave 14904-1759 (Mail to: 380 Pennsylvania Ave 14904-1759) Robert Adkins (607) 733-8219

Elmira Grace Episcopal Church **P** (427) 375 W Church St 14901-2620 (Mail to: 375 W Church St 14901-2695) Donald Matthews

Elmira Trinity Episcopal Church **P** (348) 304 N Main St 14901-2710 (Mail to: 304 N Main St 14901-2778) William Lutz (607) 732-3241

Endicott St Pauls Episcopal Church **P** (319) No 200 Jefferson Ave 13760-5212 (Mail to: 200 Jefferson Ave 13760-5295) John Martinichio

Evans Mills St Andrews Church **P** (16) 8520 LeRay St 13637 (Mail to: PO Box 233 13637-3241) Anne Wichelns (315) 350-4844

Fayetteville St Davids Episcopal Church **P** (133) 14 Jamar Dr 13066-1619 (Mail to: PO Box 261 13214-0261) Katherine Day (315) 446-2112

Fayetteville Trinity Episcopal Church **P** (600) 106 Chapel St 13066-2004 (Mail to: 106 Chapel St 13066-2052) Renee Tembeckjian John Wingert (315) 637-9872

Fulton All Saints Episcopal Church **P** (155) 153 S 1st St 13069-1716 (Mail to: PO Box 542 13069-0542)

Geneva Grace Church Willowdale **P** (17) 3874 E Lake Rd 14456-9256 (Mail to: PO Box 135 14456) Ralph Locke Ralph Harter (315) 585-9852

Greene Zion Episcopal Church **P** (369) 10 N Chenango St 13778-1102 (Mail to: PO Box 88 13778-0088) David Hanselman (607) 656-9502

Hamilton St Thomas Episcopal Church **P** (129) 12 Madison St 13346 (Mail to: 12 and a half Madison St 13346) Donnel O'Flynn (315) 824-1745

Horseheads St Matthews Episcopal Church **P** (174) 408 S Main St 14845-2409 (Mail to: 408 S Main St 14845-2409) Wanda Copeland (607) 739-5226

Ithaca Episcopal Church at Cornell **CC** G3 Anabel Taylor Hall Cornell 14853 (Mail to: G3 Anabel Taylor Hall 14853) Clark West (607) 255-4219

Ithaca St Johns Episcopal Church **P** (346) 210 N Cayuga St 14850-4333 (Mail to: 210 N Cayuga St 14850-4385) Barbara Grace Schmitz Arlen Strauss (607) 273-6532

Johnson City All Saints Episcopal Church **P** (191)

475 Main St 13790-1906 (Mail to: 475 Main St 13790-1999) Christine Day (607) 797-3354

Jordan Christ Episcopal Church **P** (64) 25 N Main Street 13080-0571 (Mail to: PO Box 571 13080-0571) Joseph Bergin (315) 689-3141

Liverpool St Matthews Episcopal Church **P** (489) 900 Vine St 13088-4502 (Mail to: 900 Vine St 13088-4502) Carrie Schofield-Broadbent (315) 457-4633

Lowville Trinity Church **P** (119) 5411 Trinity Ave 13367-1315 (Mail to: 5411 Trinity Ave 13367-1315) (315) 376-3241

Manlius Christ Church **P** (266) 407 E Seneca St 13104-1910 (Mail to: 407 E Seneca St 13104-1910) Dena Cleaver-Bartholomew (315) 682-5795

✣ **Marathon** St Johns Chapel **Other** West Main St 13803 (Mail to: 21 West Main Street 13803) Elizabeth Groskoph (607) 637-4952

Marcellus St Johns Episcopal Church **P** (182) 15 Orange St 13108-1215 (Mail to: 15 Orange St 13108-1215) (315) 673-2500

Mexico Grace Episcopal Church **P** (46) 4381 Church St 13114 (Mail to: PO Box 539 13114-0539) (315) 297-0254

Moravia St Matthews Church **P** (96) 14 Church St 13118 (Mail to: 14 Church St 13118) Perry Mouncey (315) 497-1171

✣ **Nedrow** Church of the Good Shepherd **Other** US Rte 11 13120 (Mail to: PO Box 143 13120-0143) (315) 469-0247

New Berlin St Andrews Episcopal Church **P** (128) South Main St 13411 (Mail to: PO Box 370 40 S Main St 13411-2900) Lisa Busby Charles Taylor (607) 847-6361

New Hartford St Stephens Church **P** (144) 25 Oxford Rd 13413-2638 (Mail to: 25 Oxford Rd 13413-2662) Joell Szachara (315) 732-7462

Norwich Emmanuel Episcopal Church **P** (385) 37 W Main St 13815 (Mail to: PO Box 203 13815-0203) Lisa Busby Charles Taylor (607) 334-8801

Oneida St Johns Church **P** (232) 341 Main St 13421-2144 (Mail to: 341 Main St 13421-2144) Arthur Smith (315) 363-1940

Oswego Church of the Resurrection **P** (174) 120 W 5th St 13126-2037 (Mail to: 120 W 5th St 13126-2096) Anne Wichelns

Owego St Pauls Episcopal Church **P** (148) 117 Main St 13827-1587 (Mail to: 117 Main St 13827-1587) Geoffrey Doolittle (607) 687-2830

Oxford St Pauls Church **P** (150) 36 Main St 13830 (Mail to: PO Box 72 13830-0721) David Hanselman

Parishville St Pauls Chapel **SC** 310 Montgomery St #200 13429 (Mail to: C/O Grace Church 201 E Main St 13480) (315) 733-7575

Pierrepont Manor Zion Church **P** (113) 15639 NY State Rt 193 13674 (Mail to: PO Box 782 13674-0782) Charles Henderson John Throop (315) 232-2916

Port Leyden St Marks Episcopal Church **P** (14) 6988 Main St 13433 (Mail to: PO Box 31 13433-0031) (315) 942-4726

Pulaski St James Episcopal Church **P** (150) 24 Lake St 13142-3243 (Mail to: PO Box 433 13142-0433) Bridget McManus (315) 298-2106

Rome Zion Episcopal Church **P** (107) 140 W Liberty St 13440-5718 (Mail to: 140 W Liberty St 13440-5718) James Heidt

Sackets Hbr Christ Church **M** 207 E Main St 13685-3158 (Mail to: PO Box 34 13685-0034) (315) 646-2217

Seneca Falls Trinity Episcopal Church **P** (105) 27 Fall St 13148-1428 (Mail to: PO Box 507 13148-0507) Polly Kasey (315) 568-5145

Sherburne Episcopal Church of the Epiphany **P** (106) 5 Classic Street 13830 (Mail to: PO Box 538 13460-0538) Bruce MacDuffie (607) 674-4312

Sherrill Gethsemane Episcopal Church **P** (98) 320 Park St 13461-1253 (Mail to: 320 Park St 13461-1253) (315) 363-3244

Skaneateles St James Episcopal Church **P** (591) 96 E Genesee St 13152-1328 (Mail to: 96 E Genesee St 13152-1372) Rebecca Coerper (315) 685-7600

Slaterville Springs St Thomas Episcopal Church **P** (37) 2729 Slaterville Rd (Rte 79) 14881 (Mail to: PO Box 51 14817) Gary Gruberth (607) 227-5118

South New Berlin St Matthews Church **P** (43) State Hwy 8 13843 (Mail to: State Hwy 8 13843) Lisa Busby Charles Taylor (607) 847-6361

Syracuse Church of the Saviour **Chapel** 437 James St 13203-2224 (Mail to: 437 James St 13203-2224) Gerard Beritela (315) 474-3359

Syracuse Ephphatha Parish for the Deaf **P** 310 Montgomery Ste 250 13202-2010 (Mail to: 210 Hazel St 13088-5116) Peter Williams

Syracuse Grace Church **P** (172) 819 Madison St 13210-1736 (Mail to: 819 Madison St 13210-1793) Johanna Marcure (315) 478-0901

Syracuse St Albans Episcopal Church **P** (79) 1308 Meadowbrook Dr 13224-1718 (Mail to: 1308 Meadowbrook Dr 13224-1718) Julie Calhoun-Bryant (315) 446-3490

Syracuse St Mark the Evangelist **P** (286) 1612 W Genesee St 13204-1950 (Mail to: 1612 W Genesee St 13204-1950) Adrian Amaya (315) 488-8511

✣ **Syracuse** St Pauls Episcopal Cathedral **O** (163) 220 E Fayette St 13202-1904 (Mail to: 310 Montgomery St 13202-2010) Georgina Hegney (315) 474-6053

Trumansburg Church of the Epiphany **P** (104) 11 Elm St 14886 (Mail to: PO Box 459 14886-0459) John Brewster (607) 387-6274

Utica Grace Episcopal Church **P** (492) 193 Genesee St 13501-2263 (Mail to: 6 Elizabeth St 13501-2263) Leon Mozeliak (315) 733-7575

Waterloo St Pauls Episcopal Church **P** (168)

101 E Williams St 13165-1412 (Mail to: 101 E Williams St 13165-1458) (315) 539-3897

Watertown Trinity Episcopal Church **P** (372) 227 Sherman St 13601-3611 (Mail to: 227 Sherman St 13601-3691) Richard Laribee Jennifer Kenna

Waverly Grace Episcopal Church **P** (99) 441 Park Ave 14892-1446 (Mail to: PO Box 123 14892-0123) Benjamin Lentz (607) 565-2608

Whitesboro St Johns Episcopal Church **P** (92) 135 Main St 13492-1216 (Mail to: 135 Main St 13492-1216) Sara Heiligman John Lavoe (315) 736-2659

Willard Christ Episcopal Church **P** (35) 1393 Main St 14588 (Mail to: PO Box 275 14588-0275) Lesley Adams Arlen Strauss (607) 869-9250

Windsor Zion Episcopal Church **P** (94) 21 Chapel St 13865-4307 (Mail to: PO Box 85 13865-0085) (607) 655-5533

NON-PAROCHIAL CLERGY

Avery HD *ret* Syracuse NY
Ayers RC *ret* Cazenovia NY
Banner SA *dcn* Oswego NY
Barker DW *ret* Vestal NY
Barrett JH *ret* Westerly RI
Bates MK *ret* Skaneateles NY
Baxter J *dcn* Ferrisburgh VT
Benson EH *ret* Ilion NY
Betz NE *ret* Clayton NY
Beveridge RH *ret* Seattle WA
Birkby CH *ret* Minoa NY
Bliss VP *ret* Montague MA
Bollinger DG *ret* Binghamton NY
Bower RA *ret* Ludlow VT
Budney KV Dover MA
Butler CR *ret* Albemarle NC
Corl JA *ret* Auburn NY
De Wetter RE Snowmass Village CO
Derbyshire JE *dcn* Syracuse NY
Dirghalli SG *ret* Syracuse NY
Eden KO *ret* Oswego NY
Fish CH Mystic CT
Flocken R *ret* Cazenovia NY
Foerster FH Centerville MA
Forisha ML *ret* San Antonio TX
Gay MW *ret*
Giles WE *ret* Adams Center NY
Gillett ERH *ret* Hamilton NY
Groves BT *dcn* Whitesboro NY
Guthrie SE *ret* Woodstock NY

Haugaard JJ Waterloo NY
Hoffman JP
Houck KM
Humphries JC *ret* Elmira NY
Kessler JM Binghamton NY
Kirkpatrick D *dcn*
Knox JD *ret* Fulton NY
Kuenkler RF *ret* Elmira NY
Laedlein GR *ret* Guilford CT
Lane NJ *ret* Elmira NY
Lewis RH *ret* none NY
Little HR *ret* Carthage NY
Logan LM Pierre SD
Love LL *ret* Waverly NY
Luck GT *ret* Syracuse NY
Messenger RS *ret* Moravia NY
Messenger-Harris BA *ret* Sherrill NY
Metzler PA Saint Louis MO
Mihalyi DR *ret* Geneva NY
Moore SP Napa CA
Mowers CL *ret* Brooktondale NY
Nagel VOW *ret* Syracuse NY
Nagle GO *ret* Saranac Lake NY
Parsons TH *ret* Norway ME
Pierce DK *dcn* Chenango Bridge NY
Redfield WC *ret* Syracuse NY
Reger TS Fayetteville NY
Sanders MM *ret* Lewes DE
Schiess BB Cicero NY
Shaffer JA Oswego NY
Shelton JA *ret* Washington DC
Skinner JM *dcn* Utica NY
Smith HA *ret* Manlius NY
Snyder PW *ret* Lititz PA
Stillman AA Deansboro NY
Storey WA Watertown NY
Stuhlman BD *ret* Round Pond ME
Taylor-Weiss DS *ret* Auburn NY
Toof JJ *ret* Wheaton IL
Tottey AG *ret* Clinton NY
Towers RA Ithaca NY
Tulis E
Turner DL *ret* Barnegat Light NJ
Turner WJ *ret* Biltmore Forest NC
Twyman TW *ret* Ashland MA
Van den Blink AJ Elmira NY
Wichelns JB *ret* Carthage NY
Williams CH Portland OR
Williams JA *ret* Cazenovia NY
Wilson KW *ret* Manlius NY

DIOCESE OF CENTRAL PENNSYLVANIA
(PROVINCE III)
Comprises 24 counties in Central Pennsylvania
DIOCESAN OFFICE 101 Pine St Harrisburg PA 17101 (MAIL: Box 11937 Harrisburg PA 17108-1937)
TEL (717) 236-5959   FAX (717) 236-6448
E-MAIL officemailbox@diocesecpa.org   WEB www.diocesecpa.org

Previous Bishops—
Central Pennsylvania: Mark AD
Howe 1871-95, Nelson S Rulison
coadj 1884 Bp 1895-97, Ethelbert
Talbot 1898-1928. *Harrisburg:* James
H Darlington 1905-30, Hunter Wyatt-Brown 1931-43, John T Heistand
1943-66, Earl M Honaman suffr
1956-69. *Central Pennsylvania:* Dean T Stevenson
1966-82, Charlie F McNutt coadj 1980 Bp 1982-95,
Michael W Creighton Bp 1995-2006, Nathan D Baxter Bp 2006-2014, Robert R Gepert Prov Bp 2014-
2015

Bishop—Rt Rev Audrey C Scanlan (1089) (Dio
12 September 2015)

Cn to Ord W Graffius; *Archd for Dcns* Ven J Miron;
Sec T Powell Esq; *Treas* B Chambers; *Treas Emer*
CH Fromer; *Reg* D Robelen; *Chanc* B McLemore;
V Chanc C Banks; *Asst to Bp for Leadership
Development* Very Rev R Szoke; *Ecum* Rev S Claytor;
Deploy Rev P Collins

Stand Comm—Cler: Pres B Hutchinson G Hinton L
Watkins P Pierce K Harrigan C Pinder *Lay:* S Ward
S Schwartz B Johnson C Weaver-Gelzer J Stevenson
S Weedon

Dio Conv: 16 Oct 2015 Altoona PA

PARISHES, MISSIONS, AND CLERGY

Altoona St Luke Episcopal Church **P** (87) 806
13th Street 16602-2422 (Mail to: 806 13th St
16602-2486) Michael Shipman (814) 942-1372
Bedford St James Episcopal Church **P** (59) 309 S
Richard St 15522-1029 (Mail to: 309 S Richard
St 15522-1029) (814) 623-8822
Bellefonte St John's Episcopal Church **P** (249)
120 W Lamb St 16823-1609 (Mail to: 120 W
Lamb St 16823-1609) Christopher Pyles (814)
355-0497
Benton St Gabriel Episcopal Church **P** (18) 7 Saint
Gabriel's Road 17814 (Mail to: PO Box 347
17814-0347) (570) 752-6205
Berwick Christ Episcopal Church **P** (130) 712
E 16th St 18603-2302 (Mail to: 712 E 16th St
18603-2302) Mary Kisner (570) 752-6205
Bloomsburg St Pauls Episcopal Church **P** (136)
101 E Main St 17815-1806 (Mail to: PO Box
764 17815-0764) Howell Sasser (570) 784-3316
Blue Ridge Summit Calvary Chapel **P** (80) 13646
Summit Avenue 17214-0922 (Mail to: PO Box
B 17214-0922) John Mcdowell (717) 794-2229
Blue Ridge Summit Church of the Transfiguration

P (101) 13646 Summit Ave 17214-9758 (Mail
to: PO Box B 17214-0922) John McDowell
(717) 794-2229
Brookland All Saints Episcopal Church **P** (51)
1568 Fox Hill Rd 16948 (Mail to: PO Box 52
16915-0052) Janis Yskamp (814) 274-8391
Camp Hill Mount Calvary Church **P** (539) 125
N 25th St 17011-3609 (Mail to: 125 N 25th St
17011-3609) Duncan Johnston (717) 737-3764
Carlisle St Johns Episcopal Church **P** (634) 1 N
Hanover St # A 17013-3014 (Mail to: PO Box
612 17013-0612) (717) 243-4220
Chambersburg Trinity Episcopal Church **P** (234)
58 S 2nd St 17201-2208 (Mail to: 58 S 2nd St
17201-2208) (717) 264-6351
Columbia St Pauls Episcopal Church **P** (86) 340
Locust St 17512-0096 (Mail to: PO Box 96
17512-0096) J Patrick Peters
Coudersport Christ Episcopal Church **P** (85) 601
N Main St 16915-1703 (Mail to: PO Box 52
16915-0052) Janis Yskamp
Danville Christ Memorial Episcopal Church **P**
(127) 120 E Market St 17821-1942 (Mail to:
PO Box 363 17821-0363) Nancy Shank (570)
275-3903
Eagles Mere St Johns Episcopal Church **SC** 50
Jones Ave 17731-0042 (Mail to: PO Box 352
17731-0352) (215) 242-2945
Exchange St James Episcopal Church **P** (17)
White Hall Rd State Route 44 17772 (Mail to:
PO Box 95 17766-0095) (570) 546-6470
Gettysburg Christ Episcopal Church **SC** C/O Mrs
Jennifer Railing 50 Confederate Dr 17325-8420
(Mail to: PO Box 3005 17325-0005)
Gettysburg Prince of Peace Memorial Church **P**
(244) 20 W High St 17325-2118 (Mail to: PO
Box 3005 17325-0005) Herbert Sprouse (717)
334-6463
Hanover All Saints Church **P** (215) 890 Mccosh
St 17331-1800 (Mail to: 890 McCosh St 17331-
1800) Douglas Smith (717) 637-5772
Harrisburg St Andrews Episcopal Church **P** (280)
1852 Market St 17103-2523 (Mail to: 4620
Linglestown Rd 17112-9521) (717) 234-8815
Harrisburg St Andrews in the Valley Episcopal
P 1852 Market St 17103-2523 (Mail to: 4620
Linglestown Rd 17112-9521) (717) 657-8583
Harrisburg St Pauls Episcopal Church **P** (252)
248 Seneca St 17110-1840 (Mail to: 248 Seneca
St 17110-1840) Kimberly Brooks Katherine
Harrigan Harry Knisely (717) 233-2175
✠ **Harrisburg** St Stephens Cathedral **O** (621) 221
N Front St Ste 101 17101-1407 (Mail to: 221 N
Front St 17101-1437) Churchill Pinder Calvin

Hoyt John Sivley Patrick Strohl Alton Williams (717) 236-4059

Hawk Run Chapel of the Good Shepherd **P** (50) Leonard J Coval Sr Warden 270 Whitman St 16840-0023 (Mail to: PO Box 23 16840-0023) Clifford Johnston (814) 345-5576

Hershey All Saints Episcopal Church **P** (426) 310 Elm Ave 17033-1749 (Mail to: 310 Elm Ave 17033-1749) Susan Claytor (717) 533-2454

Hollidaysburg Church of the Holy Trinity **P** (108) Allegheny & Jones St 16648 (Mail to: 315 Jones St 16648-2007) Jeanne Jacobson (814) 695-7751

Huntingdon St Johns Episcopal Church **P** (89) Patrick A Collins 212 Penn St 16652-1444 (Mail to: 212 Penn St 16652-1444) Gene Tucker (814) 643-4732

Jersey Shore Trinity Episcopal Church **P** (64) 174 Mount Pleasant Ave 17740-1762 (Mail to: 176 Mount Pleasant Ave 17740-1762) Veronica Chappell (570) 398-4007

Lancaster Saint James Episcopal Church **P** (1133) 119 N Duke St 17602-2815 (Mail to: 119 N Duke St 17602-2891) David Peck Lauren Schoeck Robert Schoeck (717) 397-4858

Lancaster St Edward Episcopal Church **P** (387) 2453 Harrisburg Pike 17601-1719 (Mail to: 2453 Harrisburg Pike 17601) Stephen Casey Harold Morrow (717) 898-6276

Lancaster St Johns Episcopal Church **P** (423) 321 W Chestnut St 17603-3509 (Mail to: 321 W Chestnut St 17603-3591) John Morris Barbara Seras (717) 299-1188

Lancaster St Thomas Episcopal Church **P** (317) 301 Saint Thomas Rd 17601-4832 (Mail to: 301 Saint Thomas Rd 17601-4832) (717) 569-3241

Lewisburg St Andrews Episcopal Church **P** (227) 255 S Derr Dr 17837-1722 (Mail to: 255 S Derr Dr 17837-1722) (570) 524-2061

Lewistown St Mark's Episcopal Church **P** (150) 21 S Main St 17044-2116 (Mail to: 21 S Main St 17044-2116) Loretta Collins (717) 248-8327

Lock Haven St Pauls Church **HC** (50) 112 East Main Street 17745-1306 (Mail to: PO Box 206 17745-0206) Daniel Selvage (570) 748-2440

Manheim Hope Episcopal Church **P** (94) 2425 Mountain Rd 17545-8793 (Mail to: 2425 Mountain Rd 17545-8793) Timothy Small (717) 665-6311

Manheim St Pauls Episcopal Church **P** (91) 90 S Charlotte St 17545-1802 (Mail to: 90 S Charlotte St 17545-1802) (717) 665-6584

Mansfield St James Episcopal Church **P** (50) 30 E Wellsboro St 16933-1121 (Mail to: 30 E Wellsboro St 16933-1121) Rowena Gibbons (570) 662-2003

Marietta St Johns Church **P** (63) 239 E Market St 17547-1533 (Mail to: PO Box 98 17547-0098) (717) 426-3189

Mechanicsburg St Lukes Episcopal Church **P** (260) 8 E Keller St 17055-3826 (Mail to: 8 E

Keller St 17055-3826) Thomas Joyce David Ster (717) 766-5182

Milton Christ Episcopal Church **P** (28) 21 Upper Market St 17847-1225 (Mail to: 21 Upper Market St 17847) Robert Van Deusen (570) 742-4153

Montoursville Church of Our Saviour **P** (39) 31 N Loyalsock Ave 17754-1703 (Mail to: 31 N Loyalsock Ave 17754-1703) (570) 368-1860

Montoursville Church of the Good Shepherd **P** (13) 827 Good Shepherd Rd 17754-7532 (Mail to: 827 Good Shepherd Rd 17754-7532) (570) 433-3823

Mount Carmel St Stephens Church **P** (27) Fourth & Maple Sts 17851 (Mail to: PO Box 353 17851-0353) (570) 339-1307

Mount Joy St Lukes Episcopal Church **P** (163) 209 S Market St 17552-3109 (Mail to: 209 S Market St 17552-3109) Eleanor Hart Garner (717) 653-4977

Muncy St James Episcopal Church **P** (61) 215 S Main St 17756-1505 (Mail to: PO Box 95 17756-0095) David Culbertson (570) 546-6470

Narvon Bangor Episcopal Church **P** (100) 2099 Main St 17555-9521 (Mail to: 2099 Main St 17555-9521) William Murphey (717) 445-0253

Newport Nativity& St Stephens Episcopal Parish **P** (124) No 159 S 2nd St 17074-1407 (Mail to: 159 S 2nd St 17074-1407) Rebecca Myers (717) 567-6514

Northumberlnd St Mark Episcopal Church **P** (32) 187 King St 17857-1653 (Mail to: 187 King St 17857-1653) Robert Van Deusen (570) 473-3220

Philipsburg St Pauls Church **P** (267) 406 E Presqueisle St 16866 (Mail to: PO Box 170 16866-0170) (814) 342-3180

Renovo Trinity Episcopal Church **P** (22) 137 3rd St 17764-0206 (Mail to: PO Box 206 17764-0206) John Harwood (570) 923-0571

Selinsgrove All Saints Episcopal Church **P** (46) 129 N Market St 17870-1905 (Mail to: PO Box 119 17870-1905) Paul Donecker (570) 374-8289

Shamokin Holy Trinity Episcopal Church **P** (70) 150 E Lincoln St 17872-5637 (Mail to: 150 E Lincoln St 17872-5637) Sarah Weedon (570) 648-6152

Shippensburg St Andrews Episcopal Church **P** (243) 206 E Burd St 17257-1402 (Mail to: 206 E Burd St 17257-1402) Barbara Hutchinson (717) 532-8089

State College St Andrews Church **P** (908) 208 W Foster Ave 16801-4822 (Mail to: 208 W Foster Ave 16801-4822) Richard Wall Christian Brady Charles Cruikshank Douglas Dailey Joseph DeLauter (814) 237-7659

Sunbury St Matthews Episcopal Church **P** (265) 32 N Front St 17801-2140 (Mail to: 32 N Front St 17801-2140) Robin Jarrell (570) 286-7002

Thompsontown St Stephens Episcopal Church

HC East Main St 17094 (Mail to: E Main St 17094-9752) (717) 567-6514

Tioga St Andrews Episcopal Church **P** (49) Main St 16946 (Mail to: PO Box 386 16946-0386) Rudolph Van Der Hiel (570) 662-7600

Tyrone Trinity Episcopal Church **P** (99) 830 Washington Ave 16686-1345 (Mail to: 830 Washington Ave 16686-1345) Jack Hoffer (814) 684-3100

University Park St Francis Episcopal Ministry **CC** 210 Eisenhower Chapel 16802-1905 (Mail to: 210 Eisenhower Chapel 16802-1905) (814) 865-3762

Waynesboro St Marys Episcopal Church **P** (138) 112 E 2nd St 17268-1603 (Mail to: 112 E 2nd St 17268-1603) Linda Watkins (717) 762-1930

Wellsboro St Pauls Episcopal Church **HC** (246) 29 Charles St 16901-1408 (Mail to: PO Box 701 16901-0701) Gregory Hinton (570) 724-4771

Westfield St Johns Church **P** (37) 205 Elm St 16950-1507 (Mail to: 205 Elm St 16950-1507) (814) 367-2245

Williamsport All Saints Memorial Church **P** (68) 1656 Scott St 17701-4459 (Mail to: 1656 Scott St 17701-4459) (570) 326-0191

Williamsport Christ Episcopal Church **P** (117) 426 Mulberry St 17701-6312 (Mail to: 426 Mulberry St 17701-6312) (570) 322-8160

Williamsport Trinity Episcopal Church **P** (366) 844 W 4th St 17701-5824 (Mail to: 844 W 4th St 17701-5824) Kenneth Wagner-Pizza (570) 322-0126

York St Andrews Episcopal Church **P** (353) 1502 4th Ave 17403-2623 (Mail to: 1502 4th Ave 17403-2623) David Robson Carol Snell (717) 843-3868

York St John The Baptist Episcopal Church **P** (460) 140 N Beaver St 17403-5324 (Mail to: 140 N Beaver St 17401-5324) David Lovelace Janet Brown Joseph Seville (717) 848-1862

NON-PAROCHIAL CLERGY

Alford WT *ret* Centreville MD
Avcin JE Harrisburg PA
Babcock TS *ret* Mt Lebanon PA
Baker CD Shippensburg PA
Barrett RL
Bateman DS Harrisburg PA
Bond JW *ret* Grover Beach CA
Broucht ML *ret dcn* Lancaster PA
Calhoun DM Jersey Mills PA
Clark VN *ret* Tyrone PA
Cohoon RA *ret* Lock Haven PA
Collins PA Harrisburg PA
Conway N Salem SC
Cooper MS *ret* Hughesville PA
Crews ND *ret* Annapolis MD
Dyakiw AR *dcn* Bellefonte PA
Edson JB *ret* Dillsburg PA
Emmert JH *ret* Manheim PA

France AM *ret* Williamsport PA
Fritz JV *dcn* Boiling Springs PA
Gardner JE *ret* Lewisburg PA
Gdula PM *dcn* Mechanicsburg PA
Gill RC *dcn* York PA
Ginolfi PG *dcn* Lancaster PA
Greenfield PA *ret* Lancaster PA
Harer MP *ret* Lewisburg PA
Harlacher RC *ret* Palmyra PA
Harper DS *ret* Harrisburg PA
Harris SD *ret* Gettysburg PA
Hartley LH Lancaster PA
Hary BA *dcn* Middletown PA
Hofer LJ *ret* Lewes DE
Hoover JF *ret* Lewisburg PA
Imboden SF *ret* Lititz PA
Kern RA *dcn* Elliottsburg PA
Kerr LA Williamsport PA
Klimas ML *ret* Atlanta GA
Kloza WM *dcn* Harrisburg PA
Lawbaugh WM *ret* Aliquippa PA
Leigh-Koser CM Wrightsville PA
Lindberg RM *ret* Swanzey NH
Looker JE New Haven CT
McGill WJ Cornwall PA
McNamara JF *ret* Mansfield PA
Mead AC *ret* Virginia Beach VA
Mease CA *dcn* Middletown PA
Menaul MA *ret* Columbus OH
Messersmith DS *ret* Duncannon PA
Messersmith ME *ret* Mechanicsburg PA
Miller FM *ret* Mechanicsburg PA
Miller WR *dcn*
Miron JE *dcn*
Mollard EMC *ret* Elizabethtown PA
Naegele JA *ret* Annapolis MD
Peck EJ *ret* Fayetteville PA
Pierce PA *ret* Mercersburg PA
Randall RA *ret* Chambersburg PA
Rementer NS *dcn* Marietta PA
Scheneman MA *ret* Carlisle PA
Schoonmaker LK Lewistown PA
Shanahan TW *ret* Washington DC
Silverstrim EM *ret* Coudersport PA
Smits HJ *ret* York PA
Solbak MM *ret dcn* Lititz PA
Stevenson FG *ret* Hanover PA
Stiscia AR *ret* Bradenton FL
Stump DW *ret* State College PA
Szoke RJ Carlisle PA
Tallevast WD Tucson AZ
Taylor BM *ret dcn* Harrisburg PA
Thomas EE Charlottesville VA
Towers PW Endwell NY
Underwood RF *ret* Sarasota FL
Walker WR *ret* Philipsburg PA
Warne WT *ret* Lake Winola PA
Whitesel AB *dcn* Carlisle PA
Wible TL *ret* New Oxford PA
Zwifka D Lewistown PA

DIOCESE OF CHICAGO
(PROVINCE V)
Comprises Northern and Western Illinois
DIOCESAN OFFICE 65 E Huron St Chicago IL 60611
TEL (312) 751-4200   FAX (312) 787-5872
E-MAIL Bishop@episcopalchicago.org   WEB www.episcopalchicago.org

Previous Bishops—
Philander Chase 1835-52, Henry J White house coadj 1851 Bp 1852-74, Wm E McLaren 1875-1905, Chas P Anderson coadj 1900 Bp 1905-30, Wm E Toll suffr 1911-15, Sheldon M Griswold suffr 1917 Bp 1930-30, Geo C Stewart coadj 1930 Bp 1930-40, Edwin J Randall suffr 1939-47, Wallace E Conkling 1941-53, Chas L St suffr 1949-63, Gerald F Burrill 1954-71, Quintin E Primo Jr suffr 1972-84, James W Montgomery suffr 1962-65 coadj 1965 Bp 1971-87, William W Wiedrich suffr 1990-97, Frank T Griswold coadj 1985-87 Bp 1987-98, HA Donavan prov 1998-99, William D Persell Bp 1999-2008, Victor A Scantlebury asst 2000-11, John C Buchanan asst Bp 2014, C Christopher Epting asst Bp 2012-15

Bishop—Rt Rev Jeffrey D Lee (1026) (Dio 2 Feb 2008)

Dir of Min J Steen; *Treas* K Kampert; *Christian Form V* Garvey; *Yth/Young Adult Min* C Senuta; *Hist* N Smith; *Chanc* M Peregrine; *Sec Conv* Rev E Bellis; *Dir Operations* C Reid; *Dir Networking* JB Burrows *Dio Commissions: Anti-Racism:* S Soto; *Congregations* K Wagner Sherer A Mysen

Stand Comm—Cler: M Humm E Biddy V Conrado; *Lay:* K Leson D Dawson S McPhee

Deans—Aurora G Smith; *Chgo-N* J VanDooren; *Chgo-S* P Lane; *Elgin* ME Eccles; *Evanston* K White; *Joliet* K Orr; *Oak Park* C Pierce; *Peoria* Deanery R Hungerford; *Rockford* S Walker-Frontjes; *Waukegan* E Shanley-Roberts

Dio Conv: 18-19 Nov 2016

PARISHES, MISSIONS, AND CLERGY

Antioch St Ignatius of Antioch Church **P** (215) 500 E Depot St 60002-1564 (Mail to: 500 E Depot St 60002-1564) Timothy Squier (847) 395-0652

Arlington Hts St Simons Episcopal Church **P** (450) 717 W Kirchhoff Rd 60005-2339 (Mail to: 717 W Kirchhoff Rd 60005-2339) Elizabeth Jameson Larry Handwerk (847) 259-2930

Aurora St Davids Episcopal Church **P** (86) 701 N Randall Rd 60506-1923 (Mail to: 701 N Randall Rd 60506-1918) Robert Lambert (630) 896-7229

Aurora Trinity Church **P** (85) 218 E Benton St 60505-4250 (Mail to: 218 E Benton St 60505-4250) John Dolan Denzil Luckritz Thomas Rosa

Barrington St Marks Episcopal Church **P** (328) 337 Ridge Rd 60010-2331 (Mail to: 337 Ridge Rd 60010-2331) David Gibbons (847) 381-0596

Barrington St Michaels Episcopal Church **P** (880) 647 Dundee Ave 60010-4258 (Mail to: 647 Dundee Ave 60010-4258) Judith Heinrich Laurie Michaels (847) 381-2323

Batavia Calvary Episcopal Church **P** (261) 222 S Batavia Ave 60510-2564 (Mail to: 222 S Batavia Ave 60510-2564) Michael Rasicci (630) 879-3378

Belvidere Church of the Holy Trinity **P** (110) 217 E Hurlbut Ave 61008-3216 (Mail to: 217 E Hurlbut Ave 61008-3216) Randal Wakitsch (815) 544-2635

Benson Zion Episcopal Church **M** E/S Route 150 61516 (Mail to: 3601 N North St 61604-1548) (309) 685-8682

Berwyn St Michael & All Angels Episcopal Ch **P** (190) 6732 W 34th St 60402 (Mail to: 6732 34th St 60402-3412) (708) 788-2197

Bloomingdale Church of the Incarnation **M** (37) 261 W Army Trail Rd 60108-1376 (Mail to: 261 W Army Trail Rd 60108-1376) Maurice Strong Louisett Ness (630) 351-3249

Bloomingdale First Asian Church **P** (70) 261 W Army Trail Rd 60108-1376 (Mail to: 261 W Army Trail Rd 60108-1376) Simon Singh (630) 351-3293

Blue Island St Josephs & St Aidans Church **M** (67) Oak St & Greenwood Ave 60406 (Mail to: Oak St & Greenwood Ave 60406) Rebecca Sperry (708) 389-5933

Bolingbrook Episcopal Church of St Benedict **M** (130) 909 Lily Cache Ln 60440-3131 (Mail to: 909 Lily Cache Ln 60440-3131) Heidi Haverkamp (630) 759-5955

Canton St Peters Episcopal Church **M** 170 E Locust St 61520-1925 (Mail to: 3601 N North St 61604-1548) (309) 685-8673

Chicago All Saints Episcopal Church **P** (665) 4550 N Hermitage Ave 60640-5304 (Mail to: 4550 N Hermitage Ave 60640-5304) Bonnie Perry Emily Guffey (773) 561-0111

✠ **Chicago** Cathedral of St James **O** (647) No 65 E Huron St 60611-2728 (Mail to: 65 E Huron St 60611-2728) Dominic Barrington Lisa Hackney Dolores Neighbors (312) 787-7360

Chicago Church of Our Saviour **P** (627) 530 W Fullerton Pkwy 60614-5919 (Mail to: 530 W Fullerton Pkwy 60614-5919) Brian Hastings Jessica Elfring-Roberts Richard Wendel (773) 549-3832

Chicago Church of St Chrysostoms **P** (1227) 1424 N Dearborn St 60610-1506 (Mail to: 1424 N Dearborn St 60610-1506) Kevin Goodman Larry Green Walter Smedley (312) 944-1083

Chicago Church of St Pauls by-the-Lake **P** (431) 7100 N Ashland Blvd 60626-2502 (Mail to: 7100 N Ashland Blvd 60626-2502) John Heschle Matthew Kemp

Chicago Church of St Thomas **P** (170) 3801 S Wabash Ave 60653-1520 (Mail to: 3801 S Wabash Ave 60653-1520) Fulton Porter (773) 268-1900

Chicago Church of the Advent **P** (65) 2900 W Logan Blvd 60647-1732 (Mail to: 2610 N Francisco Ave 60647-1794) (773) 304-5003

Chicago Church of the Ascension **P** (208) 1133 N LaSalle Dr 60610-2601 (Mail to: 1133 N LaSalle Blvd 60610-2601) David Cobb Shane Gormley (312) 664-1271

Chicago Church of the Atonement **P** (440) 5749 N Kenmore Ave 60660-4541 (Mail to: 5749 N Kenmore Ave 60660-4541) John Van Dooren Ted Durst Barbara Henry Sterling Minturn (773) 271-2727

Chicago Church of the Holy Cross **P** (18) 1201 W 111th Pl 60643-4513 (Mail to: 1201 W 111th Pl 60643) Tyrone Fowlkes (773) 779-0777

Chicago Church of the Holy Nativity **P** (101) 9300 S Pleasant Ave 60620-5644 (Mail to: 9300 S Pleasant Ave 60643-6344) Regina Volpe (773) 445-4427

Chicago El Cristo Rey Mission **M** (322) Y814 60646-4217 (Mail to: 5101 W Devon Ave 60646-4217) Alvaro Araica (773) 561-8189

Chicago Grace Episcopal Church **P** (108) 637 S Dearborn St 60605-1839 (Mail to: 637 S Dearborn St Ste 1 60605-1839) Ethan Jewett Sunny Lopez James Mcknight (312) 922-1426

Chicago Messiah St Bartholomew Episcopal Church **P** (96) 8255 S Dante Ave 60619-4623 (Mail to: 8255 S Dante Ave 60619-4623) (773) 721-3232

Chicago Nuestra Senora de las Americas **M** (147) 2610 N Francisco Ave 60647-1704 (Mail to: 2610 N Francisco Ave 60647-1704) Maria Munoz (872) 206-2631

Chicago Santa Teresa de Avila **M** (71) No 6201 S Saint Louis Ave 60629-3713 (Mail to: 6201 S Saint Louis Ave 60629-3713) Gary Cox (773) 434-9783

Chicago St Albans Episcopal Church **P** (130) 6240 N Avondale Ave 60631-2452 (Mail to: 6240 N Avondale Ave 60631-2452) Mary Milano (773) 599-2545

Chicago St Andrews Chaplaincy **PS** (20) 48 N Hoyne Ave 60612-2358 (Mail to: 48 N Hoyne Ave 60612-2358) Edward Bird (312) 226-7205

Chicago St Edmunds Episcopal Church **P** (512) 6105 S Michigan Ave 60637-2119 (Mail to: 6105 S Michigan Ave 60637-2119) Richard Tolliver David Stanford (773) 288-0038

Chicago St Johns Episcopal Church **P** (224) 3857 N Kostner Ave 60641-2851 (Mail to: 3857 N Kostner Ave 60641-2851) Kara Wagner Sherer (773) 725-9026

Chicago St Margaret of Scotland **M** (152) 2555 E 73rd St 60649-2616 (Mail to: 2555 E 73rd St 60649-2616) (773) 221-5505

Chicago St Martins Episcopal Church **M** (80) 5710 W Midway Park 60644-1818 (Mail to: 5700 W Midway Park Ave 60644-1818) Christopher Griffin (773) 378-8111

Chicago St Pauls & Redeemer Church **P** (600) 4945 S Dorchester A 60615-2907 (Mail to: 4945 S Dorchester Ave 60615-2907) Amity Carrubba Peter Lane Daniel Puchalla (773) 624-3185

Chicago St Peters Episcopal Church **P** (182) 621 W Belmont Ave 60657-4510 (Mail to: 621 W Belmont Ave 60657-4510) Samuel Colley-Toothaker Nancy Meyer Norma Sutton Ellen Wondra (773) 525-0844

Chicago Sts George & Matthias Church **M** (70) 164 E 111th St 60628-4346 (Mail to: 11219 S Forrestville 60628-4605) Robert Cristobal Gwendolyn Dillon

Chicago Trinity Church **P** (137) 125 E 26th St 60616-2310 (Mail to: 125 E 26th St 60616-2310) (312) 842-7545

Chillicothe St Francis Episcopal Church **M** 616 W Wilmot St 61523-1134 (Mail to: 12200 N Brentfield Dr Ste J 61525-9403) (309) 685-8673

Clarendon Hls Church of the Holy Nativity **P** (256) 275 S Richmond Ave 60514-2711 (Mail to: 275 S Richmond Ave 60514-2711) Elizabeth Meade Kathie Tepavchevich (630) 323-6820

Crystal Lake St Marys Episcopal Church **P** (265) 210 McHenry Ave 60014-6009 (Mail to: 210 S McHenry Ave 60014-6009) Frances Holliday Barbara Bishop Diane Koenig (815) 459-1009

Deerfield St Gregory's Episcopal Church **P** (432) Deerfield & Wilmot Rds 60015 (Mail to: 815 Wilmot Rd 60015-2723) Scott Elliott Dennis Lietz Meredith Potter (847) 945-1678

DeKalb St Pauls Episcopal Church **P** (118) 900 Normal Rd 60115-1614 (Mail to: 900 Normal Rd 60115-1614) Stacy Walker-Frontjes Joyce Beaulieu Charles Wilson (815) 756-4888

Des Plaines St Martin's Episcopal Church **HC** (208) 1095 E Thacker St 60016-3361 (Mail to: 1095 E Thacker St 60016-3361) Margot Eccles (847) 824-2043

Dixon St Lukes Episcopal Church **P** (100) 221 W 3rd St 61021-3015 (Mail to: PO Box 494 61021-0494) Richard Frontjes (815) 288-2151

Downers Grove St Andrews Episcopal Church **P** (773) 1125 Franklin St 60515-3551 (Mail to: 1125 Franklin St 60515-3599) Gregg Morris Thomas Craighead (630) 968-9188

Dundee St James Episcopal Church **P** (174) 516 Washington St 60118-1245 (Mail to: 516 Washington St 60118-1245) Donald Frye

Darby Everhard (847) 426-5612

El Paso St Andrews Episcopal Church **M** 98 N Cherry St 61738-1160 (Mail to: 3601 N North St 61604-1548) (309) 685-8673

Elgin Church of St Hugh of Lincoln **P** (199) 36w957 Highland Ave 60123-4875 (Mail to: 36 W 957 Highland Ave 60123-4875) Marion Phipps

Elgin Church of the Redeemer **P** (679) 40 Center St 60120-5609 (Mail to: 40 Center St 60120-5609) Uriel Lopez Amity Carrubba Mary Harriss (847) 742-2428

Elk Grove Vlg St Nicholas Episcopal Church **M** (158) 1072 Ridge Ave 60007-4642 (Mail to: 1072 Ridge Ave 60007-4642) Manuel Borg (847) 439-2067

Elmhurst Church of Our Saviour **P** (176) 116 E Church St 60126-3404 (Mail to: 116 E Church St 60126-3404) Robert Petite (630) 530-1434

Evanston St Andrews Episcopal Church **M** (152) 1928 Darrow Ave 60201-3404 (Mail to: 1928 Darrow Ave 60201-3404) Chukwuemeka Nwachuku (847) 328-4751

Evanston St Lukes Episcopal Church **P** (896) 939 Hinman Ave 60202-1801 (Mail to: 939 Hinman Ave 60202-1801) Kathryn Banakis John Connelly Jeannette Defriest Robert Fite Gloria Hopewell William Waff (847) 475-3630

Evanston St Marks Episcopal Church **P** (213) 1509 Ridge Ave 60201-4135 (Mail to: 1509 Ridge Ave 60201-4135) Debra Bullock (847) 864-4806

Evanston St Matthew's Episcopal Church **P** (416) 2120 Lincoln St 60201-2282 (Mail to: 2120 Lincoln St 60201-2282) Charles De Kay

Flossmoor Church of St John the Evangelist **P** (367) 2640 Park Dr 60422-1228 (Mail to: PO Box 25 60422-0025) Kristin Orr (708) 798-4150

Freeport Grace Episcopal Church **P** (376) 10 S Cherry Ave 61032-5069 (Mail to: 10 S Cherry Ave 61032-5069) Eldred George Allen (815) 232-4422

Galena Grace Episcopal Church **P** (125) PO Box 228 61036-0228 (Mail to: 309 Hill St 61036-1803) Gloria Hopewell (815) 777-2590

Galesburg Grace Episcopal Church **HC** (24) 60 Public Square 61401 (Mail to: PO Box 218 61402-0218) (309) 255-5916

Geneseo Holy Trinity Episcopal Church **M** 201 W North St 61254-1413 (Mail to: 3601 N North St 61604-1548) (309) 685-8673

Geneva St Marks Episcopal Church **P** (1179) 320 Franklin Street 60134-2639 (Mail to: 320 Franklin Street 60134-2639) Mark Tusken David Baughman William Kruse Robert Lowe Claudia Nalven (630) 232-0133

Glen Ellyn St Barnabas Episcopal Church **P** (206) No 22 W 415 Butterfield Rd 60137 (Mail to: 22 W 415 Butterfield Rd 60137-7164) Natalie Van Kirk Carol Kraft (630) 469-1394

Glen Ellyn St Mark's Episcopal Church **P** (1628) 393 North Main Street 60137-5068 (Mail to: 393 North Main Street 60137-5068) George Smith Victor Conrado Varela Walter Dunnett (630) 858-1020

Glencoe St Elisabeths Episcopal Church **P** (131) 556 Vernon Ave 60022-1647 (Mail to: 556 Vernon Ave 60022-1647) Daphne Cody Larry Handwerk (847) 835-0458

Glenview St Davids Episcopal Church **P** (532) 2410 Glenview Rd 60025-2713 (Mail to: 2410 Glenview Rd 60025-2713) Susan Sommer Thomas Aman (847) 724-1341

Grayslake St Andrews Episcopal Church **P** (156) 31 Park Ave 60030-2334 (Mail to: 31 Park Ave 60030-2334) Jane Clark (847) 223-2310

Griggsville St James Episcopal Church **M** (20) 409 S Union St 62340 (Mail to: PO Box 463 62340-0463) William Roeger (573) 221-9111

Gurnee Annunciation of Our Lady **P** (270) 5725 Stearns School Rd 60031-4520 (Mail to: 5725 Stearns School Rd 60031-4520) Elizabeth Molitors (847) 336-3730

Hanover Park Church of St Columba of Iona **P** (36) 1800 W Irving Rd 60103-3253 (Mail to: 1800 W Irving Rd 60103-3253) Mathew Idicula (630) 289-1574

Harvey St Clements Episcopal Church **P** (125) 15245 Loomis Ave 60426-3117 (Mail to: PO Box 2307 60426-8307)

Henry St Johns Fpiscopal Church **M** 807 3rd St 61537-1448 (Mail to: 3601 N North St 61604-1548) (309) 685-8673

Highland Park Trinity Episcopal Church **P** (376) 425 Laurel Ave 60035-2652 (Mail to: 425 Laurel Ave 60035-2652) Courtlyn Williams (847) 432-6653

Hinsdale Grace Episcopal Church **P** (630) 120 E 1st St 60521-4202 (Mail to: 120 E 1st St 60521-4291) Charles Pierce Robert Wyatt (630) 323-4900

Hinsdale St Helena Episcopal Church **P** (142) 120 E First St 60521 (Mail to: 120 E First St 60521) Luis Andrade (630) 323-4900

Joliet St Edward and Christ Episcopal Church **P** (183) 206 N Midland Ave 60435-6838 (Mail to: 206 N Midland Ave 60435-6838) Kathryn White Richard Lundgren (815) 725-6800

Kankakee St Pauls Episcopal Church **P** (167) St Paul's Episcopal Church 298 South Harrison Avenue 60901-4095 (Mail to: St Paul's Episcopal Church 298 South Harrison Avenue 60901-4095) Israel Anchan (815) 932-6611

Kenilworth The Church of the Holy Comforter **P** (843) 222 Kenilworth Ave 60043-1243 (Mail to: 222 Kenilworth Ave 60043-1243) Jason Parkin John Hardman Heath Howe George Hull (847) 251-6120

Kewanee St Johns Episcopal Church **P** (54) 123 S Chestnut St 61443-2121 (Mail to: PO Box 268 61443-0268) Thomas Stone (309) 853-1421

LaGrange Emmanuel Episcopal Church **P** (371) 203 S Kensington Ave 60525-2216 (Mail to: 203 S Kensington Ave 60525-2216) William Rimkus John Thompson (708) 352-1275

Lake Forest Church of the Holy Spirit **P** (2270) 400 E Westminster Rd 60045-2258 (Mail to: 400 E Westminster Rd 60045-2258) Alan James Judith Doran Sarah Odderstol (847) 234-7633

Lake Villa Church of the Holy Family **M** (159) 25291 W Lehmann Blvd 60046-9705 (Mail to: 25291 W Lehmann Blvd 60046-9705) Jose Arroyo (847) 356-7222

LaSalle St Paul Episcopal Church **M** (51) 344 Joliet St 61301-2128 (Mail to: 344 Joliet St 61301-2128) Mark Geisler (815) 220-0238

Lewistown St James Episcopal Church **M** (69) 420 E. MacArthur Ave. 61542-1250 (Mail to: PO Box 63 61542-0063) Barbara Sinclair (309) 543-4248

Libertyville St Lawrence Episcopal Church **P** (540) 125 W Church St 60048-2149 (Mail to: 125 W Church St 60048-2149) Patricia Snickenberger Harold Toberman (847) 362-2110

Lockport St Johns Episcopal Church **M** (223) 312 E 11th St 60441-3421 (Mail to: 312 E 11th St 60441-3421) Richard Humm Roberta Molony (815) 834-1168

Lombard Calvary Episcopal Church **P** (303) 105 W Maple St 60148-2513 (Mail to: 105 W Maple St 60148-2513) Emily Mellott (630) 620-8899

Loves Park St Chad Episcopal Church **M** (101) 6245 N 2nd St 61111-4100 (Mail to: 6245 N 2nd St 61111-4100) Regina Brenmark-French Joan Clark (815) 633-6633

Macomb St Georges Church **P** (16) 321 1/2 W University Dr 61455-1144 (Mail to: 622 Beverly Ave 61455-3004) (309) 421-0142

McHenry St Paul's Episcopal Church **P** (167) 3706 W Saint Paul Ave 60050-6108 (Mail to: 3706 W Saint Paul Ave 60050-6108) Lori Lowe William McLemore

Moline All Saints Episcopal Church **M** (79) P O Box 482 91265 (Mail to: PO Box 482 61266-0482) Roger Hungerford (309) 797-2515

Moline Christ Episcopal Church **M** 1717 8th Ave 61265-2119 (Mail to: 1717 8th Ave 61265-2119) (309) 685-8673

Momence Church of the Good Shepherd **M** (46) 123 E 2nd St 60954-1501 (Mail to: 123 E 2nd St 60954-1501) (815) 472-4625

Monmouth Trinity Episcopal Church **M** 125 N 2nd St 61462-1818 (Mail to: 3601 N North St 61604-1548) (309) 685-8682

Morris St Thomas Episcopal Church **P** (80) 317 Goold Park Dr 60450-1721 (Mail to: 317 Goold Park Dr 60450-1721) James Steele Charlotte Bates (815) 942-1380

Morrison St Annes Episcopal Church **P** (68) 401 N Cherry St 61270-2606 (Mail to: 401 N Cherry St 61270-2606) James Clement (815)

772-2818

Naperville St Johns Episcopal Church **P** (701) 750 Aurora Ave 60540-6276 (Mail to: 750 Aurora Ave 60540-6276) Verna Fair (630) 355-0467

New Lenox Grace Episcopal Church **M** (128) 114 N Pine St 60451-1748 (Mail to: 209 N Pine St 60451-1765) Ellen Ekevag (815) 485-6596

Northbrook St Giles Episcopal Church **P** (113) 3025 Walters Ave 60062-4370 (Mail to: 3025 Walters Ave 60062-4370) Cynthia Hallas Belinda Chandler Lee Gaede (847) 272-6622

Northfield St James the Less Episcopal Church **P** (306) 550 Sunset Ridge Rd 60093-1027 (Mail to: 550 Sunset Ridge Rd 60093-1027) Lisa Senuta (847) 446-8430

Oak Park Grace Episcopal Church **P** (475) 924 Lake St 60301-1204 (Mail to: 924 Lake St 60301-1204) Jonathan Baumgarten Shawn Schreiner Clayton Thomason (708) 386-8036

Oak Park St Christophers Episcopal Church **P** (338) 545 S East Ave 60304-1321 (Mail to: 545 S East Ave 60304-1321) Eric Biddy (708) 386-5613

Oregon St Bride Episcopal Church **M** (92) 1000 W Il Route 64 61061-9350 (Mail to: PO Box 223 61061-0223) Barbara Seward (815) 732-7211

Ottawa Christ Episcopal Church **P** (103) C/O Fran Gibson 926 Columbus St 61350-2103 (Mail to: Attn Fran Gibson 113 E Lafayette St 61350-2114) Mark Geisler (815) 434-0627

Palatine St Philips Episcopal Church **P** (192) 342 E Wood St 60067-5336 (Mail to: 342 E Wood St 60067-5336) Laura Gottardi-Littell (847) 358-0615

Palos Park Church of the Transfiguration **P** (280) 12219 S 86th Ave 60464-1263 (Mail to: 12219 S 86th Ave 60464-1263) John Nachtrieb Nicholas Romans (708) 448-1200

Park Forest Church of the Holy Family **P** (291) Sauk Trl & Orchard Dr 60466 (Mail to: 102 Marquette St 60466-2016) Elizabeth Lloyd (708) 748-1100

Park Ridge St Marys Episcopal Church **P** (703) 306 S Prospect Ave 60068-4039 (Mail to: 306 S Prospect Ave 60068-4039) Edward Bird Joseph Czolgosz Martha Durham David Grauer Michael Kitt Patrick Skutch (847) 823-4126

Peoria St Andrews Episcopal Church **M** 1601 NE Madison Ave 61603-3454 (Mail to: 3601 N North St 61604-1548) (309) 685-8673

Peoria St Paul's Episcopal Church **P** (324) 3601 N North St 61604-1548 (Mail to: 3601 N North St 61604-1548) Jennifer Replogle Jonathan Thomas (309) 688-3436

Pontiac Grace Episcopal Church **P** (91) 410 E Torrance Ave 61764-2703 (Mail to: 900 S Manlove St 61764-2605) Mark Middleton (815) 842-1743

Preemption St Johns Episcopal Church **M** 2406 170th Ave 61276 (Mail to: 3601 N North St

61604-1548) (309) 685-8673

Princeton Church of the Transfiguration **M** 101 Bryant Woods Dr 61356-2349 (Mail to: 3601 N North St 61604-1548) (309) 685-8673

Prospect Heights One in Christ Episcopal Church **M** (158) 307 W Hintz Rd 60070-1020 (Mail to: 307 W Hintz Rd 60070-1020) Indon Joo Solomon Lee (847) 537-0590

Quincy St Clares Church **M** 1425 College Ave 62301-2634 (Mail to: 3601 N North St 61604-1548) (309) 685-8673

Quincy St Johns Episcopal Church **M** 701 Hampshire St 62301-3013 (Mail to: 3601 N North St 61604-1548) (309) 685-8673

River Forest Christ Episcopal Church **P** (54) 515 Franklin Ave 60305-1719 (Mail to: 515 Franklin Ave 60305-1719) Peter Campbell (708) 366-7730

Riverside St Pauls Episcopal Church **P** (32) 60 Akenside Rd 60546-1809 (Mail to: 60 Akenside Rd 60546-1809) Thomas Fraser Richard Daly (708) 447-1604

Rock Island Trinity Episcopal Church **M** 1818 6th Ave 61201-8120 (Mail to: 3601 N North St 61604-1548) (309) 685-8673

Rockford Emmanuel Episcopal Church **P** (262) 412 N Church St 61103-6811 (Mail to: 412 N Church St 61103-6811) Thomas Rosa Andria Skornik (815) 964-5514

Rockford St Anskar Episcopal Church **P** (94) 4801 Spring Creek Rd 61114-6321 (Mail to: 4801 Spring Creek Rd 61114-6321) Andrea Wight (815) 877-1226

Savanna St Pauls Episcopal Church **M** (13) No 305 Washington St 61074-1945 (Mail to: 304 Washington St 61074-1511) Robert North (815) 273-7672

Silvis St Marks Episcopal Church **M** 1550 7th Ave 61282-2611 (Mail to: 3601 N North St 61604-1548) (309) 685-8673

St. Charles St Charles Church Episcopal **P** (341) 994 N 5th Ave 60174-1227 (Mail to: 994 N 5th Ave 60174-1227) Elizabeth Meade (630) 584-2596

Sterling Grace EpiscopalChurch **P** (108) 707 1st Ave 61081-3622 (Mail to: 707 1st Ave 61081-3622) David Rude (815) 625-0442

Streator Christ Episcopal Church **P** (28) 132 S Vermillion St 61364-2936 (Mail to: 132 S Vermillion St 61364-2936) (815) 672-2479

Sycamore Saint Peter's Episcopal Church **P** (164) 218 Somonauk St 60178-1845 (Mail to: 218 Somonauk St 60178-1845) David Hedges Amy Fallon Desiree Goodale-Mikosz (815) 895-2227

Warsaw St Pauls Episcopal Church **M** (83) 240 S 4th St 62379-1205 (Mail to: 240 S 4th St 62379-1205) Larry Snyder (217) 256-4558

Wauconda Church of the Holy Apostles **M** (62) 26238 N Il Route 59 60084-2332 (Mail to: 26238 N Highway 59 60084-2332) Martha

Gillette (847) 526-7148

Waukegan Christ Episcopal Church **P** (410) 410 Grand Ave 60085-4227 (Mail to: 410 Grand Ave 60085-4227) Eileen Shanley-Roberts (847) 662-7081

Waukegan Nuestra Senora de Guadalupe **M** (905) 2415 N Butrick St 60087-3048 (Mail to: 2415 N Butrick St 60087-3048) Narciso Diaz (847) 599-3051

Western Sprgs All Saints Episcopal Church **P** (141) 4370 Woodland Ave 60558-1458 (Mail to: 4370 Woodland Ave 60558-1458) Katherine Spelman (708) 246-0030

Wheaton Trinity Church **P** (553) 130 N West St 60187-5062 (Mail to: 130 N West St 60187-5097) Kevin Caruso James Lanning

Wilmette St Augustines Episcopal Church **P** (292) 1140 Wilmette Ave 60091-2604 (Mail to: 1140 Wilmette Ave 60091-2670) Bryan Cones Sylvia Nebel Kristin White (847) 251-6922

Winnetka Christ Episcopal Church **P** (1494) 784 Sheridan Rd 60093 (Mail to: 470 Maple St 60093-2652) Christopher Powell Rodney Quainton (847) 446-2850

Woodstock St Anns Episcopal Church **P** (258) 503 W Jackson St 60098-3143 (Mail to: 503 W Jackson St 60098-3143) Patricia Conley (815) 338-0950

NON-PAROCHIAL CLERGY

Adams FR *dcn*
Ahn PC Chicago IL
Alan SE Chicago IL
Allemeier JE *ret* Moline IL
Amadio CM *ret* Washington Island WI
Anderson EM
Anderson ME *ret* Evanston IL
Andrews GS *ret* Longwood FL
Awan AK Chicago IL
Babenko-Longhi JP *dcn* Burlington WI
Banner DL *ret* Quincy IL
Barr NM
Barron SW Arlington Heights IL
Baskerville-Burrows JL
Bates RS *ret* Belvidere IL
Bavaro CM *ret* Chicago IL
Beers WR Lodi WI
Bellis E *dcn* Chicago IL
Benvenuti AC Chicago IL
Berry GG *ret* Pasadena CA
Bice MK Chicago IL
Blossom JD Peoria IL
Blottner WE *ret* Farmville VA
Bond MD *ret dcn* Saint John IN
Bowers TL Fort Collins CO
Briones MA Chicago IL
Britton JC Salem OR
Bro AH *ret* Mount Carroll IL
Brookman CA *dcn* Warrenville IL
Broome WB *ret* Landrum SC
Brown BO Chicago IL

Browne BW Hobe Sound FL
Caldwell JH *ret* Freeport IL
Cameron JR Chicago IL
Cameron MN Chicago IL
Cannon TK *ret* Oak Park IL
Carnes RL Chattanooga TN
Carpenter FN *dcn* Barrington Hills IL
Caskey CC *ret* Bonita Springs FL
Clarke R Evanston IL
Cockbill DJ Joliet IL
Coffey JP *ret* Oak Park IL
Conrads NA *dcn* Rockford IL
Couvillion BN *ret* Western Springs IL
Cragon MM *ret* Chicago IL
Crammer MC Decatur GA
Crawford ALL Lake Forest IL
Crist JF *ret* McNabb IL
Curtis EW *ret* Chicago IL
Dally JA Chicago IL
Dalmasso GL *ret* East Moline IL
Davenport EJL *dcn* Chicago IL
Dedmon RA *ret* Manchester TN
Dehetre DB *ret* New Haven CT
Dekker RP *ret* Noblesville IN
Dreibelbis JLV *ret* Evanston IL
Dunkerley JH *ret* Chicago IL
Dunlap DJ *ret* Peoria IL
Easter WB *ret* Rio Rancho NM
Emrich RSM *ret* Baroda MI
Engelhorn PE
Ferguson RL *dcn*
Ferguson SS *ret* Naperville IL
Fisher DH *ret* Naperville IL
Fisher DL Portland OR
Fisher SK Atlanta GA
Frias M *ret* Chicago IL
Gattis LR *ret* Olympia Fields IL
Gerdau C *ret* New York NY
Gibbs JM *ret* Birmingham
Giegler CE *ret* Punta Gorda FL
Glidden RM *ret* Southport CT
Goddard PD *ret* Sanibel FL
Goforth TR Chicago IL
Gorman JM *dcn* Oregon IL
Green DH *ret* Batavia IL
Green LF *ret* Batavia IL
Gregory PR *dcn* Naperville IL
Gregory RA Waukegan IL
Griesmeyer WJ *ret* Crete IL
Grygiel JC *dcn* Rockford IL
Guistolise KJM *ret* Chicago IL
Gustafson EM El Paso TX
Hanna DB New Orleans LA
Harrington DL *dcn* Batavia IL
Harris TG *dcn* Chicago IL
Haugaard WP *ret* Oviedo FL
Haycock RH Charlottesville VA
Hemphill MA Norwich VT
Henderson JP *ret* Evanston IL
Hensel CH *ret* Northbrook IL
Hillenbrand PM *ret* Rockford IL

Hipple JK Rockford IL
Hoelzel WN *ret* Rio Rancho NM
Holstrom SA *ret* Aurora IL
Houck JB *ret* Chicago IL
Ialongo DM
Ikenye NJB Evanston IL
Jackson JA *dcn*
Janiec TD *ret* Palatine IL
Jinete AE *ret* Franklin Park IL
Johnson AC *ret* N Barrington IL
Johnson WF *ret* Chicago IL
Jones DP *ret* Evanston IL
Jones KT *dcn* McHenry IL
Joyce TJ *ret* East Berlin PA
Judson DI *ret* Elmhurst IL
King KA Chicago IL
Knowles MD Alexandria VA
Kowalski MJ *dcn* Aurora IL
Kyger PS *ret* Kissimmee FL
Lake OL *ret* Wilmington NC
Lamb TJ *ret* Rockford IL
Lane WDF *ret* Lake Forest IL
Langdon CM *ret* Grayslake IL
Larson L *ret* Moline IL
Lawler GEA *ret* Chicago IL
Lawrence JA *ret* Kerrville TX
Lee MW Moline IL
Leswing JB *ret* Downers Grove IL
Lewellen DS *dcn* Peoria IL
L'Homme RA *ret* Lafayette IN
Liebenow RE *ret* Asheville NC
Linboom BA
Lipsey HM *ret* La Grange IL
Loch JL *dcn* Sycamore IL
Longhi AP Burlington WI
Luchs LR *ret* Cabin John MD
Lundberg RE *ret* Arlington Heights IL
Lutter LF *dcn* Gurnee IL
Lynn JG *dcn*
Macfarlane RJ *ret* Fairfax VA
Maesen WA *dcn* Chicago IL
Majkrzak AW *ret* Madison WI
Marr R Three Rivers MI
Marshall EW *ret* Bartlett IL
Martz SB Glen Ellyn IL
McClough JD *ret* Western Springs IL
McIntosh MA Chicago IL
Melin MJ *ret*
Mensah AW *dcn*
Missner HMD *dcn* Winnetka IL
Monroe GW *ret* Dallas TX
Moon DP *ret* Waukegan IL
Moore C Des Plaines IL
Moser PM *dcn* Chicago IL
Moss AA Arlington VA
Muir GD *ret* Augusta GA
Muir RD *ret* Lake Forest IL
Murray TO *dcn* Chicago IL
Musgrave DC *ret* Raleigh NC
Myers RK *ret* Chicago IL
Mysen AL Highland Park IL

Nako JW *ret*
Narain EL *ret* Chicago IL
Nesbit WR St. Charles IL
Nestrock FR *ret* Waterford MI
Norris EA *ret* Dallas TX
O'Neill WH *ret* Houston TX
Orpen JR *ret* Chicago IL
Packard LA *ret* Galena IL
Pamatmat RDR Des Plaines IL
Payson CB *ret* Fort Atkinson WI
Pham JP Washington DC
Phillips CS Roselle IL
Pitcher TL *ret* Elmhurst IL
Plazas CA *ret* Chicago IL
Pollitt MJ West Caln MI
Pooser WC *ret* San Antonio TX
Portaro SA *ret* Chicago IL
Potter LG *ret* Hillsboro OR
Prechtel DL *ret* San Pablo CA
Prevost ES *ret* Worcester MA
Quill MM *ret* Elk River MN
Ramirez ML *dcn* Glen Ellyn IL
Ramshaw LCH *ret* Ormond Beach FL
Raymond PR Barrington IL
Reed JY *ret* Chicago IL
Reese CS Chicago IL
Rex CW *dcn* Evanston IL
Rhoades MA *dcn* Dixon IL
Roberts WD *ret* Mundelein IL
Robinson VAA *ret* Northbrook IL
Rogers DK *dcn* Rockford IL
Rogers JES *ret* Chicago IL
Ryan BG *ret* Burnsville MN
Schaefer NJ *ret* Lindenhurst IL
Schauble JL *ret* Compton IL
Schuneman SL *ret* Oceanside CA
Setmeyer RC *ret* Des Plaines IL
Seville JC Winnetka IL
Sey RF Chicago IL
Seymour JD *dcn* Chicago IL
Siberine KM
Sims GB *ret* Rockford IL

Siwek PC Oak Park IL
Sloan SJ Chicago IL
Smith GC *ret* Islip NY
Smith GM *ret* Jerusalem ISRAEL
Smith JM *dcn*
Smith RN Ripon WI
Smith TG *dcn* Elk Grove Village IL
Soltys JR
Soyars JE Charlotte NC
Stanley GJ *dcn* Chicago IL
Stanwise RJF *ret* Peoria IL
Steen SJ Chicago IL
Stefko NM Chicago IL
Stieper JR *ret* Barrington IL
Swarthout JE *ret* Barrington Hills IL
Tenny CM Vails Gate NY
Thiel SE *ret* Palos Park IL
Thom AJ Chicago IL
Tiling RH *ret* The Villages FL
Townes HC *dcn* Palos Park IL
Tudela ME Lihue HI
Vaccaro AJ Chicago IL
Vail JP *ret* Durham NC
Valentine RA *ret dcn* Northfield IL
Vandercook PJ *ret* Mount Horeb WI
Vandermeer LA Antioch IL
Vollkommer MM Galena IL
Ward EH Barrington IL
Warthan FA *ret* Kankakee IL
Weaver DE *ret* Western Springs IL
Weaver SC Chicago IL
Webster WR *ret* Amherst MA
Whennen JE *dcn* Flossmoor IL
White LS *ret* Woodstock IL
Williams MA Sterling IL
Willis LJ Oakland CA
Winsett SM *ret* Streamwood IL
Wright GA *ret* York
Yeager RT Oak Park IL
Yonkers MA *dcn* Park Ridge IL
Zielinski FG *dcn* Chicago IL

DIOCESE OF COLOMBIA
(PROVINCE IX)
Comprises the Republic of COLOMBIA
DIOCESAN OFFICE Cra 6 No 49-85 Piso 2 Bogotá Colombia
(MAIL: Apartado Aéreo 52964, Bogotá)
TEL 011-57-1-288-3167 FAX 011-571-2883248
E-MAIL gaiser@bc.edu WEB www.iglesiaepiscopal.org.co

Previous Bishops-
David B Reed 1964-71 Wm A
Franklin 1972-78 Bernardo
Merino Botero 1979-2001

**Bishop—Rt Rev Francisco
José Duque Gomez (969)** (Dio
14 July 2001)

Sec Conv P Ospina (AA 52964 Bogata); *Treas*
G Santos; *Reg* J Infante (Bogota); *Chanc* E Boss
(Medellin); *Medios y Comunicaciones* E Giraldo
(Bogota); *Con Residencia Canónica* T Prichard M
Ferro; *Dir Mission Dev* Rev TJ Gaiser; *Asst to Bp* MG
Monroy; *Accountant* SV Espitia

Dio Conv: TBD

PARISHES, MISSIONS, AND CLERGY
Armenia Mision Santo Tomas Apostol **P**
Carrera 1S No. 26-19 (Mail to: Carrera 20 No.
9N-1B-B4 Apto. 301) (315) 283-6844
✠ **Bogota** Catedral de San Pablo **O** (100) Carrera
6 No. 49-85 AA 52964 (Mail to: Carrera 6 No.
49-85) (571) 288-3187
Bogota Iglesia Episcopal San Pedro **P** (80) Calle
22 BIS No. 93 AA 52964 (Mail to: Calle 22 BIS
No. 93) (312) 498-4984
Bogota Parroquia Episcopal El Divino Salvador
M Calle 58 Sur 14F78 Este (Mail to: Calle 58
Sur 14F78 Este) Carlos Guevara Rodriguez
Carlos Guevara Rodriguez (571) 371-7377
Bucaramanga Parroquia San Pedro y San Pablo
M Cra 27 # 51-55 (Mail to: Cra 27 #51-55)
6470610618
Bucaramanta Mision Santa Maria Virgen **M**
Calle O # 14-54 (Mail to: Cra 27 # 51-47)
5776718540
Buenos Aires - Zaragoza Parroquia Nuestra
Senora del Carmen **P** (50) Buenos Aires
Palizada Corregimiento AA 52964 (Mail to:
Cra. 9 No. 9A-20) (313) 526-0209
Cali La Trinidad - Cali **P** (80) Calle 7 Oeste No.
3-43 AA 52964 (Mail to: Calle 7 Oeste No.
3-43) (572) 893-5953
Cali Mision la Natividad del Señor **M** CALLE 7
OESTE # 3-43 (Mail to: Calle 53 No 12-05)
5724480013
Cali Mision la Sagrada Familia **M** Cra 8 No. 71-05
(Mail to: Cra 8 No. 71-05) 5724331828
Cartagena Iglesia Epis Nuestro Salvador **P** (80)
Piepopa Camino Arriba 22-109 AA 52964
(Mail to: Pie Popa Camino Arriba) (575) 674-

0851
Cartagena Parroquia La Santa Cruz **P** B. 7 de
Agosto Av. Colombia No. 71-15 (Mail to: B.
7 de Agosto Av. Colombia No. 71-15) (314)
506-8507
El Bagre Parroquia la Anunciacion **P** CARRERA
49 # 63 A 74/85/89 Sector Las Delicias (Mail
to: CARRERA 49 # 63 A 74/85/89) (571) 837-
0201
Facatativa Mision Santa Marta de Betania **M**
Kilometro 4 via el Rosal (Mail to: Vereda
Noruega Prado Alto Cra 3E 9A-85 INT 2
CASA) (301) 371-4508
Ibague Mision San Juan Bautista **M** (50) Cra. 6
No. 16-69-71 AA 52964 (Mail to: Cra. 6 No.
16-69-71) (571) 2883187
Malambo Nuestra Senora Del Monte Carmelo **M**
(50) Cra. 3A Sur # 11A-02 AA 52964 (Mail to:
Cra. 3A, Sur # 11A-02) (575) 3478061
Medellin Iglesia Episcopal San Lucas **P** (70)
Carrera 80 # 53A-78 (Mail to: Cra 80 # 53A-78
52964) (574) 234-3940
Quibbo - Choco Mision de Cristo Rey **M** Calle
22 #17-7 Blogue 2 (Mail to: Calle 22 #17-7 B
Jardin Sector Rosales) (316) 739-5502
Soacha Mision del Espiritu Santo Tomas **M**
Carrera 5 Este 23-73 (Mail to: Carrera 5 Este
23-73) Carlos Guevara Rodriguez Carlos
Guevara Rodriguez (310) 282-9788

INSTITUTIONS
Centro de Estudios Teológico San Bernardo Abad
(CET) Rev Ernesto Boss Cra 80 No 53 A-78 Medellín
Antioquia

NON-PAROCHIAL CLERGY
Abuchar Cury R
Arenas Toro WH Bogota, BDC
Betancur Ortiz RA Bogota, BDC
Boss Wollner ES Medellin ANTIOQUIA
Bueno Bueno FJ
Calvo Perez ADJ Bogota
Correa Amariles MO *dcn* Medellin Antioguia
Correa Galvez JW Bogota
Davila Figueroa WJ Bogota, BDC
Ferro M Bogota
Gil Restrepo S Bogota
Gonzalez Aqudelo LM Antioquia
Hernandez Rojas MA Bogota
Hincapie Loaiza DH Columbia
Mafla Silva DA Bogota

Marciales Arenas AC Bogota
Martinez Toro JDJ Antioquia
Morales Gaviria JR *ret* Antioquia
Palacio Bedoya LH *dcn* Bogota
Pardo Arciniegas AM Bogota, BDC
Perez Macias JE *ret* Atlantico
Pinzon Castro LA Bogota
Rendon Ospina GA Medelin Antioquia

Riveros Mayorga JA Bogota, BDC
Serrano Poreda NE Bogota, BDC
Sierra Echeverry GA *ret* Bogota
Suarez Elles JA Malambo ATLANTICO
Tirado H
Valderrama Sanabria JP Bogota, BDC
Vergara Grueso E Bogota

DIOCESE OF COLORADO
(PROVINCE VI)
Comprises the State of Colorado
DIOCESAN OFFICE 1300 Washington St Denver CO 80203-2008
TEL (303) 837-1173   WATS (800) 446-3081   FAX (303) 837-1311
E-MAIL colorado@coloradodiocese.org   WEB www.coloradodiocese.org

Previous Bishops—
Geo M Randall (CO and adjacent)
1865-73, John F Spalding m 1873 dio
1887-1902 Chas S Olmstead 1902-18,
Irving P Johnson coadj 1917 Bp 1918-
38, Fred Ingley coadj 1921 Bp 1938-49,
Harold L Bowen coadj 1947 Bp 1949-
55, Daniel Corrigan suffr 1958-60, Jos
S Minnis coadj 1954 Bp 1955-69, Edwin
B Thayer suffr 1960-69 Actg Eccl Auth 1968-69 Bp
1969-73, Wm C Frey coadj 1972 Bp 1973-90, Wm H
Wolfrum suffr 1981-91, William J Winterrowd Bp
1991-2004

Bishop — Rt Rev Robert J O'Neill (989) (Dio
01 Jan 2004)

Exec Asst to the Bp M Stern; *Cn to Ord Rev Cn* C
Andrews; *Exec Asst to Cn to Ord* D Draper; *Cn Miss*
Rev Cn L Blanchard; *Cong Dev and Deploy Admin* N
McClung; *Comm Dir* M Orr; *Comm Asst* R Greene;
Controller P Greenfield; *PT Acct Cl* K Ward; *Chanc* L
Hitt 5670 Greenwood Plaza Blvd Ste 417 Greenwood
Village CO 80111; *Faith Form Coord (Yth & Young
Adult Min)* Rev K Malcom; *Dir of Operations for
Cathedral* Ridge T Ryan; *Treas* C Thompson; *Dir
of Epis Serv Corps* Rev R Crummy; *Jubilee Min Off*
Rev R Jones; *Colo Episc Found Pres* A Sanborn 1300
Washington St 80203 (303) 534-6778

Stand Comm—Cler: Pres S Turner G Berlin L Burns
D Freeman L Waggoner; *Lay: VPres* R Morse *Sec* J
Wolfe A Conrad C Hallowed H Tournay

Dio Conv: TBD

PARISHES, MISSIONS, AND CLERGY
Alamosa Little Shepherd of the Hills **M** 607 4th
St 81101-2522 (Mail to: PO Box 1540 81201-
7540) (719) 539-4562
Alamosa St Thomas the Apostle Epis Church **M**
(34) 607 4th St 81101-2522 (Mail to: PO Box
837 81101-0837) (719) 589-6843

Arvada The Church of Christ the King **P** (394)
6490 Carr St 80004-3338 (Mail to: PO Box 6
80001-0006) Rebecca Brown
Aspen Christ Episcopal Church **P** (280) 536 W
North St 81611-1253 (Mail to: 536 W North St
81611-1253) Jonathan Brice
Aurora St Martin in the Fields Episcopal Church
P (194) 4740 S Buckley Rd 80015-1831 (Mail
to: 4740 S Buckley Rd 80015-1831) James
Gilchrist (303) 693-8872
Aurora St Stephens Episcopal Church **P** (256) 1
Del Mar Cir 80011-8225 (Mail to: 1 Del Mar
Cir 80011-8225) Carol Meredith Marionette
Bennett (303) 364-3186
Basalt St Peters Episcopal Church **M** (186) 200
Elk Run Drive 81621-9287 (Mail to: 200 Elk
Run Drive 81621-9287) William Fisher (970)
927-4235
Battlement Mesa All Saints Episcopal Church **M**
(54) 150 Sipprelle Dr 81635-9229 (Mail to: 150
Sipprelle Dr 81635-9229) Nancy Angle (970)
285-7908
Boulder St Aidans Episcopal Church **P** (259)
2425 Colorado Ave 80302-6806 (Mail to: 2425
Colorado Ave 80302-6806) Mary Rejouis Kay
Cook (303) 443-2503
Boulder St Ambrose Episcopal Church **P** (290)
7520 S Boulder Rd 80303-4640 (Mail to: 7520
S Boulder Rd 80303-4640) Peter Munson (303)
499-3041
Boulder St Johns Episcopal Church **P** (1249)
1419 Pine St 80304 (Mail to: 1419 Pine St
80302-4812) Susan Springer Forrest Carhartt
Theodore Howard Benjamin Newland (303)
442-5246
Boulder St Mary Magdalene Episcopal Church
P (287) 4775 Cambridge St 80301-4140 (Mail
to: 4775 Cambridge St 80301-4140) Sarah
Lapenta-H Spencer Carr Mary Hardy (303)
530-1421
Breckenridge St John the Baptist Episcopal
Church **P** (181) 100 S French St 80424 (Mail to:

PO Box 2166 80424-2166) Andrew Macbeth (970) 453-4264

Brighton St Elizabeths Episcopal Church **M** (56) 76 S 3rd Ave 80601-2008 (Mail to: 76 S 3rd Ave 80601-2008) (303) 659-2648

Broomfield Church of the Holy Comforter **P** (416) 1700 W 10th Ave 80020 (Mail to: PO Box 412 80038-0412) Kimberly Seidman Linda Brown (303) 466-2667

Buena Vista Grace Episcopal Church **P** (57) 205 W Main St 81211-9169 (Mail to: PO Box 1559 81211-1559) Catherine Tran (719) 395-8868

Canon City Christ Episcopal Church **P** (146) 802 Harrison Ave 81212-3389 (Mail to: 816 Harrison Ave 81212) Mark Meyer (719) 275-2028

Castle Rock Christ's Episcopal Church **P** (377) 615 4th St 80104-2553 (Mail to: 615 4th St 80104-2553) Brian Winter (303) 688-5185

Centennial Good Shepherd Episcopal Church **P** (744) 8545 E Dry Creek Rd 80112-2750 (Mail to: 8545 E Dry Creek Rd 80112-2750) Craig Maccoll Alwen Bledsoe William Henwood (303) 740-2688

Central City St Pauls Episcopal Church **M** (14) 226 E 1st High St 80427 (Mail to: PO Box 764 80427-0764) (303) 582-0450

Colorado Spg Church of St Michael the Archangel **P** (618) 7400 Tudor Rd 80919-2615 (Mail to: 7400 Tudor Rd 80919-2615) Peter Floyd Judith Sato (719) 598-3244

Colorado Springs Chapel of Our Saviour Episcopal Ch **P** (873) 8 Fourth St 80906-3155 (Mail to: 8 Fourth St 80906-3155) Denson Freeman Krista Dias Bethany Myers

Colorado Springs Grace and St Stephens Episcopal Church **P** (701) 601 N Tejon St 80903-1009 (Mail to: 601 North Tejon St 80903-1009) Andrew Cooley Martin Pearsall Sally Ziegler (719) 328-1125

Colorado Springs St Raphael Episcopal Church **P** (142) 802 Leta Dr 80911-1126 (Mail to: 802 Leta Dr 80911-1126) Christopher Johnson Maxine Maybin Twyla Zittle (719) 392-3563

Conifer St Laurence Episcopal Church **P** (200) 26812 Barkley Rd 80433-9101 (Mail to: PO Box 361 80433-0361) Nancy Malloy (303) 838-2457

Cortez St Barnabas of the Valley Episcopal **P** (98) 110 W North St 81321-3119 (Mail to: 110 W North St 81321-3119) Leigh Waggoner Cynthia Irvin (970) 565-7865

Craig St Marks Episcopal Church **M** (16) 657 Green St 81625-3029 (Mail to: PO Box 711 81626-0711) Arthur White (970) 824-3470

Creede St Augustine Chapel **M** (12) No 502 S Main 81130 (Mail to: PO Box 803 81130-0803) Robert Pope (719) 658-2394

Crested Butte All Saints in the Mountains Church **Chapel** (41) 401 Sopris Ave 81224 (Mail to: PO Box 701 81230-0701) William Waltz (970) 641-0429

Cripple Creek St Andrews Episcopal Church **P** (69) 373 Carr St 80813-9613 (Mail to: 373 Carr St 80813-9613) William Sermon Richard Mitchell (719) 689-2920

Delta St Lukes Episcopal Church **P** (75) 145 W 5th St 81416-1803 (Mail to: PO Box 724 81416-0724) Thomas Seibert (970) 874-9489

Denver Christ Episcopal Church **P** (673) 2950 S University Blvd 80210-6029 (Mail to: 2950 S University Blvd 80210-6029) Terence Mcgugan Chad McCabe (303) 758-3674

Denver Church of St Philip & St James **P** (233) 2797 S Lowell Blvd 80236-2249 (Mail to: 2797 S Lowell Blvd 80236-2249) George Berlin (303) 936-3992

Denver Church of the Ascension **P** (346) 600 Gilpin St 80218-3632 (Mail to: 600 Gilpin St 80218-3632) Lucas Grubbs (303) 388-5978

Denver Church of the Epiphany **P** (241) 100 Colorado Blvd 80206-5533 (Mail to: 100 Colorado Blvd 80206-5533) Stacey Tafoya

Denver Church of the Holy Redeemer **P** (86) 2552 Williams St 80205-5526 (Mail to: 2552 Williams St 80205-5526) Stephen Wilson (303) 831-8963

Denver Intercession Episcopal Church **P** (261) 3101 E 100th Ave 80229-2687 (Mail to: 3101 E 100th Avenue 80229-2687) Curtis Wait (303) 451-8085

Denver Our Merciful Savior Episcopal Church **P** (318) 2222 W 32nd Ave 80211-3318 (Mail to: 2222 W 32nd Ave 80211-3318) Janice Pearson (303) 477-4555

Denver St Andrews Episcopal Church **P** (303) 2015 Glenarm Pl 80205-3121 (Mail to: 2015 Glenarm Pl 80205-3121) Elizabeth Randall Melissa Adzima (303) 296-1712

Denver St Barnabas Episcopal Church **P** (480) 1280 Vine St 80206-2912 (Mail to: 1630 E 14th Ave 80218-2503) Morris Garrett Debra Angell (303) 388-6469

Denver St Bede Episcopal Church **P** 2201 S University Blvd 80210 (Mail to: Iliff School of Theology 80210) (303) 744-1287

✠ **Denver** St Francis Episcopal Chapel **Other** (18) 2323 Curtis St 80205-2627 (Mail to: 2323 Curtis St 80205-2627) (303) 244-0766

✠ **Denver** St Johns Episcopal Cathedral **O** (2261) 1350 Washington St 80203-2008 (Mail to: 1350 Washington St 80203-2008) Elizabeth Costello Jadon Hartsuff Robert Hendrickson Charles La Fond Patrick Malloy Elizabeth Melchionna (303) 831-7115

Denver St Lukes Episcopal Church **P** (456) 1270 Poplar St 80220-3023 (Mail to: 1270 Poplar St 80220-3023) Douglas Dunn (303) 355-2331

Denver St Michael and All Angels' Episcopal Church **P** (399) 1400 S University Blvd 80210-2407 (Mail to: 1400 S University Blvd 80210-2407) Richard Fraser William Campbell Neal Dow James Johnson Edward Morgan (303)

777-5181

Denver St Peters & St Marys Church **P** (42) 126 W 2nd Ave 80223-1434 (Mail to: 126 W 2nd Ave 80223-1434) Rebecca Crummey (303) 722-8781

Denver St Thomas Episcopal Church **P** (318) 2201 Dexter St 80207-3756 (Mail to: 2201 Dexter St 80207-3756) Daniel Hopkins Michael Humber Sally Megeath (303) 388-4395

✠ **Denver** Sudanese Community Church **Other** 1350 Washington St 80203-2008 (Mail to: 1350 Washington St 80203-2008) (303) 831-7115

Durango St Marks Episcopal Church **P** (399) 910 E 3rd Ave 81301-5213 (Mail to: 910 E 3rd Ave 81301-5213) Linda Lilley (970) 247-1129

Elizabeth Peace in Christ Epis-Lutheran Min **M** (120) 236 Tabor St 80107 (Mail to: PO Box 2098 80107)

Englewood St Gabriel the Archangel Episcopal **P** (457) 6190 E Quincy Ave 80111-1002 (Mail to: 6190 E Quincy Avenue 80111-1002) Christopher Ditzenberger Marilyn Schneider (303) 771-1063

Estes Park Parish Church of St Bartholomew **P** (283) 880 Macgregor Ave 80517-9065 (Mail to: PO Box 1559 80517-9065) Seth Richmond Robert Burger William Shirey (970) 586-4504

Evergreen Church of the Transfiguration **P** (150) 27640 Highway 74 80439-5820 (Mail to: PO Box 1630 80437-1630) Michael McManus (303) 674-4904

Fort Collins St Lukes Episcopal Church **P** (792) 2000 Stover St 80525-1545 (Mail to: 2000 Stover St 80525-1545) Lupton Abshire Gregory Foraker (970) 493-7512

Fort Collins St Pauls Episcopal Church **P** (312) 1208 W Elizabeth St 80521-4509 (Mail to: 1208 W Elizabeth St 80521-4509) Bonnie Spencer Austin Leininger (970) 482-2668

Fort Lupton St Andrews Episcopal Church **M** (16) 204 Park Ave 80621-1928 (Mail to: 204 Park Ave 80621-1928) (303) 857-6502

Fort Morgan St Charles the Martyr Epis Church **P** (104) 505 E 8th Ave 80701-3227 (Mail to: 505 E 8th Ave 80701-3227) (970) 867-6228

Frederick St Brigit Episcopal Church **M** (102) 110 Johnson St 80530-8022 (Mail to: 110 Johnson St 80530-8022) Felicia Smith Graybeal (720) 208-0280

Georgetown Grace Church **M** (17) 408 Taos St 80444 (Mail to: PO Box 133 80444-0133) David Morgan (303) 569-2790

Glenwood Spgs St Barnabas Episcopal Church **P** (154) 546 Hyland Park Drive 81601-4276 (Mail to: 546 Hyland Park Drive 81601-4276) (970) 945-6423

Golden Calvary Episcopal Church **P** (852) 1320 Arapahoe St 80401-1815 (Mail to: 1320 Arapahoe St 80401-1815) Thomas Danitschek Catherine Hitch Timothy Phenna Bethany Thomas John Wengrovius (303) 279-2188

Golden St John Chrysostom Episcopal Church **P** (171) 13151 W 28th Ave 80401-1601 (Mail to: 13151 W 28th Ave 80401-1601) Timothy Thaden Janice Pearson (303) 279-2760

Granby Cranmer Memorial Chapel **Chapel** 75 High Country Dr 80446-0954 (970) 887-2742

Granby St John the Baptist Episcopal Church **P** (121) 390 Garnet Avenue 80446 (Mail to: PO Box 954 80446-0954) Diane Bielski Michael Briggs (970) 887-2742

Grand Jct St Matthew Episcopal Church **P** (517) 3888 27 1/2 Rd 81506-4186 (Mail to: 3888 27 1/2 Rd 81506-4186) Judith Schneider Hollis Wright (970) 242-3293

Grand Jct The Church of the Nativity **P** (141) 2175 Broadway 81503-1086 (Mail to: 2175 Broadway 81507-1086) Nature Johnston Teri Shecter

Greeley Trinity Episcopal Church **P** (367) 3800 W 20th St 80634-3418 (Mail to: 3800 W 20th St 80634-3418) Jack Stapleton (970) 330-1877

Gunnison Church of the Good Samaritan **P** (136) 307 W Virginia Ave 81230-3038 (Mail to: PO Box 701 81230-0701) William Waltz (970) 641-0429

Kremmling Trinity Episcopal Church **M** (37) 805 Central Ave 80459 (Mail to: PO Box 996 80459-0996) Karen Smith (970) 724-3626

La Junta St Andrew Epis & Holy Cross Lutheran Ch **P** (36) 621 Raton Ave 81050-2425 (Mail to: 621 Raton Ave 81050-2425) Mary Hendricks (719) 383-3504

La Veta St Benedict Episcopal Church **M** (85) 113 W Field St 81055 (Mail to: PO Box 1186 81055-1186) William Howard (719) 742-5202

Lake City St James Episcopal Chapel **M** (66) 5th St & Hwy 149 81235 (Mail to: PO Box 832 81235-0832) (970) 641-0429

Lakewood St Joseph Episcopal Church **P** (246) 11202 W Jewell Ave 80232-6140 (Mail to: 11202 W Jewell Ave 80232-6140) Michele Quinn-Miscall (303) 985-7170

Lakewood St Pauls Episcopal Church **P** (288) 9200 W 10th Ave 80215-4701 (Mail to: 9200 W 10th Avenue 80215-4701) Allan Cole (303) 233-4991

Lamar St Pauls Episcopal Church **M** (35) 200 E Parmenter St 81052-3241 (Mail to: PO Box 814 81052-0814) Mary Hendricks (719) 336-4522

Leadville St George Episcopal Church **M** (38) 200 W 4th St 80461-3632 (Mail to: PO Box 243 80461-0243) Alison Lufkin (719) 486-3087

Littleton St Timothys Episcopal Church **P** (661) 1401 E Dry Creek Rd 80122-3087 (Mail to: 1401 E Dry Creek Road 80122-3087) Michael Carney Karen Henwood William Riedell (303) 794-1565

Littleton The Episcopal Parish of St Gregory **P** (401) 6653 W Chatfield Ave 80128-5834 (Mail to: 6653 W Chatfield Ave 80128-5834) Todd Sorensen (303) 979-5236

Longmont St Stephens Episcopal Church **P** (650) 1303 S Bross Ln 80501-6803 (Mail to: 1303 S Bross Ln 80501-6803) Ralph Bailey Dana Solomon (303) 776-1072

Loveland All Saints Episcopal Church **P** (342) 3448 Taft Ave 80538-2556 (Mail to: 3448 N Taft Ave 80538-2596) Jean Churchman Jean D'Aoust (970) 667-0303

Mancos St Pauls Church **M** (18) 479 Bauer Ave 81328-9241 (Mail to: PO Box 226 81328-0226) (970) 533-9104

Manitou Springs St Andrews Episcopal Church **P** (65) 808 Manitou Ave 80829 (Mail to: PO Box 466 80829-0466) Susan Merrin Frances Mutolo (719) 685-9259

Meeker St James Episcopal Church **P** (91) 368 4th St 81641 (Mail to: PO Box 641 81641-0641) Scott Hollenbeck (970) 878-5823

Monte Vista St Stephen the Martyr **M** (26) 729 3rd Ave 81144-1442 (Mail to: PO Box 489 81144-0489) (719) 852-3274

Montrose St Paul Episcopal Church **P** (32) (Mail to: PO Box 3238 81402-3238) (970) 249-2535

Monument St Matthias Episcopal Church **P** (134) 18320 Furrow Rd 80132-8790 (Mail to: PO Box 1223 80132-1223) Andrew McMullen (719) 359-9204

New Castle St Johns Episcopal Church **M** (50) First & Main St 81647 (Mail to: PO Box 82 81647-0082) Thomas White Edmond-Joseph Rivet (970) 984-2780

Ouray St Johns Episcopal Church **P** (94) 329 Fifth Ave 81427 (Mail to: PO Box 563 81427-0563) David Vickers (970) 325-4655

Pagosa Springs St Patrick Episcopal Church **P** (144) 225 S Pagosa Blvd 81147-8396 (Mail to: 225 S Pagosa Blvd 81147-8396) Douglas Neel

Parker St Matthews Episcopal Church **P** (465) 19580 Pilgrims Pl 80138-7354 (Mail to: 19580 Pilgrims Pl 80138-7354) Michael Richardson (303) 841-0121

Pueblo Ch of the Ascension & Holy Trinity **P** (426) 420 W 18th St 81003-2625 (Mail to: 420 W 18th St 81003-2625) Karen Burnham Kenneth Butcher John Gardner Rachel Wenner (719) 543-4253

Pueblo St Peter the Apostle Epis Church **P** (67) 3939 W Pueblo Blvd 81005-2721 (Mail to: 3939 W Pueblo Blvd 81005-2721) William Howard (719) 561-4567

Salida Church of the Ascension **P** (117) 349 E St 81201-2631 (Mail to: PO Box 1540 81201-7540) Michael Fay (719) 539-4562

Sedalia St Philip in the Field Epis Church **P** (117) PO Box 142 80135-0142 (Mail to: PO Box 142 80135-0142) Janet Fullmer (303) 688-5444

South Fork St Francis of Assisi Mission **M** (9) 1 Church St 81154 (Mail to: PO Box 1175 81154) (719) 873-5358

Steamboat Sprngs St Pauls Episcopal Church **P** (488) 846 Oak St 80477 (Mail to: PO Box

770722 80477-0722) Arthur White Margaret Greene James Turner (970) 879-0925

Sterling Prince of Peace Episcopal Church **M** (34) 201 Phelps St 80751-4044 (Mail to: 201 Phelps Street 80751-4044) (970) 522-0539

Vail Church of the Transfiguration **P** (364) 19 Vail Rd 81657 (Mail to: PO Box 1000 81658-1000) Stuart Keith Joseph Forinash (970) 476-0618

Westcliffe St Lukes Episcopal Mission **M** (49) 201 S 3rd St 81252-9502 (Mail to: PO Box 208 81252-0208) (719) 783-2477

Westminster St Marthas Episcopal Church **P** (98) 4001 W 76th Ave 80030 (Mail to: PO Box 271 80036-0271) Stephen Wengrovius (303) 429-0495

Wheat Ridge St James Episcopal Church **P** (96) 8235 W 44th Ave 80033-4426 (Mail to: PO Box 537 80034-0537) Bruce Swinehart (303) 424-1118

Windsor St Albans Episcopal Church **P** (279) 525 Walnut St 80550-5145 (Mail to: PO Box 697 80550-0697) Rex Chambers David Tweedale Janice Windsor (970) 686-9658

Woodland Park St David of the Hills Epis Church **P** (47) 36 Edlowe Rd 80863-8226 (Mail to: 36 Edlowe Rd 80863-8226) (719) 687-9195

NON-PAROCHIAL CLERGY

Allen WD Vail CO
Anderson BG *ret* Golden CO
Andrews C Denver CO
Andrews JJ *ret* Littleton CO
Andrews RF *ret* Colorado Springs CO
Austin MS *ret* Baton Rouge LA
Baird SE *dcn* Vail CO
Beaty MK *dcn* Boulder CO
Berlin SA *ret* Wheat Ridge CO
Berryman JW *ret* Greenwood Village CO
Bevens ME *ret* Colorado Springs CO
Blake SJ *ret*
Blanchard LS Arvada CO
Blend JD Boulder CO
Boeschenstein KC *ret*
Bookstein NJ *dcn* Frederick CO
Boswell FP *ret* Lakewood CO
Bourgeault CW *ret* Sunset ME
Bowersox SA Denver CO
Boyd SH *ret* Englewood CO
Bradford LJ *ret* Denver CO
Brady SJ *dcn*
Brereton TF *ret* Colorado Springs CO
Brisbane PO *ret* Coldwater MI
Brower GR Denver CO
Brown SS *dcn*
Brown VW *dcn* Durango CO
Brownlee AG Pueblo CO
Buck RA *ret* Golden CO
Bunyan FS *ret* Loveland CO
Burdekin EA *dcn*
Burns AL La Veta CO
Burton KWF *ret* Manitou Springs CO

Campbell SD Monument CO
Casey DA *ret* Colorado Springs CO
Cella RL *dcn* Loveland CO
Chan CYLPF Mukwonago WI
Christopher M *dcn* Lakewood CO
Clift JD Denver CO
Clift WB *ret* Olympia WA
Crews WE *ret* Minneapolis MN
Danson MA Longmont CO
Darrow RM *ret* Denver CO
Davidson RP Loveland CO
Delzell CKC *ret* Santa Fe NM
Demmon MDS Hinesville GA
Denton MA *dcn* Larkspur CO
Dewlen JM *dcn* Longmont CO
Douglas AD *ret* Fort Collins CO
Dumke BA *ret* Coon Rapids MN
Duraikannu Y Goshen NY
Ebert B
Engels AR *ret* Grand Junction CO
Fhuere BL Clifton CO
Ford DB *ret* Jacksonville FL
Ford JT *ret* Jacksonville FL
Franken RA *ret dcn*
Franklin CL *ret* Denver CO
Freeman SB *ret* Littleton CO
Frensley JM *ret* Dallas TX
Gafour AB Denver CO
Garfield EA *dcn* Denver CO
Genty MD *dcn* Fort Collins CO
Girardin BJ *dcn* Aurora CO
Gray C *ret* Denver CO
Greenwood SA Golden CO
Griffin PC Denver CO
Grimes EL *dcn* Pueblo CO
Grundy SA *ret* Westminster CO
Hall AK Greeley CO
Halverstadt AN *ret* Denver CO
Hammond MJ *ret* Santa Fe NM
Hardwick LE *ret* Boulder CO
Harrison MM *dcn* Canon City CO
Hart LD *ret* Lakewood CO
Hart RL *ret* Birmingham MI
Henderson DK *ret* Superior CO
Heron MS *dcn* Centennial CO
Hicks SS *dcn* Granby CO
Hobson TP *ret* Denver CO
Hogue KG *ret* Scottsbluff NE
Hollowell JR *dcn* Lafayette CO
Hook EL *ret* Green Valley AZ
Horle GL *ret* Denver CO
Houlik MA *ret* Longmont CO
Houpt CW *dcn* Littleton CO
Hubbell S Healdsburg CA
Huber FA *ret* Lakewood CO
Humphrey GL *ret* Clive IA
Jesse H *ret* Denver CO
Jones R *dcn* Denver CO
Jones SH Denver CO
Kempf VN *ret* Fort Collins CO
Kindel WH Fort Morgan CO

King G *ret* Erie CO
Kline AF *ret* Greenwood Village CO
Koskela DM *ret* Colorado Springs CO
Laird IB *ret* Ouray CO
Larson RA *dcn* Ouray CO
Laudisio PD *ret dcn* Boulder CO
Lautenschlager PJ *ret* Colorado Springs CO
Leclair AA *ret* Englewood CO
Long TM *ret* Denver CO
Lufkin GS Leadville CO
Lukens AM *ret* Cortez CO
Lycett HA *ret* Goodland KS
Macgowan KA Falls Church VA
Magnuson GP Denver CO
Malcolm KA Durango CO
Marquand BH *dcn* Racine WI
Marsh A *dcn* Denver CO
Mason PC *ret* San Marcos TX
McNab CB *ret* Bozeman MT
McNab JT *dcn* Aspen CO
McTernan VD *ret* Colorado Springs CO
Melton JK Bronx NY
Meyers FW *ret* Castle Rock CO
Miles FW *ret* Denver CO
Mitchell WL *ret* Pueblo CO
Moore DL *dcn* Colorado Springs CO
Moore RA *ret* Aurora CO
Muller J *ret* Delta CO
Munroe SG *ret* Colorado Springs CO
Munsell RF
Need MAD Englewood CO
Nelson AJ *ret* Colorado Springs CO
Nettleton EB *ret* Lake City CO
Newby RLV *ret* Durango CO
Neyland TA *ret* Hygiene CO
O'Rourke DC *dcn* Boulder CO
Palmer RR *ret* Broomfield CO
Percival MJ *ret* Aptos CA
Peters DW *ret* Thornton CO
Radner EL *ret* Pueblo CO
Ragsdale JL *ret* Aurora CO
Ralston BM *ret dcn* Steamboat Springs CO
Ray DE *ret* Miami Beach FL
Reller WH *ret* Golden CO
Rosendale ME
Rouffy EA *ret* Portland OR
Sawicky BA St. Louis MO
Saxon MM *ret* Kansas City MO
Schelling RL *ret* Jefferson TX
Seils DD *ret* Parker CO
Shadle JL
Shain-Hendricks CA Silverthorne CO
Shepard AH *ret* Rio Rancho NM
Shepic CL *dcn* Lakewood CO
Shipman MJ
Short JH *ret* Appomattox VA
Sigafoos RV *ret* Grand Junction CO
Simpson DM Monte Vista CO
Sitton GW *ret* Westminster CO
Smith RR *ret* Aurora CO
Spurlock PA *ret* Denver CO

Stackhouse MK *dcn* Denver CO
Stanton WB Boulder CO
Steeves JA *dcn* Arvada CO
Stewart PF *dcn* Denver CO
Street CP *ret* Hamden CT
Strotheide CJ Aurora CO
Thompson DJ Monument CO
Thompson EA *ret* Pahrump NV
Thompson RG *ret* Lakewood CO
Troeger TH Woodbridge CT
Vosburgh LA *dcn* Broomfield CO
Wahl ER Boulder CO

Wallis HW *ret* Denver CO
Walton SL *dcn*
Warner DN *ret* Littleton CO
Warren HR *ret* Fort Collins CO
Weir SM *dcn* Evergreen CO
Weston SR *ret* Denver CO
Williams DM *ret* Peterborough NH
Womack EM *ret* Denver CO
Wood DR *ret* Greeley CO
Woodliff-Stanley RM Denver CO
Wright ES *ret* Helena AL
Zimmerman SF *ret* Colorado Springs CO

THE EPISCOPAL CHURCH IN CONNECTICUT
(PROVINCE I)
Comprises the State of Connecticut
DIOCESAN OFFICE 290 Pratt St Meriden CT 06450
TEL (203) 639-3501   FAX (203) 2035-1008
E-MAIL info@episcopalct.org   WEB www.episcopalct.org

Previous Bishops—
Samuel Seabury 1784-96, Abraham Jarvis 1797-1813, Thomas C Brownell 1819-65, John Williams coadj 1851 Bp 1865-99, Chauncey B Brewster coadj 1897 Bp 1899-1928, Edward C Acheson suffr 1915 coadj 1926 Bp 1928-34, Fredk G Budlong coadj 1931 Bp 1934-51, Walter H Gray suffr 1940 coadj 1945 Bp 1951-69, Robert M Hatch suffr 1951-57, John H Esquirol suffr 1958 Bp 1969-71, J Warren Hutchens suffr 1961 Bp 1971-77, Morgan Porteus suffr 1971 coadj 1976 Bp 1977-1981, W Bradford T Hastings suffr 1981-86, Jeffrey W Rowthorn suffr 1987-93, Arthur E Walmsley coad 1979-81 Bp 1981-93, Clarence N Coleridge suffr 1981-93 Bp 1993-99, Andrew D Smith suffr 1996-99 Bp 1999-2010

Bishop — Rt Rev Ian T Douglas (1042) (Dio 17 Apr 2010)

Bishop Suffragan — Rt Rev James E Curry (959) (Suffr 14 Oct 2000)

Bishop Suffragan — Rt Rev Laura J Ahrens (1018) (Suffr 30 Jun 2007)

Cn for Mission Collaboration Cn T Hodapp; *Cn for Mission Ldrshp* Cn LA Tolzmann; *Cn for Mission Integrity + Training* R Hammeal-Urban; *Cn for Mission Fin + Ops* Cn L Fuertes; *Treas* L Brooks; *Chanc* BS Babbitt; *Sec of Dio* Rev S Cosman; *Sec of Conv* Rev A Yates; *Bps Exec Sec*

Stand Comm—Cler: Pres A Dyer G Welin M Maxwell D Rogers T Russell Johnson; *Lay: Sec* B Lyons N Noyes J Carroll Jr E Seibert K Polhemus

Dio Conv: 13-14 Nov 2015 Cromwell CT

PARISHES, MISSIONS, AND CLERGY

Ansonia Christ Church Episcopal **P** (260) 56 South Cliff St 06401-1910 (Mail to: 56 South Cliff St 06401-1910) (203) 734-2715

Bantam St Pauls Episcopal Church **P** (90) 802 Bantam Rd 06750-1603 (Mail to: PO Box 449 06750-0449) Peter Stebinger (860) 567-8838

Bethany Christ Church Episcopal **P** (177) 526 Amity Rd 06524-3015 (Mail to: 526 Amity Rd 06524-3015) Elsa Worth (203) 393-3399

Bethel Church of St Thomas **P** (198) 95 Greenwood Ave 06801-2528 (Mail to: 95 Greenwood Ave 06801-2528) Norma Schmidt (203) 743-1494

Bethlehem Christ Episcopal Church **P** (90) Main St 06751 (Mail to: PO Box 520 06751-0520) (203) 266-7698

Bloomfield Old St Andrews Episcopal Church **P** (240) 59 Tariffville Rd 06002-1136 (Mail to: 59 Tariffville Rd 06002-1136)

Bloomfield St Stephens Episcopal Church **P** (150) 590 Bloomfield Ave 06002-3044 (Mail to: 590 Bloomfield Ave 06002-3044) Wilborne Austin

Bolton St Georges Episcopal Church **P** (58) 1150 BostonTpke 06043-7439 (Mail to: PO Box 9158 06043-9158) (860) 643-9203

Branford Trinity Episcopal Church **P** (493) 1109 Main St 06405-3715 (Mail to: 1109 Main St 06405-3770) Sharon Gracen (203) 488-2681

Bridgeport Calvary-St George Episcopal Church **P** (46) 755 Clinton Ave 06604-2302 (Mail to: 755 Clinton Ave 06604-2302)

Bridgeport St John's Episcopal Parish **P** (341) 768 Fairfield Ave 06604-3701 (Mail to: 768 Fairfield Ave 06604-3701) Geoffrey Hahneman José Mestre (203) 335-2528

Bridgeport St Lukes-St Pauls Episcopal Church **P** (1208) PO Box 2156 06608-0156 (Mail to: PO Box 2156 06608-0156) (203) 367-7009

Bridgeport St Marks Episcopal Church **P** (328) 401 Newfield Ave 06607-2218 (Mail to: 401 Newfield Ave. 06607-0182) (203) 335-5655

Bridgewater St Marks Episcopal Church **P** (49) 5 Main St S 06752-1521 (Mail to: PO Box 143 06752-0143) Daniel Mattila Robert Woodroofe (860) 354-8269

Bristol St Johns Episcopal Church **P** (237) 851 Stafford Ave 06010-3848 (Mail to: 851 Stafford Ave 06010-3848) Diane Caggiano Ellen Tillotson

Broad Brook Grace Episcopal Church **P** (66) 44 Old Ellington Rd 06016-9735 (Mail to: PO Box 405 06016-0405) Edward Goetz (860) 623-1574

Brookfield St Pauls Episcopal Church **P** (380) Attn K Kumerle 174 Whisconier Road 06804-3307 (Mail to: 174 Whisconier Road 06804-3307) Joseph Shepley George Crocker William Loring (203) 775-9587

Brooklyn Trinity Episcopal Church **P** (63) 7 Providence Rd 06234-0276 (Mail to: PO Box 276 06234-0276) (860) 774-9352

Cheshire St Peters Episcopal Church **P** (1134) 59 Main St 06410-2405 (Mail to: 59 Main St 06410-2468) David Stayner Sandra Stayner (203) 272-4041

Clinton Church of the Holy Advent **P** (310) 81 E Main St 06413-2139 (Mail to: PO Box 536 06413-0536) (860) 669-2232

Collinsville Trinity Church Collinsville **P** (407) 55 River Rd 06022 (Mail to: PO Box 374 06022-0374) Linda Spiers (860) 693-8172

Danbury St James Episcopal Church **P** (556) 25 West St 06810-7824 (Mail to: 25 West St 06810-7877) Joseph Krasinski (203) 748-3561

Danielson St Albans Episcopal Church **P** (62) 254 Broad St 06239-2903 (Mail to: 254 Broad St 06239-2903) (860) 774-8833

Darien Ascension Church For Deaf **M** (6) 1882 Post Rd 06820-5802 (Mail to: PO Box 271124 96127-1124) (203) 272-9958

Darien St Luke Episcopal Church **P** (2852) 1864 Post Rd 06820-5802 (Mail to: 1864 Post Rd 06820-5802) David Anderson Daniel Lennox Dawn Stegelmann Donald Thompson Denise Trogdon (203) 655-1456

Darien St Pauls Episcopal Church **P** (335) 471 Mansfield Ave 06820-2116 (Mail to: 471 Mansfield Ave 06820-2198) Novella Lawrence John Whitnah (203) 655-8773

Derby Immanuel St James Church Episcopal **P** (85) 105 Minerva St 06418-1896 (Mail to: PO Box 859 06418-0859) George Brower (203) 734-4149

Durham Church of the Epiphany **P** (226) 196 Main St 06422-2106 (Mail to: PO Box 337 06422-0337) Anthony Dinoto (860) 349-9644

East Berlin St Gabriels Church **P** (122) 68 Main St 06023-1130 (Mail to: PO Box 275 06023-0275) Audrey Scanlan Robert Watson (860) 828-3735

East Haddam St Stephens Episcopal Church **P** (417) 29 Main St 06423-1305 (Mail to: PO Box 464 06423-0464) Adam Yates (860) 873-9547

East Hartford All Saints Episcopal Church **P** (51) 444 Hills St 06118-2922 (Mail to: 444 Hills St 06118-2998) Michelle Hansen (860) 568-6175

✠ **East Hartford** Greater Hartford Regional Ministry **Other** 12 Rector St 06108-2261 (860) 528-1474

East Hartford St Johns Church **P** (36) 12 Rector Street 06108-2261 (Mail to: 12 Rector Street 06108-2261) Mark Santucci (860) 528-1474

East Haven Christ and the Epiphany Church **P** (54) 39 Park Pl 06512-2517 (Mail to: 39 Park Pl 06512-2517) (203) 467-2310

East Windsor St Johns Episcopal Church **P** (187) 92 Main St 06088-9651 (Mail to: 92 Main St 06088) Julia Fritts (860) 623-3273

Easton Christ Church **P** (317) 59 Church Rd 06612-1411 (Mail to: 59 Church Rd 06612-1411) Ellen Huber (203) 268-3569

Enfield Holy Trinity Episcopal Church **P** (299) 383 Hazard Ave 06082-4718 (Mail to: 379 Hazard Ave 06082-4718) Peter Bushnell Peter Vaughn (860) 749-2722

Essex St John's Episcopal Church **P** (447) 25 Main St 06426 (Mail to: PO Box 422 06426-0422) Jonathan Folts Mary-Lloyd Brainard Charlotte Laforest

Fairfield St Pauls Episcopal Church **P** (982) 661 Old Post Rd 06824-6648 (Mail to: 661 Old Post Rd 06824-6648) Paul Carling Stephanie Johnson (203) 259-3013

Fairfield St Timothys Church **P** (245) 4670 Congress St 06824-1721 (Mail to: 4670 Congress St 06824-1721) Richard Maxwell Alice Mindrum (203) 255-2740

Fairfield Trinity St Michaels Episcopal Church **P** (44) 554 Tunxis Hill Rd 06825-4412 (Mail to: 554 Tunxis Hill Rd 06825-4412) (203) 368-3225

Farmington St James Episcopal Church **P** (293) 3 Mountain Rd 06032-2339 (Mail to: 3 Mountain Rd 06032-2339) George Roberts (860) 677-1564

Gales Ferry St Davids Episcopal Church **P** (282) 284 Stoddards Wharf Rd 06335-1130 (Mail to: 284 Stoddards Wharf Rd 06335-1130) Rachel Thomas (860) 464-6516

Glastonbury St James Episcopal Church **P** (540) 2584 Main St 06033-4220 (Mail to: PO Box 206 06033-0206) Denise Cabana (860) 633-8333

Greenwich Christ Church Greenwich **P** (1981) 254 E Putnam Ave 06830-4801 (Mail to: 254 E Putnam Ave 06830-4871) James Lemler Ian Cron Suzanne Culhane Andrew Moore Jennifer Owen (203) 869-6600

Greenwich St Barnabas Episcopal Church **P** (416) 954 Lake Ave 06831-3032 (Mail to: 954 Lake Ave 06831-3099) Edward Pardoe Margaret Finnerud (203) 661-5526

Guilford Christ Episcopal Church **P** (453) 11 Park St 06437-2629 (Mail to: PO Box 574 06437-0574) Randolph West

Guilford St Johns Episcopal Church **P** (95) 129 Ledge Hill Rd 06437-1024 (Mail to: 129 Ledge Hill Rd 06437-1024) Maureen Lederman (203) 457-1094

Hamden Grace and St Peters Church **P** (147) 2927 Dixwell Ave 06518-3135 (Mail to: PO Box 185065 06518-0065) Amanda Gott (203) 248-4338

✣ **Hartford** Christ Church Cathedral **O** (458) 45 Church St 06103-1202 (Mail to: 45 Church St 06103-1299) Robert Carroon Miguelina Howell Stanley Kemmerer Geoffrey Ward Jervis Zimmerman (860) 527-7231

Hartford Good Shepherd El Buen Pastor **P** (181) 155 Wyllys St 06106-1957 (Mail to: 155 Wyllys St 06106-1957) Jose Irizarry Valerie Miller (860) 525-4289

Hartford Grace Episcopal Church **P** (102) Grace Episcopal Church 55 New Park Ave 06106-2123 (Mail to: Grace Episcopal Church 55 New Park Ave 06106-2123) Robert Carroon John Conners John Mitman Wayne Pokorny (860) 233-0825

Hartford St Martin Episcopal Church **M** (209) 290 Cornwall St 06112-1427 (Mail to: 290 Cornwall St 06112-1427) (860) 242-0318

Hartford St Monicas Church **P** (250) 3575 Main Street 06120-2326 (Mail to: PO Box 2184 06145-2184) Tracy Russell

Hartford Trinity College Chapel **CC** 300 Summit St 06106-3100 (Mail to: 300 Summit St 06106-3186) Allison Read (860) 297-2013

Hartford Trinity Episcopal Church **HC** (588) 120 Sigourney St 06105-2755 (Mail to: 120 Sigourney St 06105-2755) Donald Hamer Frank Kirkpatrick (860) 527-8133

Hebron St Peters Episcopal Church **P** (297) 30 Church St 06248-1427 (Mail to: 30 Church St 06248-1427) Everett Perine

Higganum Middlesex Area Cluster Ministry **P** PO Box 829 06441-0829 (Mail to: PO Box 829 06441-0829) Nathan Ives (860) 345-0058

Higganum St James Episcopal Church **P** (78) 498 Killingworth Rd 06441 (Mail to: PO Box 574 06441-0574) (860) 345-0058

Ivoryton All Saints Episcopal Church **P** (119) 129 Main St 06442-1103 (Mail to: PO Box 576 06442-0576) Brendan McCormick (860) 767-1698

Kent St Andrews Church **P** (381) 1 N Main St 06757-1512 (Mail to: PO Box 309 06757-0309) Roger White David Mcintosh Amy Reichman

Killingworth Emmanuel Episcopal Church **P** (48) PO Box 686 06419-0686 (Mail to: 50 Emanuel Church Rd 06419-1019) (860) 663-1800

Lakeville Trinity Church (Lime Rock) **P** (144) 484 Lime Rock Rd 06039-2404 (Mail to: 484 Lime Rock Rd 06039-2404) Heidi Truax (860) 435-2627

Litchfield St Michaels Church Episcopal **P** (420) 25 South St 06759-4005 (Mail to: PO Box 248 06759-0248) E Bevan Stanley (860) 567-9465

Madison St Andrews Church **P** (397) 232 Durham Rd 06443-2451 (Mail to: 232 Durham Rd 06443-2451) (203) 245-2584

Manchester St Marys Episcopal Church **P** (1154) 41 Park St 06040-5913 (Mail to: 41 Park St 06040-5913) Karen Fedorchak Marjorie Roccoberton (860) 649-4583

Marble Dale St Andrews Episcopal Church **P** (133) 247 New Milford Tpke 06777-0007 (Mail to: PO Box 2007 06777-0007) (860) 868-2275

Meriden All Saints Church **P** (65) 201 W Main St 06450 (Mail to: C/O Immanuel Lutheran Church 164 Hanover St 06451-5499) Michael Carroll (203) 235-9596

Meriden St Andrews Episcopal Church **P** (459) 20 Catlin St 06450-4204 (Mail to: 20 Catlin St 06450-4294) Marissa Rohrbach (203) 237-7451

Middle Haddam Christ Church **P** (118) 60 Middle Haddam Rd 06456 (Mail to: PO Box 81 06456-0081) Mary Anne Osborn

Middlebury St George Episcopal Church **P** (161) Tucker Hill Rd 06762-2517 (Mail to: PO Box 162 06762-0162) Andrew Zeman (203) 758-9864

Middletown Holy Trinity Church **P** (277) 381 Main St 06457-3309 (Mail to: 381 Main St 06457-3309) Dana Campbell (860) 347-2591

Milford St Andrew's Episcopal Church **P** (93) 283 Bridgeport Avenue 06460-5431 (Mail to: PO Box 2454 06460-5431) Patricia Leonard-Pasley (203) 874-2701

Milford St Peters Church **P** (327) 71 River St 06460-3315 (Mail to: 71 River St 06460-3315) Cynthia Knapp Angela Rowley (203) 874-8562

Monroe St Peters on the Green **P** (270) 175 Old Tannery Rd 06468-1932 (Mail to: 175 Old Tannery Rd 06468-1932) Kurt Huber

Mystic St Marks Episcopal Church **P** (485) 15 Pearl St 06355-2513 (Mail to: 15 Pearl St 06355-2599) Adam Thomas

N Branford Zion Episcopal Church **P** (248) 326 Notch Hill Rd 06471-1858 (Mail to: 326 Notch Hill Rd 06471-1858) Lucy Larocca

Naugatuck St Michaels Episcopal Parish **P** (277) 210 Church St 06770-4120 (Mail to: 210 Church St 06770-4197) Juliusz Jodko (203) 729-8249

New Britain St Marks Episcopal Church **P** (452) 147 W Main St 06052-1316 (Mail to: 147 W Main St 06052-1316) William Eakins Joseph Pace (860) 225-7634

New Canaan St Marks Episcopal Church **P** (1380)

111 Oenoke Rdg Ste 1 06840-4199 (Mail to: 111 Oenoke Ridge Rd 06840-4105) Peter Walsh Justin Crisp Martha Klein-Larsen Michael Rau (203) 966-4515

New Haven Christ Episcopal Church **P** (340) 84 Broadway 06511-3412 (Mail to: 84 Broadway 06511-3499) Ann Broomell Matthew Larsen Kent Smith Kenneth Thomas (203) 865-6354

New Haven Church of St Thomas **P** (225) 830 Whitney Ave 06511-1316 (Mail to: 830 Whitney Ave 06511-1316) Keri Aubert Amanda Gott Maureen Lederman William Loutrel

New Haven Episcopal Church at Yale **CC** No PO Box 201955 06520-1955 (Mail to: PO Box 201955 06520-1955) Paul Carling Bruce Shipman (203) 432-5401

New Haven St Andrews Episcopal Church **P** (82) 266 Shelton Ave 06511-1847 (Mail to: 262 Shelton Ave 06511-1847) (203) 562-1080

New Haven St Johns Church **P** (149) 400 Humphrey St 06511-3711 (Mail to: 400 Humphrey St 06511-3711) (203) 562-1487

New Haven St Lukes Episcopal Church **P** (224) 111 Whalley Ave 06511-3220 (Mail to: 111 Whalley Ave 06511-3293) Richard Meadows Paul Jacobson Betsey Lewis (203) 865-0141

New Haven St Paul - St James Episcopal Church **P** (182) 57 Olive St 06511-5739 (Mail to: 57 Olive St 06511-5739) (203) 562-2143

New Haven Trinity Church on the Green **P** (835) 950 Chapel Street, 2nd Floor 06510-2515 (Mail to: 950 Chapel St Fl 2 06510-2515) Luk De Volder Rowena Kemp (203) 624-3101

New London St James Episcopal Church **P** (313) 76 Federal St 06320-6601 (Mail to: 76 Federal St 06320-6601) (860) 443-4989

New Milford St Johns Episcopal Church **P** (236) 7 Whittlesey Ave 06776-3023 (Mail to: PO Box 179 06776-0179) John Gilpin Amy Reichman

Newington Grace Episcopal Church **P** (226) 124 Maple Hill Ave 06111-2719 (Mail to: 124 Maple Hill Ave 06111-2719) Robert Stocksdale (860) 666-3331

Newtown Trinity Church Episcopal **P** (741) Attn Ellsworth Stringer 36 Main St 06470-2106 (Mail to: 36 Main St 06470-2106) Kathleen Adams-Shepherd (203) 426-9070

Niantic St Johns Episcopal Church **P** (414) 400 Main St 06357 (Mail to: PO Box 810 06357-0810) Anthony Dinoto Dianne Warley (860) 739-2324

North Haven St Johns Episcopal Church **P** (331) 3 Trumbull Pl 06473-2522 (Mail to: 3 Trumbull Pl 06473-2522) Louise Kalemkerian (203) 239-0156

Northford St Andrew Episcopal Church **P** (63) Middletown Ave 06472 (Mail to: PO Box 96 06472-0096) (203) 484-0895

Norwalk Christ Episcopal Church **P** (174) 2 Emerson St 06855-1330 (Mail to: 2 Emerson

St 06855-1330) Patricia Coller (203) 866-7442

Norwalk Iglesia Betania Episcopal **P** (83) 1 Union Park 06850-3316 (Mail to: 1 Union Park 06850-3316) Eddie Lopez (203) 853-6767

Norwalk St Paul's on the Green **P** (621) 60 East Ave Ste 1 06851-4891 (Mail to: 60 East Ave 06851-4909) Nicholas Lang Holley Slauson Peter Thompson (203) 847-2806

Norwich Christ Episcopal Church **P** (192) 78 Washington St 06360-5039 (Mail to: 78 Washington St 06360-5039) John Hugh James (860) 887-4249

Oakville All Saints Episcopal Church **P** (280) 262 Main St 06779-1742 (Mail to: PO Box 33 06779-0033) Donna Downs (860) 274-2352

Old Greenwich St Saviours Church **P** (209) 350 Sound Beach Ave 06870-1930 (Mail to: 350 Sound Beach Ave 06870-1930) Victoria Miller (203) 637-2262

Old Lyme St Anns Episcopal Church **P** (213) 82 Shore Rd 06371-1726 (Mail to: 82 Shore Road 06371-1726) Mark Robinson (860) 434-1621

Old Saybrook Grace Episcopal Church **P** (311) 336 Main St 06475-2350 (Mail to: 336 Main St 06475-2350) Ellendale Hoffman (860) 388-0895

Orange Church of the Good Shepherd **P** (252) 680 Racebrook Rd 06477-1931 (Mail to: 680 Racebrook Rd 06477-1931) (203) 795-6577

Oxford Christ Church Quaker Farms **P** (249) 470 Quaker Farms Rd 06478-1307 (Mail to: 470 Quaker Farms Rd 06478-1398) John Donnelly (203) 888-4936

Oxford St Peters Episcopal Church **P** (65) No 421 Oxford Rd 06478-1692 (Mail to: C/O Lee Gill 421 Oxford Rd 06478-1236) Frances Donnelly (203) 888-5279

Pine Meadow St Johns Episcopal Church **P** (242) 51 Church St 06061 (Mail to: PO Box 27 06061-0027) Sandra Cosman (860) 379-3062

Plainfield St Pauls Episcopal Church **P** (111) 27 Babcock Ave 06374-1222 (Mail to: 27 Babcock Ave 06374-1222) Victoria Baldwin Scott Stevens (860) 564-3560

Plainville Church of Our Saviour **P** (148) 115 W Main St 06062-1905 (Mail to: 115 W Main St 06062-1905) (860) 747-3109

Pomfret Christ Church Episcopal **P** (436) 521 Pomfret St 06258 (Mail to: PO Box 21 06258-0021) David Carter Virginia Army (860) 928-7026

Portland Trinity Church **P** (285) 345 Main St 06480-1561 (Mail to: 345 Main St 06480-1561) Steven Ling (860) 342-0458

Preston St James Church **P** (157) 95 Route 2a 06365-8538 (Mail to: 95 Route 2A 06365-8538) Ronald Kolanowski (860) 889-0150

Putnam St Philip Episcopal Parish **P** (24) 63 Grove St 06260-2109 (Mail to: 63 Grove St 06260-2109) (860) 928-3510

Redding Christ Church Parish **P** (336) 184 Cross

Hwy 06896-2101 (Mail to: PO Box 54 06876-0054) Marilyn Anderson Nicki Kimes (203) 938-2872

Ridgefield St Stephens Church **P** (658) 351 Main St 06877-4601 (Mail to: 351 Main St 06877-4601) Whitney Altopp Leslie Hughs (203) 438-3789

Riverside St Paul's Church **P** (545) 200 Riverside Ave 06878-2210 (Mail to: 200 Riverside Ave 06878-2210) Harry Roark K Alon White (203) 637-2447

Rocky Hill St Andrew the Apostle **P** (503) 331 Orchard St 06067-2022 (Mail to: 331 Orchard St 06067-2022) William Veinot John Rogers (860) 529-7622

Roxbury Christ Church **P** (162) 1 Church St 06783-1702 (Mail to: PO Box 4 06783-0004) Robert Clements (860) 355-3695

Salisbury St Johns Episcopal Church **P** (198) 12 Main St 06068-1800 (Mail to: PO Box 391 06068-0391) Lance Beizer David Sellery (860) 435-9290

Sandy Hook St Johns Church **P** (35) Washington Ave 06482 (Mail to: 5 Washington Ave 06482)

Seymour Trinity Episcopal Church **P** (153) 91 Church St 06483-2611 (Mail to: 91 Church St 06483-2611)

Sharon Christ Episcopal Church **P** (72) 9 S Main St 06069-1778 (Mail to: PO Box 1778 06069-1778) Carl Widing (860) 364-5260

Shelton Church of the Good Shepherd **P** (190) 182 Coram Ave 06484-3347 (Mail to: 182 Coram Ave 06484-3347) Ballard Dorsee

Shelton St Pauls Episcopal Church **P** (293) 25 Church St 06484-5802 (Mail to: 25 Church St 06484-5897) Knute Hansen Amjad Samuel (203) 929-1722

Simsbury St Albans Episcopal Church **P** (211) 197 Bushy Hill Rd 06070-2604 (Mail to: 197 Bushy Hill Rd 06070-2699) Rebekah Hatch (860) 658-0406

South Glastonbury St Lukes Episcopal Church **P** (284) PO Box 155 06073-0155 (Mail to: PO Box 155 06073-0155) Kim Litsey Marian Stinson (860) 633-7175

South Windsor St Peters Episcopal Church **P** (181) 109 Sand Hill Rd 06074-2026 (Mail to: 109 Sand Hill Rd 06074-2051) Thomas White (860) 644-8548

Southbury Church of the Epiphany **P** (78) 262 Main St N 06488-1808 (Mail to: 262 Main St N 06488-1808) Marston Price (203) 264-8150

Southington St Pauls Episcopal Church **P** (339) 145 Main St 06489-2505 (Mail to: 145 Main St 06489-2505) Suzannah Rohman (860) 628-8486

Southport Trinity Episcopal Church **P** (898) PO Box 400 06890-0400 (Mail to: PO Box 400 06890-0400) Margaret Hodgkins Matthew Lindeman Leslie Smith

Stafford Springs Grace Church Parish Episcopal

P (85) 5 Spring St 06076 (Mail to: PO Box 65 06076-0065) Bennett Brockman (860) 684-2824

Stamford Church of Christ the Healer **P** (103) 20 Brookdale Rd 06903-4117 (Mail to: 20 Brookdale Rd 06903-4117) Katherine Heichler (203) 322-6991

Stamford Eglise De L'Epiphanie **M** (91) 628 Main St 06901-2011 (Mail to: 628 Main St 06901-2011) (203) 964-1517

Stamford St Andrews Church **P** (120) 1231 Washington Blvd 06901 (Mail to: 1231 Washington Blvd 06902-2402) Bartlett Gage

Stamford St Francis Church **P** (350) 2810 Long Ridge Road 06903-1110 (Mail to: 503 Old Long Ridge Rd 06903-1110) Mark Lingle Mark Lingle Debra Slade (203) 322-2949

Stamford St Johns Church **P** (991) 628 Main St 06901-2011 (Mail to: 628 Main St 06901-2094) James Wheeler Kathleen Berkowe Elizabeth Skaleski (203) 348-2619

Stonington Calvary Church **P** (589) 33 Church St 06378-1344 (Mail to: 27 Church St 06378-1344) William Tisdale Douglass Lind Alan Murchie (860) 535-1181

Storrs St Marks Chapel **P** (158) 42 N Eagleville Rd 06268-1710 (Mail to: 42 N Eagleville Rd 06268-1710) Hilary Greer (704) 782-2024

Stratford Christ Episcopal Church **P** (359) 2000 Main St 06615-6340 (Mail to: 2000 Main St 06615-6397) Scott Lee (203) 378-1445

Tariffville Trinity Episcopal Church **P** (643) 11 Church Street 06081-9624 (Mail to: 11 Church Street 06081) Thomas Furrer Patrick Bush Shaw Mudge (860) 651-0201

Thomaston St Peters Trinity Church **Chapel** (233) 160 Main St 06787-1720 (Mail to: 160 Main St 06787-1720) Mark Byers (203) 268-2809

Torrington Trinity Episcopal Church **P** (332) 220 Prospect St 06790-5314 (Mail to: 220 Prospect St 06790-5314) Ann Johnson Amy Reichman (860) 482-6027

Trumbull Christ Episcopal Church Tashua **P** (134) 5170 Madison Ave 06611-1110 (Mail to: 5170 Madison Ave 06611-1110) Robert Neville (203) 268-5566

Trumbull Grace Episcopal Church **P** (91) 5958 Main St 06611-2413 (Mail to: 5958 Main St 06611-2497) Robert Neville (203) 268-2809

Trumbull Trinity Episcopal Church (Nichols) **P** (178) 1734 Huntington Tpk 06611-5114 (Mail to: 1734 Huntington Tpke 06611-5114) Ellen Kennedy (203) 375-1503

Vernon Rockville St Johns Episcopal Church **P** (357) 523 Hartford Tpke 06066-4900 (Mail to: 523 Hartford Tpke 06066-4900) Virginia Army William Byers (860) 872-0517

Wallingford St John Evangelist Episcopal **P** (123) 360 Church St 06492-2200 (Mail to: 360 Church St 06492-2200) Peter Quinn (203) 269-9526

Wallingford St Pauls Episcopal Church **P** (860) 65 N Main St 06492-3709 (Mail to: 65 N Main St 06492-3795) Debra Dodd (203) 269-5050

Washington St Johns Church **P** (354) 78 Green Hill Rd 06793-1217 (Mail to: PO Box 1278 06793-0278) Susan McCone (860) 868-2527

Waterbury Christ Church **P** (70) 2030 E Main St 06705-2607 (Mail to: 2030 E Main St 06705-2607) (203) 753-6921

Waterbury St Johns Episcopal Church **P** (420) 16 Church St 06702-2103 (Mail to: 16 Church St 06702-2103) Amy Welin (203) 754-3116

West Hartford St James Church Episcopal **P** (1062) 1018 Farmington Ave 06107-2105 (Mail to: 19 Walden St 06107-1822) Robert Hooper Curtis Farr Molly Louden (860) 521-9620

West Hartford St Johns Church Episcopal **P** (874) 679 Farmington Ave 06119-1895 (Mail to: 679 Farmington Ave 06119-1895) Hope Eakins John Gedrick Susan Pinkerton (860) 523-5201

West Hartford St Pauls Mission of the Deaf **M** (6) c/o St. Johns Church 679 Farmington Ave 06119-1811 (Mail to: c/o St. Johns Church 679 Farmington Ave 06119-1811) (860) 756-5601

West Haven Church of the Holy Spirit **P** (216) 28 Church St 06516-4927 (Mail to: 28 Church St 06516-4927) Lisa Hahneman

Westbrook St Pauls Episcopal Church **P** (70) 53 S Main St 06498-1902 (Mail to: PO Box 598 06498-0598) (860) 669-7681

Weston Emmanuel Episcopal Church **P** (193) 285 Lyons Plain Rd 06883-2401 (Mail to: 285 Lyons Plain Rd 06883-2441) Katherine Herron-Piazza (203) 227-8565

Westport Christ and Holy Trinity Church **P** (1187) 75 Church Lane 06880-3510 (Mail to: 55 Myrtle Ave 06880-3510) Colin Chapman Whitney Edwards Peter Powell (203) 227-0827

Wethersfield Trinity Episcopal Church **P** (380) 300 Main St 06109-1826 (Mail to: 300 Main St 06109-1892) Lois Keen (860) 529-6825

Willimantic St Pauls Episcopal Church **P** (80) 220 Valley St 06226-2332 (Mail to: 220 Valley St 06226-2399) Jaclyn Sheldon (860) 423-8455

Wilton St Matthews Episcopal Church **P** (1230) 36 New Canaan Rd 06897-3310 (Mail to: 36 New Canaan Rd 06897-3310) Mary Grace Williams Richard Mayberry (203) 762-7400

Windham St Pauls Church **P** (110) 26 Plains Rd 06280-1324 (Mail to: PO Box 82 06280-0082) John Burton (860) 423-9653

Windsor Grace Church Episcopal **P** (299) 311 Broad St 06095-2906 (Mail to: 311 Broad St 06095-2906) Harry Elliott Denise Adessa (860) 688-1232

Winsted St James Episcopal Church **P** (133) 160 Main St 06098-1735 (Mail to: 160 Main St 06098-1735) (860) 379-5657

Wolcott All Saints Episcopal Church **P** (168) 282 Bound Line Rd 06716-2508 (Mail to: PO Box 6015 06716-0015) Susan Davidson Sonnie Fish (203) 879-2800

Woodbury St Pauls Episcopal Church **P** (353) 249 Main St S 06798-3408 (Mail to: PO Box 5002 06798-5002) Frederick Kuhlmann Gregory Welin (203) 263-3541

Yantic Grace Church Episcopal **P** (58) PO Box 126 06389-0126 (Mail to: 4 Chapel Hill Road 06389) Peter D'Alesandre (860) 887-2082

NON-PAROCHIAL CLERGY

Adams EE *dcn* Norwich CT
Agbo G Putnam CT
Aiken RL *ret* Truro MA
Alexis J
Allen DF *dcn* Wallingford CT
Allen RH *ret* Harwich MA
Alling R *ret* Camp Hill PA
Anderheggen GC *ret* Monroe CT
Andersen RW *ret* Cheshire CT
Anderson-Krengel WE Middletown CT
Archer CS *dcn*
Baker CM *ret* Gales Ferry CT
Balmer R Norwich VT
Barden AA Norridgewock ME
Barfield DOE *dcn* Bridgeport CT
Barnum E *dcn* Stamford CT
Barnum MM *dcn* Stamford CT
Beattie RE *ret* Orange CT
Beattie RS *ret* Old Greenwich CT
Beck TF *ret*
Bedrosian M *ret* Spring Hill FL
Belcher SA *ret* Woodbury CT
Belt M *ret* New London CT
Bergner RA Bloomfield CT
Bersin RAH *ret* Boxford MA
Birdsall JA *ret*
Black RE *ret* Bradford CT
Bottone DA *dcn* Berlin CT
Bradley J *ret* Cheshire CT
Branson JH *ret* Pittsboro NC
Briggs PR *ret* East Longmeadow MA
Brison WS *ret* Bury
Brooks RJ *ret* Kyle TX
Brown DW *ret* Charlestown RI
Burdick HC *ret* Edenton NC
Burke CC *ret* Bloomfield CT
Canavan MA Cumberland RI
Cannon DL *ret* Preston CT
Carter JF *ret* Salisbury CT
Cheney BT *ret* Hamden CT
Cheney KD *ret* Hamden CT
Chuboff EL *ret* Clinton CT
Ciriello MA *ret* Leland NC
Collamore HB *dcn*
Congdon WH
Connors BM *dcn* Saint Helens OR
Cooke DT *ret* West Hartford CT
Cooke JD Higganum CT
Coolidge EC *ret* Cromwell CT
Coughlin CF *ret* Bloomfield CT
Cowper JA *ret* Middletown CT

Cox RL *ret* Southport CT
Crysler F *ret* Louisville KY
Cudworth RW *dcn* Bloomfield CT
Dalton HL *ret* Hartford CT
Davidson PF *ret* Lyme CT
Davis VM *ret* New Haven CT
Daw C *ret* Watertown MA
De Chambeau FA *ret* Lakeville CT
De La Torre C
De Lanerolle NC New Haven CT
De Wolf MA *ret* Bristol RI
Debboli WA *ret* Plainville CT
Deming R *ret* Orange CT
Deragon RL *ret* Cocoa FL
Dezhbod ES Woodbury CT
Dixon VW *ret* Niantic CT
Domienik S Madison CT
Donnelly RC *ret* York PA
Dorr KE *ret* East Haven CT
Dugan JS *ret* Bloomfield CT
Duval RJ *ret* Whitehall PA
Dyer CA New Haven CT
Ellis RA *ret* Scarborough ME
Engwall DB *dcn* Collinsville CT
Feyrer DA *ret* Southern Shores NC
Ficks RL *ret* Columbus OH
Fiddler A *ret* New Haven CT
Fish CC *ret* Albuquerque NM
Floyd PW *ret* Higganum CT
Folts KS Essex CT
Forshaw L *dcn* Stratford CT
Frederick JBM *ret* Princeton NJ
Friedrich RE *ret* Wenham MA
Gage NE *dcn* Trumbull CT
Gallagher PMP *ret* Hamden CT
Gary HJ *ret* Fort Lauderdale FL
Gatta JM Sewanee TN
Gilbert MD Grosse Pointe Farms MI
Gilchrist JR *ret* Winter Harbor ME
Gilkes OW New Haven CT
Gillen MW *dcn*
Given ME Richardson TX
Glaude RA *ret* Brooklyn CT
Glazier WS *ret* Mystic CT
Gossling NE *ret* Glastonbury CT
Greene J *ret* Bridgeport CT
Greene-McCreight K New Haven CT
Greenlee MB Wilton CT
Grifo LA Bay Head NJ
Gurniak DF *ret* Southbury CT
Hall GE *ret* Southbury CT
Hames P *ret* New Britain CT
Hardwick W *ret* Norwalk CT
Harris RS *ret* Waterford CT
Heischman DR New York NY
Hodapp T Hartford CT
Hoffman CL *ret* Old Saybrook CT
Hoidra CA New York NY
Howard FC *ret* Simsbury CT
Hulme SE *ret* East Lyme CT
Hummel VK *ret* Hartford CT

Jackson PG *dcn* Hartford CT
James MF West Hartford CT
Jenkins GW *ret* Southington CT
Jeuland EV Shelton CT
Jeuland JCE Wethersfield CT
Jimenez-Irizarry E *ret* San Juan PR
Johnson HS *ret* Ormond Beach FL
Johnson MME Westport CT
Johnston PN Lafayette LA
Jones AL Norwalk CT
Kane DE *dcn* West Hartford CT
Keene KC *ret* Auburn MA
Keeney-Mulligan GD *ret* Oklahoma City OK
Kelderman KE Kent CT
Kellaway JL *ret* Pomfret Center CT
Kelsey JV *ret* Branford CT
Kelsey PT *ret* Hanover NH
Kilbourn TL *ret* Bethlehem CT
Kimball AB *ret* Fort Myers FL
Knauff EA *dcn* Hartford CT
Knisely HL *ret* Carlisle PA
Lamkin MW
Lapre AC *dcn* Fredericksburg VA
Larsen GS *ret* Dunnellon FL
Lavallee AA *ret* Charlotte NC
Leary KD *dcn* Woodbridge CT
Leighton C *ret* Bridgeport CT
Lewis CJ
Lewis KD Seymour CT
Libby RA *ret* Annapolis MD
Lillpopp DR *ret* Spring Hill FL
Limpitlaw JD *ret* Wellfleet MA
Little GA New Haven CT
Lloyd EA Stonington CT
Logue MAW New Haven CT
Lora JB *ret* Danbury CT
Low JR *ret* Saco ME
Low SM *ret* Pine Meadow CT
Macort JG *ret* Sarasota FL
Mallory R *ret* Stamford CT
Manderbach A *ret* Redding CT
Mann MA
Mansfield RH *ret* Avon CT
Mariconda TN *dcn* Newtown CT
Martinez J Hartford CT
Mason AN *ret* Woodstock CT
Mason B *dcn* Litchfield CT
Matheson MJJ *ret* Litchfield CT
Matthews BA *dcn* Hartford CT
Mayorga-Gonzalez M *ret* Lawrence MA
McGee KM *ret* Hamden CT
McGee-Street EL *ret* Hamden CT
McKenney W *dcn* West Hartford CT
McKinley EB
Meachen JW *dcn* Winooski VT
Miles KK Fairfield CT
Miller AC *ret* West Hartford CT
Miller BW *ret* West Hartford CT
Miner RJ *ret* Wallingford CT
Minnick M *ret* Middletown CT
Moore HM *ret* Hartford CT

Moore MR *ret* Milford CT
Morgan D Darien CT
Morris AJ *ret* Dunnellon FL
Munro JAR *ret* Bloomfield CT
Murdock AJ *ret*
Myers MA *ret* Marble Dale CT
Neel-Richard JL *ret* New Haven CT
Nixon BE Sacramento CA
Nolan RT Pompano Beach FL
Normann MEM *dcn* Southbury CT
Norris D Stamford CT
Oglesby PA Trumbull CT
Osmun AG *ret* Milford CT
Owen DA *ret* Canton CT
Page DR *ret* Somers Point NJ
Painter BW West Hartford CT
Parachini DC *ret* Northford CT
Parker SD *ret* Sarasota FL
Paul W *ret* Port-Au-Prince
Peet DH *ret* Sandisfield MA
Peterson DM *dcn* Trumbull CT
Phelps JP *ret* Niantic CT
Pople D *ret* Bethel CT
Porter NT Southport CT
Pritchard DG *ret* Wallingford CT
Purnell EG *ret* Simsbury CT
Randall CL Woodbury CT
Ray MF *ret* New Haven CT
Razee GW *ret* Essex CT
Rhodes JL Fairfield CT
Richards R *ret* Berlin NH
Richey DD *dcn* Cromwell CT
Rick JW Los Angeles CA
Robertshaw AB *ret* North Branford CT
Robinson FK *ret* Salisbury MD
Rodgers PR *ret* New Haven CT
Rogers EP *ret* Niantic CT
Rogers MB *ret* Granville NY
Rogers MD Middletown CT
Rogers V *ret* New Haven CT
Rose C *ret* Hartford CT

Ross RM *ret* Danbury CT
Rupp T
Seddon AC *ret* Suffield CT
Sharp CJ New Haven CT
Silbereis R *ret* Hartford CT
Smith A Vinalhaven ME
Speck-Ewer NS Bradenton FL
Speer JD *ret* Waterbury CT
Spellman RGW *ret* Bloomfield CT
St Louis JA Alexandria VA
Starbuck E Kent CT
Stevens H *ret* Killingworth CT
Stickney JB *ret* Higganum CT
Stuhlmann R *ret* Stratford CT
Taylor RE *ret* Essex CT
Tedesco WN *ret* South Yarmouth MA
Tessman M *ret*
Toffey JE *ret* Watertown CT
Tolzmann LAD Riverside CT
Tombaugh RF *ret* Hartford CT
Torrey BN *ret* East Windsor CT
Tuchols FJ Fairfield CT
Tudor-Foley HW *ret* Studio City CA
Tumminio Hansen DE Quincy MA
Tyson L Madison CT
Van Wely RF *ret* Greenwich CT
Viechweg EV *dcn* Stamford CT
Voets KA Irvington NY
Wagenseller JP *ret* Westport CT
Warren AL Hartford CT
Webb EC *ret* Hamden CT
Webber CL *ret* San Francisco CA
Wellner RH *ret* Schnecksville PA
West BF *ret* Manchester CT
White-hassler MJ *ret* Newington CT
Williams PM *ret* Hanover NH
Wilson JG *ret* Stratford CT
Wolff PM Wallingford CT
Wood M Providence RI
Wyper SC Bedford NY
Wysong TM *ret* Marion CT

DIOCESE OF DALLAS

(PROVINCE VII)
Comprises 25 counties in Northeast Texas
DIOCESAN OFFICE 1630 N Garrett Ave Dallas TX 75206
TEL (214) 826-8310   FAX (214) 826-5968
E-MAIL info@edod.org   WEB www.edod.org

Previous Bishops—
Alexander C Garrett 1874-1924, Harry T Moore coadj 1917 Bp 1924-46, Chas A Mason coadj 1945 Bp 1946-70, Gerald F Burrill suffr 1950-54, John JM Harte suffr 1954-62, Theology H McCrea suffr 1962-75, William Paul Barnds suffr 1966-73, A Donald Davies 1970-82, Robt E Terwilliger suffr 1975-86, Donis D Patterson 1983-92, David Bruce MacPherson suffr 1999-02, James Monte Stanton 1993-2014

Bishop — Rt Rev George Robinson Sumner (1090) (Dio 14 Nov 2015)

Bishop Suffragan — Rt Rev Paul Emil Lambert

Treas T Graves; *Chanc* T Mack; *Comm* K Durnan; *Misn/ChrEd & Yth Min* PW Dunbar; *Sec Conv* RR D'Antoni; *Dio Serv* SL Mills; *Evang* C Headington; *Budg & Fin* T Young; *Archdcn* R Trei

Stand Comm—Cler: Pres W Cavanaugh M Gilton T Reisner; *Lay:* T Graves C Dolt J LaCour

Dio Conv: TBD November 2016 Parish Episcopal School

PARISHES, MISSIONS, AND CLERGY

Allen Church of the Savior **P** (87) 1223 N Alma Dr 75013-4695 (Mail to: 2717 S Colfax Circle 75075-3159) Michael Hurst (214) 785-1612

Athens Church of St Matthias **P** (55) Attn Charlene Tucker 205 Willowbrook Dr 75751-3537 (Mail to: 205 Willowbrook Dr 75751-3537) (903) 675-3210

Atlanta All Saints Episcopal Church **M** (22) 404 N Louise St 75551-2240 (Mail to: PO Box 513 75551-0513) (903) 796-7200

Bonham Church of the Holy Trinity **M** (15) 617 Star St 75418-3630 (Mail to: PO Box 81 75418-0081) (903) 375-3859

Canton St Justin Martyr **PS** (61) 977 W Highway 243 75103-2021 (Mail to: PO Box 87 75103-0087) Ronald Studenny (903) 567-4959

Cedar Hill Church of the Good Shepherd **P** (235) 915 Straus Rd 75104-5317 (Mail to: PO Box 429 75106-0429) Marc Dobson (972) 291-4528

Coppell Church of the Apostles **P** (438) 322 S Macarthur Blvd 75019-3605 (Mail to: PO Box 1700 75019-1700) Timothy Cherry (972) 462-0234

Corsicana St Johns Episcopal Church **P** (333) 101 N 14th St 75110-5110 (Mail to: 101 N 14th St 75110-5110) Edward Monk (903) 874-5425

✠ **Dallas** Cathedral Church of St Matthew **O** (920) 5100 Ross Ave 75206-7709 (Mail to: 5100 Ross Ave 75206-7709) Neal Michell Maria Barrios George Conger Johnny Cook Diana Luck David Miller Bonnie Morrill Antonio Munoz (214) 823-8134

Dallas Christ Episcopal Church **P** (461) 534 West 10th Street 75208-4720 (Mail to: 534 West 10th Street 75208-4720) Fabian Villalobos (214) 941-0339

Dallas Church of the Good Shepherd **P** (961) 11122 Midway Rd 75229-4118 (Mail to: 11122 Midway Rd 75229-4199) Michael Mills Thomas Hotchkiss Perry Mullins (214) 351-6468

Dallas Church of the Incarnation **P** (4674) 3966 McKinney Ave 75204-8230 (Mail to: 3966 McKinney Ave 75204-2099) Anthony Burton Dorothy Budd Joseph Hermerding Harry Hill Robert Johnston Matthew Larsen Christopher Yoder (214) 521-5101

Dallas Church of the Resurrection **P** 11540 Ferguson Rd 75228-1806 (Mail to: 11540 Ferguson Rd 75228-1825)

Dallas Church of the Transfiguration **P** (1783) 14115 Hillcrest Rd 75254-8622 (Mail to: 14115 Hillcrest Rd 75254-8622) James Barber Michael Merriman Elizabeth O'Donnell Terence Roper Robert Shobe Erin Warde (972) 233-1898

Dallas Emmanuel Anglican **PS** St Luke's Episcopal Church 5923 Royal Ln 75230-3841 (Mail to: C/O St Luke's Episcopal Church 5923 Royal Ln 75230-3841)

Dallas Episcopal Church of Ascension **D** (533) § 8787 Greenville Ave 75243 (Mail to: 8787 Greenville Ave 75243) Paul Klitzke Ernest McAfee Sue Ross (214) 340-4196

Dallas Episcopal Church of Our Saviour **M** (67) 1616 N Jim Miller Rd 75217-1320 (Mail to: 1616 N Jim Miller Rd 75217-1320) (214) 391-2824

Dallas Episcopal Church of the Holy Cross **P** (46) 4052 Herschel Ave 75219-2930 (Mail to: 4052 Herschel Ave 75219-2930) George Brown (214) 528-3855

Dallas Good Samaritan Episcopal Church **M** (55) 1522 Highland Rd 75218-4420 (Mail to: 1522 Highland Rd 75218-4420) Mary Lessmann (214) 328-3883

Dallas Holy Faith **PS** Trinity Episcopal 12727 Hillcrest Rd 75230-2007 (Mail to: C/O Trinity Episcopal 12727 Hillcrest Rd 75230-2007)

Dallas Resurrection Grace Episcopal Church **M** (83) 11540 Ferguson Road 75228 (Mail to: PO Box 851800 75185-1800) Gordon Miltenberger (972) 285-5824

Dallas Saint Michael and All Angels Church **P** (6926) 8011 Douglas Avenue 75225-0385 (Mail to: PO Box 12385 75225-0385) Oliver Butler William Murray Lisa Musser Gregory Pickens Charles Ruffin Douglas Travis (214) 363-5471

Dallas San Francisco de Asis **P** (155) 11540 Ferguson Rd 75228-1825 (Mail to: 11540 Ferguson Rd 75228-1825) Juana Lara (972) 279-6501

Dallas St Albans Canterbury House at SMU **CC** 3308 Daniel Ave 75205-1440 (Mail to: 3308 Daniel Ave 75205-1440) (214) 363-2911

Dallas St Andrews Episcopal Church **P** (220) 2783 Valwood Pkwy 75234-3529 (Mail to: 2783 Valwood Pkwy 75234-3529) Craig Reed (972) 247-7702

Dallas St Christophers Episcopal Church **P** (93) 7900 Lovers Ln 75225-8200 (Mail to: 7900 W Lovers Ln 75225-8200) Pleasant Murphy (214) 363-2792

Dallas St James Episcopal Church **P** (387) 9845 Mccree Rd 75238-3444 (Mail to: 9845 McCree Rd 75238-3444) Eugene Gardner Rebecca Tankersley (214) 348-1345

Dallas St Johns Episcopal Church **P** (503) 848 Harter Rd 75218-2751 (Mail to: 848 Harter Rd 75218-2792) David Houk Herbert DeWees John Thorpe (214) 321-6451

Dallas St Lukes Episcopal Church **P** (313) 5923

Royal Ln 75230-3812 (Mail to: 5923 Royal Ln 75230-3841) James Loughren Rosemary Trei (214) 368-6304

Dallas St Peters Anglican Church **PS** 3617 Abrams Rd 75214-3009 (Mail to: 11540 Ferguson 75228) (214) 460-0094

Dallas St Thomas the Apostle Church **P** (405) 6525 Inwood Rd 75209-5314 (Mail to: 6525 Inwood Rd 75209-5314) Joy Daley (214) 352-0410

Dallas Trinity Anglican Church **M** (138) 12727 Hillcrest Road c/o Trinity Episcopal Church 75230-2007 (Mail to: 12727 Hillcrest Rd c/o Trinity Episcopal Church 75230-2007) (972) 991-3601

Dallas Trinity Episcopal Church **P** (41) 12727 Hillcrest Rd 75230-2007 (Mail to: 12727 Hillcrest Rd 75230-2007) James Lee Robin Smith Philip Snyder (972) 991-3601

Denison St Lukes Church **P** (178) 427 W Woodard St 75020 (Mail to: 427 W Woodard St 75020-3138) Donald Perschall (903) 465-2630

Denton St Barnabas Episcopal Church **P** (337) 1200 N Elm St 76201-2941 (Mail to: 1200 N Elm St 76201-2941) Donald Johnson (940) 382-2748

Denton St Davids Church **P** (416) 623 Ector St 76201-2423 (Mail to: 623 Ector St 76201-2423) Herbert Herrmann Clinton Wilson (940) 387-2622

Desoto St Anne Episcopal Church **P** (441) 1700 N Westmoreland Rd 75115-2272 (Mail to: 1700 N Westmoreland Rd 75115-2272) James Harris George Udell (972) 709-0691

Ennis St Thomas Episcopal Church **M** (93) 901 Park St 75119-1607 (Mail to: PO Box 475 75120-0475) Mark Given (972) 875-2423

Flower Mound Saint Nicholas Church **P** (362) 4800 Wichita Trl 75022-5121 (Mail to: 4800 Wichita Trl 75022-5121) Mark Wright (972) 318-7070

Frisco St Philips Church **P** (1430) 8102 Stonebrook Pkwy Ste 300 75034-7220 (Mail to: 6400 Stonebrook Pkwy 75034-5711) Thomas Methvin Janice Krause (214) 387-4700

Garland Holy Trinity Episcopal Church **P** (236) 3217 Guthrie Rd 75043-6121 (Mail to: 3217 Guthrie Rd 75043-6121) John Brown (972) 226-1283

Garland St Barnabas Episcopal Church **P** (276) 1200 N Shiloh Rd 75042-5724 (Mail to: 1200 N Shiloh Rd 75042-5769) Alyce Schrimsher Alfredo Williams (972) 494-6600

Garland St Davids Church **P** (91) 2022 Saturn Rd 75041-1640 (Mail to: 2022 Saturn Rd 75041-1640) David Krause

Gilmer St Davids Episcopal Church **P** 211 E Marshall St 75644-2227 (Mail to: PO Box 1085 75644-1085) (903) 843-3838

Greenville St Pauls Episcopal Church **P** (302) 8320 Jack Finney Blvd 75402-3004 (Mail to: 8320 Jack Finney Blvd 75402-3004) Gary Herbst (903) 455-5030

Irving Episcopal Church of the Redeemer **P** (258) 2700 Warren Cir 75062-9242 (Mail to: 2700 Warren Cir 75062-9242) Michael Wallens

Irving St Marks Episcopal Church **P** (144) 516 S O Connor Rd 75060-4059 (Mail to: 516 S O'Connor Rd 75060-4088) Robert Corley (972) 253-7124

Irving St Marys Episcopal Church **P** (957) 635 N Story Rd 75061-6732 (Mail to: 635 N Story Rd 75061-6728) Jose Bernal Christopher Steele (972) 790-4644

Kaufman Church of Our Merciful Saviour **M** (90) 500 S Jackson St 75142-2330 (Mail to: PO Box 520 75142-0520) David Petrash (972) 932-4646

Kemp St James Episcopal Church **P** (119) 10707 C R 4022 75143 (Mail to: 10707 County Road 4022 75143-4217) Jerry Morriss (903) 498-8080

Lancaster St Martins Episcopal Church **M** (15) 700 Westridge Ave 75146-2248 (Mail to: PO Box 550 75146-0550) Nancy Hood (972) 227-1311

Lewisville Church of the Annunciation **P** (709) 602 N Old Orchard Ln 75077-2869 (Mail to: PO Box 292365 75029-2365) Catherine Thompson Ralph Masters Leslie Stewart Ames Swartsfager (972) 221-3531

McKinney Church of the Holy Family **M** (275) 406 Lincoln St 75069-4263 (Mail to: PO Box 693 75070-8142) (972) 542-5799

McKinney St Peters Episcopal Church **P** (492) 400 S College St 75069 (Mail to: 511 Foote St 75069-2707) Michael Hoffman Elizabeth Breyfogle Kathy Garrett (972) 562-1166

McKinney St Andrews Episcopal Church **M** (550) 6400 McKinney Ranch Pkwy 75070-9601 (Mail to: 6400 McKinney Ranch Pkwy 75070) Michael Michie Andrew Van Kirk (972) 548-7990

Mineola St Dunstan Episcopal Church **P** (158) 800 N Johnson St 75773-1816 (Mail to: PO Box 81 75773-0081) Archibald Young (903) 569-2478

Mt Pleasant St Mark Episcopal Church **P** (93) 205 E Pecan St 75455-5403 (Mail to: PO Box 1837 75456-1837) Ethel Channon (903) 572-3211

Murphy St Timothy's Episcopal Church **P** 201 N Murphy Rd 75094-3513 (Mail to: 2700 Arbor Ct 75082-3802) Brendan Kimbrough (972) 235-3434

Paris Church of the Holy Cross **P** (268) 322 S Church St 75460-5853 (Mail to: 400 S Church St 75460-5844) (903) 784-6194

Pittsburg St William Laud Epis Church **P** (64) 601 Lafayette St 75686-3057 (Mail to: PO Box 1057 75686-3057) Mary Matthews

Plano Church of the Holy Nativity **P** (309) C/O Dk Andersen 2200 18th St 75074-4920 (Mail to: 2200 18th St 75074-4920) Garrin Dickinson

James Evans John Kline Noe Mendez (972) 424-4574

Pottsboro St John the Apostle Episcopal Church **M** (157) PO Box 972 75076-0972 William Forrest Nancy Powers

Prosper St Pauls Episcopal Church **M** (194) 800 Sommerville Dr 75078-8435 (Mail to: 420 S Coit Rd 75078-2907) Michael Gilton (972) 347-9700

Richardson Church of the Epiphany **P** (612) 421 Custer Rd 75080-5628 (Mail to: PO Box 830218 75083-0218) William Cavanaugh Brenda Kroll Anne Randall (972) 690-0095

Rockwall Holy Trinity Episcopal Church **P** (339) 1524 Smirl Dr 75032-7638 (Mail to: 1524 Smirl Dr 75032-7638) Norman Turbeville (972) 771-8242

Sherman St Stephens Episcopal Church **P** (154) 401 S Crockett St 75090-7171 (Mail to: 401 S Crockett St 75090-7171) James Evans William Forrest (903) 892-6610

Sulphur Spgs St Philips Episcopal Church **P** (66) 1206 College St 75482-3018 (Mail to: PO Box 636 75483-0636) Barbara Kelton

Terrell Church of the Good Shepherd **P** (164) 200 W. College St. 75160-2625 (Mail to: 200 W College St 75160-2625) Diana Freeman (972) 563-2412

The Colony St Peters by the Lake **M** 5200 Paige Rd Ste 106 75056-2121 (Mail to: 1630 N Garett Ave 75206-7702) (972) 625-5788

Waxahachie St Pauls Episcopal Church **M** (421) 624 Ovilla Rd 75167-4801 (Mail to: 624 Ovilla Rd 75167-4801) Terry Reisner (972) 938-2126

Winnsboro St Francis Episcopal Church **M** (21) 103 W Sage St 75494-2541 (Mail to: PO Box 1082 75494-1082) (903) 342-7240

NON-PAROCHIAL CLERGY

Ahlenius RO *ret* Dallas TX
Anderson DE Texarkana TX
Anschutz MS *ret* South Yarmouth MA
Baker PE *ret* Addison TX
Ball RC *ret* Dallas TX
Bergstrom JW Savannah GA
Biegler JC *ret* Westchester IL
Button RD *dcn* Dallas TX
Cady MS *ret* Alpharetta GA
Chambers SH *ret* Dallas TX
Chapman JW Austin TX
Classen AM Irving TX
Clement BC *dcn* Paris TX
Coke HC *ret* Dallas TX
Comegys DP *ret* Laguna Niguel CA
Copeland RG *ret* San Antonio TX
Cover MB Mishawaka IN
Dailey BH Dallas TX
Dalton WT Bonham TX
Daly RR Chicago IL
Dannals RS *ret* Dallas TX
Darden JW *ret* Prescott Valley AZ

Denison RE *ret* Georgetown TX
Dollahite DDWG *ret* Grand Prairie TX
Dunbar PVW *dcn* Dallas TX
Frick MM Alexandria LA
Frizzell JA *ret dcn* Granbury TX
Gateley GN *ret* Tigard OR
George JE *dcn* Frisco TX
Getz PRR *ret* Rockwall TX
Gores AF *dcn* Dallas TX
Hall MR *dcn* Dallas TX
Harmuth KM *ret* Dallas TX
Heard VRT Dallas TX
Heller AG Dallas TX
Hern GN *ret* Dallas TX
Hickman DR *ret* Livingston TX
Hiebert CA Dallas TX
Hill JE *ret* Waxahachie TX
Hobson CG *dcn*
Holland CT *ret* Denison TX
Holland DW *ret* Lewisville TX
Holleman VF *ret* Dallas TX
Hollenbeck JN *ret* Killeen TX
Hough CA *ret* Fort Worth TX
Hunter VE *ret* Mesquite TX
Izadi S Dallas TX
Keen CF *ret* Sunnyvale TX
Keithly TG *ret* Dallas TX
Kent SM *ret* Dallas TX
Kincaid ST La Porte IN
Klickman JM *ret* Plano TX
Kraemer CJ *ret* Prosper TX
Krumenacker GW Dallas TX
LaCrosse DP *dcn* Irving TX
Lara A Dallas TX
Lee S Farmers Branch TX
Leonczyk KG Washington DC
Lowe HC McKinney TX
Luck GE *ret* Dallas TX
Malone MJ *ret* Petersburg VA
Martin KE *ret* Georgetown TX
McCarthy BA *ret* Dallas TX
McCune HR *ret* Dallas TX
Metcalf MP *ret*
Murphree JW *ret* Dallas TX
Neitzel AC *ret dcn* Dallas TX
Nesta PA Denison TX
Norman HG *ret* Duncanville TX
Odom RM Dallas TX
Ofoegbu DO Dallas TX
Okereke NS Dallas TX
Olver MSC Dallas TX
Pantle TA *ret* Bonham TX
Parker MR
Payne NMJ *dcn* Garland TX
Philputt FC *ret* Dallas TX
Pounders MJ Dallas TX
Power WJA Dallas TX
Raffalovich FD *ret* Georgetown TX
Salik LG *ret* Hereford TX
Sargent AL *ret* San Marcos TX
Seitz CR Toronto ON

Sholty HE Dallas TX
Slack JCS *ret* Niles MO
Smalley NT Waxahachie TX
Smith LP *ret* Dallas TX
Smither GG *ret* Dallas TX
Somodevilla RF *ret* Memphis TN
Spafford DW *ret* Dallas TX
Springer AE *dcn* Rockwall TX
Swann SB *ret* Dallas TX

Theodore PH *ret* Dallas TX
Thomas JA *ret* Fort Ord CA
Thomas JP *dcn* Irving TX
Turner SKR *ret* La Grange TX
Waller SJ *ret* Irving TX
Watts RW *dcn* Pottsboro TX
Wetzel TH *ret* Cedar Hill TX
Woods JM *ret* Mount Vernon TX
Yost MC Providence RI

DIOCESE OF DELAWARE
(PROVINCE III)
Comprises State of Delaware
DIOCESAN OFFICE 913 Wilson Road, Wilmington, DE 19803
Tel (302) 256-0374 FAX (302) 543-8084
E-MAIL mabrillhart@dioceseofdelaware.net   WEB www.dioceseofdelaware.net

Previous Bishops—
Alfred Lee 1841-87, Leighton Coleman 1888-1907, Fredk J Kinsman 1908-19, Philip Cook 1920-38, Arthur R McKinstry 1939-54, J Brooke Mosley 1955-68, Wm H Mead 1968-74, Wm H Clark 1975-85, Q Primo *Int* 1985-86, C Cabell Tennis 1986-97

Bishop—Rt Rev Wayne P Wright (941) (Dio 20 June 1998)

Cn to Ord Rev G Rowe; *Bus Mgr* J Gregory; *Asst to Bp* M Brillhart; *Chanc* A Foster Box 551 Wilmington DE 19899

Stand Comm—Cler: M Allen R Bohner P Downing M Wolf; *Lay: Pres* R Harra C Kunz M Lyons B Vrana

Dio Conv: 29-30 Jan 2016 Newark DE

PARISHES, MISSIONS, AND CLERGY

Bethany Beach St Martha's Episcopal Church **P** (206) Maplewood & Pennsylvania Aves 19930 (Mail to: PO Box 1478 19930-1478) Mary Allen (302) 539-7444

Bridgeville St Marys Episcopal Church **P** (41) 114 Delaware Ave 19933-1141 (Mail to: PO Box 21 19933-0021) (302) 337-8981

Camden Wyoming St Pauls Episcopal Church **P** (105) Old North Rd At West St 19934 (Mail to: PO Box 157 19934-0157) John Desaulniers (302) 697-7904

Claymont The Church of the Ascension **P** (279) 3717 Philadelphia Pike 19703-3413 (Mail to: 3717 Philadelphia Pike 19703-3413) (302) 798-6683

Delaware City Christ Church Delaware City **P** (73) 222 Third And Clint 19706 (Mail to: PO Box 523 19706-0523) (302) 834-3328

Delmar All Saints Church Delmar **P** (60) 10th St 19940 (Mail to: PO Box 88 19940-0088)

Kenneth Athey Dorothy Vuono

Dover Christ Church Dover **P** (396) S State & Water Sts 19903 (Mail to: PO Box 1374 19903-1374) Charles Weiss Ronald Gerber Patricia Malcolm (302) 734-5731

Georgetown St Pauls Church Georgetown **P** (182) 122 East Pine Street 19947 (Mail to: PO Box 602 19947-0602) Joseph Rushton (302) 856-2894

Harrington St Stephens Church **P** (74) 190 Raughley Hill Rd 19952-3152 (Mail to: 2020 N Tatnall St 19802-4821) John Wright

Laurel St Philips Episcopal Church **P** (270) 600 S Central Ave 19956-1410 (Mail to: 600 S Central Ave 19956-1410) Howard Backus (302) 875-3644

Lewes St Georges Chapel **SC** Beaver Dam Rd & Chapel Branch 19958 (Mail to: 18 Olive Ave 19971-2806) Max Wolf

Lewes St Peters Church Lewes **P** (540) 211 Mulberry Street PO Box 464 19958-0464 (Mail to: PO Box 464 19958-0464) Jeffrey Ross Jule Gill Mark Harris Larry Hofer (302) 645-8479

Middletown St Andrews School Chapel **School** 350 Noxontown Rd 19709-1621 (Mail to: 350 Noxontown Rd 19709-1605) John Hutchinson (302) 378-9511

Middletown St Annes Episcopal Church **P** (433) 15 E Green St PO Box 421 19709-0421 (Mail to: 19 E Cochran St. 19709-0421) Charles Bohner (302) 378-2401

Milford Christ Episcopal Church Milford **P** (185) No 200 N Church Ave 19963-1123 (Mail to: PO Box 191 19963-0191) Thomas Davis (302) 422-8466

Millsboro St Marks Church **P** (128) 50 Ellis St 19966-0422 (Mail to: PO Box 422 19966-0422) David Archibald (302) 934-9464

Milton St John The Baptist **P** (144) 307 Federal St 19968-1606 (Mail to: PO Box 441 19968-0441)

(302) 856-6844

New Castle Church of the Nativity **P** (51) 206 Sykes Rd 19720-1814 (Mail to: PO Box 662 Manor Branch 19720-0662) Margaret Pumphrey (302) 328-3445

New Castle Immanuel Church On The Green **P** (204) 50 Market St 19720 (Mail to: 100 Harmony Street 19720-0047) Christopher Keene (302) 328-2413

Newark St Nicholas Episcopal Church **P** (93) 10 Old Newark Rd 19713-3944 (Mail to: 10 Old Newark Rd 19713-3944) (302) 368-4655

Newark St Thomas Parish **P** (263) 276 S College Ave 19711-5235 (Mail to: 276 S College Ave 19711-5235) Paul Gennett (302) 368-4644

Newport St James Church Newport **P** (110) 2 S Augustine St 19804-2504 (Mail to: 2 S Augustine Street 19804-2504) Sarah Nelson (302) 994-2029

Rehoboth Bch All Saints and St Georges Church **P** (766) 18 Olive Ave 19971-2806 (Mail to: 18 Olive Ave 19971-2899) Max Wolf Eunice Dunlap Elizabeth Kaeton (302) 227-7202

Seaford St Lukes Episcopal Church **P** (54) 202 N North St 19973-2728 (Mail to: 202 N North St 19973-2728) Marianne Ell (302) 629-7979

Smyrna St Peters Church **P** (71) 22 N Union St 19977-1147 (Mail to: 22 N Union St 19977-1198) Donna Jean Kiessling (302) 653-9691

Wilmington Calvary Church Hillcrest **P** (94) 304 Lore Ave 19809-3134 (Mail to: 304 Lore Ave 19809-3134)

Wilmington Christ Church Christiana Hundred **HC** (1938) § 505 E Buck Rd 19807-2167 (Mail to: PO Box 3510 19807-0510) Ruth Kirk George Karney Amanda Molina-Moore Stephen Setzer (302) 655-3379

Wilmington Episcopal Church of Sts Andrew and Matthew **P** (346) 719 N Shipley St 19801-1711 (Mail to: 719 N Shipley St 19801-1711) David Andrews (302) 656-6628

Wilmington Grace Church Brandywine Hundred **P** (313) 4900 Concord Pike 19803-1412 (Mail to: 4906 Concord Pike 19803-1412)

Wilmington Immanuel Church Highlands **P** (203) 2400 W 17th St 19806-1343 (Mail to: 2400 W 17th St 19806-1343) Kim Capwell Kathleen Benson Sheila Sharpe

Wilmington St Barnabas Episcopal Church **P** (467) 2800 Duncan Rd 19808-2306 (Mail to: 2800 Duncan Rd 19808-2313) Martha Kirkpatrick

Wilmington St Davids Episcopal Church **P** (334) 2320 Grubb Rd 19810-2702 (Mail to: 2320 Grubb Rd 19810-2798) Bradley Hinton (302) 475-4688

Wilmington St James Episcopal Church Mill Creek **HC** (409) 2106 Saint James Ch 19808-5225 (Mail to: 2106 Saint James Church Rd 19808-5225) James Bimbi Louise Howlett (302) 994-1584

Wilmington St Martins in the Field Church **P** (77) C/O Diocese Of Delaware 2020 N Tatnall St 19802-4821 (Mail to: PO Box 697 19975-0697) (302) 436-8921

Wilmington Trinity Parish **P** (870) 1108 N Adams St 19801-1327 (Mail to: 1108 N Adams St 19801-1327) Patricia Downing Juan George Virginia Wilder (302) 652-8605

NON-PAROCHIAL CLERGY

Archer AW *ret* Lancaster PA
Barker JAD *ret* Sewanee TN
Bird PA *ret* Millsboro DE
Brownell LW *ret* Wilmington DE
Calhoun NE Boothwyn PA
Casson LS *ret* Wilmington DE
Cox COH *ret* Dover DE
Culton D *ret* Goldsboro NC
Desalvo DP Middletown DE
Field WO *ret* Louisville KY
Godden EE *ret* Wilmington DE
Hanson NH *ret* Asheville NC
Hohlt AH *ret* Plymouth NH
Holland AL *ret* Pasadena CA
Howe GM *ret* Provincetown MA
Hudson JRK *ret* Villanova PA
Huiner PB *ret* Wilmington DE
Kerr TA *ret* Wilmington DE
Kunz CN *ret* Wilmington DE
Lane WB *ret* Hockessin DE
Lewis AM *ret* New York NY
Lewis EJ *ret* Charleston WV
Lowe JF *ret* Richmond VA
Manion JE *ret* Rehoboth Beach DE
Martiner JW *ret* Harwich MA
Masterson ER *ret* Newark DE
McCormick TR *dcn* Bethany Beach DE
Neilson AP *ret* Topsham ME
Nelson RB *ret* Millsboro DE
Patterson MP *ret* Wilmington DE
Peters AFR *ret* Seaford DE
Phillips SE *dcn* Rehoboth Beach DE
Powell BL *ret* Hurlock MD
Pumphrey JB *ret*
Ramshaw LA Concord MA
Rodriguez-Yejo R *ret* Wilmington DE
Rosenberg EP Vienna MD
Rowe GL Wilmington DE
Sawyer Harmon CJ *dcn* Newark DE
Schulz DA *ret* Frederica DE
Sheehan D *ret* West Grove PA
Sullivan MC *ret* Smyrna DE
Tate MK *dcn* Rehoboth Beach DE
Thornton NE Northfield MA
Turner EH *ret dcn* Millsboro DE
Waid ANM *ret* Wilmington DE
Walton JBE *ret* Ellicott City MD
White JL *ret* Lewes DE
Wick CW *ret* Wilmington DE
Wickham WH *ret* Richmond VA

DISTRICT OF COLUMBIA

Diocese of Washington

DIOCESE OF THE DOMINICAN REPUBLIC

IGLESIA EPISCOPAL DOMINICANA
(PROVINCE IX)
Comprises the Dominican Republic
DIOCESAN OFFICE Calle Santiago No 114
Gazcue District National Santo Domingo DOMINICAN REPUBLIC
(MAIL: Iglesia Episcopal Dominicana DMG 13602 100 Airport Ave Venice FL 34285 USA)
TEL (809) 688-6016, (809) 686-7493   FAX (809) 686-6364
E-MAIL iplepidom@codetel.net.do   WEB www.dominicanepiscopalchurch.org

Previous Bishops—
James T Holly (Haiti) in charge
1897-1911 Charles B Colmore
(PR) in charge 1913-22, Harry R
Carson (Haiti) in charge 1923-48
(dio 1934-40) Mis Dist Haiti and
Dom Rep) Charles Alfred Voegeli
(Haiti) Bp Coadjutor 1943-48 Bp
1943-60, Paul A Kellogg Bp 1960-
72, Telésforo A Isaac Bp 1972-91.

Bishop—Rt Rev Julio C Holguín (870) (Dio 16
Aug 1991)

Asst Bishop—Rt Rev Luis Fernando Ruiz

Archdcns: Central Reg A Sanchez; *East Reg* Cn R
Potter; *South Reg* J Mosquea; *North Reg* RA Garcia

Exec Off: Vicar General Rev Cn JI Marquez; *Treas*
ME Perez; *Fin Admin* DI Valdez; *Exec Sec to Bishop*
A Salcedo; *Reg* A Richardson; *Team Coord* K Carroll;
Asst Team Coord P Martin; *Sec* P Sanchez; *Concierge*
N Cabrera

Exec Council: Cler: J Holguin V Pena M Quezada
A Yepes; *Lay:* E Guerrero M Acevedo M Puello
J Mosquea M Brown G Reynoso

PARISHES, MISSIONS, AND CLERGY

Andrés Boca Chica Iglesia Episcopal San Jose
M Calle El Peso # 25 (Mail to: Calle Santiago
#114) (809) 686-7493

Azua Iglesia Episcopal San Jorge **PS** Calle Hernan
Cortez No. 24 (Mail to: Calle Santiago No. 114
Gazcue 764) (809) 686-7493

Bani Iglesia Episcopal La Transfiguracion **M**
(400) Las Violetas #2 Urb Brisas del Canal
(Mail to: Las Violetas #2 Urb Brisas del Canal)
(809) 522-9957

Bani Iglesia Episcopal San Antonio de Padua **P**
(100) Calle Principal #80 Carretón (Mail to:
Carretón) (809) 396-5101

Bani Iglesia Episcopal San Bernabe **PS** Principal
Barrio Pizarrete (Mail to: Apdo 764) (809)
522-9957

Bani Iglesia Episcopal San Timoteo **P** Mella #60
Nizao (Mail to: Igelesia Episcopal Dominicana
Calle Santiago 114, Gazcue) (809) 688-6016

Barahona Iglesia Episcopal El Peregrino **M**
Primera Los Blocks Batey Central (Mail to:
Calle Santiago No. 114 Gazcue #764) (809)
686-7493

Bonao Iglesia Episcopal San Juan Bautista
M (100) Padre Billini #116 (Mail to: Calle
Santiago #114 Gazcue 764) (809) 686-7493

Consuelo Iglesia Episcopal San Gabriel **M** (100)
Duarte #1 Box 70 S.P.M. (Mail to: Duarte #1)
(809) 553-7522

Consuelo La Gran Comision **PS** Calle Hato
Mayor Batey Doña Lila (Mail to: Calle Duarte
#1-A Apdo 70) (809) 753-4666

Haina Iglesia Episcopal San Juan Evangelista
PS (100) Tercera # 25 Barrio Piedra Blanca
(Mail to: Calle Penetracion A, Casa # 3, Barrio
Chino) (809) 957-0035

Haina Iglesia Episcopal San Marcos **M** (200)
Avenida Central Rio Haina #46 (Mail to: Calle
Penetracion A # 3 Barrio Chino) (809) 957-
2550

Hato Mayor del Ray Iglesia Episcopal San Mateo
PS Batey Jalonga (Mail to: Calle Duarte #1-A
Apdo. 70) (809) 753-4666

Jarabacoa Iglesia Episcopal Monte de la
Transfiguracion **PS** El Pedregal Abajo (Mail
to: Calle Santiago #114 Gazcue #764) (809)
686-7493

La Romana Iglesia Episcopal de Todos los Santos
HC (300) Calle Dr. Teofilo Ferry #75 (Mail to:
Apartado Postal #215) Moises Quezada Mota
(809) 556-5057

La Romana Iglesia Episcopal la Encarnacion **PS**
Calle Principal (Mail to: Apartado Postal #
215) Moises Quezada Mota (809) 612-4576

Las Carreras Bani Iglesia Episcopal Espiritu
Santo **P** La Cruz de Ocoa - Carreras (Mail to:
Las Carreras, Cruce de Oroa) (809) 686-7493

Municipio de Gautier Iglesia Episcopal San Tomas
PS (200) 1 No. 7 Villa Gautier (Mail to: Calle
Santiago #114 Gazcue 764) (809) 797-5392

Nizao Iglesia Episcopal San Matias **PS** (400) Sanchez Vieja # 73 (Mail to: Sanchez # 73) Juan Rosario De La Cruz (809) 451-9164

Puerto Plata Iglesia Episcopal Cristo el Rey **M** (100) Sanchez #21 Esq Jose del C. Ariza (Mail to: Sanchez Esq Jose del C. Ariza) Miguel Kingsley Murray (829) 586-6575

Puerto Plata Iglesia Episcopal Divina Gracia **PS** Principal Mosoví (Mail to: Principal, Barrio Invi- CEA # 36) (809) 574-9085

Puerto Plata Iglesia Episcopal Santa Maria Virgen **M** Principal Barrio Invi- CEA #36 Montillano (Mail to: Principal Barrio Invi-CEA #36 Montillano) Daniel Samuel (809) 574-9085

San Antonio de Guerra Iglesia Epis Divina Providencia **P** Marcos del Rosario #39 (Mail to: Calle Santiago 114 Gazcue) (809) 688-6016

San Cristobal Iglesia Episcopal San Bartolome **PS** Segunda #3, Barrio Las Flores (Mail to: Barrio Chino, Calle Penetracion A, Casa #3) (809) 957-0035

✠ **San Francisco de Macoris** Iglesia Episcopal El Buen Samaritano **Other** Calle Cesar Agosto Sandino #8 Ensanche S. Martin (Mail to: Calle Cesar Agosto Sandino #8) (809) 725-5101

San Francisco de Macoris Iglesia Episcopal Jesus Nazareno **M** Calle La Cruz # 26 Esq. Ing. Guzmán Abreu (Mail to: Calle La Cruz #26) (809) 290-1771

San Pedro de Macoris Iglesia de la Santa Cruz **M** (300) Salvador Ross Santa Fe (Mail to: Calle Salvador Ross, Santa Fe) (809) 246-0403

San Pedro de Macoris Iglesia Episcopal de Santiago el Apostol **PS** Principal Ingenio Angelina (Mail to: Calle Santiago #114 Gazcue 764) (809) 246-0403

San Pedro de Macoris Iglesia Episcopal El Buen Pastor **PS** Dra. Ana Betances Barrio Las Flores (Mail to: Dra. Ana Betances Barrio Las Flores) Jeannene Wright (809) 526-7004

San Pedro de Macoris Iglesia Episcopal San Esteban **HC** (300) Sanchez #9, Miramar 128 (Mail to: Sanchez #9 Apartado Postal# 128 128) (809) 529-4863

Santiago Cristo Salvador **M** § Calle Proyecto # 52 Ensanche Mirador NA (Mail to: Calle 10 No. 30 Villa Olga) (809) 582-8213

Santiago Iglesia Episcopal San Lucas **M** Calle Cuba # 128 Esq. Calle Pedro Fco. Bono (Mail to: Calle Cuba # 128) (809) 734-0776

Santiago Iglesia Episcopal de la Anunciacion **M** Calle 6, Esq Calle 3 #16 Llanos de Gurabo (Mail to: Calle 6, Esq Calle 3 #16 Llanos de Gurabo) (809) 734-0776

Santo Domingo Iglesia Episcopal la Epifania **HC** (100) Ave Independencia 253, Gazcue (Mail to: Ave Independencia # 253) (809) 689-2070

Santo Domingo Iglesia Episcopal San Andres **M** (600) Marcos Ruiz No. 26 Villa Consuelo (Mail to: Apartado No. 764) (809) 245-1853

Santo Domingo Este Iglesia Episcopal Santa Ana **P** Mendoza - Preaching Station (Mail to: Ens Libertad Apdo 1021) (809) 788-2957

Santo Domingo Este Iglesia Episcopal Santisima Trinidad **M** Costa Rica # 21 Ensanche Ozama (Mail to: Costa Rica # 21 Ensanche Ozama) (809) 788-2957

Santo Domingo Este Iglesia Episocopal Sagrada Familia **M** Calle 4 de Agosto # 37 Los Minas (Ensanche Felicidad) (Mail to: Calle 4 de Agosto # 37 Los Minas) (809) 532-6052

Santo Domingo Norte Iglesia Episcopal San Felipe Apostol **M** Cl Manzana C #1 Barrio INVI, Sabana Perdida (Mail to: Cl Manzana C #1 Barrio INVI, Sabana Perdida) (809) 590-0842

Santo Domingo Norte Mision San Pedro y San Pablo **PS** Calle Valera #60 La Barquita (Mail to: Calle Valera #60) (809) 350-3707

NON-PAROCHIAL CLERGY

Almonte S Santo Domingo
Amparo Tapia MM Santo Domingo
Brito NR *ret* Santo Domingo
Bruno JM *ret* Port-Au-Prince
Canela Canela RA Dominican Republic
Castro JR
Chesterman TC *ret* Santa Rosa CA
Desir JN Santo Domingo
Diaz Estevez M
Encarnacion-Caraballo FA Santo Iomingo
Fernandez-Liranzo HS *ret* Santiago
Floyd MH *ret* Austin TX
Garcia De Los Santos RA La Romana
Gil Jimenez RA
Gomez Almonte L Hato Mayor Del Rey
Guaillas Carangui RO Quito
Lopez BT Republica Dominicana
Marquez JI Santo Domingo
Martin Fumero ES
Mendoza Marmolejos MR
Moronta Vasquez BA
Mosquea J
Paraison EM Barahona
Pena Tavarez VA La Romna Dominical Republic
Peralta E
Potter-Norman RT *ret* San Pedro De Macoris
Robles-Garcia D *ret*
Romero Marte FA
Ruiz LF Colombia
Sanchez Pujol AS Santo Domingo
Santana CE
Sheen Rodriguez JE
Soto LF
Yepes Lopez AN Santo Domingo
Zaya L

DIOCESE OF EAST CAROLINA
(PROVINCE IV)
Comprises eastern North Carolina
DIOCESAN OFFICE 705 Doctors Drive Kinston NC 28501 (MAIL: Box 1336, Kinston, NC 28503)
TEL (252) 522-0885   FAX (252) 523-5272
WEB www.diocese-eastcarolina.org

Previous Bishops—
Alfred A Watson 1884-1905, Robert Strange coadj 1904 Bp 1905-14, Thomas C Darst 1915-45, Thomas H Wright 1945-73, Hunley A Elebash 1973-83, B Sidney Sanders 1979-1997 Clifton Daniel coadj 1996 Bp 1997-2013, Peter James Lee Bp Prov (2013-2014)

Bishop—Rt Rev Robert Stuart Skirving (Dio 8 November 2014)

Stand Comm—Cler: J Horton J Day *Lay:* T Judge J Parrott N Broadwell

Dio Conv: 4-6 Feb 2016 New Bern NC

PARISHES, MISSIONS, AND CLERGY

Ahoskie Church of St Thomas **P** (139) PO Box 263 27910-0263 (Mail to: PO Box 263 27910-0263) Jeffrey Douglas (252) 332-3263

Bath St Thomas Episcopal Church **P** (117) 101 Craven St 27808 (Mail to: PO Box 257 27808-0257) Diane Tomlinson (252) 923-9141

Beaufort St Pauls Episcopal Church **P** (681) 215 Ann St 28516-2103 (Mail to: 215 Ann St 28516-2103) John Carlisto (252) 728-3324

Belhaven St James Episcopal Church **P** (37) 545 E Main St NC 27810-1547 (Mail to: PO Box 1336 27810-1547) August Wiesner (252) 943-6977

Burgaw St Marys Episcopal Church **P** (57) 506 S McNeil St 28425-5036 (Mail to: PO Box 841 28425-0841) (910) 259-5541

Chocowinity Trinity Episcopal Church **P** (178) 182 NC Highway 33 W 27817 (Mail to: PO Box 332 27817-0332) Joseph Browne (252) 946-9958

Clinton St Pauls Episcopal Church **P** (91) 110 W Main St 28328-4047 (Mail to: 110 W Main St 28328-4047) Daniel Cenci (910) 592-3220

Columbia St Andrews Episcopal Church **P** (24) 106 North Road St 27925 (Mail to: PO Box 615 27925-0615) William Smyth (252) 441-8542

Creswell Christ Episcopal Church **M** (11) 100 S 6th St 27928-8960 (Mail to: PO Box 185 100 6th St 27928-0185) (252) 482-8581

Creswell Galilee Mission / Lake Phelps **M** (3) 323 Park Rd 27928-9803 (Mail to: 2323 Lake Shore Rd 27928-9179) (252) 441-8542

Currituck St Lukes Episcopal Mission **M** (30) 2864 Caratoke Hwy 27929-9611 (Mail to: 2864 Caratuck Highway 27929) Hubert McGee (252) 435-0530

Edenton St Pauls Episcopal Church **P** (405) 101 W Gale St 27932-1815 (Mail to: PO Box 548

27932-0548) John Malone Gilliam James Reed (252) 482-3522

Elizabeth City Christ Episcopal Church **P** (223) 200 S McMorrine St 27909-4831 (Mail to: 200 S McMorrine St 27909-4831) Walter Broadfoot John Horner Edward Mullins

Elizabethtown St Christophers Episcopal Church **P** (32) 2606 W Broad St 28337-9031 (Mail to: PO Box 1841 28337-1841) (910) 879-2777

Engelhard St Georges Episcopal Church **P** (142) PO Box 101 31655 Hwy 264 27824 (Mail to: PO Box 101 27824-0101) James Lupton (252) 943-6318

Farmville Emmanuel Episcopal Church **P** (27) 108 S Walnut St 27828-1658 (Mail to: 3505 S Walnut St 27828-1698) (252) 753-3737

Fayetteville Church of the Good Shepherd **P** (26) PO Box 64008 28306-0008 (Mail to: PO Box 64008 28306-4008) (910) 323-1512

Fayetteville Holy Trinity Episcopal Church **P** (606) 1601 Raeford Rd 28305-5031 (Mail to: 1601 Raeford Rd 28305-5097) Jeffrey Thornberg (910) 484-2134

Fayetteville St Johns Episcopal Church **P** (774) 302 Green St 28301-5028 (Mail to: PO Box 722 28302-0722) Robert Alves (910) 483-7405

Fayetteville St Josephs Episcopal Church **P** (47) 509 Ramsey St 28301-4911 (Mail to: PO Box 694 28302-0694) (910) 323-0161

Fayetteville St Pauls in the Pines Epis Ch **P** (134) 1800 Saint Paul Ave 28304-5238 (Mail to: 1800 Saint Paul Ave 28304-5238) John Frazier (910) 485-7098

Gatesville St Marys Episcopal Church **P** (24) Attn Edith Bridger PO Box 174 27938-0174 (Mail to: PO Box 447 27938-0447) (252) 794-3277

Goldsboro St Andrews Episcopal Church **P** (25) 901 Harris St. 27530-6666 (Mail to: PO Box 1333 27533-1333) Mary Reese (919) 734-0550

Goldsboro St Francis Episcopal Church **P** (122) 503 Forest Hill Drive 27534-1824 (Mail to: PO Box 11406 27532-1406) Douglas Culton (919) 735-9845

Goldsboro St Stephens Church **P** (323) 200 North James Street 27530-3631 (Mail to: PO Box 984 27533-0984) Jill Beimdiek (919) 734-4263

Greenville St Pauls Episcopal Church **P** (1053) 401 E 4th St 27858-1916 (Mail to: PO Box 1924 27835-1924) Robert Hudak Andrew Cannan (252) 752-3482

Greenville St Timothy's Episcopal Church **P** (254) 107 Louis St 27858-8660 (Mail to: 107 Louis St 27858-8660) John Robertson (252) 355-2125

Grifton St John & St Mark Episcopal Church **P** (33) 2016 Price Cannon Rd 28530 (Mail to: PO Box 937 28530) James Cooke (252) 524-5860

Hampstead Holy Trinity Episcopal Church **P** (102) No 107 Deerfield Dr 28443-2135 (Mail to: 107 Deerfield Dr 28443-2135) Pamela Stringer (910) 270-4221

Havelock St Christopher's Episopal Church **P** (85) 1000 E Main St 28532-2317 (Mail to: PO Box 626 28532-0626) Christine Carlin (252) 447-3912

Hertford Holy Trinity Episcopal Church **P** (151) PO Box 125 207 S Church St 27944-1113 (Mail to: PO Box 125 27944-0125) (910) 270-4221

Holly Ridge St Philips Episcopal Church **P** (56) 661 Tar Landing Rd 28445-7671 (Mail to: PO Box 155 28445-0155) (910) 329-1514

Jacksonville St Annes Episcopal Church **P** (252) 711 Henderson Dr 28540-4477 (Mail to: 711 Henderson Dr 28540-4477) (910) 347-3774

Kinston St Augustines Episcopal Church **P** (38) 707 E Lenoir Ave 28502 (Mail to: PO Box 2263 28502-2263) Bonnie Smith (252) 523-4032

Kinston St Marys Episcopal Church **P** (426) 800 Rountree St 28501-3655 (Mail to: 800 Rountree Ave 28501-3655) Allen Singer Thomas Warren (252) 523-6146

Leland All Souls Episcopal Church **P** (35) 5087 Blue Banks Loop Rd NE 28451-4009 (Mail to: 5087 Blue Banks Loop Rd NE 28451-4009) Nan Chandler

Lewiston Grace Episcopal Church **P** (15) PO Box 429 27849-0429 (Mail to: Post Office Box 537 27849) (252) 348-3116

Lumberton Trinity Episcopal Church **P** (364) 1202 N Chestnut St 28358-4713 (Mail to: 1202 N Chestnut St 28358-4713) (910) 739-3717

Morehead City St Andrew's Church **P** (222) 3003 Bridges St 28557-3329 (Mail to: 2005 Arendell St 28557-3999) John Pollock (252) 727-9093

Nags Head Church of St Andrews by the Sea **P** (398) 4212 South Va Dare Trail 27959-0445 (Mail to: PO Box 445 27959-0445) Phillip Glick (252) 441-5382

New Bern Christ Episcopal Church **P** (1020) 320 Pollock St 28560-4945 (Mail to: PO Box 1246 28563-1246) Hoyt Canady Cortney Dale (252) 633-2109

New Bern St Cyprians Episcopal Church **P** (48) 604 Johnson St 28563 (Mail to: PO Box 809 28563-0809) (252) 633-3816

Newton Grove La Iglesia de la Sagrada Familia **M** (474) 2989 Easy St 28334-7994 (Mail to: PO Box 318 28366-0318) Marilyn Mitchell (919) 658-1819

Oriental St Thomas Episcopal Church **P** (154) 402 Freemason St 28571-9206 (Mail to: PO Box 461 28571-0461) Jeremiah Day (252) 249-0256

Plymouth Grace Episcopal Church **P** (72) 107 Madison St 27962-1432 (Mail to: 106 Madison St 27962-1432) Henry Burdick (252) 793-3295

Roper St Lukes & St Annes Epis Church **P** (27) 206 S Bank St 27970-9181 (Mail to: PO Box 119 27970-0119) (252) 793-3295

Salter Path St Francis by the Sea **P** (168) 920 Salter Path Rd 28575 (Mail to: PO Box 7 28575-0007) Leonard Thomas James Sproul (252) 240-2388

Seven Springs Church of the Holy Innocents **P** (90) 6861 Hwy 55 W 28578-9493 (Mail to: 6861 Hwy 55 W 28578-9493) Bonnie Smith (252) 569-3011

Shallotte St James the Fisherman Church **P** (334) 4941 Main St 28470-4503 (Mail to: PO Box 68 28459-0068) David Davis Jean Miller (910) 754-9313

Southern Shores All Saints Episcopal Church **P** (416) 40 Pintail Trl 27949-3847 (Mail to: 40 Pintail Trl 27949-3847) Thomas Wilson Robert Morisseau (252) 261-6674

Southport St Philips Episcopal Church **P** (670) 205 E Moore St 28461-3927 (Mail to: PO Box 10476 28461-0476) Margaret Finnerud (910) 457-5643

Sunbury St Peters Episcopal Church (Sunbury) **P** (38) 61 NC Highway 32 N 27979-9447 (Mail to: PO Box 153 27979-0153) (252) 326-4757

Swansboro St Peters by the Sea Church **P** (246) 503 W Broad St 28584-9651 (Mail to: PO Box 337 28584-0337) Albert Eaton (910) 326-4757

Trenton Grace Episcopal Church **P** (12) PO Box 126 28585-0126 (Mail to: PO Box 126 28585-0126) (252) 448-3241

Vanceboro St Pauls Episcopal Church **P** (34) PO Box 466 28586 (Mail to: PO Box 466 28586-0466) (252) 244-2317

Washington St Peters Episcopal Church **HC** (733) 101 N Bonner St 27889-5016 (Mail to: PO Box 985 27889-0985) James Reed (252) 946-8151

Washington Zion Episcopal Church **P** (55) PO Box 1329 27889-9802 (Mail to: PO Box 1329 27889-1329) Sarah Saxe (252) 946-3367

Whiteville Grace Episcopal Church **P** (72) 105 S Madison St 28472-4119 (Mail to: 105 S Madison St 28472-4119) (910) 642-4724

Williamston Church of the Advent **P** (137) 124 W Church St 27892-2402 (Mail to: PO Box 463 27892-0463) (252) 792-2244

Wilmington Church of the Good Shepherd **P** (53) 515 Queen St 28401-5243 (Mail to: PO Box 928 28402-0928) (910) 763-6080

Wilmington Church of the Servant **P** (534) 4925 Oriole Dr. 28403-1759 (Mail to: 4925 Oriole Dr. 28403-1759) (910) 395-0616

Wilmington Holy Cross Episcopal Church **P** (166) 5820 Myrtle Grove Rd 28409-4322 (Mail to: 5820 Myrtle Grove Rd 28409-4322) (910) 799-6347

Wilmington St Andrews on-the-Sound Church **P** (832) 101 Arlie Road 28403 (Mail to: 101 Airlie Rd 28403-3701) Richard Elliott Christopher Adams (910) 256-3034

Wilmington St James Episcopal Church **P** (1949)

25 S 3rd St 28401-4530 (Mail to: 25 S 3rd St 28401-4530) Ronald Abrams Catherine Davis James Franklin Pauline Griffin John Sidebotham (910) 763-1628

Wilmington St John Episcopal Church **P** (565) 1219 Forest Hills Dr 28403-2555 (Mail to: 1219 Forest Hills Dr 28403-2555) Thomas Barnett Charles Barton Eric Moulton (910) 762-5273

Wilmington St Mark Episcopal Church **P** (79) 600 Grace St 28401-4127 (Mail to: 600 Grace St 28401-4127) Victor Frederiksen (910) 763-3858

Wilmington St Pauls Church **P** (271) 16 N 16th St 28401-4905 (Mail to: 16 N 16th St 28401-4905) Dena Bearl (910) 762-4578

Windsor St Thomas Episcopal Church **P** (126) 302 S Queen St 27983 (Mail to: PO Box 400 27983-0400) (252) 794-3420

NON-PAROCHIAL CLERGY

Atkinson AJ *dcn* Wilmington NC
Bean RA *dcn* Goldsboro NC
Birdsey BB *ret* Richmond VA
Blackburn GJ *ret* Wilmington NC
Bonner JH *ret* Hertford NC
Both MB *ret* Wilmington NC
Brettmann WS *ret* Pittsboro NC
Brown RF *ret* Fayetteville NC
Buck ES *dcn* Bolivia NC
Carpenter ME *ret* Goldsboro NC
Chaffee BB *ret* Raleigh NC
Chamberlain DM *ret* Perry GA
Clark RO Fayetteville NC
Conners JH Norwalk CT
Cooper JW *ret* Wilmington NC
Craig C *ret* Asheville NC
Craig CP *ret* Davidson NC
Curns MS North Adams MA
Dale AE
Dornemann DM Philadelphia PA
Drewry JC *dcn* Wilmington NC
Eaton CA *dcn*
Fordham JF *ret* Bath NC
Fornea SW Arlington VA
Fulton JG *ret* Farmville NC
Gaskill JJ *dcn* Beaufort NC
Glover BM Rocky Mount NC
Hairston RD *ret* Decatur GA
Hobgood RB *ret* Greenville NC

Hogg D *ret* Osprey FL
Horton JR *ret* Williamston NC
Houston BP *dcn* Grifton NC
Hunt AS
Hussey-Smith TR Denmark SC
Hutchins MS *ret* Wilmington NC
Joseph A *ret* Fayetteville NC
Kappel RD *ret* Lumberton NC
Kirby EM *dcn* New Bern NC
Kubler BP *ret* Woodstock GA
Kuhn TR *ret* Oak Hill WV
Lacy MC Greenville NC
Ligon MM *dcn* Greenville NC
Macswain RC Sewanee TN
McCarty MMD *ret* Havelock NC
Midyette CT *ret* Beaufort NC
Mitchell KN *dcn* Wellesley MA
Morrison RD *ret* Lynchburg VA
Murchison JW *ret* Chattanooga TN
Natoli AM *ret* Whiteville NC
Ogus MH New York NY
Overton DE *ret* Louisville KY
Page MR South Bend IN
Perdue TH Fairfax VA
Peterman LC Swansboro NC
Powell CR Wilmington NC
Powell MM Wilmington NC
Price GM *dcn* Dudley NC
Privette WH *ret* Jacksonville NC
Rickenbaker TM *ret* Edenton NC
Roberts HP *ret* Blacksburg SC
Roberts M *ret* New Bern NC
Robinson SD *dcn* Wilmington NC
Rodman JL *dcn* Washington DC
Rojas Poveda JA *ret* Coats NC
Running JM *ret* Fayetteville NC
Smith JO *dcn* Greenville NC
Souza RM *ret* Bath NC
Stockard ME Kinston NC
Swindell KH *ret dcn* Jacksonville NC
Taylor WS *ret* Rockingham NC
Thomas PM *ret* New Bern NC
Thompson MB Cambridge
Turner SD Fort Rucker AL
Warner RW *ret* Calabash NC
Webster AE Mount Savage MD
West HM *ret*
Whiteside HB Shelburne Falls MA
Williams DA *ret* Oak Island NC
Wood GM *dcn* Elizabeth City NC

DIOCESE OF EAST TENNESSEE
(PROVINCE IV)
Comprises the eastern third of the State of Tennessee
DIOCESAN OFFICE 814 Episcopal School Way Knoxville TN 37932
TEL (865) 966-2110   FAX (865) 966-2535
E-MAIL editor@dioet.org   WEB http://dioet.org

Previous Bishops—
Wm E Sanders 1985-91, Robert G Tharp 1992-99; Charles G vonRosenberg 1999-2011

Bishop—Rt Rev George D Young III (1059) (Dio 25 June 2011)

Cn to Ord Rev P Grace; *Sec* L Nichols; *Treas* W Selden; *Asst Treas* M Keyser; *Chanc* SY Sheppeard Esq; *Comm* V Myers; *Yth* A Haralson; *Dep for Min & Cong Dev* R Govan; *Shared Min Facilitator* R Govan; *com* H Harrison; *Ecum* W Farnum

Stand Comm—Cler: Pres J Minarik P Keese J Mills; *Lay:* C Robinson A Odle Sr MJ Davidson

Dio Conv: 5-6 Feb 2016 Knoxville TN

PARISHES, MISSIONS, AND CLERGY

Athens St Pauls Episcopal Church **P** (376) 123 S Jackson St 37303-4710 (Mail to: PO Box 326 37371-0326) G Hendree Harrison (423) 745-2224

Battle Creek St John the Baptist **P** (38) 12757 Ladds Cove Rd 37380 (Mail to: 1603 Gudger Ln 37347-5610) (931) 598-9546

Bristol St Columbas Episcopal Church **P** (121) 607 Greenfield Pl 37620-6124 (Mail to: 607 Greenfield Pl 37620-6124) (423) 764-2251

Chattanooga Christ Episcopal Church **P** (174) 663 Douglas St (at McCallie Ave.) 37403 (Mail to: 663 Douglas St 37403-2015) Harry Lawrence (423) 266-4263

Chattanooga Grace Episcopal Church **P** (486) 20 Belvoir Ave 37411-4501 (Mail to: 20 Belvoir Ave 37411-4599) (423) 698-2433

Chattanooga St Martin of Tours Epis Church **P** (549) 7547 E Brainerd Rd 37421-3166 (Mail to: 7547 E Brainerd Rd 37421-3166) James Wallace (423) 892-9131

Chattanooga St Pauls Episcopal Church **P** (1959) 305 W 7th St 37402-1717 (Mail to: 305 W 7th St 37402-1787) Fritz Parman Leigh Preston Ann Weeks Bradford Whitaker (423) 266-8195

Chattanooga St Peters Episcopal Church **P** (467) 848 Ashland Ter 37415-3538 (Mail to: 848 Ashland Ter 37415-3538) Robert Nichols (423) 877-2428

Chattanooga St Thaddaeus Episcopal Church **P** (189) 4300 Locksley Ln 37416-2908 (Mail to: PO Box 16305 37416-0305) (423) 892-2377

Chattanooga Thankful Memorial Church **P** (115) 1607 W 43rd St 37409-1344 (Mail to: PO Box 2274 37409-0274) Leyla King (423) 821-3135

Cleveland St Lukes Episcopal Church **P** (543) 320 Broad St NW 37311-5038 (Mail to: P O Box 5 37364-0005) Joel Huffstetler (423) 476-5541

Copperhill St Marks Episcopal Church **P** (41) 124 West Hill Street 37317-0576 (Mail to: PO Box 579 37317-0579) (423) 496-4681

Crossville St Raphaels Episcopal Church **P** (204) 1038 Sparta Hwy 38572-5746 (Mail to: 1038 Sparta Hwy 38572-5746) Felicity Peck (931) 484-2407

Elizabethton St Thomas Church **P** (59) 815 E 2nd St 37643-2324 (Mail to: 815 E 2nd St 37643-2324) Harry Shaefer (423) 543-3081

Ft Oglethorp Episcopal Church of the Nativity **P** (132) 1201 Cross St 30742-3230 (Mail to: PO Box 2356 30742-2356) (706) 866-9773

Gatlinburg Trinity Episcopal Church **P** (96) 509 Historic Nature Trail 37738-0055 (Mail to: PO Box 55 37738-0055) Barbara Harper (865) 436-4721

Greeneville St James Episcopal Church **P** (223) 107 W Church St 37745-3803 (Mail to: 107 W Church St 37745-3803) Carolyn Isley (423) 638-6583

Harriman St Andrews Episcopal Church **P** (79) 190 Circle Dr 37748-7304 (Mail to: 190 Circle Dr 37748-7304) Stephen Jones

Hixson St Albans Episcopal Church **P** (106) 7514 Hixson Pike 37343-1721 (Mail to: 7514 Hixson Pike 37343-1721) Mark Bigley (423) 842-1342

Jefferson City St Barnabas Episcopal-Lutheran Ch **PS** (28) 807 E Ellis St 37760-2526 (Mail to: 807 E Ellis St 131 Sequoiah Lane 37760-2526) (865) 397-3678-9859

Johnson City St Johns Episcopal Church **P** (416) 500 N Roan St 37601-4741 (Mail to: 500 N Roan St 37601-4717) Hal Hutchison (423) 926-8141

Jonesborough St Mary the Virgin Episcopal Church **PS** (19) 109 S 2nd Ave 37659-1105 (Mail to: PO Box 273 37659-1105) (423) 753-2350

Kingsport St Christophers Episcopal Church **P** (126) 584 Lebanon Rd 37663-2908 (Mail to: 584 Lebanon Rd 37663-2908) Margaret Zeller (423) 239-6751

Kingsport St Pauls Episcopal Church **P** (302) 161 E Ravine Rd 37660-3807 (Mail to: 161 E Ravine Rd 37660-3839) Christopher Harpster William White (423) 245-5187

Kingsport St Timothys Episcopal Church **P** (108) 2152 Hawthorne St 37664-3563 (Mail to: PO Box 3248 37664-0248) Richard Shackleford

Knoxville Church of the Good Samaritan **P** (629) 425 N Cedar Bluff Rd 37923-3600 (Mail to: 425 N Cedar Bluff Rd 37923-3600) Joseph Calhoun Taylor Dinsmore Caroline Vogel (865) 693-9591

Knoxville Church of the Good Shepherd **P** (389) 5409 Jacksboro Pike 37918-3330 (Mail to: PO Box 5104 37928-0104) John Asel Richard Carter (865) 687-9420

Knoxville Episcopal Church of the Ascension **P** (1299) 800 S Northshore Dr 37919 (Mail to: 800 S Northshore Dr 37919-7550) Brett Backus Robert Gieselmann Amy Morehous (865) 588-0589

Knoxville St Elizabeths Episcopal Church **P** (327) 110 Sugarwood Dr 37922-4662 (Mail to: 110 Sugarwood Dr 37934-4662) Carol Westpfahl John Dukes (865) 675-0450

Knoxville St James Episcopal Church **P** (512) 1101 N Broadway St 37917-6528 (Mail to: 1101 N Broadway St 37917-6592) John Wiggers Robert Powell (865) 523-5687

✠ **Knoxville** St Johns Episcopal Cathedral **O** (1090) 413 Cumberland Ave 37902-2302 (Mail to: PO Box 153 37901-0153) John Ross Christopher Hackett Thomas Rasnick (865) 525-7347

Knoxville St Lukes Episcopal Church **P** (90) 600 S Chestnut St 37914-5829 (Mail to: 600 S Chestnut St 37914-5829) Kay Reynolds (865) 522-4244

Knoxville St Thomas Episcopal Church **P** (100) 5401 Tiffany Ln 37912-4736 (Mail to: 5401 Tiffany Ln 37912-4736) Howard Bowlin (865) 688-2741

La Follette St Clare Episcopal Church **P** (18) 1720 Jacksboro Pike 37766-3226 (Mail to: 1720 Jacksboro Pike 37766-3226) (423) 566-6707

Lookout Mtn Church of the Good Shepherd **P** (927) 211 Franklin Rd 37350-1223 (Mail to: PO Box 145 37350-1223) Robert Childers Fred Brown Janice Robbins (423) 821-1583

Loudon Episcopal Church of the Resurrection **P** (161) 917 Pond Rd 37774-6401 (Mail to: 917 Pond Rd 37774-6401) Ruth Keene

Maryville St Andrews Church **P** (388) 314 W Broadway Ave 37801-4708 (Mail to: 314 W Broadway Ave 37801-4708) Steven Mosher (865) 983-3512

Morristown All Saints Episcopal Church **P** (436) 601 W Main St 37814-4508 (Mail to: 601 W Main St 37814-4508) Donna Brown Kenneth Brown John Dukes (423) 586-6201

Newport Church of the Annunciation **P** (87) 304 Cosby Hwy 37821-1916 (Mail to: PO Box 337 37822-0337) David Garrett (423) 625-1864

Norris St Francis Episcopal Church **P** (254) 158 W Norris Rd 37828 (Mail to: PO Box 29 37828-0029) Harry Minarik (865) 494-7167

Oak Ridge St Stephens Episcopal Church **P** (494) 212 N Tulane Ave 37830-6308 (Mail to: 212 N Tulane Ave 37830-6308) Craig Kallio Gerald Lovett Patricia Reuss Robert Reuss John Wilson (865) 483-8497

Ooltewah St Francis of Assisi Epis Church **P** (128) 7555 Ooltewah Georgetown Rd 37363-9582 (Mail to: 7555 Ooltewah Georgetown Rd 37363-9582) Martha Tucker Parsons (423) 238-7708

Rugby Christ Church **P** (48) 1332 Rugby Parkway 37733-0025 (Mail to: PO Box 25 37733-0025) Peter Keese (423) 628-5627

S Pittsburg Christ Episcopal Church **P** (134) 302 3rd St 37380-1318 (Mail to: PO Box 347 37380-0347) Kim Hobby (423) 837-7715

Sevierville St Joseph the Carpenter **P** (142) 345 Hardin Ln 37862-4507 (Mail to: 345 Hardin Ln 37862-4507) (865) 403-9327

Seymour St Pauls Episcopal Church **PS** (72) 1028 Boyds Creek Hwy 37865-4532 (Mail to: PO Box 907 37865-0907) (865) 577-1255

Signal Mtn St Timothys Episcopal Church **P** (752) 630 Mississippi Ave 37377-2293 (Mail to: 630 Mississippi Ave 37377-2293) Derrick Hill (423) 886-2281

NON-PAROCHIAL CLERGY

Anderson JR Chattanooga TN
Bahlow H *ret* Evans GA
Beach JL *dcn* Kingsport TN
Beasley R *ret* Maryville TN
Bell J *ret* Chattanooga TN
Bergeron ML Knoxville TN
Blanchard M Harriman TN
Bone PJ Church Hill TN
Brewer LG *dcn* Kingsport TN
Brewer VG *dcn* Monteagle TN
Brown RJ *ret* Knoxville TN
Buchholz PR *ret* Knoxville TN
Buckley AJ McMinnville OR
Burch S *dcn* Chattanooga TN
Butler SJ Chattanooga TN
Cahill PAB *ret* Chattanooga TN
Caldwell MM *ret* Chattanooga TN
Callahan GE *ret* Chattanooga TN
Carter SE *ret* Sevierville TN
Choyce G *ret* Signal Mountain TN
Cooke CA *ret* Maryville TN
Crippen DW *ret* Florence CO
Crisp JE New Canaan CT
Crump CC *dcn* Hudson FL
Dunn MEG Chattanooga TN
Eichler S *ret* Sewanee TN
England EG *dcn* South Pittsburg TN
Ewing WB *ret* Ten Mile TN
Fels CW *ret*
Fishburne DA *ret* Chattanooga TN
Fisher JC *dcn* Chattanooga TN
Fouke SV *ret* Morristown TN
Fraser WC *ret* Nashville TN
Frye JW *dcn* Knoxville TN
Garcia LF *dcn* Lookout Mountain TN

Gibson CS *ret* Aberdeenshire, Scotland
Grace PM Knoxville TN
Green KM *ret* Meridian ID
Hackett DR *ret* Ooltewah TN
Hagler JR Newark NJ
Hartmans RG Chattanooga TN
Hawley CN Knoxville TN
Haws HE *ret* Maryville TN
Henley RP *ret* Sevierville TN
Hess H *ret* Knoxville TN
Hill JA Knoxville TN
Howard HL Maryville TN
Huckabay HH *ret* Chattanooga TN
Humphreys WL
Hutson TM *ret* Nashville TN
Jekabsons WSS *ret* Bristol TN
Jones HB *ret* Anniston AL
Kanyi P Signal Mtn TN
Larkin P *ret*
Latham BC *ret* Chattanooga TN
LeCroy AK *dcn* Johnson City TN
Leopold RK Chattanooga TN
Lewis AD *ret* Kingston TN
Livermore CW *ret* Powell TN
Markle AE *ret* Crossville TN
Marquis JF *ret* Memphis TN
Mathewson KC *ret* Pittsboro NC
Mayfield EO *ret* Sewanee TN

McGee WE *dcn* Signal Mountain TN
Metz S Sewanee TN
Mills EJ *ret* Kingsport TN
Minor AN *ret* Knoxville TN
Moore MN *ret* Lookout Mountain TN
Morgan WC *ret* Cleveland TN
Morton RD *dcn* Knoxville TN
Osborne CE *dcn* Kingsport TN
Parry JW *dcn* Knoxville TN
Pinner J *ret* Kingston TN
Rizner AR *ret* Sevierville TN
Robbins BH *ret* Chattanooga TN
Rouser JR *dcn* Ooltewah TN
Scott NE *dcn* Soddy Daisy TN
Scruggs CP *ret* Chattanooga TN
Seavey SE *ret* Lenoir City TN
Sharp JL *dcn* Morristown TN
Smith RW *ret* Mountain Home TN
Smitherman G *ret* Chattanooga TN
Smitherman SN *ret* Kingsport TN
Swann AH *ret* Walland TN
Talbird JD *ret* Chattanooga TN
Temple GC *ret* Hixson TN
Thompson SL *dcn* Newport TN
Warren HDL *ret* Chattanooga TN
Weddle KG *ret* Danville KY
Weeks WIB *dcn* Chattanooga TN

DIOCESE OF EASTERN MICHIGAN
(PROVINCE V)
Comprises the eastern portion of the lower peninsula of Michigan
DIOCESAN OFFICE 924 N Niagara St Saginaw MI 48602
TEL (989) 752-6020   FAX (989) 752-6120
E-MAIL diocese@eastmich.org   WEB www.eastmich.org

Previous Bishops—
Edwin M Leidel Jr 1996-2006

Bishop—Rt Rev S Todd Ousley (1006) (Dio 9 Sept 06)

Bps Admin Asst A Krueger; *Admin* M Girard; *Financial Asst* K Rose; *Treas* M Turnbull; *Chanc* E Henneke; *Cn to Ord* M Spencer; *Comm* K Forsyth

Stand Comm—Cler: B Cavin L Speller D Scheid; *Lay:* S King B Barkley W Thewalt

Dio Conv: 11-12 Nov 2016

PARISHES, MISSIONS, AND CLERGY
Alma St John Episcopal Church **P** (92) PO Box 605 48801-9693 (Mail to: PO Box 605 48801-0605) (989) 752-6020
Alpena Trinity Episcopal Church **P** (384) 124 E Washington Ave 49707-2837 (Mail to: 124 E Washington Ave 49707-2869) William Mc-

Clure (989) 752-6020
Atlanta St Marks Episcopal Mission **P** (45) 11847 M 33 N 48638 (Mail to: 11847 M 33 49709-9206) Philip Seitz (989) 752-6020
Bad Axe St Pauls Episcopal Church **P** (66) 139 W Huron Ave 48413-1102 (Mail to: 139 W Huron Ave 48413-1102) (989) 752-6020
Bay City St Albans Episcopal Church **P** (187) 105 S Erie St 48706-4431 (Mail to: 105 S Erie St 48706-4431) Sharon Voelker (989) 752-6020
Bay City Trinity Episcopal Church **P** (195) 815 N Grant St 48708-6084 (Mail to: 815 N Grant St 48708-6084) Ann Grady (989) 892-5813
Cheboygan St James Church **P** (110) 202 S Huron St 49721-1920 (Mail to: PO Box 253 49721-0253) (989) 752-6020
Corunna St Paul Episcopal Church **P** (47) 111 S Shiawassee St 48817-1357 (Mail to: 111 S Shiawassee St 48817-1357) Russell Merrill (989) 752-6020
Davison St Dunstans Episcopal Church **P** (61) 1523 N Oak Rd 48423-9101 (Mail to: 1523

N Oak Rd 48423-9101) Linda Colavincenzo (989) 752-6020

Dryden St Johns Episcopal Church **P** (55) 4074 S Mill Rd 48428-9233 (Mail to: PO Box 86 48428-0086) Susan Rich (989) 752-6020

East Tawas Christ Church **P** (93) 202 W Westover St 48730-1238 (Mail to: 202 W Westover St 48730-1238) Rebecca Owsley (989) 752-6020

Fenton St Judes Episcopal Church **P** (266) 106 E Elizabeth St 48430-2322 (Mail to: 106 E Elizabeth St 48430-2322) Heather Barta (810) 629-5681

Flint St Andrews Episcopal Church **P** (291) 1922 Iowa Ave 48506-3539 (Mail to: 1922 Iowa Ave 48506-3539) Jay Gantz (989) 752-6020

Flint St Pauls Episcopal Church **P** (305) 711 S Saginaw St 48502-1507 (Mail to: 711 S Saginaw St 48502-1589) Daniel Scheid Sharon Naughton (810) 234-8637

Flushing Trinity Episcopal Church **P** (68) 745 E Main St 48433-2009 (Mail to: 745 E Main St 48433-2009) (989) 752-6020

Gaylord St Andrews Episcopal Church **P** (80) 525 Weiss Rd 49735-1637 (Mail to: PO Box 920 49734-0920) Pamela Lynch (989) 752-6020

Gladwin St Pauls Church **P** (111) 211 E Cedar Ave 48624-2207 (Mail to: 211 E Cedar Ave 48624-2207) Joseph Downs (989) 752-6020

Grand Blanc St Christophers Episcopal Church **P** (552) 9020 S Saginaw Rd 48439-9576 (Mail to: 9020 S Saginaw Rd 48439-9576) Donald Davidson (989) 752-6020

Grayling St Francis Episcopal Church **P** (88) PO Box 501 6441 West M-72 Highway 49738-7787 (Mail to: PO Box 501 49738-0501) Elizabeth Chace

Harrisville St Andrews by the Lake **P** (32) 745 N US 23 PO Box 52 48740-0052 (Mail to: PO Box 52 48740-0052) Nancy Harpfer Joe Jenney (989) 752-6020

Harsens Island St Paul Episcopal Church **P** (54) 208 Orchid Blvd 48028-9556 (Mail to: PO Box 144 48028-0144) Rebecca Lepley (989) 752-6020

Hillman Calvary Episcopal Church of Hillman **P** (72) 330 N State Street 49746-0158 (Mail to: PO Box 158 49746-0158) (989) 752-6020

Indian River Church of the Transfiguration **P** (152) PO Box 460 49749-0460 (Mail to: PO Box 460 49749-0460) James Harrison Audrey Bauer John Wallace (989) 752-6020

Lachine Grace Episcopal Church **P** (87) 13488 Long Rapids Rd 49753-9632 (Mail to: 13488 Long Rapids Rd 49753-9632) John Laycock (989) 752-6020

Lapeer Grace Episcopal Church **P** (96) 735 W Nepessing St 48446-2006 (Mail to: 735 W Nepessing St 48446-2006) Susan Rich (810) 664-2841

Lexington Trinity Episcopal Church **P** (167) 5646 S Main Street 48450-0315 (Mail to: 5646 S Main St 48450-8842) Kay Houck (810) 359-8741

Marine City St Marks Episcopal Church **P** (217) 527 N William St 48039-3708 (Mail to: 527 N William St 48039-3708) (989) 752-6020

Marysville All Saints Episcopal Church **P** (142) 543 Michigan Ave 48040-1111 (Mail to: 543 Michigan Ave 48040-1111) Tracie Little (989) 752-6020

Midland Holy Family Episcopal Church **P** (24) 4611 Swede Ave 48642-3861 (Mail to: 4611 Swede Ave 48642-3861) (989) 752-6020

Midland St Johns Episcopal Church **P** (604) 405 N Saginaw Rd 48640-6339 (Mail to: 405 N Saginaw Rd 48640-6339) Kenneth Hitch (989) 631-2260

Mio St Bartholomews Episcopal Church **P** (43) PO Box 787 48647-0787 (Mail to: PO Box 787 48647-0787) Allan Feltner (989) 752-6020

Oscoda Hope-St Johns Parish **P** (45) 223 E. Mill Street 48750-0338 (Mail to: PO Box 338 48750-0338) (989) 752-6020

Otter Lake St Johns Episcopal Church **P** (57) 5811 Forest Ave 48464-9790 (Mail to: PO Box 217 48764) (989) 752-6020

Owosso Christ Episcopal Church **P** (115) 120 Goodhue St 48867-2320 (Mail to: 120 Goodhue St 48867-2320) Alice Lewis (989) 752-6020

Port Huron Grace Episcopal Church **P** (470) 1213 6th St 48060-5348 (Mail to: 1213 6th St 48060-5348) Lydia Speller (810) 985-9539

Port Huron St Pauls Episcopal Church **P** (67) 3201 Gratiot Ave 48060-2240 (Mail to: 3201 Gratiot Ave 48060-2240) Jane Diehl Robert Diehl Shirley Seely (989) 752-6020

Rogers City St Lukes Episcopal Church **P** (23) 120 N First St 49779-1602 (Mail to: PO Box 184 49779-2017) (989) 752-6020

Roscommon St Elizabeths Episcopal Church **P** (118) 2936 E Higgins Lake Dr 48653-7622 (Mail to: PO Box 517 48653-0517) Charles Curtis Mary Shortt (989) 752-6020

Rose City St Andrews Episcopal Church **P** (32) 200 E Page Ave 48654 (Mail to: PO Box 247 48654-0247) Donnis Reese (989) 752-6020

Saginaw St Johns Episcopal Church **P** (240) 123 N Michigan Ave 48602-4235 (Mail to: 123 N Michigan Ave 48602-4235) Daniel Cannon (989) 793-9575

Saginaw St Matthews Episcopal Church **P** (92) 1501 N Center Rd 48603-5563 (Mail to: 1501 N Center Rd 48638-5563) Marlene Clark (989) 752-6020

Saginaw St Pauls Episcopal Church **P** (182) 720 Tuscola St 48607-1583 (Mail to: 720 Tuscola St 48607-1583) Judith Boli (989) 752-6020

Saint Clair St Pauls Episcopal Church **HC** (173) 115 N 6th St 48079-4829 (Mail to: 115 N 6th St 48079-4829) (810) 329-3821

Sand Point St Johns Episcopal Church **P** (25) 8271 Crescent Beach Rd 48755-9648 (Mail to:

PO Box 1882 48725-1882) (989) 752-6020

Sandusky St Johns Church **P** (27) 41 N Delaware St 48471-1006 (Mail to: 41 N Delaware St PO Box 266 48471-0266) (989) 752-6020

Standish Grace Episcopal Church **P** (25) PO Box 721 48658-0721 (Mail to: PO Box 721 48658-0721) (989) 752-6020

West Branch Trinity Episcopal Church **P** (64) 100 East Houghton Ave. 48661-0083 (Mail to: PO Box 83 48661-0083) Brian Chace Robert Finn (989) 752-6020

NON-PAROCHIAL CLERGY

Anderson RR *ret* Alma MI
Ash LD *dcn* Corunna MI
Bennett FP *ret* Marysville MI
Breznau JC Caseville MI
Breznau NA Caseville MI
Carlsen VS *dcn* Flushing MI
Carver SF Greensboro NC
Cavin B *ret* Flint MI
Clapp SL *ret* Traverse City MI
Clark SM *ret* Menomonee Falls WI
Cleaves GL *ret* Grand Blanc MI
Cominos PM *ret* Essexville MI
Crandell H *ret* Grand Blanc MI
Crane LS *dcn* Port Huron MI
Delaney MTK *ret* Alma MI
Downie EM *ret* Winnetka IL
Dressel MK *ret* Traverse City MI
Elliott WT *ret* Hope MI
Fargo VM
Farmer JM *dcn* Saginaw MI

Graham HJ *ret* Ann Arbor MI
Hartman AE Midland MI
Haynes FJ *ret* Port Huron MI
Hoover J Rochester NY
Houghton FL *ret* Sanford MI
Houle MA *ret* Birch Run MI
Johnson LE Flushing MI
King DD *dcn* Port Huron MI
Kubbe AL *dcn* Saginaw MI
Kusky DLS *dcn* Birch Run MI
MacDonald GJ *ret* Oscoda MI
Michaud BA *ret* Alpena MI
Norton AE Otter Lake MI
Otto RL Harrisville MI
Otto SW Harrisville MI
Parks LJ *dcn* Otter Lake MI
Parks SJ Otter Lake MI
Pressentin EA *ret* Freeland MI
Rehagen GA *ret* Gaylord MI
Renna PS Saginaw MI
Schneider EN *ret* Glendale AZ
Schuetz MJR *ret* Sanford MI
Smith TE *dcn* Dryden MI
Sorenson JR *ret* Marquette MI
Sorenson SM *dcn* Marquette MI
St Pierre JM *dcn* Otter Lake MI
Steele NJ Chesaning MI
Stuart CM *ret* Saginaw MI
Tepe DJ *ret* Saginaw MI
Thompson KE *dcn* Presque Isle MI
Trask RP *ret* Wheaton IL
Vince GL *ret* West Branch MI
Wood RL *dcn* Yale MI
Young SL *dcn* Kimball MI

DIOCESE OF EASTERN OREGON
(PROVINCE VIII)
Comprises Oregon east of the Cascade Mountains and Klickitat County Washington
DIOCESAN OFFICE 1104 Church St (Box 236) Cove OR 97824
TEL (541) 568-4514   FAX (541) 568-5000
E-MAIL diocese@episdioeo.org   WEB www.episdioeo.org

Previous Bishops—
Robert L Paddock 1907-22, Wm P Remington 1922-45, Lane W Barton 1946-68, Wm B Spofford 1967-79, Rustin R Kimsey 1980-2000, Wm O Gregg 2000-2007

Provisional Bishop—Rt Rev Bavi E Rivera (1001) (Dio 2009–)

BP Sec L Boquist; *Sec of Conv* D Harder; *Treas* J Frazier; *Exec Dir Asc Camp* P Lindsey

Dio coun—Cler: A Bonebrake K Macek, G Giacobbe; *Lay:* V Mosier, R Heise K Nash B Spell B Taylor M Thelen

Stand Comm—Cler: Pres A Carmichael N Sargent-Green J Holdorph *Lay:* J Reynolds, C Cagle K McClain

Dio Conv: 7-9 October 2016 La Grande, OR

PARISHES, MISSIONS, AND CLERGY

Baker City St Stephens Episcopal Church **P** (67) 2177 First Street 97814-2606 (Mail to: PO Box 1146 97814-2606) Aletha Bonebrake

Bend All Saints of the Cascades **P** (69) 18143 Cottonwood Rd 97707-9317 (Mail to: 18160 Cottonwood Rd PMB 266 97707-9317) Nancy Sargent Green (541) 593-5991

Bend Trinity Episcopal Church **P** (499) 469 NW Wall St 97701-2605 (Mail to: 469 NW Wall St 97701) Jedediah Holdorph (541) 382-5542

Bonanza St Barnabas Episcopal Church **P** (54) 12201 W Langell Valley Rd 97623-9781 (Mail to: 12201 W Langell Valley Rd 97623-9781) Martha Hurlburt (541) 545-1705

Burns St Andrews Episcopal Church **P** (18) 393 E A St 97720-1605 (Mail to: PO Box 627 97720-0627) (541) 573-2632

Canyon City St Thomas Episcopal Church **P** (58) 139 S Washington St 97820-6125 (Mail to: PO Box 164 97820-0164) Daniel Gardner

Enterprise St Patricks Episcopal Church **P** (19) 100 NE 3rd St 97828 (Mail to: PO Box 301 97828-0301) Rich Attebury (541) 426-3439

Heppner All Saints Memorial Epis Church **P** (97) 460 N Gale St 97836 (Mail to: PO Box 246 97836-0246) (541) 676-9970

Hermiston St Johns Episcopal Church **P** (72) 665 E Gladys Ave 97838-1915 (Mail to: 665 E Gladys Ave 97838-1915) Daniel Lediard Charles Barnes (541) 567-6672

Hood River St Marks Episcopal Church **P** (187) 400 11th Street 97031-1547 (Mail to: 400 11th Street 97031-1547) Anna Carmichael (541) 386-2077

Klamath Fall St Pauls Episcopal Church **P** (106) 801 Jefferson St 97601-2929 (Mail to: 801 Jefferson St 97601-2929) Martha Hurlburt Thomas Osgood (541) 884-3585

La Grande St Peters Episcopal Church **P** (53) 1001 O Ave 97850-2424 (Mail to: PO Box 1001 97850-1001) Kathryn Macek (541) 963-3623

Lakeview St Lukes Episcopal Church **P** (14) 614 S F St 97630-1751 (Mail to: 614 S F St 97630-1751) Richard Landrith (541) 947-2360

✠ **Madras** St Marks Episcopal Church **Other** (20) 13 SW F St 97741-1301 (Mail to: PO Box 789 97741-0110) Laurence Mahon Carol McClelland (541) 475-3578

Milton Frwtr St James Episcopal Church **P** (34) 719 Pierce St 97862-1434 (Mail to: 719 Pierce St 97862-1434) Rebecca Hendricks (541) 938-7268

Nyssa St Pauls Episcopal Church **P** (41) 505 Bower Ave 97913-3943 (Mail to: PO Box 2395 97913-0395)

Ontario St Matthews Episcopal Church **P** (147) 802 SW 5th St 97914-3417 (Mail to: 802 SW 5th St 97914-3417) (541) 889-6943

Pendleton Church of the Redeemer **P** (131) 241 SE 2nd St 97801-2222 (Mail to: 241 SE 2nd St 97801-2222) Jean Cupp Charlotte Wells (541) 276-3809

Prineville St Andrews Episcopal Church **P** (49) 807 E 1st St 97754-2007 (Mail to: PO Box 299 97754-0299) Stephen Uffelman Janet Warner (541) 447-5813

Redmond St Albans Episcopal Church **P** (24) 724 SW 14th St 97756-2619 (Mail to: 3277 NW 10th St 97756-1012) Lee Kiefer (541) 548-4212

Sisters Church of the Transfiguration **P** (198) 68825 Brooks Camp Rd 97759 (Mail to: PO Box 130 97759-0130) Theodore Rodrigues (541) 549-7087

The Dalles St Pauls Episcopal Church **P** (210) 1805 Minnesota St 97058-3319 (Mail to: 1805 Minnesota St 97058-3319) Georgia Giacobbe Lewis Hodgkins (541) 296-9587

NON-PAROCHIAL CLERGY

Barrett RC Bonanza OR
Boone CL *dcn* Baker City OR
Christopher CH *ret* Bend OR
Collins JR Sisters OR
Crum RJH *ret* Gresham OR
Crysler KW *ret*
Erskine J Sisters OR
Fairfield RL *dcn* Sisters OR
Ferguson LC *ret* Prineville OR
Fredrick LE Sunnyvale CA
Gilsdorf JW Pendleton OR
Green RD *ret*
Hoffer WM *ret dcn* Bend OR
Jerome DD Pendleton OR
Kaye RPS *ret* College Place WA
King KV *ret* Summit MS
Kozak JM *ret* Madras OR
Langfeldt JA *ret* The Dalles OR
Lujan MR Hood River OR
Meech MM Detroit MI
Miller AF Hermiston OR
Morton WP Bend OR
Mosier JD *ret* Ontario OR
Nesbitt JR Portland OR
Parker CA Prineville OR
Rose CB Casa Grande AZ
Roth ML *dcn* The Dalles OR
Schafroth SL *dcn* The Dalles OR
Schiering JC Hood River OR
Scissons AM *ret* Burns OR
Smith-Allen SV Union OR
Stanton SM *ret* Olympia WA
Thew RH *ret* Cove OR
Williams RV Nyssa OR
Young GJ *ret* Hood River OR

DIOCESE OF EASTON
(PROVINCE III)
Comprises 9 counties on the eastern shore of Maryland
DIOCESAN OFFICE 314 North St Easton MD 21601
TEL (410) 822-1919   FAX (410) 763-8259
E-MAIL diocese@dioceseofeaston.org   WEB www.dioceseofeaston.org

Previous Bishops—
Henry C Lay 1869-85, Wm F Adams 1887-1920, Geo W Davenport 1920-38, Wm McClelland 1939-49, Allen J Miller 1949-66, George A Taylor 1967-75, W Moultrie Moore Jr 1975-83, Elliott L Sorge 1983-93, Martin G Townsend 1993-2001, Charles L Longest asst 2002-03, James J Shand 2003-2014

Bishop — Rt Rev Henry Nutt Parsley Jr DD
(Bishop Provisional 2014-)

Cn to Ord Vacant; *Treas* R Geesey; *Chanc* E Cornbrooks; *Sec to Bp* L Anstatt; *Fin Admin* A Kendall; *Dio Youth* J Fisher; *Reg* L Anstatt; *Stew* Vacant; *ECW* R Eller R Kemp B Anderson; *Hist* A Leiby; *UTO* M Atwood C Meyer; *Deploy* Vacant; *ER&D* K Bainbridge; *COM* M Moyer

Deans—Northern H Sabetti; *Middle* C Osberger; *Southern* F Malcolm

Stand Comm—Cler: K Cross C Osberger W Ortt; *Lay: Pres* H Snyder S Harwood E Rice,

Dio Conv: 26-27 Feb 2016, Cambridge MD, Special Conv: Jun 11, 2016, Easton MD

PARISHES, MISSIONS, AND CLERGY

Berlin St Pauls Church **P** (132) 3 Church St 21811-1209 (Mail to: PO Box 429 21811-0429) Michael Moyer

Cambridge Christ Church - Great Choptank Paris **P** (452) 601 Church St 21613-1729 (Mail to: 601 Church St 21613-1729) (410) 228-3161

Cambridge St Johns Chapel **M** (98) 1213 Hudson Rd 21613-3237 (Mail to: 1213 Hudson Rd 21613-3237) (410) 228-5056

Centreville St Pauls Parish **P** (303) 301 S Liberty St 21617-1221 (Mail to: PO Box 278 21617-0278) Mary Garner (410) 758-1553

Chesapeake City Augustine Parish **P** (120) 310 George St 21915-1223 (Mail to: PO Box 487 21915-0487) (410) 885-5375

Chestertown Emmanuel Episcopal Church **P** (290) 101 N Cross St 21620-1527 (Mail to: PO Box 875 21620-0875) Florence Williams (410) 778-3477

Chestertown St Paul Episcopal Church **P** (119) 7579 Sandy Bottom Rd 21620-4520 (Mail to: 7579 Sandy Bottom Rd 21620-4520) (410) 778-1540

Church Creek Old Trinity Church - Dorchester Parish **P** (40) 1716 Taylors Island Rd 21622

(Mail to: 1716 Taylors Island Rd 21622) Daniel Dunlap (410) 228-2940

Church Hill St Luke's Parish **P** (104) 105 Church Ln 21623 (Mail to: PO Box 38 21623-0038) Todd Kissam (410) 556-6644

Denton Christ Church **P** (140) 105 Gay St 21629-1019 (Mail to: PO Box 428 21629-0428) (410) 479-0419

Earleville St Stephens Episcopal Church **P** (143) 10 Glebe Rd 21919-2144 (Mail to: 10 Glebe Rd 21919-2144) Robert Goldsmith (410) 275-8785

Easton All Faith Chapel **P** (54) 26281 Tunis Mills Rd 21601-5523 (Mail to: 26281 Tunis Mills Rd 21601-5523) Abigail Nestlehutt (410) 822-1464

Easton Christ Church - St Peters Parish **P** (936) 111 S Harrison St 21601-2907 (Mail to: 111 S Harrison St 21601-2998) William Ortt (410) 822-2677

✣ **Easton** Trinity Cathedral Episcopal **O** (256) 314 Goldsborough St 21601-3669 (Mail to: 314 North St 21601-3665) Gregory Powell

Elkton Trinity Episcopal Church **P** (165) 105 N Bridge St 21921-5326 (Mail to: 105 N Bridge St 21921-5326)

Hebron St Pauls Episcopal Church **P** (24) 8700 Memory Gardens Ln 21830 (Mail to: PO Box 28 21830) Ronald Knapp (443) 614-5410

Hurlock St Andrews Episcopal Church **M** (77) 303 S Main St 21643 (Mail to: PO Box 152 21643-0152) Bryan Glancey (443) 366-4652

Kennedyville Shrewsbury Parish Church **P** (399) 12824 Shrewsbury Church Rd 21645 (Mail to: PO Box 187 21645-0187) Henry Sabetti Stephan Klingelhofer (410) 348-5944

Massey St Clements **P** (41) 32940 Maryland Line Rd 21650-1703 (Mail to: PO Box 158 21650-0158) (410) 928-5051

North East St Mary Anne's Episcopal Church **P** (494) 315 S Main St 21901-3915 (Mail to: 315 S Main St 21901-3915) (410) 287-5522

Ocean City Church of St Pauls By The Sea **P** (123) 302 N Baltimore Ave 21842-3923 (Mail to: 302 North Baltimore Ave 21842-3923) Barbara Bassuener Mark Cyr (410) 289-3453

Ocean City The Church of the Holy Spirit **P** (316) 10001 Coastal Hwy 21842-2649 (Mail to: 10001 Coastal Hwy 21842-2649) George Lamontagne (410) 723-1973

Oxford Holy Trinity Church **P** (320) 502 S Morris St 21654 (Mail to: PO Box 387 21654-0387) Kevin Cross (410) 226-5134

Perryville St Marks Episcopal Church **P** (123) 175 Saint Marks Church Rd PO Box 337 21903-

2519 (Mail to: PO BOX 337 21903-0337) Patricia Drost (571) 331-2618

Pocomoke City St Mary the Virgin Epis Church **P** (82) (Mail to: PO Box 383 21851-0383) (410) 957-1518

Princess Anne St Andrews Episcopal Church **P** (83) 30513 Washington St 21853-1143 (Mail to: 30513 Washington St 21853-1143) Robert Laws (410) 651-2882

Princess Anne St Pauls Episcopal Church **P** (92) 29618 Polks Rd 21853-3228 (Mail to: 26417 Silver Ln 21817-2458) Michael Lokey (410) 651-1507

Quantico St Philips Episcopal Church **P** (43) 6457 Quantico Rd 21856 (Mail to: PO Box 92 21856-0092) Nathaniel Pierce (410) 251-8299

Queenstown St Lukes Chapel **P** C/O Wye Parish 7208 Main St 21658-1628 (Mail to: C/O Wye Parish PO Box 98 21679-0098) (410) 827-8488

Saint Michael Christ Church St Michaels Parish **P** (596) 301 S Talbot St 21663 (Mail to: PO Box S 103 Willow St 21663) Mark Nestlehutt (410) 745-9076

Salisbury St Albans Episcopal Church **HC** (120) No 302 Saint Albans Dr 21804-5267 (Mail to: 302 Saint Albans Dr 21804-5267) Frieda Malcolm (410) 742-6595

Salisbury St Peters Church **P** (728) 115 Saint Peters St 21801-4901 (Mail to: 115 Saint Peters St 21801-4901) David Michaud (410) 742-5118

Snow Hill All Hallows Episcopal Church **P** (116) 109 W Market St 21863-1047 (Mail to: 109 W Market St 21863-1047) Nanese Hawthorne

Stevensville Christ Church Parish Kent Island **P** (569) 830 Romancoke Rd 21666-2790 (Mail to: 830 Romancoke Rd 21666-2790) Mark Delcuze Melody Sutherland (410) 643-5921

Trappe St Pauls White Marsh Parish **P** (61) 3936 Main St 21673 (Mail to: PO Box 141 21673-0141) (410) 476-3048

Tyaskin St Marys - St Bartholomews Episcopal **P** (12) 21865 Nanticoke Rd 21865-2020 (Mail to: PO Box 76 21865-0076) Dennis Morgan (410) 873-2790

Vienna St Pauls Episcopal Church **P** (36) 203 Church St 21869 (Mail to: PO Box 3 21869-0003) Dennis Morgan (410) 376-3376

Worton Christ Episcopal Church **P** (38) 25328 Lambs Meadow Rd 21678-1923 (Mail to: PO Box 161 21678-0161) Frank Adams (410) 778-2821

Wye Mills Wye Parish **P** (279) 14084 Old Wye Mills Rd 21679-2004 (Mail to: PO Box 98 21679-0098) Charles Osberger (410) 827-8484

NON-PAROCHIAL CLERGY

Bast RL *ret* Peachtree City GA
Beasley CH *ret* Colora MD
Birdsall JB *ret* Williamsville NY
Bond MB *ret* Hagerstown MD
Brown EA *ret* Baltimore MD
Brown RK *ret* Millsboro DE
Bunting NR *dcn* Berlin MD
Burgess WF *ret* Denton MD
Callaghan CL *ret dcn* Easton MD
Chilton WP *ret* Easton MD
Dorsey LM Princess Anne MD
Duffy GA *ret* Berlin MD
Fitts RS *ret* Rock Hall MD
Frederic EG *ret* Hampton Bays NY
Garrity CP *dcn* Pahrump NV
Girardeau MD *ret* Salisbury MD
Gribbon RT *ret* Salisbury MD
Hartman SH *ret* North East MD
Hughes TR *ret* Fredericksburg VA
Mandell CH *ret* Stafford VA
Mason JM Easton MD
Moore CE *ret* Chesapeake City MD
Moore DE North Garden VA
Morrow P *dcn* Ocean City MD
Mosley CE *dcn* Ocean City MD
Murray GR *dcn* Salisbury MD
Nettleton JP *dcn* Cookeville TN
Neville BP *dcn* Berlin MD
Porteus BS *ret* Elkton MD
Porteus C *ret* Elkton MD
Reuschling WE *ret* Cambridge MD
Rickards RS *dcn* Fruitland MD
Robinson CD Rock Hall MD
Robinson DG Rock Hall MD
Smith RR *ret* Elkton MD
Stanton BR *ret* Kent WA
Straub GS *ret* Fort Lauderdale FL
Thom KS *ret* Snow Hill MD
Tontonoz DC *ret* Salisbury MD
Walthall CL *ret* Wilton Manors FL
Whalen D *dcn* Stuart FL

DIOCESE OF EAU CLAIRE

(PROVINCE V)

Comprises the 26 counties of northwestern Wisconsin

DIOCESAN OFFICE 510 S Farwell St Eau Claire WI 54701

TEL (715) 835-3331

E-MAIL administrator@dioec.net   WEB episcopaldioceseofeauclaire.com/

Previous Bishops—
Frank E Wilson 1929-44, Wm W Horstick 1944-69, Stanley Atkins 1969-80, William C Wantland 1980-99, Keith B Whitmore 1999-2008, Edwin M Leidel Jr 2008-2012

Bishop—Rt Rev William Jay Lambert III (Dio 16 March 2013)

Assisting Bishop—James M Adams Jr

Dio Admin A Zook; *Treas* B Weathers; *Chanc* J Pelish Box 31 Rice Lake WI 54868; *Ecum* Rev A Hancock PO Box 637 Hayward WI 54843

Stand Comm—Cler: Pres K Charles M Greene P Augustine; *Lay:* E Yeakley G Conover J Chumas

Dio Conv: 13-14 Nov 2015

PARISHES, MISSIONS, AND CLERGY

Ashland St Andrews Episcopal Church **M** (28) 620 3rd St W 54806 (Mail to: PO Box 427 54806-0427) Mark Ricker (715) 682-5067

Bayfield Christ Episcopal Church **SC** (12) 125 N 3rd St 54814-4872 (Mail to: PO Box 816 54814-0816) Elsa Harmon Dennis Michno (715) 813-0764

Chippewa Falls St Simeons Church **M** (42) 19058 190th St 54729 (Mail to: PO Box 194 54729-0194) Claudia Hogan Aaron Zook (715) 723-0050

Chippewa Falls Christ Episcopal Church **P** (51) 624 Bay St 54729-2425 (Mail to: 624 Bay St 54729-2425) Aaron Zook (715) 723-7667

Clear Lake St Barnabas Episcopal Church **M** (28) 365 5th Ave 54005-3738 (Mail to: PO Box 218 54005-0218) Robert Lyga

Conrath Holy Trinity Church **M** (58) North 1643 County Hwy G 54731 (Mail to: PO Box 152 54731-0152) (715) 748-2280

✠ **Eau Claire** Christ Church Cathedral **O** (489) 510 S Farwell St 54701-4994 (Mail to: 510 S Farwell St 54701-4994) Michael Greene James Lorenze Kenneth Van Es Louis Wilson (715) 835-3734

Hayward Church of the Ascension **M** (122) 10612 N California Ave 54843 (Mail to: PO Box 637 54843-0637) Arthur Hancock (715) 634-3283

Hudson St Pauls Episcopal Church **M** (193) 502 County Road UU 54016-7583 (Mail to: 502 County Road UU 54016-7583) Guy Usher

(715) 386-2348

La Crosse Christ Episcopal Church **P** (356) 111 9th St N 54601-3485 (Mail to: 111 9th St N 54601-3485) Patrick Augustine Peter Augustine Kathleen Charles Joanne Glasser Thomas Winkler (608) 784-0697

Menomonie Grace Episcopal Church **M** (110) 1002 6th St E 54751-2627 (Mail to: E4357 451st Ave 54751-5449) Jacalyn Broughton (715) 235-7072

New Richmond Church of St Thomas & St John **M** (14) 354 N 3rd St 54017-1114 (Mail to: 354 N 3rd St 54017-1114) (715) 246-6602

Owen St Katherine Episcopal Church **M** (29) 206 E 3rd St 54460-9763 (Mail to: PO Box 148 54460-0148) (715) 229-2643

Phillips Church of Our Saviour **M** (11) Attn Kenneth Johnson N11211 Rocky Carrie 54555-7234 (Mail to: Attn Kenneth Johnson N11547 Popple Hill Rd 54555-7140) William Radant (715) 339-4281

Rice Lake Grace Episcopal Church **M** (80) 119 W Humbird St 54868 (Mail to: PO Box 477 54868-0477) Harry Kirby (715) 234-4226

Sparta St Johns Episcopal Church **M** (74) 322 N Water St 54656-1741 (Mail to: 322 N Water St 54656-1741) Peter Augustine (608) 269-4266

Spooner St Albans Episcopal Church **M** (49) 220 Elm St 54801-1328 (Mail to: PO Box 281 54801-0281) (715) 635-4704

Springbrook St Lukes Church **M** (27) N8571 County Highway 54875-9404 (Mail to: W3399 Highway 63 54875-9409) (715) 635-4707

Superior St Alban the Martyr Episcopal **M** (51) 1510 New York Ave 54880-2082 (Mail to: PO Box 1384 54880-0220) Steven Burns (715) 392-2536

Tomah St Mary Episcopal Church **M** (55) 1001 McLean Ave 54660-1941 (Mail to: 1001 McLean Ave 54660-1941) Kathleen Charles Elna McDaniel Mary Rezin (608) 372-5174

NON-PAROCHIAL CLERGY

Agner GE *dcn* Chippewa Falls WI
Ambelang JE *ret* Sheboygan WI
Barber VH Hudson WI
Bauer CD
Dwyer BM Eau Claire WI
Edson LN Stanley WI
Frye LL *dcn* Tomah WI
Gardner BN *ret* Hayward WI
Hoekstra RB Chippewa Falls WI
Hogue MCH *dcn* Hayward WI

Huber AW *dcn* La Crosse WI
Limbach ME Port Washington WI
Michaud EJ
Penick FM *dcn* River Falls WI
Rasmus JE *ret* Madison WI
Ring AR *dcn* Thorp WI

Sola GE Hurley WI
Stamm GW *ret* Chippewa Falls WI
Sterken JL *dcn* Sparta WI
Van Gorden SH *dcn* Eau Claire WI
Washington DW River Falls WI
Webb JB *ret* San Antonio TX

DIOCESES OF ECUADOR
Iglesia Episcopal del Ecuador
(PROVINCE IX)

CENTRAL DIOCESE OF ECUADOR

Previous Bishop—
Adrián Cáceres 1971-90, Wilfrido Ramos-Orench 2006-09

Bishop — Rt Rev Luis Fernando Ruiz (1036)(Dio 1 Aug 2009)

PARISHES, MISSIONS, AND CLERGY

Cuenca Iglesia Sagrada Familia **P** (50) No Bartolome de las Casas #534 y Tirso Moliba NO534 (Mail to: Bartolome de las Casas # 534 y Tirso Moliba)
Guaranda Iglesia San Jose **P** Comunidad San Bartolo (Mail to: Comunidad "San Bartolo")
La Hondonada Iglesia Episcopal Resurreccion **P** San Pedro de Echaleche (Mail to: Oficina Central de la Iglesia Episcopal de Ecuador 00017) (593) 245-6948
La Libertad Iglesia de la Santisima Trinidad **P** Avenida 23 entre calle 30-31 (Mail to: Avda 26 y Calle 40 Esquina) Hector Perez Moreira
Pelileo Iglesia Nueva Jerusalem **P** Via La Libertad El Tambo-P. (Mail to: Cascajal de la Libertad)
Pilahuin, Ambato Iglesia San Lucas de Pilahuin **P** Prinicpal San Lucas (Mail to: Oficina Central Iglesia Episcopal del Ecuador 00017) Raul Herrera Chagna (593) 245-6948
Puyo La Ascencion **P** Manabi y Galapagos (Mail to: Manabi y Galapagos)
✠ **Quito** Catedral de El Senor **O** Av. Real Audiencia #63-47 Y Sabanilla (Mail to: Av. Real Audiencia #63-47 Y Sabanilla) Juan Salvatierra Serian (2) 534419
Quito Cristo Liberador (Iasa-Refugio) **P** Jose Enriquez 63-55 y Camilo Echanique (Mail to: Jose Enriquez 63-55 y Camilo Echanique) Raul Guaillas Carangui
Quito Iglesia de la Epifania **P** Herman Cortez N58-2 Y Vaca De Castro (Mail to: Herman Cortez N58-2 Y Vaca De Castro)
Quito Iglesia del Buen Pastor **P** Palemon Morroy S45-75 Y Av. Ecatoriana (Mail to: Palemon Morroy S45-75 Y Av. Ecatoriana) Gladys Vasquez-Vera

Quito Iglesia Episcopal Reconciliacion **P** Guayabamba E2-29 y Quilotoa (Mail to: Guayabamba E2-29 y Quilotoa)
Quito Mision Emanuel **P** Avenida Simon Bolivar s/n Guajalo (Mail to: Avenida Simon Bolivar s/n Guagalo)
Santo Domingo de los Tscahila San Pedro del Pupusa-Paraiso **P** Coop 15 de Sep. Calle Julio Jaramillo Pasaje 7 (Mail to: Coop 15 de Sep. Calle Julio Jaramillo Pasaje 7)

NON-PAROCHIAL CLERGY

Alonso Marina JD *ret* Guayaquil
Ayala Torres CA *ret* Guayaquil
Espinosa-Arevalo C *ret* Atuntaqui-Imbabura
Freire-Solorzano LH Pelileo
Guaman Ayala F Ambato
Hurtado H *ret* Cuenca
Inapanta Paez LE
Jara FG
Leon-Lozano CO Manta
Llerena Fiallos AP Provincia De Bolivar
Llumiguano Arevalo N Quito
Mantilla-Benitez H *ret* Esmeralda
Mejia Espinosa JV *ret* Guatemala City
Montoya Carpio SL *ret* Quito
Onate-Alvarado GA Guayaquil
Ortega GA Casilla
Pita-Parrales UA *ret* Puyo
Quila Garcia PP Tena
Quinonez-Mera JC
Reeson GD *ret* Quito
Reeson ML Quito
Romero-Guevara AN Quito
Serpa-Ordonez PA *ret* Riobamba
Torres Martinez WO *ret* Guaranda
Trujillo Nieto JD
Vaca Tapia HA Tulcan Carchi
Valle-Plaza JN
Veintimilla CJ *ret* Duran
Villamarin-Gutierrez WR
Vizcaino R Quito
Zapata-Garcia CA *dcn*

LITORAL DIOCESE OF ECUADOR

Previous Bishops—
Adrián D Cáceres 1971-88, Luis Caizapanta 1988-91, M García Montiel 1992-94

Bishop—Alfredo Morante (Dio 12 Oct 94)

Diocesan Office Calle Amarilis Fuentes 603 entre Av JV Trujillo y Calle D Barrio Centenario (Mail: Box 0901-5250) Guayaquil, Ecuador. From the US 011 (593-4) 2443050, 2446699 *Fax* 011 (593-4) 2443088 *E-mail* iglesia_litoral@hotmail.com

Treas Lcda E Calderon; *Chanc* Rvdo C Leon; *Sec Conv* Joselyn Contreras Q.; *Sec Dio* Sra M Zambrano; *Contadora* CPA Srta S Garcia

Comité Permanente: Pres Rvda M Loor Rvdo C León G Angulo *Sec* Sra M Barros Sra A Loor Sra. S Carrión

Comité de Ministerio: Rvda B Juárez Rvda G Angulo Rvdo G Alava Sra M Mariduena Sra J León Sr D Olvera

Comité de Disciplina: Rvda B Juarez Rvdo G Alava Rvda G Angulo Sr C Mora Srta E Velasquez Sr F Macias

Comité de Nominaciones Y Resoluciones: Pres Rvdo J Davila C Zuleta F Orrala J Vivar

Comité de Compañerismo: Rvdo A Morante Rvda M Loor Rvda B Juarez Rvdo C Leon Rvda G Angulo Rvdo G Álava Mis J Cantos.

Secretariados: Comuny Relac Públic Rvdo E Giraldo; *Educ Cristiana* Sr C Villacis; *Mujeres Episcopales* Sra E Calderon; *UTO* Sra T Mendoza; *Fondo Desarr Emergente* Sra M Zambrano; *Himnología* Rvda B Juarez y Sra. M Juárez; *Ecumenismo* Rvdo H Mendoza; *Justicia y Paz* Rvda M Loor; *Educ Teológica* Rvdo G Alava; *Estadísticas* Rvdo C Leon *Ministerio Juvenil* Rvda G Angulo

PARISHES, MISSIONS, AND CLERGY

Babahoyo Iglesia de Belen **M** Rcto Pueblo Nuevo 09015250 (Mail to: Rcto Pueblo Nuevo 0901-5250)

Duran Iglesia de Jesus Obrero de Duran **M** Cooperativa 12 de Noviembre Pedro Vicente Maldonado 0901-5250 (Mail to: Box 0901-5250)

Guayaquil Iglesia de la Resurreccion **P** Shushufindi y Paján Pascuales 0901-5250 (Mail to: Amarilis Fuertes 603 y Jose V. Trujillo 0901-5250)

Guayaquil Iglesia de la Transfiguracion **M** 33 Ava y Maldonado 0901-5250 (Mail to: 33 Ava y Maldonado 0901-5250)

Guayaquil Iglesia Espiritu Santo **M** Letamendi entre 38 y 39 0901-5250 (Mail to: Box 090-15250 Amarilis Fuentes 603 y Vicente Trujillo 0901-5250)

Guayaquil Iglesia Jesus El Senor **M** Guasmo Sur Cooperativa Battalla de Tarqui 09015250 (Mail to: Amarilis Fuente 603 y V. Trujillo/ Postal 09015250 09015250)

Guayaquil Iglesia Jesus Obrero **M** Guasmo Norte 0901-5250 (Mail to: RitA LecumBerri y 10 Callejon/ Postal# 09-01-5250 Amarilis Fuentes 603 y Vicente Trujillo)

Guayaquil Iglesia San Pedro **M** 18 y la N Plan Piloto/ Postal# 09015250 (Mail to: 18 y la N Plan Piloto/ Postal# 09015250) Eugenio Noboa Viteri

Guayaquil Iglesia Santa Maria **M** 12do. Paseo 17 NE, Sauces 3 (Mail to: Amarllis Fuente 603 y Vicente Trujillo)

Guayaquil Iglesia Santiago de Jerusalem **M** Coop. Luz del Guayas Km 10 1/2 Via Daule (Mail to: Coop. Luz del Guayas Km 10 1/2 Via Daule)

Guayaquil Iglesia Todos los Santos **M** 25 y la "Q" 0901-5250 (Mail to: Amarilis Fuertes 603 y Jose V. Trujillo 0901-5250) Eugenio Noboa Viteri

Guayaquil Iglesia Virgen Maria **M** Calle 23 Y Tercer Callejon P 0901-5250 (Mail to: Amarilis Fuentes 603 y Vicente Trujillo 0901-5250)

Guayaquil Mision de Jesus **M** Mapasinguie (Coop la Esperanza) 0901-5250 (Mail to: 09-01-5250 Amarilis Fuentes 603 y Vicente Trujillo 0901-5250)

Guayaquil San Mateo **M** Callejon "O" Entre 23 y 24 0901-5250 (Mail to: Callejon "O" entre Calle 23 y 24 Amarilis Fuentes 603 y Vicente Trujillo 0901-5250)

Manta San Esteban-Manabi **M** Sector 10 de Agosto 0901-5250 (Mail to: Parroquia Eloy Alfara Barrio Santa Ana)

Manta San Jose Obrero-Manabi **M** Ciudadela 15 de Abril Parroquiz E Afaro (Mail to: Ciudadela 15 de Abril Parroquiz E Afaro 0901-5250)

Manta San Pablo **M** (50) § Calle 19 #208 y Ave 10 Barrio Cordova 0901-5250 (Mail to: 19 #208 y Ave 10 0901-5250)

MonteCristi Igl Santiago el Apostolo **M** Parroquia La Pila Mexico y Paquisha 0901-5250 (Mail to: Parroquia la Pila 0901-5250)

Santa Elena Iglesia Virgen Maria Salanguillo **M** 10 de Agosto Comuna de Salanguillo (Mail to: Apdo 0901-5250 Guayaquil) Hector Perez Moreira

Ventanas Iglesia San Eduardo **M** Recinto San Eduardo Canton Ventana Vía Panamericana 0901-5250 (Mail to: AMarilis Fuentes 603 y Jose V. Trujillo 0901-5250)

Ventanas Iglesia San Gerardo **M** Recinto San Gerardo, Canton Ventanas Vía Panamericana 0901-5250 (Mail to: Amarilis Fuentes 603 y

Jose Vicente Trujillo 0901-5250)
Ventanas La Gracia de Dios **M** Sixto Escolona y Pablo Palacios 0901-5250 (Mail to: Amarilis Fuertes 603 y Jose V. Trujillo 0901-5250)

INSTITUTIONS

Colegio Epis Transfiguración Box 0901-5250 Guayaquil
Escuela Jardin Transfiguracion Box 0901-5250 Guayaquil
Escuela Jardín Anne Steven, Box. 0901-5250 San Eduardo, Ventanas
Escuela Jardín Stma Trinidad Box 0901-5250 Guayaquil
Campamento Episcopal en Playas Box 0901-5250 Guayaquil

Centro de Estudios Teologicos San Patricio
IMEL Instituto para el Ministerio Episcopal Laico

NON-PAROCHIAL CLERGY
Alava Villareal GJ Guayaquil
Angulo Zamora GM Guayaquil Ecuador
Chavez Franco JE Guayaquil Ecuador
Giraldo Orozco E
Juarez Villamar BM Canton Catarama
Loor Cedeno MDJ Bahia De Caraquez
Macias Perez FO GUAYAQUIL
Mendoza Cedeno E
Mendoza Quiroz HE *ret* Calderon
Mora Villega CD Guayaquil
Orrala Moncada F
Villacis Macias CE

DIOCESE OF EL CAMINO REAL
(PROVINCE VIII)
Comprises 5 counties in central coastal CA except St Mark's Palo Alto and Christ Church Los Altos
DIOCESAN OFFICE 154 Central Ave Salinas, CA 93901 (MAIL: Box 689 Salinas CA 93902)
TEL (831) 394-4465 FAX (831) 394-7133
E-MAIL marybeth@realepiscopal.org WEB www.realepiscopal.org

Previous Bishops—
Wm I Kip m 1853 dio 1857-93, Wm F Nichols coadj 1890 Bp 1893-1924, Edward L Parsons coadj 1919 Bp 1924-40, Karl M Block coadj 1933 Bp 1941-58, Henry H Shires suffr 1950-58, James A Pike 1958-66, G Richard Millard suffr 1960-76, C Kilmer Myers 1966-79, William E Swing coadj 1979 Bp 1980 (California), C Shannon Mallory 1980-90, R Shimpfky 1990-2004; S Romero asst 2004-2007

Bishop—Rt Rev Mary Gray-Reeves (1022) (Dio 10 Nov 07)

Conv Sec Rev M Hughes; *Treas* J Shreve; *Dio Admin* Rev B Nordwick; *Admin Asst* MB Powell; *Chanc* N Cohen; *Archdcn* Ven J Weber; *Cong Growth & Dev* J Reyes *Board of Trustees—Cler:* J WeberJ Ezell E Boyer M Juarez S Symington L McConnell B Palmer; *Lay:* V Pres J J HeadL Enns G Lockwood M Coffin D Parks

Stand Comm—Cler: Pres M Hughes C. Hall T Sramek C Smith; *Lay: VP* W Fernald R Jones L Gonzalez E Rosenthal

Dio Conv: 4-5 Nov 2016 Sherwood Hall Salinas CA

PARISHES, MISSIONS, AND CLERGY

Aptos Epis Ch of St John the Baptist **P** (233) 125 Canterbury Dr 95003-4367 (Mail to: 125 Canterbury Dr 95003-4367) Merritt Greenwood Eliza Linley Stuart Schlegel (831) 708-2278

Arroyo Grande St Barnabas Episcopal Church **P** (232) 301 Trinity Ave 93420-3384 (Mail to: 301 Trinity Ave 93420-3384) Jeremy Bond Merritt Greenwood Robert Keim (805) 489-2990

Atascadero St Lukes Episcopal Church **P** (114) 5318 Palma Ave 93422-3338 (Mail to: 5318 Palma Ave 93422-3338) Matthew Conrad (805) 466-0379

Ben Lomond St Andrew Episcopal Church **P** (183) 101 Riverside Ave 95005-9509 (Mail to: PO Box 293 95005-0293) Blaine Hammond (831) 336-5994

Cambria St Paul Episcopal Church **P** (77) 2700 Eton Rd 93428-4106 (Mail to: 2700 Eton Rd 93428-4106) Brian Palmer (805) 927-3239

Carmel All Saints Episcopal Church **P** (867) 100 Lincoln St 93923 (Mail to: PO Box 1296 93921-1296) John Burk (831) 624-3883

Carmel Valley St Dunstan's Episcopal Church **P** (220) 28005 Robertson Canyon Rd 93923 (Mail to: 28005 Robinson Canyon Rd 93923) Robert Fisher Marcia Lockwood (831) 624-6646

Cupertino St Jude the Apostle Episcopal **P** (477) 20920 McClellan Rd 95014-2967 (Mail to: 20920 McClellan Rd 95014-2967) Wilma Jakobsen Stephanie Tramel

Gilroy St Stephen Episcopal Church **P** (119) 651 Broadway 95020-4304 (Mail to: 651 Broadway 95020-4398) Clarence Burley (408) 842-4415

Hollister St Lukes Episcopal Church **P** (132) 720 Monterey St 95023-3826 (Mail to: 720 Monterey St 95023-3826) Amy Denney-Zuniga

Jolon St Lukes Church Episcopal **M** (50) Jolon Rd & Mission Rd 93928 (Mail to: PO Box 233 93928-0233) Robert Seifert (831) 227-1202

King City St Mark Church **M** (45) 301 Bassett St 93930-2901 (Mail to: 301 Bassett St 93930-2901) (831) 385-5119

Los Gatos St Luke Episcopal Church **P** (567) 20 University Ave 95030-6009 (Mail to: 20 University Ave 95030-6009) Richard Emerson

Los Osos St Benedict Episcopal Church **P** (88) 2220 Snowy Egret Ln 93402 (Mail to: PO Box 6877 93412-6877) Caroline Hall Donna Ross Carlton Turner

Marina Epiphany Lutheran/Episcopal Church **PM** 425 Carmel Ave 93933-3305 (Mail to: 425 Carmel Ave 93933) Jon Perez Patricia Catalano

Milpitas Church of St Joseph the Worker **P** (50) 355 Dixon Rd 95035-2634 (Mail to: PO Box 360832 95036-0832) Ernest Boyer (408) 946-8701

Monterey St James Episcopal Church **P** (92) 381 High St 93940-2161 (Mail to: 381 High St 93940-2199) George Kohn (831) 375-8476

Monterey St John Episcopal Chapel **P** (167) 1490 Mark Thomas Dr 93940-4919 (Mail to: 1490 Mark Thomas Dr 93940-4919) Robert Ott (831) 375-4463

Morgan Hill St John the Divine Epis Church **P** (226) 17740 Peak Ave 95037-4121 (Mail to: 17740 Peak Ave 95037-4121) Philip Cooke (408) 779-9510

Morro Bay St Peters by the Sea Epis Church **P** (84) 545 Shasta Ave 93442-2541 (Mail to: 545 Shasta Ave 93442-2541) Sidney Symington (805) 772-2368

Mountain View Saint Timothy's Episcopal Church **P** (308) 2094 Grant Rd 94040-3802 (Mail to: 2094 Grant Rd 94040-3899) Ronald Griffin (650) 967-4724

Pacific Grove Church of St Marys by the Sea **P** (462) 146 12th St 93950-2749 (Mail to: 146 12th St 93950-2760) Vincent Raj Michael Reid (831) 373-4441

Palo Alto All Saints Episcopal Church **P** (223) 555 Waverley St 94301-1721 (Mail to: 555 Waverley St 94301-1721) Terence Gleeson (650) 322-4528

Paso Robles St James Episcopal Church **P** (122) 1335 Oak Street 93446-2262 (Mail to: 514 14th St 93446-2262) Barbara Miller Jacqueline Sebro

Salinas Church of the Good Shepherd **P** (281) 301 Corral De Tierra Rd 93908-8917 (Mail to: 301 Corral De Tierra Rd 93908) Linda Campbell Cynthia Montague (831) 484-2153

Salinas St Georges Episcopal Church **P** (177) 98 Kip Dr 93906-2909 (Mail to: 98 Kip Dr 93906-2909) Lawrence Robles (831) 449-6709

Salinas St Paul's/San Pablo Episcopal Church **P** (215) 1071 Pajaro St 93901-3001 (Mail to: 1071 Pajaro St 93901-3099) James Ezell Mario Hauttecoeur Arnold Hedlund (831) 424-7331

San Ardo St Matthews Church **M** (23) Jolon St &

Railroad St 93450 Susan Allen (805) 740-2024

San Jose Episcopal Church in Almaden **P** (220) 6581 Camden Ave 95120-1908 (Mail to: 6581 Camden Ave 95120-1908) Shelley Denney (408) 268-0243

San Jose Holy Child Episcopal Church **M** (321) 2650 Aborn Rd 95121-1203 (Mail to: 5038 Hyland Ave 95127) Ruth Paguio Stephenie Cooper (404) 821-5961

San Jose St Francis Episcopal Church **P** (364) 1205 Pine Ave 95125-3459 (Mail to: 1205 Pine Ave 95125-2400) Mary London Hughes Richard Bender Stephenie Cooper Katherine Doar John Palmer (408) 292-7090

San Jose St Philip Episcopal Church **P** (84) 5038 Hyland Ave 95127-2212 (Mail to: 5038 Hyland Ave 95127-2299) Margaret Thomas (408) 251-8621

San Jose St Stephens in the Field Episcopal **P** (167) 7269 Santa Teresa Blvd 95139-1352 (Mail to: 7269 Santa Teresa Blvd 95139-1352) Kenneth Wratten

✣ **San Jose** Trinity Episcopal Cathedral **O** (691) 81 N 2nd St 95113-1205 (Mail to: 81 N 2nd St 95113) David Bird Lance Beizer Jerry Drino (408) 293-7953

Santa Clara St Mark Episcopal Church **P** (189) 1957 Pruneridge Ave 95050-6515 (Mail to: 1957 Pruneridge Ave 95050-6515) Michael Hiller Karin White (408) 296-8383

Santa Cruz Calvary Episcopal Church **P** (376) 532 Center St 95060-4313 (Mail to: 532 Center St 95060-4313) Joel Miller Robert Keim (831) 423-8787

Saratoga St Andrew Episcopal Church **P** (2011) 13601 Saratoga Ave 95070-5055 (Mail to: PO Box 2789 95070-0789) Channing Smith Roger Barney Peggy Bryan Kathleen Crowe Floyd Frisch Fellow Stearns (408) 867-3493

Scotts Valley St Philip the Apostle in Scotts Valley **M** (385) 5271 Scotts Valley Dr 95066-3514 (Mail to: 5271 Scotts Valley Dr 95066) Mary Blessing (831) 438-4360

Seaside El Cristo Rey **M** (146) 1092 Noche Buena St 93955-6221 (Mail to: PO Box 1903 93942-1903) Michael Dresbach (831) 394-4465

✣ **Seaside** La Iglesia de San Pablo **Other** (240) 1092 Noche Buena St 93955-6221 (Mail to: 1092 Noche Buena St 93955-6221) Rachel Bennett Jose Juarez

Sn Luis Obispo St Stephens Episcopal Church **P** (283) 1344 Nipomo St 93401-3935 (Mail to: 1344 Nipomo St 93401-3987) Thomas Tarwater Anne Wall (805) 543-7212

Sunnyvale St Thomas Episcopal Church **P** (318) 231 Sunset Ave 94086-5969 (Mail to: 231 Sunset Ave 94086-5938) Sheldon Hutchison Robert Keim Michael Ridgway (408) 736-4155

Watsonville All Saints Episcopal Church **P** (141) 437 Rogers Ave 95076-3320 (Mail to: 437 Rogers Ave 95076-3398) Michael Dresbach (831) 724-5338

NON-PAROCHIAL CLERGY

Adams GJ *ret* Carson City NV
Adams JS *ret* Carmel CA
Ahlvin JL *dcn* Morgan Hill CA
Ain JP *dcn* Watsonville CA
Anderson JW *dcn* Marina CA
Anderson R *ret* Boulder Creek CA
Arnold SL *dcn* Morro Bay CA
Bacigalupo JA San Jose CA
Barford LA *dcn* Reno NV
Barnard NAS Nipomo CA
Beason KG *ret* Cheney WA
Blundell GA *dcn* Cambria CA
Booth JA *dcn* Carmel Valley CA
Bourne-Raiswell ML Saratoga CA
Bramlett BR *ret* El Cerrito CA
Breuer DR *ret* Los Gatos CA
Buck M *dcn* Pacific Grove CA
Buenz JF *ret* Cupertino CA
Carrington JH *ret*
Cockrell EW *ret* San Jose CA
Collins JE Salinas CA
Coverston HS Orlando FL
Cowans WM *ret* Reno NV
Crawley CD New York NY
Creed CD *ret* Hillsborough CA
Cuffie KA San Jose CA
Danielson PE *ret* Salinas CA
Dod DS *ret* Atascadero CA
Duffty B *dcn* Gilroy CA
Edwards DW *ret* Pacific Grove CA
Elder-Holifield DEC *dcn* Salinas CA
Ellis SM *ret* Santa Cruz CA
Eustace WP *dcn* Lompoc CA
Ferrito ML Santa Clara CA
Fuselier DP *dcn* Monterey CA
Garcia HJ *dcn* Salinas CA
Gardner JM *ret* Hollister CA
Getchell PA *ret* San Jose CA
Glaser GS Tucson AZ
Gonzales R *ret* Nipomo CA
Grosjean LW *ret* Paso Robles CA
Hansen CR *ret* Paso Robles CA
Hansen RF *ret* Asheville NC
Hart VA *ret* Laguna Niguel CA
Heard FW *ret* Salem OR
Heidmann TJ *dcn* Salinas CA
Higgitt N Menlo Park CA
Howe WS *ret* Pacific Grove CA
Hudson-Louis H Carmel CA
Johnston LA Thousand Oaks CA
Jones DG *ret* Santa Barbara CA
Jones DJ *ret* Duras
King JC *ret* Long Beach NY
Lentz JC *ret* Plainfield NJ

Leslie RB *ret* Pacific Grove CA
Levine PH *ret* San Jose CA
Lieb JM *dcn* Ben Lomond CA
Linville HB *ret* Portland OR
Lucas AC *dcn* Saratoga CA
Mann LW Scotts Valley CA
Mather-Hempler PA *ret* Port Townsend WA
Matters RB *ret* Lodi CA
Mayer RJ Cupertino CA
McCoid DB *dcn* San Jose CA
McKenney MLR *ret*
McLeod JW *ret* Union City CA
Mejia J Carmel Valley CA
Merrill RH *ret* Palm Springs CA
Miller AB Mountain View CA
Miller SH *ret* Carmel CA
Mills SH *ret* Hollister CA
Montgomery IB New York NY
Morrison MK *ret* Los Gatos CA
Neal L *dcn* Waimanalo HI
Nelson JM Mountain View CA
Newlin MD *dcn* Seaside CA
Nordwick BP *dcn* Hollister CA
Pace DF *ret* Menlo Park CA
Parab EA Redwood City CA
Pearce WPD *ret* Seaside CA
Percival JV
Philips JK Monterey CA
Pinkerton PEL *ret* Gloucestershire ENGLAND
Pratt-Horsley ME *ret* Los Osos CA
Reyes J Monterey CA
Rice RJ *ret* San Jose CA
Shan BKC *ret* Sunnyvale CA
Smith WM *ret* Palo Alto CA
Somes NF *ret* Jacksonville OR
Sommer RL *dcn* Watsonville CA
Spencer CM *ret* Tucson AZ
Sramek TF San Jose CA
Stewart NA *dcn* Aromas CA
Strasburger RW *ret* Los Gatos CA
Swanson K San Bruno CA
Tavernetti S *dcn* El Dorado Hills CA
Taylor LS *ret* Campbell CA
Thomas JM *ret* Somoma CA
Thompson PR *dcn* Watsonville CA
Weber CJ *dcn* Paso Robles CA
Wharton RE *ret* San Jose CA
White CC *ret* Castroville CA
Whitten WR *ret* Nevada City CA
Williams DE *ret* Milpitas CA
Williams RE *dcn* Sunnyvale CA
Wilson CA Indianapolis IN
Wilson EA *ret* San Jose CA
Wiltsee LL *ret* Carmel Valley CA

CONVOCATION OF EPISCOPAL CHURCHES IN EUROPE
(PROVINCE II)
Under the Jurisdiction of the Presiding Bishop
Convocation Office American Cathedral of the Holy Trinity
23 Ave George F-75008 Paris
TEL +33 1 53 23 84 06   FAX +33 1 49 52 96 85
E-MAIL office@tec-europe.org   WEB www.tec-europe.org

Previous Bishops in Charge—EL Browning 1971-74, AE Swift 1974-77, R Millard 1979-80, JM Krumm 1980-83, RB Appleyard 1983-86, AD Davies 1986-88, MP Bigliardi 1988-91, JM Krumm int 1992, MP Bigliardi int 1992-93 JM Rowthorn 1994-2001

Bishop—The Presiding Bishop 815 Second Ave New York NY 10017

Bishop in Charge—Rt Rev Pierre W Whalon (973) (18 Nov 2001)

Convocation Adm: S Plé

Convocation Officers: Treas M Faigle (France); *Sec Rev* R Cole Dcn (Geneva); *COMB Chair* Dr L Williams; *Chris Ed Chair* Rev Cn E Hendrick (Paris) S March (Nuremberg); *Ecumenical Rep* Rev J Dauphin Dcn (Paris)

Council of Advice: Cler: Rev Dr M Barwick Rev M Dunnam Rev Cn E Hendrick Rev A Rios; *Lay* C Wilson D'Alimonte D Case Dr Y Cockcroft M Mueller-Roemer; *Ex-Off* Rt Rev P Whalon Rev R Cole Dcn M Faigle D Le Moullac Cn J Skipper S Plé

Youth Commission Chair J Döbler

Dio Conv: TBD

PARISHES, MISSIONS, AND CLERGY
Austria

Muhlbach Am Hochkonig Ecumenical Chapel of the Holy Family Mandlwandstrasse 437, 05505 (Mail to: Mandlwandstrasse) +43 664 539 3530 Clair Ullmann

Belgium

Braine-l'Alleud All Saints Episcopal Church **P** (200) Chaussée de Charleroi #2 1420 (Mail to: Chaussée de Charleroi #2 1420) Sunny Hallanan L Mark Barwick +32 2 384-7780
Charleroi Christ Church **M** Boulevard Audent, 20

France

Montpellier Grace Church **M** Rue Leon Blum c/o Eglise Don Bosco 34000 (Mail to: 10 rue Moilere)
✠ **Paris** Cathedral of the Holy Trinity **O** (1068) 23, Avenue George V 75008 (Mail to: 23, Avenue George V) Lucinda Laird Mary Haddad +33 1 5323-8400,

Royat Christ Church Clermont **P** (118) 1 bis, Avenue du Dr. Jean Heitz 63130 (Mail to: 42, avenue Albert et Elizabeth, 63000 Clermont-Ferrand) Robert Warren +33 4 6322 5035

Germany

Frankfurt am Main Church of Christ the King **P** (394) Sebastian-Rinz Strasse 22 (Mail to: Sebastian-Rinz-Straße 22) John Perris Jennifer Adams-Massmann +49 69 55 01 84
Munich Church of the Ascension **P** (587) Seybothstrasse 4 81545 (Mail to: Seybothstrasse 4 81545) Steven Smith +49 89 648 185
Nuremberg St James the Less **M** St. Jakob Kirche Jakobsplatz 1 90402 (Mail to: C/O Sonja March Schillerstrasse 17, 90402 Dennis Krumlauf +49 8964-8185
Wiesbaden St Augustine of Canterbury **P** (272) Frankfurter Strasse 3, 65189 (Mail to: Frankfurter Strasse 3) Christopher Easthill +49 611 306674
Augsburg St Boniface **M** Garmischer Str. 2a, 86163 Augsburg, Dennis Krumlauf
Karlsruhe, St. Columban's **M** Röntgenstraße 1, 76133 Hanns Engelhardt

Italy

Florence St James Episcopal Church **P** (210) Via Bernardo Rucellai 9, 50123 (Mail to: Via Bernardo Rucellai 9) Mark Dunnam +39 055 294417
Orvieto Church of the Resurrection **M** In care of St Pauls Via Napoli 58 00184 (Mail to: c/o St Pauls Church Via Napoli 58, 00184) Francisco Alberca +39 06 488 3339
Rome St Pauls within the Walls **P** (177) Via Napoli 58 00184 (Mail to: Via Napoli 58 00184) Austin Rios Mercedes Tutasig +39 06 488 3339
Milan Capella del Buon Pastore **M** via Boccaccio, 1 Archdeacon Maria Vittoria Longhitano

Switzerland

Geneva Emmanuel Episcopal Church **P** (349) 3 Rue de Monthoux 1201 (Mail to: 3, Rue de Monthoux) Richard Cole +41 22 732-80-78

NON-PAROCHIAL CLERGY

Baer WJ *ret* Vienna AUSTRIA
Baldridge KD Paducah KY
Belanger FS
Bell KE *ret* Fifty Lakes MN
Brondsted LJ *ret dcn* Winter Park FL
Dauphin JC *dcn* Paris FRANCE
Dolan MET *ret* Wiesbaden GERMANY
Engelhardt HCJ Karlsruhe GERMANY
Featherston WR *ret* Florence ITALY
Gill CH *ret* Titusville FL
Glasgow LA
Hahn DE New York NY

Hobson GH Paris FRANCE
Hsieh N *ret* Chatillon Sur Seine FRANCE
Hunt EE *ret* Dallas TX
Kitts J *ret* Shropshire ENGLAND
Laughlin LI *ret* West Cornwall CT
Littman VJ *ret* Sora
Litwinski A *ret* Wiesbaden MI
Mills-Powell MOM
Moser GS *ret* Cape Town SOUTH AFRICA
Ruffino RG *ret* Orvieto ITALY
Todd EP *ret* Copake NY
Wilson HH *ret* Finnas

STATE OF FLORIDA

Dioceses of Central Florida (CF), Central Gulf Coast (CGC), Florida (FL), Southeast Florida (SeF),
and Southwest Florida (SwF)

Apalachicola—CGC
Apopka—CF
Arcadia—SwF
Auburndale—CF
Avon Pk—CF
Bartow—CF
Belleview—CF
Big Pine Key—SeF
Biscayne Park—SeF
Boca Grande—SwF
Boca Raton—SeF
Bonita Spgs—SwF
Boynton Bch—SeF
Bradenton—SwF
Brooksville—SwF
Bushnell—CF
Cantonment—CGC
Cape Coral—SwF
Carrabelle—FL
Cedar Key—FL
Chiefland—FL
Chipley—CGC
Clearwater—SwF
Clermont—CF
Clewiston—SeF
Cocoa—CF
Cocoa Bch—CF
Coral Gables—SeF
Crescent City—FL
Crestview—CGC
Crystal River—CF
Dade City—SwF
Daytona Bch—CF
Deerfield Bch—SeF
DeFuniak Spgs—CGC
DeLand—CF
Delray Bch—SeF
Deltona—CF
Destin—CGC
Dunedin—SwF
Dunnellon—CF

E Palatka—FL
Englewood—SwF
Eustis—CF
Fernandina Bch—FL
Ft Lauderdale—SeF
Ft Meade—CF
Ft Myers—SwF
Ft Pierce—CF
Ft Walton Bch—CGC
Fruitland Pk—CF
Gainesville—FL
Green Cove Spgs—FL
Gulf Breeze—CGC
Haines City—CF
Hallandale Beach—SeF
Hawthorne—FL
Hialeah—SeF
High Spgs—FL
Hilliard—FL
Hobe Sound—SeF
Hollywood—SeF
Holmes Bch—SwF
Homestead—SeF
Hudson—SwF
Indian Rocks Bch—
    SwF
Interlachen—FL
Inverness—CF
Islamorada—SeF
Jacksonville—FL
Jacksonville Bch—FL
Jensen Bch—SeF
Key Biscayne—SeF
Key West—SeF
Kissimmee—CF
LaBelle—SwF
Lady Lake—CF
Lake City—FL
Lake Mary—CF
Lake Placid—CF
Lake Wales—CF

Lake Worth—SeF
Lakeland—CF
Largo—SwF
Lecanto—CF
Leesburg—CF
Lehigh Acres—SwF
Live Oak—FL
Longboat Key—SwF
Longwood—CF
Madison—FL
Maitland—CF
Marathon—SeF
Marco Is—SwF
Marianna—CGC
Mayo—FL
Melbourne—CF
Melbourne Bch—CF
Melrose—FL
Merritt Is—CF
Miami—SeF
Miami Bch—SeF
Micanopy—FL
Milton—CGC
Monticello—FL
Mt Dora—CF
Mulberry—CF
Naples—SwF
Navarre—CGC
Newberry—FL
New Pt Richey—SwF
New Smyrna—CF
Niceville—CGC
N Ft Myers—SwF
N Miami Bch—SeF
N Port—SwF
Ocala—CF
Okahumpka—CF
Okeechobee—CF
Opa Locka—SeF
Orange City—CF
Orange Pk—FL

Orlando—CF
Ormond Bch—CF
Osprey—SwF
Oviedo—CF
Palatka—FL
Palm Bay—CF
Palm Bch—SeF
Palm Bch Gdns—SeF
Palm City—SeF
Palm Coast—FL
Palm Hbr—SwF
Palmetto—SwF
Panama City—CGC
Panama City Bch—
    CGC
Pensacola—CGC
Perry—FL
Pinellas Pk—SwF
Plant City—SwF
Pompano Bch—SeF
Ponte Vedra—FL
Pt Charlotte—SwF
Pt Orange—CF
Pt St Joe—CGC
Pt St Lucie—CF
Punta Gorda—SwF
Quincy—FL
Riviera Beach—SeF
Rockledge—CF
Safety Hbr—SwF
St Augustine—FL
St Cloud—CF
St James City—SwF
St Johns—FL
St Petersburg—SwF
Sanford—CF
Sanibel—SwF
Santa Rosa Bch—
    CGC
Sarasota—SwF
Satellite Bch—CF

Sebastian—CF
Sebring—CF
Seminole—SwF
Spring Hill—SwF
Starke—FL
Stuart—SeF
Sun City Ctr—SwF
Tallahassee—FL
Tampa—SwF
Tarpon Spgs—SwF
Temple Terrace—SwF
Tequesta—SeF
The Villages—CF

Titusville—CF
Valrico—SwF
Venice—SwF
Vero Bch—CF
Wauchula—CF
Welaka—FL
W Palm Bch—SeF
Wewahitchka—CGC
Williston—FL
Winter Garden—CF
Winter Haven—CF
Winter Pk—CF
Zephyrhills—SwF

DIOCESE OF FLORIDA

(PROVINCE IV)
Comprises the northern part of the State of Florida
DIOCESAN OFFICE 325 N Market St Jacksonville FL 32202
TEL (904) 356-1328   FAX (904) 355-1934
E-MAIL diocese@diocesefl.org   WEB www.diocesefl.org

Previous Bishops—
Francis H Rutledge 1851-66, John F Young 1867-85, Edwin G Weed 1886-24, Frank A Juhan 1924-56, Ed Hamilton West 1956-74, Frank S Cerveny coadj 1974-75 Bp 1975-92, Stephen H Jecko 1994-2004

Bishop—Rt Rev Samuel J Howard (992) (Dio 1 Nov 03)

Assisting Bishop—Rt Rev Dorsey F. Henderson (902)

Cn to Ord & DDO A DeFoor; *Reg Cns: First Coast East* M Ellis; *First Coast West* N Suellau; *River* D Weidner; *Santa Fe* L Horne; *Apalachee* T Monica; *Sec* L Horne; *Treas* G Hinchliffe; *Dn* K Moorehead; *Comp* M Showalter; *Bp Exec Asst* V Haskew; *Chanc* Hon F Isaac; *Ecum & Outrch* Rev Cn RV Lee III; *Dir of Yth Min* R Clark; *Interim Camp & Conf Ctr* C Wallace

Stand Comm—Cler: Pres D Killeen N Suellau S Mazingo; *Lay:* L Gregory P Anderson M O'Neill

Dio Conv: 22-23 Jan 2016 Jacksonville, FL

PARISHES, MISSIONS, AND CLERGY

Carrabelle Church of the Ascension **M** (42) 110 1st St 32322 (Mail to: PO Box 546 32322-0546) (850) 545-2578

Cedar Key Christ Episcopal Church **M** (64) Corner of Hwy 24 & 5th Street 32625-5154 (Mail to: PO Box 210 32625-0210) James Wright (352) 543-6407

Chiefland St Alban Episcopal Church **M** (123)

7550 NW 149th Pl 32626 (Mail to: PO Box 997 31644-0997) Hope Koski James Parks Harold Ritchie (352) 493-2770

Crescent City Church of the Holy Comforter **M** (71) 223 N Summit St 32112-2301 (Mail to: 223 N Summit St 32112-2301) Fred Beebe

East Palatka St Paul Episcopal Church **P** (85) 124 Commercial Ave 32131-4363 (Mail to: PO Box 6 32145-0006) Donald Dinwiddie (904) 692-1967

Fernandina Bch St Peter's Episcopal Church **P** (642) 801 Atlantic Ave 32034-3628 (Mail to: 801 Atlantic Ave 32034-3628) Stephen Mazingo Patricia Sheppard (904) 261-4293

Gainesville Chapel of the Incarnation **CC** (70) 1522 W University Ave 32603-1812 (Mail to: PO Box 15116 32603-1812) Richard Clark (352) 372-8506

Gainesville Holy Trinity Episcopal Church **P** (1160) 100 NE 1st St 32601-5379 (Mail to: 100 NE 1st St 32601-5379) Connie Loch Jeremy Hole (352) 372-4721

Gainesville St Michael Episcopal Church **P** (51) 4315 NW 23rd Ave 32606-6542 (Mail to: 4315 NW 23rd Ave 32606-6587) Dale Warner (352) 376-8184

Green Cv Spg St Mary Episcopal Church **P** (123) 400 Saint Johns Ave 32043-3051 (Mail to: PO Box 1346 32043-1346) Celeste Tisdelle (904) 284-5434

Hawthorne Church of the Holy Communion **M** (37) 21810 SE 69th Ave 32640-3959 (Mail to: PO Box 655 32640-0655) Lester Singleton (352) 481-3600

High Springs St Bartholomews Episcopal Church **M** (115) 105 NW 2nd St 32643 (Mail to: PO

Box 906 32655-0906) (386) 454-9812

Hilliard Bethany Episcopal Church **M** (34) PO Box 1005 15860 CR 108 32046-1005 (Mail to: PO Box 1005 32046-1005) William Smith (904) 845-2304

Interlachen St Andrew's Episcopal Church **M** (152) 111 S. Francis St 32148-7305 (Mail to: PO Box 41 32148-0041) Diane Reeves (386) 684-4506

Jacksonville All Saints Episcopal Church **P** (357) 4171 Hendricks Ave 32207-6323 (Mail to: 4171 Hendricks Ave 32207-6398) Donavan Cain Christopher Martin (904) 737-8488

Jacksonville Church of Our Saviour **P** (1348) 12236 Mandarin Rd 32223-1813 (Mail to: 12236 Mandarin Rd 32223-1813) Joseph Gibbes Karen Booth (904) 268-9457

Jacksonville Resurrection Episcopal Church **P** (115) 12355 Fort Caroline Rd 32225-1708 (Mail to: 12355 Fort Caroline Rd 32225-1708) Carrie English

Jacksonville Saint George Episcopal Church **P** (186) 10560 Fort George Rd 32226-2442 (Mail to: 10560 Fort George Rd 32226-2442) Raymond Daly George Henderson (904) 251-9272

Jacksonville San Jose Episcopal Church **HC** (467) 7423 San Jose Blvd 32217-3429 (Mail to: 7423 San Jose Blvd 32217-3498) Stephen Britt (904) 733-1811

Jacksonville St Andrew's Episcopal Church **P** (418) 7801 Lone Star Rd 32211-6001 (Mail to: 7801 Lone Star Rd 32211-6001) Mark Atkinson (904) 725-6566

Jacksonville St Catherine Episcopal Church **P** (190) 4758 Shelby Ave 32210-1716 (Mail to: 4758 Shelby Ave 32210-1716) (904) 387-2061

Jacksonville St Elizabeths Episcopal Church **P** (100) 1735 Leonid Rd 32218-4727 (Mail to: 1735 Leonid Rd 32218-4727) William Smith (904) 751-2626

Jacksonville St Gabriel Episcopal Church **M** (72) 5235 Moncrief Rd W 32209-1042 (Mail to: PO Box 12252 32209-0252) (904) 765-0964

✠ **Jacksonville** St John Episcopal Cathedral **O** (1466) 256 E Church St 32202-3132 (Mail to: 256 E Church St 32202-3186) Kate Moorehead Jean Dodd David Erickson Carl Saxton (904) 356-5507

Jacksonville St Lukes Episcopal Church **P** (184) 2961 University Boulevard N. 32211-3398 (Mail to: 2961 University Boulevard N. 32211-3398) (904) 744-2133

Jacksonville St Mark Episcopal Church **P** (2018) 4129 Oxford Ave 32210-4425 (Mail to: 4129 Oxford Ave 32210-4404) Thomas Murray Nancy Suellau (904) 388-2681

Jacksonville St Marys Episcopal Church **M** (127) 1924 N Laura St PO Box 3243 32206-3633 (Mail to: 325 N Market St 32202-2732) (904) 354-5075

Jacksonville St Pauls Episcopal Church **P** (142) 5616 Atlantic Blvd 32207-2204 (Mail to: 5616 Atlantic Blvd 32207-2204) Michael Snider (904) 725-1150

Jacksonville St Peters Episcopal Church **P** (894) 5043 Timuquana Rd 32210-7440 (Mail to: 5042 Timuquana Rd 32210-7475) Anthony Ferguson (904) 778-1434

Jacksonville St Philips Episcopal Church **P** (220) 321 Union St W 32202-4020 (Mail to: 321 Union St W 32202-4020) Hugh Chapman (904) 354-1053

Jacksonville The Church of the Good Shepherd **P** (184) 1100 Stockton St 32204-4237 (Mail to: 1100 Stockton St 32204-4237) Jeffrey Reichmann Benjamin Ammons (904) 387-5691

Jacksonville The Church of the Redeemer **P** (244) 7500 Southside Blvd 32256-7095 (Mail to: 7500 Southside Blvd 32256-7095) (904) 642-4575

Jaxville Bch St Pauls by the Sea Episcopal **P** (609) 465 11th Ave N 32250-4722 (Mail to: 465 11th Ave N 32250-4722) Reed Freeman (904) 249-4091

Lake City St James Episcopal Church **P** (204) 2423 SW Bascom-Norris Dr 32025-4912 (Mail to: 2423 SW Bascom Norris Dr 32025-4912) Douglas Hodsdon (386) 752-2218

Live Oak St Luke's Episcopal Church **P** (339) 1391 SW 11th Street 32064 (Mail to: PO Box 1238 32064-1238) George Hinchliffe Phyllis Doty (386) 362-1837

Madison St Mary Episcopal Church **M** (86) 104 N Horry ave 32340 (Mail to: PO Box 611 32341-0611) David Boyles (850) 973-8338

Mayo St Matthew Episcopal Church **M** (9) PO Box 1570 32066-1570 (Mail to: PO Box 1570 32066-1570) (386) 294-1839

Melrose Trinity Episcopal Church **P** (150) 204 State Road 26 32666-3901 (Mail to: PO Box 361 32666-0361) Anthony Powell (352) 475-2177

Micanopy Church of the Mediator **M** (99) PO Box 184 32667-4108 (Mail to: 401 NE Cholokka Blvd 32667-4108) Diane Whallon (352) 466-3364

Monticello Christ Church Episcopal **P** (180) 425 N Cherry St 32344-2001 (Mail to: 425 N Cherry St 32344-2001) James May (850) 997-4116

Newberry St Joseph Episcopal Church **P** (234) 16921 W Newberry Rd 32669-2811 (Mail to: 16921 W Newberry Rd 32669-2811) Richard Pelkey Hope Koski (352) 472-2951

Orange Park Grace Episcopal Church **P** (425) 151 Kingsley Ave 32073-5640 (Mail to: 245 Kingsley Ave 32073-5695) Kedron Nicholson (904) 264-9981

Palatka St Mark's Episcopal Church **P** (196) 211 Main Street 32177-3508 (Mail to: PO Box 370

32178-0370) (386) 328-1474

Palatka St Marys Episcopal Church **M** (18) Mrs Edith Alexander 809 Saint Johns Ave 32177-4647 (Mail to: 919 Carr St 32177-5119) Kenneth Martin (386) 328-6394

Palm Coast St Thomas Episcopal Church of Flagle **P** (671) 5400 Belle Terre Pkwy 32137-8824 (Mail to: 5400 Belle Terre Pkwy 32137-8824) Horace Johnson Alfred Stefanik (386) 446-2300

Perry St James Episcopal Church **P** (79) 1100 W Green St 32347-3107 (Mail to: 1100 W Green St 32347-3107) Aquilla Hanson (850) 584-7636

Ponte Vedra Christ Episcopal Church **M** (6123) PO Box 1558 32004-1558 (Mail to: PO Box 1558 32004-1558) Richard Westbury Edward Chalfant Marsha Holmes Caroline Kramer Thomas Reeder Amy Slater Thomas Slone Justin Yawn (904) 285-6127

Ponte Vedra San Francisco del Campo **M** 895 Palm Valley Rd 32081-4315 (Mail to: 895 Palm Valley Rd 32081-4315) (904) 615-2130

Ponte Vedra St Francis in the Field **P** (394) PO Box 3218 32004-3218 (Mail to: 895 Palm Valley Rd 32081-4315) Michael Ellis Ian Mccarthy (904) 615-2130

Quincy St Paul Episcopal Church **P** (77) 10 W King St 32351-1702 (Mail to: 10 W King St 32351-1702) (850) 627-6257

Saint Johns St Patricks Episcopal Church **P** (130) 1221 State Road 13 32259-3184 (Mail to: 1221 State Road 13 32259-3184) Rhonda Willerer

St Augustine St Cyprian Episcopal Church **M** (101) 37 Lovett St 32084-4858 (Mail to: 37 Lovett St 32084-4858) Edwin Voorhees (904) 829-8828

St Augustine Trinity Episcopal Parish **P** (1213) 215 Saint George St 32084-4410 (Mail to: 215 Saint George St 32084-4410) David Weidner Kenneth Herzog (904) 824-2876

Starke St Mark Episcopal Church **P** (89) 212 N Church St 32091-3414 (Mail to: PO Box 487 32091-0487) (904) 964-6126

Tallahassee Church of the Holy Comforter **P** (511) 2015 Fleischmann Rd 32308 (Mail to: 2015 Fleischmann Rd 32308) Ted Monica Teri Monica (850) 877-2712

Tallahassee Episcopal Church of the Advent **P** (298) 815 Piedmont Dr 32312-2422 (Mail to: 815 Piedmont Dr 32312-2422) George Sartin Roy Lima (850) 386-5109

Tallahassee Episcopal University Center **University** (1) 655 W Jefferson St 32304-8013 (Mail to: 325 N. Market St 32202) Brian Smith (850) 296-7843

Tallahassee Grace Mission Church **M** (143) 303 W Brevard St 32301-1117 (Mail to: PO Box 10472 32302-2472) Amanda Nickles

Tallahassee St John's Episcopal Church **P** (1321) 211 N Monroe St 32301-7619 (Mail to: 211 N Monroe St 32301-7691) David Killeen Richard

Effinger Donald Fishburne Abigail Moon (850) 222-2636

Tallahassee St Michael & All Angels Episcopal Ch **P** (143) 1405 Melvin St 32301-4232 (Mail to: 1405 Melvin St 32301-4232) (850) 681-0844

Welaka Emmanuel Episcopal Church **M** (31) PO Box 302 672 Third Ave 32193-0302 (Mail to: PO Box 302 32193-0302) Fred Beebe (386) 698-1983

Williston St Barnabas Episcopal Church **M** (33) PO Box 615 32696-2050 (Mail to: 521 NW 1st Ave 32696-2050) Joanne O'Neill (352) 528-2593

NON-PAROCHIAL CLERGY

Adams-Riley GD
Alexander GG *ret* Jacksonville FL
Anderson MS
Armstrong MN *ret* Lake City FL
Askren RD *ret* Jacksonville FL
Barr DL *ret* Jacksonville FL
Barrus DS *ret* St Augustine FL
Batkin JA *ret*
Beasley TE Jacksonville FL
Beazley RW
Beyer JT *dcn* Tallahassee FL
Billingslea WW Ponte Vedra Beach FL
Birch LK *dcn* Windermere FL
Boyd WM *ret* Carrabelle FL
Brown LB Jacksonville FL
Bryan J *ret* Ponte Vedra Beach FL
Busse MR *ret* Jacksonville FL
Caley Bowers EAA *dcn* Jacksonville FL
Capaldo CJ Fernandina Beach FL
Carroll WW *dcn* Jacksonville FL
Chilton FE Crescent City FL
Clance BB *dcn* Jacksonville FL
Coffey JB *ret* Jacksonville FL
Cooper JH *ret* Ponte Vedra Beach FL
Cordoba G Jacksonville FL
Cowperthwaite RW *ret* St. Augustine FL
Crocker EI *dcn* Jacksonville FL
Damon DR *ret* Jacksonville FL
Daniel-Turk P *ret* Beaufort SC
Davis RC *ret*
Defoor JA Tallahassee FL
Dileo JM *ret* Gainesville FL
Drake BL *dcn* Green Cove Springs FL
Dunkle KH
Flory CI *dcn*
Fulton CB *ret* Marietta GA
Galantowicz DMH *ret* Saint Augustine FL
Goodlett JC *ret* Tallahassee FL
Gray MK *ret* Houston TX
Greenman ETR Tallahassee FL
Griffiths RS *ret* Saint Augustine FL
Grob BR Black Mountain NC
Hardman LOK *dcn* Jacksonville FL
Henderson MJ *ret* Tallahassee FL
Henderson SA *ret* Tallahassee FL
Holston GW Harker Heights TX

Horne LC *ret* Havana FL
Hoskins JAS *ret dcn* Jacksonville Beach FL
Huddleston NG
Huguenin R Crawfordville FL
Hull WF *ret*
Hunsinger JRC *dcn* Lake City FL
Jackson DM Jacksonville FL
Jeffery DL *ret* Atlantic Beach FL
Jones EE *ret* Ponte Vedra Beach FL
Jopling WM *ret*
King MC *ret* Nashville TN
Lee RV Jacksonville FL
Liverpool HO *ret* Lauderdale Lakes FL
Mackey JA *ret* Melrose FL
Marsh RF *ret* Saint Augustine FL
Mazza J Jacksonville FL
McCarty WBC *ret* Jacksonville FL
McGinnis RH *ret* Hudson WI
Miller AC Gainesville FL
Miller WT Farmington Hills MI
Miner DR Tallahassee FL
Minerva RE *dcn*
Moore MD *ret* Jacksonville FL
Morris RL *ret* Ponte Vedra Beach FL
Moulton JA *ret* Jacksonville Beach FL
Moyle SK Pawleys Island SC
Murdoch JC *dcn* Martinez GA
Murray MH *ret* Atlanta GA
Nanton-Marie AA Fort Lauderdale FL
Owen RM Gainesville FL

Owens JA Jacksonville FL
Palarine JR *ret* Jacksonville FL
Pfab MW *ret* Ponte Vedra Beach FL
Pfab PL *ret* Ponte Vedra Beach FL
Roach KM *ret* Waynesville NC
Robinson HJ *ret* Temple Terrace FL
Rosengren LW *ret dcn* Jacksonville FL
Schroder EA *ret* Amelia Island FL
Seagle TR Jacksonville FL
Silver GM *ret* Jacksonville FL
Smith BE Fairfax VA
Smith JP *ret* Jacksonville FL
Sorey GC *ret dcn* Jacksonville FL
Spicer JT *ret* Crawfordville FL
Spruill WA *ret* Jacksonville FL
Stafford WS *ret* San Jose CA
Still KS
Tappe EP *ret* Fernandina Beach FL
Thomas LD *ret* Tallahassee FL
Thomas VB *dcn* Melrose FL
Tjoflat ME Jacksonville FL
Tremaine GH *ret* Gainesville FL
Tull SCA Saint Augustine FL
Turk DL *ret* Jacksonville FL
Walston GW *ret* Jacksonville Beach FL
Watson JL *ret* Flat Rock NC
Weltsek GJ *ret* Jacksonville FL
Woodrum DL *ret* Live Oak FL
Young EP *dcn* Gainesville FL
Young KM Sewanee TN

DIOCESE OF FOND DU LAC
(PROVINCE V)
Comprises the northeast part of Wisconsin
DIOCESAN OFFICE 1051 N Lynndale Dr Ste 1B
Appleton WI 54914-3094
TEL (920) 830-8866   FAX (920) 830-8761
E-MAIL diofdl@diofdl.org   WEB www.diofdl.org

Previous Bishops—
John HH Brown 1875-88, Chas C Grafton 1889-1912, Reginald H Weller coadj 1900 Bp 1912-33, Harwood Sturtevant coadj 1929 Bp 1933-56, William H Brady coadj 1953 Bp 1956-80, William L Stevens 1980-94; Russell E Jacobus 1994-2013

Bishop—Rt Rev Matthew A Gunter (1081)
(Dio 26 Apr 2014)

Sec J Smith; *Admin* MP Payne; *Treas* A Peterson; *Reg* Rev P Twomey; *Chanc* G Stillings; *Cursillo* D Annis; *Trans Min* Ven E Smith; *Dcn Cncl* Ven M Whitford; *Sisterhood of the Hly Nat* Sr Abigail; *Order of Julian* Sr Hilary; *UTO* C Feller Gottard; *Yth Min* T Walter; *Comm* B Jacobson; *Com Min* Rev J Johnson; *Com Cong Vit* Rev E Mills; *Abuse Prevention* S Steinhilber; *CPC* K Powers; *Res Ctr* D Murray; *EFM* Rev R

Patience; *Trustees* vacant; *Sum Cmp* T Walter; *Const & Cns* B Sajna; *Fin Rvw Tm* R Wilson; *Archivist* MP Payne; *Historiographer* MP Payne; *Aging* C Gottard; *Chaps Ret Clergy* Rev W & B Johnston; *Intake Ofcr* Rev R Osborne; *Safety Mngr* Linda Wallenfang; *ERD* Rev S Burman *Deaneries Chairs: Lake Winnebago* Rev K Schaffenburg; *Green Bay* Rev B Sajna; *Wisconsin River* Rev V Natzke

Stand Comm—Cler: Pres Rev R Osborne B Beno V Natzke M Scolare; *Lay*: D Annis J Sachs E Schaffenburg E Wolf

Dio Conv: 22 Oct 2016

PARISHES, MISSIONS, AND CLERGY
Algoma St Agnes by the Lake **M** (27) 806 4th St 54201-1348 (Mail to: 806 4th St 54201-1348) Robert Hoppe (920) 487-2015

Amherst St Olafs Episcopal Church **M** (21) 277 N Main St 54406-9101 (Mail to: 277 N Main St 54406-9101) (715) 824-2577

Antigo St Ambrose Episcopal Church **M** (33) 800 6th Ave 54409-1856 (Mail to: PO Box 134 54409-0134) (715) 623-5532

Appleton All Saints Episcopal Church **P** (656) 100 N Drew St 54911-5421 (Mail to: 100 N Drew St 54911-5421) (920) 734-3656

De Pere St Anne Episcopal Church **P** (534) 347 Libal St 54115-3460 (Mail to: 347 S. Libal Street 54115-3460) Eric Mills Mary Adams Dale Hutjens (920) 336-9571

Eagle River St Francis Episcopal Church **M** (25) No 120 N Silver Lake Rd 54521-8017 (Mail to: PO Box 1625 54521-1625) (715) 480-4237

Fish Creek Church of the Atonement **SC** No 9415 Cottage Row Rd 54212 (Mail to: PO Box 241 54212-0241) (920) 498-8831

✠ **Fond Du Lac** Cathedral Church of Saint Paul **O** (181) 51 W Division St 54935-4028 (Mail to: 51 W Division St 54935-4028) Brian Beno Michael Hackbarth (920) 921-3363

Gardner Church of the Precious Blood **M** (14) No 9696 Gravel Pit Rd PO Box 2 54204 (Mail to: 8933 Pine Ln 54204-9789) Robert Hoppe (920) 487-2015

Green Bay Church of the Blessed Sacrament **P** (163) 825 N Webster Ave 54302-1436 (Mail to: 825 N Webster Ave 54302-1436) Michael Scolare Brien Beck (920) 432-4688

Manitowoc St James Episcopal Church **P** (137) 434 N 8th St 54220-4010 (Mail to: 434 N 8th St 54220-4010) Diane Murray (920) 684-8256

Marinette St Paul Episcopal Church **P** (130) 917 Church St 54143-2408 (Mail to: 917 Church St 54143-2408) Meredyth Albright Patrick Rudolph (715) 735-3719

Menasha St Thomas Episcopal Church **P** (804) 226 Washington St 54952-3353 (Mail to: 226 Washington St 54952-3396) Ralph Osborne Rodger Patience Aran Walter (920) 725-5601

Merrill Church of the Ascension **M** (73) 216 Pier St 54452-2449 (Mail to: 216 Pier St 54452-2449) Linda Schmidt (715) 539-0857

Minocqua St Matthias Episcopal Church **P** (185) 403 E Chicago Ave 54548-9307 (Mail to: PO Box 936 54548-0936) Erin Kirby (715) 356-6758

Mosinee St James Episcopal Church **M** (22) 409 2nd St 54455-1420 (Mail to: PO Box 24 54455-0024) Amanda Sampey (715) 693-2720

New London St Johns Episcopal Church **M** (234) 1513 Pinewood Ln 54961-2449 (Mail to: 1513 Pinewood LN 54961) Paul Feider (920) 982-0970

Oneida Church of the Holy Apostles **M** (570) 2937 Freedom Rd 54155-8926 (Mail to: 2937 Freedom Rd 54155-8926) Deborah Heckel (920) 869-2565

Oshkosh Trinity Episcopal Church **P** (328) 203 Algoma Blvd 54901 (Mail to: 311 Division St 54901-4884) Nancy Behm Sandra Muinde

(920) 231-2420

Plymouth St Paul Episcopal Church **M** (86) 312 E Main St 53073-1817 (Mail to: PO Box 192 53073-0192)

Rhinelander St Augustine's Episcopal Church **P** (80) 39 S Pelham St 54501-3458 (Mail to: 39 S Pelham St 54501-3458) (715) 362-3184

Ripon St Peter's Episcopal Church **P** (108) 217 Houston St 54971-1566 (Mail to: 217 Houston St 54971-1566) (920) 748-2422

Shawano St John's Episcopal Church **M** (63) 141 S Smalley St 54166-2347 (Mail to: 141 S Smalley St 54166-2347) (715) 526-3686

Sheboygan All Saints Chapel **SC** C/O Grace Church 1011 N 7th St 53081-4019 (Mail to: 1011 N 7th St 53081-4019) Karl Schaffenburg (920) 452-9659

Sheboygan Grace Episcopal Church **P** (217) 1011 N 7th St 53081-4019 (Mail to: 1011 N 7th St 53081-4019) Karl Schaffenburg Michael Burg Michele Whitford (920) 452-9659

Sheboygan Falls St Peters Episcopal Church **P** (123) 104 Elm St 53085-1592 (Mail to: 632 Buffalo St 53085-1592) John Throop Gregory Schultz (920) 467-6639

Sister Bay St Lukes Episcopal Church **P** (71) 316 Smith Drive 54234-0559 (Mail to: 316 Smith Dr 54234) (920) 854-9600

Stevens Point Church of the Intercession **P** (194) 1417 Church St 54481-2902 (Mail to: 1417 Church St 54481-2902) Jane Johnson (715) 344-3879

Sturgeon Bay Christ the King Holy Nativity Episcopal Church **M** (133) 512 Michigan St 54235 (Mail to: PO Box 828 54235-0828) Jerome Kuehn (920) 743-3286

Sturgeon Bay Church of the Holy Nativity **M** 3434 County Road V 54235-8832 (Mail to: PO Box 828 54235-0828) George Hillman (920) 743-3286

Suamico St Pauls Episcopal Church **M** (120) 2809 Flintville Rd 54173 (Mail to: PO Box 225 54173-0225) James Conradt (920) 434-2247

Tomahawk St Barnabas Episcopal Church **M** (9) 201 W Merrill Ave 54487-1209 (Mail to: 201 W Merrill Ave 54487-1209) (715) 453-0789

Waupaca St Mark's Episcopal Church **P** (117) 415 S Main St 415 S Main St 54981-1746 (Mail to: PO Box 561 54981-0561) Nigel Bousfield Bruce McCallum (715) 258-5125

Waupun Holy Trinity Episcopal Church **M** (40) 315 East Jefferson Street 53963-0488 (Mail to: P O Box 488 53963-0488) (920) 324-5700

Wausau Church of St John the Baptist **P** (160) 330 McClellan St 54403-4841 (Mail to: 330 McClellan St 54403-4841) David Klutterman (715) 845-6947

Wautoma St Mary's Chapel **Chapel** Hwy 21 & Bughs Lake Rd 54982 (Mail to: 217 Houston St 54971-1566) Thomas McAlpine (920) 748-2422

Wisconsin Rapids Church of St John the Evangelist **P** (82) 320 Oak St 54494-4363 (Mail to: 320 Oak St 54494-4363) Vicki Natzke

NON-PAROCHIAL CLERGY

Bennet RW *ret* Hazelhurst WI
Bippus WL *ret* Marinette WI
Bird PR *ret* Waupun WI
Brown RJC *ret* Ripon WI
Burkert-Brist MA
Burman SC *dcn* Waupun WI
Cason CE *ret* Oshkosh WI
Cell JA *ret* Green Bay WI
Coenen SA *dcn*
Crupi H Waukesha WI
Cunningham MT Sedan KS
Cusic GH *dcn* Marshfield WI
Daily CW Shawano WI
Einerson DA *ret* Rhinelander WI
Forrest W Three Rivers MI
Franks LEA *ret* Boston MA
Fruehwirth GA Norwich
Glenn LG *ret* Rockton IL
Glidden C Three Rivers MI
Good AA *dcn* De Pere WI
Gray MT Hartland WI
Guy KG *ret* Tomahawk WI
Henning KL *ret* Franklin WI
Hughes MA *ret* Shawano WI

Johnston WM *ret* Neenah WI
Lang AA *dcn*
Mazza JE *ret* Sturgeon Bay WI
Meyer RB *ret* Tremont IL
Minnis JA *ret* Boulder Junction WI
Minter MW *ret* Highland NY
Mionske WAR *ret* Wauwatosa WI
Montgomery I *ret* Chester VT
Morehouse MD *dcn* Washington Island WI
Morrison SW *ret* Pentwater MI
Neal WE
Okkerse KH *ret* Sturgeon Bay WI
Pearson AL *ret* Neenah WI
Peterson JH *ret* Neenah WI
Reimer SE *dcn* Appleton WI
Roane WK *ret* Waupaca WI
Ryerson RW *ret* De Pere WI
Sajna BJR *ret* Baileys Harbor WI
Smith EB Oshkosh WI
Splinter JT *ret* Janesville WI
Thayer CC *ret* Sioux Falls SD
Trainor MS *ret* Waupaca WI
Trainor RJ *ret* Waupaca WI
Twomey PT *ret* Appleton WI
Walter VL *ret* Sonora CA
Ward GF Bloomfield CT
Wessell DE *ret* Durham NC
Whenal B *ret* Lake Tomahawk WI
Zakrzewski JL *dcn* Sister Bay WI

DIOCESE OF FORT WORTH
(PROVINCE VII)
Comprises 24 North Central counties
DIOCESAN OFFICE 4301 Meadowbrook Dr Fort Worth TX 76103
TEL (817) 534-1900   FAX (817) 534-1904
E-MAIL: contact@edfw.org   WEB www.edfw.org

Previous Bishops—
A Donald Davies 1983-85, Clarence C Pope Jr 1986-94, Jack Leo Iker 1995-2008, Edwin F Gulick Jr 2009 (Provisional), C Wallis Ohl 2009-12 (Provisional), Rayford B High, Jr 2012-2015 (Provisional)

Provisional Bishop—Rt Rev J Scott Mayer (1035) (1 Jul 2015)

Trans Min Off & Cn to Ord J Waggoner; *Dio Sec* Rev A Wright; *Treas* D Lowder; *Hist* K Shepherd; *Reg* T Middleton; *Chanc* S Liser; *Adm Asst* M King; *Min Supp & Comm Off* T Middleton; *Dir of Comm* K Sherrod

Stand Comm—Cler: C Hughes A Haynie K Johnson; *Lay:* J Walker M Westfall J Dennis

Dio Conv: 11-12 Nov 2016

PARISHES, MISSIONS, AND CLERGY

Aledo St Francis of Assisi Epis Church **M** (26) 2 Dean Road 76008 (Mail to: 325 N Market St 32202-2732) (817) 637-0846

Arlington St Alban Episcopal Church **P** (177) 305 W Main Street 76010-7115 (Mail to: PO Box 13601 76094-0601) Kevin Johnson Sharla Marks Judith Upham (817) 264-3083

Fort Worth All Saints Episcopal Church **P** (1608) 5001 Crestline Rd 76107-3663 (Mail to: 5001 Crestline Rd 76107-3663) Christopher Jambor Melanie Barbarito Christopher Jambor Jordan Ware (817) 732-1424

Fort Worth Christ the King Episcopal Church **P** (48) 5910 Black Oak Lane 76114 (Mail to: 5910 Black Oak Ln 76114-2800)

Fort Worth St Andrew Episcopal Church **M** (30) Meeting at University Christian Church 2720 S. University Drive 76109 (Mail to: 3550 SW Loop 820 76133-2197) Edwin Barnett (817) 926-8277

Fort Worth St Anne Episcopal Church **PS** 6916 Miramar Circle 76126 (Mail to: c/o Barbara Lind 6916 Miramar Circle 76126) (817) 738-2658

Fort Worth St Christophers Church **P** (281) 3550 SW Loop 820 76133-2197 (Mail to: 3550 SW Loop 820 76133-2198) William Stanford Edwin Barnett Andrew Benko (817) 926-8277

Fort Worth St Elisabeths and Christ the King Episcopal Church **M** (89) 5910 Black Oak Ln 76114-2800 (Mail to: 5910 Black Oak Ln 76114-2800) Sandra Michels (817) 738-0504

Fort Worth St Luke-in-the-Meadow Epis Church **P** (185) 4301 Meadowbrook Dr 76103-2710 (Mail to: 4301 Meadowbrook Dr 76103-2710) Karen Calafat Susan Slaughter (817) 534-4925

Fort Worth St Simon of Cyrene Episcopal Church **PS** 3550 SW Loop 820 76133 (Mail to: C/O Diocese of Fort Worth 4301 Meadowbrook Drive 76103-2710)

Fort Worth Trinity Episcopal Church **P** (1056) 3401 Bellaire Dr S 76109-2133 (Mail to: 3401 Bellaire Dr S 76109-2133) Carlye Hughes Andrew Wright (817) 926-4631

Granbury Church of the Good Shepherd **P** (74) Seventh Day Adventist Church 2016 Acton Hwy 76049 (Mail to: PO Box 232 76048-0232) Karen Robertson (817) 219-5382

Hamilton St Mary Episcopal Church **M** (33) 1101 South Rice St 76531 (Mail to: 1101 South Rice St. 76531-3832) Linda Sutherland (254) 386-4412

Hillsboro St Mary Episcopal Church **M** (15) 200 N Abbott St 76645-3015 (Mail to: c/o David Skelton, MD 109 Corsicana Street 76645-2133) (254) 582-2255

Hurst St Stephen Episcopal Church **P** (123) 463 W Harwood Road 76054 (Mail to: PO Box 54864 76054) Robert Gross Slaven Manning (915) 479-4669

Keller St Martin in-the-Fields Church **P** (719) 223 S Pearson Ln 76248-5348 (Mail to: 223 S Pearson Ln 76248-5348) Scot McComas Henry Penner (817) 431-2396

Stephenville St Luke Episcopal Church **P** (235) 595 N Mcilhaney St 76401-5625 (Mail to: 595 N McIlhaney St 76401-5625) Curtis Norman (254) 968-6949

Weatherford All Saints Episcopal Church **PS** 121 S Waco St 76086-4327 (Mail to: 125 S Waco St 76086-4327) (817) 637-0846

Wichita Falls All Saints Episcopal Church **P** (36) 5023 Lindale Drive 76310-2551 (Mail to: 5023 Lindale Drive 76310-2551) Amy Haynie (940) 692-3982

Wichita Falls Church of the Good Shepherd **M** 5023 Lindale 76310-3551 (Mail to: 5023 Lindale Drive 76310-2551) Amy Haynie (940) 692-3982

Wichita Falls The Episcopal Church of Wichita Falls **M** (55) 5023 Lindale Dr 76310-2551 (Mail to: 5023 Lindale Dr 76310-2551) Amy Haynie John Payne (940) 692-3982

NON-PAROCHIAL CLERGY

Akinkugbe FO *ret dcn* Grand Prairie TX
Allen RB *ret* Fort Worth TX
Barber JF *ret* Fort Worth TX
Bechtold BC Fort Worth TX
Benko HT Fort Worth TX
Bridge MA Fort Worth TX
Bye TF *ret* Bedford TX
Catir NJ *ret* Providence RI
Coggin BW *ret* Fort Worth TX
Edman DA *ret* Ardmore OK
Estes WT Monroe LA
Fisher RE *ret* Santa Anna TX
Giles WC Alvarado TX
Gotcher VA *ret* Euless TX
Gough LA *ret* Fort Worth TX
Hayden LH *ret* Germantown TN
Hazel JA Fort Worth TX
Hiatt AR Fort Worth TX
Horton JT *ret* Benbrook TX
Huerta E *ret* Houston TX
Kesler WW *ret* Fort Worth TX
Komstedt WA *ret* Grand Junction CO
Kreymer DN *ret* Santa Maria CA
Logan JA Fpo AE
Madison DA Fort Worth TX
McClain MRS *ret* Fort Worth TX
McHenry RE *ret* Cleburne TX
McKenzie BK
Middleton TG *dcn* Euless TX
Moffat AD *ret*
Moore CM *ret* Plano TX
Morrow QG *ret* Fort Worth TX
Morse DR Grapevine TX
Nocher JG *dcn* Fort Worth TX
Parker RM *dcn* Fort Worth TX
Pool MG *ret* Fort Worth TX
Reeves FB *ret* Roanoke TX
Reynolds JR *ret* Fort Worth TX
Rogers JA *ret* Wichita Falls TX
Rogers S *ret* Menomonie WI
Ruiz-Riquer CS River Oaks TX
Saxton CM Jacksonville FL
Schley JH *ret* Amarillo TX
Shadow BA Fort Worth TX
Shannon MB *ret* Laguna Park TX
Smith JG *ret* Hurst TX
Smith SH *ret*
Stanley JH *ret* Fort Worth TX
Taylor WJ *ret* Irving TX
Waggoner JC Fort Worth TX
Wilson DJG *dcn* Weatherford TX
Winston WS *ret* Fort Worth TX

FRANCE
See Europe

STATE OF GEORGIA
Dioceses of Atlanta and Georgia

DIOCESE OF GEORGIA
(PROVINCE IV)
Comprises South Georgia
DIOCESAN OFFICE 611 E Bay St Savannah GA 31401-1296
TEL (912) 236-4279   FAX (912) 236-2007
E-MAIL vschuster@GAEpiscopal.org   WEB www.gaepiscopal.org

Previous Bishops—
Stephen Elliott 1841-66, John W Beckwith 1868-90, Cleland K Nelson 1892-1907, Frederick F Reese 1908-36, Middleton S Barnwell 1936-54, Albert R Stuart 1954-71, Paul Reeves 1972-85, Harry W Shipps 1985-94, Henry I Louttit 1995-2010

Bishop—Rt Rev Scott Benhase (1039) (Dio 23 Jan 2010)

Cn to Ord Rev FS Logue; *Chanc* Rev J Elliott 3016 N Patterson St Valdosta 31402; *Min Com* Rev L Lacy PO Box 889 Tift on GA 31793; *Cong Dev Dio Ofc* Rev Cn FS Logue; *Comm Off & Reg Dio Ofc* V Schuster; *Const & Can* B Cheatham 2 Sandy Point Savannah 31404; *ECW* C Baker PO Box 638 Darien GA 31305;

Hist Rev Cn F Logue; *Treas* J Draffin PO Box 642 Darien GA 31305; *Yth Progs* R Stewart *E-mail:* rstewart@gaepiscopal.org *Web:* youth.georgiaepiscopal.org *Addiction Rec Dio Off* Rev RK Kelly; *Anti-Racism Dio Off* Dcn Y Owens; *Conf Ctr* J Coble; *Cursillo* Rev K Brinson; *ER&D* Rev J Parker

Deans: Albany Rev HL Lowery *Augusta* Rev B Alford 2321 Lumpkin Rd Augusta 30906 *Central* Rev J Kilian *Savannah* W Willoughby III *Southeastern* Rev T Clarkson *Southwestern* Rev D Ronn PO Box 3226 Vald 31604

Stand Comm—Cler: Pres T Clarkson W Willoughby BJ Alford D Ronn; *Lay:* RM Lilly Jr C Hough N Threlkeld M Stevenson

Dio Conv: 10-12 Nov 2016 Augusta GA

PARISHES, MISSIONS, AND CLERGY

Albany St John and St Marks Episcopal Church **P** (104) 2425 Cherry Laurel Ln 31705-4507 (Mail to: 2425 Cherry Laurel Ln 31705-4507) Ridenour Lamb Jonathan Tuttle

Albany St Patricks Episcopal Church **P** (237) 4800 Old Dawson Rd 31721 (Mail to: 4800 Old Dawson Rd 31721-9151) James Weldon Kedron Nicholson (229) 432-7964

Albany St Pauls Episcopal Church **P** (505) 212 N Jefferson St 31701-2523 (Mail to: 212 N Jefferson St 31701-2523) Dudley Lippitt Hermon Lowery James Purks (229) 436-0196

Americus Calvary Episcopal Church **P** (235) 408 Lee St 31709-3918 (Mail to: 408 S Lee St 31709-3918) Dianne Hall Johnny Lane

Augusta Christ Church **P** (62) 1904 Greene St 30904-3906 (Mail to: PO Box 2965 30914-2965) (706) 736-5165

Augusta Church of Our Savior **P** (178) 4227 Columbia Rd 30907-1466 (Mail to: 4227 Columbia Road 30907-1466) John West Saundra Turner (706) 863-1718

Augusta Church of the Good Shepherd **P** (1702) 2230 Walton Way 30904-4302 (Mail to: 2230 Walton Way 30904-4302) Robert Fain Lisa Barrowclough Talmadge Bowden Lucius Johnson Matthew Lewis James Menger Lynn Prather (706) 738-3386

Augusta St Albans Episcopal Church **P** (161) 2321 Lumpkin Rd 30906-3014 (Mail to: 2321 Lumpkin Rd 30906) Billy Alford Rosalyn Panton (706) 798-1482

Augusta St Augustine Canterbury Episcopal Ch **P** (315) 3321 Wheeler Rd 30909-3104 (Mail to: 3321 Wheeler Rd 30909-3104) Jason Haddox James Aton Elizabeth Forbes John Warner (706) 738-6676

Augusta St Marys Church **M** (55) 1114 12th St 30901-2706 (Mail to: PO Box 2303 30903-2303) James Menger (706) 722-6061

Augusta St Pauls Church **P** (774) 605 Reynolds St 30901-1431 (Mail to: 605 Reynolds St 30901-1431) Kelsey Hutto John William Jenkins George Muir Erwin Veale (706) 724-2485

Bainbridge St Johns Episcopal Church **P** (91)

516 E Broughton St 39817-4040 (Mail to: 516 E Broughton St 39817-4040) Marcia McRae (229) 246-3554

Baxley St Thomas Aquinas Church **M** (16) 5686 Golden Isle W 31513-7937 (Mail to: PO Box 1283 31515-1283) Phillip Runge (912) 705-0287

Blakely Holy Trinity Episcopal Church **M** (8) PO Box 186 39823-0186 (Mail to: PO Box 186 39823-0186) (229) 723-3971

Brunswick Good Shepherd Church **M** (26) 1601 Macon Ave 31520-6653 (Mail to: 780 Pennick Rd 31525-5358) (912) 265-2663

Brunswick St Athanasius Episcopal Church **P** (171) C/O Mr Charles L Scott PO Box 977 31521-0977 (Mail to: PO Box 977 31521-0977) Iane Sastre (912) 342-8461

Brunswick St Marks Church **P** (468) 900 Gloucester Street 31520 (Mail to: PO Box 1155 31521-1155) Alan Akridge Gary Jackson Edward Williams (912) 265-0600

Cochran Trinity Episcopal Church **M** (82) Corner of 5th & Cherry St 31014 (Mail to: PO Box 294 31014-0294) Joy Fisher Dale Jones George Porter Eschol Wiggins (478) 934-2771

Cordele Christ Episcopal Church **M** (90) 408 S 1st St 31015-1573 (Mail to: PO Box 264 31015-1573) William Stewart (229) 273-2439

Darien St Andrews Episcopal Church **P** (215) PO Box D929 31305-0930 (Mail to: PO Drawer 929 31305-0929) Ted Clarkson

Darien St Cyprian Episcopal Church **M** (67) C/O Drawer Box 929 Fort King George Dr 31305 (Mail to: PO Drawer 929 31305-0929) Ted Clarkson (912) 437-4562

Dawson Church of the Holy Spirit **M** (15) 1170 Georgia Ave SE 39842-2112 (Mail to: PO Box 645 39842-0645) (229) 995-4729

Douglas St Andrews Episcopal Church **P** (23) 204 Coffee Ave S 31533-0006 (Mail to: PO Box 1523 31543-1523) (912) 384-1712

Dublin Christ Church **P** (88) PO Box 417 31040-0417 (Mail to: PO Box 417 31040-0417) (478) 272-3003

Fitzgerald St Matthews Episcopal Church **M** (24) 212 W Pine St 31750-5800 (Mail to: PO Box 1153 31750-1153) Frank Christian (229) 423-5268

Harlem Trinity Episcopal Church **M** (18) 345 N Louisville St 30814-5356 (Mail to: PO Box 275 30814) Kenneth Rowland (706) 556-6282

Hawkinsville St Lukes Episcopal Church **P** (136) Dooley At Broad Sts 31036 (Mail to: PO Box 273 31036-0273) Aaron Brewer (478) 892-9373

Hephzibah Church of the Atonement **M** (87) 2616 Tobacco Rd 30815-7015 (Mail to: PO Box 5785 30916-5785) (706) 796-3545

Hinesville St Philips Episcopal Church **P** (153) 302 E General Stewart Way 31313-2640 (Mail to: 302 E General Stewart Way 31313-2640) Adrianna Shaw (912) 876-2744

Jekyll Island St Richards of Chichester Episcopal Mission **M** (27) PO Box 13007 31527-0007 (Mail to: PO Box 13007 31527-0007) (912) 230-6341

Jesup St Pauls Episcopal Church **M** (279) PO Box 1291 31598-1291 (Mail to: PO Box 1291 31598-1291) Deborah Shaffer (912) 427-3900

Kingsland King of Peace **P** (235) 6230 Laurel Island Pkwy 31548-6056 (Mail to: 6230 Laurel Island Pkwy 31548-6056) Alvin Crumpton (912) 510-8958

Louisville Epis Church of St Mary Magdalene **M** (30) 321 W 7th St 30434-1307 (Mail to: PO Box 562 30434-0562) (478) 685-7019

Martinez Holy Comforter Church **M** (408) 473 Fury's Ferry Road 30907-8236 (Mail to: 473 Fury's Ferry Road 30907-8236) Lynn Prather Cynthia Taylor (706) 210-1133

Moultrie St Margaret of Scotland Church **M** (40) 1499 S Main St 31768-5811 (Mail to: PO Box 925 31776-0925) Walter Hobgood (229) 616-1116

Pooler St Patricks Church **M** (76) PO Box 576 31322-0576 (Mail to: 1285 Pine Barren Rd 31322) (912) 748-6016

✣ **Quitman** St James Episcopal Church **M** (54) 306 N Court St 31643-2036 (Mail to: PO Box 864 31643-0864) James Elliott Ned Simmons (229) 263-5053

Richmond Hill St Elizabeths Episcopal Church **P** (239) 16491 GA Highway 144 31324-5367 (Mail to: 16491 GA Highway 144 31324-5367) Charles Hubbard (912) 727-2650

Rincon St Lukes Episcopal Church **M** (116) 155 Goshen Rd 31326-5546 (Mail to: PO Box 1912 31326-5546) (912) 826-3332

Saint Marys Christ Episcopal Church **P** (127) 305 Wheeler St 31558-8431 (Mail to: 305 Wheeler St 31558-7255) Dedra Bell-Wolski (912) 882-5308

Sandersville Grace Episcopal Church **M** (31) 114 2nd Ave W PO Box 771 31082 (Mail to: PO Box 771 31082) Carlton Shuford (478) 552-5295

Savannah Christ Church Episcopal **P** (398) 28 Bull Street 31401 (Mail to: 18 Abercorn Street 31401) Michael White Patricia Davis Helen White Julia Wilkinson (912) 236-2500

Savannah St Bartholomews Church **HC** C/O Dio of Georgia 611 E Bay St 31401-1238 (Mail to: 1802 Abercorn St 31401-8122) William Willoughby (912) 232-0274

Savannah St Francis of Islands Episcopal Ch **P** (257) 590 Walthour Rd 31410-2610 (Mail to: 590 Walthour Rd 31410) Bruce Fehr Lauren Flowers (912) 897-5725

Savannah St Georges Episcopal Church **P** (256) 15 Willow Rd 31419-2627 (Mail to: PO Box 61297 31420-1297) James Parker (912) 925-6517

Savannah St Johns Episcopal Church **P** (1721) 1

W Macon St 31401-4307 (Mail to: 1 W Macon St 31401-4307) Gavin Dunbar Gavin Dunbar Craig O'Brien (912) 232-1251

Savannah St Matthew's Episcopal Church **P** (263) 1401 Martin Luther King Blvd 31415-7201 (Mail to: 1401 Martin Luther King Jr Blvd 31415-7201) (912) 233-5965

Savannah St Michael & All Angels Episcopal Ch **P** (166) 3101 Waters Ave 31404-6259 (Mail to: 3101 Waters Ave 31404) Roger Kelly (912) 354-7230

Savannah St Peters Episcopal Church **P** (635) 3 Westridge Rd 31411-2951 (Mail to: 3 W Ridge Rd Skidaway Island 31411) Zachary Fleetwood William Lea Paschal Mingledorff (912) 598-7242

Savannah St Thomas Episcopal Church **P** (380) 2 Saint Thomas Ave 31406-7533 (Mail to: 2 Saint Thomas Ave 31406-7533) Richard Nelson William Collins (912) 355-3110

Savannah The Collegiate Church of St Paul the Apostle **P** (349) 1802 Abercorn St 31401-8122 (Mail to: Canon T Porter Ball House 1802 Abercorn St 31401-8122) Charles Todd Robert Bagwell Michael Chaney Susan Gahagan George Salley Harry Shipps William Willoughby (912) 232-0274

St Simons Is Christ Church Frederica **P** (897) 6329 Frederica Rd 31522-5812 (Mail to: 6329 Frederica Rd 31522-5812) Thomas Purdy Leigh Hall Rebecca Rowell Jan Saltzgaber James Wethern (912) 638-8683

St Simons Is Church of the Holy Nativity **M** (61) 615 Mallory St 31522-4018 (Mail to: 615 Mallery Street 31522-4018) June Johnson (912) 638-3733

Statesboro Trinity Episcopal Church **P** (144) 4401 Country Club Rd 30458-9188 (Mail to: PO Box 2005 30459-2005) Joan Kilian (912) 489-4208

Swainsboro Episcopal Ch of the Good Shepherd **M** (46) 621 W. Main St 30401-0074 (Mail to: PO Box 74 30401-0074) Lucius Johnson (478) 237-7122

Thomasville All Saints Episcopal Church **P** (297) 443 S Hansell St 31792-5512 (Mail to: PO Box 2626 31799-2626) Paul Hancock (229) 228-9242

Thomasville Church of the Good Shepherd **M** (23) 515 N Oak St 31792-5046 (Mail to: PO Box 3136 31799-3136) (229) 403-7515

Thomasville St Thomas Episcopal Church **P** (268) PO Box 33 31799-0033 (Mail to: PO Box 33 31799-0033) Judith Keith Dwayne Varas (229) 226-5145

Thomson Holy Cross Episcopal Church **M** (13) 515 Fluker St 30824-3018 (Mail to: PO Box 211 30824-0211) Erwin Veale (706) 595-4342

Tifton St Annes Episcopal Church **P** (506) 2411 Central Ave N 31794 (Mail to: PO Box 889 31793-0889) Thomas Lacy Ellen Richardson (229) 386-5989

Tybee Island All Saints Episcopal Church **M** (100) 804 Jones Ave 31328-8735 (Mail to: 804 Jones Ave 31328-8735) Edna Adkins (912) 786-5845

Valdosta Christ Episcopal Church **P** (538) 1521 N Patterson St 31602-3848 (Mail to: 1521 N Patterson St 31602-3848) David Johnson Daniel Shoemake (229) 242-5115

Valdosta Christ the King Episcopal Church **P** (380) 101 E Central Ave Fl 3 31601-5500 (Mail to: 101 E Central Ave 31601-5546) Stanley White (229) 247-6859

Valdosta St Barnabas Episcopal Church **M** (82) 3565 Bemiss Rd 31605-6074 (Mail to: 3565 Bemiss Rd 31605-6074) Denise Ronn (229) 242-5332

Vidalia Church of the Annunciation **P** (134) 1512 Meadows Ln 30474-4425 (Mail to: PO Box 1311 30475-1311) Denise Vaughn (912) 537-3776

Waycross Grace Episcopal Church **P** (152) 401 Pendleton St 31501-3645 (Mail to: 401 Pendleton St 31501-3645) Katherine Brinson (912) 283-8582

Waynesboro St Michaels Episcopal Church **P** (127) 515 S Liberty St 30830-1508 (Mail to: PO Box 50 30830-0050) (706) 554-3465

Woodbine St Marks Episcopal Church **M** (22) PO Box 626 31569-0626 (Mail to: PO Box 626 31569-0626) (912) 576-5005

NON-PAROCHIAL CLERGY

Abbott GL *ret* Hawkinsville GA
Acree NP Saint Simons Island GA
Anderson CK *dcn* Evans GA
Andrew C Augusta GA
Andrews LC Hinesville GA
Angus JL *ret* Hardeeville SC
Arboleda GA
Atwood TO *ret* San Diego CA
Buechner FA *ret*
Bullion JR *ret* Albany GA
Butin JM St Simons Island GA
Byers SS *dcn* Moultrie GA
Cantrell LQ *ret* Valdosta GA
Carreker ML Savannah GA
Carter JR *ret* Savannah GA
Castles CW *dcn* Decatur GA
Chaffee AR *dcn* Hinesville GA
Clendinen JH Brunswick GA
Clift JW *ret* Dawson GA
Cox JS *ret* Valdosta GA
Crook JV *ret* Memphis TN
Cross FG *ret* Albany GA
Culbreath LD *dcn* Tifton GA
Darby SL *dcn* Statesboro GA
Davis JR *dcn* Albany GA
Degenhardt TW *dcn* Waynesboro GA
Derrick JB *dcn* Vidalia GA
Dolack CA Savannah GA
Dolen WK Augusta GA
Doster DH Dublin GA

Dunn GM *ret* Kanata ON
Dupree HD Jacksonville FL
Ethridge FE *ret* Fort Payne AL
Evans SA *ret* Savannah GA
Evans W *ret* Marietta GA
Fehr LL Savannah GA
Fitzgerald WT *ret* Lakemont GA
Green FL *ret* Brunswick GA
Gunn RR *ret* Tiger GA
Habiby SJ *ret* Swanzey NH
Hall SM *ret* Clayton GA
Harris JE *ret* Holden MA
Hay CH *ret* Leesburg FL
Heinemann AE *ret* Albany GA
Henderson CAG *dcn* Savannah GA
Highsmith JL *dcn*
Hill SD *dcn* Savannah GA
Hoskins CL *ret* Savannah GA
Hurst HJ *ret* Nashville TN
Ingeman PL *ret* Valdosta GA
Jackson IL Sandersville GA
Jesion LM *dcn* Augusta GA
Jones MS *ret* Albany GA
Koelliker KT *dcn*
Larson SS Swainsboro GA
Lasch LV Augusta GA
Lee DKC Hinesville GA
Leroux GM *ret* Atlanta GA
Lightsey PSW *dcn* Valdosta GA
Littleton WH *ret* Saint Simons Island GA
Logue FS Saint Marys GA
Lowe EC *ret* Saint Marys GA
Lucas WB *dcn* Savannah GA
Marks SP *dcn* Valdosta GA

Maury JL Savannah GA
Maxwell GM *ret* Savannah GA
McDonnell RP Hilton Head Island SC
McGowen WH *dcn* Brunswick GA
Meuschke MO *dcn* Hortense GA
Miller KD Augusta GA
Mills NT Thomasville GA
Mirate GA Valdosta GA
Mithen TS *dcn* Bainbridge GA
Moreschi AT Savannah GA
Nelson GL *ret dcn* Hendersonville NC
Norris SA Valdosta GA
Owens UNY *dcn* Valdosta GA
Paradise GH *ret* Atlanta GA
Parris CAE Savannah GA
Renegar DM *ret* Waterloo SC
Robinson JR *dcn* Valdosta GA
Rose DJ Tifton GA
Sanders RE *ret* Augusta GA
Sartin NA *dcn* Valdosta GA
Scales L *dcn* Evans GA
Scales LG *ret* Evans GA
Scott GM *dcn* Cochran GA
Shumard JB Savannah GA
Somerville DJ *ret* Brunswick GA
Steele KA
Stewart DS Douglas GA
Taylor CH *dcn*
Thompson E *ret* Baxley GA
Tonge SD *ret* Waycross GA
Varner JH Savannah GA
Walkley RN *ret* Cutler Bay FL
Whittle NW *dcn* Statesboro GA
Worthington WR *ret* Saint Simons Island GA

GERMANY

See Europe

DIOCESE OF HAITI

EGLISE EPISCOPALE D'HAITI
(PROVINCE II)
Comprises the Republic of Haiti
DIOCESAN OFFICE BP 1309 Port-au-Prince HAITI
(Mail: c/o Lynx Air PO Box 407139 Ft. Lauderdale, FL 33340)
Tel 011 (509) 257-8116   FAX 011 (509) 257-3412
E-mail epihaiti@hotmail.com; epihaiti@egliseepiscopaledhaiti.org
WEB www.egliseepiscopaledhaiti.org

Previous Bishops—
James Theodore Holly (106A) 1874-1911, Harry R Carson (327) 1923-43, Spence Burton SSJE (417) suffr 1939-42, C Alfred Voegeli (441) 1943-71, Luc Anatole Jacques Garnier (660) 1971-94

Bishop—Jean-Zaché Duracin (881) (Dio 1994)

Bishop Suffragan—Rt Rev Ogé Beauvoir (1064) (Dio 2012)

Marie-Jose Joseph; *Acct* Frantz Antilus; Jean-Marie Jean Gilles; *Dir Off of Dev* Rev Frantz Cole; *Asst Admn* Nedgie Vixamar; *Hist* Rev Jean McDonald;

Chr Ed Off Rev M Jean; *Prep of Dio Synods* Rev Fritz Desire Marc Leon Nicole Vixamar; *Comm to Examine Chap* Rev McDonald Jean Rev Kesner Ajax Sister Marie Margaret; *COM* RP Valdema Fritz RP Mathieu Brutus Madame Nicole Vixamar M Dubic Osse RP Phanord J Berhol

Coun Advice—Cler Ven Diegue Joseph Tancrel RP Bernier Noe RP Ajax Kesner; *Lay* Soeur M Raphael SSM Neptune Joubert Joseph Emmanuel

PARISHES, MISSIONS, AND CLERGY

Anse-A-Galets St Francois D'Assise **M** (100) Bas Bureau # 20 (Mail to: PO Box 1309)

Arcahaie Christ-Roi (Leger) **M** (100) Leger (Mail to: Leger)

Arcahaie St Jean L'Evangeliste **P** Jean Dumas (Mail to: Jean Dumas)

Arcahaie St Thomas Episcopal Church **M** (200) 131 Jersusalem (Mail to: 464 Jerusalem)

Bainet Ascension **M** #13, Rue St Faustin (Mail to: St Faustin)

Bainet St Cyprien **M** Labiche (Mail to: Labiche)

Bainet St Luc **SC** La Bresilienne (Mail to: La Bresilienne)

Bainet St Matthieu **SC** Begin-Laurent

Cange Bon Sauveur **M** (400) Plateau Central Rte#3

Cap-Haitien Notre Dame, Molas **PS** (200) Molas (Mail to: PO Box 38)

Cap-Haitien Paroisse St-Esprit **M** (700) 12 et 13A 1309 (Mail to: Rues 12-13A 1309)

Carrefour Ascension **M** Thor 67 (Mail to: PO Box 1309)

Carrefour Sainte Croix **M** (100) Taifer (Mail to: PO Box 1309)

Cayes St Jn Baptiste **M** Savanette

Cayes St Sauveur **M** 96 Rue Simon Bolivar et Prospere Faines (Mail to: PO Box 70)

Cayes Ste Croix **M** Ravine-a-L'Anse

Cazale St Andre **M** (700) Route Port Salut

Ganthier St Sacrement **SC** 1 Cite Rurale (Mail to: 1 Cite rurale Fonds parisien)

Ganthier Transfiguration **SC** Gorman (Mail to: 1 Cite rurale Fonds Parisien)

Gde Colline St Barthelemy **M** Nan Mangot (Mail to: PO Box 1309)

Gonaives La Resurrection **M** (200) 135 Stenio Vincent

Gonaives St Barnabas **M** (200) Treille (Mail to: Treille)

Gonaives St Mathieu **SC** Bayonnais (Mail to: Bayonnais)

Gonaives (Gros-Morne) Bon Samaritain **M** L 'Acul Beaudois (Mail to: L Acul)

Grand Goave St Matthias **M** (400) Cherident - Grande Colline (Mail to: PB 1309)

Hinche St Andre **M** (500) 6 Toussaint Louverture (Mail to: Toussaint Louverture)

Il de La Tortue St Aidan **SC** Montry (Mail to: La Tortue)

Jacmel Mission St Joseph Embouchure **SC** Embouchure (Mail to: Boite Postal # 1309)

La Gonave Saint Jacques **M** No address given (Mail to: No Address given)

La Gonave Sainte Croix **M** (300) Nouvelle Cite Anse-a-Galets (Mail to: PO Box 1309)

La Gonave St Innocents **M** Anse-a-Galets (Mail to: PO Box 1309)

La Gonave (Bois Brule) St Jacques **P** Bois Brule Anse-A-Galets (Mail to: PO Box 1309)

Lascahobas Ascension **M** (200) Pouly (Mail to: Pouly)

Lascahobas St Andre **M** (200) Flande (Mail to: Flande)

Lascahobas St Esprit **M** (200) Stenio Vincent # 1 (Mail to: Stenio Vincent# 1)

Leogane Bonne Nouvelle **M** (300) Bigonet (Mail to: PO Box 1309)

Leogane Epiphanie **M** (200) Nationale #2, Km 42 1309 (Mail to: 86 RUE RIGAUD 1309) (509) 872-1906

Leogane Mission Saint Pierre **M** Gros Morne (Mail to: Boite Postale 1309)

Leogane Mission St Andre **M** (200) Citronnier Mithon (Mail to: Boite Postale 1309)

Leogane Mission St Luc **M** (100) L'Azile Citronier (Mail to: Boite Postale 1309)

Leogane Mission St Michel **M** (300) Petit, Orangers (Mail to: Boite Postale 1309)

Leogane Mission St Timothee **M** (300) Chateau Gaillard (Mail to: Boite Postale 1309)

Leogane Paroisse Annonciation **M** (400) Darbonne (Mail to: Boite Postale 1309)

Leogane Sainte Croix **M** (400) 1 Rue La Croix (Mail to: PO Box 1309)

Leogane St Barthelemy **M** (100) Campan (Mail to: Campan)

Leogane St Etienne **M** (400) Route de L'Amitte (Mail to: PO Box 1309)

Leogane St Jean Baptiste **M** (200) Ave. Mathieu (Mail to: JeanJean)

Leogane St Jean L'Evangeliste **M** (400) Durendisse (Mail to: PO Box 1309)

Leogane St Joseph D'Arimathee **SC** Jasmin Morne a Chandelle (Mail to: PO Box 1309)

Leogane St Matthieu **M** (500) Avenue St Mathieu (Mail to: Matthieu)

Leogane St Nicolas **M** Rue Nicolas (Mail to: PO Box 1309)

Leogane Ste Marguerite **M** (200) Latournelle (Mail to: Latournelle)

Maniche St Augustin **M** (200) Maniche

Miragoane St Marc **M** Jeannette/Paillant (Mail to: PO Box 1309)

Mirebalais St Jacques **M** (200) Rte de Boucan Carre Les Bayes (Mail to: Les Bayes)

Mirebalais St Luc **M** (200) Pouille

Mirebalais St Matthias **M** (400) Deslandes (Mail to: Deslandes)

Mirebalais St Paul **M** (100) Gascogne (Mail to: Gascogne)

Mirebalais St Pierre Episcopal Church **M** (500) Grand Rue 68 Boulevard JJ Desaling (Mail to: PO Box 1309)

Petionvile St Jacques Le Juste **M** Angle Lamarre et Moise #2

Petit Trou de Nippes St Paul **SC** Chevalier (Mail to: PO Box 1309)

Plaine Mapou St Jean Baptiste **M** (Mail to: PO Box 1309)

Port-au-Prince Cathedrale Sainte Trinite **M** (2800) Angle des Rues Mgr Guilloux & Pavee (Mail to: PO Box 1309)

Port-Au-Prince Notre Dame de L Annonciation **P** (500) 4eme Ave/Bolosse

Port-Au-Prince Paroisse Epiphanie **M** (700) Place Carl Brouard (Mail to: Place Carl Brouard)

Port-Au-Prince St Alban **M** (100) Crochu (Mail to: 10 Rue Stenio Vincent Croix des Bouquets)

Port-Au-Prince St Marc **P** Lilavois 40 (Mail to: 10 Rue Stenio Vincent 1309)

Port-au-Prince St Martin de Tours **M** (400) 83 Route de Delmas (Mail to: PO Box 1309)

Port-Au-Prince St Michel & Tous Les Anges **M** Thomazeau (Mail to: Stenio Vincent #10 Croix Des Bouquets)

Port-au-Prince St Paul **M** Rte Nationale # 1 (Mail to: Rte Nationale #1)

Port-Au-Prince St Simeon **M** (200) Rue Stenio Vincent #10 (Mail to: 10 Rue Stenio Vincent Croix des Bouquets)

Rosette St Jacques **M** (200) Morne (Mail to: Morne Rosette)

Savanette Mission St Philippe & St Jacques **M** (200) Corosse (Mail to: PO Box 1309)

Thomonde St Patrick **M** (200) Locorbe (Mail to: Locorbe)

Torbeck Incarnation **M** (100) Route Platon (Le Pretre) (Mail to: Route Platon (Le Pretre))

Torbeck St Barthelemy **M** Route Ducis (Dubreuil) (Mail to: c/o St Paul, Paroisse Torbeck)

Torbeck St Hilaire **M** Route de Saint Jean (Mail to: PO Box 1309)

Torbeck St Paul **M** Rue Saint Joseph

Trouin St Marc **M** 10 Rue St Christophe (Mail to: PO Box 1309)

Trouin St Simeon et St Jude **M** Platon Balai Duny, Leogane (Mail to: PO Box 1309)

NON-PAROCHIAL CLERGY

Accime M Fort Lauderdale FL
Ais JN
Ajax K Venice FL
Alexandre S
Andre W

Auguste P
Auguste R
Avril W
Beauvoir J
Bernier N
Brutus JM *ret* Port-Au-Prince
Celestin JG
Cesar GD Port-Au-Prince
Cherisme CM *ret* Roslindale MA
Chery JF
Chery MC
Cole F Port-Au-Prince
Coriolan S *ret* Port-Au-Prince
Dalzon W
Darisme JW Port-Au-Prince
Decamps W
Dejardin W
Delicat JK
Deravil JJ Carrefour
Desir SCR *ret* Port-Au-Prince
Desire F
Diegue JT Port-Au-Prince
Duveaux I Port-Au-Prince
Estil C
Francois YG *ret* Port-Au-Prince
Gracia K
Guerrier MM
Jean M *ret* Port-Au-Prince
Jean-Jacques HM Port-Au-Prince
Jean-Philippe JA Fort Lauderdale FL
Joseph JJ Port-Au-Prince
Lafontant FR *ret* Mirebalais
Lazard A
Leon S
Lozama A
Lucas R Port-Au-Prince
McNeeley DF Teaneck NJ
Medela JM
Menelas F
Metellus D
Michaud JF
Millien JE *ret* Carrefour
Paraison M *ret* Fort Lauderdale FL
Phanord JB
Quatorze JL
Racine JJ *ret* Port-Au-Prince
Remy JMJ *ret* Sunrise FL
Rosanas LT Port-Au-Prince
Saintilver M
Sonley J
St Louis JM
St Louis S
Valdema PHF Port-Au-Prince
Vil JM Fort Lauderdale FL

DIOCESE OF HAWAII
(PROVINCE VIII)
DIOCESAN OFFICE 229 Queen Emma Sq Honolulu HI 96813
Tel (808) 536-7776 FAX (808) 538-7194
E-mail imartikainen@episcopalhawaii.org   WEB www.episcopalhawaii.org

Previous Bishops—
Eng Bps: Thomas N Staley 1862-70, Alfred Willis 1872-1902. US Bps: Henry B Restarick 1902-20, John D La Mothe 1921-28, S Harrington Littell 1930-42, Chas P Gilson suffr 1961-67, Harry S Kennedy 1944-69, E Lani Hanchett 1967-75, Edmond L Browning 1976-85, Donald P Hart 1986-94, Richard SO Chang 1997-2007

Bishop—Rt Rev Robert L Fitzpatrick (1015)
(Dio 10 Mar 2007)

Chanc W Yoshigai; *Treas & Fin Off* P Pereira; *Conv Sec* R Hino; *Reg* K Luksovsky; *Hist* S Ching

Stand Comm—Cler: M Hino K Harding D Kennedy R Taylor *Lay: Pres* G Madison P Chang A Null J Decker

Dio Conv: 28-29 Oct 2016 Honolulu HI

PARISHES, MISSIONS, AND CLERGY

Island of Hawaii

Hilo Church of the Holy Apostles **P** (184) 1407 Kapiolani St 96720 (Mail to: 1407 Kapiolani St 96720-4026) Robert Hino (808) 935-5545

Kamuela St James' Episcopal Church **P** (225) 65-1237 Kawaihae Rd 96743 (Mail to: Attn: Parish Administrator PO Box 1908 96743-1908) David Stout (808) 885-4923

Kapaau St Augustines Episcopal Church **M** (153) 54-3801 Akoni Pule Hwy 96755 (Mail to: PO Box 220 96755-0220) Diana Akiyama Heather Mueller (808) 889-5390

Ocean View St Jude Episcopal Mission **M** (53) Paradise Circle Hov 96737 (Mail to: PO Box 6026 96737) (808) 939-7000

Island of Kauai

Eleele Episcopal Church on West Kauai **M** (124) 322 A Mehana Rd 96705 (Mail to: PO Box 247 96705-0247) Maurice Goldsmith (808) 335-5533

Kapaa All Saints Episcopal Church **P** (256) 1065 Kuhio Hwy 96746 (Mail to: PO Box 248 96746-0248) Ryan Newman (808) 822-4267

Kilauea Christ Memorial Church **M** (98) 2509 Kolo Street 96754 (Mail to: PO Box 293 96754) Roberta Taylor (808) 482-4824

Lihue St Michael and All Angels Church **P** (414) 4364 Hardy St 96766 (Mail to: 4364 Hardy St 96766) (808) 245-3796

Island of Maui

Kihei Trinity by-the-Sea Episcopal Church **P** (137) 100 Kulanihakoi St 96753 (Mail to: PO Box 813 96753-0813) Austin Murray

Kula St Johns Episcopal Church **P** (299) 8992 Kula Hwy 96790-7420 (Mail to: 8992 Kula Hwy 96790-7420) Kerith Harding

Lahaina Holy Innocents Episcopal Church **P** (100) 561 Front St 96761 (Mail to: PO Box 606 96767-0606) Amy Crowe (808) 661-4202

Wailuku Church of the Good Shepherd **P** (452) 2140 Main St 96793 (Mail to: 2140 Main St 96793) Linda Decker (808) 244-4656

Island of Molokai

Hoolehua Grace Episcopal Church **M** (37) 2210 Farrington Ave 96729 (Mail to: PO Box 217 2210 Farrington Avenue 96729-0217) (808) 567-6420

Island of Oahu

Aiea St Nicholas Episcopal Church **M** (61) Christ's Gathering Place 98-939 Moanalua Rd 96701-5012 (Mail to: PO Box 700501 96709) Baldo Patterson (808) 753-7788

Aiea St Timothys Church **P** (197) 98-939 Moanalua Rd 96701 (Mail to: 98-939 Moanalua Rd 96701-5012) (808) 488-5747

✣ **Honolulu** Cathedral Church of St Andrew **O** (781) 229 Queen Emma Sq 96813-2334 (Mail to: 229 Queen Emma Sq 96813-2334) Walter Brownridge (808) 524-2822

Honolulu Church of the Epiphany **P** (187) 1041 10th Ave 96816-2210 (Mail to: 1041 10th Ave 96816-2210) Irene Tanabe Ernesto Pasalo (808) 734-5706

Honolulu Church Of The Holy Nativity **P** (192) 5286 Kalanianaole Hwy 96821 (Mail to: 5286 Kalanianaole Hwy 96821) Debra Vanover (808) 373-2131

Honolulu Good Samaritan Episcopal Church **M** (71) 1801 10th Ave 96816 (Mail to: 1801 10th Ave 96816) (808) 735-5944

Honolulu Parish of St Clement **P** (359) 1515 Wilder Ave 96822-4614 (Mail to: 1515 Wilder Ave 96822-4614) Elizabeth Zivanov (808) 955-7745

✣ **Honolulu** St Albans Chapel Iolani School **Other** 563 Kamoku St 96826 (Mail to: 563 Kamoku St 96826) Daniel Leatherman (808) 943-2205

Honolulu St Elizabeths Episcopal Church **P** (285)

720 N King St 96817-4511 (Mail to: 720 N King St 96817-5791) David Gierlach Imelda Padasdao

Honolulu St Luke Episcopal Church **M** (24) 45 N Judd St 96817-1761 (Mail to: 45 N Judd St 96817-1792) Raymond Woo (808) 533-3481

Honolulu St Mark Episcopal Parish **HC** (140) 539 Kapahulu Ave 96815-3855 (Mail to: 539 Kapahulu Ave 96815) Paul Lillie (808) 732-2333

Honolulu St Mary Episcopal Church **P** (57) 2062 S King St 96826-2219 (Mail to: 2062 S King St 96826-2219) Gregory Johnson (808) 949-4655

Honolulu St Paul Episcopal Church **M** (640) 229 Queen Emma Sq 96813-2334 (Mail to: 229 Queen Emma Sq 96813-2334) Randolph Albano Peter Wu (808) 538-3275

Honolulu St Peters Episcopal Church **P** (222) 1317 Queen Emma St 96813-2301 (Mail to: 1317 Queen Emma St 96813-2301) (808) 533-1943

Kailua Emmanuel Episcopal Church **M** (98) 780 Keolu Dr 96734-3508 (Mail to: 780 Keolu Dr 96734-3508) Matthew Lukens (808) 262-4548

Kailua St Christophers Church **P** (237) No 93 North Kainalu Dr 96734 (Mail to: PO Box 456 96734) Giovan King (808) 262-8176

Kaneohe Calvary Episcopal Church **PS** 45-435 Aumoku St 96744 (Mail to: 45-435 Aumoku St 96744) Malcolm Chun Leo Loyola

Kaneohe St John's By-the-Sea Episcopal Church **M** (114) 47-074 Lihikai Dr 96744 (Mail to: 47-074 Lihikai Dr 96744-4762) Malcolm Chun Leo Loyola (808) 239-7198

Kealakekua Christ Church Episcopal **P** (148) 81-1004 Konawaena School Rd 96750 (Mail to: PO Box 545 96750-0545) Richard Tardiff (808) 323-3429

Wahiawa St Stephen's Episcopal Church **P** (61) 1679 California Ave 96786 (Mail to: 1679 California Ave 96786) Teresa Bowden (808) 621-8662

Waianae St Philip Episcopal Church **M** (50) 87-227 St Johns Rd 96792-3259 (Mail to: 87-227 Saint Johns Rd 96792-3259) Helen Harper Marilyn Watts (808) 696-5772

Waimanalo St Matthew Episcopal Church **M** (59) 41-054 Ehukai St 96795-0070 C S Becker (808) 259-8664

NON-PAROCHIAL CLERGY

Akina EMG *dcn* Kailua HI
Akiyama DD Los Angeles CA

Albinger WJ
Aulenbach WH *ret* Irvine CA
Blanchett DH *ret* Wasilla AK
Bonsey WE *ret* Oakland CA
Buechele TJ *ret* Pahoa HI
Cannon CW *ret* Point Roberts WA
Coan BFS *dcn* Kapaa HI
Connell JB *ret* Mililani HI
Coon DP *ret* Kamuela HI
Crane CT *ret* Mesa AZ
Decker DB *ret* Ocean View HI
Duncan RA *ret* Kaneohe HI
Edson HL Lakewood CO
Geston AS *ret* Ewa Beach HI
Gifford GG *ret* Honolulu HI
Ginson IG Houston TX
Grieves BJ *ret* Honolulu HI
Hathaway DC *ret* Honolulu HI
Hawkins JS *ret* Kihei HI
Holmes JA *dcn*
Johnson FKC *ret* Houston TX
Johnson RM *ret* Hilo HI
Kennedy DK *ret* Honolulu HI
Leach DL *dcn* Kahuku HI
Lee G *ret* Honolulu HI
Leo AP *dcn* Kailua HI
Longo JA *ret* Tuscon AZ
Macneice AD *ret* Phnom Penh
Maliaman IE Tamuning GU
Moore JR *dcn* Tamuning GU
Myers JAH *ret* Petaluma CA
Nakatsuji DMK *dcn* Honolulu HI
Nurding BF *ret* Honolulu HI
O'Neill VD *ret* Aiea HI
Pang LA *dcn* Tamuning GU
Piltz GH *ret* Kamuela HI
Reynolds EW *ret* Bend CA
Sasaki N *ret* Honolulu HI
Schaefer LG *ret* Kaunakakai HI
Sewell E *dcn* Honolulu HI
Sexton TW *ret* Raton NM
Shoemaker JG *ret* Salem OR
Stevens WA *ret*
Thornton CT FPO AP
Tiapula IS Pago Pago AS
Tinnon B Aiea HI
Tinnon MS Aiea HI
Turner JE Sun City AZ
Ueda ALK Niiza-shi, Saitama
Van Culin TM *ret* Honolulu HI
Walmisley AJ *ret* Point Reyes Station CA
Watson JM *dcn* Tamuning GU
Winkler RE *ret* Harker Heights TX
Yoshida TK *ret* Honolulu HI

DIOCESE OF HONDURAS
IGLESIA EPISCOPAL DE HONDURAS
(PROVINCE IX)
(Comprises the Republic of Honduras)
DIOCESAN OFFICE Colonia Trejo 23 Ave 21 Calle (MAIL: Apdo 586) San Pedro Sula Cortés 21105
TEL: 011 (504) 556-6155   FAX 011 (504) 556-6467
International Mail: IMC-SAP Dept 215 PO Box 523900 Miami FL 33152-3900
E-MAIL: honduras@anglicano.hn   WEB: www.avanzamedia.net/anglicano/

Previous Bishops—
Bishops in Charge: David E Richards 1968, Wm C Frey 1968-72, Albert E Swift 1973, Anselmo Carral 1973-78; Diocesan Bishops: Hugo L Pina 1978-83, Leopold Frade 1984-2000 James H Ottley int 2000-01

Bishop — Rt Rev Lloyd Emmanuel Allen (971)
(Dio 20 Oct 2001)

Cn to Ord Rev Cn A Brooks; *Oficina Pastoral* V Rev Oscar López; *Dn Atlántida e Islas de la Bahía* V Rev Rosa Angélica Gámez-Cordona; *Dn Tegucigalpa* M Consuelo Cartegena de Arevalo; *Dn Comayagua* V Rev H Madrid-Paz; *Dn Copán* V Rev JA Mejia; *Dn El Paraíso* V Rev Dagobert Chacón-Rodríguez; *Dn Omoa y Puerto Cortéz* V Rev F Midence; *Dn San Pedro Sula* V Rev O López; *Dn St Bárbara* V Rev José Luis Mendoza-Barahona-y-Rodríguez; *Treas* C Antunez; *Sec* Rev J Francisco Lone; *ECW* R de Allen; *Com Min* Rev A Brooks; *Social Min* JJ Calerón; *Comm & Pub Rel* Cn E Monzón; *Finances* Dr G Frazier; *Global Rel* C de Brooks; *Theology Ed* V Rev Pascual Torres; *Faith* V Rev H Madrid-Paz; *Chris Ed* Lic Elizabeth P de Torres; *Exam Chap* RA Gómez-Cordona; *Stew* Rev F Midence-Valdés; *Bd Gov El Hogar Proj* Rev H Madrid; *Cursillo* LP Consuelo de Brenes; *Const and Can* V Rev P Torres; *Ecum* V Rev P Torres; *Yth* Prof W Barret; *Reg* V Madisson de Molina; *Chanc* V Rev P Torres; *Health* EM Galindo MD Jose Arnaldo Mejia

Stand Comm–Cler: Pres Maria Consuelo Cartagena de Arevalo Juan José Dîaz Jose Alejandro Chirinos; *Lay* Claudia Castro Wendy Avila Nativi Jethy Yolanda Portillo Pedro Herrera

To call Honduras from the US, dial (011) 504, then the number.

PARISHES, MISSIONS, AND CLERGY
Deanato Atlantida e Islas de la Bahia

La Ceiba Iglesia Episcopal Santisima Trinidad **M** § Avenida Morazan # 1175 28 (Mail to: Avenida Morazan # 1175 28) Ethelridge Brooks (504) 440-2772

Roatan Iglesia Episcopal San Pedro del Mar **P** Brick Bay (Mail to: Apartado Postal 193) (504) 445-3891

Tela Iglesia Episcopal Espiritu Santo **P** § Carretera a Telamar 6 (Mail to: Carretera A Telamar) (504) 448-2064

Deanato Comayagua

Pozo Azul el Rosario Santo Tomas Apostol **M** § Principal (Mail to: Apartado Postal # 30)

Siguatepeque Igl Epis San Bartolome Apostol **PS** (60) § Calle Principal la Esperanza Barrio Buena Vista (Mail to: Apartado Postal 30 21105) Hector Madrid 5047735660

Siguatepeque Iglesia Epis Santiago Apostol **M** Barrio Zaragoza 2 cuadras al este de la gasolinera uno (Mail to: Barrio Zaragoza) Hector Madrid

Siguatepeque Mision Episcopal San Matias Apostol **M** Aldea La Laguna (Mail to: La Laguna Siguatepeque) Hector Madrid

Deanato Copán

Capan, Florida Mision Brisas del Chamelecon **PS** Las Brisas (Mail to: Apartado Postal 586)

Copan Misión Episcopal San Mateo **PS** § San Jose Miramar (Mail to: San Jose Miramar)

Florida Misión Episcopal en El Encantadito **PS** El Encantadito (Mail to: El Encantadito)

La Entrada Misión Episcopal Suyapa **PS** Barrio Suyapa (Mail to: Barrio Suyapa Copan)

Nueva Arcadia Cristo Salvador **M** § Chalmeca (Mail to: Apartado Postal # 586)

Proteccion Misión Episcopal en El Zarzal **PS** El Zarzal (Mail to: El Zarzal Santa Barbara)

Proteccion Misión Episcopal en Nuevas Delicias **PS** Nuevas Delicias (Mail to: Nuevas Delicias)

Proteccion Misión Episcopal en Nuevo Porvenir **PS** Pueblo Nuevo (Mail to: Pueblo Nuevo)

Proteccion Santo Tomás Cranmer **SC** § Comunidad Los Mayas (Mail to: Apartado 856)

Deanato El Paraiso

Cabanas Mision "San Francisco de Asis" **M** San Francisco de Asis (Mail to: San Francisco de Asis)

Cabanas Misión Episcopal Cristo Rey **PS** El Barbasco (Mail to: El Barbasco)

Danli Iglesia Episcopal Cristo Rey **M** (100) § Barrio El Carmelo (Mail to: El Carmelo)

El Paraiso Misión Episcopal la Resurrección **PS** (100) Barrio San Jose (Mail to: Barrio San Jose)

Jacaleapa Misión Episcopal la Cena del Señor **PS** Barrio El Centro (Mail to: Barrio, El Centro)

Oropoli Misión Episcopal la Anunciación **PS** Melaisipio Oropoli (Mail to: La Anunciacion)

Yuscaran Iglesia Epis San Miguel Arcangel **P** Aldea Ojo de Agua (Mail to: Oficina del Deanato de El Paraiso)

Yuscaran Iglesia Episcopal San Antonio **M** § Aldea Los Lainez (Mail to: Apdo 56 Danli Lainez)

Yuscaran Iglesia Episcopal San Jose **M** (100) § Aldea Corral Quemado (Mail to: Aldea Corral Quemado)

Yuscaran Misión Episcopal la Ascensión **PS** Aldea Agua Viva (Mail to: Aldea Agua Viva)

Yuscaran Misión Episcopal la Presentación **SC** Barrio San Juan (Mail to: Barrio San Juan)

Yuscaran Misión Episcopal la Santa Cruz **PS** Aldea Chaguite Oriente (Mail to: Aldea Chaguite Oriente)

Yuscaran Misión Episcopal la Transfiguración **PS** Aldea Las Crucitas (Mail to: Aldea Las Crucitas)

Yuscaran Misión Episcopal la Visitación **PS** Aldea del Ocotal (Mail to: El Ocotal)

Yuscaran Santa María Virgen de Las Mercedes **M** § Aldea Rancho del Obispo (Mail to: Aldea Rancho del Obispo)

Deanato Francisco Morazán

Comayaguela, MDC Iglesia Epis Cristo Redentor **P** (200) § Col. America (Mail to: Lomas Miraflores Sur Bloque "D" #4318) (504) 236-7116

Guaimaca Misión Episcopal la Transfiguración **PS** § Barrio Arriba (Mail to: Barrio Arriba)

Miravalle Misión Episcopal Emmanuel **PS** Mision Episcopal Emmanuel (Mail to: Bo Nueva Progreso)

Pueblo Viejo Misión Episcopal San Esteban **PS** § Pueblo Viejo (Mail to: Pueblo Viejo)

Santa Ana Iglesia Episcopal San Isidro **M** § El Cruce 11001 (Mail to: Iglesia Episcopal San Isidro Apdo. Postal 15023)

Soroguara Iglesia Episcopal San Isidro **M** (100) § Santa Cruz Arriba 4063 (Mail to: Col. Florencia Norte 1era Entrada 1era calle 4063)

Talanga Misión Episcopal San Felipe **M** § Calle Agua Blanca Bo Sabanetilla (Mail to: Residencial San Miguel Agua Blanca)

Tegucigalpa Iglesia San Pedro Cerca del Rio **M** § Km 9. Carretera a Salida Talanga El Guanabano (Mail to: Km 9. Carretera a Talanga)

Tegucigalpa Iglesia Santa Maria de los Angeles **P** (200) 1era Entrada, Col. Florencia Norte 1100 (Mail to: Iglesia Episcopal Santa Maria Apartado Postal 15023 11101) (504) 232-0353

Tegucigalpa Mision en Col Villeda Morales **PS** Villeda Morales (Mail to: Villeda Morales)

Tegucigalpa Mision Episcopal "Nueva Esperanza" **PS** § Col Nueva Esperanza Amarateca (Mail to: Catedral Santa Maria de los Angeles)

Tegucigalpa Misión Episcopal Emmanuel **PS** § Las Moritas, Aldea Yaguacire Germania Carreterra al Sur (Mail to: Germania Carreterra al Sur Las Moritas)

Tegucigalpa Misión Santa María del Valle **PS** § Alpea de Amarateca (Mail to: Alpea de Amarateca)

Tegucigalpa, A.M.D.C. Misión Episcopal San Esteban **SC** § El Mulular, Quiscamote, A.M.D.C. (Mail to: Catedral Santa Maria de los Angeles)

Tegucigalpa, A.M.D.C. Misión Episcopal San Simón **PS** El Jocomico, Nueva Aldea Santa Cruz Arriba (Mail to: Catderal Santa Maria de los Angeles)

Tegucigalpa, M.D.C Iglesia San Juan Evangelista **P** (200) Terminal de buses, Mano derecha 4063 (Mail to: Apartado Postal #4063)

Tegucigalpa, M.D.C. Iglesia Episcopal "La Anunciacion" **M** § Rincon de Dolores A.M.D.C. (Mail to: Catedral "Santa Maria de los Angeles" Aptdo. 15023)

Tegucigalpa, M.D.C. Misión Episcopal Mesías **PS** Caserio Laguna del Pedregal (Mail to: Col. Florencia Norte 1era entrada, 1era calle Boulevard Suyapa)

Tegucigalpa, M.D.C. St Mary of the Angels Episcopal Church **M** 1st St. Col. Florencia N. y Blvd. Suyapa (Mail to: 1st St. Col. Florencia N. y Blvd. Suyapa)

Villa De San Francisco Natividad Nuestro Señor Jesucristo **M** § La Natividad de Nuestra Sr. Jesucristo (Mail to: Bo Nuevo Progreso)

Deanato Maya

Agua Caliente Misión Episcopal San Antonio **PS** San Antonio (Mail to: San Antonio)

Buena Vista Misión Episcopal San Agustín **PS** Mision San Agustin (Mail to: Mision San Agustin)

Carrizalito Misión Episcopal San Juan Bautista **SC** Calle Central San Juan Bautista (Mail to: San Juan Bautista)

Cedral Misión Episcopal San José **SC** Mision San Jose La Union (Mail to: La Union, Cedral)

Copan Ruinas Misión Episcopal San Jorge **SC** § Agua Caliente (Mail to: Agua Caliente)

Copan Ruinas Misión Episcopal San Lucas **PS** Rio Amarillo (Mail to: Rio Amarillo)

Copan Ruinas Misión Episcopal Santa María Virgen **PS** § Santa María Virgen 000000 (Mail to: Santa María Virgen 000000)

Copan Ruinas Misión San Juan Evangelista **SC** Sesemil II Principal (Mail to: Sesemil Segundo)

Copan Ruinas, Copan Misión Epíscopal Santísima Trinidad **PS** § Sesesmil I (Mail to: Sesesmil I)

Corralitos Misión Episcopal San Miguel Arcángel **PS** § San Miguel Arcangel (Mail to:

San Miguel Arcangel)

Dona Ana Iglesia Episcopal San Miguel **M §** Andres Bremo (Mail to: Andres Bremo) (809) 420-1867

El Cordoncillo Iglesia Episcopal San Marcos **SC** El Cordoncillo (Mail to: El Cordoncillo)

El Quebracho Mision Episcopal San Nicolas **SC §** El Quebracho (Mail to: El Quebracho)

El Tigre Misión Episcopal San Ignacio **PS §** San Ignacio (Mail to: San Ignacio)

El Zapote Misión Episcopal Santo Tomás **PS §** Santo Tomas (Mail to: Santo Tomas)

La Laguna Misión Episcopal San Felipe **SC** San Felipe La Laguna (Mail to: San Felipe La Laguna)

Naranjal Misión Episcopal la Sagrada Familia **PS** Mision Sagrada Familia (Mail to: Naranjal)

Nueva Esperanza Misión Episcopal Emmanuel **PS §** Mision Episcopal Emmanuel (Mail to: Mision Episcopal Emmanuel)

Nueva Esperanza Misión Episcopal Santa Cruz **SC §** Mision Santa Cruz (Mail to: Mision Santa Cruz)

Pinalito Misión Episcopal San Matías **PS** San Matias (Mail to: San Matias)

Porvenir II San Andres Porvonis II **PS** San Andres Porvenir II (Mail to: San Andres Porvenir II)

Rio Negro Misión Episcopal Pentecostés **PS §** Mision Pentecostes (Mail to: Mision Pentecostes)

San Pedro Sula Iglesia Episcopal Cristo Redentor **M** Vado Ancho (Mail to: Vado Ancho DCPN 06-52)

Santa Rita Misión Episcopal San Juan Apóstol **PS §** Londres (Mail to: Mision San Juan Apostol)

Santa Rita Misión Episcopal Santiago Ápóstol **PS §** La Castellana (Mail to: La Castellana)

Deanato Omoa y Puerto

Omoa Conversion de San Pablo **M §** Principal, Frente al Centro Comunal (Mail to: Principal, Frente al Centro Comunal)

Omoa Iglesia "Santa Margarita de Escocia" **M** (100) Principal Chachahuala (Mail to: Principal, Chachahuala)

Omoa Iglesia Episcopal San Fernando Rey **M** Principal, Frente al Castillo (Mail to: Bo. San Martin 12 Calle 6/7 Ave Puerto C) Antonio Carcel-Martinez 658-9062

Omoa Iglesia Episcopal San Francisco de Asis **SC §** Principal Muchilena 586 (Mail to: Apartado Postal # 35)

Omoa Iglesia Episcopal San Marcos **M** (200) **§** Principal (Mail to: Principal)

Omoa La Natividad de la Bendita Virgen Maria **M §** Real Asia Guatemala Centsica N-O 35 (Mail to: San Pedro Sula 35)

Omoa Nuestra Señora de Suyapa **SC §** Suyapa Frontera (Mail to: Suyapa Frontera)

Puerto Cortes Iglesia Episcopal "San Juan Bautista **M** 6 Calle 4 Ave Barrio El Centro (Mail to: Bo El Centro 6 Calle 4 Ave) Pascual Torres Fuentes (504) 665-0200

Puerto Cortes Jesús El Salvador **M** 15 Calle, 4ta Avenida, La Curva Barrio Buenos Aires (Mail to: 15 Calle, 4ta Avenida, La Curva Bo. Buenos Aires) 665-5859

Puerto Cortes Misión Nuestra Señora de Suyapa **PS** Col. Episcopal Chameleconcito (Mail to: Col. Episcopal Chameleconcito)

Puerto Cortes Nuestra Senora de los Desamparados **PS** Autopista Region el Chile (Mail to: Colonia Episcopal)

Deanato San Pedro Sula

Choloma Iglesia Episcopal Cristo Rey **M** (100) **§** Col. Exitos de Anach No. 2 (Mail to: Apartado # 586)

El Progreso Iglesia Episcopal "San Patricio" **M** (100) Barrio San Jose #1, 4 ave. 9 calle N.E. SPS 586 (Mail to: Barrio San Jose #1, 4 ave. 9 calle N.E. SPS 586) 5046474444

✠ **San Pedro Sula** Catedral Episcopal El Buen Pastor **O** (300) **§** 21 Calle, 23 Ave. "C" S.O. Colonia Trejo Colonia Trejo (Mail to: Apartado 586) John Park (504) 556-7140

San Pedro Sula Igl Epis San Jose de la Montana **M** (60) Calle Principal (Mail to: Col. Nueva Primavera)

San Pedro Sula Iglesia Episcopal "Fe y Alegria" **M §** Calle Principal, Colonia Episcopal El Ocotillo (Mail to: 23 Ave "C" 21 Calle Trejo)

San Pedro Sula Iglesia Episcopal San Andres **M** (200) **§** 12 Calle, 10-11 Ave, SE Barrio Cabañas (Mail to: Apartado 586) Oscar Lopez (504) 554-2292

San Pedro Sula Iglesia Episcopal San Lucas **M** (200) **§** Delicias del Norte (Mail to: Col. Trejo 23 Ave "C" Calle 21 Apartado 586) Oscar Lopez

San Pedro Sula Iglesia Episcopal San Pablo Apostol **M** (100) **§** 3 y 4 Calle, 2nd Ave Col Satelite II Etapa 586 (Mail to: Iglesia Episcopal Hondurena 586) Roberto Martinez Amengual (504) 559-3055

San Pedro Sula Misión Episcopal la Divina Gracia **PS §** Colonia Stibys (Mail to: Apartado 586)

Villanueva Iglesia Episcopal de la Epifania **M §** Barrio El Centro (Mail to: Apartado Postal No. 586) Jose Pena-Regalado 5046705203

Villanueva Santiago de Jerusalén **M §** Santa Ana de Chasnigua (Mail to: Apartado Postal No. 586)

Deanato Santa Bárbara

Atima Iglesia Episcopal "Jesus Nazareno" **M** (200) Barrio de Jesus (Mail to: Apdo. 586) (504) 556-6155

Chinda Mision Santa Maria Magdalena **SC §** El Retiro (Mail to: Apartado Postal #586)

Concepcion del Norte Iglesia Episcopal "Santa Lucia" **M** (200) Proteccion (Aldea) (Mail to: Apartado No. 586) Hector Madrid

Concepcion del Norte Iglesia Episcopal San Mateo **M** El Cerron (Aldea) (Mail to: Apartado No. 586)

Concepcion del Norte Iglesia Episcopal Santa Ana **M** § Apdo 24 Sta Barbara (Mail to: Apdo 24 Sta Barbara)

Concepcion del Norte La Visitacion de la Bendita Virgen Maria **M** Barrio Nuevo (Mail to: Apartado No. 586)

Petoa Iglesia Episcopal "La Santa Cruz" **M** Las Flores (Mail to: Apartado Postal 586)

Petoa Iglesia Episcopal San Joaquin **M** § San Joaquin (Mail to: Apartado 586)

Petoa Iglesia Episcopal San Pedro Apostol **P** Calle Real Principal (Mail to: Apartado Postal 1106)

Petoa La Resurrección **M** § Plan del Portillo (Aldea) (Mail to: Apartado No. 586)

Santa Barbara Iglesia Episcopal "Santa Barbara" **M** (100) § Calle Principal, Barrio Llano del Conejo 22101 (Mail to: Calle Principal, Barrio Llano del Conejo 22101) (504) 643-2754

Santa Barbara, Concepcion Norte Iglesia Episcopal "La Ascension" **PS** § Montanita (Mail to: Apartado 586)

Trinidad Iglesia Episcopal "La Trinidad" **P** (100) § Las Americas (Mail to: Apartado Postal 586)

Trinidad San Miguel Arcángel **M** § Real Principal (Matazanales) (Mail to: Apartado Postal # 586)

NON-PAROCHIAL CLERGY

Aguilar N
Alvarado-Palada C
Barrera Flores OI *dcn* Miami FL
Batiz Mejia JD Miami FL
Boghetich BA *ret* Miami FL
Buice WR Pensacola FL
Cabrera AF *dcn* Miami FL
Cartagena Mejia de Arevalo MC Tegucigalpa C
Chacon-Rodriguez D
Chavez R *ret*
Chirinos-Hernandez JA
Diaz JJ
Galindo-Paz EM
Gomez-Cardona RA
Hernandez LA *ret*
Herrera LC *dcn* Miami FL
Martinez Amengual M
Martinez Rapalo A *dcn* Miami FL
Martinez-Rapalo R *ret*
Mejia JA *ret* La Estrada HN
Midence Valdes JF Tela
Monge-Mancia I
Monzon-Molina E *ret* San Pedro
Patten KL
Rodriguez-Santos C
Sanchez Navarro JI
Trejo-Barahona O *ret*
Varela Solorzano MA Samparo Sula
Vasquez JA *dcn* Miami FL
Vasquez Sanchez VO

STATE OF IDAHO

Dioceses of Idaho and Spokane

DIOCESE OF IDAHO

(PROVINCE VIII)
Comprises Idaho South of the Salmon River
DIOCESAN OFFICE 1858 W Judith Ln Boise ID 83705
TEL (208) 345-4440   FAX (208) 345-9735
E-MAIL sledwich@idahodiocese.org   WEB www.episcopalidaho.org

Previous Bishops—
Daniel S Tuttle 1867-87, Ethelbert Talbot 1887-1898, James B Funsten 1899-1918, Herman Page 1919, Frank H Touret 1919-24, Herbert HH Fox 1925-26, Middleton S Barnwell 1926-35, Fredk B Bartlett 1935-41, Frank A Rhea 1942-57, Norman L Foote 1957-72, Hanford L King Jr 1972-81, David B Birney IV 1982-89, John S Thornton 1990-98, Harry B Bainbridge III 1998-2008

Bishop—Rt Rev Brian Thom (1032) (Dio 11 Oct 2008)

Canon to the Ord L Ashby; *Conv Sec* S Ledwich; *Treas* T Jones; *Chanc* B Alexander J Haemmerle; *Dio Coord* S Ledwich; *Camp Dir* M Beck; *Com* K Brannon

Stand Comm—Cler: Pres R Fagg *Sec* M Butler R Demarest *Lay:* J Ashton K Kissell P Rowett-Matlock

Dio Conv: 11-13 Nov 2016 Pocatello

PARISHES, MISSIONS, AND CLERGY

Alta St Francis of Tetons Episcopal Ch **P** (126) 20 Alta School Rd 83414-4518 (Mail to: 20 Alta School Rd 83414-4518) Debra Adams (307) 353-8100

American Fls St Johns Episcopal Church **P** (7) No 328 Roosevelt St 83211-1219 (Mail to: 257 Polk St 83211-1421) (208) 226-2646

Arco Church of the Epiphany **M** (9) 448 Yvonne St 83213-8760 (Mail to: PO Box 672 83213-0672) (208) 220-9785

Blackfoot St Pauls Episcopal Church **P** (69) 72 N Shilling Ave 83221-2846 (Mail to: 72 N Shilling Ave 83221-2846) (208) 785-4474

Boise All Saints Episcopal Church **P** (347) 704 S Latah St 83705-1547 (Mail to: 704 S Latah St 83705-1547) Holladay Sanderson (208) 344-2537

✣ **Boise** St Michaels Episcopal Cathedral **O** (1525) 518 N 8th St 83702-5515 (Mail to: 518 N 8th St 83702-5515) Richard Demarest James Brooks Rick Harvey Margaret Kurtz Emily Sieracki Mary Weiner (208) 342-5601

Boise St Phillips Episcopal Church **M** (7) C/O Diocese of Idaho 510 W Washington St 83702-5953 (Mail to: PO Box 1328 83226-1328) (208) 876-4291

Boise St Stephens Episcopal Church **P** (335) 2206 N Cole Rd 83704-7313 (Mail to: 2206 N Cole Rd 83704-7313) David Wettstein Scott Ellsworth Debra Greenleaf James Mahoney Eileen O'Shea Jeffrey Shankles (208) 375-3862

Buhl Holy Trinity Episcopal Church **P** (33) 229 9th Ave N 83316-1216 (Mail to: PO Box 26 83316-0026) Marilyn Butler (208) 543-8496

Caldwell St Davids Episcopal Church **P** (73) Arlington Ave & East Pine 83605 (Mail to: 1800 Arlington Ave 83605-5254) Wallace Lonergan (208) 459-9261

Emmett St Mary's Episcopal Church **P** (108) No 219 E 1st St 83617-2903 (Mail to: PO Box 215 83617-0215) (208) 365-2309

Fort Hall Church of the Good Shepherd **P** (72) PO Box 608 83203 (Mail to: PO Box 608 83203) Daniel Buchin (208) 223-7053

Glenns Ferry Grace Episcopal Church **P** (15) No 102 E Cleveland Ave 83623-2400 (Mail to: PO Box 786 83623-0786) (208) 366-7425

Gooding Trinity Episcopal Church **P** (25) 125 7th Ave W 83330-1227 (Mail to: 125 7th Ave W 83330-1227) Richard Goetsch (208) 934-4779

Hailey Emmanuel Episcopal Church **P** (141) 101 S 2nd Ave 83333-8604 (Mail to: PO Box 576 83333-0576) (208) 788-3547

Idaho Falls St Lukes Episcopal Church **P** (351) 270 N Placer Ave 83402-4021 (Mail to: 270 N Placer Ave 83402-4021) Susan Speir (208) 522-8465

Jerome Calvary Episcopal Church **P** (18) 201 S Adams St 83338-2600 (Mail to: 201 S Adams St 83338-2600) Richard Goetsch Barbara Ward (208) 324-8480

McCall St Andrews Episcopal Church **P** (74) Forest and Gamble 83638 (Mail to: PO Box 1045 83638-1045) (208) 634-2796

Meridian Church of the Holy Nativity **P** (134) 1021 W 8th St 83642-2003 (Mail to: 828 W Cherry Ln 83642-1619) Paula Egbert (208) 888-4342

Mountain Home St James Episcopal Church **P** (70) 315 N 3rd E 83647-2736 (Mail to: PO Box 761 83647-0761) Paul Walsh (208) 587-3516

Nampa Grace Episcopal Church **P** (135) 911 4th St S 83651-4104 (Mail to: 411 10th Ave S 83651-4137) Deborah Graham Karen Hunter (208) 466-0782

Payette St James Episcopal Church **P** (30) 110 N 10th St 83661-2625 (Mail to: PO Box 203 83661-0203) Deborah Graham (208) 642-4222

Placerville Emmanuel Epis Church Placerville **P** (12) 123 S Main St 83666-4065 (Mail to: 310 Granite St 83666-4022)

Pocatello Trinity Episcopal Church **P** (159) 248 N Arthur Ave 83204-3104 (Mail to: PO Box 1214 83204-1214) Diane Paulson Donald Paulson (208) 233-2640

Rupert St Matthews Episcopal Church **P** (59) 6th & I St 83350 (Mail to: PO Box 324 83350-0324) Randy Fagg Tammy Jones Barbara Ward (208) 436-4904

Salmon Church of the Redeemer **P** (101) 204 Courthouse Dr 83467-3943 (Mail to: 204 Courthouse Dr 83467-3943) Joseph Marek Robert Perry (208) 756-3720

Shoshone Christ Episcopal Church **P** (23) 106 W B St 83352-5365 (Mail to: PO Box 548 83352-0548) Kenneth Crothers (208) 886-2617

Sun Valley St Thomas Episcopal Church **P** (489) 201 Sun Valley Rd 83353 (Mail to: PO Box 1070 83353-1070) Kenneth Brannon (208) 726-5349

Twin Falls Church of the Ascension **P** (305) 371 Eastland Dr N 83301-4417 (Mail to: 371 Eastland Dr N 83301-4417) Deborah Seles (208) 733-1248

Weiser St Lukes Episcopal Church **P** (46) 106 E Liberty St 83672-2259 (Mail to: 106 E Liberty St 83672-2259) Deborah Graham (208) 549-1552

NON-PAROCHIAL CLERGY

Aggeler HG
Anttonen JP *ret* Eagle ID
Ashby L Boise ID
Atcitty JN *dcn* Fort Hall ID
Baltz AMH *dcn* Boise ID
Bardsley NL *dcn* Troy ID

Bergh PA mountain home ID
Brown WS Boise ID
Burger CS *ret* Garden Valley ID
Canning MJB Eagle ID
Case MA Boise ID
Coats BI
Cudd AG *ret* Gainesville FL
Davis JH *ret*
Dembi ME Bethesda MD
Downer GM Emmett ID
Duncan HC *ret* Boise ID
Dwyer MJ *ret* Garden Valley ID
Farnes JE Pittsfield MA
Farquhar-Mayes AF *ret* Boise ID
Farquhar-Mayes T Meridian ID
Finch RL
Flanigen JM *ret* Tuscaloosa AL
Gallagher ER *ret* Boise ID
Gallagher MET *dcn* Boise ID
Harrelson LE *ret* Meridian ID

Hayashi K *ret* Boise ID
Herlocker JR *ret* Terrebonne OR
Herndon JC *dcn* Blackfoot ID
Hetrick BA *dcn*
Holmes FM *ret* Nampa ID
Kelly MI *dcn* Boise ID
Kennedy AT *ret* Twin Falls ID
King JGF *dcn* Rupert ID
Matthew JC Boise ID
McKay JA
Mills WW
More JE Emmett ID
Nelson EA
Roberts WA *ret* Blackfoot ID
Slakey AEM Payette ID
Smalley HB Pocatello ID
Speir EL Idaho Falls ID
Thompson-Uberuaga W Boise ID
Yarbrough DW *ret* Nampa ID

STATE OF ILLINOIS
Dioceses of Chicago (C) and Springfield (Sp)

Albion—Sp
Alton—Sp
Antioch—C
Arlington Hts—C
Aurora—C
Barrington—C
Batavia—C
Belleville—Sp
Belvidere—C
Benson—C
Berwyn—C
Bloomingdale—C
Bloomington—Sp
Blue Is—C
Bolingbrook—C
Cairo—Sp
Canton—C
Carbondale—Sp
Carlinville—Sp
Centralia—Sp
Champaign—Sp
Chesterfield—Sp
Chicago—C
Chillicothe—C
Clarendon Hills—C
Crystal Lake—C
Danville—Sp
Decatur—Sp
Deerfield—C
DeKalb—C
Des Plaines—C
Dixon—C
Downers Grove—C

Dundee—C
Edwardsville—Sp
El Paso—C
Elgin—C
Elk Grove Village—C
Elkhart—Sp
Elmhurst—C
Evanston—C
Flossmoor—C
Freeport—C
Galena—C
Galesburg—C
Genesco—C
Geneva—C
Glen Carbon—Sp
Glen Ellyn—C
Glencoe—C
Glenview—C
Granite City—Sp
Grayslake—C
Griggsville—C
Gurnee—C
Hanover Pk—C
Harrisburg—Sp
Harvey—C
Havana—Sp
Henry—C
Highland Pk—C
Hinsdale—C
Jacksonville—Sp
Joliet—C
Kankakee—C
Kenilworth—C

Kewanee—C
La Grange—C
Lake Forest—C
Lake Villa—C
LaSalle—C
Lewistown—C
Libertyville—C
Lincoln—Sp
Lockport—C
Lombard—C
Loves Pk—C
Macomb—C
Marion—Sp
Mattoon—Sp
McHenry—C
Moline—C
Momence—C
Monmouth—C
Morris—C
Morrison—C
Morton—Sp
Mt Carmel—Sp
Mt Vernon—Sp
Naperville—C
New Lenox—C
Normal—Sp
Northbrook—C
Northfield—C
Oak Pk—C
O'Fallon—Sp & C
Oregon—C
Ottawa—C
Palatine—C

Palos Pk—C
Pk Forest—C
Pk Ridge—C
Pekin—Sp
Peoria—C
Pontiac—C
Preemption—C
Princeton—C
Prospect Heights—C
Quincy—C
Rantoul—Sp
River Forest—C

Riverside—C
Robinson—Sp
Rockford—C
Rock Island—C
St Charles—C
Salem—Sp
Savanna—C
Silvis—C
Springfield—Sp
St Charles—C
Sterling—C
Streator—C

Sycamore—C
Warsaw—C
Wauconda—C
Waukegan—C
W Frankfort—Sp
Western Springs—C
Wheaton—C
Wilmette—C
Winnetka—C
Woodstock—C

STATE OF INDIANA
Dioceses of Indianapolis and Northern Indiana

DIOCESE OF INDIANAPOLIS
(PROVINCE V)
Comprises central and southern Indiana
DIOCESAN OFFICE 1100 W 42nd St Indianapolis IN 46208
TEL (317) 926-5454
TOLL FREE (800) 669-5786   FAX (317) 926-5456.
E-MAIL cassidy@indydio.org   WEB www.indydio.org

Previous Bishops—
Jackson Kemper (MO and IN) 1835-49, Geo Upfold 1849-72, Jos C Talbot coadj 1865 Bp 1872-83, David B Knickerbocker 1883-94, John H White 1895-99, Jos M Francis 1899-1939, Richard A Kirchhoffer coadj 1939 Bp 1939-59, John P Craine coadj 1957 Bp 1959-77, Edward W Jones coadj 1977 Bp 1977-97

Bishop — Rt Rev Catherine M Waynick (929)
(Dio 10 Sept 1997)

Cn to Ord Rev Cn BW Gray; *Cn for Trans Min and Ldrshp Dev* Rev Cn DJ Kissinger; *Treas* T Wood Box 137 Unionville IN 47468; *Chanc* G Plews 1346 N Delaware Indianapolis IN 46202; *Sec* S Sullivan; *Cn Admin* M Gebuhr; *Comm* K Copas; *Coord Yth Min* D Fuller; *Stew* JV Oaks; *Hist* vacant; *Bps Exec Sec* S Cassidy; *Admin Sec* K Christopher

Stand Comm—Cler: S Bennett; J Hulen; M Slenski; *Lay:* P Smith

Dio Conv: 22-24 Oct Indianapolis IN

PARISHES, MISSIONS, AND CLERGY

Anderson Trinity Episcopal Church **P** (161) 1030 Delaware St 46016 (Mail to: 1030 Brown-Delaware St 46016-1428) William Smalley (765) 644-2566

Beanblossom St Davids Episcopal Church **P** (86) 11 State Road 45 46160 Kelsey Hutto (812) 988-1038

Bedford St Johns Episcopal Church **P** (111) 1219 14th St 47421-3228 (Mail to: 1219 14th St 47421-3228) (812) 275-6620

Bloomington Episcopal Campus Ministry at IU **Campus Ministry** (18) 719 E 7th St 47408 (Mail to: PO Box 127 47402-0127) (812) 361-7971

Bloomington Trinity Episcopal Church **P** (596) 111 S. Grant Street 47408 (Mail to: 111 S Grant St 47408-4031) Charles Dupree Henrietta Grossoehme Connie Peppler (812) 336-4466

Cannelton St Lukes Episcopal Church **P** (16) 101 S 3rd St 47520-1504 Donald Overton

Carmel St Christophers Episcopal Church **P** (1178) 1402 W Main St 46032-1442 (Mail to: 1402 W Main St 46032-1442) Stephen Fales Jennifer Hulen Susan McBeath (317) 846-8716

Columbus St Pauls Episcopal Church **P** (193) 2651 California St 47201-3650 (Mail to: 2651 California St 47201-3650) Marcus Vance (812) 372-7869

Connersville Trinity Episcopal Church **P** (5) 211 E 6th St 47331-1908 (Mail to: PO Box 127 47331-0127)

Crawfordsvlle St Johns Episcopal Church **P** (139) 212 S Green St 47933-2508 (Mail to: PO Box 445 47933-0445) Janet Oller (765) 362-2331

Danville St Augustine Episcopal Church **P** (249) 600 N Washington St 46122-1246 (Mail to: PO Box 141 46122-0141) William Barfield (317)

745-2741

Elwood St Stephens Episcopal Church **P** (13) 11706 N State Rd 37 46036-8318 (Mail to: PO Box 291 46036-0291) (765) 552-5356

Evansville St Pauls Episcopal Church **P** (237) 301 SE 1st St 47713-1003 (Mail to: 301 SE 1st St 47713-1003) Larry Minter (812) 422-9009

Fishers Holy Family Episcopal Church **M** (249) 11445 Fishers Point Blvd 46038-2997 (Mail to: 11445 Fishers Point Blvd 46038-2997) Michael Galvin (317) 842-4133

Franklin St Thomas Episcopal Church **P** (94) 600 Paul Hand Blvd 46131 (Mail to: 600 Paul Hand Blvd 46131-6922) Whitney Rice (317) 535-8985

Greencastle St Andrews Episcopal Church **P** (108) 520 E Seminary St 46135-1745 (Mail to: 520 E Seminary St 46135-1745) John Rumple (765) 653-3921

Indianapolis All Saints Episcopal Church **P** (140) 1559 Central Ave 46202-2606 (Mail to: 1559 Central Avenue 46202-2698) Tanya Beck Daniel Billman Elizabeth Wille (317) 635-2538

✛ **Indianapolis** Christ Church Episcopal Cathedral **O** (735) 125 Monument Cir 46204-2921 (Mail to: 125 Monument Cir 46204-2993) Stephen Carlsen William Curtis Shannon Macvean-Brown Zoila Manzanares (317) 636-4577

Indianapolis Church of the Nativity **P** (303) 7300 Lantern Rd 46256-2118 (Mail to: 7300 Lantern Rd 46256-2118) Mary Slenski Catherine Wilson (317) 915-1020

Indianapolis St Albans Episcopal Church **P** (58) 4601 N Emerson Ave 46226-2218 (Mail to: 4601 N Emerson Ave 46226-2218) Jean Smith (317) 546-8037

Indianapolis St Johns Episcopal Church **P** (147) 5625 W 30th St 46224-3013 (Mail to: 5625 W 30th Street 46224-3013) Jeffrey Bower (317) 293-0372

Indianapolis St Matthews Episcopal Church **P** (140) 8320 E 10th St 46219-5331 (Mail to: 8320 E 10th St 46219-5399) Mark Van Wassenhove Jacqueline Means (317) 898-7807

Indianapolis St Paul's Episcopal Church **HC** (908) 6050 N Meridian St 46208-1549 (Mail to: 6050 N Meridian St 46208-1549) John Denson Nicholas Myers Sarah Ginolfi Barbara Kempf (317) 253-1277

Indianapolis St Philips Episcopal Church **P** (71) 720 Dr Martin Luther King Jr 46202-3116 (Mail to: 720 Dr Martin Luther King Jr St 46202-3116) Michelle Roos Jean Smith Karen Sullivan (317) 636-1133

Indianapolis St Timothys Episcopal Church **P** (164) 2601 East Thompson Road 46227-4496 (Mail to: 2601 East Thompson Road 46227-4496) Rebecca Nickel (317) 784-6925

Indianapolis Trinity Episcopal Church **P** (809) 3243 N Meridian St 46208-4645 (Mail to: 3243 N Meridian St 46208-4645) Thomas Kryder-Reid Lea Colvill Karen King Karen King Larae Rutenbar (317) 926-1346

Jeffersonvlle St. Pauls Episcopal Church **P** (95) 321 E Market St 47130-3309 (Mail to: 321 E Market St 47130-3309) Nancy Woodworth-Hill Donald Hill (812) 282-1108

Lafayette St Johns Episcopal Church **P** (365) 600 Ferry St 47901-1142 (Mail to: 600 Ferry St 47901-1142) Bradley Pace Hilary Cooke Robert L'Homme (765) 742-4079

Lawrenceburg Trinity Episcopal Church **P** (53) 101 W. Center St. 47025-1942 (Mail to: PO Box 3883 47025-3883) Mary Taflinger (812) 537-2619

Lebanon St Peters Episcopal Church **M** (138) 950 E Washington St 46052-1901 (Mail to: 950 E Washington St 46052-1901) Christopher Beasley Mary Coufal (765) 482-2322

Madison Christ Episcopal Church **P** (154) 506 Mulberry St 47250-3440 (Mail to: 506 Mulberry St 47250-3440) Evelyn Wheeler (812) 265-2158

Martinsville St Marys Episcopal Church **M** (31) 1109 E Morgan St 46151-1746 (Mail to: 1109 E Morgan St 46151-1746) (765) 342-1682

Mount Vernon St Johns Episcopal Church **P** (80) 602 Mulberry Street 47620 (Mail to: PO Box 503 47620-0503) Allen Rutherford (812) 838-5445

Muncie Grace Episcopal Church **P** (193) 300 S Madison St 47305-2464 (Mail to: 300 S Madison St 47305-2489) Thomas Blake (765) 289-7931

New Albany St Pauls Episcopal Church **P** (216) 1015 E Main St 47150-5842 (Mail to: 1015 E Main St 47150-5842) Richard Kautz Gordon Anderson (812) 944-0413

New Castle St James Episcopal Church **P** (46) 2020 Bundy Ave 47362-2920 (Mail to: 2020 Bundy Ave 47362-2920) (765) 529-5309

New Harmony St Stephens Episcopal Church **P** (57) 318 Main St 47631 (Mail to: PO Box 173 47631-0173) Elizabeth Macke (812) 682-4604

Noblesville St Michaels Episcopal Church **P** (201) 444 S Harbour Dr 46062-9107 (Mail to: 444 S Harbour Dr 46062-9107) Lee Schaefer (317) 773-6157

Plainfield St Marks Episcopal Church **P** (199) 710 E Buchanan St 46168-1514 (Mail to: 710 E Buchanan St 46168-1514) Kirsteen Wilkinson (317) 839-6730

Richmond St Pauls Episcopal Church **P** (74) 800 N A St 47374-3120 (Mail to: 800 N A St 47374-3120) (765) 962-6988

Rockport Peace Episcopal Church **M** (28) 818 Madison St 476351241 (Mail to: PO Box 127 47635-0127) Donald Overton (812) 6495500

Shelbyville St Lukes Church **P** (33) 1201 N Riley Hwy 46176-9432 (Mail to: 1201 N Riley Hwy 46176-9432) (317) 392-1379

Terre Haute St Stephens Episcopal Church **P** (149) 215 N 7th St 47807-3103 (Mail to: 215 N 7th St 47807-3103) Andrew Downs (812) 232-5165

Vincennes St James Episcopal Church **HC** (33) 610 Perry St 47591-2130 (Mail to: 610 Perry St 47591-2130) Dennis Latta Mary Becker (812) 882-9640

W Lafayette Church of the Good Shepherd **Campus Ministry** (125) 610 Meridian St 47906-2656 (Mail to: 610 Meridian St 47906-2656) (765) 743-1347

Washington St Johns Episcopal Church **P** (38) 509 E Walnut St 47501-2766 (Mail to: 509 E Walnut St 47501-2766) Dennis Latta (812) 726-5333

West Terre Haute St George Episcopal Church **M** (58) 1337 Smith Pl 47885 (Mail to: 1120 East Davis Drive Apt 243 47802-4025) (812) 242-4893

Zionsville St Francis in the Fields Epis Church **P** (424) 1525 Mulberry St 46077-1146 (Mail to: 1525 Mulberry St 46077-1146) C Reed (317) 873-4377

NON-PAROCHIAL CLERGY

Allen CW Indianapolis IN
Andres AF *ret* Afton VA
Balke SM Waco TX
Bargiel MV Indianapolis IN
Barrow JCH *ret* Indianapolis IN
Bell DA *ret* Indianapolis IN
Benner ST Princeton IL
Bennett SP Vincennes IN
Berdahl PG *ret* Indianapolis IN
Bessler JL
Boodt MI *ret* Mooresville IN
Boss BW *ret* Indianapolis IN
Bradbury JS
Bradley RE *ret* Fishers IN
Brockman JM *ret* Brazil IN
Brown RD *ret* Old Fort NC
Bunder PJ West Lafayette IN
Carpenter CM *ret* Mitchell IN
Chastain GL *ret* Indianapolis IN
Chillington JH *ret* Terre Haute IN
Christian CE *dcn* Vincennes IN
Costas JK North East MD
Cramer B *dcn*
Culpepper JA *ret* Indianapolis IN
Culpepper P *ret* Washington NC
Denton JM *ret* Indianapolis IN
Dobyns NK *ret* Richmond IN
Dobyns RK *ret* Richmond IN
Dorr EJ *ret* Palmetto FL
Draper RT *ret* Eagle Harbor MI
Ferner DR *ret*
Ferriani NA *ret* Indianapolis IN
Gable SL Bloomington IN
Giannini RE *ret* Indianapolis IN
Giovangelo SM *ret* Indianapolis IN
Godbold RR *ret* Evansville IN

Goldfarb RA *dcn* New Whiteland IN
Goshorn AEG *dcn* Franklin IN
Gray BW Indianapolis IN
Gray CJ *ret* Whittier CA
Gutgsell JK
Haberkorn VM Speedway IN
Hall VB *ret* Bloomington IN
Halladay RA *ret* Nashville IN
Hempstead JB *ret* Petoskey MI
Honaker MA *ret* Sparta NC
Honderich TE *ret* Indianapolis IN
Hutchison JS *ret* Questa NM
Imara M Atlanta GA
Impicciche FS
Johnson LC Bloomington IN
Jones DA *ret* Bloomington IN
Kissinger DJ Indianapolis IN
Kleffman TA *ret* Indianapolis IN
Lamborn AB New York NY
Leehan JE *ret* Santa Fe NM
Lesesne WG Indianapolis IN
Lowe JL *ret* Dunedin FL
Lowney J *dcn* Columbus IN
MacDowell BS *dcn* Richmond IN
Mason CT *ret* Muncie IN
Mattson SR *ret* Eagle Harbor MI
McGee H Elizabeth City NC
Michels SB *ret* Ft Worth TX
Mohringer JRC *ret* Lebanon IN
Morford NL Indianapolis IN
Morrison EA *dcn* Indianapolis IN
Mosso KA *ret* Jeffersonville IN
Mote DE *ret* New Albany IN
Myers RW *ret* Indianapolis IN
Olsen DJH *dcn* Indianapolis IN
Parker DC *ret* Elkins WV
Phillips DC
Ponader MD *dcn* Sanibel FL
Purvis RD *ret* Noblesville IN
Richardson JB *ret* Lady Lake FL
Rickards JA *ret* Falling Waters WV
Roberts JS Englewood FL
Roeschlaub RF *ret* Cumbria
Roos CA *ret* Indianapolis IN
Roos RJ *ret* Atlantic Beach FL
Schomaker KE *ret* Richmond IN
Scime M *dcn*
Scott CA *dcn* Fishers IN
Shoulders DI *ret* Indianapolis IN
Smith HV *ret* Indianapolis IN
Smith WB Martinsville IN
Snyder RP *dcn* Bedford IN
Stanton J *dcn*
Thornberg AC Exeter NH
Tourangeau EJ *ret* Troy VA
Tudor WE *ret* Edgewood WA
Veach DJ *dcn* Terre Haute IN
Walton H Indianapolis IN
Webb RJ *ret* Madison IN
Wiecking FA Silver Spring MD
Wieland WD *ret* Greencastle IN

Williams HRS *dcn* Oak Island NC
Williams LC
Williams MA *ret* Indianapolis IN
Winkler AL

Winters RH Indianapolis IN
Woollen NS *dcn*
Yakubua-Madus F *dcn* Speedway IN

DIOCESE OF IOWA
(PROVINCE VI)
Comprises the State of Iowa
DIOCESAN OFFICE 225 37th St Des Moines IA 50312-4305
TEL (515) 277-6165   FAX (515) 277-0273
E-MAIL diocese@iowaepiscopal.org   WEB www.iowaepiscopal.org

Previous Bishops—
Henry W Lee 1854-74, Wm S Perry 1876-98, Theodore N Morrison 1899-1929, Harry S Longley suffr 1912 coadj 1917 Bp 1929-44, Elwood L Haines 1944-49, Gordon V Smith 1950-71, Walter C Righter 1972-88 C Christopher Epting 1988-2001

Bishop—Rt Rev Alan Scarfe (983) (Dio 5 Apr 2003)

Sec/Conv KS Milligan; *Fin Ofc* A Wagner; *Exec Asst to Bp* J Allaway; *Co-Chanc* T Carpenter Box 10434 Des Moines 50306; *Co-Chanc* L Neuman 28218 218th St Le Claire 52753; *Hist* T Colber D Kaiser 1717 Manor Dr Grinnell, IA 50112; *Treas* B Smith; *Ecum Off* J McCarthy; *ER&D* S Blake; *Prison Min* Rev A Moats Williams; *UTO* M Powell; *Yth* L Howard; *Young Adult Miss* L Bucklin; *Op Mgr* J Doherty; *Theol Ed* A Haugen; *Dio Asst* E Adams; *Jubilee* J Jones; *Altar Guild* M Hippee

Stand Comm—Cler: Pres K Milligan E Popplewell W Abrahamson; *Lay:* R Dublinske W Early M Tinsman

Dio Conv: 28-29 Oct 2016 Des Moines

PARISHES, MISSIONS, AND CLERGY

Albia Grace Episcopal Church **M** (8) 205 S. Second St. 52531 (Mail to: C/O James D Jenkins 1801 625Th Ave 52531-8805) (641) 932-2560

Algona Church of St Thomas **M** (62) 213 E Call St 50511-2453 (Mail to: PO Box 611 50511-0611) (515) 295-2113

Ames Iowa State University Chaplaincy **CC** 2338 Lincoln Way 50014-7113 (Mail to: 2338 Lincoln Way 50014) (515) 292-6655

Ames St Johns by the Campus **P** (475) 2338 Lincoln Way 50014-7113 (Mail to: 2338 Lincoln Way 50014-7113) Alexander Aiton (515) 292-6655

Anamosa St Marks Episcopal Church **M** (19) 107 W 1st St 52205-1831 (Mail to: PO Box 33 52205-0033) (319) 462-2933

Ankeny St Annes by the Fields **P** (143) 2110 W 1st

St 50023-2487 (Mail to: 2110 W 1st St 50023-2487) Robert Kem Kathleen Tripses (515) 964-5152

Bettendorf St Peters Episcopal Church **P** (287) 2400 Middle Rd 52722-3250 (Mail to: 2400 Middle Rd 52722-3250) Mary Wagner

Boone Grace Episcopal Church **M** (40) 707 8th St 50036-2727 (Mail to: 707 8th St 50036-2727) Sheryl Hughes-Empke (515) 432-7586

Burlington Christ Episcopal Church **P** (190) 623 N Fifth St 52601 (Mail to: 623 N 5th St 52601-5029) Patricia Cashman (319) 752-1381

Carroll Trinity Episcopal Church **M** (13) 127 W 9th St 51401-2305 (Mail to: 1700 Pike Ave 51401-1627) Diana Wright (712) 792-2836

Cedar Falls St Luke's Episcopal Church **P** (199) 2410 Melrose Dr 50613-5234 (Mail to: 2410 Melrose Dr 50613-5234) Elizabeth Popplewell Liane Nichols Ruth Ratliff (319) 277-8520

Cedar Rapids Christ Episcopal Church **P** (588) 220 40th St NE 52402-5616 (Mail to: 220 40th St NE 52402-5616) Mark Eccles Randall Lyle Melody Rockwell Benjamin Webb (319) 363-2029

Cedar Rapids Grace Episcopal Church **P** (108) 525 A Ave NE 52401-1015 (Mail to: 525 A Ave NE 52401-1015) (319) 362-1929

Chariton St Andrews Episcopal Church **M** (16) 1112 N 7th St 50049-1208 (Mail to: PO Box 838 50049-0838) Frederick Steinbach (641) 774-4911

Charles City Grace Episcopal Church **M** (13) 902 5th Ave 50616-3006 (Mail to: 902 5th Ave 50616-3006) (641) 228-4519

Clermont Church of the Saviour **M** (13) 610 - 702 Mill St 52135 (Mail to: PO Box 301 52135-0301) (563) 423-5508

Clinton Christ Episcopal Church **P** (152) 2100 N 2nd St 52732-2418 (Mail to: PO Box 3052 52732-3052)

Coralville New Song Episcopal Church **P** (132) 912 20th Ave 52241-1404 (Mail to: 912 20th Ave 52241-1404) Jennifer Masada (319) 351-3577

Council Blfs St Pauls Episcopal Church **P** (96) 22 Dillman Dr 51503-1641 (Mail to: 22 Dillman

Dr 51503-1641) Aaron Hudson (712) 323-7188

Davenport St Albans Episcopal Church **P** (167) 3510 W Central Park Ave 52804-2753 (Mail to: 3510 W Central Park Ave 52804-2753) (563) 386-4087

✠ **Davenport** Trinity Cathedral **O** (579) 121 W 12th St 52803-5227 (Mail to: 121 W 12th St 52803-5227) John Horn Judith Dalmasso (563) 323-9989

Decorah Grace Episcopal Church **M** (38) 506 W Broadway St 52101-1704 (Mail to: 506 W Broadway St 52101-1704) (563) 382-4246

Denison Trinity Episcopal Church **M** (5) No 12 S 16th St 51442-2011 (Mail to: 801 1st Ave S 51442-2603) Diana Wright (712) 263-6907

Des Moines All Angels Episcopal Church **M** (15) 225 37th Street 50312 (Mail to: 225 37th St 50312) (515) 277-6165

✠ **Des Moines** Cathedral Church of St Paul **O** (669) 815 High St 50309-2714 (Mail to: 815 High St 50309-2714) Troy Beecham John Doherty (515) 288-7297

Des Moines St Andrews Episcopal Church **P** (140) 5720 Urbandale Ave 50310-1250 (Mail to: 5720 Urbandale Ave 50310-1295) Steven Godfrey (515) 255-2101

Des Moines St Lukes Episcopal Church **P** (401) 3424 Forest Ave 50311-2615 (Mail to: 3424 Forest Ave 50311-2615) Martha Kester (515) 277-0875

Des Moines St Marks Episcopal Church **P** (138) 3120 E 24th St 50317-3609 (Mail to: 3120 E 24th St 50317-3609) Kathleen Travis (515) 266-1304

Dubuque St Johns Episcopal Church **P** (215) 1410 Main St 52001-4740 (Mail to: 1458 Locust St 52001-4714) Kathleen Milligan Diane Eddy (563) 556-0252

Durant St Pauls Episcopal Church **P** (45) 206 6th St 52747-9742 (Mail to: PO Box 865 52747-0865) Alice Haugen (563) 785-6228

Emmetsburg Trinity Episcopal Church **M** (21) 2219 Main St 50536-2446 (Mail to: PO Box 332 50536-0332) (712) 852-3809

Fort Dodge St Marks Episcopal Church **P** (71) 1007 1st Ave S 50501-4801 (Mail to: 1007 1st Ave S 50501-4801) Elaine Caldbeck

Fort Madison St Lukes Episcopal Church **P** (62) 605 Avenue E 52627-4805 (Mail to: 605 Avenue E 52627-4805) Lyle Brown (319) 372-6409

Glenwood St Johns Episcopal Church **M** (10) 111 N Vine St 51534-1516 (Mail to: PO Box 109 51534-0109) (712) 527-2971

Grinnell St Pauls Episcopal Church **P** (78) 1026 State St 50112 (Mail to: PO Box 365 50112-0365) Wendy Abrahamson Sallie Verrette

Harlan St Pauls Episcopal Church **M** (23) 712 Farnam St 51537-1637 (Mail to: PO Box 526 51537-0526) Diana Wright (712) 755-2793

Independence St James Episcopal Church **M** (22) 202 2nd Ave NE 50644-1905 (Mail to: 202

Second Ave NE 50644-1905) Sean Burke Sue Ann Raymond (319) 334-4297

Indianola All Saints' Church **M** (24) 501 N Jefferson Way 50125-1762 (Mail to: 102 E Main St 50001-7704) Ronald Osborne (515) 491-7966

Iowa City Trinity Episcopal Church **P** (509) 320 E College St 52240-1628 (Mail to: 320 E College St 52240-1628) Judith Crossett Lori Erickson Alice Haugen Jan Horn Thomas Hulme Elizabeth Koffron-Eisen Lauren Lyon William Moorhead Catherine Quehl-Engel Barbara Schlachter

Iowa City University of Iowa Chaplaincy **CC** 26 E Market St 52245-1742 (Mail to: 320 E College St 52240) Jan Horn (319) 337-3333

Iowa Falls St Matthews-by-the-Bridge **M** (22) No 507 Railroad St 50126-2240 (Mail to: PO Box 206 50126-0206) Elliot Blackburn (641) 648-6779

Keokuk St Johns Episcopal Church **P** (102) 208 N 4th St 52632-5602 (Mail to: 208 N 4th St 52632-5602) Larry Snyder (319) 524-4672

Le Mars St Georges Episcopal Church **M** (7) 400 1st Ave SE 51031-2045 (Mail to: 400 1st Ave SE 51031-2045) (712) 546-4604

Maquoketa St Marks Episcopal Church **M** (29) 208 W Maple St 52060-2929 (Mail to: 208 W Maple St 52060-2929) (563) 652-4970

Marshalltown St Pauls Episcopal Church **P** (77) 201 E Church St 50158-2944 (Mail to: 201 E Church St 50158-2944) (641) 753-6317

Mason City St Johns Episcopal Church **P** (158) 120 1st St NE 50401-3302 (Mail to: 120 1st St NE 50401-3302) (641) 424-1300

Mt Pleasant St Michaels Episcopal Church **P** (37) 202 E Washington St 52641-1933 (Mail to: PO Box 624 52641-0624) Mary Christopher Dian Ong (319) 385-2633

Muscatine Trinity Episcopal Church **P** (130) 211 Walnut St 52761-4130 (Mail to: 211 Walnut St 52761-4130) Cathi Bencken Martha Lang (563) 263-2177

Newton St Stephens Episcopal Church **P** (216) 223 E 4th St N 50208-3214 (Mail to: 223 E 4th St N 50208-3214) Merle Smith (641) 792-6971

Orange City Church of the Savior **M** (49) 415 Third St NW 51041-1313 (Mail to: 530 Arizona Ave SW 51041-1935) Karen Wacome (712) 737-3930

Oskaloosa St James Episcopal Church **P** (67) 207 S 3rd St 52577-3137 (Mail to: PO Box 545 52577-0545) Terence Kleven

Ottumwa Trinity Episcopal Church **M** (45) 204 E 5th St 52501-2626 (Mail to: 204 E 5th St 52501-2626) Vincent Bete (641) 682-5624

Perry St Martins Episcopal Church **P** (57) & 10th Iowa Sts 50220 (Mail to: PO Box 486 50220-0486) Sheryl Hughes-Empke (515) 465-3468

Shenandoah St Johns Episcopal Church **M** (43) 401 Church St 51601-1959 (Mail to: 1304

Southmoreland Pl 51601-2248) Holly Scherff (712) 246-4790

Sioux City Calvary Episcopal Church **M** (32) 1308 S Cleveland St 51106-1942 (Mail to: 1308 S Cleveland St 51106-1942) (712) 276-3561

Sioux City St Pauls Indian Mission **M** (569) 524 Center St 51103-3648 (Mail to: PO Box 895 51102-0895) (712) 255-5162

Sioux City St Thomas Episcopal Church **P** (197) 406 12th St 51105-1305 (Mail to: 406 12th St 51105-1305) Patricia Johnson (712) 258-0141

Spirit Lake St Alban's Episcopal Church **P** (97) 2011 23rd & Zenith 51360 (Mail to: PO Box 85 51360-0085) Carl Mann (712) 336-1117

Storm Lake All Saints Episcopal Church **P** (34) 121 W Marina Rd 50588-7473 (Mail to: 121 W Marina Rd 50588-7473) (712) 732-1314

W Des Moines St Timothys Episcopal Church **P** (502) 1020 24th St 50266-2107 (Mail to: 1020 24th St 50266-2107) Mary Cole-Duvall Jeanie Smith

Waterloo Trinity Episcopal Parish **P** (133) 4535 Kimball Ave 50701-9087 (Mail to: 4535 Kimball Ave 50701-9087) Sally Peterson (319) 232-4714

Waverly St Andrews Episcopal Church **M** (38) 717 W Bremer Ave 50677-2926 (Mail to: PO Box 176 50677-0176) Judith Jones (319) 352-1489

Webster City Church of the Good Shepherd **M** (37) 1100 Mary Ln 50595-2746 (Mail to: PO Box 108 50595-0108)

NON-PAROCHIAL CLERGY

Adney JG *dcn* Cedar Rapids IA
Bascom CC Des Moines IA
Beach KJ *dcn* Marshalltown IA
Berger F *dcn* Pleasant Valley IA
Brada NN Iowa Falls IA
Bucklin LK Des Moines IA
Campbell KS *ret* Charles City IA
Carver LT *ret* Bettendorf IA
Cornthwaite HE
Coulter E *ret* Iowa City IA
Crawford K Newton IA
Doherty MC *ret* Cedar Falls IA
Dowling S *dcn*
Eades ST Dillon MT
Easley BA Fort Madison IA
Easley JK *ret* Iowa City IA
Elfvin RR *ret* Palm Coast FL
Emge KR *dcn*
Ferrel AL Council Bluffs IA
Frelund WF *ret dcn* Mason City IA
Fuessel PA *ret* Tennessee Ridge TN
Gamble RD *ret* Poznan
Gatrel LG *ret* Carroll IA
Genereux PE *ret* Sioux Falls SD
Gerhart S
Goodfellow WM *ret* Coralville IA

Gowdy-Jaehnig CA
Graves RW *ret* Fort Dodge IA
Greve JH Coralville IA
Griesheimer J
Haack MJ *dcn*
Hall JL *ret* Davenport IA
Halverson-Rigatuso K
Harmon EW *dcn* Des Moines IA
Harper JB *dcn* Iowa City IA
Harris MS *dcn*
Hoffman ME *dcn* Davenport IA
Hughes LM *ret* Elizabethtown KY
Jackson MRB
Kamm WK *ret* Salem IA
Kannenberg JG Fort Madison IA
Keeler DF *dcn* Storm Lake IA
Kem RW *ret* Des Moines IA
Kilby JI *ret* Omaha NE
Kirkland PA *dcn*
Kramer FF *ret* Newton IA
Leaman KK
Lopez S *dcn*
Low ML *ret*
Magie WW *dcn* Polk City IA
Mahood SM *ret* Des Moines IA
McCarthy JER *ret* Des Moines IA
McCaulley BM Mason City IA
McKinney BJ *dcn* Des Moines IA
McVey JB Davenport IA
Messer KB
Moermond CR *ret*
Norton JF
Oakland MJK *ret* Ames IA
Payer DR *dcn* Ames IA
Pelkey WL *ret* West Plains MO
Pfotenhauer LH *dcn* Sioux City IA
Pillsbury J
Pope CM *ret* Saint Albans WV
Pugliese WJ *ret* Cranberry Twp PA
Pumphrey CM Portsmouth VA
Putnam TC Cambridge MA
Rankin GE *ret* Denison IA
Roberts PJ *dcn* Sioux City IA
Rogers MC *ret* Marion IA
Rogerson GW *dcn* West Burlington IA
Rollins RB *ret* Grand Rapids MI
Sanderson PO Alamogordo NM
Schlachter MH *ret* Iowa City IA
Sickels PL Davenport IA
Smith KK *ret* Castle Rock CO
Stanley AP *ret* Frome Somerset
Stewart JL Coralville IA
Summers CR *ret* Springfield MA
Thayer JA *dcn* Coralville IA
Titus FD *ret* Garden City KS
Tramel S Berkeley CA
Triska PI *dcn* Boone IA
Twentyman DG *dcn* Spirit Lake IA
Valentine Davis MR
Vann TE *ret* Papillion NE
Walker PE *ret* Burlington IA

Watson Epting SK *ret dcn* Davenport IA
Webster RL Burlington IA
Weiner MY *ret* Urbandale IA
Wentzein M *dcn*

Wharton GF *ret* Decorah IA
Whitmer ML *ret* De Witt IA
Wilkerson BC Fort Madison IA
Williams A

ITALY
See Europe

STATE OF KANSAS
Dioceses of Kansas and Western Kansas

DIOCESE OF KANSAS
(PROVINCE VII)
Comprises eastern Kansas
DIOCESAN OFFICE Bethany Pl 835 SW Polk Topeka KS 66612-1688
TEL (785) 235-9255   FAX (785) 235-2449
E-MAIL receptionist@episcopal-ks.org   WEB www.episcopal-ks.org

Previous Bishops—
Thomas H Vail 1864-89, Elisha S
Thomas coadj 1887 Bp 1889-95,
Frank R Millspaugh 1895-1916,
James Wise coadj 1916 Bp 1916-
39, Goodrich R Fenner coadj 1937
Bp 1939-59, Edward C Turner
coadj 1956 Bp 1959-81, Richard F
Grein 1981-88, William E Smalley
Bp 1989-2003

Bishop—Rt Rev Dean E Wolfe DD (994) (Dio
1 Jan 04)

Cn to Ord & Deploy Off T Lightcap; *Bp Assist* J Atha;
Comp J Currie; *Yth Off* K Schlabach; *Sec Conv* K
Clowers; *Comm* M Woerman; *Campus Missioner*
vacant; *Chanc* LF Taylor Box 550 Olathe 66051; *V
Chanc* M Francis 5100 SW 10th Ave Ste 100 Topeka
KS 66604-2279; *V Chanc* K Harper 833 N Waco
Wichita KS 67203; *Treas* D Anning 700 W 47th St Ste
1000 Kansas City MO 64112-1805; *Hist* M Woerman

Stand Comm—Cler: S Billman P Funston R Harris L
Lewis R Matney F Mays T Wilson *Lay:* F Connizzo
T Flynn L Hannan M LaRue S Mann S O'Connor
R Wheeler

Dio Conv: 27-29 Oct 2016 Wichita KS

PARISHES, MISSIONS, AND CLERGY

Abilene St Johns Episcopal Church **P** (4267) 519
N Buckeye Ave 67410-2531 (Mail to: PO Box
461 Abilene KS 67410) Jerry Rankin Frank
Holtz (785) 263-3592

Arkansas City Trinity Episcopal Church **P** (8486)
PO Box 544 67005-0544224 North A St 67005-
2204 (Mail to: PO Box 544 Arkansas City KS
67005-0544) Laurie Lewis Thomas Herlocker

Atchison Trinity Episcopal Church **P** (7090) 300
S 5th St 66002-2809 (Mail to: 300 S 5th St
Atchison KS 66002-2809) Jon Hullinger (913)
367-3171

Blue Rapids St Marks Church **P** (6168) 601
Lincoln St 66411 (Mail to: 400 E 4th703 East
Ave. St Blue Rapids KS 664111-1545) Arthur
Rathbun

Chanute Grace Episcopal Church **P** (70102) No
209 S Lincoln Ave 66720-2463 (Mail to: 209
S Lincoln Ave Chanute KS 66720-2463) Joyce
Holmes Helen Hoch (620) 431-1210

Clay Center St Pauls Episcopal Church **P** (8785)
No 1010 6th St 67432-2506 (Mail to: PO
Box 625 Clay Center KS 67432-0625) Rex
MatneyVacant (785) 632-3200

Coffeyville St Paul's Episcopal Church **P** (9891)
No 613 Elm St 67337-4935 (Mail to: 613 Elm
St Coffeyville KS 67337-4935) Antoinette
Tackkett Vacant (620) 251-4890

Derby St Andrews Episcopal Church **P** (157136)
1062 E Chet Smith Ave 67037-2354 (Mail to:
PO Box 8 Derby KS 67037-0008) John Roper
Leland Allen Thomas Wilson (316) 788-2595

Edwardsville St Martin in the Fields Church
P (7995) 1501 Edwardsville Dr 66111-1127
(Mail to: PO Box 13012 Edwardsville KS
66113-0012) Joseph Alford (913) 422-5879

El Dorado Trinity Episcopal Church **P** (24490)
No 400 W Ash Ave 67042-2803 (Mail to: PO
Box 507 El Dorado KS 67042-0507) Mary
Ware Christine Gilson (316) 321-6606

Emporia St Andrew's Episcopal Church **P** (183130) No 828 Commercial St 66801-2915 (Mail to: 828 Commercial St Emporia KS 66801-0644) Christopher Arnold Kay Dagg (620) 342-1537

Galena St Marys Episcopal Church **P** (29) 415 S. Washington St 66739-1733 (Mail to: 415 S Washington St Galena KS 66739-1733) JW Stephenson Gary Kennedy (620) 783-5075

Holton Church of St Thomas **P** (193) 512 Wisconsin Ave 66436-1645 (Mail to: PO Box 333 Holton KS 66436-0333) Raymond Hartjen (785) 979-8411

Independence Church of the Epiphany **P** (130129) 400 E Maple St 67301-3822 (Mail to: PO Box 655 Independence KS 67301-0655) Gerald Eytcheson David Butler

Iola St Timothys Episcopal Church **P** (3235) 202 S Walnut St 66749-3245 (Mail to: 202 S Walnut Ststop Box 802 Iola KS 66749-3245) David Kent (620) 365-7306

Junction City Church of the Covenant **P** (200195) 314 N Adams St 66441-3071 (Mail to: PO Box 366 Junction City KS 66441-0366) David Jenkins Rex Matney William Jenkins (785) 238-2897

Kansas City St Pauls Episcopal Church **P** (119162) 1300 N 18th St 66102-2733 (Mail to: 1300 N 18th St Kansas City KS 66102-2733) Dixie Junk Don Compier Gail Reynolds Stevie Carter (913) 321-3535

Lawrence St Margarets Episcopal Church **P** (422378) No 5700 W 6th St 66049-4829 (Mail to: 5700 W 6th St Lawrence KS 66049-4829) Matthew Zimmermann Robert Honse Robert Schwaller (785) 865-5777

Lawrence Trinity Episcopal Church **P** (539540) 1011 1027 Vermont Street 66044-2921 (Mail to: 1027 Vermont St Lawrence KS 66044-2921) Carolyn Graham Rita Tracy Dick Tracy Robert Baldwin Stephen Segerbrecht (785) 843-6166

Leavenworth St Pauls Episcopal Church **P** (380398) 209 N 7th St 66048-1930 (Mail to: PO Box 233 Leavenworth KS 66048-0233) Michael Munro (913) 682-15261033

Manhattan St Pauls Episcopal Church **P** (233232) 601 Poyntz Ave 66502-6006 (Mail to: 601 Poyntz Ave PO Box 1034 Manhattan KS 66505-10346006) Robert Charles Pearce Aidan Patrick Funston (785) 776-9427

Marysville St Pauls Episcopal Church **P** (2220) 309 N 17th St Marysville KS 66508-1405 10th and Alston 66508-1677 (Mail to: 309 306 N 17th St Marysville KS 66508-1405) (785) 562-5182

Mission St Michael and All Angels Church **P** (23192463) No 6630 Nall Ave 66202-4325 (Mail to: 6630 Nall Ave Mission KS 66202-4325) Donald Williams James Robertson Monte Giddings Samuel Cox Kevin Huddleston David Cox Monte Giddings Donald Williams Karen Wichael Doreen Rice (913) 236-8600

Neodesha Church of the Ascension **P** (4137) No 702 Osage St 66757-1466 (Mail to: PO Box 446 Neodesha KS 66757-0446) Gerald Eytcheson (620) 331-4794

Newton St Matthews Episcopal Church **P** (204123) No 2001 Windsor Dr 67114-1250 (Mail to: 2001 Windsor Dr Newton KS 67114-1250) Michael Bernard Mary Siegmund (316) 283-3310

Olathe St Aidans Episcopal Church **P** (158179) 14301 S Blackbob Rd 66062-2537 (Mail to: 14301 S Blackbob Rd Olathe KS 66062-2537) Robert Streepy (913) 764-3050

Ottawa Grace Episcopal Church **P** (1834) 315 W 5th St 66067-2842Po Box 601 66067-0601 (Mail to: PO Box 601 Ottawa KS 66067-0601315 W 5th St Ottawa KS 66067-2842) Robert Harris (785) 242-5390

Overland Park St Francis of Assisi Episcopal Church (P) (38) 17890 Metcalf Ave. 66085-9326 (Mail to PO Box 118 Stilwell KS 66085-0118) Amy Cox (913) 897-2588

Overland Park Church of St Thomas the Apostle **P** (715804) 12251 Antioch Rd 66213-1517 (Mail to: 12251 Antioch Rd Overland Park KS 66213-1517) Steven King Benedict Varnum Clifford Davis Gar Demo Kevin Schmidt Kelly Demo Barbara Adam Fran Wheeler (913) 451-0512

Parsons St Johns Episcopal Church **P** (131105) 1801 Corning 67357-4265 (Mail to: PO Box 882 Parsons KS 67357-0882) Sharon Billman (620) 421-37754540

Pittsburg St Peters Episcopal Church **P** (119108) No 306 W Euclid St 66762-5106 (Mail to: 306 W Euclid St Pittsburg KS 66762-5106) William Wolff (620) 231-3790

Sedan Church of the Epiphany Episcopal Church **P** (5538) No 309 W Elm St 67361-1216 (Mail to: PO Box 367 Sedan KS 67361-0367) Foster Mays (620) 725-3701

Shawnee St Lukes Episcopal Church **P** (399198) No 5325 Nieman Rd 66203-1939 (Mail to: 5325 Nieman Rd Shawnee KS 66203-1939) Mary Siegmund (913) 631-8597

Stilwell St Francis of Assisi Epis Church **P** (57) 17890 Metcalf 66085 (Mail to: PO Box 118 Overland Park KS 66085-0118) (913) 897-2588

Topeka Grace Cathedral **O** (742774) No 701 SW SW 8th Ave 66603-3219 (Mail to: 701 SW 8th Ave Topeka KS 66603-3219) Donald Chubb Randall Lipscomb Anne Flynn (785) 235-3457

Topeka St Davids Episcopal Church **P** (478516) 3916 SW 17th St 66604-2438 (Mail to: 3916 SW 17th St Topeka KS 66604-2438) Barbara Bloxsom Betty Glover Harry Craig Annie Hedquist Craig Klein Donald Davidson (785) 272-5144

Wamego St Lukes Episcopal Church **P** (92100) 700 Lincoln St 66547-1638 (Mail to: PO Box 109 Wamego KS 66547-0109) Matthew Cobb (785) 456-9310

Wellington St Judes Episcopal Church **P** (21) 1323 North Jefferson 67152 (Mail to: PO Box 222 Wellington KS 67152-0222) Catherine Shield (620) 326-6406

Wichita Good Shepherd Episcopal Church **P** (410409) No 8021 W 21st St N 67205-1743 (Mail to: 8021 W 21st St N Wichita KS 67205-1743) Robert Hirst Andrew O'Connor Arland Wallace (316) 721-8096

Wichita St Bartholomews Episcopal Church **P** (3429) No 2799 S Meridian Ave 67217-1461 (Mail to: 2799 S Meridian Ave Wichita KS 67217-1461) Walter Miescher (316) 941-4744

Wichita St James Episcopal Church **P** (872939) 3750 E Douglas Ave 67208-3708 (Mail to: 3750 E Douglas Ave Wichita KS 67208-3784) Jon Hullinger Caryllou Evans Catherine Shield Dawn Frankfurt Jeff Roper Peg Flynn (316) 683-5686

Wichita St Johns Episcopal Church **P** (312324) No 402 N. Topeka St 67202-2414 (Mail to: 402 N Topeka St Wichita KS 67202-2414) James Blakley Barbara Gibson Charles Mahan (316) 262-0897

Wichita Wichita Minis of Sts Alban & Stephen St Stephens Episcopal Church **P** (620160) No 7404 E. Killarney Pl 67206-1627 (Mail to: 7404 E Killarney Pl Wichita KS 67206-1627) Karen Wichael Mary Korte Robert Mitchell (316) 634-2513

Winfield Grace Episcopal Church **P** (178184) 715 Millington St 67156-2838 (Mail to: PO Box 490 Winfield KS 67156) Laurie Lewis Thomas Herlocker (620) 221-4252

Yates Center Calvary Episcopal Church **P** (3835) No 200 S Grove St 66783 (Mail to: PO Box 214 Yates Center KS 66783-0214) Helen Hoch (620) 625-2358

NON-PAROCHIAL CLERGY

Abshier PA *dcn* Wichita KS
Adam BA *dcn* Overland Park KS
Adinolfi JD *ret* Greenville NY
Akins KE *dcn* Topeka KS
Allen LE *dcn* Clearwater KS
Anderson CMW *dcn* Alma KS
Arnold CJ Emporia KS
Ash EA *ret* Olathe KS
Babcock MK Independence KS
Baguyos AT *ret* Overland Park KS
Barber BJ *dcn* Topeka KS
Bayles JA *ret* Wichita KS
Blakely WA *ret* Louisville KY
Broach MK *ret* New Orleans LA
Bunker OF *dcn* Chanute KS
Burns DS *dcn* Lawrence KS

Butler DF *dcn* Independence KS
Clowers GH Lawrence KS
Cohoon FN *ret* Topeka KS
Coleton JM *dcn* Prairie Village KS
Compier DH Topeka KS
Cowell CL *ret* Topeka KS
Criss CP *ret* Wichita KS
Davidson DF Topeka KS
Davis G *ret* Durham NC
Demo K Lenexa KS
Drumm EP *dcn*
Drury SR *dcn* Shawnee KS
D'Wolf JF *ret* Fishers IN
Eiman AB Lansdale PA
Flynn AR *dcn* Charleston IL
Flynn PR *dcn*
Gilhousen DR Mission KS
Gomes E *ret* Wichita KS
Gooch GD *ret* San Marcos TX
Graham CJ *dcn* Lawrence KS
Grosso AT Nashotah WI
Hartjen RC *ret* Leavenworth KS
Honse RW *dcn*
Horton-Smith S *dcn* Manhattan KS
Jenkins SR Topeka KS
John JH *dcn* Wichita KS
Layne NS *dcn* McPherson KS
Layne RP *ret dcn* McPherson KS
Lee MDP *ret* Denver CO
Lightcap TL Topeka KS
Macintosh NK *ret* The Oaks, NSW
McCandless RW *ret* Parsons KS
McQuin RL Falls Church VA
McVey AW *ret* Leawood KS
Mendenhall EE *ret* Topeka KS
Milan J *dcn* Kansas City KS
Miles TD *ret* Manhattan KS
Minx PA *dcn* Olathe KS
Mitchell RJ *ret* Wichita KS
Montes E Wichita KS
Moses DH *ret* Topeka KS
Mouille DR *ret* Shawnee KS
Mudge HT West Park NY
Mues SW *ret* Boulder City NV
Murphy PA *dcn* Overland Park KS
Northway DP Topeka KS
Ohlstein AM *dcn* Leavenworth KS
Oldfather SK Kingsville MD
Orndorff V The Woodlands TX
Papanek N Covington KY
Peak RR *ret* Key Largo FL
Pedersen JC *ret* Albuquerque NM
Petty TC Topeka KS
Reed RL *ret* Prairie Village KS
Robertson FW *ret* Springfield MO
Roper JH *dcn* Wichita KS
Sawyer SC *ret* Clay Center KS
Seifert SL Olathe KS
Shacklett RL *ret* Mission KS
Shaw AS Hinesville GA
Spratt GC *ret* Fulton MO

Stephenson JW Riverton KS
Stone DP Overland Park KS
Tackkett AV Coffeyville KS
Terrill RA *ret* Topeka KS
Terry SP *ret* Lawrence KS
Tilson AR *ret* Kansas City MO

Wallace AL *dcn*
Wheeler FM *dcn* Olathe KS
Wichael K *dcn* Overland Park KS
Wiley GB Lawrence KS
Wolff WG *dcn* Pittsburg KS
Wood WJ *ret* Trevett ME

STATE OF KENTUCKY
Dioceses of Kentucky and Lexington

DIOCESE OF KENTUCKY
(PROVINCE IV)
Comprises western Kentucky
DIOCESAN OFFICE 425 S 2nd St Ste 200 Louisville KY 40202
TEL (502) 584-7148   FAX (502) 587-8123
WEB www.episcopalky.org

Previous Bishops—
Benj B Smith 1832-84, Geo D
Cummins asst 1866-74, Thomas U
Dudley coadj 1875 Bp 1884-1904,
Chas E Woodcock 1905-35, Chas
Clingman 1936-54, CG Marmion
1954-74, DB Reed coadj 1972 Bp
1974-94, Edwin F Gulick Jr Bp
1994-2010

Bishop—Terry Allen White (1051) (Dio 25
Sept 2010)

Cn to Ord Rev AR Coultas *Chanc* W Robinson Beard
400 W Market St Ste 1800 Louisville; *Sec of Dio* KS
Wilkinson; *Treas* D Brooks; *Bp's Staff: All Saints Epis
Center Compt* B Meyer; *Comm* Brian Kinnaman;
Yth K Badgett; *Transition* M Linder; *Ecum* Rev A
Coultas; *Ch Form* Rev K Doyle; *Fin & Stew* D Brooks
4010 Fox Meadow Way Prospect KY 40059; *Evang
& Cong Dev* B Blodgett 57 Ironwood Dr Murray
KY 42071; *COM* Rev P Connell 720 Ford Ave
Owensboro 42301; *Cn for Cong Vitality* Rev J Lewis

Stand Comm—Cler: Pres A Vouga J Trimble
E Markham; *Lay:* C Stone J Donahue

Dio Conv: 13-14 November 2015 Calvary Church
Louisville KY

PARISHES, MISSIONS, AND CLERGY

Bardstown Episcopal Church of the Ascension **P**
(109) 211 N 3rd St 40004-1527 (Mail to: 211 N
3rd St 40004-1527) Karl Lusk (502) 348-4317

Bowling Green Christ Episcopal Church **P** (636)
1215 State St 42101-2650 (Mail to: 1215 State St
42101-2650) Judith Reese (270) 843-6563

Brandenburg Holy Trinity Episcopal Church **M**
(95) 319 Oaklawn Dr 40108-1033 (Mail to: PO
Box 645 40108-0645) Edward Peoples (270)
422-3721

Campbellsvlle St Thomas Church **M** (59) 116
S Columbia Ave 42718-1339 (Mail to: 116 S
Columbia Ave 42718-1339) (270) 789-1601

Elizabethtown Christ Episcopal Church **P** (140)
206 W Poplar St 42701-1537 (Mail to: PO Box
1054 42702-1054) (270) 765-5606

Fulton Trinity Church **M** (58) 1104 Vine Street
42041-1758 (Mail to: 1104 Vine St 42041-1758)
(270) 472-1870

Gilbertsville St Peters of the Lakes Epis Church
M (56) 47 Black River Rd 42044-9053 (Mail
to: PO Box 183 42044-0183) Meghan Holland
(270) 362-8301

Glasgow St Andrews Episcopal Church **M** (67)
910 Columbia Ave 42141-3336 (Mail to: PO
Box 905 42142-0905) Suzanne Barrow Eugene
Ward (270) 651-6931

Harrods Creek St Francis in the Fields Epis
Church **P** (1606) 6710 Wolf Pen Branch Rd
40027 (Mail to: PO Box 225 40027-0225) John
Koch Nicholas Lannon (502) 228-1176

Henderson St Pauls Episcopal Church **P** (191) 5
S Green St 42420-3536 (Mail to: 5 S Green St
42420-3536) Richard Martindale (270) 826-
2937

Hickman St Paul Episcopal Church **M** (6) 611
Church St 42050 (Mail to: 611 Church St
42050) Barbara Burgess Ellen Ekevag (270)
236-3619

Hopkinsville Grace Episcopal Church **P** (173)
216 E 6th St 42240-3433 (Mail to: 216 E 6th St
42240-3433) Alice Nichols Benjamin Hart

Louisville Calvary Church **P** (438) 821 S 4th St
40203-2115 (Mail to: 821 S 4th St 40203-2115)
Jonathan Erdman Heather Back (502) 587-
6011

✠ **Louisville** Christ Church Cathedral **O** (248) 421 S 2nd St 40202-1417 (Mail to: 421 S 2nd St 40202-1417) Joan Pritcher (502) 587-1354

Louisville Church of Our Merciful Saviour **P** (48) 473 S 11th St 40203-1875 (Mail to: 473 S 11th St 40203-1875) Harold Price (502) 587-6129

Louisville Church of the Advent **P** (186) 901 Baxter Ave 40204-2046 (Mail to: 901 Baxter Ave 40204-2046) Timothy Mitchell Drusilla Kemp

Louisville Resurrection Episcopal Church **P** (149) 4100 Southern Pkwy 40214-1648 (Mail to: 4100 Southern Pkwy 40214-1698) Eva Markham (502) 368-1146

Louisville St Albans Episcopal Church **P** (49) 9004 Beulah Church Rd PO Box 91152 40291-2789 (Mail to: PO Box 91152 40291-0152) (502) 239-3444

Louisville St Andrews Episcopal Church **P** (375) 2233 Woodbourne Ave 40205-2105 (Mail to: 2233 Woodbourne Ave 40205-2105) Mary Jane Cherry William Parker (502) 452-9581

Louisville St Clement Episcopal Church **M** (30) 4112 Wimpole Rd 40218-2369 (Mail to: 4112 Wimpole Rd 40218-2369) (502) 491-6085

Louisville St George Episcopal Church **P** (44) PO Box 3652 40201-3652 (Mail to: PO Box 3652 40210-3652) (502) 776-2030

Louisville St Lukes Chapel **NH** (21) C/O Joy Moll 1201 Lyndon Ln 40222-4319 (Mail to: 7504 Westport Rd 40222-4319) John Allen Mary Jane Cherry Lisa Tolliver (502) 736-7800

Louisville St Lukes Episcopal Church **P** (300) § 1206 Maple Ln 40223-2406 (Mail to: PO Box 23336 40223-0336) Arthur Chard Michael Delk Michelle Ryan (502) 245-8827

Louisville St Marks Episcopal Church **P** (396) 2822 Frankfort Ave 40206-2640 (Mail to: 2822 Frankfort Ave 40206-2640) (502) 895-2429

Louisville St Matthew Episcopal Church **P** (781) 330 N Hubbards Ln 40207-2253 (Mail to: 330 N Hubbards Ln 40207-2200) Emily Crouch Helen Jones Kelly Kirby (502) 895-3485

Louisville St Pauls Episcopal Church **P** (232) 4700 Lowe Rd 40220-1532 (Mail to: 4700 Lowe Rd 40220-1532) Kunihito Shirota

Louisville St Peter Episcopal Church **P** (161) 8110 Saint Andrews Church Rd 40258-3832 (Mail to: 8110 Saint Andrews Church Rd 40258-3832) John Hines

Louisville St Thomas Episcopal Church **P** (173) 9616 Westport Rd 40241-2224 (Mail to: 9616 Westport Rd 40241-2224) (502) 425-3727

Madisonville St Marys Episcopal Church **P** (209) 163 N Main St 42431-1952 (Mail to: PO Box 768 42431-0016) Candyce Loescher (270) 821-3674

Murray St Johns Episcopal Church **P** (122) 1620 Main St 42071-2275 (Mail to: 1620 W Main St 42071-2275) Rosemarie Bogal-Allbritten

Matthew Bradley (270) 753-6908

Owensboro Trinity Church Episcopal **P** (400) 720 Ford Ave 42301-4632 (Mail to: 720 Ford Ave 42301-4632) George Connell (270) 684-5326

Paducah Grace Episcopal Church **P** (485) 820 Broadway St 42001-6808 (Mail to: 820 Broadway 42001-6887) Meghan Holland Richard Paxton Charles Uhlik (270) 443-1363

Pewee Valley St James Episcopal Church **P** (304) 401 Lagrange Rd 40056 (Mail to: PO Box 433 40056-0433) Jerry Cappel (502) 241-8136

Russellville Trinity Episcopal Church **M** (62) PO Box 162 42276-0162 (Mail to: PO Box 162 42276-0162) Geoffrey Butcher (270) 726-3481

Shelbyville St James Episcopal Church **P** (131) 230 Main St 40065-1026 (Mail to: PO Box 166 40066-0166) Richard Galloway Peter Whelan (502) 633-2718

NON-PAROCHIAL CLERGY

Abrams ME *dcn* Louisville KY
Badgett BR
Banks FD Lexington KY
Bojarski MT Campbellsville KY
Brosend WF Sewanee TN
Brown WD *ret* Louisville KY
Browne TJ *ret* Louisville KY
Buckwalter G *ret* Louisville KY
Buie DS *dcn* Louisville KY
Coppick GC *ret* Owensboro KY
Coultas ACR Louisville KY
Dale CH
Doyle AK Louisville KY
Dykstra DJ *dcn* Louisville KY
England GW *dcn* Louisville KY
Fritschner JB *ret* Anchorage KY
Hasen ES Spokane WA
Humke RH *ret* Louisville KY
Jaeger GMN *ret* Paducah KY
Jennings RT *ret* Louisville KY
King RA *ret* Clayton NY
Kuol DK *dcn* Louisville KY
Lane EJ *dcn* KY
Lewis JD Belton MO
Linder MA *ret* Bowling Green KY
Lord JR *ret* Pensacola FL
Merrick BR *dcn* Louisville KY
Mills FT *dcn* Madisonville KY
Minter LC Louisville KY
Momberg TA *ret* Memphis TN
Morell EJ *ret* Louisville KY
Pike SP FPO AP
Revel AC *dcn* Paducah KY
Sanders EB *ret* Louisville KY
Shands AR *ret* Crestwood KY
Smith JA *ret* Louisville KY
Smith PW *ret* Louisville KY
Stodghill MW Louisville KY
Tachau CB *ret* Louisville KY
Tederstrom JP *ret* Louisville KY

Thompson KD Taylorsville KY
Thompson RW Anchorage KY
Trevathan WA *ret* Philadelphia PA
Vouga AF Louisville KY

Wade EAT *ret*
Warner SMC Louisville KY
Wilkinson JR *ret* Louisville KY
Wilson JB *ret* Louisville KY

DIOCESE OF LEXINGTON
(PROVINCE IV)
Comprises eastern Kentucky
DIOCESAN OFFICE 203 E Fourth St
(MAIL: Box 610 Lexington KY 40588-0610) Lexington KY 40508-1515
TEL (859) 252-6527   FAX (859) 231-9077
E-MAIL diocese@diolex.org   WEB www.diolex.org

Previous Bishops—
Lewis W Burton 1896- 1928, Henry PA Abbott 1929-45, Wm R Moody 1945-71, Addison Hosea coadj 1970 Bp 1971-85, Don A Wimberly coadj 1984 Bp 1985-99, Rogers S Harris asst 1999-2000, Stacy F Sauls Bp 2000-2011 Chilton R Knudsen asst 2011-2012

Bishop—W Douglas Hahn (2012-)

Dn of Lex C Wade; *Dio Admin* Ven B Kibler; *Chanc* MT Yeiser; *Cn to Ord* E Johnstone; *Fin* vacant; *Treas* D Sevigny *Hist* M Brinkman; *Bp Sec* E Darnall; *Depts and Comms: Yth* C Sigmon

Stand Comm—Cler: Pres C Wade M Shanks P D'Angio; *Lay:* C Johnson B Stockton D Hart

Dio Conv: 20 Feb 2016 Lexington KY

PARISHES, MISSIONS, AND CLERGY

Ashland Calvary Episcopal Church **P** (310) 1337 Winchester Ave 41101-7553 (Mail to: PO Box 109 41105-0109) Antoinette Azar (606) 325-2328

Beattyville St Thomas Episcopal Church **M** (29) 1 Madison St 41311 (Mail to: PO Box 25 41311-0025) Bryant Kibler (606) 464-9714

Corbin St Johns Episcopal Church **D** (33) 701 Engineer St 40701-1037 (Mail to: PO Box 1512 40702) Rebecca Myers (606) 528-1659

Covington Trinity Episcopal Church **P** (348) 16 E 4th St 41011 (Mail to: 16 E 4th St 41011) Peter D'Angio Linda Young (859) 431-1786

Cynthiana Episcopal Church of the Advent **P** (51) 122 N Walnut St 41031-1224 (Mail to: PO Box 308 41031-0308) Gardner Hartling (859) 234-4163

Danville Trinity Episcopal Church **P** (210) 320 W Main St 40422-1814 (Mail to: 320 W Main St 40422-1814) Amy Meaux (859) 236-3374

Flemingsburg Chapel of St Francis of Flemingsburg **M** (35) 444 Fountain Ave 41041-1032 (Mail to: 153 Westwind Drive 41041-1032) Mary Kilbourn-Huey (606) 845-4001

Florence Grace Episcopal Church **HC** (111) 7111 Price Pike 41042-1665 (Mail to: PO Box 6590 41022-6590) (859) 371-5951

Fort Thomas St Andrews Episcopal Church **P** (604) 3 Chalfonte Pl 41075-1927 (Mail to: PO Box 75027 41075-0027) Jeffrey Queen (859) 441-1092

Frankfort Episcopal Church of the Ascension **P** (285) 311 Washington St 40601-1823 (Mail to: 311 Washington St 40601-1823) William Neat (502) 223-0557

Georgetown Church of the Holy Trinity **P** (235) 209 S Broadway St PO Box 1433 40324-6433 (Mail to: PO Box 1433 40324-1340) Linda McCloud (502) 863-0505

Harlan Christ Episcopal Church **P** (57) 119 E Central St 40831-2348 (Mail to: PO Box 858 40831-0858) Bryant Kibler Bryant Kibler

Harrodsburg St Philips Episcopal Church **HC** (109) 118 W Poplar St 40330-1641 (Mail to: 118 W Poplar St 40330-1641) Peter Doddema (859) 734-3569

Hazard St Marks Episcopal Church **M** (31) 317 Walnut St 41701-1853 (Mail to: 317 Walnut St 41701-1853)

Irvine St Timothys Church **M** (7) 170 St. Timothy's Rd. 40336 (Mail to: 607 Highway 1746 40336-8701) Bryant Kibler (606) 726-0607

✠ **Lexington** Christ Church Cathedral **O** (1116) 166 Market St 40507-1139 (Mail to: 166 Market St 40507-1173) Katherine Byrd Brent Owens Carol Wade (859) 254-4497

Lexington Church of the Good Shepherd **P** (753) 533 E Main St 40508-2341 (Mail to: 533 E Main St 40508-2341) Brian Cole Andrew Hege Jeffrey Howe (859) 252-1744

Lexington St Agnes House **Chapel** 635 Maxwelton Ct 24300 (Mail to: 635 Maxwelton Ct 40508-4012) Rebecca Myers

Lexington St Andrews Episcopal Church **P** (61) 401 N Upper St 40508-1450 (Mail to: 401 N Upper St 40508-1450) Mary Kilbourn-Huey Carol Ruthven (859) 254-8325

Lexington St Augustine Episcopal Chapel **Campus Ministry** 472 Rose St University of

Kentucky 40508-3342 (Mail to: 472 Rose St 40508-3342) (859) 254-3726

Lexington St Huberts Episcopal Church **P** (88) 7559 Grimes Mill Rd 40391 (Mail to: PO Box 21987 40522-1987) Duane Smith Charles Ellestad (859) 527-6440

Lexington St Marthas Episcopal Church **P** (48) 930 Jouett Creek Dr. 40509 (Mail to: PO Box 21944 40522-1987) Sandra Stone (859) 271-7641

Lexington St Michael the Archangel Epis Church **P** (540) 2025 Bellefonte Dr 40503-2601 (Mail to: 2025 Bellefonte Dr 40503-2601) Laurie Brock (859) 277-7511

Lexington St Raphael Episcopal Church **P** (300) 1891 Parkers Mill Rd 40504-2041 (Mail to: 1891 Parkers Mill Rd 40504) Johnnie Ross Robert Slocum

Maysville Episcopal Church of the Nativity **P** (96) 31 E 3rd St 41056-1149 (Mail to: 31 E 3rd St 41056-1149) Michael Henderson (606) 564-5850

Middlesboro St Marys Episcopal Church **P** (73) 131 Edgewood Rd 40965-2840 (Mail to: PO Box 744 40965-0744) Peter Helman (606) 248-6450

Morehead St Albans Church **M** (40) 145 E 5th St 40351-1205 (Mail to: 145 E 5th St 40351-1205) Arthur Conaway (606) 784-6427

Mt Sterling Church of the Ascension **P** (79) 48 W High St 40353-0653 (Mail to: PO Box 653 40353-0653)

Newport St Pauls Episcopal Church **P** (121) 7 Court Pl 41071-1005 (Mail to: 7 Court Pl 41071-1098) Stephen Young Thomas Runge

Nicholasville Epis Church of the Resurrection **P** (290) 3220 Lexington Rd 40356-9798 (Mail to: 3220 Lexington Rd 40356-9798) Margaret Shanks (859) 885-6391

Paris St Peters Episcopal Church **P** (136) 311 High St 40361-2002 (Mail to: PO Box 27 40362-0027) Christina Brannock

Prestonsburg St James Episcopal Church **P** (14) 562 University Dr 41653-1800 (Mail to: 562 University Dr 41653-1800) Judy Yunker Stanley McGraw (606) 886-8046

Richmond Episcopal Church of Our Saviour **M** (85) 2323 Lexington Rd 40475-9135 (Mail to: 2323 Lexington Rd 40475-9135) (859) 623-1226

Somerset St Patricks Episcopal Church **P** (119) 206 West Columbia Street 42501-1674 (Mail to: PO Box 633 42502-0633) Marcia Hunter Amanda Musterman (606) 678-4262

Versailles St Johns Episcopal Church **P** (411) 210 N Main St 40383-1206 (Mail to: 210 N Main St 40383-1206) David Faupel Philip Linder (859) 873-3481

Winchester Emmanuel Episcopal Church **P** (78) 2410 Lexington Rd 40391-9522 (Mail to: 2410 W Lexington Rd 40391) Chana Tetzlaff (859) 744-4889

NON-PAROCHIAL CLERGY

Alexander SG *ret* Cincinnati OH
Bailey CJ
Barr DF *dcn* Lexington KY
Bezy BA Hanahan SC
Brown WG *ret* Frankfort KY
Burkhart JD Corbin KY
Carlisle ME *ret* Sewanee TN
Cavendish JC *ret* Waco KY
Cook HG *ret* Surprise AZ
Cottrell JM Lexington KY
Dawson MA *dcn* Midway KY
Duffus CS Mt Sterling KY
Eklund VJR *dcn* Danville KY
Farley NS *ret* Sadieville KY
Gilbertsen GE
Hamby TC Alexandria VA
Hardwick D *ret* Raleigh NC
Haug PR *ret* Richmond KY
Hinxman FW Granville Ferry NS
Holbrook PE *dcn* Lexington KY
Howard LW *dcn* Lexington KY
Hughes JR Lexington KY
Johnstone EB
Kirkpatrick RF *ret* Lafayette Hill PA
Lawrence CKC *ret* Lexington KY
Montgomery JA *dcn*
Ott PL *dcn* Winchester KY
Pennington JJ *ret* Ft Mitchell KY
Perkins D Montgomery AL
Pierce JR Versailles KY
Purcell MFF *ret* Lexington KY
Saager RA *dcn* Frankfort KY
Sessum RL *ret* Lexington KY
Suit MW Flemingsburg KY
Summers RW *ret* Lexington KY
Thomas KC Morehead KY
Villemuer-Drenth L *dcn* Lexington KY
Washam CW Crestview Hills KY
Willis AC Cincinnati OH
Zwick PD *dcn* Ashland KY

DIOCESE OF LONG ISLAND
(PROVINCE II)
Comprises the 4 counties of Brooklyn, Queens, Nassau, and Suffolk
DIOCESAN HOUSE 36 Cathedral Ave Garden City NY 11530
TEL (516) 248-4800   FAX (516) 877-1349
E-MAIL communication@dioceseli.org   WEB www.dioceselongisland.org

Previous Bishops—
Abram N Littlejohn 1868-1901, Fredk Burgess 1901-25, Ernest M Stires 1925-42, John I Larned suffr 1929-47, Frank W Creighton suffr 1933-37, James P DeWolfe 1942-66, Jonathan G Sherman suffr 1949-65 Bp 1966-77, Richd B Martin suffr 1967-74, Chas W MacLean suffr 1962-75, C Shannon Mallory asst bp 1979-80, Henry B Hucles III suffr 1981-88, Robert C Witcher coadj 1975 Bp 1977-91, Rodney R Michel suffr 1997-2007, Orris G Walker Jr coadj 1991-2009, Rt Rev James H Ottley Asst Bp 2007-09

Bishop—Rt Rev Lawrence C Provenzano (1037) (Dio 14 Nov 09)

Cn to Ord & Deploy Off Rev Cn JD Betit; *Chanc* R Fardella; *Dir of Yth Min* M Garnes Shuler; *Sec* Rev KDM Davis-Lawson; *Treas* R Cole; *Hist* Very Rev JE Walker; *Reg* C Egleston

Stand Comm–Cler: Pres GD Miles S Foster EC Nesmith CD Hofer; *Lay:* VH Crosdale JP Nightingale-Holder CP Wright PG Stewart

Dio Conv: TBD

PARISHES, MISSIONS, AND CLERGY

Amagansett St Thomas Episcopal Chapel **SC** Rt 27 & Indian Wells Hwy 11930 (Mail to: PO Box 103 11930-0103) (313) 242-7356

Amityville St Marys Episcopal Church **P** (418) 175 Broadway 11701-2703 (Mail to: 175 Broadway 11701-2703) Randolph Geminder (631) 264-0004

Astoria Church of the Redeemer **P** (706) 30-14 Crescent St 11102 (Mail to: 3014 Crescent St S 11102-3249) Juan Quevedo-Bosch (718) 278-8093

Astoria St George's Episcopal Church **P** (57) 14-02 27th Ave 11102 (Mail to: 1420 27th Ave 11102-3873) Karen Davis-Lawson (718) 721-5154

Babylon Christ Episcopal Church **P** (244) 12 Prospect St 11702-3407 (Mail to: 12 Prospect St 11702-3407) Elizabeth Nesmith (631) 661-5757

Baldwin All Saints' Episcopal Church **P** (457) 2375 Harrison Ave 11510-3214 (Mail to: 2375 Harrison Ave 11510-3214) (516) 223-3731

Bay Shore St Peters by the Sea Epis Church **P** (429) 500 S Country Rd 11706-8295 (Mail to: 500 S Country Rd 11706-8295) Johncy Itty (631) 665-0051

Bayside All Saints Episcopal Church **P** (246) 21435 40th Ave 11361-2145 (Mail to: 21435 40th Ave 11361-2145) Laurence Byrne (718) 229-5631

Bellmore St Matthias Episcopal Church **M** (8) 2856 Jerusalem Ave 11710 (516) 783-0558

Bellport Christ Episcopal Church **P** (207) 64 S Country Rd 11713-2519 (Mail to: 64 S Country Rd 11713-2519) (631) 286-0299

Brentwood Christ Episcopal Church **M** (169) 155 3rd Ave 11717-5322 (Mail to: 155 3rd Ave 11717-5322) (631) 273-9504

Bridgehampton St Anns Episcopal Church **P** (292) 2463 Main Street 11932 (Mail to: PO Box 961 11932-0961) Timothy Lewis (631) 537-1527

Brookhaven St James Episcopal Church **M** (94) 260 Beaver Dam Rd 11719-9756 (Mail to: 260 Beaver Dam Rd 11719-9756) Hickman Alexandre (631) 286-0726

Brooklyn All Saints Church **P** (173) 286-88 7th Ave 11215-3601 (Mail to: 286 7th Ave 11215-3601) Steven Paulikas (718) 768-1156

Brooklyn Bushwick Abbey **P** 22 Wyckoff Ave 11237 (Mail to: 22 Wyckoff Ave 11237)

Brooklyn Christ Church Bay Ridge **P** (179) 7301 Ridge Blvd 11209 (Mail to: 7301 Ridge Blvd 11209-2194) Joel Ireland (718) 745-3698

Brooklyn Christ Church Cobble Hill **P** (116) 180 Kane St 11231-3760 (Mail to: 180 Kane St 11231) Ronald Lau Anthony Bowen (718) 624-0083

Brooklyn Church of Calvary & St Cyprian **P** (246) 966 Bushwick Ave 11221 (Mail to: 966 Bushwick Ave 11221-3740) Charles Holdbrooke (347) 663-8120

Brooklyn Church of St Luke and St Matthew **P** (439) 520 Clinton Ave 11238-2211 (Mail to: 520 Clinton Ave 11238-2211) Edwin Chase (718) 638-0686

Brooklyn Church of St Mark **P** (3416) 1417 Union St 11213 (Mail to: 1417 Union St 11213-4337) Kino Vitet (718) 756-6607

Brooklyn Church of St Thomas **P** (543) 1405 Bushwick Ave 11207-1408 (Mail to: 1405 Bushwick Ave 11207-1408) Sully Guillaume-Sam (718) 452-2332

Brooklyn Church of the Ascension **P** (161) 127 Kent St 11222 (Mail to: 127 Kent St 11222-2103) (718) 383-5402

Brooklyn Church of the Holy Apostles **P** (116) 612 Greenwood Ave 11218 (Mail to: 612 Greenwood Ave 11218-1302) Sarah Kooperkamp (718) 871-1615

Brooklyn Church of the Holy Spirit **M** (115) 81-17 Bay Pkwy 11214 (Mail to: 8117 Bay Pkwy 11214-2513) (718) 837-0412

Brooklyn Church of the Nativity **M** (214) 121 Amersfort Pl 11210-2321 (Mail to: 1099 Ocean Ave 11230-1905) Kimberlee Auletta (718) 859-8654

Brooklyn Church The Epiphany & St Simon **P** (147) 2910 Avenue M 11210 (Mail to: 2910 Avenue M 11210-4617) Allen George (718) 258-1166

Brooklyn Emmanuel Episcopal Church **P** (206) 2635 E 23rd St 11235 (Mail to: 2635 E 23rd St 11235-2825) (718) 934-0189

Brooklyn Grace Episcopal Church **P** (1055) 254 Hicks St 11201 (Mail to: 254 Hicks St 11201-4097) Stephen Muncie Julie Hoplamazian (718) 624-1850

Brooklyn Iglesia de la Santa Cruz **M** (20) 172 St Nicholas Ave 11237 (Mail to: 172 St Nicholas Ave 11237) (917) 507-7088

Brooklyn St Albans Episcopal Church **P** (1576) 9408 Farragut Rd 11236-2028 (Mail to: 9408 Farragut Rd 11236-2028) George Bonner (718) 342-5215

Brooklyn St Andrew Episcopal Church **P** (419) 4917 4th Ave 11220-1819 (Mail to: 4917 4th Ave 11220-1819) Francisco Rodriguez-Padron (718) 439-6056

Brooklyn St Ann and the Holy Trinity Church **P** (111) 157 Montague St 11201-3587 (Mail to: 157 Montague St 11201-3587) John Denaro John Denaro Katherine Salisbury (718) 875-6960

Brooklyn St Augustines Episcopal Church **P** (2180) 4301 Ave D 11203 (Mail to: 4301 Avenue D 11203-5723) Howard Williams (718) 629-0930

Brooklyn St Barnabas Episcopal Church **P** (476) 417 Elton St 11208 (Mail to: 417 Elton St 11208-2129) Sylvester Taylor

Brooklyn St Bartholomews Church **P** (109) 1227 Pacific St 11216 (Mail to: PO Box 160297 11216) Pierre Damus (718) 467-8750

Brooklyn St Gabriels Episcopal Church **P** (1121) 331 Hawthorne St 11225-5909 (Mail to: 331 Hawthorne St 11225-5909) Edmund Alleyne (718) 774-5248

Brooklyn St Georges Episcopal Church **P** (1174) 800 Marcy Ave 11216 (Mail to: 800 Marcy Ave 11216-1513) Glenworth Miles (718) 789-6036

Brooklyn St Johns Park Slope **P** (200) 139 St Johns Pl 11217-3401 (Mail to: 139 Saint Johns Pl 11217-3401) Shelley Mcdade (718) 783-3928

Brooklyn St Marys Episcopal Church **P** (91) 230 Classon Ave 11205-1441 (Mail to: 230 Classon Ave 11205-1441) Gerald Keucher (718) 638-2090

Brooklyn St Pauls Episcopal Church **P** (312) 199 Carroll St 11231-4203 (Mail to: 199 Carroll St 11231-4203) Peter Cullen Nell Archer Robert Griffith (718) 625-4126

Brooklyn St Philips Episcopal Church **P** (519) 334 MacDonough St 11233-1704 (Mail to: 265 Decatur St 11233-1704) Carver Israel (718) 778-8700

Brooklyn St Philip's Episcopal Church **P** (64) 1072 80th St 11228 (Mail to: 1072 80th St 11228-2620) (718) 745-2505

Brooklyn St Stephen & St Martin Church **P** (241) PO Box 210160 11221-0160 (Mail to: PO Box 210160 11221-0160) Audley Donaldson (718) 453-0651

Brooklyn St. Paul's Episcopal Church-In-The-Village-Of-Flatbush **P** (915) 157 St Pauls Pl 11226-2708 (Mail to: 157 Saint Pauls Pl 11226-2708) Sheldon Hamblin (718) 282-2100

Cambria Heights St Davids Episcopal Church **P** (517) 117-35 235th St 11411 (Mail to: 11735 235th St 11411-1821) Joshua Nisbett (718) 528-2095

Carle Place St Marys Episcopal Church **P** (71) 252 Rushmore Ave 11514-1431 (Mail to: 252 Rushmore Ave 11514-1431) Peter Lai (516) 333-2290

Ctr Moriches Church of St John the Baptist **P** (195) 33 Railroad Ave 11934 (Mail to: PO Box 602 11934-0602) (631) 878-0022

Central Islip Church of the Messiah **M** (217) 53 Carleton Ave 11722 (Mail to: PO Box 161 11722-0161) Frank Elcock (631) 234-5161

Cold Spring Harbor St John's Church **P** (1185) 1675 Route 25A 11724 (Mail to: PO Box 266 11724-0266) Jesse Lebus Frederic Miller (516) 692-6368

Corona Grace Episcopal Church **P** (64) 34-34 98th St 11368 (Mail to: 3434 98th St 11368-1028)

Deer Park St Patricks Episcopal Church **P** (141) 305 Carlls Path 11729-5415 (Mail to: 305 Carlls Path 11729-5415) (631) 242-7530

Douglaston Zion Episcopal Church **P** (282) 243-01 Northern Blvd 11363 (Mail to: 24301 Northern Blvd 11363) Lindsay Lunnum Lynne Grifo (718) 225-0466

East Elmhurst Church of the Resurrection **P** (451) 100-17 32nd Ave 11369 (Mail to: 100-17 32nd Ave 11369-2501) Gilberto Hinds (718) 899-5227

East Hampton St Lukes Episcopal Church **P** (552) 18 James Ln 11937 (Mail to: 18 James Lane 11937-2796) Denis Brunelle (631) 329-0990

East Hampton St Peter Episcopal Summer Chapel **SC** 463 Old Stone Hwy 11937 (Mail to: 18 James Ln 11937-2710) (631) 329-0990

East Setauke Caroline Church of Brookhaven **P** (697) 1 Dyke Rd 11733-3014 (Mail to: 1 Dyke Rd 11733-3014) Richard Visconti Farrell Graves (631) 941-4245

Elmhurst St James Episcopal Church **P** (105) 84-07 Broadway 11373 (Mail to: 8407 Broadway 11373-5727) Winfred Vergara (718) 592-2555

✢ **Far Rockaway** Bishop Charles Maclean Nursing Home **Other** 1711 Brookhaven Ave

11691-4406 (Mail to: 1711 Brookhaven Ave 11691-4406) (718) 869-8022

Far Rockaway St Joseph Episcopal Chapel **SC** 327 Beach 19th St 11691-4423 (Mail to: 327 Beach 19th St 11691-4423) Cecily Broderick y Guerra Richard Liew Barbara Jean Maxwell (718) 869-7320

Farmingdale St Thomas Episcopal Church **P** (217) 298 Conklin St 11735-2609 (Mail to: 298 Conklin St 11735-2609) Christine Petersen-Snyder (516) 752-9254

Fishers Island St Johns Episcopal Church **SC** Oriental Ave 06390 (Mail to: PO Box 505 06390-0505) Michael Spencer (631) 788-7497

Floral Park St Elisabeths Episcopal Church **P** (104) 6 Harvard St 11001-2822 (Mail to: 6 Harvard St 11001-2822) T Abigail Murphy (516) 354-6867

Floral Park St Thomas Episcopal Church **P** (132) 6 Commonwealth Blvd 11001-4141 (Mail to: 6 Commonwealth Blvd 11001-4141) T Abigail Murphy (516) 354-6866

Flushing St Georges Episcopal Church **P** (1166) 135-32 38th Ave 11354 (Mail to: 13532 38th Ave 11354-4483) Wilfredo Benitez Songling Xie (718) 359-1171

Flushing St John's Episcopal Church **P** (169) 149-49 Sanford Ave 11355-1038 (Mail to: 14949 Sanford Ave 11355-1038) Dario Palasi (718) 961-1333

Forest Hills St Lukes Episcopal Church **P** (270) 85 Greenway S 11375 (Mail to: 85 Greenway S 11375-5942) Thomas Reese William Doubleday (718) 268-6021

Freeport Church of the Transfiguration **P** (386) Pine St & S Long Beach Ave 11520-3433 (Mail to: 69 South Long Beach Ave 11520) Raymond Wilson (516) 379-1230

✠ **Garden City** Cathedral of the Incarnation **O** (1106) 50 Cathedral Ave 11530-4435 (Mail to: 50 Cathedral Avenue 11530) Michael Sniffen Michael Delaney Steve Foster John Greco Bruce Griffith (516) 746-2955

Garden City Christ Episcopal Church **P** (118) 33 Jefferson St 11530-3929 (Mail to: 33 Jefferson St 11530-3929) Matthew Oprendek (516) 775-2626

Garden City Good Shepherd Episcopal Chapel **CC** 65 4th St 11530-4313 (Mail to: 65 4th St 11530-4313) John Mcginty

Glen Cove St Pauls Episcopal Church **P** (103) 28 Highland Rd 11542-2630 (Mail to: 28 Highland Rd 11542-2698) Shawn Williams (516) 676-0015

Great Neck All Saints Episcopal Church **P** (110) 855 Middle Neck Rd 11024-1441 (Mail to: 855 Middle Neck Rd 11024-1441) Joseph Pae (516) 482-5392

Great River Emmanuel Episcopal Church **HC** (104) 320 Great River Rd 11739-0571 (Mail to: 320 Great River Rd PO Box 586 11739-3010)

Lauren McLeavey

Greenport Church of the Holy Trinity **P** (111) 768 Main St 11944 (Mail to: PO Box 502 11944-0502) Patrick McNamara (631) 477-0855

Hampton Bays Church of St Marys **P** (425) 165 Ponquogue Ave 11946-0701 (Mail to: PO Box 782 11946-0701) Philip Hubbard (631) 728-0776

Hempstead St Georges Episcopal Church **P** (477) 319 Front St 11550-4024 (Mail to: 319 Front St 11550-4024) Patrick Rawlins (516) 483-2771

Hempstead St Johns Episcopal Church **P** (168) 536 S Franklin St 11550-7622 (Mail to: 536 S Franklin St 11550-7622) Lynn Collins

Hewlett Trinity St Johns Epis Church **P** (651) 1142 Broadway 11557 (Mail to: 1142 Broadway 11557-2395) John Ballard (516) 374-1415

Hicksville Holy Trinity Episcopal Church **P** (337) 130 Jerusalem Ave 11801-4918 (Mail to: 130 Jerusalem Ave 11801-4996) Joan Grimm (516) 931-1920

Hollis St Gabriels Episcopal Church **P** (313) 196-10 Woodhull Ave 11423 (Mail to: 19610 Woodhull Ave 11423-2984) Terence Lee (718) 465-2876

Huntington St Johns Episcopal Church **P** (368) 12 Prospect St 11743-3375 (Mail to: 12 Prospect St 11743-3375) Duncan Burns John Morrison (631) 427-1752

Islip St Marks Episcopal Church **P** (1276) 754 Montauk Hwy 11751-3696 (Mail to: 754 Montauk Hwy 11751-3696) Richard Simpson Lauren McLeavey (631) 581-4950

Jackson Heights St Marks Church **P** (122) 33-50 82nd Street 11372-1499 (Mail to: 3350 82nd St 11372-1436) Antonio Checo Jason Moskal

Jamaica Church of St James the Less **P** (640) 107-66 Merrick Blvd 11433 (Mail to: 107-66 Merrick Blvd 11433) Dennison Richards (718) 262-0535

Jamaica Grace Episcopal Church **P** (323) 155-24 90th Ave 11432-3825 (Mail to: 15524 90th Ave 11432-3825) Darryl James Charles Nelson (718) 291-4901

Jamaica St Stephens Episcopal Church **P** (204) 89-26 168th St 11432-4334 (Mail to: 8926 168 Street 11432) Donovan Leys Charles Nelson

Kew Gardens Church of the Resurrection **P** (156) 85-09 118th St 11415-2907 (Mail to: 85-09 118th St 11415-2907) (718) 847-2649

Lindenhurst St Boniface Episcopal Church **P** (180) 100 46th St 11757-2050 (Mail to: 100 46th St 11757-2051) Peter Lai (631) 957-2666

Locust Valley St John's Church of Lattingtown **P** (515) 325 Lattingtown Rd 11542 (Mail to: 325 Lattingtown Rd 11560-1022) Mark Fitzhugh (516) 671-3226

Long Beach St James of Jerusalem Episcopal Church **P** (120) 220 W Penn St 11561-3933 (Mail to: 220 W Penn St 11561-3933) John King (516) 432-1080

Long Island City All Saints Episcopal Church **P** (158) 4312 46th St 11104-2002 (Mail to: 4312 46th St 11104-2002) Joseph Jerome (718) 784-8031

Manhasset Christ Episcopal Church **P** (345) 1351 Northern Blvd 11030-3007 (Mail to: 1351 Northern Blvd 11030-3007) David Sibley (516) 627-2184

Massapequa Grace Episcopal Church **P** (323) 23 Cedar Shore Dr 11758 (Mail to: 23 Cedar Shore Dr 11758-7318) Walter Hillebrand (516) 798-1122

Mastic Beach St Andrews Episcopal Church **M** (38) PO Box 488 250 Neighborhood Rd 11951-3623 (Mail to: PO Box 488 11951-0488) John Purchal (631) 281-9133

Mattituck Church of the Redeemer **P** (155) 13225 Sound Ave 11952 (Mail to: PO Box 906 11952) Edward Blatz Patrick McNamara (631) 298-4277

Medford St Marks Episcopal Church **P** (60) 208 Jamaica Ave 11763-3290 (Mail to: 208 Jamaica Ave 11763-3290) (631) 475-7406

New Hyde Park St Philip and St James Church **M** (25) 432 Lakeville Rd 11042-1121 (Mail to: 432 Lakeville Rd 11042-1121) Edwin Chase

New York St Andrews-by-the-Sea **SC** (35) 300 W End Ave # 8b 10023-8156 (Mail to: 100 W 89th St Apt 2A 10024-1933) (631) 583-8382

North Bellmore St Francis Episcopal Church **P** 1692 Bellmore Ave 11710-5530 (Mail to: 1692 Bellmore Ave 11710-5530) Mark Genszler

Northport Trinity Episcopal Church **P** (268) 130 Main St 11768-1723 (Mail to: 130 Main St 11768-1784) Michael Bartolomeo (631) 261-7670

Oakdale St Johns Episcopal Church **M** (11) 1 Berard Blvd 11769-1701 (Mail to: 1 Berard Blvd 11769-1701) (631) 589-0213

Oceanside St Andrew Episcopal Church **P** (30) 50 Anchor Ave 11572-3031 (Mail to: 50 Anchor Ave 11572-3031) (516) 536-7677

Oyster Bay Christ Episcopal Church **P** (444) 55 East Main St 11771-2400 (Mail to: 55 East Main St 11771-2493) (516) 922-6377

Patchogue St Pauls Episcopal Church **P** (114) 31 Rider Ave 11772-3915 (Mail to: 31 Rider Ave 11772-3999) Elisabeth Tunney (631) 475-3078

Plainview St Margarets Church **P** (190) 1000 Washington Ave 11803-1831 (Mail to: 1000 Washington Ave 11803-1831) Jennifer Andrews-Weckerly (516) 692-5268

Prt Jefferson Christ Episcopal Church **P** (130) 127 Barnum Ave 11777-1621 (Mail to: 127 Barnum Ave 11777-1621) Anthony Di Lorenzo (631) 473-0273

Prt Washington St Stephens Episcopal Church **P** (452) 9 Carlton Ave 11050-3105 (Mail to: 9 Carlton Ave 11050-3105) Gary Parker

Queens Vlg St Josephs Episcopal Church **P** (926) 9910 217th Ln 11429-1214 (Mail to: 9910 217th Ln 11429-1214) Kassinda Ellis (718) 465-4193

Quogue Church of the Atonement **SC** 17 Quogue St 11959 (Mail to: PO Box 244 11959-0244) (631) 653-6798

Riverhead Grace Episcopal Church **P** (177) 573 Roanoke Ave 11901-2760 (Mail to: 573 Roanoke Ave 11901-2760) Mary Garde (631) 727-3900

Rockville Ct The Church of the Ascension **P** (510) 71 N Village Ave 11570-4605 (Mail to: 71 N Village Ave 11570-4605) Kevin Morris (516) 766-0693

Ronkonkoma St Marys Episcopal Church **P** (696) 315 Lake Shore Rd 11779-3180 (Mail to: 315 Lake Shore Rd 11779-3147) Elizabeth O'Callaghan (631) 588-1888

Roosevelt St Pauls Episcopal Church **M** (129) 25 W Centennial Ave 11575-2028 (Mail to: 18 W Centennial Ave 11575-2029) (516) 546-2754

Rosedale St Peters Episcopal Church **P** (245) 13728 244th St 11422-1828 (Mail to: 13728 244th St 11422-1828) Steve Foster (718) 528-1356

Roslyn Trinity Episcopal Church **P** (148) 1579 Northern Blvd 11576-1103 (Mail to: 1579 Northern Blvd 11576-1137) Margaret Peckham Clark (516) 621-7925

Sag Harbor Christ Episcopal Church **P** (142) 5 Hampton St 11963-4242 (Mail to: PO Box 570 11963-0012) Karen Campbell (631) 725-0128

Saint Albans St Alban the Martyr Church **P** (229) 11642 Farmers Blvd 11412-3026 (Mail to: 11642 Farmers Blvd 11412-3026) Kirtley Yearwood (718) 528-1891

Saint James St James Episcopal Church **P** (458) 490 Route 25a 11780-1953 (Mail to: 490 Route 25a 11780-1953) Raewynne Whiteley (631) 584-5560

Sayville St Ann's Episcopal Church **HC** (682) 262 Middle Rd 11782-3242 (Mail to: 2620 Middle Road 11782-3221) Tina Britt (631) 589-6522

Sea Cliff St Lukes Episcopal Church **P** (230) 253 Glen Avenue 11579-1544 (Mail to: 253 Glen Ave 11579-1544) David Macdonald (516) 676-4222

Seaford St Michael & All Angels **P** (46) 2197 Jackson Ave 11783-2607 (Mail to: 2197 Jackson Ave 11783-2607) (516) 785-3762

Selden St Cuthberts Episcopal Church **P** (63) 18 Magnolia Pl 11784-2902 (Mail to: PO Box 1367 11784-0995) John Madden (631) 475-4555

Shelter Island St Marys Church **P** (137) 26 St Marys Rd 11964 (Mail to: PO Box 1660 11964-1660) Charles Mccarron (631) 749-0770

Shoreham St Anselms Episcopal Church **P** (506) § 4 Woodville Road 11786 (Mail to: PO Box 606 11786-0606) Lyndon Shakespeare (631) 744-7730

Smithtown St Thomas of Canterbury Church **P** (641) 29 Brookside Drive 11787-3495 (Mail to: 90 Edgewater Ave 11787-3495) Lawrence De Lion Judith Carrick

South Ozone Park St Johns Church **P** (342) 133-04 109th Ave 11420 (Mail to: 13304 109th Ave 11420-1703) Frederick Opare-Addo (718) 529-0366

Southampton St Johns Episcopal Church **P** (481) No 100 S Main St 11968-4804 (Mail to: PO Box 5068 11969-5068) Stephen McWhorter

Sprngfld Gdnd St Johns Episcopal Church **P** (113) 13767 Belknap St 11413-2619 (Mail to: 13767 Belknap St 11413-2619) (718) 525-1444

Stony Brook All Souls Episcopal Church **M** (82) 61 Main Street 11790-1816 (Mail to: 10 Mill Pond Rd 11790-1816) (631) 751-0034

Valley Stream Holy Trinity Episcopal Church **P** (85) 87 7th St 11581-1214 (Mail to: 87 7th St 11581-1290) Jon Richardson (516) 825-2903

Wading River St Lukes Chapel **SC** 408 N Side Rd 11792 (Mail to: PO Box 487 11792) (631) 929-4325

Wantagh Church of St Jude **P** (626) 3606 Lufberry Ave 11793-3031 (Mail to: 3606 Lufberry Ave 11793-3031) Christopher Hofer Maxine Barnett (516) 221-2505

Westbury Church of the Advent **P** (344) 555 Advent St 11590-1309 (Mail to: 555 Advent St 11590-1309) (516) 333-0081

Westhampton Beach St Marks Episcopal Church **P** (325) 40 Main Street 11978-2673 (Mail to: PO Box 887 11978-0887) Michael Ralph (631) 288-2111

Whitestone Grace Episcopal Church **P** (122) 14-15 Clintonville Street 11357 (Mail to: 1415 Clintonville St 11357-1825) Brian Blayer (718) 767-6305

Williston Pk Resurrection **P** (59) 147 Campbell Ave 11596-1606 (Mail to: 147 Campbell Ave 11596-1606) Christina Van Liew (516) 746-5527

Woodhaven All Saints Episcopal Church **P** (189) 85-45 96th Street 11421 (Mail to: 85-45 96th Street 11421) Norman Whitmire (718) 849-2352

Woodside St Paul Episcopal Church **M** (39) 39-04 61st St 11377 (Mail to: PO Box 23 11377-0023) Anandsekar Manuel (718) 672-8565

Yaphank St Andrew Episcopal Church **P** (126) 244 E Main St 11980-9656 (Mail to: PO Box 249 11980-0249) John Purchal (631) 924-5083

NON-PAROCHIAL CLERGY

Ackerson CG *ret* Mastic Beach NY
Amend AE *ret* North Fort Myers FL
Anthony LL *ret* Queens Village NY
Baynes LC *ret*
Belasco EA *ret dcn* Massapequa NY
Bell WA *ret* Winston Salem NC
Belmontes ML *ret* Bay Shore NY
Betit JD Sutton MA
Blunt HE *ret* Brooklyn NY
Bramble PWD *ret* Brooklyn NY
Brandt RG Port Saint Lucie FL

Brewer RF *ret* Whitehall NY
Brown PG *ret* Valley Stream NY
Busler GW *ret* Westhampton Beach NY
Butler MH *ret* Hendersonville NC
Cabrero-Oliver JM *ret*
Campbell RM *ret* Louisville OH
Carmiencke BC *ret* Bohemia NY
Casparian PF *ret* Oyster Bay NY
Cayless FA *ret* Chapel Hill NC
Chan HA *ret* Kennesaw GA
Chin ML *dcn* Fresh Meadows NY
Coleman B *ret* Hollis NY
Crain LB *dcn* Brightwaters NY
Creamer FB *ret* Waldoboro ME
Cross SO *ret* New York NY
Crowson SF *ret* Leeds ME
David CL *ret* Salem NY
Deblasio DL Lindenhurst NY
Duncan SP Brooklyn NY
Duncan VD New York NY
Durbidge AJ Garden City NY
Edmiston AJ *ret* Vero Beach FL
Edwards J *ret* Lewisburg PA
Farrell JT *ret* Yonkers NY
Foster ML *ret* New York NY
Foster S *ret* Brooklyn NY
Fuller WH *dcn* North Bellmore NY
Gilbert P *ret* Mount Pleasant SC
Gill-Lopez JH *ret* New York NY
Godfrey WC *ret* Greenport NY
Golden PP *ret* Brooklyn NY
Goorahoo EB *ret* South Ozone Park NY
Gunthorpes A *ret* Brooklyn NY
Hamblin JL New York NY
Hamilton PEC *ret* Hamden NY
Harte KA *dcn*
Haynes WE *ret* New York NY
Henry LI *ret* Brooklyn NY
Hollett RT *ret* Chestertown MD
Holtkamp PJ *ret* Jackson Heights NY
Hoopes DB *ret* New York NY
Hughs LC *ret* Danbury CT
Huntley SM Port Washington NY
Hutchings DW *ret* San Antonio TX
Jackson RF *dcn* Brooklyn NY
James RA *ret* Homosassa FL
Johnson KW *ret* Maspeth NY
Johnston FN *ret* Onset MA
Jones AE *dcn* Huntington NY
Jones EU *ret* Brooklyn NY
Kertland GE *dcn* Garden City NY
Kim YGN *ret* Astoria NY
Koski HGP *ret* Gainesville FL
Kraft HB *ret* Jamaica NY
Krantz JH *ret* Massapequa NY
Krantz SC *ret* Westbury NY
Lai PC College Point NY
Lam P *ret* Waldwick NJ
Lam VP Bay Shore NY
Larsen PM *ret* Muscle Shoals AL
Latham DC *ret* Ballston Spa NY

Lee TC *ret* Pittsboro NC
Lester EW *ret* Fort Myers FL
Lewis LA *ret* Falls Church VA
Lorenson RL *dcn* Garden City NY
Lorenz C *ret dcn* Richmond Hill NY
Lowry DB *ret* New Orleans LA
Luttrell JS *ret* Downingtown PA
Lutz RH *ret* Bay Village OH
MacLean PD *ret* Colchester VT
Martino RM *ret dcn* Massapequa NY
Martin-Rhodes LR *dcn* Wesley Chapel FL
Mayhood GW
McCall RD *ret* Bloomington IN
McDermott JP Montreal QC
McDowell HC *ret* Medford MA
Melton HL Bronxville NY
Merz J Brooklyn NY
Meyer JA *ret* Sheridan WY
Mills JE Santa Monica CA
Moise J *ret* Brooklyn NY
Montrose RS *dcn* Westbury NY
Mooney NOC *ret* Oakdale NY
Moreau JR *ret* Jamaica NY
Moreno JS Brentwood NY
Murray LSE Brooklyn NY
Mushorn RC *ret* Cleveland TN
Nedelka JJ *ret* Miller Place NY
Newbery CG *ret* Berkeley CA
Nuamah R Brooklyn NY
Occhiuto JJ
O'Steen JA *ret* Lewisville TX
Parsons BE *ret* Sedona AZ
Perrin CL *dcn* Jamaica NY
Peverley SR *ret* Babylon NY
Plank DB *ret* Hampton NH
Plested RWH *ret* San Antonio TX
Powers CH *ret* Brooklyn NY
Pratt EW *ret* Lecanto FL

Price DL *ret* Brewster MA
Quiroga LA *ret* Miami FL
Ramirez-Miller GC *ret* New York NY
Raskopf RW *ret* Oconomowoc WI
Reeves JW *ret* White Plains NY
Ritter N Westfield NJ
Ross RW *ret* Punta Gorda FL
Schiff PT *ret* Miller Place NY
Schnabel CE *ret* Ridge NY
Schwarz RL *ret* North Charleston SC
Sellery D Salisbury CT
Shackleford RN *ret* Jonesborough TN
Shamhart LR *ret* New York NY
Sigamoney C
Spellers S Boston MA
Spencer AD *ret* Hobe Sound FL
Spencer AJ Hobe Sound FL
Stoute BL Elmont NY
Sullivan B *ret* Hampton Bays NY
Swartsfager AK *ret* Olympia WA
Tatro MA Brooklyn NY
Taylor LH *ret* South Ozone Park NY
Tillitt JL *ret* Redlands CA
Trillos A Huntington NY
VanCooten-Webster JE *dcn* Brooklyn NY
Von Gonten KP *ret* Ellendale DE
Von Roeschlaub WK *ret* Port Washington NY
Walker JE *ret* Bellport NY
Walton WDH *ret* Mount Sinai NY
Walworth JC *ret* Highland Park NJ
Wancura PF *ret* Shelter Island Heights NY
Watson SBJ Richmond VA
Waweru CG Fort Hood TX
Waweru DG Harker Heights TX
Weaver EJ *ret* Northport NY
Williams TM *ret* Woodhaven NY
Young BOD *ret* Saint Albans NY

DIOCESE OF LOS ANGELES
(PROVINCE VIII)
Comprises southern California, except San Diego
DIO OFC 840 Echo Pk Ave Los Angeles CA 90026 (MAIL Box 512164 Los Angeles CA 90051-0164)
TEL (213) 482-2040   FAX (213) 482-5304
E-MAIL communications@ladiocese.org   WEB www.ladiocese.org
The Bishop of the Protestant Episcopal Church in the Diocese of Los Angeles, a Corporation Sole

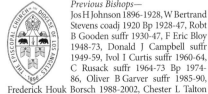

Previous Bishops—
Jos H Johnson 1896-1928, W Bertrand Stevens coadj 1920 Bp 1928-47, Robt B Gooden suffr 1930-47, F Eric Bloy 1948-73, Donald J Campbell suffr 1949-59, Ivol I Curtis suffr 1960-64, C Rusack suffr 1964-73 Bp 1974-86, Oliver B Garver suffr 1985-90, Frederick Houk Borsch 1988-2002, Chester L Talton suffr 1991-2010

Bishop—Rt Rev J Jon Bruno (953) (Dio 1 Feb 2002)

Bishop Suffragan—Rt Rev Diane Jardine Bruce (1044) (Dio 15 May 2010)

Sec Conv Cn MJ Wylie; *Treas* Rev KM Smith; *Ex for Ops* Cn D Tumilty; *CFO* Canon T Forbath; *Chanc* TBD; *Cn Form/Deploy* Rev Cn J Satorius; *COM* Very Rev Cn M Bamberger & Cn JB White; *Sch* Dr S Beeks; *Missions* C Bangao

Stand Comm—Cler: Pres M McCarthy R Nyback A Lopex M Archer; *Lay:* B Ferrell, L Headley P Brierley JD Larsen

Dio Conv: 2-3 December 2016 Ontario, CA

PARISHES, MISSIONS, AND CLERGY

Alhambra Holy Trinity & St Benedict Episcopal **P** (219) 412 No Garfield Ave 91801 (Mail to: 412 N Garfield Ave 91801-2498) Brent Quines (626) 282-9118

Altadena St Marks Episcopal Church **P** (623) 1014 E Altadena Dr 91001-2041 (Mail to: 1014 E Altadena Dr 91001-2041) Carri Grindon Graham Berry Elizabeth Hooper Joseph Lane (626) 798-6747

Anaheim St Michaels Episcopal Church **M** (2376) 311 W South St 92805-4517 (Mail to: 311 W South St 92805-4598) (714) 535-4654

Apple Valley St Timothy's Episcopal Church **P** (259) 15757 St Timothy Rd 92307-2554 (Mail to: 15757 Saint Timothy Rd 92307-2554) Nicholas Carpenter Jeffrey Martinhauk

Arcadia Church of the Transfiguration **P** (228) 1881 S 1st Ave 91006-4618 (Mail to: 1881 S 1st Ave 91006-4618) Julie Bryant (626) 445-3340

Barstow St Paul's Episcopal Church **M** (91) 512 E Williams St 92311-2941 (Mail to: PO Box 726 92312-0726) Emilie Bush (760) 256-1624

Beaumont St Stephens Church Episcopal **M** (173) 225 E 8th St 92223-5903 (Mail to: 225 E 8th St 92223-5903) William Dunn (951) 845-1358

Beverly Hills All Saints Episcopal Parish **P** (1702) 504 N Camden Dr 90210-3299 (Mail to: 504 N Camden Dr 90210-3299) Andrew Barnett Allison English Stephen Huber David Norgard Scott Taylor (310) 275-0123

Big Bear Lake St Columbas Episcopal Church **M** (193) (Mail to: PO Box 1681 92315-1681) Stuart Swann (909) 866-7239

Buena Park St Joseph Episcopal Church **P** (91) 8300 Valley View St 90620-2738 (Mail to: 8300 Valley View St 90620-2738) Matthew Parker (714) 828-8950

Burbank St Jude's Church **P** (95) 111 S 6th St 91501-2118 (Mail to: 111 S 6th St 91501-2118) Charles Mitchell (818) 842-7461

Camarillo St Columbas Church **P** (336) 1251 Las Posas Rd 93010-3001 (Mail to: 1251 Las Posas Rd 93010-3001) Gregory Larkin (805) 482-8831

Claremont St Ambrose Episcopal Church **P** (175) 830 W Bonita Ave 91711-4113 (Mail to: 830 W Bonita Ave 91711-4113) Deborah McKean George Silides (909) 626-7170

Compton St Timothys Episcopal Church **P** (130) 312 S Oleander Ave 90220 (Mail to: 312 S Oleander Ave 90220-3118) George Okusi (310) 638-6319

Corona St John's Church **P** (382) 526 Magnolia Ave 92879-3113 (Mail to: PO Box 152 92878-

0152) Arthur Wolford (951) 737-1363

Corona Dl Mar Saint Michael and All Angels Parish **P** (508) 3233 Pacific View Dr 92625-1109 (Mail to: 3233 Pacific View Dr 92625-1109) Peter Haynes Jefferson Hulet (949) 644-0463

Costa Mesa St John The Divine Church **P** (114) 183 E Bay St 92627-2145 (Mail to: 183 E Bay St 92627-2145) Barbara Stewart Sue Beck Philip Devaul (949) 548-2237

Covina Holy Trinity Episcopal Church **P** (328) 100 Third Ave 91723 (Mail to: PO Box 4195 91723-1904) Steven De Muth Mark Stuart Jared Tucker (626) 967-3939

Downey St Marks Episcopal Church **P** (99) § 10354 Downey Ave 90241-2512 (Mail to: 10354 Downey Ave 90241-2597) Sharon Sheffield (562) 862-3268

El Monte Immanuel Episcopal Church **M** (371) 4366 Santa Anita Ave 91731-1606 (Mail to: 4366 Santa Anita Ave 91731-1606) Hector Limatu (626) 448-1908

El Segundo St Michael the Archangel Parish **P** (141) 361 Richmond St 90245-3729 (Mail to: 361 Richmond St 90245-3729) Dina Ferguson (310) 322-2589

Encino St Nicholas Episcopal Church **P** (310) No 17114 Ventura Blvd 91316-4003 (Mail to: 17114 Ventura Blvd 91316-4003) Michael Cooper (818) 788-4486

Fillmore Trinity Episcopal Church **P** (97) 600 Saratoga St 93016-0306 (Mail to: PO Box 306 93016-0306) Lawrence Brown Cynthia Jew (805) 524-1910

Fullerton Emmanuel Episcopal Church **P** (703) 1145 W Valencia Mes 92833-2218 (Mail to: 1145 W Valencia Mesa Dr 92833-2218) Arthur Bethancourt Lynda Crow (714) 879-8070

Fullerton St Andrew's Episcopal Church **P** (306) 1231 E Chapman Ave 92831-3908 (Mail to: 1231 E Chapman Ave 92831-3908) Beth Arnold (714) 870-4350

Garden Grove St Anselm of Canterbury Episcopal Ch **P** (192) 13091 Galway St 92844-1633 (Mail to: 13091 Galway St 92844-1633) Jeffrey Clawson (714) 537-0604

Gardena Church of the Holy Communion **M** (80) 1160 W 141st St 90247-2220 (Mail to: 1160 W 141st St 90247-2220) Arthur Toro (310) 324-1441

Glendale Iglesia de la Magdalena **M** (144) 1011 S Verdugo Rd 91205-3831 (Mail to: 1011 S Verdugo Rd 91205-3831) Roberto Martinez-Morales (818) 243-8670

Glendale St Marks Episcopal Church **P** (580) 1020 N Brand Blvd 91202-2907 (Mail to: 1020 N Brand Blvd 91202-2907) Mark Weitzel Susie Kenny Andrea Maier Mark Weitzel (818) 240-3860

Glendora Grace Episcopal Church **P** (302) 555 E Mountain View 91741-2764 (Mail to: 555 E Mountain View Ave 91741-2764) Susan

Scranton (626) 335-3171

Granada Hills St Andrew & Charles Episcopal **P** (305) 16651 Rinaldi St 91344-3632 (Mail to: 16651 Rinaldi St 91344-3632) Gregory Frost (818) 366-7542

Hacienda Hgts St Thomas Episcopal Church **M** (287) 15694 Tetley St 91745-4543 (Mail to: 15694 Tetley St 91745-4543) Joshua Chan-Foo Ng Roger Rose (626) 330-7649

Hawthorne St Georges Episcopal Church **M** (57) 4679 W El Segundo Blvd 90250-4349 (Mail to: PO Box C 90251-0165) (310) 324-1617

Hermosa Beach St Cross Episcopal Church **P** (1052) No 1818 Monterey Blvd 90254-2906 (Mail to: 1818 Monterey Blvd 90254-2906) Rachel Nyback Gregory Brown (310) 376-8989

Hesperia St Hilarys Episcopal Church **M** (86) 11305 Hesperia Rd 92345-2170 (Mail to: 11305 Hesperia Rd 92345-2170) (760) 244-6444

Huntington Beach St Wilfrid of York Episcopal Church **P** (556) 18631 Chapel Ln 92646-1831 (Mail to: 18631 Chapel Ln 92646-1831) Michael Archer Karen Maurer (714) 962-7512

Huntington Park St Clement's Church **M** (283) 6909 Rugby Ave 90255-4721 (Mail to: 6909 Rugby Ave 90255-4721) (323) 587-1277

Inglewood Church of the Holy Faith **P** (174) 260 N Locust St 90301-1204 (Mail to: 260 N Locust St 90301-1204) Kathryn Derose Francisco Garcia Becky Tinnon (310) 674-7700

Irvine St Andrew Episcopal Church **M** (281) 4400 Barranca Pkwy 92604-4739 (Mail to: 4400 Barranca Pkwy 92604-4739) Peter Browning Richard Whittaker (949) 559-4699

Isla Vista St Michaels University Epis Church **M** (80) 6586 Picasso Rd 93117-4651 (Mail to: 6586 Picasso Rd 93117-4651) Scott Claassen Toni Stuart (805) 968-2712

La Canada St Georges Episcopal Church **P** (216) 808 Foothill Blvd 91011-3336 (Mail to: 808 Foothill Blvd 91011-3336) Amy Pringle Anthony Keller (818) 790-3323

La Crescenta St Luke's of the Mountains Church **M** (24) 2563 Foothill Blvd 91214-3508 (Mail to: 2563 Foothill Blvd 91214-3508) Jorge Enrique Pallares Arellano Kirby Smith (818) 248-3639

La Verne St John's Episcopal Church **M** (240) 4745 Wheeler Ave 91750-1960 (Mail to: 4745 Wheeler Ave 91750-1960) Kelli Kurtz Robert Van Buren (909) 596-1321

Laguna Beach St Marys Church Episcopal **P** (352) 428 Park Ave 92651-2337 (Mail to: 480 Park Ave 92651-2337) (949) 494-3542

Laguna Hills St Georges Episcopal Church **P** (334) 23802 Ave De La Carlota 92653-3117 (Mail to: 23802 Avenida De La Carlota 92653-3117) Patricia McCaughan (949) 837-4530

Laguna Niguel Faith Episcopal Church **M** (95) 27802 El Lazo 92677-3915 (Mail to: 27802 El Lazo Rd 92677-3915) Emily Bell (949) 448-8114

Lancaster St Pauls Episcopal Church **P** (372) 502 W Avenue K 93534 (Mail to: PO Box 3386 93539) Nancy Brown (661) 945-6704

Lompoc St Marys Episcopal Church **P** (440) 2800 Harris Grade Rd 93436-2211 (Mail to: 2800 Harris Grade Rd 93436-2211) Michael Cunningham (805) 733-4400

Long Beach St Gregorys Episcopal Church **P** (423) 6201 E Willow St 90815-2247 (Mail to: 6201 E Willow St 90815-2296) (562) 420-1311

Long Beach St Lukes Episcopal Church **P** (530) 525 E 7th St 90813-4559 (Mail to: PO Box 20038 90801-3038) Gary Commins Steven Alder Ricardo Avila Holway Farrar Beryl Nyre-Thomas (562) 436-4047

Long Beach St Thomas of Canterbury Church **P** (136) 5306 E Arbor Rd 90808-1109 (Mail to: 5306 E Arbor Rd 90808-1109) George Okusi (562) 425-4457

Los Angeles All Saints Episcopal Church **P** (836) 5619 Monte Vista St 90042-3425 (Mail to: 5619 Monte Vista St 90042-3425) W Clarke Prescott (323) 255-6806

✠ **Los Angeles** Cathedral Congregation of St Athanasius **O** (326) 840 Echo Park Ave 90026-4209 (Mail to: PO Box 512164 90051-0164) (213) 482-2040

Los Angeles Christ the Good Shepherd Church **P** (261) 3303 W Vernon Ave 90008-5229 (Mail to: 3303 W Vernon Ave 90008-5295) Joseph Oloimooja (323) 295-4139

Los Angeles Church of the Epiphany **M** (220) 2808 Altura St 90031-2305 (Mail to: 2808 Altura St 90031-2399) Thomas Carey (323) 227-9931

Los Angeles Episcopal Chapel of St Francis **M** (11) 3621 Brunswick Ave 90039-1727 (Mail to: 3621 Brunswick Ave 90039-1727) (323) 663-2063

Los Angeles Episcopal Church of the Advent **P** (308) 4976 W Adams Blvd 90016-2852 (Mail to: 2614 S Longwood Ave 90016-2811) Vanessa Mackenzie (323) 731-8831

Los Angeles Holy Nativity Church **P** (177) 6700 W 83rd St 90045-2730 (Mail to: 6700 W 83rd St 90045-2730) Peter Rood Margaret Mccauley (310) 670-4777

Los Angeles St Albans Episcopal Church **M** (339) 580 Hilgard Ave 90024-3234 (Mail to: 580 Hilgard Ave 90024-3234) Susan Klein Warner Traynham (310) 208-6516

Los Angeles St Barnabas Episcopal Church **P** (73) 2109 Chickasaw Ave 90041-1904 (Mail to: 2111 Chickasaw Ave 90041-1904) (323) 254-7569

Los Angeles St Bedes Episcopal Church **P** (235) 3590 Grand View Blvd 90066-1904 (Mail to: 3590 Grand View Blvd 90066-1904) James Newman (310) 391-5522

Los Angeles St James Episcopal Church **P** (1493) 3903 Wilshire Blvd 90010-3301 (Mail to: 3903 Wilshire Blvd 90010-3301) Jenifer Chatfield

Thomas Discavage John Kim (213) 388-3417

✣ **Los Angeles** St John's Pro-Cathedral **O** (390) 514 W Adams Blvd 90007-2616 (Mail to: 514 W Adams Blvd 90007-2616) Mark Kowalewski Daniel Ade Gwynne Guibord Margaret McCauley James Walker (213) 747-6285

Los Angeles St Mary in Palms **P** (158) 3647 Watseka Ave 90034-3914 (Mail to: 3647 Watseka Ave 90034-3914) Otto Anderson Vincent Shamo (310) 558-4124

Los Angeles St Marys Episcopal Church **P** (463) 961 S Mariposa Ave 90006-1413 (Mail to: 961 S Mariposa Ave 90006-1413) Floyd Naters-Gamarra Anna Olson (213) 387-1334

Los Angeles St Philips Church **P** (126) 801 E 28th St 90011-5506 (Mail to: 2800 Stanford Ave 90011-2018) Glenn Libby Cindy Voorhees (323) 232-3494

Los Angeles St Stephen's Episcopal Church **P** (171) 6128 Yucca St 90028-5214 (Mail to: 6128 Yucca St 90028-5214) James Edwards-Acton (323) 469-3993

Los Angeles St Thomas the Apostle Hollywood **P** (544) 7501 Hollywood Blvd 90046-2813 (Mail to: 7501 Hollywood Blvd 90046-2813) Ian Davies Walter Johnson Gary London Mark Stuart (323) 876-2102

Los Angeles Trinity Episcopal Church **P** (200) 650 N Berendo St 90004-2104 (Mail to: 650 N Berendo Ave 90004-2104) Nancy Frausto (323) 660-1110

Los Olivos St Marks in the Valley Episcopal Church **P** (466) 2905 Nojoqui 93441 (Mail to: 2901 Nojoqui Ave 93441) Randall Day (805) 688-4454

Malibu St Aidan's Episcopal Church **P** (222) 28211 Pacific Coast Hwy 90265-3911 (Mail to: 28211 Pacific Coast Hwy 90265-3999) Joyce Stickney (310) 457-7966

Monrovia St Lukes Episcopal Church **P** (64) 122 S California Ave 91016-2948 (Mail to: 122 S California Ave 91016-2948) Elizabeth Dumolt Neil Tadken (626) 357-7071

Monterey Park St Gabriels Episcopal Church **P** (165) 133 E Graves Ave 91755-3915 (Mail to: 133 E Graves Ave 91755-3915)

Moreno Valley Grace Episcopal Church **M** (158) 11349 Perris Blvd 92557-5657 (Mail to: 11349 Perris Blvd 92557-5657) Barbara Barnum Enrico Gnasso William Redmon (951) 924-6760

Needles St John the Evangelist Church **M** (35) 2020 J St 92363-2630 (Mail to: PO Box 817 92363-0817) Janet Hurley (760) 326-6673

Norwalk St Francis Episcopal Church **M** (111) 12700 Paddison Ave 90650-3059 (Mail to: 12700 Paddison Ave 90650-3059) (562) 863-9212

Oak Park Episcopal Church of Epiphany **M** (832) 5450 Churchwood Dr 91377-4797 (Mail to: 5450 Churchwood Dr 91377-4797) Melissa

McCarthy (818) 991-4797

Ojai St Andrews Episcopal Church **P** (233) 409 Topa Topa Dr 93023-3233 (Mail to: 409 Topa Topa Dr 93023-3233) Mikel Morrison (805) 646-1885

Ontario Christ Church Parish **P** (130) 1127 N San Antonio Ave 91762-1803 (Mail to: 1127 N San Antonio Ave 91762-1899) Richard Rubin Walter Donaldson Phillip Strange (909) 983-1859

Orange Trinity Episcopal Church **P** (628) 2400 N Canal St 92865-3614 (Mail to: 2400 N Canal St 92865-3614) Jeannie Martz Ann Calhoun (714) 637-1390

Oxnard All Saints Episcopal Church **P** (111) 144 S C St 93030-5615 (Mail to: 144 S C St 93030-5615) Melissa Campbell-Langdell (805) 483-2347

Pacific Plsds St Matthew's Episcopal Church **P** (1323) Attn Craig Ehlers 1031 Bienveneda Ave 90272-2314 (Mail to: PO Box 37 90272-0037) Kristin Barberia George Daisa Bruce Freeman Lester Mackenzie Michael Seiler William Wallace (310) 454-1358

Palos Verdes Estates St Francis Episcopal Church **P** (402) 2200 Via Rosa PO Box 772 90274-1075 (Mail to: 2200 Via Rosa PO Box 772 90274-0772) Peter Huang James Lander Paula Vukmanic (310) 375-4617

Pasadena All Saints Episcopal Church **P** (7967) 132 N Euclid Ave 91101-1722 (Mail to: 132 N Euclid Ave 91101-1722) James Bacon Frances Crean Jonathan Dephouse Sally Howard Zelda Kennedy Susan Russell Janine Schenone (626) 583-2741

Pasadena Church of the Angels **P** (183) 1100 Avenue 64 91105-2712 (Mail to: 1100 Avenue 64 91105-2712) Robert Gaestel (323) 255-3878

Pasadena St Barnabas Episcopal Church **P** (84) 1062 N Fair Oaks Ave 91103-3011 (Mail to: PO Box 93096 91109-3096) Jamesetta Glosson Hammons (626) 798-2996

Pico Rivera St Bartholomews Episcopal Church **M** (285) 7540 Passons Blvd 90660-4233 (Mail to: 7540 Passons Blvd 90660-4233) Juan Barragan (562) 949-5228

Placentia Blessed Sacrament Church **P** (203) 1314 N Angelina Dr 92870-3442 (Mail to: 1314 N Angelina Dr 92870-3442) Paul Potter (714) 528-2995

Pomona St Pauls Episcopal Church **P** (136) 242 E Alvarado St 91767-4634 (Mail to: 242 E Alvarado St 91767-4634) Thomas Hallahan (909) 622-2015

Rcho Sta Marg St John Chrysostom Church and School **M** (375) § 30382 Via Con Dios 92688-1518 (Mail to: 30382 Via Con Dios 92688-1518) John Taylor (949) 888-4595

Redlands Trinity Church **P** (917) 419 S 4th St 92373-5952 (Mail to: 419 S 4th St 92373-5952) Paul Price (909) 793-2014

Redondo Beach Christ Episcopal Church **P** (192) No 408 S Broadway 90277-3717 (Mail to: 408 S Broadway 90277-3717) Bonnie McNaughton Marilyn Omernick (310) 540-1722

Rialto St Peter's Episcopal Church **P** (99) 777 N Acacia Ave 92376-5246 (Mail to: 777 N Acacia Ave 92376-5246) (909) 875-5689

Riverside All Saints Episcopal Church **P** (436) 3847 Terracina Dr 92506-0149 (Mail to: 3847 Terracina Dr 92506-0149) John Conrad Conrad Nordquist Benjamin Orozco Lisa Schoonmaker (951) 683-8466

Riverside St Georges Episcopal Church **P** (121) 950 Spruce St 92507-2503 (Mail to: 950 Spruce St 92507-2503) Khushnud Azariah (951) 686-9936

San Bernrdno St Johns Episcopal Church **M** (96) 1407 N Arrowhead Ave 92405-4813 (Mail to: 1407 N Arrowhead Ave 92405-4813) (909) 889-1195

San Clemente St Clements by the Sea **P** (544) 202 Avenida Aragon 92672-5015 (Mail to: 202 Avenida Aragon 92672-5098) Patrick Crerar Shireen Baker William Wells (949) 492-3401

San Fernando St Simons Episcopal Church **P** (387) 623 N Hagar St 91340-2005 (Mail to: 623 N Hagar St 91340-2005) Jorge Enrique Pallares Arellano (818) 361-3317

San Gabriel Church of Our Saviour **P** (606) 535 W Roses Rd 91775-2205 (Mail to: 535 W Roses Rd 91775-2205) Garyley Bradley Margaret Bradley William Doulos Dennis Gibbs Ada Nagata Huiliang Ni (626) 282-5147

San Juan Capo St Margaret of Scotland Church **P** (926) 31641 La Novia Ave 92675-2752 (Mail to: 31641 La Novia Ave 92675-2752) Linda Ahron Ronald Bauer Robert Edwards Earl Gibson James Livingston (949) 661-0110

San Marino St Edmunds Episcopal Church **P** (519) 1175 S San Gabriel Blvd 91108-2226 (Mail to: PO Box 80038 91118-8038) George Woodward (626) 793-9167

San Pedro St Peters Episcopal Church **P** (210) 1648 W 9th St 90732-3404 (Mail to: 1648 W 9th St 90732-3404) Jeanette Repp Lucinda Voien (310) 831-2361

Santa Ana Church of the Messiah **P** (786) 614 North Bush Street 92701-4157 (Mail to: 614 North Bush Street 92701-4157) James Lee Abel Lopez Katharine MacKenzie (714) 543-9389

Santa Barbara Christ the King Episcopal Church **P** (124) 5073 Hollister Ave 93111-2637 (Mail to: PO Box 6188 93160-6188) Frederick Cox (805) 964-9966

Santa Barbara Church of All Saints-by-the-Sea **P** (845) § 83 Eucalyptus Ln 93108-2901 (Mail to: 83 Eucalyptus Ln 93108-2901) Aimee Eyer-Delevett Victoria Mouradian (805) 969-4771

Santa Barbara Trinity Episcopal Church **P** (768) 1500 State St 93101-2514 (Mail to: 1500 State St 93101-2569) Mark Asman Anne Howard

Thomas Jayawardene Carren Sheldon Judith Stevens (805) 965-7419

Santa Maria St Peter Episcopal Church **P** (280) 402 S Lincoln St 93454 (Mail to: 402 S Lincoln St 93458-5596) Deborah Dunn Faye Hogan (805) 922-3575

Santa Monica St Augustines by the Sea **P** (278) 1227 4th St 90401-1303 (Mail to: 1227 4th St 90401-1390) Nathan Rugh Katherine Cadigan Kathryn Derose (310) 395-0977

Santa Paula St Pauls Episcopal Church **P** (119) 117 N 7th St 93060-2615 (Mail to: 117 N 7th St 93060-2615) Michael Fincher (805) 525-3811

Seal Beach St Theodore of Canterbury Church **M** (42) 1240 Oakmont Rd Ste 52b 90740-3650 (Mail to: 1240 Oakmont Rd Ste 52B 90740-3689) (562) 430-8619

Sierra Madre Church of the Ascension **P** (452) 25 E Laurel Ave 91024-1915 (Mail to: 25 E Laurel Ave 91024-1915) Michael Bamberger Edward Sniecienski

Simi Valley Church of St Francis of Assisi **M** (353) 280 Royal Ave 93065 (Mail to: PO Box 940516 93094-0516) Sarah Kitch (805) 526-5141

Skyforest St Richards Episcopal Church **M** (82) 28708 Hwy 18 92385 (Mail to: PO Box 1317 92352-1317) (909) 337-3889

South Gate St Margaret's Episcopal Church **P** (365) 4704 Tweedy Blvd 90280-5208 (Mail to: 4704 Tweedy Blvd 90280-5208) Eduardo Bresciani (323) 569-9901

South Pasadena St James Episcopal Church **P** (750) 1325 Monterey Rd 91030-3228 (Mail to: 1325 Monterey Rd 91030-3291) Anne O'Hara-Tumilty Michelle Baker-Wright Todd Blackham Brian O'Rourke (626) 799-9194

Studio City St Michael & All Angels **P** (356) 3646 Coldwater Canyon Ave 91604-4062 (Mail to: 3646 Coldwater Canyon Ave 91604-4062) Daniel Justin Stefanie Wilson (818) 763-9193

Thousand Oaks St Patricks Church & Day School **P** (304) 1 Church Rd 91362-1809 (Mail to: 1 Church Rd 91362-1809) Sarah Kitch James Sprague (805) 495-6441

Torrance St Andrews Church **P** (176) 1432 Engracia Ave 90501-3201 (Mail to: 1432 Engracia Ave 90501-3201) Bonnie Brandon (310) 328-3781

Tustin St Pauls Episcopal Church **P** (407) 1221 Wass St 92780-2855 (Mail to: 1221 Wass St 92780-2855) Valerie Hart Kathleen Sylvester Karen Wojahn (714) 544-3141

Twentynine Palms St Martin in-the-Fields Church **M** (41) 72348 Larrea Ave 92277-2181 (Mail to: PO Box 173 92277-0173) Margaret Ventris (760) 367-7133

Upland St Marks Episcopal Church **P** (239) 330 E 16th St 91784-2050 (Mail to: 330 E 16th St 91784-2050) Keith Yamamoto Lee Harris Sally Monastiere (909) 920-5565

Valencia St Stephen's Episcopal Church **P** (387)

24901 Orchard Village Rd 91355-3074 (Mail to: 24901 Orchard Village Rd 91355-3074) Kelly O'Connell

Van Nuys St Marks Episcopal Church **P** (460) 14646 Sherman Way 91405-5860 (Mail to: 14646 Sherman Way 91405-5860) Joy Magala Vincent Schwahn (818) 785-4251

Ventura St Pauls Episcopal Church **P** (328) 3290 Loma Vista Rd 93003-3002 (Mail to: 3290 Loma Vista Rd 93003-3002) Susan Bek Douglas Edwards Raymond Steever Richard Swanson (805) 643-5033

Whittier Episcopal Parish of St Stephen **M** (61) 10925 Valley Home Ave 90603-3041 (Mail to: 10925 Valley Home Ave 90603-3041) Mary Trainor Paul Potter Mary Trainor (562) 947-0394

Whittier St Matthias Episcopal Church **P** (239) 7056 Washington Ave 90602-1415 (Mail to: 7056 Washington Ave 90602-1415) William Garrison Gordon Taylor (562) 698-9741

Wilmington St Johns & Holy Child Epis Church **M** (378) 1537 N Neptune Ave 90744-2003 (Mail to: PO Box 1716 90748-1716) (310) 835-7870

Winnetka St Martin in-the-Fields **P** (166) 7136 Winnetka Ave 91306-3647 (Mail to: 7136 Winnetka Ave 91306-3695) Christopher Eade (818) 348-1419

Woodland Hls Church of the Prince of Peace **P** (973) 5700 Rudnick Ave 91367-6238 (Mail to: 5700 Rudnick Ave 91367-6299) Rand Reasoner Onesmus Tayebwa (818) 346-6968

Yucaipa St Alban's Episcopal Church **M** (112) 12692 5th St 92399-2571 (Mail to: PO Box 695 92399-0695) Lawrence Steele Elizabeth Williams (909) 797-3266

Yucca Valley St Joseph of Arimathea Church **M** (44) 56312 Onaga Trl 92284-3636 (Mail to: PO Box 1989 92286) Jane Crase (760) 365-7133

NON-PAROCHIAL CLERGY

Adams MM New Haven CT
Adams WR Edwards CA
Ahn MY *ret* Cherry Valley CA
Allen EP *ret* Mashpee MA
Alton FM Los Angeles CA
Anderson BA *ret* Ashland OR
Anderson BN *ret* Los Angeles CA
Anderson HR *ret* Pacific Palisades CA
Anderson JR *ret* Los Angeles CA
Anschutz MM Los Angeles CA
Asher CW
Atwood MH *ret* Claremont CA
Avery RN *ret* Placentia CA
Bacagan MK *ret* Glendora CA
Backer KA Fullerton CA
Baldwin-Mcginnis CE Houston TX
Barnhouse DH Pittsburgh PA
Barraza R *ret* Los Angeles CA
Bayaca GG *ret*

Beal JD Concord MA
Bechtel AG *ret* Yucaipa CA
Beckett NJ *ret* Lancaster LA
Belknap C *ret* Salt Spring Island BC
Belknap SK *ret* South Pasadena CA
Bell MS Rancho Palos Verdes CA
Belliss RG *ret* Santa Clarita CA
Benson VH Torrance CA
Bethea M San Juan Capistrano CA
Biornstad NA Monrovia CA
Bohler LP *ret* Augusta GA
Brennom KM El Monte CA
Brown C Altadena CA
Brown RM Glendale CA
Bull JP Encino CA
Bullock JL *ret* Oro Valley AZ
Burgdorf DH *ret* Cathedral City CA
Busch RA *ret* Arlington VA
Byrum RY Castaic CA
Caffrey DL *ret* Joshua Tree CA
Calafat KA Arcadia CA
Callaghan AD Los Angeles CA
Campbell-Langdell AL Oxnard CA
Cantella FF Castaic CA
Capellaro JJ *ret* Marina del Rey CA
Card SJC *dcn* Dana Point CA
Cartwright HM *ret* Victorville CA
Cavalcante JI Mount Sinai NY
Chandler JH Los Angeles CA
Chang HF Hacienda Heights CA
Chavez KS *dcn* Corona CA
Chee DTH *ret* El Sobrante CA
Churchill GH *ret* Lompoc CA
Clark KH *ret* Thousand Oaks CA
Clarke TG *ret* Palm Springs CA
Collins GD Rancho Palos Verdes CA
Collis SJ Hesperia CA
Conrads AK Los Angeles CA
Corbett FJB *ret* Portland OR
Cornell AL Carlsbad CA
Cornner R *ret* Playa Del Rey CA
Corrigan ME Santa Barbara CA
Cox JL Silver Spring MD
Crawford KA *ret* Dallas OR
Crean JE *ret* Altadena CA
Crist MF Riverside CA
Crist WH *ret* Irvine CA
Crump DA *ret* Montara CA
Dale KA *ret* Palm Desert CA
D'Amico SR *ret* Lake Forest CA
David R Los Angeles CA
Davidson-Methot DG
Davis AP Los Angeles CA
Dean SJ *ret* Santa Clarita CA
DiCarlo MJ *ret* Upland CA
Duncan D *ret* Salt Lake City UT
Duncan JB *ret* North Adams MA
Edwards PD *ret* Fullerton CA
Elder PR *dcn* Los Angeles CA
Ensor PC *ret* Dubois WY
Erickson DL Hermosa Beach CA

Erickson FD *dcn* Philadelphia PA
Erickson HB San Juan Capistrano
Erickson JA *ret* Claremont CA
Erwin VG *ret* Banning CA
Estrada CS *ret* Signal Hill CA
Estrada RR Los Angeles CA
Factor BA *ret* Altadena CA
Ferrer GV Beverly Hills CA
Finley RS Tucson AZ
Fleming RE *ret* Laguna Beach CA
Flynn MT *ret* Camarillo CA
Forney JC *ret* Claremont CA
Freeman NR *ret* Laguna Hills CA
Friedrich JL Bainbridge Island WA
Fulgoni DL *dcn* Big Bear Lake CA
Fuller JP *ret* Oxnard CA
Furman JE *ret* Sherman Oaks CA
Galipeau SA *ret* West Hills CA
Galletly DP Thousand Oaks CA
Gardner MW San Marcos CA
Gordon JD Hermleigh TX
Goshert ML *ret* Benicia CA
Graves FD Sayville NY
Griffith DM *ret* La Canada CA
Gugliermetto GL
Guillen JA Ventura CA
Habecker EA *ret* Bristol RI
Haddad ME San Francisco CA
Halapua S *ret* Sunland CA
Hall RC *ret* Pasadena CA
Hampton RK *ret* Corpus Christi TX
Hand GD *ret* Pathum Thani Thailand
Hanley ID Yucca Valley CA
Harms RB *ret* Escondido CA
Harriot C *ret* Huntington Beach CA
Hatch VT *ret* Banning CA
Hauert RH *ret* Ann Arbor MI
Haynes AE Pasadena CA
Heffron JAW *ret* La Verne CA
Hegedus FM *ret* Seal Beach CA
Hemmers LE *ret* Redlands CA
Hendrickson PD *dcn* Thousand Oaks CA
Henrickson M Auckland
Hernandez G *ret* Downey CA
Herzog CR *ret* La Habra Heights CA
Hill ER *ret* Irvine CA
Honeychurch JR *ret* Altadena CA
Horn SH *ret* Pasadena CA
Hubbard TB *ret* Claremont CA
Hubinsky-Phelps SE Cary NC
Hulbert ER Lake Arrowhead CA
Hull NS Studio City CA
Ishizaki NY *ret* Los Angeles CA
Janelle NS Isla Vista CA
Jay LAD *ret* Valencia CA
Jewiss AH *ret* Brooklyn NY
Jimenez J
Johns MD Rancho Santa Margarita CA
Johns RG *ret* Vancouver BC
Johnson BD Palm Springs CA

Jones BW *ret* Long Beach CA
Jones JD *dcn* San Pedro CA
Judson HD *ret* Harbor City CA
Kahler JE *ret* Ventura CA
Kaisch KB *ret* Fullerton CA
Karelius BL *ret* Laguna Niguel CA
Katz NP Los Angeles CA
Keester JC *ret* Claremont CA
Kim A Garden Grove CA
Kim SY *ret* Lancaster CA
Kim YE
Kimura GWM Eagle River AK
Knowles HF *ret* South Pasadena CA
Koh AY Studio City CA
Kowalewski PJ *ret* La Quinta CA
Kreitler PG *ret* Pacific Palisades CA
Kujawa-Holbrook SA Claremont CA
Lafon AP *ret* Albany OR
Lance PJ Los Angeles CA
Landers KM *dcn* Upland CA
Larson JM *ret* Santa Barbara CA
Laske H Koeln
Law EHF Palm Desert CA
Lawson PD *ret* Palm Desert CA
Lebrija L Los Angeles CA
Lee DKH South Gate CA
Leemhuis GA *dcn* Inglewood CA
Leeson GW *ret* Los Angeles CA
Leslie J *dcn* Santa Monica CA
Lewis KA Thousand Oaks CA
Lieske MS *ret* Spanish Springs NV
Lim YLL Garden Grove CA
Lincoln RK *ret* Van Nuys CA
Lo K *ret* Monterey Park CA
Locke CA *dcn* Pasadena CA
Loewe R Santa Ana CA
London DD Berkeley CA
Lozano BA *dcn* Whittier CA
Lynn CK *ret* Los Angeles CA
Mackey GR *ret* Santa Maria CA
Mackey JP *dcn* Santa Maria CA
MacQueen KB Diamond Bar CA
Maronde JA
Mason MJS *ret* Bristol RI
McKaig BJ *ret* Lake Isabella CA
McKee MD Laguna Beach CA
McKinney DW *ret* Los Angeles CA
Mettler GM Pleasantville NY
Miles RAK Reidsville NC
Miller AG Pasadena CA
Miller DW *ret* Santa Monica CA
Miller JP
Millikin GL Alexandria VA
Mitchel GHH *ret* Carpinteria CA
Monette RA Vancouver BC
Moon RM Pasadena CA
Morris JH Camarillo CA
Morris RL Los Angeles CA
Mountford HH *dcn* Santa Ynez CA
Mulac PA *ret* Prescott Valley AZ
Mungoma SM Los Angeles CA

Munoz ME Chicago IL
Murasaki-Wekall ES Pasadena CA
Murphy H *ret* Los Angeles CA
Neckermann EC *ret* Newberg OR
Nguyen DX *ret* Fountain Valley CA
Nguyen HX *ret* Garden Grove CA
Nichols SW Pasadena CA
Norro HP *ret* Klamath Falls OR
Nyback WS *ret* Pomona CA
Nyberg KY Monrovia CA
Odekirk DR *ret* San Luis Obispo CA
O'Reilly P *ret* Pasadena CA
Paddock AL *dcn* Laguna Beach CA
Phalen JR *ret* Westminster CA
Pillsbury SH *dcn* Los Angeles CA
Prendergast JD South Pasadena CA
Purnell SA Yorba Linda CA
Queen LV New York NY
Ramsey-Musolf MJ Amherst MA
Rao CDS Los Angeles CA
Rechter EI Atlanta GA
Redmon CS *ret* Palm Springs CA
Regas GF *ret* Pasadena CA
Reynolds RS *ret* Killeen TX
Richards MG *ret* Newhall CA
Riley RM *ret* Santa Ana CA
Rodriguez R Pico Rivera CA
Romo-Garcia G Hesperia CA
Rose SJ *ret* Aliso Viejo CA
Rotchford LM *ret* Mission Viejo CA
Rouse AC *ret* Montrose CA
Rowins CH *ret* Baltimore MD
Rubel CS Glendora CA
Sacquety CW *ret* Huntington Beach CA
Satorius JR Los Angeles CA
Saville JK *ret* Corona CA
Schneider MJ *ret* Virginia Beach VA
Schrider JE Washington DC
Seipel JR *ret* Valencia CA
Sheridan DA *dcn* Pomona CA
Shier MW *ret* Fullerton CA
Shier NK *ret* San Gabriel CA
Sierra F *ret* Alhambra CA
Silides HP Juneau AK
Sinclair NP *ret* Fountain Valley CA
Six G *ret*
Smith AH *ret* San Diego CA
Smith AL *ret* Riverside CA
Smith DL *ret* Hopewell VA

Smith RC *ret*
Smythe CN *ret* Altadena CA
Stacy CH *ret* Solvang CA
Starr DH San Bernardino CA
Sterne CK Santa Barbara CA
Sterry SC *dcn* Placentia CA
Stingley EA *ret* Victorville CA
Stivers DA *ret* Santa Barbara CA
Stump CS *dcn* Upland CA
Sweeney SA Claremont CA
Swift DW Los Altos CA
Sy JJ Huntington Beach CA
Symington AP *dcn*
Thomson RD *ret* Mount Pleasant SC
Tiff RO
Touchstone GR *ret* Los Angeles CA
Two Bulls RW
Tyler PH Taos NM
Underhill R *ret* Lockerbie SCOTLAND
Valdes FJ *dcn*
Van Horn RS *ret* Los Angeles CA
Verdi BE *ret* Sylmar CA
Vest DC *ret* Green Valley AZ
Vukich DE Mission Viejo CA
Wagar C *dcn* South Los Angeles CA
Wagner RA *ret* Murrieta CA
Walker DC *ret* Long Beach CA
Wallace GR *ret* Upland CA
Walls AS
Ward SM *ret* Santa Barbara CA
Ward VK *dcn* Santa Maria CA
Warren TG Redlands CA
Wauters JW *ret* San Antonio TX
Weaver LE *ret* Upland CA
Weeks JA *ret* Moreno Valley CA
White KS *ret* Savannah GA
Wilhelm J *ret* Ojai CA
Willems JR *ret* Oakland CA
Williams EF *ret* Los Angeles CA
Williams JE *ret* Los Angeles CA
Williams SL *ret* Westminster CA
Wood RH *ret* Sierra Madre CA
Woodhouse MM *ret* Santa Barbara CA
Worthley C Santa Barbara CA
Wright JO Redlands CA
Yoon PH *ret* Taejon
Young AL *ret* Los Osos CA
Young JJ Studio City CA
Zahn VRM Huntington Beach CA

STATE OF LOUISIANA

Dioceses of Louisiana and Western Louisiana

DIOCESE OF LOUISIANA

(PROVINCE IV)
Comprises all parishes east of the Atchafalaya River and including all of St Mary's Parish
DIOCESAN OFFICE 1623 Seventh St New Orleans LA 70115
TEL (504) 895-6634 FAX (504) 895-6637 WEB www.edola.org

Previous Bishops—
Leonidas Polk 1841-64, Jos PB Wilmer 1866-78, John N Galleher 1880-91, Davis Sessums coadj 1891 Bp 1891-1929, James C Morris 1930-39, John L Jackson 1940-48, Girault M Jones 1949-69, Iveson B Noland suffr 1952-61 coadj 1961 Bp 1969-75, R Heber Gooden asst 1972-75 acting 1975-76, James B Brown 1976-98, Charles Edward Jenkins III Bp 1998-2010

Bishop—Rt Rev Morris K Thompson Jr (1043)
(Dio May 8 2010)

Cn to Ord Rev Cn S Manning *Sec/Reg* M Wade; *Treas* L Bradfield; *Chanc* CJ Geary 201 St Charles New Orleans LA 70170-5100; *Hist* H Murrell; *Com* Rev P Bailey

Stand Comm—Cler: Pres AJ Heine B Owen D Lasiter; *Lay:* A Ball J Girault Jr K Martin R Whitley

Dio Conv: 27-28 February 2015 Trinity Church, New Orleans LA

PARISHES, MISSIONS, AND CLERGY

Amite Episcopal Church of the Incarnation **M** (27) 111 E Olive St 70422-2539 (Mail to: PO Box 722 70422-0722) (985) 748-9706

Angola Transfiguration at Angola State Pris **M** Angola State Prison 70712 (Mail to: 3112 Green Acres Rd 70003-1820) (225) 387-0396

Baton Rouge St Albans Episcopal Chapel Campus Ministry (328) Corner of Dalrymple & Highland, LSU 70808 (Mail to: 5261 Highland Rd PMB 376 70808-6547) Andrew Rollins (225) 343-2070

Baton Rouge St Augustines Episcopal Church **M** (39) 12954 Joor Rd 70837 (Mail to: PO Box 78123 70837-8123) (225) 261-4344

Baton Rouge St James Episcopal Church **P** (2306) 205 N 4th St 70801-1403 (Mail to: PO Box 126 70821-0126) J Mark Holland Mary Ann Garrett Ralph Howe (225) 387-5141

Baton Rouge St Lukes Episcopal Church **P** (1800) 8833 Goodwood Blvd 70806-7919 (Mail to: 8833 Goodwood Blvd 70806-7995) Charles Owen Watson Lamb Reese Wiggins (225) 926-5343

Baton Rouge St Margaret's Episcopal Church **P** (164) 12663 Perkins Rd 70810-1909 (Mail to: 12663 Perkins Rd 70810-1909) William Edwards (225) 766-8314

Baton Rouge St Michael & All Angels **M** (89) 1666 77th Ave 70807-5405 (Mail to: 1620 77th Ave 70807-5405) (225) 357-8852

Baton Rouge Trinity Episcopal Church **HC** (1048) 3552 Morning Glory Ave 70808-2865 (Mail to: 3552 Morning Glory Ave 70808-2865) Sharon Alexander Ashley Freeman (225) 387-0396

Bogalusa St Matthews Church **P** (81) 208 Georgia Ave 70427-3824 (Mail to: 208 Georgia Ave 70427-3824)

Clinton St Andrews Episcopal Church **M** (96) 1 St Andrew St 70722 (Mail to: PO Box 8259 70722-1259) (225) 683-5498

Covington Christ Episcopal Church **P** (949) § 120 S New Hampshire St 70433 (Mail to: 120 S New Hampshire St 70433-3545) William Miller Morgan Macintire Anne Maxwell (985) 892-3177

Denham Spgs St Francis Church **P** (162) 726 Maple St 70726-3026 (Mail to: 726 Maple St 70726-3026) (225) 665-2707

Franklin St Marys Episcopal Church **P** (43) No 805 1st St 70538-5415 (Mail to: PO Box 95 70538-0095) Stephen Crawford (337) 828-0918

Hammond Grace Memorial Episcopal Church **P** (497) 100 W Church St 70401-3205 (Mail to: PO Box 1086 70404-1086) Paul Bailey (985) 345-2764

Harvey St Marks Episcopal Church **P** (106) 3245 Manhattan Blvd 70058-5112 (Mail to: 3245 Manhattan Blvd 70058-5112) Percy Bates John Kellogg (504) 366-0123

Houma St Matthew Episcopal Church **P** (325) 239 Barrow St 70360-4403 (Mail to: 239 Barrow St 70360-4403) Craig Dalferes

Innis St Stephens Episcopal Church **P** (211) 9795 Highway 418 70747 (Mail to: PO Box 1020 70747-1020) (225) 492-2234

Kenner St Johns Episcopal Church **M** (52) 2109 17th St 70062-6351 (Mail to: 2109 17th St 70062-6351) Charmaine Kathmann (504) 469-4535

La Place St Timothys Episcopal Church **M** (45) 1101 Belle Alliance Dr 70068-3201 (Mail to: 1101 Belle Alliance Dr 70068-3201) (985) 652-2121

Luling St Andrews Episcopal Church **M** Audbon & Early St 70070 (Mail to: PO Box 621 70070-0621) (985) 758-1607

Mandeville St Michael's Episcopal Church **M** (247) 4499 Sharp Rd 70471-8919 (Mail to: 4499 Sharp Rd 70471-8919) (985) 626-5781

Metairie St Augustines Episcopal Church **P** (947) 3412 Haring Rd 70006-3902 (Mail to: 3412 Haring Rd 70006-3902) William Heine Michael Hackett (504) 887-4801

Metairie St Martin's Episcopal Church **P** (566) 2216 Metairie Rd 70001-4205 (Mail to: 2216 Metairie Rd 70001-4205) Frederick Devall Ford Millican (504) 835-7357

Morgan City Trinity Episcopal Church **P** (116) PO Box 1776 70381-1776 (Mail to: PO Box 1776 70381-1776) Douglas Lasiter (985) 384-7629

Morganza St Marys Episcopal Church **M** (25) 331 W Tircuit St 70759 (Mail to: PO Box 386 70760-0386) Peggy Scott (225) 694-3609

Napoleonville Christ Episcopal Church **PS** 4829 Highway 1 70390-2002 (Mail to: PO Box 27 70390) (985) 369-2106

New Orleans All Saints' Episcopal Church **P** (273) 100 Rex Dr 70123-3531 (Mail to: 100 Rex Dr 70123-3531) John Angerer (504) 737-2421

New Orleans All Souls Episcopal Church and Community Center **PS** (90) 5500 Saint Claude Ave 70117-2506 (Mail to: 5500 Saint Claude Ave 70117-2506) Edward Thompson (504) 218-8995

New Orleans Chapel of the Holy Comforter **CC** (36) 2220 Lakeshore Dr 70122-3502 (Mail to: 2220 Lakeshore Dr 70122-3502) Kathleen Comer (504) 282-4593

New Orleans Chapel of the Holy Spirit **CC** (35) No 1100 Broadway St 70118-5243 (Mail to: 1100 Broadway St 70118-5243) Minka Sprague (504) 866-7438

✢ **New Orleans** Christ Church Cathedral **O** (700) No 2919 Saint Charles Ave 70115-4421 (Mail to: 2919 Saint Charles Ave 70115-4498) David Duplantier William Gayle Travers Koerner Steven Roberts Bridget Tierney

New Orleans Grace Episcopal Church **P** 3700 Canal St 70119-6141 (Mail to: 3700 Canal St 70119-6189) (504) 482-5242

New Orleans Mt Olivet Episcopal Church **P** (80) 530 Pelican Avenue 70114-1051 (Mail to: 530 Pelican Avenue 70114-1051) Merrill Broach (504) 366-4650

New Orleans St Andrew Episcopal Church **P** (376) 1116 Short St 70118-2712 (Mail to: 1031 S Carrollton Ave 70118) James Morrison Charles Ziegenfuss (504) 866-0123

New Orleans St Annas Episcopal Church **P** (183) 1313 Esplanade Ave 70116-1836 (Mail to: 1313 Esplanade Ave 70116-1836) William Terry (504) 947-2121

New Orleans St George's Episcopal Church **P** (177) 4600 Saint Charles Ave 70115-4834 (Mail to: 4600 Saint Charles Ave 70115-4897) Richard Easterling (504) 899-2811

New Orleans St Lukes Episcopal Church **P** (129) 1222 N Dorgenois St 70119-3445 (Mail to: 1222 N Dorgenois St 70119-3445) Donald Muth Edward Thompson (504) 821-0529

New Orleans St Pauls Episcopal Church **P** (337) 6249 Canal Blvd 70124-3099 (Mail to: 6249 Canal Blvd 70124-3099) Robert Courtney (504) 488-3749

New Orleans St Philips Episcopal Church **P** (324) 3643 Aurora Dr 70131-5507 (Mail to: 3643 Aurora Dr 70131-5599) Stephen Craft (504) 394-2408

New Orleans The Church of the Annunciation **P** (112) 4505 S Claiborne Ave 70125-5007 (Mail to: 4505 S Claiborne Ave 70125-5007) Duane Nettles (504) 895-8697

New Orleans Trinity Episcopal Church **P** (2670) 1329 Jackson Ave 70130-5131 (Mail to: 1329 Jackson Ave 70130-5198) Henry Hudson Katherine McLean Mitchell Smith Edgar Taylor (504) 522-0276

New Roads St Pauls Holy Trinity **P** (81) 607 E Main St 70760-3641 (Mail to: PO Box 386 70760-0386) Peggy Scott (225) 638-8433

Plaquemine Church of the Holy Communion **P** (124) 58040 Court St 70764-2704 (Mail to: PO Box 474 70765-0474) (225) 687-2611

Ponchatoula All Saints Episcopal Church **M** (49) 250 W Hickory St 70454-3218 (Mail to: Episcopal Diocese of Louisiana 1623 7th Street 70115) George Tennison (985) 386-8126

Rosedale Church of the Nativity **M** (54) 302 Laurel St 70772 (Mail to: PO Box 195 70772-0195) (225) 241-2556

Slidell Christ Episcopal Church **P** (375) 1534 7th St 70458-2847 (Mail to: 1534 7th St 70458-2897) Richard Almos Harry Jenkins

St Francisvlle Grace Church **P** (371) 11621 Ferdinand St 70775-4339 (Mail to: PO Box 28 70775-0028) Roman Roldan Hi-Jae Kang (225) 635-4065

Theriot St Andrews Episcopal Church **M** (292) 3027 Bayou Dularge Rd 70397-9743 (Mail to: 3027 Bayou Dularge Rd 70397-9743) (985) 872-2508

Thibodaux St Johns Episcopal Church **P** (93) 718 Jackson St 70301-2732 (Mail to: 718 Jackson St 70301-2732)

Zachary St Patricks Episcopal Church **P** (243) § 1322 Church St 70791-2743 (Mail to: 1322 Church St 70791-2743) Stephen Jones Camille Wood (225) 654-4091

NON-PAROCHIAL CLERGY

Adams JR New Orleans LA
Albert JG *dcn* New Orleans LA

Banks RA New Orleans LA
Barnwell WH *ret* New Orleans LA
Blackmon AT *ret* Covington LA
Brown DR *ret* New Roads LA
Bushey HW *ret* Baton Rouge LA
Cage SB Baton Rouge LA
Campbell JD Amite LA
Cannon CT *ret* Clermont FL
Clements EG *dcn* New Orleans LA
Clingenpeel RH *ret* New Orleans LA
Craft JH New Orleans LA
Daunt FT *ret* San Antonio TX
Davidson SLM *ret* Torrington CT
Dawson MG *dcn* Metairie LA
Dawson TE *ret* Bay Saint Louis MS
De Gravelles CN *dcn* Baton Rouge LA
Deakle DW *ret* Portland OR
Douglass JH *ret* Miami FL
Dunn PC
Eskamire-Jackson J *dcn* New Orleans LA
Estes DM
Fargo DR *ret* Hendersonville NC
Garma JM *dcn* Mandeville LA
Gasquet MC *ret* Jefferson LA
Gaumer SS *ret* New Orleans LA
Gay KR Plaquemine LA
Griffis TH *ret* Meridian MS
Haddock GM *ret* Denison TX
Hardy MEH *ret* Durango CO
Heine MAR *ret* Ponchatoula LA
Hicks RW *ret* Livermore CA
Holbert JR *dcn* Terrytown LA
Holzhalb L *ret* Covington LA
Hood WR Houston TX
Hopkins LE *dcn*
Hudson DM *dcn* New Orleans LA
Jefferson AL *dcn* New Orleans LA
Jenkins JS *ret* Brandon MS
Johnston MS *dcn* St Francisvle LA

Klaas AR *ret* Daphne AL
Knight KA Mandeville LA
Knight KW Baton Rouge LA
Knox FL Baton Rouge LA
Krutz CD *ret* Baton Rouge LA
Kuhn MC New Orleans LA
Lane LC Franklin LA
Lindsay SH *ret* Houma LA
Lyle PR *dcn* Baton Rouge LA
Manning SR Jackson MS
Maumus PG *dcn* New Orleans LA
Mellish RW *ret* Morgan City LA
Mesa PE *ret* Metairie LA
Miller JS Baton Rouge LA
Mkhize DE *ret* New Orleans LA
Moore RW *ret* Metairie LA
Obier CA *dcn* Baton Rouge LA
Ogle LK *dcn* Covington LA
Owens DP *ret* Wimberley TX
Petterson TR *ret* Brunswick ME
Phillips JR *ret* Rosedale LA
Plater O *dcn* New Orleans LA
Rice WE *ret* Covington LA
Riddle HC *ret* New Orleans LA
Ritter KP Baton Rouge LA
Roark HA Riverside CT
Robertson ER *ret* New Orleans LA
Rogers RG *ret* Clinton LA
Scalia DW *dcn* River Ridge LA
Stevenson FM Little Elm TX
Thomas PL *ret* New Orleans LA
Tilley DJ *ret* Baton Rouge LA
Webster EC *ret* Eros LA
Whitmer RD *ret* Gonzales LA
Wild PC *dcn* Covington LA
Williams AS Baton Rouge LA
Wood CA *ret* Baton Rouge LA
Wright L San Diego CA

DIOCESE OF MAINE
(PROVINCE I)
Comprises the State of Maine
DIOCESAN OFFICE 143 State St Portland ME 04101-3799
TEL (207) 772-1953   FAX (207) 773-0095
E-MAIL info@episcopalmaine.org   WEB www.episcopalmaine.org

Previous Bishops—
Geo Burgess 1847-66, Henry A Neely 1867-99, Robt Codman 1900-15, Benj Brewster 1916-40, Oliver L Loring 1941-68, Fredk B Wolf 1968-86, Edward C Chalfant coadj 1984-86 Bp Elizabeth ME 04107 1986-1996, Chilton R Knudsen 1998-2008

Bishop — Rt Rev Stephen T Lane (1028) (Dio 13 Sept 2008)

Cn to the Ordinary M Ambler; *Cn Fin & Stew* T Reimer; *Cn Comm & Adv* H Shott; *Cn Form* J Hartwell; *Exec Asst to Bp, Reg & Arch* B Martin; *Camp Dir* M Douglass; *Sec Conv* L Spahr; *Treas* R Rozene; *Chanc* G Gayer 16 Mare's Hollow Ln Cape Elizabeth ME 04107

Stand Comm—Cler: Pres B Shambaugh A Kellogg M Hoecker *Lay:* B Hamilton E Praul B Dalbeck

Dio Conv: Oct 2016 Portland ME

PARISHES, MISSIONS, AND CLERGY

Auburn St Michaels Episcopal Church **P** (153) 78 Pleasant St 04210-5940 (Mail to: 78 Pleasant St. 04210-5988) Daniel Warren (207) 782-1346

Augusta St Barnabas Church **M** (61) 60 Bangor St 04330 (Mail to: 60 Bangor St 04330-4804) David Matson (207) 248-2687

Augusta St Marks Church **P** (90) 9 Summer St 04330-5128 (Mail to: 9 Summer St 04330-5128) (207) 622-2424

Bailey Island All Saints by the Sea Summer Chapel **SC** Washington Ave 04003 (207) 772-1953

Bangor St Johns Episcopal Church **P** (359) 225 French St 04401 (Mail to: 225 French St 04401-5012) Thomas Benson Marguerite Steadman (207) 947-0156

Bar Harbor St Saviours Church **P** (132) 41 Mount Desert St 04609-1753 (Mail to: 41 Mount Desert St 04609-1753) Timothy Fleck Kathleen Killian Jennifer Reece (207) 288-4215

Bath Grace Episcopal Church **P** (425) 1100 Washington St 04530-2762 (Mail to: 1100 Washington St 04530-2762) Lois Hart George Lambert (207) 443-3792

Belfast St Margarets Episcopal Church **P** (259) 95 Court St 04915-6135 (Mail to: 95 Court St 04915-6135) Christopher Szarke (207) 338-2412

Biddeford Christ Episcopal Church **P** (22) 18 1/2 Crescent St 04005-2520 (Mail to: 35 South St 04005-2473) Shirley Bowen (207) 283-1783

Biddeford Pool St Martins in Field Summer Chpl **SC** St Martins Ln 04006 (Mail to: PO Box 274 04006) Daniel Meck

Blaine St Annes Episcopal Church **P** (14) 5 Military Rd 04734-4300 (Mail to: PO Box 682 04758-0682) Robert Smith (207) 749-2421

Blue Hill St Francis By The Sea **P** (360) 330 Hinckley Ridge Rd 04614-5816 (Mail to: PO Box 76 04614-0076) Claudia Smith Carlton Russell (207) 374-5200

Brewer St Patricks Episcopal Church **P** (81) 21 Holyoke St 04412-1905 (Mail to: 21 Holyoke St 04412-1905) Myrick Cross (207) 989-1308

Bridgton St Peters Episcopal Church **P** (148) 98 Main St 04009-1129 (Mail to: PO Box 143 04009) Craig Hacker (207) 647-8549

Brownville St Johns Episcopal Church **M** (41) 26 Henderson St 04415 (Mail to: PO Box 751 04414-0751) Kevin Holsapple (207) 943-5168

Brunswick St Pauls Church Episcopal **P** (635) 27 Pleasant St 04011-2222 (Mail to: PO Box 195 04011-0195) Carolyn Eklund Mary Lee Wile (207) 725-5342

Calais St Annes Church **P** (86) 29 Church St 04619-1636 (Mail to: 29 Church St 04619-1669) (207) 454-8016

Camden Christ Church Dark Harbor **SC** No Attn Stephen D Russell Schatz Fletcher Assoc 87 Elm St Ste 215 04843-1959 (Mail to: PO Box 147 04848-0147) (207) 734-8207

Camden Church of St Thomas **P** (220) PO Box 631 04843-0631 (Mail to: PO Box 631 04843-0631) Rosalee Glass (207) 236-3680

Cape Elizabeth St Alban Episcopal Church **P** (800) 885 Shore Rd 04107-1540 (Mail to: 885 Shore Rd 04107-1540) Timothy Boggs Reed Loy (207) 799-4014

Caribou St Luke Episcopal Church **P** (25) 471 Main St 04736-4411 (Mail to: 471 Main St 04736-4411) (207) 492-4211

Castine Trinity Episcopal Church **P** (73) Perkins And Tarrant 04421 (Mail to: PO Box 433 04421-0433) Richard Armstrong (207) 326-4180

Damariscotta St Cuthbert Summer Chapel **SC** C/O Jane Kennedy Hc 61 Box 124 04543 (Mail to: MacMahon Island 04548) (207) 371-2517

Deer Isle Saint Brendan's Episcopal Church **P** (44) PO Box 305 04627-0305 (Mail to: PO Box 305 04627-0305) Virginia Peacock (207) 348-6240

Dovr Foxcroft St Augustines Episcopal Church **M** (64) PO Box 504 04426-0504 (Mail to: PO Box 504 04426-0504) Kevin Holsapple (207) 564-7075

East Boothbay St Columbas Episcopal Church **P** (138) 32 Emery Ln 04538-1965 (Mail to: 32 Emery Ln 04538-1965) Maria Hoecker William Wood (207) 633-6313

Eastport Christ Episcopal Church **P** (54) PO Box 12 04631-0012 (Mail to: PO Box 12 04631) Lynn Rutledge

Ellsworth St Dunstans Episcopal Church **P** (99) 134 State Stree 04605-1832 (Mail to: PO Box 711 04605-0711) Johanna-Karen Johannson (207) 667-5495

Falmouth St Mary the Virgin Episcopal Church **P** (577) 43 Foreside Rd 04105-1708 (Mail to: 43 Foreside Rd 04105-1708) Nathan Ferrell Jack Haney (207) 781-3366

Farmington St Lukes Church **P** (104) High And School Sts 04938 (Mail to: PO Box 249 04938-0249) Robert Walmer (207) 645-2639

Ft Fairfield St Pauls Episcopal Church **P** (56) 170 Main St 04742-1220 (Mail to: PO Box 737 04742) (207) 492-4211

Gardiner Christ Church Episcopal **P** (151) 2 Dresden Ave 04345-2633 (Mail to: 2 Dresden Ave 04345-2633) Gary Drinkwater (207) 582-3354

Hallowell St Matthews Episcopal Church **P** (217) 20 Union St 04347-1369 (Mail to: 20 Union St 04347-1369) David Matson Mary Bourque Alicia Kellogg (207) 623-3041

Harborside Our Lady of Evrgrns Summer Chpl **SC** 44 Emerson Pt Rd 04642

Houlton Church Of The Good Shepherd **P** (115) 116 Main St 04730-2113 (Mail to: PO Box 1672 04730-5672) Jessie Drysdale Virginia Urbanek (207) 532-2927

Hulls Cove Church of Our Father **P** (87) State Hwy #3 3 04644 (Mail to: PO Box 186 04644-0186) Suzanne Cole (207) 288-4849

Jefferson St Giles Episcopal Church **P** (84) 72

Gardiner Rd 04348-3973 (Mail to: PO Box 34 04348-0034) Susan Kraus (207) 549-3158

Kennebunk St Davids Episcopal Church **P** (336) 138 York St 04043-7108 (Mail to: 138 York St 04043) (207) 985-3073

Kennebunk Beach Trinity Summer Chapel **SC** 3 Woodland Ave 04043 (Mail to: PO Box 1307 04043-1307) (207) 967-3056

Kennebunkport St Anns Episcopal Church **SC** 1 Ocean Ave 04046-6003 (Mail to: PO Box 44 04046-0044) Peter Cheney

Lewiston Trinity Episcopal Church **P** (32) 247 Bates St 04240-7331 (Mail to: 247 Bates St 04240-7331) Steven Crowson (207) 312-9410

Limestone Church of the Advent **M** (10) 37 Church St 04750 (Mail to: 471 Main Street 04736-4422) (207) 492-4211

Lisbon Falls St Matthews Episcopal Church **P** (147) 496 Lisbon St 04250 (Mail to: PO Box 879 04250-0879) William Wagner (207) 353-8453

Machias St Aidans Episcopal Church **M** (51) 36 Hill St 04654-1310 (Mail to: PO Box 271 04654-0271) Lynn Rutledge (207) 255-4995

Millinocket St Andrews Episcopal Church **P** (87) 40 Highland Ave 04462-1413 (Mail to: 40 Highland Ave 04462-1413) Robert Landry (207) 723-5893

Newcastle St Andrews Episcopal Church **P** (308) PO Box 234 04553-3401 (Mail to: PO Box 234 04553-0234) Lu-Anne Conner (207) 563-3533

North Haven North Haven Summer Services **SC** Church St 04853 (Mail to: PO Box 318 04853) (207) 867-4876

Northeast Harbor The Parish of St Mary & St Jude **P** (233) PO Box 105 04662-0105 (Mail to: PO Box 105 04662-0105) Jane Cornman (207) 276-5588

Norway Christ Episcopal Church **P** (101) 35 Paris St 04268-5630 (Mail to: 35 Paris St 04268-5630) Nancy Moore Elizabeth Wenthe (207) 743-6782

Old Town St James Episcopal Church **P** (69) 149 Center St 04468 (Mail to: PO Box 183 04468-0183) Richard Johnson (207) 827-5013

Orrs Island All Saints Summer Chapel **SC** 9 Cooper Ln 04066-2112 (Mail to: PO Box 114 04066) (207) 833-7745

Palmyra St Martins Episcopal Church **M** (48) 900 Main St 04965-3408 (Mail to: PO Box 107 04965) Leslie Nesin Laura Peckham (207) 938-3385

Peaks Island Holy Trinity Episcopal Summer Chapel **SC** 69 Knickerbocker Lane 04108 (207) 766-3376

✣ **Portland** Cathedral Church of St Luke **O** (682) 143 State St 04101-3701 (Mail to: 143 State St 04101) Benjamin Shambaugh David Glendinning Suzanne Roberts (207) 772-5434

Portland St Peters Church **P** (283) 10 Alton St 04103-4906 (Mail to: 10 Alton St 04103-4906) Bennett Barnes

Portland Trinity Episcopal Church **P** (460) 113 Coyle St 04103-4402 (Mail to: 580 Forest Ave 04101-1509) Lawrence Weeks (207) 772-7421

Presque Isle St Johns Episcopal Church **P** (32) 52 2nd St 04769-2636 (Mail to: PO Box 8 04769-0008) Judith Burleigh Stephen Summerson (207) 764-4298

Rangeley Church of the Good Shepherd **P** (99) 2614 Main St 04970-4114 (Mail to: PO Box 156 04970-0156) (207) 864-3381

Rockland St Peters Episcopal Church **P** (301) White St 04841 (Mail to: 11 White St 04841-2982) Lael Sorensen Arthur Karker (207) 594-8191

Rumford St Barnabas Episcopal Church **P** (19) 71 Rumford Ave 04276-1973 (Mail to: PO Box 591 04276-0591) Timothy Parsons (207) 364-2193

Saco Trinity Episcopal Church **P** (252) 403 Main St 04072-1522 (Mail to: 403 Main St 04072-1522) David Robinson Linda Cappers (207) 284-4852

Sanford St Georges Episcopal Church **P** (209) 1 Emerson St 04073-3903 (Mail to: 3 Emerson St 04073-3903) Susan Murphy (207) 324-8119

Scarborough St Nicholas Episcopal Church **M** (186) 348 US Route 1 04074-9774 (Mail to: 350 US Route 1 04070-8307) David Heald (207) 883-9437

Skowhegan All Saints Episcopal Church **M** (38) 169 Malbons Mills Rd 04976-4122 (Mail to: PO Box 412 04976-0412) William Blaine-Wallace (207) 474-2629

Sorrento Church of the Redeemer Summer Chapel **SC** 62 Bayview Ave 04677 (Mail to: PO Box 123 04677-0123) (207) 422-3955

Southport All Saints by the Sea Summer Chapel **SC** PO Box 377 04576-0377 (Mail to: General Delivery 04576-9999) (207) 633-7301

Southwest Hbr Sts Andrew & John Episcopal Church **P** (103) 315 Main St 04679-4403 (Mail to: 315 Main St 04679-0767) Timothy Fleck (207) 244-3229

Thomaston Episcopal Church of St John Baptist **P** (212) 200 Main St 04861-3800 (Mail to: 200 Main St 04861-3800) Peter Jenks (207) 354-8734

Waterville St Marks Church **P** (317) 60 Eustis Pkwy 04901-4932 (Mail to: 60 Eustis Pkwy 04901-4932) John Balicki (207) 872-7869

Windham St Anns Episcopal Church **P** (395) 40 Windham Center Rd 04062 (Mail to: PO Box 911 04062) Timothy Higgins Wendy Rozene (207) 892-8477

Winn St Thomas Episcopal Church **M** (28) 14 Main Street 04495 (Mail to: PO Box 76 04495-0076) (207) 736-2010

Winter Harbor St Christopher Summer Chapel **SC** 9 Clubhouse Rd 04693 (Mail to: PO Box 388 04693) Thomas Van Culin Ralph Warren (207) 963-5554

Winthrop St Andrews Episcopal Church **M** (54) 219 Winthrop Center Rd. 04364 (Mail to: PO Box 66 04364) (207) 395-2015

Wiscasset St Philips Episcopal Church **P** (97) 12 Hodge St 04578-4021 (Mail to: 12 Hodge St 04578-4021) Paul Tunkle (207) 882-7184

Yarmouth St Bartholomews Episcopal Church **P** (469) 396 Gilman Rd 04096-5731 (Mail to: 396 Gilman Rd 04096-5731) Nina Pooley (207) 846-9244

York St George's Episcopal Church **P** (543) 407 York St 03909-1060 (Mail to: PO Box 364 03911-0364) Calvin Sanborn Susan Blanchard Aaron Perkins

York Harbor Trinity Church **SC** No 546 York Street 03911 (Mail to: P O Box 323 03911) (207) 363-5095

NON-PAROCHIAL CLERGY

Alexander BA Dresden ME
Ambler MN Bath ME
Appleyard JB *ret* Woolwich ME
Babson KE *ret* Brunswick ME
Bamforth RA *ret* Augusta ME
Barth BL Auburn ME
Beal ME *dcn* Chesterville ME
Beaven JC *ret* Brunswick ME
Bennett CA *dcn* Raymond ME
Birney EH *dcn* Topsham ME
Birney JG *ret* North Yarmouth ME
Bittner M *ret* Newry ME
Black VK *dcn* Damariscotta ME
Bockus IL *ret* Prospect ME
Bowen PS *dcn* Biddeford ME
Bradshaw CR *ret* Ambridge PA
Bruce DA *ret* West Bath ME
Burns LF *dcn* Chelsea ME
Butler RM *ret* Zephyrhills FL
Carroll CM *dcn* Brunswick ME
Chandler GS *dcn* Kennebunk ME
Chatfield JS *dcn* Rockland ME
Chornyak CJ *ret* Ellsworth ME
Clarke BJ *ret* Brewer ME
Colby RE *ret* Kingwood TX
Conley KM *dcn* Kennebunk ME
Cyr GA Bangor ME
Day MA *dcn* Old Town ME
Dean JJ Dover NH
Delafield AS *dcn* South Portland ME
Deleuse BW *dcn* Portland ME
Deschaine TC *dcn* Augusta ME
Duplessie TF *dcn* Exeter ME
Estey LM *ret* Stonington ME
Farrar CT *ret*
Fles JC *ret* Gardiner ME
Foote SW *ret* Bremen ME
Gaiser TJ *dcn*
Gallagher R *ret* Seattle WA
Geiger CT *ret* Stuart FL
Gibson ES *ret* Wilmington DE
Gilbert TF *dcn* Pittsfield ME
Gilmore EL *ret* Portland ME
Grant RA *dcn* Augusta ME
Griffin MCA *dcn* Bar Harbor ME

Hagen AA *ret* Millinocket ME
Halkett TR *ret* Machias ME
Hall RH *ret* Brunswick ME
Hargreaves RA *ret* Nobleboro ME
Hedger JS *ret* Naples FL
Hemenway HJ *ret* Hanover NH
Henderson DB *dcn* Waterville ME
Henderson SG *ret* Portland ME
Holroyd DD *ret* South Berwick ME
Hoy MAC *ret* Freeport ME
Huntington CL *dcn* Bath ME
Illingworth DP *ret* Portland ME
Ineson JH *ret* Damariscotta ME
Keggi JJ *ret* Wellesley MA
Knox RG Portland ME
Kowalski VM *ret*
Lanctot MJ Winnipeg MB
Lathrop J *ret* Santa Fe NM
Lewis JW *dcn* Camden ME
Lindsey KL *ret* Augusta ME
Longstaff TRW Waterville ME
Maclin CW *ret* Portland ME
Maleri KD Milton MA
Matter JL *dcn* Billerica MA
McAlhany JA *dcn* Bangor ME
McCall JKW *ret* San Francisco CA
McIlveen RW
McKean DA *dcn* Cushing ME
Metzler CW Albuquerque NM
Miller ES *ret* South Portland ME
Miller JP *ret* Pawleys Island SC
Moore RM *ret* Rockland ME
Moughty KP Cape Elizabeth ME
Murdoch WH *ret* Damariscotta ME
Nickerson DA *ret* Intervale NH
O'Donnell EG *dcn* Dallas TX
O'Sullivan AK *dcn*
Otis VL *ret* Falmouth ME
Partridge HR Scarborough ME
Pealer JP *ret* Rangeley ME
Pettee AB *dcn* Camden ME
Peyton L Freeport ME
Phelps JE *ret* Kennebunk ME
Pierce GT *ret* Scarborough ME
Platt NGVD *ret* Augusta ME
Pollock EG York Harbor ME
Potter RK *ret* Augusta ME
Preble JN *dcn* Ellsworth ME
Price GN *ret* Portland ME
Radley CP *ret* Washington DC
Rafter JW *ret* Camden ME
Rasner RL *dcn* Portland ME
Reynolds GA *ret*
Richardson MAK *dcn* Westport Is ME
Riggall DJ *ret* Kennebunk ME
Rincon VM South Portland ME
Rollins EW Portland ME
Russell CA *ret* Boothbay Harbor ME
Russell ME *ret* Boothbay Harbor ME
Schuyler W *ret* Sanford ME
Seekins SA Rockland ME

Serfes PM *dcn* New Port Richey FL
Shaver EM *ret* Harpswell ME
Sherman LB *ret* Bangor ME
Sivret DO *ret* Alexander ME
Smith RS *ret* Manchester ME
Sniffen ET *ret* Readfield ME
Stanley AG *ret* Paris ME
Stiles KM Cambridge MA
Studdiford LH *ret* Brunswick ME
Sunderland ESS *ret* Providence RI

Taylor MAD *ret* Frankfort ME
Thomas MA *ret* Penobscot ME
Van Siclen JR *ret* Damariscotta ME
Walmer CA *dcn* Farmington ME
Wang KM East Waterboro ME
Wetherill BW *dcn* Rangeley ME
White SJ *ret* Newcastle ME
White WDA *ret* Brunswick ME
Widdows JH *ret* Portland ME
Woodsum M Fallbrook CA

STATE OF MARYLAND
Dioceses of Easton (E), Maryland (MD), and Washington (W)

Abingdon—MD
Annapolis—MD
Aquasco—W
Avenue—W
Baltimore—MD
Bel Air—MD
Beltsville—W
Berlin—E
Bethesda—W
Boonsboro—MD
Bowie—W
Braddock Hts—MD
Brandywine—W
Brookeville—W
Brownsville—MD
Brunswick—MD
California—W
Cambridge—E
Centreville—E
Chaptico—W
Charlotte Hall—W
Chesapeake City—E
Chestertown—E
Chevy Chase—W
Church Creek—E
Church Hill—E
Churchville—MD
Clear Spg—MD
Clinton—W
Cockeysville—MD
College Pk—W
Columbia—MD
Crownsville—MD
Cumberland—MD
Damascus—W
Darlington—MD

Deale—MD
Denton—E
District Hts—W
Dundalk—MD
Earleville—E
Easton—E
Edgewater—MD
Elkridge—MD
Elkton—E
Ellicott City—MD
Essex—MD
Forest Hill—MD
Ft Washington—W
Frederick—MD
Frostburg—MD
Gaithersburg—W
Germantown—W
Glen Burnie—MD
Glencoe—MD
Glenwood—MD
Glenn Dale—W
Gwynn Oak—MD
Hagerstown—MD
Halethorpe—MD
Hampstead—MD
Hancock—MD
Havre de Grace—MD
Hebron—E
Highland—MD
Hughesville—W
Hurlock—E
Hyattsville—W
Indian Head—W
Joppatowne—MD
Kennedyville—E
Kensington—W

Kingsville—MD
LaPlata—W
Laurel—W
Leonardtown—W
Lexington Pk—W
Linthicum Hts—MD
Lonaconing—MD
Long Green—MD
Lothian—MD
Lusby—MD
Lutherville Timon—
    MD
Massey—E
Mayo—MD
Monkton—MD
Mt Airy—MD
Mt Rainier—W
Mt Savage—MD
Nanjemoy—W
New Market—MD
Newburg—W
North East—E
Oakland—MD
Ocean City—E
Odenton—MD
Olney—W
Owings Mills—MD
Oxford—E
Parkton—MD
Pasadena—MD
Perryville—E
Pikesville—MD
Pocomoke City—E
Pt of Rocks—MD
Poolesville—W
Pt Republic—MD

Potomac—W
Prince Frederick—MD
Princess Anne—E
Quantico—E
Queenstown—E
Reisterstown—MD
Ridge—W
Rockville—W
St Michael—E
Salisbury—E
Severna Pk—MD
Sharpsburg—MD
Silver Spg—W
Smithsburg—MD
Snow Hill—E
Stevensville—E
Street—MD
Sunderland—MD
Sykesville—MD
Temple Hills—W
Thurmont—MD
Towson—MD
Trappe—E
Tyaskin—E
Upper Marlboro—W
Vienna—E
Waldorf—W
Washington—W
W River—MD
Westernport—MD
Westminster—MD
Worton—E
Wye Mills—E

DIOCESE OF MARYLAND
(PROVINCE III)
Comprises western shore of Maryland excluding Charles,
Montgomery, Prince George's & St Mary's Counties
DIOCESAN OFFICE 4 E University Pkwy Baltimore MD 21218
TEL (410) 467-1399, (800) 443-1399 FAX (410) 554-6387
E-MAIL feedback@episcopalmaryland.org WEB www.episcopalmaryland.org

Previous Bishops—
Thomas J Claggett 1792-1816,
James Kemp suffr 1814 Bp 1816-
27, Wm M Stone 1830-38, Wm
R Whittingham 1840-79, Wm
Pinkney coadj 1870 Bp 1879-
83, Wm Paret 1885-1911, John
G Murray coadj 1909 Bp 1911-
29, Edward T Helfenstein coadj
1926 Bp 1929-44, Noble C Powell coadj 1941 Bp
1944-63, Harry L Doll suffr 1955 coadj 1958 Bp 1963-
71, William J Cox suffr 1972-80, David K Leighton
Sr coadj 1968 Bp 1972-85, Barry Valentine asst
1986-88, A Theodore Eastman coadj 1982 Bp 1986-
94, Charles L Longest suffr 1989-97, Robert W Ihloff
Bp 1995-2007, John L Rabb Bp-in-Charge 2007-
08 Suffr 1998-2010, Joe G Burnett asst 2011-2013

Bishop—Rt Rev Eugene Taylor Sutton (1030)
(Dio 28 June 2008)

Assistant Bishop—Rt Rev Chilton R. Knudsen

Staff: Cn to the Ord Rev SG Slater; *Cn for Mission*
Rev AF Shepherd; *Cn for Evan & Media* Rev D
Webster; *Cn for Transitions and Human Resources*
Rev SW Wright; *Missioner for Yth & Young Adults*
TK Riley *Latino Missioner* Rev RM Santana;
Archivist M Klein

Officers: CFO KK Stewart; *Treas* D Vaughan; *Chanc*
J Ayres c/o Venable 210 W Pennsylvania Ave Ste
500 Towson MD 21204; *Sec of Convention* Rev AO
Weatherholt

Stand Comm—Cler: M Gatza T Slawson D
vanKlaveren N Conway; *Lay: Pres* P Durham A Bell
C Fallin M Garcia

Archdeacons: Archdcn for Form Rev M Doran;
Archdcn for Deployment Rev Carl Wright

Dio Conv: 13-14 May 2016 Ellicott City MD

PARISHES, MISSIONS, AND CLERGY

Abingdon St Marys Episcopal Church **P** (484) 1
Saint Marys Church Rd 21009-1565 (Mail to:
1 Saint Marys Church Rd 21009-1569) Thomas
Allen (410) 569-0180

Annapolis St Annes Episcopal Parish **P** (2219) 199
Duke Of Gloucester St 21401-2520 (Mail to:
199 Duke Of Gloucester St 21401-2520) Amy
Richter William Bell John Kenny Richardson
Libby Joseph Pagano (410) 267-9333

Annapolis St Lukes Church **P** (108) No 1101
Bay Ridge Ave 21403-2901 (Mail to: 1101 Bay
Ridge Ave 21403-2901) Diana Carroll (410)
263-5419

Annapolis St Margarets Episcopal Church **P**
(1242) 1601 Pleasant Plains Rd 21401-5928
(Mail to: 1601 Pleasant Plains Rd 21409-5928)
Peter Mayer Jane Hague (410) 974-0200

Annapolis St Philips Episcopal Church **P** (284)
730 Bestgate Rd 21401-2137 (Mail to: 730
Bestgate Rd 21401-2137) Randy Callender
John Naegele (410) 266-9755

✠ **Baltimore** Cathedral of the Incarnation **O**
(945) 4 E University Pkwy 21218-2437 (Mail
to: 4 E University Pkwy 21218-2490) Robert
Boulter Jane Mayrer (410) 467-3750

Baltimore Christ the King Episcopal Church **P**
(124) 1930 Brookdale Rd 21244-1704 (Mail
to: 1930 Brookdale Rd 21244-1704) Mary Eliot
(410) 944-6683

Baltimore Church of St Mary the Virgin **P** (100)
3121 Walbrook Ave 21216-3031 (Mail to: 3121
Walbrook Ave 21216-3031) Charles Mercer

Baltimore Church of St Michael & All Angels
P (131) 2013 Saint Paul St 21218-5929 (Mail
to: 2013 Saint Paul St 21218-5998) Ramelle
McCall (410) 685-3128

Baltimore Church of the Advent - Federal Hill **P**
(172) 1234 Patapsco St Apt 2 21230-4246 (Mail
to: 1301 S Charles St 21230-4218) Timothy
Kroh (410) 539-7804

Baltimore Church of the Guardian Angel **P** (68)
2629 Huntingdon Ave 21211-3111 (Mail to:
2629 Huntingdon Ave 21211-3111) Alice
Jellema Jane O'Leary (443) 879-9453

Baltimore Church of the Holy Covenant **P** (97)
5657 The Alameda 21239-2738 (Mail to: 5657
the Alameda 21239-2738) M Dion Thompson
(410) 435-3707

Baltimore Church of the Holy Nativity **M** (82)
4238 Pimlico Rd 21215-6961 (Mail to: 4238
Pimlico Rd 21215-6961) (410) 542-9554

Baltimore Church of the Holy Trinity **P** (228)
2300 W Lafayette Ave 21216-4816 (Mail to:
2300 W Lafayette Ave 21216-4898) Eddie Blue
(410) 945-0002

Baltimore Church of the Messiah **P** (140) 5801
Harford Rd 21214-1848 (Mail to: 5801 Harford
Rd 21214-1848) Timothy Grayson (410) 426-
0709

Baltimore Church of the Nativity **P** (120) 419
Cedarcroft Rd 21212-2523 (Mail to: 419
Cedarcroft Rd 21212-2599) Anthony Hollis
Thomas Lucas (410) 433-4811

Baltimore Church of the Redeemer **P** (3264) 5603 N Charles St 21210-2006 (Mail to: 5603 N Charles St 21210-2097) Maria Cristina Paglinauan Caroline Stewart David Ware (410) 435-7333

Baltimore Church of the Redemption **P** (98) 1401 Towson St 21230-5301 (Mail to: 1401 Towson St 21230-5301) Mary Davisson (410) 539-8270

Baltimore Church of the Resurrection **M** (80) 2900 E Fayette St 21224-1316 (Mail to: 4 E University Pkwy 21218-2437) (443) 631-0115

Baltimore Emmanuel Episcopal Church **P** (569) 811 Cathedral St 21201-5201 (Mail to: 811 Cathedral St 21201-5201) (410) 685-1130

Baltimore Grace & St Peters Church **P** (411) 707 Park Ave 21201-4703 (Mail to: 707 Park Ave 21201-4799) Frederick Thomas (410) 539-1395

Baltimore Memorial Episcopal Church **P** (474) 1407 Bolton St 21217-4202 (Mail to: 1407 Bolton St 21217-4202) Ervin Brown William Sell-Lee (410) 669-0220

Baltimore Old St Pauls **P** (436) 233 N Charles St 21201 (Mail to: 309 Cathedral St 21201-4410) Mark Stanley Daniel Meck Mary Stanley (410) 685-3404

Baltimore St Bartholomews Episcopal Church **P** (411) 4711 Edmondson Ave 21229-2404 (Mail to: 4711 Edmondson Ave 21229-1440) Florence Ledyard Neva Brown Maria Fedock Thelma Smullen (410) 945-7263

Baltimore St Davids Church **P** (769) 4700 Roland Ave 21210-2320 (Mail to: 4700 Roland Ave 21210-2399) Scott Bellows Anna Noon

Baltimore St James' Episcopal Church **P** (454) 829 N Arlington Ave 21217-2534 (Mail to: 1020 W Lafayette Ave 21217-2555) Allen Robinson Carole Douglas Melvin Truiett (410) 523-4588

Baltimore St Johns Church **P** (136) 3001 Old York Rd 21218-3544 (Mail to: 3009 Greenmount Ave 21218-3939) Jesse Parker Natalie Conway

Baltimore St Johns Episcopal Church **P** (100) 1702 South Rd 21209-4504 (Mail to: 1702 South Rd 21209-4504) Lori Babcock (410) 367-7287

Baltimore St Katherine of Alexandria **P** (233) 2001 Division St 21217-3323 (Mail to: 2001 Division St 21217-3323) Allston Jacobs (410) 523-2207

Baltimore St Lukes Franklin Square **P** (31) 217 N Carey St 21223-1836 (Mail to: PO Box 20596 21223-0596) (410) 523-6272

Baltimore St Matthias Episcopal Church **P** (69) 6400 Belair Rd 21206-1840 (Mail to: 6400 Belair Rd 21206-1899) Ann Copp (410) 426-1002

Bel Air Emmanuel Episcopal Church **P** (391) Main St & Broadway 21014 (Mail to: PO Box 628 21014-0628) Mark Gatza (410) 838-7699

Boonsboro St Marks Episcopal Church **P** (449) 18313 Lappans Rd 21713-1918 (Mail to: 18313 Lappans Rd 21713-1918) Charles McGinley

Anne Weatherholt John Cozzoli (301) 582-0417

Braddock Heights Church of the Transfiguration **P** (151) 6909 Maryland Ave 21714 (Mail to: PO Box 87 21714-0087) Gordon De La Vars

Brownsville St Lukes Episcopal Church **M** (29) 2150 Boteler Rd 21715-2008 (Mail to: 2150 Boteler Rd 21758-1002) Thomas Hudson (301) 432-4209

Brunswick Grace Episcopal Church **P** (74) 114 E A St 21716-1406 (Mail to: 114 E A St 21716-1406) Anjel Scarborough (301) 843-8540

Churchville Holy Trinity Church **P** (146) 2929 Level Rd 21028-1820 (Mail to: PO Box 25 21028-0025) Arthur Ingalls (410) 836-2227

Clear Spring St Andrew's Episcopal Church **M** (82) 22 Cumberland St 21722 (Mail to: PO Box 189 21722-0189) Steven McCarty (301) 842-2433

Cockeysville Sherwood Episcopal Church **P** (108) 5 Sherwood Rd 21030-2323 (Mail to: 5 Sherwood Rd 21030-2346) (410) 666-2180

Columbia Christ Episcopal Church **P** (1066) 6800 Oakland Mills Rd 21045-4706 (Mail to: 6800 Oakland Mills Rd 21045-4706) (410) 381-9365

Crownsville St Stephens - Severn Parish **P** (499) 1112 Saint Stephens Church Rd 21032-1908 (Mail to: 1110 Saint Stephens Church Rd 21032-1908) Steven Hagerman (410) 721-2881

Cumberland Emmanuel Episcopal Church **P** (643) 16 Washington St 21502-2924 (Mail to: 16 Washington St 21502-2976) Martha Macgill (301) 777-3364

Darlington Grace Memorial Church **P** (103) 1022 Main St 21034-1434 (Mail to: PO Box 35 21034-0035) (410) 836-3587

✠ **Deale** St Marks Chapel **Other** 361 Deale Rd 20779 (Mail to: c/o St James' 5757 Solomons Island 20711) William Ticknor Amanda Knouse (410) 867-2838

Dundalk St George & St Matthew Episcopal Ch **P** (308) 2900 Dunleer Rd 21222-5112 (Mail to: 2900 Dunleer Road 21222-5112) Jansen String (410) 284-6242

Edgewater All Hallows Episcopal Church **P** (289) 3600 Solomons Island Rd 21037 (Mail to: 3604 Solomons Island Rd 21037-3620) Alistair So (410) 798-0808

Elkridge Grace Episcopal Church **P** (570) 6725 Montgomery Rd 21075-5723 (Mail to: 6725 Montgomery Rd 21075-5723) Travis Smith (410) 796-3270

Elkridge Trinity Episcopal Church **P** (157) 7474 Washington Blvd 21075-6330 (Mail to: 7474 Washington Blvd 21075-6330) Anne Macnabb (410) 220-3628

Ellicott City St Johns Episcopal Church **P** (1798) 9120 Frederick Rd 21042-3912 (Mail to: 9120 Frederick Rd 21042-3978) Carol Oak Emmett Anderson Wan Lee Miriam Mathews Anna Noon Jennifer Ovenstone (410) 461-7793

Ellicott City St Peters Church **P** (278) 3695 Rogers Ave 21043-4125 (Mail to: 3695 Rogers Ave 21043-4175) H Thomas Slawson (410) 465-2273

Essex Holy Trinity Episcopal Church **P** (234) C/O The Reverend Eric Zile 1131 Mace Ave 21221-3316 (Mail to: 1131 Mace Ave 21221-3316) Eric Zile (410) 687-5531

Forest Hill Christ Episcopal Church **P** (398) 2100 Rock Spring Rd 21050-2632 (Mail to: PO Box 215 21050-0215) Frances Le Blanc (410) 838-6606

Frederick All Saints Church **P** (1115) 108 W Church St 21701-5411 (Mail to: 106 W Church St 21701-5411) Jessica Holthus Walter Mullins (301) 663-5625

Frederick St Timothy's Episcopal Church **M** (58) 36 Franklin St 21701-5710 (Mail to: C/O Irene Cole 8404 Grossnickle Ct. 21793-8600) (301) 448-7157

Frostburg St Johns Episcopal Church **P** (35) 52 S Broadway 21532-1710 (Mail to: PO Box 229 21532-0229) Karen Crosby (301) 689-6634

Glen Burnie St Albans Episcopal Parish **P** (231) 105 1st Ave 21060-7627 (Mail to: 105 1st Ave SW 21061) Paula Barker (410) 766-1455

Glencoe Immanuel Episcopal Church **P** (176) 1509 Glencoe Rd 21152-9439 (Mail to: 1509 Glencoe Rd 21152-9349) Megan Stewart-Sicking

Glenwood St Andrews Episcopal Church **P** (606) Rte 97 At Union Chapel Rd 21738 (Mail to: PO Box 52 21738-0052) Dina Van Klaveren Charles Shaffer (410) 489-4035

Gwynn Oak St Mary Episcopal Church **P** (66) 5610 Dogwood Rd 21207-5906 (Mail to: 5610 Dogwood Rd 21207-5985) William Anderson Susan Oldfather

Hagerstown St Johns Episcopal Church **P** (487) 101 S Prospect St 21740-5409 (Mail to: 101 S Prospect St 21740-5495) Kim Baker

Halethorpe The Church of the Holy Apostles **P** (133) 4922 Leeds Ave 21227-2412 (Mail to: 4922 Leeds Ave 21227-2412) (410) 242-5477

Hampstead St Georges Episcopal Church **P** (333) 2434 Cape Horn Rd 21074-1123 (Mail to: 2434 Cape Horn Rd 21074-1172) Mario Conliffe Anthony Warner

Hancock St Thomas Church **P** (823) 2 E High St 21750-1216 (Mail to: 2 E High St 21750-1216) Floyd Weatherholt (301) 678-6569

Havre De Grace St Johns Episcopal Church **P** (59) 114 N Union Ave 21078-3008 (Mail to: PO Box 306 21078-3008) T James Snodgrass (410) 939-2107

Highland St Marks Episcopal Church **P** (438) 12700 Hall Shop Rd 20777-9544 (Mail to: 12701 Hall Shop Rd 20777-9547) Taylor Smith (301) 854-2304

Joppatowne Copley Parish **P** (90) 700 Anchor Dr 21085-0222 (Mail to: PO Box 222 21085-0222)

Matthew D'Amario (410) 679-8700

Kingsville St Johns Episcopal Church **P** (257) 11901 Belair Rd 21087-1155 (Mail to: PO Box 187 21087-0187) Daniel Hinkle (410) 592-8570

Linthicum Hts St Christopher Episcopal Church **P** (73) 116 Marydel Rd 21090-2130 (Mail to: 116 Marydell Rd 21090-2130) Monique Ellison (410) 859-5633

Lonaconing St Peters Episcopal Church **M** (74) 6 Saint Peters Place 21562 (Mail to: 6 Saint Peters Place 21562) Thomas Hudson (301) 463-6144

Long Green Trinity Episcopal Church **P** (198) 12400 Manor Rd 21092 (Mail to: PO Box 4001 21057-1001) Virginia Stanford Charles Pugh (410) 592-6224

Lothian St James Parish **P** (594) 5757 Solomons Island Rd 20711-9707 (Mail to: 5757 Solomons Island Rd 20711-9792) William Ticknor (410) 867-2838

Lusby Middleham & St Peters Parish **P** (572) 10210 H G Trueman Rd 20657 (Mail to: PO Box 277 20657-0277) David Showers Erin Shank (410) 326-4948

Luthvle Timon Epiphany Episcopal Church **P** (335) 2216 Pot Spring Rd 21093-2724 (Mail to: 2216 Pot Spring Road 21093-2797) Kathryn Wajda Kristofer Lindh-Payne (410) 252-4465

Luthvle Timon The Church of the Holy Comforter **P** (378) 130 W Seminary Ave 21093-5523 (Mail to: 130 W Seminary Ave 21093-5523) Christopher Tang William Dunning (410) 252-2711

Mayo St Andrew the Fisherman **P** (123) Central Ave & Carrs Wharf Rd 21106 (Mail to: PO Box 175 21106-0175) Rock Schuler (410) 798-1533

Monkton St James Episcopal Church **P** (1403) 3100 Monkton Rd 21111-2113 (Mail to: 3100 Monkton Rd 21111-2113) Charles Barton Charles Barton Victor Hailey (410) 771-4466

Mount Airy St James' Episcopal Church **P** (327) 1307 N Main Street 21771-0416 (Mail to: 1307 N Main Street 21771-7499) Kristin Krantz (301) 829-0325

Mount Airy St Pauls Episcopal Church **P** (63) 16457 Old Frederick Rd 21771-3331 (Mail to: 16457 Old Frederick Rd 21771-3331) Susan Keller (410) 489-4411

Mount Savage St Georges Episcopal Church **P** (32) 12811 Saint Georges Ln NW 21545-1001 (Mail to: PO Box 655 21545-0655) Theresa Brion (301) 264-3524

New Market Grace Episcopal Church **P** (250) 4 E Main St 21774 (Mail to: PO Box 17 21774-0017) Sharon Watts

Oakland Garrett County Episcopal Church **P** 5234 Maryland Hwy 21550-4807 (Mail to: Route 135 21550)

Oakland Our Fathers House **SC** 109 C St 21550-3507 (Mail to: PO Box 414 21550-4414) William Lee (301) 334-1197

Oakland St Johns Church **M** (135) 5234 Maryland

Hwy 21550-4807 (Mail to: PO Box 414 21550-4414) William Lee (301) 334-2510

Oakland St Matthews Church **P** (195) PO Box 303 21550-0303 (Mail to: PO Box 303 21550-4807) William Lee Anne Byrne Pamela Fahrner Gloria Stromwell (301) 334-2510

Odenton Epiphany Episcopal Church **P** (809) PO Box 110 21113-0110 (Mail to: PO Box 110 21113-0110) Phebe Mcpherson (410) 674-8819

Owings Mills St Thomas Episcopal Church **P** (1321) 232 Saint Thomas Ln 21117-3806 (Mail to: 232 Saint Thomas Ln 21117-3800) Malcolm Ellis Nathan Erdman (410) 363-1044

Parkton St James Episcopal Church **P** (258) 19200 York Rd 21120-9207 (Mail to: PO Box 420 21120-0420) (410) 357-4473

Pasadena St Andrews Episcopal Church **P** (149) 7859 Tick Neck Rd 21122-2264 (Mail to: 7859 Tick Neck Rd 21122-2264) John Kenny Carl Wright (410) 255-1070

Pikesville Church of St Marks on the Hill **P** (388) 1620 Reisterstown Rd 21208-2902 (Mail to: 1620 Reisterstown Rd 21208-2900) Adrien Dawson (410) 486-3016

Port Of Rocks St Pauls Episcopal Church **P** (51) 1914 Ballenger Creek Rd 21777 (Mail to: PO Box 216 21777-0216) Grayce Rowe (301) 874-2995

Port Republic Christ Church **P** (234) 3100 Broomes Island Rd 20676-2101 (Mail to: 3100 Broomes Island Rd 20676) (410) 586-0565

Prnc Frederck St Pauls Episcopal Church **P** (185) 25 Church St 20678-4116 (Mail to: PO Box 99 20678-0099) M Joanna White (410) 535-2897

Reisterstown All Saints Episcopal Church **P** (461) 203 E Chatsworth Ave 21136-1305 (Mail to: 203 E Chatsworth Ave 21136-1305) Melvin Turner (410) 833-0700

Reisterstown St Johns Church **P** (425) 3738 Butler Rd 21136-3830 (Mail to: Western Run Parish 3738 Butler Road 21136-3830) Tracy Bruce Joseph Cochran (410) 429-4690

Severna Park St Martins-in-the-Field Episcopal Ch **P** (1261) 375 Benfield Rd 21146-2794 (Mail to: 375 Benfield Rd 21146-2794) (410) 647-6248

Sharpsburg St Pauls Episcopal Church **P** (113) 209 W Main St 21782 (Mail to: PO Box 364 21782-0364) Mark Wastler (301) 432-7098

Smithsburg St Anns Episcopal Church **P** (48) 9 N Maple Ave 21783-9702 (Mail to: 9 N Maple Ave 21783-9702) Sandra Kline-Mortimer (301) 824-3033

Street Church of the Ascension **P** (60) 3460 Mill Green Rd 21154-1724 (Mail to: 3460 Mill Green Rd 21154-1724) (410) 836-3587

Street Holy Cross Episcopal Church **M** (132) 4603 Rocks Rd 21154-1210 (Mail to: PO Box 103 21154-0103) Marta Johnson (410) 452-5502

Sunderland All Saints Parish **P** (243) 100 Lower Marlboro Rd 20689 (Mail to: PO Box 40

20689-1692) Kenneth Phelps Michelle Doran Margaret VanAuker (410) 257-6306

Sykesville St Barnabas Episcopal Church **P** (238) 13135 Forsythe Rd 21784-5818 (Mail to: 13135 Forsythe Rd 21784-7337) Martha Watson (410) 489-2800

Thurmont Catoctin Parish Harriet Chapel **P** (120) 12625 Catoctin Furnace Rd 21788-3008 (Mail to: 12625 Catoctin Furnace Rd 21788-3008) Sally Joyner-Giffin (301) 271-4554

Towson Church of the Good Shepherd **P** (866) 1401 Carrollton Ave 21204-6518 (Mail to: 1401 Carrollton Avenue 21204-6518) Arianne Weeks Joshua Rodriguez-Hobbs (410) 823-0122

Towson St Thomas Episcopal Church **P** (304) 1108 Providence Rd 21286-1743 (Mail to: 1108 Providence Rd 21286-1743) Loree Penner (410) 821-5489

Towson Trinity Episcopal Church **P** (471) § 120 Allegheny Ave 21204-4019 (Mail to: 120 Allegheny Ave 21204-4095) Kenneth Saunders Diane Fadely (410) 823-3588

West River Christ Episcopal Church **P** (294) 220 Owensville Rd 20778-9704 (Mail to: 220 Owensville Rd 20778-9704) Nicholas Szobota (410) 867-0346

Westernport St James Episcopal Church **P** (75) 32 Main St 21539 (Mail to: 32 Main Street 21539) Garrett Carskadon (301) 359-6001

Westminster Church of the Ascension **P** (563) 23 N Court St 21157-5109 (Mail to: 23 N Court St 21157-5352) Samuel Nsengiyumva Barbara Sears

NON-PAROCHIAL CLERGY

Arents G *dcn* Lutherville MD
Ash GA *ret* Cincinnati OH
Babin AED *ret* Sedona AZ
Bailey FH *dcn* Elkridge MD
Bauer TW *ret* Silver Spring MD
Billups BM *ret* Annapolis MD
Bishop HE Quincy PA
Blackburn JC *ret* Baltimore MD
Bolin WE *ret* Walkersville MD
Bonadie LRR Cumberland ND
Bourdeau ME *dcn* Lonaconing MD
Boyd VAL *ret* Frederick MD
Braine BB *ret* Monkton MD
Brunett HE *ret* Littleton CO
Bryant RG *ret* Covington KY
Burroughs JP *ret* Sykesville MD
Burt WR
Bustard-Burnside C Baltimore MD
Butts RP *ret* Finksburg MD
Cammack DW *ret* Sykesville MD
Carter TB *ret* Baltimore MD
Cassell JS *ret* Baltimore MD
Cawthorne JH *ret* Dunedin FL
Chappell AM *ret*
Claggett TW *dcn* Knoxville MD

Clark DN *ret* Clear Spring MD
Cloughen CE *ret* Hunt Valley MD
Coerper MG Chevy Chase MD
Cox FF Greensboro NC
Crowder JR *ret* Cockeysville MD
Culbertson TL *ret* Lutherville MD
Daly RE *ret* Cockeysville MD
Dawson FP *dcn*
Dawson PS *ret* Vineyard Haven MA
DeVore KE *dcn* Hancock MD
Dreisbach C Baltimore MD
Dunnan DS Saint James MD
Eads CC *ret* Swanton MD
Edleman SW *ret* Westminster MD
Edwards CN *ret*
Elder RA *dcn* Baltimore MD
Ellis MW *ret* Hilliard OH
Evans JM *ret* Portsmouth NH
Eversley WVL *ret* Baltimore MD
Fallowfield WH *ret* Baltimore MD
Fernandez LJP Baltimore MD
Fishbaugh-Looney KF Timonium MD
Fisher RS *ret* Severna Park MD
Flintom JG *ret* Hayes VA
Foote NB *dcn* Baltimore MD
Fortkamp FE *ret* Columbus OH
Frederick RJ *dcn* Baltimore MD
Fulghum PC *ret* Smithsburg MD
Gardner VH *ret* Baltimore MD
Geer CG Stonington CT
Gifford LAB *ret* Baltimore MD
Gillard GL
Gilliss C *ret* Adamstown MD
Ginnever RA *ret* Columbia MD
Goldbloom RA *dcn* Frostburg MD
Gordon-Barnes JE *ret* The Villages FL
Grusell KL Ellicott City MD
Hamill JE *ret* Bel Air MD
Hamilton JG Baltimore MD
Hammond HL *ret* Baltimore MD
Harmon JR *ret* Saint Ann MO
Harris CB *ret* Crofton MD
Hart JJ Towson MD
Hawkins JB Alexandria VA
Hayek HT Baltimore MD
Hayes JM Baltimore MD
Hirschman PRC *ret* Monrovia MD
Holder CR *ret* Rohrersville MD
Holland EL *ret* Baltimore MD
Howanstine JE *ret* Port Republic MD
Huber GJ Baltimore MD
Hudgen CR Baltimore MD
Hurwitz ES Myersville MD
Israel F *ret* Williamsburg VA
Johnson DB *ret* Arnold MD
Jones DA *ret* Highland MD
Jones TG *ret* Baltimore MD
Kaval LM Laurel MD
Klein JW *ret* Opelika AL
Knight WA *ret* Chester NH
Kratovil MEIJ *dcn* Williamsburg IA

Krulak WM *ret* Baltimore MD
Kubicek KA *ret* Stevenson MD
Lamming SR Annapolis MD
Landers GJ *dcn* Glen Arm MD
Larson WH Baltimore MD
Laveroni AF Hvre De Grace MD
Lewis SE Eldersburg MD
Lodder HK *ret* Lutherville MD
MacDonald HH *ret* Charlottesville VA
Maniyatt JK Baltimore MD
Martin JC *dcn* Cumberland MD
Martin LAP *dcn* Lavale MD
Martin RE Adamstown MD
McCoy RM *dcn* Annapolis MD
McDermott JR Concord CA
McDonald NH Bel Air MD
McDonnell BK *ret dcn* Sparks MD
McGarvey PP
McIntyre JG *ret* Havre De Grace MD
McNamara BC Towson MD
McPherson WB *ret* Annapolis MD
Merrill GR *ret* Saint Michaels MD
Miller RH *ret* Baltimore MD
Montjoy G *ret* Murrells Inlet SC
Moser PH *ret* Bel Air MD
Munro EH *dcn* Bowie MD
Newcomb BD *ret* Center Sandwich NH
Neylon JC *dcn*
Nicholson AL Washington DC
Olsen MDK Marietta GA
Orens EMP *ret*
Patterson RP *ret* Topsham ME
Peridans D Parkville MD
Perra JF Baltimore MD
Poling JA
Price JR *ret* Severna Park MD
Prince E *ret* Hagerstown MD
Pruitt GR *ret* Roanoke VA
Radcliffe WE *dcn* Molino FL
Ramsay FJ *ret* Glendale AZ
Ransom JC *ret* Wilmot NH
Raye JM *dcn* Westernport MD
Redmon WJ *ret* Palm Springs CA
Reid-Levy S *dcn*
Rice SK *dcn* Frederick MD
Rodriguez HR Columbia MD
Rogers MA Monkton MD
Rokos MG *ret* Baltimore MD
Rosenzweig EC *ret* Brooklin ME
Salmon AD *ret* Frederick MD
Santana RM San Pedro De Macoris
Saxe SE Alexandria VA
Scarlett WG *dcn*
Schirmacher MG *ret* Houston TX
Schmidt EW *ret* Catonsville MD
Sears B *dcn* Adamstown MD
Seras BJ Lancaster PA
Shahinian KA *dcn* Severna Park MD
Shematek JP *dcn* Ellicott City MD
Shepherd AF Baltimore MD
Shields JM *ret* Columbia MD

Shiflet WR *ret* Ellicott City MD
Shisler SL Baltimore MD
Simmons WC *ret* Lutherville Timonium MD
Slater SG Baltimore MD
Smith BH *ret* Baltimore MD
Smith JT *ret* Annapolis MD
Smith KJ *dcn* Tracys Landing MD
Smith ML *ret* Mountain Lake Park MD
Smith PK *ret* Towson MD
Smith WL *ret* Bel Air MD
Solon RF Baltimore MD
Speer RH *ret* Baltimore MD
Spicer CA *ret* Towson MD
Standiford SE *dcn*
Steiner J *ret* Elkridge MD
Stenner DA *ret* Reisterstown MD
Stewart-Sicking J Columbia MD
Swift SA *ret* Parkville MD
Tchamala TK Baltimore MD
Testa DA *ret* Linthicum MD
Thomas WE *ret* Thomaston ME
Tilden R *ret* Denton MD

Tipton-Zile C *ret* Perry Hall MD
Tongue MJ *dcn* Abingdon MD
Tunkle PD *ret* Dresden ME
Urquidi AE Virginia Beach VA
Vilar-Santiago ME *ret* Brooklanville MD
Wahl HE *dcn* Chesapeake Beach MD
Wakeman NA *dcn*
Walton MF *dcn* Richmond VA
Ward GB *dcn*
Warfield ES *ret* Sykesville MD
Webster DJ Baltimore MD
Welch LM *dcn* Baltimore MD
Wheeler JB *ret* Annapolis MD
White NA *ret dcn* Edgewater MD
Wiley HL Baltimore MD
Wilkerson CE *dcn* Annapolis MD
Willard JD Annapolis MD
Wizorek JC *ret* Prince Frederick MD
Woolley AE *ret* Catonsville MD
Wright SW Baltimore MD
Wubbenhorst W *ret* Baltimore MD

STATE OF MASSACHUSETTS

Dioceses of Massachusetts and Western Massachusetts

DIOCESE OF MASSACHUSETTS

(PROVINCE I)
Comprises eastern Massachusetts
DIOCESAN OFFICE 138 Tremont St Boston MA 02111-1318
TEL (617) 482-5800   FAX (617) 451-6446
E-MAIL info@diomass.org   WEB www.diomass.org

Previous Bishops—
Edward Bass 1797-1803, Samuel Parker 1804-04, Alexander V Griswold (Eastern Dio) 1811-43, Manton Eastburn coadj 1842 Bp 1843-72, Benj H Paddock 1873-91, Phillips Brooks 1891-93, Wm Lawrence 1893-1927, Charles L Slattery coadj 1922 Bp 1927-30, Saml G Babcock suffr 1913-38, Henry K Sherrill 1930-47, Raymond A Heron suffr 1938-54, Norman B Nash coadj 1947 Bp 1947-56, Frederic C Lawrence suffr 1956-68, Anson P Stokes Jr coadj 1954 Bp 1956-70, John M Burgess suffr 1962-69 coadj 1969 Bp 1970-75, Morris F Arnold suffr 1972-82, John B Coburn 1976-86, David E Johnson coadj 1985 Bp 1986-1995, Barbara C Harris suffr 1989-2002, Roy F Cederholm Jr suffr 2001-11, M Thomas Shaw III SSJE 1995-2014

Bishop—Rt Rev Alan M. Gates (1082) (Dio 13 Sep 2014)

Bishop Suffragan—Rt Rev Gayle Elizabeth Harris (981)

Chanc E Notis-McConarty; *Sec* LA Brathwaite; *Asst Sec* L Simons; *Treas* L Garcia; *Reg-Hist* L Smith; *Asst Treas* G Sullivan; *Dean* V Rev JP Streit Jr; *Bps Exec Asst* D Pound

Stand Comm—Cler: P Werntz A McCreath C Wendell A Stoessel; *Lay: Pres* J Nelson Dilday A McConney Scheepers J Iredale W Kennard

Dio Conv: 4-5 Nov 2016 Mansfield MA

PARISHES, MISSIONS, AND CLERGY

Acton Church of the Good Shepherd **P** (458) 164 Newtown Rd 01720-3114 (Mail to: 164 Newtown Rd Acton MA 01720-3114) Gareth Evans (978) 263-5782

Amesbury St James's Episcopal Church **P** (238) 120 Main St 01913-2809 (Mail to: PO Box 25 Amesbury MA 01913-0001) John Satula (978)

388-0030

Andover Christ Church **P** (1266) 33 Central St 01810-3737 (Mail to: 33 Central St Andover MA 01810-3737) Michael Hodges (978) 475-0529

Arlington Church of Our Saviour **P** (119) 21 Marathon St 02474-6940 (Mail to: 21 Marathon St Arlington MA 02474-6940) Malia Crawford (781) 648-5962

Arlington St John's Church **P** (235) 74 Pleasant St 02476-6516 (Mail to: 74 Pleasant St Arlington MA 02476-6516) Diane Wong (781) 648-4819

Attleboro All Saints' Episcopal Church **P** (48) 121 N Main St 02703-2221 (Mail to: 121 N Main St Attleboro MA 02703-2221) Meghan Sweeney Billie Gordon (508) 222-2233

Ayer St Andrew's Episcopal Church **P** (201) 7 Faulkner St 01432-1611 (Mail to: 7 Faulkner St Ayer MA 01432-1611) Joyce Scherer-Hoock (978) 772-2615

Barnstable St Mary's Episcopal Church **P** (576) 3055 Main St 02630-1119 (Mail to: PO Box 395 Barnstable MA 02630-0395) Elizabeth Gibson Michael Bousquet (508) 362-3977

Bedford St Paul's Episcopal Church **P** (310) 100 Pine Hill Rd 01730-1641 (Mail to: 100 Pine Hill Rd Bedford MA 01730-1698) Christopher Wendell Rachel Wildman (781) 275-8262

Belmont All Saints' Episcopal Church **P** (138) 17 Clark St 02478-2448 (Mail to: 17 Clark Street Belmont MA 02478-2448) Cheryl Minor Paul Minor (617) 484-2228

Beverly Farms St John's Church **P** (965) 705 Hale St 01915-2118 (Mail to: PO Box 5610 Beverly Farms MA 01915-2118) Stephanie Chase Bradbury Stephen Scarff (978) 927-0229

Beverly St Peter's Episcopal Church **P** (267) 4 Ocean St 01915-5220 (Mail to: 4 Ocean St Beverly MA 01915-5220) Manuel Faria (978) 922-3438

✠ **Boston** Cathedral Church of St Paul **O** 138 Tremont St C/O Diocese Of Massachusetts 02111-1318 (Mail to: 138 Tremont St Boston MA 02111) Marsha Hoecker John Streit Cristina Rathbone Katharine Black (617) 482-5800

Boston Emmanuel Episcopal Church **P** (237) 15 Newbury St 02116-3105 (Mail to: 15 Newbury St Boston MA 02116-3185) Susanne George Pamela Werntz (617) 536-3355

Boston Old North Christ Church **P** (140) 193 Salem St 02113-1123 (Mail to: 193 Salem St Boston MA 02113-1123) Eleanor Terry Stephen Ayres (617) 523-6676

Boston Parish of All Saints **P** (323) 209 Ashmont St 02124-3803 (Mail to: 209 Ashmont St Dorchester MA 02124-3803) Michael Godderz Frank Jarvis (617) 436-6370

Boston Church of St Augustine and St Martin **P** (117) 29 Lenox St 02118-3201 (Mail to: 31 Lenox St Boston MA 02118-3201) Evan

Thayer (617) 442-6395

Boston St Cyprian's Episcopal Church **P** (175) 1073 Tremont St 02120-2163 (Mail to: 1073 Tremont St Roxbury MA 02120-2163) Monrelle Williams Julian Fredie (617) 427-6175

Boston St John St James Church **P** (111) 149 Roxbury St 02119-1525 (Mail to: 149 Roxbury St Roxbury MA 02119-1525) Rospignac Ambroise (617) 445-8843

Boston St Mary's Episcopal Church **P** 14 Cushing Ave 02125-2009 (Mail to: 14 Cushing Ave Dorchester MA 02125-2009) Edwin Johnson (617) 282-3181

Boston St Stephen's Episcopal Church **M** (225) 419 Shawmut Ave 02118-3822 (Mail to: 419 Shawmut Ave Boston MA 02118-3825) Timothy Crellin Elizabeth Steinhauser (617) 262-9070

Boston Church of the Advent **P** (659) 30 Brimmer St 02108-1002 (Mail to: 30 Brimmer St Boston MA 02108-1002) Daphne Noyes Allan Warren Sammy Wood (617) 523-2377

Boston Trinity Church **P** (922) 206 Clarendon St 02116- (Mail to: 206 Clarendon St Boston MA 02116-3784) Patrick Ward Susan Rainey Dankel Rita Powell William Rich Samuel Lloyd (617) 536-0944

Braintree Emmanuel Episcopal Church **P** (137) 519 Washington St 02184-4655 (Mail to: 519 Washington St Braintree MA 02184) Thomas Mulvey (781)843-0170

Bridgewater Trinity Episcopal Church **P** (234) 91 Main Street 02324-1406 (Mail to: 91 Main St Bridgewater MA 02324-1406) Natasha Stewart (508) 697-4311

Brockton Grace Chapel **M** 900 Main St 02301 (Mail to: c/o First Evangelical Lutheran Church 900 Main St Brockton MA 02301) Moses Sowale James Kangethe (508)649-3161

Brookline All Saints Parish **P** (395) 1773 Beacon St 02445-4214 (Mail to: 1773 Beacon St Brookline MA 02445-4214) Richard Burden Anoma Abeyaratne (617) 738-1810

Brookline Boston University Episcopal Chapel **CC** 40 Prescott St 02446-4038 (Mail to: 40 Prescott St Brookline MA 02446-4038) Cameron Partridge (617) 596-2022

Brookline Church of Our Saviour **P** (150) 25 Monmouth St 02446-5604 (Mail to: 25 Monmouth St Brookline MA 02446-5604) Joel Ives (617) 277-7334

Brookline St Paul's Episcopal Church **P** (268) 15 Saint Paul St 02446-6501 (Mail to: 15 Saint Paul St Brookline MA 02446-6501) Jeffrey Mello Megan Holding (617) 566-4953

Burlington St Mark's Episcopal Church **P** (262) 10 Saint Marks Rd 01803-3622 (Mail to: 10 Saint Marks Rd Burlington MA 01803-3622) Bryan Pearson (781) 272-1586

Buzzards Bay St Peters Church **P** (124) 165 Main

St 02532 (Mail to: PO Box 265 Buzzards Bay MA 02532-0265) Susan Lederhouse (508) 759-5641

Cambridge Christ Church **P** (1023) 0 Garden St 02138-3631 (Mail to: Zero Garden St Cambridge MA 02138) Joseph Robinson Jonathan Eden Kevin Sparrow (617) 876-0200

Cambridge Episcopal Chapel at MIT **CC** 77 Massachusetts Ave 02139-4307 (Mail to: MIT W11 77 Massachusetts Ave Cambridge MA 02139-4307) Thea Keith-Lucas (617) 253-2983

Cambridge Episcopal Chaplaincy at Harvard **CC** 2 Garden St 02138-3631 (Mail to: 2 Garden St Cambridge MA 02138-3631) Luther Zeigler (617) 495-4340

Cambridge St James's Episcopal Church **P** (300) 1991 Massachusetts Ave 02140-1306 (Mail to: 1991 Massachusetts Ave Cambridge MA 02140-1342) Robert Massie Judith Gay Holly Antolini Eric Litman(617) 547-4070

Cambridge St John's Chapel **CC** 99 Brattle St 02138-3402 (Mail to: 99 Brattle St Cambridge MA 02138-3402)

Cambridge St Peter's Episcopal Church **P** (240) 838 Massachusetts Ave at Sellers St 02139-3004 (Mail to: 838 Massachusetts Ave at Sellers St Cambridge MA 02139-3004) Christian Brocato Bruce Nickerson (617) 547-7788

Cambridge St. Bartholomew's Episcopal Church **P** (117) 239 Harvard St 02139-2640 (Mail to: 239 Harvard St Cambridge MA 02139-2640) Leslie Sterling Patricia Zifcak (617) 354-8582

Canton Trinity Church Episcopal **P** (107) 1 Blue Hill River Rd 02021-1001 (Mail to: 1 Blue Hill River Rd Canton MA 02021-1001) Philip Jacobs (781) 828-1810

Charlestown St John's Episcopal Church **P** (83) 27 Devens St 02129-3735 (Mail to: 27 Devens St Charlestown MA 02129-3735) Thomas Mousin (617) 242-1272

Chatham St Christopher's Church **P** (577) 625 Main St 02633-2233 (Mail to: 625 Main St Chatham MA 02633) Brian McGurk (508) 945-2832

Chelmsford All Saints' Church **P** (568) 10 Billerica Rd 01824-3011 (Mail to: 10 Billerica Rd Chelmsford MA 01824-3097) William Bradbury (978) 256-5673

Chelsea St Luke's-San Lucas Episcopal Church **M** (100) 201 Washington Ave 02150-3914 (Mail to: 201 Washington Ave Chelsea MA 02150-3914) Edgar Gutierrez-Duarte (617) 884-4278

Chestnut Hill Church of the Redeemer **P** (1041) 379 Hammond St 02467-1224 (Mail to: 379 Hammond St Chestnut Hill MA 02467-1224) Michael Dangelo Margery Kennelly (617) 566-7679

Chestnut Hill Boston College Campus Ministry **CC** 379 Hammond St 02467 (Mail to: 379 Hammond St Chestnut Hill MA 02467) Judith Stuart 617-285-6577

Cohasset St Stephen's Episcopal Church **P** (573) 16 Highland Ave 02025-1819 (Mail to: 16 Highland Ave Cohasset MA 02025-1819) Margot Critchfield (781) 383-1083

Concord Trinity Episcopal Church **P** (940) 81 Elm St 01742-2252 (Mail to: 81 Elm St Concord MA 01742-2252) Rebecca Gettel Anthony Buquor Maureen Kemeza (978) 369-3715

Danvers All Saints Episcopal Church of the North Shore **P** (247) 46 Cherry St 01923-2820 (Mail to: PO Box 393 Danvers MA 01923-0693) Marya DeCarlen David Prentice (978) 774-1150

Dartmouth St Peter's Episcopal Church **P** (60) 351 Elm St 02748-3407 (Mail to: 351 Elm St Dartmouth MA 02748-3407) Scott Ciosek (508) 997-0903

Dedham Church of the Good Shepherd **P** (126) 62 Cedar St 02026-3222 (Mail to: 62 Cedar St Dedham MA 02026-3237) Chitral deMel (781) 326-3052

Dedham St Paul's Church Episcopal **P** (287) 59 Court St 02026-4301 (Mail to: 59 Court St Dedham MA 02026-4301) Melanie McCarley (781) 326-4553

Dorchester St Mark's Episcopal Church **P** (170) 73 Columbia Rd 02121-3347 (Mail to: 73 Columbia Rd Dorchester MA 02121) James Githitu Joseph Mumita (617) 436-4319

Dover St Dunstan's Episcopal Church **P** (180) 18 Springdale Ave 02030-2353 (Mail to: PO Box 515 Dover MA 02030-0515) Audrey Stewart (508) 785-0879

Duxbury Church of St John the Evangelist **P** (1066) 410 Washington St 02332-4552 (Mail to: PO Box 2893 Duxbury MA 02331-2893) Sharon Powers Roy Tripp (781) 934-6523

East Boston Grace Federated Church **M** (6) 760 Saratoga St 02128-1513 (Mail to: 760 Saratoga St East Boston MA 02128-1513) (617) 569-5358

Edgartown St Andrew's Episcopal Church **P** (217) 34 North Summer St 02539-1287 (Mail to: PO Box 1287 Edgartown MA 02539-1287) Vincent Seadale (508) 627-5330

Everett Grace Episcopal Church **P** (59) 67 Norwood St 02149-2722 (Mail to: PO Box 490285 Everett MA 02149-0004) (617) 387-7526

Fairhaven Church of the Good Shepherd **P** (134) 357 Main St 02719-3405 (Mail to: 357 Main St Fairhaven MA 02719) (508) 992-2281

Fall River Church of the Holy Spirit **P** 160 Rock Street 02720-3233 (Mail to: 160 Rock St Fall River MA 02720-3283) Jeremi Colvin Matthew Stewart (508) 672-5571

Fall River St Luke's Episcopal Church **P** (69) 315 Warren St 02721-3919 (Mail to: 315 Warren St Fall River MA 02721-3919) Susan Lee (508) 678-5118

Falmouth St Barnabas's Church **P** (718) 91 Main St 02540-2652 (Mail to: PO Box 203 Falmouth MA 02541-0203) Patricia Barrett Matthew Potts (508) 548- 3863

Foxborough St Mark's Episcopal Church **P** (194) 116 South St 02035-1760 (Mail to: 116 South St Foxborough MA 02035-1760) Edward Cardoza (508) 543- 8191

Framingham St Andrew's Episcopal Church **P** (468) 3 Maple St 01702-2915 (Mail to: 3 Maple St Framingham MA 01702-2915) Julie Carson Lorraine Mills-Curran (508) 875-5095

Franklin St John's Episcopal Church **P** (338) 237 Pleasant St 02038-3620 (Mail to: PO Box 287 Franklin MA 02038-0287) Paula Toland Chris Beukman (508) 528-2387

Gloucester St John's Episcopal Church **P** (541) 48 Middle St 01930-5716 (Mail to: 48 Middle St Gloucester MA 01930-5795) Bret Hays (978) 283-1708

✤ **Groton** St John's Chapel **O** 282 Farmers Row 01450-1848 (Mail to: Groton School Groton MA 01450) Beth Humphrey (978) 448-5271

Groveland St James's Episcopal Church **P** (238) 119 Washington St 01834-1535 (Mail to: 119 Washington St Groveland MA 01834-1535) Kathleen Lonergan (978) 373-1270

Hanover St Andrew's Church **P** (277) 17 Church St 02339-2315 (Mail to: 17 Church St Hanover MA 02339-2315) Elizabeth Wheatley Dyson (781) 826-2062

Harwich Port Christ Church **P** (140) 671 Route 28 02646-1913 (Mail to: 671 Main St (Rt. 28) Harwich Port MA 02646-1913) Judith Davis (508) 432-1787

Haverhill Trinity Episcopal Church **P** (187) 26 White St 01830-5702 (Mail to: 26 White St Haverhill MA 01830-5702) Jane Bearden Brian Raiche (978) 372-4244

Hingham Parish of St John the Evangelist **P** (1299) 172 Main St 02043-1911 (Mail to: 172 Main St Hingham MA 02043-1999) Timothy Schenck Noah VanNiel (781) 749-1535

Holbrook St John's Episcopal Church **P** (67) 322 S Franklin St 02343-1430 (Mail to: PO Box 323 Holbrook MA 02343-0323) Timothy Rogers (781) 767-4656

Holliston St Michael's Church **P** (285) 1162 Highland St 01746-1602 (Mail to: 1162 Highland St Holliston MA 01746-1602) Sarah Robbins-Cole (508) 429-4248

Hopkinton St Paul's Church **P** (75) 61 Wood St 01748 (Mail to: 61 Wood St Hopkinton MA 01748) Gordon Schultz (508) 435-4536

Hudson St Luke's Episcopal Church **P** (190) 5 Washington St 01749-2409 (Mail to: 5 Washington St Hudson MA 01749-2409) James Kodera Jennifer Beal (978) 562-2701

Hyannis Port St Andrew's Chapel **SC** Irving Ave 02647 (Mail to: Irving Ave Hyannis Port MA 02647) Robert Anthony 508-362-9465

Hyde Park Christ Church **P** (140) 1220 River St 02136-0022 (Mail to: PO Box 366202 Hyde Park MA 02136-0022) Kapya John Kaoma (617) 361-2457

Hyde Park Iglesia de San Juan **M** (75) 1220 River St 02136-0022 (Mail to: PO Box 366202 Hyde Park MA 02136-0022) Kapya John Kaoma (617) 361- 2457

Ipswich Ascension Memorial Church **P** (375) 31 County St 01938-2224 (Mail to: PO Box 547 Ipswich MA 01938-0547) Bradford Clark (978) 356-2560

Jamaica Plain St John's Episcopal Church **P** (135) 1 Roanoke Ave 02130-2828 (Mail to: 24 Alveston St Jamaica Plain MA 02130-2817) Ted Cole (617) 524-2999

Lawrence Grace Episcopal Church **P** (364) 35 Jackson St 01840-1626 (Mail to: PO Box 467 Lawrence MA 01842-0967) Joel Almono (978) 682-6003

Lexington Church of Our Redeemer **P** (469) 6 Meriam St 02420-5309 (Mail to: 6 Meriam St Lexington MA 02420) Katherine Ekrem Andrew Goldhor (781) 862-6408

Lincoln St Anne's in-the-Fields Church **P** (400) 147 Concord Rd 01773-4108 (Mail to: PO Box 6 Lincoln MA 01773-0006) Daniel MacDonald Katherine Malin (781) 259-8834

Lowell St Anne's Episcopal Church **P** (142) 8 Kirk St 01852-1005 (Mail to: 8 Kirk St Lowell MA 01852-1086) Ennis Duffis (978) 452-2150

Lowell St John's Episcopal Church **P** (66) 260 Gorham St 01852 (Mail to: 260 Gorham St Lowell MA 01852-3345) Ennis Duffis Richard Lewis Sarah Lewis(978) 453-5423

Lynn St Stephen's Memorial Church **P** (315) 74 S Common St 01902 (Mail to: 74 S Common St Lynn MA 01902-4594) Sarah van Gulden Jane Gould Joseph Ngotho George Gitau (781) 599-4220

Lynnfield St Paul's Episcopal Church **P** (193) 127 Summer St 01940-1827 (Mail to: 127 Summer St Lynnfield MA 01940-1827) Robert Bacon (781) 334-4594

Malden St Paul's Church **P** (30) 26 Washington St 02148-4903 (Mail to: 26 Washington St Malden MA 02148-8299) John Clarke (781) 324-9544

Manchester Emmanuel Chapel **SC** 24 Masconomo St 01944 (Mail to: PO Box 705 Manchester MA 01944) Luther Zeigler (978) 526-0085

Marblehead St Michael's Church Episcopal **P** (285) 26 Pleasant St 01945-3432 (Mail to: 26 Pleasant St Marblehead MA 01945-3432) Andrew Stoessel (781) 631-0657

Marblehead Wyman Memorial Church of St Andrew **P** (469) 135 Lafayette St 01945 (Mail to: 135 Lafayette St Marblehead MA 01945-1113) Charles (Clyde) Elledge (781) 631-4951

Marion St Gabriel's Episcopal Church **P** (400) 124 Front St 02738-1634 (Mail to: PO Box 545

Marion MA 02738-0010) Catherine Harper Geoffrey Piper (508) 748-1507

Marshfield Trinity Episcopal Church **P** (222) 229 Highland St 02050-6202 (Mail to: PO Box 388 Marshfield Hills MA 02051-0388) Noble Scheepers (781) 834- 8575

Mattapan Church of the Holy Spirit **P** (300) 525 River St 02126-3013 (Mail to: 525 River St Mattapan MA 02126-3013) Zenetta Armstrong Harry Jean-Jacques (617) 298-0577

Mattapoisett St Philip of Bethsaida **SC** 34 Water St 02739 (Mail to: PO Box 1884 Mattapoisett MA 02739) (508) 758-1346

Medfield Church of the Advent **P** (270) 28 Pleasant St 02052-2613 (Mail to: 28 Pleasant St. Medfield MA 02052-0461) Marc Eames (508) 359-6303

Medford Grace Episcopal Church **P** (149) 160 High St 02155-3818 (Mail to: 160 High St Medford MA 02155-3818) Noah Evans Maggie Arnold (781) 396-7215

Medway Christ Church **P** (150) 14 School St 02053-1306 (Mail to: 14 School Street Medway MA 02053-0156) Rebecca Black (508) 533-7171

Melrose Trinity Parish **P** (227) 131 W Emerson St 02176-3136 (Mail to: 131 W Emerson St Melrose MA 02176-3136) Bruce Lomas (781) 665-3890

Methuen St Andrew's Church **P** (96) 90 Broadway 01844-3838 (Mail to: 90 Broadway Methuen MA 01844-3838) Joseph Wilkes (978) 689-0463

Middleboro Church of Our Saviour **P** (278) 120 Centre St 02346-2233 (Mail to: PO Box 89 Middleboro MA 02346-0089) David Milam (508) 947-1900

Milton Church of Our Saviour **P** (86) 453 Adams St 02186-4359 (Mail to: 453 Adams St Milton MA 02186-4359) Rachael Pettengill-Rasure (617) 698-4757

Milton St Michael's Church **P** (635) 112 Randolph Ave 02186-3401 (Mail to: 112 Randolph Ave Milton MA 02186-3401) Hall Kirkham Joyce Caggiano (617) 698-1813

Nantucket St Paul's Episcopal Church **P** (553) 20 Fair St 02554-3705 (Mail to: PO Box 278 Nantucket MA 02554-0278) John Beach (508) 228-0916

Natick St Paul's Episcopal Church **P** (462) 39 E Central St 01760-4612 (Mail to: PO Box 238 Natick MA 01760-0003) Jon Strand Paul Kolbet (508) 655-5880

Needham Christ Episcopal Church **P** (929) 1132 Highland Ave 02494-1131 (Mail to: PO Box 920372 Needham MA 02492-0005) Lynn Campbell Nicholas Morris-Kliment (781) 444-1469

New Bedford Grace Church **P** (383) 422 County St 02740 (Mail to: 133 School St New Bedford

MA 02740-5928) Christopher Morck Andrea Wyatt (508) 993-0547

New Bedford St Andrew's Church **P** (85) § 169 Belleville Rd 02745-5220 (Mail to: 169 Belleville Rd New Bedford MA 02745) Rebecca Blair (508) 992-9274

New Bedford St Martin's Episcopal Church **P** (111) 136 Rivet St 02744-1814 (Mail to: 136 Rivet St New Bedford MA 02744) Scott Ciosek (508) 994-8972

Newburyport St Paul's Episcopal Church **P** (627) 166 High St 01950-3948 (Mail to: 166 High St Newburyport MA 01950-3948) Martha Hubbard (978) 465-5351

Newton Grace Episcopal Church **P** (350) 76 Eldredge St 02458-2017 (Mail to: 76 Eldredge St Newton MA 02458-2017) Regina Walton (617) 244-3221

Newton Center Trinity Episcopal Church **P** (94) 11 Homer St 02459 (Mail to: 11 Homer St Newton Centre MA 02459) Todd Miller James LaMacchia (617) 527-2790

Newton Highlands Parish of St Paul **P** (91) 1135 Walnut St 02161 (Mail to: 1135 Walnut St Newton Highlands MA 02461-1242) Gretchen Grimshaw (617) 527-6642

Newton Lower Falls St Mary's Episcopal Church **P** (379) 258 Concord St 02462-1315 (Mail to: 258 Concord St Newton Lower Falls MA 02462) George Stevens (617) 527-4769

Newtonville St John's Episcopal Church **P** (136) 297 Lowell Ave 02460-1826 (Mail to: 297 Lowell Ave Newtonville MA 02460-1826) Mark Edington (617) 964-2591

✠ **North Andover** Brooks School **O** 1160 Great Pond Rd 01845-1298 (Mail to: 1160 Great Pond Rd North Andover MA 01845-1298) Robert Flanagan (978) 725-6300

North Andover St Paul's Episcopal Church **P** (361) 390 Main St 01845-3952 (Mail to: 390 Main St North Andover MA 01845-3952) Sarah Kelb (978) 683-0671

North Attleboro Grace Episcopal Church **P** (612) 104 N Washington St 02760-1633 (Mail to: 104 N Washington St North Attleborough MA 02760-1686) Phillip Kutta (508) 695-5471

North Billerica St Anne's Episcopal Church (240) 14 Treble Cove Rd 01862-0134 (Mail to: PO Box 134 North Billerica MA 01862-0134) Louise Forest (978) 663-4073

North Easton Bristol Trinity Episcopal Church **P** (50) 143 Lincoln St 02356 (Mail to: 143 Lincoln St North Easton MA 02356 Susan Schwab Janice Walden (508) 230-2684

Norwood Grace Episcopal Church **P** (183) 150 Chapel St 02062-3130 (Mail to: 150 Chapel St Norwood MA 02062-3130) John Brockmann (781) 762-0959

Oak Bluffs Trinity Episcopal Church **SC** (100) Ocean Ave 02557 (Mail to: PO Box 2147 Oak Bluff s MA 02557-2147) (508) 693-3780

Orleans Church of the Holy Spirit **P** (570) 204 Monument Rd 02653-3512 (Mail to: 204 Monument Rd Orleans MA 02653-3512) Adam Linton Liza Spangler (508) 255-0433

Osterville St Peter's Church **P** (603) 421 Wianno Ave 02655-1918 (Mail to: PO Box 437 Osterville MA 02655-0437) Bill Eddy (508) 428-3561

Plymouth Christ Church **P** (718) 149 Court St 02360-4003 (Mail to: 149 Court St Plymouth MA 02360-4003) David Fredrickson (508) 746-4959

Provincetown Church of St Mary of the Harbor **P** (165) 517 Commercial St 02657-2412 (Mail to: 517 Commercial St Provincetown MA 02657-2412) Terry Pannell (508) 487-2622

Quincy Christ Church **P** (100) 12 Quincy Ave 02169-6712 (Mail to: 12 Quincy Ave Quincy MA 02169-6712) Clifford Brown (617) 773-0310

Quincy Parish of St Chrysostom **P** (105) 1 Linden St 02170-1809 (Mail to: 1 Linden St Quincy MA 02170-1809) Eric Hillegas (617) 472-0737

Randolph Trinity Church **P** (342) 120 North Main St 02368 (Mail to: 120 North Main St Randolph MA 02368-4629) Philip Kuhn (781) 963-2366

Reading Church of the Good Shepherd **P** (309) 95 Woburn St 01867-2907 (Mail to: 95 Woburn St Reading MA 01867-2907) Mary Wagner (781) 944-1572

Rockland Trinity Episcopal Church **P** (100) 3 Goddard Ave 02370-2325 (Mail to: 3 Goddard Ave Rockland MA 02370-2325) Sarah Brockmann (781) 871-0096

Rockport St Mary's Episcopal Church **P** (254) 24 Broadway 01966-1537 (Mail to: PO Box 299 Rockport MA 01966-0399) Karin Wade (978) 546-3421

Salem Grace Episcopal Church **P** (420) 385 Essex St 01970-3260 (Mail to: 385 Essex St Salem MA 01970-3260) Deborah Phillips (978) 744-2796

Salem St Peter's Episcopal Church **P** (182) 24 Saint Peter St 01970-3820 (Mail to: 24 Saint Peter St Salem MA 01970-3820) Silvestre Romero 978-745-2291

Sandwich St John's Episcopal Church **P** (525) 159 Main St 02563-2283 (Mail to: 159 Main St Sandwich MA 02563-2283) Paul Bresnahan (508) 888-2828

Saugus St John's Episcopal Church **P** (260) 8 Prospect St 01906 (Mail to: 8 Prospect St Saugus MA 01906-2155) Kevin Olds (781) 233-1242

Scituate St Luke's Episcopal Church **P** (288) 465 First Parish Rd 02066-3334 (Mail to: PO Box 291 Scituate MA 02066-0291) Grant Barber (781) 545-9482

Sharon St John's Church **P** (33) 23 High St 02067-1417 (Mail to: 23 High St Sharon MA 02067-

1417) Jerry Morrow (781) 784-3400

Shirley Trinity Chapel **P** (78) 188 Center Rd 01464-2115 (Mail to: 188 Center Rd Shirley MA 01464-2115) Marsha Hoecker (978) 425-9041

Somerset Church of Our Saviour **P** (343) 2112 County St 02726-5501 (Mail to: 2112 County St Somerset MA 02726-5501) Virgilio Fortuna Katherine Cress (508) 678-9663

Somerville St James's Episcopal Church **P** (164) 1170 Broadway 02144 (Mail to: PO Box 440185 Somerville MA 02144-1704) Karen Coleman (617) 666-1063

South Dartmouth St Aidan's Chapel **SC** 188 Smith Neck Rd 02748-1310 (Mail to: PO Box P183 South Dartmouth MA 02748) (508) 996-2008

South Hamilton Christ Church **P** (300) 149 Asbury St 01982-1813 (Mail to: 149 Asbury St South Hamilton MA 01982) Susan Russell Dean Borgman Patrick Gray (978) 468-4461

South Weymouth Church of the Holy Nativity **P** (439) 8 Nevin Rd 02190-1611 (Mail to: 8 Nevin Rd South Weymouth MA 02190-1611) Harold Birkenhead (781) 335-2030

South Yarmouth St David's Church **P** (250) § 205 Old Main St 02664-4529 (Mail to: 205 Old Main St South Yarmouth MA 02664-4529) Cynthia Hubbard (508) 394-4222

Southborough St Mark's Church **P** (858) 27 Main St 01772-1508 (Mail to: 27 Main St Southborough MA 01772) Philip LaBelle (508) 481-1917

Southborough St Mark's Episcopal Chapel/School **School** 25 Marlboro Rd 01772-1207 (Mail to: St Marks School 25 Marlboro Rd Southborough MA 01772-1299) Barbara Talcott (508) 786-6000

Stoneham All Saints' Episcopal Church **P** (76) 79 Central St 02180-2042 (Mail to: 79 Central St Stoneham MA 02180-2042) Kathryn Elledge (781) 438-2776

Stoughton Trinity Episcopal Church **P** (130) 414 Sumner St 02072 (Mail to: 414 Sumner St Stoughton MA 02072-3430) Harry Walton (781) 344-4592

Sudbury St Elizabeth's Episcopal Church **P** (408) 1 Morse Rd 01776-1746 (Mail to: 1 Morse Rd Sudbury MA 01776-1746) Jacqueline Clark Barbara Williamson (978) 443-6035

Swampscott Church of the Holy Name **P** (104) 60 Monument Ave 01907-1968 (Mail to: 40 Hardy Rd Swampscott MA 01907-1981) Mark Templeman (781) 595-1674

Swansea Christ Episcopal Church **P** (225) 57 Main St 02777-4624 (Mail to: 57 Main St Swansea MA 02777-4624) Alan Hesse (508) 678-0923

Taunton St Thomas's Church **P** (150) 111 High St 02780-3901 (Mail to: PO Box 149 Taunton MA 02780-0149) Richard Bardusch (508) 824-

9595

Topsfield Trinity Church **P** (450) 124 River Rd 01983-2111 (Mail to: PO Box 308 Topsfield MA 01983-0408) Daniel Weir Johanna Barrett (978) 887-5570

Vineyard Haven Grace Episcopal Church **P** (148) 36 Woodlawn Ave 02568 (Mail to: PO Box 1197 Vineyard Haven MA 02568-0903) Brian Murdoch (508) 693-0332

Waban Church of the Good Shepherd **P** (351) 1671 Beacon St 02468-1401 (Mail to: 1671 Beacon St Waban MA 02468-1401) Sarah Conner (617) 244-4028

Wakefield Emmanuel Episcopal Church **P** (219) 5 Bryant St 01880-5008 (Mail to: 5 Bryant St Wakefield MA 01880-5008) Matthew Cadwell (781) 245-1374

Walpole Epiphany Church **P** (545) 62 Front St 02081-2810 (Mail to: 62 Front St Walpole MA 02081-2810) Bailey Whitbeck (508) 668-2353

Waltham Christ Church **P** (100) 750 Main St 02451-0603 (Mail to: 750 Main St Waltham MA 02451-0603) Sara Irwin Christine Nakyeyune (781) 891-6012

Wareham Church of the Good Shepherd **P** (218) 74 High St 02571-2014 (Mail to: PO Box 719 Wareham MA 02571-0719) Daniel Bernier (508) 295-2840

Watertown Church of the Good Shepherd **P** (150) 9 Russell Ave 02472-3452 (Mail to: 9 Russell Ave Watertown MA 02472-3452) Amy McCreath (617) 924-9420

Wellesley St Andrew's Episcopal Church **P** (1600) 79 Denton Rd 02482-6404 (Mail to: 79 Denton Rd Wellesley MA 02482-6404) Adrian Robbins-Cole Karen Budney Margaret Schwarzer Catherine Healy (781) 235-7310

Wellfleet St James the Fisherman Church **SC** 2317 State Hwy Rte 6 02667 (Mail to: PO Box 1334 Route 6 Wellfleet MA 02667-1334) (508) 349-2188

West Newbury All Saints' Episcopal Church **M** (47) 893 Main St 01985-1302 (Mail to: 893 Main St West Newbury MA 01985-1307) Derrick Muwina (978) 462-4244

West Roxbury Emmanuel Church **P** (40) 21 Stratford St 02132-2008 (Mail to: 21 Stratford St West Roxbury MA 02132-2020) Robert Edson (617) 323-1440

Westford St Mark's Episcopal Church **P** (229) 75 Cold Spring Rd 01886-2410 (Mail to: 75 Cold Spring Rd Westford MA 01886-2410) Suzanne Wade (978) 692-7849

Weston St Peter's Church **P** (175) 320 Boston Post Rd 02493-1540 (Mail to: 320 Boston Post Rd Weston MA 02493-1540) Christen Mills Stephen Voysey (781) 891-3200

Westwood St John's Episcopal Church **P** (285) 95 Deerfield Ave 02090-1612 (Mail to: 95 Deerfield Ave Westwood MA 02090-1612) Jennifer Phillips (781) 329-2442

Whitman All Saints' Church **P** (129) 44 Park Ave 02382-1419 (Mail to: 44 Park Ave Whitman MA 02382-1419) Colette Bachand-Wood (781) 447-6106

Wilmington St Elizabeth's Episcopal Church **P** (150) 4 Forest St 01887-2811 (Mail to: PO Box 294 Wilmington MA 01887-0294) Christopher Fike (978) 658-2487

Winchester Parish of the Epiphany **P** (984) 70 Church St 01890-2523 (Mail to: 70 Church St Winchester MA 01890-2523) Thomas Brown Miriam Gelfer (781) 729-1922

Winthrop St John's Episcopal Church **P** (200) 222 Bowdoin St 02152-3123 (Mail to: 222 Bowdoin St Winthrop MA 02152-3123) Walter Connelly (617) 846-2363

Woburn Trinity Episcopal Church **P** (194) 535 Main St 01801-2923 (Mail to: 535 Main St Woburn MA 01801-2923) John Conn (781) 935-0219

Woods Hole Church of the Messiah **P** (209) 13 Church St 02543-1007 (Mail to: 13 Church St Woods Hole MA 02543-1007) Deborah Warner (508) 548-2145

Wrentham Trinity Episcopal Church **P** (280) 47 East St 02093-1369 (Mail to: PO Box 55 Wrentham MA 02093-0055) Elise Feyerherm (508) 384-3958

NON-PAROCHIAL CLERGY

Abeyaratne KA Brookline MA
Allen AC Marlborough MA
Allen DE *ret* Cambridge MA
Allen DE *ret* Barnstable MA
Almquist CG *ret* Cambridge MA
Anderson JC *ret* Cambridge MA
Andrews SM *ret* Barrington RI
Angelica DM *ret* Boynton Beach FL
Appleyard RB *ret* Acton ME
Armstrong RS *ret* Castine ME
Ayers RC *ret* Alexandria VA
Aymerich RI *ret*
Bagwell RRMD Savannah GA
Baker FD *ret* Waterville ME
Balcom JM *ret* Amherst MA
Barney DM *ret* Concord MA
Barns GS *ret* Cambridge MA
Barrington ET North Chelmsford MA
Barton CDH *ret* Wilmington NC
Beale NV Ramsey NJ
Bela RJ *ret* Breeding KY
Bell MC Rochester MA
Bennett RA *ret* Cambridge MA
Benshoff BL *ret* Middleboro MA
Bergstrom CE *ret* Edmonton AB
Berman EES Lexington MA
Besse A *ret* Vineyard Haven MA
Bettacchi KZ *ret* Lexington MA
Bloom BM
Bond WD *ret* Cambridge MA
Bonnyman AB *ret* Asheville NC

Bonsey SC Boston MA
Boyd JH Bethany CT
Breeden JP *ret* Hanover NH
Brome HLV *ret* Canton MA
Bronk HR *ret* Milton MA
Brown RM *ret* Cambridge MA
Burhoe AR *ret* Somerset MA
Burke RE Hernando Beach FL
Burr WH *ret* Chatham MA
Cardoza EM Foxboro MA
Carpenter JP Rockland ME
Caruso F *dcn* Hopkinton MA
Chambliss RA Jamaica Plain MA
Chandler SE *ret* Rowley MA
Chandler-Ward C Tenants Harbor ME
Chapman GM *ret* West Roxbury MA
Chapman JD *dcn* Chelsea MA
Chapman T *ret* Mendocino CA
Chase PGO *ret* Newton MA
Chase R *ret* Barnstable MA
Cheek AM
Cheney MR *ret* Malden MA
Cheng PS New York NY
Child KH *ret* New London NH
Ciannella JDK *ret* West Springfield MA
Ciccarelli SL
Clark JF *ret* Worcester MA
Clark RT *ret* Fairhaven MA
Cleveland TG *ret* Tamworth NH
Coburn AS *ret* Berkeley CA
Conn JH *ret* Brookline MA
Cook J Roxbury MA
Corrigan M *ret* Mt. Hermon MA
Cramer RW *ret* Amesbury MA
Crandall JD *ret* Tavares FL
Crane RM *dcn* Danvers MA
Crapsey MT *ret* Derry NH
Crowley DF *ret* West Chatham MA
D'Alcaravela JA *ret* Palmela
Daley AS *ret* North Andover MA
David CWL Delray Beach FL
Davis EG *ret* Andover MA
Day RC *ret* West Tisbury MA
De Beer JM *ret* Greensboro NC
De Mel CS
Deery LP *dcn* Manchester MA
Deyoung LA Lexington MA
Dickson ER *ret* Greensboro NC
Dodge JA San Francisco CA
Dolnikowski EW Boston MA
Donohue MJ *ret* Melrose MA
Duerr RE
Dunbar DM *ret* Fairfield CT
Ebens RF *ret* Hudson MA
Eckel MD Brookline MA
Eddy WW *ret* Waquoit MA
Edmunds R *ret* Edgartown MA
Engels J *ret* Dorchester Center MA
Evans KC *ret* Ipswich MA
Faramelli NJ *ret* Waltham MA
Fesq JA *ret* Fredericksburg VA

Flaherty JB
Flanders AB *ret* North Andover MA
Fornaro F *ret* Bedford MA
Fortune DC *ret* North Attleboro MA
Foster PLM *ret* Wareham MA
Fowler AC *ret* Portland ME
Foxx LN *ret* Cambridge MA
Franklin AH *ret* Brevard NC
Freeman WG *ret* Mashpee MA
Fregeau SA *ret* Hobe Sound FL
Frothingham CS North Reading MA
Garbarino HW *ret* Laurel Park NC
Gardner AE Andover MA
Garrett GK *ret* Fairhaven MA
Geissler-O'Neil SL Pleasanton CA
Gelfer MC *ret* Cambridge MA
George CAH Chestnut Hill MA
Githitu JK *ret* Lowell MA
Glenn CL *ret* Boston MA
Gober PD *ret* Attleboro MA
Gober WG *ret* Attleboro MA
Good E *dcn* Hanover MA
Goshgarian MJ *ret* Somerville MA
Gowen EL *dcn*
Gracey CB *ret* Brookline MA
Grumhaus JW *dcn* Milton MA
Gunness MB *ret* Belmont MA
Hall AC *ret* Wellesley MA
Hall LJ South Woodstock VT
Hall LG *ret* South Woodstock VT
Hamilton WM *dcn* North Billerica MA
Hammett RL *ret* Oak Bluff MA
Handloss PD *ret* Duxbury MA
Hardy J *ret* Haverhill MA
Hardy SP *ret* Humarock MA
Harrison MR *ret* Cambridge MA
Hartman HH *dcn* Needham MA
Hartwell M *ret* Thomasville NC
Hastie CW *ret* Jamaica Plain MA
Hayden DF
Hefling CC *ret* Cambridge MA
Helferty SH *ret* Salt Lake City UT
Hesse AR Walpole MA
Heuss WB *ret* South Yarmouth MA
Heyward IC *ret* Cedar Mountain NC
Ho EHC Malden MA
Horgan DE *dcn* Orleans MA
Hornberger-Brown SL Hudson MA
Houghton AB *ret* Pawleys Island SC
Howell MA *ret* North Billerica MA
Hughes JS Berkeley CA
Hultman EB *ret* Quincy MA
Hunt DA *ret* Marblehead MA
Hunt MW *ret* East Harwich MA
Hunt VW *ret* East Harwich MA
Ijams CP *ret* Tucson AZ
Jackson RS *ret* Woodstock IL
Jaikes DW *ret* Saint Petersburg FL
Jeffrey PL *dcn* Lowell MA
Jerauld PE *ret* Litchfield NH
Johnson JC *ret* Naples FL

Johnson KW *dcn* Reston VA
Johnston DK *ret* Framingham MA
Jones KL *ret* Mt Pleasant SC
Kazanjian RC *ret* Sonoita AZ
Kazanjian VH Wellesley MA
Kelley BS *ret* Boston MA
Kennedy TB *ret* Brookline MA
King AB *ret* Princeton NJ
King B Sewanee TN
Kinney E
Kondrath WM *ret* Sharon MA
Koulouris BAC *ret* Plymouth MA
Kreft AJ *ret* Palm Springs CA
Krumme JS Concord MA
Laforest CH Essex CT
Lam CN Boston MA
Landreth RD Marblehead MA
Lawrence GM *ret* Redmond WA
Lewis KE *ret* Jersey City NJ
Lindeman MJ Southport CT
Litman ER Cambridge MA
Littlepage DM Lynn MA
Lloyd ME Cambridge MA
Loring RT *ret* Bedford MA
Louise SC Boston MA
Lucas ML Hamilton
Mackie RA *ret* Somerville MA
Mann AB *ret* Haverhill MA
Mann L *ret* Edmonton KY
Marrone MJ *ret* Duxbury MA
Marsh E Haddonfield NJ
Mathews RK Randolph MA
McAlpine JP *ret* Newton Highlands MA
McCall TA *ret* Bloomington IN
McCarthy SJ Birmingham AL
McCue AH *ret* Wenham MA
McFarlane RB *ret* Lynn MA
McGinn JE *ret* Sandwich MA
McGrady JA Nantucket MA
McKinnon MJ Worcester MA
McLachlan DS Cambridge
McLaughlin JN *ret* Swampscott MA
Melendez MP *dcn* Boston MA
Messenger WG Belmont MA
Meyer WW *ret* Naples FL
Milholland NE San Francisco CA
Milligan DA *ret* Winthrop MA
Minton AM *ret* Lowell MA
Montagno KAB Medford MA
Moulton RC *ret* Arlington MA
Nelson JL *ret* Yarmouth Port MA
Newberry JL *ret* Wayland MA
Ntagengwa JB Boston MA
Outman-Conant RE *ret* Rockland MA
Page WR *ret* Somerville MA
Panasevich EJ Weston MA
Pang PKT *ret* Boston MA
Pape CD *dcn* Quincy MA
Parini BDB Ashland OR
Parker DH *ret* Smithfield RI
Parker RE West Park NY

Parthum CF *ret* Elm Grove WI
Partridge CE Medford MA
Payne RL *ret* Brewster MA
Pease EC *ret* Walpole MA
Peterson BA *ret* East Sandwich MA
Piccard KA *ret* Charlestown MA
Pinho JT *ret* Reading MA
Pitt LW *ret* Bedford MA
Pizzonia WS Darien CT
Povey JM *ret* Sarasota FL
Prentice DR Wakefield MA
Price PA Lake Ridge VA
Privitera LF *ret* Arlington MA
Radtke WR *ret* Chelsea MA
Ragsdale KH Cambridge MA
Ralph SL *ret* Reading MA
Randall SA Duxbury MA
Rebholtz BL Wellesley MA
Reece NT *ret* Raynham MA
Reiley JBS North Andover MA
Retamal MR *ret* Framingham MA
Richmond SO *ret* Charlestown MA
Ricketts LH *ret* San Antonio TX
Rimer KP Boston MA
Robinson ME Brookline MA
Rodgers PB Dartmouth MA
Rodman EW *ret* Framingham MA
Rodman SS Milton MA
Roeske MJ Boston MA
Rofinot LA Somerville MA
Rolfe-Boutwell SJ Tucson AZ
Rolle YA
Rosero-Nordalm E *dcn* Boston MA
Russell CT Stockton Springs ME
Ryan AM *ret* Duxbury MA
Schmidt KJ *dcn*
Schmitt J *ret* Fayetteville NY
Schneider WJ *ret* New York NY
Schwenzfeier PM *ret* Wareham MA
Sears AN *ret* Rocky Hill CT
Seeger SF *dcn* Cambridge MA
Shepherd NH *ret* Stow MA
Shepherd TC *ret* Fort Lauderdale FL
Shirley MO *ret* Lawrence MA
Siegenthaler DJ *ret* Cambridge MA
Signore RS *ret* Bourne MA
Simson JE Woodland Hills CA
Skelly HC *ret* Eastham MA
Smith CA *ret* Norwell MA
Smith GS *ret* Chatham MA
Smith NS Boston MA
Smith-Moran BP *ret* Concord MA
Snyder SJ Cambridge MA
Soughers TK Plainville MA
Stair A *ret* Amherst MA
Stowe BE *dcn* Topsfield MA
Stuart JL Chatham MA
Sullivan M *ret* North Attleboro MA
Sullivan PD *dcn* Boston MA
Taylor AS Arlington MA
Thomas JH *ret* Sandwich MA

Tobin RW *ret* Sunset ME
Torres MA Medford MA
Townsend JT *ret* Newton MA
Trever S Berkeley CA
Van Dusen DB *ret* Tucson AZ
Viereck A
Walberg EP *ret*
Wan SK Newton Center MA
Way R *ret* Rockford MI
Weiss JME Chestnut Hill MA
Welch GT *ret* Waban MA
Welles GH *ret* Myrtle Beach SC
Wenner PW *ret* West Newton MA
Westerberg GA *ret* Lovell ME
Whitaker JS *ret* Westford MA

Whitbeck MBO *ret* West Newton MA
White KG *ret* Sabattus ME
Whitmore EN *dcn* Barnstable MA
Whittaker-Navez CR *ret* Hopkinton MA
Williams S Boxford MA
Wilson DR *ret* Berwick ME
Windsor RG *ret* West Newton MA
Wood PP *ret* Framingham MA
Woods J *ret* Malden MA
Woods JC *ret* Toms River NJ
Woodward DM *ret* Milton MA
Wyman DL *ret* Cambridge MA
Young BA *ret*
Zalneraitis HB *ret* Brattleboro VT

STATE OF MICHIGAN
Dioceses of Eastern Michigan (EMI), Michigan (MI), Northern Michigan (NMI),
and Western Michigan (WMI)

Adrian—MI
Albion—WMI
Allegan—WMI
Allen Pk—MI
Alma—EMI
Alpena—EMI
Ann Arbor—MI
Atlanta—EMI
Bad Axe—EMI
Battle Creek—WMI
Bay City—EMI
Beaver Is—WMI
Belleville—MI
Belmont—WMI
Benton Hbr—WMI
Beulah—WMI
Big Rapids—WMI
Birmingham—MI
Bloomfield Hills—MI
Bloomfield Township—MI
Boyne City—WMI
Brighton—MI
Brooklyn—MI
Cadillac—WMI
Charlevoix—WMI
Charlotte—WMI
Cheboygan—EMI
Chelsea—MI
Clarkston—MI
Clinton—MI
Coldwater—WMI
Corunna—EMI
Crystal Falls—NMI
Davison—EMI
Dearborn—MI
DeTour Vil—NMI
Detroit—MI

Dewitt—MI
Dexter—MI
Dowagiac—WMI
Dryden—EMI
Eagle Harbor—NMI
E Lansing—MI
E Tawas—EMI
Ecorse—MI
Elk Rapids—WMI
Escanaba—NMI
Farmington Hills—MI
Fenton—EMI
Ferndale—MI
Flint—EMI
Flushing—EMI
Fremont—WMI
Gaylord—EMI
Gladstone—NMI
Gladwin—EMI
Grand Blanc—EMI
Grand Haven—WMI
Grand Ledge—WMI
Grand Rapids—WMI
Grayling—EMI
Greenville—WMI
Grosse Ile—MI
Grosse Pte—MI
Grosse Pte Farms—MI
Gwinn—NMI
Hamburg—MI
Harbert—WMI
Harbor Spgs—WMI
Harrisville—EMI
Harsens Is—EMI
Hastings—WMI
Hillman—EMI
Hillsdale—MI
Holland—WMI

Houghton—NMI
Howell—MI
Indian River—EMI
Inkster—MI
Ionia—WMI
Iron Mtn—NMI
Iron River—NMI
Ironwood—NMI
Ishpeming—NMI
Jackson—MI
Kalamazoo—WMI
Kentwood—WMI
Lachine—EMI
Lake Orion—MI
Lansing—MI and WMI
Lapeer—EMI
Larium—NMI
Leland—WMI
Lexington—EMI
Lincoln Pk—MI
Livonia—MI
Ludington—WMI
Mackinac Is—NMI
Madison Hts—MI
Manistee—WMI
Manistique—NMI
Marine City—EMI
Marquette—NMI
Marshall—WMI
Marysville—EMI
Mason—MI
Menominee—NMI
Michigan Ctr—MI
Midland—EMI
Milford—MI
Mio—EMI
Monroe—MI
Montague—WMI

Mt Clemens—MI
Mt Pleasant—WMI
Munising—NMI
Muskegon—WMI
Negaunee—NMI
Newaygo—WMI
Newberry—NMI
Niles—WMI
Northport—WMI
Norton Shores—WMI
Novi—MI
Onekama—WMI
Ontonagon—NMI
Oscoda—EMI
Otter Lake—EMI
Owosso—EMI
Paw Paw—WMI
Pentwater—WMI
Petoskey—WMI
Plainwell—WMI
Pleasant Lake—MI
Plymouth—MI
Pte Aux Pins—NMI
Pontiac—MI
Pt Huron—EMI
Portage—WMI
Redford Chtr
Twnshp—MI
Richland—WMI
Rochester—MI
Rogers City—EMI
Romeo—MI
Roscommon—EMI
Rose City—EMI
Royal Oak—MI
Saginaw—EMI
St Clair—EMI
St Clair Shores—MI

St Joseph—WMI
Saline—MI
Sand Pt—EMI
Sandusky—EMI
Saugatuck—WMI
Sault Ste Marie—NMI
Shelbyville—WMI

Southfield—MI
Southgate—MI
S Haven—WMI
Standish—EMI
Sturgis—WMI
Taylor—MI
Three Rivers—WMI

Traverse City—WMI
Trenton—MI
Troy—MI
Utica—MI
Walled Lake—MI
Waterford—MI
W Bloomfield—MI

W Branch—EMI
Westland—MI
Williamston—MI
Wyandotte—MI
Wyoming—WMI
Ypsilanti—MI

DIOCESE OF MICHIGAN
(PROVINCE V)
Comprises the southeastern and southcentral portion of Michigan's lower peninsula
DIOCESAN OFFICE 4800 Woodward Ave Detroit MI 48201
TEL (313) 832-4400   TOLL FREE (866) 545-6424   FAX (313) 831-0259
E-MAIL info@edomi.org   WEB www.edomi.org

Previous Bishops—
Samuel A McCoskry 1836-78, Samuel S
Harris 1879-88, Thomas F Davies 1889-
1905, Chas D Williams 1906-23, Herman
Page 1923-39, Frank W Creighton coadj
1937 Bp 1940-48, Donald B Aldrich
coadj 1945-46, Russell S Hubbard suffr
1948-54, Archie H Crowley suffr 1954-
72, Richard S Emrich suffr 1946-48 coadj 1948 Bp
1948-73, Robt I. DeWitt suffr 1960-64, C Kilmer Myers
suffr 1964-66, WJ Gordon Jr asst 1976-86, H Coleman
McGehee Jr coadj 1971 Bp 1973-89, H Irving Mayson
suffr 1976-92, R Stewart Wood Jr coadj 1989-90 Bp
1990-2000

Bishop—Rt Rev Wendell N Gibbs Jr (950) (Dio
4 Nov 2000)

Cn for Cong Life J Gettel; *Cn Admin* J Hardy; *Dir of
Fin* M Miliotto; *Accountant* K Chapman; *Miss for
Yth & Young Adults* E Travis; *Dir Comm* E Schulte;
Bishop's Ex Asst B Rowley; *Sec for Admin* J Michalak;
Dir Whitaker Institute E Williams; *Asst Whitaker
Institute* K Causey; *Min Dev* M Meech *Chanc* S Ott;
Asst Chanc M Norris N Yaw

Stand Comm—Cler: Chair C Mader P Miller W
Roberts J Kennedy Slater; *Lay:* K Lindquist P
Trumbore G Swan G Smereck

Dio Conv: 21-22 Oct 2016 Lansing, MI

PARISHES, MISSIONS, AND CLERGY

Adrian Christ Episcopal Church **P** (35) 720
Riverside Ave 49221-1445 (Mail to: 720
Riverside Ave 49221-1445) (517) 263-1162
Allen Park St Lukes Episcopal Church **P** (45) 15603
Wick Rd 48101-1532 (Mail to: 15603 Wick Rd
48101-1532) William Hale (313) 381-6345
Ann Arbor Canterbury House **Campus Ministry**
No 721 E Huron St 48104-5903 (Mail to: 721
E Huron St 48104-5903) Reid Hamilton (734)
665-0606

Ann Arbor Church of the Incarnation **M** (124)
3257 Lohr Rd 48108-9515 (Mail to: 3257
Lohr Rd 48108-9515) Joseph Summers Thalia
Johnson (734) 769-7900
Ann Arbor St Aidans Episcopal Church **P** (55)
1679 Broadway St 48105-1811 (Mail to: 1679
Broadway St 48105-1811) Judith Harmon
(734) 663-5503
Ann Arbor St Andrews Episcopal Church **HC**
(972) 306 N Division St 48104-1441 (Mail to:
306 N Division St 48104-1497) Alan Gibson
Robert Bickley Walter Labatt Lewis Towler
Edward Witke (734) 663-0518
Ann Arbor St Clare of Assisi Episcopal Church
P (486) 2309 Packard St 48104-6321 (Mail
to: 2309 Packard St 48104-6321) James
Rhodenhiser (734) 662-2449
Belleville Trinity Episcopal Church **P** (266) 11575
Belleville Rd 48111-2401 (Mail to: 11575
Belleville Rd 48111-2401) Ian Twiss Richard
Boulter (734) 699-3361
Birmingham St James Episcopal Church **P** (500)
§ 355 W Maple Rd 48009-3347 (Mail to: 355
W Maple Rd 48009-3347) Joshua Hoover (248)
644-0820
Bloomfield Hills Christ Church Cranbrook **P**
(1596) 470 Church Rd 48304-3400 (Mail to:
470 Church Rd 48304-3400) William Danaher
Joyce Matthews (248) 644-5210
Bloomfield Township Nativity Episcopal Church
P (47) 21220 W 14 Mile Rd 48302 (Mail to:
21220 W 14 Mile Rd 48302) William Bales
(248) 646-4100
Brighton St Pauls Episcopal Church **P** (298) 200
W Saint Paul St 48116-1202 (Mail to: 200 W
Saint Paul St 48116-1202) Deon Johnson Jenny
Housner-Ritter Carl Russell (810) 229-2821
Brooklyn All Saints Episcopal Church **P** (72) 151
N Main St 49230-8979 (Mail to: PO Box 367
49230-0367)
Brooklyn St Michaels and All Angels Episcopal
P (44) 11646 Old Monroe Pike 49230-8706

(Mail to: PO Box 287 49265-0287) Winifred Cook Cynthia Corner Mark Hastings Diana Walworth (517) 467-7855

Chelsea St Barnabas Episcopal Church **M** (46) 20500 W Old US Highway 12 48118-1309 (Mail to: 20500 W Old US Highway 12 48118-1309) David Glaser Ernest Stech (734) 475-8818

Clarkston Church of the Resurrection **P** (41) 6490 Clarkston Rd 48346-1500 (Mail to: 6490 Clarkston Rd 48346-1500) (248) 625-2325

Clinton St Johns Episcopal Church **M** (251) 122 E Church St 49236-9762 (Mail to: PO Box 518 49236-0518) Susan Shaefer (517) 456-4828

Dearborn Christ Episcopal Church **P** (437) 120 N Military St 48124-1035 (Mail to: 120 N Military St 48124-1035) Terri Pilarski Maryjane Peck (313) 565-8450

Detroit All Saints Episcopal Church **P** (82) 3837 West Seven Mile Road 48221-2218 (Mail to: 3837 West Seven Mile Road 48221-2218) (313) 341-5320

✙ **Detroit** Cathedral Church of St Paul **O** (429) 4800 Woodward Ave 48201-1310 (Mail to: 4800 Woodward Ave 48201-1399) S Scott Hunter Robert Alltop Frederick Nestrock Jonathan Sams Brian Shaffer Sharon Watton (313) 831-5000

Detroit Christ Episcopal Church **P** (465) 960 E Jefferson Ave 48207-3102 (Mail to: 960 E Jefferson Ave 48207-3102) (313) 259-6688

Detroit Church of the Messiah **P** (301) 231 E Grand Blvd 48207-3739 (Mail to: 231 E Grand Blvd 48207-3739) (313) 567-1158

Detroit Grace Episcopal Church **P** (38) 1926 Virginia Park St 48206-2422 (Mail to: 1926 Virginia Park St 48206-2422) (313) 895-6442

Detroit St Cyprians Episcopal Church **P** (56) 6114 28th St 48210-1400 (Mail to: 6114 28th St 48210-1400) Donald Lutas (313) 896-7515

Detroit St Johns Episcopal Church **P** (246) 50 E Fisher Fwy 48201-3405 (Mail to: 50 E Fisher Fwy 48201-3405) Steven Kelly Michael Bedford (313) 962-7358

Detroit St Matthews and St Josephs Church **P** (156) 8850 Woodward Ave 48202-2137 (Mail to: 8850 Woodward Ave 48202-2137) Cece Loua (313) 871-4750

Detroit St Peters Episcopal Church **P** (42) 1950 Trumbull St 48216-1529 (Mail to: 1950 Trumbull St 48216-1529) (313) 496-0938

Detroit Trinity Episcopal Church **P** (153) 1519 Martin Luther King Jr Bl 48208-2867 (Mail to: 1519 M L King Jr Blvd 48208-2867) Robert Smith (313) 964-3113

Dewitt Christ United (St Annes) **M** (38) 1000 W Webb Rd 48820-8396 (Mail to: 1000 W Webb Rd 48820-8396) (517) 669-9308

Dexter St James Episcopal Church **P** (84) 3279 Broad St 48130-1016 (Mail to: 3279 Broad St 48130-1016) Jenny Housner-Ritter Carol Mader (734) 426-8247

East Lansing All Saints Episcopal Church **P** (593) 800 Abbott Rd 48823-3103 (Mail to: 800 Abbot Rd 48823-3194) Katherine Carlson (517) 351-7160

East Lansing Canterbury at Michigan State Univ **CC** 1020 S Harrison Rd 48823-5102 (Mail to: 1020 S Harrison Rd 48823-5102) Sarah Midzalkowski (517) 351-1885

Ecorse Episcopal Church of the Resurrection **M** (42) 27085 W Outer Dr 48229-1282 (Mail to: 27085 W Outer Dr 48229-1282) (313) 382-1781

Farmington Hills Trinity Episcopal Church **P** (251) 26880 La Muera St 48334-4614 (Mail to: 26880 La Muera St 48334-4614) Julia Huttar Bailey (248) 474-2860

Ferndale St Lukes Episcopal Church **P** (122) 540 W Lewiston Ave 48220-1204 (Mail to: 540 W Lewiston Ave 48220-1204) Clare Hickman (248) 543-5900

Grosse Ile St James Episcopal Church **P** (372) 25150 East River 48138 (Mail to: 25150 East River 48138) Philip Dinwiddie (734) 676-1727

Grosse Pointe St Michaels Episcopal Church **P** (542) 20475 Sunningdale Park 48236-1637 (Mail to: 20475 Sunningdale Park 48236-1637) Jimmie Sue Deppe Marianna Gronek Jack Trembath (313) 884-4820

Grosse Pointe Farms Christ Episcopal Church **P** (1459) 61 Grosse Pointe Blvd 48236-3712 (Mail to: 61 Grosse Pointe Blvd) Thomas Van Culin Areeta Bridgemohan Virginia Hesse Paul Spann (313) 885-4841

Hamburg St Stephens Episcopal Church **P** (102) 10585 Hamburg Rd 48139 (Mail to: PO Box 436 48139-0436) John Franklin (810) 231-3220

Hillsdale St Peters Episcopal Church **P** (42) 3 N Broad St 49242-1601 (Mail to: 3 N Broad St 49242-1601) (517) 437-2833

Howell St Johns Episcopal Church **P** (126) 504 Prospect St 48843-1440 (Mail to: 504 Prospect St 48843-1440) (517) 546-3660

Inkster St Clements Episcopal Church **P** (79) 4300 Harrison St 48141-2963 (Mail to: 4300 Harrison St 48141-2963) Ellis Clifton (734) 728-0790

Jackson St Pauls Episcopal Church **P** (353) 309 S Jackson St 49201-2214 (Mail to: Attn: Ms Diane Billingsley, Treasurer 309 S Jackson St 49201-2214) Richard Ressler (517) 787-3370

Lake Orion St Marys-in-the-Hills Epis Church **P** (249) 2512 Joslyn Ct 48360-1938 (Mail to: 2512 Joslyn Ct 48360-1938) Laurel Dahill

Lansing St Michael Episcopal Church **P** (183) 6500 Amwood Dr 48911-5955 (Mail to: 6500 Amwood Dr 48911-5955) Nikki Seger Roger Walker (517) 882-9733

Lansing St Paul's Episcopal Church **P** (569) 218 W Ottawa St 48933-1309 (Mail to: 218 W Ottawa St 48933-1374) Karen Lewis (517) 482-9454

Lincoln Park St Michaels & All Angels Epis

Church **P** (197) 1325 Champaign Rd 48146-3302 (Mail to: 1325 Champaign Rd 48146-3302) Paula Miller (313) 382-5525

Livonia St Andrews Episcopal Church **P** (75) 16360 Hubbard St 48154-6100 (Mail to: 16360 Hubbard St 48154-6100) John Lohmann

Madison Hts St Patrick's Episcopal Church **P** (97) 1434 E 13 Mile Rd 48071-1515 (Mail to: 1434 E 13 Mile Rd 48071-1515) Judith Marinco Vincent Marinco (248) 585-9591

Mason St Augustine of Canterbury **P** (36) 546 W South St 48854-1914 (Mail to: 546 W South St 48854-1914) (517) 676-2525

Michigan Ctr St Aidans Episcopal Church **P** (38) 361 E Grove Ave 49254-1511 (Mail to: 361 E Grove Ave 49254-1511) (517) 764-2950

Milford St George's Episcopal Church **P** (144) 801 E Commerce St 48381-1727 (Mail to: 801 E Commerce St 48381-1727) Thomas Hawkins (248) 684-0495

Monroe Trinity Episcopal Church **P** (61) 11 W 3rd St 48161-6536 (Mail to: 11 W Third St 48161) Carol Bullard (734) 242-3113

Mount Clemens Grace Episcopal Church **P** (308) 115 S Main St 48043-2379 (Mail to: 115 S Main St 48043-2379) Susan Bock

Novi Church of the Holy Cross **P** (137) 46200 W 10 Mile Rd 48374-3004 (Mail to: 40700 W 10 Mile Rd 48375-3510) Alexander Babin Elizabeth Webber (248) 427-1175

Pleasant Lake Christ Church **P** (89) 9900 N Meridian Rd 49272-9630 (Mail to: 9900 N Meridian Rd 49272-9630) (517) 769-2333

Plymouth St Johns Episcopal Church **P** (655) 574 S Sheldon Rd 48170-1565 (Mail to: 574 S Sheldon Rd 48170-1587) Lisa Gray Jeanne Hansknecht (734) 453-0190

Pontiac All Saints Episcopal Church **P** (232) 171 W Pike St 48341-1750 (Mail to: PO Box 430357 48343-0357) (248) 334-4571

Redford Charter Township St Elizabeths Episcopal Church **P** (28) 26431 W Chicago 48239-1897 (Mail to: 26431 W Chicago Rd 48239-1897) Richard Iwick (313) 937-2880

Rochester St Philips Episcopal Church **P** (244) 100 Romeo Rd St. 48307-1557 (Mail to: 100 Romeo Rd 48307-1557) Cynthia Garman (248) 651-6188

Romeo St Pauls Episcopal Church **P** (79) 11100 W St Clair St 48065 (Mail to: PO Box 148 48065-0148) (586) 752-3212

Royal Oak St John's Episcopal Church **P** (378) 26998 Woodward Ave 48067-0923 (Mail to: 26998 Woodward Ave 48067-0923) Robert Hart Jeffernell Howcott Marjorie Taylor Sharon Watton (248) 546-1255

Saline Holy Faith Episcopal Church **M** (134) 6299 Saline Ann Arbor Rd 48176-8805 (Mail to: 6299 Saline Ann Arbor Rd 48176-8805) Donald Dersnah

Southfield Episcopal Church of the Redeemer **P** (151) 18140 Cornell Rd 48075-4146 (Mail to:

18140 Cornell Rd 48075-4146) (248) 569-4418

Southfield St Davids Episcopal Church **P** (550) 16200 W 12 Mile Rd 48076-2959 (Mail to: 16200 W 12 Mile Rd 48076-7357) Christopher Yaw (248) 557-5430

Southgate Grace Episcopal Church **P** (122) 15650 Reeck Rd 48195-3237 (Mail to: 15650 Reeck Rd 48195-3237) Lynda Carter (734) 285-0380

St Clair Shrs Trinity Episcopal Church **P** (76) 30205 Jefferson Ave 48082-1787 (Mail to: 30205 E Jefferson Ave 48082-1787) (586) 294-0740

Taylor Church of Christ the King **M** (44) 23045 Wick Rd 48180-3504 (Mail to: 23045 Wick Rd 48180-3504) William Hale (313) 291-4570

Trenton St Thomas Episcopal Church **M** (136) 2441 Nichols St 48183-2419 (Mail to: 2441 Nichols St 48183-2486) Shirley Mcwhorter (734) 676-3122

Troy St Stephens Episcopal Church **P** (507) 5500 North Adams Road 48098-2399 (Mail to: 5500 North Adams Road 48098-2399) Susan Williams (248) 641-8080

Utica St Lukes Episcopal Church **P** (278) 7700 22 Mile Rd 48317-2312 (Mail to: 7700 22 Mile Rd 48317-2312) (586) 731-1221

Walled Lake St Anne's Episcopal Church **M** (46) 430 E. Nicolet St 48390-3589 (Mail to: 430 E Nicolet St 48390-3589) Janis Stevenson (248) 624-3817

Waterford St Andrews Episcopal Church **P** (180) 5301 Hatchery Rd 48329-3440 (Mail to: 5301 Hatchery Rd. 48329-3440) (248) 673-7635

West Bloomfield Spirit of Grace Luth-Epis Ch **P** (139) 2399 Figa Avenue 48324-1808 (Mail to: 2399 Figa Avenue 48324-1808) Stephen Bancroft (248) 338-3505

Westland St Johns Episcopal Church **P** (209) 555 S Wayne Rd 48186-4301 (Mail to: 555 S Wayne Rd 48186-4301) Steven Domienik (734) 721-5023

Williamston St Katherines Episcopal Church **P** (213) 4650 Meridian Rd 48895-9317 (Mail to: 4650 N Meridian Rd Rte #2 48895-9317) Ronald Byrd (517) 349-4120

Wyandotte St Stephens Episcopal Church **P** (169) 2803 1st St 48192-5113 (Mail to: 2803 1st St 48192-5113) Andrea Morrow

Ypsilanti Episcopal Chaplaincy at E Michigan **Campus Ministry** 120 N Huron St 48197-2610 (Mail to: C/O St. Lukes Church, 120 N Huron 48197) (734) 483-4253

Ypsilanti St Lukes Episcopal Church **P** (369) 120 North Huron St. 48197-2610 (Mail to: 120 North Huron St. 48197-2610) JoAnn Slater

NON-PAROCHIAL CLERGY

Albrecht JH *ret* Troy MI
Baum NL Green Cove Springs FL
Baxter RL Walled Lake MI
Behnke CA *dcn* Detroit MI

Benes SS Brooklyn MI
Berg JC *ret* Waterford MI
Bird RD *dcn* Adrian MI
Boyer GT *ret* Decatur GA
Brogan BJ *dcn* Clinton Township MI
Brook RC *ret* East Lansing MI
Brown IF *ret* Saline MI
Buchin DA Idaho Falls ID
Bump AG *ret* Pittsburgh PA
Burke GF *dcn* Warren MI
Buxo DC *ret* Royal Oak MI
Caguiat CJ *ret* Redmond WA
Campbell BA *ret* Wyandotte MI
Campbell RW Ann Arbor MI
Carlson DJ *dcn* Madison Heights MI
Carr ML *ret* Grand Blanc MI
Carter LS East Lansing MI
Case DM Gregory MI
Castelli PH
Clabuesch WH *ret* Rochester Hills MI
Clark MM *ret* Lennon MI
Clausen RL *ret* Brevard NC
Cobden EAM *ret* South Egremont MA
Colvin MA Chelsea MI
Cook HT *ret* Royal Oak MI
Cox AE Tenants Harbor ME
Curry GE *ret* Ann Arbor MI
Davinich GL *ret* Plymouth MI
Dawson WW *ret* Presque Isle MI
Dempz JA *ret* Grosse Pointe Farms MI
Dennison BW *ret* Grosse Pointe MI
Derby RS *ret* Bloomfield Hills MI
Dieter DD *ret* Grosse Pointe Park MI
Duford DJ *ret* Southgate MI
Eichenlaub P *ret* Saint Joseph MI
Eidson RG *ret* Bloomfield Hills MI
Elwood FC *ret* Buhl ID
Engdahl FR *ret* Clarkston MI
Erdman DLR *ret* Webb City MO
Erickson KL Bloomfield Hills MI
Ericson WD *ret* Dewitt MI
Evans DH *ret* Sarasota FL
Fineout WH *dcn* East Lansing MI
Fitzpatrick MC Detroit MI
Fox SMR *ret* Shreveport LA
Francis JW Detroit MI
Gallagher RJ *ret* Maynard MA
Gelineau F *ret* Roscommon MI
Glennie JT *ret* Mason MI
Goldacker GW *ret* Belleville IL
Goodrich DH *ret* Mount Clemens MI
Gowing MLV Pinckney MI
Gray SB *dcn* Ann Arbor MI
Groh CH
Groschner PK *ret* Grosse Pointe Woods MI
Guthrie HH *ret* Fillmore CA
Haas MA Ypsilanti MI
Hamlin WR *ret* Lansing MI
Hartley HA Rogers City MI
Heath GE *ret* Southfield MI
Herrington WJ Garden City MI

Hiyama PS *ret* Ann Arbor MI
Hooper JK *ret* West Lebanon NH
Horning DJ *ret* Leadville CO
Humphrey CA *ret* Pontiac MI
Izutsu MW Arlington MA
Kerr RA Taylor MI
Keydel JF Beverly Hills MI
Kim R *ret* Grosse Pointe MI
Klein JC Detroit MI
Knight ST *ret* Lathrup Village MI
Knockel W Mason MI
Knotts HW *ret* Redford MI
Krell TW Southfield MI
Lawson D
Laycock JE *ret* Presque Isle MI
Leas BE *dcn* Corryton TN
Leclair PJ Madison Heights MI
Ledford ML Ypsilanti MI
Lillvis DM *ret* Interlochen MI
Linder CM *dcn* Tulsa OK
Logan WS *ret* Detroit MI
MacDonald LJ *dcn* Haslett MI
MacDonald WY Ann Arbor MI
Mack AR *ret* Hendersonville NC
Mackey PD *ret* Adrian MI
Maxwell J *ret* Ferndale MI
Mayers TWO Detroit MI
McDonald WK *ret* Fenton MI
McGimpsey RG *ret* Sarasota FL
McGlannan DL *ret* Edmonds WA
Melcher JR *ret* Trenton MI
Menzi DW New York NY
Meyer JP *ret* Detroit MI
Midzalkowski SF East Lansing MI
Millar CW *ret* Perry MI
Morgan DE *ret* Redford MI
Morrison GD *dcn* Pontiac MI
Morse AJ *ret* Monroe MI
Mullins EL *ret* Corolla NC
Muray LA Lansing MI
Mutzelburg MK *ret* Fenton MI
Nancarrow AP *ret* Maple Grove MN
Neily RE *ret* Durham NC
Norris RB *ret* Detroit MI
Northcraft LL *ret* Southfield MI
Paran WJ *ret* Sarasota FL
Pashturro JJ
Patton DC *ret*
Pennington JG *ret* Ypsilanti MI
Perez JF
Pressey SP *ret* Youngstown OH
Randolph BT Detroit MI
Rasnick KW *dcn*
Renfrew WF *dcn* Lansing MI
Rexford WN Clarksville MD
Reynolds EC Ann Arbor MI
Rhodenhiser IL Durham NC
Roberts WT Walled Lake MI
Roby J *dcn* Detroit MI
Salles SD Washington MI
Sauerzopf RC Charlotte MI

Savage JL *ret* Sanford MI
Schellhammer JL
Seelye Forest EJ *dcn* Sterling Heights MI
Semon-Scott DA *ret* Hillsdale MI
Shaefer HF *ret* Johnson City TN
Shafer LJ *dcn* Brooklyn MI
Shelton ES *dcn* Detroit MI
Sherwood ZO Arcadia FL
Shinn RE *ret* Stanwood MI
Shirota K Louisville KY
Singleton RO *ret* Scottsville VA
Slocombe IR *ret* Ajijic Jalisco
Smucker JR *ret* Alexandria VA
Steiner SA
Stout AJ *ret dcn* Cameron WI
Strang RH Howell MI
Stuart LE Richmond VA
Sullivan HP
Swinehart CH *ret* East Lansing MI
Taylor EN *ret* Toronto

Tetz WE
Tiffany RL *ret* Medina OH
Treppa JL *dcn* Venice FL
Vandercook RA Pleasant Lake MI
Vandercook SE Pleasant Lake MI
Walters JL Westhampton MA
Walters LR *ret*
Weikert RC
Weinreich G Chelsea MI
Weller GF *ret* Lansing MI
Werner FJE *dcn* Utica MI
Whitaker BG Grosse Pointe MI
Williams EM Bloomfield Hills MI
Williams LH West Chester PA
Willoughby RG *ret* Clinton Township MI
Wills RM *ret* Prescott AZ
Wilson GI Austin TX
Wollard RF *ret* Waterford MI
Wood CL *ret* Southern Pines NC
Zull AB *ret* Detroit MI

EPISCOPAL CHURCH IN MICRONESIA
Under the jurisdiction of the Presiding Bishop
BISHOP'S OFFICE The Episcopal Church in Hawaii 229 Queen Emma Square Honolulu HI 96813
TEL (808) 536-7776　FAX (808) 538-7194　WEB www.episcopalhawaii.org; episcopalmicronesia.org/guam/
LOCAL ADMINISTRATIVE OFFICES 911 N Marine Dr Tamuning GU 96913-4302
TEL (671) 649-0690　FAX (671) 649-0690

Previous Bishops—
HS Kennedy 1957-69, L Hanchett 1969, EL Browning 1969-71, L Hanchett 1971-75, EL Browning 1975-78, CL Burgreen 1978-86, JF Ashby 1986-87, DP Hart 1987-94, CL Keyser 1994-99, GE Packard 1999-2009

Bishop-in-charge—Rt Rev RL Fitzpatrick (1015)

Archdcn Ven Irene Egmalis Maliaman

MISSIONS AND CLERGY
Agat St Andrew of the Philippine Sea **M** (79) Rt 2 Marine Corps Dr 96928 (Mail: 911 N Marine Corps Dr Agat GU 96913) (671) 649-0690
Dededo St Michael and All Angels Church **M**

(207) § 177 Ahu Ln 96929 (Mail: 911 N Marine Corps Dr Tamuning GU 96913-4302) (671) 649-0690
Saipan St Pauls Episcopal Church **M** (42) Gualo Rai Middle Rd 96950 (Mail: PO Box 506610 Saipan MP 96950-4339) (670) 233-6081
Tamuning Epis Ch of St John the Divine **M** (60) § 911 N Marine Corps Dr 96913-4302 (Mail: 911 N Marine Corps Dr Tamuning GU 96913-4302) James Moore Irene Maliaman (671) 646-1708

NON-PAROCHIAL CLERGY
Valdez PA *ret* Carthage MO

DIOCESE OF MILWAUKEE
(PROVINCE V)
Comprises Southern Wisconsin
DIOCESAN OFFICE 804 E Juneau Ave Milwaukee WI 53202-2798
TEL (414) 272-3028   FAX (866) 499-1973
E-MAIL info@diomil.org   WEB www.diomil.org

Previous Bishops—
Jackson Kemper 1854-70, Wm E
Armitage coadj 1866 Bp 1870-73,
Edward R Welles 1874-88, Cyrus F
Knight 1889-91, Isaac L Nicholson
1891-1906, Wm W Webb 1906-33,
Benj FP Ivins coadj 1925 Bp 1933-
53, Donald HV Hallock coadj 1952
Bp 1953-73, Charles T Gaskell
coadj 1973 Bp 1974-85, Roger J White coadj 1984
Bp 1984-03

Bishop—Rt Rev Steven A Miller (991)
(Dio 18 Oct 2003)

Fin Off M Udovich; *Treas* C Bachand; *Chanc* S
Parsons; *Bp Asst Chr Form* C McCook; *Hist* Rev E
Payson; *Bp Asst for Cong Dev* P Bean; *Archdcn* C
Zellermayer

Stand Comm—Cler: P Harris, K Carroll SA
Raymond D Simmons; *Lay:* M Cairo P Koss K Bush
V McAuliffe

Dio Conv: 7-8 Oct 2016 Marriott West 1313 John Q
Hammond Drive Middleton WI

PARISHES, MISSIONS, AND CLERGY

Baraboo Trinity Episcopal Church **P** (138) 111
6th St 53913-2157 (Mail to: 111 6th St 53913-
2177) Scott Seefeldt (608) 356-3620

Beaver Dam St Marks Episcopal Church **P** (60)
700 E Mill St 53916-2435 (Mail to: PO Box 126
53916-0126) (920) 885-3536

Beloit St Pauls Episcopal Church **P** (106) 212 W
Grand Ave 53511-6109 (Mail to: 212 W Grand
Ave 53511-6193) Gregg Schneider (608) 362-
4312

Brookfield St Bartholomews Episcopal Church
P (385) Carl Bardenwerper 21020 Highland
Pass 53045-4544 (Mail to: N27W24000 Paul
Ct 53072-6239) Gregory Wilde (262) 691-0836

Burlington Church of St John the Divine **P** (161)
216 E Chandler Blvd 53105-1901 (Mail to: 216
E Chandler Blvd 53105-1901) Jason Lavann
Loretta Mendoza (262) 763-7482

Delafield St John Chrysostom Church **P** (139)
1111 Genesee St 53018-1411 (Mail to: PO Box
180082 53018-0082) Philip Cunningham (262)
646-2727

Delavan Christ Church **P** (93) 503 E Walworth
Ave 53115-1209 (Mail to: PO Box 528 53115-
0528) William Pelnar Joel Prather Marlyne
Seymour (262) 728-5292

Elkhorn St Johns in the Wilderness **P** (52) 13 S
Church St 53121-1707 (Mail to: 13 S Church St
53121-1707) (262) 723-4229

Fort Atkinson St Peters Episcopal Church **P**
(88) 302 Merchants Ave 53538-2248 (Mail
to: 302 Merchants Ave 53538-2248) Andrew
Hanyzewski

Greendale St Thomas of Canterbury Church **P**
(255) No 7255 W Grange Ave 53129-1132
(Mail to: 7255 W Grange Ave PO Box 342
53129-0342) Margaret Kiss Mark Moore (414)
421-0130

Hartford St Aidans Episcopal Church **SC** (152)
670 E Monroe Ave 53027-2574 (Mail to: 670 E
Monroe Ave 53027-2574) (262) 673-7273

Hartland St Anskars Episcopal Church **P** (76)
N48W31340 State Road 83 53029 (Mail to:
N48W31340 State Road 83 53029-8501)
Thomas Buchan (262) 367-2439

Hartland St Peters Episcopal Church **P** (37)
14N7412 Hwy 83 53029 (Mail to: PO Box 267
53064-0267) (262) 966-7312

Janesville Trinity Episcopal Church **P** (310) 419
E Court St 53545-4009 (Mail to: 409 E Court
St 53545-4009) Kathleen Lutes (608) 754-3402

Kenosha St Andrews Church **P** (51) 6609 26th
Ave 53143-4728 (Mail to: 6609 26th Ave
53143-4728) (262) 652-5118

Kenosha St Matthews Church **P** (216) 5900 7th
Ave 53140-4133 (Mail to: 5900 7th Ave 53140-
4162) Matthew Buterbaugh (262) 605-5526

Lake Geneva Church of the Holy Communion
P (96) 320 Broad St 53147-1812 (Mail to: 320
Broad St 53147-1812)

Madison Grace Episcopal Church **P** (430) 116
W Washington Ave 53703-2740 (Mail to: Attn
Financial Administrator 116 W Washington
Ave 53703-2740) Dale Grieser Margaret Irwin
Carol Smith (608) 255-5147

Madison St Andrews Episcopal Church **P** (387)
1833 Regent St 53726-4119 (Mail to: 1833
Regent St 53726-4198) Andrew Jones Dorota
Pruski

Madison St Dunstans Episcopal Church **P** (363)
6205 University Ave 53562 (Mail to: 6205
University Ave 53705-1056) Miranda Hassett
Sybil Robinson

Madison St Francis House **Chaplaincy** 1011
University Ave 53715-1092 (Mail to: 1011
University Ave 53715-1041) Jonathan Melton
(608) 257-0688

Madison St. Luke's Church **P** (132) 4011 Major
Ave 53716-1133 (Mail to: 4011 Major Ave

53716-1133) Paula Harris (608) 222-6921

Menomonee Falls St Francis Episcopal Church **P** (81) N84 W16525 Menomonee Ave 53051 (Mail to: PO Box 194 53052-0194) Martha Berger (262) 251-7420

✠ **Milwaukee** All Saints Cathedral **O** (222) 818 E Juneau Ave 53202-2714 (Mail to: 818 E Juneau Ave 53202-2714) Kevin Carroll Theodore Parks (414) 271-7719

Milwaukee Christ Church Episcopal **P** (668) 5655 N Lake Dr 53217-4849 (Mail to: 5655 N Lake Drive 53217-4849) Thomas Binder Seth Dietrich Edwin Leidel Seth Raymond (414) 964-3368

Milwaukee St Christophers Church **P** (354) 7845 N River Rd 53217-3025 (Mail to: 7845 N River Road 53217-3025) (414) 352-0380

Milwaukee St James Episcopal Church **P** (108) 833 W Wisconsin Ave 53233-2308 (Mail to: 833 W Wisconsin Ave 53233-2308)

Milwaukee St Lukes Episcopal Church **P** (63) 3200 S Herman St 53207-2852 (Mail to: 3200 S Herman St 53207-2899)

Milwaukee St Marks Episcopal Church **P** (306) 2618 N Hackett Ave 53211-3832 (Mail to: 2618 N Hackett Ave 53211-3832) Michelle Mooney (414) 962-0500

Milwaukee St Martins Episcopal Church **P** (70) 8401 N 60th St 53223 2852 (Mail to: 8401 N 60th St 53223-2852) Oswald Bwechwa (414) 354-4249

Milwaukee St Pauls Church **P** (351) 914 E Knapp St 53202-2825 (Mail to: 914 E Knapp St 53202-2825) Charles Teague (414) 276-6277

Milwaukee St Peters Episcopal Church **P** (103) 7929 W Lincoln Ave 53219-1752 (Mail to: 7929 W Lincoln Avenue 53219) Karen Buker Theodore Parks (414) 543-6040

Milwaukee Trinity Episcopal Church **P** (537) 1717 Church St 53213-2105 (Mail to: 1717 Church St 53213-2199) Gary Manning Kevin Stewart (414) 453-4540

Mineral Point Trinity Church **P** (34) 409 High St 53565-1220 (Mail to: 409 High Street 53565-1220) (608) 987-3019

Monroe St Andrews Episcopal Church **P** (15) 2810 6th St 53566-1901 (Mail to: 2810 6th St 53566-1901) (608) 328-8265

Oconomowoc St Pauls Episcopal Church **P** (46) N982 County Road P 53066-9517 (Mail to: N982 County Road P 53066-9517) Thomas Holtzen (920) 474-4797

Oconomowoc Zion Episcopal Church **P** (130) 135 Rockwell St 53066-2854 (Mail to: 135 Rockwell St 53066-2854) Charles Burch Michael Caldwell (262) 567-7507

Platteville Trinity Episcopal Church **P** (42) 250 Market St 53818-2543 (Mail to: 250 Market St 53818-2543) (608) 348-6402

Portage St John the Baptist Episcopal Church **P** (70) 211 W Pleasant St 53901-1744 (Mail to: 211 W Pleasant St 53901-1744) (608) 742-6054

Prairie Du Chien Church of the Holy Trinity **P** (31) 220 S Michigan St 53821-1713 (Mail to: 724 S Beaumont Rd 53821-1912) Carson Culver (608) 326-6085

Prt Washington St Simon the Fisherman Epis Ch **SC** (62) 3448 Green Bay Rd 53074-9765 (Mail to: PO Box 34 53074-0034) Julian Hills Mary Pain (262) 284-0510

Racine St Lukes Episcopal Church **P** (97) 614 Main St 53403-1210 (Mail to: 614 Main St 53403-1210) Robert Lambert

Racine St Michaels Episcopal Church **P** (319) 4701 Erie St 53402-2513 (Mail to: 4701 Erie St 53402-2513) Dustin Fecht (262) 639-2507

Richland Ctr St Barnabas Episcopal Church **P** (73) 297 N Main St 53581-2240 (Mail to: PO Box 487 53581-0487) Donald Fleischman (608) 649-6003

S Milwaukee St Marks Church **P** (292) 1314 Rawson Ave 53172-1939 (Mail to: 1314 Rawson Ave 53172-1939) Robert Rohleder Carl Wilke (414) 762-1772

Summit St Marys Episcopal Church **P** (284) 36014 Sunset Dr 53066 (Mail to: PO Box 126 53118-0126) Scott Leannah Charles Zellermayer (262) 965-3924

Sun Prairie Church of the Good Shepherd **D** (244) 3416 Swansee Ridge 53590 (Mail to: 3416 Swansee Ridge 53590-9495) Michael Tess (608) 837-3308

Sussex St Albans Episcopal Church **P** (60) W239 N5924 Maple Ave 53089 (Mail to: PO Box 202 53089-0202) Stephen Capitelli (262) 246-4430

Thiensville St Boniface Episcopal Church **P** (368) 3906 W Mequon Rd 53092-2728 (Mail to: 3906 W Mequon Road 53092-2799) Kenneth Miller Terrance Garner Thomas Niehaus (262) 242-2994

Watertown St Pauls Episcopal Church **P** (104) 413 S 2nd St 53094-4420 (Mail to: 413 S 2nd St 53094-4420) Elizabeth Tester

Waukesha St Matthias Episcopal Church **P** (379) 111 E Main St 53186 (Mail to: PO Box 824 53187-0824) David Simmons Richard Fox (262) 547-4838

West Bend St James Episcopal Church **P** (221) 148 S 8th Ave 53095-3207 (Mail to: 148 S 8th Ave 53095-3207) Richard Craig Cathleen Mccurry Milliken (262) 334-4242

Whitewater St Luke Episcopal Church **P** (33) 146 S Church St 53190-1950 (Mail to: 146 S Church St 53190-1950) Evelyn Payson (262) 473-8980

Wisconsin Dells Holy Cross Episcopal Church **P** (59) 322 Unity Dr 53965-9761 (Mail to: 322 Unity Dr 53965-9761) Kenneth Foster (608) 254-8623

NON-PAROCHIAL CLERGY

Abbott GE *ret*
Ackerman TD *ret* Hartland WI
Allen JT *ret* South Milwaukee WI
Anderson JA *ret* Pickerington OH
Apker D *dcn* Oconomowoc WI
Backstrand BE Milwaukee WI
Bagley RC *dcn* Racine WI
Barrett CY Shorewood WI
Berard JJ *dcn* Racine WI
Berends AL Milwaukee WI
Braden A Milwaukee WI
Bramlett RG *ret* Janesville WI
Braun JR *ret*
Bunting MA Sewanee TN
Burch IC Chicago IL
Burmeister ML Monticello IN
Caballero D *ret* Madison WI
Carnes VB Chattanooga TN
Cheesman BP *ret* Milwaukee WI
Cirves JM *dcn*
Couper DC *ret* Blue Mounds WI
Cunningham AL *ret* Delafield WI
Davis JL *ret* Johnston IA
Dinges JA *dcn* West Allis WI
Doherty AC Hartford WI
Downing JW *ret*
Downs LD *ret* Menomonee Falls WI
Du Priest TT *ret* Racine WI
Dunlop WH *dcn* Watertown WI
Dunst EW *dcn* Milwaukee WI
Farina GM *dcn* Hudson FL
Fehr WL *ret* Wauwatosa WI
Ferguson TC Columbus OH
Fessler RH *ret* Brookfield WI
Fischer JD *ret* Milwaukee WI
Grady AN Bay City MI
Gray-Fow MJG *ret* Whitewater WI
Green GJ *ret* Kenosha WI
Hands DR *ret* Savannah GA
Hekel UD *ret* Madison WI
Henery CR *ret* Delafield WI
Hickey JD
Himmerich MF *ret* Watertown WI
Hohenfeldt RJ *dcn* South Milwaukee WI
Kelly SM Columbus OH
Keough CJ Hartland WI
Kimball GA *ret* Oconomowoc WI
Koskela RN Madison WI
Koskela RA Madison WI
Kuhlman DH *dcn* Janesville WI

Kwiatkowski JJ Milwaukee WI
Lambert GP *ret* Monona WI
Lebron RE *ret* Janesville WI
Lewis MA *ret* Fort Worth TX
Lund VUS *ret* Missoula MT
Mail M *ret* Bloomington IN
Markevitch DM *ret* Madison WI
Matlak DJ Richmond VA
Maxfield CD Prairie Du Chien WI
May LE *ret* Sun Prairie WI
Mccook CB Waukesha WI
Misner MJB *dcn* Walworth WI
Morey GH Brodhead WI
Mueller SR *dcn* Madison WI
Myrick WH *ret* Delavan WI
Norby LL *dcn* Waunakee WI
Oliver KM Alexandria VA
Pfaff D
Probert WL *dcn*
Radant WF *ret* Manitowish Waters WI
Rozo OA Watertown WI
Schlafer DJ *ret* Bethesda MD
Schwartz WE Doha
Scott SM *dcn* Brown Deer WI
Secaur SC *ret* Mayfield Village OH
Shaw RC *ret* Asheville NC
Shemayev RA Middleton WI
Simpson GS *ret*
Sinclair EA Kansas City MO
Size PB *ret* Madison WI
Skidmore JL *ret* Sister Bay WI
Smith CH *dcn*
Smoke JC *ret* Wisconsin Dells WI
Starr NB Auckland NZ
Stephens WE *ret* Milwaukee WI
Stoner DS Milwaukee WI
Swanson JJ *ret* Hartland WI
Thompson CA *ret* Nanaimo BC
Trakel DL *ret* Menomonee Falls WI
Trigleth JP *dcn* Baraboo WI
Troutman-Miller JL Milwaukee WI
Van Deusen RW *ret* Milwaukee WI
Vicens LC Sioux Falls SD
Vine WJ *dcn* Milwaukee WI
Waff WDR *ret* Gurnee IL
Walker WD *dcn* Durham NC
Westberg DA Nashotah WI
Wilcox MQ
Woodbury RL *ret* Whitefish Bay WI
Wosikowski TJ *ret* Madison WI

DIOCESE OF MINNESOTA
(PROVINCE VI)
Comprises the State of Minnesota
DIOCESAN OFFICE 1730 Clifton Pl #201 Minneapolis MN 55403-3242
TEL (612) 871-5311; In MN (800) 596-3839   FAX (612) 871-0552
E-MAIL info@episcopalmn.org   WEB www.episcopalmn.org

Previous Bishops— Henry B Whipple 1859-1901, Mahlon N Gilbert coadj 1886 1900, Samuel C Edsall 1901-17, Frank A Mc Elwain suffr 1912 Bp 1917-43, Benj T Kemerer suffr 1944-48, Stephen E Keeler coadj 1931 Bp 1944-56, Hamilton H Kellogg coadj 1952 Bp 1956-70, Philip F McNairy suffr 1958 coadj 1968 Bp 1971-78, Robert M Anderson 1978 93, Sanford ZK Hampton suffr 1989-95, James L Jelinek 1993-2010

Bishop—Rev Brian Prior (1040) (Dio 13 Feb 2010)

Miss for Missional-Management Rev Cn M Pipkin; *Miss for Min* Cn K Olson A Ziebell-Finley; *Miss for Comm Engagement* R Lowenberg-DeBoer; *Miss for Indian Work and Multicultural Min* Rev Cn R Two Bulls; *Miss for Yth Min* C O'Leary; *Miss for Young Adult and College Min* S Mullaney; *Miss for the School for Form* Rev DM Salmon; *Miss for Admin* L Turner-Opanga; *Miss for Comm* H Copley-Woods; *Miss for Fin* J Gamberg; *Miss for the Bp* S Cadiz

Stand Comm—Cler: B Grace M Jacobs S Moss C Schmidt J Nelson; *Lay:* B Edstrom H Sims S Tobah J Galich M Moore A Norman

Dio Conv: 26-27 TBD

PARISHES, MISSIONS, AND CLERGY

Aitkin St Johns Church **M** (14) 222 1st St SE 56431-1706 (Mail to: 417 1st Ave SW 56431-1818) (218) 927-6040

Albert Lea Christ Church **P** (64) 204 W Fountain St 56007-2406 (Mail to: 204 W Fountain St 56007-2406) Henry Doyle

Alexandria Emmanuel Episcopal Church **P** (48) PO Box 231 56308-0231 (Mail to: PO Box 231 56308-0231) Thomas Sinning (320) 763-3201

Annandale St Marks Church **SC** (9) 10536 108th St NW 55302-2912 (Mail to: C/O Jon Papas 4839 Nason Pkwy NE 55376) (320) 230-6337

Anoka Trinity Episcopal Church **P** (288) 1415 6th Ave 55303-5250 (Mail to: 1415 6th Ave S 55303-5250) Mary Phelps (763) 421-1196

Austin Christ Episcopal Church **P** (118) 301 3rd Ave NW 55912-3023 (Mail to: 301 3rd Ave NW 55912-3023) Catherine Lemons (507) 433-3782

Bemidji St Bartholomews Episcopal Church **M** (110) 1800 Irvine Ave NW 56601-2552 (Mail to: 1800 Irvine Ave NW 56601-2552) (218) 444-6831

Brainerd St Pauls Church **P** (56) 408 N 7th St 56401-3019 (Mail to: 408 N 7th St 56401-3019) Gretchen Pickeral (218) 829-3834

Burnsville Episcopal Church of the Nativity **M** (516) 15601 Maple Island Rd 55306-5541 (Mail to: 15601 Maple Island Rd 55306-5541) Dana Strande (952) 435-8687

Cannon Falls Church of the Redeemer **P** (39) 123 3rd St N 55009-2012 (Mail to: C/O Rue Boykin PO Box 122 55009-2500) (507) 263-3469

Cass Lake St Peters Church **M** (101) 301 Cedar Ave NW 56633 (Mail to: PO Box 222 56633-0222) (218) 536-0834

Chatfield St Matthew Episcopal Church **P** (59) 100 Fillmore St SE 55923-1219 (Mail to: 100 Fillmore St SE 55923-1219) Alice Applequist (507) 867-3707

Cloquet St Andrews Episcopal Church **P** (18) 204 8th St 55720-1811 (Mail to: 128 Canterbury Cir 56058-2101) (218) 879-6100

Detroit Lakes St Lukes Episcopal Church **M** (100) 1400 Corbett Rd 56501-4508 (Mail to: PO Box 868 56502-0868) Loxley Koshnick (218) 847-5858

Duluth St Andrews by the Lake **M** (156) 2802 Minnesota Ave 55802-2526 (Mail to: 2802 Minnesota Ave 55802-2526) Marta Maddy (218) 727-1262

Duluth St Pauls Episcopal Church **P** (753) 1710 E Superior St 55812-2045 (Mail to: 1710 E Superior St 55812-2045) William Van Oss David Hill (218) 724-3535

Edina St Albans Episcopal Church **P** (403) 6716 Gleason Rd 55439-1130 (Mail to: 6716 Gleason Rd 55439-1130) John Peters (952) 941-3065

Elk River Holy Trinity Episcopal Church **P** (95) 1326 4th St 55330-1809 (Mail to: PO Box 65 1326 4th Street NW 55330-0065) Robert Cavanna Kenneth Toven (763) 441-5482

Ely St Mary's Church **M** (14) 715 S. Central Avenue 55731-0513 (Mail to: PO Box 513 55731-0513) (218) 365-4914

Eveleth St John's Episcopal Church **P** (38) 210 McKinley Avenue 55734-1600 (Mail to: 210 McKinley Avenue 55734-1600) (218) 341-4195

Excelsior Trinity Episcopal Church **P** (558) 221 Center St 55331-1817 (Mail to: 322 2nd St 55331-1806) Devon Anderson (952) 474-5263

Fairmont St Martins Episcopal Church **P** (76) 102 N Park St 56031-2822 (Mail to: 102 N Park St 56031-2822)

✠ **Faribault** Cathedral of Our Merciful Saviour **O** (151) 515 2nd Ave NW PO Box 816 55021-4203 (Mail to: PO Box 816 55021-0816) Justin

Chapman Jane Holt (507) 334-7732

Farmington Church of the Advent **P** (31) 412 Oak St 55024-1326 (Mail to: 412 Oak St 55024-1326) (651) 460-6636

Fergus Falls St James Episcopal Church **P** (78) 321 S Lakeside Dr 56537-2219 (Mail to: 321 S Lakeside Dr 56537-2219) (218) 736-6736

Frontenac Christ Episcopal Church **M** (53) 29036 Westervelt Ave. Way 55026-0058 (Mail to: PO Box 58 55026-0058) (651) 345-5986

Grand Marais Spirit of the Wilderness **M** (78) PO Box 1115 55604-1115 (Mail to: PO Box 1115 55604) Mary Ellen Ashcroft Carolyn Schmidt (218) 387-1536

Grand Rapids Christ Episcopal Church **P** (122) 520 N Pokegama Ave 55744-2646 (Mail to: 520 N Pokegama Ave 55744-2646) Kenneth Toven (218) 326-6279

Hastings St Lukes Episcopal Church **P** (153) 615 Vermillion St 55033-1939 (Mail to: PO Box 155 55033-0155) Elizabeth Herman Robert Langenfeld Darcy Valentine Franklin Van De Steeg Katherine Wanamaker (651) 437-9855

Hastings St Mary's Afton-Basswood Grove **P** (83) 8435 Saint Croix Trl S 55033-9495 (Mail to: 8435 Saint Croix Trl S 55033-9495) Scott Monson (651) 338-5364

Hermantown Trinity Episcopal Church **M** (85) 4903 Maple Grove Rd 55811-1446 (Mail to: 4903 Maple Grove Road 55811-1446) Cheryl Harder David Hill (218) 729-7957

Hibbing St James Episcopal Church **P** (75) 2028 7th Ave E 55746-1706 (Mail to: 2028 Bob Dylan Dr 55746-1706) Sally Maxwell (218) 263-5764

Hinckley Trinity Episcopal Church **M** (44) 305 1st St NW 55037-8712 (Mail to: PO Box 204 55037-0204) (320) 245-2575

Intl Falls Holy Trinity Episcopal Church **P** (79) 820 4th St 56649-2213 (Mail to: PO Box 170 56649-0170) Lynn Naeckel (218) 283-8606

Kasson St Peter's Episcopal Church **P** (105) 101 1st St NE 55944-1419 (Mail to: PO Box 205 55944-0205) (507) 634-6081

Lake City St Marks Episcopal Church **P** (51) 110 S Oak St 55041-1629 (Mail to: 110 S Oak St 55041-1629) (651) 345-2674

Le Center St Pauls Episcopal Church **P** (7) Rr 2 Box 140 56057-9631 (Mail to: 18647 State Highway 99 56057-4099)

Litchfield Trinity Episcopal Church **P** (33) 3 E 4th St 55355-2121 (Mail to: 3 E 4th St 55355-2121) (320) 693-6035

Little Falls Church of Our Saviour **P** (24) 113 4th Ave NE 56345-2625 (Mail to: ATTN Christy Bintz 1111 Joy Lane 56345-0344) Randy Welsand (320) 632-2209

Luverne Church of the Holy Trinity **P** (6) 220 N Cedar St 56156-1601 (Mail to: 220 North Cedar St 56156)

Mankato St Johns Episcopal Church **P** (222) Warren & Broad St 56002 (Mail to: PO Box

1119 56002-1119) Paul Rider (507) 388-1969

Marshall St James Episcopal Church **P** (50) 101 N 5th St 56258-1303 (Mail to: 101 N 5th St 56258-1303) Marilyn Leach (507) 532-6632

Minneapolis All Saints Episcopal Indian Mission **M** (165) 3044 Longfellow Ave 55407-1811 (Mail to: 3044 Longfellow Ave 55407-1811) Robert Two Bulls James Shoulak (612) 722-2342

✣ **Minneapolis** Cathedral Church of St Mark **O** (877) 519 Oak Grove St 55403-3230 (Mail to: 519 Oak Grove St 55403-3230) Paul Lebens Englund Siri Hustad Anna Ostenso Moore (612) 870-7800

Minneapolis Church of the Epiphany **P** (373) 4900 Nathan Ln N 55442-3156 (Mail to: 4900 Nathan Lane N 55442-3156) Alissa Smith (763) 559-3144

Minneapolis Gethsemane Church **M** (76) 905 Fourth Avenue South 55404-1093 (Mail to: 905 Fourth Avenue South 55404-1020) Phillip Boelter Sandra Obarski (612) 332-5407

Minneapolis Holy Trinity - St Anskars Church **P** (47) 1808 Riverside Ave 55454-1022 (Mail to: 1219 University Ave SE # 309 55414-2038) (612) 331-1544

Minneapolis St Andrews Episcopal Church **P** (197) 1832 James Ave N 55411-3164 (Mail to: PO Box 11745 55411-0745) (612) 529-1320

Minneapolis St George's Episcopal Church **P** (244) 5224 Minnetonka Blvd 55416-2104 (Mail to: 5224 Minnetonka Blvd 55416-2104) Paul Allick Diane McGowan

Minneapolis St James on the Parkway **P** (238) 3225 E Minnehaha Pkwy 55417-1431 (Mail to: 3225 E Minnehaha Pkwy 55417-1498) James Young (612) 724-3425

Minneapolis St John the Baptist Episcopal Church **P** (710) 4201 Sheridan Ave S 55410-1618 (Mail to: 4201 Sheridan Ave S 55410-1699) Susan Barnes (612) 922-0396

Minneapolis St Lukes Episcopal Church **P** (356) 4557 Colfax Ave S 55419-4736 (Mail to: 4557 Colfax Ave S 55409-1798) Warren Domenick (612) 824-2697

Minneapolis St Nicholas Episcopal Church **P** (186) 7227 Penn Ave S 55423-2820 (Mail to: 7227 Penn Avenue S 55423-2899) Thomas Eklo (612) 869-7551

Minneapolis St Pauls Episcopal Church **P** (240) 1917 Logan Ave S 55403-2846 (Mail to: 1917 Logan Ave S 55403-2846) Marlene Jacobs (612) 377-1273

Minneapolis St Stephen the Martyr Church **P** (1204) 4439 W 50th St 55424-1327 (Mail to: 4439 W 50th St 55424-1399) Thomas Cook (952) 920-0595

Minneapolis University Episcopal Center **CC** 317 17th Ave SE 55414-2012 (Mail to: 324 Harvard St SE 55414-2920) (612) 331-3552

Minnetonka The Episcopal Parish of St David **P** (440) 13000 St Davids Rd 55305-4119 (Mail to:

13000 St Davids Road 55305-4119) Leonard Freeman Lindsay Freeman Katherine Lewis (952) 935-3336

Minnetonka Beach Church of St Martins by the Lake **P** (575) 2801 Westwood Rd 55391 (Mail to: PO Box 38 55361-0038) David Langille David Mowers (952) 471-8429

Moose Lake St Andrews Episcopal Church **M** (13) 114 Elm Ave 55767-0840 (Mail to: PO Box 840 55767-0840) (218) 485-4945

Morton Bishop Whipple Mission **M** (313) 38378 Reservation Hwy 101 56270 (Mail to: PO Box 369 56270-0369) (507) 697-6433

Naytahwaush Samuel Memorial Church **M** (105) 36 Church Street 56566 (Mail to: PO Box 8 56566-0008) (218) 935-2192

New Ulm St Peters Episcopal Church **P** (5) 125 S Broadway St 56073-3114 (Mail to: 125 S Broadway St 56073-3114) (507) 354-3241

Northfield All Saints Episcopal Church **P** (111) 419 Washington St 55057-2028 (Mail to: PO Box 663 55057-0663) Gayle Marsh (507) 645-7417

Owatonna St Pauls Episcopal Church **P** (278) 222 S Cedar Ave 55060-2915 (Mail to: 220 S Cedar Ave 55060-2915) Steven Judd Michael Tippett (507) 451-5319

Park Rapids Trinity Church **M** (50) 212 Court Avenue 56470-0262 (Mail to: 212 Court Ave 56470-0262) (218) 732-4393

Paynesville St Stephens Episcopal Church **P** (10) 320 Wendell St 56362-1248 (Mail to: 320 Wendell St 56362-1248) (320) 243-2012

Ponsford Breck Memorial Mission **M** (70) PO Box 141 56575-0141 (Mail to: PO Box 141 56575-0141) (218) 255-1535

Red Lake St John in the Wilderness **M** (24) 15341 St Marys Mission Rd 56671 (Mail to: PO Box 64 56671-0054) (218) 679-4330

Red Wing Christ Episcopal Church **P** (279) 321 West Ave 55066-2250 (Mail to: 321 West Ave 55066-2250) Tristan English Barbara Von Haaren (651) 388-0411

Redby St Antipas Episcopal Church **M** (43) 19050 State Highway 1 56670 (Mail to: PO Box 273 56670-0273) (218) 679-3900

Rice Lake St Philips Church **M** (176) 16101 290th St 56621-9503 (Mail to: PO Box 8 56566-0008) (218) 358-0723

Rochester Calvary Episcopal Church **P** (614) 111 3rd Ave SW 55902-3150 (Mail to: 111 3rd Ave SW 55902-3198) Nicklas Mezacapa (507) 282-9429

Rochester St Lukes Episcopal Church **P** (539) 1884 22nd St NW 55901-0618 (Mail to: 1884 22nd St NW 55901-0618) Douglas Sparks Wesley Crowle (507) 288-2469

Rushford Emmanuel Episcopal Church **P** (49) 217 W Jessie St 55971-9103 (Mail to: PO Box 443 55971-0443) (507) 864-2164

Saint Cloud St Johns Episcopal Church **P** (164) 1111 Cooper Ave S 56301-4829 (Mail to: 1111

Cooper Ave S 56301-4829) Priscilla Gray (320) 251-8524

Saint Paul Christ Church Episcopal Parish **P** (430) 7305 Afton Rd 55125-1501 (Mail to: 7305 Afton Rd 55125-1501) (651) 735-8790

Saint Paul Church of the Epiphany **P** (45) Attn Kenneth Johnson Treasurer 1636 Van Buren Ave 55104-1818 (Mail to: 1636 Van Buren Ave 55104-1818) (612) 645-4466

Saint Paul Church of the Holy Apostles **M** (931) 2200 Minnehaha Ave 55119-3932 (Mail to: 2200 Minnehaha Ave E 55119-3932) M Letha Wilson-Barnard (651) 735-3016

Saint Paul Holy Trinity Episcopal Church **P** (139) 1636 Van Buren Ave 55104-1818 (Mail to: 501 Dale St N Ste 201 55103-1914) James Wilson (651) 228-0930

Saint Paul La Mision El Santo Nino Jesus **M** (180) 463 Maria Ave 55106-4428 (Mail to: 463 Maria Ave 55106-4428) Neptali Rodriguez Espinel (651) 295-7481

Saint Paul Messiah Episcopal Church **P** (477) 1631 Ford Pkwy 55116-2130 (Mail to: 1631 Ford Pkwy 55116-2130)

Saint Paul St Annes Episcopal Church **P** (285) 2035 Charlton Rd 55118-4704 (Mail to: 2035 Charlton Rd 55118-4704) Joan Delamater Theodore Park (651) 455-9449

Saint Paul St Christophers Episcopal Church **P** (444) 2300 Hamline Ave N 55113-4200 (Mail to: 2300 Hamline Ave N 55113-4290) John Dwyer Janet MacNally (651) 633-4589

Saint Paul St Clements Episcopal Church **P** (442) 901 Portland Ave 55104-7032 (Mail to: 901 Portland Ave 55104-7032) Joy Caires (651) 228-1164

Saint Paul St John in the Wilderness Episcopal **P** (550) 2175 1st St 55110-3462 (Mail to: 2175 1st St 55110-3462) Mark Kelm Randy Johnson (651) 429-5351

Saint Paul St John the Evangelist Epis Church **P** (463) 60 Kent Street 55102-2232 (Mail to: 60 Kent Street 55102-2232) Katharine Stebinger Jered Weber-Johnson (651) 228-1172

Saint Paul St Mary Episcopal Church **P** (417) 1895 Laurel Ave 55104-5938 (Mail to: 1895 Laurel Ave 55104-5998) Leeanne Watkins (651) 646-6175

Saint Paul St Matthews Episcopal Church **P** (361) 2136 Carter Ave 55108-1708 (Mail to: 2136 Carter Ave 55108-1708) Blair Pogue Lisa Wiens Heinsohn Dwight Zscheile (651) 645-3058

Saint Paul St Pauls on the Hill Church **P** (402) 1524 Summit Ave 55105-2292 (Mail to: 1830 University Ave W 55104-3578) Mark Thompson (651) 698-0371

Saint Paul Sts Martha & Mary Church **M** (223) 4180 Lexington Ave S 55123-1534 (Mail to: 4180 Lexington Ave S 55123-1534) Bruce Henne Alfred Hopwood (651) 681-0219

Saint Peter Church of the Holy Communion **HC**

(98) 118 North Minnesota Ave 56082-2412 (Mail to: PO Box 176 56082-0176) Thomas Harries (507) 934-2542

Sauk Centre Church of the Good Samaritan **P** (16) 529 S Main St 56378-0205 (Mail to: PO Box 205 56378-0205) Roger Phillips (320) 352-6882

Squaw Lake Gifillan Memorial **M** (30) 51497 Townhall Rd 56681-2029 (Mail to: 51497 Townhall Rd 56681-2029) (218) 335-2646

Stillwater Ascension Episcopal Church **P** (604) 214 4th St N 55082-4807 (Mail to: 215 N 4th St 55082) Marilyn Baldwin Holt Grace (651) 439-2609

Virginia St Pauls Episcopal Church **P** (46) 231 3rd St S 55792-2619 (Mail to: PO Box 376 55792-0376) (218) 741-1379

Wabasha Grace Memorial Church **P** (119) 936 Gambia Ave 55981-1011 (Mail to: 936 Gambia Ave 55981-1011) (651) 565-4827

Wadena St Helens Episcopal Church **M** (69) 22 Dayton Ave SW 56482-1450 (Mail to: PO Box 175 56482-0311) (218) 583-2206

Walker St Johns Episcopal Church **M** (104) 8819 Onigum Rd NW PO Box 1192 56484-2673 (Mail to: Pastor Mark Olson PO Box 84 56484-0084) (218) 547-2570

Warroad St Peters Church **M** (37) PO Box 117 56763-0875 (Mail to: Karen Hontvet PO Box 117 56763-0117) (218) 386-4334

Waterville St Andrews Episcopal Church **P** (27) 210 Lake St W 56096-1320 (Mail to: 210 Lake St W 56096-1320)

Wayzata St Edward the Confessor Episcopal Ch **P** (74) 865 Ferndale Road N 55391-1011 (Mail to: 865 Ferndale Rd N 55391-1011) Jason Lucas (952) 473-2262

Welch Church of the Messiah **M** (92) 1760 Chakya St 55089-9416 (Mail to: 21449 County 18 Blvd 55089-6402) Martin Balfe (612) 388-7531

White Earth St Columbas Church **M** (87) 26094 370th Street 56591-0388 (Mail to: PO Box 388 56591-0388) (218) 935-0259

Willmar St Lukes Episcopal Church **P** (12) 422 6th St SW 56201-3225 (Mail to: PO Box 887 56201-0887) (320) 235-5808

Windom Church of the Good Shepherd **P** (19) 453 10th St 56101-1407 (Mail to: PO Box 69 56101-0069) (507) 831-1797

Winona St Pauls Episcopal Church **P** (119) 265 Lafayette St 55987-3535 (Mail to: 265 Lafayette St 55987-3535) (507) 452-5355

NON-PAROCHIAL CLERGY

Abbott GH *ret* Saint Paul MN
Adwell L Tempe AZ
Ashcroft E *ret* Edina MN
Babler EJ *dcn* Sun Lakes AZ
Bamford MH *dcn* Duluth MN
Barber EERC Minnetonka MN
Bauman WJ Minneapolis MN

Beaulieu DJ *dcn* Bagley MN
Becherer CJ Saint Paul MN
Becker AP *ret* Brooklyn Park MN
Bedard CM *dcn* Brainerd MN
Bellaimey JE Minneapolis MN
Bernacchi JA Minneapolis MN
Bland JD *dcn* Mendota Heights MN
Bormes RJ *ret* Edina MN
Bozarth AR Sandy OR
Brantingham NM Long Lake MN
Brickson CJ Minneapolis MN
Brown DE *ret* Eagan MN
Brown LH North Oaks MN
Brusco KK Burnsville MN
Bulson WL Minnetonka MN
Burley AEJT Arlington Heights IL
Butler BT *dcn* Duluth MN
Carlson RA Cambridge MA
Ceynar MH *dcn* Wadena MN
Cherry CS *ret* Breckenridge MN
Christopherson PC New Vernon NJ
Clark PC Le Sueur MN
Claxton CC *ret* Audubon IA
Claxton LC *ret* Truman MN
Cogill RL Cape Town
Cook JH Red Wing MN
Cox ML Minneapolis MN
Cressman LSK Lake Elmo MN
Crockett LJ Inver Grove Heights MN
Cummings SA Grand Rapids MN
Daughtry SL Richmond VA
Deetz SM *dcn* Duluth MN
Dehler DR Crystal MN
Dodds DA Paynesville MN
Doherty JC *ret* Stillwater MN
Donovan WP Saint Paul MN
Dostal Fell MA Inver Grove Heights MN
Dougherty JH *dcn* Woodbury MN
Drysdale-Schruth S Wabasha MN
Eaglebull HL *ret* Cass Lake MN
Edwards KL *dcn*
Elliott BA Duluth MN
Elliott RN White Bear Lake MN
Emery DK Detroit Lakes MN
Fairbanks BJ Minneapolis MN
Fait HC Barnum MN
Feely MJ *dcn* Stillwater MN
Fenton GRC *ret* Minneapolis MN
Fontaine HD *ret* Minnetonka MN
Forbes MP Rochester MN
Froiland PV Eden Prairie MN
Furniss RH Woodbury MN
Garrison TM Eagan MN
Gears WE *dcn* Minneapolis MN
Gehlsen TJ *ret* Woodbury MN
Gifford-Cole IM *ret* Qualicum Beach
Gillman PR Grand Rapids MN
Goodwin MM Naytahwaush MN
Gordon WJ *ret* Saint Paul MN
Grabner-Hegg LM Fargo ND
Green LJ Winona MN

Grim LH *dcn* International Falls MN
Haack CA *dcn* Saint Paul MN
Hanson JD *ret* Minneapolis MN
Hanten HB *dcn* Duluth MN
Haptonstahl SR *ret* Cumberland MD
Hardman RR *ret* Saint Paul MN
Harris ER *dcn* Rochester MN
Hauck BH *dcn* Duluth MN
Hecock GI Detroit Lakes MN
Hennessy JK Burnsville MN
Hill NT *ret* Duluth MN
Hillger CL *dcn* Minnetonka Beach MN
Hiza DW *ret* London
Holmberg SA *ret* Detroit Lakes MN
Hoover JV *ret* Golden Valley MN
Hopkins TR *dcn* Monticello MN
Husband JF *ret* Detroit Lakes MN
Jankowski JA Woodbury MN
Jenkins JL *ret* Edina MN
Jones MF *dcn*
Joos HL *ret* Minneapolis MN
Kelm WE *dcn* Red Wing MN
Koch EJ *dcn* Ely MN
Kruger SM
Kunz PA *dcn* Kasson MN
Lalor DJ *dcn*
Lander SK Minneapolis MN
Larson FJ *dcn* Wheaton MN
Lawyer EV *ret dcn* Arden Hills MN
Lee BA Golden Valley MN
Lemming CP Saint Paul CO
Lennon EC *dcn* Saint Paul MN
Lesch RA *ret* Minneapolis MN
Loper JD *dcn* Albert Lea MN
Loud JD *ret* Prescott WI
Lundgren LL Proctor MN
Lyga RM *ret* Independence WI
Maltbie CS Faribault MN
Markie PG *dcn* Saint Paul MN
Martin GH *ret*
Mathias BH Lake City MN
Matthews RL *ret* Eden Prairie MN
Mattlin MB *dcn* Saint Paul MN
McAllister LW *dcn*
McDonald CJW Eden Prairie MN
McNairy PE *ret* Red Wing MN
McNally JS Sunfish Lake MN
Mercure JC Minneapolis MN
Merriman MW *ret* Plano TX
Miller RW *ret* Venice FL
Miner-Pearson AA *ret* Burnsville MN
Moore RA *ret* Chorley, Lancs
Morgan K Saint Paul MN
Morgan MH Minneapolis MN
Morley AJ *ret* Minneapolis MN
Morrigan CA Little Falls MN
Morrison-Cleary DV
Moses MD Chatfield MN
Moss SM *ret* Saint Paul MN
Mraz BE *dcn* Minneapolis MN
Muldoon MR Cloverdale BC

Nairn FW *ret* Minnetonka MN
Nelson CN *dcn* Park Rapids MN
Nesheim DO *ret* Eden Prairie MN
Neuhaus TJ *ret* Saint Paul MN
Newton JD *ret* Saint Paul MN
Olson AI *dcn* Two Harbors MN
Onkka MR *dcn* Faribault MN
Onkka PW *dcn* Faribault MN
O'Pray DM *ret* Minneapolis MN
Overgaard EL Luverne MN
Padzieski VS *dcn* Grand Marais MN
Pearson D *ret* W. St. Paul MN
Peterson-Wlosinski CME *ret* Duluth MN
Piette JL Cloquet MN
Pipkin M Minneapolis MN
Polyard KM Wabasha MN
Preble CW *ret* Saint Joseph MN
Preston SE Alexandria VA
Provine MK *ret* White Bear Lake MN
Punnett IC *dcn* Saint Paul MN
Quesenberry-Nelson JE *dcn* Hermantown MN
Raasch TD Brainerd MN
Ramnaraine BA *dcn* Minneapolis MN
Ramos MS Minneapolis MN
Ramstad PR *ret* Osceda WI
Rettger JH *ret* Coon Rapids MN
Reynolds KS *ret* Minneapolis MN
Rich ND *ret* Alexandria MN
Riley JF *ret* Christchurch
Robertson JE Morton MN
Robinson GH *ret* Saint Paul MN
Rock JS Bemidji MN
Roeck GE Minneapolis MN
Rose PJ
Ross GM *ret* Cass Lake MN
Roy RR Saint Paul MN
Rush JA Brainerd MN
Salmon MJ *ret* Saint Paul MN
Sams DL *dcn* Redwood Falls MN
Scarpace R Sunfish Lake MN
Schaffner PP *dcn* Minneapolis MN
Schaitberger SH *ret* Brainerd MN
Scheible ACE
Schubert JM *dcn* Grand Rapids MN
Schulenberg MA *ret* Lake City MN
Scott BI *ret* Byron MN
Selden EA MN Edina
Seward BJ Excelsior MN
Shaver J *ret* Anoka MN
Simmons KW *ret* Saint Paul MN
Skau LJ Brooklyn Center MN
Smith BL *ret* Northfield MN
Smith CD Detroit Lakes MN
Sonnesyn RE *ret*
Sowah CK Eagan MN
Spears ML *ret* Minneapolis MN
Sprick LA *dcn* Lake City MN
Strong EA *dcn* Saint Paul MN
Studley CKM *dcn* Litchfield Park AZ
Studley RE *dcn* Sun City AZ
Swenson RC

Swesey JE *dcn* Roseville MN
Tan WC
Teska WJ *ret* Minneapolis MN
Thao CM *dcn* Saint Paul MN
Thomas MW *ret* Duluth MN
Thor MC *dcn* Saint Paul MN
Todd RA *dcn* North Branch MN
Tollefson JJC *dcn* Northfield MN
Tully CM Marshall MN
Turner ID *ret* Waubun MN
Turner ME *ret* Owings Mills MD
Tuttle PEW *ret* Palm Beach Gardens FL
Vang T Saint Paul MN
Vogt CM *ret* Edina MN
Wafler DS *dcn* Faribault MN
Warren PSM Crystal MN

Weaver RW *ret* Tower MN
Webster PB Ely MN
Wells JE *dcn* Oberlin OH
Wheclock J Minneapolis MN
Whitney MJ *ret* Windom MN
Willms J *ret* Duluth MN
Wilson FE *ret* Lakeland MN
Windal CL St. Paul, MN
Winkler TE *ret* Winona MN
Wlosinski SS Duluth MN
Wojciehowski AA Cloquet MN
Wright MK *ret* Northfield MN
Wyman IM *dcn* Saint Paul MN
Zosel JR *ret* Minneapolis MN
Zotalis J Faribault MN

DIOCESE OF MISSISSIPPI
(PROVINCE IV)
Comprises the State of Mississippi
DIOCESAN OFFICE 118 N Congress St PO Box 23107 Jackson 39225-3107
TEL (601) 948-5954   FAX (601) 354-3401
E-MAIL info@dioms.org   WEB www.dioms.org

Previous Bishops—
Wm M Green 1850-87, Hugh M
Thompson coadj 1883 Bp 1887-
1902, Theodore D Bratton 1903-
38, Wm M Green II coadj 1919
Bp 1938-42, Duncan M Gray
1943-66, Jn M Allin coadj 1961 Bp
1966-74, Duncan M Gray Jr coadj
1974 Bp 1974-93, AC Marble Jr
coadj 1991 Bp 1993-2003, Duncan
M Gray III coadj 2000 Bp 2003-15

Bishop—Rt Rev Brian R. Seage (1085) (Dio
Feb 2015)

**Bishop Coadjutor—Rt Rev Brian R. Seage
(1085)** (Coadj 27 Sept 2014)

Cn to Ord Rev D Johnson; *Sec* B Ponder; *Treas* F
Page; *Cn Adm & Fin* B Ponder; *Reg* P Jones; *Chanc*
G Tate; *Chm Fin* B Howard; *Ecum* Rev J Switzer; *Yth
Adv* W Robinson

Stand Comm—Cler: A Fraser L Ott W Jones; *Lay:* D
Meadors A Perry E Sisson LD Thames

Dio Conv: 29-31 Jan 2016 Biloxi MS

PARISHES, MISSIONS, AND CLERGY
Aberdeen St Johns Episcopal Church **M** (109) 402
W Commerce St 39730-2523 (Mail to: PO Box
54 39730-0054) (662) 369-4854
Bay Saint Louis Christ Episcopal Church **P** (152)
912 S Beach Blvd 39520-4105 (Mail to: 912 S
Beach Blvd 39520) Tucker Dawson
Belzoni Mission of St Thomas **M** (19) 210
Castleman PO Box 145 39038 (Mail to: PO Box

401 39038-0401) (662) 746-5082
Biloxi Church of the Redeemer **P** (361) 1904
Popps Ferry Road 39532 (Mail to: 1904 Popps
Ferry Road 39532) Robert Wetherington
✠ **Bolton** St Mary Episcopal Church **Other** (1)
209 E Madison St 39041 (Mail to: C/O David
McCain PO Box 566 39041) (601) 209-8044
Brandon St Lukes Church **P** (138) 104 N College
St 39042-3180 (Mail to: PO Box 1899 39043-
1899) (601) 825-5839
Brandon St Peters by the Lake **P** (220) 1954
Spillway Rd 39047-6064 (Mail to: PO Box
39047) Carol Mead Roy Wilson (601) 992-2691
Brookhaven Church of the Redeemer **P** (196) 230
W Monticello St 39601-3204 (Mail to: PO Box
804 39602-0804) Emily Matthews (601) 833-
7399
Canton Grace Episcopal Church **P** (106) 161
E Peace St 39046-4519 (Mail to: PO Box 252
39046-0252) Elizabeth Foose (601) 859-2680
Carrollton Mission of Grace **M** (20) Washington
St 38917 (Mail to: PO Box 203 38917) (601)
445-8432
Clarksdale St Georges Episcopal Church **P** (216)
106 Sharkey Ave 38614-4402 (Mail to: 106
Sharkey Ave 38614-4402) Charles Keeler Jason
Shelby (662) 627-7875
Cleveland Calvary Episcopal Church **P** (177) 409
S Court St 38732 (Mail to: 107 S Victoria Ave
38732) Sylvia Czarnetzky Julia Moore (662)
843-5964
Clinton Episcopal Church of the Creator **P** (126)
1445 Clinton Raymond Rd 39056-5443 (Mail
to: 1445 Clinton Raymond Rd 39056-5443)

William Hanna

Collins St Elizabeths Mission **M** (23) 1200 S 4th St 39428 (Mail to: PO Box 873 39428-0873) Susan Hrostowski (601) 765-6809

Columbia St Stephens Episcopal Church **M** (55) 1300 Church St 39429 (Mail to: PO Box 761 39429-0761) Joycelyn Stabler-Tippett (601) 736-5496

Columbus Epis Church of the Good Shepherd **M** (100) 321 Forrest Blvd 39702-5313 (Mail to: PO Box 2023 39704-2023) Sandra Depriest (662) 327-1953

Columbus St Pauls Episcopal Church **P** (344) 318 College St 39701-5701 (Mail to: 318 College St 39701-5701) Anne Harris Morris Thompson (662) 328-6673

Como Holy Innocents Episcopal Church **M** (58) 311 N Main St 38619-7305 (Mail to: PO Box 391 38619-0391) Donald Chancellor (662) 526-5166

Corinth St Pauls Episcopal Church **P** (74) 250 Hwy 2 NE 38834 (Mail to: PO Box 1225 38835) Ann Fraser (662) 286-2922

Crystal Springs Mission of Holy Trinity **M** (54) 204 W Railroad Ave S 39059 (Mail to: PO Box 812 39059-0812) (601) 892-5142

Diamondhead St Thomas Episcopal Church **P** (196) 5303 Diamondhead Cir 39525-3203 (Mail to: 5303 Diamondhead Cir 39525-3203) (228) 255-9213

Enterprise Mission of St Mary **M** (17) 106 Saint John St 39330-8909 (Mail to: PO Box 177 39330-0177) (601) 656-2938

Forest Mission of St Matthew **M** (7) E Third St 39074 (Mail to: Ron Walsh 108 Azalea Dr 39074-3008) (601) 469-4669

Gautier St Pierre Episcopal Church **M** (108) 4412 Gautier Vancleave Rd 39553-4807 (Mail to: 4412 Gautier Vancleave Rd 39553-4807) (228) 497-9819

Greenville Church of the Redeemer **M** (18) 632 W Ohea St 38701-3663 (Mail to: PO Box 494 38702-0494) David Langdon (601) 332-8658

Greenville St James Episcopal Church **P** (234) 1026 S Washington Ave 38701-6307 (Mail to: 1026 S Washington Ave 38701-6307) Brandt Dick (662) 334-4582

Greenwood Church of the Nativity **P** (318) 400 Howard St 38930-4338 (Mail to: PO Box 1006 38935-1006) Peter Gray (662) 453-7786

Grenada All Saints Episcopal Church **P** (179) 469 S Main St 38901-3816 (Mail to: PO Box 345 38902-0345) Elizabeth Wheatley-Jones (662) 226-8234

Gulfport St Marks Episcopal Church **P** (672) 11322 West Taylor St 39503 (Mail to: 11322 West Taylor St 39503) Stephen Kidd (228) 896-7597

Gulfport St Peters by the Sea **P** (500) 1909 15th St 39501-2117 (Mail to: 1909 15th St 39501-2117) Diane Livingston Patrick Sanders

Hattiesburg Episcopal Church of the Ascension **P** (249) 3600 Arlington Loop 39402-1618 (Mail to: 3600 Arlington Loop 39402-1618) Susan Bear (601) 264-6773

Hattiesburg Trinity Episcopal Church **P** (519) PO Box 1483 39403-1483 (Mail to: PO Box 1483 39403-1483) Marian Fortner (601) 544-5551

Holly Spring Christ Episcopal Church **P** (145) 100 N Randolph St 38635-2411 (Mail to: PO Box 596 38635-0596) Bruce McMillan (662) 252-2435

Indianola St Stephens Episcopal Church **P** (92) PO Box 1004 38751-1004 (Mail to: 205 E Gresham St 38751-2424) Giulianna Gray (662) 887-4365

Inverness All Saints Episcopal Church **M** (18) Us Hwy 49 W 38753 (Mail to: PO Box 9 38753-0009) (662) 265-5775

Jackson All Saints Episcopal Church **P** (103) 147 Daniel Lake Blvd 39212-4942 (Mail to: 147 Daniel Lake Blvd 39212-4942) William Ndishabandi (601) 372-5185

✠ **Jackson** St Andrews Episcopal Cathedral **O** (1211) 305 East Capitol Street 39201 (Mail to: 305 East Capitol Street 39201-3404) Edward O'Connor Hailey Allin Joseph Burnett Jennifer Deaton David Elliott (601) 354-1535

Jackson St Christophers Church **M** (52) 643 Beasley Rd 39206-3827 (Mail to: 643 Beasley Rd 39206-3827) (601) 366-6768

Jackson St James Episcopal Church **P** (2655) 3921 Oakridge Dr 39216-3412 (Mail to: PO Box 4463 39296-4463) James McElroy Ann McLemore Jennifer Southall Seth Walley (601) 982-4880

Jackson St Marks Episcopal Church **P** (130) 903 Dr. Robert Smith, Sr. Pkwy 39203-3036 (Mail to: PO Box 3191 39207-3191) Robert Spencer (601) 353-0246

Jackson St Philips Episcopal Church **P** (537) 5400 Old Canton Rd 39211-4254 (Mail to: 5400 Old Canton Rd 39211-4277) Bruns Myers Kyle Seage (601) 956-5788

Kosciusko St Matthews Church **P** (36) St. Matthew Street 39090-3455 (Mail to: PO Box 1455 39090-1455) Mary Berry (662) 289-5326

Laurel St Johns Episcopal Church **P** (209) 541 N 5th Ave 39440 (Mail to: PO Box 1766 39441-1766) Jeffrey Reich (601) 428-7252

Leland St Johns Episcopal Church **M** (47) 405 California 38756 (Mail to: PO Box 267 38756-0267) (662) 686-4260

Leland St Pauls Episcopal Church **M** (19) C/O The Rev R E Sanders PO Box 267 38756-0267 (Mail to: PO Box 25 38748-0025) (662) 822-4863

Lexington St Mary Episcopal Church **M** (40) 402 Hillside St 39095 (Mail to: PO Box 63 39095-0063) (662) 834-2973

Long Beach St Patricks Episcopal Church **P** (134) 310 N Cleveland Ave 39560-4739 (Mail to: 310 N Cleveland Ave 39560-4739) Betsy

Baumgarten (228) 863-7882

Macon Mission of the Nativity **M** (5) 3376 Jefferson St 39341 (Mail to: C/O Joseph S Maury 301 N Washington St 39341-2523) (662) 726-4387

Madison The Chapel of the Cross **P** (635) 674 Mannsdale Rd 39110-7991 (Mail to: 674 Mannsdale Rd 39110-7991) William Compton Benjamin Robertson Robert Spencer (601) 856-2593

McComb Mediator - Redeemer Episcopal Church **P** (135) 215 N Broadway 39648-3905 (Mail to: 217 N Broadway 39648-3905) David Lemburg

Meridian Church of the Mediator **P** (404) 3825 35th Ave 39305-3617 (Mail to: PO Box 3400 39303-3400) Charles Floyd Terrell Griffis Joshua Messick (601) 483-3959

Meridian St Pauls Episcopal Church **P** (244) 1116 23rd Ave 39301-4017 (Mail to: 1116 23rd Ave 39301-4091) (601) 693-2502

Michigan City Mission of Calvary **M** (24) 43 Fort St 38647-8554 (Mail to: Mrs Jane Foster Matthews 22776 Highway 5 38647-9435) (662) 401-3089

Natchez Trinity Episcopal Church **P** (377) PO Box 1323 39121-1323 (Mail to: 305 S Commerce St 39120-3503) Walton Jones (601) 445-8432

Newton Trinity Episcopal Church **M** (5) PO Box 418 39345-0418 (Mail to: Edmund Phillips PO Box 178 39345-0178)

Ocean Springs St Johns Episcopal Church **P** (615) 705 Rayburn Ave 39564-3762 (Mail to: 705 Rayburn Ave 39564-3762) Charles Hawkins Robert Lenoir (228) 875-4454

✠ **Okolona** Mission of St Bernard **Other** (8) 400 W Main St 38860-1305 (Mail to: PO Box 375 38860-0375) (662) 447-2752

Olive Branch Holy Cross Episcopal Church **M** (117) 8230 Highway 178 38654-1116 (Mail to: 8230 Highway 178 38654-1116) (662) 895-5029

Oxford St Peters Episcopal Church **P** (749) 113 S 9th St 38655-3916 (Mail to: 113 S 9th St 38655-3916) David Elliott Bruce McMillan Christopher Robinson Penny Sisson Ann Whitaker (662) 234-1269

Pascagoula St Johns Episcopal Church **P** (480) 3507 Pine St 39567-3117 (Mail to: 3507 Pine St 39567-3100) Thomas Fanning (228) 762-1705

Pass Christian Trinity Episcopal Church **P** (365) PO Box 459 39571-0459 (Mail to: PO Box 459 39571-0459) David Faulkner (228) 452-4563

Philadelphia Mission of St Francis of Assisi **M** (35) 10701 St Francis Drive 39350 (Mail to: 10701 St Francis Drive 39350) (601) 656-2938

Picayune St Pauls Episcopal Church **P** (38) 1421 Goodyear Blvd 39466-3152 (Mail to: 1421 Goodyear Blvd 39466-3152) Arthur Johnson (601) 798-2802

Port Gibson St James Episcopal Church **M** (72) 305 Jackson St 39150-2327 (Mail to: PO Box

494 39150-0494) Margaret Ayers (601) 437-4244

Raymond St Marks Church **M** (15) 201 Main St 39154-9712 (Mail to: PO Box 10 39154) Janet Ott (601) 826-2128

Ridgeland St Columbs Episcopal Church **P** (645) 550 Sunnybrook Rd 39157-1810 (Mail to: 550 Sunnybrook Rd 39157-1810) Katie Bradshaw Melanie Lemburg (601) 853-0205

Rolling Fork Chapel of the Cross **P** (77) 35 McLaurin Ave 39159 (Mail to: PO Box 276 39159-0276) Frederick Proctor Robert Weatherly (662) 873-2226

Rosedale Mission of Grace **M** (13) Main St 38769 (Mail to: PO Box 712 38769-0712) Sylvia Czarnetzky

Southaven St Timothy Episcopal Church **P** (649) 8245 Getwell Rd 38672-6420 (Mail to: PO Box 325 38671-0004) Clelie McCandless (662) 393-3100

Starkville Church of the Resurrection **P** (332) 105 N Montgomery St 39759-2903 (Mail to: 105 N Montgomery St 39759-2903) Lynn Phillips-Gaines Laurence Wainwright-Maks

Sumner Episcopal Church of the Advent **P** (89) 224 Monroe St 38957 (Mail to: PO Box 366 38957-0366) Lynn Ronaldi (662) 375-8848

Terry Mission of the Good Shepherd **M** (76) 109 E Claiborne St 39170-7805 (Mail to: PO Box 325 39170-0325) (601) 878-5612

Tunica Church of the Epiphany **P** (70) 1061 Shady Ln 38676-9499 (Mail to: PO Box 224 38676-0224) William Lowry (662) 363-2393

Tupelo All Saints' Episcopal Church **P** (376) 608 W Jefferson St 38804-3736 (Mail to: 608 W Jefferson St 38804-3736) Paul Stephens (662) 842-4386

Vicksburg Christ Episcopal Church **P** (199) 1115 Main St 39183-2527 (Mail to: 1115 Main St 39183-2527) Samuel Godfrey (601) 638-5899

Vicksburg Church of the Holy Trinity **HC** (257) 900 South St 39180-3256 (Mail to: 930 South Street 39180-3256) Beth Palmer Elizabeth Hunter (601) 636-0542

Vicksburg St Albans Episcopal Church **P** (161) 5930 Warriors Trl 39180-0878 (Mail to: 5930 Warriors Trl 39180-0878) Billie Abraham Josie Williams (601) 636-6687

Vicksburg St Marys Episcopal Church **M** (42) 900 First North St 39183-2616 (Mail to: 900 First North St 39183-2699) Denny Allman (601) 636-4811

West Point Church of the Incarnation **P** (120) 103 W Broad St 39773-2801 (Mail to: PO Box 316 39773-0316) Patricia Cantrell (662) 494-1378

Woodville St Pauls Episcopal Church **P** (118) 259 S Church St 39669 (Mail to: PO Box 207 39669-0207) Mary Anne Heine (601) 888-6704

Yazoo City Trinity Church **P** (53) 323 N Main St 39194-4262 (Mail to: PO Box 145 39194-0145) George Woodliff (662) 746-5082

NON-PAROCHIAL CLERGY

Adams HS Tupelo MS
Allain TA Birmingham AL
Barker LK *ret* Purvis MS
Bell GM *ret* Florence AL
Biggers JC *ret* Pensacola FL
Bircher VM *ret* Columbia MS
Black RBW *ret* Jackson MS
Boney SA *ret* Pensacola FL
Branscome DA *dcn* Jackson MS
Bryant BH *ret* Mableton GA
Burns JO *ret* Carriere MS
Cheney BD Sikeston MO
Crawford SK *ret* Greenville MS
De Bary EO *ret* Asheville NC
Deaton CM Meridian MS
DeDeaux JT *dcn* Diamondhead MS
Disharoon SC *dcn* Port Gibson MS
Dunn PH *ret* Mobile AL
Dykes DW *ret dcn* Jackson MS
Elliott AKC Ridgeland MS
Elliott GS Jackson MS
Falconer A Fairfax VA
Fellhauer E *ret* Nashville KS
Fellhauer SR *ret* Nashville TN
Foncree RMI *dcn* Jackson MS
Freeman RH *ret* Jacksonville FL
Galbraith JMA *ret* Gulfport MS
Gieseler MM *dcn*
Guillaume S Pompano Beach FL
Halford CN *dcn* Jackson MS
Hanson DA *dcn* Jackson MS
Horner WMK *dcn* Goodyear AZ
Hunt WG *ret* Bristol TN
Johnson DH Jackson MS
Jones CB *ret* Canton MS
Jones EG *ret* Gulfport MS
Kellum RE *dcn*

Knight JD Delray Beach FL
LaFon KD Knoxville TN
Lancaster JM *dcn* Ocean Springs MS
Livingston WV *ret* Brevard NC
Luckett DS *ret* Niceville FL
Lundin GE *ret* Hattiesburg MS
McInnis VE Lexington MS
Meaders CJ Natchez MS
Meaders CJ *ret* Canton MS
Middleton RT *ret* Jackson MS
Moore WT *ret* Oxford MS
Moses SM
Myers AH Sewanee TN
Naef L Jackson MS
Ott LS Jackson MS
Ponder JB Meridian MS
Potts KK *ret* Picayune MS
Ray WA *ret* Ocean Springs MS
Reese FW *ret* Brookhaven MO
Rhea PT *dcn* Columbus MS
Roberts HF *ret* Ocean Springs MS
Roberts JB *ret* Biloxi MS
Ryan DL *ret* Pascagoula MS
Seney RW *ret* Lakewood CO
Simmons HP *ret* Meridian MS
Spencer CB *ret dcn* Jackson MS
Tester HW *ret* Meridian MS
Tomlinson SA *ret* Natchez MS
Travis SM *ret* Brentwood TN
Wade MM Jackson MS
Walling CE *ret* Fayetteville AR
Walton BR *dcn* Tupelo MS
Warwick ER *dcn* Madison MS
Webb JW *ret* Indianola MS
Williams AL *ret* Summerville SC
Williams SE *dcn* Gulfport MS
Winter JL *ret* Starkville MS

DIOCESE OF MISSOURI
(PROVINCE V)
Comprises eastern Missouri
DIOCESAN OFFICE 1210 Locust St Louis MO 63103
TEL (314) 231-1220   FAX (314) 231-3373
E-MAIL info@diocesemo.org   WEB www.diocesemo.org

Diocese of Missouri
THE EPISCOPAL CHURCH

Previous Bishops— Jackson Kemper 1835-44, Cicero S Hawks 1844-68, Chas F Robertson 1868-86, Daniel S Tuttle 1886-1932, Fredk F Johnson coadj 1912 Bp 1923-32, Wm Scarlett coadj 1930 Bp 1932-52, Arthur Lichtenberger coadj 1951 Bp 1952-59, George L Cadigan 1959-75, WA Jones Jr 1975-93 Hays H Rockwell 1993-2002 Bishop—Rt Rev George Wayne Smith (975) (Dio 6 June 2002)

Cn to Ord JMC Chambers; *Exec Dir Fin/Admin* D Viliocco; *Chanc* HR Burroughs 211 N Broadway St Louis MO 63102; *Treas* T Hedrick; *Sec of Conv* The Rev M Smith; *Comm* B Felice

Stand Comm—Cler: *VP* J Birdsong *Sec* M Smith K Carlson P Dolan S Robin D Goldfeder J Stratton J Chambers GW Smith; *Lay:* *Pres* R Entenmann D Belcher S Camp A Pearson S Goodlow H Burroughs

Diocesan Council—Cler: *Chair* T Whistler R Ard E Bird J Chambers GW Smith; *Lay:* *Vice-Chair* T Hedrick K Baker A Bullock H Burroughs B Click

B Forsyth W Gilbert P Heeter A Ludwig M Rowe S Thomas E Yount

Diocesan Committees and Commissions—Companion Diocese Committee *Chair Dcn* D Goldfeder (314) 231-1220 *E-mail:* info@diocesemo.org; Task Force for the Hungry *Chair Dcn* K McGrane (314) 231-1220 *E-mail:* info@diocesemo.org; *United Thank Offering Dio Coord* J King (314) 231-1220 *E-mail:* info@diocesemo.org

Dio Conv: 18-19 Nov 2016 Chesterfield MO

PARISHES, MISSIONS, AND CLERGY

Cape Girardeau Christ Episcopal Church **P** (163) 101 N Fountain St 63701-7338 (Mail to: 38 N Fountain St 63701-7315) Edith Bird (573) 335-2997

Columbia Calvary Episcopal Church **P** (809) 123 S 9th St 65201-4815 (Mail to: 123 S Ninth St 65201) Harold Jacobson (573) 449-3194

De Soto Trinity Episcopal Church **M** (35) PO Box 9 63020-0009 (Mail to: PO Box 9 63020-0009) (636) 586-2542

Ellisville St Martins Episcopal Church **P** (467) 15764 Clayton Rd 63011-2330 (Mail to: 15764 Clayton Road 63011-2330) Jon Hall Emily Davis Christopher Slane (636) 227-1484

Eolia Saint John's Church Prairieville **P** (9) Hwy H 63344 (Mail to: PO Box 528 63353) Patricia Glenn (573) 754-6423

Eureka St Francis' Episcopal Church **M** (90) 210 S. Central Ave. 63025 (Mail to: 210 S Central Ave 63025-3739) Sally Weaver

Farmington All Saints Episcopal Church **M** (36) 1151 W. Columbia 63640 (Mail to: PO Box 651 63640-0651) Catherine Hillquist (573) 756-3225

Florissant St Barnabas Episcopal Church **P** (133) 2900 Saint Catherine St 63033-3628 (Mail to: 2900 St Catherine St 63033) Renee Fenner (314) 837-7113

Fulton St Albans Episcopal Church **M** (54) 6 W 9th & Nichols St 65251 (Mail to: PO Box 6065 65251-6065) Marshall Crossnoe (573) 291-9886

Hannibal Trinity Episcopal Church **P** (134) 213 N 4th St 63401-3508 (Mail to: C/O Bob Leicht 1520 Central Ave 63401) Dawn-Victoria Mitchell Michael Kyle (573) 221-0298

Ironton St Pauls Episcopal Church **M** (36) 106 N Knob St 63650-1219 (Mail to: PO Box 62 63650-0062) Catherine Hillquist (573) 546-2397

Jefferson City Grace Episcopal Church **P** (411) 217 Adams St 65101-3203 (Mail to: 217 Adams St 65101-3298) Niranjani Molegoda Paula Hartsfield (573) 635-4405

Kirksville Trinity Episcopal Church **M** (81) PO Box 652 63501-0652 (Mail to: PO Box 652 63501-0652) Johnnette Shane (660) 665-6155

Kirkwood Saint Thomas Church For The Deaf **M** (12) C/O Grace Episcopal Church 514 E Argonne Dr 63122-4526 (Mail to: C/O Grace Episcopal Church 514 E Argonne Dr 63122-

4526) Emily Davis (314) 560-6731

Lake Saint Louis Church of the Transfiguration **P** (398) 1860 Lake Saint Louis Blvd 63367-1318 (Mail to: 1860 Lake Saint Louis Boulevard 63367-1318) Charles Morris Howard Park (636) 561-8951

Louisiana Calvary Episcopal Church **P** (30) 706 Georgia St 63353-1612 (Mail to: PO Box 528 63353-0528) Patricia Glenn

Manchester St Lukes Episcopal Church **P** (246) 1101 Sulphur Spring Rd 63021-7419 (Mail to: 1101 Sulphur Spring Rd 63021-7498) Doris Westfall (636) 227-1227

Mexico St Matthews Episcopal Church **P** (41) 1100 S Grove St 65265-2292 (Mail to: 1100 Grove St 65265-2292) Christina Cobb Janet Schisser (573) 581-1498

Northwoods Church of the Ascension **M** (68) 4520 Lucas and Hunt Rd 63121-2737 (Mail to: 4520 Lucas and Hunt Rd 63121-2737) Marc Smith (314) 361-0105

Poplar Bluff Church of the Holy Cross **P** (103) 420 N Main St 63901-5108 (Mail to: 420 N Main St 63901-5108) Annette Joseph (573) 785-1098

Portland St Marks Episcopal Church **M** (63) 8645 Co Road 466 65067 (Mail to: PO Box 5 65067) (573) 291-9886

Rolla Christ Episcopal Church **P** (217) 1000 N Main St 65401-2865 (Mail to: PO Box 845 65402-0845) Aune Strom (573) 364-1499

Saint Charles Trinity Episcopal Church **P** (366) 318 S Duchesne Dr 63301-1655 (Mail to: 318 S Duchesne Drive 63301-1655) Tamsen Whistler (314) 949-0160

Saint James Trinity Episcopal Church **M** (65) 120 E Scioto St 65559-1718 (Mail to: PO Box 126 65559-0126) James Barber (573) 265-7667

Saint Louis All Saints Episcopal Church **P** (194) 5010 Terry Ave 63115-1540 (Mail to: 5010 Terry Ave 63115-1540) Michael Dunnington (314) 367-2314

✠ **Saint Louis** Christ Church Cathedral **O** (632) 1210 Locust St 63103-2322 (Mail to: 1210 Locust St 63103-2322) Michael Kinman Amy Cortright Robert Franken (314) 231-3454

Saint Louis Church of the Advent **P** (172) 9373 Garber Rd 63126-2849 (Mail to: 9373 Garber Rd 63126-2849) Daniel Handschy (314) 843-0123

Saint Louis Church of the Good Shepherd **P** (130) No 1166 S Mason Rd 63131-1039 (Mail to: 1166 S Mason Rd 63131-1039) Pamela Dolan (314) 576-5502

Saint Louis Church of the Holy Communion **P** (315) 7401 Delmar Blvd 63130-4035 (Mail to: 7401 Delmar Blvd. 63130-4093) Michael Angell (314) 721-7401

Saint Louis Emmanuel Episcopal Church **P** (834) 9 S Bompart Ave 63119 (Mail to: 9 S Bompart Ave 63119-3282) Daniel Appleyard Martha Metzler Melanie Slane (314) 961-2393

Saint Louis Grace Episcopal Church **HC** (692) 514 E Argonne Dr 63122-4526 (Mail to: 514 E Argonne Dr 63122-4526) Todd McDowell Virginia Bennett (314) 821-1806

Saint Louis St Johns Church **P** (279) 3664 Arsenal St 63116-4801 (Mail to: St Johns Offices 3672-B Arsenal St 63116-4801) Teresa Danieley (314) 772-3970

Saint Louis St Marks Episcopal Church **P** (251) 4714 Clifton Ave 63109-2701 (Mail to: 4712 Clifton Ave 63109-2701) Mark Kozielec (314) 832-3508

Saint Louis St Michael And St George **P** (1471) PO Box 11887 63105-0687 (Mail to: PO Box 11887 63105-0687) Andrew Archie (314) 721-1502

Saint Louis St Pauls Episcopal Church **P** (77) 6518 Michigan Ave 63111-2803 (Mail to: 6518 Michigan Ave 63111-2803) Robert Ard (314) 352-0370

Saint Louis St Peters Episcopal Church **P** (1540) 110 N Warson Rd 63124-1327 (Mail to: 110 N Warson Rd 63124-1327) Louis Jernagan Kelly Carlson (314) 993-2306

Saint Louis St Stephens Episcopal Church **P** (294) 33 N Clay Ave 63135-2418 (Mail to: 33 N Clay Avenue 63135-2484) Steven Lawler (314) 521-0138

Saint Louis St Timothys Episcopal Church **P** (478) 808 N Mason Rd 63141-6306 (Mail to: 808 N Mason Road 63141-6306) Marvin Foltz Suzanne Eastes (341) 434-5909

Saint Louis Trinity Episcopal Church **HC** (244) 600 N Euclid Ave 63108-1606 (Mail to: 600 N Euclid Ave 63108-1606) Jonathan Stratton Harry Leip Beverly Van Horne (314) 361-4655

Sikeston St Pauls Episcopal Church **P** (41) 1010 N Main St 63801-5044 (Mail to: PO Box 428 63801-0428) Bruce Cheney (573) 471-2680

Ste Genevieve St Vincents-in-the-Vineyard **M** (27) 24345 State Route WW 63670-9022 (Mail to: 23 The Villages at Chaumette 24345 State Rte WW 63670-9022) (314) 397-3050

Sullivan St John and St James Church **M** (15) 463 N Church St 63080-1505 (Mail to: 463 N Church St 63080) Carol Wesley (573) 468-3753

NON-PAROCHIAL CLERGY

Baker RH Saint Louis MO
Bartlett SM *dcn* Rolla MO
Belcher NS *dcn* Fulton MO
Benson DH *ret* Inver Grove Heights MN
Birdsong JE *dcn* Saint Louis MO
Bowden GE *ret* Myrtle Beach SC
Bowen EA *dcn* Saint Charles MO
Bruns TC *ret* Seguin TX
Cadigan CR *ret* DeSoto TX
Caldwell WF *ret* Harrisonburg VA
Campbell CA *ret* Milwaukee WI
Cassell JL *ret* Cedar Rapids IA
Chambers JMC Columbia MO
Cherbonnier ELB *dcn* Hartford CT

Chollet MJ Chesterfield MO
Crews WE *ret* Saint Louis MO
Danforth JC Saint Louis MO
Davenport CK Kirksville MO
Doyle RT *ret* El Cerrito CA
Esbenshade BT *dcn* Saint Louis MO
Fleming JC *ret* Kirkwood MO
Fly DK *ret* St. Louis MO
Goldfeder DB *dcn* Saint Louis MO
Hardwick LC Rolla MO
Heathcock JE *ret* Chesterfield MO
Heigham LM *ret* Ballwin MO
Hines C *dcn* St. Louis MO
Jewson D *dcn* Saint Louis MO
Johnston CL *dcn* Kingsport TN
Kanzler JL Clayton MO
Kelsey AH *ret* Saint Louis MO
Kilgore JW Saint Louis MO
Labatt WB *ret* Dexter MI
Ludbrook HC *ret* Des Peres MO
Luley WT *ret* Manchester MO
Macarthur RS Center Sandwich NH
Marta DC Maryville MO
McGrane KJ *dcn* Saint Louis MO
Metzger JP *ret* Cincinnati OH
Morgan HM Columbia MO
Myers B *ret* Saint Louis MO
Nabe CM Saint Petersburg FL
Nanny SK *ret* Saint Louis MO
Naylor SB *dcn* Saint Louis MO
Noel VL *ret* Ellisville MO
Nowlin BG *ret* Ferguson MO
O'Neil JA *dcn* Saint Louis MO
Orme-Rogers CA Madison WI
Peabody WN *ret* Saint Johnsbury VT
Peets PAD *dcn* Albany GA
Purdy JH *ret* Saint Louis MO
Pyron WN *ret* Saint Louis MO
Ragland RB University City MO
Raske LK *ret* Saint Louis MO
Robinson PP *ret* Columbia MO
Roeger WD *ret* Hannibal MO
Sanders HR *ret* Sedalia MO
Sarkissyian SK Ballwin MO
Scriven EA Ann Arbor MI
Skinner S *ret* Saint Louis MO
Sluss MD *dcn* Saint Louis MO
Smith ED *ret* Saint Louis MO
Stansbery MW *dcn* Saint Louis MO
Stuart CTB *ret* Saint Louis MO
Thomas WT *ret* Saint Louis MO
Towner RA *ret* Cape Girardeau MO
Tudor RB *ret* Florissant MO
Valantasis RL *ret* Santa Fe NM
Van Horne PE *ret* St. Louis MO
Vandivort PM Des Peres MO
Weissman SE *ret* Asheville NC
Welles HV Jacksonville FL
Wilkinson DC *ret* San Antonio TX
Williams PS *ret* Cape Girardeau MO
Wiltse RD *ret* Chesterfield MO
Yerkes KB *ret* Haddon Township NJ

DIOCESE OF MONTANA
(PROVINCE VI)
Comprises the State of Montana
DIOCESAN OFFICE 515 N Park Ave Helena MT 59601 (MAIL: PO Box 2020 Helena MT 59624)
TEL (800) 247-1391   FAX (406) 442-2238
E-MAIL admin@diomontana.com   WEB www.diomontana.com

Previous Bishops—
Daniel S Tuttle 1866-1880, Leigh R Brewer m 1880 dio 1904-16, Wm F Faber coadj 1914 Bp 1916-34, Herbert HH Fox suffr 1920 coadj 1925 Bp 1934-39, Henry H Daniels coadj 1939 Bp 1939-57, Chandler W Sterling coadj 1956 Bp 1957-68, Jackson E Gilliam 1968-85, Charles I Jones, 1986-2001, Charles L Keyser Bp asst 2001-2003

Bishop—Rt Rev C Franklin Brookhart (987)
(Dio 27 Sept 2003)

Cn to Ord & Deploy Off Rev Canon JC Roberts; *Dio Adm* B Hagen; *Sec* G Archey; *Treas* M Winford *Ecum* Rev V Webster; *Chanc* J Shuler; *Yth Dir* The Rev Canon W Blessing

Stand Comm—Cler: Pres S Eades K Axberg J Yetter *Lay:* D DeHart P Randall M Messina

Dio Conv: 7-9 Oct 2016, Great Falls

PARISHES, MISSIONS, AND CLERGY

Absarokee St Pauls of the Stillwater Episcopal **M** (44) 111 S Woodard Ave 59001-6316 (Mail to: PO Box 605 59001-0605) (406) 328-4163

Anaconda St Marks Episcopal Church **P** (44) 600 Main St 59711-2937 (Mail to: 601 Main St 59711-2941) Theresa Kelley (405) 563-3625

Big Sky All Saints in Big Sky **P** (69) Meadow Village Big 59716 (Mail to: PO Box 161026 59716-1026) Valarie Webster (406) 995-7988

Big Timber St Marks Episcopal Church **P** (78) 203 W 4th Ave 59011 (Mail to: PO Box 626 59011-0626) (406) 932-5712

Bigfork St Patricks Episcopal Church **P** (99) 105 S Crane Mountain Rd 59911 (Mail to: PO Box 431 59911-0431) Ruth Baker (406) 849-5465

Billings St Lukes Church **P** (254) 119 N 33rd St 59101-2018 (Mail to: 119 N 33rd St 59101-2018) (406) 252-7186

Billings St Stephens Church **P** (335) 1241 Crawford Dr 59102-2442 (Mail to: 1241 Crawford Dr 59102-2442) Jacob Knee Gerald Jasmer (406) 259-5017

Bozeman St James Episcopal Church **P** (598) 5 West Olive St 59715-4624 (Mail to: 5 W Olive St 59715-4624) Clark Sherman Constance Campbell-Pearson (406) 586-9093

Butte St John's Episcopal Church **P** (50) 15 N Idaho St 59701-9229 (Mail to: 15 N Idaho St 59701)

Columbia Falls All Saints' Episcopal Church **P** (196) 2048 Conn Road 59912 (Mail to: PO Box

1923 59937-1923) Bradley Wirth (406) 862-2863

Deer Lodge St James-Pintler Cluster **P** (37) 307 Cottonwood Ave 59722-1040 (Mail to: 307 Cottonwood Ave 59722-1040) (406) 563-3625

Dillon St James Episcopal Church **P** (65) 203 E Glendale St 59725-2707 (Mail to: PO Box 1374 59725-1374) Susan Eades (406) 683-2735

Emigrant St Johns Episcopal Church **P** (71) 8 Story Rd 59027 (Mail to: PO Box 176 59027-0176) (406) 222-0222

Ennis Trinity Episcopal Church **P** (86) 93 Jeffers Rd 59729 (Mail to: PO Box 336 59729-0336) Keith Axberg (406) 600-1128

Eureka St Michael & All Angels Church **P** (54) PO Box 342 59917-0342 (Mail to: PO Box 342 59917-0342) Pattiann Bennett (406) 297-7233

Forsyth Church of the Ascension **M** (19) 380 15th Ave N 59327 (Mail to: PO Box 105 59327-0105) (406) 234-5188

Fort Benton St Paul Episcopal Church **P** (9) 1112 14th 59442 (Mail to: PO Box 463 59442-0463) (406) 265-2638

Glasgow St Matthew Episcopal Church **P** (19) 539 3rd Ave S 59230-2427 (Mail to: PO Box 506 59230-0506) (406) 228-4789

Great Falls Church of the Incarnation **P** (172) 600 3rd Ave N 59401-2426 (Mail to: PO Box 3046 59403-3046) Timothy Ljunggren (406) 453-4167

Hamilton St Pauls Episcopal Church **P** (135) No 600 S 3rd St 59840-2730 (Mail to: PO Box 758 59840-0758) (406) 360-2661

Havre St Mark's Episcopal Church **M** (25) 539 3rd Ave 59501-3915 (Mail to: PO Box 950 59501-0950) (406) 265-2161

✢ **Helena** St Peters Cathedral **O** (452) 511 N Park Ave 59601-2703 (Mail to: PO Box 819 59624) Heidi Kinner Raymond Brown Raymond Brown Donna Gleaves Richard Johnson John Moran Gabriel Morrow (406) 442-5175

Kalispell Christ Church Episcopal **P** (199) 215 3rd Ave E 59901 (Mail to: 215 3rd Ave E 59901-4531) (406) 257-6182

Lewistown St James Episcopal Church **P** (64) 502 W Montana St 59457-2631 (Mail to: PO Box 744 59457-0744) Jean Collins

Livingston St Andrews Episcopal Church **P** (183) 310 W Lewis St 59047-3015 (Mail to: PO Box 835 59047-0835) (406) 222-0222

Manhattan Gethsemane Episcopal Church **P** (10) 305 5th Ave 59741 (Mail to: PO Box 95 59741-0095) (406) 282-0049

Miles City Emmanuel Episcopal Church **M** (18) 208 North 11th 59301 (Mail to: PO Box 1526 59301-1526) (406) 234-5188

Missoula Church of the Holy Spirit **P** (842) 130 S 6th St E 59801-4222 (Mail to: 130 S 6th St E 59801-4222) Douglas Anderson Judith Anderson Myrna Chaney Terri Grotzinger

Philipsburg St Andrews Episcopal Church **P** (19) 101 E Kearney St 59858 (Mail to: PO Box 601 59858-0601) (406) 563-3625

Polson St Andrews Episcopal Church **P** (86) 110 6th Ave E 59860-2728 (Mail to: 110 6th Ave E 59860-2728) Steven Yurosko (406) 883-5524

Red Lodge Calvary Episcopal Church **M** (93) PO Box 348 59068-0348 (Mail to: PO Box 368 59068) (406) 425-0388

Sheridan Christ Episcopal Church **P** (42) 304 S Main St 59749 (Mail to: PO Box 152 59749-0152) Janis Hansen (406) 842-7539

Stevensville St Stephens Episcopal Church **M** (19) 203 Main St 59870-2112 (Mail to: PO Box 35 59870-0035) (406) 777-0028

Troy Holy Trinity Episcopal Church **P** (11) 218 E Missoula Ave 59935 (Mail to: PO Box 637 59935-0637) (406) 297-7233

Virginia City St Paul Episcopal Church **P** (16) 102 E Idaho St 59755 (Mail to: PO Box 206 59755-0206) (406) 600-1128

NON-PAROCHIAL CLERGY

Aker ES *ret* Polson MT
Baumgarten WP *ret* Kalispell MT
Blessing WT Helena MT
Board JC *dcn* Helena MT
Brehe SL *ret* Helena MT
Champion-Garthe MV *ret* Columbia MO
Colvill LN Indianapolis IN
Conklin CE *dcn* Seattle WA
Dooling TA Helena MT
Gleaves GL *ret* Livingston MT

Guthrie DA *ret* Missoula MT
Hall KE *ret* Watertown SD
Jacques MM *ret* Dillon MT
Jett MJ New York NY
Johnson FO *ret* Jackson WY
Johnson M Red Lodge MT
Kelley JT *dcn* Butte MT
King KG Troy MT
Klingensmith REP *ret dcn* Bozeman MT
Knapp GB *dcn* Hilger MT
Knox JM *dcn* Sheridan MT
Kuhr CS *ret* Boise ID
Lauzon ML *dcn* Great Falls MT
Lindell JA *ret* Naples FL
McCloud L Billings MT
McLean JM
McLellan BJ *ret* Stuart FL
Morgan MT Spokane WA
Naumann JF *ret* Billings MT
Neeley HE *ret* Dillon MT
Oreskovich SJ *ret* Missoula MT
Peel RC
Pendergraft RS Red Lodge MT
Roberts JC *ret* Helena MT
Roberts LL *ret* Plattsmouth NE
Rognas AA *dcn* Lewiston ID
Rowe MS
Scheeler JL Helena MT
Shipp MJM *ret* Dillon MT
Sisk RB Wilsall MT
Smith DG
Smith JE Butte MT
Travis MH
Vardemann BJ *ret* Helena MT
Waddingham GB *ret* Billings MT
Yetter JM *ret* Billings MT
Zabriskie G *ret* Bozeman MT

NAVAJOLAND AREA MISSION

(PROVINCE VIII)

Comprises portions of Navajo Reservation in Arizona, New Mexico, and Utah

OFFICE: 1257 Mission Ave Farmington NM 87499-0720 (MAIL: Box 720 Farmington NM 87499-0720)

TEL (505) 327-7549 FAX (505) 327-6904

E-MAIL ceaton@ec-n.org WEB www.episcopal-navajo.org

Previous Bishops— Frederick W Putnam 1979-83, Wesley Frensdorff int 1983-88, Wm F Wolfrum int 1988-90, Wm C Wantland int 1990-2005 Steven T Plummer 1990-2005, Rustin R Kimsey 2005-06, Mark L MacDonald 2006-2009.

Bishop—Rt Rev David E Bailey (1049) (Dio 7 Aug 2010)

Admin The Rt Rev David E Bailey Box 720 Farmington NM 87499; *Sec* C Eaton Box 720 Farmington NM 87499

Dio Coun—Cler: R Stevens P Cook K Nuehardt P Henson I Velarde C Plummer; *Lay:* A Fowler A Mason L Sampson G Buck L Hardy M Benally;

Deacons: C Eaton L Sampson CA Plummer

Standing Committee—Cler: Pres R Stevens, R Chan Anaya R Kerry Nuehardt; *Lay:* A Mason C Westin A Fowler

Dio Conv: TBD

PARISHES, MISSIONS, AND CLERGY

Bluff St Christophers Church **M** (61) 3315 East Old Mission Rd 1.7 Mile Utah Route 162 84512 (Mail to: PO Box 28 84512-0028) Merrill Stevens Patricia Cook (435) 672-9940

Bluff Utah Region **P** St. Christopher Mission PO Box 720 97499 (Mail to: PO Box 720 87499-0720) Merrill Stevens Patricia Cook (435) 672-2296

Farmington All Saints Church **M** (106) 1271 Mission Ave 87401 (Mail to: PO Box 720 87499-0720) Cathlena Plummer Rosella Jim (505) 327-7549

Farmington San Juan/New Mexico Region **M** 1257 Mission Ave 87499 (Mail to: PO Box 720 87499-0720) (505) 327-7549

Farmington St Luke-in-the-Desert **M** (46) PO Box 720 87499-0720 (Mail to: PO Box 720 87499-0720) Inez Velarde (505) 327-7549

Fort Defiance Church of the Good Shepherd **M** (187) No 618 Kit Carson Drive 86504 (Mail to: PO Box 618 86504-0618) Cynthia Hizer Paula Henson (928) 729-2322

Fort Defiance Southeast Region **HC** Kit Carson Dr 86504 (Mail to: PO Box 618 86504-0618) (928) 729-2322

Fort Defiance St Mark Church **M** (77) Coalmine 86504 (Mail to: PO Box 618 86504-0618) (928) 729-2322

Many Farms St Joseph Church **M** (9) Indian Route 59 86538 (Mail to: PO Box 618 86504-0618) (928) 729-2322

Montezuma Creek St John the Baptizer Church **M** (60) Mile 12.9 Route 162 3599 W Hwy 162 84534 (Mail to: c/o St Christopher's Mission PO Box 28 84512-0028) Merrill Stevens Patricia Cook (435) 444-0484

Oljato St Mary of the Moonlight **M** (39) Rte 6420 Oljato Wash Road 84536 (Mail to: PO Box 360397 84536-0397) Merrill Stevens Patricia Cook (435) 727-0200

Upper Fruitland St Michaels Episcopal Church **M** (75) Highway N36 87416 (Mail to: PO Box 720 87499-0720) Archie Osborn De Anaya (505) 327-7549

NON-PAROCHIAL CLERGY

Corbett ID *ret* Bluff UT
Eaton CK Farmington NM
Plummer CB Farmington NM
Sampson L Bluff UT
Snyder RH *ret* Carson City NV
Sosa GR Bluff UT
Tookey CR Aztec NM

DIOCESE OF NEBRASKA
(PROVINCE VI)
Comprises the State of Nebraska
DIOCESAN OFFICE 109 N 18th St Omaha NE 68102
TEL (402) 341-5373   FAX (402) 341-8683
WEB www.episcopal-ne.org

Previous Bishops— Robt H Clarkson 1865-84, George Worthington 1885-1908, Arthur L Williams coadj 1899 Bp 1908-19, Ernest V Shayler 1919-38, Howard R Brinker 1940-62, Russell T Rauscher coadj 1961 Bp 1962-72, Robert P Varley coadj 1971 Bp 1972-75, Jas D Warner 1976-89, James E Krotz, 1990-03, Joe Goodwin-Burnett 2003-2011

Bishop—Rt Rev J Scott Barker (Dio 8 Oct 2011)

Archdcn B Bennett; *Cn to Ord* Rev Cn E Easton; *Chanc* D Bradford III; *Sec Reg* Rev Cn E Easton; *Treas* S Reagan; *Dio Admin* L Rowe; *Dir of Fin* B Byrne

Stand Comm—Cler: Pres Rev J Emerson Very Rev C Scott Rev E Medina Rev J Long; *Lay:* B Reno ML Martin C Schrader J Wisniewski

Comm on Min—Cler: Rev R Goeke Rev K Watson Rev E Thober Rev N Huston; *Lay: Chair* M Schaefer D Hendricks P Van Dyne C Simmons B Agar R Behrens

Dio Conv: 7-8 Oct 2016

PARISHES, MISSIONS, AND CLERGY

Alliance St Matthews Episcopal Church **P** (102) 312 W 16th St 69301-2205 (Mail to: PO Box 430 69301-0430) Robert McClure John Adam Cheryl Harris

Arapahoe St Pauls Episcopal Church **P** (42) 909 4th St 68922-2776 (Mail to: PO Box 583 68922-0583) (308) 962-7271

Bassett St Marys Episcopal Church **M** (48) 212 Clark St 68714-5503 (Mail to: PO Box 361 68714-0361) Randall Goeke (402) 684-3943

Beatrice Christ Episcopal Church **P** (148) 524 North 5th St 68310-2903 (Mail to: 524 North 5th St 68310-2903) Frank Smith (402) 223-5515

Bellevue Church of the Holy Spirit **P** (258) 1305 Thomas Dr 68005-2973 (Mail to: 1305 Thomas Dr 68005-2973) Thomas Jones

Blair St Marys Episcopal Church **P** (131) 1743 Grant St 68008-1916 (Mail to: 1743 Grant St 68008-1916) John Symonds (402) 426-2057

Broken Bow St Johns Episcopal Church **P** (54) 602 N 10th Ave 68822-1222 (Mail to: PO Box 353 68822-0353) (308) 872-5900

Central City Christ Church **P** (15) 1414 15th St 68826-1416 (Mail to: 1414 15th St 68826-1416) (308) 946-2640

Chadron Grace Episcopal Church **P** (52) 450 Bordeaux St 69337-2607 (Mail to: 450 Bordeaux St 69337-2607) (308) 432-2229

Columbus Grace Episcopal Church **P** (69) 2053 23rd Ave 68601-3329 (Mail to: PO Box 306 68601) Ellen Thober (402) 564-0116

Cozad St Christophers Church **P** (20) 1520 Avenue B 69130-1645 (Mail to: PO Box 88 69130-0088) (308) 784-2056

Creighton St Marks Church **P** (10) 901 Garfield St 68739 (Mail to: PO Box 653 68729-0653) (402) 358-3295

Crete Trinity Memorial Chruch **P** (18) 14th & Juniper Sts 68333 (Mail to: 1175 Driftwood Dr 68355) (402) 826-3390

DeWitt St Augustines Episcopal Church **P** (24) 108 N Quince St 68341 (Mail to: PO Box 201 68341-0201) (402) 683-4110

Elkhorn St Augustine of Canterbury **P** (228) 285 S 208th St 68022-1811 (Mail to: 285 S 208th St 68022-1811) Benedict Varnum Patricia Sheldon

Falls City St Thomas Episcopal Church **P** (24) 1602 Harlan St 68355-2655 (Mail to: PO Box 117 68355-0117) Larry Parrish (402) 245-2868

Fremont St James Episcopal Church **P** (130) 301 E 5th St 68025-5025 (Mail to: PO Box 2421 68026) Maureen May (402) 721-3327

Gordon St Marks Episcopal Church **P** (52) Attn Amy Moore 116 E Lariet St 69343-1135 (Mail to: 116 E Lariet St 69343-1143) (308) 282-1303

Grand Island St Stephens Episcopal Church **P** (311) 422 W 2nd Street 68801 (Mail to: PO Box 2317 68802-2317) Robert Lewis (308) 382-4961

Harrisburg Good Shepherd of Plains **P** (17) Maryland Avenue 69345-0025 (Mail to: 3050 County Rd 33 69345) (308) 436-4465

Harvard St Johns Episcopal Church (Harvard) **P** (13) 410 North Harvard 68944 (Mail to: 422 N Burlington Ave 68901-5059) (402) 462-4126

✠ **Hastings** St Marks Pro Cathedral **O** (245) 422 N Burlington Ave 68901-5059 (Mail to: 422 N Burlington Ave 68901-5059) Catherine Scott

Holdrege St Elizabeths Church **P** (78) 512 Tilden St 68949-2245 (Mail to: PO Box 864 68949-0864) Karen Watson (308) 995-4528

Hyannis Calvary Church Hyannis **M** (32) 302 E Highway 2 69350 (Mail to: PO Box 80 69350-

0080) Robert McClure (308) 458-2336

Kearney St Lukes Church **P** (202) 2304 Second Ave 68847-5317 (Mail to: 2304 Second Ave 68847-5317) Jerry Ness (308) 236-5821

Kimball St Hilda Church **P** (23) 601 S. Chesnut 69145-1423 (Mail to: C/O Beverly Dunkin 509 S Adams 69145) Christine Plantz (308) 235-4588

Lexington St Peters in the Valley Church **P** (9) 903 E 13th St 68850-1741 (Mail to: 905 E 13th St 68850-1741) Kay Knudson (308) 324-6199

Lincoln Church of the Holy Trinity **P** (285) 6001 A St 68510-5006 (Mail to: 6001 A St 68510-5006) Susanna Desmarais Daniel Coffman John Long (402) 488-7139

Lincoln St David of Wales Epis Church **P** (127) 8800 Holdrege St 68505-9417 (Mail to: 8800 Holdrege St 68505) (402) 489-2772

Lincoln St Marks on the Campus Church **P** (269) 1309 R St 68508-1219 (Mail to: 1309 R St 68508-1219) Jerrold Thompson

Lincoln St Matthews Church **P** (418) 2325 S 24th St 68502-4005 (Mail to: 2325 S 24th St 68502-4099) Mark Hatch Stephen Lahey (402) 435-2226

McCook St Albans Episcopal Church **P** (129) 509 W 1st St 69001-3102 (Mail to: 509 W 1st Street 69001-3102)

Mitchell Holy Apostles Church **P** (129) 1730 18th St 69357-1138 (Mail to: 1730 18th St 69357-1138) Carol Bullard (308) 623-1969

Mullen St Josephs Church **P** (36) 402 Northwest 1st St 69152 (Mail to: PO Box 453 69152-0453) (308) 546-2262

Nebraska City Grace Episcopal Church **P** (4) 1416 1st Corso 68410-2238 (Mail to: 392 North 4th 68450) Richard Swenson (402) 335-2331

Nebraska City St Mary Episcopal Church **P** (78) 116 S 9th St 68410-2403 (Mail to: 116 S 9th St 68410-2403) (402) 873-6517

Norfolk Trinity Episcopal Church **P** (246) 111 S 9th St 68701-5166 (Mail to: 111 S 9th St 68701-5166) Robert Schlismann Sylvia Landers (402) 371-3080

North Platte Church of Our Savior **P** (192) No 203 W 4th St 69101-3916 (Mail to: 203 W 4th St 69101-3916) Jeffrey Nelson (308) 532-0515

Ogallala St Pauls Episcopal Church **P** (20) 318 E A St 69153-2609 (Mail to: 318 E A St 69153-2609) (308) 203-1141

Omaha All Saints Episcopal Church **P** (1204) 9302 Blondo St 68134-6036 (Mail to: 9302 Blondo St 68134-6036) Marisa Thompson Lynne Bacon Robert Brown Stephanie Ulrich (402) 393-8612

Omaha Church of the Resurrection **P** (256) 3004 Belvedere Blvd 68111-1232 (Mail to: 3004 Belvedere Blvd 68111-1232) Jason Emerson Mary Forsythe Juanita Johnson

Omaha St Andrews Episcopal Church **P** (677) 925 S 84th St 68114-5207 (Mail to: 925 S 84th St

68114-5207) Otto Schaefer (402) 391-1950

Omaha St Martin of Tours Church **P** (35) 2312 J St 68107-1815 (Mail to: 2324 J St 68107-1815) (402) 733-8815

✠ **Omaha** Trinity Cathedral **O** (477) 113 N 18th St 68102-4903 (Mail to: 113 N 18th St 68102-4903) Craig Loya (402) 342-7010

Oshkosh St Georges Church **P** (6) 421 West 5th Street 69154 (Mail to: PO Box 254 69154) (308) 778-7177

Papillion St Marthas Episcopal Church **P** (295) 801 Magnolia Ave 68046-6264 (Mail to: 780 Pinnacle Dr 68046-6268) Ernesto Medina Ralph Agar

Plattsmouth St Lukes Church **P** (90) 302 Ave A 68048 (Mail to: PO Box 446 68048-0446) Phillip Chapman Mavis Hall (402) 296-4718

Rushville St Marys Church **M** (22) 6919 State Highway 87 69360 (Mail to: PO Box 71 69360-0071) William Graham (308) 327-2506

Scottsbluff St Francis Episcopal Church **P** (195) 14 E 20th St 69361-2050 (Mail to: PO Box 1201 69363-1201) Mark Selvey Karen Anderson Robert Manasek (308) 632-4626

Seward St Andrews Church **P** (66) 1014 N 6th St 68434-1243 (Mail to: C/O Donald R Nelson 1014 N 6th St 68434-1243) Verneda Kelly Pamela Williams (402) 643-3829

Sidney Christ Episcopal Church **P** (27) 1205 10th Ave 69162-2045 (Mail to: PO Box 141 69162) Charles Cook Edna Drazdowski (308) 254-2166

Valentine St Johns Episcopal Church **P** (15) 372 North Main Street 69201-0261 (Mail to: PO Box 261 69201-0261) (402) 376-1723

Wymore St Lukes Episcopal Church **P** (6) 114 N 10th St 68466-1728 (Mail to: 114 N 10th St 68466-1728) (402) 645-3231

NON-PAROCHIAL CLERGY

Adams JD Omaha NE
Amsden HP *dcn* Omaha NE
Anderson TL *ret* Ashland NE
Andrews AJ *dcn* Sidney NE
Austin HW *dcn* Papillion NE
Bee RD *ret* Gladstone MO
Bennett BB *dcn* Hastings NE
Benson GA *ret* Lincoln NE
Boman SR *ret* Lincoln NE
Boyd LR *ret* Lincoln NE
Churchman MA *ret* Council Bluffs IA
Cool OM *dcn* Omaha NE
Crawford SW Lincoln NE
Easton EL Omaha NE
Funk DG *ret* Columbus NE
Gabb JN *ret* Centennial CO
Gaston KE *dcn* Omaha NE
Gavin CE *ret* Lincoln NE
Gearhart RJ *ret* Syracuse NE
Gerhard EJ *dcn* Omaha NE
Gilchrist JE

Gockley MJ Broken Bow NE
Grosh CM *dcn* Lincoln NE
Grubb SA *dcn* Lincoln NE
Hanway DG *ret* Lincoln NE
Henrichsen RA *dcn*
Holmquist DW *dcn* Elkhorn NE
Howell-Burke UJ
Huber DM *ret* Cattaraugus NY
Hurley TJ *ret* Omaha NE
Huston NW *dcn* Omaha NE
Jaynes RLMK Omaha NE
Johanson NL *dcn* Monrovia CA
Jones AL *dcn* Mitchell NE
Kirby RA *dcn*
Kuschel CM *ret* Grand Island NE
Marsh KE *ret* Suttons Bay MI
Martin LF Gregory SD
McConney JA *ret* Omaha NE
McNutt RL *dcn* Omaha NE
Merritt FD *dcn*
Moon RW West Plains MO
Moore OM *dcn* Omaha NE
Morford SA *dcn* Omaha NE
Mottl PE *ret* Crisfield MD
Naugle GR *ret* Lincoln NE
Nerud BJ *dcn*
Norris MJP West Monroe LA
Odgers MCH *dcn* Lincoln NE
Olson EE *dcn* Plattsmouth NE
Parrish DLR *ret* Janesville WI
Peek CA *ret* Kearney NE
Raybourn FL *ret* Bellevue NE
Roberts KE Omaha NE
Robson JM *dcn* Lincoln NE
Ross EM *ret dcn* Council Bluffs IA
Royal DK *dcn* Nebraska City NE
Scott RW *ret* Bellevue NE
Scribner JM *ret* Asheville NC
Shepard KR *ret* Lincoln NE
Slane CDT
Snow RG *ret* Fort Lauderdale FL
Spencer OJ *ret* Raleigh NC
Sturgeon MS *dcn* Omaha NE
Sturgis JE *ret* Kearney NE
Tan Creti MJ *ret* Omaha NE
Tomlinson RM *ret* Omaha NE
Upton TL *dcn* Omaha NE
Van Beveren EC *ret* Pendleton OR
Visger JR *dcn* Lincoln NE
Wait RL *dcn* Lincoln NE
Walker AK
Warner DE *dcn* Grand Island NE
Warren JL *ret* Scottsbluff NE
Whitted WR *dcn* Omaha NE
Wiley RL *ret* Fremont NE
With JL Bassett NE
Wolcott SE *dcn*
Wolfe DA *dcn* Bayard NE
Yeates JA *ret* Omaha NE
Young GR *ret* Scottsbluff NE

DIOCESE OF NEVADA
(PROVINCE VIII)
Comprises the State of Nevada and 1 church in Arizona
DIOCESAN OFFICE 9480 S Eastern Ave Ste 236 Las Vegas NV 89123-8037
TEL (702) 737-9190   FAX (702) 737-6488
E-MAIL michelle@episcopalnevada.org   WEB www.episcopalnevada.org

Previous Bishops—
Ozi W Whitaker (NV and AZ) 1869-86, Henry D Robinson 1908-13, Geo C Hunting 1914-24, Thomas Jenkins 1929-42, Wm F Lewis 1942-59, Wm G Wright 1960-72, Wesley Frensdorff 1972-85, Stewart C Zabriskie 1986-99, Katharine Jefferts Schori 2001-06

Bishop—Rt Rev Dan T Edwards (1023) (Dio 5 Jan 2008)

Conv Sec C Moore; *Treas* M Estes; *Finan Off* W O'Brien; *Chanc* A Morgan; *Cn to Ord* RM Nelson Jr; *Cn for Cong Vit* C Gregg

Stand Comm—Cler: Pres B Polley N Janess W Millsap M Asson R Sims; *Lay: Sec* C Moore *Treas* M Estes L Baca C Hess C Marks D Kesner L Negrete

Dio Staff—Admin and Comm Off: M McCarragher; *Finance Officer:* W O'Brien; *Can Lat/Hisp Min* B Iniesta-Avila; *Cn for Cong Vit* C Gregg

Dio Conv: 6-8 Oct 2016, Las Vegas, NV

PARISHES, MISSIONS, AND CLERGY

Austin St George Episcopal Church **P** (9) 156 Main St 89310-0181 (Mail to: PO Box 181 89310-0181) (775) 964-1477

Boulder City St Christophers Episcopal Church **P** (99) 812 Arizona St 89005-2604 (Mail to: 812 Arizona St 89005-2604) James Lyons (702) 293-4275

Bullhead City Church of the Holy Spirit **P** (40) 580 Hancock Rd 86442-4902 (Mail to: 580 Hancock Rd 86442-4902) (928) 763-1881

Carson City St Nicholas Mission **PM** 1721 Snyder Ave 89701-7812 (Mail to: PO Box 7000 89702) (775) 882-9203

Carson City St Peters Episcopal Church **P** (205) 314 S Division St 89703-4172 (Mail to: 305 N Minnesota St 89703-4172) Jeffrey Paul Kimberly Morgan (775) 882-1534

Elko St Pauls Episcopal Church **P** (95) 777 Sage St 89801-3318 (Mail to: 777 Sage St 89801-3318) Karen Albrethsen David Grube Kenneth Jewell (775) 738-3264

Ely St Bartholomews Church **P** (63) 209 7th St 89301-1583 (Mail to: PO Box 151585 89315-1207) Mary Bianchi Richard Sims

Eureka St James Episcopal Church **HC** (4) 101 S Spring St 89316 (Mail to: PO Box 473 89316-0473) (775) 289-0557

Fallon Holy Trinity Episcopal Church **P** (94) 507 Churchill Street 89406-3902 (Mail to: 507

Churchill Street 89406-3902) Virginia Hart Patrick Leclaire (775) 423-3551

Glenbrook St Johns in the Wilderness Church **P** (57) 1776 Us Highway 50 89413 (Mail to: 1776 Us Highway 50 89413-9714) Victoria Warren (775) 588-6793

Henderson Episcopal Church of the Epiphany **P** (120) 9041 S Pecos Rd Ste 4000 89074-6600 (Mail to: 9041 S Pecos Rd Ste 4000 89074-6602) (702) 427-9588

Henderson St Timothys Episcopal Church **P** (160) 43 W Pacific Ave 89015-7351 (Mail to: 43 W Pacific Ave 89015-7351) John Jordan Carol Walton (702) 565-8033

Incline Vlg St Patrick's Episcopal Church **P** (213) 341 Village Blvd 89451-8237 (Mail to: 341 Village Blvd 89451-8237) Eric Heidecker David Mussatti (775) 831-1418

Las Vegas All Saints Episcopal Church **P** (455) 4201 W Washington Ave 89107-2005 (Mail to: 4201 W Washington Ave 89107-2005) Michael Engfer (702) 878-2373

Las Vegas Christ Episcopal Church **P** (1014) 2000 S Maryland Pkwy 89104-3200 (Mail to: 2000 S Maryland Pkwy 89104-3200) Richard O'Brien James Vaughn (702) 735-7655

Las Vegas Grace in the Desert Episcopal Church **P** (484) 2004 Spring Gate Ln 89134-6246 (Mail to: 2004 Spring Gate Ln 89134-6246) Mary Bredlau Sherman Frederick Clelia Garrity Shannon Leach Barbara Lewis Barbara Preas James Wallis (702) 838-7444

Las Vegas St Lukes Episcopal Church **P** (351) 832 N Eastern Ave 89101-2345 (Mail to: 832 N Eastern Ave 89101-2345) Antonio Lopez (702) 642-4459

Las Vegas St Matthews Episcopal Church **P** (144) 4709 S Nellis Blvd 89121-3113 (Mail to: 4709 S Nellis Blvd 89121-3113) Christie Leavitt Lionel Starkes (702) 451-2483

Las Vegas St Thomas Episcopal Church **P** (85) 5383 E Owens Ave 89110-1624 (Mail to: 5383 E Owens Ave 89110-1624) Timothy Swonger (702) 452-1199

Lovelock Grace - St Francis Episcopal Church **P** (15) 801 Cornell Ave 89419 (Mail to: PO Box 1043 89419-1043) (775) 273-7720

Minden Coventry Cross Episcopal Church **P** (39) 1631 Esmeralda Ave 89423-4202 (Mail to: PO Box 518 89423-0518) (775) 782-4161

Nixon St Mary the Virgin Episcopal Church **P** (78) 240 Church St 89424 (Mail to: PO Box 207 89424-0207) (775) 574-0280

Pahrump St Martins in the Desert Episcopal **P** (75) 631 W Irene St 89060-3929 (Mail to: PO Box

1385 89041-1385) Julie Platson (775) 537-1115

Pioche Christ Episcopal Church **P** (30) Cedar St 89043 (Mail to: PO Box 126 89043-0126) (775) 962-5835

Reno St Catherine of Siena **M** (180) 110 Bishop Manogue Dr 89511-4809 (Mail to: PO Box 6791 89513-6791) Laurinda Chappelle (775) 771-4168

Reno Trinity Episcopal Church **P** (795) 200 Island ave 89505-2246 (Mail to: PO Box 2246 89505-2246) William Millsap Patricia Pumphrey William Stomski (775) 329-4279

Sparks St Pauls Episcopal Church **P** (299) 1135 12th St 89431-3607 (Mail to: PO Box 737 89432-0737) Kirk Woodliff William Arnold (775) 358-4474

Tonopah St Marks Episcopal Church **P** (14) 210 University St 89043 (Mail to: PO Box 447 89049-0447) (775) 482-5546

Virginia City Old St Pauls Episcopal Church **P** (16) F & Taylor St 89440 (Mail to: PO Box 13 89440-0013) (775) 847-9700

Wadsworth St Michael & All Angels Church **P** (39) 445 Reservation Rd 89442 (Mail to: PO Box 310 89442-0310) (775) 835-6440

Wells St Barnabas Episcopal Church **P** 367 4th St 89835 (Mail to: PO Box 339 89835-0339) (775) 752-3416

Winnemucca St Marys Episcopal Church **P** 350 Melarkey St 89445-3146 (Mail to: PO Box 2088 89446-2088) (775) 623-3296

Yerington St Albans Episcopal Church **P** (6) Van Ness & West St 89447 (Mail to: PO Box 207 89447-0207) (775) 463-1276

NON-PAROCHIAL CLERGY

Addiego JC Boulder City NV
Almodiel AD Las Vegas NV
Appolloni SL *dcn* Reno NV
Armstead DW *dcn*
Asson ML *dcn* Huntsville AL
Augustin DL *ret* Las Vegas NV
Beebe JR *ret* Akron OH
Belmore CDS Las Vegas NV
Belmore K *ret* Las Vegas NV
Bernardez TK Las Vegas NV
Bertolozzi MA *dcn* Las Vegas NV
Boivin BA *dcn*
Cantrell D Austin NV
Cole MJ *dcn* Las Vegas NV
Cowell FB *ret* West Richland WA
Crites KD Reno NV
Curtis WS *ret* Minden NV
Davidson JP *ret* Incline Village NV
Dockery NL *dcn* Las Vegas NV
Dulgar SL *dcn*
Dunn SKE Reno NV
Edmonds CM
Edwards JP Reno NV
Erquiaga TN Fallon NV
Ferguson VA *dcn* Las Vegas NV
Foraker-Thompson J Gardnerville NV
Ford JC *dcn*

Frowe JS Reno NV
Goddard JR *ret* Gleneden Beach OR
Gregg CC Saint George UT
Gregory EJ *dcn* Las Vegas NV
Groubert GH *dcn* Las Vegas NV
Gustafson KE *dcn* Las Vegas NV
Henry RL Henderson NV
Hernandez JA Las Vegas NV
Hiatt KM *dcn* Pioche NV
Holly FE Chimacum WA
Hopner KA Sparks NV
Hunt TL *ret* Chico CA
Iniesta-Avila B Las Vegas NV
Janess NK *dcn*
Jeffery VJ *ret* Reno NV
Johnson TA South Lake Tahoe CA
Kalas SC North Las Vegas NV
Kasio JL
Kelly JL Incline Village NV
Kempson-Thompson D Glenbrook NV
Lagana GL *dcn* Spokane WA
Langevin AE *dcn* Las Vegas NV
Lassiter RB Boulder City NV
Lawrence EJ Reno NV
Link MR *ret* Las Vegas NV
Margerum MC *dcn* Reno NV
McCarroll SK Boulder City NV
McNaul RG *ret* North Las Vegas NV
Merfy FM *dcn* Davis CA
Morgan EL *dcn* Carson City NV
Nelson RM Las Vegas NV
Netzler SK Minden NV
Nye MO *ret* Brentwood CA
Oetjen SL *dcn* North Las Vegas NV
Olandese JS Las Vegas NV
Patterson MS Fernley NV
Petzak RR Reno NV
Polley BB *dcn* Las Vegas NV
Putz SJB *dcn* Boulder City NV
Quinton DL Anthony TX
Radke PK *dcn* Las Vegas NV
Rogina JM *ret* Reno NV
Ruggaber MP Virginia City NV
Rupp LG *ret* Henderson NV
Scott NJ Hawthorne NV
Shanks E Austin NV
Shannon CL *dcn* Henderson NV
Shortridge DJ Denver CO
Slater MA *dcn* Stagecoach NV
Smallwood RL Las Vegas NV
Smith LB *dcn* Sparks NV
Sorensen RT Sparks NV
Steinfeld JW *ret* Reno NV
Supin CR *ret* Jefferson NC
Tattersall EAR Stateline NV
Towner PE *ret* Colorado Springs CO
Ward HA *ret* Boulder City NV
Watson M Ellicott City MD
Whitfield AA *ret* Vancouver WA
Woomer HG
Yoder JH *ret* Fort Pierce FL
Zaiss JD

DIOCESE OF NEW HAMPSHIRE
(PROVINCE I)
Comprises the State of New Hampshire
DIOCESAN OFFICE 63 Green St Concord NH 03301
TEL (603) 224-1914   FAX (603) 225-7884
E-MAIL info@nhepiscopal.org   WEB www.nhepiscopal.org

Previous Bishops—
Alexander V Griswold 1811-43, Carlton Chase 1844-70, Wm W Niles 1870-1914, Edward M Parker coadj 1906 Bp 1914-25, John T Dallas 1926-48, Chas F Hall 1948-73, Philip A Smith 1973-86, Douglas E Theuner 1986-2004, V Gene Robinson 2004-13

Bishop—Rt Rev A Robert Hirschfeld (1067)
(Dio 5 Jan 2013)

Cn to Ord H Anderson; *Cn for Mission* Res K Nichols; *Sec* E Rotch; *Treas* C Porter; *Fin Mgr* G Gallant; *Chanc* RA Wells Jr; *Bps Exec Asst* T Pickering; *Admin Asst* L Eaton

Stand Comm—Cler: Pres C Hemingson G Collins TP Gocha; *Lay:* M Porter J Esmay T Knowles

Dio Conv: 7 Nov 2015 Concord NH

PARISHES, MISSIONS, AND CLERGY

Ashland St Marks Episcopal Church **M** (47) 18 Highland St 03217-4337 (Mail to: PO Box 737 03217-0737) Richard Belshaw James Ransom (603) 968-7640

Berlin St Barnabas Church **P** (72) 1 Main St 03570-2414 (Mail to: PO Box 545 03570-0545) (603) 752-3504

Bretton Woods Church of the Transfiguration **SC** No Rt 302 03860-0382 (Mail to: C/O Christ Church PO Box 382 03860) Susan Buchanan (603) 356-2062

Canterbury Church of the Woods **M** 92 Foster Rd 03224-2517 (Mail to: C/O Kairos Earth 92 Foster Rd 03224-2517) (603) 731-5013

Claremont Trinity Episcopal Church **P** (149) 120 Broad St 03743-3621 (Mail to: PO Box 172 03743-0172) Janet Lombardo (603) 542-2103

Claremont Union-St. Luke's Episcopal Church **P** (58) 133 Old Church Rd 03743 (Mail to: PO Box 326 03603-0326) Marthe Dyner (603) 542-7209

Colebrook St Stephens Episcopal Mission **M** (23) 16 Parsons St 03576 (Mail to: PO Box 85 03576) Marlyn Neary (603) 237-8229

Concord Chapel of St Peter and Paul **CC** 325 Pleasant St 03301 (Mail to: 325 Pleasant St 03301) (603) 229-4659

Concord Grace Episcopal Church **M** (163) 30 Eastman St 03301-5409 (Mail to: 30 Eastman St 03301-5409) Jason Wells (603) 224-2252

Concord St Pauls Church **P** (489) 21 Centre St 03301-6301 (Mail to: 21 Centre St 03301-6301)

Kate Atkinson Charles Leclerc Keith Patterson (603) 224-2523

Contoocook St Andrews Episcopal Church **P** (796) 354 Main St 03229-2627 (Mail to: 354 Main Street 03229-2627) John McCausland Luis Rodriguez (603) 746-3415

Derry Church of the Transfiguration **P** (146) 1 Hood Rd 03038-2046 (Mail to: 1 Hood Rd 03038-2046) Raymond Bonin (603) 432-2120

Dover Church of St Thomas **P** (320) 5 Hale St 03820-3712 (Mail to: 5 Hale St 03820-3773) Gail Avery (603) 742-3155

Dublin Emmanuel Church **SC** Dublin Rd 03444 (Mail to: 8 Main St Apt 6 03452-6203) (603) 563-8029

Dunbarton Church of St John the Evangelist **M** (53) 270 Stark Hwy N 03046-4714 (Mail to: 270 Stark Hwy N 03046-4714) Winifred Skeates (603) 774-3678

Durham St Georges Episcopal Church **P** (312) 1 Park Ct 03824-2407 (Mail to: 1 Park Ct 03824-2407) Michael Bradley (603) 868-2785

Exeter Christ Church Episcopal **P** (1158) 43 Pine St 03833-2720 (Mail to: 43 Pine St 03833-2797) Mark Pendleton David Holroyd (603) 772-3332

Goffstown St Matthews Episcopal Church **P** (1204) 7 N Mast St 03045-1709 (Mail to: 7 N Mast St 03045-1709) William Exner (603) 497-2003

Hampstead St Christophers Episcopal Church **M** (340) 187 East Rd 03841-5302 (Mail to: 187 East Rd 03841-5340) Miriam Acevedo Gail Avery (603) 329-4674

Hampton Trinity Episcopal Church **M** (119) 200 High St 03842-2286 (Mail to: 200 High St 03842-2286) David Robinson (603) 926-5688

Hanover St Thomas Episcopal Church **P** (633) 9 W Wheelock St 03755-1710 (Mail to: 9 W Wheelock St 03755-1710) Guy Collins Kelly Seaman (603) 643-4155

Holderness Chapel of Holy Cross **M** Holderness School 33 Chapel Lane 03245 (Mail to: Holderness School PO Box 1879 03264-1879) (603) 536-1257

Keene Parish of St James Church **P** (289) 44 West St 03431-3371 (Mail to: 44 West St 03431-3371) Caroline Hines Geoffrey Smith (603) 352-1019

Laconia St James Episcopal Church **P** (191) 2238 Parade Rd 03246-1520 (Mail to: 2238 Parade Rd 03246) Tobias Nyatsambo William Gannon (603) 524-5800

Lancaster St Pauls Church **P** (131) 113 Main St 03584-3028 (Mail to: 113 Main St 03584-3028) John Hutchinson (603) 788-4654

Lisbon Church of the Epiphany **M** (12) 90 School St 03585-6514 (Mail to: PO Box 126 03585) (603) 838-8961

Littleton All Saints Episcopal Church **P** (246) 35 School St 03561-4820 (Mail to: 35 School St 03561-4820) Susan Garrity Paul Higginson (603) 444-3414

Londonderry St Peters Episcopal Church **P** (276) 3 Peabody Row 03053-3302 (Mail to: 3 Peabody Row 03053-3302) Sarah Rockwell (603) 437-8222

Lost Nation St Timothys Chapel **SC** Lost Nation Road 03584 (Mail to: C/O St Pauls Church 113 Main St 03584) (603) 788-4654

Manchester Grace Episcopal Church **P** (317) 106 Lowell St 03101-1625 (Mail to: 106 Lowell St 03101-1625) Marjorie Gerbracht-Stagnaro William Knight Jane Van Zandt Wesley Wasdyke (603) 622-9813

Manchester St Andrews Episcopal Church **P** (100) 102 Main St 03102-4028 (Mail to: 102 N Main St 03102-4028) Sarah Rockwell Thomas Vanderslice (603) 622-8632

Marlborough St Francis Chapel **SC** Stone Pond 03444 Anne Webb (603) 876-4407

Meredith Trinity Episcopal Church **P** (110) 93 Route 25 East 03253-0635 (Mail to: PO Box 635 03253-0635) Robin Soller (603) 279-6689

Merrimack Faith Episcopal Church **M** (80) 590 Daniel Webster Hwy 03054-3429 (Mail to: PO Box 422 03054-0422) Patricia Henking (603) 424-6806

Milford Church of Our Saviour **P** (160) 10 Amherst St 03055-4009 (Mail to: PO Box 237 03055-0237) Hays Junkin (603) 673-3309

Nashua Church of the Good Shepherd **P** (1148) 214 Main St 03060-2939 (Mail to: PO Box 412 03061-0412) Robert Odierna Alanna Van Antwerpen (603) 882-5352

New London St Andrews Church **P** (385) 15 Gould Rd 03257-5533 (Mail to: PO Box 294 03257-0294) John Macleod Kelly Seaman (603) 526-6344

Newport Church of the Epiphany **P** (58) 55 Cheney St 03773 (Mail to: PO Box 624 03773-0624) Alice Roberts (603) 863-1786

North Conway Christ Episcopal Church **P** (225) 16 Pine St 03860-5210 (Mail to: PO Box 382 03860-0382) (603) 356-2062

North Woodstock Church of the Messiah **M** (97) School St 03262 (Mail to: PO Box 267 03262-0267) Teresa Gocha (603) 745-3148

Peterborough All Saints Church **P** (299) 51 Concord St 03458-1510 (Mail to: 51 Concord St 03458-1510) Jamie Hamilton (603) 924-3202

Pittsfield St Stephens Episcopal Church **P** (72) 50 main st 03263 (Mail to: PO Box 435 03263-0435) Curtis Metzger Stephen Blackmer (603) 435-7908

Plymouth Church of the Holy Spirit **P** (174) 170 Main St 03264-1526 (Mail to: PO Box 68 03264-0068) Grace Burson (603) 536-1321

Portsmouth Christ Church **M** (82) 1035 Lafayette Rd 03801-5468 (Mail to: 1035 Lafayette Rd 03801-5468) David Robinson (603) 436-8842

Portsmouth St John's Episcopal Church **P** (1153) 100 Chapel St 03801-3808 (Mail to: 100 Chapel St 03801-3808) Robert Stevens Anne Williamson (603) 436-8283

Rye Beach St Andrews by the Sea **SC** Church Rd 03871 (Mail to: Tom Gage PO Box 555 03871) (207) 964-8432

Salem St Davids Episcopal Church **P** (89) 231 Main St 03079-3186 (Mail to: 231 Main St 03079-3186) Carolyn Stevenson (603) 893-0342

Sanbornville Church of St John the Baptist **P** (179) 118 High St 03872-4367 (Mail to: PO Box 249 03872-0249) Suzanne Poulin (603) 522-3329

Sugar Hill St Matthews Summer Chapel **SC** Rte 117 03585 (Mail to: 71 Sunset Hill Rd 03586-4235) (603) 823-5667

Sunapee St James Episcopal Church **SC** 378 Lake Avenue 03782-0178 (Mail to: PO Box 116 01810-0002) (603) 526-9070

Tamworth Church of St Andrew in Valley **P** (97) 678 Whittier Road 03886-0436 (Mail to: PO Box 436 03886-0436) Heidi Frantz-Dale (603) 323-8515

Tilton Trinity Episcopal Church **P** (45) Trinity Episcopal Church 274 Main Street 03276 (Mail to: Trinity Church Tilton c/o Diocese of NH 63 Green Street 03301) Marcus Crapsey (603) 224-1914

Walpole St Johns Episcopal Church **P** (51) Westminister And Elm Sts 03608 (Mail to: PO Box 179 03608-0179) Susan De Puy Kershaw (603) 756-4533

Weare Church of the Holy Cross **M** (89) 118 Center Rd 03281-4605 (Mail to: PO Box 161 03281-0161) (603) 529-1042

Whitefield Church of the Transfiguration **SC** 277 Water St 03598 (Mail to: PO Box 277 03598-0277) Gordon Owen (603) 837-2098

Wolfeboro All Saints Episcopal Church **P** (428) 359 S Main St 03894-4413 (Mail to: PO Box 359 03894-0359) (603) 569-3453

Woodsville St Lukes Episcopal Church **M** (75) 3 Church St 03785-1259 (Mail to: PO Box 167 03785-0167) William Watts (603) 747-2670

NON-PAROCHIAL CLERGY

Ackley SM *ret* Ashland NH
Allen GR *ret* South Berwick ME
Allen JS *ret* Laconia NH
Anderson HP Concord NH
Babcock HRM *ret* Montgomery Center VT
Bailey M *ret* Kennebunkport ME
Ballew TJ *dcn* Durham NH
Beale MI *ret* Manchester NH
Bidwell MA Bristol VT
Blauvelt CJ *ret* Manchester NH

Bonell JW *ret* Wareham MA
Brooks WT Lancaster NH
Cipolla AM Woodbridge NJ
Clark CH *ret* Exeter NH
Coffin PR *ret* Keene NH
Collier DR Billerica MA
Courtright AH
Crosby DP *ret* Peterborough NH
Cruse WC North Conway NH
Cullen KM *ret* Manchester NH
Custer MG *ret* Chocorua NH
Dales RK *ret* Wolfeboro NH
Davenport CR Colebrook NH
Evans JH *ret* Tiverton RI
Fairless CS *ret* Wilmont NH
Ferry DW *ret* Hooksett NH
Folsom HT *ret* Randolph NH
Freeman RA *ret* Poultney VT
Gould JR Watertown MA
Greene FE *ret* Laconia NH
Greenleaf RE Concord NH
Hague SA *ret* Lebanon NH
Hall TL *ret* Milan NH
Haney JH *ret* Fairhaven MA
Hemingson CA *ret* Hopkinton NH
Hildebrandt ML Longmont CO
Hulse GG Colebrook NH
Hurst WG *ret* Fort Myers FL
Jacobson BH *ret* Groveland MA
Jenkins MA *ret* Gregory MI
Langle S Claremont NH
Le Sueur SD *ret* Derry NH
Loy RJ Cape Elizabeth ME

MacKenzie J *ret* Chelmsford MA
McIlhiney DB *ret* Charlottesville VA
McLaughlin EL *ret* Randolph NH
McNamara P Greenport NY
Mears PK *ret* Upper Marlboro MD
Moore MO *ret* Falls Church VA
Nichols KD Bow NH
O'Donnell JJ Milford NH
Opel WA *ret* Eastham MA
Park SR *ret* Nisswa MN
Potter FD *ret* Lexington MA
Reinheimer JJ *ret* Port Clinton OH
Rice EG *ret* Wolfeboro NH
Romer WM *ret* ACTON MA
Sherrill EK Exton PA
Siener GR *ret* Exeter NH
Slawnwhite VA *dcn* Portsmouth NH
Spencer ME Concord NH
Spinella LJ Dunbarton NH
Stecker F *ret* New London NH
Stelz PA West Chester PA
Stevenson AW *ret* North Berwick ME
Stiefel JH *dcn* Dover NH
Stiefel RE *ret* Dover NH
Stone LS *ret* Peterborough NH
Talcott BG Southborough MA
Vogele NAG White River Junction VT
Vorkink P Exeter NH
Webb RCL *ret* Jaffrey NH
Weymouth RC Plymouth NH
Whittaker BJ *ret* Guildhall VT
Woodward BW *ret* Plymouth NH

STATE OF NEW JERSEY
Dioceses of Newark and New Jersey

DIOCESE OF NEW JERSEY
(PROVINCE II)
Comprises 14 counties in central and southern New Jersey
DIOCESAN OFFICE 808 W State St Trenton NJ 08618-5326
TEL (609) 394-5281, (877) 394-5281   FAX (609) 394-9546   BISHOP'S FAX (609) 394-8015
E-MAIL diocese@dioceseofnj.org WEB www.dioceseofnj.org

Previous Bishops—
John Croes 1815-32, Geo W Doane
1832-59, Wm H Odenheimer 1859-
74, John Scarborough 1875-1914,
Paul Matthews 1915-37, Albion
W Knight coadj 1923-35, Ralph
E Urban suffr 1932-35, Wallace J
Gardner 1937-54, Alfred L Banyard
suffr 1945-55 Bp 1955-73, Albert
W Van Duzer suffr 1966-72 Bp 1973-82, VK Pettit
suffr 1983-91, GPM Belshaw suffr 1975-82 coadj
1982 Bp 1983-94, Joe Morris Doss Bp 1995-2001,

David B Joslin asst 2000-03, Sylvestre D Romero
2008-10, George E Councell, DD 2003-2013

Bishop—Rt Rev William H. Stokes, D.D. (Dio
2 Nov 2013)

Cn to Ord Rev Cn JW Sosnowski; *Dep Off* Cn
C Alvarez; *CFO* Cn Phyllis Jones; *Sec of Conv* C
Browne; *Treas* J Bathurst; *Chanc* P Ambos; Esq; *COP
Co-Chairs:* Rev J Belmont C White; *Dir of Comm* J
Elliott; *Com Chair* Rev J Belmont; *Dir of Yth Min* Cn
D Clarke

Stand Comm—Cler: Pres R Pollock LG Caton Valerie Balling; *Lay:* CH Perfater C Browne D Kirk K Moore

Dio Conv: 4-5 March 2015 Cherry Hill NJ

PARISHES, MISSIONS, AND CLERGY

Absecon St Marks and All Saints Church **P** (307) 429 S Pitney Rd 08205-9780 (Mail to: 429 S Pitney Rd 08205-9780) Martha Bradley Thomas Sweeny (609) 652-6222

Allenhurst Church of St Andrews by the Sea **SC** 150 Norwood Ave 07711 (Mail to: 14 Knight Rd 01701) (508) 740-2115

Asbury Park St Augustine Episcopal Church **P** (129) Atlantic And Prospect Aves 07712 (Mail to: PO Box 245 07712-0245) Eddie Lillard (732) 774-3069

Asbury Park Trinity Church **P** (411) 503 Asbury Ave 07712-6104 (Mail to: 503 Asbury Ave 07712-6189) Michael Way Gail Bennett (732) 775-5084

Atlantic City Historic Church of Ascension **P** (27) 30 S Kentucky Ave 08401-7008 (Mail to: PO Box 1686 08404) (609) 344-0615

Atlantic City St Augustines Church **P** (147) 1709 Arctic Ave PO Box1657 08401-4304 (Mail to: PO Box 1657 08404-1657) (609) 345-0718

Avalon St Johns by the Sea **SC** 25th & Avalon Ave 08202 (Mail to: PO Box 256 19406-1986) (609) 996-7715

Avon By Sea St Johns Episcopal Church **SC** 100 Woodland Ave 07717-1341 (Mail to: PO Box 375 07717-0375) (732) 988-9577

Barnegat Light St Peters at the Light Church **M** (94) 607 Central Ave 08006 (Mail to: 700 Central Ave 08006) Donald Turner (609) 494-2398

Basking Ridge St Marks Church **P** (292) 140 S Finley Ave 07920-1428 (Mail to: 140 S Finley Ave 07920-1428) Richard Morley (908) 766-9058

Bay Head All Saints Episcopal Church **P** (359) 500 Lake Ave 08742-0053 (Mail to: 500 Lake Ave 08742-0053) Neil Turton (732) 892-7478

Beach Haven Holy Innocents Church **P** (478) 1 Marine St 08008-1635 (Mail to: 410 S Atlantic Ave 08008-1699) Frank Crumbaugh Charles Arlin Judith Krom Gretchen Zimmerman (609) 492-7571

Bellmawr Church of the Holy Spirit **M** (85) 20 E. Browning Rd 08031 (Mail to: 20 E Browning Rd 08031-2315) (856) 931-0990

Berlin Church of the Good Shepherd **P** (136) 108 W Broad St 08009-1438 (Mail to: 108 W Broad St 08009-1438) Frances Clark Jonathan Deacon (856) 767-0160

Bernardsville St Bernards Episcopal Church **P** (80) 88 Claremont Rd 07924-2210 (Mail to: 88 Claremont Rd 07924-2210) Elizabeth Sciaino (908) 766-0602

Bernardsville St John on the Mountain **P** (361) 379 Mount Harmony Rd 07924-1414 (Mail to:

379 Mount Harmony Rd 07924-1414) Susan Ironside Patrick Malloy

Beverly St Stephens Episcopal Church **P** (167) 158 Warren St 08010-1342 (Mail to: 158 Warren St 08010-1342) Frederick Pray Anne Wrede (609) 387-0169

Blackwood St John Episcopal Church **P** (414) 1720 Old Black Horse Pk 08012-5218 (Mail to: 1720 Old Black Horse Pike 08012-5218) Margaret Sterchi

Bordentown Christ Church **P** (194) 124 Prince St 08505-1318 (Mail to: 130 Prince St 08505-1318) James Tucker (609) 298-2348

Bound Brook St Pauls Episcopal Church **P** (174) 214 Church St 08805-1934 (Mail to: 214 Church St 08805-1934) Reginald Nuamah (732) 356-0247

Bradley Beach St James Episcopal Church **P** (305) 605 4th Ave 07720-1250 (Mail to: PO Box 1 07720-0001) Frank Goss (732) 775-5414

Brick St Raphael the Archangel **P** (74) 1520 Route 88 08724-2320 (Mail to: 1520 Route 88 08724-2320) Nancy Hite Speck (732) 458-5743

Bridgeton Church of the Resurrection **P** 186 E Commerce St 08302-2606 (Mail to: 186 E Commerce St 08302-2606) Ellen Rutherford (856) 451-3233

Bridgewater St Martins Episcopal Church **P** (412) 1350 Washington Valley Rd 08807-1418 (Mail to: 1350 Washington Valley Rd 08807-1418) Bruce Montgomery

Burlington St Barnabas Church **P** (125) 309 E Broad St 08016-1723 (Mail to: 309 E Broad St 08016-1794) (609) 386-9119

Burlington St Marys Episcopal Church **P** (305) 145 W Broad St 08016-1341 (Mail to: 145 W Broad St 08016-1341) John Haynes (609) 386-0902

Camden Church of St Andrew the Apostle **M** (452) 3050 River Rd 08105-4134 (Mail to: PO Box 1333 08105-0333) Pedro Guzman (856) 365-0111

Camden St Augustine Episcopal Church **P** (160) Broadway & Royden St 08101 (Mail to: PO Box 1925 08101-1925) Earlie Clemons (856) 365-3243

Camden St Pauls Episcopal Church **P** (185) 422 Market St 08102-1526 (Mail to: PO Box 1551 08101-1551) (856) 365-5880

Camden St Wilfreds Church **M** (37) 83 N Dudley St 08105-2425 (Mail to: PO Box 1506 08105-2425) (856) 365-4924

Cape May Church of the Advent **P** (331) Washington & Franklin Sts 08204 (Mail to: PO Box 261 08204-0261) John Mitchell Daniel Hall (609) 884-3065

Cape May Point St Peters by the Sea **SC** No 102 Lake Dr 08212-0261 (Mail to: PO Box 261 08212-0261) (609) 898-4318

Cherry Hill St Bartholomews Episcopal Church **P** (682) 1989 Marlton Pike E 08003-1830 (Mail to: 1989 Marlton Pike E 08003-1830) Peter

Manzo Lynn Johnson Arthur Knight Colleen Spaeth

Clarksboro St Peter's Episcopal Church **P** (68) 304 Kings Hwy 08020-1404 (Mail to: 302 Kings Hwy 08020-1404) Daniel Gunn (856) 423-4116

Clementon St Mary Episcopal Church **M** (85) 33 Berlin Rd 08021-4501 (Mail to: PO Box 219 08021-0222) Douglas Reans (856) 435-2009

Collingswood Holy Trinity Church **P** (247) 839 Haddon Ave 08108-1941 (Mail to: 839 Haddon Ave 08108-1993) Mark Chattin (856) 858-0491

Cranbury St Davids Episcopal Church **P** (396) 90 S Main St 08512-3144 (Mail to: 90 S Main St 08512-3144) Karin Mitchell Henry Bristol (609) 655-4731

Cranford Trinity Church **P** (239) 205 North Avenue East 07016-2040 (Mail to: 205 North Avenue East 07016-2040) (908) 276-4047

Dunellen St Francis Episcopal Church **P** (167) 400 New Market Rd 08812-1505 (Mail to: 400 New Market Rd 08812-1505) John Zamboni Margaret Forsythe (732) 968-6781

Eatontown St James Memorial Episcopal Church **P** (161) 69 Broad St # O 07724-1528 (Mail to: 69 Broad St 07724-1528) Agostino Rivolta

Edison St James Episcopal Church **HC** (61) 2136 Woodbridge Ave 08817-4421 (Mail to: PO Box 1286 08818-1286) Kristen Foley (732) 985-2023

Elizabeth San Jose Episcopal Church **M** (985) 38 W End Pl 07202-1724 (Mail to: 38 W End Pl 07202-1724) Toribio Rodriguez-Santos

Elizabeth St Elizabeths Church **P** (185) 305 N Broad St 07208-3704 (Mail to: PO Box 510 07207-0510) Andy Moore Andy Moore Theodore Moore

Elizabeth St Johns Episcopal Church **P** (375) 61 Broad St 07201-2205 (Mail to: PO Box 278 07207-0278) (908) 352-1218

Flemington Calvary Episcopal Church **P** (359) 44 Broad St 08822-1404 (Mail to: 44 Broad St 08822-1404) Harry Mazujian John Hain Ann Holt (908) 782-7227

Florence St Stephens Church **M** (62) Second & Spring Sts 08518 (Mail to: PO Box 365 08518-0365) Linda Moeller (609) 499-0998

Freehold St Peters Episcopal Church **P** (258) 33 Throckmorton St 07728-1946 (Mail to: 33 Throckmorton St 07728-1946) Dirk Reinken (732) 431-8383

Gibbsboro St Johns in the Wilderness Church **M** (214) 77 Hilliards Road 08026-0126 (Mail to: PO Box 126 08026-0126) Eric Brechner Martha Dooley (856) 783-8480

Gladstone St Lukes Episcopal Church **P** (702) 182 Main St 07934-2063 (Mail to: PO Box 605 07934-0605) Kent Walley (908) 234-0002

Glassboro St Thomas Episcopal Church **P** (287) 212 N Main St 08028-1919 (Mail to: 212 N Main St 08028-1919) Idalia Craig Louis De Sheplo (856) 881-9144

Gloucester City Church of the Ascension **P** (142) 110 S Sussex St 08030-1942 (Mail to: 110 S Sussex St 08030-1942) (856) 456-4394

Haddon Heights St Marys Episcopal Church **P** (253) 70 White Horse Pike 08035 (Mail to: 501 Green St 08035-1903) (856) 547-3240

Haddonfield Grace Episcopal Church **P** (1073) 19 Kings Hwy E 08033-2001 (Mail to: 19 Kings Hwy E 08033-2001) Patrick Close (856) 429-0007

Hammonton St Marks Church **M** (143) Peach St & Central Ave 08037 (609) 898-6071

Keansburg St Marks Episcopal Church **M** (65) 247 Carr Ave 07734-1452 (Mail to: 247 Carr Ave 07734-1452) Kathleen Murray (732) 787-1075

Keyport St Mary the Virgin **M** (20) 10 E Front St 07735-1525 (Mail to: PO Box 2 07735-0002) Walter Leigh (732) 264-5288

Lakewood All Saints Church **P** (267) 213 Madison Ave 08701-3316 (Mail to: 213 Madison Ave 08701-3316) Jose Ubiera Juan Monge-Santiago (732) 367-0933

Lambertville St Andrews Episcopal Church **P** (235) 50 York St 08530-2024 (Mail to: 50 York St 08530-2024) Richard Townley (609) 397-2425

Laurel Springs Church of the Atonement **P** (121) 233 Fairmount Ave 08021-2115 (Mail to: 233 Fairmount Ave 08021-2115) Elizabeth Oasin (856) 784-8666

Lawnside Church of the Annunciation **M** (18) 18 Warwick Rd 08045 (Mail to: 12 Warwick Rd N 08045-1539)

Lebanon Church of the Holy Spirit **P** (567) 3 Haytown Rd 08833-4009 (Mail to: 3 Haytown Rd 08833-4009) Philip Carr-Jones Johnine Byrer (908) 236-6301

Linden St John the Baptist Episcopal Church **P** (109) 2018 Dewitt Ter 07036-3700 (Mail to: 2018 Dewitt Ter 07036-3700) Terry Blackburn Donald Caron (908) 925-1535

Little Silver St John's Episcopal Church **P** (267) 325 Little Silver Point Rd 07739-1757 (Mail to: 325 Little Silver Point Road 07739-1757) Valerie Redpath (732) 741-7826

Long Branch St James Church **P** (201) 300 Broadway 07740-6930 (Mail to: 300 Broadway 07740-6930) Robert Sullivan (732) 222-1411

Longport Church of the Redeemer **SC** 108 S 20th Ave 08403-1135 (Mail to: 1013 W 9th Ave Ste 9E 19406-1208) (609) 822-7222

Lumberton St Martin in the Fields **P** (173) 489 Main St 08048-1101 (Mail to: 485 Main Street 08048-1101) Margaret Smyth (609) 261-4882

Magnolia Christ Church **M** (85) 413 Evesham Ave W 08049-1726 (Mail to: PO Box 67 08049-0067) (856) 783-4281

Manchester Twp St Stephens Episcopal Church **P** (270) 180 Route 539 08759-1248 (Mail to: 180 Route 539 08759-1248) Paul Van Sant (732) 350-2121

Maple Shade St Johns Episcopal Church **M** (90) 41 E Linwood Avenue 08052-2535 (Mail to: 41 E Linwood Avenue 08052-2535) John Powell (856) 779-0389

Matawan Trinity Episcopal Church **P** (266) 18 Ryers Ln 07747-3417 (Mail to: 18 Ryers Ln 07747-3417) Maria Sanzo (732) 591-9210

Medford St Peters Episcopal Church **P** (634) 1 Hartford Rd 08055-9051 (Mail to: 1 Hartford Rd 08055-9051) Donald Muller Ronald Albury (609) 654-2963

Merchantville Grace Episcopal Church **P** (334) 7 E Maple Ave 08109-5005 (Mail to: 7 E Maple Ave 08109-5005) Jeffrey Kirk (856) 665-4117

Metuchen St Lukes Episcopal Church **P** (272) 17 Oak Ave 08840-1529 (Mail to: 17 Oak Ave 08840-1529) Edmund Zelley (732) 548-4308

Middletown Christ Church **P** (282) 90 Kings Hwy 07748-2025 (Mail to: 90 Kings Hwy 07748-2025) Donald Caron William Thomas (732) 671-2524

Millville Christ Episcopal Church **M** (21) 225 Sassafras Street 08332-3353 (Mail to: PO Box 357 08332-0357) Donald Richey (856) 825-1163

Mnchstr Twp St Elisabeths Chapel by-the-Sea **SC** 2 Stonybrook Ct 08759-2032 (Mail to: 31 Ocean Bay Blvd 08735-1922) (732) 830-0450

Monmouth Jct St Barnabas Episcopal Church **HC** (251) 142 Sand Hills Rd 08852-3103 (Mail to: 142 Sand Hills Rd 08852-3103) Valerie Balling William Breedlove (732) 297-4607

Moorestown Evergreens Chapel **Chapel** 309 Bridgeboro Rd 08057-1419 (Mail to: 309 Bridgeboro Rd 08057-1419) Douglas Halvorsen (856) 439-2000

Moorestown Trinity Church Episcopal **P** (669) 207 W Main St 08057-2325 (Mail to: 207 W Main St 08057-2381) Henry Elek Douglas Halvorsen Henrietta Lavengood Leslie Mazzacano John Salmon (856) 235-0811

Mount Holly St Andrews Church Episcopal **P** (472) 121 High St 08060-1401 (Mail to: 121 High St 08060-1401) David Snyder (609) 267-0225

Mullica Hill St Stephen's Episcopal Church **M** (100) 51 N Main St 08062-9414 (Mail to: 51 N Main St 08062-9414) Frank St Amour

Navesink All Saints Memorial Church **P** (196) 202 Navesink Ave 07752-0326 (Mail to: PO Box 326 07752) Deborah Cook

New Brunswick Christ Church **P** (459) 5 Paterson St 08901-1204 (Mail to: 5 Paterson St 08901-1204) Joanna Hollis Peter Cornell (732) 545-6262

New Brunswick Church of St John the Evangelist **P** (139) 189 George St 08901-1319 (Mail to: 189 George St 08901-1319) Joyce Scheyer (732) 545-5619

New Brunswick Episcopal Campus Ministry at Rutgers **CC** 5 Mine St 08901-1111 (Mail to:

Canterbury House 5 Mine St 08901-1111) Gregory Bezilla (732) 932-1278

New Brunswick St Albans Episcopal Church **M** (189) 148 Lee Ave 08901-2919 (Mail to: 148 Lee Ave 08901-2919) (732) 247-0808

New Providence St Andrews Episcopal Church **P** (312) 419 South St 07974-2131 (Mail to: 419 South St 07974-2194) Thomas Haverly

Ocean City Holy Trinity Episcopal Church **P** (378) 2998 Bay Ave 08226-2263 (Mail to: 2998 Bay Ave 08226-2263) Elizabeth Ohlson George Wong

Palmyra Christ Church **M** (62) 638 Parry Ave 08065-2502 (Mail to: 638 Parry Ave 08065-2599) Elly Brown (856) 829-1764

Paulsboro St James Episcopal Church **M** (80) 190 E Jefferson St 08066 (Mail to: 968 Kings Hwy Apt V15 08086) (856) 845-4878

Pemberton Grace Episcopal Church **P** (126) 43 Elizabeth St 08068-1215 (Mail to: 43 Elizabeth St 08068-1215) Jane Brady (609) 894-8001

Pennington St Matthews Episcopal Church **P** (1320) § 300 S Main St 08534-2804 (Mail to: 300 S Main St 08534-2804) Barbara Briggs John Merz (609) 737-0985

Penns Grove Church of Our Merciful Saviour **P** (176) 110 E Maple Ave 08069-2066 (Mail to: 110 E Maple Ave 08069-2065) Petrina Pyatt (856) 299-6038

Pennsville St Georges Church **P** (75) 305 N Broadway 08070-1216 (Mail to: 305 N Broadway 08070-3010) William Boatwright (856) 678-7979

Perth Amboy Church of the Holy Cross **M** (50) 351-355 Lawrie Street 08861-3342 (Mail to: 351-355 Lawrie Street 08861-3342) Francis Cho (732) 738-0862

Perth Amboy St Peters Episcopal Church **P** (486) 183 Rector St 08861-4739 (Mail to: 183 Rector St 08861-4739) Anne-Marie Jeffery Kathleen Dejohn (732) 826-1594

Pitman Church of the Good Shepherd **P** (728) 315 Highland Ter 08071-1550 (Mail to: 315 Highland Ter 08071-1550) (856) 589-8209

Pittstown St Thomas Episcopal Church **P** (313) 98 Sky Manor Rd 08867-4032 (Mail to: PO Box 348 08867-0348) Carol Horton Debra Clarke

Plainfield Church of the Holy Cross **P** (210) 40 Mercer Ave 07060-4630 (Mail to: 103 Grove St 07060-4737) Kwabena Owusu-Afriyie (908) 756-2438

Plainfield Grace Episcopal Church **P** (337) 600 Cleveland Ave 07060-1727 (Mail to: 600 Cleveland Ave 07060-1727) Theodore Moore Gideon Uzomechina (908) 756-1520

Plainfield St Marks Episcopal Church **P** (449) 1430 Park Ave 07060-2911 (Mail to: 1430 Park Ave 07060-2911) (908) 754-9483

Pleasantville St Marys Episcopal Church **M** (90) 118 W Bayview Ave 08232-3106 (Mail to: 118 W Bayview Ave 08232-3106) (609) 646-1604

Princeton All Saints Church **P** (444) 16 All Saints Rd 08540-3634 (Mail to: 16 All Saints Rd 08540-3634) Hugh Brown John Frederick Karl Morrison (609) 921-2420

Princeton Episcopal Church at Princeton **Campus Ministry** (290) C/O Diocese Of New Jersey 808 State Rd 08540-1416 (Mail to: 53 University Pl 08540-5100) Peter French (609) 252-9469

Princeton Trinity Episcopal Church **P** (2023) 33 Mercer St 08540-6807 (Mail to: 33 Mercer St 08540-6893) Paul Jeanes Nancy Hagner (609) 924-2277

Pt Pleas Bch St Marys by the Sea **P** (398) 804 Bay Ave 08742-3006 (Mail to: 804 Bay Ave 08742-3006) Victoria Duncan (732) 892-9254

Rahway Church of the Good Shepherd **P** (170) 749 Seminary Ave 07065-3413 (Mail to: 749 Seminary Ave 07065-3413) Salvador Ros (732) 388-3460

Red Bank St Thomas Episcopal Church **P** (153) 26 East Sunset Ave 07701-1408 (Mail to: PO Box 502 07701-0502) Eddie Lillard (732) 747-1039

Red Bank Trinity Episcopal Church **P** (204) 65 W Front St 07701-1621 (Mail to: 65 W Front St 07701-0742) Kenneth Gluckow John Lock (732) 741-4581

Riverside St Stephens Episcopal Church **P** (83) 324 Bridgeboro St 08075 (Mail to: 324 Bridgeboro St 08075) Sharon Sutton Anne Wrede (856) 461-1037

Riverside Trinity Church **M** (47) 6023 Us Route 130 08075 (Mail to: 51 Shawmont Ln 08046-1033) (856) 461-9124

Riverton Christ Church **P** (494) 500 4th St 08077-1214 (Mail to: 500 4th St 08077-1214) Richard Wrede (856) 829-1634

Rocky Hill Trinity Episcopal Church **M** (165) 1 Crescent Ave 08553 (Mail to: PO Box 265 08553-0265) Paul Rimassa (609) 921-8971

Rumson St Georges-by-the-River **P** (1136) 7 Waterman Ave 07760 (Mail to: 7 Lincoln Ave 07760-2051) Ophelia Laughlin James Jones Jeffrey Roy (732) 842-0596

Salem St Johns Church **HC** (110) 76 Market St 08079-1911 (Mail to: 76 Market St 08079-1911) (856) 935-1798

Scotch Plains All Saints Episcopal Church **P** (408) 559 Park Ave 07076-1705 (Mail to: 559 Park Ave 07076-1777) (908) 322-8047

Sea Girt The Ch of St Uriel the Archangel **P** (402) 219 Philadelphia Blvd 08750-2799 (Mail to: 219 Philadelphia Blvd 08750) Russell Griffin Kenneth Gluckow (732) 449-6173

Sewaren St Johns Church **M** (156) 7 Woodbridge Ave 07077-1423 (Mail to: 17 Woodbridge Ave 07077-1423) (732) 634-2397

Shrewsbury Christ Episcopal Church **P** (367) 380 Sycamore Ave 07702-4513 (Mail to: 380 Sycamore Ave 07702-4513) Lisa Mitchell William Balmer Victoria Cuff Mary Schjonberg

(732) 741-2220

Somers Point Christ Church Episcopal **P** (230) 157 Shore Rd 08244-2752 (Mail to: PO Box 97 08244) Justin Falciani (609) 927-6262

Somerville St Johns Episcopal Church **P** (727) 158 W High St 08876-1818 (Mail to: 158 W High St 08876-1881) Ronald Pollock William McCoy (908) 722-1250

South Amboy Christ Church **P** (129) 220 Main Street 08879-1304 (Mail to: 257 4th St 08879-1304) Robert Shearer (732) 721-6262

South River Holy Trinity Episcopal Church **P** (217) 90 Leonardine Ave 08882-2507 (Mail to: 90 Leonardine Ave 08882-2507) Gregory Bezilla (732) 254-1734

Spotswood St Peters Episcopal Church **P** (464) 505 Main St 08884-1734 (Mail to: 505 Main St 08884-1797) Marshall Shelly (732) 251-2449

Spring Lake Holy Trinity Episcopal Church **SC** 301 Monmouth Ave 07762-1128 (Mail to: 301 Monmouth Ave 07762-1128) Peter Stimpson (734) 477-4363

Stone Harbor St Marys Episcopal Church **P** (194) 9425 3rd Ave 08247-1926 (Mail to: 9425 3rd Ave 08247-1926) Ronald Lockhart Victoria Pretti (609) 368-5922

Summit St Simons by the Sea Church **SC** C/O Mr Sandy White 206 Oak Ridge Ave 07901-3237 (Mail to: c/o Mr. Sandy Diehl 7 Norwood Road 06117) (860) 236-5321

Swedesboro Trinity Episcopal Old Swedes Church **M** (91) No 1208 Kings Hwy 08085-0031 (Mail to: PO Box 31 08085-0031) Frank St Amour (856) 467-1227

Toms River Christ Episcopal Church **P** (768) 415 Washington St 08753-6742 (Mail to: 415 Washington St 08753-6742) Joan Mason Theodore Foley Emily Holman Lewis McCrum (732) 349-5506

Trenton Christ Church-Cristo Rey **M** (1083) 331 Hamilton Ave 08609-2716 (Mail to: 331 Hamilton Ave 08609-2716) Francisco Pozo (609) 394-8926

Trenton Grace St Pauls Church **P** (252) 3715 E State St Ext 08619-2447 (Mail to: 3715 E State Street Ext 08619-2447) Amy Cornell (609) 586-6004

Trenton Holy Apostles Episcopal Church **P** (237) 1040 Yardville-Allentown Rd 08620 (Mail to: 1040 Yardville Allentown Rd 08620-9711) Arthur Powell Denise Cavaliere (609) 208-0228

Trenton St Lukes Episcopal Church **P** (158) 1620 Prospect St 08638-3031 (Mail to: 1620 Prospect St 08638-3031) Megan Thomas (609) 882-7614

Trenton St Michaels Episcopal Church **M** (93) 140 N Warren St 08608-1308 (Mail to: 140 N Warren St 08608-1308) (609) 392-8086

Trenton St Peters IGBO Church **M** (110) 1300 Brunswick Ave 08638-3316 (Mail to: 1300 Brunswick Ave 08638-3316) (609) 599-2880

✠ **Trenton** Trinity Cathedral **O** (508) 801 W State St 08618-5325 (Mail to: 801 W. State St 08618-5390) Rene John Marilyn Adams Shawn Armington Peter Bridge Carol Gilbert Andy Moore Alan Salmon (609) 392-3805

Tuckerton Church of the Holy Spirit **M** (204) 220 E. Main 08087-2627 (Mail to: PO Box 174 08087-0174) Martha McKee Richard Wisniewski (609) 296-9618

Union St Luke & All Saints Epis Church **P** (73) 398 Chestnut St 07083-9413 (Mail to: 398 Chestnut St 07083-9413) James Kollin (908) 688-7253

Ventnor City Church of the Epiphany **P** (117) 6605 Atlantic Ave 08406-2617 (Mail to: 21 S Troy Ave 08406-2649) (609) 822-0285

Villas St Barnabas by the Bay Church **M** (138) 13 W Bates Ave 08251-2502 (Mail to: PO Box 77 08251-0077) Lisa Hoffman Susan Cushinotto (609) 886-5960

Vincentown Trinity Episcopal Church **M** (66) 18 Mill St 08088-8824 (Mail to: 18 Mill Street 08088-8824) Robert Haller (609) 859-2299

Wall Township St Michaels Episcopal Church **P** (548) 2015 Allenwood Rd 07719-4633 (Mail to: 2015 Allenwood Rd 07719-4633) (732) 681-1863

Waretown St Stephens Episcopal Church **P** (374) 367 Route 9 08758-1702 (Mail to: 367 Route 9 08758-1702) Terry Martin (609) 698-8561

Wenonah Holy Trinity Episcopal Church **P** (396) 11 N Monroe Ave 08090-1735 (Mail to: 11 N Monroe Ave 08090-1735) (856) 468-0295

Westfield St Pauls Episcopal Church **P** (1427) 414 E Broad St 07090-2124 (Mail to: 414 E Broad St 07090-2124) Andrew Hamersley Nathan Ritter (908) 232-8506

Wildwood St Simeons by the Sea Church **P** (126) 2502 Central Ave 08260-5235 (Mail to: 119 E 26th Ave 08260-5217) (609) 522-8389

Williamstown St Marks at the Crossing Church **M** (99) 131 W Malaga Rd 08094-3852 (Mail to: 131 W Malaga Rd 08094-3852) (856) 629-8762

Willingboro Church of Christ the King **M** (306) C/O Clint Jackson 40 Charleston Rd 08046-2066 (Mail to: 40 Charleston Rd 08046-2066) (609) 877-2987

Woodbridge Trinity Episcopal Church **P** (678) 650 Rahway Ave 07095-3530 (Mail to: 650 Rahway Ave 07095-3530) Angela Cipolla

Woodbury Christ Episcopal Church **P** (816) 62 Delaware St 08096-5912 (Mail to: 62 Delaware St 08096-5989) Brian Burgess (856) 845-0190

Woodstown St Lukes Episcopal Church **M** (76) 37 E Grant St 08098-1401 (Mail to: PO Box 197 37 E Grant St 08098-1401) Edward Cook (856) 769-0760

NON-PAROCHIAL CLERGY

Adams DR *ret*
Adams FG Chestertown MD

Aders MM *dcn* Matawan NJ
Aldrich KD *ret* Huntingdon PA
Anderson TL *ret* Little Egg Harbor NJ
Atkins HL *ret* Houston TX
Auer DK Fayetteville NC
Baker DM
Baldwin FS *ret* Charleston SC
Belmont JC *ret* Pennington NJ
Benedict RAD *ret* Fort Lauderdale FL
Bickerton FCB Fair Haven NJ
Bird JE *ret* Woodbury NJ
Bishop KG Point Pleasant Beach NJ
Blacklock MGG *ret* Silver City NM
Bollinger MD Los Angeles CA
Bradley CA *dcn* Asbury Park NJ
Broderick R *dcn* Navesink NJ
Brown B *ret* Tinton Falls NJ
Brunson CE *dcn* Somerset NJ
Buntaine RE *ret* Cherry Hill NJ
Campbell GL *ret* South Amboy NJ
Carroll SE *ret* Salem NJ
Castellon PF *dcn* Mechanicsville VA
Caton LG Pennington NJ
Cesaretti CA *ret* New Milford PA
Chalakani PS *dcn* Rumson NJ
Chamberlain EY *dcn* Little Silver NJ
Chinery ET Metuchen NJ
Civalier GR *ret* Deptford NJ
Code DA State College PA
Cogan TB *ret* Edgartown MA
Cohen GS *ret* Blawenburg NJ
Collis G *ret* Rumson NJ
Conway TB *ret* Interlaken NJ
Cooke PS *ret* Brielle NJ
Counselman RL *ret* Sabinal TX
Cox CE *dcn* Trenton NJ
Cressman LA *dcn* Hammonton NJ
Cressman NM *dcn* Riverton NJ
Critelli RJ *ret* Sicklerville NJ
Croes JR *ret* South River NJ
Cromwell R *ret* Kailua HI
Cummings CJ *ret dcn* Surf City NJ
Daniels J *dcn* Point Pleasant NJ
Deatrick GE *ret* Sea Girt NJ
Deavours CA *dcn* Montclair NJ
deBussy MS *ret* Hockessin DE
Deppen GD *ret* Wellfleet MA
Dower RW *ret* Zanesville OH
Downs AL *ret* Southwest Harbor ME
Droste RE San Leandro CA
Druce GE *ret* Tijuana Baja California
Dubois CH *ret* Warminster PA
Duffy CG *ret* Trenton NJ
Dunn CW *dcn* Mount Holly NJ
Eberly GD *ret* Ocean City NJ
Eddy JE *ret* Pacifica CA
Edwards LA Metuchen NJ
Engleby MS Bernardsville NJ
Englund HC *ret* Washington Crossing PA
Epply-Schmidt J Princeton NJ
Esposito CP *dcn* Matawan NJ

Fisher JA *ret* South Seaville NJ
Fleming JE *ret* Princeton NJ
French AC *ret* Berkeley Heights NJ
French PA Princeton NJ
Fuller LB *ret* Nutley NJ
Funk PVK *dcn* Princeton NJ
Gammons EB *ret* Warren RI
Gauvin JHA *ret* Saint Catharine's
Geitz ER *ret* Shohola PA
Gerhardt MJ Bogota NJ
Gerhart WJ *ret* Edison NJ
Gorman WK *ret* Avalon NJ
Gowland JD Wenonah NJ
Griesmann DA *ret* Pago Pago AS
Gutwein M *ret* Camden NJ
Hardman RJ *ret* Stuart FL
Harris LD
Harris SL *ret* Wilson WY
Hartt WF *ret* Tuckerton NJ
Hawkes DWP *ret* Princeton NJ
Hayden ARM Asbury Park NJ
Hebert FN Freehold NJ
Henry D *ret* Southwest Harbor ME
Hermanson DH *ret* Old Bridge NJ
Holder TS *ret* Seaside Heights NJ
Hospador DC *dcn* Keansburg NJ
Hubbard FA *ret* Berkeley Heights NJ
Hulbert JE *ret* Winter Park FL
Hulet JR Newport Coast CA
Hunt JP *ret* Delhi NY
Immel OW *ret* Tybee Island GA
Jaenke KA *dcn* Fairfax CA
Jensen BA *dcn*
Johnson JH *ret* Annapolis MD
Johnston HV *ret* Indian Land SC
Kahl RM *ret* Villas NJ
Kasey PH *ret* Geneva NY
Kasey PM *ret* Geneva NY
Kerbel CA *ret dcn* Santa Fe NM
Kingston LL *ret* Princeton NJ
Koenig JT *ret* San Diego CA
Krieger KS *dcn* Galloway NJ
Laquintano DL *ret*
Lavengood MB Medford NJ
Lawson-Beck DR *dcn* Rahway NJ
Legnani RH *ret* Delran NJ
Lemay AR *dcn* Sewaren NJ
Liriano Martinez JA *dcn* Camden NJ
Lloyd JE *ret* Ajijic Chiapas
Lochner CN *ret* Spring Lake NJ
Lyons LA *ret* Plainfield NJ
Maddison BB
Manola JE *dcn*
Marshall HR Pennsauken NJ
Martin EE *ret* Vineland NJ
Maurer SB *dcn* Salem NJ
May FB *dcn* Mantoloking NJ
May TR Red Bank NJ
McHugh JM Albuquerque NM
Moore JI *ret* Pennsville NJ
Moreau WJ *ret* Lancaster PA

Morrison LC *ret* Front Royal VA
Morrow JT *ret* Pine Beach NJ
Murphy EJ Clinton NJ
Myers CT *ret* North Wildwood NJ
Nancekivell D *ret* Bridport VT
Neilson JR *ret* Scotch Plains NJ
Nelson JRP *ret* Elizabeth NJ
Niese AM *ret* Brunswick ME
Noble WC *ret* Tinton Falls NJ
Norris SBP *ret* Chincoteague VA
O'Connor T Ocean City NJ
Oguike MU Sewaren NJ
Orlando HM *dcn* Marlton NJ
Osborne-Mott SE Asbury Park NJ
Ottaway RN *ret* Bernardsville NJ
Parker WC Lincoln University PA
Parodi LM *ret* San Juan PR
Parrish JR *ret* New York NY
Patterson JW *ret* Naples FL
Pepe CA *dcn*
Percival JB *ret* Sarasota FL
Pierce PD *ret* Pitman NJ
Piggins DH
Powers L *ret* Galloway NJ
Pritts CE *ret* Merchantville NJ
Puca AJ
Rauscher WV *ret* Woodbury NJ
Raven MH Toms River NJ
Reeman KB *dcn* Eatontown NJ
Reiss GA *ret* Hellertown PA
Rockman JL *ret* Scotch Plains NJ
Roman JM *dcn* West Trenton NJ
Rosheuvel TW *ret* Red Bank NJ
Rowe JG Pine Beach NJ
Runner PW *ret* Wakefield RI
Sakin CR Wall NJ
Sang CO *dcn* Cranford NJ
Sasso-Crandall R *ret* Hammonton NJ
Saunders JL *ret* Philadelphia PA
Scholer LC Chincoteague Island VA
Sheay VM *ret* Stockton NJ
Sherrill CR *ret* Southport ME
Shockley SE New York NY
Sink TL
Smith JR *ret* Brattleboro VT
Smith LC *ret* Princeton NJ
Smith MD *ret* Nashville TN
Sosnowski JW Trenton NJ
Speer WR *ret* Millville NJ
Spencer WD *dcn* Freehold NJ
Spoor CP *dcn* Roosevelt NJ
Steed JG *ret* Whiting NJ
Stone JC *ret* Highlands NJ
Stone MR Highlands NJ
Stowe DA *ret* Doylestown PA
Stowell PW *ret* Moorestown NJ
Stoy CB *dcn* Princeton NJ
Strasburger FC *ret* Brunswick ME
Sullivan EL *ret* Ewing NJ
Sumner ER *ret* Hackettstown NJ
Suruda TA *dcn* Matawan NJ

Swartzentruber AO *ret* Sarasota FL
Sweeney JF *dcn* Westampton NJ
Taylor ASB *dcn* Montrose NY
Thayer SA Jamison PA
Thorme TA *dcn* Trenton NJ
Troncale JE *ret* Forest VA
Trull CS *ret* Philadelphia PA
Turner PK *ret* Hillburn NY
Turner R *dcn* Piscataway NJ
Urinoski AK
Van Kuiken AM Trenton NJ
Van Sant MR *ret* Monmouth Beach NJ

Viola CJ *dcn* Mullica Hill NJ
Webber BM Flushing NY
Wedderburn DH Cadmen NJ
West GG Jeffersonville PA
White SL *ret* Williamstown MA
Wible CKK *dcn* Clinton NJ
Wiesner AD *ret* Washington NC
Wildsmith JN Philadelphia PA
Wisner SF *ret* Wall Township NJ
Zeilfelder EW *ret* Apo AP
Zelley EW *ret* Copake Falls NY

STATE OF NEW MEXICO
Diocese of Rio Grande (RG)

STATE OF NEW YORK
Dioceses of Albany (A), Central New York (CNY), Long Island (LI), New York (NY), Rochester (Roch),
and Western New York (WNY)

Adams—CNY
Addison—Roch
Afton—CNY
Albany—A
Albion—WNY
Alden—WNY
Alexandria Bay—CNY
Amagansett—LI
Amityville—LI
Amsterdam—A
Angelica—Roch
Angola—WNY
Arden—NY
Ardsley—NY
Armonk—NY
Astoria—LI
Attica—WNY
Auburn—CNY
Aurora—CNY
Au Sable Forks—A
Avon—Roch
Babylon—LI
Bainbridge—CNY
Baldwin—LI
Baldwinsville—CNY
Ballston Spa—A
Barneveld—CNY
Barrytown—NY
Batavia—WNY
Bath—Roch
Bay Shore—LI
Bayside—LI
Beacon—NY
Bedford—NY

Bellmore—LI
Bellmont—Roch
Bellport—LI
Berkshire—CNY
Binghamton—CNY
Black River—CNY
Bloomfield—Roch
Bloomville—A
Blue Mountain
  Lake—A
Bolton Landing—A
Bovina—A
Branchport—Roch
Brant Lake—A
Brentwood—LI
Brewster—NY
Briarcliff Manor—NY
Bridgehampton—LI
Brockport—Roch
Bronx—NY
Bronxville—NY
Brookhaven—LI
Brooklyn—LI
Brownville—CNY
Buffalo—WNY
Burnt Hills—A
Burt—WNY
Cairo—A
Caledonia—Roch
Callicoon—NY
Cambria Hts—LI
Cambridge—A
Camden—CNY
Camillus—CNY

Canajoharie—A
Canandaigua—Roch
Canaseraga—Roch
Canastota—CNY
Candor—CNY
Canton—A
Cape Vincent—CNY
Carle Pl—LI
Carthage—CNY
Castleton—A
Catskill—A
Cazenovia—CNY
Central Islip—LI
Chadwicks—CNY
Champlain—A
Chappaqua—NY
Chatham—A
Chautauqua—WNY
Chelsea—NY
Cherry Valley—A
Chester—NY
Chittenango—CNY
Clark Mills—CNY
Clayton—CNY
Clifton Park—A
Clifton Spgs—Roch
Clinton—CNY
Cobleskill—A
Cohoes—A
Cold Spg—NY
Cold Spg Hbr—LI
Colton—A
Columbiaville—A
Constableville—CNY

Constantia—CNY
Cooperstown—A
Copake Falls—A
Copenhagen—CNY
Corning—Roch
Cornwall—NY
Corona—LI
Cortland—CNY
Coxsackie—A
Croton on Hudson—
  NY
Cuba—Roch
Dansville—Roch
Deer Pk—LI
Delhi—A
Delmar—A
Deposit—A
Dobbs Ferry—NY
Douglaston—LI
Dover Plains—NY
Downsville—A
Duanesburg—A
Dunkirk—WNY
Eastchester—NY
E Aurora—WNY
E Elmhurst—LI
E Hampton—LI
E Setauke—LI
E Syracuse—CNY
Elizabethtown—A
Ellenville—NY
Ellicottville—WNY
Elmhurst—LI
Elmira—CNY

Endicott—CNY
Essex—A
Evans Mills—CNY
Fairport—Roch
Far Rockaway—LI
Farmingdale—LI
Fayetteville—CNY
Fishers Is—LI
Fishkill—NY
Floral Pk—LI
Flushing—LI
Forest Hills—LI
Ft Edward—A
Franklin—A
Franklinville—WNY
Fredonia—WNY
Freeport—LI
Fulton—CNY
Garden City—LI
Garnerville—NY
Garrison—NY
Gates—Roch
Geneseo—Roch
Geneva—Roch & CNY
Gilbertsville—A
Glen Cove—LI
Glens Falls—A
Goshen—NY
Gouverneur—A
Gowanda—WNY
Grand Is—WNY
Granite Spgs—NY
Granville—A
Great Neck—LI
Great River—LI
Greene—CNY
Greenport—LI
Greenville—A
Greenwich—A
Greenwood Lake—NY
Guilderland—A
Hamburg—WNY
Hamilton—CNY
Hammondsport—Roch
Hampton Bays—LI
Harrison—NY
Hartsdale—NY
Hastings on Hudson—NY
Hempstead—LI
Henrietta—Roch
Herkimer—A
Hewlett—LI
Hicksville—LI
Highland Falls—NY
Hilton—Roch
Holley—WNY
Hollis—LI
Honeoye Falls—Roch
Hoosick Falls—A
Hopewell Jct—NY
Hornell—Roch

Horseheads—CNY
Hudson—A
Hudson Falls—A
Huntington—LI
Hyde Park—NY
Ilion—A
Irving—WNY
Irvington—NY
Islip—LI
Ithaca—CNY
Jackson Hts—LI
Jamaica—LI
Jamestown—WNY
Johnson City—CNY
Johnstown—A
Jordan—CNY
Katonah—NY
Keeseville—A
Keuka Park—Roch
Kew Gardens—LI
Kinderhook—A
Kingston—NY
Lake George—A
Lake Luzerne—A
Lake Placid—A
Lakeview—WNY
Lancaster—WNY
Larchmont—NY
Latham—A
LeRoy—WNY
Lewiston—WNY
Lindenhurst—LI
Little Falls—A
Liverpool—CNY
Lockport—WNY
Locust Valley—LI
Long Bch—LI
Long Is City—LI
Lowville—CNY
Lyons—Roch
Mahopac—NY
Malone—A
Mamaroneck—NY
Manhasset—LI
Manlius—CNY
Marathon—CNY
Marcellus—CNY
Margaretville—A
Marlboro—NY
Massapequa—LI
Massena—A
Mastic Bch—LI
Mattituck—LI
Mayville—WNY
Mechanicville—A
Medford—LI
Medina—WNY
Mexico—CNY
Middletown—NY
Millbrook—NY
Mohawk—A

Mohegan Lake—NY
Monroe—NY
Montgomery—NY
Monticello—NY
Montour Falls—Roch
Montrose—NY
Moravia—CNY
Morris—A
Morristown—A
Mt Kisco—NY
Mt Vernon—NY
Nedrow—CNY
Newark—Roch
New Berlin—CNY
New City—NY
New Hamburg—NY
New Hartford—CNY
New Hyde Park—LI
New Lebanon—A
New Paltz—NY
New Rochelle—NY
New Windsor—NY
New York—NY & LI
Newburgh—NY
Newcomb—A
Niagara Falls—WNY
N Belmore—LI
N Creek—A
N Granville—A
N Salem—NY
N Tonawanda—WNY
Northport—LI
Norwich—CNY
Norwood—A
Nyack—NY
Oakdale—LI
Oceanside—LI
Odessa—Roch
Ogdensburg—A
Old Forge—A
Olean—WNY
Oneida—CNY
Oneonta—A
Orchard Pk—WNY
Ossining—NY
Oswego—CNY
Owego—CNY
Oxford—CNY
Oyster Bay—LI
Palenville—A
Palmyra—Roch
Parishville—CNY
Patchogue—LI
Patterson—NY
Paul Smiths—A
Pawling—NY
Pearl River—NY
Peekskill—NY
Pelham—NY
Penfield—Roch
Penn Yan—Roch

Perry—WNY
Philmont—A
Pierrepont Manor—
   CNY
Pine Plains—NY
Pittsford—Roch
Plainview—LI
Plattsburgh—A
Pleasant Valley—NY
Pleasantville—NY
Pt Chester—NY
Pt Jefferson—LI
Pt Jervis—NY
Pt Leyden—CNY
Pt Washington—LI
Potsdam—A
Pottersville—A
Poughkeepsie—NY
Pulaski—CNY
Queens Village—LI
Quogue—LI
Randolph—WNY
Red Hook—NY
Rensselaer—A
Rensselaerville—A
Rhinebeck—NY
Richfield Spgs—A
Riverhead—LI
Rochester—Roch
Rockville Ctr—LI
Rome—CNY
Ronkonkoma—LI
Roosevelt—LI
Roosevelt Is—NY
Rosedale—LI
Roslyn—LI
Round Lake—A
Rye—NY
Sackets Hbr—CNY
Sag Hbr—LI
St Albans—LI
St James—LI
Salamanca—WNY
Salem—A
Saranac Lake—A
Saratoga Spgs—A
Saugerties—NY
Savona—Roch
Sayville—LI
Scarsdale—NY
Schenectady—A
Schenevus—A
Schroon Lake—A
Schuylerville—A
Scottsville—Roch
Sea Cliff—LI
Seaford—LI
Selden—LI
Seneca Falls—CNY
Shelter Is—LI
Sherburne—CNY

Sherrill—CNY	Stamford—A	Utica—CNY	W Middleburgh—A
Shoreham—LI	Star Lake—A	Valley Cottage—NY	W Park—NY
Sidney—A	Staten Is—NY	Valley Stream—LI	Westbury—LI
Silver Creek—WNY	Stockport—A	Waddington—A	Westfield—WNY
Skaneateles—CNY	Stone Ridge—NY	Wading River—LI	Westford—A
Slaterville Spgs—CNY	Stony Brook—LI	Walden—NY	Westhampton Bch—LI
Smithtown—LI	Stony Pt—NY	Walton—A	White Plains—NY
Sodus—Roch	Suffern—NY	Wantagh—LI	Whitehall—A
Somers—NY	Syracuse—CNY	Wappingers Falls—NY	Whitesboro—CNY
So Fallsburgh—NY	Tannersville—A	Warrensburg—A	Whitestone—LI
Southampton—LI	Tarrytown—NY	Warsaw—WNY	Willard—CNY
So New Berlin—CNY	Ticonderoga—A	Warwick—NY	Williamsville—WNY
S Ozone Park—LI	Tivoli—NY	Washingtonville—NY	Williston Pk—LI
So Salem—NY	Tomkins Cove—NY	Waterford—A	Wilson—WNY
Sparkill—NY	Tonawanda—WNY	Waterloo—CNY	Windsor—CNY
Spring Valley—NY	Troy—A	Watertown—CNY	Woodhaven—LI
Springfield Ctr—A	Trumansburg—CNY	Watervliet—A	Woodside—LI
Springfield Gdns—LI	Tupper Lake—A	Watkins Glen—Roch	Woodstock—NY
Springville—WNY	Tuxedo Park—NY	Waverly—CNY	Yaphank—LI
Staatsburg—NY	Twilight Park—A	Webster—Roch	Yonkers—NY
Stafford—WNY	Unadilla—A	Wellsville—Roch	Youngstown—WNY

DIOCESE OF NEW YORK

(PROVINCE II)

Comprises 10 counties in southern New York
DIOCESAN OFFICE 1047 Amsterdam Ave New York NY 10025
TEL (212) 316-7400   FAX (212) 316-7405
E-MAIL info@dioceseny.org   WEB www.dioceseny.org

Previous Bishops—
Samuel Provoost 1787-1815, Benj Moore asst 1801 Bp 1815-16, John H Hobart asst 1811 Bp 1816-30, Benj T Onderdonk 1830-61, Jonathan M Wainwright provis 1852-54, Horatio Potter provis 1854 Bp 1861-87, Henry C Potter asst 1883 Bp 1887-1908, David H Greer coadj 1904 Bp 1908-19, Chas S Burch suffr 1911 Bp 1919-20, Wm T Manning 1921-46, Arthur S Lloyd suffr 1921-36, Herbert Shipman suffr 1921-30, Chas K Gilbert suffr 1930 Bp 1947-50, Chas F Boynton suffr 1951-69, Horace WB Donegan suffr 1947-50, coadj 1950 Bp 1950-72, Harold L Wright suffr 1974-78, James S Wetmore suffr 1960-87, Paul Moore Jr coadj 1969 Bp 1972-89, Walter D Dennis suffr 1979-1998, Richard F Grein coadj 1989 Bp 1989-2001, Mark S Sisk coadj 1995-2001 Bp 2001-2013, Catherine S Roskam suffr 1996-2012

Bishop—Rt Rev Andrew ML Dietsche (Dio 2 Feb 2013)

Bishop Suffragan—Rt Rev Allen K Shin

Chanc G Wade; *V-Chanc* R Vandenburg Jr A Yurke; *Treas* Sr F Margaret CHS; *Sec of Conv & Reg* JA Forde Sr; *Asst Sec of Conv* S Saavedra; *Cn to Ord* Rev Cn

WB Rider; *Hist Rev Cn* JE Lindsley; *Cn Theologian* Rev Cn JR Wright; *Cong Sup Plan Coord & Stew* Rev Dr R Sloan; *Cn Min* Rev Cn C Simmons; *Cn Deploy* Rev Cn D Tammearu; *Cn Pastor* Rev Cn KJ Person; *Cn for Congregational Vitality* Rev Cn A Perez-Bullard

Stand Comm—Cler: M Sullivan S Gerth R Cole S Fortunato; *Lay:* J Kramer R Ingram J Gunnison D Levitt

Dio Conv: 4-5 November 2016

PARISHES, MISSIONS, AND CLERGY

Arden St Johns Church **P** (44) 26 Homestead Dr 10910-0051 (Mail to: c/o Michael Trabulsy 375 Park Ave. Arden Asset Mgt.—32nd Floor 10152) (845) 351-4696

Ardsley St Barnabas Church **P** (97) 2 Revolutionary Rd 10502 (Mail to: 2 Revolutionary Rd 10502-1511) Richard Spencer (914) 693-3366

Armonk St Stephen's Church **P** (233) 50 Bedford Rd 10504-1830 (Mail to: 50 Bedford Rd 10504-1814)

Barrytown St John the Evangelist **P** (180) 1114 River Rd 12571-2938 (Mail to: 1114 River Road 12571-0537) (845) 758-6433

Beacon St Andrews Church **P** (64) 17 South Ave

12508-3114 (Mail to: 17 South Ave 12508-3114) John Williams (845) 831-1369

Beacon St Lukes Church **P** (181) 543 Wolcott Ave 12508-4033 (Mail to: PO Box 507 12508-0507) Edwin Cromey John Williams (845) 831-2643

Bedford St Matthews Church **P** (1523) 382 Cantitoe St 10507 (Mail to: PO Box 293 10506-0293) Broaddus Johnson Richard Pike Susan Wyper (914) 234-9636

Brewster St Andrews Church **P** (273) 26 Prospect St 10509-1216 (Mail to: 26 Prospect St 10509-1216) (845) 279-4325

Briarcliff All Saints Church **P** (192) 201 Scarborough Rd 10510-2043 (Mail to: 201 Scarborough Rd 10510-2043) Ann Douglas Yejide Peters

Briarcliff St Marys Church **P** (65) 669 Albany Post Rd 10510-2428 (Mail to: PO Box 8805 10510-8805) (914) 941-3030

Bronx Christ Church Riverdale **P** (339) 5030 Henry Hudson Pkwy 10471-3297 (Mail to: 5030 Henry Hudson Pkwy E 10471-3216) Andrew Butler (718) 543-1011

Bronx Church of the Atonement **P** (102) 1344-44 Beach Ave 10472-1909 (Mail to: 1344 Beach Ave 48 10472-1909)

Bronx Church of the Good Shepherd **P** (328) 4401 Matilda Ave 10470-1502 (Mail to: 4401 Matilda Ave 10470-1502) Calvin McIntyre (718) 324-2347

Bronx Church of the Holy Nativity **P** (161) 3061 Bainbridge Ave 10467-3904 (Mail to: 3061 Bainbridge Ave 10467-3999) (718) 652-0443

Bronx Church of the Mediator **P** (305) 260 W 231st St 10463-3904 (Mail to: 260 W 231st St 10463-3904) (718) 548-0944

Bronx Grace Church (City Island) **P** (56) 104 City Island Ave 10464-1660 (Mail to: 116 City Island Ave 10464) Ruth Anne Garcia (718) 885-1080

Bronx Grace Church (West Farms) **P** (112) 1909 Vyse Ave 10460-4343 (Mail to: 1909 Vyse Ave 10460-4343) (718) 542-1946

Bronx Haitian Cong of Good Samaritan **P** (109) 777 E 222nd St 10467-5105 (Mail to: 777 E 222nd St 10467-5105) Sam Owen

Bronx Iglesia de San Juan Bautista **M** (45) 948 E 156th St 10455-1998 (Mail to: 948 E 156th St 10455-1998) Maria Servellon (718) 893-0376

Bronx St Andrews Episcopal Church **P** (346) 781 Castle Hill Ave 10473-1330 (Mail to: 781 Castle Hill Ave 10473-1330) Yesupatham Duraikannu (718) 863-2244

Bronx St Anns Church **P** (470) 295 St Ann Ave 10454 (Mail to: 295 Saint Anns Ave 10454-2588) Martha Overall (718) 585-5632

Bronx St Davids Church **P** (152) 384 E 160th St #200 10451-4404 (Mail to: PO Box 200 10451-0200) Bertram Bennett (718) 665-2747

Bronx St Edmunds Church **P** (55) 1905 Morris Ave 10453-5903 (Mail to: 1905 Morris Ave 10453-5903)

Bronx St James Church Fordham **P** (697) 2500 Jerome Ave 10468-4300 (Mail to: 2500 Jerome Ave 10468-4300) William Cusano (718) 367-0655

Bronx St Josephs Church **P** (174) 155 Dreiser Loop 10475-2703 (Mail to: 155 Dreiser Loop 10475-2703) (718) 320-0844

Bronx St Lukes Episcopal Church **P** (865) Attn Mr Bookal 777 E 222nd St 10467-5105 (Mail to: 777 E 222nd St 10467-5105) Pierre-Andre Duvert (718) 882-3060

Bronx St Margarets Church (Longwood) **P** (136) 940 E 156th St 10455-1914 (Mail to: 940 E 156th St 10455-1998) Theodora Brooks (718) 589-4430

Bronx St Marthas Church **P** (45) 1858 Hunt Ave 10462-3623 (Mail to: 1858 Hunt Ave 10462-3623) Percy Brathwaite Eliza Davies-Aryeequaye (718) 792-3681

Bronx St Pauls Church **P** (100) 489 Saint Pauls Pl 10456-1935 (Mail to: PO Box 507 10456-0520) Horton Scott Ralph Smith (347) 269-7604

Bronx St Peters Church **P** (159) 2500 Westchester Ave 10461-3543 (Mail to: 2500 Westchester Ave 10461-3543) Joade Dauer-Cardasis Howard Blunt (718) 931-9270

Bronx St Simeons Church **P** (105) 1858 Hunt Ave 10462-3623 (Mail to: 1858 Hunt Ave 10462-3623) Vincent Ackaah (718) 824-9188

Bronx St Stephens Church (Woodlawn) **P** (65) 439 E 238th St 10470-1701 (Mail to: 439 E 238th St 10470-1701) (718) 324-5427

Bronx Trinity Church of Morrisania **P** (181) 698 East 166th Street 10456-5699 (Mail to: 698 E 166th St 10456-5625) Howard Blunt Andrew Kadel (718) 542-1309

Bronxville Christ Church **P** (606) 17 Sagamore Rd 10708-1502 (Mail to: 17 Sagamore Rd 10708-1599) Michael Bird Jennifer Brown (914) 337-3544

Callicoon St James Church **P** (25) Route 17b 12723 (Mail to: PO Box 296 12723-0296) Elizabeth Groskoph Ralph Groskoph (845) 887-4742

Chappaqua Church of St Mary the Virgin **P** (373) 191 South Greeley Avenue 10514 (Mail to: PO Box 380 10514-0380) (914) 238-8751

Chelsea St Marks Church (Chelsea on Hudson) **P** (9) 9 Liberty St 12512 (Mail to: PO Box 252 12512-0252) (845) 838-1886

Chester St Pauls Church **P** (98) 101 Main St 10918-1328 (Mail to: 101 Main St 10918-1328) (845) 469-2616

Cold Spring St Marys Church in the Highlands **P** (234) 1 Chestnut St 10516-2516 (Mail to: 1 Chestnut St 10516-2598) Shane Scott-Hamblen (845) 265-2539

Cornwall St John's Church **P** (210) 66 Clinton St 12518-1558 (Mail to: PO Box 783 12518-0783) Suzanne Toro (845) 534-5475

Croton Hdsn St Augustines Episcopal Church **P**

(278) 6 Old Post Rd N 10520-2016 (Mail to: 6 Old Post Rd N 10520-2016) Bradley Dyche Beth Glover Sharon Manning-Lew (914) 271-3501

Dobbs Ferry Zion Church **P** (98) 55 Cedar St 10522-1711 (Mail to: 55 Cedar St 10522-1711) Mary Grambsch (914) 693-9320

Dover Plains Mision Ep Santiago Apostol **P** (30) 12 Reimer Ave 12522-5136 (Mail to: PO Box 336 12522-0336) (203) 605-0090

Eastchester St Lukes Church **P** (44) 100 Stewart Ave 10709-5799 (Mail to: 100 Stewart Ave 10709-5799) Charles Pridemore (914) 961-3856

Ellenville St Johns Memorial Church **P** (120) 40 Market St 12428-2132 (Mail to: 40 Market St 12428-2132) Jeffrey Golliher (845) 647-7084

Fishkill Trinity Church **P** (346) 1200 Main St 12524-1890 (Mail to: PO Box 484 12524-0484) Garrett Mettler

Garnerville Trinity Church **P** (113) 28 Chapel St 10923 (Mail to: 28 Chapel St 10923-1209) (845) 947-1090

Garrison St Philips in the Highlands **P** (310) 1101 Route 9d 10524-3638 (Mail to: PO Box 158 10524-0158) Francis Geer (845) 424-3571

Goshen St James Church **P** (528) 1 Saint James Pl 10924-2013 (Mail to: 1 Saint James Pl 10924-2013) Michael Lunden Thomas Liotta (845) 294-6225

Granite Spgs Church of the Good Shepherd **P** (161) 39 Granite Springs Rd 10527-1108 Gwyneth Murphy (914) 248-5631

Greenwood Lake Church of the Good Shepherd **P** (31) 62 Windermere Ave 10925-0011 (Mail to: PO Box 11 10925-0011) Peter Turner (845) 477-2191

Harrison All Saints Church **P** (148) 300 Harrison Ave 10528-3328 (Mail to: 300 Harrison Ave 10528-3360) David Rider

Hartsdale St Andrews Episcopal Church **P** (47) 101 N Central Ave 10530-1912 (Mail to: 101 N Central Ave 10530-1912) (914) 946-7931

Hastings Hds Grace Episcopal Church **P** (246) 78 Main St 10706-1602 (Mail to: 78 Main St 10706-1602) Anna Pearson (914) 478-1779

Highland Falls Church of the Holy Innocents **P** (234) 401 Main St 10928-0116 (Mail to: PO Box 116 10928-0116) Judith Ferguson (845) 446-2197

Highland Falls St Marks Church **M** 9 St Marks Place Ft. Montgomery 10928 (Mail to: 40 Main St PO Box 887 11978-0887)

Hopewell Junction Church of the Resurrection **P** (89) 182 Route 376 12533 (Mail to: 182 Route 376 12533) (845) 226-5727

Hyde Park St James Episcopal Church **P** (204) 4526 Albany Post Rd 12538-1564 (Mail to: 4526 Albany Post Rd 12538-1564) Charles Kramer David Bender Gail Ganter-Toback (845) 229-2820

Irvington St Barnabas Church **P** (559) 15 N Broadway 10533-1802 (Mail to: 15 N Broadway 10533-1898) Lenora Smith Keith Voets (914) 591-8194

Katonah St Luke's Episcopal Church **P** (159) 68 Bedford Rd 10536-2117 (Mail to: PO Box 602 10536-0602) (914) 232-5220

Kingston Church of the Holy Cross **P** (265) 30 Pine Grove Ave 12401-5408 (Mail to: 30 Pine Grove Ave 12401-5408) Maria Servellon

Kingston St Johns Episcopal Church **P** (300) 207 Albany Ave 12401-2511 (Mail to: PO Box 1221 12402-1221) (845) 331-2252

Larchmont St Johns Church **P** (766) 4 Fountain Sq 10538-4106 (Mail to: 4 Fountain Sq 10538-4106) Joseph Greene Dorothy Greene (914) 834-2981

Mahopac Church of the Holy Communion **P** (96) 1055 Route 6 10541-3402 (Mail to: 1055 Route 6 10541-3402) David Morris Claudia Wilson (845) 628-6144

Mamaroneck St Thomas Church **P** (224) 168 W Boston Post Rd 10543-3605 (Mail to: 168 W Boston Post Rd 10543-3605) Carol Gadsden (914) 698-0300

Marlboro Christ Church **P** (122) 222 Old Post Rd 12542-6211 (Mail to: PO Box 27 12542-0027) (845) 220-7478

Middletown Grace Church **P** (385) 58 North St 10940-5011 (Mail to: 12 Depot St. 10940-5011) John Warfel (845) 343-6101

Millbrook Grace Church **D** (547) 3328 Franklin Ave 12545-5969 (Mail to: PO Box 366 12545-0366) Matthew Calkins (845) 677-3064

Millbrook St Peters Church Lithgow **P** (363) 692 Deep Hollow Rd 12545-1502 (Mail to: PO Box 1502 12545-1502) Albert Ogle Cameron Hardy (845) 677-9286

Mohegan Lake St Marys Church **P** (256) 1836 E Main St 10547 (Mail to: 1836 E Main St 10547-1226) Claire Woodley (914) 528-3972

Monroe Grace Episcopal Church **P** (55) 1 Forest Ave 10950-2809 (Mail to: 1 Forest Ave 10950-2809) (845) 782-8535

Montgomery St Francis of Assisi **P** (28) 74 Wallkill Ave 12549 (Mail to: 74 Wallkill Ave 12549-1115) (845) 457-7545

Monticello St Johns Episcopal Church **P** (91) 15 St John St 12701-2118 (Mail to: 13 Saint John St 12701-2117) (845) 807-3050

Montrose Church of the Divine Love **P** (193) 80 Sunset Rd 10548 (Mail to: 80 Sunset Rd 10548-1334) Imlijungla Sojwal (484) 737-1080

Mount Kisco St Marks Church **P** (350) 85 E Main St 10549 (Mail to: 85 E Main St 10549-2313) William Doubleday (914) 666-8058

Mount Vernon Church of the Ascension **P** (182) 104 Park Ave 10550-1410 (Mail to: 104 Park Ave 10550-1410) (914) 668-4851

Mount Vernon Episcopal Church Of Sts John Paul And Clement **P** (67) 126 S 9th Ave 10550-

3019 (Mail to: PO Box 1067 10550-1067) (914) 668-0551

Mount Vernon Trinity Church **P** (113) 335 S 4th Ave 10550 (Mail to: 335 S 4th Ave 10550-4103) (914) 667-8409

New City St Johns Church **P** (246) No 365 Strawtown Rd 10956-6632 (Mail to: 365 Strawtown Rd 10956-6632) Karen Henry (845) 634-3601

New Hamburg St Nicholas on the Hudson **M** (215) 37 Point St 12590-5529 (Mail to: 37 Point St 12590) Astrid Storm (845) 297-2010

New Paltz St Andrews Episcopal Church **P** (172) 163 Main St 12561-1116 (Mail to: 163 Main St 12561-1116) Robin James (845) 255-5098

New Rochelle Church of St Simon the Cyrenian **P** (91) 135 Remington Pl 10801 (Mail to: 135 Remington Pl 10801-3925) John Morgan Paulette Remppel (914) 632-5911

New Rochelle St Johns Church Wilmot **P** (94) 11 Wilmot Rd 10804 (Mail to: 11 Wilmot Rd 10804-1514) Jennie Talley (914) 636-0047

New Rochelle Trinity St Pauls Episcopal **P** (163) 311 Huguenot St 10801-7208 (Mail to: 311 Huguenot St 10801-7295) Robert Gahler Hollis Galgano Hyacinth Lee

New Windsor St Thomas Episcopal Church **P** (103) 47 Old Route 9w 12553-5480 (Mail to: PO Box 4221 12553-4221) (845) 562-4712

New York All Angels Church **P** (456) 251 W 80th St 10024-5743 (Mail to: 251 W 80th St 10024-5798) Milind Sojwal (212) 362-9300

New York All Saints Church **P** (225) 230 E 60th St 10065 Steven Yagerman Andrew Mullins (212) 758-0447

New York All Souls Church **P** (65) 88 Saint Nicholas Ave 10026-2926 (Mail to: 88 Saint Nicholas Ave 10026-2926) Frank Morales William Murrell (212) 663-2351

New York Calvary & St George Church **P** (600) 61 Gramercy Park N 10010 (Mail to: 61 Gramercy Park N 10010) Benjamin Dehart Jacob Smith (646) 723-4178

✠ **New York** Cathedral of St John the Divine **O** 1047 Amsterdam Ave 10025-1747 (Mail to: 1047 Amsterdam Ave 10025-1798) James Kowalski Constance Coles Edward Johnston Thomas Pike Victoria Sirota Julia Whitworth Steven Yagerman (212) 316-7401

New York Christ & St Stephens Church **P** (567) 120 W 69th St 10023 (Mail to: 120 W 69th St 10023-5194) Linda Liles Jay Gordon James Hagen (212) 787-2755

New York Church of St Edward the Martyr **P** (239) 14 E 109th St 10029-3402 (Mail to: 14 E 109th St 10029-3402) William Derby Alejandra Trillos (212) 369-1140

New York Church of St Mary the Virgin **P** (380) 145 W 46th St 10036-8591 (Mail to: 145 W 46th St 10036-8502) Stephen Gerth Peter Powell James Smith Rebecca Weiner Tompkins

(212) 869-5830

New York Church of St Matthew and St Timothy **P** (337) 26 West 84th St 10024-4702 (Mail to: 26 West 84th St 10024-4702) Carla Roland George Diaz (212) 362-6750

New York Church of the Ascension **P** (177) 12 W 11th St 10011-8602 (Mail to: 12 W 11th St 10011-8695) Edwin Chinery Elizabeth Maxwell (212) 254-8620

New York Church of the Crucifixion **P** (144) 459 W 149th St 10031 (Mail to: 459 W 149th St 10031-2704) (212) 281-0900

New York Church of the Good Shepherd **P** (98) 240 E 31st St 10016 (Mail to: 236 E 31st St 10016-6303) Mary Grambsch Erika Meyer (212) 689-1595

New York Church of the Heavenly Rest **P** (1794) 2 E 90th St 10128 (Mail to: 2 E 90th St 10128-0674) Euan Cameron Elizabeth Garnsey Matthew Heyd Cynthia Stravers (212) 289-3400

New York Church of the Holy Apostles **P** (142) 296 9th Ave 10001-5703 (Mail to: 296 9th Ave 10001-5703) Peter Carey Glenn Chalmers Luis Gomez Susan Hill Robert Jacobs Andrew Kadel (212) 807-6799

New York Church of the Holy Trinity **P** (704) 316 E 88th St 10128-4909 (Mail to: 316 E 88th St 10128-4909) John Beddingfield Mark Collins Paul Feuerstein (212) 289-4100

New York Church of the Holyrood **P** (196) 715 W 179th St 10033 (Mail to: 715 W 179th St 10033-6096) James Hagen (212) 923-3770

New York Church of the Incarnation **P** (464) 209 Madison Ave 10016-3814 (Mail to: 209 Madison Ave 10016-3814) John Ousley (212) 689-6350

New York Church of the Intercession **P** (215) 550 W 155th St 10032 (Mail to: 550 W 155th Street 10032-7801) Adrian Dannhauser William Murrell (212) 283-6200

New York Church of the Resurrection **P** (148) 119 E 74th St 10021 (Mail to: 119 E 74th St 10021-3299) Barry Swain E Michael Allen James Harkins Horace Hitchcock Sean Wallace (212) 879-4320

New York Church of the Transfiguration **P** (639) 1 E 29th St 10016-7405 (Mail to: 1 E 29th St 10016-7405) Andrew St John Ian Betts Patrick Cheng David Fleenor Clair McPherson Paul Metzler (212) 684-6770

New York Congregation of St Saviour **P** (847) 1047 Amsterdam Ave 10025-1747 (Mail to: 1047 Amsterdam Ave 10025-1747) (212) 316-7483

New York Eglise Du St Esprit **P** (146) 109-111 E 60th St 10022-1113 (Mail to: 111 E 60th St 3F 10022-1113) Nigel Massey (212) 838-5680

New York Episcopal Church of Our Savior **P** (201) 48 Henry Street 10002-6901 (Mail to: 48 Henry Street 10002-6901) Noel Bordador (212) 233-

2899

New York Grace Church **P** (799) 802 Broadway 10003 (Mail to: 802 Broadway 10003-4831) James Waring Stephen Arbogast Nicholas Danford Stephen Holton (212) 254-2000

New York Holy Trinity Church - Inwood **P** (51) 20 Cumming St 10034-4804 (Mail to: 20 Cumming St 10034-4804) Rebecca Barnes (212) 567-1177

New York St Ambrose Church **P** (105) 9 W 130th St 10037 (Mail to: 9 W 130th St 10037-3638) Wayne Dodson (212) 283-2175

New York St Andrews Church **P** (149) 2067 5th Ave 10035-1219 (Mail to: 2067 5th Ave 10035-1297) Terry Jackson (212) 534-0896

New York St Ann's Church For the Deaf **M** (34) 209 E 16th St 10003-3702 (Mail to: 209 E 16th St 10003-3702) (347) 458-9571

New York St Augustines Church **P** (342) 290 Henry St 10002 (Mail to: 333 Madison St 10002-5706) Nathanael Saint-Pierre (212) 673-5300

New York St Bartholomews Church **P** (5506) 325 Park Ave 10022-6814 (Mail to: 325 Park Ave 10022-6814) Clayton Crawley Matthew Moretz Lynn Sanders Edward Sunderland (212) 378-0265

New York St Clements Church **P** (54) 423 W 46th St 10036-3510 (Mail to: 423 W 46th St 10036-3592) Jeffrey Hamblin (212) 246-7277

New York St James Church **P** (3148) 865 Madison Ave 10021-4103 (Mail to: 865 Madison Ave 10021-4195) Brenda Husson Craig Townsend Ryan Fleenor William Peyton Sarah Stewart (212) 774-4240

New York St Johns in Village Church **P** (185) 224 Waverly Pl 10014-2405 (Mail to: 224 Waverly Pl 10014-2405) Samuel Cross Alan Dennis Denise Lavetty

New York St Luke in the Fields Church **P** (857) No 487 Hudson St 10014-2851 (Mail to: 487 Hudson St 10014-2851) Caroline Stacey Lisa Krakowsky Gabriel Lamazares Emily Lloyd (212) 924-0562

New York St Lukes Church **P** (53) 435 W 141st St 10031-6401 (Mail to: 435 W 141st St 10031-6401) (212) 926-2713

New York St Marks Church in the Bowery **P** (205) 131 E 10th St 10003 (Mail to: 131 E 10th St 10003-7590) Allison Moore (212) 674-6377

New York St Martins Church **P** (166) 230 Lenox Avenue 10027-6340 (Mail to: 230 Lenox Ave 10027-6396) Johan Johnson (212) 534-4531

New York St Marys Church (Manhattanville) **P** (195) 521 W 126th St 10027-2496 (Mail to: 521 W 126th St 10027-2496) Patricia Ackerman Douglas Clark Gordon Duggins Stephanie Shockley (212) 864-4013

New York St Michaels Church **P** (714) 225 W 99th St 10025-5014 (Mail to: 225 W 99th St 10025-5014) Katharine Flexer Leigh Mackintosh

(212) 222-2700

New York St Peters Church **P** (70) 346 W 20th St 10011 (Mail to: 346 W 20th St 10011-3398) Stephen Harding (212) 929-2390

New York St Philip's Church **P** (204) 204 W 134 St 10030 (Mail to: 204 W 134th St 10030-3098) Sidney Blake Chloe Breyer Fitzroy Edwards Joyce Washington Patrick Williams (212) 862-4940

New York St Thomas Church Fifth Avenue **P** (2666) 1 W 53rd St 10019 (Mail to: 1 W 53rd St 10019-5496) Carl Turner Victor Austin Joel Daniels David McNeeley William Norgren Michael Spurlock Samuel Weiser (212) 757-7013

New York The Church of St Ignatius of Antioch **P** (266) 552 W End Ave 10024-2707 (Mail to: 552 W End Ave 10024-2707) Andrew Blume Paul Kahn

New York The Church of the Epiphany **P** (220) 1393 York Ave 10021 (Mail to: 1393 York Ave 10021-3407) R Anne Auchincloss Jennifer Reddall Horace Whyte Joseph Zorawick (212) 737-2720

New York Trinity Parish **P** (970) 120 Broadway 38th Fl 10271-0002 (Mail to: 120 Broadway 38th Fl 10271-0002) Phillip Jackson Mark Bozzuti-Jones Clayton Crawley William Lupfer Kristin Miles Benjamin Musoke-Lubega William Norgren Daniel Simons Winnie Varghese Robert Zito (212) 602-0800

Newburgh Church of the Good Shepherd **P** (27) 271 Broadway 12550-5452 (Mail to: PO Box 2865 12550-0119) (845) 562-8545

Newburgh Iglesia del Buen Pastor **M** (42) 270 Broadway & Mill St 12550 (Mail to: PO Box 2865 12550-0119) (845) 562-8545

Newburgh St Georges Episcopal Church **P** (160) 105 Grand St 12550 (Mail to: 105 Grand St 12550-4613) Dustin Trowbridge (845) 561-5355

North Salem St James Church **P** (334) 296 Titicus Road 10560 (Mail to: PO Box 459 10560-0459)

Nyack Grace Church **P** (803) 130 First Ave 10960 (Mail to: 130 1st Ave 10960-2633) Owen Thompson Anne Ross (845) 358-1297

Ossining St Pauls on the Hill Epis Church **P** (144) 40 Ganung Dr 10562-3936 (Mail to: 40 Ganung Dr 10562-3944) (914) 941-6627

Ossining Trinity Church **P** (117) 7 South Highland Avenue Post Office Box # 108 10562-4803 (Mail to: PO Box 108 10562-0108)

Patterson Christ Church **P** (24) 590 Route 11 12563-0569 (Mail to: PO Box 569 1056 Route 311 12563-0569) (845) 878-8027

Pawling Holy Trinity Church **P** (232) 22 Coulter Ave 12564-1109 (Mail to: 22 Coulter Ave 12564-1109) (845) 855-5276

Pearl River St Stephens Church **P** (356) 84 Ehrhardt Rd 10965 (Mail to: 84 Ehrhardt Rd 10965-1930) Stephen Hagerty (845) 735-8588

Peekskill St Peters Episcopal Church **P** (216) 137 N Division St 10566 (Mail to: 137 N Division St 10566-2788) Robert Hamlyn Janet Nunley (914) 737-6312

Pelham Parish of Christ the Redeemer **P** (625) 1415 Pelhamdale Ave 10803-3698 (Mail to: 1415 Pelhamdale Ave 10803-3698) Matthew Mead John Zacker (914) 738-5516

Pine Plains Church of the Regeneration **P** (81) 18 Pine St 12567-5209 (Mail to: PO Box 321 12567-0321)

Pleasant Valley St Pauls Episcopal Church **P** (119) 808 Traver Rd 12569 (Mail to: PO Box 1449 12569-1449) Megan Sanders (845) 635-2854

Pleasantville St Johns Church **P** (273) 8 Sunnyside Ave 10570-3125 (Mail to: 8 Sunnyside Ave 10570-3125) Mary Gregorius

Port Chester St Peters Church **P** (210) Westchester Ave at Pearl St 10573 (Mail to: 19 Smith St 10573-4505) Hilario Albert Kristin Saylor (914) 939-1244

Port Jervis Grace Church **P** (126) 84 Seward Ave 12771 (Mail to: 84 Seward Ave 12771-2006) David Carlson (845) 856-3026

Poughkeepsie Christ Church **P** (267) 20 Carroll St 12601-4314 (Mail to: 20 Carroll St 12601-4396) Arnulfo Arambulo J Cooper Conway Susan Fortunato (845) 452-8220

Poughkeepsie Iglesia de la Virgen de Guadalupe **M** (159) 20 Carroll St 12601 (Mail to: 20 Carroll St 12601-4314) (845) 452-8225

Poughkeepsie St Andrews Episcopal Church **P** (20) 110 Overlook Rd 12603-6200 (Mail to: 110 Overlook Rd 12603-6200) (845) 452-6832

Poughkeepsie St Pauls Church **P** (179) 161 Mansion St 12601-2524 (Mail to: 161 Mansion St 12601-2524) Bradley Jones (845) 452-8440

Red Hook Christ Church of Red Hook **P** (126) 7423 S Broadway 12571-1747 (Mail to: 7423 S Broadway 12571-1747) Ryan Lesh (845) 758-1591

Rhinebeck Church of the Messiah **P** (625) 6436 Montgomery St 12572 (Mail to: PO Box 248 12572-0248) Richard McKeon (845) 876-3533

Roosevelt Island Good Shepherd Ch Roosevelt Isl **M** (66) 543 Main St 10044 (Mail to: PO Box 361 10044) (917) 843-3338

Rye Christ's Church **P** (2140) 2 Rectory St 10580-3818 (Mail to: Rectory St 10580-3830) Susan Harriss Dorothee Caulfield Sanford Key Catherine Lawrence

Saugerties Trinity Church **P** (35) 32 Church St 12477-1809 (Mail to: 32 Church St 12477-1809) Michael Phillips (845) 246-6312

Scarsdale Church of St James the Less **P** (443) 10 Church Lane 10583-5604 (Mail to: 10 Church Lane 10583) Robert Flanagan (914) 723-6100

Somers Saint Luke's Church **P** (234) 331 Rte 100 10589-3204 (Mail to: 331 Rte 100 10589-3204) Amy Lamborn James Melton

South Fallsburgh St Andrews Church **M** (10) 5277 St. Rt 42 12779 (Mail to: PO Box 55 12788-0055) (845) 436-7539

South Salem St Johns Church **P** (205) 82 Spring St 10590-1417 (Mail to: PO Box 394 10590-0394) Joseph Campo (914) 763-8273

Sparkill Christ Church **P** (60) New St 10976-1203 (Mail to: PO Box 177 10976-0177) Karen Lynn Depue (646) 373-6013

Spring Valley St Pauls Church **P** (345) 26 S Madison Ave 10977-5512 (Mail to: 26 S Madison Ave 10977-5512) Cheryl Parris (845) 356-1857

Staatsburg St Margarets Church **P** (83) 68 Old Post Rd 12580 (Mail to: PO Box 395 12580-0395) Charles Ford (845) 889-4181

Staten Island All Saints Church **P** (109) 2329 Victory Blvd 10314-6621 (Mail to: 2329 Victory Blvd 10314-6689) Lewis Marshall (718) 698-1338

Staten Island Christ Church New Brighton **P** (239) 76 Franklin Ave 10301-1239 (Mail to: 76 Franklin Ave 10301-1239) Victoria Duncan Geraldine Swanson

Staten Island Church of St Andrew **P** (297) 40 Old Mill Rd 10306 (Mail to: 40 Old Mill Rd 10306-1197) Frederick Fausak (718) 351-0900

Staten Island Church of the Ascension **P** (167) No 1 Kingsley Ave 10314-2420 (Mail to: 1 Kingsley Ave 10314-2420) R Richard Marchand (718) 442-4187

Staten Island St Albans Episcopal Church **P** (208) 76 Saint Albans Pl 10312-5131 (Mail to: 76 Saint Albans Pl 10312-5199) Daniel Gross

Staten Island St Johns Church **P** (250) 1333 Bay St 10305 (Mail to: 1333 Bay St 10305-3199) Roy Cole Rhoda Treherne-Thomas (718) 447-1605

Staten Island St Mary's Church Castleton **P** (133) 347 Davis Ave 10310 (Mail to: 347 Davis Ave 10310-1557) Horace Free (718) 442-1527

Staten Island St Pauls Church **P** (110) C/O Gwendloyn Simmons 77 Bard Ave 10310-1605 (Mail to: 225 Saint Pauls Ave 10304-2246) (718) 273-9572

Staten Island St Simons Church **P** (63) 1055 Richmond Rd 10304 (Mail to: 1055 Richmond Rd 10304-2401) (718) 987-5252

Staten Island St Stephens Church **P** (178) 7516 Amboy Rd 10307-1423 (Mail to: 7516 Amboy Rd 10307-1423) (718) 984-1722

Stone Ridge Christ the King Church **P** (187) 3021 St Rt 213 E 12484-5101 (Mail to: 3021 State Route 213 E 12484-5101) Alison Quin Robin Beveridge Judith Borzumato (845) 687-9414

Stony Point St Johns in the Wilderness Church **M** (63) 119 St John's Rd 10980-3624 (Mail to: PO Box 641 10980) (845) 578-6036

Suffern Christ Church of Ramapo **P** (174) 65 Washington Ave 10901 (Mail to: 65 Washington Ave 10901) Dale Cranston (845) 357-1615

Tarrytown Christ Church **P** (262) 43 S Broadway

10591-4012 (Mail to: 43 S Broadway 10591-4095) Susan Copley Joanne Izzo (914) 631-2074

Tivoli St Pauls Church **P** (46) 39 Woods Rd 12583-5433 (Mail to: 39 Woods Rd 12583-5433) Sharon Clayton (845) 757-3131

Tomkins Cove Church of St John the Divine **P** (52) 170 Mott Farm Rd 10986 (Mail to: PO Box 92 10986-0092) (845) 786-5203

Tuxedo Park St Marys Church **P** (490) 10 Fox Hill Rd 10987-4224 (Mail to: PO Box 637 10987-0637) Bruce Woodcock (845) 351-5122

Valley Cottage All Saints Episcopal Church **P** (64) 182 Ridge Rd 10989-2351 (Mail to: 3 Daken Ct. 10989-2609) Jacob Nanthicattu (845) 268-9542

Walden St Andrews Church **P** (177) 15 Walnut St 12586 (Mail to: 20 Maidstone Dr 12586-2425) (845) 778-5310

Wappingers Falls Zion Church **P** (650) 12 Saterlee Pl 12590-2600 (Mail to: 12 Satterlee Pl 12590-2600) Deborah Magdalene (845) 297-9797

Warwick Christ Church **P** (671) 50 South St 10990-1638 (Mail to: 50 South St 10990-1638) James Erwin (845) 986-3440

Washingtonville St Annes Church **P** (157) 179 E Main St 10992 (Mail to: 175 E Main St 10992-1723) (845) 496-3961

West Park Ch of Ascension & Holy Trinity **P** (108) 1585 Rte 9W 12493 (Mail to: PO Box 1512 12528-8512) Jennifer Barrows Teresa Jones (845) 384-6723

White Plains Grace Church **P** (648) 33 Church St 10601 (Mail to: 33 Church St 10601-1995) Richard Kunz Martha-Jane Dunphy (914) 949-2874

White Plains St Bartholomews Church **P** (57) 82 Prospect St 10606-3421 (Mail to: 82 Prospect St 10606-3499) Gawain De Leeuw (914) 949-5577

White Plains St Francis & St Marthas Church **P** (74) 575 Tarrytown Rd 10607 (Mail to: 575 Tarrytown Rd 10607-1335) John Farrell (914) 946-8846

White Plains St Joseph of Arimathea Church **P** (78) 2172 Saw Mill River Rd 10607 (Mail to: 2172 Saw Mill River Rd Route 9A 10607-2205) Claire Lofgren (914) 592-7163

Woodstock St Gregorys Episcopal Church **P** (94) 2578 Rte 212 12498 (Mail to: PO Box 66 12498-0066) H William Benson Matthew Wright (845) 679-6394

Yonkers Church of the Holy Cross **P** (59) 81 Locust Hill Ave 10701 (Mail to: 81 Locust Hill Ave 10701-2801)

Yonkers St Andrews Church/Iglesia San Andres **P** (258) 22 Post St 10705 (Mail to: 22 Post St 10705-2241) (914) 963-9523

Yonkers St Johns Church (Gettys Sq) **P** (130) 1 Hudson St 10701 (Mail to: 1 Hudson St 10701-3601) John Hamilton (914) 963-3033

Yonkers St Johns Church of Tuckahoe **P** (231) 100

Underhill St 10710 (Mail to: 100 Underhill St 10710-3615) Kristin Kopren (914) 779-7024

Yonkers St Marks Church **P** (27) 1373 Nepperham Ave 10703-1011 (Mail to: 1373 Nepperham Ave 10703-1011) Maxine Cleghorn (914) 965-3455

Yonkers St Pauls Church **P** (18) 636 Palisade Ave 10703-2122 (Mail to: 636 Palisade Ave 10703-2122) (914) 965-4967

NON-PAROCHIAL CLERGY

Abernathy WH *ret*
Alagna FJ *ret* Rhinecliff NY
Ampah RA Augusta GA
Anderson CL *ret* New York NY
Anderson RJ *ret* San Diego CA
Anderson WM *ret*
Andrews JA *ret* Lima NY
Armstrong GM
Arnold DWH Indianapolis IN
Askew AV Brooklyn NY
Auchincloss SC *ret* Woodstock NY
Auletta K
Avila-Nativi R Poughkeepsie NY
Bailey AV Bronx NY
Ballantine LP *ret* North Salem NY
Baltus DB *ret* New York NY
Bane JD *ret* Camden DE
Baroody RA *ret* Covington VA
Barrie DP New York NY
Barrios L Bronx NY
Bartholomew AGL *ret* New York NY
Bass-Choate Y Yonkers NY
Batchelder KC *ret*
Batson SR Montgomery AL
Beckles WA *ret* Mount Vernon NY
Beery WS *ret* New Bern NC
Bercovici HR Greenwich CT
Bloomer NH *ret* Essex Junction VT
Boatright-Spencer AR *ret* Wadesboro NC
Bodie PMD *ret* New York NY
Bolle SM *ret* Greenville SC
Bonsteel SL *dcn* Kingston NY
Bourhill JW *dcn* Yonkers NY
Bowers TD *ret* Morehead City NC
Bowes B *ret* Lagrangeville NY
Boynton CC *dcn*
Brandt GW *ret* New York NY
Breiner BF *ret* New York NY
Brewer AA
Bronson DL *ret* Stone Ridge NY
Brooks RB *dcn* Hyde Park NY
Brooks TG *ret* Highland NY
Brown DC *ret* Hackensack NJ
Broyles ER *ret* Kerhonkson NY
Burnham FB *ret* Asheville NC
Burns JL *ret* Hillsdale NY
Buzzard HL White Plains NY
Callaway JG *ret* New York NY
Campbell JC *ret* Poughkeepsie NY
Campbell-Dixon RA West Park NY

Campo JAC South Salem NY
Cartier FC *ret* Red Hook NY
Chambers RK
Chilton B *ret* Annandale-on-Hudson NY
Chinlund SJ *ret* New York NY
Chisholm AL *ret* Nyack NY
Chittenden NP Armonk NY
Choate H *ret* Yonkers NY
Choi SYS *ret* North Bergen NJ
Clark AS *ret* Monroe OH
Clarke JDB *ret dcn* New York NY
Clayton PB *ret* Lagrangeville NY
Cobden EAM Bedford Corners NY
Coggi LMM San Antonio TX
Coleman FG *ret* Akron OH
Coleman HD *ret* Pearl River NY
Colwell CR *ret* Oyster Bay NY
Combs LD *ret* Concord NH
Conger GM *ret* New Paltz NY
Copley DM Tarrytown NY
Corney RW *ret* Glens Falls NY
Cosentino EF *ret* Peekskill NY
Covington JE *ret* New York NY
Crafton BC *ret* Metuchen NJ
Crawford RL Camden ME
Crothers JM *ret* Toms River NJ
Crouch BG *dcn* Austin TX
Culhane SM Greenwich CT
Cumming J Katonah NY
Curtis KJ *dcn* New York NY
Cushman MT *ret* Chebeague Island ME
Cushman TS *ret*
Cutler DR *ret* Salem MA
Darves-Bornoz DY New York NY
De Champlain MM New York NY
De Fontaine-Stratton JB *ret* Poughkeepsie NY
Dearman WB *ret* Peekskill NY
Delaney MF Garden City NY
Delgado-Miller DA Bronx NY
Dell JW New York NY
Desueza EF *ret* Newburgh NY
Dewey SD *ret* London
Dias KK Bronxville NY
Diaz G Bronx NY
Dingle JH *ret* West Palm Beach FL
Dorrien GJ New York NY
Draesel HG *ret* New York NY
Dresser D *ret* Newburgh NY
Drobin FA Hopewell Junction NY
Dulfer JG *ret* New York NY
Duncanson FP Airmont NY
Duval LM *dcn* Kingston NY
Edmonds JB *ret* Blue Hill ME
Edward BJ Pleasantville NY
Ekizian HJ *dcn* Peekskill NY
Elisee JR *ret* West Orange NJ
Elsberry TL *ret* Bedford NY
Ewart CK
Eylers DE *ret* Harwinton CT
Faulkner TD *ret* New York NY
Fenton GD Vancouver BC

Ferlo RA Chicago IL
Fernandez JP *ret* Stuart FL
Fitzpatrick RJ Washingtonville NY
Flores N *dcn* New York NY
Forbes BW *ret* New York NY
Fortna RT *ret* New York NY
Foster AW *ret* Claremont CA
Foster GR *ret* Wilton Manors FL
Foulke ML New York NY
Fox CR New York NY
Fox CL New York NY
Francks RC *ret* New York NY
Frew RL *ret* New York NY
Fulton CN *ret* New York NY
Fulton NH *dcn* Katonah NY
Gallagher DP Millbrook NY
Gallagher GJ *ret* Leland NC
Gatch MM *ret* New York NY
George AWS Bronx NY
George CDD San Francisco CA
Girard JA *ret dcn* Staten Island NY
Glover MB *ret* White Plains NY
Godley RJ *ret* Murrells Inlet SC
Goodness DR *ret* Alexandria VA
Grab VL *ret* Tivoli NY
Graham SH Nyack NY
Greenlaw WA *ret* New York NY
Gressle RL *ret* Nyack NY
Griffith DW Virginia Beach VA
Haller TS *ret* Bronx NY
Hanna NW *ret* Lawrence NY
Hare ADB *dcn* Bronx NY
Harrington LB *ret* Pound Ridge NY
Hart CW *ret* Tarrytown NY
Hart WG *dcn* Mount Kisco NY
Harvey EA *ret* Miami FL
Hayes EP *ret* Lewes DE
Haynes LL *dcn* New Hamburg NY
Healey JP Grosse Pointe MI
Hellman GL New York NY
Heron J *ret* Beacon NY
Herrick RF *ret* New York NY
Hesse RW *ret* Bethany Beach DE
Hewitt EC
Heyduk MTM Chicago IL
Hildesley CH *ret* New York NY
Hill RL New York NY
Hoag DS *ret* New Smyrna Beach FL
Hoeltzel GA *ret* Yonkers NY
Hoke SH *ret* Pittsboro NC
Holmes FR Oak Park CA
Holton SC White Plains NY
Hopper EW *dcn*
Hubbard MA *dcn* Beacon NY
Hummell MW
Huntington FC *ret* Saint James NY
Johannsen CA *ret* Bedford Hills NY
Johannson JK *ret* Bucksport ME
Johnson FH Oakland Park FL
Johnson JR *ret* Charleston SC
Johnson SO Staten Island NY

Johnson WA Scarsdale NY
Jones CA
Joseph AE *ret* New York NY
Kanellakis T *ret* Camden ME
Kassebaum JA *dcn* Hastings On Hudson NY
Kaswarra GA *ret* Montclair NJ
Kavros PM New York NY
Kearney JA *dcn* Houston TX
Keech AI
Kemmler RS *ret* Sarasota FL
Kendall MS *ret* New York NY
Keyes CD *ret* Pittsburgh PA
Kimmey JE *ret* Denton TX
King JLR *ret* Ridgewood NJ
Knight FL *ret* Allentown PA
Krauss HE *ret* New York NY
Kunhardt PB Waccabuc NY
Landers GL Wall Township NJ
Lane KC New York NY
Larom RU *ret* Ivoryton CT
Larson LAA *ret* New Fairfield CT
Lathrop BA New York NY
Lawrence NE *dcn* Staten Island NY
Lee CK New York NY
Leseure LJ *ret* Bronx NY
Levy WT Canoga Park CA
Lewis MB *ret* Newburgh NY
Liew R *ret* Oakland NJ
Lindsley JE *ret* Millbrook NY
Lloyd JJ *ret* Yonkers NY
Lodwick JN *ret* South Bend IN
Lofman DS *dcn* Middletown NY
Logan YL New York NY
Lowe EY Evanston IL
Lutz AW Cange Haiti
Maas JA *ret* Alexandria VA
Macinnis EG Beijing
Magliula RJ *ret* West Park NY
Mallary RDW *ret* Hanover NH
Mallonee A New York NY
Mandeville KC Tivoli NY
Margrave TEC *ret* Cortland NY
Marran PM *dcn* Hanover NH
Martin KA New York NY
Martin MJ New York NY
Mason JC *ret* Chappaqua NY
Matlack DR *ret* Southwest Harbor ME
Matthews DP *ret* New York NY
Mayer CD
McCloghrie KL *ret* Fortuna CA
McCoy AD *ret* Santa Barbara CA
McDade SD New York NY
McDonald JR Austin TX
McElroy CDL Teaneck NJ
McGehee LE New York NY
McKenna K *dcn* Putnam Valley NY
McQuade LJ *ret* Bronxville NY
McWhorter ES *ret* Tuxedo Park NY
Mead AC *ret* Narragansett RI
Mercer TR *ret*
Mesler RC *ret* Milwaukee WI

Miller EC New York NY
Miller JL *ret* Katonah NY
Miller JL Princeton NJ
Miller TP *ret* New York NY
Minifie CJ *ret* Hilton Head Island SC
Minturn SM *ret* Chicago IL
Mitchell PRS Tuckahoe NY
Montalto AP *ret* St. Petersburg FL
Moody JW *ret* New York NY
Moquete CR *ret* Bronx NY
Morales LE Kissimmee FL
Morehouse TL New York NY
Morisseau REL *ret* Pompton Plains NJ
Morton JP *ret* New York NY
Mukhwana-Nafuma JE *ret*
Muncie MA *ret* Greenville SC
Newcomb TL *ret* Bronxville NY
Newcombe DG Cambridge
Nicoll TE *ret* Greenville SC
Northup LA Miami FL
Ogwal-Abwang BY *ret* New Rochelle NY
O'Hara E *ret* Poughkeepsie NY
Orso TR *ret* Yonkers NY
Osgood JA *ret*
Owen JM
Pace JC New York NY
Pagliaro LA *ret dcn* Hollis NY
Palmer JM *ret* New York NY
Parnell WC New York NY
Peacock C New York NY
Pellaton TJP *ret* New York NY
Perez-Bullard A New York NY
Perrin RVO
Person KJ Brooklyn NY
Peterson FL *dcn* New York NY
Peterson RE *ret* Lenox MA
Pfaff BH *ret* New York NY
Phillips RO *ret* Littleton NH
Pietsch LP *ret* Hanover NH
Place DLA Pittsburgh PA
Platt WC New York NY
Pollard R *ret*
Powell SR *ret* Bronx NY
Prator LE *ret* New York NY
Price SM *ret* Peterborough NH
Pritchett HH *ret* Atlanta GA
Reddimalla SR *ret* Chantilly VA
Reid FL Bronx NY
Reiners D
Reinhard KL New Haven CT
Relyea MJ Atlantic Beach NC
Rice RV Pikesville MD
Richards AF *ret* New york NY
Rider WB New York NY
Riley GD Long Beach NY
Rivera-Rivera LA *dcn* New York NY
Roadman BJ *ret* Ossining NY
Rock JBK Bronx NY
Rodgers SM *ret* Beaverton OR
Rose MR New York NY
Roundtree EL *dcn* New Rochelle NY

Rubinson RJ New York NY
Ruschmeyer HC *ret* Stuart FL
Rutledge F *ret* Rye Brook NY
Sabune PAN *ret* Newark NJ
Sanborn VBM *ret* Cincinnati OH
Sanon JLF *ret* Douglasville GA
Santiviago-Espinal MI *ret* East Elmhurst NY
Scantlebury CA *ret* Mashpee MA
Schacht LA *dcn* New York NY
Schaeffer SE *ret* Northampton MA
Scheide DS Callicoon NY
Schmidt WR *ret* Newburgh NY
Schnitzer WL *ret* New Paltz NY
Schraplau FW *ret* Staten Island NY
Seaborn SL Scarborough NY
Seipp V *dcn* Fishkill NY
Selfe-Verrone AC Los Angeles CA
Shafer MG *ret* Stanfordville NY
Shepherd RG *ret*
Shriver FH *ret* New York NY
Signorelli BM Jersey City NJ
Simmons CW Bronx NY
Slauson HB *ret* Norwalk CT
Sloan RD Ho-Ho-Kus NJ
Smith JC *ret* New York NY
Smith SR *ret* Chapel Hill NC
Smith TP New York NY
Speeks MW
Springer LL *ret* Deltona FL
Sserwadda EK Bronxville NY
Stafford RH *ret* Palm Springs CA
Stallings FM *ret* New York NY
Starr WF *ret* Chilmark MA
Stelk LF *ret* Yarmouth ME
Stowe HTW *ret* Miami Shores FL
Strickland V New York NY
Strobel PO *ret* Greenwich CT
Sturtevant HH *ret* New York NY
Sullivan MP Walden NY
Swain S
Sword CR *ret* New York NY

Syedullah MI *ret* Hyde Park NY
Tammearu DG New York NY
Taylor GW New Rochelle NY
Taylor WS *ret* Mount Vernon NY
Temple CS *ret* New York NY
Toomey DC *ret* Norwich VT
Torres JO *ret* New York NY
Towner PH New York NY
Trapp JE *ret* Portland OR
Tully WM *ret* Santa Barbara CA
Turczyn JR *ret* Scarborough ME
Turner PA New York NY
Tweedy JE *ret* Peacham VT
Vincent J *ret* Washington DC
Volkmann JE *dcn* Valatie NY
Wachner E New York NY
Wade JA *ret* Hampton VA
Walker RL
Ward PJ *ret* Ossining NY
Wayne DB *ret* Rowe MA
Webber MB *ret* Paradox NY
Weglarz EE Eastchester NY
Wegman JD New York NY
Wells EF *ret* New York NY
Werdal EP *dcn* Mamaroneck NY
White KA Nyack NY
Wildman RP Bedford MA
Wilking SVB Concord MA
Williams AWL *dcn* Corona NY
Williams EE
Wilson ET *dcn* Bronx NY
Wing AK *ret* Suffern NY
Winkler WE *dcn*
Winslow KD *ret* Rensselaerville NY
Witt RC Accord NY
Wolsoncroft AM New York NY
Wood GD *ret* Wawarsing NY
Woods SI *ret* Above NM
Wright JR *ret* New York NY
Young MC New York NY

DIOCESE OF NEWARK

(PROVINCE II)
Comprises Northern New Jersey
DIOCESAN OFFICE 31 Mulberry St Newark NJ 07102
TEL (973) 430-9900   FAX (973) 622-3503
E-MAIL jking@dioceseofnewark.org   WEB www.dioceseofnewark.org

Previous Bishops—
Wm H Odenheimer 1874-79, Thomas A Starkey 1880-1903, Edwin S Lines 1903-27, Wilson R Stearly suffr 1915 coadj 1917 Bp 1927-35, Benj M Washburn coadj 1932 Bp 1935-58, Theodore R Ludlow suffr 1936-53, Donald MacAdie suffr 1958-63, Leland Stark coadj 1953 Bp 1958-73, George E Rath suffr 1964 coadj 1970 Bp 1974-78, John S Spong coadj 1976 Bp 1979-2000, JM McKelvey suffr 1991-99, John P Croneberger coadj 1998 Bp 2000-2007

Bishop—The Rt Rev Mark M Beckwith (1012)
(Dio 27 Jan 2007)

Bp Exec Asst K Lark; *Dio Admin Off* JA King; *Asst* R Johnson; *Cn to Ord* Rev GA Jacobs; *CFO* P

Shackford; *Chanc* DE Sammons

Stand Comm—Cler: P Bakal J Mennell L Wurm; *Lay: Pres* P Yankus P Henderson N Horsky R Simmons

Dio Conv: 29-30 Jan 2016 Parsippany NJ

PARISHES, MISSIONS, AND CLERGY

Allendale Trinity Episcopal Church of Bergen County **P** (111) 55 George St 07401-1426 (Mail to: 55 George St 07401-1426) E Michael Allen (201) 327-3012

Bayonne Calvary Episcopal Church **P** (37) 956 Avenue C 07002-3022 (Mail to: 956 Avenue C 07002-3022) (201) 339-3112

Bayonne Trinity Parish in Bergen Point **P** (144) 141 Broadway 07002-2459 (Mail to: 23 La Tourette Pl 07002-2407) Gregory Perez (201) 858-4460

Belvidere St Marys Church Belvidere **M** (67) 408 3rd St 07823-1834 (Mail to: 408 3rd St 07823-1834) Rosemarie Hassan (908) 475-5494

Bergenfield All Saints Episcopal Korean Church **M** (98) 12 W Central Ave 07621-1302 (Mail to: 12 West Central Ave 07621) Ho Gil Won (201) 244-1004

Boonton St Johns Episcopal Church **P** (213) 226 Cornelia St 07005-1712 (Mail to: 226 Cornelia St 07005-1712) Timothy Carr (973) 334-3655

Budd Lake Christ Episcopal Church **P** (98) 369 Sand Shore Rd 07828-2215 (Mail to: 369 Sand Shore Rd 07828-2215) Ellen Kohn-Perry (973) 347-1866

Chatham St Pauls Episcopal Church **P** (326) 200 Main St 07928-2406 (Mail to: 200 Main St 07928-2467) Mary Davis (973) 635-8085

Chester Church of the Messiah **P** (186) 50 State Route 24 07930-2410 (Mail to: 50 State Route 24 07930-2410) Margaret Otterburn Linda Phillips (908) 879-7208

Cliffside Pk Trinity Church **P** (40) 555 Palisade Ave 07010-3035 (Mail to: 555 Palisade Ave 07010-3035) Willie Smith (201) 943-1034

Clifton St Peters Episcopal Church **P** (145) 380 Clifton Ave 07011-2643 (Mail to: 380 Clifton Ave 07011-2643) Peter De Franco (973) 546-5020

Denville The Church of the Saviour **P** (761) 155 Morris Ave 07834-1736 (Mail to: 155 Morris Ave 07834-1736) (973) 627-3304

Dover St Johns Episcopal Church **P** (83) 11 S Bergen St 07801-4634 (Mail to: 11 S Bergen St 07801-4634) John Habecker

East Orange Christ Episcopal Church **P** (315) Attn John Taylor 422 Main St 07018-3210 (Mail to: 422 Main St 07018-3295) Joseph Harmon (973) 678-1160

East Orange St Agnes & St Pauls Church **P** (65) 206 Renshaw Ave 07017-3313 (Mail to: 206 Renshaw Ave 07017-3313) Esar Budhu (973) 678-6716

Englewood St Pauls Episcopal Church **P** (418) 113 Engle St 07631-2508 (Mail to: 113 Engle St 07631-2508) William Allport (201) 568-3276

Essex Fells St Peters Episcopal Church **P** (1010) 271 Roseland Ave 07021-1313 (Mail to: PO Box 96 07021-0096) J Barrington Bates Anthony Puca (973) 226-6500

Fair Lawn Church of the Atonement **P** (55) No 1-36 30th St 07410-3946 (Mail to: 1-36 30th St 07410) Kevin Coffey (201) 797-0760

Fort Lee Church of the Good Shepherd **COO** (96) 1576 Palisade Ave 07024-6929 (Mail to: 1576 Palisade Ave 07024-6993) Hosea Lee

Glen Ridge Christ Episcopal Church **P** (216) 74 Park Ave 07028 (Mail to: 74 Park Ave 07028-2309) Diana Wilcox Robert Solon

Glen Rock All Saints Episcopal Church **P** (332) 40 Central Ave 07452-1837 (Mail to: 40 Central Ave 07452-1837) Mark Collins (201) 444-6874

Hackensack Christ Episcopal Church **P** (217) 251 State St 07601-5512 (Mail to: PO Box 1097 07601-1097) Michael Gerhardt (201) 342-2365

Hackensack Church of St Anthony Padua **P** (692) 72 Lodi St 07601-5350 (Mail to: 72 Lodi St 07601-5363) Brian Laffler (201) 489-3286

Hackensack St Cyprians Church **M** (49) 269 1st St 07601-3434 (Mail to: 269 1st St 07601-3434) (201) 342-5560

Hackettstown St James Episcopal Church **P** (330) 214 Washington St 07840-2146 (Mail to: 214 Washington St 07840-2146) (908) 852-3968

Harrington Park St Andrews Episcopal Church **P** (123) Lynn St and La Roche Ave 07640 (Mail to: 31 Lynn Street 07640-0161) Diane Rhodes (201) 768-0819

Harrison Christ Church **M** (52) 100 Frank E Rodgers Blvd N 07029-1402 (Mail to: 100 Frank E Rodgers Blvd N 07029) (973) 483-1260

Hasbrouck Hts Church of St John the Divine **M** (140) 229 Terrace Ave 07604-1917 (Mail to: 229 Terrace Ave 07604-1917) Alexei Khamin (201) 288-0002

Haworth St Lukes Episcopal Church **P** (69) 43 Massachusetts Ave 07641-1950 (Mail to: 43 Massachusetts Ave 07641-1950) Elizabeth Golub (201) 384-0706

Hawthorne St Clements Episcopal Church **P** (183) 271 Lafayette Ave 07506-1921 (Mail to: 271 Lafayette Ave 07506-1921) Susan Schink (973) 427-8118

Hillsdale Holy Trinity Episcopal Church **P** (315) 326 Hillsdale Ave 07642-2209 (Mail to: 326 Hillsdale Ave 07642-2209) Briggett Keith (201) 664-2428

Ho Ho Kus St Bartholomews Episcopal Church **P** (190) 70 Sheridan Ave 07423-1541 (Mail to: 70 Sheridan Ave 07423-1541) Daniel Kreller (201) 444-5025

Hoboken All Saints Episcopal Parish **P** (568) 707 Washington St 07030-5001 (Mail to: 707 Washington St 07030-5001) Daniel Lennox

(201) 792-3563

Hope St Lukes Church **P** (54) 346 High St 07844-0292 (Mail to: PO Box 292 07844-0292)

Jersey City Church of the Incarnation **P** (100) 68 Storms Ave 07306-3316 (Mail to: 68 Storms Ave 07306-3316) (201) 434-4810

Jersey City Grace Van Vorst Church **P** (343) 39 Erie St 07302-2821 (Mail to: 39 Erie St 07302-2821) Laurie Wurm (201) 659-2211

Jersey City St Paul's Episcopal Church **P** (134) 38 Duncan Ave 07304-0176 (Mail to: 38 Duncan Ave 07304-2102) Thomas Murphy (201) 433-4922

Kinnelon St Davids Episcopal Church **P** (166) 91 Kinnelon Rd 07405-2335 (Mail to: 91 Kinnelon Rd 07405-2335) David Desmith (973) 838-6696

Leonia All Saints Episcopal Church **P** (98) 150 Park Ave 07605-2012 (Mail to: 150 Park Ave 07605-2091) Dean Weber (201) 947-1233

Little Falls St Agnes Episcopal Church **P** (106) 65 Union Ave 07424-1321 (Mail to: 65 Union Ave 07424-1397) Deborah Drake

Livingston St Peter's Episcopal Church **P** (108) 94 E Mount Pleasant Ave 07039-3004 (Mail to: 94 E Mount Pleasant Ave 07039-3004) Elizabeth Wigg-Maxwell (973) 992-1932

Lyndhurst St Thomas Episcopal Church **P** (48) 300 Forest Ave PO Box 207 07071-2330 (Mail to: 300 Forest Ave PO Box 207 07071-0207) (201) 438-5668

Madison Grace Church **P** (1099) 4 Madison Ave 07940-1433 (Mail to: 4 Madison Ave 07940-1433) Lauren Ackland Paul Adler Lesley Hay (973) 377-0106

Maplewood St Georges Episcopal Church **P** (425) 550 Ridgewood Rd 07040-2135 (Mail to: 550 Ridgewood Rd 07040-2198) Bernard Poppe (973) 762-1319

Maywood St Martins Episcopal Church **P** (53) 29 Parkway 07607-1558 (Mail to: 29 Parkway 07607-1558) Ruben Jurado

✠ **Mendham** St John Baptist Convent **Other** 82 W Main St 07945-1230 (Mail to: PO Box 240 07945-0240) (973) 543-4641

Mendham St Marks Church **P** (148) 9 E Main St 07945-1501 (Mail to: 9 E Main St 07945) Shawn Carty Charles Rice (973) 543-4471

Millburn St Stephens Church **P** (269) 119 Main St 07041-1115 (Mail to: 119 Main St 07041-1115) Sheelagh Clarke Derek Darves-Bornoz

Millington All Saints Church **P** (262) 15 Basking Ridge Rd 07946-1407 (Mail to: PO Box 415 07946-0415) Victoria McGrath (908) 647-0067

Montclair St James Episcopal Church **P** (444) 581 Valley Rd 07043-1826 (Mail to: 581 Valley Rd 07043-1826) David Casto Charlotte Hall Audrey Hasselbrook (973) 744-0270

Montclair St Johns Episcopal Church **P** (438) 55 Montclair Ave 07042-4109 (Mail to: 55 Montclair Ave 07042-4109) Candace Sandfort

Montclair St Lukes Episcopal Church **P** (698) 73 S Fullerton Ave 07042-2627 (Mail to: 73 S Fullerton Ave 07042-2618) John Mennell (973) 744-6220

Montvale St Pauls Episcopal Church **P** (387) 4 Woodland Rd 07645-2134 (Mail to: 4 Woodland Rd 07645-2134) Edward Hasse (201) 391-3181

Morris Plains St Pauls Episcopal Church **P** (218) No 29 Hillview Ave 07950 (Mail to: 29 Hillview Ave 07950-2114) Paul Olsson (973) 285-0884

Morristown Church of the Redeemer **P** (347) 36 South St 07960-4136 (Mail to: 36 South St 07960-7260) Cynthia Black (973) 539-0703

Morristown St Peters Episcopal Church **P** (1036) 121 South Street 07960 (Mail to: 70 Maple Ave 07960-9600) Janet Broderick (973) 538-0555

Mountain Lks St Peters Episcopal Church **P** (350) 215 Boulevard 07046-1209 (Mail to: 215 Boulevard 07046-1209) Adele Hatfield Charles Hatfield (973) 334-4429

Mt Arlington St Peters Episcopal Church **P** (69) 50 Edgemere Ave 07856-1164 (Mail to: PO Box 403 50 Edgemere Avenue 07856-0403) Elizabeth Myers Wayne Sherrer (973) 398-1890

N Arlington St Pauls Church **M** (21) 11 York Rd 07031-5811 (Mail to: 11 York Rd 07031-5811) (201) 199-1725

Newark Grace Episcopal Church **P** (168) 950 Broad St 07102-2614 (Mail to: 950 Broad St 07102-2684) James Bates Marjorie Lindstrom Randy Webster (973) 623-1733

Newark House of Prayer Episcopal Church **M** (93) 407 Broad St 07104-3310 (Mail to: 407 Broad St 07104-3310) Valerie Bailey Fischer Kathleen Ballard Wade Renn

Newark St Andrews Episcopal Church **M** (110) 933 S 17th St 07108-1136 (Mail to: 933 S 17th St 07108-1136) James Hagler (973) 375-3012

✠ **Newark** Trinity & St Philips Cathedral **O** (206) 24 Rector St 07102-4512 (Mail to: 24 Rector St 07102-4588) George Bowen Thomas Pike Wade Renn Sandra Wilson (973) 622-3505

Newton Christ Episcopal Church **P** (606) 62 Main St 07860-2024 (Mail to: 62 Main St 07860-2024) Robert Griner (973) 383-2245

Norwood Church of the Holy Communion **P** (135) 66 Summit St 07648-1841 (Mail to: 66 Summit St 07648-1841) James Petroccione (201) 768-0634

Nutley Grace Episcopal Church **P** (539) 200 Highfield Ln 07110-2448 (Mail to: 200 Highfield Ln 07110-2448) Pamela Bakal Nancy Read (973) 235-1177

Oak Ridge St Gabriels Episcopal Church **M** (40) 153 Milton Rd 07438-9598 (Mail to: 153 Milton Rd 07438-9596) (973) 697-5688

Oakland St Albans Episcopal Church **P** (162) 1 Church Ln 07436-4036 (Mail to: 1 Church Ln 07436-4036) Kathryn King (201) 337-4909

Oradell The Church of the Annunciation **P** (89)

343 Kinderkamack Rd 07649-2123 (Mail to: 343 Kinderkamack Rd 07649-2123) Archie Palmer (201) 262-7222

Orange Church of the Epiphany **P** (148) 105 Main St 07050-4026 (Mail to: 105 Main St PO Box 93 07051-0093) Elizabeth Golub (973) 676-8886

Paramus St Matthews Episcopal Church **M** (153) 167 Spring Valley Rd 07652-5333 (Mail to: 167 Spring Valley Rd 07652-5333) Bruce Woodcock (201) 262-5286

Parsippany St Gregorys Episcopal Church **M** (89) 480 S Beverwyck Rd 07054-3328 (Mail to: 480 S Beverwyck Rd 07054-3328) Susan Saucedo Sica (973) 887-5879

Passaic St Johns Episcopal Church **P** (143) 215 Lafayette Ave 07055-4711 (Mail to: 215 Lafayette Ave 07055-4711) William Thiele (973) 779-0966

Paterson Church of the Holy Communion **P** (38) 219 Carroll St 07501-2319 (Mail to: 99 Pearl St 07501-2319) (973) 742-5553

Paterson St Pauls Episcopal Church **P** (408) 451 Van Houten St 07501-2119 (Mail to: 451 Van Houten St 07501-2119) Rosa Brown (973) 278-7900

Phillipsburg St Luke Episcopal Church **P** (237) 500 Hillcrest Blvd 08865-1407 (Mail to: 500 Hillcrest Blvd 08865-1499) Thomas Mathews (908) 859-1479

Pompton Lake Christ Episcopal Church **P** (429) 400 Ramapo Ave 07442-1825 (Mail to: 400 Ramapo Ave 07442-1825) Stephen Rozzelle (973) 835-2207

Ramsey St Johns Memorial Episcopal Church **P** (609) 301 E Main St 07446 (Mail to: 301 E Main St 07446-1902) Julian Eibin (201) 327-0703

Randolph Mar Thoma Church **P** 790 State Route 10 07869-1903 (Mail to: 790 State Route 10 07869-1903)

Ridgefield St James Episcopal Church **P** (248) 514 Abbott Ave 07657-2413 (Mail to: 514 Abbott Ave 07657-2413) Mariano Gargiulo

Ridgewood Christ Episcopal Church **P** (462) 105 Cottage Pl 07450-3213 (Mail to: 105 Cottage Pl 07450-3213) William Coats Daniel Gunn Elizabeth Sciaino (201) 652-2350

Ridgewood St Elizabeths Church **P** (988) 169 Fairmount Rd 07450-1422 (Mail to: 169 Fairmount Rd 07450-1422) John Hartnett Maylin Biggadike Joan Conley Catherine Quinn (201) 444-2299

Ringwood Church of the Good Shepherd **M** (78) 80 Margaret King Ave 07456-1703 (Mail to: PO Box 727 07456-0727) (973) 962-9510

Rutherford Grace Episcopal Church **P** (139) 128 W Passaic Ave 07070-1935 (Mail to: 128 W Passaic Ave 07070-1935) Robert Browning (201) 438-8623

Secaucus Church of Our Saviour **M** (150) 191 Flanagan Way 07094-3435 (Mail to: 191 Flanagan Way 07094-3435) Barbara Lewis

(201) 863-1449

Short Hills Christ Episcopal Church **P** (624) 66 Highland Ave 07078-2829 (Mail to: 66 Highland Ave 07078-2829) Timothy Mulder (973) 379-2898

South Orange St Andrew and Holy Communion Church **P** (649) 160 W South Orange Ave 07079-1731 (Mail to: 160 W South Orange Ave 07079-1731) Sandra Wilson Anne Bolles-Beaven (973) 763-2355

Sparta St Marys Episcopal Church **P** (299) 85 Conestoga Trl 07871-2537 (Mail to: 85 Conestoga Trl 07871-2537) Elizabeth Ostuni

Succasunna St Dunstans Church **P** (107) 179 S Hillside Ave 07876-1147 (Mail to: 179 S Hillside Ave 07876-1147) (973) 927-1485

Summit Calvary Church **P** (1339) Attn Dolores Hofmann 31 Woodland Ave 07901-2157 (Mail to: 31 Woodland Ave 07901-2149) Matthew Corkern (908) 277-1814

✠ **Summit** Interweave **Other** 31 Woodland Ave 07901-2157 (Mail to: 31 Woodland Ave 07901-2157) Robert Morris (908) 277-2120

Sussex Church of the Good Shepherd **M** (88) 200 State Rt 23 07461-3100 (Mail to: 200 State Rt 23 07461-3100) Elizabeth Ostuni David Rude (973) 875-0919

Teaneck Christ Church **M** (145) 480 Warwick Ave 07666-2926 (Mail to: 480 Warwick Ave 07666-2926) Ramon Aymerich Michelle White (201) 833-4502

Teaneck St Marks Episcopal Church **P** (504) 118 Chadwick Rd 07666-4204 (Mail to: 118 Chadwick Rd 07666-4282) (201) 836-7275

Tenafly Church of the Atonement **P** (219) 97 Highwood Ave 07670-1834 (Mail to: 97 Highwood Ave 07670-1834) Lynne Weber (201) 568-1763

Towaco Good Shepherd Episcopal Church **P** of Lincoln Park and Montville Twp. 9 Two Bridges Road 07082-1318 (Mail to: 9 Two Bridges Rd 07082-1318) (973) 334-2882

Union City Grace Episcopal Church **P** (100) 3901 Park Ave 07087-6127 (Mail to: 3901 Park Ave 07087-6127) Arthur Fouts Juan Rosario De La Cruz

Union City St Johns Episcopal Church **P** (5) 1514 Palisade Ave 07087-4322 (Mail to: 1516 Palisade Ave 07087-4322) Ellen Barrett (201) 348-3966

Vernon St Thomas Church **M** (209) 307 Rte 94 07462 (Mail to: 307 State Rt 94 07462-3164) Howard Whitaker (973) 764-7506

Verona The Church of the Holy Spirit **P** (141) 36 Gould St 07044-1928 (Mail to: 36 Gould St 07044-1928) Gerard Racioppi (973) 239-2850

Washington St Peters Church **P** (170) 127 Broad St 07882-1801 (Mail to: 127 Broad St 07882-1801) Edward Murphy (908) 689-1019

Wayne St. Michael's Episcopal Church **P** (230) 1219 Ratzer Rd 07470-2310 (Mail to: 1219

Ratzer Rd 07470-2310) Frederick Duncanson Keith Gentry (973) 694-1026

West Orange Church of the Holy Innocents **P** (77) 681 Prospect Ave 07052-3212 (Mail to: 681 Prospect Ave 07052-3212) Anne Bolles-Beaven Trevor Thomas (973) 731-0259

West Orange Church of the Holy Trinity **M** (45) 315 Main St 07052-5630 (Mail to: 315 Main St 07052-5624) Miguel Hernandez

Westwood Grace Episcopal Church **P** (576) 9 Harrington Ave 07675-1801 (Mail to: 9 Harrington Ave 07675-1899) James Delaney (201) 664-0407

Wood Ridge Church of St Paul and Resurrection **P** (123) 483 Center St 07075-2311 (Mail to: 483 Center St 07075-2311) Jacob Nanthicattu Charles Nelson (201) 438-8333

NON-PAROCHIAL CLERGY

Alling FA *ret* Marblehead MA
Andersen RB *ret* Ho Ho Kus NJ
Arlin CN *ret* Long Beach Twp NJ
Austin DA Cambridge MA
Baldwin JA *ret* Millburn NJ
Barrett TL Montclair NJ
Batson LS *dcn* South Orange NJ
Beach DL *ret* Thomaston ME
Bendall RD *ret* Newark NJ
Bennett RD *ret* Jackson NJ
Boccino KR *dcn* Maplewood NJ
Boyle P *ret* Rensselaer NY
Brant GH *ret* Bordentown NJ
Braxton L Teaneck NJ
Brdlik CMF *ret* Newton NJ
Brundige AP Wallingford CT
Byrum EE *ret* Solebury PA
Cabush DW *ret* Morristown NJ
Carlson WD *ret* Somerset NJ
Carroll C Maplewood NJ
Chang MCM *ret* Ajax
Chasse RP *ret* Jersey City NJ
Chrystal SP Short Hills NJ
Clark DD *ret* Montclair NJ
Clarke GAM *ret* Meadowbrook Mews Kingston 19
Curtiss GB *ret* Bradley Beach NJ
David JT *ret* Dayton NJ
Davis OW *ret* Canton NC
Dinsmore VC Succasunna NJ
Dixon RK *ret* Delmar NY
Donnelly F *ret* Southbury CT
Dughi LM
Dure LA Verona NJ
Eberhardt KA *dcn* Lake Hiawatha NJ
Edman EM New York NY
Ellis JF *dcn* Huntington CT
Fox FC *ret* Lake George NY
Gable DL *ret* Pt Jefferson Station NY
Galleher SC *ret* North Bergen NJ
Gambrill JH *ret* York Beach ME
Gannon WS *ret* Bedford NH
Gat MA *ret* Sarasota FL

Glover BF Nyack NY
Groff AK *ret*
Guthrie WA *ret* Haines City FL
Hamilton AW *ret* West Orange NJ
Hamilton DH *ret* Manahawkin NJ
Harper F Hackensack NJ
Harriman BJ *dcn*
Hile JT *dcn* Landing NJ
Hinman AA *ret* Passaic NJ
Hogue RH
Holland JC *ret* Youngsville NC
Holtman KE Chicago IL
Hoogerhyde SM *ret* Mendham NJ
Huck BJ Littleton NC
Jackson P *dcn* Bloomfield NJ
Jacobs GA Newark NJ
Kaeton EMC *ret* Millsboro DE
Karda MR Port Orange FL
Keller CE *ret* Miles City MT
Kern DP *ret* North Eastham MA
Kimmick DW *ret* Raleigh NC
Koehler AE *ret* East Orleans MA
Koeniger MS *ret* Maplewood NJ
Lannon NJ Jersey City NJ
Lantz FW *ret* Mt Pleasant SC
Laws TR *ret* Montclair NJ
Lewis MA Rensselaerville NY
Lewis WE *ret* Montclair NJ
Lincoln TC *ret* Vero Beach FL
Locke KN Summit NJ
Louis RM *ret* Mahwah NJ
MacDonell AH *ret* Hackettstown NJ
Marcantonio J
Matarazzo LR *ret* Belvidere NJ
McCloud CL *dcn*
McGirr JB
McIntosh KL New York NY
Mockridge OA *ret* West Orange NJ
Moore AS Fort Lee NJ
Morgan-Higgins SE *ret* Decatur GA
Neglia DL *ret* Mays Landing NJ
Nelson SL Glen Mills PA
Nicolosi GG London ON
Oh DY Carmichael CA
O'Neill JC *dcn* Tenafly NJ
Packer BJ Mendham NJ
Pae KJ Newark OH
Partridge EB *ret* Sherwood MD
Partridge IH *ret* Cotuit MA
Perez-Vega R Hackettstown NJ
Phelan S Haworth NJ
Pickard JS *ret* Ormond Beach FL
Pisani GA *ret* Apex NC
Polglase KA *ret* Annapolis MD
Powers SF *ret* Claremont CA
Rawson WL *ret* Jasper GA
Reynolds EF Mendham NJ
Rezach KB Maywood NJ
Riker WC *ret* Locust NJ
Riley DN *dcn*
Rollins JA *ret* High Bridge NJ

Salmon JF *ret* Lumberton NJ
Salt AL *ret* Naples FL
Schembs LJ *ret* Westfield NJ
Schjonberg MF Neptune NJ
Schwab AW *ret* Hinesburg VT
Searle SE *ret* New York NY
Shearer DR *ret* Greentown PA
Shearer RL *ret* Fort Lee NJ
Shike CW *ret* Bronx NY
Shuford SC *dcn* Randolph NJ
Sickles CW *ret* Hackettstown NJ
Smith LP *dcn* Madison VA
Smith SH *ret* Madison VA
Soldwedel EG *dcn* Newark NJ
Soucek P
St George D *ret* Old Lyme CT
Stanton JF *ret* North Bay Village FL
Steele RE *dcn* College Park MD
Stopfel BL *ret* Mifflinburg PA
Stout-Kopp RT Mahwah NJ
Strain WH *ret* Boynton Beach FL
Swanson GG *ret* Manset ME

Swetman MO *ret* New Orleans LA
Tarplee C *ret* Key West FL
Taylor DK *ret* Flemington NJ
Thomas DR *ret* Port Hope MI
Tittle DAD *ret* Budd Lake NJ
Tomaine JA *ret* Mountainside NJ
Tuttle MC Maplewood NJ
Van Dine J *dcn*
Vilas FE *ret* Lakewood NJ
Wajnert TA Calistoga CA
Waldon MW *ret* Clifton NJ
Warnke JW Teaneck NJ
Warrington JM *ret* Falls Church VA
Waters SE Budd Lake NJ
Webb FM *ret* Columbia NJ
Wethered SK *ret* Boonton NJ
Williams CD *ret* Newark NJ
Wilson PD *ret* Morristown NJ
Witte WW *ret* Vineyard Haven MA
Won JSH *ret* Norwalk CA
Woodrum LP *ret* Brooklyn NY
Yoon Y

STATE OF NORTH CAROLINA
Dioceses of East Carolina (EC), North Carolina (NC), and Western North Carolina (WNC)

Advance—NC
Ahoskie—EC
Albemarle—NC
Ansonville—NC
Asheboro—NC
Asheville—WNC
Bat Cave—WNC
Bath—EC
Battleboro—NC
Beaufort—EC
Belhaven—EC
Bessemer City—WNC
Black Mtn—WNC
Blowing Rock—WNC
Boone—WNC
Brevard—WNC
Burgaw—EC
Burlington—NC
Burnsville—WNC
Canton—WNC
Cary—NC
Cashiers—WNC
Chapel Hill—NC
Charlotte—NC
Cherokee—WNC
Chocowinity—EC
Clayton—NC
Clemmons—NC
Cleveland—NC
Clinton—EC
Columbia—EC
Concord—NC

Cooleemee—NC
Creswell—EC
Cullowhee—WNC
Currituck—EC
Davidson—NC
Denver—WNC
Durham—NC
Eden—NC
Edenton—EC
Edneyville—WNC
Elizabeth City—EC
Elizabethtown—EC
Elkin—NC
Engelhard—EC
Erwin—NC
Farmville—EC
Fayetteville—EC
Flat Rock—WNC
Fletcher—WNC
Franklin—WNC
Fuquay Varina—NC
Garner—NC
Gastonia—WNC
Gatesville—EC
Glendale Spgs—WNC
Goldsboro—EC
Greensboro—NC
Greenville—EC
Grifton—EC
Hamlet—NC
Hampstead—EC
Havelock—EC

Haw River—NC
Hayesville—WNC
Henderson—NC
Hendersonville—WNC
Hertford—EC
Hickory—WNC
High Pt—NC
Highlands—WNC
Hillsborough—NC
Holly Ridge—EC
Huntersville—NC
Jackson—NC
Jacksonville—EC
Kernersville—NC
Kinston—EC
Laurinburg—NC
Leland—EC
Lenoir—WNC
Lewiston—EC
Lexington—NC
Lincolnton—WNC
Linville—WNC
Little Switzerland—WNC
Littleton—NC
Louisburg—NC
Lumberton—EC
Marion—WNC
Marshall—WNC
Mars Hill—WNC
Matthews—NC
Mayodan—NC

Mills River—WNC
Monroe—NC
Mooresville—NC
Morehead City—EC
Morganton—WNC
Mt Airy—NC
Murphy—WNC
Nags Head—EC
New Bern—EC
Newland—WNC
Newton—WNC
Newton Grove—EC
Oriental—EC
Oxford—NC
Pittsboro—NC
Plymouth—EC
Raleigh—NC
Reidsville—NC
Ridgeway—NC
Roanoke Rapids—NC
Robbinsville—WNC
Rockingham—NC
Rocky Mt—NC
Roper—EC
Roxboro—NC
Rutherfordton—WNC
Salisbury—NC
Salter Path—EC
Saluda—WNC
Sanford—NC
Scotland Neck—NC
Seven Sprs—EC

Shallotte—EC	Statesville—NC	Vanceboro—EC	Whiteville—EC
Shelby—WNC	Sunbury—EC	Wadesboro—NC	Wilkesboro—WNC
Smithfield—NC	Swansboro—EC	Wake Forest—NC	Williamston—EC
Southern Pines—NC	Sylva—WNC	Walnut Cove—NC	Wilmington—EC
Southern Shores—EC	Tarboro—NC	Warrenton—NC	Wilson—NC
Southport—EC	Trenton—EC	Washington—EC	Windsor—EC
Sparta—WNC	Troy—NC	Waxhaw—NC	Winston-Salem—NC
Speed—NC	Tryon—WNC	Waynesville—WNC	
Spruce Pine—WNC	Valle Crucis—WNC	Weldon—NC	

DIOCESE OF NORTH CAROLINA
(PROVINCE IV)
Comprises central North Carolina
DIOCESAN OFFICE 200 W Morgan St Ste 300 Raleigh NC 27601-1338
Tel (919) 834-7474 FAX (919) 834-7546
GREENSBORO OFFICE (Suffragan location): 301 N Elm St Ste 308-C Greensboro NC 27401
Tel (336) 273 5770 FAX (336) 273 9253
E-Mail communications@episdionc.org WEB www.episdionc.org

Previous Bishops—
John S Ravenscroft 1823-30, Levi S Ives 1831-53, Thomas Atkinson 1853-81, Theodore B Lyman coadj 1873 Bp 1881-93, Jos B Cheshire coadj 1893 Bp 1893-1932, Henry B DeLny suffr 1918-28, Edwin A Penick coadj 1922 Bp 1932-59, Richard H Baker coadj 1950 Bp 1959-65, W Moultrie Moore Jr suffr 1967-75, Thomas A Fraser coadj 1960 Bp 1965-83, Frank H Vest Jr suffr 1985-89, Robt W Estill coadj 1980 Bp 1983-94, Huntington Williams Jr suffr 1990-96, Robert C Johnson Jr 1994-2000, J Gary Gloster suffr 1996-2004; Michael B Curry (955) (2000-14)

Bishop Diocesan Pro Tempore —The Rt Rev Anne E Hodges-Copple (1076) (Dio 15 June 2013)

Bishop Assisting – The Rt. Rev. Peter Lee

Cn Admin M Weigert; *Cn for Trans and Pastoral Mins* C Massey; *Reg Cn* R Lee *(South)* E Graham *(Northwest)* vacant *(East); Exec Asst to Bishops* E Dawkins S Kappauf; *Acct* M Gillespie; *Ins Adm* D Warner; *Comm Dir* C McTaggart; *Comm Coord* S Walter; *Lead Yth Miss* B Crow; *Yth Miss* L Aycock A Campbell; *Archdcn* WH Joyner Jr; *Sec* JS Ferrell; *Treas* W Gresham; *Chanc* E Embree; *Hist* B Graebner; *Ecum & Interfaith Off* K Brown; *Lit* D Umphlett; *North Carolina Council of Churches Liaison* J Bullard

Stand Comm—Cler: M Stebbins J Wilson D Umphlett R Black BJ Owens; *Lay:* T Womble J Ferrell Z Smith M Alexander

Diocesan Council—Cler: A Abt M Thompson J Kendall M Saxon B Armstrong J Taylor *Lay:* L Holden J Kutrow GP Macon N Coghill W Mabe R Quackenbush A Freeman J Branch J Fussell

Deans of Convoc—Rocky Mt G Greer; *Raleigh* V Smith; *Durham* B Graebner; *Sandhills* R Foster; *Greensboro* R Miles; *Winston-Salem* D Kinser; *Charlotte* K Brown

Lay Wardens of Convoc—Rocky Mt E Pope; *Raleigh* M Harvey; *Durham* M Gardner-Woods; *Sandhills* R Hyers; *Greensboro* L Seymour; *Winston-Salem* B Morphis; *Charlotte* W Lorenz

Dio Conv: (201st) TBD

PARISHES, MISSIONS, AND CLERGY

Advance Church of the Ascension **M** (67) 183 Fork Bixby Rd 27006-7217 (Mail to: 183 Fork Bixby Rd 27006-7217) Chantal McKinney (336) 998-0857

Albemarle Christ Episcopal Church **P** (152) 428 Pee Dee Ave 28001-4934 (Mail to: PO Box 657 28002-0657) James Bernacki (704) 982-1428

Ansonville All Souls Episcopal Church **M** (6) 52 Highway 52 N 28007-9798 (Mail to: 207 White Store Rd 28170-2657) (704) 694-3223

Asheboro Episcopal Church of the Good Shepherd **P** (243) 505 Mountain Rd 27205-4219 (Mail to: 505 Mountain Rd 27205-4219) Joe Mitchell Douglas Remer (336) 625-5234

Battleboro St Johns Episcopal Church **M** (12) 211 E Main Street 27809 (Mail to: PO Box 577 27809-0577)

Burlington Church of the Holy Comforter **P** (633) 320 East Davis Street 27215 (Mail to: PO Box 1336 27216-1336) Adam Shoemaker Janet Fuller (336) 227-4251

Cary St Pauls Episcopal Church **P** (1065) § 221 Union St 27511-3763 (Mail to: 221 Union St 27511-3763) George Adamik Cathy Deats Jule Holland Candace Snively Antoinette Wike (919) 467-1477

Chapel Hill Church of the Advocate **M** (101) 8410 Merin Road 27516 (Mail to: 8410 Merin Road 27516) Lisa Fischbeck (919) 933-3221

Chapel Hill Church of the Holy Family **P** (800) 200 Hayes Rd 27517-5633 (Mail to: 200 Hayes Rd 27517-5633) Clarke French Sarah Ball-Damberg (919) 942-3108

Chapel Hill The Chapel of the Cross **P** (1863) 304 E Franklin St 27514-3619 (Mail to: 304 E Franklin St 27514-3624) Martha Brimm David Frazelle Victoria Jamieson-Drake William Joyner John Keith Tambria Lee William Morley (919) 929-2193

Charlotte Chapel of Christ the King **M** (35) 425 E 17th St 28206-3407 (Mail to: 425 E 17th St 28206-3407) (704) 334-3097

Charlotte Christ Episcopal Church **P** (4525) § 1412 Providence Rd 28207-2543 (Mail to: 1412 Providence Rd 28207) Henry Edens Martha Hedgpeth Matthew Holcombe John Porter-Acee Elizabeth Saunders Ann Willett (704) 333-0378

Charlotte Church of St Michael & All Angels **M** (59) 750 East 9th Street 28202-3102 (Mail to: PO Box 11318 28220-1318) (704) 399-3151

Charlotte Church of the Holy Comforter **P** (800) 2701 Park Rd 28209-1311 (Mail to: 2701 Park Rd 28209-1357) Kevin Brown Deborah Blackwood Jacob Pierce Amanda Robertson (704) 332-4171

Charlotte St Johns Episcopal Church **P** (2896) 1623 Carmel Rd 28226-5015 (Mail to: 1623 Carmel Rd 28226-5097) Paul Winton Suzanne Cate Nancee Cekuta (704) 366-3034

Charlotte St Martins Episcopal Church **P** (777) 1510 E 7th St 28204-2410 (Mail to: 1510 E 7th St 28204-2410) Joshua Bowron Armand Lavallee Jonathan Soyars (704) 376-8441

Charlotte St Peters Episcopal Church **P** (757) 115 W 7th St 28202-2127 (Mail to: 115 W 7th St 28202-1514) Ollie Rencher Joslyn Schaefer Jonathan Soyars (704) 332-7746

Clayton Grace Episcopal Mission **M** (200) 111 Lee Court 27520 (Mail to: PO Box 752 27528-0752) John Gibson (919) 553-2810

Clemmons St Clements Episcopal Church **P** (217) 3600 Harper Rd 27012-8681 (Mail to: PO Box 1547 27012-1547) Jamie Edwards (336) 766-4323

Cleveland Christ Episcopal Church **P** (108) 3430 Old US Highway 27013-9733 (Mail to: PO Box 37 27013-0037) Sarah Blaies-Diamond

Concord All Saints Episcopal Church **P** (423) 525 Lake Concord Rd NE 28025-2925 (Mail to: 525 Lake Concord Rd NE 28025-2925) Nancy Cox

Cooleemee Church of the Good Shepherd **P** (9) 141 Church St 27014 (Mail to: PO Box 1047 27014-1047) (336) 284-4359

Davidson St Albans Episcopal Church **P** (573) 301 Caldwell Ln 28036 (Mail to: PO Box 970 28036-0970) David Buck Gregory McIntyre Rebecca Yarbrough

Durham Church of St Titus **P** (165) 400 Moline St 27707-2348 (Mail to: 400 Moline St 27707-2348) Stephanie Yancy (919) 682-5504

✠ **Durham** Episcopal Center at Duke University **Other** 505 Alexander Ave 27705-4707 (Mail to: 505 Alexander Ave 27705-4707) (919) 286-0624

Durham Iglesia El Buen Pastor **M** (358) 1852 Liberty St 27703-2271 (Mail to: 1852 Liberty St 27703-2271) Jose Sierra (919) 682-3301

Durham St Josephs Episcopal Church **M** (47) 1902 W Main St 27705-4838 (Mail to: 1902 W Main St 27705-4838) Karen Barfield (919) 286-1064

Durham St Lukes Church **P** (360) 1737 Hillandale Rd 27705-3045 (Mail to: 1737 Hillandale Rd 27705-3045) James Craven Daniel Laird Daniel Reeves Helen Svoboda-Barber (919) 286-2273

Durham St Philips Episcopal Church **P** (1464) 403 E Main St 27701-3719 (Mail to: 403 E Main St 27702) Jill Bullard Sally French Michael Kendall (919) 682-5708

Durham St Stephens Church **P** (582) 82 Kimberly Dr 27707-5446 (Mail to: 82 Kimberly Dr 27707-5446) Robert Kaynor Gail Davis Louane Frey William Shows (919) 493-5451

Eden Church of the Epiphany **P** (149) 538 Henry St 27288-6103 (Mail to: 538 Henry St 27288-6103) Linda Nye (336) 623-9410

Eden St Lukes Episcopal Church **P** (92) 604 Morgan Rd 27288-2526 (Mail to: 600 Morgan Rd 27288) Wheigar Bright (336) 627-4668

Elkin Galloway Memorial Chapel **M** (42) 310 W Main St 28621 (Mail to: PO Box 747 28621-0747) Wanda Brown (336) 526-2172

Erwin St Stephens Episcopal Church **P** (142) 201 Denim Dr 28339 (Mail to: 209 Denim Dr 28339) David Mcguinness (910) 897-5291

Fuquay Varina Trinity Episcopal Church **M** (100) 1128 S Main St 27526-9700 (Mail to: PO Box 821 27526-0821) Roxane Gwyn (919) 552-1056

Garner St Christophers Episcopal Church **M** (80) 1101 Vandora Springs Rd 27529-3746 (Mail to: 1101 Vandora Springs Rd 27529) (919) 772-7125

Greensboro All Saints Church **P** (237) 4211 Wayne Rd 27407-7314 (Mail to: 4211 Wayne Rd 27407-7314) Kenneth Kroohs (336) 299-0705

Greensboro Church of the Holy Spirit **M** (58) 3910 Yanceyville St 27405-3350 (Mail to: 3910 Yanceyville St 27405-3350) Stephen Smith (336) 621-7321

Greensboro Church of the Redeemer **P** (184) 901 E Friendly Ave 27401-3103 (Mail to: 901 E Friendly Ave 27401-3103) Alicia Alexis (336) 275-0033

Greensboro Holy Trinity Episcopal Church **P** (2377) 607 N Greene St 27401-2023 (Mail to: 607 N Greene St 27401-2023) Sarah Carver Virginia Inman Timothy Patterson Susan Sherard (336) 272-6149

Greensboro St Andrews Episcopal Church **P** (765) 2105 W Market St 27403-1718 (Mail to: 2105 W Market St 27403-1799) Bernard Owens Audra Abt Robert Hamilton (336) 275-1651

Greensboro St Barnabas Episcopal Church **M** (241) 1300 Jefferson Rd 27410-3529 (Mail to: 1300 Jefferson Rd 27410-3529) Randall Keeney (336) 294-1282

Greensboro St Francis Episcopal Church **P** (669) 3506 Lawndale Dr 27408-2804 (Mail to: 3506 Lawndale Dr 27408-2804) Milton Williams (336) 288-4721

✣ **Greensboro** St Marys House **Other** (26) 930 Walker Ave 27403-2530 (Mail to: 930 Walker Ave 27403-2530) Kevin Matthews (336) 334-5219

Hamlet All Saints Episcopal Church **M** (63) 217 Henderson St 28345-3311 (Mail to: PO Box 687 28345-0687)

Haw River St Andrews Episcopal Church **M** (65) Route 70 27258 (Mail to: PO Box 1088 27258-1088) Miriam Saxon (336) 578-3623

Henderson Church of the Holy Innocents **P** (361) 210 S Chestnut St 27536-4223 (Mail to: 210 S Chestnut St 27536-4223) Donald Lowery Harrel Johnson

Henderson St James Church **M** (13) 3415 Cameron Dr 27536-3820 (Mail to: PO Box 245 27544-0245) (252) 257-3542

Henderson St Johns Episcopal Church **M** (28) N Church & Main Sts 27536 (Mail to: PO Box 974 27536-0974) (252) 492-0082

High Point St Christophers Episcopal Church **P** (192) Corner of Eastchester & High 27262 (Mail to: 303 Chester Dr 27265-7547) Barbara Cooke (336) 869-5311

High Point St Marys Episcopal Church **P** (794) 108 W Farriss Ave 27262-3008 (Mail to: 108 W Farriss Ave 27262-3099) David Umphlett Nathan Finnin Sara Palmer (336) 886-4756

Hillsborough St Matthews Parish Church **P** (389) 210 Saint Marys Rd 27278-2518 (Mail to: PO Box 628 27278-0628) Norman Graebner Carl Edwards Lisa Frost-Phillips Jean Vail (919) 732-9308

Huntersville St Marks Episcopal Church **P** (461) 8600 Mount Holly Hntrsvlle Rd 28078-8475 (Mail to: 8600 Mt Holly-Huntersville Rd 28078-8475) Sarah Hollar Foss Smithdeal

Jackson The Church of The Saviour **M** (54) Calhoun & Church Sts 27845 (Mail to: PO Box 613 27845-0613) (919) 534-0911

Kernersville St Matthews Episcopal Church **M** (103) 1110 Salisbury St 27284-3302 (Mail to: PO Box 1173 27285-1173) Frances Cox (336) 996-4422

Laurinburg St Davids Episcopal Church **Cluster** (50) Covington & Azure 28353 (Mail to: PO Box 334 28353-0334) Kara Slade (919) 276-1757

Lexington Grace Episcopal Church **P** (280) 419 S Main St 27292-3234 (Mail to: 419 S

Main St 27292-3234) Mark Plummer Bonnie Duckworth Bonnie Duckworth (336) 249-7211

Littleton St Alban Episcopal Church **M** (40) 300 Mosby Avenue 27850-0955 (Mail to: PO Box 955 27850-0117) Beverly Huck (252) 586-4700

Louisburg St Matthias Episcopal Church **M** (10) Attn Miss Mary L Hill Treas 102 Harris St 27549-2722 (Mail to: 907 George Leonard Rd 27549-7190) (919) 853-2278

Louisburg St Pauls Episcopal Church **M** (74) 301 North Church Street 27549-2417 (Mail to: PO Box 247 27549-0247) Lauren Winner (919) 496-4180

Matthews Thompson Child and Family Focus **P** 6800 Saint Peters Ln 28105 (Mail to: 6800 Saint Peters Ln 28105-8458) (704) 536-0375

Mayodan Church of the Messiah **M** (46) 114 S 2nd Ave 27027-2712 (Mail to: 114 S 2nd Ave 27027-2712) Robert Rachal (336) 548-2801

Monroe St Paul's Episcopal Church **P** (217) 116 S Church St 28112-5605 (Mail to: PO Box 293 28111-0293) Bradford Smith (704) 289-8434

Mooresville Saint Patrick's Episcopal Church **P** (476) 164 Fairview Rd 28117-9512 (Mail to: PO Box 1491 28115-1491) Mark Forbes Sally Brower (704) 663-5659

Mooresville St James Episcopal Church **M** (47) 851 Shinnville Rd 28115-7111 (Mail to: 851 Shinnville Rd 28115-7111) (704) 664-7115

Mount Airy Trinity Episcopal Church **P** (259) 472 N Main St # 1043 27030-3814 (Mail to: PO Box 1043 27030-1043) Raymond Hanna (336) 786-6067

Oxford St Cyprians Episcopal Church **M** (98) 408 Granville St 27565-3673 (Mail to: PO Box 2337 27565-2337) Harriette Sturges (919) 693-1351

Oxford St Stephens Episcopal Church **P** (207) 140 College St 27565-2947 (Mail to: 140 College St 27565-2947) James Pahl (919) 693-9740

Pittsboro St Bartholomews Episcopal Church **P** (216) 204 W Salisbury St 27312-9483 (Mail to: 204 W Salisbury St 27312-9483) Wilberforce Mundia (919) 542-5679

Raleigh Christ Episcopal Church **P** (2923) 120 E Edenton St 27601-1014 (Mail to: PO Box 25778 27611-5778) James Adams Jennifer Brown Margaret Hunn Callie Swanlund (919) 834-6259

Raleigh Church of the Good Shepherd **P** (1485) 121 Hillsborough St 27603-1762 (Mail to: 121 Hillsborough St 27603-1762) William Bennett Robert Sawyer Miriam Saxon (919) 831-2000

Raleigh Church of the Nativity **P** (542) 8849 Ray Rd 27613-1232 (Mail to: 8849 Ray Rd 27613-1232) Stephanie Allen Nancy Allison Ann Burts George Clifford (919) 846-8338

Raleigh NC State Campus Ministry **P** 2208 Hope St 27607-7334 (Mail to: 2208 Hope St 27607-7334) Deborah Fox Nancy Titus (919) 834-2428

Raleigh St Ambrose Episcopal Church **P** (374) 813 Darby St 27610-4017 (Mail to: 813 Darby

St 27610-4017) Nita Byrd Robert Taylor (919) 833-8055

Raleigh St Augustines Chapel **P** (8) 1315 Oakwood Ave 27610-2247 (Mail to: 1315 Oakwood Ave 27610-2298) (919) 516-4000

Raleigh St Marks Episcopal Church **P** (461) 1725 N New Hope Rd 27604-8304 (Mail to: 1725 N New Hope Rd 27604-8304) Margaret Ljunggren John Wall (919) 231-6767

Raleigh St Marys School Chapel **School** 900 Hillsborough St 27603-1610 (Mail to: 900 Hillsborough St 27603-1689) Ann Bonner-Stewart (919) 424-4122

Raleigh St Michaels Episcopal Church **P** (1885) 1520 Canterbury Rd 27608-1106 (Mail to: 1520 Canterbury Rd 27608-1197) Samuel Jones Richard Callaway Meta Ellington Holly Gloff Jane Gurry Christopher Hogin (919) 782-0731

Raleigh St Timothys Church **P** (816) 4523 Six Forks Rd 27609-5709 (Mail to: PO Box 17787 27619-7787) Jay James Henry Presler (919) 787-7590

Reidsville St Thomas Episcopal Church **P** (167) 315 Lindsey St 27320-3649 (Mail to: PO Box 72 27323) Richard Miles (336) 349-3511

Ridgeway Chapel of the Good Shepherd **M** (4) 1202 Ridgeway-Warrenton Road 27570-0070 (Mail to: PO Box 70 27570-0070) (252) 456-2412

Roanoke Rapids All Saints Episcopal Church **P** (224) 635 Hamilton Street 27870-2703 (Mail to: 635 Hamilton St 27870-2703) (252) 537-3610

Roanoke Rapids St Mark Episcopal Church **P** (19) C/O Senior Warden PO Box 234 27870-0234 (Mail to: PO Box 234 27870-0234) Ben Duffey (252) 537-8835

Rockingham Church of the Messiah **P** (19) 202 N Lawrence St 28379-3668 (Mail to: PO Box 1313 28380-1313)

Rocky Mount Church of the Epiphany **M** (11) 500 N Fairview Rd 27801 (Mail to: PO Box 1471 27802-1471) (252) 442-7516

Rocky Mount Church of the Good Shepherd **P** (496) 231 N Church St 27804-5404 (Mail to: 231 N Church St 27804-5404) Louise Anderson Matthew Johnson (252) 442-1134

Rocky Mount St Andrews Episcopal Church **P** (493) 301 S Circle Dr 27804-3613 (Mail to: 301 S Circle Dr 27804-3613) George Greer (252) 443-2070

Roxboro St Marks Episcopal Church **M** (66) 422 N Main St 27573-5037 (Mail to: PO Box 1071 27573-1071) (336) 597-2171

Salisbury St Lukes Episcopal Church **P** (589) 131 W Council St 28144-4320 (Mail to: 131 W Council St 28144-4320) Robert Black (704) 633-3221

Salisbury St Matthew Episcopal Church **M** (54) 4401 Statesville Blvd 28147-7463 (Mail to: 4401 Statesville Blvd 28147-7463) (704) 636-0821

Salisbury St Pauls Church **M** (44) 930 S Main St 28144-6453 (Mail to: PO Box 1852 28145-1852) (704) 637-9404

Sanford St Thomas Episcopal Church **P** (402) 312 N Steele St 27330-3922 (Mail to: 312 N Steele St 27330-3922) Melanie Mudge (919) 774-8644

Scotland Neck Trinity Episcopal Church **P** (37) 1305 Main St 27874-1346 (Mail to: PO Box 372 27874-0372) Elmer Malone John Fulton (252) 826-4616

Smithfield San Jose Mission **M** (120) 218 South Second St 27577 (Mail to: 218 S 2nd St 27577-4532) (910) 989-9742

Smithfield St Paul's Episcopal Church **P** (245) 218 S 2nd St 27577-4532 (Mail to: 218 S 2nd St 27577-4532) James Melnyk (919) 934-2675

Southern Pines Emmanuel Parish Episcopal Church **P** (745) 340 S Ridge St 28387-6036 (Mail to: 340 S Ridge St 28387-6036) Randal Foster John Talk (910) 692-3171

Southern Pines Transfiguration (Penick Village) **Chapel** Rhode Island Ave Extension 28387 (Mail to: PO Box 2001 28388-2001) (910) 692-0355

Speed St Marys Episcopal Church **M** (41) 169 Kilquick Rd 27886 (Mail to: 108 Mill Pond Rd 27843-9785) (252) 903-3555

Statesville Trinity Episcopal Church **P** (271) 801 Henkel Rd 28677-3215 (Mail to: PO Box 1103 28687-1103) Robert Mullis

Tarboro Calvary Episcopal Church **P** (332) 411 E Church St 27886-4403 (Mail to: PO Box 1245 27886-1245) Velinda Hardy Jane Wilson (252) 823-8192

Tarboro St Luke Episcopal Church **M** (24) PO Box 64 27886-0064 (Mail to: PO Box 64 27886-0064) Jane Wilson Louise Anderson (252) 641-5853

Tarboro St Michael Episcopal Church **M** (114) 3204 Western Blvd 27886 (Mail to: PO Box 331 27886-0331) (252) 823-4926

Troy St Mary Magdalene Episcopal Church **M** (58) PO Box 613 27371-0613 (Mail to: PO Box 456 27376-0456) Robert Brown Carol Burgess Fred Thompson (910) 673-3838

Wadesboro Calvary Episcopal Church **P** (149) 223 E Morgan St 28170-2222 (Mail to: PO Box 942 28170-0942) (704) 694-3223

Wake Forest St Johns Episcopal Church **P** (767) 830 Durham Rd 27587-8792 (Mail to: 834 Durham Road 27587) John Linscott Margaret Silton Vicki Smith (919) 556-3656

Walnut Cove Christ Church **P** (52) 412 Summit Ave. 27052-0476 (Mail to: PO Box 476 27052-0476) (336) 591 7727

Warrenton All Saints Episcopal Church **M** (5) Front And Franklin Sts 27589 (Mail to: PO Box 578 27589-0578) (252) 257-9194

Warrenton Emmanuel Episcopal Church **M** (57) 133 N Main St 27589-1921 (Mail to: PO Box 704 27589-0704) (252) 257-2557

Waxhaw St Margarets Episcopal Church **P** (796) 8515 Rea Rd 28173-6801 (Mail to: 8515 Rea Rd 28173-6801) Suzanne Bruno Todd Dill Elenito Santos (704) 243-3523

Weldon Grace Episcopal Church **P** (26) Washington Ave & 5th St 27890 (252) 536-4312

Wilson La Iglesia de la Guadalupana **M** (974) 106 Reid St SE 27893-6230 (Mail to: PO Box 4032 27893-0032) (252) 206-9996

Wilson St Marks Episcopal Church **M** (91) C/O Louie Tabron 2404 Nash St N 27896-1309 (Mail to: PO Box 4405 27893-0405) Philip Byrum (252) 291-6076

Wilson St Timothys Church **P** (641) 202 N Goldsboro Street 27893 (Mail to: PO Box 1527 27894-1527) Martha Stebbins Robert Thomas (252) 291-8220

Winston Salem St Annes Episcopal Church **P** (377) 2690 Fairlawn Dr 27106-3802 (Mail to: PO Box 11437 27116) Lawrence Womack (336) 768-0174

Winston Salem St Pauls Episcopal Church **P** (2876) 520 Summit St 27101-1115 (Mail to: 520 Summit St 27101-1195) Sara Ardrey-Graves Darby Everhard David Kinser Lauren Villemuer-Drenth (336) 723-4391

Winston Salem St Stephen Episcopal Church **P** (119) 810 Highland Ave 27101-4209 (Mail to: 810 N Highland Ave 27101-4209) Hector Sintim (336) 724-2614

Winston Salem St Timothys Episcopal Church **P** (1058) 2575 Parkway Dr 27103-3522 (Mail to: 2575 Parkway Dr 27103-3522) Steven Rice Mary Kroohs (336) 765-0294

NON-PAROCHIAL CLERGY

Aiken W *ret* Eden NC
Armstrong BK *ret dcn* Apex NC
Aycock MB *ret* Albemarle NC
Backus HG *ret* Laurel DE
Bailey DM *ret*
Bailey EP *ret* Southern Pines NC
Bandy TG *dcn* Whispering Pines NC
Barker CD *dcn* Statesville NC
Barwick FE *dcn* Roxboro NC
Battle M Raleigh NC
Benz CF Durham NC
Bergstrom FM *ret* Umina Beach NSW NC
Bland LR *dcn* Greensboro NC
Bland TJ *dcn* Greensboro NC
Boyd JW Charlotte NC
Bradshaw MR *dcn* Winston Salem NC
Broome JT *ret* Greensboro NC
Brown DA *ret* Grovetown GA
Browne FL *dcn* High Point NC
Bruce CJ *ret* Chapel Hill NC
Burgess BC Clemmons NC
Busch GE *ret* Lynchburg VA
Bye M *ret* Wadesboro NC
Cahoon VJ *dcn* Albemarle NC

Caimano CA Raleigh NC
Charles WB *ret* Raleigh NC
Clarkson JC *ret* Charlotte NC
Coles CC *ret* Raleigh NC
Connelly CR *ret* Charlotte NC
Cook RB *ret* Browns Summit NC
Coolidge WMC *ret* Asheville NC
Cooper GH *ret* Charleston SC
Coram JM *ret* Woodbridge VA
Corlett DB *ret* Raleigh NC
Cox EM *ret* Greensboro NC
Crabtree DR *dcn*
Cross ES *ret* Winston Salem NC
Cummings SR *ret* Tallahassee FL
Cunningham JC
Curtis MP *ret* Southern Pines NC
Cushing NCM *dcn* Durham NC
Davis CM *dcn* Charlotte NC
Davis-Shoemaker CE Burlington NC
Dowling-Sendor E Chapel Hill NC
Droppers T *ret* Greensboro NC
Durant JD *dcn* Raleigh NC
Earle PAT *ret* Statesville NC
Eastman SG Hurdle Mills NC
Ehrich TL *ret* New York NY
Elkins-Williams SJ *ret* Chapel Hill NC
Ely EW *ret* Columbus NC
Feamster TO *ret* Tavares FL
Finnerud MA Greenwich CT
Fisher JW *ret* Wake Forest NC
Fleischer MM *ret* Raleigh NC
Franklin JD Wilmington NC
Frazier SK *ret* Durham NC
Freeman M *ret* Smyrna GA
Georgi GM Rougemont NC
Gilmer LW *ret*
Going VL *dcn* Raleigh NC
Goodheart DP *ret* Satellite Beach FL
Graham EN Suffolk VA
Grant EW *dcn* Chapel Hill NC
Green RP *ret* Boone NC
Haden RL *ret* Hendersonville NC
Harbold SL *ret* Cary NC
Hawes CM *ret* Greensboro NC
Haynes RF *ret* Davidson NC
Hayworth JA *ret* High Point NC
Henry GK *ret* Brevard NC
Herring VN *ret* Greensboro NC
Hilsabeck PH *ret* Durham NC
Hocking CE *ret* Hampstead NC
Hodges DB Winston Salem NC
Hodgkins NB *ret* Pilot Mountain NC
Holder LR New York NY
Holm MH Roanoke Rapids NC
Holmes JVF *dcn* Charlotte NC
Holmes RE *ret* Charlotte NC
Horton FL Winston Salem NC
Howard NB Tarboro NC
Huacani AJ Durham NC
Hudson KK *dcn*
Humphreys EL *dcn* Charlotte NC

Hunn MC Raleigh NC
Jenner HML *dcn* Clayton NC
Jennings WW *ret* Garner NC
Johnson JB *dcn* Winston Salem NC
Johnson KAB *dcn* Durham NC
Joiner JM Portland OR
Jones DH *dcn*
Jones RM *ret* Greensboro NC
Kebba EMB *ret* Greensboro NC
Kerr WV *ret* Charlotte NC
Kilbourn LM Cary NC
King TE Moore OK
Kirkpatrick NE Chapel Hill NC
Lamb JM *dcn* Durham NC
Langston MG Erwin NC
Lasley JD
Lawrence BB Durham NC
Lee RM Durham NC
Lindenberg JT Rocky Mount NC
Lister CJ *ret* Sanford NC
Lynch WD *dcn* Raleigh NC
Maddox WE *ret* Durham NC
Magoon GA *ret* Centennial CO
Marchl WH *ret* Smithfield NC
Mason SA *ret*
McCarthy MF *ret* Charlotte NC
McKee ES *dcn* Greensboro NC
Menjivar N *ret* Durham NC
Mitchell MD *dcn* Washington Depot CT
Moore AL *dcn* Raleigh NC
Morales CO *ret* Greensboro NC
Morales ER *dcn* High Point NC
Morrison PC *ret* Phoenix AZ
Moulden MM *ret* Greenborough NC
Oakes LK *ret* Madison WI
Oats L *ret* Dandridge TN
Ogburn JN *dcn* Asheboro NC
Oglesby CL *dcn* Cary NC
Paschall FW *ret* Charlotte NC
Patterson WB *ret* Sewanee TN
Payne-Wiens RA Austin TX
Pendleton WB *dcn* Winston Salem NC
Pfaff RW Chapel Hill NC
Phillips WR *ret* Charlotte NC
Pilcher WE *ret* Mount Airy NC
Pinkston FW Charlotte NC
Pittman DW *ret* Inman SC
Pittman WL *ret* Greensboro NC

Platt-Hendren BM *ret* Clayton NC
Pogoloff SM *ret* Durham NC
Poulos GW *ret* Greensboro NC
Powell WL *ret* Moncure NC
Prevatt JT *ret* Greensboro NC
Rachal PC Greensboro NC
Rea RA San Francisco CA
Reardin LA *ret* Cary NC
Reeve KJ *ret* Raleigh NC
Reinecke RL *ret* Burlington NC
Schelb HG *dcn* Winston Salem NC
Schneider GA *dcn* Beloit WI
Scott EC Concord NC
Settles RL *dcn* Charlotte NC
Sherrill J *dcn*
Shields JE *ret* Winston Salem NC
Shoemaker PRP *dcn* Lexington NC
Short MMG Sewanee TN
Simpson SOK *dcn* Raleigh NC
Smith HL Durham NC
Smith LM *ret*
Smith LL *ret* Roanoke VA
Smith MM New Haven CT
Smith RB *ret* Greensboro NC
Smyth WE Columbia NC
Spencer LP *ret* Greensboro NC
Steber GD *ret* Davidson NC
Stewart JM Nichols Hills OK
Tabor HCC Oxford NC
Taylor RG *ret* Pemaquid ME
Thompson MK *ret* Williamsburg VA
Thullbery MF Durham NC
Tilson HA *dcn* Chapel Hill NC
Tola EM *dcn*
Umeofia CC Goldsboro NC
Vaders NJ *dcn* Winston Salem NC
Walker TC *ret* Raleigh NC
Wall DS
Warnecke FJ *ret* Greensboro NC
Warren HA Earlysville VA
Watrous JC *ret* Raleigh NC
Webster TH *ret* Wilson NC
Whitesell HA *ret* Lebanon OH
Wiehe PF *ret* Hendersonville NC
Williams DR *ret* Elon NC
Williams RA *ret* Salisbury NC
Woodard SW *dcn* Durham NC
Zumpf MJ *ret* Eden NC

DIOCESE OF NORTH DAKOTA
(PROVINCE VI)
Comprises the State of North Dakota and Clay County, Minnesota
DIOCESAN OFFICE 3600 South 25th St Fargo ND 58104-6861
TEL (701) 235-6688   FAX (701) 232-3077
WEB http://www.ndepiscopal.org/

Previous Bishops—
Wm D Walker 1883-96, Samuel C
Edsall 1899-1901, Cameron Mann
1901-13, John P Tyler 1914-31, Fredk
B Bartlett 1931-35, Douglass H Atwill
1937-51, Richard R Emery 1951-64,
George T Masuda 1965-79, Harold
A Hopkins Jr 1980-88 Andrew H
Fairfield 1989-2003

Bishop—The Rt Rev Michael G Smith (998)
(Dio 18 May 04)

Conv Sec J Helgaas; *Treas* C Peterson; *Chanc* K
Venhuizen; *Dio Admin* L Woltjer; *Indian Work* C
Goodhouse; *Fin* vacant; *ER&D* C Robbins and E
Morlan; *Evang Off* vacant; *UTO* P Fearing and O
Henley

Stand Comm—Cler: Pres B Davis D Fox J Shannon;
Lay: C Goodhouse D Henderson C Iverson

Dio Conv: 14-15 Oct 2016 Bismarck ND

PARISHES, MISSIONS, AND CLERGY
Bismarck St George Episcopal Church **P** (325)
601 N 4th St 58501-3685 (Mail to: PO Box 1241
58502-1241) Zanne Ness Jane Towne James
Zotalis (701) 223-1942
Cartwright St Michael & All Angels Church **P**
(47) 14 Route 1 Box Box 58838 (Mail to: 3032
160th Ave NW 59221-9346) (701) 572-9278
Devils Lake Episcopal Church of the Advent **P**
(24) 501 6th St NE 58301-2523 (Mail to: PO
Box 703 58301-0703) (701) 662-3726
Dickinson St Johns Episcopal Church **P** (27) 822
5th Ave W 58601-3832 (Mail to: PO Box 48
58602-0048) (701) 225-5026
Dunseith St Sylvans Church **P** (77) 1025 61st Ave
NW 58329 (Mail to: PO Box 159 58329-0159)
(701) 891-2911
✠ **Fargo** Gethsemane Cathedral **O** (371) No 3600
25th St S 58104-6861 (Mail to: 3600 25th St S
58104-6861) Mary Gokey Charlotte Robbins
Glenn Williams (701) 232-3394
Fargo St Stephens Episcopal Church **P** (153) 120
21st Ave N 58102-2015 (Mail to: 120 21st Ave
N 58102-2015) Jamie Parsley (701) 232-2076
Fort Totten St Thomas Church **P** (119) PO Box 43
58335-0043 (Mail to: General Delivery 58335-
9999) (701) 766-4630
Fort Yates St James Episcopal Church **P** (122)
General Delivery 58538-9999 (Mail to: PO Box
612 58538-0612) Neil Two Bears (701) 854-7425
Fort Yates St Lukes Church **P** (297) 501 S River
Rd 58538 (Mail to: 820 W Central Ave 58501)

Lindsey Dwarf Sloane Floberg Virginia Luger
Neil Two Bears (701) 854-2323
Garrison St Pauls Church **P** (86) 1025 61st Ave
NW 58540-9384 (Mail to: 1025B 61st Ave NW
58540-9384)
Grand Forks St Pauls Episcopal Church **P** (202)
319 S 5th St 58201-4607 (Mail to: 319 S 5th St
58201-4607) James Shannon (701) 775-7955
Jamestown Grace Episcopal Church **P** (135) 405
2nd Ave NE 58401-3308 (Mail to: 405 2nd Ave
NE 58401-3308) Christian Senyoni (701) 252-
4499
Minot All Saints' Episcopal Church **P** (58) 301
Main St S 58701-3917 (Mail to: 301 S Main St
58701-3917) Mary Johnson (701) 839-1037
Moorhead St John the Divine Episcopal Church **P**
(265) 120 8th St S 56560-2809 (Mail to: 120 8th
St S 56560-2809) (218) 233-0423
Oakes St Mary and St Mark Epis Church **M** (26)
211 N 6th St 58474-1218 (Mail to: 224 S 8th St
58474-1701) (701) 742-2213
Selfridge Church of the Cross **P** (29) Main St
58568 (Mail to: Box 73 58568-0073) John
Floberg (701) 891-2911
Valley City All Saints Episcopal Church **P** (19)
516 Central Ave N 58072-2544 (Mail to: PO
Box 366 58072-0366) (701) 845-0819
Walhalla St Peters Church **P** 508 Delano Ave
58282 (Mail to: PO Box 704 58282-0704) Elsie
Magnus
Williston St Peters Episcopal Church **P** (96) 111
East 14th Street 58802-1181 (Mail to: PO Box
1181 58802-1181) Michael Paul (701) 572-
9278

NON-PAROCHIAL CLERGY
Anderson AJ Fargo ND
Baggett HK Bismarck ND
Broadhead AJ *ret* Lansdale PA
Christensen BM *dcn* Sarasota FL
Coomber MJM
Cowardin EB Jamestown ND
Davis JB Jamestown ND
Edward GM *dcn* Moorhead MN
Fox WD *ret* Garrison ND
Goodrich K Jamestown ND
Henderson HG Wahpeton ND
Henley CW *ret* Valley City ND
Horn MJ *ret* Scottsdale AZ
Hylden JL Saint Louis MO
Johnson WK Bismarck ND
Keehn RP
Kenyi AL *ret* San Diego CA
Lander BT *dcn* Grand Forks ND

Leroux DF *dcn* Grand Forks ND
Lipp BA *dcn* Bismarck ND
Luntsford SL Alexander ND
Mathew C
Mauai BL *dcn* Sioux Falls SD
Pettitt RR Fargo ND
Richards EK Minot ND
Schulenberg GW *ret* Fergus Falls MN
Slanger GC Lakeville MN

Smythe SL *dcn* Minot ND
Starkweather B Merced CA
Walters DM *dcn* Fort Yates ND
Whitehead DR Devils Lake ND
Whitnah JC Fargo ND
Williams MR
Wolfe A
Yeager AE *dcn* Minot ND
Zaharia PM Minot ND

DIOCESE OF NORTHERN CALIFORNIA
(PROVINCE VIII)
Comprises the northern third of the State of California
DIOCESAN OFFICE 350 University Avenue, Ste 280, Sacramento CA 95825
TEL (916) 442-6918   FAX (916) 442-6927
E-MAIL info@norcalepiscopal.org   WEB www.norcalepiscopal.org

Previous Bishops—
John HD Wingfield 1874-98; William
H. Moreland m 1899 Bp 1910-33;
Archie WN Porter coadj 1933 Bp
1933-57; Edward McNair suffr 1967-
73; Clarence R. Haden coadj 1957
Bp 1958-78; John L. Thompson III
1978-91; Jerry A. Lamb coadj 1991
Bp 1992-2006; Barry L. Beisner coadj
2006 Bp 2006

Bishop—Rt. Rev Barry Leigh Beisner (1008)
(Dio Sep 2006)

Sec Conv Rev E Armstrong; *Cn to Ord* Rev. Canon
A McMillin; *Treas* C Chapman; *Chanc* C Mack; *Dir
of Fin & Admin* L Bruno; *Board of Trustees* Rt Rev
B Beisner; *Commission on Min* R Simas; *Cong Dev*
Very Rev C Haggenjos; *Christian Form Chairs* Rev R
Davis A Clarke; *Lit & Music* Very Rev L Holben; *Epis
Comm Serv* Rev L Jevne; *Health Min* S Wahlstrom;
Companion Diocese Rev E Howell; *MDGs* Rev
L Jevne; *ERD* J Snibbe; *Chap to Ret Clergy* Rev J
Schively

Stand Comm—Pres J Sargent *Cler: Sec* E Armstrong
S Carpenter C Haggenjos E Lewis *Lay:* R Frie C Hill
L Maxwell

Diocesan Conv: 3-5 Nov 2016 – Sacramento, CA

PARISHES, MISSIONS, AND CLERGY

Alturas St Michaels Episcopal Church **M** (27) 310
W North St 96101 (Mail to: 310 W North St
96101) David Cohen James Young (530) 233-
2251

Anderson St Michaels Episcopal Church **P** (82)
3001 Rupert Rd 96007-3746 (Mail to: PO Box
144 96007-0144) Royston Auelua (530) 365-
4344

Antelope St Andrews in the Highlands Mssn **M**
(56) 7850 Watt Ave 95843-2001 (Mail to: 7850

Watt Ave 95843-2001) Peter Rodgers Diana
Turner (916) 332-1476

Arcata St Albans Episcopal Church **P** (257) 1675
Chester Ave 95521-6827 (Mail to: 1675 Chester
Ave 95521-6827) Sara Potter Nancy Streufert
(707) 822-4102

Auburn St Lukes Church **P** (193) 124 Orange St
95603-5233 (Mail to: 124 Orange St 95603-
5233) Brian Rebholtz

Benicia St Pauls Episcopal Church **P** (281) 120 E J
St 94510-3235 (Mail to: 120 E J St 94510-3298)
Phyllis Forte Arthur Holder (707) 745-0307

Calistoga St Lukes Episcopal Church **M** (94) 1504
Myrtle St 94515-1633 (Mail to: PO Box 381
94515-0381) Mary Goshert (707) 942-6007

Cameron Park Faith Episcopal Church **P** (523)
2200 Country Club Dr 95682-7703 (Mail to:
2200 Country Club Dr 95682-7703) Sean Cox
Andrea Baker (530) 676-5348

Carmichael St Georges Church **P** (82) 5600
Winding Way 95608-1213 (Mail to: 5600
Winding Way 95608-1213) Robert Gould
Raymond Hess Robert Olsen (916) 487-5600

Carmichael St Michaels Episcopal Church **P**
(678) 2140 Mission Ave 95608-5635 (Mail to:
2140 Mission Ave 95608-5699) Mary Hudak
Rodney Davis George Foxworth Cynthia Long
(916) 488-3550

Chico St John the Evangelist Church **P** (325) 2341
Floral Ave 95926-7311 (Mail to: 2341 Floral
Ave 95926-7311) Richard Yale (530) 894-1971

Cloverdale Good Shepherd Episcopal Church **M**
(38) 122 N Main St 95425-3346 (Mail to: PO
Box 337 95425-0337) Edward Howell (707)
891-6015

Colusa St Stephens Episcopal Church **P** (49)
642 5th St 95932-2611 (Mail to: PO Box 1044
95932-1044) John Vafis (530) 458-2470

Corning St Andrew Episcopal Church **M** (14)
820 Marin St 96021-3230 (Mail to: PO Box 276
96021-0276) (530) 680-0353

Crescent City St Pauls Episcopal Church **M** (69) 220 E Macken Ave 95531-2745 (Mail to: 220 E Macken Ave 95531-2745) David Shewmaker (707) 464-2708

Davis Church of St Martin **P** (559) 640 Hawthorne Ln 95616-3463 (Mail to: 640 Hawthorn Lane 95616-3463) Mark Allen Anne Beatty Margaret Grayden Ernest Lewis (530) 756-0444

Eureka Christ Episcopal Church **P** (194) 625 15th St 95501-2328 (Mail to: PO Box 861 95502-0861) Susan Armstrong Nancy Streufert (707) 442-1797

Fair Oaks St Francis Episcopal Church **P** (143) 11430 Fair Oaks Blvd 95628-5157 (Mail to: 11430 Fair Oaks Blvd 95628-5157) Aileen Aidnik Joseph Duggan Raymond Hess Diana Lueckert (916) 966-2261

Fairfield Grace Episcopal Church **P** (352) 1405 Kentucky St 94533-4715 (Mail to: 1405 Kentucky St 94533-4715) David Cavanagh Perry Polk (707) 425-4481

Ferndale St Mary Episcopal Church **M** (6) 400 Shaw Ave 95536 (Mail to: PO Box 366 95536-0366) (707) 786-9843

Folsom Trinity Episcopal Church **P** (374) 803 Figueroa St 95630-2404 (Mail to: 801 Figueroa St 95630-2404) Jason Bruce Thomas Johnson (916) 985-2495

Fort Bragg St Michael & All Angels Parish **P** (72) 201 Fir St 95437-3110 (Mail to: PO Box 124 95437-0124) Tansy Chapman Randy Knutson Blake Leighton (707) 964-1900

Fortuna St Francis Episcopal Church **M** (130) 568 16th St 95540-2415 (Mail to: 568 16th St 95540-2415) Kathleen McCloghrie (707) 725-4686

Galt St Lukes Episcopal Church **M** (78) 200 Third St 95632 (Mail to: PO Box 897 95632-0897) Barbara Nixon (209) 745-2784

Grass Valley Emmanuel Episcopal Church **P** (415) 235 S Church St 95945-6703 (Mail to: 235 S Church St 95945-6793) Alan Kellermann Anne Powell Lewis Powell (530) 273-7876

Gridley St Timothys Episcopal Church **M** (87) 410 Jackson St 95948-2513 (Mail to: PO Box 176 95948-0176) (530) 846-4147

Gualala Shepherd by the Sea MIssion **M** (62) 39141 Church Street 95445 (Mail to: PO Box 691 95445-0691) James Knutsen (707) 785-3682

Healdsburg St Pauls Episcopal Church **P** (294) 209 Matheson St 95448-4109 (Mail to: 209 Matheson St 95448-4109) Sally Hubbell (707) 433-2107

Kenwood St Patricks Episcopal Church **P** (378) 9000 Sonoma Hwy 95452-9028 (Mail to: PO Box 247 95452-0247) Jennifer Hornbeck George Hunt Clifford Kent Karen King Leslie King (707) 833-4228

Lake Almanor Holy Spirit Mission **M** (11) 3767 Hwy A 13 96137 (Mail to: 3767 State Route A13 96137-9700) John Palmer Matthew Warren (530) 375-0994

Lakeport St Johns Episcopal Church **P** (82) 1190 N Forbes St 95453-3824 (Mail to: 1190 N Forbes St 95453-3824) (707) 263-4785

Lincoln St James Episcopal Church **P** (122) 479 L St 95648-1633 (Mail to: 490 K St 95648-1627) William Rontani Richard Henry (916) 645-1739

Marysville St Johns Episcopal Church **P** (86) 800 D St 95901-5321 (Mail to: 800 D St 95901-5321) Sara Aseltine John Mangels (530) 742-8829

Monte Rio St Andrews in the Redwoods **M** 20329 Highway 116 95462-9747 (Mail to: PO Box 721 95462-0721) Pamela Moore (707) 865-0834

Mount Shasta St Barnabas **M** (95) 701 Lassen Ln 96067-9711 (Mail to: 701 Lassen Ln 96067-9711) Lawrence Holben George Ridgway (530) 926-5326

Napa St Marys Episcopal Church **P** (391) 1917 Third St 94558 (Mail to: 1917 3rd St 94559-2312) Stephen Carpenter John Morris (707) 255-0991

Nevada City Holy Trinity Episcopal Church **P** (401) 201 Nevada St 95959-2605 (Mail to: 202 High St 95959-2605) William Christopher Seal Davis Ferrell Bradley Helmuth (530) 265-8836

Oroville St Pauls Episcopal Church **P** (58) 1430 Pine St 95965-4836 (Mail to: 1430 Pine St 95965-4836) David Englund Susan Fay (530) 533-5035

Paradise Church of St Nicholas **P** (159) 5872 Oliver Rd 95969-3835 (Mail to: 5872 Oliver Rd 95969-3835) Ann Sullivan David Alves (530) 877-7006

Petaluma St Johns Episcopal Church **P** (100) 40 5th St 94952-3042 (Mail to: 40 5th St 94952-3042) Daniel Green (707) 762-8872

Placerville Episcopal Church of Our Saviour **P** (155) 2979 Coloma St 95667-4440 (Mail to: PO Box 447 95667-0447) Debra Warwick-Sabino Susan Plucker Stephen Shortes (530) 622-2441

Quincy Christ the King Episcopal Church **M** (35) 545 Lawrence St 95971-9432 (Mail to: 545 Lawrence St 95971) Matthew Warren (530) 283-0254

Rancho Cordova St Clements Episcopal Church **P** (130) 2376 Zinfandel Dr 95670-4953 (Mail to: 2376 Zinfandel Dr 95670-4953) David Davidson-Methot Charles Rines (916) 635-5282

Red Bluff St Peters Episcopal Church **P** (91) 510 Jefferson St 96080-3408 (Mail to: PO Box 705 96080-0705) Maryly Adair (530) 527-5205

Redding All Saints Episcopal Church **P** (291) 2150 Benton Dr 96003-2151 (Mail to: 2150 Benton Dr 96003-2151) Paul Blanch Harold Clinehens (530) 243-1000

Rio Vista St Brigid of Kildare **P** 218 California Street 94571-1923 (Mail to: PO Box 580 94571-

0580) Lucretia Jevne Walter Phelps Susan Reeve (707) 374-2667

Rocklin St Augustine of Canterbury Church **P** (146) 1800 Wildcat Blvd 95765 (Mail to: 1800 Wildcat Blvd 95765-5471) Elizabeth Armstrong Maryellen Garnier (916) 435-9552

Roseville St Johns Episcopal Church **P** (439) 2351 Pleasant Grove 95747-8918 (Mail to: 2351 Pleasant Grove 95747-8918) Clifford Haggenjos Sarah Quinney Bettye Reynolds John Schively (916) 786-6911

Sacramento All Saints' Memorial Episcopal Church **P** (207) 2076 Sutterville Rd 95822-1320 (Mail to: 2076 Sutterville Rd 95822-1384) Virginia McNeely Elizabeth Monnot Michael Monnot (916) 455-0643

Sacramento St Marys Church **P** (128) 9085 Calvine Rd 95829-9451 (Mail to: 9085 Calvine Rd 95829-9451) Raymond Potter Anne Slakey Anne Smith

Sacramento St Matthews Episcopal Church **P** (112) 2300 Edison Ave 95821-1714 (Mail to: 2300 Edison Ave 95821-1796) Cynthia Long Chana Tetzlaff (916) 927-0115

Sacramento St Pauls Episcopal Church **P** (129) 1430 J St 95814-2918 (Mail to: 1430 J St 95814-2918) Michael Backlund Rik Rasmussen Anne Slakey Lynell Walker (916) 446-2620

✠ **Sacramento** Trinity Episcopal Cathedral **O** (1749) 2620 Capitol Ave 95816-5905 (Mail to: 2620 Capitol Ave 95816-5991) Brian Baker Megan Anderson Grant Carey Kathryn Hopner Steven Skiffington Jesse Vaughan Lynell Walker (916) 446-2513

Saint Helena Grace Episcopal Church **P** (460) 1314 Spring St 94574-2050 (Mail to: 1314 Spring St 94574-2050) William McIlmoyl Michael Erhard (707) 963-4157

Santa Rosa Episcopal Church of the Incarnation **P** (612) 550 Mendocino Ave 95401-5213 (Mail to: 550 Mendocino Ave 95401) Margaret Moore Pamela Moore James Richardson (707) 579-2604

Sebastopol St Stephens Episcopal Church **P** (140) 500 Robinson Rd 95472-4110 (Mail to: PO Box 98 95473-0098) Christy Laborda Harris (707) 823-3281

Sonoma Trinity Episcopal Church **P** (159) 275 E Spain St 95476-5732 (Mail to: 275 E Spain St 95476-5732) James Thomas (707) 938-4846

Susanville Good Shepherd Episcopal Church **M** (26) 1155 North St 96130-4051 (Mail to: 1155 North St 96130-4051) David Cohen (530) 257-6002

Sutter Creek Trinity Episcopal Church **P** (124) 430 Highway 49 95685 (Mail to: 430 State Highway 49 95685-4144) Karen Siegfriedt (209) 267-0255

Tahoe City St Nicholas Episcopal Church **M** (93) 855 W. Lake Blvd Hwy 89 96145 (Mail to: PO Box 855 96145-0855) Jennifer Liem John

Steinfeld (530) 583-4713

Ukiah Holy Trinity Episcopal Church **P** (77) 640 S Orchard Ave 95482-5012 (Mail to: 640 S Orchard Ave 95482-5012) (707) 462-8042

Vacaville Epiphany Episcopal Church **P** (292) 300 West St 95688-4516 (Mail to: 300 West St 95688-4516) Thomas Olson Beatryce Clark (707) 448-2275

Vallejo Ascension Episcopal Church **P** (167) 2420 Tuolumne St 94589-2345 (Mail to: 2420 Tuolumne St 94589-2345) Bayani Rico Richard Von Grabow (707) 644-5505

Wheatland Grace Episcopal Church **M** (27) 610 3rd St 95692-9459 (Mail to: 610 3rd St 95692-9459) Paul Hancock (530) 483-7050

Willits St Francis in the Redwoods Mission **M** (91) 1 N Main Street 95490 (Mail to: 66 E Commercial St 95490-3102) Betsy Bruneau Mary Fisher Donnalee Hart (707) 459-3066

Willows Holy Trinity Episcopal Church **P** (33) 556 E Sycamore St 95988-3250 (Mail to: PO Box 1116 95988-1116) (530) 934-3778

Woodland St Lukes Episcopal Church **P** (126) 515 2nd St 95695-4029 (Mail to: 515 2nd St 95695-4029) Terri Hobart Frank Chacon George Foxworth (530) 662-7152

Yuba City St James of Jerusalem Mission **M** (37) 556 N George Washington Blvd 95993 (Mail to: 556 N George Washington Blvd 95993-8995) (530) 673-1790

NON-PAROCHIAL CLERGY

Adams WJ *ret* Ukiah CA
Allagree HR *ret* Cotati CA
Ardley EL *ret* San Francisco CA
Arthur AT Sacramento CA
Beal ST *ret* San Francisco CA
Benesh JB Redwood City CA
Boeger DE *dcn*
Boeger MRS *dcn*
Bogart JL *ret* Benicia CA
Bowers MN *ret* Healdsburg CA
Brannon SN *ret* Sonoma CA
Bridges DL
Brown GN *dcn*
Cafferata GL *ret* Santa Rosa CA
Campbell ER *dcn* Sacramento CA
Christianssen PJ *ret*
Clader LL *ret* Vallejo CA
Clemons DD *ret* Yucca Valley CA
Cornell CW *ret* Folsom CA
Cram NL *ret* Vineburg CA
Doncaster DL Cincinnati OH
Duff ETM Sacramento CA
Duncan JL *ret* Aptos CA
Eckstein CG *dcn* Bayside CA
Edwards NB *ret*
Elliott JT *ret* Auburn WA
Felsovanyi A Menlo Park CA
Gaines WB *ret* Sacramento CA
Grayden MM *dcn*

Hallisey LA Davis CA
Hargis JF *ret* Half Moon Bay CA
Hart D *dcn* Willits CA
Hartley RH *dcn* Tucson AZ
Hauck ME *ret* Sacramento CA
Hefti WJ *dcn* Auburn CA
Henson DR North Augusta SC
Hobart TL Novato CA
Howell DS Toa Baja PR
Jenks SM *dcn* Albuquerque NM
Johnson TS *ret* Folsom CA
Joseph LM *ret* Kelseyville CA
Jurkovich-Hughes J Davis CA
Kendrick WB *ret* Chico CA
Kerrick MW Placerville CA
Knutson RA Lodi CA
Kuehn CC *ret* Placerville CA
Leigh-Taylor CH Placerville CA
Leininger A Fort Collins CO
Leonetti SJ *ret* Vacaville CA
Levensaler KH Danville CA
Lillicropp AR *ret* Sacramento CA
MacKenzie AJ *ret* Los Gatos CA
Maloney RB Windsor CA
Mangels JF *ret* Fair Oaks CA
McClain WA *ret* Montague CA
McClenaghan ME *ret* Roseville CA
McKeever AD Sacramento CA
McNair KS *ret* Cameron Park CA
Metheny LE *ret* Rancho Cordova CA
Miller JB *ret* Oceanside CA
Moore FA *dcn* Arcata CA

Moore SP Napa CA
Moore LT *ret* Susanville CA
Moore PE *ret* Santa Rosa CA
Muth DP *ret* Roseville CA
Nolta HG Willows CA
Owren D *ret* Fortuna CA
Page RL *ret* Sacramento CA
Powell DR *ret* Cloverdale CA
Quinney SH
Rasmussen RL Sacramento CA
Reinheimer P Penn Valley CA
Sassman WA *ret* Citrus Hts CA
Schenone JL Pasadena CA
Sheldon C San Francisco CA
Sigler JM *ret* Wimberley TX
Skiffington SW *dcn* Sacramento CA
Steadman DW *dcn* Sebastopol CA
Stevenson RH *ret* Santa Rosa CA
Straukamp JE Carmichael CA
Streufert NS Eureka CA
Stuart TF *ret* Carpinteria CA
Symons FR *ret* Carmichael CA
Taylor TH *ret* Sun City AZ
Thompson WD *ret* Eureka CA
Tilden GB
Torrey DE *ret* Yuba City CA
Wallace KM *dcn* Mount Shasta CA
Westphal EH Benicia CA
Whitmore EN *dcn* San Francisco CA
Wright CW Ramstein
Ziemann JJ *ret* Wheat Ridge CO

DIOCESE OF NORTHERN INDIANA
(PROVINCE V)
Comprises Northern Indiana
DIOCESAN OFFICE 117 N Lafayette Blvd South Bend IN 46601
TEL (574) 233-6489　FAX (574) 287-7914
E-MAIL info@ednin.org　WEB www.ednin.org

Previous Bishops—
John H White 1895-1925, Campbell Gray 1925-44, Reginald Mallett 1944-63, Walter Conrad Klein 1963-72, William CR Sheridan 1972-87, Francis C Gray 1987-98

Bishop—Rt Rev Edward Stuart Little II (952)
(Dio 18 Mar 00)

Cn to Ord: S Silla

Officers: Sec Rev JH Warnock; *Treas* D Kroll; *Chanc* Daniel H Pfeifer 53600 N Ironwood Dr South Bend IN 46635 (574) 272-2870

Stand Comm: Cler: M Cowden C Hodges S Haynes; *Lay:* P Harris T McLaughlin T Gray

Depts: COM Rev JH Warnock

Dio Conv: 22 Oct 2016 South Bend IN

PARISHES, MISSIONS, AND CLERGY

Angola Church of the Holy Family **P** (81) 909 A S Darling St 46703-1857 (Mail to: 909 S Darling St 46703-1857) (260) 665-5067

Berne St George Episcopal Church **M** (31) 1195 Hendricks St 46711-2391 (Mail to: PO Box 269 46711-0269) (260) 589-3315

Bristol St John of the Cross Epis Church **P** (127) No 601 E Vistula St 46507-8904 (Mail to: PO Box 433 46507-0433) Jennifer Fulton

Chesterton St Francis Episcopal Church **P** (90) 237 E 1200 N 46304-9360 (Mail to: PO Box 621 46304-0621) David Pearson (219) 926-3497

Crown Point St Christophers Episcopal Church **P** (72) 12718 Marshall St 46307-8386 (Mail to: 12718 Marshall St 46307-8386) Spencer Thiel (219) 663-0559

Culver St Elizabeths Episcopal Church **M** (18) 820 Academy Rd 46511-1106 (Mail to: 515 State St. 46511-1131) Clark Miller (574) 339-0235

East Chicago Church of the Good Shepherd **P** (149) 4525 Baring Ave 46312-3208 (Mail to: 4525 Baring Ave 46312-3208) (219) 397-4597

Elkhart Church of St John the Evangelist **P** (238) 226 W Lexington Ave 46516-3128 (Mail to: 226 W Lexington Ave 46516-3128) Daniel Repp (574) 295-1725

Elkhart St David Episcopal Church **P** (135) 26824 County Road 4 46514-5851 (Mail to: 26824 County Road 4 46514-5851) Henry Randolph (574) 264-4039

Fort Wayne Grace Episcopal Church **P** (132) 10010 Aurora Pl 46804-8500 (Mail to: 10010 Aurora Pl 46804) Kathryn Thomas (260) 432-9221

Fort Wayne St Alban Episcopal Church **P** (165) 7308 Saint Joe Rd 46835-1581 (Mail to: 7308 Saint Joe Rd 46835-1596) Daniel Layden (260) 485-8022

Fort Wayne Trinity Episcopal Church **P** (391) 611 W Berry St 46802-2105 (Mail to: 611 W Berry St 46802) Thomas Hansen Gordon Samra

Gary St Augustine Episcopal Church **P** (128) 2425 W 19th Ave 46404-2749 (Mail to: PO Box 4156 46404-4156)

Gary St Barnabas in the Dunes **P** (38) PO Box 2608 46403-0608 (Mail to: PO Box 2608 46403-0608) Michael Dwyer (219) 938-2834

Gas City St Paul Episcopal Church **P** (15) 121 E South A St 46933-1706 (Mail to: 121 E South A St, PO Box 46 46933-1706) (765) 674-2670

Goshen St James Episcopal Church **P** (70) 105 S 6th St 46528-3303 (Mail to: 105 S 6th St 46528-3398)

Griffith St Timothy Episcopal Church **P** (87) 1115 N Cline Ave 46319-1563 (Mail to: PO Box 347 46319-0347) (219) 838-8379

Hobart St Stephen Episcopal Church **P** (52) 1360 State St 46342-6056 (Mail to: 1360 State St 46342) John Blakslee (219) 696-4819

✠ **Howe** St Mark's Episcopal Church **Other** (35) 5755 N State Road 9 46746-9228 (Mail to: PO Box 336 46746-0336) David Douglass (260) 497-9718

Huntington Church of Christ the King **P** (64) 1224 N Jefferson St 46750-1848 (Mail to: 1224 N Jefferson St 46750-1848) Theodore Neidlinger (260) 356-3570

Kokomo St Andrew Episcopal Church **HC** (242) 602 W Superior Street 46901-5299 (Mail to: 514 W Superior St 46901-5299) Richard Lightsey (765) 457-2075

Laporte St Pauls Episcopal Church **P** (238) 708 Harrison St 46350-3418 (Mail to: 708 Harrison St 46350-3418) Samuel Kincaid Paul Nesta (219) 362-2784

Logansport Trinity Episcopal Church **P** (114) 319 7th St 46947-3128 (Mail to: 319 7th St 46947-3128) Clark Miller (574) 753-2733

Marion Gethsemane Episcopal Church **P** (186) 111 E 9th St 46953-1968 (Mail to: 803 S Washington St 46953-1968) James Warnock (765) 664-4638

Michigan City St Andrew by the Lake Episcopal Ch **P** (29) 1007 Moore Rd 46360-1762 (Mail to: PO Box 8766 46361-8766) Robert Dorow (219) 872-6984

Michigan City Trinity Episcopal Church **P** (109) 600 Franklin Sq 46360 (Mail to: 614 Franklin St 46360-3492) Tanya Scheff

Mishawaka St Paul Episcopal Church **P** (163) 616 Lincoln Way E 46544-2210 (Mail to: 616 Lincolnway E 46544-2210) Susan Haynes Stewart Clem Michael Cover (574) 255-9090

Munster St Paul Episcopal Church **P** (71) 1101 Park Dr 46321-2544 (Mail to: 1101 Park Dr 46321-2544) Michael Dwyer

Plymouth St Thomas Church Episcopal **HC** (144) N Center Street at Adams 46563-1728 (Mail to: PO Box 421 46563-0421) Thomas Haynes (574) 936-2735

Rensselaer St Peter Episcopal Church **M** (6) 402 S Melville St 47978-3202 (Mail to: 402 S Melville St 47978) (219) 866-8225

✠ **South Bend** Cathedral of St James **O** (223) 117 N Lafayette Blvd 46601-1507 (Mail to: 117 N Lafayette Blvd 46601-1587) Brian Grantz Terri Bays Joseph Illes Janice Miller Hugh Page (574) 232-4837

South Bend Church of the Holy Trinity **P** (51) 915 N Olive St 46628-2521 (Mail to: PO Box 3679 46619-0679) Stewart Clem (574) 234-9582

South Bend St Michael & All Angels Episcopal Ch **P** (231) 53720 Ironwood Rd 46635-1532 (Mail to: 53720 Ironwood Rd 46635-1532) Matthew Cowden Cynthia Van Parys

Syracuse All Saints Episcopal Church **M** (77) 7812 E Vawter Park Rd 46567-9515 (Mail to: 7812 E Vawter Park Rd 46567-9515) (574) 457-2178

Valparaiso St Andrew's Episcopal Church **P** (259) No 505 Bullseye Lake Rd. 46383-4813 (Mail to: 505 Bullseye Lake Rd. 46383-1951) Roger Bower (219) 462-4946

Warsaw St Anne Episcopal Church **P** (246) 424 W Market St 46580-2831 (Mail to: 424 W Market St 46580-2831) Corinne Hodges

NON-PAROCHIAL CLERGY

Berkley JCA *dcn* Elkhart IN
Biller L *ret* Syracuse IN
Blubaugh SJ Lafayette IN
Bradshaw PF London
Carpenter MG *dcn* Warsaw IN
Finster MR *dcn* Kokomo IN
Fleming CAS *ret* Union MI

Frolick BR *ret* Fort Wayne IN
Fulk MT *ret* Angola IN
Greve PA Fort Wayne IN
Haas MJ *ret* Logansport IN
Harker MAG *ret* Marion IN
Houghton JW Culver IN
Hyndman DL *ret* Gary IN
Irvine PB *ret* Homewood IL
Kallenberg RA *ret* Elkhart IN
King FH *ret* Marion IN
Kohlbecker EE *ret* Hilton NY
Mack RJ *ret* Valparaiso IN
Miller MR Lowell IN
Minnix GM *ret* Elkhart IN
Patston JRA *ret* Ludington MI
Peeler AL Geneva IL

Phelps CR *ret* East Chicago IN
Reid RP Palm Desert CA
Schramm JE *ret* Plymouth IN
Seger DL *ret* Rapid City SD
Silla SM *ret* South Bend IN
Stanley JM Geneva IL
Taylor GA *dcn* Munster IN
Tiffany SJ South Bend IN
Tracy PJ *ret* Mishawaka IN
Velthuizen T *ret* South Bend IN
Wiens DF *ret* Wheaton IL
Wietstock AK *dcn* South Bend IN
Wineland RK Goshen IN
Wolford AC *dcn* Corona CA
Woodruff Tait JL Huntington IN

DIOCESE OF NORTHERN MICHIGAN
(PROVINCE V)
Comprises the northernmost part of the State of Michigan
DIOCESAN OFFICE 131 E Ridge St Marquette MI 49855
TEL (906) 228-7160　FAX (906) 228-7171
E-MAIL diocese@upepiscopal.org　WEB www.upepiscopal.org

Previous Bishops—
Gershom M Williams 1896-1919, Robt L Harris coadj 1918 Bp 1919-29, Hayward S Ablewhite 1930-39, Herman Page prov 1940-42, Herman R Page 1942-64, George R Selway 1964-71, Sam J Wylie 1972-74, Wm A Dimmick 1975-82, Thomas K Ray 1982-99, James A Kelsey 1999-2007

Bishop—Rayford J Ray (April 1, 2011)

Treas R Graybill; *Chanc* P Micklow; *Liturgy* K Thew Forrester; *Comm* RT Forrester; *Stewardship* C Kleber; *District Ministry Developers* Rev M Padilla Rev R Thew Forrester Rev K Thew Forrester Rev Cathy Clark *COM* G Graybill; *Deploy* M Padilla; *Dio Ops Coord* J Cisluycis

Dio Conv: 29-30 Oct 2016 Marquette MI

PARISHES, MISSIONS, AND CLERGY

Crystal Falls St Marks Church **P** (29) 809 Crystal Ave 49920-1104 (Mail to: 127 Iron St 49920-1124) Christine Mello-Maki Carolyn Orchard Margaret Padilla (906) 875-3921
De Tour Village St Stephens Episcopal Church **P** (17) 124 S Ontario St 49725 (Mail to: PO Box 413 49725-0413) (906) 297-3207
Eagle Harbor St Peters by the Sea **SC** (7) 435 Front St 49950-9682 (Mail to: 13266 M-26 49950) (906) 289-4567
Escanaba St Stephens Episcopal Church **P** (301) 500 Ogden Ave 49829-3930 (Mail to: 500

Ogden Ave 49829-3930) (906) 786-7970
Gladstone Trinity Episcopal Church **P** (135) 901 Dakota Ave 49837-1616 (Mail to: PO Box 428 49837-0428) Dale Jamison Maria Maniaci Suzanne Ray (906) 428-4116
Gwinn Holy Innocents Episcopal Church **P** (19) Canale-Gwinn Funeral Home 96 E Stephenson Ave 49841-9153 (Mail to: 131 E Ridge Street 49855) (906) 942-7178
Houghton Trinity Episcopal Church **P** (49) 205 E Montezuma Ave 49931-2110 (Mail to: 205 E Montezuma Ave 49931-2110) Laura Eaton (906) 482-2010
Iron Mountain Church of the Holy Trinity **P** (78) PO Box 805 49801-0805 (Mail to: PO Box 805 49801-0805) Candice Lauk Norris Satterly (906) 774-3722
Iron River St Johns Church **P** (17) 527 N 2nd Ave 49935-1446 (Mail to: 527 N 2nd Ave 49935-1446) (906) 265-9013
Ironwood Church of the Transfiguration **P** (52) 336 E Aurora St 49938-2114 (Mail to: 336 E Aurora St 49938-2114) Geri Sola John Kangas (906) 932-4395
Ishpeming Grace Episcopal Church **P** (83) & 1st Canda Sts 49849 (Mail to: PO Box 601 49849-0601) (906) 485-1623
Larium Christ Episcopal Church **P** (74) 57031 Fifth St 49913 (Mail to: PO Box 687 49913-0687) Laura Eaton (906) 337-5242
Mackinac Island Trinity Episcopal Church **P** (32) 1623 Fort St 49757 (Mail to: PO Box 472 49757-0472) (906) 847-3798

Manistique St Albans Church **P** (35) 301 Range St 49854-1562 (Mail to: PO Box 302 49854-0302) (906) 286-2881

Marquette St Pauls Episcopal Church **P** (340) 201 E Ridge St 49855-4210 (Mail to: 201 E Ridge St 49855-4210) Marcia Franz Coralie Hambleton Kevin Thew Forrester (906) 226-2912

Menominee Grace Episcopal Church **P** (54) 922 10th Ave 49858-3033 (Mail to: 922 10th Ave 49858-3033) Bonnie Turner (906) 863-2385

Munising St Johns Church **P** (18) 121 W Onota Street 49862-1119 (Mail to: 121 W Onota Street 49862-1119) Marion Luckey Kimberly Moote (906) 387-2468

Negaunee St Johns Episcopal Church **P** (56) 101 W Main St 49866-1607 (Mail to: PO Box 29 49866-0029) John Lenten James Martindale (906) 475-4012

Newberry All Saints Church **P** (23) 314 W Truman St 49868-1227 (Mail to: PO Box 53 49868-0053)

Pointe Aux Pins Church of the Tranfiguration **SC** (3) Island Rd 49775 (Mail to: PO Box 934 49775-0934) (231) 634-7323

Sault Ste Marie St James Episcopal Church **P** (86) 533 Bingham Ave 49783-2141 (Mail to: 533 Bingham Ave 49783-2141) Dawn Aldrich Robert Aldrich Susan Harries Diane Horst Lawrence Rice (906) 632-2451

NON-PAROCHIAL CLERGY

Andersen JA *dcn* Escanaba MI
Auer NA
Bauer AT *dcn* Pellston MI
Berry JE
Britton JA *dcn* Gwinn MI
Church SJ Calumet MI
Clark CR Rapid River MI
Clark CA *dcn* Ishpeming MI
Collins ES Pickford MI
Creten CD *dcn*
Cutaiar ML *dcn*
Cutler PC *dcn* Wetmore MI
Dansdill DN Sault Sainte Marie MI
Darlington DL *dcn* Ishpeming MI
Deneau EA *dcn* Escanaba MI
DeWitt EL *dcn* Negaunee MI
DeWitt PM Ishpeming MI
DeWitt WH *dcn* Ishpeming MI
Diller SW *dcn* Gulliver MI
Engle MC *ret* Battle Creek MI
Erickson WJ Crystal Falls MI
Ettenhofer KR *dcn* Escanaba MI
Evans GT Houghton MI

Ford CL Newberry MI
Ford SE Newberry MI
Fritsche JY *dcn* Iron River MI
Graybill RM Ishpeming MI
Graybill VK Ishpeming MI
Hannabass KT *dcn*
Hay AL *dcn* Escanaba MI
Hetler GK Skandia MI
James SP *dcn* Iron Mountain MI
Jarvis LG Marquette MI
Jennings RP *ret* Sault Sainte Marie MI
Johns LM *dcn* Escanaba MI
Johnson DG Iron Mountain MI
Johnson MR *dcn* Iron Mountain MI
Kopera DJ Newberry MI
Korn EL *dcn* Wallace MI
Kozikowski MC *dcn* Menominee MI
Lee JE *dcn* Newberry MI
Lippart TE *ret* Vero Beach FL
Livingston JL Skandia MI
Luckey TH Munising MI
Manning JL Ontonagon MI
Mannisto VL Chatham MI
McClellan RF Saint Helena CA
Mineau CD
Nygaard SB *dcn* Gladstone MI
Peacock MA *dcn* Saint Ignace MI
Peacock VA *ret* Deer Isle ME
Perry RG Crystal Falls MI
Person DJ Kingsford MI
Piper CE *ret* Lafayette CO
Piper LL Lafayette CO
Purrington SJ Marquette MI
Rafferty RD Iron River MI
Railey RM Marquette MI
Robertson BE Marquette MI
Sand DA Iron Mountain MI
Sand LA Iron Mountain MI
Schuiling AC *dcn* Saint Johns MI
Shell LS *dcn* Marquette MI
Simmons DC Gladstone MI
Simmons MR *dcn* Gladstone MI
Slater J Mackinac Island MI
Smith BL *dcn* Naubinway MI
Spencer DJ *dcn* Manistique MI
Spencer RP Manistique MI
Sullivan MP *dcn* Marquette MI
West JT *dcn* Ishpeming MI
Weston MM Marquette MI
Wils DM *dcn* Gladstone MI
Wingert ALV *ret* Sault Sainte Marie MI
Winkler BJ *dcn* Iron Mountain MI
Woodworth LT Gladstone MI
Wright AD Manistique MI

DIOCESE OF NORTHWEST TEXAS
(PROVINCE VII)
Comprises 80 counties of Texas
DIOCESAN OFFICE The Hulsey Episcopal Center 1802 Broadway Lubbock TX 79401-3016
TEL (806) 763-1370   FAX (806) 472-0641
E-MAIL diocese@nwtdiocese.org   WEB www.nwtdiocese.org

Previous Bishops— Edward A Temple 1910-24, Eugene C Seaman 1925-45, George H Quarterman 1946-72, Willis R Henton 1972-80, Sam B Hulsey 1980-1997, Charles Wallis Ohl Jr 1997-2008

Bishop—J Scott Mayer (1035) (Dio 21 Mar 09)

Cn to Ord JM Ehmer; *Dio Adm* E Thames; *Fin Mgr* A Mora; *Treas* C Holley; *Reg* E Thames; *Chanc* T Choate; *COM* JM Ehmer; *Communications and HR* N Igo

Stand Comm—Cler: R Pace M Rowe C Cowden; *Lay:* K McLoughlin B Jowell J Wolf

Dio Conv: TBD Oct 2016 Lubbock Texas

PARISHES, MISSIONS, AND CLERGY

Abilene Church of the Heavenly Rest **P** (1216) 602 Meander St 79602-1027 (Mail to: 602 Meander St 79602-1099) Nathaniel Back Susanna Cates Eric Mancil (325) 677-2091

Abilene St Marks Episcopal Church **P** (53) 3150 Vogel St 79603-2128 (Mail to: 3150 Vogel St 79603-2128) Mary Glover James Smart Peggy Valentine (325) 677-1471

Albany Trinity Episcopal Church **M** (15) 140 N Ave B 76430 (Mail to: PO Box 3041 76430-8051) (325) 513-7983

Amarillo St Andrews Episcopal Church **P** (1102) 1601 Georgia St S 79102-2315 (Mail to: 1601 S Georgia St 79102-2315) Todd Baxley Claire Cowden Nina Jo Craig Patricia Knight Robert Pace Jill Walters-Pace Christopher Wrampelmeier (806) 376-6316

Amarillo St Peters Episcopal Church **P** (152) 4714 NW 4th Ave 79106-5220 (Mail to: 4714 NW 4th Ave 79106-5220) (806) 353-9594

Big Spring St Mary the Virgin Episcopal Church **P** (66) 1001 S Goliad St 79720 (Mail to: PO Box 2949 79721-2949) Janice Byrd Connetta Fowler John Marshall (432) 267-8201

Borger St Peters Church **P** (22) 620 Hemlock St 79007-4554 (Mail to: PO Box 138 79008-0138)

Brownfield Good Shepherd Mission **M** (41) 304 E. Lanny 79316-0334 (Mail to: PO Box 334 79316-0334) John Corbett James Haney (806) 637-9464

Canyon St Georges Episcopal Church **M** (27) 2516 4th Ave 79015-4146 (Mail to: 2516 4th Ave 79015-4146) Beverly Couzzourt (806) 655-3121

Clarendon St John the Baptist Mission **M** (29) 301 South Park 79226 (Mail to: PO Box 1078

79226-1078) (806) 874-2511

Coleman St Marks Episcopal Church **M** (61) 601 S Neches St 76834-4026 (Mail to: PO Box 838 76834-0838) Russell Fisher (325) 625-4995

Colorado City All Saints Episcopal Church **M** (25) 304 Locust St 79512-6428 (Mail to: 304 Locust St 79512-6428) Jared Houze (325) 728-2243

Dalhart St James Church **P** (158) 801 Denver Ave 79022-3625 (Mail to: 801 Denver Ave 79022-3625) (806) 244-2396

Dumas St Pauls Episcopal Church **M** (22) 815 E 3rd St 79029-4155 (Mail to: PO Box 71 79029-0071) (806) 935-3139

Hereford Church of St Thomas the Apostle **M** (12) 601 W Park Ave 79045-4105 (Mail to: 601 W Park Ave 79045-4105) (806) 344-2018

Levelland St Lukes Episcopal Church **M** (19) 1103 Sundown Hwy 79336 (Mail to: 1103 W Fm 300 79336-6229) (804) 894-8097

Lubbock Canterbury At Texas Tech **CC** 2407 16th St 79401-4434 (Mail to: 2407 16th St 79401-4434) Jennifer Holder (806) 765-0037

Lubbock St Christophers Episcopal Church **P** (581) 2807 42nd St 79413-3223 (Mail to: 2807 42nd St 79413-3223) Jimmy Jackson Melissa Wafer-Cross (806) 799-8208

Lubbock St Pauls Church on the Plains **P** (782) No 1510 Ave X 79401 (Mail to: 1510 Avenue X 79401-4423) James Haney (806) 762-2893

Lubbock St Stephens Episcopal Church **HC** (290) No 1101 Slide Rd 79416-5419 (Mail to: 1101 Slide Rd 79416-5419) James Perdue

Midland Episcopal Church of the Holy Trinity **P** (431) 1412 W Illinois Ave 79701-6537 (Mail to: 1412 W Illinois Ave 79701-6537) David Galletly Barbara Kirk-Norris (432) 683-4207

Midland St Nicholas Episcopal Church **P** (201) 4000 W Loop 250 N 79707-3419 (Mail to: 4000 W Loop 250 N 79707-3419) Thomas Burns David Huxley

Odessa San Miguel Arcangel Episcopal Church **M** (375) 907 Adams Ave 79761-4111 (Mail to: 1802 Broadway 79401-3016) Alberto Casas (432) 332-2074

Odessa St Barnabas Episcopal Church **P** (122) 4141 Tanglewood Ln 79762-7224 (Mail to: 4141 Tanglewood Ln 79762-7224) David Mossbarger

Odessa St Johns Episcopal Church **P** (179) 401 N County Road West 79763 (Mail to: PO Box 3346 79760-3346) Jimmy Jackson

Pampa St Matthews Episcopal Church **P** (215) 727 W Browning Ave 79065-6204 (Mail to:

727 W Browning Ave 79065-6204) Mark Lang (806) 665-0701

Perryton All Saints Mission **M** (8) 2001 Jefferson St 79070-5051 (Mail to: 1518 S Fordham St 79070-4546) (806) 435-4516

Plainview St Marks Episcopal Church **P** (31) 710 Joliet St 79072-7716 (Mail to: 710 Joliet St 79072-7716) (806) 296-7185

San Angelo Church of the Good Shepherd **P** (41) 720 S. Abe Street 76903 (Mail to: 720 S. Abe Street 76903) Celia Ellery (325) 659-3800

San Angelo Emmanuel Episcopal Church **P** (417) 3 S Randolph St 76903-5828 (Mail to: 3 S Randolph St 76903-5828) Matthew Rowe (325) 653-2446

Shamrock St Michaels & All Angels Church **PS** (7) 304 S Madden St 79079-2518 (Mail to: 300 S Madden St 79079-2518) (806) 256-5181

Sweetwater St Stephens Episcopal Church **M** (31) 505 Locust St 79556-3249 (Mail to: 502 Locust St 79556-3250) Jared Houze Nikki Jones (325) 235-8408

Vernon Grace Episcopal Church **M** (20) 3207 Indian St 76384-5923 (Mail to: PO Box 1404 76385-1404) (940) 552-7008

NON-PAROCHIAL CLERGY

Aveni JV Clarendon TX
Ballou DS *dcn*
Betty CW Perryton TX
Bilby GE *dcn* Perryton TX
Bonnington RL *ret* Midland TX
Bowyer CL *ret* Lubbock TX
Cashell DH *dcn* Lubbock TX
Cobb JK *dcn* Odessa TX
Collier MA *dcn*
Creswell CE *ret* Amarillo TX
Ehmer JM Lubbock TX
Ferguson DP *ret* Dallas TX
Finn AM *ret* Abilene TX
Girvin CS *ret* Colorado City TX
Goolsbee AL *dcn* Abilene TX
Gregory LA *ret* Dalhart TX
Holder JS Abilene TX
Houghton WC *ret* The Woodlands TX
Igo NE *dcn* Lubbock TX
Jimenez DS

Jones RE *dcn* Lubbock TX
Keith TA
Kelly LL *ret* Kerrville TX
Lee SR Conroe TX
Liggett JE *ret* Midland TX
Logsdon TD *dcn* Amarillo TX
Loving JH *ret* Austin TX
Manley DB *ret* Cottonwood AZ
Masterman PD *dcn* Amarillo TX
McIntyre CE *ret* Odessa TX
McKay PH *dcn* Lubbock TX
Morrison LO *dcn* Odessa TX
Nelson RL Burton TX
Nix WD *ret* Canadian TX
Orem BJT *dcn* Lubbock TX
Prehn WL Midland TX
Ray PC Dalhart TX
Ricketts MCC *dcn* Tuscola TX
Rose JR *ret* Saint Petersburg FL
Russell PG *ret* Lubbock TX
Sanford GL *dcn* San Angelo TX
Scott DT Perryton TX
Scott JP Lubbock TX
Seidman KA Broomfield CO
Shafer JL *dcn* Lubbock TX
Sinclair GL *dcn*
Slayter MF *ret* Midland TX
Smith RA *dcn* Amarillo TX
Smith WC Pampa TX
Spannagel LE *ret* Meridian ID
Swindle FM *ret* Pioneer LA
Taliaferro RD Amarillo TX
Thomas DP
Tothill MG
Vaughn JLHE *dcn* Vernon TX
Veal DL *ret* Lubbock TX
Walker JA
Way JE Lubbock TX
Wedgwood-Greenhow SJF *ret* Midland TX
Whitfield MD Quanah TX
Wilkins AP *dcn* Conroe TX
Wilkinson EB *dcn* Pampa TX
Wilkinson MS *dcn* Pampa TX
Williams JD Borger TX
Wilson CA *ret* Amarillo TX
Wischmeyer KL Lubbock TX
Wright WB *ret* San Angelo TX

DIOCESE OF NORTHWESTERN PENNSYLVANIA
(PROVINCE III)
Comprises 13 counties in Northwest PA
DIOCESAN OFFICE 145 W 6th St Erie PA 16501
TEL (814) 456-4203   FAX (814) 454-8703
WEB www.dionwpa.org

Previous Bishops—
Rogers Israel 1911-21, John C Ward 1921-43, Edward P Wroth 1943-46, Harold E Sawyer 1946-51, Wm Crittenden 1952-1973, Donald J Davis coadj 1973 Bp 1974-91 Robt D Rowley Jr coadj 1989-1991 Bp 1991-2007

Bishop—Rt Rev Sean Rowe (1019) (Dio 8 Sep 07)

Archdcn GG Winslow; *Cn for Miss Dev & Trans* Rev M Ishman; *Cn for Admin* V Butler; *Treas* R Armstrong 381 Armstrong Dr New Castle PA 16101; *Chanc* J Steadman 24 Main St Girard PA 16417; *Deans: SW* Rev D Blauser *NE* Rev S Fussell *NW* Rev M Norton *SE* Rev B Ellis; *Cn for Fin* C Dougan; *Asst for Form* Rev J Piatko; *Cn for Cong Vit & Innovation* Rev A Johnson; *Asst for Comm & Admin* J Goulet; *Asst for Finance* S Schuette

Stand Comm—Cler: DA Blauser S Fussell B Reid E Fitzgibbons *Lay: Pres* J Malovich C Pryts K Reib *Sec* A Bardol

Dio Conv: 4-5 Nov 2015 Warren PA

PARISHES, MISSIONS, AND CLERGY

Bradford Church of the Ascension **P** (139) 26 Chautauqua Pl 16701-1915 (Mail to: PO Box 337 16701-0337) Stacey Fussell Gail Winslow (814) 368-8915

Brookville Church of the Holy Trinity **M** (52) 62 Pickering St 15825-1246 (Mail to: 62 Pickering St 15825-1246) (814) 849-7235

Clearfield St Andrews Church **M** (25) 102 E Cherry St 16830-2350 (Mail to: 102 E Cherry St 16830-2350) (814) 849-7235

Corry Emmanuel Episcopal Church **P** (48) 327 N Center St 16407-1628 (Mail to: 327 N Center St 16407-1676) Mary Norton (814) 665-7535

DuBois Church of Our Saviour **P** (130) 400 Liberty Blvd. 15801 (Mail to: PO Box 503 15801-0503) Melinda Hall (814) 371-8810

Edinboro St Augustine of Canterbury Church **M** (74) 427 W Plum St 16412-2145 (Mail to: PO Box 213 16412-0213) David Fulford (814) 734-4116

Emporium Emmanuel Episcopal Church **P** (75) 144 E 4th St 15834-1445 (Mail to: PO Box 88 15834-0088) Matthew Ryan (814) 486-0711

✥ **Erie** Cathedral of St Paul **O** (484) 134 W 7th St 16501-1004 (Mail to: 134 W 7th St 16501-

1004) John Downey (814) 452-3779

Erie Church of the Holy Spirit **M** (88) 501 W 31st St 16508-1742 (Mail to: 501 W 31st St 16508-1742) (814) 452-4040

Erie St Marks Episcopal Church **P** (207) 4701 Old French Rd 16509-3631 (Mail to: 4701 Old French Rd 16509-3631) (814) 868-9704

Erie St Marys Episcopal Church **M** (62) 662 Silliman Ave 16511-2057 (Mail to: 662 Silliman Ave 16511-2057) Shawn Clerkin Zachary Irwin (814) 899-0118

Fairview St Stephens Church **P** (221) 1070 Dutch Rd 16415-1627 (Mail to: 1070 Dutch Rd 16415-1627) Elisabeth Fitzgibbons (814) 474-5490

Foxburg Memorial Church of Our Father **M** (39) 110-136 Church Rd R 16036 (Mail to: PO Box 332 16036-0332) Patricia Lavery (724) 659-4541

Franklin St Johns Episcopal Church **P** (232) 1145 Buffalo St 16323-1254 (Mail to: PO Box 550 16323-0550)

Greenville St Clements Episcopal Church **P** 103 Clinton St 16125-2051 (Mail to: PO Box 1714 16148) (724) 588-6440

Grove City Church of the Epiphany **M** (47) 870 Liberty St Ext 16127-6438 (Mail to: PO Box 287 16127-0287) Geoffrey Wild Patricia Lavery (724) 458-6720

Hermitage Church of the Redeemer **P** 5130 E State St 16148-9447 (Mail to: PO Box 1714 16148)

Houtzdale Church of the Holy Trinity **M** (40) 222 Brisbin St 16651-1301 (Mail to: Donna Ellis 203 Dorthea Street 16651-1751) William Ellis (814) 378-8543

Kane St Johns Episcopal Church **P** (9) 427 Chase St 16735-1320 (Mail to: 427 Chase St 16735-1320) (814) 837-6351

Lake City Grace Episcopal Church **M** (39) 10121 Hall Avenue 16423 (Mail to: 10121 Hall Avenue 16423-0208) Donald Baxter (814) 774-8288

Meadville Christ Episcopal Church **P** (103) 870 Diamond Park 16335-2606 (Mail to: 870 Diamond Park 16335-2606) Rebecca Lash (814) 724-7389

New Castle St Jude's Episcopal Church **Cluster** (230) 212 N Mill St 16101-3612 (Mail to: PO Box 1714 16148-0714) Dennis Blauser Douglas Dayton (724) 654-8761

New Castle Trinity Episcopal Church **P** 212 N Mill St 16101-3612 (Mail to: PO Box 1714 16148) Robert Reed

North East Holy Cross Episcopal Church **M** (44) 51 W Main St 16428-1103 (Mail to: 51 W Main St 16428-1103) (814) 725-2910

Oil City Christ Church **P** (56) 16 Central Ave 16301-2734 (Mail to: 16 Central Ave 16301-2734) Charl Kapp (814) 677-3023

Osceola Mills St Laurence Episcopal Church **M** (43) 501 Lingle St 16666-1121 (Mail to: PO Box 128 16666-0128) (814) 342-2379

Port Allegan St Joseph Church **M** (38) 116 E Arnold Ave 16743-1247 (Mail to: 116 E Arnold St 16743-1247) Joann Piatko (814) 558-5876

Ridgway Grace Episcopal Church **P** (63) 216 Center St 15853-1203 (Mail to: PO Box 404 15853-0404) Alan Coudriet (814) 776-6132

Saint Marys St Agnes Episcopal Church **P** (57) 209 N Saint Marys St 15857-1237 (Mail to: 209 N Saint Marys St 15857-1271) (814) 781-1909

Sharon St Johns Episcopal Church **P** (545) 226 W State St 16146-1341 (Mail to: 226 W State St 16146-1395) Adam Trambley Randall Beck (724) 347-4501

Smethport St Lukes Episcopal Church **P** (74) 600 W Main & Church 16749 (Mail to: PO Box 1475 16749-0475) (814) 887-5841

Titusville St James Memorial Church **P** (98) 112 E Main St 16354-1849 (Mail to: 112 E Main St 16354-1849) Martha Ishman (814) 827-3590

Warren Trinity Memorial Church **P** (122) 444 Pennsylvania Ave W 16365-2238 (Mail to: 444 Pennsylvania Ave W 16365-2238) Matthew Scott Timothy Dyer (814) 723-9360

Waterford St Peters Church **M** (42) 100 E 3rd St 16441-9766 (Mail to: PO Box 452 16441-0452) (814) 796-9011

Youngsville St Francis of Assisi Epis Church **P** (62) 343 E Main St 16371-1125 (Mail to: 343 E Main St 16371-1177) (814) 563-7586

NON-PAROCHIAL CLERGY

Akin MB
Baker JM Brookville PA
Bauschard MRT *dcn* Warren PA
Buell SD *ret* New York City NY
Burke RT Lake City PA
Carlson CE *ret* Mount Jewett PA
Cavagnaro DD *dcn* Smethport PA
Chango G *dcn* Punxsutawney PA
Considine HJ *ret* Miramar FL
Donahue LC *ret* Bradford PA
Duncan JE *ret* Hermitage PA
Elberfeld R *ret* Erie PA
Evans CD *ret* Erie PA
Field NG Erie PA
French WA Brookville PA
Harris GJ *ret* McAllen TX
Harris WH *ret* Emporium PA
Herald EC *dcn* Hermitage PA
Hough GW *ret* Hollidaysburg PA
Johnson NE Williamsville NY
Juchter MR Killeen TX
Kline JW *ret* Plano TX
Lord MG *dcn* Erie PA
Lowrey ES *ret* Foxburg PA
Macdougall MB Youngsville PA
McDermot J *dcn* Meadville PA
McKay R *ret* Du Bois PA
Nelson JF *ret* Falmouth MA
Orville LD Ellsworth ME
Reid BS *ret* Warren PA
Rowe RC Hermitage PA
Scofield LF *ret* Corry PA
Scofield SM Corry PA
Shank EB
Shuart RS *ret* South Harwich MA
Skellen BJ *dcn* Ridgway PA
Wareham GL *ret* New Castle PA
Williams RS *ret* Pleasantville PA
Ziegenhine KR Erie PA

STATE OF OHIO
Dioceses of Ohio and Southern Ohio

DIOCESE OF OHIO
(PROVINCE V)
Comprises the northern portion of Ohio
DIOCESAN OFFICE Trinity Commons 2230 Euclid Ave Cleveland OH 44115-2499
TEL (216) 771-4815   FAX (216) 623-0735
WEB www.dohio.org

Previous Bishops—
Philander Chase 1819-31, Chas P McIlvaine 1832-73, Gregory T Bedell coadj 1859 Bp 1873-89, Wm A Leonard 1889-30, Frank De Moulin coadj 1914-24, Warren L Rogers coadj 1925 Bp 1930-38, Beverley D Tucker coadj 1938 Bp 1938 -52, Nelson M Burroughs coadj 1949 Bp 1952-68, John H Burt coadj 1967 Bp 1968-1984, William Davidson asst 1980-86, James R Moodey coadj 1983 Bp 1984-93, Arthur Benjamin Williams Jr Bp Suffr 1986-2002, J Clark Grew II Bp 1994-2004

Bishop—Rt Rev Mark Hollingsworth Jr (997) (Dio 17 Apr 04)

Assisting Bishop—Rt Rev William D Persell (999)

Assisting Bishop—Rt Rev Arthur B Williams Jr (812)

Cn to Ord WA Powel III; *Sec* D Arrington; *Treas* PT Austin; *Chanc* WA Powel III; *Archiv* B Wilbert; *Cn for Cong* B Purdom; *Cn for Min* P Grant; *Cn for Chr Frm* V Black; *Cn for Mission* M D'Anieri; *CFO* S Leishman; *Comm* J Rocha; *Development* L Hnat; *Camp & Retreat Proj Dir* K Ong-Landini; *Admin Asst* E Cole

Stand Comm—Cler: J Ashby J Bunke G Catinella B Wilbert; *Lay:* D Coughlin J Freeman D Shamlin J West

Dio Conv: Nov 2016 Cleveland OH

PARISHES, MISSIONS, AND CLERGY

Akron Church of Our Saviour **P** (213) 471 Crosby St 44302-1518 (Mail to: 471 Crosby St 44302-1518) Debra Bennett (330) 535-9174

Akron St Andrews Church **P** (52) 765 Thayer St 44315-0001 (Mail to: 765 Thayer St 44310-3003) (330) 253-6447

Akron St Pauls Church **P** (2109) 1361 W Market St 44313-7123 (Mail to: 1361 W Market St 44313-7123) Mark Pruitt Polly Glanville (330) 836-9327

Akron St Philips Church **P** (94) 1130 Mercer Ave 44320-3646 (Mail to: 1130 Mercer Ave 44320-

3646) Melanie Sunderland (330) 535-7295

Alliance Trinity Church **P** (84) 1200 S Union Ave 44601-4021 (Mail to: 1200 S Union Ave 44601-4021) Jerome Colegrove (330) 821-8498

Ashland St Matthews Church **P** (89) 1515 Mifflin Ave 44805-3648 (Mail to: 1515 Mifflin Ave 44805-3648) Alice Kay Ashby (419) 281-1420

Ashtabula St Peters Church **P** (231) 4901 Main Ave 44004-7018 (Mail to: PO Box 357 44005-0357) C David Evans Peter Nielsen (440) 992-8100

Barberton St Andrews Church **P** (156) 267 5th St NW 44203-2103 (Mail to: 583 W Hopocan Ave 44203-2256) Michael Petrochuk (330) 7459026

Bellevue St Pauls Church **P** (77) 285 W Main St 44811-1333 (Mail to: 285 Main St 44811-1333) John Reinheimer (419) 483-4628

Berea Church of St Thomas **P** (285) 50 E Bagley Rd 44017-2009 (Mail to: 50 E Bagley Rd 44017-2009)

Boardman St James Church **P** (110) 7640 Glenwood Ave 44512-5897 (Mail to: 7640 Glenwood Ave 44512-5821) Shawn Dickerson Mary Vidmar John Wigle (330) 758-2727

Bowling Green St Johns Church **P** (29) 1505 E Wooster St 43402-3392 (Mail to: 1505 E Wooster St 43402-3392) (419) 353-0881

Brecksville St Matthews Church **P** (190) 9549 Highland Dr 44141-2729 (Mail to: 9549 Highland Dr 44141-2799) Stephanie Pace (440) 526-9865

Brunswick St Patricks Church **P** (100) 3611 Center Rd 44212-0397 (Mail to: PO Box 397 44212-3619) (330) 220-2777

Canton St Marks Church **P** (340) 515 48th St NW 44709-1369 (Mail to: 515 48th St NW 44709-1369) Dustin Berg (330) 449-2662

Canton St Pauls Church **P** (217) 425 Cleveland Ave SW 44702-1625 (Mail to: PO Box 21333 44701-1333) Barbara Bond (330) 455-0286

Chagrin Fall St Martin's Episcopal Church **P** (482) 6295 Chagrin River Rd 44022-3544 (Mail to: 6295 Chagrin River Rd 44022) John Cerrato (440) 247-7406

Chardon St Lukes Church **P** (223) 11519 Wilson Mills Rd 44024-9406 (Mail to: PO Box 244 44024-0244) Christopher McCann (440) 285-4641

Cleveland All Saints Church **P** (272) 8911 W Ridgewood Dr 44130-4122 (Mail to: 8911 W Ridgewood Dr 44130-4100) Heather Hill (440) 888-4055

Cleveland St Albans Church **P** (30) 2555 Euclid Heights Blvd 44106-2709 (Mail to: 2555 Euclid Heights Blvd 44106-2799)

Cleveland St Andrews Church **P** (132) 2171 E 49th St 44103-4401 (Mail to: 2171 E 49th St 44103-4401) Himie-Budu Shannon (216) 391-2632

Cleveland St Bartholomew's Episcopal Church **P** (107) 435 Som Center Rd 44143-1519 (Mail to: 435 Som Center Road 44143-1519) Stephen Secaur (440) 449-2290

Cleveland St Johns Church **P** (216) 781-5546

Cleveland St Pauls Episcopal Church **P** (1643) 2747 Fairmount Blvd 44106-3606 (Mail to: 2747 Fairmount Blvd 44106-3696) Philip Anderson Jeanne Leinbach (216) 932-5815

✣ **Cleveland** Trinity Cathedral **O** (1031) 2021 E 22nd St 44115-2401 (Mail to: 2230 Euclid Ave 44115-2405) Tracey Lind Geoffrey Curtiss Mary Kathryn Rackley (216) 771-3630

Coshocton Trinity Episcopal Church **P** (85) 705 Main St 43812-1616 (Mail to: 705 Main St 43812-1616) (740) 622-0860

Cuyahoga Fls St Johns Episcopal Church **P** (128) 2220 2nd St 44221-2502 (Mail to: 2220 Second St 44221) Christopher Coughlin William Tompkin (330) 928-2139

Defiance Grace Church **P** (62) 308 W 2nd St 43512-2131 (Mail to: 308 W 2nd St 43512-2131) (419) 782-0766

E Liverpool St Stephens Church **P** (109) 220 W 4th St 43920-4510 (Mail to: 220 W 4th St 43920-4510) Mary Vidmar (330) 385-3828

Elyria St Andrews Church **P** (271) 300 3rd St 44035-5618 (Mail to: 300 3rd St 44035-5693) Martha June Dorsey (440) 322-2126

Euclid Church of the Epiphany **P** (313) 21000 Lakeshore Blvd 44123-1800 (Mail to: 21000 Lakeshore Blvd 44123-1800) Rosalind Hughes (216) 731-1316

Findlay Trinity Episcopal Church **P** (253) 128 W Hardin St 45840-3104 (Mail to: 128 W Hardin St 45840-3104) (419) 422-3214

Fremont St Pauls Church **P** (170) 206 N Park Ave 43420-2430 (Mail to: 206 N Park Ave 43420-2430) (419) 332-3032

Gambier Harcourt Parish **P** (123) Church of the Holy Spirit, Kenyon Campus 102 College-Park St 43022 (Mail to: PO Box 377 43022-0377) (740) 427-2187

Gates Mills St Christophers by the River Church **P** (249) 7601 Old Mill Rd 44040 (Mail to: PO Box 519 44040-0519) Ann Kidder (440) 423-4451

Geneva Christ Church **P** (96) 66 South Eagle St 44041-1547 (Mail to: 66 South Eagle St 44041-1547)

Hudson Christ Church **P** (308) 21 Aurora St 44236-2902 (Mail to: 21 Aurora St 44236-2902) Larry Minter (330) 650-4359

Huron Christ Episcopal Church **P** (260) 120 Ohio St 44839-1537 (Mail to: 120 Ohio St 44839-1599) Michael Floyd (419) 433-4701

Kent Christ Episcopal Church **P** (191) 118 S Mantua St 44240-3437 (Mail to: 118 South Mantua Street 44240) Julie Fisher William Lyle (330) 673-4604

Lakewood Church of the Ascension **P** (105) 13216 Detroit Ave 44107-2842 (Mail to: 13216 Detroit Ave 44107-2894) (216) 521-8727

Lakewood St Peters Episcopal Church **P** (609) 18001 Detroit Ave 44107-3417 (Mail to: 18001 Detroit Ave 44107-3491) Gordon Owen Nancy Wittig (216) 226-1772

Lisbon Holy Trinity Church **P** (43) 310 E Lincoln Way 44432-1420 (Mail to: PO Box 323 44432-0323) (330) 424-5442

Lorain Church of the Redeemer **P** (164) 647 Reid Ave 44052-1737 (Mail to: PO Box 521 44052-0521) Mary Carson (440) 244-3134

Lyndhurst Church of the Good Shepherd **P** (285) 23599 Cedar Rd 44122-1065 (Mail to: 23599 Cedar Rd 44122-1065) Aaron Collins Anne Pillot

Macedonia St Timothys Church **P** (300) 8667 Shepard Rd 44056-2010 (Mail to: PO Box 204 44056-2010) Albert Jennings Anne Pillot (330) 467-1103

Mansfield Grace Church **P** (319) 41 Bowman St 44903-1650 (Mail to: 41 Bowman St 44903-1650) Joe Ashby Daniel Orr (419) 524-2661

Marion St Pauls Episcopal Church **P** (25) 197 E Center St 43302-3813 (Mail to: 197 E Center St 43302-3876)

Massillon St Timothys Church **P** (442) 226 3rd St SE 44646-6702 (Mail to: 226 3rd St SE 44646-6702) (330) 833-3183

Maumee St Pauls Church **P** (523) 310 Elizabeth St 43537-3322 (Mail to: 310 Elizabeth St 43537-3322) John Board (419) 893-3381

Medina St Pauls Church **P** (539) 317 E Liberty St 44256-2108 (Mail to: 317 E Liberty St 44256-2108) Charles Funston (330) 725-4131

Mentor St Andrews Church **P** (256) 7989 Little Mountain Rd 44060-7802 (Mail to: 7989 Little Mountain Rd 44060-7802) Marie Phillips (440) 255-8842

Mentor St Huberts Church **P** (293) 8870 Baldwin Rd 44060-7835 (Mail to: 8870 Baldwin Rd 44060-7835) Daniel Schoonmaker John Hayden (440) 256-1280

Mount Vernon St Paul's Episcopal Church **HC** (99) 100 E High St 43050-3402 (Mail to: 100 E High St 43050) David Kendall-Sperry (740) 392-8601

Napoleon St Johns Church **P** (26) 1400 Glenwood Ave 43545-9032 (Mail to: PO Box 227 43545-0227)

New Phila Trinity Church **P** (66) 122 3rd St NW 44663-3719 (Mail to: 122 3rd St NW 44663-3719) (330) 339-6439

Niles St Lukes Church **P** (118) 348 Robbins Ave 44446-2408 (Mail to: 348 Robbins Ave 44446-2489) Vernon Hall (330) 652-2952

Norwalk St Pauls Church **P** (65) 87 W Main St 44857-1439 (Mail to: 87 W Main Street 44857-1439) Margaret D'Anieri Barbara Mudge (419) 668-1937

Oberlin Christ Church **P** (90) 162 S Main St 44074-1699 (Mail to: 162 S Main St 44074-1699) Brian Wilbert (440) 775-2501

Oregon St Pauls Church **P** (146) 798 S Coy Rd 43616-3008 (Mail to: 798 S Coy Rd 43616-3008) (419) 691-9400

Painesville St James Church **P** (216) 131 N State St 44077-3939 (Mail to: 131 N State St 44077-3991) Vanessa Clark

Perrysburg St Timothys Church **D** (212) 871 E Boundary St 43551-2451 (Mail to: 871 E Boundary St 43551-2451) Jeffry Bunke (419) 874-5704

Port Clinton Church of St Thomas **P** (57) 214 E 2nd St 43452-1117 (Mail to: 214 E 2nd St 43452-1117)

Put-In-Bay St Pauls Church **P** (46) 623 Catawba Ave 43456-0248 (Mail to: PO Box 248 43456-0248) Mary Staley (419) 285-5981

Ravenna Grace Church **P** (180) 250 Cedar Ave 44266-2740 (Mail to: 250 Cedar Ave 44266-2740) Carol Evans William Snyder James Wichman (330) 296-3443

Salem Church of Our Saviour **P** (51) 870 E State St 44460-2224 (Mail to: PO Box 120 44460-0120) Jerome Colegrove (330) 332-5701

Sandusky Grace Church **P** (244) 315 Wayne St 44870-2619 (Mail to: 315 Wayne St 44870-2658) Jan Wood (419) 625-6919

Shaker Heights Christ Church **P** (305) 3445 Warrensville Center Rd 44122-5206 (Mail to: 3445 Warrensville Center Rd 44122-5206) Peter Faass James Greer (216) 991-3432

Shelby St Marks Episcopal Church **P** (87) 31 N Gamble St 44875-1201 (Mail to: 31 N Gamble St 44875-1201) (419) 347-7701

Sidney St Mark's Episcopal Church **P** (54) 231 N Miami Ave 45365-2707 (Mail to: 231 N Miami Ave 45365-2707) Stephanie Brugger Arthur Good (937) 492-8584

Steubenville St Pauls Church **P** (98) 415 Adams St 43952-2809 (Mail to: 415 Adams St 43952-2809) (740) 282-5366

Steubenville St Stephens Episcopal Church **P** (104) 284 Lovers Ln 43953-3401 (Mail to: 284 Lovers Ln 43953-3401) (740) 264-5005

Tiffin Old Trinity Church **P** (79) 125 E Market St 44883-3903 (Mail to: 125 E Market St 44883-3903) Aaron Gerlach (419) 447-0728

Toledo All Saints Episcopal Church **P** (135) 563 Pinewood Ave 43602-1009 (Mail to: 563 Pinewood Ave 43604-8009) Nancy Graumlich Beverly Tasy (419) 246-2461

Toledo St Andrew's Episcopal Church **P** (202) 2770 W. Central Ave 43606-3462 (Mail to: 2770 W. Central Ave 43606-3462) Jeremiah Williamson (419) 473-1367

Toledo St Matthews Church **P** (307) 5240 Talmadge Rd 43623-2138 (Mail to: 5240 Talmadge Rd 43623-2138) Joseph Keblesh (419) 473-1187

Toledo St Michaels in the Hills Church **P** (483) 4718 Brittany Rd 43615-2314 (Mail to: 4718 Brittany Rd 43615-2314) Jennifer Leider (419) 531-1616

Toledo Trinity Church **P** (177) 1 Trinity Plz 43604-1503 (Mail to: 316 Adams St 43604-1565) Elizabeth Hoster (419) 243-1231

Uniontown New Life Episcopal Church **P** (132) 13118 Church Ave NW 44685-8452 (Mail to: 13118 Church Ave NW 44685-8452) Elizabeth Frank (330) 699-3554

Wadsworth St Marks Episcopal Church **P** (52) 146 College St 44281-1852 (Mail to: 146 College St 44281-1852) Allan Belton (330) 336-0212

Warren Christ Episcopal Church **P** (344) 2627 Atlantic St NE 44483-4423 (Mail to: 2627 Atlantic St NE 44483-4498) J Jeffrey Baker (330) 372-4998

Westlake Church of the Advent **P** (139) 3760 Dover Center Rd 44145-5433 (Mail to: 3760 Dover Center Rd 44145-5433) Ronald Johnson (440) 871-6685

Willoughby Grace Church **P** (94) 36200 Ridge Rd 44094-4161 (Mail to: 36200 Ridge Rd 44094-4161) Rose Anne Lonsway (440) 942-1015

Wooster St James Episcopal Church **P** (271) 201 N Market St 44691-3511 (Mail to: 127 W North Street 44691) Evelyn Manzella

Youngstown St Augustines Church **P** (40) C/O Leonard Mc Cormick Treas 614 Parmalee Ave 44510-1603 (Mail to: 614 Parmalee Ave 44510-1603) Jane McDermott (330) 747-7225

Youngstown St Johns Church Episcopal **P** (304) 323 Wick Ave 44503-1003 (Mail to: 323 Wick Ave 44503-1095) Gayle Catinella (330) 743-3175

NON-PAROCHIAL CLERGY

Anderson MS *ret* Cleveland Heights OH
Angus CH *ret* Cleveland Heights OH
Bailey LC *dcn* Euclid OH
Bargetzi DM Lakewood OH
Baum GR Cleveland OH
Beamer CW *ret* Cleveland OH
Beeman PH *dcn* Bryn Mawr PA
Black VE Cleveland OH
Brewster W *ret* Kittery Point ME
Brown JL *dcn*
Butler JG *dcn* Akron OH
Cole AD *ret* Akron OH
Colwell KP *ret dcn* Chagrin Falls OH
Cooney JF Kent OH

Creasy WC *ret* New Concord OH
D'Alesandre PJ *ret* Chepachet RI
Dautel TP Gates Mills OH
Dell ML Shaker Heights OH
Dudley MD *ret* Canandaigua NY
Elliott RJ *ret* Tampa FL
Eversman KL Avon OH
Falcone JF *ret* Tulsa OK
Froehlich MF Akron OH
Gaston PL Hudson OH
Gibbs LW Springfield VA
Gillooly BC *dcn* Cleveland OH
Gingher RH *ret* Toledo OH
Grant PR Cleveland OH
Green GH *dcn* Hudson OH
Greenwood M Arroyo Grande CA
Griffith GE *ret* Coshocton OH
Grose FP *ret* Lisbon OH
Hanen PL *ret* Cleveland OH
Harding SM Omaha NE
Harig RO *ret* Akron OH
Harris HG *ret* Massillon OH
Hawkins TE Detroit MI
Hays DL *ret* Waverly OH
Herkner RT *ret* Huron OH
Hobbs WE *ret* Toronto ON
Holliger JC *ret* Delaware OH
Horner JS *ret* Elizabeth City NC
Horton CB
Hubbell GL *ret* Akron OH
Humphrey HM *ret* Chagrin Falls OH
Hunt JC *dcn* Oberlin OH
Ifill AS Yonkers NY
Isaac FR *ret* Cleveland OH
Jennings GC *ret* Sagamore Hills OH
Jones WH *ret* Toledo OH
Keller JS *ret* Rocky River OH
Kelly SE Pandora OH
Knaup DJ Cleveland Heights OH
MacDonald TC New Canaan CT
Mason DR *ret* Cleveland Heights OH
Maughan MW *ret* Sandusky OH
Maxwell BJ *dcn* Elyria OH
Mayfield DW *ret* Aurora OH
McCandless RL *ret* Akron OH
McCoy EK *ret* Cleveland OH
McElroy GA *ret* Chagrin Falls OH
Mitchener GA *ret* Cleveland Heights OH
Moore JA *ret* Albuquerque NM
Moorer DD *ret* Euclid OH

Morris RM *ret* Cumberland RI
Nevels HV *ret* Richmond VA
Nusser-Telfer HM Perrysburg OH
O'Keefe LF *ret* Kent OH
O'Rear LE
Patnaude RJ *ret* Warrenton VA
Pearson CE *ret* Perrysburg OH
Perkinson EM *ret* Plymouth MA
Petty JJ *ret* Marblehead MA
Pitman RW *ret* Cleveland Heights OH
Prater WG *ret* Thomaston ME
Pumphrey DW *ret* Akron OH
Purdom AB Cleveland OH
Ralston DD *ret* Lima OH
Rankin DT *ret* Cuyahoga Falls OH
Ransom CW *ret* Mount Vernon OH
Ray WL *ret* Huron OH
Reece HA Evanston IL
Reed BP *dcn* East Hampton CT
Rich NW *ret* Cleveland Heights OH
Richards JM *ret* Akron OH
Richey LE *ret* Toledo OH
Roosevelt NA *ret* Shaker Heights OH
Roth NL *ret* Oberlin OH
Sammons GP *ret* Toledo OH
Sammons MDH *ret* Kettering OH
Schutz CE *ret* Findlay OH
Sedgwick RS *ret* Lorain OH
Selnick T Gates Mills OH
Sipes DS *ret* Mansfield OH
Sloan CE *ret* Bolivar OH
Smercina EE *ret* Huron OH
Smith ME *ret* Toledo OH
Smith SJ New York NY
Smith-Criddle LC Madison CT
Sobol W *ret* Sylvania OH
Stewman KJ Bonita Springs FL
Tarsis LM *ret* Barberton OH
Taylor TR *ret* Danville KY
Trager J *dcn* Elyria OH
Trumble JL *ret* Tiffin OH
Turney NJ *ret* Hilltown PA
Ullman RL *ret* Philadelphia PA
Voorhees EH *ret* St. Augustine FL
Walcott R *ret* Cleveland OH
Watts CM *ret* Wilmington OH
Weaver RC *ret* Cleveland Heights OH
White NB *ret* Charlotte NC
Wrenn WC *ret* East Sandwich MA

DIOCESE OF OKLAHOMA
(PROVINCE VII)
Comprises the State of Oklahoma
DIOCESAN OFFICE 924 N Robinson Oklahoma City 73102
TEL (405) 232-4820   FAX (405) 232-4912
WEB www.epiok.org

Previous Bishops—
Theology P Thurston 1919-27, Thomas Casady m 1927 dio 1937-53, WR Chilton Powell 1953-77, Frederick W Putnam suffr 1963-79, Gerald N McAllister 1977-89, William J Cox asst 1980-88, Robert Manning Moody 1988-2007

Bishop—Rt Rev Dr Edward Joseph Konieczny DMin (1020) (Dio 15 Sep 07)

Staff: Cn to Ord J McLoughlin; *Cn Missioner* M Stephenson; *Bp Exec Asst* M Crawford; *Admin Asst to Cn to Ord* D Ellsworth; *Prison Missioner* N Brock; *Ch Form Dir* S Evans; *Comp E Morgan*; *Sr Acct* J Price; *Payroll & Benefits* M Smith; *Admin Comm* N Baxley; *Disaster Coordinator* A Kueteman.

Officers: Conv Sec M Wignall 9177 E 117th Pl Bixby OK; *Chanc* W Cathcart 2807 Classen Blvd OK; *Vice Chanc* G Derrick, T Williams; *Treas* H Baer

Stand Comm—Cler: Pres W Carroll W Holly T Baer. *Lay:* G Derrick M Whaley J Menzer

Dio Conv: TBD

PARISHES, MISSIONS, AND CLERGY

Ada St Lukes Episcopal Church **P** (148) 110 E 17th St 74820-7802 (Mail to: PO Box 890 74821-0890) John Norvell (580) 332-6429

Altus St Pauls Episcopal Church **P** (58) 721 N Thomas St 73521-2871 (Mail to: 721 N Thomas St 73521-2871) Carol Mollison Michael Trachman (580) 482-2102

Antlers St James Episcopal **M** (51) 700 N High St 74523-2245 (Mail to: 600 N High St 74523-2246) (580) 298-5123

Ardmore St Philips Episcopal Church **P** (464) 516 Mclish St 73401-4710 (Mail to: 516 McLish St 73401-4710) Stephen Bilsbury Joyce Spurgin (580) 226-2191

Bartlesville St Lukes Episcopal Church **P** (390) 210 E 9th St 74003-4905 (Mail to: 210 E 9th St 74003-4961) Thomas Stephens Sean Ekberg Laurel Watkins (918) 336-1212

Broken Arrow St Patricks Episcopal Church **P** (550) 4250 W Houston St 74012-4538 (Mail to: 4250 W Houston St 74012-4538) Shelby Scott Laura Beck Thomas Dahlman (918) 294-9444

Chickasha St Lukes Episcopal Church **M** (83) 124 S 6th St 73018-3420 (Mail to: 124 S 6th St 73018-3420) Justin Fletcher (405) 224-1296

Claremore St Pauls Episcopal Church **P** (130) 1310 N Sioux Ave 74017-4416 (Mail to: 1310 N Sioux Ave 74017-4416) Lisa Goforth

Clinton St Pauls Episcopal Church **M** (54) 321 S 7th St 73601-3903 (Mail to: PO Box 144 73601) Lynn Borrego (580) 323-2160

Coalgate St Peters Episcopal Church **M** (16) 107 W Hanover Ave 74538-1839 (Mail to: PO Box 165 74538-0165) (580) 927-3310

Cushing St Albans Episcopal Church **M** (8) 112 S Thompson Ave 74023-4040 (Mail to: 112 S Thompson Ave 74023-4040) Paul Ostrander (918) 225-2170

Duncan All Saints' Episcopal Church **P** (131) 809 W Cedar Ave 73533-4135 (Mail to: 809 W Cedar Ave 73533-4135) Anita Slovak Gary Templeton (580) 255-6165

Durant St Johns Episcopal Church **P** (96) 515 W Beech St 74701-4335 (Mail to: PO Box 1168 74702-1168) James Blagg (580) 924-1332

Edmond St Marys Episcopal Church **P** (754) 325 E 1st St 73034-4544 (Mail to: 325 E 1st St 73034-4500) Mark Story Nancy Bridges William Hesse Scott Lee (405) 341-3855

El Reno Christ Memorial Episcopal Church **M** (59) 500 S Bickford Ave 73036-3844 (Mail to: 500 S Barker Ave 73036-3801) Hillyer Jackson Sylvia Shirley (405) 262-1710

Enid St Matthews Church **P** (200) 518 W Randolph Ave 73701-3828 (Mail to: 518 W Randolph Ave 73701-3897) John Toles

Eufaula Trinity Episcopal Church **M** (74) S 3rd & High Sts 74432 (Mail to: PO Box 759 74432-0759) William Ellington Therese Starr (918) 689-2369

Grove St Andrews Episcopal Church **P** (185) 555 E 3rd St 74344-7139 Philip Lawrence Melissa Harris (918) 786-4113

Guthrie Trinity Church **P** (117) 310 E Noble Ave 73044-3311 (Mail to: 310 E Noble Ave 73044-3311)

Guymon St Stephens Episcopal Church **M** (19) 1803 N Lelia St 73942-2832 (Mail to: PO Box 1952 73942-1952) (580) 338-8747

Holdenville St Pauls Episcopal Church **M** (11) 8th And Oak Sts 74848 (Mail to: PO Box 69 74848-0069) Elizabeth Davis Cyntha Gilks (405) 379-5879

Hugo St Mark's Episcopal Church **P** (43) 803 S 3rd St 74743-6809 (Mail to: 803 S 3rd St 74743-6809) Arlen Fowler (580) 326-9197

Idabel St Luke the Beloved Physician **M** (22) 211 SE Ave N 74745 (Mail to: 211 SE Ave N 74745-5728)

Langston Holy Family Episcopal Church **M** (6) 308 West Hale 73050 (Mail to: PO Box 727 73050-0727) (405) 521-8839

Lawton St Andrews Episcopal Church **P** (252) 1313 SW D Ave 73501-4252 (Mail to: PO Box 1256 73502-1256) Shelley Forrester Katherine Dutcher Patricia Kardaleff (580) 355-9543

Lindsay St Michael & All Angels **M** (10) 1505 NW 4th St 73052-1803 (Mail to: PO Box 134 73052-0134) (405) 756-3433

Mcalester All Saints Episcopal Church **P** (116) 325 E Washington Ave 74501-4757 (Mail to: PO Box 534 74502-0534) Stephanie Swinnea (918) 423-1915

Miami All Saints Episcopal Church **P** (103) 225 B St NW 74354-5806 (Mail to: 225 B St NW 74354-5806) Mary Koppel Ruth Boman (918) 542-3662

Midwest City St Christophers Church **P** (226) 800 S Midwest Blvd 73110-4730 (Mail to: PO Box 10722 73140-1722) Emily Schnabl (405) 732-4802

Muskogee Grace Episcopal Church **HC** (235) Attn Mary Emily Basolo 218 N 6th St 74401-6209 (Mail to: 218 N 6th St 74401-6200) Charles Wickizer Thomas Harrington

Norman St Anselm Canterbury Assn **Campus Ministry** 800 Elm Ave 73069-8837 (Mail to: 800 Elm Ave 73069-8837) Kay Greenshields Joshua Woods (405) 360-6453

Norman St Johns Episcopal Church **P** (1018) 235 W Duffy St 73069-5827 (Mail to: PO Box 2088 73070-2088) Dwight Helt (405) 321-3020

Norman St Michaels Episcopal Church **P** (261) 1601 W Imhoff Rd 73072-7408 (Mail to: 1601 W Imhoff Rd 73072-7408) Tommy King (405) 321-8951

Oklahoma City All Souls Episcopal Church **P** (1667) 6400 N Pennsylvania Ave 73116-5626 (Mail to: 6400 N Pennsylvania Ave 73116-5694) Patrick Bright James Easter Dale Petley James Stewart (405) 842-1461

Oklahoma City Church of the Redeemer **P** (152) 2100 N Martin Luther King Ave 73111 (Mail to: PO BOX 11272 73136-1272) (405) 427-2106

Oklahoma City Church of the Resurrection **P** (317) 13112 N Rockwell Ave 73142-2717 (Mail to: 13112 N Rockwell Ave 73142-2700) Beth Bell Melva Bridges Nicolette Papanek (405) 721-2929

Oklahoma City Santa Maria Virgen **M** (863) 5500 S Western Ave 73109 (Mail to: 5500 S Western Ave 73109-4511) (405) 631-6747

Oklahoma City St Augustine of Canterbury **M** (247) 14700 N May Ave 73134-5009 (Mail to: 14700 N May Ave 73134-5008) Joseph Alsay Anthony Moon Robert Trammell (405) 751-7874

Oklahoma City St Davids Episcopal Church **M** (52) 3333 No Meridian Ave 73112 (Mail to: 3333 N Meridian Ave 73112-3198) Tracey Carroll (405) 942-1740

Oklahoma City St James Episcopal Church **M** (111) 8400 S Pennsylvania Ave 73159-5205 (Mail to: 8400 S Pennsylvania Ave 73159-5292) Nathan Carr Jeffrey Huston (405) 682-3405

Oklahoma City St Johns Episcopal Church **P** (296) 5401 N Brookline Av 73112-3514 (Mail to: 5401 N Brookline Ave 73112-3598) David Stock George Back Lisa Chronister Dana Orwig

✣ **Oklahoma City** St Pauls Cathedral **O** (1070) 127 NW 7th St 73102-6004 (Mail to: 127 NW 7th St 73102-6004) Justin Lindstrom Susan Joplin Marilyn Robertson (405) 235-3436

Okmulgee Church of the Redeemer **M** (44) 213 N Seminole Ave 74447-7334 (Mail to: PO Box 1012 74447-1012) (918) 756-2384

Owasso Church of the Holy Cross **M** (47) 9309 N 129th East Ave 74055-5314 (Mail to: 9309 N 129th East Ave 74055-5314) (918) 271-1075

Pauls Valley St Timothys Church **M** (23) 1820 S Walnut St 73075-6902 (Mail to: PO Box 485 73075-0485) Stanley Upchurch (405) 238-2133

Pawhuska St Thomas Episcopal Church **M** (44) 817 Leahy Ave 74056-3219 (Mail to: PO Box 1476 74056-1476) Kathleen Jones (918) 287-3513

Pawnee Church of the Ascension **M** (11) Seventh And Ash Sts 74058 (Mail to: PO Box 26 74058-0026) (918) 762-2771

Perry St Mark Episcopal Church **M** (22) 701 N 7th St 73077-4227 (Mail to: PO Box 507 73077-0507) William Powell (580) 336-9720

Ponca City Grace Episcopal Church **P** (208) 109 N 13th St 74601-7314 (Mail to: 109 N 13th St 74601-7314) Dee Bright Steven Mallory

✣ **Poteau** St Barnabus Episcopal Church **Other** 506 College Ave 74953-3114 (918) 647-9092

Pryor St Martin of Tours Episcopal Church **M** (65) 612 SE 1st St 74361-4614 (Mail to: PO Box 1153 74362-1153) William Martin (918) 825-1115

Sand Springs St Matthews Episcopal Church **M** (27) 601 N Lake Dr 74063-8716 (Mail to: 601 North Lake Drive 74063)

Sapulpa Church of the Good Shepherd **P** (191) 1420 E Dewey Ave 74066 (Mail to: 1420 E Dewey Ave 74066-3742) Joseph Farber Nancy Brown

Seminole St Marks Episcopal Church **M** (21) 800 N Highland St 74868 (Mail to: PO Box 1304 74818-1304) Lynn Borrego William Bales Elizabeth Davis (405) 382-2192

Shawnee Emmanuel Episcopal Church **P** (345) 501 N Broadway Ave 74801-6926 (Mail to: PO Box 1905 74802-1905) Roland Carroll John Belzer (405) 273-1374

Stillwater St Andrews Church **P** (397) 516 W 3rd Ave 74074-3001 (Mail to: 516 W 3rd Ave 74074-3001) James Cook Jeffrey Huston (405) 372-3357

Stillwater St Augustine Canterbury Center **Campus Ministry** 519 W University Ave 74074-3033 (Mail to: 519 W University Ave 74074-3033)

Tahlequah St Basils Episcopal Church **M** (81) 814 N Vinita Ave 74464-2235 (Mail to: 814 N Vinita Ave 74464-2235) Debora Jennings (918) 456-3649

✠ **Tulsa** Chapel of All Saints **Other** 5666 E 81st St 74136 (Mail to: 4040 E 91st St 74137) Robert Bibens (918) 481-1111

Tulsa Christ Episcopal Church **M** (148) 10901 S Yale Ave 74137-7211 (Mail to: 10901 S Yale Ave 74137-7211) Everett Lees Judith Gann (918) 299-7510

Tulsa St Adrian of Canterbury **Campus Ministry** 1115 S Florence Ave 74104-4104 (Mail to: 1115 S Florence Ave 74104-4104) (918) 631-2993

Tulsa St Aidans Episcopal Church **M** (35) 4045 N MLK, Jr. Blvd 74106-1541 (Mail to: 4045 N MLK, Jr. Blvd 74106-1541) William Holly (918) 425-7882

Tulsa St Dunstans Episcopal Church **P** (523) 5635 E 71st St 74136-6538 (Mail to: 5635 E 71st St 74136-6500) Alan Barrow Lois Gatchell Mary Hill (918) 492-7140

Tulsa St Johns Episcopal Church **P** (1186) 4200 S Atlanta Pl 74105-4331 (Mail to: 4200 S Atlanta Pl 74105-4300) Irving Cutter Susanne Methven John Rule (918) 742-7381

Tulsa St Lukes Episcopal Church **P** (124) 4818 E 9th St 74112-4240 (Mail to: 4818 E 9th St 74112-4240) Georges Jallouf (918) 834-4800

Tulsa St Peters Episcopal Church **P** (89) 9100 E 21st St 74129-1421 (Mail to: 9100 E 21st St 74129-1421) Heber Papini Mary Lord (918) 627-2713

Tulsa Trinity Church **P** (1859) 501 S Cincinnati Ave 74103-4801 (Mail to: 501 S Cincinnati Ave 74103-4800) Stephen McKee Kristina Maulden (918) 582-4128

Vinita St Johns Church **M** (51) 522 W Canadian Ave 74301-3612 (Mail to: PO Box 165 74301-0165) (918) 256-3766

Wagoner St James Church **M** (41) 303 E Church St 74467-5209 (Mail to: 303 E Church St 74467-5209) Edmund James (918) 485-5681

Watonga Whirlwind Mission of the Holy Family **M** (64) 1000 E Russworm Dr 73772 (Mail to: PO Box 26 73772-0026) James Kee-Rees (580) 623-5585

Westport St Bedes Episcopal Church **M** (55) 1 2 Miles North Hwy 64 74020 (Mail to: 6960 W Old Keystone Rd 74020-3506) John Powers (918) 743-2686

Woodward St Johns Episcopal Church **M** (73) 917 Texas St 73801-3125 (Mail to: 917 Texas St 73801-3125) Mary Davis (580) 256-7713

Yukon Grace Church - Episcopal **P** (54) 720 S Yukon Parkway 73099-3300 (Mail to: 720 S Yukon Pkwy 73099-4585) Kirsten Baer Timothy Baer (405) 354-7277

NON-PAROCHIAL CLERGY

Alexander WD
Anderson OH *ret* Culver City CA
Beard BB Owasso OK
Blanco-Monterroso L *ret* Oklahoma City OK
Blazek LS *dcn* Norman OK
Borrego JE *ret* Guthrie OK
Bradley CE *dcn*
Brewer RE *ret* Tulsa OK
Brown CH *ret* Ardmore OK
Burris RR *ret* Norman OK
Butcher GA *dcn* Chickasha OK
Carlin WB *ret* Duncan OK
Castillo SA *ret* Sparta WI
Clark CS *dcn* Indianola OK
Clem SD Mishawaka IN
Connell SLC *ret* Monkey Island OK
Daharsh FA Hugoton KS
Davis D *dcn* Shawnee OK
Disbrow JL *ret* Oklahoma City OK
Doherty NJ *ret* Tulsa OK
Dugan HW *ret* Altus OK
Edwards HD *ret* Oklahoma City OK
Egbert DA *ret* Edmond OK
Epple JF *ret* Saint Paul MN
Fellows RH *ret* Stillwater OK
Fox DC *ret* Cody WY
Freebern DW *dcn* Bartlesville OK
Gates RJ *ret*
Glandon CC *ret* Tulsa OK
Glenn ME Palestine TX
Gonzales PM *dcn* Watonga OK
Granger CI *ret* Midwest City OK
Greenwood HLH *ret*
Hampton CMD Oklahoma City OK
Hansen KS *dcn* Guthrie OK
Hileman ME *ret* Stillwater OK
Holley JP *dcn* Lawton OK
Hunkins OJ *ret* Edmond OK
Ibe MK Edmond OK
Jasper MA *ret* Oklahoma City OK
Jones SR *ret* Asheville NC
Kenney CS Georgetown TX
Kiker NW *dcn* Shawnee OK
Kinney RS *ret* Granbury TX
Labarre BLR *dcn* Tulsa OK
Lewis SC *dcn*
Lierle DK *ret* Phoenix AZ
Lindley SS *ret* Duncan OK
Maddon EC *ret* Keller TX
Marlin JH *ret* Oklahoma City OK
McEwen MT *ret* Medicine Park OK
McKenna CA Boerne TX
McLoughlin JA Oklahoma City OK
Menjivar N Alexandria VA
Metivier CA
Miller EL *ret* Oklahoma City OK
Miller JT *ret* Norman OK
Mullin MH *ret* Charlottesville VA
Murray KF Altus OK
Nesbitt ML Oklahoma City OK

Norris JR *ret* Tulsa OK
Orsburn KR
Paul LJ *dcn* Tulsa OK
Rahhal MD *ret dcn* Ardmore OK
Ray MA *ret* Tulsa OK
Ritter CA *dcn* Broken Arrow OK
Rockabrand WR *ret* Dallas TX
Rogers LS Claremore OK
Rosenbaum RL Manassas VA
Saunkeah BR *dcn* Ada OK
Scrutchins AP Tulsa OK
Servais JN Coalgate OK
Shackelford LC *ret* Sand Springs OK
Snyder PL *dcn* Midwest City OK
Spangler RJ *ret* Arden NC
Stephenson MP Norman OK
Sutherland A *ret* Norman OK
Thompson DJ
Thomson JV *ret* Tulsa OK

Tlucek LR *ret* Edmond OK
Underwood DA *dcn* Tulsa OK
Urmson-Taylor R *ret*
Waddle HA *dcn* Oklahoma City OK
Wakely NK *dcn* Norman OK
Walker ML *ret* Guthrie OK
Walters GL Hugo OK
Watkins MM *dcn* Bartlesville OK
Welch JD *dcn* Broken Arrow OK
Wilcox JF *ret* Norman OK
Williams GW *dcn* Norman OK
Wilson HL *ret* Laramie WY
Woltz CM *ret dcn* Oklahoma City OK
Woodward LC *dcn* Tulsa OK
Wooliver T Noble OK
Wright JAS *ret* Vinita OK
Youmans TS Oklahoma City OK
Young JO *dcn* Ardmore OK

DIOCESE OF OLYMPIA
(PROVINCE VIII)
Comprises western Washington
DIOCESAN OFFICE 1551 10th Ave E Seattle WA 98102
TEL (206) 325-4200   FAX (206) 325-4631
E-MAIL info@ecww.org   WEB ecww.org

Previous Bishops—
John A Paddock 1880-94, Wm M Barker 1894-1901, Frederic W Keator 1902-24, S Arthur Huston 1925-47, Stephen F Bayne Jr 1947-60, Wm F Lewis 1960-64, Ivol I Curtis 1964-76, Robt H Cochrane 1976-89, Sanford ZK Hampton asst 1996-2004, Vincent W Warner 1990-2007, Bavi Edna Rivera Suff 2004-10

Bishop—Rt Rev Gregory H Rickel (1021)
(Dio 15 Sep 2007)

Cn to Ord M Steedman Sanborn; *Treas* B Fox; *Sec* K Gusse; *Chanc* J Andrews; *V Chanc* M Reynvaan; *Hist Br* C Griffin n; *Archiv* D Wells; *Cn for Stew & Dev* L Ousley; *Cn for Finance & Property* L Humason; *Cn for Faith Formation: 35 & Under* R Kirkpatrick; *Cn for Operations* D Moore; *Dir Resource Ctr* S Tait; *Cn for Multicultural Min* A Davison; *Refugee Resettl* G Hope; *Mission to Seafarers Exec Dir* K Hawkins; *Ecum Off* vacant; *Huston Ctr Dir* B Tubbs; *SA Hse Mgr* C Corrigan

Stand Comm—Cler: Pres J Maynard C Espeseth B Fulton; *A* Feregrino *Lay:* K Rickert A Reid D Woods K Casey

Dio Conv: 21-22 Oct 2016 SeaTac WA

PARISHES, MISSIONS, AND CLERGY

Aberdeen St Andrews Episcopal Church **P** (431) 400 E 1st St 98520-4116 (Mail to: 400 E 1st St 98520-4116) Evan Clendenin Sarah Monroe (360) 533-2511

Allyn St Hugh of Lincoln Episcopal Church **M** (86) 280 E Wheelwright St S 98524 (Mail to: PO Box 156 98524-0156) Sylvia Haase Christie Logan James Neal Jennifer Pratt

Anacortes Christ Episcopal Church **M** (113) 1216 7th St 98221-1809 (Mail to: 1216 Seventh Street 98221-1809) Eric Johnson (360) 293-5790

Auburn St Matthews Episcopal Church **P** (278) 123 L St NE 98002-4434 (Mail to: 123 L St NE 98002-4434) Patricia Trytten (253) 833-0890

Bainbridge Island Grace Episcopal Church **M** (1011) 8595 NE Day Rd 98110-1395 (Mail to: 8595 NE Day Rd E 98110-1395) Mary Anderson Tommy Dillon Eric Mason William Maxwell (206) 842-9997

Bainbridge Island St Barnabas Episcopal Church **P** (480) 1187 Wyatt Way NW 98110-2722 (Mail to: 1187 Wyatt Way NW 98110-2722) Daniel Fowler Patricia Robertson Nancy Tiederman Dennis Tierney (206) 842-5601

Battle Ground Church of the Holy Spirit **M** (118) 2400 NW 9th Ave 98604-1117 (Mail to: PO Box 1117 98604-1117) (360) 687-3301

Bellevue All Saints Episcopal Church **M** (29) 1307 120th Ave NE 98005-2124 (Mail to: 1307 120th Ave NE 98005-2124) Stephen Moore (425) 646-1136

Bellevue Church of the Holy Apostles **M** (76) 15220 Main St 98007-5228 (Mail to: 15220 Main St 98007-5228) Jeffrey Sharp (425) 351-1423

Bellevue Church of the Resurrection **P** (138) 15220 Main St 98007-5228 (Mail to: 15220 Main St 98007-5228) Jeffrey Sharp (425) 746-0322

Bellevue St Margarets Episcopal Church **P** (898) 4228 Factoria Blvd SE 98006-1929 (Mail to: 4228 Factoria Blvd SE 98006-1929) Christina Jillard Christine Demura Robert Ford Frank Spina (425) 746-6650

Bellingham St Paul's Episcopal Church **P** (1041) 2117 Walnut St 98225-2836 (Mail to: 2117 Walnut St 98225-2836) Todd Foster Joshua Hosler Jonathan Weldon Charles Whitmore (360) 733-2890

Blaine Christ Episcopal Church **M** (78) 382 Boblett St 98230-4003 (Mail to: 382 Boblett St 98230-4003) (360) 332-4113

Bremerton St Pauls Episcopal Church **P** (321) 700 Callahan Dr 98310-3304 (Mail to: 700 Callahan Dr 98310-3304) Kathleen Kingslight Susan Stroup (360) 377-0106

Castle Rock St Matthew Church **M** (55) 412 Pioneer Ave NE 98611-9234 (Mail to: PO Box 1467 98611-1467) Elizabeth Cochran Suzanne Streiff (360) 274-9393

Cathlamet St James Episcopal Church **M** (43) 1134 Columbia St 98612-9535 (Mail to: 1134 Columbia St 98612-9535) Irene Martin Joann Prestegard Rachael Wolford

Chehalis St Timothy Episcopal Church **P** (128) 1826 SW Snively Ave 98532-4022 (Mail to: PO Box 277 98532-0277) (360) 748-8232

Darrington Church of the Transfiguration **M** (23) 836 Commercial St 98241 (Mail to: PO Box 55 98241-0055) Janet Loyd David Price (360) 436-1552

Eastsound Emmanuel Episcopal Church **P** (189) 242 Main St 98245 (Mail to: PO Box 8 98245-0008) Jose Gandara-Perea Kathleen Kinney (360) 376-2352

Edmonds St Albans Episcopal Church **P** (225) 21405 82nd Pl W 98026-7434 (Mail to: 21405 82nd Pl W 98026-7434) (425) 778-0371

Edmonds St Hilda-St Patrick Church **M** (147) 15224 52nd Ave W 98026-4304 (Mail to: 15224 52nd Ave W 98026-4304) Cynthia Espeseth Brian Wright (425) 743-4655

Elma St Lukes Episcopal Church **M** (20) 626 E Young St 98541-9357 (Mail to: 103 Heritage Dr 98541-9339) Steven Brill John Nemes (360) 482-3231

Everett Trinity Episcopal Church **P** (332) 2301 Hoyt Ave 98201-2898 (Mail to: 2301 Hoyt Ave 98201-2898) Rachel Taber-Hamilton (425) 252-4129

Federal Way Church of the Good Shepherd **P** (180) 345 S 312th St 98003-4031 (Mail to: PO Box 3108 98063-3108) Esther Poirier (253) 839-6100

Forks St Swithin **M** Prince of Peace Lutheran Church 98362-6938 (Mail to: 660 G St 98331) (360) 457-4862

Freeland St Augustines in-the-Woods Episcopal **P** (147) 5217 Honeymoon Bay Rd 98249-9712 (Mail to: PO Box 11 98249-0011) Nigel Taber-hamilton Malcolm Davis (360) 331-4887

Friday Harbor St Davids Episcopal Church **P** (101) 780 Park St 98250-9609 (Mail to: PO Box 2714 98250-2714) Margaret Lewis-Headden Douglas Simonsen (360) 378-5360

Gig Harbor St Johns Episcopal Church **P** (361) 7701 Skansie Ave 98335-8330 (Mail to: 7701 Skansie Ave 98335-8330) Marilyn Behrens Laura Murray Eric Stelle

Hoodsport St Germain Episcopal Church **M** (21) 600 N Lake Cushman Rd 98548-9781 (Mail to: PO Box 222 98548-0222) Peter Van Zanten (360) 866-9870

Issaquah St Michael and All Angels Church **P** (286) 325 SE Darst St 98027-4326 (Mail to: 325 SE Darst St 98027-4326) Katherine Sedwick John Schaeffer (425) 392-3215

Kenmore Church of the Redeemer **P** (687) 6211 NE 182nd St 98028-9419 (Mail to: PO Box 82677 98028-0677) Jedediah Fox Jill Zimmerschied (425) 486-3777

Kent St Columba's Episcopal Church **M** (88) 26715 Military Rd S 98032-7011 (Mail to: 26715 Military Rd S 98032-7011) Alissabeth Newton (253) 854-9912

Kent St James Episcopal Church **P** (856) 24447 94th Ave S 98030-4746 (Mail to: 24447 94th Ave S 98030-4746) (253) 852-4450

Kingston Faith Episcopal Church **M** (59) 9900 NE Shorty Campbell Road 98346 (Mail to: PO Box 505 98346-0505) Raymond Sheldon (360) 471-7522

Kirkland St Johns Episcopal Church **P** (273) 105 State St S 98033-6610 (Mail to: 127 State St S 98033-6687) Glen Deshaw Patrick Ousley Christina Robertson (425) 827-3077

Lacey St Benedicts Episcopal Church **M** (344) 910 Bowker St SE 98503-1212 (Mail to: PO Box 3811 98509-3811) George Anne Mcdonnell Anthony Irving John Van Eenwyk (360) 456-2240

Lakewood St Joseph & St John Church **P** (90) 11111 Old Military Rd SW 98498 (Mail to: PO Box 88550 98388-0550) Sheila Crisp Zula Johnston (253) 584-6143

Lakewood St Marys Episcopal Church **P** (305) 10630 Gravelly Lake Dr SW 98499-1328 (Mail to: 10630 Gravelly Lake Dr SW 98499-1328) Genevieve Grewell Eldwin Lovelady Robert

Mayor (253) 588-6621

Longview St Stephens Episcopal Church **P** (289) 1428 22nd Ave 98632-2828 (Mail to: 1428 22nd Ave 98632-2828) Kathleen Patton (360) 423-5600

Lopez Island Grace Church **P** (156) 70 Sunset Ln 98261 (Mail to: PO Box 324 98261-0324) Nancy Wynen (360) 468-3477

Maple Valley St Georges Episcopal Church **M** (201) 24219 Witte Rd SE 98038-6827 (Mail to: PO Box 510 98038-0510) Bonnie Malone (425) 432-5481

Marysville St Philip Episcopal Church **P** (72) 4312 84th St NE 98270-3447 (Mail to: 4312 84th St NE 98270-3447) (360) 659-1727

Medina St Thomas Episcopal Church **P** (1164) 8398 NE 12th St 98039-3100 (Mail to: PO Box 124 98039-0124) Alexander Breckinridge Kathryn Ballinger Stephen Best Martha Haig (425) 454-9541

Mercer Island Emmanuel Episcopal Church **P** (357) 4400 86th Ave SE 98040-4146 (Mail to: 4400 86th Ave SE 98040-4146) William Priest Beverly Hosea Jonathan Myers (206) 232-1572

Monroe Church of Our Saviour Episcopal **M** (50) 331 S Lewis St 98272-2320 (Mail to: PO Box 99 98272-0099) Nanette Waldie (360) 794-4816

Montesano St Marks Episcopal Church **M** (32) 124 N Sylvia St 98563-3717 (Mail to: 124 N Sylvia St 98563-3717) Joyce Avery F Lorraine Dierick (360) 249-3281

Mount Vernon St Pauls Episcopal Church **P** (97) 415 S 18th St 98273 (Mail to: 415 S 18th St 98274-4658) (360) 424-1822

Oak Harbor St Stephens Episcopal Church **P** (34) 555 SE Regatta Dr 98277-3981 (Mail to: PO Box 2754 98277-6754) Rilla Barrett Richard Scott (360) 279-0715

Olympia St Christophers Community Church **M** (169) 3320 79th Ave NW 98502-9693 (Mail to: 7902 Steamboat Island Road NW 98502) Patricia Sells James Thibodeaux (360) 866-2111

Olympia St John's Episcopal Church **P** (537) 114 20th Ave SE 98501-2923 (Mail to: 114 20th Ave SE 98501-2923) Albin Fogelquist June Johnson Robert Laird (360) 352-8527

Port Angeles St Andrews Church **P** (217) 510 E Park Ave 98362-8687 (Mail to: 510 E Park Ave 98362-6938) Gail Wheatley

Port Orchard St Bede Episcopal Church **M** (175) 1578 SE Lider Rd 98367-7516 (Mail to: PO Box 845 98366-0845) Arienne Davison (360) 876-1182

Port Townsend St Pauls Episcopal Church **P** (350) 1020 Jefferson St 98368-6618 (Mail to: PO Box 753 98368-0753) Dianne Andrews Francis Holly William Maxwell (360) 385-0770

Puyallup Christ Episcopal Church **P** (305) 422 W Meeker 98371-5380 (Mail to: 210 5th Street SW 98371) Rachel Endicott

Redmond Church of the Holy Cross **P** (826)

11526 162nd Ave NE 98052-2645 (Mail to: 11526 162nd Ave NE 98052-2645) James Eichner Carlos Caguiat Jane Rohrer (425) 885-5822

Renton St Luke Episcopal Church **P** (230) 99 Wells Ave S 98055-2153 (Mail to: 99 Wells Ave S 98057-2191) Kevin Pearson (425) 255-3323

Rockport St Martin-St Francis **M** 55223 Conrad Rd 98283-9740 (Mail to: 55223 Conrad Rd 98283-9740)

Sammamish Good Samaritan Episcopal Church **P** (458) 1757 244th Ave NE 98074-3323 (Mail to: 1757 244th Ave NE 98074-3323) Charles Danzey Gerald Garman (425) 868-4379

Seattle All Saints Episcopal Church **M** (65) 5150 S Cloverdale Pl S 98118-4711 (Mail to: 5150 S Cloverdale Pl 98118-4711) (206) 721-0285

Seattle Christ Episcopal Church **P** (181) 4548 Brooklyn Ave NE 98105-4509 (Mail to: 4548 Brooklyn Ave NE 98105-4537) Shelly Fayette (206) 633-1611

Seattle Church of St John the Baptist **P** (221) 3050 California Ave SW 98116-3302 (Mail to: 3050 California Ave SW 98116-3302) Michael Carroccino (206) 937-4545

Seattle Church of the Apostles **M** 4272 Fremont Avenue N 98103 (Mail to: 4272 Fremont Ave N 98103) (206) 851-8962

Seattle Church of the Ascension **P** (308) 2330 Viewmont Way W 98199 (Mail to: 2330 Viewmont Way W 98199-3939) Marilyn Cornwell Carla Robinson (206) 283-3967

Seattle Epiphany Parish of Seattle **P** (710) 1805 38th Ave 98122-3447 (Mail to: 1805 38th Ave 98122-3447) Doyt Conn Kate Wesch (206) 324-2573

Seattle St Andrews Episcopal Church **P** (747) 111 NE 80th St 98115-4033 (Mail to: 111 NE 80th St 98115-4033) Constance Carlson Kay Kessel-Hanna George Steig (206) 523-7476

Seattle St Clement of Rome Episcopal Church **P** (85) 1501 32nd Ave S 98144-3917 (Mail to: 1501 32nd Ave S 98144-3917) Thomas Bigelow Robert Gallagher (206) 324-3072

Seattle St Elizabeths Episcopal Church **P** (196) 1005 SW 152nd St 98166-1845 (Mail to: PO Box 66579 98166-0579) John Forman (206) 243-6844

Seattle St Lukes Episcopal Church **P** (39) 5710 22nd Ave NW 98107-3144 (Mail to: 5710 22nd Ave NW 98107-3144) Britt Olson (206) 784-3119

✠ **Seattle** St Marks Episcopal Cathedral **O** (2708) 1245 10th Ave E 98102-4323 (Mail to: 1245 10th Ave E 98102-4323) Steven Thomason Jennifer Daugherty Nancee Martin Richard Weyls (206) 323-0300

Seattle St Pauls Episcopal Church **P** (261) No 15 Roy St 98109-4019 (Mail to: PO Box 9070 98109-0070) Sara Fischer Stephen Crippen Kerry Kirking Alissabeth Newton Charles

Ridge Jay Rozendaal (206) 282-0786

Seattle St Peter's Episcopal Parish **P** (107) 1610 S King St 98144-2115 (Mail to: 1610 S King St 98144-2115) Richard Buhrer Edmund Harris (206) 323-5250

Seattle St Stephen's Episcopal Church **P** (457) 4805 NE 45th St 98105-3803 (Mail to: 4805 NE 45th St 98105-3803) Stephanie Parker Danae Ashley David Storm (206) 522-7144

Seattle Trinity Church Episcopal **P** (385) 609 8th Ave 98104-1921 (Mail to: 609 8th Ave 98104-1997) Malcolm Davis Jeffrey Gill (206) 624-5337

Seaview St Peters Episcopal Church **M** (17) 5000 N Place 98644 (Mail to: PO Box 268 98644-0268) (360) 642-3115

Sedro Woolley St James Church **P** (25) 1013 Polte Rd 98284-1142 (Mail to: PO Box 864 98284-1142) (360) 424-1822

Sequim St Lukes Episcopal Church **P** (260) 525 N 5th Ave 98382-3079 (Mail to: PO Box 896 98382-0896) Robert Rhoads (360) 683-4862

Shelton Church of St David of Wales **P** (114) 324 W Cedar St 98584-0339 (Mail to: PO Box 339 98584-0339) (360) 426-8472

Shoreline St David Emmanuel Episcopal Church **M** (58) 18842 Meridian Ave N 98133-4232 (Mail to: PO Box 77322 98177-0322) (206) 362-2565

Shoreline St Dunstans Church **P** (310) 722 N 145th St 98133-6502 (Mail to: 722 N 145th St 98133-6502) David Marshall (206) 363-4319

Silverdale St Antony of Egypt Episcopal Church **P** (166) 10239 Old Frontier Rd NW 98383-8895 (Mail to: PO Box 2822 98383-2822) William Fulton Craig Vocelka (360) 698-0555

Snohomish St John's Episcopal Church **P** (252) 913 2nd St 98290-2918 (Mail to: 913 2nd St 98290-2918) Mark Miller (360) 568-4622

Snoqualmie St Clare of Assisi Episcopal Church **M** (113) 8650 Railroad Ave SE 98065 (Mail to: PO Box 369 98065-0369) Patricia Baker (425) 831-6175

South Bend St Johns Episcopal Church **M** (28) 103 Adams St S 98577 (Mail to: PO Box 531 98586-0531) Gretchen Gunderson (360) 875-5326

Stanwood St Aidans Episcopal Church **M** (168) 1318 E State Route 532 98292 (Mail to: PO Box 145 98292-0145) Stephen Foisie

Tacoma All Saints' Episcopal Church **M** (107) 205 E 96th St 98445-2003 (Mail to: 205 E 96th St 98445-2003) Robert Biever (253) 537-2970

Tacoma Christ Church **P** (253) 310 N K St 98403-1617 (Mail to: 310 N K St 98403-1617) Janet Campbell Robert Carver Samuel Torvend (253) 383-1569

Tacoma Holy Family of Jesus Epis Church **M** (13) 1427 E 40th St 98411-2376 (Mail to: Sue Bernstein PO Box 112376 98411-2376) (253) 471-9838

Tacoma St Andrews Episcopal Church **P** (239) 7410 S 12th St 98465-1500 (Mail to: 7410 S 12th St 98465-1500) Martin Yabroff Edward Sterling (253) 564-4402

Tacoma St Lukes Episcopal Church **P** (469) 3615 N Gove St 98407-4815 (Mail to: 3615 N Gove St 98407-4815) Marlene Jacobs (253) 759-3534

Tacoma St Matthews Episcopal Church **P** (134) 6800 E Side Dr NE 98422-1116 (Mail to: 6800 E Side Dr NE 98422-1116) Kendall Haynes (253) 927-9808

Tahuya St Nicholas Episcopal Church **M** (27) 15000 NE North Shore Rd 98588 (Mail to: PO Box 101 98588-0101) Robert Williams (360) 275-7141

Vancouver All Saints Episcopal Church **M** (68) 2206 NW 99th St 98665-6253 (Mail to: PO Box 65825 98665-0028) (360) 573-8106

Vancouver Church of the Good Shepherd **P** (606) 805 SE Ellsworth Rd 98664-5120 (Mail to: 805 SE Ellsworth Rd 98664-5120) William Warne (360) 892-7770

Vancouver St Lukes Church **P** (472) 426 E Fourth Plain Blvd 98663-3040 (Mail to: 426 E Fourth Plain Blvd 98663-3040) Jaime Case Dennis Cole Willis Lonergan Eliacin Rosario-Cruz (360) 696-0181

Vashon Church of the Holy Spirit **P** (200) 15420 Vashon Hwy SW 98070 (Mail to: PO Box 508 98070-0508) Carla Pryne

Washougal St Anne Episcopal Church **M** (116) 2350 Main St 98671 (Mail to: PO Box 62 98671-0062) Jessica Smith

Westport St Christopher's Episcopal Church **M** (13) 281 W Spokane Ave 98595 (Mail to: PO Box 1248 98595-1248) (360) 268-0503

NON-PAROCHIAL CLERGY

Ackermann JF *dcn*
Adams RC *ret* Hinesburg VT
Adams WS *ret* Langley WA
Allen JM *ret* Lacey WA
Amburgey CG *dcn* Puyallup WA
Anthony JM *ret* Seattle WA
Appling EF *ret* Port Townsend WA
Armer SC *ret* Auburn WA
Arnold-Boyd AR *ret* Portland OR
Astleford EL *ret* Vancouver WA
Atcheson CB *ret* Seattle WA
Barber GA Washougal WA
Bartels JT *dcn* Lacey WA
Bayles RA *ret* South Bend WA
Beecher JC *ret*
Bell JR *ret* Palm Springs CA
Berge WC Mount Sinai NY
Besheer KA *ret* Seattle WA
Betsinger VL Allyn WA
Bigford JN *dcn* Kent WA
Bogel M *ret* Helotes TX
Bond LW *ret* Everett WA
Borders CL Longview WA
Bower A

Brelsford DB Seattle WA
Brentnall B *dcn* Blaine WA
Caguiat J *dcn* Saranac Lake NY
Campbell A
Carlson SS *dcn* Vashon WA
Carmichael MJ *dcn*
Carpenter GH *ret* Medina WA
Chrisman R *ret* Long Beach WA
Christie RL *ret* Ferndale WA
Clark DC Beaverton OR
Cleveland JB McMinnville OR
Collins PM *ret* Summerland CA
Conklin DG *ret* Berlin
Corrigan CL Austin MN
Craighead JT Vashon WA
Creighton S *ret* Bellingham WA
Davis WR *ret* Friday Harbor WA
Dean SC Mercer Island WA
Dearing T *ret* Stamford
Dement TE *ret* Spokane WA
Deng Deng W Renton WA
Devine WAJ Bellevue WA
Dills RS Seattle WA
Dogaru VA Battle Ground WA
Donohue-Adams A Austin TX
Dunn RE *ret* Granite Falls WA
Eaton KLA *dcn* Port Townsend WA
Ensor AJ *dcn* Seattle WA
Eustis PA *ret* Grants NM
Fageol SA Langley WA
Farr CA West Hartford CT
Fast TH *ret* Seattle WA
Feregrino A
Fergueson JF *ret* Bothell WA
Foisie DAC Lothian MD
Forbes CA *ret* Marysville WA
Fowler SG *ret* Seattle WA
Francis MJ *ret* Seattle WA
French RC *ret* Cupertino CA
Garlichs RW *ret* Seattle WA
Garratt SR *ret* Lake Forest Park WA
Gehrig SJ Renton WA
Gillett RW *ret* Seattle WA
Godwin JD *ret* Seattle WA
Goode C *ret* Lopez Island WA
Gorsuch JP *ret* Milwaukee WI
Gould MD *dcn* Maple Valley WA
Grabinski KL *dcn* Seattle WA
Green RL *ret* Longview WA
Grout EL *dcn* Seattle WA
Hakiel NE Sultan WA
Halbrook TR *ret* Aberdeen WA
Hanna GB *ret* Seattle WA
Harper WR *ret* Bainbridge Island WA
Hayman RF *ret* Seattle WA
Helgeson GM *ret* Port Townsend WA
Heller J Poulsbo WA
Hickey-Tiernan JJ *ret* Tacoma WA
Hoebermann CM *dcn* Auburn WA
Hopkins VL *dcn* Federal Way WA
Houi-Lee SS Federal Way WA

Hubbard LM *dcn* Port Angeles WA
Jackson EMC *ret* Kingston WA
Jessett FE *ret* Spokane WA
Jimenez-Mesenbring MJ *dcn* Seattle WA
Johns NS *ret* Bremerton WA
Johnson JL *ret* Tumwater WA
Johnson LM Westport WA
Johnson WC *ret* Shoreline WA
Keller P *ret* Cody WY
Kennedy K *dcn*
Kirkpatrick RB Seattle WA
Knowles WR Kirkland WA
Kolbet PR Wellesley MA
Korathu AM *ret* Seattle WA
Lambert JP *ret* Kent WA
Lane JC *dcn* Port Townsend WA
Leche ED *ret* Friday Harbor WA
Leech JR Tucson AZ
Lewis PG *dcn*
Lindsey BK *ret* Spokane WA
Lobdell GT Mount Vernon WA
Lolcama TA *dcn* Lakewood WA
Luethe RL *ret* Chehalir WA
Lukens AP *ret* Bellevue WA
Mack AE *ret*
Mackay D *ret* Kirkland WA
Mackenzie MC Bellevue WA
Maddux DJ *ret* Shelton WA
Maier AR North Hollywood OR
Maynard JF *ret* Tacoma WA
McCaw MA Wellesley MA
McClain RL *ret* San Diego CA
McCulloch KT *ret* Lakewood WA
McDaniel JM *ret* Bainbridge Island WA
McNamara K Allyn WA
McQueen DL *ret* Lake Havasu city AZ
Mesenbring DG Seattle WA
Mikel JF
Miller AS *ret* Palm Desert CA
Miller JJW *dcn* Westport WA
Minifie TR *ret* Snohomish WA
Moore DC *ret* Eastsound WA
Moore MD *dcn* Centennial CO
Moore RA *ret* Grapeview WA
Moorehead CFP *dcn* Seattle WA
Morrison MA *dcn* Santa Barbara CA
Mullins JP *dcn* Seattle WA
Murray VD Port Angeles WA
Nakayama TM *ret* Seattle WA
Novak MA *dcn* Shoreline WA
Ortung TE Kirkland WA
O'Shea SJ *ret* Bainbridge Island WA
Ostertag EF *ret* Burien WA
Paolozzi JL *ret*
Pearson JN Steilacoom WA
Peters GW Seattle WA
Phinney JM *ret* Port Townsend WA
Pollock DS *ret* Gig Harbor WA
Porter GW *ret* Santa Rosa CA
Radcliffe ES *ret* Port Orchard WA
Ramerman DG Anacortes WA

Rankin EH *ret* Vancouver WA
Reddell RK *ret* Bellingham WA
Reid CB Seattle WA
Reid MS *ret* Williamsburg VA
Rhodes RW *ret* Vancouver WA
Richards FI *ret* Burlington WA
Rietmann PD *ret* Tacoma WA
Ringland RL *dcn* Mount Vernon WA
Rodin CJS Anacortes WA
Rogers HSF *ret* Bellevue WA
Ruder JW *ret* Castlegar BC
Saunderson AM Tacoma WA
Schmaling PJ *dcn* Blaine WA
Schnack PE
Scott RJ *dcn*
Seeger EA *ret* SeaTac WA
Sells JE *ret* Salt Lake City UT
Shaver SR
Shehane MK *ret dcn* Seattle WA
Sherman GC *ret* Seattle WA
Shigaki JM *ret* Seattle WA
Shigaki PY *dcn*
Smith DL *ret* Beulah CO
Smith JK *dcn* Lakewood WA
Smith KC Seattle WA
Snow PD *ret* Seattle WA
Steedman Sanborn ML Kent WA
Steele CC *ret* Seattle WA
Stewart DR *ret* Kailua HI

Stewart RR *ret* New Paltz NY
Strimer PM *ret* Seattle WA
Stroo EE *dcn* Seattle WA
Taylor ND *dcn* Mount Vernon WA
Taylor PL *ret* Seattle WA
Taylor RV Benton City WA
Tench JM *ret* Poulsbo WA
Thomas JM Durham NC
Thompson JK *ret* Vashon WA
Tomter PA *ret* Portland OR
Trelease ML *ret* Lopez Island WA
Tyree-Cuevas SMC *ret* Tacoma WA
Vervynck JR *ret dcn* Oceanside CA
Ward KM Seattle WA
Weller EB Seattle WA
Wesen VJS *ret* Mount Vernon WA
Williams HR *ret* Seattle WA
Williams RH *ret* Seattle WA
Wills CE *ret* Seattle WA
Wilson GS *ret* Brier WA
Wilton GWP Canterbury ENGLAND
Winn JB *ret* Silverdale WA
Wolfe VE *ret* Milton Freewater OR
Wong PYM *ret* Rockville Centre NY
Woods JE *dcn* Des Moines WA
Wright MA Longview WA
Wright SR *ret* Bellevue WA
Yearwood K Saint Albans NY
Zimmerman CR *ret* Kirkland WA

STATE OF OREGON
Dioceses of Oregon and Eastern Oregon

DIOCESE OF OREGON
(PROVINCE VIII)
Comprises Oregon west of the Cascade Mountains
DIOCESAN OFFICE 11800 SW Military Ln Portland OR 97219-8436
TEL (503) 636-5613   FAX (503) 636-5616
E-MAIL marieb@diocese-oregon.org   WEB www.diocese-oregon.org

Previous Bishops—
Thomas F Scott 1854-67, Benj W
Morris m 1868 (OR and WA) 1880
(OR) dio 1889-1906, Chas Scadding
1906-14, Walter T Sumner 1915-
35, Benj D Dagwell 1936-58, James
WF Carman 1958-74, Hal R Gross
suffr 1965-79, Matthew P Bigliardi
1974-85, Robert L Ladehoff coadj 1985 Bp 1986-2003,
Johncy Itty 2003-08

Bishop—Rt Rev Michael Joseph Hanley (1041)
(Dio 10 Apr 2010)

Cn Ord N Ellgren; *Treas* S Morris; *Ex Asst* M Bagwell;
Chanc PA Dakopolos PO Box 749 Salem OR 97308;
Fin M Macy; *Archdcns* B Mallon & C Hawley; *C Ed* B
Ross; *Comm* J Quanbeck; *Prog/Budg* T Hutchinson;
COM P Hale; *Archivist* M Bagwell

Deans: Metro-East Rev D Morrow; *Columbia* Rev D
Sweeney; *Sunset* Rev J Littlefield; *Will* pending; *Cen*
Rev B Powell; *Sou* Rev T Young; *S Coast* Rev A Hazen

Stand Comm—Cler: D Sweeney S Justice R Bryant
N Gallager; *Lay: Pres* S Brewster J Simpson J Walker
S Rogers

Dio Conv: 3-5 Nov 2016 Eugene OR

PARISHES, MISSIONS, AND CLERGY

Albany St Albans Episcopal Church **M** (137) 1730 Hill St SE 97322-4246 (Mail to: PO Box 1556 97321-0465)

Ashland Trinity Episcopal Church **P** (317) 44 N 2nd St 97520-1927 (Mail to: 44 N 2nd St 97520-1927) Bert Anderson Anne Bartlett Anthony Hutchinson Meredith Pech (541) 201-3418

Astoria Grace Episcopal Church **P** (92) 1545 Franklin Ave 97103-3717 (Mail to: 1545 Franklin Ave 97103-3717) Patricia Morris-Rader Lance Peeler (503) 325-4691

Bandon Church of St John by the Sea **M** (70) 795 Franklin Avenue 97411-0246 (Mail to: PO Box 246 97411-0246) Beth Hoffmann Jo Miller Thomas Murdock (541) 347-2152

Beaverton St Bartholomews Episcopal Church **P** (456) 11265 SW Cabot St 97005-2295 (Mail to: 11265 SW Cabot St 97005-2295) Jeffrey Littlefield Janis Hansen Philippa Lindwright Mikel Mcclain Roger Reynolds (503) 644-3468

Boring Holy Cross Episcopal Church **M** (82) 10351 SE Orient Dr 97009 (Mail to: PO Box 1462 97009-1462) Roberto Maldonado-Mercado (503) 663-4223

Brookings St Timothy Episcopal Church **M** (123) 401 Fir St 97415-9222 (Mail to: PO Box 1237 97415-0115) James Lindley (541) 469-3314

Cave Junction Church of St Matthias **M** (7) 25904 97523-0805 (Mail to: PO Box 805 97523-0805) James Boston (541) 592-2006

Coos Bay Emmanuel Episcopal Church **P** (214) 370 Market Ave 97420-2229 (Mail to: PO Box 1028 97420-0226) Christine Close Erskine (541) 269-5829

Coquille St James Episcopal Church **M** (38) 210 E 3rd St 97423-1871 (Mail to: 210 E 3rd St 97423-1871) Alba Hazen (541) 396-2322

Corvallis Church of the Good Samaritan **P** (649) 333 NW 35th St 97330-4908 (Mail to: 333 NW 35th St 97330-4908) Simon Justice Abigail Buckley Lance Peeler (541) 757-6647

Corvallis St Anselm of Canterbury Episcopal Ch **CC** No 2615 NW Arnold Way 97330-5308 (Mail to: 2615 NW Arnold Way 97330-5308) Douglas Hale (541) 752-3734

Cottage Grove St Andrews Episcopal Church **M** (23) 1301 W Main St 97424-1802 (Mail to: 1301 W Main St 97424-1802) Lawrence Crumb (541) 767-9050

Dallas Church of St Thomas **M** (72) 1486 SW Levens St 97338-0144 (Mail to: PO Box 144 97338-0144) Addyse Palagyi (503) 623-8522

Drain St Davids Episcopal Church **M** (5) 239 East B Ave 97436 (Mail to: PO Box 97 97435-0097) (541) 972-7085

Eugene Church of the Resurrection **P** (236) 3925 Hilyard St 97405-3957 (Mail to: 3925 Hilyard St 97405-3957) Brent Was Nancy Gallagher Maron Van (541) 686-8462

Eugene St Marys Episcopal Church **P** (631) 1300 Pearl St 97401-3539 (Mail to: 1300 Pearl St 97401-3539) Thomas English Douglas Hale Nancy Muhlheim Robert Powell Ann Rose Warren Toebben

Eugene St Matthews Episcopal Church **P** (174) 4110 River Rd 97404-1235 (Mail to: 4110 River Rd 97404-1235) Patricia Hale (541) 689-4010

Eugene St Thomas Episcopal Church **P** (163) 1465 Coburg Rd 97401-5006 (Mail to: 1465 Coburg Rd 97401-5006) (541) 343-5241

Florence St Andrews Episcopal Church **M** (108) 2135 19th St 97439 (Mail to: PO Box 15 97439-0001) John Crocker Georgia Dubose (541) 997-6600

Forest Grove St Bede Episcopal Church **M** (130) 1609 Elm St 97116-2503 (Mail to: 1609 Elm St 97116-2503) (503) 357-5300

Gardiner St Mary Episcopal Church **M** (29) North 2nd & High Sts 97441 (Mail to: PO Box 208 97441-0208) (541) 271-0413

Gold Beach St Matthews Episcopal Church **M** (43) 94261 Moore St 97444 (Mail to: PO Box 651 97444-0651) George Walter (541) 247-7878

Grants Pass St Lukes Episcopal Church **P** (192) 244 NW D St 97526-2042 (Mail to: 224 NW D St 97526-2042) Gary Young Joan Bristol (541) 476-2493

Gresham St Luke the Physician Epis Church **P** (119) 120 SW Towle Ave 97080-6750 (Mail to: 120 SW Towle Ave 97080-6750) Jennifer Creswell

Hillsboro All Saints Parish of Hillsboro **P** (111) 372 NE Lincoln St 97124-3146 (Mail to: 372 NE Lincoln St 97124-3146) David Brownmiller

✢ **Hillsboro** San Pablo Church **Other** (137) 372 NE Lincoln St 97124-3146 (Mail to: 372 NE Lincoln St 97124-3146) Wilson Ferreira-Sandoval (503) 640-9425

Lake Oswego Christ Episcopal Church **P** (1189) 1060 Chandler Rd 97034-2874 (Mail to: PO Box 447 97034-0048) Carolynne Fairweather Shannon Leach Jeremy Lucas Alison Schultz Thomas Stanwood (503) 636-5618

Lebanon St Martins Episcopal Church **P** (162) 257 E Milton St 97355-3493 (Mail to: 257 E Milton St 97355-3493) Carol Sedlacek Helen Richard Charlotte Wells (541) 451-1159

Lincoln City St James Episcopal Parish **P** (82) 2490 NE Highway 101 97367-4148 (Mail to: PO Box 789 97367-0789) Kristina Burbank Christine Hertlein (541) 994-2426

McMinnville St Barnabas Episcopal Church **P** (261) 822 W Second St 97128 (Mail to: PO Box 539 97128-0539) (503) 472-5831

Medford St Marks Episcopal Parish **P** (369) 140 N Oakdale Ave 97501-2629 (Mail to: 426 W 6th St 97501-2713) Jedediah Holdorph Thomas Murphy Betty Pinnock Linda Potter (541) 773-3111

Monmouth St Hildas Episcopal Church **M** (67) 245 Main St W 97361-2024 (Mail to: 245 Main St W 97361-2024) William Mosier Ronald Wynn (503) 838-6087

Nehalem St Catherine Episcopal Church **M** (182) 36335 Highway 101 N 97131-9732 (Mail to: PO Box 251 97130-0251) Patricia Steagall (503) 368-7890

Newberg St Michael/San Miguel **M** (195) 110 S Everest Rd 97132-2113 (Mail to: PO Box 358 97132-0358) Roberto Arciniega Juan Guerra-Diaz (503) 538-3080

Newport St Stephens Episcopal **P** (88) 331 SW 9th St 97365-0076 (Mail to: PO Box 1014 97365-0076) Susan Church Janis Calhoun George Goold (541) 265-5251

Oregon City St Pauls Episcopal Church **P** (191) 822 Washington St 97045-1945 (Mail to: 822 Washington St 97045-1945) Davis Fisher Daniel Morrow

Port Orford St Christophers Church **M** (48) 9th & Washington Sts 97465 (Mail to: PO Box 214 97465-0214) Norman Goldman (541) 347-1504

Portland All Saints Episcopal Church **P** (303) 4033 SE Woodstock Blvd 97202-7661 (Mail to: 4033 SE Woodstock Blvd 97202-7661) Laura Truby (503) 777-3829

Portland Ascension Parish **P** (235) 1823 SW Spring St 97201-2345 (Mail to: 1823 SW Spring St 97201-2345) Claude Craig Robert Ladehoff (503) 227-7806

Portland Church of St John the Evangelist **P** (404) 2036 SE Jefferson St 97222-7660 (Mail to: 2036 SE Jefferson St 97222-7660) Stephen Denny William Lupfer Richard Simpson (503) 653-5880

Portland Grace Memorial Church **P** (474) 1535 NE 17th Ave 97232-1417 (Mail to: 1535 NE 17th Ave 97232-1417) Darrah Clark Esme Jo Culver Martin Elfert Lucy Houser (503) 287-0418

Portland Parish of St John the Baptist **P** (469) 6300 SW Nicol Rd 97223-7566 (Mail to: 6300 SW Nicol Rd 97223-7566) Robert Bryant Julia Jensen Heather Wenrick Colin Williams

Portland Saints Peter and Paul **P** (426) 8147 SE Pine St 97215-1554 (Mail to: 8147 SE Pine St 97215-1554) Tracy LeBlanc Marla McGarry-Lawrence (503) 254-8168

Portland St Aidan's Episcopal Church **P** (168) 17405 NE Glisan St 97230-6414 (Mail to: PO Box 1319 97030-0277) (503) 252-6128

Portland St Andrew Episcopal Church **M** (75) 7600 N Hereford Ave 97203-3432 (Mail to: 7600 N Hereford Ave 97203-3432) Karen Ward (503) 285-0631

Portland St Barnabas Episcopal Church **P** (151) 2201 SW Vermont St 97219-1935 (Mail to: 2201 SW Vermont St 97219-1935) Sean Wall (503) 246-1949

Portland St Davids Episcopal Church **P** (183) 2800 SE Harrison St 97214-5650 (Mail to: 2800 SE Harrison St 97214-5650) John Nesbitt P Joshua Griffin James Joiner (503) 232-8461

Portland St Gabriel the Archangel Episcopal **M** (411) 17435 NW West Union Rd 97229-2190 (Mail to: 17435 NW West Union Rd 97229-2190) Louann Pickering Thomas Lang (503) 645-0744

Portland St James Episcopal Church **P** (185) 11511 SW Bull Mountain Rd 97224-2716 (Mail to: 11511 SW Bull Mountain Road 97224-2716) Robert Williams (503) 639-3002

Portland St Matthews Episcopal Church **P** (59) 11229 NE Prescott St 97220-2457 (Mail to: 11229 NE Prescott St 97220-2457) Joshua Kingsley (503) 252-5720

Portland St Michael & All Angels Church **P** (796) 1704 NE 43rd Ave 97213-1402 (Mail to: 1704 NE 43rd Ave 97213-1402) Christopher Craun Samuel Borbon Sallie Bowman Arlan Bullock James Joiner David Perry John Scannell Bonnie Stewart (503) 284-7141

Portland St Philip the Deacon Epis Church **P** (81) 120 NE Knott St 97212-3010 (Mail to: 120 NE Knott St 97212-3010) Deborah Brown (503) 281-5802

Portland St Stephens Episcopal Parish **P** (193) 1432 SW 13th Ave 97201-3356 (Mail to: 1432 SW 13th Ave 97201-3390) Dennis Parker Dale Carr (503) 223-6424

✣ **Portland** Trinity Episcopal Cathedral **O** (1818) 147 NW 19th Ave 97209-1901 (Mail to: 147 NW 19th Ave 97209-1901) Phillip Ayers Valerie Ivey Nathanael Lerud Sandra Ragan John Scannell Maureen Tighe Patrick Tomter (503) 222-9811

Prospect Church of the Good Shepherd **M** (14) No 13 Mill Creek Dr 97536-9728 (Mail to: 431 Red Blanket Rd 97536-9718) John Brown (541) 560-3571

Riddle Church of the Ascension **M** (14) 135 N D St 97469 (Mail to: PO Box 460 97469-0460) Robert Lonergan (541) 874-2936

Roseburg St Georges Episcopal Church **P** (221) 1024 SE Cass Ave 97470-4912 (Mail to: 1024 SE Cass Ave 97470-4984) (541) 673-4048

Saint Helens Christ Episcopal Church **M** (102) 35350 E Division Rd 97051-3202 (Mail to: PO Box 478 97051-0478) (503) 397-1033

Salem Prince of Peace Episcopal Church **M** (148) 1525 Glen Creek Rd NW PO Box 5757 97304-2726 (Mail to: PO Box 5757 97304-0757) Margaret McMurren Anne Moore (503) 585-1479

Salem St Pauls Episcopal Church **P** (1059) 1444 Liberty St SE 97302-4344 (Mail to: 1444 Liberty St SE 97302-4344) Anne Emry Zachary Harmon (503) 362-3661

Salem St Timothys Episcopal Church **P** (160) 3295 Ladd Ave NE 97301-1750 (Mail to: PO Box 7416 97303-0089) Brandon Filbert Donald Wilson

Seaside Calvary Parish **P** (146) 503 N Holladay Dr 97138-6923 (Mail to: 503 N Holladay Dr 97138-6923) David Sweeney (503) 738-5773

Shady Cove St Martins Church **M** (55) 95 Cleveland St 97539-9730 (Mail to: PO BOX

786 97539-9730) Randel Livingood (541) 878-2166

Silverton St Edwards Episcopal Church **M** (108) 211 W Center St 97381-1905 (Mail to: PO Box 344 97381-0344) Shana Mccauley (503) 873-6188

Springfield Church of St John the Divine **P** (50) 2537 Game Farm Rd 97477-7577 (Mail to: PO Box 1537 97477-0166) (541) 746-3322

Stayton Christ the King on the Santiam **M** (12) 550 W Regis St 97383-1164 (Mail to: PO Box 403 97383-0403) Thomas Moehl (503) 394-4113

Sutherlin Church of the Holy Spirit **M** (22) 120 S Umatilla St 97479-9548 (Mail to: PO Box 1398 97479-1398) Nancy Gallagher (541) 459-4697

Tillamook St Albans Episcopal Parish **P** (169) 2102 6th St 97141-3900 (Mail to: PO Box 285 97141-0285) (503) 842-6192

Toledo St Johns Episcopal Church **M** (38) 110 NE Alder St 97391-1520 (Mail to: 110 NE Alder St 97391-1520) Pauline Morrison (541) 336-3161

Waldport St Luke by the Sea Episcopal Church **M** (79) 1353 Highway 101 S 97394 (Mail to: PO Box 422 97394-0422) Susan Church (541) 563-4812

Wilsonville St Francis of Assisi Episcopal **P** (607) 8818 SW Miley Rd 97070 (Mail to: PO Box 445 97070-0445) Beth Mallon Anthony Petrotta Kenneth Russell (503) 678-5422

Woodburn St Marys Episcopal Church **M** (78) 1560 W Hayes St 97071-4314 (Mail to: PO Box 362 97071-0362) Samuel Borbon (503) 982-6262

NON-PAROCHIAL CLERGY

Alexander JR Berkeley CA
Andrews AE *ret* Portland OR
Avery SW *dcn* Florence OR
Barthelemy PB *ret* Lake Oswego OR
Bennett J Roseburg OR
Berktold BC *ret dcn* Eugene OR
Berktold TA *ret* Eugene OR
Bernhard MM *ret dcn* Corvallis OR
Bishop EL *ret* Henrico VA
Blinman CL *ret* Oro Valley AZ
Boozer AEC *ret* Portland OR
Borg MW *ret* Portland OR
Borsch KA *dcn*
Brown MM *ret* Auburn WA
Brown RE *ret*
Brubaker Garrison TV Eugene OR
Bruce JA *ret* Wilsonville OR
Carlson RB Beaverton OR
Cartwright TL *ret* Woodburn OR
Clark TB *dcn* Salem OR
Close DW *ret* Clinton WA
Coulter CR *ret* Portland OR
Crawford NR *ret dcn* Eugene OR
Cummins TW Portland OR
Dinovo DR Milwaukie OR

Dolph SMM Portland OR
Dorsch KJ *ret* Beaverton OR
Drynan TS *dcn*
Dubay JA *ret* Portland OR
Eick MH *dcn* Tigard OR
Ellgren NA Portland OR
Finch BJ *dcn* Tualatin OR
Floyd TA *dcn* Forest Grove OR
Fones PA Springfield OR
Fritsch PL *ret* Las Vegas NV
Galvin KMAM *ret* McMinnville OR
Gard MA Portland OR
Goertz LR *dcn*
Goman JG *ret* Corvallis OR
Gonzalez-Mesa G *ret* Gresham OR
Gray CD *dcn* Newberg OR
Hadley DJ *ret* Charlevoix MI
Hagen ME *dcn* Portland OR
Hammon LRR *ret* Lake Oswego OR
Hammond CA *ret* Portland OR
Harrell LJ *ret* Cambridge MA
Harris MH *ret* Pinehurst NC
Hawley CR *dcn* Eugene OR
Hazelett JR *ret* Portland OR
Healy C
Heverly CB *ret* Portland OR
Higgins-Shaffer DH *dcn* Seaside OR
Hilyard JL *ret* Portland OR
Holland KG *dcn* Portland OR
Howard CG *dcn* Gresham OR
Howser CLJ *dcn* Ashland OR
Jenkins JM *dcn* Eugene OR
Knight HT *ret* Sausalito CA
Krueger AP *ret* Portland OR
Laing CA *ret* Portland OR
Lambert SA *dcn* Portland OR
Leach JZ *ret* Las Vegas NV
Likowski JB *ret* Longview WA
Likwartz JS *dcn* Casper WY
Litzenberger CJ *ret* Portland OR
Loop RB *ret* Astoria OR
Mackendrick GW *ret* Forest Grove OR
Maris ME *ret* Portland OR
McCarthy WR *ret* Corvallis OR
McKenzie WB *ret* Portland OR
McKinley MST *dcn* Waldport OR
McMurren JJ *ret* Salem OR
Meier KI Atlantic Beach FL
Morrison RP Lincoln City OR
Morse EB *ret* Dallas OR
Mudge BDC *ret* Bandon OR
Neilson KB Portland OR
Norcross SC *ret* Portland OR
Nunez CE *ret* Portland OR
Olsen DL *ret* Tigard OR
Pace DT *ret* Portland OR
Pardington GP *ret* Portland OR
Parr HK Eugene OR
Peck DM *dcn* Eugene OR
Peck FW *ret* Vancouver WA
Pero DE *dcn* Forest Grove OR

Piper MM Eagle Point OR
Ramey LF *dcn* Salem OR
Richter KJ Brooklyn NY
Roddy BJ *ret* Salt Lake City UT
Roddy JE *dcn* Salt Lake City UT
Rodman RC *ret* Bainbridge Island WA
Rothauge AJ *ret* Friday Harbor WA
Sanders JM Lake Oswego OR
Scannell AU *ret* Portland OR
Schneider SV *ret* Portland OR
Sedlacek WH Lebanon OR
Semes RL *ret* Palm Springs CA
Shippey EE *ret* Coquille OR
Shulda DL *dcn* Eugene OR
Sipe RB *ret* Saint Helens OR
Smith JH Portland OR

Smith WA *ret* Sandy Spring MD
Stevenson TE *ret* Alsea OR
Stewart CT *dcn* Lake Oswego OR
Thurston AC *ret* Lake Oswego OR
Tiegs KSB Riverside CA
Toll RK *ret* Milwaukie OR
Treadwell RA *ret* McMinnville OR
Trewhella CK *ret* Yamhill OR
Tyndall JH Farnborough Hants
Tyson SA *ret* Coos Bay OR
Veale DM *ret* Carlsbad CA
Voyle RJ Hillsboro OR
Whitney-Wise SD *ret* Portland OR
Wood KR *ret* Denver CO
Wood-Hull LD Houston TX

STATE OF PENNSYLVANIA

Dioceses of Bethlehem (Be), Central Pennsylvania (CPA), Northwestern Pennsylvania (NWPA),
Pennsylvania (PA), and Pittsburgh (Pgh)

Abington—PA
Allentown—Be
Altoona—CPA
Ambler—PA
Archbald—Be
Ardmore—PA
Ashland—Be
Athens—Be
Bala Cynwyd—PA
Bedford—CPA
Bellefonte—CPA
Benton—CPA
Berwick—CPA
Bethlehem—Be
Blairsville—Pgh
Bloomsburg—CPA
Blue Bell—PA
Blue Ridge Summit—
　CPA
Boothwyn—PA
Brackenridge—Pgh
Bradford—NWPA
Bridgeport—PA
Brighton Heights—Pgh
Bristol—PA
Brookland—CPA
Brookville—NWPA
Bryn Mawr—PA
Buckingham—PA
Camp Hill—CPA
Canonsburg—Pgh
Carbondale—Be
Carlisle—CPA
Carnegie—Pgh
Chambersburg—CPA
Chester—PA
Clarks Summit—Be

Clearfield—NWPA
Clifton Hts—PA
Coatesville—PA
Collegeville—PA
Columbia—CPA
Conshohocken—PA
Corry—NWPA
Coudersport—CPA
Dallas—Be
Danville—CPA
Donora—Pgh
Downingtown—PA
Douglassville—Be
Doylestown—PA
Drexel Hill—PA
Drifton—Be
Dubois—NWPA
Eagles Mere—CPA
East Liberty—Pgh
Easton—Be
Edinboro—NWPA
Elkins Pk—PA
Emmaus—Be
Emporium—NWPA
Erie—NWPA
Essington—PA
Exchange—CPA
Exton—PA
Fairview—NWPA
Forest City—Be
Ft Washington—PA
Foxburg—NWPA
Frackville—Be
Franklin—NWPA
Franklin Park—Pgh
Gap—PA
Gettysburg—CPA

Gladwyne—PA
Glen Mills—PA
Glenmoore—PA
Glenside—PA
Greensburg—Pgh
Greenville—NWPA
Grove City—NWPA
Hamlin—Be
Hanover—CPA
Harleysville—PA
Harrisburg—CPA
Hatboro—PA
Havertown—PA
Hawk Run—CPA
Hazelwood—Pgh
Hazleton—Be
Hellertown—Be
Hermitage—NWPA
Hershey—CPA
Highland Park—Pgh
Hilltown—PA
Hollidaysburg—CPA
Homestead—Pgh
Honesdale—Be
Honey Brook—PA
Houtzdale—NWPA
Hulmeville—PA
Huntingdon—CPA
Huntingdon Valley—PA
Indiana—Pgh
Jeannette—Pgh
Jenkintown—PA
Jersey Shore—CPA
Jim Thorpe—Be
Johnstown—Pgh
Kane—NWPA
Kennett Sq—PA

King of Prussia—PA
Kingston—Be
Kittanning—Pgh
Kutztown—Be
Lafayette Hill—PA
Lake City—NWPA
Lancaster—CPA
Langhorne—PA
Lansdale—PA
Lansdowne—PA
Lansford—Be
Lebanon—Be
Lehighton—Be
Levittown—PA
Lewisburg—CPA
Lewistown—CPA
Ligonier—Pgh
Lock Haven—CPA
Lower Gwynedd—PA
Malvern—PA
Manheim—CPA
Mansfield—CPA
Maple Glen—PA
Marietta—CPA
McKeesport—Pgh
Meadville—NWPA
Mechanicsburg—CPA
Media—PA
Milford—Be
Milton—CPA
Monogehela—Pgh
Montoursville—CPA
Montrose—Be
Morgantown—Be
Morrisville—PA
Moscow—Be
Mountaintop—Be

Mt Carmel—CPA	Osceola Mills—NWPA	St Marys—NWPA	Troy—Be
Mt Joy—CPA	Oxford—PA	Sayre—Be	Tunkhannock—Be
Mt Lebanon—Pgh	Palmerton—Be	Schuylkill Haven—Be	Tyrone—CPA
Mt Pocono—Be	Paoli—PA	Scottdale—Pgh	University Pk—CPA
Muncy—CPA	Parkesburg—PA	Scranton—Be	Valley Forge—PA
Nanticoke—Be	Pen Argyl—Be	Selinsgrove—CPA	Villanova—PA
Narvon—CPA	Penn Hills—Pgh	Shamokin—CPA	Warren—NWPA
Nazareth—Be	Peters Township—Pgh	Sharon—NWPA	Waterford—NWPA
New Castle—NWPA	Philadelphia—PA	Shippensburg—CPA	Wayne—PA
New Hope—PA	Philipsburg—CPA	Smethport—NWPA	Waynesboro—CPA
New Milford—Be	Phoenixville—PA	Solebury—PA	Wayne Township—CPA
Newport—CPA	Pittston—Be	Somerset—Pgh	& Pgh
Newtown—PA	Pittsburgh—Pgh	Southampton—PA	Wellsboro—CPA
Newtown Sq—PA	Pt Alleghany—NWPA	Springfield—PA	W Chester—PA
Norristown—PA	Pottstown—PA	Squirrel Hill—Pgh	Westfield—CPA
North East—NWPA	Pottsville—Be	State College—CPA	Whitehall—Be
North Hills—Pgh	Prospect Pk—PA	Stroudsburg—Be	Wilkes-Barre—Be
North Side—Pgh	Quakertown—PA	Sunbury—CPA	Williamsport—CPA
North Versailles—Pgh	Reading—Be	Susquehanna—Be	Wind Gap—Be
Northern Cambria—Pgh	Renovo—CPA	Swarthmore—PA	Wrightstown—PA
Northumberland—CPA	Ridgway—NWPA	Tamaqua—Be	Wyncote—PA
Norwood—PA	Ridley Pk—PA	Thompsontown—CPA	Wynnewood—PA
Oakmont—Pgh	Rockledge—PA	Tioga—CPA	Yardley—PA
Oaks—PA	Rosemont—PA	Titusville—NWPA	York—CPA
Oil City—NWPA	Royersford—PA	Towanda—Be	Youngsville—NWPA
Oreland—PA	St Clair—Be	Trexlertown—Be	

DIOCESE OF PENNSYLVANIA

(PROVINCE III)

Comprises Bucks, Chester, Delaware, Montgomery, and Philadelphia Counties
DIOCESAN OFFICE Church House 3717 Chestnut Street, Suite 300, Philadelphia 19104
Tel (215) 627-6434 FAX (267) 900-2928
E-MAIL mail@diopa.org   WEB www.diopa.org

Previous Bishops—
Wm White 1787-1836, Henry U Onderdonk coadj 1827 Bp 1836-44, Alonzo Potter 1845-65, Samuel Bowman suffr 1858-61, Wm B Stevens coadj 1862 Bp 1865-87, Ozi W Whitaker coadj 1886 Bp 1887-1911, Alexander Mackay-Smith coadj 1902 Bp 1911, Philip McRhinelander coadj 1911 Bp 1911-23, Thomas J Garland suffr 1911 Bp 1924-31, Francis M Taitt coadj 1929 Bp 1931-43, Wm P Remington suffr 1945-51, Oliver J Hart coadj 1942 Bp 1943-63, J Gillespie Armstrong suffr 1949 coadj 1960 Bp1963-64, Robert L DeWitt coadj 1964 Bp 1964-73, Lyman C Ogilby coadj 1973 Bp 1974-87, Allen L Bartlett Jr coadj 1986 Bp 1987-98, Franklin D Turner suffr 1988-2000, Charles E. Bennison Jr, coadj 1997-98, Bp 1998-2012 retired

Bishop Provisional—Clifton Daniel, 3rd (922)

Chanc M Kohart; *V Chanc* F Helminski; *Treas* J Pope; *Bp's Staff :* Bp R Michel *Asst Bp; Exec Asst* L Hollingsworth; *Fin Off* R Rogers; *Cn for Trans Min* J Mathis; *Ch Ed* H Carnes; *Property Chair* S McCauley;

Yth Min A Kuhn; *Cn to Ord* NJ Deming; *Cn to Ord* L Amerman; *Conv Sec* J Buescher

Deans: Brandywine RT Morgan; *Bucks* M Ruk; *Delaware* FM Knight; *Merion* F Wallner; *Montgomery* EB Richards, P Reid; *Pennypack* J Clodfelter *Schuylkill* M Shaw; *Southwark* D Maree; *Valley Forge* K Mathews; *Wissahickon* J Kerbel

Stand Comm—Cler: Pres K Andonian H Raining S Mullen D Whitfield E Colton; *Lay:* G Vosburgh J Cosby P Smith N McCausland D Brown

Dio Conv: 5 Nov 2016 Philadelphia PA

PARISHES, MISSIONS, AND CLERGY

Abington St Annes Episcopal Church **P** (433) 2119 Welsh Rd 19001-1013 (Mail to: 2119 Old Welsh Rd 19001-1013) Kempton Hastings (215) 659-1674

Ambler Trinity Episcopal Church **P** (506) 708 S Bethlehem Pike 19002-5809 (Mail to: 708 S Bethlehem Pike 19002-5899) David Canan Mary McCullough (215) 646-0416

Ardmore Nevil Memorial Church of St George **P** (350) 1 W Ardmore Ave 19003-1017 (Mail to: 1 W Ardmore Ave 19003-1017) Ryan Whitley (610) 642-3500

Ardmore St Marys Episcopal Church **P** (254) 36 Ardmore Ave 19003-1334 (Mail to: PO Box 86 19003-0086) Michael Giansiracusa Joseph Schaller (610) 649-1486

Bala Cynwyd Church of St Asaphs **P** (296) 27 Conshohocken State Rd 19004-2400 (Mail to: 27 Conshohocken State Rd 19004-2496) Barry Harte (610) 664-0966

Bala Cynwyd St Johns Episcopal Church **P** (119) 404 Levering Mill Rd 19004-2703 (Mail to: 404 Levering Mill Rd 19004-2700) Frank Wallner (610) 664-4517

Blue Bell St Dunstans Episcopal Church **P** (161) 750 Skippack Pike 19422-1712 (Mail to: 750 Skippack Pike 19422-1712) (215) 643-0522

Boothwyn Trinity Church **P** (103) 700 Meetinghouse Rd 19061-3503 (Mail to: 700 Meetinghouse Rd 19061-3503) Aaron Manderbach Paul Gitimu (610) 213-9587

Bridgeport Christ Episcopal Church **P** (44) 740 Schuylkill River Rd 19405-1761 (Mail to: 740 Schuylkill River Rd 19405-1761) Theodore Henderson (610) 272-6036

Bristol St James Church Episcopal **P** (120) 225 Walnut St 19007-4940 (Mail to: 225 Walnut St 19007-4940) Marlee Norton (215) 788-2228

Bryn Mawr Church of the Redeemer **P** (2349) 230 Pennswood Rd 19010 (Mail to: 230 Pennswood Rd 19010) Peter Vanderveen David Romanik Melissa Wilcox (610) 525-2486

Buckingham Trinity Episcopal Church **P** (305) 2631 Durham Rd 18912 (Mail to: PO Box 387 18912-0387) Barbara Abbott Nancy Dilliplane (215) 794-7921

Chester St Mary Episcopal Church **M** (85) 703 Edwards St 19013 (Mail to: PO Box 595 19016-0595) Deirdre Whitfield (610) 874-8565

Chester St Pauls Episcopal Church **P** (90) 301 E 9th St 19013-6020 (Mail to: 301 E 9th St 19013-6088) John Hudson (610) 872-5711

Clifton Hgts St Stephen Episcopal Church **P** (114) 119 W Baltimore Ave 19018-1405 (Mail to: 199 W Baltimore Ave 19018-1405) Jill McNish (610) 622-3636

Coatesville The Church of the Trinity **P** (111) 323 E Lincoln Hwy 19320-3409 (Mail to: 323 E Lincoln Hwy 19320-3409) Sherry Deets (610) 384-4771

Collegeville St James Church Collegeville **P** (428) 3768 Germantown Pike 19426-3151 (Mail to: 3768 Germantown Pike 19426-3151) William Sowards (610) 489-7564

Conshohocken Calvary Episcopal Church **P** (119) 325 Fayette St 19428-0546 (Mail to: PO Box 546 19428-0546) Stephen Price (610) 825-5959

Downingtown St James Episcopal Church **P** (503) 409 E Lancaster Ave 19335-2722 (Mail to: 409 E Lancaster Ave 19335-2722)

Doylestown St Pauls Episcopal Church **P** (616) 84 E Oakland Ave 18901-4647 (Mail to: 84 E Oakland Ave 18901-4647) Gerald Collins (215) 348-5511

Drexel Hill Incarnation Holy Sacrament Episcopal **P** (244) 3000 Garrett Rd 19026-2217 (Mail to: 3000 Garrett Rd 19026-2217) Benjamin Wallis (610) 259-5148

Drexel Hill The Church of the Holy Comforter **P** (253) 1000 Burmont Rd 19026-4533 (Mail to: 1000 Burmont Rd 19026-4533) Jonathan Mitchican Benjamin Wallis (610) 789-6754

Elkins Park St Paul's Episcopal Church **P** (181) 7809 Old York Rd 19027-2508 (Mail to: 7809 Old York Rd 19027-2593) Paul Reid (215) 635-4185

Essington Church of St John the Evangelist **P** (172) 16 W 3rd St 19029-1200 (Mail to: 16 W 3rd St 19029-1200) Denise Leo Harry White

Exton St Pauls Episcopal Church **P** (420) 901 E Lincoln Hwy 19341-2806 (Mail to: 1105 E Lincoln Hwy 19341-2824) Deanna Dornemann (610) 363-2363

Fort Washington St Thomas Church Whitemarsh **P** (1379) 7020 Camp Hill Rd 19034-2202 (Mail to: Church Rd and Bethlehem Pike 19034) Marek Zabriskie Daniel Stroud Lara Stroud (215) 233-3970

Gap St Johns Episcopal Church **P** (122) 1520 W Kings Hwy 17527-9009 (Mail to: 1520 W Kings Hwy 17527) John Obenchain (717) 442-4302

Gladwyne St Christophers Church **P** (618) 226 Righters Mill Rd 19035-1533 (Mail to: 226 Righters Mill Rd 19035-1597) Hillary Raining (610) 642-8920

Glen Mills St Johns Episcopal Church **P** (753) 576 Concord Rd 19342-1402 (Mail to: 576 Concord Rd 19342-1402) John Sorensen Jill Laroche Wilson (610) 459-2994

Glenmoore St Andrews Episcopal Church **P** (509) 7 Saint Andrews Ln 19343-9559 (Mail to: 7 Saint Andrews Ln 19343-9559) Robert Smith (610) 458-5277

Glenside St Peters Episcopal Church **P** (332) 654 N Easton Rd 19038-4310 (Mail to: 654 N Easton Rd 19038-4310) Emily Richards (215) 887-1765

Harleysville The Church of the Holy Spirit **P** (632) 2871 Barndt Rd 19438-1150 (Mail to: PO Box 575 19438-0575) Kathryn Andonian (215) 234-8020

Hatboro Church of the Advent **P** (243) 12 Byberry Rd 19040-3405 (Mail to: 12 Byberry Rd 19040-3405) Lynn Hade Louis Temme

Havertown St Faith Episcopal Church **P** (139) 1208 Allston Rd 19083-3817 (Mail to: 1208 Allston Rd 19083-3894) Aaron Manderbach (610) 446-9450

Hilltown Good Shepherd Epis Church **P** (131) 1634 Hilltown Pike 18927-9701 (Mail to: PO

Box 132 18927-0132) Catherine Kerr (215) 822-3930

Honey Brook St Marks Church **P** (83) 1040 Chestnut Tree Rd 19344-9645 (Mail to: 1040 Chestnut Tree Rd 19344-9645) (610) 942-2365

Hulmeville Grace Episcopal Church **P** (134) 313 Main St 19047-5801 (Mail to: 313 Main Street 19047-5801) E F Michael Morgan Marlee Norton (215) 757-6025

Huntingdon Valley St John the Evangelist **P** (90) 1333 Welsh Rd 19006-5829 (Mail to: 1333 Old Welsh Rd 19006-5829) Eric Bond (215) 947-3212

Jenkintown Church of Our Saviour **P** (81) Old York & Homestead Rds 19046 (Mail to: 821 Homestead Rd 19046-2805) Eric Bond (215) 887-0500

Kennet Sq Church of the Advent **P** (1067) 401 N Union St 19348-2427 (Mail to: 201 Crestline Dr 19348) Nancy Hauser Linda Kapurch (610) 444-4624

King of Prussia Grace Church and the Incarnation **P** (89) C/O John Loftus 966 Trinity Lane 19406 (Mail to: 966 Trinity Lane 19406) John Atkins (610) 828-1500

Kng of Prussia Trinity Church Gulph Mills **P** (199) 966 Trinity Ln 19406-3636 (Mail to: 966 Trinity Ln 19406-3636) Elizabeth Colton Deborah Payson (610) 828-1500

Lafayette Hill Church of St Jude and the Nativity **P** (90) 203 Germantown Pike 19444-1323 (Mail to: 203 Germantown Pike 19444-1323) Judith Meckling (610) 941-6666

Langhorne St James Episcopal Church **P** (240) 330 S Bellevue Ave 19047-2808 (Mail to: 330 S Bellevue Ave 19047-2899) Barbara Kelley (215) 757-3766

Lansdale Holy Trinity Church **P** (171) 407 N Broad St 19446-2413 (Mail to: 407 N Broad St 19446-2450) (215) 855-4431

Lansdowne St Michaels Episcopal Church **P** (71) 813 Longacre Blvd 19050-3319 (Mail to: 813 Longacre Blvd 19050-3319) (610) 259-7871

Levittown All Saints Episcopal Church **P** (58) 9 Old Locust Ave 19054-1107 (Mail to: 9 Old Locust Avenue 19054-1107) Sean Slack (215) 295-5196

Levittown St Paul Church **P** (128) 89 Pinewood Dr 19054-3609 (Mail to: 89 Pinewood Dr 19054-3609) Sean Slack (215) 946-8559

Lower Gwynedd Church of the Messiah **P** (929) 1001 Dekalb Pike 19002-1941 (Mail to: 1001 Dekalb Pike 19002-1941) Keith Marsh MaryJo Melberger (215) 699-9204

Malvern St Francis in the Fields **P** (524) 689 Sugartown Rd 19355-3305 (Mail to: 689 Sugartown Rd 19355-3305) Barbara Abbott (610) 647-0130

Malvern St Peters Church in the Great Valley **P** (622) 2475 Saint Peters Rd 19355-8791 (Mail to: 2475 Saint Peters Rd 19355-8791) (610)

644-7967

Maple Glen St Matthews Episcopal Church **P** (670) 919 Tennis Ave 19002-2312 (Mail to: 919 Tennis Ave 19002-2312) David Robinson James Walton (215) 646-4092

Media Christ Episcopal Church **P** (402) 311 S Orange St 19063-3111 (Mail to: 311 S Orange St 19063-3190) Adam Kradel (610) 566-7525

Morrisville Church of the Incarnation **P** (145) 1505 Makefield Rd 19067-3149 (Mail to: 1505 Makefield Rd 19067-3149) Linda Kerr (215) 295-2259

New Hope St Philips Episcopal Church **P** (149) 10 Chapel Rd 18938-1006 (Mail to: 10 Chapel Rd 18938-1006) Michael Ruk (215) 862-5782

Newtown St Lukes Church **P** (402) 100 E Washington Ave 18940-1980 (Mail to: 100 E Washington Ave 18940-1980) Ernest Curtin (215) 968-2781

Newtown Square St Albans Episcopal Church **P** (210) 3625 Chapel Rd 19073-3602 (Mail to: 3625 Chapel Rd 19073-3698)

Norristown All Saints Episcopal Church **P** (183) 535 Haws Ave 19401-4542 (Mail to: 535 Haws Ave 19401-4542) Sandra Etemad Geoffrey West (610) 279-3990

Norristown St Augustine of Hippo Church **P** (126) 1208 Green St 19401-3402 (Mail to: 1208 Green St 19401-3402) (610) 279-8890

Norristown St Johns Episcopal Church **P** (88) 23 E Airy St 19401-4815 (Mail to: 23 E Airy St 19401-4815) Scott Albergate (610) 272-4092

Norwood St Stephen Episcopal Church **P** (126) 128 Chester Pike 19074-1702 (Mail to: 128 Chester Pike 19074-1702) Frank Knight (610) 461-0490

Oaks St Pauls Episcopal Church **P** (134) 126 Black Rock Rd 19456 (Mail to: PO Box 404 19456-0404) Daniel Olsen (610) 650-9336

Oreland St Philip in the Fields **P** (136) Lorraine Ave & Oreland Mill Rd 19075 (Mail to: 317 Oreland Mill Rd 19075-2256) Robin Smith (215) 233-0409

Oxford St Christophers Episcopal Church **P** (242) 116 Lancaster Pike 19363-1171 (Mail to: 116 Lancaster Pike 19363-1171) Mary Mertz (610) 932-8134

Paoli Church of the Good Samaritan **P** (1104) 212 W Lancaster Ave 19301-1723 (Mail to: 212 W Lancaster Ave 19301-1758) Beverly Berry Carolyn Huff Richard Morgan Geoffrey Simpson (610) 644-4040

Parkesburg Church of the Ascension **P** (94) 406 W 2nd Ave 19365-1402 (Mail to: 2nd & West Sts 19365) Gail Tomei (610) 857-9176

Philadelphia All Saints Church (Rhawnhurst) **P** (71) 7939 Frontenac St 19111 (Mail to: 1811 Loney St 19111-2911) James Morris (215) 342-6310

Philadelphia All Saints Church Torresdale **P** (372) 9601 Frankford Ave 19114-2813 (Mail to: 9601 Frankford Ave 19114-2895) Bradley Hauff (215) 637-8787

Philadelphia Calvary-St Augustine Church **P** (189) 814 N 41st St 19104-4813 (Mail to: 814 N 41st St 19104-4813) Isaac Miller (215) 222-2070

✣ **Philadelphia** Cathedral Church of Our Saviour **O** (150) 13-19 S 38th St 19104 (Mail to: 3701 Chestnut St Ste 6W 19104) Judith Sullivan Phillip Bennett Emily Richards Robert Tate (215) 386-0234

Philadelphia Christ Church **P** (544) 20 N American St 19106-4509 (Mail to: 20 N American St 19106-4592) Timothy Safford Susan Richardson (215) 922-1695

Philadelphia Christ Church & St Michaels Church **P** (227) 29 W Tulpehocken St 19144-2607 (Mail to: 29 W Tulpehocken St 19144-2607) (215) 844-7274

Philadelphia Church of St John the Free **M** (77) 3089 Emerald St 19134-0498 (Mail to: PO Box 14798 19134-0498) (215) 425-2933

Philadelphia Church of St Luke & the Epiphany **P** (253) 330 S 13th St 19107-5916 (Mail to: 330 S 13th St 19107-5916) Rodger Broadley (215) 732-1918

Philadelphia Church of St Martin in the Fields **P** (800) 8000 Saint Martins Ln 19118-4101 (Mail to: 8000 Saint Martins Ln 19118-4101) Walter Kerbel Carol Duncan Callie Swanlund James Taylor Anne Thatcher (215) 247-7466

Philadelphia Church of the Annunciation **P** (94) 324 Carpenter Ln 19119-3003 (Mail to: 324 Carpenter Ln 19119-3003) (215) 844-3059

Philadelphia Church of the Crucifixion **P** (69) 620 S 8th St 19147-2038 (Mail to: 620 S 8th St 19147-2038) (215) 922-1128

Philadelphia Emmanuel/Resurrection Episcopal Ch **P** (92) 8201 Frankford Ave 19136-2735 (Mail to: 8201 Frankford Ave 19136-2735) (215) 624-8520

Philadelphia George W South Ch of Advocate **P** (75) 2121 Gratz Street 19121 (Mail to: PO Box 50480 19132-6480) Renee McKenzie-Hayward (215) 978-8000

Philadelphia Gloria Dei Episcopal Church **P** (220) 916 S Swanson St 19147-4332 (Mail to: 916 S Swanson St 19147-4332) Danna Segal (215) 389-1513

Philadelphia Grace Epiphany Church **P** (174) 224 E Gowen Ave 19119-1020 (Mail to: 224 E Gowen Ave 19119-1020) Nazareno Javier (215) 248-2950

Philadelphia Holy Apostles and the Mediator **P** (210) Spruce & 51st Sts 19139 (Mail to: 260 S 51st St 19139-4120) Joseph Garrigan Charles Messer (215) 472-3000

Philadelphia Holy Innocents St Pauls Church **P** (150) 7001 Torresdale Ave 19135-1914 (Mail to: 7001 Torresdale Ave 19135-1914) Harriet Kollin (215) 624-1144

Philadelphia House of Prayer **P** (99) 1747 Church Ln 19141-1309 (Mail to: 1747 Church Ln 19141-1309) (215) 549-7650

Philadelphia La Iglesia de Christo y San Ambrosio **M** (2172) 3552 N 6th St 19140-4506 (Mail to: 3552 N. 6th St. 19140-4506) (215) 226-1444

Philadelphia Memorial Church of St Luke **P** (112) 1946 Welsh Rd 19115-4654 (Mail to: 1946 Welsh Rd 19115-4654) Timothy Griffin (215) 969-3645

Philadelphia Memorial Church of the Good Shepherd **P** (121) 3820 The Oak Road 19129-1030 (Mail to: 3820 The Oak Road 19129-1030)

Philadelphia St Albans Church Roxborough **P** (160) 6769 Ridge Ave 19128-2444 (Mail to: 6769 Ridge Ave 19128-2444) Kyle Tomlin Paul Adler (215) 482-2627

Philadelphia St Andrew & St Monica Church **M** (181) 3600 Baring St 19104-2333 (Mail to: 3600 Baring St 19104-2333) Samuel Adu-Andoh (215) 222-7606

Philadelphia St Andrews in the Field Church **P** (117) 500 Somerton Ave 19116-2027 (Mail to: 500 Somerton Ave 19116-2027) (215) 673-5938

Philadelphia St Clements Church **P** (105) 2013 Appletree St 19103-1409 (Mail to: 2013 Appletree St 19103-1409) Richard Alton (215) 563-1876

Philadelphia St Davids Episcopal Church **P** (44) 156 Dupont St 19127 (Mail to: PO Box 29102 19127-0102) Frank Wallner (215) 482-2345

Philadelphia St Dismas Episcopal Mission **M** (20) 3717 Chestnut St 19104 (Mail to: 3717 Chestnut Street 19104) George Master

Philadelphia St Gabriels Episcopal Church **M** (125) 101 E Roosevelt Blvd 19120-4243 (Mail to: 101 E Roosevelt Blvd 19120-4299) Nancy Deming Joseph Schaller (215) 329-3807

Philadelphia St George & St Barnabas **P** (191) 520 S 61st St 19143-2234 (Mail to: 520 S 61st St 19143-2234) James Wynn (215) 747-2605

Philadelphia St James of Kingsessing Episcopal Ch **P** (207) 6838 Woodland Ave 19142-1822 (Mail to: 6838 Woodland Ave 19142-1822) George Master (215) 727-5265

Philadelphia St Lukes Church Germantown **P** (615) 5421 Germantown Ave 19144-2223 (Mail to: 5421 Germantown Ave 19144-2223) David Morris (215) 844-8544

Philadelphia St Marks Church Frankford **P** (190) 4442 Frankford Ave 19124-3659 (Mail to: 4442 Frankford Ave 19124-3659) Jonathan Clodfelter (215) 535-0635

Philadelphia St Mark's Episcopal Church **P** (392) 1625 Locust St 19103-6304 (Mail to: 1625 Locust St 19103-6388) Sean Mullen Nicholas Phelps Marie Swayze Erika Takacs (215) 735-1416

Philadelphia St Marys Church Cathedral Road **P** (189) 630 E Cathedral Rd 19128-1935 (Mail to: 630 E Cathedral Rd 19128-1935) (215) 482-6300

Philadelphia St Marys Church Hamilton Village **P** (205) 3916 Locust Walk 19104-6152 (Mail to: 3916 Locust Walk 19104-6152) Mariclair Partee (215) 386-3916

Philadelphia St Marys Episcopal Church **P** (35) 1831 Bainbridge St 19146-1429 (Mail to: 1831 Bainbridge St 19146-1429) (215) 985-0360

Philadelphia St Pauls Church Chestnut Hill **P** (486) 22 E Chestnut Hill Ave 19118-2715 (Mail to: 22 E Chestnut Hill Ave 19118-2715) E Clifford Cutler Robert Davidson Emmanuel Mercer (215) 242-2055

Philadelphia St Peter's Church **P** (413) 313 Pine St 19106-4212 (Mail to: 313 Pine St 19106-4299) Sean Lanigan Claire Nevin-Field (215) 925-5968

Philadelphia St Simon the Cyrenian Church **P** (106) 22nd And Reed Sts 19146 (Mail to: 1401 S 22nd St 19146-4530) Betsy Ivey (215) 468-1926

Philadelphia St Stephens Church **HC** (29) 19 S 10th St 19107-4224 (Mail to: PO Box 1103 19105-1103) Charles Flood (215) 922-3807

Philadelphia St Timothy Episcopal Church **HC** (320) 5720 Ridge Ave 19128-1734 (Mail to: 5720 Ridge Ave 19128-1734) Kirk Berlenbach (215) 483-1529

Philadelphia The African Epis Ch of St Thomas **P** (983) 6361 Lancaster Ave 19151-2622 (Mail to: 6361 Lancaster Ave 19151-2622) Martini Shaw Angelo Wildgoose (215) 473-3065

Philadelphia The Church of the Holy Trinity **HC** (531) 1904 Walnut St 19103-5733 (Mail to: 1904 Walnut St 19103-5796) Alan Neale Zachary Smith (215) 567-1267

Philadelphia Trinity Church Oxford **P** (147) No 6900 Oxford Ave 19111-3903 (Mail to: 601 Longshore Ave 19111-4330) Richard Robyn (215) 745-1258

Philadelphia Trinity Memorial Church **P** (99) 2212 Spruce St 19103-6503 (Mail to: 2212 Spruce St 19103-6503) Donna Maree (215) 732-2515

Phoenixville St Peters Episcopal Church **P** (381) 121 Church St 19460-3438 (Mail to: 121 Church St 19460-3438) Joseph Dietz Koshy Mathews (610) 933-2195

Pottstown Christ Episcopal Church **P** (326) 316 E High St 19464-5538 (Mail to: 316 E High St 19464-5538) John Houghton (610) 323-2895

Prospect Park St James Church Episcopal **P** (153) 11th & Lincoln Aves 19076 (Mail to: 732 11th Ave 19076-1313) John Wallace (610) 461-6698

Quakertown Emmanuel Episcopal Church **P** (100) 560 S Main St 18951-1570 (Mail to: 560 S Main St 18951-1570)

Ridley Park Christ Church Episcopal **P** (1130) 104 Nevin St 19078-2108 (Mail to: 104 Nevin St 19078-2195) Douglas Tompkins Judith Buck-Glenn (610) 521-1626

Rockledge Memorial Ch of the Holy Nativity **P** (223) Michael Rau (215) 663-9903

Rosemont The Church of the Good Shepherd **P** (40) 1116 E Lancaster Ave 19010-2615 (Mail to: 1116 E Lancaster Ave 19010-2615) Ian Montgomery (610) 525-7070

Royersford Church of the Epiphany **P** (103) 209 S 3rd Ave 19468-2551 (Mail to: 209 S 3rd Ave 19468-2551) Beth Hixon (610) 948-9655

Solebury Trinity Episcopal Church **P** (490) 6587 Upper York Rd 18963 (Mail to: PO Box 377 18963-0377) Emory Byrum Virginia Sheay Richard Vinson (215) 297-5135

Southampton Church of the Redemption **P** (161) 1101 2nd Street Pike 18966-3956 (Mail to: 1101 2nd Street Pike 18966-3956) Emmanuel Williamson (215) 357-0303

Springfield Church of the Redeemer **P** (326) 145 W Springfield Rd 19064-1414 (Mail to: 145 W Springfield Rd 19064-1414) Edward Shiley (610) 544-8113

Swarthmore Trinity Church **P** (203) N Chester Rd & College Ave 19081 (Mail to: 301 N Chester Rd & College Av 19081) Joyce Tompkins (610) 544-2297

Valley Forge Washington Memorial Chapel **P** (206) RR 23 19481-0098 (Mail to: PO Box 98 19481-0098) (610) 783-0120

Villanova Christ Church **P** (275) 536 Conestoga Rd 19085-1131 (Mail to: 536 Conestoga Rd 19085-1131) (610) 688-1110

Wayne St David Episcopal Church **P** (3330) 763 Valley Forge Rd 19087-4724 (Mail to: 763 South Valley Forge Rd 19087-4794) William Allen Amanda Eiman Alexander Mccurdy Dennis Reid Martha Tucker Matthew Welch William Wood (610) 688-7947

Wayne St Martins Church **P** (238) 400 King Of Prussia Rd 19087-2342 (Mail to: 400 King of Prussia Rd 19087-2342) Christopher Bishop (610) 688-4830

Wayne St Marys Episcopal Church **P** (449) 104 Louella Ave 19087-4121 (Mail to: 104 Louella Ave 19087-4195) Joseph Smith (610) 688-1313

West Chester The Church of the Holy Trinity **P** (399) 212 S High St 19382-3404 (Mail to: 212 S High St 19382-3499) Paul Hunt Karen Kaminskas (610) 696-4640

Wrightstown Church of the Holy Nativity **M** (46) 749 Durham Rd 18940-9679 (Mail to: 749 Durham Rd 18940-9679) Lisa Keppeler (215) 598-3405

Wyncote All Hallows Church **P** (192) 262 Bent Road 19095 (Mail to: 262 Bent Rd 19095-1503) Mark Ainsworth (215) 885-1641

Wynnewood All Saints Episcopal Church **P** (148) Montgomery Ave & Gypsy Ln 19096 (Mail to: 1325 Montgomery Ave 19096-1037) (610) 642-4098

Wynnewood Church of the Holy Apostles **P** (243) 1020 Remington Rd 19096-2326 (Mail to: 1020

Remington Rd 19096-2326) Dennis Lloyd (610) 642-6617

Yardley St Andrews Church Episcopal **P** (458) 47 W Afton Ave 19067-1444 (Mail to: 47 W Afton Avenue 19067-1444) Daniell Hamby Lloyd Winter (215) 493-2636

NON-PAROCHIAL CLERGY

Aalan JC *ret* Philadelphia PA
Adebonojo MB *ret* Durham NH
Amerman LSL Buckingham PA
Anderson JM Royersford PA
Anderson JF *ret* Sarasota FL
Anthony CR Philadelphia PA
Austin VA *ret*
Baker JLR *dcn* Wayne PA
Batson SC *ret* Malvern PA
Beck JLT *ret* Philadelphia PA
Bennett VRK Meshoppen PA
Betts RH *ret* Gwynedd PA
Brinkman CR *ret* Phoenixville PA
Brown RH Whispering Pines NC
Brunner AF *ret* N Cape May NJ
Bullock KR *ret* Carrboro NC
Bullock MA *ret* Columbia SC
Carpenter JP *ret* Philadelphia PA
Carter CA *ret* Philadelphia PA
Chamberlain CM *ret* Newport News VA
Coble RH *ret* Harleysville PA
Cole HM *ret* West Des Moines IA
Coleman DE *dcn* Phoenixville PA
Constant DR *ret* Middleburg PA
Craighill PG *ret* Lexington VA
Cunningham MT *ret* Haverford PA
Czarniecki L *dcn* Watchung NJ
Davidson CA *ret* Philadelphia PA
Davis AK *ret* Kimberton PA
Davis BG Newtown Square PA
Deane WB
Diaz JA Philadelphia PA
Dickinson AH *ret* Grand Rapids MI
Ditterline RC *ret* Bethlehem PA
Dobbins T Radnor PA
Duffey W *ret* Haverford PA
Dull SL *ret* Punta Gorda FL
Eisenstadt-Evans EA Glenmoore PA
Elek H Newtown Square PA
Eoyang TT Philadelphia PA
Evans HB *ret* Philadelphia PA
Evans JE *ret* Phoenixville PA
Evans ND Media PA
Fackler PJ Raleigh NC
Faison DD *dcn* West Chester PA
Fenn RK *ret* Princeton NJ
Fox S *ret dcn* Phoenixville PA
Fulks WB *ret* Hurricane WV
Fulton SA *ret* Gwynedd PA
Funkhouser DF *ret* Oakland CA
Gafney WC Philadelphia PA
Galganowicz HC *ret* Lake Harmony PA
Gardner AL *ret* Philadelphia PA

Gavin T Newtown Square PA
Geliebter PL *dcn* Phila PA
Giles RS *ret* Lansdowne PA
Gooding LE *ret* Philadelphia PA
Graff DT *ret* Philadelphia PA
Grandell PF Philadelphia PA
Granfeldt RC *ret* Buford GA
Graves RB *dcn* Philadelphia PA
Greene ER *dcn* Philadelphia PA
Haines M *ret* Phoenixville PA
Haley-Ray J *dcn*
Hardenstine AH *ret* Schuylkill Haven PA
Hargrove TJ *ret* Ewing NJ
Harris PS Philadelphia PA
Hawkins RT *ret* Oconomowoc WI
Hedgis SE Philadelphia PA
Herrera M *ret*
Highland T *ret*
Hockensmith DA *ret* Morgan VT
Hockridge AE
Hoffacker MPN *ret* Devon PA
Holcombe MP Charlotte NC
Holland ME *ret* Morrisville PA
Hughes A *ret* Gresham OR
Hurtt AL Philadelphia PA
Hyatt DW *ret* Phoenixville PA
Igarashi PH *ret* Philadelphia PA
Jackson J *ret* Collingdale PA
Jacobson SK *ret* Summerfield FL
Jaynes RP *ret* Lancaster PA
Jessup DMP *ret dcn* Paoli PA
Keefer JS Sharon Hill PA
Keener EM *ret* Stonington ME
Kelly AJ *ret* Doylestown PA
Keshgegian FA *ret* Oakland CA
Kessler ES Sheffield
Kim JJK *ret* Drexel Hill PA
Kimball JC *ret* Collegeville PA
Kirk RJ *ret* Kennett Square PA
Knapp CJ *dcn* Philadelphia PA
Kostic EM *dcn* Philadelphia PA
Kountz PJ
Larsen RJ *ret* Dayton OH
Lefebvre EF *ret* Lancaster PA
Lewis BJ *ret* Lawrenceville NJ
Ley JL *dcn* West Chester PA
Liddle VT *ret* Ambler PA
Liddy JT *ret* Lynchburg VA
Littrell JH *ret* South Newfane VT
Lockhart RW *ret* Malvern PA
Lolk OLM *ret* Lewes DE
Longstreth WM *ret* Pottstown PA
Maguire BL *ret* Plymouth Meeting PA
Martin JG *ret* Wyncote PA
Martin RP *ret* Wyncote PA
Matis GM *ret* Doylestown PA
McCaslin HK *dcn* Wayne PA
McClellan TL *ret* Lafayette Hill PA
McGuire M *ret* Philadelphia PA
Mellon RE *ret dcn* San Antonio FL
Metzger C *ret* Philadelphia PA

Midwood JE *ret* Philadelphia PA
Miller RA *ret* Paoli PA
Miller RM *ret* Schwenksville PA
Mills JAM *ret* Paoli PA
Mintz EH *ret* Mount Pleasant SC
Mitchell SS Philadelphia PA
Mole JF *ret* Waynesboro PA
Molina-Moore AE Wilmington DE
Monnat TL *ret* Havertown PA
Moore CO *ret* Naples FL
Moore CC *ret* Harbeson DE
Morin GS West Chester PA
Moroney KJ Villanova PA
Morris AE *ret* Chambersburg PA
Morton K *ret*
Mottl CE *ret* Crisfield MD
Murgani S
Murray CA *dcn* Philadelphia PA
Musselman WS *ret* Lansdale PA
Ndai DM *ret* Collingdale PA
Nelson LS Norristown PA
Nesbit PM *dcn* Wycombe PA
Newman MW *ret* Garnet Valley PA
Newman RB *ret dcn* Newtown PA
Oughton MK *dcn* Chester PA
Owusu-Afriyie K Yeadon PA
Parker RW *ret* Bryn Mawr PA
Partenheimer GH Northfield MA
Partington RO *ret* Blue Bell PA
Peabody SW *ret* Dahlonega GA
Pearson MA *ret* Barrington RI
Penniman CF *ret* Philadelphia PA
Pike CAH *ret* Lawrenceburg KY
Platt TW *ret* West Chester PA
Proud J *ret* Philadelphia PA
Rajagopal DE Wayne PA
Reed AW *ret* Doylestown PA
Reed TL *ret* Middleboro MA
Reid WG *ret* Philadelphia PA
Richards SM Bryn Mawr PA
Richardson J Philadelphia PA
Riegel JW *ret* Bailey Island ME
Ritchie RJ *dcn* Philadelphia PA
Ritchings FA *ret* Placitas NM
Ritter CE *ret* Meadowbrook PA
Rivers B *ret* Paoli PA
Rivers DB *ret* Wyncote PA
Rivers JT *ret* Springfield PA

Roper TC *ret* Philadelphia PA
Ruby LD *ret* Columbia PA
Ruppe-Melnyk GL *ret* Malvern PA
Santos-Rivera C *ret* Philadelphia PA
Schwoyer RLV *dcn* Richboro PA
Scott DG *ret* Ranchos De Taos NM
Secor NA *ret* Philadelphia PA
Shannon JL *ret* Lansdowne PA
Shaw WE *ret* Charlottesville VA
Shepherd WJ *ret* Philadelphia PA
Simpson JP *ret* Narberth PA
Sipple PW *ret* Cornwall on Hudson NY
Smart JA *ret* Tucson AZ
Smart LM *ret* Folsom PA
Smiraglia RP Philadelphia PA
Smith AR Bryn Mawr PA
Smith EESC *ret* Glen Mills PA
Smith HG *ret* Philadelphia PA
Smith RW *ret* New York NY
Snider SB *ret* Wynnewood PA
Squire JR Newtown Square PA
St Claire EK *ret* Furlong PA
Steeves T *ret* Downingtown PA
Stevick DB *ret* Philadelphia PA
Stroh NM *ret* Holland PA
Stube PB Wayne PA
Sykes R *ret* Lansdale PA
Taylor PG *ret* Cheltenham PA
Tinklepaugh JR *ret* North East MD
Toia FP *ret* Lansdale PA
Trimble JA *ret* Philadelphia PA
Urban PL *ret* Haverford PA
Van Atta RS *ret* Philadelphia PA
Vanucci AJ *ret* Albuquerque NM
Von Dreele JD *ret* Wilmington DE
Wand TC *ret* Phoenixville PA
Waters EM Alexandria VA
Weedon SL Shamokin PA
Wehmiller PJL Swarthmore PA
Welty WW *ret* Chapala Jalisco
Williams HN *ret* Shermans Dale PA
Williamson RL *ret* Swarthmore PA
Wilson GM Media PA
Wissink CJ *ret* Levittown PA
Wissler KJ *ret* Philadelphia PA
Wittig NCH *ret* Fairview Park OH
Wood HF *ret* Hulmeville PA
Zug AER Media PA

DIOCESE OF PITTSBURGH
(PROVINCE III)
Comprises the southwestern portion of Pennsylvania
DIOCESAN OFFICE 325 Oliver Avenue, Suite 300, Pittsburgh, PA 15222
TEL (412) 721-0853
E-MAIL office@episcopalpgh.org   WEB www.episcopalpgh.org

Previous Bishops—
John B Kerfoot 1866-81, Cortlandt Whitehead 1881-1922, Alexander Mann 1923-43, Austin Pardue 1944-68, William S Thomas suffr 1954-70, Robert B Appleyard 1968-82, Alden M H athaway 1983-97, Robert Duncan 1997-2008, Kenneth L Price 2009-2012

Bishop—Rt Rev Dorsey McConnell (1070) (Dio 21 Oct 2012)

Dir of Admin T Babcock; *Treas* K Workman: *Cn Pastor* S Quinn; *Can for Form* J Geisler; *Cn for Miss* K Karashin; *Exec Asst* J Rogers; *Fin and Prop Admin* M Rihn; *Archivist* J Gundersen; *Dir of Comm* R Creehan; *Web Admin* A Muhl; *Chanc* A Roman, Cohen & Grigsby PC 625 Liberty Ave Pittsburgh PA 15222 (412) 297-4867; *Pres Brd of Trustees* J Karas; *Child Min Team Coord* L Brown; *College Min* Rev P Wainwright; *Comm on Arch & Hist Chr* G Fisher; *Comm on Min Chr* Rev L Hays; *Comm on Race and Reconciliation Chr* N Bolden; *Disaster Prep Coords* J Gundersen & Rev H Gillette; *Ed for Min Coord* V Sterling; *Epis Ch Women Pres* B Duckstein; *Epis Relief & Dev Rep* D Duntley; *Social Justice Comm* N Lapp

Stand Comm—Cler: W Geiger K McInnes J Simons TJ Freeman; *Lay:* D Phillips J Adams K Baird D Powell

Dio Conv: 4-5 Nov 2016

PARISHES, MISSIONS, AND CLERGY

Blairsville St Peters Episcopal Church P (24) 36 W Campbell St 15717-1312 (Mail to: 36 W Campbell St 15717-1312) Arthur Dilg (724) 459-8804

Brackenridge St Barnabas Episcopal Church P (80) 989 Morgan St 15014-1164 (Mail to: 989 Morgan St 15014-1197) (724) 224-9280

Brighton Heights All Saints Episcopal Church P (91) 3577 McClure Ave 15212-2147 (Mail to: 3577 McClure Ave 15212-2147) John Schaeffer (412) 766-8112

Canonsburg St Thomas Episcopal Church P (116) 139 N Jefferson Ave 15317-1307 (Mail to: 139 N Jefferson Ave 15317-1307) Catherine Brall (724) 745-2013

Carnegie Church of the Atonement P (27) 618 Washington Ave 15106-2837 (Mail to: 618 Washington Ave 15106-2837) (412) 279-1944

Donora St Johns Episcopal Church P (29) 998 Thompson Ave 15033-2146 (Mail to: 998 Thompson Ave 15033-2146) Gwen Santiago (724) 379-8871

East Liberty Calvary Episcopal Church P (1530) 315 Shady Ave 15206-4388 (Mail to: 315 Shady Ave 15206-4388) Jonathon Jensen TJ Freeman Carol Henley Leslie Reimer Walter Szymanski (412) 661-0120

Franklin Park St Brendans Episcopal Church P (251) 2365 McAleer Rd 15143-8762 (Mail to: 2365 McAleer Rd 15143-8762) Daniel Russell (412) 364-5974

Greensburg Christ Episcopal Church P (34) 132 Sherwood Drive 15601 (Mail to: 132 Sherwood Drive 15601) (724) 216-4717

Hazelwood Church of the Good Shepherd P (25) 124 Johnston Avenue 15207 (Mail to: PO Box 55054 15207-0054) Huett Fleming (412) 421-8497

Highland Park St Andrews Episcopal Church P (465) 5801 Hampton St 15206-1615 (Mail to: 5801 Hampton St Highland Park 15206-1615) Bruce Robison Jean Chess Philip Wainwright (412) 661-1245

Homestead St Matthews Episcopal Church P (63) 336 E 10th Ave 15120-1613 (Mail to: 336 E 10th Ave 15120-1613) (412) 461-5291

Homewood Church of the Holy Cross P (113) 7507 Kelly St 15208-1914 (Mail to: 7507 Kelly St 15208-1914) Moni McIntyre (412) 242-3209

Indiana Christ Episcopal Church P (114) 902 Philadelphia St 15701-3912 (Mail to: 902 Philadelphia St 15701-3912) William Geiger (724) 465-6129

Jeannette Church of the Advent P (36) 101 Clay Ave 15644-2116 (Mail to: 51 South First Street 15644-2102) Vicente Santiago (724) 523-9390

Johnstown St Marks Episcopal Church P (145) 335 Locust St 15901-1606 (Mail to: 335 Locust St 15901-1606) Nancy Threadgill

Kittanning St Pauls Episcopal Church P (109) 112 N Water St 16201-1516 (Mail to: 112 N Water St 16201-1516) Herbert Daly (724) 543-5402

Ligonier St Michaels of the Valley P (245) 2535 Route 381 15658 (Mail to: PO Box 336 15658-0336) James Simons (724) 238-9411

Mckeesport St Stephens Episcopal Church P (78) 220 8th St 15132-2744 (Mail to: 220 8th Street 15132-2744) (412) 664-9379

Monongahela St Pauls Episcopal Church P (42) 130 W Main Street 15063-2332 (Mail to: 130 W Main Street 15063) Teresa Hunt (724) 258-7792

Mt Lebanon St Pauls Episcopal Church P (1443) 1066 Washington Rd 15228-2061 (Mail to:

1066 Washington Rd 15228-2026) Louis Hays Michelle Boomgaard Christopher Yates (412) 531-7153

North Hills Christ Episcopal Church **P** (1425) 5910 Babcock Blvd 15237-2548 (Mail to: 5910 Babcock Blvd 15237-2548) James Shoucair Charles Hamill Jean McIlvain

North Side Emmanuel Episcopal Church **P** (204) 957 W North Ave 15233-1693 (Mail to: 957 W North Ave 15233-1693) Don Youse

North Versailles All Souls Church **P** (26) 215 Canterbury Ln 15137-2111 (Mail to: 215 Canterbury Ln 15137-2198) Linda Wilson (412) 823-1440

Northern Cambria St Thomas Episcopal Church **P** (20) 1201 Chestnut Ave 15714 (Mail to: PO Box 91 15714-0091) Ann Staples (814) 948-5230

Oakmont St Thomas Memorial Church **P** (686) 378 Delaware Ave 15139 (Mail to: 378 Delaware Ave 15139) Jeffrey Murph (412) 828-9680

Penn Hills St James Episcopal Church **P** (18) 11524 Frankstown Rd 15235-3199 (Mail to: 11524 Frankstown Rd 15235-3199) Eric Mcintosh (412) 242-2300

Peters Township St Davids Episcopal Church **P** (134) 905 E McMurray Rd 15367-1094 (Mail to: 905 E McMurray Rd 15367-1094) Kristian Opat (724) 941-4060

Pittsburgh All Saints Episcopal Church **M** (59) 1548 Pineview Dr 15241-3204 (Mail to: 1548 Pineview Dr 15241-3204) (412) 564-5620

Pittsburgh Church of the Nativity **P** (263) 33 Alice St 15205-2801 (Mail to: 33 Alice St 15205-2801) Shawn Malarkey (412) 921-4103

Pittsburgh Old St Luke's Church **P** (Mail to: PO Box 9089 15224-0089)

Pittsburgh St Peters Episcopal Church **P** (380) 4048 Brownsville Rd 15227-3499 (Mail to: 4048 Brownsville Rd 15227-3499) William Geisler (412) 884-5225

Pittsburgh St Stephens Episcopal Church **P** (128) 600 Pitt St 15221-3136 (Mail to: 600 Pitt Street 15221-3136) Nancy Chalfant-Walker (412) 243-6100

Pittsburgh Trinity Cathedral **O** (154) 325 Oliver Avenue 15222-2403 (Mail to: 325 Oliver Ave 15222-2403) Michelle Boomgaard Timothy Hushion Scott Quinn (412) 232-6404

Scottdale St Bartholomew Trinity Church **P** (28) 149 Walnut Ave 15683-1936 (Mail to: 149 Walnut Ave 15683-1936) (724) 832-5110

Somerset St Francis in the Fields Epis Church **P** (59) 2081 Husband Rd 15501-7253 (Mail to: 2081 Husband Rd 15501-7253) Lennel Anderson

Squirrel Hill Church of the Redeemer **P** (231) 5700 Forbes Ave 15217-1526 (Mail to: 5700 Forbes Ave 15217-1526) Michael Foley (412) 422-7100

Wayne Township St Michaels Episcopal Church **P** (11) 274 Saint Michaels Rd 16249-0218 (Mail to: PO Box 544 16249-0544) (724) 783-7194

NON-PAROCHIAL CLERGY

Barker CH *ret* Gibsonia PA
Bell RC *ret* Three Rivers MI
Blessing KA *ret* Wilington NC
Brewer T Pittsburgh PA
Carnahan PK *ret* Murrysville PA
Casto DC *ret* Woodland Park NJ
Davies RW *ret* Pittsburgh PA
Edwards LC *ret* Pittsburgh PA
Else JD *ret* Pittsburgh PA
Fanguy MM Canonsburg PA
Fetterman JJ *ret* Verona PA
Feuerstein JM *dcn* Mt Lebanon PA
Gentle JM *ret* North Andover MA
Gillette HD *dcn* Coraopolis PA
Golden JA *ret* Lawrenceville NJ
Hall DE Pittsburgh PA
Haslett WW *ret* Windber PA
Hays LPW *ret* Ambridge PA
Hurd AA *ret* Cabot PA
Isadore DJ Pittsburgh PA
Jackson JJ Gibsonia PA
Jacobson MR Waxhaw NC
Johnston PM Pittsburgh PA
Johnston TL St Francisvle LA
Koehler NE Pittsburgh PA
LaLonde KN *ret* Albuquerque NM
LaLonde WJ Canonsburg PA
Lewis HT *ret*
Lockett TL Ambridge PA
Martin CP *ret* Johnstown PA
Miller WC Olathe KS
Ogburn WL North Kingstown RI
Park JH *ret* Ambridge PA
Pocalyko RP *ret* Atlanta GA
Pollard RA Pittsburgh PA
Pozzuto KA Mckeesport PA
Prichard TM *ret* Ambridge PA
Ray AM Pittsburgh PA
Ringle LM *dcn*
Ritchie SL *dcn* Pittsburgh PA
Shepard DER *ret* Pittsburgh PA
Smalley SM *ret* Cranberry Township PA
Starr CM Bakerstown PA
Stinson RL *ret* Indiana PA
Sweigert CB *ret* Pittsburgh PA
Visminas CE Framingham MA
Watt GM *ret* Verona PA
Weatherwax EM Pittsburgh PA
Werner GLW *ret* Sewickley PA
Wright ML Shanksville PA
Yesko FM Monroeville PA
Younkin RJ *dcn* Youngstown OH
Younkin RW *ret* Fayetteville AR
Zubieta AT *ret* Clifton VA

DIOCESE OF PUERTO RICO

IGLESIA EPISCOPAL PUERTORRIQUENA
(Province IX)
Comprises the Island of Puerto Rico
DIOCESAN OFFICE Carr 848 Km 1.1 Saint Just, Trujillo Alto, Puerto Rico
(Mail: PO Box 902 Saint Just PR 00978-0902)
TEL (787)761-9800   FAX (787)761-0320
E-MAIL iep@episcopalpr.org   WEB www.episcopalpr.org

Previous Bishops—
WW Jackson (Antigua) in charge
1860-1895, James H Van Buren
1902-1912, Charles B Colmore 1913-
1947, Charles F Boynton 1948-1950,
Albert E Swift 1951-1964, Francisco
Reus Froylan 1964-1986, David
Andres Alvarez 1986-2013

Bishop—Rt Rev Wilfrido Ramos Orench (960)
(Dio 4 Nov 2013)

Bp Exec Asst J Pinto; *Tesorero Diocesano* N Lopez;
Secretario de la Asamblea Rvdo PR Zorrilla; *Asuntos
Extra Diocesanos* Rev PA Rivera; *Oficial Desarrollo
Congregacional e Institucional* Rev P C Ramirez;
Oficina de Mayordomia F Molina; *Oficina de
Evangelismo y Educacion Cristiana* Rev PC Ramirez;
Oficina de Servicios Comunitarios Rev AR Mendez;
Oficina de Comunicaciones Sra Y Torres; *Oficina de
Juventud* Rvdo PA Davila; *Oficina de Propiedad y
Expansion* Rvdo PC Ramirez

Dean: Rt Rev JA Ramos Orench

Stand Comm (Comite Permanente)—Cler: Rvdo PF
Morales Rvdo P JP Gonzalez, Rvdo P A Liz Rvdo
PA Araque; *Lay:* E Cruz F Quiñones A Rodriguez
M Ponce

Dio Conv: 21-22 Oct 2016

PARISHES, MISSIONS, AND CLERGY

Aibonito Espiritu Santo la Tea **M** Bo. Caonillas
Sector La Tea Carr. 726, Km 4.2 00705 (Mail
to: PO Box 127 00705-0127) (787) 313-7015

Aibonito Mision San Judas Tadeo **M** (114) Barrio
Pasto Carr. 717 Km. 0.9 Sector La Playita
00705 (Mail to: PO Box 612 00705-0612) (787)
735-2299

Añasco San Jose de Arimatea **P** Carr. 109 Km. 2.4
00610 (Mail to: PO Box 239 00610-0239) (787)
645-3971

Arecibo Mision San Pablo **M** (158) Carr. 653
Avenida Universidad Barrio Villa Los Santos
00613 (Mail to: Apartado 1051 00613) (787)
878-2084

Bayamon Mision San Bernabe **M** (18) Carr. 167
Km 14.7 Bo. Buena Vista 00956 (Mail to: RR
5, Box 8100 Bo. Buena Vista 00956) (787) 730-
8265

Bayamon Parroquia San Pedro y San Pablo **P** (61)
No IC33 Ave Lomas Verdes 00956 (Mail to:

IC33 Ave. Lomas Verdes 00956) (787) 785-6472

Bayamon San Timoteo **P** 49-13 Calle 36, Esq.
North Main Urb Sierra Bayamon 00961 (Mail
to: 49-13 Calle 36, Esq. North Main Urb Sierra
Bayamon 00961)

Cabo Rojo Nuestra Senora de Walsingham **M**
Carr. 103 Residencia #3 Bario Bajura Sector
Coqui 00623 (Mail to: PO Box 1271 00623)
(787) 685-6766

Caguas Mision Cristo Rey **M** (64) No Calle
Mayagüez, Esquina Ponce Urb Villa del
Carmen 00725 (Mail to: PO Box 6271 00726)
Juan Garcia De Jesus (787) 746-2543

Carolina Mision El Adviento **M** (42) No Urb
Villa Fontana Calle Via 19 QR 16 00985 (Mail
to: Condominio La Rada Ashford 1020 Apt. 23
Condado 00907) (787) 724-9217

Carolina Mision Santo Tomas Apostol **M** (50) Bo
Martin Gonzalez Carr 860 KM 1.1 00987 (Mail
to: PO Box 757 00986-0757) (787) 276-1283

Coamo Nueva Mision San Simon de Cirineo **M**
(9) Bo. Las Flores #47 A Paseo Los Tulipanes
00769 (Mail to: Urb. Valle de Andalucia 3143
Calle Almeria 00728) (787) 387-0889

Dorado Mision Emmanuel **M** (46) Bo Maguayo,
Sector Maysonet II Carr 694 00646 (Mail to:
HC 46 Box 5667 00646) (787) 466-8970

Ensenada Mision Santa Cecilia **M** (62) Calle
Brandon #1 00647 (Mail to: PO Box 445
00647-0445) Jacqueline Ponce Martinez (787)
821-1201

Fajardo Mision El Buen Pastor **M** (50) No 399
Ave. General Valero 00738 (Mail to: 399 Ave.
General Valero 00738) Juan Monge-Santiago
(939) 400-1278

Guayama Mision San Pedro **M** (41) Hospital
Episcopal San Lucas Guayama Ave Pedro
Albizu Campos 00785 (Mail to: Hospital
Episcopal San Lucas Guayama Ave Pedro
Albizu Campos 00784) (787) 989-2369

Guaynabo Mision San Esteban El Martir **M** (43)
Urb. San Ramón Calle Nogal Final 00970
(Mail to: Urb Santiago Iglesias 1308 Ave Paz
Granela Pmb 160 00921-4183) (787) 367-1128

Hato Rey Parroquia la Encarnacion **P** (45) Calle
Juan A. Davila Esq. Juan B. R Urb. Roosevelt
00918 (Mail to: GPO Box 361067 00936-1067)
(787) 459-8374

Humacao Mision San Gabriel Arcangel **M** (49)
Ave. Los Sauces Lote B 00792 (Mail to: Villa
Humacao A-2 00791) (787) 645-3971

Lares Mision la Santa Cruz **M** (73) Carr 135 KM 64.4 Poblado de Castañer 00631 (Mail to: PO Box 1012 00631-1012) Tomas Pixcar-Pol (787) 439-7111

Lares Mision San Bartolome **M** (40) Carr. 128 KM. 37.9 Bo. Bartolo 00631 (Mail to: PO Box 1005 00631-1005) (787) 553-0401

Lares Mision San Matias **M** (62) Carr 111 KM 2.4 Ave. Los Patriotas 00669 (Mail to: PO Box 499 00669) (787) 800-3960

Levittown Mision Santa Maria Magdalena **M** (100) No Ave Boulevard Esq Paseo Conde 00949 (Mail to: PO Box 580497 00950) (787) 604-3135

Loiza Mision San Felipe y Santiago Apostol **M** (53) Carr 187 KM 5.8 Mediania Alta 00772 (Mail to: HC - 01 Buzon 5460 00772-9726) (787) 536-1700

Manati Parroquia la Resurreccion **P** (160) Bo. Cantera Carr. 2 KM 47 00674 (Mail to: PO Box 2292 00674) (787) 368-1625

Maricao Mision la Epifania **M** (44) Barrio Indiera Alta, Sector El Treinta Km. 128 Carr 428 00606 (Mail to: HC-01 Box 4766 00606) (787) 553-0401

Maricao Mision la Transfiguracion **M** (78) Carr. 365, Int 105 Sector Indiera Baja 00606 (Mail to: PO Box 551 00606-0551) (787) 838-2629

Mayaguez Parroquia San Andres **P** (205) 156 Calle Santiago R Palmer 00680 (Mail to: PO Box 4297 00681-4297) (787) 832-1116

Morovis Parroquia Ayudada La Ascencion **P** (112) Carr 633 Km 3.9 Bo. Barahona 00674 (Mail to: HC-02 Box 5830 00687) (787) 862-4206

Penuelas San Mateo Apostol y Evangelista **M** (65) KM 2.3 Sector La Gelpa Bo Quebrada Ceiba 00624 (Mail to: HC - 01 Buzon 8219 00624) (787) 969-0164

Ponce Mision Principe de Paz **M** (31) 469 Calle 13 Urb Brisas del Caribe El Tuque 00728 (Mail to: PO Box 271 Brisas del Caribe 00728-5312) (787) 514-5994

Ponce Mision San Lucas Evangelista **M** 909 Ave Tito Castro Torre Medica Hospital Episcopal San Lucas 00716 (Mail to: 2703 Paseo De La Reina 00717) (787) 996-4504

Ponce Mision San Marcos Evangelista **M** (72) Carr 123 Km. 10 Hm. 5 Bo. Magueyes 00731 (Mail to: PO Box 8453 00732-8453) (787) 844-4681

Ponce Mision San Miguel Arcangel **M** (76) Calle Lolita Tizol #49 00731 (Mail to: HC - 01 Box 10100 00624) (787) 470-5894

Ponce Parroquia Ayudada La Reconciliacion **P** (235) Bo. Quebrada Limon Carr. 502, Km. 4.5 00728 (Mail to: Parcelas Pastillo Canas 818 Calle Jesus T Pineiro 00728-3601) (787) 612-0381

Ponce Parroquia Ayudada Santa Maria Virgen **M** (196) Bo. Clausells Calle Central #15 00780 (Mail to: PO Box 10010 00732-0010) (787) 454-9161

Ponce Parroquia Santisima Trinidad **P** (389) Calle Marina Esq Abolicion 732 (Mail to: Apartado 335693 00732) (787) 841-6719

Ponce Parroquia Santo Nombre de Jesus **P** (120) Parcelas Pastillos Canas 806 Calle Jesus T Pineiro 00728-3601 (Mail to: Parcelas Pastillo Canas 806 Calle Jesus T Pineiro 00728-3601) (787) 844-3955

Rio Piedras Mision San Francisco de Asis **M** (17) Urb El Comandante 876 Calle Manuel Guerra 00924-2534 (Mail to: Urb El Comandante 876 Calle Manuel Guerra 00924) (787) 762-0835

Rio Piedras Parroquia San Jose **P** (80) No Carr 842 KM 2.4 Caimito 00926 (Mail to: RR 6 Box 9615 00926) (787) 720-5834

Sabana Grande Mision Santa Ana **M** (41) Urb El Arrendado 97 Calle A 00637 (Mail to: PO Box 445 00647) (787) 821-1201

✣ **Santurce** Catedral San Juan Bautista **O** (171) Ave Ponce de León Esq. Calle Canals Pda. 20 00908 (Mail to: PO Box 9262 00908-9262) Emilia Morales-Vega (787) 721-2395

✣ **Santurce** Cathedral St John the Baptist **O** (175) 1401 Ponce de Leon Ave Esquina Calle Canals Parada 20 00907 (Mail to: PO Box 9373 00908-9373) (787) 722-3254

Trujillo Alto Parroquia la Sagrada Familia **P** (65) Carr 848 KM 1.1 Bo Saint Just 00978 (Mail to: PO Box 360145 00936-0145) (787) 616-9174

Trujillo Alto Parroquia Ayudada Santa Hilda **P** (106) Carr 848 Bo Saint Just 00978 (Mail to: Apartado 902 00978) (787) 755-7675

Utuado Los Santos Apostoles **M** Calle Dr Cueto 81 00641 (Mail to: PO Box 2729 00613) (787) 516-9438

Vieques Mision Todos los Santos **M** (62) Calle Plinion Peterson 557 765 (Mail to: PO Box 308 00765-0308) (787) 741-2668

Yauco Mision la Anunciacion a la Virgen **M** (99) Bo Rancheras Carr. 371, Km. 12.2 00698 (Mail to: Urb Alta Vista 1925 Calle Afrodita 00716) (787) 856-6256

Yauco Mision San Juan Apostol y Evangelist **M** (39) Calle Marcial Santana, #73 Parcelas Viejas,Barinas 00698 (Mail to: HC 03 Box 15683 00698) (787) 460-1001

Yauco Mision San Rafael Arcangel **M** (114) Calle Barbosa #21 00698 (Mail to: PO Box 1967 00698-1967) (787) 460-1001

NON-PAROCHIAL CLERGY

Adorno Andino HL Saint Just PR
Alvarado Figueroa LA
Alvarez-Adorno AL
Anthony TM *ret*
Araque Galvis A Saint Just PR
Arques R *ret*
Arroyo-Sanchez J
Ausas-Combes J *ret*

Aybar-Marte P
Cedeno Medina OA *ret*
Cintron J *ret*
Colon Torres L Saint Just PR
Cruz H *ret*
Davila Colon AM
de Anaya NL *ret* Silver Spring MD
De Jesus-Jimenez J Ponce PR
Del Valle-Ortiz EE San Juan RP
Del Valle-Tirado JA
Desueza-Savinon EG San Juan PR
Ebel AT
Fernandez-Pola R *ret*
Franceschi D
Franco Estevez JB Saint Just PR
Garces Torres GG Saint Just PR
Garcia DA *ret*
Garcia-Aponte J
Garcia-Perez JR
Gonzalez Garavito JP Saint Just PR
Gonzalez Santos RA
Gonzalez-Figueroa E *ret*
Gutierrez H Caguas PR
Guzman Velez FI Saint Just PR
Kidder FE
Lago AM *ret*
Linares-Rivera I
Liz Lopez RA Elizabeth NJ
Malave Torres H *ret*
Marrero Camacho LF
Martinez Toledo E
Medina FR *ret* Bridgeport CT
Mendez-Colon AR San Juan PR
Mercado Galarza W *ret*
Millien W *ret*

Morales Colon FJ
Morales Maldonado RL Saint Just PR
Muñoz Peña JA Ponce PR
Muñoz Quintana DD Humacao PR
Muñoz-Labra MJ *ret*
Narvaez Adorno JA *ret*
Padilla-Morales LF
Palacin ME *ret*
Perez-Quinones JP
Ramirez L *ret*
Ramirez-Segarra CE Yauco PR
Ramos L *ret*
Ramos WF *ret*
Ramos-Garcia R *ret*
Rivera JJ *ret*
Rivera Perez FJ Saint Just PR
Rivera Rivera LG *ret*
Rivera-Rodriguez A
Rodriguez Sanchez MH San Juan PR
Rojas-Arroyo S
Salcedo FB *ret*
Sanchez Nunez CA *ret* Manati PR
Santana-Ruiz B *ret* Sarasota FL
Santiago-Padilla G Loiza PR
Santos-Montes M
Silva-Gonzalez A
Snodgrass TJ *ret* Baltimore MD
Stevens WC
Torres JA *ret*
Vallenilla De La Rosa AR
Vazquez-Geli JR *ret*
Velazquez-Morales JA *ret*
Vilar Mendez JF
Vilar-Santiago JE *ret*
Wainwright RF *ret*

DIOCESE OF RHODE ISLAND
(PROVINCE I)
Comprises the State of Rhode Island
DIOCESAN OFFICE 275 N Main St Providence 02903-1298
TEL (401) 274-4500   FAX (401) 331-9430
E-MAIL diocese@episcopalri.org   WEB www.episcopalri.org

Previous Bishops—
Samuel Seabury 1790-96, Edward Bass 1798-1803, Alexander V Griswold 1811-43, John PK Henshaw 1843-52, Thomas M Clark 1854-1903, Wm M McVickar coadj 1898 Bp 1903-10, James D Perry 1911-46, Granville G Bennett suffr 1939 Bp 1946-54, John S Higgins coadj 1953 Bp 1955-72, Frederick H Belden coadj 1971 Bp 1972-79, George N Hunt 1980-94, Geralyn Wolf 1996-2012

Bishop—The Very Rev W Nicholas Knisely SOSc (1071) (Dio 17 Nov 2012)

Bps Exec Asst/Sec E Crawley; *Cn for Program* B Fornal; *Comm Dir* B Sibielski; *Epis Char* P Amatore; *Sec Conv Rev* K Lloyd; *Hist Rev* L Bradner; *Treas* R Batchelor 275 N Main Providence 02903; *Cn to Ord* L Grenz; *CFO* Dennis Burton

Stand Comm—Cler: J Bocchino K Lloyd P Greene G Getlein; *Lay:* Pres L MacFall L Sibielski J Gelatii N McNamara

Dio Conv: 11-12 Nov 2016

PARISHES, MISSIONS, AND CLERGY
   Barrington St Johns Episcopal Church **P** (996) 191 County Rd 02806-4501 (Mail to: 191

County Rd 02806-4501) Robert Marshall (401) 245-4065

Barrington Sts Matthew & Mark Episcopal Church **P** (182) 3 Chapel Rd 02806-1807 (Mail to: 5 Chapel Rd 02806-1861) Patrick Greene (401) 245-3690

Block Island St Anns-by-the-Sea Episcopal Church **M** (69) 25 Spring St 02807-0622 (Mail to: PO Box 622 02807-0622) Eileen Lindeman (401) 466-2911

Bristol St Michaels Church **P** (260) 399 Hope St 02809-1803 (Mail to: PO Box 414 02809-0414) Paul Twelves (401) 253-7717

Central Falls St George & San Jorge **P** (710) 12 Clinton St 02863-2906 (Mail to: 12 Clinton St 02863-2906) Jose Roberts (401) 722-9449

Charlestown Church of the Holy Spirit **M** (75) 4150 Old Post Rd 02813-2551 (Mail to: PO Box 241 02813-0241) (401) 364-6368

Coventry St Francis Episcopal Church **M** (252) 132 Peckham Ln 02816-5125 (Mail to: PO Box 142 02816-0003) Sean Manchester (401) 397-7757

Cranston Church of the Ascension **P** (400) 390 Pontiac Ave 02910-3322 (Mail to: 390 Pontiac Ave 02910-3322) Michael Coburn Mercedes Julian

Cranston St Davids on the Hill Epis Ch **P** (546) 200 Meshanticut Valley Pkwy 02920-3917 (Mail to: 200 Meshanticut Valley Pkwy 02920-3997) Peter Lane (401) 942-4368

Cranston Trinity Episcopal Church **P** (453) 139 Ocean Ave 02905-3628 (Mail to: 139 Ocean Avenue 02905-3628) (401) 941-4324

Cumberland Emmanuel Episcopal Church **P** (439) 120 Nate Whipple Hwy 02864-1410 (Mail to: 120 Nate Whipple Hwy 02864-1410) Joan Testin (401) 658-1506

E Greenwich St Lukes Episcopal Church **P** (1182) 99 Peirce St 02818-3814 (Mail to: 99 Peirce St 02818-3814) Noel Bailey Timothy Rich

E Providence St Marys Episcopal Church **M** (73) 81 Warren Ave 02914-5119 (Mail to: 81 Warren Ave 02914-5199) Peter Michaelson Michele Matott (401) 434-7456

Greenville St Thomas Episcopal Church **P** (350) 1 Smith Avenue 02828 (Mail to: PO Box 505 02828-0505) Susan Carpenter Donald Parker (401) 949-0261

Hope Valley St Elizabeths Church **M** (115) 63 Canonchet Rd 02832-2401 (Mail to: PO Box 48 63 Canonchet Rd 02832-0048) Richard Schweinsburg (401) 539-7346

Jamestown St Matthews Parish **P** (418) 87 Narragansett Ave PO Box 317 02835-0317 (Mail to: PO Box 317 02835-0317) Kevin Lloyd (401) 423-1762

Kingston St Augustines Church **P** (139) 35 Lower College Rd 02881-1307 (Mail to: 15 Lower College Rd 02881-1307) William Dobbins Janice Grinnell (401) 783-2153

Lincoln Christ Church in Lonsdale **P** (199) 1643 Lonsdale Ave 02865-1707 (Mail to: 1643 Lonsdale Ave 02865-0245) (401) 725-1920

Little Compton St Andrew's by-the-Sea **P** (248) 182 Willow Ave 02837-1535 (Mail to: PO Box 491 02837-0491) Robert Brooks William Locke

Middletown Church of the Holy Cross **M** (62) 1439 West Main Rd 02842-7315 (Mail to: PO Box 4121 02842-0121) (401) 846-7076

Middletown St Columbas Chapel **P** (486) 55 Vaucluse Ave 02842-5742 (Mail to: 55 Vaucluse Ave 02842-5742) Everett Greene Erik Larsen (401) 847-5571

N Kingstown St Pauls Wickford **P** (1960) 55 Main St 02852-5017 (Mail to: 55 Main St 02852-5017) Virginia Heistand William Ogburn (401) 294-4357

N Providence St James Episcopal Church **M** (55) 474 Fruit Hill Ave 02911-2636 (Mail to: 474 Fruit Hill Ave 02911-2636) (401) 353-2079

N Scituate Trinity Episcopal Church **P** (556) 251 Danielson Pike 02857-1906 (Mail to: 251 Danielson Pike 02857) Pamela Gregory (401) 647-2322

Narragansett St Peters-by-the-Sea Church **P** (453) 72 Central St 02882-3647 (Mail to: 72 Central St 02882-3647) Craig Swan (401) 783-4623

Newport Emmanuel Church **P** (297) 42 Dearborn St 02840-3408 (Mail to: 42 Dearborn St 02840-3408) Anita Schell

Newport St Johns Church **P** (63) 61 Poplar St 02840-2434 (Mail to: 61 Poplar St 02840-2434) Nathan Humphrey Peter Spencer (401) 848-2561

Newport Trinity Church **P** (402) 1 Queen Anne Sq 02840-6855 (Mail to: 1 Queen Anne Sq 02840-6855) Anne Richards Paul Koumrian (401) 846-0660

Pawtucket Church of the Good Shepherd **P** (167) 490 Broadway 02860-1340 (Mail to: 490 Broadway 02860-1340) (401) 723-0408

Pawtucket St Lukes Episcopal Church **P** (234) 670 Weeden St 02860-1649 (Mail to: 670 Weeden St 02860-1649) Dennis Bucco Joyce Thorne (401) 723-9216

Pawtucket St Pauls Church **P** (333) 50 Park Pl 02860-4010 (Mail to: 50 Park Pl 02860-4010) Greta Getlein (401) 728-4300

Portsmouth St Marys Episcopal Church **P** (995) 324 East Main Rd 02871-2113 (Mail to: 324 East Main Rd 02871-2113) Jennifer Pedrick (401) 846-9700

Portsmouth St Pauls Episcopal Church **P** (32) 2679 E Main Rd 02871-2613 (Mail to: 2679 E Main Rd 02871-2613) (401) 683-1164

Providence All Saints Memorial Church **P** (84) 674 Westminster St 02903-4066 (Mail to: 674 Westminster St 02903-4066) David Ames (401) 751-1747

Providence Cathedral of St John **P** (384) 271 N Main St 02903-1237 (Mail to: 275 N Main St 02903-1237) (401) 274-4500

Providence Church of the Redeemer **P** (81) 655 Hope St 02906-2652 (Mail to: 655 Hope St 02906-2652) Patrick Campbell (401) 331-0678

Providence Church of the Transfiguration **P** (929) 1665 Broad St 02905-2727 (Mail to: 1665 Broad Street 02905-2727) Michele Matott (401) 461-3142

Providence Grace Episcopal Church **P** (429) 175 Mathewson St 02903-3410 (Mail to: 175 Mathewson St 02903-3499) Jonathan Huyck (401) 331-3225

Providence St Martins Episcopal Church **P** (630) 50 Orchard Ave 02906-5418 (Mail to: 50 Orchard Ave 02906-5418) Mark Sutherland Lawrence Bradner Linda Griggs (401) 751-2141

Providence St Peters & St Andrews Episcopal **P** (122) 25 Pomona Ave 02908-5255 (Mail to: 25 Pomona Ave 02908-5244) Joyce Penfield (401) 272-9649

Providence St Stephens Church **P** (134) 114 George St 02906-1189 (Mail to: 114 George St 02906-1189) John Alexander Leroy Close Peter D'Alesandre Blake Sawicky Martin Yost (401) 421-6702

Rumford Church of the Epiphany **P** (301) 1336 Pawtucket Ave 02916-1412 (Mail to: 1336 Pawtucket Ave 02916-1412) Dorothy Brightman Maryalice Sullivan Jennifer Zogg (401) 434-5012

Saunderstown Chapel of St John the Divine **P** (184) 10 Church Way 02874-3807 (Mail to: PO Box 541 02874-0541)

Tiverton Church of the Holy Trinity **P** (242) 1956 Main Rd 02878-4637 (Mail to: 1956 Main Rd 02878-4698) John Higginbotham (401) 624-4759

Wakefield Church of the Ascension **P** (218) 370 Main St 02879-7407 (Mail to: 370 Main St 02879) Robert Travis

Warwick All Saints Church in Pontiac **P** (63) 111 Greenwich Ave 02886-1279 (Mail to: 111 Greenwich Ave 02886-1279) Philip Devens (401) 739-1238

Warwick St Barnabas Episcopal Church **P** (414) 3257 Post Rd 02886-7145 (Mail to: 3257 Post Rd 02886-7196) James Bocchino (401) 737-4141

Warwick St Marks Church **P** (460) 111 W Shore Rd 02889-1102 (Mail to: 111 W Shore Rd 02889-1102) Susan Wrathall (401) 737-3127

Westerly Christ Church **P** (508) 7 Elm St 02891 (Mail to: 7 Elm St 02891-2125) Kuruvilla Chandy John Barrett Sandra Haines-Murdocco David Joslin Richard Morgan Amy Spagna

Wood River Jct St Thomas Episcopal Church **M** (73) 322 Church St 02894-1119 (Mail to: PO Box 33 02894-0033) Bettine Besier (401) 364-3113

Woonsocket St James Church **P** (201) 24 Hamlet Ave 02895-4408 (Mail to: 24 Hamlet Ave 02895-4427) Peter Tierney (401) 762-2222

NON-PAROCHIAL CLERGY

Almon AA *dcn* Pawtucket RI
Anderson EB *ret* Bristol RI
Anthony HF *ret* Vero Beach FL
Anthony RW *ret* Centerville MA
Bailey PA *dcn* Riverside RI
Barr GR Providence RI
Boucher EC *ret* Swansea MA
Brower MM Providence RI
Buote-Greig EA *ret* North Scituate RI
Burger DC Woonsocket RI
Burke AB *dcn* Westerly RI
Burlington RC *ret* Delray Beach FL
Burton CH *dcn* Hope Valley RI
Carney SR Ocean Springs MS
Chaplin GM *ret* Newport RI
Chrisman JA *ret* Sarasota FL
Collins JT *dcn* Providence RI
Decarvalho ME Providence RI
Drake JAJ *ret* Pawtucket RI
Fairman HF *ret* Swansea MA
Fischer-Davies CI *ret* Providence RI
Fraioli KA *ret* Sharon MA
Frink JP *ret* Smithfield RI
Gillespie DM *ret* Rochester VT
Gordon HM *ret* Warwick RI
Grenz LL Providence RI
Hallenbeck EF *dcn* Warwick RI
Harris EI Rumford RI
Harris M *ret* North Kingstown RI
Hitt M *dcn* Providence RI
Jacob JN
Johnson MM *ret* Silver Spring MD
Johnstone MBMA *ret* Newport RI
Kirby JW Jamestown RI
Kuehl HA *ret* Warren RI
Laremore RT *ret* Barrington RI
LaVallee DA *ret* Cranston RI
Lemery GC *ret* Jamestown RI
Lesieur BA *ret dcn* Cumberland RI
Lewis JC Newport RI
Lucey DJ Bristol RI
Marcetti AJ East Providence RI
Matthews MT Mckinney TX
Mauney JP *ret* Sagamore Beach MA
Mays-Stock BL *dcn* Cranston RI
Mello IE *dcn* Cranston RI
Mello MA *dcn*
Miller NF *dcn* Westwood MA
Millette CL *dcn* Warwick RI
Mitchell JN *ret* Providence RI
Neilsen E *dcn* Narragansett RI
Nestor EM Wakefield RI
Olmsted NKY *ret* Lincoln RI
Olsen JB *dcn* Charlestown RI
Pappas CA Edmonton AB
Peckham AH *ret* Portsmouth RI
Pelletier AD *dcn* Wakefield RI
Perry CC *ret* Bristol RI
Prior JG *ret* Hilton Head Island SC
Purcell CF Westerly RI

Rannenberg PL *ret* North Kingstown RI
Rogers JS *ret* Saint Marys GA
Scott KE *ret* Delmar NY
Sessions MA *ret* Greenville RI
Shattuck GH *ret* Warwick RI
Shippee RC *ret* Mesa AZ
Shobe MW Cranston RI
Shoemaker HSC *ret* Newport RI
Simonian MJ *dcn* North Port FL
Simpson RR *ret* Portland OR
Spulnik FJ *ret* San Diego CA
Stahl DW *ret* providence RI
Stenning GJ *ret* Portsmouth RI

Stiles-randak S *ret* Peace Dale RI
Strahan LC *ret* Newport RI
Tarrant PJ Edinburgh
Tierney PJ *ret* Charlotte NC
Tierney VM Newport RI
Trafford EJ *dcn* West Warwick RI
Turnbull HG *ret* Jamesville NY
Vanderau RJ *ret* Orlando FL
Westhorp PH Maryland Heights MO
Wheelock LG *dcn* Jamestown RI
Willis NA *ret* Wakefield RI
Wright EL *dcn* Newport RI

DIOCESE OF THE RIO GRANDE
(PROVINCE VII)
Comprises New Mexico and Far West Texas
DIOCESAN OFFICE 6400 Coors Blvd NW Albuquerque NM 87120
TEL (505) 881-0636   FAX (505) 883-9048
E-MAIL mjewell@dioceserg.org   WEB www.dioceserg.org

Previous Bishops—
John M Kendrick 1889 (NM and AZ) 1892-1911, Fredk B Howden 1914-40, James M Stoney M 1942 dio 1952-56, Charles James Kinsolving III 1956-72, Richard M Trelease Jr 1972-87 Terence Kelshaw 1989-2005, Jeffrey N Steenson 2005-07

Bishop—Rt Rev Michael L Vono DD (1052)
(Dio 22 Oct 2010)

Assisting Bishop—Rt Rev Jerry Lamb

Treas G Gronquist V Rizzo C Frost; *Chanc for NM* K Aubrey; *Chanc for TX* C Pine; *Archivist* CE Davies; *Reg* M Jewell; *ECW* C Davis; *Faith Alive!* N McMillian; *Recov Min* R Murphy; *Stew; Jubliee* Min D Martin; *Inv Bd* G Gronquist; *Cn to Ord* Rev Cn D Gutierrez; *Cn Lit* Rev Dcn P Soukup; *Cn Theol* Very Rev Cn C McGowan; *Trans Off* Rev Cn R Raney; *Bosque Ctr* Rev Cn D Gutierrez; *Bishop's Ridge: Stoney Camp and Rec Ctr* K Telehany; *Yth Min; Border Min* S Hutchins; *Comm* Rev Cn R Rancy; *Hispano Min* Rev Cn D Gutierrez; *School for Min* Rev Cn C McGowan; *Disciplinary Board* S Pine; *COMB* J Alarid

Stand Comm—Cler: Pres K Sermon P Moore R Hurst; *Lay:* P Mote C Johnson K Pittman

Regional Deans: NE Very Rev M Olsen; *NW* Very Rev Cn R Mundy; *SE* Very Rev J Burgess; *SW* Very Rev M St. Clair

Dio Conv: 27-29 Oct 2016 Santa Fe NM

PARISHES, MISSIONS, AND CLERGY

Alamogordo St Johns Episcopal Church **P** (187) 1114 Indiana Ave 88310-6720 (Mail to: PO Box 449 88311-0449) Thomas Arrowsmith-Lowe (575) 437-3891

✠ **Albuquerque** Cathedral Church of St John **O** (1995) 318 Silver Ave SW 87102-3328 (Mail to: PO Box 1246 87103-1246) James Goodman Michael Drinkwater Arthur Lovekin Shawn Wamsley (505) 247-1581

Albuquerque Church Of Our Savior Episcopal **M** (28) 2805 Don Felipe Rd 87105-6748 (Mail to: 2805 Don Felipe Rd SW 87105) (505) 873-2011

Albuquerque Hope-in-the-Desert Episcopal Church **P** (136) 8700 Alameda Blvd NE 87122-3789 (Mail to: 8700 Alameda Blvd NE 87122-3789) Daniel Tuton Ruth Morgan (505) 830-0572

Albuquerque St Chads Episcopal Church **P** (382) 7171 Tennyson St NE 87122-1081 (Mail to: 7171 Tennyson St NE 87122-1081) Janice Hosea

Albuquerque St Marks Episcopal Church **P** (239) 431 Richmond Pl NE 87106-2150 (Mail to: 431 Richmond Pl NE 87106-2150) Christopher Mclaren Patricia Soukup (505) 262-2484

Albuquerque St Marys Episcopal Church **P** (308) 1500 Chelwood Park Blvd NE 87112-4620 (Mail to: 1500 Chelwood Park Blvd NE 87112-4620) James Hunter Ernest St Johns Samuel Stearns (505) 293-1911

Albuquerque St Michael and All Angels Church **P** (1339) 601 Montano Rd NW 87107-5226 (Mail to: 601 Montano Rd NW 87107-5226) Mary Allison-Hatch Joseph Britton Judith Jenkins Paul Strid (505) 345-8147

Albuquerque St Thomas of Canterbury Church **P** (341) 425 University Blvd NE 87106-4521 (Mail to: 425 University Blvd NE 87106-4556) Linda Lilley Sylvia Miller-Mutia (505) 247-2515

Alpine St James Church **M** 510 N 6th St # 877 79830-3510 (Mail to: PO Box 1319 79831) (432) 837-7313

Anthony St Luke's Episcopal Church **P** (218) 7050 Mcnutt Rd 88021-9221 (Mail to: 7050 McNutt Rd 88021-9221) Daniel Cave (575) 874-3972

Artesia St Pauls Church **P** (24) 807 S 10th St 88210-2388 (Mail to: PO Box 1308 88211-1308) Maurice Geldert

Carlsbad Grace Episcopal Church **P** (169) 508 W Fox St 88220-5721 (Mail to: PO Box PP 88221-7529) Rodney Hurst (575) 885-6200

Chama St Jeromes Church **M** (25) 331 North Pine 87520 (Mail to: PO Box 1072 331 Pine Ave 87520-1072) (575) 753-1503

Cloudcroft Church of the Ascension **SC** (7) 60 Chipmunk Ave 88317 (Mail to: PO Box 263 88317-0263) (575) 404-1590

Clovis Curry St James Episcopal Church **P** (142) 1117 N. Main St 88102-0249 (Mail to: PO Box 249 88102-0249)

Corrales San Gabriel the Archangel **P** (54) 4908 Corrales Rd Suite B 87048-9312 (Mail to: 4908 Corrales Rd Ste B 87048-8613) Rhonda Mcintire (505) 933-5931

Deming St Lukes Episcopal Church **M** (30) No 419 W Spruce Street 88030-3640 (Mail to: PO Box 1258 88031-1258) Donald Heacox (575) 546-8088

Edgewood Church of the Holy Cross **P** (222) 367 State Road 344 87015-1090 (Mail to: PO Box 1090 87015-1090) Arthur Raney

El Paso All Saints Episcopal Church **P** (131) 3500 McRae Blvd 79925-2807 (Mail to: 3500 McRae Blvd 79925-2807) Melinda St Clair (915) 598-0721

El Paso Holy Spirit Episcopal Church **P** (90) 10500 Kenworthy St 79924-1738 (Mail to: 10500 Kenworthy St 79924-1738) (915) 821-1362

El Paso St Albans Episcopal Church **P** (120) 1810 Elm St 79930-3110 (Mail to: 1810 Elm St 79930-3110) Francis Perko (915) 565-2727

El Paso St Christophers Episcopal Church **P** (91) 300 Riverside Dr 79915-4527 (Mail to: 300 Riverside Dr 79915-4527) Jose Bernal (915) 859-9329

El Paso St Francis on the Hill Episcopal Church **M** (116) 6280 Los Robles Dr 79912-1958 (Mail to: 6280 Los Robles Dr 79912-1958) James Brzezinski (915) 581-9500

Espanola St Stephens Episcopal Church **M** (35) 703 Bond St 87532-2729 (Mail to: PO Box 1303 87532-1303) Douglas Bleyle Constance Delzell (505) 753-3010

Farmington St Johns Episcopal Church **P** (312) 312 N Orchard Ave 87401-6227 (Mail to: 312

N Orchard Ave 87401-6227) Robert Bailey Guy Mackey George Peacock (505) 325-5832

Fort Sumner St Johns Episcopal Church **M** (21) 113 S 7th St 88119-9218 (Mail to: PO Box 392 88119-0392) (575) 355-2800

Gallup Church of the Holy Spirit **M** (73) 1334 S Country Club Dr 87301-5665 (Mail to: 1334 S Country Club Dr 87301-5665) Lynn Perkins Roger Perkins (505) 863-4695

Glencoe St Anne Chapel **HC** Highway 70 88355-7367 (Mail to: 121 Mescalero Trail 88355-7367) (575) 257-2356

Hillsboro Christ Episcopal Church **M** (5) Eleanora St 88042 (Mail to: Christ Church P O Box 514 88042) (575) 895-5644

Hobbs St Christophers Church **M** (30) 207 E Permian Dr 88240-4434 (Mail to: 207 E Permian Dr 88240-4434) (575) 393-3237

Hurst St Stephens Episcopal Church **M** (52) No 463 W Harwood Rd 76054-2941 (Mail to: PO Box 54864 76054-4864) (915) 479-4669

Las Cruces St Andrews Episcopal Church **P** (487) Canon Scott A Ruthven 518 N Alameda Blvd 88005 (Mail to: PO Box 266 88004-0266) Scott Ruthven Walter LaLonde (575) 526-6333

Las Cruces St James Episcopal Church **P** (457) 102 Saint James 88005-3713 (Mail to: PO Box 2427 88047-2427) Nicholas Funk Francis Williams (575) 526-2389

Las Vegas St Pauls Peace Church **M** (53) 810 8th St 87701-4242 (Mail to: PO Box 2576 87701-2576) Madelynn Johnston William McKay Thomas Woodward (505) 425-8479

Los Alamos Trinity on the Hill Episcopal Church **P** (474) 3900 Trinity Dr 87544-1871 (Mail to: 3900 Trinity Dr 87544-1871) Christopher Adams Gary Baldwin Alicia Pope Louise Weiss (505) 662-5107

Los Lunas St Matthews Episcopal Church **M** (166) 400 Huning Ranch Loop West 87031 (Mail to: 400 Huning Ranch Loop West 87031) Robert Mundy (505) 865-6548

Lovington St Marys Episcopal Church **M** (4) 417 W Avenue C 88260-4337 (Mail to: PO Box 883 88260-0883) (575) 396-5222

Marfa St Paul's Church **M** (35) 101 E Washington 79843-0175 (Mail to: PO Box 175 79843-0175) Jeremiah Griffin (830) 660-2971

Milan All Saints Episcopal Church **M** (33) 600 Hwy 605 87021 (Mail to: PO Box 157 87020-0157) Patricia Eustis (505) 285-5074

Pecos St Marks Episcopal Church **M** (8) 416 S Plum St 79772-3832 (Mail to: 416 S Plum St 79772-3832) Charles McIntyre (915) 445-3812

Portales Trinity Episcopal Church **M** (7) 1116 W 3rd St 88130-6618 (Mail to: 1116 W 3rd St 88130-6618) Larry Mote (575) 356-6860

Raton Holy Trinity Episcopal Church **HC** (74) 240 Rio Grande Ave 87740-3945 (Mail to: PO Box 1016 87740-1016) Timothy Sexton (575) 445-9884

Rio Communities St Philips Episcopal Church **M** (98) 113 La Luna Pl 87002 (Mail to: 113 LaLuna Pl 87002) Diane Figge

Rio Rancho St Francis Episcopal Church **P** (162) 2903 Cabezon Blvd SE 87124-1741 (Mail to: 2903 Cabezon Blvd SE 87124-1741) Alexander Lenzo (505) 896-1999

Roswell St Andrews Church **P** (250) 505 N Pennsylvania Ave 88201-4736 (Mail to: PO Box 1495 88202-1495) Dale Plummer (575) 622-1353

Ruidoso Epis Church in Lincoln County **P** (210) 121 Mescalero Trl 88345-6090 (Mail to: 121 Mescalero Trail 88345-6090) Judith Burgess Laurie Benavides (575) 257-2356

Santa Fe Church of the Holy Faith **P** (866) 311 E Palace Ave 87501-2221 (Mail to: 311 E Palace Ave 87501-2221) Kenneth Semon James Gordon Margaret Patterson (505) 982-4447

Santa Fe Church of the Holy Family **M** (36) 4 Estambre Pl 87508-2105 (Mail to: 10A Bisbee Ct 87508-1338) Florence Kay Anders Elisabeth Noland (505) 424-0095

Santa Fe St Bedes Episcopal Church **P** (245) 1601 S Saint Francis Dr 87505-4051 (Mail to: 1601 S Saint Francis Dr 87505-4051) Randall Lutz George Kunkle Mary Volland (505) 982-1133

Silver City Church of the Good Shepherd **P** (145) 615 N Texas St 88061-5422 (Mail to: PO Box 2795 88062-2795) Paul Moore Thomas Bates Francoise Gelineau Maurice Hutchins (575) 538-2015

Socorro Church of the Epiphany **M** (108) 908 Leroy Pl 87801-4744 (Mail to: PO Box 692 87801-0692) Morrill Peabody (575) 835-1818

Taos St James Episcopal Church **P** (223) 214 Camino De Santiago 87571-4306 (Mail to: 5794 Ndcbu 87571-6129) Walter Allen Loren Olsen Pamela Tyler (575) 758-2790

Terlingua Santa Inez Episcopal Church **M** Terlingua Ghost Town and Ivey Rd 79852 (Mail to: PO Box 88 79830) (432) 371-4399

Truth Consq St Pauls Episcopal Church **M** (47) 407 N Cedar St 87901-2335 (Mail to: PO Box 949 87901-0949) (575) 894-9596

Tucumcari St Michaels Episcopal Church **M** (41) 2602 S 2nd St 88401-4221 (Mail to: 2602 S 2nd St 88401-4221) Mark Lake (575) 461-4222

NON-PAROCHIAL CLERGY

Albers BA *ret dcn* Empire MI
Anderson KE *dcn* El Paso TX
Bachschmid EK *dcn* New Market VA
Bales JS *ret dcn* Albuquerque NM
Batton RN Albuquerque NM
Bayang ME *ret* Gallup NM
Boldine CS *ret* Albuquerque NM
Brandon KD White Sands Missile Range NM
Brockmeier AL Clovis NM
Brockmeier SC Clovis NM
Cacoperdo PA *ret* Elephant Butte NM
Caldwell SR *ret* Albuquerque NM

Canterbury ML *ret* Albuquerque NM
Carman CC *ret* Nellysford VA
Carter GL Phoenix AZ
Caruso CW Austin TX
Case MT
Conroe JW
Cook LLL *dcn* Albuquerque NM
Cram DO Rio Rancho NM
Croft CC *ret* Silver City NM
Daughtry JR *ret* Melbourne FL
Dixon JH *ret* Alicante
Ellingboe SK *ret* Taos NM
Gaddy AL
Gray TW *ret* Carlsbad NM
Green PLOB *ret* Albuquerque NM
Guck SSJ Silver City NM
Gutierrez DGP Albuquerque NM
Hall SL *ret* Albuquerque NM
Hassemer DW Medanales NM
Hobden BC *ret* Las Cruces NM
Hupf JL Minnetonka Beach MN
Hutchins S
Kelly CP *ret* Los Alamos NM
Kerr KA *dcn* Tesuque NM
King CW *ret* El Paso TX
Kinsolving JA *ret* Santa Fe NM
Koch WC *ret* Blue Hill ME
Lutz RJEM *ret* Las Cruces NM
Marr JA *ret* Santa Fe NM
Martin WH *ret* El Paso TX
Martinez KR
McDowell AS Clovis NM
McFarland EE *dcn* Las Cruces NM
McGowan CJ *ret* Albuquerque NM
McNellis KK *ret* Albuquerque NM
Molnar AJ *dcn* Sudbury MA
Murphy RW *ret* Santa Fe NM
Myrick HE *ret* Alpine TX
Oesterlin PW *ret* Rio Rancho NM
Orbaugh PR *dcn* Cochiti Lake NM
Osborne RL *ret* Pottsboro TX
Parham AP *ret* El Paso TX
Penn JW *ret* Ruidoso NM
Polk TR *ret* The Woodlands TX
Reed RW Las Vegas NM
Rehberg GI *dcn* Albuquerque NM
Robbins HJ *ret* Ruidoso Downs NM
Rollinson JT *ret* Clovis NM
Ross RJ *dcn*
Rowland TD Truth Or Consequences NM
Schneider TC Crossville TN
Schuster FP *ret* Edwardsburg MI
Shafer SH Oakland CA
Shepherd KA *ret dcn* Algodones NM
Smith WF *ret* Albuquerque NM
Taylor BC *ret* Albuquerque NM
Thomson RR *ret* El Paso TX
Tripp AD *ret* Raton NM
Turner AR *ret* Traphill NC
Turrie AE *dcn* Mesilla Park NM
Weiser SI *ret* Santa Fe NM
West P *ret* Albuquerque NM

Whitaker M San Mateo CA
Williams BMK *ret* Albuquerque NM
Williams SJC *ret* Pittsfield MA
Wilson FK *ret* Alamogordo NM
Winter BW Albuquerque NM

Winter LR *ret* Ruidoso NM
Worthington CM San Antonio TX
Wright BR *ret* Beaver PA
Zachritz JL *ret* Espanola NM

DIOCESE OF ROCHESTER
(PROVINCE II)
Comprises 8 western New York counties
DIOCESAN OFFICE 935 East Ave Rochester NY 14607
TEL (585) 473-2977   FAX (585) 473-3195
E-MAIL communications@episcopaldioceseofrochester.org   WEB www.episcopalrochester.org

Previous Bishops—
David L Ferris 1931-38, Bartel H
Reinheimer coadj 1936 Bp 1938-
49, Dudley S Stark 1950-62, Geo
W Barrett 1963-69, Robt R Spears
Jr 1970-84, William G Burrill 1984-
99, Jack M McKelvey 1999-2008

Bishop—Rt Rev Prince Grenville Singh (1029)
(Dio 31 May 2008)

Cn Miss & Cong Dev J Cicora; *CFO* T Rubiano;
Operations K Estey; *Staff:* C McConnell, C
Shoemaker, M Townsend, K Woodward; *Sec to Conv*
S Woodhouse; *Treas* T Butwid; *Asst Treas* B Owen;
Chanc PR Fileri; *Asst Chanc* CT Wright, FP Greene;
Reg K Estey

Stand Comm— Cler: L Adams, R Hamlin, Michael
Hartney, V Mazzarella; *Lay:* C Moore, Lois Giess, S
Peters

Dio Conv: November 13-14 2015 Hobart William
Smith College, Geneva NY

PARISHES, MISSIONS, AND CLERGY

Addison Church of the Redeemer **P** (60) 1
Wombaugh Sq 14801 (Mail to: 1 Wombaugh
Sq 14801-1032) (607) 359-2300
Angelica St Pauls Church **P** (15) 1 Park Cir 14709
(Mail to: Park Circle 14709) (585) 466-3546
Avon Zion Church **P** (110) 10 Park Pl 14414-1055
(Mail to: 10 Park Pl 14414-1055) Kelly Ayer
(585) 226-3722
Bath St Thomas Church **P** (199) 122 Liberty St
14810-1509 (Mail to: 122 Liberty St 14810-
1509) J Brad Benson (607) 776-4503
Belmont Christ Church Belvidere **HC** 5781
County Road W 20 14813-9525 (Mail to: Acem
12 E Genesee St 14895-1032) (585) 593-5592
Bloomfield St Peters Episcopal Church **P** (45)
44 Main St 14469-9231 (Mail to: PO Box 67
14469-0067) C Denise Yarbrough (585) 657-
6715
Branchport St Lukes Church **P** (63) 121 West
Lake Rd 14418-9754 (Mail to: 187 W Lake Rd
14418-9768) Philip Kasey (315) 595-6162

Brockport St Lukes Episcopal Church **P** (191) 14
State St 14420-1922 (Mail to: 14 State St 14420-
1922) Krista Cameron (585) 637-6650
Caledonia St Andrews Episcopal Church **M** (53)
175 North St 14423-1036 (Mail to: 175 North
St 14423-1036) (585) 538-2112
Canandaigua St Johns Church **P** (305) 183 N
Main St 14424-1226 (Mail to: 183 N Main St
14424-1226) David Hefling (585) 394-4818
Canaseraga Trinity Church **P** (5) 20 N Church St
14822 (Mail to: PO Box 202 14822-0202) Bruce
Torrey (607) 545-6211
Clifton Spgs St Johns Church **P** (68) No 32 East
Main Street 14432-1120 (Mail to: PO Box 622
14432-0622) Andrew Vanburen (315) 462-
6611
Corning Christ Episcopal Church **P** (219) 33 East
First St 14830-2620 (Mail to: 33 East First St
14830-2620) (607) 937-5449
Cuba Christ Church **P** (13) 19 South St 14727-
1411 (Mail to: PO Box 112 14727-0112) (585)
268-7622
Dansville St Peters Memorial **P** (22) 25 Clara
Barton Street 14437 (Mail to: PO Box 127
14437) (585) 335-5434
Fairport St Lukes Church **P** (216) 77 Country
Corner Ln 14450-3034 (Mail to: PO Box 146
14450-0146) Deven Hubert (585) 223-2796
Gates Ephphatha Mission of the Deaf **M** 3285
Buffalo Rd 14624-2413 (Mail to: C/O Church
of the Epiphany 3285 Buffalo Rd 14624-2483)
Suzanne Johnston Nancy Stevens (585) 247-
4190
Gates The Church of the Epiphany **P** (269) 3285
Buffalo Rd 14624-2413 (Mail to: 3285 Buffalo
Rd 14624-2413) (585) 247-4190
Geneseo Saint Michael's Episcopal Church **P**
(228) 23 Main St 14454-1213 (Mail to: 23 Main
St 14454-1213) William Daniel Terrell Price
(585) 243-1220
Geneva St Johns Chapel **M** South Main St 14456
(Mail to: 300 Pulteney St 14456-3304) Lesley
Adams (315) 781-3671
Geneva St Peters Memorial **P** (370) 149 Genesee
St 14456 (Mail to: PO Box 147 14456-0147)
James Adams (315) 789-4910

Geneva Trinity Church **P** (77) 520 S Main St 14456-3107 (Mail to: 520 S Main St 14456-3196) (315) 789-2919

Hammondsport St James Church **P** (119) 38 Lake St 14840 (Mail to: PO Box 249 14840-0249) Lynne Sharp (607) 569-2647

Henrietta St Peter's **P** (154) 3825 E Henrietta Rd 14467-9147 (Mail to: 3825 E Henrietta Rd 14467-9147) Catherine Tatem (585) 334-1110

Hilton St Georges Church **P** (92) 635 Wilder Rd 14468-9701 (Mail to: 635 Old Wilder Rd 14468-9701) Paul Frolick (585) 392-4099

Honeoye Falls St Johns Episcopal Church **P** (105) 11 Episcopal Ave 14472-1001 (Mail to: 11 Episcopal Ave 14472-1001)

Hornell Christ Episcopal Church **P** (92) Main And Center St 14843 (Mail to: PO Box 336 14843-0336) John Andrews (607) 324-3620

Keuka Park Garrett Chapel **SC** C/O John Barden 213 West Main St 14478 (Mail to: Skyline Dr 14478) (315) 536-3955

Lyons Grace Episcopal Church **P** (44) 7 Phelps St 14489-1420 (Mail to: 9 Phelps St 14489-1509) Andrew White Sara White (315) 946-9687

Montour Falls St Paul's Mission **HC** (7) 108 S Genesee St 14865-9637 (Mail to: 112 6th St 14891-1359) Michael Hartney (607) 535-2321

Newark St Marks Church **P** (88) No 400 S Main St 14513-1723 (Mail to: 400 S Main St 14513-1700) Andrew White Sara White (315) 331-3610

Odessa Saint John's Church **HC** (52) 4938 County Route 14 14869-9729 (Mail to: 112 6th Street 14891-1359) Michael Hartney (607) 535-2321

Palmyra Zion Episcopal Church **P** (134) 120 E Main St 14522-1018 (Mail to: 120 East Main St 14522-1018) Susan Kohlmeier (315) 597-9236

Penfield Church of the Incarnation **P** (233) 1957 Five Mile Line Rd 14526-1000 (Mail to: 1957 Five Mile Line Rd 14526-1000) Miriam Owens Christopher Streeter (585) 586-7860

Penn Yan St Marks Episcopal Church **P** (80) 179 Main St 14527-1202 (Mail to: PO Box 424 14527-1202) Dan Burner (315) 536-3955

Pittsford Christ Church **P** (1051) 36 S Main St 14534-1939 (Mail to: 36 South Main St 14534-1939) Joshua Walters Ronald Young (585) 586-1226

Rochester Chapel of the Good Shepherd **Chapel** 505 Mount Hope Ave 14620-2251 (Mail to: 505 Mount Hope Ave 14620-2251) (585) 546-8400

Rochester Christ Church **P** (253) 141 East Ave 14604-2521 (Mail to: 141 East Ave 14604-2597) Ruth Ferguson Mary Alonzo (585) 454-3878

Rochester Church of the Ascension **P** (137) 2 Riverside St 14613-1222 (Mail to: 2 Riverside St 14613-1222) Dahn Gandell Philip Schaefer (585) 458-5423

✠ **Rochester** Memorial Chapel Diocesan House **Other** 935 East Ave 14607-2216 (Mail to: 935 East Ave 14607-2216) (585) 473-2977

Rochester St Luke & St Simon Cyrene Episcopal **P** (205) 17 Fitzhugh St S 14614-1401 (Mail to: 17 South Fitzhugh St 14614-1401) John Burr

Saundra Cordingley (585) 546-7730

Rochester St Marks & St Johns Church **P** (88) 1245 Culver Rd 14609-5340 (Mail to: 1245 Culver Rd 14609-5340) Michael Finn Cynthia Rasmussen

Rochester St Pauls Church **P** (745) 41 Westminster Rd 14607-2223 (Mail to: 25 Westminster Rd 14607-2223) Jay Burkardt Robert Picken (585) 271-2240

Rochester St Stephens Episcopal Church **P** (55) 350 Chili Ave 14611-2555 (Mail to: 350 Chili Ave 14611-2596) Mary Brody Gloria Fish Lynne McNulty

Rochester St Thomas Episcopal Church **P** (705) 2000 Highland Ave 14618-1125 (Mail to: 2000 Highland Ave 14618-1125) Leslie Burkardt Christa Levesque Craig Uffman (585) 442-3544

Rochester Trinity Episcopal Church **P** (239) 3450 Ridge Rd W 14626 (Mail to: 3450 Ridge Rd W 14626-3432) (585) 225-7848

Savona Church of the Good Shepherd **HC** (55) 31 Church St 14879-9658 (Mail to: PO Box 466 14879-0466) Lynne Sharp (607) 569-2647

Scottsville Grace Episcopal Church **P** (105) 9 Browns Ave 14546-1345 (Mail to: PO Box 158 14546-0158) Kenneth Pepin (585) 889-2028

Sodus Christ Church **SC** 54 W Main St 14551-1134 (Mail to: 54 W Main St 14551-1134) (315) 331-8251

Sodus St Johns Episcopal Church **P** (56) 54 West Main St 14551-1134 (Mail to: 54 W Main St 14551-1134) Andrew White Sara White (315) 483-4235

Watkins Glen Saint James' Church **HC** (78) 597 S Decatur St 14891-1610 (Mail to: 112 Sixth Street 14891-1359) Michael Hartney (607) 535-2321

Webster Church of the Good Shepherd **P** (458) 1130 Webster Rd 14580-9320 (Mail to: 1130 Webster Rd 14580-9320) Lance Robbins

Webster St Andrews by the Lake **SC** 1206 Lake Rd 14580-9708

Wellsville St John Episcopal Church **P** (34) 12 E Genesee St 14895-1032 (Mail to: PO Box 1336 14895-4156) Carol Stewart (585) 593-5592

NON-PAROCHIAL CLERGY

Arrington SC *ret* Pittsford NY
Bedell BD Honeoye Falls NY
Bennett DH *ret* Clifton Springs NY
Bordner KE *ret* Santa Fe NM
Bryant PF Scio NY
Butler CE *ret* Watertown MA
Carney GM *dcn* Rochester NY
Carroll DJ *ret* Cohocton NY
Charles DM Oakland CA
Cicora JA Webster NY
Collin WN *ret* Pittsford NY
Cripps DR Rochester NY
Culp RS *ret* Fairport NY
Curtis SK *ret* Hammondsport NY
Darling M Oakland CA

Dennis LA Philadelphia PA
Eckart RJ *ret* Rochester NY
English WH *ret* Foster City CA
Fornalik BH *dcn* Webster NY
Garrenton LW *ret* Brooklyn NY
Gramley TS *ret* Canisteo NY
Groskoph EM *ret* Hancock NY
Groskoph RG *ret* Hancock NY
Grover CL *ret* Chittenango NY
Gutierrez JM *ret* Boxborough MA
Hamlin RL *ret* Miami FL
Harter RMP Pittsford NY
Henshaw RA *ret* Rochester NY
Hill DB *ret* Jeffersonville IN
Hopkins MW *ret* Hornell NY
James MG
Johnson A *dcn* Penfield NY
Johnson WJ
Johnson-Toth LM *ret* Rochester NY
Karl JC *ret* Rochester NY
Karl SL *ret* Rochester NY
Keeney AJ *ret* Canandaigua NY
Krapf RD *dcn* Canandaigua NY
Leibhart LD *ret* Richmond VA
Lewis CB *ret* Williamson NY
Lillis RH *ret* Asbury Park NJ
Linnenberg DM Rochester NY
Luedde CS *ret* Pittsford NY
Lumbard CMD *ret* Rochester NY
Mazzarella VT Pittsford NY
McCart TK *ret* Indianapolis IN
Meister SG *dcn* Newark NY

Mothersell LL Geneseo NY
Mroczka MAC Dansville NY
Page MS *ret* Rochester NY
Perry KM *dcn* Geneva NY
Peters PW *ret* Rochester NY
Petersen WH *ret* Fairport NY
Pope DS *ret* Palmyra NY
Prescott VL *ret* Rochester NY
Purcell-Chapman DB Wellsville NY
Reynolds FW *ret* Portsmouth NH
Richards GR *ret* Scotia NY
Rorke SE *ret* Alexandria VA
Roy BW *ret* Penfield NY
Sawtelle GD *ret* Scottsville NY
Schneider MH Friendship NY
Seufert CR *ret* Newark NY
Shannon RL Orleans MA
Sinnott LD
Smith DG Penn Yan NY
Smith DH *ret* Cape Coral FL
Steinhauer RK *ret* Rochester NY
Stiegler MA *ret* Lima NY
Stridiron AR *dcn* Rochester NY
Thompson JE Geneseo NY
Tobin FL Corning NY
Tyler Smith VS Honeoye Falls NY
Tyo CH Friendship NY
Van Deventer AR *ret* Rochester NY
Van Eenwyk JR Olympia WA
Wheaton PE *ret* Takoma Park MD
Wienk DL *ret* Rochester NY
Wyland RR Redding CT

DIOCESE OF SAN DIEGO
(PROVINCE VIII)
Comprises San Diego, Imperial and part of Riverside Counties, CA and Yuma County, AZ
DIOCESAN OFFICE 2083 Sunset Cliffs Blvd, San Diego CA 92107
TEL (619) 291-5947   FAX (619) 481-3091
E-MAIL info@edsd.org   WEB www.edsd.org

Previous Bishops—
Robert M Wolterstorff 1974-82, C
Brinkley Morton 1982-92, Gethin
B Hughes 1992-2005

**Bishop—Rt Rev James R
Mathes (1002)** (Dio 5 March
2005)

Assisting Bishop—Rt Rev John B Chane

Cn to Ord A Thomas; *Ecum Off* E Ellsworth; *Sec* D
Peralta; *Treas* J Young; *Reg* K Rodriguez; *Hist* J Will;
Chanc CH Dick

Standing Comm—Cler: P Blair S Mainwaring K Kelly
G Lynch; *Lay: Pres* A Sweet J Westaway H Astleford
J Stiven

Dio Conv: 11-12 Nov 2016, St. Margaret's Episcopal
Church, Palm Desert, CA

PARISHES, MISSIONS, AND CLERGY

Alpine Church of Christ the King **P** (66) 1460
Midway Dr 91901-3714 (Mail to: 1460 Midway
Dr 91901-3714) Mitchell Bojarski (619) 445-3419

Bonita Epis Church of the Good Shepherd **P** (109)
3990 Bonita Rd 91902-1260 (Mail to: 3990
Bonita Rd 91902-1260) George Calvert (619)
479-8391

Borrego Spgs St Barnabas Episcopal Church **P**
(121) 2680 Country Club Rd 92004 (Mail to:
PO Box 691 92004-0691) Laura Brecht (760)
767-4038

Brawley All Saints Episcopal Church **M** (20) 305
H St 92227-2517 (Mail to: PO Box 1811 92227-
1308) (760) 344-8806

Carlsbad Church of St Michaels-by-the-Sea **P**
(473) 2775 Carlsbad Blvd 92008-2210 (Mail
to: 2775 Carlsbad Blvd 92008-2210) Kenneth
Simon Doran Stambaugh (760) 729-8901

Carlsbad Holy Cross Episcopal Church **M** (66) 2510 Gateway Road 92009-1727 (Mail to: 2510 Gateway Road 92009-1727) Laura Sheridan-Campbell (760) 930-1270

Chula Vista St Johns Epis Ch **P** (477) 760 1st Ave 91910 (Mail to: 760 1st Ave 91910) David Marshall

Coronado Christ Episcopal Church **P** (581) 1114 Ninth St 92118 (Mail to: 1114 Ninth St 92118-2602) Anne Bridgers Monica Mainwaring (619) 435-4561

Del Mar St Peters Episcopal Church **P** (891) 334 14th St 92014-2519 (Mail to: PO Box 336 92014-0336) Paige Blair-Hubert Martha Anderson Frank Munoz (858) 755-1616

Desert Hot Springs St Anthony of-the-Desert Mission **M** (96) 19990 Mountain View Rd. 92240 (Mail to: PO Box 40 92240-0040) (760) 329-2755

Desert Shores Santa Rosa Del Mar **M** (107) 20 Monterey Ave 92274 (Mail to: 61 Coronado Ave 92274) (760) 554 2640

El Cajon St Albans Episcopal Church **P** (203) 490 Farragut Cir 92020-5203 (Mail to: 490 Farragut Circle 92020) David Madsen (619) 444-8212

El Centro Sts Peter & Paul Episcopal Church **P** (50) 500 S 5th St 92243-3333 (Mail to: PO Box 3446 92244-3446)

Encinitas St Andrew-the-Apostle Church **D** (781) 890 Balour Dr 92024-3943 (Mail to: 890 Balour Dr 92024-3943) Brenda Sol (760) 753-3017

Escondido Trinity Episcopal Church **P** (300) 845 Chestnut St 92025-5257 (Mail to: 845 Chestnut St 92025-5257) Margaret Decker Robert Lucent (760) 743-1629

Fallbrook St Johns Episcopal Church **P** (133) 434 N. Iowa St 92028-2109 (Mail to: PO Box 1576 92088-1576) Leland Jones (760) 728-2908

Hemet The Church of the Good Shepherd **P** (214) 308 E Acacia Ave 92543-4228 (Mail to: 308 E Acacia Ave 92543-4228) Kathleen Kelly (951) 929-1152

Idyllwild St Hugh of Lincoln Episcopal Church **M** (37) 25525 Tahquitz Rd 92549 (Mail to: PO Box 506 92549-0506) (951) 659-4471

Indio St Johns Episcopal Church **P** (133) 45319 Deglet Noor St 92201-4315 (Mail to: 45319 Deglet Noor St 92201-4315) (760) 347-3265

La Jolla St James by-the-Sea Episcopal Church **P** (1174) 743 Prospect St 92037-4229 (Mail to: 743 Prospect St 92037-4290) Eleanor Ellsworth Steven Strane (858) 459-3421

La Mesa St Andrews Episcopal Church **P** (239) 4816 Glen St 91941-5498 (Mail to: 4816 Glen St 91941-5498) (619) 460-7272

Lake Elsinore St Andrews by the Lake Epis Church **M** (51) 111 S Kellogg St 92530-3538 (Mail to: 111 S Kellogg St 92530) W Clarke Prescott (951) 674-4087

Lemon Grove Church of St Philip the Apostle **P** (416) 2660 Hardy Dr 91945-2936 (Mail to: 2660 Hardy Dr 91945-2936) Carlos Garcia-

Tuiran (619) 466-8055

Menifee St Stephen's Episcopal Church **M** (49) 26704 Murrieta Rd 92585-9545 (Mail to: 26704 Murrieta Rd 92585-9545) W Clarke Prescott Thomas Wilson (951) 679-3010

National City St Matthews Episcopal Church **P** (242) 521 E 8th St 91950-2343 (Mail to: 521 E 8th St 91950-2398) Maria Borges (619) 474-8916

Oceanside St Annes Episcopal Church **M** (40) 701 West St 92054-5021 (Mail to: 701 West St 92054-5021) Larry Hart (760) 966-2950

Palm Desert St Margarets Episcopal Church **P** (807) 47-535 Highway 74 92260 (Mail to: 47-535 Highway 74 92260-5946) Lane Hensley Kathleen Dale Joseph Lund Clark Trafton Richard Wilmington

Palm Springs St Paul in the Desert **P** (537) 125 W El Alameda 92262-5662 (Mail to: 125 W El Alameda 92262-5662) Marvin Green (760) 320-7488

Pauma Valley St Francis Episcopal Church **P** (128) 16608 State Highway 76 92061 (Mail to: PO Box 1220 92061-1220) (760) 742-1738

Poway St Bartholomews Episcopal Church **P** (1739) 16275 Pomerado Rd 92064-1826 (Mail to: 16275 Pomerado Rd 92064-1826) James Kellett Mark Mckone-Sweet (858) 487-2159

Ramona St Marys in the Valley Church **M** (159) 1010 12th St 92065-2848 (Mail to: PO Box 491 92065-0491) Gwynn Lynch Ellen Deuel (760) 789-0890

San Diego All Saints Church **P** (182) 625 Pennsylvania Ave 92103-4321 (Mail to: 625 Pennsylvania Ave 92103-4393) Victor Krulak James Mcqueen (619) 298-7729

San Diego All Souls' Episcopal Church **P** (386) 1475 Catalina Blvd 92107-3763 (Mail to: 1475 Catalina Blvd 92107-3798) James Carroll Joseph Dirbas (619) 223-6394

✠ **San Diego** Cathedral Church of St Paul **O** (1156) No 2728 6th Ave 92103-6301 (Mail to: 2728 6th Ave 92103-6301) Penelope Bridges Jeffrey Martinhauk Brooks Mason Colin Mathewson Laurel Mathewson (619) 298-7261

San Diego Good Samaritan Episcopal Church **P** (282) 4321 Eastgate Mall 92121-2102 (Mail to: 4321 Eastgate Mall 92121-2102) Monica Mainwaring (858) 458-1501

San Diego St Andrews by the Sea Church **P** (147) 1050 Thomas Ave 92109-4161 (Mail to: 1050 Thomas Ave 92109-4194) Simon Mainwaring (858) 273-3022

San Diego St Davids Episcopal Church **P** (175) § 5050 Milton St 92110-1250 (Mail to: 5050 Milton St 92110-1250) Jason Samuel (619) 276-4567

San Diego St Dunstans Episcopal Church **P** (568) 6556 Park Ridge Blvd 92120-3236 (Mail to: 6556 Park Ridge Blvd 92120-3236) Robert Eaton Henry Mann (619) 460-6442

San Diego St Lukes Episcopal Church **P** (215)

3725 30th St 92104-3607 (Mail to: 3725 30th St 92104-3697) Susan Astarita (619) 298-2130

San Diego St Marks Episcopal Church **P** (167) 4227 Fairmount Ave 92105-1243 (Mail to: PO Box 5788 92165-5788) Marvin Collins (619) 283-6242

San Diego St Timothy's Episcopal Church **P** (120) 10125 Azuaga St 92129-4000 (Mail to: 10125 Azuaga St 92129-4000) Wilfredo Crespo Edward Busch (858) 538-1267

San Marcos Grace Episcopal Church **M** (182) 1020 Rose Ranch Rd 92069-1161 (Mail to: 1020 Rose Ranch Rd 92069-1161) Clayola Gitane William Lieber (760) 744-7667

Santee St Columbas Episcopal Church **M** (35) 9720 Cuyamaca St 92071-2626 (Mail to: 9720 Cuyamaca St 92071-2626) (619) 857-6749

Temecula Saint Thomas of Canterbury Epis Church **M** (488) 44651 Avenida de Missiones 92592-3098 (Mail to: 44651 Avenida de Missiones 92592-3098) (951) 302-4566

Vista All Saints Episcopal Church **P** (78) 651 Eucalyptus Ave 92084-6241 (Mail to: 651 Eucalyptus Ave 92084-6298) Virginia Benson (760) 726-4280

Yuma St Pauls Episcopal Church **P** (187) 1550 S 14th Ave 85364-4414 (Mail to: 1550 S 14th Ave 85364-4498) Paul Gambling Timothy True (928) 782-5155

NON-PAROCHIAL CLERGY

Acosta JM *ret* San Diego CA
Allison JA *ret*
Allman MK *ret* La Jolla CA
Barker HJ *ret* Valley Center CA
Blair-Loy MF San Diego CA
Blessing RA *ret* San Diego CA
Broughton W *ret* Coronado CA
Bush P *ret* San Diego CA
Canter MA Carlsbad CA
Carey BH
Carmona PB *ret* San Diego CA
Carr MG *ret* Vista CA
Chisham AB *dcn* San Diego CA
Christian JW *ret* Bermuda Dunes CA
Collins JM *ret* San Diego CA
Colmore CB *ret* Jacksonville VT
Crafts R *ret* Poway CA
Dexter BL *ret* Spring Valley CA
Dirbas TS Coronado CA
Dowdle CE Chula Vista CA
Edelman WL *ret* San Diego CA
Estes JG *ret* Escondido CA
Fenton AA *ret* El Cajon CA
Fenton DH *ret* Eugene OR
Fidler BE La Jolla CA

Ford JB *ret*
Franklin AA *ret* San Diego CA
Harrison EH *ret* Coronado CA
Hayes WLR *ret* San Diego CA
Heaney DL *ret* Chula Vista CA
Hills W *ret* Athens OH
Holding SV San Diego CA
Hunt BJW San Diego CA
Jacobsen LC
Johnson FT *ret* Vista CA
Kaehr MG *ret* La Jolla CA
Keith GA *ret* San Diego CA
Kellogg ES San Diego CA
Knight SH *ret* Prescott AZ
Lacey M *ret* San Diego CA
Lief RC *ret* San Diego CA
Mackillop AB *ret* Manchester NH
Marcussen BB *ret* Chula Vista CA
Maynard DR *ret* Rancho Mirage CA
McCullough BD *ret* Winfield KS
Meairs BM *ret* San Diego CA
Milner RJ *dcn* Roswell NM
Morelli TCA *dcn* Coronado CA
Murray AJ Palm Springs CA
Myers FE *ret* Palm Springs CA
Nagy RA Temecula CA
Nelson RA *dcn* Del Mar CA
Noble AN *ret* San Diego CA
Orozco BM *ret* Riverside CA
Ovenstone J Towson MD
Pacheco J *ret* Weed CA
Patronik JA *ret* Pauma Valley CA
Phelps SD Del Mar CA
Randall CC *ret*
Rank APR San Diego CA
Remboldt CA *dcn* Palm Deset CA
Rhodes DH *dcn* Palm Desert CA
Richardson CG Escondido CA
Riebe NW *ret* Charlotte NC
Rieger PA *dcn*
Rondeau DJ *ret* La Quinta CA
Sanders WFM *ret* San Diego CA
Scheible GK *ret* Canyon Lake TX
Shears SH *ret* Lompoc CA
Stephenson-Diaz L Carlsbad CA
Suter VL *ret* Cathedral City CA
Teed LB *ret* San Diego CA
Thayer FW *ret* San Diego CA
Thomas AL San Diego CA
Thrumston RE *ret* San Diego CA
Watson SE
Weatherford DW *ret* San Diego CA
Wehrs JM *ret* San Diego CA
Wendfeldt SH *ret*
Woodridge DE *ret* Lake Oswego OR
Zettinger WH *ret dcn* Escondido CA

DIOCESE OF SAN JOAQUIN
(PROVINCE VIII)
Comprises the central third of California
DIOCESAN OFFICE 1528 Oakdale Rd Modesto CA 95355
TEL (209) 576-0104   FAX (209) 576-0114
E-MAIL emeyer@diosanjoaquin.org   WEB www.diosanjoaquin.org

Previous Bishops—
Louis C Sanford 1911-42, Sumner
FD Walters 1944-68, Victor M Rivera
1968-88,   John-David   Schofield
1989-2008, Jerry A Lamb 2008-11,
Chester L Talton (861) (2011-14)

Bishop—Rt Rev. David C. Rice (2014)

Cn to Ord Rev K Cullinane; *Chanc* MO Glass 1101
Fifth Avenue Suite 100 San Rafael CA 94901; *Treas*
M Austin; *Dio Admin* E Meyer

Stand Comm—Cler: G Kanestrom; K Galicia R
Woods *Lay: Pres* C Smith K Olds N Voorhees E
Raush

Dio Coun—Cler: P Colbert L Morlan H Mueller;
Lay: J Kuykendall D Dunlop J Dunlap D Austin G
Sitts D Karcher

Com on Min: Chair Rev G Kanestrom N Silva Rev
Dcn G Cano Rev J McDonald E Berg T March H
Webb Rev K Galicia

Deaneries—Southern: Pres R Hendricks; *VPres* Rev T
Vivian; *Central: Pres* Rev Deacon G Bernthal*V Pres*
M Corollo; *Northern: Pres* D Dunlop *VPres* Rev. N
Lorenzetti

Dio Conv: TBD Oct 2016 Modesto CA

PARISHES, MISSIONS, AND CLERGY

Atwater St Nicholas Episcopal Church **M** (7) No
1216 3rd St 95301-4041 (Mail to: PO Box 368
95301-0368) (209) 761-8180

Avery St Clare of Assisi **M** (41) 4351 Highway 4
95224 (Mail to: PO Box 278 95224-0278) (209)
795-5970

Bakersfield St Paul's Episcopal Church **P** (209)
2216 17th St 93301-3605 (Mail to: 2216 17th St
93301-3605) Tim Vivian (661) 869-1630

Fresno Episcopal Church of the Holy Family **P**
(306) 1135 E Alluvial Ave 93720-2605 (Mail to:
PO Box 27591 93729-7591) Michele Racusin
(559) 439-5011

Hanford Church of the Saviour Parish **P** (106) 519
N Douty St 93230-3910 (Mail to: 519 N Douty
St 93230-3910) (559) 584-7706

Kernville St Sherrian Episcopal Church **M** (18)
Meets at 251 Big Blue Road 93238 (Mail to: PO
Box 1837 93238-1837) Robert Woods (760)
376-2455

Lodi Church of St John The Baptist **P** (299) 1055
S Lower Sacramento Rd 95242 (Mail to: 1055
S Lower Sacramento Rd 95242-9339) Elaine
Breckenridge Randy Knutson (209) 369-3381

Madera Holy Trinity Episcopal Church **M** (24)
500 Sunset Ave 93637-3012 (Mail to: PO Box
517 93639-0517) Paul Colbert (559) 975-9037

Modesto St Pauls Episcopal Church **P** (170) §
1528 Oakdale Rd 95355-3306 (Mail to: 1528
Oakdale Rd 95355-3306) Glenn Kanestrom
Dominick Lorenzetti (209) 522-3267

Oakhurst St Raphael Episcopal Church **M** (17)
PO Box 13 93644 (Mail to: PO Box 13 93644-
0013) (559) 683-4023

Ridgecrest St Michael's Episcopal Church **M** (57)
200 Drummond Ave 93555-3119 (Mail to: 200
Drummond Ave 93555-3119) (760) 446-5816

San Andreas St Matthews Episcopal Church **P**
(62) 414 Oak Street 95249-9612 (Mail to: PO
Box 520 95249-0520) John Shumaker (209)
754-3878

Sonora St James Episcopal Church **P** (60) No 42
Snell St 95370-5600 (Mail to: 42 Snell St 95370-
5600) Carolyn Woodall (209) 532-1580

Stockton Church of St Anne **P** (226) 1020 W
Lincoln Rd 95207-2516 (Mail to: 1020 W
Lincoln Rd 95207-2516) Justo Andres Lynette
Morlan (209) 473-2313

Taft St Andrews Mission **M** (32) 703 5th Street
93268 (Mail to: 703 5th Street 93268) Heather
Mueller (661) 765-2378

Tulare St Johns Episcopal Church **P** (70) 1701 E
Prosperity Ave 93274-2345 (Mail to: 1701 E
Prosperity Ave 93274-2345) (559) 631-3663

Turlock St Francis Episcopal Church **M** (54) Light
of Christ Lutheran Church 4510 Crowell Rd
95381 (Mail to: PO Box 3632 95381-3632)
Ellen Deuel Kathryn Galicia Donald Rees
(209) 324-1677

Visalia St Pauls Epis Fellowship **P** (71) 1039 S
Chinowth St 93277-1609 (Mail to: PO Box
7446 93290-7446) Suzanne Ward (559) 627-
8265

NON-PAROCHIAL CLERGY

Anderson EW Jamestown CA
Bakker GK Southampton
Barrow JT *ret* Mammoth Lakes CA
Bentley SR *dcn* Stockton CA
Bernardi FA Visalia CA
Bernthal GE Hanford CA
Brown KB *ret* Fresno CA
Burk JH *ret* Monterey CA
Callender FC Manteca CA
Campbell MB *dcn* Sheridan WY
Cano GL *dcn* Modesto CA
Colbert PA Coarsegold CA
Collins SP *ret* Modesto CA

Cooke HM *dcn* Stockton CA
Coppel SG Twain Harte CA
Correa TC *ret* Clovis CA
Cullinane KJ Modesto CA
Davis MS Bakersfield CA
Duval RH *ret* Lake Almanor CA
Eaton RG Tulare CA
Edwards JS *ret* Arroyo Grande CA
Galagan JM *ret* Tehachapi CA
German KL *ret* Shafter CA
Gleason DJ *dcn* Ambridge PA
Gowett RJ Fresno CA
Hall MH *ret* Stockton CA
Hamilton TE *ret* Wenatchee WA
Henry RA *ret* Lincoln CA
Hill VW Bakersfield CA
Jacobs CH *ret dcn* Oakhurst CA
Johnson L *dcn* Lodi CA
Karcher SM Bakersfield CA
Key NA *dcn* Visalia CA
Lawson NJ Stockton CA
Livingston PIC *ret* Monterey CA

Matthews AMB Vallecito CA
McDonald JW *ret* Clovis CA
McNiel DL Albuquerque NM
Monreal AA Fresno CA
Murray RS Shiga
Patterson J *ret* North Lincolnshire
Phillips-Matson WA *ret*
Rice D Modesto CA
Risard FW *ret* Hanford CA
Shaubach SK *dcn* Raymond CA
Short JR *ret* Carmel CA
Singer-Hedlund SM *ret dcn* Stockton CA
Smith AL Sacramento CA
Smith JB W Roxbury MA
Statezni GG *dcn* Bakersfield CA
Thompson JE *ret* Portland OR
Van Huss TH Visalia CA
Van Walterop NP *ret* Modesto CA
Vongsanit SC Fresno CA
West KF *ret* Pasadena CA
Wilcox JM *ret* Bakersfield CA
Williams RA *ret* Sun City CA

STATE OF SOUTH CAROLINA

Diocese of Upper South Carolina and The Episcopal Church in South Carolina

THE EPISCOPAL CHURCH IN SOUTH CAROLINA

(PROVINCE IV)
Comprising churches in Southern and Eastern South Carolina
DIOCESAN OFFICE: 98 Wentworth St Charleston SC 29401 (MAIL: Box 20485 Charleston SC 29413)
TEL: (843) 259-2016   E-MAIL: info@episcopalchurchsc.org   WEB: www.episcopalchurchsc.org

Provisional Bishop: The Right Reverend Charles G von Rosenberg (944) (Dio Jan 2013)

Archdcn Calhoun Walpole; *Chancellor* T S Tisdale; *Treas* J Taylor; *Exec Asst to Bp* L Kinard; *Comm* H Behre; *Admin Asst* A McKellar

Stand Comm: Cler— M Brinkmann J Dannals C Huff J McGraw J Yarsiah J Zahl; *Lay—* T Armstrong D Billings F Elmore B Mann S Shaffer V Wilder

Diocesan Council—Cler: P Fahrner C Lee R Lindsey M Wright DA Williams A Votaw; *Lay:* H Douglas C Grish P Guess S Cavanaugh V Weaver J Gettys

Trustees—Lay: C Carpenter J Gilbert R Moffit B Pinkerton B Walker; *Cler:* J Taylor J Nietert D McPhail

Comm on Ministry—Cler: D Sanderson W Keith R Lindsey J McGraw C Walpole; *Lay:* M Wright C Hayes MA Foy

Dio Conv: 13-14 Nov 2016 Grace Church Cathedral, Charleston, SC

PARISHES, MISSIONS, AND CLERGY

Allendale Church of Holy Communion **M** (24) 401 Main St N 29810-3717 (Mail to: PO Box 202 29810-0202) William Rose (803) 812-9912

Charleston Calvary Episcopal Church **P** (268) 106 Line St 29403-5305 (Mail to: 104 Line St 29403-5305)

Charleston Church of the Holy Communion **P** (499) 218 Ashley Ave 29403-5245 (Mail to: 218 Ashley Ave 29403-5245) Marshall Sanderson Michael Smith (843) 722-2024

Charleston Grace Church Cathedral **P** (1886) 98 Wentworth St 29401-1424 (Mail to: 115 Wentworth St 29401-1736) Jonathan Wright Lisa Walpole Alberry Cannon Paul Gilbert Caleb Lee Charles Minifie John Zahl (843) 723-4575

Charleston St Francis Episcopal Church **M** (51) No Stuhr's Chapel 3360 Glenn McConnell Pkwy 29414-5759 (Mail to: 2341 Wofford Rd 29414-7034) Jean Mcgraw Gregory Smith (843) 442-2692

Charleston St Marks Episcopal Church **P** (100) 18 Thomas St 29403-6024 (Mail to: 18 Thomas St 29403-6839) John Lantz

Charleston St Stephens Church **P** (307) 67 Anson St 29401-1529 (Mail to: 67 Anson St 29401-1529) William Coyne John Johnson

Cheraw St Davids Church **P** (115) 420 Market St 29520-2637 (Mail to: PO Box 926 29520-0926)

Conway St Anne's Episcopal Church **P** (110) Lackey Chapel 105 University Dr 29526-8832 (Mail to: PO Box 752 29578-0752) Barry Stopfel (843) 246-1247

Denmark Christ Episcopal Church **M** (43) 5266 Carolina Highway 29042-1643 (Mail to: PO Box 237 29042-0237) William Mcswain

Denmark St Philip Episcopal Church **CC** (18) 386 Porter Dr 29042 (Mail to: PO Box 678 29042-0678) (803) 780-1264

Edisto Island Episcopal Church on Edisto **P** (208) 1650 Hwy 174 29438 (Mail to: PO Box 239 29438-0239) (843) 869-3568

Estill Church of the Heavenly Rest **M** (7) 152 Corley Rd 29918-0152 (Mail to: PO Box 1190 29918-1190) William Rose (843) 524-1644

Florence St Catherine's Episcopal Church **P** (49) Back Swamp School House 502 East Pocket Road 29506 (Mail to: 4205 Byrnes Blvd 29506-8335) (843) 259-2016

Hampton All Saints Episcopal Church **M** (42) 511 Jackson Ave E 29924-3605 (Mail to: 511 Jackson Ave E 29924-3605) (803) 943-2300

Hilton Head Island All Saints Episcopal Church **P** (411) 3001 Meeting St 29926-1673 (Mail to: 3001 Meeting St 29926-1673) Richard Lindsey Mark Brinkmann (843) 681-8333

Kingstree St Albans Church **M** (37) 305 Hampton Ave 29556-3417 (Mail to: PO Box 866 29556-0866) Jeffrey Richardson (843) 355-7575

McClellanville St James Santee **M** (139) (Mail to: PO Box 123 29458-0123) Jennie Olbrych (843) 887-4386

Mount Pleasant The East Cooper Episcopal Church **M** No 690 Coleman Blvd 29464-4018 (Mail to: 604 Hamlet Square Ln 29464-5194)

Myrtle Beach Episcopal Church of the Messiah **M** 6200 N Kings Hwy 29572-3001 (Mail to: PO Box 70367 29572-0025) Randolph Ferebee (843) 582-2866

N Charleston St Thomas Episcopal Church **P** (249) 1150 E Montague Ave 29405-4719 (Mail to: 1150 E Montague Ave 29405-4719) James Taylor Charles Jett (843) 747-0479

N Myrtle Bch St Stephens Episcopal Church **P** (203) 801 11th Ave N 29582-2644 (Mail to: 801 11th Ave N 29582-2644) Wilmot Merchant (843) 249-1169

Orangeburg Church of the Redeemer **P** (292) 1606 Russell St 29115-6065 (Mail to: PO Box 9 29116-0009) (803) 534-3794

Pawleys Island Holy Cross Faith Memorial Episcopal **P** (497) 88 Baskervill Dr 29585-6191 (Mail to: PO Box 990 29585-0990) William Keith Sandra Moyle

Pinewood St Augustines Episcopal Church **M** (46) 5450 Milford Plantation Rd 29125 (Mail to: PO Box 247 29168-0247) (803) 259-2016

Port Royal St Mark's Episcopal Church **M** (167) 1110A Paris Ave 29935 (Mail to: PO Box 761 29935-0761) (843) 379-1020

Ridgeland The Episcopal Church in Okatie **M** 231 Hazzard Creek Drive, Ste 1 & 2 29936 (Mail to: 231 Hazzard Creek Drive, Ste 1 &2 29936) (843) 259-2016

Saint Stephen St Stephens Episcopal Church **M** (45) 245 Mendel St 29479 (Mail to: PO Box 517 29479-0517) Jeffrey Richardson (843) 567-3419

Summerville Church of the Epiphany **M** (95) 212 Central Ave 29483-6004 (Mail to: 212 Central Ave 29483-6004) Robert Switz (843) 851-3467

Summerville Church of the Good Shepherd **P** (952) 119 W Luke Ave # B 29483-6423 (Mail to: PO Box 7 29484-0007) Verling Votaw (843) 873-1991

Summerville St Georges Episcopal Church **P** (390) 9110 Dorchester Rd 29485-8647 (Mail to: 9110 Dorchester Rd 29485-8647) Richard Luoni Christopher Huff

Sumter Church of the Good Shepherd **M** (39) 401 Dingle St 29150-5155 (Mail to: PO Box 1701 29151-1701) (803) 773-8341

NON-PAROCHIAL CLERGY

Barron CA Jr *ret* Pawleys Island SC
Beckwith JQ III *ret* Charleston SC
Bird JC *dcn*
Burton JM *ret* Goose Creek SC
Cheves HM *ret* Edisto Island SC
Cockrell JG *ret* Bluefield WV
Cole MG *ret* Crozet VA
Dewey ER Mount Pleasant SC
Dover JR III *ret* Chapel Hill NC
Dubose JD *ret* Barnwell SC
Fahrner PH Deer Park MD
Finch FW Jr *ret* Charleston SC
Fisher JC *ret* Edisto Island SC
Free HD Johns Island SC
Grant SM *dcn*
Gray DA Summerville SC
Hills WL Jr *ret* Mt Pleasant SC
Johnson EW *ret* Ashburn VA
Lent MJ *ret* Charleston SC
Lewis TR Jr *ret* Charleston SC
McPhail DS *ret* Charleston SC
Mills LF III *ret* Johns Island SC
Morgan RC *ret* Walterboro SC
Moyser GH *ret* Bluffton SC
Nietert JF *ret* Beaufort SC
Oswald TD Mount Pleasant SC
Porcher PG *ret* Mount Pleasant SC
Powell M *dcn* Charleston SC
Putnam ST *ret* Marion SC

Rathman WE *dcn* Hilton Head Island SC
Russ FD Jr Charleston SC
Smith CM III *ret* Charleston SC
Smith RW *ret* Beaufort SC
Sosnowski FS *ret* Wadmalaw Island SC

Thompson HL III *ret* Moon Township PA
Tindall BC *ret* Waleska GA
Tompkins GJ III *ret* Charleston SC
Turnage RW *dcn* Myrtle Beach SC
Wiseley JL *ret* Hot Springs SD

DIOCESE OF SOUTH DAKOTA
(PROVINCE VI)
Comprises South Dakota, 2 churches in Nebraska, and 1 church in Minnesota
DIOCESAN OFFICE 500 S Main Ave Sioux Falls SD 57104-6814
TEL (605) 338-9751   FAX (605) 336-6243
E-MAIL office.diocese@midconetwork.com   WEB www.diocesesd.org

Previous Bishops—
Wm H Hare 1873-1909, Fredk F
Johnson asst 1905 Bp 1910-11, Geo
Biller Jr 1912-15, Hugh L Burleson
1916-31, Wm P Remington suffr
1918-22, W Blair Roberts suffr
1922 Bp 1931-53, Conrad H Gesner
coadj 1945-54 Bp 1954-69, Lyman
C Ogilby coadj 1967-70, Harold S Jones suffr 1970-
75, Walter H Jones 1970-83, Craig B Anderson
1984-92, Creighton L Robertson Bp 1994-2009

Bishop—Rt Rev John T Tarrant (1038) (Dio 31
Oct 09)

Admin R Barnhardt; *Admin Asst* M Armin; *Archdcn*
P Sneve; *Cn to Ord* D Hussey; *Treas* C Clem; *Chanc*
S Sanford PO Box 2498 Sioux Falls SD 57105; *Hist*
A Brooks 1332 Trail Ridge Circle Brookings SD
57006; *Missioner for Yth & YAs* P Corbin

Stand Comm—Cler: Pres W Simpson A Henninger
M Watson P White Horse Carda; *Lay:* T Fonder P
LeBeau J Sanford D Stands

Counc: V Cloud B Hill K Fonder A Montileaux
M Fratzke P LeBeau S Lyman F Haukaas

Departments: COM; *Ecum* M Hobbs; *Litur*
G Parmeter; *Theology Edu* P Sneve; *Chm Niobrara
Council* D Eagle

Dio Conv: 30 Sept-1 Oct 2016 Pierre SD

PARISHES, MISSIONS, AND CLERGY
Aberdeen St Marks Episcopal Church **P** (137)
1410 N Kline St 57401-2103 (Mail to: 1410 N
Kline St 57401-2103) (605) 225-0474
Batesland St Michaels Episcopal Church **M** (129)
Hwy 18 57716 (Mail to: PO Box 74 57752-
0074) (605) 455-2140
Bear Creek St James Church **M** 5 Miles North of
Hwy 212 57636 (Mail to: PO Box 534 57625-
0534) (605) 964-6180
Belle Fourche St James Episcopal Church **P** (47)
806 6th Ave 57717-1707 (Mail to: PO Box 414
57717-0414) (605) 892-2446

Blackfoot Church of the Ascension **M** Blackfoot
57601 (Mail to: PO Box 80 57625-0080) (605)
964-6180
Brookings St Pauls Episcopal Church **P** (130) 725
5th St 57006-2102 (Mail to: 726 6th St 57006-
2108) Larry Ort (605) 692-2617
Browns Valley St Johns Church **M** (278) Browns
Valley 56219 (Mail to: 716 7th Ave W 57262-
1248) (605) 698-6528
Bullhead St John the Baptist **PS** (15) Bullhead Rd
57642 (Mail to: 500 S Main Ave 57104-6814)
(605) 338-9751
Chamberlain Christ Episcopal Church **M** (21)
207 S Main St 57325-1420 (Mail to: 209 S Main
St 57325-1420) (605) 234-6327
Cherry Creek St Andrews Station **M** Cherry
Creek 57623 (Mail to: PO Box 80 57625-0080)
(605) 964-6180
Deadwood St Johns Episcopal Church **P** (57) 401
Williams St 57732-1113 (Mail to: PO Box 130
57732-0130) Michael Johnson (605) 920-8818
DeSmet St Stephens Church **M** (20) 411 Calumet
Ave NW 57231 (Mail to: 43604 Francis Rd
57231-6425) (605) 338-9751
Dupree St Philips Church **M** Main St 57623 (Mail
to: PO Box 80 57625-0080) (605) 964-6180
Eagle Butte Cheyenne River Episcopal Mission
Other Eagle Butte 57625 (Mail to: PO Box 80
57625) (605) 964-7283
Eagle Butte St John the Evangelist **M** (417) N
Main Street 57625-0080 (Mail to: PO Box 80
57625) (605) 964-6180
Firesteel Church of the Holy Spirit **M** (101) State
Rte 20 57633 (Mail to: c/o John Red Bear PO
Box 336 57642-0336) (605) 338-9751
Flandreau St Mary & Our Blessed Redeemer **M**
(47) 217 E 2nd St 57028 (Mail to: 217 E 2nd
57105-7122) (605) 270-3560
Fort George Holy Name Church **M** (24) Iron
Nation St 57548 (Mail to: 209 S Main St 57325-
1420) (605) 730-0626
Fort Pierre St Peters Episcopal Church **M** (36)
713 S 1st St 57532-2074 (Mail to: PO Box 391
57532-0391) (605) 670-7195

Fort Thompson Christ Episcopal Church **M** (147) Ft Thompson 57339 (Mail to: PO Box 457 57339-0457) (605) 730-0626

Gregory Church of the Incarnation **M** (17) 1117 Main St 57533-1147 (Mail to: 105 E 12th Street 57533) (605) 835-8144

Herrick All Saints Episcopal Church **M** (26) 352 Avenue 57538 (Mail to: 105 E 12th St 57533-1140) (605) 835-8144

Hot Springs St Lukes Episcopal Church **M** (69) Hammond Ave & Minnekah 57747 (Mail to: 1915 Washington Ave 57747-1911) (605) 745-3323

Huron Grace Episcopal Church **P** (83) 1617 McClellan Dr 57350-1361 (Mail to: PO Box 1361 57350-1361) Jean Mornard (605) 352-3096

Ideal Church of the Holy Spirit **M** (88) Rural Tripp Co Gravel Rd 57541 (Mail to: 105 E 12th Street 57533) (605) 842-2211

Iron Lightning St Lukes Church **SC** Iron Lightning 57623 (Mail to: PO Box 80 57625) (605) 964-6180

Kyle Church of the Mediator **M** (414) Kyle Village Rd 57752 (Mail to: PO Box 74 57752-0074) (605) 455-2140

Lake Andes Church of St Philip the Deacon **M** (24) 29273 383rd Ave 57356 (Mail to: PO Box 686 57380) (605) 384-5294

Lead Christ Episcopal Church **P** (59) 631 W. Main Avenue 57754 (Mail to: PO Box 675 57754-0675) (605) 584-3607

Little Eagle St Pauls Episcopal Church **M** (43) Little Eagle 57639 (Mail to: PO Box 14 57639-0014) (605) 338-9751

Little Oak Creek Church of the Good Shepherd **M** (87) Little Oak Creek 57639 (Mail to: PO Box 84 57639-0084) (605) 338-9751

Lower Brule Holy Comforter Episcopal Church **M** (450) 412 Spotted Tail Lane 57548 (Mail to: 209 S Main St 57325-1420) (605) 441-6812

Lower Brule Messiah Episcopal Church **P** Iron Nation 57548 (Mail to: PO Box 227 57548-0227)

Madison Grace Episcopal Church **M** (17) 306 NW 3rd St 57042-2115 (Mail to: c/o PO Box 410 57042) (605) 256-2325

Martin St Katharines Episcopal Church **M** (214) 4th Avenue & School Street 57551-0207 (Mail to: PO Box 207 57551-0207) (605) 685-6173

McLaughlin St Peters Episcopal Church **M** (100) 307 3rd Ave W 57642 (Mail to: PO Box 534 57642-0534) (605) 823-2269

Milbank Christ Episcopal Church **M** (36) 203 N 4th St 57252 (Mail to: 302 S Maple 57201) Marion Paulis (605) 438-2101

Mission Rosebud Episcopal Mission **Other** No Bishop Hare Rd 57555 (Mail to: PO Box 188 57555-0188)

Mission St Philip and St James Station **M** (36) PO Box 256 57579 (Mail to: PO Box 256 57555-0256) (605) 828-3892

Mission Trinity Episcopal Church **M** (207) 180 Main Street 57601 (Mail to: PO Box 188 57555-0188) (605) 828-3892

Mitchell St Marys Episcopal Church **P** (132) 214 W 3rd Ave 57301-2547 (Mail to: PO Box 866 57301-0866) (605) 996-3025

Mobridge St James Episcopal Church **P** (59) 802 N Main St 57601 (Mail to: 401 1st Ave W 57601-2578) (605) 845-3281

Niobrara Church of the Blessed Redeemer **M** (39) 535 Ave Howe Creek 68760 (Mail to: PO Box 686 57380-0686) (605) 384-5294

Norris Tiwahe ed wacekiyapi **M** S Main St 57560 (Mail to: S Main St 57560)

Okreek Calvary Episcopal Church **M** (29) Highway 18 57563 (Mail to: 105 E 12th St 57533) (605) 835-8144

On The Tree St Thomas Station **PS** Green Grass-Whitehorse Rd Rural Dewey County 57265 (Mail to: PO Box 80 57625-0080) (605) 964-6180

Parmelee Holy Innocents Episcopal Church **M** (237) 7 1st St 57566 (Mail to: PO Box 188 57555-0188) (605) 828-3892

Peever St Marys Episcopal Church **M** (106) 12889 Whipple Rd 57257-7628 (Mail to: 716 7th Ave W 57262-1248) (605) 698-6528

Pierre Trinity Episcopal Church **P** (158) 408 N Jefferson Ave 57501-2626 (Mail to: 408 N Jefferson Ave 57501-2626) Mercy Hobbs (605) 224-5237

Pine Ridge Church of the Advent **PS** (102) Calico 57770 (Mail to: PO Box 229 57794-0229) (605) 685-6631

Pine Ridge Holy Cross Episcopal Church **M** (95) Highway 407 57770 (Mail to: PO Box 855 57770-0855) (605) 685-6631

Pine Ridge Pine Ridge Episcopal Mission **Other** Pine Ridge Reservation 57551 (Mail to: PO Box 532 57551-0532) (605) 685-6173

Porcupine St Julias Episcopal Church **PS** (50) 92 Main St 57772 (Mail to: PO Box 229 57794-0229) (605) 685-6631

Promise St Marys Episcopal Church **M** Whitehorse-Promise Rd 57625 (Mail to: PO Box 80 57625-0085) (605) 964-6180

Pukwana St John the Baptist Episcopal Church **M** (62) Crow Creek Reservation 57370 (Mail to: Box 46 57370) (605) 730-0626

Rapid City Emmanuel Episcopal Church **P** (540) 717 Quincy St 57701-3631 (Mail to: 717 Quincy St 57701-3697) Christopher Roussell (605) 342-0909

Rapid City St Andrew's Episcopal Church **P** (321) 3435 W South St 57702-8163 (Mail to: 910 Soo San Dr 57702-8115) (605) 343-4210

Rapid City St Matthews Episcopal Church **M** (430) 620 N Haines Ave 57701 (Mail to: PO Box 1606 57709-1606) (605) 342-6199

Red Scaffold St Stephens Station **SC** Red Scaffold 57626 (Mail to: PO Box 80 57625) (605) 964-6180

Red Shirt Table Christ Episcopal Church **SC** (214) RR 57701 (Mail to: PO Box 168 57744-0168) (605) 255-4914

Reliance St Albans Episcopal Church **P** 23792 340th Ave 57569-5622 (Mail to: 209 S Main St 57325-1420) (605) 730-0626

Rosebud Church of Jesus **M** (187) Rosebud Mission 57570 (Mail to: PO Box 188 57555-0188) (605) 828-3892

Santee Church of Our Most Merciful Savior **M** (209) 65 Santee Rt 22 68760 (Mail to: PO Box 686 57380-0686) (605) 384-5294

Sioux Falls Calvary Cathedral Episcopal **P** (774) 500 S Main Ave 57104-6814 (Mail to: 500 S Main Ave 57104-6814) Christina O'Hara Ward Simpson (605) 336-3486

Sioux Falls Church of the Good Shepherd **P** (417) No 2707 W 33rd St 57105-4302 (Mail to: 2707 W 33rd St 57105-4302) (605) 332-1474

Sioux Falls Church of the Holy Apostles **M** (188) 1415 S Bahnson Ave 57103-3443 (Mail to: 1415 S Bahnson Ave 57103-3443)

Sioux Falls Dow Rummel Village **NH** 1321 W Dow Rummel St 57104-7808 (Mail to: 1321 W Dow Rummel St 57104-7808) (605) 336-1491

Sioux Falls Waterford At All Saints **NH** 111 W 17th St 57104-4972 (Mail to: 111 W 17th St 57104-4972)

Sisseton Gethsemane Episcopal Church **M** (52) Sisseton 57262 (Mail to: 716 7th Ave W 57262-1248) (605) 698-6528

Soldier Creek Grace Station **PS** (32) Soldier Creek Rd 57570 (Mail to: PO Box 188 57555) (605) 382-3892

Spearfish Church of All Angels **P** (192) 1044 N 5th St 57783-2009 (Mail to: 1044 N 5th St 57783-2009) (605) 642-4349

Sturgis St Thomas Episcopal Church **P** (105) 1222 Junction Ave 57785-1937 (Mail to: 1222 Junction Ave 57785-1937) (605) 347-5683

Thunder Butte St Peters Church **M** Thunder Butte Rd 57623 (Mail to: PO Box 80 57625-0080) (605) 964-6180

Vermillion St Pauls Episcopal Church **M** (53) 10 Linden Ave 57069-3203 (Mail to: 10 Linden Ave 57069-3203) (605) 624-3379

Wagner Woniya Wakan (Holy Spirit) **M** (105) 613 S Main St 57380 (Mail to: PO Box 686 57380) (605) 384-5294

Wakpala St Elizabeths Episcopal Church **M** (131) Standing Rock Mission 57658 (Mail to: PO Box 105 57658-0105) (605) 845-7131

Wanblee Gethsemane Episcopal Church **M** (90) 210 1st St 57577 (Mail to: PO Box 532 57551) (605) 685-6631

Watertown Trinity Episcopal Church **P** (34) 202 E Kemp 57201-3642 (Mail to: 202 E Kemp 57201-3642) (605) 280-4927

Waubay St James Episcopal Church **M** (259) Enemy Swim Lake 57273 (Mail to: 716 7th Ave W 57262-1248) (605) 698-6528

Webster St Marys Episcopal Church **M** (19) 8th & Main 57275 (Mail to: PO Box 71 57261-0071) (605) 486-4587

White Horse Emmanuel Episcopal Church **M** White Horse 57661 (Mail to: PO Box 5 57661-0005) (605) 964-6180

Yankton Christ Episcopal Church **P** (227) Attn Richard Unruh 513 Douglas Ave 57078-4030 (Mail to: 517 Douglas Ave 57078-4030) James Pearson

NON-PAROCHIAL CLERGY

Barnes JP *ret* Bend OR
Bird VL *dcn* Rapid City SD
Bryan EP *ret* Rapid City SD
Cameron DA *ret* Rapid City SD
Campbell LR *ret* Mobridge SD
Campbell TW *ret* Spearfish SD
Ciesel BB *dcn* Wagner SD
Ciesel CH *ret* Lake City SD
Cimijotti JA Spokane WA
Cloud VL *dcn* Waubay SD
Corbin PR Sioux Falls SD
Donovan NL *dcn* Silver City SD
Flagstad JM Pierre SD
Fonder KM Lower Brule SD
Fountain TL Sioux Falls SD
Garwood MJ *dcn* Rapid City SD
Hall RA Brookings SD
Hedin JC *dcn*
Henninger A Gregory SD
Hill RJ *ret* Sturgis SD
Hollingsworth-Graves JL *dcn* Sioux Falls SD
Husby MEB *dcn* Sioux Falls SD
Hussey DP Vermillion SD
Jennings MK *ret* Wagner SD
Keyes JI *dcn* Yankton SD
King CM New Milford CT
Kramer LJ *ret* Hill City SD
Lang ED *ret* Sioux Falls SD
Lewis AL *ret* Sioux Falls SD
Makes Good DH *ret* Wanblee SD
Mayen JM *dcn* Sioux Falls SD
Mayom AM
McIntosh WS Watertown SD
Mesteth RY
Montileaux CT Kyle SD
Nelson JD Vincennes
Newman TF *ret* Shawnee OK
Noisy Hawk LM *ret* Rapid City SD
Parmeter GE *ret* Huron SD
Pearsall AE *dcn* Sioux Falls SD
Petersen J *dcn* Brookings SD
Pitt-Hart BT *dcn* Sioux Falls SD
Potts DG *dcn* Rapid City SD
Powers EA *ret* Chamberlain SD
Raschke VJ *ret* Lead SD
Rectenwald MB *ret* Sewanee TN
Red Owl C Porcupine SD
Regan TF *dcn* Lead SD
Ressler R Jackson MI

Schwarz RC *ret* Sioux Falls SD
Shoberg WE *ret* Sioux Falls SD
Skinner B *dcn*
Sneve PM Vermillion SD
Spruhan JH *ret* Salem VA
Spruhan JB *ret* Salem VA
Stanley LR Mission SD
Takes War Bonnett RL *dcn*
Taylor Lyman SM *dcn* Vermillion SD
Two Hawk WA *ret* Fort Pierre SD
Tyon BR *ret* Pine Ridge SD
Valandra LB *dcn* Hot Springs SD

Vander Lee JN *dcn* Sioux Falls SD
Vershure CE Custer SD
Voorhees JM *dcn* Belle Fourche SD
Walker CH *dcn* Wilmot SD
Watson MH Richmond VA
Weaver EJ Belle Fourche SD
Weaver IM *dcn*
West CA Martin SD
White Horse-Carda PA Sioux Falls SD
Williams JA *dcn* Caribou ME
Williams SK Belle Fourche SD
Zephier RG Aberdeen SD

DIOCESE OF SOUTHEAST FLORIDA
(PROVINCE IV)
Comprises 7 counties in SE Florida
DIOCESAN OFFICE 525 NE 15th St Miami FL 33132
TEL (305) 373-0881   FAX (305) 375-8054
E-MAIL info@diosef.org   WEB www.diosef.org

Previous Bishops—
Wm C Gray 1892-1913, Cameran Mann m 1913 dio 1922-32, John D Wing coadj 1925 Bp 1932-50, Martin J Bramm suffr 1951-56, Wm F Moses suffr 1956-61, Henry I Louttit suffr 1945 coadj 1948 Bp 1951-69, Wm L Hargrave suffr 1961-69, James L Duncan suffr 1961-69 Bp 1970-80, Calvin O Schofield Jr Bp 1980-2000, James Ottley Asst Bp 2002-2006

Bishop — Rt Rev Leopold Frade (780) (Dio Sept 2000)

Bishop Coadjutor — Rt Rev Peter Eaton 1087 (2015)

Archdcn for Cong Dev Ven BA Hobbs; *Archdcn for Deploy Ven* TA Bruttell; *Archdcn for Imm and Soc Just Ven* JF Bazin; *Sec Cn* R Miller; *Treas Cn* T Huston; *Chanc* C Johnson ESQ; *Vice Chanc* B Reid; K Grantham; WT Muir ESQ; D Anderson ESQ; *Chanc Em;* RD Tylander; JR Gillespie; *COO* C Valdes; *Interim Pres Episc Charities* Rev DA Maconaughey; *Comm* Rev P Rasmus

Deans: N Palm Beach Very Rev D Wilt; *South Palm Beach* Very Rev W Tobias; *Broward* Very Rev E Henry; *North Dade* Very Rev G Mansfield; *South Dade* Very Rev W Allen-Faiella; *Keys* Very Rev C Todd; *Trinity Cathedral* Very Rev D McCaleb

Stand Comm—Cler: Pres J Tidy A Sherman M Conroy T Cederberg; *Lay:* R Miller G Outler J Smith K Neely

Dio Conv: 11-12 Nov 2016 North Palm Beach Deanery Palm Beach Gardens

PARISHES, MISSIONS, AND CLERGY

Big Pine Key St Francis in the Keys Church **M** (29) 1600 Key Deer Blvd 33043 (Mail to: PO Box 430645 33043-0645) Christopher Todd (305) 872-2547

Biscayne Park Santa Cruz-Resurrection Episcopal Church **M** (613) 11173 Griffing Blvd 33161 (Mail to: 11173 Griffing Blvd 33161) Jose Ortez (305) 893-8523

Boca Raton Chapel of St Andrew **M** (149) 2707 NW 37th St 33434-4497 (Mail to: 2707 NW 37th St 33434-4497) Winnie Bolle Charles Browning Anne Harris Faye Somers Charles Wissink (561) 210-2700

Boca Raton St Gregorys Episcopal Church **P** (1071) 100 NE Mizner Blvd 33432-4008 (Mail to: PO Box 1503 33429-1503) Andrew Sherman Angela Cortinas Anita Thorstad (561) 395-8285

Boynton Beach St Cuthberts Episcopal Church **M** (46) Attn Mrs Barbara Smith 417 NW 7th Ave 33435-3754 (561) 732-7422

Boynton Beach St Josephs Episcopal Church **P** (871) 3300a S Seacrest Blvd 33435-8661 (Mail to: 3300a S Seacrest Blvd 33435-8661) Martin Zlatic Gwendolyn Tobias (561) 732-3060

Clewiston St Martins Episcopal Church **M** (97) 207 NW Cowen Ave 33440 (Mail to: 207 North W C Owens Ave 33440-3030) (863) 983-7960

Coral Gables St Philips Episcopal Church **P** (440) 1121 Andalusia Avenue 33134-4799 (Mail to: 1121 Andalusia Avenue 33134-4799) Mary Conroy Mercedes Busto David Karcher

Deerfield Beach St Marys Episcopal Church **M** (122) 417 S Dixie Hwy 33441-4627 (Mail to: 417 S Dixie Hwy 33441-4627) Lynne Jones (954) 428-3040

Delray Beach St Matthews Episcopal Church **M** (140) 404 SW 3rd St 33444-2402 (Mail to: 404 SW 3rd St 33444-2402) Marcia Beam (561) 272-4143

Delray Beach St Pauls Church **P** (973) 188 S Swinton Ave 33444-3656 (Mail to: 188 S Swinton Ave 33444-3656) Paul Kane Kathleen Gannon (561) 276-4541

Fort Lauderdale St Mark the Evangelist Church **P** (551) 1750 E Oakland Park Blvd 33334 (Mail to: 1750 E Oakland Park Blvd 33334-5299) Ronald Hayde Eliza Ragsdale Robert Trache (954) 563-5155

Ft Lauderdale All Saints Episcopal Church **P** (1087) 333 Tarpon Dr 33301-2337 (Mail to: 333 Tarpon Dr 33301-2337) (954) 467-6496

Ft Lauderdale Episcopal Church of the Atonement **P** (718) 4401 W Oakland Park Blvd 33313-1826 (Mail to: 4401 W Oakland Park Blvd 33313-1826) Earl Henry (954) 731-6100

Ft Lauderdale St Ambrose Episcopal Church **M** (110) 2250 SW 31st Ave 33312 (Mail to: 2250 SW 31st Ave 33312) Andrew Hudson Rosa Lindahl Jose Memba Emilio Rosolen Fred Sands (954) 583-0603

Ft Lauderdale St Benedicts Episcopal Church **P** (1200) No 7801 NW 5th St 33324-1911 (Mail to: 7801 NW 5th Street 33324-1999) Albert Cutie (954) 473-6578

Ft Lauderdale St Christophers Episcopal Church **M** (117) 318 NW 6th Ave 33311-9154 (Mail to: PO Box 228 33302-0228) Leonel Charles Fred Sands (954) 306-6148

Hallandale Beach St Anne's Episcopal Church **M** (181) 705 NW 1st Ave 33009-2301 (Mail to: 705 NW 1st Ave 33009-2301) (954) 454-2811

Hialeah St Margarets & San Francisco de Asis Epis Ch **M** (160) 15650 Miami Lakeway N 33014-5517 (Mail to: 15650 Miami Lakeway N 33014-5517) Modesto Mursuli (305) 558-3961

Hobe Sound Christ Memorial Chapel **SC** (46) 52 S Beach Rd 33455-2225 (Mail to: PO Box 582 33475-0582) (772) 546-8329

Hollywood Holy Sacrament Episcopal Church **P** (665) 2801 N University Dr 33024-2547 (Mail to: 2801 N University Drive 33024-2547) Anthony Holder William Eaton (954) 432-8686

Hollywood St Andrews Episcopal Church **M** (60) 2800 N 23rd Ave 33020-1616 (Mail to: PO Box 695 33004-0695) (954) 922-8444

Hollywood St James in the Hills Church **P** (151) 3329 Wilson St 33021-4836 (Mail to: 3329 Wilson St 33021-4836) (954) 987-2203

Hollywood St Johns Episcopal Church **P** (136) 1704 Buchanan St 33020-4030 (Mail to: 1704 Buchanan St 33020-4030) Matthew Faulstich (954) 921-3721

Homestead St Johns Episcopal Church **M** (506) 145 NE 10th St 33030-4633 (Mail to: 145 NE 10th St 33030-4698) (305) 247-5343

Islamorada St James the Fisherman **P** (232) 87500 Overseas High 33036 (Mail to: PO Box 509 33036-0509) Thomas Graf (305) 852-2161

Jensen Beach All Saints Episcopal Church **P** (554) 2303 NE Seaview Dr 34957-5533 (Mail to: 2303 NE Seaview Dr 34957-5533) Alan Gellert Walter Hendricks (772) 334-0610

Key Biscayne St Christophers By The Sea Church **P** (148) 95 Harbor Dr 33149-1411 (Mail to: 95 Harbor Dr 33149-1499) Susan Bruttell Miguel Baguer Natalie Blasco (305) 361-5080

Key West St Pauls Episcopal Church **P** (400) 401 Duval St 33040-6550 (Mail to: 401 Duval Street 33040) Larry Hooper (305) 296-5142

Key West St Peters Episcopal Church **M** (100) 807 Center St 33040-7435 (Mail to: 800 Center St 33040-7435) (305) 296-2346

Lake Worth Holy Redeemer Episcopal Church **M** (257) 3730 Kirk Rd 33461-3431 (Mail to: 3730 Kirk Rd 33461-3431) Christina Encinosa (561) 965-8632

Lake Worth St Andrews Episcopal Church **P** (390) 100 N Palmway 33460-3515 (Mail to: 100 N Palmway 33460-3515) Brenda Masterman (561) 582-6609

Lake Worth St Johns Episcopal Church **M** (34) 810 Washington Ave 33460-5555 (Mail to: George Glinton 1524 Douglas St 33460-5510) (561) 547-4480

Marathon St Columba Episcopal Church **P** (110) 451 52nd Street Gulf 33050-2614 (Mail to: 451 52nd St 33050-0426) Debra Andrew-maconaughey Virginia Landwer (305) 743-6412

Miami All Angels Episcopal Church **M** (215) 1801 Ludlam Dr 33166-3165 (Mail to: 1801 Ludlam Dr 33166-3165) Ann Kathleen Goraczko Susan Keedy (305) 885-1780

Miami Chapel of the Venerable Bede **CC** (88) 1150 Stanford Dr 33146-2002 (Mail to: 1150 Stanford Drive 33146-2002) Frank Corbishley (305) 284-2333

Miami Christ Church **P** (595) 3481 Hibiscus St 33133-5717 (Mail to: 3481 Hibiscus St 33133-5717) Jonathan Archer Vivian Hopkins

Miami Church of St Matthew the Apostle **P** (172) 7410 Sunset Dr 33143-4130 (Mail to: 7410 Sunset Dr 33143-4130) James Jones (305) 665-7333

Miami Church of the Holy Family **P** (595) 18501 NW 7th Ave 33169-4441 (Mail to: 18501 NW 7th Ave 33169-4441) Horace Ward Ledly Moss

Miami Episcopal Church of the Ascension **P** (498) 11201 SW 160th St 33157-2701 (Mail to: 11201 SW 160th St 33157-2701) Norbert Cooper (305) 238-5151

Miami Episcopal Church of the Incarnation **P** (863) 1835 NW 54th St 33142-3065 (Mail to: PO Box 420050 33142-0050) John Jarrett (305) 633-2446

Miami Historic St Agnes Episcopal Church **P** (483) 1750 NW 3rd Ave 33136-1610 (Mail to:

PO Box 12943 33101-2943) Doris Ingraham
Denrick Rolle (305) 573-5330

Miami Holy Comforter Episcopal Church **M**
(483) 150 SW 13th Ave 33135-2412 (Mail to:
150 SW 13th Ave 33135-2491) Sixto Garcia
(305) 643-2711

Miami Iglesia Epis de Todos Los Santos **P** (378)
1023 SW 27th Ave 33135-4614 (Mail to:
1023 SW 27th Ave 33135-4614) Alejandro
Hernandez (305) 642-2951

Miami Iglesia Episcopal Santisima Trinidad **P**
(79) 6744 N Miami Ave 33150-4030 (Mail
to: 6744 N Miami Ave 33150-4030) Marivel
Milien (305) 758-8546

Miami St Andrews Episcopal Church **P** (545)
14260 Old Cutler Rd 33158-1347 (Mail to:
14260 Old Cutler Road 33158-1347) Spencer
Potter George Ronkowitz (305) 238-2161

Miami St Faith Episcopal Church **P** (251) 10600
Caribbean Blvd 33189-1361 (Mail to: 10600
Caribbean Blvd 33189-1361) Jennie Reid Cyril
White (305) 235-3621

Miami St Luke the Physician **M** (346) 12355 SW
104th St 33186-3602 (Mail to: 12355 SW 104th
St 33186-3602) Corinna Olson (305) 279-4265

Miami St Paul et Les Martyrs D'Haiti **M** (179)
6744 N Miami Ave 33150-4030 (Mail to: 6744
N Miami Ave 33150-4000) Marivel Milien
Smith Milien (305) 758-8546

Miami St Simons Episcopal Church **M** (112)
10950 SW 34th St 33165-3542 (Mail to: 10950
SW 34th St 33165-3542) Carlos Sandoval Cros
Rohani Weger (305) 221-4753

Miami St Stephens Episcopal Church **P** (535)
2750 McFarlane Rd 33133-6026 (Mail to: 2750
McFarlane Rd 33133-6026) Wilifred Allen-
Faiella Jo-Ann Murphy (305) 448-2601

Miami St Thomas Episcopal Church **P** (957)
5690 SW 88th St 33156-2199 (Mail to: 5690 N
Kendall Dr 33156-2132) Amanda Lippe Mario
Milian Modesto Mursuli Harold Walker (305)
661-3436

✣ **Miami** Trinity Cathedral **O** (985) 464 NE 16th
St 33132-1222 (Mail to: 464 NE 16th St 33132-
1222) Douglas McCaleb Richard Benedict
Elaine Jessup Grey Maggiano John Stanton
(305) 374-3372

Miami Beach All Souls' Episcopal Church **P** (106)
4025 Pine Tree Dr 33140-3601 (Mail to: 4025
Pine Tree Dr 33140-3677) John Tidy Charles
Humphries (305) 520-5410

N Miami Beach St Bernard de Clairvaux
Episcopal Church **P** (729) 16711 W Dixie Hwy
33160-3714 (Mail to: 16711 W Dixie Hwy
33160-3714) Gregory Mansfield

Opa Locka Church of the Transfiguration **M**
(146) 15260 NW 19th Ave 33054-2960 (Mail
to: PO Box 272 33054) Terrence Taylor (305)
681-1660

Opa Locka St Kevins Episcopal Church **M** (120)
3280 NW 135th St 33054-4812 (Mail to: PO

Box 540668 33054) Simeon Newbold (305)
688-8517

Palm Beach Church of Bethesda-by-the-Sea **P**
(1643) 141 S County Rd 33480 (Mail to: 141
S. County Rd 33480-1057) James Harlan
Timothy Cogan Walter Salmon Kimberly Still
Clayton Waddell (561) 655-4554

Palm Beach Garden St Marks Episcopal Church
P (1361) 3395 Burns Rd 33410-4322 (Mail
to: 3395 Burns Rd 33410-4322) James Cook
Sanford Groff Jean Wright (561) 622-0956

Palm City Church of the Advent **M** (184) 4484
SW Citrus Blvd 34990 (Mail to: 4484 SW
Citrus Blvd 34990) Robert Shires (772) 283-
6221

Pompano Beach St Martins Episcopal Church **P**
(349) 140 SE 28th Ave 33062-5441 (Mail to:
140 SE 28th Ave 33062-5441) Bernard Pecaro
Ralph Klingenberg (954) 941-4843

Pompano Beach St Mary Magdalene Episcopal **P**
(840) 1400 Riverside Dr 33071-6070 (Mail to:
1400 Riverside Drive 33071-6070) Cynthia Gill
Lorna Goodison Ruth Hahne Todd Hoover
Mark Sims (954) 753-1400

Pompano Beach St Nicholas Episcopal Church
P (433) 1111 E Sample Rd 33064-5113 (Mail
to: 1111 E Sample Rd 33064-5113) Mark Jones
Ralph Klingenberg (954) 942-5887

Pompano Beach St Philips Episcopal Church **M**
(50) 465 NW 15th St 33060-5416 (Mail to: 465
NW 15th St 33060-5416) Joseph Joseph (954)
785-2437

Riviera Beach St Georges Episcopal Church **P**
(70) 21 W 22nd St 33404-5509 (Mail to: PO
Box 10584 33419-0584) (561) 844-7713

Stuart St Lukes Episcopal Church **P** (400) 5150 SE
Railway Ave 34997-3305 (Mail to: PO Box 1127
34992-1127) Carol Barron (772) 286-5455

Stuart St Marys Episcopal Church **P** (1377) 623
East Ocean Blvd 34994-2329 (Mail to: 623
East Ocean Boulevard 34994-2376) Todd
Cederberg Stephen Fregeau (772) 287-3244

Stuart St Monicas Episcopal Church **M** (59) PO
Box 1798 34995-1798 (Mail to: PO Box 1798
34995-1798) Allison Spencer Arthur Spencer
(772) 221-0552

Tequesta Church of the Good Shepherd **P** (1516)
400 Seabrook Road 33469-2685 (Mail to: 400
Seabrook Rd 33469-2685) (561) 746-4674

West Palm Bch Grace Episcopal Church **P** (561)
3600 N Australian Ave 33407-4513 (Mail to:
3600 N Australian Ave 33407-4599) Winston
Wright (561) 845-6060

West Palm Bch Holy Spirit Episcopal Church **P**
(304) 1003 Allendale Rd 33405-1347 (Mail
to: 1003 Allendale Rd 33405-1347) Hallock
Martin Donna Hall

West Palm Bch Holy Trinity Episcopal Church **P**
(532) 211 Trinity Pl 33401-6119 (Mail to: 211
Trinity Pl 33401-6119) David Wilt Howarth
Lewis (561) 655-8650

West Palm Bch St Christophers Episcopal Church
   M (220) 1063 Haverhill Rd N 33417-5805
   (Mail to: PO Box 222068 33422-2068) Willie
   Davila (561) 683-8167
West Palm Bch St David in the Pines Epis Church
   P (431) 465 W Forest Hill Blvd 33414-4705
   (Mail to: 465 W Forest Hill Blvd 33414-4705)
   William Thomas (561) 793-1976
West Palm St Patricks Episcopal Church **P** (321)
   418 North Sapodilla Avenue 33401-4138 (Mail
   to: 418 North Sapodilla Avenue 33401-4138)
   Winston Joseph (561) 833-1903

NON-PAROCHIAL CLERGY

Allee RG *ret* Ft. Lauderdale FL
Ames RK *ret* San Antonio TX
Andrews GE Marion MA
Bambrick BN *ret dcn* Perry IA
Banks RA *ret*
Baptiste-Williams BJ *ret* Miami FL
Barrowclough LS Palm Beach Gardens FL
Barry-Marquess RL *ret* Miami FL
Bazin JF *ret* Miami FL
Beebe JS Palm Beach FL
Beebe SR Palm Beach FL
Beniste JC Washington DC
Blackburn G *dcn* Coral Gables FL
Browne SJ *ret* Lake Park FL
Brusso LG *ret* Venice FL
Bruttell TA Plantation FL
Campbell SS Nassau
Cassell WM *ret* Boynton Beach FL
Casseus FJ *ret* Montreal QC
Cassini MED Boca Raton FL
Clark DB Brooklyn NY
Clarke JV *ret dcn* Leesburg FL
Clawson DR *ret* Vero Beach FL
Collins DW Miami Springs FL
Crawford HG *ret* Saint Petersburg FL
Cruz R *dcn* Biscayne Park FL
Dambrot DL Fort Lauderdale FL
Damon RE *dcn* Hollywood FL
De Miranda ME Miami Lakes FL
Deshaies RJ *ret* Plantation FL
Dougherty EA *ret* Albany NY
Douglas HB *ret* Crawfordville FL
Effinger RW Palm Beach FL
Fox RN *ret* Miami FL
Froehlich BH *ret* St Augustine FL
Froyen JC
Gabaud PS Miami FL
Galeano Franco GA
Gay JR Miami Shores FL
Gilbert SE *dcn* Miami FL
Glendenning AG *dcn* Palm Beach Gardens FL
Graff SJ Boca Raton FL
Grant BH *ret* Baton Rouge LA
Graves CC *dcn*
Griffith BM *ret* Miami FL
Gutierrez JP *dcn* West Palm Beach FL
Hamilton WE *ret* Lake Worth FL

Hammatt EA *dcn* Miami FL
Hobbs BA *ret* Pembroke Pines FL
Howard MM *ret dcn*
Hudson AG *dcn* Fort Lauderdale FL
Hudspeth DW Belle Glade FL
Hurley HO *dcn* West Palm Beach FL
Johnson RF *ret* Islamorada FL
Johnson RN *ret* Hardy VA
Katon JC *ret dcn* Miami FL
Kelly CD *ret* Gansevoort NY
Kennedy DC *ret* Boynton Beach FL
Killian KE Southwest Harbor ME
Kinard GO *dcn*
Klein JH *ret* Lake Worth FL
Kozlowski MW Stuart FL
Krickbaum DW *ret* Harpers Ferry WV
LaCrone FP *ret* Palm Beach Gardens FL
Laine J Delray Beach FL
Laremore DL Austin TX
Libby RMG *ret* Key Biscayne FL
Major JK *ret* Miami FL
Mallin CSD *dcn* Coral Gables FL
Mallow SE *ret* Fort Lauderdale FL
Martin DA *ret* Buffalo NY
Masterman FJ *ret* Tucson AZ
McCarthy IF Stuart FL
McCarthy NH *ret* Asheville NC
McCloskey RJ *ret* West Jefferson NC
McGregor PC Ambridge PA
McLaughlin DK *dcn* Hollywood FL
McPhee GV *dcn* Miami FL
Minich HNF *ret* Earlysville VA
Minshew JK *ret* Port Salerno FL
Morgan DD *ret* Coconut Grove FL
Moyer DL *ret* Dover PA
Murray LT Miami Beach FL
Naughton MA Boynton Beach FL
Noetzel JL *dcn* West Palm Beach FL
Ostlund HL Loxahatchee FL
Paul ME *dcn* Cutler Bay FL
Perrino RA *dcn* Palm Beach Gardens FL
Peterson Zubizarreta DC
Picou MD Coconut Grove FL
Preston RG *ret* Hallandale Beach FL
Price GH *ret* Boca Raton FL
Rasmus PA *ret* Palm Beach Gardens FL
Reece MS Madrid
Reeves JL Kansas City MO
Regisford SHA *ret* Shakopee MN
Reid RW *ret* Frisco TX
Robb GK *ret* Palm Beach Gardens FL
Ruffin CH Dallas TX
Ryan TF *ret* Clermont FL
Sanchez JDJ Miami FL
Scupholme A *dcn* Charlottesville VA
Sheldon PA Palm City FL
Shives BM *dcn* Tampa FL
Simmons WR Washington DC
Sims KH *dcn* Opa Locka FL
Sligh JL *ret* Tampa FL
Stathers BS *ret* Lewisburg WV

Stennette LR *ret*
Strainge RT
Sullivan MR *dcn* West Palm Beach FL
Surgeon OA Miami Gardens FL
Taylor RS *ret* Jupiter FL
Thomas SS *ret* Clewiston FL
Thomas TB *ret* Flagler Beach FL
Tiller MJ *ret* Lantana FL
Tirado V *dcn* Miami FL
Titcomb CJ *ret dcn* Palm Beach FL

Tobin RM *ret* Miami FL
Valovich SA *dcn* Palm Beach Gardens FL
Verell GA *ret* Miami FL
Vernon VV *dcn*
Warren RR *ret* Palm Beach Gardens FL
Weeks Wulf MJ Palmetto Bay FL
Wells MB *ret dcn* Gordonsville VA
Williams SE *dcn* Miami FL
Williams WA *ret* Tequesta FL
Woodcock BW Nyack NY

DIOCESE OF SOUTHERN OHIO
(PROVINCE V)
Comprises 40 counties of Southern Ohio
DIOCESAN OFFICE 412 Sycamore St Cincinnati OH 45202-4179
TEL (513) 421-0311; (800) 582-1712   FAX (513) 421-0315
WEB www.diosohio.org

Previous Bishops—
Thomas A Jaggar 1875-1904, Boyd Vincent coadj 1889 Bp 1904-29, Theodore I Reese coadj 1913 Bp 1929-31, Henry W Hobson coadj 1930 Bp 1931-59, Roger W Blanchard coadj 1958 Bp 1959-70, John M Krumm 1971-80, WG Black coadj 1979 Bp 1980-91, Herbert Thompson Jr coadj 1988 Bp 1992-05, Kenneth Price Jr suffr 1994-2012

Bishop—Rt Rev Thomas E Breidenthal (1016)
(Dio 28 April 2007)

Cn to Ord Rev Cn J Koepke; *Cn for Mission* Rev Cn A Reed; *Cn for Formation & Transitions* Rev Cn L Carter-Edmands; *CFOD* Robinson; *Yth Min & Sum Camp* R Konkol; *Dir of Comm* D Dreisbach; *Pres of Trustees* J Boss; *Sec to Conv* D Morris; *Chanc* JJ Dehner 3300 Great American Tower 301 E Fourth St Cincinnati 45202; *Hist* Rev AW Wilson; *Ecum & Interfaith* M Zacharia 318 E Fourth St Cincinnati OH 45202; *Treas* J Harris 846 E Mitchell Ave Cincinnati OH 45229

Stand Comm—Cler: Pres S Smith P College E Cook; *Lay:* D Parker C Bagot J Rucker

Dio Conv: 11-12 Nov 2016 Crowne Plaza North, Columbus OH

PARISHES, MISSIONS, AND CLERGY

Amelia Church of the Good Samaritan **M** (31) 25 Amelia-Olive Branch Rd 45102-0889 (Mail to: PO Box 889 45102) (513) 753-4115

Athens Church of the Good Shepherd **P** (153) 64 University Ter 45701-2913 (Mail to: 64 University Ter 45701-2913) Deborah Woolsey (740) 593-6877

Bellaire Trinity Episcopal Church **M** (39) 4310 Noble St 43906-1448 (Mail to: 4310 Noble St

43906-1448) (740) 676-4472

Cambridge St Johns Episcopal Church **M** (33) 1025 Steubenville Ave 43725-2401 (Mail to: PO Box 1044 43725-6044) Robert Howell (740) 432-7508

Chillicothe St Pauls Episcopal Church **P** (94) 33 E Main St 45601-2504 (Mail to: 33 E Main St 45601-2595) Paul Daggett (740) 772-4105

Cincinnati All Saints Episcopal Church **P** (171) 6301 Parkman Pl 45213-1123 (Mail to: 6301 Parkman Pl 45213-1123) Eileen O'Reilly (513) 531-6333

Cincinnati Calvary Episcopal Church **P** (411) 3766 Clifton Ave 45220-1238 (Mail to: 3766 Clifton Ave. 45220-1299) Jason Leo Gary Givler Wilson Willard (513) 861-4437

Cincinnati Christ Church (Glendale) **P** (512) 965 Forest Ave 45246-4405 (Mail to: 965 Forest Ave 45246-4405) John Keydel (513) 771-1544

✣ **Cincinnati** Christ Church Cathedral **O** (599) 318 E 4th St 45202-4202 (Mail to: 318 E 4th St 45202-4299) Gail Greenwell Gary Goldacker Noel Julnes-Dehner Sherilyn Pearce Anne Reed Robert Rhodes Manoj Zacharia (513) 621-1817

Cincinnati Church of Our Saviour **P** (103) 65 E Hollister St 45219-1703 (Mail to: 65 E Hollister St 45219-1796) Paula Jackson (513) 241-1870

Cincinnati Church of the Advent **HC** (66) No 2366 Kemper Lane 45206-2686 (Mail to: 2366 Kemper Lane 45206-2686)

Cincinnati Church of the Redeemer **P** (1347) 2944 Erie Ave 45208-2404 (Mail to: 2944 Erie Ave 45208-2404) Charles Brumbaugh Nancy Hopkins-Greene Michael Smith (513) 321-6700

Cincinnati Grace Episcopal Church **M** (49) 5501 Hamilton Ave 45224-3111 (Mail to: 5501 Hamilton Ave 45224-3195) (513) 541-2415

Cincinnati Holy Child Chapel-Childrens Hospital **PS** 3333 Burnet Ave MLC 5022 45229

(Mail to: 3333 Burnet Ave 45229-3026) (513) 636-4200

Cincinnati Holy Trinity Episcopal Church **M** (36) 7190 Euclid Ave 45243-2544 (Mail to: 7190 Euclid Ave 45243-2544) Theresa Thornton (513) 984-8400

Cincinnati Indian Hill Church **P** (165) 6000 Drake Rd 45243-3308 (Mail to: 6000 Drake Rd 45243-3308) (513) 561-6805

Cincinnati St Andrews Episcopal Church **P** (238) 1809 Rutland Ave 45207-1219 (Mail to: 1809 Rutland Ave 45207-1219) Anne Reed (513) 531-4337

Cincinnati St Barnabas Church **P** (705) 10345 Montgomery Rd 45242-5113 (Mail to: 10345 Montgomery Rd 45242-5113) Nancy Turner-Jones (513) 984-8401

Cincinnati St James Episcopal Church **P** (218) James Strader Blake Sawicky (513) 661-1154

Cincinnati St Simon of Cyrene Episcopal **P** (206) 810 Matthews Dr 45215-1837 (Mail to: 810 Matthews Dr 45215-1837) Trevor Babb Theorphlis Borden Colenthia Hunter James Mobley (513) 771-4828

Cincinnati St Timothys Episcopal Church **P** (1045) 8101 Beechmont Ave 45255-3190 (Mail to: 8101 Beechmont Ave 45255-3196) Roger Greene Alexander Martin (513) 474-4445

Circleville St Philips Episcopal Church **HC** (142) 129 W Mound St 43113-1623 (Mail to: PO Box 484 43113-0484) David Getreu (740) 474-4525

Columbus Saint Mark's Episcopal Church **P** (783) 2151 Dorset Rd 43221-3103 (Mail to: 2151 Dorset Road 43221-3103) Kenneth St Germain Christopher Richardson (614) 486-9452

Columbus St Albans Epis Church of Bexley **P** (506) 333 S Drexel Ave 43209-2139 (Mail to: 333 S Drexel Ave 43209-2139) Harry Harper John Jupin Meribah Mansfield Susan Marie Smith (614) 253-8549

Columbus St Edwards Church Whitehall **M** (108) 214 Fairway Blvd 43213-2012 (Mail to: 214 Fairway Blvd 43213-2012) Fredric Shirley (614) 861-1777

Columbus St James Episcopal Church **P** (334) 3400 Calumet St 43214-4106 (Mail to: 3400 Calumet St 43214-4106) Elise Feyerherm Phillip Harris (614) 262-2360

Columbus St Johns Episcopal Church **M** (293) 1003 W Town St 43222-1438 (Mail to: 1003 W Town St 43222-1438) Craig Foster Meribah Mansfield Lee Reat (614) 221-9328

Columbus St Philip Episcopal Church **P** (289) 166 Woodland Ave 43203-1774 (Mail to: 166 Woodland Ave 43203-1774) Karl Ruttan Brenda Taylor Charles Wilson (614) 253-2771

Columbus St Stephens Episcopal Church **P** (254) 30 W Woodruff Ave 43210-1118 (Mail to: PO Box 82263 43202) Pamela Elwell Faith Perrizo

Columbus Trinity Episcopal Church **P** (355) 125 E Broad St 43215-3605 (Mail to: 125 E Broad

St 43215-3605) Richard Burnett Brian Shaffer (614) 221-5351

Dayton Christ Episcopal Church **P** (434) 20 W 1st St 45402-1213 (Mail to: 20 W 1st St 45402-1269) John Paddock Robert Dwight Charles Watts (937) 223-2239

Dayton St Andrews Episcopal Church **P** (121) 1060 Salem Ave 45406-5130 (Mail to: 1060 Salem Ave 45406-5198) Connie McCarroll (937) 278-7345

Dayton St Georges Episcopal Church **P** (585) 5520 Far Hills Ave 45429-2204 (Mail to: 5520 Far Hills Ave 45429-2232) Benjamin Phillips C David Cottrill Lewis Lane (937) 434-1781

Dayton St Margarets Episcopal Church **P** (286) 3010 McCall St 45417-2034 (Mail to: 5301 Free Pike 45426-2441) Benjamin Speare-Hardy Jeanette Manning (937) 837-7741

Dayton St Marks Episcopal Church **P** (102) 456 Woodman Dr 45431-2099 (Mail to: 456 Woodman Dr 45431-2099) Michael Kreutzer George Snyder (937) 256-1082

Dayton St Pauls Church Episcopal **P** (625) 33 W Dixon Ave 45419-3431 (Mail to: 33 W Dixon Ave 45419-3431) Michael Kreutzer (937) 293-1154

Delaware St Peters Episcopal Church **P** (208) 45 W Winter St 43015-1947 (Mail to: 15 N Franklin St 43015-1913) (740) 369-3175

Dublin St Patricks Episcopal Church **P** (901) 7121 Muirfield Dr 43017-2863 (Mail to: 7121 Muirfield Dr 43017-2863) Stephen Smith Robert Rideout (614) 766-2664

Fairborn St Christophers Church **P** (161) 1501 N Broad St 45324-5575 (Mail to: PO Box 1026 45324-1026) Ruth Paulus (937) 878-5614

Gallipolis St Peters Episcopal Church **P** (58) 541 2nd Ave 45631-1250 (Mail to: 541 2nd Ave 45631-1250) Gene Stack (740) 446-2483

Granville St Luke Episcopal Church **P** (394) 107 Broadway E 43023-1303 (Mail to: PO Box 82 43023-0082) Stephen Applegate (740) 587-0167

Greenville St Pauls Episcopal Church **P** (67) 201 S Broadway St 45331-1978 (Mail to: 201 S Broadway St 45331-1978) David Brower Richard Larsen (937) 548-5575

Hamilton Trinity Episcopal Church **P** (165) 115 N 6th St 45011-3541 (Mail to: 115 N 6th St 45011-3541) Suzanne Levesconte (513) 896-6755

Hillsboro St Marys Episcopal Church **P** (91) 234 N High St 45133-1129 (Mail to: 234 N High St 45133-1129) Judi Wiley (937) 393-2043

Ironton Christ Episcopal Church **M** (72) 501 Park Ave 45638-1546 (Mail to: PO Box 555 45638-0555) Sallie Schisler (740) 532-3528

Lancaster St Johns Episcopal Church **P** (271) 134 N Broad St 43130-3701 (Mail to: 134 N Broad St 43130-3701) George Pursley (740) 653-3052

Lebanon St Patricks Church **P** (217) 232 E Main St 45036-2230 (Mail to: 232 E Main St 45036-2230) Jacqueline Matisse (513) 932-7691

Logan St Pauls Episcopal Church **M** (36) 375 E Main St 43138-1307 (Mail to: PO Box 736 43138-0736) (740) 385-1005

London Christ Chapel **SC** 11235 State Route 38 SE 43140-9716 (Mail to: 11235 State Route 38 SE 43140-9716)

London Trinity Episcopal Church **P** (74) Corner of 4th and Main St 43140-0468 (Mail to: PO Box 468 43140-0468) Frank Edmands

Maineville St Mary Magdalene Church **M** (29) 2757 W US Route 22 45039 (Mail to: 2757 W US Route 22 45039-0325) (513) 677-1777

Marietta St Luke's Episcopal Church **P** (241) 320 2nd St 45750-2919 (Mail to: 320 2nd St 45750-2919) David Ruppe William Field (740) 373-5132

McArthur Trinity Church **M** (8) 202 W High St 45651-1009 (Mail to: 202 W High St 45651-1009) (740) 596-5562

Mechanicsburg Church of Our Saviour **M** (65) 56 S Main St 43044-1111 (Mail to: 56 S Main St 43044-1111) (937) 653-3497

Middletown Church of the Ascension **P** (186) 2709 McGee Ave 45044-4836 (Mail to: 2709 McGee Ave 45044-4836) Joanna Leiserson Hugh Whitesell (513) 424-1254

Nelsonville Church of the Epiphany **M** (32) 193 Jefferson St 45764-1207 (Mail to: 193 Jefferson St 45764-1207) William Mccleery (740) 753-3434

New Albany All Saints Episcopal Church **P** (366) PO Box 421 5101 Johnstown Road 43054-0421 (Mail to: PO Box 421 5101 Johnstown Rd 43054-8964) Jason Prati (614) 855-8267

Newark Trinity Episcopal Church **P** (191) 76 E Main St 43055-5604 (Mail to: 76 E Main St 43055-5604) (740) 345-5643

Oxford Holy Trinity Episcopal Church **P** (236) 25 E Walnut St. 45056-1892 (Mail to: 25 E. Walnut St. 45056-1892) Thomas Kryder-Reid (513) 523-7559

Pickerington St Andrews Episcopal Church **P** (156) 8630 Refugee Rd 43147-9509 (Mail to: 8630 Refugee Rd 43147-9509) Paul Williams (614) 626-2720

Piqua St James Episcopal Church **P** (138) 200 W High St 45356-2218 (Mail to: 200 W High St 45356-2218) Jeffrey Bessler (937) 773-1241

Pomeroy Grace Episcopal Church **M** (31) 326 E Main St 45769-1023 (Mail to: 326 E Main St 45769-1023) (740) 992-3968

Portsmouth All Saints' Episcopal Church **P** (222) 610 4th St 45662-3921 (Mail to: 610 4th St 45662-3921) Stephen Cuff Richard Schisler (740) 353-7919

Springboro St Francis Episcopal Church **P** (143) 225 N Main St 45066-9255 (Mail to: 225 N Main St 45066-9255)

Springfield Christ Church Episcopal **P** (374) 409 E High St 45505-1007 (Mail to: 409 E High St 45505-1007) Charlotte Reed Otto Anderson (937) 323-8651

Terrace Park St Thomas Episcopal Church **P** (1467) 100 Miami Ave 45174-1175 (Mail to: 100 Miami Ave 45174-1175) Darren Elin Daniel Grossoehme Robert Reynolds (513) 831-2052

Troy Trinity Episcopal Church **P** (123) 60 S Dorset Rd 45373-5616 (Mail to: 60 S Dorset Rd 45373-5616) Joan Smoke (937) 335-7747

Urbana Church of the Epiphany **M** (84) 230 Scioto St 43078-2128 (Mail to: 230 Scioto St 43078-2128) (937) 653-3497

Waynesville St Marys Episcopal Church **M** (28) No 107 S 3rd St 45068-9011 (Mail to: PO Box 653 45068-0653) Pamela Gaylor (513) 897-2435

West Chester St Anne Episcopal Church **P** (441) 6461 Tylersville Rd 45069-1435 (Mail to: 6461 Tylersville Rd 45069-1435) Phyllis Spiegel (513) 779-1139

Westerville St Matthews Episcopal Church **M** (98) 23 East College Avenue 43081 (Mail to: 23 East College Avenue 43081) Joseph Kovitch

Worthington St Johns Episcopal Church **P** (494) 700 High St 43085-4137 (Mail to: 700 High St 43085-4137) Philip College Alice Herman (614) 846-5180

Wshngtn Ct Hs St Andrews Episcopal Church **M** (92) 733 State Route 41 SW 43160-8797 (Mail to: 733 State Route 41 SW 43160) Gayle Browne Jennifer Oldstone-Moore (740) 335-2129

Wyoming Ascension and Holy Trinity **P** (458) Eric Miller (513) 821-5341

Xenia Christ Episcopal Church **P** (74) 63 E Church St 45385-3001 (Mail to: 68 E Church St 45385-3002) Lynn Sinnott (937) 372-1594

Zanesville St James Episcopal Church **P** (142) 155 N 6th St 43701-3603 (Mail to: 155 N 6th St 43701-3603) Robert Willmann (740) 453-9459

NON-PAROCHIAL CLERGY

Agbaje JO Portsmouth VA
Albert EE Loveland OH
Allen GC *ret* Cincinnati OH
Argue D *dcn* Columbus OH
Armstrong P *dcn* Cincinnati OH
Bailey DB *ret* West Chester OH
Baldwin JM *ret* Brown Deer WI
Bales WO *dcn* Logan OH
Barrow CV *ret* Sandy Springs GA
Betts AR *ret* Cincinnati OH
Bondurant SB *ret* Cincinnati OH
Bower JA *ret* Springdale OH
Bowers JE *ret* Lancaster OH
Brandenburg JP Bridgeport OH
Brandenburg NLH *dcn* Worthington OH
Brentley DJ *dcn* Cincinnati OH
Brugger SB *dcn* Troy OH
Bumiller WN *ret* Dayton OH
Burdick EN *ret* Newark OH
Burnard KK *ret* Oxford OH

Burns JM *dcn* Worthington OH
Burns JW *ret* Columbus OH
Burton JC *ret* Edgartown MA
Carberry TO *ret* Orrs Island ME
Carter-Edmands L Fort Thoms KY
Christian CJ *dcn*
Clark JL *ret* Windsor ON
Clarke KG *dcn* Maineville OH
Clausen KP *ret* Millersport OH
Cobb JP *ret* Gloucester MA
Cogar CC *dcn* Gallipolis OH
Coleman BEG *ret* Englewood OH
Connor AE Cincinnati OH
Cook EP *dcn* Cincinnati OH
Cotter BL *ret* Evanston IL
Crockett JL *dcn* Columbus OH
Cross MT *ret* Freedom ME
Crowell LA
Decker CF *ret* Columbus OH
Delfs CB *ret* Delaware OH
Denton EM *dcn* Waynesville OH
Eager DB *dcn* Lancaster OH
Everett SB *dcn* Columbus OH
Fehr TJ Cincinnati OH
Fenwick RD *ret* Centerville OH
Fisher JR *ret* Columbus OH
Flemming LA *ret* Athens OH
Foote RL *ret* Cincinnati OH
Foster KK Athens OH
Frees MC *dcn* Amelia OH
Gamble DE *ret* Cincinnati OH
Gartig WG Cincinnati OH
Gerdsen EJ Dayton OH
Gill JN *ret* Columbus OH
Glazier GH *ret* Columbus OH
Greenwood DR *ret* Vancouver WA
Gunn SA Cincinnati OH
Hadley AC *ret* McAllen TX
Hampton CM Cincinnati OH
Hanisian JA *ret* Cincinnati OH
Hansel RR *ret* Little Switzerland NC
Hatch AH *ret* Edisto Island SC
Helms DC
Hill GA *ret* Cincinnati OH
Hinton WW *ret* Milford OH
Hobson PS *ret* Cincinnati OH
Hoover MA *dcn*
Howard DZ *ret*
Hufford RA *ret* Cincinnati OH
Hughes RD *ret* Sewanee TN
Hull CW *ret* Lake Oswego OR
Jergens AM *ret* Cincinnati OH
Johanssen JR *ret* Thornville OH
Keeshin JJ Cincinnati OH
Kinsey TB *ret* Minneapolis MN
Koepke J Cincinnati OH
Krieger FG *ret* Halifax

Leary CR *ret* Medway OH
Lilly EL *ret* Columbus OH
Lyle WE *ret* Kent OH
Mackenzie AH *ret* Washington NC
Martin CA *dcn* Middletown OH
Matheus RD *ret* Columbus OH
Mathews KE *ret* Firth ID
Maynard JP *dcn* Columbus OH
McCoy DO *ret* Athens OH
McCracken-Bennett RJ *ret* Johnstown OH
McGavran FJ *dcn* Cincinnati OH
Michelfelder SR The Plains VA
Mills AD *dcn* Beavercreek OH
Mills DK *ret* Southwest Harbor ME
Mills SP *ret* Dayton OH
Miner JS *ret* Columbus OH
Morrison JA *ret* Cincinnati OH
Mueller DR *dcn* Cincinnati OH
Mycoff WJ *ret* Summersville WV
Neely CF *ret* Cincinnati OH
Newberry HW Worthington OH
Oh K Cincinnati OH
Payne ET *ret* West Chester OH
Perrin HK *ret* Cincinnati OH
Potterton CT *dcn* Cincinnati OH
Puopolo AJ *ret* Cincinnati OH
Radcliff IE *dcn*
Raysa MG *dcn*
Riis SH *ret dcn* Thornville OH
Robbins AW *ret* Bonita Springs FL
Rupp LD *ret* New London NH
Sangrey WF *dcn*
Saville M *ret* Cincinnati OH
Schlachter BJH *ret* Iowa City IA
Schmitt BJ *dcn* Hamilton OH
Scrivener WE *ret* Cincinnati OH
Shaver TR *ret* Saint Johns FL
Shirley DF *dcn* Westerville OH
Smith AB *ret* Columbus OH
Snodgrass CJ Gainesville FL
Southerland TR *dcn* Cincinnati OH
Stearns HJ *ret* Moraine OH
Stevens KPB Columbus OH
Stevenson FB *ret* Oxford
Turner BW Fredericksburg VA
Van Brunt TH *ret* Amelia OH
West JK *ret* Westerville OH
West JT *ret* Urbana OH
Williams JM *dcn* West Chester OH
Williams MS *ret* Troy OH
Wilson AW Cincinnati OH
Wiseman HB *ret* Cincinnati OH
Wiseman PM *dcn* Cincinnati OH
Wood GA *ret* Pawleys Island SC
Wooden L *ret* Cincinnati OH
Wrider AJ *ret* Cincinnati OH
Wright PJ *dcn*

DIOCESE OF SOUTHERN VIRGINIA
(PROVINCE III)
Comprises 26 southern VA counties
DIOCESAN OFFICE 11827 Canon Blvd Ste 101 Newport News VA 23606
TEL (757) 423-8287   In VA only (800) 582-8292   FAX (757) 595-0783
E-MAIL 600@diosova.org   WEB www.diosova.org

Previous Bishops—
Alfred M Randolph 1892-1918, Beverley D Tucker coadj 1906 Bp 1918-30, Arthur C Thomson suffr 1917 coadj 1919 Bp 1930-37, Wm A Brown 1938-50, Geo P Gunn coadj 1948 Bp 1950-71, David S Rose suffr 1958 coadj 1964 Bp 1971-1978, C Charles Vaché coadj 1976 Bp 1978-91, O'Kelley Whitaker asst 1992-97 Frank H Vest Jr coadj 1989 Bp 1991-98 Donald P Hart asst 1998-2001, Carol Joy WT Gallagher suffr 2002-2005, David C Bane coadj 1997 Bp 1998-2006, John C Buchaman Bp Int 2006-09

Bishop—Herman Hollerith IV (1034) (Dio 13 Feb 2009)

Sec Rev RE Haines; *Chanc* S Webster; *Vice Chancs* T Coyle; *Cn for Deploy* M Spear-Jones; *Treas* J Meek

Stand Comm—Cler: Pres R Randall J Rohrs E Felicetti; *Lay:* A Parker I Burch C Shield

Deans: 1st or Eastern Shore V Rev B Ford; *2nd or Virginia Beach* V Rev S Sawyer; *3rd or Norfolk* V Rev J Rohrs; *4th* V Rev K Emerson; *5th or Jamestown* V Rev C Robinson; *6th or Petersburg* V Rev D Teschner; *7th or South Richmond* V Rev D Custer; *8th or Farmville* V Rev N Meck; *9th or Danville* V Rev S Grimm

Dio Conv: 5-6 Feb 2016 Williamsburg Lodge VA

PARISHES, MISSIONS, AND CLERGY

Accomac St James Episcopal Church **P** (52) 23309 Back St 23301-1742 (Mail to: PO Box 540 23301-0540) (757) 787-4892

Amelia Ct Hs Christ Church **P** (82) 16401 Court St 23002-4870 (Mail to: PO Box 468 23002-0468) (804) 561-2441

Appomattox St Anne Episcopal Church **P** (72) 311 Oakleigh Ave 24522 (Mail to: PO Box 387 24522-0387) (434) 352-8296

Baskerville St Andrew Episcopal Church **M** (8) 4118 Baskerville Rd 23915-2045 (Mail to: 4188 Baskerville Rd 23915-2045) (434) 447-4914

Blackstone St Lukes Episcopal Church **P** (68) Corner of S Main & Church 23824 (Mail to: PO Box 36 23824-0036) (434) 292-4265

Bracey St Mark Episcopal Church **M** (30) 3906 Highway 903 23919-9997 (Mail to: PO Box 227 23919-0227) (434) 689-2219

Buckingham Emmanuel Episcopal Church **M** (18) 7825 Howardsville Rd 23921-2459 (Mail to: 7825 Howardsville Rd 23921-2459)

Cape Charles Emmanuel Episcopal Church **M** (31) 601 Tazewell Ave 23310-0601 (Mail to: 601 Tazewell Ave 23310) Robert Coniglio (757) 678-7802

Cartersville St James Episcopal Church **P** (52) C/O Mr John R Martin 35 Boone Trl 23027-9630 (Mail to: PO Box 24 23027-0024) (804) 375-3019

Chase City St John Episcopal Church **P** (33) 338 E 4th St 23924-1226 (Mail to: 338 E 4th St 23924-1226) (434) 372-3318

Chatham Emmanuel Episcopal Church **P** (65) 66 North Main Street 24531-0026 (Mail to: PO Box 26 24531-0026) (434) 432-0316

✠ **Chatham** St Marys Chapel **Other** 800 Chatham Hall Cir 24531-3084 (Mail to: 800 Chatham Hall Cir 24531-3084) (757) 489-9096

Chesapeake Church of the Messiah **M** 816 Kempsville Rd 23320-5002 (Mail to: 816 Kempsville Rd 23320-5002) (757) 436-2545

Chesapeake St Bride Episcopal Church **P** (118) 621 Sparrow Rd 23325-2504 (Mail to: 621 N Sparrow Rd 23325-2504)

Chesapeake St Thomas Episcopal Church **P** (567) 233 Mann Dr 23322-5215 (Mail to: 233 Mann Dr 23322-5215) Fletcher Wells (757) 547-4662

Chester St John's Episcopal Church **P** (336) 12201 Richmond St 23831-4440 (Mail to: PO Box 3886 23831-4440) Raymond Custer (804) 748-2182

Chesterfield St Matthew Episcopal Church **P** (175) 9300 Shawonodasee Rd 23832-6330 (Mail to: PO Box 2187 23832-9111) Mary Hansley (804) 790-1211

✠ **Claremont** Ritchie Memorial Episcopal Church **Other** 115 Virginian 23899 (Mail to: PO Box 27 23899-0027) (804) 866-8629

Clarksville St Timothy Episcopal Church **P** (100) No 111 6th St 23927-9285 (Mail to: 111 6th St 23927-9285) Susan Grimm (434) 374-8611

Colonial Hgt St Michael Episcopal Church **P** (303) 501 Old Town Dr 23834-1734 (Mail to: 501 Old Town Dr 23834-1734) (804) 526-1790

Courtland St Luke Episcopal Church **M** (38) 22430 Main St 23837-1027 (Mail to: PO Box 156 23837-0156) (757) 653-2442

Danville Christ Episcopal Church **P** (174) 9 Ridgecrest Dr 24540-0115 (Mail to: PO Box 10355 24543) Cleon Ross

Danville Church of the Epiphany **P** (291) 781 Main St 24541-1803 (Mail to: 115 Jefferson Ave 24541-1921) K Drew Baker Rebecca Crites (434) 792-4321

Disputanta Brandon Episcopal Church **P** (34) 18706 James River Dr 23842-9045 (Mail to: 18706 James River Dr 23842-9045) Macon Walton (757) 866-8977

Drakes Branch Grace Episcopal Church **M** (5) 250 Proctor St 23937-2936 (Mail to: PO Box 467 23937-0467) (434) 568-5861

Eastville Christ Church **P** (80) 16304 Courthouse Rd 23347 (Mail to: PO Box 367 23347-0367)

Emporia St James Episcopal Church **M** (41) 609 Halifax St 23847-1305 (Mail to: PO Box 821 23847-0821) (434) 634-5351

Farmville Johns Memorial Episcopal Church **P** (228) 400 High St 23901-1812 (Mail to: 400 High St 23901-1812) Nancy Meck (434) 392-5695

Franklin Emmanuel Episcopal Church **P** (280) 400 N High St 23851-1420 (Mail to: PO Box 146 23851-0146) Edmund Pickup (757) 562-4542

Freeman St Thomas Episcopal Church **M** (58) 6271 Belfield Rd 23856-2413 (Mail to: PO Box 71 23856-0071) (434) 336-1132

Gretna St Johns Episcopal Church **M** (16) 1357 Hickeys Rd 24557-4689 (Mail to: 6772 East Gretna Road 24557-1943) (434) 656-1735

Halifax Christ Episcopal Church **M** (10) 545 N Main St 24558 (Mail to: 545 North Main St 24558) (434) 476-4421

Halifax Emmanuel Episcopal Church **M** 3120 Mountain Road 24558-0905 (Mail to: PO Box 905 24558-0905)

Halifax St John Episcopal Church **P** (141) 197 Mountain Rd 24558-2010 (Mail to: PO Box 905 24558-0905) Cleon Ross (434) 476-6696

Hampton Emmanuel Episcopal Church **P** (367) 179 E Mercury Blvd 23669-2461 (Mail to: 179 E Mercury Blvd 23669-2461) Rhonda Wheeler (757) 723-8144

Hampton St Cyprian Episcopal Church **P** (215) 1242 W Queen St 23669-3843 (Mail to: PO Box 65 23669-0065) Ronald Ramsey (757) 723-8253

Hampton St John Church **P** (436) 100 W Queens Way 23669-4014 (Mail to: 100 W Queens Way 23669-4014) James Hutton Mark Riley Samantha Vincent-Alexander (757) 722-2567

Hampton St Mark Episcopal Church **P** (129) 2605 Cunningham Dr 23666-2370 (Mail to: PO Box 7430 23666-0430) (757) 826-3515

Hopewell St John Episcopal Church **P** (184) 505 Cedar Ln 23860-1517 (Mail to: 505 Cedar Ln 23860-1517) William Taylor (804) 458-8142

Java St Paul Episcopal Church **M** (9) 13953 Halifax Rd 24565 (Mail to: PO Box 43 24565-0043) (804) 432-3776

Kenbridge Church of St Paul and St Andrew **P** (115) 512 S Broad St 23944-2012 (Mail to: PO Box 248 23944-0248) Virginia Distanislao (434) 676-3448

Lawrenceville St Andrew Episcopal Church **P** (37) 400 Windsor 23868-1202 (Mail to: PO Box 26 23868-0026) (434) 848-3939

Lawrenceville St Pauls Memorial Chapel **CC** (76) 115 College Dr 23868-1299 (Mail to: PO Box 268 23868-0268) (434) 848-2544

Machipongo Hungars Parish **P** (181) 10107 Bayside Rd 23405 (Mail to: PO Box 367 23347-0367) Harry Crandall Daniel Crockett (757) 678-7837

McKenney Church of the Good Shepherd **P** (61) 7800 Lew Jones Rd 23872 (Mail to: PO Box 357 23872-0357) (804) 478-4280

Midlothian Church of Our Saviour **P** (40) 4000 Stigall Dr 23112-3208 (Mail to: 4000 Stigall Dr 23112-3208) John Stanton (804) 744-2164

Midlothian Episcopal Church of the Redeemer **P** (949) 2341 Winterfield Rd 23113-4157 (Mail to: 2341 Winterfield Rd 23113-4157) Douglas Dunn John Newell

Midlothian Manakin Episcopal Church **P** (494) 985 Huguenot Trl 23113-9224 (Mail to: 985 Huguenot Trl 23113-9224) Rebecca Dean Judith Lee (804) 794-6401

Midlothian St Matthias Episcopal Church **P** (667) 11300 W Huguenot Rd 23113-1121 (Mail to: 11300 W Huguenot Rd 23113-1121) Brenda Overfield (804) 272-8588

Newport News St Andrew Episcopal Church **P** (716) 45 Main St 23601-4011 (Mail to: 45 Main St 23601-4011) Elizabeth Greenman Richard Holley Betty Hudson David Perkins (757) 595-0371

Newport News St Augustine Episcopal Church **P** (160) No 2515 Marshall Ave 23607-4605 (Mail to: 2515 Marshall Ave 23607-4605) Terry Edwards (757) 245-4613

Newport News St George Episcopal Church **P** (75) No 15446 Warwick Blvd 23608-1506 (Mail to: 15446 Warwick Blvd 23608-1506) Anne Kirchmier (757) 877-0088

Newport News St Paul Episcopal Church **P** (90) 221 34th St 23607-2903 (Mail to: 221 34th St 23607-2903) (757) 247-5086

Newport News St Stephen Episcopal Church **P** (273) 372 Hiden Blvd 23606-2934 (Mail to: 372 Hiden Blvd 23606-2934) Joseph Baker Lauren McDonald (757) 595-5521

Norfolk Christ & St Lukes Epis Church **P** (1340) 560 W Olney Rd 23507-2135 (Mail to: 560 W Olney Rd 23507-2135) Irwin Lewis Grant Stokes (757) 627-5665

Norfolk Church of the Good Shepherd **P** (527) 7400 Hampton Blvd 23505-1775 (Mail to: 7400 Hampton Blvd 23505-1780) James Medley (757) 423-3230

Norfolk Episcopal Church of the Advent **P** (102) 9620 Sherwood Pl 23503-1723 (Mail to: 9629 Norfolk Ave 23503-1701) Anne Dale (757) 587-0125

Norfolk Episcopal Church of the Ascension **P** (290) 405 Talbot Hall Rd 23505-4309 (Mail to: 405 Talbot Hall Rd 23505-4309) Alan Mead Stewart Tabb

Norfolk Episcopal Church of the Epiphany **P** (106) 1530 Lafayette Blvd 23509-1112 (Mail to: 1530 Lafayette Blvd 23509-1112) Julia Ashby (757) 622-7672

Norfolk Grace Episcopal Church **P** (857) 1400 E Brambleton Ave 23504-4394 (Mail to: 1400 E Brambleton Ave 23504-4394) Harold Cobb (757) 625-2868

Norfolk St Andrew Episcopal Church **P** (458) 1009 W Princess Anne Rd 23507-1219 (Mail to: 1009 W Princess Anne Rd 23507-1219) John Rohrs Andrea Wigodsky (757) 622-5530

Norfolk St Paul Episcopal Church **P** (459) 201 St Pauls Blvd 23510 (Mail to: 201 St Pauls Blvd 23510-4205) Frank Hennessy (757) 627-4353

Norfolk St Peter's Episcopal Church **P** (542) 224 S Military Hwy 23502-5231 (Mail to: 224 S Military Hwy 23502-5231) John Eidam (757) 466-9392

Norfolk St Stephen's Episcopal Church **P** (79) 1445 Norview Ave 23513-1552 (Mail to: 1445 Norview Ave 23513-1552) Gwynneth Mudd (757) 855-2788

North Chesterfield St Barnabas Episcopal Church **P** (113) 5155 Iron Bridge Rd 23234-4703 (Mail to: 5155 Iron Bridge Road 23234-4703) (804) 275-1648

North Chesterfield St David Episcopal Church **P** (285) 1801 Camborne Rd 23236-2126 (Mail to: 1801 Camborne Rd 23236-2126) Elizabeth Felicetti (804) 276-4348

North Prince George Merchants Hope Episcopal Church **M** (96) 11500 Merchants Hope Rd 23860-8933 (Mail to: 11500 Merchants Hope Rd 23860-8933) Charles Moore (804) 458-1356

Onancock Holy Trinity Episcopal Church **P** (140) 66 Market St 23417-4224 (Mail to: PO Box 338 23417-0338) Calvin Ford (757) 787-4430

Petersburg Christ & Grace Epis Church **P** (389) 1545 S Sycamore St 23805-1314 (Mail to: 1545 S Sycamore St 23805-1314) David Teschner (804) 733-7202

Petersburg St John Episcopal Church **P** (64) 842 W Washington St 23804-1187 (Mail to: PO Box 1187 23804-1187) (804) 732-8107

Petersburg St Paul's Episcopal Church **P** (323) 110 N Union St 23803 (Mail to: PO Box 564 23804-0564) Daniel Greenwood (804) 733-3415

Petersburg St Stephen Episcopal Church **P** (121) 228 Halifax St 23803-6312 (Mail to: 228 Halifax St 23803-6312) Willis Foster (804) 733-6228

Portsmouth St Christopher Episcopal Church **P** (164) 3300 Cedar Ln 23703-4104 (Mail to: 3300 Cedar Ln 23703-4104) Eileen Walsh (757) 484-5155

Portsmouth St James Episcopal Church **M** (118) 928 Effingham St 23704-3438 (Mail to: 928 Effingham St 23704-3438) Frederick Walker (757) 399-7707

Portsmouth St John Episcopal Church **P** (250) 424 Washington St 23704-2435 (Mail to: 424 Washington St 23704-2435) J Derek Harbin (757) 399-4967

Portsmouth Trinity Episcopal Church **P** (434) 500 Court St 23704-3606 (Mail to: 500 Court

St 23704-3606) James Sell Charles Smith (757) 393-0431

Powhatan Emmanuel Episcopal Church **P** (36) PO Box 481 23139-0481 (Mail to: PO Box 481 23139-0481) Stephan Beatty Michael Murphy (804) 212-5845

Powhatan St Luke Episcopal Church **P** (252) 2245 Huguenot Trl 23139-4403 (Mail to: 2245 Huguenot Trl 23139-4403) Sandra Kerner (804) 794-6953

Pungoteague St George Episcopal Church **P** (70) 30241 Bobtown Rd 23422 (Mail to: PO Box 540 23301-0540) Cameron Randle (757) 787-4892

Richmond Church of the Good Shepherd **P** (347) 4206 Springhill Ave 23225-3345 (Mail to: 4206 Springhill Ave 23225-3345) Ross Wright (804) 233-2278

Richmond St Michael Episcopal Church **P** (261) 8706 Quaker Ln 23235-2918 (Mail to: 8706 Quaker Ln 23235-2918) Jeunee Godsey (804) 272-0992

Smithfield Christ Episcopal Church **P** (141) 111 S Church St 23430-1332 (Mail to: 111 S Church St 23430-1332) Charles Pringle (757) 357-2826

South Boston Trinity Episcopal Church **P** (95) No 520 Yancey St 24592-3322 (Mail to: 520 Yancey St 24592-3322) Susan Grimm (434) 572-4513

South Hill All Saints Episcopal Church **P** (71) 203 Franklin St 23970-2009 (Mail to: PO Box 58 23970-0058) Terrence Walker (434) 955-2271

South Hill Trinity Episcopal Church **P** (49) 926 Thomason Ln 23970 (Mail to: PO Box 903 23970-0903) Terrence Walker (434) 447-6533

Suffolk Glebe Episcopal Church **P** (143) 4400 Nansemond Pkwy 23435-2136 (Mail to: PO Box 5042 23435-0042) Ross Keener (757) 538-8842

Suffolk St John Episcopal Church **P** (126) 828 Kings Hwy 23432-1112 (Mail to: 828 Kings Hwy 23432-1112) Leslie Ferguson (757) 255-4168

Suffolk St Mark Episcopal Church **P** (74) 142 Tynes St 23434-4625 (Mail to: 142 Tynes St 23434-4625) Frederick Walker (757) 934-0830

Suffolk St Paul Episcopal Church **P** (221) No 213 North Main Street 23434-4420 (Mail to: 213 North Main Street 23434-4420) Keith Emerson (757) 539-2478

Surry St Paul Episcopal Church **M** (63) 11891 Rolfe Hwy 23883-2738 (Mail to: PO Box 298 23883-0298) (757) 569-6280

Temperanceville Emmanuel Episcopal Church **M** (70) 26405 Horsey Rd 23442 (Mail to: PO Box 186 23416-0186) Claire Hunkins (757) 824-5043

Toano Hickory Neck Episcopal Church **P** (509) 8300 Richmond Rd 23168-9206 (Mail to: 8300 Richmond Rd 23168-9206) Henry Mcqueen

Victoria St Luke Episcopal Church **M** (9) C/O Charlie W Allen 601 Mecklenburg Avenue 23974-0437 (Mail to: C/O Charlie Allen PO Box 437 23974-0437) (434) 676-3432

Virginia Bch Church of the Holy Apostles **P** (114) 1598 Lynnhaven Pkwy 23453-2008 (Mail to: 1593 Lynnhaven Pkwy 23453-2054) Michael Ferguson (757) 427-0963

Virginia Bch Galilee Episcopal Church **P** (865) 3928 Pacific Ave 23451-2636 (Mail to: 3928 Pacific Ave 23451-2636) Andrew Buchanan Mark Riley (757) 428-3573

Virginia Bch Good Samaritan Episcopal Church **P** (35) 848 Baker Rd 23462-1035 (Mail to: 848 Baker Rd 23462-1035) Wendy Wilkinson (757) 497-0729

Virginia Bch Old Donation Episcopal Church **P** (973) 4449 N Witchduck Rd 23455-6151 (Mail to: 4449 N Witchduck Rd 23455-6151) Robert Randall Peggy Luhring Henry Poteet Ashley Urquidi (757) 497-0563

Virginia Bch St Aidan Episcopal Church **P** (458) 3201 Edinburgh Dr 23452-5803 (Mail to: 3201 Edinburgh Dr 23452-5803) Mark Wilkinson Josephine Taylor (757) 340-6459

Virginia Bch St Francis Episcopal Church **P** (274) 509 S Rosemont Rd 23452-4131 (Mail to: 509 S Rosemont Rd 23452-4131) Conor Alexander (757) 340-6884

Virginia Bch St Simons by the Sea **M** (43) 308 Sandbridge Rd 23456-4522 (Mail to: 308 Sandbridge Rd 23456-4522) Marni Schneider (757) 426-5427

Virginia Bch All Saints' Episcopal Church **P** (603) 1969 Woodside Ln 23454-1031 (Mail to: 1969 Woodside Ln 23454-1031) Stanley Sawyer Jacqueline Gravatt (757) 481-0577

Virginia Bch Eastern Shore Chapel **P** (1109) 2020 Laskin Rd 23454-4208 (Mail to: 2020 Laskin Rd 23454-4208) Thomas Deppe Julia Messer (757) 428-6763

Virginia Bch Emmanuel Episcopal Church **P** (824) 5181 Singleton Way 23462-4241 (Mail to: 5181 Singleton Way 23462-4241) Mary Lacy (757) 499-1271

Warfield St James Episcopal Church **M** (39) 275 Waqua Creek Rd 23889-2048 (Mail to: 910 Pine Ridge Rd 23889-2206) Allan Wentt (434) 949-7720

Waverly Christ Episcopal Church **M** (27) 203 E Main St 23890-3240 (Mail to: PO Box 928 23890-0928) Macon Walton (804) 834-2393

Williamsburg Bruton Parish Church **HC** (1994) 331 E Duke Of Gloucester St 23185-4251 (Mail to: PO Box 3520 23187-3520) Christopher Epperson Charles Robinson Tyler Montgomery (757) 229-2891

Williamsburg St Martins Episcopal Church **P** (920) 1333 Jamestown Rd 23185-3335 (Mail to: 1333 Jamestown Rd 23185-3335) John Riley (757) 229-1111

Yorktown Christ the King Church **P** (220) 4109 Big Bethel Rd 23693-3821 (Mail to: 4109 Big Bethel Rd 23693-3821) John Lynch (757) 865-7227

Yorktown Grace Episcopal Church **P** (540) § 111 Church St 23690-4002 (Mail to: PO Box 123 23690-0123) Carleton Bakkum Constance Jones (757) 898-3261

NON-PAROCHIAL CLERGY

Alley MC *dcn* Virginia Beach VA
Armstrong RH *ret* Chester VA
Avery DT Williamsburg VA
Bailey TH *ret* Williamsburg VA
Baillargeon HA *ret* Tampa FL
Bakely CM *dcn* Oak Hall VA
Baldwin JA *ret* Virginia Beach VA
Ballentine GY *ret* Venice FL
Bledsoe SC Jupiter FL
Bobbitt KM *ret* Virginia Beach VA
Booher DL *ret* Elizabethton TN
Boucher JP *ret* Richmond VA
Bridgford RO *ret* Norfolk VA
Brockenbrough ML Williamsburg VA
Browder JW *ret* Courtland VA
Budd RW *dcn* Williamsburg VA
Buelow PJ *ret* Carrollton VA
Bushong ES *ret* Richmond VA
Butler-Gee E Disputanta VA
Caulkins RLR *ret* Palmyra VA
Christian ER *dcn* Hampton VA
Cochran CB Chesapeake VA
Cowardin SP *ret* Richmond VA
Craft CM *ret* Farmville VA
Crommelin-Dell SH Portsmouth VA
Cunningham CT Farmville VA
Davenport DW *ret* Norfolk VA
Davenport RA Norfolk VA
Delk ML Williamsburg VA
Duffey BR *ret* Franklin VA
Emery HA *ret* Salina KS
Farkas HDM *dcn* Williamsburg VA
Flaherty JF *ret* Alton IL
Frazier AW *ret* Charlottesville VA
Friedrich RP San Francisco CA
Gardner CG Virginia Beach VA
Gay RG *dcn*
Gordon RE North Chesterfield VA
Gray DA Virginia Beach VA
Gray KT *dcn* Newport News VA
Green JN *ret* Norfolk VA
Haines RE *ret* Newport News VA
Hall JH *ret* Antioch TN
Hall SJ *ret* Clemson SC
Hanchey H *ret* Williamsburg VA
Harper WR *ret* Norfolk VA
Harris DB Williamsburg VA
Hayden RS *ret* Farmville VA
Hirst DE Norfolk VA
Hodge WC *ret* Suffolk VA
Hodgson GS *ret* Midlothian VA
Hoffman RE Newport RI
Hoffman WC *ret* Chesapeake VA
Hogg P *ret* Hayes VA
Holder MR *ret* South Hill VA

Howell ME *dcn* Norfolk VA
Huffman RN *ret* Wilmington NC
Jenkins MJL *ret* Richmond VA
Johnson RG *ret* Galveston TX
Johnston RO *ret* Petersburg VA
Jones WO *dcn* Bon Air VA
Joy CA *ret* Norfolk VA
Kahle GF Houston TX
Kellam PM *ret* Amelia Court House VA
Kellett JW *ret* San Diego CA
Kenney M *ret* Virginia Beach VA
Lassalle DF *ret* Norfolk VA
Lewis T *ret* Greensboro NC
Long GA *ret* Albany GA
Loomis JDR *ret* Portsmouth VA
Marston RD *ret* Newport News VA
Mason LW *ret* Richmond VA
Mathieson JW *ret* Danville VA
May RL *ret* Williamsburg VA
McKee HL Danville VA
Miles JP *ret* Williamsburg VA
Miller CB Williamsburg VA
Mumford NWD *ret*
Munday SB *dcn* Chester VA
Murdoch RD *ret* Williamsburg VA
Nelson RA Richmond VA
New RH *ret* Midlothian VA
Noon ACC Hampton VA
Partlow R *ret* North Chesterfield VA
Powers RS *ret* Virginia Beach VA

Purvis HB Chesapeake VA
Riddle CM *ret* Norfolk VA
Ruef JS *ret* Chatham VA
Ryder BH *ret* Decatur GA
Scherer AJKM McLean VA
Siderius DA *ret* Hampton VA
Sims CC *ret* Virginia Beach VA
Slemp DC *ret* North Chesterfield VA
Smith JD *ret* Powhatan VA
Smith JH *ret* Salem VA
Spangenberg RW *ret* Norfolk VA
Spear-Jones MW Crossville TN
Steilberg IF *ret* Newport News VA
Stone ML *ret* Midlothian VA
Teasley R
Tetrault DJ *ret* Williamsburg VA
Thompson JC *ret* Midlothian VA
Tracy EJ Norfolk VA
Tucker J *dcn* Virginia Beach VA
Turner CS *ret* Williamsburg VA
Turner MD *ret* Williamsburg VA
VanVliet-Pullin DM *dcn* Norfolk VA
Walters KG *ret* No Venice FL
Watson RA *ret* East Haddam CT
Williams BF *dcn* Virginia Beach VA
Willis FW *ret* Chincoteague Island VA
Wimbush CS Williamsburg VA
Winborn JH *ret* Bonita Springs FL
Wood NC *dcn* Virginia Beach VA

DIOCESE OF SOUTHWEST FLORIDA

(PROVINCE IV)
Comprises 12 counties of SW Florida
DIOCESAN OFFICE 8005 25th St E Parrish FL 34219
TEL (941) 556-0315   FAX (941) 556-0321
E-MAIL jnothum@episcopalswfl.org   WEB www.episcopalswfl.org

Previous Bishops–
Francis H Rutledge 1851–1866, John F Young 1867-1885, Edwin G Weed 1886-1924, Wm C Gray 1892-1913, Cameron Mann 1914-1932, John D Wing coadj 1925 Bp 1932-1950, Martin J Bramm suffr 1951-1956, Wm F Moses suffr 1956-1961, Henry I Louttit suffr 1945 coadj 1948 Bp 1951-1969, James L Duncan suffr 1961-1969, Wm L Hargrave suffr 1961-1969 Bp 1970-1975, E Paul Haynes 1975-1988, Rogers S Harris 1989-1997, Telesforo A Issac assist 1991-1996, John B Lipscomb 1997-2007

Bishop—Rt Rev Dabney T Smith (1014) (Dio 15 Sep 07)

*Assisting Bishops—*Rt Rev J Michael Garrison and Rt Rev Barry R Howe

Chanc TL Tripp, Jr; *Sec and Treas/CFO* A Vickers; *Cn to Ord* MP Durning; *COM Chair* EM Sloan; *Cn for Development* CN Gray; *Cn for Mission and Outreach* V DR McManis; *Diocesan Missioner/ Campus Ministries* ES Cooter; *Ex Dir DaySpring* CJ Odell

Deans: Clearwater V Rev RK Hehr; *Ft Myers* V Rev Dr E Sloan; *St Petersburg* V Rev J Suhar; *Manasota* V Rev F Robinson; *Tampa* V Rev D Scharf; *Naples* V Rev KV Bennett; *Venice* V Rev R Tuff

Stand Comm–Cler: VP C Olivero C Connelly F Robinson L Wallace R Hehr; *Lay: Pres* K Fitzgerald W Ford G Hileman D Maldonado

Dio Conv: 15 Oct 2016 Punta Gorda

PARISHES, MISSIONS, AND CLERGY

Arcadia Church of St Edmund the Martyr **M**

(123) 327 W Hickory St 34266-3905 (Mail to: 327 W Hickory St 34266-3905) Lisa Hamilton (863) 494-0485

Boca Grande St Andrews Church **P** (347) 4th Street and Gilchrist Ave. 33921 (Mail to: PO Box 272 33921-0272) Michelle Robertshaw (941) 964-2257

Bonita Springs St Marys Episcopal Church **P** (373) 9801 Bonita Beach Rd 34135-4628 (Mail to: PO Box 1923 34135-1923) Michael Rowe George Curt (239) 992-4343

Bradenton Christ Church **P** (964) 4030 Manatee Ave West 34205-1789 (Mail to: 4030 Manatee Ave West 34205-1789) Joel Morsch Alexander Andujar (941) 747-3709

Bradenton St George's Episcopal Church **P** (130) 912 63rd Ave W 34207-4849 (Mail to: 912 63rd Ave West 34207-4849) Bryan O'Carroll (941) 755-3606

Bradenton St Mary Magdalene **P** (330) No 11315 Palmbrush Trail 34202-2938 (Mail to: 11315 Palmbrush Trl 34202-2938) James Hedman Edward Fiebke (941) 751-5048

Brooksville St John Episcopal Church **P** (173) 200 S Brooksville Ave 34601-3311 (Mail to: 200 S Brooksville Ave 34601-3311) (352) 796-9112

Cape Coral Church of the Epiphany **P** (205) 2507 Del Prado Blvd South 33904-5768 (Mail to: 2507 Del Prado Blvd S 33904-5768) Aubrey Cort Susan Henderson Mary Piper Nancy Smith Ryan Wright (239) 574-3200

Clearwater Epis Ch of Good Samaritan **M** (285) 2165 NE Coachman Rd 33765-2616 (Mail to: 2165 NE Coachman Rd 33765-2616) (727) 461-1717

Clearwater Episcopal Church of the Ascension **P** (985) 701 Orange Ave 33756-5232 (Mail to: 701 Orange Ave 33756-5232) John Hiers Hugh Bell Leo Crawford (727) 447-3469

Clearwater Holy Trinity Episcopal Church **P** (440) 3200 N McMullen Booth Rd 33761-2009 (Mail to: 3200 N McMullen Booth Rd 33761-2009) Randall Hehr Sandra Jamieson (727) 796-5514

Clearwater St Johns Episcopal Church **P** (512) 1676 South Belcher Rd 33764-6517 (Mail to: 1676 South Belcher Rd 33764-6517) Kathleen Walter (727) 531-6020

Dade City St Marys Episcopal Church **P** (311) Attn Sandra Sartain 37637 Magnolia Ave 33523-3744 (Mail to: 37637 Magnolia Ave 33523-3744) Dewey Brown Robin Murray (352) 567-3888

Dunedin Church of the Good Shepherd **P** (227) 639 Edgewater Dr 34698-6916 (Mail to: 639 Edgewater Dr 34698-6916) Sylvia Robbins-Penniman (727) 733-4125

Englewood St Davids Episcopal Church **P** (264) 401 South Broadway 34223-3802 (Mail to: 401 S Broadway 34223-3802) James Popham (941) 474-3140

Fort Myers Iona-Hope Episcopal Church **P** (161) 9650 Gladiolus Drive 33908-7616 (Mail to: 9650 Gladiolus Drive 33908-7616) Herman Buchanan (239) 454-4778

Fort Myers Lamb of God Lutheran Episcopal Church **P** (480) 19691 Cypress View Dr 33967-6217 (Mail to: 19691 Cypress View Dr 33967-6217) James Reho (239) 267-3525

Fort Myers St Hilarys Episcopal Church **P** (509) 5011 McGregor Blvd 33901-8840 (Mail to: 5011 McGregor Blvd 33901-8840) Charles Cannon Bercry Leas (239) 936-1000

Fort Myers St Lukes Episcopal Church **P** (846) 2635 Cleveland Ave 33901-5803 (Mail to: 2635 Cleveland Ave 33901-5803) Philip Read (239) 334-2479

Fort Myers Bch St Raphaels Church **M** (51) 5601 Williams Dr 33931-4031 (Mail to: 5601 Williams Dr 33931-4097) John Adler (239) 463-6057

Holmes Beach Episcopal Church of Annunciation **P** (150) No 4408 Gulf Dr 34217-1829 (Mail to: 4408 Gulf Dr 34217-1829) Matthew Grunfeld (941) 778-1638

Hudson St Martins Episcopal Church **P** (168) 15801 US Highway 19 34667-3602 (Mail to: PO Box 7199 34667-3602) Elaine Cole Ronald Kowalski (727) 863-8560

Indian Rk Bch Calvary Episcopal Church **P** (520) 1615 1st St 33785-2809 (Mail to: 1615 1st St 33785-2809) Charles Roberts (727) 595-2374

Labelle The Church of the Good Shepherd **M** (73) 1098 Collingswood Pkwy 33935-2306 (Mail to: 1098 Collingswood Pkwy 33935-2306) David Jackson (863) 675-0385

Largo St Dunstans Episcopal Church **M** (74) No 10888 126th Ave N 33778-2710 (Mail to: 10888 126th Ave N 33778-2710) Nathan Speck-Ewer (727) 586-6968

Lehigh Acres St Anselms Church **M** (124) 2201 E 6th Street 33936-4376 (Mail to: 2201 6th St East 33972-4376) Marcel Algernon (239) 369-1916

Longboat Key All Angels by the Sea **P** (214) 563 Bay Isles Rd 34228-3142 (Mail to: 563 Bay Isles Rd 34228-3142) David Danner Frederick Emrich (941) 383-8161

Marco Island St Mark's Episcopal Church **P** (626) 1101 N Collier Blvd 34145-2507 (Mail to: 1101 N Collier Blvd 34145-2507) Kyle Bennett Alden Burhoe John Ineson Susan Price (239) 394-7242

Naples St Johns Episcopal Church **P** (485) 500 Park Shore Dr 34103-3537 (Mail to: 500 Park Shore Dr 34103-3537) Joseph Maiocco Christian Maxfield (239) 261-2355

Naples St Monica Episcopal Church **P** (482) 7070 Immokalee Rd 34119-8845 (Mail to: 7070 Immokalee Rd 34119-8845) Kathryn Schillreff Hipolito Fernandez-Reina (239) 591-4550

Naples St Pauls Episcopal Church **P** (190) 3901 Davis Blvd 34104-5010 (Mail to: 3901 Davis Blvd 34104-5010) Panel Guerrier Tara McGraw

(239) 643-0197

Naples Trinity by the Cove **P** (1416) 553 Galleon Dr 34102-7639 (Mail to: 553 Galleon Dr 34102-7639) Edward Gleason Jean Hite (239) 262-6581

New Prt Rchy St Stephens Episcopal Church **P** (219) 5326 Charles St 34652-3906 (Mail to: 5326 Charles St 34652-3906) Walcott Hunter (727) 849-4330

North Fort Myers All Souls Episcopal Church **M** (47) 14640 N Cleveland Ave 33903-3806 (Mail to: 14640 N Cleveland Ave 33903-3806) David Jackson Sandra Johnson Nancy Smith (239) 997-7685

North Port St Nathaniel Episcopal Church **P** (180) 4200 S Biscayne Dr 34287-1626 (Mail to: 4200 S Biscayne Dr 34287-1626) Margaret Koor Jo Popham (941) 426-2520

Osprey Church of the Holy Spirit **P** (109) 129 S Tamiami Trl 34229-9211 (Mail to: 129 S Tamiami Trl 34229-9211) Michael Todd (941) 966-1924

Palm Harbor St Alfreds Episcopal Church **P** (441) 1601 Curlew Rd 34683-6515 (Mail to: 1601 Curlew Rd 34683-6515) Gina Walsh-Minor (727) 785-1601

Palmetto St Marys Episcopal Church **P** (212) 1010 24th Ave W 34221-3540 (Mail to: 1010 24th Ave W 34221-3540) William De la Torre Glen Graczyk (941) 722-5292

Pinellas Park St Giles Episcopal Church **P** (342) 8271 52nd St North 33781-1518 (Mail to: 8271 52nd St North 33781-1518) Marion Brown William De la Torre Deborah Self (727) 544-6856

Plant City St Peters Episcopal Church **P** (562) 302 N Carey St 33563-4316 (Mail to: 302 N. Carey St 33563-4316) Thomas Thoeni (813) 752-5061

Pt Charlotte St James Episcopal Church **P** (448) 1365 Viscaya Dr 33952-2519 (Mail to: 1365 Viscaya Dr 33952-2519) Arthur Lee Cesar Olivero (941) 627-4000

Punta Gorda Church of the Good Shepherd **P** (525) 401 W Henry St 33950-5905 (Mail to: 401 W Henry St 33950-5905) Roy Tuff Jane Kelly Judith Roberts (941) 639-2757

Safety Harbor Church of the Holy Spirit **P** (131) 601 Phillippe Pkwy 34695-3148 (Mail to: 601 Phillippe Pkwy 34695-3148) Raynald Bonoan (727) 725-4726

Sanibel Church of Saint Michael & All Angels Episcopal Church **P** (327) 2304 Periwinkle Way 33957-3209 (Mail to: 2304 Periwinkle Way 33957-3209) Ellen Sloan Alan Kelmereit

Sarasota Church of the Nativity **P** (481) 5900 N Lockwood Ridge Rd 34243-2523 (Mail to: 5900 N Lockwood Ridge Rd 34243-2523) Charles Mann (941) 355-3262

Sarasota Church of the Redeemer **P** (1976) 222 S Palm Ave 34236-6727 (Mail to: 222 S Palm Ave 34236-6727) Fredrick Robinson Mario Castro Richard Marsden Charleston Wilson

(941) 955-4263

Sarasota St Boniface Church **P** (883) 5615 Midnight Pass Rd 34242-1721 (Mail to: 5615 Midnight Pass Rd 34242-1721) John Chrisman Ralph McGimpsey Andrea Taylor (941) 349-5616

Sarasota St Margaret of Scotland Church **P** (232) 8700 State Rd #72 7 34241 (Mail to: 8700 State Road 72 34241-9578) Kathlyn Gilpin Richard Kemmler (941) 925-2525

Sarasota St Wilfred Episcopal Church **P** (199) 3773 Wilkinson Rd 34233-3607 (Mail to: 3773 Wilkinson Rd 34233-3607) Virginia Herring

Seminole St Anne of Grace Church **M** (335) 6650 113th St North 33772-6214 (Mail to: 6650 113th St 33772-6214) Stephen Ankudowich John Hyde (727) 392-4483

Spring Hill St Andrews Episcopal Church **P** (383) 2301 Deltona Blvd 34606 (Mail to: PO Box 5026 34611-5026) Lance Wallace

St James City St Johns Episcopal Church **M** (60) 7771 Stringfellow Rd 33956-2805 (Mail to: 7771 Stringfellow Road 33956-2805) Mary Piper (239) 283-1820

St Petersburg St Albans Episcopal Church **P** (157) 330 85th Ave 33706-1525 (Mail to: 330 85th Ave 33706-1525) (727) 360-8406

St Petersburg St Augustine's Episcopal Church **P** (83) No 2920 26th Ave South 33712-3328 (Mail to: 2920 26th Ave S 33712-3328) Robert Whitlock

St Petersburg St Bartholomews Episcopal Church **P** (298) 3747 34th St South 33711-3836 (Mail to: 3747 34th St S 33711-3836) William Burkett Lucien Watkins (727) 867-7015

St Petersburg St Matthews Church **M** (78) 738 Pinellas Point Dr S 33705-6255 (Mail to: 738 Pinellas Point Dr S 33705-6255) Harry Parsell (727) 866-2187

St Petersburg St Thomas Episcopal Church **P** (1116) 1200 Snell Isle Blvd NE 33704-3036 (Mail to: 1200 Snell Isle Blvd NE 33704-3099) John Suhar Janet Tunnell (727) 896-9641

St Petersburg St Vincents Episcopal Church **P** (303) 5441 Ninth Ave N 33710-6546 (Mail to: 5441 Ninth Ave N 33710-6546)

St. Petersburg St Bede Episcopal Church **P** (162) 2500 16th St N 33704-3132 (Mail to: 2500 16th St N 33704-3132) William Bosbyshell Frederick Mann (727) 823-7649

St. Petersburg St Peters Episcopal Cathedral **O** (915) 140 4th St N 33701-3807 (Mail to: PO Box 1581 33731-1581) Richard Earle Lynde May Stephen Morris Samuel Tallman Thomas Williams

Sun City Center St John the Divine Episcopal Church **P** (329) 1015 Del Webb East 33573 (Mail to: 1015 Del Webb Blvd. E. 33573) Leewin Miller Kevin Warner (813) 633-3970

Tampa Grace Episcopal Church **P** (478) 15102 Amberly Drive 33647-1618 (Mail to: 15102

Amberly Drive 33647-1618) Benjamin Twinamaani Ricardo Leanillo (813) 971-8484

Tampa Saint Mark's Episcopal Church Of Tampa **P** (260) 13312 Cain Rd 33625-4004 (Mail to: 13312 Cain Rd 33625-4004) Charles Allison (813) 962-3089

Tampa St Andrews Episcopal Church **P** (889) 509 E Twiggs St 33602-3916 (Mail to: 509 E Twigg Street 33602-3916) John Reese Jerold Stadel (813) 221-2035

Tampa St Chads Episcopal Church **M** (111) 5609 N Albany Ave 33603-1005 (Mail to: 5609 North Albany Avenue 33603-1005) Christian Villagomeza (813) 872-7545

Tampa St Clement's Church **P** (228) 706 W 113th Ave 33612-5605 (Mail to: 706 W 113th Ave 33612-5605) Andrew Heyes (813) 932-6204

Tampa St Francis Episcopal Church **M** (234) 912 E Sligh Ave 33604-5636 (Mail to: PO Box 9332 33674-9332) Livan Echazabal Martinez (813) 238-1098

Tampa St James House of Prayer **P** (161) 2708 N Central Avenue 33602-1602 (Mail to: 2708 N Central Avenue 33602-1602) Ernestein Flemister (813) 223-6090

Tampa St Johns Episcopal Church **P** (1667) 906 S Orleans Ave 33606-2941 (Mail to: 906 S Orleans Ave 33606-2941) Charles Connelly Robert Baker Alice Sadler (813) 259-1570

Tampa St Marys Episcopal Church **P** (300) 4311 W San Miguel St 33629-5623 (Mail to: 4311 W San Miguel St 33629-5623) Lester Durst (813) 251-1660

Tarpon Spgs All Saints Episcopal Church **P** (286) 1700 Keystone Rd 34688-4928 (Mail to: 1700 Keystone Rd 34689-8928) Wayne Farrell (727) 937-3881

Temple Terrace St Catherine of Alexandria Ch **P** (479) 502 Druid Hills Rd 33617-3853 (Mail to: 502 Druid Hills Road 33617-3853) Susan Latimer Alisa Carmichael (813) 988-6483

Valrico Church Of the Holy Innocents **P** (596) 604 N Valrico Rd 33594 (Mail to: 604 N Valrico Rd 33594-6874) Douglas Scharf (813) 689-3130

Venice Episcopal Ch of the Good Shepherd **P** (346) 1115 Center Rd 34292-3812 (Mail to: 1115 Center Rd 34292-3812) Gary Wilde (941) 497-7286

Venice St Marks Episcopal Church **P** (711) 513 Nassau St South 34285-2816 (Mail to: 513 Nassau St S 34285-2816) James Puryear Oliver Backhaus John Lawrence Joyce Treppa (941) 488-7714

Zephyrhills St Elizabeths Episcopal Church **P** (111) 5855 16th St 33542-3761 (Mail to: 5855 16th St 33542-3761) Ricardo Leanillo Edward Scully Hugh Wilkes (813) 782-1202

NON-PAROCHIAL CLERGY

Arnold WB *dcn* Greenwood SC
Ayerbe R Sarasota FL

Barley LE *dcn* Largo FL
Barnes BH *ret* Brunswick ME
Basden MP *ret* Naples FL
Bauknight MM *dcn* Saint Petersburg FL
Bennett GL *ret* Bradenton FL
Benter HW *ret* Sun City Center FL
Beshears ED *ret* St Petersburg FL
Birtch JEMK *ret* Lakeland FL
Bowers DD Venice FL
Branscombe MP Clearwater FL
Bretscher RG *ret* Athens GA
Brewer FW Franklin TN
Browning RGS *ret* Fort Myers FL
Brust JC *dcn* Naples FL
Bumsted DS Sarasota FL
Burchill GS *ret* Tampa FL
Cain GR *ret*
Carey PM Richmond VA
Carlton-Jones AH *dcn* Fort Myers FL
Carson BR *ret* Saint Petersburg FL
Carter JL *ret dcn* Largo FL
Carter RD *ret* Tampa FL
Cartwright GE *dcn* Valrico FL
Cathers RE *ret* Hendersonville NC
Cave GH *ret* Nashville TN
Chapman AJ *ret* Tampa FL
Conner GD *ret* Gulfport FL
Cooter ES Rotonda West FL
Copland EM *ret* Sarasota FL
Cummer EW *dcn*
Currea LA *ret* Tampa FL
Dakan KN *dcn* Sarasota FL
Davenport MEMC *ret* Arnold MD
Davis CL *ret* Venice FL
Davis PA *dcn* Bradenton FL
Day MH *ret* Saint Petersburg FL
De Montmollin DA *ret* Rutherfordton NC
Diaz JH *ret* Clearwater FL
Diefenbacher FH *ret* Valrico FL
Doing RB *ret* Fort Myers FL
Dopp WF *ret* San Marcos CA
Dorner MA *ret* Wesley Chapel FL
Durning MP Bradenton FL
Echols MW *dcn* Naples FL
Edwards TW *ret* Williamsburg VA
Ennis KK *dcn* Naples FL
Evans VC Okinawa
Faupel DW Naples FL
Fellows RG *ret* Tampa FL
Fisher EW *dcn* Saint Petersburg FL
Fleming PW *ret* Saint Petersburg FL
Frazier RM *dcn* Tampa FL
Gamble JR FL
Grady RC *ret* Fort Myers FL
Gray CN *ret* Parrish FL
Greene LT *dcn* Nokomis FL
Green-Witt MEA *dcn* Spring Hill FL
Grinnell LD *dcn* Tampa FL
Griscom DW *dcn* Bradenton FL
Hall JC Sarasota FL
Harris MWH *ret* Port Charlotte FL

Harrison FC *ret* Saint Augustine FL
Healy DC *dcn* Plant City FL
Henley EJ *ret* Temple Terrace FL
Herlihy PC *dcn* Bradenton FL
Heydt CR *ret* Sarasota FL
Howard N *ret* Clearwater FL
Jackson-McKinney SF *dcn*
Johansen PC *ret* New Philadelphia OH
Johns EW *ret* Port Charlotte FL
Johnson RL *ret* Clearwater FL
Kerr DR *ret* Tampa FL
Kezar DD *ret* Bradenton FL
Kircher KL Naples FL
Kress RP *ret* Apollo Beach FL
Kulp JE *ret* Phoenix AZ
Lacey JH *ret* Brooksville FL
Lampert RB *ret* Sarasota FL
Lewis SLG *ret* Sarasota FL
Linzel CB *dcn* Arlington TX
Lockley LS *dcn*
Lopez MA *dcn* Tampa FL
Lopez-Chaverra H *ret* Tampa FL
Loughran EJ *ret* Fort Myers FL
Mahurin SM *ret* Spring Hill FL
Martin RJ *ret* Riverview FL
Massey HB *ret* Franklin NC
Matijasic EG *ret* Sandusky OH
McCormick PA *dcn* Palm Harbor FL
McCurtain GR *ret* Largo FL
McDowell JL *ret* Little Rock AR
McManis DR *dcn* Lakewood Ranch FL
McPherson TD *dcn* Valdosta GA
Millott DL *dcn* Cumming GA
Millott DE *dcn*
Millott RT *dcn* Cumming GA
Monsour JV *ret* St George UT
Montooth CH *dcn* Decatur GA
Moore VS
Mort KD *dcn* St Petersburg FL
Mosher DR *ret* Seminole FL
Moyers WR *dcn* Naples FL
Murphy JTJ Walhalla SC
Neal MF Clearwater FL

O'Brien DR
O'Reilly JTJ *dcn* Sarasota FL
Ortiz MA Valrico FL
Ostenson RO *ret* Boulder CO
Paul RA *dcn* Palmetto FL
Peterson JR *ret* Tampa FL
Platt GM *dcn* Gladwin MI
Post SM *ret* Fort Myers FL
Powers PA *ret*
Remer DE *ret* Tampa FL
Rich ER *ret* Tampa FL
Riggle JF *ret* Saint Petersburg FL
Rogers AD *dcn* Sarasota FL
Rosenberg EJVF *dcn* Saint Petersburg FL
Rubright EAS *dcn* Clearwater FL
Rudacille SL *ret* Valrico FL
Ruth AR *dcn* Pensacola FL
Santosuosso JE *dcn* Lakeland FL
Scharf FE *ret* Hudson FL
Schuller CD Venice CA
Schwenke CF *ret* Tampa FL
Scotto VF *ret* Port Charlotte FL
Sircy MJ *dcn* Bradenton FL
Straughn RD *ret* Cape May NJ
Taber KW *ret* Grand Rapids MI
Terry MC *dcn* Sarasota FL
Tremmel MA *dcn* Parrish FL
Trively TC *ret* Asheville NC
Vaguener M *ret* Zephyrhills FL
Vasquez OA *ret* Naples FL
Vella JA *ret* Saint Petersburg FL
Vilord CL *dcn*
Wagenseil RA *ret* Largo FL
Walk EP *ret* Sarasota FL
Walker EM *ret* Mount Pleasant SC
Warner KW *ret* Boca Grande FL
Wilder TH *ret* Wamauma FL
Williamson JG *ret* Parrish FL
Willow MMG *dcn* Linden NJ
Wilson MH *ret* Midland MI
Wolfe JM *dcn* Tampa FL
Yates RG *dcn* Dade City FL
Zimmerman DL Tampa FL

DIOCESE OF SOUTHWESTERN VIRGINIA

(PROVINCE III)
Comprises 32 Southwestern VA counties
DIOCESAN OFFICE 1002 1st St. SW Roanoke VA 24016 (MAIL: Box 2279 Roanoke VA 24009-2279)
TEL (540) 342-6797, (800) 346-7982   FAX (540) 343-9114
E-MAIL lrobertson@dioswva.org   WEB www.dioswva.org

Previous Bishops—
Robt C Jett 1920-38, Henry D Phillips 1938-54, Wm H Marmion 1954-79, A Heath Light 1979-96, F Neff Powell 1996-2013

Bishop—Rt Rev Mark Allen Bourlakas (1077)
(Dio 20 Jul 2013)

Cn Admin AN Boyce; *Treas* J Hall 614 Academy Salem 24153; *Chanc* M Loftis PO Box 14125 Roanoke VA 24038; *Reg* L Robertson PO Box 2279

Roanoke VA 24009; *Hist* KL Brown 25 S Washington St Staunton 24401; *Ecum* Rev SR Stanley 1826 Mount Vernon Road SW Roanoke VA 24015

Stand Comm—Cler: H Beasley K Chase J Heck; *Lay: Pres* C Harveycutter M Cox N Moga

Dio Conv: 29-31 Jan 2016

PARISHES, MISSIONS, AND CLERGY

Abingdon Church of St Thomas **P** (151) Attn Elizabeth K Hurley 124 E Main St 24210-2808 (Mail to: 124 E Main St 24210-2808) Katherine Dunagan (276) 628-3606

Altavista St Peters Episcopal Church **P** (37) 1010 Broad St 24517-1806 (Mail to: PO Box 207 24517) Karen Kelly (434) 369-5291

Amherst Ascension Episcopal Church **P** (38) 253 S. Main St 24521-0810 (Mail to: PO Box 810 24521-0810) (434) 946-5498

Amherst St Marks Episcopal Church **P** (53) 670 Patrick Henry Hwy 24521-3982 (Mail to: PO Box 36 24533-0036) James Hubbard (434) 946-1121

Amherst St Pauls Episcopal Mission **M** (155) 2009 Kenmore Road 24521-3239 (Mail to: 2009 Kenmore Rd 24521-3239) (434) 946-2531

Arrington Trinity Episcopal Church **P** (37) 475 Oak Ridge Rd 22922-2610 (Mail to: 475 Oak Ridge Rd 22922-2610) (434) 263-5721

Bedford St Johns Episcopal Church **P** (207) 314 N Bridge St 24523-1928 (Mail to: 314 N Bridge St 24523-1928) Francis Brown (540) 586-9582

Bedford St Thomas Episcopal Church **M** (21) 9575 Big Island Highway 24523 (Mail to: PO Box 695 24523-0695) (540) 586-4768

Big Stone Gap Christ Episcopal Church **P** (44) 106 Clinton Avenue PO Box 778 24219 (Mail to: PO Box 778 24219-0778) Robert Moore (276) 523-0401

Blacksburg Christ Episcopal Church **P** (632) 120 Church St NE 24060-3923 (Mail to: PO Box 164 24063-0164) Scott West Emily Lukanich (540) 552-2411

Blue Grass Epis Church of the Good Shepherd **P** (34) 3678 Blue Grass Valley Rd 24413-0007 (Mail to: PO Box 7 24413-0007) Robert Gilman (540) 474-2175

Bluefield St Marys Episcopal Church **P** (69) 30 Logan St 24605-1404 (Mail to: PO Box 990 24605-0990) (276) 322-0487

Bristol Emmanuel Episcopal Church **P** (237) 700 Cumberland Street 24201 (Mail to: 700 Cumberland St. 24203-4124) Joe Dunagan (276) 669-9488

Buchanan Trinity Episcopal Church **P** (27) 19460 Main St 24066-2701 (Mail to: PO Box 459 24066-0459)

Buena Vista Christ Episcopal Church **P** (27) 2246 Walnut Ave 24416-2702 (Mail to: 2246 Walnut Ave 24416-2702) (540) 261-3929

Callaway St Peters Episcopal Church **P** (109) 65 Rock Ridge Rd 24067-5701 (Mail to: 65 Rock Ridge Rd 24067-5701) (540) 483-5370

Christiansbrg St Thomas Episcopal Church **P** (238) 103 E Main St 24073-3032 (Mail to: PO Box 236 24068-0236) (540) 382-4365

Clifton Forg St Andrews Episcopal Church **P** (11) 516 McCormick Blvd 24422-1137 (Mail to: 516 McCormick Blvd 24422-1137) (540) 863-3041

✠ **Covington** All Saints Chapel **Other** 414 Boys' Home Rd 24426-5539 (Mail to: 414 Boys' Home Rd 24426-5539) Connie Gilman (540) 965-7700

Covington Emmanuel Episcopal Church **P** (41) 138 N Maple Ave 24426-1545 (Mail to: PO Box 709 24426-0709) Lebaron Taylor (540) 965-5626

Fincastle St Marks Episcopal Church **P** (123) 111 S Roanoke St 24090 (Mail to: PO Box 277 24090-0277) (540) 473-2370

Forest St Stephens Episcopal Church **P** (113) 1695 Perrowville Rd 24551-2258 (Mail to: 1695 Perrowville Rd 24551-2258) Ralph Laycock (434) 525-5511

Galax Church of the Good Shepherd **P** (71) 9441 Grayson Parkway 24333 (Mail to: PO Box 1266 24333-1266) (276) 236-4957

Glasgow St John Episcopal Church **M** (16) 1002 Blue Ridge Rd 24555-2160 (Mail to: PO Box 507 24555-0607) (540) 258-2959

Hot Springs St Lukes Episcopal Church **P** (93) Rte 220 24445 (Mail to: PO Box 779 24445-0779) Jerry Heidel (540) 839-2279

Lexington R E Lee Memorial Church **P** (426) 123 W Washington St 24450-2122 (Mail to: 123 W Washington St 24450-2122) Francis Crittenden Robert Crewdson (540) 463-4981

Lynchburg Grace Memorial Episcopal Church **P** (226) 1021 New Hampshire Ave 24502-1216 (Mail to: 1021 New Hampshire Ave 24502-1216) Catharine Montgomery (434) 846-3156

Lynchburg St Johns Episcopal Church **P** (1256) 200 Boston Ave 24503-0123 (Mail to: PO Box 3123 24503-0123) William Watson Kimberly Glenn

Lynchburg St Pauls Episcopal Church **P** (510) 7th & Clay St 24504 (Mail to: 605 Clay St 24504-2460) William Bumgarner Diane Vie Todd Vie

Lynchburg Trinity Episcopal Church **P** (128) 104 Walnut Hollow Rd 24503-4213 (Mail to: PO Box 3278 24503-4778) James Young (434) 384-2257

Marion Christ Episcopal Church **P** (103) 401 W Main St 24354-2417 (Mail to: 401 W Main St 24354-2417) Emily Edmondson (276) 783-8050

Martinsville Christ Episcopal Church **P** (287) 321 E Church Street 24112-2981 (Mail to: 311 E Church St 24112-2927)

Martinsville St Pauls Episcopal Church **M** (27) 904 Fayette St 24112-3432 (Mail to: 904 Fayette

St 24112-3432) Gene Anderson (276) 790-2612

Massies Mill Grace Church Massies Mill **P** (50) 1934 Crab Tree Falls Hwy 22967 (Mail to: PO Box 148 22967) Marion Kanour (434) 277-8926

Massies Mill Peace in the Valley Church **M** (2) 1934 Crabtree Falls Hwy 22967 (Mail to: 395 Goodwin Creek Trl 22920-2853) Marian Windel (540) 456-6746

Moneta Trinity Ecumenical Parish **P** (118) 40 Lakemount Dr 24121-1915 (Mail to: 40 Lakemount Dr 24121-1915)

Monroe St Lukes Episcopal Church **M** (5) 3788 Buffalo Springs Tpke 24574-3104 (Mail to: PO Box 222 24572-0222) (434) 845-3446

Norton All Saints Episcopal Church **P** (64) Virginia Ave & 11th St 24273 (Mail to: PO Box 227 24273-0227) Robert Beauchamp (276) 679-3185

Pearisburg Christ Episcopal Church **P** (39) 529 Wenonah Ave. 24134 (Mail to: PO Box 360 24134-0360) Sarah Morris (540) 921-3033

Pocahontas Christ Episcopal Church **M** (23) Water St 24635-0322 (Mail to: PO Box 127 24635-0127) (276) 322-0487

Pulaski Christ Episcopal Church **P** (76) 144 N Washington Ave 24301-0975 (Mail to: PO Box 975 24301-0975) (540) 980-2413

Radford Grace Episcopal Church **P** (150) 210 4th St 24141-1523 (Mail to: 210 4th St 24141-1523) David Rose Sarah Morris (540) 639-3494

Richlands Trinity Episcopal Church **P** (46) 107 Hill Creek Rd 24641-2032 (Mail to: 2518 2nd St 24641-2222)

Roanoke Christ Episcopal Church **P** (408) 1101 Franklin Rd SW 24016-4309 (Mail to: 1101 Franklin Rd SW 24016-4397) Alexander MacPhail Melissa Hays-Smith (540) 343-0159

Roanoke St Elizabeths Episcopal Church **P** (73) 2339 Grandin Rd SW 24015-3916 (Mail to: PO Box 4706 24015-0706) Jonathan Harris (540) 774-5183

Roanoke St James Episcopal Church **P** (228) 4515 Delray St NW 24012-2209 (Mail to: 4515 Delray St NW 24012-2209) Susan Bentley William Eanes (540) 366-4157

Roanoke St John Episcopal Church **P** (1672) 1 Mountain Ave SW 24016-5109 (Mail to: PO Box 257 24002-0257) Whitney Burton Eric Long (540) 343-9341

Rocky Mount Trinity Episcopal Church **P** (160) 15 East Church Street 24151 (Mail to: PO Box 527 24151-0527) David Taylor (540) 483-5038

Saint Paul St Marks Episcopal Church **P** (23) Broad And Fifth Ave 24283 (Mail to: PO Box 227 24273) Robert Beauchamp (276) 679-3185

Salem St Pauls Episcopal Church **P** (360) 42 E Main St 24153-3807 (Mail to: 42 E Main St 24153-3807) James Lively David Dixon

Saltville St Pauls Episcopal Church **M** (15) 370 E Main St 24370 (Mail to: c/o The Rev Dr

Christopher Mason PO Box 96 28684) (276) 791-3175

Staunton Emmanuel Episcopal Church **P** (192) 300 W Frederick St 24401-3328 (Mail to: 300 W Frederick St 24401-3328) Shelby Owen

Staunton Good Shepherd Folly Mills **M** (44) 809 Lee Jackson Hwy 24401-5510 (Mail to: 809 Lee Jackson Hwy 24401-5510) (540) 377-9449

Staunton Trinity Episcopal Church **P** (482) 214 W Beverley St 24401-4205 (Mail to: PO Box 208 24402-0208) Paul Nancarrow John Lane (540) 886-9132

Tazewell Stras Memorial Epis Church **P** (67) 211 N Central Ave 24651-1005 (Mail to: PO Box 342 24651-0342)

Waynesboro St Johns Episcopal Church **P** (398) 473 S Wayne Ave 22980-4739 (Mail to: PO Box 945 22980-0693) Alan Webster (540) 942-4136

Wytheville St John's Episcopal Church **P** (209) 275 E Main St 24382-2323 (Mail to: 275 E Main St 24382-2323) (276) 228-2562

NON-PAROCHIAL CLERGY

Ambler JJ *ret* Amherst VA
Baker KD Charleston SC
Beasley HR *ret* Galax VA
Brodie RE *ret* Salem VA
Bunn GS *ret* Bristol TN
Burchard RC *ret* Dawsonville GA
Carroll VJ Richlands VA
Chase KB *dcn*
Copenhaver RT *ret* Daleville VA
Covert EM *ret* Fort Defiance VA
Cox RD *ret* Lexington VA
Crews NA *ret* Virginia Beach VA
Crites RT Glasgow VA
Curran CD *ret* Henrico VA
Elphee DT *ret*
Fife RH *ret* Roanoke VA
Frazier MW Bristol VA
Fuller JF Burlington NC
Furgerson JA *ret* Lexington VA
Furlow MD Arrington VA
Gilman JE *dcn* Staunton VA
Guinta DG Fort Myers FL
Hanckel EJ *ret* Martinsville VA
Heck JH Callaway VA
Henry JR *ret* Williamsburg VA
Hershbell JP *ret* Lexington VA
Houk VL *ret* Pulaski VA
Howard KD *ret* Kernersville NC
Hunley DH *ret* Roanoke VA
Jones RJ *ret* Alexandria VA
Kramer CA
Lawrence RJ *ret* Niskayuna NY
Lehman SC *ret* Cincinnati OH
Lipscomb CL *ret* Lynchburg VA
Litzenburg TV Lexington VA
Lloyd RB *ret* Blacksburg VA
Mackin MR Roanoke VA
Mackintosh LP Lynchburg VA

Mannschreck MLC Bartlesville OK
Mason CP *ret* Todd NC
Mathews E Richmond VA
McCoy FJ *ret* Norton VA
McNeer CC *ret* Abingdon VA
Milam TR
Mitchell PW *dcn*
Moritz BE *ret* Richmond VA
Mustard GT *ret* Hoschton GA
Novak-Scofield EP *dcn* Abingdon VA
Parrish JK *ret* Roseland VA
Parrish WP *ret* Lynchburg VA
Payden-Travers CA *ret* Lynchburg VA
Peyton SC *dcn*
Pollina RG *ret*

Renick VT *ret* Rocky Mount VA
Riddick DH *ret* Glade Hill VA
Sigloh JE *ret* Crozet VA
Sinclair RD *ret* Charlottesville VA
Stanley SR *ret* Fincastle VA
Streever HB Abingdon VA
Tarpley KW *ret* Wytheville VA
Thacker JR *ret* Osprey FL
Trapp GJ *ret* Harpswell ME
Tyree RD *ret* Holyoke MA
Vance TK *ret* Sewanee TN
Waff KC *dcn* Bedford VA
Wells LD Martinsville VA
Wilkinson JP *dcn* Staunton VA
Wylie CR *ret* Abingdon VA

DIOCESE OF SPOKANE

(PROVINCE VIII)
Comprises Eastern Washington and Northern Idaho
DIOCESAN OFFICE 245 E 13th Ave Spokane WA 99202-1114
TEL (509) 624-3191   FAX (509) 747-0049
E-MAIL malloryw@spokanediocese.org   WEB www.spokanediocese.org

Previous Bishops—
Lemuel H Wells 1892-1913, Herman
Page 1915-23, Edward M Cross
1924-54, Russell S Hubbard m 1954
dio 1964-67, John R Wyatt 1967-78,
Leigh A Wallace Jr 1979-90, Frank J
Terry coadj 1990-91 Bp 91-99

Bishop — James E Waggoner Jr (961) (Dio 21
Oct 2000)

Cn to Ord Rev Cn K Schomberg; *Trans Min* Rev
Cn S Cleveley; *Sec Conv* Rev J Neuberger; *Treas* G
Durrie; *Chanc* S Miller of J Scott Miller, PS 201 W
No River Dr Ste 500 Spokane WA 99201; *Arch and
Reg* G Lund; *Arch dcn* Rev T Nitz; *Trustee Bd Chair
Foundation* M Henneberry; *Fin Off* L Boss; *B Exec
Asst* M Ware; *COM Chair* Rev G Rehberg

Stand Comm The Rev MaryBeth Rivetti

Dio Conv: 14-16 Oct 2016 Lewiston ID

PARISHES, MISSIONS, AND CLERGY

Bonners Ferry St Marys Church **Chapel** (23) No
6633 Buchanan St 83805-8616 (Mail to: 113
Kullyspell Dr 83836-9754) (208) 267-3202

Cashmere St James Episcopal Church **M** (68)
222 Cottage Ave 98815-1004 (Mail to: 222
Cottage Ave 98815-1004) Carol Forhan Robert
Hasseries (509) 782-1590

Chelan St Andrews Episcopal Church **P** (69) 120
East Wooden Ave 98816 (Mail to: PO Box 1226
98816-1226) Linda Mayer

Cheney St Pauls Episcopal Church **M** (38) 625 C
St 99004-1747 (Mail to: 625 C St 99004-1747)
Judith Soule (509) 235-6150

Coeur D Alene St Lukes Episcopal Church **P**
(293) 501 E Wallace Ave 83814-2955 (Mail to:
501 E Wallace Ave 83814-2955) Patrick Bell
Robert Runkle (208) 664-5533

Colville St Johns Episcopal Church **M** (14) 2000 E
Hawthorne Ave 99114-9357 (Mail to: PO Box
601 99114-0601) (509) 684-2839

Dayton Grace Episcopal Church **M** (17) 301 S 3rd
St 99328-1332 (Mail to: 301 S 3rd St 99328-
1332) (509) 382-4795

Dover Holy Spirit Episcopal Church **M** (57) 55
Rocky Point Road 83825 (Mail to: 217 Cedar
St #336 83864-1410) Marjorie Stanley (208)
263-7078

Ellensburg Grace Episcopal Church **P** (158) 1201
N B Street 98926-2578 (Mail to: PO Box 644
98926-1918) (509) 962-2951

Ephrata St John the Baptist Epis Church **M** (68)
701 1st Ave NW 98823-1504 (Mail to: PO Box
295 98823-0295) Anthony Green (509) 754-
4949

Grand Coulee St Dunstans Episcopal Church **M**
(48) 328 Grand Coulee E 99133 (Mail to: PO
Box 125 99133-0125) (509) 989-9672

Grangeville Holy Trinity Episcopal Church **M**
(32) 311 S Hall St 83530-2011 (Mail to: 311 S
Hall St 83530-2011) Chris Hagenbuch (208)
451-0645

Kennewick St Pauls Episcopal Church **P** (357)
1609 W 10th Ave 99336-5200 (Mail to: PO Box
6857 99336-0529) Jo Anne Lediard Marilynn
Yule (509) 582-8635

Lewiston Church of the Nativity **P** (112) 731 8th
St 83501-2626 (Mail to: 731 8th St 83501-2626)
Gretchen Rehberg

Moscow St Marks Episcopal Church **P** (134) 111 S Jefferson St 83843-2859 (Mail to: 111 S Jefferson St 83843-2859) Robin Biffle (208) 882-2022

Moses Lake St Martins Episcopal Church **P** (88) 416 E Nelson Rd 98837-2383 (Mail to: 416 E Nelson Rd 98837-2383) Gayle Gaither (509) 765-3369

Omak St Annes Episcopal Church **M** (72) 639 W Ridge Dr 98841-3251 (Mail to: PO Box 3251 98841-3251) Stanalee Wright (509) 826-5815

Oroville Trinity Episcopal Church **M** (103) 604 Central Ave. 98844-0186 (Mail to: PO Box 1270 98844-1270) (509) 476-2230

Pomeroy St Peters Church **P** (39) 710 High St 99347 (Mail to: PO Box 82 99347-0082) William Totten (509) 843-1871

Prosser St Matthews Episcopal Church **M** (61) 317 7th St 99350-1180 (Mail to: PO Box 828 99350-0828) (509) 830-6318

Pullman St. James Episcopal Church **P** (172) 1410 NE Stadium Way 99163-3841 (Mail to: 1410 NE Stadium Way 99163-3897) Mary Rivetti Dianne Lowe Theodore Nitz Wilhelmina Sarai-Clark (509) 332-1742

Republic Episcopal Church of the Redeemer **M** (6) 3 Klondike Rd 99166-9701 (Mail to: PO Box 342 99166-0342) (509) 775-3096

Richland All Saints Episcopal Church **P** (447) 1322 Kimball Ave 99354-3206 (Mail to: 1322 Kimball Ave 99354-3206) Jane Schmoetzer (509) 943-1169

Ritzville St Marks Episcopal Church **M** (5) W 4th Ave & S Adams St 99169 (Mail to: 309 W 10th Ave 99169-2257) (509) 659-0453

South Cle Elum Church of the Resurrection **M** (82) Kelly Clift PO Box 23 98943-0023 (Mail to: PO Box 701 98941-0701) (509) 649-2283

✠ **Spokane** Cathedral of St John the Evangelist **O** (739) 127 E 12th Ave 99202-1105 (Mail to: 127 E 12th Ave 99202-1105) William Ellis John Hay Nicholas Mather

Spokane St Andrews Episcopal Church **P** (145) 2404 N Howard St 99205-3215 (Mail to: 2404 N Howard St 99205-3215) Margaret Fisher (509) 325-5252

Spokane St Davids Episcopal Church **P** (373) 7315 N Wall St 99208-6102 (Mail to: PO Box 18917 99228-0917) (509) 466-3100

Spokane St Stephens Episcopal Church **P** (268) 5720 S Perry St 99223-6349 (Mail to: 5720 S Perry St 99223-6349) William Osborne Elaine Pitzer (509) 448-2255

Spokane West Central Episcopal Mission **M** (81) 1832 W Dean Ave 99201-1829 (Mail to: PO Box 8508 99203) Kris Christensen (509) 326-6471

Sunnyside Holy Trinity Episcopal Church **P** (117) 327 E Edison Ave 98944 (Mail to: 327 E Edison Ave 98944) Peter Kalunian (509) 837-4727

Veradale Church of the Resurrection **P** (196) 15319 E 8th Ave 99037-8828 (Mail to: PO Box 14771 99214-0771) Linda Bartholomew (509) 926-6450

Walla Walla St Pauls Church **P** (502) 323 Catherine St 99362-3021 (Mail to: 323 Catherine St 99362-3082) Thomas Rambo Ernest Campbell Robert Kaye (509) 529-1083

Wallace Holy Trinity Episcopal Church **M** (27) 312 4th St 83873-2202 (Mail to: 312 4th St 83873-2202) (208) 752-7031

Wenatchee St Luke's Episcopal Church **P** (150) 428 King St 98801-2846 (Mail to: PO Box 1642 98807-1642) Frances Twiggs (509) 662-5635

Yakima St Michaels Episcopal Church **P** (67) 5 S Naches Ave 98901-2726 (Mail to: 5 S Naches Ave 98901-2726) Frank Cowell (509) 453-4881

Yakima St Timothys Episcopal Church **P** (473) 4105 Richey Rd 98908-2662 (Mail to: 4105 Richey Rd 98908-2662) Anne Barton (509) 966-7370

Zillah Christ Episcopal Church **M** (28) Second & 4th 98953 (Mail to: PO Box 356 98953-0356) Joan Dahl David Hacker Elisabeth Kuhr (509) 829-3020

NON-PAROCHIAL CLERGY

Biggers HH *dcn* Spokane WA
Bowman AC *ret* Ellensburg WA
Boyle PL *ret* Wenatchee WA
Campbell RD *ret* Colorado Springs CO
Campbell WE *ret* Denver CO
Carver BS *dcn* Sandpoint ID
Carver JP *ret* Sandpoint ID
Chandler PG
Cleveley SL Moscow ID
Coppen CJ Spokane WA
Day JE *ret* Elk Grove CA
Doll MC *ret* Tucson AZ
Empsall GM *dcn* Coeur D Alene ID
English AC *dcn* Touchet WA
Feerer JE
Fitzgibbons MJ *ret* Kennewick WA
Fogelquist AH Fircrest WA
Ford SE *ret*
Grabner JD Pullman WA
Green KW *ret* Havre MT
Griffin J *ret* Richland WA
Hale LM *dcn* Sunnyside WA
Harland MF Medical Lake WA
Harrelson ES *ret* Yakima WA
Hawkins MA *dcn*
Hodgkins L *ret* The Dalles OR
Johnson VL *dcn* Richland WA
Kiefer LR *ret* Wenatchee WA
Killingstad ML Yakima WA
Kirking KC Seattle WA
Lamphere MK Spokane Valley WA
Larive AE *ret* Bellingham WA
Loposer EF *dcn* Spokane WA
Magee FH *ret* ST. ANDREWS -
McKee CL Ellensburg WA

Murphy TE *ret* Ashland OR
Nelson-Low J *ret* Spokane WA
Neuberger JL Spokane WA
Novak BEH *dcn* Spokane WA
Oshry MA Spokane WA
Philip K *ret* Spokane WA
Pollock C *dcn* Spokane WA
Pond FR *dcn* Spokane WA
Prehm KAT Yakima WA
Price SM
Redman NB *ret* Mead WA
Robison SLH *dcn* Richland WA

Schomburg KA Spokane WA
Shapton EL Ephrata WA
Stoffregen DLJ Spokane WA
Stoffregen MA Spokane WA
Totten JK *dcn* Florence OR
Walker DB *dcn* Spokane WA
Ward RP *ret* Eugene OR
Whitmore PM *ret* Pendleton OR
Wilder M *ret* Oroville WA
Wood CE *ret* Olympia WA
Woolley SE *ret* Walla Walla WA
Wysock CP Silverton OR

DIOCESE OF SPRINGFIELD
(PROVINCE V)
Comprises 60 counties of central and southern Illinois
DIOCESAN CENTER 821 S Second St Springfield IL 62704
TEL (217) 525-1876   FAX (217) 525-1877
E-MAIL diocese@episcopalspringfield.org   WEB www.episcopalspringfield.org

Previous Bishops—
Geo F Seymour 1878-1906, Chas R Hale coadj 1892-1900, Edward W Osborne coadj 1904 Bp 1906-16, Granville H Sherwood 1917-23, John C White 1924-47, Richard T Loring 1947-48, Chas A Clough 1948-61, Albert A Chambers 1962-72, Albert W Hillestad 1972-81, Donald M Hultstrand 1982-91, Peter H Beckwith 1992-2010

Bishop—The Rt Rev Daniel H Martins (Dio 19 March 2011)

Assisting Bishop—Rt Rev Donald J Parsons (691)

Archdcn The Ven SW Denney; *V Pres* The Rev DJ Halt; *Sec* The Rev GW Howard III; *Asst Sec* Rev S Howard; *Treas* R Matthews; *Chanc* KJ Babb; *Trustee* D Monty; *COM* The Very Rev JR Henry; *ECW* J Goossens; *Dio Admin* S Spring; *Depts—Chr Ed* B Techau; *Comm* M Coffman; *Evan & Spir Enrich* The Rev DJ Halt; *Fin* The Very Rev ME Evans; *Gen Miss Strat* Rev BU DeGooyer; *Chr Soc Conc* The Rev SL Black; *Stew* R Winn; *Ecum* The Rev GEL Scanlon; *Yng Adlt & Higher Ed Min* The Rev SD Ferrell; *Yth Wk* B Hankinson; *Nat & World Miss* S Moore

Stand Comm—Cler: Pres DJ Halt CL Ashmore RA Swan IC Wetmore *Lay:* R Matthews C DeWitt A Waight C McCrary

Deans—Darrow DD Coleman; *Eastern* DM Baumann; *Hale* KG Jeffrey; *Northern* ME Evans; *Northeastern* BH Maynard; *Northwestern* JR Henry

Dio Conv: 21-22 Oct 2016 St Andrew's Edwardsville

PARISHES, MISSIONS, AND CLERGY

Albion St Johns Episcopal Church **M** (15) 20 E Cherry St 62806-1302 (Mail to: C/O The Rev Bill Howard PO Box 1810 62864-0036) George Howard (618) 242-6594

Alton St Pauls and Trinity Chapel **P** (352) 10 E 3rd St 62002-6201 (Mail to: 10 E 3rd St 62002-6201)

Alton Trinity Chapel **SC** 1901 State St 62002-6201 (Mail to: 10 E 3rd St 62002-6201) (618) 465-9149

Belleville St Georges Episcopal Church **P** (539) 105 E D St 62220-1205 (Mail to: 105 E D St 62220-1205) Dale Coleman Margaret Coleman (618) 233-6320

Bloomington St Matthews Episcopal Church **P** (513) 1920 E Oakland Ave 61701-5755 (Mail to: 1920 E Oakland Ave 61701-5755) David Halt (309) 662-4646

Cairo Church of the Redeemer **M** (8) 6th & Washington Ave 62914 (Mail to: 821 S 2nd Street 62704-2601) James Muriuki (618) 734-1443

Carbondale St Andrews Episcopal Church **P** (72) 402 W Mill St 62901-2728 (Mail to: 402 W Mill St 62901-2728) Kathryn Jeffrey (618) 529-4316

Carlinville St Pauls Episcopal Church **P** (48) 415 S Broad St 62626-2111 (Mail to: 415 S Broad St 62626-2111) John Henry (217) 854-6431

Centralia St Johns Episcopal Church **M** (21) 700 E Broadway 62801-3261 (Mail to: PO Box 1512 62801) Sylvia Howard Gene Tucker (618) 532-3767

Champaign Chapel of St John the Divine **P** (207) 1011 S. Wright St 61820-6249 (Mail to: 1011 S

Wright St 61820-6249) Sean Ferrell (217) 344-1924

Champaign Emmanuel Memorial Episcopal Church **P** (407) 102 N State St 61820-3908 (Mail to: 208 W University Ave 61820-3912) Beth Maynard Christine Hopkins (217) 352-9827

Chesterfield St Peters Episcopal Church **M** 110 East Lincoln Ave 62630 (Mail to: C/O St Paul's Church 415 S Broad St 62626-2111) (217) 854-6431

Danville Church of the Holy Trinity **P** (154) 308 N Vermilion St 61832-4770 (Mail to: 308 N Vermilion St 61832-4770) (217) 442-3498

Decatur St Johns Episcopal Church **P** (232) 130 W Eldorado St 62522-2111 (Mail to: 130 W Eldorado St 62522-2111) Richard Swan (217) 428-4461

Edwardsville St Andrews Episcopal Church **P** (227) 406 Hillsboro Ave 62025-1730 (Mail to: 406 Hillsboro Ave 62025-1730) Ralph McMichael (618) 656-1929

Elkhart Church of St John the Baptist **SC** PO Box 386 62634 (Mail to: PO Box 386 62656-0386) James Cravens (217) 732-7609

Glen Carbon St Thomas Episcopal Church **M** (54) 182 Summit St 62034 (Mail to: 182 Summit St 62034) (618) 288-5620

Granite City St Bartholomews Episcopal Church **M** (25) 2167 Grand Ave 62040-4724 (Mail to: 2167 Grand Ave 62040-4724) (618) 876-9097

Harrisburg St Stephens Episcopal Church **M** (32) 101 E Church St 62946-1704 (Mail to: 101 E Church St 62946-1704) Timothy Goodman (618) 252-8239

Havana St Barnabas Episcopal Church **M** (38) 420 N Plum St 62644-1129 (Mail to: PO Box 343 62644-0343) (309) 543-2430

Jacksonville Trinity Episcopal Church **P** (87) 359 W State St 62650-2007 (Mail to: PO Box 488 62651-0488) Christopher Ashmore Thomas Langford (217) 245-5901

Lincoln Trinity Episcopal Church **P** (61) 402 Pekin St 62656-2033 (Mail to: PO Box 386 62656-0386) Mark Evans (217) 732-7609

Marion St James Episcopal Church **Chapel** (8) 301 E Thorn St 62959 (Mail to: 301 E Thorn St 62959-3159) (618) 993-2074

Mattoon Trinity Episcopal Church **M** (27) PO Box 302 61938-0302 (Mail to: PO Box 302 61938-0302) Anne Flynn Jeffrey Kozuszek (217) 234-4514

Morton All Saints Episcopal Church **M** (63) 201 W Chicago St 61550-1909 (Mail to: 329 S Plum Ave 61550-1856) Laurie Kellington (309) 266-9894

Mount Carmel St John the Baptist Episcopal Church **P** (39) 600 N Mulberry St 62863-2045 (Mail to: PO Box 674 62863-0674) Brant Hazlett (618) 262-7382

Mount Vernon Trinity Episcopal Church **P** (90) 1100 Harrison St 62864-3814 (Mail to: 1100 Harrison St 62864-3814) Benjamin Hankinson (618) 242-3434

Normal Christ the King Episcopal Church **P** (77) 1210 S Fell Ave 61761-3641 (Mail to: 1210 S Fell Ave 61761-3641) (309) 310-9574

O'Fallon St Michaels Episcopal Church **M** (169) 111 O'Fallon Troy Rd 62269-6703 (Mail to: 111 O'Fallon Troy Rd 62269-6703) Ian Wetmore (618) 632-6168

Pekin St Pauls Church Episcopal **P** (48) 349 Buena Vista Ave 61554-4288 (Mail to: 343 Buena Vista Ave 61554-4227) Laurie Kellington (309) 346-2615

Rantoul St Christopher Episcopal Church **M** (24) 1501 E Grove Ave 61866-2735 (Mail to: 1501 E Grove Ave 61866-2735) Steven Thorp (217) 892-2476

Robinson St Marys Episcopal Church **M** (17) 8996 E 1050th Ave 62454-4822 (Mail to: PO Box 442 62454-0442) Ann Tofani Kenneth Truelove (618) 544-8974

Salem St Thomas Episcopal Church **M** (41) 512 W Main St PO Box 622 62881-0622 (Mail to: PO Box 622 62881-0622) (618) 548-3560

✠ **Springfield** Cathedral Church of St Paul **O** (414) 815 So 2nd St 62704 (Mail to: 815 S 2nd St 62704-2601) Martha Bradley Gus Franklin Andrew Hook Gerald Raschke (217) 544-5135

Springfield Christ Episcopal Church **P** (141) 611 E Jackson St 62701 (Mail to: 611 E Jackson St 62701-1898) Gregory Tournoux (217) 523-1871

Springfield St Lukes Episcopal Church **M** (165) 1218 S Grand Ave E 62703-2621 (Mail to: 1218 S Grand Ave E 62703-2621) Shawn Denney (217) 528-5915

W Frankfort St Marks Episcopal Church **M** (48) 212 N Ida St 62896-2311 (Mail to: PO Box 97 62896-0097) Sheryl Black

NON-PAROCHIAL CLERGY

Alley AL *dcn* Champaign IL
Baumann DM *ret* Salem IL
Bennett VL *ret* Saint Charles MO
Bergner MJ South Hamilton MA
Blackburn EH *ret* Mason City IA
Bloom CR *ret* Chandler AZ
Boase DJ *ret* Godfrey IL
Boeve PD *ret* Fort Atkinson WI
Clavier AFM *ret* Glen Carbon IL
Coventry DE *dcn* Decatur IL
DeGooyer BU *dcn* Bloomington IL
Dicks PR *ret* Carlinville IL
Fedosuk JH *ret* Havana IL
Griffin JE West Frankfort IL
Hall EE Champaign IL
Hallett TJ *ret* Bloomington IN
Harmon RD *ret* Mount Vernon IL

Hoffman AR *ret* Saint Louis MO
Karanja DN Blythewood SC
Kellington BT *ret* Pekin IL
Koehler RB *ret* San Antonio TX
Langlois DH *ret* Chandler AZ
Lee MC *ret* Atlanta GA
Lewis PM Havana IN
Moore WH Wallace NC
Patton TD
Pence GE *ret* Edwardsville IL
Peters DW Mount Vernon IL
Phillips TL *ret* Champaign IL

Pugliese RA *ret* West Glover VT
Reischman CJ Decatur IL
Richmond JD Bartonville IL
Scanlon GEL *ret* Urbana IL
Schroeder DJ *ret* Brunswick ME
Sheldon JV Kings Bay GA
Stormer EA *ret* Springfield IL
Toland WL *ret* Springfield IL
Wall JF *ret* Fredericksburg VA
Ward MCM Bloomington IL
Wells DL Springfield IL
Winward MS Saco ME

SWITZERLAND

See Europe

DIOCESE OF TAIWAN

(PROVINCE VIII)
Comprises Taiwan and neighboring islands
DIOCESAN OFFICE 7 Ln 105 Hangchow S Rd Sec 1 Taipei Taiwan 10060 ROC
TEL 886-2-2341-1265   FAX 886-2-2396-2014
E-MAIL skh.tpe@msa.hinet.net   WEB www.episcopalchurch.org.tw

Previous Bishops—
Harry S Kennedy 1954-60, Chas
P Gilson suffr 1961-64, James CL
Wong 1965-70, James TM Pong
1971-79, PY Cheung 1980-87
John Chien 1988-2001

Bishop—Rt Rev David Jung-Hsin Lai (962) (Dio 25 Nov
2000) *Sec Conv* CN Yang *Treas* Amy BH Lin *Chanc* HHP Ma

Stand Comm—Cler: SY C Lin YR Chang LL Chang CC Lee LF Lin ML Wu *Lay:* CN Yang YH Ti YY Kuo BS Hu G Chern HW Chuang *Honorable Chairperson* HHP Ma

Dio Conv: TBD

PARISHES, MISSIONS, AND CLERGY

✠ **Taipei** St John Cathedral **O** 280 Fu-Hsing S Rd Sec 2 TAIWAN 10663 (Mail to: 280 Fu-Hsing S Rd Sec 2 Taipei TAIWAN 10663) Elizabeth Wei

Keelung Holy Trinity **P** 163 Tung-Ming Road TAIWAN 20141 (Mail to: 163 Tung-Ming Road Keelung TAIWAN 20105) Justin Lin

Keelung St Stephen **M** 1F No29 Aly 6 Ln 168 Zhonghe Rd Zhongshan Dist TAIWAN 20347 (Mail to: 1F No29 Aly 6 Ln 168 Zhonghe Rd Zhongshan Dist Keelung TAIWAN 20347) Julia Lin

Taipei Good Shepherd **P** 509 Chung-Cheng Rd Shihlin Dist TAIWAN 11168 (Mail to: 509 Chung-Cheng Rd Shihlin Dist Taipei TAIWAN 11168) Philip Lin

New Taipei City Advent **P** 499 Sec 4 Tam King Rd 25135 Tamsui TAIWAN 25135 (Mail to: 499 Sec 4 Tam King Rd 25135 Tamsui New Taipei City TAIWAN 25135) Lennon Chang

Taoyuan City Christ **M** 1F No29 Ln 282 Wenhua St Pingzhen Dist TAIWAN 32450 (Mail to: 1F No29 Ln 282 Wenhua St Pingzhen Dist Taoyuan City TAIWAN 32450) Joseph Ho

Taichung St James **P** No 23 Wu-Chuan West Road Sec 1 TAIWAN 40348 (Mail to: No 23 Wu-Chuan West Road Sec 1 Taichung TAIWAN 40348) Lily Chang

Taichung Leading Star **M** No8 Ln 530 Guangxing Rd Taiping Dist TAIWAN 41148 (Mail to: No8 Ln 530 Guangxing Rd Taiping Dist Taichung TAIWAN 41148) Sam Cheng

Chiayi St Peters **M** 8 Hsing Chung St TAIWAN 60047 (Mail to: 8 Hsing Chung St Chiayi TAIWAN 60047) Simon Tsou

Chiayi County Goubei Mission **PS** No 70-1 Goubei Village Dalin Township TAIWAN 62245 (Mail to: No 70-1 Goubei Village Dalin Township Chiayi County TAIWAN 62245) Simon Tsou

Tainan Grace **M** No24 Ln 550 Chongde Rd East Dist TAIWAN 70171 (Mail to: No24 Ln 550 Chongde Rd East Dist Tainan TAIWAN 70171) Keith Lee

Kaohsiung St Andrew **PS** No311 Sec 2 Jiading Rd Qieding Dist TAIWAN 85241 (Mail to: No311 Sec 2 Jiading Rd Qieding Dist Kaohsiung TAIWAN 85241) Chen-Chang Cheng

Kangshan All Saints **P** No5 Jieshou Rd Gangshan Dist TAIWAN 82044 (Mail to: No5 Jieshou Rd Gangshan Dist Kaohsiung TAIWAN 82044) Leo Tzeng

Kaohsiung St Paul **M** 200 Tzu Chiang 1 Rd San Min Dist TAIWAN 80749 (Mail to: 200 Tzu Chiang 1 Rd San Min Dist Kaohsiung

TAIWAN 80749) Philip Ho

Kaohsiung St Timothy **P** 3F # 262 Chung-Hsiao 1 Rd Hsin-Hsing Dist TAIWAN 80055 (Mail to: 3F # 262 Chung-Hsiao 1 Rd Hsin-Hsing Dist Kaohsiung TAIWAN 80055) Richard Lee

Pingtung St Mark **M** 120-11 Chung Hsiao Rd TAIWAN 90063 (Mail to: 120-11 Chung Hsiao Rd Pingtung Taiwan 90063)

Hualien St Lukes **M** No 1-6 Ming Hsin St TAIWAN 97050 (Mail to: 1-6 Ming Hsin St Hualien TAIWAN 97050) Joseph Wu

---

STATE OF TENNESSEE
Dioceses of East Tennessee (ETN), Tennessee (TN), and West Tennessee (WTN)

Antioch—TN	Dickson—TN	Lebanon—TN	Rogersville—ETN
Athens—ETN	Dyersburg—WTN	Lookout Mtn—ETN	Rossview—TN
Atoka—WTN	Elizabethton—ETN	Loudon—ETN	Rugby—ETN
Battle Creek—ETN	Fayetteville—TN	Madison—TN	Saint Andrews—TN
Bolivar—WTN	Franklin—TN	Manchester—TN	Sevierville—ETN
Brentwood—TN	Ft Ogelthorpe—ETN	Maryville—ETN	Sewanee—TN
Bristol—ETN	Gallatin—TN	Mason—WTN	Seymour—ETN
Brownsville—WTN	Gatlinburg—ETN	McMinnville—TN	Shelbyville—TN
Chattanooga—ETN	Germantown—WTN	Memphis—WTN	Sherwood—TN
Clarksville—TN	Greeneville—ETN	Millington—WTN	Signal Mtn—ETN
Cleveland—ETN	Harriman—ETN	Monteagle—TN	Smyrna—TN
Collierville—WTN	Hendersonville—TN	Morristown—ETN	Somerville—WTN
Columbia—TN	Hixson—ETN	Murfreesboro—TN	So Pittsburg—ETN
Cookeville—TN	Humboldt—WTN	Nashville—TN	Spring Hill—TN
Copperhill—ETN	Jackson—WTN	Newport—ETN	Springfield—TN
Cordova—WTN	Jefferson City—ETN	New Johnsonville—TN	Tracy City—TN
Covington—WTN	Johnson City—ETN	Norris—ETN	Tullahoma—TN
Cowan—TN	Jonesborough—ETN	Oak Ridge—ETN	Union City—WTN
Crossville—ETN	Kingsport—ETN	Ooltewah—ETN	Winchester—TN
Cumberland Furnace—	Knoxville—ETN	Paris—WTN	
TN	LaFollette—ETN	Pulaski—TN	
Dechard—TN	La Grange—WTN	Ripley—WTN	

DIOCESE OF TENNESSEE
(PROVINCE IV)
Comprises the middle section of the State of Tennessee
DIOCESAN OFFICE 3700 Woodmont Blvd Nashville TN 37215
TEL (615) 251-3322   FAX (615) 251-8010
E-MAIL info@edtn.org   WEB http://edtn.org/

Previous Bishops—
James H Otey 1834-63, Chas T Quintard 1865-98, Thomas F Gailor coadj 1893 Bp 1898-1935, Troy Beatty coadj 1919-22, James hM Maxon coadj 1922 Bp 1935-47, Edmund P Dandridge coadj 1938 Bp 1947-53, Theodore N Barth coadj 1948 Bp

1953-61, John Vander Horst suffr 1955-1961 coadj 1961 Bp 1961-1977, William E Sanderscoadj 1962 Bp 1977-1984, W Fred Gates Jr suffr 1966-1982, Geo L Reynolds 1985-91, Bertram N Herlong 1993-2006

Bishop—Rt Rev John C Bauerschmidt (1013) (Dio 27 Jan 2007)

Cn to Ord Rev Cn PP Snare; *Cn for Spec Proj Rev Cn* F Dettwiller; *Treas* WA Stringer; *Chanc* GS Aden; V

Chanc J Ramsey; *Asst Treas* D Shriver; *COM Chair* E Arning; *CFO* J Pate; *Comm* C Hendrix; *Exec Asst* A Stephenson

Stand Comm—Cler: B Barton B Dennler R Dunnavant; *Lay:* C Clark D Clayton B Smith

Dio Conv: 22-23 Jan 2016 St. George's Church Nashville TN

PARISHES, MISSIONS, AND CLERGY

Antioch St Marks Episcopal Church **P** (135) 3100 Murfreesboro Pike 37013-2202 (Mail to: PO Box 741 37011-0741) Battle Beasley (615) 361-4100

Brentwood Church of the Good Shepherd **P** (953) 1420 Wilson Pike 37027-7701 (Mail to: 1420 Wilson Pike 37027-7701) Charles Dunnavant (615) 661-0890

Clarksville Trinity Episcopal Church **P** (401) 317 Franklin St 37040-3421 (Mail to: 317 Franklin St 37040-3421) Meghan Holland

Columbia St Peters Episcopal Church **P** (432) 311 W 7th St 38401-3132 (Mail to: 311 W Seventh St 38401-3132) Christopher Bowhay

Cookeville St Michael Episcopal Church **P** (300) 640 N Washington Ave 38501-2659 (Mail to: 640 N Washington Ave 38501-2659) Joseph Weatherly

Cowan St Agnes Mission **M** (38) England At Cherry 37318 (Mail to: PO Box 356 37318-0356) (931) 636-6313

Cumberland Furnace Calvary Episcopal Church **M** (22) 1086 Old Highway 48 N 37051-5000 (Mail to: 1199 Cauthern Rd 37082-9221) Joseph Davis (615) 789-4782

Decherd Christ Episcopal Church **M** (22) 9616 Old Alto Hwy 37324 (Mail to: 9616 Old Alto Hwy 37324) (931) 967-0898

Dickson St James Episcopal Church **M** (41) 205 Church Street 37055 (Mail to: PO Box 1196 37056-1196) (615) 446-8916

Fayetteville St Mary Magdalene Episcopal Church **P** (155) 106 Washington St E 37334-2544 (Mail to: PO Box 150 37334-0150) James Pappas (931) 433-2911

Franklin Church of the Resurrection **P** (186) 1216 Sneed Rd W 37069-6927 (Mail to: 1216 Sneed Rd W 37069-6927) (615) 377-9144

Franklin St Pauls Episcopal Church **P** (1442) 510 W Main St 37064-2722 (Mail to: 510 W Main St 37064-2722) William Barton Monna Mayhall William Rogers (615) 790-0527

Gallatin Church of Our Saviour **P** (115) 704 Hartsville Pike 37066-2525 (Mail to: PO Box 307 37066-0307) Joseph Woodfin (615) 452-7146

Hendersonvlle St Joseph of Arimathea Episcopal Church **P** (129) 103 Country Club Dr 37075-4024 (Mail to: 103 Country Club Dr 37075-4024) Joseph Howard (615) 824-2910

Lebanon Episcopal Church of the Epiphany **P** (112) 1500 Hickory Ridge Rd 37087-5702

(Mail to: 1500 Hickory Ridge Rd 37087-5702) Kira Schlesinger (615) 444-7336

Madison St James The Less **P** (83) 411 W Due West Ave 37115-4403 (Mail to: 411 W Due West Ave 37115-4403) Robin Courtney (615) 865-4496

Manchester St Bedes Episcopal Church **P** (67) 93 Saint Bede's Dr 37355 (Mail to: PO Box 305 37349-0305) Mariann Hassell (931) 728-4463

McMinnville St Matthews Episcopal Church **M** (143) 105 Edgewood Ave 37110-1565 (Mail to: 105 Edgewood Ave 37110-1565) (931) 473-8233

Monteagle Church of the Holy Comforter **M** (9) 1st Ave & Fairmont 37356 (Mail to: PO Box 1205 37356-1205) (931) 967-0898

Murfreesboro Church of the Holy Cross **M** (146) 1140 Cason Ln 37128-7660 (Mail to: 1140 Cason Ln 37128-7660) Carolyn Coleman (615) 867-7116

Murfreesboro St Pauls Episcopal Church **P** (986) 315 E Main St 37130-3826 (Mail to: 116 N Academy St 37130-3717) James Van Zandt Colin Ambrose (615) 893-3780

✠ **Nashville** Christ Church Cathedral **O** (2025) 900 Broadway 37203-3807 (Mail to: 900 Broadway 37203-3854) Joshua Caler Timothy Kimbrough Gene Manning Aleathia Nicholson (615) 255-7729

Nashville Church of the Advent **P** (623) 5501 Franklin Pike 37220-2115 (Mail to: 5501 Franklin Pike 37220-2115) James McVey (615) 373-5630

Nashville Church of the Holy Spirit **P** (140) 222 Franklin Limestone Rd 37217-3004 (Mail to: 5325 Nolensville Pike 37211-6415) Paul Mun (615) 333-9979

Nashville Church of the Holy Trinity **P** (102) 615 6th Ave S 37203 William Dennler (615) 256-6359

Nashville Saint David's Episcopal Church **P** (380) 6501 Pennywell Dr 37205-3005 (Mail to: 6501 Pennywell Dr 37205-3005) Mary Smith (615) 352-0293

Nashville St Anns Episcopal Church **P** (208) 419 Woodland St 37206-4207 (Mail to: 419 Woodland St 37206-4207) Richard Britton Charles Burdeshaw (615) 254-3534

Nashville St Anselms Episcopal Chapel **M** (78) 2008 Meharry Blvd 37208-2916 (Mail to: 2008 Meharry Blvd 37208-2916) Cynthia Seifert (615) 329-9640

Nashville St Augustine Episcopal Chapel **CC** (603) 200 24th Ave S 37235 (Mail to: PO Box 6330B 37235-0001) Alison Lutz Charles Peerman Melissa Smith Rebecca Stevens-Hummon (615) 322-4483

Nashville St Bartholomews Episcopal Church **P** (1091) 4800 Belmont Park Terr 37215-4422 (Mail to: 4800 Belmont Park Ter 37215-4422) Jerry Smith Travis Hines Harold Wilson (615) 377-4750

Nashville St Georges Episcopal Church **P** (3443) § 4715 Harding Pike 37205-2809 (Mail to: 4715 Harding Pike 37205-2809) Robert Spruill Samuel Adams William Kew Sarah Puryear Roger Senechal Timus Taylor Clinton Wilson (615) 385-2150

Nashville St Philip's Episcopal Church **P** (355) 85 Fairway Dr 37214-2148 (Mail to: 85 Fairway Dr 37214-2148) Vicki Burgess (615) 883-4595

New Johnsonville St Andrews Episcopal Church **M** (30) 539 Hillcrest Dr 37134-9668 (Mail to: PO Box 522 37134-0522) David Yancey (931) 363-1454

Pulaski Church of the Messiah **P** (104) 114 N 3rd St 38478-3203 (Mail to: 114 N 3rd St 38478-3203) Carolyn Keck (931) 363-1454

Rossview Grace Chapel **M** (25) 1950 Rossview Rd 37043 (Mail to: C/O Trinity Episcopal Church 317 Franklin St 37040-3421) Dorothy Hartzog

Saint Andrews St Andrews-Sewanee **SC** 290 Quintard Rd 37375-3000 (Mail to: 290 Quintard Rd 37375-3000)

Sewanee Otey Memorial Episcopal Church **P** (420) 216 University Ave 37375-2202 (Mail to: PO Box 267 37375-0267) Elizabeth Carpenter Robert Lamborn (931) 598-5926

Sewanee St James Episcopal Church **P** (88) 898 Midway Rd 37375-2701 (Mail to: PO Box 336 37375-0336) Linda Hutton (931) 598-0153

Shelbyville Church of the Redeemer **P** (55) 203 E Lane St 37160-3429 (Mail to: PO Box 274 37162-0274) Peter Whalen (931) 684-5506

Sherwood Church of the Epiphany **M** (102) 62 Mountain Ave E 37376 (Mail to: PO Box 41 37376-0041) (931) 967-0898

Smyrna All Saints Episcopal Church **M** (273) 1401 Lee Victory Pkwy 37167-6299 (Mail to: 1401 Lee Victory Pkwy 37167-6299) (615) 400-3824

Spring Hill Grace Episcopal Church **M** (80) 5291 Main St 37174-2449 (Mail to: 5291 Main St 37174-2449) William Martin (931) 486-3223

Springfield St Lukes Church **M** (36) 103 7th Ave W 37172-2826 (Mail to: 103 7th Ave W 37172-2826) Hassell Hurst (615) 382-7505

Tracy City Christ Episcopal Church **M** (147) 530 10th Street 37387-0457 (Mail to: PO Box 457 37387-0457) (931) 592-6336

Tullahoma St Barnabas Episcopal Church **P** (234) 110 E Lincoln St 38388-3631 (Mail to: 110 E Lincoln St 38388-3632) Michael Murphy (931) 455-3170

Winchester Trinity Episcopal Church **P** (27) 213 1st Ave NW 37398-1645 (Mail to: 213 1st Avenue NW 37398-1645) William Barton (931) 967-0898

NON-PAROCHIAL CLERGY

Abstein WR *ret* Nashville TN
Adams ML Nashville TN
Arnhart JR Murfreesboro TN
Baker MC *ret* Sewanee TN
Ballard JH *ret* Sewanee TN
Batarseh PB Franklin TN
Bender J *ret* Gallatin TN
Bryan MJC *ret* Sewanee TN
Carden LE *ret* Sewanee TN
Coleman EC *ret* Nashville TN
Dalglish WA *ret* Lebanon TN
Dettwiller GF Nashville TN
Fishbeck NB
Fraley AM Lebanon TN
Greenwood ES *ret* Nashville TN
Grimes CG *dcn* Franklin TN
Hethcock WH *ret* Sewanee TN
Holt WM *ret* Dickson TN
Hoover-Dempsey HLG Madison TN
Ingalls CD Nashville TN
Johnson JA Fayetteville TN
Keys JT *ret* Saint Simons Island GA
Kochtitzky RM Nashville TN
Kuenneth JR *ret* Nashville TN
Landers EL *ret* Nashville TN
Lee TM La Vergne TN
Lloyd BJ *dcn* Brentwood TN
Macfie TE Sewanee TN
Marek JJ Salmon ID
Miller MR Monterey CA
Phillips SJT *ret* Goodlettsville TN
Regen CLE Dickson TN
Rhea RE
Rice FG *ret* Nashville TN
Richaud RH *ret* Townsend TN
Rogers JL *ret* Columbia TN
Runkle JA Sewanee TN
Schane CE *ret* Atlanta GA
Scott DJ Nashville TN
Snare PLP Nashville TN
Stevenson AB *ret* Nashville TN
Terhune JS Nashotah WI
Thomas JT Sewanee TN
Van Dervoort VA *ret* Nashville TN
Von Wrangel C *ret* Nashville TN
Wade WSC *ret* East Kingston NH
Walling AB Nashville TN
Ward TR *ret* Sewanee TN
Wells Miller TJ Franklin TN
Wilson MK *ret* Nashville TN
Wilson TS *ret* Columbia TN
Wise EF *ret* Murfreesboro TN
Young KM *ret* Austin TX
Zalesak RJ Galveston TX

STATE OF TEXAS

Dioceses of Dallas (Dal), Fort Worth (FtW), Northwest Texas (NT), Rio Grande (RG), Texas (TX), and West Texas (WT)

Abilene—NT
Albany—NT
Alamogordo—RG
Albuquerque—RG
Aledo—FtW
Alice—WT
Allen—Dal
Alpine—RG
Alvin—TX
Amarillo—NT
Angleton—TX
Anthony—RG
Aransas Pass—WT
Arlington—FtW
Artesia—RG
Athens—Dal
Atlanta—Dal
Austin—TX
Bandera—WT
Bastrop—TX
Bay City—TX
Baytown—TX
Beaumont—TX
Beeville—WT
Bellville—TX
Big Spg—NT
Blanco—WT
Boerne—WT
Bonham—Dal
Borger—NT
Bracketville—WT
Brady—WT
Brenham—TX
Brownfield—NT
Brownsville—WT
Bryan—TX
Buda—WT
Burnet—TX
Calvert—TX
Cameron—TX
Canton—Dal
Canyon—NT
Canyon Lake—WT
Carlsbad—RG
Carrizo Spgs—WT
Carthage—TX
Cedar Hill—Dal
Cedar Pk—TX
Center—TX
Chama—RG
Clarendon—NT
Cloudcroft—RG
Clovis—RG
Coleman—NT
College Sta—TX
Colorado City—NT

Columbus—TX
Comfort—WT
Conroe—TX
Coppell—Dal
Copperas Cove—TX
Corpus Christi—WT
Corrales—RG
Corsicana—Dal
Cotulla—WT
Crockett—TX
Cuero—WT
Cypress—TX
Cypress Mill—WT
Dalhart—NT
Dallas—Dal
Del Rio—WT
Deming—RG
Denison—Dal
Denton—Dal
De Soto—Dal
Devine—WT
Dickinson—TX
Dripping Spgs—WT
Dumas—NT
Eagle Lake—TX
Eagle Pass—WT
Edgewood—RG
Edinburg—WT
Edna—WT
El Paso—RG
Ennis—Dal
Espanola—RG
Farmington—RG
Fort Sumner—RG
Flower Mound—Dal
Ft McKavett—WT
Ft Worth—FtW
Fredericksburg—WT
Freeport—TX
Friendswood—TX
Frisco—Dal
Gallup—RG
Galveston—TX
Garland—Dal
Georgetown—TX
George West—WT
Gilmer—Dal
Glencoe—RG
Goliad—WT
Gonzales—WT
Granbury—FtW
Greenville—Dal
Hallettsville—WT
Hamilton—FtW
Harlingen—WT
Hearne—TX

Hebbronville—WT
Hempstead—TX
Henderson—TX
Hereford—NT
Hillsboro—FtW & RG
Hitchcock—TX
Hobbs—RG
Houston—TX
Humble—TX
Huntsville—TX
Hurst—FtW & RG
Irving—Dal
Jacksonville—TX
Jasper—TX
Jefferson—TX
Junction—WT
Katy—TX
Kaufman—Dal
Keller—FTW
Kemp—Dal
Kenedy—WT
Kerrville—WT
Kilgore—TX
Killeen—TX
Kingsville—WT
LaGrange—TX
LaMarque—TX
LaPorte—TX
Lake Corpus Christi—WT
Lake Jackson—TX
Lampasas—TX
Lancaster—Dal
Laredo—WT
Las Cruces—RG
Las Vegas—RG
League City—TX
Leander—TX
Levelland—NT
Lewisville—Dal
Liberty—TX
Lindale—TX
Livingston—TX
Llano—WT
Lockhart—WT
Longview—TX
Los Alamos—RG
Los Lunas—RG
Lovington—RG
Lubbock—NT
Lufkin—TX
Luling—WT
Madisonville—TX
Manor—TX
Marble Falls—TX
Marfa—RG

Marlin—TX
Marshall—TX
Matagorda—TX
McAllen—WT
McKinney—Dal
Menard—WT
Mexia—TX
Midland—NT
Milan—RG
Mineola—Dal
Mission—WT
Missouri City—TX
Montell—WT
Mt Pleasant—Dal
Murphy—Dal
Nacogdoches—TX
Navasota—TX
New Braunfels—WT
Odessa—NT
Orange—TX
Palacios—TX
Palestine—TX
Pampa—NT
Paris—Dal
Pasadena—TX
Pearland—TX
Pecos—RG
Perryton—NT
Pflugerville—TX
Pharr—WT
Pittsburg—Dal
Plainview—NT
Plano—Dal
Pleasanton—WT
Portales—RG
Pt Aransas—WT
Pt Isabel—WT
Pt Lavaca—WT
Portland—WT
Pt Neches—TX
Pottsboro—Dal
Prairie View—TX
Prosper—Dal
Raton—RG
Raymondville—WT
Refugio—WT
Richardson—Dal
Richmond—TX
Rio Communities—RG
Rio Rancho—RG
Rockdale—TX
Rockport—WT
Rockwall—Dal
Roswell—RG
Round Rock—TX
Ruidoso—RG

Salago—TX
San Antonio—WT
San Angelo—NT
San Augustine—TX
San Benito—WT
San Marcos—WT
San Saba—WT
Santa Fe—RG
Sealy—TX
Seguin—WT
Shamrock—NT
Sherman—Dal
Silsbee—TX

Silver City—RG
Socorro—RG
Sonora—WT
Spring—TX
Stafford—TX
Stephenville—FtW
Sugar Land—TX
Sulphur Spgs—Dal
Sweetwater—NT
Taos—RG
Taylor—TX
Temple—TX
Terlingua—RG

Terrell—Dal
Texas City—TX
The Colony—Dal
The Woodlands—TX
Tomball—TX
Truth Consq—RG
Tucumcari—RG
Tyler—TX
Universal City—WT
Uvalde—WT
Vernon—NT
Victoria—WT
Waco—TX

Waxahachie—Dal
Weatherford—FtW
Weslaco—WT
W Columbia—TX
Wharton—TX
Wichita Falls—FtW
Wimberley—WT
Windcrest—WT
Winnie—TX
Winnsboro—Dal
Woodville—TX

DIOCESE OF TEXAS

(PROVINCE VII)
Comprises 57 counties of southeast and central Texas
DIOCESAN OFFICE 1225 Texas Ave Houston TX 77002-3504
TEL (713) 520-6444, (800) 318-4452   FAX (713) 520-5723
E-MAIL Individual e-mail addresses may be found on the diocesan website   WEB www.epicenter.org

Previous Bishops—
Alexander Gregg 1859-93, Geo H Kinsolving coadj 1892 Bp 1893-1928, Clinton S Quin coadj 1918 Bp 1928-55, F Percy Goddard suffr 1955-72, James P Clements suffr 1956-60, Scott Field Bailey suffr 1964-75, John E Hines coadj 1945 Bp 1955-64, James M Richardson 1965-80, Roger H Cilley suffr 1976-85, Gordon T Charlton suffr 1982-89, Maurice M Benitez 1980-95, William E Sterling suffr 1989-99 James B Brown asst Bp 2000-2003, Claude E Payne Bp 1995-2003, Leopoldo J Alard suffr 1995-2003, Rayford B High Jr suffr 2003-2011, Don A Wimberly Bp 2003-09

Bishop—Rt Rev C Andrew Doyle (1033) (Dio 7 June 09)

Bishop Suffragan—Rt Rev Dena A Harrison (1009) (7 Oct 2006)

Bishop Suffragan—Rt Rev Jeff W Fisher (1068) (6 Oct 2012)

Cn to Ord Rev Cn KM Ryan; *Sec* Rev Cn JA Logan Jr; *Treas* RJ Biehl; *Chanc* DT Harvin; *Chief of Staff* Rev Cn J Newton; *Cn for Wellness & Care* Rev Cn C Petty; *Dir Fdns* D Fisher; *Chr Ed* J Martin-Currie; *Yth* A Mireles-Paz; *Comm* C Barnwell; *Camps* G Dehan; *Cn Cong Vitality* M MacGregor; *Archdcn* R Oechsel; *Intercultural Dev* D Trevino

Deans: Austin M Allen; *Central* D Hay; *Northeast* M Tollett; *Northwest* B St. Romain; *San Jacinto* G Sevick; *Southeast* N DeForest; *Southwest* J Soard; *West Harris* T Bryant; *East Harris* V Thomas; *Galveston* S Stringer

Stand Comm—Cler: Pres M Crawford B Baetz P Lopez; *Lay: Sec* J Higgins R Fanning G Vincent

Dio Conv: 12-13 Feb 2016 The Woodlands

PARISHES, MISSIONS, AND CLERGY

Alvin Grace Episcopal Church **P** (234) 200 W Lang St 77511-2396 (Mail to: 112 W Lang St 77511-2408) David Price Carol Mills Joseph Mills (281) 331-5657

Angleton Church of the Holy Comforter **P** (178) 234 South Arcola 77515 (Mail to: PO Box 786 77516-0786) Travis Smith (979) 849-1269

Austin All Saints Episcopal Church **P** (1377) 209 W 27th St 78705-1043 (Mail to: 209 W 27th St 78705-1043) Michael Adams Miles Brandon Cynthia Caruso (512) 476-3589

Austin Church of the Resurrection **P** (321) 2200 Justin Ln 78757-2417 (Mail to: 2200 Justin Ln 78757-2417) William Tweedie (512) 459-0027

Austin Iglesia San Francisco de Asis **M** (997) 7000 Woodhue Dr 78745-5454 (Mail to: 7000 Woodhue Dr 78745-5454) Albert Pearson (512) 439-0721

Austin St Albans Episcopal Church **P** (597) 11819 S I H 35 78747-1804 (Mail to: PO Box 368 78652-0368) Erin Hensley (512) 282-5631

Austin St Christophers Episcopal Church **P** (244) 8724 Travis Hills Dr 78735-8171 (Mail to: 8724 Travis Hills Dr 78735-8171) Bowman Townsend Sharon Williams (512) 288-0128

Austin St Davids Episcopal Church **P** (2410) 301 E 8th St 78701-3203 (Mail to: 301 E 8th St 78701-3280) Chad McCall Catherine Wright (512) 610-3500

Austin St Georges Episcopal Church **P** (128) 4301 N I-35 78722-1103 (Mail to: 4301 N Interstate

35 78722-1197) Kevin Schubert (512) 454-2523

Austin St James' Episcopal Church **P** (700) 1941 Webberville Rd 78721-1679 (Mail to: 1941 Webberville Rd 78721-1679) Albert Rodriguez Madeline Shelton-Hawley (512) 926-6339

Austin St Johns Episcopal Church **P** (237) 11201 Parkfield Dr 78758-4264 (Mail to: 11201 Parkfield Dr 78758-4264) Matthew Seddon (512) 836-3974

Austin St Lukes on the Lake Epis Church **P** (953) 5600 Ranch Road 620 N 78732-1823 (Mail to: 5600 Ranch Road 620 N 78732-1823) Michael Wyckoff John Jameson (512) 266-2455

Austin St Marks Episcopal Church **P** (758) 2128 Barton Hills Dr 78704-4651 (Mail to: 2128 Barton Hills Dr 78704-4651) Elizabeth Turner (512) 444-1449

Austin St Matthews Episcopal Church **P** (1404) 8134 Mesa Dr 78759-8615 (Mail to: 8134 Mesa Dr 78759-8678) John Wade Jerry Chapman Christian Hawley George Wilson (512) 345-8314

Austin St Michaels Episcopal Church **P** (678) 6317 Bee Caves Rd 78746-5148 (Mail to: 1500 N Capital of Texas Hwy 78746-3320) Robert Vickery Brin Bon Nancy Ricketts Sharon Williams (512) 327-1474

Austin The Church of the Good Shepherd **P** (3307) 3201 Windsor Dr 78703 2239 (Mail to: PO Box 5176 78763-5176) Morgan Allen Anne Jolly Cynthia Kittredge Christine Mendoza Kathleen Pfister Michael Russell (512) 476-3523

Bastrop Calvary Episcopal Church **P** (488) 603 Spring St 78602-3226 (Mail to: PO Box 721 78602-0721) Lisa Hines Kenneth Kesselus (512) 303-7515

Bay City St Marks Episcopal Church **P** (372) 2200 Avenue E 77414-5009 (Mail to: 2200 Avenue E 77414-5009) Bradley Sullivan (979) 245-2557

Baytown Trinity Episcopal Church **P** (442) 5010 N Main St 77521-9606 (Mail to: 5010 N Main St 77521-9606) Nicky Novak Lajunta Rios Rebecca Smith Booth

Beaumont St Mark's Episcopal Church **P** (763) 680 Calder St 77701-2303 (Mail to: 680 Calder St 77701-2398) Mark Crawford (409) 832-3405

Beaumont St Stephens Episcopal Church **P** (531) 4090 Delaware St 77706-7801 (Mail to: 4090 Delaware St 77706-7801) Nancy Deforest Patricia Ritchie

Bellville St Marys Episcopal Church **P** (103) 24 N Masonic St 77418-1444 (Mail to: 24 N Masonic St 77418-1444) James Pevehouse (979) 865-2330

Brenham St Peters Episcopal Church **P** (232) 2310 Airline Dr 77833 (Mail to: PO Box 937 77834-0937) David Ottsen (979) 836-7248

Bryan St Andrews Episcopal Church **P** (343) 217 W 26th St 77803-3215 (Mail to: PO Box 405

77806-0405) Daryl Hay David Hoster (979) 822-5176

Burnet Church of the Epiphany **P** (247) 601 N Wood St 78611-0002 (Mail to: PO Box 2 78611-0002)

Calvert Church of the Epiphany **M** (21) 700 E Gregg St 77837-7801 (Mail to: PO Box 99 77837-0099) (512) 217-6314

Cameron All Saints Episcopal Church **M** (30) 200 N Travis St 76520 (Mail to: 200 N Travis Ave 76520-3312) Durwood Bagby

Carthage St Johns Episcopal Church **M** (52) Attn Maudie Leach 904 N Daniels St 75633-1126 (Mail to: 308 Cottage Rd 75633-1512) Jennene Laurinec Richard Mcleon (903) 693-5566

Cedar Park Christ Episcopal Church **P** (293) 3520 W Whitestone Blvd 78613 (Mail to: PO Box 638 78630-0638) Trawin Malone (512) 267-2428

Center St Johns Episcopal Church **M** (26) 1063 Southview Circle 75935 (Mail to: PO Box 1026 75935-1026)

College Station St Francis Episcopal Church **P** (95) 1101 Rock Prairie Rd 77845-8344 (Mail to: 1101 Rock Prairie Rd 77845-8344) James Lawrence

College Station St Thomas Episcopal Church **P** (562) 906 George Bush Dr 77840-3056 (Mail to: 906 George Bush Dr 77840-3056) James Said (979) 696-1726

Columbus St Johns Episcopal Church **P** (33) (Mail to: PO Box 746 78934-0746) (979) 732-2590

Conroe St James the Apostle Epis Church **P** (524) 1803 Highland Hollow Dr 77304-4092 (Mail to: 1803 Highland Hollow Dr 77304-4092) Jerald Hyche Phyllis Hartman (936) 756-8831

Copperas Cove St Martins Episcopal Church **M** (67) 1602 S Fm 116 76522-4204 (Mail to: 1602 S FM 116 76522-4204) (254) 547-0331

Crockett All Saints Episcopal Church **M** (26) 1301 E Houston Ave 75835-1749 (Mail to: PO Box 103 75835-0103)

Cypress St Aidans Episcopal Church **M** (406) 13131 Fry Rd 77433 (Mail to: 13131 Fry Rd 77433) Leslie Carpenter Warren Miedke (281) 373-3203

Cypress St Marys Episcopal Church **P** (520) 15415 N Eldridge Pkwy 77429-2005 (Mail to: 15415 N Eldridge Pkwy 77429-2005) Beth Fain Katherine Churchwell Kellaura Johnson Russell Oechsel (281) 370-8000

Dickinson Holy Trinity Episcopal Church **P** (273) 4613 Highway 3 77539-6852 (Mail to: 4613 Highway 3 77539-6852) Stacy Stringer Michael Gemignani (281) 337-1833

Eagle Lake Christ Church **P** (106) 304 E Stockbridge St 77434-1839 (Mail to: PO Box 577 77434-0577) Stephen Spicer (979) 234-3437

Freeport St Pauls Episcopal Church **P** (95) 1307 W 5th St 77541-5311 (Mail to: 1307 W 5th St

77541-5311) Robert Dohle (979) 233-3673

Friendswood Church of the Good Shepherd **P** (720) 1207 Winding Way Dr 77546-4808 (Mail to: 1207 Winding Way Dr 77546-4808) Geoffrey Gwynne (281) 482-7630

Galveston Grace Episcopal Church **P** (289) 1115 36th St 77550-4113 (Mail to: 1115 36th St 77550-4113) Meredith Holt (409) 762-9676

Galveston St Augustine of Hippo Church **M** (89) 1410 Jack Johnson Blvd. (41st Street) 77550-3953 (Mail to: 1410 Jack Johnson Blvd 77550-3953) Chester Makowski (409) 763-4254

Galveston Trinity Episcopal Church **P** (522) 2216 Ball St 77550-2224 (Mail to: 2216 Ball St 77550-2224) Susan Kennard David Dearman (409) 765-6317

✣ **Galveston** William Temple Episcopal Center **Other** (Mail to: 2216 Ball St 77550-2224) Kyle Stillings (409) 539-2077

Georgetown Grace Episcopal Church **P** (509) 1314 E University Ave 78626-6115 (Mail to: 1314 E University Ave 78626-6115) John Garland David Peters

Hearne St Philips Episcopal Church **M** (3) 408 Cedar St 77859-2545 (Mail to: 408 Cedar St 77859-2545) (979) 279-3234

Hempstead St Bartholomews Church **P** (87) No 811 14th St 77445-5146 (Mail to: PO Box 961 77445-0961) Elizabeth Huber (979) 826-2525

Henderson St Matthews Episcopal Church **P** (70) 214 College Ave 75654-4131 (Mail to: 214 College Ave 75654-4131) Patsy Barham (903) 657-3154

Hitchcock All Saints Episcopal Church **M** (41) 10416 Highway 6 77563-4580 (Mail to: 10416 Highway 6 77563-4580) Mark Marmon (409) 925-2544

✣ **Houston** Christ Church Cathedral **O** (3608) 1117 Texas St 77002-3113 (Mail to: 1117 Texas Ave 77002-3183) Barkley Thompson Arthur Callaham Simon Bautista Genevieve Razim Glenice Robinson-Como (713) 590-3308

Houston Christ the King Episcopal Church **M** (251) 15325 Bellaire Blvd 77083-3110 (Mail to: 15325 Bellaire Blvd 77083-3110) Johannes George

Houston Church of the Ascension **P** (425) 2525 Seagler Rd 77042-3119 (Mail to: 2525 Seagler Rd 77042-3119) Todd Bryant (713) 781-1330

Houston Church of the Epiphany **P** (704) 9600 S Gessner Dr 77071-1002 (Mail to: 9600 S Gessner Dr 77071-1099) Christine Faulstich (713) 774-9619

Houston Church of the Holy Spirit **P** (1207) 12535 Perthshire Rd 77024-4106 (Mail to: 12535 Perthshire Rd 77024-4186) Joshua Condon Elizabeth Yale (713) 468-7796

Houston Church of the Redeemer **M** (75) 5700 Lawndale 77023-1898 (Mail to: PO Box 9564 77261) James Kearney Lacy Largent (713) 928-3221

Houston Emmanuel Episcopal Church **P** (662) 15015 Memorial Dr 77079-4301 (Mail to: 15015 Memorial Drive 77079-4301) Christy Shain-Hendricks (281) 493-3161

Houston Grace Episcopal Church **M** (157) 4040 W Bellfort St 77025-5307 (Mail to: 4040 W Bellfort St 77025-5397) Gena Davis (713) 666-1408

Houston Hope Episcopal Church **P** (145) 1613 W 43rd St 77018-1849 (Mail to: PO Box 920564 77292-0564) Roberta Knowles (713) 681-6422

Houston Lord of the Streets Episcopal Church (23) 3401 Fannin St 77004-3806 (Mail to: 3401 Fannin St 77004-3806) (713) 526-0311

Houston Palmer Memorial Episcopal Church **P** (2648) 6221 Main St 77030-1506 (Mail to: 6221 Main St 77030-1506) William Brooks Alexandra Easley William O'Neill John Price Linda Shelton Henry Strobel Katharine Wallingford Neil Willard (713) 529-6196

Houston Santa Maria Virgen Episcopal Church **M** (1028) 9600 Huntington Place Dr 77099-2316 (Mail to: 9600 Huntington Place Dr 77099-2316) Uriel Osnaya-Jimenez (281) 879-6000

Houston St Albans Episcopal Church **M** (141) 420 Woodard St 77009-1824 (Mail to: 420 Woodard St 77009-1824) William Laucher

Houston St Andrews Episcopal Church **P** (282) 1819 Heights Blvd 77008-4025 (Mail to: 1811 Heights Blvd 77008-4025) James Grace (713) 861-5596

Houston St Barnabas Episcopal Church **P** (107) 107 E Edgebrook Dr 77034-1401 (Mail to: 107 E Edgebrook Dr 77034-1401) (713) 946-8058

Houston St Christophers Episcopal Church **P** (185) 1656 Blalock Rd 77080-7396 (Mail to: 1656 Blalock Rd 77080-7396) Robert Goolsby (713) 465-6015

Houston St Cuthbert Episcopal Church **P** (1108) 17020 West Rd 77095-7758 (Mail to: 17020 West Rd 77095-5579) Bruce Bonner Margaret Williams (281) 463-7330

Houston St Dunstans Episcopal Church **P** (1240) 14301 Stuebner Airline Rd 77069-3529 (Mail to: 14301 Stuebner Airline Rd 77069-3529) Robert Price Brian Tarver Randall Trego (281) 440-1600

Houston St Francis Episcopal Church **P** (1187) § 345 Piney Point Rd 77024-6505 (Mail to: 345 Piney Point Rd 77024-6599) Stuart Bates Richard Elwood Robert Wismer (713) 782-1270

Houston St James Episcopal Church **P** (519) 3129 Southmore Boulevard 77004-6298 (Mail to: 3129 Southmore Boulevard 77004-6298) Elizabeth Divine Victor Thomas (713) 526-9571

Houston St John the Divine Episcopal Church **P** (4486) 2450 River Oaks Blvd 77019-5826 (Mail to: 2450 River Oaks Blvd 77019-5898) Reagan Cocke Janet Dantone Clay Lein Matthew Marino Douglas Richnow (713) 622-3600

Houston St Luke the Evangelist Church **P** (164) 3530 Wheeler St 77004-5527 (Mail to: 3530 Wheeler St 77004-5527) Francene Young (713) 748-5974

Houston St Marks Episcopal Church **P** (838) 3816 Bellaire Blvd 77025-1209 (Mail to: 3816 Bellaire Blvd. 77025-1296) Patrick Miller Mary Ann Huston Murray Powell (713) 664-3466

Houston St Martin's Episcopal Church **P** (8664) 717 Sage Rd 77056-2111 (Mail to: 717 Sage Rd 77056-2111) Russell Levenson Martin Bastian Sarah Condon James Cunningham Robert Dixon Rutger-Jan Heijmen Alexander Large Chad Martin Susannah Mcbay Mary Wilson (713) 621-3040

Houston St Matthews Church **M** (1282) 6635 Alder Dr 77081-5201 (Mail to: PO Box 277 77401-0277) Alejandro Montes (713) 664-7792

Houston St Pauls Episcopal Church **P** (514) 7843 Park Place Blvd 77087-4639 (Mail to: 7843 Park Place Blvd 77087-4639) (713) 645-5031

Houston St Stephens Episcopal Church **P** (433) 1805 W Alabama St 77098-2601 (Mail to: 1805 W Alabama St 77098-2601) Lisa Hunt Brandon Peete (713) 528-6665

Houston St Thomas Episcopal Church **P** (411) 4900 Jackwood St 77096-1505 (Mail to: 4900 Jackwood St 77096-1599) David Browder Mathew Fenlon (713) 666-3111

Houston St Thomas the Apostle Episcopal Churchh **P** (1091) 18300 Upper Bay Rd 77058-4110 (Mail to: 18300 Upper Bay Rd 77058-4199) Michael Stone (281) 333-2384

Houston St Timothys Episcopal Church **P** (202) 13125 Indianapolis St 77015-3600 (Mail to: 13125 Indianapolis St 77015-3600) Frederick Clarkson (713) 451-2909

Houston Trinity Episcopal Church **P** (677) 1015 Holman St 77004-3810 (Mail to: 1015 Holman St 77004-3899) Hannah Atkins Richard Houser (713) 528-4100

Humble Christ the King (Atascocita) **P** (207) 19330 Pinehurst Trail Dr 77346-2224 (Mail to: 19330 Pinehurst Trail Dr 77346-2224) David Nelson (281) 852-1990

Humble Church of the Good Shepherd **P** (606) 2929 Woodland Hills Dr 77339-1406 (Mail to: 2929 Woodland Hills Dr 77339-1496) William Richter (281) 358-3154

Huntsville St Stephens Episcopal Church **P** (295) 5019 Sam Houston Ave 77340-6653 (Mail to: PO Box 388 77342-0388) (936) 295-7226

Jacksonville Trinity Episcopal Church **M** (63) 1000 S Jackson St 75766-3016 (Mail to: PO Box 472 75766-0472) (903) 586-4336

Jasper Trinity Episcopal Church **P** (22) 800 N Main St 75951-3018 (Mail to: PO Box 1598 75951-0016) (409) 384-3719

Jefferson Christ Episcopal Church **M** (18) 703 S Main St 75657-2227 (Mail to: 703 S Main St 75657-2227) (903) 665-2693

Katy Holy Apostles Episcopal Church-Katy **P** (597) 1225 S Grand Pkwy 77494-8283 (Mail to: 1225 W Grand Pkwy S 77494-8283) Darrel Proffitt

Katy St Pauls Episcopal Church **P** (259) 5373 Franz Rd 77493-1732 (Mail to: 5373 Franz Rd 77493) Christopher Duncan Gillian Keyworth

Kilgore St Pauls Episcopal Church **P** (58) 314 N Henderson Blvd 75662-2712 (Mail to: 314 N Henderson Blvd 75662-2712) (903) 984-3929

Killeen St Christophers Episcopal Church **P** (435) 2800 Trimmier Rd 76542 (Mail to: 2800 Trimmier Rd. 76542) Janice Jones (254) 634-7474

LaGrange St James Episcopal Church **P** (129) 156 N Monroe St 78945-2651 (Mail to: PO Box 507 78945-0507) Eric Hungerford (979) 968-3910

Lake Jackson St Timothys Episcopal Church **P** (593) 200 Oyster Creek Dr 77566-4402 (Mail to: 200 Oyster Creek Dr 77566-4402) Andrew Parker Elizabeth Parker (979) 297-6003

LaMarque St Michaels Episcopal Church **HC** (102) 1601 Lake Rd 77568-5242 (Mail to: 1601 Lake Rd 77568-5242) Robert Moore (409) 935-3559

Lampasas St Marys Episcopal Church **P** (147) 501 S Chestnut St 76550-3225 (Mail to: PO Box 29 76550-0001) Susanne Comer Mildred Williams (512) 556-5433

LaPorte St Johns Episcopal Church **P** (244) 815 S Broadway St 77571-5323 (Mail to: 815 S Broadway Street 77571-5323) Viktoria Gotting (281) 471-0383

League City St Christopher Episcopal Church **P** (358) 2100 Saint Christopher Ave 77573-4234 (Mail to: PO Box 852 77574-0852) Thomas Day Viktoria Gotting (281) 332-5553

Leander St Peters Episcopal Church **P** (49) 3305 Pinnacle Cv 78645-6567 (Mail to: 3305 Pinnacle Cove 78645-6567) (512) 267-2744

Liberty St Stephens Episcopal Church **P** (139) 2041 Trinity St 77575-4831 (Mail to: PO Box 10357 77575) Ted Smith Glennda Hardin (936) 336-3762

Lindale St Luke's Episcopal Church **M** (51) 16292 FM 849 75771 (Mail to: PO Box 1766 75771-1766) John Carr Kenneth Martin (903) 882-8118

Livingston St Lukes Episcopal Church **P** (70) 832 W Jones St 77351-2721 (Mail to: 836 W Jones St 77351-2721) Leonard Hullar (936) 327-8467

Longview St Michael & All Angels Episcopal Ch **P** (168) 909 Reel Rd 75604-2528 (Mail to: 909 Reel Rd 75604-2528) (903) 759-2051

Longview Trinity Episcopal Church **P** (402) 906 Padon St 75601-6734 (Mail to: 906 Padon St 75601-6797) Kevin Wittmayer (903) 753-3366

Lufkin St Cyprians Episcopal Church **P** (588) 919 S John Redditt Dr 75904-4326 (Mail to: 919 S John Redditt Dr 75904-4326) Ralph Morgan (936) 639-1253

Madisonville Holy Innocents Episcopal Church

M (25) 600 N McIver St 77864-3270 (Mail to: PO Box 1344 77864-1344) (936) 348-2034

Manor St Mary Magdalene Episcopal Church **M** (67) 12800 Lexington St 78653-3333 (Mail to: PO Box 33 78653) Alex Montes (512) 423-8897

Marble Falls Trinity Episcopal Church **P** (170) 909 Ave D 78654 (Mail to: 909 Ave D 78654-0580) David Sugeno Catherine Boyd (830) 693-2822

Marlin St Johns Episcopal Church **P** (59) 514 Carter St 76661-2326 (Mail to: 514 Carter St 76661-2326) Judy Filer Elizabeth Huber

Marshall St Pauls Church **P** (11) Fm Rd 134 75670 (Mail to: 317 Swendson Road 75657-8297) (903) 407-0117

Marshall Trinity Episcopal Church **P** (427) 106 N Grove St 75670-3237 (Mail to: 106 N Grove St 75670-3237) John Himes (903) 938-4246

Matagorda Christ Episcopal Church **M** (68) 206 Cypress St 77457 (Mail to: PO Box 673 77457-0673) Lawrence Gwin (979) 863-7239

Mexia Christ Episcopal Church **M** (50) 505 E Commerce St 76667-2862 (Mail to: 505 E Commerce St 76667-2862) (254) 562-5918

Missouri City St Catherine of Sienna Epis Church **M** (437) 4747 Sienna Pkwy 77459 (Mail to: 4747 Sienna Pkwy 77459) Michael Besson (281) 778-2046

Nacogdoches Christ Church **P** (394) 1430 N Mound St 75961-4052 (Mail to: 1320 N Mound St 75961-4029) Howard Castleberry Wanda Cuniff (936) 564-0421

Navasota St Pauls Episcopal Church **P** (76) 414 E McAlpine St 77868-3645 (Mail to: 414 E McAlpine St 77868-3645) Cynthia Engle (936) 825-7726

Orange St Pauls Episcopal Church **P** (105) 1401 W Park Ave 77630 (Mail to: 1401 W Park Ave 77630) Petroula Ruehlen (409) 883-2969

Palacios St Johns Episcopal Church **M** (55) 3rd & Main Sts 77465 (Mail to: PO Box 895 77465-0895) (361) 972-2744

Palestine St Philips Episcopal Church **P** (213) 106 E Crawford St 75801-2805 (Mail to: 106 E Crawford 75801) (903) 729-4214

Pasadena St Peters Episcopal Church **M** (290) 705 Williams St 77506-3639 (Mail to: 705 Williams St 77506-3639) Pedro Lopez (713) 473-8090

Pearland St Andrews Episcopal Church **P** (762) 2535 Broadway St 77581-4901 (Mail to: 2535 Broadway St 77581-4901) James Liberatore (281) 485-3843

Pflugerville St Paul's Episcopal Church **M** (91) 507 E Pflugerville Loop 78660-1904 (Mail to: 511 E Pflugerville Pkwy PO Box 28 78691-0028) Kelly Koonce (512) 990-1350

Port Neches Holy Trinity Episcopal Church **P** (242) 2425 Nall St 77651-4703 (Mail to: 2425 Nall St 77651-4703) James Rucker (409) 722-6238

Prairie View St Francis of Assisi Epis Church **P**

(29) PO Box 246 77446-0246 (Mail to: PO Box 246 77446-0246) Cynthia Engle (936) 857-3272

Richmond Calvary Episcopal Church **P** (337) 806 Thompson Rd 77469-3334 (Mail to: 806 Thompson Rd 77469-3334) Paul Wehner Neil Innes Kellaura Johnson (281) 342-2147

Richmond St Marks Episcopal Church **P** (135) § 7615 FM 762 77469 (Mail to: 7615 Fm 762 Rd 77469-9505) Bertrand Baetz (281) 545-1661

Rockdale St Thomas Episcopal Church **M** (27) 302 E Davilla Ave 76567-2986 (Mail to: PO Box 997 76567-0997) (512) 446-5932

Round Rock St Julian of Norwich Episcopal Church **M** (220) 7700 Cat Hollow Drive Suite 204 78681-5796 (Mail to: 7700 Cat Hollow Drive Suite 204 78681-5796) Miles Brandon Kelly Koonce (512) 284-7983

Round Rock St Richards Episcopal Church **P** (898) 1420 E Palm Valley Blvd 78664-4549 (Mail to: 1420 E Palm Valley Blvd 78664-4549) Franck Shelby Zachary Koons (512) 255-5436

Salado St Joseph's Episcopal Church **M** (63) 881 North Main Street 76571-0797 (Mail to: PO Box 797 76571-0797) Robert Bliss (254) 947-3160

San Augustine Christ Episcopal Church **M** (29) 201 N Ayish St 75972-2105 (Mail to: PO Box 85 75972-0085) (936) 275-6993

Sealy St Johns Episcopal Church **M** (83) 311 6th St 77474-2719 (Mail to: PO Box 1477 77474-1477) Eric LeBrocq (979) 885-2359

Silsbee St Johns Episcopal Church **P** (225) 1305 Roosevelt Dr 77656-3309 (Mail to: PO Box 636 77656-0636) (409) 385-4371

Spring Holy Comforter Episcopal Church **P** (250) 2322 Spring Cypress Rd 77388-4717 (Mail to: 2322 Spring Cypress Rd 77388-4717) James Abbott (281) 288-8169

Stafford All Saints Episcopal Church **P** (239) 605 Dulles Ave 77477-5222 (Mail to: 605 Dulles Ave 77477-5222) Stephen Whaley

Sugar Land Holy Cross Episcopal Church **P** (223) 5653 W River Park Dr 77479-7900 (Mail to: 5653 W River Park Dr 77479-7900) Scott Thompson (281) 633-2000

Taylor St James Episcopal Church **M** (35) 612 Davis St 76574-2729 (Mail to: PO Box 268 76574-0268) Terry Pierce (512) 352-2330

Temple Christ Episcopal Church **P** (497) 300 N Main St 76501-3210 (Mail to: PO Box 966 76503-0966) William Fowler James Wilburn (254) 773-1657

Temple St Francis Episcopal Church **P** (151) 5001 Hickory Rd 76502-3012 (Mail to: 5001 Hickory Rd 76502-3099) John Saint Romain Tamara Clothier (254) 773-4255

Texas City St Georges Episcopal Church **P** (218) 510 13th Ave N 77590-6250 (Mail to: 510 13th Ave N 77590-6250) Robin Reeves (409) 945-2583

The Woodlands Trinity Episcopal Church **P**

(1353) 3901 S Panther Creek Dr 77381-2736 (Mail to: 3901 S Panther Creek Dr 77381-2736) Gerald Sevick Robert Horner Vivian Orndorff Sean Steele

Tomball Church of the Good Shepherd **P** (211) 715 Carrell St 77375-4899 (Mail to: 715 Carrell St 77375-4808) Cecil McGavern

Tyler Christ Episcopal Church **P** (1607) 118 S Bois D Arc Ave 75702-7101 (Mail to: 118 S Bois D Arc Ave 75702-7199) David Luckenbach Matthew Boulter Keith Pozzuto Stephen Stine (903) 597-9854

Tyler St Francis Episcopal Church **P** (257) 3232 Jan Ave 75701-9115 (Mail to: 3232 Jan Ave 75701-9115) Robert DeWolfe Fenton Kovic Mitchell Tollett (903) 593-8459

Tyler St John's Episcopal Church **M** (34) 514 W Vance St 75702-3251 (Mail to: 514 W Vance St 75702-3251) ML Agnew (903) 597-5923

Waco Episcopal Church of the Holy Spirit **P** (338) 1624 Wooded Acres Dr 76710-2852 (Mail to: 1624 Wooded Acres Dr 76710-2852) Jason Ingalls (254) 772-1982

Waco St Albans Episcopal Church **P** (519) 305 N 30th St 76710-7225 (Mail to: 305 N 30th St 76710-7299) Aaron Zimmerman Benjamin Maddison (254) 752-1773

Waco St Pauls Episcopal Church **P** (1118) 515 Columbus Ave 76701-1347 (Mail to: 601 Columbus Ave 76701-1347) William Treadwell Steven Balke Sharron Cox (254) 753-4501

West Columbia St Marys Episcopal Church **P** (32) 16th & Clay Sts 77486 (Mail to: PO Box 786 77486-0786) Peter Conaty (979) 345-3456

✠ **Wharton** St Thomas Church **P** (129) 207 Bob O Link Lane 77488-3205 (Mail to: PO Box 586 77488-0586) John Soard (979) 532-1723

Winnie Trinity Episcopal Church **M** (82) 1324 Highway 124, 77665-0630 (Mail to: PO Box 777 77514-0777) (409) 267-6582

Woodville St Pauls Episcopal Church **M** (110) Hwy 190 W 75979 (Mail to: 1703 W Bluff 75979-0546) (409) 283-3710

NON-PAROCHIAL CLERGY

Abernathey JM *ret* Palacios TX
Adam BC *ret* Houston TX
Agim EN Houston TX
Alcorn JK *ret* Sugar Land TX
Alwine DW *ret* Charleston SC
Appelberg HMW *ret* Galveston TX
Aurand BK *ret* Two Harbors MN
Barrett JR Copperas Cove TX
Beeley CA South Bend IN
Beer DF *ret* Austin TX
Bell HO *ret*
Bennett SG Austin TX
Bennett WM *ret* Austin TX
Benson RL *ret* Galveston TX
Bentley JR *ret* Houston TX
Bethell TJ *ret* Oceanside OR

Blaine CMG *ret* Marlin TX
Bowen PR *ret* Staunton VA
Boyd DA Austin TX
Boyd SL *ret* Chandler TX
Brotherton EA *ret* Manchaca TX
Brown FM Galveston TX
Buffone GJ *dcn*
Burgos JA North Manchester IN
Butler GH *ret* Berlin MD
Butts SJ *ret* Kilgore TX
Buxton EH *ret* Clearwater FL
Cadwallader DS *ret* Houston TX
Cain EH *ret* Austin TX
Calcote AD *ret* Beaumont TX
Canion GY *ret* Houston TX
Capper SM Houston TX
Chabot BG College Station TX
Chase JG Crockett TX
Clark CL Calvert TX
Coe WN *ret* Houston TX
Coke PT *ret* Boca Raton FL
Conklin AC *dcn* Houston TX
Cook AM *dcn* Lufkin TX
Cook CJ *ret* Austin TX
Cook WE *ret* Tyler TX
Cooper RR *ret* Rosenberg TX
Craven SH *ret* Houston TX
Critchlow FSCJ *dcn* Kingwood TX
Crocker BG *ret* Beaumont TX
Daigle DH Madisonville TX
Dannelley JP *ret* Llano TX
Davis RJ
Deforest JW *ret* Beaumont TX
Deleery SM *ret* Austin TX
Dimmick KR *ret* Stuttgart
Dixon ML *dcn* College Station TX
Doerr NL *ret* Alvin TX
Dolan-Henderson SM *ret* Austin TX
Donovan JC *ret* Galveston TX
Dowell ER Columbus TX
Driskill LE Anahuac TX
Dyke NRD *ret* Humble TX
Ellis WL *ret* Pearland TX
Ely JE Bay City TX
Falls ML *ret* Austin TX
Felton PD *ret* Sugar Land TX
Ferguson SK *ret* Houston TX
Fields KL *ret* Katy TX
Fields LB *ret* Hendersonville NC
Fikes GD Arlington VA
FitzGerald TR Austin TX
Flick RT *ret* Friendswood TX
Fotinos DG *ret* Mills River NC
Frances M *ret* Houston TX
Fredholm EL *ret* Asheville NC
Fuller FE *ret* Corpus Christi TX
Geib LR *ret* Colorado Springs CO
Gentry BM *ret* Fairhope AL
Gerding SA Livingston TX
Gervais SJ *ret* Round Rock TX
Giblin KF Orange TX

Goldsmith ML *ret* Birmingham AL
Gomez E Austin TX
Goonesekera DJP *ret* Katy TX
Gowty RN
Graham JK *ret* Houston TX
Green ME *ret* Clinton WA
Greene AS Houston TX
Gremillion DA *ret* Pflugerville TX
Gribble RL *ret* Austin TX
Gudger GB *ret*
Hall LA *ret* Houston TX
Hall PM Houston TX
Halstead JF *dcn* Cedar Park TX
Hamilton JE *ret* Houston TX
Harris-Bayfield MH *ret* Winchester VA
Hartwell EM *ret* Austin TX
Havens HMM *ret* Houston TX
Hawkins FJ *ret* Rosenberg TX
Henderson PA *dcn* Georgetown TX
Hervey TE *ret* Bertram TX
Hill GD *ret* Dallas TX
Hines JC *ret* College Station TX
Hoey AK *ret* Austin TX
Holden EG Bellaire TX
Holloway EAC Houston TX
Holman JE Spring TX
Hubby TE *ret* San Antonio TX
Huerta Garcia O Tlaquepaque Jalisco
Huff CK *ret* San Marcos TX
Huffman CH *ret* Austin TX
Hyde LW Houston TX
Hyde RW *ret* Galveston TX
Jackson MT Austin TX
Jennings KK
Jennings NG Austin TX
Jensen JD *ret* Dayton TX
Johnson JB Silsbee TX
Johnson PA Dripping Springs TX
Jones GH *ret* Missouri City TX
Jones JG Pflugerville TX
Khoo OC *ret* Houston TX
Kinney SW Austin TX
Kirkaldy D La Marque TX
Knoll-Williams SJ Lawrence KS
Lawrence AS *ret* The Woodlands TX
Leacock RJ Austin TX
Legge DE Austin TX
Leighton JL *ret* Beaumont TX
Lewis B *ret* Houston TX
Lewis GF *ret* Spartanburg SC
Linscott S Houston TX
Liro JR *ret* Austin TX
Littlejohn LM *ret* Windcrest TX
Logan JA *ret* Houston TX
Long BI Austin TX
Lopez U Elgin IL
Lowry RL *dcn* The Woodlands TX
Lyle JR *dcn* Salado TX
Magill EA Austin TX
Magnuson PW Copperas Cove TX
Mangum FB *ret* Waco TX

Mason VA *dcn* Austin TX
Masquelette ES *ret* Houston TX
Masters RL *ret* Highland Village TX
McDonald DR *ret* Austin TX
McGehee JP *ret* Austin TX
McGill JC *ret* Houston TX
Melis AM *dcn* Waco TX
Merrill RC Houston TX
Miller CI *ret* Clearwater FL
Miller SHT Washington DC
Minter RD *ret* Port Townsend WA
Mizirl SM College Station TX
Moore EF Cypress TX
Morgan JC *ret* Huntsville TX
Morris JLK *ret* Oklahoma City OK
Morris TR Sewanee TN
Nazro AP *ret* Austin TX
Newton JW Austin TX
Nichols RG Mobile AL
Normand AD *ret* Houston TX
North WM *ret* Swarthmore PA
Nutter JW *ret* Houston TX
O'Brien EE Houston TX
Onyendi ME
Osborne JA *ret* Austin TX
Parker RC *ret* Livingston TX
Petty CR Angleton TX
Picot KF Cirencester TX
Pierce RJ *ret* Springfield MO
Pitts JR *ret* Houston TX
Pogue RD Arlington TX
Pope SM *ret* Georgetown TX
Porter LB *ret* Houston TX
Poteet DB *ret* Katy TX
Powell AC *ret* Jackson MS
Presler TL *ret* Montgomery VT
Preston JM *ret* Spring TX
Puckett DFK *ret* Houston TX
Rardin TM *ret* Hewitt TX
Reddick MJ *dcn* Houston TX
Reynolds JD *ret* Houston TX
Robbins ME Huntsville TX
Robertson CJ Kirkland WA
Robinson DL Austin TX
Russell JD *ret* Tyler TX
Russell KS Austin TX
Ryan KM Dallas TX
Sachers CS *ret* Boerne TX
Saunders LA Milwaukee WI
Savage HS Bay City TX
Scheider DM
Schiffmayer JP *ret* Houston TX
Scott JE *ret* Houston TX
Sellers RC *ret* Daytona Beach FL
Seracuse LK *ret* Conroe TX
Shannon CS *ret* Houston TX
Sheffield EJ *ret* Wallisville TX
Sheffield JJ *ret* San Antonio TX
Skyles BH *ret* Deer Park TX
Smith CB *ret* Austin TX
Smith CR *ret* Memphis TN

Smith RN *ret* Austin TX
Smith SM Greensboro NC
Sonnen JA *ret* Pasadena TX
Sotomayor RS *ret*
Stein EL *ret* Houston TX
Stockton JV Pflugerville TX
Sullivan KL
Sweet PAS *dcn* Houston TX
Taft PE *ret* Tyler TX
Tarbet RM *ret* Mc Gregor TX
Taylor WH *ret* Lenox MA
Terhune RD *ret* Austin TX
Thames DB Alexandria VA
Thomas CJ Friendswood TX
Thomas PG *ret* Pittsboro NC
Tirrell CD *ret* Houston TX
Tobola CP Palacios TX
Todd SR *ret* Houston TX
Travis D Albuquerque NM
Tubbs SF *ret* Tyler TX
Tucker AE Austin TX
Tucker DJ *ret* Galveston TX
Tucker JT *ret* Chapel Hill NC
Turner PW *ret* Austin TX
Udell GME *ret* DeSoto TX
Vaszuez-Juarez PE *ret* Columbus TX
Viggiano RP Malvern PA

Wallace TA *ret* Belton TX
Wallens MG Dallas TX
Walling AC *ret* Round Rock TX
Ward J *ret* Spring TX
Warde EJ Waco TX
Wareing RE *ret* Friendswood TX
Waters MH *ret* Austin TX
Watson JD Longview TX
Watt JH *ret* Mission TX
Wells JT *ret* Woodway TX
Wells RL *ret* Pearland TX
Welty TA Palestine TX
Whitfield RP *ret* Austin TX
Whitfield SR *ret* Leander TX
Whitmore BG *ret* Huntsville TX
Whittington RC *dcn*
Wigmore WJ Round Rock TX
Wilburn MI Houston TX
Williams JA *ret* Austin TX
Williams JG *ret* College Station TX
Willke HA *ret* Austin TX
Wilson RE Lenox MA
Wingfield VG *ret* Houston TX
Wise CM San Antonio TX
Woolery-Price ER *dcn* Austin TX
Yawn JS Ponte Vedra Beach FL
Younger LK *ret* Johnson City TX

DIOCESE OF UPPER SOUTH CAROLINA
(PROVINCE IV)
Comprises Northwestern South Carolina
DIOCESAN OFFICE 1115 Marion St Columbia SC 29201
TEL (803) 771-7800   FAX (803) 799-5119
E-MAIL diocese@edusc.org   WEB www.edusc.org

Previous Bishops—
Kirkman G Finlay 1922-38; John
J Gravatt 1939-53; C Alfred Cole
1953-63; John A Pinckney 1963-
72; George M Alexander 1973-79;
Rogers S Harris suffr 1985-89;
Wm A Beckham 1979-94; Wm
F Carr asst 1991-94; Dorsey F
Henderson Jr 1995-2009

Bishop—Rt Rev W Andrew Waldo (1046) (Dio
22 May 2010)

Chanc K Shealy; *Asst Chanc* JP Lee; *Sec* Rev S
Fleischer; *Asst to BP* M Sweet; *Cn for Cong Dev/
Admin* Rev DM Hazel; *Cn for Lead/Chr Form* Rev
K Wilson; *Cn for Communications* C Graves; *Aging
Min* Rev W Kinyon; *Pres ECW* W Evans; *Cursillo* G
Keller; *DOK* C Armstrong; *ER&D* P/B Ewing; *Com*
M Richards; *Treas* Rev J Neuberger; *Sec to Conv* B
Hendrix

Stand Comm—Cler: M Abdelnour S Anderson J
Barnhill D Deaderick S Fleischer J Gettys N Morris

A Pilat G Wiseman; *Lay:* E Burch J Clarkson J
Coleman R Dent E Greenleaf M Richards T Stepp
B Williamson

Dio Conv: 4-5 Nov 2016 St John's, Columbia, SC

PARISHES, MISSIONS, AND CLERGY

Abbeville Trinity Episcopal Church **M** (40) No 200
Church Street 29620-0911 (Mail to: PO Box 911
29620-0911) Kenneth Tucker (864) 366-5186

Aiken St Augustine of Canterbury **M** (132) 1630
Silver Bluff Rd 29803-9200 (Mail to: 1630 Silver
Bluff Rd 29803-9200) Dale Klitzke (803) 641-
1913

Aiken St Thaddeus Episcopal Church **P** (569) 125
Pendleton St SW 29801-3861 (Mail to: 125
Pendleton St SW 29801-3861) Grant Wiseman
Joseph Whitehurst (803) 648-5497

Anderson Grace Episcopal Church **P** (410) 711
S McDuffie St 29624-2334 (Mail to: 711 S
McDuffie St 29624) John Hardaway (864) 225-
8011

Anderson St George Episcopal Church **P** (80) 2206 N Highway 81 29621-2548 (Mail to: 2206 N Highway 81 29621-2548) (864) 224-1104

Batesburg St Pauls Episcopal Church **PS** 116 S Perry St 29006-2244 (Mail to: 116 S Perry St 29006-2244) Teddy Higgins (803) 532-0950

Beech Island All Saints Episcopal Church **M** (31) 305 Williston Rd 29842-8407 (Mail to: 305 Williston Rd 29842-8407) (803) 302-9900

Boiling Spgs St Margarets Episcopal Church **P** (222) 4180 Highway 9 29316-8580 (Mail to: PO Box 160024 29316-0002) Henry Leonard (864) 578-3238

Camden Grace Episcopal Church **P** (507) 1315 Lyttleton St 29020-3617 (Mail to: 1315 Lyttleton St 29020-3600) James Barnhill Michael Bullock (803) 432-7621

Cayce All Saints' Episcopal Church **P** (150) 1001 12th St 29033-3302 (Mail to: 1001 12th St 29033-3302) Patricia Sexton (803) 796-5735

Chapin St Francis of Assisi **P** (542) 735 Old Lexington Hwy 29036-7980 (Mail to: PO Box 265 29036-0265) (803) 345-1550

Chester St Marks Episcopal Church **M** (12) 132 Center St 29706-1703 (Mail to: PO Box 572 29706-0572) William Feus (803) 581-3273

Clemson Holy Trinity Episcopal Parish **P** (474) 193 Old Greenville Hwy 29631-1335 (Mail to: 193 Old Greenville Hwy 29631-1335) (864) 654-5071

Clinton All Saints Episcopal Church **P** (122) 505 Calvert Ave 29325-2620 (Mail to: 505 Calvert Ave 29325-2620) Harold Morgan (864) 833-1388

Columbia Church of the Cross **M** (69) 7244 Patterson Rd PO Box 9561 29209-2626 (Mail to: PO Box 9561 29209-2626) Simon Bautista J Blaney Pridgen Herbert Johnson (803) 776-1864

Columbia Church of the Good Shepherd **P** (353) 1512 Blanding St 29201-2907 (Mail to: 1512 Blanding St 29201-2907) James Lyon (803) 779-2960

Columbia Finlay House **Other** 2100 Blossom St 29205-2248 (Mail to: 2100 Blossom St 29205-2248) Brice Kinyon (803) 799-6524

Columbia St Davids Episcopal Church **P** (373) 605 Polo Rd 29223-2905 (Mail to: 605 Polo Rd 29223-2905) William Brock (803) 736-0866

Columbia St Johns Episcopal Church **P** (1385) 2827 Wheat St 29205-2515 (Mail to: 2827 Wheat St 29205-2515) John Montgomery Scott Fleischer Louis Wheeler William Wight (803) 799-4767

Columbia St Lukes Episcopal Church **P** (266) 1300 Pine St 29204-1846 (Mail to: 1300 Pine St 29204-1846) Calvin Griffin (803) 254-2327

Columbia St Martins-in-the-Fields **P** (757) 5220 Clemson Ave 29206-3011 (Mail to: 5220 Clemson Ave 29206-3098) Sarah Johnston Charles Petit Susan Prinz Henry Wall (803) 787-0392

Columbia St Marys Episcopal Church **P** (680) 170 Saint Andrews Rd 29210-4107 (Mail to: 170 St Andrews Road 29210-4412) Phillip Webster Alfredo Gonzalez Alice Ray (803) 798-2776

Columbia St Michael and All Angels **P** (190) § 6408 Bridgewood Rd 29206-2126 (Mail to: 6408 Bridgewood Rd 29206-2198) Margaret Jennings Todd Jill Zook-Jones (803) 782-8080

Columbia St Timothys Episcopal Church **P** (117) 900 Calhoun St 29201-2308 (Mail to: 900 Calhoun St 29201-2308) Dimitrula Henson (803) 765-1519

✠ **Columbia** Trinity Cathedral **O** (3834) 1100 Sumter St 29201-3717 (Mail to: 1100 Sumter St 29201-3795) Dane Boston Charles Davis Charles Davis Emily Hylden Timothy Jones Patricia Malanuk (803) 771-7300

Easley St Michaels Episcopal Church **P** (196) 1200 Powdersville Rd 29642-2422 (Mail to: 1200 Powdersville Rd 29642-2422) Thomas Dudley (864) 859-6296

Eastover St Thomas Church **M** (59) No 115 Yelton Road 29044-0614 (Mail to: PO Box 614 29044-0614) Brice Kinyon (803) 479-4101

Fort Mill St Pauls Episcopal Church **P** (329) 501 Pine St 29715-1750 (Mail to: PO Box 753 29716-0753) Sarah Franklin (803) 547-5968

Gaffney Episcopal Church of the Incarnation **P** (110) 308 College Dr 29340-3007 (Mail to: 308 College Dr 29340-3007) Jeannette Gettys (864) 489-6183

Graniteville St Pauls Episcopal Church **P** (82) 111 Hard St 29829 (Mail to: PO Box 276 29829-0276) Douglas Puckett (803) 663-9457

Great Falls St Peters Episcopal Church **M** (32) 30 Hampton St 29055-1636 (Mail to: PO Box 521 29055-0521) Charles Davis (803) 482-6755

Greenville Christ Episcopal Church **P** (3498) § 10 N Church St 29601-2809 (Mail to: 10 N Church St 29601-2864) Harrison McLeod Robert Chiles John Eichelberger Donald Hultstrand (864) 271-8773

Greenville Church of the Redeemer **P** (335) 120 Mauldin Rd 29605-1257 (Mail to: 120 Mauldin Rd 29605-1257) Scott Anderson (864) 277-4562

Greenville St Andrews Episcopal Church **P** (187) 1002 S Main St 29601-3335 (Mail to: 1002 South Main St 29601-3335) Stephen Bolle David Taylor (864) 235-5884

Greenville St Francis Episcopal Church **P** (378) 301 Piney Mountain Rd. 29609 (Mail to: C/O St James Church 301 Piney Mountain Rd 29609-3035) (864) 268-2845

Greenville St James Episcopal Church **P** (651) 301 Piney Mountain Rd 29609-3035 (Mail to: 301 Piney Mountain Rd 29609-3035) Stephen Rhoades (864) 244-6358

Greenville St Peters Episcopal Church **P** (555) 910 Hudson Rd 29615-3430 (Mail to: PO Box 25817 29616-0817) Furman Buchanan Micah Del Priore (864) 268-7280

Greenville St Philips Church **M** (44) 31 Allendale Ln 29607-2208 (Mail to: PO Box 17521 29606-8521) John Zellner (864) 271-1382

Greenwood Church of the Resurrection **P** (484) 700 Main St W 29646-3211 (Mail to: PO Box 3283 29648-3283) Nicholas Beasley Timothy Ervolina (864) 223-5426

Greer Church of the Good Shepherd **P** (189) 200 Cannon St 29651-3705 (Mail to: PO Box 1408 29652-1408) Michael Schnatterly (864) 877-2330

Hopkins St Johns Episcopal Church **P** (168) 1151 Elm Savannah Road 29061-8938 (Mail to: 1151 Elm Savannah Road 29061-8938) Daniel Hank (803) 776-9292

Irmo St Simon and St Jude Episcopal Church **P** (278) 1110 Kinley Rd 29063-9633 (Mail to: 1110 Kinley Rd 29063-9633) Mark Abdelnour (803) 732-0153

Jenkinsville St Barnabas Episcopal Church **M** (71) 1056 St. Barnabas Church Road 29065 (Mail to: PO Box 18 29065-0018) (803) 635-4995

Lancaster Christ Episcopal Church **P** (111) 534 Plantation Rd 29720 (Mail to: PO Box 488 29721-0488) Gordon Hamilton (803) 286-5224

Laurens Church of the Epiphany **P** (81) 225 W Main St 29360-2940 (Mail to: 225 W Main St 29360-2940) (864) 984-7000

Lexington St Albans Episcopal Church **P** (343) 403 Park Rd 29072-9060 (Mail to: PO Box 882 29071-0882) Thomas Dimarco (803) 359-2444

Newberry St Lukes Episcopal Church **P** (108) 1605 Main St 29108-3456 (Mail to: 1605 Main St 29108-3456) Mamie Morgan (803) 276-8513

North August St Bartholomews Episcopal Church **P** (539) 471 W Martintown Rd 29841-3105 (Mail to: 471 W Martintown Rd 29841-3105) Geoffrey Coupland David Henson (803) 279-4622

Pauline Calvary Episcopal Church **M** (55) C/O Claude Finney 305 Quinn Rd 29374-2834 (Mail to: PO Box 549 29374-0549) Louis Miller (864) 582-3952

Ridgeway St Stephens Episcopal Church **M** (67) 335 Longtown Rd 29130-6814 (Mail to: PO Box 26 29130-0026)

Rock Hill Church Of Our Saviour **P** (565) 144 Caldwell St 29730-4534 (Mail to: 144 Caldwell St 29730-4534) Janice Chalaron (803) 327-1131

Seneca Church of the Ascension **P** (159) 214 Northampton Road 29672-2221 (Mail to: 214 Northampton Road 29672-2221) Carol Marshall (864) 882-2006

Simpsonville Holy Cross Episcopal Church **P** (696) 205 E College St 29681-2616 (Mail to: PO Box 187 29681-0187) Michael Flanagan Linda Gosnell Susan Hardaway

Spartanburg Episcopal Church of the Advent **P** (1446) 141 Advent St 29302-1904 (Mail to: 141 Advent St 29302-1904) Jonathan Morris Deborah Apoldo Stephen McGehee (864) 585-2268

Spartanburg Episcopal Church of the Epiphany **M** (53) 121 W Park Dr 29306-5010 (Mail to: PO Box 726 29304-0726)

Spartanburg St Christophers Church Episcopal **M** (169) 400 Dupre Dr 29307-2976 (Mail to: 400 Dupre Dr 29307-2976) Leslie Horvath James Trimble (864) 585-2858

Spartanburg St Matthews Episcopal Church **P** (501) 101 Saint Matthews Ln 29301-1378 (Mail to: 101 Saint Matthews Ln 29301-1378) Robert Brown (864) 576-0424

Trenton Episcopal Church of the Ridge **M** (105) 117 Watson St 29847-0206 (Mail to: PO Box 206 29847) Thomas Dimarco (803) 275-3934

Union Church of the Nativity **M** (61) 320 S Church St 29379-2307 (Mail to: PO Box 456 29379-0456) Louis Miller (864) 427-8610

Winnsboro St Johns Episcopal Church **P** (105) 301 W Liberty St 29180-1423 (Mail to: 301 W Liberty St 29180-1423) (803) 635-4398

York Church of the Good Shepherd **P** (202) 108 E Liberty St 29745-1549 (Mail to: PO Box 437 29745-0437)

NON-PAROCHIAL CLERGY

Anderson FE *ret* San Antonio TX
Bethell JC Clemson SC
Blauvelt JD Pass Christian MS
Bridgforth DE *ret* Columbia SC
Brown JA Columbia SC
Bryce CDF *ret* Cross SC
Byrd FC *ret* Columbia SC
Cannon AC *ret* Flat Rock NC
Carter HR Everett WA
Chassey GI *ret* West Columbia SC
Clements CC *ret* West Columbia SC
Cockrell R *ret* Anderson SC
Cole RW *ret* Spartanburg SC
Cooling DA *ret* Lambertville NJ
Cope MS Spartanburg SC
Crozier RL Aiken SC
Crum GM *ret* Helena MT
Culliper JR *ret* Balsam Grove NC
Davis JM West Columbia SC
Davis TC *ret* Clemson SC
Davis TP Columbia SC
Deaderick DLM *dcn* Columbia SC
Diggs TT *ret* Rock Hill SC
Drake LS Aiken SC
Dunbar RB *ret* Rock Hill SC
Earls JG
Edwards JL *ret* Columbia SC
Eldridge RW Fort McPherson GA
Fitch WB *ret* Columbia SC
Foss CS *ret* Troutdale OR
Goodkind CC *ret* Murrells Inlet SC
Gotautas PM *dcn*
Gould GH *ret* Sumter SC

Greeley PW *ret* York SC
Grimball RB Greenville SC
Harris H *dcn* Elgin SC
Hawes PW *ret* Tryon NC
Haynes AS *ret* West Columbia SC
Hazel DM *dcn* Columbia SC
Heath SB Columbia SC
Henry WW *ret* Easley SC
Hipp TA *dcn* Greenville SC
Holmes AR Fountain Inn SC
Hostetter J *dcn* Jensen Beach FL
Huntley PB *ret* Cheraw SC
Ireland CL *ret* Columbia SC
Jackson DH Greenville SC
Jeffers ME *dcn* Anderson SC
Kirk PL *dcn*
Libbey EW *ret* Saluda NC
Libbey RE *ret* Asheville NC
Manning SL Prosperity SC
Marks WP *ret* Easley SC
McCreary EC *ret* Cleveland SC
McDowell MCD Spartanburg SC
Meadowcroft JW *ret* Laurens SC
Meeks EG *ret* Baltimore MD
Nead PE *ret* Evans GA
Neuburger JE *ret* Winnsboro SC
Nieman JS Clemson SC
Oswald TD Mount Pleasant SC
Parlier ST *dcn* West Columbia SC
Parrott SF Greer SC
Perrin SE *dcn*
Phillips RL *ret* Fort Mill SC
Pilat AF *dcn* Columbia SC

Poisson EH North Augusta SC
Purser JP *ret* Chapin SC
Quinn CES *dcn* Greenville SC
Retzlaff G *ret* West Columbia SC
Riegel RG *ret* Columbia SC
Roberson MMM *ret* Columbia SC
Rowell EM *ret* Ocklawaha FL
Ruggles R York SC
Schnaufer DE *ret* Greenville SC
Smith DL *ret* SC
Stricker DW *ret* Huntsville AL
Stricklin PE *ret* Columbia SC
Tarbox JE Lexington SC
Taylor RC Greenville SC
Thompson DFO *ret* North Augusta SC
Thompson WE *ret* Taylors SC
Tipton TH *ret* Pawleys Island SC
Tollison HE *ret* Greenville SC
Turner CH *ret* Marion NC
Upton DH *ret* Greenville SC
Waldrop CME *ret* Aiken SC
Walters FA *dcn* Cayce SC
Walters WH *ret* Lancaster SC
Webb RA Rock Hill SC
Webster KS Dallas TX
Werner M Columbia SC
Weston EH *ret* Hopkins SC
Whiddon EH *dcn* Greenville SC
White LD Pendleton OR
Whitehead PH *ret* Columbia SC
Wight SM *ret* Blythewood SC
Wilson KC Columbia SC
Workman JK *ret* Easley SC

DIOCESE OF UTAH

(PROVINCE VIII)

Comprises the State of Utah, excluding Navajoland and including Page, AZ
DIOCESAN OFFICE 75 South 200 East Salt Lake City UT 84111-2147
TEL (801) 322-4131, 800-343-4756   FAX (801) 322-5096
E-MAIL arogers@episcopal-ut.org   WEB www.episcopal-ut.org

Previous Bishops—
Daniel S Tuttle 1867-86, Abiel Leonard 1888-1903, Franklin S Spalding 1904-14, Paul Jones 1914-18, Arthur W Moulton 1920-46, Stephen C Clark 1946-50, Richard S Watson 1951-71, E Otis Charles 1971-86, George E Bates 1986-97, Carolyn T Irish coadj 1996-97 Bp 1997-2010

Bishop—Rt Rev Scott B Hayashi (1038) (Dio 6 Nov 2010)

Bp Adm Asst M Daly; *Comm* C Wirth; *Chanc* S Hutchinson; *Treas* S Garrard; *Conv Sec* D Sakrison; *Fin Off* S Andersen; *Cn for Min Form & Exec Off* MJ Nestler; *Latino Missioner* P Ramos

Stand Comm—Cler: Pres L Briggs; *Lay: VP* L Watt

Dio Conv: 29-30 April 2016 The Cathedral Church of St. Mark, Salt Lake City UT

PARISHES, MISSIONS, AND CLERGY

Brigham City St Michaels Episcopal Church **M** (96) 589 S 200 E 84302-2903 (Mail to: 589 S 200 E 84302-2903) (801) 391-2185

Cedar City St Judes Episcopal Church **M** (35) 70 N 200 W 84720-2570 (Mail to: 70 N 200 W 84720-2570) (435) 586-3623

Centerville Church of the Resurrection **P** (76) 1131 S Main St 84014-2217 (Mail to: 1131 S Main St 84014-2217) (801) 295-1360

Clearfield St Peters Episcopal Church **P** (116) 1204 E 1450 S 84015-1643 (Mail to: 1579 S State St 84015-1649)

Ivins Spirit of the Desert **M** (20) 873 Coyote Gulch Ct Ste D 84738-6708 (Mail to: 873 Coyote Gulch Ct Ste D 84738-6708) (435) 592-0034

Logan St Johns Episcopal Church **P** (130) No 85 East 100 North 84321-4624 (Mail to: 85 East 100 North 84321-4624) (435) 752-0331

Midvale St James Episcopal Church **P** (510) 7486 Union Park Ave 84047-4164 (Mail to: 7486 Union Park Ave 84047-4164) John Dillon Marie Therese Heyduk (801) 566-1311

Moab Mision de San Francisco **P** (143) 250 Kane Creek Blvd 84532-2538 (Mail to: PO Box 596 84532-0596) (435) 259-3113

Moab St Francis Episcopal Church **P** (156) 250 Kane Creek Blvd 84532-2950 (Mail to: PO Box 96 84532-0096) (435) 259-5831

Ogden Church of the Good Shepherd **P** (314) 2374 Grant Ave 84401-1408 (Mail to: 2374 Grant Ave 84401-1408) Vanessa Cato Nancy Groshart Lewis Poggemeyer (801) 392-8168

Page St Davids Episcopal Church **M** (162) 421 S Lake Powell Blvd 86046 (Mail to: PO Box 125 86040-0125)

Park City St Lukes Church **P** (283) 4595 N. Silver Springs Dr. 84098 (Mail to: PO Box 981208 84098-1208) (435) 649-4900

Price Ascension St Matthew's Episcopal Church **M** (143) 522 Homestead Blvd 84501-2261 (Mail to: 522 N Homestead Blvd 84501) (435) 637-0106

Provo St Marys Episcopal Church **P** (51) 50 W 200 N 84601-2806 (Mail to: 50 W 200 N 84601) Craig Klein Peter Van Hook (801) 373-3090

Randlett Church of the Holy Spirit **M** (221) 4250 South 10000 E 84063 (Mail to: HC 69 Box 630016 84063) (435) 545-2400

Salt Lake City All Saints Episcopal Church **P** (394) 1710 Foothill Dr 84108-3052 (Mail to: 1710 Foothill Dr 84108) Tracy Browning Ernest Bebb Ronald Belnap Antoinette Catron Miner Deborah Hughes-Habel (801) 581-0380

✠ **Salt Lake City** Cathedral Church of St Mark **O** (971) 231 East 100 South 84111-1604 (Mail to: 231 East 100 South 84111-1604) Raymond Waldon Michael Milligan Jennifer Tucker (801) 322-3400

Salt Lake City St Pauls Episcopal Church **P** (680) 261 S 900 E 84102-2308 (Mail to: 261 S 900 E 84102-2308) Kurt Wiesner Tracy Browning Christine Contestable (801) 322-5869

St George Grace Episcopal Church **P** (360) 1072 East 900 South 84790-4042 (Mail to: 1072 East 900 South 84790-4042)

Tooele St Barnabas Episcopal Church **M** (62) 286 N 7th St 84074-2479 (Mail to: 1784 N Aaron Dr 84074-8221) (435) 882-4721

Vernal St Pauls Episcopal Church **P** (63) 226 W Main St 84078-2506 (Mail to: 226 W Main St 84078-2506) (435) 781-1806

West Valley City Iglesia Episcopal San Esteban **P** (98) 4615 S 3200 W 84119-5943 (Mail to: 4615 S 3200 W 84119-5943) (801) 968-2731

West Valley City St Stephens Episcopal Church **P** (153) 4615 S 3200 W 84119-5943 (Mail to: 4615 S 3200 West 84119-5943) (801) 968-2731

Whiterocks St Elizabeths Episcopal Church **P** (122) 11700 N 3900 E 84085 (Mail to: PO Box 100 84085-0100) (435) 353-4279

NON-PAROCHIAL CLERGY

Adams DS *dcn* Perry UT
Alder ST *dcn* Signal Hill CA
Allman SG *ret* Cedar City UT
Altizer AM
Andersen SC Salt Lake City UT
Atem GG
Barbuto JS South Jordan UT
Beacham AB Vernal UT
Beery SB *ret* Alexandria VA
Beitzel WD Ben Lomond CA
Belsky EE *ret* Grand Junction CO
Briggs LZ Salt Lake City UT
Brock EA Randlett UT
Buckley HW *ret* Helena MT
Carter FL *ret* Tooele UT
Cendese WI *ret* Salt Lake City UT
Clevenger MR Shoreham NY
Cook KK Boulder CO
Crocker JAF *ret* Florence OR
Doherty TB Salt Lake City UT
Duffield SEM *ret* Whiterocks UT
Eller RE *ret* Ridgecrest CA
Evans LD *ret* Salt Lake City UT
Fabre JK *dcn* West Valley City UT
Filler JA *ret* Box Elder SD
Fox RS *dcn* New York NY
Frank RL *ret dcn* Phoenix AZ
Giacoma CL Park City UT
Gonzalez IT West Valley City UT
Gordon CL Tooele UT
Hatch JA *ret* Salt Lake City UT
Heath CH *dcn*
Hunter ES *ret dcn* Salt Lake City UT
Janda MS
Johnson DP *ret* Salt Lake City UT
Johnson MJ *dcn* Logan UT
Jones SLS *dcn* Park City UT
Kotuby J Midvale UT
Lawson FQ Salt Lake City UT
Lea GA Moab UT
Lee JC Keelung
Marsh CA *ret* Salt Lake City UT
Maxwell WF *ret* Port Townsend WA
Mendez R *ret* Pocatello ID
Montgomery LA Cedar City UT
Moore CP Salt Lake City UT
Nestler MJ Cottonwood Heights UT
Potter JC *ret* Salt Lake City UT
Rabago-Nunez LA Salt Lake City UT

Ramos P Salt Lake City UT
Roberts SJ Salt Lake City UT
Robinson CE Park City UT
Sakrison DL Moab UT
Seiter CD Brigham City UT
Shucker CA *ret* Salida CO
Smith BJ *ret* Cordova AK
Stasser NL *ret* Tucson AZ
Stephens J *ret* St George UT

Sturgeon SC *dcn* Logan UT
Tendick JR *ret* Moab UT
Toone SK Clearfield UT
Two Bulls RG *ret* Hermosa SD
Ure LR Salt Lake City UT
Van Oss ET Orem UT
Walling CM
Whittaker RR Tooele UT
Winder FLP *ret* Salt Lake City UT

DIOCESE OF VENEZUELA
IGLESIA ANGLICANA/EPISCOPAL EN VENEZUELA
(PROVINCE IX)
DIOCESAN OFFICE Centro Diocesano, Ave Caroni No 100, Colinas de Bello Monte Caracas
(Mail: 49-143 Colinas de Bello Monte Caracas 1042-a Venezuela)
TEL: (58) 212-7513046 or (58) 212-7530723   FAX (58) 212-7513180
E-MAIL: obispoguerrero@iglesianglicanavzla.org WEB www.iglesianglicanavzla.org

Previous Bishops—
Guy Marshall 1967-76, Hyden Jones 1976-1986, Onell Soto 1987-1995

Bishop—Rt Rev Orlando JT Guerrero (1004)

Dio Admin: Sr Marco A Ramos C; *Treas:* Sr José Francisco; *Chris Ed:* Lic Adrián E Cárdenas T

PARISHES, MISSIONS, AND CLERGY
Barquisimeto Mision San Judas Tadeo **M** Av. Florencio Jimenez - KM14 Via Quibor (Mail to: Ave Florencio Jimenez Manzana Caja No. L-95)
Caraballeda Mision Anglicana San Mateo **M** Vista al Mar (Mail to: Centro Diocesano) (212) 615-4440
Caracas Capilla de la Reconciliacion **P** Ave Caroni #100, Colinas Bello Monte (Mail to: Ave Caroni #100, Colinas Bello Monte) (212) 753-0723
Caripe Mision de la Sagrada Familia **M** El Potrero de Teresen (Mail to: Calle El Cementerio Arriba No. 27- Teresen) 2925551022
Caripe Mision de San Miguel Arcangel **M** Sector Alto de las Brisas (Mail to: Sector Alto de las Brisas) (281) 808-0882
Caripe 6224 Mision Bendita Virgen Maria **M** Sector La Sabana (Mail to: Sector La Sabana) 2925551022
El Callao, 8017 Mision de San Agustin de Cantorbery **M** Via Santa Elena de Uairen Km 72 (Mail to: Calle Orinoco #3) 2887621206
El Callao, 8056 Iglesia de la Resurreccion **M** Calle Heres Con Bolivar #14 (Mail to: Calle Heres # 14) 2887621206

Puerto La Cruz, 6023 Iglesia de la Santisima Trinidad **M** Valdez No. 46- Tierra Adentro (Mail to: Valdez No. 102- Tierra Adentro)
San Felix, 8050 Iglesia de la Santisima Cruz **M** Tumutu, Urb Bella Vista (Mail to: Calle Bakairies, Detras Semaforo El Roble) (414) 894-9254
San Flaviano Mision de San Flaviano **M** Carretera Nacional via la Gran Sabana (Mail to: Calle Orinoco #3) 2887621206
Steenrijk, Curacao Iglesia de Todos los Santos **P** Heelsumstraat #18 (Mail to: Heelsumstraat #18)

INSTITUTIONS
ISTESAC Insituto Superior de Teología San Agustine de Cantórbery *E-mail* istesac@iglesianglicanavzla.org; *Web* www.iglesianglicanavzla.org/ISTESAC.htm

NON-PAROCHIAL CLERGY
Anthony-Charles AG
Camacho-Osorio N
Carreno-Gamboa BF
Colmenarez GA Caracas
Delgado-Marksman AF
Joseph PJ Sta Elena Venezuela
Mendoza Perez JC Colinas de Bello Monte Caracas 1042-A
Salazar-Sotillo OR
Salazar-Vasquez JF
Sucre-Cordova GA *ret*
Vesga-Ardila R *ret*
Williams WD Colinas de Bello Monte Caracas 1042-A

DIOCESE OF VERMONT
(PROVINCE I)
Comprises the State of Vermont
DIOCESAN OFFICE 5 Rock Pt Rd Burlington VT 05408-2735
TEL (802) 863-3431   FAX (802) 860-1562
E-MAIL adminasst@dioceseofvermont.org   WEB www.dioceseofvermont.org

Previous Bishops—
John H Hopkins 1832-68, Wm HA Bissell 1868-93, Arthur AC Hall 1894-1929, Wm F Weeks coadj 1913-14, Geo Y Bliss coadj 1915-24, Samuel B Booth coadj 1925 Bp 1929-35, Vedder Van Dyck 1936-60, Harvey D Butterfield 1961-74 Robert S Kerr 1974-86, Daniel L Swenson coadj 1986 Bp 1987-93, Mary Adelia R McLeod Bp 1993-2001

Bishop—Rt Rev Thomas Clark Ely (965) (Dio 28 April 2001)

Cn to Ord L Bates; *Archdcn* C Cooke; *Fin-Property Adm* J Giguere; *Bishop Booth Conf Ctr Mgr* A Drapelick; *Reg/Hist* E Allison; *Off Asst* D Crabtree; *Bishop's Asst* S Kremer; *Off Admin* M Sandul; *Comm Min* K Moore; *Conv Sec* N Robinson; *Treas* WH Good Jr; *Chanc* T Little; *V Chanc* W Meub; *Deploy Off /Trans Min* L Bates; *COM COD Chair* LA Crawford; *Dio Altar Guild Co-Chairs* A Davis, C Murray; *Earth Stew Convener* W Grace; *Dismantling Racism Chair* vacant; *Outreach & Social Just Chair* LA Crawford; *Oversight & Audit Comm* D Ganter; *UTO Coord* W. Grace

Stand Comm—Cler: *Pres* LA Crawford L Baxter M Lindquist T Bennett; *Lay:* E Van Dyk H Kendrick M Neal B Murphy

Dio Conv: 6-7 Nov 2016 Cathedral Church of St Paul Burlington VT

PARISHES, MISSIONS, AND CLERGY

Alburg St Lukes Episcopal Mission **M** (11) 33 N Main St 05440-9726 (Mail to: PO Box 113 05440-0113) Thora Chadwick (802) 863-8036

Arlington St James Episcopal Church **P** (166) 46 Church St 05250 (Mail to: PO Box 25 05250-0025) Scott Neal Christopher David

Barre Church of the Good Shepherd **P** (84) 39 Washington St 05641-4236 (Mail to: PO Box 726 05641-0726) William Kooperkamp (802) 476-3929

Bellows Falls Immanuel Episcopal Church **HC** (40) 20 Church St 05101-1515 (Mail to: PO Box 64 05101-0064) Steven Fuller Charles Mansfield

Bennington St Peters Episcopal Church **P** (443) 200 Pleasant St 05201-2526 (Mail to: 200 Pleasant St 05201-2526) Justin Lanier Penelope Hawkins (802) 442-2911

Bethel Christ Episcopal Church **P** (30) 5 Main St 05032-9002 (Mail to: PO Box 383 05032-0383) (802) 234-5680

Brandon St Thomas and Grace Church **P** (62) 19 Conant Sq 05733-1011 (Mail to: 19 Conant Sq 05733-1011)

Brattleboro St Michaels Episcopal Church **P** (314) 16 Bradley Ave 05301-3429 (Mail to: 16 Bradley Ave 05301-3429) Mary Lindquist Jean Jersey Jean Smith (802) 254-6048

✠ **Burlington** Cathedral Church of St Paul **O** (345) 2 Cherry St 05401-7304 (Mail to: 2 Cherry St 05401-7304) Alice Finan Joseph Baker Diane Nancekivell

Canaan St Paul-Border Parish **P** (3) 55 Power House Rd 05903 (Mail to: 51 Park St 05903-9708) Robert Lee (802) 266-8269

Chester St Lukes Episcopal Church **P** (142) 313 Vermont 11 05143 (Mail to: PO Box 8 05143-0008) Heidi Edson (802) 875-6000

Colchester St Andrews Episcopal Church **P** (188) 1063 Prim Rd 05446 (Mail to: PO Box 78 05446-0078) Lisette Baxter (802) 658-0533

East Middlebury Jerusalem Gathering **SC** PO Box 554 05740-0554 (Mail to: PO Box 554 05740-0554) Mary Bidwell Catherine Nichols

Enosburg Fls St Matthews Episcopal Church **P** (24) C/O Michael Burfoot Md 1650 Water Tower Rd 05450-5422 (Mail to: PO Box 276 05450-0276) Jane Presler (802) 933-6127

Essex Jct St James Episcopal Church **P** (328) 4 St James Pl 05452-3223 (Mail to: 4 St James Pl 05452-3223) G David Ganter (802) 878-4014

Fair Haven St Marks-St Lukes Episcopal Mission **M** (24) 13 East Main St 05743 (Mail to: PO Box 293 05743) John Miller (203) 788-6965

Fairlee St Martins Episcopal Church **P** (90) 1 Lake Morey Rd 05045-9595 (Mail to: PO Box 158 05045-0158) Mark Preece (802) 333-9725

Hardwick Church of St John the Baptist **P** (43) PO Box 424 05843-0424 (Mail to: PO Box 424 05843-0424) Zarina O'Hagin (802) 472-5979

Island Pond Christ Church Episcopal Mission **M** (26) 5 Walnut Ave 05846 (Mail to: PO Box 341 05846-0341) (802) 723-6381

Killington Church of Our Saviour **M** (22) 316 Mission Farm Rd 05751-9451 (Mail to: P O Box 272 05056) Lee Crawford (802) 422-9064

Lyndonville St Peter Episcopal Mission **M** (46) 51 Elm St 05851-0041 (Mail to: PO Box 41 05851-0041) (802) 626-5705

Manchestr Ctr Zion Church **P** (631) 5167 Main St 05255-9772 (Mail to: PO Box 717 05255-0717) John Mitchell (802) 362-1987

Middlebury St Stephens Episcopal Church **P** (464) 3 Main St 05753-1450 (Mail to: 3 Main St 05753-0223) Susan McGarry Donald Morris Lucy Pellegrini (802) 388-7200

Montpelier Christ Episcopal Church **P** (229) 64 State St 05602-2933 (Mail to: 64 State St 05602-2933) Paul Habersang (802) 223-3631

Newport St Marks Episcopal Church **HC** (183) 44 2nd St 05855-2178 (Mail to: PO Box 125 05855-0125) Robert Miller (802) 334-7365

Northfield St Marys Episcopal Church **P** (42) 203 S. Main St. 05663-5670 (Mail to: 203 S Main St 05663-5670) M P Schneider (802) 485-8221

Norwich St Barnabas Episcopal Church **P** (58) 262 Main St 05055 (Mail to: PO Box 306 05055-0306) Todd McKee (802) 649-1923

Proctorsville Gethsemane Church **P** (41) Depot St 05153 (Mail to: PO Box 217 05153-0217) Todd Mckee (802) 226-7967

Randolph St Johns Episcopal Church **P** (80) 15 Summer St 05060-1162 (Mail to: PO Box 278 05060-0278) Susan Taylor (802) 728-9910

Rutland Trinity Episcopal Church **P** (471) 85 West St 05701-3452 (Mail to: 85 West St 05701-3452) William Muller (802) 775-1004

S Burlington All Saints Episcopal Church **P** (207) 1250 Spear St 05403-7407 (Mail to: 1250 Spear St 05403-7407) David Hamilton Daniel MacDonald Margaret Mathauer (802) 862-9750

Saint Albans St Lukes Church **P** (165) 8 Bishop St 05478-1639 (Mail to: 8 Bishop St 05478-1639) James Ballard (802) 524-6212

Shelburne Trinity Episcopal Church **P** (475) 5171 Shelburne Rd 05482-6509 (Mail to: 5171 Shelburne Rd 05482-6509) (802) 985-2269

Sheldon Grace Church **M** (12) Beth Crane Senior Warden 215 Pleasant St 05483-9801 (Mail to: 215 Pleasant St 05483) (802) 899-1188

Springfield St Marks Church **P** (37) 33 Fairground Rd 05156-2112 (Mail to: 33 Fairground Rd 05156-2112) (802) 885-2723

St Johnsbury St Andrews Episcopal Church **P** (40) 1265 Main St 05819-2697 (Mail to: 1265 Main Street 05819-2697) Jean Macdonald (802) 748-2121

Stowe St Johns in the Mountains **P** (125) 1994 Mountain Road 05672-1175 (Mail to: PO Box 1175 05672-1175) Richard Swanson (802) 253-7578

Swanton Holy Trinity Episcopal Church **P** (141) 38 Grand Ave 05488-0273 (Mail to: 38 Grand Ave 05488-1427) Craig Smith John Spainhour (802) 868-7185

Underhill Calvary Episcopal Church **P** (80) 372 Vermont Route 15 05489-0057 (Mail to: PO Box 57 05489-0057) Regina Christianson (802) 899-2326

Vergennes St Paul's Episcopal Church **P** (117) 6 Park St 05491-1129 (Mail to: PO Box 196 05491-0196) Alan Kittelson (802) 877-3322

Waitsfield St Dunstans Episcopal Mission **M** (14) 6307 Main Street 05673 (Mail to: PO Box 1133 05673-1133) Laurian Seeber (802) 479-7920

Wells St Pauls Episcopal Church **M** (45) 587 E Wells Rd 05774-3847 (Mail to: PO Box 726 05774-0726) William Davidson (518) 499-1850

White Riv Jct St Pauls Episcopal Church **P** (204) 749 Hartford Ave 05001-8037 (Mail to: 749 Hartford Ave 05001) Scott Neal Judith Marquess (802) 295-5415

Wilmington St Marys in the Mountains Episcopal **P** (53) 13 E Main St 05363 (Mail to: PO Box 1366 05363-1366) Nicholas Porter (802) 464-9341

Windsor St Pauls Episcopal Church **P** (29) 27 State St 05089-1201 (Mail to: PO Box 725 05089-0725) Donna Reidt (802) 674-6576

Woodstock St James Episcopal Church **P** (213) 2 St. James Place 05091-1214 (Mail to: 2 St James Place 05091-1214) Norman Macleod (802) 457-1727

NON-PAROCHIAL CLERGY

Arbuckle JF *dcn*
Atkinson WH *ret* Meredith NH
Aubert KT Berkeley CA
Austin JE *ret* Digby NS
Bardos GA *ret* Sun City AZ
Barre JL *ret* Wilmington NC
Beebe-Bove P *dcn* Burlington VT
Bennett TA *ret* Newfane VT
Berlenbach BL *ret* Perkinsville VT
Boone AR *ret* Berkeley CA
Borden RB East Middlebury VT
Boyer MM
Brannock-Wanter HP *ret* Hartland VT
Braun EH *dcn* Stowe VT
Brown FR Long Beach CA
Brown JK *ret* Jericho VT
Brown RH *ret* South Burlington VT
Chase BO *ret* Worcester VT
Collins DG *dcn* Springfield VT
Comeau MS *ret* Alburg VT
Cooke CCH *dcn* Burlington VT
Corklin SE *ret* West Glover VT
Coyne MC *ret* Bellows Falls VT
Cramer A *ret* Brattleboro VT
Deppe JS Grosse Pointe Woods MI
Dyson ML
Eberhardt TC *ret* Braintree VT
Eley GW *ret* Burlington VT
Ellis RR *ret* Burlington VT
Emerson EA White River Junction VT
Farrell RD *ret* Swanton VT
Ferry ML *ret* East Bridgewater MA
Flanagan JR
Fletcher MAL Bennington VT
Garrett JN Leeds MA
Genszler M
Gratz LP *ret*

Hayward DE *ret* Mabou NS
Henault AJ *dcn* St Johnsbury VT
Hilgartner E Orford NH
Hitch KR Essex Junction VT
Horton SC *ret* West Lebanon NH
Horvath VJ Bellows Falls VT
Irving SH *ret* Saint Albans VT
Keenan JP *ret* Newport VT
Keizer GJ Sutton VT
Kingdon AM *ret* Vassalboro ME
Lanigan S Long Beach CA
Larcombe DJ Roxbury VT
Laura RS *dcn*
Lawson RA
Lloyd SL *ret* Middlebury VT
Macauley RC Charlotte VT
Maier BA *dcn* Berkeley CA
Maloney LM *ret* Enosburg Falls VT
Mansfield MR *ret* North Middlesex VT
Maranville IW *dcn* Bradenton FL
Maranville JM *dcn* Bradenton FL
McKnight LJZ *ret* Lyndonville VT
McLeod HM *ret* Charleston WV
Meacham CH *ret* Washburn IL
Morris JC *ret* East Corinth VT
Ohlidal SM Burlington VT

Osborn SE Charlotte VT
Patterson KF
Perry JW *ret* Hudson NY
Pickup EA *ret* Alburgh VT
Pierson S *ret* Hinesburg VT
Poppe KW *ret* Burlington VT
Pratt MFC *ret dcn* New Haven VT
Ransom LM Waterbury VT
Reid RW *ret* North Dartmouth MA
Reynes SA *dcn*
Root DE *ret* West Lebanon NH
Rose-Crossley R *ret* Sewanee TN
Rose-Crossley R
Shatagin TI Ardmore OK
Sheldon KS *ret* Hanover NH
Sherwin LA *ret* Montpelier VT
Smith MJ *dcn* Reading VT
St. Germain BAL *dcn* Burlington VT
Stefanik AT *ret* Palm Coast FL
Thompson PM *ret* Cummaquid MA
Urang G *ret* Norwich VT
Veale DS Saint Albans VT
Wageman CA *ret* North Ferrisburgh VT
Watersong AL Montpelier VT
Woods HD *ret* South Hero VT
Yarbrough OL Middlebury VT

DIOCESE OF THE VIRGIN ISLANDS

(PROVINCE II)
Comprises the American and British Virgin Islands
DIOCESAN OFFICE #13 Commandant Gade Charlotte Amalie St Thomas
US Virgin Islands 00801
(MAIL: PO Box 7488 St Thomas VI 00801)
TEL (340) 776-1797   FAX (340) 777-8485
E-MAIL episcopal@vipowernet.net   WEB www.episcopalvi.org

Previous Bishops—
Cedric E Mills 1963-72, Edward
M Turner 1972-86, Richard B
Martin int 1985-87, E Don Taylor
1987-94, Telesforo A Isaac int
(1996-May 1997) Theodore A
Daniels 1997-2003 Telesforo Issac
2004-05

Bishop—E Ambrose Gumbs (1003) (Dio 11
June 05)

Cn to Ord Rev JM Clarke; *Treas* J Williams; *Hist* B
Hodge-Smith; *Chanc* Atty R Simmonds-Ballentine;
Conv Sec E Haynes-Lake; *Fin Comm Chr* G Walters;
COM Chr Rev E Georges

Stand Comm—Cler: Pres Dcn E Francis; Rev G
Gibson *Lay:* L Claxton M Jacobs M Hennessey

Dio Conv: 30 Sept-1 Oct 2016 St Croix

PARISHES, MISSIONS, AND CLERGY

Christiansted St Croix St Johns Episcopal Church
P (605) 27 King St 00820 (Mail to: PO Box 486
00821-0486) Gregory Gibson Dwight Ogier
(340) 773-1581

Christiansted St Croix St Peters Episcopal
Church **P** (228) Castle Coakley 38-40 00820
(Mail to: PO Box 7974 00823-7974) Alric
Francis (340) 778-6471

Cruz Bay St John St Ursula Church **M** (50) 295
Contant 00831 (Mail to: PO Box 199 00831-
0199) (340) 777-6306

Frederiksted St Croix Iglesia San Francisco
Episcopal **M** (29) 20 Estate Diamond 00840
(Mail to: PO Box 1796 00851-1796) (340) 776-
1797

Frederiksted St Croix St Pauls Episcopal Church
P (322) 25-26-27 Prince St 00841-0745 (Mail
to: PO Box 745 00841-0745) (340) 772-0818

Kingshill St Croix Episcopal Church of the Holy Cross **P** (35) Estate Upper Love 00850 (Mail to: RR 1 Box 8005 00850-9860) (340) 778-3272

Roadtown St Paul's Episcopal Church **M** (85) (Mail to: PO Box 3066 Tortola VG1110) (284) 494-4732

St Thomas Cathedral Church of All Saints **P** (400) § PO Box 1148 Charlotte Amalie Street 00801 Peter Courtney John George (340) 774-0217

St Thomas Church of the Holy Spirit **M** (36) (Mail to: PO Box 301827 00803-1827) (340) 776-5833

St Thomas St Andrews Episcopal Church **P** (950) 31-33 Frist Ave Sugard Estate 00802 (Mail to: PO Box 7386 008010386) Lenroy Cabey Jane Davis (340) 774-1223

St Thomas St Lukes Episcopal Church **P** (74) Smith Bay #10A & 115A 00801 (Mail to: PO Box 7335 00801-0335) (340) 715-1020

Tortola St George the Martyr Church **P** (400) 170 Main St Road Town VG1110 (Mail to: PO Box 28 Road Town VG1110) Ronald Branche (284) 494-4574

Virgin Gorda VG 1150 St Mary the Virgin Church **P** Church Hill Road South Valley VG 1150 (Mail to: PO Box 65 South Valley VG 1150) (284) 495-5769

NON-PAROCHIAL CLERGY

Abbott R *ret* Frederiksted VI
Bartlett BA *dcn* St Thomas VI
Clarke JM *ret* Saint Simons Island GA
Daniel WA *ret* Christiansted, Saint Croix VI
Dawson EE
Doward AR *dcn* Christiansted VI
Francis EC *dcn* St Thomas VI
George EA St. Thomas Virgin Islands
Georges EM
Gibson JNK *ret*
Gumbs DE *dcn* St Croix VI
Henry DW *ret* Christiansted VI
Hinton M Saint John VI
Hodge RR *dcn*
Huggins AH *ret* St. Vincent
Lee SWR Frederiksted VI
Naughton EA Washington DC
Ramirez-Nieves AI *dcn* Kingshill
Rock IE Tortola VI
Russell AV *dcn* Sea Cow's Bay, Tortola British Virgin Island
Rymer LS *ret* St Thomas VI
Scipio CT *dcn* St Thomas VI
Taylor BW *ret* Virgin Gorda VI
Walters Malone SA Road Town, Tortola British Virgin Islands
Williams WS St Thomas VI
Woodbury KJ St Thomas VI

STATE OF VIRGINIA

Dioceses of Southern Virginia (SV), Southwestern Virginia (SwV), and Virginia (VA)

Abingdon—SwV	Bluefield—SwV	Chester—SV	Fairfax—VA
Accomac—SV	Bluemont—VA	Chesterfield—SV	Fairfax Sta—VA
Afton—VA	Boonesville—VA	Christchurch—VA	Falls Church—VA
Aldie—VA	Bowling Green—VA	Christiansburg—SwV	Farmville—SV
Alexandria—VA	Bracey—SV	Claremont—SV	Farnham—VA
Altavista—SwV	Brandy Sta—VA	Clarksville—SV	Fincastle—SwV
Amelia Court House—SV	Bremo Bluff—VA	Clifton Forge—SwV	Forest—SwV
Amherst—SwV	Bristol—SwV	Colonial Bch—VA	Franconia—VA
Annandale—VA	Buchanan—SwV	Colonial Hts—SV	Franklin—SV
Appomattox—SV	Buckingham—SV	Columbia—VA	Fredericksburg—VA
Arlington—VA	Buena Vista—SwV	Courtland—SV	Freeman—SV
Arrington—SwV	Burke—VA	Covington—SwV	Front Royal—VA
Ashburn—VA	Callaway—SwV	Culpeper—VA	Galax—SwV
Ashland—VA	Cape Charles—SV	Danville—SV	Glasgow—SwV
Aylett—VA	Cartersville—SV	Delaplane—VA	Glen Allen—VA
Baskerville—SV	Casanova—VA	Disputanta—SV	Gloucester—VA
Bedford—SwV	Catlett—VA	Doswell—VA	Goochland—VA
Berryville—VA	Centreville—VA	Drakes Branch—SV	Gordonsville—VA
Big Stone Gap—SwV	Charles City—VA	Dunn Loring—VA	Great Falls—VA
Blacksburg—SwV	Charlottesville—VA	Earlysville—VA	Greenwood—VA
Blackstone—SV	Chase City—SV	Eastville—SV	Gretna—SV
Blue Grass—SwV	Chatham—SV	Elkton—VA	Grottos—VA
	Chesapeake—SV	Emporia—SV	Hague—VA

Halifax—SV	Marion—SwV	Petersburg—SV	Staunton—SwV
Hampton—SV	Markham—VA	Pocahontas—SwV	Sterling—VA
Hanover—VA	Martinsville—SwV	Pt Royal—VA	Suffolk—SV
Harrisonburg—VA	Massies Mill—SwV	Portsmouth—SV	Surry—SV
Haymarket—VA	Mathews—VA	Powhatan—SV	Tappahannock—VA
Heathsville—VA	McKenney—SV	Pulaski—SwV	Tazewell—SwV
Henrico—VA	McLean—VA	Pungoteague—SV	Temperanceville—SV
Herndon—VA	Mechanicsville—VA	Purcellville—VA	The Plains—VA
Hopewell—SV	Middleburg—VA	Radford—SwV	Toano—SV
Hot Spgs—SwV	Midlothian—SV	Rapidan—VA	Upperville—VA
Ivy—VA	Millers Tavern—VA	Reedville—VA	Victoria—SV
Java—SV	Millwood—VA	Remington—VA	Vienna—VA
Kenbridge—SV	Mineral—VA	Reston—VA	Virginia Bch—SV
Keswick—VA	Moneta—SwV	Richlands—SwV	Warfield—SV
Kilmarnock—VA	Monroe—SwV	Richmond—VA & SV	Warrenton—VA
King and Queen	Montpelier—VA	Rixeyville—VA	Warsaw—VA
Cthse—VA	Montross—VA	Roanoke—SwV	Washington—VA
King George—VA	Mt Jackson—VA	Rocky Mt—SwV	Waverly—SV
Lancaster—VA	Mt Vernon—VA	St Paul—SwV	Waynesboro—SwV
Lawrenceville—SV	New Kent—VA	Salem—SwV	West Pt—VA
Leesburg—VA	Newport News—SV	Saltville—SwV	White Marsh—VA
Lexington—SwV	Norfolk—SV	Scottsville—VA	White Post—VA
Loretto—VA	Norton—SwV	Shenandoah—VA	Wicomico Church—VA
Lorton—VA	N Chesterfield—SV	Smithfield—SV	Williamsburg—SV
Louisa—VA	N Prince George—SV	S Boston—SV	Winchester—VA
Luray—VA	Oak Grove—VA	S Hill—SV	Woodbridge—VA
Lynchburg—SwV	Oak Hill—VA	Spotsylvania—VA	Woodstock—VA
Machipongo—SV	Onancock—SV	Springfield—VA	Wytheville—SwV
Madison—VA	Orange—VA	Stafford—VA	Yorktown—SV
Manakin Sabot-VA	Orkney Spgs—VA	Stanardsville—VA	
Manassas—VA	Pearisburg—SwV	Stanley—VA	

DIOCESE OF VIRGINIA

(PROVINCE III)

Comprises 38 northern and northwestern VA counties
DIOCESAN OFFICE 110 W Franklin St Richmond VA 23220
TEL (804) 643-8451, (VA) 1-800-DIOCESE   FAX (804) 644-6928
E-MAIL bishopsoffice@thediocese.net

NORTHERN VA OFFICE 115 E Fairfax St Falls Church VA 22046
TEL (703) 241-0441   FAX (703) 531-0082
WEB www.thediocese.net

Previous Bishops—
James Madison 1790-1812, Richard C Moore 1814-41, Wm Meade coadj 1829 Bp 1842-62, John Johns coadj 1842 Bp 1862-76, Francis M Whittle coadj 1868 Bp 1876-1902, Alfred M Randolph coadj 1883- 1892, John B Newton coadj 1894-97, Robt A Gibson coadj 1897 Bp 1902-19, Arthur S Lloyd coadj 1909-10, Wm C Brown coadj 1914 Bp 1919-27, Henry StG Tucker coadj 1926 Bp 1927-44, Wiley R Mason suffr 1942-50, Fredk D Goodwin coadj 1930 Bp 1944-60, Robt F Gibson Jr suffr 1949-54 coadj 1954 Bp 1960-74, Samuel B Chilton suffr 1960-69, Phil A Smith suffr 1970-73, John A Baden suffr 1973-79, Robt B Hall coadj 1966 Bp 1974-85, David H Lewis Jr suffr 1980-87, Robt P Atkinson asst 1989-93, FC Matthews suff 1993-9, Francis C Gray ret asst 1999-2006, Peter James Lee coadj 1984 Bp 1985-2009, David C Jones suff 1995-2012

Bishop—Rt Rev Shannon S Johnston (1017)
(Coadjutor 2007, Bp 1 Oct 2009)

Bishop Suffragan—Rt Rev Susan E Goff (1066)

Asst Bishop—Rt Rev Edwin F Gulick Jr (891)

Chanc JP Causey Jr Esq; *Pres Exec Bd* Rt Rev S Johnston; *Dio Sec* dcn E Jones; *Treas* T Smith; *Cn to Ord* Rev P Wingo; *Dir Chr Form* P Ball; *Dep Off* Rev M Thorpe; *Stew* J Simonton; *Comm Off* A Michel

Stand Comm—Cler: Pres C Campbell K Coleman L Hutton J Piver J Belser H Jones; *Lay:* S Van Voorhees A Getlein B Allison-Bryan C Anderson R Inger W Pennell

Deans of Regions: A Greenwood R Hollerith J Hortum L Hutchson S Shepherd S Williams D Duncan-Probe A Hallmark J Piver P Roaf J Shankles M Windel D Brown T Harman C Brock

Dio Conv: 22-23 Jan 2016 Reston VA

PARISHES, MISSIONS, AND CLERGY

Afton Holy Cross Church **M** (85) 190 Rockfish School Ln 22920 (Mail to: PO Box 12 22924-0012) Anthony Andres (540) 456-6305

Aldie Church of Our Redeemer **M** (548) PO Box 217 20105-0217 (Mail to: PO Box 217 20105-0217) John Sheehan (703) 327-4060

Alexandria All Saints Sharon Chapel **P** (222) 3421 Franconia Rd 22310-2320 (Mail to: 3421 Franconia Rd 22310-2320) Valerie Hayes Bernard Ramey (703) 960-4808

Alexandria Christ Church **P** (2496) 118 N Washington St 22314-3023 (Mail to: 118 N Washington St 22314-3078) John Branson Ann Gillespie Timothy Hamby Diane Murphy Heather VanDeventer (703) 549-1450

Alexandria Church of St Clement **P** (276) 1701 N Quaker Ln 22302-2339 (Mail to: 1701 N Quaker Ln 22302-2339) John Hortum Cynthia Park (703) 998-6166

Alexandria Church of the Resurrection **P** (131) 2280 N Beauregard St 22311-2200 (Mail to: 2280 N Beauregard St 22311-2299) Jo Belser Ann Truitt (703) 998-0888

Alexandria Church of the Spirit **P** (172) 5775 Barclay Dr Ste G 22315-5731 (Mail to: 5775 Barclay Dr Ste G 22315-5710) Cornelia Weierbach (703) 971-5242

Alexandria Emmanuel Church **P** (648) 1608 Russell Rd 22301-1926 (Mail to: 1608 Russell Rd 22301-1998) Charles McCoart Joan Peacock (703) 683-0798

Alexandria Grace Episcopal Church **P** (885) 3601 Russell Rd 22305-1731 (Mail to: 3601 Russell Rd 22305-1731) Robert Malm Elizabeth Locher Leslie Steffensen (703) 549-1980

Alexandria Immanuel Church on the Hill **P** (1004) 3606 Seminary Rd 22304-5200 (Mail to: 3606 Seminary Rd 22304-5200) Joseph Alexander David Crosby (703) 370-6555

Alexandria La Iglesia de San Marcos **M** (100) 6744 S Kings Hwy 22306-1318 (Mail to: 6744 S Kings Hwy 22306-1318) (703) 765-3949

Alexandria Meade Memorial Church **P** (120) 322 N Alfred St 22314-2423 (Mail to: 322 N Alfred St 22314-2423) Collins Asonye (703) 549-1334

Alexandria St Aidans Church **P** (277) 8531 Riverside Rd 22308-2206 (Mail to: 8531 Riverside Rd 22308-2200) John Baker Elizabeth Rees (703) 360-4220

Alexandria St Luke's Church **P** (439) 8009 Fort Hunt Road 22308-1207 (Mail to: 8009 Fort Hunt Road 22308-1293) Ellis Bowerfind Michael Moore Grace Pratt (703) 765-4342

Alexandria St Marks Church **P** (262) 6744 S Kings Hwy 22306-1318 (Mail to: 6744 S Kings Hwy 22306-1318) John Weatherly Buddelov Moronta Vasquez Meredith Heffner (703) 765-3949

Alexandria St Pauls Church **P** (2714) 228 S. Pitt Steet 22314 (Mail to: 228 S Pitt St 22314-3742) Oran Warder Rosemary Beales Edward Kane Anne Mertz Gregory Millikin Anne Monahan Judith Proctor (703) 549-3312

Annandale St Albans Church **P** (526) 6800 Columbia Pike 22003-3431 (Mail to: 6800 Columbia Pike 22003-3431) Jeffrey Shankles (703) 256-2966

Annandale St Barnabas' Church **P** (420) 4801 Ravensworth Rd 22003-5551 (Mail to: 4801 Ravensworth Rd 22003-5551) Linda Hawkins (703) 941-2922

Arlington La Iglesia de Cristo Rey **M** (147) 415 S Lexington St 22204-1226 (Mail to: 415 S Lexington St 22204-1226) (703) 524-4716

Arlington San Jose Church **M** (192) 911 N Oakland St 22203-1916 (Mail to: 911 N Oakland St 22203-1916) (703) 524-4716

Arlington St Andrews Church **P** (200) 4000 Lorcom Ln 22207-3937 (Mail to: 4000 Lorcom Ln 22207) Jennifer Montgomery Alfred Moss (703) 522-1600

Arlington St Georges Church **P** (481) 915 N Oakland St 22203-1916 (Mail to: 915 N Oakland St 22203-1916) Shearon Williams Stephen Rorke John Shellito (703) 525-8286

Arlington St Johns Episcopal Church **P** (67) 415 S Lexington St 22204-1226 (Mail to: 415 S Lexington St 22204-1226) Ann Barker (703) 671-6834

Arlington St Marys Church **P** (1606) 2609 N Glebe Rd 22207-3501 (Mail to: 2609 N Glebe Rd 22207-3501) Andrew Merrow Timothy Malone Anne Turner (703) 527-6800

Arlington St Michaels Church **P** (225) No 1132 N Ivanhoe St 22205-2445 (Mail to: 1132 N Ivanhoe St 22205-2445) Leslie Hague (703) 241-2474

Arlington St Peters Episcopal Church **P** (1079) 4250 N Glebe Rd 22207-4508 (Mail to: 4250 N Glebe Rd 22207-4500) Craig Phillips Elyse Gustafson Howard Kempsell Ann Martens (703) 536-6606

Arlington Trinity Church **P** (183) 2217 Columbia Pike 22204-4405 (Mail to: 2217 Columbia Pike 22204-4497) Kim Coleman Elliott Waters (703) 920-7077

Ashburn St Davids Church **P** (732) 43600 Russell Branch Pkwy 20147-2903 (Mail to: 43600 Russell Branch Pkwy 20147-2903) Mary Brown Emmanuel Johnson (703) 729-0570

Ashland Church of St James the Less **P** (441) 125 Beverly Rd 23005-1821 (Mail to: 125 Beverly Rd 23005-1821) Claudia Merritt (804) 798-6336

Aylett St Davids Church **M** (45) 11291 W River Rd 23009-3000 (Mail to: PO Box 68 23009-0125) (804) 737-6685

Berryville Grace Episcopal Church **P** (360) 110 N Church St 22611-1109 (Mail to: PO Box 678 22611-0678) Dwight Brown (540) 955-1610

Berryville St Marys Church **M** (31) N Buckmarsh St 22611 (Mail to: PO Box 252 22611-0252) Dwight Brown (540) 955-1610

Bluemont Church of the Good Shepherd **M** (37) 27 Good Shepherd Rd 20135-4725 (Mail to: PO Box 324 20135-0324) Ralph Bayfield (540) 554-8351

Boonesville Good Shepherd-of-the-Hills **M** (23) Intersection of SR-601 and SR-810 22940 (Mail to: PO Box 31 22940-0031) (434) 973-7688

Bowling Green St Asaphs Church **P** (109) 130 S Main St 22427-9424 (Mail to: PO Box 1178 22427-1178) Barbara Willis (804) 633-5660

Brandy Station Christ Church **P** (73) 14586 Alanthus Rd 22714-0025 (Mail to: PO Box 25 22714-0025) Peter Way (434) 286-3914

Bremo Bluff Grace Episcopal Church **M** (55) 754 Bremo Bluff Rd 23022-2104 (Mail to: General Delivery Region 15 23022-9999) Thomas Hendrickson (804) 266-1410

Burke Church of the Good Shepherd **P** (1529) 9350 Braddock Rd 22015-1521 (Mail to: 9350 Braddock Rd 22015-1521) Philip Johnston (703) 323-5400

Burke St Andrews Church **P** (1237) 6509 Sydenstricker Rd 22015-4210 (Mail to: 6509 Sydenstricker Rd 22015-4210) Timothy Heflin Alexander Graham Howard Kempsell (703) 455-2500

Casanova Grace Church Emmanuel Parish **P** (47) 5108 Weston Rd 20139 (Mail to: PO Box 18 20139-0018) James Cirillo

Catlett St Stephens Church **P** (206) 8695 Old Dumfries Road 20119-1922 (Mail to: 8695 Old Dumfries Road 20119-1922)

Centreville St Johns Church **P** (175) 5649 Mount Gilead Rd 20120-1906 (Mail to: PO Box 2360 20122-2360) Carol Hancock (703) 803-7500

Charles City Westover Parish Church **P** (296) 6401 John Tyler Mem High 23030 (Mail to: 6401 John Tyler Memorial Hwy 23030-3310) April Greenwood (804) 829-2488

Charlottesville McIlhany Parish **M** (66) 960 Monacan Trail Rd 22903-7704 (Mail to: 960 Monacan Trail Rd 22903-7704) Kelly Jennings (434) 293-3455

Charlottesville St Paul's Ivy Church **P** (796) No 773 Neves Lane 22901 (Mail to: PO Box 37

22945-0037) Eric Liles Sarah Gaventa (434) 979-6354

Charlottesvlle Christ Episcopal Church **P** (1453) 120 W High St 22902 (Mail to: 100 W Jefferson St 22902-5023) Paul Walker George Logan (434) 977-1227

Charlottesvlle Church of Our Saviour **P** (566) 1165 Rio Rd E 22901-1810 (Mail to: 1165 Rio Rd E 22901-1810) David Stoddart Allison Liles (434) 973-6512

Charlottesvlle St Lukes Episcopal Church **M** (92) 1333 Thomas Jefferson Pkwy 22902-7518 (Mail to: PO Box 694 22902-0694) Ann Willms (434) 970-5020

Charlottesvlle St Paul's Memorial Church **P** (1662) 1700 University Ave 22903-2619 (Mail to: 1700 University Ave 22903-2619) Elaine Thomas (434) 295-2156

Charlottesvlle Trinity Episcopal Church **M** (120) 1118 Preston Ave 22903-2002 (Mail to: 1118 Preston Ave 22903-2002) Bertram Bailey (434) 293-3157

Christchurch Christ Church Parish **P** (155) 56 Christchurch Labe Rt 33 & 638 23031 (Mail to: PO Box 476 23149-0476) Paul Andersen Stuart Wood (804) 758-2006

Colonial Beach St Mary's Church **P** (313) 203 Dennison St 22443-2311 (Mail to: 203 Dennison St 22443-0420) Thomas Hughes (804) 224-7186

Columbia St Johns Church **M** (28) 43 Washington St 23038 (Mail to: PO Box 853 23038-0853) Richard Singleton (434) 842-3715

Culpeper St Stephens Episcopal Church **P** (287) 115 N East St 22701-3021 (Mail to: 115 N East St 22701-3021) Benson Shelton (540) 825-8786

Delaplane Emmanuel Episcopal Church, Delaplane **P** (180) 9668 Maidstone Rd 20144-2211 (Mail to: PO Box 126 20144-0126) Amanda Knouse (540) 364-2772

Doswell St Martins Church **M** (11) 10523 Doswell Rd 23047-1800 (Mail to: PO Box 214 23047-0214) (804) 233-8120

Doswell The Fork Church **P** (154) 12566 Old Ridge Rd 23047 (Mail to: 12566 Old Ridge Rd 23047) Kenneth Forti (804) 227-3413

Dunn Loring Church of the Holy Cross **P** (481) 2455 Gallows Road 22027-1225 (Mail to: 2455 Gallows Road 22027-1225) Robert Becker Jamie Samilio Denise Trogdon (703) 698-6991

Earlysville Buck Mountain Church **P** (189) 4133 Earlysville Rd 22936-2504 (Mail to: PO Box 183 22936-0183) Constance Clark (434) 973-2054

Elkton St Stephen & the Good Shepherd **P** (36) 7078 Rocky Bar Rd 22827-3503 (Mail to: 7120 Ore Bank Rd 24471) Stuart Wood (540) 249-4121

Fairfax Holy Cross Korean Epis Church **M** (37) 10520 Main St 22030-3380 (Mail to: 4060 Championship Dr 22003-2418) Nievalentine Han (703) 563-6333

Fairfax Station St Peters in the Woods **M** (374) 5911 Fairview Woods Dr 22039-1427 (Mail to: 5911 Fairview Woods Dr 22039-1427) DeDe Duncan-Probe Susan Hartzell (703) 503-9210

Falls Church La Iglesia de Santa Maria **M** (314) 7000 Arlington Blvd 22042-1827 (Mail to: 7000 Arlington Blvd 22042-1827) Roberto Orihuela (703) 533-9220

Falls Church St Patricks Episcopal Church **M** (126) 3241 Brush Dr 22042-2569 (Mail to: 3241 Brush Dr 22042-2569) (703) 532-5656

Falls Church St Pauls Episcopal Church **P** (73) 3439 Payne St 22041-2019 (Mail to: 3439 Payne St 22041-2019) Elizabeth Tomlinson (703) 820-2625

Falls Church The Falls Church Episcopal **P** (266) 115 E. Fairfax St 22046-2903 (Mail to: 115 E Fairfax St 22046-2903) John Ohmer Michael Hinson Kelly Moughty (703) 241-0003

Farnham North Farnham Parish Church **P** (37) 231 N Farnham Church Rd 22460 (Mail to: PO Box 1093 22572-1093) (804) 333-4333

Franconia Olivet Church **P** (82) No 6107 Franconia Rd 22310-2542 (Mail to: 6107 Franconia Rd 22310) Jeanie Martinez-Jantz (703) 971-4733

Fredericksbrg Church of the Messiah **M** (135) 5875 Plank Rd 22407-6229 (Mail to: 12201 Spotswood Furnace Ln 22407-2265) Kyle Tomlin (540) 786-3100

Fredericksbrg Trinity Church **P** (794) 825 College Ave 22401-5469 (Mail to: PO Box 3400 22402-3400) Kent Rahm (540) 373-2996

Fredericksburg St George's Episcopal Church **P** (1195) 905 Princess Anne St 22401 (Mail to: 905 Princess Anne St 22401) Joseph Hensley Carey Chirico Gaynell Rahn (540) 373-4133

Front Royal Calvary Church **P** (362) 132 N Royal Avenue 22630-2603 (Mail to: PO Box 62 22630-0002) Deborah Rutter (540) 635-2763

Glen Allen Christ Episcopal Church **P** (1990) 5000 Pouncey Tract Rd 23059-5301 (Mail to: 5000 Pouncey Tract Rd 23059-5301) Shirley Smith Graham Robin Teasley (804) 364-0394

Gloucester Ware Episcopal Church **P** (318) 7825 John Clayton Mem Hwy 23061 (Mail to: PO Box 616 23061-0616) (804) 693-3821

Goochland Grace Church **P** (228) 2955 River Road West 23063-0698 (Mail to: PO Box 698 23063-0698) Rhonda Baker (804) 556-3051

Gordonsville Christ Church **P** (78) No 310 N High Street 22942 (Mail to: PO Box 588 22942-0588) Richard Fichter Mary Wells (540) 832-3209

Great Falls St Francis Church **P** (625) 9220 Georgetown Pike 22066-2726 (Mail to: 9220 Georgetown Pike 22066-2726) Tracey Kelly David Lucey (703) 759-2082

Greenwood Emmanuel Episcopal Church **P** (576) 7500 Rockfish Gap Tpk 22943-1802 (Mail to: 7599 Rockfish Gap Tpke 22943-1802) Mignon

Brockenbrough Christopher Garcia (540) 456-6334

Grottoes Grace Memorial Church **P** (57) C/O Sally Jensen 1203 Randall Rd Apt A6 24441-2433 (Mail to: 7120 Ore Bank Rd 24471-2206) Stuart Wood (540) 249-4121

Hague Cople Parish **P** (162) 72 Coles Point Rd 22469 (Mail to: PO Box 110 22469-0110) Rita White (804) 472-2593

Hanover Calvary Episcopal Church **P** (104) 13312 Courthouse Road 23069-0307 (Mail to: PO Box 307 23069-0307) (804) 537-5061

Hanover St Paul's Episcopal Church **P** (391) 8050 St Paul's Church Rd 23069 (Mail to: 8050 Saint Pauls Church Rd 23069-1522) Connor Newlun (804) 537-5516

Harrisonburg Emmanuel Church **P** (510) 660 S Main St 22801-5819 (Mail to: 660 S Main St 22801-5819) Daniel Robayo-Hidalgo Edward Bachschmid (540) 434-2357

Haymarket St Pauls Church **P** (132) No St. Paul's Episcopal Church 6750 Fayette Street 20169-2916 (Mail to: 6750 Fayette St 20169-2913) (703) 753-2443

Heathsville St Stephens Episcopal Church **P** (71) 6807 Northumberland Hwy 22473 (Mail to: PO Box 40 22473-0040) Lucia Lloyd (804) 724-4238

Henrico Varina Church **P** (232) 2385 Mill Rd 23231-7019 (Mail to: 2385 Mill Rd 23231-7019) Catherine McKinney (804) 795-5340

Herndon St Timothys Church **P** (1380) § 432 Van Buren St 20170-5104 (Mail to: 432 Van Buren St 20170-5104) Bradford Rundlett Leslie Chadwick Mark Michael (703) 437-3790

Ivy St John the Baptist Church **M** (56) State Route 637 22945 (Mail to: PO Box 351 22945-0351) Kathleen Sturges (434) 295-0744

Keswick Grace Church **P** (220) 5607 Gordonsville Rd 22947-1906 (Mail to: PO Box 43 22947-0043) Gary Smith Donald Cady (434) 293-3549

Kilmarnock Grace Church **P** (533) 303 S Main St 22482-9595 (Mail to: PO Box 1059 22482-1059) David May Megan Limburg (804) 435-1285

King and Queen Courthouse Immanuel Church **M** (5) 190 Allens Cir 23085 (Mail to: 17651 The Trail 23085) (804) 785-6461

King George Emmanuel Church **P** (8) 17062 James Madison Parkway 22485-2543 (Mail to: PO Box 134 22485-0134) (540) 775-3635

King George St Johns Church **P** (69) 9403 Kings Highway 22485-0134 (Mail to: PO Box 134 22485-0134) Diane Carroll (540) 775-3635

King George St Pauls Church **P** (173) 5486 Saint Pauls Rd 22485-5436 (Mail to: 5486 Saint Pauls Rd 22485-5436) Brian Turner (540) 663-3085

Lancaster St Marys Whitechapel **P** (75) 5940 White Chapel Rd 22503-3029 (Mail to: 5940 White Chapel Rd 22503-3029) (804) 462-5908

Lancaster Trinity Episcopal Church **P** (66) 8484 Mary Ball Rd, Lancaster 22503 (Mail to: PO Box 208 22503-0208) (804) 462-0610

Leesburg Christ Church Lucketts **M** (35) 14861 New Valley Church Rd 20176 (Mail to: 14861 New Valley Church Rd 20176-6024) Stephen Becker (703) 771-2196

Leesburg St Gabriels Episcopal Church **M** (95) 14 Cornwall St NW 20176-2801 (Mail to: 14 Cornwall St NW. 20176-2801) Daniel Velez-Rivera (703) 779-3616

Leesburg St James Church **P** (1100) § 14 Cornwall St NW 20176-2801 (Mail to: 14 Cornwall St NW 20176-2801) Mark Feather Katherine Bryant (703) 777-1124

Loretto Vauters Church **P** (81) 3661 Tidewater Trl 22438 (Mail to: PO Box 154 22438-0154) (804) 443-4788

Lorton Pohick Church **P** (637) 9301 Richmond Hwy 22079-1519 (Mail to: 9301 Richmond Hwy 22079-1519) Donald Binder Ruth Correll (703) 339-6572

Louisa St James Church **P** (183) 102 Ellisville Dr 23093-6550 (Mail to: PO Box 1216 23093-1216) Rodney Caulkins Charles Riffee (540) 967-1665

Luray Christ Church **P** (79) PO Box 231 22835-0231 (Mail to: PO Box 231 22835-0231) Catherine Tibbetts

Madison Piedmont/Bromfield Parish **P** (174) 214 Church St 22727-3013 (Mail to: PO Box 305 22727-0305) William Miller

Manakin Sabot St Francis Episcopal Church **P** (58) 1484 Hockett Rd 23103 (Mail to: PO Box 303 23103-0303) John Maher (804) 784-6116

Manassas Trinity Church **P** (1156) 9325 West St 20110-5128 (Mail to: 9325 West St 20110-5128) Stuart Schadt Vinnie Lainson Dennis Reid (703) 368-4231

Markham Episcopal Church of Leeds Parish **P** (299) 4332 Leeds Manor Rd 22643-1906 (Mail to: 4332 Leeds Manor Rd 22643-1906) Justin McIntosh (540) 364-2849

Mathews Kingston Parish **P** (245) 370 Main Street 23109-0471 (Mail to: PO Box 471 23109-0471) Gary Barker (804) 725-2175

McLean St Dunstans Church **P** (659) 1830 Kirby Rd 22101-5323 (Mail to: 1830 Kirby Rd 22101-5323) Stephen Shepherd Fanny Belanger (703) 356-7533

McLean St Johns Episcopal Church **P** (1302) 6715 Georgetown Pike 22101-2243 (Mail to: PO Box 457 22101-0457) Edward Miller Justin Ivatts (703) 356-4902

McLean St Francis Korean Church **M** (30) 1830 Kirby Rd 22101-5323 (Mail to: 1830 Kirby Rd 22101-5323)

McLean St Thomas Church **P** (444) 8991 Brook Rd 22102-1510 (Mail to: 8991 Brook Rd 22102-1510) Stephen Edmondson Mary Emerson William Newland (703) 442-0330

Mechanicsville All Souls Episcopal Church **M** (189) 9077 Atlee Rd 23116-2501 (Mail to: PO Box 2798 23116-0021) Amelie Wilmer (804) 229-4998

Mechanicsvlle Church of the Creator **P** (280) 7159 Mechanicsville Tpke 23111-3663 (Mail to: 7159 Mechanicsville Tpke 23111-3663) William Burk (804) 746-8765

Mechanicsville Immanuel Church **P** (281) 3263 Old Church Rd 23111 (Mail to: 3263 Old Church Rd 23111) (804) 779-3454

Middleburg Emmanuel Church **P** (141) 105 E Washington St 20117 (Mail to: PO Box 306 20118-0306) Charlotte Hallmark (540) 687-6297

Millers Tavern Grace Church **P** (33) 604 Howerton Road 23115 (Mail to: PO Box 126 23115-0126)

Millers Tavern St Paul's Episcopal Church **P** (175) 360 Highway 23115 (Mail to: PO Box 278 23115-0278) (804) 443-2341

Millwood Cunningham Chapel Parish **P** (135) 809 Bishop Meade Road 22646-0153 (Mail to: PO Box 153 22646-0153) (540) 837-1112

Mineral Church of the Incarnation **M** (115) Rt 552 & Lee St 23117 (Mail to: C/O Marian Windel PO Box 307 23117-0307) Marian Windel (540) 894-0136

Montpelier Church of Our Saviour **M** (148) 17102 Mountain Rd 23192-2550 (Mail to: PO Box 11 23192-0011) Herbert Jones

Montross St James Church **P** (146) 15870 Kings Hwy 22520 (Mail to: PO Box 177 22520-0177) Alan Hooker (804) 493-8285

Montross St Pauls Church Nomini Grove **P** (34) 21983 Kings Hwy 22520-2912 (Mail to: 1819 Neenah Rd 22520-3115) (804) 493-8994

Mount Jackson St Andrews Church **P** (52) 5890 Main St 22842-9406 (Mail to: PO Box 117 22842-0117) (540) 477-3335

Mount Vernon St James' Episcopal Church **P** (114) 5614 Old Mills Rd 22309 (Mail to: 5614 Old Mill Road 22309-3332) Charles Brock (703) 780-3081

New Kent St Peters Parish Church **P** (332) No 8400 Saint Peters Ln 23124-2718 (Mail to: 8400 St Peters Ln 23124-2718) Stephen Rowles (804) 932-4846

Oak Grove St Peters **P** (114) 2961 Kings Hwy 22443-5310 (Mail to: 601 Colonial Avenue 22443) Rodney Gordon Linda Murphy (804) 224-0163

Oak Hill Church of the Epiphany **P** (126) 3301 Hidden Meadow Drive 20171 (Mail to: 3301 Hidden Meadow Drive 20171-0995) Hillary West (703) 466-5200

Orange St Thomas Episcopal Church **P** (179) 119 Caroline St 22960-1532 (Mail to: 119 Caroline St 22960-1532) Linda Hutton (540) 672-3761

✠ **Orkney Springs** Cathd Shrine of the Transfiguration **O** (9) 221 Shrine Mont Cir

22845 (Mail to: PO Box 10 22845) (540) 856-2141

Port Royal St Peters Church **P** (66) 823 Water St 22535 (Mail to: PO Box 399 22535) Catherine Hicks (804) 742-5908

Purcellville St Peters Church **P** (306) 37018 Glendale St 20132-3422 (Mail to: PO Box 546 20134-0546) Thomas Simmons (540) 338-7307

Rapidan Emmanuel Church **P** (60) 28279 Rapidan Rd 22733-2431 (Mail to: PO Box 81 22733-0081) Philip Morgan (540) 672-1395

Reedville St Marys Church **P** (65) 3020 Fleeton Rd 22539-4221 (Mail to: PO Box 278 22539-0278) Sandra Mizirl Harold White (804) 453-6712

Remington St Lukes Church **P** (56) 400 N Church St 22734-9708 (Mail to: PO Box 267 22734-0267) Nancy Betz (540) 439-3733

Reston St Annes Church **P** (1318) Attn Susan Allen 1700 Wainwright Dr 20190-5500 (Mail to: 1700 Wainwright Dr 20190-5500) James Papile Laura Cochran Harold Johnson (703) 437-6530

Richmond All Saints Church **P** (1608) 8787 River Rd 23229-8303 (Mail to: 8787 River Rd 23229-8303) Judith Davis Brent Melton William Queen (804) 288-7811

Richmond Christ Ascension Church **P** (123) 1704 W Laburnum Ave 23227-4312 (Mail to: 1704 W Laburnum Ave 23227-4312) David Keill (804) 264-9474

Richmond Church of the Holy Comforter **P** (293) 4819 Monument Ave 23230-3615 (Mail to: 4819 Monument Ave 23230-3615) J Fletcher Lowe Hilary Smith (804) 355-3251

Richmond Emmanuel Church at Brook Hill **P** (349) 1214 Wilmer Ave 23227-2405 (Mail to: 1214 Wilmer Ave 23227-2405) Sara Wingo

Richmond Epiphany Church **P** (340) 8000 Hermitage Rd 23228-3704 (Mail to: PO Box 9544 23228-0544) (804) 266-2503

Richmond Grace and Holy Trinity Church **P** (900) 8 N Laurel St 23220-4704 (Mail to: 8 N Laurel St 23220-4797) Bollin Millner Kimberly Reinholz (804) 359-5628

Richmond St Andrews Church **P** (195) 240 S Laurel St 23220 (Mail to: 236 S Laurel St 23220-6229) S Abbott Bailey Barbara Ambrose (804) 648-7980

Richmond St Bartholomews Episcopal Church **P** (229) 10627 Patterson Ave 23238-4701 (Mail to: PO Box 29626 23242) Andrew Dunks (804) 740-2101

Richmond St Jamess Church **P** (2891) 1205 W Franklin St 23220-3711 (Mail to: 1205 W Franklin St 23220-3711) Randolph Hollerith Carmen Germino Caroline Parkinson Hilary Streever (804) 355-1779

Richmond St Johns Church **P** (220) No 2401 E Broad St 23223-7128 (Mail to: 2319 E Broad St 23223-7126) Laura Inscoe Sandra Levy (804) 649-7938

Richmond St Johns Episcopal Church **P** (267) 2401 E Broad St 23223 (Mail to: 2401 E Broad St 23223) Robert Friend (804) 649-7938

Richmond St Marks Church **P** (300) 520 N Boulevard 23220-3309 (Mail to: 520 N Boulevard 23220-3309) John Niemeyer (804) 358-4771

Richmond St Martins Episcopal Church **M** (297) 9000 Saint Martin Ln 23294-4448 (Mail to: 9000 St Martins Lane 23294-4448) Lee Hutchson (804) 270-6786

Richmond St Mary's Episcopal Church **P** (1902) Attn Gina M Alexander 12291 River Rd 23238-6112 (Mail to: 12291 River Rd 23238-6112) Louise Blanchard Emily Rowell Eleanor Wellford (804) 784-5678

Richmond St Matthews Episcopal Church **P** (702) 1101 Forest Ave 23229-5845 (Mail to: 1101 Forest Ave 23229-5845) Charles Alley Mario Gonzalez Del Solar

Richmond St Pauls Church **P** (934) 815 E Grace St 23219-3409 (Mail to: 815 E Grace St 23219-3409) Daniel Adams-Riley Molly Bosscher Melanie Mullen (804) 643-3589

Richmond St Peters Episcopal Church **M** (50) 1719 N 22nd St 23223-4431 (Mail to: 1719 N 22nd St 23223-4431) Andrew Terry (804) 643-2686

Richmond St Philips Church **P** (293) 2900 Hanes Avenue 23222-3607 (Mail to: 2900 Hanes Avenue 23222-3607) Phoebe Roaf (804) 321-1266

Richmond St Stephens Church **P** (4200) 6000 Grove Ave 23226-2601 (Mail to: 6000 Grove Ave 23226-2601) Gary Jones Eugene Lecouteur Edward Mathews Penny Nash William Sachs Mary Sulerud (804) 288-2867

Richmond St Thomas Church **P** (654) § 3602 Hawthorne Ave 23222-1824 (Mail to: 3602 Hawthorne Ave 23222-1824) Susan Buchanan Jeffrey Higgins

Rixeyville Little Fork Episcopal Church **P** (144) 16471 Oak Shade Rd 22737-2927 (Mail to: PO Box 367 22737-0367) Emmetri Beane Brad Jackson

Scottsville St Annes Parish **P** (179) 410 Harrison St 24590 (Mail to: PO Box 337 24590-0337) Randall Haycock

Shenandoah St Pauls Church **P** (12) 3075 Comertown Rd 22849-4047 (Mail to: PO Box 332 22849-0332) (540) 962-7112

Spotsylvania Christ Church **P** (577) 8951 Courthouse Rd 22553-2517 (Mail to: 8951 Courthouse Rd 22553-2517) Jeffrey Packard (540) 582-5033

Springfield St Christophers Church **P** (561) 6320 Hanover Ave 22150-4009 (Mail to: 6320 Hanover Ave 22150-4099) Peter Ackerman (703) 451-1088

Stafford Aquia Church **P** (1131) 2938 Jefferson Davis Hwy 22554-1730 (Mail to: PO Box 275

22555-0275) John Morris Connor Newlun (540) 659-4007

Stanardsville Grace Church **M** (117) 97 Main St 22973 (Mail to: PO Box 112 22973-0112) Jane Piver (434) 985-7716

Stanley St Georges Church **M** (34) The Diocese Of Virginia 3380 Pine Grove Rd 22851-5411 (Mail to: 3392 Pine Grove Rd 22851) Stuart Smith (540) 778-3462

Sterling St Matthews Church **P** (738) 201 E Frederick Dr 20164-2387 (Mail to: 201 E Frederick Dr 20164-2387) Carl Merola Carl Merola (703) 430-2121

The Plains Grace Church **P** (609) 6507 Main St 20198 (Mail to: PO Box 32 20198-0032) Susan Michelfelder (540) 253-5177

Upperville Trinity Church **P** (458) 9108 John Mosby Highway 20184 (Mail to: PO Box 127 20185-0127) Robert Banse (540) 592-3343

Vienna Church of the Holy Comforter **P** (2045) 543 Beulah Rd NE 22180-3510 (Mail to: 543 Beulah Rd NE 22180-3599) Richard Lord Valerie Hayes Margaret Peel (703) 938-6521

Warrenton St Andrews Church **M** (65) Attn Mr Ordie L Frazier 75 Frazier Rd 20186-2704 (Mail to: PO Box 931 20116) (540) 675-3616

Warrenton St James Church **P** (641) 73 Culpeper St 20186-3321 (Mail to: 73 Culpeper St 20186-3321) Benjamin Maas Lynda Youll Marshall (540) 347-4342

Warsaw St Johns Church **P** (138) 5987 Richmond Rd 22572-1093 (Mail to: PO Box 1093 22572-1093) (804) 333-4333

Washington Trinity Church **P** (208) 379 Gay St 22747 (Mail to: PO Box 299 22747-0299) William Queen (540) 675-3716

West Point St Johns Episcopal Church **P** (90) C/O H V Perry 916 Main St 23181-0249 (Mail to: PO Box 629 23181-0629) Barbara Marques (804) 843-4594

West Point St Pauls Church **P** (57) 532 15th St 23181-0767 (Mail to: PO Box 767 23181-0767) (804) 843-3587

White Marsh Abingdon Church **P** (271) 4645 Geo Washington Mem Hwy 23183 (Mail to: PO Box 82 23183-0082) Sven Vanbaars Mary Turner (804) 693-3035

White Post Meade Memorial Church **M** (36) 192 White Post Road 22663-0007 (Mail to: PO Box159 22663-0007) Charles Kettlewell (540) 837-2354

Wicomico Church Wicomico Parish Church **P** (219) 5195 Jessie Ball Dupont Memorial Hwy 22579-0321 (Mail to: PO Box 70 22579-0070) James Silcox (804) 580-6445

Winchester Christ Episcopal Church **P** (642) 114 W Boscawen St 22601-4116 (Mail to: 114 W Boscawen St 22601-4116) Webster Gibson Bridget Coffey (540) 662-5843

Winchester St Pauls on the Hill Church **P** (184) 1527 Senseny Rd 22602-6423 (Mail to: 1527

Senseny Rd 22602-6423) Susan Macdonald (540) 667-8110

Woodbridge St Margaret's Episcopal Church **P** (120) 5290 Saratoga Ln 22193-3455 (Mail to: 5290 Saratoga Ln 22193-3455) Kathy Rowe-Guin (703) 590-3990

Woodstock Emmanuel Church **P** (93) 122 E Court St 22664-1727 (Mail to: 122 E Court St 22664-1727) Stephen Rowles (540) 459-2720

NON-PAROCHIAL CLERGY

Adams JD *ret* Richmond VA
Agnew CM *ret*
Aiken CD *ret* Richmond VA
Ambrose TG Arlington VA
Andrews PM *ret* Gainesville VA
Ardrey-Graves SC Harrisonburg VA
Barr JW *ret* Alexandria VA
Baxter PR *ret* Lakeland FL
Beatty SP Ashland VA
Berberich GCK Charlottesville VA
Biddle C *ret* Annapolis MD
Birnbaum RE *ret* Southbury CT
Bitsberger DE *ret* Bethesda MD
Blair TW *ret* Kilmarnock VA
Blakemore BK *ret* Mechanicsville VA
Brake MW
Brenneis MJ Arlington VA
Brookfield CM *ret* Charlottesville VA
Brooks PH *ret* Vienna VA
Brown AW *ret* Cape Coral FL
Brown WH *ret* Richmond VA
Bryan J *ret* Alexandria VA
Burgoyne DG *ret*
Cadaret JM Richmond VA
Caldwell GM Alexandria VA
Campbell BP *ret* Richmond VA
Campbell CM Woodbridge VA
Cangialosi GL *ret* Richmond VA
Carter JCM *ret* Richmond VA
Cavanaugh SH Marietta GA
Chipps KDM *ret* Dumfries VA
Cobb-Anderson V *ret* Richmond VA
Cochran JM
Coffey EA *ret* Mechanicsville VA
Cooke BH *ret* Moneta VA
Corry RS *ret* Quincy FL
Coupland GD Richmond VA
Crocker RC *ret* Uxbridge MA
Davila MF Leesburg VA
Davis AD *ret* Luray VA
Davis GB *ret* Richmond VA
DeGavre SW *ret* Aurora CO
DeMott RA *ret* Banner Elk NC
Desaulniers JJ *ret* Milford DE
Dickey RW *ret* Stevensville MD
Dickson PJ
Dillard WS *ret* Luray VA
Dols TW *ret* Wilmington NC
Dols WL *ret* Alexandria VA
Dunlap GE *ret* Winchester VA

Duvall RW *ret* North Myrtle Beach SC
Eade KC *ret* Cumming GA
Eaves LJ Richmond VA
Eaves SN *ret* Richmond VA
Eberle WE *ret* Rixeyville VA
Elder RM *ret* Huntingdon PA
Epes GE *ret* Alexandria VA
Faeth MA *ret* Alexandria VA
Fishwick JP *ret* Charlottesville VA
Foughty DL Alexandria VA
Frank WG *ret* Asheville NC
Garcia CJ *dcn* Richmond VA
Garza FE *dcn* Richmond VA
Geddes RD *ret* Hallieford VA
Glenn KB Lynchburg VA
Glover JF *ret* Grottoes VA
Gray BA *ret* Richmond VA
Gray MF *ret* Culpeper VA
Gray PH *ret* McLean VA
Griffin EA McLean VA
Grumbine EE *ret* Richmond VA
Guffey AR Annandale VA
Guffey EW Chicago IL
Gustin PR Leesburg VA
Gwin CB Roanoke VA
Haddix TR *ret* Cincinnati OH
Hager MM *dcn* McLean VA
Hallock HH *ret* Charlottesville VA
Hammond JA *ret* Winchester VA
Han HD
Hanback H *dcn* Leesburg VA
Harman TM *ret* Richmond VA
Harris CB *ret* Seattle WA
Hartl KP *ret* Philadelphia PA
Hatcher JH *ret* San Jose
Hayes CT *ret* Culpeper VA
Hearn RD Alexandria VA
Henderson SH *ret* Carolina Shores NC
Hergenrather LMS Alexandria VA
Hetherington RG *ret* Richmond VA
Higgins WH *dcn* Richmond VA
Hobson JW *ret* Washington VA
Hodge VS *ret* West Point VA
Hogin CW Raleigh NC
Holland CL Kilmarnock VA
Hollerith MKZ Richmond VA
Holliday CT *ret* Richmond VA
Horne MJ *ret* Alexandria VA
Howell SC *ret* Monticello FL
Hummel TC Alexandria VA
Hunter HM *ret* Ivy VA
Huntington FDB *ret* Alexandria VA
Huynh TT *ret* Columbus NJ
Iswariah JC *ret* King William VA
Jackson CT *ret* Conneaut OH
Jenkins KE Midlothian VA
Johnson CE
Johnson CL *ret* Irvington VA
Jones EW *dcn* Richmond VA
Keeler EF Washington DC
Kettlewell PS *ret* Charlottesville VA

Kiblinger CE *ret* Osprey FL
Kimball JW Ashland VA
Klam WP
Klemmt PW *ret* Alexandria VA
Knight DH *ret* Richmond VA
Krejci RS *ret* Urbanna VA
Kunz AG *ret* Richmond VA
Kuratko RP Mechanicsville VA
La Rue HA *ret* Searsport ME
Ledgerwood MJ McLean VA
Lee DE *ret* Charlottesville VA
Lubelfeld NPN *ret* Annandale VA
Lukens MM Kailua HI
MacPhail KL Woodstock VA
Mansella TG *ret* Falls Church VA
Manson ALY *ret* Richmond VA
Markham IS Alexandria VA
Marshall MAC *ret* Richmond VA
Mattia JP *ret* Debrecen
Mattia LJ *ret* Herndon VA
May RE Campton NH
Maycock RW *ret* Williamsburg VA
Maypole SC *ret* Fayetteville NY
McConnell TH *ret* Mechanicsville VA
McCusker TB *ret* Chonburi
McDonald JS Free Union VA
McKenzie JG Alexandria VA
McWhorter SD *ret* Southampton GA
Miller CH Alexandria VA
Miller JE *ret* Richmond VA
Milliken JL *ret* Arlington VA
Minnich-Lockey LK Harrisonburg VA
Mohn MC *ret* Winchester VA
Moore DT Naples FL
Moore ML *ret* Locust Grove VA
Morales R *ret*
Morris RL
Morton WB Leesburg VA
Mullaly CF *ret* Charlottesville VA
Murphy GM *ret* Earlysville VA
Murphy JAR *ret* Miami FL
Murray MH *ret* Easton MD
Myers WF *ret* Reston VA
Neville RM Alexandria VA
Newbold SE Opa Locka FL
Newcomb DJ *ret* Dexter NY
Newman ML *ret* Mitchellville MD
Noe WS *ret* Ashland VA
Norton MR Arlington VA
Nunn FL
Okrasinski RS *ret* Colonial Beach VA
Packard LK *ret* Burke VA
Paradine PJ *ret* Charlottesville VA
Parker B Richmond VA
Peyton WP New York NY
Phillips KA Mountain View CA
Phipps RS *ret* San Antonio TX
Pickering WT *ret* Richmond VA
Poist DH *ret* Charlottesville VA
Pollach GLK Brooklyn NY
Pollock M Laytonsville MD

Ponsoldt MH Kilmarnock VA
Praktish CR
Prest APL *ret* Richmond VA
Prichard RW Alexandria VA
Prior RL *ret* Burke VA
Pruitt AC *ret* Richmond VA
Pulimootil CP Alexandria VA
Reed JG Fredericksburg VA
Reeves W *ret* Richmond VA
Reiners A *ret* Richmond VA
Rice JF *ret* South Yarmouth MA
Ritchie AG *ret* Alexandria VA
Robillard RM *ret* Highland Springs VA
Rousseau SK Haymarket VA
Rowe GON *ret* Hagerstown MD
Schaller WA *ret* Galena IL
Schellenberg RT *ret* Kingstowne VA
Schroeder CC Leesburg VA
Schroeder HBW
Seiler JH Williamsburg VA
Seiler RS *ret* Richmond VA
Siefferman NC *ret* Fredericksburg VA
Skala K *ret* Winchester VA
Smith DH Chatham VA
Smith JM *ret* Pasadena CA
Smith TR *ret* Richmond VA
Solak KA Alexandria VA
Sonderegger KA Middlebury VT
Spagna AL Bethlehem PA
Spangler HB Charlottesville VA
Spigner CB Ashland VA
Staley ML Put In Bay OH
Stewart JB Annandale VA
Strasser G Leesburg VA
Strawbridge JR Oxford
Stribling AJ *ret* Markham VA
Stribling JH *ret* Norfolk VA
Sullivan RG *ret* Alexandria VA
Sutor JT *ret* Hanover VA
Swann CW *ret* Reedville VA
Sydnor CR *ret* Heathsville VA
Taylor GB *ret* Charlottesville VA
Tedesco RL *ret* Gaithersburg MD

Thomas JA Falls Church VA
Thomas KP *dcn* Madison VA
Thomas SH *ret* Louisa VA
Thompson CE Alexandria VA
Thomson JC *ret* Vienna VA
Thorpe MB Richmond VA
Tollison ABB *ret* Gum Spring VA
Trimble SM *ret* Pensacola FL
Trumbore FR *ret* Woodstock VA
Tuller SS *ret* Reston VA
Turnbull ME *ret* N Chesterfield VA
Turner LAS *ret* Broad Run VA
Van Scoyoc GW *ret* Alexandria VA
Vandevelder FR *ret* Woodbridge VA
Voorhees JA Charlottesville VA
Waddell TR *ret* Alexandria VA
Wade SH *ret* Middleburg VA
Walsh RD *ret* Dumfries VA
Wandall FS *ret* Springfield VA
Ward EM *ret* Hilton Head SC
Warner DM *ret* Richmond VA
Washington LE Mechanicsville VA
Wayland DF *ret* Charlottesville VA
Webb J *ret* Williamsburg VA
Webb PC *ret* Williamsburg VA
Weiher JMC *ret* Warrenton VA
Weiler WL *ret* Arlington VA
Wells WS *ret* Richmond VA
Wentt AR *ret* Richmond VA
Wheeler ED *ret* Mathews VA
White DA Richmond VA
White HC *ret* White Stone VA
Wigner JD *ret* Henrico VA
Wilmoth DS *dcn* Falls Church VA
Winchell RS *ret* Locust Grove VA
Wingo PJ Richmond VA
Witt AL Kilmarnock VA
Wood HH *ret* Charlottesville VA
Wood SA New York NY
Woodruff KB *ret* Lively VA
Worthington DO *ret* Gloucester VA
Wyer GW *ret* Ivy VA
Yung BY

STATE OF WASHINGTON

Dioceses of Olympia and Spokane

DIOCESE OF WASHINGTON

(PROVINCE III)
Comprises DC and 4 counties of Maryland
DIOCESAN OFFICE Episcopal Church House Mt S Alban Washington DC 20016-5094
TEL (202) 537-6555 (800) 642-4427   FAX (202) 364-6605
E-MAIL newspaper@edow.org   WEB www.edow.org

Previous Bishops—
Henry Y Satterlee 1896-1908, Alfred Harding 1909-23, James E Freeman 1923-43, Angus Dun 1944-62, William F Creighton coadj 1959 Bp 1962-77, Paul Moore Jr suffr 1964-70, John T Walker suffr 1971-76 coadj 1976 Bp 1977-89, Ronald H Haines suffr 1986-90 Bp 1990-2000, Jane H Dixon suffr 1992-2002; John Bryson Chane 2002-2011

Bishop —Rt Rev Mariann Edgar Budde (1061)
(Dio 12 Nov 2011)

Cn to Ord P Cooney; *Cler Dev & Multicultural Rev Cn* P Clark; *Cong Vit* Cn J Rick; *Chanc* M Kostel; *Treas* P Barkett; *Hist* S Stonesifer; *Sec* K Roachford; *Latino Missioner* Rev S Goodwin; *Yth* I Green; *Yng Adult* J Evans

Stand Comm—Cler: K Baker J Beilstein V Brown-Nolan S Nagley; *Lay:* H Bale K Camara C Hartley S Stonesifer

Dio Conv: 30 Jan 2016 Washington Cathedral Washington DC

PARISHES, MISSIONS, AND CLERGY

Accokeek Christ Church, Saint John's Parish **P** (123) 600 Farmington Rd W 20607-9732 (Mail to: 600 Farmington Road West 20607-9732) Brian Vander Wel (301) 292-5633

✠ **Aquasco** St Mary **Other** 13500 Baden Westwood Rd 20608 Mary McCarty (301) 579-2643

Avenue All Saints Church **P** (218) 22598 Oakley Rd 20609 (Mail to: PO Box 307 20609-0307) (301) 769-4288

Beltsville St Johns Church **P** (293) 11040 Baltimore Ave 20705-2118 (Mail to: PO Box 14 20704-0014) Joseph Constant John Price (301) 937-9242

Bethesda Church of the Redeemer **P** (327) 6201 Dunrobbin Dr 20816-1044 (Mail to: 6201 Dunrobbin Dr 20816-1044) Ciritta Park Robin Razzino David Schlafer (301) 229-3770

Bethesda St Dunstans Episcopal Church **P** (369) 5450 Massachusetts Ave 20816-1653 (Mail to: 5450 Massachusetts Ave 20816-1653) Jeffrey Macknight Linda Von Rautenkranz (301) 229-2960

Bethesda St Lukes Church Trinity Parish **P** (369) 6030 Grosvenor Ln 20814-1852 (Mail to: 6030 Grosvenor Ln 20814-1852) Stephanie Nagley Jessica Hitchcock Owen Thompson (301) 530-1800

Bowie Holy Trinity Episcopal Church **P** (390) 13106 Annapolis Rd 20720-3829 (Mail to: 13106 Annapolis Rd 20720-3829) Leslie St Louis (301) 262-5353

Brandywine St Pauls Parish **P** (111) 13500 Baden Westwood Rd 20613-8419 (Mail to: 13500 Baden Westwood Rd 20613-8419) Charles Hoffacker Harry Harper (301) 579-2643

Brandywine St Philips Church **P** (120) 13801 Baden Westwood Rd 20613-8426 (Mail to: 13801 Baden Westwood Rd 20613-8426) (301) 888-1536

Brookeville St Lukes Church **P** (125) PO Box 131 20833-0131 (Mail to: PO Box 131 20833-0131) Kathleen Corbett-welch (301) 570-3834

California St Andrews Church **P** (341) 44078 St Andrews Church Rd 20619 (Mail to: 44078 St Andrews Church Rd 20619-2100) Beverly Weatherly (301) 862-2247

Chaptico Christ Church King & Queen Parish **P** (369) 25390 Maddox Rd 20621 (Mail to: P O Box 8 20621) (301) 884-3451

Charlotte Hall All Faith Episcopal Church **P** (106) 38885 New Market Turner Rd 20659 (Mail to: PO Box 24 20622-0024) Noreen Seiler-Dubay (301) 884-3773

Chevy Chase All Saints Episcopal Church **P** (1580) 3 Chevy Chase Cir 20815-3408 (Mail to: 3 Chevy Chase Cir 20815-3400) Edward Kelaher Theodore Lewis Thomas Malionek (301) 654-2488

Chevy Chase St Barnabas Church of the Deaf **M** (44) 6701 Wisconsin Ave 20815-5351 (Mail to: 6701 Wisconsin Ave 20815-5351) (301) 907-2955

Chevy Chase St Johns Church **P** (1175) 6701 Wisconsin Ave 20815-5351 (Mail to: 6701 Wisconsin Ave 20815-5351) Sari Ateek Elizabeth Anne Tesi (301) 654-7767

Clinton Christ Church **P** (106) 8710 Old Branch Ave 20735-2522 (Mail to: 8710 Old Branch Ave 20735-2522) Cassandra Burton (301) 868-1330

College Park St Andrews Episcopal Church **P** (477) 4510 College Ave 20740-3302 (Mail to: 4512 College Ave 20740-3302) Carol Jablonski Sarah Lamming (301) 864-8881

College Park University of Maryland Mission **CC** University of Maryland 2116 Memorial Chapel 20742 (Mail to: 2116 Memorial Chapel 20742) (301) 405-8453

Damascus St Anne's Church **P** (280) 25100 Ridge Rd 20872-1832 (Mail to: 25100 Ridge Rd 20872-1832) Ronald Davis

Ft Washington St Johns, Broad Creek **P** (169) 9801 Livingston Rd 20744-4925 (Mail to: 9801 Livingston Rd 20744-4925) (301) 248-4290

Gaithersburg Church of the Ascension **P** (1084) 205 S Summit Ave 20877-2315 (Mail to: 205 S Summit Ave 20877-2399) Kimberly Becker Randall Lord-Wilkinson (301) 948-0122

Gaithersburg St Bartholomews Church **P** (160) 21615 Laytonsville Rd 20882-1627 (Mail to: 21611 Laytonsville Road 20882-0005) Linda Calkins Margaret Pollock (301) 355-7189

Germantown St Nicholas Episcopal Church **P** (591) 15575 Germantown Road 20874-3012 (Mail to: 15575 Germantown Road 20874-3012) Kenneth Howard Kenneth Howard Shivaun Wilkinson (240) 631-2800

Glenn Dale St Georges Church Glenn Dale Parish **P** (266) 7010 Glenn Dale Rd 20769 (Mail to: PO Box 188 20769-0188) Constance Reinhardt (301) 262-3285

✠ **Hughesville** Old Fields Chapel **Other** 15837 Prince Frederick Road 20637-9801 (Mail to: PO Box 178 20637-0178) (301) 934-1424

Hughesville Trinity Parish **P** (215) PO Box 178 20637-1178 (Mail to: PO Box 178 20637-0178) (301) 934-1424

Hyattsville St Matthews Episcopal Church **P** (650) 5901 36th Ave 20782-2925 (Mail to: 5901 36th Ave 20782-2925) Vidal Rivas (301) 559-8686

Hyattsville St Michael & All Angels Epis Church **P** (250) 8501 New Hampshire Ave 20783-2411 (Mail to: 8501 New Hampshire Avenue 20783-2411) Clinton Esonu

Indian Head St James' Church **P** (153) 7 Potomac Ave 20640 (Mail to: 7 Potomac Ave 20640) Nancy Hildebrand (301) 743-2366

Kensington Christ Church Parish **P** (663) 4001 Franklin St 20895-3827 (Mail to: 4001 Franklin St 20895-3827) Emily Guthrie (301) 942-4673

La Plata Christ Church **P** (101) 112 E Charles Street 20646-0760 (Mail to: PO Box 760 20646-0760) Timothy Johnson Eric Shoemaker

Laurel St Philips Church **P** (479) 522 Main St 20707-4118 (Mail to: 522 Main St 20707-4118) Sheila McJilton (301) 776-5151

Leonardtown St Georges Church **P** (264) 44965 Blake Creek Rd 20650 (Mail to: PO Box 30 20692-0030) Gregory Syler

Lexingtn Park The Church of the Ascension **P** (267) 21641 Great Mills Rd 20653-1239 (Mail to: 21641 Great Mills Rd 20653-1239) Melinda Artman Harry Harper (301) 863-8551

Mount Rainier St Johns Episcopal Church **P** (285) 4104 34th St 20712-1948 (Mail to: 4112 34th St 20712-1948) (301) 927-1156

Nanjemoy Christ Church (Durham Parish) **P** (182) 8700 Ironsides Rd 20662-3430 (Mail to: 8700 Ironsides Rd 20662-3430) Mary McCarty Arnold Taylor

New Carrollton St Christophers Church **P** (324) 8001 Annapolis Rd 20784-3009 (Mail to: 8001 Annapolis Road 20784-3009) Melana Nelson-Amaker (301) 577-1281

Newburg Christ Church Wayside William and Mary Parish **P** (99) 13050 Rock Point Rd 20664 (Mail to: PO Box 177 20664-0177) (301) 259-4327

Olney St Johns Church **P** (1153) 3427 Olney Laytonsville Rd 20832-1743 (Mail to: PO Box 187 20830-0187) Carol Flanagan John Price (301) 774-6999

Poolesville St Peters Parish **P** (333) 20100 Fisher Ave 20837-2080 (Mail to: PO Box 387 20837-0387) Ann Ritonia

Potomac St Francis Church **P** (1200) 10033 River Rd 20854-4902 (Mail to: 10033 River Rd 20854-4975) William Shand Phillip Ellsworth (301) 365-2055

Potomac St James Church **P** (268) 11815 Seven Locks Rd 20854-3340 (Mail to: 11815 Seven Locks Rd 20854-3340) William Doggett James Isaacs (301) 762-8040

✠ **Ridge** St Marys Chapel **Other** 12960 Point Lookout Road 20687 (Mail to: PO Box 207 20686-0207) John Ball (301) 862-4597

Rockville Christ Church, Rockville **P** (592) 107 S Washington St 20850-2319 (Mail to: 107 S Washington St 20850-2319) John McDuffie Cynthia Simpson (301) 762-2191

Silver Spring Church of the Ascension **P** (735) 633 Sligo Ave 20910-4764 (Mail to: 634 Silver Spring Ave 20910-4657) Joan Beilstein Terri Murphy (301) 587-3272

Silver Spring Church of the Transfiguration **P** (641) 13925 New Hampshire Ave 20904-6218 (Mail to: 13925 New Hampshire Ave 20904) Margaret Ingalls (301) 384-6264

Silver Spring Good Shepherd Episcopal Church **P** (281) 818 University Blvd W 20901-1039 (Mail to: 818 University Boulevard West 20901-1039) David Wacaster (301) 593-3282

Silver Spring Grace Church **P** (702) 1607 Grace Church Rd 20910-1509 (Mail to: 1607 Grace Church Rd 20910-1509) Andrew Walter Amanda Akes (301) 585-3515

Silver Spring Our Saviour Hillandale **P** (958)

1700 Powder Mill Rd 20903-1514 (Mail to: 1700 Powder Mill Rd 20903-1514) Robert Harvey Jose Valle (301) 439-5900

Silver Spring St Marks Church Fairland **P** (231) 12621 Old Columbia Pike 20904-1614 (Mail to: 12621 Old Columbia Pike 20904-1614) Isaac Bonney

Silver Spring St Mary Magdalene Church **P** (185) 3820 Aspen Hill Rd 20906-2904 (Mail to: 3820 Aspen Hill Rd 20906-2904) Ann Moczydlowski John Stonesifer (301) 871-7660

St Marys City St Marys Parish **HC** (316) PO Box 145 20686-0145 (Mail to: PO Box 207 47477 Trinity Church Road 20686-0207) John Ball Nathan Beall (301) 862-4597

Temple Hills St Barnabas Episcopal Church **P** (117) 5203 St Barnabas Rd 20748-5837 (Mail to: 5203 Saint Barnabas Rd 20748-5837) Shell Kimble (301) 894-9100

✠ **Uppr Marlboro** Chapel of the Incarnation **Other** No 14300 Thomas Church 20772 (Mail to: c/o St Thomas Parish 14300 St Thomas Church Rd 20772) Debra Brewin-Wilson (301) 627-8469

Uppr Marlboro St Barnabas Church **P** (252) 14111 Oak Grove Rd 20774-8424 (Mail to: 14111 Oak Grove Road 20774-8424) Phillip Cato Robyn Franklin-Vaughn

Uppr Marlboro St Thomas Parish **P** (96) 14300 Saint Thomas Church Rd 20772 (Mail to: 14300 Saint Thomas Church Road 20772-8222) Debra Brewin-Wilson (301) 627-8469

Uppr Marlboro Trinity Episcopal Church **P** (351) 14515 Church St 20772-3039 (Mail to: PO Box 187 20773-0187) Martha Bonwitt (301) 627-2636

Waldorf St Pauls Episcopal Church **P** (368) Piney Church Rd @ St Pauls Dr 20604 (Mail to: 4535 Piney Church Rd 20602-3262) Maria Kane (301) 645-5000

Washington All Souls Memorial Church **P** (406) 2300 Cathedral Ave NW 20008-1505 (Mail to: 2300 Cathedral Ave NW 20008-1505) John Beddingfield Elizabeth Orens

Washington Calvary Church **P** (334) 509 I St NE 20002-4345 (Mail to: 509 I St NE 20002-4345) Peter Schell (202) 546-8011

✠ **Washington** Cathedral of St Peter & St Paul **O** (1126) Attn Human Resources Dept 3101 Wisconsin Ave NW 20016 (Mail to: 3101 Wisconsin Ave NW 20016-5098) Eva Maria Cavaleri Jeannette Cope Patricia Dickson Eleanor Ellsworth Preston Hannibal Mary Humphrey Brooks Hundley Stuart Kenworthy Richard Kukowski Richardson Libby (202) 537-6200

Washington Christ Church Georgetown **P** (1469) 3116 O St NW 20007-3116 (Mail to: 3116 O St NW 20007-3198) Kristen Hawley Elizabeth Keeler Peter Lee (202) 333-6677

Washington Christ Church Washington Parish **P** (357) 620 G St SE 20003-2722 (Mail to: 620 G

St SE 20003-2722) Cara Spaccarelli (202) 547-9300

Washington Church of Our Saviour **P** (102) 1616 Irving St NE 20018-3826 (Mail to: 1616 Irving St NE 20018-3826) (202) 635-7804

Washington Church of the Ascension & St Agnes **P** (211) 1217 Massachusetts Ave NW 20005-5301 (Mail to: 1217 Massachusetts Ave NW 20005-5396) Shawn Strout (202) 347-8161

Washington Church of the Atonement **P** (281) 5073 E Capitol St SE 20019-5327 (Mail to: 5073 E Capitol St SE 20019-5327) Hannah Irving (202) 582-4200

Washington Church of the Epiphany **P** (163) Rock Creek Church Rd & Webster St. NW 20747-4434 (Mail to: Rock Creek Church Rd & Webster St NW 20747-4434) Prince Decker (202) 726-2080

Washington Church of the Holy Comforter **P** (287) 701 Oglethorpe St NW 20011-2021 (Mail to: 701 Oglethorpe St NW 20011-2021) Joseph Constant (202) 726-1862

Washington Church of the Holy Communion **P** (46) 3640 Martin Luther King Jr Ave 20032-1546 (Mail to: PO Box 54707 20032-9307) Rondesia Jarrett (202) 562-8153

Washington Grace Church **P** (365) 1041 Wisconsin Ave NW 20007-3635 (Mail to: 1041 Wisconsin Ave NW 20007-3635) John Graham Sarah Fischer Shearon Williams (202) 333-7100

Washington Howard University Episcopal Mission **CC** 2225 Georgia Ave 20059-1014 (Mail to: Howard University MS 59017 20059-0001) (202) 806-5747

Washington Saint Mark's Church **P** (700) 118 3rd St SE 20003-1007 (Mail to: 301 A St SE 20003-3812) Michele Morgan Rebecca Schunior (202) 543-0053

Washington St Albans Episcopal Parish **P** (1857) 3001 Wisconsin Ave NW 20016-5095 (Mail to: 3001 Wisconsin Ave NW 20016-5046) Deborah Meister Emily Griffin Matthew Hanisian Deborah Kirk Loren Mead James Quigley (202) 363-8286

Washington St Augustines Episcopal Church **P** (119) 617 I St SW Ste A 20024-2431 (Mail to: 617 I St SW Ste A 20024-2431) Martha Clark (202) 554-3222

Washington St Columba's Episcopal Church **P** (3996) § 4201 Albemarle St NW 20016-2009 (Mail to: 4201 Albemarle St NW 20016-2098) Ledlie Laughlin Peter Antoci Jason Cox Rosemarie Duncan Margaret Guenther (202) 363-4119

Washington St Davids Episcopal Church **P** (407) 5150 Macomb St NW 20016-2612 (Mail to: 5150 Macomb St NW 20016-2699) Robin Dodge (202) 966-2093

Washington St Georges Church **P** (241) 160 U St NW 20001-1606 (Mail to: 160 U St NW 20001-

1699) John Hayden Stephen Marcoux (202) 387-6421

Washington St Johns Church **P** (457) Georgetown Parish 3240 O St NW 20007-2842 (Mail to: 3240 O St NW 20007-2880) Sarah Duggin Virginia Gerbasi (202) 338-1796

Washington St Johns Church **P** (1737) 1525 H St NW 20005-1005 (Mail to: 1525 H St NW 20005-1098) Luis Leon David Olivo Juan Reyes (202) 347-8766

Washington St Lukes Church **P** (312) 1514 15th St NW 20036 (Mail to: 1514 15th St NW 20005-1922) Raymond Massenburg (202) 667-4394

Washington St Margarets Church **P** (449) 1820 Connecticut Ave NW 20009-5732 (Mail to: 1830 Connecticut Ave NW 20009-5706) Kimberly Lucas Anne Nicholson (202) 232-2995

Washington St Marys Church **P** (108) 728 23rd St NW 20037-2501 (Mail to: 728 23rd St NW 20037-2598) Michael Hamilton (202) 333-3985

Washington St Monicas and St James Capitol Hill **P** (80) 222 8th St NE 20002-6106 (Mail to: 222 8th St NE 20002-6188) William Stafford-Whittaker (202) 546-1746

Washington St Patricks Church **P** (472) 4700 Whitehaven Pkwy NW 20007-1554 (Mail to: 4700 Whitehaven Pkwy NW 20007-1554) Kurt Gerhard Loren Lasch Katrina Solter (202) 342-2800

Washington St Pauls Parish **P** (750) 2430 K St NW 20037-1703 (Mail to: 2430 K St NW 20037-1797) James Anderson Jean Beniste Douglas Greenaway Jeffrey Hual James Jelinek Lloyd Lewis Kyle Oliver John Pham Richard Wall (202) 337-2020

Washington St Pauls Rock Creek Parish **P** (159) 201 Allison St NW 20011-7305 (Mail to: 201 Allison St NW 20011-7305) Allan Johnson-Taylor Douglas Greenaway (202) 726-2080

Washington St Philip the Evangelist Episcopal **P** (109) 2001 14th St SE 20020-4817 (Mail to: 2001 14th St SE 20020-4817) Louis Wheeler (202) 678-4300

Washington St Stephen & the Incarnation Parish **P** (210) 1525 Newton St NW 20010-3103 (Mail to: 1525 Newton St NW 20010-3103) Frank Dunn Sarabeth Goodwin Linda Kaufman (202) 232-0900

Washington St Thomas Parish **P** (344) 1772 Church St NW 20036-1302 (Mail to: 1772 Church St NW 20036-1327) Nancy Jose Rebecca Zartman (202) 332-0607

Washington St Timothys Church **P** (310) 3601 Alabama Ave SE 20020-2425 (Mail to: 3601 Alabama Ave SE 20020-2425) Caron Gwynn (202) 582-7740

Washington The Church of the Epiphany **P** (320) 1317 G St NW 20005-3102 (Mail to: 1317 G St NW 20005-3102) Timothy Johnson (202) 347-2635

Washington Trinity Church **P** (604) 7005 Piney Branch Rd NW 20012-2417 (Mail to: 7005 Piney Branch Rd NW 20012-2417) Anita Braden John Harmon (202) 726-7036

NON-PAROCHIAL CLERGY

Abernathy PR *ret* Spartanburg SC
Alexander PAP Potomac MD
Allen B *ret* Bethesda MD
Amuzie CC *ret* Washington DC
Anderson JD *ret* Chestertown MD
Andrews DT *ret* Millersville MD
Arbogast SD Washington DC
Arpee ST *ret* Washington DC
Astarita SG *ret* Del Mar CA
Babnis MC Lewes DE
Baker KT Washington DC
Baskin CO *ret* N Potomac MD
Beck JD *ret* Thurmont MD
Billow WP *ret* Barboursville VA
Blackwell NL *ret* Fairfax VA
Blue SN *ret* Durango CO
Booker VPL *ret* Alexandria VA
Booth EK *ret* Huntingtown MD
Boulter RJ Washington DC
Britt ML *ret* Pittsfield MA
Brock VE *ret* Syracuse NY
Brown D *ret* Knoxville TN
Brown ES Alexandria VA
Brown ER *ret* Washington DC
Brown KE *ret* Knoxville TN
Brown Douglas KD Germantown MD
Brown-Nolan V *ret* Silver Spring MD
Bunch LL
Carl E Washington DC
Catchings RM *ret*
Charles R *ret* Arlington VA
Clark DCFG Hertfordshire
Clark JM *ret* Washington Grove MD
Clark PE Upper Marlboro MD
Clarkson W Atlanta GA
Clay TD *ret* Accokeek MD
Clayton VH Poolesville MD
Colvin SM Charlottesville VA
Croft JL *ret* Montgomery AL
Crumley CA Washington DC
Daniels JD Exton PA
Darko DD *ret* Takoma Park MD
Davenport SR *ret* Washington DC
Davis DHK *ret* Kensington MD
DeLaney CT
Denham J *ret* Claremont CA
Donald J *ret* Atlanta GA
Donathan WL Washington DC
Downing RE *ret* Wilmington DE
Downs DD *ret* Poinciana FL
Duncan BT *ret* Glen Allen VA
Early ND Catonsville MD
Eberman JF *ret* Elizabeth City NC
Eckian D *ret* Washington DC
Edwards LMF Silver Spring MD

Edwards TH *ret* Bethesda MD
Evans JF *ret* Mitchellville MD
Fisher-Stewart GA
Flanders JW Washington DC
Flanders SM *ret* Washington DC
Flett C *ret* Washington DC
Flowers MM
Fouts AG *ret* Pompton Lakes NJ
Gardner EB McLean VA
Gill J *ret* Lewes DE
Gillespie RS *ret* Accokeek MD
Gilson AB Harwich MA
Gleason DT *ret* Evergreen CO
Gonzalez EC Alexandria VA
Gortner DT Alexandria VA
Grieb AK Alexandria VA
Hadler JB *ret* Washington DC
Hagans MV Washington DC
Hague EA *ret* Chevy Chase MD
Hague JM
Hague W *ret* Kensington MD
Hall GR *ret* Washington DC
Halter KS *ret*
Harding RR *ret*
Harris JC *ret* Washington DC
Harris L *ret* Mitchellville MD
Harris V *ret* Silver Spring MD
Harrison CR The Hague
Harron FM *ret* North Bethesda MD
Hayward SH *ret* Brooksville ME
Henry BD *ret* IL
Hensley-Echols BM San Antonio TX
Hilton OPL
Hogan LAL Washington DC
Holmes JC *ret* Baltimore MD
Humphrey MT Fort Washington MD
Hunter RFB *ret* Bowie MD
Ilogu ECO Crofton MD
Irvin HS *ret* Asheville NC
Jackson PJE London
Jaekle CR *ret* Springfield VA
James NC Washington DC
Jenneker BWB *ret* Cape Town
Jenson C *ret* Cobb Island MD
Johnson HV *ret* Lake Ridge VA
Johnson KB *ret* Gaithersburg MD
Johnson TW *ret* Basye VA
Johnson WP *ret* Richmond VA
Jones JT *dcn* Beltsville MD
Jordan KH *ret* Silver Spring MD
Jubinski CD Chaptico MD
Karefa-Smart RJW Chevy Chase MD
Karpf T *ret* Santa Fe NM
Lawrence JE *ret* Venice FL
Lee NJC Waco TX
Lewis WB *ret* Silver Spring MD
Lund JW *ret* Rancho Mirage CA
Lundelius CS *ret* Rockville MD
Lusignan LJC *ret* Mitchellville MD
Lyons PM
Malone TJ Arlington VA

Martin AB Hillsdale MI
McNaughton M Alexandria VA
Minturn BB *ret* Hendersonville NC
Monahan AD *ret* Alexandria VA
Moriyama JT *ret* Co. Cork
Mullen MB Richmond VA
Murphy TC *ret* Arlington VA
Neal DD
Neil EA *ret* Washington DC
Noall NJ *ret* Silver Spring MD
Noble MMA *ret* Moneta VA
Owen HH *ret*
Palmer A Wellfleet MA
Peete NOA *ret* Washington DC
Peters AW *ret* Catonsville MD
Peterson JL *ret* Hendersonville NC
Peyton FB Timonium MD
Phillips RT Washington DC
Pinzon S *ret* Miami FL
Pittman AC *ret* Gaithersburg MD
Pregnall WS *ret* Irvington VA
Price K *ret* Williamsburg VA
Quinn EF Chevy Chase MD
Rogge JJ Ipswich MA
Rose LAP Alexandria VA
Sandoe DE *ret* Deland FL
Schmidt FW Dallas TX
Scott JS *ret* Falling Waters WV
Sell-Lee WM *ret* Bainbridge Island WA
Shakespeare L
Shirley SA Fort Walton Beach FL
Slater SE
Smith ML *ret* Washington DC
Smith PM *ret* Baltimore MD
Stephenson R *ret* Rockville MD
Stewart S
Stribling EB Washington DC
Sturges HH *ret dcn* Washington DC
Suarez EN
Tait CWS *ret* Seattle WA
Talbott JT *ret* Old Saybrook CT
Tartt JC *ret* Washington DC
Thon SC *ret* Glen Echo MD
Tielking CG McLean VA
Trainor HC *ret dcn* Charlottesville VA
Trigg J *ret* La Plata MD
Truelove KE *ret* Champaign IL
Tutu MA Alexandria VA
Underhill WD *ret* Kingston MA
Van Culin S *ret* Washington DC
Wade FH *ret* Alexandria VA
Wagnon WS Indianapolis IN
Walker SC *ret* Chaptico MD
Walker SK *dcn* Washington DC
Wallace ME *ret* Washington DC
Weaver JC *ret* Aiken SC
Welch MH Wayne PA
Welsh CW *ret* Annapolis MD
Wilkins CI St Marys City MD
Williams MC Chicago IL
Williams-Duncan S Atherton CA

Woggon KM Hickory NC
Wolf DB Washington DC
Yount AC Washington DC

Zahl PFM *ret* Winter Garden FL
Zaina LM New Canaan CT
Ziobro AF *ret* Washington DC

DIOCESE OF WEST MISSOURI
(PROVINCE VII)
Comprises counties of the western half of Missouri
DIOCESAN OFFICE 420 W 14th St Kansas City MO 64105
TEL (816) 471-6161, (800) 471-6160
E-MAIL info@diowestmo.org   WEB www.diowestmo.org

Previous Bishops—
Edward R Atwill 1890-1911, Sidney C Partridge 1911-30, Robert N Spencer 1930-49, Robt R Spears Jr suffr 1967-70, Edward R Welles 1950-72, Arthur A Vogel 1973-89, John C Buchanan coadj 1989 Bp 1989-99 Barry R Howe 1998-2011

Bishop—Martin Scot Field (Dio 5 March 11)

Cn Ord & Cong Dev S Rottgers; *Sec* C Hamilton *Comm Dir* dG Allman; *Treas* C Cordonnier; *Assoc Treas* J Gilligan; *Chanc* RW Wagstaff; *Reg Min Dev* WF Fasel T Coppinger S Breese

Stand Comm—Cler: P DeVeau M Castellan R Verhaeghe K Hall; *Lay: Pres* C Horner S Danielson G Leabo J Morrow

Deans: D Kendrick P Miller M Castellan

Chairs: COM R Maynard; *Yth* K Snodgrass; *Lit*; *Hist* C Neuman; *Campus Min* B Marshall; *ECW* J Turner; *Comp Dio* D Robinson; *Christian Form* J Kile

Dio Conv: TBD 2016 Ramada Plaza Springfield Hotel and Oasis Convention Center

PARISHES, MISSIONS, AND CLERGY

Blue Springs Church of the Resurrection **P** (225) 1433 NW R D Mize Rd 64015-3666 (Mail to: 1433 NW RD Mize Rd 64015-3666) David Lynch (816) 228-4220

Bolivar St Albans Episcopal Church **M** (61) 201 South Killingsworth 65613 (Mail to: PO Box 844 65613-0844) Catherine Cox Brenda Sickler (417) 777-2233

Boonville Christ Episcopal Church **M** (37) 524 4th St 65233-1552 (Mail to: 524 4th St 65233-1552) Martha Byer (660) 882-6444

Branson Shepherd of the Hills Church **P** (55) 107 Walnut Ln 65616-2220 (Mail to: 107 Walnut Ln 65616-2220) (417) 334-3968

Camdenton St George Episcopal Church **Chapel** (89) 423 North Business Route 5 65020-9591 (Mail to: PO Box 1043 65020-1043) Luther Henderson (573) 346-4686

Carthage Grace Episcopal Church **P** (808) No 820 Howard St 64836 (Mail to: PO Box 596 64836-0596) Steven Wilson Robert Estes Jose Palma (417) 358-4631

Cassville St Thomas a Becket Epis Ch **M** (30) 13628 State Highway AA 65625-8529 (Mail to: PO Box 613 65625-0613) (417) 846-2155

Chillicothe Grace Episcopal Church **P** (62) 421 Elm St 64601-2610 (Mail to: 421 Elm St 64601-2610) (660) 646-4288

Clinton St Pauls Episcopal Church **M** (78) 181 E Highway 7 64735-9504 (Mail to: PO Box 453 64735-0453) (660) 885-8008

Excelsior Springs St Luke Episcopal Church **M** (97) 404 Regents Street 64024-2649 (Mail to: PO Box 551 64024-0551) John Coil (816) 630-2309

Fayette St Marys Episcopal Church **M** (21) 104 W Davis St 65248-1453 (Mail to: PO Box 57 65248-0057)

Harrisonville St Peters Episcopal Church **P** (106) 400 W Wall St 64701-2251 (Mail to: PO Box 425 64701-0425) John Richardson

Independence St Michaels Episcopal Church **M** (174) 4000 S Lees Summit Rd 64055-4005 (Mail to: 4000 S Lees Summit Rd 64055-4005) Patricia Miller (816) 373-5333

Independence Trinity Episcopal Church **P** (130) 409 N Liberty St 64050-2701 (Mail to: PO Box 58 64051) (816) 254-3644

Joplin St Philips Episcopal Church **P** (250) 706 Byers Ave 64801-4304 (Mail to: 706 Byers Ave 64801-4304) Francisco Sierra (417) 623-6893

Kansas City Bishop Spencer Place Inc **Retirement Home** 4301 Madison Ave 64111-3488 (Mail to: 4301 Madison Ave 64111-3488) William Crain Kathleen Hall (816) 931-4277

Kansas City Church of the Good Shepherd **P** (355) 4947 NE Chouteau Dr 64119-4815 (Mail to: 4947 NE Chouteau Dr 64119-4815) Galen Snodgrass (816) 452-0745

Kansas City Church of the Redeemer **P** (263) 7110 N State Route 9 64152-2930 (Mail to: 7110 N State Route 9 64152-2930) Ralph Behen Elisabeth Sinclair (816) 741-1136

Kansas City Grace and Holy Trinity Cathedral **O** (977) 415 W 13th St 64105-1350 (Mail to: PO Box 412048 64141-2048) Peter Deveau Christy

Dorn (888) 902-4482

Kansas City Saint Lukes Chapel **Other** 4401 Wornall Rd 64111-3220 (Mail to: 4401 Wornall Rd 64111-3220) Marshall Scott

Kansas City Saint Mary's Episcopal Church **P** (218) 1307 Holmes St 64106-2845 (Mail to: 1307 Holmes St 64106-2845) Charles Marks Cecil Perkins (816) 842-0975

Kansas City St Andrews Episcopal Church **P** (1478) 6401 Wornall Ter 64113-1755 (Mail to: 6401 Wornall Ter 64113-1755) John Spicer Marcus Halley

Kansas City St Augustines Church **P** (84) 2732 Benton Blvd 64128-1130 (Mail to: 2732 Benton Blvd 64128-1130) David Angus (816) 921-8534

Kansas City St Matthews Episcopal Church **P** (105) 9349 E 65th St 64133-4907 (Mail to: 9349 E 65th Street 64133-4907) Arthur McVey (816) 353-4592

Kansas City St Pauls Church **P** (659) 11 E 40th St 64111-4909 (Mail to: 11 E 40th St 64111-4909) Rufus Runnels (816) 931-2850

Kansas City St Peter & All Saints Epis Ch **P** (187) 100 E Red Bridge Rd 64114-5412 (Mail to: 100 E Red Bridge Rd 64114-5412) Kathleen Hall Evelyn Hornaday (816) 942-1066

Kimberling City St Marks Episcopal Church **M** (64) 3 Northwoods Blvd 65686 (Mail to: PO Box 153 65686-0153) (417) 739-2460

Lebanon Trinity Episcopal Church **M** (41) PO Box 1615 65536-1615 (Mail to: PO Box 1615 65536-1615) Jerry Miller (417) 532-3433

Lees Summit St Annes Church **P** (249) 1815 NE Independence Ave 64086-5415 (Mail to: 1815 NE Independence Ave 64086) Margaret Rhodes (816) 524-5552

Lees Summit St Pauls Episcopal Church **P** (166) 416 Grand St 64063 (Mail to: PO Box 372 64063-0372) Mark Mcguire Nancy Nevins Joan Zoller (816) 524-3651

Lexington Christ Episcopal Church **P** (96) 13th and Franklin St 64067 (Mail to: PO Box 307 64067-0307) (660) 259-3605

Liberty Grace Episcopal Church **P** (217) 520 S State Route 2 64068-1915 (Mail to: 520 S 291 Hwy 64068-1915) John McCann (816) 781-6262

Loch Lloyd St Mary Magdalene **P** (302) 16808 S Holmes Road 64012-9661 (Mail to: 16808 S State Route D 64012-9661) David Lynch (816) 331-2222

Maryville St Pauls Episcopal Church **M** (23) 901 N Main St 64468 (Mail to: 901 N Main St 64468-1435) (660) 582-5832

Monett St Stephens Episcopal Church **M** (58) 601 E Benton St 65708-1770 (Mail to: 601 E Benton St 65708-1770) (417) 235-3330

Mountain Grove Church of the Transfiguration **M** (57) 215 N Wall St 65711-1766 (Mail to: 215 N Wall St 65711-1766) Bradford Ellsworth

(417) 926-5217

Neosho St Johns Church **M** (36) 305 W Spring St 64850-1762 (Mail to: 305 W Spring St 64850-1762) Daniel Erdman (417) 451-3644

Nevada All Saints Episcopal Church **P** (135) 425 E Cherry St 64772-3418 (Mail to: PO Box 456 64772-0456) (417) 667-2607

Noel St Nicholas Episcopal Church **M** (95) 101 Sulphur St 64854 (Mail to: PO Box 248 64854-0248) (417) 475-3852

Overland Park St Luke's South Chapel **Chapel** 12300 Metcalf Ave 66213-1324 (Mail to: Spiritual Wellness Department 12300 Metcalf Ave 66213-1324) Ronald Verhaeghe (816) 932-2190

Ozark St Matthews Episcopal Church **P** 203A E Brick St 65721-8906 (Mail to: 203A E Brick St 65721-8906) (417) 581-1350

Saint Joseph Christ Episcopal Church **P** (128) 207 N 7th St 64501-1905 (Mail to: 207 N 7th St 64501-1975) Charles Caskey (816) 279-6351

Savannah St Marys Episcopal Church **M** (18) 401 W Chestnut St 64485-1439 (Mail to: 401 W Chestnut Street 64485-0350) (816) 324-5532

Sedalia Calvary Episcopal Church **P** (140) 713 S Ohio Ave 65301-4415 (Mail to: 713 S Ohio Ave 65301-4415)

Skidmore St Oswalds in the Field Church **M** (7) 30996 X Ave 64487-8191 (Mail to: 30996 X Ave 64487-8191) (660) 442-5897

Springfield Christ Episcopal Church **P** (1144) 601 E Walnut St 65806-2419 (Mail to: 601 E Walnut St 65806-2419) Kenneth Chumbley Jonathan Frazier (417) 866-5133

Springfield St James Episcopal Church **P** (117) 2645 E Southern Hill Blvd 65804-3433 (Mail to: 2645 E Southern Hills Blvd 65804-3433) Suzanne Lynch

Springfield St Johns Episcopal Church **P** (229) 515 E Division St 65803-2815 (Mail to: 515 E Division St 65803-2815) David Kendrick (417) 869-6351

Trenton St Philips Church **M** (10) 205 E 9th St 64683-2202 (Mail to: PO Box 46 64683-0046) (660) 359-5309

Warrensburg Christ Episcopal Church **P** (161) 136 E Gay St 64093-1810 (Mail to: PO Box 3 64093-0003) (660) 429-1133

West Plains All Saints Church **P** (74) 107 S Curry St 65775-3943 (Mail to: PO Box 1012 65775-1012) (417) 256-2215

NON-PAROCHIAL CLERGY

Allen LJ *dcn* Independence MO
Anderson EA Newton KS
Armer MCC *ret* Lenexa KS
Babcock LM *dcn*
Bauer KA Kremmling CO
Beachy WN *ret* Kansas City MO
Beam BJW *ret* Lathrop MO

Bellais WF *ret* Chillicothe MO
Biggs JW *ret* Springfield MO
Bishop NR Blue Springs MO
Bower BE *dcn* Kansas City MO
Breese MS *ret* Saint Joseph MO
Breese SS *ret* Saint Joseph MO
Brown VD *ret* Houston TX
Castellan ML Kansas City MO
Cheffey AD Kimberling City MO
Cook PR
Coppinger TR San Antonio TX
Cox AE Overland Park KS
Easter MK *dcn* Hollister MO
Egger JA *dcn* Kansas City MO
Eick JD *dcn* Kansas City MO
England OB *dcn* Independence MO
Fasel WJ Kansas City MO
Firth HW *ret* Overland Park KS
Fritsch AJ *dcn* Joplin MO
Gilbertson GR *ret* Overland Park KS
Grabher J *dcn* Kansas City MO
Harris NJ *ret* Springfield MO
Heathman SG *dcn* Lexington MO
Hinson JA Fredericksburg VA
Hoover GT Branson MO
Hughes LK Ozark MO
Hutchens HB *ret* Drumnadrochit SCOTLAND
Hutcherson AV *ret* Kansas City MO
Hutcherson RM *ret* Kansas City MO
Jewson AJ *ret* Saint Louis MO
Johnson DP *ret* Ponca City OK
Johnson RW *ret* Independence MO
Johnston LT *ret* Lawrence KS
Keel RD *ret*
Kolb JW *ret* Prairie Village KS
Kyle AM
Leed RA *ret* Clinton MO
Lewis LB *ret* Osceola MO
Lively PK Monett MO
Long RC *dcn* Kansas City MO
McCann SG *ret* Liberty MO
Mesley GW *dcn* Independence MO
Milholen LS *dcn* Houston MO

Moon JF *ret* South Greenfield MO
Moore JW *dcn* Stilwell KS
Murphy RA *dcn* Lees Summit MO
Myers DJ *dcn* Garfield AR
Mynatt BC *dcn* Independence MO
O'Hearne JJ Kansas City MO
Pulliam JM *ret* Warrensburg MO
Punzo TE *ret* Gladstone MO
Robertson JB *dcn* Kansas City MO
Rottgers SR Lees Summit MO
Roumas PG *dcn* Kansas City MO
Russell SA *dcn* Kansas City MO
Ruth MF *ret dcn* Kansas City MO
Sanford CW
Saribay E Kansas City MO
Savidge KF *ret* St. Joseph MO
Schubert RM *dcn* Prairie Village KS
Scott MS Kansas City MO
Shaffer JM Friday Harbor WA
Shepherd TE *ret* Euless TX
Siegel CDH Baltimore MD
Skillicorn GA *ret* Somerset NJ
Smith KW *ret* Kimberling City KS
Spencer RD *ret* Angel Fire NM
Stanford DL *dcn* Kansas City MO
Stinnett RA *ret* Carthage MO
Stockwell-Tangeman CL *dcn*
Stuckey RW *ret* Springfield MO
Swift JK *ret* Guilford CT
Taube KL *dcn* Boonville MO
Ticknor PH *ret dcn* Oro Valley AZ
Tyndall CF *dcn* Springfield MO
Uhlik CR Springfield MO
Vaughn DC Austin TX
Verhaeghe RE Kansas City MO
Whelan EJ *ret* Parkville MO
Whelan JK *dcn* Parkville MO
White KG *dcn*
Whitsitt HB *dcn* Fayette MO
Wilke CE *ret* Aliso Viejo CA
With DF *ret* Lake Quivira KS
Wood RE *ret* Kansas City MO
Yeager LS *ret dcn* Overland Park KS

DIOCESE OF WEST TENNESSEE
(PROVINCE IV)
Comprises twenty counties lying west of the Tennessee River including all of Hardin County
DIOCESAN OFFICE 692 Poplar Ave Memphis TN 38105
TEL (901) 526-0023   FAX (901) 526-1555
E-MAIL diocese@episwtn.org   WEB www.episwtn.org

Previous Bishops—
Alex D Dickson 1983-94, James M
Coleman 1994-2001

**Bishop — Rt Rev Don E Johnson
(967)** (Dio 30 June 01)

Cn to Ord ZA Davis II; *Sec* Rev D
Wells; *Asst Sec* E Gassler; *Treas* MR
Crow; *Asst Treas* PA Calame Jr; *Asst Treas* B Rolfes
Jr; *Chanc* CB Foster II; *V Chanc* L Leach; *V Chanc*
MA Cobb Jr; *Hist* P McFarland; *Reg* L Stone

Stand Comm—Cler: R McCloy T Rhoads J Rogers
JW Sewell; *Lay:* B Falvey J McGehee B Steinhauser
C Walsh

Bishop's Council—Cler: R Fletcher C McMillen
GJ Meade R Van Doren S Webb D Wells; *Lay:* R
Edmonds S Haight L Harris M Mangum M Miller
M Shaw

Dio Conv: 20-21 Nov 2015 Germantown TN

PARISHES, MISSIONS, AND CLERGY

Atoka Ravenscroft Chapel **M** (41) C/O Shelly
Nichols 33 Sarah Cove 38004-4904 (Mail to:
8219 Holly Grove Rd 38011-6241) (901) 837-
1312

Bolivar St James Episcopal Church **M** (50) 223 W
Lafayette St PO Box 85 38008-0085 (Mail to:
PO Box 85 38008-0085) Walter Gordon (731)
658-4439

Brownsville Christ Episcopal Church **HC** (28)
140 N Washington Ave 38012-2519 (Mail to:
140 N Washington Ave 38012-2519) (901)
772-9156

Collierville Church of the Holy Apostles **P** (547)
1380 Wolf River Blvd 38017-8687 (Mail to:
1380 Wolf River Blvd 38017-8687) John Leach
(901) 937-3830

Collierville Saint Andrew's Episcopal Church
P (357) 106 Walnut St 38017-2672 (Mail to:
PO Box 626 38027-0626) Jeffery Marx David
Carletta (901) 853-0425

Cordova Church of the Annunciation **P** (150)
8282 Macon Rd 38018-8532 (Mail to: 8282
Macon Rd 38018-8532) (901) 753-0142

Covington St Matthew Episcopal Church **HC**
(41) 303 S Munford St 38019-2555 (Mail to:
303 S Munford St 38019-2555) (901) 476-6577

Dyersburg St Mary's Episcopal Church **P** (161)
108 N King Ave 38024-4610 (Mail to: 108 N
King Ave 38024-4610) Gary Meade (731) 285-
3522

Germantown St George Episcopal Church **P** (540)
§ 2425 S Germantown Rd 38138-5946 (Mail to:
2425 S Germantown Rd 38138-5946) Dorothy
Wells Marian Whitman (901) 754-7282

Humboldt St Thomas the Apostle **M** (38) 6
Esquire Lewis Road 38343 (Mail to: PO Box
442 38343-0442) Bill Burks (901) 784-2872

Jackson St Lukes Episcopal Church **HC** (373)
309 E Baltimore St 38301-6304 (Mail to: 309
E Baltimore St 38301-6304) Tommy Rhoads
(731) 424-0556

La Grange Immanuel Episcopal Church **HC** (37)
PO Box 21 38046-0021 (Mail to: PO Box 21
38046-0021)

Mason St Paul Episcopal Church **M** (38) 2406
Highway 59 38049-7522 (Mail to: PO Box 158
38049-0158) (901) 294-2641

Mason Trinity Episcopal Church **M** (9) 260 N
Main St 38049 (Mail to: PO Box 99 38049-
0099) (901) 594-5012

Memphis All Saints Episcopal Church **P** (49) 1508
S White Station Rd 38117-6826 (Mail to: 1508
S White Station Rd 38117-6899) (901) 685-
7333

Memphis Calvary Episcopal Church **HC** (1005)
102 N 2nd St 38103-2203 (Mail to: 102 N 2nd
St 38103-2287) Christopher Girata Robert
Bartusch Eyleen Farmer Lewis McKee Paul
Mclain (901) 525-6602

Memphis Church of the Good Shepherd **P** (51)
1971 Jackson Ave 38107-4614 (Mail to: 1971
Jackson Ave 38107-4614) William Fry (901)
725-9768

Memphis Church of the Holy Communion **P**
(1153) 4645 Walnut Grove Rd 38117-2537
(Mail to: 4645 Walnut Grove Rd 38117-2537)
Benjamin Badgett Hester Mathes Alexander
Webb (901) 767-6987

Memphis Emmanuel Episcopal Church **P** (109)
4150 Boeingshire Dr 38116-6007 (Mail to:
4150 Boeingshire Dr 38116-6007) Colenzo
Hubbard (901) 346-7434

Memphis Grace - St Lukes Church **P** (1086) 1720
Peabody Ave 38104 (Mail to: 1720 Peabody
Ave 38104) Richard Lawson Broderick Greer
James Snapp (901) 272-7425

Memphis Holy Trinity Episcopal Church **P** (42)
3749 Kimball Ave 38111-6420 (Mail to: 3745
Kimball Ave 38111-6496) (901) 743-6421

Memphis St Elisabeths Episcopal Church **P** (246)
6033 Old Brownsville Rd 38135-0722 (Mail
to: 6033 Old Brownsville Rd 38135-0722) Jack
Rogers (901) 372-2753

Memphis St Johns Episcopal Church **P** (864) 3245 Central Ave 38111-4409 (Mail to: 3245 Central Ave 38111-4409) John Sewell James Biedenharn Robert VanDoren (901) 323-8597

Memphis St Joseph Episcopal Church **Other** (6) 604 Saint Paul Ave 38126-2865 (Mail to: 604 St Paul Ave 38126)

Memphis St Mary's Episcopal Cathedral **O** (702) 692 Poplar Ave 38105-4512 (Mail to: 692 Poplar Ave 38105-4512) William Andrews Laura Gettys (901) 527-3361

Memphis St Philip Episcopal Church **P** (256) 9380 Davies Plantation Rd 38133-4250 (Mail to: 9380 Davies Plantation Rd E 38133-4250) Terry Street Marian Whitman (901) 388-9830

Millington St Annes Church **P** (111) 4063 Sykes Rd 38053-7930 (Mail to: 4063 Sykes Rd 38053-7930) (901) 872-0303

Paris Grace Episcopal Church **P** (107) 103 S Poplar St 38242-4103 (Mail to: PO Box 447 38242-0447) (731) 642-1721

Ripley Immanuel Episcopal Church **M** (51) 153 Highland St Ro Winslow 38063-1815 (Mail to: 134 South Jefferson St PO Box 513 38063) Nancy O'Shea (731) 635-5593

Somerville St Thomas Episcopal Church **M** (49) Attn Rev William Fry 203 W Market St 38068-1593 (Mail to: PO Box 368 38068-0368) (901) 465-7112

Union City St James Episcopal Church **P** (80) 422 E Church St 38261-3906 (Mail to: PO Box 838 38281-0838) William Mcmillen (731) 885-9575

NON-PAROCHIAL CLERGY

Allen CT *ret* Nashville TN
Altizer CJ Federal Way WA
Blakley RL Roseville CA
Boyd JR *ret* Memphis TN
Brooks DE *ret* Union City TN
Burruss JB Cordova TN

Bush KMQ Memphis TN
Cheney RS *ret* Memphis TN
Christian DV *dcn* Cordova TN
Connolly EF *ret dcn* Memphis TN
Crook SC *ret* Memphis TN
Cubine JW *ret* Memphis TN
Davis ZA Memphis TN
Donelson FT *dcn* Memphis TN
DuGard DH *dcn* Memphis TN
Fletcher RJ *dcn* Dyersburg TN
Gardner CH *dcn* Nashville TN
Greathouse WM Paris TN
Hart FM *ret* Brevard NC
Hatzenbuehler RR Memphis TN
Ince EE Memphis TN
Johnson IJ *ret* Memphis TN
Jones MW *dcn* Memphis TN
Kneipp LB Pineville LA
Kolb WA *ret* Memphis TN
Macbeth AJ *ret* Memphis TN
McCarty PG Memphis TN
McCloy RMK *dcn* Memphis TN
Montiel RM *ret* Paris TN
Moore AY Greenwich CT
Mowery D *ret* Memphis TN
Murray WS Dallas TX
Musser LF Dallas TX
Newsom J *ret* Memphis TN
Porter JT *ret* Sewanee TN
Powell BC *dcn* Memphis TN
Reese J Bowling Green KY
Rutenbar CM *ret* Presque Isle MI
Ryan WW Cordova TN
Snyder BAW *ret* Memphis TN
Stillings KD Galveston TX
Sturni GK *ret* Germantown TN
Walker NR *ret* Olive Branch MS
Wallace-Williams JA Memphis TN
Watson GS Richardson TX
White PD Memphis TN

DIOCESE OF WEST TEXAS

(PROVINCE VII)
Comprises 60 West Texas counties
DIOCESAN OFFICE 111 Torcido Dr San Antonio TX 78209 (MAIL: Box 6885)
TEL (210) 824-5387 (888) 824-5387   FAX (210) 824-2164
E-MAIL general.mail@dwtx.org   WEB www.dwtx.org

Previous Bishops—
Robt WB Elliott miss 1874-87, James S Johnston miss 1888-1904 dio 1905-16, Wm T Capers 1916-43, Everett H Jones 1943-69, R Earl Dicus suffr 1955-75, Harold C Gosnell coadj 1968 dio 1969-77, Scott Field Bailey 1976-87, Stanley F Hauser suffr 1979-87, John H MacNaughton coadj 1986, dio 1987-95 Earl N McArthur suffr 1988-93, James Folts coadj 1994-96, dio 1996-2006, Robert B Hibbs 1996-2003

Bishop—Rt Rev Gary R Lillibridge (995) (coadj 2004; Dio 24 Feb 2006)

Bishop Suffragan—Rt Rev David M Reed (1005) (Cons 26 Aug 2006)

Bishop Coadjutor—Rt Rev David M Reed (1005) (28 Feb 2015)

Lay Cn K Mason; *Sec* Rev D Read; *Treas* T Burkhart; *Reg* L Woodall; *Chanc* D Cauthorn 300 Austin Hwy Ste 100 San Antonio TX 78209; *Asst Chanc* K Kimble J Norman; *Comm* L Shaver; *Stew* N Stinson; *Camps & Conf* R Watson; *Cong Dev* J Saylors; *Hisp Off* vacant; *Hist* S Johnson; *Deploy Off* J Saylors

Stand Comm—Cler: Pres R Hardaway, L Mason, D Read *Lay:* M Duffy J Warren, R Mosty

Deans: Central C Cole; *Eastern* S Carson; *North Eastern* D Chalk; *Northern* L Tyler; *Southern* P May ; *Valley* J Nelson ; *Western* J Fritts

Dio Conv: 18-20 Feb 2016 McAllen TX

PARISHES, MISSIONS, AND CLERGY

Alice The Epis Church of the Advent **P** (82)
  Alice The Epis Church of the Advent **P** (30) 200 N Wright 78332 (Mail to: PO Box 1937 78333-1937) Thomas Turner (361) 664-7881
Aransas Pass The Episcopal Church of Our Saviour **M** (59) 822 S McCampbell St 78336-2316 (Mail to: 406 Champions Dr 78352-6908) Thomas Keith (361) 727-9101
Bandera St Christophers Church **P** (156) 395 State Highway 173 N 78003 (Mail to: PO Box 314 78003-0314) Allan Conkling (830) 796-4387
Beeville St Philip's Episcopal Church **P** (142) 311 E Corpus Christi St 78102 (Mail to: 311 E Corpus Christi St 78102-4899) Clayton Elder (361) 358-2730
Blanco St Michaels and All Angels Episcopal **M** (77) 218 Pittsburg St 78606-5768 (Mail to: PO Box 684 78606-0684) (830) 833-4816
Boerne St Helenas Episcopal Church **P** (570) 410 N Main St 78006 (Mail to: PO Box 1765 78006-6765) Brian Cannaday Patrick Soule (830) 249-3228
Brackettville St Andrews Episcopal Church **M** (27) 300 E Henderson St 78832 (Mail to: Ford & Henderson St 78832) (830) 563-3666
Brady St Pauls Episcopal Church **P** (67) 1111 S Blackburn 76825 (Mail to: PO Box 1148 76825-1148) Shanna Neff (325) 597-1330
Brownsville Church of the Advent **P** (472) 104 W Elizabeth St 78520-5547 (Mail to: 104 W Elizabeth St 78520-5594) Laurie McKim (956) 542-4123
Brownsville St Pauls Episcopal Church **M** (50) 16th and Taft St 78521-3132 (Mail to: 960 Toledo Dr 78526) Charles Sharrow (956) 542-3869
Buda St Elizabeths Episcopal Church **M** (116) 723 Ranch Road 967 78610-9297 (Mail to: PO Box 292 78610-0292) Jennifer Brooke-Davidson (512) 295-3674
Canyon Lake St Francis-by-the-Lake Epis Church **P** (304) 13250 Farm to Market 306 78133 (Mail

to: PO Box 2031 78133-0023) David Chalk (830) 964-3820
Carrizo Springs Holy Trinity Episcopal Church **M** (49) 1807 Pena 78834 (Mail to: PO Box 919 78834-6919) Nicholas Mayer (830) 876-9729
Comfort St Boniface Episcopal Church **Chapel** (81) 116 US 87 78013 (Mail to: PO Box 676 78013) Lera Tyler
Corpus Christi All Saints Episcopal Church **P** (300) 3026 S Staples 78404 (Mail to: 3026 S Staples St 78404-3691) Jonathan Wickham
Corpus Christi Church of the Good Shepherd **P** (1171) 700 S Upper Broadway 78401-3521 (Mail to: 700 S Upper Broadway St 78401-3521) Milton Black Philip May (361) 882-1735
Corpus Christi St Andrews Episcopal Church **M** (193) 13026 Leopard St 78410-4515 (Mail to: 13026 Leopard St 78410-4515)
Corpus Christi St Bartholomews Episcopal Church **P** (345) 622 Airline Rd 78412 (Mail to: 622 Airline Rd 78412-3156) Sean Maloney (361) 991-2954
Corpus Christi The Church of the Reconciliation **P** (90) 4518 Saratoga Blvd 78413-2151 (Mail to: 4518 Saratoga Blvd 78413-2151) Conrad Wilson (361) 852-9677
Cotulla St Timothys Church **M** (18) 305 North Choctaw Ave 78014 (Mail to: 305 North Choctaw Ave 78014)
Crp Christi St Marks Episcopal Church **P** (225) 2727 Airline Rd 78414-3306 (Mail to: 2727 Airline Rd 78414-3306) John Hardie
Cuero Grace Episcopal Church **P** (57) 102 E Live Oak St 77954 (Mail to: 102 E Live Oak St 77954-2957) (361) 275-3423
Cypress Mill St Lukes Episcopal Church **M** (121) 263 Spur 962 East 78663-8486 (Mail to: 263 Spur 962 East 78663-8486) Tommy Bye (830) 825-8001
Del Rio St James Episcopal Church **P** (294) 206 W Greenwood St 78841-1129 (Mail to: PO Box 1129 78841-1129) John Fritts (830) 775-7292
Devine St Matthias **M** (31) 901 N. Teel Dr. 78016-1701 (Mail to: PO Box 682 78016-0681) (210) 385-7668
Dripping Spgs Holy Spirit Episcopal Church **P** (203) § 301 Hays Country Acres Rd 78620-4282 (Mail to: 301 Hays Country Acres Rd 78620-4282) Christopher Caddell (512) 858-4924
Eagle Pass Church of the Redeemer **P** (150) 648 Madison St 78852 (Mail to: 648 Madison St 78852-4246) Matthew Frey (830) 773-5122
Edinburg St Matthews Episcopal Church **P** (123) 2620 Crestview Dr 78539-6296 (Mail to: 2620 Crestview Dr 78539-6296) (956) 383-4202
Edna Trinity Episcopal Church **P** (29) 102 W Church St 77957 (Mail to: PO Box 305 77957-0305) (361) 782-2204
Fort McKavett St James Episcopal Church **M** (29) 3232 Runge Ranch Rd 76841 (Mail to: HC 84

Box 57 76841-9702) Christopher Roque (325) 387-2955

Fredricksburg St Barnabas Episcopal Church **P** (613) 601 W Creek St 78624 (Mail to: 601 W Creek St 78624-3117) Richard Elwood Jeffrey Hammond (830) 997-5762

George West Church of the Good Shepherd **Chapel** (75) 809 N San Antonio St 78022 (Mail to: PO Box 1582 78022-1582) John Rayls George Keeble (361) 449-2737

Goliad St Stephens Episcopal Church **M** (13) 152 N Chilton Ave 77963-3906 (Mail to: PO Box 739 77963-0739) (361) 645-2234

Gonzales Episcopal Church of the Messiah **P** (50) 721 St Louis St 78629-4154 (Mail to: PO Box 139 78629-0139) Mark Melton (830) 672-3407

Hallettsville St James Episcopal Church **M** (24) 1103 E 4th St 77964-3219 (Mail to: 1103 E 4th St 77964-3219)

Harlingen St Albans Episcopal Church **P** (890) 1417 E Austin Ave 78550 (Mail to: 1417 E Austin Ave 78550-8855) Scott Brown William Clark (956) 428-2305

Hebbronville St James Episcopal Church **M** (44) 112 W North 78361 (Mail to: PO Box 68 78361-0068) Kristine Graunke (361) 527-3433

Junction Trinity Episcopal Church **M** (74) 1119 Main 76849 (Mail to: PO Box 3 76849-0003) (325) 446-4416

Kenedy St Matthews Episcopal Church **M** (25) 309 S 5th 78119 (Mail to: 315 S 5th St 78119-2607) (830) 583-2589

Kerrville St Peters Episcopal Church **P** (968) 956 Main St 78028-3549 (Mail to: 320 Saint Peter St 78028-4650) Jerre Williams Thomas Murray (830) 257-8162

Kingsville Episcopal Church of the Epiphany **P** (171) 206 N 3rd St 78363 (Mail to: 206 N 3rd St 78363-4409)

Lake Corpus Christi St Michaels Episcopal Church **M** (3) 99109 FM 534 78383 (Mail to: PO Box 180 78383-0180) (361) 547-6658

Laredo Christ Episcopal Church **P** (187) 2320 Lane St 78043-2711 (Mail to: 2320 Lane St 78043-2711) Paul Frey (956) 723-5714

Llano Grace Episcopal Church **P** (98) 1200 Oatman St 78643-2730 (Mail to: 1200 Oatman St 78643-2730)

Lockhart Emmanuel Episcopal Church **P** (132) 118 N Church St 78644 (Mail to: 118 N Church St 78644-2102) Thomas Bruns (512) 398-3342

Luling Church of the Annunciation **P** (87) 301 S Walnut 78648 (Mail to: Post Office Box 106 78648-0106) Burford Dobbins (830) 875-5155

McAllen St Johns Episcopal Church **P** (651) 2500 N 10th St 78501-4008 (Mail to: 2500 N 10th St 78501-4008) James Nelson Nancy Springer (956) 687-6191

Menard Calvary Episcopal Church **M** (12) 201 Callan St 76859 (Mail to: PO Box 237 76859) (325) 396-2696

Mission St Peter & St Paul Church **M** (166) 2310 N Stewart Rd 78574 (Mail to: 2310 N Stewart Rd 78574-8842) Michael Bertrand (956) 585-5005

Montell Church of the Ascension **M** (33) 27851 N Hwy 55 78802-0808 (Mail to: PO Box 808 78802-0808) (830) 597-4284

New Braunfels St Johns Episcopal Church **P** (242) 312 S Guenther Ave 78130-5639 (Mail to: 312 S Guenther Ave 78130-5639) Ripp Hardaway (830) 625-2532

Pharr Trinity Episcopal Church **P** (171) 210 W Caffery St 78577 (Mail to: PO Box 692 78577-1613) Roger Penrod (956) 787-1243

Pleasanton All Saints Episcopal Church **M** (40) 1435 W Oaklawn Rd 78064 (Mail to: PO Box 732 78064-0732) (830) 277-2222

Port Aransas Trinity by the Sea **M** (127) 431 Trojan St 78373 (Mail to: PO Box 346 78373-0346) John Derkits Douglas Schwert (361) 749-6449

Port Isabel St Andrews by the Sea **HC** (87) 1022 N Yturria 78578 (Mail to: PO Box 1168 78578-1168) Beverly Patterson (956) 943-1962

Port Lavaca Grace Episcopal Church **P** (43) 213 E Austin St 77979 (Mail to: PO Box 172 77979-0172) Robert DeWolfe

Portland St Christophers by the Sea **P** (154) 720 7th St 78374 (Mail to: PO Box 386 78374-0386)

Raymondville Church of the Epiphany **M** (92) 688 W Kimball Ave 78580-2309 (Mail to: PO Box 82 78580-0082) Robert McAllen (956) 689-9582

Refugio Church of the Ascension **M** (20) 602 E Plasuela St 78377-3241 (Mail to: PO Box 903 78377-0903) (361) 526-4262

Rockport St Peter's Episcopal Church **P** (339) 412 N Liveoak St 78382-2747 (Mail to: 412 N Live Oak St 78382-2747) James Friedel (361) 729-2649

San Antonio Christ Episcopal Church **P** (1108) 510 Belknap Pl 78212-3400 (Mail to: 510 Belknap Pl 78212-3493) William Gahan Robert Harris Scott Kitayama Robert Koehler (210) 736-3132

San Antonio Church of Reconciliation **P** (460) 8900 Starcrest Dr 78217-4741 (Mail to: 8900 Starcrest Dr 78217-4741) Robert Woody (210) 655-2731

San Antonio Church of the Holy Spirit **P** (215) 11093 Bandera Road 78250-6814 (Mail to: 11093 Bandera Road 78250-6814) Jason Roberts Kelly Conkling (210) 314-6729

San Antonio Grace Episcopal Church **M** (52) All Saints Chapel at TMI 20955 W Tejas Trail 78257 (Mail to: 6275 Camp Bullis Rd 78257) Jacob George (210) 462-6901

San Antonio Sante Fe Episcopal Church **M** (175) 1108 Brunswick Blvd 78211-1502 (Mail to: 1108 Brunswick Blvd 78211-1502) John Wauters Donald Wilkinson (210) 923-0822

San Antonio St Andrews Episcopal Church **P** (278) 6110 NW Loop 410 78238-3305 (Mail to: 6110 NW Loop 410 78238-3305) David Archibald (210) 684-0845

San Antonio St Davids Episcopal Church **P** (583) 1300 Wiltshire Ave 78209-6049 (Mail to: 1300 Wiltshire Ave 78209-6049) Lisa Mason

San Antonio St Francis Episcopal Church **Chapel** (272) No 4242 Bluemel Rd 78240-1063 (Mail to: 4242 Bluemel Rd 78240) Cristopher Robinson

San Antonio St George Episcopal Church **P** (743) 6904 West Ave 78213-1820 (Mail to: 6904 West Ave 78213-1820) Ramiro Lopez (210) 342-4261

San Antonio St Lukes Episcopal Church **P** (1648) Jane Crowley 11 Saint Lukes Ln 78209-4445 (Mail to: 11 Saint Lukes Ln 78209-4499) John Badders David Read (210) 828-6425

San Antonio St Margarets Episcopal Church **M** (141) 5310 Stahl Rd 78247-1522 (Mail to: 5310 Stahl Rd 78247-1522) John Hill (210) 657-3328

San Antonio St Marks Episcopal Church **P** (1475) 315 E Pecan St 78205-1819 (Mail to: 315 E Pecan St 78205-1819) Elizabeth Knowlton Carol Morehead Christopher Wise (210) 226-2426

San Antonio St Pauls Episcopal Church **P** (164) 1018 E Grayson St 78208-1224 (Mail to: 1018 E Grayson St 78208-1224) Robert Carabin Bradley Landry Joseph Webb (210) 226-0345

San Antonio St Philips Episcopal Church **P** (94) 1310 Pecan Valley Dr 78210-3416 (Mail to: 1310 Pecan Valley Dr 78210-3416) Patricia Riggins (210) 333-6256

San Antonio St Stephens Episcopal Church **P** (53) 3726 S. New Braunfels Ave. 78223 (Mail to: 3726 S. New Braunfels Ave 78223-1706) (210) 534-5400

San Antonio St Thomas Epis Church & School **P** (1228) 1416 N Loop 1604 E 78232-1427 (Mail to: 1416 N Loop 1604 E 78232-1400) Charles Woehler Beth Wyndham (210) 494-3507

San Benito All Saints Episcopal Church **P** (47) 499 N Reagan 78586 (Mail to: PO Box 1948 78586-0041) Antonio Illas (956) 399-1795

San Marcos St Marks Episcopal Church **P** (519) 3039 Ranch Road 12 78666-2488 (Mail to: 3039 Ranch Road 12 78666-2488) Benjamin Nelson (512) 353-1979

San Saba St Lukes Episcopal Church **P** (34) 601 W Dry St 76877-5611 (Mail to: 601 W Dry St 76877-5611) William Grusendorf

Seguin St Andrews Episcopal Church **P** (569) 201 E Nolte 78155 (Mail to: 201 E Nolte St 78155-6123) Kevin Dellaria (830) 372-4330

Sonora St Johns Episcopal Church **P** (158) 404 E Poplar St 76950 (Mail to: PO Box 1100 76950-1100) Christopher Roque (325) 387-2955

Universal City St Matthews Episcopal Church **P** (162) 810 Kitty Hawk Rd 78148-3822 (Mail to:

PO Box 2337 78148-1337) Timothy Vellom (210) 658-5956

Uvalde St Philips Episcopal Church **P** (244) 343 N Getty St 78801-4609 (Mail to: 343 N Getty St 78801-4690) Michael Marsh Casey Berkhouse (830) 278-5223

Victoria St Francis Episcopal Church **P** (168) 3002 Miori Ln 77901-3618 (Mail to: 3002 Miori Ln 77901-3618) Stephen Carson

Victoria Trinity Episcopal Church **P** (602) 1501 N Glass St 77901 (Mail to: 1501 N Glass St 77901-5130) James Kee-Rees (361) 573-3228

Weslaco Grace Episcopal Church **P** (186) 701 S Missouri 78596 (Mail to: 701 S Missouri Ave 78596-6941) Richard Speer (956) 968-7014

Wimberley St Stephens Episcopal Church **P** (722) 6000 Fm 3237 78676-5832 (Mail to: 6000 FM 3237 Unit A 78676-6386) Sandra Casey-Martus (512) 847-9956

Windcrest Church of the Resurrection **P** (390) 5909 Walzem Rd 78218-2197 (Mail to: 5909 Walzem Rd 78218-2197) Christopher Cole (210) 655-5484

NON-PAROCHIAL CLERGY

Arroyo ME
Barrett JH Dallas TX
Berry C *ret* Boerne TX
Blavier DC *ret* Victoria TX
Bledsoe FE
Bostian NL San Antonio TX
Bowersox NF *ret* Austin TX
Brown HF *ret* Boerne TX
Burkardt LS Portland TX
Calhoun R Boerne TX
Calhoun WB *ret* Port Aransas TX
Cannell JE San Antonio TX
Carter DB Aberdeen MS
Chalk MD *ret* San Antonio TX
Cole RE *ret* San Antonio TX
Collins CB *ret* Albuquerque NM
Conley AB *ret* Hunt TX
Coon NG *ret* Dripping Springs TX
Cunningham PJ McAllen TX
Davis MMK *ret* Austin TX
Davis M *ret* San Antonio TX
Dawson GH *ret* Corpus Christi TX
Delgado-Vera RM *ret* Raymondville TX
DiRaddo JA *ret* Charleston SC
Dohoney EL *ret* San Antonio TX
Dunham RE *ret* Corpus Christi TX
Earle CD *ret* San Antonio TX
Earle MEC *ret* San Antonio TX
England LD Pflugerville TX
Fenton ED *ret* Cuero TX
Friedman ML *ret* Brownsville TX
Fuller BW *ret* Corpus Christi TX
Gottlich SG *ret* Corpus Christi TX
Griffith NE *ret* Georgetown TX
Harrison S *ret* Santa Clara CA
Hartzog HG *ret* Sacramento CA

Harvey EE *ret* Cochran GA
Hawley FM *dcn* San Antonio TX
Heard W *ret* Galveston TX
Innes NF *ret* Sugar Land TX
Johnston RH Cuero TX
Jones JM *ret* San Angelo TX
Koehler MAC Wimberley TX
Lauer DD San Antonio TX
Lee DDA *ret* Bandera TX
Lewis JG San Antonio TX
Luna EG *ret* San Antonio TX
Magers JH *ret* Brownsville TX
Matthews AR *ret* Luling TX
McLean R *ret* Plano TX
McLeon RA Henderson TX
Mueller MM *ret* San Antonio TX
Murguia JR San Antonio TX
Narvaez AA *ret* Reston VA
Ormos CP *ret* Austin TX
Padgett JE *ret* San Antonio TX
Patterson JL Austin TX
Pitman OW *ret* San Antonio TX
Regist AA Antonio TX

Reynolds MM *ret* Kerrville TX
Riggs KG *ret* San Antonio TX
Rose ES *ret* Fulton TX
Saylors JL San Antonio TX
Sessions JK *ret* Harlingen TX
Shepherd BH *ret* Saint Augustine FL
Sherman RE *ret* San Antonio TX
Sneary JM *ret* Canyon Lake TX
Snyder AL *ret* San Antonio TX
Soper RA *ret* Edinburg TX
Spanutius WF Corpus Christi TX
Spear LE *ret* Crockett TX
Sproat JL *ret* Spring TX
Storment JD *ret* San Antonio TX
Sumners CA *ret* Cuero TX
Tapley WC *ret* Midland TX
Taylor PJ *ret* Boerne TX
Thiering BB *ret* Cedar Park TX
Thomas DE *ret* San Antonio TX
Turner TJ San Antonio TX
Waller CS *ret* San Antonio TX
Worley JP *ret* Cibolo TX
Yarborough JH *ret* Brunswick GA

DIOCESE OF WEST VIRGINIA

(PROVINCE III)
Comprises State of West Virginia
DIOCESAN OFFICE 1608 Virginia St E Charleston WV 25311-2114
(MAIL: PO Box 5400 Charleston WV 25361-0400)
TEL (304) 344-3597; Toll-free (866) 549-8346   FAX (304) 343-3295
E-MAIL [use first initial and last name]@wvdiocese.org   WEB www.wvdiocese.org

Previous Bishops—
Geo W Peterkin 1878-1916, Wm L Gravatt coadj 1899 Bp 1916-39, Robt EL Strider coadj 1923 Bp 1939-55, WC Campbell coadj 1950 Bp 1955-76, Robt P Atkinson coadj 1973 Bp 1976-88, W Franklin Carr suffr 1985-90, John H Smith 1989-99

Bishop—Rt Rev W Michie Klusmeyer (970)
(Dio 13 Oct 2001)

Treas TC Farnsworth 111 McCulloch Dr Wheeling WV 26003; *Chanc* K Klein; *VChanc* T Dinsmore; *Fin Asst* A Combs; *CFO* D Ramkey; *COM* M Hussell; *Dio Admin* M Bailey; *Yth & Young Adult Min* S Gunter

Stand Comm—Cler: C Graves P Shier C Slater J Valentine; *Lay: Pres* D Lumsden J Beall J Sturgeon

Dio Conv: TBD

PARISHES, MISSIONS, AND CLERGY

Ansted Church of the Redeemer **M** (25) 102 Taylor St 25812 (Mail to: PO Box 625 25812-0625) Roy Crist

Beckley St Andrews Episcopal Church **M** (13) c/o St Stephens 200 Virginia St. 25801 (Mail to: c/o St Stephen's 200 Virginia St 25801) (304) 294-7030

Beckley St Stephens Episcopal Church **P** (149) 200 Virginia St 25801-5243 (Mail to: 200 Virginia St 25801-5299) Jon White (304) 253-9672

Berkeley Spg St Marks Episcopal Church **P** (76) 180 S Washington St 25411-1646 (Mail to: 180 S Washington St 25411-1646) David Shoda (304) 258-2440

Bluefield Christ Episcopal Church **P** (195) 200 Duhring St 24701-2910 (Mail to: 200 Duhring St 24701-2910) Chadwick Slater

Buckhannon Church of the Transfiguration **M** (42) 65 S Kanawha St 26201-2636 (Mail to: 65 S Kanawha St 26201-2636) Frederick Bird (304) 472-4418

Bunker Hill Christ Episcopal Church **HC** Runnymeade Rd 25413 (Mail to: c/o Diocesan Office PO Box 5400 25361) (304) 344-3597

Charles Town St Philips Episcopal Church **M** (25) 411 S Lawrence St 25414 (Mail to: PO Box 368 25414-0368) Elwyn Mackov (304) 725-4236

Charles Town Zion Episcopal Church **P** (424) 301 East Congress Street 25414 (Mail to: 221 E

Washington St 25414-1073) Melanie McCarley (304) 725-5312

Charleston Chapel of the Resurrection **Other** 1608 Virginia St E 25311-2114 (Mail to: PO Box 5400 25361-0400) (304) 344-3597

Charleston St Christopher Episcopal Church **P** (170) 821 Edgewood Dr 25302-2811 (Mail to: 821 Edgewood Dr 25302-2811) Melissa Remington (304) 342-3272

Charleston St Johns Episcopal Church **P** (430) 1105 Quarrier St 25301-2410 (Mail to: 1105 Quarrier St 25301-2493) Marquita Hutchens (304) 346-0359

Charleston St Matthews Episcopal Church **P** (504) 36 Norwood Rd 25314-1327 (Mail to: 36 Norwood Rd 25314-1399) John Hagan (304) 343-3837

Clarksburg Christ Episcopal Church **P** (92) 123 S 6th St 26302 (Mail to: PO Box 1492 26302-1492)

Colliers Olde St John Episcopal Church **M** (61) 2308 Eldersville Rd 26035 (Mail to: PO Box 347 26035-0347) (304) 527-4746

Elkins Grace Episcopal Church **P** (78) 212 John St 26241-3823 (Mail to: 212 John St 26241-3823) Frederick Bird (304) 636-4251

Fairmont Christ Church **P** (182) 824 Fairmont Avenue 26554-5138 (Mail to: 824 Fairmont Ave 26554) (304) 366-3471

Glenville St Mark Episcopal Church **M** (9) 607 Main St 26351 (Mail to: 607 Main St 26351) Teresa Wayman (304) 462-7455

Grafton St Matthias Episcopal Church **M** (13) 330 W Francis St 26354-1720 (Mail to: PO Box 27 26354-0027) Frederick Bird (304) 265-3112

Hansford Church of the Good Shepherd **P** (78) 1203 Center St 25103 (Mail to: PO Box 41 25103-0041) (304) 595-6224

Harpers Ferry St Johns Episcopal Church **M** (33) 898 W Washington St 25425-6910 (Mail to: 898 W Washington St 25425-6910) (304) 579-5586

Hedgesville Mt Zion Episcopal Church **M** (28) PO Box 2246 1 Zion Street 25427 (Mail to: PO Box 2246 25427-2246) (304) 702-7111

Hinton Ascension Episcopal Church **M** (29) 222 5th Ave 25951-2210 (Mail to: 222 5th Ave 25951-2210) (304) 627-1232

Huntington St John Episcopal Church **P** (266) 3000 Washington Blvd 25705-1633 (Mail to: 3000 Washington Blvd 25705-1633) Lisa Graves (304) 525-9105

Huntington St Peters Episcopal Church **P** (136) 2248 Adams Ave 25704-1424 (Mail to: 2261 Washington Ave 25704) (304) 429-2241

Huntington Trinity Episcopal Church **P** (297) 520 11th St 25701-2211 (Mail to: 520 11th St 25701-2292) Jon Graves James Morgan (304) 529-6084

Hurricane Church St Timothys in the Valley **P** (243) 3434 Teays Valley Rd 25526-0424 (Mail to: PO Box 424 25526-0424) Cheryl Winter (304) 562-9325

Kearneysville Grace Episcopal Church **M** (62) East & Church St 25430 (Mail to: 159 East St 25430-5691) (304) 725-7073

Kearneysville St Bartholomews Church **M** (18) PO Box 896 25430 (Mail to: PO Box 896 25430-0896) (304) 725-1707

Keyser Emmanuel Episcopal Church **P** (57) 303 S Mineral St 26726-2641 (Mail to: 303 S Mineral St 26726-2641) Martin Townsend (304) 788-4475

Kingwood St Michaels Episcopal Church **M** (38) 107 McDonald St 26537-1017 (Mail to: PO Box 543 26537-0543) (304) 329-3207

Lewisburg St James Episcopal Church **P** (126) 218 Church St 24901-1330 (Mail to: 218 Church St 24901-1330) Joshua Saxe (304) 645-2588

Logan Holy Trinity Church **P** (32) 604 Stratton St 25601-4029 (Mail to: 604 Stratton Street 25601-0507) George Kostas (304) 752-6900

Marlinton St Johns Church **M** 415 9th St 24954-1236 (Mail to: 717 8th Ave 24954-1214) James Lanter (304) 704-2014

Martinsburg Trinity Episcopal Church **P** (264) 200 West King Street 25401-3212 (Mail to: 200 W King St 25401-3212) Julie Harris (304) 263-0994

Moorefield Emmanuel Episcopal Church **M** (31) 309 Winchester Ave 26836 (Mail to: PO Box 692 26836-0692) Stephen Haptonstahl (304) 530-5226

Morgantown St Thomas a Becket Episcopal **P** (366) Old Cheat Rd And Rt 26505 (Mail to: 75 Old Cheat Rd 26508-4103) Julie Murdoch (304) 296-0270

Morgantown Trinity Episcopal Church **P** (198) 247 Willey St 26505-5522 (Mail to: 247 Willey St 26505-5522) Michael Hadaway (304) 292-7364

Moundsville Trinity Church **P** (114) 1 Oak Ave 26041-1107 (Mail to: PO Drawer P 26041-0966) Bruce Bevans (304) 845-5982

N Martinsvlle St Anns Episcopal Church **P** (74) 453 Maple Ave 26155-1340 (Mail to: PO Box 161 26155-0161) Richard Heller (304) 455-5143

Oak Hill St Andrew's Episcopal Church **P** (131) 345 Kelley Ave 25901-2916 (Mail to: 345 Kelly Ave 25901-2916) Roy Crist

Parkersburg Memorial Church of the Good Shepherd **P** (575) 903 Charles St 26101-4825 (Mail to: 903 Charles St 26101-4825) Marjorie Bevans (304) 428-1525

Parkersburg Trinity Episcopal Church **P** (203) No 430 Juliana St 26101-5335 (Mail to: 430 Juliana St 26101-5335) Paul Hicks (304) 422-3362

Point Pleasat Christ Church **P** (104) C/O Jack Sturgeon 804 Main St 25550-1229 (Mail to: PO Box 419 25550-0419) Katharine Foster Raymond Hage (304) 675-3120

Princeton Church of the Heavenly Rest **M** (62) 1207 Mercer St 24740-3031 (Mail to: 1207 Mercer St 24740-3031) William Armstrong (304) 425-9345

Ravenswood Grace Episcopal Church **M** (32) 405 Walnut St 26164-1649 (Mail to: 405 Walnut St 26164-1649) Marie Mulford (304) 273-0980

Ripley St Johns Episcopal Church **M** (30) 702 W Main St 25271-1118 (Mail to: PO Box 558 25271-0558) Katharine Foster (304) 372-9183

Romney St Stephens Church **M** (42) 316 E Main St 26757-1822 (Mail to: 316 E Main St Apt A 26757-1822) (304) 822-5054

Ronceverte Church of the Incarnation **M** (34) 707 W Main St 24970-1754 (Mail to: PO Box 276 24970-0276) (304) 536-3320

Salem Prince of Peace Episcopal Church **M** (25) 53 Sacred Heart Ln 26426-8647 (Mail to: PO Box 215 26426-0215) Pamela Shier (304) 906-7540

Shepherdstown Trinity Church **P** (470) 200 W German St 25443 (Mail to: PO Box 308 25443-0308) George Schramm (304) 876-6990

Sistersville St Pauls Episcopal Church **P** (24) 313 N Wells St 26175-1437 (Mail to: PO Box 79 26175-0079) (304) 652-1801

Snowshoe Chapel on the Mount **Other** (16) 10 Snowshoe Dr. 26209 (Mail to: 354 Locust Glen Drive 26291) James Lanter (304) 572-3333

St Albans St Marks Episcopal Church **P** (141) 405 B St 25177-2716 (Mail to: 405 B St 25177-2716) (304) 722-4284

St Marys Grace Episcopal Church **P** (25) 317 Riverside Dr 26170-1030 (Mail to: 317 Riverside Dr 26170-1030) Richard Heller (304) 684-7976

Summersville St Martins in the Fields **M** (29) 221 McKees Creek Rd 26651-1601 (Mail to: 221 McKees Creek Rd 26651-1601) (304) 872-5594

Union All Saints Church **M** (50) 1 Greenhill Rd 24983 (Mail to: PO Box 401 24983-0401) (304) 772-3120

Weirton St Thomas Episcopal Church **P** (38) 300 Three Springs Dr 26062-4922 (Mail to: PO Box 2232 26062-1432) (304) 723-4120

Welch St Lukes Episcopal Church **M** PO Box 204 24801-2414 (Mail to: PO Box 204 24801-0204) (304) 436-2641

Wellsburg Christ Episcopal Church **P** (61) 1014 Main St 26070-1632 (Mail to: 1014 Main St 26070-1632) (304) 737-1866

Weston St Pauls Church **P** (195) 206 E 2nd St 26452-1927 (Mail to: 206 E 2nd St 26452-1927) John Valentine (304) 269-5266

Wheeling Lawrencefield Parish Church **P** (133) No Table Rock Ln 44 Kirkside Dr 26003 (Mail to: PO Box 4063 26003-0414) Cynthia Walter (304) 277-2353

Wheeling St Lukes Episcopal Church **M** (79) 200 S Penn St 26003-2028 (Mail to: 200 S Penn St 26003-2097) James Kelley Theresa Kelley (304) 232-2395

Wheeling St Matthews Church **P** (397) PO Box 508 26003-0064 (Mail to: PO Box 508 26003-0064) Mark Seitz Richard Skaggs (304) 233-0133

Wht Sphr Spgs St Thomas Episcopal Church **P** (128) 205 W Main St 24986-2411 (Mail to: PO Box 148 24986-0148) (304) 536-3320

Williamson St Pauls Episcopal Church **M** (36) 411 Prichard St 25661-3140 (Mail to: 411 Prichard St 25661-3140) Nick England (304) 235-4056

Williamstown Christ Memorial Episcopal Church **M** (57) 409 Columbia Ave 26187-1122 (Mail to: 409 Columbia Ave 26187-1122) Richard Heller (304) 375-6506

NON-PAROCHIAL CLERGY

Aird IM *dcn* Parkersburg WV
Alfriend JD *ret* Charles Town WV
Anderson RJ
Bailey SE *ret* Berkeley Springs WV
Barnes RD
Bennett AL *ret* Vienna WV
Bicking D *ret* Front Royal VA
Chard AC *ret* Anchorage KY
Coe FS Harpers Ferry WV
Davis-Heller LA
Drennen ZP Amagoro
Dubose GC Harpers Ferry WV
Geerdes PS *ret* Raleigh NC
Geesey BS *ret* Conyers GA
Giardina DD *dcn*
Greene ER *ret* Bath ME
Haas KB *ret* Morgantown WV
Hadaway ELP Morgantown WV
Hawkins GA New Windsor MD
Higgins SK Charleston WV
Jackson LD *ret* Parkersburg WV
James RM Union WV
Jenks AW Morgantown WV
Jones SB Shepherdstown WV
Kennedy HL *ret dcn* Northfork WV
Kevern JR *ret* Moundsville WV
Khalil AM *ret* Beckley WV
Lawson VF *ret* Charles Town WV
Lynch DL Scott Depot WV
Macgill WD Wilmington NC
Martin JM Huntington WV
Martin ND *dcn* Hinton WV
Mazgaj MS *ret* Valley Grove WV
Moses GD *ret* Morgantown WV
Paine MJ Boston MA
Partlow JMO
Perrizo FC Marietta OH
Prichard AH *dcn* Morgantown WV
Raih DR *ret* Romney WV
Reece RD *ret* Romney WV
Shaffer DB Keyser WV
Sheppard DE *ret* Follansbee WV
Sherrill G Hurricane WV
Sherrill KF Huntington WV
Strohm RW *ret* Huntington WV
Thabet DG *ret* Huntington WV
Thomas RL *ret* Huntington WV
Turner AP
Vinson DK *ret* Huntington WV
Walker EA Fairlea WV

Waple G *dcn* Lewisburg WV
Watkins GH *ret* Saint Albans WV
Weise JWT *ret* Parkersburg WV
West AK Clarksburg WV

Wilkinson JM Killeen TX
Wood RT *ret* Coraopolis PA
Wood WR *ret* Williamstown WV

DIOCESE OF WESTERN KANSAS
(PROVINCE VII)
Comprises Western Kansas
DIOCESAN OFFICE 1 North Main Ste 502 Hutchinson KS 67504
TEL (620) 669-0006   FAX (620) 669-9783
WEB http://www.diowks.org

Previous Bishops—
Sheldon M Griswold 1903-17, John C Sage 1918-19, Robt H Mize 1921-38, Shirley H Nichols 1943-55, Arnold M Lewis 1956-64, Wm Davidson mb 1966-71, Bp 1971-80, John F Ashby 1981-95, Vernon E Strickland 1995-2002, James M Adams Jr 2002-10

Bishop—Rt Rev Michael P Milliken (Dio 19 Feb 2011)

Dio Admin Toni Cottrell; *Chanc* J Cowell 501 W 5th St Larned KS 67550; *Treas* M Wamsley; *Asst Treas* L Carver; *Bus & Fin* M Wamsley; *COM* The Rev K Lemon; *Sec Dio Conv* S Denton; *Dispatch of Business for Dio Conv* C Peterson; *ECW* L Mederos; *UTO Chair* K Milliken; *Yth* M Cowell *Cn to Ord* The Rev P Flory 1551 Briargate Salina KS 67401 (785) 493-2760

Stand Comm—Cler: Pres M Cowell J Jones K Lemon *Lay:* M Wamsley S Denton H Smith

Dio Conv: 28-29 Oct 2016 Wichita (joint conv with Diocese of Kansas)

PARISHES, MISSIONS, AND CLERGY

Anthony Grace Episcopal Church **M** (19) 401 N Anthony Ave 67003-2012 (Mail to: 401 N Anthony Ave 67003-2012) (620) 842-3254

Bavaria St Onesimus Chapel **Other** St Francis Academy 5097 W Cloud St 67401-9743 (Mail to: 5097 W Cloud St 67401-9743) (913) 825-0563

Colby Ascension-on-the-Prairie Episcopal **P** (31) 1170 Wheat Ridge Rd 67701-3530 (Mail to: PO Box 842 67701-0842) Donald Martin (785) 462-7198

Concordia Church of the Epiphany **M** (17) 117 W 8th St 66901-3401 (Mail to: PO Box 466 66901-0466) Dale Lumley (785) 243-2947

Dodge City St Cornelius Episcopal Church **P** (159) 200 W Spruce St 67801-4425 (Mail to: PO Box 1414 67801-1414) Kathleen Hargis (620) 227-6975

Ellsworth Holy Apostles Church **M** (21) 104 W 4th St 67439-3212 (Mail to: 1298 Hwy 14 67439) Phyllis Flory (785) 472-5477

Garden City St Thomas Episcopal Church **M** (57) 710-712 N Main St 67846-5433 (Mail to: PO Box 2410 67846-2410) (620) 276-3173

Goodland St Pauls Episcopal Church **M** (31) 121 W 13th St 67735-2926 (Mail to: PO Box 452 67735-0452) Donald Martin (785) 890-2115

Great Bend St Johns Episcopal Church **M** (21) 2701 17th St 67530-2303 (Mail to: 3100 25th St. 67530-2303) Phyllis Flory Kevin Schmidt (620) 792-4288

Hays St Andrews Episcopal Church **M** (24) 2422 Hyacinth Ave 67601 (Mail to: PO Box 247 67601-0247) Harvey Hillin (785) 625-6476

Hays St Michaels Episcopal Church **P** (39) 2900 Canal Blvd 67601-1704 (Mail to: PO Box 1352 67601-1352) Harvey Hillin (785) 628-8442

Hutchinson Grace Episcopal Church **P** (418) 2 Hyde Park Dr 67502-2824 (Mail to: 2 Hyde Park Dr 67502-2824) James Blakley Larry Carver Georgia Decker Andrew Hook Larry Steadman (620) 662-8024

Kingman Christ Episcopal Church **M** (10) 332 N Spruce St 67068-1651 (Mail to: PO Box 323 67068-0323) Charles Kerschen (620) 532-2488

Kinsley Holy Nativity Episcopal Church **M** (10) 714 E 8th St 67547-1326 (Mail to: 403 Elizabeth Ave 67547-1200) (620) 659-2539

Lakin Epis Church of the Upper Room **M** (29) 406 W Kingman Ave 67860-9463 (Mail to: PO Box 634 67860-0634) (620) 355-6077

Larned Sts Mary and Martha of Bethany **M** (45) PO Box 333 67550-0333 (Mail to: PO Box 333 67550-0333) Mark Cowell Kevin Schmidt (620) 285-6503

Liberal St Andrews Church **M** (44) 521 N Sherman Ave 67901-3205 (Mail to: PO Box 250 67905-0250) Charles Schneider (620) 624-3944

Logan Church of the Transfiguration **HC** (13) 20 Washington St 67646 (Mail to: PO Box 445 67646-0445) (785) 689-4627

Lyons St Marks Episcopal Church **M** (28) 524 East Ave S 67554 (Mail to: 524 East Ave S 67554)

Brian Viel Kevin Schmidt (620) 257-5955

McPherson St Annes Episcopal Church **M** (75) 105 W Sutherland St 67460-4719 (Mail to: PO Box 577 67460-0577) Laird MacGregor (866) 363-8850

Meade St Augustine Episcopal Church **M** (6) 2127 18 Road 67864 (Mail to: 2127 18 Road 67864) (620) 646-5420

Medicine Ldg St Marks Episcopal Church **M** (7) 204 N Walnut St 67104-1325 (Mail to: 200 S Cherry Apt 225 67104) Karen Lemon (620) 866-5131

Norton Trinity Episcopal Church **M** (61) 319 N. State St 67654 (Mail to: 319 N State St 67654) Charles Schneider (785) 877-2589

Pratt All Saints Episcopal Church **M** (44) 218 N Main St 67124-1739 (Mail to: 542 Terrace Dr 67124-1354) Karen Lemon (620) 672-2308

Russell St Elizabeth's Episcopal Church **M** (8) No 66 S Culp St 67665-3134 (Mail to: 629 E Margaret Ave 67665-3110) (785) 483-4889

Russell Springs St Francis Episcopal Church **M** (18) 525 Hilts Ave 67764 (Mail to: 1509 County Rd. 220 67764) Donald Martin (785) 751-4278

Salina Armstrong Memorial Chapel **CC** 110 E Otis Ave 67402 (Mail to: PO Box 827 67402-0827) (785) 823-7231

✠ **Salina** Christ Cathedral Church **O** (188) 138 S 8th St 67401 (Mail to: 138 S 8th St 67401) Bruce Le Barron Charles Schneider Robert Seaton Benjamin Thomas (785) 825-0974

Salina Church of the Incarnation **M** (58) 639 Max Ave 67401-6662 (Mail to: 639 Max 67401) Randy McIntosh (785) 823-2850

Salina St Francis of Assisi Chapel **Special Needs**

Ministry 509 E Elm St 67401-2348 (Mail to: PO Box 1340 67402-1340) (800) 423-1342

Scott City St Lukes Episcopal Church **M** (35) 303 Epperson Dr 67871-1841 (Mail to: 303 Epperson Dr 67871-1841) Donald Martin (620) 872-3666

Ulysses St Johns Episcopal Church **M** (26) 104 S Maxwell St 67880-2327 (Mail to: 104 S Maxwell St 67880-2327) Floyd Daharsh (620) 356-3690

NON-PAROCHIAL CLERGY

Ballinger CT
Bridge MJ
Brooks RS Concordia KS
Brown CH Hays KS
Calhoun OA *ret* Bay Village OH
Cox JR *ret* Salina KS
English L *ret* Phoenix AZ
Goodpankratz G *dcn* Liberal KS
Griffith C *ret* Ozark AR
Heden EM *ret* Sterling KS
Hixson ML Anthony KS
Jones JS *ret* Hays KS
Keith TF *ret* Rockport TX
Kemp MB Salina KS
Kline TE *ret* Graford TX
Knox JM Lenexa KS
Lampe CK Garden City KS
Nissen PB *ret* Norton KS
Null JA Salina KS
Rapp PJ *ret* Clifton VA
Rock JK Hutchinson KS
Stockton MG Lakin KS

DIOCESE OF WESTERN LOUISIANA
(PROVINCE VII)
Comprises Forty-One Civil Parishes in Western Louisiana
DIOCESAN OFFICE 335 Main St Pineville LA 71360 (MAIL: Box 2031 Alexandria LA 71309)
TEL (318) 442-1304   FAX (318) 442-8712
E-MAIL bishopjake@diocesewla.org   WEB www.diocesewla.org

Previous Bishops—
Willis R Henton 1980-90, Robert J Hargrove 1990-2002, D Bruce MacPherson 2002-12

Bishop—Rt Rev Jacob W Owensby
(21 July 2012)

Sec N Shaw; *Chanc* K McInnis 1080 Avery St Shreveport 71106; *Treas* G Easterling 128 Versailles Blvd Alexandria 71303; *Reg* H Davis; *Ecum* Rev WE Carter; *Comm* R Harwell

Standing Comm—Cler: Pres M George R Norman R Snow; *Lay: Sec* N Shaw L Davis R Lafargue

Deans: Acadiana M Woollett; *Alexandria* E Ratcliff; *Lake Charles* A Perry; *Monroe* B Easterling; *Shreveport* M Richard

Dio Conv: 23-24 Oct 2015

PARISHES, MISSIONS, AND CLERGY

Abbeville St Pauls Episcopal Church **P** (80) 101 E Vermilion St 70510 (Mail to: PO Box 1101 70511-1101) R Christopher Heying (337) 893-3195

Alexandria St James Episcopal Church and School **P** (385) 1620 Murray Street 71301-6882 (Mail to: 1620 Murray Street 71301-6882) Deborah

Heathcock (318) 445-9845

Alexandria St Timothy's Episcopal Church **P** (309) 2627 Horseshoe Dr 71301-2664 (Mail to: 2627 Horseshoe Dr 71301-2664) George Snow (318) 487-0875

Bastrop Christ Episcopal Church **P** (133) 204 S Locust St 71220-4554 (Mail to: PO Box 52 71221-0052) Edward Head (318) 281-5276

Bossier City St Georges Episcopal Church **P** (226) 1959 Airline Dr 71112-2407 (Mail to: 1959 Airline Dr 71112-2407) James Flowers

Bunkie Calvary Church **P** (53) 401 S Lexington Ave 71322-1842 (Mail to: PO Box 679 71322-0679) (318) 445-7651

Cheneyville Trinity Episcopal Church **M** (15) PO Box 223 71325-0223 (Mail to: 5704 Monroe Hwy 71405-3359) Joseph Bordelon (318) 473-9811

Crowley Trinity Episcopal Church **P** (46) 1303 Hoffpauir Ave 70526-2625 (Mail to: PO Box 342 70527-0342) Herman Ogea (337) 783-3615

Deridder Trinity Episcopal Church **P** (46) C/O Marjorie H Adams PO Box 661 70634-0661 (Mail to: PO Box 661 70634-0661) (337) 463-6322

Grambling St Lukes Chapel **M** (26) 1991 S Main & Adams St 71245 (318) 247-6669

Jennings St Lukes Mission Episcopal Church **M** (21) PO Box 461 70546-0461 (Mail to: 1818 N State St 70546-3743) Johnny Clark (337) 824-4397

Lafayette Episcopal Church of The Ascension **P** (722) 1030 Johnston St 70501-7810 (Mail to: 1030 Johnston St 70501-7810) Joseph Daly Peter Johnston Duane Petersen Duane Petersen (337) 232-2732

Lafayette St Barnabas Episcopal Church **HC** (546) 400 Camellia Blvd 70503-4316 (Mail to: 400 Camellia Blvd 70503-4316) John Bedingfield Mitzi George (337) 984-3848

Lake Charles Church of the Good Shepherd **P** (438) 715 Kirkman St 70601-4350 (Mail to: 715 Kirkman St 70601-4350) John Myers David Donald Frances Kay (337) 433-5244

Lake Charles St Andrews Episcopal Church **M** (108) 1532 Sam Houston Jones Pkwy 70611 (Mail to: PO Box 12326 70612-2326) (337) 855-1344

Lake Charles St Michael & All Angels Episcopal Ch **P** (296) 123 W Sale Rd 70605-2821 (Mail to: 123 W Sale Rd 70605-2821) (337) 477-1881

Lecompte Holy Comforter Episcopal Church **M** (67) 1708 Hardy St 71346 (Mail to: C/O The Rev Borderlon 5704 Monroe Hwy 71405-3359) Joseph Bordelon (318) 776-5287

Leesville Leonidas Polk Memorial Church **M** (23) PO Box 1546 71496-1546 (Mail to: PO Box 1546 71496-1546) (337) 239-3083

Lk Providence Grace Episcopal Church **M** (26) PO Box 566 71254-0566 (Mail to: PO Box 566 71254) William Echols (318) 559-1620

Mansfield Christ Memorial Episcopal Church **P** (114) 401 Washington Ave 71052-3103 (Mail to: 401 Washington St 71052) Michael Millard (318) 872-1144

Mer Rouge St Andrews Episcopal Church **P** (112) 201 Davenport Ave 71261 (Mail to: PO Box 65 71261-0065) (318) 647-3683

Minden St Johns Episcopal Church **P** (181) 1107 Broadway St 71055-3314 (Mail to: 1107 Broadway St 71055-3314) Frank Hughes

Monroe Grace Episcopal Church **P** (697) 405 Glenmar Ave 71201-5307 (Mail to: 405 Glenmar Ave 71201-5307) Richard Norman (318) 387-6646

Monroe St Albans Episcopal Church **P** (167) 2816 Deborah Dr 71201-1942 (Mail to: 2816 Deborah Dr 71201-1942) Thomas Stodghill Bette Kauffman (318) 323-3139

Monroe St Thomas Episcopal Church **P** (68) 3706 Bon Aire Dr 71203-3009 (Mail to: 3706 Bon Aire Dr 71203-3009) Dawnell Stodghill (318) 343-4089

Natchitoches Trinity Episcopal Church **P** (147) 533 Second Street 71457-4619 (Mail to: 148 Rue Touline 71457-4639) (318) 352-3113

New Iberia Episcopal Church of the Epiphany **P** (224) No 303 W Main St 70560-3642 (Mail to: 303 W Main St 70560-3642) Donald Woollett (337) 369-9966

Oak Ridge Church of the Redeemer **M** (21) 206 N Oak St 71264-9385 (Mail to: PO Box 238 71264) (318) 647-3683

Oakdale St Johns Episcopal Church **M** (1) 220 Pelican Highway 71463 (Mail to: PO Box 2031 71309) (318) 442-1304

Opelousas Church of the Epiphany **P** (153) 1103 S. Union St 70570-5972 (Mail to: 1103 S. Union St 70570-5952) Anne Etheredge (337) 942-3336

Pineville Mount Olivet Chapel **HC** 335 Main St 71360-6929 (Mail to: PO Box 2031 71309) Jacob Owensby (318) 442-1304

Pineville St Michael's Episcopal Church **P** (323) 500 Edgewood Dr 71360-4525 (Mail to: 500 Edgewood Dr 71360-4525) George Gennuso (318) 640-0030

Rayville St Davids Episcopal Church **P** (77) 834 Louisa St 71269-2633 (Mail to: PO Box 276 71269-0276) (318) 728-2367

Ruston Church of the Redeemer **P** (122) 504 Tech Dr 71270-4938 (Mail to: 504 Tech Dr 71270-4938) William Easterling (318) 255-3925

Shreveport Church of the Holy Cross **P** (83) 875 Cotton St. 71101 (Mail to: PO Box 1627 71165-1627) Mary Richard Susan Bell Donald Heacock

Shreveport St James Episcopal Church **P** (137) 2050 Bert Kouns Loop 71118-3315 (Mail to: 2050 W Bert Kouns Industrial Loop 71118-3315) (318) 686-1261

Shreveport St Marks Episcopal Cathedral **O**

(1774) 908 Rutherford St 71104-4246 (Mail to: 908 Rutherford 71104-4297) William Bryant Wayne Carter Alston Johnson Thomas Nsubuga Rowena White (318) 221-3360

Shreveport St Matthias Episcopal Church **P** (252) 3301 St Matthias Dr 71119-5600 (Mail to: 3301 St Matthias Dr 71119-5600) (318) 635-5354

Shreveport St Pauls Episcopal Church **P** (648) 275 Southfield Rd 71105-3608 (Mail to: 275 Southfield Rd 71105-3608) Paul Martin (318) 865-8469

St Joseph Christ Episcopal Church **P** (25) 120 Hancock St 71366 (Mail to: PO Box 256 71366-0256) Gregg Riley (318) 766-3518

Sulphur Church of the Holy Trinity **P** (173) C/O Mrs Heather Reddoch 1700 Maplewood Dr 70663-6002 (Mail to: 1700 Maplewood Dr 70663-6002) Ally Perry (337) 625-4288

Tallulah Trinity Episcopal Church **P** (57) PO Box 208 71284-0208 (Mail to: PO Box 208 71284-0208) William Echols (318) 362-9728

Vidalia Church of the Good Shepherd **M** (33) 806 Concordia Ave 71373-2620 (Mail to: 806 Concordia Ave 71373-2620) (318) 336-7405

West Monroe St Patricks Episcopal Church **P** (97) 1712 Wellerman Rd 71291 (Mail to: 1712 Wellerman Rd 71291-7429) (318) 396-1341

Winnfield St Pauls Episcopal Church **M** (5) 206 Pecan St 71483-3363 (Mail to: PO Box 206 71483-0206) Richard Taylor (318) 628-6971

Winnsboro St Columbas Episcopal Church **M** (11) 201 N Franklin St 71295-2245 (Mail to: PO Box 972 71295-0972) (318) 435-6269

NON-PAROCHIAL CLERGY

Agnew ML *ret* Bullard TX
Alexander JB *ret* Jackson MS

Anderson PC *dcn* Calhoun LA
Bordelon M Alexandria LA
Breckenridge EH *ret* Alexandria LA
Caudle SJ *ret*
Comeaux AA *ret* Bossier LA
Cook PJA *ret* Lake Charles LA
Cooper RN *ret* Comfort TX
Dandridge RF Minden LA
Dennis WJ *ret* Eutaw AL
Doherty-Ogea KL Bastrop LA
Fetterman JH *ret* South Ozone Park NY
Friese WE *ret* Pineville LA
Greer DJ *ret* Shreveport LA
Hall PC *ret* Farmerville LA
Hunter KS *dcn* Mansfield LA
Johnston RW *ret* Rome GA
Leger DC *dcn* Opelousas LA
Lueckenhoff JJ *ret* Lake Charles LA
McBride WG *ret* Shreveport LA
Montgomery BL Lafayette LA
Moore DM *ret dcn* New Iberia LA
Myers RC *ret* Bastrop LA
Newby WRM *ret* Joplin MO
Paul KW *ret* Shreveport LA
Phillips AW Alexandria VA
Raish JW *ret* Shreveport LA
Ratcliff ER
Rollins BF *dcn* Pineville LA
Schmitt G *ret* Princeton LA
Smith JP *ret* Opelousas LA
Stitt DW *ret* Hastings NE
Theus JG *ret* Alexandria LA
Thweatt RF *ret* Oklahoma City OK
Tinsley FH *ret* Corpus Christi TX
Verbeck GF *ret* Shreveport LA
White KO
Wolfenbarger MS Belleville IL

DIOCESE OF WESTERN MASSACHUSETTS
(PROVINCE I)
Comprises the central and western half of the state of Massachusetts
DIOCESAN OFFICE 37 Chestnut St Springfield MA 01103
TEL (413) 737-4786, 737-4787, (800) 332-8513   FAX (413) 746-9873
E-MAIL diocese@diocesewma.org   WEB www.diocesewma.org

Previous Bishops—
Alexander H Vinton 1902-11, Thomas F Davies 1911-36, William A Lawrence 1937-57, Robert M Hatch 1957-70, Alexander D Stewart 1970-84, Andrew F Wissemann 1984-92, Robert S Denig 1993-95, Gordon P Scruton 1996-2012

Bishop—Rt Rev Douglas John Fisher (1073) (Dio 1 Dec 2012)

Sec of Conv Rev Wm Murray; *Cns to Ord* Rev Dr R Simpson Rev P Mott; *Cn for Mission Resources* S Abdow; *Exec Asst to Bp Dio* C Haggerty; *Treas* W Gass; *Asst Treas* S Abdow; *Chanc* H Doherty 1550 Main St Suite 2700 Springfield MA 01103; *Exec Dir Trustees* N Kalber

Stand Comm—Cler: Chair C Munz D Fetz C Jones N Webb Stroud; *Lay:* L Cheek P Kite N Lowry C Loy

Dio Conv: 28-29 Oct 2016 Marriott Springfield MA

PARISHES, MISSIONS, AND CLERGY

Amherst Grace Episcopal Church **P** (635) 14 Boltwood Ave 01002-2301 (Mail to: 14 Boltwood Ave 01002-2301) (413) 256-6754

Ashfield St Johns Episcopal Church **M** (133) Main & South St 01330-9602 (Mail to: Main & South St 01330-9602) J Eliot Moss (413) 628-4402

Athol St Johns Episcopal Church **P** (93) 15 Park Ave 01331-2515 (Mail to: 15 Park Ave 01331-2515) (978) 249-9553

Auburn Church of St Thomas **P** (96) 35 School St 01501-2917 (Mail to: 35 School St 01501-2917) David Hall (508) 832-2598

Chicopee Grace Episcopal Church **P** (73) 156 Springfield St. 01013-2637 (Mail to: 156 Springfield St 01013-2637) Donna Larson (413) 594-4017

Chicopee St Christophers Episcopal Church **P** (130) 27 Streiber Dr 01020-3055 (Mail to: 27 Streiber Dr 01020-3055) Scott Seabury (413) 533-7872

Clinton Church of the Good Shepherd **P** (263) 209 Union St 01510-2903 (Mail to: 209 Union St 01510-2903) William Bergmann (978) 365-5169

Dalton Grace Episcopal Church **P** (87) 791 Main St 01226-2201 (Mail to: 791 Main St 01226-2201) (413) 684-0016

E Longmeadow St Marks Episcopal Church **P** (353) 1 Porter Rd 01028-1348 (Mail to: 1 Porter Rd 01028-1348) James Swarr (413) 525-6341

Easthampton St Philips Episcopal Church **P** (169) 128 Main St 01027-2023 (Mail to: 128 Main St 01027-2023) (413) 527-0862

Feeding Hills St Davids Episcopal Church **P** (128) 699 Springfield St 01030-2134 (Mail to: 699 Springfield St 01030-2134) Benjamin Hill (413) 786-6133

Fitchburg Christ Episcopal Church **P** (697) 569 Main St 01420-8012 (Mail to: 569 Main St 01420-8012) Carolyn Jones (978) 342-0007

Gardner St Pauls Episcopal Church **P** (140) 79 Cross St 01440-2214 (Mail to: 79 Cross St 01440-2214) (978) 632-0925

Great Barrington Grace Church in the Southern Berkshires **P** (111) 67 State Road 01230 (Mail to: PO Box 114 01230-0114) Frances Hills Ray Wilson (413) 644-0022

Greenfield Saint James Episcopal Church **P** (228) 8 Church St 01301-2901 (Mail to: 8 Church Street 01301) Heather Blais (413) 773-3925

Holden St Francis Episcopal Church **P** (695) 70 Highland St 01520-2594 (Mail to: 70 Highland St 01520-2594) Richard Simpson Jill Williams

Holyoke St Pauls Episcopal Church **P** (309) 485 Appleton St 01040-3255 (Mail to: 485 Appleton St 01040-3255) Barbara Thrall (413) 532-5060

Lanesboro St Lukes Episcopal Church **M** (39) 20 S Main St 01237-9656 (Mail to: PO Box 593 01237-0593) Noreen Suriner (413) 443-0165

Lenox St Helenas Chapel **M** (137) 245 New Lenox Rd 01240-2242 (Mail to: 245 New Lenox Rd 01240-2223) (413) 637-1483

Lenox Trinity Parish **P** (203) 88 Walker St 01240-2725 (Mail to: Attn Eugine Fawcett 88 Walker St 01240-2725) (413) 637-0073

Leominster St Marks Episcopal Church **P** (572) 60 West St 01453-5653 (Mail to: 60 West St 01453-5653) James Craig (978) 537-3560

Longmeadow St Andrews Episcopal Church **P** (542) 335 Longmeadow St 01106-1367 (Mail to: 335 Longmeadow St 01106-1399) Robert Fetz Benjamin Hill Francis Howard (413) 567-5901

Milford Trinity Episcopal Church **HC** (515) 17 Congress St 01757-4152 (Mail to: 17 Congress St 01757-4152) William Murray Donna Kingman

Millville St Johns Episcopal Church **M** (149) 49 Central St 01529-1714 (Mail to: PO Box 395 01529-0395) John Stubbs (508) 883-4480

North Adams All Saints Episcopal Church **P** (218) 59 Summer St 01247-4009 (Mail to: PO Box 374 01247-0374) James Duncan Stephen White (413) 664-9656

North Adams St Andrews Episcopal Church **M** (23) PO Box 327 01247-0327 (Mail to: 1438 Massachusetts Ave 01247-2294) (413) 662-2775

North Brookfield Christ Memorial Church **P** (92) 133 N Main St 01535-1413 (Mail to: PO Box 43 01535) (508) 867 2789

North Grafton St Andrews Episcopal Church **P** (192) 53 N Main St 01536-1519 (Mail to: 53 N Main St 01536-1519) Laura Goodwin (508) 839-3453

Northampton St Johns Episcopal Church **P** (587) 48 Elm St 01060-2903 (Mail to: 48 Elm St 01060-2932) Catherine Munz (413) 584-1757

Northborough Church of the Nativity **P** (363) 45 Howard St 01532-1441 (Mail to: 45 Howard St 01532-1441) (508) 393-3146

Oxford Grace Episcopal Church **P** (165) 270 Main St 01540-2359 (Mail to: 270 Main St 01540-2359) Alfred Zadig (508) 987-1004

Pittsfield St Martins Church **M** (25) 133 Dalton Ave 01201-3509 (Mail to: 133 Dalton Ave 01201-3509) (413) 442-8018

Pittsfield St Stephens Episcopal Church **P** (969) 67 East St 01201-5313 (Mail to: 67 East St 01201-5383) Charlotte Cooper Jennifer Gregg Gwen Sears (413) 448-8276

Rochdale Christ Episcopal Church **P** (154) 1089 Stafford St 01542-1003 (Mail to: PO Box 142 01542-0142) Mary Scherm (508) 892-8460

Sheffield Christ Episcopal Trinity Lutheran Church **P** (105) 180 S Main St 01257 (Mail to: PO Box 127 01257-0127) Anne Ryder (413) 229-8811

Shrewsbury Trinity Episcopal Church **P** (197) 440 Main St 01545-2208 (Mail to: 440 Main St 01545-2208) (508) 842-6040

South Hadley All Saints Church **P** (335) 7 Woodbridge St 01075-1117 (Mail to: 7 Woodbridge St 01075-1117) Tanya Wallace

Southbridge Holy Trinity Episcopal Church **P** (81) 446 Hamilton St 01550-1859 (Mail to: 446 Hamilton St 01550-1859)

Southwick Southwick Community Episcopal Ch **M** (196) PO Box 1069 01077-1069 (Mail to: 660 College Hwy 01077-9260) John Albright (413) 569-9650

Springfield Christ Church Cathedral **O** (558) 35 Chestnut St 01103-1705 (Mail to: 35 Chestnut St 01103-1705) J Eliot Moss (413) 736-2742

Springfield St Barnabas & All Saints Church **P** (133) 41 Oakland St 01108-1701 (Mail to: 41 Oakland St 01108-1701) (413) 732-2981

Springfield St Lukes Episcopal Church **M** (40) 961 St James Ave 01104-2816 (Mail to: PO Box 3762 01101-3762) (413) 734-8388

Springfield St Peters Church **P** (198) 45 Buckingham St 01109-3926 (Mail to: 45 Buckingham St 01109-3926) Michael Devine (413) 736-8567

Stockbridge St Pauls Episcopal Church **P** (163) 29 Main St 01262 (Mail to: PO Box 704 01262-0704) (413) 298-4913

Sutton St Johns Episcopal Church **P** (392) 3 Pleasant St 01590-3890 (Mail to: 3 Pleasant St 01590-3890) Elizabeth Green (508) 865-6448

Thorndike St Marys Episcopal Church **M** (49) 4080 Main St 01079 (Mail to: PO Box 487 01079-0487) (413) 283-3501

Turners Fall St Andrews Church **P** (67) 2 Prospect St 01376-1304 (Mail to: 2 Prospect St 01376-1304) (413) 863-4602

W Springfield Church of the Good Shepherd **P** (150) 214 Elm St 01089-2709 (Mail to: PO Box 483 01090-0483) (413) 734-1976

Ware Trinity Episcopal Church **P** (106) PO Box 447 01082-0447 (Mail to: PO Box 447 01082-0447) (413) 967-6100

Webster The Church of the Reconciliation **P** (310) 5 N Main St 01570-2229 (Mail to: 5 N Main St 01570-2229) Janice Ford (508) 943-8714

Westborough St Stephens Episcopal Church **P** (278) 3 John St 01581-2510 (Mail to: 3 John St 01581-2510) Jesse Abell (508) 366-4134

Westfield Church of the Atonement **P** (374) No 36 Court St 01085-3503 (Mail to: 36 Court St 01085-3594) Nancy Stroud (413) 562-5461

Whitinsville Trinity Episcopal Church **P** (285) 33 Linwood Ave 01588-2309 (Mail to: 33 Linwood Ave 01588-2309) John Stubbs

Wilbraham Church of the Epiphany **P** (272) 10 Highland Ave 01095-1932 (Mail to: 20 Highland Ave 01095-1932) (413) 596-6080

Williamstown St Johns Church **P** (466) 35 Park St 01267-2114 (Mail to: 35 Park St 01267-2114) Peter Elvin (413) 458-8144

Worcester All Saints Episcopal Church **P** (1020) 10 Irving St 01609-3210 (Mail to: 10 Irving St 01609-3229) Kevin Bean Gregory Lisby Jose Reyes Perez (508) 752-3766

Worcester St Lukes Episcopal Church **P** (275) 921 Pleasant St 01602-1908 (Mail to: 921 Pleasant

St 01602-1908) (508) 756-1990

Worcester St Marks Episcopal Church **P** (74) 0 Freeland St 01603-2603 (Mail to: 0 Freeland St 01603-2603) William Hobbs (508) 791-6027

Worcester St Matthews Church **P** (261) 695 Southbridge St 01610-2914 (Mail to: 695 Southbridge St 01610-2914) Nancy Strong (508) 755-4433

Worcester St Michaels on the Heights **P** (167) 340 Burncoat St 01606-3101 (Mail to: 340 Burncoat St 01606-3101) David Woessner (508) 853-9400

NON-PAROCHIAL CLERGY

Anderson RW *dcn* Shrewsbury MA
Aubrey NE *dcn* South Hadley MA
Bain RW
Baldwin A *ret*
Bellows CH *dcn* Wilton ME
Bellows RS *ret* Westfield MA
Bogert-Winkler HM Amherst MA
Booth SP *ret*
Bullitt-Jonas MM Northampton MA
Burger TH Glen Rock NJ
Byers W Tolland CT
Callard TA Springfield MA
Campbell KSB *ret* South Orleans MA
Carlisle CAE *ret* Amherst MA
Cerrato JA Raleigh NC
Chace AR *ret* Brewster MA
Chamberlain DF *ret* Worcester MA
Cheney AM *ret* West Greenwich RI
Clarke RK *ret* Hopedale MA
Cowan LC *ret* Worcester MA
Crampton SH *ret* Williamstown MA
Cronin AA *dcn*
Damrosch TH *ret* Stockbridge MA
Davis MF *ret* Freeland WA
Dean GJ *ret* Shelburne Falls MA
Dunbar JB Cambridge MA
Dunn SA Amherst MA
Dunning JR *ret* Shelburne Falls MA
Elley EM *dcn* Somersville CT
Emrich FE *ret* North Haven ME
Evans TH *ret* Lenox MA
Finkenstaedt HS *ret* Gainesville VA
Fowle EH *ret* Hancock NH
Frederick WC *ret* Worcester MA
Freeman JE
Ginn RJ Templeton MA
Goranson PW *ret* Worcester MA
Griesbach J *dcn*
Gustafson MD *ret* Saint Paul MN
Hall AB *ret* Port Charlotte FL
Hatch MH Florence MA
Hicks MK *dcn* Charlton MA
Hicks WE Worcester MA
Hooke RB Alexandria VA
Hooker JL *ret* Springfield MA
Hurlbut TJ *dcn* South Hadley MA
Johnson SR *ret* Marlborough NH
Jones BG Fitchburg MA

Kayigwa BM *dcn* Clinton MA
Keator MK *ret* South Londonderry VT
Kilfoyle JR *ret* Worcester MA
King EA *ret* East China MI
Kingman PA *ret* Worcester MA
Kitagawa C *ret* Amherst MA
Knapp CL *ret* Sarasota FL
Kunhardt DB *ret* Brunswick ME
Long BA *ret* Sandwich MA
McCue ME *ret* Susanville CA
Morrissette PE *ret* Worcester MA
Moss FH *ret* Portland OR
Mott PJ Portsmouth RI
Munroe JG *ret* Springfield MA
O'Brien CH Williamstown MA
Parke JH *ret* Springfield MA
Perkins P West Hartford CT
Perry PT *dcn* Worcester MA
Place DG *ret* Pownal VT
Porter P *ret* Heath MA
Ramsey HE West Hartford CT
Rierdan JE Easthampton MA
Rockwell CVK *ret* Springfield MA
Schieffelin JJ *ret*

Schreiber MF *ret* Shelburne Falls MA
Senechal RE *ret* Joelton TN
Smith SJ New York NY
Stevens AG Santa Barbara CA
Stevens JP *ret* Santa Barbara CA
Strong DR *ret* Auburn MA
Synan TNJ New York NY
Taylor PN *ret* Shrewsbury MA
Tillman JG
True JE *ret* Cape Coral FL
Tuck MG Providence RI
Venkatesh CR Arlington MA
Vidmar MB *ret* Lake Milton OH
Walters RC *ret* Worcester MA
Ward MW Worcester MA
Warren GH *ret* Pascoag RI
Watts WJ *ret* Chicopee MA
White KS *ret* Woodstock CT
Wood AP *dcn* South Deerfield MA
Woolley SM *ret* Livingston SC
Wright AML *ret*
Zimmerman JW Great Barrington MA
Zink JA

DIOCESE OF WESTERN MICHIGAN
(PROVINCE V)
Comprises the western half of the Lower Peninsula
DIOCESAN OFFICE Episcopal Center Diocese of Western Michigan
535 S Burdick Ste 1 Kalamazoo MI 49007
TEL (269) 381-2710   Bishop's Office (269) 381-2710 x14   FAX (269) 381-7067
E-MAIL info@edwm.org   WEB www.edwm.org

Previous Bishops—
Geo deN Gillespie 1875-1909, John McCormick coadj 1906 Bp 1909-37, Lewis B Whittemore coadj 1936 Bp 1937-53, Dudley B McNeil 1953-59, Chas E Bennison 1960-84, Howard S Meeks coadj 1984 Bp 1984-88, Edward L Lee Jr 1989-2002, Robert R Gepert 2002-2013

Bishop—Rt Rev Whayne M Hougland Jr (1078)
(Dio 28 Sept 2013)

Sec Conv WJ Spaid; *Chanc* WJ Fleener Jr *Admin Staff: Bp Admin Asst* M Ettwein; *Cn to Ord* WJ Spaid; *Asst to the Bp for Bus & Fin* T Mazure; *Asst to the Bp for Child Yth & Young Adult Min* G Callard; *Asst to the Bp for Comm* K Puzzuoli; *Fin Asst* C Rhodes; *Young Adult Miss* K Day

Stand Comm—Cler: M Perrin V Ambrose P Finn A Schnaare; *Lay:* B Tillman A Davidson E Stoffan J Henry

Council: Pres The Bishop; D Croal B Edwards D Hawley-Lowry R Mast N Parish T Perrin J Smith

J Turmo G Stackhouse M Schlotterbeck J Baron A Evans R Hagan C Lopez M Wernick

Extended Staff: Past Couns K Reid; *Dcn for MDGs* B Drew; *Dcn for Health Min* K McDonald; *Dcn for Dom Miss* C Nawrocki

Deanery Chairs: Eastern J Turmo; *Grand Valley N Parish*; *Lakeshore* D Hawley-Lowry; *St Jos* T Perrin; *Traverse* R Hagan

Deans: Lakeshore J Cramer; *St Jos* R Crise; *Grand Valley* J Croom; *Traverse* D Richards; *Eastern* B Coleman

Comm on Ministry—Cler: Chair M Ryan; A Schnaare D Kuhn M Fedewa; *Lay:* J DeGoede M Simpson L Cox M Hirt C Thomas

Dio Conv: 4-5 Nov 2016 Battle Creek

PARISHES, MISSIONS, AND CLERGY
Albion St James Church **P** (86) 119 W Erie St 49224-1756 (Mail to: 119 W Erie St 49224-1756) Darlene Kuhn (517) 629-8710
Allegan Church of the Good Shepherd **P** (79) 101 N Walnut St 49010-1249 (Mail to: 101 N

Walnut St 49010-1249) Thomas Toeller-Novak (269) 673-2254

Battle Creek Church of St Thomas **P** (334) 16 E Van Buren St 49017-3916 (Mail to: 16 Van Buren St E 49017-3916) Brian Coleman

Battle Creek Church of the Resurrection **P** (30) 2589 Capital Ave SW 49015-4160 (Mail to: 2589 Capital Ave SW 49015-4160) (269) 965-2840

Beaver Island St James Episcopal Mission **M** 26055 Pine St 49782 (Mail to: PO Box 281 49782-0281)

Belmont Church of the Holy Spirit **P** (103) 1200 Post Dr NE 49306 (Mail to: 1200 Post Dr NE 49306) David Meyers James Croom (616) 784-1111

Benton Harbor St Augustine's Church **P** (150) 1753 Union St 49022-6261 (Mail to: 1753 Union Ave 49022-6298) Barbara Wilson

Beulah St Philips Church **P** (96) 785 Beulah Hwy 49617-9297 (Mail to: PO Box 26 49617-0026) Richard Sauerzopf Marilou Schlotterbeck

Big Rapids St Andrew's Episcopal Church **P** (47) 323 S State St 49307-1760 (Mail to: 323 S State St 49307-1760) Gary Hamp (231) 796-5473

Boyne City Church of the Nativity **P** (16) 209 E Main St 49712-1306 (Mail to: PO Box 228 49712-1306) (231) 582-5045

Cadillac St Marys Church **P** (60) 815 Lincoln St 49601-2033 (Mail to: 815 Lincoln St 49601-2033)

Charlevoix Christ Church **P** (76) PO Box 385 49720-0385 (Mail to: PO Box 385 49720-0385)

Charlotte St Johns Episcopal Church **P** (47) 201 W Shepherd St 48813-1868 (Mail to: 201 W Shepherd St 48813-1868) (517) 543-4430

Coldwater St Marks Church **P** (256) 27 E Chicago St 49036-1605 (Mail to: 27 E Chicago St 49036-1605) Frederick Schark (517) 278-5752

Dowagiac St Pauls Episcopal Church **P** (82) 306 Courtland St 49047-1198 (Mail to: 306 Courtland St 49047-1198)

Elk Rapids St Pauls Episcopal Church **P** (102) 403 Traverse St 49629-9721 (Mail to: 403 Traverse St 49629-9721)

Fremont St Johns Episcopal Church **P** (56) 124 S Sullivan Ave 49412-1546 (Mail to: 124 S Sullivan Ave 49412-1546) William Fleener

Grand Haven St Johns Episcopal Church **P** (379) 524 Washington Ave 49417-1455 (Mail to: 524 Washington Ave 49417-1455) Jared Cramer (616) 842-6260

Grand Ledge Trinity Church **P** (104) 201 E Jefferson St 48837-0116 (Mail to: PO Box 116 48837-0116) (517) 627-6287

Grand Rapids Grace Church **P** (434) 1815 Hall St SE 49506-4005 (Mail to: 1815 Hall St SE 49506-4099) Stephen Holmgren (616) 241-4631

Grand Rapids St Andrews Church **P** (498) 1025 3 Mile Rd NE 49505-3419 (Mail to: 1025 3 Mile Rd NE 49505-3419) Michael Fedewa Nurya

Parish (616) 361-7887

Grand Rapids St Marks Episcopal Church **P** (876) 134 Division Ave N 49503-3103 (Mail to: 134 Division Ave N 49503-3103) Brenton Carey Albert Dickinson Susan York

Grand Rapids St Philips Church **P** (84) 550 Henry Ave SE 49503-5547 (Mail to: 550 Henry Ave SE 49503-5547) John English (616) 451-9865

Greenville St Pauls Church **P** (120) 305 S Clay St 48838-1917 (Mail to: 305 S Clay St 48838-1917) (616) 754-3163

Harbert Church of the Mediator **P** (102) 14280 Red Arrow Hwy 49115 (Mail to: PO Box 223 49115-0223) Paula Durren (269) 469-1441

Harbor Spgs St Johns Chapel **SC** Third & Traverse 49740 (Mail to: PO Box 52 49740-0052) Phillip Ellsworth (231) 526-3914

Hastings Emmanuel Church **P** (125) 315 W Center St 49058-1615 (Mail to: 315 W Center St 49058-1615) William Ericson (269) 945-3014

Holland Grace Church **P** (665) 555 Michigan Ave 49423-4748 (Mail to: 555 Michigan Ave 49423-4794) Jennifer Adams Christian Baron Jodi Baron Henry Idema (616) 396-7459

Ionia St John the Apostle Episcopal Church **P** (71) 107 W Washington St 48846-1623 (Mail to: PO Box 307 48846-0307) (616) 527-2290

Kalamazoo St Lukes Church **P** (416) 247 W Lovell St 49007-5207 (Mail to: 247 W Lovell St 49007-5276) Randall Warren (269) 345-8553

Kalamazoo St Martin of Tours Episcopal Church **P** (118) 2010 Nichols Rd 49004-3200 (Mail to: 2010 Nichols Rd 49004-3200) Mary Perrin Linnea Stifler (269) 381-3188

Kentwood Church of the Holy Cross **P** (125) 4252 Breton Rd SE 49512-3858 (Mail to: 4252 Breton Rd SE 49512-3858) Michael Wernick (616) 949-7034

Lansing St Davids Church **P** (303) 1519 Elmwood Rd 48917-1543 (Mail to: 1519 Elmwood Rd 48917-1543) David Pike Andrew Downs Carol Spangenberg (517) 323-2272

Leland St Peters Chapel **SC** PO Box 3 49654-0003 (Mail to: 3309 N Lake Leelanau Dr 49654) (231) 271-3081

Ludington Grace Church **P** (57) 301 N James St 49431-1723 (Mail to: 301 N James St 49431-1723) Domingo Shriver (231) 843-9366

Manistee Holy Trinity Episcopal Church **P** (105) 410 2nd St 49660-1534 (Mail to: PO Box 577 49660-0577) (231) 723-2078

Marshall Trinity Episcopal Church **P** (156) 101 E Mansion St 49068-1117 (Mail to: 101 E Mansion St 49068-1186) Anne Schnaare (269) 781-7881

Montague St Peters by the Lake Episcopal **P** (102) 8435 Old Channel Trl 49437-1360 (Mail to: 8435 Old Channel Trl 49437-1360) David Meyers

Mt Pleasant St Johns Church Episcopal **P** (193)

206 W Maple St 48858-3103 (Mail to: 206 W Maple St 48858-3103) Wayne Nicholson Nancy Fulton (989) 773-7448

Muskegon St Pauls Episcopal Church **P** (170) 1006 3rd St 49440-1206 (Mail to: 1006 3rd St 49440-1206) Patrick Finn (231) 722-2112

Newaygo St Marks Church **P** (100) 30 Justice St 49337-8519 (Mail to: PO Box 211 49337-0211) Mary Frens (231) 652-7284

Niles Trinity Episcopal Church **P** (99) 9 S 4th St 49120-2708 (Mail to: 9 S 4th St 49120-2708) (269) 683-6060

Northport St Christophers Church **P** (38) 701 N Warren St 49670 (Mail to: PO Box 98 49670-0098) (231) 386-5037

Norton Shores St Gregorys Episcopal Church **P** (167) 1200 Seminole Rd 49441-4375 (Mail to: 1200 Seminole Rd 49441-4375) (231) 780-2955

Onekama St Johns by the Lake Chapel **SC** 4663 Highway 22 49675-9748 (Mail to: 17046 Lloyds Bayou Dr Apt 403 49456-9271) (231) 935-1898

Paw Paw St Marks Episcopal Church **P** (73) 412 Cedar St 49079 (Mail to: PO BOX 307 49079) Rebecca Crise

Pentwater St James Church **P** (48) 82 S Wythe St 49449-7526 (Mail to: PO Box 412 49449-0412) Samuel Morrison (231) 869-7351

Petoskey Emmanuel Episcopal Church **P** (298) 1020 E Mitchell St 49770-2636 (Mail to: Attn Office Manager 1020 E Mitchell St 49770-2636) Gregory Brown

Plainwell St Stephens Episcopal Church **P** (155) 309 Union St 49080-1248 (Mail to: 309 Union St 49080-1248) (269) 685-8230

Portage St Barnabas Episcopal Church **P** (256) 929 E Centre Ave 49002-5571 (Mail to: 929 E Centre Ave 49002-5571) Bonnie Edwards (269) 327-7878

Richland St Timothys Church **P** (68) 9800 E BC Ave 49083-9577 (Mail to: 9800 East BC Ave 49083-9577) Joel Turmo

Saugatuck All Saints Episcopal Church **P** (276) 252 Grand St 49453-9627 (Mail to: PO Box 189 49453-0189) Gerald Stoppel (269) 857-5201

Shelbyville St Francis Episcopal Church **P** (34) 11850 9 Mile Rd 49344-9441 (Mail to: 11850 9 Mile Rd 49344-9441) (269) 664-4345

South Haven Church of the Epiphany **P** (62) 410 Erie St 49090-1324 (Mail to: 410 Erie St 49090-1324) Michael Ryan

St Joseph St Pauls Episcopal Church **P** (114) 914 Lane Dr 49085-2053 (Mail to: 914 Lane Drive 49085-2053) (269) 983-4761

Sturgis St John Episcopal Church **P** (135) 110 S Clay St 49091-1711 (Mail to: 110 S Clay St 49091-1711) Aaron Evans (269) 651-5811

Three Rivers Trinity Episcopal Church **P** (85) 321 N Main St 49093-1422 (Mail to: 321 N Main St 49093-1422) Carlton Kelley (269) 273-3795

Traverse City Grace Episcopal Church **P** (576)

341 Washington St 49684-2547 (Mail to: 341 Washington St 49684-2547) Kathryn King Louise Kountze (231) 947-2330

Wyoming Holy Trinity Episcopal Church **P** (155) 5333 Clyde Park Ave SW 49509-9527 (Mail to: 5333 Clyde Park Avenue SW 49509-9527) James Croom Bradley Allard (616) 538-0900

NON-PAROCHIAL CLERGY

Ambrose VG *ret* Grand Rapids MI
Anei AM *dcn*
Bartlett S *ret* Shelby MI
Bell JM *ret* Manistee MI
Breakey PJ *ret* Dowagiac MI
Brinkmoeller LJ *ret* Paw Paw MI
Brower DA *ret* Zeeland MI
Brower KM *ret dcn* Grand Rapids MI
Burke CA *ret* Bend OR
Carlson GB *dcn* Petoskey MI
Carter PL *ret* Boulder CO
Char Z Comstock Pk MI
Clark RN *ret* Eureka Springs AR
Comer HL *ret* Frankfort MI
David JS *ret* Fairbanks AK
Draeger WR *ret* Traverse City MI
Dukes LAS *ret* Jacksonville Beach FL
Eickwort KR *ret* Ocala FL
Emenheiser DE *ret* Traverse City MI
Evans RN Muskegon MI
Flentje GL *dcn* Ada MI
Fout JA Bexley OH
Frandsen CF *ret* Saint Joseph MI
Green PA Somerset MA
Grubb DS New Era MI
Guback TH *ret* Northport MI
Harris LK *ret* Beverly Hills FL
Haughn TL *ret* Plainwell MI
Hector JR *ret* Drake CO
Hills JB *ret* Grand Haven MI
Homeyer CF *ret* Ada MI
Hoop KA *dcn* Grand Rapids MI
Hostetler HS *ret* Surfside Bch SC
Hotra NL *ret* Richland MI
Hunt M *ret* Interlochen MI
Inman JW *ret* New Hope PA
Kirkman JR *ret* Grand Rapids MI
Klein EH *ret* Whitehall MI
Lawlor J Kalamazoo MI
McCabe CP *ret* Hastings MI
McDonald KL *dcn* Lawton MI
McLaren BA Kalamazoo MI
Meengs JR *dcn* Holland MI
Mikaya HC *ret* Gabrone
Murphy WMK *ret* Lodi WI
Nattermann MA Charlevoix MI
Nawrocki CL *dcn* Grand Rapids MI
Neiman J *dcn* Paw Paw MI
Nickerson AM *dcn* Battle Creek MI
O'Dell TP *ret* Lexington VA
Potts ML Falmouth MA

Reishus JW *ret* Kokomo IN
Richards DP Traverse City MI
Rutenbar LJ Cordova TN
Schiesler RA *ret* Grand Rapids MI
Scott TCH *ret* Evanston IL
Sherfick KL *ret* Knoxville TN
Smith RA *ret* Dowagiac MI
Smith WH Port St Lucie FL
Smith-Kurtz MB *dcn* Williamsburg MI
Sten PV *ret* Buchanan MI
Stravers RL
Thomson MD

Tillman CW *dcn* Wyoming MI
Tomczak BL *dcn* Three Rivers MI
Van Hooser JB *ret* Knoxville TN
Van Valkenburgh WB *ret* Angola IN
Wagner BJ *dcn* Harbor Springs MI
Walton RH *ret* Okemos MI
Weller GK *ret* Mayfield Village OH
White WC *ret* Burlington VT
Whiting WR *ret* Grand Rapids MI
Williams GP *ret* Traverse City MI
Wolterstorff CK Grand Rapids MI

DIOCESE OF WESTERN NEW YORK
(PROVINCE II)
Comprises 7 Western New York counties
DIOCESAN OFFICE 1064 Brighton Rd Tonawanda NY 14150
TEL (716) 881-0660   FAX (716) 881-1724
E-MAIL diocesanoffice@episcopalwny.org   WEB www.episcopalwny.org

Previous Bishops—
Wm H Delancey 1839-65, Arthur C
Coxe coadj 1865 Bp 1865-96, Wm
D Walker 1897-1917, Chas H Brent
1918-29, David L Ferris suffr 1920-
24 coadj 1924 Bp 1929-31, Cameron
J Davis coadj 1930 Bp 1931-47,
Lauriston L Scaife 1948-70, Harold
B Robinson coadj 1968 Bp 1970-1987, David C
Bowman coadj 1986 Bp 1987-98, J Michael Garrison
1999-2011

Bishop—Rt Rev R William Franklin (1057) (Dio
30 Apr 2011)

Ex Sec Trustees H Gondree; *Sec* H Gondree; *Treas* R
Matson; *Chanc* JS Fanning; *Archdcn* T Tripp

Standing Comm—Cler: Pres S Leonard P Dempesy-
Sims E King E Brauza; *Lay:* J Isaac T Ashford N
Consedine B Fortune

Deans: Cattaraugus T Broad; *Central Erie* G Payne-
Carter; *Chautauqua* T Broad; *Eastern Erie* B Price;
Genesee Region C O'Connor; *Niagara*; *Northern Erie*
E King; *Southern Erie* G Schindler

Dio Conv: 28-29 Oct 2016 Niagara Falls, NY

PARISHES, MISSIONS, AND CLERGY
Albion Christ Episcopal Church **P** (29) 26 S Main
St 14411-1401 (Mail to: 26 S Main St 14411-
1401) (585) 589-5314
Alden St Aidans Church **M** (45) 13021 Main St
14004-1225 (Mail to: 13021 West Main St
14004-1225) (716) 937-6922
Angola St Pauls Episcopal Church **P** (117) 930
Lake St 14006-9200 (Mail to: PO Box 344
14006-0344) (716) 549-0063
Attica St Luke's Episcopal Church **P** (340) 30

Favor St 14011-1257 (Mail to: PO Box 178
14011-0178) Christopher O'Connor (585) 591-
0301
Batavia St James Church **P** (262) 405 E Main St
14020-2496 (Mail to: 405 E Main St 14020-
2496) Steven Metcalfe (585) 343-6802
Buffalo Church of the Advent **P** (332) 54
Delaware Rd 14217-2402 (Mail to: 54 Delaware
Road 14217-2402) Terry Bull Penelope Foster
(716) 876-6504
Buffalo Church of the Ascension **P** (39) 96 Jewett
Parkway 14214 (Mail to: 96 Jewett Parkway
14214) Lucinda Cornell Catherine Dempesy
(716) 884-6362
Buffalo St Andrews Church **P** (34) 3107 Main
St 14214-1305 (Mail to: 3105 Main St 14214-
1305) Ellen Brauza
Buffalo St Davids Episcopal Church **P** (246) 3951
Seneca St 14224-3412 (Mail to: 3951 Seneca
Street 14224-3412) Allen Farabee (716) 674-
4670
Buffalo St Johns Grace Church **P** (108) 51
Colonial Cir 14222-1399 (Mail to: 51 Colonial
Cir 14222-1399)
Buffalo St Judes Episcopal Church **P** (192)
124 Macamley St 14220-1242 (Mail to: 124
Macamley St 14220-1242) (716) 824-4322
Buffalo St Marks and All Saints Episcopal Church
P (63) 311 Ontario St 14207-1548 (Mail to: 311
Ontario St 14207-1548) (716) 875-8374
Buffalo St Matthews Church **P** (48) 1182 Seneca
St 14210-1545 (Mail to: 1182 Seneca St 14210-
1545) Judith Hefner Patricia Guinn (716) 822-
4830
Buffalo St Michael and All Angels Church **P** (75)
81 Burke Dr 14215-1305 (Mail to: 81 Burke Dr
14215-1305) John Marshall (716) 836-0220
Buffalo St Patricks Episcopal Church **P** (102) 1395

George Urban Blvd 14225-3807 (Mail to: 1395 George Urban Blvd. 14225-3807) (716) 684-4206

Buffalo St Pauls Cathedral in Buffalo **O** (217) 4 Cathedral Park 14202-4094 (Mail to: 4 Cathedral Park 14202-4094) Willie Mebane Daniel Pinti (716) 855-0900

Buffalo St Pauls Episcopal Church **P** (448) 4275 Harris Hill Rd 14221-7437 (Mail to: 4275 Harris Hill Road 14221-7437) Vicki Zust Leann McConchie (716) 632-8221

Buffalo St Peters Episcopal Church **P** (217) 205 Longmeadow Rd 14226-2905 (Mail to: 205 Longmeadow Road 14226-2905) (716) 832-9764

Buffalo St Philips Episcopal Church **P** (184) 18 Sussex Street 14215 (Mail to: PO Box 1254 14215-6254) Katherine Lwebuga-Mukasa Gloria Payne-Carter (716) 833-0444

Buffalo St Simons Episcopal Church **P** (140) 200 Cazenovia St 14210-2451 (Mail to: 200 Cazenovia St 14210-2499) Ralph Strohm Linda Malia

Buffalo The Church of the Good Shepherd **P** (152) 96 Jewett Pkwy 14214-2322 (Mail to: 96 Jewett Pkwy 14214-2322) Leann McConchie (716) 833-1151

Buffalo Trinity Episcopal Church **P** (628) 371 Delaware Ave 14202-1601 (Mail to: 371 Delaware Ave 14202-1699) Stephen Lane Matthew Lincoln (716) 852-8314

Burt St Andrews Episcopal Church **P** (159) 2239 W Creek Rd 14028-9724 (Mail to: PO Box 133 14028-0133) (716) 778-7633

Chautauqua Chapel of the Good Shepherd **SC** Clark Ave 14722 (Mail to: Clark Ave 14722)

Dunkirk Church of St John the Baptist **P** (96) 16 W 4th St 14048-2056 (Mail to: PO Box 14 14048-0014) Lawrence Schuster (716) 366-1979

East Aurora St Matthias Episcopal Church **P** (125) No 374 Main St 14052-1715 (Mail to: 374 Main St 14052-1715) Ann Tillman Pauline Bowen William Wipfler (716) 652-0377

Ellicottville St Johns Episcopal Church **P** (16) Washington & Jefferson Sts 14731 (Mail to: PO Box 137 14731-0137) Michael Lonto (716) 945-1820

Franklinville St Barnabas Episcopal Church **M** (14) 81 N Main St PO Box 105 14737-1032 (Mail to: PO Box 105 14737-0105) (716) 676-3468

Fredonia Trinity Episcopal Church **P** (214) 11 Day St 14063-1813 (Mail to: PO Box 467 14063-0467) Robert Arnold (716) 679-7901

Gowanda St Marys Episcopal Church **P** (41) 75 Center St 14070-1106 (Mail to: PO Box 166 14070-0166) W David Noves (716) 532-4352

Grand Island Church of St Martin in the Fields **P** (272) 2587 Baseline Rd 14072-1656 (Mail to: 2587 Baseline Rd 14072-1656) Earle King

(716) 773-3335

Hamburg Trinity Episcopal Church **P** (340) 261 E Main St 14075-5345 (Mail to: 261 E Main St 14075-5345) Blane Van Pletzen-Rands (716) 649-4320

Holley St Pauls Episcopal Church **P** (39) 2 Jackson St 14470-1106 (Mail to: 2 Jackson St 14470-1106) John Boyer (585) 638-5142

Irving Church of the Good Shepherd **M** (105) 12114 Route 438 Extension 14081 (Mail to: PO Box 179 14081-0179) (716) 934-3328

Jamestown St Lukes Episcopal Church **P** (375) 410 N Main St 14701 (Mail to: 410 N Main St 14701) Barbara Baxter Lucas Fodor Cathleen Smith (716) 483-6405

Lake View Church of the Holy Communion **M** (122) 5381 Old Lake Shore Rd. 14085-0158 (Mail to: PO Box 158 14085-0158) Frieda Webb (716) 627-5951

Lancaster Trinity Episcopal Church **P** (198) 5448 Broadway 14086-2124 (Mail to: 5448 Broadway 14086-2124) Karen Gough (716) 683-1111

LeRoy St Marks Episcopal Church **P** (203) 1 E Main St 14482-1209 (Mail to: 1 E Main St 14482-1209) Mary O'Connor (585) 768-7200

Lewiston St Pauls Episcopal Church **P** (128) 400 Ridge St 14092-1206 (Mail to: PO Box 354 14092-0354) Neil Johnson Alison Martin (716) 754-4591

Lockport Christ Church **P** (245) 7145 Fieldcrest Dr 14094-1613 (Mail to: 7145 Fieldcrest Dr 14094-1613) Jeffery Edmister Thomas Mitchell

Lockport Grace Episcopal Church **P** (109) 100 Genesee St 14094-4318 (Mail to: 100 Genesee St 14094-4318) Cynthia Sever (716) 433-2878

Mayville St Pauls Episcopal Church **P** (141) 99 S Erie St 14757-1120 (Mail to: 99 S Erie St 14757-1120) Claudia Scheda (716) 753-2172

Medina St Johns Church **P** (51) 200 E Center St 14103-1623 (Mail to: PO Box 699 14103) Nancy Guenther (585) 798-0920

Niagara Falls Niagara Falls Episcopal Urb Ministry **Ministry** (109) 140 Rainbow Blvd 14303-1214 (Mail to: 140 Rainbow Blvd 14303-1214) (716) 282-1717

Niagara Falls St Stephen's Episcopal Church **P** (244) 616 Cayuga Drive 14304-3499 (Mail to: 616 Cayuga Drive 14304-3499) (716) 283-2774

North Tonawanda St Mark Episcopal Church **P** (340) 61 Payne Ave 14120-6012 (Mail to: 61 Payne Ave 14120-6012) (716) 692-3735

Olean St Stephens Church **P** (108) 109 S Barry St 14760-3626 (Mail to: PO Box 446 14760-0446) Kim Rossi (716) 372-5628

Orchard Park St Marks Episcopal Church **P** (616) 6595 E Quaker St 14127-2501 (Mail to: 6595 E Quaker St 14127-2585) Sean Leonard Leland Rose (716) 662-4418

Perry Holy Apostle Episcopal Church **P** (50) 88 S Main St 14530-1524 (Mail to: 88 S Main St 14530-1524) (585) 237-5883

Randolph Grace Episcopal Church **P** (101) 21 N Washington St 14772 (Mail to: 21 N Washington St 14772-1207) Thomas Broad (716) 358-6124

Salamanca St Marys Episcopal Church **P** (112) 99 Wildwood Ave 14779-1523 (Mail to: 99 Wildwood Ave 14779-1523) Michael Lonto (716) 945-1820

Silver Creek St Albans Episcopal Church **P** (57) 4 Lake Ave 14136-1012 (Mail to: PO Box 214 14136-0214) (716) 934-2174

Springville St Pauls Episcopal Church **M** (138) 591 E Main St 14141-1437 (Mail to: 591 E Main St 14141-1437) Gary Schindler Gerald Hilfiker (716) 592-2153

Stafford St Pauls Episcopal Church **P** (39) 6188 Main Rd 14143-9546 (Mail to: PO Box 786 14143-0786) (585) 356-0769

Tonawanda St Anthony of Padua Chapel **Other** 1064 Brighton Road 14150 (Mail to: 1064 Brighton Road 14150) (716) 881-0660

Warsaw Trinity Church **P** (26) 62 W Buffalo S 14569 (Mail to: PO Box 396 14569-1209) Sarah Anuszkiewicz (585) 786-5285

Westfield St Peters Episcopal Church **P** (110) 12 Elm St 14787-1402 (Mail to: 12 Elm St 14787-1402) Virginia Carr (716) 326-2064

Williamsville Calvary Episcopal Church **P** (1226) 20 Milton Street 14221-6704 (Mail to: 20 Milton Street 14221-6704) Judith Lee (716) 633-7800

Wilson St Johns Episcopal Church **P** (61) 431 Lake St 14172-9798 (Mail to: PO Box 28 14172-0028) (716) 751-6109

Youngstown St Johns Episcopal Church **P** (86) 110 Chestnut St 14174-1002 (Mail to: PO Box 366 14174-0366) Alison Martin (716) 745-3369

NON-PAROCHIAL CLERGY

Amend RJ *ret* Amherst NY
Bencken CF *ret* Muscatine IA
Boyd-Ellis S *dcn*
Bridgford PW *ret* Buffalo NY
Budez JH
Buxton-Smith SW *ret* Buffalo NY
Carney PL *dcn*
Carr JJ Kenmore NY
Choi BT *ret* Buffalo NY
Cole EJ Clarence NY
Crittenden WS *ret* Chautauqua NY
Curtis YM Dunkirk NY
Cutolo MA
Davis-Wilson L *dcn*
Deacon CA *ret* Amherst NY
Dedde JC *ret* Amherst NY
Dougharty PW *ret* Albuquerque NM
Dower SN
Dugger RJC *dcn*
Farone M *dcn*
Feagin JW *ret* Williamsville NY
Fenn RL *ret* Edgartown MA

Foster MR *dcn* Buffalo NY
Fuller GC *ret*
Gillies C *dcn* Buffalo NY
Grace HT *ret* Buffalo NY
Greene KH *dcn* Buffalo NY
Guenther JH Hilton NY
Haines HJ *ret* Rochester NY
Hardy K *ret* Buffalo NY
Hass CV *dcn* Alexander NY
Holmes PW Buffalo NY
Houghton PG *ret* Olean NY
Hovencamp O *ret* Irving NY
Ihiasota II *ret* Niagara Falls NY
Irsch LM *ret* Edwardsville PA
Johnson RC *ret* Glendale AZ
Keppy SC *ret* Lewiston NY
Kim JJH Kumi Kyungbuk
Kozlowski JF
Lancaster RV *ret* Sante Fe NM
Lord PW *ret* Dunkirk NY
Lullo M *dcn* Buffalo NY
Mackenzie JAR Richmond VA
Middleton EB *dcn* Palm Beach Gardens FL
Montanari AU *ret* Williamsville NY
Montgomery EM *ret* Buffalo NY
Morris BF Williamsville NY
Newbert RA *ret* Buffalo NY
Outwin EM *ret* Medina NY
Peek GR *ret* East Amherst NY
Pike DM Springfield NJ
Polvino AR Waco TX
Pond WE Warsaw NY
Potter LH Buffalo NY
Price BJ *ret* Buffalo NY
Rayburg-Elliott JA *dcn* Buffalo NY
Russell JA *ret* Buffalo NY
Sam AS *ret* Lockport NY
Sam H Dunkirk NY
Samuels RM *ret* Green Bay WI
Selzer DO *ret* Ottawa ON
Smith DL *dcn* Lancaster NY
Smith EO *ret* Washington DC
Smith SJ *ret* Buffalo NY
Spangler ND *ret* Buffalo NY
Stedman DA *ret* St Thomas VI
Steffenhagen LR *dcn* Niagara Falls NY
Stubbs JD Whitinsville MA
Szymanski MS *dcn* Lackawanna NY
Thomas MJ *ret* Buffalo NY
Trail SE *dcn* Buffalo NY
Tripp TN *dcn* Amherst NY
Turner AC *dcn* Lackawanna NY
Walser GC *dcn* Williamsville NY
Webb WC Angola NY
Weir DS *ret* Danvers MA
Wheeler CR *dcn* Westfield NY
Whiteford CS *dcn* Williamsville NY
Whitmore CW *ret* Bellingham WA
Witt BR *dcn* Gasport NY
Wolter JM *ret* Prescott AZ

DIOCESE OF WESTERN NORTH CAROLINA
(PROVINCE IV)
Comprises the 28 westernmost counties of North Carolina
DIOCESAN OFFICE 900-B Centre Park Dr Asheville NC 28805
TEL (828) **225-6656**   FAX (828) 225-6657
E-MAIL bishop@diocesewnc.org   WEB www.diocesewnc.org

Previous Bishops—
Junius M Horner 1898-1933, Robt
E Gribbin 1934-47, Matt G Henry
1948-75, Wm G Weinhauer coadj
1973 Bp 1975-89, Robert H Johnson
1990-2004

**Bishop — Rt Rev Granville Porter
Taylor (999)** (Dio 18 Sept 2004)

Cn to Ord and Deploy Rev Cn J Pritchett Jr; *Chr Form
and Min (co-chairs)* Rev T Murphy P Redd; *Sec Rev*
Rev C Criag; *Treas* H Cole; *Chanc* GS Hilderbran 72
Patton Ave Asheville NC 28801; *Ecum* Rev B Norris;
Outreach Min A Ware; *Prog Min* E Clarke; *Cn Yth
Min* Rev J Myers; *Cong Dev* Rev C Beebe & Rev G
Butterworth; *Archdcn* K Neal

Stand Comm—Cler: Chair A Anderson L Walton
M Morrow; *Lay:* A Fullwood R Murray R Rios N
Wilson

Deans: Asheville Rev S Oxford; *Foothills* Rev K
Woggon; *Hendersonville* Rev W Shields; *Mountain*
Rev Dn G Erickson; *Piedmont* Rev C Beebe; *Western*
Rev B Walker

Dio Conv: 11-13 November 2016

PARISHES, MISSIONS, AND CLERGY

Asheville Cathedral of All Souls **O** (909) 9 Swan
St 28803-2674 (Mail to: 9 Swan St 28803-2674)
Todd Donatelli Rosa Harden Delmas Hare
Mildred Morrow Thomas Murphy (828) 274-
2681

Asheville Church of the Advocate **Other** (225) 60
Church St 28801-3622 (Mail to: 60 Church St.
28801-3622) (828) 243-3932

Asheville Church of the Redeemer **P** (144)
1201 Riverside Dr 28804-3019 (Mail to: 1201
Riverside Dr 28804-3019) Alexander Hanks
(828) 253-3588

Asheville Grace Episcopal Church **P** (454) 871
Merrimon Ave 28804-2404 (Mail to: 871
Merrimon Ave 28804-2492) Gary Coffey
Wendy Porter Cade Robert Reese (828) 254-
1086

Asheville St Georges Episcopal Church **P** (33) 1
School Rd 28806-1633 (Mail to: 1 School Rd
28806-1633) Elizabeth Darling Harry Woggon
(828) 258-0211

Asheville St Johns Episcopal Church **P** (76) 290
Old Haw Creek Rd 28805-1436 (Mail to: 290
Old Haw Creek Rd 28805-1436) (828) 298-
3553

Asheville St Lukes Episcopal Church **P** (152) 219
Chunn's Cove Rd 28805-1210 (Mail to: 219
Chunn's Cove Rd 28805-1210) Patricia Mouer
(828) 254-2133

Asheville St Marys Church **P** (167) 337 Charlotte
Street 28801-1437 (Mail to: 337 Charlotte
Street 28801) Michael Norris William Austin
Otis Edwards Gary Kovach Stephen Weissman
Harry Woggon (828) 254-5836

Asheville St Matthias Episcopal Church **P** (82) 1
Dundee Street 28802-7375 (Mail to: PO Box
7375 28802-7375) Gerald Prickett David Sailer
(828) 285-0033

Asheville Trinity Episcopal Church **P** (1049) 60
Church St 28801-3622 (Mail to: 60 Church St
28801-3690) Robert White Margaret Buchanan
Carol Hubbard (828) 253-9361

Bat Cave Church of the Transfiguration **P** (97)
106 Saylor Lane 28710 (Mail to: PO Box 130
28710-0130) John Shields (828) 625-9244

Bessemer City St Andrews Episcopal Church **P**
(50) 1303 N 12th St 28016-6739 (Mail to: PO
Box 611 28016-0611) (704) 629-3021

Black Mtn St James Episcopal Church **P** (372) 424
W State St 28711-3345 (Mail to: PO Box 1087
28711-1087) Scott Oxford (828) 669-2754

Blowing Rock St Mary of the Hills Church **P** (276)
140 Chestnut Cir 28605-9214 (Mail to: PO
Box 14 28605-0014) Richard Lawler Richard
DeMott James Gloster Samuel Tallman (828)
295-7323

Boone St Lukes Episcopal Church **P** (342) 170
Councill St 28607-3727 (Mail to: 170 Councill
St 28607-3727) Cynthia Banks (828) 264-8943

Brevard St Philip's Episcopal Church **P** (554) 317
E Main St 28712-3834 (Mail to: 256 E Main St
28712-3724) Robert Field (828) 884-3666

Burnsville St Thomas Episcopal Church **P** (96)
372 Reservoir Rd PO Box 591 28714-0591
(Mail to: 372 Reservoir Rd PO Box 591 28714-
0591) (828) 682-0037

Canton St Andrews Church **P** (271) 99 Academy
St 28716-4445 (Mail to: PO Box 947 28716-
4445) Timothy McRee Harlan Bemis Raymond
Escott Curruth Smith (828) 648-7550

Cashiers Church of the Good Shepherd **P** (581)
1448 Highway 107 S 28717 (Mail to: PO Box 32
28717-0032) Douglas Remer

Cherokee St Francis of Assisi Church **P** (40) Hwy
441 At Oconaluftee Bridge 28719 (Mail to: PO
Box 585 28719-0585) (828) 507-5992

Cullowhee St Davids Episcopal Church **P** (122)
PO Box 152 28723 (Mail to: PO Box 152

28723-0152) Michael Hudson Alice Mason (828) 293-9496

Denver Epis Ch of St Peters by the Lake **P** (492) 8433 Fairfield Rd 28037-9130 (Mail to: 8433 Fairfield Forest Rd 28037-9166) Ronald Taylor Judith Cole (704) 483-3460

Edneyville St Pauls Episcopal Church **P** (76) 1659 St Pauls Rd 28727 (Mail to: PO Box 70 28727-0070) Harriet Shands (828) 685-3644

Flat Rock St John in the Wilderness **P** (482) 1895 Greenville Hwy 28731-9646 (Mail to: PO Box 185 28731-0185) John Morton Joyce Beschta Harry Viola (828) 693-9783

Fletcher Calvary Episcopal Church **P** (388) PO Box 187 Hwy 25 28732-0187 (Mail to: PO Box 187 28732-0187) William Frank (828) 684-6266

Franklin All Saints Parish **P** 216 Roller Mill Rd 28734-9089 (Mail to: 84 Church St 28734-2946) Dorothy Pratt

Franklin St Agnes Episcopal Church **P** (113) 84 Church St 28734-2946 (Mail to: 84 Church St 28734-2946) (828) 524-4910

Franklin St Cyprians Episcopal Church **P** (86) PO Box 5 28744-0005 (Mail to: PO Box 5 28734-0005) Dorothy Pratt (828) 524-4910

Franklin St John's Episcopal Church **P** (75) 542 St John's Church Rd 28734-8201 (Mail to: 542 Saint John's Church Rd 28734-8201) (828) 524-6370

Gastonia All Saints Episcopal Church **P** (162) 1201 S New Hope Rd 28054-5833 (Mail to: 1201 S New Hope Rd 28054-5833) Gary Butterworth Anita Ware

Gastonia St Marks Episcopal Church **P** (540) 258 W Franklin Blvd 28052-4108 (Mail to: 258 W Franklin Blvd 28052-4108) Shawn Griffith (704) 864-4531

Glendale Springs Parish of Holy Communion **P** (98) 120 Glendale School Rd 28629 (Mail to: PO Box 177 28629-0177) Kimberly Becker Shirley Long (336) 982-3076

Hayesville Church of the Good Shepherd **P** (282) 495 Herbert Hills Dr 28904-4716 (Mail to: PO Box 677 28904-0677) William Breedlove

Hendersonvlle La Capilla de Santa Maria **P** (165) PO Box 296 28793 (Mail to: PO Box 2906 28793-2906) Hilario Cisneros (828) 697-5292

Hendersonvlle St James Episcopal Church **P** (809) 766 N Main St 28792-5078 (Mail to: 766 N Main St 28792-5078) Joel Hafer Timothy Jones Christiana Olsen (828) 693-7458

Hickory Church of the Ascension **P** (374) 726 1st Ave NW 28601-6062 (Mail to: 726 1st Ave NW 28601-6062) Karla Woggon (828) 328-5393

Hickory St Albans Episcopal Church **P** (739) 130 39th Ave Pl NW 28601-8029 (Mail to: 130 39th Ave Pl NW 28601-8029) Tryggvi Arnason Randolph Ferebee (828) 324-1351

Highlands Church of the Incarnation **P** (307) 520 Main St 28741 (Mail to: Post Office Box 729

28741-0729) Stephen Walker (828) 526-2968

Lenoir St James Episcopal Church **P** (249) 806 College Ave SW 28645-5426 (Mail to: 806 College Ave SW 28645-5426) Janis Costas (828) 754-3712

Lincolnton Our Saviour Episcopal Church **P** (21) P O Box 203 28092 (Mail to: PO Box 203 28093-0203) (704) 732-3585

Lincolnton St Lukes Church **P** (161) 325 N Cedar St 28092-2802 (Mail to: 315 N Cedar St 28092-2802)

Linville All Saints Episcopal Chapel **SC** Carolina Ave 28646 (Mail to: Carolina Ave 28646) (828) 733-4311

Little Switzerland Church of the Resurrection **SC** 160 Highridge Rd 28749 (Mail to: 160 High Ridge Rd 28749) Robert Hansel (828) 765-1808

Marion St Johns Episcopal Church **P** (117) 311 S Main St 28752-4526 (Mail to: PO Box 968 28752-0968) Richard Rowe (828) 652-4144

Mars Hill Church of the Holy Spirit **P** (176) 433 Bone Camp Rd 28753 (Mail to: PO Box 956 28754-0956) David McNair Otis Edwards Robert Magnus (828) 689-2517

Mills River Church of the Holy Family **P** (80) No 419 Turnpike Rd 28729 (Mail to: 419 Turnpike Rd 28759-9548) Robert Lundquist

Morganton Grace Episcopal Church **P** (216) 303 S King St 28655-3536 (Mail to: 303 S King St 28655-3536) Michael Jenkins Marshall Jolly (828) 437-1133

Morganton St Marys & St Stephen's Episcopal Ch **P** (140) 140 St Mary's Church Rd 28655-9096 (Mail to: 140 Saint Marys Church Rd 28655-9096) James Dahlin (828) 448-8490

Morganton St Pauls Episcopal Church **P** (92) 4656 E Shores Dr 28655-8278 (Mail to: 1865 N Powerhouse Rd 28655-7849) Harry Rains (704) 584-0955

Murphy Church of the Messiah **P** (119) 76 Peachtree St 28906-2940 (Mail to: PO Box 67 28906-0067)

Newland Church of the Savior **P** (17) 2118 Elk Park Hwy 28657-8827 (Mail to: 2118 Elk Park Hwy 28657-8827) David Booher (828) 733-2513

Newton Episcopal Church of the Epiphany **P** (104) 750 W 13th St 28658-3826 (Mail to: PO Box 270 28658-0270) (828) 464-1876

Robbinsville Grace Mountainside Lutheran Episcopal Church **P** (20) 129 S Main St. 28771-9802 (Mail to: PO Box 1208 28771-1208) (828) 479-1184

Rutherdforton St Gabriels Episcopal Church **P** (52) PO Box 2121 28139 (Mail to: PO Box 2121 28139-4321) Bobby Lynch (828) 980-1466

Rutherfordton St Francis Episcopal Church **P** (130) 395 N Main Street 28139-2415 (Mail to: 395 North Main Street 28139-0046) Christine Beebe

Saluda Church of the Transfiguration **P** (133) 72 Church St 28773-9716 (Mail to: PO Box 275 28773-0275) Augusta Anderson (828) 749-9740

Shelby Church of the Redeemer **P** (183) 502 W Sumter St 28150-4329 (Mail to: 502 W Sumter St 28150-4329) Valori Sherer (704) 487-5404

Sparta Christ Episcopal Church **P** (108) 2543 US Hwy 21 S 28675 (Mail to: PO Box 1866 28675-1866) (336) 372-7983

Spruce Pine Trinity Episcopal Church **P** (211) 15 Hemlock Ave 28777-2981 (Mail to: 15 Hemlock Ave 28777-2981) Richard Biega (828) 520-1151

Sylva St Johns Episcopal Church **P** (93) 18 Jackson St 28779-3034 (Mail to: PO Box 175 28779-0175) Patricia Curtis (828) 586-8358

Tryon Church of the Good Shepherd **P** (75) 814 Markham Rd 28782-2819 (Mail to: PO Box 893 28782-0893)

Tryon Church of the Holy Cross **P** (164) 150 Melrose Ave 28782-3327 (Mail to: PO Box 279 28782-0279) Marie Cope Robert Mugan (828) 859-9741

Valle Crucis Church of the Holy Cross **P** (320) 122 Skiles Way 28604 (Mail to: PO Box 645 28691-0645) Robert McCaslin (828) 963-4609

Waynesville Grace Church in the Mountains **P** (256) 394 N Haywood St 28786-5718 (Mail to: 394 N Haywood St 28786-5718) (828) 456-6029

Wilkesboro St Pauls Episcopal Church **P** (371) 200 W Cowles St 28697-2410 (Mail to: PO Box 95 28697-0095) Ann Dieterle John Shields Nancy Whittington (336) 667-4231

NON-PAROCHIAL CLERGY

Abbott SFJ *ret* Asheville NC
Alvarez-Estrada M Las Vegas NV
Ashmore RM *dcn* Mars Hill NC
Barry ECM *dcn* Asheville NC
Beschta GT *dcn* Hendersonville NC
Blanck CK *ret* Sparta NC
Boone RA *ret* Asheville NC
Brackett TL Asheville NC
Bright BP *dcn* Shelby NC
Britt LA *ret* Morganton NC
Bryan WL *ret* Columbus NC
Calloway NL *dcn* Old Fort NC
Canham EJ *ret* Black Mountain NC
Cheshire GP *dcn* Gastonia NC
Cleghorn CD *ret* Arden NC
Cogsdale MH Lenoir NC
Comfort AF *ret* Mars Hill NC
Cosslett A *ret* Asheville NC
Curl JF Asheville NC
Doty DM *ret* Landrum SC
Dowdeswell EH *dcn* Flat Rock NC
Downing GL *ret* Hendersonville NC
Earl JK *dcn* Hickory NC

Edwards WG *ret* Asheville NC
Erickson GC *dcn* Hendersonville NC
Farmer GC *ret* Arden NC
Fisher RL *ret* Rockport ME
Fritschner AR *dcn* Hendersonville NC
Fuller PH *ret* Mills River NC
Gardner EM *ret* Asheville NC
Gorday PJ *ret* Atlanta GA
Grant JL Kalispell MT
Greiser RE *ret* New Port Richey FL
Guidry RT *dcn* Hayesville NC
Hetzel AD *dcn* Highlands NC
Hines JS *ret* Asheville NC
Holcomb SA Marble NC
Hovey FF *ret* Ormond Beach FL
Hoyt TL *ret* Saluda NC
Hughes TD *ret* Asheville NC
Hull-Ryde NA *dcn* Gastonia NC
Ingersoll RW *ret* Greensboro NC
Jackson RH *ret* Zirconia NC
Jamieson WS *dcn* Asheville NC
Johnson HA *dcn* Franklin NC
Jones PW *dcn* Hickory NC
Jones RM *ret* Highlands NC
Keller DGR *ret* Alexander NC
Kempster JL *ret* Mitchellville MD
King FMC *ret* Morganton NC
King FW Gastonia NC
Le Roy MLP *dcn* Arden NC
Lilly E Newton NC
Lukas A *ret* Waynesville NC
Mann HV *ret* Asheville NC
Mansfield VC *ret* Skyland NC
Matthews JH *ret* Gastonia NC
McDowell GI *dcn* Asheville NC
McElrath JD *dcn*
McIntyre GE Gastonia NC
Meservey NR *ret* Franklin NC
Miller SA *ret* Jefferson NC
Moore LF *ret* Asheville NC
Morton PK *ret* Saluda NC
Myers JE Seattle WA
Myhr LP *ret* Marion NC
Neal KH *dcn* Black Mountain NC
Niehaus TK *ret* Mequon WI
O'Malley DR Hayesville NC
Parmley IC *ret* Lenoir NC
Petersen BJ *ret* Mars Hill NC
Pfeiffer DK *dcn* Hilton Head SC
Plimpton BW Marion
Poteat ST *dcn*
Price JE Fairview NC
Price RE Asheville NC
Pritchett JH Arden NC
Reuss PAO *ret*
Reuss RJ *ret* Oak Ridge TN
Rice DH *ret* Franklin NC
Rice JDS *ret* Hayesville NC
Rightmyer TN *ret* Asheville NC
Rivers J *ret* Black Mountain NC

Ryan KA *ret* Aubrey TX
Seaver MB *dcn* Charlotte NC
Smith JG *ret* Asheville NC
Southern JC *ret* Asheville NC
Stokes GA Norfolk VA
Stoudemire SM *dcn* Hickory NC
Stroud RL *dcn*
Summerfield LJ Connellys Springs NC
Summerour WW *ret* Lake Toxaway NC

Taylor CH *ret* Asheville NC
Thomsen WR *dcn*
Turner AB Asheville NC
Vella JC *ret* State Road NC
Walker JF *ret* Richmond VA
Walker P *ret* New Orleans LA
Whelchel JH Asheville NC
Whisenhunt WA *ret* Asheville NC
Winters CL *ret* Asheville NC

STATE OF WISCONSIN
Dioceses of Eau Claire (EauC), Fond du Lac (FdL), and Milwaukee (Mil)

Algoma—FdL
Amherst—FdL
Antigo—FdL
Appleton—FdL
Ashland—EauC
Baraboo—Mil
Bayfield—EauC
Beaver Dam—Mil
Beloit—Mil
Brookfield—Mil
Brown Deer—Mil
Burlington—Mil
Chippewa Falls—EauC
Clear Lake—EauC
Conrath—EauC
Delafield—Mil
Delavan—Mil
De Pere—FdL
Eagle River—FdL
Eau Claire—EauC
Elkhorn—Mil
Fish Creek—FdL
Fond du Lac—FdL
Ft Atkinson—Mil

Gardner—FdL
Green Bay—FdL
Greendale—Mil
Hartford—Mil
Hartland—Mil
Hayward—EauC
Hudson—EauC
Janesville—Mil
Kenosha—Mil
La Crosse—EauC
Lake Geneva—Mil
Madison—Mil
Manitowoc—FdL
Marinette—FdL
Menasha—FdL
Menomonee Falls—Mil
Menomonie—EauC
Merrill—FdL
Milwaukee—Mil
Mineral Pt—Mil
Minocqua—FdL
Monroe—Mil
Mosinee—FdL
New London—FdL

New Richmond—EauC
Oconomowoc—Mil
Oneida—FdL
Oshkosh—FdL
Owen—EauC
Pewaukee—Mil
Phillips—EauC
Platteville—Mil
Plymouth—FdL
Pt Washington—Mil
Portage—Mil
Prairie du Chien—Mil
Racine—Mil
Rhinelander—FdL
Rice Lake—EauC
Richland Ctr—Mil
Ripon—FdL
Shawano—FdL
Sheboygan—FdL
Sheboygan Falls—FdL
Sister Bay—FdL
So Milwaukee—Mil
Sparta—EauC
Spooner—EauC

Springbrook—EauC
Stevens Pt—FdL
Sturgeon Bay—FdL
Suamico—FdL
Summit—Mil
Sun Prairie—Mil
Superior—EauC
Sussex—Mil
Thiensville—Mil
Tomah—EauC
Tomahawk—FdL
Watertown—Mil
Waukesha—Mil
Waupaca—FdL
Waupun—FdL
Wausau—FdL
Wautoma—FdL
W Bend—Mil
Whitefish Bay—Mil
Whitewater—Mil
Wis Dells—Mil
Wis Rapids—FdL

DIOCESE OF WYOMING
(PROVINCE VI)
Comprises the State of Wyoming
DIOCESAN OFFICE 123 S Durbin Casper WY 82601
TEL (307) 265-5200   FAX (307) 577-9939
E-MAIL jessica@wyomingdiocese.org   WEB www.wyomingdiocese.org

Previous Bishops—
Ethelbert Talbot 1887-98, Nathaniel S Thomas 1909-27, Elmer N Schmuck 1929-36, Winifred H Ziegler 1936-49, James W Hunter 1949-69, David R Thornberry 1969-77, Bob G Jones 1977-96, Bruce Caldwell 1997-2010

Bishop — Rt Rev John S Smylie (1048) (Dio 31 July 2010)

Deploy Rev T English; *Sec/Treas* J Hotle; *Chanc* P Nicolaysen; *Comm* T English; *Admin* J Reynolds; *Can for Min* J Dingman; *Ed* L Modesitt; *Rec* K. Corbin; *Youth* K Flores

Stand Comm—Cler: Pres M Erickson J Inserra B Gross; *Lay:* C King S Massey T Trosper

COM—Cler: L Modesitt L Fleming C Clarke D Wasinger J Zimmerschied *Lay: Sec* J Reynolds J Dominick J Prokos M Tepper

Diocesan Council: *Cler* C Moore S Askew L Davenport D Wasinger *Lay:* J Wildman L Galloway R Friday S Wildman W Owens T Kuiva T Soller D Land

Dio Conv: 7-9 Oct 2016 Sheridan WY

PARISHES, MISSIONS, AND CLERGY

Atlantic City St Andrews Episcopal Church **M** (20) 50 E Forbes St 82520-8812 (Mail to: PO Box 1028 82520-1028) (307) 332-4327

Basin St Andrews Episcopal Church **P** (75) 401 S 8th St 82410-9550 (Mail to: PO Box 407 82410-0407) Jean McLean (307) 568-2072

Big Piney St John the Baptist Episcopal Church **M** (46) 340 Smith Ave 83113 (Mail to: PO Box 205 83113-0205) Jami Anderson (307) 276-3805

Bondurant St Hubert the Hunter **SC** US 191 189 82922 (Mail to: PO BOX 3485 83001) (307) 733-4166

Buffalo St Lukes Episcopal Church **P** (335) 178 S Main St 82834-0909 (Mail to: PO Box 909 82834-0909) Douglas Wasinger (307) 684-7529

Casper St Marks Church **P** (576) 701 S Wolcott St 82601-3159 (Mail to: 701 S Wolcott St 82601-3159) Philip Major

Casper St Stephens Church **P** (50) 4700 S Poplar St 82601-6257 (Mail to: 4700 S Poplar St 82601-6257) Katherine Flores Judy Likwartz (307) 265-4105

Cheyenne St Christophers Church **P** (178) 2602 Deming Blvd 82001-5708 (Mail to: 2602 Deming Blvd 82001-5708) (307) 632-4488

Cheyenne St Marks Episcopal Church **P** (247) 1908 Central Ave 82001-3743 (Mail to: 1908 Central Ave 82001-3743) Richard Veit David Mcelwain James Stewart (307) 634-7709

Cody Christ Church **P** (597) 825 Simpson Avenue 82414-1718 (Mail to: PO Box 1718 82414-1718) Mary Caucutt David Fox Douglas Sunderland (307) 587-3849

Cokeville St Bartholomews Church **M** (7) 220 Pine St 83114 (Mail to: PO Box 365 83114-0365) (307) 279-3519

Dixon St Pauls Episcopal Church **M** (123) PO Box 68 82323-0068 (Mail to: PO Box 68 82323-0068) (307) 383-7645

Douglas Christ Episcopal Church **P** (92) 411 E Center St 82633-2438 (Mail to: PO Box 1419 82633-1419) (307) 358-5609

Dubois St Thomas Episcopal Church **P** (80) 5 S 1st St 82513 (Mail to: PO Box 735 82513-0735) Melinda Bobo Lyndie Duff (307) 455-2313

Encampment St James Church **M** (6) 812 McCaffrey 82325 (Mail to: c/o Yvonne Asbell 2996 N Kilt Ln 82301-4341) (307) 710-5464

Evanston St Pauls Episcopal Church **P** (160) 10th and Sage Sts 82930 (Mail to: PO Box 316 82931-0316) Constance Clark Suzanne Mac Ewen George Snow (307) 444-2601

Fort Bridger St Davids Episcopal Church **M** (3) 95 Carter St 82933 (Mail to: PO Box 144 82933-0144) (307) 782-3454

Fort Washakie Shoshone Mission **M** (179) 189 Trout Creek Rd 82514 (Mail to: PO Box 175 82514-0175) Velma Chavez Carl Means (307) 332-7925

Gillette Holy Trinity Episcopal Church **P** (120) 5101 Tanner Drive 82718 (Mail to: 5101 Tanner Drive 82718) Thomas Fiske (307) 682-4296

Glendo St John the Baptist Church **M** (29) Attn Mrs John H Hughes PO Box 412 82213-0008 (Mail to: PO Box 412 82213-0412) (307) 331-8405

Glenrock Christ Episcopal Church **M** (128) 415 W Cedar St 82637-0849 (Mail to: PO Box 298 82637-0298) (307) 436-8804

Green River St Johns Episcopal Church **P** (74) 350 Mansface St 82935-4904 (Mail to: PO Box 400 82935-4904) (307) 875-3419

Hartville Our Saviour Church **M** (40) 9 Lincoln St 82215 (Mail to: PO Box 64 82215-0064) Rex Martin William Walker (307) 836-2321

Jackson Chapel of the Transfiguration **SC** No 170 N Glenwood 83001 (Mail to: PO Box 1690 83001-1690) (307) 733-2603

Jackson St Johns Episcopal Church **P** (1035) 170 N Glenwood St 83001 (Mail to: PO Box 1690 83001-1690) John Asel Ronald Pogue Trenton Moore (307) 733-2603

Kaycee All Souls Episcopal Church **M** (37) 414 Sullivan St 82639 (Mail to: PO Box 12 82639-0012) (307) 738-2416

Kemmerer St James Episcopal Church **M** (76) 506 Cedar Ave 83101-3015 (Mail to: 506 Cedar Ave 83101-3015) Walter Seeley (307) 877-3652

Kinnear Holy Nativity Church **M** (30) 10925 US Hwy 26 82516-0160 (Mail to: PO Box 160 82516-0160)

Lander Our Fathers House/St Michaels **M** (144) 3 Saint Michael Cir 82520-9373 (Mail to: PO Box 160 82514-0160) Patricia Bergie

Lander Trinity Episcopal Church **P** (125) 806 S 3rd St 82520-3712 (Mail to: 860 S 3rd St 82520-3712) Raymond Price Terry Robeson (307) 332-5977

Laramie St Matthews Episcopal Cathedral **O** (300) No 104 S 4th St 82070 (Mail to: 104 S 4th St 82070-3102) Stephen Askew Richard Naumann (307) 742-6608

Lusk St Georges Episcopal Church **P** (61) 120 West 5th St 82225 (Mail to: PO Box 38 82225-0038) (307) 334-2870

Medicine Bow St Lukes Church **M** (12) 220 Pine Street 82329 (Mail to: PO Box 1194 82073) (307) 745-8472

Meeteetse St Andrews Episcopal Church **M** (50) 1116 Park Ave 82433 (Mail to: PO Box 88 82433-0088) (307) 868-2534

Newcastle Christ Episcopal Church **M** (23) 310 S Summit Ave 82701-0519 (Mail to: PO Box 519 82701-0519) (307) 746-9684

Pinedale St Andrews in the Pines **P** (289) 524 West Pine St 82941 (Mail to: PO Box 847 82941-0847) Jami Anderson Raleigh Denison (307) 367-2674

Powell St Johns Episcopal Church **M** (77) 308 Mountain View St 82435-2231 (Mail to: PO Box 846 82435-0846) Megan Nickles (307) 754-4000

Rawlins St Thomas Episcopal Church **P** (84) 6th And Pine Sts 82301 (Mail to: PO Box 608 82301-0608) Karen Buckingham (307) 324-5447

Riverton St James Episcopal Church **P** (169) 519 E Park Ave 82501-3652 (Mail to: 519 E Park Ave 82501) (307) 856-2369

Rock Springs Church of the Holy Communion **P** (147) 205 2nd St 82901 (Mail to: PO Box 567 82902-0567) (307) 362-3002

Saratoga St Barnabas Episcopal Church **M** (27) 204 West Main 82331 (Mail to: PO Box 250 82331-0250) (307) 326-8514

Sheridan St Peters Episcopal Church **P** (692) One S Tschirgi St 82801 (Mail to: 1 S Tschirgi St 82801-4229) John Inserra Elizabeth Bentley-Shelton (307) 674-7655

Sundance Good Shepherd Episcopal Church **M** (31) 120 North 6th St 82729 (Mail to: PO Box 246 82729-0246) Katherine Moore (307) 283-1863

Thermopolis Holy Trinity Episcopal Church **P** (122) 642 Arapahoe St 82443-2712 (Mail to: PO Box 950 82443-0950) Joseph Galligan Anetta Davenport (307) 864-3629

Torrington All Saints Episcopal Church **P** (195) 2601 Main St 82240-1925 (Mail to: 2601 Main St 82240-2054) Brian Gross (307) 532-5495

Wheatland All Saints Episcopal Church **P** (150) 605 11th Street 82201-2805 (Mail to: PO Box 997 82201-0997) Lori Modesitt Jill Zimmerschied (307) 322-9067

Worland St Albans Episcopal Church **P** (102) 1126 Us Highway 16 82401-3011 (Mail to: PO Box 84 82401-0084) Edward Farmer (307) 347-4704

Wright St Francis Episcopal Church **M** (51) 357 Willow Creek Dr 82732 (Mail to: PO Box 161 82732-0161) Sally Boyd (307) 464-0028

NON-PAROCHIAL CLERGY

Aaron SC Evanston WY
Adams-Harris AJ *dcn* Santa Barbara CA
Babcock MA *ret* Casper WY
Baldwin GR *ret* Greybull WY
Brown RW *ret* Casper WY
Bub SL *ret* Kinnear WY
Buckingham CS Kaycee WY
Burger RF *ret* Estes Park CO
Caldwell BA *ret dcn* Laramie WY
Carleton ED Riverton WY
Chance RL *ret* Cheyenne WY
Christy SJ Sundance WY
Clarke CR Lander WY
Cliver SC *ret* Sundance WY
Craft BL Rock Springs WY
Cunningham LE Washington DC
Day JW *ret* Bellingham WA
Denison CW Laramie WY
Dingman J Gillette WY
Duprey DL Sheridan WY
Dyer SJ *dcn* Saratoga WY
Earle LC *dcn* Casper WY
English TC Casper WY
Engstrom MJ *ret* Laramie WY
Erickson MC Jackson WY
Fitzhugh BK Douglas WY
Fleming LL Dixon WY
Fontaine AKH *ret* Cannon Beach OR
Galagan CK *dcn* Cody WY
Grieb RK *ret* Wheatland WY
Grimes DB Cody WY
Herring DL *dcn* Kaycee WY
Hudson LA *dcn* Lander WY
Jellison ML *ret* Bellingham WA
Johnson DL *dcn* Jackson WY
Ketner TH Douglas WY
Lohse DM Kaycee WY
Lytle RD *ret* Powell WY
MacConnell JS *ret* Dallas Center IA
March BA *dcn* Cody WY
Mayes AK Riverton WY
Moore CA *ret* Sundance WY
Murphy RE *ret* Kansas City MO
Murphy WC *ret* Cody WY
Palmer RW Fort Myers Beach FL
Peterson CE *dcn* Cheyenne WY
Philips RK Thermopolis WY
Robinson KS *ret* Casper WY
Rounds JA Laramie WY
Salbador GW *ret* Mount Vernon WA
Seeley JL Kemmerer WY
Sims RF *ret* Keller TX
Smith JW Laramie WY
Smith JD *dcn* Sheridan WY
Solon TT *ret* Cheyenne WY
Spencer RD *ret* Cheyenne WY
Stuber RL Yakima WA
Walworth RC *ret* Evanston WY
Wilson LR *ret* Socorro NM

The Succession of American Bishops

See end of list for lettered entries.

		Consecrators			Born	Date Consecrated	Died
1	SEABURY SAMUEL	AAA	AAB	AAC	1729	1784	1796
2	WHITE WILLIAM	AAD	AAE	AAF	1748	1787	1836
3	PROVOOST SAMUEL	AAD	AAE	AAF	1742	1787	1815
4	MADISON JAMES	AAG	AAD	AAH	1749	1790	1812
5	CLAGGETT THOMAS JOHN	3	1	2	1743	1792	1816
6	SMITH ROBERT	2	3	4	1732	1795	1801
7	BASS EDWARD	2	3	5	1726	1797	1803
8	JARVIS ABRAHAM	2	3	7	1739	1797	1813
9	MOORE BENJAMIN	2	5	8	1748	1801	1816
10	PARKER SAMUEL	2	5	8	1744	1804	1804
11	HOBART JOHN HENRY	2	3	8	1775	1811	1830
12	GRISWOLD ALEXANDER V	2	3	8	1766	1811	1843
13	DEHON THEODORE	2	8	11	1776	1812	1817
14	MOORE RICHARD C	2	11	12	1762	1814	1841
15	KEMP JAMES	2	11	14	1764	1814	1827
16	CROES JOHN	2	11	15	1762	1815	1832
17	BOWEN NATHANIEL	2	11	15	1779	1818	1839
18	CHASE PHILANDER	2	11	15	1775	1819	1852
19	BROWNELL THOMAS C	2	11	12	1779	1819	1865
20	RAVENSCROFT JOHN S	2	12	15	1772	1823	1830
21	ONDERDONK HENRY U	2	11	15	1789	1827	1858
22	MEADE WILLIAM	2	11	12	1789	1829	1862
23	STONE WILLIAM MURRAY	2	14	21	1779	1830	1838
24	ONDERDONK BENJAMIN T	2	19	21	1791	1830	1861
25	IVES LEVI SILLIMAN	2	21	24	1797	1831	1867
26	HOPKINS JOHN HENRY	2	12	17	1792	1832	1868
27	SMITH BENJAMIN B	2	19	21	1794	1832	1884
28	MCILVAINE CHARLES P	2	12	22	1799	1832	1873
29	DOANE GEORGE W	2	24	25	1799	1832	1859
30	OTEY JAMES HERVEY	2	21	24	1800	1834	1863
31	KEMPER JACKSON	2	14	18	1789	1835	1870
32	MCCOSKRY SAMUEL ALLEN	21	29	31	1804	1836	1886
33	POLK LEONIDAS	22	27	28	1806	1838	1864
34	DELANCEY WILLIAM H	12	21	24	1797	1839	1865
35	GADSDEN CHRISTOPHER E	12	29	32	1785	1840	1852
36	WHITTINGHAM WILLIAM R	12	14	24	1805	1840	1879
37	ELLIOT STEPHEN	22	25	35	1806	1841	1866
38	LEE ALFRED	12	14	18	1807	1841	1887
39	JOHNS JOHN	12	22	25	1796	1842	1876
40	EASTBURN MANTON	12	19	24	1801	1842	1872
41	HENSHAW JOHN P K	19	24	26	1792	1843	1852
42	CHASE CARLTON	18	19	24	1794	1844	1870
43	COBBS NICHOLAS HAMNER	18	22	28	1795	1844	1861
44	HAWKS CICERO STEPHENS	18	31	32	1812	1844	1868
45	BOONE WILLIAM JONES	18	29	30	1811	1844	1864
46	FREEMAN GEORGE W	18	31	33	1789	1844	1858
47	SOUTHGATE HORATIO	18	36	37	1812	1844	1894
48	POTTER ALONZO	18	19	29	1800	1845	1865
49	BURGESS GEORGE	18	19	40	1809	1847	1866
50	UPFOLD GEORGE	27	28	31	1796	1849	1872
51	GREEN WILLIAM MERCER	30	33	43	1798	1850	1887
52	PAYNE JOHN	22	38	39	1815	1851	1874
53	RUTLEDGE FRANCIS H	35	37	43	1799	1851	1866
54	WILLIAMS JOHN	19	26	34	1817	1851	1899
55	WHITEHOUSE HENRY JOHN	19	38	40	1803	1851	1874
56	WAINWRIGHT JONATHAN M	19	29	31	1792	1852	1854
57	DAVIS THOMAS F	19	26	27	1804	1853	1871
58	ATKINSON THOMAS	19	28	29	1807	1853	1881
59	KIP WILLIAM INGRAHAM	31	38	45	1811	1853	1893
60	SCOTT THOMAS FIELDING	37	43	57	1807	1854	1867
61	LEE HENRY WASHINGTON	26	32	34	1815	1854	1874
62	POTTER HORATIO	19	26	29	1802	1854	1887
63	CLARK THOMAS MARCH	19	26	29	1812	1854	1903
64	BOWMAN SAMUEL	31	34	38	1800	1858	1861
65	GREGG ALEXANDER	26	27	30	1819	1859	1893
66	ODENHEIMER WILLIAM H	22	32	39	1817	1859	1879

		Consecrators			Born	Cons.	Died
67	BEDELL GREGORY T	22	28	39	1817	1859	1892
68	WHIPPLE HENRY B	31	34	43	1822	1859	1901
69	LAY HENRY C	22	28	33	1823	1859	1885
70	TALBOT JOSEPH C	31	27	44	1816	1860	1883
71	STEVENS WILLIAM B	26	38	48	1815	1862	1887
72	WILMER RICHARD H	22	37	39	1816	1862	1900
73	VAIL THOMAS H	31	55	61	1812	1864	1889
74	COXE ARTHUR CLEVELAND	26	49	58	1818	1865	1896
75	QUINTARD CHARLES T	26	49	58	1824	1865	1898
76	CLARKSON ROBERT H	26	31	32	1826	1865	1884
77	RANDALL GEORGE M	26	27	40	1810	1865	1873
78	KERFOOT JOHN B	26	28	36	1816	1866	1881
79	WILLIAMS CHANNING M	26	38	39	1829	1866	1910
80	WILMER JOSEPH P B	26	51	72	1812	1866	1878
81	CUMMINS GEORGE D	26	27	61	1822	1866	1876
82	ARMITAGE WILLIAM E	31	32	61	1830	1866	1873
83	NEELY HENRY A	26	54	62	1830	1867	1899
84	TUTTLE DANIEL S	26	62	66	1837	1867	1923
85	YOUNG JOHN F	26	52	65	1820	1867	1885
86	BECKWITH JOHN W	51	58	72	1831	1868	1890
87	WHITTLE FRANCIS M	39	38	67	1823	1868	1902
88	BISSELL WILLIAM H A	32	54	62	1814	1868	1893
89	ROBERTSON CHARLES F	27	32	39	1835	1868	1886
90	MORRIS BENJAMIN W	38	66	73	1819	1868	1906
91	LITTLEJOHN ABRAM N	62	39	66	1824	1869	1901
92	DOANE WILLIAM C	62	66	83	1832	1869	1913
93	HUNTINGTON FREDERIC D	27	40	62	1819	1869	1904
94	WHITAKER OZI W	28	38	40	1830	1869	1911
95	PIERCE HENRY N	51	55	72	1820	1870	1899
96	NILES WILLIAM W	27	54	83	1832	1870	1914
97	PINKNEY WILLIAM	27	39	58	1810	1870	1883
98	HOWE WILLIAM B W	27	36	57	1823	1871	1894
99	HOWE MARK A DE W	27	28	38	1809	1871	1895
100	HARE WILLIAM H	27	38	54	1838	1873	1909
101	AUER JOHN GOTTLIEB	27	38	52	1832	1873	1874
102	PADDOCK BENJAMIN H	27	38	54	1828	1873	1891
103	LYMAN THEODORE B	36	58	69	1815	1873	1893
104	SPALDING JOHN F	32	67	70	1828	1873	1902
105	WELLES EDWARD R	27	54	58	1830	1874	1888
106	ELLIOTT ROBERT W B	65	72	75	1840	1874	1887
A	HOLLY JAMES THEODORE	27	38	62	1829	1874	1911
107	WINGFIELD JOHN H D	39	58	69	1833	1874	1898
108	GARRETT ALEXANDER C	76	84	100	1832	1874	1924
109	ADAMS WILLIAM F	51	80	86	1833	1875	1920
110	DUDLEY THOMAS U	27	39	71	1837	1875	1904
111	SCARBOROUGH JOHN	62	71	78	1831	1875	1914
112	GILLESPIE GEORGE D	32	70	88	1819	1875	1909
113	JAGGAR THOMAS A	27	38	62	1839	1875	1912
114	MC LAREN WILLIAM E	32	67	68	1831	1875	1905
115	BROWN JOHN H H	62	88	92	1831	1875	1888
116	PERRY WILLIAM S	71	74	78	1832	1876	1898
117	PENICK CHARLES C	58	87	97	1843	1877	1914
118	SCHERESCHEWSKY SAMUEL	27	62	67	1831	1877	1906
119	BURGESS ALEXANDER	27	54	63	1819	1878	1901
120	PETERKIN GEORGE W	67	78	87	1841	1878	1916
121	SEYMOUR GEORGE F	62	66	69	1829	1878	1906
B	RILEY HENRY CHAUNCEY	38	67	71		1879	1904
122	HARRIS SAMUEL S	72	70	76	1841	1879	1888
123	STARKEY THOMAS A	63	73	91	1818	1880	1903
124	GALLEHER JOHN N	51	71	89	1839	1880	1891
125	DUNLOP GEORGE K	68	89	102	1830	1880	1888
126	BREWER LEGH R	93	84	88	1839	1880	1916
127	PADDOCK JOHN A	27	38	62	1825	1880	1894
128	WHITEHEAD CORTLANDT	71	67	99	1842	1882	1922
129	THOMPSON HUGH M	51	72	122	1830	1883	1902
130	KNICKERBACKER DAVID B	74	89	103	1833	1883	1894
131	POTTER HENRY C	27	54	63	1835	1883	1908
132	RANDOLPH ALFRED M	38	98	110	1836	1883	1918
133	WALKER WILLIAM D	63	74	76	1839	1883	1917
134	WATSON ALFRED A	51	83	98	1818	1884	1905
135	BOONE WILLIAM J	79	AAK	AAL	1846	1884	1891

		Consecrators			Born	Cons.	Died
136	RULISON NELSON S	38	99	114	1842	1884	1897
137	PARET WILLIAM	38	71	99	1826	1885	1911
138	WORTHINGTON GEORGE	74	100	114	1840	1885	1908
139	FERGUSON SAMUEL DAVID	38	71	91	1842	1885	1916
140	WEED EDWIN GARDNER	75	98	106	1847	1886	1924
141	GILBERT MAHLON NORRIS	38	67	68	1848	1886	1900
142	THOMAS ELISHA SMITH	68	73	84	1834	1887	1895
143	TALBOT ETHELBERT	68	73	84	1848	1887	1928
144	JOHNSTON JAMES S	72	110	122	1843	1888	1924
145	LEONARD ABIEL	73	75	84	1848	1888	1903
146	COLEMAN LEIGHTON	99	94	109	1837	1888	1907
147	KENDRICK JOHN MILLS	84	110	130	1836	1889	1911
148	VINCENT BOYD	104	110	117	1845	1889	1935
149	KNIGHT CYRUS F	114	116	119	1831	1889	1891
150	GRAFTON CHARLES C	114	119	121	1832	1889	1912
151	LEONARD WILLIAM A	54	68	92	1848	1889	1930
152	DAVIES THOMAS F	54	68	84	1831	1889	1905
153	GRAVES ANSON ROGERS	84	100	119	1842	1890	1931
154	NICHOLS WILLIAM FORD	54	75	83	1849	1890	1924
155	ATWILL EDWARD ROBERT	84	114	121	1840	1890	1911
156	JACKSON HENRY M	72	98	120	1848	1891	1900
157	SESSUMS DAVIS	75	84	108	1858	1891	1929
158	BROOKS PHILLIPS	54	63	68	1835	1891	1893
159	NICHOLSON ISAAC LEA	114	94	109	1844	1891	1906
160	NELSON CLELAND K	75	98	103	1852	1892	1917
161	HALE CHARLES REUBEN	116	121	133	1837	1892	1900
162	KINSOLVING GEORGE H	72	75	94	1849	1892	1928
163	WELLS LEMUEL HENRY	54	83	90	1841	1892	1936
164	GRAY WILLIAM CRANE	75	110	140	1835	1892	1919
165	BROOKE FRANCIS KEY	84	95	104	1852	1893	1918
166	BARKER WILLIAM MORRIS	90	104	114	1854	1893	1901
167	MCKIM JOHN	91	103	110	1852	1893	1936
168	GRAVES FREDERICK R	91	103	110	1858	1893	1940
169	CAPERS ELLISON	103	134	140	1837	1893	1908
170	GAILOR THOMAS FRANK	75	110	116	1856	1893	1935
171	LAWRENCE WILLIAM	54	63	83	1850	1893	1941
172	CHESHIRE JOSEPH B	103	134	169	1850	1893	1932
173	HALL ARTHUR CRAWSHAY	83	96	146	1847	1894	1930
174	NEWTON JOHN B	87	110	120	1839	1894	1897
175	WHITE JOHN HAZEN	84	114	128	1849	1895	1925
176	MILLSPAUGH FRANK R	68	84	104	1848	1895	1916
177	ROWE PETER TRIMBLE	92	94	123	1856	1895	1942
178	BURTON LEWIS WILLIAM	110	120	132	1852	1896	1940
179	JOHNSON JOSEPH H	152	138	143	1847	1896	1928
180	SATTERLEE HENRY YATES	74	93	110	1843	1896	1908
181	WILLIAMS GERSHOM MOTT	84	75	114	1857	1896	1923
182	MORRISON JAMES DOW	92	93	111	1844	1897	1934
183	BREWSTER CHAUNCEY B	91	92	94	1848	1897	1941
184	GIBSON ROBERT A	87	117	120	1846	1897	1919
185	MC VICKAR WILLIAM N	92	94	113	1843	1898	1910
186	BROWN WILLIAM M	114	121	128	1855	1898	1937
187	HORNER JUNIUS MOORE	172	134	169	1859	1898	1933
C	KINSOLVING LUCIEN LEE	110	92	111	1862	1899	1929
188	MORELAND WILLIAM HALL	154	145	147	1861	1899	1946
189	EDSALL SAMUEL COOK	114	121	133	1860	1899	1917
190	MORRISON THEODORE N	114	121	133	1850	1899	1929
191	FUNSTEN JAMES BOWEN	84	94	117	1856	1899	1918
192	FRANCIS JOSEPH M	114	121	152	1862	1899	1939
193	WILLIAMS ARTHUR L	138	104	153	1853	1899	1919
194	GRAVATT WILLIAM L	87	117	120	1858	1899	1942
195	PARTRIDGE SIDNEY C	167	118	168	1857	1900	1930
196	CODMAN ROBERT	96	92	93	1859	1900	1915
197	ANDERSON CHARLES P	114	112	121	1863	1900	1930
198	BARNWELL ROBERT W	129	140	144	1849	1900	1902
199	WELLER REGINALD H	150	114	159	1857	1900	1935
200	TAYLOR FREDERICK W	121	150	159	1853	1901	1903
201	MANN CAMERON	84	143	155	1851	1901	1932
202	BRENT CHARLES H	92	131	171	1862	1901	1929
203	KEATOR FREDERIC W	114	100	159	1855	1902	1924
204	BURGESS FREDERICK	131	92	111	1853	1902	1925
205	INGLE JAMES A	168	167	195	1867	1902	1903

		Consecrators			Born	Cons.	Died
206	VINTON ALEXANDER H	152	93	173	1852	1902	1911
207	OLMSTED CHARLES S	84	144	145	1853	1902	1918
208	MACKAY SMITH A	92	111	128	1850	1902	1911
209	VAN BUREN JAMES H	120	171	173	1850	1902	1917
210	RESTARICK HENRY B	154	113	147	1854	1902	1933
211	OLMSTED CHARLES T	93	96	131	1842	1902	1924
212	BECKWITH CHARLES M	110	108	157	1851	1902	1928
213	GRISWOLD SHELDON M	92	121	133	1861	1903	1930
214	BRATTON THEODORE D	110	140	144	1862	1903	1944
215	LINES EDWIN S	84	92	111	1845	1903	1927
216	FAWCETT EDWARD	84	121	150	1865	1904	1935
217	GREER DAVID H	131	92	94	1844	1904	1919
218	NELSON RICHARD H	92	94	133	1859	1904	1931
219	OSBORNE EDWARD W	121	131	150	1845	1904	1926
220	STRANGE ROBERT	169	132	172	1857	1904	1914
221	ROOTS LOGAN H	168	167	171	1870	1904	1945
222	SPALDING FRANKLIN S	84	94	111	1865	1904	1914
223	AVES HENRY D	108	144	157	1853	1904	1936
224	KNIGHT ALBION W	84	140	157	1859	1904	1936
225	WOODCOCK CHARLES E	84	121	138	1854	1905	1940
226	DARLINGTON JAMES H	94	121	128	1856	1905	1930
227	JOHNSON FREDERIC F	84	94	113	1866	1905	1943
228	WILLIAMS CHARLES D	84	113	148	1860	1906	1923
229	PARKER EDWARD M	96	171	173	1855	1906	1925
230	MC CORMICK JOHN N	84	112	160	1863	1906	1939
231	WEBB WILLIAM W	159	150	175	1857	1906	1933
232	SCADDING CHARLES	84	121	128	1861	1906	1914
233	TUCKER BEVERLEY D	132	120	172	1846	1906	1930
234	GUERRY WILLIAM A	84	140	170	1861	1907	1928
235	PADDOCK ROBERT L	84	131	180	1869	1907	1939
236	KNIGHT EDWARD J	111	143	208	1864	1907	1908
237	ROBINSON HENRY D	84	150	189	1859	1908	1913
238	REESE FREDERICK F	160	140	170	1854	1908	1936
239	KINSMAN FREDERICK J	84	94	96	1868	1908	1944
240	HARDING ALFRED	84	109	111	1852	1909	1923
241	THOMAS NATHANIEL S	84	94	111	1867	1909	1937
242	BREWSTER BENJAMIN	84	154	183	1860	1909	1941
243	MURRAY JOHN G	137	109	132	1857	1909	1929
244	LLOYD ARTHUR S	84	120	132	1857	1909	1936
245	BEECHER GEORGE A	84	108	153	1868	1910	1951
246	TEMPLE EDWARD A	84	108	144	1867	1910	1924
247	PERRY JAMES D	84	126	171	1871	1911	1947
248	ATWOOD JULIUS W	171	173	183	1857	1911	1945
249	THURSTON THEODORE P	84	126	165	1867	1911	1941
250	SANFORD LOUIS C	154	179	188	1867	1911	1948
251	BURCH CHARLES S	217	92	111	1855	1911	1920
252	ISRAEL ROGERS	128	143	148	1854	1911	1921
253	WINCHESTER JAMES R	84	140	162	1852	1911	1941
254	DAVIES THOMAS F	84	171	183	1872	1911	1936
255	RHINELANDER PHILIP M	84	128	171	1869	1911	1939
256	GARLAND THOMAS J	84	111	128	1866	1911	1931
257	TOLL WILLIAM E	84	151	175	1843	1911	1915
258	TUCKER HENRY ST G	167	AAM	AAN	1874	1912	1959
259	HUNTINGTON DANIEL T	168	221	AAO	1868	1912	1950
260	BILLER GEORGE JR	84	126	165	1874	1912	1915
261	LONGLEY HARRY S	84	190	193	1868	1912	1944
262	MC ELWAIN FRANK A	84	189	193	1875	1912	1957
263	WEEKS WILLIAM F	173	218	229	1859	1913	1914
264	REESE THEODORE I	148	151	171	1873	1913	1931
265	BABCOCK SAMUEL G	171	196	202	1851	1913	1942
266	COLMORE CHARLES B	84	140	170	1879	1913	1950
267	TYLER JOHN P	84	120	132	1862	1914	1931
268	DU MOULIN FRANK	151	128	148	1870	1914	1947
269	HOWDEN FREDERICK S	84	143	148	1869	1914	1940
270	CAPERS WILLIAM T	84	140	144	1867	1914	1943
271	BROWN WILLIAM C	84	132	184	1861	1914	1927
272	FABER WILLIAM F	84	126	151	1860	1914	1934
273	HUNTING GEORGE C	84	154	179	1871	1914	1924
274	JONES PAUL	84	154	179	1880	1914	1941
275	DARST THOMAS C	84	172	187	1875	1915	1948
276	SUMNER WALTER T	197	151	175	1873	1915	1935

		Consecrators			Born	Cons.	Died
277	HULSE HIRAM RICHARD	217	151	163	1868	1915	1938
278	MATTHEWS PAUL	148	151	192	1866	1915	1954
279	PAGE HERMAN	84	163	171	1866	1915	1942
280	BLISS GEORGE YEMENS	173	196	229	1864	1915	1924
281	FISKE CHARLES	84	199	211	1868	1915	1942
282	STEARLY WILSON REIFF	215	128	143	1869	1915	1941
283	ACHESON EDWARD C	183	171	215	1858	1915	1934
284	WISE JAMES	84	162	177	1875	1916	1939
285	BURLESON HUGH LATIMER	84	171	189	1865	1916	1933
286	JOHNSON IRVING PEAKE	84	189	193	1866	1917	1947
287	TOURET FRANK HALE	84	270	272	1875	1917	1945
288	SHERWOOD GRANVILLE H	84	190	193	1878	1917	1923
289	SAPHORE EDWIN W	84	162	195	1854	1917	1944
290	THOMSON ARTHUR C	84	132	172	1871	1917	1946
291	MOORE HARRY TUNIS	84	108	162	1874	1917	1955
292	MIKELL HENRY JUDAH	170	140	164	1873	1917	1942
293	REMINGTON WILLIAM P	84	228	249	1879	1918	1963
294	SAGE JOHN CHARLES	84	190	193	1866	1918	1919
295	HARRIS ROBERT LE ROY	84	151	175	1874	1918	1948
296	DEMBY EDWARD THOMAS	84	170	195	1869	1918	1957
297	QUIN CLINTON SIMON	84	223	225	1883	1918	1956
298	DELANY HENRY B	172	233	275	1858	1918	1928
299	GREEN WILLIAM M	84	157	170	1876	1919	1942
300	SHAYLER ERNEST V	203	163	272	1868	1919	1947
301	BEATTY TROY	84	170	253	1866	1919	1922
302	PARSONS EDWARD L	154	179	188	1868	1919	1960
303	OVERS WALTER H	84	226	252	1870	1919	1934
304	MORRIS JAMES C	84	170	224	1870	1920	1944
305	MOSHER GOUVERNEUR F	168	259	258	1871	1920	1941
306	JETT ROBERT C	84	233	194	1865	1920	1950
307	MOULTON ARTHUR W	84	171	173	1873	1920	1962
308	DAVENPORT GEORGE W	84	233	151	1870	1920	1956
309	STEVENS WILLIAM B	179	154	167	1884	1920	1947
310	FERRIS DAVID L	202	128	173	1864	1920	1947
311	COOK PHILIP	84	143	201	1875	1920	1938
312	FOX HERBERT H H	84	184	262	1871	1920	1943
313	BENNETT GRANVILLE G	84	151	192	1882	1920	1975
314	MIZE ROBERT HERBERT	84	213	245	1870	1921	1956
315	FINLAY KIRKMAN GEORGE	234	172	238	1877	1921	1938
316	MANNING WILLIAM T	84	148	171	1866	1921	1949
317	INGLEY FRED	84	286	128	1878	1921	1951
318	GARDINER THEOPHILUS M	84	170	244	1870	1921	1941
319	LA MOTHE JOHN D	84	243	233	1868	1921	1928
320	WARD JOHN C	84	128	148	1873	1921	1949
321	SHIPMAN HERBERT	84	316	215	1869	1921	1930
322	PENICK EDWIN A	172	234	275	1887	1922	1959
323	MAXON JAMES M	170	216	225	1875	1922	1948
324	MC DOWELL WILLIAM G	170	210	233	1882	1922	1938
325	OLDHAM GEORGE A	218	151	316	1877	1922	1963
326	SLATTERY CHARLES L	171	233	265	1867	1922	1930
327	ROBERTS WILLIAM BLAIR	84	285	286	1881	1922	1964
328	CARSON HARRY R	84	170	316	1869	1923	1948
329	MANN ALEXANDER	201	171	215	1860	1923	1948
330	FREEMAN JAMES E	170	171	243	1866	1923	1943
331	STRIDER ROBERT E L	194	271	329	1887	1923	1969
332	STERRETT FRANK W	143	226	194	1885	1923	1976
D	FERRANDO MANUEL	170	316	244	1866	1923	1934
333	REIFSNIDER CHARLES S	167	179	151	1875	1924	1958
334	CROSS EDWARD MAKIN	262	261	330	1880	1924	1965
335	WHITE JOHN CHANLER	143	216	197	1867	1924	1956
336	COLEY EDWARD H	143	244	310	1861	1924	1949
337	JUHAN FRANK A	143	253	315	1887	1924	1967
338	SEAMAN EUGENE CECIL	170	162	270	1881	1925	1950
339	BOOTH SAMUEL B	173	229	247	1883	1925	1935
340	GILMAN ALFRED A	168	259	221	1878	1925	1966
341	ROGERS WARREN L	151	279	148	1877	1925	1938
342	GRAY CAMPBELL	199	216	231	1879	1925	1944
343	IVINS BENJAMIN F P	231	199	213	1884	1925	1962
344	HUSTON SIMEON A	162	270	309	1876	1925	1963
345	WING JOHN D	201	238	170	1882	1925	1960
346	STIRES ERNEST M	143	243	316	1866	1925	1951

		Consecrators			Born	Cons.	Died
347	CAMPBELL ROBERT E	143	170	303	1884	1925	1977
348	THOMAS WILLIAM M M	143	172	C	1878	1925	1951
349	BARNWELL MIDDLETON S	143	170	212	1882	1925	1957
350	MITCHELL WALTER	243	278	248	1876	1926	1971
351	CREIGHTON FRANK W	243	218	256	1879	1926	1948
352	NICHOLS SHIRLEY HALL	167	333	AAN	1884	1926	1964
353	DALLAS JOHN T	243	173	171	1880	1926	1961
354	HELFENSTEIN EDWARD T	243	194	233	1865	1926	1947
355	CASADY THOMAS	243	190	245	1881	1927	1958
356	THOMAS ALBERT S	243	172	214	1873	1928	1967
357	BINSTED NORMAN S	243	167	258	1890	1928	1961
358	JENKINS THOMAS	243	177	250	1871	1929	1955
359	LARNED JOHN I B	243	177	250	1883	1929	1955
360	WILSON FRANK E	243	170	197	1885	1929	1944
361	ABBOTT HENRY P A	243	178	225	1881	1929	1945
362	TAITT FRANCIS M	256	226	241	1862	1929	1943
363	STURTEVANT HARWOOD	199	213	231	1888	1929	1977
364	SCHMUCK ELMER N	197	238	241	1882	1929	1936
365	DAVIS CAMERON J	310	281	285	1873	1930	1952
366	LITTELL SAMUEL H	285	167	210	1873	1930	1967
367	ABLEWHITE HAYWARD S	285	230	279	1887	1930	1964
368	HOBSON HENRY W	148	151	194	1891	1930	1983
369	SCARLETT WILLIAM	148	227	248	1883	1930	1973
370	GOODEN ROBERT B	309	188	250	1874	1930	1976
371	STEWART GEORGE C	247	213	225	1879	1930	1940
372	SHERRILL HENRY KNOX	247	171	221	1890	1930	1980
373	GOODWIN FREDERICK D	258	194	244	1888	1930	1968
374	GILBERT CHARLES K	247	224	244	1878	1930	1958
375	SPENCER ROBERT N	270	216	227	1877	1930	1961
376	KEMERER BENJAMIN T	269	230	262	1874	1930	1960
377	WYATT BROWN HUNTER	247	310	320	1884	1931	1952
378	KEELER STEPHEN E	269	230	262	1887	1931	1956
379	BENTLEY JOHN B	247	170	177	1896	1931	1989
380	SALINAS Y VELASCO E	247	170	244	1886	1931	1968
381	BUDLONG FREDERICK G	247	183	242	1881	1931	1953
382	BARTLETT FREDERICK B	285	250	317	1882	1931	1941
383	WASHBURN BENJAMIN M	247	224	244	1887	1932	1966
384	URBAN RALPH E	247	224	278	1875	1932	1935
385	PORTER ARCHIE W N	188	250	302	1885	1933	1963
386	GRIBBIN ROBERT E	247	322	275	1887	1934	1976
387	NICHOLS JOHN WILLIAMS	AAI	168	340	1878	1934	1940
388	LUDLOW THEODORE R	247	282	311	1883	1936	1961
389	DAGWELL BENJAMIN D	278	177	250	1890	1936	1963
390	KROLL LEOPOLD	247	244	316	1874	1936	1946
391	VAN DYCK VEDDER	247	353	372	1889	1936	1960
392	REINHEIMER BARTEL H	247	281	310	1889	1936	1949
393	CLINGMAN CHARLES	247	178	225	1883	1936	1971
394	WHITTEMORE LEWIS B	247	230	342	1885	1936	1965
395	GARDNER WALLACE J	278	188	311	1883	1936	1954
396	ESSEX WILLIAM L	247	192	261	1886	1936	1959
397	ZIEGLER WINFRED H	371	177	245	1885	1936	1972
398	LAWRENCE WILLIAM A	171	247	242	1889	1937	1968
399	BEAL HARRY	309	250	370	1885	1937	1944
400	ATWILL DOUGLASS H	378	261	262	1881	1937	1960
401	FENNER GOODRICH R	284	270	286	1891	1937	1966
402	ROBERTS WILLIAM P	AAI	168	AAJ	1888	1937	1971
403	WILNER ROBERT F	305	333	AAK	1889	1938	1960
404	HERON RAYMOND A	258	171	242	1886	1938	1960
405	BROWN WILLIAM A	258	275	306	1878	1938	1965
406	CARPENTER CHARLES C J	258	214	270	1899	1938	1969
407	DANDRIDGE EDMUND P	258	214	266	1881	1938	1961
408	PHILLIPS HENRY D	258	275	292	1882	1938	1955
409	TUCKER BEVERLEY D	258	194	275	1882	1938	1969
410	PEABODY MALCOLM E	258	248	307	1888	1938	1974
411	BLOCK KARL M	302	309	358	1886	1938	1958
412	MITCHELL RICHARD B	350	214	289	1887	1938	1961
413	KIRCHHOFFER RICHARD A	258	342	349	1890	1939	1977
414	MC KINSTRY ARTHUR R	258	309	320	1894	1939	1991
415	BLANKINGSHIP A H	258	266	328	1894	1939	1975
416	BURTON SPENCE	258	247	286	1881	1939	1966
417	GRAVATT JOHN J	258	194	275	1881	1939	1965

		Consecrators			Born	Cons.	Died
418	MC CLELLAND WILLIAM	258	268	308	1883	1939	1949
419	DANIELS HENRY HEAN	312	307	344	1885	1939	1958
420	RANDALL EDWIN J	258	177	262	1869	1939	1962
421	BRINKER HOWARD R	258	245	300	1893	1940	1965
422	PITHAN ATHALICIO T	348	380	415	1898	1940	1966
423	JACKSON JOHN L	258	275	292	1884	1940	1948
424	GRAY WALTER H	258	247	381	1898	1940	1973
425	CRAIGHILL LLOYD R	402	AAI	AAL	1886	1940	1971
426	CONKLING WALLACE E	258	347	395	1896	1941	1979
427	LORING OLIVER L	258	247	391	1904	1941	1979
428	POWELL NOBLE C	258	354	330	1891	1941	1968
429	STONEY JAMES M	258	406	412	1888	1942	1965
430	RHEA FRANK A	307	334	358	1887	1942	1963
431	DE WOLFE JAMES P	258	316	346	1895	1942	1966
432	LEWIS WILLIAM F	258	307	358	1902	1942	1964
433	MASON WILEY R	258	306	373	1879	1942	1967
434	WALKER JOHN M	258	337	412	1888	1942	1951
435	HART OLIVER J	258	330	362	1892	1942	1977
436	PAGE HERMAN R	258	351	394	1892	1942	1977
437	GRAY DUNCAN M	258	214	412	1898	1943	1966
438	HEISTAND JOHN T	258	332	435	1895	1943	1979
439	WROTH EDWARD P	258	329	331	1889	1943	1946
440	JONES EVERETT H	258	401	414	1902	1943	1995
441	VOEGELI CHARLES A	258	325	383	1904	1943	1984
442	BOYNTON CHARLES F	266	343	395	1906	1944	1999
443	WALTERS SUMNER F D	258	250	309	1898	1944	1979
444	KENNEDY HARRY S	258	317	350	1901	1944	1986
445	PARDUE AUSTIN	258	365	421	1899	1944	1981
446	DUN ANGUS	258	372	368	1892	1944	1971
447	CARRUTHERS THOMAS N	258	323	356	1900	1944	1960
448	HAINES ELWOOD L	258	406	423	1893	1944	1949
449	HORSTICK WILLIAM W	258	363	420	1902	1944	1973
450	MALLETT JAMES R	343	363	395	1893	1944	1965
451	HARRIS BRAVID W	258	405	322	1896	1945	1965
452	GESNER CONRAD H	258	327	378	1901	1945	1993
453	ALDRICH DONALD B	258	251	374	1892	1945	1961
454	GOODEN REGINALD H	258	370	415	1910	1945	2003
455	LOUTTIT HENRY I	345	350	416	1903	1945	1984
456	KINSOLVING II ARTHUR	258	350	409	1894	1945	1964
457	BARRY FREDERICK L	258	325	346	1897	1945	1960
458	MASON CHARLES A	258	291	426	1904	1945	1970
459	BANYARD ALFRED L	258	383	395	1908	1945	1992
460	WRIGHT THOMAS H	258	275	428	1904	1945	1997
461	HINES JOHN E	258	297	411	1910	1945	1997
462	MOODY WILLIAM R	258	393	368	1900	1945	1986
463	EMRICH RICHARD S M	258	262	351	1910	1946	1997
464	SAWYER HAROLD E	258	320	410	1890	1946	1969
465	BARTON Ln W	258	368	378	1899	1946	1997
466	QUARTERMAN GEORGE H	258	355	401	1906	1946	2002
467	CLARK STEPHEN C	258	307	309	1892	1946	1950
468	NASH NORMAN B	372	353	398	1888	1947	1963
469	BAYNE JR STEPHEN F	372	344	424	1908	1947	1974
470	BOWEN HAROLD L	372	317	426	1886	1947	1967
471	LORING JR RICHARD T	372	335	426	1900	1947	1948
472	DONEGAN HORACE W B	372	374	468	1900	1947	1991
473	GUNN GEORGE P	372	306	405	1903	1948	1973
474	HALL CHARLES F	372	353	468	1908	1948	1992
475	MELCHER LOUIS C	372	407	417	1898	1948	1965
476	HUNTER JAMES W	372	397	440	1904	1948	1987
477	BLOY FRANCIS E I	258	302	370	1904	1948	1993
478	SCAIFE LAURISTON L	372	365	420	1907	1948	1970
479	GORDON JR WILLIAM J	372	322	379	1918	1948	1994
480	HUBBARD RUSSELL S	343	335	445	1902	1948	1972
481	CLOUGH CHARLES A	343	335	427	1903	1948	1961
482	BARTH THEODORE N	372	323	407	1898	1948	1961
483	HENRY MATTHEW G	258	408	447	1910	1948	1975
484	WEST EDWARD H	372	337	349	1906	1948	1977
485	HIGLEY WALTER M	372	336	410	1899	1948	1969
486	SHERMAN JONATHAN G	372	394	431	1907	1949	1989
487	CAMPBELL DONALD J	372	302	477	1903	1949	1973
488	JONES GIRAULT M	372	337	417	1904	1949	1998

		Consecrators			Born	Cons.	Died
489	CLAIBORNE RANDOLPH R	258	406	428	1906	1949	1986
490	GIBSON JR ROBERT F	258	373	433	1906	1949	1990
491	ARMSTRONG JOSEPH G	372	293	435	1901	1949	1964
492	St CHARLES L	372	343	426	1891	1949	1968
493	MILLER ALLEN J	428	446	464	1901	1949	1991
494	BURROUGHS NELSON M	258	368	408	1899	1949	1998
495	KRISCHKE EGMONT M	475	379	422	1909	1950	1972
496	STARK DUDLEY S	372	368	378	1894	1950	1971
497	WELLES EDWARD R	372	375	428	1907	1950	1991
498	SMITH GORDON V	372	327	394	1906	1950	1997
499	CAMPBELL WILBURN C	258	331	373	1910	1950	1997
500	BURRILL G FRANCIS	258	291	432	1906	1950	2001
501	SHIRES HENRY H	372	370	411	1886	1950	1961
502	BAKER RICHARD H	372	322	428	1897	1951	1981
503	LICHTENBERGER A C	372	340	369	1900	1951	1968
504	HATCH ROBERT M	372	381	424	1910	1951	2009
505	WATSON RICHARD S	372	307	430	1902	1951	1987
506	SWIFT A ERVINE	372	379	442	1913	1951	2003
507	EMERY RICHARD R	372	378	400	1910	1951	1964
508	RICHARDS DAVID E	372	347	451	1921	1951	
509	BRAM MARTIN J	455	458	416	1897	1951	1956
510	POWELL CHILTON	372	355	421	1911	1951	1994
511	WALTHOUR JOHN B	372	322	435	1904	1952	1952
512	HALLOCK DONALD H V	343	426	363	1908	1952	1996
513	KELLOGG HAMILTON H	372	297	378	1899	1952	1977
514	CRITTENDEN WILLIAM	372	368	409	1908	1952	2003
515	NOLAND IVESON B	488	412	437	1916	1952	1975
516	OGILBY LYMAN C	357	403	424	1922	1953	1990
517	HIGGINS JOHN S	372	313	378	1904	1953	1992
518	WARNECKE FREDERICK J	372	332	383	1906	1953	1977
519	BRADY WILLIAM H	363	481	343	1912	1953	1996
520	STARK LELAND	372	378	383	1907	1953	1986
521	MURRAY GEORGE M	406	393	498	1919	1953	2006
522	MC NEIL DUDLEY B	372	394	470	1908	1953	1977
523	THOMAS WILLIAM S	445	435	478	1901	1953	1986
524	COLE CLARENCE ALFRED	322	417	447	1909	1953	1963
525	KINSOLVING III C J	429	401	456	1904	1953	1984
526	MOSLEY J BROOKE	372	368	414	1915	1953	1988
527	MARMION CHARLES G	372	393	458	1905	1954	2000
528	MARMION WILLIAM H	372	408	414	1907	1954	2002
529	HARTE JOSEPH M	500	297	510	1914	1954	1999
530	MINNIS JOSEPH S	470	421	449	1904	1954	1977
531	CROWLEY ARCHIE H	372	436	468	1907	1954	1996
532	STUART ALBERT R	372	347	488	1906	1954	1973
533	STOKES JR ANSON P	372	368	468	1905	1954	1986
534	VANDERHORST JOHN	372	407	482	1912	1955	1980
535	DOLL HARRY L	372	373	428	1903	1955	1984
536	DICUS RICHARD E	440	350	412	1910	1955	1996
537	GODDARD FREDERICK P	297	440	461	1903	1955	1983
538	BROWN ROBERT R	412	414	373	1910	1955	1994
539	LEWIS ARNOLD M	372	337	484	1904	1956	1994
540	CARMAN JAMES W F	372	389	293	1903	1956	1979
541	HONAMAN EARL M	372	438	435	1904	1956	1982
542	SIMOES PLINIO L	475	379	495	1915	1956	1994
543	TURNER EDWARD C	401	470	421	1915	1956	1997
544	CLEMENTS JAMES P	372	297	461	1911	1956	1977
545	MOSES WILLIAM F	372	455	345	1898	1956	1961
546	STERLING CHANDLER W	419	421	530	1911	1956	1984
547	LAWRENCE FREDERIC C	372	398	533	1899	1956	1989
548	FOOTE NORMAN L	372	430	449	1915	1957	1974
549	CRAINE JOHN P	413	411	368	1911	1957	1977
550	HADEN CLARENCE R	372	385	497	1910	1957	2000
551	SAUCEDO JOSE G	372	380	440	1924	1958	
552	MC NAIRY PHILIP F	372	368	513	1911	1958	1989
553	ESQUIROL JOHN HENRY	372	424	504	1900	1958	1970
554	CORRIGAN DANIEL	372	530	449	1900	1958	1994
555	PIKE JAMES ALBERT	372	302	472	1913	1958	1969
556	ROSE DAVID S	372	473	405	1913	1958	1997
557	LICKFIELD FRANCIS W	500	396	519	1908	1958	1997
558	MACADIE DONALD	383	520	503	1899	1958	1963
559	BLANCHARD ROGER W	372	368	484	1909	1958	1998

		Consecrators			Born	Cons.	Died
560	SHERRILL EDMUND K	372	495	542	1925	1959	
561	BROWN ALLEN W	503	457	410	1908	1959	1990
562	CABANBAN BENITO C	516	444	587	1911	1959	1990
563	CADIGAN GEORGE L	503	496	538	1910	1959	2005
564	CREIGHTON WILLIAM F	503	446	480	1909	1959	1987
565	MILLARD G RICHARD	503	432	443	1914	1960	
566	WRIGHT WILLIAM G	503	432	443	1904	1960	1973
567	BENNISON SR CHARLES E	503	394	470	1917	1960	2004
568	KELLOGG PAUL A	503	441	506	1910	1960	1999
569	WETMORE JAMES STUART	503	472	478	1915	1960	1999
570	CURTIS IVOL I	503	370	477	1908	1960	1994
571	CHILTON SAMUEL B	503	373	490	1900	1960	1984
572	FRASER JR THOMAS A	503	373	502	1915	1960	1989
573	DE WITT ROBERT L	503	446	468	1916	1960	2003
574	THAYER EDWIN B	530	470	498	1905	1960	1989
575	TEMPLE GRAY	503	424	427	1914	1961	1999
576	BUTTERFIELD HARVEY D	503	424	427	1908	1961	1998
577	RAUSCHER RUSSELL T	503	421	510	1908	1961	1989
578	GILSON CHARLES P	503	444	402	1899	1961	1980
579	GONZALEZ AGUEROS R	503	415	379	1906	1961	1966
580	BROWN JR DILLARD H	503	446	564	1912	1961	1969
581	ALLIN JOHN M	503	488	437	1921	1961	1998
582	HUTCHENS JOSEPH W	424	427	553	1913	1961	1979
583	DUNCAN JAMES L	503	455	534	1913	1961	2000
584	HARGRAVE WILLIAM L	503	455	424	1903	1961	1975
585	MAC LEAN CHARLES W	431	472	486	1903	1962	1985
586	SANDERS WILLIAM E	503	534	532	1919	1962	
587	MONTGOMERY JAMES WINCHESTER	503	500	492	1921	1962	
588	CHAMBERS ALBERT A	503	472	450	1906	1962	1993
589	MCCREA THEODORE H	503	458	500	1908	1962	1986
590	BURGESS JOHN MELVILLE	503	526	446	1909	1962	2003
591	LONGID EDWARD G	503	516	533	1908	1963	1993
592	PERSELL JR CHARLES B	503	561	478	1909	1963	1988
593	MILLS CEDRIC EARL	428	379	506	1903	1963	1992
594	BARRETT GEORGE W	472	496	554	1908	1963	2000
595	PUTNAM JR FREDERICK W	538	510	543	1917	1963	2007
596	KLEIN WALTER C	450	500	549	1904	1963	1980
597	PINCKNEY JOHN A	483	356	417	1905	1963	1972
598	MOORE JR PAUL	503	549	564	1919	1964	2003
599	ROMERO LEONARDO	503	551	506	1930	1964	1986
600	SAUCEDO MELCHOR	503	551	506	1920	1964	
601	RATH GEORGE E	503	472	520	1913	1964	1995
602	COLE JR NED	503	410	485	1917	1964	2000
603	REED DAVID B	503	454	529	1927	1964	
604	BAILEY SCOTT FIELD	461	466	537	1916	1964	2005
605	MYERS C KILMER	549	463	531	1914	1964	1981
606	RUSACK ROBERT C	477	370	570	1926	1964	1986
607	SELWAY GEORGE R	549	529	436	1905	1964	1989
608	REUS FROYLAN F	503	506	442	1919	1964	2008
609	WONG JAMES CHANG L	AAK	AAO	AAP		1960	1970
610	MASUDA GEORGE T	452	476	546	1913	1965	1995
611	RICHARDSON J MILTON	461	604	537	1913	1965	1980
612	GROSS HAL R	461	540	550	1914	1965	2002
613	DAVIDSON WILLIAM	461	466	610	1919	1966	2006
614	VAN DUZER ALBERT W	461	459	486	1917	1966	1999
615	GATES JR WILLIAM F	461	534	586	1912	1966	1987
616	BARNDS WILLIAM PAUL	461	458	589	1904	1966	1973
617	STEVENSON DEAN T	461	438	518	1915	1966	1994
618	HALL ROBERT BRUCE	461	490	500	1921	1966	1985
619	TAYLOR GEORGE A	461	493	414	1903	1966	1978
620	MARTIN RICHARD B	461	486	478	1913	1967	2012
621	BURT JOHN HARRIS	461	494	409	1918	1967	2009
622	MOORE JR WILLIAM M	532	572	502	1916	1967	1998
623	WYATT JOHN R	461	529	605	1913	1967	2004
624	SPEARS JR ROBERT R	461	472	497	1918	1967	2008
625	WOOD JR MILTON L	461	406	489	1922	1967	2015
626	KELLER CHRISTOPH JR	461	581	538	1916	1967	1995
627	FREY WILLIAM C	461	508	608	1930	1967	
628	MCNAIR EDWARD	461	477	550	1913	1967	1986
629	HANCHETT EDWIN LANI	461	444	540	1919	1967	1975
630	BROWNING EDMOND LEE	461	AAQ	444	1929	1968	

		Consecrators			Born	Cons.	Died
631	APPLEYARD ROBERT B	461	445	523	1917	1968	1999
632	ROBINSON HAROLD B	461	478	AAR	1922	1968	1994
633	GOSNELL HAROLD C	461	440	494	1908	1968	1999
634	GILLIAM JACKSON EARL	461	521	546	1920	1968	2000
635	RIVERA VICTOR MANUEL	461	443	570	1916	1968	2005
636	ELEBASH HUNLEY AGEE	461	460	484	1923	1968	1993
637	WOLF FREDERICK BARTO	461	424	517	1922	1968	1998
638	MEAD WILLIAM HENRY	461	414	526	1921	1968	1974
639	LEIGHTON DAVID K SR	461	535	523	1922	1968	2013
640	HAYNSWORTH GEORGE E	608	508	510	1925	1969	2012
641	RAMOS JOSE ANTONIO	461	608	508	1937	1969	
642	MANGURAMAS C B	562	591	630	1933	1969	
643	SPOFFORD WILLIAM B J	461	548	465	1921	1969	2013
644	THORNBERRY DAVID R	461	368	476	1911	1969	1995
645	ATKINS STANLEY H	449	512	519	1912	1969	1996
646	REEVES GEORGE PAUL	532	455	Nassau	1918	1969	2010
647	SMITH PHILIP A	461	490	618	1920	1970	2010
648	FOLWELL WILLIAM H	455	583	646	1924	1970	
649	HOSEA ADDISON	462	527	488	1914	1970	1986
650	DAVIES A DONALD	461	577	581	1920	1970	
651	JONES WALTER H	498	452	610	1925	1970	2003
652	BROWNE GEORGE D	461	520	441	1933	1970	1993
653	STEWART ALEXANDER D	461	590	504	1926	1970	1999
654	GRESSLE LLOYD EDGAR	461	526	518	1918	1970	1999
655	PONG JAMES T M	461	AAK	AAJ	1911	1971	1988
656	HOBGOOD CLARENCE E	461	539	572	1914	1971	2008
657	CACERES V ADRIAN D	461	627	600	1922	1971	2006
658	STOUGH FURMAN C	461	521	581	1928	1971	2004
659	KRUMM JOHN MC GILL	461	474	559	1913	1971	1995
660	GARNIER LUC A J	461	527	620	1928	1971	1999
661	VARLEY ROBERT P	461	577	619	1921	1971	2000
662	VOGEL ARTHUR ANTON	461	497	512	1924	1971	2012
663	HENTON WILLIS RYAN	461	466	599	1925	1971	2006
664	WALKER JOHN THOMAS	461	564	590	1925	1971	1989
665	CHARLES EDGAR OTIS	461	505	582	1926	1971	
666	BELDEN FREDERICK H	461	517	561	1909	1971	1979
667	MCGEHEE HARRY C JR	461	490	463	1923	1971	2013
668	PORTEUS MORGAN	461	582	424	1917	1971	
669	TRELEASE JR RICHARD M	461	526	621	1921	1971	2005
670	JONES HAROLD STEPHEN	461	452	651	1909	1972	2002
671	RIGHTER WALTER C	461	474	498	1923	1972	2011
672	ARNOLD MORRIS F	461	590	659	1915	1972	1992
673	FRANKLIN WILLIAM A	603	514	454	1916	1972	1998
674	HILLESTAD ALBERT W	461	588	637	1924	1972	
675	SHIRLEY LEMUEL B	454	603	584	1916	1972	1999
676	SIMS BENNETT J	461	489	613	1920	1972	2006
677	FRENSDORFF WESLEY	461	505	566	1926	1972	1988
678	ISAAC TELESFORO A	461	568	441	1929	1972	
679	WYLIE SAMUEL J	461	472	659	1918	1972	1974
680	TURNER EDWARD MASON	461	593	506	1918	1972	1996
681	KING HANFORD L JR	461	548	651	1921	1972	1986
682	SHERIDAN WILLIAM CR	461	587	AAQ	1917	1972	2005
683	PRIMO QUINTIN E JR	461	587	463	1913	1972	1998
684	COX WILLIAM JACKSON	461	639	535	1921	1972	
685	ALEXANDER GEORGE M	461	521	583	1914	1973	1983
686	CARRAL-SOLAR ANSELMO	600	675	514	1925	1973	2002
687	ATKINSON ROBERT P	461	499	586	1927	1973	2012
688	BADEN JOHN ALFRED	490	618	556	1913	1973	1983
689	GASKELL CHARLES T	461	512	645	1919	1973	2000
690	WEINHAUER WILLIAM G	461	636	572	1924	1973	
691	PARSONS DONALD JAMES	461	587	512	1922	1973	
692	DAVIS DONALD JAMES	461	514	549	1929	1973	2007
693	BIGLIARDI MATTHEW P	540	612	570	1920	1974	1996
694	WRIGHT HAROLD LOUIS	598	590	472	1929	1974	1978
695	HOGG WILBUR EMORY JR	461	561	637	1918	1974	1986
696	KERR ROBERT SHAW	461	576	624	1917	1974	1988
697	WOLTERSTORFF ROBERT M	461	477	552	1914	1974	
698	GRAY DUNCAN M JR	461	581	515	1926	1974	
699	CERVENY FRANK S	461	543	484	1933	1974	
700	COCHRAN DAVID REA	581	479	610	1915	1974	2001
701	HAYNES EMERSON PAUL	581	584	455	1918	1974	1988

		Consecrators			Born	Cons.	Died
702	BELSHAW GEORGE PHELPS MELLICK	581	614	444	1928	1975	
703	WITCHER ROBERT CAMPBELL	581	486	515	1926	1975	
704	JONES WILLIAM AUGUSTUS JR	581	563	614	1927	1975	
705	CLARK WILLIAM HAWLEY	581	590	613	1919	1975	1997
706	DIMMICK WILLIAM ARTHUR	581	534	582	1919	1975	1984
707	ABELLON RICHARD ABELARDO	562	591	614	1924	1975	
708	TERWILLIGER ROBERT ELWIN	581	560	699	1917	1975	1991
709	COCHRANE ROBERT HUME	581	570	677	1924	1976	2010
710	CILLEY ROGER HOWARD	581	611	537	1918	1976	1986
711	BROWN JAMES BARROW	581	488	454	1932	1976	
712	VACHE CLAUDE CHARLES	581	556	564	1926	1976	2009
713	SPONG JOHN SHELBY	581	601	618	1931	1976	
714	HEISTAND JOSEPH THOMAS	581	438	618	1924	1976	2008
715	COBURN JOHN BOWEN	581	590	472	1914	1976	2009
716	MAYSON HENRY IRVING	581	667	683	1925	1976	1995
717	WARNER JAMES DANIEL	581	519	543	1924	1976	2009
718	McALLISTER GERALD NICHOLAS	581	613	633	1923	1977	2014
719	JONES EDWARD WITKER	581	549	617	1929	1977	2007
720	LUMPIAS MANUEL CAPUYAN	562	707	655	1930	1977	
721	JONES BOBBY GORDON	581	644	479	1932	1977	
722	ANDERSON ROBERT MARSHALL	581	552	665	1933	1978	2011
723	CHILD CHARLES JUDSON	581	676	489	1923	1978	2004
724	BURGREEN CHARLES LEE	581	539	633	1924	1978	2006
725	PINA HUGO LUIS	581	675	648	1938	1978	
726	THOMPSON JOHN LESTER	581	550	635	1926	1978	2004
727	WALLACE LEIGH ALLEN	581	623	634	1927	1979	2010
728	SCHOFIELD CALVIN ONDERDONK	581	583	455	1933	1979	
729	LIGHT ARTHUR HEATH	581	528	516	1929	1979	
730	MERINO BERNARDO	581	675	657	1930	1979	
731	HAUSER STANLEY FILLMORE	581	604	670	1922	1979	1989
732	SWING WILLIAM EDWIN	581	605	664	1936	1979	
733	BECKHAM WILLIAM ARTHUR	581	685	586	1927	1979	2005
734	DENNIS WALTER DECOSTER	598	472	569	1932	1979	2003
735	SANDERS BRICE SIDNEY	581	460	636	1930	1979	1997
736	WALMSLEY ARTHUR EDWARD	581	668	637	1928	1979	
737	BLACK WILLIAM GRANT	581	368	659	1920	1979	2013
738	CHEUNG PUI-YEUNG	581	655	642	1919	1980	1987
739	LEWIS DAVID H JR	581	618	490	1918	1980	2002
740	HOPKINS HAROLD A JR	581	610	637	1930	1980	
741	ESTILL ROBERT W	581	572	650	1927	1980	
742	MARTINEZ-RESENDEZ ROBERTO	581	551	600	1938	1980	
743	HUERTA-RAMOS CLARO	581	551	600	1929	1980	
744	HUNT GEORGE N III	581	732	517	1931	1980	
745	KIMSEY RUSTIN R	581	465	643	1935	1980	2015
746	STEVENS WILLIAM L	581	519	689	1932	1980	1997
747	BENITEZ MAURICE M	581	461	604	1928	1980	2014
748	DONOVAN HERBERT A JR	581	626	538	1931	1980	
749	ALLISON C FITZSIMONS	581	575	685	1927	1980	
750	WANTLAND WILLIAM C	581	645	718	1934	1980	
751	MALLORY C SHANNON				1936	1972	
752	McNUTT CHARLIE FULLER JR	581	617	687	1931	1980	
753	HULSEY SAM BYRON	581	466	663	1932	1980	
754	WOLFRUM WILLIAM H	581	627	574	1926	1981	2007
755	DUVALL CHARLES F	581	521	733	1935	1981	
756	WHITAKER O'KELLEY	581	602	648	1926	1981	2015
757	ASHBY JOHN F	581	718	750	1929	1981	2001
758	GREIN RICHARD F	581	543	552	1932	1981	
759	HARRIS GEORGE C	581	700	651	1925	1981	2000
760	HUCLES HENRY B III	581	703	486	1923	1981	1989
761	HATHAWAY ALDEN M	581	631	618	1933	1981	
762	ESPINOZA-VENEGAS SAMUEL	581	600	551	1942	1981	2013
763	COLERIDGE CLARENCE L	581	736	AAA	1930	1981	
764	HASTINGS W BRADFORD	581	736	AAA	1919	1981	1992
765	GUERRA-SORIA ARMANDO R	675	686	678	1949	1982	
766	HULTSTRAND DONALD M	581	689	719	1927	1982	
767	EASTMAN ALBERT THEODORE	581	639	535	1928	1982	
768	BIRNEY DAVID B IV	581	654	681	1929	1982	2004
769	RAY THOMAS K	581	567	706	1934	1982	
770	CHARLTON GORDON T JR	581	747	650	1923	1982	
771	MORTON CHARLES B	581	697	658	1926	1982	1994
772	DYER JM MARK	581	654	590	1930	1982	2014

		Consecrators			Born	Cons.	Died
773	DICKSON ALEX D JR	581	698	586	1926	1983	
774	MOODEY JAMES R	581	621	494	1932	1983	2005
775	SORGE ELLIOTT L				1929	1971	2011
776	PATTERSON DONIS D	581	604	724	1930	1983	2006
777	LONGID ROBERT LEE OMENGAN	707	591	720	1935	1983	1996
778	SHIPPS HARRY WOOLSTON	581	646	773	1926	1984	
779	OTTLEY JAMES HAMILTON	581	730	599	1936	1984	
780	FRADE LEOPOLD	581	711	765	1943	1984	
781	PETTIT VINCENT KING	581	702	734	1924	1984	2006
782	BALL DAVID STANDISH	581	508	695	1926	1984	
783	WISSEMANN ANDREW FREDERICK	581	782	504	1928	1984	2014
784	BURRILL WILLIAM GEORGE	581	500	550	1934	1984	
785	LEE PETER JAMES	581	741	618	1938	1984	
786	ANDERSON CRAIG BARRY	581	452	634	1942	1984	
787	WHITE ROGER JOHN	581	766	587	1941	1984	
788	CHALFANT EDWARD COLE	581	559	659	1937	1984	
789	WIMBERLY DON ADGER	581	749	699	1937	1984	
790	MEEKS HOWARD SAMUEL	581	567	776	1932	1984	
791	POPE CLARENCE CULLAM JR	581	645	711	1929	1985	
792	GARCIA-MONTEIL MARTINIANO	581	650	762	1933	1985	
793	DOWNS-HIGGS STURDIE WYMAN	599	787	678	1947	1985	
794	GRISWOLD FRANK TRACY III	581	500	587	1937	1985	
795	HARRIS ROGERS SANDERS	581	733	773	1930	1985	
796	VEST FRANK HARRIS JR	581	741	572	1936	1985	2008
797	GARVER OLIVER BAILEY JR	581	745	746	1925	1985	1996
798	CARR WILLIAM FRANKLIN	581	687	499	1938	1985	
799	REYNOLDS GEORGE LAZENBY JR	581	722	773	1927	1985	1991
800	JOHNSON DAVID ELLIOT	581	538	500	1933	1985	1995
801	LADEHOFF ROBERT LOUIS	581	693	755	1932	1985	
802	MacNAUGHTON JOHN HERBERT	630	604	731	1929	1986	
803	JONES CHARLES IRVING	630	634	603	1943	1986	
804	BARTLETT ALLEN LYMAN JR	630	516	603	1929	1986	
805	THEUNER DOUGLAS EDWIN	630	647	736	1938	1986	2013
806	SWENSON DANIEL LEE	630	722	696	1928	1986	2014
807	TICOBAY NARCISCO VALENTIN	692	707	777	1932	1986	2014
808	MILLER ROBERT ORAN	630	698	608	1935	1986	2009
809	ZABRISKIE STEWART CLARK	677	740	771	1936	1986	1999
A810	VALENTINE BARRY						
811	BOWMAN DAVID CHARLES	630	494	621	1932	1986	2015
812	WILLIAMS ARTHUR BENJAMIN JR	630	774	621	1935	1986	
813	BATES GEORGE EDMOND	677	745	643	1933	1986	1999
814	HAINES RONALD HAYWARD	630	664	690	1934	1986	2008
815	GRAY FRANCIS CAMPBELL	630	648	719	1940	1986	
816	TENNIS CALVIN CABELL	729	804	712	1932	1986	
817	HART DONALD PURPLE	630	479	647	1937	1986	
818	ALLAN FRANK KELLOGG	723	586	676	1935	1987	
819	TAYLOR EGBERT DON	630	632	680	1937	1987	2014
820	MARTINEZ-MARQUEZ GERMAN	802	779	551	1933	1987	
821	ROWTHORN JEFFERY WILLIAM	630	657	736	1934	1987	
822	McARTHUR EARL NICHOLAS	630	802	718	1925	1988	
823	MacBURNEY EDWARD HARDING	630	746	813	1927	1988	
824	MOODY ROBERT MANNING	630	718	785	1939	1988	
825	CHIEN JOHN CHIH-TSUNG	630	817		1923	1988	2013
826	WALKER ORRIS GEORGE	630	812	703	1942	1988	2015
827	CAISAPANTA LUIS	779	692	657	1932	1988	1991
828	BORSCH FREDERICK HOUK	630	702	664	1935	1988	
829	THOMPSON HERBERT	630	737	620	1933	1988	2006
830	EPTING C CHRISTOPHER	630	648	671	1946	1988	
831	TURNER FRANKLIN D	630	804	664	1933	1988	2013
832	SCHOFIELD DAVID MERCER	630	635	732	1938	1988	
833	WOOD RAYMOND STEWART	664	667	659	1934	1988	
834	HARRIS BARBARA CLEMENTINE	630	800	804	1930	1989	
835	BUCHANAN JOHN CLARK	630	755	622	1933	1989	
836	KELSHAW TERENCE	630	761	747	1936	1989	
837	JOHNSON ROBERT HODGES	630	690	723	1934	1989	
838	HAMPTON SANFORD ZANGWILL KAYE	630	722	834	1935	1989	
839	HOWE JOHN W	630	761	627	1942	1989	
840	ROWLEY ROBERT D	630	692	772	1941	1989	2010
841	SMITH JOHN H	630	690	774	1939	1989	2012
842	HARGROVE ROBERT JEFFERSON	630	663	711	1937	1989	2005
843	WARNER VINCENT WAYDELL JR	709	637	800	1940	1989	

		Consecrators			Born	Cons.	Died
844	CARRANZA-GOMEZ SERGIO	678	826	675	1941	1989	
845	STERLING WILLIAM E	630	747	686	1927	1989	2005
846	KROTZ JAMES E	630	717	830	1948	1989	
847	LEE EDWARD L JR	719	769	516	1934	1989	
848	LONGEST CHARLES L	630	639	767	1933	1989	
849	ZABALA ARTEMIO MASLENG	707	777	807		1989	
850	FAIRFIELD ANDREW H	630	610	740	1943	1989	
851	SMALLEY WILLIAM E	630	758	767	1940	1989	
852	SALMON EDWARD L JR	630	749	640	1934	1990	
853	PLUMMER STEVEN T	630	670	595	1944	1990	2005
854	KEYSER CHARLES L	630	699	785	1930	1990	
855	WILLIAMS HUNTINGTON JR	630	741	676	1925	1990	2013
856	LARREA-MORENO JOSE N	630	779	780	1949	1990	
857	THORNTON JOHN STUART	658	745	801	1932	1990	
858	SHIMPFKY RICHARD LESTER	630	834	713	1940	1990	
859	TERRY FRANK JEFFREY	630	516	623	1939	1990	1999
860	WINTERROWD WILLIAM JERRY	630	627	754	1938	1991	
861	TALTON CHESTER LOVELLE	630	722	826	1941	1991	
862	WIEDRICH WILLIAM W	719	587	794	1931	1991	2014
863	ROCKWELL HAYS HAMILTON	630	758	704	1936	1991	
864	SCANTLEBURY VICTOR A	630	779	675	1945	1991	
865	CHARLESTON STEVEN	630	853	750	1949	1991	
866	MCKELVEY JACK MARSTON	756	713	831	1941	1991	
867	THARP ROBERT G	630	648	586	1928	1991	2003
868	LAMB JERRY A	630	726	801	1940	1991	
869	MARBLE ALFRED CLARK JR	581	698	735	1936	1991	
870	HOLGUIN-KHOURY JULIO CESAR	856	779	678	1948	1991	
871	JOSLIN DAVID BRUCE	630	631	838	1936	1991	
872	BECKWITH PETER HESS	630	829	794	1939	1991	
873	BARAHONA-PASCASIO MARTIN DE JESUS	630	779	856	1943	1992	
874	HUGHES GETHIN BENWIL	630	828	842	1942	1992	
875	SHAHAN ROBERT R	630	529	714	1939	1992	2012
876	DIXON JANE HOLMES	630	814	834	1937	1992	
877	TOWNSEND MARTIN GOUGH	630	775	772	1943	1992	
878	DENIG ROBERT S	630	847	783	1946	1993	1995
879	STANTON JAMES M	630	828	832	1946	1993	
880	IKER JACK L	630	791	659	1949	1993	
881	DURACIN JEAN Z	630	660	867	1947	1993	
882	HERLONG BERTRAM N	630	785	752	1934	1993	2011
883	MATTHEWS FRANK CLAY	630	785	687	1947	1993	
884	PAYNE CLAUDE E	630	461	581	1932	1993	
885	JELINEK JAMES L	630	722	838	1942	1993	
886	DOSS JOE MORRIS	630	732	780	1943	1993	
887	MCLEOD MARY ADELIA R	630	808	834	1938	1993	
888	COLEMAN JAMES MALONE	630	711	773	1929	1993	
889	FOLTS JAMES EDWARD	630	802	604	1940	1994	
890	GREW JOSEPH CLARK	630	812	794	1939	1994	
891	GULICK EDWIN FUNSTEN JR	630	796	883	1948	1994	
892	JECKO STEPHEN HAYS	630	699	661	1940	1994	2007
893	JOHNSON ROBERT CARROLL JR	630	741	855	1938	1994	2014
894	JACOBUS RUSSELL EDWARD	630	746	787	1944	1994	
895	MAZE LARRY EARL	630	698	748	1943	1994	
896	ROBERTSON CREIGHTON LELAND	630	786	670	1944	1994	2014
897	ACKERMAN KEITH LYNN	630	691	823	1946	1994	
898	SHAW MARVIL THOMAS III SSJE	630	800	834	1945	1994	
899	ESPAÑA ALFREDO TERENCIO MORANTE	D A906		856	1947	1994	
900	PRICE KENNETH LESTER	630	829	841	1943	1994	
901	LOUTITT HENRY IRVING JR	630	778	675	1938	1995	
902	HENDERSON DORSEY FELIX JR	630	583	746	1939	1995	
903	SAID JOHN LEWIS	630	728	583	1932	1995	
904	STRICKLAND VERNON EDWARD	630	721	830	1938	1995	
905	HAYES CLARENCE WALLACE	630	454	730	1928	1995	
A906	SOTO ONELL ASISELO	779	648	730	1932	1987	2015
907	JONES DAVID COLIN	630	785	687	1943	1995	
908	ALARD LEOPOLDO J	630	884	845	1941	1995	2003
909	IHLOFF ROBERT W	630	763	834	1941	1995	
910	CREIGHTON MICHAEL W	630	752	843	1940	1995	
911	HIBBS ROBERT B	630	889	802	1932	1996	
912	ROSKAM CATHERINE A	630	834	758	1943	1996	
913	WOLF GERALYN	630	794	744	1947	1996	
914	LIPSCOMB JOHN B	630	888	795	1950	1996	

		Consecrators			Born	Cons.	Died
915	SKILTON WILLIAM J	630	852	575	1940	1996	
916	DUNCAN ROBERT WILLIAM	630	761	785	1948	1996	
917	SMITH ANDREW DONNAN	630	763	736	1944	1996	
918	IRISH CAROLYN TANNER	630	813	665	1940	1996	
919	MARSHALL PAUL VICTOR	840	772	654	1947	1996	
920	GLOSTER JAMES GARY	630	893	741	1936	1996	
921	LEIDEL JR EDWIN MAX	630	833	719	1938	1996	
922	DANIEL III CLIFTON	630	735	712	1947	1996	
923	PARSLEY JR HENRY NUTT	630	808	785	1948	1996	
924	SCRUTON GORDON PAUL	630	653	783	1947	1996	
925	POWELL FRANK NEFF	630	729	796	1947	1996	
926	CHANG RICHARD SUI ON	630	744	745	1941	1997	
927	BENNISON JR CHARLES ELLSWORTH	630	804	831	1943	1997	
928	MICHEL RODNEY RAE	630	826	703	1943	1997	
929	WAYNICK CATHERINE MAPLES	812	719	667	1948	1997	
930	OHL JR CHARLES WALLIS	752	753	860	1943	1997	
931	DANIELS THEODORE ATHELBERT	734	819	675	1944	1997	
932	BANE JR DAVID CONNER	829	796	687	1942	1997	
933	MACDONALD MARK LAWRENCE	630	853	750	1954	1997	
934	CALDWELL BRUCE EDWARD	846	721	850	1947	1997	
935	HERZOG DANIEL	630	782	924	1941	1997	
936	JENKINS CHARLES EDWARD III	794	711	852	1951	1998	
937	HOWE BARRY ROBERT	794	835	795	1942	1998	
938	KNUDSEN CHILTON ABBIE RICHARDSON	794	637	913	1946	1998	
939	SISK MARK SEAN	794	758	734	1942	1998	
940	BAINBRIDGE HARRY BROWN	812	867	857	1939	1998	2010
941	WRIGHT WAYNE PARKER	840	936	887	1951	1998	
942	RABB JOHN LESLIE	840	909	767	1944	1998	
943	CRONEBERGER JOHN PALMER	812	713	866	1938	1998	
944	VONROSENBERG CHARLES GLENN	867	586	733	1947	1999	
945	PERSELL WILLIAM D	794	812	890	1943	1999	
946	WHITMORE KEITH BERNARD	794	750	904	1945	1999	
947	GARRISON J MICHAEL	794	811	809	1945	1999	
948	KELSEY JAMES ARTHUR	794	769	847	1952	1999	2007
949	MACPHERSON DAVID BRUCE	851	879	828	1940	1999	
950	GIBBS WENDELL NATHANIEL	812	587	834	1954	2000	
951	PACKARD GEORGE ELDEN	794	854	758	1944	2000	
952	LITTLE EDWARD STUART	812	815	832	1947	2000	
953	BRUNO JOSEPH JON	858	828	861	1946	2000	
954	BENA DAVID JOHN	794	935	782	1943	2000	
955	CURRY MICHAEL BRUCE	837	920	834	1953	2000	
956	GRAY III DUNCAN MONTGOMERY	794	869	698	1949	2000	
957	GREGG WILLIAM OTIS	630	745	801	1951	2000	
958	SAULS STACY FRED	837	789	891	1955	2000	
959	CURRY JAMES E.	805	917	763	1948	2000	
960	RAMOS-ORENCH WILFRIDO	805	917	763	1940	2000	
961	WAGGONER JAMES EDWARD	868	687	900	1947	2000	
962	LAI DAVID JUNG-HSIN	926	825		1948	2000	
963	SCHORI KATHARINE JEFFERTS	868	801	918	1954	2001	
964	CEDARHOLM ROY FREDERICK JR	805	898	834	1944	2001	
965	ELY THOMAS CLARK	805	887	806	1951	2001	
966	DUNCAN PHILIP MENZIE II	794	755	937	1944	2001	
967	JOHNSON DON EDWARD	794	888	586	1949	2001	
968	ALEXANDER JOHN NEIL	794	818	723	1954	2001	
969	DUQUE FRANCISCO JOSÉ	794	730	856	1950	2001	
970	KLUSMEYER WILLIAM MICHIE	794	945	687	1955	2001	
971	ALLEN LLOYD EMMANUEL	779	780		1956	2001	
972	ADAMS GLADSTONE BAILEY III	866	671	891	1952	2001	
973	WHALON PIERRE WELTÉ	794	821	839	1952	2001	
974	ANDRUS MARK HANDLEY	794	923	785	1956	2002	
975	SMITH GEORGE WAYNE	890	863	830	1955	2002	
976	ADAMS JAMES MARSHALL JR	851	904	894	1948	2002	
977	GALLAGHER CAROL JOY WT	840	932	834	1955	2002	
978	GEPERT ROBERT R	812	847	772	1948	2002	
979	CHANE JOHN BRYSON	794	876	814	1944	2002	
980A	SCRIVEN HENRY WM	AAD			1951	1995	
981	HARRIS GAYLE ELIZABETH	812	898	834	1951	2003	
982	SHAND JAMES JOSEPH	909	877	775	1946	2003	
983	SCARFE ALAN	885	830	981	1950	2003	
984A	ALVAREZ DAVID ANDRES	779	772	608	1941	1987	
985	BURNETT JOE GOODWIN	885	717	846	1948	2003	

		Consecrators			Born	Cons.	Died
986	ITTY JOHNCY	794	630	801	1963	2003	
987	BROOKHART C FRANKLIN	794	970	854	1948	2003	
988	HIGH RAYFORD BAINES JR	949	789	884	1941	2003	
989	O'NEILL ROBERT JOHN	885	860	898	1955	2003	
990	COUNCELL GEORGE EDWARD	794	783	945	1949	2003	
991	MILLER STEVEN ANDREW	950	787	662	1957	2003	
992	HOWARD SAMUEL JOHNSON	936	892	699	1951	2003	
993	ROBINSON V GENE	794	630	767	1947	2003	
994	WOLFE DEAN ELLIOTT	949	851	758	1956	2003	
995	LILLIBRIDGE GARY	794	889	911	1956	2004	
996	HOLLINGSWORTH MARK JR	950	890	898	1954	2004	
997	SMITH KIRK STEVAN	794	875	953	1951	2004	
998	SMITH MICHAEL GENE	794	850	740	1955	2004	
999	TAYLOR GRANVILLE PORTER	893	968	818	1950	2004	
1000	STEENSON JEFFREY NEIL	794	836	791	1952	2005	
1001	RIVERA BAVI EDNA	940	843	732	1946	2005	
1002	MATHES JAMES ROBERT	926	874	995	1959	2005	
1003	GUMBS EDWARD AMBROSE	812	678	826	1949	2005	
1004A	GUERRERO ORLANDO JESUS	AAS	870	AAT		2005	
1005	REED DAVID MITCHELL	949	995	889	1957	2006	
1006	OUSLEY STEVEN TODD	950	921	948	1961	2006	
1007	LOVE WILLIAM H	794	935	954	1957	2006	
1008	BEISNER BARRY L	940	963	868	1951	2006	
1009	HARRISON DENA A	949	789	988	1947	2006	
1010	BAXTER NATHAN D	794	910	979	1948	2006	
1011	BENFIELD LARRY R	963	748	895	1955	2007	
1012	BECKWITH MARK M	963	722	943	1951	2007	
1013	BAUERSCHMIDT JOHN C	922	882	711	1959	2007	
1014	SMITH DABNEY T	922	914	648	1953	2007	
1015	FITZPATRICK ROBERT L	963	926	962	1958	2007	
1016	BREIDENTHAL THOMAS E	963	900	737	1951	2007	
1017	JOHNSTON SHANNON S	963	785	907	1958	2007	
1018	AHRENS LAURA J	963	959	912	1962	2007	
1019	ROWE SEAN W	963	840	772	1975	2007	
1020	KONIECZNY EDWARD J	963	952	824	1954	2007	
1021	RICKEL GREGORY	926	843	1001	1963	2007	
1022	GRAY-REEVES MARY	963	1027	728	1962	2007	
1023	EDWARDS DAN	963	968	868	1950	2008	
1024	SLOAN JOHN MCKEE	963	923	808	1955	2008	
1025	LAWRENCE MARK	922	870	897	1950	2008	
1026	LEE JEFFREY	963	950	938	1957	2008	
1027A	ROMERO SYLVESTRE	AAU			1943	1994	
1028	LN STEPHEN	963	866	938	1949	2008	
1029	SINGH PRINCE	963	866	1012	1962	2008	
1030	SUTTON EUGENE	963	979	1010	1954	2008	
1031	LAMBERT PAUL	949	879	998	1950	2008	
1032	THOM BRIAN	963	940	868	1955	2008	
1033	DOYLE CHARLES A	963	789	1009	1966	2008	
1034	HOLLERITH HERMAN	963	785	925	1955	2009	
1035	MAYER J SCOTT	963	753	930	1955	2009	
1036	RUIZ LUIS F	963	969	960	1956	2009	
1037	PROVENZANO LAWRENCE	963	924	990	1955	2009	
1038	TARRANT JOHN J	963	896	786	1952	2009	
1039	BENHASE SCOTT A	963	901	1030	1957	2010	
1040	PRIOR BRIAN N	963	885	961	1959	2010	
1041	HANLEY MICHAEL J	963	1021	1001	1954	2010	
1042	DOUGLAS IAN T	963	955	952	1958	2010	
1043	THOMPSON MORRIS K	963	958	956	1955	2010	
1044	BRUCE DIANE	963	953	1037	1956	2010	
1045	GLASSPOOL MARY D	963	953	997	1954	2010	
1046	WALDO ANDRE W	963	881	923	1953	2010	
1047	MAGNESS JAMES B	963	891	951	1947	2010	
1048	SMYLIE JOHN S	963	1040	955	1952	2010	
1049	BAILEY DAVID E	963	918	745	1940	2010	
1050	LATTIME MARK A	963	1029	866	1966	2010	
1051	WHITE TERRY ALLEN	963	891	937	1959	2010	

		Consecrators			Born	Cons.	Died
1052	VONO MICHAEL LOUIS	963	906	973	1949	2010	
1053	HAYASHI SCOTT B	963	918	1008	1953	2010	
1054	MILLIKEN MICHAEL P	963	994	1011	1947	2011	
1055	FIELD MARTIN S	963	937	994	1956	2011	
1056	MARTINS DANIEL H	963	952	894	1951	2011	
1057	FRANKLIN RALPH WILLIAM	963	939	973	1947	2011	
1058	RAY RAYFORD JEFFREY	963	1006	950	1956	2011	
1059	YOUNG GEORGE DIBRELL III	963	1013	967	1955	2011	
1060	BARKER JOSEPH SCOTT	963	985	939	1964	2011	
1061	BUDDE MARIANN EDGAR	963	1040	1012	1959	2011	
1062	DIETSCHE ANDREW ML	963	939	990	1953	2012	
1063	BREWER GREGORY O	922	839	1007	1951	2012	
1064	BEAUVOIR OGÉ	963	881	939	1956	2012	
1065	OWENSBY JACOB W	963	949	975	1957	2012	
1066	GOFF SUSAN E	963	1017	891	1953	2012	
1067	HIRSCHFELD ALFRED ROBERT	963	993	924	1961	2012	
1068	FISHER JEFF W	963	1033	1009	1964	2012	
1069	WRIGHT ROBERT C	963	968	955	1964	2012	
1070	MCCONNELL DORSEY WM	963	900	898	1953	2012	
1071	KNISELY W NICHOLAS JR	963	996	1028	1960	2012	
1072	MARRAY SANTOSH KUMAR					2005	
1073	FISHER DOUGLAS J	963	924	939	1954	2012	
1074	HAHN WILLIAM DOUGLAS	963	968	1051	1952	2012	
1075	LAMBERT WILLIAM JAY III	963	894	1063	1948	2013	
1076	HODGES-COPPLE ANNIE ELLIOTT	963	955	1039	1957	2013	
1077	BOURLAKAS MARK ALLEN	963	955	968	1963	2013	
1078	HOUGLAND WHAYNE MILLER JR	963	955	958	1962	2013	
1079	STOKES WILLIAM HALLOCK	963	990	780	1957	2013	
1080	RICE DAVID	963			1961	2014	
1081	GUNTER MATTHEW ALAN	963	1026	991	1957	2014	
1082	SHIN ALLEN KUNHO	963	1062	1037	1956	2014	
1083	COOK HEATHER ELIZABETH	963	1030	982		2014	
1084	GATES ALAN MCINTOSH	1028	898	990	1958	2014	
1085	SEAGE BRIAN RICHARD	963	956	953	1963	2014	
1086	SKIRVING ROBERT	963	1006	870	1960	2014	
1087	EATON PETER DAVID	963	780	989	1958	2015	
1088	KENDRICK JAMES RUSSELL	963	966	1033	1960	2015	
1089	SCANLAN AUDREY CADY	963	1042	1018	1958	2015	
1090	SUMNER GEORGE ROBINSON	955	1031	1013	1955	2015	

Codes for other Anglican and Old Catholic Consecrators

AAA Aberdeen	AAE York	AAI North China	AAM Rangoon	AAQ Rowinski (PNC)
AAB Ross	AAF Bath and Wells	AAJ Singapore	AAN Kyushu	AAR Zielinski (PNC)
AAC Skinner	AAG London	AAK Hong Kong	AAO Borneo	AAS Costa Rica
AAD Canterbury	AAH Rochester	AAL Honan	AAP Korea	AAT Colombia
				AAU Belize

Key to Single-Letter Entries

These entries refer to Bishops consecrated for foreign lands which subsequently became missionary jurisdictions of this church: A Haiti; B Mexico; C Brazil; D Puerto Rico.

Key to "A" + Number

These entries refer to Bishops consecrated outside the American episcopate, later transferred in as Assistant Bishops under Canon III.12.(b)(2) or a Bishop whose diocese has joined The Episcopal Church under Article V of the Constitution.

A Table of Presiding Bishops*

1. WILLIAM WHITE (2) (Bishop of Pennsylvania), from July 28, 1789, to October 3, 1789.
2. SAMUEL SEABURY (1) (Bishop of Connecticut), from October 5, 1789 to September 8, 1792.
3. SAMUEL PROVOOST (3) (Bishop of New York), from September 13, 1792, to September 8, 1795.
4. WILLIAM WHITE (2) (Bishop of Pennsylvania), from September 8, 1795, to July 17, 1836.
5. ALEXANDER VIETS GRISWOLD (12) (Bishop of the Eastern Diocese), from July 17, 1836, to February 15, 1843.
6. PHILANDER CHASE (18) (Bishop of Illinois), from February 15, 1843, to September 20, 1852.
7. THOMAS CHURCH BROWNELL (19) (Bishop of Connecticut), from September 20, 1852, to January 13, 1865.
8. JOHN HENRY HOPKINS (26) (Bishop of Vermont), from January 13, 1865, to January 9, 1868.
9. BENJAMIN BOSWORTH SMITH (27) (Bishop of Kentucky), from January 9, 1868, to May 31, 1884.
10. ALFRED LEE (38) (Bishop of Delaware), from May 31, 1884, to April 12, 1887.
11. JOHN WILLIAMS (54) (Bishop of Connecticut), from April 12, 1887, to February 7, 1899.
12. THOMAS MARCH CLARK (63) (Bishop of Rhode Island), from February 7, 1899, to September 7, 1903.
13. DANIEL SYLVESTER TUTTLE (84) (Bishop of Missouri), from September 7, 1903, to April 17, 1923.
14. ALEXANDER CHARLES GARRETT (108) (Bishop of Dallas), from April 17, 1923, to February 18, 1924.
15. ETHELBERT TALBOT (143) (Bishop of Bethlehem), from February 18, 1924, to January 1, 1926.

ELECTIVE

16. JOHN GARDNER MURRAY (243) (Bishop of Maryland), from January 1, 1926, to October 3, 1929 (died in office).
17. CHARLES PALMERSTON ANDERSON (197) (Bishop of Chicago), from November 13, 1929, to January 30, 1930 (died in office).
18. JAMES DEWOLF PERRY (247) (Bishop of Rhode Island), from March 26, 1930, to serve until General Convention of 1931. Reelected September 25, 1931, at General Convention held in Denver, Colo., for a term of six years to end December 31, 1937.

19. HENRY ST. GEORGE TUCKER (258) (Bishop of Virginia, resigned** in 1944), from January 1, 1938, to December 31, 1946.
20. HENRY KNOX SHERRILL (372) (Bishop of Massachusetts, resigned June 1, 1947), from January 1, 1947, to November 14, 1958.
21. ARTHUR LICHTENBERGER (503) (Bishop of Missouri, resigned in 1959), from November 15, 1958. Resigned for ill health, October, 1964.
22. JOHN ELBRIDGE HINES (461) (Bishop of Texas, resigned December 31, 1964), from January 1, 1965 to May 31, 1974.
23. JOHN MAURY ALLIN (581) (Bishop of Mississippi, resigned 1974), from June 1, 1974 to December 31, 1985.
24. EDMOND LEE BROWNING (630) (Bishop of Hawaii, resigned 1986) from January 1, 1986 to December 31, 1997.
25. FRANK TRACY GRISWOLD III (794) (Bishop of Chicago, resigned 1998) from January 1, 1998 to October 31, 2006.
26. KATHARINE JEFFERTS SCHORI (963) (Bishop of Nevada, resigned October 31, 2006) from November 1, 2006, to October 31, 2015.
27. MICHAEL BRUCE CURRY (955) (Bishop of North Carolina, resigned October 31, 2015), from November 1, 2015.

*NOTE—The title *Presiding Bishop* was not used in the Journals of General Convention until 1795. This table is based on the premise that the Bishop who was President of General Convention or of the House of Bishops before 1795 was *de facto* Presiding Bishop.

The General Convention of 1789 during its first session (July 28-August 8), and for the first five days (September 29-October 3) of its second session (September 29-October 16), consisted of one House only. Bishop White was *President of the General Convention* throughout its first session and for the first five days of its second session, and as such signed the minutes of the first session.

When, on October 5, 1789, a separate House of Bishops was first organized, Bishop Seabury became President of the House of Bishops in accordance with the rule of seniority, based on the date of consecration to the episcopate.

On September 13, 1792, Bishop Provoost became President of the House of Bishops by the adoption of the rule that the office should "be held in rotation, beginning from the North."

In 1795, under the above rule, Bishop White automatically became President of the House of Bishops, and for the first time the title *Presiding Bishop* appears in the signing of the minutes of that

House. In 1799, "the Bishop whose turn it would have been to preside" not being present, "Bishop White was requested to preside." In 1801 the rule of rotation was suspended. On September 12, 1804, the rule of seniority was again adopted and continued in effect for 115 years.

The General Convention of 1919 provided for the election of the Presiding Bishop by the Convention. The first such election took place at the General Convention of 1925.

**NOTE—The Presiding Bishop is currently elected by and from the House of Bishops and confirmed by the House of Deputies. The Presiding Bishop resigns from being a Diocesan within six months of taking office and retires after nine years (or at age seventy). The term begins on the first day of November following the election. (See Canon I.2 for further detail.)

RECENTLY CONSECRATED BISHOPS

PETER EATON

Peter Eaton was elected the Bishop Coadjutor of the Diocese of Southeast Florida on January 31, 2015 at a special convention of the Diocese at Trinity Cathedral, Miami. He was ordained to the episcopate on May 9, 2015, and he became the Bishop of Southeast Florida on the retirement of the Right Reverend Leo Frade on January 9, 2016. At the time of his retirement, Bishop Frade was the longest-serving active bishop in The Episcopal Church, having pastored the Diocese of Honduras and the Diocese of Southeast Florida for a total of 31 years. Bishop Eaton was seated as the diocesan bishop at a special liturgy at Trinity Cathedral, Miami, on January 30, 2016, at which over 20 bishops from The Episcopal Church, the Anglican Communion, and our full communion partner churches were present, including Archbishop Josiah Idowu-Fearon, the Secretary General of the Anglican Communion Office. Lord Williams of Oystermouth, the 104th Archbishop of Canterbury, was the preacher.

At his episcopal ordination, over 40 co-consecrating bishops joined in the laying-on-of-hands. In addition to a number of Episcopal bishops, there were bishops from the wider Anglican Communion, including the current and former Primates of the West Indies. The preacher was the Bishop of Ely in the Church of England. Among the principal co-consecrators were Bishop Hans Gerny, the retired Bishop of the Old Catholic Church of Switzerland (The Old Catholic Union of Utrecht); Mar Theodosius, the Bishop of the North America-Europe diocese of the Mar Thoma Syrian Church of Malabar; Bishop Robert Schaefer, Bishop of the Florida-Bahamas Synod of the Evangelical Lutheran Church in America; and Bishop Graham Rights, a Bishop of the Moravian Church in America. Bishop Eaton is the first bishop in the history of The Episcopal Church to have among his principal co-consecrators the bishops of these full communion partners from both Western and Eastern successions.

Among the local and international ecumenical and inter-religious guests at the ordination were official representatives of His All-Holiness Bartholomew I, the Ecumenical Patriarch; His Beatitude Theophilos III, the Patriarch of Jerusalem; and His Beatitude Nourhan Manougian, the Armenian Patriarch in Jerusalem. The Archbishop of Miami and the Bishop of Palm Beach sent representatives, and Dr. Marcie Lenk represented the Shalom Hartman Institute in Jerusalem, where Bishop Eaton was a fellow in 2008-2009. At Bishop Eaton's seating in January 2016, both the Patriarch of Constantinople and the Patriarch of Jerusalem were once again represented, and Archbishop Vicken Aykazian was present to remind the congregation of the long and close relationship between The Episcopal Church and the Armenian Orthodox Church.

Bishop Eaton was born on August 28, 1958 in Washington, DC. A life-long Episcopalian, he is the son, grandson, and nephew of priests, and he has lived and served in three provinces of the Anglican Communion. His father was the late Reverend Dr. Wade Eaton, who taught at Codrington College, Barbados, and the Seminario Episcopal and the

Seminario Evangélico in Puerto Rico. His grandfather was the late Senator Wayne Morse, who represented Oregon in the US Senate from 1944 to 1969, and his uncle was the late Right Reverend Francisco Reus-Froylán, the first native-born bishop of Puerto Rico. Raised in New England, Barbados, Puerto Rico, and London, he read classics at King's College, London; Theology at Queens' College, Cambridge; and was trained for the priesthood at Westcott House, Cambridge. Between university and theological college, he served for a year as the pastoral assistant at Saint George's Anglican Church in Paris (France). He has twice been a Fellow-in-Residence at the School of Theology, Sewanee (1995 and 2014).

Bishop Eaton was ordained to the diaconate on the Feast of Saint Peter and Saint Paul, June 29, 1986, by his uncle, Bishop Reus, at the Cathedral of Saint John the Baptist in Santurce, PR, by Letters Dimissory from the Archbishop of Canterbury. He was ordained to the priesthood on the same feast in 1987 by Archbishop Robert Runcie in Canterbury Cathedral.

He served as the Assistant Curate of the Parish of All Saints, Maidstone, Kent, UK, from 1986 to 1989; the Fellows' Chaplain of Magdalen College, Oxford, UK, from 1989 to 1991, where he also did graduate research in early Christian history and literature; the Associate Rector of Saint Paul's, Salt Lake City, UT, from 1991 to 1995, where he was also Canon Theologian to the Bishop of Utah until 2001; the Rector of Saint James, Lancaster, PA, from 1995 to 2001; and the Dean of Saint John's Cathedral, Denver, CO, from 2002 to 2015. In Denver he was also an adjunct faculty member of Iliff School of Theology from 1995 to 2015, where he taught Anglican theology and liturgy.

In 2004 he and Kate Gleason were married at Saint John's Cathedral. A fourth-generation Coloradoan and life-long Episcopalian, Kate is a resource development professional, and has worked for many organizations, including the University of Denver, Habitat for Humanity, and Mercy Housing. She was part of the development team of *the Wilderness* in 2007, one of the most innovative and longest-lived new worshipping communities in the Church, and in 2010 she founded *Mishkhah*, an organization that seeks "to reveal the mystery of God by stirring the senses and opening the heart." She has helped a number of congregations across the Church develop new worshipping communities.

Throughout his priestly ministry, Bishop Eaton has been primarily a pastor and teacher, and is deeply committed to the strength and vitality of congregations and their leaders. He seeks to broaden the Church's visible presence in the wider community wherever he lives and works. He has also been involved in ecumenical and inter-religious dialogue, both in the United States and abroad, and from 1999 to 2015 he was a member of the Church's

Standing Commission on Ecumenical and Inter-religious Relations.

RUSSELL KENDRICK

The Rt. Rev. Russell Kendrick was elected to be the 4th Bishop of the Central Gulf Coast in February of 2015, and was ordained Bishop on July 25th, 2015.

A native of Fort Walton Beach, Florida, Bishop Russell earned a Bachelor of Arts in architecture and marketing from Auburn University in 1984. Then in 1995, he received a Master of Divinity from Virginia Theological Seminary. At the time of his election, Bishop Russell was Rector of St. Stephen's in Birmingham, Alabama since 2007. Russell is married to Robin, and they have two children, Aaron and Hannah.

AUDREY SCANLAN

The Rt. Rev. Dr. Audrey Scanlan is the Bishop of the Episcopal Diocese of Central Pennsylvania. She was elected to this position on March 14, 2015, and ordained and consecrated as the eleventh bishop of the diocese of Central Pennsylvania on Sept. 12, 2015, in Harrisburg.

Audrey comes to Pennsylvania from Connecticut where she served on diocesan staff as the Canon for Mission Collaboration and Congregational Life. Before that, Audrey was the Rector of two yoked congregations in central Connecticut and has also served two other local congregations in her ministerial life. She has a particular interest in congregational vitality, creative and adaptive use of church buildings, local mission, and community engagement. Audrey is the co-founder of Rhythms of Grace, a worship and formation program for children with special needs, has co-authored three volumes of lesson plans, and holds a doctorate in the Theology of Disability.

Audrey and her husband Glenn have been married for thirty-one years and are the parents of three adult children—Emma, William, and Harriet. Hiking, cooking, running, and playing the cello are among Audrey's hobbies.

She blogs for the Diocese of Central Pennsylvania at compasspointsmappingtheway.blogspot.com

of capacities: youth minister, missionary teacher in east Africa, curate in an inner-city Anglo-Catholic parish, vicar on a Native American reservation in New Mexico and Arizona, and rector in a small town. Sumner has a PhD in theology from Yale, and has written a book about priestly calling and a commentary on Daniel. He also has a MDiv from Yale Divinity School and a BA from Harvard College.

Sumner and his wife, Stephanie, a psychotherapist, have a son, 18 and a daughter, 26. He plays squash and follows Boston sports.

GEORGE SUMNER

The Rt. Rev. George Sumner was elected as the 7th bishop for the Diocese of Dallas during a Special Convention in May 2015. He was consecrated on November 14, 2015. As bishop he oversees the administrative needs throughout the diocese and is chief pastor for more than 31,000 Episcopalians, 200 clergy, and 100 congregations.

Prior to his election, Sumner served as principal of Wycliffe College in Toronto, Canada. He was the dean of a growing seminary and was the chief administrator responsible for strategic planning, encouraging young, future priests, stewardship, building relations with bishops, and overseeing clergy's continuing education.

Ordained as an Episcopal priest in western Massachusetts in 1981, Sumner served in a variety

The Anglican Communion

Introduction

The Anglican Communion comprises 38 self-governing *Member Churches* or *Provinces* that share several things in common including doctrine, ways of worshipping, mission, and a focus of unity in the Archbishop of Canterbury. Formal mechanisms for meeting include the Lambeth Conference, the Anglican Consultative Council, and the Primates' Meeting, together with the Archbishop, known as the *Instruments of Communion*.

Most Communion life, however, is found in the relationships between Anglicans at all levels of church life and work around the globe; dioceses linked with dioceses, parishes with parishes, people with people, all working to further God's mission. There are around 85 million people on six continents who call themselves Anglican (or Episcopalian), in more than 165 countries. These Christian brothers and sisters share prayer, resources, support and knowledge across geographical and cultural boundaries.

As with any family, the Anglican Communion's members have a range of differing opinions. The Anglican Christian tradition has long valued its diversity, and has never been afraid to tackle publicly the hard questions of life and faith.

History

In continuity with the ancient Celtic and Saxon churches of the British Isles, and Britain's place within Catholic Europe, Anglicanism found its distinctive identity in the 16th and 17th centuries. At the Reformation national Churches emerged in England, Ireland and Scotland. With the American Revolution an autonomous Episcopal Church was founded in the United States and later Anglican or Episcopal Churches were founded across the globe as a result of the missionary movements of the 18th and 19th centuries. Many of these Churches became autonomous Provinces in the course of the 19th and 20th centuries. In South Asia, the United Churches formed between Anglican and Protestant denominations, joined the Anglican Communion, as did Churches elsewhere such as the Spanish Episcopal Reformed Church and the Lusitanian Church of Portugal.

Official structures

It was in 1867 that Lambeth Palace hosted the first conference for Anglican bishops from around the world. From 1948 each Archbishop of Canterbury has called a *Lambeth Conference* every ten years. The last, in 2008, saw more than 800 bishops from around the world invited to Canterbury. The Conference has no authority of itself: rather it is a chance for bishops to meet and explore aspects of Anglican Communion life and ministry.

Bishops attending the 1968 Lambeth Conference called for a body representative of all sections of the churches—laity, clergy and bishops—to co-ordinate aspects of international Anglican ecumenical and mission work. The resulting body was the *Anglican Consultative Council*. This council comprising elected and appointed members from around the globe meets approximately every three years.

Since 1979 the Archbishop of Canterbury has also regularly invited the chief bishops of the Provinces (known as *Primates*) to join him in a meeting for consultation, prayer and reflection on theological, social and international matters. These *Primates' Meetings* take place approximately every two years.

These Instruments of Communion are served by a secretariat with staff based at the Anglican Communion Office in London, England, and New York.
(See below for more information on the Anglican Communion Office)

Beliefs

There can be many differences between individual Anglican churches, but all uphold and proclaim the Catholic and Apostolic faith, proclaimed in the Scriptures, interpreted in the light of tradition and reason. Anglicans hold these things in common:

- The Holy Bible, comprising the Old and New Testament, as a basis of our faith;

- The Nicene and Apostles' Creeds as the basic statements of Christian belief;

- Recognition of the Sacraments of Baptism and Holy Communion; and

- The Historic Episcopate—ours is a Christian tradition with bishops.

This *quadrilateral*, drawn up in the 19th Century, is one of the definitions of Anglican faith and ministry. Another is a style of worship which has its roots in the Book of Common Prayer and the Services of Ordination (the Ordinal). Anglicans also celebrate the Eucharist (also known as the Holy Communion, the Lord's Supper or the Mass), the Sacrament of Baptism and other rites including Confirmation, Reconciliation, Marriage, Anointing of the Sick, and Ordination.

Anglicanism rests on the three pillars of Scripture, Tradition and Reason as it seeks to chart 'a middle way' among the other Christian traditions.

Mission

Following the teachings of Jesus Christ, Anglicans are committed to proclaiming the good news of the Gospel to all creation as expressed in the Marks of Mission:

- To proclaim the Good News of the Kingdom;

- To teach, baptise and nurture new believers;

- To respond to human need by loving service;

- To seek to transform unjust structures of society, to challenge violence of every kind and to pursue peace and reconciliation

- To strive to safeguard the integrity of creation and sustain and renew the life of the earth.

These Marks are to be expressed in all areas of a Christian's life: their words and their actions. Therefore, members of the Anglican Communion around the world are involved with a range of life-changing activities that include evangelism and church growth; providing food, shelter and clothing to those in need; speaking out with and for the oppressed; and setting up schools, hospitals, clinics and universities.

PROVINCES

The Anglican Church in Aotearoa,
New Zealand & Polynesia
The Anglican Church of Australia
The Church of Bangladesh
Igreja Episcopal Anglicana do Brasil
The Anglican Church of Burundi
The Anglican Church of Canada
The Church of the Province of Central Africa
Iglesia Anglicana de la Region Central de America
Province de L'Eglise Anglicane Du Congo
The Church of England
Hong Kong Sheng Kung Hui
The Church of the Province of the Indian Ocean
The Church of Ireland
The Nippon Sei Ko Kai
(The Anglican Communion in Japan)
The Episcopal Church in Jerusalem &
the Middle East
The Anglican Church of Kenya
The Anglican Church of Korea
The Church of the Province of Melansia
La Iglesia Anglicana de Mexico
The Church of the Province of Myanmar (Burma)
The Church of Nigeria (Anglican Communion)
The Church of North India (United)
The Church of Pakistan (United)
The Anglican Church of Papua New Guinea
The Episcopal Church in the Philippines
Province de l'Eglise Episcopal au Rwanda
The Scottish Episcopal Church
Church of the Province of South East Asia
The Church of South India (United)
The Anglican Church of Southern Africa

The Anglican Church of South America
Province of the Episcopal Church
of South Sudan and Sudan
The Anglican Church of Tanzania
The Church of the Province of Uganda
The Episcopal Church *(Includes 100 dioceses*
in the United States, and 12 additional dioceses
or jurisdictions in 15 nations)
The Church in Wales
The Church of the Province of West Africa
The Church in the Province of the West Indies

Extra-Provincial Churches and other dioceses
The Church of Ceylon
(Extra-Provincial to Canterbury)
Iglesia Episcopal de Cuba
Bermuda (Extra-Provincial to Canterbury)
The Lusitanian Church(Extra-Provincial
to Canterbury)
The Reformed Episcopal Church of Spain
(Extra-Provincial to Canterbury)
Falkland Islands (Extra-Provincial to Canterbury)

Churches in Communion
The Mar Thoma Syrian Church of Malabar
The Old Catholic Churches of the Union of Utrecht
The Philippine Independent Church (Iglesia
Filipina Independiente - IFI)
NB: Anglicans/Episcopalians in certain parts of
the Communion are in full communion with some
Lutheran Churches.

THE ANGLICAN COMMUNION OFFICE

Sec Gen for Ang Com Archbishop Dr Josiah Idowu-Fearon; *Dir for Unity Faith and Order* Revd Cn Dr John Gibaut; *Co-Executive Dir for Anglican Alliance* Revd Andy Bowerman *and* Revd Rachel Carnegie; *Dir for Com* vacant; *Dir Cont Indaba* Revd Cn Dr Phil Groves; *Dir for Fin and Admin* Tim Trimble; *Dir for Mission* Rev John Kafwanka; *Dir for Women in Church and Society* Revd Terrie Robinson; *Rep to UN institutions in Geneva* Revd Cn Flora Winfield - Anglican Communion; *Wdn of the Gst Hse* Ann Quirke

Anglican Communion Office: St Andrew's House, 16 Tavistock Crescent, London, W11 1AP
Tel: +44 (0)207 313 3900   *Fax:* +44 (0)207 313 3999
E-mail: aco@anglicancommunion.org
Web: www.anglicancommunion.org   ACNS: www.anglicannews.org/

The permanent secretariat (the Anglican Communion Office) serves the Anglican Communion and is responsible for facilitating all meetings of the conciliar Instruments of Communion as well as the commissions, working groups and networks of the Communion. Anglican Communion Office staff from countries including Canada, Colombia, Latvia, Nigeria and Zambia also maintain the Anglican Communion website where visitors can find the official prayer cycle (daily prayer intentions for the dioceses of the Communion) and vast amounts of official information and documentation about the Anglican Communion's Instruments and its ministries. The very latest news from around the Anglican world is available via the Anglican Communion News Service (ACNS) website. Most of the funding for the work of the office comes from the Inter-Anglican budget supported by all Member Churches according to their means.

The Anglican Episcopate

THE ANGLICAN CHURCH IN AOTEAROA, NEW ZEALAND AND POLYNESIA
General Secretary The Revd Michael M Hughes PO BOX 87188 Meadowbank Auckland 1742 NEW ZEALAND *Tel:* +64 (0)9 521 4439 *Email:* gensecm@anglicanchurch.org.nz *Web:* www.anglican.org.nz

Aotearoa The Most Revd William Brown Turei Pihopa o Aotearora and Primate and Archbishop of the Anglican Church in Aotearoa, New Zealand & Polynesia PO Box 568 Gisborne 4040 NEW ZEALAND *Tel:* +64 (0)6 867 8856 *Fax:* +64 (0)6 867 8859 *Email:* bishop@tairawhiti.org.nz

Aotearoa-Central North Island The Rt Revd Ngarahu N Katene Pihopa ki Te Manawa o Te Wheke (Bp Central North Island Region) PO Box 146 Rotorua 3040 New Zealand *Tel:* +64 (0)7 348 4043 *Email:* ngarahukatane@ihug.co.nz

Aotearoa-Northern Region The Rt Revd Te Kitohi Wiremu Pikaahu Pihopa ki Te Tai Tokerau (Bp, Northern Region) PO Box 25 Paihia Bay of Islands 247 New Zealand *Tel:* +64 (0)9 402 6788 *Fax:* +64 (0)9 402 6663 *Email:* tkwp@tokerau.ang.org.nz

Aotearoa-South Island The Rt Revd John Robert Kuru Gray Pihopa ki Te Waipounamu (Bp, South Island) PO Box 10 086 Christchurch 8145 NEW ZEALAND *Tel:* +64 (0)3 389 1683 *Fax:* +64 (0)3 389 0912 *Email:* bishopgray@hawaipounamu.co.nz

Aotearoa-Wellinton/Taranaki The Rt Revd Muru Walters Pihopa o Te Upoko o Te Ika (Bp, Wellington/Taranaki Region) 14 Amesbury Drive Churton Park Wellington 6037 NEW ZEALAND *Tel:* +64 (0)4 478 3549 *Email:* muru.walters@xtra.co.nz

Auckland The Rt Revd Ross Bay Bishop of Auckland PO Box 37 242 Parnell Auckland 1151 New Zealand *Tel:* +64 (0)9 302 7201 *Email:* bishop.office@auckanglican.org.nz

Christchurch The Rt Revd Victoria Matthews Bishop of Christchurch PO Box 4438 Christchurch 8140 New Zealand *Tel:* +64 (0)3 379 5950 *Fax:* +64 (0)3 372 3357 *Email:* bishopspa@anglicanlife.org.nz *Web:* www.anglicanlife.org.nz

Dunedin The Rt Revd Dr Kelvin Peter Wright Bishop of Dunedin PO Box 13-170 Green Island Dunedin 9052 New Zealand *Tel:* +64 (0)3 488 0820 *Fax:* +64 (0)3 488 2038 *Email:* bishop@dn.anglican.org.nz

Nelson The Rt Revd Victor Richard Ellena Bishop of Nelson PO Box 100 Nelson 7040 New Zealand *Tel:* +64 (0)3 548 3124 *Fax:* +64 (0)3 548 2125 *Email:* bprichard@nelsonanglican.org.nz *Web:* www.nelsonanglican.org.nz

Polynesia The Most Revd Dr Winston Halapua Bishop of Polynesia and Primate and Archbishop of the Anglican Church in Aotearoa, New Zealand & Polynesia Box 35 Suva Fiji *Tel:* +679 3 304 716 *Fax:* +679 3 302 553 *Email:* bishoppolynesia@connect.com.fj *Web:* www.dioceseofpolynesia.org

Polynesia-Vanua Levu and Taveuni The Rt Revd Apimeleki Nadoki Qiliho Bishop of Vanua Levu and Taveuni, Fiji PO Box 117 Lautoka FIJI *Tel:* +679 666 0124 *Email:* qiliho@gmail.com *Web:* www.dioceseofpolynesia.org

Polynesia-Viti Levu West The Rt Revd Apimeleki Qiliho Bishop of Viti Levu West, Fiji PO Box 117 Lautoka FIJI *Email:* qiliho@gmail.com *Web:* www.dioceseofpolynesia.org

Waiapu The Rt Revd Andrew Hedge Bishop of Waiapu PO Box 227 Napier 4140 New Zealand *Tel:* +64 (0)6 835 8230 *Fax:* +64 (0)6 835 0680 *Email:* *Web:* www.waiapu.anglican.org.nz

Waikato & Taranaki The Most Revd Philip Richardson Primate and Bishop of Taranaki PO Box 547 566 Mangorei Road New Plymouth 4340 NEW ZEALAND *Tel:* +64 (0)6 759 1178 *Fax:* +64 (0)6 759 1180 *Email:* bishop@taranakianglican.org.nz

Waikato & Taranaki The Rt Revd Helen-Ann Hartley Bishop of Waikato PO Box 21 Hamilton 3240 New Zealand *Tel:* +64 (0)7 857 0020 *Email:* bishop@hn-ang.org.nz *Web:* www.waikatotaranakianglican.org.nz/

Wellington The Rt Revd Justin Duckworth Bishop of Wellington PO Box 12-046 Wellington 6144 New Zealand *Tel:* +64 04 472 1057 *Fax:* +64 04 499 1360 *Email:* reception@wn.ang.org.nz *Web:* wn.anglican.org.nz

THE ANGLICAN CHURCH OF AUSTRALIA
General Secretary Ms Anne Hywood General Synod Office Suite 4 Level 5 189 Kent Street Sydney NSW 2000 Australia *Tel:* +61 (0)2 8267 2701 *Fax:* +61 (0)2 8267 2727 *Email:* general.secretary@anglican.org.au

Finance and Administration Manager Mr Michael Nicholls General Synod Office Suite 4 Level 5 189 Kent Street Sydney NSW 2000 Australia *Tel:* +61 2 8267 2700 *Fax:* +61 2 8267 2727 *Email:* reception@anglican.org.au *Web:* www.anglican.org.au

Adelaide-South Australia The Most Revd Jeffrey William Driver Archbishop of Adelaide 18 King William Road North Adelaide South Australia 5006 Australia *Tel:* +61 (0)8 305 9350 *Fax:* +61 (0)8 305 9399 *Email:* jdriver@adelaide.anglican.com.au *Web:* www.adelaide.anglican.com.au

Adelaide-South Australia The Rt Revd Tim Harris Bishop for Mission and Evangelism 18 King William Road North Adelaide South Australia 5006 Australia *Tel:* +61 8 8305 9352 *Email:* tharris@adelaide.anglican.com.au

Adelaide-South Australia The Rt Revd Christopher McLeod Assistant Bishop of Adelaide 18 King William Road North Adelaide South Australia 5006 Australia *Tel:* +61 (0)8 305 9350 *Web:* www.adelaide.anglican.com.au

Armidale-New South Wales The Rt Revd Richard Lewers Bishop of Armidale Anglican Diocesan Registry PO Box 198 Armidale NSW 2350 Australia *Tel:* +61 (02) 6772 4491 *Fax:* +61 (02) 6772 9261 *Email:* bishop@armidaleanglicandiocese.com *Web:* www.armidaleanglicandiocese.com

Ballarat-Victoria The Rt Revd Garry Weatherill Bishop of Ballarat PO Box 89 Ballarat Victoria 3352 Australia *Tel:* +61 (0)35 331 1183 *Fax:* +61 (0)35 333 2982 *Email:* bishop@ballaratanglican.org.au *Web:* www.ballaratanglican.org.au

Bathurst-New South Wales The Rt Revd Ian Palmer Bishop of Bathurst PO Box 23 Bathurst NSW 2795 Australia *Tel:* +61 (0)26 331 1722 *Fax:* +61 (0)26 332 2772 *Email: Web:* www.bathurst.anglican.org

Bendigo-Victoria The Rt Revd Andrew William Curnow Bishop of Bendigo PO Box 2 Post office Bendigo Victoria 3552 Australia *Tel:* +61 (0)35 443 4711 *Fax:* +61 (0)35 441 2173 *Email:* bishop@bendigoanglican.org.au *Web:* www.bendigoanglican.org.au/

Brisbane-Queensland The Most Revd Dr Phillip John Aspinall Archbishop of Brisbane PO Box 421 Brisbane QLD 4001 Australia *Tel:* +61 (0)7 3835 2218 *Fax:* +61 (0)7 3832 5030 *Email:* ajoseph@anglicanbrisbane.org.au *Web:* www.brisbane.anglican.org

Brisbane-Queensland The Rt Revd Ian Keese Lambert Anglican Bishop to the Australian Defence Force PO Box 421 Brisbane QLD 4001 Australia

Brisbane-Northern Region-Queensland The Rt Revd Dr Jonathan Holland Bishop of Brisbane-Northern Region GPO Box 421 Brisbane Queensland 4001 Australia *Tel:* +61 (0)7 3835 2213 *Fax:* +61 (0)7 3832 5030 *Email:* jholland@anglicanbrisbane.org.au

Brisbane-Southern Region-Queensland The Rt Revd Alison Taylor Bishop of Brisbane-Southern Region PO Box 5384 Gold Coast Mail Centre 9726 Queensland Australia

Brisbane-Western Region-Queensland The Rt Revd Cameron Venables Bishop of Brisbane-Western Region PO Box 2600 Toowoomba QLD 4350 Australia *Tel:* +61 (0)7 4639 1875 *Fax:* +61 (0)7 4632 6882

Bunbury-Western Australia The Rt Revd Alan Ewing Bishop of Bunbury Bishopscourt PO Box 15 Bunbury W Australia 6231 Australia *Tel:* +61 9721 2100 *Email:* office@bunbury.org.au *Web:* www.bunbury.org.au

Canberra & Goulburn-New South Wales The Rt Revd Stuart Robinson Bishop of Canberra & Goulburn Jamieson House 43 Constitution Avenue Reid ACT 2612 Australia

Canberra & Goulburn-New South Wales The Rt Revd Trevor W Edwards Assistant Bishop of Canberra & Goulburn 28 McBryde Crescent Wanniassa ACT 2903 Australia *Tel:* +61 (0)2 6231 7347 *Fax:* +61 (0)2 6231 7500 *Email:* trevor@stmattswanniassa.org.au

Canberra & Goulburn-Wagga Wagga Region-New South Wales Vacant Regional Bishop in Wagga Wagga Jamieson House 43 Constitution Avenue Reid ACT 2612 Australia

Gippsland-Victoria The Rt Revd Kay Goldsworthy Bishop of Gippsland PO Box 928 Gippsland Victoria 3853 Australia *Tel:* +61 (0)35 144 2044 *Fax:* +61 (0)35 144 7183 *Email:* bishop@gippsanglican.org.au *Web:* www.gippsanglican.org.au

Grafton-New South Wales The Rt Revd Sarah Macneil Bishop of Grafton Bishopsholme PO Box 4 Grafton NSW 2460 Australia *Tel:* +61 (0)2 6642 4122 *Fax:* +61 (0)2 6643 1814 *Email:* sarah@chapmac.com *Web:* www.graftondiocese.org.au

Melbourne-Victoria The Most Revd Philip Leslie Freier Archbishop of Melbourne & Primate of Australia The Anglican Centre 209 Flinders Lane Melbourne Victoria 3000 Australia *Tel:* +61 (0)3 9653 4204 *Email:* primate@anglican.org.au *Web:* www.melbourne.anglican.com.au/

Melbourne-Eastern Region-Victoria The Rt Revd Genieve Blackwell Bishop of Melbourne-Eastern Region The Anglican Centre 209 Flinders Lane Melbourne Victoria 3000 Australia *Tel:* +61 (0)3 9653 4220

Melbourne-Northern & Western Region-Victoria The Rt Revd Philip J Huggins Bishop of Melbourne- Northern & Western Region The Anglican Centre 209 Flinders Lane Melbourne Victoria 3000 Australia *Tel:* +61 (0)3 9653 4220 *Fax:* +61 (0)3 9653 4266 *Email:* phuggins@melbourne.anglican.com.au

Melbourne-Southern Region-Victoria The Rt Revd Paul White Bishop of Melbourne-Southern Region The Anglican Centre 209 Flinders Lane Melbourne Victoria 3000 Australia *Tel:* +61 3 9653 4220 *Fax:* +61 3 9650 2184 *Email:* pwhite@melbourne.anglican.com.au

Newcastle (AUS)-New South Wales The Rt Revd Greg E Thompson Bishop of Newcastle The Bishop's Registry PO Box 817 Newcastle NSW 2300 Australia *Tel:* +61 (0)2 4926 3733 *Fax:* +61 (0)2 4926 1968 *Web:* www.newcastleanglican.org.au

Newcastle (AUS)-New South Wales The Rt Revd Peter Stuart Assistant Bishop of Newcastle The Diocesan Office PO Box 817 Newcastle NSW 2300 AUSTRALIA *Tel:* +61 (02) 4926 3733 *Email:* bishoppeter@newcastleanglican.org.au *Web:* www.newcastleanglican.org.au

North Queensland-Queensland The Rt Revd William J Ray Bishop of North Queensland PO Box 1244 Townsville QLD 4810 Australia *Tel:* +61 (0)7 4771 4175 *Fax:* +61 (0)7 4721 1756 *Email:* bishop@anglicannq.org *Web:* www.anglicannq.com

North Queensland-Queensland The Rt Revd Saibo Mabo Assistant Bishop of North Queensland (Torres Islander) PO Box 714 Thursday Island Qld 4875 Australia *Tel:* +61 (0)7 4069 1960 *Email:* bishopti@bigpond.com

North West Australia-Western Australia The Rt Revd Gary Nelson Bishop of North West Australia PO Box 2783 Geraldton WA 6531 Australia *Tel:* +61 (0)8 9921 7277 *Fax:* +61 (0)8 9964 2220 *Email:* bishop@anglicandnwa.org *Web:* www.anglicandnwa.org

Northern Territory, The-Queensland The Rt Revd Greg Anderson Bishop of the Northern Territory GPO Box 2950 Darwin NT 801 Australia *Tel:* +61 (0)8 8941 7440 *Fax:* +61 (0)8 8941 7446 *Email:* ntdiocese@internode.on.net *Web:* www.anglicanchurchnt.org.au

Perth-Western Australia The Most Revd Roger A Herft Archbishop of Perth GPO Box W2067 Perth Western Australia 6846 Australia *Tel:* +61 (0)8 9425 7201 *Fax:* +61 (0)8 9325 6741 *Email:* archbishop@perth.anglican.org *Web:* www.perth.anglican.org/

Perth-Eastern and Rural Region-Western Australia The Rt Revd Tom Wilmot Assistant Bishop of Perth, Eastern and Rural Region GPO Box W2067 Perth Western Australia 6846 Australia *Tel:* +61 08 9325 7455 *Fax:* +61 08 9325 6741 *Email:* twilmot@perth.anglican.org

Perth-Goldfields-Country Region-Western Australia The Rt Revd Jeremy James Assistant Bishop of Perth Goldfields-Country Region GPO Box W2067 Perth Western Australia 6846 Australia *Tel:* +61 (0)8 9430 7224 *Fax:* +61 (0)8 9336 3374

Riverina-New South Wales The Rt Revd Rob Gillion Bishop of Riverina PO Box 10 58 Arthur Street Narrandera NSW 2700 Australia *Tel:* +61 (0)2 6959 1648 *Fax:* +61 (0)2 6959 2903 *Web:* www.riverina.anglican.org

Rockhampton-Queensland The Rt Revd David Robinson Bishop of Rockhampton PO Box 6158 Central Queensland Mail Centre Rockhampton QLD 4702 Australia *Tel:* +61 (0)7 4927 3188 *Fax:* +61 (0)7 4922 4562 *Email:* bishop@anglicanrock.org.au *Web:* www.anglicanrock.org.au

Sydney-New South Wales The Most Revd Dr Glenn N Davies Archbishop of Sydney PO Box 190 Q.V.B Post Office Sydney NSW 1230 Australia *Tel:* +61 2 9265 1527 *Fax:* +61 2 9265 1543 *Email:* gdavies@sydney.anglican.asn.au *Web:* www.sydneyanglicans.net

Sydney-Liverpool-New South Wales The Rt Revd Peter J Tasker Assistant Bishop of Sydney-Liverpool PO Box Q190 QVB Post Office Sydney NSW 1230 Australia *Tel:* +61 2 9265 1572 *Fax:* +61 2 9265 1543 *Email:* ptasker@sydney.anglican.asn.au

Sydney-North-New South Wales The Rt Revd Chris Edwards Assistant Bishop of Sydney-North PO Box Q190 QVB Post Office Sydney NSW 1230 Australia *Tel:* +61 2 9265 1527 *Fax:* +61 2 9265 1543 *Email:* *Web:* www.sydneyanglicans.net

Sydney-South-New South Wales The Rt Revd Robert C Forsyth Assistant Bishop of Sydney-South PO Box Q190 QVB Post Office Sydney NSW 1230 Australia *Tel:* +61 (0)292 651 523 *Fax:* +61 (0)292 651 543 *Email:* robforsyth@sydney.anglican.asn.au *Web:* www.anglicanmediasydney.asn.au/

Sydney-West-New South Wales The Rt Revd Ivan Y Lee Assistant Bishop of Sydney-West St John's Church Buildings PO Box 1443 Parramatta NSW 2124 Australia *Tel:* +61 (0)296 353 186 *Fax:* +61 (0)296 333 636 *Email:* office@westernsydney.anglican.asn.au

Sydney-Wollongong-New South Wales The Rt Revd Al Stewart Assistant Bishop of Sydney-Wollongong 74 Church Street PO Box A287 Wollongong NSW 2500 Australia *Tel:* +61 (0)2 4225 2800 *Fax:* +61 (0)2 4228 4296 *Email:* office@wollongong.anglican.asn.au *Web:* www.anglicanmediasydney.asn.au

Tasmania-Ex-P Vacant Bishop elect of Tasmania GPO 748H Hobart Tasmania 7001 Australia *Fax:* +61 (0)3 6223 8968 *Email:* bishop@anglicantas.org.au *Web:* www.anglicantas.org.au

Tasmania-Ex-P The Rt Revd Christopher R Jones Assistant Bishop of Tasmania GPO Box 1620 Hobart Tasmania 7001 AUSTRALIA *Tel:* +61 (0)3 6231 9602 *Fax:* +61 (0)3 6231 9589 *Email:* c.jones@anglicare-tas.org.au *Web:* www.anglicare-tas.org.au

Tasmania-Ex-P The Rt Revd Ross J Nicholson Assistant Bishop of Tasmania 157 St John Street Launceston Tasmania 7250 AUSTRALIA *Tel:* +61 (0)3 6331 4896 *Fax:* +61 (0)3 6334 1719 *Email:* rnicholson@stjohns.net.au

The Murray-South Australia The Rt Revd John Frank Ford Bishop of The Murray PO Box 269 Murray Bridge SA 5253 Australia *Tel:* +61 (0)8 8532 2270 *Fax:* +61 (0)8 8532 5760 *Email:* registry@murray.anglican.org *Web:* www.murray.anglican.org

Wangaratta-Victoria The Rt Revd John Parkes Bishop of Wangaratta Bishop's Lodge PO Box 457 Wangaratta Victoria 3677 Australia *Tel:* +61 (0)3 5721 3643 *Email:* bishop@wangaratta.anglican.org *Web:* www.wangaratta-anglican.org.au

Willochra-South Australia The Rt Revd John Stead Bishop of Willochra PO Box 96 Gladstone South Australia 5497 Australia *Tel:* +61 (0)8 8662 2249 *Fax:* +61 (0)8 8662 2027 *Email:* bishop@diowillochra.org. au *Web:* www.willochra.anglican.org

THE CHURCH OF BANGLADESH

Provincial Secretary Mr Joseph M Mondal Church of Bangladesh 54/1 Baro Bagh Mirpur-2 Dhaka 1216 BANGLADESH *Tel:* +880 2 802 0876 *Email:* emondal012@gmail.com

Dhaka The Most Revd Paul Shishir Sarker Moderator, Church of Bangladesh & Bishop of Dhaka 54/1 Barobag Mirpur-2 Dhaka 1216 Bangladesh *Tel:* +880 2 805 3729 *Email:* pssarker19@ gmail.com

Kushtia The Rt Revd Sunil Mankhin Bishop of Kushtia St Thomas Church 391 New Eskaton Road Moghbazar Dhaka 1000 Bangladesh *Tel:* +880 2 711 6546 *Fax:* +880 2 712 1632 *Email:* sunil_mankhin@ yahoo.com

IGREJA EPISCOPAL ANGLICANA DO BRASIL

Provincial Secretary The Revd Arthur P Cavalcante Praça Olavo Bilac nº 63-Campos Elseos São Paulo SP 01201-050 BRAZIL *Email:* arthurieab@gmail.com

Provincial Treasurer Mrs Silvia Fernandes Campos Elíseos São Paulo SP 01201-050 BRAZIL *Tel:* +55 (0)11 3667 8161 *Fax:* +55 (0)11 3667 8161 *Email:* sec.geral@ieab.org.br

Amazon The Rt Revd Saulo Mauricio de Barros Bishop of the Amazon Avenida Serzedelo Corrêa 514 Batista Campos Belem PA 66033-265 Brazil *Tel:* +55 (0)91 3241 9720 *Email:* saulomauricio@gmail. com *Web:* www.daa.ieab.org.br/

Brasilia The Rt Revd Maurício Jose Araujo De Andrade Bishop of Brasilia Gabinete Episcopal-Catedral Anglicana EQS 309/310 sala 1- Asa Sul Brazilia DF 70362-400 Brazil *Tel:* +55 (0)61 3443 4305 *Fax:* +55 (0)61 3443 4337 *Email:* mandrade@ ieab.org.br *Web:* www.dab.ieab.org.br

Curitiba The Rt Revd Naudal Alves Gomes Bishop of Curitiba Av. Sete de Setembro 3927 sl. 8 Centro Curitiba PR 80250-210 Brazil *Tel:* +55 (0)41 3079 9992 *Fax:* +55 (0)41 3079 9992 *Email:* naudal@ yahoo.com.br *Web:* www.dac.ieab.org.br

Missionary District of Oeste-Brasil Vacant The Most Revd Francisco de Assis da Silva is currently Bishop in Charge Av. Rio Branco 880 Santa Maria RS 97010-422 Brazil *Tel:* +55 (0)55 3221 4328 *Fax:* +55

(0)55 8131 0709 *Email:* xicosilva@gmail.com *Web:* www.dmo.ieab.org.br/

Pelotas The Rt Revd Renato Da Cruz Raatz Bishop of Pelotas Rua Goncalves Chaves, 665 Pelotas RS 96015-560 Brazil *Tel:* +55 (0)53 3202 8618 *Email:* rcaatz@ieab.org.br *Web:* www.dapsul.com.br/

Recife The Rt Revd João Cancio Peixoto Bishop of Recife Av. Boa Viagem 5130 apto 701 Recife PE 51.030-000 Brazil *Tel:* +55 (0)81 33410791 *Fax:* +55 (0)81 88330791 *Email:* joao.peixoto01@uol.com.br *Web:* www.dar.ieab.org.br

Rio de Janeiro The Rt Revd Filadelfo Oliviera Neto Bishop of Rio de Janeiro Rua Haddock Lobo 258 RIO DE JANEIRO RJ 20260-142 Brazil *Tel:* +55 (0)21 2220 2148 *Fax:* +55 (0)21 2252 9686 *Email:* oliveira.ieab@gmail.com *Web:* www.anglicanarj.org

Sao Paulo The Rt Revd Flavio Augusto Borges Irala Bishop of São Paulo Rua Borges Lagoa 172 Vila Clementino Sao Paulo SP 04038-030 Brazil *Tel:* +55 (0)11 5549 9086

South Western Brazil The Most Revd Francisco De Assis Da Silva Primate of Brazil & Bishop of South-Western Brazil Av. Rio Branco 880 Santa Maria RS 97010-422 Brazil *Tel:* +55 55 3221 4328 *Fax:* +55 55 3221 4328 *Email:* xicoasilva@gmail.com *Web:* www.ieab.org.br

Southern Brazil The Rt Revd Humberto Maiztegue Bishop of Southern Brazil Av Eng Ludolfo Boehl 278 Teresópolis PORTO ALEGRE RS 91720-150 Brazil *Tel:* +55 (0)51 3318 6199 *Fax:* +55 (0)51 3318 6199 *Email:* humbertox@uol.com.br *Web:* www.dm.ieab. org.br

THE ANGLICAN CHURCH OF BURUNDI

The Most Revd Dr Thabo C Makgoba Archbishop of Capetown and Primate of Southern Africa 20 Bishopscourt Drive Bishopscourt Claremont Cape Town Western Cape 7708 South Africa *Tel:* +27 021 763 1320 *Fax:* +27 021 761 4193 *Email:* archpa@anglicanchurchsa.org.za *Web:* www. anglicanchurchsa.org/

Provincial Secretary The Revd Canon Seth Ndayirukiye BP 2098 Bujumbura Burundi *Tel:* +257 22 22 9129 *Fax:* + *Email:* canonseth@gmail.com

Provincial Treasurer Mrs Christine Niyonkuru BP 2098 Bujumbura Burundi *Email:* peab@cbinf.com

Bujumbura The Rt Revd Eraste Bigirimana Bishop of Bujumbura BP 1300 Bujumbura Burundi *Tel:* +257 22 249 104 *Fax:* +257 22 227 496 *Email:* bigirimanaeraste@yahoo.fr

Buye The Rt Revd Sixbert Macumi Bishop of Buye Eglise Episcopale du Burundi BP 94 Ngozi Burundi *Tel:* +257 22 302 210 *Fax:* +257 22 302 317 *Email:* buyedioc@yahoo.fr

Gitega The Rt Revd John W Nduwayo Bishop of Gitega BP 23 Gitega Burundi *Tel:* +257 22 402 247 *Fax:* +257 22 402 247 *Email:* eab.diogitega@gmail.com

Makamba The Rt Revd Martin B Nyaboho Bishop of Makamba BP 96 Makamba Burundi *Tel:* +257 22 508 080 *Fax:* +257 22 229 129 *Email:* bishopnyaboho@yahoo.fr

Matana The Most Revd Bernard Ntahoturi Archbishop of the Province of Burundi & Bishop of Matana BP447 Bujumbura Burundi *Email:* ntahober@yahoo.co.uk *Web:* www.anglicanburundi.org

Muyinga The Rt Revd Paisible Ndacayisaba Bishop of Muyinga BP 55 Muyinga Burundi *Tel:* +257 22 306 019 *Fax:* +257 22 306 157 *Email:* ndacp@yahoo.com *Web:* www.anglicanchurchmuyinga.moonfruit.com

Rumonge The Rt Revd Pedaculi Birakengana Bishop of Rumonge Awaiting Details *Tel:* +257 79 970 926 *Email:* birakepeda@yahoo.fr

THE ANGLICAN CHURCH OF CANADA

Primate of the Anglican Church of Canada The Most Revd Frederick J Hiltz Primate of the Anglican Church of Canada 80 Hayden Street Toronto ON M4Y 3G2 Canada *Tel:* +1 416 924 9199 *Fax:* +1 416 924 0211 *Email:* primate@national.anglican.ca *Web:* www.anglican.ca/

General Secretary of the General Synod The Ven Dr Michael Thompson 80 Hayden Street Toronto ON M4Y 3G2 Canada *Tel:* +1 416 924 9199 *Fax:* +1 416 924 0211 *Email:* mthompson@national.anglican.ca

General Treasurer of the General Synod Ms Hanna Goschy 80 Hayden Street Toronto ON M4Y 3G2 Canada *Tel:* +1 416 924 9199 *Fax:* + *Email:* hgoschy@national.anglican.ca

Algoma-Ontario The Rt Revd Stephen Andrews Bishop of Algoma PO Box 1168 619 Wellington Street East Sault Ste. Marie ON P6A 5N7 Canada *Tel:* +1 705 256 5061 *Fax:* +1 705 673 4979 *Email:* bishop@dioceseofalgoma.com *Web:* www.dioceseofalgoma.com/

Anglican Parishes of the Central Interior (formerly Cariboo)-British Columbia & the Yukon The Rt Revd Barbara Jean Andrews Bishop of Anglican Parishes of the Central Interior 250-546 Saint Paul Street Kamloops BC V2C 5T1 Canada *Tel:* +1 778 471 5573 *Fax:* +1 778 471 5586 *Email:* apcibishop@shaw.ca *Web:* www.apcionline.ca/

Athabasca-Rupert's Land The Rt Revd Fraser W Lawton Bishop of Athabasca Box 6868 Peace River AB T8S 1S6 Canada *Tel:* +1 780 624 2767 *Fax:* +1 780 624 2365 *Email:* bpath@telusplanet.net *Web:* www.dioath.ca

Brandon-Rupert's Land The Rt Revd James Dusan Njegovan Bishop of Brandon Box 21009 W.E.P.O Brandon MB R7B 3W8 Canada *Tel:* +1 204 727 7550 *Fax:* +1 204 724 4135 *Email:* bishopbdn@mts.net *Web:* www.dioceseofbrandon.org/

British Columbia-British Columbia & the Yukon The Rt Revd Logan McMenamie Bishop of British Columbia 900 Vancouver Street Victoria BC V8V 3V7 Canada *Tel:* +1 250 386 7781 *Fax:* +1 250 386 4013 *Email:* bishop@bc.anglican.ca *Web:* www.bc.anglican.ca

Caledonia-British Columbia & the Yukon The Rt Revd William John Anderson Bishop of Caledonia #201- 4716 Lazelle Avenue Terrace BC V8G 1T2 Canada *Tel:* +1 250 635 6016 *Fax:* +1 250 635 6026 *Email:* Synodofc@citytel.net *Web:* www.caledonia.anglican.org

Calgary-Rupert's Land The Rt Revd Gregory Kerr-Wilson Bishop elect of Calgary 180 1209- 59th Avenue SE Calgary Alberta T2H 2P6 Canada *Tel:* +1 403 243 3673 *Fax:* +1 403 243 2182 *Email:* info@calgary.anglican.ca *Web:* www.calgary.anglican.ca

Central Newfoundland-Canada The Rt Revd Frederick David Torraville Bishop of Central Newfoundland 34 Fraser Road Gander NL A1V 2E8 Canada *Tel:* +1 709 256 2372 *Fax:* +1 709 256 2396 *Email:* bishopcentral@nfld.net *Web:* www.centraldiocese.org/

Eastern Newfoundland & Labrador-Canada The Rt Revd Geoffrey Peddle Bishop of Eastern Newfoundland & Labrador 16 King's Bridge Road St John's NL A1C 3K4 Canada *Tel:* +1 709 576 6697 *Fax:* +1 709 576 7122 *Email:* geoffpeddle48@gmail.com *Web:* www.anglicanenl.net

Edmonton-Rupert's Land The Rt Revd Jane Alexander Bishop of Edmonton 10035-103 Street Edmonton AB T5J 0X5 Canada *Tel:* +1 780 439 7344 *Fax:* +1 780 439 6549 *Email:* bishop@edmonton.anglican.ca *Web:* www.edmonton.anglican.org

Fredericton-Canada The Rt Revd David Edwards Bishop of Fredericton 115 Church Street Fredericton NB E3B 4C8 Canada *Tel:* +1 506 459 1801 *Fax:* +1 506 460 0520 *Email:* bishop@anglican.nb.ca *Web:* www.fredericton.anglican.org

Huron-Ontario The Rt Revd Robert Franklin Bennett Bishop of Huron 190 Queen's Avenue London ON N6A 6H7 Canada *Tel:* +1 519 434 6893 *Fax:* +1 519 673 4151 *Email:* bishops@huron.anglican.ca *Web:* www.diohuron.org

Huron-Ontario The Rt Revd Terrance Arthur Dance Suffragan Bishop of Huron 190 Queens Avenue London ON N6A 6H7 Canada *Tel:* +1 519 434 6893 *Fax:* +1 519 673 1451 *Email:* bishops@huron.anglican.ca *Web:* www.diohuron.org

Keewatin-Rupert's Land The Most Revd David Norman Ashdown Metropolitan of Rupert's Land and Archbishop of Keewatin 915 Ottawa Street PO Box 567 Keewatin ON P0X 1C0 Canada *Tel:* +1 807 547 3353 *Fax:* +1 807 547 3356 *Email:* keewatinbishop@shaw.ca *Web:* www.dioceseofkeewatin.ca/

Kootenay-British Columbia & the Yukon The Most Revd John Elswood Privett Metropolitan of BC and Yukon and Archbishop of Kootenay 1876 Richter Street Kelowna BC V1Y 2M9 Canada *Tel:* +1 250 762 3306 *Fax:* +1 250 762 4150 *Email:* diocese_of_kootenay@telus.net *Web:* www.kootenay.anglican.ca/

Mishamikoweesh-Rupert's Land The Rt Revd Lydia Mamakwa Bishop of Indigenous Spiritual Ministry of Mishamikoweesh PO Box 65 Kingfisher Lake ON P0V 1Z0 Canada *Tel:* +1 807 532 2085 *Fax:* +1 807 532 2344 *Email:* lydiam@kingfisherlake.ca

Montreal-Canada The Rt Revd Mary Irwin-Gibson Bishop of Montreal 1444 Union Avenue Montreal QC H3A 2B8 Canada *Tel:* +1 514 843 6577 *Fax:* +1 514 843 3221 *Email:* bishops.office@montreal.anglican.ca *Web:* www.montreal.anglican.ca

Moosonee-Ontario The Rt Revd Thomas A Corston Bishop of Moosonee Box 841 Schumacher ON P0N 1G0 Canada *Tel:* +1 705 360 1129 *Fax:* +1 705 360 1120 *Email:* bishop@moosoneeanglican.ca *Web:* www.moosonee.anglican.org

National Indigenous Bishop-Ontario The Rt Revd Mark Lawrence MacDonald National Indigenous Anglican Bishop 80 Hayden Street Toronto ON M4Y 3G2 Canada *Tel:* +1 416 924 9199 *Fax:* +1 416 968 7983 *Email:* mmacdonald@national.anglican.ca *Web:* www.anglican.ca

New Westminster-British Columbia & the Yukon The Rt Revd Melissa M Skelton Bishop of New Westminster Suite 580 401 W Georgia Street Vancouver BC V6B 5A1 Canada *Tel:* +1 604 684 6306 *Fax:* +1 604 684 7017 *Email:* bishop@vancouver.anglican.ca *Web:* www.vancouver.anglican.ca

Niagara-Ontario The Rt Revd Michael Allan Bird Bishop of Niagara Cathedral Place 252 James Street North Hamilton ON L8R 2L3 Canada *Tel:* +1 905 527 1316 *Fax:* +1 905 527 1281 *Email:* bishop@niagara.anglican.ca *Web:* www.niagara.anglican.ca

Nova Scotia & Prince Edward Island-Canada The Rt Revd Ronald Wayne Cutler Bishop of Nova Scotia & Prince Edward Island 6017 Quinpool Road Halifax NS B3K 5J6 Canada *Tel:* +1 902 420 0717 *Fax:* +1 902 425 0717 *Email:* rcutler@nspeidiocese.ca *Web:* www.nspeidiocese.ca

Ontario-Ontario The Rt Revd George Lindsey Russell Bruce Bishop of Ontario 90 Johnson Street Kingston ON K7L 1X7 Canada *Tel:* +1 613 544 4774 *Fax:* +1 613 547 3745 *Email:* gbruce@ontario.anglican.ca *Web:* www.ontario.anglican.ca

Ontario-Ontario The Rt Revd Michael D Oulton Coadjutor Bishop of Ontario 90 Johnson Street Kingston ON K7L 1X7 Canada *Tel:* +1 613 544 4774 *Fax:* +1 613 547 3745 *Email:* moulton@ontario.ca *Web:* www.ontario.anglican.ca

Ottawa-Ontario The Rt Revd John Holland Chapman Bishop of Ottawa 71 Bronson Avenue Ottawa ON K1R 6G6 Canada *Tel:* +1 613 232 7124 *Fax:* +1 613 232 7088 *Email:* bishopsoffice@ottawa.anglican.ca *Web:* www.ottawa.anglican.ca

Ottawa-Ontario The Rt Revd Peter Robert Coffin Bishop Ordinary to the Canadian Armed Forces 42 Bridle Park Drive Ottawa ON CANADA *Tel:* +1 613 232 7124 *Fax:* +1 613 232 7088 *Email:* petercoffin@rogers.com *Web:* www.ottawa.anglican.ca

Qu'Appelle-Rupert's Land The Rt Revd Robert Hardwick Bishop of Qu'Appelle 1501 College Avenue Regina SK S4P 1B8 Canada *Tel:* +1 306 522 1608 *Fax:* +1 306 352 6808 *Email:* bishop.rob@sasktel.net *Web:* www.quappelle.anglican.ca/

Quebec-Canada The Rt Revd Dennis Paul Drainville Bishop of Quebec 31 rue des Jardins Quebec QC G1R 4L6 Canada *Tel:* +1 418 692 3858 *Fax:* + *Email:* bishopqc@quebec.anglican.ca *Web:* www.quebec.anglican.org

Rupert's Land-Rupert's Land The Rt Revd Donald David Phillips Bishop of Rupert's Land 935 Nesbitt Bay Winnipeg MB R3T 1W6 Canada *Tel:* +1 204 992 4200 *Fax:* +1 204 992 4219 *Email:* dphillips@rupertsland.anglican.ca *Web:* www.rupertsland.ca/

Saskatchewan-Rupert's Land The Rt Revd Michael William Hawkins Bishop of Saskatchewan 1308 Fifth Avenue East Prince Albert SK S6V 2H7 Canada *Tel:* +1 306 763 2455 *Fax:* +1 306 764 5172 *Email:* synod@sasktel.net *Web:* www.saskatchewan.anglican.org

Saskatchewan-Rupert's Land The Rt Revd Adam Halkett Suffragan Bishop of Saskatchewan-Indigenous Ministry 1308 Fifth Avenue East Prince Albert SK S6V 2H7 Canada *Tel:* +1 306 763 2455 *Fax:* +1 306 764 5172 *Email:* *Web:* www.saskatchewan.anglican.org

Saskatoon-Rupert's Land The Rt Revd David M Irving Bishop of Saskatoon PO Box 1965 1403 9th Avenue North Saskatoon SK S7K 3S5 Canada *Tel:* +1 306 244 5651 *Fax:* +1 306 933 4606 *Email:* bishopdavid@sasktel.net *Web:* www.saskatoon.anglican.org

The Arctic-Rupert's Land The Rt Revd David Parsons Bishop of the Diocese of the Arctic Box 190 Yellowknife NT X1A 2N2 Canada *Tel:* +1 867-873-5432 *Fax:* + *Email:* arctic@arcticnet.org *Web:* www.arcticnet.org

The Arctic-Rupert's Land The Rt Revd Darren McCartney Suffragan Bishop of the Diocese of the

Arctic PO Box 57 Iqaluit NU X0A 0H0 Canada *Tel:* +1 867-979-5595 *Fax:* + *Email:* darren@arcticnet.org

Toronto-Ontario The Most Revd Colin Robert Johnson Metropolitan of Ontario and Archbishop of Toronto 135 Adelaide St East Toronto ON M5C 1L8 Canada *Tel:* +1 416 363 6021 *Fax:* +1 416 363 7678 *Email:* cjohnson@toronto.anglican.ca *Web:* www.toronto.anglican.ca

Toronto-Trent-Durham Area-Ontario The Rt Revd Linda Carol Nicholls Suffragan Bishop of Toronto-Trent-Durham Area Suite 207 965 Dundas St. West Whitby ON L1P 1G8 CANADA *Tel:* +1 905 668 1558 *Fax:* +1 905 668 8216 *Email:* bishoptrentdurham@bellnet.ca *Web:* www.trent-durhamanglicans.ca

Toronto-York-Credit Valley Area-Ontario The Rt Revd Maurice Philip Poole Suffragan Bishop of Toronto-York-Credit Valley Area 135 Adelaide St East Toronto ON M5C 1L8 Canada *Tel:* +1 416 363 6021 *Fax:* +1 416 363 7678 *Email:* ppoole@toronto.anglican.ca

Toronto-York-Scarborough-Ontario The Rt Revd Patrick Tin-Sik Yu Suffragan Bishop of Toronto-York- Scarborough 135 Adelaide St East Toronto ON M5C 1L8 Canada *Tel:* +1 416 497 7750 *Fax:* +1 416 497 4103 *Email:* patyu@toronto.anglican.ca

Toronto-York-Simcoe-Ontario The Rt Revd Peter Fenty Suffragan Bishop of Toronto-York-Simcoe 2174 King Road Unit 2 King City ON L7B 1L5 Canada *Tel:* +1 905 833 8327 *Fax:* +1 905 833 8329 *Email:* ysimcoe@toronto.anglican.ca

Western Newfoundland-Canada The Rt Revd Percy David Coffin Bishop of Western Newfoundland 25 Main Street Corner Brookl NF A2H 1C2 Canada *Tel:* +1 709 639 8712 *Fax:* + *Email:* dsown@nf.aibn.com *Web:* www.westernnewfoundland.anglican.org/

Yukon-British Columbia & the Yukon The Rt Revd Larry David Robertson Bishop of Yukon Box 31136 Whitehorse YK Y1A 5P7 Canada *Tel:* +1 867 667 7746 *Fax:* +1 867 667 6125 *Email:* synodoffice@klondiker.com *Web:* www.yukon.anglican.org

THE CHURCH OF THE PROVINCE OF CENTRAL AFRICA

Mr R Kanja *Provincial Treasurer* CPCA PO Box 22317 Kitwe Zambia *Tel:* +267 351 081 *Fax:* +267 351 668

Botswana The Rt Revd Metlhayotlhe Rawlings Belemi Bishop of Botswana PO Box 769 Gaaborone Botswana *Tel:* +267 (0)3 953 779 *Fax:* +267 (0)3 913 015 *Email:* angli_diocese@info.bw *Web:* www.diobot.org

Central Zambia The Rt Revd Derek Gary Kamukwamba Bishop of Central Zambia PO Box 70172 Ndola Zambia *Tel:* +260 (0)2 612 431 *Fax:* +260 (0)2 615 954 *Email:* adcznla@zamnet.zm

Central Zimbabwe The Rt Revd Ishmael Mukuwanda Bishop of Central Zimbabwe PO Box 25 Gweru Zimbabwe *Tel:* +263 (0)5 421 030 *Fax:* +263 (0)5 421 097 *Email:* diocent@telconet.co.zw

Eastern Zambia The Rt Revd William Mchombo Bishop of Eastern Zambia & Acting Provincial Secretary PO Box 510154 Chipata Zambia *Tel:* +260 216 221 294 *Email:* dioeastzm@zamnet.zm

Harare The Rt Revd Dr Chad Nicholas Gandiya Bishop of Harare 9 Monmouth Road Avondale Harare Zimbabwe *Tel:* +263 4 308 042 *Email:* chadgandiya@gmail.com

Lake Malawi The Rt Revd Francis Kaulanda Bishop of Lake Malawi PO Box 30349 Lilongwe 3 Malawi *Tel:* +265 1 797 858 *Fax:* +265 1 797 548

Luapula The Rt Revd Robert Mumbi Bishop of Luapula PO Box 710 210 Mansa Zambia *Tel:* +260 (0)2 821 680 *Email:* diopula@zamtel.zm

Lusaka The Rt Revd David Njovu Bishop of Lusaka Bishop's Lodge PO Box 30183 Lusaka Zambia *Tel:* +260 (0)1 264 515 *Fax:* +260 (0)1 262 379

Manicaland The Rt Revd Erick Ruwona Bishop of Manicaland 146 Herbert Chitepo Street Mutare Zimbabwe *Email:* ruwonaerick@gmail.com

Masvingo The Rt Revd Godfrey Tawonezwi Bishop of Masvingo PO Box 1421 Masvingo Zimbabwe *Tel:* +263 39 362 536 *Email:* bishopgodfreytawonezvi@gmail.com *Web:* www.masvingo.anglican.org/

Matabeleland The Rt Revd Cleophas Lunga Bishop of Matabeleland PO Box 2422 Bulawayo Zimbabwe *Tel:* +263 09 613 70 *Fax:* +263 09 683 53 *Email:* clunga@aol.com

Northern Malawi The Rt Revd Fanuel Emmanuel Magangani Bishop of Northern Malawi PO Box 120 Mzuzu Malawi *Tel:* +265 (0) 1312 858 *Email:* magangani@sdnp.org.mw *Web:* www.nmalawianglican.org

Northern Zambia The Most Revd Albert Chama Archbishop of Central Africa & Bishop of Northern Zambia PO Box 20798 Kitwe Zambia *Tel:* +260 2 223 264 *Fax:* +260 2 224 778 *Email:* chama_albert@yahoo.ca

Southern Malawi The Rt Revd Alinafe Kalemba Bishop of Southern Malawi PO Box 30220 Chichiri Blantyre 3 Malawi *Tel:* +265 1 841 218 *Fax:* +265 1 841 235 *Email:* dean@sdnp.org.mw

Upper Shire The Rt Revd Brighton Vitta Malasa Bishop of Upper Shire Bishop's House Private Bag 1 Chilema Zomba Malawi *Email:* malasab@yahoo.co.uk *Web:* www.malawipartnership.co.uk/uppershire/

IGLESIA ANGLICANA DE
LA REGION CENTRAL DE AMERICA

Mr Harold Charles *Provincial Treasurer* Apartado R Balboa REPUBLIC OF PANAMA *Tel:* +507 262 2052 *Email:* iarcahch@sinfo.net

Costa Rica The Rt Revd Hector Monterroso Gonzalez Bishop of Costa Rica & Provincial Secretary Apartado 2773-1000 San José Costa Rica *Tel:* +506 22250209 *Fax:* +506 22538331 *Email:* iarca@me.com

El Salvador The Rt Revd Juan David Alvarado Melgar Bishop of El Salvador 47 Avenida Sur 723 Col Flor Blanca Apt Postal (01) San Salvador 274 El Salvador *Tel:* +503 2 223 2252 *Email:* anglican.es@gmail.com

Guatemala The Most Revd Armando R Guerra Soria Bishop of Guatemala Apartado 58a Avenida La Castellana 40-06 Guatemala City Zona 8 Guatemala *Tel:* +502 (0)2 472 0852 *Fax:* +502 (0)2 472 0764 *Email:* agepiscopal@yahoo.com

Nicaragua The Most Revd Sturdie Downs Primate of IARCA & Bishop of Nicaragua Apartado 1207 Managua Nicaragua *Tel:* +505 22225174 *Fax:* +505 22545248 *Email:* secretaria_diocesana@hotmail.com

Panama The Rt Revd Julio Murray Bishop of Panama Box R Balboa Republic of Panama *Tel:* +507 212 0062 *Email:* bpmurray@hotmail.com

PROVINCE DE L'EGLISE ANGLICANE
DU CONGO

The Ven Anthonio Kibwela *Provincial Secretary* The Province of the Anglican Church of Congo 11 AV Basalakala Commune de Kalamu Kinshasa DR CONGO *Tel:* +243 995412138

Mr Alain Batondela *Provincial Treasurer* C/O PO Box 25586 Kampala Uganda

Aru The Rt Revd Dr Georges Titre Ande Bishop of Aru PO Box 226 Arua Uganda *Tel:* +243 8 1039 3071 *Email:* revdande@yahoo.co.uk

Boga The Rt Revd Mugenyi William Bahemuka Bishop of Boga Awaiting Details *Email:* mugenywilliam@yahoo.com

Bukavu The Rt Revd Sylvestre Bahati Bishop of Bukavu Evache Anglican Av. Pagni No2 Q/ Nyalukemba, C/ Ibanda Bukavu Democratic Republic of the Congo*Email:* bahati_bali@yahoo.fr

Kasai The Rt Revd Marcel Kapinga Bishop of Kasai No. 05, Avenue Makenga District Bonzola Common Dibindi Mbuji-Mayi Kasai Oriental Democratic Republic of Congo *Tel:* +243 8160 61423 *Email:* anglicanekasai2@gmail.com

Katanga The Rt Revd Muno Kasima Bishop of Katanga C/O U.M.M PO Box 22037 Kitwe Zambia *Tel:* +342 97 047 173 *Email:* kasimamuno@yahoo.fr

Kindu The Rt Revd Zacharie Masimango Katanda Bishop of Kindu Av. Penemisenga No 4, C/ Kasuku Kindu Maniema Rwanda *Tel:* +243 08 1328 6255 *Email:* angkindu@yahoo.fr

Kinshasa The Most Revd Kahwa Henri Isingoma Archbishop of the Congo & Bishop of Kinshasa C/O PO Box 25586 Kampala Uganda *Email:* peac_isingoma@yahoo.fr

Kinshasa The Rt Revd Molanga Jean Botola Suffragan Bishop of Kinshasa PO Box 16482 Kinshasa 1 D R Congo *Email:* molangab@gmail.com

Kisangani The Rt Revd Lambert F Botolome Bishop of Kisangani Bowane Street, No 10 Quartier des Musiciens C/ Makiso BP 861 Kisangani Democratic Republic of Congo

Nord Kivu The Rt Revd Muhindo Isesomo Bishop of Nord Kivu CAZ Butembo PO Box 506 Bwera-Kasese Uganda *Fax:* +871 166 1121

Nord Kivu The Rt Revd Enoch WM Kayeeye Assistant Bishop of Nord Kivu C/O PO Box 506 Bwera/Kasese Uganda *Tel:* +243 09 9414 8579 *Email:* bpkayeeye@hotmail.com

THE CHURCH OF ENGLAND

Provincial Secretary Mr William Fittall Church House Great Smith Street London SW1P 3AZ England *Tel:* +44 (0)207 898 1360 *Fax:* +44 (0)207 898 1369 *Email:* william.fittall@churchofengland.org

Bath & Wells-Canterbury The Rt Revd Peter Hancock Bishop of Bath & Wells The Palace Wells Somerset BA5 2PD England *Tel:* +44 (0)1749 672 341 *Fax:* +44 (0)1749 679 355 *Email:* bishop@bathwells.anglican.org *Web:* www.bathwells.anglican.org

Bath & Wells-Taunton-Canterbury The Rt Revd Ruth Worsley Suffragan Bishop of Taunton The Palace Wells Somerset BA5 2PD England *Tel:* +44 (0)1749 672 341 *Fax:* +44 (0)1749 679 355 *Email:* bishop.taunton@bathwells.anglican.org *Web:* www.bathandwells.org.uk

Birmingham-Canterbury The Rt Revd David Andrew Urquhart Bishop of Birmingham Birmingham Diocese Office 1 Colmore Row Birmingham B3 2BJ England *Tel:* +44 (0)121 427 1163 *Fax:* +44 (0)121 426 1322 *Email:* bishop@birmingham.anglican.org *Web:* www.birmingham.anglican.org

Birmingham-Aston-Canterbury The Rt Revd Anne Elizabeth Hollinghurst Suffragan Bishop of Birmingham-Aston Birmingham Diocese Office 1 Colmore Row Birmingham B3 2BJ England *Tel:* +44 (0)121 426 0400 *Fax:* +44 (0)121 428 1114 *Email:* bishopofaston@birmingham.anglican.org *Web:* www.birmingham.anglican.org

Blackburn-York The Rt Revd Julian Tudor Henderson Bishop of Blackburn Bishop's House Ribchester Road Clayton-le-Dale Blackburn BB1 9EF England *Tel:* +44 (0)1254 248 234 *Fax:* +44 (0)1254 246 668 *Email:* bishop@bishopofblackburn. org.uk *Web:* www.blackburn.anglican.org

Blackburn-Burnley-York The Rt Revd Philip North Suffragan Bishop of Blackburn-Burnley Church House Cathedral close Blackburn Lancs BB1 5AA England *Tel:* +44 01254 503087 *Email:* bishop. burnley@blackburn.anglican.org

Blackburn-Lancaster-York The Rt Revd Geoffrey Seagrave Pearson Suffragan Bishop Lancaster The Vicarage Whinney Brow Lane Shireshead, Forton Preston PR3 0AE England *Tel:* +44 (0)1524 799 900 *Fax:* +44 (0)1524 799 901 *Email:* bishop.lancaster@ ukonline.co.uk

Bristol-Canterbury The Rt Revd Michael Arthur Hill Bishop of Bristol 58a High Street Winterbourne Bristol BS36 1JQ England *Tel:* +44 (0)1454 777 728 *Fax:* +44 (0)1454 777 814 *Email:* bishop@ bristoldiocese.org *Web:* www.bristol.anglican.org

Bristol-Swindon-Canterbury The Rt Revd Lee Stephen Rayfield Bishop of Swindon Mark House Field Rise Swindon SN1 4HP England *Tel:* +44 (0)1793 538 654 *Fax:* +44 (0)1793 525 181 *Email:* bishop.swindon@bristoldiocese.org

Canterbury-Canterbury The Most Revd and Rt Hon Justin Welby Archbishop of Canterbury Lambeth Palace London SE1 7JU United Kingdom *Tel:* +44 (0)20 7898 1200 *Fax:* +44 (0)20 7261 9836 *Email:* pa.archbishop@lambethpalace.org.uk *Web:* www.archbishopofcanterbury.org/

Canterbury-Dover-Canterbury The Rt Revd Trevor Willmott Bishop in Canterbury and Bishop of Dover The Old Palace The Precincts Canterbury CT1 2EE England *Tel:* +44 (0)1227 459 382 *Fax:* +44 (0)1227 784 985 *Email:* bishop@bishcant.org

Canterbury-Ebbsfleet-Canterbury The Rt Revd Jonathan Goodall Suffragan Bishop of Ebbsfleet Hill House The Mount Caversham Reading RG4 7RE UK *Tel:* +44 (0)1865 288 030 *Email:* bishop@ebbsfleet. org.uk

Canterbury-Maidstone-Canterbury The Rt Revd Roderick Charles Howell Thomas Suffragan Bishop of Maidstone Bishop's House Pett Lane Charing Ashford TN27 0DL England *Tel:* +44 (0)1233 712 950 *Fax:* +44 (0)1233 713 543 *Email:* bishop@ bishmaid.org *Web:* www.bishopofmaidstone.org

Canterbury-Richborough-Canterbury The Rt Revd Norman N Banks Suffragan Bishop of Rich-borough Parkside House Abbey Mill Lane St Albans AL3 4HE England *Tel:* +44 (0)1727 836 358 *Email:* bishop@richborough.org.uk

Carlisle-York The Rt Revd James Scobie W Newcome Bishop of Carlisle Bishop's House Ambleside Road Keswick CA12 4DD England *Tel:* +44 (0)1768 773 430 *Email:* bishop.carlisle@ carlislediocese.org.uk *Web:* www.carlislediocese.org. uk

Carlisle-Penrith-York The Rt Revd Robert Freeman Suffragan Bishop of Penrith Bishop's House Ambleside Road Keswick CA12 4DD England *Tel:* +44 (0)1539 727 836 *Email:* bishop.penrith@ carlislediocese.org.uk

Chelmsford-Canterbury The Rt Revd Stephen Geoffrey Cottrell Bishop of Chelmsford Bishopscourt Main Road Margretting Ingatestone Essex CM4 0HD England *Tel:* +44 (0)1277 352 001 *Fax:* +44 (0)1277 355 374 *Email:* bishopscourt@chelmsford. anglican.org *Web:* www.chelmsford.anglican.org

Chelmsford-Barking-Canterbury The Rt Revd Peter Hill Bishop of Barking Barking Lodge 35A Verulam Avenue Walthamstow London E17 8ES England *Tel:* +44 (0)20 8509 7377 *Fax:* +44 (0)20 8514 6049 *Email:* b.barking@chelmsford.anglican. org

Chelmsford-Bradwell-Canterbury The Rt Revd John Wraw Suffragan Bishop of Bradwell Bishop's House Orsett Road Hordon-on-the-Hill Stanford-le-Hope Essex SS17 8NS England *Tel:* +44 (0)1375 673 806 *Fax:* +44 (0)1375 674 222 *Email:* b.bradwell@ chelmsford.anglican.org

Chelmsford-Colchester-Canterbury The Rt Revd Anthony Brett Morris Bishop of Colchester 1 Fitzwalter Road Colchester CO3 3SS England *Tel:* +44 (0)1206 576 648 *Fax:* +44 (0)1206 763 868 *Email:* b.colchester@chelmsford.anglican.org *Web:* www.chelmsford.anglican.org

Chester-York The Rt Revd Dr Peter Robert Forster Bishop of Chester Bishop's House Abbey Square Chester CH1 2JD England *Tel:* +44 (0)1244 350 864 *Fax:* +44 (0)1244 314 187 *Email:* bpchester@chester. anglican.org *Web:* www.chester.anglican.org/

Chester-Birkenhead-York The Rt Revd Keith Sinclair Bishop of Birkenhead Bishops Lodge 67 Bidston Road Prenton Wirral CH43 6TR ENGLAND *Tel:* +44 (0)151 652 2741 *Fax:* +44 (0)151 651 2330 *Email:* bpbirkenhead@chester.anglican.org

Chester-Stockport-York The Rt Revd Libby L Lane Suffragan Bishop of Chester-Stockport Bishop's Lodge Back Lane Dunham Town Altrincham WA14 4SG England *Tel:* +44 (0)161 928 5611 *Fax:* +44 (0)161 929 0692 *Email:* bpstockport@chester. anglican.org

Chichester-Canterbury The Rt Revd Martin C Warner Bishop of Chichester The Palace Canon Lane Chichester West Sussex PO19 1PY England

Tel: +44 (0)1243 782 161 *Fax:* +44 (0)1243 531 332 *Email:* bishop@chichester.anglian.org *Web:* www. chichester.anglican.org

Chichester-Horsham-Canterbury The Rt Revd Mark Sowerby Suffragan Bishop of Horsham Bishop's House 21 Guildford Road Horsham Sussex RH12 1LU England *Tel:* +44 (0)1403 211 139 *Fax:* +44 (0)1403 217 349 *Email:* bishop.horsham@ chichester.anglican.org

Chichester-Lewes-Canterbury The Revd Richard Charles Jackson Suffragan Bishop of Lewes The Palace Canon Lane Chichester West Sussex PO19 1PY England

Coventry-Canterbury The Rt Revd Christopher J Cocksworth Bishop of Coventry Bishop's House 23 Davenport Road Coventry CV5 6PW England *Tel:* +44 (0)2476 672 244 *Fax:* +44 (0)24 76 713 271 *Email:* bishop@bishop-coventry.org *Web:* www. dioceseofcoventry.org

Coventry-Warwick-Canterbury The Rt Revd John R A Stroyan Suffragan Bishop of Warwick Warwick House 139 Kenilworth Road Coventry W Midlands CV4 7AP England *Tel:* +44 (0)2476 412 627 *Fax:* +44 (0)2476 415 254 *Email:* Bishop.Warwick@covcofe. org

Derby-Canterbury The Rt Revd Alastair Redfern Bishop of Derby The Bishop's House 6 King Street Duffield Belper DE56 4EU England *Tel:* +44 (0)1332 840 132 *Fax:* +44 (0)1332 842 743 *Email:* pa@ bishopofderby.org *Web:* www.derby.anglican.org/

Derby-Repton-Canterbury The Rt Revd Humphrey Southern Suffragan Bishop of Derby-Repton Repton House Lea Matlock Derby DE4 5JP England *Tel:* +44 (0)1629 534 644 *Fax:* +44 (0)1629 534 003 *Email:* bishop@repton.free-online.co.uk

Diocese in Europe-Canterbury The Rt Revd David Hamid Suffragan Bishop of the Diocese in Europe 14 Tufton Street Westminster London SW1P 3QZ ENGLAND *Tel:* +44 (0)20 7898 1160 *Fax:* +44 (0)20 7898 1166 *Email:* david.hamid@ churchofengland.org

Diocese in Europe-Gibralter-Canterbury The Rt Revd Robert Innes Bishop of Gibraltar in Europe 47 rue Capitaine Crespel-boite 49 Brussels 1050 Belgium *Tel:* +32 2 213 7480 *Email:* robert.innes@ churchofengland.org *Web:* www.europe.anglican.org

Durham-York The Rt Revd Paul R Butler Bishop elect of Durham Auckland Castle Bishop Auckland Co Durham DL14 7NR England *Tel:* +44 (0)1388 602 576 *Fax:* +44 (0)1388 605 264 *Email:* bishop.of. durham@durham.anglican.org *Web:* www.durham. anglican.org

Durham-Jarrow-York The Rt Revd Mark Watts Bryant Suffragan Bishop of Jarrow Bishop's House

Ivy Lane Low Fell Gateshead NE9 6QD ENGLAND *Tel:* +44 (0)191 491 0917 *Fax:* +44 (0)191 491 5116 *Email:* bishop.of.jarrow@durham.anglican.org *Web:* www.durham.anglican.org

Ely-Canterbury The Rt Revd Stephen David Conway Bishop of Ely The Bishop's House Ely Cambs CB7 4DW England *Tel:* +44 (0)1353 662 749 *Fax:* +44 (0)1353 669 477 *Email:* bishop@ely. anglican.org *Web:* www.ely.anglican.org

Ely-Huntingdon-Canterbury The Rt Revd David Thomson Suffragan Bishop of Huntingdon 14 Lynn Road Ely CB6 1DA England *Tel:* +44 (0)1353 662 137 *Fax:* +44 (0)1353 662 137 *Email:* bishop. huntingdon@ely.anglican.org

Exeter-Canterbury The Rt Revd Robert Atwell Bishop of Exeter The Palace Exeter EX1 1HY England *Tel:* +44 (0)1392 272 362 *Fax:* +44 (0)1392 430 923 *Email:* sarah.johnson@exeter.anglican.org *Web:* www.exeter.anglican.org

Exeter-Crediton-Canterbury The Rt Revd Sarah Mullally Suffragan Bishop of Crediton 32 The Avenue Tiverton Devon EX16 4HW England *Tel:* +44 (0)1884 250 002 *Fax:* +44 (0)1884 257 454 *Email:* Sarah.mullally@exeter.anglican.org

Exeter-Plymouth-Canterbury The Rt Revd Nick McKinnel Suffragan Bishop of Plymouth 31 Riverside Walk Tamerton Foliot Plymouth PL5 4AQ England *Tel:* +44 (0)1752 769 836 *Fax:* +44 (0)1752 769 818 *Email:* bishop.of.plymouth@exeter.anglican. org

Gloucester-Canterbury The Rt Revd Rachel Treweek Bishop of Gloucester Church House 2 College Green Gloucester GL1 2LR England *Tel:* +44 (0)1452 835 512 *Fax:* + *Email:* bshpglos@glosdioc. org.uk *Web:* www.gloucester.anglican.org

Gloucester-Tewksury-Canterbury The Rt Revd Martyn James Snow Suffragan Bishop of Tewkesbury Bishop's House Church Road Staverton Gloucester GL51 0TW England *Tel:* +44 (0)1242 680 188 *Email:* bshptewk@glosdioc.org.uk

Guildford-Canterbury The Rt Revd Andrew John Watson Bishop of Guildford Willow Grange Woking Road Guildford Surrey GU4 7QS England *Tel:* +44 01483 590 500 *Fax:* +44 01483 590 501 *Email:* bishop.guildford@cofeguildford.org.uk *Web:* www. cofeguildford.org.uk

Guildford-Dorking-Canterbury The Rt Revd Ian James Brackley Suffragan Bishop of Dorking Dayspring 13 Pilgrims Way Guildford Surrey GU4 8AD ENGLAND *Tel:* +44 (0)1483 570 829 *Fax:* +44 (0)1483 567 268 *Email:* bishop.ian@cofeguildford. org.uk *Web:* www.guildford.anglican.org

Hereford-Canterbury The Rt Revd Richard M C Frith Bishop of Hereford Bishop's House The Palace

Hereford HR4 9BN England *Tel:* +44 (0)1432 373 300 *Email:* diooffice@hereford.anglican.org

Hereford-Ludlow-Canterbury The Rt Revd Alistair James Magowan Suffragan Bishop of Ludlow Bishops' House Corvedale Road Cavern Arms Shropshire SY7 9BT England *Tel:* +44 (0)1588 673 571 *Fax:* +44 (0)1588 673 571 *Email:* bishopalistair@btinternet.com

Leicester-Canterbury The Rt Revd Timothy John Stevens Bishop of Leicester Bishop's Lodge 10 Springfield Road Leicester LE2 3BD England *Tel:* +44 (0)116 270 8985 *Fax:* +44 (0)116 270 3288 *Email:* bishop.tim@leccofe.org *Web:* www.leicester. anglican.org

Leicester-Canterbury The Rt Revd Christopher John Boyle Assistant Bishop in the Diocese of Leicester Church House St Martin's East Leicester LE1 5FX ENGLAND *Tel:* +44 (0) 116 248 7411 *Email:* bishop.boyle@leccofe.org

Lichfield-Canterbury Vacant Bishop elect of Lichfield The Bishop's House 22 The Close Lichfield WS13 7LG England *Tel:* +44 (0)1543 306 000 *Fax:* +44 (0)1543 306 009 *Email:* bishop.lichfield@lichfield.anglican.org *Web:* www.lichfield.anglican. org

Lichfield-Shrewsbury-Canterbury The Rt Revd Mark James Rylands Bishop of Shrewsbury Athlone House 68 London Road Shrewsbury SYZ 6PG England *Tel:* +44 (0)1743 235 867 *Fax:* +44 (0)1743 243 296 *Email:* bishop.shrewsbury@lichfield. anglican.org *Web:* www.lichfield.anglican.org

Lichfield-Stafford-Canterbury The Rt Revd Geoffrey Peter Annas Suffragan Bishop of Stafford Ash Garth 6 Broughton Crescent Barlaston Stoke on Trent ST12 9DD England *Tel:* +44 01782 373 308 *Fax:* +44 01782 373 705 *Email:* bishop.stafford@lichfield.anglican.org

Lichfield-Wolverhampton-Canterbury The Rt Revd Clive Gregory Bishop of Wolverhampton 61 Richmond Road Merridale Wolverhampton WV3 9JH ENGLAND *Tel:* +44 (0)1902 824 503 *Fax:* +44 (0)1902 824 504 *Email:* bishop.wolverhampton@lichfield.anglican.org

Lincoln-Canterbury The Rt Revd Christopher Lowson Bishop of Lincoln The Old Palace Minster Yard Lincoln LN2 1PU England *Tel:* +44 (0)1522 504 090 *Fax:* +44 (0)1522 511 095 *Email:* bishop. lincoln@lincoln.anglican.org *Web:* www.lincoln. anglican.org

Lincoln-Grantham-Canterbury The Revd Nicholas Alan Chamberlain Suffragan Bishop elect of Grantham Saxonwell Vicarage Church Street Long Bennington Newark NG23 5ES England *Tel:* +44 (0)1400 283 344 *Fax:* +44 (0)1400 283 321 *Email:* bishop.grantham@lincoln.anglican.org

Lincoln-Grimsby-Canterbury The Rt Revd David Eric Court Suffragan Bishop of Grimsby Bishop's House Church Lane Irby Upon Humber Grimsby DN37 7JR ENGLAND *Tel:* +44 (0)1472 371 715 *Fax:* +44 (0)1472 371 716 *Email:* bishop.grimsby@lincoln.anglican.org

Liverpool-York The Rt Revd Paul Bayes Bishop of Liverpool Bishop's Lodge Woolton Park Liverpool L25 6DT England *Tel:* +44 (0)151 421 0831 *Fax:* +44 (0)151 428 3055 *Email:* Bishopslodge@liverpool. anglican.org *Web:* www.liverpool.anglican.org

Liverpool-Warrington-York The Rt Revd Richard Finn Blackburn Suffragan Bishop of Warrington St James House 20 St James Road Liverpool L1 7BY England *Tel:* +44 (0)151 705 2140 *Fax:* +44 (0)151 709 2885 *Email:* bishopofwarrington@liverpool. anglican.org

London-Canterbury The Rt Revd & Rt Hon Richard John Carew Chartres Bishop of London The Old Deanery Dean's Court London EC4V 5AA ENGLAND *Tel:* +44 (0)20 7248 6233 *Fax:* +44 (0)20 7248 9721 *Email:* bishop@londin.clara.co.uk *Web:* www.london.anglican.org

London-Edmonton-Canterbury The Rt Revd Robert Wickham Suffragan Bishop of London-Edmonton 27 Thurlow Road Hampstead London NW3 5PP ENGLAND *Tel:* +44 (0)20 7435 5890 *Fax:* +44 (0)20 7435 6049 *Email:* bishop.edmonton@london.anglican.org

London-Fulham-Canterbury The Rt Revd Jonathan Mark Richard Baker Suffragan Bishop of Fulham The Old Deanery Dean's Court London EC4V 5AA ENGLAND *Tel:* +44 (0)20 7932 1130 *Email:* bishop. fulham@london.anglican.org

London-Islington-Canterbury The Rt Revd Ric Thorpe Suffragan Bishop of London-Islington

London-Kensington-Canterbury The Rt Revd Graham Tomlin Suffragan Bishop of London-Kensington Dial House Riverside Twickenham Middlesex TW1 3DT England *Tel:* +44 (0)208 8892 7781 *Fax:* +44 (0)208 8891 3969 *Email:* bishop. kensington@london.anglican.org

London-Stepney-Canterbury The Rt Revd Adrian Newman Suffragan Bishop of London-Stepney 63 Coborn Road Bow London Kent E3 2DB ENGLAND *Tel:* +44 (0)1634 843 366 *Fax:* +44 (0)1634 401 410 *Email:* bishop.stepney@london.anglican.org

London-Willesden-Canterbury The Rt Revd Peter Allan Broadbent Bishop of Willesden 173 Willesden Lane London NW6 7YN ENGLAND *Tel:* +44 (0)20 8451 0189 *Fax:* +44 (0)20 8451 4606 *Email:* bishopwillesden.pa@btinternet.com

Manchester-York The Rt Revd David S Walker Bishop of Manchester Bishopscourt Bury New Road

Salford Manchester M7 4LE England *Tel:* +44 (0)161 792 2096 *Fax:* +44 (0)161 792 6826 *Email:* bishop@bishopscourt.manchester.anglican.org *Web:* www.manchester.anglican.org

Manchester-Bolton-York The Rt Revd Christopher Paul Edmondson Suffragan Bishop of Bolton Bishop's Lodge Walkden Road Worsley Manchester M28 2WH England *Tel:* +44 (0)161 790 8289 *Fax:* +44 (0)1204 882 988 *Email:* bishopchris@manchester.anglican.org

Manchester-Middleton-York The Rt Revd Mark Davies Suffragan Bishop of Middleton The Hollies Manchester Road Rochdale OL11 3QY England *Tel:* +44 (0)1706 358 550 *Fax:* +44 (0)1706 354 851 *Email:* bishopmark@manchester.anglican.org

Newcastle-York The Ven Christine Hardman Bishop elect of Newcastle Bishop's House 29 Moor Road South Gosforth Newcastle upon Tyne NE3 1PA England *Tel:* +44 (0)191 285 2220 *Fax:* +44 (0)191 284 6933 *Email:* bishop@newcastle.anglican.org *Web:* www.newcastle.anglican.org

Newcastle-York The Rt Revd Francis White Assistant Bishop of Newcastle C/O Bishops House 29 Moor Road South Newcastle upon Tyne NE3 1PA England *Tel:* +44 (0)191 285 2220 *Fax:* +44 (0)191 284 6933 *Email:* bishopfrank@newcastle.anglican.org

Norwich-Canterbury The Rt Revd Graham James Bishop of Norwich Bishop's House Norwich Norfolk NR3 1SB England *Tel:* +44 (0)1603 629 001 *Fax:* +44 (0)1603 761 613 *Email:* bishop@norwich.anglican.org *Web:* www.norwich.anglican.org

Norwich-Lynn-Canterbury The Rt Revd Jonathan Meyrick Suffragan Bishop of Lynn The Old Vicarage Castle Acre King's Lynn Norfolk PE32 2AA England *Tel:* +44 (0)1760 755 553 *Fax:* +44 (0)1760 755 085 *Email:* bishop.lynn@norwich.anglican.org

Norwich-Thetford-Canterbury The Rt Revd Alan Peter Winton Suffragan Bishop of Thetford The Red House 53 Norwich Street Stoke Holy Cross Norwich Norfolk NR14 8AB England *Tel:* +44 (0)1508 491 014 *Fax:* +44 (0)1508 492 105 *Email:* bishop.thetford@norwich.anglican.org

Oxford-Canterbury Vacant Bishop elect of Oxford Diocesan Church House North Hinksey Oxford OX2 0NB England *Tel:* +44 (0)1865 208 222 *Fax:* +44 (0)1865 790 470 *Email:* bishopoxon@dch.oxford.anglican.org *Web:* www.oxford.anglican.org

Oxford-Buckingham-Canterbury The Rt Revd Dr Alan Thomas Lawrence Wilson Suffragan Bishop of Buckingham Sheridan Grimms Hill Great Missenden Bucks HP16 9BD England *Tel:* +44 (0)1494 862 173 *Fax:* +44 (0)1494 890 508 *Email:* bishopbucks@oxford.anglican.org

Oxford-Dorchester-Canterbury The Rt Revd Colin William Fletcher Suffragan Bishop of Dorchester Arran House Sandy Lane Yarnton Kidlington OX5 1PB ENGLAND *Tel:* +44 (0)1865 208 218 *Fax:* +44 (0)1865 379 890 *Email:* bishopdorchester@oxford.anglican.org

Oxford-Reading-Canterbury The Rt Revd Andrew Proud Suffragan Bishop of Reading Bishop's House Tidmarsh Lane Reading Berks RG8 8HA England *Tel:* +44 (0)118 984 1216 *Fax:* +44 (0)118 984 1218 *Email:* bishopreading@oxford.anglican.org

Peterborough-Canterbury The Rt Revd Donald Spargo Allister Bishop of Peterborough Bishop's Lodging The Palace Peterborough Cambs PE1 1YA England *Tel:* +44 (0)1733 562 492 *Fax:* +44 (0)1733 890 077 *Email:* bishop@peterborough-diocese.org.uk *Web:* www.peterborough-diocese.org.uk

Peterborough-Brixworth-Canterbury The Rt Revd John E Holbrook Suffragan Bishop of Brixworth Orchard Acre 11 North Street Mears Ashby Northampton NN6 0DW England *Tel:* +44 (0)1733 562 492 *Email:* bishop.brixworth@peterborough-diocese.org.uk

Portsmouth-Canterbury The Rt Revd Christopher R J Foster Bishop of Portsmouth Bishopsgrove 26 Osborn Road Fareham Hants PO16 7DQ England *Tel:* +44 (0)1329 280 247 *Fax:* +44 (0)1329 231 538 *Email:* bishports@portsmouth.anglican.org *Web:* www.portsmouth.anglican.org/

Rochester-Canterbury The Rt Revd James H Langstaff Bishop of Rochester Bishopscourt 24 St Margaret's Street Rochester Kent ME1 1TS England *Tel:* +44 (0)1634 842 721 *Fax:* +44 (0)1634 831 136 *Email:* bishop.rochester@rochester.anglican.org *Web:* www.rochester.anglican.org/

Rochester-Tonbridge-Canterbury The Rt Revd Dr Brian Castle Suffragan Bishop of Tonbridge Bishop's Lodge 48 St Botolph's Road Sevenoaks TN13 3AG England *Tel:* +44 (0)1732 456 070 *Fax:* +44 (0)1732 741 449 *Email:* bishop.tonbridge@rochester.anglican.org

Salisbury-Canterbury The Rt Revd Nicholas R Holtam Bishop of Salisbury South Canonry 71 The Close Salisbury Wiltshire SP1 2ER England *Tel:* +44 (0)1722 334 031 *Fax:* +44 (0)1722 413 112 *Email:* bishop.salisbury@salisbury.anglican.org *Web:* www.salisbury.anglican.org

Salisbury-Ramsbury-Canterbury The Rt Revd Edward Condry Suffragan Bishop of Ramsbury Diocesan Office Church House Crane Street Salisbury Wilts SP1 2QB ENGLAND *Tel:* +44 (0)1722 438 662 *Fax:* +44 (0)1380 848 247 *Email:* ramsbury.office@salisbury.anglican.org

Salisbury-Sherborne-Canterbury Vacant Suffragan Bishop elect of Sherborne The Sherborne Area

Office St Nicholas' Church Centre 30 Wareham Road Corfe Mullen Dorset BH21 3LE England *Tel:* +44 (0)1202 691 418 *Fax:* + *Email:* gsherborne@ salisbury.anglican.org *Web:* www.salisbury.anglican. org

Sheffield-York The Rt Revd Steven Croft Bishop of Sheffield Church Hosue 95-99 Effingham Road Rotheram South Yorks S65 1BL England *Tel:* +44 (0)114 230 2170 *Fax:* +44 (0)114 263 0110 *Email:* bishop@sheffield.anglican.org *Web:* www.sheffield. anglican.org/

Sheffield-Doncaster-York The Rt Revd Peter Burrows Suffragan Bishop of Doncaster Doncaster House Church Lane Fishlake Doncaster DN7 5JW England *Tel:* +44 (0)1302 846 610 *Fax:* +44 (0)1709 730 230 *Email:* bishoppeter@bishopofdoncaster.org.uk

Sodor & Man-York The Rt Revd Robert Paterson Bishop of Sodor and Man Thie yn Aspick 4 The Falls Tromode Road Douglas IM4 4PZ Isle of Man *Tel:* +44 (0)1624 622 108 *Fax:* +44 (0)1624 672 890 *Email:* bishop@sodorandman.im

Southwark-Canterbury The Rt Revd Christopher T Chessun Bishop of Southwark Trinity House 4 Chapel Court Borough High Street London SE1 1HW England *Tel:* +44 (0)207 939 9241 *Fax:* + *Email:* bishop.christopher@southwark.anglican.org *Web:* www.southwark.anglican.org

Southwark-Croydon-Canterbury The Rt Revd Johnathan Clark Suffragan Bishop of Croydon St Matthew's House 100 George Street Croydon Surrey CR0 1PE England *Tel:* +44 (0)208 256 9630 *Fax:* +44 (0)208 256 9631 *Email:* bishop.johnathan@ southwark.anglican.org

Southwark-Kingston-Canterbury The Rt Revd Richard I Cheetham Suffragan Bishop of Kingston 620 Kingston Road Raynes Park London SW20 8DN England *Tel:* +44 (0)20 8545 2440 *Fax:* +44 (0)20 8545 2441 *Email:* bishop.richard@southwark. anglican.org

Southwark-Woolwich-Canterbury The Rt Revd Michael Ipgrave Suffragan Bishop of Woolwich Trinity House 4 Chapel Court Borough High Street London SE1 1HW England *Tel:* +44 (0)207 939 9405 *Fax:* +44 (0)207 939 9467 *Email:* bishop.michael@ southwark.anglican.org

Southwell & Nottingham-York The Rt Revd Paul Gavin Williams Bishop elect of Southwell & Nottingham Bishop's Manor Southwell Notts NG25 0JR England *Tel:* +44 (0)1636 812 112 *Fax:* +44 (0)1636 815 401 *Email:* bishop@southwell.anglican. org *Web:* www.southwell.anglican.org

Southwell & Nottingham-Sherwood-York The Rt Revd Anthony Porter Suffragan Bishop of Southwell-Sherwood Dunham House 8 Westgate Southwell Notts NG25 0JL England *Tel:* +44 (0)1636 819 133

Fax: +44 (0)1636 819 085 *Email:* bishopsherwood@ southwell.anglican.org

St Albans-Canterbury The Rt Revd Alan G C Smith Bishop of St Albans Abbey Gate House 4 Abbey Mill Lane St Albans Herts AL3 4HD England *Tel:* +44 (01727 853 305 *Fax:* +44 (01727 846 715 *Email:* bishop@stalbans.anglican.org *Web:* www. stalbans.anglican.org/

St Albans-Bedford-Canterbury The Rt Revd Richard Atkinson Bishop of Bedford Bishop's Lodge Bedford Road Cardington MK44 3SS England *Tel:* +44 (0)1234 831 432 *Fax:* +44 (0)1234 831 484 *Email:* bishopbedford@stalbans.anglican.org

St Albans-Bishopswood-Canterbury The Rt Revd Michael Beasley Suffragan Bishop of Hertford Bishopswood 3 Stobarts Close Knebworth Herts SG3 6ND England *Tel:* +44 (0)1438 817 260 *Fax:* + *Email:* bishophertford@stalbans.anglican.org

St Edmundsbury & Ipswich-Canterbury The Rt Revd Martin Seeley Bishop of St Edmundsbury & Ipswich The Bishop's House 4 Park Road Ipswich Suffolk IP1 3ST England *Tel:* +44 01473 252829 *Fax:* +44 01473 232552 *Email:* bishops.office@cofesuffolk. org *Web:* www.stedmundsbury.anglican.org

St Edmundsbury & Ipswich-Dunwich-Canterbury Vacant Suffragan Bishop elect of Dunwich Awaiting Details *Tel:* +44 (0)1473 222 276

Truro-Canterbury The Rt Revd Timothy M Thornton Bishop of Truro Lis Escop Feock Truro Cornwall TR3 6QQ England *Tel:* +44 01872 862 657 *Fax:* +44 01872 862 037 *Email:* bishop@truro. anglican.org *Web:* www.truro.anglican.org/

Truro-St Germans-Canterbury The Revd Christopher David Goldsmith Suffragan Bishop of St Germans 32 Falmouth Road Truro Cornwall TR1 2HX England *Tel:* +44 (0)1872 273 190 *Fax:* +44 (0)1872 277 883 *Email:* bishop@stgermans.truro. anglican.org

West Yorkshire & the Dales-Bradford-York The Rt Revd Toby Howarth Area Bishop of Bradford Kadugli House Elmsley Street Keighley West Yorkshire BD20 6SE England *Email:* toby.howarth@ lambethpalace.org.uk

West Yorkshire & the Dales-Huddersfield-York The Rt Revd Jonathan J Gibbs Area Bishop of Huddersfield See Wakefield Area

West Yorkshire & the Dales-Leeds-York The Rt Revd Nicholas Baines Bishop of Leeds St Mary's Street Leeds West Yorkshire LS9 7DP England *Tel:* +44 01274 545414 *Fax:* +44 01274 544831 *Email:* bishop.nick@westyorkshiredales.anglican.org *Web:* www.westyorkshiredales.anglican.org

West Yorkshire & the Dales-Richmond-York The Rt Revd Paul Slater Suffragan Bishop of

Richmond St Mary's Street Leeds West Yorkshire LS9 7DP England

West Yorkshire & the Dales-Ripon-York The Rt Revd James H Bell Bishop of Ripon Thistledown Exelby Bedale DL8 2HD England *Tel:* +44 (0)1677 423 525 *Fax:* +44 (0)1677 427 515 *Email:* bishop. knaresb@btinternet.com

West Yorkshire & the Dales-Wakefield-York The Rt Revd Anthony W Robinson Bishop of Wakefield 181A Manygates Lane Sandal Wakefield WF2 7DR England *Tel:* +44 (0)1924 250 781 *Fax:* +44 (0)1924 240 490 *Email:* bishop.tony@westyorkshiredales. anglican.org

Winchester-Canterbury The Rt Revd Tim Dakin Bishop of Winchester Wolvesey Winchester Hampshire SO23 9ND England *Tel:* +44 (0)1962 854 050 *Fax:* +44 (0)1962 897 088 *Email:* joyce.cockell@ winchester.anglican.org   *Web:* www.winchester. anglican.org

Winchester-Basingstoke-Canterbury The Rt Revd David Grant Williams Suffragan Bishop of Basingstoke Bishop's Lodge Colden Lane Old Alresford Hampshire SO24 9DY England *Tel:* +44 (0)1962 737 330 *Email:* lindsey.demaudave@ winchester.anglican.org

Winchester-Southampton-Canterbury The Rt Revd Jonathan H Frost Suffragan Bishop of Southampton Bishop's House St Mary's Church Close Wessex Lane Southampton Hants SO18 2ST England *Tel:* +44 (0)23 8067 2684 *Fax:* + *Email:* bishop.jonathan@winchester.anglican.org

Worcester-Canterbury The Rt Revd John G Inge Bishop of Worcester The Bishop's Office The Old Palace Deans Way Worcester Worcs WR1 2JE England *Tel:* +44 (0)1905 731 599 *Fax:* +44 (0)1299 250 027 *Email:* generalinfo@cofe-worcester.org.uk

Worcester-Dudley-Canterbury The Rt Revd Graham B Usher Suffragan Bishop of Dudley Bishop's House Bishop's Walk Cradley Heath Warley West Midlands B64 7RH ENGLAND *Tel:* +44 (0)121 550 3407 *Fax:* +44 (0)121 550 7340

York-York The Most Revd & Rt Hon Dr John T M Sentamu Archbishop of York Bishopthorpe Palace Bishopthorpe York North Yorks YO23 2GE England *Tel:* +44 (0)1904 707 021 *Fax:* +44 (0)1904 709 204 *Email:* alison.cundiff@archbishopofyork.org *Web:* www.dioceseofyork.org.uk/

York-Beverly-York The Rt Revd Glyn Webster Suffragan Bishop of Beverley Holy Trinity Rectory Micklegate York YO1 6LE England *Tel:* +44 (0)113 265 4280 *Fax:* +44 (0)113 265 4281 *Email:* bishopofbeverley@yorkdiocese.org

York-Hull-York The Rt Revd Alison White Suffragan Bishop of Hull Hullen House Woodfield Lane Hessle

HU13 0ES ENGLAND *Tel:* +44 (0)1482 649 019 *Fax:* +44 (0)1482 647 449 *Email:* bishopofhull@ yorkdiocese.org

York-Selby-York The Rt Revd John Bromilow Thomson Bishop of Selby Bishop's House Barton-le-Street Malton YO17 6PL England *Tel:* +44 (0)1653 627 191 *Fax:* +44 (0)1653 627 193 *Email:* bishselby@ clara.net

York-Whitby-York The Rt Revd Paul John Ferguson Bishop of Whitby Handyside 60 West Green Stokesley Middlesborough North Yorks TS9 5BD England *Tel:* +44 (0)1642 714 475 *Fax:* +44 (0)1642 710 685 *Email:* julie.elphee@yorkdiocese.org

HONG KONG SHENG KUNG HUI

Provincial Secretary The Revd Peter D Koon 71 Bonham Road Shek Tong Tsui Hong Kong People's Republic of China *Tel:* +852 25 265 355 *Fax:* +852 25 212 199 *Email:* peter.koon@hkskh.org

Eastern Kowloon The Rt Revd Timothy Kwok Bishop of Eastern Kowloon Diocesan Office Bradbury Center 139 Ma tau Chung Road Kowloon Hong Kong People's Republic of China *Tel:* +852 27 139 983 *Fax:* +852 27 111 609 *Email:* ekoffice@ ekhkskh.org.hk *Web:* dek.hkskh.org

Hong Kong Island The Most Revd Dr Paul Kwong Archbishop of Hong Kong Sheng Kung Hui & Bishop of Hong Kong Island 71 Bonham Road Shek Tong Tsui Hong Kong People's Republic of China *Tel:* +852 2526 5366 *Fax:* +852 2523 3344 *Email:* do.dhk@hkskh.org *Web:* dhk.hkskh.org

Western Kowloon The Rt Revd Andrew Chan Bishop of Western Kowloon 11 Pak Po Street Mongkok Kowloon Hong Kong People's Republic of China *Tel:* +852 27 830 811 *Fax:* +852 27 830 799 *Email:* dwk@hkskh.org *Web:* dwk.hkskh.org

THE CHURCH OF THE PROVINCE OF THE INDIAN OCEAN

Provincial Secretary The Revd Canon Samitiana J Razafindralambo Jhonson Diocesan Church House 37th St Paul Road Vacoas Mauritius *Tel:* +230 686 5158 *Email:* indian.ocean.psec@gmail.com

Provincial Treasurer Mr Philip Tse Rai Wai 21 Dr, J. Riviere St Port Louis Republic of Mauritius *Tel:* +230 465 1235 *Email:* pptrw@intnet.mu

Antananarivo The Rt Revd Samoela Jaona Ranarivelo Bishop of Antananarivo Evêché Anglican Lot VK57 ter Ambohimanoro 101 Antananarivo Madagascar *Tel:* +261 (0)20 222 0827 *Fax:* +261 (0)2 226 1331 *Email:* eemdanta@yahoo.com

Antananarivo-Tulear The Rt Revd Todd Andrew McGregor Bishop of Tulear and Assistant Bishop of Antananarivo Evêché Anglican Lot VK57 ter

Ambohimanoro 101 Antananarivo Madagascar *Email:* revmctodd@yahoo.com

Antsiranana The Rt Revd Theophile Botomazava Bishop of Antsiranana Evêché Anglican BP 278 4 Rue Grandidier Antsiranana 201 Madagascar *Tel:* +261 (0)20 822 2776

Fianarantsoa The Rt Revd Gilbert Rateloson Rakotondravelo Bishop of Fianarantsoa Eveque du Diocese Fianarantsoa BP 1418 Fianarantsoa 301 Maagascar *Tel:* +261 20 755 1583 *Email:* eemdiofianara@yahoo.fr

Mahajanga The Rt Revd Jean Claude Andrianjafimanana Bishop of Mahajanga Eveche Anglican 401 Mahajanga B.P 570 Mahajanga 501 Madagascar *Email:* andrianjajc@yahoo.fr

Mauritius The Most Revd Ian Gerald James Ernest Archbishop, Province of Indian Ocean & Bishop of Mauritius Bishops House Nallatamby Road Phoenix Mauritius *Tel:* +230 686 5158 *Fax:* +230 697 1096 *Email:* dioang@intnet.mu

Seychelles The Rt Revd James Richard R Wong Yin Song Bishop of the Seychelles PO Box 44 Victoria Mahe Seychelles *Tel:* +248 321 977 *Fax:* +248 323 879 *Email:* angdio@seychelles.net

Toamasina The Rt Revd Jean Paul Solo Bishop of Toamasina Evêché Anglican Lot VK57 ter Ambohimanoro Antananarivo 101 Madagascar *Tel:* +261 20 533 1663 *Fax:* +261 20 533 1689 *Email:* eemdtoam@wanadoo.mg

Toliara New Diocese Awaiting Details Bishop elect of Toliara Awaiting Details

THE CHURCH OF IRELAND

Chief Officer and Secretary Mr Adrian Clements Church of Ireland House Church Avenue Rathmines Dublin 6 REPUBLIC OF IRELAND *Tel:* +353 (0)1 497 8422 *Fax:* +353 (0)1 497 8792 *Email:* chiefofficer@rcbdub.org *Web:* www.rcb.ireland. anglican.org

Armagh-Dublin The Most Revd Dr Richard Lionel Clarke Archbishop of Armagh and Primate of All Ireland and Metropolitan Church House 46 Abbey Street Armagh BT61 7DZ Northern Ireland *Tel:* +44 (0)28 375 27144 *Fax:* +44 (0)28 375 1059 *Email:* archbishop@armagh.anglican.org *Web:* www. armagh.anglican.org/

Cashel & Ossory-Dublin The Rt Revd Michael Andrew James Burrows Bishop of Cashel, Ferns & Ossory Bishop's House Troysgate Kilkenny Republic of Ireland *Tel:* +353 (0)56 778 6633 *Fax:* +353 (0)56 775 1813 *Email:* cashelossorybishop@eircom.net *Web:* www.cashel.anglican.org/

Clogher-Armagh The Rt Revd John McDowell Bishop of Clogher The See House 152A Ballagh

Road Fivemiletown Co Tyrone BT75 0QP Northern Ireland *Tel:* +44 (0)28 6634 7879 *Fax:* +44 (0)28 8952 2475 *Email:* bishop@clogher.anglican.org *Web:* www.clogher.anglican.org

Connor-Armagh The Rt Revd Alan Francis Abernethy Bishop of Connor Bishop's House 1 Marlborough Gate Marlborough Park Malone, Belfast BT9 6GB Northern Ireland *Tel:* +44 (0)28 902 33188 *Fax:* +44 (0)28 902 37802 *Email:* bishop@ connor.anglican.org *Web:* www.connor.anglican. org/

Cork, Cloyne & Ross-Dublin The Rt Revd William Paul Colton Bishop of Cork, Cloyne & Ross The Palace Bishop Street Cork Republic of Ireland *Tel:* +353 (0)21 5005 080 *Fax:* +353 (0)21 4320 960 *Email:* bishop@ccrd.ie *Web:* www.cork.anglican.org

Derry & Raphoe-Armagh The Rt Revd Kenneth Raymond Good Bishop of Derry & Raphoe The See House 112 Culmore Road Londonderry BT48 8JF Northern Ireland *Tel:* +44 (0)28 7135 1206 *Fax:* +44 (0)28 7135 2554 *Email:* bishop@derry.anglican.org *Web:* www.derry.anglican.org

Down & Dromore-Armagh The Rt Revd Harold Creeth Miller Bishop of Down & Dromore The See House 32 Knockdene Park South Belfast BT5 7AB Northern Ireland *Tel:* +44 (0)28 9082 8850 *Fax:* +44 (0)28 902 31902 *Email:* bishop@down.anglican.org *Web:* www.down.anglican.org

Dublin & Glendalough-Dublin The Most Revd Michael Geoffrey St Aubyn Jackson Archbishop of Dublin & Glendalough The See House 17 Temple Road Dartry Dublin 6 Republic of Ireland *Tel:* +353 (0)1 497 6981 *Fax:* +353 (0)1 497 6355 *Email:* archbishop@dublin.anglican.org *Web:* www.dublin. anglican.org

Kilmore, Elphin & Ardagh-Armagh The Rt Revd Ferran F Glenfield Bishop of Kilmore, Elphin & Ardagh 48 Carrickfern Road Cavan Co Cavan Ireland *Tel:* +44 (0)49 437 2759 *Email:* bishop@ kilmore.anglican.org *Web:* www.kilmore.anglican. org

Limerick & Killaloe-Dublin The Rt Revd Kenneth Kearon Bishop of Limerick & Killaloe Rien Roe Adare Co Limerick Republic of Ireland *Tel:* +353 (0)61 396 244 *Fax:* +353 (0)66 451 100 *Email:* bishop@limerick.anglican.org *Web:* www.limerick. anglican.org

Meath & Kildare-Dublin The Rt Revd Patricia Louise Storey Bishop of Meath & Kildare Bishop's House Mayglare Maynooth Co Kildare Republic of Ireland *Tel:* +353 (0)1 629 2163 *Fax:* +353 (0)1 628 9354 *Email:* bishop@meath.anglican.org *Web:* www. meath.anglican.org

Tuam, Killala & Achonry-Armagh The Rt Revd Patrick William Rooke Bishop of Tuam, Killala &

Achonry Bishop's House 2 Summerfield Cahergowan Claregalway Co Galway Ireland *Tel:* +353 (0)91 799 359 *Email:* bishop@tuam.anglican.org *Web:* www.tuam.anglican.org

THE NIPPON SEI KO KAI
(THE ANGLICAN COMMUNION IN JAPAN)

General Secretary The Revd Jesse Shin-Ichi Yahagi 65-3 Yarai Cho Shinjuku-Ku Tokyo 162-0805 Japan *Tel:* +81 (0)3 5228 3171 *Fax:* +81 (0)3 5228 3175 *Email:* general-sec.po@nskk.org

Provincial Treasurer Mr Shigeo Ozaki Provincial Office 65-3 Yarai-cho Shinjuku-ku Tokyo 162-0805 JAPAN *Tel:* +81 (0)3 5228 3171 *Fax:* +81 (0)3 5228 3175

Chubu The Rt Revd Peter Ichiro Shibusawa Bishop of Chubu 2-28-1 Meigetsu-cho Showa-ku Nagoya-shi Aichi-ken 466-0034 Japan *Tel:* +81 (0)52 858 1007 *Fax:* +81 (0)52 858 1008 *Email:* bishop.chubu@nskk.org

Hokkaido The Most Revd Nathaniel Makoto Uematsu Primate of The Nippon Sei Ko Kai & Bishop of Hokkaido Kita 15 Jo Nishi 5-1-12 Kita-Ku Sapporo 001-0015 Japan *Tel:* +81 (0)11 717 8181 *Fax:* +81 (0)11 736 8377 *Email:* fwjh6169@mb.infoweb.ne.jp *Web:* www.nskk.org/hokkaido

Kita Kanto The Rt Revd Zerubbabel Katsuichi Hirota Bishop of Kita Kanto 2-172 Sakuragi-cho Omiya-ku Saitama-shi Saitama-ken 330-0854 Japan *Tel:* +81 (0)48 642 2680 *Fax:* +81 (0)48 648 0358 *Email:* horotaz@nifty.com

Kobe The Rt Revd Andrew Yatuka Nakamura Bishop of Kobe 5-11-1 Shimo Yamate Dori Chuo-ku Kobe City Hyogo 650 0011 JAPAN *Tel:* +81 (0)78 351 5469 *Fax:* +81 (0)78 382 1095 *Email:* nakamurayutaka6@msn.com *Web:* www.kobe.anglican.org

Kyoto The Rt Revd Stephen Takashi Kochi Bishop of Kyoto 380 Okakuen-cho, Shimotachiuri-agaru Karasumadori Kamikyo-ku Kyoto-shi Kyoto-hu 602-8011 Japan *Tel:* +81 (0)75 431 7204 *Fax:* +81 (0)75 441 4238 *Email:* aset@kje.biglobe.ne.jp *Web:* www.nskk.org/kyoto

Kyushu The Rt Revd Luke Ken-ichi Muto Bishop of Kyushu 2-9-22 Kusagae Chuo-ku Fukuoka-shi Fukuoka-ken 810-0045 Japan *Tel:* +81 (0)92 771 2050 *Fax:* +81 (0)92 771 9857 *Web:* www.kyushu.anglican.org

Okinawa The Rt Revd David Eisho Uehara Bishop of Okinawa 3-3-5 Aza Meada Urasoe-shi Okinawa-ken 901-2102 Japan *Tel:* +81 (0)98 942 1101 *Fax:* +81 (0)98 942 1102 *Email:* rtrev.david-uehara@anglican-okinawa.jp

Osaka The Rt Revd Andrew Haruhisa Iso Bishop of Osaka 2-1-8 Matsuzaki-cho Abeno-ku Osaka-shi Osaka-fu 545-0053 Japan *Tel:* +81 (0)6 621 2179 *Fax:*

+81 (0)6 6621 3097 *Email:* office.osaka@nskk.org *Web:* www.nskk.org/osaka/

Tohoku The Rt Revd John Hiromichi Kato Bishop of Tohoku 2-13-15 Kokubun-cho Aoba-ku Sendai-shi Miyagi-ken 980-0803 Japan *Tel:* +81 (0)22 223 2349 *Fax:* +81 (0)22 223 2387 *Email:* bishop.tohoku@nskk.org *Web:* www.tohoku.anglican.org

Tokyo The Rt Revd Andrew Yoshimichi Ohata Bishop of Tokyo 3-6-18 Shiba Koen Minato-ku Tokyo Tokyo-to 105-0011 Japan *Tel:* +81 (0)3 3433 0987 *Fax:* +81 (0)3 3433 8678 *Email:* bishop.tko@nskk.org *Web:* www.tokyo.anglican.org

Yokohama The Rt Revd Laurence Yutaka Minabe Bishop of Yokohama 14-57 Mitsuzawa Shimo-cho Kanagawa-ku Yokohama-shi Kanagawa-ken 221-0852 Japan *Tel:* +81 (0)45 321 4988 *Fax:* +81 (0)45 321 4978 *Email:* laurence.yokohama@anglican.jp *Web:* www.anglican.jp/yokohama/

THE EPISCOPAL CHURCH IN JERUSALEM
AND THE MIDDLE EAST

Provincial Secretary Ms Georgia Katsantonis 2 Grigori Afxentiou Nicosia 1515 P O Box 22075 CYPRUS *Email:* georgia@spidernet.com.cy

Provincial Treasurer The Ven Canon William Schwartz PO Box 3210 Doha Qatar *Tel:* +974 4416 5726 *Email:* archdeacon.bill@cypgulf.org

Cyprus and the Gulf The Rt Revd Michael Augustine Owen Lewis Bishop of Cyprus and the Gulf Bishop's Office PO Box 22075 CY 1517 Nicosia Cyprus *Tel:* +357 (0)22 332 206 *Fax:* +357 (0)22 672 241 *Email:* bishop@spidernet.com.cy *Web:* www.cypgulf.org/

Egypt The Most Revd Dr Mouneer Hanna Anis Archbishop, Jerusalem & the Middle East & Bishop in Egypt with North Africa and the Horn of Africa Diocesan Office PO Box 87 Zamalek Distribution 11211 Cairo Egypt *Tel:* +20 (0)2 738 0821/3/9 *Fax:* +20 (0)2 735 894 *Email:* bishopmouneer@gmail.com *Web:* www.dioceseofegypt.org/

Egypt-Horn of Africa Area The Rt Revd Grant Lemarquand Area Bishop for the Horn of Africa Gambella Anglican Centre Gambella Town Gambella Ethiopia *Tel:* +20 (0)2 738 0821/3/9 *Fax:* +20 (0)2 735 894 *Email:* bishopgrant777@gmail.com

Egypt-North Africa Vacant Assistant Bishop elect for North Africa Diocesan Office PO Box 87 Zamalek Distribution 11211 Cairo Egypt *Tel:* +20 (0)2 738 0821/3/9

Iran The Rt Revd Azad Marshall Bishop in Iran St Thomas Center Raiwind Road PO Box 688 Lahore Punjab 54000 Pakistan *Tel:* +92 (0)42 542 0452 *Email:* bishop@saintthomascenter.org

Jerusalem The Rt Revd Suheil S Dawani Archbishop in Jerusalem St George's Cathedral Close Nablus

Road Box 19122 Jerusalem 91191 Israel *Tel:* +972 (0)2 627 1670 *Fax:* +972 (0)2 627 3847 *Email:* bishop@j-diocese.org *Web:* www.j-diocese.org

THE ANGLICAN CHURCH OF KENYA

Provincial Secretary The Revd Canon Rosemary Mbogo Bishops Road Off Ngong Road PO Box 40502- 00100 Nairobi Kenya *Tel:* +254 20 271 4752/3/4 *Fax:* +254 20 2718442 *Email:* ackpsoffice@ackenya.org

Provincial Treasurer Mr William Ogara PO Box 40502 Bishop's Gardens Bishop's Road Nairobi KENYA *Tel:* +254 (0)20 2333 324/5 *Fax:* +254 (0)20 2728 139

Provincial Accountant Mr John Muhoho PO Box 40502 Bishop's Gardens Bishop's Road Nairobi KENYA *Tel:* +254 (0)20 2714 755 *Fax:* +254 (0)20 2718 442

All Saints Cathedral Diocese The Most Revd Dr Eliud Wabukala Primate and Archbishop of All Kenya PO Box 40502 Nairobi 100 Kenya *Tel:* +254 (0)20 2714 752/3/5 *Fax:* +254 (0)20 2718 442 *Email:* archoffice@ackenya.org

All Saints Cathedral Diocese-Garissa Missionary Area The Rt Revd David Mutisya Suffragan Bishop of All Saints Cathedral Diocese-Garissa Missionary Area All Saints Cathedral PO Box 60 Garissa 70100 KENYA

All Saints Cathedral Diocese The Rt Revd Cleti Ogeto Suffragan Bishop-All Saints Cathedral Diocese PO Box 40502 Nairobi 100 Kenya

Bondo The Rt Revd Johannes O Angela Bishop of the Diocese of Bondo PO Box 240 Bondo 40601 Kenya *Tel:* +254 (0)335 20415 *Email:* ackbondo@swiftkenya.com

Bungoma The Revd George Mechumo Bishop elect of Bungoma PO Box 2392 Bungoma 50200 Kenya *Tel:* +254 (0)337 30 481 *Fax:* +254 (0)337 30 481 *Email:* ackbungoma@swiftkenya.com

Butere The Rt Revd Timothy Wambunya Bishop of Butere PO Box 54 Butere 50101 Kenya *Tel:* +254 056 620 412 *Fax:* +254 056 620 038 *Email:* ackbutere@swiftkenya.com

Eldoret The Rt Revd Dr Christopher Ruto Bishop of Eldoret PO Box 3404 Eldoret 30100 KENYA *Email:* ackeldoret@africaonline.co.ke

Embu The Rt Revd David Muriithi Ireri Bishop of Embu PO Box 189 Embu 60100 Kenya *Tel:* +254 068 30614 *Email:* ack-embu@swiftkenya.com

Kajiado The Rt Revd Gadiel Katanga Lenini Bishop of Kajiado PO Box 203-01100 Kajiado 1100 Kenya *Tel:* +254 (0)45 21105 *Email:* ackajiado@swiftkenya.com

Katakwa The Rt Revd Dr Zakayo I Epusi Bishop of Katakwa PO Box 68 Amagoro 50244 Kenya *Tel:* +254 (0)337 54 079 *Fax:* +254 (0)337 54 017 *Email:* ackatakwa@swiftkenya.com

Kericho The Rt Revd Jackson Ole Sapit Bishop of Kericho PO Box 678 Kericho 20200 KENYA *Tel:* +254 (0)52 20112 *Email:* nasoore2001@yahoo.com

Kirinyaga The Rt Revd Joseph Kibuchua Bishop of Kirinyaga PO Box 95 Kutus 10304 Kenya *Tel:* +254 (0)163 44 221 *Fax:* +254 (0)163 44 020 *Email:* ackirinyaga@swiftkenya.com

Kitale The Rt Revd Stephen Kewasis Bishop of Kitale PO Box 4176 Kitale Kenya *Tel:* +254 054 31631 *Email:* ack.ktl@gmail.com

Kitui The Rt Revd Josephat V Mule Bishop of Kitui PO Box 1054 Kitui 90200 Kenya *Tel:* +254 (0)141 226 82 *Fax:* +254 (0)141 221 19 *Email:* ackitui@swiftkenya.com

Machakos The Rt Revd Joseph Mutungi Bishop of Machakos PO Box 282 Machakos 90100 Kenya *Tel:* +254 044 21379 *Fax:* +254 044 20178 *Email:* ackmachakos@gmail.com

Makueni The Rt Revd Joseph M Kanuku Bishop of Makueni PO Box 282 Machakos *Tel:* +Bishop of Makueni 254 *Fax:* +044 21379 254 *Email:* 044 20178 *Web:* ackmachakos@swiftkenya.com

Malindi The Rt Revd Lawrence K Dena Bishop of Malindi Ukumbusho House Nkrumah Road PO Box 80072 Mombasa Kenya *Web:* www.ackenya.org

Marsabit The Rt Revd Robert Martin Bishop of Marsabit PO Box 51 Marsabit 6500 KENYA *Email:* ackbishopmarsabit@gmail.com

Maseno North The Rt Revd Simon M Oketch Bishop of Maseno North PO Box 416 Kakemega 50100 Kenya *Tel:* +254 56 2/3 *Email:* ackmnorth@jambo.co.ke

Maseno South The Rt Revd Dr Francis Abiero Bishop of Maseno South PO Box 114 Kisumu 40100 Kenya *Tel:* +254 (0)35 45 147 *Fax:* +254 (0)35 21 009 *Email:* ackmsouth@swiftkenya.com

Maseno West The Rt Revd Joseph O Wasonga Bishop of Maseno West PO Box 793 Siaya 40600 Kenya *Email:* wbishopjoseph@yahoo.com

Mbeere The Rt Revd Dr Moses Masamba Nthukah Bishop of Mbeere PO Box 122 Siakago 60104 Kenya *Tel:* +254 721423840 *Email:* bishopmbeere@gmail.com *Web:* http://www.ackenya.org/dioceses/mbeere.html

Meru The Rt Revd Charles Mwendwa Bishop of Meru PO Box 427 Meru 60200 Kenya *Tel:* +254 16 430 719 *Email:* ackmeru@swiftkenya.com

Mombasa The Rt Revd Julius R Katio Kalu Bishop of Mombasa Ukumbusho House Mkrumah Road PO Box 80072 Mombasa 80100 Kenya *Tel:* +254 (0)11 311 105 *Fax:* +254 (0)11 227 837 *Email:* ackmombasa@swiftmombasa.com

Mount Kenya Central The Rt Revd Isaac M Ng'ang'a Bishop of Mount Kenya Central PO Box 1040 Muranga 10200 Kenya *Tel:* +254 (0)60 30559 *Fax:* +254 (0)60 30148 *Email:* ackmkcentral@wananchi.com

Mount Kenya Central The Rt Revd Allen M Waithaka Suffragan Bishop of Mount Kenya Central PO Box 1040 Muranga 10200 Kenya *Tel:* +254 156 305 59

Mount Kenya South The Rt Revd Timothy Ranji Bishop of Mount Kenya South PO Box 886 Kiambu 900 Kenya *Tel:* +254 (0)154 22 997 *Fax:* +254 (0)154 22 408 *Email:* ackmtksouth@swiftkenya.com

Mount Kenya South The Rt Revd Charles Muturi Suffragan Bishop Mt Kenya South Mount Kenya South Diocese PO Box 886 Kiambu 900 KENYA *Email:* ackmtkenyasouth@swiftkenya.com

Mount Kenya West The Rt Revd Joseph M Kagunda Bishop of Mount Kenya West PO Box 229 Nyeri 10100 Kenya *Tel:* +254 (0)171 302 14 *Fax:* +254 (0)171 2954 *Email:* ackmtkwest@wananchi.com

Mumias The Rt Revd Beneah Okumu Salala Bishop of Mumias PO Box 213 Mumias 50102 Kenya *Fax:* +254 333 41232 *Email:* ackmumias@swiftkenya.com

Murang'a South The Rt Revd Julius Karanu Bishop of Murang'a South Awaiting Details

Nairobi The Rt Revd Joel Waweru Mwangi Bishop of Nairobi PO Box 72846 Nairobi 200 Kenya *Tel:* +254 2 222 6337 *Fax:* +254 2 226259 *Email:* acknairobi@swiftkenya.com

Nakuru The Rt Revd Joseph Muchai Bishop of Nakuru PO Box 56 Moi Road Nakuru 20100 Kenya *Tel:* +254 (0)37 212 155 *Fax:* +254 (0)37 44 379

Nakuru-Baringo Area The Rt Revd Musa Kamuren Suffragan Bishop of Nakuru-Baringo Area PO Box 56 Moi Road Nakuru 20100 Kenya *Tel:* +254 (0)37 212 155

Nambale The Rt Revd Dr Robert Magina Barasa Bishop of Nambale PO Box 4 Nambale 50409 Kenya *Tel:* +254 (0)336 24040 *Fax:* +254 (0)336 24071 *Email:* acknambale@swiftkenya.com

Nyahururu The Rt Revd Stephen Kabora Bishop of Nyahururu PO Box 926 Nyahururu 20300 Kenya *Tel:* +254 365 32179 *Fax:* + *Email:* nyahu_dc@africaonline.co.ke

Nyahururu-Maralal Area The Rt Revd Jacob Lesuuda Suffragan Bishop of Maralal Area PO Box 42 Maralal KENYA *Email:* jlesuuda@yahoo.com

Southern Nyanza The Rt Revd James Ochiel Bishop of Southern Nyanza PO Box 65 Homa Bay 40300 Kenya *Tel:* +254 0385 221 27 *Fax:* +254 0385 220 56 *Email:* acksnyanza@swiftkenya.com

Taita-Taveta The Rt Revd Dr Samson Mwaluda Bishop of Taita Taveta ACK Taita-taveta Diocese PO Box 75 Voi 80300 Kenya *Tel:* +254 (0)147 30 096 *Fax:* +254 (0)147 30 364 *Email:* acktaita@swiftmombasa.com

Taita-Taveta The Rt Revd Liverson Mng'onda Coadjutor Bishop of Taita-Taveta ACK Taita-taveta Diocese PO Box 75 Voi 80300 Kenya

Thika The Rt Revd Julius Njuguna Wanyoike Bishop of Thika PO Box 214 Thika 1000 Kenya *Tel:* +254 (0)151 217 35 *Fax:* +254 (0)151 315 44

THE ANGLICAN CHURCH OF KOREA

General Secretary The Revd Stephen Si-Kyung Yoo 16, Sejong-daero 19-gil Jung-gu Seoul 100-120 Korea *Tel:* +82 (0)2 738 8952 *Fax:* +82 (0)2 737 4210 *Email:* 08skyoo@naver.com *Web:* www.skh.or.kr

Busan The Rt Revd Onesimus Dongsin Park Bishop of Busan Bishop's Office 18 Daecheng-dong 2Ga Jung-Ku Busan 600-092 Korea *Tel:* +82 (0)51 463 5742 *Fax:* +82 (0)51 463 5957 *Email:* onesimus63@hanmail.net *Web:* skhpusan.onmam.com/

Daejeon The Revd Moses Nak Jun Yoo Bishop elect of Daejeon Bishop's Office 87-6 Sunhwa 2-dong Jung-gu Daejeon 301-823 Korea *Tel:* +82 (0)42 256 9988 *Fax:* +82 (0)42 255 8918 *Email:* tdio@unitel.co.kr *Web:* www.djdio.or.kr

Seoul The Most Revd Paul Kim Primate of the Anglican Church of Korea and Bishop of Seoul Bishop's Office 16 Sejong-daero 19-gil Jung-gu Seoul 100-120 Korea *Tel:* +82 (0)2 735 6157 *Fax:* +82 (0)2 723 2640 *Email:* paulkim7@hitel.net *Web:* www.skhseoul.or.kr

THE CHURCH OF THE PROVINCE OF MELANESIA

Provincial Secretary Dr Abraham Hauriasi Anglican Church of Melanesia PO Box 19 Honiara Solomon Islands *Tel:* +677 20407

Provincial Accountant Mr Jimmy Maeigoa PO Box 19 Dogura MBP Papua New Guinea *Tel:* +677 21 892 *Fax:* +677 23 301

Banks & Torres The Rt Revd Alfred P Worek Bishop of Banks & Torres C/O PO Box 19 Sola Vanualava Torba Province Vanutu *Tel:* +678 38520 *Fax:* +678 38520 *Email:* worek_p@comphq.org.sb

Central Melanesia The Most Revd David Vunagi Archbishop of Melanesia and Bishop of Central Melanesia Church of Melanesia PO Box 19 Honiara Solomon Islands *Tel:* +677 24210 *Email:* dvunagi@comphq.org.sb

Central Solomons The Rt Revd Ben Seka Bishop of Central Solomons PO Box 52 Tulagia CIP Solomon Islands *Tel:* +677 32 042 *Email:* d.bindon@xtra.co.nz

Guadalcanal The Rt Revd Nathan Tome Bishop of Guadacanal Awaiting Details *Tel:* +677 23337 *Email:* ntome4080@gmail.com

Hanuato'o The Rt Revd Alfred Karibongi Bishop of Hanuato'o C/O Post Office Kirakira Makira/Ulawa Province Solomon Islands

Malaita The Rt Revd Samuel Sahu Bishop of Malaita Bishops House PO Box 7 Auki Malaita Province Solomon Islands *Tel:* +611 45 121 071 *Fax:* +677 21 098

Malaita The Rt Revd Alfred Hou Assistant Bishop of Malaita C/O Bishop's House PO Box 7 Auki Malaita Province Solomon Islands

Temotu The Rt Revd George Takeli Bishop of Temotu PO Box 50 Lata Santa Cruz Temotu Province Solomon Islands *Tel:* +677 530 80 *Fax:* +677 530 92

Vanuatu The Rt Revd James M Ligo Bishop of Vanuatu Bishop's House PO Box 238 Luganville Santo Vanuatu *Tel:* +678 370 65 *Fax:* +678 363 31 *Email:* comdov@vanuatu.com.vu

Ysabel The Revd Ellison Quity Bishop elect of Ysabel Bishop's House PO Box 6 Buala Jejevo Ysabel Province Solomon Islands *Tel:* +677 350 34 *Fax:* +677 350 71

LA IGLESIA ANGLICANA DE MEXICO

Provincial Secretary The Revd Canon Alfonso Walls Acatlán 102 Oriente Col. Mitras Centro Monterrey Nuevo Leon 64460 Mexico *Tel:* +52 81 8333 0992 *Fax:* +52 81 8348 7362 *Email:* awalls@mexico-anglican.org

Provincial Treasurer Ms Laura Gracia Acatlán 102 Ote Mitras Centro Monterrey NL 64460 MEXICO *Tel:* +52 (0)81 8333 0992 *Email:* laura.gracia@gmail.com *Web:* www.mexico-anglican.org

Cuernavaca The Rt Revd Enrique Treviño Cruz Bishop of Cuernavaca Minerva #1 Fracc. Delicias Cuernavaca Morelos 62330 Mexico *Tel:* +52 777 315 2870 *Email:* diocesisdecuernavaca@hotmail.com

Mexico The Rt Revd Carlos Touche-Porter Bishop of Mexico San Jeronimo #117 Col. San Angel Delegacion Alvaro Obregón Mexico City DF 1000 Mexico *Tel:* +52 (0)33 5616 2205 *Email:* diocesisdemexico@gmail.com

Northern Mexico The Most Revd Francisco Moreno Presiding Bishop of La Iglesia Anglicana de Mexico & Bishop of Northern Mexico Acatlán 102 Oriente Col. Mitras Centro Monterrey Nuevo Leon 64460 Mexico *Tel:* +52 81 8333 0992 *Fax:* +52 81 8348 7362 *Email:* primado@mexico-anglican.org *Web:* www.mexico-anglican.org

Southeastern Mexico The Rt Revd Benito Juarez-Martinez Bishop of Southeastern Mexico Av Las Americas #73 Col. Aguacatal Xalapa Veracruz 91130 Mexico *Tel:* +52 (0)228 814 6951 *Email:* obispobenito.49@gmail.com

Western Mexico The Rt Revd Lino Rodriguez-Amaro Bishop of Western Mexico Torres Quintero # 15 Col. Seattle Zapopan Jalisco 45150 Mexico *Tel:* +52 333 560 4727 *Fax:* +52 333 560 4726 *Email:* obispolino@hotmail.com *Web:* www.iamoccidente.org.mx

THE CHURCH OF
THE PROVINCE OF MYANMAR (BURMA)

Provincial Secretary The Revd Canon Saw Maung Doe 140 Pyidaungsu Yeiktha Road Dagon PO 11191 Yangon MYANMAR *Tel:* +95 1 395 279 *Email:* markmgdoe@gmail.com

Provincial Treasurer Ms Helen Myint Htwe Yee 140 Pyidaungsu-Yeiktha Road Dagon PO Yangon MYANMAR *Tel:* +95 (0)1 395 279 *Email:* cpm.140@mptmail.com.mm

Hpa-an The Rt Revd Saw Stylo Bishop of Hpa-an Bishop Kone: Ward 4 Hpa-an Kayin State Myanmar *Tel:* +95 58 216 96

Mandalay The Rt Revd David Nyi Nyi Naing Bishop of Mandalay Diocesan Office 22 Pinya Road Mandalay Myanmar *Tel:* +95 (0)2 341 10 *Email:* davidnaing@gmail.com

Mytikyina The Rt Revd John Zau Li Bishop of Mytikyina 147 Thankin Net Pe Road Thinda Quarters Mytikyina Kachin State Myanmar *Tel:* +95 (0)74 231 04 *Email:* john.zauli@gmail.com

Mytikyina The Rt Revd Vacant Assistant Bishop elect of Mytikyina Diocesan Office 147 Thakin Net Pe Road Thida Quarter Mytikyina Kachin State Myanmar *Tel:* +95 074 25428

Sittwe The Rt Revd Dr James Min Dein Bishop of Sittwe May Yu Stree Sittwe Rakhine State Myanmar *Tel:* +95 43 536 22 *Email:* mindein3@gmail.com

Toungoo The Rt Revd Dr Saw Wilme Bishop of Toungoo Diocesan Office Nat-shin-Naung Street Ward 20 Toungoo Myanamar *Tel:* +95 54 231 59 *Email:* bishop.wilme@gmail.com

Yangon The Most Revd Stephen Than Myint Oo Archbishop of Myanmar and Bishop of Yangon No 140 Pyidaungsu Yeiktha Street PO Box 11191 Yangon Myanmar *Tel:* +95 (0)1 395 314 *Email:* stephenthan777@gmail.com

Yangon The Rt Revd Samuel Htang Oak Assistant Bishop of Yangon No 44 Bishop Home Pyay Road Yangon Myanmar *Tel:* +95 1 372 300 *Email:* sthangoak40@gmail.com

THE CHURCH OF NIGERIA (ANGLICAN COMMUNION)

Provincial Secretary The Ven Prof Israel 'Kelue F Okoye Episcopal House 24 Doula Street PO Box 212 ADCP Abuja Nigeria *Tel:* +234 9 5236950 *Email:* communicator1@anglican-nig.org

Provincial Treasurer Chief O O A Adekunle PO Box 78 Lagos NIGERIA *Tel:* +234 (0)1 263 3581

The Rt Revd Michael Olurohunbi Episcopal House 24 Douala Street Wuse District, Zone 5 PO Box 212 ADCP, Garki, Abuja NIGERIA *Tel:* +234 (0)9 523 6950 *Email:* mikefarohunbi08@gmail.com

Aba-Province of Niger Delta The Most Revd Ugochukwu U Ezuoke Archbishop of the Province of Niger Delta & Bishop of Aba Bishopscourt 70-72 St Michael's Road PO Box 212 Aba Nigeria *Tel:* +234 (0)82 227 666 *Email:* aba@anglican-nig.org

Aba Ngwa North-Province of Niger Delta The Rt Revd Nathan C Kanu Bishop of Aba Ngwa North Bishopscourt-All Saints Cathedral Abayi-Umuocham No. 161-165 Owerri Road PO Box 43 Aba Abia State Nigeria *Email:* odinathnfe@sbcglobal.net

Abakaliki-Province of Enugu The Rt Revd Monday C Nkwoagu Bishop of Abakaliki All Saints Cathedral PO Box 112 Abakaliki Ebonyi State Nigeria *Tel:* +234 (0)43 20 762 *Email:* abakaliki@anglican-nig.org

Abuja-Province of Abuja The Most Revd Nicholas Okoh Metropolitan & Primate of all Nigeria & Bishop of Abuja Episcopal House 24 Douala Street Wuse District, Zone 5, PO Box 212 Abuja ADCP Garki Abuja *Tel:* +234 (0)56 280 682 *Email:* nickorogodo@yahoo.com

Afikpo-Province of Enugu The Rt Revd Paul Uduogu Bishop of Afikpo Bishop's House PO Box 699 Afikpo Ebonyi State Nigeria *Email:* udogupaul@yahoo.com

Aguata-Province of Niger The Most Revd Christian O Efobi Archbishop of the Province of the Niger & Bishop of Aguata Bishopscourt PO Box 1128 Ekwulobia Anambra State Nigeria *Tel:* +234 (0)803 750 1077 *Email:* christianefobi@yahoo.com

Ahoada-Province of Niger Delta The Rt Revd Clement Ekpeye Bishop of Ahoada Bishopscourt PO Box 4 Ahoada Rivers State Nigeria *Tel:* +234 (0)806 357 6242 *Email:* ahoada@anglican-nig.org

Ajayi Crowther-Province of Ibadan The Rt Revd Olugbenga Oduntan Bishop of Ajayi Crowther Bishopscourt PO Box 430 Iseyin Oyo State Nigeria *Tel:* +234 (0)803 719 8182 *Email:* ajayicrowther-diocese@yahoo.com

Akoko-Province of Ondo The Rt Revd Gabriel Akinbiyi Bishop of Akoko Bishopscourt PO Box 572

Ikare-Akoko Ondo State Nigeria *Tel:* +234 (0)31 801 011 *Email:* bishopgabrielakinbiyi@yahoo.com

Akoko Edo-Province of Bendel The Rt Revd Jolly Oyekpen Bishop of Akoko Edo Bishopscourt PO Box 10 Igarra Edo State Nigeria *Tel:* +234 (0)803 470 5941 *Email:* venjollye@yahoo.com

Akure-Province of Ondo The Rt Revd Simeon O Borokini Bishop of Akure Bishopscourt PO Box 1622 Akure Ondo state Nigeria *Tel:* +234 (0)34 241 572 *Fax:* +234 (0)34 241 572

Amichi-Province of Niger The Rt Revd Ephraim Ikeakor Bishop of Amichi Bishopscourt PO Box 13 Amichi Anambra State Nigeria *Tel:* +234 (0)803 317 0916 *Email:* eoikeakor@yahoo.com

Arochukwu/Ohafia-Province of Aba The Rt Revd Johnson Onuoha Bishop of Arochukwu/Ohafia Bishopscourt PO Box 193 Arochukwu Abia State Nigeria *Tel:* +234 (0)802 538 6407 *Email:* aroohafia@anglican-nig.org

Asaba-Province of Bendel The Rt Revd Justus N Mogekwu Bishop of Asaba Bishopscourt PO Box 216 Asaba Delta State Nigeria *Tel:* +234 (0)802 819 2980 *Email:* justusmogekwu@yahoo.com

Awgu/Aninri-Province of Niger The Rt Revd Emmaunuel Ugwu Bishop of Awgu/Aniniri Bishopscourt PO Box 305 Agwu Enungu State Nigeria *Tel:* +234 (0)803 334 9360 *Email:* afamnonye@yahoo.com

Awka-Province of Niger The Rt Revd Alexander C Ibezim Bishop of Awka Bishopscourt PO Box 130 Awka Anambra State Nigeria *Tel:* +234 (0)48 550 058 *Email:* chioma1560@aol.com

Awori-Province of Lagos The Rt Revd J Akin Atere Bishop of Awori Bishopscourt PO Box 10 Ota Ogun State Nigeria *Tel:* +234 (0)803 553 7284 *Email:* dioceseofawori@yahoo.com

Badagry-Province of Lagos The Rt Revd Joseph B Adeyemi Bishop of Badagry Bishopscourt PO Box 7 Badagry Lagos State Nigeria *Email:* badagry@anglican-nig.org

Bari-Province of Kaduna The Rt Revd Idris A Zubairu Bishop of Bari Bishopscourt Gidan Mato Bari Kano State Nigeria *Tel:* +234 (0)808 559 7183

Bauchi-Province of Jos The Rt Revd Musa Tula Bishop of Bauchi Bishop's House 2 Hospital Road PO Box 2450 Bauchi Nigeria *Tel:* +234 (0)77 543 460 *Email:* bauchi@anglican-nig.org

Benin-Province of Bendel The Rt Revd Peter J Imasuen Bishop of Benin Bishopscourt PO Box 82 Benin City Edo State Nigeria *Tel:* +234 (0)52 250 552

Bida-Province of Abuja The Rt Revd Jonah G Kolo Bishop of the Missionary Diocese of Bida Bishop's

House St John's Mission Compound PO Box 14 Bida Nigeria *Tel:* +234 (0)66 461 694

Bukuru-Province of Jos The Rt Revd Jwan Zhumbes Bishop of Bukuru Bishopscourt Citrus Estate PO Box 605 Sabon Bariki Plateau State Nigeria

Calabar-Province of Niger Delta The Rt Revd Tunde Adeleye Bishop of Calabar Bishopscourt PO Box 74 Calabar Cross Rivers State Nigeria *Tel:* +234 (0)87 232 812 *Fax:* +234 (0)88 220 835 *Email:* calabar@anglican-nig.org

Damaturu-Province of Jos The Rt Revd Abiodun Ogunyemi Bishop of Damaturu PO Box 312 Damaturu Yobe State Nigeria *Tel:* +234 (0)74 522 142 *Email:* damaturu@anglican-nig.org

Diocese on the Coast formerly (Ikale-Ilaje)-Province of Ondo The Rt Revd Joshua E Ogunele Bishop of the Diocese on the Coast Bishopscourt Ikoya Road PMB 3 Ilutitun-Osooro Ondo State Nigeria *Tel:* +234 (0)803 467 1879 *Email:* joshuaonthecoast@yahoo.ca

Doko-Province of Lokoja The Rt Revd Uriah Kolo Bishop of Doko PO Box 1513 Bida Niger State Nigeria *Tel:* +234 (0)803 590 6327 *Email:* uriahkolo@gmail.com

Dutse-Province of Kaduna The Rt Revd Yesufu I Lumu Bishop of Dutse PO Box 67 Yadi Dutse Jigawa State Nigeria *Tel:* +234 (0)64 721 379 *Email:* dutse@anglican-nig.org

Egba-Province of Lagos The Rt Revd Emmanuel O Adekunle Bishop of Egba Bishopscourt Cathedral of St Peter PO Box 46 Ile-oluji Ondo State Nigeria

Egba West-Province of Lagos The Rt Revd Samuel O Ajani Bishop of Egba-West Bishopscourt Oke-Ata Housing Estate PO Box 6204 Sapon Abeokuta Nigeria *Tel:* +234 (0)80 5518 4822 *Email:* samuelajani@yahoo.com

Egbu-Province of Owerri The Rt Revd Geoffrey E Okoroafor Bishop of Egbu PO Box 1967 Owerri Imo State Nigeria *Tel:* +234 (0)83 231 797 *Email:* egbu@anglican-nig.org

Eha- Amufu-Province of Enugu The Rt Revd Daniel Olinya Bishop of Eha-Amufu St Andrews Cathedral Bishopscourt PO Box 85 Eha-Amufu Enugu State Nigeria *Tel:* +234 (0)803 089 2131 *Email:* dankol@yahoo.com

Ekiti-Province of Ondo The Most Revd Samuel Abe Archbishop of the Province of Ondo & Bishop of Ekiti Bishopscourt PO Box 12 Okesa Street Ado-Ekiti Ekiti State Nigeria *Tel:* +234 (0)30 250 305 *Email:* adedayoekiti@yahoo.com

Ekiti Kwara-Province of Ibadan The Rt Revd Andrew O Ajayi Bishop of Ekiti Kwara Awaiting

Details *Tel:* +234 (0)803 470 3522 *Email:* andajayi@yahoo.com

Ekiti Oke-Province of Ondo The Rt Revd Isaac Olubowale Bishop of Ekiti-Oke PMB 207 Usi-Ekiti Ekiti State Nigeria *Email:* ekitioke@anglican-nig.org

Ekiti West-Province of Ondo The Rt Revd Samuel Oke Bishop of the Diocese of Ekiti West Bishop's Residence 6 Ifaki Street PO Box 477 Ijero-Ekiti Nigeria *Tel:* +234 (0)30 850 314

Enugu-Province of Niger The Rt Revd Dr Emmanuel O Chukwuma Bishop of Enugu Bishop's House PO Box 418 Enugu Nigeria *Tel:* +234 (0)42 435 804 *Fax:* +234 (0)42 259 808 *Email:* enugu@anglican-nig.org

Enugu North-Province of Niger Delta The Rt Revd Sosthenes Eze Bishop of Enugu North Bishopscourt St Marys Cathedral Ngwo-Enugu Nigeria *Tel:* +234 (0)803 870 9362 *Email:* bishopsieze@yahoo.com

Esan-Province of Bendel The Most Revd Friday J Imaekhai Archbishop of Bendel Province & Bishop of Esan Bishopscourt Ojoelen PO Box 921 Ekpoma Edo State Nigeria *Tel:* +234 (0)55 981 079 *Email:* bishopimaekhai@yahoo.com

Etche-Province of Niger Delta The Rt Revd Precious Nwala Bishop of Etche Bishopscourt PO Box 89 Okehi Etche Rivers State Nigeria

Etsako-Province of Bendel The Rt Revd Jacob Bada Bishop of Etsako Bishopscourt PO Box 11 Jattu Auchi Edo State Nigeria

Evo-Province of Niger Delta The Rt Revd Innocent Ordu Bishop of Evo Bishopscourt PO Box 3576 Port Harcourt Rivers State Nigeria *Tel:* +234 (0)803 715 2706 *Email:* innocent-ordu@yahoo.com

Gboko-Province of Abuja The Rt Revd Emmanuel Nyitsse Bishop of Gboko Awaiting Details

Gombe-Province of Jos The Rt Revd Henry Ndukuba Bishop of Gombe Cathedral Church of St Peter PO Box 39 Gombe Nigeria *Tel:* +234 (0)72 221 212 *Fax:* +234 (0)72 221 141 *Email:* gombe@anglican-nig.org

Gusau-Province of Kaduna The Rt Revd John Garba Bishop of Gusau PO Box 64 Gusau Zamfara State Nigeria *Tel:* +234 (0)63 204 747 *Email:* gusau@anglican.skannet.com

Gwagwalada-Province of Abuja The Rt Revd Moses Tabwaye Bishop of Gwagwalada Diocesan Headquarters Secretariat Road PO Box 287 Gwagwalada Abuja Nigeria *Tel:* +234 (0)9 882 2083 *Email:* anggwag@skannet.com.ng

Ibadan-Province of Ibadan The Most Revd Joseph Akinfenwa Archbishop of Province of Ibadan & Bishop of Ibadan PO Box 3075 Mapo Ibadan Nigeria

Tel: +234 (0)2 810 1400 *Fax:* +234 (0)2 810 1413 *Email:* ibadan@anglican.skannet.com.ng

Ibadan North-Province of Ibadan The Rt Revd Dr Segun Okubadejo Bishop of Ibadan North Bishopscourt Moyede PO Box 182 Dugbe Ibadan Nigeria *Tel:* +234 (0)2 810 7482 *Email:* angibn@ skannet.com

Ibadan South-Province of Ibadan The Rt Revd Jacob Ajetunmobi Bishop of Ibadan South Bishopscourt PO Box 166 St David's Compound Kudeti Ibadan Nigeria *Tel:* +234 (0)2 231 9141 *Fax:* +234 (0)2 231 9141 *Email:* jacajet@skannet.com.ng

Idah-Province of Abuja The Rt Revd Joseph Musa Bishop of Idah Bishopscourt PO Box 25 Idah Kogi State Nigeria *Email:* idah@anglican-nig.org

Ideato-Province of Owerri The Rt Revd Caleb A Maduoma Bishop of Ideato Bishopscourt PO Box 2 Ndizuogu Imo State Nigeria *Email:* bpomacal@ hotmail.com

Idoani-Province of Ondo The Rt Revd Ezekiel B Dahunsi Bishop of Idoani Bishopscourt PO Box 100 Idoani Ondo State Nigeria *Tel:* +234 (0)803 384 4029 *Email:* bolaezek@yahoo.com *Web:* www. dioceseofidoani.org

Ife-Province of Ibadan The Rt Revd Oluwole Odubogun Bishop of Ife Bishopscourt PO Box 312 Ife Osun State Nigeria *Tel:* +234 (0)36 230 046 *Email:* rantiodubogun@yahoo.com

Ife East-Province of Ibadan The Rt Revd Oluseyi Oyelade Bishop of Ife East Bishop's House PMB 505 Modakeke-Ife Osun State Nigeria *Tel:* +234 (0)802 332 4962 *Email:* seyioyelade@yahoo.com

Ifo-Province of Lagos The Rt Revd Nathaniel Oladejo Ogundipe Bishop of Ifo Bishopscourt Trinity House KM1 Ibogun Road Ifo Ogun State Nigeria *Tel:* +234 (0)802 778 4377 *Email:* dioceseofifo@gmail. com

Igbomina-Province of Kwara The Most Revd Michael O Akinyemi Archbishop of Province of Kwara & Bishop of Igbomina Bishopscourt PO Box 102 Oro Kwara State Nigeria *Tel:* +234 (0)803 669 1940 *Email:* oluakinyemi2000@yahoo.com

Igbomina- West-Province of Kwara The Rt Revd James O Akinola Bishop of Igbomina West Bishop's House PO Box 32 Oke Osin Kwara State Nigeria *Tel:* +234 (0)803 392 3720 *Email:* olaotimuyiwa@ yahoo.com *Web:* www.dioceseofigbominawest.org/ igbomina/

Ihiala-Province of Niger The Rt Revd Ralph Okafor Bishop of Ihiala Bishopscourt St Silas Cathedral PMB 11 Ihiala Anambra State 431003 Nigeria *Tel:* +234 (0)803 711 2408 *Email:* raphoka@yahoo.com

Ijebu-Province of Lagos The Rt Revd Ezekiel Awosoga Bishop of Ijebu Bishopscourt Ejirin Road PO Box 112 Ijebu-Ode Nigeria

Ijebu-North-Province of Lagos The Rt Revd Solomon Kuponu Bishop of Ijebu- North Bishopscourt Oke-Sopen Ijebu-Igbo Nigeria *Tel:* +234 (0)803 741 9372 *Web:* www.ijebunorthdiocese. org

Ijesa North East-Province of Ibadan The Rt Revd Joseph A Olusola Bishop of Ijesa North East PO Box 40 Ipetu Ijesa Osun State Nigeria *Tel:* +234 (0)803 942 8275 *Email:* bpjafsola@gmail.com *Web:* www. ijesanortheastdiocese.org

Ijesha North-Province of Ibadan The Rt Revd Isaac I Oluyamo Bishop of Ijesha North Bishopscourt PO Box 4 Ijebu-Jesa Osun State Nigeria *Tel:* +234 (0)802 344 0333

Ijumu-Province of Lokoja The Rt Revd Ezekiel Ikupolati Bishop of Ijumu Bishopscourt PO Box 90 Iyara-Ijumi Kogi State Nigeria *Tel:* +234 (0)807 500 8780 *Email:* efikupolati@yahoo.com

Ikara-Province of Kaduna The Rt Revd Yusuf I Janfalan Bishop of Ikara Bishopscourt PO Box 23 Ikara Kaduna State Nigeria *Tel:* +234 (0)803 679 3865 *Email:* ikara@anglican-nig.org

Ikeduru-Province of Owerri The Rt Revd Emmanuel C Maduwike Bishop of Ikeduru Bishop's House PO Box 56 Atta Imo State Nigeria *Tel:* +234 (0)803 704 4686 *Email:* emmamaduwike@yahoo. com

Ikka-Province of Bendel The Rt Revd Peter Onekpe Bishop of Ikka St John's Cathedral PO Box 5 Agbor Delta State Nigeria *Tel:* +234 (0)55 250 14

Ikwerre-Province of Niger Delta The Rt Revd Blessing Enyindah Bishop of Ikwerre Bishopscourt St Peter's Cathedral PO Box 14229 Port Harcourt Rivers State Nigeria *Tel:* +234 (0)802 321 2824 *Email:* blessingenyindah@yahoo.com

Ikwo-Province of Enugu The Rt Revd Kenneth K C Ifemene Bishop of Ikwo Bishops Residence PO Box 998 Agubia Ikwo Abakaliki Ebonyi State Nigeria *Tel:* +234 (0)805 853 4849 *Email:* bishopikwoanglican@ yahoo.com

Ikwuano-Province of Aba The Rt Revd Chigozirim Onyegbule Bishop of Ikwuano Bishopscourt St Phillip's Cathedral PO Box 5 Ahaba-Oloko Abia State Nigeria *Tel:* +234 (0)803 085 9319 *Email:* ikwuano@anglican-nig.org

Ilaje-Province of Ondo The Rt Revd Fredrick I Olugbemi Bishop of Iiaje Bishopscourt PO Box 147 Igbokoda Ondo State Nigeria *Tel:* +234 (0)806 624 8662 *Email:* forogbemi@yahoo.com

Ile-Oluji-Province of Ondo The Rt Revd Samson O Adekunle Bishop of Ile-Oluji Bishopscourt Cathedral of St PEter PO Box 46 Ile-Oluji Ondo State Nigeria *Tel:* +234 (0)803 454 1236 *Email:* adekunlesamson86@yahoo.co.uk

Ilesa-Province of Ibadan The Rt Revd Dr Olubayu Sowale Bishop of Ilesa Diocesan Headquarters Muroko Road PO Box 237 Ilesa Osun State Nigeria *Tel:* +234 (0)36 460 138 *Email:* ilesha@anglican-nig.org

Ilesa South West-Province of Ibadan The Rt Revd Samuel Egbebunmi Bishop of Ilesa South West Bishopscourt Cathedral of the Holy Trinity Imo Ilesa Osun State Nigeria *Tel:* +234 (0)803 307 1876 *Email:* segbebunmi@yahoo.com

Irele- Eseodo-Province of Ondo The Rt Revd Felix O Akinbuluma Bishop of Irele-Eseodo Bishopscourt Sabomi Road Ode Irele Ondo State Nigeria *Tel:* +234 (0)805 671 2653 *Email:* felixgoke@yahoo.com

Isiala-Ngwa-Province of Aba The Rt Revd Owen N Azubuike Bishop of Isiala-Ngwa Bishopscourt St Georges Cathedral Compound PNB 2033 Mbawsi Abia State Nigeria *Tel:* +234 (0)805 467 0528 *Email:* bpowenazubuike@yahoo.com

Isial-Ngwa South-Province of Aba The Rt Revd Isaac Nwaoha Bishop of Isiala-Ngwa South St Peter's Cathedral Compound PO Box 15 Owerrinta Abia State Nigeria *Tel:* +234 (0)803 711 9317 *Email:* isialangwasouth@anglican-nig.org

Isikwuato-Province of Aba The Rt Revd Manasses Chijiokem Okere Bishop of Isikwuato Bishopscourt PO Box 350 Ovim Abia State Nigeria *Tel:* +234 (0)803 386 221 *Email:* isiukwuato@anglican-nig.org

Jalingo-Province of Jos The Rt Revd Timothy Yahaya Bishop of Jalingo PO Box 4 Magami Jalingo Tabara State Nigeria *Tel:* +234 806 594 4694 *Email:* timothyyahaya@yahoo.com

Jebba-Province of Kwara The Rt Revd Timothy S Adewole Bishop of Jebba Bishopscourt PO Box 2 Jebba Kwara State Nigeria *Tel:* +234 (0)803 572 5298 *Email:* bishopadewole@yahoo.com

Jos-Province of Jos The Most Revd Benjamin A Kwashi Archbishop of the Province of Jos & Bishop of Jos Bishopscourt PO Box 6283 Jos Plateau State Nigeria *Email:* benkwashi@gmail.com

Kabba-Province of Lokoja The Rt Revd Steven K Akobe Bishop of Kabba Bishopscourt Obara Way PO Box 62 Kabba Kogi State Nigeria *Tel:* +234 (0)58 300 633 *Fax:* +234 (0)803 471 4759

Kaduna-Province of Kaduna Vacant Bishop elect of Kaduna PO Box 72 Kaduna Nigeria *Tel:* +234 (0)62 240 085 *Fax:* +234 (0)62 244 408

Kafanchan-Province of Abuja The Rt Revd Marcus Dogo Bishop of Kafanchan Bishopscourt PO Box 29 Kafanchan Kaduna State Nigeria *Tel:* +234 (0)61 20 634 *Web:* www.anglicankafanchan.blogspot.co.uk

Kano-Province of Kaduna The Rt Revd Zakka L Nyam Bishop of Kano Bishopscourt PO Box 362 Kano Kano State Nigeria *Tel:* +234 (0)64 647 816 *Fax:* +234 (0)64 647 816 *Email:* kano@anglican.skannet.com.ng

Katsina-Province of Kaduna The Rt Revd Jonathan S Bamaiyi Bishop of Katsina Bishop's Lodge PO Box 904 Katsina Katsina State Nigeria

Kebbi-Province of Kaduna The Most Revd Edmund E Akanya Archbishop of the Province of Kaduna & Bishop of Kebbi Bishops Residence PO Box 701 Birnin Kebbi Kebbi State Nigeria *Tel:* +234 (0)68 321 179 *Fax:* +234 (0)803 586 1060 *Email:* eekanya@yahoo.com

Kontagora-Province of Lokoja The Rt Revd Jonah Ibrahim Bishop of Kontagora Bishop's House GPA PO Box 1 Kontagora Niger State Nigeria *Tel:* +234 (0)803 625 2032 *Email:* jonahibrahim@yahoo.co.uk

Kubwa-Province of Abuja The Rt Revd Duke Akamisoko Bishop of Kubwa Bishop's House PO Box 67 Kubwa Abuja FCT Nigeria *Tel:* +234 (0)803 451 9437 *Email:* dukesoko@yahoo.com

Kutigi-Province of Lokoja The Rt Revd Jeremiah N Kolo Bishop of Kutigi Bishop's House St John's Mission Compound PO Box 14 Bida Nigeria *Tel:* +234 (0)803 625 2032 *Email:* bishopkolo@yahoo.com

Kwara-Province of Kwara The Rt Revd Olusegun S Adeyemi Bishop of Kwara Bishopscourt Fate Road PO Box 1884 Ilorin Kwara State Nigeria *Tel:* +234 (0)31 220 879 *Fax:* +234 (0)803 325 8068 *Email:* bishopolusegun@yahoo.com

Kwoi-Province of Abuja The Rt Revd Paul S Zamani Bishop of Kwoi Bishop's Residence Cathedral Compound Samban Gida PO Box 173 Kwoi Kaduna State Nigeria *Tel:* +234 (0)80 651 8160 *Email:* paulzamani@yahoo.com

Lafia-Province of Abuja The Rt Revd Miller K Maza Bishop of the Missionary Diocese of Lafia PO Box 560 Lafia Nasarawa State Nigeria *Tel:* +234 (0)803 973 5973 *Email:* anglicandioceseoflafia@yahoo.com

Lagos-Province of Lagos The Most Revd Ephraim A Ademowo Archbishop of the Province of Lagos & Bishop of Lagos 29 Marina PO Box 13 Lagos Nigeria *Tel:* +234 (0)1 263 6026 *Fax:* +234 (0)803 403 1358 *Email:* adebolaademowo@dioceseoflagos.org

Lagos Mainland-Province of Lagos The Rt Revd Adebayo Akinde Bishop of Lagos Mainland Bishops

House PO Box 849 Ebute Lagos State Nigeria *Tel:* +234 (0)703 390 5522 *Email:* adakinde@gmail.com

Lagos West-Province of Lagos The Rt Revd James Odedeji Bishop of Lagos West Vining House 3rd Floor Archbishop Vining Memorial Cathedral Oba Akinjobi Road GRA Ikeja Nigeria *Tel:* +234 (0)1 493 7333 *Fax:* +234 (0)1 493 7337 *Email:* dioceseoflagoswest@yahoo.com

Langtang-Province of Jos The Rt Revd Stanley D Fube Bishop of Langtang No 87 Solomon Lar Road PO Box 38 Langtang Plateau State Nigeria *Tel:* +234 (0)803 605 8767 *Email:* stanleyfube@gmail.com

Lokoja-Province of Lokoja The Most Revd Emmanuel Sokowamju E S Egbunu Archbishop of the Province of Lokoja & Bishop of Lokoja Bishopscourt PO Box 11 Bethany Lokoja Koji State Nigeria *Tel:* +234 (0)58 220 588 *Fax:* +234 (0)803 592 5698 *Email:* emmanuelegbunu@yahoo.co.uk *Web:* www.anglican-lokojadiocese.org

Maiduguri-Province of Jos The Rt Revd Emmanuel Kana Mani Bishop of Maiduguri Bishopscourt PO Box 1693 Maiduguri Borno State Nigeria *Tel:* +234 (0)76 234 010 *Email:* bishope-45@yahoo.com

Makurdi-Province of Abuja The Rt Revd Nathan Nyitar Inyom Bishop of Makurdi Bishopscourt PO Box 1 Makurdi Benue State Nigeria *Tel:* +234 (0)44 533 349 *Fax:* +234 (0)803 614 5319 *Email:* makurdi@ anglican.skannet.com.ng

Mbaise-Province of Owerri The Rt Revd Chamberlain Chinedu Ogunedo Bishop of Mbaise Bishopscourt PO Box 10 Ife Imo State Nigeria *Tel:* +234 (0)803 336 9836 *Fax:* + *Email:* ogunedochi@ yahoo.com

Mbamili-Province of Niger The Rt Revd Henry Okeke Bishop of Mbamili Bishopscourt PO Box 2653 Onitsha Anambra State Nigeria *Tel:* +234 (0)803 644 9780 *Fax:* + *Email:* bishopokeke@yahoo. com

Minna-Province of Lokoja The Rt Revd Daniel Abu Yisa Bishop of Minna Bishopscourt Dutsen Kura PO Box 2469 Minna Nigeria *Tel:* +234 (0)803 588 6552 *Email:* danyisa2007@yahoo.com

Ndokwa-Province of Bendel The Rt Revd David Obiosa Bishop of Ndokwa Bishopscourt 151 Old Sapele Road Obiaruka Delta State Nigeria *Tel:* +234 (0)803 776 9464 *Email:* dfao1963@yahoo.com

New Busa-Province of Kwara The Rt Revd Israel Amoo Bishop of New Busa Bishoscourt PO Box 208 New Busa Niger State Nigeria *Tel:* +234 (0)803 677 3839 *Email:* bishopamoo@yahoo.com

Ngbo-Province of Enugu The Rt Revd Christian Ebisike Bishop of Ngbo Bishop's House PO Box 93 Abakaliki Ebonyi State Nigeria *Tel:* +234 (0)806 979 4899 *Email:* vendchris@yahoo.com

Niger Delta North-Province of Niger Delta The Most Revd Ignatius C O Kattey Archbishop of Niger Delta Province & Bishop of Niger Delta North PO Box 53 Diobu Port Harcourt Rivers State Nigeria *Tel:* +234 (0)803 309 4331 *Email:* bishopicokattey@ yahoo.com

Niger Delta West-Province of Niger Delta The Rt Revd Emmanuel Oko-Jaja Bishop of Niger Delta West PO Box 10 Yenagoa Bayelsa Nigeria *Tel:* +234 (0)803 870 2099 *Email:* nigerdelta-west@anglican-nig.org

Niger Delta, The-Province of Niger Delta The Rt Revd Ralph Ebirien Bishop of the Niger Delta Bishopscourt PO Box 115 Port Harcourt Rivers State Nigeria *Tel:* +234 (0)708 427 9095 *Email:* revralph_ ebirien@yahoo.com

Niger West-Province of Niger The Rt Revd Johnson Ekwe Bishop of Niger West Bishop's House Anambra Anambra State Nigeria *Tel:* +234 (0)803 384 3339

Nike-Province of Enugu The Rt Revd Evans Jonathan Ibeagha Bishop of Nike Bishopscourt Trans-Ekulu PO Box 2416 Enugu Enugu State Nigeria *Tel:* +234 (0)803 324 1387 *Email:* pnibeagha@ yahoo.com

Nnewi-Province of Niger The Rt Revd Dr Godwin Izundu Nmezinwa Okpala Bishop of Nnewi Bishopscourt (opp Total filling station) PO Box 2630 Uruagu-Nnewi Anambra State Nigeria *Tel:* +234 (0)803 348 5714 *Fax:* +234 (0)46 462 676 *Email:* okpalagodwin@yahoo.co.uk

Northern Izon-Province of Niger Delta The Rt Revd Fred Nyanabo Bishop of Northern Izon Bishopscourt PO Box 705 Yenagoa Bayelsa State Nigeria *Tel:* +234 (0)803 316 0938 *Email:* fred_ nyanabo@yahoo.co.uk

Nsukka-Province of Enugu The Rt Revd Aloysius Agbo Bishop of Nsukka Bishopscourt St Cypran's Compound PO Box 516 Nsukka Enugu State Nigeria *Tel:* +234 (0)803 932 7840 *Email:* nsukka@anglican-nig.org

Offa-Province of Kwara The Rt Revd Akintunde Popoola Bishop of Offa Bishop's House 78-80 Ibrahim Road PO Box 21 Offa Kwara State Nigeria *Tel:* +234 (0)805 925 0011 *Email:* tpopoola@ anglican-nig.org

Ogbaru-Province of Niger The Rt Revd Samuel Ezeofor Bishop of Ogbaru Bishopscourt PO Box 46 Atani Anambra State Nigeria *Email:* *Web:* www. ogbaruanglicandiocese.org

Ogbia-Province of Niger Delta The Rt Revd James Oruwori Bishop of Ogbia Bishop's House No 10 Queens Street Ogbia Town Bayelsa State Nigeria *Tel:* +234 (0)803 73 4746 *Email:* jaoruwori@yahoo.com

Ogbomoso-Province of Ibadan The Rt Revd Matthew Osunade Bishop of Ogbomoso Bishopscourt St David's Anglican Cathedral PO Box 1909 Ogbomoso Nigeria *Tel:* +234 (0)805 593 6164 *Email:* maaosunade@yahoo.com

Ogoni-Province of Niger Delta The Rt Revd Solomon S Gberegbara Bishop of Ogoni Bishopscourt PO Box 73 Bori Rivers State Nigeria *Tel:* +234 (0)803 339 2545 *Email:* ogoni@anglican-nig.org

Ogori-Magongo-Province of Lokoja The Rt Revd Festus Davies Bishop of Ogori-Magongo Bishop's House St Peter's Cathedral Ogori Kogi State Nigeria *Tel:* +234 (0)803 451 0378 *Email:* fessyoladiran@yahoo.com

Ohaji/Egbema-Province of Owerri The Rt Revd Chidi Collins Oparaojiaku Bishop of Ohaji/Egbema Bishop's House PO Box 8026 New Owerri Imo State Nigeria *Tel:* +234 (0)803 312 1063 *Email:* chidioparachiaku@yahoo.com

Oji River-Province of Enugu The Most Revd Amos Amankechinelo Madu Archbishop of the Province of Enugu & Bishop of Oji River St Paul's Cathedral Church PO Box 123 Oji River Enuga Nigeria *Tel:* +234 (0)803 670 4888 *Email:* amosmadu@yahoo.com

Okene-Province of Lokoja The Rt Revd Emmanuel Bayo Ajulo Bishop of Okene Bishopscourt PO Box 43 Okene Kogi State Nigeria *Tel:* +234 (0)803 700 0016 *Email:* okenediocese@yahoo.com

Oke-Ogun-Province of Ibadan The Rt Revd Solomon Amusan Bishop of Oke-Ogun Bishopscourt PO Box 30 Saki Oyo State Nigeria *Tel:* +234 (0)802 323 3365 *Email:* solomonamusan@yahoo.com

Oke-Osun-Province of Ibadan The Rt Revd Abraham Akinlalu Bishop of Oke-Osun Bishopscourt PO Box 251 Gbongan Osun State Nigeria *Tel:* +234 (0)803 771 7194 *Email:* abrahamakinlalu@yahoo.com *Web:* www.okeosunanglicandiocese.org

Okigwe-Province of Owerri The Rt Revd Edward Osuegbu Bishop of Okigwe Bishopscourt PO Box 156 Okigwe Imo State Nigeria *Tel:* +234 (0)803 724 6374 *Email:* edchuc@justice.com

Okigwe North-Province of Owerri The Rt Revd Godson Udochukwu Ukanwa Bishop of Okigwe North Bishopscourt PO Box 127 Anara Imo State Nigeria *Tel:* +234 (0)803 672 4314 *Email:* venukanwa@yahoo.com

Okigwe South-Province of Owerri The Rt Revd David Onuoha Bishop of Okigwe South Bishopscourt PO Box 235 Nsu Imo State Nigeria *Email:* okisouth@yahoo.com

Okrika-Province of Niger Delta The Rt Revd Tubokosemie Atere Bishop of Okrika Bishopscourt PO Box 11 Okrika Rivers State Nigeria *Tel:* +234 (0)803 312 5226 *Email:* dioceseofokrika@yahoo.com

Oleh-Province of Bendel The Rt Revd John Usiwoma Aruakpor Bishop of Oleh Bishopscourt PO Box 8 Oleh Delta State Nigeria *Tel:* +234 (0)53 701 062 *Fax:* +234 (0)802 307 4008 *Email:* angoleh2000@yahoo.com

Omu-Aran-Province of Kwara The Rt Revd Philip Adeyemo Bishop of Omu-Aran Bishop's House PO Box 224 Omu-Aran Kwara State Nigeria *Tel:* +234 (0)806 592 4891 *Fax:* + *Email:* rtrevadeyemo@yahoo.com

On the Lake-Province of Owerri The Rt Revd Chijioke Oti Bishop of on the Lake Bishopscourt PO Box 36 Oguta Imo State Nigeria *Tel:* +234 (0)802 788 8738 *Email:* chijiokeoti72@yahoo.com

On the Niger-Province of Niger The Rt Revd Owen Chidozie Nwokolo Bishop of On the Niger Bishopscourt Ozala Road Onitsha Anambra State Nigeria *Tel:* +234 (0)803 726 0548 *Email:* owenelsie@yahoo.com

Ondo-Province of Ondo The Rt Revd George Lasebikan Bishop of Ondo Bishopscourt PO Box 265 Ife Road Ondo Ondo State Nigeria *Tel:* +234 (0)34 610 718 *Fax:* +234 (0)803 472 1813 *Email:* ondoanglican@yahoo.co.uk

Ondo-Province of Ondo The Rt Revd Christopher Tayo Omotunde Suffragan Bishop of Ondo Bishopscourt PO Box 265 Ife Road Ondo Ondo State Nigeria *Tel:* +234 (0)802 919 1866 *Email:* chrisomotunde@yahoo.com

Orlu-Province of Owerri The Most Revd Bennett C I Okoro Archbishop of Province of Owerri & Bishop of Orlu Bishopscourt PO Box 260 Nkwerre Imo State Nigeria *Tel:* +234 (0)82 440 538 *Fax:* +234 (0)803 671 1271 *Email:* anglicannaorlu@yahoo.com

Oru-Province of Owerri The Rt Revd Geoffrey Chukwunenye Bishop of Oru PO Box 191 Mgbidi Imo State Nigeria *Tel:* +234 (0)803 308 1270 *Email:* geoinlagos@yahoo.com

Osun-Province of Ibadan The Rt Revd James Afolabi Jopoola Bishop of Osun Bishopscourt PO Box 285 Osogbo Osun State Nigeria *Tel:* +234 (0)35 240 325 *Fax:* +234 (0)803 356 1628 *Email:* folapool@yahoo.com

Osun North East-Province of Ibadan The Rt Revd Humphery Olumakaiye Bishop of Osun North East Bishopscourt PO Box 32 Otan Ayegbaju Osun State Nigeria *Tel:* +234 (0)803 388 2678 *Email:* bamisebi2002@yahoo.co.uk *Web:* www.osunnortheastdiocese.org

Otukpo-Province of Abuja The Rt Revd David Bello Bishop of Otukpo Bishopscourt PO Box 360

Otukpo Benue State Nigeria *Tel:* +234 (0)803 309 1778 *Email:* bishopkbello@yahoo.com

Owerri-Province of Owerri The Rt Revd Dr Cyril Chukwunonyerem Okorocha Bishop of Owerri Bishop's Bourne PMB 1063 Owerri Imo State Nigeria *Tel:* +234 (0)83 230 784 *Fax:* +234 (0)803 338 9344 *Email:* owerri_anglican@yahoo.com

Owo-Province of Ondo The Rt Revd James Adedayo Oladunjoye Bishop of Owo Bishopscourt PO Box 472 Owo Ondo State Nigeria *Tel:* +234 (0)51 241 463 *Fax:* +234 (0)803 475 4291 *Email:* bishopoladunjoye@yahoo.co.uk

Oyo-Province of Ibadan The Rt Revd Williams Oluwarotimi Aladekugbe Bishop of Oyo PO Box 23 Oyo Oyo State Nigeria *Tel:* +234 (0)38 240 225 *Fax:* +234 (0)803 857 2120 *Email:* oyo@anglican-nig.org

Pankshin-Province of Jos The Rt Revd Olumuyiwa Ajayi Bishop of Pankshin Diocesan Secretariat PO Box 196 Pankshin Plateau State Nigeria *Tel:* +234 (0)803 344 7318 *Email:* olumijayi@yahoo.com

Remo-Province of Lagos The Rt Revd Michael Fape Bishop of Remo Bishopscourt PO Box 522 Sagama Ogun State Nigeria *Tel:* +234 (0)37 640 598 *Fax:* +234 (0)803 726 7949 *Email:* remo@anglican-nig.org

Sabongidda-Ora-Province of Bendel The Rt Revd John Akao Bishop of Sabongidda-Ora Bishopscourt PO Box 13 Sabongidda-Ora Edo State Nigeria *Tel:* +234 (0)57 54 132 *Fax:* +234 (0)806 087 7137 *Email:* akaojohn@yahoo.com

Sapele-Province of Bendel The Rt Revd Blessing A Erifeta Bishop of Sapele Bishopscourt PO Box 52 Sapele Delta State Nigeria *Tel:* +234 (0)803 662 4282 *Email:* dioceseofsapele@yahoo.com

Sokoto-Province of Kaduna The Rt Revd Augustin Omole Bishop of Sokoto Bishop's Lodge 68 Shuni Road PO Box 3489 Sokoto Sokoto State Nigeria *Tel:* +234 (0)60 234 639 *Fax:* +234 (0)803 542 3765 *Email:* akin_sok@yahoo.com *Web:* www.dosac.org

Udi-Province of Enugu The Rt Revd Chjioke Augustine Aneke Bishop of Udi Bishopscourt PO Box 30 Udi Enugu State Nigeria *Tel:* +234 (0)806 908 9690 *Email:* bpchijiokeudi@yahoo.com

Ughelli-Province of Bendel The Rt Revd Cyril C Odutemu Bishop of Ughelli Bishopscourt PO Box 760 Ughelli Delta State Nigeria *Tel:* +234 (0)53 600 403 *Fax:* +234 (0)803 530 7114 *Email:* ughellianglican@yahoo.com

Ukwa-Province of Aba The Rt Revd Samuel Kelechi Eze Bishop of Ukwa PO Box 20468 Aba Abia State Nigeria *Tel:* +234 (0)803 789 2431 *Email:* kelerem53878@yahoo.com

Umuahia-Province of Aba The Most Revd Dr Ikechi Nwachukwu Nwosu Archbishop of Province

of Aba & Bishop of Umuahia St Stephen's Cathedral Church Compound PO Box 96 Umuahia Abia State Nigeria *Tel:* +234 (0)88 221 037 *Fax:* +234 (0)803 549 9066

Uyo-Province of Niger Delta The Rt Revd Prince Asukwo Antai Bishop of Uyo Bishopscourt PO Box 70 Uyo Akwa Ibom State Nigeria *Tel:* +234 (0)802 916 2305 *Email:* uyo@anglican-nig.com

Warri-Province of Bendel The Rt Revd Christian Esezi Ideh Bishop of Warri Bishopscourt 17 Mabiaku Road PO Box 4571 Warri Delta State Nigeria *Tel:* +234 (0)53 255 857 *Fax:* +234 (0)805 102 2680 *Email:* angdioceseofwarri@yahoo.com

Western Izon-Province of Bendel The Rt Revd Edafe B Emamezi Bishop of Western Izon Bishopscourt PO Box 5 Patani Delta State Nigeria *Tel:* +234 (0)822 05 6228 *Email:* anglizon@yahoo.co.uk

Wusasa-Province of Kaduna The Rt Revd Ali Buba Lamido Bishop of Wusasa PO Box 28 Wusasa Zaria Kaduna State Nigeria *Tel:* +234 (0)69 334 594 *Fax:* +234 (0)803 727 2504 *Email:* lamido2sl@aol.co.uk

Yewa (form. Egbado)-Province of Lagos The Rt Revd Michael Adebayo Oluwarohunbi Bishop of Yewa Bishopscourt PO Box 484 Ilaro Ogun State Nigeria *Tel:* +234 (0)39 440 695

Yola-Province of Jos The Rt Revd Markus A Ibrahm Bishop of Yola PO Box 601 Yola Adamawa State Nigeria *Tel:* +234 (0)75 624 303 *Fax:* +234 (0)803 045 7576 *Email:* marcusibrahim2002@yahoo.com

Zaki-Biam-Province of Abuja The Rt Revd Benjamin A Vager Bishop of Zaki-Biam Bishopscourt PO Box 600 Yam Market Road Zaki-biam Benue State Nigeria *Tel:* +234 (0)803 676 0018 *Email:* rubavia@yahoo.com

Zaria-Province of Kaduna The Rt Revd Cornelius Salifu Bello Bishop of Zaria Bishopscourt PO Box 507 Zaria Kaduna State Nigeria *Tel:* +234 (0)802 708 9555 *Email:* cssbello@hotmail.com

Zonkwa-Province of Abuja The Rt Revd Jacob W Kwashi Bishop of Zonkwa Bishop's Residence PO Box 26 Zonkwa Kaduna State 802002 Nigeria *Tel:* +234 (0)803 331 0252 *Email:* zonkwa@anglican-nig.org

THE CHURCH OF NORTH INDIA

Provincial Secretary Mr Alwan Masih CNI Synod Post Box 311 16 Pandit Pant Marg New Delhi 110 001 INDIA *Tel:* +91 11 2373 1079 *Fax:* +91 11 2371 6901 *Email:* alwanmasih@cnisynod.org *Web:* www.cnisynod.org

Provincial Treasurer Mr Prem Masih CNI Synod Post Box 311 16 Pandit Pant Marg New Delhi 110

001 INDIA *Tel:* +91 11 4321 4000 *Fax:* +91 11 4321 4006 *Email:* cnitr@cnisynod.org

Agra The Rt Revd Prem Prakash Habil Bishop of Agra Bishop's House 4/116-B Church Road Civil Lines Agra Uttarr Pradesh 282 002 India *Tel:* +91 (0)562 285 4845 *Fax:* +91 (0)562 252 0074 *Email:* doacni@gmail.com

Amritsar The Most Revd Pradeep K Samantaroy Moderator of CNI & Bishop of Amritsar 26 R B Prakash Chand Road Opp Police Ground Amritsar Punjab 143 001 India *Tel:* +91 (0)183 222 2910 *Fax:* +91 (0)183 222 2910 *Email:* bunu13@rediffmail.com *Web:* www.amritsardiocese.org/

Andaman & Car Nicobar Islands The Rt Revd Christopher Paul Bishop of Andaman & Car Nicobar Islands Cathedral Church Compound Car Nicobar MUS 744 301 Andaman & Nicobar Islands *Tel:* +91 (0)319 223 1362 *Fax:* +91 (0)319 223 1362 *Email:* cniportblair@yahoo.co.in

Barrackpore The Rt Revd Brojen Malakar Bishop of Barrackpore Bishop's Lodge 86 Middle Road Barrackpore Kolkata West Bengal 700 120 India *Tel:* +91 (0)332 593 1852 *Fax:* +91 (0)332 593 1852 *Email:* malakar.brojen@rediffmail.com *Web:* www.barrackporediocesecni.org

Bhopal The Rt Revd Robert Ali Bishop of Bhopal Bishop's House 57 Residency Area Behind Narmada Water Tank Indore Madhya Pradesh 452 001 India *Tel:* +91 (0)731 271 0551 *Fax:* +91 (0)731 405 5452 *Email:* bhopal_diocese@yahoo.com

Calcutta The Rt Revd Ashok Biswas Bishop of Kolkatta Bishop's House 51 Chowringhee Road Kolkatta West Bengal 700 071 India *Tel:* +91 (0)336 534 7770 *Fax:* +91 (0)332 282 6340 *Email:* ashoke.biswas@vasnl.net

Chandigarh The Rt Revd Younas Massey Bishop of Chandigarh Bishop's House CNI Mission Compound Brown Road Ludhiana Punjab 141 008 India *Tel:* +91 (0)161 222 5706 *Fax:* +91 (0)161 222 5706 *Email:* massey.younas@yahoo.in

Chhattisgarh The Rt Revd Purna Sagar Nag Bishop of Chhattisgarh Opp. Rajbhavan Gate No 1 Civil Lines Raipur Chhattisgarh 492 001 India *Tel:* +91 (0)771 221 0015 *Email:* doccni@reiffmail.com

Chotanagpur The Rt Revd BBaskey Bishop of Chotanagpur Bishop's Lodge PO Box 1 Old Hazari Bagh Road Ranchi Jharkhand 834 001 India *Tel:* +91 651 235 1181 *Fax:* +91 651 235 1184 *Email:* rch_cndta@sancharnet.in

Cuttack The Rt Revd Dr Samson Das Bishop of Cuttack Bishop's House Mission Road Cuttack Orissa 753 001 India *Tel:* +91 (0)671 230 0102 *Email:* bishopsamsondas@gmail.com

Delhi Vacant Bishop elect of Delhi 1 Church Lane Off North Avenue New Delhi Delhi 110 001 India

Tel: +91 (0)112 371 7471 *Fax:* +91 (0)112 335 8006

Durgapur The Rt Revd Dr Probal K Dutta Bishop of Durgapur St Michael's Church Compound Alderin Path Bidhan Nagar Durgapur West Bengal 713 212 India *Tel:* +91 (0)343 253 4552 *Email:* probaldutta@ymail.com

Eastern Himalayas Vacant Bishop elect of Eastern Himalayas Bishop's House 1B K Gongba Road Darjeeling West Bengal 734 001 India *Tel:* +91 (0)354 225 8183 *Email:* easternhimalaya2004@yahoo.co.in

Gujarat The Rt Revd Silvans S Christian Bishop of Gujarat Bishop's House I.P Mission Compound Ellis Bridge Ahmedabad Gujarat State 380 006 India *Tel:* +91 (0)792 656 1950 *Fax:* +91 (0)792 656 1950 *Email:* gujdio@yahoo.co.in

Jabalpur The Rt Revd Dr Prem C Singh Deputy Moderator of CNI & Bishop of Jabalpur Bishop's House 2131 Napier Town Jabalpur Madhya Pradesh 482 001 India *Tel:* +91 (0)761 262 2109 *Fax:* +91 (0)761 262 2109 *Email:* bishoppcsingh@yahoo.co.in

Kolhapur The Rt Revd Bathuel R Tiwade Bishop of Kolhapur Bishop's House EP School Compound Nagala Park Kolhapur Maharashatra 416 003 India *Tel:* +91 (0)231 265 4832 *Fax:* +91 (0)231 265 4832 *Email:* kdcdbss@yahoo.com

Lucknow The Rt Revd Peter Baldev Bishop of Lucknow Bishop's House 25/11 Mahatma Gandhi Marg Allahabad Uttar Pradesh 211 001 India *Tel:* +91 (0)532 242 7053

Marathwada The Rt Revd Madhukar Kasab Bishop of Marathwada Bungalow 28/A Mission Compound Cantt Aurangabad Maharashtra 431 002 India *Tel:* +91 (0)240 237 3136 *Email:* revmukasab@yahoo.co.in

Mumbai (Form. Bombay) The Rt Revd Prakash D Patole Bishop of Mumbai Bishop's House 19 Hazarimal Somani Marg Mumbai Maharashtra 400 001 India *Tel:* +91 (0)222 206 0248 *Fax:* +91 222 206 0248 *Email:* cnibombaydiocese@yahoo.com

Nagpur The Rt Revd Paul B Dupare Bishop of Nagpur Bishop's House Cathedral House, Opp Indian Coffee House Sadar Nagpur Maharashtra 440 001 India *Tel:* +91 (0)712 255 3351 *Fax:* +91 (0)712 255 3351 *Email:* nagpurdiocese@rediffmail.com

Nasik The Rt Revd Pradip Kamble Bishop of Nasik Bishop's House 1 Outram Road Tarakpur Ahmednagar Maharashtra 414 003 India *Tel:* +91 (0)241 241 1806 *Fax:* +91 (0)241 242 2314 *Email:* bishopofnasik@rediffmail.com

North East India The Rt Revd Michael Herenz Bishop of North East India Bishop's Kuti Shillong 1 Meghalaya 793 001 India *Tel:* +91 (0)364 222 3155 *Fax:* +91 (0)364 250 1178

Patna The Rt Revd Dr Philip P Marandih Bishop of Patna Bishop's House Christ Church Compound Bhagalpur Bihar 812 001 India *Tel:* +91 (0)641 240 0033 *Email:* cnipatna@rediffmail.com

Phulbani The Rt Revd Bijay K Nayak Bishop of Phulbani Bishop's House, Mission Compound Gudripori G. Udayagiri Phulbani Kandhmal 762 100 India *Tel:* +91 (0)684 726 0569 *Email:* bpnayakbijaykumar@gmail.com *Web:* www.cniphulbanidiocese.org

Pune The Rt Revd Andrew B Rathod Bishop of Pune 1A Stavley Road General Bhagat Marg Pune Maharashtra 411 001 India *Tel:* +91 (0)202 633 4374 *Email:* punediocese@yahoo.co.in

Rajasthan The Rt Revd Warris Masih Bishop of Rajasthan 2/10 Civil Lines Opp. Bus Stand Jaipur Road Ajmer Rajasthan 305 001 India *Tel:* +91 (0)145 242 0633 *Fax:* +91 (0)145 262 1627 *Email:* wkmasih@yahoo.co.in

Sambalpur The Rt Revd Pinuel P Dip Bishop of Sambalpur Bishop's House Mission Compound Bolangir Orissa 767 001 India *Tel:* +91 (0)665 223 0625 *Email:* pinuel_dip@rediffmail.com

THE CHURCH OF PAKISTAN (UNITED)

Provincial Secretary Lt Col Kanwal Isaacs St Johns Cathedral 1 Sir Syed Road Peshawar 25000 Pakistan *Tel:* +92 91 527 8643 *Email:* kanwal4454@gmail.com

Provincial Treasurer Mr Irshad Nawab 113 Quasim Road PO Box 204 Multan Cantt Pakistan *Email:* treasurersynod.cop@gmail.com

Faisalabad The Rt Revd John Samuel Bishop of Faisalabad Bishop's House PO Box 27 Mission Road Gojra Dist Toba Tek Sing Pakistan *Tel:* +92 (0)46 351 4689 *Fax:* + *Email:* jsamuel51@hotmail.com

Hyderabad The Rt Revd Kaleem John Bishop of Hyderabad 27- Liaqat Road Civil Lines Hyderabad 71000 Pakistan *Email:* kaleemjohn@aol.com

Karachi The Rt Revd Saddiq Daniel Bishop of Karachi and Deputy Moderator of the Church of Pakistan Trinity Close Abdullah Haroon Road Karachi 4 Pakistan *Tel:* +92 021 356556913 *Email:* sadiqdaniel@hotmail.com

Lahore The Rt Revd Irfan Jamil Bishop of Lahore Bishopsbourne Cathedral Close The Mall Lahore 54000 Pakistan *Tel:* +92 (0)42 3723 3560 *Fax:* +92 (0)42 3712 0766 *Email:* 9thbishopoflahore@gmail.com *Web:* www.dol.com.pk

Multan The Rt Revd Leo Roderick Paul Bishop of Multan 113 Quasim Road PO Box 204 Multan Cantt Pakistan *Tel:* +92 (0)61 458 3694 *Email:* bishop_mdcop@live.com

Peshawar The Rt Revd Humphrey S Peters Bishop of Peshawar St Johns Cathedral 1 Sir Syed Road Peshawar 25000 Pakistan *Tel:* +92 (0)91 527 6519 *Email:* bishopdop@hotmail.com

Raiwind The Most Revd Samuel Robert Azariah Bishop of Raiwind & Moderator of the Church of Pakistan 17 Warris Road Lahore 54000 Pakistan *Tel:* +92 (0)42 3758 8950 *Email:* sammyazariah@yahoo.com

Sialkot The Rt Revd Alwin Samuel Bishop of Sialkot Christian Town Sialkot 2 Pakistan *Tel:* +92 052 4264828 *Email:* alwinsialkot@gmail.com

THE ANGLICAN CHURCH OF PAPUA NEW GUINEA

Provincial Secretary Mr Samson Chicki PO Box 673 Lae 411 Morobe Province PAPUA NEW GUINEA *Tel:* +675 472 4111 *Fax:* +675 472 1852 *Email:* schicki@acpng.org.pg

Dogura The Rt Revd Clyde M Igara Archbishop of Papua New Guinea & Bishop of Dogura PO Box 19 Dogura MBP Papua New Guinea *Tel:* +675 641 1530 *Fax:* +675 641 1129 *Email:* clydemigara@gmail.com

Aipo Rongo The Rt Revd Dr Nathan Ingen Bishop of Aipo Rongo. PO Box 893 Mount Hagen Western Highlands Province Papua New Guinea *Tel:* +675 54 211 31 *Fax:* +675 54 211 81 *Email:* bishopnathan2@gmail.com

New Guinea Islands, The The Rt Revd Allan Migi Bishop of The New Guinea Islands Bishop's House PO Box 806 Kimbe NGIP Papua New Guinea *Tel:* +675 9 835 120 *Fax:* +675 9 835 120 *Email:* AllanRirmeMigi@gmail.com

Popondota The Rt Revd Lindsley Ihove Bishop of Popondota Diocese of Popondota PO Box 26 Popondetta Oro Province Papua New Guinea *Tel:* +675 329 7194 *Fax:* +675 329 7476 *Email:* bplndsleyihove@gmail.com

Port Moresby The Rt Revd Denny Bray Guka Bishop of Port Morsby PO Box 6491 Boroko NCD Papua New Guinea

Aipo Rongo The Rt Revd Denys Ririka Suffragan Bishop of Aipo Rongo PO Box 1178 Goroka Eastern Highlands Province Papua New Guinea *Email:* acpngair@global.net.pg

THE EPISCOPAL CHURCH IN THE PHILIPPINES

The Most Revd Renato Mag-Gay R M Abibico *Prime Bishop of the Episcopal Church in the Philippines* The ECP Mission Center #275 E. Rodriguez Sr. Avenue Quezon City 1112 Philippines *Tel:* +63 (0)2 722 8481 *Fax:* +63 (0)2 721 1923 *Email:* reneabibico@yahoo.com

Provincial Secretary Mr Floyd Lalwet P.O Box 10321 Broadway Centrum Quezon City 1112 PHILIPPINES *Fax:* +63 (0)2 721 1923 *Email:* flaw997@gmail.com

Provincial Treasurer Mrs Bridget B Lacdao Provincial Office PO Box 10321 Broadway Centrum 1112 Quezon City PHILIPPINES *Tel:* +63 (0)2 722 8510 *Fax:* +63 (0)2 721 1923

Central Philippines The Rt Revd Dixie Copanut Taclobao Central Philippines 281 E Rodriguez Sr Avenue 1102 Quezon City Philippines *Tel:* +63 (0)2 412 8561 *Fax:* +63 (0)2 721 1923 *Email:* central@i-next.net

Davao The Rt Revd Jonathan Labasan Casimina Bishop of Davao Km. 3 McArthur Highway Matina Davao City Philippines *Tel:* +63 82 299 1511 *Fax:* +63 82 296 9629 *Email:* episcopaldioceseofdavao@ yahoo.com *Web:* www.eddphilippines.com

North Central Philippines The Rt Revd Joel Atiwag Pachao Bishop of North Central Philippines 358 Magsaysay Avenue Baguio City 2600 Philippines *Tel:* +63 (0)74 443 7705 *Fax:* +63 (0)74 442 2432 *Email:* edncp@digitelone.com

Northern Luzon Vacant Bishop elect of Northern Luzon Bulanao Tabuk Kalinga-Apayao 3800 Philippines

Northern Philippines The Rt Revd Brent W Alawas Bishop of Northern Philippines Diocesan Office Bontoc Mt Province 2616 Philippines *Tel:* +63 (0)74 602 1026 *Fax:* +63 (0)74 462 4099 *Email:* ednpvic@ hotmail.com

Northern Philippines The Rt Revd Miguel P Yamoyam Suffragan Bishop of the Northern Philippines PO Box 10321 Broadway Centrum Quezon City 1112 Philippines *Tel:* +63 (0)2 722 8481/8460 *Fax:* +63 (0)2 721 1923 *Email:* ecpnational@yahoo.co.ph

Santiago The Rt Revd Alexander A A Wandag Bishop of Santiago Episcopal Diocese of Santiago Maharlika Highway 3311 Divisoria Santiago City Isabela 3311 Philippines *Tel:* +63 (0)78 682 3756 *Fax:* +63 (0)78 682 1256 *Email:* alexwandageds@ yahoo.com

Southern Philippines The Rt Revd Danilo Labacanacruz Bustamante Bishop of Southern Philippines 186 Sinsuat Avenue Cotabato City 9600 Philippines *Tel:* +63 (0)64 421 2960 *Fax:* +63 (0)64 421 1703 *Email:* edsp_ecp@yahoo.com *Web:* www. edspphilippines.com

L'EGLISE EPISCOPAL AU RWANDA

Provincial Secretary The Revd Francis F Karemera PO Box 2487 Kigali Rwanda *Email:* frkaremera@ yahoo.co.uk

Butare The Rt Revd Nathan K Gasatura Bishop of Butare BP 255 Butare Rwanda *Tel:* +250 30 710 *Fax:* +250 30 504 *Email:* nathan.gasatura@gmail.com

Byumba The Rt Revd Emmanuel Ngendahayo Bishop of Byumba BP 17 Byumba Rwanda *Tel:* +250

64 242 *Fax:* +250 64 242 *Email:* engendahayo@ ymail.com

Cyangugu The Rt Revd Nathan Amooti Rusengo Bishop of Cyangugu PO Box 52 Cyangugu Rwanda *Tel:* +250 788 409 061 *Email:* nathanamooti@gmail. com

Gahini The Rt Revd Alexis Bilindabagabo Bishop of Gahini BP 22 Gahini Rwanda *Tel:* +250 67 422 *Fax:* +250 77 831 *Email:* abilindabagabo@gmail.com

Gasabo The Most Revd Dr Onesphore Rwaje Archbishop of L'Eglise Episcopal au Rwanda and Bishop of Gasabo PO Box 2487 Kigali Rwanda *Fax:* +250 64 242 *Email:* onesphorerwaje@yahoo.fr

Kibungo The Rt Revd Emmanuel Ntazinda Bishop of Kibungo BP 719 Kibungo Rwanda *Tel:* +250 566 194

Kigali The Rt Revd Louis Muvunyi Bishop of Kigali PO Box 61 Kigali Rwanda *Tel:* +250 576 340 *Fax:* +250 573 213 *Email:* louismuvunyi@hotmail.com

Kigeme The Rt Revd Augustin Mvunabandi Bishop of Kigeme BP 67 Gikongoro Rwanda *Tel:* +250 535 086 *Email:* dkigemeear@yahoo.fr

Kivu The Rt Revd Augustin Ahimana Bishop of Kivu PO Box 166 Gisenyi Rwanda *Tel:* +250 78 830 5119 *Email:* aamurekezi@gmail.com

Shyira The Rt Revd Dr Laurent Mbanda Bishop of Shyira EER-Shyira PO Box 52 Ruhengeri Rwanda *Tel:* +250 466 02 *Fax:* +250 546 449 *Email:* mbandalaurent@yahoo.com

Shyogwe The Rt Revd Jered Kalimba Bishop of Shyogwe BP 27 Gitarama Rwanda *Tel:* +250 62 372 *Fax:* +250 62 460 *Email:* kalimbaj60@yahoo.fr

THE SCOTTISH EPISCOPAL CHURCH

Secretary General Mr John Stuart 21 Grosvenor Crescent Edinburgh EH12 5EE SCOTLAND *Tel:* +44 (0)131 225 6357 *Fax:* +44 (0)131 346 7247 *Email:* secgen@scotland.anglican.org

Provincial Treasurer Mr Malcolm G Bett 21 Grosvenor Crescent Edinburgh EH12 5EE SCOTLAND *Tel:* +44 (0)131 225 6357 *Fax:* +44 (0)131 346 7247

Aberdeen & Orkney The Rt Revd Dr Robert Gillies Bishop of Aberdeen & Orkney Diocesan Office St Clement's Church House Mastrick Drive Aberdeen AB16 6UF Scotland *Tel:* +44 (0) 1224 662 247 *Fax:* +44 (0)1224 662 168 *Email:* bishop@aberdeen. anglican.org *Web:* www.aberdeen.anglican.org

Argyll & The Isles The Rt Revd Kevin Pearson Bishop of Argyll & The Isles St Moluag's Diocesan Centre Croft Avenue Oban Argyll PA34 5JJ Scotland *Tel:* +44 (0)1631 570 870 *Fax:* +44 (0)1631 570 411 *Email:* bishop@argyll.anglican.org *Web:* www. argyllandtheisles.org.uk

Brechin The Rt Revd Dr Nigel Peyton Bishop of Brechin The Brechin Diocesan Office Unit 14 Prospect III Technology Park Gemini Crescent Dundee DD2 1SW Scotland *Tel:* +44 (0)1382 562 24 *Email:* office@brechin.anglican.org *Web:* www. thedioceseofbrechin.org

Edinburgh The Rt Revd John Armes Bishop of Edinburgh Diocesan Centre 21A Grosvenor Crescent Edinburgh EH12 5EL Scotland *Tel:* +44 (0)131 538 7044 *Fax:* +44 (0)131 538 7088 *Email:* bishop@edinburgh.anglican.org *Web:* www. edinburgh.anglican.org

Glasgow & Galloway The Rt Revd Dr Gregor Duncan Bishop of Glasgow & Galloway Bishop's Office Diocesan Centre 5 St Vincent Place Glasgow G1 2DH Scotland *Tel:* +44 (0)141 221 6911 *Fax:* +44 (0)141 221 7014 *Email:* bishop@glasgow.anglican. org *Web:* www.glasgow.anglican.org

Moray, Ross & Caithness The Rt Revd Mark Strange Bishop of Moray, Ross & Caithness St Duthac's Centre Arpafeelie North Kessock Ross-Shire IV1 3XD Scotland *Tel:* +44 (0)1463 811 333 *Email:* bishop@moray.anglican.org *Web:* www. moray.anglican.org

St Andrews Dunkeld & Dunblane The Most Revd David R Chillingworth Primus of the Scottish Episcopal Church & Bishop of St Andrews Dunkeld & Dunblane Diocesan Office 28A Balhousie Street Perth PH1 5HJ Scotland *Tel:* +44 (0)1738 580 426 *Fax:* +44 (0)1738 443 174 *Email:* bishop@standrews. anglican.org *Web:* www.standrews.anglican.org

CHURCH OF THE PROVINCE OF SOUTHEAST ASIA

Provincial Secretary Mr Leonard David Shim Messrs. Reddi & Co Advocates No. 393 Jalan Datuk Abang Abdul Rahim Kuching Sarawak 93450 MALAYSIA *Tel:* +60 82 484 466 *Fax:* +60 82 484 467 *Email:* leonard.shim@reddi.com.my

Provincial Treasurer Mr Keith Chua 35 Ford Avenue Singapore 268714 SINGAPORE *Tel:* +65 (0)2 6235 3344 *Fax:* +65 (0)2 6736 1201 *Email:* keithchu@ singnet.com.sg

Kuching The Most Revd Bolly A Lapok Archbishop of South East Asia & Bishop of Kuching Bishop's House PO Box 347 Kuching Sarawak 93704 Malaysia *Tel:* +60 (0)82 240 187 *Fax:* +60 (0)82 426 488 *Email:* bpofkuching@gmail.com *Web:* www. diocesekuching.org

Kuching The Rt Revd Solomon Cheong Sung Voon Assistant Bishop of Kuching Bishop's House PO Box 347 Kuching Sarawak 93704 Malaysia *Tel:* +60 (0)82 429 755

Sabah The Rt Revd Melter Jiki Tais Bishop of Sabah PO Box 10811 88809 Kota Kinabalu Sabah 88809

Malaysia *Tel:* +60 (0)89 521 448 *Fax:* +60 (0)89 521 448 *Email:* uskupmjtais@gmail.com

Sabah The Rt Revd John Yeo Assistant Bishop of Sabah 201 Jalan Dunlop Tawau sabah 91000 Malaysia *Tel:* +60 (0)89 772 212 *Fax:* +60 (0)89 761 451 *Email:* ad.johnyeo@gmail.com

Singapore The Rt Revd Rennis Ponniah Bishop of Singapore St Andrew's Village 1 Francis Thomas Drive #01-01 Singapore 359340 Singapore *Tel:* +65 6288 7585 *Fax:* +65 6288 5574 *Email:* bpoffice@ anglican.org.sg

West Malaysia The Rt Revd Ng Moon Hing Archbishop elect of South East Asia & Bishop of West Malaysia 16 Jalan Pudu Kuala Lumpur 50200 Malaysia *Tel:* +60 (0)32 031 3213 *Fax:* +60 (0)32 031 2728 *Email:* canonmoon@gmail.com

West Malaysia The Rt Revd Charles K. Samuel Assistant Bishop of West Malaysia St George's Church 1 Lebuh Farquhar Georgetown Pulau Pinang 10200 Malaysia *Tel:* +60 (0)16 922 1618 *Email:* vencan.cs@gmail.com

West Malaysia The Rt Revd Jason Selvaraj Assistant Bishop of West Malaysia Christ Church Melaka 48 Jalan Gereja Melaka 75000 West Malaysia *Tel:* +60 06 2848 804 *Email:* jasondaphne101@gmail.com

CHURCH OF THE PROVINCE OF SOUTH INDIA

General Secretary CSI The Revd Dr D R Sadananda CSI Centre, No 5 Whites Road Royapettah Chennai 6000 014 INDIA *Tel:* +91 044 2852 1566 *Email:* synodcsi@gmail.com

Provincial Treasurer Advocate Robert Bruce Star Cottage Sarai Vila Kattathurai Kanyakumari Dist INDIA *Tel:* +91 044 2852 1566 *Email:* csisnd_tr@ sify.com

Coimbatore The Rt Revd Timothy Ravinder Bishop of Coimbatore Bishop's House 256 Race Course Road Coimbatore TN 1 641018 India *Tel:* +91 (0)422 221 3605 *Fax:* +91 (0)422 221 3369 *Email:* csi. bpcbe@gmail.com

Dornakal The Rt Revd Vadapalli Prasada Rao Bishop of Dornakal Bishop's House Epiphany Cathedral Compound SC Railway Dornakal Andhra Pradesh 506 381 India *Tel:* +91 (0) 8719 227 535 *Fax:* +91 (0) 8719 227 376 *Email:* dkbpoff@ hotmail.com

East Kerala The Rt Revd Dr Kayalakkakathu George Daniel Bishop of East Kerala CSI Bishop's House Melukavumattom- 686 652 Kerala India *Tel:* +91 (0)4822 219 044 *Email:* bishopkgdaniel@ rediffmail.com

Jaffna The Rt Revd Dr Daniel Selvaratnam Thiagarajah Bishop of Jaffna Bishop's House

Vaddukoddai Sri Lanka *Tel:* +94 (0)60 221 2424 *Email:* dsthiagarajah@yahoo.com

Kanyakumari The Rt Revd Gnanasigamony Devakadasham Bishop of Kanyakumari 71-A Dennis Street Nagercoil Tamil Nadu 629 001 India *Tel:* +91 (0)4652 231 539 *Fax:* +91 (0)4652 226 560 *Email:* csikkd@bsnl.com

Karimnagar The Rt Revd Reuben Mark Bishop of Karimnagar 2-8-95 CV Raman Road PO Box 40 Makarampura Karimnagar 505 001 Andhra Pradesh India *Tel:* +91 878 226 2971 *Fax:* +91 878 226 2972

Karnataka Central The Rt Revd Prasana Kumar Samuel Bishop of Karnataka Central Diocesan Office 20 Third Cross CSI Compound Bangalore 560 027 Karnataka India *Tel:* +91 (0)80 2222 3766 *Email:* admin@csikcd.org

Karnataka North The Rt Revd Ravikumar J. R J Niranjan Bishop of Karnataka North Bishop's House All Saints Church Compound Dharwad- 580 008 Karnataka India *Tel:* +91 (0)836 244 7733 *Email:* haradoni.rn@gmail.com

Karnataka South The Rt Revd Mohan Manoraj Bishop of Karnataka South Bishop's House Balmatta Mangalore 575 001 India *Tel:* +91 (0)824 2432 657 *Fax:* +91 (0)824 2432 363

Krishna-Godavari The Most Revd Govada Dyvasirvadam Moderator of CSI & Bishop of Krishna-Godavari St Andrew's Cathedral Compound Main Road Machilipatnam- 521 002 Krishna-Godaviri District Andhra Pradesh India *Tel:* +91 (0)8672 220 623 *Fax:* +91 (0)8672 220 771 *Email:* bishopkrishna@yahoo.com

Madhya Kerala The Rt Revd Thomas Kanjirappally T K Oommen Deputy Moderator of CSI & Bishop of Madhya Kerala CSI Bishop's House Cathedral Road Kottayam Kerala State 686 001 India *Tel:* +91 (0)481 2566 536 *Fax:* +91 (0)481 2566 531 *Email:* csimkdbishop@sancharnet.in

Madras The Rt Revd Dr Vedanayagam Devasahayam Bishop of Madras Diocesan Office PB No 4914 226 Cathedral Road Chennai Tamil Nadu 600 086 India *Tel:* +91 (0)44 2811 3933 *Fax:* +91 (0)44 2811 0608 *Email:* bishopdeva@hotmail.com *Web:* www.csimadrasdiocese.org

Madurai-Ramnad The Rt Revd Marialouis Joseph Bishop of Madurai-Ramnad #5 Bhulabai Road Chockikulam Madurai District Tamil Nadu 625 002 India *Tel:* +91 (0)452 256 3196 *Fax:* +91 (0)452 256 0864 *Email:* bishop@csidmr.net

Medak Vacant Bishop elect of Medak 10-3-65, Church House Golden Jubilee Bhavan Old Lancer Lane Secunderabad Andhra Pradesh 500 025 India *Tel:* +91 (0)40 2783 3151 *Fax:* +91 (0)40 2782 0843 *Email:* medakdiocese@yahoo.com

Nandyal The Rt Revd Eggoni Pushpalalitha Bishop of Nandyal Bishop's House Nandyal RS Kurnool District Andhra Pradesh 518 502 India *Tel:* +91 (0)8514 222 477 *Fax:* +91 (0)8514 242 255

North Kerala The Rt Revd B N Fenn Bishop of North Kerala CSI Diocesan Office PB 104 Shoranur Kerala 679 121 India *Tel:* +91 (0)466 222 4454 *Fax:* +91 (0)466 222 2545 *Email:* csinkd@gmail.com

Rayalaseema The Rt Revd B D Prasada Rao Bishop of Rayalaseema CSI Compound Kadapa Andhra Pradesh 516 001 India *Tel:* +91 (0) 8562 325320 *Fax:* +91 (0) 8562 275200 *Email:* lbd_prasad@yahoo.com

South Kerala The Rt Revd Dharmaraj Rasalam Bishop of South Kerala Bishop's House LMS Compound Trivandrum Kerala State 695 033 India *Tel:* +91 (0)471 231 5490 *Fax:* +91 (0)471 231 6439

Thoothukudi-Nazareth Vacant Bishop elect of Thoothukudi-Nazareth Diocesan Road Caldwell Hr. Sec. School Campus Beach Road Thoothukudi Tamil Nadu 628 001 India *Tel:* +91 (0) 461 2329 408 *Fax:* +91 (0)461 2328 408 *Email:* csitnd@bsnl.in

Tirunelveli The Rt Revd Jayaraj J Christdoss Bishop of Tirunelveli Bishopstowe PO Box 118 Palayamkottai Tirunelveli Tamil Nadu 627 002 India *Tel:* +91 (0)462 2578 744 *Fax:* +91 (0)462 2574 525

Trichy-Tanjore The Rt Revd Dr Gnanamuthu Paul Vasanthakumar Bishop of Trichy-Tanjore CSI Diocesan Office Allithurai Road Palhur Tiruchirappalli Tamil Nadu 620 017 India *Tel:* +91 (0)431 771 254 *Email:* csittd@tr.net.in

Vellore The Rt Revd A Rajavelu Bishop of Vellore 3/1 Anna Salai Vellore Tamil Nadu 632 001 India *Tel:* +91 (0)416 2232 160 *Fax:* +91 (0)416 2223 835 *Email:* csi.vlrdiocese@gmail.com

THE CHURCH OF THE PROVINCE OF SOUTHERN AFRICA

Provincial Executive Officer The Revd Willie Mostert 20 Bishopscourt Drive Bishopscourt Claremont Western Cape 7708 South Africa *Tel:* +27 (0)21 763 1328 *Fax:* +27 (0)21 797 1329 *Email:* peo@ anglicanchurchsa.org.za

Provincial Treasurer and Diocesan Secretary of Cape Town Mr Rob S Rogerson P O Box 53014 KENILWORTH 7745 SOUTH AFRICA *Tel:* +27 (0)21 797 8324 *Fax:* +27 (0)21 683 4603 *Email:* rogerson@cpsa-province.org.za

Angola (Missionary Diocese) The Rt Revd Andre Soares Bishop of Angola Off Caixa Postal No. 10498 Luanda Angola *Tel:* +244 23 957 92 *Fax:* +244 23 967 94 *Email:* anglican@ebonet.net

Cape Town The Rt Revd Garth Q Counsell Bishop of Table Bay PO Box 1932 Cape Town 8000 South

Africa *Tel:* +27 (0)21 469 3774 *Fax:* +27 (0)21 469 3774 *Email:* bishop.suffragan@ctdiocese.org.za

Christ the King The Rt Revd Peter J Lee Bishop of Christ the King Diocese of Christ the King PO Box 1653 Rosettenville Gauteng 2130 South Africa *Tel:* +27 (0)11 435 0097 *Fax:* +27 (0)11 435 2868 *Email:* bishop@ctkdiocese.co.za *Web:* www.christthekingdiocese-anglican.org

Diocese of the Free State (formerly Bloemfontein) The Rt Revd Dintoe Letloenyane Bishop of Diocese of the Free State PO Box 411 Bloemfontein 9300 South Afrcia *Tel:* +27 (0)51 447 6053 *Fax:* +27 (0)51 447 5874 *Email:* bishopdintoe@dsc.co.za *Web:* www.dsc.co.za

False Bay The Rt Revd Margaret Brenda Vertue Bishop of False Bay PO Box 2804 Somerset West 7129 South Africa *Tel:* +27 (0)21 852 5243 *Fax:* +27 (0)21 852 9430 *Email:* bishopm@falsebaydiocese. org.za *Web:* www.falsebaydiocese.org.za

George The Rt Revd Brian Marajh Bishop of George PO Box 227 George Cape Province 6530 South Africa *Tel:* +27 (0)44 873 5680 *Fax:* +27 (0)44 873 5680 *Email:* glynis@georgediocese.co.za

Grahamstown The Rt Revd Ebenezer StM Ntlali Bishop of Grahamstown Bishopsbourne PO Box 181 Grahamstown Eastern Cape 6140 South Africa *Tel:* +27 (0)46 636 1996 *Fax:* +27 (0)46 622 5231 *Email:* bpgtn@intekom.co.za

Highveld The Rt Revd David H Bannerman Bishop of the Highveld PO Box 17642 Benoni West Gauteng 1503 South Africa *Tel:* +27 (0)11 422 2231/2 *Fax:* +27 (0)11 420 1336 *Email:* diohveld@iafrica.com *Web:* www.diocesehighveld.org.za

Johannesburg The Rt Revd Stephen Mosimanegape Moreo Bishop of Johannesburg Diocesan Office P O Box 157 Westhoven Gauteng 2142 South Africa *Tel:* +27 (0)11 375 2700 *Fax:* +27 (0)11 477 1337 *Email:* steve.moreo@anglicanjoburg.org.za

Kimberley & Kuruman The Rt Revd Oswald P P. Swartz Bishop of Kimberley and Kuruman PO Box 45 Kimberley 8300 South Africa *Tel:* +27 (0)53 833 2433 *Fax:* +27 (0)53 831 2730 *Email:* oppswartz@onetel.com

Lebombo The Rt Revd Carlos Simao Matsinhe Bishop of Lebombo Caixa Postale 120 Maputo Mozambique *Tel:* +258 21 404 885 *Fax:* +258 21 401 093

Lesotho The Rt Revd Adam Mallane A Taaso Bishop of Lesotho PO Box 87 Maseru 100 Losotho *Tel:* +266 (0)22 3311 974 *Fax:* +266 (0)22 310 161 *Email:* dioceselesotho@ecoweb.co.ls

Matlosane (formerly Klerksdorp) The Rt Revd Stephen M Diseko Bishop of Matlosane PO Box

11417 Klerksdorp 2570 South Africa *Tel:* +27 (0)18 464 2260 *Fax:* +27 (0)18 462 4939 *Email:* diocesematlosane@telkomsa.net

Mbhashe The Rt Revd Elliot S Williams Bishop of Mbhashe PO Box 1184 Butterworth 4960 South Africa *Tel:* +27 (0)47 491 8127 *Fax:* +27 (0)47 491 9218 *Email:* dioceseofmbhashe@telkomsa.net

Mpumalanga The Rt Revd Daniel M Kgomosotho Bishop of Mpumalanga PO Box 4327 White River 1240 South Africa *Tel:* +27 (0)13 751 1960 *Fax:* +27 (0)13 751 3638 *Email:* bishopdan@telkomsa.net

Mthatha (formerly St John's) The Rt Revd Dr Sitembele T Mzamane Bishop of Mthatha PO Box 25 Umtata Transkei 5100 South Africa *Tel:* +27 (0)47 532 4450 *Fax:* +27 (0)47 532 4191 *Email:* anglicbspmthatha@intekom.co.za *Web:* www.mthatha.anglican.org

Namibia The Rt Revd Natanael Nakwatumba Bishop of Namibia PO Box 57 Windhoek 9000 Namibia *Tel:* +264 (0)61 238 920 *Fax:* +264 (0)61 225 903 *Email:* bishop@anglicanchurchnamibia.com

Namibia The Rt Revd Petrus Hilukiluah Suffragan Bishop of Namibia PO Box 65 Windhoek NAMIBIA *Tel:* +264 (0)61 236 009 *Fax:* +264 (0)61 225 903 *Email:* bpertus@iafrica.com.na

Natal The Rt Revd Dino Gabriel Bishop elect of Natal PO Box 47439 Greyville Durban 4023 South Africa *Tel:* +27 (0)31 308 9302 *Fax:* +27 (0)31 308 9316 *Email:* bishop@dionatal.org.za

Natal-North West Episcopal Area The Rt Revd Tsietse Edward Seleoane Suffragan Bishop of the North West Episcopal Area P O Box 463 Ladysmith 3370 South Africa *Tel:* +27 (0)36 631 4650 *Fax:* +27 (0)36 637 4949 *Email:* seleoanet@vodamail.co.za

Natal-South Episcopal Area The Rt Revd Dr Hummingfield C Ndwandwe Suffragan Bishop of the South Episcopal Area PO Box 889 Pietermaritzburg 3200 South Africa *Tel:* +27 (0)33 394 1560 *Fax:* +27 (0)33 394 8785 *Email:* bishopndwandwe@dionatal.org.za

Niassa The Rt Revd Mark A van Koevering Bishop of Niassa Diocese of Niassa CP 264 Lichinga Niassa Mozambique *Tel:* +258 27120735 *Fax:* +258 7 120 735 *Email:* bishop.niassa@gmail.com

Niassa The Ven Manuel Ernesto Suffragan Bishop elect of Niassa Diocese of Niassa CP 264 Lichinga Niassa Mozambique *Tel:* +258 27 121 377 *Email:* mernesto.diocese.niassa@gmail.com

Port Elizabeth The Rt Revd Nceba B Nopece Bishop of Port Elizabeth PO Box 7109 Newton Park 6055 South Africa *Tel:* +27 (0)41 365 1387 *Fax:* +27 (0)41 365 2049 *Email:* pebishop@iafrica.com *Web:* www.anglicandiocesepe.org.za

Pretoria The Rt Revd Dr Johannes T Seoka Bishop of Pretoria PO Box 1032 Pretoria 1 South Africa *Tel:* +27 (0)12 322 2218 *Fax:* +27 (0)12 322 9411 *Email:* ptabish@dioceseofpretoria.org *Web:* www.dioceseofpretoria.org/

Saldanha Bay The Rt Revd Raphael B V Hess Bishop of Saldanha Bay PO Box 420 Malmesbury Cape Province 7299 South Africa *Tel:* +27 (0)22 487 3885 *Fax:* +27 (0)22 487 3187 *Email:* bishop@dioceseofsaldanhabay.org.za

St Helena The Rt Revd Richard D Fenwick Bishop of St Helena Bishopsholme PO Box 62 St Helena Island South Atlantic *Tel:* +290 4471 *Fax:* +290 4728 *Email:* bishop@helanta.sh *Web:* www.sthelena.anglican.org

St Mark the Evangelist The Rt Revd Martin A Breytenbach Bishop of St Mark the Evangelist PO Box 643 Polokwane 700 South Africa *Tel:* +27 (0)15 297 3297 *Fax:* +27 (0)15 297 0408 *Email:* martin@stmark.org.za

Swaziland The Rt Revd Ellinah Ntfombi E Wamukoya Bishop of Swaziland PO Box 118 Mbabane Swaziland *Tel:* +268 4 04 3624 *Fax:* +268 404 6759 *Email:* bishopen@swazilanddiocese.org.sz

Ukhahlamba The Rt Revd Mazwi E Tisani Bishop of Ukhahlamba PO Box 1673 Queenstown Eastern Cape 116 South Africa *Tel:* +27 (0)45 838 3261 *Fax:* +27 (0)45 838 2874 *Email:* bishopmazwi@mweb.co.za

Umzimvubu The Rt Revd Mlibo M Ngewu Bishop of Umzimvubu PO Box 644 Kokstad 4700 South Africa *Tel:* +27 (0)39 727 4117 *Fax:* +27 (0)39 727 4117 *Email:* mzimvubu@futurenet.co.za

Zululand Vacant Bishop elect of Zululand PO Box 147 Eshowe Zululand 3815 South Africa *Tel:* +27 (0)35 474 2047 *Fax:* +27 (0)35 474 2047

IGLESIA ANGLICANA DEL CONO SUR DE AMERICA

Provincial Secretary The Revd Daniel Ramón Genovesi Cro. Gral. Belgrano 946 Hurlingham Buenos Aires 1686 ARGENTINE *Tel:* +54 11 4452 7555 *Email:* danielgenovesi@gmail.com

Provincial Treasurer Miss Elisa Aguilar Rojas Victoria Subercaseaux 41Of 301 Santiago 50675 CHILE *Tel:* +56 (0)2 2638 3009 *Email:* eaguilar@iach.cl

Argentina The Rt Revd Gregory James Venables Bishop of Argentina 25 de Mayo 282 Capital Federal Buenos Aires 1001 Argentina *Tel:* +54 11 4342 4618 *Fax:* +54 11 4784 1277 *Email:* diocesisanglibue@fibertel.com.ar *Web:* www.anglicana.org.ar

Bolivia The Rt Revd Raphael Samuel Bishop of Bolivia Inglesia Anglicana Episcopal de Bolivia Casilla 848 Cochabamba Bolivia *Tel:* +591 4440 1168 *Email:* raphaelsamuel@gmail.com

Chile The Most Revd Hector Zavala Muñoz Presiding Bishop of the Anglican Church of South America & Bishop of Chile Casilla 50675 Correo Central Santiago Chile *Tel:* +56 (0)2 638 3009 *Fax:* +56 (0)2 639 4581 *Email:* tzavala@iach.cl *Web:* www.iach.cl

Chile The Rt Revd Abelino Manuel Apeleo Suffragan Bishop of Chile Pasaje Viña Poniente 4593 Puente Alto Santiago CHILE *Tel:* +56 (0)2 638 3009 *Email:* aapeleo@gmail.com *Web:* www.iach.cl

Northern Argentina The Rt Revd Nicholas James Quested Q Drayson Bishop of Northern Argentina Iglesia Anglicana Casilla 187 Salta 4400 Argentina *Tel:* +54 387 431 1718 *Fax:* +54 371 142 0100 *Email:* nicobispo@gmail.com *Web:* www.iglesiaanglicanasalta.org

Paraguay The Rt Revd Peter John Henry Bartlett Bishop of Paraguay Iglesia Anglicana Paraguya Casilla de Correo 1124 Asuncion Paraguya Paraguay *Tel:* +595 (0)21 200 933 *Fax:* +595 (0)21 214 328 *Email:* peterparaguay@gmail.com

Paraguay The Rt Revd Andrés Rodríguez Erben Assistant Bishop of Paraguay España # 1357 (casi Gral. Santos) Asuncion 1124 PARAGUAY *Tel:* +59 5331 242 533

Peru The Rt Revd Dr Harold William Godfrey Bishop of Peru Calle Doña María 141 Los Rosales Surco Lima 33 Peru *Tel:* +51 (0)1 449 0600 *Email:* hwgodfrey@gmail.com *Web:* www.peru.anglican.org

Peru The Rt Revd Michael Alexander Chapman Suffragan Bishop of Peru Calle Doña María 141 Los Rosales Lima 33 PERU *Tel:* +51 (1)1 449 0600 *Email:* thwmac@juno.com

Peru The Rt Revd Eulogio Alejandro Mesco Suffragan Bishop of Peru Residencial Monte Bello D4 Cerro Colorado Arequipa Peru *Tel:* +51 054 9943 51781 *Email:* alejandromesco@hotmail.com

Peru The Rt Revd Juan Carlos Revilla Suffragan Bishop of Peru Calle Doña María 141 Los Rosales Surco Lima 33 Peru *Tel:* +51 (0)1 449 0600 *Fax:* + *Email:* jucareli1208@hotmail.es

Peru The Rt Revd Jorge Luis Aguilar Suffragan Bishop of Peru Calle Doña María 141 Los Rosales Surco Lima 33 Peru *Tel:* +51 (0)1 449 0600 *Email:* cocosac59@hotmail.com

Uruguay The Rt Revd Michael Pollesel Bishop of Uruguay Reconquista # 522 Montevideo 11000 Uruguay *Tel:* +598 (0)2 915 9627 *Fax:* +598 (0)2 916 2519 *Email:* iglesiaau@gmail.com *Web:* www.uruguay.fedigitales.org

Uruguay The Rt Revd Gilberto Obdulio Porcal Martínez Suffragan Bishop of Uruguay Reconquista

522 Montevideo 11000 Uruguay *Tel:* +598 (0)2 915 9627 *Fax:* +598 (0)4 732 8237 *Email:* gilbertoporcal@hotmail.com

THE EPISCOPAL CHURCH OF THE SUDAN

Acting Provincial Secretary Mr John Augustino Lumori PO Box 110 Juba South Sudan *Email:* provincialsecretary@sudan.anglican.org

Provincial Treasurer Mr Evans Sokiri PO Box 110 Juba South Sudan *Email:* ecsprovince@hotmail.com

Abyei The Rt Revd Michael Deng Bishop of Abyei Awaiting Details *Email:* mbol55@hotmail.com

Akot The Rt Revd Isaac Dhieu Ater Bishop of Akot PO Box 110 Juba South Sudan *Email:* bishop@akot. anglican.org *Web:* www.akot.anglican.org

Attooch The Rt Revd Moses Anur Ayom Bishop of Attooch Awaiting Details *Email:* mosesanurayom@gmail.com

Aweil The Rt Revd Abraham Yel Nhial Bishop of Aweil e/o ECS PO Box 110 Northern Bah el Ghazal South Sudan *Tel:* +211 (0)955 621 584 *Email:* bishop@aweil.anglican.org *Web:* www.aweil.anglican.org

Ayod The Rt Revd Thomas Tut Bishop of Ayod Awaiting Details *Email:* tutgany@gmail.com

Bor The Rt Revd Ruben Akurdid Ngong Bishop of Bor C/O ECS PO Box 110 Juba South Sudan *Tel:* +211 (0)926 572 471 *Fax:* + *Email: Web:* www.bor. anglican.org

Cueibet The Rt Revd Elijah Matueny Awet Bishop of Cueibet C/O ECS PO Box 110 Juba South Sudan *Tel:* +211 (0)926 572 471 *Email:* bishop@cueibet. anglican.org *Web:* www.cueibet.anglican.org

Duk The Rt Revd Daniel Deng Abot Bishop of Duk Awaiting Details *Email:* danieldengabot@gmail.com

El-Obeid The Rt Revd Ismail Gabriel Abudigin Bishop of El-Obeid PO Box 211 El Obeid Sudan *Web:* www.elobeid.anglican.org

Ezo The Rt Revd John Kereboro Zawo Bishop of Ezo C/O ECS PO Box 110 Juba South Sudan *Tel:* +211 (0)818 593 217 *Email: Web:* www.ezo.anglican.org

Ibba The Rt Revd Wilson Elisa Kamani Bishop of Ibba C/O ECS PO Box 110 Juba South Sudan *Email:* bishopkamani@gmail.com *Web:* www.ibba.anglican.org

Juba The Most Revd Dr Daniel B Y Deng Bul Yak Archbishop of the Province of the Episcopal Church of South Sudan & Sudan & Bishop of Juba Province of the Episcopal Church of South Sudan & Sudan PO Box 110 Juba South Sudan *Email:* archbishopdeng@gmail.com *Web:* www.juba.anglican.org

Juba The Rt Revd Fraser Yugu Elias Assistant Bishop of Juba Episcopal Church of Sudan PO Box 110 Juba South Sudan *Email:* bishopyugu@gmail.com

Kadugli & Nuba Mountains The Rt Revd Andudu Adam Elnail Bishop of Kadugli and Nuba Mountains PO Box 35 Kadugli Sudan *Tel:* +249 63 182 2898 *Fax:* +249 63 182 2898 *Email:* bpkadugli@gmail.com *Web:* www.kadugli.anglican.org

Kajo Keji The Rt Revd Anthony Poggo Dangasuk Bishop of Kajo Keji C/O ECS PO Box 110 Juba South Sudan *Email:* bishop@kajokeji.anglican.org *Web:* www.kajokeji.anglican.org

Khartoum The Most Revd Ezekiel Kumir Kondo Archbishop of the Internal Province of Sudan & Bishop of Khartoum C/O ECS PO Box 110 Juba South Sudan *Email:* esc_bishop_khartoum@kastanet.org *Web:* www.khartoum.anglican.org

Kongor The Rt Revd Gabriel Thuch Agoth Bishop of Kongor Awaiting Details *Email:* gabrielthuchagoth@yahoo.com

Lainya The Rt Revd Eliaba Lako Obed Bishop of Lainya C/O ECS PO Box 110 Juba South Sudan *Email:* eliabalakoobed@gmail.com

Lomega The Rt Revd Paul Yugusuk Bishop of Lomega Awaiting Details *Email:* lomegarea@yahoo.com

Lui The Rt Revd Stephen Dokolo Ismail Bishop of Lui C/O ECS PO Box 110 Juba South Sudan *Email:* stephen.dokolo@gmail.com *Web:* www.lui.anglican.org

Magwi Vacant Bishop elect of Magwi Awaiting Details

Malakal The Rt Revd Hilary Garang Deng Bishop of Malakal PO Box 114 Malakal South Sudan *Email:* bishop@malakal.anglican.org *Web:* www.malakal.anglican.org

Malakal The Rt Revd John Gattek Assistant Bishop of Malakal- Bentiu Area PO Box 114 Malakal South Sudan *Email:* Jg2012w2015@gmail.com

Malek The Rt Revd Peter Joh Mayom Bishop of Malek Awaiting Details *Email:* johabraham@yahoo.com

Maridi The Rt Revd Justin Badi Arama Bishop of Maridi C/O ECS Office PO Box 7576 Kampala Uganda *Tel:* +256 41 343 497 *Email:* bishop@maridi.anglican.org *Web:* www.maridi.anglican.org

Mundri The Rt Revd Bismark Monday Avokaya Bishop of Mundri PO Box 127 Juba Sudan *Tel:* +88 216 2197 4812 *Email:* bishop@mundri.anglican.org *Web:* www.mundri.anglican.org

Nasir The Rt Revd Peter Gatbel Kunen Bishop of Nasir Awaiting Details *Email:* pgkunen2014@gmail.com

Nzara The Rt Revd Samuel Enosa Peni Bishop of Nzara c/o ECS PO Box 110, WES/Yambio South Sudan *Email:* samuelpeni@yahoo.com *Web:* www.nzara.anglican.org

Olo The Rt Revd Tandema O Andrew Bishop of Olo Awaiting Details *Email:* bishopolo65@gmail.com

Pacong The Rt Revd Joseph Maker Atot Bishop of Pacong C/O CMS PO Box 40360 Nairobi Kenya *Email:* ecs.pacongdiocese@yahoo.com *Web:* www.pacong.anglican.org

Port Sudan The Rt Revd Abdu Elnur Kodi Bishop of Port Sudan PO Box 278 Red Sea State Sudan *Tel:* +249 31 212 24 *Email:* bunukaa@live.com *Web:* www.portsudan.anglican.org

Rejaf The Rt Revd Enock Tombe Bishop of Rejaf PO Box 110 Juba South Sudan *Tel:* +249 811 20040 *Fax:* +249 183 20065 *Email: Web:* www.rejaf.anglican.org

Renk The Rt Revd Joseph Garang Atem Bishop of Renk c/o ECS PO Box 110 Uppe Nile State SOUTH SUDAN *Email:* josephatem@gmail.com *Web:* www.renk.anglican.org

Rokon The Rt Revd Francis Loyo Mori Bishop of Rokon c/o ECS PO Box 110 CES-Juba SOUTH SUDAN *Tel:* +211 928 122 065 *Email:* bployo@yahoo.co.uk *Web:* www.rokon.anglican.org

Rumbek The Rt Revd Alapayo Manyang Kuctiel Bishop of Rumbek c/o ECS PO Box 110 Lake State SOUTH SUDAN *Email:* kuctiel@yahoo.com *Web:* www.rumbek.anglican.org

Terekeka The Rt Revd Paul Modi Bishop of Terekeka PO Box 110 Juba South Sudan *Email:* modipaul5@gmail.com *Web:* www.terekeka.anglican.org

Torit The Rt Revd Bernard Oringa Balmoi Diocesan Bishop of Torit Diocese of Torit PO Box 26157 Kampala Uganda *Email:* bishop@torit.anglican.org *Web:* www.torit.anglican.org

Twik East The Rt Revd Ezekiel Diing Ajang Bishop of Twic East c/o ECS PO Box 110 Jonglei State SOUTH SUDAN *Email:* ezekieldiing@yahoo.co.uk *Web:* www.twiceast.anglican.org

Twik East Vacant Bishop elect of Twik East Awaiting Details

Wad Medani The Rt Revd Saman Farajalla Mahdi Bishop of Wad Medani Awaiting Details *Email:* bishop@wadmedani.anglican.org *Web:* www.wadmedani.anglican.org

Wau The Rt Revd Moses Deng Bol Bishop of Wau c/o ECS PO Box 110 Western Bahr El Ghazal South Sudan *Email:* mosesdengbol@gmail.com *Web:* www.wau.anglican.org

Wondurba The Rt Revd Matthew Taban Peter Bishop of Wondurba Awaiting Details *Email:* bp.matthewpeter@gmail.com

Yambio The Rt Revd Peter Munde Yacoub Bishop of Yambio c/o ECS PO Box 110 WES/Yambio South Sudan *Email:* mundepeter@gmail.com *Web:* www.yambio.anglican.org

Yei The Rt Revd Hilary Luate Adeba Bishop of Yei c/o ECS PO Box 110 CES-Juba South Sudan *Email:* hill_shepherd@yahoo.com *Web:* www.yei.anglican.org

Yirol The Rt Revd David D Akau Bishop of Yirol C/O ECS PO Box 110 Lakes State South Sudan *Email:* ecsyiroldiocese@yahoo.com *Web:* www.yirol.anglican.org

THE ANGLICAN CHURCH OF TANZANIA

Provincial Secretary The Revd Canon Capt. Johnson J Chinyong'ole PO Box 899 Dodoma Tanzania *Tel:* +255 (0) 26 232 4574 *Fax:* +255 (0) 26 232 4565 *Email:* Chinyongole@anglican.or.tz *Web:* www.anglican.or.tz

Central Tanganyika The Rt Revd Dickson Chilongani Bishop elect of Central Tanganyika Makay House PO Box 15 Dodoma Tanzania *Tel:* +255 (0)26 232 4518 *Email:* chilongani@anglican.or.tz *Web:* www.d-c-t.org

Dar-es-Salaam The Rt Revd Valentino Mokiwa Bishop of Dar-es-Salaam St Mark's Theological College pO Box 25016 Dar es Salaam Tanzania *Fax:* +255 (0)22 286 5840 *Email:* mokiwa_valentine@hotmail.com *Web:* www.diodar.org

Kagera The Rt Revd Aaron Kijanjali Bishop of Kagera PO Box 18 Ngara Tanzania *Tel:* +255 (0)28 222 3624 *Fax:* +255 (0)28 222 2518 *Email:* dkagera@gmail.com *Web:* www.kageradiocese.info

Kibondo The Rt Revd Awaiting Details Bishop of Kibondo PO Box 15 Kibondo Kigoma Tanzania

Kiteto The Rt Revd Isaiah Chambala Bishop of Kiteto PO Box 74 Kibaya Kiteto Tanzania *Email:* bishopiofkiteto@yahoo.com

Kondoa The Rt Revd Given Gaula Bishop of Kondoa PO Box 7 Kondoa Tanzania *Tel:* +255 687424428 *Fax:* +255 762080083 *Email:* gmguala@gmail.com

Lake Rukwa The Rt Revd Mathayo Kasagara Bishop of Lake Rukwa PO Box 19 Mpanda Tanzania *Email:* kasagarajr@gmail.com

Lweru The Rt Revd Jackton Yeremiah Lugumira Bishop of Lweru PO Box 12 Muleba Tanzania *Tel:* +255 (0)28 222 2796 *Email:* act@bukobaonline.com

Mara The Rt Revd Hilkiah Omindo Deya Bishop of Mara PO Box 131 Musoma Tanzania *Tel:* +255 (0)28 262 2376 *Fax:* +255 (0)28 262 2414 *Email:* omindo@anglican.or.tz

Masasi The Rt Revd James J` Almasi Bishop of Masasi Private Bag PO Masasi Mtwara Region

Tanzania *Tel:* +255 (0)23 251 0016 *Fax:* +255 (0)23 251 0351 *Email:* Bishopjamesalmasi@yahoo.com

Morogoro The Rt Revd Godfrey D Sehaba Bishop of Morogoro PO Box 320 Morogoro Tanzania *Tel:* +255 (0)23 260 3356 *Fax:* +255 (0)23 260 4602 *Email:* bishopgsehaba@yahoo.com

Mount Kilimanjaro The Rt Revd Stanley Elilekia Hotay Bishop of Mount Kilimanjaro PO Box 1057 Arush Tanzania *Tel:* +255 (0)27 254 8396 *Fax:* +255 (0)27 254 4187 *Email:* hotaystanley@gmail.com *Web:* www.mountkilimanjaro.anglican.org

Mpwapwa The Most Revd Jacob Erasto Chimeledya Archbishop of Tanzania & Bishop of Mpwapwa PO Box 2 Mpwapwa Tanzania *Tel:* +255 (0)26 232 0117 *Fax:* +255 (0)26 232 0063 *Email:* jacobchimeledya@hotmail.com

Newala The Rt Revd Oscar Mnung'a Bishop of Newala PO Box 92 Newala Tanzania *Email:* oscarnewala.diocese@yahoo.com

Rift Valley The Rt Revd John Daudi Lupaa Bishop of the Rift Valley PO Box 16 Manyoni Tanzania *Tel:* +255 (0)26 254 0013 *Fax:* +255 (0)26 250 3014 *Email:* jlupaa@yahoo.com *Web:* www.dioceseofriftvalley.weebly.com

Rorya The Rt Revd John Adiema Bishop of Rorya PO Box 38 Musoma Tanzania *Tel:* +255 (0)752 893957

Ruaha The Rt Revd Joseph D Mgomi Bishop of Ruaha PO Box 1028 Iringa Tanzania *Email:* sanbalatchisewo@yahoo.com

Ruvuma The Rt Revd Dr Maternus K Kapinga Bishop of Ruvuma Bishop's Office PO Box 1357 Songea Tanzania *Tel:* +255 (0)25 260 0090 *Fax:* +255 (0)25 260 2987 *Email:* matemask@gmail.com

Shinyanga The Rt Revd Charles Kija Ngusa Bishop of Shinyanga C/O PO Box 421 Shinyanga Tanzania *Tel:* +255 (0)28 276 3584 *Fax:* + *Email:* ckngusa@yahoo.com

South West Tanganyika The Rt Revd Matthew Mhagama Bishop of South West Tanganyika Bishop's House PO Box 32 Njombe Tanzania *Tel:* +255 (0)26 278 2010 *Fax:* +255 (0)26 278 2403

Southern Highlands The Rt Revd John Mwela Bishop of Southern Highlands PO Box 198 Mbeya Tanzania *Tel:* +255 (0)25 250 0216 *Email:* mwelajohn@yahoo.co.uk

Tabora The Rt Revd Elias S Chakupewa Bishop of Tabora Diocese of Tabora PO Box 1408 Tabora Tanzania *Tel:* +255 (0)26 260 4124 *Fax:* +255 (0)26 260 4899 *Email:* chakupewalucy@yahoo.com *Web:* www.anglicantabora.wordpress.com

Tanga The Rt Revd Maimbo Mndolwa Bishop of Tanga PO Box 35 Korogwe Tanga Tanzania *Tel:* +255 (0)27 264 0631 *Fax:* +255 (0)27 264 0631

Tarime The Rt Revd Dr R Mwita Akiri Bishop of Tarime PO Box 410 Tarime Tanzania *Tel:* +255 (0)28 269 0153 *Fax:* +255 (0)28 269 0153 *Email:* bishop.tarime@gmail.com *Web:* www.anglicantarime.org/

Victoria Nyanza The Rt Revd Boniface Kwangu Bishop of Victoria Nyanza PO Box 278 Mwanza Tanzania *Tel:* +255 (0)75 439 6020 *Fax:* +255 (0)28 250 0676 *Email:* bandmkwangu@yahoo.co.uk

Western Tanganyika The Rt Revd Sadock Makaya Bishop of Western Tanganyika PO Box 13 Kasulu Tanzania *Tel:* +255 (0)26 260 4124 *Fax:* +255 (0)26 260 4899

Zanzibar The Rt Revd Michael Hafidh Bishop of Zanzibar PO Box 5 Mkunazini Zanzibar Tanzania *Tel:* +255 (0)24 223 5348 *Fax:* +255 (0)24 223 6772 *Email:* secactznz@zalink.com

THE CHURCH OF THE PROVINCE OF UGANDA

Provincial Secretary The Revd Canon Amos Magezi Wills Road Namirembe PO Box 14123 Kampala Uganda *Tel:* `+256 414 272 757 *Fax:* + *Email:* pschurchofuganda@gmail.com

Provincial Treasurer Mr Richard Obura Box 14123 Kampala Uganda *Tel:* +256 (0)41 270 218 *Fax:* +256 (0)41 251 925 *Email:* richardobura@gmail.com

Ankole The Rt Revd Sheldon F Mwesigwa Bishop of Ankole PO Box 14 Mbarara Uganda *Tel:* +256 787 084 301 *Email:* ruharo@utlonline.co.ug

Bukedi The Rt Revd Samuel Egesa Bishop of Bukedi PO Box 170 Tororo Uganda *Tel:* +256 772 542 164

Bunyoro-Kitara The Rt Revd Nathan Kyamanywa Bishop of Bunyoro-Kitara PO Box 20 Hoima Uganda *Tel:* +256 465 40128 *Email:* nathan_nathan@yahoo.co.uk

Busoga Thr Rt Revd Naimanhye Paul Bishop of Busoga PO Box 1658 Jinja Uganda *Tel:* +256 0752 598 955 *Fax:* +256 (0)43 20 547 *Email:* busogadiocese@gmail.com

Central Buganda The Rt Revd Jackson Matovu Bishop of Central Buganda PO Box 1200 Kanoni-Gomba Mpigi Uganda *Tel:* +256 772 475 640 *Fax:* +256 772 242 742 *Email:* mapetovurusi@yahoo.com

East Ruwenzori The Rt Revd Edward Bamucwanira Bishop of East Ruwenzori PO Box 1439 Kamwenge Uganda *Tel:* +256 772 906 236

Kampala The Most Revd Stanley Ntagali Archbishop of Uganda & and Bishop of Kampala Box 335 Kampala Uganda *Tel:* +256 (0)41 270 218 / 9 *Fax:* +256 (0)41 251 925 *Email:* abpcou@gmail.com *Web:* www.kampaladiocese.org

Kampala The Rt Revd Hannington Mutebi Assistant Bishop of Kampala Box 335 Kampala Uganda *Tel:* +256 (0)414 342 601

Karamoja The Rt Revd Joseph Abura Bishop of Karamoja PO Box 44 Moroto Uganda *Tel:* +256 782 658 502 *Email:* karamojadiocese@yahoo.co.uk

Kigezi The Rt Revd George Bagamuhunda Bishop of Kigezi PO Box 3 Kabale Uganda *Tel:* +256 772 450 019 *Email:* bishopkigezi@infocom.co.ug

Kinkiizi The Rt Revd Dan J Zoreka Bishop of Kinkizi PO Box 77 Kanungu Uganda *Tel:* +256 782 316 238 *Email:* zoekadan@gmail.com

Kitgum Vacant Bishop elect of Kitgum PO Box 187 Kitgum Uganda *Tel:* +256 772 959 924

Kumi The Rt Revd Thomas E Irigei Bishop of Kumi PO Box 18 Kumi Uganda *Tel:* +256 772 659 460 *Fax:* +256 (0)45 613 25 *Email:* kumimothersunion@yahoo.com

Lango The Rt Revd John Charles Odurkami Bishop of Lango PO Box 6 Lira Uganda *Tel:* +256 772 614 000 *Email:* bishoplango@yahoo.com

Luwero The Rt Revd Eridard Kironde Nsubuga Bishop of Luwero PO Box 125 Luwero Uganda *Tel:* +256 772 349 669 *Email:* eridard.nsubuga@gmail.com

Madi & West Nile The Rt Revd Dr Joel Obetia Bishop of Madi & West Nile PO Box 370 Arua Uganda *Tel:* +256 785 513 333 *Email:* jobetia@yahoo.com

Masindi-Kitara The Rt Revd George Kasangaki Bishop of Masindi-Kitara PO Box 515 Masindi Uganda *Tel:* +256 772 618 822

Mbale The Rt Revd Patrick M Gidudu Bishop of Mbale Bishop's House PO Box 473 Mbale Uganda *Tel:* +256 782 625 619 *Email:* patrickgidudu@yahoo.com

Mityana The Rt Revd Stephen Kaziimba Bishop of Mityana PO Box 102 Mityana Uganda *Tel:* +256 772 512 175 *Fax:* + *Email:* skaziimba@yahoo.com

Muhabura The Rt Revd Cranmer Mugisha Bishop of Muhabura PO Box 22 Kisoro Uganda *Tel:* +256 712 195 891 *Email:* cranhopmu@yahoo.co.uk

Mukono The Rt Revd William K Ssebaggala Bishop of Mukono PO Box 39 Mukono Uganda *Tel:* +256 712 860 742 *Email:* jamesebagala@yahoo.co.uk *Web:* www.mukonodiocese.or.ug

Namirembe The Rt Revd Wilberforce Kityo Luwalira Bishop of Namirembe PO Box 14297 Kampala Uganda *Tel:* +256 712 942 161 *Email:* omulabirizi@gmail.com *Web:* www.namirembediocese.org

Nebbi The Rt Revd Alphonse Watho-kudi Bishop of Nebbi PO Box 27 Nebbi Uganda *Tel:* +256 772 650 032 *Email:* bpalphonse@ekk.org

North Ankole The Rt Revd Stephen Namanya Bishop of North Ankole PO Box 1 Rushere-Kiruhura

Uganda *Tel:* +256 772 622 116 *Email:* stevnam@yahoo.com

North Karamoja The Rt Revd James Nasak Bishop of North Karamoja PO Box 26 Kotido Uganda *Tel:* +256 772 660 228 *Email:* jnasak@yahoo.com

North Kigezi The Rt Revd Patrick Tugume-Tusingwire Bishop of North Kigezi PO Box 23 Kinyasano-Rukungiri Uganda *Tel:* +256 777 912 010 *Email:* northkigezi@infocom.co.ug

North Mbale The Rt Revd Samuel Gidudu Bishop of North Mbale PO Box 2357 Mbale Uganda *Tel:* +256 752 655 225 *Email:* northmbalediocese@yahoo.com

Northern Uganda The Rt Revd Johnson Gakumba Bishop of Northern Uganda PO Box 232 Gulu Uganda *Email:* dnu@utlonline.co.ug

Ruwenzori The Rt Revd Reuben Kisembo Bishop of Northern Uganda PO Box 37 Fort Portal Uganda *Tel:* +256 (0)45 51 072 *Email:* dioruwenzori@yahoo.com

Sebei The Rt Revd Paul Kiptoo Masaba Bishop of Sebei PO Box 23 Kapchorwa Uganda *Tel:* +256 772 550 520

Soroti The Rt Revd George Erwau Bishop of Soroti Soroti Diocese PO Box 107 Soroti Uganda *Tel:* +256 772 653 607 *Email:* georgeerwau@yahoo.com

South Ankole The Rt Revd Nathan Ahimbisibwe Bishop of South Ankole PO Box 39 Ntungamo Uganda *Tel:* +256 772 660 636 *Email:* revnathan2000@yahoo.com *Web:* www.southankolediocese.com

South Rwenzori The Rt Revd Jackson Nzerebende Bishop of South Rwenzori PO Box 142 Kasese Uganda *Tel:* +256 772 713 736 *Email:* bpbende@gmail.com *Web:* www.southrd.org

West Ankole The Rt Revd Yona M Katoneene Bishop of West Ankole PO Box 140 Bushenyi Uganda *Tel:* +256 752 377 192 *Email:* wad@westankolediocese.org *Web:* www.westankolediocese.org

West Buganda Vacant Bishop elect of West Buganda PO Box 242 Masaka Uganda *Tel:* +256 772 413 400 *Email:* mapetovurusi@yahoo.com

THE CHURCH IN WALES

Provincial Secretary Mr John M Shirley 39 Cathedral Road Cardiff CF11 9XF WALES *Tel:* +44 (0)2920 348 200 *Fax:* +44 (0)2920 387 835 *Email:* johnshirley@churchinwales.org.uk

Bangor The Rt Revd Andrew T G John Bishop of Bangor Ty'r Esgob Upper Garth Road Bangor Gwynedd LL57 2SS Wales *Tel:* +44 (0)1248 362 895 *Email:* bishop.bangor@churchinwales.org.uk *Web:* www.esgobaethbangordiocese.org/

Llandaff The Most Revd Dr Barry C Morgan Archbishop of Wales & Bishop of Llandaff Llys

Esgob The Cathedral Green Llandaff Cardiff CF5 2YE Wales *Tel:* +44 (0)292 056 2400 *Fax:* +44 (0)292 057 7129 *Email:* archbishop@churchinwales.org.uk *Web:* www.churchinwales.org.uk

Llandaff The Rt Revd David J Wilbourne Assistant Bishop of Llandaff Llys Esgob The Cathedral Green Llandaff Cardiff CF52YE Wales *Tel:* +44 (0)292 056 2400 *Email:* asstbishop@churchinwales.org.uk

Monmouth The Rt Revd Richard Pain Bishop of Monmouth Bishopstow 91 Stow Hill Newport Gwent NP20 4EA Wales *Tel:* +44 (0)1633 263 510 *Fax:* +44 (0)1633 259 946

St Asaph The Rt Revd Gregory K Cameron Bishop of St Asaph Esgobty St Asaph Denbighshire LL17 0TW Wales *Tel:* +44 (0)1745 583 503 *Fax:* +44 (0)1745 584 301 *Email:* Bishop.stasaph@churchinwales.org.uk

St David's The Rt Revd Wyn J W Evans Bishop of St David's Llys Esgob Abergwili Carmarthen SA31 2JG Wales *Tel:* +44 (0)1267 236 145 *Fax:* +44 (0)1267 237 482 *Email:* Bishop.StDavids@ChurchInWales.org.uk

Swansea & Brecon The Rt Revd John E Davies Bishop of Swansea & Brecon Bishop's House Ely Tower Castle Square Brecon Powys LD3 9DJ Wales *Tel:* +44 (0)1874 622 008 *Fax:* +44 (0)1874 610 927 *Email:* bishop.swanbrec@churchinwales.org.uk

THE CHURCH IN THE PROVINCE OF WEST AFRICA

Provincial Secretary The Revd Canon Anthony M Eiwuley PO Box KN 2023 Kaneshie Accra GHANA *Email:* morkeiwuley@gmail.com

Provincial Treasurer Mr Samuel A Twum St Mary's Church Hall Bannerman Road Akoto Lante PO Box LT 226 Accra Ghana *Tel:* +233 21 225 777 *Fax:* +233 21 225 781 *Email:* cpwa@4u.com.gh

Accra (Ghana) The Rt Revd Dr Daniel Sylvanus Mensah Torto Bishop of Accra Bishopscourt PO Box 8 Accra 233 Ghana *Tel:* +233 302 662 292 *Fax:* +233 277 496 479 *Email:* dantorto@yahoo.com *Web:* http://www.accraanglican.org/

Asante-Mampong (Ghana) The Rt Revd Dr Cyril K Ben-Smith Bishop of Asante-Mampong PO Box 220 Mampong Ashanti Ghana *Email:* bishop.mampong@yahoo.co.uk *Web:* www.mampong.anglican.org

Bo (Sierra Leone) (West Africa) The Rt Revd Emmanuel J S Tucker Bishop of Bo PO Box 21 Bo Southern Province Sierra Leone *Fax:* +232 (0)32 605 *Email:* ejstucker@gmail.com

Cameroon (West Africa) The Rt Revd Dibo T B Elango Bishop of Cameroon BP 15705 Akwa Douala Cameroon *Tel:* +237 7 555 8276 *Email:* revdibo2@yahoo.com

Cape Coast (Ghana) The Rt Revd Dr Victor R Atta-Baffoe Bishop of Cape Coast Bishopscourt PO Box A233 Adiadel Estates Cape Coast Ghana *Tel:* +233 20 818 9528 *Email:* victorattabaffoe@yahoo.com

Dunkwa-on-Offin (Ghana) The Rt Revd Edmund K Dawson Ahmoah Bishop of Dunkwa-on-Offin PO Box DW42 Dukwa-on-Offin Ghana *Tel:* +233 244 464 764 *Email:* papacy11@yahoo.co.uk

Freetown (Sierra Leone) West Africa The Rt Revd Thomas Arnold Ikunika Wilson Bishop of Freetown (Sierra Leone) Bishopscourt PO Box 537 105 Fourah Bay Road Freetown Sierra Leone *Tel:* +232 (0)22 251 307 *Email:* vicnold2003@gmail.com

Gambia (West Africa) Vacant Bishop elect of the Gambia Bishopscourt PO Box 51 Banjul The Gambia *Tel:* +220 990 5227 *Web:* www.gambiadiocese.org

Guinea (West Africa) The Rt Revd Jacques Boston Bishop of Guinea BP 1187 Conakry Guinea *Tel:* +224 632 204 660 *Email:* dioceseanglicanguinee@yahoo.fr

Ho (Ghana) The Rt Revd Matthias K Mededues-Badohu Bishop of Ho Bishopslodge PO Box MA300 Ho Volta Region Ghana *Tel:* +233 20 816 2246 *Email:* matthiaskwab@gmail.com

Koforidua (Ghana) The Rt Revd Francis B Quashie Bishop of Koforidua PO Box 980 Koforidua Ghana *Tel:* +233 26 681 9414 *Email:* fbquashie@yahoo.com

Kumasi (Ghana) The Most Revd Dr Daniel Y Sarfo Primate & Metropolitan, CPWA; Archbishop of the Internal province of Ghana and Bishop of Kumasi Bishop's House PO Box 144 Kumasi Ghana *Tel:* +233 32 204 7717 *Email:* anglicandioceseofkumasi@yahoo.com *Web:* www.anglicandioceseofkumasi.com

Liberia (West Africa) The Most Revd Jonathan Bau-Bau Bonaparte Hart Archbishop for the internal province of West Africa and Bishop of Liberia PO Box 10-0277 1000 Monrovia 10 Liberia West Africa *Tel:* +231 88 651 6343*Email:* bishopecl12@yahoo.com *Web:* www.episcopalchurchofliberia.org

Sekondi (Ghana) The Rt Revd Col John K Otoo Bishop of Sekondi PO Box 85 Sekondi Ghana *Tel:* +233 20 820 0887 *Email:* angdiocesek@yahoo.co.uk

Sunyani (Ghana) The Rt Revd Dr Festus Yeboah-Asuamah Bishop of Sunyani PO Box 23 Sunyani Ghana *Tel:* +233 208 124 378 *Email:* fyasuamah@yahoo.com

Tamale (Ghana) The Rt Revd Dr Jacob K Ayeebo Bishop of Tamale PO Box 110 Tamale NR Ghana *Tel:* +233 24 341 9864 *Email:* ayeebojacob@gmail.com

Wiawso (Ghana) The Rt Revd Abraham K Ackah Bishop of Wiawso PO Box 4 Sefwi Wiawso Ghana

Tel: +233 20 816 1826 *Email:* bishopackah@yahoo. com

THE CHURCH IN THE PROVINCE OF THE WEST INDIES

Provincial Secretary Mrs Elenor I Lawrence Bamford House Society Hill St John BB2008 BARBADOS *Tel:* +1 246 423 0842 *Fax:* +1 246 423 0855 *Email:* cpwi@caribsurf.com

Barbados The Most Revd & The Hon Dr John W D Holder Archbishop of West Indies & Bishop of Barbados Mandeville House Henry's Lane Collymore Rock St Michael Barbados *Tel:* +1 246 426 2761 *Fax:* +1 246 426 0871 *Email:* jwdh@outlook.com *Web:* www.barbados.anglican.org

Belize The Rt Revd Philip S Wright Bishop of Belize Diocesan Office 2 Rectory Lane PO Box 535 Belize City Belize *Tel:* +11 501 227 3029 *Fax:* +11 501 227 6898 *Email:* bzediocese@btl.net *Web:* www.sites.google.com/site/dioceseofbelizecpwi

Guyana Vacant Bishop elect of Guyana Diocesan Office 49 Barrack Street PO Box 10949 Georgetown Guyana *Tel:* +11 592 226 3862 *Fax:* +11 592 226 6091 *Email:* dioofguy@networksgy.com

Jamaica & The Cayman Islands The Rt Revd Dr Howard K A Gregory Bishop of Jamaica & The Cayman Islands Church House 2 Caledonia Avenue Kingston Jamaica *Tel:* +1 876 920 2712 *Email:* hkagregory@hotmail.com *Web:* www.anglicandioceseja.org

Jamaica & The Cayman Islands-Kingston The Rt Revd Dr Robert M Thompson Suffragan Bishop of Kingston 3 Duke Street Kingston Jamaica *Tel:* +1 876 924 9044 *Fax:* +1 876 948 5362 *Email:* bishop.kingston@anglicandiocese.com

Jamaica & The Cayman Islands-Mandeville Vacant Suffragan Bishop elect of Mandeville 8 Morningside Drive PO Box 346 Montego Bay Jamaica *Tel:* +1 876 625 6817 *Fax:* +1 876 625 6819

Jamaica & The Cayman Islands-Montego Bay The Rt Revd Leon Paul Golding Suffragan Bishop of Montego Bay 8 Clieveden Avenue Kingston 6 Jamaica *Tel:* +876 920 2712

Nassau & The Bahamas The Rt Revd Laish Z Boyd Bishop of Bahamas and The Turks and Caicos Islands Addington House Sands Road PO Box N-7107 Nassau New Providence Bahamas *Tel:* +1 (0)242 322 3015/6/ *Fax:* +1 (0)242 322 7943 *Email:* bishop@bahamasanglican.org *Web:* www.bahamasanglicans.org

North Eastern Caribbean & Aruba The Rt Revd Leroy E Brooks Bishop of North Eastern Caribbean & Aruba Bishop's Lodge Redcliffe Street PO Box 23 St John's Antigua *Tel:* +1 268 462 0151 *Fax:* +1 268 462 2090 *Email:* brookx@anguillanet.com

Trinidad & Tobago The Rt Revd Claude Berkley Bishop of Trinidad & Tobago Diocesian Office 21 Maraval Road Port of Spain Trinidad *Email:* claberk@yahoo.com

Windward Islands The Rt Revd Calvert L Friday Bishop of the Windward Islands Diocesan Pastoral Centre Montrose PO Box 502 Kingstown St Vincent *Tel:* +1 784 456 1895 *Fax:* +1 784 456 2591 *Email:* diocesewi@vincysurf.com

THE CHURCH OF CEYLON

Secretary to General Assembly Mrs Barbara M T Praesoody 154D S Senanayake Vidiya Kandy 20000 Sri Lanka *Tel:* +94 81 222 2016 *Fax:* +94 1 684 811 *Email:* barbpraesoody@sltnet.lk

Colombo The Rt Revd Dhiloraj Ranjit D R Canagasabey Bishop of Colombo Bishop's Office 368/3A Bauddhaloka Mawatha Colombo- 07 Sri Lanka *Fax:* +94 (0)11 268 4811

Kurunagala Vacant Bishop elect of Kurunagala Bishop's House 31 Kandy Road Kurunagala 60000 Sri Lanka *Tel:* +94 (0)37 222 2191 *Email:* bishopkg@sltnet.lk

IGLESIA EPISCOPAL DE CUBA

Provincial Secretary Mr Francisco De Arazoza Calle 6 No 273 Vedado Plaza de la revolucion Ciudad de la Habana CUBA *Tel:* +53 7 832 1120 *Fax:* +53 7 834 3293 *Email:* episcopal@enet.cu

Cuba The Rt Revd Griselda Delgado Del Carpio Bishop of Cuba Calle 6 No 273 Vedado Plaza Cuidad de La Habana CP 10400 Cuba *Tel:* +53 (0)7 833 5760 *Fax:* + *Email:* griselda@enet.cu

Cuba The Rt Revd Ulises A Prendes Suffragan Bishop of Cuba Calle Escario No. 459 entre 3 Y 4 Santiago de Cuba CP 90100 Cuba *Tel:* +53 (0)22 627 815 *Fax:* + *Email:* bpulises@enet.cu

BERMUDA (EXTRA-PROVINCIAL TO CANTERBURY)

Provincial Treasurer Mr Campbell Mcbeath PO Box HM769 Hamilton HM CX Bermuda *Tel:* +1 441 292 6987 *Fax:* +1 441 292 5421 *Email:* diocese@anglican.bm *Web:* www.anglican.bm

Bermuda The Rt Revd Nicholas Dill Bishop of Bermuda Diocesan Office PO Box HM769 Hamilton HM CX Bermuda *Tel:* +1 441 292 6987 *Fax:* +1 441 292 5421 *Email:* bishop@anglican.bm *Web:* www.anglican.bm

THE LUSITANIAN CHURCH
(EXTRA-PROVINCIAL TO CANTERBURY)

Provincial Treasurer The Revd Dr Sérgio Filipe Pinho Alves Diocesan Centre of Lusitanian Church Rua Afonso de Albuquerque, No 86 4430-003 Vila Nova de Gaia PORTUGAL *Tel:* +351 22 375 4018 *Fax:* +351 22 375 2016 *Email:* sergioalves@igreja-lusitana.org *Web:* www.igreja-lusitana.org

Lusitanian Church The Rt Revd José Jorge De Pina Cabral Bishop of the Lusitanian Church Diocesan Centre of Lusitanian Church Rua Afonso de Albuquerque, No 86 4430-003 Vila Nova de Gaia PORTUGAL *Tel:* +351 (0)22 375 4018 *Fax:* +351 (0)22 375 2016 *Email:* bispopinacabral@igreja-lusitana.org *Web:* www.igreja-lusitana.org

THE REFORMED CHURCH OF SPAIN
(EXTRA-PROVINCIAL TO CANTERBURY)

Provincial Treasurer Senor Jose Antonio Rodriguez Calle Beneficencia 18 Madrid 28004 Spain *Tel:* +34 91 445 25 60 *Email:* secretario@anglicanos.org *Web:* www.anglicanos.org

The Reformed Episcopal Church of Spain The Rt Revd Carlos C López-Lozano Bishop of Spanish Reformed Episcopal Church Calle Beneficencia 18 Madrid 28004 Spain *Tel:* +34 (0)91 445 2560 *Fax:* +34 (0)91 594 4572 *Email:* eclesiae@arrakis.es

PARISH OF THE FALKLAND ISLANDS

Falkland Islands (Parish of) Canterbury The Rt Revd Nigel William Stock Bishop to the Forces and Bishop to the Falkland Islands Lambeth Palace London SE1 7JU United Kingdom *Email:* nigel.stock@lambethpalace.org.uk   *Web:* www.anglicanparishfalklands.co.uk

CHURCHES IN FULL COMMUNION WITH
THE EPISCOPAL CHURCH

The Episcopal Church seeks the full, visible unity of Christ's church in one Eucharistic fellowship—a communion of communions. The Episcopal Church has further clarified that in full communion, "churches become interdependent while remaining autonomous. Diversity is preserved, but this diversity is not static. Neither church seeks to remake the other in its own image, but each is open to the gifts of the other as it seeks to be faithful to Christ and his mission." (*Called to Common Mission*, para. 2)

The Office of Ecumenical and Interreligious Relations, located at the Episcopal Church Center, seeks to promote ecumenical relationships between the Episcopal Church and other Christian communities of faith as well as to support interreligious relationships globally and locally. The Rev. Margaret Rose is the deputy to the Presiding Bishop for ecumenical and interreligious relations. *Email: mrose@episcopalchurch.org. The Presiding Bishop is the Ecumenical Officer of the Episcopal Church.*

EVANGELICAL LUTHERAN CHURCH IN AMERICA (ELCA)

In 2001, the Episcopal Church and the Evangelical Lutheran Church in America entered into a relationship of full communion on the basis of the document *Called to Common Mission*, culminating thirty years of dialogue with one another. The two churches have committed themselves to joint mission and witness in the world, including mutual participation in consecrations and installations of bishops and the free movement of clergy between the two churches.

THE MORAVIAN CHURCH

In 1997, the Episcopal Church established an official dialogue with the Moravian Church in America. In 2003, the two churches entered into interim Eucharistic sharing. In 2009, the General Convention approved *Finding Our Delight in the Lord*, a proposal for full communion between the two churches. While presbyters and bishops may be shared interchangeably, Moravian and Episcopal deacons may not be interchanged because of differences over the nature and role of the diaconate. The ELCA is also in full communion with the Moravian Church.

THE CHURCH OF BANGLADESH, THE CHURCH OF NORTH INDIA, THE CHURCH OF SOUTH INDIA, AND THE CHURCH OF PAKISTAN

Full communion has been established between provinces of the Anglican Communion and these churches, resulting from the union of Anglicans in these countries with Christians from other traditions.

THE OLD CATHOLIC CHURCHES

In 1934, the Episcopal Church entered full communion with the Old Catholic Churches in communion with the See of Utrecht during the ratification of the Bonn Agreement of 1931, which stipulated that:

1. Each Communion recognizes the catholicity of the other and maintains its own.

2. Each Communion agrees to admit members of the other communion to participate in the sacraments.

3. Intercommunion does not require from either communion the acceptance of all doctrinal opinion, sacramental devotion, or liturgical practice characteristic of the other, but implies that each believes the other to hold all the essentials of the Christian faith.

PHILIPPINE INDEPENDENT CHURCH

In 1961, the Philippine Independent Church (PIC), also known as the Iglesia Filipina Independiente (IFI), and the Episcopal Church agreed to "establish a concordat of full communion. As part of that agreement, the Episcopal Church is called to assist the PIC in its efforts to minister to PIC members in the U.S., and PIC members are called to assist and participate in the broader life and work of the Episcopal Church.

MAR THOMA SYRIAN CHURCH OF MALABAR

When requested by the Metropolitan of the Mar Thoma Church, bishops of the diocese of the Episcopal Church shall exercise episcopal oversight of clergy and laity of the Mar Thoma Church within their jurisdictions. Members of the Mar Thoma Church in the jurisdiction of an Episcopal diocese shall be treated as members of the Episcopal Church, with the understanding that they remain members of the Mar Thoma Church.

ECUMENICAL RELATIONS

The Episcopal Church maintains ecumenical relations by (1) dialogues and visits with the Orthodox, Roman Catholic, Lutheran, Presbyterian, Methodist, and Moravian churches supported by the Standing Commission on Ecumenical Relations and the Anglican Consultative Council; (2) membership in the World Council of Churches and the National Council of Churches supported through the Executive Council; (3) local ecumenism conducted within the dioceses and the network of Episcopal Diocesan Ecumenical and Interreligious Officers (EDEIO).

ECUMENICAL DIALOGUES

The Episcopal Church is engaged in formal bilateral talks with the following churches. These dialogues have been established by act of General Convention and are provided with oversight by the Office of Ecumenical and Interreligious Relations (EIR) in conjunction with clergy and laity selected by the EIR and the Standing Commission.

Churches Uniting in Christ

After 40 years of study and prayer through the Consultation on Church Union, nine churches—the African Methodist Episcopal Church, the African Methodist Episcopal Zion Church, the Christian Church (Disciples of Christ), the Christian Methodist Episcopal Church, the Episcopal Church, International Council of Community Churches, the Presbyterian Church USA, the United Church of Christ, and the United Methodist Church—in 2002 agreed to start living their unity in Christ more fully through a relationship called Churches Uniting in Christ (CUIC). In 2006, the Moravian Church (Northern Province) became a full member. The ELCA is a CUIC partner in mission and dialogue. Each church maintains its own identity and decision-making structures, but each also pledges to draw closer in sacred things and common mission, especially the mission to combat racism. Each church is also committed to an intensive dialogue toward the day when ministers are authorized when invited to serve and lead worship in each of the communions. The efforts of the CUIC are overseen by the Coordinating Council which is comprised of ecumenical and appointed representatives of the participating church bodies.

United Methodist-Episcopal Dialogue

The United Methodist-Episcopal dialogue was established by act of the 2000 General Convention and began meeting in 2002. The 2006 General Convention approved interim Eucharistic sharing with the United Methodist Church. Episcopal parishes are now authorized to hold joint celebrations of the Eucharist with United Methodist churches under the guidelines established by General Convention. The Episcopal Church participated with the United Methodist Church as part of the Consultation on Church Union. The ecumenical work of the United Methodist Church is carried out by the General Board of Christian Unity and Interreligious Concerns.

Presbyterian-Episcopal Dialogue

The Episcopal Church has participated in the ecumenical dialogue with the Presbyterian Church, USA within the context of the Consultation on Church Union. A bilateral dialogue was established in 2000 and began meeting in 2002. General Convention in 2009 approved an agreement with the Presbyterian Church, USA. While not full communion or Eucharistic sharing, the agreement encourages cooperation and joint ministry. General Convention also authorized a second round of dialogue. The Presbyterian Church, USA was formed in 1983 through the merger of the United Presbyterian Church and the Presbyterian Church in the United States.

Anglican-Roman Catholic Dialogue

The Episcopal Church has been in dialogue with the Roman Catholic Church for more than 40 years through the Anglican-Roman Catholic Dialogue in the USA (ARC-USA), and on the international level through the Anglican Communion Office in the Anglican-Roman Catholic International Consultations (ARCIC). In a common declaration signed in 2006 by Dr. Rowan Williams, then Archbishop of Canterbury, and Pope Benedict XVI, the two leaders renewed the historic commitment to the goal of "full visible communion in the truth of Christ."

OTHER ECUMENICAL RELATIONS

The Church of Sweden

The Episcopal Church maintains close relations with the Church of Sweden. Most recently, both churches agreed to work together to mitigate climate change; in 2013, Presiding Bishop Katharine Jefferts Schori and Church of Sweden Archbishop Anders Wejryd, along with then-ELCA Presiding Bishop Mark Hanson, signed a joint statement affirming their commitment to advocate for governmental policies that encourage renewable energy and support fair and just economic systems. Through the Lutheran World Federation, the Church of Sweden is in fellowship with all other Lutheran member churches.

The Polish National Catholic Church

The Episcopal Church was in a relationship of full communion with the Polish National Catholic Church (PNCC) on the basis of the Bonn Agreement and a supplemental concordat of intercommunion by the 1946 General Convention. In 1978, the PNCC terminated this full communion agreement after the ordination of women in the Episcopal Church. The Episcopal Church did not take a similar action. In 2003, the PNCC ceased to be in communion with the Archbishop of Utrecht and is no longer a member of the Old Catholic Churches of the Union of Utrecht. The PNCC is a member of the World Council of Churches.

WORLD COUNCIL OF CHURCHES

The World Council of Churches (WCC) is a fellowship of churches which confess the Lord Jesus Christ as God and Savior according to the Scriptures and therefore seeks to fulfill together their common calling to the glory of the one God: Father, Son, and Holy Spirit. The WCC is constituted by member churches to serve the one ecumenical movement. It incorporates the work of the world movements for Faith and Order and Life and Work, the International Missionary Council, and the World Council of Christian Education. The primary purpose of the fellowship of churches in the WCC is to call one another to visible unity in one faith and in one Eucharistic fellowship, expressed in worship and common life in Christ, through witness and service to the world.

In seeking *koinonia* in faith and life, witness and service, the churches throughout the Council commit to:

- Promote the prayerful search for forgiveness and reconciliation in a spirit of mutual accountability, the development of deeper relationships through theological dialogue, and the sharing of human, spiritual, and material resources with one another; facilitate common witness in each place and in all places, and support each other in their work for mission and evangelism;
- Express their commitment to *diakonia* in serving human need, breaking down barriers between people, promoting one human family in justice and peace, and upholding the integrity of creation, so that all may experience the fullness of life;
- Nurture the growth of an ecumenical consciousness through processes of education and a vision of life in community rooted in each particular cultural context;
- Assist each other in their relationships to and with people of other faith communities;
- Foster renewal and growth in unity, worship, mission, and service.

In order to strengthen the ecumenical movement, the Council will:

- Nurture relations with and among churches, especially within but also beyond its membership;
- Establish and maintain relations with national councils, regional conferences of churches, organizations of Christian World Communions and other ecumenical bodies;
- Support ecumenical initiatives at regional, national, and local levels;
- Work towards maintaining the coherence of the one ecumenical movement in its diverse manifestations.

As the result of recent restructuring, the work of the WCC is carried out through four clusters which focus on:

- The issues and themes with which the WCC is concerned, including teams on faith and order, mission evangelism, justice, peace and creation, and education and ecumenical formation;
- The relationship the WCC maintains, including teams on ecumenical relations, regional relations, inter-religious relations and dialogue, and documentation;
- Communication, including teams on public information and publications and documentation;
- Finance, services and administration, including teams on finance, income monitoring and development, human resources, house services, and computer and information technology services.

Coordination of the staff's work is the responsibility of a deputy general secretary and a staff leadership team made up of the general secretary, deputy general secretary, and the directors of the four clusters. The WCC has more than 342 member churches. Almost every province of the Anglican Communion is included, together with all independent Orthodox churches and most Protestant traditions. The Roman Catholic Church is not in membership but has sent official observers to all main WCC meetings since 1960. In the U.S., nearly all the churches that belong to the National Council of Churches belong to the WCC, as well as the Apostolic Catholic Assyrian Church of the East, Religious Society of Friends, Friends General Conference, and Friends United Meeting.

NATIONAL COUNCIL OF CHURCHES OF CHRIST IN THE USA

The National Council of Churches is the preeminent expression in the U.S. of the movement toward Christian unity. The NCC's 37 member communions, including Protestant, Orthodox, and Anglican church bodies, work together on a wide range of activities that further Christian unity, that witnesses to the faith, that promote peace and justice, and that serve people throughout the world. The council was formed in 1950 by the action of representatives of the member churches and by the merger of 12 previously existing ecumenical agencies, each of which had a different program focus.

CHRISTIAN CHURCHES TOGETHER IN THE USA

In 2006, 34 churches and national Christian organizations officially formed the broadest, most inclusive fellowship of Christian churches and traditions in the U.S. Those participating as founding members represent the Episcopal Church, Orthodox, Roman Catholic, Evangelical, Pentecostal, and charismatic churches, among others. Christian Churches Together (CCT) provides a context in which churches can develop relationships with other churches with which they presently have little contact. CCT strives to speak to contemporary culture on issues of life, social justice, and peace.

INTERRELIGIOUS RELATIONS

The Episcopal Church in the past 40 years has made public and formal efforts toward establishing positive relationships with other religious traditions. In 2003, General Convention officially located oversight of the church's interreligious work with the Standing Commission on Ecumenical Relations, which was renamed the Standing Commission on Ecumenical and Interreligious Relations (SCEIR). During the 2006-2009 triennium, the Interreligious Relations Subcommittee of the SCEIR worked to develop a more substantive statement to clarify the theological and historical rationale for the Episcopal Church's interreligious engagement, and in 2009 a resolution was adopted by General Convention— and reaffirmed in 2012—establishing a canonical teaching on interreligious relations known as "Toward Our Mutual Flourishing."

The Episcopal Church's primary participation in interreligious dialogue focuses principally on:

- Ecumenical efforts with other Christians through the Interfaith Relations Commission of the National Council of Churches of Christ (NCC). The 1999 Assembly of the NCC unanimously approved a policy statement giving a theological rationale for participating in interreligious dialogue;

- International efforts through the Anglican Communion Office, including the Network for Interfaith Concerns;
- Particular initiatives taken by the Presiding Bishop as primate and chief pastor of the church;
- Task force initiatives and programs created by Episcopal institutions, such as Episcopal Relief and Development, which in response to the terrorist attacks of September 11, 2001, funded the Interfaith Education Initiative, a three-year program in conjunction with the Office of the Ecumenical and Interfaith Relations that surveyed the interfaith work of the Episcopal Church and developed educational resources for interreligious dialogue;
- Diocesan, congregational, and individual efforts in peace making and interreligious dialogue.

RELIGIONS FOR PEACE USA

The Episcopal Church actively participates with Religions for Peace USA, the largest and most broadly-based, multi-religion forum in the U.S. Religions for Peace USA works to contribute to the well being of civil society and to advance peace building efforts and reconciliation in the U.S. and internationally.   Religions for Peace USA is part of a network of Religions for Peace with nearly 100 affiliates globally. The Presiding Bishop is a member of the organization's Council of Presidents, and representatives from the Episcopal Church are members of its Executive Council.

NATIONAL INTERRELIGIOUS LEADERSHIP INITIATIVE FOR PEACE IN THE MIDDLE EAST

The National Interreligious Leadership Initiative for Peace in the Middle East (NILI) unites a high range of Jewish, Christian, and Muslim national organizations in support of a common message for peace between Israelis and Palestinians. NILI coordinates advocacy in a bipartisan manner with policy makers to build public support for lasting peace. The Episcopal Church commonly endorses NILI statements as they relate to peace advocacy.

Clergy List of
The Episcopal Church

Any changes to this list should be addressed to the
Recorder of Ordinations, Church Pension Group,
19 East 34th Street, New York, NY 10016.

The symbol ✚ indicates bishop.

CLERGY LIST

The names, addresses, and canonical residences in the Clergy List section are supplied by The Recorder of Ordinations and reflect changes reported by **31 December 2015**. Any request for a change in the Clergy List should be addressed to The Recorder of Ordinations, CHURCH PENSION GROUP, 19 East 34th Street, New York, NY 10016.

NECROLOGY
1/15-12/15

Bishops

BOWMAN, David Charles	7/10/15
KIMSEY, Rustin Ray	4/10/15
SOTO, Onell Asiselo	8/5/15
WALKER JR, Orris George	2/28/15
WHITAKER, O'Kelley	6/25/15
WOOD, Milton Legrand	7/16/15

Priests and Deacons

ADAMS, Edgar George	2/13/15
ALKINS, David Stanley	5/4/15
ANGEVINE, Leo G	2/11/15
ARIS-PAUL, Maria Marta	10/7/15
ASBURY, Eldridge Eugene	11/16/15
ASBURY, Giles Lee	3/12/15
AUSTILL, Stephen P	2/15/15
AVALOS, Abdias C	2/11/15
AVERY III, Gilbert Stiles	8/10/15
AYALA-PORFIL, Eugenio	5/27/15
BAGGETT, Edward Allen	6/27/15
BAIN, Caroline Margaret	2/25/15
BALDWIN JR, Harry Webster	2/3/15
BALK, Roger Allen	10/10/15
BARBOUR, Norman Hugh	1/2/15
BARCLAY, David Laird	2/18/15
BARNES, Brian J	9/5/15
BECKWITH III, John Quintus	1/24/15
BELIVEAU, Harold Edmond	2/24/15
BELL, Benjamin Franklin	6/23/15
BERGMANN, J(Ohn) Stephen	11/7/15
BETHEA, Robert	10/30/15
BILLINGS, Stephen Robb	7/1/15
BINFORD, John Edward	10/4/15
BIRDWELL, Harland Bryan	2/5/15
BIRNEY, James Gillespie	6/13/15
BLACKLOCK JR, Charles William	2/13/15
BOGART, John Lawrence	4/9/15
BONES JR, William Lyle	10/22/15
BOSSIERE, Jacques Paul	5/9/15
BOWERS, George Franklin	8/20/15
BOYD, Malcolm	2/27/15
BRADLEY, Nancy B	4/24/15
BRADY JR, Thomas Joseph	8/19/15
BRETZ, Donald Walter Andrew	9/5/15
BROTHERTON, Curt Paul	4/11/15

BRUMBAUGH, George William	5/21/15
BUITRAGO-VALENCIA, Roberto Anibal	3/25/15
BURDEN, William Robertson	9/19/15
BURKE, Joseph Daniel	1/20/15
BURKERT, Alfred Paul	4/16/15
BUTLER-NIXON, Grahame Gordon	1/19/15
CALVERT, Cara J	11/15/15
CANON, Cham	1/30/15
CAREY, Amos Clark	3/31/15
CARLISLE, Charles Richard	5/29/15
CARLISLE, Dorothy(Dutch) Mae	4/7/15
CARLSON, Robert John	6/24/15
CARLSON, Robert Warren	6/24/15
CARTER, Wilson Rosser	3/3/15
CHEN, Samuel Ta-Tung	9/25/15
CHUNG, Jae W	12/16/15
CIANNELLA, Domenic Kenneth	12/11/15
CLAY, Frederick Guion	2/3/15
COLBOURNE, Albert George	10/1/15
CONKLIN, Edward Wilbur	10/30/15
COOK, Diane Elizabeth	12/19/15
CORRIGAN, Gertrude Lane	10/29/15
COSAND, Dale Wayne	9/7/15
CRAIG, Hugh Burnette	10/15/15
CRAMPTON, Barbara Amelia	9/13/15
CRANE, Charles Tarleton	12/7/15
CROOK, Clifford	6/24/15
CROWTHER JR, James Pollard	9/9/15
CUNNINGHAM, James Harry	7/6/15
CURRY, Norval Henry	6/25/15
DAVENPORT, Lane	7/30/15
DAVIS, Thomas Anthony	8/30/15
DEACON, Robert	6/23/15
DENNEY, Curtis Stetson	11/1/15
DENNISTON, Marjanne Manlove	9/20/15
DIETEL, Robert G.	12/17/15
DOOLY, Robert Wallace Bernard	5/31/15
DOUCETTE, Lee Francis	8/31/15
DRESSER, Robert Merrill	2/27/15
DURANT, Jennifer Ronan	2/18/15
DURGIN, Ralph Thayer	10/9/15
DWYER, William Daniels	2/11/15
DYER, Edward John	1/23/15
EBRIGHT, Howard Sefton	3/7/15
ECKMAN JR, Daniel Willard	2/28/15
EDWARDS JR, John Richard	8/10/15
EILERTSEN, Edwin John	5/16/15
ELLIOTT, Nathaniel R	5/28/15
ENGLISH, William Lawson	8/27/15
ERWIN, William Portwood	11/23/15
ETHELSTON, Frank Geoffrey	12/14/15

ETTLING, Albert John	11/16/15	**KARSHNER**, Donald Lee	12/2/15
FITTERER, John Angus	5/28/15	**KATNER**, Kirk Vaughan Chris	8/19/15
FLESHER, Hubert Louis	7/21/15	**KEATEN**, Robert W	3/11/15
FLYNN, Bernard Thomas	5/6/15	**KEEL**, Robert Donald	1/29/15
FOGG JR, Ralph Everett	6/14/15	**KELLEY**, John Beverley Leffingwell	1/2/15
FORMAN, Bernard Kim	5/10/15	**KEPHART**, Arthur Keith D'Arcy	1/12/15
FRANCE, Robert Lyle	8/20/15	**KIMBLE**, John Raymond	7/26/15
FREDENBURGH, John Cole	2/17/15	**KINNETT**, Kenneth	9/26/15
FREEMAN, Robert W	12/21/15	**KINNEY**, John Mark	7/6/15
FULLER, Margaret Jane Haas	2/4/15	**KLINE**, Harold Emmett	7/25/15
GAINES, Winifred B	9/30/15	**KNAPP**, Kate S	9/16/15
GARRETT III, Edwin Atlee	7/2/15	**KNIGHT**, David Edward	6/17/15
GARY, Richard Ellis	11/11/15	**KOOSER**, Robert Lee	8/3/15
GILMORE, Paul Michael	7/13/15	**KRIEGER**, William F	3/28/15
GLASGOW, Joseph Rodney	1/2/15	**KRUG**, Philip Sinclair	3/11/15
GONZALEZ, Oscar	10/29/15	**KURTZ**, Robert Guy	11/24/15
GORDON, John Douglas	6/9/15	**LA FOLLETTE**, Melvin Walker	7/4/15
GORDY, Zane Wesley	3/7/15	**LANSFORD**, Theron George	9/10/15
GRAY, David Dodson	6/4/15	**LATHROP**, John Campbell	12/9/15
GREEN, Bruce	1/5/15	**LEOVY**, James G	2/19/15
GREENE, Robert B	11/17/15	**LIGUORI**, Robert David	1/6/15
GRISWOLD, Edwin A	9/28/15	**LIMEHOUSE**, Capers H	5/25/15
HAAS, Mary Elizabeth	5/10/15	**LLOYD II**, Arthur Selden	8/4/15
HACKLEY, Staley Paxton	11/7/15	**LOWRY**, Linda Louise	7/20/15
HAIFLEY, Thomas Leo	5/14/15	**LUTHRINGER**, George Francis	10/26/15
HALL, Everett	10/29/15	**MADDOX JR**, H(Ubert) Carter	1/25/15
HANSEN, Robert John	7/6/15	**MALOTTKE**, William Neill	9/16/15
HARDIN JR, Hugh Fletcher	5/7/15	**MARKHAM**, Richard Benedict	1/2/15
HARDING, Leslie Frank	8/18/15	**MARTIN**, Richard Cornish	7/27/15
HARTLEY, Sherry L	10/22/15	**MASON**, Judith Ann	11/13/15
HARTNETT, John L	8/15/15	**MASON**, Keith Wentworth	9/17/15
HATCHETT JR, Jefferson Bryan	9/26/15	**MATTHEWS**, Alan Montague Basil	12/3/15
HELSEL, Verle Eugene	6/21/15	**MCALEER**, Ruth Bresnahan	8/19/15
HEMINGWAY, George Thomson	11/8/15	**MCCAULEY**, Claud Ward	12/28/15
HENDERSON, Anna Martin	5/5/15	**MCDOUGALL**, Robert Franklin	11/16/15
HEWETT, Clayton Kennedy	8/1/15	**MC GEE**, Vern Wesley	9/23/15
HEWITT JR, Arch M(Erille)	2/1/15	**MCGREEVY**, Molly Paine	11/1/15
HEWITT, Susan Miller	7/20/15	**MCQUEEN**, Duncan Robert	3/10/15
HICKS, Phyllis Branham	3/14/15	**MILLER**, Luther Deck	3/21/15
HILL, Barbara Jeanne	5/13/15	**MILLER JR**, Merrill Cushing	1/22/15
HOLLOWAY, Jonathan Aldrich	7/8/15	**MILLER**, Richard Sevier	10/4/15
HOLMES, Douglas	10/15/15	**MILLS**, Charlotte Ann	6/25/15
HOLT, David Lewis	10/22/15	**MINNIS**, William H	7/6/15
HOLTZ, Frank John	12/17/15	**MIRACLE**, David Robert	6/18/15
HOLZHAMMER, Robert Ernest	3/24/15	**MITCHELL III**, James Franklin	10/6/15
HOUGH, Johnnie Lynne	12/22/15	**MONTES**, Gesner Roger	5/4/15
HOVERSTOCK, Rolland William	10/2/15	**MOORE**, Michael Stanley	7/22/15
HOWELL, Charles Henry	7/5/15	**MORGAN III**, Edward	7/25/15
HOWLETT, Gail Edward	3/22/15	**MORGAN III**, Ray Reid	4/14/15
HUGHES II, Theron Rex	10/9/15	**MOSS**, R Benjamin	3/14/15
HUMPHREY, Barbara Myers	7/8/15	**MYERS**, Henry Lee Hobart	5/13/15
HUTCHINSON JR, Robert Henri	6/10/15	**NEDS**, Walter Eugene	12/22/15
IHLEFELD, Robert Lee	2/2/15	**NEILSON**, Jack Drew	1/29/15
INGE, F Coleman	1/27/15	**NEIMAN**, Joseph Clayton	4/15/15
IRISH, Charles Manning	10/12/15	**NEUHAUS**, Beverly Ruth	12/11/15
JACKSON, Terry Wightman	12/26/15	**NEWBURY**, Edwards B	7/19/15
JACOBSEN, Peter Arthur	5/27/15	**NEWMAN JR**, Harry George	8/30/15
JANEWAY IV, John Livingston	7/4/15	**NEWTON**, Willoughby	4/18/15
JAYNES, Larry W.	3/27/15	**NICHOLSON**, David Owen	7/20/15
JENKINS, Hedley Percy	3/15/15	**NICHOLSON**, Donald Robert	8/10/15
JIMENEZ, Dario M	6/30/15	**NOYES**, Roger Bow	4/8/15
JOBES, Amy Louise Carle	8/23/15	**OEHMIG**, Henry King	5/23/15
JOHANNS, Karen	8/31/15	**OLER**, Clarke Kimberly	4/6/15
JOHNSON, James Arthur	8/8/15	**OLIVER**, Eugene Emery	11/26/15
JOHNSON, Rudolph	3/25/15	**O'NEILL**, Dennis Topliss	4/18/15
JOHNSTON, Michael Adair	12/3/15	**ORMOND**, John James	3/31/15
JONES JR, Vernon A.	11/14/15	**OTTERY JR**, Willis Dee	10/2/15
JOSEPH, Leo	1/23/15	**OUZTS**, Peter Daniel	5/6/15

PAGE, Herman	9/17/15
PAGE, Sherrill Lee	1/29/15
PARADISE, Scott Ilsley	9/13/15
PARTLOW, Robert Greider	5/9/15
PENDLETON JR, Eldridge H	8/26/15
POFFENBARGER II, George	2/5/15
POLK JR, Rollin Saxe	3/16/15
PRICE, Gary Kilmer	4/10/15
PRICE, Robert David	1/27/15
PRIEBE JR, Charles M	6/24/15
PRUEHER JR, Roi Francis	8/23/15
QUILLMAN, Bard	6/5/15
RAYMOND, Robert Martin	3/15/15
REED, Kenneth Courter	7/11/15
REEVES JR, C(Harles) Edward	12/30/15
REINHART, Rodney Eugene	11/24/15
REYNOLDS V, Elsbery Washington	8/29/15
REYNOLDS, Mary Lou Corbett	10/19/15
RHODES, William Chester	9/2/15
RIVERS, John Charles	1/8/15
ROBBINS, Geoffrey Thayer	1/13/15
ROBINSON, David Wendell	6/13/15
ROBINSON, Robert Nesbitt	5/31/15
ROBISON, Ronald Livingston	1/5/15
ROGAN, Donald Lynn	9/18/15
ROGERS, David Beebe	7/30/15
ROULETTE, Philip Burwell	11/7/15
ROWLAND, Richard William	7/18/15
RUNNION, Norman Ray	6/19/15
RUTLAND, Edward Cumpston	8/12/15
RUTLEDGE, Theodore Elsworth	12/10/15
RYAN, David Andrew	11/5/15
RYAN, John Prime	9/28/15
SACCO, Ronald John	8/12/15
SAMPSON, Timothy Warren	8/13/15
SAMUEL JR, Morris Vaughn	6/13/15
SANDERSON, Joseph Wesley	11/9/15
SASAKI, Norio	9/8/15
SASSO-CRANDALL, Charles David	10/1/15
SCALES JR, Sherrill	12/21/15
SCHAEFFER, Phillip Negley	1/20/15
SCHUYLER, Janice Macfarland	10/26/15
SEEBECK, William Bernard	12/13/15
SHARP, Robert Elven	7/24/15
SHAW, Joan Elizabeth	3/31/15
SHAW, W. Lee	6/27/15
SHERRILL II, Franklin Goldthwaite	7/26/15
SILAS, Berkman	10/5/15
SIMMONS, C Douglas	9/26/15
SITES, William Kilmer	5/8/15
SKIRVEN JR, James French	6/18/15
SMITH JR, Alfred Hersey	12/26/15
SMITH, Joan Barr	3/21/15
SMITH, Wesley Hugh	1/1/15
SONGY, Benedict Gaston	1/2/15
SOTO, Pedro S	1/18/15
SOUTHWORTH, Richard Louis	7/20/15
STAUP, Thomas Peter	1/4/15
STEUP, Harold Wilbur	2/20/15
STEVENS JR, Ernest Lee	8/16/15
STEVENSON, James Paul	1/25/15
STEVENSON JR, Phillip Marion	5/28/15
STEWART JR, Claude York	12/13/15
STILLINGS, Eugene Nelson	12/6/15
SWAN JR, William Orr	3/6/15
SWANNER-MONTGOMERY, Rhoda J	10/25/15
TAYLOR, Harold Edwin	2/16/15
THOMAS, John Walter Riddle	10/12/15

THOMAS, Owen Clark	6/29/15
TIMBERLAKE, Roland Ashley	1/6/15
TO, Albany Shiu-Kin	4/18/15
TOMLIN, Billy Frank	7/17/15
TOMPKINS III, George Johnson	11/17/15
TRAVERSE, Alfred	9/15/15
TREGARTHEN, Doran Woodrow	8/5/15
TRIMPE, Herbert William	4/13/15
TYON, Agnes Lucille	10/3/15
VALDES, Paul Anthony	8/26/15
VOTH, Murray Howard	1/26/15
WALKER, Robert Howard	4/6/15
WALSH JR, Harry Joseph	1/17/15
WARE, Mary Jane Casper	4/4/15
WARING, William Davis	5/2/15
WASHINGTON SR, Emery	9/21/15
WATSON III, John R	12/5/15
WEBB SR, Donald Ray	2/16/15
WEBNER, Marie Louise	2/3/15
WENTZ, Herbert Stephenson	10/16/15
WHITE, William R	1/20/15
WHITLEY, Harry Brearley	8/16/15
WHITTEMORE, James R	12/30/15
WIGHT-HOLBY, Patricia Ann Page	4/22/15
WILHITE JR, Macdonald	10/14/15
WILKINS, Leon Ray	2/22/15
WILLIAMS, Robert Carson	5/2/15
WILLIAMSON JR, Wayne Bert	12/16/15
WILSON, Mark Howard	1/7/15
WILSON, Tom Stacey	11/30/15
WINSOR, Edward Stiness	4/10/15
WINSOR, J(Ames) Michael	4/10/15
WRIGHT, Hugh Maxwell	7/29/15

CLERGY RECEIVED FROM ROMAN CATHOLIC CHURCH OR OTHER CHURCHES IN FULL COMMUNION 1/15-12/15

CUBILLAS, Angelito (RC)	3/1/15
ESTRADA, Richard Roger (RC)	5/13/15
HART, J. Joseph (RC)	9/12/15
LASLEY, Jerry Drew (RC)	2/19/15
MALARKEY, Shawn O (RC)	6/22/15
MEMBA, Jose Luis (RC)	5/30/15
RAICHE, Brian Michael (RC)	6/6/15
SILVA-GONZALEZ, Alvaro (RC)	1/24/15
SMITH, David Gregory (RC)	11/22/15
THOMPSON-UBERUAGA, William (RC)	7/11/15
VALLE, Jose Francisco (RC)	2/28/15
WOO, Raymond A (RC)	6/14/15

CLERGY RECEIVED FROM EVANGELICAL LUTHERAN CHURCH IN AMERICA 1/15-12/15

(None during this time period.)

Clergy List [For Corrections see p. C1]

CLERGY TRANSFERRED FROM OTHER PROVINCES OF THE ANGLICAN COMMUNION
1/15-12/15

BARRINGTON, Dominic M J (Ch Of Engl)	8/24/15
BORGES, Maria Cristina	1/27/15
(Iglesia Epis de Cuba)	
CONLIFFE, Mario Romain Marvin	10/6/15
(Ch in the Prov Of The W Indies)	
JACOB, James Neithelloor (Ch of No India)	11/16/15
KOVOOR, George Iype (Ch Of Engl)	6/18/15
LIMO, John Edward (Angl Ch Of Kenya)	6/16/15
MARCETTI, Alvin Julian (Ch Of Engl)	5/14/15
MORRIS, Roberta Louise	5/12/15
(Epis Ch in the Philippines)	
PESSAH, Elisabeth Jayne (Angl Ch of Can)	7/8/15
PESSAH, Stephen Michael (Angl Ch of Can)	5/27/15
ROCK, Ian Eleazar	11/5/15
(Ch in the Prov Of The W Indies)	
STAFFORD-WHITTAKER, William Paul	6/3/15
(Ch Of Engl)	

RESTORATIONS
1/15-12/15

BANE JR, David Conner (SVa)	4/8/15
BUCHIN, Daniel Arthur (Mich)	5/28/15
HINES, Travis S (Tenn)	1/26/15
KALAS, Steven Curtis (Nev)	9/29/15
LOCKETT, Tina Lynn (Pgh)	10/14/15
PURCELL, Mary Frances Fleming (Lex)	12/8/15
WALLACE, Hugh J (SC)	3/24/15
WATSON JR, Clyde M (Va)	3/10/15

SUSPENSIONS
1/15-12/15

HENSLEY, Robert E (Chi)	2/13/15
KRAMER, Aron M (Minn)	1/6/15
SMITH, Stephen Vaughn (Mass)	5/26/15
VILLALOBOS-MATUTE, Fidencio (Hond)	1/1/15

DEPOSITIONS
1/15-12/15

BECKER, Elizabeth Coleman (La)	1/6/15
BONEY, Lois (NC)	1/13/15
COOK, Heather E (Md)	5/1/15
HANSEN, Jonathan David (Ia)	1/30/15
QUITO-PAGUAY, Luis Eulogio (EcuC)	11/21/15
SAIK, Ernest William (La)	1/6/15
TAMPA, John Grey (NC)	10/28/15
TUAZA CASTRO, Luis Alberto (EcuC)	11/21/15

REMOVALS
1/15-12/15

ARMSTRONG, Linda Joyce (La)	10/5/15
ATTAS III, Michael (Tex)	3/25/15
BARBEE JR, William Thomas (Tex)	6/19/15
BASSETT, John William (Alb)	10/5/15
BOMBARD, Thom H (Alb)	11/10/15
BOSLEY, Dennis Vaughn (NwT)	3/25/15
BROWN, Donald Franklin (RG)	7/21/15
BURWELL, John Beckett (CFla)	3/26/15
COLBY, Christopher Gage (Miss)	9/2/15
DUFFY, Kirk Mallory (Ga)	11/10/15
EYBERG, Carl Joseph (Pgh)	5/11/15
FITZPATRICK, Paul Elliot (Nwk)	7/14/15
FRANCKE, Paul (WVa)	2/2/15
GADDIS III, Otis (WA)	11/5/15
HAZZARD SR, Richard Augustus (CPa)	8/19/15
LOBSINGER, Eric John (Mo)	3/6/15
LOVE, Sean David (RG)	12/15/15
MATHER, John L. (Az)	12/10/15
MCCASKILL, James Calvin (Va)	7/9/15
MCREYNOLDS, James Craig (NJ)	1/15/15
MERCHANT JR, Livingston Tallmadge (RI)	9/16/15
MILLER, Colin Douglas (NC)	12/21/15
MORGAN, James Patrick (RG)	7/21/15
MORRISSEY, Mike (Oly)	10/13/15
PAULUS II, Garrett Keith (RG)	3/24/15
POLLOCK, Alma Harward (Ct)	4/29/15
RODRIGUEZ, Katherine Renee (RG)	4/14/15
SEDDON, Barbara Cynthia (Mont)	1/20/15
SETZER, Eleanor Scott Johnson (RG)	12/15/15
SHOOK, Janis Helen (WVa)	8/18/15
TAYLOR, Robert Martin (NI)	8/25/15
WELTY IV, Terrence Anthony (Dal)	4/14/15
WHITACRE, Rodney Alan (Pgh)	5/11/15
WRIGHT, Melanie Barnett (FtW)	3/31/15

CLERGY REPORTED AS ORDAINED
Not included in the Clergy List

The following is a list of names of Clergy who have been reported as ordained. At deadline date no data had been received from them. Because they could not be properly entered in the files of THE CHURCH PENSION FUND, they are not a part of the Clergy List.

ADAMS, David (Spr)	**BAKER**, Thomas (Ark)	**BLINDHEIM**, Mark (Oly)
ADAMS, Enoch (Ak)	**BALABANIS**, Achilles (Spok)	**BOYDEN-EDMONDS**, Marjorie (LI)
ALDANA ROJAS, Javier (Colom)	**BARGER**, Rebecca (Mo)	**BRADEN**, Lawrence (Ark)
ALEXANDER, Brantley (Ind)	**BASS**, Francis (ETenn)	**BRASWELL**, James (Fla)
ANDERSON, Kent (Ia)	**BENNETT**, Dale (WMich)	**BROWNE**, Marigold (VI)
ARSENIE, Linda (Ct)	**BIRD**, Robert (Los)	**BUXEDA-DIAZ**, Ivan (PR)
ASH, Patricia (Los)	**BLANCO**, Patricia (Los)	**CALLAHAN**, Carol (SO)

C4

CHAPMAN, Jennifer (NMich)
CHAVEZ, Chloe (RG)
CLARAGE, Thelma (NMich)
COLLINS, Jason (SC)
COOK-QUARRY, Cassandra (Minn)
COULTER, Linda (CFla)
COX, Amy (Los)
CROSS, Carol (SwVa)
DAVIS, Gae (EC)
DAY, James (Eur)
DENT, David (Az)
DILLON, Karla (Okla)
DOSHER, Joy (EC)
DOYLE, Lawrence (Colo)
DUBOVENKO, Sandra (NMich)
EASTER, James (WMo)
ELDRIDGE, Buel (EMich)
ENGLAND, Nicholas (SO)
EVERSON, Jacquelyn (NMich)
FERGUSON, Linda (Mich)
FLAMINIO, Robert (NMich)
FRANCISCO VILAR, Jose (PR)
FRIDAY, Rawlin (Wyo)
GALEY, Hilary (NMich)
GALEY, Patrick (NMich)
GOODHOUSE-MAUAI, Angela (ND)
GRAY, Donna (Ct)
GREELEY, Horace (Cal)
GREENEY, Dawnlynn (Minn)
GROENINGER, Mary (Minn)
HARDIN, Nancy (SO)
HART, Robert (Ala)
HEIGHTON, Robert (Alb)
HENSLEY, Paul (Episcopal SJ)
HINDLE, Darren (RG)
HODGSON, Carla (Minn)
HOLMS, Christopher (Ct)
HOXIE, George (Dal)
HUGHES, J Daniel (Chi)
HUMPERT, David (EMich)
IISTOWANOHPATAAKIIWA,
   Timothy (The Episcopal NCal)
JAMES, Reynelda (Nev)
JOE-KINALE, Rose Mary (Nev)
JOHNSON, Nora (Pa)
JONES, Harriet (NMich)

LADUC, Shaun (Mich)
LAITE, Robert (Me)
LANE, Charles (Ia)
LAWSON, Shirley (NY)
LEBEAU, Philip (ECR)
LENNE, Laurent (Eur)
LOR, Cher (Minn)
LOR, Nor (Minn)
LORE, Harry (CFla)
LORIO, John (RG)
LOVELESS, Phillip (SanD)
LUBIN, Gary (SO)
MADDUX, Christine (CFla)
MARIE, Christine (Ak)
MARIN, Mario (Cal)
MARIN, Nora (Cal)
MARTIN, Douglas (RG)
MARTIN, Patricia (NMich)
MARVIC, Paula (NMich)
MASON, John (RG)
MCEWEN, Billy (ND)
MCGILL, Dennis (Ga)
METRO, Michael (Be)
MICKLOW, Patricia (NMich)
MIRON, Mary (NMich)
MOISE, Burnet (SeFla)
MONREAL, Linda (Episcopal SJ)
MORETZSOHN, Jeffrey (Pa)
MORGAN, Carroll
   (The Episcopal NCal)
MOSELEY, Hiriam (SC)
MOUA, Bao (Minn)
MUMLEY, Joanne (CFla)
MURPHY, Susan (Ind)
NEWCOMB, Timothy (CPa)
NIEMANN, Joan (Oly)
NORTHRUP, Michael (Nev)
NWANKWO, Chizoba (NJ)
NYSTROM, Brian (Wyo)
OLOIMOOJA, Edith (Los)
OLSON, Barbara (ND)
OVERBO, Terry (ND)
PALMERHALL, Juanita (Minn)
PAYNE, Samuel (ETenn)
PINZON, John (WMich)

POST VAN DER BURG, Melissa
   (Me)
REAMSNYDER, David (Md)
RED BIRD, Hazel (SD)
REINKE, Saundra (Ga)
RENG, Zecharia (ND)
RILEY, Linda (Ak)
ROSADA, Miguel (Fla)
ROWAN, Mary (Minn)
RUDER, Rhonda (Minn)
SABOGAL-GUTIERREZ, Diego
   (Colom)
SALAZAR TAPIAS, Julio (Colom)
SANTMAN, Linda (Oly)
SAUNDERS, John (Ga)
SCOTT, Michael (NMich)
SEUTTER, Jennifer (Ak)
SHIELDS, Kelly (Ia)
SHIODE, Jimmy (Los)
SIMPLE, Margaret (Ak)
SIRENO, Robert (Ct)
SMITH, Thomas (Alb)
TESKE, Evelyne (Spok)
THAO, Thomas (Minn)
THOR, Peter (Minn)
THURBER, Lorraine (Alb)
TINGLEY, Harry (Chi)
TOWERS, Crystal (ND)
UEDA, Noriaki
   (The Episcopal Church in Haw)
UNDEM, John (Minn)
VAN BLACK, Barbara (Tex)
VAUGHN, Robert (SeFla)
VENTURA, Gregory (NJ)
VOLLMAN, Michael (Ky)
WALDING, Jennifer (Minn)
WALKER, Randolf (Oly)
WALTERS, Marilyn (WNC)
WASHINGTON, Vant (Minn)
WATKINS, LindaMay (SO)
WELLBORN, Gay (RG)
WEST, Russell (EC)
WESTBROOK, Carl (Tex)
WIRENIUS, John (NY)
WODEHOUSE, Priscilla (WNC)

CLERGY:
BISHOPS, PRIESTS, AND DEACONS

The names, addresses, and canonical residences in the Clergy List, as well as the preceding list (Necrology, Receptions, Transfers, Restorations, Suspensions, Depositions, Removals, and Clergy Reported as Ordained), are supplied by The Recorder of Ordinations and reflect changes reported by 31 December 2015. Any request for a change in the Clergy List should be addressed to The Recorder of Ordinations, CHURCH PENSION GROUP, 19 East 34th Street, New York, NY 10016.

A

AALAN, Joshua Canon (Pa) 2013 Appletree St, Philadelphia, PA 19103
AARON, Stephen Craig (Wyo) 618 Saunders Cir, Evanston, WY 82930

ABBOTT, Barbara Leigh (Pa) 110 Llanfair Rd, Ardmore, PA 19003
ABBOTT, Gail Eoline (Mil)
ABBOTT SR, Gary Louis (Ga) 92 Camden Way, Hawkinsville, GA 31036
ABBOTT, Grant H (Minn) 2163 Carter Ave, Saint Paul, MN 55108

ABBOTT, James Michael (Tex) 6507 Allentown Dr, Spring, TX 77389
ABBOTT, Richard (VI) PO Box 686, Frederiksted, VI 00841
ABBOTT, Samuel Bassett (Alb) 1 Church St, Cooperstown, NY 13326

ABBOTT, Sefton Frank James (WNC) 27 Hildebrand St, Asheville, NC 28801
ABDELNOUR, Mark Anthony (USC) St. Simon & St. Jude Epis Church, 1110 Kinley Rd., Irmo, SC 29063
ABELL, Jesse W (WMass) 3 John Street, Westborough, MA 01581
ABER, Jack Albert (Q)
ABERNATHEY, James Milton (Tex) 1903 E. Bayshore Dr., Palacios, TX 77465
ABERNATHY, Paul Roberts (WA) 1050 Willis Rd, Spartanburg, SC 29301
ABERNATHY JR, W Harry (NY)
ABERNETHY-DEPPE, David Edward (Cal) 19938 Josh Pl, Castro Valley, CA 94546
ABERNETHY-DEPPE, Jonathan (Cal) 2322 Oakcrest Dr, Palm Springs, CA 92264
ABEYARATNE, Keshini Anoma (Mass) 4 Greenough Cir, Brookline, MA 02445
ABIDARI, Mehrdad (Cal) Cathedral School for Boys, 1257 Sacramento St, San Francisco, CA 94108
ABRAHAM, Billie Patterson (Miss) P.O. Box 921, Vicksburg, MS 39181
ABRAHAM, John (Az) 9138 North Palm Brook Dr., Tucson, AZ 85743
ABRAHAMSON, Wendy Kay (Ia) St. John's Episcopal Church, 120 First St. NE, Mason City, IA 50401
ABRAMS, Mary Elizabeth (Ky) 4100 Southern Pkwy, Louisville, KY 40214
ABRAMS, Ronald George (EC) 3309 Upton Ct, Wilmington, NC 28409
ABSHIER, Patsy Ann (Kan) Po Box 1175, Wichita, KS 67201
ABSHIRE, Lupton P (Colo) Saint Luke's Episcopal Church, 2000 Stover St, Fort Collins, CO 80525
ABSTEIN II, W(lliam) Robert (Tenn) 9210 Sawyer Brown Rd, Nashville, TN 37221
ABT, Audra M (NC) 2105 W Market St, Greensboro, NC 27403
ABUCHAR CURY, Rafael Cury (Colom)
ACANFORA, Joseph Gerard (Alb) 561 Copes Corners Rd, South New Berlin, NY 13843
ACCIME, Max (Hai) C/O Lynx Air, PO Box 407139, Fort Lauderdale, FL 33340
ACEVEDO, Miriam (NH) 92 Nashua Rd, Pelham, NH 03076
ACKAAH, Vincent Abisi (NY) PO Box 950A, Bronx, NY 10451
ACKER, Patricia Small (CFla) PO Box 290245, Pt Orange, FL 32129
ACKERMAN, Patricia Elizabeth (NY) 86 Piermont Ave, Nyack, NY 10960
ACKERMAN, Peter (Va) 101 N. Quaker Ln, Alexandria, VA 22304
ACKERMAN, Thomas Dieden (Mil) 4875 Easy St, Unit # 12, Hartland, WI 53029
ACKERMANN, John Frederick (Oly)
ACKERSON, Charles Garrett (LI) Po Box 113, Mastic Beach, NY 11951

ACKLAND III, Lauren Dreeland (Nwk) 6 Madison Ave, Madison, NJ 07940
ACKLEY, Susan M (NH) 28 River St, Ashland, NH 03217
ACOSTA, Juan Maria (SanD) 3552 Hatteras Ave, San Diego, CA 92117
ACREE, Nancy Pickering (Ga) 207 High Pt, Saint Simons Island, GA 31522
ADAIR, Maryly S (The Episcopal NCal)
ADAM, Barbara Ann (Kan) 10500 W 140th Ter, Overland Park, KS 66221
ADAM, Betty (Tex) 3501 Chevy Chase Dr, Houston, TX 77019
ADAM, John Todd (Neb) 2621 CR 59, Alliance, NE 69301
ADAMIK, George F (NC) 221 Union St, Cary, NC 27511
ADAMS, Christopher M (RG) 231 Amberleigh Dr Apt 102, Wilmington, NC 28411
ADAMS, David Robert (NJ)
ADAMS, Deanna Sue (U) 603 W 2350 S, Perry, UT 84302
ADAMS, Debra Jeanne (Ida) 20 Alta School Rd, Alta, WY 83414
ADAMS, Eloise Ellen (Ct) 495 Laurel Hill Rd Apt 4B, Norwich, CT 06360
ADAMS, Frank George (NJ) 107 Devon Dr, Chestertown, MD 21620
ADAMS, Gary Jay (ECR) 3002 Hauser Ct, Carson City, NV 89701
✠ **ADAMS III**, Gladstone Bailey (Bp of CNY 2001-) 1020 7th North St Ste 110, Suite 200, Liverpool, NY 13088
ADAMS, Helen (CFla) 103 Shady Branch Trl, Ormond Beach, FL 32174
ADAMS JR, Holmes Stanford (Miss) All Saints' Church, 608 W Jefferson St, Tupelo, MS 38804
ADAMS, James Harold (Roch) 517 Castle St, Geneva, NY 14456
✠ **ADAMS JR**, James Marshall (Resigned Bp of WK 2010-) 428 W Cobblestone Loop, Hernando, FL 34442
ADAMS, James Patrick (NC) 120 East Edenton Street, Raleigh, NC 27601
ADAMS, Jennifer Lin (WMich) 536 College Ave, Holland, MI 49423
ADAMS JR, Jesse Roland (La) 6306 Prytania St, New Orleans, LA 70118
ADAMS, John David (Neb) 109 N 18th St, Omaha, NE 68102
ADAMS JR, John Davry (Va) 1731 Cloister Dr, Richmond, VA 23238
ADAMS, John Stockton (ECR) 24745 Summit Field Road, Carmel, CA 93923
ADAMS, John Torbet (Alb) 262 Center Rd, Lyndeborough, NH 03082
ADAMS, Lesley Margaret (Roch) 630 S Main St, Geneva, NY 14456
ADAMS, Margaret Louise (Tenn) 411 Annex Ave Apt F-1, Nashville, TN 37209
ADAMS, Marilyn (Los) Po Box 208306, New Haven, CT 06520
ADAMS, Mary Lynn (FdL)

ADAMS, Michael K (Tex) 209 W 27th St, Austin, TX 78705
ADAMS, Patricia Anne (Ak) 3506 Cherokee Dr S, Salem, OR 97302
ADAMS, Richard Carl (Oly) Po Box 336, Hinesburg, VT 05461
ADAMS, Samuel Bowman (Tenn) 4715 Harding Pike, Nashville, TN 37205
ADAMS JR, Thomas Edwin (Mass) PO Box 522, Falmouth, MA 02541
ADAMS, William J (The Episcopal NCal) 95 Malaga Ct, Ukiah, CA 95482
ADAMS, William Rian (Los) 10 Chamberland Loop, Edwards, CA 93524
ADAMS, William Seth (Oly) 2707 Silver Crest Court, Langley, WA 98260
ADAMS-HARRIS, Anne Jane (Wyo) Po Box 4086, Santa Barbara, CA 93140
ADAMS-MASSMANN, Jennifer Helen (Eur) Sebastian-Rinz-Str 22, Frankfurt, Germany, Germany
ADAMS-RILEY, Daniel W (Va) 815 E Grace St, Richmond, VA 23219
ADAMS-RILEY, Gena D (Fla)
ADAMS-SHEPHERD, Kathleen Elizabeth (Ct) 64 Main St, Newtown, CT 06470
ADDIEGO, Jeffrey Clark (Nev) 1429 Bronco Rd, Boulder City, NV 89005
ADDISON, Orlando Joseph (CFla) 6990 S US Highway 1, Port St Lucie, FL 34952
ADE, Daniel Gerard George (Los) 242 E Alvarado St, Pomona, CA 91767
ADEBONOJO, Mary (Pa) 50 Bagdad Rd, Durham, NH 03824
ADELIA, Laura A (Az) 100 W Roosevelt St, Phoenix, AZ 85003
ADER, Thomas Edmund (At) 3596 Liberty Ln, Marietta, GA 30062
ADERS, Magdalena Mary (NJ) 18 Ryers Ln, Matawan, NJ 07747
ADESSA, Denise Mcgovern (Ct) 311 Broad St, Windsor, CT 06095
ADINOLFI, Debora L (Az) 12111 N La Cholla Blvd, Oro Valley, AZ 85755
ADINOLFI JR, Jerry Domenick (Kan) 131 Country Estates Rd, Greenville, NY 12083
ADKINS, Edna (Ga) Po Box 1601, Tybee Island, GA 31328
ADKINS JR, Robert Frederick (CNY) 956 Graylea Cir, Elmira, NY 14905
ADLER, John Stuart (SwFla) 1406 S. Larkwood Square, Fort Myers, FL 33919
ADLER, Paul E (Pa) 6769 Ridge Ave, Philadelphia, PA 19128
ADOLPHSON, Donald Richard (Cal) 552 Old Orchard Dr, Danville, CA 94526
ADORNO ANDINO, Hector Luis (PR) Iglesia Episcopal Puertoriquena, PO Box 902, Saint Just, PR 00978-0902, Puerto Rico
ADU-ANDOH, Samuel (Pa) 1121 Serrill Ave, Yeadon, PA 19050
ADWELL, Lynn (Minn) 334 E Fremont Dr, Tempe, AZ 85282

ADZIMA, Melissa Lian (Colo) 2015 Glenarm Pl, Denver, CO 80205
AFANADOR-KAFURI, Hernan (Ala) 176 Ridgewood Dr., Remlap, AL 35133
AFFER, Licia (At) 3098 Saint Annes Ln NW, Atlanta, GA 30327
AGAR JR, Ralph Wesley (Neb) 2315 Georgetown Pl, Bellevue, NE 68123
AGBAJE, John Olasoji (SO) 1 Paddle Ct, Portsmouth, VA 23703
AGBO, Godwin (Ct) 61 Grove St, Putnam, CT 06260
AGGELER, Harold Griffith (Ida)
AGIM, Emeka Ngozi (Tex) 16203 Dryberry Ct, Houston, TX 77083
AGNER, Georgia Ellen (Eau) 17823 57th Ave, Chippewa Falls, WI 54729
AGNEW, Christopher Mack (Va)
AGNEW JR, ML (WLa) 113 Whispering Pines Dr, Bullard, TX 75757
AGUILAR, Norman (Hond)
AGUILAR, Richard Joseph (Az) 15650 Miami Lakeway N, Miami Lakes, FL 33014
AGUILAR DE RAMIREZ, Ana Roselia (Hond)
AHLENIUS, Robert Orson (Dal) 2541 Pinebluff Drive, Dallas, TX 75228
AHLVIN, Judith L (ECR) 18325 Crystal Dr, Morgan Hill, CA 95037
AHN, Matthew Y (Los) 10555 Bel Air Dr, Cherry Valley, CA 92223
AHN, Paul C (Chi) 5801 N Pulaski Rd #348, Chicago, IL 60646
✠ **AHRENS**, Laura (Bp Suffr of Ct 2007-) 2 Cannondale Dr, Danbury, CT 06810
AHRON, Linda W (Los) 31641 La Novia Ave, San Juan Capistrano, CA 92675
AIDNIK, Aileen Marie (The Episcopal NCal) 988 Collier Dr, San Leandro, CA 94577
AIKEN JR, Charles Duval (Va) 4210 Hanover Ave, Richmond, VA 23221
AIKEN, Richard L (Ct) P.O. Box 1130, Truro, MA 02666
AIKEN JR, Warwick (NC) 700 Riverside Dr, Eden, NC 27288
AIN, Judith Pattison (ECR) 286 Thompson Rd Unit B, Watsonville, CA 95076
AINSLEY, Matthew Brian (CFla) 4950 S Apopka Vineland Rd, Orlando, FL 32819
AINSWORTH, Mark J (Pa) 262 Bent Road, Wyncote, PA 19095
AIRD, Isabel May (WVa) 1209 1/2 Williams St, Parkersburg, WV 26101
AIS, Jean Nesly (Hai) c/o Diocese of Haiti, Boite Postale 1309, Port au Prince, Haiti
AITON JR, Alexander Anthony (Ia) 717 10th St, Ames, IA 50010
AJAX, Kesner (Hai) C/O Agape Flights Acc. #2519, 100 Airport Avenue, Venice, FL 34285

AKAMATSU, Mary Catherine (Ala) St Matthew's Episcopal Church, 786 Hughes Rd, Madison, AL 35758
AKER, Edwina Sievers (Mont) 32413 Skidoo Ln, Polson, MT 59860
AKES, Amanda Ann (WA) Grace Church, 1607 Grace Church Rd, Silver Spring, MD 20910
AKIN, Mary Barbara (NwPa)
AKIN, Mary Anne (Ala) 3525 Great Oak Lk Ln, Birmingham, AL 35223
AKINA, Eleanore Mayo (The Episcopal Church in Haw) 1237 Mokulua Dr, Kailua, HI 96734
AKINKUGBE, Felix Olagboye (FtW) 2995 Celian Dr, Grand Prairie, TX 75052
AKINS, Keith Edward (Kan) 900 Sw 31st St Apt 219, Topeka, KS 66611
AKIYAMA, Diana D (The Episcopal Church in Haw) 2745 Glendower Ave, Los Angeles, CA 90027
AKRIDGE, Alan M (Ga) 108 Worthing Rd, St Simons Island, GA 31522
ALAGNA, Frank J (NY) Po Box 1, Rhinecliff, NY 12574
ALAN, Stacy (Chi) 5540 S Woodlawn Ave, Chicago, IL 60637
ALAVA VILLAREAL, Geronimo Javier (Litoral Ecu) Casilla 0901-5250, Guayaquil, Ecuador
ALBANO, Randolph Vicente Nolasco (The Episcopal Church in Haw) St. Paul's Episcopal Church, 229 Queen Emma Square, Honolulu, HI 96813
ALBERGATE, Scott P (Pa) 249 N. Belfield Ave, Havertown, PA 19083
ALBERS, Barbara Ransom (RG) 8540 S Southpoint Rd, Empire, MI 49630
ALBERT II, Edwin Edward (SO) 1924 Timberidge Dr., Loveland, OH 45140
ALBERT, Hilario Alejandro (NY) 535 King St, Port Chester, NY 10573
ALBERT III, Jules Gilmore (La) 6249 Canal Blvd, New Orleans, LA 70124
ALBINGER JR, William Joseph (The Episcopal Church in Haw)
ALBRECHT, John Herman (Mich) 293 Scottsdale Dr, Troy, MI 48084
ALBRETHSEN, Karen Anne (Nev) 777 Sage St, Elko, NV 89801
ALBRIGHT, John Taylor (WMass) 525 Suffield St, Agawam, MA 01001
ALBRIGHT, Meredyth L (FdL)
ALBRIGHT, Timothy S (Be) 383 N Hunter Hwy, Drums, PA 18222
ALBURY, Ronald Graham (NJ) 28 Maine Trl, Medford, NJ 08055
ALCORN, James Krammer (Tex) 906 Sugar Mountain Ct, Sugar Land, TX 77478
ALDAY, Kristen Nowell (CFla) 1017 E. Robinson Street, Orlando, FL 32801
ALDER, Steve (U) 2215 Molino Ave Apt A, Signal Hill, CA 90755
ALDRICH, Dawn Marie (NMich) 1310 Ashmun St, Sault Sainte Marie, MI 49783
ALDRICH JR, Kenneth Davis (NJ) 400 4th St., Huntingdon, PA 16652

ALDRICH, Robert Paul (NMich)
ALEXANDER, Bruce Ames (Me) 292 Alexander Rd, Dresden, ME 04342
ALEXANDER, Conor Matthew (SVa)
ALEXANDER, George Wilson (At) 3468 Summerford Ct, Marietta, GA 30062
ALEXANDER, Gerald G (Fla) 4311 Ortega Forest Dr, Jacksonville, FL 32210
ALEXANDER, Jane Biggs (WLa) 2015 East Northside Dr., Jackson, MS 39211
ALEXANDER, Jason L (Ark) The Episcopal Diocese of Arkansas, P.O. Box 164668, Little Rock, AR 72216
ALEXANDER, John David (RI) 974 Pine St, Seekonk, MA 02771
✠ **ALEXANDER**, J(ohn) Neil (Ret Bp of At 2012-) 335 Tennessee Avenue, Sewanee, TN 37383
ALEXANDER, Jonna Ruth (Ore) 2220 Cedar St, Berkeley, CA 94709
ALEXANDER JR, Joseph Randolph (Va) 3606 Seminary Rd, Alexandria, VA 22304
ALEXANDER, Kathryn Bellm (Ark) CHRIST CHURCH, 509 SCOTT ST, LITTLE ROCK, AR 72201
ALEXANDER, Patricia Phaneuf (WA) 8804 Postoak Rd, Potomac, MD 20854
ALEXANDER, Sharon Ann (La) 3552 Morning Glory Ave, Baton Rouge, LA 70808
ALEXANDER, Stephen Gray (Lex) 5300 Hamilton Ave Apt 906, Cincinnati, OH 45224
ALEXANDER, William David (Okla)
ALEXANDRE, Hickman (LI) 260 Beaver Dam Road, Brookhaven, NY 11719
ALEXANDRE, Soner (Hai)
ALEXIS, Alicia (NC) PO Box 20427, Greensboro, NC 27420
ALEXIS, Judith (Ct)
ALFORD, Billy J (Ga) 3041 Hummingbird Ln, Augusta, GA 30906
ALFORD JR, H(arold) Bennett (Ala) 680 Calder St, Beaumont, TX 77701
ALFORD, Joseph Stanley (Kan) 2618 W 24th Terrace, Lawrence, KS 66047
ALFORD, William T (CPa) 302 S Liberty St, Centreville, MD 21617
ALFRIEND, John Daingerfield (WVa) 224 Muirfield Ct, Charles Town, WV 25414
ALGERNON, Marcel Glenford (SwFla) 2055 Woodsong Way, Fountain, CO 80817
ALLAGREE, The Rev. Harry R. (The Episcopal NCal) 361 Lincoln Avenue, Cotati, CA 94931
ALLAIN, Thomas Alexander (Miss) 615 18th St S, Birmingham, AL 35233
✠ **ALLAN**, Frank Kellogg (Ret Bp of At 2001-) 1231 Briarcliff Rd Ne, Atlanta, GA 30306
ALLARD, Bradley Richard (WMich) 114 Union Ave Ne # 1, Grand Rapids, MI 49503

ALLEE, Roger G (SeFla) All Saints Episcopal Church, 333 Tarpon Dr., Ft. Lauderdale, FL 33301

ALLEMAN, Timothy Lee (Be)

ALLEMEIER, James Elmer (Chi) 4306 34th Avenue Pl, Moline, IL 61265

ALLEN, Abraham Claude (Mass) 17 Winthrop St, Marlborough, MA 01752

ALLEN, Barbara Ann (WA) 6919 Strathmore St Apt C, Bethesda, MD 20815

ALLEN, Charles William (Ind) 4118 Byram Ave, Indianapolis, IN 46208

ALLEN, Curtis Tilley (WTenn) 133 Jefferson Sq, Nashville, TN 37215

ALLEN, David Eastman (Mass) 980 Memorial Dr, Cambridge, MA 02138

ALLEN, David Edward (Mass) PO Box 1052, Barnstable, MA 02630

ALLEN, Donald Frederick (Ct) 34 Ashlar Vlg, Wallingford, CT 06492

ALLEN, E(arl) Michael (Nwk) 55 George St, Allendale, NJ 07401

ALLEN, Edward Powell (Los) 49 Captains Row, Mashpee, MA 02649

ALLEN II, George Curwood (SO) 988 Duxbury Ct, Cincinnati, OH 45255

ALLEN, Gordon Richard (NH) 237 Emerys Bridge Rd, South Berwick, ME 03908

ALLEN JR, John Gwin (Ky) 1512 Valley Brook Rd, Louisville, KY 40222

ALLEN, John M (Oly) 4415 Colebrooke Lane SE, Lacey, WA 98513

ALLEN, John Shepley (NH) 229 Shore Dr, Laconia, NH 03246

ALLEN, John Tait (Mil) 515 Oak St., South Milwaukee, WI 53172

ALLEN, Larry Joe (WMo) 3212 S. Jeffrey Cir., Independence, MO 64055

ALLEN, Leland Eugene (Kan) 811 E Wood St, Clearwater, KS 67026

✠ **ALLEN**, Lloyd Emmanuel (Bp of Hond 2001-) Diocese of Honduras, PO Box 523900, Miami, FL 33152

ALLEN, Mark Frederick (The Episcopal NCal)

ALLEN, Mary Louise (Del) 3 Thornberry Dr, Ocean View, DE 19770

ALLEN, Morgan S (Tex) 3201 Windsor Rd, Austin, TX 78703

ALLEN, Patrick Scott (SC) 886 Seafarer Way, Charleston, SC 29412

ALLEN JR, Radford B. (FtW) 1804 Dakar Rd W, Fort Worth, TX 76116

ALLEN, Robert Edward (Ark) 1101 Glenwood Dr, El Dorado, AR 71730

ALLEN, Roger D (At) St. James Episcopal Church, 161 Church St NE, Marietta, GA 30060

ALLEN, Russell Harvey (Ct) 28 Seaward Ln, Harwich, MA 02645

ALLEN, Stephanie Perry (NC) Church of the Nativity, 8849 Ray Road, Raleigh, NC 27613

ALLEN, Susan Van Leunen (ECR) PO Box 173, King City, CA 93930

ALLEN, T Scott (Be) 713 Cherokee St, Bethlehem, PA 18015

ALLEN, Thomas Wynn (Md) 1 St. Mary's Church Rd., Abingdon, MD 21009

ALLEN, W Frank (Pa) 763 Valley Forge Rd, Wayne, PA 19087

ALLEN, Walter Drew (Colo) Po Box 5958, Vail, CO 81658

ALLEN-FAIELLA, Wilifred Sophia Nelly (SeFla) 16745 Southwest 74th Avenue, Miami, FL 33157

ALLEN-HERRON, Dawn (Ak) 3886 S Tongass Hwy, Ketchikan, AK 99901

ALLEY, Ann Leonard (Spr) 913 W Washington St, Champaign, IL 61821

ALLEY, Charles Dickson (Va) 1101 Forest Ave, Richmond, VA 23229

ALLEY, Marguerite Cole (SVa) 1917 Indian Run Rd, Virginia Beach, VA 23454

ALLEYNE, Edmund Torrence (LI) 972 E 93rd St, Brooklyn, NY 11236

ALLICK, Paul (Minn) 2841 Florida Ave S, St. Louis Park, MN 55426

ALLIN, Hailey Wile (Miss) PO Box 1366, Jackson, MS 39215

ALLING, Fred Augustus (Nwk) 3 Mariners Ln, Marblehead, MA 01945

ALLING JR, Roger (Ct) 125 N 28th St, Camp Hill, PA 17011

ALLISON II, Charles Roy (SwFla) St Mary's Episcopal Church, 9801 Bonita Beach Rd SE, Bonita Springs, FL 34135

✠ **ALLISON**, C(hristopher) FitzSimons (Ret Bp of SC 1990-) 1081 Indigo Ave, Georgetown, SC 29440

ALLISON, Judith Anne (SanD)

ALLISON, Nancy Jean (NC) 3110 Belvin Dr, Raleigh, NC 27609

ALLISON-HATCH, Mary Susan (RG) 1625 Escalante Ave SW, Albuquerque, NM 87104

ALLMAN, Denny Paul (Miss) 8008 Bluebonnet Blvd Apt 13-2, Baton Rouge, LA 70810

ALLMAN, Mary Katherine (SanD) 7946 Calle De La Plata, La Jolla, CA 92037

ALLMAN, Susan G (U) 1016 E. High Cedar Highlands Dr., Cedar City, UT 84720

ALLPORT II, William H (Nwk) 113 Engle St, Englewood, NJ 07631

ALLTOP, Robert William (Mich) Cathedral Church of St Paul, 4800 Woodward Ave, Detroit, MI 48201

ALMODIEL JR, Arsolin Diones (Nev) Dioces of Nevada, 9480 S Eastern Ave, Las Vegas, NV 89123

ALMON JR, Austin Albert (RI) 116 Daggett Ave, Pawtucket, RI 02861

ALMONO ROQUE, Joel A(ntonio) (Mass) 1524 Summit Ave, Saint Paul, MN 55105

ALMONTE, Salvador (DR (DomRep)) Calle Santiago #114 Gazcue, Santo Domingo, Dominican Republic

ALMOS, Richard Wayne (La) 996 Marina Dr, Slidell, LA 70458

ALMQUIST, Curtis Gustav (Mass) Society of St. John the Evangelist, 980 Memorial Drive, Cambridge, MA 02138

ALONGE-COONS, Katherine Grace (Alb) Grace Church, 34 3rd St, Waterford, NY 12188

ALONSO MARINA, Jesus Daniel (EcuC) Ava Y Maldonado, Guayaquil, Ecuador

ALONZO, Mary (Roch) 541 Linden St, Rochester, NY 14620

ALONZO MARTINEZ, Gerardo Antonio (Hond)

ALSAY, Joseph Caldwell (Okla) 14700 N MAY AVE, OKLAHOMA CITY, OK 73134

ALTENBACH, Julie Kay (CFla)

ALTIZER, Aimee Marie (U)

ALTIZER, Caryl Jean (WTenn) 1830 S 336th St Apt C-202, Federal Way, WA 98003

ALTON, Frank Mitchell (Los) 840 Echo Park Ave, Los Angeles, CA 90026

ALTON, Richard (Pa) St. Clement's Church, 2013 Appletree Street, Philadelphia, PA 19103

ALTOPP, Whitney Lynn (Ct) Saint Stephen's Church, 351 Main St, Ridgefield, CT 06877

ALVARADO FIGUEROA, Luis (PR)

ALVARADO-PALADA, Carlos (Hond)

ALVAREZ-ADORNO, Aida-Luz (PR)

ALVAREZ-ESTRADA, Miguel (WNC) 5383 E Owens Ave, Las Vegas, NV 89110

✠ **ALVAREZ-VELAZQUEZ**, David Andres (Ret Bp of PR 2003-) 4735 Ave. Isla Verde, Cond. Villas del Mar Oeste, Apt. 3-E, Carolina, PR 00979

ALVES, David Alan (The Episcopal NCal) 13840 Tulsa Ct, Magalia, CA 95954

ALVES, Robert (EC) St John's Episcopal Church, 302 Green St, Fayetteville, NC 28301

ALVEY JR, John Thomas (Ala) 110 W Hawthorne Rd, Birmingham, AL 35209

ALWINE, David W (Tex) 527 Shem Butler Ct., Charleston, SC 29414

AMADIO, Carol Margaret (Chi) Po Box 51, Washington Island, WI 54246

AMAYA, Adrian A (CNY) 1612 W Genesee St, Syracuse, NY 13219

AMBELANG, John Edward (Eau) 506 Fairway Dr, Sheboygan, WI 53081

AMBLER V, John Jaquelin (SwVa) 507 Sunset Dr, Amherst, VA 24521

AMBLER JR, Michael Nash (Me) 912 Middle St, Bath, ME 04530

AMBROISE, Rospignac (Mass) Box 1309, Port-Au-Prince, Haiti

AMBROSE, Barbara Lockwood (Va) 236 S Laurel St, Richmond, VA 23220

AMBROSE, Colin Moore (Tenn) 116 N. Academy St., Murfreesboro, TN 37130

AMBROSE, Theodore Grant (Va) 2609 N Glebe Rd # P, Arlington, VA 22207

AMBROSE, Valerie Twomey (WMich) 6308 Greenway Drive SE, Grand Rapids, MI 49546

AMBURGEY, Cristina Goubaud (Oly) 3213 17th Street Pl Se, Puyallup, WA 98374

AMEND, Albert Edward (LI) 13821 Willow Bridge Dr, North Fort Myers, FL 33903

AMEND, Russell Jay (WNY) 25 Caspian Ct, Amherst, NY 14228

AMERMAN, Lucy S L (Pa) PO Box 57, Buckingham, PA 18912

AMES, David A (RI) 130 Slater Ave, Providence, RI 02906

AMES, Richard Kenneth (SeFla) 4917 Ravenswood Dr Apt 1709, San Antonio, TX 78227

AMMONS JR, B Wiley (Fla) 325 N Market St, Jacksonville, FL 32202

AMPAH, Rosina Rhoda Araba (NY) 3042 Eagle Dr, Augusta, GA 30906

AMPARO TAPIA, Milton Mauricio (DR (DomRep)) Juan Luis Franco Bido #21, Santo Domingo, Dominican Republic

AMSDEN, Helen (Neb) 9459 Jones Cir, Omaha, NE 68114

AMUZIE, Charles C (WA) 3601 Alabama Ave SE, Washington, DC 20020

ANCHAN, Israel D (Chi) 298 S. Harrison Ave., Kankakee, IL 60901

ANDERHEGGEN, George Curtis (Ct) 6 Rosewood Cir, Monroe, CT 06468

ANDERS, Florence Kay (RG) Holy Family Episcopal Church, 10 A Bisbee Court, Santa fe, NM 87508

ANDERSEN, Francis Ian (Cal) 5 Epsom Court, Donvale Victoria, VI 3111, Australia

ANDERSEN, John Day (CNY) 2702 W Old State Road 34, Lizton, IN 46149

ANDERSEN, Judith Ann (NMich) 500 Ogden Ave, Escanaba, MI 49829

ANDERSEN, Paul John (Va)

ANDERSEN, Raynor Wade (Ct) 199 Eastgate Dr, Cheshire, CT 06410

ANDERSEN, Richard Belden (Nwk) 275 E Franklin Tpke, Ho Ho Kus, NJ 07423

ANDERSEN, Steven C (U) 75 South 200 East, P.O. Box 3090, Salt Lake City, UT 84110

ANDERSON, Ann Johnston (ND) 2405 W Country Club Dr S, Fargo, ND 58103

ANDERSON, Augusta A (WNC) 2 Cedarcliff Road, Asheville, NC 28803

ANDERSON JR, Bert A (Los) 612 Chestnut St, Ashland, OR 97520

ANDERSON, Betsy Neville (Los) 315 Lorraine Blvd, Los Angeles, CA 90020

ANDERSON, Bettina (Colo) 822 Fox Hollow Ln, Golden, CO 80401

ANDERSON, Carmen Marie (Kan) 375 Lake Shore Drive, Alma, KS 66401

ANDERSON, Carol Linda (NY) 115 E 87th St Apt 6B, New York, NY 10128

ANDERSON, Carolyn Kinsey (Ga) 4221 Blue Heron Ln, Evans, GA 30809

ANDERSON JR, C Newell (At) 1884 Rugby Ave, College Park, GA 30337

✠ **ANDERSON**, Craig Barry (Ret Bp of SD 1993-) PO Box 1316, Ranchos de Taos, NM 87557

ANDERSON, David R (Ct) Saint Luke's Parish, 1864 Post Rd, Darien, CT 06820

ANDERSON, Devon Elizabeth (Minn) 4644 Upton Ave S, Minneapolis, MN 55410

ANDERSON, Douglas Evan (Dal) 413 Olive St, Texarkana, TX 75501

ANDERSON, Douglas Reid (Mont) 408 Westview Dr, Missoula, MT 59803

ANDERSON, Eldon Wayne (Episcopal SJ) 208 E Smoke St, Jamestown, CA 95327

ANDERSON III, Elenor Lucius (Ala) 447 McClung Ave SE, Huntsville, AL 35801

ANDERSON, Elizabeth May (Chi)

ANDERSON JR, Emmett Bernard (Md) 9120 Frederick Rd, Ellicott City, 21042

ANDERSON, Eric A (WMo) 2001 Windsor Dr, Newton, KS 67114

ANDERSON, Evangeline (RI) 719 Hope St Apt 1, Bristol, RI 02809

ANDERSON, Forrest Ewell (USC) 3333 Oakwell Ct Apt 529, San Antonio, TX 78218

ANDERSON, Gene Ray (SwVa) 5631 Warwood Dr, Roanoke, VA 24018

ANDERSON, George Michael (CFla) Grace Episcopal Church, 503 SE Broadway St, Ocala, FL 34471

ANDERSON, Gordon James (Ind) 2522 E Elm St, New Albany, IN 47150

ANDERSON, Hannah Pedersen (NH) 54 Dunklee St, Concord, NH 03301

ANDERSON, Howard Rae (Los) PO Box 37, Pacific Palisades, CA 90272

ANDERSON, James Arthur (Mil) 10041 Beckford St, Pickerington, OH 43147

ANDERSON, James Desmond (WA) 9556 Chantilly Farm Ln, Chestertown, MD 21620

ANDERSON, James Russell (WA) 3111 Ritchie Rd, Forestville, MD 20747

ANDERSON, Jami Andrea (Wyo) PO Box 847, Pinedale, WY 82941

ANDERSON, Jennie M (Pa) 209 S. 3rd Ave., Royersford, PA 19468

ANDERSON, Jerry Ray (Los) 339 West Avenue 45, Los Angeles, CA 90065

ANDERSON JR, Jesse Fosset (Pa) 4848 Carrington Cir, Sarasota, FL 34243

ANDERSON, Joan Wilkinson (ECR) 425 Carmel Ave, Marina, CA 93933

ANDERSON, Jon R (ETenn) 663 Douglas Street, Chattanooga, TN 37403

ANDERSON, Judith Kay Finney (Mont) 408 Westview Dr, Missoula, MT 59803

ANDERSON, Juliana (Mass) 1770 Massachusetts Ave, Cambridge, MA 02140

ANDERSON, Karen Sue (Neb) 1517 Broadway Ste 104, Scottsbluff, NE 69361

ANDERSON, Kenneth Edwin (RG) 258 Riverside Dr, El Paso, TX 79915

ANDERSON III, Lenny (Pgh) 2081 Husband Rd, Somerset, PA 15501

ANDERSON, Louise Thomas (NC) 901 N Main St, Tarboro, NC 27886

ANDERSON, Marilyn Lea (Ct) 180 Cross Highway, Redding, CT 06896

ANDERSON, Mark Sargent (Fla)

ANDERSON, Martha O (SanD) P. O. Box 334, Del Mar, CA 92014

ANDERSON, Mary Petty (Oly) 10450 NE Yaquina Ave, Bainbridge Island, WA 98110

ANDERSON, Mary Sterrett (O) 2581 Norfolk Rd, Cleveland Heights, OH 44106

ANDERSON, Megan Elizabeth (The Episcopal NCal) Trinity Cathedral, 2620 Capitol Ave, Sacramento, CA 95816

ANDERSON, Michael E (Chi) 1225 Asbury Ave, Evanston, IL 60202

ANDERSON JR, Otto Harold (Okla) 5901 Canterbury Dr Unit 1, Culver City, CA 90230

ANDERSON, Otto S. (SO) 409 E High St, Springfield, OH 45505

ANDERSON III, Paul Kemper (At) 1210 Wooten Lake Rd NW, Kennesaw, GA 30144

ANDERSON, Philip Alden (O) 2581 Norfolk Rd, Cleveland Heights, OH 44106

ANDERSON, Polly Chambers (WLa) 4037 Highway 15, Calhoun, LA 71225

ANDERSON JR, Ralph W (WMass) 114 Lake St, Shrewsbury, MA 01545

ANDERSON, Richard John (NY) 2635 2nd Ave Apt 203, San Diego, CA 92103

ANDERSON, Richard Rupert (EMich) 221 Purdy Dr, Alma, MI 48801

ANDERSON, Robert Jay (WVa)

ANDERSON, Robert M(elville) (CFla)

ANDERSON, Rosemarie (ECR) 355 Redwood Dr, Boulder Creek, CA 95006

ANDERSON, Scott Crawford (USC) Episcopal Church Of The Redeemer, 120 Mauldin Rd, Greenville, SC 29605

ANDERSON JR, Theodore Lester (NJ) 47 S Ensign Dr, Little Egg Harbor, NJ 08087

ANDERSON, Timothy Lee (Neb) P.O. Box 64, Ashland, NE 68003

ANDERSON III, William (NY)

ANDERSON, William Alvin (At) 2510 Two Oaks Dr, Charleston, SC 29414

ANDERSON, William Clarence (Md) 415 Helmsman Way, Severna Park, MD 21146

ANDERSON-KRENGEL, William Erich (Ct) 191 Margarite Rd, Middletown, CT 06457

ANDERSON-SMITH, Susan (Az) Imago Dei Middle School, PO Box 3056, Tucson, AZ 85702

ANDONIAN, Kathryn Ann (Pa) 942 Masters Way, Harleysville, PA 19438

ANDRADE, Luis E (Chi) 40 Center St, Elgin, IL 60120

ANDRE, Wildaine (Hai)

ANDRES, Anthony Francis (Ind) 795 Elk Mountain Rd, Afton, VA 22920

ANDRES, Justo Rambac (Episcopal SJ) 115 E Miner Ave, Stockton, CA 95202

ANDREW, Carol (Ga) 3042 Eagle Dr, Augusta, GA 30906

ANDREW SR, Robert Nelson (O) 3800 W 33rd St, Cleveland, OH 44109

ANDREW-MACONAUGHEY, Debra Elaine (SeFla) 111 W Indies Dr, Ramrod Key, FL 33042

ANDREWS, Alfred John (Neb) PO Box 141, Sidney, NE 69162

ANDREWS, Arthur Edward (Ore) 1704 Se 22nd Ave, Portland, OR 97214

ANDREWS, Carl Machin (Colo) The Diocese of Colorado, 1300 Washington Street, Denver, CO 80203

ANDREWS JR, David Tallmadge (Del) 732 Nottingham Rd, Wilmington, DE 19805

ANDREWS, David Thomas (WA) 500 Merton Woods Way, Millersville, MD 21108

ANDREWS, Dianne Peterson (Oly) 1613 California Ave SW #301, Seattle, WA 98116

ANDREWS II, George Edward (SeFla) 20 Vine St, Marion, MA 02738

ANDREWS II, George Strafford (Chi) 102 Starling Ln, Longwood, FL 32779

ANDREWS, John Anthony (NY) PO Box 547, Lima, NY 14485

ANDREWS, John Joseph (Colo) 5968 S Zenobia Ct, Littleton, CO 80123

ANDREWS, Lyde Coley (Ga) St Philips Episcopal Church, 302 E General Stewart Way, Hinesville, GA 31313

ANDREWS, Pati Mary (Va) 8217 Roxborough Loop, Gainesville, VA 20155

ANDREWS, Robert Forrest (Colo) 30 Hutton Ln, Colorado Springs, CO 80906

ANDREWS, Shirley May (Mass) 2 Palmer St, Barrington, RI 02806

ANDREWS III, William E (WTenn) St Mary's Cathedral, 692 Poplar Ave, Memphis, TN 38105

ANDREWS-WECKERLY, Jennifer N. (LI) 1000 Washington Ave, Plainview, NY 11803

ANDRUS, Archie Leslie (HB) 2701 Bellefontaine St, Houston, TX 77025

✠ **ANDRUS**, Marc Handley (Bp of Cal 2006-) Episcopal Diocese Of California, 1055 Taylor St, San Francisco, CA 94108

ANDUJAR, Alexander (SwFla) 4030 Manatee Ave W, Bradenton, FL 34205

ANEI, Abraham Muong (WMich)

ANGELICA, David M (Mass) 15 Colonial Club Dr Apt 300, Boynton Beach, FL 33435

ANGELL, Debra L (Colo) 13866 W 2nd Ave, Golden, CO 80401

ANGELL, Michael R (Mo) 1525 H St NW, Washington, DC 20005

ANGERER JR, Jay (La) 112 Hazel Drive, River Ridge, LA 70123

ANGLE, Nancy Scott (Colo) 150 Sipprelle Dr, Battlement Mesa, CO 81635

ANGULO ZAMORA, Gina Mayra (Litoral Ecu) Iglesia Episcopal del Ecuador Diocese Litoral, Amarilis Fuente 603, Avenida 09015250, Guayaquil, Ecuador, Ecuador

ANGUS, Caroline Helen (O) 2716 Colchester Rd, Cleveland Heights, OH 44106

ANGUS, David E (WMo) Grace Cathedral, 415 W 13th St, Kansas City, MO 64105

ANGUS, J Lloyd (Ga) 88 Oakwood Dr., Hardeeville, SC 29927

ANKUDOWICH, Stephen (SwFla) 197 Corsica St, Tampa, FL 33606

ANSCHUTZ, Mark Semmes (Mass) 162 Pleasant Street, South Yarmouth, MA 02664

ANSCHUTZ, Maryetta Madeleine (Los) P.O. Box 691404, Los Angeles, CA 90069

ANTHONY, Benjamin Jay (At)

ANTHONY, Carol R (Pa) 627 Kenilworth St, Philadelphia, PA 19147

ANTHONY II, Henry F (RI) 727 Hampton Woods Ln SW, Vero Beach, FL 32962

ANTHONY, Joan Marie (Oly) 1549 MW 57th St., Seattle, WA 98107

ANTHONY JR, Joseph Daniel (At) 389 Dorsey Cir Sw, Lilburn, GA 30047

ANTHONY, Lloyd Lincoln (LI) 9910 217th Ln, Queens Village, NY 11429

ANTHONY, Robert Williams (RI) 104 Old Stage Rd, Centerville, MA 02632

ANTHONY, Thomas Murray (PR)

ANTHONY-CHARLES, Ana Graciela (Ve)

ANTOCI, Peter M (WA) St Columba's Parish, 4201 Albemarle St NW, Washington, DC 20016

ANTOLINI, Holly Lyman (Mass) 11 Quincy St, Arlington, MA 02476

ANTTONEN, Jennifer (Ida) 288 E Kite Dr, Eagle, ID 83616

ANUSZKIEWICZ, Sare (WNY) St Paul's Episcopal Church, 4275 Harris Hill Rd, Williamsville, NY 14221

APKER, David (Mil) 4400 Deer Park Rd, Oconomowoc, WI 53066

APOLDO, Deborah D (USC)

APPELBERG, Helen Marie Waller (Tex) 301 University Blvd, Galveston, TX 77555

APPLEGATE, Stephen Holmes (SO) 360 E Sharon Rd, Glendale, OH 45246

APPLEQUIST, Alice Mae (Minn) 17221 Highway 30 SE, Chatfield, MN 55923

APPLETON, Mary Ellen (CFla) 200 Saint Andrews Blvd Apt 1406, Winter Park, FL 32792

APPLEYARD, Daniel Scott (Mo) 9 S Bompart Ave, Webster Groves, MO 63119

APPLEYARD, Jonathan Briggs (Me) 26 Montsweag Road, Woolwich, ME 04579

APPLEYARD JR, Robert Bracewell (Mass) 2036 Acton Ridge Rd, Acton, ME 04001

APPLING, Elizabeth Faragher (Oly) St. Paul's Episcopal Church, P.O. Box 753, Port Townsend, WA 98368

APPOLLONI, Sharyn L (Nev) 1965 Golden Gate Dr, Reno, NV 89511

ARAICA, Alvaro (Chi) 4609 Main St, Skokie, IL 60076

ARAMBULO, Arnulfo (NY) 231 City View Ter, Kingston, NY 12401

ARAQUE GALVIS, Alirio (PR) Iglesia Episcopal Puertorriquena, PO Box 902, Saint Just, PR 00978-0902, Puerto Rico

ARASE-BARHAM, Michael Preston (Cal) PO Box 555, Half Moon Bay, CA 94019

ARBOGAST, Stephen Daniel Kirkpatrick (WA) National Cathedral School, Mount Saint Alban, Washington, DC 20016

ARBOLEDA, Guillermo Alejandro (Ga)

ARBUCKLE, Jacquelyn (Vt)

ARCHER, A(rthur) William (Del) 650 Willow Valley Sq # K-401, Lancaster, PA 17602

ARCHER, Carolyn (Ct)

ARCHER, John Richard (Cal) 80 Harmon St, Hamden, CT 06517

ARCHER, Jonathan Gurth Adam (SeFla) 3481 Hibiscus St, Miami, FL 33133

ARCHER, Melinda (Az) 5265 NE 3rd Court, Lincoln City, OR 97367

ARCHER, Michael (Los) 18631 Chapel Ln, Huntington Beach, CA 92646

ARCHER, Nell B (LI) 199 Carroll St, Brooklyn, NY 11231

ARCHIBALD, David Jost (Del) 32216 Bixler Rd, Selbyville, DE 19975

ARCHIBALD, David Roberts (WTex) 6110 NW Loop 410, San Antonio, TX 78238

ARCHIE, Andrew John (Mo) 6345 Wydown Blvd, Saint Louis, MO 63105

ARCINIEGA, Roberto (Ore) 2065 Se 44th Ave Apt 248, Hillsboro, OR 97123

ARD, Eddie Jackson (At) 3880 Glenhurst Dr Se, Smyrna, GA 30080

ARD JR, Robert Francis (Mo) 6518 Michigan Ave, St. Louis, MO 63111
ARD, Roger Hoyt (At) 104 Sequoia Dr SE, Rome, GA 30161
ARDLEY, Evan Lloyd (The Episcopal NCal) 435 43rd Ave, #301, San Francisco, CA 94121
ARDREY-GRAVES, Sara C (Va) 660 S Main St, Harrisonburg, VA 22801
ARENAS TORO, William Henry (Colom) c/o Diocese of Colombia, Cra 6 No. 49-85 Piso 2, Bogota, BDC, Colombia
ARENTS, Gina (Md) 1511 Long Quarter Ct, Lutherville, MD 21093
ARGUE, Douglas (SO) 22 Glencoe Rd, Columbus, OH 43214
ARLEDGE JR, Thomas Lafayette (At) 909 Massee Ln, Perry, GA 31069
ARLIN, Charles Noss (Nwk) 1078B Long Beach Blvd, Long Beach Twp., NJ 08008
ARMENTROUT, Katharine Jacobs (At) 202 Griffith Rd, Jasper, GA 30143
ARMER, Mary Carolyn (WMo) 8170 Halsey St, Lenexa, KS 66215
ARMER, Susan Charlee (Oly) 5551 S 300th Pl, Auburn, WA 98001
ARMINGTON, Shawn Aaron (NJ) 118 Jefferson Rd, Princeton, NJ 08540
ARMSTEAD, Delaney Wendell (Nev)
ARMSTRONG, Barbara (NC) 509 Sleepy Valley Rd, Apex, NC 27523
ARMSTRONG, Elizabeth (The Episcopal NCal) 1008 Linier Ct., Roseville, CA 95678
ARMSTRONG, Geoffrey Macgregor (NY)
ARMSTRONG, Michael N (Fla) 2349 SW Bascom Norris Dr, Lake City, FL 32025
ARMSTRONG, Phyllis Elaine (SO) 2841 Urwiler Ave, Cincinnati, OH 45211
ARMSTRONG, Richard Sweet (Mass) 35 Old Fields Way, Castine, ME 04421
ARMSTRONG, Robert Hancock (SVa) 4600 Bruce Rd, Chester, VA 23831
ARMSTRONG, Susan J (The Episcopal NCal) 1765 Virginia Way, Arcata, CA 95521
ARMSTRONG, William Henry (WVa) 320 Old Bluefield Rd, Princeton, WV 24740
ARMSTRONG, Zenetta M (Mass) 58 Crawford St Apt 2, Dorchester, MA 02121
ARMY, Virginia Wilson (Ct) The Rectory School, Pomfret, CT 06258
ARNASON, Tryggvi G. (WNC) 130 39th Avenue Pl NW, Hickory, NC 28601
ARNEY, Carol Mary (The Episcopal Church in Haw) 1840 University Ave W, Apt. 104, Saint Paul, MN 55104
ARNHART, James Rhyne (Tenn) 1710 Riverview Dr, Murfreesboro, TN 37129
ARNOLD, Beth Kelly (Los) 1231 E. Chapman Ave., Fullerton, CA 92831

ARNOLD, Christopher John (Kan) St Andrew's, 828 Commercial Street, Emporia, KS 66801
ARNOLD, Donna J (Alb) 4 Pine Ledge Ter, Gansevoort, NY 12831
ARNOLD, Duane Wade-Hampton (NY) 5815 Lawrence Dr., Indianapolis, IN 46226
ARNOLD, Kimball Clark (Az) 3150 Spence Springs Rd, Prescott, AZ 86305
ARNOLD, Margaret L (Mass) 149 High St Apt 1, Wareham, MA 02571
ARNOLD, Robert D (WNY) 29 University Park, Fredonia, NY 14063
ARNOLD, Robyn Elizabeth (Ala) 2146 Santa Clara Ave Apt 1, Alamed, CA 94501
ARNOLD, Scott A (Ala) 1204 Valridge N, Prattville, AL 36066
ARNOLD, Susan Louise (ECR) Church Divinity School Of The Pacific, Morro Bay, CA 93442
ARNOLD, William Bruce (SwFla) 114 Fairway Ct, Greenwood, SC 29649
ARNOLD JR, William Stevenson Maclaren (Nev) 1855 Baring Blvd Apt 301, Sparks, NV 89434
ARNOLD-BOYD, Annette Ruth (Oly) 12420 SW Tremont St, Portland, OR 97225
ARPEE, Stephen T(Rowbridge) (WA) 3810 39th St NW Apt A-121, Washington, DC 20016
ARQUES, Rafael (PR)
ARRINGTON, Sandra Clark (Roch) 20 Trumbull Lane, Pittsford, NY 14534
ARROWSMITH-LOWE, Thomas (RG) Episcopal Church of St. John, P.O. Box 449, Alamogordo, NM 88310
ARROYO, Jose Del Carmen (Chi) 25291 W Lehmann Blvd, Lake Villa, IL 60046
ARROYO, Margarita (WTex)
ARROYO-SANCHEZ, Jose (PR)
ARRUNATEGUI, Herbert (CFla) 3468 Capland Ave, Clermont, FL 34711
ARTHUR, Anne Tilley (The Episcopal NCal) 2620 Capitol Ave, Sacramento, CA 95816
ARTMAN, Melinda M (WA)
ARTRESS, Lauren (Cal) 309 Coleridge St, San Francisco, CA 94110
ASEL, J(Ohn) Kenneth (Wyo) 407 F Street Suite 104, North Wilkesboro, NC 28659
ASELTINE, Sara Jane (The Episcopal NCal) 18215 Challenge Cut Off Rd, Forbestown, CA 95941
ASGILL, Edmondson Omotayo (CFla) 381 N Lincoln St, Daytona Beach, FL 32114
ASH JR, Evan Arnold (Kan) 1114 E Northview St, Olathe, KS 66061
ASH, Gerald Arnold (Md) 2206 Endovalley Dr, Cincinnati, OH 45244
ASH, Linda D (EMich) 111 S Shiawassee St, Corunna, MI 48817
ASHBY, Alice Kay (O) 344 Shepard Rd, Mansfield, OH 44907
ASHBY, Joe Lyn (O) 402 Channel Rd, N Muskegon, MI 49445

ASHBY, Julia (SVa) 4205 Cheswick Ln, Virginia Beach, VA 23455
ASHBY, Lucinda Beth (Ida) 1858 Judith Ln, Boise, ID 83705
ASHCROFT, Ernest (Minn) 4015 Sunnyside Road, Edina, MN 55424
ASHCROFT, Mary Ellen (Minn) PO Box 1093, Grand Marais, MN 55604
ASHER, Charles William (Los)
ASHLEY, Danae M (Oly) 865 Ferndale Road North, Wayzata, MN 55391
ASHMORE, Christopher Lee (Spr) 17 Forest Park W, Jacksonville, IL 62650
ASHMORE JR, Robert Michael (WNC) PO Box 956, Mars Hill, NC 28754
ASIS, Debra (Az) 6715 N. Mockingbird Ln., Scottsdale, AZ 85253
ASKEW, Angela V (NY) 659 E 17th St, Brooklyn, NY 11230
ASKEW, Stephen H (Wyo) 104 S 4th St, Laramie, WY 82070
ASKREN, Robert D. (Fla) 11366 Tacito Creek Dr. South, Jacksonville, FL 32223
ASMAN, Mark Elliott (Los) 1500 State St, Santa Barbara, CA 93101
ASONYE, Collins Enyindah (Va)
ASSON, Marla Lynn (Nev) Holy Cross/ St Christopher, 3740 Meridian St N, Huntsville, AL 35811
ASTARITA, Susan Gallagher (WA) PO Box 816, Del Mar, CA 92014
ASTLEFORD, Elise Linder (Oly) 2515 NE 80th St, Vancouver, WA 98665
ASTON, Geraldine Patricia (Ala) 544 S Forest Dr, Homewood, AL 35209
ATAMIAN, Thomas Michael (Chi) 272 Presidential Ln, Elgin, IL 60123
ATCHESON, Chuck (Oly) 8529 Caroline Ave N, Seattle, WA 98103
ATCITTY, Janice (Ida) Po Box 388, Fort Hall, ID 83203
ATEEK, Sari N (WA) 6701 Wisconsin Ave, Chevy Chase, MD 20815
ATEM, Garang G (U)
ATHEY JR, Kenneth F (Del) PO Box 88, 10719 Grove St, Delmar, DE 19940
ATKINS, Hannah E (Tex) Trinity Episcopal Church, 1015 Holman St, Houston, TX 77004
ATKINS JR, Henry Lee (NJ) 3210 Louisiana St, Apt 1413, Houston, TX 77006
ATKINS, John Merritt (Pa) 749 Durham Rd., Wrightstown, PA 18940
ATKINSON, Andy (EC) 321 Pettigrew Dr, Wilmington, NC 28412
ATKINSON, Herschel Robert (At) 509 Rhodes Dr, Elberton, GA 30635
ATKINSON JR, Joel Walter (Be) 321 Wyandotte St, Bethlehem, PA 18015
ATKINSON, Kate Bigwood (NH)
ATKINSON, Mark W (Fla) 7801 Lone Star Rd, Jacksonville, FL 32211
ATKINSON, William Harold (Vt) 40 Water St, Meredith, NH 03253

ATON JR, James Keyes (Ga) 3321 Wheeler Rd, Augusta, GA 30909
ATTEBURY, Rich Earl (EO) Po Box 123, Lostine, OR 97857
ATWELL, John Joseph (Az) 6043 E Ellis St, Mesa, AZ 85205
ATWOOD, Mary Hill (Los) 546 Bradford Ct, Claremont, CA 91711
ATWOOD JR, Theodore Oertel (Ga) 6785 El Banquero Pl, San Diego, CA 92119
AUBERT, Keri T (Vt) 1700 Le Roy Ave Apt 7, Berkeley, CA 94709
AUBREY, Norman Edward (WMass) 5 College View Hts, South Hadley, MA 01075
AUCHINCLOSS, R Anne (NY) 250 W 94th St # 4F, New York, NY 10025
AUCHINCLOSS, Susan Carpenter (NY) 2342 Glasco Tpk., Woodstock, NY 12498
AUELUA, Royston Toto'A Stene (The Episcopal NCal) 6963 Riata Dr, Redding, CA 96002
AUER, Dorothy Kogler (NJ) 320 Glenburney Dr Apt 106, Fayetteville, NC 28303
AUGUSTE, Pierre (Hai)
AUGUSTE, Roldano (Hai)
AUGUSTIN, Dale Lee (Nev) 422 Red Canvas Pl, Las Vegas, NV 89144
AUGUSTINE, Patrick Parvez (Eau) 427 14th St S, La Crosse, WI 54601
AUGUSTINE, Peter John (Eau) 111 9th St N, La Crosse, WI 54601
AULENBACH JR, Bil (The Episcopal Church in Haw) The Groves 59, 5200 Irvine Blvd, Irvine, CA 92620
AULETTA, Kimberlee (NY)
AURAND, Benjamin Kyte (Tex) 2421 Gate 11 Rd, Two Harbors, MN 55616
AUSAS-COMBES, Jose (PR)
AUSTIN, Dorothy A (Nwk) Harvard Yard, Cambridge, MA 02138
AUSTIN, Evette Eliene (Alb) 9 E Main St, Canton, NY 13617
AUSTIN, Henry Whipple (Neb) 4509 Anderson Cir, Papillion, NE 68133
AUSTIN, Jean E (Vt) 545 Shore Road, Digby, NS B0V 1A0, Canada
AUSTIN, Margaret Sutton (Colo) 2526 Gates Cir, Apt. 2611, Baton Rouge, LA 70809
AUSTIN JR, Vernon Arthur (Pa)
AUSTIN, Victor Lee (NY) 1 W 53rd St, New York, NY 10019
AUSTIN, Wilborne Adolphus (Ct) 18 Richard Rd, East Hartford, CT 06108
AUSTIN, William Bouldin (CFla) 3508 Lakeshore Dr SW, Smyrna, GA 30082
AUSTIN, William Paul (WNC) 112 Trotter Pl, Asheville, NC 28806
AVCIN, Janet Elaine (CPa) 228 Charles St, Harrisburg, PA 17102
AVENI JR, James Vincent (NwT) Po Box 1064, Clarendon, TX 79226
AVERY, Daniel Thomas (SVa) 118 Nina Lane, Williamsburg, VA 23188

AVERY, Gail (NH) Seafarer's Friend, 77 Broadway, Chelsea, MA 02150
AVERY, Harold Dennison (CNY) 112 Arbordale Pl, Syracuse, NY 13219
AVERY, Joyce Marie (Oly) 1022 Monte Elma Rd, Elma, WA 98541
AVERY, Richard Norman (Los) 1026 Goldenrod St, Placentia, CA 92870
AVERY, Steven Walter (Ore) PO Box 2617, Florence, OR 97439
AVILA, Ricardo (Cal) 600 Colorado Ave, Palo Alto, CA 94306
AVILA-NATIVI, Rigoberto (NY) PO Box 3786, Poughkeepsie, NY 12603
AVRIL, Wilky (Hai)
AWAN, Abraham Kuol (Chi) 7100 N Ashland Blvd, Chicago, IL 60626
AXBERG, Keith Frederick (Mont) Trinity Church Jeffers, PO Box 336, Ennis, MT 59729
AYALA TORRES, Carlos Anibal (EcuC) Bogota S/N Jose Vicente Trujillo, Guayaquil, Ecuador
AYBAR-MARTE, Pantaleon (PR)
AYCOCK, David H (CFla) 726 Phoenix Ln, Oviedo, FL 32765
AYCOCK JR, Marvin B(rady) (NC) 669 N. 6th St., Albemarle, NC 28001
AYER, Kelly Lane (Roch) 10 Park Pl, Avon, NY 14414
AYERBE, Reynaldo (SwFla) 4012 Penhurst Park, Sarasota, FL 34235
AYERS, Barbara (Alb)
AYERS, John Cameron (Cal) 13601 Saratoga Ave, Saratoga, CA 95070
AYERS, Margaret Susan (Miss) St James Episcopal Church, PO Box 494, Port Gibson, MS 39150
AYERS, Phillip Wallace (Ore) 3232 NE 12th Ave, Portland, OR 97212
AYERS, Robert Curtis (CNY) 6010 E. Lake Rd., Cazenovia, NY 13035
AYERS, Russell C (Mass) 3737 Seminary Rd, Alexandria, VA 22304
AYMERICH, Ramon Ignacio (Mass)
AYRES, Stephen T (Mass) 193 Salem St, Boston, MA 02113
AZAR, Antoinette Joann (Lex) 201 Providence Hill, Ashland, KY 41101
AZARIAH, Khushnud M (Los) 6563 East Ave, Etiwanda, CA 91739

B

BAAR, David Josef (The Episcopal Church in Haw)
BABB, Trevor Roosevelt (SO) 401 Newfield Ave, Bridgeport, CT 06607
BABCOCK, Harold Ross Manly (NH) Old Rossier Farm, 238 Rossier Rd., Montgomery Center, VT 05471
BABCOCK, Jessica H (CGC) St Marks Episcopal Church, 4129 Oxford Ave, Jacksonville, FL 32210
BABCOCK, Linda Mae (WMo)
BABCOCK, Lori Hale (Md) 1700 South Rd, Baltimore, MD 21209
BABCOCK, Margaret Anderson (Wyo) 4230 S Oak St, Casper, WY 82601

BABCOCK, Mary Kathleen (Kan) 400 E. Maple St, Independence, KS 67301
BABCOCK, Ted (CPa) 1214 Driftwood Dr, Mt. Lebanon, PA 15243
BABENKO-LONGHI, Julie P (Chi) 1850 Landre Ct, Burlington, WI 53105
BABIN, Alexander Raymond (Mich) 69440 Brookhill Dr, Romeo, MI 48065
BABIN, Alice Elizabeth Duffy (Md) 65 Verde Valley School Rd Apt C-13, Sedona, AZ 86351
BABLER, Emmett John (Minn) 9411 E Parkside Dr, Sun Lakes, AZ 85248
BABNIS, Mariann C (WA) 33203 W Batten St, Lewes, DE 19958
BABSON, Katharine E (Me) 149 Pennellville Rd, Brunswick, ME 04011
BACAGAN, Magdaleno K (Los) 225 W Linfield St, Glendora, CA 91740
BACHAND-WOOD, Colette (Mass) 16 Highland Ave., Cohasset, MA 02025
BACHMANN, Douglas P (Cal) 419 Orchard View Ave, Martinez, CA 94553
BACHSCHMID, Edward Karl (RG) 9024 N Congress St, New Market, VA 22844
BACIGALUPO, Joseph Andrew (ECR) 1343 Wylie Way, San Jose, CA 95130
BACK, George Henry (Okla) 2520 NW 59 St, Oklahoma City, OK 73112
BACK, Heather Back (Ky) 744 Sherwood Dr, Bowling Green, KY 42103
BACK, Luke (NwT) 602 Meander St, Abilene, TX 79602
BACKER, Karri Anne (Los) 1231 E. Chapman Ave., Fullerton, CA 92832
BACKHAUS, Oliver Keith (SwFla) St Mark's Episcopal Church, 513 Nassau St S, Venice, FL 34285
BACKLUND, Michael Anders (Cal) 10449 Oak Valley Rd, Angels Camp, CA 95222
BACKSTRAND, Brian E (Mil) 804 E Juneau Ave, Milwaukee, WI 53202
BACKUS, Brett Paul (ETenn) The Episcopal Church of the Ascension, 800 S. Northshore Drive, Knoxville, TN 37919
BACKUS, Howard G (NC) 600 South Central Avenue, Laurel, DE 19956
BACKUS, Timothy Warren (CGC) PO Box 12683, Pensacola, FL 32591
BACON JR, J(ames) Edwin (Los) 132 N Euclid Ave, Pasadena, CA 91101
BACON, Lynne Lazier (Neb) 719 Crestridge Rd, Omaha, NE 68154
BACON JR, Robert (Mass) 51 Ledgelawn Ave, Lexington, MA 02420
BADDERS JR, John David (WTex) 11 Saint Lukes Ln, San Antonio, TX 78209
BADE, James Robert (Az) 6300 N Central Ave, Phoenix, AZ 85012
BADER-SAYE, Demery Letisha (Be) 334 Knapp Rd, Clarks Summit, PA 18411
BADGETT, Benjamin R (WTenn)

BAER, Kirsten Herndon (Okla) 13316 SW 3rd St, Yukon, OK 73099

BAER, Timothy Christopher (Okla) 13316 SW 3rd St, Yukon, OK 73099

BAER, Walter Jacob (Eur) Graf Seilern-Gasse 20, Vienna, 1120, Austria

BAETZ III, Bert (Tex) 7307 Quiet Glen Dr, Sugar Land, TX 77479

BAGAY, Martin John (At)

BAGBY, D. Ray (Tex) PO Box 510, Cameron, TX 76520

BAGBY, John B. (Ala) 3516 Country Club Road, Birmingham,, AL 35213

BAGGETT, Heather Kathleen (ND) 601 N 4th St, Bismarck, ND 58501

BAGLEY, Robert Chambers (Mil) 4701 Erie St, Racine, WI 53402

BAGUER II, Miguel A (SeFla) 300 Sunrise Dr Apt 1b, Key Biscayne, FL 33149

BAGUYOS, Avelino T (Kan) PO Box 40222, Overland Park, KS 66204

BAGWELL, Robert Randall McDonald (Mass) 401 E 60th St, Savannah, GA 31405

BAHLOW, Harold (ETenn) 4026 Starview Lane, Evans, GA 30809

BAILEY, Anne Cox (Cal) 1944 Tice Valley Blvd., Walnut Creek, CA 94595

BAILEY, Audrey Veronica (NY) 777 E 222nd St, Bronx, NY 10467

BAILEY, B(Ertram) Cass (Va) 1118 Preston Ave, Charlottesville, VA 22903

BAILEY, Charles James (Lex)

BAILEY, Charles Leroy (Alb) 15 Richards Ave, Oneonta, NY 13820

BAILEY, David Bruce (SO) 9097 Cascara Dr, West Chester, OH 45069

✠ **BAILEY**, David Earle (Bp of NAM 2010-) PO Box 720, Farmington, NM 87499

BAILEY III, Douglass Moxley (NC)

BAILEY, Edwin Pearson (NC) Po Box 2001, Southern Pines, NC 28388

BAILEY, Frank Hudson (Md) 7474 Washington Blvd, Elkridge, MD 21075

BAILEY, Gregory Bruce (Alb) Trinity Episcopal Church, 30 Park St, Gouverneur, NY 13642

BAILEY, Jefferson Moore (Az) PO Box 492, Tucson, AZ 85702

BAILEY, Lydia Collins (O) 21000 Lake Shore Blvd, Euclid, OH 44123

BAILEY, Marjean (NH) 21 Kings Ln, Kennebunkport, ME 04046

BAILEY, Noel Ahlbum (RI) St Luke's Episcopal Church, 99 Pierce St, East Greenwich, RI 02818

BAILEY, Patricia Ann (RI) 1357 Wampanoag Trl, Apt 130, Riverside, RI 02915

BAILEY, Paul Milton (La) Po Box 1086, Hammond, LA 70404

BAILEY, Pauline Rose (Alb) 15 Richards Ave, Oneonta, NY 13820

BAILEY, Ralph Lomax (Colo) 1303 S Bross Ln, Longmont, CO 80501

BAILEY, Ricardo Z (At) 2744 Peachtree Rd NW, Atlanta, GA 30305

BAILEY SR, Robert Jerome (RG) 1505 Knudsen Ave, Farmington, NM 87401

BAILEY, Sarah (WVa) 401 S Washington St, Berkeley Springs, WV 25411

BAILEY, S(tephanie) Abbott (Va) 423 1/2 S Laurel St., Richmond, VA 23220

BAILEY III, Theodore Harbour (SVa) 133 Leon Dr, Williamsburg, VA 23188

BAILEY FISCHER, Valerie Dianne (Nwk) 283 Herrick Avenue, Teaneck, NJ 07666

BAILLARGEON JR, Henri Albert (SVa) 4604 Sewaha St, Tampa, FL 33617

BAIN, Robert Walker (WMass)

BAIRD, Gary Clifton (Ark) 617 Tahleguah, Siloan Springs, AR 72761

BAIRD, Kathryn Jo Anne (Az) 4442 E Bermuda St, Tucson, AZ 85712

BAIRD, Lynn (Cal) 1026 Springhouse Dr, Ambler, PA 19002

BAIRD, Stephen Earl (Colo) PO Box 1000, Vail, CO 81658

BAKAL, Pamela (Nwk) 200 Highfield Ln, Nutley, NJ 07110

BAKELY, Catherine Mae (SVa) P.O. Box 186, Oak Hall, VA 23416

BAKER, Andrea (The Episcopal NCal) 2620 Capitol Ave, Sacramento, CA 95816

BAKER, Brian Neal (The Episcopal NCal) 1160 Los Molinos Way, Sacramento, CA 95864

BAKER, Brock (Alb) PO Box 1374, Lake Placid, NY 12946

BAKER, Bruce D'Aubert (Be) St Mary's Episcopal Church, 100 W Windsor St, Reading, PA 19601

BAKER, Carenda D (CPa) 206 E Burd St, Shippensburg, PA 17257

BAKER JR, Charles Mulford (Ct) PO Box 296, Gales Ferry, CT 06335

BAKER, Clarence Dawson (Ark) 692 Poplar Ave, Memphis, TN 38105

BAKER, Douglas Macintyre (NJ)

BAKER, Frank Danforth (Mass) 7 Sturtevant St, Waterville, ME 04901

BAKER, Gene Powell (Dal) 14500 Marsh Lane, Apt. 176, Addison, TX 75001

BAKER, J Jeffrey (O) 160 Keagler Dr, Steubenville, OH 43953

BAKER, Johanna Michelle (NwPa) 62 Pickering St., Brookville, PA 15825

BAKER, John Marcus (Va) 8531 Riverside Rd, Alexandria, VA 22308

BAKER JR, John Thurlow (Cal) 2055 Northshore Rd, Bellingham, WA 98226

BAKER, Joseph Scott (SVa) St. Stephen's Episcopal Church, 372 Hiden Blvd., Newport News, VA 23606

BAKER, Josephine Louise (Pa) Po Box 429, Wayne, PA 19087

BAKER, K. Drew (SwVa) 2411 Shiraz Lane, Charleston, SC 29414

BAKER, Kim Turner (WA) St. Peter and St. Paul, Mt. St. Albans, Washington, DC 20016

BAKER, Mark James (At) 126 wild horse cove circle, cleveland, GA 30528

BAKER, Mathew Scott (Alb) PO Box 183, Greenwich, NY 12834

BAKER, M Clark (Tenn) 780 Laurel Branch Trl, Sewanee, TN 37375

BAKER, Milledge Leonard (CGC) 699 S Hwy 95A, Cantonment, FL 32533

BAKER, Patricia Thomas (Oly) PO Box 369, Snoqualmie, WA 98065

BAKER, Paul Edgar (Alb) 4 St Lukes Pl, Cambridge, NY 12816

BAKER, Rhonda (Va) Po Box 59, Goochland, VA 23063

BAKER, Richard Henry (Mo) 3139 Barrett Station Rd, Saint Louis, MO 63122

BAKER, Robert O (SwFla) 906 S Orleans Ave, Tampa, FL 33606

BAKER, Ruth Louise (Mont) 52120 Lake Mary Ronan Rd, Proctor, MT 59929

BAKER, Shireen Ruth (Los) 202 Avenida Aragon, San Clemente, CA 92672

BAKER, Stannard (Vt) 2 Cherry St., Burlington, VT 05401

BAKER-BORJESON, Susan C (Alb) 3425 South Atlantic Avenue, #1006, Daytona Beach Shores, FL 32118

BAKER-WRIGHT, Michelle (Los) 1325 Monterey Rd, South Pasadena, CA 91030

BAKKER, Cheryl Anne (CFla) 7416 W Seven Rivers Dr, Crystal River, FL 34429

BAKKER, Greg (Episcopal SJ) 41 Station Road, Sholing, Southampton, SO19 8FN, Great Britain (UK)

BAKKUM, Carleton Benjamin (SVa) PO Box 123, Yorktown, VA 23690

BALCOM, John Murray (Mass) 2 Autumn Ln, Amherst, MA 01002

BALDRIDGE SR, Kempton Dunn (Eur) 605 Woodland Drive, Paducah, KY 42001

BALDWIN, Allan (WMass)

BALDWIN, Charles Walter (At) P.O. Box 123, Madison, GA 30650

BALDWIN, Frederick Stephen (NJ) 1710 Restoration Court, Charleston, SC 29414

BALDWIN, Gary Lee (CGC) 126 Alexander Drive, Brewton, AL 36426

BALDWIN, Gayle R (Wyo) ????, Greybull, WY 82426

BALDWIN, Jerome Maynard (SO) 9477 N Maura Ln., Brown Deer, WI 53223

BALDWIN, John Anson (SVa) 5181 Singleton Way, Virginia Beach, VA 23462

BALDWIN, Judith (Nwk) 119 Main St, Millburn, NJ 07041

BALDWIN, Marilyn Elizabeth (Minn) 1387 Park St, White Bear Lake, MN 55110

BALDWIN, Robert Evan (Kan) 1011 Vermont St, Lawrence, KS 66044

BALDWIN, Victoria Evelyn (Ct) 27 Babcock Ave, Plainfield, CT 06374

BALDWIN-MCGINNIS, Carissa E. (Los) 1220 Omar St, Houston, TX 77008

BALDYGA, Andrea Paula (Be) 69 Pleasant St, Sayre, PA 18840

BALES, Janice (RG) 3112 La Mancha Pl Nw, Albuquerque, NM 87104

BALES, Joshua M (CFla)

BALES, William Oliver (SO) 29405 Blosser Rd, Logan, OH 43138

BALFE, Martin Kevin (Minn) 315 State St W, Cannon Falls, MN 55009

BALICKI, John Andrew (Me) 104 Echo Rd, Brunswick, ME 04011

BALKE JR, Steven M (Ind) 601 Columbus Ave, Waco, TX 76701

✠ **BALL**, David Standish (Ret Bp of Alb 1998-) 3 Park Hill Dr Apt 5, Albany, NY 11204

BALL, Edwin (CFla) 3740 Pinebrook Cir, Bradenton, FL 34209

BALL, John Arthur (WA) 46455 Hyatt Ct, Drayden, MD 20630

BALL JR, John Coming (SC) 1 Bishop Gadsden Way, Apt 155, Charleston, SC 29412

BALL, Raymond Carl (Dal) 5421 Victor St, Dallas, TX 75214

BALLANTINE, Lucia P (NY) 402 Route 22, North Salem, NY 10560

BALLARD, J. Christopher (LI) St Lukes and St Matthew's Episcopal Church, 520 Clinton Ave, Brooklyn, NY 11238

BALLARD, James David (Vt) 139 Sanderson Rd, Milton, VT 05468

BALLARD JR, Joseph Howard (Tenn) 216 University Ave, Sewanee, TN 37375

BALLARD, Kathleen Miller (Nwk)

BALL-DAMBERG, Sarah (NC) 1014 Monmouth Ave, Durham, NC 27701

BALLENTINE JR, George Young (SVa) 305 Park Blvd N, Venice, FL 34285

BALLENTINE, Jabriel Simmons (CFla) 1000 Bethune Dr, Orlando, FL 32805

BALLERT JR, Irving Frank (Alb) 25 Sharon St, Sidney, NY 13838

BALLEW, Thelma Johnanna (NH) 1 Park Ct, Durham, NH 03824

BALLING, Valerie L (NJ) 142 Sand Hill Road, Monmouth Junction, NJ 08852

BALLINGER, Carolyn Tucker (WK)

BALLINGER, Kathryn Elisabeth (Oly) 9210 Ne 123rd St, Kirkland, WA 98034

BALLOU, Diedre Schuler (NwT)

BALMER, Randall (Ct) 720 Pattrell Road, Norwich, VT 05055

BALMER, William John (NJ) 380 Sycamore Ave, Shrewsbury, NJ 07702

BALTUS, D(onald) Barrington (NY) 123 E 15th St # 1504, New York, NY 10003

BALTZ, Ann Marie Halpin (Ida) 8947 Springhurst Dr, Boise, ID 83704

BALTZ, Francis Burkhardt (At) 369 Merrydale Dr SW, Marietta, GA 30064

BAMBERGER, Michael Andrew (Los) 241 Ramona Ave, Sierra Madre, CA 91024

BAMBRICK, Barbara Ann (SeFla) 1802 Pine St, Perry, IA 50220

BAMFORD, Marilyn Halverson (Minn) PO Box 3247, Duluth, MN 55803

BAMFORTH, Richard Anderson (Me) Po Box 5068, Augusta, ME 04332

BANAKIS, Kathryn Loretta (Chi) 939 Hinman Ave, Evanston, IL 60202

BANCROFT, John Galloway (At) 1865 Highway 20 W, Mcdonough, GA 30253

BANCROFT, Stephen Haltom (Mich) 27310 Wellington Rd, Franklin, MI 48025

BANDY, Talmage Gwaltney (NC) 22 Bogie Dr, Whispering Pines, NC 28327

✠ **BANE JR**, David Conner (Ret Bp of SVa 2006-) 163 Pelican Pointe Dr, Elizabeth City, NC 27909

BANE, Jack Donald (NY) 210 Old North Rd, St Paul's Episcopal Church, Camden, DE 19934

BANKOWSKI, Thomas (CFla) 1250 Paige Pl, The Villages, FL 32159

BANKS, Cynthia Kay (WNC) 272 Maple Ridge Dr, Boone, NC 28607

BANKS JR, Frederick David (Ky) 2541 Southview Dr, Lexington, KY 40503

BANKS JR, Ralph Alton (SeFla)

BANKS, Richard Allan (La) 1444 Cabrini Ct, New Orleans, LA 70122

BANKSTON, Van A (Be) 509 W Pine St, Hattiesburg, MS 39401

BANNER, Daniel Lee (Chi) 2431 Bradmoor Dr, Quincy, IL 62301

BANNER, Shelly Ann (CNY) 41 Highmore Dr, Oswego, NY 13126

BANSE JR, Robert Lee (Va) 221 Orr Rd, Pittsburgh, PA 15241

BAPTISTE-WILLIAMS, Barbara Jeanne (SeFla) 6041 Sw 63rd Ct, Miami, FL 33143

BARBARITO, Melanie Repko (FtW) 5005 Dexter Ave, Fort Worth, TX 76107

BARBER, Barbara Jean (Kan) 5518 Sw 17th Ter, Topeka, KS 66604

BARBER, Elaine Elizabeth Clyborne (Minn) 4830 Acorn Ridge Rd, Minnetonka, MN 55345

BARBER, Grant Woodward (Mass) 102 Branch St., Scituate, MA 02066

BARBER, Grethe Hallberg (Oly) 690 N Shepherd Rd, Washougal, WA 98671

BARBER, James Frederick (FtW) 3217 Chaparral Ln, Fort Worth, TX 76109

BARBER, James S (Mo) 313 W Hardy St, Saint James, MO 65559

BARBER JR, Vernon H (Eau) 502 County Road Ff, Hudson, WI 54016

BARBERIA, Kristin Neily (Los) c/o St. Matthew's Parish School, 1031

Bienveneda Avenue, Pacific Palisades, CA 90272

BARBOUR, Grady Frederic Waddell (Ala) 565 12th Ct, Pleasant Grove, AL 35127

BARBUTO, Judith Steele (U) 11146 S Heather Grove Ln, South Jordan, UT 84095

BARDEN III, Albert A (Ct) 254 Father Rasle Rd, Norridgewock, ME 04957

BARDOS, Gordon A (Vt) 9449 N 110th Ave, Sun City, AZ 85351

BARDSLEY, Nancy Louise (Ida) 1154 Camps Canyon Rd, Troy, ID 83871

BARDUSCH JR, Richard Evans (Mass) PO Box 149, Taunton, MA 02780

BARFIELD, David S (Ala) 156 S 9th St, Gadsden, AL 35901

BARFIELD, DeOla Edwina (Ct) 744 Lakeside Dr, Bridgeport, CT 06606

BARFIELD, Karen Clay (NC) 501 E Poplar Ave, Carrboro, NC 27510

BARFIELD, William G (Ind) PO Box 141, Danville, IN 46122

BARFORD, Lee Alton (ECR) 561 Keystone Ave #434, Reno, NV 89503

BARGETZI, David Michael (O) 1417 Larchmont Ave, Lakewood, OH 44107

BARGIEL, Mary Victoria (Ind) 3243 N Meridian St, Indianapolis, IN 46208

BARHAM, Patsy Griffin (Tex) St Matthew's Episcopal Church, 214 College Ave, Henderson, TX 75654

BARKER, Ann Biddle (Va) 6231 Kilmer Ct, Falls Church, VA 22044

BARKER, Christie Dalton (NC) 981 Valiant Dr., Statesville, NC 28677

BARKER, Christopher Haskins (Pgh) 1062 Old Orchard Dr, Gibsonia, PA 15044

BARKER, Daniel W (CNY) 324 Harding Ave, Vestal, NY 13850

BARKER, Gary Joseph (Va) 111 S Church St, Smithfield, VA 23430

BARKER, Herbert James (SanD) 11727 Mesa Verde Dr, Valley Center, CA 92082

✠ **BARKER**, J. Scott (Bp of Neb 2011-) 109 N 18th St, Omaha, NE 68102

BARKER, Joann D (Del) 241 Louisiana Circl, Sewanee, TN 37375

BARKER, Kenneth Lee (CGC) 9409 E 65th St, Tulsa, OK 74133

BARKER, Lynn Kay (Miss) 29 Melody Ln, Purvis, MS 39475

BARKER, Patrick Morgan (Ark) 1521 Mcarthur Dr, Jacksonville, AR 72076

BARKER, Paula Suzanne (Md) St Alban's Church, 105 1st Ave SW, Glen Burnie, MD 21061

BARLEY, Linda Elizabeth (SwFla) 10922 106th Ave, Largo, FL 33778

BARLOWE, Michael (Cal) 815 Second Avenue, New York, NY 10017

BARNARD, N. Sandra (ECR) 1267 Black Sage Cir, Nipomo, CA 93444

BARNES JR, Bennett Herbert (SwFla) 7 Fiddlehead Fern TRL, Brunswick, ME 04011

BARNES, Charles Richard (EO) Po Box 317, Hermiston, OR 97838
BARNES, Jeffry Parker (SD) 21285 E Highway 20 Apt 127, Bend, OR 97701
BARNES, John David (Ala) P.O. Box 560, 401 N Main Ave, Demopolis, AL 36732
BARNES, Rebecca A (Be) 20 Cumming St, New York, NY 10034
BARNES, Robert Dean (WVa)
BARNES, Susan Johnston (Minn) St John The Baptist Episc Ch, 4201 Sheridan Ave S, Minneapolis, MN 55410
BARNETT, Andrew Kreussel (Los) 4705 Laurel Canyon Blvd Ste 200, Valley Village, CA 91607
BARNETT, Becca Fleming (Cal) 435 Euclid Ave Apt 1, San Francisco, CA 94118
BARNETT, Edwin Wilson (FtW) 808 Voltamp Dr., Fort Worth, TX 76108
BARNETT, Maxine (LI) Church Of Saint Jude, 3606 Lufberry Ave, Wantagh, NY 11793
BARNETT, Thomas C (EC) 1219 Forest Hills Dr., Wilmington, NC 28403
BARNEY, David Marshall (Mass) 310 Hayward Mill Rd, Concord, MA 01742
BARNEY, Roger Alexander (ECR) 19040 Portos Dr, Saratoga, CA 95070
BARNHILL JR, James Wallance (USC) Grace Episcopal Church And Kindergarten, 1315 Lyttleton St, Camden, SC 29020
BARNHOUSE, David H (Los) 6844 Penham Pl, Pittsburgh, PA 15208
BARNS, G(eorge) Stewart (Mass) Po Box 381164, Cambridge, MA 02238
BARNUM, Barbara Coxe (Los) 11359 Perris Blvd, Moreno Valley, CA 92557
BARNUM, Elena (Ct) 112 Bentwood Dr, Stamford, CT 06903
BARNUM, Malcolm McGregor (Ct) 112 Bentwood Dr, Stamford, CT 06903
BARNWELL, William (La) 1917 Audubon St, New Orleans, LA 70118
BARON, Christian John (WMich) 555 Michigan Ave, Holland, MI 49423
BARON, Jodi Lynn (WMich) 555 Michigan Ave, Holland, MI 49423
BAROODY, Roger Anis (NY) 218 Luke Mountain Rd, Covington, VA 24426
BARR, David Lee (Fla) 8227 Bateau Rd S, Jacksonville, FL 32216
BARR, Donna (Lex) 2140 Woodmont Dr, Lexington, KY 40502
BARR, Gillian Rachel (RI) 275 N Main St, Providence, RI 02903
BARR, Jane Wallace (Va) 209 Macarthur Rd, Alexandria, VA 22305
BARR, Norma M (Chi)
BARRAGAN, Juan (Los) 9046 Gallatin Rd., Pico Rivera, CA 90660
BARRAZA, Rene (Los) St Athanasius and St Paul's, 840 Echo Park Ave, Los Angeles, CA 90026

BARRE, James Lyman (Vt) 1009 Robert E. Lee Drive, Wilmington, NC 28412
BARRERA FLORES, Olga I (Hond) IMS SAP Dept 215. PO BOX 523900, Miami, FL 33152-3900, Honduras
BARRETT, Constance Yvonne (Mil) 3560 N Summit Ave, Shorewood, WI 53211
BARRETT, J Richard (Tex) St Martin's Episcopal Church, 1602 S Fm 116, Copperas Cove, TX 76522
BARRETT, Johanna Elizabeth Langley (Mass) Trinity Church, 124 River Road, Topsfield, MA 01983
BARRETT, John Hammond (WTex) 3527 Vancouver Dr, Dallas, TX 75229
BARRETT JR, John Henry (CNY) 41 S Woody Hill Rd, Westerly, RI 02891
BARRETT, Patricia (Mass)
BARRETT, Regina Leigh (CPa)
BARRETT, Rilla Diane (Oly) 670 Rainbow Dr, Sedro-Woolley, WA 98284
BARRETT, Robin Carter (EO) 9310 Parakeet Dr, Bonanza, OR 97623
BARRETT, Sr Helena (Nwk)
BARRETT, Timothy Lewis (Nwk) 10 Crestmont Rd, Montclair, NJ 07042
BARRIE, David Paul (NY) 2109 Broadway # 1241, New York, NY 10023
BARRINGTON, Dominic M J (Chi) 65 E Huron St, Chicago, IL 60611
BARRINGTON JR, E Tom (Mass) 27 6th Ave, North Chelmsford, MA 01863
BARRIOS, Luis (NY) 295 Saint Anns Ave, Bronx, NY 10454
BARRIOS, Maria Trevino (Dal) 534 W 10th St, Dallas, TX 75208
BARRON JR, Caldwell Alexander (SC) 168 Club Cir, Pawleys Island, SC 29585
BARRON, Carol Dunn (SeFla) 3954 SE Fairway E, Stuart, FL 34997
BARRON, Scott William (Chi) 1148 N Douglas Ave, Arlington Heights, IL 60004
BARROW, Alan Lester (Okla) 5635 E. 71st St., Tulsa, OK 74136
BARROW, Colin Vere (SO) 8592 Roswell Rd Apt.218, Sandy Springs, GA 30350
BARROW, John Condict Hurst (Ind) 8920 Washington Blvd West Dr, Indianapolis, IN 46240
BARROW, John Thomas (Episcopal SJ) Po Box 3231, Mammoth Lakes, CA 93546
BARROW, Suzanne Hurst (Ky)
BARROWCLOUGH, Lisa Shirley (SeFla) St. Mark's Episcopal Church and School, 3395 Burns Road, Palm Beach Gardens, FL 33410
BARROWS, Jennifer Eve (NY) 1585 Route 9 West, West Park, NY 12493
BARRUS, Donald Sidney (Fla) 516 Balmora Dr, St Augustine, FL 32092
BARRY, Eugenia (WNC) 11 Lone Pine Rd, Asheville, NC 28803

BARRY, Peggy Sue (Ark) 400 Hill St, Forrest City, AR 72335
BARRY-MARQUESS, Richard Livingston (SeFla) 19540 Nw 8th Ave, Miami, FL 33169
BARTA, Heather Marie (EMich) 156 Guanonocque St, Auburn Hills, MI 48326
BARTELS, Judith Tallman (Oly) none----moved from there, lacey, WA 98117
BARTH, Barbara L (Me) 42 Tailwind Ct Apt 78 D, Auburn, ME 04210
BARTHELEMY, Paul Berge (Ore) 4524 Trillium Woods, Lake Oswego, OR 97035
BARTHOLOMEW, Gilbert Leinbach (NY) 802 Broadway, New York, NY 10003
BARTHOLOMEW, Linda M (Spok) Church Of The Resurrection, 15319 E 8th Ave, Spokane Valley, WA 99037
BARTLE, Edward Bartholomew (CFla) 330 Hickory Ave, Orange City, FL 32763
BARTLE, John Dixon (Alb) Po Box E, Richfield Springs, NY 13439
BARTLE, Leonard William (CFla) 3520 Curtis Dr, Apopka, FL 32703
BARTLE, Phyllis Ann (CFla) 330 Hickory Ave, Orange City, FL 32763
✠ **BARTLETT JR**, Allen Lyman (Ret Bp of Pa 1998-) 600 E. Cathedral Rd., Apt. L-209, Philadelphia, PA 19128
BARTLETT, Anne Kristin (Ore) 281 Talent Ave, Talent, OR 97540
BARTLETT, Basil A (VI) PO Box 7386, St Thomas, VI 00801
BARTLETT, Harwood (At) 4345 Erskine Rd, Clarkston, GA 30021
BARTLETT, Laurie Lee (Alb) Calvary Church, PO Box 41, Burnt Hills, NY 12027
BARTLETT, Lois Sherburne (Be) 2716 Tennyson Ave, Sinking Spring, PA 19608
BARTLETT, Stephen I(Ves) (WMich) 8975 Shawbacoung Trail, Shelby, MI 49455
BARTLETT, Susan Mansfield (Mo) 906 Mallard Sq, Rolla, MO 65401
BARTOLOMEO, Michael Edward (LI) 124 Balaton Ave, Lake Ronkonkoma, NY 11779
BARTON, Anne Whitlock (Spok) 5205 Sycamore Dr, Yakima, WA 98901
BARTON, Charles D H (Mass) 3602 Stembridge Ct, Wilmington, NC 28409
BARTON, Charles Lee (Md) 3101 Monkton Rd, Monkton, MD 21111
BARTON JR, John Clib (Ark) 1024 Stanford Dr Ne, Albuquerque, NM 87106
BARTON JR, Lane Wickham (Cal) 12616 Se 11th St, Vancouver, WA 98683
BARTON III, William Henderson (Tenn) Trinity Episcopal Church, 213 1st Ave NW, Winchester, TN 37398

BARTUSCH, Robert Frederic (WTenn) 2851 Neeley St # 113, Batesville, AR 72501

BARTZ, James Perkins (Los) 6343 W 82nd St, Los Angeles, CA 90045

BARWICK III, Frederick Ernest (NC) 5941 Leasburg Rd., Roxboro, NC 27574

BARWICK, Mark (Eur) avenue du Préau 16, Brussels, 01040, Belgium

BASCOM, Cathleen (Ia) Cathedral Church of St. Paul, 815 High Street, Des Moines, IA 50309

BASDEN, Michael Paul (SwFla) 495 Galleon Dr, Naples, FL 34102

BASINGER JR, Elvin David (Ala) 21526 Silver Oaks Circle, Athens, AL 35613

BASKERVILLE-BURROWS, Jennifer Lynn (Chi)

BASKIN, Cynthia (WA) 10924 Citreon Ct, N Potomac, MD 20878

BASS-CHOATE, Yamily (NY) 4 Gateway Rd, Unit 1-D, Yonkers, NY 10703

BASSUENER, Barbara A. (Eas) 20 3rd St, Pocomoke City, MD 21851

BAST, Robert Lee (Eas) 201 Crosstown Dr Apt 3013, Peachtree City, GA 30269

BASTIAN, Martin James (Tex) 6623 Minola St, Houston, TX 77007

BATARSEH, Peter Bahjat (Tenn) 312 Battle Avenue, Franklin, TN 37064

BATCHELDER JR, Kelsey (NY)

BATEMAN, David S (CPa) 3312 Brisban St, Harrisburg, PA 17111

BATES, Allen Layfield (Ark) 1902 W Magnolia St, Rogers, AR 72758

BATES, (Charlotte) Chere (Chi) 15136 S. Dillman, Plainfield, IL 60544

BATES, J Barrington (Nwk) 15 Warren St Unit 117, Jersey City, NJ 07302

BATES, James Brent (Nwk) 31 Woodland Ave, Summit, NJ 07901

BATES, Margaret Knop (CNY) 5623 Mack Rd, Skaneateles, NY 13152

BATES, Percy Quin (La)

BATES, Robert Seaton (Chi) 121 W Macomb St, Belvidere, IL 61008

BATES, Steven Byron (CGC) 508 S Market St, Scottsboro, AL 35768

BATES, Stuart Alan (Tex) 345 Piney Point Rd, Houston, TX 77024

BATES, Thomas Justin (RG)

BATIZ MEJIA, Jose David (Hond) IMS SAP Dept 215, PO BOX 523900, Miami, FL 33152-3900, Honduras

BATKIN, Jeffrey Alan (Fla)

BATSON, Lloyd Samuel (Nwk) 160 W South Orange Ave, South Orange, NJ 07079

BATSON, Sara Chapman (Pa) 117 Sagewood Dr, Malvern, PA 19355

BATSON III, Stephen Radford (NY) 3721 Wares Ferry Rd Apt 500, Montgomery, AL 36109

BATTLE, Michael Jesse (NC) 1611 East Millbrook Rd, Raleigh, NC 27609

BATTON JR, Robert Nolton (RG) 4304 Carlisle Blvd NE, Albuquerque, NM 87107

BAUER, Audrey (NMich) 6837 Lahti Ln, Pellston, MI 49769

BAUER, Kathryn Ann (WMo) Po Box 996, Kremmling, CO 80459

BAUER, Ronald Coleman (Los) 27292 Via Callejon Unit B, San Juan Capistrano, CA 92675

BAUER, Thomas William (Md) 3148 Gracefield Rd Apt CL412, Silver Spring, MD 20904

✠ **BAUERSCHMIDT**, John Crawford (Bp of Tenn 2007-) 50 Vantage Way Ste 107, Nashville, TN 37228

BAUGHMAN, David Lee (Chi) 804 James Court, Wheaton, IL 60189

BAUKNIGHT JR, Mack Miller (SwFla) 2440 26th Ave S, Saint Petersburg, FL 33712

BAUM, Denis Blaine (CGC) 532 Skyline Drive, N Little Rock, AR 72116

BAUM, George R (O) 13415 Ardoon Ave, Cleveland, OH 44120

BAUM, Nancy Louise (Mich) 411 Walnut St, Green Cove Springs, FL 32043

BAUMAN, Dwayne Ray (Ark) 176 State Road YY, Tunas, MO 65764

BAUMAN, Ward J (Minn) 1111 Upton Ave N, Minneapolis, MN 55411

BAUMANN, David Michael (Spr) PO Box 303, Salem, IL 62881

BAUMGARTEN, Betsy Ann (Miss) 14294 John Lee Road, Biloxi, MS 39532

BAUMGARTEN, Jonathan David (Chi) 41 E. 8th St. Apt. 2001, Chicago, IL 60605

BAUMGARTEN, William Paul (Mont) 845 2nd Ave E, Kalispell, MT 59901

BAUSCHARD, Michael Robert Thomas (NwPa) 5 Cottage Pl, Warren, PA 16365

BAUSTIAN, Donald Edward (Ark) 1801 20th St Unit K-15, Ames, IA 50010

BAUTISTA, Simon (Tex) Christ Church Cathedral, 1117 Texas St, Houston, TX 77002

BAVARO, Carolyn Margaret (Chi) P.O. Box 30247, Chicago, IL 60630

BAXLEY, Todd Lee (NwT) 1601 S Georgia St, Amarillo, TX 79102

BAXTER, Barbara (WNY) 16 N Phetteplace St, Falconer, NY 14733

BAXTER JR, Donald Leslie (NwPa) 300 Hilltop Rd, Erie, PA 16509

BAXTER, Jane (CNY) 151 Hawkins Rjoad, Ferrisburgh, VT 05456

BAXTER, Lisette Dyer (Vt) 112 Lakewood Pkwy, Burlington, VT 05408

BAXTER, Nancy Julia (At) 1223 Clifton Rd NE, Atlanta, GA 30307

✠ **BAXTER**, Nathan Dwight (Ret Bp of CPa 2014-) 115 N Duke St, Lancaster, PA 17602

BAXTER, Philip Roland (Va) 612 South Ingraham Avenue, Lakeland, FL 33801

BAXTER, Rae Lee (Mich) 430 Nicolet St, Walled Lake, MI 48390

BAYACA, Greg G(uerrero) (Los)

BAYANG, Martin Eugenio (RG) 1406 S Cliff Dr, Gallup, NM 87301

BAYFIELD, Ralph Wesley (Va) 300 Westminster Canterbury Dr Apt 405, Apt 405, Winchester, VA 22603

BAYLES, Joseph Austin (Kan) 1341 N River Blvd, Wichita, KS 67203

BAYLES, Richard Allen (Oly) Po Box 1115, South Bend, WA 98586

BAYNE, Bruce George Cuthbert (Cal) 2875 Idledwild Dr, #108, Reno, NV 89505

BAYNES, Leopold Cornelius (LI)

BAYS, Terri (NI) 84 Broadway, New Haven, CT 06511

BAZIN, Jean Jacques Emmanuel Fritz (SeFla) 525 NE 15 Street, Miami, FL 33132

BEACH, Deborah Elizabeth (Alb) 132 Duanesburg - Churches Road, Duanesburg, NY 12056

BEACH, Diana Lee (Nwk) 88 Main Street, Thomaston, ME 04861

BEACH, John Tappan (Eur) 39, Route De Malagnou, Geneva, 01208, Switzerland

BEACH, Joseph Lawrence (ETenn) 4768 Edens View Rd, Kingsport, TN 37664

BEACH, Kay Joan (Ia) 201 E Church St, Marshalltown, IA 50158

BEACHAM III, Albert Burton (U) 1420 N 3000 W, Vernal, UT 84078

BEACHY, William Nicholas (WMo) 431 W 60th Ter, Kansas City, MO 64113

BEAL, Jennifer D (Los) 1745 Wedgewood Cmn, Concord, MA 01742

BEAL, M(adeleine) Elizabeth (Me) 35 Beal Rd, Chesterville, ME 04938

BEAL, Stephen Thomas (The Episcopal NCal) 2301 Polk St, Apt 3, San Francisco, CA 94109

BEALE, Mary I (NH) 45 Derryfield Ct, Manchester, NH 03104

BEALE, Norman Victor (Mass) 141 W. Oak St., Ramsey, NJ 07446

BEALES, Rosemary E (Va) St Stephen's & St Agnes School, 400 Fontaine St, Alexandria, VA 22302

BEALL, Nathan Andrew (WA) PO Box 207, St Marys City, VA 20686

BEAM, Barbara Jean (WMo) 6336 SE Hamilton Rd, Lathrop, MO 64465

BEAM, Marcia Mckay (SeFla)

BEAMER, Charles Wesley (O) 3920 Spokane Ave, Cleveland, OH 44109

BEAN, Kevin D (WMass) All Saints Church, 10 Irving St., Worcester, MA 01609

BEAN, Rebecca Anne (EC) PO Box 1333, Goldsboro, NC 27533

BEANE, Emmetri Monica (Va) PO Box 367, Rixeyville, VA 22737

BEAR, Susan Dowler (Miss) 3600 Arlington Loop, Hattiesburg, MS 39402

BEARD, Bryan Benjamin (Okla) 9309 N 129th East Ave, Owasso, OK 74055

BEARDEN, Jane Bostick (Mass) 77 Westchester Dr, Haverhill, MA 01830

BEASLEY, Battle Alexander (Tenn) 1613 Fatherland St, Nashville, TN 37206

BEASLEY, Carl H (Eas) 1196, Apt B Firetower Rd, Colora, MD 21917

BEASLEY, Christopher Ryan (Ind)

BEASLEY, Helen Roberts (SwVa) Po Box 1266, Galax, VA 24333

BEASLEY, Nicholas Madden (USC) 126 Blyth Avenue, Greenwood, SC 29649

BEASLEY, Robert (ETenn) 121 E. Harper Avenue, Maryville, TN 37804

BEASLEY JR, Thomas Edward (Fla) 6003 Brookridge Rd, Jacksonville, FL 32210

BEASON, Kenneth G (ECR) 438 N 5th St, Cheney, WA 99004

BEATTIE, Richard Edward (Ct) 438 Old Tavern Rd, Orange, CT 06477

BEATTIE, R(ichard) Sherman (Ct) 25 Stuart Dr, Old Greenwich, CT 06870

BEATTY, Anne M (The Episcopal NCal) 1908 Humboldt Ave, Davis, CA 95616

BEATTY, Stephan P (Va) 10267 Lakeridge Square CT, Apt B, Ashland, VA 23005

BEATY, Maureen Kay (Colo) St Mary Magdalene, 4775 Cambridge St, Boulder, CO 80301

BEAUCHAMP, Robert William (SwVa) PO Box 227, Norton, VA 24273

BEAUHARNOIS, Patricia Ann (Alb) 18 Butternut St, Champlain, NY 12919

BEAULAC, David Armand (Alb) St Mary's Church, PO Box 211, Lake Luzerne, NY 12846

BEAULIEU, Cynthia Rae (Me) 650 Main St, Caribou, ME 04736

BEAULIEU, Delores Joyce (Minn) Rr 2 Box 246, Bagley, MN 56621

BEAULIEU, Joyce Elaine (Chi) 223 W Royal Dr, Dekalb, IL 60115

BEAUMONT, Jerrold Foster (CFla) 8494 Ridgewood Ave Apt 4201, Cape Canaveral, FL 32920

BEAUMONT, Katharine Jenetta (Az)

BEAUVOIR, Jonas (Hai) c/o Diocese of Haiti, Boite Postale 1309, Port au Prince Haiti, Haiti

✠ **BEAUVOIR**, Oge (Bp Suffr of Hai 2012-)

BEAVEN, John Clinton (Me) 22 Willow Grove Rd, Brunswick, ME 04011

BEAZLEY, Robert William (Fla)

BEBB JR, Ernest Leo (U) 6452 South 1650 East, Murray, UT 84121

BEBBER, Gerald King (Q) 1821 Mcgougan Rd, Fayetteville, NC 28303

BECHERER, Carl John (Minn)

BECHTEL, A(Lpha) Gillett (Los) 36176 Golden Gate Dr, Yucaipa, CA 92399

BECHTOLD, Bryant Coffin (FtW) 3290 Lackland Rd, Fort Worth, TX 76116

BECK, Brien Patrick (FdL) 347 Libal St, De Pere, WI 54115

BECK, Jacob David (WA) 13 Victor Dr, Thurmont, MD 21788

BECK, Judith Taw (Pa) 3300 W Penn St, Philadelphia, PA 19129

BECK, Laura Eileen (Okla)

BECK, Randall Alan (NwPa) St John's Episcopal Church, 226 W State St, Sharon, PA 16146

BECK, Sue Ann (Los) St. John The Divine, 183 E. Bay St., Costa Mesa, CA 92627

BECK, Tanya (Ind) 5810 Kingsley Dr., Indianapolis, IN 46220

BECK, Thomas Francis (Ct)

BECKER, Arthur Paul (Minn) 2901 Pearson Pkwy, Brooklyn Park, MN 55444

BECKER, C S Honey (The Episcopal Church in Haw) PO Box 819, Kailua, HI 96734

BECKER, Kim (WNC) PO Box 177, Glendale Springs, NC 28629

BECKER, Mary Elizabeth (Ind) 2076 E County Rd 375 S, Winslow, IN 47598

BECKER, Robert Andrew (Va) 1124 Handlebar Rd, Reston, VA 20191

BECKER, Stephen David (Va) 13 Braxton Dr, Sterling, VA 20165

BECKETT, Kimberly Youngblood (Ala) 113 Brown Ave, Rainbow City, AL 35906

BECKETT JR, Norman James (Los) 3157 E Avenue, #B-4, Lancaster, LA 93535, Costa Rica

BECKHAM JR, M. Edwin (At) 1140 Brookwood Dr, Watkinsville, GA 30677

BECKLES, William Anthony (NY) Po Box 1067, Mount Vernon, NY 10551

✠ **BECKWITH**, Mark M (Bp of Nwk 2007-) Episcopal Diocese of Newark, 312 Mulberry St, Newark, NJ 07102

✠ **BECKWITH**, Peter Hess (Ret Bp of Spr 2010-) 7451 E Bacon Rd, Hillsdale, MI 49242

BEDARD, Caren Marie (Minn) 408 N 7th St, Brainerd, MN 56401

BEDDINGFIELD, John (WA) 2745 29th St NW Apt 416, Washington, DC 20008

BEDELL, Bryan Douglas (Roch) 28 Village Trl, Honeoye Falls, NY 14472

BEDFORD, Michael John (Mich) 25831 Lexington Dr Unit 1, South Lyon, MI 48178

BEDINGFIELD, John Davis (WLa) 400 Camellia Blvd, Lafayette, LA 70503

BEDROSIAN, Magar (Ct) 6283 Darien Way, Spring Hill, FL 34606

BEE, Robert D (Neb) 5109 N Jefferson St, Gladstone, MO 64118

BEEBE, Christine Fair (WNC) 395 N Main St, Rutherfordton, NC 28139

BEEBE SR, Fred H (Fla) 124 Peninsular Dr, Crescent City, FL 32112

BEEBE, James Russell (Nev) 205 Mackinaw Ave, Akron, OH 44333

BEEBE SR, Jeffrey Scott (SeFla) 151 S County Rd, Palm Beach, FL 33480

BEEBE, Susan Rafter (SeFla) 151 S County Rd, Palm Beach, FL 33480

BEEBE-BOVE, Polly (Vt) 3 Cathedral Sq Apt 2G, Burlington, VT 05401

BEECHAM, Troy C (Ia) 815 High St, Des Moines, IA 50309

BEECHER, Josefina Cameron (Oly)

BEELEY, Christopher Alfred (Tex) 1527 Sunnymede Ave, South Bend, IN 46615

BEEM, Charles Lee (Be) 9 Plymouth Pl, Wyomissing, PA 19610

BEEMAN, Patricia Houston (O) 220 Pennswood Rd, Bryn Mawr, PA 19010

BEER, David Frank (Tex) 6810 Thistle Hill Way, Austin, TX 78754

BEERS, William Rogers (Chi) 120 1st St, Lodi, WI 53555

BEERY, Susan (U) 228 S Pitt St, Alexandria, VA 22314

BEERY, William Stocktill (NY) 905 Osprey Ct, New Bern, NC 28560

BEHEN, Ralph Joseph (WMo)

BEHM, Nancy Anne (FdL) 1703 Doemel St, Oshkosh, WI 54901

BEHNKE, Cathleen Ann (Mich) 4800 Woodward Ave, Detroit, MI 48201

BEHNSTEDT, Patrice Faith (CFla) 500 W Floral Ave, Bartow, FL 33830

BEHRENS, Marilyn Jean (Oly) 7417 Hill Ave Apt 2, Gig Harbor, WA 98335

BEIKIRCH, Paula Marie (CFla) 4915 Deter Rd, Lakeland, FL 33813

BEILSTEIN, Joan Elizabeth (WA) 400 Hinsdale Ct, Silver Spring, MD 20901

BEIMDIEK, Jill (EC) St. Stephen's Episcopal Church, 200 North James St, Goldsboro, NC 27530

BEIMES, Phyllis Mahilani (The Episcopal Church in Haw)

✠ **BEISNER**, Barry Leigh (Bp of NCal 2006-) Episcopal Diocese Of Northern California, 350 University Ave Ste 280, Sacramento, CA 95825

BEITZEL, Wallace D (U) 9475 Brookside Ave, Ben Lomond, CA 95005

BEIZER, Lance Kurt (ECR) P.O. Box 1047 (9 Blackberry Way), Canaan, CT 06018

BEK, Susan (Los) 3290 Loma Vista Rd, Ventura, CA 93003

BELA, Robert Joseph (Mass) 475 Breeding Loop, Breeding, KY 42715

BELANGER, Fanny Sohet (Eur)

BELASCO, Elizabeth Anne (LI) 612 Forest Ave, Massapequa, NY 11758

BELCHER, Nancy Spencer (Mo) PO Box 6065, Fulton, MO 65251

BELCHER, Sandra Alves (Ct) 165 Grassy Hill Rd, Woodbury, CT 06798

BELKNAP, Charles (Los) 1386 Beddis Road, Salt Spring Island, BC V8K 2C9, Canada

BELKNAP, Sarah Koelling (Los) 2066 Empress Ave, South Pasadena, CA 91030

BELL, Beth Ann (Okla) 13112 N Rockwell Ave, Oklahoma City, OK 73142

BELL, David Allen (Ind) 8320 E 10th St, Indianapolis, IN 46219

BELL, Emily Susan Richardson (Los) 190 Avenida Aragon, San Clemente, CA 92672

BELL, G(erald) Michael (Miss) 602 Riverview Dr, Florence, AL 35630

BELL JR, Hugh Bell (Tex)

BELL, Jocelyn (ETenn) 643 Westview Rd, Chattanooga, TN 37415

BELL, John Michael (WMich) 406 2nd St, Manistee, MI 49660

BELL JR, John Robinson (Oly) 2454 E Palm Canyon Dr # 4d, Palm Springs, CA 92264

BELL, Karl Edwin (Eur) Po Box 171, Fifty Lakes, MN 56448

BELL, (Mary) Cynthia (Mass) 22 Hathaway Pond Circle, Rochester, MA 02770

BELL, Michael S (Los) 5801 Crestridge Rd, Rancho Palos Verdes, CA 90275

BELL, Patrick William (Spok) 501 E Wallace Ave, Coeur D Alene, ID 83814

BELL, Roger Craig (Pgh) 56500 Abbey Rd, Three Rivers, MI 49093

BELL, Susan Endicott (WLa) 403 East Flournoy Lucas Road, 04/01/0158, Shreveport, LA 71115

BELL JR, William R (Md) 2901 Boston St Apt 601, Baltimore, MD 21224

BELL, Winston Alonzo (LI) 2263 Sedgemont Dr, Winston Salem, NC 27103

BELLAIMEY, John Edward (Minn) 4233 Linden Hills Blvd, Minneapolis, MN 55410

BELLAIS, William Frank (WMo) 440 Dickinson St, Chillicothe, MO 64601

BELLIS, Elaine (Chi) 1747 E 93rd St, Chicago, IL 66017

BELLISS, Richard Guy (Los) 25454 Via Heraldo, Santa Clarita, CA 91355

BELLNER, Elisabeth Ann (CFla)

BELLOWS, Carol Hartley (WMass) 33 Fernald Street, Wilton, ME 04294

BELLOWS, Richard S. (WMass) 21 Briarcliff Dr, Westfield, MA 01085

BELLOWS, Scott P (Md) Saint Davids Church, 4700 Roland Ave, Baltimore, MD 21210

BELL-WOLSKI, Dedra Ann (Ga)

BELMONT JR, John C (NJ) 300 S Main St, Pennington, NJ 08534

BELMONTES, Mervyn Lancelot (LI) 812 Nebraska Ave, Bay Shore, NY 11706

BELMORE, Constance (Nev) 4626 Grand Drive #2, Las Vegas, NV 89169

BELMORE JR, Kent (Nev) 4626 Grand Dr Unit 2, Las Vegas, NV 89169

BELNAP, Ron(ald) Victor (U) 8952 Golden Field Way, Sandy, UT 84094

BELSER, Jo J (Va) 2280 N Beauregard St, Alexandria, VA 22311

✠ **BELSHAW**, George Phelps Mellick (Ret Bp of NJ 1995-) 15 Boudinot St, Princeton, NJ 08540

BELSHAW, Richard W (NH) 18 Highland Street, Ashland, NH 03217

BELSKY, Emil Eugene (U) 2714 Sierra Vista Road, Grand Junction, CO 81503

BELT, Michel (Ct) 119 Huntington St, New London, CT 06320

BELTON, Allan Edgar (O) 3490 E Prescott Cir, Cuyahoga Falls, OH 44223

BELTON, Colin Charles (Alb) 18 Trinity Pl., Plattsburgh, NY 12901

BELZER, John Alfred (Okla) 13 Lake Ln, Shawnee, OK 74804

BEMIS, Harlan Arnold (WNC) 30 Hidden Meadow Dr, Candler, NC 28715

BENAVIDES, Laurie Pauline (RG) 112 Goldenrod Ln, Alto, NM 88312

BENCKEN, Cathi Head (Ia) 211 Walnut St., Muscatine, IA 52761

BENCKEN, Charles F (WNY) 2461 Longhurst Ct., Muscatine, IA 52761

BENDALL, R Douglas (Nwk) 26 Howard Court, Newark, NJ 07103

BENDER, David R (NY)

BENDER, Jane Arrington (Be) 557 W 3rd St Apt K, Bethlehem, PA 18015

BENDER, John Charles (Tenn) Our Saviour Episcopal Church, 704 Hartsville Pike, Gallatin, TN 37066

BENDER, Richard E (ECR) P.O. Box 2400, Saratoga, CA 95070

BENDER, William Dexter (Ala) 402 S Scott St, Scottsboro, AL 35768

BENDER-BRECK, Barbara (Cal) 3226 Adeline St, Oakland, CA 94608

BENEDICT, Richard Alan Davis (NJ) 1625 SE 10th Ave Apt 602, Fort Lauderdale, FL 33316

BENES, Sandra S (Mich) 122 White Lake Dr, Brooklyn, MI 49230

BENESH, Jimi Brown (The Episcopal NCal) 334 D St, Redwood City, CA 94063

✠ **BENFIELD**, Larry R (Bp of Ark 2007-) Episcopal Diocese Of Arkansas, 310 W 17th St, Little Rock, AR 72206

BENHAM, David D (Ark) 2701 Old Greenwood Rd, Fort Smith, AR 72903

✠ **BENHASE**, Scott Anson (Bp of Ga 2010-) 611 E Bay St, Savannah, GA 31401

BENISTE, Jean C (SeFla) 2430 K St NW, Washington, DC 20037

BENITEZ, Wilfredo (LI) St George's Church, 13532 38th Ave, Flushing, NY 11354

BENJAMIN, Judith Benjamin (Cal) 1400 Loma Drive, Ojai, CA 93023

BENKO, Andrew Grayson (FtW) 908 Rutherford St, Shreveport, LA 71104

BENKO, Hope Tinsley (FtW) 9700 Saints Cir, Fort Worth, TX 76108

BENNER, Stephen Thomas (Ind) 1923 1935 East St, Princeton, IL 61356

BENNET, Richard Wilson (FdL) 7220 Newell Road, Hazelhurst, WI 54531

BENNETT III, Arthur Lasure (WVa) 16 Ashwood Dr, Vienna, WV 26105

BENNETT JR, Bertram George (NY) 384 E 160th St, Bronx, NY 10451

BENNETT, Betsy Blake (Neb) 325 W. 11th St., Hastings, NE 68901

BENNETT, Bill (Tex) 3711 Hidden Holw, Austin, TX 78731

BENNETT, Christine Aikens (Me) 30 Turtle Cove Rd, Raymond, ME 04071

BENNETT, Debra Q (O) 1933 Kingsley Ave, Akron, OH 44313

BENNETT, Denise Harper (Roch) 2882 Country Road 13, Clifton Springs, NY 14432

BENNETT, E Gene (Miss) 981 S Church St, Brookhaven, MS 39601

BENNETT, Ernest L (CFla) Diocese of Central Florida, 1017 E Robinson St, Orlando, FL 32801

BENNETT JR, Franklin Pierce (EMich) 1051 Virginia Ave, Marysville, MI 48040

BENNETT, Gail Louise (NJ) 803 Prospect Ave, Spring Lake, NJ 07762

BENNETT, Gerald L (SwFla) 5134 Wedge Ct E, Bradenton, FL 34203

BENNETT, JoAnne (Ore) PO Box 1791, Roseburg, OR 97470

BENNETT, Kyle Vernon (SwFla) St. Mark's Episcopal Church, 1101 N. Collier Blvd, Marco Island, FL 34145

BENNETT, Marionette Elvena (Colo) 15625 E Atlantic Cir, Aurora, CO 80013

BENNETT, Pattiann Benner (Mont) 200 Terning Dr W, Eureka, MT 59917

BENNETT, Phillip C (Pa) 2001 Hamilton St Apt 303, Philadelphia, PA 19130

BENNETT, Rachel Marybelle (ECR) 201 Glenwood Cir Apt 19e, Monterey, CA 93940

BENNETT, R Dudley (Nwk) 16 Warwick Way, Jackson, NJ 08527

BENNETT, Robert Avon (Mass) Po Box 380367, Cambridge, MA 02238

BENNETT, Sarah (Tex) 7002 Rusty Fig Dr, Austin, TX 78750

BENNETT, Susan P (Ind) 610 Perry St, Vincennes, IN 47591

BENNETT, Thaddeus Albert (Vt) 17 Lane Dr, Newfane, VT 05345

BENNETT, Virginia Lee (Spr) 1404 Gettysburg Lndg, Saint Charles, MO 63303

BENNETT, Vivian Rose (Pa) 934 Overfield RD, Meshoppen, PA 18630

BENNETT JR, William Doub (NC) Po Box 28024, Raleigh, NC 27611

✠ **BENNISON JR**, Charles Ellsworth (Ret Bp of Pa 2012-) 279 S 4th St, Philadelphia, PA 19106

BENO, Brian Martin (FdL) 17 Yorkshire Dr, Fond du Lac, WI 54935

BENOIT, Arlette Dierdre (At) 2005 S Columbia Pl, Decatur, GA 30032

BENSHOFF, Bruce L (Mass) 11 Meadowlark Dr, Middleboro, MA 02346

BENSON, David Howard (Mo) 6309 Burnham Cir Apt 323, Inver Grove Heights, MN 55076

BENSON, E. Heather (CNY) 60 Elm St, Ilion, NY 13357

BENSON, George Andrew (Neb) 8800 Holdrege St, Lincoln, NE 68505

BENSON, H William (NY) 1 Tongore Kill Rd, Olivebridge, NY 12461

BENSON, J(Ohn) Bradley (Roch) 110 Robie St, Bath, NY 14810

BENSON, Kathleen (Del) 4830 Kennett Pike Apt 2537, Wilmington, DE 19807

BENSON, Ricky Lynn (Tex) 1616 Driftwood Ln, Galveston, TX 77551

BENSON, Thomas Earle (Me) 21 Boyd St. Apt. 1406, Bangor, ME 04401

BENSON, Virginia H (Los) 1432 Engracia Ave, Torrance, CA 90501

BENTER JR, Harry William (SwFla) 1010 American Eagle Blvd, Apt 348, Sun City Center, FL 33573

BENTLEY JR, John R (Tex) 15410 Misty Forest Ct., Houston, TX 77068

BENTLEY, Stephen Richard (Episcopal SJ) 316 N El Dorado St, Stockton, CA 95202

BENTLEY, Susan Emmons (SwVa) 4515 Delray St Nw, Roanoke, VA 24012

BENTLEY-SHELTON, Elizabeth Michael (Wyo) 2511 Coffeen Ave, Sheridan, WY 82801

BENVENUTI, Anne Cecilia (Chi) 4945 S Dorchester Ave, Chicago, IL 60615

BENZ, Charles Frederick (NC) 4118 Pin Oak Dr, Durham, NC 27707

BERARD, Jeffrey Jerome (Mil) 1622 Quincy Ave, Racine, WI 53405

BERBERICH, Gloria Carroll (Va) 673 Evergreen Ave, Charlottesville, VA 22902

BERCOVICI, Hillary Rea (NY) 8 Sound Shore Dr Ste 130, Greenwich, CT 06830

BERDAHL, Peder Grant (Ind) 4810 Crystal River Ct, Indianapolis, IN 46240

BERENDS, April L (ETenn) St. Mark's Episcopal Church, 2618 N. Hackett Ave., Milwaukee, WI 53211

BERESFORD, Ruth Lawson (Del) P. O. Box 3510, Greenville, 507 East Buck Road, Wilmington, DE 19807

BERG, Dustin D (O) Saint Mark's Church, 515 48th St NW, Canton, OH 44709

BERG, James Christopher (Mich) 642 Woodcreek Dr, Waterford, MI 48327

BERGE JR, Clark (Oly) P.O. Box 399, Mount Sinai, NY 11766

BERGEN, Franklyn Joseph (Az) 4076 N Hidden Cove Pl, Tucson, AZ 85749

BERGER, Fred (Ia) 25111 Valley Drive, Pleasant Valley, IA 52767

BERGER, Jere Schindel (Alb) Montvert Road #1125, Middletown Springs, VT 05757

BERGER, Martha Branson (Mil) 1616 Martha Washington Dr, Wauwatosa, WI 53213

BERGERON, Mary Lee (ETenn) 6823 Sheffield Dr, Knoxville, TN 37909

BERGH JR, P A (Ida) 180 kings court, mountain home, ID 83647

BERGIE, Patricia (Wyo) Po Box 903, Fort Washakie, WY 82514

BERGIN, Joseph Alphonsus (CNY) 6312 N Manlius Rd, Kirkville, NY 13082

BERGMANN, William Carl (WMass) 85 E Main St, Ayer, MA 01432

BERGMANS, Susan Estelle (Cal) 1320 Addison St Apt C130, Berkeley, CA 94702

BERGNER, Mario Joseph (Spr) 149 Asbury St, South Hamilton, MA 01982

BERGNER, Robert Allen (Ct) 200 Seabury Dr, Bloomfield, CT 06002

BERGSTROM, Carl Edwin (Mass) 2914-109 Street, #1211, Edmonton AB, T6J 7E8, Canada

BERGSTROM, Fiona M (NC) 11 Fleet St, Umina Beach NSW, NC 02257, Australia

BERGSTROM, Jeremy W (Dal) St John's Church, 1 W Macon St, Savannah, GA 31401

BERITELA, Gerard Frederick (CNY) 360 S Collingwood Ave, Syracuse, NY 13206

BERK, Dennis Bryan Alban (Be)

BERKHOUSE, Casey Stephen (WTex) 343 N Getty St, Uvalde, TX 78801

BERKLEY, John Clayton Ashton (NI) 26824 County Road 4, Elkhart, IN 46514

BERKOWE, Kathleen Hawkins (Ct) 628 Main St, Stamford, CT 06901

BERKTOLD, Penny (Ore) 170 Brookside Dr, Eugene, OR 97405

BERKTOLD, Theodore Anthony (Ore) 170 Brookside Dr, Eugene, OR 97405

BERLENBACH, Betty Lorraine (Vt) 1961 Plains Rd., Perkinsville, VT 05151

BERLENBACH, Kirk Thomas (Pa) 5720 Ridge Ave, Philadelphia, PA 19128

BERLIN II, George Albert (Colo) 3155 Kendall St, Wheat Ridge, CO 80214

BERLIN, Sarah Aline (Colo) 3155 Kendall St, Wheat Ridge, CO 80214

BERMAN, Elizabeth Sievert (Mass) 6 Heritage Dr, Lexington, MA 02420

BERNACCHI, Jacqueline A (Minn) 1730 Clifton Pl Ste 201, Minneapolis, MN 55403

BERNACKI, James Bernard (NC) P.O. Box 657, Albemarle, NC 28002

BERNAL, Jose Juan (RG) 635 N Story Rd, Irving, TX 75061

BERNARD, Michael Allen (Kan) 305 Old Colony Ct, North Newton, KS 67117

BERNARDEZ JR, Teogenes Kalaw (Nev) 832 N Eastern Ave, Las Vegas, NV 89101

BERNARDI, Frank Alan (Episcopal SJ) 1815 S Teddy St, Visalia, CA 93277

BERNHARD, Margaret (Ore) 1180 NW Country Ct, Corvallis, OR 97330

BERNIER, Daniel L (Mass) PO Box 719, Wareham, MA 02571

BERNIER, Noe (Hai)

BERNTHAL, Gail Elizabeth (Episcopal SJ) 519 N Douty St, Hanford, CA 93230

BERRA, Robert M (Az) St Augustine's Episcopal Church, 1735 S College Ave, Tempe, AZ 85281

BERRY, Beverly D (Pa) 212 W Lancaster Ave, Paoli, PA 19301

BERRY JR, Charles Herbert (WTex) 1100 Grand Blvd Apt 223, Boerne, TX 78006

BERRY JR, Graham Pete (Chi) 1021 S Orange Grove Blvd, Unit 107, Pasadena, CA 91105

BERRY, John Emerson (NMich)

BERRY, Mary Helen (Miss)

BERRYMAN II, Jerome Woods (Colo) 5455 Landmark PL Unit 807, Greenwood Village, CO 80111

BERSIN, Ruth Hargrave (Ct) 4 Holmes Rd, Boxford, MA 01921

BERTOLOZZI, Michael Alan (Nev) 3625 Marlborough Ave, Las Vegas, NV 89110

BERTRAND, Michael Elmore (WTex) 2310 N Stewart Rd, Mission, TX 78574

BESCHTA, Gerald Thomas (WNC) 175 Mimosa Way, Hendersonville, NC 28739

BESCHTA, Joyce Marie (WNC) 65 Mimosa Way, Hendersonville, NC 28739

BESENBRUCH, Peter Ray (The Episcopal Church in Haw) 1679 California Ave, Wahiawa, HI 96786

BESHEARS, Earl D (SwFla) 331 56th Ave S, St Petersburg, FL 33705

BESHEER, Kimbrough Allan (Oly) 600 1st Ave Ste 632, Seattle, WA 98104

BESIER, Bettine Elisabeth (RI) 30 Scotch Cap Rd, Quaker Hill, CT 06375

BESS JR, Walter (Cal) 118 Tamalpais Rd, Fairfax, CA 94930

BESSE, Alden (Mass) 86 Weaver Ln # 4069, Vineyard Haven, MA 02568

BESSLER, Jeffrey Lee (Ind)

BESSON JR, Michael Wallace (Tex) 9610 Roarks Psge, Missouri City, TX 77459

BEST, Stephen Warren (Oly) 17421 Ne 139th Pl, Redmond, WA 98052

BETANCES, Ramon Antonio (At) 925 Whitlock Ave Apt 1308, Marietta, GA 30064

BETANCUR ORTIZ, Ricardo Antonio (Colom) c/o Diocese of Colombia, Cra 6 No. 49-85 Piso 2, Bogota, BDC, Colombia
BETE, Vincent Songaben (Ia) 204 E. 5th St., Ottumwa, IA 52501
BETENBAUGH, Helen R (CGC)
BETHANCOURT JR, A Robert (Los) 1145 W Valencia Mesa Dr, Fullerton, CA 92833
BETHEA, Mary (Los) 31641 La Novia Ave, San Juan Capistrano, CA 92675
BETHELL, John Christian (USC) Holy Trinity, 193 Old Greenville Hwy, Clemson, SC 29631
BETHELL, T(albot) James (Tex) 290 Fall Creek Dr., Oceanside, OR 97134
BETIT, John David (LI) 5 Pleasant St, Sutton, MA 01590
BETSINGER, Vicki Lynn (Oly) 280 E Wheelright St, Allyn, WA 98524
BETTACCHI, Karen Zahniser (Mass) 6 Garfield St, Lexington, MA 02421
BETTINGER, Robert Louis (Cal) 3940 Park Blvd Apt 911, San Diego, CA 92103
BETTS III, A(Lbert) Raymond (SO) 5810 Mccray Ct, Cincinnati, OH 45224
BETTS, Ian Randolph (NY) 6515 Palisade Ave Apt 201, West New York, NJ 07093
BETTS, Robert Hamilton (Pa) 1126 Foulkeways, Gwynedd, PA 19436
BETTY, Claude William (NwT) 2200 S Jefferson St, Perryton, TX 79070
BETZ, Nancy Elizabeth (CNY) 412 Hugunin St, Clayton, NY 13624
BETZ-SHANK, Erin L (NwPa)
BEUKMAN, Christian Arnold (Mass) 12 Quincy Ave, Quincy, MA 02169
BEVANS, Bruce Sinclair (WVa) PO Box P, Moundsville, WV 26041
BEVANS, Marjorie Salling (WVa) 903 Charles St, Parkersburg, WV 26101
BEVENS, Myrna Eloise (Colo) 46 N Albion St, Colorado Springs, CO 80911
BEVERIDGE, Robert Hanna (CNY) 1416 34th Ave, Seattle, WA 98122
BEVERIDGE, Robin Lorraine (NY)
BEYER, Jeanie Tillotson (Fla) 2872 N. Hannon Hill Dr., Tallahassee, FL 32309
BEZILLA, Gregory (NJ) 39 Ross Stevenson Cir, Princeton, NJ 08540
BEZY, Bernard Anthony (Lex) 1407 Gemstone Blvd, Hanahan, SC 29410
BIANCHI, Mary Elizabeth (Nev) 1674 Harper Drive, Carson City, NV 89701
BIBENS, Robert Lee (Okla) 4642 E 57th Pl, Tulsa, OK 74135
BICE, Michael Kenneth (Chi) 1244 N Astor St, Chicago, IL 60610
BICKERTON, Frances Catherine (NJ) 164 Buttonwood Dr, Fair Haven, NJ 07704
BICKFORD, Wayne Elva (HB) 8212 Kelsey Whiteface Rd, Cotton, MN 55724

BICKING, David Darlington (WVa) 813 Bowling Green Rd, Front Royal, VA 22630
BICKLEY, Robert James (Mich) Oakwood Common, 16351 Rotunda Dr #311, Grosse Pointe Park, MI 48120
BIDDLE, Blair Charles (Alb) Po Box 1029, Plattsburgh, NY 12901
BIDDLE III, Craig (Va) 364 Friar Trl, Annapolis, MD 21401
BIDDY, Eric Coleman (Chi) 545 S East Ave, Oak Park, IL 60304
BIDWELL, Mary Almy (NH) 1145 Jerusalem Rd, Bristol, VT 05443
BIDWELL-WAITE, Davidson (Cal) 3641 20th St., San Francisco, CA 94110
BIEDENHARN III, James Phelan (WTenn) 3245 Central Ave, Memphis, TN 38111
BIEGA, Richard A (WNC) 426 English Rd, Spruce Pine, NC 28777
BIEGLER, James Cameron (Dal) 11202 Prairie View Ct, Westchester, IL 60154
BIELSKI, Diane Irene (Colo) P O Box 1558, Fraser, CO 80442
BIEVER, Robert Ray (Oly) 3310 N Bennett St, Tacoma, WA 98407
BIFFLE, Robin Lee (Spok) 111 S. Jefferson St., Moscow, ID 83843
BIGELOW, Thomas Seymour (Oly) Box 20489, Seattle, WA 98102
BIGFORD, Jack N(orman) (Oly) 520 Scenic Way, Kent, WA 98030
BIGGADIKE, Maylin Tercsa (Nwk) 398 Shelbourne Ter, Ridgewood, NJ 07450
BIGGERS, Helen Hammond (Spok) 4803 W Shawnee Ave, Spokane, WA 99208
BIGGERS, Jackson Cunningham (Miss) 10100 Hillview Dr Apt 537, Pensacola, FL 32514
BIGGS, Carolyn K (CFla) 6071 Sabal Hammock Cir, Port Orange, FL 32128
BIGGS, John Winston (WMo) 2632 S Wallis Smith Blvd, Springfield, MO 65804
BIGLEY, Mark Charles (ETenn) 792 Keith Salem Rd., Ringgold, GA 30736
BILBY, Gary Eugene (NwT) 1501 S Grinnell St, Perryton, TX 79070
BILLER, Larry Ray (NI) 9064 E Koher Rd S, Syracuse, IN 46567
BILLINGSLEA, Wendy Ward (Fla) 400 San Juan Dr, Ponte Vedra Beach, FL 32082
BILLINGSLEY, Michael (Mass) Saint Paul's Episcopal Church, 61 Wood St., Hopkinton, MA 01748
BILLINGTON, James Hadley (Cal) 1 S El Camino Real, San Mateo, CA 94401
BILLMAN, Daniel Robert (Ind) 8165 Gwinnett Pl., Indianapolis, IN 46250
BILLMAN, Sharon Lynn (Kan) 1738 24000 Rd, Parsons, KS 67357
BILLOW JR, William Pierce (WA) PO Box 242, Barboursville, VA 22923

BILLUPS, Beatrice (Md) 1514 Gordon Cove Dr, Annapolis, MD 21403
BILSBURY, Stephen Robert (Okla) St. Philip's Episcopal Church, 516 McLish St, Ardmore, OK 73401
BIMBI, James Michael (Del) 4828 Hogan Dr, Wilmington, DE 19808
BINDER, Donald Drew (Va) 9301 Richmond Hwy, Lorton, VA 22079
BINDER, Thomas Francis (Mil)
BINGHAM, John Pratt (The Episcopal NCal) 17538 Caminito Balata, San Diego, CA 92128
BINGHAM, Patricia M (Cal) 1 Key Capri 713 East, Treasure Island, FL 33706
BINGHAM, Sally Grover (Cal) 7 Laurel St, San Francisco, CA 94118
BIORNSTAD, Nathan Allan (Los) 122 S California Ave, Monrovia, CA 91016
BIPPUS JR, William Lloyd (FdL) 917 Church St, Marinette, WI 54143
BIRCH, Lucene Kirkland (Fla) 6812 Mapperton Drive, Windermere, FL 34786
BIRCHER, Victor Malcolm (Miss) 102 Edie St, Columbia, MS 39429
BIRD, David John (ECR) 81 North 2 Street, San Jose, CA 95113
BIRD, Edith S (Mo) 1325 Margaret, Cape Girardeau, MO 63701
BIRD IV, Edward T (Chi) 306 S Prospect Ave, Park Ridge, IL 60068
BIRD, Frederick Lee (WVa) 1009 S Henry Ave, Elkins, WV 26241
BIRD JR, John Edwin (NJ) 304 S Girard St, Woodbury, NJ 08096
BIRD, Julie Childs (SC)
BIRD, Michael Andrew (NY) 7 Library Ln, Bronxville, NY 10708
BIRD, Patricia A (Del) 30851 Crepe Myrtle Dr Unit 60, Millsboro, DE 19966
BIRD, Peter (FdL) 315 E. Jefferson St., Waupun, WI 53963
BIRD, Robert Dale (Mich) 824 W Maple Ave, Adrian, MI 49221
BIRD, Virginia Lee (SD) Po Box 9412, Rapid City, SD 57709
BIRDSALL, James Andrew (Ct)
BIRDSALL, John Burton (Eas) 419a Evans St Apt 2, Williamsville, NY 14221
BIRDSEY, Bruce B (EC) 2206 Rosewood Ave, Richmond, VA 23220
BIRDSONG, Jerre Eugene (Mo) 4714 Clifton Ave, Saint Louis, MO 63109
BIRKBY, Charles H (CNY) 79 Ripplebrook Lane, Minoa, NY 13116
BIRKENHEAD, Harold George (Mass) 8 Nevin Rd, South Weymouth, MA 02190
BIRNBAUM, Rachelle Eskenaizi (Va) 942A Heritage Vlg, Southbury, CT 06488
BIRNEY, Edith Hazard (Me) 11 Perkins St, Topsham, ME 04086
BIRNEY III, James Gillespie (Me) 1110 North Rd, North Yarmouth, ME 04097

BIRTCH, John Edward McKay (SwFla) 1001 Carpenters Way Apt H108, Lakeland, FL 33809

BISHOP, Barbara Elaine (Chi) 827 Canterbury Dr, Crystal Lake, IL 60014

BISHOP, Christopher (Pa)

BISHOP, Edwin (Ore) 1900 Lauderdale Dr Apt D115, Henrico, VA 23238

BISHOP JR, Harold Ellsworth (Md) Box 128, Cottage 505-B, Quincy, PA 17247

BISHOP, Kathleen Gayle (NJ) St Mary's by-the-sea, 804 Bay Ave, Point Pleasant Beach, NJ 08742

BISHOP, Nila Ruth (WMo) 1433 NW R D Mize Rd, Blue Springs, MO 64015

BISSELL-THOMPSON, Geraldine Vina (Alb) 11 E Main St, Lebanon, VA 24266

BISSOONDIAL, Din (CFla) St Peter's Episcopal Church, 700 Rinehart Rd, Lake Mary, FL 32746

BITSBERGER, Donald Edward (Va) 4970 Sentinel Dr Apt 505, Bethesda, MD 20816

BITTNER, Merrill (Me) 118 Lone Pine Rd, Newry, ME 04261

BLACK, Cynthia Louise (Nwk) 36 South St, Morristown, NJ 07960

BLACK, G(Eorge) Donald (At) 215 N Edenfield Ridge Dr, Rome, GA 30161

BLACK, Katharine C (Mass) 13 Louisburg Sq, Boston, MA 02108

BLACK JR, Milton England (WTex) 149 Cordula St, Corpus Christi, TX 78411

BLACK, Rebecca Lynn (Mass) 128 Village St, Millis, MA 02054

BLACK, Robert E. (Ct) 21Jerimoth Dr., Bradford, CT 06405

BLACK JR, Robert William (NC) 131 W Council St, Salisbury, NC 28144

BLACK, Ruth Buck (Miss) 1704 Poplar Blvd, Jackson, MS 39202

BLACK, Sherry Leonard (Spr) 12806 Mallard Dr., Whittington, IL 62897

BLACK, Timothy H (At) 4393 Garmon Rd NW, Atlanta, GA 30327

BLACK, Vicki Kay (Me) 73 Bristol Rd, Damariscotta, ME 04543

BLACK, Vincent E (O) 2230 Euclid Ave, Cleveland, OH 44115

BLACKBURN, Elliot Hillman (Spr) 603 South Grant, Mason City, IA 50401

BLACKBURN, Gerald Jackson (EC) 4212 Stratton Village Ln, Wilmington, NC 28409

BLACKBURN, Gregory (SeFla) 1121 Andalusia Ave, Coral Gables, FL 33134

BLACKBURN, James Clark (Md) 105 Tunbridge Rd, Baltimore, MD 21212

BLACKBURN, Terry Gene (NJ) 35-50 85th Street 5J, Jackson Heights, NY 11372

BLACKERBY JR, William S (Ala) 4307 Clairmont Ave S, Birmingham, AL 35222

BLACKHAM, Todd Patten (Los) 1325 Monterey Rd, South Pasadena, CA 91030

BLACKLOCK, Martha Grace (NJ) POBox 2973, Silver City, NM 88062

BLACKMER, Stephen D (NH) Kairos Earth, 107 Hackleboro Road, Canterbury, NH 03224

BLACKMON, A(ndrew) Thomas (La) 120 S New Hampshire St, Covington, LA 70433

BLACKWELL, Norma Lee (WA) 10754 Main St Apt 202, Fairfax, VA 22030

BLACKWELL, Robert Hunter (Ala) 305 Arnold Street, Cullman, AL 35055

BLACKWOOD, Deb (NC) 14103 Wilford Ct, Charlotte, NC 28277

BLADON, Doyle Gene (Az) 310 W Union Ave, Monticello, AR 71655

BLAESS, Kristine A (Tenn)

BLAESS, Michael (Tenn)

BLAGG, James Raymond (Okla) 117 Sandpiper Cir, Durant, OK 74701

BLAIES-DIAMOND, Sarah (NC) 3430 Old US 70 PO BOX 37, Cleveland, NC 27013

BLAINE, Carol (Tex) 307 Palm Dr, Marlin, TX 76661

BLAINE-WALLACE, William Edwards (Me) 161 Wood Street, Lewiston, ME 04240

BLAIR, Alexander (Cal) 1801 Marin Ave, Berkeley, CA 94707

BLAIR, Rebecca H (Mass) 40 Hoppin Hill Avenue, North Attleboro, MA 02760

BLAIR JR, Thom Williamson (Va) Po Box 1059, Kilmarnock, VA 22482

BLAIR-HUBERT, Paige Michele (SanD) PO Box 336, Del Mar, CA 92014

BLAIR-LOY, Mary Frances (SanD) 747 W University Ave, San Diego, CA 92103

BLAIS, Heather Jeanette (WMass) 12 Hodge St, Wiscasset, ME 04578

BLAKE, Sandra Jean (Colo)

BLAKE, Sidney Spivey (NY) 204 W 134th St, New York, NY 10030

BLAKE, Susan Lynn (CFla) 460 N Grandview St, Mount Dora, FL 32757

BLAKE JR, Thomas William (Ind)

BLAKELOCK, Douglas Paul (Alb) 295 Main St, Unadilla, NY 13849

BLAKELY, W(ayne) A(llen) (Kan) 2805 Woodmont Dr, Louisville, KY 40220

BLAKEMORE, Barbara Keller (Va) 8499 Anderson Ct, Mechanicsville, VA 23116

BLAKLEY, Dave Edward (NwT)

BLAKLEY, J. Ted (WK) 402 N Topeka St, Wichita, KS 67202

BLAKLEY, Raymond Leonard (WTenn) 761 Spaulding Dr, Roseville, CA 95678

BLAKSLEE, John Charles (NI) 15606 W 103rd Lane, Dyer, IN 46311

BLANCH, Paul F (The Episcopal NCal) 2150 Benton Dr, Redding, CA 96003

BLANCHARD, Louise Browner (Va) St. Mary's Episcopal Church, 12291 River Road, Richmond, VA 23238

BLANCHARD, Louise Sharon (Colo) 6774 Tabor St, Arvada, CO 80004

BLANCHARD, Mary Margaret (ETenn) 100 Steven Ln., Harriman, TN 37748

BLANCHARD, Sudie Mixter (Me) 25 Southside Rd, York, ME 03909

BLANCHETT, David Harvey (The Episcopal Church in Haw) 1100 Pullman Dr, Wasilla, AK 99654

BLANCK, Charles Kenneth (WNC) 977 Collins Rd, Sparta, NC 28675

BLANCO-MONTERROSO, Leonel (Okla) 5500 S Western Ave., Oklahoma City, OK 73109

BLAND, John D (Minn) 1431 Cherry Hill Rd, Mendota Heights, MN 55118

BLAND, Leslie Rasmussen (NC) 1300 Jefferson Rd, Greensboro, NC 27410

BLAND SR, Thomas James (NC) 4608 Pine Cove Rd, Greensboro, NC 27410

BLASCO, Natalie (SeFla) 1801 Ludlam Dr, Miami Springs, FL 33166

BLASDELL, Machrina Loris (Cal) 804 Cottonwood Dr., Lansing, KS 66043

BLATZ, Nils (LI) 79 Zophar Mills Road, Wading River, NY 11792

BLAUSER, Dennis Alan (NwPa) 215 Dermond Rd, Hermitage, PA 16148

BLAUVELT II, Charles Joseph (NH) 162 Sagamore St., Manchester, NH 03104

BLAUVELT, Jeremy David (USC) 125 Church Ave, Pass Christian, MS 39571

BLAVIER JR, Donald Charles (WTex) 404 Salisbury Ln, Victoria, TX 77904

BLAYER, Brian David (LI) 15117 14 Rd, Whitestone, NY 11357

BLAZEK, Laura Sue (Okla) 1601 W Imhoff Rd, Norman, OK 73072

BLEDSOE, Alwen (Colo)

BLEDSOE, Faith Elizabeth (WTex)

BLEDSOE, Sharon C (SVa) 116 Victorian Lane, Jupiter, FL 33458

BLEND, Jennifer (Colo) 4775 Cambridge St, Boulder, CO 80301

BLESSING, Kamila Abrahamova (Pgh) 6211 Wrightsville Ave. Unit 147, Wilington, NC 28403

BLESSING, Mary Elizabeth Brunner (ECR) 5271 Scotts Valley Dr, Scotts Valley, CA 95066

BLESSING, Robert Alan (SanD) 12539 Sundance Ave, San Diego, CA 92129

BLESSING, Wren Tyler (Mont) Diocese Of Montana, PO Box 2020, Helena, MT 59624

BLEYLE, Douglas Karl (RG) 318 Silver Ave SW, Albuquerque, NM 87102

BLINMAN, Clifford Louis (Ore) 2092 E. Bighorn Mountain Dr, Oro Valley, AZ 85755

BLISS, John Derek Clegg (Cal) 4 Edgewater Hillside, Westport, CT 06880

BLISS, Robert Francis (Tex) 881 North Main Street, PO Box 797, Salado, TX 76571

BLISS, Vernon Powell (CNY) 86 E Taylor Hill Rd, Montague, MA 01351

BLIZZARD, Charles Fortunate-Eagle (Okla) 1301 Andover Ct, Oklahoma City, OK 73120

BLOOM, Barry Moffett (Mass)

BLOOM, Carl Richard (Spr) 1989 East Gleneagle Drive, Chandler, AZ 85249

BLOOMER, Nancy H (NY) 4 Grant St, Essex Junction, VT 05452

BLOSSOM JR, John Dickson (Chi) 125 Sw Jefferson Ave, Peoria, IL 61602

BLOTTNER, William Eugene (Chi) 510 First Ave, Farmville, VA 23901

BLUBAUGH, Susan Jo (NI) 1305 S 2nd St, Lafayette, IN 47905

BLUE, Eddie Michael (Md) Church Of The Holy Trinity, 2300 W. Lafayette Ave., Baltimore, MD 21216

BLUE, Gordon Kenneth (Ak) 2902 Sawmill Creek Rd, Sitka, AK 99835

BLUE, Susan Neff (WA) 270 El Diente Dr., Durango, CO 81301

BLUME, Andrew Charles (NY) 160 West 95th Street, Apt. 8B, New York, NY 10025

BLUMER, Gary R (Be) Po Box 623, Portland, PA 18351

BLUNDELL, Gayle (Gay) A(nn) (ECR) 2100 Emmons Rd, Cambria, CA 93428

BLUNT, Elizabeth E (Az) Christ Church of the Ascension, 4015 E Lincoln Dr, Paradise Valley, AZ 85253

BLUNT JR, Howard Elton (LI) 125 Eastern Parkway #5D, Brooklyn, NY 11238

BOARD, John C (Mont) 2704 Gold Rush Ave, Helena, MT 59601

BOARD III, J(ohn) Paul (O) 313 E Wayne St, Maumee, OH 43537

BOASE, David John (Spr) 4902 Blu Fountain Dr, Godfrey, IL 62035

BOATRIGHT-SPENCER, Angela (NY) 801 Willow St, Wadesboro, NC 28170

BOATWRIGHT, William Emanuel (NJ) 1901 N. DuPont Highway, New Castle, DE 19720

BOBBITT, Kathleen Morrisette (SVa) 1005 Windsor Rd, Virginia Beach, VA 23451

BOBO, Melinda (Wyo) P.O. Box 1177, Dubois, WY 82513

BOCCHINO, James Robert (RI) 589 Smithfield Rd, North Providence, RI 02904

BOCCINO, Kenneth Robert (Nwk) 550 Ridgewood Rd, Maplewood, NJ 07040

BOCK, Susan Kay (Mich) 529 E Kirby St, Detroit, MI 48202

BOCKUS, Ian Lawrence (Me) 496 N Searsport Rd, Prospect, ME 04981

BODIE, Park McDermit (NY) 235 W 56th St Apt 11m, New York, NY 10019

BOEGER, Daniel Edward (The Episcopal NCal)

BOEGER, Mary Rose Steen (The Episcopal NCal)

BOELTER, Phillip R (Minn) Gethsemane Episcopal Church, 905 4th Avenue South, Minneapolis, MN 55404

BOELTER, Sarah (Cal) 41485 S. I-94 Service Drive, Belleville, MI 48111

BOESCHENSTEIN, Kathryn C (Colo)

BOESSER, Mark Alan (Ak) 17585 Point Lena Loop Rd, Juneau, AK 99801

BOEVE, Phillip Dale (Spr) 303 Merchants Avenue, Fort Atkinson, WI 53538

BOGAL-ALLBRITTEN, Rose (Ky) 1504 Kirkwood Dr, Murray, KY 42071

BOGAN III, Leslie Eugene (CGC) 1336 Greenvista Ln, Gulf Breeze, FL 32563

BOGEL, Marianne (Oly) 11844 Bandera Rd #148, HELOTES, TX 78023

BOGERT-WINKLER, Hilary M (WMass) 14 Boltwood Ave., Amherst, MA 01002

BOGGS, Timothy A (Me) 12 Oakhurst Road, Cape Elizabeth, ME 04107

BOGHETICH, Barbara Ann (Hond) IMC-SAP 564, PO Box 52-3900, Miami, FL 33152

BOHLER JR, Lewis Penrose (Los) PO Box 16216, Augusta, GA 30919

BOHNER, Charles Russell (Del) 1309 Grinnell Rd # N33, Wilmington, DE 19803

BOIVIN, Barbara Ann (Nev)

BOJARSKI, Mitchell T (Ky) 116 S. Columbia St., Campbellsville, KY 42718

BOLAND, Geoffrey Allan (CFla) 1861 Peninsular Dr, Haines City, FL 33844

BOLDINE, Charles Stanley (RG) 6009 Costa Brava Ave NW, Albuquerque, NM 87114

BOLI, Judith (EMich) 4444 State St Apt F-318, Saginaw, MI 48603

BOLIN, William Eugene (Md) 244 Braeburn Cir, Walkersville, MD 21793

BOLLE, Stephen M (NY) 1 Chipping Ct, Greenville, SC 29607

BOLLE, Winnie Mckenzie Hoilette (SeFla) 6055 Verde Trl S Apt H316, Boca Raton, FL 33433

BOLLES-BEAVEN, Anne Elizabeth (Nwk) 32 Yale St, Maplewood, NJ 07040

BOLLINGER II, David Glenn (CNY) 206 John St, Binghamton, NY 13905

BOLLINGER, Matthew D (NJ) 514 W Adams Blvd, Los Angeles, CA 90007

BOLT, Michelle Warriner (ETenn) 413 Cumberland Ave, Knoxville, TN 37902

BOLTON, Carolyn Marie (Cal) 1125 Brush St, Oakland, CA 94607

BOLTON, John Donald (At) 16245 Birmingham Hwy, Milton, GA 30004

BOMAN, Ruth Kay (Okla) 424 E St Nw, Miami, OK 74354

BOMAN, Samuel Ratliff (Neb) 262 Parkside Ln, Lincoln, NE 68521

BON, Brin Carol (Tex) 3901 Bee Caves Rd, Austin, TX 78746

BONADIE, LeRoy Rowland (Md) 609 Wellington Ln, Cumberland, ND 21502

BOND, Barbara Lynn (O) 455 Santa Clara St Nw, Canton, OH 44709

BOND, Eric B (Pa) 2122 Washington Ln, Huntingdon Valley, PA 19006

BOND, Jeremy William (CPa) 676 N 12th Street Unit 25, Grover Beach, CA 93433

BOND, L(eonard) Wayne (Oly) 5810 Fleming St Unit 66, Everett, WA 98203

BOND, Michael David (Chi) 10550 Knickerbocker Ct, Saint John, IN 46373

BOND, Michele (Eas) 19524 Meadowbrook Rd, Hagerstown, MD 21742

BOND JR, Walter Douglas (Mass) 10 Dana St Apt 212, Cambridge, MA 02138

BONDURANT, Stephen Bryce (SO) 785 Ludlow Ave, Cincinnati, OH 45220

BONE, Patrick Joseph (ETenn) Po Box 129, Church Hill, TN 37642

BONEBRAKE, Aletha Green (EO) 2347 Campbell St, Baker City, OR 97814

BONELL, John W. (NH) 3 Bodfish Av, Wareham, MA 02571

BONEY, Samuel Ashford (Miss) 10100 Hillview Dr. Apt 433, Pensacola, FL 32514

BONIN, Raymond Thomas (NH) 1 Hood Rd, Derry, NH 03038

BONNER, Bruce (Tex) 3520 W. Whitestone Blvd., Cedar Park, TX 78613

BONNER, George Llewellyn (LI) 783 E 35th St, Brooklyn, NY 11210

BONNER III, John Hare (EC) Holy Trinity Episcopal Church, 207 S Church St, Hertford, NC 27944

BONNER-STEWART, Ann Pinckney (NC) St Mary's Chapel, 900 Hillsborough St, Raleigh, NC 27603

BONNEY, Isaac Kojo Nyame (WA) Saint Mark's Church, 12621 Old Columbia Pike, Silver Spring, MD 20904

BONNINGTON, Robert Lester (NwT) 2820 Goddard Pl, Midland, TX 79705

BONNYMAN, Anne Berry (Mass) 50 Sonnet Lane, Asheville, NC 28804

BONOAN, Raynald Sales (SwFla) 18612 Chemille Dr, Lutz, FL 33558

BONSEY, Steven Charles (Mass) 138 Tremont St, Boston, MA 02111

BONSEY, W(Illiam) Edwin (The Episcopal Church in Haw) 401 SAnta Clara Av e Apt 309, Oakland, CA 94610

BONSTEEL, Susan (NY) 94 Clifton Ave, Kingston, NY 12401

BONWITT, Martha (WA) 14303 Old Marlboro Pike, Upper Marlboro, MD 20772

BOODT, Mary Ione (Ind) 100 Oakview Dr, Mooresville, IN 46158

BOOHER, David Lewis (SVa) 724 West H St., Elizabethton, TN 37643

BOOK, Robert TM (At) 170 Trinity Ave SW, Atlanta, GA 30303

BOOKER JR, James Howard (Az) 700 E Georgia Ave, Deland, FL 32724

BOOKER, Vaughan P L (WA) 5537 Holmes Run Pkwy, Alexandria, VA 22304

BOOKSTEIN, Nancey Johnson (Colo) 110 Johnson St, Frederick, CO 80530

BOOMGAARD, Michelle C (Pgh)

BOONE, Arthur Robinson (Vt) 1616 Harmon St, Berkeley, CA 94703

BOONE, Connie Louise (EO) 42893 Pocahontas Rd, Baker City, OR 97814

BOONE JR, Robert Augustus (WNC) 900b Centre Park Dr, Asheville, NC 28805

BOOTH, Errol Kent (WA) 2811 Deep Landing Rd, Huntingtown, MD 20639

BOOTH, James Alexander (ECR) 48 Miramoute Rd., Carmel Valley, CA 93924

BOOTH, Karen Workman (Fla) 7423 San Jose Blvd, Jacksonville, FL 32217

BOOTH, Stephen P (WMass)

BOOZER, Alcena Elaine (Ore) 5256 NE 48th Ave, Portland, OR 97218

BORBON, Samuel (Ore) 1704 NE 43rd Ave, Portland, OR 97213

BORDADOR, Noel Estrella (NY)

BORDELON, Joseph Ardell (WLa) 5704 Monroe Hwy, Ball, LA 71405

BORDELON, Michael (WLa) 1620 Murray St, Alexandria, LA 71301

BORDEN, Robert Bruce (Vt) P0 Box 554, East Middlebury, VT 05740

BORDEN, Theorphlis Marzetta (SO) St Simon Of Cyrene, 810 Matthews Dr, Cincinnati, OH 45215

BORDENKIRCHER, Amanda Jane (CFla) 942 Cobbler Ct, Longwood, FL 32750

BORDERS, Calvin Leroy (Oly) 602 24th Ave, Longview, WA 98632

BORDIN, Richard F (CFla) 832 Summeroaks Rd, Winter Garden, FL 34787

BORDNER, Kenneth Edward (Roch) 3471 Cerrillos Rd Trlr 78, Santa Fe, NM 87507

BORG, Manuel (Chi) 1072 Ridge Ave, Elk Grove Village, IL 60007

BORG, Marianne (Ore) 1133 Nw 11th Ave Apt 403, Portland, OR 97209

BORGEN, Linda Suzanne Cecelia (CGC) Episcopal Church of the Nativity, 205 Holly Lane, Dothan, AL 36301

BORGES, Maria Cristina (SanD) 521 E 8th St, National City, CA 91950

BORGESON, Josephine (The Episcopal NCal) 458 Occidental Cir, Santa Rosa, CA 95401

BORGMAN, Dean Wylie (Mass) 5 Heritage Dr, Rockport, MA 01966

BORMES, Richard Joseph (Minn) 4350 Brookside Ct Apt 117, Edina, MN 55436

BORREGO, John Edward (Okla) 422 E Noble Ave, Guthrie, OK 73044

BORREGO, Lynn Griffith (Okla) 422 E Noble Ave, Guthrie, OK 73044

✠ **BORSCH**, Frederick Houk (Ret Bp of Los 2002-) 2930 Corda Ln, Los Angeles, CA 90049

BORSCH, Kathleen Ann (Ore)

BORZUMATO, Judith Alice (NY) 500 State Rte 299 Apt 24C, Highland, NY 12528

BOSBYSHELL, William Allen (SwFla) 106 21st Ave Ne, Saint Petersburg, FL 33704

BOSLER, Sarah Mather (Be) 1188 Ben Franklin Hwy E, Douglassville, PA 19518

BOSS, Bruce William (Ind) 8846 Spinnaker Ct, Indianapolis, IN 46256

BOSSCHER, Molly Boscher (CFla) 251 E Lake Brantley Dr, Longwood, FL 32779

BOSS WOLLNER, Ernesto Sieghard (Colom) Cra 86 # 46-38 Apto 202, Medellin, ANTIOQUIA, Colombia

BOST, Emily Catherine (Ark) 217 N East Ave, Fayetteville, AR 72701

BOSTIAN, Nathan Louis (WTex) 20955 W Tejas Trl, San Antonio, TX 78257

BOSTON, Dane E (USC) Trinity Cathedral, 1100 Sumter St, Columbia, SC 29201

BOSTON, James Terrell (Ore) 518 NE Dean Dr, Grants Pass, OR 97526

BOSWELL JR, Frederick Philip (Colo) 9200 W 10th Ave, Lakewood, CO 80215

BOSWELL, Kathryn Mary (Alb) 21 Cherry St., Potsdam, NY 13676

BOTH, M Blair (EC) 305 S 5th Ave, Wilmington, NC 28401

BOTT, Harold Ray (At) 3750 Peachtree Rd NE Apt 905, Atlanta, GA 30319

BOTTONE, Doreen Ann (Ct) 68 Main St, Berlin, CT 06037

BOUCHER, Edward Charles (RI) 341 Seaview Ave, Swansea, MA 02777

BOUCHER, John Paul (SVa) 12020 Smoketree Dr, Richmond, VA 23236

BOULTER, Matthew Rutherford (Tex) 118 S. Bois d'Arc, Tyler, TX 77702

BOULTER, Richard Ottmuller (Mich) 11575 Belleville Rd, Belleville, MI 48111

BOULTER, Robert James (WA) St. Columba's Episcopal Church, 4201 Albemarle St NW, Washington, DC 20016

BOURDEAU, Mary Ellen (Md) 2 Saint Peters Pl, Lonaconing, MD 21539

BOURGEAULT, Cynthia Warren (Colo) HC 2 Box 16, Sunset, ME 04683

BOURHILL, John William (NY) 26 Huron Rd, Yonkers, NY 10710

✠ **BOURLAKAS**, Mark Allen (Bp of SwVa 2013-) 421 S 2nd St, Louisville, KY 40202

BOURNE-RAISWELL, Margaret Lafayette (ECR) 20025 Glen Brae Dr, Saratoga, CA 95070

BOURQUE, Mary Elizabeth (Me) 20 Union St., Hallowell, ME 04347

BOUSFIELD, Nigel J (FdL) 1432 Foxfire Ct, Waupaca, WI 54981

BOUSQUET, Vincent Michael (Mass) Po Box 395, Barnstable, MA 02630

BOWDEN, George Edward (Mo) 624 Saffron Ct, Myrtle Beach, SC 29579

BOWDEN JR, Talmadge Arton (Ga) 3409 Wheeler Rd, Augusta, GA 30909

BOWDEN, Teresa Thomas (The Episcopal Church in Haw) 2573 California Ave, Wahiawa, HI 96786

BOWDISH, Lynn Eastman (Cal) 172 Northgate Ave, Daly City, CA 94015

BOWEN, Anthony DeLisle (LI) 180 Kane St, Brooklyn, NY 11231

BOWEN, Carol (Cal)

BOWEN, Elizabeth Anne (Mo) Trinity Episcopal Church, 318 S Duchesne Dr, Saint Charles, MO 63301

BOWEN, George Harry (Nwk) 308 River Oaks Dr, Rutherford, NJ 07070

BOWEN, Paul (Tex) 324 Sherwood Ave, Staunton, VA 24401

BOWEN, Pauline Mason (WNY) 138 Castle Hill Rd, East Aurora, NY 14052

BOWEN, Peter Scott (Me) 20 Sky Harbor Dr, Biddeford, ME 04005

BOWEN, Shirley Williams (Me)

BOWER, Bruce E (WMo) 6401 Wornall Ter, Kansas City, MO 64113

BOWER, Jeffrey L (Ind) 4160 Broadway St, Indianapolis, IN 46205

BOWER, John A(Llen) (SO) 418 Sugar Maple Ln, Springdale, OH 45246

BOWER, Richard Allen (CNY) 681 N Hill Cross Rd, Ludlow, VT 05149

BOWER, Roger Andrew (NI) 505 Bullseye Lake Rd, Valparaiso, IN 46383

BOWERFIND, Ellis Tucker (Va) 8727 Bluedale St, Alexandria, VA 22308

BOWERS, Albert Wayne (Alb) 17 Woodbridge Ave, Sewaren, NJ 07077

BOWERS, David Douglas (SwFla) 513 Nassau St S, Venice, FL 34285

BOWERS, J(ohn) E(dward) (SO) 1276 Coonpath Rd Nw, Lancaster, OH 43130

BOWERS, Marvin Nelson (The Episcopal NCal) 202 Tucker St, Healdsburg, CA 95448

BOWERS, Terry L. (Chi) 1900 Etton Dr, Fort Collins, CO 80526

BOWERS, Thomas Dix (NY) 304 Lord Granville Dr, Morehead City, NC 28557

BOWERSOX, Ned Ford (WTex) 8607 Tomah Dr, Austin, TX 78717

BOWERSOX, Sally Ann (Colo) 605 S Alton Way 10A, Denver, CO 80247

BOWES, Bruce Orin (NY) 254 Bloomer Rd, Lagrangeville, NY 12540

BOWHAY, Christopher Andrew (Tenn) Saint George's Church, 4715 Harding Pike, Nashville, TN 37205

BOWLIN, Howard B (ETenn) PO Box 6259, Maryville, TN 37802

BOWMAN, Andrea C (Spok) 104 E 17th Ave, Ellensburg, WA 98926

BOWMAN, Sallie Wirt (Ore) Department Of Spiritual Care, 1015 NW 22nd Ave, Portland, OR 97210

BOWMAN, Susan Blount (Alb) 16 Mansion Blvd, Apt B, Delmar, NY 12054

BOWRON, Joshua Dan (At) 1623 Carmel Rd, Charlotte, NC 28226

BOWYER, Charles Lester (NwT) 5806 Emory St, Lubbock, TX 79416

BOYD, Catherine Tyndall (Tex) 13401 Galleria Cir Apt 335, Austin, TX 78738

BOYD, David A (Tex) 13401 Galleria Cir Apt 335, Austin, TX 78738

BOYD, James R (WTenn) 6367 Shadowood Ln, Memphis, TN 38119

BOYD, Jeffrey Howard (Mass) 57 Bethany Woods Rd, Bethany, CT 06524

BOYD, Julia Woolfolk (NC) Po Box 6124, Charlotte, NC 28207

BOYD, Lawrence Robert (Neb) 2325 S 24th St, Lincoln, NE 68502

BOYD, Sally Ann (Wyo) 436 Sundance Circle, Wright, WY 82732

BOYD, Samuel Lee (Tex) Po Box 1884, Chandler, TX 75758

BOYD, Sandra Hughes (Colo) 8251 E Phillips Pl, Englewood, CO 80112

BOYD, Virginia Ann (Md) 10901 Farrier Rd, Frederick, MD 21701

BOYD, William Marvin (Fla) 338 River Rd, Carrabelle, FL 32322

BOYD, William Orgill (At) 210 E Robert Toombs Ave, Washington, GA 30673

BOYD-ELLIS, Sue (WNY)

BOYER JR, Ernest Leroy (ECR) PO Box 360832, Milpitas, CA 95036

BOYER, Geoffrey Thomas (Mich) 1130 N. Jamestown Road, Apt. #401, Decatur, GA 30033

BOYER, John Paul (WNY) 3885 Teachers Ln Apt 8, Orchard Park, NY 14127

BOYER, Marcia M (Vt)

BOYER, William James (CFla) 126 E Palmetto Ave, Howey in the Hills, FL 34737

BOYLE, Patton Lindsay (Spok) 1342 Bartlett Ave, Wenatchee, WA 98801

BOYLE, Peter (Nwk) 10 Lindbergh Ave, Rensselaer, NY 12144

BOYLES, David Joseph (Fla) St Mary's Episcopal Church, PO Box 611, Madison, FL 32341

BOYNTON, Caroline Cochran (NY)

BOZARTH, Alla Renée (Minn) 43222 SE Tapp Rd, Sandy, OR 97055

BOZZUTI-JONES, Mark Francisco (NY) 74 Trinity Place, New York, NY 10006

BRACKETT, Thomas L (WNC) 13 Kent Pl, Asheville, NC 28804

BRADA, Netha Nadine (Ia) 345 Lincoln Ave, Iowa Falls, IA 50126

BRADBURY, John Saferian (Ind)

BRADBURY, Stephanie C (Mass) 390 Main St, North Andover, MA 01845

BRADBURY, William John (Mass) 133 School Street, New Bedford, MA 02740

BRADEN, Anita (Mil) N26 W24150 River Park Drive, Milwaukee, WI 53072

BRADFORD, Kathleen Diane (Cal) 1713 Daisy Way, Antioch, CA 94509

BRADFORD, Lawrence J (Colo) 4131 E 26th Ave, Denver, CO 80207

BRADLEY, Carolyn Ann (NJ) 503 Asbury Ave, Asbury Park, NJ 07712

BRADLEY, Charles Eldwyn (Okla)

BRADLEY, Garyley J (Los) Immanuel Mission, 4366 Santa Anita Ave., El Monte, CA 91731

BRADLEY, James (Ct) 95 Cornwall Ave, Cheshire, CT 06410

BRADLEY, M Mantelle (NJ) 318 Elton Ln, Galloway, NJ 08205

BRADLEY, Margaret (Los) 619 W Roses Rd, San Gabriel, CA 91775

BRADLEY, Martha Jean (Spr) 3621 Troon DR, Springfield, IL 62712

BRADLEY, Matthew Bryant (Ky) St. John's Episcopal Church, 1620 Main St, Murray, KY 42071

BRADLEY, Michael Lee (NH) 15 Park Court, Durham, NH 03824

BRADLEY, Patrick John (WNY) 505 Riverdale Ave, Lewiston, NY 14092

BRADLEY, Raymond Earle (Ind) 15914 Blush Drive, Fishers, IN 46037

BRADNER, Lawrence Hitchcock (RI) 500 Angell St Apt 504, Providence, RI 02906

BRADSEN, Kate (Az)

BRADSHAW, Charles Robbins (Me) PO Box 399, Ambridge, PA 15003

BRADSHAW, Katie Ann (Miss) 550 Sunnybrook Rd, Ridgeland, MS 39157

BRADSHAW, Michael Ray (NC) St Paul's Episcopal Church, 520 Summit St, Winston Salem, NC 27101

BRADSHAW, Paul F (NI) University of Notre Dame, 1 Suffolk Street, London, SW1Y 4HG, Great Britain (UK)

BRADY, Amanda B Mandy (At)

BRADY, Christian Mark (CPa) 18 Hampton Ct, State College, PA 16803

BRADY, Jane Tanaskovic (NJ)

BRADY, Susan Jane (Colo)

BRADY II, William Donald (CFla) 9870 W Fort Island Trl, Crystal River, FL 34429

BRAINARD, Mary-Lloyd (Ct) 3A Gold St, Stonington, CT 06378

BRAINE, Beverly (Md) 2132 Corbett Rd., Monkton, MD 21111

BRAKE, Mary Wood (Va)

BRAKEMAN, Lyn G (Mass) 203 Pemberton St Unit #, Cambridge, MA 02140

BRALL, Catherine Mary (Pgh) 321 Parkside Ave, Pittsburgh, PA 15228

BRAMBILA, Gerardo Brambila (Az) 483 W. 80Th. Avenue, Denver, CO 80221

BRAMBLE, Peter Wilkin Duke (LI) 1417 Union St, Brooklyn, NY 11213

BRAMLETT, Bruce Richard (ECR) 6028 El Dorado Street, El Cerrito, CA 94530

BRAMLETT, Robert Gordon (Mil) 419 E Court St, Janesville, WI 53545

BRANCH, Caroline E (At) 2089 Ponce De Leon Ave NE, Atlanta, GA 30307

BRANCHE, Ronald Clifford (VI)

BRANDENBURG, John Paul (SO) 56482 Boyd Avenue, Bridgeport, OH 43912

BRANDENBURG, Nancy Lee (SO) Saint John'S Church, Worthington, OH 43085

BRANDON, Bonnie P (Los) 1874 W Nutwood Pl, Anaheim, CA 92804

BRANDON, Karen Dale (RG) 226 Jupiter Dr, White Sands Missile Range, NM 88002

BRANDON II, Miles Raymond (Tex) 1501 W 30th St, Austin, TX 78703

BRANDT JR, George Walter (NY) 16 Park Ave, Apt 9C, New York, NY 10016

BRANDT, Robert George (LI) 414 SW Horseshoe Bay, Port Saint Lucie, FL 34986

BRANNOCK, Christina Combs (Lex) PO Box 27, Paris, KY 40362

BRANNOCK-WANTER JR, Henry Paul (Vt) 257 Us Route 5, Hartland, VT 05048

BRANNON, Kenneth Hoffman (Ida) St. Thomas Episcopal Church, PO Box 1070, Sun Valley, ID 83353

BRANNON, Stephen Nave (The Episcopal NCal) 19275 Robinson Rd, Sonoma, CA 95476

BRANSCOMB JR, Wm (Ala) 532 W Ariel Ave, Foley, AL 36535

BRANSCOMBE, Mike (SwFla) 1010 Charles St, Clearwater, FL 33755

BRANSCOME III, Dexter Arno (Miss) 1 Oakleigh Pl, Jackson, MS 39211

BRANSON, John H (Ct) 827 Fearrington Post, Pittsboro, NC 27312

BRANSTETTER, Kent Alan (At) 3332 James Harbor Way, Lawrenceville, GA 30044

BRANT, George Henry (Nwk) 601 Park St Apt 11-D, Bordentown, NJ 08505

BRANTINGHAM, Nancy Marie (Minn) 3185 County Road 6, Long Lake, MN 55356

BRATHWAITE, Christopher Ethelbert (CFla) 102 North 9Th Street, Haines City, FL 33844

BRATHWAITE, Percy Alphonso (NY) 17 Granada Cres Apt 6, White Plains, NY 10603

BRAUN, Elise (Vt) Wood Road, Box 1033, Stowe, VT 05672

BRAUN, James Richard (Mil)

BRAUZA, Ellen Lederer (WNY) 4210 Gunnville Road, Clarence, NY 14031

BRAWLEY, Anna P (Ala) 1900 Darby Drive, Florence, AL 35630

BRAWLEY, Joan Biddles (CFla) 631 W Lake Elbert Dr, Winter Haven, FL 33881

BRAXTON JR, Louis (Nwk) 480 Warwick Ave, Teaneck, NJ 07666

BRAY, Doris S (Be) 443 Franklin Ave, Palmerton, PA 18071

BRDLIK, Christopher M F (Nwk) 914 Ridge Rd, Newton, NJ 07860

BREAKEY, Pamela Jean (WMich) 54581 California Rd, Dowagiac, MI 49047

BRECHNER, Eric Lonell (NJ) Po Box 126, Gibbsboro, NJ 08026

BRECHT, Laura Berger (SanD) 3425 Santa Saba Rd, Borrego Springs, CA 92004

BRECKENRIDGE, Elaine Howlett (Episcopal SJ) 31 W 37th Ave, Spokane, WA 99203

BRECKENRIDGE, Ella Huff (WLa) 1825 Albert Street, Alexandria, LA 71301

BRECKENRIDGE, William Allen (Az) 2721 N Dos Hombres Rd, Tucson, AZ 85715

BRECKINRIDGE IV, Alexander Negus (Oly) 8398 NE 12th St, Medina, WA 98039

BREDLAU, Mary Theresa (Nev) 8520 W Hammer Ln, Las Vegas, NV 89149

BREEDEN, James Pleasant (Mass) 29 Rope Ferry Rd # 3755, Hanover, NH 03755

BREEDLOVE, William L (WNC) Church Of The Good Shepherd, PO Box 677, Hayesville, NC 28904

BREEDLOVE II, William Otis (NJ) 10 Winthrop Road, Somerset, NJ 08873

BREESE, Mary Schrom (WMo) 2533 Francis St, Saint Joseph, MO 64501

BREESE, Sidney Samuel (WMo) 2533 Francis St, Saint Joseph, MO 64501

BREHE, Stephen Louis (Mont) 912 Stuart St., Helena, MT 59601

✠ **BREIDENTHAL**, Thomas Edward (Bp of SO 2007-) Diocese Of Southern Ohio, 412 Sycamore St, Cincinnati, OH 45202

BREINER, Bert Fredrick (NY) 401 W 24th St, New York, NY 10011

BRELSFORD, Diane (Oly) 507 5th Ave W, Seattle, WA 98119

BRENEMEN, Betty Jo (CGC) 18 West Wright Street Street, Pensacola, FL 32501

BRENMARK-FRENCH, Regina Kay (Chi) 2105 Cumberland St, Rockford, IL 61103

BRENNEIS, Michael Joseph (Va) 2309 N Kentucky St, Arlington, VA 22205

BRENNOM, Kesha Mai (Los) 4366 Santa Anita Ave., La Canada, CA 91731

BRENTLEY, David J (SO) 804 Clearfield Ln, Cincinnati, OH 45240

BRENTNALL, Burden (Oly) 9086 Chickadee Way, Blaine, WA 98230

BRENY, Judith Mary (WNY) 745 Ashland Ave, Buffalo, NY 14222

BRERETON, Thomas F (Colo) 2741 Freedom Heights, Colorado Springs, CO 80904

BRESCIANI, Eduardo Roberto (Los) 9037 Park St, Bellflower, CA 90706

BRESNAHAN, Paul B (Mass) 17 King Street, Unit 1, Lynn, MA 01902

BRETSCHER, Robert George (SwFla) 240 Hancock Ln, Athens, GA 30605

BRETTMANN, William Sims (EC) 557 Fearnington Post, Pittsboro, NC 27312

BREUER, David R (ECR) 20 University Ave, Los Gatos, CA 95030

BREWER, Aaron Keith (Ga) PO Box 273, Hawkinsville, GA 31036

BREWER, Anne (NY)

BREWER, Floyd William (SwFla) 910 Murfreesboro Rd Apt 314, Franklin, TN 37064

✠ **BREWER**, Gregory Orrin (Bp of CFla 2012-) 1017 East Robinson St, Orlando, FL 32801

BREWER, Johnny Lyvon (CGC) 7810 Navarre Pkwy, Navarre, FL 32566

BREWER JR, Luther Gordon (ETenn) 1417 Warpath Dr Ste B, Kingsport, TN 37664

BREWER, Richard Elliott (Okla) 6606 E 99th Pl, Tulsa, OK 74133

BREWER III, Richard Frederick (LI) Prestwick Farm, 2260 County Route 12, Whitehall, NY 12887

BREWER, Todd (Pgh) 4048 Brownsville Rd, Pittsburgh, PA 15227

BREWER, Virginia Gale (ETenn) Po Box 427, Monteagle, TN 37356

BREWIN-WILSON, Debra M (WA) 14300 Saint Thomas Church Rd, Upper Marlboro, MD 20772

BREWSTER, John Gurdon (CNY) 376 Shaffer Rd, Newfield, NY 14867

BREWSTER, John Pierce (At) 1064 Can Tex Dr, Sewanee, TN 37375

BREWSTER JR, William (O) 7 Bond Rd, Kittery Point, ME 03905

BREYER, Chloe Anne (NY) 1800 Adam Clayton Powell Blvd., Apartment 7B, New York, NY 10026

BREYFOGLE, Elizabeth Elain (Dal) 511 Foote St., McKinney, TX 75069

BREZNAU, Jack Charles (EMich) PO Box 1882, Caseville, MI 48725

BREZNAU, Nancy Ann (EMich) PO Box 1882, Caseville, MI 48725

BRICE, Jonathan Andrew William (Colo) Christ Episcopal Church, 536 W North St, Aspen, CO 81611

BRICE, Theresa (At) 302 West Avenue, Cedartown, GA 30125

BRICKSON, Cynthia Jean (Minn) 905 4th Ave S, Minneapolis, MN 55404

BRIDGE, Melvin Alden (FtW) 729 Carette Dr, Fort Worth, TX 76108

BRIDGE, Michael James (WK)

BRIDGE, Peter James (NJ) 1509 Esther Ln, Yardley, PA 19067

BRIDGEMOHAN, Areeta D (Mich)

BRIDGERS, Anne (SanD) 1114 9th St, Coronado, CA 92118

BRIDGES, David Leslie (The Episcopal NCal) 2376 Zinfandel Dr, Rancho Cordova, CA 95670

BRIDGES, Melva Gayle (Okla) 12719 S Couts Dr, Mustang, OK 73064

BRIDGES, Nancy (Okla) 408 Ridge Rd, Edmond, OK 73034

BRIDGES, Penelope Maud (SanD) 6935 Camino Pacheco, San Diego, CA 92111

BRIDGFORD, Peter W (WNY) 18 Harbour Pointe Cmn, Buffalo, NY 14202

BRIDGFORD, Richard Oliver (SVa) 707 Steiner Way, Norfolk, VA 23502

BRIDGFORTH, David Elgin (USC) 900 Calhoun St, Columbia, SC 29201

BRIGGS, Barbara K (NJ) 126 Lakewood Cir N, Manchester, CT 06040

BRIGGS, Lyn Zill (U) 661 Redondo Ave, Salt Lake City, UT 84105

BRIGGS, Michael E (Ark) PO Box 954, Granby, CO 80446

BRIGGS, Paul R (Ct) 14 Melody Ln, East Longmeadow, MA 01028

BRIGHAM, Richard Daniel (At) 208 Edgewater Way, Peachtree City, GA 30269

BRIGHT, Barbara Pamela (WNC) Episcopal Church of the Redeemer, 502 W Sumter St, Shelby, NC 28150

BRIGHT, Carl Connell (CGC) 198 Beardsley Court, Muscle Shoals, AL 35661

BRIGHT SR, Dee Wellington (Okla) 511 South Cabin Lake Drive, San Antonio, TX 78244

BRIGHT, John Adams (Cal) 812 Southwest Saint Clair Ave. Apt 1, Portland, OR 97209

BRIGHT, Patrick Edmund (Okla) 11901 Maple Hollow Ct, Oklahoma City, OK 73120

BRIGHT, Wheigar J (NC) PO Box 858, Yanceyville, NC 27379

BRIGHTMAN, Dorothy Louise (RI) 17 N Country Club Dr, Warwick, RI 02888

BRILL, Steven G (Oly) St Luke's Episcopal Church, PO Box 1294, Elma, WA 98541

BRIMM, Martha Carol (NC) 7 Surrey Ln, Durham, NC 27707

BRINDLEY, Thomas (Cal) 704 Sutro Ave, Novato, CA 94947

BRINKMAN, Charles Reed (Pa) 219 Hanover Rd, Phoenixville, PA 19460

BRINKMANN, Mark Ransom (SC) All Saints Episcopal Church, 3001 Meeting St, Hilton Head Island, SC 29926

BRINKMOELLER, Leonard Joseph (WMich) 312 Maple Street, Paw Paw, MI 49079

BRINSON, Katherine Herrington (Ga) 4227 Columbia Rd, Martinez Branch, GA 30907

BRION, Theresa Markley (Md) Episcopal Diocese of Maryland, 4 E University Parkway, Baltimore, MD 21218

BRIONES, Miguel Angel (Chi) 5101 W Devon Ave, Chicago, IL 60646

BRISBANE, Paul Owen (Colo) 513 N. Union City Rd., Coldwater, MI 49036

BRISBIN, James A (Alb) 2647 Brookview Rd., Castleton, NY 12033

BRISON, William Stanly (Ct) 2 Scott Ave, Bury, BL9 9RS, Great Britain (UK)

BRISSON JR, James L (Az) 868 Satinwood Ct, Fayetteville, NC 28312

BRISTOL II, Henry Platt (NJ) St David's Church, 90 S Main St, Cranbury, NJ 08512

BRISTOL, Joan Esther (Ore) 2529 Bel Abbes Ave, Medford, OR 97504

BRITCHER, Sharon Ann (CFla) 1010 Pennsylvania Ave, Fort Pierce, FL 34950

BRITNELL, Offie Wayne (Ak) 18609 S. Lowrie Loop, Eagle River, AK 99577

BRITO, Antonio Peguero (At) 1015 Old Roswell Rd, Roswell, GA 30076

BRITO, Napoleon Ramon (DR (DomRep)) Box 764, Santo Domingo, Dominican Republic

BRITT, Diane (LI) St Ann's Church, 257 Middle Rd, Sayville, NY 11782

BRITT, Lawrence Albert (WNC) 236 Camelot Dr, Morganton, NC 28655

BRITT, Marc Lawrence (WA) 2 Amy Ct, Pittsfield, MA 01201

BRITT, Sarah Eugenia (Swiss) (At) 253 Lake Somerset Dr Nw, Marietta, GA 30064

BRITT, Stephen (Fla) San Jose Episcopal, 7423 San Jose Blvd., Jacksonville, FL 32217

BRITTON, John Clay (Chi) 680 Madrona Ave S, Salem, OR 97302

BRITTON, Joseph Harp (Cal) St. Michael and All Angels Church, 601 Montano Road, NW, Albuquerque, NM 87107

BRITTON SR, Judith A (NMich) 365 Kirkpatrick Ln, Gwinn, MI 49841

BRITTON JR, Richard Carlisle (Tenn) 419 Woodland St., Nashville, TN 37206

BRO, Andrew Harmon (Chi) Po Box 111, Mount Carroll, IL 61053

BROACH, Merrill Kilburn (Kan) 3401 Plymouth Pl, New Orleans, LA 70131

BROAD, Thomas Michael (WNY) 19 N Washington St, Randolph, NY 14772

BROADFOOT III, Walter Marion (EC) 200 S. McMorrine Street, Elizabeth City, NC 27909

BROADHEAD, Alan John (ND) 107 Heartwood Drive, Lansdale, PA 19446

BROADLEY, Rodger Charles (Pa) 336 S Camac St, Philadelphia, PA 19107

BROCATO, Christian F (Mass) St. Peter's Episcopal Church, 838 Mass Ave., Cambridge, MA 02139

BROCHARD, Philip Thomas (Cal) 2729 Kinney Dr, Walnut Creek, CA 94595

BROCK, Charles F. (Va) St. James' Episcopal Church, Alexandria, VA 22309

BROCK, Elizabeth Ann (U) HC 69 Box 630016, Randlett, UT 84063

BROCK, Laurie M (Lex) 2025 Bellefont Dr, Lexington, KY 40503

BROCK, Velma Elaine Wooten (WA) 233 Cambridge St, Syracuse, NY 13210

BROCK, William Marshall (USC) 230 Pinecrest Dr Apt 25, Fayetteville, NC 28305

BROCKENBROUGH, Mignon L (SVa) PO Box 3520, Williamsburg, VA 23187

BROCKMAN, Bennett A(lbert) (Ct) 362 Lake St, Vernon, CT 06066

BROCKMAN, John Martin (Ind) 82 E. Colony Acres Dr., Brazil, IN 47834

BROCKMANN, R John (Mass) 78 Mann Hill Rd, Scituate, MA 02066

BROCKMANN, Sarah (Mass) 78 Mann Hill Road, Scituate, MA 02066

BROCKMEIER, Alan Lee (RG) 8516 N Prince St, Clovis, NM 88101

BROCKMEIER, Suzanne Carroll (RG) St James Episcopal Church, PO Box 249, Clovis, NM 88102

BRODERICK, Janet (Nwk) 268 2nd St, Jersey City, NJ 07302

BRODERICK, Rosemarie (NJ) P.O. Box 326, Navesink, NJ 07752

BRODERICK Y GUERRA, Cecily Patricia (LI) 3495 Hawthorne Dr N, Wantagh, NY 11793

BRODIE, Robert Earle (SwVa) 1612 Valhalla Ct, Salem, VA 24153

BRODY, Mary A (Roch) 190 Penarrow Rd., Rochester, NY 14618

BROGAN, Betty Jean (Mich) 17665 E Kirkwood Dr, Clinton Township, MI 48038

BROGAN, Margaret (Cal) 1432 Eastshore Dr, Alameda, CA 94501

BROKAW, Ronald Gene (CFla) 1106 Dorchester St, Orlando, FL 32803

BROME, Henderson Levere (Mass) 1201 Davenport Ave, Canton, MA 02021

BROMILEY, Hugh Philip (CFla) 1250 Paige Pl, The Villages, FL 32159

BRONDSTED, Linda Cole Judd (Eur) 1880 Taylor Ave, Winter Park, FL 32789

BRONK JR, Harold R (Mass) 27 Curtis Road, Milton, MA 02186

BRONOS, Sarah L. (CFla) 7718 White Ash Street, Orlando, FL 32819

BRONSON, David Louis (NY) 414 Cottekill Rd, Stone Ridge, NY 12484

BROOK, Robert Charles (Mich) 6112 W Longview Dr, East Lansing, MI 48823

BROOKE-DAVIDSON, Jennifer (WTex) 6000 Fm 3237 Unit A, Wimberley, TX 78676

BROOKFIELD, Christopher Morgan (Va) 1870 Field Rd, Charlottesville, VA 22903

✠ **BROOKHART JR**, Charles Franklin (Bp of Mont 2003-) PO Box 2020, Helena, MT 59624

BROOKMAN, Cathleen Anne (Chi) 29 West 410 Emerald Green Drive, Warrenville, IL 60555

BROOKS, Ashton Jacinto (VI) C/O Cathedral Church of the Epiphany, P O BOX 764, Santo Domingo, Dominican Republic

BROOKS, Donald Edgar (WTenn) 1436 Forest Drive, Union City, TN 38261

BROOKS, Ethelridge Albert (Hond) Aptd 28, La Ceiba Atlantida, 31101, Honduras

BROOKS, James Buckingham (Ida) Po Box 36, Letha, ID 83636

BROOKS, Kimberly (CPa) 248 Seneca St., Harrisburg, PA 17110

BROOKS, Porter Harrison (Va) 9797 Kedge Ct, Vienna, VA 22181

BROOKS, Richard Smith (WK) 1333 Crescent Ln, Concordia, KS 66901

BROOKS JR, Robert Brudon (NY) 4 Quail Ridge Rd, Hyde Park, NY 12538

BROOKS, Robert Johnson (Ct) 149 Mood Lake Drive, Kyle, TX 78640

BROOKS, Robert Thomas (RI) 285 West Main, 285 W Main Rd, Little Compton, RI 02837

BROOKS, Theodora Nmade (NY) 750 Kelly St, Bronx, NY 10455

BROOKS, Thomas Gerald (NY) 35 Cambridge Ct, Highland, NY 12528

BROOKS, Weldon Timothy (NH) 113 Main St, Lancaster, NH 03584

BROOKS, William Earl (Tex) 1718 Wentworth St, Houston, TX 77004

BROOME, John Tol (NC) 3009 Round Hill Rd, Greensboro, NC 27408

BROOME JR, William Bridges (Chi) 504 E Earle Street, Landrum, SC 29356

BROOMELL, Ann Johnson (Ct) 28 Long Hill Farm, Guilford, CT 06437

BROSEND II, William Frank (Ky) 335 Tennessee Ave., Sewanee, TN 37383

BROTHERTON, E Ann (Tex) 112101 Bluebonnet L, Manchaca, TX 78652

BROUCHT, Mary Louise (CPa) 126 N. Water St., Lancaster, PA 17603

BROUGHTON, Jacalyn Irene (Eau) E4357 451st Ave, Menomonie, WI 54751

BROUGHTON, William (SanD) 1830 Avenida Del Mundo Unit 712, Coronado, CA 92118

BROWDER, David O'Neal (Tex) St Dunstan's Episcopal Church, 14301 Stuebner Airline Rd, Houston, TX 77069

BROWDER III, James Wilbur (SVa) Po Box 133, Courtland, VA 23837

BROWER, David Angus (WMich) 7895 Adams St, Zeeland, MI 49464

BROWER, Gary Robert (Colo) 2050 E Evans Ave Ste 29, Denver, CO 80208

BROWER, George C (Ct) 503A Heritage Village, Southbury, CT 06488

BROWER, Katherine Moore (WMich) 335 Bridge St NW Apt 2301, Grand Rapids, MI 49504

BROWER, Meaghan M (RI) Episcopal Diocese of Rhode Island, 275 N Main St, Providence, RI 02903

BROWER, Sally Morgan (NC) 164 Fairview Rd, Mooresville, NC 28117

BROWN JR, Allen Webster (Va) 3625 SE 17th Pl, Cape Coral, FL 33904

BROWN, Barton (NJ)

BROWN, Bernard Owen (Chi) 5417 S Blackstone Ave, Chicago, IL 60615

BROWN, Charles Homer (Okla) 1416 Stoneridge Pl, Ardmore, OK 73401

BROWN, Christopher Aubrey (Alb) 437 Old Potsdam Parishville Road, Potsdam, NY 13676

BROWN, Clifford Ross (Mass) 351 Pearl St # 1, Cambridge, MA 02139

BROWN, Colin (Los) 1024 Beverly Way, Altadena, CA 91001

BROWN, Craig Howard (WK) 3710 Summer Ln, Hays, KS 67601

BROWN, Daniel Aaron (NC) 936 Cannock St, Grovetown, GA 30813

BROWN, Daniel Barnes (At) Po Box 490, Clarkesville, GA 30523

BROWN, David Churchman (WNC) 500 Christ School Rd, Arden, NC 28704

BROWN, David Crane (NY) 125 Prospect Ave Apt 9G, Hackensack, NJ 07601

BROWN, David Wooster (Ct) 729 W Beach Rd, Charlestown, RI 02813

BROWN, Deborah Eleanor (Minn) 1297 Wilderness Curv, Eagan, MN 55123

BROWN, Deborah Renee (Ore) Diocese of Oregon, 11800 SW Military Ln, Portland, OR 97219

BROWN, Dennis Roy Alfred (CGC) 306 Grant St, Chickasaw, AL 36611

BROWN JR, Dewey Everrett (SwFla) 37637 Magnolia Ave, Dade City, FL 33523

BROWN, Don (La) 224 Pecan Ave, New Roads, LA 70760

BROWN, Donald Gary (Cal) 2821 Claremont Blvd, Berkeley, CA 94705

BROWN, Donn H (At) 217 Booth St Apt 119, Gaithersburg, MD 20878

BROWN, Donna Hvistendahl (WA) 1318 Charlottesville Blvd, Knoxville, TN 37922

BROWN, Dorothy Lynne (At) 1197 Skyline Drive, Toccoa, GA 30577

BROWN, Dwight Larcom (Va) 115 North Church St, Berryville, VA 22611

BROWN, Elly (WA) 5006-B Barbour Dr, Alexandria, VA 22304

BROWN, Enrique Ricardo (WA) 5248 Colorado Ave Nw, Washington, DC 20011

BROWN III, Ervin Adams (Eas) 2212 E Baltimore St, Baltimore, MD 21231

BROWN JR, F Wilson (SwVa) 715 Sunset Drive, Bedford, VA 24523

BROWN, Fred Mckelder (ETenn) Good Shepherd Episcopal Church, 211 Franklin Rd, Lookout Mountain, TN 37350

BROWN, Freda Marie (Tex) St. Vincent's Episcopal House, 2817 Alfreda Houston Place, Galveston, TX 77550

BROWN, Frederick Ransom (Vt) 346 Gladys Avenue, Long Beach, CA 90814

BROWN, Gary Neil (The Episcopal NCal)

BROWN III, George Willcox (Dal) 409 Prospect St, New Haven, CT 06511

BROWN, Ginny (Colo) 706 E. 3rd Avenue, Durango, CO 81301

BROWN, Gregory Bryan Francis (WMich) 1020 E Mitchell St, Petoskey, MI 49770

BROWN, Gregory Michael (Los) St Cross Episcopal Church, 1818 Monterey Blvd, Hermosa Beach, CA 90254

BROWN III, Henry William (CFla) Po Box 1420, Homosassa Springs, FL 34447

BROWN JR, H (Horace) Frederick (WTex) 309 S Someday Dr, Boerne, TX 78006

BROWN III, Hugh Eldridge (NJ) 16 All Saints Rd, Princeton, NJ 08540

BROWN, Ian Frederick (Mich) 26 Tower Dr., Saline, MI 48176

✠ **BROWN**, James Barrow (Resigned Bp of La 1998-) 2136 Octavia St, New Orleans, LA 70115

BROWN, James Louis (O)

BROWN, James Thompson (Cal) 6225 Vine Hill School Rd, Sebastopol, CA 95472

BROWN, Janet Easson (CPa) 140 N Beaver St, York, PA 17401

BROWN, Janet Kelly (Vt) Po Box 351, Jericho, VT 05465

BROWN, Jennifer Clarke (NC) 2212 Tyson Street, Raleigh, NC 27612

BROWN, Jennifer Elaine (NY) 1558 Unionport Rd Apt 7E, Bronx, NY 10462

BROWN JR, John Ashmore (USC) 9 Sweet Branch Ct, Columbia, SC 29212

BROWN, John Clive (Ore) 431-A Red Blanket Rd, Prospect, OR 97536

BROWN, John Daniel (Dal) 7610 Rockingham Rd, Prospect, KY 40059

BROWN, John Thompson (Ala) 4157 Winston Way, Birmingham, AL 35213

BROWN, Keith Burton (Episcopal SJ) 1776 S Homsy Ave, Fresno, CA 93727

BROWN, Kenneth E (WA) 1318 Charlottesville Blvd, Knoxville, TN 37922

BROWN, Kevin S (NC) Church of the Holy Comforter, 2701 Park Rd, Charlotte, NC 28209

BROWN, Lawrence Mitchell (Los) 2095 Stoneman St, Simi Valley, CA 93065

BROWN, Lila Byrd (Fla) 2358 Riverside Ave. #704, Jacksonville, FL 32204

BROWN, Linda Josephine (Colo) 1700 W 10th Ave, Broomfield, CO 80020

BROWN, Lydia Huttar (Minn) 10 Buffalo Rd, North Oaks, MN 55127

BROWN, Lyle L (Ia) 605 Avenue E, Fort Madison, IA 52627

BROWN, Marilynn M(arie) (Ore) 332338 109Th Pl SE Apt 102, Auburn, WA 98092

BROWN, Marion Mackey (SwFla) 208 Ne Monroe Cir N Apt 103-C, Saint Petersburg, FL 33702

BROWN, Mark (Mass) 980 Memorial Dr, Cambridge, MA 02138

BROWN, Mary K (Va) 228 Pitt St, Alexandria, VA 22314

BROWN, Nancy (Los) 2095 Stoneman St, Simi Valley, CA 93065

BROWN, Nancy Elisabeth (Okla) 3914 E. 37th Street, Tulsa, OK 74135

BROWN, Neva Wilkins (Md)

BROWN, Percival George (LI) 926 Dana Ave, Valley Stream, NY 11580

BROWN, Ralph Douglas (Ind) Po Box 1596, Old Fort, NC 28762

BROWN, Raymond Dutson (Mont) 6162 Lazy Man Gulch, Helena, MT 59601

BROWN, Raymond Francis (EC) 205 Bedell Pl, Fayetteville, NC 28314

BROWN, Rebecca Susan (Colo) 6832 W 69th Ave, Arvada, CO 80003

BROWN, Reed Haller (Vt) 49 Brewer Pkwy, South Burlington, VT 05403

BROWN III, Richard Julius (ETenn) 1431 Armiger Lane, Knoxville, TN 37932

BROWN, Rob (USC) 531 Old Iron Works Rd, Spartanburg, SC 29302

BROWN, Robert Eugene (Ore)

BROWN, Robert Henry (Pa) 117 Pine Lake Dr, Whispering Pines, NC 28327

BROWN, Robert James Crawford (FdL) 778 Hillside Ter, Ripon, WI 54971

BROWN, Robert Labannah (Neb) 9302 Blondo St, Omaha, NE 68134

BROWN, Rodney K (Eas) 32659 Seaview Loop, Millsboro, DE 19966

BROWN, Rosa Maria (Los) 1011 S Verdugo Rd, Glendale, CA 91205

BROWN, Royce Walter (Wyo) Central Wyoming Hospice, 319 S Wilson, Casper, WY 82601

BROWN, Ruth Ellen (Az) 9071 E Old Spanish Trl, Tucson, AZ 85710

BROWN, Sally Sims (Colo)

BROWN, Scott Jeffrey (WTex) 1417 E Austin Ave, Harlingen, TX 78550

BROWN, Thomas James (Mass) 70 Church St., Winchester, MA 01890

BROWN, Virginia Dabney (WMo) 874 Yorkchester, # 108, Houston, TX 77079

BROWN JR, Walter R (Ark) 12415 Cantrell Rd, Little Rock, AR 72223

BROWN, Wanda Gaye (NC) 308 W Main St, Elkin, NC 28621

BROWN, William Garland (Lex) 311 Washington St, Frankfort, KY 40601

BROWN III, William Hill (Va) 5103 Harlan Cir, Richmond, VA 23226

BROWN, William Stewart (Ida) 5605 Lynwood Pl., Boise, ID 83706

BROWN, Willis Donald (Ky) 2402 Glenview Ave, Louisville, KY 40222

BROWN DOUGLAS, Kelly Delaine (WA) 12519 Hawks Nest Ln, Germantown, MD 20876

BROWNE, Bliss Williams (Chi) 7743 SE Loblolly Bay Dr, Hobe Sound, FL 33455

BROWNE, Frances Louise (NC) 303 Eastchester Dr, High Point, NC 27262

BROWNE, Gayle (SO) 212 Tulane Ave, Oak Ridge, TN 37830

BROWNE III, Joseph M (EC) 200 NC Highway 33 W, Chocowinity, NC 27817

BROWNE, Joy Elizabeth (Ky) 922 Milford Ln, Louisville, KY 40207

BROWNE, Samuel Jonathan (SeFla) 426 Cypress Dr, Lake Park, FL 33403

BROWNELL, Leona Weiss (Del) 4830 Kennett Pike #3504, Wilmington, DE 19807

BROWNING JR, Bob (Nwk) Grace Church, 128 W Passaic Ave, Rutherford, NJ 07070

BROWNING II, Charles Alex (SeFla) 2707 NW 37th Street, Boca Raton, FL 33434

✠ **BROWNING**, Edmond Lee (Ret PBp) of The Episcopal Church 1997-) 5164 Imai Rd, Hood River, OR 97031

BROWNING, Peter Sparks (Los) 2 HIdalgo, Irvine, CA 92620

BROWNING JR, robert guy (SwFla) 7038 West Brandywine Circle, Fort Myers, FL 33919

BROWNING, Trace (U) Rowland Hall St Marks School, 720 Guardsman Way, Salt Lake City, UT 84108

BROWNLEE, Annette Geoffrian (Colo) 410 W 18th St, Pueblo, CO 81003

BROWNMILLER, David Clark (Ore) 16379 Nw Charlais St, Beaverton, OR 97006

BROWN-NOLAN, Virginia (WA) 12613 Meadowood Dr, Silver Spring, MD 20904

BROWNRIDGE, Walter B.A. (The Episcopal Church in Haw) The Cathedral Church of St. Andrew, 229 Queen Emma Square, Honolulu, HI 96813

BROYLES, Elizabeth Ruth (NY) 37 Chipmunk Hollow Rd, Kerhonkson, NY 12446

BRUBAKER GARRISON, Tasha (Ore) 418 Stonewood Dr, Eugene, OR 97405

BRUCE, David Allison (Me) Brigham'S Cove Road, Box 243 HCR 63, West Bath, ME 04530

✠ **BRUCE**, Diane M Jardine (Bp Suffr of Los 2010-) 5 W Trenton, Irvine, CA 92620

BRUCE, Jane (NC) 750 Weaver Dairy Rd Apt 1225, Chapel Hill, NC 27514

BRUCE, John Allen (Ore) 31877 SW Village Crest Ln, Wilsonville, OR 97070

BRUCE, Todd (The Episcopal NCal)

BRUCE, Tracy Ann (Md) 5814 19th St N, Arlington, VA 22205

BRUCKART, Robert Monroe (CFla) 2327 Saint Andrews Cir, Melbourne, FL 32901

BRUGGER, Stephanie Black (SO) 335 Lincoln Ave, Troy, OH 45373

BRUMBAUGH, Charles Fredrick (SO) 72 Reily Rd, Cincinnati, OH 45215

BRUNDIGE, Allyson Paige (Nwk) 333 Christian St, Wallingford, CT 06492

BRUNEAU, Betsy (The Episcopal NCal) 66 E. Commercial St., Willits, CA 95490

BRUNELLE, Denis Charles (LI) PO Box 2733, East Hampton, NY 11937

BRUNETT, Harry Edgar (Md) 9855 S Iris Ct, Littleton, CO 80127

BRUNNER, Arthur F (Pa) Po Box 1190, N Cape May, NJ 08204

BRUNO, Jean M (DR (DomRep)) Box 1309, Port-Au-Prince, Haiti

✠ **BRUNO**, Joseph Jon (Bp of Los 2002-) 3505 Grayburn Rd., Pasadena, CA 91107

BRUNO, Suzanne Lee (NC) 9528 Spurwig Ct, Charlotte, NC 28278

BRUNS, Thomas Charles (Mo) 222 Montwood, Seguin, TX 78155

BRUNSON, Catherine E (NJ) 124 Harrow Dr, Somerset, NJ 08873

BRUSCO, Kathleen (Minn) 112 Crestridge Dr, Burnsville, MN 55337

BRUSSO, Leonard George (SeFla) 1225 Knollcrest Ct, Venice, FL 34285

BRUST, John Costello (SwFla) 1201 Yellowstone Dr, Naples, FL 34110

BRUTTELL, Susan Margaret (SeFla) 706 Glenwood Ln, Plantation, FL 33317

BRUTTELL, Thomas Allen (SeFla) 706 Glenwood Ln, Plantation, FL 33317

BRUTUS, Joseph Mathieu (Hai) Box 1309, Port-Au-Prince, Haiti

BRYAN, Christopher (Tenn) The School of Theology, The University of the South, 335 Tennessee Ave, Sewanee, TN 37398

BRYAN, Elizabeth Persis (SD) 1521 Forest Dr, Rapid City, SD 57701

BRYAN, Joan Carr (Fla) PO Box 1584, Ponte Vedra Beach, FL 32004

BRYAN, Jonathan (Va) 7815 Midday Ln, Alexandria, VA 22306

BRYAN, Nancy Ann (Cal) 2111 Hyde St # 404, San Francisco, CA 94109

BRYAN, Peggy L (ECR) 5038 Hyland Ave, San Jose, CA 95127

BRYAN, Walter Lee (WNC) PO Box 1356, Columbus, NC 28722

BRYANT, Bronson Howell (Miss) 5408 Vinings Lake View, SW, Mableton, GA 30126

BRYANT, Julie Diane (Los) Church of the Transfiguration, 1881 South First Avenue, Arcadia, CA 91006

BRYANT, Katherine Seavey (Va) 14 Cornwall St NW, Leesburg, VA 20176

BRYANT, Laura Annette (At) 2456 Tanglewood Rd, Decatur, GA 30033

BRYANT, Peter F (Roch) 4160 Back River Rd, Scio, NY 14880

BRYANT, Richard Gordon (Md) 678 Dave Ct, Covington, KY 41015

BRYANT, Robert Harrison (Ore) 6300 Sw Nicol Rd, Portland, OR 97223

BRYANT, Todd Alan (Tex) 5826 Doliver Dr, Houston, TX 77057

BRYANT, William Reid (WLa) 715 Lewisville Rd, Minden, LA 71055

BRYCE, Christopher David Francis (USC) 819 Angela Ln, Cross, SC 29436

BRYSON, Nancy Gretchen (CFla)

BRZEZINSKI, James (RG)

BUB, Sally Letchworth (Wyo) 30 Diversion Dam Rd, Kinnear, WY 82516

BUCCO, Dennis M (RI) 58 Arrowhead Ln, West Greenwich, RI 02817

BUCHAN, Thomas Nicholson (CFla) 1716 River Lakes Rd N, Oconomowoc, WI 53066

BUCHANAN, Andrew (SVa) 3928 Pacific Ave, Virginia Beach, VA 23451

BUCHANAN, Furman Lee (USC) 910 Hudson Road, Greenville, SC 29615

BUCHANAN, H Ray (SwFla) 9650 Gladiolus Dr, Fort Myers, FL 33908

✠ **BUCHANAN**, John Clark (Asst Bp of Chi 2013-2015) 1Bishop Gadsden Way Apt 332, Charleston, SC 29412

BUCHANAN, Margaret Grace (WNC) 827 Montreat Rd, Black Mountain, NC 28711

BUCHANAN, Susan Jill (Va) PO Box 1135, Glen, NH 03838

Clergy List

BUCHHOLZ, Paige Randolph (ETenn) 1211 Oakdale Trl, Knoxville, TN 37914

BUCHIN, Daniel Arthur (Mich) 2260 Baltic Ave, Idaho Falls, ID 83404

BUCK, David E (NC) 616 Watson St., Davidson, NC 28036

BUCK, Elizabeth (EC) 744 Lakeside Dr Se, Bolivia, NC 28422

BUCK, Leonard Frank (HB)

BUCK, Martha (ECR) 651 Sinex Ave Apt L115, Pacific Grove, CA 93950

BUCK, Robert Allen (Colo) 3070 Indiana St, Golden, CO 80401

BUCK-GLENN, Judith (Pa) 1031 N Lawrence St, Philadelphia, PA 19123

BUCKINGHAM, Carole Sylmay (Wyo) PO Box 12, Kaycee, WY 82639

BUCKINGHAM, Karen Burnquist (Wyo) 608 6th St, Rawlins, WY 82301

BUCKLEY, Abigail J (ETenn) St Barnabas Episcopal Church, 822 SW 2nd St, Mcminnville, OR 97128

BUCKLEY, Herbert Wilkinson (U) 1964 Colorado Gulch Dr, Helena, MT 59601

BUCKLIN, Lydia Kelsey (Ia) 225 37th St, Des Moines, IA 50312

BUCKWALTER, Georgine (Ky) 2511 Cottonwood Dr, Louisville, KY 40242

BUCKWALTER, Paul William (Az) 927 N 10th Ave, Tucson, AZ 85705

BUDD, Dorothy Reid (Dal) 3707 Crescent Ave, Dallas, TX 75205

BUDD, Richard Wade (SVa) 120 Cypress Crk, Williamsburg, VA 23188

✠ BUDDE, Mariann Edgar (Bp of WA, DC 2011-) Diocese of Washington, Episcopal Church House-Mount St Alban, Washington, DC 20016

BUDEZ, Jorge Horacio (WNY)

BUDHU, Esar (Nwk) 206 Renshaw Ave, East Orange, NJ 07017

BUDNEY, Karen Vickers (CNY) 18 Cross St., Dover, MA 02030

BUECHELE, Thomas J (The Episcopal Church in Haw) 15-2686 Hinalea St, Pahoa, HI 96778

BUECHNER, Deborah Ann (CFla) 1078 Coastal Cir, Ocoee, FL 34761

BUECHNER, Frederick Alvin (Ga)

BUEHLER, Lynnsay Anne (At) 147 Shadowmoor Dr, Decatur, GA 30030

BUEHRENS, Gwen Langdoc (Mass) 1333 Gough St. Apt 1-D, San Francisco, CA 94109

BUELL, Susan Davies (NwPa) 75 Perry St. 2A, New York City, NY 10014

BUELOW, Peggy Butterbaugh (SVa) 23397 Owen Farm Road, Carrollton, VA 23314

BUENO BUENO, Francisco Javier (Colom)

BUENTING, Julianne (Chi) 3857 N Kostner Ave, Chicago, IL 60641

BUENZ JR, John Frederick (ECR) 22115 Dean Ct, Cupertino, CA 95014

BUFFONE, Gregory James (Tex)

BUHRER, Richard Albert (Oly)

BUICE, Bonnie Carl (At) 115 Maplewood Ave Sw, Milledgeville, GA 31061

BUICE, Samuel Walton (At) 3 Westridge Rd, Savannah, GA 31411

BUICE, William Ramsey (Hond) 10100 Hillview Dr #4A, Pensacola, FL 32514

BUIE, Delinda (Ky) 2341 Strathmoor Blvd, Louisville, KY 40205

BUISSON, Pierre-Henry (Az) 375 Benfield Rd, Severna Park, MD 21146

BUKER, Karen Elaine (Mil) 3380 S Jeffers Dr, New Berlin, WI 53146

BULL, Julian Patrick (Los) 5049 Gloria Ave, Encino, CA 91436

BULL, Terry Wayne (WNY) 633 Harrison Ave, Buffalo, NY 14223

BULLARD, Carol Ann (Neb) 1603 17th St, Mitchell, NE 69357

BULLARD, Jill Staton (NC) 403 E Main St, Durham, NC 27701

BULLARD, Lynn Huston (Ala) 8020 Whitesburg Dr S, Huntsville, AL 35802

BULLION, James Regis (Ga) 512 Flamingo Ln., Albany, GA 31707

BULLITT-JONAS, Margaret (WMass) 83 Bancroft Rd, Northampton, MA 01060

BULLOCK, A(rlan) Richard (Ore) 22346 Se Hoffmeister Rd, Damascus, OR 97089

BULLOCK, Debra K (Chi) St. Mark's Episcopal Church, 1509 Ridge Avenue, Evanston, IL 60201

BULLOCK, Jeffrey L (Los) 13182 N Deergrass Drive, Oro Valley, AZ 85755

BULLOCK, Kenneth R (Pa) 213 Stable Rd, Carrboro, NC 27510

BULLOCK, Michael Anderson (Pa) 1040 Brentwood Dr, Columbia, SC 29206

BULSON, William Lawrence (Minn) 13000 Saint Davids Rd, Minnetonka, MN 55305

BUMGARNER, William Ray (SwVa)

BUMILLER, William Norton (SO) 320 Lonsdale Ave, Dayton, OH 45419

BUMP, Anne Glass (Mich) 1708 Jamestown Place, Pittsburgh, PA 15235

BUMSTED, David S (CFla) Church Of The Redeemer, 222 S Palm Ave, Sarasota, FL 34236

BUNCH, Wilton H. (Ala) Samford University, Birmingham, AL 35229

BUNDER, Peter J (Ind) 610 Meridian St, West Lafayette, IN 47906

BUNKE, Jeff L (O) 871 E Boundary St, Perrysburg, OH 43551

BUNKER, Oliver Franklin (Kan) Grace Episcopal Church, 209 S Lincoln Ave, Chanute, KS 66720

BUNN III, George Strother (SwVa) 518 Beech Forest Rd, Bristol, TN 37620

BUNSY, Martin (Episcopal SJ) 1327 N Del Mar Ave, Fresno, CA 93728

BUNTAINE, Raymond Earl (NJ) 106 Palmwood Ave, Cherry Hill, NJ 08003

BUNTING, Michael Andrew (Mil) 290 Quintard Rd # 19, Sewanee, TN 37375

BUNTING SR, Norman Richard (Eas) St Paul's Episcopal Church, 3 Church St, Berlin, MD 21811

BUNYAN, Frederick Satyanandam (Colo) 1749 Stove Prairie Cir, Loveland, CO 80538

BUOTE-GREIG, Eletha A (RI) Po Box 192, North Scituate, RI 02857

BUQUOR, Anthony Francis (Mass) 1357 Old Marlboro Rd, Concord, MA 01742

BURBANK, Kristina Dawn (Ore)

BURCH, Charles Francis (Mil) W356 N5928 Meadow Court, Oconomowoc, WI 53066

BURCH, Ian C (Mil) 1424 N Dearborn St, Chicago, IL 60610

BURCH, Suzanne (ETenn) 4111 Albemarle Ave, Chattanooga, TN 37411

BURCHARD, Russell Church (SwVa) 51 Mayapple Gln, Dawsonville, GA 30534

BURCHILL, George Stuart (SwFla) 2611 Bayshore Blvd, Tampa, FL 33629

BURDEKIN, Edwina Amelia (Colo)

BURDEN, Richard James (Mass) 2323 Lexington Rd, Richmond, KY 40475

BURDESHAW, Charles Abbott (Tenn) 139 Brighton Close, Nashville, TN 37205

BURDETT, Audrey (At) 3223 Rilman Rd Nw, Atlanta, GA 30327

BURDICK II, Edward Noyes (SO) 2437 Swans Rd Ne, Newark, OH 43055

BURDICK III, Henry Carlyle (Ct) 152 Wharf Landing Dr Unit A, Edenton, NC 27932

BURG, Michael John (FdL) 2515 Lakeshore Dr, Sheboygan, WI 53081

BURGDORF, David H (Los) 36270 Avenida De Las Montanas, Cathedral City, CA 92234

BURGER, Charles Sherman (Ida) 9640 W. Sleepy Hollow Ln, Garden Valley, ID 83714

BURGER, Douglas Clyde (RI) 214 Oakley Rd, Woonsocket, RI 02895

BURGER, Robert Franz (Wyo) Po Box 579, Estes Park, CO 80517

BURGER, Timothy H (WMass) 11 Berkeley Pl, Glen Rock, NJ 07452

BURGESS, B(arbara) Candis (NC) Po Box 1547, Clemmons, NC 27012

BURGESS, Brian Kendall (NJ) The Rectory of Christ Church, 62 Delaware Street, Woodbury, NJ 08096

BURGESS, Carol Jean (NC) 721 7 Lks N, Seven Lakes, NC 27376

BURGESS, Judith Fleming (RG) 134 Hillcrest Loop, Capitan, NM 88316

BURGESS, Vicki Tucker (Tenn) 4016 Brush Hill Rd, Nashville, TN 37216

BURGESS, Walter F (Eas) 105 Gay St, Denton, MD 21629

BURGOS, Joe A (Tex) 305 Sunset Drive, North Manchester, IN 46962

BURGOYNE, Douglas G (Va)

BURHANS III, Charles F (CFla)

BURHOE, Alden Read (Mass) 54 Grant Ave, Somerset, MA 02726

BURK, John Harry (Episcopal SJ) 599 Colton St, Monterey, CA 93940

BURK, William H (Va) 7159 Mechanicsville Tpke, Mechanicsville, VA 23111

BURKARDT, Jay P (Roch) Episcopal Churc St Paul, 25 Westminster Rd, Rochester, NY 14607

BURKARDT, Leslie S (Roch) 2000 Highland Ave, Rochester, NY 14618

BURKE, Anne B (RI) 66 Elm St Apt 1, Westerly, RI 02891

BURKE, Celine Ann (WMich) 1033 NW Stannium Rd, Bend, OR 97701

BURKE, Cyril Casper (Ct) 26 Hoskins Rd, Bloomfield, CT 06002

BURKE, Geneva Frances (Mich) 21514 Deguindre, #202, Warren, MI 48091

BURKE, Michael Edward (Ak) 3221 Amber Bay Loop, Anchorage, AK 99515

BURKE, Norman Charles (Az) 9552 West Wild Turkey Lane, Strawberry, AZ 85544

BURKE, Richard Early (Mass) 3279 Flamingo Blvd, Hernando Beach, FL 34607

BURKE, Robert Thomas (NwPa) Grace Episcopal Church, 10121 Hall Ave, Lake City, PA 16423

BURKE, Sean D (Ia) 201 Hollihan St, Decorah, IA 52101

BURKETT, William Vernard (SwFla) 2902 Weset San Rafael Street, Tampa, FL 33629

BURKHART, John Delmas (Lex) 701 E Engineer St, Corbin, KY 40701

BURKS, Bill Edward (WTenn) 98 Jim Dedmon Rd., Dyer, TN 38330

BURLEIGH, Judith Cushing (Me) PO Box 8, Presque Isle, ME 04769

BURLEY, Aloysius Englebert John Timothy (Minn) 615 W Tanglewood Dr, Arlington Heights, IL 60004

BURLEY III, Clarence Augustus (ECR) 651 Broadway, Gilroy, CA 95020

BURLINGTON, R(obert) Craig (RI) 2070 Homewood Blvd Apt 306, Delray Beach, FL 33445

BURMAN, Susan Crandall (FdL) 315 E Jefferson St, Waupun, WI 53963

BURMEISTER, Melissa Lynne (Mil) 5556 E. Colonial Oaks Dr., Monticello, IN 47960

BURNARD, Karen (SO) 6073 Contreras Rd, Oxford, OH 45056

BURNER, Dan E (Roch)

☩ **BURNETT**, Joe Goodwin (Form Asst Bp of Md 2014-) 932 N 145th Circle, Omaha, NE 68154

BURNETT, Joseph or Jody Goodwin (Miss) Cathedral Parish Of St Andrew, 305 E Capitol St, Jackson, MS 39201

BURNETT, Richard Alvin (SO) 125 E Broad St, Columbus, OH 43215

BURNETTE, William Marc (Ala) 1930 Fairfax Dr, Florence, AL 35630

BURNHAM, Frederic Bradford (NY) 556 Lakeshore Drive Ext, Asheville, NC 28804

BURNHAM, Karen Lee (Colo) 2029 Pine St, Pueblo, CO 81004

BURNS, A(Nn) Lyn (Colo) PO Box 635, La Veta, CO 81055

BURNS, Deborah Stanbrough (Kan) 3021 Steven Dr, Lawrence, KS 66049

BURNS, Duncan Adam (LI) 209 Albany Ave, Kingston, NY 12401

BURNS, Jacquelyn Mae (SO) St John's Episcopal Church, 700 High St, Worthington, OH 43085

BURNS, James Lee (NY) 111 Hunt Road, Hillsdale, NY 12529

BURNS, Jerome Wilson (SO) 6130 Gioffre Woods Ln, Columbus, OH 43232

BURNS JR, Jervis Oliver (Miss) 204 Donnybrook Dr, Carriere, MS 39426

BURNS, Leonetta Faye (Me) 52 Dondero Rd, Chelsea, ME 04330

BURNS, Steven Thomas (Eau)

BURNS, Thomas Dale (NwT) 3402 W Ohio Ave, Midland, TX 79703

BURR, John Terry (Roch) 594 Stearns Rd, Churchville, NY 14428

BURR, Whitney Haight (Mass) 175 Shane Dr, Chatham, MA 02633

☩ **BURRILL**, William George (Ret Bp of Roch 1999-) 7550 N. 16th Street #5204, Phoenix, AZ 85020

BURRIS, Richard R (Okla) 900 Schulze Dr., Norman, OK 73071

BURROUGHS, Joseph Parker (Md) 7236 Gaither Rd, Sykesville, MD 21784

BURROWS, Judith Anne (WNY) 106 Hickory Hill Rd Apt A, Buffalo, NY 14221

BURROWS, Paul Anthony (Cal) 474 48th Avenue, Apt 23A, Long Island City, NY 11109

BURRUSS, John Bailey (WTenn) 8282 Macon Rd, Cordova, TN 38018

BURSON, Grace Pritchard (NH) 20 Winter Street, Episcopal Church of the Holy Spirit, Plymouth, NH 03264

BURT, William R (Md)

BURTENSHAW, Noel C (At) 2813 Greenhouse Pkwy, Alpharetta, GA 30022

BURTON, Anthony John (Dal) 3966 McKinney Ave, Dallas, TX 75204

BURTON, Bob (Az) 9502 W. Hutton Drive, Sun City, AZ 85351

BURTON, Cassandra Yvonne (WA)

BURTON, Christine Hazel (RI) PO Box 48, Hope Valley, RI 02832

BURTON, Jack C(alvin) (SO) Norton Orchard Rd, PO Box 5195, Edgartown, MA 02539

BURTON, James M (SC) 126 Taylor Cir, Goose Creek, SC 29445

BURTON, JOHN DRYDEN (Ark) 807 COUNTY ROAD 102, EUREKA SPRINGS, AR 72632

BURTON, John L (Ct)

BURTON, John Peter (Chi) 4839 W Howard, Skokie, IL 60076

BURTON, Kenneth William Fowler (Colo) 472 Crystal Hills Blvd, Manitou Springs, CO 80829

BURTON, Laurel Arthur (Ark)

BURTON, Whitney A (At)

BURTON-EDWARDS, Grace (At) St Thomas Episcopal Church, 2100 Hilton Ave, Columbus, GA 31906

BURTS, Ann Horton (NC) 8804 Broadmore Ct, Raleigh, NC 27613

BUSBY, Lisa Jo (CNY) 37 W Main St, Norwich, NY 13815

BUSCH, Edward Leonard (SanD) 11650 Calle Paracho, San Diego, CA 92128

BUSCH, Glenn Edward (NC) 3024 Cardinal Pl, Lynchburg, VA 24503

BUSCH, Richard Alan (Los) 4125 36th St S, Arlington, VA 22206

BUSH JR, Arnold Arlington (CGC) 1109 Bristol Way, Birmingham, AL 35242

BUSH, Emilie Chaudron (Los) St. Paul's, PO Box 726, Barstow, CA 92312

BUSH, Katherine McQuiston (WTenn) 718 Charles Place, Memphis, TN 38112

BUSH, Patricia (SanD) 4642 Utah Street #1, San Diego, CA 92116

BUSH, Patrick M (Ct) 11 Church St, Tariffville, CT 06081

BUSHEE, Grant Sartori (Cal) 1225 Rosefield Way, Menlo Park, CA 94025

BUSHEY JR, Howard Wallace (La) 8833 Goodwood Blvd, Baton Rouge, LA 70806

BUSHNELL, Peter Emerson (Ct) Holy Trinity Church, 383 Hazard Ave., Enfield, CT 06082

BUSHONG JR, Edward S (SVa) 2806 E. Marshall St., Richmond, VA 23223

BUSLER, George Warren (LI) P. O. Box 55, Westhampton Beach, NY 11978

BUSSE, Mary Ruth (Fla) 3580 Pine St, Jacksonville, FL 32205

BUSTARD-BURNSIDE, Carol (Md) 1106 Woodheights Ave, Baltimore, MD 21211

BUSTO, Mercedes (SeFla)

BUSTRIN, Robert C (Az) 118 Lafayette Ave, Brooklyn, NY 11217

BUTCHER, Geoffrey (Ky) 607 5th Ave W, Springfield, TN 37172

BUTCHER, Gerald Alfred (Okla) 1720 W Carolina Ave, Chickasha, OK 73018

BUTCHER, Kenneth P F (Colo) 3306 Morris Ave, Pueblo, CO 81008

BUTERBAUGH, Matthew L (Mil) St Matthew's Church, 5900 7th Ave, Kenosha, WI 53140

BUTIN, John Murray (Ga) 303 Cannon Ct, St Simons Island, GA 31522

BUTLER III, Andrew Garland (NY) 59 Montclair Ave, Montclair, NJ 07042

BUTLER, Barbara Thayer (Minn) 2324 Branch St, Duluth, MN 55812

BUTLER, C(harles) Roger (CNY) 28205 Nc 73 Hwy, Albemarle, NC 28001

BUTLER, Clarence Elliot (Roch) 19 Russell Ave., Watertown, MA 02472

BUTLER, David (Kan) PO Box 65, Independence, KS 67301

BUTLER, Guy Harry (Tex) 10019 Beaverdam Creek Rd, Berlin, MD 21811

BUTLER, Josh (O) 471 Crosby St, Akron, OH 44302

BUTLER, Marilyn M (Ida) 4251 N 1800 E, Buhl, ID 83316

BUTLER, Mark Hilliard (LI) 225 Arbutus Ln, Hendersonville, NC 28739

BUTLER, Oliver Martin (Dal) 8011 Douglas Ave, Dallas, TX 75225

BUTLER, Pauline Felton (CFla) 815 E Graves Ave, Orange City, FL 32763

BUTLER, Robert Mitchell (Me) 35821 Pradera Dr, Zephyrhills, FL 33541

BUTLER, Susan J (ETenn) 20 Belvoir Ave, Chattanooga, TN 37411

BUTLER, Tony Eugene (Cal) Po Box 4380, Sparks, NV 89432

BUTLER-GEE, Eve (SVa) Martin's Brandon Episcopal Church, 18706 James River Dr, Disputanta, VA 23842

BUTTERBAUGH, Anna Marie (CGC) 401 Live Oak Ave, Pensacola, FL 32507

BUTTERWORTH, Gary Wayne (WNC) 3587 Fieldstone Dr, Gastonia, NC 28056

BUTTON, Roger Dee (Dal) 9845 McCree Rd, Dallas, TX 75238

BUTTS, Roger Paul (Md) 2206 Pheasant Run Dr, Finksburg, MD 21048

BUTTS, Stephen Jack (Tex) 314 N Henderson Blvd, Kilgore, TX 75662

BUXO, David Carlysle (Mich) 3601 W 13 Mile Rd, Royal Oak, MI 48073

BUXTON JR, Eugene Harvey (Tex) 514 Belleair Pl, Clearwater, FL 33756

BUXTON-SMITH, Sarah Wallace (WNY) 100 Beard Ave, Buffalo, NY 14214

BUZZARD, Henry Lewis (NY) 71 Wayne Ave, White Plains, NY 10606

BWECHWA, Oswald (Mil) 3400 E Debbie Drive, Oak Creek, WI 53154

BYE, Michael (NC) P.O. Box 942, wadesboro, NC 28170

BYE, Tommy Frank (FtW) 1201 Overhill St, Bedford, TX 76022

BYER, Martha Russell (WMo) 3907 Ivanhoe Blvd, Columbia, MO 65203

BYERS, Mark Harrison (Ct) 38 Grove St, Thomaston, CT 06787

BYERS, Sara Shovar (Ga) PO Box 925, Moultrie, GA 31776

BYERS, William (WMass) 35 Nedwied Rd, Tolland, CT 06084

BYRD, Frederick Colclough (USC) 1115 Marion St, Columbia, SC 29201

BYRD, Janice Lovinggood (NwT) 430 Dallas St, Big Spring, TX 79720

BYRD, Jeffrey Yona (CGC) 403 W College St, Troy, AL 36081

BYRD, Katherine Hahn (Lex) 166 Market St, Lexington, KY 40507

BYRD, Nita C (NC) St Paul Episcopal Church, 221 Union St, Cary, NC 27511

BYRD, Ronald Charles (Mich) 634 Canoga, Haslett, MI 48840

BYRER, Johnine Vaughn (NJ) 6 Juniper Dr, Whitehouse Station, NJ 08889

BYRNE, Anne Sc (Md) 126 E. Liberty St., Oakland, MD 21550

BYRNE, Laurence Goodwin (LI) 21433 40th Ave., Bayside, NY 11361

BYRUM, Emory Etheridge (Nwk) Trinity Episcopal Church, 6587 Upper York Rd. PO Box 377, Solebury, PA 18963

BYRUM, Philip Robert (NC)

BYRUM, Rick Yervant (Los) 28648 Greenwood Pl, Castaic, CA 91384

C

CABALLERO, Daniel (Mil) 4305 Rolla Ln, Madison, WI 53711

CABANA, Denise E (Ct) 2584 Main St, Glastonbury, CT 06033

CABEY, Lenroy Kirtley (VI)

CABRERA, Amador Fredy (Hond) IMS SAP Dept 215. PO Box 523900, Miami, FL 22152-3900, Honduras

CABRERO-OLIVER, Juan M (LI)

CABUSH, David Walter (Nwk) 2 Pond Hill Rd # 7960, Morristown, NJ 07960

CACOPERDO, Peter A(Nthony) (RG) PO Box 1747, Elephant Butte, NM 87935

CADARET, John Michael (Va) 8411 Freestone Ave, Richmond, VA 23229

CADDELL, Christopher Len (WTex) The Episcopal Church of the Holy Spirit, 301 Hays Country Acres Rd, Dripping Springs, TX 78620

CADENA, Enrique (Az) 2801 N 31st Street, Phoenix, AZ 85008

CADIGAN, C(harles) Richard (Mo) 1625 Masters Drive, DeSoto, TX 75115

CADIGAN, Katherine (Los) 1227 4th St, Santa Monica, CA 90401

CADWALLADER, Douglas Stephen (Tex) PO Box 35303, Houston, TX 77235

CADWELL, Matthew P (Mass) 94 Newbury Ave #309, North Quincy, MA 02171

CADY, Donald Holmes (Va) PO Box 38, Greenwood, VA 22943

CADY III, Mark Stone (Dal) 650 Copper Creek Circle, Alpharetta, GA 30004

CAFFERATA, Gail Lee (The Episcopal NCal) 4794 Hillsboro Cir, Santa Rosa, CA 95405

CAFFREY, David Leslie (Los) PO Box 514, Joshua Tree, CA 92252

CAGE JR, Stewart Bernard (La) 8932 Fox Run Ave, Baton Rouge, LA 70808

CAGGIANO, Diane Ruth (Ct) 11 Overvale Rd, Wolcott, CT 06716

CAGGIANO, Joyce C (Mass) 27 Curtis Rd., Milton, MA 02186

CAGUIAT, Carlos J (Mich) 10901 176 Circle NE apt 2421, Redmond, WA 98052

CAGUIAT, Julianna (Oly) 20 Oakwood Road, Saranac Lake, NY 12983

CAHILL, Patricia Ann Bytnar (ETenn) 317 Windy Hollow Dr, Chattanooga, TN 37421

CAHOON, Vernon John (NC) 428 Pee Dee Ave, Albemarle, NC 28001

CAIMANO, Catherine Anne (NC) 200 W Morgan St Ste 300, Raleigh, NC 27601

CAIN, Donavan Gerald (Fla) St Mark's Episcopal Church, 4129 Oxford Ave, Jacksonville, Fl 32210

CAIN JR, Everett Harrison (Tex) 7705 Merrybrook Circle, Austin, TX 78731

CAIN, George Robert (SwFla)

CAIRES, Joy MarieLouise (Minn) 12671 Woodside Drive, Chesterland, OH 44026

CAIRNS, John C (Alb) 316 Valentine Pond Road, Pottersville, NY 12860

CALAFAT, Karen A (Los) 2647 Mayflower Ave, Arcadia, CA 91006

CALCOTE, A(Lan) Dean (Tex) 5615 Duff St, Beaumont, TX 77706

CALDBECK, Elaine S (Ia) 2709 McGee Ave., Middletown, OH 45044

CALDWELL, Brenda Ann (Wyo) 1167 Hidalgo Dr, Laramie, WY 82072

✠ **CALDWELL**, Bruce E (Ret Bp of Wyo 2010-) 104 S 4th St, Laramie, WY 82070

CALDWELL, Edward Frederick (Alb) 100 Farmington Dr, Camillus, NY 13031

CALDWELL, George M (Va) 501 Slaters Ln Apt 521, Alexandria, VA 22314

CALDWELL, James Hardy (Chi) 1307nW Logan St, Freeport, IL 61032

CALDWELL, Margaret Caldwell (ETenn) 1264 Duane Rd, Chattanooga, TN 37405

CALDWELL, Michael Lee (Mil) 3401 Bellaire Dr S, Fort Worth, TX 76109

CALDWELL, Stephen Russell (RG) 9632 Allande Rd. NE, Albuquerque, NM 87109

CALDWELL, Wallace Franklin (Mo) 1115 Woodleigh Ct, Harrisonburg, VA 22802

CALER, Joshua Morgan (Tenn) 900 Broadway, Nashville, TN 37203

CALEY BOWERS, Elizabeth Ann (Fla) 9252 San Jose Blvd. Apt. 3703, Jacksonville, FL 32257

CALHOUN, Ann Brant (Los) 2400 N Canal St, Orange, CA 92865

CALHOUN III, Bill (WTex) 355 Marina Dr, Port Aransas, TX 78373

CALHOUN, Dolores Moore (CPa) Po Box 32, Jersey Mills, PA 17739

CALHOUN, Janis Leigh (Ore) 16530 Nottingham Dr, Gladstone, OR 97027

CALHOUN JR, Joseph (Cal) William (ETenn) 9420 States View Dr, Knoxville, TN 37922

CALHOUN, Nancy Ellen (Del) 31 Dresner Cir, Boothwyn, PA 19061

CALHOUN, Ora Albert (WK) 26627 Midland Rd, Bay Village, OH 44140

CALHOUN, Royce (WTex) 103 Bluff Vista, Boerne, TX 78006

CALHOUN-BRYANT, Julie Elizabeth (CNY) Po Box 91, Camillus, NY 13031

CALKINS, Linda (WA) 10617 Eastwood Ave, Silver Spring, MD 20901

CALKINS, Matthew H(amilton)) (NY) PO Box 366, Millbrook, NY 12545

CALLAGHAN, Alice Dale (Los) 307 E 7th St, Los Angeles, CA 90014

CALLAGHAN, Carol Lee (Eas) 308 Elm Ave, Easton, MD 21601

CALLAHAM, Arthur A (Tex) 6167 Olympia Drive, Houston, TX 77057

CALLAHAN, Gary Edward (ETenn) Po Box 21275, Chattanooga, TN 37424

CALLARD, Tom Adams (WMass) 35 Chestnut St, Springfield, MA 01103

CALLAWAY, James Gaines (NY) 549 W 123rd St Apt 13A, New York, NY 10027

CALLAWAY, Richard H (At)

CALLENDER, Francis Charles (Episcopal SJ) 1060 Cottage Ave, Manteca, CA 95336

CALLENDER, Randy Kyle (Md) Saint Philip's Church, 730 Bestgate Rd, Annapolis, MD 21401

CALLOWAY, N(ancy) (WNC) 1119 Old Fort Sugar Hill Rd, Old Fort, NC 28762

CALVERT, George Morris (SanD) 3990 Bonita Rd, Bonita, CA 91902

CALVO, Gustavo Alberto (Alb)

CALVO PEREZ, Antonis De Jesus (Colom) C165 No. 36 A-30, Bogota, Colombia

CAMACHO-OSORIO, Nabor (Ve)

CAMERON, David Albert (SD) 2417 Holiday Ln, Rapid City, SD 57702

CAMERON, Euan Kerr (NY)

CAMERON, Jacqueline Rene (Chi) 513 W Aldine Ave Apt 2h, Chicago, IL 60657

CAMERON, Krista Ann (Roch) 3345 Edgemere Dr, Rochester, NY 14612

CAMERON, Meigan Cameron (Chi) 4140 N Lavergne Ave, Chicago, IL 60641

CAMERON JR, Robert Speir (CFla)

CAMMACK, David Walker (Md) 7200 3rd Ave, Sykesville, MD 21784

CAMPBELL, Anne (Oly)

CAMPBELL, Benjamin Pfohl (Va) Richmond Hill, 2209 E Grace St, Richmond, VA 23223

CAMPBELL, Bruce Alan (Mich) 160 Walnut St, Wyandotte, MI 48192

CAMPBELL, Catherine Mary (Va) 3420 Flint Hill Place, Woodbridge, VA 22192

CAMPBELL, Claude Alan (Mo) 2831 N Prospect Ave, Milwaukee, WI 53211

CAMPBELL, Dana L(Ou) (Ct) 58 Greenwood St, East Hartford, CT 06118

CAMPBELL, Dennis Gail (Ark) 1501 32nd Ave S, Seattle, WA 98144

CAMPBELL, Ernest Francis (Spok) 825 Wauna Vista Dr, Walla Walla, WA 99362

CAMPBELL, Ernestina (The Episcopal NCal) 1617 32nd Ave, Sacramento, CA 95822

CAMPBELL III, George Latimer (NJ) 257 4th St, South Amboy, NJ 08879

CAMPBELL, James Donald (La) 525 N Laurel St, Amite, LA 70422

CAMPBELL, Janet Bragg (Oly) 1556 NE 148th St, Shoreline, WA 98155

CAMPBELL, Jean C (NY) 42 Timberline Dr, Poughkeepsie, NY 12603

CAMPBELL, Karen Ann (LI) PO Box 570, Hampton & East Union Street, Sag Harbor, NY 11963

CAMPBELL, Kathryn S. (Ia) 106 3rd Ave, Charles City, IA 50616

CAMPBELL, Kenneth Stuart Bradstreet (WMass) 5 Peace Lane, Box 306, South Orleans, MA 02653

CAMPBELL, Leslie R (SD) Po Box 722, Mobridge, SD 57601

CAMPBELL, Linda McConnell (ECR) 2065 Yosemite St., Seaside, CA 93955

CAMPBELL, Lynn Marie (Mass) 1132 Highland Ave, Needham, MA 02494

CAMPBELL, Maurice Bernard (Episcopal SJ) 1151 Park View Ct, Sheridan, WY 82801

CAMPBELL, Patrick Alan (RI) St Paul's Church, 50 Park Pl, Pawtucket, RI 02860

CAMPBELL, Peter Nelson (Chi) 519 Franklin Ave, River Forest, IL 60305

CAMPBELL II, Ralph Marion (LI) 9825 Georgetown St. N.E., Louisville, OH 44641

CAMPBELL, Robert Dean (Spok) 16007 Red Fox Ln, Colorado Springs, CO 80921

CAMPBELL, Ross W (Mich) 899 Greenhills Dr, Ann Arbor, MI 48105

CAMPBELL, Scott D. (Colo) PO Box 1961, Monument, CO 80132

CAMPBELL, Solomon Sebastian (SeFla) P.O. Box 50222, Nassau, Bahamas

CAMPBELL, Thomas Wellman (SD) 234 W. Kansas Street, Spearfish, SD 57783

CAMPBELL, William Edward (Spok) 1421 S Josephine Street, Denver, CO 80210

CAMPBELL-DIXON, Robert A (NY) PO Box 99, West Park, NY 12493

CAMPBELL-LANGDELL, Alene L (Los) 144 S C St, Oxnard, CA 93030

CAMPBELL-LANGDELL, Melissa Christina (Los) 144 S. C St, Oxnard, CA 93030

CAMPBELL-PEARSON, Constance Anne (Mont) 5 W Olive St, Bozeman, MT 59715

CAMPO, JoAnne Crocitto (NY) 48 Spring St S, South Salem, NY 10590

CAMPO, Joseph John (NY)

CANADY III, Hoyt Paul (EC) Christ Church, P.O. Box 1246, New Bern, NC 28563

CANAN, David A (Pa) 708 S Bethlehem Pike, Ambler, PA 19002

CANAVAN, Mary A (Ct)

CANDLER, Samuel Glenn (At) 2744 Peachtree Rd Nw, Atlanta, GA 30305

CANELA CANELA, Ramon Antonio (DR (DomRep)) Ms Digna Valdez, Box 764, Dominican Republic, Dominican Republic

CANGIALOSI, Grace Louise (Va) 2209 E Grace St, Richmond, VA 23223

CANHAM, Elizabeth Jean (WNC) 51 Laurel Ln, Black Mountain, NC 28711

CANION, Gary Yates (Tex) 5435 Whispering Creek Way, Houston, TX 77017

CANNADAY, Brian Wallace (WTex) 410 N Main St, Boerne, TX 78006

CANNAN, Andrew (EC) St Lukes Episc Church, 435 Peachtree St NE, Atlanta, GA 30308

CANNELL, John Edward (WTex) 11107 Wurzbach Rd Ste 401, San Antonio, TX 78230

CANNING, Michael Jacob (Ida) 2333 W Duck Alley Rd, Eagle, ID 83616

CANNON JR, Alberry Charles (USC) 51 Roper Rd, Flat Rock, NC 28731

CANNON, Carl Thomas (La) 10622 Masters Dr, Clermont, FL 34711

CANNON III, Charles (SwFla) 87500 Overseas Highway, Islamorada, FL 33036

CANNON, Charles Wilcken (The Episcopal Church in Haw) 291 Shady Glen Ave., Point Roberts, WA 98281

CANNON, Daniel M (EMich)

CANNON, David Lawrence (Ct) #93 Route 2-A Pouquetanuck, Preston, CT 06365

CANNON, Justin R (Cal) PO Box 187, Moraga, CA 94556

CANNON, Thomas Kimball (Chi) 141 S Taylor Ave, Oak Park, IL 60302

CANO, George Luciano (Episcopal SJ) 3605 Shady Valley Ct, Modesto, CA 95355

CANTELLA, Frances French (Los) 30015 Buchanan Way, Castaic, CA 91384

CANTER, Matthew A (SanD) PO Box 127, Carlsbad, CA 92018

CANTERBURY, Marion Lucille (RG) 5304 Rincon Rd Nw, Albuquerque, NM 87105

CANTOR, Este Gardner (Cal) 1105 High Ct, Berkeley, CA 94708

CANTRELL, Darla (Nev) PO Box 181, Austin, NV 89310

CANTRELL, Laura Quattlebaum (Ga) Christ Church, 1521 N Patterson St, Valdosta, GA 31602

CANTRELL, Patricia Martin (Miss) PO Box 316, West Point, MS 39773

CAPALDO, Christopher James (Fla) 801 Atlantic Ave, Fernandina Beach, FL 32034

CAPELLARO, John (Los) 13900 Marquesas Way, Apt 5104, Marina del Rey, CA 90292

CAPITELLI, Stephen Richard (Mil) St John in the Wilderness, 13 S Church St, Elkhorn, WI 53121

CAPPEL, Jerry Jay (Ky) 5719 Prince William St, Louisville, KY 40207

CAPPER, Steve (Tex) 4405 McKinney St, Houston, TX 77023

CAPPERS, Linda Frances (Me) 30 Hemlock Dr, Saco, ME 04072

CAPWELL, Kim F (Del) 2400 W 17th St, Wilmington, DE 19806

CARABIN, Robert Jerome (WTex) 203 Panama Ave, San Antonio, TX 78210

CARADINE, Billie Charles (Ala) Po Box 787, Asotin, WA 99402

CARBERRY, Timothy Oliver (SO) 49 Dipper Cove Rd, Orrs Island, ME 04066

CARCEL-MARTINEZ, Antonio (Hond) Apdo 52, Camino Rio Mar, Puerto Cortes, Honduras

CARD, June (Los) 24102 Avenida Corona, Dana Point, CA 92629

CARDEN, Larry Edward (Tenn) University Of The South, Spo, Sewanee, TN 37375

CARDOZA, Edward M (Mass) 116 South St, Foxboro, MA 02035

CAREY, Brenton H (SanD)

CAREY, Grant S (The Episcopal NCal) 2701 Capitol Ave Apt 302, Sacramento, CA 95816

CAREY, Pamela Hann (Cal) 525 29th St, Oakland, CA 94609

CAREY, Peter Michael (SwFla) 5602 Cary Street Rd, Richmond, VA 23226

CAREY, Peter R (NY) 150 9th Ave Apt 1, New York, NY 10011

CAREY, Tom (Los) 2449 Sichel St., Los Angeles, CA 90031

CARHARTT, Forrest Andrew (Colo) 4737 Mckinley Dr, Boulder, CO 80303

CARL, Elizabeth (WA) 1414 Montague St NW, Washington, DC 20011

CARLETON, Ellen Diane (Wyo) 519 E Park Ave, Riverton, WY 82501

CARLETTA, David M (WTenn) St Andrew's Church, 17 South Ave, Beacon, NY 12508

CARLIN, Christine (EC) 810 Fisher St Apt 4, Morehead City, NC 28557

CARLIN II, William B (Okla) 3508 Robert Drive, Duncan, OK 73533

CARLING, Paul Joseph (Ct) Saint Paul's Episcopal Church, 661 Old Post Road, Fairfield, CT 06824

CARLISLE, Christopher Arthur Elliott (WMass) 758 N Pleasant St, Amherst, MA 01002

CARLISLE, Michael Emerson (Lex) 85 Mikell Ln, Sewanee, TN 37375

CARLISTO, John Bradley (EC) 121 Radley Ln, Beaufort, NC 28516

CARLOZZI, Carl Gillman (Az) 10801 East Happy Valley Road, Lot #53, Scottsdale, AZ 85255

CARLSEN, Gail Melin (Az) 3756 E Marble Peak Pl, Tucson, AZ 85718

CARLSEN, Stephen Earl (Ind) 55 Monument Cir Ste 600, Indianapolis, IN 46204

CARLSEN, Vause Smith (EMich) 745 E Main St, Flushing, MI 48433

CARLSON, Carol Emma (NwPa) Po Box 328, Mount Jewett, PA 16740

CARLSON, Constance Jo (Oly) St Andrew's Episc Church, 111 NE 80th St, Seattle, WA 98115

CARLSON, David John (Mich) 28217 Edward Ave, Madison Heights, MI 48071

CARLSON, David Lee (NY) 84 Seward Ave, Port Jervis, NY 12771

CARLSON, Geraldine Beatrice (WMich) 1287 La Chaumiere Drive # 5, Petoskey, MI 46770

CARLSON, Katherine Ann (Mich) 907 Southlawn Ave, East Lansing, MI 48823

CARLSON, Kelly B (Mo) Saint Peter's Episcopal Church, 110 N Warson Rd, Saint Louis, MO 63124

CARLSON, Monica Alexandra (Ala) 2310 Skyland Blvd E, Tuscaloosa, AL 35405

CARLSON, Philip Lawrence (Az) 7147 N 78th St, Scottsdale, AZ 85258

CARLSON, Reed Anthony (Minn) 1991 Massachusetts Ave, Cambridge, MA 02140

CARLSON, Robert Bryant (Ore) 15242 Sw Millikan Way Apt 517, Beaverton, OR 97006

CARLSON, Sara Sessions (Oly) 17320 97th Pl Sw Apt 603, Vashon, WA 98070

CARLSON, Walter Donald (Nwk) 11 Avalon Ct, Somerset, NJ 08873

CARLSON, William Douglas (At) 114 Grady Ridge Dr, Ashville, NC 28806

CARLTON-JONES, Anne Helen (SwFla) 15608 Fiddlesticks Blvd, Fort Myers, FL 33912

CARLYON, Robert David (Be) P.O.Box 262, Orwigsburg, PA 17961

CARMAN, Charles Churchill (RG) 94 Winterhaven Drive, Nellysford, VA 22958

CARMICHAEL, Alisa Roberts (SwFla) 502 Druid Hills Rd, Temple Terrace, FL 33617

CARMICHAEL, Anna Roope (EO) 400 11th St, PO Box 25, Hood River, OR 97031

CARMICHAEL, (Mary) Jean (Oly)

CARMIENCKE JR, Bayard Collier (LI) 1145 Walnut Ave, Bohemia, NY 11716

CARMODY, Alison Cutter (Ala) 1708 Wickingham Cv, Vestavia, AL 35243

CARMONA, Paul Bernard (SanD) 4658 El Cerrito Dr, San Diego, CA 92115

CARNAHAN, Patricia King (Pgh) 4201 Saltsburg Rd, Murrysville, PA 15668

CARNES, Ralph Lee (Chi) 4507 Dayton Blvd, Chattanooga, TN 37415

CARNES, Valerie Folts (Mil) 4507 Dayton Blvd, Chattanooga, TN 37415

CARNEY, Georgia Martyn (Roch) 350 Chili Ave, Rochester, NY 14611

CARNEY, Michael Rex (Colo) 1401 E Dry Creek Rd, Centennial, CO 80122

CARNEY, Paul Martin (Alb) 146 1st St, Troy, NY 12180

CARNEY, Paulette Louise (WNY)

CARNEY, Susan Roberta (RI) 9924 Pointe Aux Chenes Road, Ocean Springs, MS 39564

CARON, Donald Raymond (NJ) 116 Forte Dr Nw, Milledgeville, GA 31061

CARON II, Joseph Auridas (Alb) 271 Stevenson Rd, Greenwich, NY 12834

CARPENTER, Allen Douglas (Alb) 62 S. Swan St., Albany, NY 12210

CARPENTER, Catherine E (CNY) PO Box 6, Baldwinsville, NY 13027

CARPENTER, Charles Monroe (Ind) 91 Smiths Rd, Mitchell, IN 47446

CARPENTER, Douglas Morrison (Ala) 3037 Overton Rd, Birmingham, AL 35223

CARPENTER, Elizabeth Kincaid (Tenn) 216 University Ave, Sewanee, TN 37375

CARPENTER, Francis Newton (Chi) 337 Ridge Rd, Barrington Hills, IL 60010

CARPENTER, George Harrison (Oly) Po Box 343, Medina, WA 98039

CARPENTER, John Paul (Pa) 3937 Netherfield Rd, Philadelphia, PA 19129

CARPENTER, Judith (Mass) 192 N. Main Street, Rockland, ME 04841

CARPENTER, Leslie Scott (Tex) 6050 N. Meridian St., Indianapolis, IN 46208

CARPENTER II, Marion George (NI) Saint Annes, 424 W Market St, Warsaw, IN 46580

CARPENTER, Morton Eugene (EC) 1603 E Walnut St, Goldsboro, NC 27530

CARPENTER, Nicholas (Los) 15757 Saint Timothy Rd, Apple Valley, CA 92307

CARPENTER, Stephen Morris (The Episcopal NCal) 1020 Westview Dr, Napa, CA 94558

CARPENTER, Susan Morrison (RI) PO Box 505, Greenville, RI 02828

CARR, Clifford Bradley (Be) 526 11th Avenue, Bethlehem, PA 18018

CARR, Dale Robert (Ore) 5223 NE Everett St, Portland, OR 97213

CARR, John Joseph (WNY) 56 Mckinley Ave, Kenmore, NY 14217

CARR, John Philip (Tex)

CARR, Michael Gordon (SanD) 651 Eucalyptus Ave, Vista, CA 92084

CARR, Michael Leo (Mich) 9132 Pine Valley Dr, Grand Blanc, MI 48439

CARR, Nathan Daniel (Okla) 6400 N Pennsylvania Ave, Nichols Hills, OK 73116

CARR, Spencer David (Colo) 4661 Wilson Dr, Broomfield, CO 80023

CARR, Timothy Patrick (Nwk) St John's Episcopal Church, 226 Cornelia St, Boonton, NJ 07005

CARR, Virginia Rose (WNY) 12 Elm St, Westfield, NY 14787

✠ **CARR**, William Franklin (Ret Bp Suffr of WVa 1994-) 4249 Cedar Grove Rd, Murfreesboro, TN 37127

✠ **CARRANZA-GOMEZ**, Sergio (Asst Bp of Los 2003-) PO Box 512164, Los Angeles, CA 90051

CARREKER, Michael Lyons (Ga) 1 West Macon Street, Savannah, GA 31401

CARRENO-GAMBOA, Bladimir Francisco (Ve)

CARRICK, Judith Trautman (LI) 4 Kenny St, Hauppauge, NY 11788

CARRIERE, Anne Stone (Ark) 31 Stonecrest Ct, Mountain Home, AR 72653

CARRINGTON, James Henry (ECR)

CARR-JONES, Philip Bohdan (NJ) 3 Haytown Rd, Lebanon, NJ 08833

CARROCCINO, Michael Jonathan (Oly)

CARROLL, Charles Moisan (Me) PO Box 155, Brunswick, ME 04011

CARROLL, Christian (Nwk) 173 Oakland Rd, Maplewood, NJ 07040

CARROLL, Diana E (Md) St. Luke's Church, 1101 Bay Ridge Avenue, Annapolis, MD 21403

CARROLL, Diane Phyllis (Va) 10360 Rectory Ln, King George, VA 22485

CARROLL, Douglas James (Roch) 3387 County Route 6, Cohocton, NY 14826

CARROLL, James Earle (SanD) 3750 Amaryllis Dr, San Diego, CA 92106

CARROLL, Kevin Charles (Mil) 3309 N Knoll Terrace, Wauwatosa, WI 53222

CARROLL, Michael Edward (Ct) 16 Church St, Waterbury, CT 06702

CARROLL III, R. William (Okla) 501 N Broadway Ave, Shawnee, OK 74801

CARROLL, Steven E (NJ) 76 Market Street, Salem, NJ 08079

CARROLL, Tracey Fiore (Okla)

CARROLL, Vincent John (SwVa) 2518 2nd St, Richlands, VA 24641

CARROLL, William Wesley (Fla) 465 11th Ave N, Jacksonville, FL 32250

CARROON, Robert Girard (Ct) 24 Park Pl, Apt 8F, Hartford, CT 06106

CARRUBBA, Amity Lynn (Chi) 1434 W Thome Ave Apt 1A, Chicago, IL 60660

CARSKADON, Garrett Harvey (Md) 32 Main St, Westernport, MD 21562

CARSON, Boyd Rodney (SwFla) 1875 Massachusetts Ave Ne, Saint Petersburg, FL 33703

CARSON, Julie Ann (Mass) 500 Brook St, Framingham, MA 01701

CARSON, Mary (O) 14523 Lake Ave, Lakewood, OH 44107

CARSON, Rebecca Jayne (CGC) 1707 Government St, Mobile, AL 36604

CARSON, Stephen Wilson (WTex) 3002 Miori Ln, Victoria, TX 77901

CARSWELL, Amber Brooke (Ark) 531 W College Ave, Jonesboro, AR 72401

CARTAGENA MEJIA DE AREVALO, Maria Consuelo (Hond) San Angel B-26, C4202, Tegucigalpa, C, Honduras

CARTER, Bente (Cal) 60 Pinehurst Way, San Francisco, CA 94127

CARTER III, Charles Alexander (Pa) 8018 Navajo St, Philadelphia, PA 19118

CARTER, David Morgan (Ct) 521 Pomfret Street (Box 21), Pomfret, CT 06258

CARTER, Davis Blake (WTex) Po Box 707, Aberdeen, MS 39730

CARTER JR, Frederick LeRoy (U) 472 Gordon Cir, Tooele, UT 84074

CARTER, Grayson Leigh (RG) 1602 Palmcroft Dr Sw, Phoenix, AZ 85007

CARTER, Halcott Richardson (USC) 4708 Seahurst Ave, Everett, WA 98203

CARTER, James Currie Mackechnie (Va) 4413 W Franklin St, Richmond, VA 23221

CARTER, James Lee (SwFla) 9925 Ulmerton Rd Lot 40, Largo, FL 33771

CARTER III, James Robert (Ga) 601 Washington Ave, Savannah, GA 31405

CARTER, John F (Ct) Po Box 391, Salisbury, CT 06068

CARTER, L. Susan (Mich) 1102 Portage Path, East Lansing, MI 48823

CARTER, Lynda Anne (Mich) 2803 1st St, Wyandotte, MI 48192

CARTER III, Philander Lothrop (WMich) 1296 Siena Way, Boulder, CO 80301

CARTER, R Douglas (SwFla) Berkeley Preparatory School, 4811 Kelly Road, Tampa, FL 33615

CARTER JR, Richard Blair (ETenn) PO Box 5104, Knoxville, TN 37928

CARTER, Stanley Edward (ETenn) 1930 Chelsea Jo Ln., Sevierville, TN 37876

CARTER, Thomas Brooke (Md) 105 Dunkirk Rd, Baltimore, MD 21212

CARTER, Wayne Ervin (WLa) 396 Country Club Circle, Minden, LA 71055

CARTER-EDMANDS, Lynn (SO) 55 S. Vernon Lane, Fort Thoms, KY 41075

CARTIER, Fred Claire (NY) 222 Starbarrack Rd, Red Hook, NY 12571

CARTWRIGHT, Gary Earle (SwFla) 2202 Wildwood Hollow Dr, Valrico, FL 33594

CARTWRIGHT JR, Howard Mott (Los) 15997 Molino Dr, Victorville, CA 92395

CARTWRIGHT, Thomas Lisson (Ore) 1720 Ten Oaks Ln, Woodburn, OR 97071

CARTY, Shawn (Nwk) PO Box 117, Bellevue, ID 83313

CARUSO, Cynthia Woodham (RG) 209 W 27th St, Austin, TX 78705

CARUSO, Frank (Mass) 112 Spring St, Hopkinton, MA 01748

CARUSO, Kevin Garrett (Chi) 647 Dundee Avenue, Barrington, IL 60010

CARUTHERS, Mary C (Ark)

CARVER, Barbara (Spok) 1904 Browning Way, Sandpoint, ID 83864

CARVER, John Phillip (Spok) 1904 Browning Way, Sandpoint, ID 83864

CARVER, Larry Alfred (WK) 18 E 28th Ave, Hutchinson, KS 67502

CARVER, Lynne (Ia) St. Peter's Episcopal Church, 2400 Middle Rd., Bettendorf, IA 52722

CARVER, Robert Cody (Oly) 1701 N Juniper St, Tacoma, WA 98406

CARVER, Sarah Frances (EMich) 4795 Silver Creek Dr., Greensboro, NC 27410

CASAS, Alberto Moreno (NwT) San Miguel Arcangel, 907 N Adams Ave, Odessa, TX 79761

CASE, Doris May (Mich) 10242 Joslin Lake Rd, Gregory, MI 48137

CASE, Jaime J (Oly) 426 E Fourth Plain Blvd, Vancouver, WA 98663

CASE, James Joshua (At) Holy Innocents Episcopal Church, 805 Mount Vernon Hwy, Atlanta, GA 30327

CASE, Margaret Timothy (RG)

CASE, Michael Allen (Ida) 704 S Latah St, Boise, ID 83705

CASEY, Dayle Alan (Colo) 2059 Glenhill Rd, Colorado Springs, CO 80906

CASEY, Stephen Charles (CPa) 429 Camp Meeting Rd, Landisville, PA 17538

CASEY-MARTUS, Sandra (WTex) St. Stephen's Episcopal Church, Wimberley, TX 78676

CASHELL, Douglas Hanson (NwT) 2807 42nd St, Lubbock, TX 79413

CASHMAN, Patricia (Ia) 2 Riverside St, Rochester, NY 14613

CASILLAS, Laina Wood (Cal) 4942 Thunderhead Ct, El Sobrante, CA 94803

CASKEY, Charles C (Chi) 24410 Reserve Ct Apt 103, Bonita Springs, FL 34134

CASON JR, Charles Edward (FdL) 1805 Arlington Dr, Oshkosh, WI 54904

CASPARIAN, Peter Frasius (LI) 65 East Main St, Oyster Bay, NY 11771

CASSELL JR, John Summerfield (Md) 708 Milford Mill Rd, Baltimore, MD 21208

CASSELL, Jonnie Lee (Mo) 2015 Rockford Rd SW Apt 5, Cedar Rapids, IA 52404

CASSELL JR, Warren Michael (SeFla) 2718 Sw 6th St, Boynton Beach, FL 33435

CASSEUS, Frantz Joseph (SeFla) 7835 Jean Vincent, Montreal, QC H1E 3C4, Canada

CASSINI, Mary Ellen Dakin (SeFla) 2805 Duncan Dr Apt C, Boca Raton, FL 33434

CASSON, Lloyd Stuart (Del) 902 N Market St Apt 1327, Wilmington, DE 19801

CASTELLAN, Megan Laura (WMo) 11 E 40th St, Kansas City, MO 64111

CASTELLI, Paul Henry (Mich)

CASTELLON, P. Frank (NJ) 7403 Dress Blue Cir, Mechanicsville, VA 23116

CASTILLO, Guillermo Antonio (Ark) 406 W Central Ave, Bentonville, AR 72712

CASTILLO, Sandra Ann (Okla) 322 N Water St, Sparta, WI 54656

CASTLEBERRY, Howard Glen (Tex) 300 N Main St, Temple, TX 76501

CASTLES, Charles William (Ga) 1552 Pangborn Station Dr, Decatur, GA 30033

CASTO, David Cameron (Pgh) 9 Cliff Rd. Apt. B2, Woodland Park, NJ 07424

CASTO, R Richard (CFla) Po Box 2068, Dunnellon, FL 34430

CASTRO, Jose Roberto (DR (DomRep))

CASTRO, Mario (SwFla) Church of the Redeemer, 222 S Palm Ave, Sarasota, FL 34236

CASTRO, Reinel (CFla) 29655 Circle R Greens Drv, Escondido, CA 92026

CATALANO, Patricia (ECR)

CATCHINGS, Robert Mitchell (WA)

CATE, Suzanne Lowe (NC) Saint Johns Church, 1623 Carmel Rd, Charlotte, NC 28226

CATES, Susanna P (NwT) 602 Meander St, Abilene, TX 79602

CATHERS, Robert Earl (SwFla) 2291 Hebron Rd, Hendersonville, NC 28739

CATINELLA, Gayle Louise (O) 16507 S Red Rock Dr, Strongsville, OH 44138

CATIR JR, Norman Joseph (FtW) 31 John St, Providence, RI 02906

CATO, Brooks Arthur (Ark) Christ Church, 509 Scott Street, Little Rock, AR 72201

CATO, Phillip Carlyle (WA) 8617 Hidden Hill Ln, Potomac, MD 20854

CATO, Vanessa Gisela (U) 2374 Grant Ave, Ogden, UT 84401

CATON, Lisa Elfers (NJ) 23 E Welling Ave, Pennington, NJ 08534

CATRON MINER, Antoinette (U) 1710 Foothill Dr, Salt Lake City, UT 84108

CAUCUTT, Mary Allison (Wyo) 820 River View Dr, Cody, WY 82414

CAUDLE, Stephen (WLa)

CAUGHEY, Robert Grover (Cal) 721 E 16th Ave, San Mateo, CA 94402

CAULFIELD, Dorothee Renee (NY)

CAULKINS, Rodney LeRoy (SVa) 267 Jefferson Dr, Palmyra, VA 22963

CAVAGNARO, Deborah Daggett (NwPa) St Luke's Church, 600 W Main St, Smethport, PA 16749

CAVALCANTE, Jose Ivanildo (Los) 48 Old Post Rd, Mount Sinai, NY 11766

CAVALERI, Eva Maria K (WA) 3612 Woodley Rd Nw, Washington, DC 20016

CAVALIERE, Denise B(Ourgeois) (NJ) 15 Paper Mill Rd., Cherry Hill, NJ 08003

CAVANAGH, David Nathan (The Episcopal NCal) 2901 Owens Ct, Fairfield, CA 94534

CAVANAUGH, Sean Harris (Va) 1795 Johnson Ferry Rd, Marietta, GA 30062

CAVANAUGH, William Jeffrey (Dal) 421 Custer Road, Richardson, TX 75080

CAVANNA, Robert Charles (Minn) 6910 43rd Ave Se, Saint Cloud, MN 56304

CAVE, Daniel Eugene (RG) 7052 McNutt Rd, La Union, NM 88021

CAVE JR, George Harold (SwFla) 14 Old Club Ct, Nashville, TN 37215

CAVE, Jeffrey Paull (At) 3550 Wyoming St, Kansas City, MO 64111

CAVENDISH, John Claude (Lex) 240 Cedar Cliff Rd, Waco, KY 40385

CAVIN, Barbara (EMich) Saint Paul's Episcopal Church, 711 S Saginaw St, Flint, MI 48502

CAWTHORNE, John Harry (Md) 1597 Amberlea Dr. S, Dunedin, FL 34698

CAYLESS, F(Rank) Anthony (LI) 108 Woodbridge Ln, Chapel Hill, NC 27514

CAZDEN, Jan Steward (Cal) 2901 Verona Ct, Arlington, TX 76012

CEDENO MEDINA, Oscar Antonio (PR)

CEDERBERG, Todd Lee (SeFla) 623 SE Ocean Blvd, Stuart, FL 34994

✠ **CEDERHOLM JR**, Roy Frederick (Ret Bp Suffr of Mass 2011-) 499 Webster St, Needham, MA 02494

CEKUTA, Nancee A (NC) 1413 Carmel Rd, Charlotte, NC 28226

CELESTIN, Jois Gourrse (Hai)

CELL, John Albert (FdL) 825 N Webster Ave, Green Bay, WI 54302

CELLA, Richard Louis (Colo) 4935 Hahns Peak Dr Apt 104, Loveland, CO 80538

CEMBALISTY INNES, Susan Eve (Be) 108 Fern Way, Clarks Summit, PA 18411

CENCI, Daniel M (EC) 110 W Main St, Clinton, NC 28328

CENDESE, William Ivan (U) 521 9th Ave, Salt Lake City, UT 84103

CERRATO, John A (WMass) 2813 Market Bridge Ln Unit 101, Raleigh, NC 27608

CERTAIN, Robert Glenn (At) 3776 Loch Highland Pkwy NE, Roswell, GA 30075

✠ **CERVENY**, Frank Stanley (Ret Bp of Fla 1998-) 3711 Ortega Blvd, Jacksonville, FL 32210

CESAR, Gerard David (Hai) Box 1309, Port-Au-Prince, Haiti

CESARETTI, Charles Antony (NJ) Po Box 408, New Milford, PA 18834

CEYNAR, Marlene (Minn) 1811 Southbrook Ln, Wadena, MN 56482

CHABOT, Bruce Guy (Tex) 5919 Wild Horse Run, College Station, TX 77845

CHACE, Alston R (WMass) 144 Pine Bluff Rd, Brewster, MA 02631

CHACE, Brian David (EMich) Trinity Episcopal Church, PO Box 83, West Branch, MI 48661

CHACE, Elizabeth Marian Maxwell (EMich) PO Box 109, 5313 Trails End, Frederic, MI 49733

CHACON, Frank Joe (The Episcopal NCal)

CHACON-RODRIGUEZ, Dagoberto (Hond)

CHADWICK, Leslie Elizabeth (Va) 11290 Spyglass Cove Lane, Reston, VA 20191

CHADWICK, Loring William (CFla) 11440 SW 84th Avenue Rd, Ocala, FL 34481

CHADWICK, Thora L (Vt) 267 Hildred Dr, Burlington, VT 05401

CHAFFEE, Adna Romanza (Ga) 302 E General Stewart Way, Hinesville, GA 31313

CHAFFEE, Barbara B (EC) 10618 Peppermill Dr, Raleigh, NC 27614

CHALAKANI, Paul Scott (NJ) 7 Lincoln Ave, Rumson, NJ 07760

CHALARON, Janice Belle Melbourne (USC) 144 Caldwell St, Rock Hill, SC 29730

✠ **CHALFANT**, Edward Cole (Ret Bp of Me 1996-) PO Box 2056, Ponte Vedra Beach, FL 32004

CHALFANT-WALKER, Nancy Oliver (Pgh) 33 Thorn St, Sewickley, PA 15143

CHALK, David Paul (WTex) 651 Pecan St, Canyon Lake, TX 78133

CHALK, Michael Dulaney (WTex) 155 El Rancho Way, San Antonio, TX 78209

CHALKER, Gae Marguerite (Az) 400 S. Old Litchfield Rd., Litchfield Park, AZ 85340

CHALMERS, Glenn Burr (NY) 296 9th Ave, New York, NY 10001

CHAMBERLAIN, Carol Moore (Pa) 22 Pin Oak Rd, Newport News, VA 23601

CHAMBERLAIN, David Morrow (EC) 136 Fairway Oaks Dr, Perry, GA 31069

CHAMBERLAIN, Donald Fred (WMass) 340 Burncoat St, Worcester, MA 01606

CHAMBERLAIN, Eve Yorke (NJ) 325 Little Silver Point Rd, Little Silver, NJ 07739

CHAMBERLAIN-HARRIS, Naomi Redman (Cal) 4467 Crestwood Cir, Concord, CA 94521

CHAMBERS, Joseph Michael Cortright (Mo) 3906 Tropical Ln, Columbia, MO 65202

CHAMBERS, Rex (Colo) PO BOX 237, WINDSOR, CO 80550

CHAMBERS, Richard Graeff Mark (CFla) 91 Church St, Seymour, CT 06483

CHAMBERS, Robert Karl (NY)

CHAMBERS, Stanford Hardin (Dal) PO Box 540562, Dallas, TX 75354

CHAMBLISS, Rebecca Arrington (Mass) 7 Eldridge Rd, Jamaica Plain, MA 02130

CHAMPION, Peter O (Cal) 703 Mariposa Avenue, Rodeo, CA 94572

CHAMPION, Susan Manley (Cal) 703 Mariposa Ave., Rodeo, CA 94572

CHAMPION-GARTHE, Maurice Vinck (Mont) 2101 W Broadway, #103-190, Columbia, MO 65203

CHAMPLIN, Jeffrey Fletcher (Ark) 2701 Old Greenwood Rd, Fort Smith, AR 72903

CHAN, Charles Yang-Ling Ping-Fai (Colo) Po Box 662, Mukwonago, WI 53149

CHAN, Henry Albert (LI) 3410 Silver Stream Way NW, Kennesaw, GA 30144

CHANCE, Robin Leea (Wyo) 6516 Weaver Rd, Cheyenne, WY 82009

CHANCELLOR JR, Donald Wood (Miss) PO Box 391, Como, MS 38619

CHANDLER, Archie Lee (SC) 103 Woodland Dr, Darlington, SC 29532

CHANDLER, Belinda (Chi) 3025 Walters Ave, Northbrook, IL 60062

CHANDLER, Gail Stearns (Me) St. David's Episcopal Church, 138 York St, Kennebunk, ME 04043

CHANDLER, John Herrick (Los) 2286 Vasanta Way, Los Angeles, CA 90068

CHANDLER, Nan Elizabeth (EC) 301 Bretonshire Rd, Wilmington, NC 28405

CHANDLER, Paul Gordon (Spok)

CHANDLER JR, Richard Anthony (Alb) 224 Main St, Hudson Falls, NY 12839

CHANDLER, Susan Esco (Mass) 195 Patmos Rd., Sawyer's Island, Rowley, MA 01969

CHANDLER-WARD, Constance (Mass) 16 School St., Tenants Harbor, ME 04860

CHANDY, Kuruvilla Kulangana (RI) 1115 New Pear St, Vineland, NJ 08360

✠ CHANE, John Bryson (Ret Bp of WA, DC 2011-) 5309 Pendleton St, San Diego, CA 92109

CHANEY JR, Michael Jackson (Ga) 1802 Abercorn St, Savannah, GA 31401

CHANEY, Myrna Faye (Mont) 14 September Dr, Missoula, MT 59802

CHANG, Hsin Fen (Los) 15694 Tetley St, Hacienda Heights, CA 91745

CHANG, Lennon Yuan-Rung (Tai) Wen-Hua 3rd Road, 4th Place #75, Pei-Tan, Taiwan

CHANG, Ling-Ling (Tai) 280 Fu-Hsing South Road, Sec 2, Taipei, Taiwan

CHANG, Mark Chung-Moon (Nwk) 11 Foakes Drive, Ajax, LIT 3K5, Canada

✠ CHANG, Richard Sui On (Ret Bp of Haw 2007-) 1760 S. Beretania Street, Apt. 11C, Honolulu, HI 96826

CHANGO, Georgianna (NwPa) Rr 6 Box 324, Punxsutawney, PA 15767

CHANNON, Ethel M (Dal) 2304 County Ave, Texarkana, AR 71854

CHAPLIN, George Manton (RI) 1201 Capella South, Goat Island, Newport, RI 02840

CHAPMAN, Alton James (SwFla) 12905 Forest Hills Dr, Tampa, FL 33612

CHAPMAN JR, Chuck (Ark) 525 N Madison Ave, El Dorado, AR 71730

CHAPMAN, Colin M (Ct) Christ Church, 2 Rectory St, Rye, NY 10580

CHAPMAN, George Memory (Mass) 41 Garth Road, West Roxbury, MA 02132

CHAPMAN, Hugh William (Fla) 13 Bb Misgunsi, St. Thomas, VI 802

CHAPMAN, James Dreger (Mass) 201 Washington Ave, Chelsea, MA 02150

CHAPMAN, Jerry Wayne (Dal) 11201 Pickfair Dr, Austin, TX 78750

CHAPMAN, Justin P (Minn) 1430 15th Ave NW, Rochester, MN 55901

CHAPMAN, Michael (Alb) 22 Bergen St, Brentwood, NY 11717

CHAPMAN, Phillip (Neb) 322 S 15th St, Plattsmouth, NE 68048

CHAPMAN, Tansy (Mass) PO Box 832, Mendocino, CA 95460

CHAPPELL, Annette Mary (Md)

CHAPPELL, Veronica Donohue (CPa) 1118 State Route 973 E, Cogan Station, PA 17728

CHAPPELLE, Laurinda (Nev) 1230 Riverberry Dr, Reno, NV 89509

CHAR, Zachariah (WMich) 4232 Alpinehorn Dr Nw, Comstock Pk, MI 49321

CHARD JR, Arthur Cameron (WVa) 1206 Maple Lane, Anchorage, KY 40223

CHARLES, D Maurice (Roch) 412 Euclid Avenue, Oakland, CA 94610

CHARLES, Kathleen Jane (Eau) 1001 McLean Ave, Tomah, WI 54660

CHARLES, Leonel (SeFla) Box 1309, Port-Au-Prince, Haiti

CHARLES, Randolph (WA) 1331 19th Rd S, Arlington, VA 22202

CHARLES, Winston Breeden (NC) 114 East Drewry Lane, Raleigh, NC 27609

✠ CHARLESTON, Steven (Ret Bp of Ak 1996-) 2702 Silvertree Dr, Oklahoma City, OK 73120

✠ CHARLTON, Gordon Taliaferro (Ret Bp Suffr of Tex 1989-) 132 Lancaster Dr Apt 310, Irvington, VA 22480

CHASE, Alexis M (At) PO Box 286, Decatur, GA 30031

CHASE JR, Benjamin Otis (Vt) 95 Worcester Village Rd, Worcester, VT 05682

CHASE, Christopher (Cal) 10885 Caminito Cuesta, San Diego, CA 92131

CHASE IV, Edwin Theodore (Ted) (LI) 432 Lakeville Road, The Church of St. Philip and St. James, Lake Success, NY 11042

CHASE JR, John Garvey (Tex) P.O. Box 103, Crockett, TX 75835

CHASE, Katharine Barnhardt (SwVa)

CHASE, Peter Gray Otis (Mass) 258 Concord St, Newton, MA 02462

CHASE JR, Randall (Mass) PO Box 924, Barnstable, MA 02630

CHASSE, Richard P (Nwk) 176 Palisade Ave, Jersey City, NJ 07306

CHASSEY JR, George Irwin (USC) 9b Exum Dr, West Columbia, SC 29169

CHASTAIN, Gordon Lee (Ind) 1769 Dunaway Ct, Indianapolis, IN 46228

CHATFIELD, Jane Sheldon (Me) 11 White St, Rockland, ME 04841

CHATFIELD, Jenifer (Los)

CHATHAM, Charles Erwin (Az) 500 S Jackson St, Wickenburg, AZ 85390

CHATTIN, Mark Haney (NJ) 839 Haddon Ave., Collingswood, NJ 08108

CHAVEZ, Karen Sue (Los) 3160 Graceland Way, Corona, CA 92882

CHAVEZ, Rafael (Hond)

CHAVEZ, Velma (Wyo) 29 Shipton Lane, Fort Washakie, WY 82514

CHAVEZ FRANCO, Juan Eloy (Litoral Ecu) Iglesia Episcopal del Ecuador-Diocesis Litoral, Amarilis Fuente 603, Avenida 09015250, Guayaquil, Ecuador, Ecuador

CHECO, Antonio (LI) 2510 30th Rd Apt 2L, Astoria, NY 11102

CHEE, David Tsu Hian (Los) 700 Devils Drop Ct, El Sobrante, CA 94803

CHEEK, Alison Mary (Mass)

CHEESMAN JR, Benbow Palmer (Mil) 2501 S 60th St, Milwaukee, WI 53219

CHEFFEY, Anne Davis (WMo) 3 Northwoods Dr, Kimberling City, MO 65686

CHEN, Charles Chin-Ti (Tai) 23 Wu-Chuan West Road, 403, Taichung, Taiwan

CHEN, Luke H H (Tai) No 67 Lane 314 Ming Shen Rd, Shin Hua County, Tainan Hsien, 71246, Taiwan

CHENEY III, A(rthur) Milton (WMass) 38 Barnes Ln, West Greenwich, RI 02817

CHENEY, Barbara June (Ct) 90 Rogers Rd, Hamden, CT 06517

CHENEY SR, Bruce David (Miss) 1004 Pine St, Sikeston, MO 63801

CHENEY, Knight Dexter (Ct) 90 Rogers Rd, Hamden, CT 06517

CHENEY, Michael Robert (Mass) 117 Forest St, Malden, MA 02148

CHENEY, Peter Gunn (Az) 5090 N Via Gelsomino, Tucson, AZ 85750

CHENEY II, Reynolds Smith (WTenn) 60 Eastland Dr, Memphis, TN 38111

CHENG, Chen Chang (Tai) 499, Sec 4 Tam King Rd, Tamsui Dist, New Taipei City Taiwan, 25135, Taiwan

CHENG, Ching-Shan (Tai) 40 Ta Tung Rd, Wu Feng, Taichung County, 852, Taiwan

CHENG, Patrick S (Mass) 19 E 34th St, New York, NY 10016

CHERBONNEAU, Allen Robert (Ala) 4367 East River Road, Box 282, Mentone, AL 35984

CHERBONNIER, Edmond La Beaume (Mo) 843 Prospect Ave, Hartford, CT 06105

CHERISME, Charles M. (Hai) 472 Beech St, Roslindale, MA 02131

CHERISOL, Burnet (CFla) Chemin Des Dalles #76, Port-Au-Prince, BP 365, Haiti

CHERRY, Charles Shuler (Minn) 734 7th St S, Breckenridge, MN 56520

CHERRY, Jacqueline A (Cal) 1076 De Haro St, San Francisco, CA 94107

CHERRY, Mary Jane (Ky) 425 S 2nd St Ste 200, Louisville, KY 40202

CHERRY, Timothy B (Dal) 56 Cedar Ln, Osterville, MA 02655

CHERY, Jean Fils (Hai)

CHERY, Marie Carmel (Hai)

CHESHIRE, G(rady) Patterson (WNC) 1131 S Edgemont Ave, Gastonia, NC 28054

CHESNEY, Jonathan C (Ala) 608 Harper Ave, Auburn, AL 36830

CHESNUT, Mark Douglas (Alb) 1 N Market St, Johnstown, NY 12095

CHESS, Jean D (Pgh) 1500 Cochran Rd Apt 901, Pittsburgh, PA 15243

CHESTERMAN JR, Thomas Charles (DR (DomRep)) 2418 Hidden Valley Dr, Santa Rosa, CA 95404

CHEVES, Henry Middleton (SC) 635 Foredeck Lane, Edisto Island, SC 29438

CHILD, Kendrick H (Mass) Po Box 2085, New London, NH 03257

CHILDERS, Robert T J (ETenn) Church of the Good Shepherd, P.O. Box 145, Lookout Mountain, TN 37350

CHILDRESS JR, John Robinson (Ark) 10702 Crestdale Ln, Little Rock, AR 72212

CHILES, Robert Lee (USC) The Reverend Robert L Chiles, 103 Underwood Dr, Hendersonville, NC 28739

CHILESE, Sandra Lee (Az)

CHILLINGTON, Joseph Henry (Ind) 215 N 7th Street, Terre Haute, IN 47807

CHILTON, Bruce (NY) Bard College, Annandale-on-Hudson, NY 12504

CHILTON, Frank Eugene (Fla) 107 Golf Course Ln, Crescent City, FL 32112

CHILTON, Mary Habel (Alb) 3 Woods Edge Ln, West Sand Lake, NY 12196

CHILTON, William Parish (Eas) 214 Wye Ave, Easton, MD 21601

CHIN, Mary Louise (LI) Po Box 650397, Fresh Meadows, NY 11365

CHINERY, Edwin Thomas (NJ) 165 Essex Ave Apt 102, Metuchen, NJ 08840

CHINLUND, Stephen James (NY) 445 W 19th St, New York, NY 10011

CHIPPS, Kathleen Dawn (Va) 3604 Secret Grove Ct, Dumfries, VA 22025

CHIRICO, Carey D (Va) 905 Princess Anne St, Fredericksburg, VA 22401

CHIRINOS-HERNANDEZ, Jose A (Hond)

CHISHAM, Anne (SanD) 47568 Hawley Boulevard, San Diego, CA 92116

CHISHOLM, Alan Laird (NY) 209 S Broadway, Nyack, NY 10960

CHITTENDEN, Nils Philip (NY) St Stephens Church, 50 Bedford Rd, Armonk, NY 10504

CHO, Francis Soonhwan (NJ) 16 Rodak Cir, Edison, NJ 08817

CHOATE JR, Horace (NY) 4 Gateway Rd., Unit 1-D, Yonkers, NY 10703

CHOI, Beryl (WNY) 51 Virginia Pl, Buffalo, NY 14202

CHOI, Stephen Young Sai (NY) 5 7th St # 7047, North Bergen, NJ 07047

✠ **CHOI**, William Chul-Hi (Ret Bp of Pusan Korea 1987-) 8105 232nd St Se, Woodinville, WA 98072

CHOI, YoungKwon (Va) 1830 Kirby Rd, Mclean, VA 22101

CHOLLET, Mari (Mo) 232 South Woods Mill Rd., Chesterfield, MO 63017

CHORNYAK, Christopher John (Me) 3 Spring House Ln, Ellsworth, ME 04605

CHOYCE, George (ETenn) 27 Cool Springs Rd, Signal Mountain, TN 37377

CHRISMAN JR, John Aubrey (RI) 7118 Treymore Ct, Sarasota, FL 34243

CHRISMAN, Robert Edwin (Oly) 1214 184th Pl, Long Beach, WA 98631

CHRISNER, Marlen Ronald (At) 2320 Nw 53rd Avenue Rd, Ocala, FL 34482

CHRISTENSEN, Bonniejean (ND) 4001 Beneva Rd Apt 334, Sarasota, FL 34233

CHRISTENSEN, Kris Cay (Spok) PO Box 8508, Spokane, WA 99203

CHRISTIAN, Carol Jean (SO)

CHRISTIAN, Charles Ellis (Ind) 3627 E Crystal Valley Dr, Vincennes, IN 47591

CHRISTIAN, David Victor (WTenn) 8282 Macon Rd, Cordova, TN 38018

CHRISTIAN, Earl Rix (SVa) 25 Tripp Ter, Hampton, VA 23666

CHRISTIAN JR, Frank Stanaland (Ga) 212 W Pine St, Fitzgerald, GA 31750

CHRISTIAN, Julia Wadsworth (SanD) 78482 Bent Canyon Court, Bermuda Dunes, CA 92203

CHRISTIANSON, Regina Lee (Vt) PO Box 57, Underhill, VT 05489

CHRISTIANSSEN, Paul Jerome (The Episcopal NCal) 1016 W. Arrow Hwy, Apt. C, Upland, CA 91786

CHRISTIE, (Bob) (Oly) 6350 Portal Way Unit 72, Ferndale, WA 98248

CHRISTOFFERSEN, Timothy Robert (Cal) 611 Foxwood Way, Walnut Creek, CA 94595

CHRISTOPHER JR, Charles Harry (EO) 61157 Princeton Loop, Bend, OR 97702

CHRISTOPHER, John S (Az) 5143 E Karen Dr, Scottsdale, AZ 85254

CHRISTOPHER, Mary (Ia) 2110 Summit St, Sioux City, IA 51104

CHRISTOPHER, Melanie (Colo) 371 Upham St, Lakewood, CO 80226

CHRISTOPHERSON, Paul Conrad (Minn) Wildlife Run, New Vernon, NJ 07976

CHRISTY, Stephen James (Wyo) PO Box 246, Sundance, WY 82729

CHRONISTER, Lisa Marie (Okla)

CHRYSTAL, Susan (Nwk) 33 Woodstone Cir, Short Hills, NJ 07078

CHUBB JR, Donald Allen (Kan) 1011 SW Cambridge Ave, Topeka, KS 66604

CHUBOFF, Esther Lois (Ct) 83 E Main St, Clinton, CT 06413

CHUMBLEY, Kenneth Lawrence (WMo) 601 E Walnut St, Springfield, MO 65806

CHUN, Franklin Seu Hook (The Episcopal Church in Haw) 1163 Lunaanela St, Kailua, HI 96734

CHUN, Malcolm N (The Episcopal Church in Haw)

CHURCH, Susan Campbell (Ore) Po Box 1014, Newport, OR 97365

CHURCH, Susan Jean (NMich) Christ Church, 3906 5th St, Calumet, MI 49913

CHURCHILL, Gregg Hardison (Los) Po Box 1082, Lompoc, CA 93438

CHURCHMAN, Jean (Nina) Wood (Colo) All Saints Episcopal Church, 3448 N. Taft Ave., Loveland, CO 80538

CHURCHMAN, Michael Arthur (Neb) 300 W Broadway Ste 108, Council Bluffs, IA 51503

CHURCHWELL, Katherine Carlsen (Tex)

CIANNELLA, J(oseph) Domenic Kennith (Mass) 13 Park Dr, West Springfield, MA 01089

CICCARELLI, Sharon Lynn (Mass)

CICORA, Julie Anne (Roch) 556 Forest Lawn Dr, Webster, NY 14580

CIESEL, Barbara (Bitsey) Bitney (SD) 126 N Park St Ne, Wagner, SD 57380

CIESEL, Conrad Henry (SD) Po Box 216, Lake City, SD 57247

CIHAK, Susan Elizabeth (Az) 12990 E Shea Blvd, Scottsdale, AZ 85259

CILLEY, Norman H (CFla) 23 E Hampton Dr, Auburndale, FL 33823

CIMIJOTTI, Jerry Anthony (SD) 2822 S Division St, Spokane, WA 99203

CINTRON, Julio A (PR)

CIOSEK, Scott Andrew (Mass) 351 Elm St, South Dartmouth, MA 02748

CIPOLLA, Angela Marie (NJ) 650 Rahway Dr., Woodbridge, NJ 07095

CIRIELLO, Mary Anne (Ct) 3768 Anslow Drive, Leland, NC 28451

CIRILLO, James Hawthorne (Va) Po Box 847, Buckingham, PA 18912

CIRVES, Judith Melanie (Mil)

CISNEROS, Hilario (WNC) 2657 Chimney Rock Rd, Hendersonville, NC 28792

CIVALIER, Gordon Richard (NJ) 161 Lakebridge Dr., Deptford, NJ 08096

CLAASSEN, Scott Allen (Los) 1316 3rd St Ste B4, Santa Monica, CA 90401

CLABUESCH, Ward Henry (Mich) 3176 Topview Ct, Rochester Hills, MI 48309

CLADER, Linda Lee (The Episcopal NCal) 5555 Montgomery Dr Apt N201, Santa Rosa, CA 95409

CLAGGETT III, Thomas West (Md) 1123C Jefferson Pike, Knoxville, MD 21758

CLANCE, Bennett Bolton (Fla) 256 E Church St, Jacksonville, FL 32202

CLAPP JR, Schuyler L (EMich) 1102 W Front St, Traverse City, MI 49684

CLARK, Adelaide Sampselle (NY) 45 Miami Dr. Unit B, Monroe, OH 45050

CLARK, Anthony P (CFla) 108 Ludlow Dr, Longwood, FL 32779

CLARK, Beatryce Arlene (The Episcopal NCal) 581 Ridgewood Dr, Vacaville, CA 95688

CLARK, Bradford Duff (Mass) Po Box 25, Arlington, VT 05250

CLARK, Carol Ruth (NMich) 10401 V.05 Rd, Rapid River, MI 49878

CLARK, Carole Sue (Okla) Hc 67 Box 82, Indianola, OK 74442

CLARK, C(aroline) Robbins (Cal) 36 Larkhay Road, Hucclecote Gloucester, AE GL3 3NS, Great Britain (UK)

CLARK, Cathy A (NMich) P.O. Box 601, Ishpeming, MI 49849

CLARK, Charles Halsey (NH) 5 Timber Ln Apt 228, Exeter, NH 03833

CLARK, Cheryl Lynn (Ark) 1106 Deer Run N, Pine Bluff, AR 71603

CLARK, Cindy Lou (Tex) 501 E Gregg St, Calvert, TX 77837

CLARK, Constance Lee (Va) PO Box 183, Earlysville, VA 22936

CLARK, D(arrah) Corbet (Oly) 11520 Sw Timberline Dr, Beaverton, OR 97008

CLARK, David Norman (Md) 12265 Boyd Rd, Clear Spring, MD 21722

CLARK, Diana (Nwk) 59 Montclair Ave, Montclair, NJ 07042

CLARK, Diane Catherine (WA) 13 Eleanor Avenue, Saint Albans, Hertfordshire, AL35TA, Great Britain (UK)

CLARK, Douglas Burns (SeFla) 116 Prospect Park W # 2r, Brooklyn, NY 11215

CLARK, Frances M (NJ) 201 Penbryn Rd, Berlin, NJ 08009

CLARK, Frank Herbert (Az) 7810 W Columbine Dr, Peoria, AZ 85381

CLARK, Jacqueline Ann (Mass) St Elizabeth's Episcopal Church, 1 Morse Rd, Sudbury, MA 01776

CLARK, Jane Alice (Chi) 1608 W Plymouth Dr, Arlington Heights, IL 60004

CLARK II, Jim B. (Az) 6715 N Mockingbird Lane, Paradise Valley, AZ 85253

CLARK, Joan Bonnell (CFla) 5961 W Dedham Trl, Crystal River, FL 34429

CLARK, John Leland (SO) #1712 - 8888 Riverside Dr E, Windsor, ON N8S 1H2, Canada

CLARK SR, Johnny (John) Warren (WLa) 321 Horseshoe Drive, Crowley, LA 70526

CLARK, Joseph Madison (WA) 402 Grove Ave, po box 1098, Washington Grove, MD 20880

CLARK, Judith Freeman (Mass) 10 Ida Rd., Worcester, MA 01604

CLARK, Katherine Hampton (Los) 3969 Bucklin Pl, Thousand Oaks, CA 91360

CLARK, Marlene Mae (Mich) 1180 S Durand Rd, Lennon, MI 48449

CLARK, Martha K (WA) 600 M St SW, Washington, DC 20024

CLARK, Paula E (WA) 3001 Orion Ln, Upper Marlboro, MD 20774

CLARK, Philip C (Minn) 128 Canterbury Cir, Le Sueur, MN 56058

CLARK, Ralph (EC) 801 Bobby Jones Drive, Fayetteville, NC 28312

CLARK JR, Richard Johnston (Fla) 1623 7th St, New Orleans, LA 70115

CLARK, Richard Neece (WMich) 900 Pivot Rock Rd, Eureka Springs, AR 72632

CLARK, Richard Tilton (Mass) 16 Timothy St, Fairhaven, MA 02719

CLARK, Susan Mccarter (Mich) W180N7890 Town Hall Rd Apt D315, Menomonee Falls, WI 53051

CLARK, Taylor Brooks (Ore) 991 Normandy Ave S, Salem, OR 97302

CLARK, Vance Norman (CPa) 925 S. Lincoln Ave., Apt. G, Tyrone, PA 16686

CLARK, Vanessa E. B. (O) St. James Episcopal Church, 131 N State St, Painesville, OH 44077

CLARK, William Roderick (WTex) 1417 E Austin Ave, Harlingen, TX 78550

CLARK, William Whittier (Alb) Po Box 56, Medusa, NY 12120

CLARKE, Barbara Jean (Me) 11 Daisey Ln, Brewer, ME 04412

CLARKE, Charles Ray (Wyo) 796 Garner Dr, Lander, WY 82520

CLARKE JR, Daniel L (SC) 94 Willow Oak Cir, Charleston, SC 29418

CLARKE, Debra (NJ) 187 Aster Ct, Whitehouse Station, NJ 08889

CLARKE, Gervaise Angelo Morales (Nwk) 34 Orane Ave, Meadowbrook Mews, Kingston 19, Jamaica

CLARKE, James Munro (Alb) Po Box 405, Downsville, NY 13755

CLARKE, Janet Vollert (SeFla) 33406 Fairway Rd, Leesburg, FL 34788

CLARKE, John David (NY) 790 11th Ave Apt 29a, New York, NY 10019

CLARKE, John Robert (Mass) 2 Ridgewood Rd, Malden, MA 02148

CLARKE, Julian Maurice (VI) 123 Circle Dr, Saint Simons Island, GA 31522

CLARKE, Kenneth Gregory (SO) 3090 Montego Ln. Apt. 1, Maineville, OH 45039

CLARKE, Richard Kent (WMass) 162 Laurelwood Dr, Hopedale, MA 01747

CLARKE, Robert (Chi) 524 Sheridan Sq Apt 3, Evanston, IL 60202

CLARKE, Sheelagh Alison (Nwk) 119 Main St, Millburn, NJ 07041

CLARKE, Thomas George (Los) 1549 E Lobo Way, Palm Springs, CA 92264

CLARKSON, Frederick C (Tex) 4401 Statesville Blvd., Salisbury, NC 28147

CLARKSON, Julie Cuthbertson (NC) 1420 Sterling Rd, Charlotte, NC 28209

CLARKSON, Ted Hamby (Ga) Po Drawer 929, Darien, GA 31305

CLARKSON IV, William (WA) 1424 W Paces Ferry Rd Nw, Atlanta, GA 30327

CLASSEN, Ashley Molesworth (Dal) 635 N Story Rd, Irving, TX 75061

CLAUSEN, Kathryn Pearce (SO) 3623 Sellers Drive, Millersport, OH 43046

CLAUSEN, Ruth Lucille (Mich) 100 N. College Row Apt. 165, Brevard, NC 28712

CLAVIER, Anthony Forbes Moreton (Spr) 193 Summit Avenue, Glen Carbon, IL 62034

CLAWSON, Donald Richard (SeFla) 1605 Paseo Del Lago Ln, Vero Beach, FL 32967

CLAWSON, Jeffrey David (Los) 3 Bayview Ave., Belvedere, CA 94920

CLAXTON, Constance Colvin (Minn) 312 Church St, Audubon, IA 50025

CLAXTON, Leonard Cuthbert (Minn) RR #2, Box 207, Truman, MN 56088

CLAY, Thomas Davies (WA) 15003 Reserve Rd, Accokeek, MD 20607

CLAYTON JR, Paul Bauchman (NY) 4 Townsend Farm Rd, Lagrangeville, NY 12540

CLAYTON, Sharon Hoffman Chant (NY) 4 Townsend Farm Rd, Lagrangeville, NY 12540

CLAYTON, Victoria Helen (WA) 20100 Fisher Ave, Poolesville, MD 20837

CLAYTOR, Susan Quarles (CPa) 310 Elm Avenue, Hershey, PA 17033

CLEAVER-BARTHOLOMEW, Dena Marcel (CNY) 4566 Stoneledge Ln, Manlius, NY 13104

CLEAVES JR, George Lucius (EMich) 9020 South Saginaw Road, Grand Blanc, MI 48439

CLECKLER, Michael Howard (Ala) 1513 Edinburgh Way, Birmingham, AL 35243

CLEGHORN, Charlotte Dudley (WNC) 37 Cherry St., Arden, NC 28704

CLEGHORN, Maxine Janetta (NY) 4401 Matilda Ave, Bronx, NY 10470

CLELAND, Carol Elaine (Cal) 1550 Portola Avenue, Palo Alto, CA 94306

CLEM, Stewart Douglas (Okla) 616 Lincolnway E, Mishawaka, IN 46544

CLEMENT, Betty Cannon (Dal) 4120 Jasmine St, Paris, TX 75462

CLEMENT, James Marshall (Chi) 3411 N Harvard Ave, Peoria, IL 61614

CLEMENTS, C(Harles) Christopher (USC) 1523 Delmar St, West Columbia, SC 29169

CLEMENTS, Elaine Gant (La) St Andrew's Episcopal Church, 1101 S Carrollton Ave, New Orleans, LA 70118

CLEMENTS, Robert (Ct) PO Box 809, Litchfield, CT 06759

CLEMMONS, Geraldine Dobbs (Alb) 105 23rd St., Troy, NY 12180

CLEMONS, D David (The Episcopal NCal) 8148 Emerson Ave, Yucca Valley, CA 92284

CLEMONS, E(arlie) Roland (NJ) 132 S Adelaide Ave Apt 1b, Highland Park, NJ 08904

CLENDENIN, Evan Graham (Oly) 719 West 2nd St, Erie, PA 16507

CLENDINEN JR, James H. (Ga) 51 Hornet Dr., Brunswick, GA 31525

CLERKIN, Shawn Jeffrey (NwPa) 662 Silliman Ave, Erie, PA 16510

CLEVELAND, Jennifer B (Oly) 125 SW Eckman St, McMinnville, OR 97128

CLEVELAND, Thomas Grover (Mass) 28 Grover Ln, Tamworth, NH 03886

CLEVELEY, Susan Lynn (Spok) 1005 E B St, Moscow, ID 83843

CLEVENGER, Mark R (U) PO Box 606, Shoreham, NY 11786

CLIFF, F(rank) Graham (Be) 15 Bede Circle, Honesdale, PA 18431

CLIFF, Wendy Dawson (Cal) 3 Bayview Ave, Belvedere, CA 94920

CLIFFORD III, George Minott (The Episcopal Church in Haw)

CLIFT, Jean Dalby (Colo) 2130 E Columbia Pl, Denver, CO 80210

CLIFT, Joe Walter (Ga) 343 Gander Rd, Dawson, GA 39842

CLIFT JR, Wallace B (Colo) 2328 Lakemoor Dr SW, Olympia, WA 98512

CLIFTON JR, Ellis Edward (Mich) St. Clement'S Episcopal Church, 4300 Harrison Road, Inkster, MI 48141

CLIFTON, Steve (CFla) 3137 Denham Ct, Orlando, FL 32825

CLINEHENS JR, Harold O (The Episcopal NCal) 714 Lassen Lane, Mount Shasta, CA 96067

CLINGENPEEL, Ronald Harvey (La) 1911 Cypress Creek Road #222, New Orleans, LA 70123

CLIVER, Stanley Cameron (Wyo) Po Box 176, Sundance, WY 82729

CLODFELTER, Jonathan Norwood (Pa) 4442 Frankford Ave, Philadelphia, PA 19124

CLOSE, David Wyman (Ore) 7990 Headlands Way, Clinton, WA 98236

CLOSE, Leroy Springs (RI) 316 W Main Rd, Little Compton, RI 02837

CLOSE, Patrick Raymond (NJ) Grace Episcopal Church, 19 Kings Hwy E, Haddonfield, NJ 08033

CLOSE ERSKINE, Christine Elaine (Ore) 60960 Creekstone Loop, Bend, OR 97702

CLOTHIER, Tamara A (Tex) 5001 Hickory Rd, Temple, TX 76502

CLOUD, Vernon Luther (SD) 13696 448th Ave, Waubay, SD 57273

CLOUGHEN JR, Charles Edward (Md) PO Box 313-, Hunt Valley, MD 21030

CLOWERS, Grantland Hugh (Kan) 2007 Miller Dr, Lawrence, KS 66046

CLUETT JR, Richard (Be) 119 W. Johnston St., Allentown, PA 18103

COAN, Barbara Frances Smith (The Episcopal Church in Haw) 1311 Nahele Pl, Kapaa, HI 96746

COATS, Bleakley Irving (Ida)

COATS, Christopher Vincent (CGC) Wharf Marina Slip #38, Orange Beach, AL 36561

COATS, John Rhodes (Cal) 15814 Champion Forest Dr, Spring, TX 77379

COATS, William Russell (Nwk) 19 Elmwood Ave., Ho Ho Kus, NJ 07423

COBB, Christina Rich (Mo) 1212 Ringo St, Mexico, MO 65265

COBB, David C (Chi) 1133 N La Salle Blvd, Chicago, IL 60610

COBB JR, Harold James (SVa) 1931 Paddock Rd, Norfolk, VA 23518

COBB, John Pierpont (SO) 36 Ledge Rd, Gloucester, MA 01930

COBB, Julia (NwT) St Barnabas Episcopal Church, 4141 Tanglewood Ln, Odessa, TX 79762

COBB, Matthew Mickey (Kan) 1915 Montgomery Dr, Manhattan, KS 66502

COBB-ANDERSON, Vienna (Va) 1138 West Ave, Richmond, VA 23220

COBDEN JR, Edward Alexander Morrison (Mich) Po Box 295, South Egremont, MA 01258

COBDEN JR, Edward Alexander Morrison (NY) 374 Sarles St, Bedford Corners, NY 10549

COBLE JR, John Reifsnyder (Be) 1929 Pelham Rd, Bethlehem, PA 18018

COBLE, Robert Henry (Pa) 36 Crescent Cir, Harleysville, PA 19438

COBURN, Ann Struthers (Mass) PO Box 1988, Berkeley, CA 94709

COBURN, Michael (RI) 55 Linden Road, Barrington, RI 02806

COCHRAN, Carlotta B (SVa) 713 Seagrass Reach, Chesapeake, VA 23320

COCHRAN, Elizabeth Jane (Oly) St Matthew's Episcopal Church, 412 Pioneer Ave, Castle Rock, WA 98611

COCHRAN, Joseph M (Md)

COCHRAN, Laura Doud (Va) 1700 Wainwright Dr, Reston, VA 20190

COCHRAN, Paul Coleman (Be)

COCKBILL, Douglas J (Chi) 3310 Coventry Ct, Joliet, IL 60431

COCKE, Reagan Winter (Tex) 2450 River Oaks Blvd, Houston, TX 77019

COCKRELL, Ernest William (ECR) 1538 Koch Ln, San Jose, CA 95125

COCKRELL, John Grafton (SC) 275 Warden Ave, Bluefield, WV 24701

COCKRELL, Richard (USC) 2104 E North Ave, Anderson, SC 29625

CODE, David Arthur (NJ) 729 Partridge Ln, State College, PA 16803

CODY, Daphne Ceil (Chi) 380 Hawthorn Ave, Glencoe, IL 60022

COE III, Frank S (WVa) 74 Rhodes Court, Harpers Ferry, WV 25425

COE, Wayland Newton (Tex) 5934 Rutherglenn Dr, Houston, TX 77096

COENEN, Susan Ann (FdL)

COERPER, Milo George (Md) 7315 Brookville Rd, Chevy Chase, MD 20815

COERPER, Rebecca Blackshear (CNY) 98 East Genesee St, Skaneateles, NY 13152

COFFEY, Bridget Eileen (Va) 5 School House Ln, North East, MD 21901

COFFEY, E Allen (Va) 10231 Fenholloway Dr, Mechanicsville, VA 23116

COFFEY, Gary Keith (WNC) 23 Forest Knoll Dr, Weaverville, NC 28787

COFFEY, J(anet) Paris (Chi) 240 S. Marion St., 1N, Oak Park, IL 60302

COFFEY JR, Jonathan Bachman (Fla) 4903 Robert D Gordon Rd, Jacksonville, FL 32210

COFFEY, Kevin Patrick Joseph (Nwk) 2-06 31st St, Fair Lawn, NJ 07410

COFFIN, Peter R (NH) 35 Woodbury St, Keene, NH 03431

COFFMAN, Daniel Brian (Neb) Holy Trinity Episcopal Church, 6001 A St, Lincoln, NE 68510

COGAN, Timothy Bernard (NJ) 38 The Blvd/RFD659, Edgartown, MA 02539

COGAR, Carolyn Christine (SO) 541 2nd Ave, Gallipolis, OH 45631

COGGI, Lynne Marie Madeleine (NY) 3206 Cripple Creek St Apt 39b, San Antonio, TX 78209

COGGIN, Bruce Wayne (FtW) 3700 Ellsmere Ct, Fort Worth, TX 76103

COGILL, Richard Leonard (Minn) Cathedral of St George the Martyr, 5 Wales St, Cape Town, 8001, South Africa

COGSDALE, Michael H (WNC) 845 Cherokee Place, Lenoir, NC 28645

COHEE, William Patrick (Az) 114 W Roosevelt St, Phoenix, AZ 85003

COHEN, David Michael (The Episcopal NCal) 310 W North St, Alturas, CA 96101

COHEN, Georgia Shoberg (NJ) Po Box 5, Blawenburg, NJ 08504

COHOON, Frank Nelson (Kan) 44 Sw Pepper Tree Ln, Topeka, KS 66611

COHOON, Richard Allison (CPa) 500 E Guardlock Dr, Lock Haven, PA 17745

COIL, John Albert (WMo) 7917 Lamar Ave, Prairie Village, KS 66208

COIL, Paul Douglas (At) 4141 Wash Lee Ct Sw, Lilburn, GA 30047

COKE III, Henry Cornick (Dal) 5433 N Dentwood Dr, Dallas, TX 75220

COKE, Paul T (Tex) 9426 Peabody Ct, Boca Raton, FL 33496

COLANGELO, Preston Hart (Ala) 1663 Bradford Ln, Bessemer, AL 35022

COLAVINCENZO, Sue (EMich) St Dunstan's Episcopal Church, 1523 N Oak Rd, Davison, MI 48423

COLBERT, Paul A (Episcopal SJ) 42274 Long Hollow Dr, Coarsegold, CA 93614

COLBURN, Suzanne Funk (Mass) Po Box 185, Boothbay Harbor, ME 04538

COLBY, Richard Everett (Me) 3702 Haven Pines Dr, Kingwood, TX 77345

COLE, Allan Hunter (Colo) 9200 W 10th Ave, Lakewood, CO 80215

COLE, Anson Dean (O) 565 S Cleveland Massillon Rd, Akron, OH 44333

COLE, Brian Lee (Lex) Church of the Good Shepherd, 533 E Main St, Lexington, KY 40508

COLE JR, C Alfred (CFla) 125 Larkwood Dr, Sanford, FL 32771

COLE, Cecil (Mass) 2210 E Tudor Rd, Anchorage, AK 99507

COLE, Christopher Alan (At) Holy Innocents Episcopal Church, 805 Mt Vernon Hwy NW, Atlanta, GA 30327

COLE, Christopher Owen (WTex) 5909 Walzem Rd, San Antonio, TX 78218

COLE, Dennis C (Oly) 3917 Ne 44th St, Vancouver, WA 98661

COLE, Elaine Agnes (SwFla) 330 Forest Wood Ct, Spring Hill, FL 34609

COLE, Ethan J (WNY) 5083 Thompson Rd, Clarence, NY 14031

COLE, Frantz (Hai) Box 1309, Port-Au-Prince, Haiti

COLE JR, H(oward) Milton (Pa) 2001 S. 40th Court, West Des Moines, IA 50265

COLE, Judith Poteet (WNC) 8015 Island View Ct, Denver, NC 28037

COLE, Marguerite June (Nev) 5268 Jodilyn Ct Apt 150, Las Vegas, NV 89103

COLE, Michael George (SC) 1202 Stonegate Way, Crozet, VA 22932

COLE JR, Raymond Elden (WTex) 3614 Hunters Dove, San Antonio, TX 78230

COLE, Roy Allen (NY) 1333 Bay St, Staten Island, NY 10305

COLE III, Roy W (USC) 184 Clifton Ave, Spartanburg, SC 29302

COLE, Suzanne Louise (Me) 41 Gardiner Pl, Walton, NY 13856

COLE-DUVALL, Mary Duvall (Ia) 2001 S. 40th Court, West Des Moines, IA 50265

COLEGROVE, Jerome 'Kip' (O) 551 Rockwell Street, Kent, OH 44240

COLEMAN, Bernice (LI) 10206 Farmers Blvd, Hollis, NY 11423

COLEMAN, Betty Ellen Gibson (SO) 4325 Skylark Dr, Englewood, OH 45322

COLEMAN, Brian Ray (WMich) 252 Chestnut St, Battle Creek, MI 49017

COLEMAN, Carolyn (Tenn) Holy Cross Episcopal Church, 1140 Cason Land, Murfreesboro, TN 37128

COLEMAN JR, Dale D (Spr) 105 E. D St., Belleville, IL 62220

COLEMAN, Dennis E (Pa) 121 Church St, Phoenixville, PA 19460

COLEMAN, Edwin Cabaniss (Tenn) 4715 Harding Pike, Nashville, TN 37205

COLEMAN JR, Fred George (NY) 2048 Lorena Ave., Akron, OH 44313

COLEMAN, Henry Douglas (NY) 39 W Lewis Ave, Pearl River, NY 10965

✠ **COLEMAN**, James Malone (Ret Bp of WTenn 2001-) 3052 Tyrone Dr, Baton Rouge, LA 70808

COLEMAN, James Patrick (CFla) 4820 Lake Gibson Park Rd, Lakeland, FL 33809

COLEMAN, John Charles (CGC) 2 Chateau Place, Dothan, AL 36303

COLEMAN, Karen (Mass) 59 Fayerweather St # 2138, Cambridge, MA 02138

COLEMAN, Kim Latice (Va) 912 S Veitch St, Arlington, VA 22204

COLEMAN, M Joan (Spr) 9 Teakwood Dr, Belleville, IL 62221

✠ **COLERIDGE**, Clarence Nicholas (Ret Bp of Ct 2002-) 29 Indian Rd, Trumbull, CT 06611

COLES, Clifford Carleton (NC) 3927 Napa Valley Dr, Raleigh, NC 27612

COLES, Constance C. (NY) 73 Waterside Lane, Clinton, CT 06413

COLETON, John Mortimer (Kan) 7224 Village Dr, Prairie Village, KS 66208

COLLAMORE JR, (Harry) Bacon (Ct)

COLLEGE, Philip Anthony (SO) 5691 Great Hall Ct, Columbus, OH 43231

COLLER, Patricia Marie (Ct) Church Pension Group, 19 E 34th St, New York, NY 10016

COLLEY-TOOTHAKER, Samuel Scott (Chi) 437 Hawthorne Drive, Danville, VA 24541

COLLIER, Catherine Hudson (Ala) 605 Lurleen B Wallace Blvd N, Tuscaloosa, AL 35401

COLLIER, Daniel R (NH) 155 Salem Rd, Billerica, MA 01821

COLLIER, Mary Anne (NwT)

COLLIN, Winifred Nohmer (Roch) 2696 Clover St, Pittsford, NY 14534

COLLINS, Aaron Paul (O) 6630 Orchard Club Pl, Louisville, KY 40291

COLLINS, Charles Blake (WTex) 431 Richmond Pl Ne, Albuquerque, NM 87106

COLLINS, David Browning (At) 132 Hearthstone Dr, Woodstock, GA 30189

COLLINS, David William (SeFla) 365 La Villa Dr., Miami Springs, FL 33166

COLLINS, Diana Garvin (Vt) 535 Woodbury Rd, Springfield, VT 05156

COLLINS, E Selden (NMich) 1628 W Town Line Rd, Pickford, MI 49774

COLLINS, Gary David (Los) 2720 Colt Rd, Rancho Palos Verdes, CA 90275

COLLINS, Gerald (Pa) 520 S 61st St, Philadelphia, PA 19143

COLLINS, Guy J(Ames) D(Ouglas) (NH) 9 W Wheelock St, Hanover, NH 03755

COLLINS, James Edward (ECR) 615 Santa Paula Dr, Salinas, CA 93901

COLLINS, Jean Griffin (Mont) 1000 Fountain Terrace, 402, Lewistown, MT 59457

COLLINS III, John Milton (SanD) 701 Kettner Blvd Unit 94, San Diego, CA 92101

COLLINS, John Robert (EO) PO Box 130, Sisters, OR 97759

COLLINS, Judith Tindall (RI) 84 Benefit St # 3, Providence, RI 02904

COLLINS, Loretta L (CPa) 21 S Main St, Lewistown, PA 17044

COLLINS, Lynn Arnetha (LI) 21 Eldridge Ave, Hempstead, NY 11550

COLLINS, M A (SanD) 3847 Balsamina Dr, Bonita, CA 91902

COLLINS, Mark R (NY) 88 Saint Nicholas Avenue, New York, NY 10026

Clergy List

COLLINS, Patrick A (CPa) 640 N
67th St, Harrisburg, PA 17111
COLLINS, Paul Michael (Oly) PO
Box 1204, Summerland, CA 93067
COLLINS, Stanley Penrose (Episcopal
SJ) 1401 Locke Rd, Modesto, CA
95355
COLLINS, Victoria Lundberg (CFla)
688 Ebony St, Melbourne, FL 32935
COLLINS, William Gerard (Ga) 209
Maple St, Saint Simons Island, GA
31522
COLLIS, Geoffrey (NJ) 32 Lafayette
St, Rumson, NJ 07760
COLLIS, Shannon Jane (Los) 11305
Hesperia Rd., Hesperia, CA 92345
COLLUM, David Joseph (Alb) 62
South Swan St., Albany, NY 12210
COLMENAREZ, Gustavo Adolfo
(Ve) Iglesia Episcopal de Venezuela,
Colinas de Bello Monte, Centro
Diocesano Av. Caroní No. 100,
Caracas, 1042-A, Venezuela
COLMORE III, C(harles) Blayney
(SanD) PO Box 516, Jacksonville, VT
05342
COLON TORRES, Lydia (PR) PO
Box 902, Saint Just, PR 00978, Puerto
Rico
COLTON, Elizabeth Wentworth (Pa)
966 Trinity Lane, King of Prussia, PA
19406
COLVILL, Lea Nadine (Mont) 3243 N
Meridian St, Indianapolis, IN 46208
COLVIN, Jeremi Ann (Mass) 160 Rock
St, Fall River, MA 02720
COLVIN, Myra Angeline (Mich) 226
Spring Lake Dr, Chelsea, MI 48118
COLVIN, Sarah Margaret (WA) 131
Waterbury Court, Charlottesville, VA
22902
COLWELL, Charles Richard (NY) 172
Ivy St, Oyster Bay, NY 11771
COLWELL II, Kirby Price (O) 4449
Lander Rd, Chagrin Falls, OH 44022
COMBS, Leslie David (NY) 123
Franklin St., Concord, NH 03301
COMBS, William (At) 2920 Landrum
Education Dr, Oakwood, GA 30566
COMEAU, Molly Stata (Vt) 70 Poor
Farm Rd, Alburg, VT 05440
COMEAUX, Andrew Anthony (WLa)
3728 Sabine Pass Dr, Bossier, LA
71111
COMEGYS JR, David Pierson (Dal)
25721 Weston Dr, Laguna Niguel, CA
92677
COMER, Fletcher (Ala) 898 Running
Brook Dr, Prattville, AL 36066
COMER, Harold Leroy (WMich) 1231
Fran Dr, Frankfort, MI 49635
COMER, Judith Walton (Ala) 2813
Godfrey Ave NE, Fort Payne, AL
35967
COMER, Kathleen Susan (La) 4105
Division St, Metairie, LA 70002
COMER, Susanne Darnell (Tex) 1941
Webberville Rd, Austin, TX 78721
COMFORT, Alexander Freeman
(WNC) 105 Sunny Ln, Mars Hill, NC
28754

COMINOS, Peter (EMich) 508 Hart
St, Essexville, MI 48732
COMMINS, Gary (Los) 1114 Opal St
Apt D, Redondo Beach, CA 90277
COMPIER, Don Hendrik (Kan) 835
SW Polk St, Topeka, KS 66612
COMPTON, William Hewlett (Miss)
674 Mannsdale Rd, Madison, MS
39110
CONANT, Louise R (Mass) 24
Bowdoin St, Cambridge, MA 02138
CONATY, Peter Michael (Tex) 404
Buena Vista Ln, West Columbia, TX
77486
CONAWAY, Arthur Clarence (Lex)
1403 Providence Rd, Richmond, KY
40475
CONDON, Joshua T (Tex) Holy Spirit
Episcopal Church, 12535 Perthshire
Rd, Houston, TX 77024
CONDON, Sarah Taylor (Tex)
CONES, Bryan Matthew (Chi) 1140
Wilmette Ave, Wilmette, IL 60091
CONGDON, William Hopper (Ct)
CONGER, George Am (CFla) Po Box
97, Vero Beach, FL 32961-097
CONGER, George Mallett (NY) 9
Angel Rd, New Paltz, NY 12561
CONGER, John Peyton (Cal)
CONIGLIO, Robert Freeman (SVa)
21313 Metompkin View Lane,
Parksley, VA 23421
CONKLIN, Andrea Caruso (Tex) 1819
Heights Blvd, Houston, TX 77008
CONKLIN, Caroline Elizabeth (Mont)
13231 15th Ave N.E., Seattle, WA
98125
CONKLIN, Daniel G (Oly) Neue
Jakob Str 1, Berlin, 10179, Germany
CONKLING JR, Allan Alden (WTex)
PO Box 314, Bandera, TX 78003
CONKLING, Kelly Schneider (WTex)
10642 Newcroft Pl, Helotes, TX 78023
CONLEY, Alan Bryan (WTex) P.O.
Box 350, 231 Cave Springs Dr. W.,
Hunt, TX 78024
CONLEY, Joan Frances (Nwk) 169
Fairmount Rd, Ridgewood, NJ 07450
CONLEY, Kris (Me) 17 Littlefield Dr,
Kennebunk, ME 04043
CONLEY, Patricia Ann (Chi) 1993
Yasgur Dr, Woodstock, IL 60098
CONLEY, Thomas Herbert (At) 2215
Cheshire Bridge Road NE, Atlanta, GA
30324
CONLIFFE, Mario Romain Marvin
(Md) 2434 Cape Horn Rd, Hampstead,
MD 21074
CONN JR, Doyt LaDean (Oly) 1805
38th Ave, Seattle, WA 98122
CONN, John Hardeman (Mass) 4
Alton Court, Brookline, MA 02446
CONN, Rodney Carl (Be) 108 N. 5th
St., Allentown, PA 18102
CONNELL, George Patterson (Ky) 11
Saint Lukes Ln, San Antonio, TX
78209
CONNELL, John Baade (The
Episcopal Church in Haw) 95-1050
Makaikai St. Apt. 17M, Mililani, HI
96789

CONNELL, Susan (Okla) 57200 E
Hwy 125, Unit 3431, Monkey Island,
OK 74331
CONNELLY III, Albert Pinckney
(CFla) 16 Hawks Lndg, Weaverville,
NC 28787
CONNELLY, Charles Evans (SwFla)
2401 Bayshore Blvd., Unit 505,
Tampa, FL 33629
CONNELLY, Constance R (NC) 1950
S Wendover Rd, Charlotte, NC 28211
CONNELLY, John Vaillancourt (Chi)
2327 Birchwood Ave, Wilmette, IL
60091
CONNELLY JR, Walter Joseph
(Mass) 231 Bowdoin St, Winthrop, MA
02151
CONNER, Georgene Davis (SwFla)
2926 57th Street S, Gulfport, FL 33707
CONNER, Lu-Anne (Me) 140 The
Kings Hwy, Newcastle, ME 04553
CONNER, Martha Hathcock (Az)
11102 W. Kolina Lane, Sun City, AZ
85351
CONNER, Sarah A (Mass) 4 Ernest
Rd # 3, Arlington, MA 02474
CONNERS, John H (EC) 6 Old Kings
Hwy, Norwalk, CT 06850
CONNOLLY, Emma French (WTenn)
480 S. Greer St., Memphis, TN 38111
CONNOR, Alice Elizabeth (SO) 5735
Lester Rd, Cincinnati, OH 45213
CONNORS, Barbara Mae (Ct) 35350
E Division Rd, Saint Helens, OR 97051
CONRAD JR, James Wallace (Az)
6069 Weeping Banyan Ln, Woodland
Hills, CA 91367
CONRAD, John William (Los) All
Saints Episcopal Church, 3847
Terracina Dr, Riverside, CA 92506
CONRAD, Matthew Mcmillan (ECR)
5318 Palma Ave., Atascadero, CA
93422
CONRADO VARELA, Victor Hugo
(Chi)
CONRADS, Alexandra Kennan (Los)
CONRADS, Nancy Alice (Chi) 4801
Spring Creek Rd, Rockford, IL 61114
CONRADT, James Robert (FdL)
W1693 Echo Valley Rd, Kaukauna, WI
54130
CONROE, Jon Wallace (RG)
CONROY, Mary E (SeFla) 1121
Andalusia Ave, Coral Gables, FL
33134
CONSIDINE, H James (NwPa) 11733
SW 17th CT, Miramar, FL 33025
CONSTANT, Donna Rittenhouse (Pa)
167 Hermit Hollow Lane, Middleburg,
PA 17842
CONSTANT, Joseph Murrenz (WA)
701 Oglethorpe St NW, Washington,
DC 20011
CONTESTABLE, Christine Marie (U)
673 Wall St, Salt Lake City, UT 84103
CONWAY, J Cooper (NY) 1514
Palisade Ave, Union City, NJ 07087
CONWAY, Nancy Jean (CPa) 6 Watch
Tower Ct, Salem, SC 29676
CONWAY, Natalie Hall (Md)

CONWAY, Thomas Bradley (NJ) 22 Wickapecko Dr, Interlaken, NJ 07712

COOK, Ashley Michele (Tex) 919 S John Redditt Dr, Lufkin, TX 75904

COOK, Carol Lee (Cal) 2235 3rd St, Livermore, CA 94550

COOK, Charles James (Tex) Po Box 2247, Austin, TX 78768

COOK, C(harles) Robert (Neb) 2666 El Rancho Rd, Sidney, NE 69162

COOK, Deborah (NJ) 202 Navesink Avenue, Atlantic Highlands, NJ 07716

COOK, Edward Richard (NJ) 130 Stoneham Dr, Glassboro, NJ 08028

COOK, Ellen Piel (SO) 2768 Turpin Oaks Ct, Cincinnati, OH 45244

COOK II, Harry Theodore (Mich) 3114 Vinsetta Blvd, Royal Oak, MI 48073

COOK, Harvey Gerald (Lex) 20129 N Painted Sky Dr, Surprise, AZ 85374

COOK, James Bonham (Okla) Saint Andrew's Church, 516 W 3rd Ave, Stillwater, OK 74074

COOK, James Brian (SeFla) 3395 Burns Road, Palm Beach Gardens, FL 33410

COOK, James Harrison (Minn) 317 Franklin St, Red Wing, MN 55066

COOK JR, Joe Jr (Mass) 28 Highland Ave, Roxbury, MA 02119

COOK, Johnny Walter (CGC) 206 Fig Ave, Fairhope, AL 36532

COOK, Kay Kellam (U) 2425 Colorado Ave, Boulder, CO 80302

COOK, Lilian Lotus Lee (RG) 2114 Hoffman Dr Ne, Albuquerque, NM 87110

COOK, Nancy Bell (Ark) 228 Spring St, Hot Springs, AR 71901

COOK, Patricia Ann (NAM) PO Box 85, Bluff, UT 84512

COOK, Paul Raymond (WMo)

COOK, Peter John Arthur (WLa) 4100 Bayou Rd, Lake Charles, LA 70605

COOK JR, Robert Bruce (NC) 8400 Goose Landing Ct, Browns Summit, NC 27214

COOK, Thomas R (Minn) 301 N. Chester Rd., Swarthmore, PA 19081

COOK, William E (Tex) 11245 Shoreline Dr., Apt 308, Tyler, TX 75703

COOK, Winifred Rose (Mich) PO Box 287, Onsted, MI 49265

COOKE, Barbara Jane (NC) 5205 Ainsworth Dr, Greensboro, NC 27410

COOKE, Bruce Henry (Va) 117 Wagon Wheel Trl, Moneta, VA 24121

COOKE, Catherine Cornelia Hutton (Vt) 500 South Union, Burlington, VT 05401

COOKE, C(hester) Allen (ETenn) 2124 Carpenter's Grade Road, Maryville, TN 37803

COOKE, Douglas Tasker (Ct) 19 Ridgebrook Dr, West Hartford, CT 06107

COOKE, Hilary Elizabeth (Ind)

COOKE, Hugh Mabee (Episcopal SJ) 67 W Noble St, Stockton, CA 95204

COOKE JR, James Coffield (EC) 309 Mary Lee Ct, Winterville, NC 28590

COOKE, James Daniel (Ct) 23 Parsonage Road, HIgganum, CT 06441

COOKE, Peter Stanfield (NJ) 16 Brandywyne, Brielle, NJ 08730

COOKE, Philip Ralph (ECR) 17740 Peak Ave, Morgan Hill, CA 95037

COOL, Opal Mary (Neb) 3525 N. 167Th Cir. Apt. 206, Omaha, NE 68116

COOLEY, Andrew A (Colo) 1415 N Franklin St, Colorado Springs, CO 80907

COOLIDGE, Edward Cole (Ct) 43 Spruce Ln, Cromwell, CT 06416

COOLIDGE, Robert Tytus (Cal) PO Box 282, Westmount, QC H3Z 2T2, Canada

COOLIDGE, William McCabe (NC) 118 Cumberland Ave, Asheville, NC 28801

COOLING, David Albert (USC) 280 Holcombe Way, Lambertville, NJ 08530

COOMBER, Matthew J.M. (ND)

COON, David Paul (The Episcopal Church in Haw) Po Box 690, Kamuela, HI 96743

COON, Nancy Galloway (WTex) 200 Crossroads Drive, Dripping Springs, TX 78620

COONEY, James Francis (O) 384 Burr Oak Dr, Kent, OH 44240

COOPER JR, A(Llen) William (Alb) 1365 County Route 60, Onchiota, NY 12989

COOPER, Cricket S (WMass) 67 East Street, Pittsfield, MA 01201

COOPER IV, Francis Marion (CGC) Po Box 1677, Santa Rosa Beach, FL 32459

COOPER, Gale Hodkinson (NC) 1636 Headquarters Plantation Drive, Charleston, SC 29455

COOPER, James Herbert (Fla) 1314 Ponte Vedra Blvd, Ponte Vedra Beach, FL 32082

COOPER, Joseph Wiley (EC) 4925 Oriole Dr, Wilmington, NC 28403

COOPER, Michael Francis (Los) 4018 Vista Ct, La Crescenta, CA 91214

COOPER, Michael Scott (CPa) 181 S 2nd St, Hughesville, PA 17737

COOPER, Miles Oliver (CFla) 423 Forest Ridge Dr, Aiken, SC 29803

COOPER, Norbert Milton (SeFla) 11201 Sw 160th St, Miami, FL 33157

COOPER, Richard Randolph (Tex) 4805 E Columbary Dr, Rosenberg, TX 77471

COOPER, Robert Norman (WLa) 108 Blue Ridge, Site 41, Comfort, TX 78013

COOPER, Stephenie Rose (ECR) 1205 Pine Ave, San Jose, CA 95125

COOPER-WHITE, Pamela (At) Union Theological Seminary, 3041 Broadway, New York, NY 10027

COOTER, Eric Shane (SwFla) 24 Clubhouse Rd, Rotonda West, FL 33947

COPE, Jan Naylor (WA) Washington National Cathedral, 3101 Wisconsin Avenue, NW, Washington, DC 20016

COPE, Marie Swann (USC) 101 St. Matthew's Ln, Spartanburg, SC 29301

COPELAND, Richard (Dal) 1141 N Loop 1604 E, Suite 105-614, San Antonio, TX 78232

COPELAND, Wanda Ruth (CNY) St Matthews Episcopal Church, 408 S Main St, Horseheads, NY 14845

COPENHAVER, Robert Thomas (SwVa) 50 Draper Place, Daleville, VA 24083

COPLAND, Edward Mark (SwFla) 5462 Shadow Lawn Dr, Sarasota, FL 34242

COPLEY, David Mark (NY) 10 West Elizabeth Street, Tarrytown, NY 10591

COPLEY, Susan Kay (NY) 10 W Elizabeth St, Tarrytown, NY 10591

COPP, Ann Humphreys (Md) 444 Garrison Forest Rd, Owings Mills, MD 21117

COPPEL JR, Stanley Graham (Episcopal SJ) Po Box 1431, Twain Harte, CA 95383

COPPEN, Christopher J (Spok) 5108 W Rosewood Ave, Spokane, WA 99208

COPPICK, Glendon Cleon (Ky) 851 Live Oak Pl, Owensboro, KY 42303

COPPINGER, Timothy R (WMo) 107 W Perimeter Dr, San Antonio, TX 78227

CORAM, James M (NC) 12109 Park Shore Ct, Woodbridge, VA 22192

CORBETT, Ian Deighton (NAM) Po Box 28, Bluff, UT 84512

CORBETT, James Byron David (Los) 10819 SE Rex St, Portland, OR 97266

CORBETT, John Philip (NwT) P.O. Box 334, Brownfield, TX 79316

CORBETT-WELCH, Kathleen Ellen (WA) 2218 Hillhouse Rd, Baltimore, MD 21207

CORBIN, Portia Renae (SD) 500 S Main Ave, Sioux Falls, SD 57104

CORBISHLEY, Frank J. (SeFla) 921 Sorolla, Coral Gables, FL 33134

CORDINGLEY, Saundra Lee (Roch) 23 Seneca Road, Rochester, NY 14622

CORDOBA, Guillermo (Fla) 2961 University Blvd N, Jacksonville, FL 32211

CORIOLAN, Simpson (Hai) Box 1309, Port-Au-Prince, Haiti

CORKERN, Matthew Thomas Locy (Nwk) 41 Woodland Avenue, Summit, NJ 07901

CORKLIN, Stanley Earl (Vt) 744 Parker Road, West Glover, VT 05875

CORL, James Alexander (CNY) 2435 Fleming Scipio Town Line Road, Auburn, NY 13021

CORLETT, Diane Bishop (NC) 6901 Three Bridges Cir, Raleigh, NC 27613

CORLEY, Kathryn S (CNY) 97 Underhill Rd, Ossining, NY 10562

CORLEY, Robert M (Dal) 10837 Colbert Way, Dallas, TX 75218

CORNELL, Allison Lee (Los) 2510 Gateway Rd, Carlsbad, CA 92009

CORNELL, Amy S (NJ)

CORNELL, Charles Walton (The Episcopal NCal) 813 Mormon St, Folsom, CA 95630

CORNELL, Lucinda Sims (WNY) Church of the Asencion, 16 Linwood Ave, Buffalo, NY 14209

CORNELL, Peter Stuart (NJ) 5 Paterson St, New Brunswick, NJ 08901

CORNER, Cynthia Ruth (Mich) PO Box 287, Onsted, MI 49265

CORNEY, Richard Warren (NY) 12 Hartford Ave Apt B, Glens Falls, NY 12801

CORNMAN, Jane Elizabeth (Me) Po Box 105, Northeast Harbor, ME 04662

CORNNER, Robert Wyman (Los) 8170 Manitoba St., Unit #1, Playa Del Rey, CA 90293

CORNTHWAITE, Hannah Elyse (Ia)

CORNWELL, Marilyn M (Oly) Church of the Ascension, 2330 Viewmont Way Weat, Seattle, WA 98199

CORREA, Trino Cortes (Episcopal SJ) 3345 Sierra Madre, Clovis, CA 93619

CORREA AMARILES, Maria Ofelia (Colom) Parroquia San Lucas, Cr 80 No 53A-78, Medellin, Antioguia, Colombia

CORREA GALVEZ, Jose William (Colom) Carrera 6 No 49-85, Piso 2, Bogota, Colombia

CORRELL, Ruth E. (Va) 15639 John Diskin Cir, Woodbridge, VA 22191

CORRIGAN, Candice Lyn (Oly) 506 21st St SW, Austin, MN 55912

CORRIGAN, Michael (Mass) Northfield Mount Hermon School, 1 Lamplighter Way #4702, Mt. Hermon, MA 01354

CORRIGAN, Michael Edward (Los) 1500 State St, Santa Barbara, CA 93101

CORRY, Richard Stillwell (Va) 214 E King St, Quincy, FL 32351

CORSELLO, Dana Colley (Cal) 1755 Clay St, San Francisco, CA 94109

CORT, Aubrey Ebenezer (SwFla) 2507 Del Prado Blvd S, Cape Coral, FL 33904

CORTINAS, Angela Maria (SeFla) 333 Tarpon Dr, Fort Lauderdale, FL 33301

CORTRIGHT, Amy Ethel Marie Chambers (Mo) Christ Church Cathedral, 1210 Locust Street, St. Louis, MO 63103

COSBY, Arlinda W (Cal) 36458 Shelley Ct, Newark, CA 94560

COSENTINO, Eric Fritz (NY) 719 Hudson Ave, Peekskill, NY 10566

COSMAN, Sandra Lee (Ct) 220 Prospect St, Torrington, CT 06790

COSSLETT, Ashley (WNC) 449 Crowfields Drive, Asheville, NC 28803

COSTA, Steven James (The Episcopal Church in Haw) St Timothy's Episcopal Church, 98-939 Moanalua Rd, Aiea, HI 96701

COSTAS, Catherine Stephenson (Cal) 905 W. Middlefield #946, Sausalito, CA 94043

COSTAS, J. Kathryn (Ind) 315 S. Main St, North East, MD 21901

COSTELLO, Elizabeth Regina (Colo) St John's Cathedral, 1350 Washington St, Denver, CO 80203

COSTIN, Richard Banks (CFla) 1601 Alafaya Trl, Oviedo, FL 32765

COTTER, Barry Lynn (SO) 1864 Sherman Ave Apt 5SE, Evanston, IL 60201

COTTRELL, Jan M. (Lex) 1445 Copperfield Court, Lexington, KY 40514-175

COTTRILL, C(harles) David (SO) 3724 Mengel Dr, Kettering, OH 45429

COUDRIET, Alan P (NwPa) 10 Woodside Ave, Oil City, PA 16301

COUFAL, M(ary) Lorraine (Ind) 3819 Green Arbor Way #812, Indianapolis, IN 46220

COUGHLIN, Christopher Anthony (O) 7640 Glenwood Ave, Boardman, OH 44512

COUGHLIN, Clark F (Ct) 400 Seabury Dr., Apt. 2126, Bloomfield, CT 06002

COULTAS, Amy Real (Ky) 612 Myrte St, Louisville, KY 40208

COULTER, Clayton Roy (Ore) 7430 Sw Pineridge Ct, Portland, OR 97225

COULTER, Elizabeth (Ia) 3148 Dubuque St. NE, Iowa City, IA 52240

COULTER, Sherry Lynn (At) 681 Holt Rd Ne, Marietta, GA 30068

✠ **COUNCELL**, George Edward (Ret Bp of NJ 2013-) Diocese of New Jersey, 808 West State Street, Trenton, NJ 08618

COUNSELMAN, Robert Lee (NJ) 119 S Hondo St, P O Box 1478, Sabinal, TX 78881

COUNTRYMAN, L(Ouis) William (Cal) 5805 Keith Avenue, Oakland, CA 94618

COUPER, David Courtland (Mil) 5282 County Road K, Blue Mounds, WI 53517

COUPLAND, Geoffrey D (Va) 5110 Park Ave., Richmond, VA 23226

COURTNEY, Michael David (Ark) 235 Caroline Acres Road, Hot Springs, AR 71913

COURTNEY, Peter (At) 127 Inverness Road, Athens, GA 30606

COURTNEY II, Robert Wickliff (La) 1025 Beverly Garden Drive, New Orleans, LA 70002

COURTNEY JR, Robin Spencer (Tenn) 7872 Harpeth View Dr, Nashville, TN 37221

COURTRIGHT, Alice Hodgkins (NH)

COUVILLION, Brian Neff (Chi) 4370 Woodland Ave, Western Springs, IL 60558

COUZZOURT, Beverly Schmidt (NwT) 2516 4th Ave, Canyon, TX 79015

COVENTRY, Donald Edgar (Spr) 246 Southmoreland Pl, Decatur, IL 62521

COVER, Michael Benjamin (Dal) 616 Lincolnway E., Mishawaka, IN 46544

COVERSTON, Harry Scott (ECR) 630 Roberta Ave, Orlando, FL 32803

COVERT, Edward Martin (SwVa) Po Box 126, Fort Defiance, VA 24437

COVINGTON, John E (NY) 410 West 24th Street, Apartment 8K, New York, NY 10011

COWAN, Leonard Chaffee (WMass) 48 Berwick Street, Worcester, MA 01602

COWANS, William Marsden (ECR) 10101 Double R Blvd Apt B10, Reno, NV 89521

COWARDIN, Eustis Barber (ND) 510 E Lake County Rd, Jamestown, ND 58401

COWARDIN, Stephen Paul (SVa) 8525 Summit Acres Dr, Richmond, VA 23235

COWART, Alan B (At)

COWDEN, Claire Meadows (NwT) 1601 S Georgia St, Amarillo, TX 79102

COWDEN, Matthew D (NI) 8385 Luce Ct, Springfield, VA 22153

COWELL, Curtis Lyle (Kan) 2601 Sw College Ave, Topeka, KS 66611

COWELL, Frank Bourne (Nev) 7300 W Van Giesen St, West Richland, WA 99353

COWELL, Mark Andrew (WK) 501 W 5th St, Larned, KS 67550

COWPER, Judith Ann (Ct) 54 Dora Dr, Middletown, CT 06457

COWPERTHWAITE, Robert W (Fla) 7001 Charles St., St. Augustine, FL 32080

COX, Amy Eleanor (WMo) St. Francis of Assisi in the Pines, 17890 Metcalf Ave, Overland Park, KS 66085

COX, Anne Elizabeth (Mich) 8 Ridge Rd, Tenants Harbor, ME 04860

COX IV, Brian (Los) 871 Serenidad Pl, Goleta, CA 93117

COX, Catherine Susanna (WMo) 365 E 372nd Rd, Dunnegan, MO 65640

COX, Celeste O'Hern (Del) Po Box 1374, Dover, DE 19903

COX, Christopher Edward (NJ) 801 W State St, Trenton, NJ 08618

COX, Edwin Manuel (NC) 4510 Highberry Rd, Greensboro, NC 27410

COX, Frances Fosbroke (Md) 4510 Highberry Rd, Greensboro, NC 27410

COX, Gary Robert (Chi)

COX, James Richard (WK) Po Box 827, Salina, KS 67402

COX JR, James Stanley (Ga) 1805 Jeanette St, Valdosta, GA 31602

COX, Jason (Los) 8201 16th St Apt 1024, Silver Spring, MD 20910

COX, Mildred Louise (Minn) 1210 Washburn Ave N, Minneapolis, MN 55411

COX, Nancy L J (NC) 525 Lake Concord Road NE, Concord, NC 28025

COX, R. David (SwVa) 107 Lee Ave., Lexington, VA 24450

COX, Raymond L (Ct) 461 Mill Hill Ter, Southport, CT 06890

COX, Samuel David (Kan) 1455 E 37th St, Sedalia, MO 65301

COX, Sean Armer (The Episcopal NCal) 3601 Sudbury Rd, Cameron Park, CA 95682

COX, Sharron Leslie (Tex) 601 Columbus Ave, Waco, TX 76701

COYNE, Margaret (Vt) 14 Church St, Bellows Falls, VT 05101

COYNE, William H (SC) 134 Stonehill Rd, East Longmeadow, MA 01028

COZZOLI, John David (Md) 17524 Lincolnshire Rd, Hagerstown, MD 21740

CRABTREE, David (NC)

CRAFT, Bernadine Louise (Wyo) Po Box 567, Rock Springs, WY 82902

CRAFT, Carolyn M (SVa) 1702 Briery Rd, Farmville, VA 23901

CRAFT, John Harvey (La) 4505 S Claiborne Ave, New Orleans, LA 70125

CRAFT, Stephen Frank (La) 3101 Plymouth Pl, New Orleans, LA 70131

CRAFTON, Barbara Cawthorne (NY) 53 McCoy Ave, Metuchen, NJ 08840

CRAFTS JR, Robert (SanD) 13030 Birch Ln, Poway, CA 92064

CRAGON JR, Miller M. (Chi) 5555 N Sheridan Rd Apt 810, Chicago, IL 60640

CRAIG, Carolyn (EC) 5302 Verde Vista Circle, Asheville, NC 28805

CRAIG SR, Claude Phillip (EC) 214 Twain Ave, Davidson, NC 28036

CRAIG JR, Claude Phillip (Ore) 6300 SW Nicol Road, Portland, OR 97223

CRAIG JR, Harry Walter (Kan) 5041 Sw Fairlawn Rd, Topeka, KS 66610

CRAIG, Idalia Simmons (NJ) 212 N Main St, Glassboro, NJ 08028

CRAIG III, James O (WMass) 11 Cotton St, Leominster, MA 01453

CRAIG, Jo Roberts (NwT) 2401 Parker St, Amarillo, TX 79109

CRAIG III, Richard Edwin (Mil) 4417 Westway Ave, Racine, WI 53405

CRAIGHEAD JR, J. Thomas (Oly) 23404 107th Ave SW, Vashon, WA 98070

CRAIGHEAD, Thomas Gray (Chi) St Andrew's Church, 1125 Franklin St, Downers Grove, IL 60515

CRAIGHILL, Peyton Gardner (Pa) 25 Sycamore Lane, Lexington, VA 24450

CRAIN II, Lee Bryan (LI) 518 Brooklyn Blvd, Brightwaters, NY 11718

CRAIN, William Henry (WMo) 9208 Wenonga Rd, Leawood, KS 66206

CRAM, Don (RG) Po Box 45000, Rio Rancho, NM 87174

CRAM JR, Norman Lee (The Episcopal NCal) Po Box 224, Vineburg, CA 95487

CRAMER, Alfred Anthony (Vt) 47 Morningside Commons, Brattleboro, VT 05301

CRAMER, Barry (Ind)

CRAMER, Jared C (WMich) 524 Washington Ave, Grand Haven, MI 49417

CRAMER, Roger W (Mass) 16 Aubin Street, Amesbury, MA 01913

CRAMMER, Margaret Corinne (Chi) 927 Scott Blvd Apt 205, Decatur, GA 30030

CRAMPTON, Susan H (WMass) 54 Grandview Dr, Williamstown, MA 01267

CRANDALL, Harry Wilson (SVa) PO Box 275, 9115 Franktown Road, Franktown, VA 23354

CRANDALL, John Davin (Mass) 404 Juniper Way, Tavares, FL 32778

CRANDELL, Herbert Charles (EMich) 3191 Hospers St, Grand Blanc, MI 48439

CRANE, Linda Sue (EMich) 1213 6th St, Port Huron, MI 48060

CRANE, Rebecca Mai (Mass) 13 Trinity St., Danvers, MA 01923

CRANSTON, Dale Lawrence (NY) 21 Stone Fence Road, Mahwah, NJ 07430

CRANSTON, Pamela Lee (Cal) 207 Taurus Ave, Oakland, CA 94611

CRAPSEY II, Marcus Trowbridge (Mass) 77 L Drew Rd, Derry, NH 03038

CRARY, Kathleen (Cal) 733 Baywood Rd, Alameda, CA 94502

CRASE, Jane L (Los) P.O. Box 1989, 56312 Onaga Trail, Yucca Valley, CA 92284

CRAUN, Christopher Brooke (Ore) 3236 NE Alberta St., Portland, OR 97211

CRAVEN III, James Braxton (NC) 17 Marchmont Ct, Durham, NC 27705

CRAVEN, Sam (Tex) 6221 Main St, Houston, TX 77030

CRAVENS, James Owen (Spr) 4 Canterbury Ln, Lincoln, IL 62656

CRAVER III, Marshall Pinnix (CGC) 613 Highland Woods Dr E, Mobile, AL 36608

CRAWFORD, Alicia Leu Lydon (Chi) 550 N Green Bay Rd, Lake Forest, IL 60045

CRAWFORD JR, Grady J (At) 2602 Oglethorpe Cir NE, Atlanta, GA 30319

CRAWFORD, Hayden G (SeFla) 701 45th Ave S, Saint Petersburg, FL 33705

CRAWFORD, Karen (Ia) 223 E 4th St N, Newton, IA 50208

CRAWFORD JR, Kelly Allen (Los) 450 NW Ivy Ave, Dallas, OR 97338

CRAWFORD, Lee Alison (Vt) POB 67, Plymouth, VT 05056

CRAWFORD, Leo Lester (SwFla) 2694 Grove Park Rd, Palm Harbor, FL 34583

CRAWFORD, Malia (Mass) 21 Marathon St., Arlington, MA 02474

CRAWFORD, Mark Taylor (Tex) PO Box 20269, Houston, TX 77225

CRAWFORD, Nancy Rogers (Ore) 1595 E 31st Ave, Eugene, OR 97405

CRAWFORD, Robert Lee (NY) Po Box 1415, Camden, ME 04843

CRAWFORD, Sidnie White (Neb) 925 Piedmont Rd, Lincoln, NE 68510

CRAWFORD, Stephen Howard (La) 3552 Morning Glory Ave, Baton Rouge, LA 70808

CRAWFORD, Susan Kaye (Miss) 1026 S Washington Ave, Greenville, MS 38701

CRAWLEY, Clayton D (ECR) 20 Pine St Apt 2106, New York, NY 10005

CREAMER JR, Francis Bunnell (LI) 715 Friendship Rd, Waldoboro, ME 04572

CREAN, Charleen (Los) 931 E. Walnut St. #114, Pasadena, CA 91106

CREAN JR, John Edward (Los) 1735 La Paz Rd, Altadena, CA 91001

CREASY, James A (Ala) 712 Sixth Ave., Opelika, AL 36801

CREASY, William Charles (O) 65 E Maple Ave, New Concord, OH 43762

CREED, Christopher Duflon (ECR) 1769 Forest View Ave, Hillsborough, CA 94010

✠ **CREIGHTON**, Michael Whittington (Ret Bp of CPa 2006-) 2716 Gingerview Lane, Annapolis, MD 21401

CREIGHTON, Susan (Oly) 15 Huckleberry Court, Bellingham, WA 98229

CRELLIN, Timothy Edward (Mass) 25 Boylston St, Jamaica Plain, MA 02130

CRERAR, Patrick T (Los) 202 Avenida Aragon, San Clemente, CA 92672

CRESPO, Wilfredo (SanD) 10125 Azuaga St, San Diego, CA 92129

CRESS, Katherine Elizabeth (Mass) 28 Pleasant St., Medfield, MA 02052

CRESSMAN, Lisa Suzanne Kraske (Minn) 4731 Lily Ave N, Lake Elmo, MN 55042

CRESSMAN, Louisel A (NJ) 25 Lakeshore Dr, Hammonton, NJ 08037

CRESSMAN, Naomi May (NJ) 305 Main St, Riverton, NJ 08077

CRESWELL, C(arl) Edward (NwT) 2113 S Lipscomb St, Amarillo, TX 79109

CRESWELL, Jennifer Marin (Ore) 4411 NE Beech St., Portland, OR 97213

CRETEN, C(laude) Dan (NMich)

CREWDSON, Robert Henry (SwVa) 6 Miley Ct, Lexington, VA 24450

CREWS, Norman Andrew (SwVa) 1125 Spindle Xing, Virginia Beach, VA 23455

CREWS, Norman Dale (CPa) 201 Porter Dr, Annapolis, MD 21401

CREWS, Warren Earl (Mo) 2 Algonquin Wood, Saint Louis, MO 63122

CREWS, William Eugene (Colo) 4042 Xerxes Ave. S., Minneapolis, MN 55410

CRICHLOW, Neville Joseph (CFla) 381 N Lincoln St, Daytona Beach, FL 32114

CRIM, Marcus Jacob (Cal) 455 Fair Oaks St, San Francisco, CA 94110

CRIMI, Lynne B (Alb) 7 Sweet Rd, Stillwater, NY 12170

CRIPPEN, David Wells (ETenn) 4617 County Road 103, Florence, CO 81226

CRIPPEN, Stephen Daniel (Oly) 1922 12th Ave W, Seattle, WA 98119

CRIPPS, David Richard (Roch) 139 Lake Bluff Rd, Rochester, NY 14622

CRISE, Rebecca Ann (WMich) Saint Mark's Episcopal Church, PO Box 307, Paw Paw, MI 49079

CRISP, Justin Ernest (ETenn) 111 Oenoke Rdg, New Canaan, CT 06840

CRISP, Sheila L A (Oly) PO Box 88550, Steilacoom, WA 98388

CRISS, Carthur Paul (Kan) 4138 E 24th St N, Wichita, KS 67220

CRIST, John Frederick (Chi) P.O. Box, 131 Fifth St., McNabb, IL 61335

CRIST, Mary Frances (Los) St Michael's Episcopal Church, 4070 Jackson St, Riverside, CA 92503

CRIST, Roy Gene (WVa) Box 602, 19958 Midland Trail, Ansted, WV 25812

CRIST JR, William Harold (Los) 2091 Business Center Dr Ste 130, Irvine, CA 92612

CRISTE-TROUTMAN, Robert Joseph (Be) 137 Trinity Hill Rd., Mt. Pocono, PA 18344

CRISTOBAL, Robert S (Chi) 1000 West Rt 64, Oregon, IL 61061

CRITCHFIELD, Margot D (Mass) St. Stephen's Church, 16 Highland Ave., Cohasset, MA 02025

CRITCHLOW II, Fitzgerald St Clair (Jerry) (Tex) 3700 Kingwood Dr Apt 1806, Kingwood, TX 77339

CRITELLI, Robert J (NJ) 13 King Arthurs Ct, Sicklerville, NJ 08081

CRITES, Karry Dean (Nev) 1035 Munley Dr, Reno, NV 89503

CRITES, Rebecca Tuck (SwVa) St Johns Episcopal Church, P O Box 607, Glasgow, VA 24555

CRITTENDEN, Francis Thomas Glasgow (SwVa) 123 W. Washinton St., Lexington, VA 24450

CRITTENDEN, William Setchel (WNY) Po Box 93, Chautauqua, NY 14722

CROCKER, Byron Grey (Tex) 2025 Hanover Cir, Beaumont, TX 77706

CROCKER, Edna Irene (Fla) 10560 Fort George Rd, Jacksonville, FL 32226

CROCKER, George Neville (Ct) 29 Powder Horn Hl, Brookfield, CT 06804

CROCKER JR, J(ohn) A(lexander) Frazer (U) 3541 Ocean View Dr, Florence, OR 97439

CROCKER, Ronald Conrad (Va) 3 Hamilton Court, Uxbridge, MA 01569

CROCKETT, Daniel L (SVa) PO Box 102, Conyers, GA 30012

CROCKETT, Jennie L (SO) 2700 Kenview Rd S, Columbus, OH 43209

CROCKETT, Larry Joe (Minn) 4525 Alicia Dr, Inver Grove Heights, MN 55077

CROES, John Rodney (NJ) 20 Claremont Ave, South River, NJ 08882

CROFT, Charles Carter (RG) 615 N Texas St, Silver City, NM 88061

CROFT, Jay Leslie (WA) 1431 Magnolia Curv, Montgomery, AL 36106

CROMEY, Edwin Harry (NY) St. Luke's Church, 850 Wolcott Ave. Box 507, Beacon, NY 12508

CROMEY, Robert Warren (Cal) 3839 - 20th, San Francisco, CA 94114

CROMMELIN-DELL, Sue (SVa) 500 Court St., Portsmouth, VA 23704

CROMWELL, Richard (NJ) 322 Aoloa St Apt 803, Kailua, HI 96734

CRON, Ian Morgan (Ct) 226 5th Ave S, Franklin, TN 37064

✠ **CRONEBERGER**, John Palmer (Ret Bp of Nwk 2007-) 1079 Old Bernville Rd, Reading, PA 19605

CRONIN, Audrey Ann (WMass)

CROOK II, Jerry V (Ga) 4027 Dumaine Way, Memphis, TN 38117

CROOK, Senter Cawthon (WTenn) 2796 Lombardy Ave, Memphis, TN 38111

CROOM, James (WMich) 2795 Riley Ridge Road, Holland, MI 49424

CROSBY, David Malcom (Va) Immanuel Church-on-the-Hill, 3606 Seminary Rd, Alexandria, VA 22304

CROSBY, Derrill Plummer (NH) 11 Central St, Peterborough, NH 03458

CROSBY, Karen Ann (Md) 52 S Broadway, Frostburg, MD 21532

CROSS II, Eugenia Sealy (NC) 1032 Wessyngton Rd, Winston Salem, NC 27104

CROSS JR, Freeman Grant (Ga) 5424 Hill Rd, Albany, GA 31705

CROSS, Kevin Michael (Eas) P.O. Box 387, Oxford, MD 21654

CROSS, Myrick Tyler (SO) 52 Pleasant St., Freedom, ME 04941

CROSS, Samuel Otis (NY) 224 W 11th St Apt 4, New York, NY 10014

CROSSETT, Judith (Ia) 320 E College St, Iowa City, IA 52240

CROSSNOE, Marshall E (Mo)

CROSSWAITE, John J (CNY) 700 Quinlan Dr., Pewaukee, WI 53072

CROTHERS, John-Michael (NY) 214 Burntwood Trl, Toms River, NJ 08753

CROTHERS, Kenneth Delbert (Ida) Po Box 374, Shoshone, ID 83352

CROUCH, Billy Gene (NY) 3604 Balcones Dr, Austin, TX 78731

CROUCH, Emily Schwartz (Ky) 821 S 4th St, Louisville, KY 40203

CROW, Lynda D (Los) 1145 W Valencia Mesa Dr, Fullerton, CA 92833

CROW, Robert B (CGC) St. Andrews By-the-Sea Episcopal Church, PO Box 1658, Destin, FL 32540

CROWDER, James Robert (Md) 13801 York Rd Apt E9, Cockeysville, MD 21030

CROWE, Amy Beth (The Episcopal Church in Haw)

CROWE, Kathleen A (ECR) The Rev Kathleen Crowe, 4271 N 1st St Spc 74, San Jose, CA 95134

CROWELL, Larry A (SO)

CROWELL, Paul L (Az) 2800 Huntsman Ct, Jamestown, NC 27282

CROWLE, Wesley Edward (Minn) 1545 Northeast 7 1/2 Avenue NE, Rochester, MN 55906

CROWLEY, Daniel Fenwick (Mass) 76 Olde Towne Lane, West Chatham, MA 02669

CROWSON, Steven Franklin (LI) Po Box 22, Leeds, ME 04263

✠ **CROWTHER**, CE (Form Bp of ECR 1988-) 289 Moreton Bay Ln Apt 2, Goleta, CA 93117

CROZIER, Richard Lee (USC) 125 Pendleton St Sw, Aiken, SC 29801

CRUIKSHANK, Charles Clark (CPa) 208 W Foster Ave, State College, PA 16801

CRUM JR, G(Eorge) Milton (USC) 9 Bumblebee Court, Helena, MT 59601

CRUM, Robert James Howard (EO) 700 SW Eastman Pkwy Ste B110, Gresham, OR 97080

CRUMB, Lawrence Nelson (Ore) 1674 Washington St, Eugene, OR 97401

CRUMBAUGH III, Frank Boyd (NJ) 410 S Atlantic Ave, Beach Haven, NJ 08008

CRUMLEY, Carole Anne (WA) 3039 Beech St Nw, Washington, DC 20015

CRUMMEY, Rebecca Jo (Colo) 967 Marion St Apt 7, Denver, CO 80218

CRUMP, Carl Calvin (ETenn) St Martin's/ St Stephen's, 15801 US Highway 19, Hudson, FL 34667

CRUMP, David Archelaus (Los) Po Box 371645, Montara, CA 94037

CRUMPTON IV, Alvin Briggs (Ga) PO Box 1155, Brunswick, GA 31521

CRUPI, Hilary (FdL) Julian House Monastery, 2812 Summit Ave., Waukesha, WI 53188

CRUSE, John Woolfolk (Ala) 4941 Montevallo Rd, Birmingham, AL 35210

CRUSE, William Clayton (NH) PO Box 382, North Conway, NH 03860

CRUZ, Hector (PR)

CRUZ, Ruby (SeFla) Church of the Resurrection, 11173 Griffing Blvd, Biscayne Park, FL 33161

CRUZ-DIAZ, Nora (At) 400 Holcomb Bridge Rd, Norcross, GA 30071

CRYSLER JR, Fred (Ct) PO Box 9324, Louisville, KY 40209

CRYSLER, Kenneth (EO)

CUBILLAS, Angelito (Az) PO Box 8667, Phoenix, AZ 85066

CUBINE, James W (WTenn) 7910 Gayle Ln, Memphis, TN 38138

CUDD, Anne (Ida) 3024 SW 98th Way, Gainesville, FL 32608

CUDWORTH, Robert Wallace (Ct) 400 Seabury Dr Apt 3142, Bloomfield, CT 06002

CUFF, Stephen James (SO) 2140 Grandview Ave, Portsmouth, OH 45662

CUFF, Victoria Slater Smith (NJ) 45 2nd St, Keyport, NJ 07735

CUFFIE, Karen Ann (ECR) 6581 Camden Ave, San Jose, CA 95120

CULBERTSON, David Paul (CPa) 210 S Washington St, Muncy, PA 17756

CULBERTSON, Thomas Leon (Md) 6 Yearling Way, Lutherville, MD 21093

CULBREATH, Leeann Drabenstott (Ga) PO Box 889, Tifton, GA 31793

CULHANE, Suzanne M (NY) 254 E Putnam Ave, Greenwich, CT 06830

CULLEN, Kathleen Mary (NH) St. Andrew's Episcopal Church, 102 N Main St., Manchester, NH 03102

CULLEN, Peter (LI) 199 Carroll St, Brooklyn, NY 11231

CULLINANE, Kathleen Jean (Episcopal SJ) 1528 Oakdale Rd, Modesto, CA 95355

CULLIPHER III, James Robert (USC) 800 Stillpoint Way, Balsam Grove, NC 28708

CULMER, Ronald D (Cal) 3350 Hopyard Rd, Pleasanton, CA 94588

CULP JR, Robert S (Roch) 19 Arbor Ct, Fairport, NY 14450

CULPEPPER, Charles Leland (Miss) 1832 Saint Ann St, Jackson, MS 39202

CULPEPPER, Judith Anne (Ind) 6736 Prince Regent Ct, Indianapolis, IN 46250

CULPEPPER, Polk (Ind) 1301 Summit Ave, Washington, NC 27889

CULTON, Douglas (Del) 1212 E Holly St, Goldsboro, NC 27530

CULVER, Carson Kies (Mil) 590 N Church St, Richland Center, WI 53581

CULVER, Esme Jo R (Ore) Grace Memorial Church, 1535 Ne 17th Ave, Portland, OR 97232

CUMBIE II, W(alter) Kenneth (CGC) 172 Hannon Ave, Moile, AL 36604

CUMMER, Edwin West (SwFla)

CUMMING, Jane (NY) 163 Todd Road, Katonah, NY 10536

CUMMINGS, Carolsue (NJ) 322 So Second St, Surf City, NJ 08008

CUMMINGS, Patricia L (Cal) 110 Wood Rd Apt C-104, Los Gatos, CA 95030

CUMMINGS, Sally Ann (Minn) 520 N Pokegama Ave, Grand Rapids, MN 55744

CUMMINGS, Sudduth Rea (NC) 3990 Meandering Ln., Tallahassee, FL 32308

CUMMINS, Thomas Woodrow (Ore) 11100 Sw Riverwood Rd, Portland, OR 97219

CUNIFF, Wanda Wood (Tex) Christ Episcopal Church, 1320 Mound St., Nacogdoches, TX 75961

CUNNINGHAM, Arthur Leland (Mil) 1320 Mill Rd, Delafield, WI 53018

CUNNINGHAM, Chris (SVa) 400 High St, Farmville, VA 23901

CUNNINGHAM, James Earl (Tex) 2227 Woodland Springs Dr, Houston, TX 77077

CUNNINGHAM, Joyce Corbin (NC)

CUNNINGHAM, Lynn Edward (Wyo) 3403 Ordway St Nw, Washington, DC 20016

CUNNINGHAM, Marcus T (FdL) 309 W Elm St, Sedan, KS 67361

CUNNINGHAM, Margaret Taylor (Pa) 138 Rose Ln, Haverford, PA 19041

CUNNINGHAM, Michael Ray (Los) St Marys Episcopal Church, 2800 Harris Grade Rd, Lompoc, CA 93436

CUNNINGHAM, Patricia (Cal) 1668 Bush St, San Francisco, CA 94109

CUNNINGHAM, Philip John (WTex) 2500 N. 10th St., McAllen, TX 78501

CUNNINGHAM, William Wallace (Ala)

CUPP, Jean Carol (EO) 1239 Nw Ingram Ave, Pendleton, OR 97801

CURL, James Fair (WNC) 461 Crowfields Dr., Asheville, NC 28803

CURNS, Mary S (WMass) All Saints Episcopal Church, PO Box 374, North Adams, MA 01247

CURRAN JR, Charles Daniel (SwVa) 1011 Francisco Road, Henrico, VA 23229

CURRAN, Michael Joseph (Ak) 4024 Ridge Way, Juneau, AK 99801

CURREA, Luis Alejandro (SwFla) Po Box 9332, Tampa, FL 33674

CURRIN JR, Beverly Madison (CGC) 510 N 20th Ave, Pensacola, FL 32501

CURRY, Dorothy Reed (Cal) 4351 Ridgeway Dr, San Diego, CA 92116

CURRY, Gene Edward (Mich) 2735 Manchester Rd, Ann Arbor, MI 48104

CURRY, Glenda (Ala) 2670 Southgate Dr, Birmingham, AL 35243

✠ **CURRY**, James Elliot (Bp Suffr of Ct 2000-) 14 Linwold Dr, West Hartford, CT 06107

✠ **CURRY**, Michael B (PBp of TEC 2015-) 200 W Morgan St Ste 300, Raleigh, NC 27601

CURT, George (SwFla) 1204 Westlake Blvd, Naples, FL 34103

CURTIN, Anne Fahy (Alb) Healing A Woman's Soul Inc, 68 S Swan St, Albany, NY 12210

CURTIN JR, Ernest A (Pa) St Luke's Episcopal Church, 100 E Washington Ave, Newtown, PA 18940

CURTIS, Charles Edward (EMich) 3260 E Midland Rd, Bay City, MI 48706

CURTIS, Edward Wells (Chi) 637 S Dearborn St Ste 1, Chicago, IL 60605

CURTIS, Frederick L (Alb) 262 Main St N, Southbury, CT 06488

CURTIS, James Dabney (At) 1100 Hampton Way NE, Atlanta, GA 30324

CURTIS, Kenton James (NY) 200 Bennett Ave #3G, New York, NY 10040

CURTIS, Lynne Marsh Piret (Alb) 912 Route 146, Clifton Park, NY 12065

CURTIS, Mary Page (NC) 212 Edinboro Dr, Southern Pines, NC 28387

CURTIS, Patricia H (WNC) St John's Episcopal Church, PO Box 175, Sylva, NC 28779

CURTIS, Sandra King (Roch) 10 Shether St # 272, Hammondsport, NY 14840

CURTIS, Sandra Olivia (Ark) Episcopal Collegiate School, 1701 Cantrell Rd, Little Rock, AR 72201

CURTIS III, William L (Ind) 2407 Cascade Rd SW, Atlanta, GA 30311

CURTIS JR, W(illiam) Shepley (Nev) 1654 County Rd, Minden, NV 89423

CURTIS, Yvonne Marie (WNY) PO Box 14, Dunkirk, NY 14048

CURTISS, Geoffrey (Nwk) 202 3RD AVE, Bradley Beach, NJ 07720

CUSANO, William Alan (NY) 2500 Jerome Ave, Bronx, NY 10468

CUSHING, Nan Chenault Marshall (NC) 69 Crystal Oaks Ct, Durham, NC 27707

CUSHINOTTO, Susan Elizabeth (NJ) 9425 3rd Ave, Stone Harbor, NJ 08247

CUSHMAN, Mary (NY) PO Box 211, Chebeague Island, ME 04017

CUSHMAN, Thomas Spaulding (NY)

CUSIC, Georgeanne Hill (FdL) 1510 N Broadway Ave, Marshfield, WI 54449

CUSTER, Margaret (Peg) Gardiner (NH) 356 Deer Hill Road, Chocorua, NH 03817

CUSTER, Raymond Dale (SVa) 14404 Roberts Mill Court, Midlothian, VA 23113

CUTAIAR, Michael Louis (NMich)

CUTIE, Albert R (SeFla) 11173 Griffing Blvd, Miami, FL 33161

CUTLER, Donald Robert (NY) 38 Chestnut St, Salem, MA 01970

CUTLER, E Clifford (Pa) 18 E Chestnut Hill Ave, Philadelphia, PA 19118

CUTLER, Howard Taylor (HB) 1124 Westhampton Glen Dr, Richmond, VA 23238

CUTLER, Paul Colman (NMich) Hc 1 Box 646, Wetmore, MI 49895

CUTOLO, Mark Anthony (WNY)

CUTTER IV, Irving Taylor (Okla) 4200 S Atlanta Pl, Tulsa, OK 74105

CYR, Gary Alan (Me) 3 J St, Bangor, ME 04401

CYR, Mark Bernard (Eas) 25 Addy Road, P.O. Box 191, Bethany Beach, DE 19930

CZARNETZKY, Sylvia Yale (Miss) 148 French Br, Madison, MS 39110

CZARNIECKI, Lynn (Pa) 30 Gildersleeve Pl, Watchung, NJ 07069

CZOLGOSZ, Joseph Tamborini (Chi) 707 S Chester Ave, Park Ridge, IL 60068

D

DAGG, Margaret Kathleen (Kan) 1427 SW Macvicar Ave, Topeka, KS 66604

DAGGETT, Paul Edward (SO) 115 North 6th Street, Hamilton, OH 45011

DAHARSH, Floyd Arthur (Okla) 112 West 9th Street, Hugoton, KS 67951

DAHILL, Laurel Anne (Mich) Saint Mary's-In-The-Hills Church, 2512 Joslyn Ct, Lake Orion, MI 48360

DAHL, Joan Elizabeth (Spok) 8991 State Route 24, Moxee, WA 98936

DAHLIN, James G (WNC) 140 Saint Marys Church Rd, Morganton, NC 28655

DAHLMAN, Thomas A (Okla) 4250 W Houston St, Broken Arrow, OK 74012

DAIGLE, Deborah Heft (Tex) PO Box 1344, Madisonville, TX 77864

DAILEY, Beulah Huffman (Dal) 2929 Hickory St, Dallas, TX 75226

DAILEY, Douglas G (At) 3603 Tradition Drive, Gainesville, GA 30506

DAILY JR, Charles Wendell (FdL) N 6945 Ash Road, Shawano, WI 54166

DAILY, Teresa Wooten (Ark) 925 Mitchell St, Conway, AR 72034

DAISA IV, George Donald John (Los) PO Box 37, Pacific Palisades, CA 90272

DAKAN, Karen Nugent (SwFla) 14 Sandy Hook Rd N, Sarasota, FL 34242

DALBY, Mary Martin Douglass (Ark)

D'ALCARAVELA, Joao A (Mass) Palmoinho, Serra do Louro, Palmela, 2950-305, Portugal

DALE, Anne Edge (EC)

DALE, Cortney H (Ky)

DALE, Kathleen Askew (Los) St. Margaret's Episcopal Church, 47-535 HWY 74 at Haystack Rd., Palm Desert, CA 92260

DALES, Randolph Kent (NH) PO Box 1363, Wolfeboro, NH 03894

D'ALESANDRE, Peter John (O) 84 Lake Washington Dr # 2814, Chepachet, RI 02814

DALEY, Alexander Spotswood (Mass) 81 Mill Pond, North Andover, MA 01845

DALEY, Joy Anne (Dal) 13355 Pandora Cir, Dallas, TX 75238

DALFERES, Craig Douglas (La) 624 Winfield Blvd, Houma, LA 70360

DALGLISH, William Anthony (Tenn) 1911 Hampton Dr, Lebanon, TN 37087

DALLY, John Addison (Chi) 2650 N Lakeview Ave Apt 2501, Chicago, IL 60614

DALMASSO, Gary Lee (Chi) 215 29th Ave, East Moline, IL 61244

DALMASSO, Judith Connie (Ia) Renewal in Christ Ministries, PO Box 94, East Moline, IL 61244

DALRYMPLE, Sharon Gladwin (Az) 5147 Show Low Lake Rd, Lakeside, AZ 85929

DALTON, Harlon Leigh (Ct) Episcopal Diocese of Connecticut, 1335 Asylum Avenue, Hartford, CT 06105

DALTON JR, James Albert (Ark) 94 Cherrywood Dr., Cabot, AR 72023

DALTON, Joyce Foley (Ark) St Stephen's Episcopal Church, 2413 Northeastern Ave, Jacksonville, AR 72076

DALTON, William Thomas (Dal) 311 W. 5th St., Bonham, TX 75418

DALY JR, Herbert T (Pgh) 112 N Water St, Kittanning, PA 16201

DALY, Joseph Erin (WLa) 1030 Johnston St, Lafayette, LA 70501

DALY III, Raymond Ernest (Fla) 160 Sea Island Dr, Ponte Vedra Beach, FL 32082

DALY, Richard R (Dal) 5323 N Mulligan Ave, Chicago, IL 60630

DALY JR, Robert Edmund (Md) 13801 York Rd Apt D5, Cockeysville, MD 21030

DALZON, Wilfrid (Hai)

D'AMARIO, Matthew Justin (Md) Bridge and Anchor Drives, Joppa, MD 21085

DAMBROT, Donna Lise (SeFla) 738 NE 7th Ave, Fort Lauderdale, FL 33304

D'AMICO, Samuel Robert (Los) 23442 El Toro Rd # 368, Lake Forest, CA 92630

DAMON, David Reid (Fla) 7930 Bellemeade Blvd S, Jacksonville, FL 32211

DAMON, Robert Edward (SeFla) 3329 Wilson St, Hollywood, FL 33021

DAMROSCH, Thomas Hammond (WMass) PO Box 612, Stockbridge, MA 01262

DAMUS, Pierre Gasner (LI) 1227 Pacific St, Brooklyn, NY 11216

DANAHER JR, William Joseph (Mich) 470 Church Rd, Bloomfield Hills, MI 48304

DANDRIDGE, Robert Floyd (WLa) 702 Elm St, Minden, LA 71055

DANFORD, Nicholas C (NY) 4 Fountain Sq, Larchmont, NY 10538

DANFORTH, John Claggett (Mo) 911 Tirrill Farms Rd, Saint Louis, MO 63124

DANGELO, Michael B (Mass) 10600 Preston Rd, Dallas, TX 75230

D'ANGIO, Peter David (Lex) 16 E 4th St, Covington, KY 41011

✠ **DANIEL III**, Clifton (Bp Provsnl of Pa 2013-) 3717 Chestnut St, Suite 300, Philadelphia, PA 19104

DANIEL, Wilfred Arthnel (VI) 112 Estate La Reine, Christiansted, Saint Croix, VI 00823

DANIEL JR, William Otis (Roch) St James School, 17641 College Rd, St James, MD 21781

DANIELEY, Teresa Kathryn Mithen (Mo) 3664 Arsenal St, Saint Louis, MO 63116

DANIELS, Janet (NJ) St Mary's by the Sea, 804 Bay Ave, Point Pleasant, NJ 08742

DANIELS, Joel C. (NY) 1 W. 53rd St., New York, NY 10019

DANIELS, John D (WA) 1001 E Lincoln Hwy, Exton, PA 19341

✠ **DANIELS**, Theodore Athelbert (Ret Bp of VI 2003-) 3208 Prairie Clover Path, Austin, TX 78732

DANIELSON JR, Paul Everett (ECR) 22481 Ferdinand Dr, Salinas, CA 93908

DANIEL-TURK, Patricia Daniel-Turk (Fla) 15 East Manor, Beaufort, SC 29906

D'ANIERI, Margaret C (O) 18369 State Route 58, Wellington, OH 44090

DANITSCHEK, Thomas K (Colo) 6930 E 4th Ave, Denver, CO 80220

DANKEL, S. Rainey Gamble (Mass) 233 Clarendon St., Boston, MA 02115

DANNALS, James Clark (SC) 1979 Long Branch Rd, Marshall, NC 28753

DANNALS, Robert Samuel (Dal) 8011 Douglas @ Colgate, Dallas, TX 75225

DANNELLEY, James Preston (Tex) 1205 Flag St, Llano, TX 78643

DANNER, David Lawrence (SwFla) All Angels by the Sea Episcopal Church, 563 Bay Isles Rd, Longboat Key, FL 34228

DANNHAUSER, Adrian F (NY) St James' Church, 865 Madison Ave, New York, NY 10021

DANSDILL, Dorothy Newton (NMich) 501 N Ravine St, Sault Sainte Marie, MI 49783

DANSON, Michelle A(nne) (Colo) 7776 Country Creek Dr, Longmont, CO 80503

DANTONE, Janet Wiley (Tex)

DANZEY, Charles Stephen (Oly) St Peter's Episcopal Church, 621 W Belmont Ave, Chicago, IL 60657

D'AOUST, Jean-Jacques (Colo) 1515 W 28th St Apt 114, Loveland, CO 80538

DARBY, Steven Lanier (Ga) 114 W Mockingbird Ln, Statesboro, GA 30461

DARDEN, John Webster (Dal) 1852 E Mulberry, PPrescott Valley, AZ 89314

DARISME, Joseph Wilkie (Hai) Boite Postale 1309, Port-Au-Prince, Haiti

DARKO, Daniel Dodoo (WA) 1510 Erskine St, Takoma Park, MD 20912

DARLING, Elizabeth Ann (WNC) 118 Clubwood Ct, Asheville, NC 28803
DARLING, Laura Toepfer (Cal) 724 Valle Vista Avenue, Vallejo, CA 94590
DARLING, Mary (Roch) 2704 Darnby Dr, Oakland, CA 94611
DARLINGTON, Diane Lillie (NMich) 301 N 1st St, Ishpeming, MI 49849
DARROW, Robert Michael (Colo) 3275 S Pontiac St, Denver, CO 80224
DARVES-BORNOZ, Derek Yves (NY) Church Pension Group, 19 E 34th St, New York, NY 10016
DASS, Stephen (CFla) 1108 SE 9th Ave, Ocala, FL 34471
DAUER-CARDASIS, Joade A (NY) 227 E 87th St Apt 1B, New York, NY 10128
DAUGHERTY, Jennifer King (Oly) 1245 Tenth Ave E, Seattle, WA 98102
DAUGHTRY, James Robert (RG) 205 Augusta Way, Melbourne, FL 32940
DAUGHTRY, Susan Laurel (Minn) 1325 Nottoway Ave, Apt. A, Richmond, VA 23227
DAUNT, Francis Thomas (La) 815 E Guenther St, San Antonio, TX 78210
DAUPHIN, Joanne Coyle (Eur) 51 rue d'Amsterdam, Paris, 75008, France
DAUTEL, Terrence Pickands (O) Po Box 62, Gates Mills, OH 44040
DAVENPORT, Anetta Lynn (Wyo) Holy Trinity Episcopal Church, PO Box 950, Thermopolis, WY 82443
DAVENPORT, Carrol Kimsey (Mo) 17 Broadview, Kirksville, MO 63501
DAVENPORT JR, Charles Richard (NH) PO Box 85, Colebrook, NH 03576
DAVENPORT, David Wendell (SVa) 6051 River Road Pt, Norfolk, VA 23505
DAVENPORT, Elizabeth Jayne Louise (Chi) 5850 S. Woodlawn Ave, Chicago, IL 60637
DAVENPORT, Marcia Ellen McC (SwFla) 1606 Chickasaw Rd, Arnold, MD 21012
DAVENPORT, Robert A (SVa) 1509 N Shore Rd, Norfolk, VA 23505
DAVENPORT III, Stephen Rintoul (WA) 4700 Whitehaven Pkwy Nw, Washington, DC 20007
DAVID, Charles Laskin (Mass) 6390 Sagewood Way, Delray Beach, FL 33484
DAVID, Christopher Leyshon (LI) PO Box 110, 482 County Route 30, Salem, NY 12865
DAVID, Jacob Thandasseril (Nwk) 1 Paddock Court, Dayton, NJ 08810
DAVID, John Spencer (WMich) 2701 Black Sheep Ln, Fairbanks, AK 99709
DAVID, Ronald (Los) 1225 Wilshire Blvd, Los Angeles, CA 90017
DAVIDSON, Charles Alexander (Pa) 814 N 41st St, Philadelphia, PA 19104
DAVIDSON, Donald F (Kan) 1809 Sw Webster Ave, Topeka, KS 66604
DAVIDSON, Jon Paul (Nev) PO Box 8822, Incline Village, NV 89452

DAVIDSON, Patricia Foote (Ct) 118 Bill Hill Rd, Lyme, CT 06371
DAVIDSON, Robert Michael (Pa) 22 E Chestnut Hill Ave, Philadelphia, PA 19118
DAVIDSON, Robert Paul (Colo) 1005 Cimmaron Dr, Loveland, CO 80537
DAVIDSON, Susan La Mothe (La) 61 Hunter Ct, Torrington, CT 06790
DAVIDSON, Thomas Walter (Az) 4041 N 164th Dr, Goodyear, AZ 85395
DAVIDSON, William Albert (Vt) Prestwick Farm, 2260 County Route 12, Whitehall, NY 12887
DAVIDSON-METHOT, David G. (Los)
DAVIES, Ian E (Los) 7501 Hollywood Blvd, Los Angeles, CA 90046
DAVIES JR, Richard Wood (Pgh) 300 Madison Ave, Apt 309, Pittsburgh, PA 15243
DAVIES-ARYEEQUAYE, Eliza Ayorkor (NY) 23 Water Grant St. Apt. 9E, Yonkers, NY 10701
DAVILA, Mary B (Va) 117 Rivana Terr SW, Leesburg, VA 20175
DAVILA, Willie Rodriguez (SeFla) 1063 Haverhill Rd N, Haverhill, FL 33417
DAVILA COLON, Angel Michael (PR)
DAVILA FIGUEROA, Wilson Jaime (Colom) c/o Diocese of Colombia, Cra 6 No. 49-85 Piso 2, Bogota, BDC, Colombia
DAVINICH, George Lawrence (Mich) 945 Palmer St, Plymouth, MI 48170
DAVIOU, Albert G (At) 432 Noelle Lane, Dahlonega, GA 30533
DAVIS JR, Albin P (Los) 209 S. Detroit St., Los Angeles, CA 90036
DAVIS, Alice Downing (Va) P.O. Box 622, Luray, VA 22835
DAVIS, Angus Kenneth (Pa) PO Box 329, Kimberton, PA 19442
DAVIS, Bancroft Gherardi (Pa) 809 Bryn Mawr Ave, Newtown Square, PA 19073
DAVIS, Calvin Lee (SwFla) 725 Nokomis Ave S, Venice, FL 34285
DAVIS, Catherine Ward (EC) St James Parish, 25 S 3rd St, Wilmington, NC 28401
DAVIS, Charles Lee (Ak) ST MATTHEW'S EPISCOPAL CHURCH, 1030 2ND AVE, FAIRBANKS, AK 99701
DAVIS SR, Charles Meyer (USC) 232 Elstow Rd, Irmo, SC 29206
DAVIS JR, Charles Meyer (USC) 3709 Greenbriar Dr, Columbia, SC 29206
DAVIS, Charlotte Murray (NC) 3120 Sunnybrook Dr, Charlotte, NC 28210
DAVIS, Clifford Bruce (Kan)
DAVIS, David Joseph (EC) 208 Country Club Dr., Shallotte, NC 28470
DAVIS, Donald Henry Kortright (WA) 11414 Woodson Ave, Kensington, MD 20895

DAVIS, Doyal (Okla) P.O. Box 1905, Shawnee, OK 74802
DAVIS, Elizabeth Hill (Okla) PO BOX 1304, Seminole, OK 74818
DAVIS, Emily Hillquist (Mo) 9441 Engel Ln, St. Louis, MO 63132
DAVIS, Fletcher (WMass) 4490 Smugglers Cove Rd, Freeland, WA 98249
DAVIS, Gail E (Kan) 1228 Auburn Village Dr, Durham, NC 27713
DAVIS, Gale Davis (Mass) 25 Central St, Andover, MA 01810
DAVIS, Gena Lynn (Tex) 5010 N Main St, Baytown, TX 77521
DAVIS, Gordon Bell (Va) 1201 Rothesay Cir, Richmond, VA 23221
DAVIS, Holly A (Az) All Saints' Episcopal Church and Day School, 6300 N Central Ave, Phoenix, AZ 85012
DAVIS, James Howard (Ida)
DAVIS, James Lloyd (Mil) 6617 Romford Ct, Johnston, IA 50131
DAVIS, Jane Lowe (VI) PO Box 7386, St Thomas, VI 00801
DAVIS, John Bartley (ND) 7940 45r Street Southeast, Jamestown, ND 58401
DAVIS, John William (Be) Church of the Good Shepherd, 1780 N Washington Ave, Scranton, PA 18509
DAVIS JR, Johnnie Manly (USC) PO Box 2959, West Columbia, SC 29171
DAVIS, Jon (CFla) 1412 Palomino Way, Oviedo, FL 32765
DAVIS, Joseph Norman (Tenn) 8215 Planters Grove Dr, Cordova, TN 38018
DAVIS, Joy Ruth (Ga) St Patrick's Episcopal Church, 4800 Old Dawson Rd, Albany, GA 31721
DAVIS, Judith Anne (Mass) 671 Route 28, Harwich Port, MA 02646
DAVIS, Judith W (Va) 236 S Laurel St, Richmond, VA 23220
DAVIS, Margaret Callender (CFla) 19924 W Blue Cove Dr, Dunnellon, FL 34432
DAVIS, Mary Alice (Okla) 3200 Shady Brook Rd, Woodward, OK 73801
DAVIS, Mary Elizabeth (Nwk) 200 Main St, Chatham, NJ 07928
DAVIS, Matthew Steven (Episcopal SJ) 1710 Verde St, Bakersfield, CA 93304
DAVIS, Michael McKean (WTex) 8401 Kearsarge Dr, Austin, TX 78745
DAVIS, Milbrew (WTex) 338 Hub Ave, San Antonio, TX 78220
DAVIS, Orion Woods (Nwk) 2 Pasadena St, Canton, NC 28716
DAVIS, Patricia Rhoads (Ga) 215 Grimball Point Rd, Savannah, GA 31406
DAVIS, Philip Arthur (SwFla) 1603 52nd St W, Bradenton, FL 34209
DAVIS, Rodney (The Episcopal NCal) 2140 Mission Ave., Carmichael, CA 95608
DAVIS, Ronald C. (Fla)

DAVIS, Ronald Lee (WA) Saint Anne's Church, 25100 Ridge Rd, Damascus, MD 20872

DAVIS, Roy Jefferson (Tex)

DAVIS JR, Thomas Clark (USC) 102 Carteret Court, Clemson, SC 29631

DAVIS, Thomas Preston (USC) 30 Lyme Bay Road, Columbia, SC 29210

DAVIS, Vicki M (Ct) 227 Church St, Apt. 8B, New Haven, CT 06510

DAVIS, West Richard (Oly) 790 Smugglers Cove Rd, Friday Harbor, WA 98250

DAVIS III, Zabron A (WTenn) 2225 Jefferson Ave, Memphis, TN 38104

DAVIS-HELLER, Lisa Ann (WVa)

DAVIS-LAWSON, Karen Dm (LI) 1420 27th Ave, Astoria, NY 11102

DAVISON, Arienne Siu Ling (Oly) 2151 4th St, Bremerton, WA 98312

DAVIS-SHOEMAKER, Courtney Elizabeth (NC) 1019 E Willowbrook Drive, Burlington, NC 27215

DAVISSON, Mary Thomsen (Md) 2363 Hamiltowne Cir., Baltimore, MD 21237

DAVY, Brian Kendall (At) 589 Martins Grove Rd, Dahlonega, GA 30533

DAW JR, Carl Pickens (Ct) 171 Highland Ave, Watertown, MA 02472

DAWSON, Adrien Portia (Md) 4412 Eastway, Baltimore, MD 21218

DAWSON, Barbara Louise (Cal) 399 Gregory Ln, Pleasant Hill, CA 94523

DAWSON, Eric Emmanuel (VI)

DAWSON JR, Frank Prescott (Md)

DAWSON, George Henry (WTex) 4426 Dolphin Pl, Corpus Christi, TX 78411

DAWSON, Margaret Grantham (La) 320 Sena Dr, Metairie, LA 70005

DAWSON JR, Marshall Allen (Lex) 1375 Weisenberger Mill Rd, Midway, KY 40347

DAWSON, Paul Sweeting (Md) 145 Main St., Apt. A1, Vineyard Haven, MA 02568

DAWSON JR, Tucker Edward (La) 321 State St, Bay Saint Louis, MS 39520

DAWSON, Walter Wesley (Mich) 18017 Grand Lake Blvd, Presque Isle, MI 49777

DAY III, Charles V. (Be) 1006 Eisenhower Way, Tobyhanna, PA 18466

DAY, Christine Jane (CNY) 35 Second St, Johnson City, NY 13790

DAY, Dennis Lee (CGC) PO Box 2066, Fairhope, AL 36533

DAY, Jeremiah Carroll (EC) 109 Skipper Circle, Oriental, NC 28571

DAY, John Edward (Spok) 9843 Derby Way, Elk Grove, CA 95757

DAY JR, John Warren (Wyo) 441 Highland Dr, Bellingham, WA 98225

DAY, Katherine Browning Lufkin (CNY) 106 Ardsley Dr, Syracuse, NY 13214

DAY, Margaret Ann (Me) 777 Stillwater Ave Lot 63, Old Town, ME 04468

DAY, Marshall Benjamin (At) 2089 Ponce de Leon Ave NE, Atlanta, GA 30307

DAY, Michael Henry (SwFla) 1070 54th St N, Saint Petersburg, FL 33710

DAY, Randall Carl Kidder (Los) 2901 Nojoqui Avenue, P.O. Box 39, Los Olivos, CA 93441

DAY, Robert Charles (Mass) 47 Willow Tree Hollow, PO Box 3000 PMB 3124, West Tisbury, MA 02575

DAY, Thomas Leighton (Tex) 320 N Kansas Ave, League City, TX 77573

DAY, Virginia Rex (Be) 1006 Eisenhower Way, Tobyhanna, PA 18466

DAYTON, Douglas Kennedy (NwPa) 3600 Mcconnell Rd, Hermitage, PA 16148

DE ACETIS, Joseph Lewis (Be) 58 Deer Path Dr, Flanders, NJ 07836

DEACON JR, Charles Alexander (WNY) 84 Rosedale Blvd., Amherst, NY 14226

DEACON, Jonathan (NJ) 12 Bryan Dr, Voorhees, NJ 08043

DEADERICK, Dianna LaMance (USC) 1300 Pine St, Columbia, SC 29204

DEAKLE, David Wayne (La) 4350 SE Brooklyn St, Portland, OR 97206

DEAN, Bobby Wayne (CGC) PO Box 1677, Santa Rosa Beach, FL 32459

DEAN, Gordon Joy (WMass) 10 Fox Rd, Shelburne Falls, MA 01370

DEAN, Jay Judson (Me) 33 Baker St, Dover, NH 03820

DEAN, Rebecca Anderson (SVa) 985 Huguenot Trl, Midlothian, VA 23113

DEAN, Steven Jay (Los) 25211 Via Tanara, Santa Clarita, CA 91355

DEAN, Susan Chanda (Oly) 3714 90th Avenue SE, Mercer Island, WA 98040

DE ANAYA, Nilda Lucca (PR) 2100 Washington Ave Apt 2c, Silver Spring, MD 20910

DEANE JR, William Boyd (Pa)

DEAR, Arthur Tyrrel (CFla) Po Box 668, New Smyrna, FL 32170

DEARING, Trevor (Oly) 4 Rock House Gardens, Radcliffe Road, Stamford, PE9 1AS, Great Britain (UK)

DEARMAN, David Coy (Tex) 90 Island Psge, Galveston, TX 77554

DEARMAN JR, William Benjamin (NY) 7 Oakridge Pkwy, Peekskill, NY 10566

DEASY, James Scott (Az) Epiphany Episcopal Church, 423 N Beaver St, Flagstaff, AZ 86001

DEATON JR, Charles Milton (Miss) 1616 52nd Ct, Meridian, MS 39305

DEATON, Jennifer Deaton (Miss) PO Box 23107, Jackson, MS 39225

DEATRICK, George Edward (NJ) 215 Philadelphia Blvd, Sea Girt, NJ 08750

DEATS, Cathy L (NC) 6625 Battleford Dr, Raleigh, NC 27613

DEAVOURS, Cipher Alston (NJ) 112 Union St, Montclair, NJ 07042

DE BARY, Edward Oscar (Miss) 11 Wakefield Dr Apt 2105, Asheville, NC 28803

DEBBOLI, Walter Anthony (Ct) 80 Rockwell Ave, Plainville, CT 06062

DE BEER, John Michael (Mass) 2905 Wynnewood Drive, Greensboro, NC 27408

DE BEER, Patricia Jean (Mass) 2905 Wynnewood Dr., Greensboro, NC 27408

DEBENHAM JR, M(artin) Warren (Cal) 143 Arlington Ave, Berkeley, CA 94707

DEBLASIO, Diane L (LI) 100 46th St, Lindenhurst, NY 11757

DEBOW, Rebecca Stephenson (Ala) 3519 W Lakeside Dr, Birmingham, AL 35243

DEBUSSY, Muriel S (NJ) 825 Summerset Dr, Hockessin, DE 19707

DEBUYS III, John Forrester (Ala) 2501 Country Club Cir, Birmingham, AL 35223

DECAMPS, Walin (Hai)

DECARLEN, Marya L (Mass) 35 King George Dr # 1921, Boxford, MA 01921

DECARVALHO, Maria Elena (RI) 18 Vassar Ave, Providence, RI 02906

DE CHAMBEAU, Franck Alsid (Ct) 163 Belgo Rd, P.O. Box 391, Lakeville, CT 06039

DE CHAMPLAIN, Mitties Mcdonald (NY) 175 9th Ave, New York, NY 10011

DECKER, Clarence Ferdinand (SO) 545 Woodsfield Dr, Columbus, OH 43214

DECKER, Dallas B (The Episcopal Church in Haw) PO Box 7105, Ocean View, HI 96737

DECKER, Georgia Ann (WK) 509 16th Ter, Hutchinson, KS 67501

DECKER, Linda McCullough (The Episcopal Church in Haw) 307 S Alu Rd, Wailuku, HI 96793

DECKER, Margaret Sharp (SanD) 1651 S Juniper St Unit 26, Escondido, CA 92025

DECKER, Prince A (WA) 3918 Wendy Ln, Silver Spring, MD 20906

DECOSS, Donald Albion (Cal) 26 Overlake Ct, Oakland, CA 94611

DEDDE, Joseph Colin (WNY) 233 Brantwood Rd, Amherst, NY 14226

DEDEAUX JR, James Terrell (Miss) 5303 Diamondhead Cir, Diamondhead, MS 39525

DEDMON JR, Robert Aaron (Chi) 1804 Sycamore Circle, Manchester, TN 37355

DEEGAN, Virginia Edna (CFla) 210 Fallen Timber Trl, Deland, FL 32724

DEERY, Laurel Pierson (Mass) 44 School St, Manchester, MA 01944

DEETHS, Margaret Edith (Cal) 576 Cedarberry Ln, San Rafael, CA 94903

DEETS, Sherry (Pa) 2717 Shelburne Road, Downingtown, PA 19335

DEETZ, Susan Maureen (Minn) 4210 Robinson St, Duluth, MN 55804

DE FONTAINE-STRATTON, James (NY) 161 Mansion St, Poughkeepsie, NY 12601

DEFOOR II, Allison (Fla) 200 W. College Ave., Tallahassee, FL 32301

DEFOREST, John William (Tex) 3535 Whittaker Ln, Beaumont, TX 77706

DEFOREST, Nancy (Tex) 3535 Whittaker Ln, Beaumont, TX 77706

DE FRANCO JR, Peter (Nwk)

DEFRIEST, Jeannette (Chi) 400 Main St Apt 5A, Evanston, IL 60202

DEGAVRE, Susan Williams (Va) 7120 S. Wenatchee Way Unit C, Aurora, CO 80016

DEGENHARDT, Terri Walker (Ga) St Michael's Episcopal Church, 515 S Liberty St, Waynesboro, GA 30830

DEGOOYER, Bruce Underwood (Spr) 2816 Greenfield Rd, Bloomington, IL 61704

DE GRAVELLES, Charles Nattons (La) 3651 Broussard St, Baton Rouge, LA 70808

DEGWECK, Stephen William (Ala) 3736 Montrose Rd, Birmingham, AL 35213

DEHART, Benjamin (NY) Calvary and St George, 61 Gramercy Park N Fl 2, New York, NY 10010

DEHART, Elsa Arp (Ak) St James the Fisherman, PO Box 1668, Kodiak, AK 99615

DEHETRE, Donna B (Chi) 31 Edgehill Rd, New Haven, CT 06511

DEHLER, Debra Rae (Minn) 3427 Utah Ave., N., Crystal, MN 55427

DEJARDIN, Wisnel (Hai)

DE JESUS, Gerardo James (CFla) 6316 Matchett Rd, Orlando, FL 32809

DE JESUS-JIMENEZ, Justo (PR) Parroquia Santo Nombre de Jesus, 806 Calle Jesus T Pineiro, Ponce, PR 00728-3601, Puerto Rico

DE JESUS LAGARES, Jose Joaquin (DR) (DomRep)

DEJOHN, Kathleen Ann Gillespie (NJ) 138 Rector St, Perth Amboy, NJ 08861

DE KAY, Charles Augustus (Chi) 901 Forest Avenue 1E, Evanston, IL 60202

DEKKER, Robert Peter (Chi) 15145 Smarty Jones Drive, Noblesville, IN 46060

DE LA CRUZ, Luis Manuel (CFla) 1709 N John Young Pkwy, Kissimmee, FL 34741

DELAFIELD, Audrey Sawtelle (Me) 32 Ship Channel Rd, South Portland, ME 04106

DELAMATER, Joanie Potvin (Minn) 6287 Crackleberry Trl, Woodbury, MN 55129

DELANCEY, Mary Louise (CFla) 510 SE Broadway St, Ocala, FL 34471

DE LANEROLLE, Nihal Chandra (Ct) 500 Prospect St Apt 2-F, New Haven, CT 06511

DELANEY, Conrad Todd (WA)

DELANEY, James William (Nwk) 26 Prescott Rd, Ho Ho Kus, NJ 07423

DELANEY, Mary Joan (Az) 5611E Alta Vista St, Tucson, AZ 85712

DELANEY, Mary T (EMich) 1038 W Center St, Alma, MI 44001

DELANEY, Michael F (NY) 191 Kensington Road, Garden City, NY 11530

DELANEY, Ryan Ray (Alb)

DE LA TORRE, Carlos (Ct)

DE LA TORRE, William Jhon (SwFla) 8271 52nd St N, Pinellas Park, FL 33781

DELAURA, Gilbert Frank (Alb) Church of the Messiah, 296 Glen St, Glens Falls, NY 12801

DELAUTER, Joe H (CPa) 598 Longbarn Rd, State College, PA 16803

DE LA VARS, Gordon John (Md) 115 S Erie St, Mayville, NY 14757

DEL BENE, Ronald Norman (Ala) 2841 Floyd Bradford Rd, Trussville, AL 35173

DEL CASTILLO, Gloria Rosa (Cal) 622 Lois Lane, El Sobrante, CA 94803

DELCUZE, Mark Stewart (Eas) 623 Cloverfields Dr, Stevensville, MD 21666

DELEERY, Seth Mabry (Tex) 9002 Clithea Cv, Austin, TX 78759

DE LEEUW, Gawain Frederik (NY) 95 Ralph Ave, White Plains, NY 10606

DELEUSE, Betsey Wilder (Me) 27 Arlington St. Unit 1, Portland, ME 04101

DELFS, Carin Bridgit (SO) 109 John St, 95 Elizabeth St Apt 412, Delaware, OH 43015

DELGADO, Joseph Anthony (Cal) 2220 Cedar St, Berkeley, CA 94709

DELGADO-MARKSMAN, Adams Felipe (Ve)

DELGADO-MILLER, Diego Antonio (NY) 260 W 231st St, Bronx, NY 10460

DELGADO-VERA, Ramiro Mario (WTex) 697 W White Ave, Raymondville, TX 78580

DELICAT, Joseph Kerwin (Hai)

DE LION, Lawrence Raymond (LI) 15 Greenwich Rd, Smithtown, NY 11787

DELK, Michael L (SVa) 205 Castle Ln, Williamsburg, VA 23185

DELL, Jacob William (NY) 504 E 79th St Apt 4H, New York, NY 10075

DELL, Mary Lynn (O) 2741 Sherbrooke Road, Shaker Heights, OH 44122

DELLARIA, Kevin (WTex) St. Andrew's Episcopal Church, 201 E. Nolte, Seguin, TX 78155

DELMAS, Hailey Lynne (Cal) 28 Cobblestone Ln, Belmont, CA 94002

DEL PRIORE, Micah Dorian (USC) 910 Hudson Rd, Greenville, SC 29615

DEL VALLE-ORTIZ, Efrain Edgardo (PR) Mansiones de San Martin #26 Las Villas, San Juan, RP 00924-4592, Puerto Rico

DEL VALLE-TIRADO, Jose A (PR)

DELZELL, Constance Kay Clawson (Colo) 3 Calle de Montanas, Santa Fe, NM 87507

DEMAREST, Richard Alan (Ida) 518 N. Eighth Street, Boise, ID 83702

DEMBI, Megan E (Be) 6030 Grosvenor Ln, Bethesda, MD 20814

DE MEL, Chitral Suranjith (Mass)

DEMENT, Thomas Erik (Oly) 1118 E Baldwin Ave, Spokane, WA 99207

DEMING, Nancy James (Pa) 518 Hilaire Rd, Saint Davids, PA 19087

DEMING, Robert (Ct) 20 Shepherd Ln, Orange, CT 06477

DE MIRANDA, Mario Eugenio (SeFla) 15650 Miami Lakeway N, Miami Lakes, FL 33014

DEMLER, Maureen Ann (Alb) 912 Route 146, Clifton Park, NY 12065

DEMMLER, Mary Reynolds Hemmer (At) 995 E Tugalo St, Toccoa, GA 30577

DEMMON, Mike (Colo) 407 Club Drive, Hinesville, GA 31313

DEMO, Gar R (Kan) 8144 Rosehill Rd, Lenexa, KS 66215

DEMO, Kelly (Kan) 8144 Rosehill Rd, Lenexa, KS 66215

DE MONTMOLLIN, D(ee) Ann (SwFla) 394 N. Main Street, Rutherfordton, NC 28139

DEMOTT, Richard Arthur (Va) 784 Alpine Dr, Seven Devils, Banner Elk, NC 28604

DEMPESY, Catherine Biggs (WNY) St Pauls Cathedral, 128 Pearl St, Buffalo, NY 14202

DEMPZ, Julia A (Mich) 61 Grosse Pointe Blvd, Grosse Pointe Farms, MI 48236

DEMURA, Christine A (Oly) 10042 Main St Apt 410, Bellevue, WA 98004

DE MUTH, Steven H (Los) Holy Trinity Parish, PO Box 4195, Covina, CA 91723

DENARO, John Edward (LI) 157 Montague St, Brooklyn, NY 11201

DENDTLER, Robert Blanchard (At) 1011 Cedar Ridge, Greensboro, GA 30642

DENEAU, Elizabeth Ann (NMich) 500 Ogden Ave, Escanaba, MI 49829

DENEKE, William Thomas (At) 515 E Ponce De Leon Ave, Decatur, GA 30030

DENG DENG, William Deng (Oly) 4759 Shattuck Pl S Unit B101, Renton, WA 98055

DENHAM, John (WA) 767 N Cambridge Way, Claremont, CA 91711

DENISON, Charles Wayne (Wyo) 2502 Overland Road, Laramie, WY 82070

DENISON JR, Raleigh Edmond (Dal) 1504 S Ash St, Georgetown, TX 78626

DENMAN, Scott Lester (Cal) 7917 Outlook Ave, Oakland, CA 94605

DENNEY, Shawn W (Spr) 3813 Bergamot Dr, Springfield, IL 62712

DENNEY, Shelley Booth (ECR) PO Box 1317, Lake Arrowhead, CA 92352

DENNEY-ZUNIGA, Amy E (ECR)

DENNIS, Alan Godfrey (NY) 45 orchard lane, Torrington, CT 06790

DENNIS, Fredrick Hogarth (Alb) 455 Park Ave, Saranac Lake, NY 12983

DENNIS, Loretta Anne (Roch) 240 S 4th St, Philadelphia, PA 19106

DENNIS, William Joseph (WLa) 501 Springfield Ave, Eutaw, AL 35462

DENNISON JR, Bryant Whitman (Mich) 420 Rivard Blvd, Grosse Pointe, MI 48230

DENNLER, William David (Tenn) 615 6th Ave. S., Nashville, TN 37203

DENNY, Stephen Michael (Ore) 10143 Se 49th Ave, Milwaukie, OR 97222

DENSON JR, John Eley (Ind) 5 Granite St, Exeter, NH 03833

DENTON, Edna Marguerite (SO) 1021 Crede Way, Waynesville, OH 45068

DENTON, Jean Margaret (Ind) 1210 E 71st St, Indianapolis, IN 46220

DENTON, Maria Anna (Colo) 7068 Kiowa Rd, Larkspur, CO 80118

DEPHOUSE, Jonathan R (Los) 1325 Monterey Rd, South Pasadena, CA 91030

DEPPE, Jimmie Sue (Roch) 20475 Sunningdale Park, Grosse Pointe Woods, MI 48236

DEPPE, Thomas W (SVa) 2020 Laskin Rd, Virginia Beach, VA 23454

DEPPEN, G(ehret) David (NJ) 35 Queens Way, Wellfleet, MA 02667

DEPRIEST, Sandra Moss (Miss) 510 7th St N, Columbus, MS 39701

DEPUE, (Karen Lynn) Joanna (NY) 7 Heather Ln, Orangeburg, NY 10962

DE PUY KERSHAW, Susan Lynn (NH) P.O. Box 485, Walpole, NH 03608

DERAGON, Russell Lelan (Ct) 871 N Indian River Dr, Cocoa, FL 32922

DERAVIL, Jean-Jacques (Hai) Diquini 63b #8, Carrefour, Haiti

DERBY, Roger Sherman (Mich) 2441 Mulberry Sq Apt 25, Bloomfield Hills, MI 48302

DERBY, William Vinton (NY) 14 E 109th St, New York, NY 10029

DERBYSHIRE, John Edward (CNY) 229 Twin Hills Dr, Syracuse, NY 13207

DE RIJK, Cornelis Johannes (Az) 28 W Pasadena Ave, Phoenix, AZ 85013

DERKITS III, J James (WTex) Trinity by the Sea Episcopal Church, PO Box 346, Port Aransas, TX 78373

DEROSE, Kathryn Pitkin (Los) 2621 6th St Apt 5, Santa Monica, CA 90405

DERRICK, John Burton (Ga) 1512 Meadows Ln, Vidalia, GA 30474

DERSNAH, Donald (Mich) 4354 Weber Rd, Saline, MI 48176

DE RUFF, Elizabeth Anslow (Cal) PO Box 1137, Ross, CA 94957

DESALVO, David Paul (Del) 350 Noxontown Rd, Middletown, DE 19709

DESAULNIERS, John J (Va) 406 Haven Lake Ave, Milford, DE 19963

DESCHAINE, Thomas Charles (Me) Po Box 467, Augusta, ME 04332

DESHAIES, Robert Joseph (SeFla)

DESHAW, Glen (Oly) 11380 NE 36th Pl Apt B135, Bellevue, WA 98004

DE SHEPLO, Louis John (NJ) 551 Saint Kitts Dr, Williamstown, NJ 08094

DE SILVA, Sumith (Az) 9533 E. Kokopelli Circle, Tucson, AZ 85748

DESIR, Jean Nephtaly (DR (DomRep)) Iglesia Episcopal Dominicana, Apartado 764, Santo Domingo, Dominican Republic

DESIR, St Clair Roger (Hai) Box 13224, Port-Au-Prince, Haiti

DESIRE, Fritz (Hai)

DESMARAIS, Susanna (Neb) 4545 S 58th St, Lincoln, NE 68516

DESMITH, David John (Nwk) 90 Kiel Ave, Kinnelon, NJ 07405

DESROSIERS JR, Norman (CFla) St Sebastian By The Sea, 2010 Oak St, Melbourne Beach, FL 32951

DESUEZA, Edmond (NY) 271 Broadway, Newburgh, NY 12550

DESUEZA-SAVINON, Edmond Guillermo (PR) Urb. Fairview, D11 Calle 10, San Juan, PR 00926

DETTWILLER II, George Frederick (Tenn) 108 Savoy Cir., Nashville, TN 37205

DEUEL, Ellen Mighells Cook (SanD) 1212 H St Spc 219, Ramona, CA 92065

DEVALL IV, Frederick D (La) St. Martin's Episcopal Church, 2216 Metairie Road, Metairie, LA 70001

DEVATY, Jean M (Alb) 508 4th Ave, Beaver Falls, PA 15010

DEVAUL, Philip H (Los) 31641 La Novia Ave, San Juan Capistrano, CA 92675

DEVEAU, Peter Jay (WMo) 3824 34th Ave Sw, Seattle, WA 98126

DEVENS, Philip (RI) 111 Greenwich Ave # 2886, Warwick, RI 02886

DEVINE, Michael Francis (WMass) 47 Ruskin St, Springfield, MA 01108

DEVINE, Whitney Alford Jones (Oly) 4420 - 137th Avenue Northeast, Bellevue, WA 98005

DE VOLDER, Luk (Ct) 950 Chapel St Fl 2, New Haven, CT 06510

DEVORE, Kirk Eugene (Md) 2 E High St, Hancock, MD 21750

DEWEES, Herbert Reed (Dal) 9511 Meadowknoll Dr, Dallas, TX 75243

DE WETTER, Robert Emerson (CNY) PO Box 5310, Snowmass Village, CO 81615

DEWEY, E Robinson (SC) 598 E Hobcaw Dr, Mount Pleasant, SC 29464

DEWEY JR, S(anford) Dayton (NY) B908 New Providence Wharf, 1 Fairmont Ave, Docklands, London, E14 9PB U.K., Great Britain (UK)

DEWITT, Edward Leonard (NMich) 90 Croix St Apt 2, Negaunee, MI 49866

DEWITT, Phyllis M (NMich) 301 N 1st St, Ishpeming, MI 49849

DEWITT, William Henry (NMich) 301 N 1st St, Ishpeming, MI 49849

DEWLEN, Janet Marie (Colo) 2500 22nd Drive, Longmont, CO 80503

DE WOLF, Mark Anthony (Ct) 9 Weetamoe Farm Druve, Bristol, RI 02809

DEWOLFE, Robert Francis (WTex) 3412 Pebblebrook Dr, Tyler, TX 75707

DEXTER, Beverly Liebherr (SanD) 325 Kempton St Apt 400, Spring Valley, CA

DEYOUNG, Lily (Mass) 12408 Main Campus Drive, Lexington, MA 02421

DEZHBOD, Esmail Shahrokh (Ct) 294 Main St S, Woodbury, CT 06798

DIAS, Krista K (NY) Christ Church, 17 Sagamore Rd, Bronxville, NY 10708

DIAZ, George Diaz (NY) 257 Clinton St Apt 19n, New York, NY 10002

DIAZ, Gladys (NY) Po Box 617, Bronx, NY 10473

DIAZ, Jose A (Pa) 3554 N 6th St, Philadelphia, PA 19140

DIAZ, Joseph Herbert (SwFla) 3396 Deerfield Ln, Clearwater, FL 33761

DIAZ, Juan Jose (Hond)

DIAZ, Narciso Antonio (Chi)

DIAZ ESTEVEZ, Manuel (DR (DomRep))

DIBENEDETTO, Aileen Elizabeth (Mass)

DICARLO, Michael Joseph (Los) 1400 W. 13th St. Spc 139, Upland, CA 91786

DICE, Daniel Sean (At) 2833 Flat Shoals Rd, Decatur, GA 30034

DICK, Brandt Allen (Miss) 1026 S. Washing Ave, Greenville, MS 38701

DICKERSON, Shawn Evan (O) 7640 Glenwood Ave, Boardman, OH 44512

DICKEY, Robert William (Va) 108 Forest Garden Rd, Stevensville, MD 21666

DICKINSON, A Hugh (Pa) 2510 Lake Michigan Dr, NW Apt. A-205, Grand Rapids, MI 49504

DICKINSON, Garrin William (Dal) 3804 Carrizo Dr, Plano, TX 75074

DICKS, Paul Richard (Spr) 422 E 1st South St, Carlinville, IL 62626

✠ DICKSON, Alex Dockery (Ret Bp of WTenn 1994-) 1F Vendue Range, Charleston, SC 29401

DICKSON JR, E(lton) Robert (Mass) 6102 Buckhorn Rd, Greensboro, NC 27410

DICKSON, Patricia Joan (Va)

DIEBEL, Mark H (Alb) 68 Troy Rd., East Greenbush, NY 12061

DIEFENBACHER, Fred H (SwFla) 3824 Twilight Dr, Valrico, FL 33594

DIEGUE, Joseph Tancrel (Hai) Box 1309, Port-Au-Prince, Haiti

DIEHL, Jane Cornell (EMich) 3201 Gratiot Ave, Port Huron, MI 48060

DIEHL, Robert Edward (EMich) 3201 Gratiot Ave, Port Huron, MI 48060

DIELY, Elizabeth Barrett Hanning (Be) 629 Glenwood St, Emmaus, PA 18049

DIERICK, Frances Lorraine (Oly) 102 Glenn Ln, Montesano, WA 98563

DIETER, David D (Mich) 847 Grand Marais St, Grosse Pointe Park, MI 48230

DIETERLE, Ann M (WNC) 200 W Cowles St, Wilkesboro, NC 28697

DIETRICH, Seth A (Mil) 4234 N Larkin St, Milwaukee, WI 53211

✠ **DIETSCHE**, Andrew Marion Lenow (Bp of NY 2013-) 1047 Amsterdam Ave, New York, NY 10025

DIETZ, Joseph Bland (Pa) 2619 N Charlotte St, Pottstown, PA 19464

DIETZ-ALLEN, Doyle Douglas (Az) Saint Alban's Episcopal Church, 3738 N Old Sabino Canyon Rd, Tucson, AZ 85750

DIGGS, Thomas Tucker (USC) 2313 Kestrel Dr, Rock Hill, SC 29732

DILEO, John Michael (Fla) 1505 NW 91st Ter, Gainesville, FL 32606

DILG, Arthur Charles (Pgh) 1371 Washington St, Indiana, PA 15701

DILL, David Stone (Ala) Church of the Good Shepherd, 3809 Spring Avenue SW, Decatur, AL 35603

DILL, Todd R (NC) 8515 Rea Rd, Waxhaw, NC 28173

DILLARD, Walter Scott (Va) 9 Deerfield Dr, Luray, VA 22835

DILLER, Sallie Winch (NMich) 733n E Gulliver Lake Rd, Gulliver, MI 49840

DILLEY, John S (HB)

DILLIPLANE, Nancy Burton (Pa) Po Box 387, Buckingham, PA 18912

DILLON, Gwendolyn J (Chi) 446 E 95th St, Chicago, IL 60619

DILLON, John Lawrence (U) 8738 Oakwood Park Cir, Sandy, UT 84094

DILLON II, Tommy J (Oly) 561 Burnett #1, San Francisco, CA 94131

DILLS, (Robert) Scott (Oly) 919 - 21st Avenue East, Seattle, WA 98112

DI LORENZO, Anthony (LI) 40 Warren Avenue, Lake Ronkonkoma, NY 11779

DIMARCO, Thomas Edgar (USC) PO Box 206, Trenton, SC 29847

DIMMICK, Kenneth Ray (Tex) Lorenzstaffel 8, Stuttgart, 70182, Germany

DINGES, John Albert (Mil) Box 27671, West Allis, WI 53227

DINGLE, John Hausmann (NY) 143 Kent I, Century Village, West Palm Beach, FL 33417

DINGLEY, Alison M. (The Episcopal Church in Haw) 1255 Nuuanu Ave., #E1513, Honolulu, HI 96817

DINGMAN, Joel Andrew (Wyo) 419 Circle Dr, Gillette, WY 82716

DINNERVILLE, Robert Raymond (CFla) 6400 N Socrum Loop Rd, Lakeland, FL 33809

DINOTO, Anthony Charles (Ct) 196 Main St., Durham, CT 06422

DINOVO, D Rebecca (Ore) St John The Evangelist Episcopal Church, 2036 SE Jefferson St, Milwaukie, OR 97222

DINSMORE, Taylor Whitehead (ETenn) 9125 Candlewood Dr, Knoxville, TN 37923

DINSMORE, Virginia Carol (Nwk) 5 Dalland Rd, Succasunna, NJ 07876

DINWIDDIE, Donald H (Fla) 130 Commercial Ave, East Palatka, FL 32131

DINWIDDIE, Philip Matthew (Mich) 25150 East River, Grosse Ile, MI 48138

DIRADDO, Joseph Andrew (WTex) 1 Bishop Gadsden Way #329, Charleston, SC 29412

DIRBAS, Joseph James (SanD) 1475 Catalina Blvd, San Diego, CA 92106

DIRBAS, Terry Shields (SanD) 1114 9th St, Coronado, CA 92118

DIRGHALLI, S George (CNY) 131 Durston Ave, Syracuse, NY 13203

DISBROW, Jimme Lynn (Okla) 1737 Churchill Way, Oklahoma City, OK 73120

DISCAVAGE, Thomas Damian (Los) 1830 Taft Ave Apt 202, Los Angeles, CA 90028

DISHAROON, Susan Clay (Miss) 3030 Highway 547, Port Gibson, MS 39150

DISTANISLAO, Virginia Gates (SVa) 512 S. Broad St., Kenbridge, VA 23944

DITTERLINE, Richard Charles (Pa) 1350 Spring Valley Rd, Bethlehem, PA 18015

DITZENBERGER, Christopher Steven (Colo) 6190 E. Quincy Avenue, Englewood, CO 80111

DIVINE, Betty Baird (Tex) 1616 Fountainview Dr #203, Houston, TX 77057

DIVIS, Mary Lou (Be) 408 E Main St, Nanticoke, PA 18634

DIXON III, David Lloyd (SwVa) 42 E Main St, Salem, VA 24153

DIXON JR, John Henry (RG) Av. C. Leon de Nicaragua 1, Esc. 3, 1-B, Alicante, 03015, Spain

DIXON, Mary Lenn (Tex) 1101 Rock Prairie Rd, College Station, TX 77845

DIXON, Robert Keith (Nwk) 73 Fernbank Ave, Delmar, NY 12054

DIXON, Robert P (CGC) Saint Stephen's Church, 1510 Escambia Ave, Brewton, AL 36426

DIXON, Valerie Wilde (Ct) 23 Bayview Ave, Niantic, CT 06357

DOAR, Katherine Baginski (ECR) 1225 Pine Ave, San Jose, CA 95125

DOBBIN, Robert A (Cal) 24 Van Gordon Pl, Danville, CA 94526

DOBBINS, Burford C (WTex) 1501 N. Glass St., Victoria, TX 77901

DOBBINS, Timothy (Pa) 292 Militia Dr, Radnor, PA 19087

DOBBINS JR, W. David (RI) 205 Lindley Ave, North Kingstown, RI 02852

DOBSON, Marc A (Dal) 6021 Shady Valley Court, Garland, TX 75043

DOBYNS, N(ancy) (Ind) 1021 Sw 15th St, Richmond, IN 47374

DOBYNS, R(ichard) (Ind) 1021 Sw 15th St, Richmond, IN 47374

DOCKERY, Nancy Lynn (Nev) 501 Bianca Bay St, Las Vegas, NV 89144

DOCTOR, Virginia Carol (Ak) P.O. Box 93, Tanana, AK 99777

DOD, David Stockton (ECR) 8294 Carmelita Ave, Atascadero, CA 93422

DODD, Debra (Dee) Anne (Ct) 37 Bailey Dr, North Branford, CT 06471

DODD, Jean Carrison (Fla) 1860 Edgewood Ave S, Jacksonville, FL 32205

DODDEMA, Peter (Lex) 118 West Poplar Street, Harrodsburg, KY 40330

DODDS, Doris Ann (Minn) 715 Paine Dr, Paynesville, MN 56362

DODGE, Jeffrey A (Mass) 1755 Clay St, San Francisco, CA 94109

DODGE, Robin Dennis (WA) 5150 Macomb Street, N.W., Washington, DC 20016

DODSON, Wayne (NY) 9 W 130th St, New York, NY 10037

DOERR, Nan Lewis (Tex) 901 S. Johnson, Alvin, TX 77511

DOGARU, Vickie A (Oly) 22405 Ne 182nd Ave, Battle Ground, WA 98604

DOGGETT, William Jordan (WA) 1209 East Capitol Street SE, Washington, DC 20003

DOHERTY, Anna Clay (Mil) 670 E Monroe Ave, Hartford, WI 53027

DOHERTY, Jerry Clay (Minn) 201 Bayberry Avenue Ct, Stillwater, MN 55082

DOHERTY, John S (Ia) CATHEDRAL CHURCH OF ST PAUL, 815 HIGH ST, DES MOINES, IA 50309

DOHERTY, Maureen Catherine (Ia) 417 Olive St, Cedar Falls, IA 50613

DOHERTY, Noel James (Okla) 6910 E 62nd St, Tulsa, OK 74133

DOHERTY, Tyler Britton (U) 231 E 100 S, Salt Lake City, UT 84111

DOHERTY-OGEA, Kathleen Lambert (WLa) 206 South Street, Bastrop, LA 71220

DOHLE, Robert Joseph (Tex) St Paul's Episcopal Church, 1307 W 5th St, Freeport, TX 77541

DOHONEY, Edmund Luther (WTex) 14906 Grayoak Frst, San Antonio, TX 78248

DOING JR, Robert Burns (SwFla) 36 Barkley Circle Apt 205, Fort Myers, FL 33907

DOLACK, Craig A (Ga) Saint Michael And All Angels, 3101 Waters Ave, Savannah, GA 31404

DOLAN, John Richard (Chi) 3925 Central Ave, Western Springs, IL 60558

DOLAN, Mary Ellen (Eur) Frankfurter Strasse 3, Wiesbaden, 65189, Germany

DOLAN, Pamela E (Mo) 9 S Bompart Ave, Saint Louis, MO 63119

DOLAN-HENDERSON, Susan (Tex) 3104 Harris Park Ave, Austin, TX 78705

DOLEN, William Kennedy (Ga) 605 Reynolds St, Augusta, GA 30901

DOLL, M(ary) Chotard (Spok) 4850 N Paseo Del Tupo, Tucson, AZ 85750

DOLLAHITE, Damian DeWitt Gene (Dal) 226 Oakhaven Dr, Grand Prairie, TX 75050

DOLLHAUSEN, Matthew Mark (CGC) 6849 Oak St, Milton, FL 32570

DOLNIKOWSKI, Edith Wilks (Mass) The Episcopal Diocese Of Massachusetts, 138 Tremont St, Boston, MA 02111

DOLPH, Scott Marshall Michael (Ore) 4233 S. E. Ash Street, Portland, OR 97215

DOLS, Timothy Walters (Va) 5705 Oak Bluff Ln, Wilmington, NC 28409

DOLS JR, William Ludwig (Va) 300 Aspen St, Alexandria, VA 22305

DOMBEK, Timothy M (Az) 11242 N 50th Ave, Glendale, AZ 85304

DOMENICK JR, W(arren) L(ee) (Minn) St Luke's Church, 4557 Colfax Ave S, Minneapolis, MN 55419

DOMIENIK, Steven (Ct) 10 Church Lane, Madison, CT 06443

DONAHOE, Melanie (Cal) Church of the Epiphany, 1839 Arroyo Avenue, San Carlos, CA 94070

DONAHUE, Lawrence Charles (NwPa) 204 Jackson Ave, Bradford, PA 16701

DONAHUE, Ray Lawrence (Alb) 24929 State Highway 206, Downsville, NY 13755

DONALD, David Seth (WLa) 715 Kirkman St, Lake Charles, LA 70601

DONALD, James (WA) 1 Peachtree Battle Ave. , NW #5, Unit #5, Atlanta, GA 30305

DONALDSON, Audley (LI) 1345 President St, Brooklyn, NY 11213

DONALDSON, Walter Alexander (Los) 7631 Klusman Ave, Rancho Cucamonga, CA 91730

DONATELLI, Todd M (WNC) Cathedral of All Souls, 9 Swan St, Asheville, NC 28803

DONATHAN, W(illiam) Larry (WA) 105 15th Street SE, Washington, DC 20003

DONCASTER, Diana Lynn (The Episcopal NCal) 495 Albion Ave, Cincinnati, OH 45246

DONDERO, Christina Downs (At) 879 Clifton Rd Ne, Atlanta, GA 30307

DONECKER, Paul Clayton (CPa) 351 Bull Run Crossing, Lewisburg, PA 17837

DONELSON JR, Frank T(aylor) (WTenn) 475 N Highland St Apt 7e, Memphis, TN 38122

DONNELLY, Ellen Alston (Nwk) 852 Bullet Hill Rd, Southbury, CT 06488

DONNELLY, Jeffrey Joseph (Cal)

DONNELLY, John Allen (Ct) 470 Quaker Farms Road, Oxford, CT 06478

DONNELLY, J(ohn) Kevin (Az) 609 Oliver Cir, Bisbee, AZ 85603

DONNELLY, Richard Colonel (Ct) 430 Quaker Drive, York, PA 17402

DONOHUE, Mary Jane (Mass) 51 Ryder Ave, Melrose, MA 02176

DONOHUE-ADAMS, Amy (Oly) 11703 Oakwood Dr, Austin, TX 78753

✠ **DONOVAN JR**, Herbert Alcorn (Ret Bp of Ark 1993-) 152 Broadway # 8, Dobbs Ferry, NY 10522

DONOVAN, John Carl (Tex) 2908 Avenue O Apt 1, Galveston, TX 77550

DONOVAN, Nancy Lu (SD) 9412 Saint Joseph St, Silver City, SD 57702

DONOVAN, William Patrick (Minn) 684 Mississippi River Blvd S, Saint Paul, MN 55116

DOOLEY, Martha Mae (NJ) 4735 Cedar Ave, Philadelphia, PA 19143

DOOLING, Thomas Alexander (Mont) 548 Breckenridge St, Helena, MT 59601

DOOLITTLE, Geoffrey D. (CNY) 117 Main St, Owego, NY 13827

DOPP, William Floyd (SwFla) 818 Chamise Ct, San Marcos, CA 92069

DORAN, Judith Ann (Chi) 1350 N Western Ave Apt 111, Apt 111, Lake Forest, IL 60045

DORAN, Michelle Stuart (Md) All Saints, PO Box 40, Sunderland, MD 20689

DORN, Christy M (WMo) 13134 Lamar Ave, Overland Park, KS 66209

DORN III, James M (CFla) 574 West Montrose St, Clermont, FL 34711

DORNEMANN, Deanna Maxine (EC) 60 Bethlehem Pike Rm 1401, Philadelphia, PA 19118

DORNER, Mary Anne (SwFla) 27127 Fordham Dr, Wesley Chapel, FL 33543

DOROW, Robert Michael (NI) 1007 Moore Rd, Michigan City, IN 46360

DORR JR, E(rwin) John (Ind) 256 51st St Cir E, Palmetto, FL 34221

DORR, Kathleen Elaine (Ct) 39 Whalers Pt, East Haven, CT 06512

DORRIEN, Gary John (NY) Union Theological Seminary, 3041 Broadway, New York, NY 10027

DORSCH, Kenneth John (Ore) 15625 Nw Norwich St, Beaverton, OR 97006

DORSEE, Ballard (Ct) 461 Mill Hill Ter, Southport, CT 06890

DORSEY, June Hardy (O) 3602 Hawthorne Ave, Richmond, VA 23222

DORSEY, Laura Miller (Eas) 28333 Mount Vernon Rd, Princess Anne, MD 21853

✠ **DOSS**, Joe Morris (Form Bp of NJ 2001-) 15 Front St, Mandeville, LA 70448

DOSTAL FELL, Margaret Ann (Minn) 1765 Upper 55th St E, Inver Grove Heights, MN 55077

DOSTER, Daniel Harris (Ga) 724 Victoria Cir, Dublin, GA 31021

DOTY, D(avid) Michael (WNC) 143 Caledonia Rd, Landrum, SC 29356

DOTY, Phyllis Marie (Fla) P.O. Box 4366, Dowling Park, FL 32064

DOUBLEDAY, William Alan (NY) 31 Croton Avenue, MOUNT KISCO, NY 10549

DOUGHARTY, Philip Wilmot (WNY) 427 Loma Hermosa Dr NW, Albuquerque, NM 87105

DOUGHERTY JR, Edward Archer (SeFla) 8 Sky Hollow Dr, Albany, NY 12204

DOUGHERTY, Jan (Minn) 5844 Deer Trail Cir, Woodbury, MN 55129

DOUGLAS, Alan David (Colo) 5409 Fossil Creek Dr, Fort Collins, CO 80526

DOUGLAS, Ann Leslie (NY) 201 Scarborough Rd, Briarcliff Manor, NY 10510

DOUGLAS, Carole Robinson (Md) 7521 Rockridge Rd, Pikesville, MD 21208

DOUGLAS, Dorothy Ruth (CGC) 5904 Woodvale Dr, Mobile, AL 36608

DOUGLAS JR, Harry Bell (SeFla) 33 Kathy Ann Dr, Crawfordville, FL 32327

✠ **DOUGLAS**, Ian Theodore (Bp of Ct 2010-) Episcopal Diocese Of Connecticut, 290 Pratt Street, Box 52, Meriden, CT 06450

DOUGLAS, Jeffrey Allen (EC) 907 Colony Ave N, Ahoskie, NC 27910

DOUGLAS, Michael John (Az) 400 S Old Litchfield Rd, Litchfield Park, AZ 85340

DOUGLAS, Roger Owen (Az) 47280 Amir Dr, Palm Desert, CA 92260

DOUGLASS, David George (NI) 6085 N 190 W, Howe, IN 46746

DOUGLASS, James Herford (La) Po Box 523900, Miami, FL 33152

DOULOS, William Lane (Los) 535 W Roses Rd, San Gabriel, CA 91775

DOVER III, John Randolph (SC) 231 Cedar Berry Ln, Chapel Hill, NC 27517

DOVER, Sara Harned (Be) 226 Ridings Cir, Macungie, PA 18062

DOW, Neal Hulce (Colo) 3296 S Heather Gardens Way, Aurora, CO 80014

DOWARD, Amonteen Ravenden (VI) PO Box 486, Christiansted, VI 00821

DOWDESWELL, Eugenia Hedden (WNC) Po Box 132, Flat Rock, NC 28731

DOWDLE, Cathey (SanD) 726 2nd Ave, Chula Vista, CA 91910

DOWELL, Elizabeth Ruth (Tex) PO Box 746, Columbus, TX 78934

DOWER, Ronny W (NJ) 3500 Penny Ln, Zanesville, OH 43701
DOWER, Sandra Nichols (WNY)
DOWLING-SENDOR, Elizabeth (NC) 6 Davie Cir, Chapel Hill, NC 27514
DOWNER, Gretchen Marie (Ida) 1419 Butte View Cir, Emmett, ID 83617
DOWNES, Richard Hill (Mass) 71 Saint Marys St Apt 1, Brookline, MA 02446
DOWNEY, John Paul (NwPa) 220 W 41st St, Erie, PA 16508
DOWNIE, Elizabeth Morris (EMich) 1091 Cherry St, Winnetka, IL 60093
DOWNING, George L (WNC) 21 Indigo Way, Hendersonville, NC 28739
DOWNING, John W (Mil)
DOWNING, Patricia S (Del) 1108 N Adams St, Wilmington, DE 19801
DOWNING, Richard E (WA) 2602 N Harrison St, Wilmington, DE 19802
DOWNS, Alice Lacey (NJ) 14 Winding Lane, Southwest Harbor, ME 04679
DOWNS, Andrew D (Ind) Saint Stephen's Church, 215 N 7th St, Terre Haute, IN 47807
DOWNS, Dalton Dalzell (WA) 703 Carmel Lane, Poinciana, FL 34759
DOWNS, Donna (Ct) 64 Philip Dr, Shelton, CT 06484
DOWNS JR, Joseph Thomas (EMich) 3225 N Branch Dr, Beaverton, MI 48612
DOWNS, Lee Daniel (Mil) N77W17700 Lake Park Dr Apt 311, Menomonee Falls, WI 53051
DOWNS, Thomas Alexander (CFla) 390 Lake Lenelle Drive, Chuluota, FL 32766
✠ **DOYLE**, C Andrew (Bp of Tex 2009-) 1225 Texas Ave, Houston, TX 77002
DOYLE, Henry Lovelle (Minn) 1000 Shumway Ave, Faribault, MN 55021
DOYLE, Katherine (Ky) Calvary Episcopal Church, 821 S 4th St, Louisville, KY 40203
DOYLE, Margaret (Ala) 429 Cloudland Dr, Hoover, AL 35226
DOYLE, Ralph Thomas (Mo) 1432 Kearney St, El Cerrito, CA 94530
DOYLE, Seamus Patrick (Ark) 1802 W Cambridge Dr, Harrison, AR 72601
DRACHLIS, David Bernard (Ala) 1103 Shades Cir Se, Huntsville, AL 35803
DRAEGER JR, Walter Raymond (WMich) 3957 Sherwood Forest Dr, Traverse City, MI 49686
DRAESEL JR, Herbert Gustav (NY) 215 W 84th St #515, New York, NY 10024
DRAKE, Betty Lorraine Miller (Fla) 100 S Palmetto Ave, Green Cove Springs, FL 32043
DRAKE, Deborah Rucki (Nwk) 380 Clifton Ave, Clifton, NJ 07011
DRAKE, Jo-Ann Jane (RI) 104 Lafayette St, Pawtucket, RI 02860

DRAKE, Lesley-Ann (At) 2160 Cooper Lake Rd SE, Smyrna, GA 30080
DRAKE, Leslie Sargent (USC) 1630 Silver Bluff Rd., Aiken, SC 29803
DRAPER, Richard Thorp (Ind) 11974 State Highway M26, Eagle Harbor, MI 49950
DRAZDOWSKI, Edna (Neb) 1217 10th Ave, Sidney, NE 69162
DREBERT, Kay Marie (CNY) 227 W Walnut Dr, Sturgeon Bay, WI 54235
DREBERT, Rebecca Ellen (CNY) Trinity Memorial Church, 44 Main St, Binghamton, NY 13905
DREIBELBIS, John LaVerne (Chi) 3317 Grant St, Evanston, IL 60201
DREISBACH, Christopher (Md) Old St. Paul's Episcopal Church, Charles & Saratoga, Baltimore, MD 21201
DRENNEN, Zachary Polk (WVa) c/o Katakwa Diocese, PO Box 68, Amagoro, 50244, Kenya
DRESBACH, Michael Garrick (ECR) 490 Vivienne Dr, Watsonville, CA 95076
DRESSEL, Marilyn Kaye (EMich) 3725 Woodside Dr, Traverse City, MI 49684
DRESSER, Deborah (NY) 105 Grand St, Newburgh, NY 12550
DREWRY, John Colin (EC) 2513 Confederate Dr, Wilmington, NC 28403
DRINKWATER, Gary G (Me) 132 Montello St., Lewiston, ME 04240
DRINKWATER, Michael Peter (RG) PO Box 1246, Albuquerque, NM 87103
DRINO, Jerry William (ECR) 14801 Whipple Ct, San Jose, CA 95127
DRISKILL, Lorinda Elizabeth (Tex) Trinity Episcopal Church, PO Box 777, Anahuac, TX 77514
DRIVER, Bess D (Az) 2137 W. University Ave., Flagstaff, AZ 86001
DROBIN, Frederick Anthony (NY) PO Box 126, Hopewell Junction, NY 12533
DROPPERS, Thomas (NC) 1503 Pepper Hill Rd, Greensboro, NC 27407
DROST, Patricia May (Eas)
DROSTE, Robert E (NJ) 911 Dowling Blvd, San Leandro, CA 94577
DRUBE, Bruce James (Ala) 1219 Quail Run Dr Sw, Jacksonville, AL 36265
DRUCE, Glenn Edward (NJ) Calle Meteoro 1169, Secc Jardines, Las Playas, Tijuana, Baja California 22500, Mexico
DRUMM, Elizabeth Prentice (Kan)
DRURY, Susan Rollins (Kan) 7311 Legler Road, Shawnee, KS 66217
DRYMON, John Aaron (Ark) P.O. Box 2255, Batesville, AR 72503
DRYNAN, Thomas Steele (Ore)
DRYSDALE, Jessie Cookson (Me) 136 Butterfield Landing Rd., Weston, ME 04424

DRYSDALE-SCHRUTH, Sherry (Minn) Grace Memorial Episcopal Church, Po Box 27, Wabasha, MN 55981
DUBAY, Joseph Arthur (Ore) 1805 NW 34th Ave, Portland, OR 97210
DUBOIS, Charles Holgate (NJ) 33509 Anns Choice Way, Warminster, PA 18974
DUBOSE, Georgia Caldwell (WVa) Po Box 999, Harpers Ferry, WV 25425
DUBOSE, Jerry Davis (SC) 9540 Marlboro Ave, Barnwell, SC 29812
DUCKWORTH, Bonnie Wagner (NC)
DUCKWORTH, Penelope Tulleys (Cal) Trinity Cathedral, 81 North Second Street, San Jose, CA 94115
DUDLEY, Michael DeVere (O) 28 Perry Place, Canandaigua, NY 14424
DUDLEY JR, Thomas Lee (USC) 134 Boscawen, Winchester, VA 22601
DUER, Don Rey (CFla) 2005 Harrison Ave, Orlando, FL 32804
DUERR, Robert Edward (Mass)
DUFF, Eric Towle Moore (The Episcopal NCal) 524 Old Wagon Road, Trinidad, CA 95570
DUFF, Lyndie (Wyo) 1117 West Ramshorn Boulevard, Box 844, Dubois, WY 82513
DUFFEY, Ben Rosebro (SVa) 1401 N High St., Apt. 102, Franklin, VA 23851
DUFFEY, William (Pa) 3300 Darby Rd, Cottage 304, Haverford, PA 19041
DUFFIELD, Suzanne Elaine (U) St Eliizabeth Episcopal Church, PO Box 100, Whiterocks, UT 84085
DUFFTY, Bryan (ECR) 3020 Daurine Ct, Gilroy, CA 95020
DUFFUS, Cynthia Slaughter (Lex) 48 W High St, Mt Sterling, KY 40353
DUFFY, Christopher Gregory (NJ) 338 Ewingville Rd., Trenton, NJ 08628
DUFFY, Glenn Alan (Eas) 63 Battersea Rd., Berlin, MD 21811
DUFORD, Donald John (Mich) 16889 Club Drive, Southgate, MI 48195
DUFOUR, Matthew John (Ak) PO Box 773223, Eagle River, AK 99577
DUGAN II, Haynes Webster (Okla) 305 Camino Norte, Altus, OK 73521
DUGAN, Jeffrey Scott (Ct) 102 Seabury Drive, Bloomfield, CT 06002
DUGAN, Raymond P (Az) 534 W Wilshire Dr, Phoenix, AZ 85003
DUGARD, Debra Harris (WTenn) Emmanuel Episcopal Church, 4150 Boeingshire Dr, Memphis, TN 38116
DUGGAN, Joe F (The Episcopal NCal) 1644 Shadow Wood Road, Reno, NV 93103
DUGGAR, Marilyn Elaine (Ak) St Mark's Episcopal Church, PO Box 469, Nenana, AK 99760
DUGGER, Clinton George (Alb) Po Box 148, New Lebanon, NY 12125
DUGGER, Rita Jacqueline Carney (WNY)
DUGGER, Tracy Michelle (CFla)

DUGGIN, Sarah Helene (WA) 3240 O St NW, Washington, DC 20007

DUGGINS, Gordon Hayes (NY) P.O. Box 670, Colfax, NC 27235

DUGHI, Lorraine Mazury (Nwk)

DUH, Michael Yung-che (Tai) 952 Sec 2 Chading Road Chading, Kaohsiung Hsien 85202, Taiwan, China

DUKE, Cecilia Bliley (At) 597 Haralson Dr Sw, Lilburn, GA 30047

DUKE, James Brandon (At) 5400 Stewart Mill Rd, Douglasville, GA 30135

DUKES, John Edmund (At) 626 Mississippi Ave, Signal Mountain, TN 37377

DUKES, Lynne Adair (Slane) (WMich) 115 3rd St S Apt 913, Jacksonville Beach, FL 32250

DULFER, John Guidi (NY) 110 W 15th St Apt 1, New York, NY 10011

DULGAR, Sandra (Nev)

DULL, Stanley Lynn (Pa) 2215 Palm Tree Dr, Punta Gorda, FL 33950

DUMKE, Barbara A (Colo) 11684 Eldorado St Nw, Coon Rapids, MN 55433

DUMKE, Edward John (Cal) 805 Barneson Ave, San Mateo, CA 94402

DUMOLT, Elizabeth Ann (Los) 122 S. California Ave., Monrovia, CA 91016

DUNAGAN, Joe K (SwVa) 116 Alabama Ave, Macon, GA 31204

DUNAGAN, Katherine K (SwVa) 1 Mountain Ave SW, Roanoke, VA 24016

DUNBAR, Donald Machell (Mass) 160 Longmeadow Rd, Fairfield, CT 06824

DUNBAR, Gavin Gunning (Ga) 1 W Macon St, Savannah, GA 31401

DUNBAR, Julia Brown (WMass) 20 Whitney Ave, Cambridge, MA 02139

DUNBAR, Pamela Virginia Waite (Dal) 9221 Flickering Shadow Dr, Dallas, TX 75243

DUNBAR, Philip Craig (CFla) 2505 Gramercy Dr, Deltona, FL 32738

DUNBAR, Robert B (USC) PO Box 36155, Rock Hill, SC 29732

DUNCAN, Barbara Tompkins (WA) 8103 Langley Dr, Glen Allen, VA 23060

DUNCAN, Carol Craig (Pa) 8031 Roanoke St, Philadelphia, PA 19118

DUNCAN, Christopher Ray (Tex) PO Box 5176, Austin, TX 78763

DUNCAN, David (Los) 4640 Wooddduck Ln, Salt Lake City, UT 84117

DUNCAN, Hugh C (Ida) 5120 W Overland Rd PMB-276, Boise, ID 83705

DUNCAN, J(ames) Bruce (Los) 45 Chestnut St Unit A, North Adams, MA 01247

DUNCAN, Janice Eileen (NwPa) 870 N Buhl Farm Dr, Hermitage, PA 16148

DUNCAN, John L (The Episcopal NCal) 110 San Benito Avenue, Aptos, CA 95003

✠ **DUNCAN II**, Philip Menzie (Ret Bp of CGC 2015-) Diocese Of The Central Gulf Coast, P.O. Box 13330, Pensacola, FL 32591

DUNCAN, Rosemarie Logan (WA) 1329 Hamilton St Nw, Washington, DC 20011

DUNCAN, Rudolph Atherton (The Episcopal Church in Haw) 46-082 Puulena St Apt 1221, Kaneohe, HI 96744

DUNCAN, Shawn P (LI) 722 E 22nd St, Brooklyn, NY 11210

DUNCAN, Victoria (LI) Office For Transition Ministry, 815 2nd Ave, New York, NY 10017

DUNCAN-O'NEAL III, Bill M. (Ark) 9669 Wedd St, Overland Park, KS 66212

DUNCAN-PROBE, DeDe (Va) 11544 Clara Barton Dr., Fairfax Station, VA 22039

DUNCANSON, Frederick Philip (NY) 6 Long Meadow Drive, Airmont, NY 10952

DUNHAM, Richard Eldon (WTex) 4137 Harry St, Corpus Christi, TX 78411

DUNKERLEY, James Hobson (Chi) 6033 N Sheridan Rd Apt 44B, Chicago, IL 60660

DUNKLE, Kurt Hughes (Fla)

DUNKS, Andrew A (Va) Saint Bartholomew's Church, 10627 Patterson Ave, Richmond, VA 23238

DUNLAP, Daniel K (Eas) 715 Carrell St., Tomball, TX 77375

DUNLAP, D(ennis) Joe (Chi) 326 W. Northland Ave, Peoria, IL 61614

DUNLAP, Eunice R (Del) 403 Northview Dr, Fayetteville, NC 28303

DUNLAP, Garland Edward (Va) 207 Branner Ave, Winchester, VA 22601

DUNLAP, Mary Balfour Van Zandt (Ala) 431 10th St NW, Fayette, AL 35555

DUNLOP, William Henry (Mil) 413 S 2nd St, Watertown, WI 53094

DUNN JR, Carlton Willard (NJ) St Andrew's Church, 121 High St, Mount Holly, NJ 08060

DUNN, Deborah (Los) 402 S Lincoln St, Santa Maria, CA 93458

DUNN III, D(ouglas) (SVa) 2000 Huguenot Trl, Powhatan, VA 23139

DUNN, Douglas Robert (Colo) 1270 Poplar St, Denver, CO 80220

DUNN, Frank Gasque (WA) St Stephen and the Incarnation Parish, 1525 Newton St NW, Washington, DC 20010

DUNN, G(eorge) Mervyn (Ga) 8 Woodbridge Crescent, Kanata, ON K2M 2N6, Canada

DUNN, Matilda Eeleen Greene (ETenn) 7013 Rocky Trl, Chattanooga, TN 37421

DUNN, Patrick Hall (Miss) 4030 Perch Point Dr, Mobile, AL 36605

DUNN, Prentiss Carroll (La)

DUNN, Robert Ellis (Oly) Po Box 1377, Granite Falls, WA 98252

DUNN, Sarah Amelia (WMass) 14 Boltwood Ave, Amherst, MA 01002

DUNN, Sharon Kay Estey (Nev) 3500 San Mateo Ave, Reno, NV 89509

DUNN, William Edward (Los) 1803 Highland Hollow Dr # 559, Conroe, TX 77304

DUNNAM, Thomas Mark (Eur) Via Bernardo Rucellai 9, Firenze, 50123, Italy

DUNNAN, Donald Stuart (Md) Saint James School, Saint James, MD 21781

DUNNAVANT, Charles Randall (Tenn) 817 Stonebrook Blvd, Nolensville, TN 37135

DUNNETT, Walter McGregor (Chi) 2127 Hallmark Ct, Wheaton, IL 60187

DUNNING, Jane Romeyn (WMass) 44 Main St, Shelburne Falls, MA 01370

DUNNING, William Melbourne (Md) 1612 Trebor Ct, Lutherville, MD 21093

DUNNINGTON, Michael Gerard (Mo) 1620 Forestview Ridge Ln, Ballwin, MO 63021

DUNPHY, Martha-Jane (NY) 190 Pinewood Rd Apt 78, Hartsdale, NY 10530

DUNST, Earl Walter (Mil) 8121 N Seneca Rd, Milwaukee, WI 53217

DUPLANTIER, David Allard (La) 2037 South Carrollton Avenue, New Orleans, LA 70118

DUPLESSIE, Thomas Frederick (Me) 27 Butters Rd, Exeter, ME 04435

DUPREE, Charles T (Ind) 111 S. Grant St., Bloomington, IN 47408

DUPREE, H(Ugh) Douglas (Ga) 325 N Market St, Jacksonville, FL 32202

DUPREY, David Luke (Wyo) 1 S Tschirgi St, Sheridan, WY 82801

DU PRIEST, Travis Talmadge (Mil) 508 DeKoven, Racine, WI 53403

✠ **DUQUE-GOMEZ**, Francisco Jose (Bp of Colom 2001-) Calle 122-A #1211, Bogota, Colombia

✠ **DURACIN**, Jean Zache (Bp of Hai 2003-) Box 1309, Port-Au-Prince, Haiti

DURAIKANNU, Yesupathan (Colo) St.James' Church, 1 St. James' Place, Goshen, NY 10924

DURAND, Sally Elaine (Az) 7813 N. Via De La Luna, Scottsdale, AZ 85258

DURANT, Jack Davis (NC) 3001 Old Orchard Rd, Raleigh, NC 27607

D'URBANO, Faith Jeanne (Be) 340 W. Orange Street, Lancaster, PA 17603

DURBIDGE, Andrew John (LI) 50 Cathedral Ave, Garden City, NY 11530

DURE, Lucy Ann Craig (Nwk) 46 Montrose Ave, Verona, NJ 07044

DURHAM, Eugenia M (Az) 1275 S Heritage Pl, Safford, AZ 85546

DURHAM, Martha Hemenway (Chi) St Mary's Episcopal Church, 306 S Prospect Ave, Park Ridge, IL 60068

DURNING, Michael Peter (SwFla) 12002 Summer Meadow Dr, Bradenton, FL 34202

DURREN, Paula Ellen (WMich) 19 S Jameson St, New Buffalo, MI 49117

DURST, Lester Earle (CGC) 5409 Twin Creeks Dr, Valrico, FL 33596

DURST, Ted E (Chi) 4900 N Marine Dr Apt 411, Chicago, IL 60640

DUTCHER, Katherine Grant (Okla) St Andrew's Episcopal Church, PO Box 1256, Lawton, OK 73502

DUTTON-GILLETT, Matthew Richard (Cal) 330 Ravenswood, Menlo Park, CA 94025

DUVAL, Linda Marie (NY) 16 Boulder Ave, Kingston, NY 12401

DUVAL JR, Richard Henri (Episcopal SJ) 813 Lassen View Dr, Lake Almanor, CA 96137

DUVAL, Robert Joseph (Ct) 3121 St. Stephens Ln., Whitehall, PA 18052

✠ **DUVALL**, Charles Farmer (Ret Bp of CGC 2001-) 104 Wildeoak Trl, Columbia, SC 29223

DUVALL, Robert Welsh (Va) 704 Holloway Circle N, North Myrtle Beach, SC 29582

DUVEAUX, Irnel (Hai) Box 1309, Port-Au-Prince, Haiti

DUVERT, Pierre-Andre (NY) 331 Hawthorne St, Brooklyn, NY 11225

DWARF, Lindsey Craig (ND)

DWIGHT, Robert Bolman (SO) 115 W Monument Ave, #1201, Dayton, OH 45402

D'WOLF JR, James Francis (Kan) 6976 Pintail Dr # 113, Fishers, IN 46038

DWYER, Beatrice Mary (Eau) Christ Church Cathedral, 510 S Farwell St, Eau Claire, WI 54701

DWYER, John F (Minn) 1772 Church St Nw, Washington, DC 20036

DWYER, Martin James (Ida) 3 Park Pl, Garden Valley, ID 83622

DWYER, Michael William (NI) 1101 Park Drive, Munster, IN 46321

DWYER, Patricia Marie (Be)

DWYER, Thomas Patrick Jonathan (CGC) 800 22nd St, Port St Joe, FL 32456

DYAKIW, Alexander Raymond (CPa) St John's Episc Ch, 120 W Lamb St, Bellefonte, PA 16823

DYCHE, Bradley Callaway (NY) 6 Old Post Road North, Croton on Hudson, NY 10520

DYER, Alex (Ct) 51 Crown St, New Haven, CT 06510

DYER, Susan Jeinine (Wyo) PO Box 399, Saratoga, WY 82331

DYER, Timothy D (NwPa) 444 Pennsylvania Ave W, Warren, PA 16365

DYER-CHAMBERLAIN, Margaret Elizabeth (Ca)

DYKE, Nicolas Roger David (Tex) 3815 Echo Mountain Dr, Humble, TX 77345

DYKES, Deborah White (Miss) 3524 Old Canton Rd, Jackson, MS 39216

DYKSTRA, Danny Jon (Ky) 9616 Westport Rd, Louisville, KY 40241

DYNER, Marthe F (NH)

DYSON, Elizabeth Wheatley (Mass) 451 Birchbark Dr, Hanson, MA 02341

DYSON, Martha Lynn (Vt)

DYSON, Thack Harris (CGC) 28788 N Main St, Daphne, AL 36526

E

EADE, Christopher K (Los) 1031 Bienveneda Ave, Pacific Palisades, CA 90272

EADE, Kenneth Charles (Va) 6465 Calamar Dr, Cumming, GA 30040

EADES, Susan Tindall (Ia) 218 E Chapman St, Dillon, MT 59725

EADS, Charles Carroll (Md) 16 Swantamont Rd, Swanton, MD 21561

EAGER, Donald Bates (SO) 2102 Scenic Dr Ne, Lancaster, OH 43130

EAGLEBULL, Harold L (Minn) Po Box 1149, Cass Lake, MN 56633

EAKINS, Hope Howlett (Ct) 25 Scarborough St, Hartford, CT 06105

EAKINS, William (Ct) 25 Scarborough St, Hartford, CT 06105

EAMES, Marc Gilbert (Mass) 28 Pleasant St., The Church of the Advent, Medfield, MA 02052

EANES II, William Raymond (SwVa) St James Episcopal Church, 4515 Delray St NW, Roanoke, VA 24012

EARL, John Keith (WNC) 1650 5th St Nw, Hickory, NC 28601

EARLE, Charles Douglas (WTex) 7302 Robin Rest Dr, San Antonio, TX 78209

EARLE, Leigh Christensen (Wyo) 1745 Westridge Ct, Casper, WY 82604

EARLE, Mary Colbert (WTex) 7302 Robin Rest Dr, San Antonio, TX 78209

EARLE, Patty Ann Trapp (NC) Po Box 1103, Statesville, NC 28687

EARLE III, Richard Tilghman (SwFla) 555 13th Avenue NE, Saint Petersburg, FL 33701

EARLS, John G (USC)

EARLY, Nancy Davis (WA) 402 Montrose Ave, Catonsville, MD 21228

EASLEY, Alexandra (Tex)

EASLEY, Barbara Ann (Ia) 605 Avenue E, Fort Madison, IA 52627

EASLEY, Julia Kathleen (Ia) 26 E Market St, Iowa City, IA 52245

EASTER, James Hamilton (Okla) 11308 N Miller Ave, Oklahoma City, OK 73120

EASTER, Mary Kathleen (WMo) 973 Evergreen Ave, Hollister, MO 65672

EASTER, William Burton (Chi) 594 Eastlake Dr Se, Rio Rancho, NM 87124

EASTERDAY, Pamela Kay (CFla) 1830 S. Babcock St, Melbourne, FL 32901

EASTERDAY, Stephen Wayne (CFla) 1830 S. Babcock St., Melbourne, FL 32901

EASTERLING JR, Richard Brooks (La) 4600 St. Charles Avenue, New Orleans, LA 70115

EASTERLING SR, William Ramsay (WLa) 504 Tech Dr, Ruston, LA 71270

EASTES, Suzanne Hardey (Mo) 312 Clayton Crossing Dr., #108, Ellisville, MO 63011

EASTHILL, Christopher Mark (Eur)

✠ **EASTMAN**, A(lbert) Theodore (Ret Bp of Md 1994-) 3440 S Jefferson St, #1481, Falls Church, VA 22041

EASTMAN, Susan Grove (NC) 4604 Brodog Ter, Hurdle Mills, NC 27541

EASTON, Elizabeth Lavender (Neb) 9302 Blondo St., Omaha, NE 68134

EASTON, Stanley Evan (Ala) 1104 Church Avenue Northeast, Jacksonville, AL 36265

EASTWOOD, John Harrison (Cal) 30 Ogden Ave, San Francisco, CA 94110

EATON, Albert Edward (EC) PO Box 337, Swansboro, NC 28584

EATON, Carol Ann (EC)

EATON, Cornelia Kay (NAM) PO Box 720, Farmington, NM 87499

EATON, Karen Lee Abraham (Oly) PO Box 753, Port Townsend, WA 98368

EATON, Laura Mary (NMich)

✠ **EATON**, Peter David (SeFla) 525 NE 15th Street, Miami, FL 33132

EATON, Robert G (Episcopal SJ) 1571 E Glenwood Ave, Tulare, CA 93274

EATON, William Albert (SeFla) 10914 Nw 8th Ct, Plantation, Fl. 33324

EAVES, Lindon John (Va) 10835 Old Prescott Rd, Richmond, VA 23238

EAVES, Susan Nuthall (Va) 3207 Hawthorne Ave, Richmond, VA 23222

EBEL, Ann Teresa (PR)

EBENS, Richard Frank (Mass) 4-C Autumn Dr, Hudson, MA 01749

EBERHARDT, Karen Anne (Nwk) 18 Ute Ave., Lake Hiawatha, NJ 07034

EBERHARDT, Timothy Charles (Vt) 2460 Braintree Hill Rd, Braintree, VT 05060

EBERLE, Bill (Va) P.O. Box 367, Rixeyville, VA 22737

EBERLY, G(eorge) Douglas (NJ) 500 19th St, Ocean City, NJ 08226

EBERMAN, John Fowler (WA) 703 Agawam St, Elizabeth City, NC 27909

EBERT, Bernhard (Colo)

ECCLES, Mark Eldon (Ia) 1619 21st St Nw, Cedar Rapids, IA 52405

ECCLES, M.E. (Chi) 4144 N. Sacramento Ave., Chicago, IL 60618

ECHAZABAL MARTINEZ, Livan (SwFla) 6709 N Nebraska Ave, Tampa, FL 33604

ECHOLS, Mary W (SwFla) 917 11th St N, Naples, FL 34102

ECHOLS, William Joseph (WLa) 104 Ingram St, Lake Providence, LA 71254

ECKARDT, Robert Remick (At) 720 Whitemere Ct Nw, Atlanta, GA 30327

ECKART JR, Richard Joseph (Roch) 38 Dale Rd, Rochester, NY 14625

ECKEL, Malcolm David (Mass) 11 Griggs Ter., Brookline, MA 02446

ECKIAN, Deirdre A (WA) 4000 Tunlaw Road NW Apt 1005, Washington, DC 20007

ECKSTEIN, Carol Garvey (The Episcopal NCal) Po Box 534, Bayside, CA 95524

EDDY, Charles H. (Ak) P.O. Box 747, Willow, AK 99688

EDDY, Diane Lynn (Ia) 1458 Locust St, Dubuque, IA 52001

EDDY, Elizabeth (NJ) 913 Fassler Ave, Pacifica, CA 94044

EDDY, William Welles (Mass) PO Box 3615, Waquoit, MA 02536

EDELMAN, Walter Lucian (SanD) 17427 Gibraltar Ct, San Diego, CA 92128

EDEN, Jonathan T (Mass) 865 Madison Ave, New York, NY 10021

EDEN, Kathryn O (CNY) 120 W 5th St, Oswego, NY 13126

EDENS III, Henry Harman (NC) 8011 Douglas Ave, Dallas, TX 75225

EDINGTON, Mark David Wheeler (Mass) PO Box 455, Hardwick, MA 01037, Dominican Republic

EDLEMAN JR, Samuel Warren (Md) 1257 Weller Way, Westminster, MD 21158

EDMAN, David Arthur (FtW) 159 Acorn Hollow Ln, Ardmore, OK 73401

EDMAN, Elizabeth Marie (Nwk) 690 Fort Washington Ave., apt 1L, New York, NY 10040

EDMANDS II, Frank A (SO) 55 S Vernon Lane, Fort Thomas, KY 41075

EDMINSTER, Beverley Beadle (Az) 1810 E Camino Cresta, Tucson, AZ 85718

EDMISTER, Jeffery Ray (WNY) Christ Episcopal Church, 7145 Fieldcrest Dr, Lockport, NY 14094

EDMISTON, Alan James (LI) 3939 Ocean Dr, Vero Beach, FL 32963

EDMONDS, Curtis M (Nev)

EDMONDS, John B (NY) Po Box 1535, Blue Hill, ME 04614

EDMONDSON, Emily F (SwVa)

EDMONDSON, Stephen Bud (Va) 3939 Seminary Rd, Alexandria, VA 22304

EDMUNDS, Robert Douglas (Mass) Po Box 2862, Edgartown, MA 02539

EDSON, Heidi L (Vt) 6795 W 19th Pl Apt 304, Lakewood, CO 80214

EDSON, John B (CPa) 622 S York Rd, Dillsburg, PA 17019

EDSON, Larry (Eau) 608 Madison St, Stanley, WI 54768

EDSON, Robert Bruce (Mass) 4 Home Meadows Ln, Hingham, MA 02043

EDWARD, Baskaran John (NY) 8 Sunnyside Ave, Pleasantville, NY 10570

EDWARD, Gadi Michael (ND) 120 8th St S, Moorhead, MN 56560

EDWARDS, Bonnie E (WMich) St. Barnabas Episcopal Church, 929 East Centre Avenue, Portage, MI 49002

EDWARDS, Carl Norris (Md)

✠ **EDWARDS**, Dan Thomas (Bp of Nev 2008-) 9480 S Eastern Ave Ste 236, Las Vegas, NV 89123

EDWARDS, Douglas Brian (Los) 4255 Harbour Island Ln, Oxnard, CA 93035

EDWARDS, Dwight Woodbury (ECR) Po Box 853, Pacific Grove, CA 93950

EDWARDS, Fitzroy Foster (NY) 72 Carnegie Ave, Elmont, NY 11003

EDWARDS, Halbert Daniel (Okla) 1728 NW 42nd St, Oklahoma City, OK 73118

EDWARDS, James Dennison (LI) 4 S Aspen Pl, Lewisburg, PA 17837

EDWARDS, James Lloyd (USC) 4628 Datura Rd, Columbia, SC 29205

EDWARDS, James Paul (Nev) 1400 Ebbetts Dr, Reno, NV 89503

EDWARDS, Jamie E (NC) 1902 N Holden Rd, Greensboro, NC 27408

EDWARDS II, J(ustin) Sargent (Episcopal SJ) 765 Mesa View Dr Spc 98, Arroyo Grande, CA 93420

EDWARDS, Kathleen Louise (Minn)

EDWARDS, Laura MacFarland (WA) 13118 Collingwood Ter, Silver Spring, MD 20904

EDWARDS, Lydia A (NJ) 81 Hillside Ave, Metuchen, NJ 08840

EDWARDS, Lynn Chester (Pgh) 611 West St, Pittsburgh, PA 15221

EDWARDS, Nancy Beltz (The Episcopal NCal)

EDWARDS JR, O(tis) C(arl) (WNC) 115 Murphy Hill Rd, Weaverville, NC 28787

EDWARDS, Paul David (Los) 734 W Maplewood Ave, Fullerton, CA 92832

EDWARDS, Rebecca (Cal) 4321 Eastgate Mall, San Diego, CA 92121

EDWARDS, Robert Daniel (Los) 31641 La Novia, San Juan, CA 92675

EDWARDS, Terry Ann (SVa) 2515 Marshall Ave, Newport News, VA 23607

EDWARDS JR, Theodore Whitfield (SwFla) 114 John Pott Dr, Williamsburg, VA 23188

EDWARDS III, Tilden Hampton (WA) 9615 Page Ave, Bethesda, MD 20814

EDWARDS, Whitney Z (Ct) St Jame's Episcopal, 1205 W Franklin St, Richmond, VA 23220

EDWARDS, William Glover (WNC) 38 Wildwood Ave, Asheville, NC 28804

EDWARDS, William Patrick (La) 12663 Perkins Rd, Baton Rouge, LA 70810

EDWARDS-ACTON, James Kendall (Los) 727 Olympic Ave, Costa Mesa, CA 92626

EFFINGER, Richard W (SeFla) 141 S County Rd, Palm Beach, FL 33480

EGAN, Adam Dj (Alb) 16 Elsmere Ave, Delmar, NY 12054

EGBERT, David Allen (Okla) 2817 Natchez Trl, Edmond, OK 73012

EGBERT, Paula Sue (Ida) 5780 Millwright Ave, Boise, ID 83714

EGERTON, Karen Campbell (CFla) 1404 Chapman Cir, Winter Park, FL 32789

EGGER, Jon Anthony (WMo) 4334 Northern Avene Apt 2911, Kansas City, MO 64133

EHMER, Joseph Michael (NwT) 1802 Broadway, Lubbock, TX 79401

EHRICH, Thomas Lindley (NC) 505 W 54th St Apt 812, New York, NY 10019

EIBIN, Julian Raymond (Nwk) 284 Island Ave., Ramsey, NJ 07446

EICH III, W Foster (Ala) St Bartholomew's Episcopal Church, 1600 Darby Dr, Florence, AL 35630

EICHELBERGER JR, J Gary (USC) 10 N Church St, Greenville, SC 29601

EICHENLAUB, Patricia (Mich) 2745 Lake Pine Path Apt 219, Saint Joseph, MI 49085

EICHLER, Stephen (ETenn) 1151 Gudger Rd, Sewanee, TN 37375

EICHNER, James F (Oly)

EICK, John David (WMo) 8030 Ward Pkwy, Kansas City, MO 64114

EICK, Mary Herron (Ore) 11511 SW Bull Mountain Rd, Tigard, OR 97224

EICKWORT, Kathleen Ruth (WMich) 501 Se 50th Ave, Ocala, FL 34471

EIDAM JR, John Mahlon (SVa) 224 S Military Hwy, Norfolk, VA 23502

EIDSON, Robert George (Mich) 6257 Telegraph Road, Apt. 102, Bloomfield Hills, MI 48301

EIMAN, Amanda B (Kan) 405 N Broad St, Lansdale, PA 19446

EINERSON, Dean Alfred (FdL) 29 S Pelham St, Rhinelander, WI 54501

EISENSTADT-EVANS (Pa) 50 Fleming Drive, Glenmoore, PA 19343

EKBERG, Sean Armington (Okla) 210 E 9th St, Bartlesville, OK 74003

EKEVAG, Ellen Poole (Chi) 209 N Pine St, New Lenox, IL 60451

EKIZIAN, Hagop J (NY) 137 N Division St, Peekskill, NY 10566

EKLO, Thomas J (Minn) 8064 Golden Valley Rd, Golden Valley, MN 55427

EKLUND, Carolyn Hassig (Me) Episcopal Churc St Paul, Po Box 195, Brunswick, ME 04011

EKLUND, Virginia Jane Rouleau (Lex) 130 Winterhawk Rd, Danville, KY 40422

EKREM, Katherine Boyle (Mass) 12 White Pine Ln, Lexington, MA 02421

EKSTROM, Ellen Louise (Cal) 1017 Virginia Street, Berkeley, CA 94710

ELAM III, Walter L (CGC) 153 Orange Ave, Fairhope, AL 36532

ELBERFELD, Katherine Ann Fockele (At) 123 Church St NE # 150, Marietta, GA 30060

ELBERFELD, Richard Bradford (NwPa) 3105 Springland Terrace, Erie, PA 16506

ELCOCK, Frank Ulric (LI) 257 Leaf Ave, Central Islip, NY 11722

ELDER, Clayton Lee (WTex) 311 E Corpus Christi St, Beeville, TX 78102

ELDER, Paul Robert (Los) 580 Hilgard Ave, Los Angeles, CA 90024

ELDER, Robert Macrum (Va) 218 2nd St, Huntingdon, PA 16652

ELDER, Ruth Annette (Md) 4238 Pimlico Rd, Baltimore, MD 21215

ELDER-HOLIFIELD, Donna Ellen Carter (ECR) 64 San Pedro St, Salinas, CA 93901

ELDRIDGE, Barbara Adelle (CFla) 2143 Kings Cross St, Titusville, FL 32796

ELDRIDGE JR, Robert William (USC) Hq Forscom, 1777 Hardee Ave Sw, Fort Mcpherson, GA 30330

ELEK, Hentzi (Pa) 3625 Chapel Rd, Newtown Square, PA 19073

ELEY, Gary W (Vt) 33 Adams Ct, Burlington, VT 05401

ELFERT, Martin (Ore) 127 E 12th Ave, Spokane, WA 99202

ELFRING-ROBERTS, Jessica Lee Christine (Chi) Church of our Saviour, 530 W Fullerton Pkwy, Chicago, IL 60614

ELFVIN, Robert Roger (Ia) 8 Poinciana Lane, Palm Coast, FL 32164

ELIN, Darren Richard Strawn (SO) 100 Miami Ave, Terrace Park, OH 45174

ELIOT, Mary Ashley (Md) 6800 Oakland Mills Rd, Columbia, MD 21045

ELISEE, Jean R (Hai) 33 Mount Pleasant Ave Rm 120, West Orange, NJ 07052

ELKINS-WILLIAMS, Stephen John (NC) 100 Black Oak Pl, Chapel Hill, NC 27517

ELL, Marianne Sorge (Del) 4751 Highway 1804, Williston, ND 58801

ELLEDGE II, C Clyde (Mass) 54 Robert Road, Marblehead, MA 01945

ELLEDGE, Kathryn Nesbit (Mass) 54 Robert Road, Marblehead, MA 01945

ELLER, Ruth Elizabeth (U) 700 S Silver Ridge St Spc 85, Ridgecrest, CA 93555

ELLERY, Celia (NwT) 2661 Yale Ave, San Angelo, TX 76904

ELLESTAD, Charles Dwight (Lex) 837 Isaac Shelby Cir E, Frankfort, KY 40601

ELLEY, Eric M (WMass) PO Box 528, Somersville, CT 06072

ELLGREN, Neysa Anne (Ore) 11800 SW Military Ln, Portland, OR 97219

ELLINGBOE, Shirley Kay (RG) 5794 Ndcbu, Taos, NM 87571

ELLINGTON, Meta Louise Turkelson (NC) 521 Marlowe Rd, Raleigh, NC 27609

ELLINGTON, William Ferrell (Cal) 303 N West St, McAlester, OK 74501

ELLIOTT, Annie Kay Cumberland (Miss) 370 Old Agency Rd, Ridgeland, MS 39157

ELLIOTT, Barbara Ann (Minn) St Paul's Episcopal Church, 1710 E Superior St, Duluth, MN 55812

ELLIOTT, Beverley Florence (At) 5458 E Mountain St, Stone Mountain, GA 30083

ELLIOTT III, David Augustus (Miss) 205 Autumn Ridge Dr, Jackson, MS 39211

ELLIOTT, Gates Safford (Miss) Episcopal Diocese of Mississippi, 118 North Congress St, Jackson, MS 39201

ELLIOTT III, Harry A (Ct) Grace Episcopal Church, 311 Broad St, Windsor, CT 06095

ELLIOTT JR, James Edward (Ala) 2714 Hilltop Cir, Gadsden, AL 35904

ELLIOTT, James Lawrence (Ga) PO Box 864, Quitman, GA 31643

ELLIOTT, James Thom (The Episcopal NCal) 32339 109th Pl SE Apt 202, Auburn, WA 98092

ELLIOTT, Neil (Minn) 1262 Birch Pond Trail, White Bear Lake, MN 55110

ELLIOTT, Norman Henry Victor (Ak) 2401 Galewood St, Anchorage, AK 99508

ELLIOTT, Paul Alexander (At) 5458 E Mountain St, Stone Mountain, GA 30083

ELLIOTT, Paul C (At)

ELLIOTT III, Richard G (EC) 2322 Metts Ave, Wilmington, NC 28403

ELLIOTT, Robert James (O) 4141 Bayshore Blvd Apt 101, Tampa, FL 33611

ELLIOTT, Scott Fuller (Chi) 2222 W Belmont Ave, # 205, Chicago, IL 60618

ELLIOTT, William Tate (EMich) 6757 Middle Rd, Hope, MI 48628

ELLIS, Jane Fielding (Ala) 556 Mohave Cir, Huntington, CT 06484

ELLIS, Kassinda Rosalinda (LI)

ELLIS, Malcolm A (Md) 232 Saint Thomas Ln, Owings Mills, MD 21117

ELLIS, Michael Elwin (Fla) 6126 Cherry Lake Dr N, Jacksonville, FL 32258

ELLIS, Michael Warren (Md) 4803 Leybourne Dr, Hilliard, OH 43026

ELLIS, Richard Alvin (Ct) 15 Piper Rd Apt J313, Scarborough, ME 04074

ELLIS, Russell Ray (Vt) 328 Shore Rd, Burlington, VT 05408

ELLIS, Steven MacDonald (ECR) 318 Lee St, Santa Cruz, CA 95060

ELLIS, Walter L. (Tex) 2419 Lansing Cir, Pearland, TX 77584

ELLIS, William Joseph (NwPa) 222 Brisbin St, Houtzdale, PA 16651

ELLIS JR, William Robert (Spok) 128 E 12th Ave, Spokane, WA 99202

ELLISON, Monique A (Md) 6060 Charles Edward Terrace, Columbia, MD 21045

ELLSWORTH, Anne Katherine (Az) 6300 N Central Ave, Phoenix, AZ 85012

ELLSWORTH, Bradford Edwin (WMo) Po Box 160, Cabool, MO 65689

ELLSWORTH, Eleanor L (SanD) 2205 Caminito Del Barco, Del Mar, CA 92014

ELLSWORTH JR, Phillip Channing (WA) 10033 River Rd, Potomac, MD 20854

ELLSWORTH, Scott Anthony (Ida) 2887 Snowflake Dr, Boise, ID 83706

ELMER-ANTHONY, Betty Lou (Ak) 11641 Hebron Dr, Eagle River, AK 99577

ELMIGER-JONES, Mary Kathleen (Cal) St Timothy's Church, 1550 Diablo Rd, Danville, CA 94526

ELPHEE, David T (SwVa)

ELSBERRY, Terence Lynn (NY) PO Box 293, Bedford, NY 10506

ELSE, John David (Pgh) 272 Caryl Dr, Pittsburgh, PA 15236

ELSENSOHN, David Dirk (Ak) 1714 Edgecumbe Dr, Sitka, AK 99835

ELVIN, Peter Thurston (WMass) 35 Park St, Williamstown, MA 01267

ELWELL, Pamela (SO) 321 East Kanawha Ave, Columbus, OH 43214

ELWOOD, Fred(erick) Campbell (Mich) 1334 Riverside Dr, Buhl, ID 83316

ELWOOD, Richard Hugh (Tex) 308 E San Antonio St, Fredericksburg, TX 78624

ELY, Elizabeth Wickenberg (NC) "Dunwyck", 64 Peniel Road, Columbus, NC 28722

ELY, James Everett (Tex) 1700 Golden Ave, Bay City, TX 77414

✠ **ELY**, Thomas C (Bp of Vt 2001-) 11 Rock Point Rd, Burlington, VT 05408

EMENHEISER, D(avid) Edward (WMich) 174 Wakulat Ln, Traverse City, MI 49686

EMERSON, E Angela (Vt) Gates Briggs Blgd. Ste. 315, White River Junction, VT 05001

EMERSON, James Carson (Q) 1625 Hershey Ct, Columbia, MO 65202

EMERSON, Jason Daniel (Neb) 9932 Bedford Ave., Omaha, NE 68134

EMERSON, Keith Roger (SVa) St. Paul's Church, 213 N. Main Street, Suffolk, VA 23434

EMERSON, Mary Beth (Va) 8991 Brook Rd, McLean, VA 22102

EMERSON, R Clark (ECR) 1412 Maysun Ct, Campbell, CA 95008

EMERY, Dana Karen (Minn) 1400 Corbett Rd, Detroit Lakes, MN 56501

EMERY, Harold Alfred (SVa) 2363 Chapel Ridge Pl Apt 2B, Salina, KS 67401

EMGE, Kevin Ray (Ia)

EMMERT, John H (CPa) 648 Laurel View Dr., Manheim, PA 17545

EMPSALL, Glenda Mascarella (Spok) 501 E Wallace Ave, Coeur D Alene, ID 83814

EMRICH III, Frederick Ernest (WMass) 7 Smith St, P.O. Box 318, North Haven, ME 04853

EMRICH III, Richard S M (Chi) 755 Hinchman Rd, Baroda, MI 49101

EMRY, Anne D (Ore) 1444 Liberty St SE, Salem, OR 97302

ENCARNACION-CARABALLO, Felix Antonio (DR (DomRep)) C/ Santiago 114, Santo Iomingo, Dominican Republic

ENCINOSA, Christina Dolores (SeFla) 68 Paxford Ln, Boynton Beach, FL 33426

ENDICOTT, Rachel Faith (Oly) 15114 SE 48th Dr., Bellevue, WA 98006

ENGDAHL JR, Frederick Robert (Mich) 6490 Clarkston Rd., Clarkston, MI 48346

ENGELHARDT, Hanns Christian Joachim (Eur) Stephanienstrasse, 72, Karlsruhe, 76133, Germany

ENGELHORN, Paula Elaine (Chi)

ENGELS, Allen Robert (Colo) 3081 Evanston Ave, Grand Junction, CO 81504

ENGELS, Jimichael (Mass) 1190 Adams St Apt 213, Dorchester Center, MA 02124

ENGFER, Michael John (Nev) 4201 W Washington Ave, Las Vegas, NV 89107

ENGLAND, Edward Gary (ETenn) 408 Oak Ave, South Pittsburg, TN 37380

ENGLAND, Gary William (Ky) 7404 Arrowwood Rd, Louisville, KY 40222

ENGLAND, Loy David (WTex) Po Box 1025, Pflugerville, TX 78691

ENGLAND, Margaret Jefferson (Az) 11058 Portobelo Dr, San Diego, CA 92124

ENGLAND JR, Nick Arnold (WVa) 411 Prichard St, Williamson, WV 25661

ENGLAND, O Bryan (WMo) 315 E Partridge Ave, Independence, MO 64055

ENGLE, Cynthia L (Tex) 414 E. McAlpine, Navasota, TX 77868

ENGLE SR, Mark (NMich) 22975 Pine Lake Rd, Battle Creek, MI 49014

ENGLEBY, Matthew S (NJ) 379 Mount Harmony Rd, Bernardsville, NJ 07924

ENGLISH, Allison Rainey (Los) 504 N Camden Dr, Beverly Hills, CA 90210

ENGLISH, Ann Cantwell (Spok) Rr 1 Box 241-B, Touchet, WA 99360

ENGLISH, Carrie R (Fla) 11601 Longwood Key Dr W, Jacksonville, FL 32218

ENGLISH, John Lyle (WMich) 1045 Woodrow Ave Nw, Grand Rapids, MI 49504

ENGLISH, Linda Jean (WK) 114 W Roosevelt, Phoenix, AZ 85003

ENGLISH, Thomas Ronald (Ore) 2530 Fairmount Blvd, Eugene, OR 97403

ENGLISH, Tristan Clifford (Wyo) 4700 S Poplar St, Casper, WY 82601

ENGLISH, William H (Roch) 248 Commons Lane, Foster City, CA 94404

ENGLUND, David (The Episcopal NCal) 1624 10th St, Oroville, CA 95965

ENGLUND, Henry C (NJ) 90 Dillon Way, Washington Crossing, PA 18977

ENGSTROM, Marilyn Jean (Wyo) 1714 Mitchell St, Laramie, WY 82072

ENGWALL, Douglas Brian (Ct) Trinity Episcopal Church, 55 River Rd, Collinsville, CT 06019

ENNIS, Kathleen Knox (SwFla) 6180 Golden Oaks Ln, Naples, FL 34119

ENSOR, A(melia) Jeanne (Oly) 8235 36th Ave Ne, Seattle, WA 98115

ENSOR, Peter Crane (Los) 111 Westview Drive, Dubois, WY 82513

EOYANG JR, Thomas (Pa) 6622 Germantown Ave Unit 3A, Philadelphia, PA 19119

EPES, Gail E (Va) 1200 N Quaker Ln, Alexandria, VA 22302

EPPERSON, Christopher (SVa) PO Box 3520, Williamsburg, VA 23187

EPPLE, Jogues Fred (Okla) 1830 University Ave W, Apt 201, Saint Paul, MN 55104

EPPLY-SCHMIDT, Joanne (NJ) 26 Nelson Ridge Rd, Princeton, NJ 08540

✠ **EPTING**, Carl Christopher (Ret Bp of Ia 2000-) 3026 Middle Rd, Davenport, IA 52803

ERB, Edward Kenneth (Be) 827 Church St., Honesdale, PA 18431

ERDMAN, Daniel Le Roy (Mich) 929 E Hawthorne Loop, Webb City, MO 64870

ERDMAN, Jonathan Mark (Ky) 821 S 4th St, Louisville, KY 40203

ERDMAN, Nathan Andrew (Md) St Thomas Episcopal Church, 232 Saint Thomas Ln, Owings Mills, MD 21117

ERHARD, Michael Edward Charles (Cal) 2300 Bay St Apt 302, San Francisco, CA 94123

ERICKSON, David L (Los) 1818 Monterey Blvd, Hermosa Beach, CA 90254

ERICKSON, Frederick David (Los) 219 Hortter Street, Philadelphia, PA 19144

ERICKSON, Gregory Charles (WNC) 1359 Lamb Mountain Rd, Hendersonville, NC 28792

ERICKSON, Heather B (Los) St Margaret's Episcopal Church, 31641 La Novia Ave, San Juan Capistrano, 92675

ERICKSON JR, Joseph Austin (Los) 764 Valparaiso Dr, Claremont, CA 91711

ERICKSON, Kenneth Lawrence (Mich) 711 Wooddale Rd, Bloomfield Hills, MI 48301

ERICKSON, Lori Jean (Ia)

ERICKSON, Mary Cobb (Wyo) PO Box 1690, Jackson, WY 83001

ERICKSON, Mary Kahrs (At) 4 Jones St, Cartersville, GA 30120

ERICKSON, Richard Paul (Alb) 901 Ridge View Circle, Castleton-On-Hudson, NY 12033

ERICKSON, Scott (Cal) 420 Eureka St, San Francisco, CA 94114

ERICKSON, Winifred Jean (NMich) 1506 Us #2 Highway West, Crystal Falls, MI 49920

ERICSON, William Delmer (Mich) Po Box 267, Dewitt, MI 48820

ERIXSON, Lorna Lloyd (At) 316 Spyglass Hill Dr, Perry, GA 31069

ERQUIAGA, Trudel Nada (Nev) 1128 Green Valley Drive, Fallon, NV 89406

ERSKINE, John (Jack) Arthur (EO) 69787 Pine Ridge Road, Sisters, OR 97759

ERVOLINA, Timothy Mark (USC) 120 Ridgewood Cir, Greenwood, SC 29649

ERWIN JR, James Walter (NY) 5 Second St, Warwick, NY 10990

ERWIN, Virginia Gilbert (Los) 2157 Birdie Dr, Banning, CA 92220

ESBENSHADE, Burnell True (Mo) 1116 E Linden Ave, Saint Louis, MO 63117

ESCOTT, Raymond Philip (WNC) 12 Misti Leigh Ln, Waynesville, NC 28786

ESKAMIRE-JACKSON, Joyce (La) 1313 Esplanade Ave, New Orleans, LA 70116

ESONU, Clinton Chukwuemeka (WA) 2031 Powhatan Rd, Hyattsville, MD 20782

ESPESETH, Cynthia A. (Oly) 13613 178TH Ave NE, Redmond, WA 98052

ESPINOSA-AREVALO, Carlos (EcuC) Apartado Postal 10-04-21, Atuntaqui-Imbabura, Ecuador

ESPOSITO, Catherine Patricia (NJ) 14 Edgemere Dr, Matawan, NJ 07747

ESTES, Diane Manguno (La)

ESTES, James Gray (SanD) 1427 Rimrock Dr, Escondido, CA 92027

ESTES, Robert Theodore (WMo) 425 East Cherry St, Nevada, MO 64772

ESTES, William Thomas (FtW) Grace Church, 405 Glenmar Ave, Monroe, LA 71201

ESTEY, Lawrence Mitchell (Me) 3 Greenhead Lane, PO Box 646, Stonington, ME 04681

ESTIL, Colbert (Hai) c/o Diocese of Haiti, Boite Postale 1309, Port au Prince, Haiti

✠ **ESTILL**, Robert Whitridge (Ret Bp of NC 1994-) 8601 Cypress Lakes Dr # A302, Raleigh, NC 27615

ESTRADA, Carolyn Sullivan (Los) 2516 E Willow St Unit 108, Signal Hill, CA 90755

ESTRADA, Richard Roger (Los) 2808 Altura St, Los Angeles, CA 90031

ESWEIN, Nancy G (Cal) 27 Grand View Ave, San Francisco, CA 94114

ETEMAD, Sandra L (Pa) 535 Haws Ave, Norristown, PA 19401

ETHEREDGE, Annie Bates (WLa) 905 Dafney Drive, Lafayette, LA 70503

ETHRIDGE, Forrest Eugene (Ga) 2408 Forest Ave NW, Fort Payne, AL 35967

ETTENHOFER, Karen Ruth (NMich) 500 Ogden Ave, Escanaba, MI 49829

EUNSON, Lisa Kei (Cal) St Ternan's Rectory, High Street, Banchory, - AB31 5TB, Great Britain (UK)

EUSTACE, Warren Paul (ECR) 1604 E. Nectarine Ave., Lompoc, CA 93436

EUSTIS, Patricia Anne (Oly) 628 Jackson Ave Apt C, Grants, NM 87020

EVANS, Aaron Jay (WMich) 1115 W Summit Ave, Muskegon, MI 49441

EVANS, Amber Stancliffe (Cal) 1357 Natoma St, San Francisco, CA 94103

EVANS, Carol S (O) 246 Cedar Ave, Ravenna, OH 44266

EVANS II, C David (NwPa) 506 Young Rd, Erie, PA 16509

EVANS, David Hugh (Mich) 1926 Morris St, Sarasota, FL 34239

EVANS, Deedee (Kan) St. James Episcopal Church, 3750 E. Douglas, Wichita, KS 67208

EVANS, Dolores Elaine (Be) 184 Meadow Lane, Conestoga, PA 17516

EVANS, Gareth Clive (Mass) 148 Newtown Rd, Acton, MA 01720

EVANS, Gary T (NMich) 1000 Bluff View Dr Apt 112, Houghton, MI 49931

EVANS, Geoffrey Parker (Ala) 1910 12th Ave S, Birmingham, AL 35205

EVANS, Haydn Barry (Pa) 214 New Street, 4N, Philadelphia, PA 19106

EVANS, Holly Sue (CNY) PO Box 319, Copenhagen, NY 13626

EVANS, J. Wesley (Dal) 2200 18th St, Plano, TX 75074

EVANS, Jacob Joseph (Alb) 5 Simpson Ave, Round Lake, NY 12151

EVANS, James Eston (Pa) 2 Emmett St, Phoenixville, PA 19460

EVANS, Jeffrey Keith (Ala) St Timothy's Episcopal Church, 207 E Washington St, Athens, AL 35611

EVANS, John Frederick (WA) 10450 Lottsford Rd Apt 3115, Mitchellville, MD 20721

EVANS, John Howard (NH) 1215 Main Rd Apt 211, Tiverton, RI 02878

EVANS, John Miles (Md) PO Box 1272, PO Box 1272, Portsmouth, NH 03802

EVANS, Karen Patricia (At) 675 Holly Drive, Marietta, GA 30064

EVANS, Katharine Cope (Mass) 18 Lafayette Rd, Ipswich, MA 01938

EVANS, Leonard D (U) 515 S 1000 E Apt 506, Salt Lake City, UT 84102

EVANS, Mark E (Spr) 402 Pekin St., P.O. Box 386, Lincoln, IL 62656

EVANS, N. Dean (Pa) 304 Lexington, Media, PA 19063

EVANS, Noah Hearne (Mass) 260 Grove St, Medford, MA 02155

EVANS, Paul Fredric (Cal) 23 Seward St Apt C2, Saratoga Springs, NY 12866

EVANS, Rachael Nichole (WMich) 1115 W Summit Ave, Muskegon, MI 49441

EVANS JR, Ralph Easen (CFla) 2804 Coral Shores Dr, Fort Lauderdale, FL 33306

EVANS, Scott Charles (Alb) 15 W High St, Ballston Spa, NY 12020

EVANS, Steve Armitage (Ga) 4625 Sussex Pl, Savannah, GA 31405

EVANS, Theodore H. (WMass) 235 Walker St. Apt. 236, Lenox, MA 01240

EVANS JR, V(ernon) Creighton (SwFla) All Souls Episcopal/Anglican Church, 101 Yoshihara, Chatan, Okinawa, 904-0105, Japan

EVANS, WILLIAM LEE (Ga) 675 Holly Drive, Marietta, GA 30064

EVENSON, Bruce John (SC) 34 Krier Ln, Mt Pleasant, SC 29464

EVERETT, Sherman Bradley (SO) 3206 Brandon Rd, Columbus, OH 43221

EVERHARD, Darby Oliver (NC) 520 Summit Street, Winston Salem, NC 27101

EVERSLEY, Walter VL (Md) 214 Lambeth Rd, Baltimore, MD 21218

EVERSMAN, Karen Lynn (O) 2041 W. Reserve Cir., Avon, OH 44011

EWART, Craig Kimball (NY)

EWING, Elizabeth Ann (CNY) St Andrew's Episcopal Church, 4512 College Ave, College Park, MD 20740

EWING, Judith Lynette (SC) 203 Magnolia Bluff Dr, Columbia, SC 29229

EWING, Ward Burleson (ETenn) P O Box 6, 213 Baker Cemetery Road, Ten Mile, TN 37880

EXNER, William Edward (NH) 19 W Union St, Goffstown, NH 03045

EYER-DELEVETT, Aimee E S (Los) All Saints By The Sea, 83 Eucalyptus Lane, Santa Barbara, CA 93108

EYLERS, David Edward (NY) PO Box 352, Harwinton, CT 06791

EYTCHESON, Gerald Leonard (Kan) 2400 Gary Ave, Independence, KS 67301

EZELL II, James V (ECR) 105 Dogwood Trl, Elizabeth City, NC 27909

F

FAASS, Peter (O) 3566 Avalon Rd, Shaker Heights, OH 44120

FABIAN, Richard Gardner (Cal) 2525 Lyon St, San Francisco, CA 94123

FABRE, John Peter (Az) 18083 W Douglas Way, Surprise, AZ 85374

FABRE, Julie Kilbride (U) 38105 Redwood Road #2191, West Valley City, UT 84119

FACCIO, David Franceschi (PR)

FACKLER, Phillip Joseph Augustine (Pa) 1104 Mayberry Place, Raleigh, NC 27609

FACTOR, Beverly A (Los) 2620 Catherine Rd, Altadena, CA 91001

FADELY, Diane Camille (Md) Trinity Episcopal Church, 120 Allegheny Ave, Towson, MD 21204

FAETH, Margaret Ann (Va) 4529 Peacock Ave, Alexandria, VA 22304

FAGEOL, Suzanne Antoinette (Oly) Po Box 303, Langley, WA 98260

FAGG, Randy Jay (Ida) PO Box 324, Rupert, ID 83350

FAHRNER, Pamela Henry (SC) Saint John's Episcopal Church, 5234 Maryland Hwy, Deer Park, MD 21550

FAIN, Beth Jernigan (Tex) 10515 Laneview Dr, Houston, TX 77070

FAIN, Robert Duncan (Ga) 2230 Walton Way, Augusta, GA 30904

FAIR, Verna Maria (Chi) 1134 Highpointe Dr, Dekalb, IL 60115

FAIRBANKS, Barbara Jean (Minn) 3044 Longfellow Ave, Minneapolis, MN 55407

FAIRFIELD, Roger Louis (EO) 69793 Pine Glen Rd, Sisters, OR 97759

FAIRLESS, Caroline S (NH) 8 Whispering Pines Rd, Wilmont, NH 03287

FAIRMAN, Henry Francis (RI) 73 Touisset Ave, Swansea, MA 02777

FAIRWEATHER, Carolynne Marie (Ore)

FAISON, Dee Doheny (Pa) 405 Warren Rd, West Chester, PA 19382

FAIT JR, Harold Charles (Minn)

FALCIANI, Justin Anthony (NJ) 16 W. Wilmont Ave, Somers Point, NJ 08244

FALCONE, John Francis (O) 7513 W 33rd St, Tulsa, OK 74107

FALCONER, Allan (Miss) 11593 Avondale Dr, Fairfax, VA 22030

FALES, Stephen Abbott (Ind) 1402 W Main St, Carmel, IN 46032

FALLON, Amy L (Chi) Grace Place Campus Ministry, 401 Normal Rd, Dekalb, IL 60115

FALLOWFIELD, William Harris (Md) 2622 N Calvert St, Baltimore, MD 21218

FALLS, Michael Lee (Tex) 5831 Secrest Dr, Austin, TX 78759

FAMULARE JR, Joseph Anthony (Alb) 119 Southern Ave, Little Falls, NY 13365

FAN, Peter Sheung-Mau (The Episcopal Church in Haw) St Elizabeth Episcopal Church, 720 N King St, Honolulu, HI 96817

FANGUY, Mabel Matheny (Pgh) 1114 1st St, Canonsburg, PA 15317

FANNING, Thomas H (Miss) 24 Greystone Dr, Madison, MS 39110

FARABEE, Allen Waldo (WNY) 310 Norwood Ave, Buffalo, NY 14222

FARAMELLI, Norman Joseph (Mass) 29 Harris St, Waltham, MA 02452

FARBER, Joseph Wade (Okla) 1420 E Dewey Ave, Sapulpa, OK 74066

FARGO, David Rolland (La) 3081 Golfside Ln, Hendersonville, NC 28739

FARGO, Valerie Mae (EMich)

FARIA III, Manuel P. (Mass) 4 Ocean St, Beverly, MA 01915

FARINA, Gaspar Miran (Mil) 154 Club Wildwood, Hudson, FL 33568

FARKAS, Hazel Daphne Martin (SVa) 111 Montrose, Williamsburg, VA 23188

FARLEY, Nancy Stone (Lex) 151 Vine St, Sadieville, KY 40370

FARMER, Edward Dean (Wyo)

FARMER, Eyleen Hamner (WTenn) 102 N 2nd St, Memphis, TN 38103

FARMER, Gary Clayton (WNC) Po Box 633, Arden, NC 28704

FARMER, Jennie Marietta (EMich) 453 S 26th St, Saginaw, MI 48601

FARNES, Joseph E (Ida) 67 East St, Pittsfield, MA 01201

FARQUHAR-MAYES, Alice F(ay) (Ida) 1560 Lenz Ln, Boise, ID 83712

FARQUHAR-MAYES, Thomas (Ida) 1115 W Clarinda Dr, Meridian, ID 83642

FARR, Beau Anthony (At)

FARR, Curtis Andrew (Oly) St James' Church, 19 Walden St, West Hartford, CT 06107

FARR, Meghan J (CFla) St Luke's Episcopal Church, PO Box 605, Gladstone, NJ 07934

FARRAR, Charles Thomas (Me)

FARRAR III, Holway Dean (Los) 4091 E La Cara St, Long Beach, CA 90815

FARRELL, John T (LI) 1155 Warburton Ave, Apt 4D, Yonkers, NY 10701

FARRELL JR, Reid Dwyer (Vt) PO Box 273, Swanton, VT 05488

FARRELL, Wayne Foil (SwFla) 1700 Keystone Rd, Tarpon Springs, FL 34688

FARWELL JR, James William (At) Virginia Theological Seminary, Alexandria, VA 22304

FASEL, William Jay (WMo) 824 W 62nd St, Kansas City, MO 64113

FAST SR, Todd Howard (Oly) 8756 Sylvan Pl Nw, Seattle, WA 98117

FAUCETTE, Chip (At) 2998 Kodiak Ct, Marietta, GA 30062

FAULKNER, David M (Miss) Saint James' Church, 413 Olive Street, Texarkana, TX 75501

FAULKNER, Thomas Dickson (NY) 131 E 66th St Apt 10b, New York, NY 10065

FAULSTICH, Christine Marie (Tex) 9600 South Gessner Rd., Houston, TX 77071

FAULSTICH, Matthew (SeFla) 1704 Buchanan St, Hollywood, FL 33020

FAUPEL, David William (SwFla) 7447 Emilia Ln, Naples, FL 34114

FAUSAK, Frederick Emil (NY) 41 Alter Ave, Staten Island, NY 10304

FAY, Michael (Colo) 349 E Street, Salida, CO 81201

FAY, Susan Delia (The Episcopal NCal) 3878 River Rd, Colusa, CA 95932

FAYETTE, Shelly Lynn (Oly) 805 SE Ellsworth Rd, Vancouver, WA 98664

FEAGIN JR, Jerre Willis (WNY) 70 Westchester Rd, Williamsville, NY 14221

FEAMSTER JR, Thomas Otey (NC) 1805 Virginia Ct, Tavares, FL 32778

FEATHER, Mark Randolph (Va) 14 Cornwall St NW, Leesburg, VA 20176

FEATHERSTON, William Roger (Eur) Via B. Rucellai 09, Florence, 50123, Italy

FECHT, Dustin Michael (Mil) St John's Episcopal Church, 405 N Saginaw Rd, Midland, MI 48640

FEDEWA, Michael Carl (WMich) 1025 3 Mile Rd Ne, Grand Rapids, MI 49505

FEDOCK, Maria Michele (Md) 2115 Southland Rd, Baltimore, MD 21207

FEDORCHAK, Karen (Ct) 48 S Hawthorne St, Manchester, CT 06040

FEDOSUK, James Henry (Spr) 415 N Plum St, Havana, IL 62644

FEELY, Mary Josephine (Minn) 8055 Morgan Ave N, Stillwater, MN 55082

FEERER, Jane Elizabeth (Spok)

FEHR, Bruce Charles (Ga) 590 Walthour St, Savannah, GA 31410

FEHR, Lori Lee (Ga) 590 Walthour Rd, Savannah, GA 31410

FEHR, Thomas James (SO) Community of the Transfiguration, 495 Albion Ave., Cincinnati, OH 45246

FEHR, Wayne L (Mil) 8220 Harwood Ave Apt 334, Wauwatosa, WI 53213

FEIDER, Paul A (FdL) 1511 Cedarhurst Dr, New London, WI 54961

FELICETTI, Elizabeth Marshall (SVa) 1217 Yarbrough Way, Virginia Beach, VA 23455

FELLHAUER, Edward William (Miss) 3737 Springwater Drive, Nashville, KS 37221

FELLHAUER, Sheila Rose (Miss) 3737 Springwater Dr, Nashville, TN 37221

FELLOWS, Richard Greer (SwFla) 15801 Country Lake Drive, Tampa, FL 33624

FELLOWS, Robert Hayden (Okla) 5820 W Garden Pointe Dr, Stillwater, OK 74074

FELS, Charles Wentworth Baker (ETenn)

FELSOVANYI, Andrea (The Episcopal NCal) 4 Bishop Ln, Menlo Park, CA 94025

FELTNER, Allan L (EMich) 1287 Adams Dr, West Branch, MI 48661

FELTON, Paul D (Tex) 707 Venice St, Sugar Land, TX 77478

FELTY, Rose Ann (Alb) PO Box 114, Columbiaville, NY 12050

FENLON, Mathew Charles (Tex) 2450 River Oaks Blvd, Houston, TX 77019

FENN, Richard Kimball (Pa) 43 Hibben Rd, Princeton, NJ 08540

FENN, Richard Lewis (WNY) 19 Pradas Way, Edgartown, MA 02539

FENNER, Renee Lynette (Mo)

FENTON, Arnold Aidan (SanD) 9815 Circa Valle Verde, El Cajon, CA 92021

FENTON, David Henry (SanD) 3962 Josh St, Eugene, OR 97402

FENTON, Eric Denis (WTex) 606 W Cleveland St, Cuero, TX 77954

FENTON, Fred (Cal) 4726 Curletto Dr, Concord, CA 94521

FENTON, Gordon Douglas (NY) #580-401 West Georgia Street, Diocese of New Westminster, Vancouver, BC V6B 5A1, Canada

FENTON, Graham R C (Minn) 4720 Zenith Ave S, Minneapolis, MN 55410

FENWICK, Robert Donald (SO) 6439 Bethany Village Dr., Box 307, Centerville, OH 45459

FEREBEE, Randolph Curtis (WNC) 127 42nd Avenue Dr NW, Hickory, NC 28601

FEREGRINO, Alfredo (Oly)

FERGUESON, John Frederick (Oly) 14449 90th Ct Ne, Bothell, WA 98011

FERGUSON, Anthony David Norman (Fla) St. Peter's Church, 5042 Timuquana Road, Jacksonville, FL 32210

FERGUSON, Dina McMullin (Los) St. George's Church, Drawer C, Hawthorne, CA 90250

FERGUSON, Dru (NwT) 510 Newell Ave, Dallas, TX 75223

FERGUSON, Fred-Munro (Alb) 6 Spences Tree, Harwich, MA 02645

FERGUSON, Judith Ann (NY) 391 Main St, Highland Falls, NY 10928

FERGUSON JR, Lawrence C (EO) Po Box 1344, Prineville, OR 97754

FERGUSON, Leslie Clark (SVa) 5537 Greenefield Dr S, Portsmouth, VA 23703

FERGUSON SR, Michael Blackburn (SVa) 900 Fleet Drive #287, Virginia Beach, VA 23454

FERGUSON, Ronald L (Chi)

FERGUSON, Ruth Ephgrave (Roch) 377 Rector Pl Apt 95, New York, NY 10280

FERGUSON, Sheila Louise Ellen (Chi) 1709 Indian Knoll Rd, Naperville, IL 60565

FERGUSON, Stephen Keith (Tex) 20171 Chasewood Park Drive, Houston, TX 77070

FERGUSON, Thomas C (Mil) 583 Sheridan Ave, Columbus, OH 43209

FERGUSON, Vergie Rae (Az) 1650 W Glendale Ave Apt 4103, Phoenix, AZ 85021

FERGUSON, Virginia Alice (Nev) 6773 W Charleston Blvd, Las Vegas, NV 89146

FERLO, Roger Albert (NY) 1700 E 56th Street, Apartment 2601, Chicago, IL 60637

FERNANDEZ, Jose Pascual (NY) 107 Se Superior Way, Stuart, FL 34997

FERNANDEZ, Linda Jean Pell (Md) 1930 Brookdale Rd, Baltimore, MD 21244

FERNANDEZ-LIRANZO, Hipolito Secundino (DR (DomRep)) Calle 10 No. 30, Villa Olga, Santiago, Dominican Republic

FERNANDEZ-POLA, Rosali (PR)

FERNANDEZ-REINA, Hipolito (SwFla)

FERNER, David Raymond (Ind)

FERREIRA-SANDOVAL, Wilson (Ore) 372 NE Lincoln St, Hillsboro, OR 97124

FERREL, Artis Louise (Ia) 15102 Pinehurst Dr, Council Bluffs, IA 51503

FERRELL, Davis Marion (The Episcopal NCal) 515 Nursery St, Nevada City, CA 95959

FERRELL, Nathan Wilson (Me) 41 Foreside Road, Falmouth, ME 04105

FERRELL, Sean Daniel (Spr) 2018 Boudreau Dr, Urbana, IL 61801

FERRER, Gabriel V (Los) All Saints Parish, 504 N Camden Dr, Beverly Hills, CA 90210

FERRIANI, Nancy Ann (Ind) 5010 Washington Blvd, Indianapolis, IN 46205

FERRITO, Michael Louis (ECR) 1391 Market St, Santa Clara, CA 95050

FERRO, Mauricio (Colom) Carrera 16 #94-A-30, Bogota, Colombia

FERRY, Daniel Whitney (NH) 1465 Hooksett Rd Unit 280, Hooksett, NH 03106

FERRY, Margaret Lee (Vt) 16 Pearl St, East Bridgewater, MA 02333

FESQ, John Alfred (Mass) 2708 Salem Church Rd Apt 217, Apt 222, Fredericksburg, VA 22407

FESSLER, Robert H (Mil) 2275 De Carlin Dr, Brookfield, WI 53045

FETTERMAN, James Harry (WLa) 11130 122nd Street, South Ozone Park, NY 11420

FETTERMAN, John J (Pgh) 1446 Maple Ave, Verona, PA 15147

FETZ, Robert Derrick (WMass) 30 Warren Ter, Longmeadow, MA 01106

FEUERSTEIN, John Mark (Pgh) 1066 Washington Rd, Mt Lebanon, PA 15228

FEUERSTEIN, Paul Bruck (NY) 431 E 118th St, New York, NY 10035

FEUS, William Frederick (USC) St. Mark's Church, 132 Center Street, Chester, SC 29706

FEYERHERM, Elise Anne (Mass) 3400 Calumet St, Columbus, OH 43214

FEYRER, David Allport (Ct) 70 S. Dogwood Trail, Southern Shores, NC 27949

FHUERE, Brenda Lee (Colo) 520 Jaylee St Unit A, Clifton, CO 81520

FICHTER JR, Richard E (Va) PO Box 322, Gordonsville, VA 22942

FICKS III, Robert Leslie (Ct) 8166 Mount Air Place, Columbus, OH 43235

FIDDLER, Andrew (Ct) 215 Highland St, New Haven, CT 06511

FIDLER, Brian Ernest (SanD) The Bishop's School, 7607 La Jolla Blvd, La Jolla, CA 92037

FIEBKE, Edward John (Alb) 6014 7th Ave W, Bradenton, FL 34209

✠ **FIELD**, Martin Scott (Bp of WMo 2011-) 420 W. 14th St, Kansas City, MO 64105

FIELD, Norman Grover (NwPa) 747 E 41st St, Erie, PA 16504

FIELD, Robert Durning (WNC) 256 E. Main St., Brevard, NC 28712

FIELD, William Overstreet (Del) 1611 Spring Dr Apt 5B, Louisville, KY 40205

FIELDS, Kenneth L (Tex) 1227 Wellshire Dr, Katy, TX 77494

FIELDS, Laddie B (Tex) 431 Pace Rd, Hendersonville, NC 28792

FIELDSTON, Heidi A (Mass) 24 Court St, Dedham, MA 02026

FIFE, Richard (SwVa) 2250 Maiden Ln Sw, Roanoke, VA 24015

FIGGE, Diane (RG) 3900 Trinity Dr, Los Alamos, NM 87544

FIKE, Christopher John (Mass) 24 Oakland St, Medford, MA 02155

FIKES, G(erald) David (Tex) PO Box 100014, Arlington, VA 22210

FILBERT, Brandon Lee (Ore) 2090 High St. SE, Salem, OR 97302

FILER, Judy Kathleen (Tex) St John's Episcopal Church, 514 Carter St, Marlin, TX 76661

FILL, Michael (Be) 1919 Chestnut St Apt 2212, Philadelphia, PA 19103

FILLER, John Arthur (U) 514 Americas Way #4603, Box Elder, SD 57719

FINAN, A(lice) Jeanne (Vt) Cathedral Church of St. Paul, 2 Cherry St, Burlington, VT 05401

FINCH, Barbara Jo (Ore) 11865 SW Tualatin Rd Apt 45, Tualatin, OR 97062

FINCH JR, Floyd William (SC) 1 Bishop Gadsden Way Apt 119, Charleston, SC 29412

FINCH, Robin Lee (Ida)

FINCHER, Michael Kevin (Los) 1040 Seamist Pl Apt 108, Ventura, CA 93003

FINEANGANOFO, Sosaia Ala (Cal) 2565 Redbridge Rd, Tracy, CA 95377

FINEOUT, William (Mich) 630 Moorland Dr, East Lansing, MI 48823

FINKENSTAEDT JR, Harry Seymour (WMass) 13761 Charismatic Way, Gainesville, VA 20155

FINLEY IV, John Huston (Mass) 717 Atlantic Ave Apt 3B, Boston, MA 02111

FINLEY, Rosamond Stelle (Los) 212 W Franklin St, Tucson, AZ 85701

FINN, Anne Marie (NwT) 2630 S 11th St, Abilene, TX 79605

FINN, Emilie Aurora (Az) 13150 W Spanish Garden Dr, Sun City West, AZ 85375

FINN, Michael John (Roch) 1245 Culver Rd, Rochester, NY 14609

FINN, Patrick Shawn (WMich) 1006 3rd Street, Muskegon, MI 49440

FINN, Robert Patrick (EMich) PO Box 83, West Branch, MI 48661

FINNERUD, Margaret A (EC) Episcopal Churc St Philip's, 205 E Moore St, Southport, NC 28461

FINNIN, Nathan McBride (NC) Canterbury School, 5400 Old Lake Jeanette Rd, Greensboro, NC 27455

FINSTER, Mary Ruth (NI) 1817 W Monroe St, Kokomo, IN 46901

FIRTH, Harry Warren (WMo) 4024 W 100th Ter, Overland Park, KS 66207

FISCHBECK, Lisa Galen (NC) 8410 Merin Rd, Chapel Hill, NC 27516

FISCHER III, Charles L (At) St. Paul's Episcopal Chur, 294 Peyton Rd., SW, Atlanta, GA 30311

FISCHER, John Denny (Mil) 920 E Courtland Pl, Milwaukee, WI 53211

FISCHER, Sara (Oly) 2800 SE Harrison Street, Portland, OR 97214

FISCHER, Sarah Motley (WA) Grace Episcopal Church, 1041 Wisconsin Ave NW, Washington, DC 20007

FISCHER-DAVIES, Clare Ilene (RI) 50 Orchard Ave, Providence, RI 02906

FISH, Cameron Hoover (CNY) 6 Canberra Ct, Mystic, CT 06355

FISH, Charles (Tad) Cramer (Ct) PO Box 67724, Albuquerque, NM 87193

FISH, Gloria Hoyer (Roch) 46 Azalea Rd, Rochester, NY 14620

FISH, Sonnie Eriksen (Ct) PO Box 67724, Albuquerque, NM 87193

FISHBAUGH-LOONEY, Kristen Fishbaugh (Md) 11232 Falls Rd, Timonium, MD 21093

FISHBECK, Nadine B (Tenn)

FISHBURNE, Donald A (ETenn) 3488 Reflecting Drive, Chattanooga, TN 37415

FISHER, David Hickman (Chi) 1012 Churchill Dr, Naperville, IL 60563

FISHER, Davis Lee (Chi) 430 SW 13th Ave, #1015, Portland, OR 97205

✠ **FISHER**, Douglas John (Bp of WMass 2012) 37 Chestnut St, Springfield, MA 01103

FISHER, Elizabeth B (NY) Po Box 974, Millbrook, NY 12545

FISHER, Ernest Wilkin (SwFla) 550 1st Ave S Apt 514, #514, Saint Petersburg, FL 33701

FISHER, James A(lfred) (NJ) 15 Maple Street, South Seaville, NJ 08246

✠ **FISHER**, Jeff Wright (Bp Suffr of Tex 2012-) 2695 S Southwest Loop 323, Tyler, TX 75701

FISHER, Jerry William (NC) 635 Galashiels Place, Wake Forest, NC 27587

FISHER, Jill Carmen (ETenn) 1175 Pineville Rd Apt 85, Chattanooga, TN 37405

FISHER, John Coale (SC) 8244 Crooked Creek Ln, Edisto Island, SC 29438

FISHER, John R(aymond) (SO) Po Box 29064, Columbus, OH 43229

FISHER, Joy (Ga) 147 SouthSecond Street, Cochran, GA 31014

FISHER, Julie Blake (O) 551 Rockwell Street, Kent, OH 44240

FISHER, Margaret Jo (Spok) 522 West Park Place, Spokane, WA 99205

FISHER, Mary Carlton (The Episcopal NCal) 72 Mill Creek Dr, Willits, CA 95490

FISHER, Paige Ford (Mass) 206 Clarendon St, Boston, MA 02116

FISHER, Richard Lingham (WNC) 175 Vinal St, Rockport, ME 04856

FISHER, Robert William (ECR) PO Box 101, Carmel Valley, CA 93924

FISHER, Ronald Spencer (Md) 24 Evergreen Trail, Severna Park, MD 21146

FISHER JR, Russell Ellsworth (FtW) Po Box 192, Santa Anna, TX 76878

FISHER, Sarah Kathleen (Chi) 4755 N Peachtree Rd, Atlanta, GA 30338

FISHER, Scott Owen (Ak) 1030 2nd Ave, Fairbanks, AK 99701

FISHER, William A (Colo) 200 Elk Run Dr, Basalt, CO 81621

FISHER-STEWART, Gayle Antoinette (WA) 820 6th St Ne, Washington, DC 20002

FISHWICK, Jeffrey Palmer (Va) 1260 River Chase Ln, Charlottesville, VA 22901

FISKE, Thomas Walton (Wyo) 123 Linden Avenue, Fairmont, MN 56031

FITCH, William Babcock (USC) 6342 Yorkshire Dr, Columbia, SC 29209

FITE, Robert Cotton (Chi) 212 Wood Ct, Wilmette, IL 60091

FITTS, Ronald Sheldon (Eas) 21103 Striper Run, Rock Hall, MD 21661

FITZGERALD, Joe (Az) 2288 W Silverbell Tree Dr, Tucson, AZ 85745

FITZGERALD III, John Henry (Mich) 1350 Berkshire Rd, Grosse Pointe Park, MI 48230

FITZGERALD, John Paul (HB)

FITZGERALD, Todd R. (Tex) St Stephens School, 6528 Saint Stephens Dr, Austin, TX 78746

FITZGERALD, William Thomas (Ga) 3168 Seed Lake Rd, Lakemont, GA 30552

FITZGIBBONS, Michael John (Spok) 8505 W Hood Ave, Kennewick, WA 99336

FITZGIBBONS, Sabeth S. (NwPa) 1070 Dutch Rd, Fairview, PA 16415

FITZHUGH, Bobbe Kay (Wyo) PO Box 1419, Douglas, WY 82633

FITZHUGH, Mark L (LI) 325 Lattingtown Road, Locust Valley, NY 11560

FITZPATRICK, Michael Carl (Mich) 24699 Grand River Ave, Detroit, MI 48219

FITZPATRICK, Robert Joseph (NY) 179 East Main st, Washingtonville, NY 10992

✠ **FITZPATRICK**, Robert Leroy (Bp of Haw 2007-) Office of the Bishop, 229 Queen Emma Sq, Honolulu, HI 96813

FITZSIMMONS, Daniel V (Be) 16 Allenberry Dr, Wilkes Barre, PA 18706

FITZSIMMONS, James (Az)

FITZSIMMONS, James Patrick (Az) 969 W Country Club Dr, Nogales, AZ 85621

FLAGSTAD, Judith Marie (SD) 101 W Prospect Ave Apt 3, Pierre, SD 57501

FLAHERTY, Jane Frances (SVa) 614 E 7th St, Alton, IL 62002

FLAHERTY, Jessica Barbara (Mass)

FLANAGAN, Carol Cole (WA) St. John's Episcopal Church & School, 3427 Olney Laytonsville Road, Olney, MD 20832

FLANAGAN, Jakki Renee (Vt)

FLANAGAN, Michael Patrick (USC) 104 Brockman Dr, Mauldin, SC 29662

FLANAGAN, Robert D (NY) PO Box 267, Bridgewater, CT 06752

FLANDERS, Alden Beaman (Mass) 145 Weyland Cir, North Andover, MA 01845

FLANDERS JR, J(ames) William (WA) 3714 Harrison St Nw, Washington, DC 20015

FLANDERS, Susan Mann (WA) Susan Flanders, 3714 Harrison St., NW, Washington, DC 20015

FLANIGEN, John Monteith (Ida) Po Box 71027, Tuscaloosa, AL 35407

FLECK, Timothy R (Me) Saint Saviour's Parish, 41 Mount Desert St, Bar Harbor, ME 04609

FLEENER SR, William Joseph (WMich) 5665 S Cherokee Bnd, New Era, MI 49446

FLEENOR, David (NY) 1 E 29th St, New York, NY 10016

FLEENOR, Ryan C (NY) 865 Madison Ave, New York, NY 10021

FLEETWOOD, Zachary (Eur) 28 Castle Terrace, Edinburgh, EH1 2EL, Great Britain (UK)

FLEISCHER, Marie Moorefield (NC) 8241 Allyns Landing Way Apt 304, Raleigh, NC 27615

FLEISCHER, Scott Ronald (USC) 2827 Wheat St, Columbia, SC 29205

FLEISCHMAN, Donald M (Mil) 297 N Main St, Richland Center, WI 53581

FLEMING, Carol Ann Spayd (NI) 70865 Wayne St, Union, MI 49130

FLEMING JR, Huett Maxwell (Pgh) 3000 William Penn Hwy, Pittsburgh, PA 15235

FLEMING, Joan Elizabeth (NJ) 183 Hartley Ave., Princeton, NJ 08540

FLEMING, John Charles (Mo) 638 Huntwood Ln, Kirkwood, MO 63122

FLEMING, Linda Lee (Wyo) St Paul's Episcopal Church, PO Box 68, Dixon, WY 82323

FLEMING JR, Peter Wallace (SwFla) 1 Beach Dr SE Apt 2214, Saint Petersburg, FL 33701

FLEMING JR, Raymond Edgar (Los) 484 Cliff Dr Apt 10, Laguna Beach, CA 92651

FLEMISTER, Ernestein Cassell (SwFla) 112 W Idlewild Avenue, Tampa, FL 33604

FLEMMING, Leslie Abel (SO) 1 Kent Dr, Athens, OH 45701

FLENTJE, Gregory Laurence (WMich) 4210 Honey Creek Ave Ne, Ada, MI 49301

FLES, Jacob C (Me) 2 Dresden Ave, Gardiner, ME 04345

FLETCHER, Justin Price (Okla) St Luke's Episcopal Church, 126 S 6th St, Chickasha, OK 73018

FLETCHER, Margaret Ann Laurie (Vt) St. Peter's Episcopal Church, 300 Pleasant St., Bennington, VT 05201

FLETCHER JR, Richard James (WTenn) 108 N King Ave, Dyersburg, TN 38024

FLETT, Carol (WA) retired, Washington, DC 20016

FLEXER, Katharine Grace (NY) 225 W 99th St, New York, NY 10025

FLICK, Robert Terry (Tex) 1410 Cambridge Dr, Friendswood, TX 77546

FLINTOM, Jack Glenn (Md) 2030 Marshall Ln, Hayes, VA 23072

FLOBERG, John F (ND) Po Box 612, Fort Yates, ND 58538

FLOBERG, Sloane R (ND) 820 West Central Ave, Bismarck, ND 58501

FLOCKEN, Robin (CNY) 1721 Stanley Rd, Cazenovia, NY 13035

FLOOD, Charles Ta (Pa) 19 S 10th St, Philadelphia, PA 19107

FLOOR, Marjorie Jacobsen (Alb) 77 Sabbath Day Point Rd, Silver Bay, NY 12874

FLORES, Kay Osborn (Wyo) 4700 S Poplar St, Casper, WY 82601

FLORES, Nydia (NY) 630 Water St Apt 4-C, New York, NY 10002

FLORY, Carol Inez (Fla)

FLORY, Phyllis Brannon (WK) 1551 Briargate Dr, Salina, KS 67401

FLOWERS JR, James Byrd (CGC)

FLOWERS JR, James Edgar (WLa) 946 Ockley Dr, Shreveport, LA 71106

FLOWERS, Lauren F (Ga) 3 Ridge Rd, Savannah, GA 31405

FLOYD JR, Charles K(amper) (Miss) 4400 King Road, Meridian, MS 39305

FLOYD, Charles Rhein (CGC) 117 Rusty Gans Dr, Panama City Beach, FL 32408

FLOYD, Michael Hinnant (DR (DomRep)) 5505 B Stuart Cir, Austin, TX 78721

FLOYD, Michael Stephen (O) 120 Ohio St, Huron, OH 44839

FLOYD, Peter M (Colo) 7408 Tudor Rd, Colorado Springs, CO 80919

FLOYD, Peter Winslow (Ct) 18 Hidden Lake Rd, Higganum, CT 06441

FLOYD, Theresa Ann (Ore) 4177 Nw Thatcher Rd, Forest Grove, OR 97116

FLY, David Kerrigan (Mo) 4400 Lindell Blvd., Apt. 11-N, St. Louis, MO 63108

FLYNN, Anne Regina (Kan) 21 Copperfield Ln, Charleston, IL 61920

FLYNN, Michael (Los) 4406 El Corazon Ct, Camarillo, CA 93012

FLYNN, Peggy Rishel (Kan)

FODOR, Luke (WNY) 410 N Main St, Jamestown, NY 14701

FOERSTER III, Frederick Henry (CNY) 183 Capn Crosby Rd, Centerville, MA 02632

FOGELQUIST, Albin Hilding (Spok) 1307 Regents Blvd Apt D, Fircrest, WA 98466

FOISIE, Dawn Ann Campbell (Oly) 5757 Solomons Island Rd, Lothian, MD 20711

FOISIE, Stephen D (Oly) 228 Wall St, Camano Island, WA 98282

FOLEY, Kristen C (NJ) 2136 Woodbridge Ave, Edison, NJ 08817

FOLEY, Michael Brian (Pgh) 5700 Forbes Ave, Pittsburgh, PA 15217

FOLEY, Theodore Archer (NJ) Christ Church, 415 Washington St, Toms River, NJ 08753

FOLSOM, Henry Titus (NH) 62 Durand Rd, Randolph, NH 03593

✠ **FOLTS**, James Edward (Ret Bp of WTex 2006-) PO Box 6885, San Antonio, TX 78209

FOLTS, Jonathan Hunter (Ct) 3 Windswept Ridge Road, Ivoryton, CT 06442

FOLTS, Kimberly Spire (Ct) 40 Main St, Essex, CT 06426

FOLTZ, Marvin Lee (Mo) 12424 Cape Cod Dr, Saint Louis, MO 63146

✠ **FOLWELL**, William Hopkins (Ret Bp of CFla 1990-) 600 Carolina Village Rd Unit 25, Hendersonville, NC 28792

FONCREE, Rose Mary Ivas (Miss) 4526 Meadow Hill Road, Jackson, MS 39206

FONDER SR, Kim Michael (SD) Holy Comforter/Messiah, PO Box 242, Lower Brule, SD 57548

FONES, Peter Alden (Ore) 723 S. 48th St, Springfield, OR 97478

FONTAINE, Ann Kristin (Wyo) PO Box 1354, Cannon Beach, OR 97110

FONTAINE, H(oward) Douglas (Minn) 3940 Auburn Dr, Minnetonka, MN 55305

FOOSE, Elizabeth Boutwell (Miss) 6697 Bee Lake Rd, Tchula, MS 39169

FOOTE, Beth (Cal) 705 Grand St, Alameda, CA 94501

FOOTE, Nancy Burns (Md) 1 Holmes Ave, Baltimore, MD 21228

FOOTE, Roger Lee (SO) 985 Forest Ave, Cincinnati, OH 45246

FOOTE, Stephen Williams (Me) 574 Turner Rd, Bremen, ME 04551

FORAKER, Gregory A (Az) PO Box 65840, Tucson, AZ 85728

FORAKER-THOMPSON, Jane (Nev) P.O. Box 2665, Gardnerville, NV 89410

FORBES, Bruce Willard (NY) 109 E 50th St, New York, NY 10022

FORBES JR, Charles Alvin (Oly) 4510 123rd Pl NE, Marysville, WA 98271

FORBES, David Reineman (Cal) 22 Delmar St, San Francisco, CA 94117

FORBES, Elizabeth Faye (Ga) 3321 Wheeler Rd, Augusta, GA 30909

FORBES, Mark S (NC) 156 Lavender Bloom Loop, Mooresville, NC 28115

FORBES, Michael Philip (Minn) 402 31st St Ne Apt 224, Rochester, MN 55906

FORD, Austin McNeill (At) 569 Cherokee Ave Se, Atlanta, GA 30312

FORD, Calvin B(erkley) (SVa) 68 Market Street, Onancock, VA 23417

FORD, Charles Allan (NY) 205 Stone Rd, West Hurley, NY 12491

FORD, Cheri Lynn (NMich) Rr 2 Box 939-A, Newberry, MI 49868

FORD, Denis B (Colo) 3231 Olive St., Jacksonville, FL 32207

FORD, Janet Carol (Nev)

FORD, Janice Celeste (WMass)

FORD, Joan Butler (SanD)

FORD, Joann (Colo) 3231 Olive St, Jacksonville, FL 32207

FORD, John Mark (Ala) PO Box 614, Chelsea, AL 35043

FORD, Richard Barlow (Cal) 2165 West Dry Creek Road, Healdsburg, CA 95448

FORD, Robert Lawrence (Oly) PO Box 3276, Bellevue, WA 98009

FORD, Russell Wayne (CGC) Po Box 5853, Gulf Shores, AL 36547

FORD, Stanley Eugene (Spok)

FORD, Steven E (NMich) Rr 2 Box 939-A, Newberry, MI 49868

FORD, Steven Richard (Az) 3436 N 43rd Pl, Phoenix, AZ 85018

FORDHAM, James Frederick (EC) 1579 Bayview Rd, Bath, NC 27808

FOREMAN JR, Harold Vandon (Ala) 3031 Boundary Oaks Drive S E, Owens Cross Roads, AL 35763

FORHAN, Carol Lynn (Spok) 9327 E Leavenworth Rd, Leavenworth, WA 98826

FORINASH JR, Joseph Lynn (Colo) PO Box 1026, Eagle, CO 81631

FORISHA, Martha Lee (CNY) 102 Delaware St, San Antonio, TX 78210

FORMAN, John P (Oly) 1005 S.W. 152nd Street, Burien, WA 98166

FORNALIK, Barbara Horn (Roch) 1130 Webster Rd, Webster, NY 14580

FORNARO, Francis (Mass) 11 Alaska Ave, Bedford, MA 01730

FORNEA, Stanley Wayne (EC) 2111 Jefferson Davis Hwy Apt603S, Arlington, VA 22202

FORNEY, John Craig (Los) 316 W Green St., Claremont, CA 91711

FORREST, E(lizabeth) Louise (Mass) 41 Hall Ave, Watertown, MA 02472

FORREST, William (FdL) 56500 Abbey Rd, Three Rivers, MI 49093

FORREST, William Clifford (Az) 24922 S Lakewood Dr, Sun Lakes, AZ 85248

FORREST, William Fred (Dal) 3029 Frances Dr, Denison, TX 75020

FORRESTER, Shelley A (Okla) St. Andrew's Church, PO Box 1256, 1313 SW D Ave, Lawton, OK 73502

FORSHAW, Lee (Ct) 2000 Main St, Stratford, CT 06615

FORSYTHE, Margaret Ann Kroy (NJ) 687 Donald Dr S, Bridgewater, NJ 08807

FORSYTHE, Mary Louise (Neb) 420 Shorewood Ln, Waterloo, NE 68069

FORTE, Jeanne (The Episcopal NCal) 700 Wellfleet Dr, Vallejo, CA 94591

FORTI, Nicholas (Va) 1700 University Ave, Charlottesville, VA 22903

FORTKAMP, Frank Edwin (Md) 1840 Canvasback Lane, Columbus, OH 43215

FORTNA, Robert Tomson (NY) 720 W End Ave Apt 818, New York, NY 10025

FORTNER, Marian Dulaney (Miss) 509 W Pine St, Hattiesburg, MS 39401

FORTUNA, Lisa Roxanne (Mass) Christ Church Iglesia San Juan, 1220 River St, Hyde Park, MA 02136

FORTUNA, Virgilio (Mass) 2112 County St, Somerset, MA 02726

FORTUNATO, Susan Boykin (NY) 82 Ehrhardt Rd, Pearl River, NY 10965

FORTUNE, Dwight Chapman (Mass) 246 Mount Hope St, North Attleboro, MA 02760

FOSS, Charles Sanford (USC) 1646 SW Spence Ave, Troutdale, OR 97060

FOSTER III, Andrew William (NY) 790 Plymouth Rd, Claremont, CA 91711

FOSTER, Craig Arthur (SO) 508 Thistle Dr, Delaware, OH 43015

FOSTER, Guy Roland (NY) 2233 Wilton Park Dr., Wilton Manors, FL 33305

FOSTER, Katharine K (SO) 7919 N Coolville Ridge Rd, Athens, OH 45701

FOSTER JR, Kenneth Earl (Mil) 1418 Valley Dr, Wisconsin Dells, WI 53965

FOSTER, Malcolm Lysle (LI) 5 Riverside Drive, Apt 8D, New York, NY 10023

FOSTER, Margaret Reidpath (WNY) 1088 Delaware Ave Apt 5a, Buffalo, NY 14209

FOSTER, Pamela LaMotte (Mass) 19 Warren Point Rd, Wareham, MA 02571

FOSTER, Penelope Hope (WNY) 54 Delaware Rd, Kenmore, NY 14217

FOSTER, Randal Arthur (NC) 105 Pettingill Pl, Southern Pines, NC 28387

FOSTER, Simon (LI) 808 Driggs Ave Apt 5B, Brooklyn, NY 11211

FOSTER, Steve Leslie (LI) 13728 244th St, Rosedale, NY 11422
FOSTER, Todd (Oly)
FOSTER, Willis Renard (SVa) 228 Halifax St, Petersburg, VA 23803
FOTCH JR, Charlton Harvey (Cal) 681 S Eliseo Dr, Greenbrae, CA 94904
FOTINOS, Dennis George (Tex) 248 Birchbark Dr., Mills River, NC 28759
FOUGHTY, Donna L (Va) 7414 Heatherfield Ln, Alexandria, VA 22315
FOUKE, Scherry Vickery (ETenn) 1601 Forest Dr, Morristown, TN 37814
FOULKE, Mary Lova (NY) 521 West 126th Street, New York, NY 10027
FOUNTAIN, Timothy Logan (SD) 2707 W. 33rd St, Sioux Falls, SD 57105
FOUT, Jason A (WMich) 591 Sheridan Ave, Bexley, OH 43209
FOUTS, Arthur Guy (WA) 603 Ramapo Ave, Pompton Lakes, NJ 07442
FOWLE, Elizabeth (WMass) 15 Old Hancock Rd., Hancock, NH 03449
FOWLER, Anne Carroll (Mass) 39 Prospect Street, Portland, ME 04103
FOWLER, Arlen Lowery (Okla) 817 Virginia Ln, Ardmore, OK 73401
FOWLER, Connetta (NwT) 430 Dallas St, Big Spring, TX 79720
FOWLER, Daniel Lewis (Oly) 4335 NE Rhodes End Rd, Bainbridge Island, WA 98110
FOWLER III, Robert F (Ala) St Margaret's Episcopal Church, 606 Newnan St, Carrollton, GA 30117
FOWLER, Stanley Gordon (Oly) 111 Ne 80th St, Seattle, WA 98115
FOWLER IV, William Young (Tex) Po Box 292, Buda, TX 78610
FOWLKES, Tyrone (Cal) 530 W Fullerton Pkwy, Chicago, IL 60614
FOX, Carol Rogers (NY) 312 West 22nd Street, New York, NY 10011
FOX, Cheryl Lynn (NY) 175 9th Ave # 262, New York, NY 10011
FOX, David Coblentz (Okla) 2455 Sulphur Creek St, Cody, WY 82414
FOX, Deborah (NC) 2208 Hope St, Raleigh, NC 27607
FOX, Donald Allan (Cal) 185 Baltimore Way, San Francisco, CA 94112
FOX III, Frederick Carl (Nwk) 441 Lockhart Mountain Rd Unit 4, Lake George, NY 12845
FOX, Jedediah W (Oly) 6345 Wydown Blvd, Saint Louis, MO 63105
FOX, Loren Charles (CFla) Tang-Lin, Minden Road, 248816, Singapore
FOX, Matthew Timothy (Cal) 287 17th St Ste 400, Oakland, CA 94612
FOX, R Steven (U) 136 E 57th St Ste 405, New York, NY 10022
FOX, Richard George (Mil) South 24 West 26826 Apache Pass, Waukesha, WI 53188
FOX, Ronald Napoleon (SeFla) 3464 Oak Ave, Miami, FL 33133

FOX, Sarah McRae (Mich) 8500 Jackson Square Blvd Apt 5D, Shreveport, LA 71115
FOX, Susann (Pa) 76 S Forge Manor Dr, Phoenixville, PA 19460
FOX SR, Wesley D (ND) HC 2, Box 176, Garrison, ND 58540
FOXWORTH, George Marion (The Episcopal NCal) 4338 Walali Way, Fair Oaks, CA 95628
FOXX, Louis Nelson (Mass) 397 Putnam Ave., Cambridge, MA 02139
✠ **FRADE**, Leopold (Bp of SeFla 2000-) 525 NE 15th St, Miami, FL 33132
FRAIOLI, Karen Ann (Mass) 20 Rhodes Ave, Sharon, MA 02067
FRALEY, Anne Mckinne (Tenn) 1500 Hickory Ridge Rd, Lebanon, TN 37087
FRANCE JR, Andrew Menaris (CPa) 651 Harding Ave, Williamsport, PA 17701
FRANCES, Martha (Tex) 6405 Westward #65, Houston, TX 77081
FRANCIS SR, Alric V (VI) PO Box 7974, Christiansted, VI 00823-7974, Virgin Islands (U.S.)
FRANCIS, Desmond C (Alb) 2011 Trotter Ln, Bloomington, IL 61704
FRANCIS, Elaine Consuela (VI) PO Box 1148, St Thomas, VI 00804
FRANCIS, Everett Warren (Be) 3200 Baker Circle Unit I131, Adamstown, MD 21710
FRANCIS, James Woodcock (Mich) 1404 Joliet Pl, Detroit, MI 48207
FRANCIS, John Robert (Be) 435 Court St, P.O. Box 1094, Reading, PA 19603
FRANCIS, Mary Jane Jane (Oly) 725 9th Ave., Apt. 2109, Seattle, WA 98104
FRANCKS, Robert Christopher (NY) 360 W 21st St, New York, NY 10011
FRANCO ESTEVEZ, Juan Bautista (PR) Iglesia Episcopal Puertorriquena, PO Box 902, Saint Just, PR 00978-0902, Puerto Rico
FRANCOIS, Yvan (Hai) Box 1309, Port-Au-Prince, Haiti
FRANDSEN, Charles Frederick (WMich) 509 Ship St, Saint Joseph, MI 49085
FRANK, Anna (Ak) 1578 Bridgewater Dr, Fairbanks, AK 99709
FRANK, Elizabeth (O) New Life Episcopal Church, 13188 Church Ave NW, Uniontown, OH 44685
FRANK, Richard Lloyd (U) 13640 N 21st Ave, Phoenix, AZ 85029
FRANK, Travis Ray (Ark) 14 Haslingden Ln, Bella Vista, AR 72715
FRANK JR, William George (Va) 11 Wakefield Dr Apt 2004, Asheville, NC 28803
FRANKEN, Robert Anton (Colo)
FRANKFURT, Dawn M (Kan) 3750 E Douglas Ave, Wichita, KS 67208
FRANKLIN, Ann Hope (Mass) 143 Gillespie Circle, Brevard, NC 28712

FRANKLIN, Arthur Alden (SanD) 2404 Loring St # 190, San Diego, CA 92109
FRANKLIN, Cecil Loyd (Colo) 2250 E Columbia Pl, Denver, CO 80210
FRANKLIN JR, Denson N (Ala) 517 Mayfair Cir, Birmingham, AL 35209
FRANKLIN III, Gus Lee (Spr) 6508 Willow Springs Rd, Springfield, IL 62712
FRANKLIN III, James D (NC) St James Parish, 25 S 3rd St, Wilmington, NC 28401
FRANKLIN, John Thomas (Mich) 2933 Dunsary Ln, Brighton, MI 48114
✠ **FRANKLIN**, Ralph William (Bp of WNY 2011-) 1064 Brighton Road, Tonawanda, NY 14150
FRANKLIN, Sarah Claire (USC) 7128 Caggy Ln, Fort Mill, SC 29707
FRANKLIN-VAUGHN, Robyn (WA) 319 Bryant St Ne, Washington, DC 20002
FRANKS, L(aurence) Edward Alexander (FdL) 299 Corey St, Boston, MA 02132
FRANTZ-DALE, Heidi Hallett (NH) 247 Pound Road, Madison, NH 03849
FRANZ, Marcia Wheatley (NMich)
FRASER, Ann Benton (Miss) St. Paul's Episcopal Church, P.O. Box 1225, Corinth, MS 38835
FRASER, R(ichard) Trent (Colo) 1400 S University Blvd, Denver, CO 80210
FRASER, Thomas A (Chi) 60 Akenside Rd, Riverside, IL 60546
FRASER SR, William Carson (ETenn) 4487 Post Place, #129, Nashville, TN 37205
FRAUSTO, Nancy Aide (Los) 861 S Mariposa Ave, Los Angeles, CA 90005
FRAZELLE, David C (NC) 304 E Franklin St, Chapel Hill, NC 27514
FRAZER, Candice Burk (Ala) St John's Episcopal Church, 113 Madison Ave, Montgomery, AL 36104
FRAZIER JR, Allie Washington (SVa) 1124 Dryden Lane, Charlottesville, VA 22903
FRAZIER, John T (EC) 5324 Bluewater Pl, Fayetteville, NC 28311
FRAZIER, Jonathan Edward (WMo) 516 S Weller Ave, Springfield, MO 65802
FRAZIER, Mark W (SwVa) 905 Highland Ave, Bristol, VA 24201
FRAZIER, Raymond Malcom (SwFla) 8017 Fountain Ave, Tampa, FL 33615
FRAZIER JR, Samuel K.(indley) (NC) 500 N Duke St. #55-202, Durham, NC 27701
FREARSON, Andrew Richard (At) 3136 Lynnray Dr, Doraville, GA 30340
FREDERIC, Eliot Garrison (Eas) 51 Columbine Ave N, Hampton Bays, NY 11946
FREDERICK, John Bassett Moore (Ct) 32 Chestnut St, Princeton, NJ 08542

FREDERICK, Robert John (Md) 1930 Brookdale Rd, Baltimore, MD 21244

FREDERICK, Sherman Richardson (Nev) 2724 Brienza Way, Las Vegas, NV 89117

FREDERICK, Warren Charles (WMass) 19 Rydal St, Worcester, MA 01602

FREDERIKSEN III, Victor (EC) Po Box 7672, Wilmington, NC 28406

FREDHOLM, Everett Leonard (Tex) 201 Nicholas Dr, Asheville, NC 28806

FREDIE JR, Julian Von Kessel (Mass)

FREDRICK, Lawrence Edward (EO) 1220 Tasman Dr Spc 1k, Sunnyvale, CA 94089

FREDRICKS, John Raymond (Cal) Po Box 296, San Mateo, CA 94401

FREDRICKSON, David A. (Mass) 149 Court Street, Plymouth, MA 02360

FREE JR, Horace D (NY) PO Box 125, Johns Island, SC 29457

FREEBERN, Douglas Wayne (Okla) 210 E 9th St, Bartlesville, OK 74003

FREEMAN, Ashley B (La) 3552 Morning Glory Ave, Baton Rouge, LA 70808

FREEMAN, Bruce A (Los) 2944 Erie Ave, Cincinnati, OH 45208

FREEMAN JR, Denson Fred (Colo) 8 Fourth Street, Colorado Springs, CO 80906

FREEMAN, Diana G(ail) (Dal) 6400 Stonebrook Pkwy, Frisco, TX 75034

FREEMAN, John (WMass)

FREEMAN, Leonard W (Minn) 190 Cygnet Pl, Long Lake, MN 55356

FREEMAN, Lindsay Hardin (Minn) 190 Cygnet Pl, Long Lake, MN 55356

FREEMAN JR, Monroe (NC) 1706 Highlands Vw SE, Smyrna, GA 30082

FREEMAN JR, Norman Reid (Los) St George's Church And Academy, 23802 Avenida de la Carlota, Laguna Hills, CA 92653

FREEMAN, Reed H. (Miss) 12614 Muirfield Blvd S, Jacksonville, FL 32225

FREEMAN, Robert Arthur (NH) Po Box 182, Poultney, VT 05764

FREEMAN, Sarah Belle (Colo) 726 W Elati Cir, Littleton, CO 80120

FREEMAN, Sollace Mitchell (At) 5194 Glenstone Ct, Gainesville, GA 30504

FREEMAN, T.J. (Pgh) 315 Shady Ave, Pittsburgh, PA 15206

FREEMAN, Warren Gray (Mass) 77 Lakeside Trailer Park, Mashpee, MA 02649

FREES, Mooydeen Claire (SO) 3826 Portrush Way, Amelia, OH 45102

FREGEAU, Stephen Alfred (Mass) 7719 SE Sugar Sand Cir, Hobe Sound, FL 33455

FREGOSO, Krista Dawn (Cal) 1707 Gouldin Rd, Oakland, CA 94611

FREIRE-SOLORZANO, Luis Hernan (EcuC) Barrio El Tambo Sector Bomba De Aqua, Pelileo, 24, Ecuador

FRELUND, Warren F (Ia) 1029 W State St, Mason City, IA 50401

FRENCH, Alan C (NJ) 15 Old Forge Ln, Berkeley Heights, NJ 07922

FRENCH, Clarke (NC) 414 Yorktown Dr, Chapel Hill, NC 27516

FRENCH, Jonathan D (CFla) 2304 SE 12th ST, Ocala, FL 34471

FRENCH, Peter (NJ) 53 University Pl., Princeton, NJ 08540

FRENCH, Richard Clement (Oly) 23500 Cristo Rey Dr Unit 520G, Cupertino, CA 95014

FRENCH, Sally (NC) 407 E. Seneca St., Manlius, NY 13104

FRENCH, William A (NwPa) 42 Oak St, Brookville, PA 15825

FRENS, Mary Jean (WMich) 934 Clubview Dr, Fremont, MI 49412

FRENSLEY, James Monroe (Colo) 3506 Armstrong Ave, Dallas, TX 75205

FREW, Randolph Lloyd (NY) 332 Bleecker St #K80, New York, NY 10014

FREY, Louane Florence Virgilio (NC) 801 Footbridge Pl, Cary, NC 27519

FREY, Matthew Vincent (WTex) 2620 Crestview Dr, Edinburg, TX 78539

FREY, Paul Anthony (WTex) 139 Kentucky St, Laredo, TX 78041

✠ FREY, William Carl (Ret Bp of Colo 1996-) 23315 Eagle Gap, San Antonio, TX 78255

FRIAS, Miguel (Chi) 941 W Lawrence Ave, Chicago, IL 60640

FRIBOURGH, Cynthia Kaye (Ark) 11123 Bainbridge Dr, Little Rock, AR 72212

FRICK, Matthew M (Dal) 2627 Horseshoe Dr, Alexandria, LA 71301

FRIEDEL, James W (WTex) 11905 E Maple Dr, Claremore, OK 74019

FRIEDMAN, Anna Russell (Ala) PO Box 27, Minter, AL 36761

FRIEDMAN, Maurice Lane (WTex) 4934 Lakeway Dr, Brownsville, TX 78520

FRIEDRICH, James Louis (Los) 4685 Taylor Ave Ne, Bainbridge Island, WA 98110

FRIEDRICH JR, Robert Edmund (Ct) 23 Friend Ct, Wenham, MA 01984

FRIEDRICH, Roger Paul (SVa) 1136 Quintara St, San Francisco, CA 94116

FRIEND, Robert Douglas (Va) 4011 College Valley Ct, Richmond, VA 23233

FRIESE JR, Walter Edward (WLa) 107 Shady Ave., Pineville, LA 71360

FRINK, James Phillip (RI) 3a Grouse Trl, Smithfield, RI 02917

FRISCH, Floyd Charles (ECR) 2 N Santa Cruz Ave, Los Gatos, CA 95030

FRITCH, Charles Oscar (CFla) 324 S Lost Lake Ln, Casselberry, FL 32707

FRITSCH, Andrew John (WMo) 3702 Poplar Dr, Joplin, MO 64804

FRITSCH, Peter Louis (Ore) 6310 W Ford Ave, Las Vegas, NV 89139

FRITSCHE, Janet Yvonne (NMich) 122 Hunter Rd, Iron River, MI 49935

FRITSCHNER, Ann Rumage (WNC) Po Box 2818, Hendersonville, NC 28793

FRITSCHNER, John B (Ky) Saint Luke's Church, 1206 Maple Ln, Anchorage, KY 40223

FRITTS, John Clinton (WTex) St Paul's Episcopal Church, PO Box 1148, Brady, TX 76825

FRITTS, Julia Anne (Ct) 628 Main St, Stamford, CT 06901

FRITZ, Janice Vary (CPa) 109 Hope Dr, Boiling Springs, PA 17007

FRIZZELL, Judith Ann (Dal) 5200 Fairway Circle, Granbury, TX 76049

FRNKA, Virginia H (WTex) 314 W Gayle St, Edna, TX 77957

FROEHLICH, Burt H (SeFla) 406-B Coopers Cove Rd, St Augustine, FL 32095

FROEHLICH, Meghan F (O) Our Saviour, Episcopal, 471 Crosby St., Akron, OH 44302

FROILAND, Paul Vincent (Minn) 12525 Porcupine Ct, Eden Prairie, MN 55344

FROLICK, Betty Roberson (NI) 6334 Bennington Dr, Fort Wayne, IN 46815

FROLICK, Paul Michael (Roch) St George's Episcopal Chruch, 635 Wilder Rd, Hilton, NY 14468

FROMBERG, Paul D (Cal) 500 De Haro Street, San Francisco, CA 94107

FRONTJES, Richard Andrew (Chi) 910 Normal Rd, DeKalb, IL 60115

FROST, Gregory Hayden (Los) 18354 Superior St, Northridge, CA 91325

FROST, Jeffrey Louis (Cal) Saint Timothy's Church, 1550 Diablo Rd, Danville, CA 94526

FROST-PHILLIPS, Lisa Ann (NC) 128 Creekview Cir, Carrboro, NC 27510

FROTHINGHAM, Christen Struthers (Mass) 6 Sunset Ave, North Reading, MA 01864

FROWE, Jeanne Shelton (Nev) 384 Sunset Dr, Reno, NV 89509

FROYEN, Jeremy Craig (SeFla)

FRUEHWIRTH, Robert Alan (FdL) 66 Ella Road, Norwich, NR1 4BS, Great Britain (UK)

FRY, Gwenneth Jeri (Ark) 7604 Apache Road, Little Rock, AR 72205

FRY, Lisa Smith (Ark) 1000 N Mississippi St, Little Rock, AR 72207

FRY III, William Nall (WTenn) 10 N Highland St, Memphis, TN 38111

FRYE, Donald Jay (Chi) 2843 Gypsum Cir, Naperville, IL 60564

FRYE III, Jacob Wade (ETenn) 332 Essex Dr, Knoxville, TN 37922

FRYE, Linda Lou (Eau) 21836 Gladestone Ave, Tomah, WI 54660

FUESSEL JR, Paul A (Ia) 2585 Hurricane Loop Rd, Tennessee Ridge, TN 37178

FULFORD, David Edward (NwPa)

FULGHUM, Charles Benjamin (At) 759 Loridans Dr Ne, Atlanta, GA 30342

FULGHUM, Peter Clopper (Md) 13007 Still Meadow Rd, Smithsburg, MD 21783

FULGONI, Dina Loreen (Los) PO Box 1681, Big Bear Lake, CA 92315

FULK, Michael Thomas (NI) 909 S. Darling St., Angola, IN 46703

FULKS, William B (Pa) 112 Elite Hts, Hurricane, WV 25526

FULLER, Betty Wl Works (WTex) 823 S Water St Apt 3G, Corpus Christi, TX 78401

FULLER, Edward Beaty (At) 3826 Courtyard Drive, Atlanta, GA 30339

FULLER III, Frank E (Tex) 823 S Water St #3G, Corpus Christi, TX 78401

FULLER, Glen C (WNY)

FULLER, Jan (SwVa) 2247 Saddle Club Rd, Burlington, NC 27215

FULLER, John Paul (Los) 940 Ivywood Dr, Oxnard, CA 93030

FULLER, Lynnette Burley (NJ) 8 Sargent Street, #4, Nutley, NJ 07110

FULLER IV, Paul Hamilton (WNC) 205 Waterford Dr, Mills River, NC 28759

FULLER SR, Steven George (Vt) 10 South St # 5101, Bellows Falls, VT 05101

FULLER, Walter Harry (LI) 1692 Bellmore Ave, North Bellmore, NY 11710

FULLMER, Janet M (Colo) 1700 Esther Way, The Dalles, OR 97058

FULTON JR, Charles Britton (Fla) 1580 Murdock Rd, Marietta, GA 30062

FULTON III, Charles Newell (NY) 815 2nd Ave, New York, NY 10017

FULTON, Jennifer (NI) 601 E. Vistula St., Bristol, IN 46507

FULTON, J(ohn) (EC) 307 N Main St, Farmville, NC 27828

FULTON, Nancy Casey (WMich) 807 South University, Mt Pleasant, MI 48858

FULTON, Norman Hamilton (NY) Macaulay Road, Rd #2, Katonah, NY 10536

FULTON, Sharline Alahverde (Pa) 1207 Foulkeways, Gwynedd, PA 19436

FULTON, William Riggs (Oly) 32 NE Tracy Ave., Bremerton, WA 98311

FUNK, Delmar Gerald (Neb) 3668 - 18th, Columbus, NE 68601

FUNK, Jeffrey Lawrence (Be) 46 S Laurel St, Hazleton, PA 18201

FUNK, Nicholas J (RG) 5125 Rock House Rd, Las Cruces, NM 88011

FUNK, Peter Van Keuren (NJ) 4825 Province Line Rd, Princeton, NJ 08540

FUNKHOUSER, David Franklin (Pa) 456 66th St, Oakland, CA 94609

FUNSTON, A Patrick K (Kan) 601 Poyntz Avenue, Manhattan, KS 66502

FUNSTON, C Eric (O) St. Paul's Episcopal Church, 317 E. Liberty Street, Medina, OH 44256

FURGERSON, John Arthur (SwVa) 11 Whitmore St, Lexington, VA 24450

FURLOW, Mark D (SwVa) Trinity Church, 475 Oak Ridge Rd, Arrington, VA 22922

FURMAN, James Edmund (Los) 13131 Moorpark St Apt 412, Sherman Oaks, CA 91423

FURNISS III, Robert Hosmer (Minn) 2132 Cameron Dr, Woodbury, MN 55125

FURRER, Thomas (Ct) 5 Trout Drive, Granby, CT 06035

FUSELIER, Donald Paul (ECR) 1017 Alameda St, Monterey, CA 93940

FUSSELL, Stacey Marie (NwPa) 462 Congress St, Bradford, PA 16701

G

GABAUD, Pierre Simpson (SeFla) St Paul et Les Martyrs d'Haiti, 6744 N Miami Ave, Miami, FL 33150

GABB, James Neil (Neb) 16604 E Crestline Pl, Centennial, CO 80015

GABEL, Mark Francis (CFla) 5139 Marbella Isle Dr, Orlando, FL 32837

GABLE, David Lee (Nwk) 24 Harmony Dr, Pt Jefferson Station, NY 11776

GABLE, Stephen Louis (Ind) 1045 E Sassafras Cir, 1129 Linden Dr, Bloomington, IN 47408

GADDY, Anna Lee (RG)

GADSDEN, Carol D (NY) 168 W Boston Post Rd, Mamaroneck, NY 10543

GAEDE, Lee A (Chi) 342 Custer Ave. Apt. 2, Evanston, IL 60202

GAEDE, Sarah Harrell (Ala) 830 Willingham Rd, Florence, AL 35630

GAESTEL, Robert J (Los) 1100 Avenue 64, Pasadena, CA 91105

GAFFORD, Donna Elizabeth Goodman (Ala) 38 Longview Ct, Seale, AL 36875

GAFFORD, Happy Lawton (CFla) 2410 Ridgeside Rd, Apopka, FL 32712

GAFNEY, Wilda Clydette (Pa) 7301 Germantown Ave, Philadelphia, PA 19119

GAFOUR, Ayyoubawaga Bushara (Colo) Sudanese Community Church, 1350 Washington St, Denver, CO 80203

GAGE, Bartlett Wright (Ct) 26 Edmond St, Darien, CT 06820

GAGE, Nancy Elizabeth (Ct) Grace Church, 5958 Main St, Trumbull, CT 06611

GAHAGAN, Susan Elisabeth (Ga) 1802 Abercorn St, Savannah, GA 31401

GAHAN III, W(Illiam) Patrick (WTex) Christ Episcopal Church, 510 Belknap Pl, San Antonio, TX 78212

GAHLER, Robert Edward (NY) 67 Woodmere Rd, Stamford, CT 06905

GAILLARD, Ann Schwarberg (Alb)

GAINES, Mary Moore Thompson (Cal) 128 Beaumont Ave, San Francisco, CA 94118

GAISER, Ted J (Me)

GAITHER, Gayle Lee (Spok) 416 E Nelson Rd, Moses Lake, WA 98837

GALAGAN, Christine Kay (Wyo) PO Box 1718, Cody, WY 82414

GALAGAN, John Michael (Episcopal SJ) 21105 Carriage Dr, Tehachapi, CA 93561

GALANTOWICZ, Deena McHenry (Fla) 49 Ocean Ct, Saint Augustine, FL 32080

GALAZ, Ernest M (Az) 969 W Country Club Dr, Nogales, AZ 85621

GALBRAITH, James MacAlpine (Miss) 2196 Saint James Blvd, Gulfport, MS 39507

GALBREATH, Janet Louise (CFla) 01236 Miller Blvd, Fruitland Park, FL 34731

GALEANO FRANCO, Gustavo (SeFla)

GALGANO, Hollis Holder (NY) 311 Huguenot St, New Rochelle, NY 10801

GALGANOWICZ, Henry C (Pa) 432 Bluestone Ct, PO Box 714, Lake Harmony, PA 18624

GALICIA, Kathryn K (Episcopal SJ) 3308 Swallow Dr, Modesto, CA 95356

GALINDO-PAZ, Elvia Maria (Hond)

GALIPEAU, Steven Arthur (Los) 8805 Azul Drive, West Hills, CA 91304

☒ **GALLAGHER**, Carol J (Form Asst Bp of Nwk 2007-) 40 Charlotte St, Haverhill, MA 01830

GALLAGHER, Daniel Paul (NY) 29 Halcyon Rd, Millbrook, NY 12545

GALLAGHER, Elvin Ross (Ida) 5605 Randolph Dr, Boise, ID 83705

GALLAGHER, Gerald J (NY) 1001 Leesburg Dr, Leland, NC 28451

GALLAGHER, John Merrill (Cal) 212 Riviera Cir, Larkspur, CA 94939

GALLAGHER, Mary Ellen Turner (Ida) 13118 W Picadilly St, Boise, ID 83713

GALLAGHER, Nancy Elizabeth (Ore) 1800 Lakewood Ct, Spc 58, Eugene, OR 97402

GALLAGHER, Patricia Portley (Ct) 9134 Town Walk Dr, Hamden, CT 06518

GALLAGHER, Robert A (Me) 1640 18th Ave, Apt 2, Seattle, WA 98122

GALLAGHER, Robert Joseph (Mich) 78 Nason St, Maynard, MA 01754

GALLEHER, Stephen Cary (Nwk) 7855 Kennedy Blvd E, Apt. 21D, North Bergen, NJ 07047

GALLETLY, David P (Los) 2812 Amber Wood Pl, Thousand Oaks, CA 91362

GALLIGAN, Joseph Edward (Wyo) PO Box 950, Thermopolis, WY 82443

GALLOWAY, David Alan (At) 845 Edgewater Dr Nw, Atlanta, GA 30328

GALLOWAY, Richard Kent (Ky) 120 Mauldin Rd, Greenville, SC 29605

GALVIN, Kathleen M (Ore) 2293 NW Mcgarey Dr, McMinnville, OR 97128

GALVIN, Michael Joseph (Ind) 9621 Claymont Ln, Fishers, IN 46037

GAMBLE, Deborah E (SO) 4234 Hamilton Ave, Cincinnati, OH 45223

GAMBLE, John Robert (SwFla) 1005 Sleepy Hollow Rd, FL

GAMBLE, Robert David (Ia) ul. Pasieka 24, Poznan, 61657, Poland

GAMBLING, Paul (Evans) (SanD) 5079 E 30th Pl, Yuma, AZ 85365

GAMBRILL, James Howard (Nwk) PO Box 1929, York Beach, ME 03910

GAME, Paul Richard (At) Trinity Episcopal Church, 1130 First Ave, Columbus, GA 31901

GAMMONS JR, Edward Babson (NJ) 7 Oak St, Warren, RI 02885

GANDARA-PEREA, Jose Roberto (Oly) 143 Lindsay Way, Eastsound, WA 98245

GANDELL, Dahn (Roch) 21 Warwick Dr, Fairport, NY 14450

GANN, Judith Fara Walsman (Okla) 6335 S 72nd East Ave, Tulsa, OK 74133

GANNON, Kathleen (SeFla) 2014 Alta Meadows Ln Apt 302, Delray Beach, FL 33444

GANNON, William Sawyer (Nwk) 11 French Dr, Bedford, NH 03110

GANTER, G David (Vt) 12 Beechwood Lane, Jericho, VT 05465

GANTER-TOBACK, Gail Sage (NY) 32 Center St, New Paltz, NY 12561

GANTZ, Jay John (EMich) 10095 E Coldwater Rd, Davison, MI 48423

GARAFALO, Robert Christopher (Los) 19988 Promenade Cir, Riverside, CA 92508

GARBARINO, Harold William (Mass) 2038 Laurel Park Hwy, Laurel Park, NC 29739

GARCEAU, John Earle (Alb) 2050 N San Clemente Rd, Palm Springs, CA 92262

GARCES TORRES, Gilberto Goen (PR) Iglesia Episcopal Puertorriquena, PO Box 902, Saint Just, PR 00978-0902, Puerto Rico

GARCIA, Christine Joyce (Va) 1704 W Laburnum Ave, Richmond, VA 23227

GARCIA, Christopher (Va) 3116 O St NW, Washington, DC 20007

GARCIA, David Allen (PR)

GARCIA JR, Francisco J (Los) All Saints Church, 132 N Euclid Ave, Pasadena, CA 91101

GARCIA, Hope Jufiar (ECR) Po Box 3994, Salinas, CA 93912

GARCIA, Louis Fernando (ETenn) 10 Fort Stephenson Pl, Lookout Mountain, TN 37350

GARCIA, Ruth Anne (NY) Grace Episcopal Church, 116 City Island Avenue, Bronx, NY 10464

GARCIA, Sixto Rafael (SeFla) 150 SW 13th Ave, Miami, FL 33135

GARCIA, Teodosio R (HB)

GARCIA-APONTE, Jorge (PR)

GARCIA CORREA, Luis Alberto (DR (DomRep))

GARCIA DE JESUS, Juan (PR)

GARCIA DE LOS SANTOS, Ramon Antonio (DR (DomRep)) Guarionex #19, Ensanche Quisqueya, La Romana, Dominican Republic

GARCIA-PEREZ, Jose Rafael (PR)

GARCIA-TUIRAN, Carlos Alfredo (SanD) 2660 Hardy Drive, Lemon Grove, CA 91945

GARD, Mary Anne (Ore) 147 NW 19th Ave, Portland, OR 97209

GARDE, Mary (LI) 573 Roanoke Ave, Riverhead, NY 11901

GARDNER, Albutt Lorian (Pa) 600 E. Cathedral Rd., # H-304, Philadelphia, PA 19128

GARDNER, Anne Elizabeth (Mass) Phillips Academy, 180 Main Street, Andover, MA 01810

GARDNER, Bruce Norman (Eau) Po Box 637, Hayward, WI 54843

GARDNER, Calvin George (SVa) 1405 Bruton Ln, Virginia Beach, VA 23451

GARDNER, Carol Hartsfield (WTenn) 215 Windsor Terrace Dr, Nashville, TN 37221

GARDNER, Daniel Wayne (EO) 571 Yakima St S, Vale, OR 97918

GARDNER, Edward Morgan (WNC) 118 Clubwood Ct, Asheville, NC 28803

GARDNER, Elizabeth Bonforte (WA) St John's Church, 6715 Georgetown Pike, McLean, VA 22101

GARDNER, E(Ugene) Clifton (Dal) 6505 Brook Lake Dr., Dallas, TX 75248

GARDNER, H Huey (Ala) 1910 12th Ave. South, Birmingham, AL 35205

GARDNER, James Edward (CPa) 839 Fraternity Rd, Lewisburg, PA 17837

GARDNER, Joan Margiotta (ECR) 1970 Cerra Vista Dr, Hollister, CA 95023

GARDNER, John (Cal) 1340 Dolores St, San Francisco, CA 94110

GARDNER, John Burke (Colo) Ch Of The Ascension & Holy Trinity, 420 W 18th St, Pueblo, CO 81003

GARDNER, Mark W (Los) 1031 Lanza Ct, San Marcos, CA 92078

GARDNER, Randal B. (Cal) Grace Cathedral Church, 1100 California St, San Francisco, CA 94108

GARDNER, Van Howard (Md) 89 Murdock Rd, Baltimore, MD 21212

GARDNER-SMITH, Fran (Cal) 2217 Koa Ct, Antioch, CA 94509

GARFIELD, Elizabeth Ann (Colo) St Luke's Episcopal Church, 1270 Poplar St, Denver, CO 80220

GARFIELD, Liston Alphonso (Ala) 2060 Mohican Dr, Auburn, AL 36879

GARGIULO, Mariano (Nwk) 384 Hilltop Ave # 7605, Leonia, NJ 07605

GARLAND III, John G (Tex) 1002 South Main Street, Greenville, SC 29611

GARLICHS, Richard Walbridge (Oly) 900 University St Apt 6G, Seattle, WA 98101

GARMA, Joann Marie (La) 1014 Marigny Ave, Mandeville, LA 70448

GARMAN, Cynthia Anne (Mich) 426 Cottonwood Ln., Saline, MI 48176

GARMAN, Gerald Roger (Oly) 11758 Meridian Ave N, Seattle, WA 98133

GARNER, Evan D (Ala) 2411 13th St SE, Decatur, AL 35601

GARNER, Jeffery Ray (CGC)

GARNER, Mary P (Eas) 302 S Liberty St, Centrevillle, MD 21617

GARNER, Terry (Mil) 10328 N Stanford Dr, Mequon, WI 53097

GARNIER, Maryellen (The Episcopal NCal) 1800 Wildcat Blvd, Rocklin, CA 95765

GARNO, Arthur Scott (Alb) 5828 State Highway 68, Ogdensburg, NY 13669

GARNO, Scott Arthur (Alb) Po Box 537, Unadilla, NY 13849

GARNSEY, Elizabeth H (NY) Church of the Heavenly Rest, 2 E 90th St, New York, NY 10128

GARRAMONE, Laurie (Alb)

GARRATT, Stephen Richard (Oly) 19247 40th Pl NE, Lake Forest Park, WA 98155

GARREN, Benjamin Nathan (Az) 715 N Park Ave, Tucson, AZ 85719

GARRENTON, Linwood Wilson (Roch) 599 E 7th St Apt 6E, Brooklyn, NY 11218

GARRETT, David (ETenn) 515 5th St, Newport, TN 37821

GARRETT, G(eorge) Kenneth (Mass) 12 Academy Ave, Fairhaven, MA 02719

GARRETT, Jane Nuckols (Vt) 206 Fairway Vlg, Leeds, MA 01053

GARRETT, Kathy Ann (Dal) 511 Foote St, McKinney, TX 75069

GARRETT, M Paul (Colo) 2530 Leyden St., Denver, CO 80207

GARRETT, Mary Ann (La) PO Box 126, Baton Rouge, LA 70821

GARRIGAN, J(oseph) Edward (Pa) PO Box 1681, Doylestown, PA 18901

✠ **GARRISON**, J Michael (Ret Bp of WNY 2011-) 207 Pineneedle Dr, Bradenton, FL 34210

GARRISON, Thomas Martin (Minn) 4180 Lexington Ave S, Eagan, MN 55123

GARRISON, William (Los) 7056 Washington Ave, Whittier, CA 90602

GARRISON, William Brian (CFla) 212 Brevity Ln, DeLand, FL 32724

GARRITY, Clelia Pinza (Eas) 3081 Margarita Ave, Pahrump, NV 89048

GARRITY, Susan E (NH) 97 Halls Mill Rd, Newfields, NH 03856

GARTIG, William George (SO) 2146 Cameron Ave Apt 5, Cincinnati, OH 45212

GARTON, Mary Pamela (CFla) 190 Interlachen Rd, Melbourne, FL 32940

GARVIN, Grayson Barry (CFla) 3000 Nw 42nd Ave Apt B401, Coconut Creek, FL 33066

GARWOOD, Martha Jayne (SD) 4640 Sturgis Rd Lot 49, Rapid City, SD 57702

GARY, Hobart Jude (Ct) 2855 West Commericial Blvd, Apartment 354, Fort Lauderdale, FL 33309

GARZA JR, Frederico Eloy (Va) 2900 Hanes Ave, Richmond, VA 23222

GASKILL JR, Joseph John (EC) 174 Windy Point Rd, Beaufort, NC 28516

GASQUET, Mark Cordes (La) 308 Central Ave, Jefferson, LA 70121

GASTON, Katherine Elizabeth (Neb) 7625 Lafayette Ave, Omaha, NE 68114

GASTON III, Paul L (O) 2389 Brunswick Lane, Hudson, OH 44236

GAT, Maggie (Nwk) 4230 Cascade Falls Dr, Sarasota, FL 34243

GATCH JR, Milton Mccormick (NY) 575 W End Ave Apt 7C, New York, NY 10024

GATCHELL, Lois Harvey (Okla) 8222 S Yale Ave Apt 321, Tulsa, OK 74137

GATELEY, Gail Nicholson (Dal) 15264 SW Peachtree Drive, Tigard, OR 97224

GATES, Alan K (Cal)

✠ **GATES**, Alan M (Bp of Mass 2014-) Episcopal Diocese of Massachusetts, 138 Tremont St, Boston, MA 02111

GATES, Mary May (Ct) 16 Church St, Waterbury, CT 06702

GATES JR, Robert J (Okla)

GATREL, Larry Gene (Ia) 1602 Edgewood Dr, Carroll, IA 51401

GATTA, Julia Milan (Ct) 243 Tennessee Ave, Sewanee, TN 37375

GATTIS, Larry Russell (Chi) 20326 Harding Ave, Olympia Fields, IL 60461

GATZA, Mark Francis (Md) Po Box 628, Bel Air, MD 21014

GAUMER, Susan Salot (La) 7820 Jeannette St., New Orleans, LA 70118

GAUVIN, Joseph Henri Armand (NJ) 25 Southwood Drive, Saint Catharine'S, L2M 4M5, Canada

GAVENTA, Sarah Kinney (Va)

GAVIN, Craig Edmonds (Neb) 4321 S 36th St, Lincoln, NE 68516

GAVIN, Timothy (Pa) The Episcopal Academy, 1785 Bishop White Dr, Newtown Square, PA 19073

GAVIT, Sara B (Ak) 2222 E Tudor Rd, Anchorage, AK 99507

GAY, Jean-Ricot Ricot (SeFla) 465 Ne 100th St, Miami Shores, FL 33138

GAY, Judith Shumway (Mass) 59 Fenno St, Cambridge, MA 02138

GAY, Karen R (La) Episcopal Church of the Holy Communion, P. O. Box 474, Plaquemine, LA 70764

GAY, Margaret Worcester (CNY)

GAY, Robert George (SVa)

GAYLE JR, William Gedge (La) 227 Helios Avenue, Metarie, LA 70005

GAYLOR, Pamela Elaine (SO) 3149 Indian Ripple Rd, Dayton, OH 45440

GDULA, Peter Mark (CPa) St Luke's Episcopal Church, 8 E Keller St, Mechanicsburg, PA 17055

GEARHART, Robert James (Neb) 665 4th St., PO Box 56, Syracuse, NE 68446

GEARING, Charles Edward (At) 6525 Gardenia Way, Stone Mountain, GA 30087

GEARS, Wallace E (Minn) 3240 Jersey Ave S, Minneapolis, MN 55426

GEDDES, Robert Douglas (Va) 269 Johnson Point Road, Hallieford, VA 23068

GEDRICK, John (At) 700 Route 22, Pawling, NY 12564

GEEN, Russell Glenn (HB) 4 Shad Bush Dr, Columbia, MO 65203

GEER, Christine Groves (Md) 23 Briar Patch Rd, Stonington, CT 06378

GEER, Francis Hartley (NY) Po Box 158, Garrison, NY 10524

GEERDES, Patricia Seney (WVa) 900 Hillsborough St, Raleigh, NC 27603

GEESEY, Barry Stephen (WVa) 3887 Carriage Ln SW, Conyers, GA 30094

GEHLSEN, Thomas J (Minn) 1232 Lakemoor Dr., Woodbury, MN 55129

GEHRIG, Stephen James (Oly) 1828 Field Place NE, Renton, WA 98059

GEIB, Lanny Roland (Tex) 5087 Galileo Dr, Colorado Springs, CO 80917

GEIGER, Clifford Theodore (Me) 2800 Se Fairway W, Stuart, FL 34997

GEIGER, William Linwood (Pgh) 3079 Warren Rd, Indiana, PA 15701

GEISLER, Mark A (Chi) 113 E. Lafayette St., Ottawa, IL 61350

GEISLER, William Fredric (Cal) PO Box 2624, San Anselmo, CA 94979

GEISLER, William Joseph (Pgh) 1283 Earlford Drive, Pittsburgh, PA 15227

GEISSLER-O'NEIL, Susan Lorraine (Mass) 3350 Hopyard Rd, Pleasanton, CA 94588

GEITZ, Elizabeth R (NJ) 431 Twin Lakes Road, Shohola, PA 18458

GELDERT, Maurice William (RG) 121 Mescalero Tr, Ruidoso, NM 88345

GELFER, Miriam Carmel (Mass) 8 Saint Johns Rd, Cambridge, MA 02138

GELIEBTER, Phillip Lincoln (Pa) 4442 Frankford Ave, Phila, PA 19124

GELINEAU, Francoise (Mich) P.O. Box 351, Roscommon, MI 48653

GELLER, Maggie (Mass) 4 Key St., Millis, MA 02054

GELLERT, Alan Cranston (SeFla) 2303 NE Seaview Dr, Jensen Beach, FL 34957

GEMIGNANI, Michael Caesar (Tex) 1816 Dublin Dr., League City, TX 77573

GEMINDER, Randolph Jon (LI) 175 Broadway, Amityville, NY 11701

GENEREUX, Patrick Edward (Ia) 3700 S Westport Ave #530, Sioux Falls, SD 57106

GENNETT JR, Paul William (Del) 413 Terra Dr, Newark, DE 19702

GENNUSO JR, George (WLa) 500 Edgewood Dr, Pineville, LA 71360

GENSZLER, Mark (Vt)

GENTLE, Judith Marie (Pgh) 315 Turnpike St, North Andover, MA 01845

GENTRY, (Bryan) Massey (Tex) 209 Orange Avenue, Fairhope, AL 36532

GENTRY, Keith A (Nwk) 11 Hinchman Avenue, Wayne, NJ 07470

GENTY, Marc Daniel (Colo) St Luke's Episcopal Church, 2000 Stover St, Fort Collins, CO 80525

GEORGE, Allen Winnie Sie (NY) 781 Castle Hill Ave, Bronx, NY 10473

GEORGE, Cathy Ann Hagstrom (Mass) 381 Hammond St, Chestnut Hill, MA 02467

GEORGE, C(larence Davis) Dominic (NY) 797 Corbett Ave Apt 3, San Francisco, CA 94131

GEORGE, Erminie A (VI) PO Box 9798 Charlotte Amalie, St. Thomas, Virgin Islands 00801

GEORGE JR, Jay Charles (WTex) 7714 Moss Brook Dr, San Antonio, TX 78255

GEORGE, Joanna Elizabeth (Dal) St Philip's Episcopal Church, 6400 Stonebrook Pkwy, Frisco, TX 75034

GEORGE, Johannes Mark Philip (Tex) 15325 Bellaire Boulevard, Houston, TX 77083

GEORGE, John (VI)

GEORGE, Juan Victor (Del) Trinity Episcopal Church, 1108 N Adams St, Wilmington, DE 19801

GEORGE, Mitzi Gae Shelton (WLa) 1020 Sutherland Rd., Lake Charles, LA 70611

GEORGE, Susanne T (Cal) 60 Brunswick Park, Melrose, MA 02176

GEORGE ALLEN, Eldred Hamilton (Chi)

GEORGE-HACKER, Nina (Alb) St Christophers Episcopal Church, PO Box 386, Cobleskill, NY 12043

GEORGES, Esther Mathilda (VI)

GEORGI, Geoffrey Mack (NC) Po Box 13, Rougemont, NC 27572

✠ **GEPERT**, Robert R (Ret Bp of WMich 2002-) Episcopal Diocese of Central Pennsylvania, 101 Pine St, Harrisburg, PA 17101

GERBASI, Virginia Kaye (WA) 1525 H St., N.W, St. John's Church, Lafayette Square, Washington, DC 20005

GERBER, Ronald D (Alb) 36 General Torbert Dr, Milford, DE 19963

GERBRACHT-STAGNARO, Marjorie Ann (NH) 106 Lowell St, Manchester, NH 03101

GERDAU, Carlson (Chi) 305 W End Ave Apt 1214, New York, NY 10023

GERDING, Susan Ann (Tex) 836 W. Jones St., Livingston, TX 77351
GERDSEN, Elizabeth Jane (SO) 1219 Amherst Pl, Dayton, OH 45406
GERHARD, Ernest J (Neb) 14214 Briggs Cir, Omaha, NE 68144
GERHARD, Kurt Joseph (WA) Saint Patrick's Episcopal Church, 4700 Whitehaven Pkwy NW, Washington, DC 20007
GERHARDT, Michael Joseph (NJ) 171 Larch Ave., Bogota, NJ 07603
GERHART JR, John James (CFla) 4315 Longshore Dr, Land O Lakes, FL 34639
GERHART, William James (NJ) 2131 Woodbridge Ave, PO Box 1286, Edison, NJ 08817
GERLACH, Aaron R (O) 125 East Market St, Tiffin, OH 44883
GERMAN, Kenneth L (Episcopal SJ) 329 Mannel Ave, Shafter, CA 93263
GERMINO, Carmen C (Va) 1205 W Franklin St, Richmond, VA 23220
GERNS, Andrew Timothy (Be) 14 Midland Dr, Easton, PA 18045
GEROLD, Donna Jane (Ala) St Stephen's Episcopal Church, 3775 Crosshaven Dr, Vestavia, AL 35223
GERTH JR, Stephen Shea (NY) Church of Saint Mary the Virgin, 145 West 46th Street, New York, NY 10036
GERVAIS JR, Sidney Joseph (Tex) 1210 E Mesa Park Dr, Round Rock, TX 78664
GESTON, Alejandro Sumadin (The Episcopal Church in Haw) 91-1746 Bond St, Ewa Beach, HI 96706
GETCHELL, Philip Armour (ECR) 6524 Hercus Ct, San Jose, CA 95119
GETLEIN, Greta (RI) Saint Paul's Church, 50 Park Pl, Pawtucket, RI 02860
GETREU, David Edward (SO) 127 W Mound Street, Circleville, OH 43113
GETTEL, Rebecca Binns (Mass) Trinity Church, 81 Elm St, Concord, MA 01742
GETTS, Sarah Jane (Az)
GETTYS, Jeannette Cooper (USC) 308 College Dr., Gaffney, SC 29340
GETTYS, Laura F (WTenn) 692 Poplar Ave, Memphis, TN 38105
GETZ, Peter Richard Remsen (Dal) 808 Oak Hollow Lane, Rockwall, TX 75087
GIACOBBE, Georgia Bates (EO) 3564 E. Second St. #26, The Dalles, OR 97058
GIACOMA, Claudia Louder (U) 7362 Tall Oaks Dr, Park City, UT 84098
GIANNINI, Robert Edward (Ind) 55 Monument Cir Ste 600, Indianapolis, IN 46204
GIANSIRACUSA JR, Michael (Pa) 225 S 3rd St, Philadelphia, PA 19106
GIARDINA, Denise Diana (WVa)
GIBBES, Joseph A (Ala) 2017 6th Ave N, Birmingham, AL 35203

GIBBONS, David Austen (Chi) 339 Ridge Rd, Barrington, IL 60010
GIBBONS, Rowena Gregg (CPa) 64 Mayflower Ln, Mansfield, PA 16933
GIBBS, Charles Philip (Cal) 9900 Kensington Pkwy, Kensington, MD 20895
GIBBS, Dennis (Los) 840 Echo Park Ave, Los Angeles, CA 90026
GIBBS, James Millard (Chi) 13 Lingfield Court, 60 High St, Birmingham, B17 9NE, Great Britain (UK)
GIBBS, Lee Wayland (O) 2413 Weymouth Dr, Springfield, VA 22151
✠ **GIBBS JR**, Wendell Nathaniel (Bp of Mich 2000-) 19594 Renfrew Rd, Detroit, MI 48221
GIBLIN, Keith Fredrick (Tex) 1401 W Park Ave, Orange, TX 77630
GIBSON, Alan Glen (Mich) St Andrew Episcopal Church, 306 N Division St, Ann Arbor, MI 48104
GIBSON, Barbara Jean (Kan) 701 SW 8th Ave, Topeka, KS 66603
GIBSON, Beverly Findley (CGC) 24 Blacklawn St, Mobile, AL 36604
GIBSON, Catherine Snyder (ETenn) Carlene Cottage, Tarland, Aboyne, Aberdeenshire, Scotland, AB34 4YX, Great Britain (UK)
GIBSON, Earl Dodridge (Az) 31641 La Novia Ave., San Juan Capistrano, CA 92675
GIBSON, Emily Stearns (Me) 732 Nottingham Rd, Wilmington, DE 19805
GIBSON, Gregory Hyvestra (VI) St John's Episcopal Church, PO Box 486, Christiansted, 00821-0486, Virgin Islands (U.S.)
GIBSON, John Kenneth (NC)
GIBSON, John Noel Keith (VI)
GIBSON, Libby (Mass) Saint Mary's Episcopal Church, 3055 Main St, Barnstable, MA 02630
GIBSON III, Owen S (HB) 2926 Maple Springs Blvd, Dallas, TX 75235
GIBSON, Robert Burrows (At) 20 Lucky Ln, Blairsville, GA 30512
GIBSON, Thomas William (CFla) Po Box 320026, 139 S. Atlantic Avenue, Cocoa Beach, FL 32932
GIBSON, Webster S (Va) 111 Stonebrook Rd, Winchester, VA 22602
GIDDINGS, Monte Carl (Kan) 26755 W 103rd St, Olathe, KS 66061
GIEGLER, Carl E (Chi) 414 Gaspar Key Ln, Punta Gorda, FL 33955
GIERLACH, David Joseph (The Episcopal Church in Haw) 231 Miloiki Pl, Honolulu, HI 96825
GIESELER, Gieseler Morgret (Miss)
GIESELMANN, Robert K (ETenn) Church of the Ascension, 800 S. Northshore Drive, Knoxville, TN 37919
GIFFORD II, Gerald Gerard (The Episcopal Church in Haw) 446 Kawaihae St Apt 119, Honolulu, HI 96825

GIFFORD, Lance Allen Ball (Md) 1700 South Rd, Baltimore, MD 21209
GIFFORD-COLE, Irene Margarete (Minn) 225 Hoylake Rd. W, Qualicum Beach, V9k 1k5, Canada
GILBERT, Carol Beverly (NJ) 34 Mystic Way, Burlington, NJ 08016
GILBERT JR, George Asbury (CGC) 10100 Hillview Dr Apt 432, Pensacola, FL 32514
GILBERT, Marilynn D (Ct) 28 Windemere Pl, Grosse Pointe Farms, MI 48236
GILBERT, Paul (LI) 1760 Parc Vue Ave, Mount Pleasant, SC 29464
GILBERT, Shedrick Edward (SeFla) 3368 Nw 51st Ter, Miami, FL 33142
GILBERT, Thomas F (Me) 118 Morrill St, Pittsfield, ME 04967
GILBERT, Trimble (Ak) General Delivery, Arctic Village, AK 99722
GILBERTSEN, George Eugene (Lex)
GILBERTSON, Gary Raymond (WMo) 12301 West 125th Terr, Overland Park, KS 66213
GILCHRIST, J Edwin (Neb)
GILCHRIST, James Fiveash (Colo) 5478 S Idalia Cir, Centennial, CO 80015
GILCHRIST, John Richard (Ct) Po Box 361, Winter Harbor, ME 04693
GILDERSLEEVE, Robert Kirk (Be) 435 Center Street, Jim Thorpe, PA 18229
GILES, James D (CFla)
GILES, Richard Stephen (Pa) 105 Lansdowne Ct, Lansdowne, PA 19050
GILES, Walter Crews (FtW) 1649 Park Ln, Alvarado, TX 76009
GILES, Walter Edward (CNY) 12914 US Route 11, Adams Center, NY 13606
GILFEATHER, Gordon Grant (Az) 12990 E Shea Blvd, Scottsdale, AZ 85259
GILHOUSEN, Dennis Ray (Kan) 6501 Mapel Dr, Mission, KS 66202
GIL JIMENEZ, Ramon Antonio (DR (DomRep))
GILKES, Overton Weldon (Ct) 262 Shelton Ave, New Haven, CT 06511
GILKEY JR, Sam (CFla) 912 Virginia Ave., St. Cloud, FL 34769
GILKS, Cyntha Ann (Okla) 903 E Main St, Holdenville, OK 74848
GILL JR, Charles Henry (Eur) 3451 South Washington Ave., Titusville, FL 32780
GILL, Cynthia Elizabeth (SeFla)
GILL, James Lawrence (Be) PO Box 214, East Winthrop, ME 04343
GILL, Jeffrey Shilling (Oly) Trinity Parish, 609 8th Ave, Seattle, WA 98104
GILL JR, John Nicholas (SO) 3429 Live Oak Place, Columbus, OH 43221
GILL, Jule Carlyle (WA) 4 Milford Ave, Lewes, DE 19958
GILL, Robert Clarence (CPa) 139 N Findlay St, York, PA 17402
GILLARD, Gary Laverne (Md)

GILLEN, Marguerite Webb (Ct)

GILLESPIE, Ann Hazard (Va) Christ Church, 118 N Washington St, Alexandria, VA 22314

GILLESPIE, David Marston (RI) 2206 N Hollow Rd, Rochester, VT 05767

GILLESPIE, Harold Stanley (Az) 501 S. La Posada Cir., Apt. 116, Green Valley, AZ 85614

GILLESPIE JR, Robert Schaeffer (WA) 14702 W Auburn Rd, Accokeek, MD 20607

GILLETT, Elizabeth Rosa Hamliton (CNY) 1213 River Rd, Hamilton, NY 13346

GILLETT, Richard W (Oly) 719 N 67th St, Seattle, WA 98103

GILLETTE, Howard Dennis (Pgh) 3414 Ventana Dr, Coraopolis, PA 15108

GILLETTE, Martha Carol (Chi) 154 Timber Ridge Ln, Lake Barrington, IL 60010

GILLIAM, John Malone (EC) 101 W Gale St, Edenton, NC 27932

GILLIES, Bruce Nelson (WNY) 1082 Brookwood Dr, Derby, NY 14047

GILLIES, Clara (WNY) 18 N Pearl St, Buffalo, NY 14202

GILLISS, Columba (Md) 3200 Baker Cir Unit I209, Adamstown, MD 21710

GILL-LOPEZ, John Herbert (LI) 80 La Salle St Apt 21-H, New York, NY 10027

GILLMAN, Paula Ruth (Minn) 520 N Pokegama Ave, Grand Rapids, MN 55744

GILLOOLY, Bryan Charles (O) 19636 Scottsdale Blvd, Cleveland, OH 44122

GILMAN, Connie W (SwVa) 306 Boys Home Rd, Covington, VA 24426

GILMAN, James Earl (SwVa) 719 Opie St, Staunton, VA 24401

GILMAN, Robert Ray (SwVa) 16918 Paynes Creek Dr, Cypress, TX 77433

GILMER, Lyonel Wayman (NC)

GILMORE, Elizabeth Lameyer (Me) 24 Fairmount St, Portland, ME 04103

GILPIN, Jack (Ct) St John's Episcopal Church, 7 Whittlesey Ave, New Milford, CT 06776

GILPIN, Kathlyn Castiglioni (SwFla)

GIL RESTREPO, Silvio (Colom) Carrera 6 No 49-85, Piso 2, Bogota, Colombia

GILSDORF, John Walter (EO) 1971 Sw Quinney Ave, Pendleton, OR 97801

GILSON, Anne Elizabeth (WA) 5 Fernwood Cir, Harwich, MA 02645

GILSON, Christine (Kan) Po Box 883, El Dorado, KS 67042

GILTON, Michael R (Dal)

GINGHER, Richard Hammond (O) 4747 Scioto #201, Toledo, OH 43615

GINN JR, Robert Jay (WMass) Oratory Of Saint Francis, Box 300, Templeton, MA 01468

GINNEVER, Richard Arthur (Md) 9259 Brush Run, Columbia, MD 21045

GINOLFI, Priscilla Grant (CPa) 156 Warren Way, Lancaster, PA 17601

GINOLFI, Sarah Catherine (Ind) 6050 N Meridian St, Indianapolis, IN 46208

GINSON, Isaias Gonzales (The Episcopal Church in Haw) 1805 W.Alabama st., Houston, TX 77098

GIOVANGELO, Steven Michael (Ind) 337 North Kenyon Street, Indianapolis, IN 46219

GIRALDO OROZCO, Edgar (Litoral Ecu)

GIRARD, Jacques Andre (Nwk) 8 Shore Rd, Staten Island, NY 10307

GIRARDEAU, Charles Michael (At) 1446 Edinburgh Dr, Tucker, GA 30084

GIRARDEAU, Malcolm Douglas (Eas) 211 E Isabella St, Salisbury, MD 21801

GIRARDIN, Barbara Jeanine (Colo) 2604 S Troy Ct, Aurora, CO 80014

GIRATA, Christopher D (WTenn) Calvary Episcopal Church, 102 N 2nd St, Memphis, TN 38103

GIROUX, Mark Alan (CNY) 355 Hyde St, Whitney Point, NY 13862

GIRVIN, Calvin Shields (NwT) 4541 County Road 127, Colorado City, TX 79512

GITANE, Clayola Hillaker (SanD) 1020 Rose Ranch Rd, San Marcos, CA 92069

GITAU, Samson Njuguna (Ark) 243 N Mcneil St, Memphis, TN 38112

GITHITU, James Kimari (Mass) 740 Princeton Blvd Apt 3, Lowell, MA 01851

GITIMU, Paul (Pa) 1747 Church Ln, Philadelphia, PA 19141

GIVEN, Mark E (Ct) 1113 Abrams Road, #4-121, Richardson, TX 75081

GIVLER, Gary Bruce (SO) 6215 Kenwood Rd, Madeira, OH 45243

GLANCEY, Bryan Eaton (Eas) 1205 Frederick Ave, Salisbury, MD 21801

GLANDON, Clyde Calvin (Okla) 4223 E 84th St, Tulsa, OK 74137

GLANVILLE, Polly Ann (O) 1945 26th Street, Cuyahoga Falls, OH 44223

GLASER, David Charles (Mich) 20500 W OLD US HIGHWAY 12, Chelsea, MI 48118

GLASER, Geoffrey Scott (ECR) 3631 W Avenida Obregon, Tucson, AZ 85746

GLASGOW, Laurette Alice (Eur) 2 Chaussee De Charleroi, Braine-l'Alleud Belgium, 1420, Belgium

GLASS, Rosalee (Me)

GLASS, Vanessa (Cal) St. Francis of Assisi Episcopal Church, 967 5th Street, Novato, CA 94945

GLASSER, Joanne Kathleen (Eau) 111 9th St N, La Crosse, WI 54601

✠ GLASSPOOL, Mary Douglas (Bp Suffr of Los 2010-) Episcopal Diocese of Los Angeles, 840 Echo Park Ave, Los Angeles, CA 90026

GLAUDE, Ronald Arthur (Ct) 125 Grand View Ter, Brooklyn, CT 06234

GLAZIER JR, George H (SO) 10 E. Weber Rd #305, Columbus, OH 43202

GLAZIER II, William Stuart (Ct) 30 Ice House Ln, Mystic, CT 06355

GLEASON, David Thomas (WA) PO Box 1617, Evergreen, CO 80437

GLEASON, Dorothy Jean (Episcopal SJ) Po Box 399, Ambridge, PA 15003

GLEASON, Edward Campbell (SwFla) 553 Galleon Dr, Naples, FL 34102

GLEAVES, Donna Jeanne (Mont) 5 West Olive St, Bozeman, MT 59715

GLEAVES, Glen Lee (Mont) 1226 Wildflower Trl, Livingston, MT 59047

GLEESON, Terence Patrick (ECR) All Saints Church, 555 Waverley Street, Palo Alto, CA 94301

GLENDENNING, Audrey Geraldine (SeFla) 3322 Meridian Way N Apt A, Palm Beach Gardens, FL 33410

GLENDINNING, David Cross (Me) 221 Shelburne Rd, Burlington, VT 05401

GLENN JR, Charles Leslie (Mass) 1 Robeson St, Boston, MA 02130

GLENN, Kimberly B (SwVa) 200 Boston Ave, Lynchburg, VA 24503

GLENN, L G (FdL) 1230 Sandpebble Dr., Rockton, IL 61072

GLENN, Michael Eugene (Okla) 106 E Crawford St, Palestine, TX 75801

GLENN, Patricia Foster (Mo) 19424 Highway 54, Louisiana, MO 63353

GLENNIE, Jannel (Mich) 294 Willoughby Rd, Mason, MI 48854

GLICK, Phillip Randall (EC) 184 Watersedge Drive, Kill Devil Hills, NC 27948

GLIDDEN, Charles Aelred (FdL) 56500 Abbey Rd, Three Rivers, MI 49093

GLIDDEN, Richard Mark (Chi) 49 Larbert Rd # 6490, Southport, CT 06890

GLOFF, Holly M (NC) 1520 Canterbury Rd, Raleigh, NC 27608

GLOSSON HAMMONS, Jamesetta Cheryl (Los) 1508 W 145th St, Compton, CA 90220

✠ GLOSTER, J(ames) Gary (Ret Bp Suffr of NC 2004-) 2236 Fernbank Dr, Charlotte, NC 28226

GLOVER, Beth Faulk (Nwk) 29 Village Gate Way, Nyack, NY 10960

GLOVER, Betty Marie (Kan) Episcopal Churc Saint David's, 3916 Sw 17th St, Topeka, KS 66604

GLOVER, Hazel Smith (At) 606 Newnan St, Carrollton, GA 30117

GLOVER, John Frederick (Va) 14449 S Eastside Hwy, Grottoes, VA 24441

GLOVER, Marsha Bacon (NY) 122 Grandview Ave, White Plains, NY 10605

GLOVER, Mary Elizabeth (NwT) 891 Davis Dr, Abilene, TX 79605

GLUCKOW, Kenneth Allan (NJ) 70 Mount Tabor Way, Ocean Grove, NJ 07756

GNASSO, Enrico Mario (Los) 10961 Desert Lawn Dr Spc 252, Calimesa, CA 92320

GOBER, Patricia Derr (Mass) 17 Leroy St, Attleboro, MA 02703

GOBER, Wallace Gene (Mass) 17 Leroy St, Attleboro, MA 02703

GOCHA, Teresa Payne (NH) 477 Main St, Plymouth, NH 03264

GOCKLEY, Mary Jane (Neb) PO Box 353, Broken Bow, NE 68822

GODBOLD, Richard Rives (Ind) 829 Wiltshire Dr, Evansville, IN 47715

GODDARD, John R (Nev) PO Box 422, Gleneden Beach, OR 97388

GODDARD, Paul Dillon (Chi) 742 Sand Dollar Dr, Sanibel, FL 33957

GODDEN, Edward Eastman (Del) 610 Lindsey Rd, Wilmington, DE 19809

GODDERZ, Michael John (Mass) 209 Ashmont Street, Boston, MA 02124

GODFREY, Samuel Bisland (Miss) 1115 Main St., Vicksburg, MS 39183

GODFREY, Steven R (Ia)

GODFREY, William Calvin (LI) 102 Thompson Blvd, Greenport, NY 11944

GODLEY, Robert James (NY) 4440 E Lady Banks Ln, Murrells Inlet, SC 29565

GODSEY, Jeunee Jerman (SVa) 8706 Quaker Ln, North Chesterfield, VA 23235

GODWIN, Jerry D (Oly) 2630 46th Ave SW, Seattle, WA 98116

GOEKE, Randall Fred (Neb) 87993 482nd Ave, Atkinson, NE 68713

GOERTZ, Linda Ruth (Ore)

GOETSCH, Richard William (Ida) 213 E Avenue D, Jerome, ID 83338

GOETZ, Edward Craig (Ct) 504 Saybrook Road, P.O. Box 121, Higganum, CT 06441

GOFF, Nancy L. (Alb) The Church of the Messiah, 296 Glen Street, Glens Falls, NY 12801

✠ **GOFF**, Susan Ellyn (Bp Suffr of Va 2012-) 110 W Franklin St, Richmond, VA 23220

GOFF, Terry Lynn (CGC) 7125 Hitt Rd, Mobile, AL 36695

GOFORTH, Lisa Anne (Az) 1310 N. Sioux Ave., Claremore, OK 74017

GOFORTH, Thomas Robert (Chi) 1126 W Wolfram St, Chicago, IL 60657

GOGLIA, Bette Mack (CFla) 9203 Glascow Dr, Fredericksburg, VA 22408

GOING, Virginia Lee (NC) 400 S Boylan Ave, Raleigh, NC 27603

GOKEY, Mary Jordheim (ND) 1742 9th St S, Fargo, ND 58103

GOLDACKER, Gary Wray (Mich) 225 Southwind Dr, Belleville, IL 62221

GOLDBERG, Michael William (CFla) 460 38th Sq Sw, Vero Beach, FL 32968

GOLDBERG, Rebecca Lee (Cal) 777 Southgate Ave, Daly City, CA 94015

GOLDBLOOM, Ruth Alice (Md) 52 S Broadway, PO Box 229, Frostburg, MD 21532

GOLDEN JR, John Anthony (Pgh) 5 Devon Ave, Lawrenceville, NJ 08648

GOLDEN, Peter Pq (LI) 2115 Albemarle Terrace, Brooklyn, NY 11226

GOLDFARB, Ronald Allen (Ind) 570 Wheat Field Lane, New Whiteland, IN 46184

GOLDFEDER, Deborah Baker (Mo) 4520 Lucas and Hunt Rd, Saint Louis, MO 63121

GOLDHOR, Andrew Colquhoun (Mass) 6 Meriam St, Lexington, MA 02420

GOLDMAN, Norman Clifford (Ore) 94416 Langlois Mountain Rd, Langlois, OR 97450

GOLDSBOROUGH, Charles Neal (CGC) PO Box 12683, Pensacola, FL 32591

GOLDSMITH, Maurice Rusty (Tex) Saint Luke's Episcopal Church, 3736 Montrose Rd., Birmingham, AL 35213

GOLDSMITH III, Robert Sidney (Eas) 314 North St, Easton, MD 21601

GOLDSMITH, Thomas Michael (Ala) 113 Brown Ave, Rainbow City, AL 35906

GOLENSKI, John Donald (Cal) 1360 Montgomery St Apt 1, San Francisco, CA 94133

GOLLIHER, Jeffrey Mark (NY) 150 W End Ave Apt 30-M, New York, NY 10023

GOLUB, Elizabeth Kress (Nwk) 18 Wittig Ter # 7470, Wayne, NJ 07470

GOMAN, Jon Gifford (Ore) 2615 Nw Arnold Way, Corvallis, OR 97330

GOMER JR, Richard Henry (CFla) 6400 N Socrum Loop Rd, Lakeland, FL 33809

GOMES, Elizabeth (Kan) 912 N Amidon Ave, Wichita, KS 67203

GOMEZ, Edward (Tex) 2404 Marcus Abrams Blvd, Austin, TX 78748

GOMEZ, Luis Enrique (NY) 26 W 84th St, New York, NY 10024

GOMEZ ALMONTE, Lorenzo (DR DomRep) Calle Las Mercedes #66, Bigalindo, Hato Mayor Del Rey, Dominican Republic

GOMEZ-CARDONA, Rosa Angelica (Hond)

GOMPERTZ, Charles Bates (Cal) PO Box 713, Nicasio, CA 94946

GONZALES, Pat Marie (Okla) PO Box 26, Watonga, OK 73772

GONZALES JR, Ricardo (ECR) 859 Jessica Pl, Nipomo, CA 93444

GONZALEZ, Alfredo P. (USC) 1115 Marion St, Columbia, SC 29201

GONZALEZ, Elizabeth Carmody (WA) 1200 N Quaker Ln, Alexandria, VA 22302

GONZALEZ, Isabel (U) 4024 Red Hawk Rd, West Valley City, UT 84119

GONZALEZ AQUDELO, Luis Manano (Colom) Carrera 84 North 50 A-112, Ap 301, Medellin, Antioquia, Colombia

GONZALEZ DEL SOLAR, Mario Sebastian (Va) 800 Brantley Rd, Richmond, VA 23235

GONZALEZ-FIGUEROA, Efrain (PR)

GONZALEZ GARAVITO, Jose Pio (PR) PO Box 902, Saint Just, PR 00978

GONZALEZ-MESA, Gustavo (Ore) 700 Se 7th St, Gresham, OR 97080

GONZALEZ SANTOS, Rosa Ari (PR)

GOOCH, Gary Duane (Kan) 117 E Sierra Cir, San Marcos, TX 78666

GOOD, Arthur Allen (FdL) 1068 Misty Meadow Circle, De Pere, WI 54115

GOOD, Elizabeth (Mass) 17 Church St, Hanover, MA 02339

GOODALE-MIKOSZ, Desiree Ann (Chi) 20913 W Snowberry Ln, Plainfield, IL 60544-416

GOODE, Colin (Oly) PO Box 276, Lopez Island, WA 98261

GOODFELLOW, Willa Marie (Ia) 1745 5th St., #8, Coralville, IA 52241

GOODHEART, Donald P (NC) 1303 Hwy A1A #201, Satellite Beach, FL 32937

GOODING, Ludwick E (Pa) 5910 Cobbs Creek Pkwy, Philadelphia, PA 19143

GOODISON, Lorna Fay (SeFla) 1400 Riverside Dr, Coral Springs, FL 33071

GOODKIND, Caroline Cox (USC) 45 Crooked Island Circle, Murrells Inlet, SC 29576

GOODLETT, James Calvin (Fla)

GOODMAN, James Mark (RG) P.O. Box 1246, Albuquerque, NM 87103

GOODMAN, Kevin M (Chi) 1137 W Leland 102A, Chicago, IL 60640

GOODMAN, Timothy Allen (Spr) 9267 HERRIN RD, JOHNSTON CITY, IL 62951

GOODNESS, Donald Roy (NY) 4800 Fillmore Ave Apt 651, Alexandria, VA 22311

GOODPANKRATZ, Gretchen (WK) Po Box 851, Liberal, KS 67905

GOODRICH III, Daniel Hillman (Mich) 39 Hubbard St, Mount Clemens, MI 48043

GOODRICH, Kevin (ND) 405 2nd Ave Ne, Jamestown, ND 58401

GOODRIDGE, Robert J (CFla) 4791 Longbow Drive, Titusville, FL 32796

GOODWIN, Joan Carolyn (Az)

GOODWIN, Laura Bishop (WMass) St Andrew's Church, 53 N Main St, North Grafton, MA 01536

GOODWIN, Marilyn Marie (Minn) 27309 County Road 4, Naytahwaush, MN 56566

GOODWIN, Sarabeth (WA) 1721 Lamont St NW, Washington, DC 20010

GOOLD, George Charles (Ore) St Stephen's Church, SW Ninth & Hurbert Sts, Newport, OR 97365

GOOLSBEE, Arthur Leon (NwT) 602 Meander St., Abilene, TX 79602

GOOLSBY, Robert Patrick (Tex) 1656 Blalock Rd., Houston, TX 77080

GOOLTZ, Janet R (Az) 12607 W Westgate Dr, Sun City West, AZ 85375

GOONESEKERA, Desmond Joel Peter (Tex) 2806 Belham Creek Dr, Katy, TX 77494

GOORAHOO, Ephraim Basant (LI) 111-16 116th St, South Ozone Park, NY 11420

GORACZKO, Ann (SeFla) 1801 Ludlam Drive, Miami Springs, FL 33166

GORANSON, Paul Werner (WMass) 130 Sachem Ave., Worcester, MA 01606

GORCHOV, Michael Ivan (Alb) 58 3rd St, Troy, NY 12180

GORDAY, Peter Joseph (WNC) 34 Lullwater Pl Ne, Atlanta, GA 30307

GORDON, Billie Mae (Mass) 4301 Pheasant Ln, Middleborough, MA 02346

GORDON, Constance Leigh (U) 789 White Pine Dr, Tooele, UT 84074

GORDON, David Walter (Cal) 130 Avenida Barbera, Sonoma, CA 95476

GORDON JR, Harrington Manly (RI) 108 Columbia Ave, Warwick, RI 02888

GORDON, Jay Holland (NY) 382 Central Park W Apt 17p, New York, NY 10025

GORDON, Jim (RG) St Paul's Episcopal Church, PO Box 175, Marfa, TX 79843

GORDON, Rodney E (SVa) 701 S Providence Rd, North Chesterfield, VA 23236

GORDON, Walt (Minn) 834 Marshall Ave, Saint Paul, MN 55104

GORDON, Walter Bernard (WTenn) PO Box 622, Grand Junction, TN 38039

GORDON-BARNES, Janice E (Md) 3117 Raven Croft Terrace, The Villages, FL 32163

GORE, Gina Lee (Los) 18631 Chapel Ln, Huntington Beach, CA 92646

GORES, Ariail Fischer (Dal) 4229 Tomberra Way, Dallas, TX 75220

GORMAN, James Michael (Chi) 5388 W Harvey Rd, Oregon, IL 61061

GORMAN, W(Illiam) Kenneth (NJ) 684 Sunrise Dr, Avalon, NJ 08202

GORMLEY, Shane P (Alb)

GORSUCH, John P (Oly) 1840 North Prospect Ave, APT 511, Milwaukee, WI 53202

GORTNER, David Timothy (WA) 3737 Seminary Road, Alexandria, VA 22304

GOSHERT, Mary Linda (Los) 882 Oxford Way, Benicia, CA 94510

GOSHGARIAN, Martin John (Mass) 85 Glenwood Rd, Somerville, MA 02145

GOSHORN, Alice Elizabeth Gill (Ind) 4921 E State Road 252, Franklin, IN 46131

GOSNELL, Linda (USC) 5 Southbridge Ct, Simpsonville, SC 29680

GOSS, Frank Michael (NJ) Po Box 1, Bradley Beach, NJ 01/01/7720

GOSS III, James Paul (Cal) 792 Penny Royal Ln, San Rafael, CA 94903

GOSSETT JR, Earl Fowler (Ala) 1811 Cedar Crest Rd, Birmingham, AL 35214

GOSSLING, Nancy E (Mass) 25 Chapman Dr, Glastonbury, CT 06033

GOTAUTAS, Patricia Marie (USC)

GOTCHER, Vernon Alfred (FtW) 1904 Westcliff Dr, Euless, TX 76040

GOTKO, Raymond Morgan (At) 501 Sweet Berry Drive, Mont Eagle, TN 37356

GOTT, Amanda Katherine (Ct)

GOTTARDI-LITTELL, Laura E (Chi) Church of Our Saviour, Chicago, IL 60614

GOTTING, Viktoria Johanna Petra (Tex) St Christopher's Episcopal Church, PO Box 852, League City, TX 77574

GOTTLICH, Samuel Grier (WTex) 5857 Timbergate Dr Apt 1149, Apt 1149, Corpus Christi, TX 78414

GOUGH, Karen E (WNY) 315 Oakbrook Dr, Williamsville, NY 14221

GOUGH, Lauren A (FtW) 3733 Whitefern Dr., Fort Worth, TX 76137

GOULD, Glenn Hamilton (USC) 30 Moise Dr, Sumter, SC 29150

GOULD, Jane Soyster (Mass) 19 Nahant Pl, Lynn, MA 01902

GOULD, Jennie Ruth (NH) 32 Templeton Pkwy, Watertown, MA 02472

GOULD, Mary Dolores (Oly) Po Box 1193, Maple Valley, WA 98038

GOULD, Robert Carwyle (The Episcopal NCal) 2528 Clearlake Way, Sacramento, CA 95826

GOWEN, Eleanore Louise (Mass)

GOWETT, Randall James (Episcopal SJ) 1224 E Sample Ave, Fresno, CA 93710

GOWING, Michael LeVern (Mich) 2696 Indian Trl, Pinckney, MI 48169

GOWLAND, James David (NJ) 11 N Monroe Ave, Wenonah, NJ 08090

GOWTY, Richard Newton (Tex)

GRAB, Virginia Lee (NY) 74 Montgomery St, Tivoli, NY 12583

GRABHER, Jerald (WMo) 4635 Campbell St, Kansas City, MO 64110

GRABINSKI, Kenneth Lee (Oly) 5240 46th Ave Sw, Seattle, WA 98136

GRABNER, John David (Spok) 165 SW Spruce St, Apt 1, Pullman, WA 99163

GRABNER-HEGG, Linnae Marie (Minn) 1619 31st Ave S, Fargo, ND 58103

GRACE JR, Harry Tyler (WNY) 36 Parkside Ct, Buffalo, NY 14214

GRACE, Holt B (Minn) 215 4th St N, Stillwater, MN 55082

GRACE SR, James McKay Lykes (Tex)

GRACE, Patricia M. (ETenn) 4753 Scepter Way, Knoxville, TN 37912

GRACEN, Sharon Kay (Ct) 1109 Main St, Branford, CT 06405

GRACEY, Colin Beal (Mass) 18 Monmouth Ct, Brookline, MA 02446

GRACIA, Kesner (Hai)

GRACZYK, Glen Gerard (SwFla) St Marys Episcopal Church, 1010 24th Ave W, Palmetto, FL 34221

GRADY, Ann Nadine (Mil) 815 N. Grant St, Bay City, MI 48708

GRADY, Richard Charles (SwFla) 6985 Edgewater Cir, Fort Myers, FL 33919

GRAEBNER, Norman B (NC) Po Box 628, Hillsborough, NC 27278

GRAF, Thomas William (SeFla) St Faith's Episcopal Church, 10600 Caribbean Blvd, Cutler Bay, FL 33189

GRAFF, Donald T (Pa) 1434 Alcott St, Philadelphia, PA 19149

GRAFF, Stephen John (SeFla) 2871 N Ocean Blvd Apt C513, Boca Raton, FL 33431

GRAHAM IV, Alexander C (Va) 3114 38th St NW, Washington, DC 20016

GRAHAM, Carolyn Jane (Kan) 1107 W 27th Ter, Lawrence, KS 66046

GRAHAM, Deborah Marie Therese (Ida) 911 4th St S, Nampa, ID 83651

GRAHAM III, Earnest N (NC) 828 Kings Hwy, Suffolk, VA 23432

GRAHAM, H(arry) James (EMich) 534 Little Lake Dr., Ann Arbor, MI 48103

GRAHAM, John Kirkland (Tex) 6231 Ella Lee Ln, Houston, TX 77057

GRAHAM, John M. (WA) 1041 Wisconsin Ave. NW, Washington, DC 20007

GRAHAM, Julie Ann (Cal) 1104 Mills Ave, Burlingame, CA 94010

GRAHAM III, Robert Lincoln (Alb) 153 Billings Ave, Ottawa, ON K1H 5K8, Canada

GRAHAM, Suzanne H (NY) 279 Piermont Ave, Nyack, NY 10960

GRAHAM, Timothy Harold (At) 1130 First Ave, Columbus, GA 31901

GRAHAM, Wells Newell (CGC) 771 Simon Park Cir, Lawrenceville, GA 30045

GRAHAM JR, William James (Neb) 607 Toluca Ave, Alliance, NE 69301

GRAMBSCH, Mary Frances (NY) 28 Seaman Ave Apt 1k, New York, NY 10034

GRAMLEY, Thomas S (Roch) 13 Prospect Ave, Canisteo, NY 14823

GRANDELL, Peter Frank (Pa) The Church Of The Crucifixion, 620 S 8Th St, Philadelphia, PA 19147

GRANFELDT SR, Robert Carl (Pa) 1400 Mall of Georgia Blvd Apt 1412, Buford, GA 30519

GRANGER JR, Charles Irving (Okla) 305 E Douglas Dr, Midwest City, OK 73110

GRANT JR, Blount Hamilton (SeFla) 8500 Bluebonnet Blvd Apt 31, Baton Rouge, LA 70810

GRANT, Elizabeth Wade (NC) 750 Weaver Dairy Rd Apt 176, Chapel Hill, NC 27514

GRANT, Hugh M (At) PO Box 632, Eastsound, WA 98245

GRANT, Joan L (WNC) 215 3rd Ave E, Kalispell, MT 59901

GRANT, Priscilla (Percy) R (O) 2230 Euclid Ave., Cleveland, OH 44115

GRANT, Rebecca Ann (Me) 16 Alton Road, Apt 219, Augusta, ME 04330

GRANT, Sandra Marceau (SC)

GRANTZ, Brian Glenn (NI) 117 N Lafayette Blvd, South Bend, IN 46601

GRATZ, L(ouis) Paul (Vt)

GRAUER, David Ernst (Chi) 808 S Seminary Ave, Park Ridge, IL 60068

GRAUMLICH, Nancy Rice (O) 7815 Hedingham Rd, Sylvania, OH 43560

GRAUNKE, Kristine Helen (WTex) PO Box 68, Hebbronville, TX 78361

GRAVATT, J Segar (SVa) 301 49th St, Virginia Beach, VA 23451

GRAVES, Carol Carson (SeFla)

GRAVES JR, Farrell Dean (Los) 257 Middle Rd, Sayville, NY 11782

GRAVES, Jon C (WVa) 210 S McHenry Ave, Crystal Lake, IL 60014

GRAVES JR, Leonard Roberts (CGC) 1302 E Avery St, Pensacola, FL 32503

GRAVES, Lisa Beyer (WVa) 290 Grove St, Crystal Lake, IL 60014

GRAVES, Rena B (Pa) 5421 Germantown Ave, Philadelphia, PA 19144

GRAVES, Richard W (Ia) 1247 7th Ave N, Fort Dodge, IA 50501

GRAY, Bruce Alan (Va) 8525 Burgundy Rd, Richmond, VA 23235

GRAY, Bruce William (Ind) Episcopal Diocese of Indianapolis, 1100 W 42nd St, Indianapolis, IN 46208

GRAY, Calvin (Colo) 1625 Larimer Street #2501, Denver, CO 80202

GRAY, Cathy Jean (Testa-Avila) (Ind) 11120 El Arco Dr, Whittier, CA 90604

GRAY, Christopher Neil (SwFla) 8005 25th Street East, Parrish, FL 34219

GRAY, Cindra Dee (Ore) PO Box 358, Newberg, OR 97132

GRAY, Douglas Alan (SVa) 3100 Shore Dr, Virginia Beach, VA 23451

✠ **GRAY JR**, Duncan Montgomery (Ret Bp of Miss 2000-) 3775 Old Canton Rd, Jackson, MS 39216

✠ **GRAY III**, Duncan Montgomery (Ret Bp of Miss 2015-) PO Box 23107, Jackson, MS 39225

✠ **GRAY**, Francis Campbell (Ret Asst Bp of Va 2012-) 3820 Nall Ct, South Bend, IN 46614

GRAY, Giulianna C (Miss) 4600 Saint Charles Ave, New Orleans, PA 70115

GRAY, Katherine Tupper (SVa) 84 Post St, Newport News, VA 23601

GRAY, Lisa (Mich) 4225 Walden Dr, Ann Arbor, MI 48105

GRAY, Marie Therese (FdL) N63W29046 Tail Band Ct, Hartland, WI 53029

GRAY, Melvin Kelly (Fla) 715 Sleepyvale Ln, Houston, TX 77018

GRAY, Michael Fred (Va) 712 Amanda Ct, Culpeper, VA 22701

GRAY, Patrick Terrell (Mass) 151 Asbury St, South Hamilton, MA 01982

GRAY, Peter Hanson (Va) 1800 Old Meadow Rd Apt 321, McLean, VA 22102

GRAY, Peter Whittlesey (Miss) Trinity Church, 1329 Jackson Ave, New Orleans, LA 70130

GRAY, Priscilla Grace-Gloria (Minn) 611 19th St N, Sartell, MN 56377

GRAY, Svea Blomquist (Mich) 306 N Division St, Ann Arbor, MI 48104

GRAY, Thomas Weddle (RG) 108 E Orchard Ln, Carlsbad, NM 88220

GRAY, Victoria Stephanie (Cal)

GRAYBILL, Richard Martin (NMich) First And Canda St, Ishpeming, MI 49849

GRAYBILL, Virginia K (NMich) 301 N 1st St, Ishpeming, MI 49849

GRAYDEN, Margaret Miller (The Episcopal NCal)

GRAY-FOW, Michael John Gregory (Mil) 120 S Ridge St, Whitewater, WI 53190

✠ **GRAY-REEVES**, Mary (Bp of ECR 2008-) PO Box 1903, Monterey, CA 33410

GRAYSON, Timothy Holiday (Md) 536 Kinsale Rd, Timonium, MD 21093

GREATHOUSE, William Matthew (WTenn) 103 S Poplar St, Paris, TN 38242

GREATWOOD, Richard Neil (CFla) 1167 Adair Park Place, Orlando, FL 32804

GRECO, John Anthony (LI) 333 E 53rd St Apt 5m, New York, NY 10022

GREELEY III, Paul William (USC) 206 Kings Mountain St, York, SC 29745

GREEN, Andrew (SanD) 2004 East Calle Lileta, Palm Springs, CA 92262

GREEN III, Anthony Roy (Spok) 1705 5th St, Wenatchee, WA 98801

GREEN, Daniel Currie (The Episcopal NCal)

GREEN, David Edward (Cal) 6103 Harwood Ave, Oakland, CA 94618

GREEN, David Keith (CGC) 4362 Lafayette St, Marianna, FL 32446

GREEN, David Robert (Be) 623 Cloverfields Dr., Stevensville, MD 21666

GREEN, Drury Hamilton (Chi) 971 First St, Batavia, IL 60510

GREEN, Elizabeth A (WMass) 66 Highland Ave #C, Short Hills, NJ 07078

GREEN, Frazier L (Ga) 1041 Fountain Lake Dr, Brunswick, GA 31525

GREEN, G J (Mil) 2030 74th Pl, Kenosha, WI 53143

GREEN, Gretchen Hall (O) 35 Cohasset Dr, Hudson, OH 44236

GREEN JR, Joseph Nathaniel (SVa) 3826 Wedgefield Ave, Norfolk, VA 23502

GREEN, Kenneth William (Spok) 539 3rd Ave, Havre, MT 59501

GREEN, Kuulei Mobley (ETenn) 3975 E Clocktower Ln Apt 236, Meridian, ID 83642

GREEN, Larry A (Chi) 1424 N Dearborn St, Chicago, IL 60610

GREEN, Lawrence Joseph (Minn) Saint Pauls Episcopal Church, 265 Lafayette St, Winona, MN 55987

GREEN, Linda Frances (Chi) 971 First St, Batavia, IL 60510

GREEN, Mary Emily (Tex) 4633 Tanner View Dr, Clinton, WA 98236

GREEN, Patricia Anne (WMich) 160 Main St, Somerset, MA 02726

GREEN, Patricia Lynn (RG) 1678 Tierra Del Rio NW, Albuquerque, NM 87107

GREEN, Randolph Patrick (NC) 343 Dogwood Knl, Boone, NC 28607

GREEN, Richard Lee (Oly) 1645 24th Avenue, Longview, WA 98632

GREEN JR, Roy Donald (EO)

GREEN, Tamara Melanie (Cal) 7211 Garden Glen Ct Apt 318, Huntington Beach, CA 92648

GREENAWAY, Douglas Andrew Gordon (WA) 1116 Lamont St Nw, Washington, DC 20010

GREENE, Adam S (Tex) 4135 Oberlin Street, Houston, TX 77005

GREENE, Dorothy Anne (NY) 27 Willow Ave, Larchmont, NY 10538

GREENE, Edward Rideout (WVa) 19 Valley Rd, Bath, ME 04530

GREENE, Elinor Robinson (Pa) 6635 Mccallum St Apt B406, Philadelphia, PA 19119

GREENE, Everett Henry (RI) 1117 Capella S, Newport, RI 02840

GREENE JR, Frank Eugene (NH) 5 Nutmeg Cir, Laconia, NH 03246

GREENE, George Burkeholder (Alb) 53 West St, Whitesboro, NY 13492

GREENE, Joseph D (NY) 1451 Carriage Ridge Dr., Greensboro, GA 30642

GREENE, Judith (Ct) 60 Bywatyr Ln, Bridgeport, CT 06605

GREENE, Kim Harlene (WNY) St Paul's Cathedral, 128 Pearl St, Buffalo, NY 14202

GREENE, Lynne Tuthill (SwFla) 1369 Vermeer Drive, Nokomis, FL 34275

GREENE, Margaret Catharine (Colo) 1300 Washington St, Denver, CO 80203

GREENE, Mary Carter (Cal) 330 Ravenswood Ave, Menlo Park, CA 94025

GREENE, Michael Paul Thomas (Eau) St Luke's Episcopal Church, 221 W 3rd St, Dixon, IL 61021

GREENE, Patrick James (RI) 55 Main St, N Kingstown, RI 02852

GREENE, Roger Stewart (SO) 8101 Beechmont Ave, Cincinnati, OH 45255

GREENE, Timothy Patrick (Cal) 4155 Cesar Chavez St Apt 13, San Francisco, CA 94131

GREENE-MCCREIGHT, Kathryn (Ct) 198 Mckinley Ave, New Haven, CT 06515

GREENFIELD, Peter Alan (CPa) 122 Greenview Dr, Lancaster, PA 17601

GREENLAW, William A (NY) 529 West 42nd St. Apt. 4J, New York, NY 10036

GREENLEAF, Debra Lynn (Ida)

GREENLEAF, Richard Edward (NH) 325 Pleasant St, Concord, NH 03301

GREENLEE, Malcolm Blake (Ct) 32 Old Wagon Rd, Wilton, CT 06897

GREENMAN, Elizabeth Travis Rees (Fla) 2959 Apalachee Parkway, Unit J6, Tallahassee, FL 32301

GREENSHIELDS, Kay Conner (Okla) 405 Roserock Dr, Norman, OK 73026

GREENWELL, Gail E. (SO) 318 E 4th St, Cincinnati, OH 45202

GREEN-WITT, Margaret Evelyn Ashmead (SwFla) 2499 Mapleleaf Ct, Spring Hill, FL 34606

GREENWOOD, April Valeria Trew (Va) Po Box 278, Millers Tavern, VA 23115

GREENWOOD, Daniel R (SVa) 2910 Stratford Rd, Richmond, VA 23225

GREENWOOD, Don Robert (SO) 10414 Nw 13th Pl, Vancouver, WA 98685

GREENWOOD JR, Eric Sutcliffe (Tenn) 404 Northridge Ct, Nashville, TN 37221

GREENWOOD, Harold Lee Hal (Okla)

GREENWOOD, Jody L (At) Christ Church Episcopal, 400 Holcomb Bridge Rd, Norcross, GA 30071

GREENWOOD, Susan Anne (Colo) 53 Paradise Rd, Golden, CO 80401

GREENWOOD, W(Alter) Merritt (O) 1473 Brighton Ave, Arroyo Grande, CA 93420

GREER, Broderick Lee (WTenn) 1720 Peabody Ave, Memphis, TN 38104

GREER, David Jay (WLa) 208 Bruce Ave, Shreveport, LA 71105

GREER JR, George H (NC) 301 S Circle Dr, Rocky Mount, NC 27804

GREER, Hilary Anne (Ct) 42 N Eagleville Rd, Storrs, CT 06268

GREER JR, James Gossett (O) 13710 Shaker Blvd Apt 404, Cleveland, OH 44120

GREGG, Catherine (Nev) 2235 S. 1400 E Unit 19, Saint George, UT 84790

GREGG, Jennifer E (WMass) St Stephen's Episcopal Church, 67 East St, Pittsfield, MA 01201

GREGG, Robert Clark (Cal) 659 Salvatierra St, Stanford, CA 94305

✠ **GREGG**, William O (Ret Bp of EO 2007-) St. Paul's Church, 220 N. Zapapta Hwy #11, PMB 141A, Laredo, TX 78043

GREGORIUS, Mary B. (NY) 378 Bedford Rd, Pleasantville, NY 10570

GREGORY, Emma Jean (Nev) 4201 W Washington Ave, Las Vegas, NV 89107

GREGORY, Leslie Burtner (NwT) 822 Keeler Ave, Dalhart, TX 79022

GREGORY, Pamela S (RI) 251 Danielson Pike, North Scituate, RI 02857

GREGORY, Phillip Richard (Chi) 2612 Gateshead Dr, Naperville, IL 60564

GREGORY, Rachael Anne (Chi) 410 Grand Ave, Waukegan, IL 60085

✠ **GREIN**, Richard Frank (Ret Bp of NY 2002-) 150 West End Avenue, Apt. 9H, New York, NY 10013

GREISER, Ronald Edmond (WNC) 5601 Oak Ridge Ave, New Port Richey, FL 34652

GREMILLION, Dorothy Ann (Tex) 2708 Butler National Dr, Pflugerville, TX 78660

GRENNEN, T Kyle (Alb) Grace Church, 32 Montgomery St, Cherry Valley, NY 13320

GRENZ, Linda L (RI) 275 N Main St, Providence, RI 02903

GRESSLE, Richard Lloyd (NY) 130 1st Ave, Nyack, NY 10960

GREVE, John Haven (Ia) New Song Episcopal Church, 912 20th Ave, Coralville, IA 52241

GREVE JR, Paul Andrew (NI) 611 W Berry St, Fort Wayne, IN 46802

✠ **GREW II**, J Clark (Ret Bp of O 2004-) One Huntington Avenue, # 304, Boston, MA 02116

GREWELL, Genevieve Michael (Oly) 1551 Tenth Ave. E, Seattle, WA 98102

GRIBBLE, Robert Leslie (Tex) 301 E 8th St, Austin, TX 78701

GRIBBON, Robert T (Eas) PO Box 1493, Salisbury, MD 21802

GRIEB, Anne Katherine (WA) 3737 Seminary Rd, Alexandria, VA 22304

GRIEB, Ray Kline (Wyo) 487 Goodrich Rd, Wheatland, WY 82201

GRIESBACH, Jane (WMass)

GRIESER, D Jonathan (Mil) 116 W Washington Ave, Madison, WI 53703

GRIESMANN, Donald Andre (NJ) Po Box 7, Pago Pago, AS 96799

GRIESMEYER, Walter Jimmy (Chi) 1468 Elizabeth St, Crete, IL 60417

GRIEVES, Brian Jervis (The Episcopal Church in Haw) 7007 Hawaii Kai Drive Apt A21, Honolulu, HI 96825

GRIFFIN, Barry Quentin (At) Po Box 169, Morrow, GA 30260

GRIFFIN, Calvin Russell (USC)

GRIFFIN, Christopher Edward (Chi) 1356 W Jarvis Ave # 1, Chicago, IL 60626

GRIFFIN, Emily A (Va) 6715 Georgetown Pike, McLean, VA 22101

GRIFFIN, Horace Leeolphus (Cal)

GRIFFIN, Janet (Spok) 803 Symons St, Richland, WA 99354

GRIFFIN, Jeremiah (RG) Po Box 175, Marfa, TX 79843

GRIFFIN, Jon Edward (Spr) 449 State Highway 37, West Frankfort, IL 62896

GRIFFIN, Mary-Carol Ann (Me) 862 Eagle Lake Rd, Bar Harbor, ME 04609

GRIFFIN, Patrick Corrigan (Colo) 127 W Archer Pl, Denver, CO 80223

GRIFFIN, Pauline Ruth (EC) 25 S 3rd St, Wilmington, NC 28401

GRIFFIN, P Joshua (Cal) St David Of Wales, 2800 SE Harrison St, Portland, OR 97214

GRIFFIN, Ronald Wayne (ECR) 1007 Persimmon Ave, Sunnyvale, CA 94087

GRIFFIN, Russell Agnew (NJ) 219 Philadelphia Blvd, Sea Girt, NJ 08750

GRIFFIN, Timothy Lee (Pa)

GRIFFIN JR, William Leonard (Len) (Ark) 40 Cliffdale Dr, Little Rock, AR 72223

GRIFFIS SR, Terrell Hathorn (La) 316 Driftwood Dr, Meridian, MS 39305

GRIFFITH, Bernard Macfarren (SeFla) 15100 Sw 141st Ter, Miami, FL 33196

GRIFFITH, Bruce Derby (LI)

GRIFFITH, Charles Jefferson (WK) 8631 Beulah Land Dr, Ozark, AR 72949

GRIFFITH, David M (Los) 821 Valley Crest St, La Canada, CA 91011

GRIFFITH, David W (NY) 1209 Proust Rd, Virginia Beach, VA 23454

GRIFFITH, Gregory Erwin (O) 705 Main St, Coshocton, OH 43812

GRIFFITH JR, Norman Early (WTex) 1601 E 19th St, Georgetown, TX 78626

GRIFFITH JR, Robert L (LI) 36 Cathedral Avenue, Garden City, NY 11530

GRIFFITH, Shawn Lynn (WNC) 3658 Gaston Day School Rd, Gastonia, NC 28056

GRIFFITHS, Robert Stephen (Fla) 2613 Vista Cove Rd, Saint Augustine, FL 32084

GRIFO, Lynne A (Ct)

GRIGG, Joel (Alb) 145 Main Street, Massena, NY 13662

GRIGGS, Linda Mackie (RI) 50 Orchard Ave, Providence, RI 02906

GRIM, Leland Howard (Minn) 2636 County Road 94, International Falls, MN 56649

GRIMBALL JR, Richard Barnwell (USC) 101 Brookside Way, Greenville, SC 29605

GRIMES, Charles Gus (Tenn) 510 W Main St, Franklin, TN 37064

GRIMES, Daphne Buchanan (Wyo) 16 Thomas The Apostle Rd, Cody, WY 82414

GRIMES, Eve Lyn (Colo) 624 W 19th St, Pueblo, CO 81003

GRIMM, Joan (LI) 124 Jerusalem Ave, Hicksville, NY 11801

GRIMM, Susan (SVa) 1104 Lakepoint Dr, Clarksville, VA 23927

GRIMSHAW, Gretchen Sanders (Mass) 28 Robbins Rd, Watertown, MA 02472

GRINDON, Carri Patterson (Los) 1014 E. Altadena Dr., Altadena, CA 91001

GRINER, Robert Tyler (Nwk) 115 Cedar Dr, Newton, NJ 07860

GRINNELL, Janice Louise (RI) 263 Orchard Woods Drive, Saunderstown, RI 02874

GRINNELL, Lynn Dean (SwFla) 15102 Amberly Dr, Tampa, FL 33647

GRISCOM, Donald Wayne (SwFla) 3324 Chicago Ave, Bradenton, FL 34207

GRISHAM JR, Lowell Edward (Ark) Po Box 1190, Fayetteville, AR 72702

✠ **GRISWOLD III**, Frank Tracy (Ret PBp of The Episcopal Church 2006-) 151 W Springfield Ave, Philadelphia, PA 19118

GRISWOLD-KUHN, Karl E (Alb) 6 Silvester St, Kinderhook, NY 12106

GROB, Bruce Russell (Fla) 151 Nc Highway 9 Pmb 227, Black Mountain, NC 28711

GROFF, Addison Keiper (Nwk)

GROFF JR, John Weldon (Ala) 12656 N Shoreland Pkwy, Mequon, WI 53092

GROFF, Mary E Worobe (Ala) 6141 Sherry Dr, Guntersville, AL 35976

GROFF JR, Sanford Harover (SeFla) 3395 Burns Rd, Palm Beach Gardens, FL 33410

GROH, Clifford Herbert (Mich)

GRONEK, Marianna (Mich) St Michael's Episcopal Chuch, 20475 Sunningdale Park, Grosse Pointe Woods, MI 48236

GRONEMAN, Leslie Joyce (Alb)

GROSCHNER, Peter Kingston (Mich) 19759 Holiday Rd, Grosse Pointe Woods, MI 48236

GROSE, Fayette Powers (O) 310 E Lincoln Way, Lisbon, OH 44432

GROSH, Christine Marie (Neb) 7921 N Hazelwood Dr, Lincoln, NE 68510

GROSHART, Nancy Louise (U) 1051 Allen Peak Cir, Ogden, UT 84404

GROSJEAN, Lyle Wood (ECR) 3255 Amber Dr, Paso Robles, CA 93446

GROSKOPH, Elizabeth May (Roch) PO Box 541, Hancock, NY 13783

GROSKOPH, Ralph Gordon (Roch) PO Box 541, 211 Somerset Lake Rd, Hancock, NY 13783

GROSS, Brian (Wyo)

GROSS, Daniel La Rue (NY) 208 E. Campus Ave., Chestertown, MD 21620

GROSS, Donald William (CFla) 800 Lake Port Blvd Apt D402, Leesburg, FL 34748

GROSS, Robert Arthur (FtW) 4200 French Lake Dr, Fort Worth, TX 76133

GROSSMAN, Stacey (Cal) Church of the Nativity, 333 Ellen Drive, San Rafael, CA 94903

GROSSO, Andrew Thomas (Kan) 2777 Mission Rd, Nashotah, WI 53058

GROSSOEHME, Daniel Huck (SO) Pulmonary Medicine Mlc2021, Cchmc, Cincinnati, OH 45229

GROSSOEHME, Henrietta H (Ind) 1078 Carraway Ln, Milford, OH 45150

GROTZINGER, Terri (Mont) 130 S 6th St E, Missoula, MT 59801

GROUBERT, Gerri Helen (Nev) 3665 Largo Verde Way, Las Vegas, NV 89121

GROUT III, Earl Leroy (Oly) 6801 30th Ave Ne, Seattle, WA 98115

GROVER III, Charles Lowell (Roch) 4006 Brick Kiln Dr, Chittenango, NY 13037

GROVES, Barbara T (CNY) 141 Main St, Whitesboro, NY 13492

GRUBB, Daniel Studd (WMich) 4770 W Park Rd, New Era, MI 49446

GRUBB, Sarah Ann (Neb) 8800 Holdrege St, Lincoln, NE 68505

GRUBBS, Lucas Michael (Colo) 630 Gilpin St, Denver, CO 80218

GRUBE, David Quinn (Nev) 777 Sage St., Elko, NV 89801

GRUBERTH, G Cole (CNY)

GRUMAN, Stephen Cowles (Ala) 131 Silver Lake Cir, Madison, AL 35758

GRUMBINE, Eugene Edmund (Va) 506 Danray Dr, Richmond, VA 23227

GRUMHAUS, Jennifer Wood (Mass) 23 Loew Cir, Milton, MA 02186

GRUNDY, Elizabeth A (Cal) 27 Caswell St, New Bedford, MA 02745

GRUNDY, Sandra A (Colo) 9345 Carr St, Westminster, CO 80021

GRUNFELD, Matthew Theodore (Ala) PO Box 3073, Montgomery, AL 36109

GRUSELL, Katrina Lynn (Md) 5057 Stone Hill Dr, Ellicott City, MD 21043

GRUSENDORF, William Connor (WTex) 401 W Dry St, San Saba, TX 76877

GRYGIEL, Janet Carol (Chi) 1415 Temple Cir, Rockford, IL 61108

GUAILLAS CARANGUI, Raul Octavio (DR (DomRep)) Cafetos Oe-3-76 Y Nazareth, Quito, 00593, Ecuador

GUAMAN AYALA, Francisco (EcuC) Brasilia Y Buenos Aires, Ambato, Ecuador

GUBACK, Thomas Henry (WMich) 6300 North ManitouTrail, Northport, MI 49670

GUCK, Sarah St John (RG) PO Box 2795, Silver City, NM 88062

GUDGER JR, Gordon B (Tex)

GUENTHER, John Howard (WNY) 88 Cedar Terrace, Hilton, NY 14468

GUENTHER, Margaret (WA) 4101 Albemarle St NW Apt 651, Washington, DC 20016

GUENTHER, Nancy Louise (WNY) 200 East Center St., Medina, NY 14103

GUERNSEY, Jacqueline Louise (CFla) 25510 Belle Alliance, Leesburg, FL 34748

GUERNSEY, Justine Marie (Alb) 563 Kenwood Ave, Delmar, NY 12054

GUERRA-DIAZ, Juan Antonio (Ore) Po Box 1731, Hillsboro, OR 97123

✠ **GUERRERO**, Orlando Jesus (Bp of Ve 2005) Centro Diocesano, Avenue Caroni No. 100, Colinas de Bello Monte, Caracas, Venezuela

GUERRERO-STAMP, Carmen Bruni (Az) 114 W Roosevelt, Phoenix, AZ 85003

GUERRIER, Michel Marguy (Hai)

GUERRIER, Panel Marc (SwFla) 3901 Davis Blvd, Naples, FL 34104

GUEVARA RODRIGUEZ, Carlos Eduardo (Colom) Calle 30 No 17-08, Barrio Armenia, Teusaquillo, Bogota, Colombia

GUFFEY, Andrew R (Va) 6800 Columbia Pike, Annandale, VA 22003

GUFFEY, Emily Williams (Va) 4550 N Hermitage Ave, Chicago, IL 60640

GUIBORD, Gwynne Marlyn (Los) 146 S Beachwood Dr, Los Angeles, CA 90004

GUIDA, Angela Gayle (Az) 2480 Virginia St Apt 4, Berkeley, CA 94709

GUIDRY, R(obert) (WNC) 869 Daylily Dr, Hayesville, NC 28904

GUILE, Frederic Corwith (Alb) 1680 Liebig Rd., Granville, NY 12832

GUILLAUME, Sebastien (Miss) 311 Nw 37th St, Pompano Beach, FL 33064

GUILLAUME-SAM, Sully (LI) 1405 Bushwick Ave, Brooklyn, NY 11207

GUILLEN, Anthony Anthony (Los) 198 Via Baja, Ventura, CA 93003

GUINN, Patricia J. (WNY) 2753 Eastwood Rd, East Aurora, NY 14052

GUINTA, Denise Gray (SwVa) 5011 McGregor Blvd, Fort Myers, FL 33901

GUISTOLISE, Kathryn Jean Mazzenga (Chi) 5555 N Sheridan Rd #608, Chicago, IL 60640

✠ **GULICK JR**, Edwin Funsten (Ret Bp of Ky 2005-) 425 S 2nd St, Louisville, KY 40202

GULLETT, John Manford (CFla) 202 Pontotoc St, Auburndale, FL 33823

GUMBS, Delores Elvida (VI) PO Box 6454, Christiansted, St Croix, VI 00823

✠ **GUMBS**, Edward Ambrose (Bp of VI 2004-) P.O. Box 7488, St Thomas, VI 00801

GUNDERSON, David John (Mont) 313 S Yellowstone St, Livingston, MT 59047

GUNDERSON, Gretchen Anne (Oly) 629 Taft Ave, Raymond, WA 98577

GUNN, Daniel Cube (Be) 180 Riverside Dr., Wilkes Barre, PA 18702

GUNN, Reginald Richard (Ga) 688 Covecrest Dr, Tiger, GA 30576

GUNN, Scott Alan (SO) Forward Movement, 412 Sycamore St, Cincinnati, OH 45202

Clergy List

GUNNESS, Margaret (Mass) 641 Pleasant St, Belmont, MA 02478

✠ **GUNTER**, Matthew A (Bp of FdL 2014-) 22w400 Hackberry Dr, Glen Ellyn, IL 60137

GUNTHORPES, Alexander (LI) 2666 E 22nd St, Brooklyn, NY 11235

GURNIAK, David Fyodor (Ct) 610a Heritage Villiage, Southbury, CT 06488

GURRY, Jane Todd (NC) 817 Rosemont Ave, Raleigh, NC 27607

GUSTAFSON, Elyse Marie (Chi) 4901 N Mesa St Apt 4206, El Paso, TX 79912

GUSTAFSON III, Karl Edmund (Nev) 4201 W Washington Ave, Las Vegas, NV 89107

GUSTAFSON II, Karl Edmund (Az) 3949 W Alexander Rd Unit 1268, Norht Las Vegas, NV 89032

GUSTAFSON, Mary Dannies (WMass) 1840 University Ave W Apt 201, Saint Paul, MN 55104

GUSTIN, Peter Rochefort (Va) 14899 James Monroe Hwy, Leesburg, VA 20176

GUTGSELL, Jessie Katherine (Ind)

GUTHRIE, Donald Angus (Mont) 1801 Selway Dr., Missoula, MT 59808

GUTHRIE, Emily (WA) 7215 Arthur Dr, Falls Church, VA 22046

GUTHRIE JR, Harvey Henry (Mich) 1486 Old Telegraph Rd, Fillmore, CA 93015

GUTHRIE, Suzanne Elizabeth (CNY) 31 Oriole Drive, 105 Federal Hill Road, Woodstock, NY 12498

GUTHRIE, William A (Nwk) 2812 Sequoyah Drive, Haines City, FL 33844

GUTIERREZ, Daniel George Policarpio (RG) 601 Montano Rd. N.W., Albuquerque, NM 87107

GUTIERREZ, Hayr (PR) Villas De Castro, Calle 25 Ee-19, Caquas, PR 00726, Puerto Rico

GUTIERREZ, Janssen Jose (Fla) 895 Palm Valley Rd, Ponte Vedra, FL 32081

GUTIERREZ, Jorge Martin (Roch) 48 Whitcomb Road, Boxborough, MA 01719

GUTIERREZ, Jorge Pablo (SeFla) 1003 Allendale Rd, West Palm Beach, FL 33405

GUTIERREZ-DUARTE, Edgar Armando (Mass) 32 Franklin Ave, Chelsea, MA 02150

GUTWEIN, Martin (NJ) 527 N 2nd St, Camden, NJ 08102

GUY, Kenneth Gordon (FdL) N11052 Norway Ln, Tomahawk, WI 54487

GUZMAN, Pedro S (NJ) 7709 Piersanti Ct, Pennsauken, NJ 08109

GUZMAN VELEZ, Francisco Inocencio (PR) PO Box 902, Saint Just, PR 00978-0902, Puerto Rico

GWIN, Connor Brindley (Va) 1002 1st St SW, Roanoke, VA 24016

GWIN JR, Lawrence Prestidge (Tex) Po Box 404, Bay City, TX 77404

GWINN, Thomas Wallace (Alb) PO Box 286, North Stratford, NH 03590

GWYN III, Lewis R. (CFla) 5855 39th Ln, Vero Beach, FL 32966

GWYN, Roxane S (NC) 1700 Clearwater Lake Rd, Chapel Hill, NC 27517

GWYNN, Caron A. (WA) St. Timothy's Episcopal Church, 3601 Alabama Avenue, S.E., Washington, DC 20020

GWYNNE, Geoffrey Carrington (Tex) 1104 Peregrine Dr, Friendswood, TX 77546

H

HAACK, Christopher Allyn (Minn) 877 Jessie St, Saint Paul, MN 55130

HAACK, Marcus John (Ia)

HAAS, Kirk Bayard (WVa) 112 South Walnut St., Morgantown, WV 26501

HAAS, Margaret Ann (Mich) 2923 Roundtree Blvd Apt A2, Ypsilanti, MI 48197

HAAS, Michael James (NI) 2006 E Broadway, Logansport, IN 46947

HAASE, Sylvia Anne (Oly) Po Box 208, Vaughn, WA 98394

HABECKER, Elizabeth A (Los) Po Box 743, Bristol, RI 02809

HABECKER, John C (Nwk) 47 Av Sur #723 Colonia Flor Blanca, Apartado (01) 274, San Salvador, CA 000

HABERKORN, Violet M(arie) (Ind) 5045 W 15th Street, Speedway, IN 46224

HABERSANG, Paul Matthew (Vt) 99 Freedom Drive, Montpelier, VT 05602

HABIBY, Samir Jamil (Ga) 24 Sawyers Crossing Rd, Swanzey, NH 03446

HACKBARTH, Michael George (FdL)

HACKER, Craig A (Me) Po Box 775, Waddington, NY 13694

HACKER, David Carl (Spok) PO Box 356, Zillah, WA 98953

HACKETT, Ann R. (At) Po Box 169, Morrow, GA 30260

HACKETT JR, Charles Dudleigh (At) 10298 Big Cnoe, Big Canoe, GA 30143

HACKETT, Christopher James (ETenn) 413 Cumberland Ave, Knoxville, TN 37902

HACKETT, David Robert (ETenn) 7994 Prince Dr., Ooltewah, TN 37363

HACKETT, Michael George (La)

HACKLER, Wendy Kaye Douglas (Az)

HACKNEY, Lisa E (Chi) 2954 Essex Rd, Cleveland Heights, OH 44118

HADAWAY, Elizabeth Leigh (WVa) 913 Briarwood Ct, Morgantown, WV 26505

HADAWAY JR, Michael Miller (WVa) PO Box 205, Kingsville, MD 21087

HADDAD, Mary E. (Los) 4505 25th St Unit B, San Francisco, CA 94114

HADDIX JR, Theodore Ray (Va) 3825 Indianview Ave, Cincinnati, OH 45227

HADDOCK, Gene Moore (La) 1122 W. Chestnut St, Denison, TX 75020

HADDOX, Jason Monroe (Ga) 80 B Maple Avenue, Morristown, NJ 07960

HADE, Lynn Augustine (Pa) Church Of The Advent, 12 Byberry Rd, Hatboro, PA 19040

HADEN JR, Robert Lee (NC) 798 Evans Rd., Hendersonville, NC 28739

HADLER JR, Jacques Bauer (WA) 1736 Columbia Rd NW Apt 201, Washington, DC 20009

HADLEY, Arthur Clayton (SO) 1500 Shasta, McAllen, TX 78504

HADLEY, Douglas J (Ore) 2261 Hidden Valley Ln, Charlevoix, MI 49720

HAFER, Joel Gilbert (WNC) 776 N. Main St., Hendersonville, NC 28792

HAGAN JR, John Ronald (WVa) 11575 Belleville Rd, Belleville, MI 48111

HAGANS, Michele Victoria (WA) 1645 Myrtle St Nw, Washington, DC 20012

HAGBERG, Joseph Alan (CGC) 9101 Panama City Beach Parkway, Panama City Beach, FL 32407

HAGE, Raymond Joseph (WVa) 2105 Wiltshire Blvd, Huntington, WV 25701

HAGEN, Amelia Ann (Me) 39 Highland Ave, Millinocket, ME 04462

HAGEN, James Barlow (NY) 21-15 34th Ave apt 14C, Astoria, NY 11106

HAGEN, Maureen Elizabeth (Ore) 3030 Se Bybee Blvd, Portland, OR 97202

HAGENBUCH, Chris Barrett (Spok) 311 South Hall St, Grangeville, ID 83530

HAGER, Marty Monroe (Va) St Thomas Episcopal Church, 8991 Brook Rd, McLean, VA 22102

HAGERMAN, Steven William (Md) 1110 Saint Stephens Church Rd, Crownsville, MD 21032

HAGERTY, Stephen (NY) 84 Ehrhardt Rd, Pearl River, NY 10965

HAGGENJOS JR, Clifford R (The Episcopal NCal) 1905 Third Street, Napa, CA 94559

HAGLER, James Robert (ETenn) 933 S. 17th St., Newark, NJ 07108

HAGNER, Nancy Jane (NJ) Trinity Church, 33 Mercer St, Princeton, NJ 08540

HAGOOD II, M(onroe) Johnson (CFla) 6525 7th Manor, Vero Beach, FL 32968

HAGUE, Betsy Ann (WA) 4507 Leland St, Chevy Chase, MD 20815

HAGUE, Jane Milliken (WA)

HAGUE, Leslie Janette (Va) 1132 N Ivanhoe St, Arlington, VA 22205

HAGUE, Sarah Anne (NH) 23 Alice Peck Day Dr Unit 247, Lebanon, NH 03766

HAGUE, William (WA) 4001 Franklin St, Kensington, MD 20895

HAHN, Dorothee Elisabeth (Eur) 815 2nd Ave, New York, NY 10017

✠ **HAHN**, William Douglas (Bp of Lex 2012-) 2134 Wells Dr, Columbus, GA 31906

HAHNE, Ruth Olive (CFla) 9260-C Sw 61st Way, Boca Raton, FL 33428

HAHNEMAN, Geoffrey Mark (Ct) 154 Jackman Avenue, Fairfield, CT 06825

HAHNEMAN, Lisa (Ct) 154 Jackman Ave, Fairfield, CT 06825

HAIG, David William (Alb) PO Box 1834, Orleans, MA 02653

HAIG, Martha Karen (Oly) 4685 Taylor Ave NE, Bainbridge Island, WA 98110

HAILEY, Victor C. (Md) 3100 Monkton Rd., Monkton, MD 21111

HAIN, John Walter (NJ) 13 Madison Ave, Flemington, NJ 08822

HAINES, Harry Jeffrey (WNY) 24 Cobb Ter, Rochester, NY 14620

HAINES, Marlene (Pa) 31 Kleyona Ave, Phoenixville, PA 19460

HAINES III, Ralph Edward (SVa) 42 Park Ave, Newport News, VA 23607

HAINES-MURDOCCO, Sandra Paula (RI) 109 Old Post Rd, Wakefield, RI 02879

HAIRSTON, Raleigh Daniel (EC) 3183 Kings Bay Cir, Decatur, GA 30034

HAKIEL, Nicholas Edward (Oly) 1014 Wildwood St, Sultan, WA 98294

HALAPUA, Sione (Los) 8614 Foothill Blvd Apt 223, Sunland, CA 91040

HALBROOK, Thomas Robert (Oly) 1805 Graves Ave, Aberdeen, WA 98520

HALE, Douglas J (Ore) 2785 Elysium Ave, Eugene, OR 97401

HALE, Linda Mosier (Spok) PO Box 456, Sunnyside, WA 98944

HALE, Patricia Ann (Ore) 2785 Elysium Avenue, Eugene, OR 97401

HALE, William Charles (Mich) 1067 Hubbard St, Detroit, MI 48209

HALEY-RAY, Judith Ray (Pa)

HALFORD, Cathrine Nance (Miss) 147 Daniel Lake Blvd, Jackson, MS 39212

HALKETT, Thomas Richmond (Me) PO Box 564, Machias, ME 04654

HALL, Addison Curtis (Mass) 79 Denton Rd, Wellesley, MA 02482

HALL, Albert Benjamin (WMass) 775 Columbia Northwest, Port Charlotte, FL 33952

HALL, Allen Keith (Colo) 3950 W 12th St Nr 10, Greeley, CO 80634

HALL, Caroline J A (ECR) Po Box 6359, Los Osos, CA 93412

HALL, Charlotte Melissa (Nwk)

HALL, Daniel Charles (NJ) 114 Willow Dr, North Cape May, NJ 08204

HALL, Daniel Emerson (Pgh) 412 Locust St, Pittsburgh, PA 15218

HALL, David A (Ala) 2753 11th Ave S, Birmingham, AL 35205

HALL, David Moreland (WMass) 20 Winchester Ave, Auburn, MA 01501

HALL, Dianne Costner (Ga) 212 N Jefferson St, Albany, GA 31701

HALL, Donna Moody (SeFla) 941 Allendale Rd, West Palm Beach, FL 33405

HALL, E Eugene (Spr) 1808 Lakeside Dr Unit A, Champaign, IL 61821

HALL, Gary Richard (WA) Cathedral of St Peter & St Paul, 3101 Wisconsin Ave NW, Washington, DC 20016

HALL, George E (Ct) 496 F Heritage Vlg, Southbury, CT 06488

HALL, James Harold (SVa) 3628 Applewood Ln, Antioch, TN 37013

HALL, John (At) 265 Mail Rd., Exeter, RI 02822

HALL, John C N (SwFla) 7440 Ridge Rd, Sarasota, FL 34238

HALL, John Liston (Ia) 20 Mcclellan Blvd, Davenport, IA 52803

HALL, Jon William (Mo) 15764 Clayton Rd, Ellisville, MO 63011

HALL, Karen Elizabeth (Mont) 302 S.Maple, Watertown, SD 57201

HALL, Kathleen (WMo) 100 E Red Bridge Rd, Kansas City, MO 64114

HALL, Laurens Allen (Tex) 3725 Chevy Chase Dr, Houston, TX 77019

HALL, Leigh Ellen (Ga) P.O. Box 74, Swainsboro, GA 30401

HALL, Lisbeth Jordan (Mass) 1239 Peterkin Hl, South Woodstock, VT 05071

HALL JR, Lyle Gillis (Mass) 1239 Peterkin Hill Road, South Woodstock, VT 05071

HALL, Mark Heathcote (Episcopal SJ) 2212 River Dr, Stockton, CA 95204

HALL, Mark Robert (Dal) 5100 Ross Ave, Dallas, TX 75206

HALL, Mavis Ann (Neb) 3214 Davy Jones Dr, Plattsmouth, NE 68048

HALL, Melinda (NwPa) Church of Our Saviour, 400 Liberty Blvd, DuBois, PA 15801

HALL, Michael Gregory (CFla) Shepherd of the Hills, 2540 W Norvell Bryant Hwy, Lecanto, FL 34461

HALL, Patrick Mckenzie (Tex) 915 Saulnier St # B, Houston, TX 77019

HALL, PaulaClaire (WLa) 361 Cypress Loop, Farmerville, LA 71241

HALL, Richard Charles (Los) 1310 E Orange Grove Blvd, Unit 107, Pasadena, CA 91104

HALL, Richard Hastings (Me) 29 Tarratine Dr, Brunswick, ME 04011

HALL, Ryan Ashley (SD) St. Paul's Episcopal Church, 726 6th St, Brookings, SD 57006

HALL, Samuel Leslie (RG) 1023 Acequia Trl Nw, Albuquerque, NM 87107

HALL, Sidney J (SVa) 218 Grove Dr, Clemson, SC 29631

HALL, Stephen M (Ga) PO Box 69, Clayton, GA 30525

HALL, Tod Latham (NH) 140 Muzzy Hill Rd, Milan, NH 03588

HALL, V(ernon) Donald (O) 2432 Romar Dr, Hermitage, PA 16148

HALL, Virginia B (Ind) 3436 E. Longview, Bloomington, IN 47408

HALLADAY, Richard Allen (Ind) 448 Freeman Ridge Rd, Nashville, IN 47448

HALLAHAN, T Mark (Los)

HALLANAN, Sunny (Eur) Chaussee de Charleroi 2, 1420 Braine-l'Alleud, Belgium

HALLAS, Cynthia Johnston (Chi) 3025 Walters Ave, Northbrook, IL 60062

HALLE, Michael Adderbrooke (Az) 241 S.Beverly Street, Chandler, AZ 85225

HALLENBECK, Edwin Forrest (RI) 101 Larchmont Rd, Warwick, RI 02886

HALLER, Robert Bennett (NJ) Trinity Episcopal Church, Vincentown, NJ 08088

HALLER, Tobias Stanislas (NY) St James Rectory, 2627 Davidson Ave, Bronx, NY 10468

HALLETT, Timothy Jerome (Spr) 3007 N Ramble Rd W, Bloomington, IN 47408

HALLEY, Marcus George (WMo) 6401 Wornall Ter, Kansas City, MO 64113

HALLISEY, L Ann (The Episcopal NCal) 1711 Westshore St, Davis, CA 95616

HALLMARK, C. Anne (Va) PO Box 306, Middleburg, VA 20118

HALLOCK JR, Harold H (Va) 920 Flordon Dr, Charlottesville, VA 22901

HALLY, Jane Eloise (At) 16A Lenox Pointe NE, Atlanta, GA 30324

HALSTEAD, Jan (Tex) Christ Episcopal Church, 3520 Whitestone Blvd, Cedar Park, TX 78613

HALT, David Jason Andrew (Spr) 2153 Crest Rd, Cincinnati, OH 45240

HALTER, Karl (WA)

HALVERSTADT JR, Albert Nast (Colo) 1244 Detroit St, Denver, CO 80206

HALVORSEN, Douglas Carl (NJ) 28 Oakhurst Ln, Mount Laurel, NJ 08054

HAMBLETON, Coralie Voce (NMich) St Paul's Episcopal Church, 201 E Ridge St, Marquette, MI 49855

HAMBLIN M.D., Fr Jeffrey L. (LI) 423 West 46th Street, New York, NY 10036

HAMBLIN, Sheldon Neilson (LI) 4301 Avenue D, Brooklyn, NY 11203

HAMBY, Daniell C (Pa) 47 W Afton Ave, Yardley, PA 19067

HAMBY, Timothy (Lex) 118 N Washington St, Alexandria, VA 22314

HAMER, Donald Lee (Ct) 240 Kenyon St, Hartford, CT 06105

HAMERSLEY, Andrew C (NJ) 414 East Broad Street, Westfield, NJ 07090

HAMES, Patricia (Ct) 330 Hart St, New Britain, CT 06052

HAMILL, Allardyce Armstrong (CFla) Church of our Saviour, 200 NW 3rd St, Okeechobee, FL 34972

HAMILL, Charles Brent Wagner (Pgh) Christ Episcopal Church North Hills, 5910 Babcock Blvd, Pittsburgh, PA 15237

HAMILL, January Elizabeth (Md) 703 Peppard Dr, Bel Air, MD 21014

HAMILTON, Abigail W (Nwk) 681 Prospect Ave # 7052, West Orange, NJ 07052

HAMILTON, David George (Vt) 129 Cumberland Rd, Burlington, VT 05408

HAMILTON, David Hendry (Nwk) 75 Summerhill Dr, Manahawkin, NJ 08050

HAMILTON, Gordon William (USC) 101 Woodside Dr, Gaffney, SC 29340

HAMILTON SR, James Edward (Tex) 13618 Brighton Park Drive, Houston, TX 77044

HAMILTON, James Gary (Md) Canton/Fells Point Church Plant, 1025 S Potomac St, Baltimore, MD 21224

HAMILTON, Jamie L (NH) 20 Main St, Exeter, NH 03833

HAMILTON, John Marshall (NY) 1 Hudson St., Yonkers, NY 10701

HAMILTON, Lisa B (SwFla) 626 Hibiscus Dr, Venice, FL 34285

HAMILTON, Michael Pollock (WA) 3111 44th St Nw, Washington, DC 20016

HAMILTON, Paul Edward Connell (LI) 176 Davis Ln, Hamden, NY 13782

HAMILTON, Reid Henry (Mich) 4657 Dexter Ann Arbor Road, Ann Arbor, MI 48103

HAMILTON, Robert Earl (NC) 1200 N Elm St, Greensboro, NC 27401

HAMILTON, Roger John (CFla) 4018 Shorecrest Drive, Orlando, FL 32804

HAMILTON, Terrell Eugene (Episcopal SJ) 401 N Marilyn Ave, Wenatchee, WA 98801

HAMILTON, William Edward (SeFla) 1728 13th Ave N, Lake Worth, FL 33460

HAMILTON, W Michael (Mass) 15 Call St, North Billerica, MA 01862

HAMLIN, Richard Lee (Roch) 9375 SW 77th Ave Apt. 4013, Miami, FL 33156

HAMLIN, W Richard (Mich) 1016 Poxson Ave, Lansing, MI 48910

HAMLYN, Robert Cornelius (NY) 127 Fulton Ave Apt J1, Poughkeepsie, NY 12603

HAMMATT JR, Edward Augustus (SeFla) 16330 Sw 80th Ave, Miami, FL 33157

HAMMETT, Robert Lee (Mass) P.O. Box 224, Oak Bluff, MA 02557

HAMMON, LeRoy Ralph (Ore) 820 Berwick Ct, Lake Oswego, OR 97034

HAMMOND, Blaine Randol (ECR) PO Box 293, Ben Lomond, CA 95005

HAMMOND, Constance Ann (Ore) 4045 S.E. Pine St., Portland, OR 97214

HAMMOND, D(avid) (Cal) 11 Mesa Ave, Mill Valley, CA 94941

HAMMOND, Henry Latane (Md) 6705 Maxalea Rd, Baltimore, MD 21239

HAMMOND, James Allen (Va) 102 Cottage Drive, Winchester, VA 22603

HAMMOND, Jeffrey Benjamin (WTex) 14526 Spaulding Dr, Corpus Christi, TX 78410

HAMMOND, Marion Junior (Colo) 9 Chusco Rd, Santa Fe, NM 87508

HAMMONDS, Joanie (Ala) 755 Plantation Dr, Selma, AL 36701

HAMNER IV, James Edward (At) 3110-A Ashford Dunwoody Rd Ne, Atlanta, GA 30319

HAMP, Gary (WMich) 245 Rose Bud Ct, Traverse City, MI 49696

HAMPTON, Carol McDonald (Okla) 1414 N Hudson Ave, Oklahoma City, OK 73103

HAMPTON, Cynthia Marie (SO) 410 Torrence Ct, Cincinnati, OH 45202

HAMPTON, Roger Keith (Los) Po Box 260304, Corpus Christi, TX 78426

✠ **HAMPTON**, Sanford Zangwill Kaye (Ret Asst Bp of Oly 1996-) La Vida Real, 11588 Via Rancho San Diego, Apt. D 3049, San Diego, CA 92019

HAN, Heewoo Daniel (Va) 4060 Championship Dr, Annandale, VA 22003

HAN, Valentine S (Va) 4060 Championship Dr, Annandale, VA 22003

HANAHAN, Gwin Hunter (At) 2744 Peachtree Rd NW, Atlanta, GA 30305

HANBACK, Holly (Va) 14 Cornwall St NW, Leesburg, VA 20176

HANCHEY, Howard (SVa) 3003 Larkspur Run, Williamsburg, VA 23185

HANCKEL, Ellen Jervey (SwVa) 1013 Oakwood Ct, Martinsville, VA 24112

HANCOCK, Arthur B (Eau) 13705 Perry Lake Road, Cable, WI 54821

HANCOCK, Carol Jean (Va) 10730 Scott Dr, Fairfax, VA 22030

HANCOCK, Paul B (Ga) 1317 Gordon Ave, Thomasville, GA 31792

HAND, Gary Dean (Los) 669/659 Moo Ban Far Rangsit, Bungyeetho, Thanyaburi, Pathum Thani Thailand, 12130, Thailand

HANDLOSS, Patricia Diane (Mass) 115 Bayridge Lane, Duxbury, MA 02332

HANDS, Donald Raymond (Mil) 6 Becks Retreat, Savannah, GA 31411

HANDSCHY, Daniel John (Mo) 9373 Garber Rd, Saint Louis, MO 63126

HANDWERK, Larry Wayne (Chi) 9517 Springfield Ave, Evanston, IL 60203

HANDY, David Allan (Alb) 2919 Maplevale Rd, Chester, VA 23831

HANEN, Patricia Ida (O) 3785 W 33rd St, Cleveland, OH 44109

HANEY, Jack Howard (NH) 2 Leeward Way, Fairhaven, MA 02719

HANEY, James Paul (NwT) 4904 14th Street, Lubbock, TX 79416

HANEY V, James Paul (NwT) St. Paul's-on-the-Plains, 1510 Avenue X, Lubbock, TX 79401

HANISIAN, James Andrew (SO) 3870 Virginia Ave, Cincinnati, OH 45227

HANISIAN, Matthew Raymond (WA) 3001 Wisconsin Ave NW, Washington, DC 20016

HANK, Daniel Hayman (USC) 1151 Elm Savannah Rd, Hopkins, SC 29061

HANKINS, Samuel Scott (Az) 2501 W. Zia Road, #8205, Santa Fe, NM 87505

HANKINSON JR, Benjamin D (Spr)

HANKS JR, Alexander Hamilton (WNC) Po Box 8893, Asheville, NC 28814

HANLEY, Ian David (Los) 59131 Wilcox Ln, Yucca Valley, CA 92284

✠ **HANLEY**, Michael J (Bp of Ore 2010-) Episcopal Diocese of Oregon, 11800 SW Military Ln, Portland, OR 97219

HANNA, Bill (Miss) 783 Rosewood Pointe, Madison, MS 39110

HANNA, Daniel Bassett (Chi) 760 Magazine Street #205, New Orleans, LA 70130

HANNA, Gerald Benson (Oly) 11527 9th Ave Ne, Seattle, WA 98125

HANNA, Nancy Wadsworth (NY) 100 Edward Bentley Rd., Lawrence, NY 11559

HANNA, Raymond J (NC) Po Box 1043, Mount Airy, NC 27030

HANNABASS, Katherine Tootle (NMich)

HANNIBAL, Preston Belfield (WA) Washington National cathedral, Mount St. Alban, Washington, DC 20016

HANNUM, Christopher Cary Lee (At) 2148 Winding Creek Ln Sw, Marietta, GA 30064

HANSCOM, John David (Ak) St. Christopher's Episcopal, 7208 Duben Ave., ANCHORAGE, AK 99504

HANSEL, Robert Raymond (SO) PO Box 217, Little Switzerland, NC 28749

HANSELL, Susan Weir (CFla) 2048 Ryan Way, Winter Haven, FL 33884

HANSELMAN, David (CNY) PO Box 88, Greene, NY 13778

HANSEN, Alan Whitney (At) 1302 Hidden Brook Ln NW, Acworth, GA 30101

HANSEN, Carl R (ECR) 959 Vista Cerro Dr., Paso Robles, CA 93446

HANSEN, Janis Lee Harney (Mont) 2430 Sw Crestdale Dr, Portland, OR 97225

HANSEN, Jessica V (Cal) 1532 Burlingame Ave, Burlingame, CA 94010

HANSEN, Karen Sue (Okla) 310 E. Noble Ave., Guthrie, OK 73044

HANSEN, Knute Coates (Ct)

HANSEN, Michael (Cal) 1055 Taylor St, San Francisco, CA 94108

HANSEN, Michelle Helena (Ct) 125 Parklawn Dr, Waterbury, CT 06708
HANSEN JR, Robert F (ECR) 16 Salisbury Dr Apt 7217, Asheville, NC 28803
HANSEN, Thomas Parker (NI) 3717 N Washington Rd, Fort Wayne, IN 46802
HANSKNECHT, Jeanne Marie (CNY) 10 Mill St, Cazenovia, NY 13035
HANSLEY, Mary Belfry (SVa) 6219 Chelsea Crescent, Williamsburg, VA 23188
HANSON III, Aquilla Brown (Fla) 406 Glenridge Rd, Perry, FL 32348
HANSON, Deborah Ann (Miss) 5400 Old Canton Rd, Jackson, MS 39211
HANSON, Jay D (Minn) 1201 Yale Pl, Apt 1007, Minneapolis, MN 55403
HANSON, Norma Halmagyi (Del) 405 Lady Huntingdon Ln, Asheville, NC 28803
HANSON-FOSS, Patricia Jean (Alb) PO Box 237, Au Sable Forks, NY 12912
HANSTINE, Barbara Ann (Alb) 287 Leonard St, Hancock, NY 13783
HANTEN, Helen Bailey (Minn) 66 E. St. Marie St. #205, Duluth, MN 55803
HANWAY JR, Donald Grant (Neb) 128 N 13th St Apt #1009, Lincoln, NE 68508
HANYZEWSKI, Andrew J (Mil) 303 Merchants Ave, Fort Atkinson, WI 53538
HAPTONSTAHL, Stephen R (Minn) 807 Louisiana Ave, Cumberland, MD 21502
HARBIN, J Derek (SVa) 424 Washington St, Portsmouth, VA 23704
HARBOLD, Stanley L (NC) 221 Union St, Cary, NC 27511
HARBORT, Raymond Louis (Be) 1841 Millard St, Bethlehem, PA 18017
HARDAWAY IV, John Benjamin (USC) 795 Wilson St, Anderson, SC 29621
HARDAWAY, Ripp Barton (WTex) 312 S Guenther Ave, New Braunfels, TX 78130
HARDAWAY, Susan Arledge Louttit (USC) 404 North St, Anderson, SC 29621
HARDEN, Rosa Lee (Cal) 15 Riparian Way, Asheville, NC 28778
HARDENSTINE, Autumn Hecker (Pa) 126 Grist Mill Rd, Schuylkill Haven, PA 17963
HARDER, Cheryl Anne (Minn) 10 E Penton Blvd, Duluth, MN 55808
HARDIE JR, John Ford (WTex) 6709 Pharaoh Dr, Corpus Christi, TX 78412
HARDIN, Glennda Cecile (Tex) PO Box 10357, Liberty, TX 77575
HARDING, Kerith (The Episcopal Church in Haw)
HARDING, Leander Samuel (Alb) Trinity School For Ministry, 311 Eleventh Street, Ambridge, PA 15003
HARDING, Rona Robertine (WA)

HARDING, Sahra Megananda (O) 3004 Belvedere Blvd, Omaha, NE 68111
HARDING, Scott Mitchell (Alb) 25 Bonner Dr, Queensbury, NY 12804
HARDING, Stephen Riker (NY) 1047 Amsterdam Ave, New York, NY 10025
HARDMAN, J(Ohn) (Chi) 222 Kenilworth Ave., Kenilworth, IL 60043
HARDMAN, Louise O'Kelley (Fla) 256 E Church St, Jacksonville, FL 32202
HARDMAN, Richard Joseph (NJ) 3902 Se Fairway W, Stuart, FL 34997
HARDMAN, Robert Rankin (Minn) 2338 Como Ave, Saint Paul, MN 55108
HARDWICK, Dana (Lex) 7620 Summerglen Dr, Raleigh, NC 27615
HARDWICK, Lada Eldredge (Colo) 4490 Hanover Ave, Boulder, CO 80305
HARDWICK, Lindy Cornelius (Mo) 1001 Pheasant Hill Drive, Rolla, MO 65401
HARDWICK, William (Ct) 19 1/2 Murray St, Norwalk, CT 06851
HARDY, Cameron Reynolds (NY) 696 Deep Hollow Rd., Millbrook, NY 12545
HARDY, Jerry (Mass) 51 John Ward Ave, Haverhill, MA 01830
HARDY, Karen (WNY) 200 Cazenovia St, Buffalo, NY 14210
HARDY, Kim (Mass) 138 W. Plain St., Wayland, MA 01778
HARDY, Mary Elizabeth Holsberry (La) Po Box 3654, Durango, CO 81302
HARDY, (Patricia) Joyce (Ark) 2114 Center St, Little Rock, AR 72206
HARDY, Stanley P (Mass) Po Box 657, Humarock, MA 02047
HARDY, Velinda Elaine (NC) P.O. Box 86, 4880 Highway 561 East, Tillery, NC 27887
HARE, Ann DuBuisson (NY) 4300 Edson Ave, Bronx, NY 10466
HARE, Delmas (At) 104 Sequoyah Hills Drive, Fletcher, NC 28732
HARER, Mark P (CPa) 251 S Derr Dr, Lewisburg, PA 17837
HARGIS, James Frederick (The Episcopal NCal) 742 El Granada Blvd, Half Moon Bay, CA 94019
HARGIS, Kathleen Anne (WK) PO Box 1414, Dodge City, KS 67801
HARGREAVES, Helen Jessica (Ark) 10 Camp Mitchell Rd, Morrilton, AR 72110
HARGREAVES, Robert Alan (Me) Po Box 96, Boothbay Harbor, ME 04555
HARGROVE, Thomas J (Pa) 1628 Prospect St, Ewing, NJ 08638
HARIG, Richard Oliver (O) 3583 Sparrow Pond Cir., Akron, OH 44333
HARING, Charlotte (Az) 3942 E Monte Vista Dr, Tucson, AZ 85712
HARKER, Margaret Ann Griggs (NI) 1364 N Pinebluff Dr, Marion, IN 46952
HARKINS, James Robert (NY) 235 Walker Street, Apt. 43, Lenox, MA 01240

HARKINS III, J(ohn) William (At) 1703 Grace Ct SE, Smyrna, GA 30082
HARLACHER, Richard Charles (CPa) 486 Fencepost Ln, Palmyra, PA 17078
HARLAN, James Robert (SeFla) 141 S County Rd, Palm Beach, FL 33480
HARLAND, Mary Frances (Spok) Po Box 1510, Medical Lake, WA 99022
HARMAN, Torrence McClure (Va) 1927 Stuart Ave, Richmond, VA 23220
HARMON, Elsa Wittmack (Ia) 3131 Fleur Dr Apt 901, Des Moines, IA 50321
HARMON, John Robert (Md) 10128 Camshire Ct Apt B, Saint Ann, MO 63074
HARMON, John TW (WA) 7005 Piney Branch Rd NW, Washington, DC 20012
HARMON, Joseph Albion (Nwk) 8 Rosemont Ct, West Orange, NJ 07052
HARMON, Jude Aaron (Cal) Grace Cathedral, 1100 California St, San Francisco, CA 94108
HARMON, Judith Lynn (Mich) 8874 Northern Ave, Plymouth, MI 48170
HARMON, Robert Dale (Spr) 1119 Oakland Ave, 1119 Oakland Ave, Mount Vernon, IL 62864
HARMON, Zachary Charles (Ore) 1444 Liberty St SE, Salem, OR 97302
HARMS, Richard Benjamin (Los) 2731 Jody Pl, Escondido, CA 92027
HARMUTH, Karl Michael (Dal) 9021 Church Rd, Dallas, TX 75231
HARNEY, Margaret Ferris (At) 4393 Garmon Rd Nw, Atlanta, GA 30327
HARPER, Anna Katherine (CFla) St Mary's Church, 5750 SE 115th St, Belleview, FL 34420
HARPER, Barbara Anne (ETenn) 1155 Woodlawn Rd, Lenoir City, TN 37771
HARPER, Catherine Ann (Mass) 124 Front St, Marion, MA 02738
HARPER, David Scott (CPa) 5598 Arminda St, Harrisburg, PA 17109
HARPER, Fletcher (Nwk) 241A Johnson Ave Apt M1, Hackensack, NJ 07601
HARPER, Harry Taylor (WA) 36303 Notley Manor Ln, Chaptico, MD 20621
HARPER, Helen Othelia (The Episcopal Church in Haw) 94-1053 Nawele St, Waipahu, HI 96797
HARPER, John Brammer (Ia) 1310 Bristol Dr, Iowa City, IA 52245
HARPER, John Harris (Ala) 2600 Arlington Ave S Apt 62, Birmingham, AL 35205
HARPER JR, William Rhoderick (SVa) 6829 Cape View Avenue, Norfolk, VA 23518
HARPER, William Roland (Oly) 5836 Packard Lane, Bainbridge Island, WA 98110
HARPFER, Nancy Jean Fuller (EMich) St Andrews Episcopal Church, PO Box 52, Harrisville, MI 48740

Clergy List

HARPSTER, Christopher Lee (ETenn) St Paul's Episcopal Church, 161 E Ravine Rd, Kingsport, TN 37660

HARRELL, Linda J (Ore) 99 Brattle St, Cambridge, MA 02138

HARRELSON JR, Ernest S (Spok) 915 S 22nd Ave, Yakima, WA 98902

HARRELSON, Larry Eugene (Ida) 3095 W. Ravenhurst St., Meridian, ID 83646

HARRES, Elisa P (At) 13479 Spring View Dr, Alpharetta, GA 30004

HARRIES, Susan Gratia (NMich) 1111 Bingham Ave, Sault Sainte Marie, MI 49783

HARRIES, Thomas Dunbar (Minn) 10520 Beard Ave S, Bloomington, MN 55431

HARRIGAN, Katherine Gunn Lester (CPa) 1105 Old Quaker Rd, Etters, PA 17319

HARRIGFELD, Chris L (Cal) 8872 Bronson Dr., Granite Bay, CA 95746

HARRIMAN, Barbara June (Nwk)

HARRINGTON, Debra L (Chi) 1250 Averill Dr, Batavia, IL 60510

HARRINGTON, Lynn Beth (NY) 203 Salem Rd, Pound Ridge, NY 10576

HARRINGTON, Thomas Anthony (Okla) 2961 N 23rd St W, Muskogee, OK 74401

HARRIOT, Cameron (Los) 5672 Castle Dr, Huntington Beach, CA 92649

HARRIS, Anne Marie (Miss) 705 Rayburn Ave, Ocean Springs, MS 39564

✠ **HARRIS**, Barbara Clementine (Ret Bp Suffr of Mass 2002-) 11 Atherton Rd., Foxboro, MA 02035

HARRIS, Carl Berlinger (Md) 1506 Eton Way, Crofton, MD 21114

HARRIS, Carl Burton (Va) 2727 Fairview Ave E Apt 3b, Seattle, WA 98102

HARRIS, Cheryl J. (Neb) 820 Weat 9th Street, Alliance, NE 69301

HARRIS, Donald Bell (SVa) 121 Jordans Journey, Williamsburg, VA 23185

HARRIS, Edmund Immanuel (Oly) 1336 Pawtucket Ave, Rumford, RI 02916

HARRIS, Edward Ridgway (Minn) 2225 Crest Ln Sw, Rochester, MN 55902

HARRIS, Gareth Scott (At) Po Box 191708, Atlanta, GA 31119

✠ **HARRIS**, Gayle Elizabeth (Bp Suffr of Mass 2003-) 138 Tremont St, Boston, MA 02111

HARRIS, Gerald Joaquin (NwPa) 2604 Toucan Ave., McAllen, TX 78504

HARRIS, Henry Gibbard (O) 226 3rd St Se, Massillon, OH 44646

HARRIS, Herman (USC) 633 Swallow Rd, Elgin, SC 29045

HARRIS JR, James Wesley (Dal) 1700 N Westmoreland Rd, Desoto, TX 75115

HARRIS, John Carlyle (WA) 3050 Military Rd NW #2104, Washington, DC 20015

HARRIS, John Edward Crane (Ga) 30 Anderson Ave., Holden, MA 01520

HARRIS, John T. (The Episcopal NCal) P.O. Box 1291, Gridley, CA 95948

HARRIS, Jonathan Fisher (SwVa) 3286 Avenham Ave Sw, Roanoke, VA 24014

HARRIS, Julie Nan (WVa) 200 W King St, Martinsburg, WV 25401

HARRIS, Ladd Keith (WMich) 5527 N Sierra Ter, Beverly Hills, CA 34465

HARRIS JR, Lawrence (WA) 10450 Lottsford Road, #1218, Mitchellville, MD 20721

HARRIS, Lee Marshall (Los) 330 E 16th St, Upland, CA 91784

HARRIS, Margaret Stilwell (Ia)

HARRIS, Mark (Del) 207 E Market St, Lewes, DE 19958

HARRIS, Mark Hugh (Ore) 385 Doral Place, Pinehurst, NC 28374

HARRIS, Marsue (RI) 99 Main St, North Kingstown, RI 02852

HARRIS, Martha Caldwell (CGC) 79 6th St., Apalachicola, FL 32320

HARRIS, Melissa (Okla)

HARRIS, Michael William Henry (SwFla) 24311 Narwhal Lane, Port Charlotte, FL 33983

HARRIS, Neal Joseph (WMo) 1636 E Grand St, Springfield, MO 65804

HARRIS JR, Paul Sherwood (Pa) 810 Pine St, Philadelphia, PA 19107

HARRIS, Paula (Mil) St. Luke's Episcopal Church, 4011 Major Ave, Madison, WI 53716

HARRIS, Phillip Jay (SO) Po Box 484, Circleville, OH 43113

HARRIS, Randall Sellers (Ct) 129 Oil Mill Rd, Waterford, CT 06385

HARRIS, Robert Carradine (WTex) 512 Belknap Pl, San Antonio, TX 78212

HARRIS, Robert Charles (Kan) 6649 Nall Dr, Mission, KS 66202

✠ **HARRIS**, Rogers Sanders (Ret Bp of SwFla 1997-) 5502 Exum Drive, West Columbia, SC 29169

HARRIS, Rory Hb (CFla) 827 Tomlinson Ter, Lake Mary, FL 32746

HARRIS, Stephen Dirk (CPa) 1138 Boyds School Rd, Gettysburg, PA 17325

HARRIS, Suzanne Love (NJ) Box 864, Wilson, WY 83014

HARRIS, Thomas G (Chi) 5749 N Kenmore Ave, Chicago, IL 60660

HARRIS, Vincent Powell (WA) 3917 Peppertree Ln, Silver Spring, MD 20906

HARRIS, William Henry (NwPa) 940 Route 46, Emporium, PA 15834

HARRIS-BAYFIELD, Maeva-Louise Beckwith Hair (Tex) 300 Westmnstr Cantrbry Dr, Apt 405, Winchester, VA 22603

HARRISON JR, Claude Robert (WA) Churchillplein 6, The Hague, 2517 JW, Netherlands

✠ **HARRISON**, Dena Arnall (Bp Suffr of Tex 2006-) 3402 Windsor Rd, Austin, TX 78703

HARRISON JR, Edward Hendree (SanD) 1114 9th St., Coronado, CA 92118

HARRISON, Elizabeth Arendt (CFla) 215 S Lake Florence Dr, Winter Haven, FL 33884

HARRISON JR, Frederick C (SwFla) 140 Bilbao Dr, Saint Augustine, FL 32086

HARRISON JR, G Hendree (ETenn) Po Box 326, Athens, TN 37371

HARRISON, Harold Donald (At) 3823 Cherokee Frd, Gainesville, GA 30506

HARRISON, James Edward (EMich) Transfiguration Church, PO Box 460, Indian River, MI 49749

HARRISON, Merle Marie (Colo) 816 Harrison Ave, Canon City, CO 81212

HARRISON, Merritt Raymond (Mass) 12 Remington St Apt 105, Cambridge, MA 02138

HARRISON, Ronald Edward (Alb) 24 Summit Ave, Latham, NY 12110

HARRISON, Sherridan (WTex) 2431 Michele Jean Way, Santa Clara, CA 95050

HARRISS, Mary L (Chi) 2338 Country Knolls Ln, Elgin, IL 60123

HARRISS, Susan Carol (NY) 2 Rectory St, Rye, NY 10580

HARRITY, Alison Propeck (CFla) 5151 Lake Howell Rd, Winter Park, FL 32792

HARRON II, Frank Martin (WA) 10708 Brewer House Rd, North Bethesda, MD 20852

HARROP, Stephen Douglas (Tai) 16 W 3rd St, Essington, PA 19029

HART, Alan (Alb) 120 Waters Rd, Scotia, NY 12302

HART, Benjamin James (Ky) Grace Episcopal Church, 216 E 6th St, Hopkinsville, KY 42240

HART, Curtis Webb (NY) 132 N Broadway 1NW, Tarrytown, NY 10591

✠ **HART**, Donald Purple (Ret Asst Bp of SVa 1998-) P.O. Box 461, Peterborough, NH 03458

HART, Donnalee (The Episcopal NCal) St Francis in the Redwoods, 66 E Commercial St, Willits, CA 95490

HART, Frederick Morgan (WTenn) 78 Ottaray Ct, Brevard, NC 28712

HART JR, George Barrow (Ark) 3802 Hwy 82 W, Crossett, AR 71635

HART, J. Joseph (Md) 6701 N Charles St, Towson, MD 21204

HART, Larry Don (Colo) 8344 W Eastman Pl, Lakewood, CO 80227

HART, Lois Ann (Me) 1100 Washington St, Bath, ME 04530

HART, Mary Carol (Alb) 120 Waters Rd, Scotia, NY 12302

HART, Robert Lee (Colo) 1471 Bennaville Ave, Birmingham, MI 48009

HART, Stephen Anthony (Alb) 49 Killean Park, Albany, NY 12205

HART, Valerie Ann (ECR) 8 Daytona Dr, Laguna Niguel, CA 92677

HART, Virginia Frances (Nev) 451 N. Broadway St. Apt. E., Fallon, NV 89406

HART, William Gardner (NY) 414 Haines Rd # 4, Mount Kisco, NY 10549

HARTE, Barry Jay (Pa) 27 Conshohocken State Rd, Bala Cynwyd, PA 19004

HARTE JR, John Joseph Meakin (Az) 1000 E. Ponderosa Parkway, Flagstaff, AZ 86001

HARTE, Kathleen Audrey (LI)

HARTE, Susan Brainard (Az) 1000 E. Ponderosa Parkway, Flagstaff, AZ 86001

HARTER, Ralph M Peter (Roch) 98 Canfield Rd, Pittsford, NY 14534

HART GARNER, Eleanor E (Be) 125 Mount Joy St, Mount Joy, PA 17552

HARTJEN JR, Raymond Clifton (Kan) 1015 S. 5th St., Leavenworth, KS 66048

HARTL, Konrad Palmer (Va) 240 South 3rd Street, Philadelphia, PA 19106

HARTLEY, Chris (Ala) 1000 W 18th St, Anniston, AL 36201

HARTLEY, Harold Aitken (Mich) 1106 Riverview St, Rogers City, MI 49779

HARTLEY, Loyde Hobart (CPa) St James Church, 119 N Duke St, Lancaster, PA 17602

HARTLEY, Melissa M (At) 735 University Ave, Sewanee, TN 37383

HARTLEY, Robert Henry (The Episcopal NCal) 14530 N Line Post Ln, Tucson, AZ 85755

HARTLING, David Charles (CFla) 1606 Fort Smith Blvd, Deltona, FL 32725

HARTLING, Gardner J (Lex)

HARTMAN, Anthony Eden (EMich) 3458 E Mckinley Rd, Midland, MI 48640

HARTMAN, Holly H (Mass) PO Box 920372, Needham, MA 02492

HARTMAN, John Franklin (Be) 30 Butler St, Kingston, PA 18704

HARTMAN, Phyllis Colleen (Tex) 1803 Highland Hollow Dr, Conroe, TX 77304

HARTMAN, Samuel Henry (Eas) 5 School House Lane, North East, MD 21901

HARTMANS, Robert Gerrit (ETenn) 5008 14th Ave, Chattanooga, TN 37407

HARTNETT, John Godfrey (Nwk) 169 Fairmount Rd, Ridgewood, NJ 07450

HARTNEY, Michael Elton (Roch) 210 Reading Rd, Watkins Glen, NY 14891

HARTSFIELD, Paula Kindrick (Mo)

HARTSUFF, Jadon D (Colo) Saint John's Cathedral, 1350 Washington St, Denver, CO 80203

HARTT, Paul Jonathan (Alb) 8 Loudon Hts S, Loudonville, NY 12211

HARTT, Walter Fred (NJ) 408 Kingfisher Rd, Tuckerton, NJ 08087

HARTWELL, Edward M. (Tex) 5502-B Buffalo Pass, Austin, TX 78745

HARTWELL, Michael (Mass) 620 Flick Cir., Thomasville, NC 27360

HARTZELL, Susan Pye (Va) 5911 Fairview Woods Dr, Fairfax Station, VA 22039

HARTZOG, Dorothy Chatham (Tenn) 211 Chip N Dale Dr., Clarksville, TN 37043

HARTZOG, Howard Gallemore (WTex) 7520 Sunwest Ln, Sacramento, CA 95828

HARVEY, Edwin E (WTex) 868 Porter Rd, Cochran, GA 31014

HARVEY, Errol Allen (NY) 800 North Miami Ave., Apt. 302, Miami, FL 33136

HARVEY, Rick E (Ida) 2080 Bodine Ct, Boise, ID 83705

HARVEY, Robert William (Az) 9901 Penn Ave S Apt 336, Bloomington, MN 55431

HARVEY, Robert William (WA) Episcopal Church of Our Saviour, 1700 Powder Mill Road, Silver Spring, MD 20903

HARWOOD, John Thomas (CPa) 137 3rd St, Renovo, PA 17764

HARY, Barbara Ann (CPa) 20 Heatherland Rd, Middletown, PA 17057

HASEN, Elizabeth Sorchan (Ky) 409 W 22nd Ave, Spokane, WA 99203

HASKELL, Robert Finch (Alb) 9 Long Creek Dr, Burnt Hills, NY 12027

HASLETT III, William Warner (Pgh) 418 Jerad Ln., Windber, PA 15963

HASS, Caroline Vada (WNY) Po Box 161, Alexander, NY 14005

HASSAN, Rose Cohen (Nwk) 954 Ave C, Bayonne, NJ 07002

HASSE III, Edward Max (Nwk) 4 Woodland Rd, Montvale, NJ 07645

HASSELBROOK, Audrey Caroline (Nwk) 18 Shepard Pl, Nutley, NJ 07110

HASSELL, Mariann Barbara (Tenn) 1204 Jackson Dr, Pulaski, TN 38478

HASSEMER, Donald William (RG) Po Box 747, Medanales, NM 87548

HASSERIES, Robert Alan (Spok) East 360 Springview Drive, Coeur D'Alene, ID 83814

HASSETT, Miranda Katherine (Mil) 6325 Shoreham Dr, Madison, WI 53711

HASSETT, Stephen (Cal)

HASTIE, Cornelius deWitt (Mass) 24 Castleton St, Jamaica Plain, MA 02130

HASTINGS, Brian J (Chi) 857 W. Margate Terrace, #1-W, Chicago, IL 60640

HASTINGS, K(Empton) (Pa) 2119 Old Welsh Rd, Abington, PA 19001

HASTINGS, Mark Wayne (Mich) PO Box 287, Onsted, MI 49265

HATCH, Bert Huntington (SO) 3108 Fort St, Edisto Island, SC 29438

HATCH, Jessica Ann (U) 2586 Elizabeth St Apt 6, Salt Lake City, UT 84106

HATCH, Mark H (WMass) 267 Locust Street, Apt 2K, Florence, MA 01062

HATCH, Rebekah Bokros (At) 2852 Kimmeridge Dr, Atlanta, GA 30344

HATCH, Victoria Theresa (Los) 1095 Dysar, Banning, CA 92220

HATCHER JR, John Harris (Va) Apdo 632- 1250, Escazu, San Jose, 10201, Costa Rica

HATFIELD, Adele Dees (Nwk) 221 Boulevard, Mountain Lakes, NJ 07046

HATFIELD JR, Charles Jerome (Nwk) 221 Boulevard, Mountain Lakes, NJ 07046

HATFIELD, Russell Allen (SwVa) 101 Logan St, Bluefield, VA 24605

✠ **HATHAWAY**, Alden Moinet (Ret Bp of Pgh 1997-) 107 Laurens St., Beaufort, SC 29902

HATHAWAY, Dale Caldwell (The Episcopal Church in Haw) 1863 Rock Glen DR Apt 103, Rock Hill, SC 29732

HATZENBUEHLER, Robin Ritter (WTenn) 1544 Carr Ave, Memphis, TN 38104

HAUCK, Barbara Horsley (Minn) 32 W College St, Duluth, MN 55812

HAUCK, Mary Rockett (The Episcopal NCal) 11489 Phoebe Ct, Penn Valley, CA 95946

HAUERT, Robert Harold (Los) 1419 Jorn Ct, Ann Arbor, MI 48104

HAUFF, Bradley Sylvan (Pa) 9601 Frankford Ave, Philadelphia, PA 19114

HAUG, Phillip Russell (Lex) 100 Daisey Dr, Richmond, KY 40475

HAUGAARD, Jeffrey James (CNY) 101 E Williams St, Waterloo, NY 13165

HAUGAARD, William P (Chi) 1365 Twin Rivers Blvd, Oviedo, FL 32766

HAUGEN, Alice (Ia) 1483 Grand Ave, Iowa City, IA 52246

HAUGH, William Walter (Okla) 10126 S Kraft Dr, Vail, AZ 85641

HAUGHN, Terry Lee (WMich) 111 W Brighton St, Plainwell, MI 49080

HAUSER, Nancy (Pa) 245 Stoughton Cir, Exton, PA 19341

HAUTTECOEUR, Mario Alberto (ECR) 95 Stillbreeze Ln, Watsonville, CA 95076

HAVENS, Helen Markley Morris (Tex) 2401 Dryden Rd, Houston, TX 77030

HAVERKAMP, Heidi R (Chi)

HAVERLY, Tom P. (NJ) Saint Andrew's Episcopal Church, 419 South St, New Providence, NJ 07974

HAWES III, Charles Morris (NC) 1848 N Elm St, Greensboro, NC 27408

HAWES, Peter Wortham (USC) 32 Locust Ln, Tryon, NC 28782

HAWKES, Daphne Wolcott Parker (NJ) 50 Patton Ave, Princeton, NJ 08540

HAWKINS, Charles Thomas (Miss) 3003 Curran Rd, Louisville, KY 40205

HAWKINS, Deborah J (Cal) 280 Country Club Dr., South San Francisco, CA 94080

HAWKINS JR, Frank Jay (Tex) 1827 Green Gate Dr, Rosenberg, TX 77471

HAWKINS, Gary Altus (WVa) 1803 New Windsor Road, New Windsor, MD 21776

HAWKINS IV, J(Ames) Barney (Md) 3737 Seminary Rd, Alexandria, VA 22304

HAWKINS, Jodene Scaylea (The Episcopal Church in Haw) 203 Kulipuu St, Kihei, HI 96753

HAWKINS, Linda Wofford (Va) 4801 Ravensworth Rd, Annandale, VA 22003

HAWKINS, Mary Alice (Spok)

HAWKINS, Penelope Elizabeth (Vt) Po Box 492, North Bennington, VT 05257

HAWKINS, Richard Thurber (Pa) W396 n5918 Meadow Ln, Oconomowoc, WI 53066

HAWKINS, Thomas Edward (O) 14900 Mark Twain St, Detroit, MI 48227

HAWLEY, Carter Ricks (Ore) St Thomas Episcopal Church, 1465 Coburg Rd, Eugene, OR 97401

HAWLEY, Christian N (ETenn) 800 S Northshore Dr, Knoxville, TN 37919

HAWLEY, Frank Martin (WTex) 4518 Winlock Dr, San Antonio, TX 78228

HAWLEY, Kristen L (WA) Christ Church, 3116 O St NW, Washington, DC 20007

HAWLEY, Oral Robers (Ak)

HAWS, Howard Eugene (ETenn) 1418 Lonas Dr, Maryville, TN 37803

HAWS, Molly Elizabeth (Cal) Episcopal Church of the Redeemer, 123 Knight Dr, San Rafael, CA 94901

HAWTHORNE, Nanese Arnold (Eas) All Hallows Episcopal Church, 109 W Market St, Snow Hill, MD 21863

HAY, Audrey Lorna (NMich) 4955 12th Rd, Escanaba, MI 49829

HAY, Charles Henry (Ga) 1014 Shore Acres Dr, Leesburg, FL 34748

HAY, Daryl Tabor (Tex)

HAY, John Gardner (Spok) 2411 E 35th Ave, Spokane, WA 99223

HAY, Lesley J H (Cal) 1100 California St, San Francisco, CA 94108

HAYASHI, Koji (Ida) 2282 S Southshore Way, Boise, ID 83706

✠ **HAYASHI**, Scott Byron (Bp of U 2011-) 2649 E. Chalet Circle, Cottonwood Heights, UT 84093

HAYCOCK, Randall Hilton (Chi) 935 Dorchester Pl Apt 301, Charlottesville, VA 22911

HAYDE, Ronald Edward (SeFla) St Mark the Evangelist, 1750 E Oakland Park Blvd, Oakland Park, FL 33334

HAYDEN, Andrea Rose-Marie (NJ) 1002 4th Ave, Asbury Park, NJ 07712

HAYDEN JR, Daniel Frank (Mass)

HAYDEN, John Carleton (WA) 3710 26th St Ne, Washington, DC 20018

HAYDEN, John Hart (O) 206 S Oval Dr, Chardon, OH 44024

HAYDEN JR, Louis Harold (FtW) 7193 Neshoba Cir, Germantown, TN 38138

HAYDEN, Robert Stoddard (SVa) 1101 Sixth Ave, Farmville, VA 23901

HAYEK, Hal T (Md) 4 East University Parkway, Baltimore, MD 21218

HAYES III, Christopher Thomas (Va) 1131 Oaklawn Dr, Culpeper, VA 22701

HAYES, E Perren (NY) 33165 W Chesapeake St, Lewes, DE 19958

HAYES, John Michael (Md) 217 N Carey St, Baltimore, MD 21223

HAYES, Margaret Leigh (CFla)

HAYES, Valerie Jean (Va) 543 Beulah Rd NE, Vienna, VA 22180

HAYES JR, Walter LeRoy (SanD) 3663 Princeton Ave, San Diego, CA 92117

HAYES-MARTIN, Gianetta Marie (Cal) 2650 Sand Hill Rd, Menlo Park, CA 94025

HAYMAN, Robert Fleming (Oly) 1102 E Boston St, Seattle, WA 98102

HAYNES, Alice Smith (USC) 3136 Cimarron Trl, West Columbia, SC 29170

HAYNES, Argola Electa (Los) 1979 Newport Ave, Pasadena, CA 91103

HAYNES, Elizabeth S (Be) 621 Prices Dr, Cresco, PA 18326

HAYNES, Frank James (EMich) 2518 Woodstock Dr, Port Huron, MI 48060

HAYNES, John Connor (NJ) 45 W Broad St, Burlington, NJ 08016

HAYNES, Kendall Thomas (Oly) PO Box 6906, Tacoma, WA 98417

HAYNES SR, Larry Lee (NY) 34 Point St, New Hamburg, NY 12590

HAYNES, Peter Davis (Los) 3233 Pacific View Dr, Corona Del Mar, CA 92625

HAYNES, Rachel Fowler (NC) Po Box 504, Davidson, NC 28036

HAYNES, Susan B (NI) 616 Lincolnway East, Mishawaka, IN 46544

HAYNES, Thomas E (NI) 515 State St, Culver, IN 46511

HAYNES, Warren Edward (LI) 429 E 52nd St Apt 27h, New York, NY 10022

HAYNIE, Amy Dawn Peden (FtW) 223 S Pearson Ln, Keller, TX 76248

HAYS, Bret (Mass) 48 Middle St, Gloucester, MA 01930

HAYS, Donald Lewis (O) 322 Wendy Ln, Waverly, OH 45690

HAYS, Joseph Spurgeon (At) 666 E College St, Griffin, GA 30224

HAYS, Lloyd Phillip Whistler (Pgh) Po Box 43, Ambridge, PA 15003

HAYS, Louis B. (Pgh) 505 Kingsberry Cir, Pittsburgh, PA 15234

HAYS, Miriam Peggy Wall (Ark) 16 Birchwood Dr., Conway, AR 72034

HAYS-SMITH, Melissa Beth (SwVa) Christ Episcopal Church, 1101 Franklin Rd SW, Roanoke, VA 24016

HAYWARD, Dennis Earl (Vt) 511 Rankinville Rd, Mabou, NS B0E1X0, Canada

HAYWARD, Stephen H (WA) Stephen H Hayward, 154 Mills Point Rd, Brooksville, ME 04617

HAYWORTH, Joseph Allison (NC) 910 Croyden St, High Point, NC 27262

HAZEL, Dorothy Massey (USC) 546 Woodland Hills West, Columbia, SC 29210

HAZEL, Jim (FtW) 6828 Woodstock Road, Fort Worth, TX 76116

HAZELETT, Jackson Reiser (Ore) 18989 Ne Marine Dr Slip 4, Portland, OR 97230

HAZELETT, William Howard (CFla) 1666 Parkgate Dr., Kissimmee, FL 34746

HAZEN, Alba (Ore) 869 N Collier St, Coquille, OR 97423

HAZEN, Susan Marcotte (Be) St John's Episcopal Church, PO Box 246, Bandon, OR 97411

HAZLETT, Brant Vincent (Spr) 600 N Mulberry St # 674, Mount Carmel, IL 62863

HEACOCK, Donald Dee (WLa) 3218 Line Ave # 101, Shreveport, LA 77104

HEACOX, Don (RG) PO Box 1863, Deming, NM 88031

HEAD JR, Edward Marvin (WLa) 407 Tulane St, Bastrop, LA 71220

HEAD, Paul Anthony (CFla) 656 Avenue L, NW, Winter Haven, FL 33881

HEALD, David Stanley (Me) 8 Pine Ln, Cumberland Foreside, ME 04110

HEALEY, Joseph Patrick (NY) 1045 Cook Rd, Grosse Pointe, MI 48236

HEALY, Catherine (Ore)

HEALY, Denise Catherine (SwFla) 1502 Paddock Dr, Plant City, FL 33566

HEALY, Ruth Tenney (At) 1403 Oakridge Cir, Decatur, GA 30033

HEANEY, David Lloyd (SanD) 690 Oxford St, Chula Vista, CA 91911

HEARD, Fred (ECR) 1239 Wigh St SE, Salem, OR 97302

HEARD, Thomas (CGC)

HEARD, Victoria R.T. (Dal) 1630 N Garrett Ave, Diocese of Dallas, Dallas, TX 75206

HEARD, William Hugh (WTex) 415 E Beach St Apt 302, Galveston, TX 77550

HEARN, Arnold Withrow (Ark) 232 Pearl St., Marianna, AR 72360

HEARN, Roger Daniel (Va) 2201 Foresthill Rd, Alexandria, VA 22307

HEATH, Claudia (U)

HEATH, Glendon Edward (Mich) 19751 Northbrook Dr, Southfield, MI 48076

HEATH, Susan Blackburn (USC) 1115 Marion Street, Columbia, SC 29201

HEATHCOCK, Deborah B (WLa) 5219 Show Low Lake Road, Lakeside, AZ 85929

HEATHCOCK, J(Ohn) Edwin (Mo) 14485 Brittania Dr, Chesterfield, MO 63017

HEATHMAN, Sharron Gae (WMo) Po Box 307, Lexington, MO 64067

HEBERT, Francis Noel (NJ) 33 Throckmorton St., Freehold, NJ 07728

HECK, John Hathaway (SwVa) 65 Rock Ridge Rd, Callaway, VA 24067

HECKEL, Deborah Lee (FdL) Church of the Holy Apostles, 2937 Freedom Rd, Oneida, WI 54155

HECOCK, Georgia Ingalls (Minn) St. Luke's Episcopal Church, P.O. Box 868, Detroit Lakes, MN 56502

HECTOR JR, John Robert (WMich) 348 Waltonia Road, Drake, CO 80515

HEDEN, Eileen May (WK) 311 N 4th St, Sterling, KS 67579

HEDGER, John Spencer (Me) 524 Lake Louise Cir Apt 501, Naples, FL 34110

HEDGES, David Thomas (Chi) 222 Somonauk Street, Sycamore, IL 60178

HEDGES, Merry Helen (Ark) 8201 Hood Rd, Roland, AR 72135

HEDGIS, Sarah Emily (Pa) 5421 Germantown Ave, Philadelphia, PA 19144

HEDGPETH, Martha Holton (NC) 1412 Providence Rd, Charlotte, NC 28207

HEDIN, Joanne Christine (SD)

HEDLUND, Arnold Melvin (ECR) PO Box 2131, Salinas, CA 93902

HEDMAN, James Edward (SwFla) 9719 33rd Ave E, Palmetto, FL 34221

HEDQUIST, Ann Whitney (Kan) 3205 Sw 33rd Ct, Topeka, KS 66614

HEE, Malcolm Keleawe (The Episcopal Church in Haw) 720 N King St, Honolulu, HI 96817

HEFFNER, John H (Be) 129 Fairfax Rd, Bryn Mawr, PA 19010

HEFFNER, Meredith Tobin (Va) 6744 S Kings Hwy, Alexandria, VA 22306

HEFFRON, Judith Ann Williams (Los) 4959 Ridgeview St, La Verne, CA 91750

HEFLIN, Tim (Va) St Andrew's Episcopal Church, 6509 Sydenstricker Rd, Burke, VA 22015

HEFLING JR, Charles (Mass) 1619 Massachusetts Ave, Cambridge, MA 02138

HEFLING, David (Roch) St. John's Episcopal Church, 183 North Main Street, Canandaigua, NY 14424

HEFNER, Judy (WNY) 1307 Ransom Rd, Grand Island, NY 14072

HEFTI, William Joseph (The Episcopal NCal) 24300 Green Valley Rd, Auburn, CA 95602

HEGE, Andrew Joseph (Lex) 533 E Main St, Lexington, KY 40508

HEGEDUS, Frank M (Los) 12340 Seal Beach Blvd Ste B, Seal Beach, CA 90740

HEGG, Camille Sessions (At) 753 College St, Macon, GA 31201

HEGLUND, Janice N (Cal) 84 San Gabriel Dr, Fairfax, CA 94930

HEGNEY, Georgina (CNY) 210 Twin Hills Dr, Syracuse, NY 13207

HEHR, Randall Keith (SwFla) 3200 McMullen Booth Road, Clearwater, FL 33761

HEICHLER, Katherine (Ct) 1689 Litchfield Tpke # 1, Woodbridge, CT 06525

HEIDECKER, Eric (Nev) 14645 Rim Rock Dr, Reno, NV 89521

HEIDEL, Harrison (SwVa) PO Box 779, Hot Springs, VA 24445

HEIDMANN, Tina Jeanine (ECR) 98 Kip Dr, Salinas, CA 93906

HEIDT, James Kevin (CNY) St John's Church, 341 Main St, Oneida, NY 13421

HEIGHAM JR, Llewellyn Maitland (Mo) 182 Ameren Way Apt 462, Ballwin, MO 63021

HEIJMEN, Rutger-Jan Spencer (Tex) St Martin's Episcopal Church, 717 Sage Rd, TX, Houston 77056

HEILIGMAN, Sara (Sally) (CNY) 187 Brookside Ave., Amsterdam, NY 12010

HEIN, Charles Gregory (CGC) 533 Woodleaf Ct, Saint Louis, MO 63122

HEINE JR, Aj (La) 436 Jefferson Ave., Metaire, LA 70005

HEINE, Mary Anne Rose (La) 15249 Brandon Dr, Ponchatoula, LA 70454

HEINEMANN, Ann E (Ga) 539 N Westover Blvd Apt 103, Albany, GA 31707

HEINRICH, Judith Capstaff (Chi) 853 Oak Hill Rd, Barrington, IL 60010

HEISCHMAN, Daniel R (Ct) 20 Park Ave, #9A, New York, NY 10016

HEISTAND, Virginia (RI) Saint Paul's Church, 55 Main St, North Kingstown, RI 02852

HEKEL, Ulis Dean (Mil) 7017 Colony Dr, Madison, WI 53717

HELFERTY, Scott Hanson (Mass) 57 Hillside Ave, Salt Lake City, UT 84103

HELGESON, Gail M (Oly) 2909 7th St, Port Townsend, WA 98368

HELLER, Amy Groves (Dal) 6119 Black Berry Ln, Dallas, TX 75248

HELLER, Jan C (Oly) 1663 Bungalow Way NE, Poulsbo, WA 98370

HELLER, Richard Charles (WVa) 266 Paw Paw Ln, Saint Marys, WV 26170

HELLMAN, Gary Lee (NY) 224 W 11th St Apt 2, New York, NY 10014

HELMAN, Peter Alan (Lex) 131 Edgewood Rd, Middlesboro, KY 40965

HELMER, Ben Edward (Ark) 28 Prospect Ave, Eureka Springs, AR 72632

HELMER, Richard Edward (Cal) Church of Our Saviour, 10 Old Mill St, Mill Valley, CA 94941

HELMS III, David Clarke (SO)

HELMUTH, Bradley Mathew (The Episcopal NCal) Holy Trinity Church, 202 High St, Nevada City, CA 95959

HELT, Dwight Neil (Okla) 130 Rue de Montserrat, Norman, OK 73071

HEMENWAY, Henry Jack (Me) 80 Lyme Rd, Apt 250, Hanover, NH 03755

HEMINGSON, Celeste A (NH) 340 Main St # 3229, Hopkinton, NH 03229

HEMMERS, Louis Emanuel (Los) 1634 Crestview Rd, Redlands, CA 92374

HEMPHILL, Margaret Ayars (Chi) 53 Loveland Rd, Norwich, VT 05055

HEMPSTEAD, James Breese (Ind) 512 Woodland Ave, Petoskey, MI 49770

HENAULT JR, Armand Joseph (Vt) 374 Spring Street, St Johnsbury, VT 05819

HENAULT, Rita Laverne (At)

HENDERSON, Catherine Ann Graves (Ga) St Francis of the Islands, 590 Walthour Rd, Savannah, GA 31410

HENDERSON III, Charles (CNY) 39 E Church St, Adams, NY 13605

HENDERSON, Don Keith (Colo) 2855 Rock Creek Cir Unit 179, Superior, CO 80027

☩ **HENDERSON**, Dorsey Felix (Ret Bp of USC 2010-) 1115 Marion St, Columbia, SC 29201

HENDERSON, Dumont Biglar (Me) 65 Eustis Pkwy., Waterville, ME 04901

HENDERSON JR, George Raymond (Fla) 1516 Marsh Inlet Ct, Jacksonville Beach, FL 32250

HENDERSON, Harvey George (ND) 801 2nd St N, Wahpeton, ND 58075

HENDERSON, Jane Pataky (Chi) 624 Colfax St, Evanston, IL 60201

HENDERSON, L Owen (WMo) 288 Cedar Glen Dr Unit 4B, Camdenton, MO 65020

HENDERSON, Mark William (Cal) 795 Buena Vista Ave W Apt 6, San Francisco, CA 94117

HENDERSON, Michael Brant (Lex) 381 Bon Haven Rd, Maysville, KY 41056

HENDERSON, Michael Jack (Fla) 1746 Hillgate Ct, Tallahassee, FL 32308

HENDERSON, Patricia Ann (Tex) Grace Episcopal Church, 1314 E University Ave, Georgetown, TX 78626

HENDERSON, Robert Bobo (Ala) 5375 US Highway 231, Wetumpka, AL 36092

HENDERSON III, Samuel Gott (Me) 134 Park St, Portland, ME 04101

HENDERSON, Sterling (Fla) 1746 Hillgate Ct, Tallahassee, FL 32308

HENDERSON, Stuart Hanford (Va) 55 Sunfield Dr, Carolina Shores, NC 28467

HENDERSON, Susan (SwFla) 12630 Panasoffkee Dr, North Fort Myers, FL 33903

HENDERSON JR, Theodore Herbert (Pa) 236 Glen Pl, Elkins Park, PA 19027

HENDRICK, Elizabeth (At) 1520 Oak Rd, Snellville, GA 30078

HENDRICKS, Mary D (Colo)

HENDRICKS, Rebecca Lanham (EO) Po Box 293, Milton Freewater, OR 97862

HENDRICKS III, Walter Frisby (SeFla) 2303 N.E. Seaview Drive, Jensen Beach, FL 34957

HENDRICKSON, Patricia Dee (Los) 265 W Sidlee St, Thousand Oaks, CA 91360

HENDRICKSON III, Robert J (Colo) Saint John's Cathedral, 1350 Washington St Fl 3, Denver, CO 80203

HENDRICKSON, Thomas Samuel (Va) 3845 Village Views Pl, Glen Allen, VA 23059

HENERY, Charles Robert (Mil) 20 Oakwood Dr, Delafield, WI 53018

HENKING, Patricia Ellen (NH) 2 Lavender Ct, Merrimack, NH 03054

HENLEY, Carol Eileen (Pgh) 1212 Trevanion Ave, Pittsburgh, PA 15218

HENLEY, Charles Wilbert (ND) PO Box 524, Valley City, ND 58072

HENLEY JR, Edward Joseph (SwFla) 404 Park Ridge Ave, Temple Terrace, FL 33617

HENLEY, Robert Pinkerton (ETenn) 351 Hardin Ln, Sevierville, TN 37862

HENNAGIN, Bob (Ala) Church Of The Holy Comforter, 2911 Woodley Rd, Montgomery, AL 36111

HENNE, Bruce Charles (Minn) 1270 118th Ave NW, Coon Rapids, MN 55448

HENNESSY, F(rank) Scott (SVa) 132 Blue Ridge Dr, Orange, VA 22960

HENNESSY, J Katherine (Minn) 13946 Echo Park Cir, Burnsville, MN 55337

HENNING, Joel Peter (HB)

HENNING, Kristina Louise (FdL) 6426 S. 35th Street, Franklin, WI 53132

HENNINGER, Annie (SD) 105 E 12th St, Gregory, SD 57533

HENRICHSEN, Robert Anton (Neb)

HENRICK, Joan (Ala) 5789 Tydan Ln, Gadsden, AL 35907

HENRICKSON, Mark (Los) 32A Wingate Street, Avondale, Auckland, 0600, New Zealand (Aotearoa)

HENRY, Barbara D. (WA) 5333 N Sheridan Rd Apt.8H, Chicago, IL 60640

HENRY, David Winston (VI) Po Box 6119, Christiansted, VI 00823

HENRY, Dean (NJ) 14 Winding Lane, Southwest Harbor, ME 04679

HENRY, Earl Fitzgerald (SeFla) 4401 W Oakland Park Blvd, Fort Lauderdale, FL 33313

HENRY, George Kenneth Grant (NC) 34 Red Fox Lane, Brevard, NC 28712

HENRY, James Russell (SwVa) 4647 Prince Trevor Dr, Williamsburg, VA 23185

HENRY, John Reeves (Spr) 415 S Broad St, Carlinville, IL 62626

HENRY II, John W (Alb) P.O. Box 175, Clifton Park, NY 12065

HENRY, Karen E J (NY) St John's Church, 365 Strawtown Rd, New City, NY 10956

HENRY, Lloyd (LI) 4607 Avenue H, Brooklyn, NY 11234

HENRY, Richard Arlen (Episcopal SJ) 1155 Leavell Park Cir, Lincoln, CA 95648

HENRY, Richard L(ynn) (Nev) 228 Hillcrest Dr, Henderson, NV 89015

HENRY JR, Wayman Wright (USC) 116 Sedgewood Ct, Easley, SC 29642

HENSARLING JR, Larry Reid (CFla) 146 Oak Sq S, Lakeland, FL 33813

HENSEL, Charles Howard (Chi) 2625 TEchny Rd Apt 620, Northbrook, IL 60062

HENSHAW, Richard Aurel (Roch) 199 Crosman Terr., Rochester, NY 14620

HENSLEY, Erin S (Tex) Po Box 368, Austin, TX 78767

HENSLEY, Joseph H (Va) 905 Princess Anne St, Fredericksbrg, VA 22401

HENSLEY, Lane Goodwin (SanD) 47535 State Highway 74, Palm Desert, CA 92260

HENSLEY-ECHOLS, Beth Marie (WA) Brooke Army Medical Center, 3851 Roger Brooke Dr, San Antonio, TX 78234

HENSON, David R (The Episcopal NCal) 471 W Martintown Rd, North Augusta, SC 29841

HENSON, Paula (The Episcopal Church In NAM) Good Shepherd Mission, PO Box 618, Fort Defiance, AZ 86504

HENSON, Tula (USC) 253 Bridleridge Rd, Lexington, SC 29073

HENWOOD, Karen Lee (Colo) 5604 E Nichols Pl, Centennial, CO 80112

HENWOOD, William A (Colo) 5604 E Nichols Pl, Centennial, CO 80112

HERALD, Erin Carol (NwPa) St Jude's Episc Church, PO Box 1714, Hermitage, PA 16148

HERBST, Gary Siegfried (Dal) 8320 Jack Finney Blvd., Greenville, TX 75402

HERGENRATHER, Lynda Stevenson (Va) 5904 Mount Eagle Dr Apt 318, Alexandria, VA 22303

HERKNER JR, Robert Thomas (O) 328 Windsor Ct, Huron, OH 44839

HERLIHY, Phyllis Cleo (SwFla) 514 50th St W, Bradenton, FL 34209

HERLOCKER SR, John Robert (Ida) 3700 NW Orchard Dr, Terrebonne, OR 97760

HERLOCKER, Thomas D. (Kan) 1704 E 10th Ave, Winfield, KS 67156

HERMAN, Alice McWreath (SO) 345 Ridgedale Dr N, Worthington, OH 43085

HERMAN, Elizabeth Frances (Minn) 615 Vermillion St, Hastings, MN 55033

HERMANSON, David Harold (NJ) 56 Grace Drive, Old Bridge, NJ 08857

HERMERDING, Joseph R (Dal) Church Of The Incarnation, 3966 Mckinney Ave, Dallas, TX 75204

HERN, George Neal (Dal) 4329 Irvin Simmons Dr, Dallas, TX 75224

HERNANDEZ, Alejandro Felix (SeFla) 9460 Fontainebleau Blvd Apt 334, Miami, FL 33172

HERNANDEZ, Gustavo (Los) Po Box 893, Downey, CA 90241

HERNANDEZ, Jorge A (Nev) 2000 S Maryland Pkwy, Las Vegas, NV 89104

HERNANDEZ, Luis Alfonso (Hond)

HERNANDEZ, Miguel Angel (Nwk)

HERNANDEZ JR, Nicolas (Alb) Trinity Episcopal Church, 1336 1st Ave, Watervliet, NY 12189

HERNANDEZ ROJAS, Martin Antonio (Colom) Carrera 6 No 49-85, Piso 2, Bogota, Colombia

HERNDON, James C (Ida) 1055 Riverton Rd, Blackfoot, ID 83221

HERON, James (NY) 54 Angela Ct, Beacon, NY 12508

HERON, Marsha Smith (Colo) 4447 E Lake Cir S, Centennial, CO 80121

HERRERA, Lourdes del Carmen (Hond) IMS SAP Dept 215. PO Box 523900, Miami, FL 33152-3900, Honduras

HERRERA, Marisa (Pa)

HERRERA CHAGNA, Raul (EcuC) Avenue Amazonas #4430, Igl Epis Del Ecuador, Quito, Ecuador

HERRICK, Robert Frank (NY) 159-00 Riverside Drive West, Apt 6K-70, New York, NY 10032

HERRING, Dianne Lerae (Wyo) PO Box 12, Kaycee, WY 82639

HERRING, John Foster (At) 634 W Peachtree St NW, Atlanta, GA 30308

HERRING, Joseph Dahlet (At) 5575 N Hillbrooke Trce, Johns Creek, GA 30005

HERRING, Virginia Norton (NC) 607 N Greene st, Greensboro, NC 27401

HERRINGTON III, Willet Jeremiah (Mich) 30420 Rush St, Garden City, MI 48135

HERRMANN, H(Erbert) W(Illiam) (Dal) 623 Ector St, Denton, TX 76201

HERRON, Daniel Peter (Az) St Mark's Church, 322 N Horne, Mesa, AZ 85203

HERRON-PIAZZA, Katherine (Ct) 22 Coulter Ave, Pawling, NY 12564

HERSHBELL, Jackson Paul (SwVa) 274 Still House Dr, Lexington, VA 24450

HERTH, Daniel Edwin (Cal) 32 Mallorie Park Drive, The Garden House, Ripon North Yorkshire, HG42QF, Great Britain (UK)

HERTLEIN, Christine R (Ore) 2490 Ne Highway 101, Lincoln City, OR 97367

HERVEY JR, Theodore E (Tex) 933 N Fm 1174, Bertram, TX 78605

HERZOG, Carole Regina (Los) 1471 Cloister Dr, La Habra Heights, CA 90631

✠ **HERZOG**, Daniel William (Ret Bp of Alb 2007-) 612 S Shore Rd, Delanson, NY 12053

HERZOG, Kenneth Bernard (Fla) 3545 Olympic Dr, Green Cove Springs, FL 32043

HESCHLE, John Henry (Chi) 7100 North Ashland Blvd, Chicago, IL 60626

HESS, George Robert (HB)

HESS, Howard (ETenn) 8500 Cambridge Woods Ln, Knoxville, TN 37923

HESS III, Raymond Leonard (The Episcopal NCal) 9001 Crowley Way, Elk Grove, CA 95624

HESS, Richard Walton (Cal) 601 Torre Malibu, 325 Calle Amapas, Puerto Vallarta, Mexico

HESSE, Alan Roger (Mass) 409 Common St, Walpole, MA 02081

HESSE JR, Rayner Wilson (NY) 415 Collins St, Bethany Beach, DE 19930

HESSE, Vicki K. (Az) St Philips in the Hills Parish, PO Box 65840, Tucson, AZ 85728

HESSE, William Arthur (Okla) 1805 N Canary Dr, Edmond, OK 73034

HETHCOCK, William Hoover (Tenn) Po Box 3310, Sewanee, TN 37375

HETHERINGTON, Robert Gunn (Va) 1500 Westbrook Ct Apt 2133, Richmond, VA 23227

HETLER, Gwendolyn Kay (NMich) 3135 County Road 456, Skandia, MI 49885

HETRICK JR, Budd A(lbert) (Ida)

HETZEL, Alan Dorn (WNC) Po Box 442, Highlands, NC 28741

HEUSS, William (Mass) 15 Thimbleberry Rd, South Yarmouth, MA 02664

HEVERLY, Craig Brian (Ore) 925 Se Center St, Portland, OR 97202

HEWETSON, Richard Walton (Cal)

HEWIS, Clara Mae (CGC) 7979 N 9th Ave, Pensacola, FL 32514

HEWITT, Emily Clark (NY)

HEYD, Matthew F (NY) 74 Trinity Pl, New York, NY 10006

HEYDT, C(harles) Read (SwFla) 5676 Lake Vista Ct, Sarasota, FL 34233

HEYDUK, Terri (NY) 7612 N Eastlake Terr Unit 2N, Chicago, IL 60626

HEYES, Andrew (SwFla) 706 W 113th Ave, Tampa, FL 33612

HEYING, R Christopher (WLa) PO Box 26, Chatham, VA 24531

HEYVAERT, Bruce T (Ark) Saint James Church, PO Box 846, Magnolia, AR 71754

HEYWARD, (Isabel) Carter (Mass) PO Box 449, Cedar Mountain, NC 28718

HIATT, Anthony Ray (FtW) 4301 Meadowbrook Dr, Fort Worth, TX 76103

HIATT, Kathleen Mary (Nev) Po Box 146, Pioche, NV 89043

✠ **HIBBS**, Robert Boyd (Bp Suffr of WTex 2006-) 1 Towers Park Ln Apt 1807, San Antonio, TX 78209

HICKENLOOPER, A(ndrew) Morgan (CGC) Po Box 27120, Panama City, FL 32411

HICKEY, John D (Mil)

HICKEY-TIERNAN, Joseph J (Oly) 3415 S 45th St Apt G, Tacoma, WA 98409

HICKMAN, Clare Louise (Mich) 241 S Franklin St, Dearborn, MI 48124

HICKMAN, Donald Royce (Dal) 183 Rainbow Dr # 8309, Livingston, TX 77399

HICKS, Catherine D (Va) PO Box 399, Port Royal, VA 22535

HICKS, John Wellborn (CGC) 502 La Rose Dr, Mobile, AL 36609

HICKS, Mary Kohn (WMass) 88 Masonic Home Rd, #R404, Charlton, MA 01507

HICKS, Paul L. (WVa) 430 Juliana St., Parkersburg, WV 26101

HICKS, Richard William (La) 2507 Portola Ave Apt 20, Livermore, CA 94551

HICKS, Sally Sue (Colo) Po Box 1590, Granby, CO 80446

HICKS, Warren Earl (WMass) 921 Pleasant St, Worcester, MA 01602

HIEBERT, Cornelius A (Dal) 8105 Fair Oaks Xing, Dallas, TX 75231

HIERS JR, John Douglas (SwFla) 1004 Woodcrest Ave, Clearwater, FL 33756

HIERS, Sharon Leigh (At) 2089 Ponce de Leon Ave NE, Atlanta, GA 30307

HIGGINBOTHAM, John E (RI) 99 Pierce St, East Greenwich, RI 02818

HIGGINBOTHAM, Stuart Craig (At) 2900 Paces Ferry Rd SE Bldg D, Atlanta, GA 30339

HIGGINS, Jeffrey David (Va)

HIGGINS, Kent (WVa) St Matthews Episcopal Church, 36 Norwood Rd, Charleston, WV 25314

HIGGINS, Pamela (Cal) 272 W I St, Benicia, CA 94510

HIGGINS, Teddy John (USC)

HIGGINS, Timothy John (Me) 25 Twilight Ln, Gorham, ME 04038

HIGGINS, William Harrison (Va) 8000 Hermitage Rd, Richmond, VA 23228

HIGGINSON, Paul Howard (NH) 472 Swazey La, Bethlehem, NH 03574

HIGGINS-SHAFFER, Diane Hazel (Ore) 503 N Holladay Dr, Seaside, OR 97138

HIGGITT, Noel (ECR) 1325 San Mateo Dr, Menlo Park, CA 94025

✠ **HIGH JR**, Rayford Baines (Ret Bp Provsnl of FtW 2015-) 4709 Marbella Cir, Fort Worth, TX 76126

HIGHLAND, Terrence Irving (Pa)

HIGHSMITH, Jennifer Lynn (Ga)

HILDEBRAND, Nancy Steakley (WA) St Nicholas Episcopal Church, 14100 Darnestown Rd Ste B, Germantown, MD 20874

HILDEBRANDT, M Lise (NH) 1400 1st Avenue, Longmont, CO 80501

HILDESLEY, Christopher Hugh (NY) 570 Park Ave Apt 6-D, New York, NY 10021

HILE, Jeanette Theresa (Nwk) 16 Day Rd, Landing, NJ 07850

HILEMAN, Mary E(sther) (Okla) 2809 W 28th Ave, Stillwater, OK 74074

HILFIKER, Gerald Milton (WNY) 10085 Pfarner Road, Boston, NY 14025

HILGARTNER, Elizabeth (Vt) Po Box 6, Orford, NH 03777

HILL, C(harleen) Diane (Ala) 1806 Meadows Dr, Birmingham, AL 35235

HILL, David Ernest (Minn) 103 West Oxford Street, Duluth, MN 55803

HILL, Derrick C (ETenn) 626 Mississippi Ave, Signal Mountain, TN 37377

HILL, Don (Roch) 321 E Market St, Jeffersonville, IN 47130

HILL, Ellen R. (Los) 5066 Berean Ln, Irvine, CA 92603

HILL, Gary Hill (Tex) 9541 Highland View Dr., Dallas, TX 75238

HILL III, George Aldrich (SO) 22 Vintage Walk, Cincinnati, OH 45249

HILL, Gordon Carman (Az) 2257 E Becker Ln, Phoenix, AZ 85028

HILL III, Harry Hargrove (Dal) Church Of The Incarnation, 3966 McKinney Ave, Dallas, TX 75204

HILL IV, Harvey (WMass) 59 Dryads Green, Northampton, MA 01060

HILL, Heather L (O) 8911 W Ridgewood Dr, Parma, OH 44130

HILL, H Michael (CGC) 2255 Valle Escondido Dr, Pensacola, FL 32526

HILL, Jerry Echols (Dal) 281 Becky Ln, Waxahachie, TX 75165

HILL, John Spencer (WTex) St Margaret's Episcopal Church, 5310 Stahl Rd, San Antonio, TX 78247

HILL, Joshua Ashton (ETenn) 950 Episcopal School Way, Knoxville, TN 37932

HILL, Jude (Cal) 573 Dolores St, San Francisco, CA 94110

HILL, Nicholas T (Minn) 4 Saint Paul Ave, Duluth, MN 55803

HILL, Ralph Julian (SD) 1224 Junction Ave, Sturgis, SD 57785

Clergy List

HILL, Renee Leslie (NY) 575 Grand St Apt 1801, New York, NY 10002
HILL, Susan Diane (Ga) 3101 Waters Ave, Savannah, GA 31404
HILL, Susan Elizabeth (NY) 225 W 99th St., New York, NY 10025
HILL, Vernon Willard (Episcopal SJ) PO Box 153, Bakersfield, CA 93302
HILLEBRAND, Walter V. (LI) 23 Cedar Shore Dr, Massapequa, NY 11758
HILLEGAS, Eric (Mass) Parish of St. Chrysostom, 1 Linden Street, Quincy, MA 02170
HILLENBRAND, Pamela M (Chi) 412 North Church St, Rockford, IL 61103
HILLER, Michael T. (Cal) 278 Hester Ave, San Francisco, CA 94134
HILLGER, Cindy Lou (Minn) 2801 Westwood Rd, Minnetonka Beach, MN 55361
HILLIARD-YNTEMA, Katharine Arnold (At) 737 Woodland Ave SE, Atlanta, GA 30316
HILLIN JR, Harvey Henderson (WK) Box 215, Sturgeon Bay, WI 54235
HILLMAN, George Evans (FdL) P O Box 215, Sturgeon Bay, WI 54235
HILLMAN, Harry Randall (Ak) PO Box 870995, Wasilla, AK 99687
HILLQUIST, Catherine Rinker (Mo) 121 Riverside St., Arcadia, MO 63621
HILLS, Frances Ann (WMass) 2 Amy Ct, Pittsfield, MA 01201
HILLS, John Bigelow (WMich) 1450 S Ferry St Apt 104, Grand Haven, MI 49417
HILLS, Julian Victor (Mil) 3046 N Cambridge Ave, Milwaukee, WI 53211
HILLS, Lindsay Marie (Cal) 1 S El Camino Real, San Mateo, CA 94401
HILLS, Wesley (SanD) 15 Old Coach Rd, Athens, OH 45701
HILLS JR, William Leroy (SC) 727 Atlantic St, Mt Pleasant, SC 29464
HILSABECK, Polly H (NC) 184 Grey Elm Trl, Durham, NC 27713
HILTON, Elizabeth Grant (At) PO Box 169, Morrow, GA 30260
HILTON, Olivia P L (WA)
HILYARD, Jack Lee (Ore) 311 NW 20th Ave, Portland, OR 97209
HIMES, John Martin (Tex) 106 N Grove St, Marshall, TX 75670
HIMMERICH, Maurice Fred (Mil) 107 Fairview St, Watertown, WI 53094
HINCAPIE LOAIZA, David Hernan (Colom) Manzana 26 Barrio Simon Bolivar, Armenia-Quindio, Columbia, Colombia
HINCHLIFFE, George Lewis (Fla) PO Box 1238, Live Oak, FL 32064
HINDS, Eric Kimball (Cal) 1 S El Camino Real, San Mateo, CA 94401
HINDS, Gilberto Antonio (LI) 9707 Horace Harding Expy Apt 8L, Corona, NY 11368
HINES, Caroline V (NH) 2 Wentworth St, Exeter, NH 03833
HINES JR, Chester (Mo) 1210 Locust St, St. Louis, MO 63103

HINES, J (ohn) Christopher (Tex) 4603 Pro Ct, College Station, TX 77845
HINES, John Moore (Ky) 5722 Coach Gate Wynde, Louisville, KY 40207
HINES, John S (WNC) 219 Chunns Cove Rd, Asheville, NC 28805
HINES, Lisa Stolley (Tex) Calvary Episcopal Church, PO Box 721, Bastrop, TX 78602
HINES, Travis S (Tenn) 4800 Belmont Park Ter, Nashville, TN 37215
HINKLE, Daniel Wayne (Be) 234 High St, Atglen, PA 19310
HINKLE, Lisa Jan (CFla) Po Box 2373, Belleview, FL 34421
HINKLE, Robin Hansen (Ala) 424 Emery Drive, Hoover, AL 35244
HINMAN, Allen (Nwk) 149 Pennington Ave, Passaic, NJ 07055
HINO, Moki (The Episcopal Church in Haw) Church of the Holy Apostles, 1407 Kapiolani Street, Hilo, HI 96727
HINRICHS, William Roger (Alb) 1201 Vineyard St., Cohoes, NY 12047
HINSE, Mary Norquist (Cal) 2230 Huron Dr., Concord, CA 94519
HINSON, Bryan T (At) 582 Walnut St, Macon, GA 31201
HINSON, Jerome Andrew (WMo) 5 Averil Ct, Fredericksburg, VA 22406
HINSON, Michael Bruce (Va) 6033 Queenston St, Springfield, VA 22152
HINTON, Brad (Del) 2320 Grubb Road, Wilmington, DE 19810
HINTON, Gregory Paul (CPa) PO Box 701, Wellsboro, PA 16901
HINTON, Michael (VI) Box 199, Cruz Bay, Saint John, VI 00831
HINTON, Wesley Walker (SO) 5907 Castlewood Xing, Milford, OH 45150
HINTZ, Mary Louise (Cal) 623 28th Street, Richmond, CA 94804
HINXMAN, Frederic William (Lex) 5639 Highway #1, Granville Ferry, NS B0S 1K0, Canada
HIPP JR, Thomas Allison (USC) 910 Hudson Rd, Greenville, SC 29615
HIPPLE, Judy Kay (Chi) 4511 Newcastle Rd, Rockford, IL 61108
HIPPLE, Maureen Atlee (Be) 298 Country View Drive, Towanda, PA 18848
✠ **HIRSCHFELD**, A Robert (Bp of NH 2013-) 103 Hedgerose Ln, Hopkinton, NH 03229
HIRSCHMAN, Portia Royall Conn (Md) 11860 Weller Hill Dr, Monrovia, MD 21770
HIRST, Dale Eugene (SVa) 4127 Columbus Ave, Norfolk, VA 23504
HIRST, Robert Lynn (Kan) Po Box 1859, Wichita, KS 67201
HITCH, Catherine Elizabeth (Colo) 1320 Arapahoe Street, Golden, CO 80401
HITCH, Kenneth R (EMich) 405 N Saginaw Rd, Midland, MI 48640
HITCHCOCK JR, H(Orace) Gaylord (The Episcopal Church in Haw) 1030

Aoloa Place, Apt 206A, Kailua, HI 96734
HITCHCOCK, Jessica Katherine (WA)
HITE, Jean A (SwFla) St Nathaniel's Episcopal Church, 4200 S Biscayne Dr, North Port, FL 34287
HITE SPECK, Nancy Jean (NJ) 201 Meadow Ave, Point Pleasant, NJ 08742
HITT, Mary (RI) 11 Beaufort St, Providence, RI 02908
HIXON, Beth Wunderlich (Pa) 1201 Lower State Rd, North Wales, PA 19454
HIXSON, Mary L (WK) 19 Deer Creek Tr, Anthony, KS 67003
HIYAMA, Paul Shoichi (Mich) 734 Peninsula Ct, Ann Arbor, MI 48105
HIZA, Douglas (Minn) 10 Meynal Crescent, South Hackney, London, E97AS, Great Britain (UK)
HIZER, Cynthia A (At) 550 Jenkins Rd, Covington, GA 30014
HLASS, Lisa (Ark) 2606 Beach Head Ct, Richmond, CA 94804
HLAVACEK, Frances (Be) 110 W Catherine St, Milford, PA 18337
HO, Edward HC (Mass) 24 Greenleaf St, Malden, MA 02148
HO, Jeng-Long Philip (Tai) #200 Ziqiang 1st Rd, Samin Dist, Kaohsiung, Taiwan
HO, Jui-En (Tai)
HOAG, David Stewart (NY) 503 North Causeway #102, New Smyrna Beach, FL 32169
HOARE, Geoffrey Michael St John (At)
HOBART, Terri Lynn (The Episcopal NCal) 967 5th St, Novato, CA 94945
HOBBS, Bryan Arthur (SeFla) 751 Sw 98th Ter, Pembroke Pines, FL 33025
HOBBS, Edward Craig (Cal) 32 Upson Road, Wellesley, MA 02482
HOBBS, Mercy Gardiner (SD) 405 N Madison Ave, Pierre, SD 57501
HOBBS, William Battersby (WMass) 45 Park Ave., Athol, MA 01331
HOBBS, William Ebert (O) 18 Donlea Dr, Toronto, ON M4G 2M2, Canada
HOBBY, Kim Annette (ETenn) Christ Church Episcopal, P.O. Box 347, South Pittsburg, TN 37380
HOBDEN, Brian Charles (RG) 3160 Executive Hills Rd, Las Cruces, NM 88011
HOBGOOD, Robert Bryan (EC) 403 S Eastern St, Greenville, NC 27858
HOBGOOD JR, Walter Palmer (Ga) 1499 S Main St, Moultrie, GA 31768
HOBSON, Carol Gordon (Dal)
HOBSON JR, George Hull (Eur) 119 Blvd. Du Montparnasse, Paris, 75006, France
HOBSON III, Jennings Wise (Va) Po Box 247, Washington, VA 22747
HOBSON, Patricia Shackelford (SO) 2955 Thrushfield Terrace, Cincinnati, OH 45238
HOBSON, Thomas P (Colo) 1236 S High St, Denver, CO 80210

HOCH, Helen Elizabeth (Kan) 314 N 3rd St, Burlington, KS 66839

HOCHE-MONG, Raymond (Cal) Box 937, Montara, CA 94037

HOCKENSMITH, David Albert (Pa) PO Box 90, Morgan, VT 05853

HOCKER, William (Cal) 6135 Laird Ave, Oakland, CA 94605

HOCKING, Charles Edward (NC) 632 Hughes Rd, Hampstead, NC 28443

HOCKRIDGE, Ann Elizabeth (Pa)

HODAPP, Timothy Leo (Ct) 1335 Asylum Ave, Hartford, CT 06105

HODGE, Reginald Roy (VI)

HODGE SR, Vincent Stafford (Va) Po Box 767, West Point, VA 23181

HODGE SR, Wayne Carlton (SVa) 114 Cross Ter, Suffolk, VA 23434

HODGES, Corinne U (NI) St. Anne's Episcopal Church, 424 W. Market St., Warsaw, IN 46580

HODGES, David Burton (NC) 520 Summit St., Winston Salem, NC 27101

HODGES, Michael (Mass) 29 Central St, Andover, MA 01810

✠ **HODGES-COPPLE**, Anne Elliott (Bp Suffr of North Caro) 1104 Watts St, Durham, NC 27701

HODGKINS, Lewis (Spok) 1000 Vey Way Apt 264, The Dalles, OR 97058

HODGKINS, Margaret S. R. (Ct) Trinity Episcopal Church, PO Box 400, Southport, CT 06890

HODGKINS, Nelson Bainbridge (NC) 874 Simmons Grove Church Rd, Pilot Mountain, NC 27041

HODGSON, Gregory Scott (SVa) 11940 Fairlington Lane, Midlothian, VA 23113

HODSDON, Douglas Graham (Fla) 1439 N Market St, Jacksonville, FL 32206

HOEBERMANN, Christine Marie (Oly) 123 L St NE, Auburn, WA 98002

HOECKER, Maria J. (Me) 32 Emery Ln, Boothbay Harbor, ME 04538

HOECKER, Marsha Hogg (Mass) 188 Center Road, Shirley, MA 01464

HOEKSTRA, Robert Bruce (Eau) 909 Summit Ave, Chippewa Falls, WI 54729

HOELTZEL, Geo(rge) Anthony (NY) 721 Warburton Ave, Yonkers, NY 10701

HOELZEL III, William Nold (Chi) 3221 Cochiti St NE, Rio Rancho, NM 87144

HOEY, Anne (Tex) 5608-A Jim Hogg Ave., Austin, TX 78756

HOEY, Lori Jean (CFla) 901 Clearmont St, Sebastian, FL 32958

HOFER, Christopher David (LI) 1400 Poulson St, Wantagh, NY 11793

HOFER, Larry John (CPa) 32801 Ocean Reach Dr, Lewes, DE 19958

HOFF, Timothy (Ala) 2601 Lakewood Cir, Tuscaloosa, AL 35405

HOFFACKER, Charles Edward Niblett (WA) 13301 Baden Westwood Rd, Brandywine, MD 20613

HOFFACKER, Michael Paul Niblett (Pa) PO Box 765, Devon, PA 19333

HOFFER, Jack Lee (CPa) 830 Washington Avenue, Tyrone, PA 16686

HOFFER, Wilma(Willie) Marie (EO) 64849 Casa Ct, Bend, OR 97701

HOFFMAN, Arnold R (Spr) 1226 Olive St Unit 505, Saint Louis, MO 63103

HOFFMAN, Charles Lance (Ct) 8 Sharon Ln, Old Saybrook, CT 06475

HOFFMAN JR, Edgar Henry (Hap) (Ark) 7 Rubra Ct, Little Rock, AR 72223

HOFFMAN, Ellendale Mccollam (Ct) 8 Sharon Ln, Old Saybrook, CT 06475

HOFFMAN, Jeffrey Paul (CNY)

HOFFMAN, Lisa A (NJ) St. Barnabas by the Bay Church, 13 W. Bates Avenue, Villas, NJ 08251

HOFFMAN, Mary Elizabeth (Ia) 2704 E garfield, Davenport, IA 52803

HOFFMAN, Michael Patrick (Dal) 1912 Fair Oaks Dr, Mission, TX 78574

HOFFMAN, Roy Everett (SVa) 2 BL Jackson Road, Newport, RI 02840

HOFFMAN, William Charles (SVa) 4101 Mingo Trl, Chesapeake, VA 23325

HOFFMANN, Beth Borah (Ore) 2409 Crescent Rd, Navarre, FL 32566

HOFMANN, Therese Marie (Mass) 108 Stratford St, West Roxbury, MA 02132

HOGAN, C (Eau)

HOGAN, F Faye (Los) 1237 Laguna Ln, San Luis Obispo, CA 93035

HOGAN, Lucy Lind (WA) 4500 Massachusetts Ave Nw, Washington, DC 20016

HOGG, Douglas Reynolds (EC) 347 South Creek Drive, Osprey, FL 34229

HOGG JR, Paul (Peter) (SVa) 7858 Sunset Dr, Hayes, VA 23072

HOGIN, Christopher Westlund (Va) 1520 Canterbury Rd, Raleigh, NC 27608

HOGUE, Kelsey Graham (Colo) 9 W 35th St, Scottsbluff, NE 69361

HOGUE, Marlene Christine Harshfield (Eau) Po Box 637, Hayward, WI 54843

HOHENFELDT, Robert John (Mil) 1310 Rawson Ave, South Milwaukee, WI 53172

HOHLT, Allan Hunter (Del) 94 Oak Ridge Rd, Plymouth, NH 03264

HOIDRA, Carol (Ct) 245 East 72nd Street, Apt. 2D, New York, NY 10021

HOKE, Stuart Hubbard (NY) 536 Fearrington Post, Pittsboro, NC 27312

HOLBEN, Lawrence Robert (The Episcopal NCal) 701 Lassen Ln, Mount Shasta, CA 96067

HOLBERT, John Russell (La) 1645 Carol Sue Ave, Terrytown, LA 70056

HOLBROOK JR, Paul Evans (Lex) 308 Madison Pl, Lexington, KY 40508

HOLCOMB, Justin S (CFla)

HOLCOMB, Steve A-Retired (WNC) 1500 Maltby Rd, Marble, NC 28905

HOLCOMBE, Matthew P (Pa) 1412 Providence Road, Charlotte, NC 28207

HOLCOMBE, Scott T (CFla) 4146 Millstone Dr, Melbourne, FL 32940

HOLDBROOKE, Charles Henry (LI) Calvary & St. Cyprian's Church, Brooklyn, NY 11221

HOLDEN, Beth (Tex) 4709 Laurel St, Bellaire, TX 77401

HOLDER, Anthony Brian (SeFla) 2801 N University Dr, Pembroke Pines, FL 33024

HOLDER, Arthur Glenn (Cal) 2400 Ridge Rd, Berkeley, CA 94709

HOLDER, Charles Richard (Md) PO Box A, 4336 Main Street, Rohrersville, MD 21779

HOLDER, Jennifer Sutton (NwT) 1318 Amarilla St, Abilene, TX 79602

HOLDER, Lauren R (NC) 74 Trinity Pl, New York, NY 10006

HOLDER, Michael Rawle (SVa) 926 Thomasson Lane, South Hill, VA 23970

HOLDER, Timothy Scott (NJ) P O Box 5, 205-A Grant Ave, Seaside Heights, NJ 08751

HOLDER-JOFFRION, Kerry Elizabeth (Ala) 3009 Barcody Rd Se, Huntsville, AL 35802

HOLDING, Megan Carr (Mass) 15 Saint Paul St, Brookline, MA 02446

HOLDING, Suzann V (SanD) 2728 6th Ave, San Diego, CA 92103

HOLDORPH, Jedediah D (EO) 2203 Dollarhide Way, Ashland, OR 97520

HOLE, Jeremy G (Fla) 4141 Nw 18th Dr, Gainesville, FL 32605

✠ **HOLGUIN-KHOURY**, Julio Cesar (Bp of DomRep 1991-) Agape Flights Dms 13602, 100 Airport Ave E, Venice, FL 34285

HOLLAND, Albert Leslie (Del) 350 E California Blvd Apt 304, Pasadena, CA 91106

HOLLAND, C Lynn (Va) P.O. Box 1626, Kilmarnock, VA 22482

HOLLAND, Clayton Theodore (Dal) 517 W Hull St, Denison, TX 75020

HOLLAND, David Wesley (Dal) Po Box 292365, Lewisville, TX 75029

HOLLAND, Eleanor Lois (Md) 3204 Bayonne Ave, Baltimore, MD 21214

HOLLAND, J Mark (La) Po Box 126, Baton Rouge, LA 70821

HOLLAND, Janet M. (Cal) 1042 Dead Indian Memorial Road, Ashland, OR 97520

HOLLAND, John Stewart (HB)

HOLLAND III, Jule Carr (Nwk) 7404 Halifax Rd, Youngsville, NC 27596

HOLLAND, Katharine Grace (Ore) 13265 Nw Northrup St, Portland, OR 97229

HOLLAND, Meghan C (Ky) 820 Broadway St, Paducah, KY 42001

HOLLAND JR, Melford Elias (Pa) 121 Penns Grant Dr, Morrisville, PA 19067

HOLLAND-SHUEY, Basye (Ala) 3740 Meridian St N, Huntsville, AL 35811

HOLLAR, Sarah Darnell (NC) 19107 Southport Drive, Cornelius, NC 28031

HOLLEMAN, Virginia Falconer (Dal) 5518 Merrimac Ave, Dallas, TX 75206

HOLLENBECK, Jon Nelson (Dal) 2215 Tracey Ann Ln, Killeen, TX 76543

HOLLENBECK, Scott Warren (Colo) 820 2nd Street, Meeker, CO 81641

✠ **HOLLERITH IV**, Herman (Bp of SVa 2009-) 600 Talbot Road, Norfolk, VA 23505

HOLLERITH, Melissa Kaye Zuber (Va) 5503 Toddsbury Rd, Richmond, VA 23226

HOLLERITH, Randolph Marshall (Va) 1205 W Franklin St, Richmond, VA 23220

HOLLETT, Robert Titus (LI) 220 Valley Rd, Chestertown, MD 21620

HOLLEY, James Paul (Okla) 7609 Nw Stonegate Dr, Lawton, OK 73505

HOLLEY, Richard Hedge (SVa) 202 Devils Den Road, Hampton, VA 23669

HOLLIDAY, Charles Thomas (Va) 3001 Stonewall Avenue, Richmond, VA 23225

HOLLIDAY, Frances M (Chi) 5057 W. Devon Ave, Chicago, IL 60646

HOLLIGER, John Charles (O) 70 Welshire Court, Delaware, OH 43015

✠ **HOLLINGSWORTH JR**, Mark (Bp of O 2004-) 2230 Euclid Ave, Cleveland, OH 44115

HOLLINGSWORTH-GRAVES, Judy Lynn (SD) 1508 S Rock Creek Dr # 168, Sioux Falls, SD 57103

HOLLIS, Anthony Wolcott Linsley (Md) 712 Murdock Rd, Baltimore, MD 21212

HOLLIS, Joanna Pauline (NJ) 5 Paterson St, New Brunswick, NJ 08901

HOLLIS, Robin Buckholtz (Az) St James the Apostle Episcopal Church, 975 E Warner Rd, Tempe, AZ 85284

HOLLOWAY, Eric Andre Cole (Tex) 9600 Huntington Place Dr, Houston, TX 77099

HOLLOWELL II, J Rhoads (Colo) 11675 Flatiron Dr, Lafayette, CO 80026

HOLLY, Francis Eugene (Nev) 2481 Anderson Lake Rd # 417, Chimacum, WA 98325

HOLLY, William David (Okla)

HOLLYWOOD, Trula Louise (Be) 701 S Main St, Athens, PA 18810

HOLM, Marjorie H (NC) 635 Hamilton St., Roanoke Rapids, NC 27870

HOLMAN, Emily Clark (NJ) 96 Fairacres Dr, Toms River, NJ 08753

HOLMAN, John(Jack) Earl (Tex) 2400 Spring Raindrive, #1018, Spring, TX 77379

HOLMAN, J(oseph) Lawrence (Be)

HOLMAN, Kathryn Daneke (At) 1883 Clinton Dr, Marietta, GA 30062

HOLMBERG, Sandra A (Minn) 14266 E Fox Lake Rd, Detroit Lakes, MN 56501

HOLMES, Anna Rilla (USC) 205 Meadowlark Ln, Fountain Inn, SC 29644

HOLMES, Forrest Milton (Ida) 1100 Burnett Dr Unit 416, Nampa, ID 83651

HOLMES, Fran R (NY) 944 Thistlegate Rd, Oak Park, CA 91377

HOLMES, James Colomb (WA) 5203 Downing Rd, Baltimore, MD 21212

HOLMES, Jane Victoria Frances (NC) 2540 Bricker Drive, Charlotte, NC 28273

HOLMES, Joyce Ann Woolever (Kan) Grace Episcopal Church, 209 South Lincoln, Chanute, KS 66720

HOLMES, Marsha Evans (Fla) 400 San Juan Dr, Ponte Vedra Beach, FL 32082

HOLMES, Martha Hixson (Ala) 5712 1st Ave N, Birmingham, AL 35212

HOLMES, Phillip Wilson (WNY) 418 Virginia St, Buffalo, NY 14201

HOLMES, Rebecca Elizabeth (NC) 237 N Canterbury Rd, Charlotte, NC 28211

HOLMES, Stanley Warren (WVa) Po Box 79, Hansford, WV 25103

HOLMGREN, Stephen Carl (WMich) 2200 Thornapple River Dr SE, MI, Grand Rapids 49546

HOLMQUIST, David Wendell (Neb) St Augustine of Canterbury, 285 S 208th St, Elkhorn, NE 68022

HOLROYD, David D (Me) 3 Elizabeth Rd, South Berwick, ME 03908

HOLSAPPLE, Kevin G (Me) 7208 W Milwe Lane, Crystal Rivet, FL 34429

HOLSTON III, George Wilson (Fla) 804 Doubles Ct, Harker Heights, TX 76548

HOLSTROM, Susan A. (Chi) 737 N Randall Rd, Aurora, IL 60506

HOLT, Ann Case (NJ) 60 Main St, Clinton, NJ 08809

HOLT, Charles Lindley (CFla) 700 Rinehart Road, Lake Mary, FL 32746

HOLT, Jane L (Bonnie) (Minn) 224 2nd St N, Cannon Falls, MN 55009

HOLT, Joseph (Cal) 2237 Fulton #103, San Francisco, CA 94117

HOLT, Meredith (Tex) 1115 36th St, Galveston, TX 77550

HOLT, William Mayes (Tenn) 202 Kimberly Dr, Dickson, TN 37055

HOLT III, William Therrel (Az) 270 17th Street Unit 1101, Atlanta, GA 30363

HOLTHUS, Jessica Trout Knowles (Md) 106 W Church St, Frederick, MD 21701

HOLTKAMP, Patrick John (LI) 7712 35th Ave Apt A64, Jackson Heights, NY 11372

HOLTMAN, Kimberly Erica (Nwk) 655 W Briar Pl, Apt 1, Chicago, IL 60657

HOLTON, Stephen Christopher (NY) Grace Church In New York, 802 Broadway, New York, NY 10003

HOLTON, Steve (NY) 91 Greenwood Lane, White Plains, NY 10607

HOLTZEN, Thomas Lee (Mil) 2777 Mission Rd, Nashotah, WI 53058

HOLZ JR, John Clifford (Ak)

HOLZHALB, Leon Stephen (La) 100 Christwood Blvd, Covington, LA 70433

HOMEYER, Charles Frederick (WMich) 3539 Quiggle Ave Se, Ada, MI 49301

HONAKER, Martha Anne (Ind) 111 Ivy Lane, Sparta, NC 28675

HONDERICH, Thomas E (Ind) 3941 N Delaware St, Indianapolis, IN 46205

HONEA, Janice Bailey (CFla) 6246 Tremayne Dr, Mount Dora, FL 32757

HONEYCHURCH, J(ohn) Robert (Los) 1000 Concha St, Altadena, CA 91001

HONNOLD, Sandra Elizabeth (The Episcopal Church in Haw) PO Box 7063, PMB 295, Ocean View, HI 96737

HONODEL, Jill (Cal) 285 Kaanapali Dr, Napa, CA 94558

HONSE, Robert Wayne (Kan)

HOOD, Nancy Elizabeth (Dal) 6883 Lagoon Dr, Grand Prairie, TX 75054

HOOD, Stephen Dale (Ala) 3648 Dabney Drive, Vesatvia Hills, AL 35243

HOOD, William Rienks (La) 1808 Prospect St, Houston, TX 77004

HOOGERHYDE, Scott Matthew (Nwk) 7 E Main St, Mendham, NJ 07945

HOOK, Andrew S (Spr) Cathedral Church of Saint Paul the Apostle, 815 South Second Street, Springfield, IL 62704

HOOK, Edward Lindsten (Colo) PO Box 1388, Green Valley, AZ 85622

HOOKE, Ruthanna Brinton (WMass) 3737 Seminary Rd, Alexandria, VA 22304

HOOKER, Alan Bruce (Va) 6645 Northumberland Hwy, Heathsville, VA 22473

HOOKER, John L (WMass) 235 State St Apt 306, Springfield, MA 01103

HOOP, Kimberly Ann (WMich) 4155 S Norway St Se, Grand Rapids, MI 49546

HOOPER, Elizabeth E (Los) 1014 E. Altadena Drive, Altadena, CA 91001

HOOPER, John K (Mich) 42 Cottage Circle, West Lebanon, NH 03784

HOOPER, Larry Donald (SeFla) 401 Duval St, Key West, FL 33040

HOOPER III, Robert Channing (Ct) 10 Cumberland Rd, West Hartford, CT 06119

HOOPER, Ruth Isabelle (Az) 1710 W. Dalehaven Cir, Tucson, AZ 85704

HOOPES, David Bryan (LI) Church of St Edward the Martyr, 14 E 109th St, New York, NY 10029

HOOVER, Greg T (WMo) 107 Walnut Ln, Branson, MO 65616
HOOVER, John Frain (CPa) 99 Willowbrook Blvd, Lewisburg, PA 17837
HOOVER, Joshua (Mich) 355 W Maple Rd, Birmingham, MI 48009
HOOVER, Judy Verne Hanlon (Minn) 2020 Orkla Dr, Golden Valley, MN 55427
HOOVER, Melvin Aubrey (SO)
HOOVER, Richard A (CFla) 209 S Iowa Ave, Lakeland, FL 33801
HOOVER, Todd Jay (SeFla) 1400 Riverside Dr, Coral Springs, FL 33071
HOOVER-DEMPSEY, Randy (Tenn) 1829 Hudson Rd, Madison, TN 37115
HOPEWELL, Gloria Grayson (Chi) 939 Hinman Ave, Evanston, IL 60202
HOPKINS, Christine Carroll (Spr) 102 E Mchenry St, Urbana, IL 61801
HOPKINS, Daniel Warren (Colo) 7127 S. Quemoy St., Aurora, CO 80016
✠ **HOPKINS JR**, Harold Anthony (Ret Bp of ND 1998-) 15 Piper Rd Apt K211, Scarborough, ME 04074
HOPKINS, John Leonard (Alb) 34 Velina Dr, Burnt Hills, NY 12027
HOPKINS, Lydia Elliott (La)
HOPKINS, Michael Warren (Roch) 67 E Main St, Hornell, NY 14843
HOPKINS, Terry Robert (Minn) P.O. Box 402, Monticello, MN 55362
HOPKINS, Vivian Louise (Oly) 32820 20th Ave S #61, Federal Way, WA 98003
HOPKINS-GREENE, Nancy (SO) 6255 Stirrup Rd, Cincinnati, OH 45244
HOPLAMAZIAN, Julie M (LI) Grace Church, 254 Hicks St, Brooklyn, NY 11201
HOPNER, Kathryn Ann (Nev) St Paul's Episcopal Church, PO Box 737, Sparks, NV 89432
HOPPE, Robert Donald (FdL) 806 4th St, Algoma, WI 54201
HOPPER, Edgar Wilson (NY)
HOPWOOD, Alfred Joseph (Minn) 1417 Blue Flag Ct, Northfield, MN 55057
HORD, Christine D (CGC)
HORGAN, Daniel E (Mass) 204 Monument Rd, Orleans, MA 02653
HORLE, Garrison Locke (Colo) 720 Downing St, Denver, CO 80218
HORN, John C (Ia) Trinity Episcopal Cathedral, 121 W. 12th St., Davenport, IA 52803
HORN, Michael John (ND) 15757 N 90th Pl Apt 2053, Scottsdale, AZ 85260
HORN, Peter Moya (Ala)
HORN, Raisin (Ia) Trinity Church, 320 E College St, Iowa City, IA 52240
HORN, S(tanley) Huston (Los) 334 S Parkwood Ave, Pasadena, CA 91107
HORNADAY, Evelyn (WMo) St. Peter & All Saints Episcopal Church, 100 E.

Red Bridge Rd., Kansas City, MO 64114
HORNBECK, Jennifer (The Episcopal NCal) PO Box 274, Kenwood, CA 95452
HORNBERGER-BROWN, Sharon Lois (Mass) 1d Autumn Dr, Hudson, MA 01749
HORNE, Lance Cameron (Fla) 3275 Tallavana Trl, Havana, FL 32333
HORNE, Martha Johnston (Va) 3809 Fort Worth Ave, Alexandria, VA 22304
HORNER, John Scott (O) 813 West Main St, Elizabeth City, NC 27909
HORNER, Robert William (Tex) 8 Coralvine Ct, The Woodlands, TX 77380
HORNER, William McKinley (Miss) 14981 W Verde Ln, Goodyear, AZ 85338
HORNING, David J (Mich) 104 Mount Homestake Dr., Leadville, CO 80461
HORNSBY, James Harmon (Mass) 260 Lake Ave, Fall River, MA 02721
HORST, Diane Elizabeth (NMich) 12769 W Lakeshore Dr, Brimley, MI 49715
HORTON, Carol J (NJ) 3 Plumstead Ct, Annandale, NJ 08801
HORTON, Cathy Lynne (O)
HORTON, Edward Robert (Cal) 6618 Taylor Dr., Woodridge, IL 60517
HORTON, Fred Lane (NC) 2622 Weymoth Rd, Winston Salem, NC 27103
HORTON, James Roy (EC) 1060 Dixie Trl, Williamston, NC 27892
HORTON JR, James Taylor (FtW) 7413 Hillstone Dr, Benbrook, TX 76126
HORTON, Sarah Catherine (Vt) 17 Mack Ave, West Lebanon, NH 03784
HORTON-SMITH, Sandra (Kan) St Paul's Episcopal Church, 601 Poyntz Ave, Manhattan, KS 66502
HORTUM, John Derek (Va) 1407 N Gaillard St, Alexandria, VA 22304
HORVATH, Leslie Ferguson (USC) 400 Dupre Dr., Spartanburg, SC 29307
HORVATH, Victor John (Vt) 6 South St, Bellows Falls, VT 05101
HOSEA, Beverly Ann (Oly) 1833 13th Ave Apt 304, Seattle, WA 98122
HOSEA, Janice Forney (RG) 7171 Tennyson St NE, Albuquerque, NM 87122
HOSKINS, Charles L (Ga) 4629 Sylvan Dr, Savannah, GA 31405
HOSKINS, JoAnn Smith (Fla) 4241 Duval Dr, Jacksonville Beach, FL 32250
HOSLER, Carol Smith (Az) PO Box 171, 408 Jamestown Road, Kearny, AZ 85137
HOSLER, Joshua Luke (Oly) 2117 Walnut St, Bellingham, WA 98225
HOSLER, Samuel Odyth (Az) 408 Jamestown Road, Kearny, AZ 85137
HOSPADOR, Dorothea Cecelia (NJ) 247 Carr Ave, Keansburg, NJ 07734

HOSTER JR, David William (Tex) 30003 Edgewood Drive, Georgetown, TX 78628
HOSTER, Elizabeth M (O) Trinity Episcopal Church, 316 Adams Street, Toledo, OH 43604
HOSTETLER, Hugh Steiner (WMich) 313B 15th Ave S, Surfside Bch, SC 29575
HOSTETTER, Jane (USC) 2303 NE Seaview Dr, Jensen Beach, FL 34957
HOTCHKISS, Thomas S (Dal) 11122 Midway Rd, Dallas, TX 75229
HOTRA, Nancy Louise (WMich) 9733 Sterling, Richland, MI 49083
HOTZE, Janice A (Ak) Po Box 91, Haines, AK 99827
HOUCK III, Ira Chauncey (Be) 120 Norse Dr, Columbia, SC 29229
HOUCK, John Bunn (Chi) 5236 S Cornell Ave, Chicago, IL 60615
HOUCK, Kay M (WMich)
HOUGH III, Charles Albert (Dal) 2900 Alemeda St, Fort Worth, TX 76108
HOUGH, George Willard (NwPa) 904 Holiday Hills Dr, Hollidaysburg, PA 16648
HOUGHTON, Alanson Bigelow (Mass) 43 Blockade Dr, Pawleys Island, SC 29585
HOUGHTON, Frederick Lord (EMich) 4138 N Francis Shores Ave, Sanford, MI 48657
HOUGHTON, John William (NI) 609 Houghton St., Culver, IN 46511
HOUGHTON, Philip G (WNY) 105 S. Clinton St., Olean, NY 14760
HOUGHTON, William Clokey (NwT) 27 Painted Canyon Place, The Woodlands, TX 77381
✠ **HOUGLAND JR**, Whayne Miller (Bp of WMich 2013-) Episcopal Diocese of Western Michigan, 535 S Burdick St, Kalamazoo, MI 49007
HOUI-LEE, Samuel Sroun (Oly) 34608 8th Ave Sw, Federal Way, WA 98023
HOUK, David Stangebye (Dal) 848 Harter Road, Dallas, TX 75218
HOUK, Vickie Lynn (SwVa) 739 Prospect Ave., Pulaski, VA 24301
HOULE, Michael Anthony (EMich) 4525 Birch Run Rd, Birch Run, MI 48415
HOULIK, Michael Andrew (Colo) 2712 Geneva Place, Longmont, CO 80503
HOUPT, Cameron Wheeler (Colo) 10222 W Ida Ave Unit 238, Littleton, CO 80127
HOUSE, Karen Ellen (CFla) 1120 Sunshine Ave, Leesburg, FL 34748
HOUSER, Lucy Anne Latham (Ore) 11476 SW Riverwoods Rd., Portland, OR 97219
HOUSER III, Richard Truett (Tex) 13131 Fry Rd, Cypress, TX 77433
HOUSNER-RITTER, Jenny Lee (Mich)

HOUSTON, Barbara Pearce (EC) 206 North Fairlane Drive, Box 939, Grifton, NC 28530

HOUZE, Jared Foster (NwT)

HOVENCAMP, Otis (WNY) 85 Wide Beach Rd, Irving, NY 14081

HOVEY JR, Frederick Franklin (WNC) 724 Cobblestone Dr, Ormond Beach, FL 32174

HOWANSTINE JR, John Edwin (Md) 3090 Broomes Island Road, Port Republic, MD 20676

HOWARD, Anne Sutherland (Los) 950 Dena Way, Santa Barbara, CA 93111

HOWARD, Coleen Gayle (Ore) PO Box 1319, Gresham, OR 97030

HOWARD, Cynthia A (CGC) 2005 Boxwood Ave, Andalusia, AL 36421

HOWARD, David Z (SO)

HOWARD, Francis Curzon (Ct) 116 Terry's Plain Road, Box 423, Simsbury, CT 06070

HOWARD III, George Williams (Spr) 1811 Highland Vw, Mount Vernon, IL 62864

HOWARD, Harry Lee (ETenn) 2668 Karenwood Dr, Maryville, TN 37804

HOWARD II, Joseph Burton (Tenn) 2458 Center Point Rd, Hendersonville, TN 37075

HOWARD, Karin Dreiske (SwVa) 903-A Park Place Drive, Kernersville, NC 27284

HOWARD, Kenneth W(ayne) (WA) 9 Liberty Heights Court, Germantown, MD 20874

HOWARD, Leonard Rice (The Episcopal Church in Haw) 98-1128 Malualua St, Aiea, HI 96701

HOWARD, Lois Waser (Lex) 713 Dicksonia Ct, Lexington, KY 40517

HOWARD, Mary Merle (SeFla)

HOWARD, Noah B (NC) 206 Maryland Ave, Tarboro, NC 27886

HOWARD, Norman (SwFla) 766 Lake Forest Rd, Clearwater, FL 33765

HOWARD, Sally (Los) 132 N Euclid Ave, Pasadena, CA 91101

✠ **HOWARD**, Samuel Johnson (Bp of Fla 2003-) 325 N Market St, Jacksonville, FL 32202

HOWARD, Sylvia Lord (Spr) 1811 Highland Vw, Mount Vernon, IL 62864

HOWARD, Theodore B (Colo) 1419 Pine St., Boulder, CO 80302

HOWARD, William Alexander (Colo) 7168 Burnt Mill Rd, Beulah, CO 81023

HOWCOTT, Jeffernell Ophelia Green (Mich) 19320 Santa Rosa Dr, Detroit, MI 48221

✠ **HOWE**, Barry Robert (Ret Bp of WMo 2011-) PO Box 413227, Kansas City, MO 64141

HOWE, Gregory Michael (Del) 7 Conway St, Provincetown, MA 02657

HOWE, Heath (Chi) 1229 Hinman Ave, Evanston, IL 60202

HOWE, Jeffrey Newman (Lex) 201 Price Rd Apt 216, Lexington, KY 40511

✠ **HOWE**, John Wadsworth (Ret Bp of CFla 2012-) 5583 Jessamine Lane, Orlando, FL 32830

HOWE, Karen Elvgren (CFla) 5583 Jessamine Ln, Orlando, FL 32839

HOWE JR, Ralph Finch (La) 8965 Bayside Ave, Baton Rouge, LA 70806

HOWE, Raymond Jordan (Be) 833 Gillinder Place, Cary, NC 27519

HOWE, Wendy Salisbury (ECR) 203 Lighthouse Ave, Pacific Grove, CA 93950

HOWELL, David Silva (The Episcopal NCal) Po Box 52008, Toa Baja, PR 00950

HOWELL, Edward Allen (The Episcopal NCal) 1953 Terry Rd, Santa Rosa, CA 95403

HOWELL, Laura (Be) 44 E Market St, Bethlehem, PA 18018

HOWELL, Margery E (SVa) 3316 Hyde Cir, Norfolk, VA 23513

HOWELL, Miguelina (Ct) Christ Church Cathedral, 45 Church St, Hartford, CT 06103

HOWELL, Peggy Ann (Mass) Po Box 134, North Billerica, MA 01862

HOWELL, Robert M (SO) 69081 Mount Herman Rd, Cambridge, OH 43725

HOWELL, S(ydney) Caitlin (Va) 495 Melrose Dr, Monticello, FL 32344

HOWELL, Terry Robert (At) 2135 Zelda Dr Ne, Atlanta, GA 30345

HOWELL-BURKE, Undine Jean (Neb)

HOWELLS, Donald Arthur (Be) 1936 Chestnut Hill Road, Mohnton, PA 19540

HOWLETT, Louise (Del) 350 Noxontown Rd, Middletown, DE 19709

HOWSER, Carol Louise Jordan (Ore) 192 Harrison St, Ashland, OR 97520

HOWZE, Lynn Corpening (CFla) 215 West Park, Lakeland, FL 33803

HOY, Lois (Cal) 36 Dos Posos, Orinda, CA 94563

HOY, Mary Ann Collins (Me) 6 Old Mast Landing Rd, Freeport, ME 04032

HOYT, Calvin Van Kirk (CPa) 1418 Walnut St, Camp Hill, PA 17011

HOYT, Timothy Lynn (WNC) 479 Whispering Woods Dr, Saluda, NC 28773

HROSTOWSKI, Susan (Miss)

HSIEH, Nathaniel Wei-Chung (Eur) 44 Rue Docteur Robert, Chatillon Sur Seine, 21400, France

HU, Kuo-hua (Tai) Chieh Shou Road 5, Kangshan, 82018, Taiwan

HUACANI, Amy J (NC) PO Box 2263, Durham, NC 27702

HUAL, Jeffrey Charles (CGC) 2430 K St NW, Washington, DC 20037

HUANG, Peter P (Los) 2200 Via Rosa, Palos Verdes Estates, CA 90274

HUBBARD, Carol Murphy (WNC) 211 Montford Ave, Asheville, NC 28801

HUBBARD JR, C(harles) Clark (Ga) 227 McDuffie Drive, Richmond Hill, GA 31324

HUBBARD, Colenzo James (WTenn) 604 Saint Paul Ave, Memphis, TN 38126

HUBBARD, Cynthia Plumb (Mass) 45 White Trellis, Plymouth, MA 02360

HUBBARD, Francis Appleton (NJ) 5 North Rd, Berkeley Heights, NJ 07922

HUBBARD, James Alan (SwVa) 384 Waughs Ferry Rd, Amherst, VA 24521

HUBBARD, Lani Marie (Oly) 225 Mar Vista Way, Port Angeles, WA 98362

HUBBARD, Martha L (Mass) St. Paul's Church, 166 High St., Newburyport, MA 01950

HUBBARD, Mavourneen Ann (NY) 17 South Ave, 855 Wolcott Ave, Beacon, NY 12508

HUBBARD, Philip R (LI) 20309 W 219th Ter, Spring Hill, KS 66083

HUBBARD, Thomas Beckwith (Los) 621 Mayflower Rd 104, Claremont, CA 91711

HUBBELL, Gilbert Leonard (O) 1094 Clifton Ave # 2, Akron, OH 44310

HUBBELL, Sally Hanes (Colo) 209 Matheson St, Healdsburg, CA 95448

HUBBY III, Turner E(rath) (Tex) 329 Meadowbrook Dr, San Antonio, TX 78232

HUBER, Amy Whitcombe (Eau) 234 Avon St, La Crosse, WI 54603

HUBER, Donald Marvin (Neb) 10807 Scott Peddler Rd, Cattaraugus, NY 14719

HUBER, E. Wendy (Tex) St John's Episcopal Church, 514 Carter St, Marlin, TX 76661

HUBER, Ellen (Ct) 171 Old Tannery Rd # 6468, Monroe, CT 06468

HUBER, Frank A (Colo) 12295 West Applewood Drive, Lakewood, CO 80215

HUBER, Glenna J (Md) 1820 Greenberry Rd., Baltimore, MD 21209

HUBER, Kurt J (Ct) 171 Old Tannery Rd, Monroe, CT 06468

HUBER, Stephen A (Los) 506 N. Camden Drive, Beverly Hills, CA 90210

HUBERT, Deven Ann (Roch) 66 Little Briggins Circle, Fairport, NY 14450

HUBERT, Lawrence William (Alb) 970 State St, Schenectady, NY 12307

HUBINSKY - PHELPS, Sarah E (Los) 306 Bayoak Dr, Cary, NC 27513

HUCK, Beverly Jean (Nwk) 668 Timber Creek Dr, Littleton, NC 27850

HUCKABAY JR, H(arry) Hunter (ETenn) 1706 Glenroy Ave., Chattanooga, TN 37405

HUDAK, Bob (EC) St Paul's Church, 401 E. 4th St, Greenville, NC 27858

HUDAK, Mary L. (The Episcopal NCal) 1240 Mission Ave., Sacramento, CA 95608

HUDDLESTON, Kevin D (Kan) PO Box 12385, Dallas, TX 75225

HUDDLESTON, Nathan (Fla)
HUDGEN, Calvin Rodney (Md) Emmanuel Church, 811 Cathedral St, Baltimore, MD 21201
HUDLOW, Alison Kelley (Ala) 431 10th St NW, Fayette, AL 35555
HUDSON, Aaron (Ia) St. Paul's Episcopal Church, 22 Dillman Drive, Council Bluffs, IA 51503
HUDSON, Andrew (SeFla) 7538 Granville Dr, Tamarac, FL 33321
HUDSON, Andrew George (SeFla) 2250 SW 31st Ave, Fort Lauderdale, FL 33312
HUDSON, Betty (SVa) 120 John Bratton, Williamsburg, VA 23185
HUDSON, Daniel Mark (La) 1329 Jackson Ave, New Orleans, LA 70130
HUDSON, Henry Lee (La) 1424 4th St, New Orleans, LA 70130
HUDSON, Joel Pinkney (At) 1225 N Shore Dr, Roswell, GA 30076
HUDSON, John Richard Keith (Del) 1300 Morris Ave, Villanova, PA 19085
HUDSON, Kimberly Karen (NC)
HUDSON, Linda Ann (Wyo) 860 S 3rd St, Lander, WY 82520
HUDSON, Mary Bowen (CFla) 4345 Indian River Dr, Cocoa, FL 32927
HUDSON, Michael Vincent (WNC) Po Box 152, Cullowhee, NC 28723
HUDSON, Thomas James (Md) St James Episcopal Church, 32 Main Street, Westernport, MD 21562
HUDSON-LOUIS, Holly (ECR) 65 Highway 1, Carmel, CA 93923
HUDSPETH, Denise Wardell (SeFla) 208 Nw Avenue H, Belle Glade, FL 33430
HUERTA, Efrain (FtW) 12607 Banchester Ct, Houston, TX 77070
HUERTA GARCIA, Oscar (Tex) Chamela 33 A, Tlaquepaque, Jalisco 45589, Mexico
HUFF, Carolyn Tuttle (Pa) 1121 N Trooper Rd, Eagleville, PA 19403
HUFF, Christopher Mercer (SC) 1612 Dryden Ln, Charleston, SC 29407
HUFF, Clark Kern (Tex) 2252 Garden Court, San Marcos, TX 78666
HUFF, Susan Ellen (At) 1031 Eagles Ridge Ct, Lawrenceville, GA 30043
HUFFMAN, Charles Howard (Tex) 8124 Greenslope Dr, Austin, TX 78759
HUFFMAN, Robert Nelson (SVa) 2212 Lynnwood drive, Wilmington, NC 28403
HUFFORD, Robert Arthur (SO) 52 Bishopsgate Dr Apt 703, Cincinnati, OH 45246
HUFFSTETLER, Joel W (ETenn) 3920 Clairmont Dr Ne, Cleveland, TN 37312
HUFT, Jerry Ray (CGC) Po Box 595, Wewahitchka, FL 32465
HUGGARD, Linda S (Episcopal SJ) 4300 Keith Way, Bakersfield, CA 93309
HUGGINS, Arthur Hoskins (VI) P.O. Box 748, St. Vincent, Saint Vincent & the Grenadines

HUGHES, A(lan) (Pa) 1408 Sw 20th Ct, Gresham, OR 97080
HUGHES, Carlye J (FtW) Trinity Episcopal Church, 3401 Bellaire Drive South, Fort Worth, TX 76109
HUGHES, Frank W. (WLa) 1107 Broadway St, Minden, LA 71055
✠ **HUGHES**, Gethin Benwil (Ret Bp of SanD 2005-) 461 Quail Run Rd, Buellton, CA 93427
HUGHES, Jennifer Scheper (Mass) 1147 Walnut St, Berkeley, CA 94707
HUGHES, John Richard (Lex) 2449 Larkin Rd, Lexington, KY 40503
HUGHES, Lauretta Kaye (WMo) 203 E Brick St # A, Ozark, MO 65721
HUGHES, Linda May (Ia) 103 Melissa St, Elizabethtown, KY 42701
HUGHES, Malcolm Albert (FdL) Saint John's Episcopal Church, 139 South Smalley, Shawano, WI 54166
HUGHES, Mary London Carswell (ECR) 902 California Ave, San Jose, CA 95125
HUGHES III, Robert Davis (SO) 335 Tennessee Ave, Sewanee, TN 37383
HUGHES, Rosalind Claire (O)
HUGHES, Thomas Downs (WNC) 16 Salisbury Dr Apt 7206, Asheville, NC 28803
HUGHES JR, Thomas Roddy (Eas) 852 Spring Valley Dr, Fredericksburg, VA 22405
HUGHES-EMPKE, Sheryl Ann (Ia) PO Box 486, Perry, IA 50220
HUGHES-HABEL, Deborah Jean (U) 4615 S 3200 W, West Valley City, UT 84119
HUGHS, Leslie Curtis (LI) 16 Birch Road, Danbury, CT 06811
HUGUENIN, Robert (Fla) 4224 Coastal Hwy, Crawfordville, FL 32327
HUINER, Peter Bruce (Del) 500 Woodlawn Rd, Wilmington, DE 19803
HULBERT, Edward R (Los) St Richard of Chichester Church, PO Box 1317, Lake Arrowhead, CA 92352
HULBERT, James Edward (NJ) 1620 Mayflower Ct Apt A405, Winter Park, FL 32792
HULEN, Jennifer Lynn (Ind) St Christopher's Episcopal Church, 1402 W. Main, Carmel, IN 46032
HULET, Jefferson R (NJ) 14 Saint Remy Ct, Newport Coast, CA 92657
HULL, Carol Wharton (SO) 14590 Wilmot Way, Lake Oswego, OR 97035
HULL, George Andrew (Chi) 509 Brier St, Kenilworth, IL 60043
HULL, Nicholas Andrew (At) PO Box 1146, Columbus, GA 31902
HULL, S (Los) 13025 Bloomfield St., Studio City, CA 91604
HULL IV, William Franklin (Fla)
HULLAR, Leonard Earl (Tex) 107 E Edgebrook Dr, Houston, TX 77034
HULLINGER, Jon M (Kan) 3750 E Douglas Ave, Wichita, KS 67208
HULL-RYDE, Norman Arthur (WNC) 2535 Sheffield Dr, Gastonia, NC 28054

HULME, Steven Edward (Ct) 26 Colony Road, East Lyme, CT 06333
HULME, Thomas Stanford (Ia) 1617 W Benton St, Iowa City, IA 52246
HULS II, Frederick Eugene (Az) 2812 N 69th Pl, Scottsdale, AZ 85257
HULS, Patricia Taylor (Az) 2310 N 56th St, Phoenix, AZ 85008
HULSE JR, Granvyl Godfrey (NH) 57 Pleasant St, Colebrook, NH 03576
✠ **HULSEY**, Sam Byron (Ret Bp of NwT 1997-) 801 Hillcrest St, Fort Worth, TX 76107
HULTMAN, Eugene Bradlee (Mass) 255 N Central Ave, Quincy, MA 02170
✠ **HULTSTRAND**, Donald Maynard (Ret Bp of Spr 1991-) 1706 Parkins Mill Rd, Greenville, SC 29607
HUMBER, Michael Reagan (Cal) 2201 Dexter St, Denver, CO 80207
HUMKE, Richard Herbert (Ky) 200 S Galt Ave, Louisville, KY 40206
HUMM, Matt (Chi) 326 E. 11th Street, Lockport, IL 60441
HUMMEL, Thomas Charles (Va) 1200 N Quaker Ln, Alexandria, VA 22302
HUMMEL, Virginia (Ct) 30 Woodland Street, #6D, Hartford, CT 06105
HUMMELL, Mark William (NY)
HUMPHREY, Christine Ann (Mich) 544 W Iroquois Rd, Pontiac, MI 48341
HUMPHREY, Georgia Lehman (Ia) 15064 Sheridan Ave, Clive, IA 50325
HUMPHREY JR, Howard Mackenzie (O) 6295 Chagrin River Rd, Chagrin Falls, OH 44022
HUMPHREY, Marian Teresa (WA) 9801 Livingston Rd, Fort Washington, MD 20744
HUMPHREY, M(ary) Beth (WA) St Albans School, Mount St Albans, Washington, DC 20016
HUMPHREY, Nathan J.A. (RI) The Zabriskie Memorial Church of Saint John the Evangelist, 61 Poplar St, Newport, RI 02840
HUMPHREYS, Eugene L (NC) 425 E 17th St, Charlotte, NC 28206
HUMPHREYS, Walter Lee (ETenn)
HUMPHRIES, Charles E (SeFla)
HUMPHRIES JR, John Curtis (CNY) 405 Euclid Avenue, Elmira, NY 14905
HUNDLEY, Brooks F (WA)
HUNGATE, Carla Valinda (At) 4318 Windmill Trce, Douglasville, GA 30135
HUNGERFORD, Eric Paul (Tex) 3901 S Panther Creek Dr, The Woodlands, TX 77381
HUNGERFORD, Roger Alan (Chi) 2805 32nd Avenue Dr, Moline, IL 61265
HUNKINS, Claire Morfit (SVa) PO Box 186, Oak Hall, VA 23416
HUNKINS, Orin James (Okla) 3724 Bonaire Pl, Edmond, OK 73013
HUNLEY, Deborah Hentz (SwVa) 2042 Lee HI Rd SW, Roanoke, VA 24018

HUNN, Meg Buerkel (NC) 412 N East Street, Raleigh, NC 27604

HUNN, Michael Cb (NC) 412 N East St, Raleigh, NC 27604

HUNSINGER, Jimmie Ruth (Fla) 350 Sw Stallion Gln, Lake City, FL 32024

HUNT, Ashley Stephen (EC)

HUNT, Barnabas John William (SanD) PO Box 34548, San Diego, CA 92163

HUNT, Donald Aldrich (Mass) 221 Atlantic Ave, Marblehead, MA 01945

HUNT, Edward Walter (Ala) 1024 12th St. S., Birmingham, AL 35205

HUNT III, Ernest Edward (Eur) 3310 Fairmount St Apt 9b, Dallas, TX 75201

✠ **HUNT III**, George Nelson (Ret Bp of RI 1995-) 1401 Fountain Grove Pkwy #107, Santa Rosa, CA 95403

HUNT, Hazel Bailey (Be) Po Box 86, Towanda, PA 18848

HUNT, John C (O) 44267 Route 511 East, Oberlin, OH 44074

HUNT, John Patrick (NJ) 55 Lake Delaware Drive, Lake Delaware, Delhi, NY 13753

HUNT, Katherine Ann (Ak) 2006 W 31st Ave, Anchorage, AK 99517

HUNT, Lisa Wynne (Tex) 419 Woodland St, Nashville, TN 37206

HUNT, Marshall William (Mass) Po Box 1205, East Harwich, MA 02645

HUNT, Meredith (WMich) 4708 State Park Hwy, Interlochen, MI 49643

HUNT, Paul Stuart (Pa) 212 S High St, West Chester, PA 19382

HUNT, Teresa Gioia (Pgh) 1335 Berryman Avenue, Bethel Park, PA 15102

HUNT, Terry Lynn (Nev) 79 Northwood Commons Pl, Chico, CA 95973

HUNT, Victoria Wells (Mass) Po Box 1205, East Harwich, MA 02645

HUNT, William Gilbert (Miss) 510 Godsey Rd., Apt. 183, Bristol, TN 37620

HUNTER, Colenthia Hill (SO) 8387 Vicksburg Dr, Cincinnati, OH 45249

HUNTER, Elizabeth Lane (Miss) 327 N First St, Rolling Fork, MS 39159

HUNTER, Elizabeth Sue (U) 231 E 100 S, Salt Lake City, UT 84111

HUNTER JR, Herschel Miller (Va) Po Box 37, Ivy, VA 22945

HUNTER, James Wallace (RG) St Mary's Church, 1500 Chelwood Park Blvd NE, Albuquerque, NM 87112

HUNTER II, J Nathaniel (Ak) 322 Cross Way, North Pole, AK 99705

HUNTER, Karen (Ida) 204 Courthouse Dr, Salmon, ID 83467

HUNTER, Kay Smith (WLa) 401 Washington Ave, Mansfield, LA 71052

HUNTER, Kenneth Eugene (Alb) 29 Walnut St., Oneonta, NY 13820

HUNTER, Lawrence Scott (Cal) 1042 Dead Indian Memorial Road, Ashland, OR 97520

HUNTER, Marcia G (Lex) 104 Dellwood Dr, Berea, KY 40403

HUNTER, Mary Veronica (Alb) 305 Main St, Oneonta, NY 13820

HUNTER, Paul A (Alb) Christ Episcopal Church, 69 Fair St, Cooperstown, NY 13326

HUNTER SR, Robert Fulton Boyd (WA) 12213 Rolling Hill Ln, Bowie, MD 20715

HUNTER, S Scott (Mich) The Cathedral Church of St. Paul, 4800 Woodward Ave, Detroit, MI 48201

HUNTER JR, Victor Edward (Dal) 1115 S. Bryan St., Mesquite, TX 75149

HUNTER, Walcott Wallace (NY) Po Box 646, Kinderhook, NY 12106

HUNTINGTON, Carol L (Me) 121 Bowery St, Bath, ME 04530

HUNTINGTON, Francis Cleaveland (NY) 11 Rassapeague, Saint James, NY 11780

HUNTINGTON, Frederic DuBois (Va) 219 Wolfe St, Alexandria, VA 22314

HUNTLEY JR, Preston Brooks (USC) 312 Powe St., Cheraw, SC 29520

HUNTLEY, Stuart Michael (LI) 9 Carlton Ave, Port Washington, NY 11050

HUPF, Jeffrey L (RG) 2801 Westwood Rd S, Minnetonka Beach, MN 55361

HUR, Won-Jae (Cal) 206 Arborway Apt 3, Boston, MA 02130

HURD JR, Austin Avery (Pgh) 102 Fountain Cv, 160 Marwood Rd Apt 3314, Cabot, PA 16023

HURLBURT, Martha Cornue (EO) 801 Jefferson St, Klamath Falls, OR 97601

HURLBUT, Terence James (WMass) 7 Woodbridge St, South Hadley, MA 01075

HURLEY, Hal Owen (SeFla) 418 N Sapodilla Ave, West Palm Beach, FL 33401

HURLEY, Janet (Los) St John the Evangelist Episcoapl Church, PO Box 183, Needles, CA 92363

HURLEY, Thomas James (Neb) 113 N 18th St, Omaha, NE 68102

HURST, Hassell J (Ga) PO Box 50555, Nashville, TN 37205

HURST, Michael W (Dal) 400 S Church St, Paris, TX 75460

HURST, Rodney Shane (RG) 508 W Fox St, Carlsbad, NM 88220

HURST, William George (NH) 108 Wecuwa Dr, Fort Myers, FL 33912

HURTADO, Homero (EcuC) Guallabamba 214, Cuenca, Ecuador

HURTT, Annie Lawrie (Pa) 659 W Johnson St, Philadelphia, PA 19144

HURWITZ, Ellen Sara (Md) 12147 Pleasant Walk Rd, Myersville, MD 21773

HUSBAND, John Frederick (Minn) 16533 Long Beach Dr, Detroit Lakes, MN 56501

HUSBY, Mary Eloise Brown (SD) 1504 S Park Ave, Sioux Falls, SD 57105

HUSHION, Timothy V (Pgh) 328 6th St, Pittsburgh, PA 15215

HUSSEY, David Payne (SD) 12 Linden Avenue, Vermillion, SD 57069

HUSSEY-SMITH, Teddra R (EC) 5071 Voorhees Rd, Denmark, SC 29042

HUSSON, Brenda G (NY) 865 Madison Ave, New York, NY 10021

HUSTAD, Siri Hauge (Minn) 519 Oak Grove St, Minneapolis, MN 55403

HUSTON, Jeffrey Clayton (Okla)

HUSTON, Julie Winn (At) 2950 Mt. Wilkinson Pkwy, Unit 817, Atlanta, GA 30339

HUSTON, Mary Ann Mcbride (Tex) 3816 Bellaire Blvd, Houston, TX 77025

HUSTON, Nancy Williams (Neb) 923 S 33rd St, Omaha, NE 68105

HUTCHENS, Holly Blair (WMo) St Ninians Cottage, Melton, Drumnadrochit, SCOTLAND IV63 6UA, Great Britain (UK)

HUTCHENS, Marquita L (WVa) St. John's Episcopal Churh, 1105 Quarrier Street, Charleston, WV 25301

HUTCHERSON, Anne V (WMo) 624 W 61st Ter, Kansas City, MO 64113

HUTCHERSON, Robert M (WMo) 624 West 64th Terrace, Kansas City, MO 64113

HUTCHINGS, Douglas Wayne (LI) 1030 Kayton Ave, San Antonio, TX 78210

HUTCHINS, Margaret Smith (EC) 7909 Blue Heron Dr W Apt 2, Wilmington, NC 28411

HUTCHINS, M(aurice) Gene (RG) Po Box 223, Tyrone, NM 88065

HUTCHINSON, Anthony A. (Ore) Trinity Episcopal Church, 44 N 2nd St, Ashland, OR 97520

HUTCHINSON, Barbara (CPa) 9 Carlton Ave, Port Washington, NY 11050

HUTCHINSON JR, Jay (Del) 350 Noxontown Rd, Middletown, DE 19709

HUTCHINSON, Ninon N (CNY) 7029 Texas Road, Croghan, NY 13327

HUTCHISON, Hal T. (ETenn) 309 Quail Dr., Johnson City, TN 37601

HUTCHISON, Jonathan Schofield (Ind) Hc 81 Box 6009, Questa, NM 87556

HUTCHISON, Sheldon Butt (ECR) 921 Eton Way, Sunnyvale, CA 94087

HUTCHSON, Lee Allen (Va) 18256 Oxshire Ct, Montpelier, VA 23192

HUTH, Harvey Checketts (Alb) St Stephen's Church, 16 Elsmere Ave, Delmar, NY 12054

HUTJENS, Dale Henry (FdL) 123 Nob Hill Ln, De Pere, WI 54115

HUTSON, Blake Robert (Ala) Church Of The Holy Apostles, 424 Emery Dr, Hoover, AL 35244

HUTSON, Linda Darlene (Az) 12111 N La Cholla Blvd, Oro Valley, AZ 85755

HUTSON, Thomas Milton (ETenn) 3502 Wood Bridge Dr, Nashville, TN 37217

HUTTAR BAILEY, Julia (Mich)

HUTTO, Kelsey L (Ind) 422 N 13th Ave, Beech Grove, IN 46107

HUTTON III, James Laurence (SVa) 3429 Boyce Court, Norfolk, VA 23509

HUTTON, Lin Vaught (Va)

HUTTON, Linda Arzelia (Tenn) Box 3167, Sewanee, TN 37375

HUXLEY, David B (NwT) Saint Luke's Church, 146 S Church St, Whitewater, WI 53190

HUYCK, Jonathan Taylor (RI) 175 Mathewson St, Providence, RI 02903

HUYNH, Tinh Trang (Va) 64 Horseshoe Ln N, Columbus, NJ 08022

HYATT, David W (Pa) 404 Donna Ln, Phoenixville, PA 19460

HYBL, Andrew David (Ark) 925 Mitchell St, Conway, AR 72034

HYCHE, Jerald Walton (Tex) 1803 Highland Hollow Drive, Conroe, TX 77304

HYDE, John Ernest Authur (SwFla) 4650 Cove Cir Apt 407, Madeira Beach, FL 33708

HYDE, Lillian (Tex) Po Box 580117, Houston, TX 77258

HYDE, Pamela Willson (Az) 75 Church Ln, Westport, CT 06880

HYDE III, Robert Willis (Tex) 208 Seawall Blvd, Galveston, TX 77550

HYER, Darin Stant (CGC) St Simon's on the Sound Episcopal Church, 28 Miracle Strip Pkwy SW, Fort Walton Beach, FL 32548

HYLDEN, Emily Rose (USC) 448 Cami Forest Ln, Columbia, SC 29209

HYLDEN, Jordan L (ND) 6345 Wydown Blvd, Saint Louis, MO 63105

HYNDMAN, David Lee (NI) 8981 E 5th Ave Apt 101, Gary, IN 46403

I

IALONGO, Donna Marie (Chi)

IBE, Morgan Kelechi (Okla) 2424 Pinon Pl, Edmond, OK 73013

IDEMA III, Henry (WMich) 13562 Redbird Ln, Grand Haven, MI 49417

IDICULA, Mathew P (Chi) The Church of St Columba of Iona, 1800 Irving Park Rd, Hanover Park, IL 60133

IFILL, Angela Sylvia S (O) 64 Bayley Ave, Yonkers, NY 10705

IGARASHI, Peter Hiroshi (Pa) 600 E Cathedral Rd # D202, Philadelphia, PA 19128

IGO, Nancy Elle (NwT) Episcopal Diocese of Northwest Texas, 1802 Broadway, Lubbock, TX 79401

IHIASOTA, Isaac Iheanyichukwu (WNY) 8283 Effie Drive, Niagara Falls, NY 14304

✠ **IHLOFF**, Robert Wilkes (Ret Bp of Md 2007-) 1200 Steuart St Unit 1020, Baltimore, MD 21230

IJAMS, Carl Phillip (Mass) 38295 S Bogie Ct, Tucson, AZ 85739

IKENYE, Ndungu John Brown (Chi) 1930 Darrow Ave, Evanston, IL 60201

ILLAS, Antonio (WTex) PO Box 1948, San Benito, TX 78586

ILLES, Joseph Paul (NI) 56869 Sundown Rd, South Bend, IN 46619

ILLINGWORTH, David Paul (Me) 28 Wayne St, Portland, ME 04102

ILOGU, Edmund Christopher Onyedum (WA) 2355 Weymouth Ln, Crofton, MD 21114

IMARA, Mwalimu (Ind) 4550 Orkney Ln Sw, Atlanta, GA 30331

IMBODEN, Stanley Franklin (CPa) 315 Dead End Rd, Lititz, PA 17543

IMMEL, Otto Wigaart (NJ) Po Box 2379, Tybee Island, GA 31328

IMPICCICHE, Frank Santo (Ind)

INAPANTA PAEZ, Lourdes Esther (EcuC)

INCE JR, Edgar Elmer (WTenn) 3749 Kimball Ave, Memphis, TN 38111

INESON JR, John Henry (Me) 53 High St., Damariscotta, ME 04543

INGALLS JR, Arthur Bradford (Md) PO Box 25, Churchville, MD 21028

INGALLS, Clayton Dean (Tenn) 5501 Franklin Pike, Nashville, TN 37220

INGALLS, Jason T (Tex) 1100 N. 15th St., Waco, TX 76707

INGALLS, Margaret Eileen Fowler (WA) Transfiguration Church, 13925 New Hampshire Ave, Silver Spring, MD 20904

INGEMAN, Peter Lyle (Ga) 3128 Huntington Ridge Circle, Valdosta, GA 31602

INGERSOLL, Russell William (WNC) 52 Sturbridge Lane, Greensboro, NC 27408

INGRAHAM, Doris Williams (SeFla) 15955 Nw 27th Ave, Opa Locka, FL 33054

INIESTA-AVILA, Bernardo (Nev) 4201 W Washington Ave, Las Vegas, NV 89107

INMAN, John Wesley (WMich) 135 Old York Road, New Hope, PA 18938

INMAN, Virginia Bain (NC) 607 N Greene St, Greensboro, NC 27401

INNES, Neil Fraser (WTex) 1702 S Medio River Cir, Sugar Land, TX 77478

INSCOE, Laura D (Va) 2319 E. Broad Street, Richmond, VA 23223

INSERRA, John Michael (Wyo) Saint Peter's Episcopal Church, 1 S Tschirgi St, Sheridan, WY 82801

IRELAND, Clyde Lambert (USC) 2517 Duncan St, Columbia, SC 29205

IRELAND, Joel T (LI) 532 E 1st St, Tucson, AZ 85705

✠ **IRISH**, Carolyn Tanner (Ret Bp of U 2011-) 1930 South State, Salt Lake City, UT 84115

IRIZARRY, J E (Ct) 200 exeter st, Hartford, CT 06106

IRONSIDE, Susan R (NJ) 414 E Broad St, Westfield, NJ 07090

IRSCH, Leona M (WNY) 108 S Thomas Ave, Edwardsville, PA 18704

IRVIN, Cynthia Diane (Colo) 546 N Elm St # 1496, Cortez, CO 81321

IRVIN, Henry (Stuart) (WA) 425 Crowfields Dr, Asheville, NC 28803

IRVINE, Peter Bennington (NI) 1601 183rd Street, Homewood, IL 60430

IRVING, Anthony Tuttle (Oly) 5445 Donnelly Dr Se, Olympia, WA 98501

IRVING, H(annah) Jocelyn (WA) 9713 Summit Cir Apt 1B, Upper Marlboro, MD 20774

IRVING, Stanley Herbert (Vt) 5205 Georgia Shore Rd, Saint Albans, VT 05478

IRWIN, Margaret Bertha (Mil) 6989 Apprentice Pl, Middleton, WI 53562

IRWIN, Sara Hariett (Mass)

IRWIN, Zachary Tracy (NwPa) 4216 E South Shore Dr, Erie, PA 16511

ISAAC, Donald Tileston (Mass) 99 Centre Avenue, Rockland, MA 02370

ISAAC III, F(rank) Reid (O) 2181 Ambleside Drive, Apartment 412, Cleveland, OH 44106

✠ **ISAAC**, Telesforo A (Ret Bp of DomRep 1991-) JP 8600, PO Box 02-5284, Miami, FL 33102

ISAACS, James Steele (WA) St James Church, 11815 Seven Locks Rd, Potomac, MD 20854

ISADORE, Daniel Joseph (Pgh) 5801 Hampton St, Pittsburgh, PA 15206

ISHIZAKI, Norman Yukio (Los) 580 Hilgard Avc, Los Angeles, CA 90024

ISHMAN, Martha S. (NwPa) 245 Valley Trails Ln, Franklin, PA 16323

ISLEY, Carolyn W (ETenn) 118 Oak Grove Rd, Greeneville, TN 37745

ISRAEL, Carver Washington (LI) 322 Clearbrook Ave, Lansdowne, PA 19050

ISRAEL JR, Fielder (Md) 4720 Winterberry Ct, Williamsburg, VA 23188

ISWARIAH, James Chandran (Va) 465 Walnut Ln, King William, VA 23086

✠ **ITTY**, Johncy (Form Bp of Ore 2008-) 10 Avalon Road, Garden City, NY 11530

IVATTS, Justin Anthony (Va)

IVES, Joel (Mass) 23 Monmouth St., Brookline, MA 02446

IVES, Nathan Warren (Ct)

IVEY, Betsy S (Pa) 1401 S 22nd St, Philadelphia, PA 19146

IVEY, Valerie Ann (Ore) 15240 Nw Courting Hill Dr, Banks, OR 97106

IWICK, Richard Edward (Mich) 25755 Kilreigh Ct, Farmington Hills, MI 48336

IZADI, Samira (Dal) 6941 kingdom estates drive, Dallas, TX 75236

IZUTSU, Margaret Widdifield (Mich) 18 Fairview Ave, Arlington, MA 02474

IZZO, Joanne (NY) 43 S Broadway, Tarrytown, NY 10591

Clergy List

J

JABLONSKI, Carol J (WA) 4512
College Ave, College Park, MD 20740
JACKSON, Brad Lee (Va) Po Box
305, Madison, VA 22727
JACKSON, Bruce A (Az) 4102 W
Union Hills Dr, Glendale, AZ 85308
JACKSON, Carl Thomas (Va) 2940
Corries Way, Conneaut, OH 44030
JACKSON, David (SwFla) All Souls
Episcopal Church, 14640 N Cleveland
Ave, North Fort Myers, FL 33903
JACKSON, David Hilton (USC) 245
Cavalier Drive, Greenville, SC 29650
JACKSON, Deborah Mitchell (Fla)
5620 Columbia Pl, Jacksonville, FL
32210
JACKSON, Eric Michael Colin (Oly)
26291 Pennsylvania Ave NE APT 105,
Kingston, WA 98346
JACKSON, Gary Jon (Ga) St Mark's
Episcopal Church, 900 Gloucester St,
Brunswick, GA 31520
JACKSON JR, Gary Leon (CFla) 500
W Stuart St, Bartow, FL 33830
JACKSON JR, Hillyer Barnett (Okla)
3149 NW 24th St, Oklahoma City, OK
73107
JACKSON, Hugo Terrance (At) 4246
Glenforest Way Ne, Roswell, GA
30075
JACKSON, Ira Leverne (Ga) Grace
Episcopal Church, PO Box 617,
Sandersville, GA 31082
JACKSON, Jared Judd (Pgh) 903
Orchard Park Dr., Gibsonia, PA 15044
JACKSON, Jeffery Rand (At) 69
Mobley Road, PO Box 752, Hamilton,
GA 31811
JACKSON, Jimmy (NwT) PO Box
3346, Odessa, TX 79760
JACKSON, Judy Ann (Chi)
JACKSON, Julius W D (Pa) 803
Macdade Blvd, Collingdale, PA 19023
JACKSON, Kimberly Sue (At)
JACKSON, Larry Dean (WVa) 2004
Maxwell Ave, Parkersburg, WV 26101
JACKSON, Margaret Ruth Brosz (Ia)
JACKSON, Micah T (Tex) 501 E
32nd St, Austin, TX 78705
JACKSON, Patricia Gladys (Ct) 120
Sigourney St, Hartford, CT 06105
JACKSON, Paul Phillip (CFla) 1620
Mayflower Ct. A-211, Winter Park, FL
32789
JACKSON, Paula Marie (SO) 65 E
Hollister St, Cincinnati, OH 45219
JACKSON, Peter (Nwk) 130 Bessida
St, Bloomfield, NJ 07003
JACKSON, Peter Jonathan Edward
(WA) 1 The Green, London, N14 7EG,
Great Britain (UK)
JACKSON, Phillip A (NY) 50 Pine
St, New York, NY 10005
JACKSON, Reginald Fitzroy (LI)
1695 E 55th St, Brooklyn, NY 11234
JACKSON, Rhea Ewing (Ark) PO
Box 36, Roland, AR 72135

JACKSON, Robert Sumner (Mass)
339 S Madison St, Woodstock, IL
60098
JACKSON, Rosemary Herrick (WNC)
145 Old Mt Olivet Rd, Zirconia, NC
28790
JACKSON, Terry Allan (NY) 600 W
246th St Apt 1515, Bronx, NY 10471
JACKSON, Thomas C (Cal) Christ
Episcopal Church, 1700 Santa Clara
Avenue, Alameda, CA 94501
JACKSON, Thomas Lee (Ala) Po Box
4155, Tyler, TX 75712
JACKSON-MCKINNEY, Statha
Frances (SwFla)
JACOB, James Neithelloor (RI)
JACOB, Jerry Elias (Ala) 305 Arnold
St NE, Cullman, AL 35555
JACOBS, Allston Alexander (Md)
2019 Division St, Baltimore, MD
21217
JACOBS, Connie Hartquist
(Episcopal SJ) PO Box 446, Oakhurst,
CA 93644
JACOBS, Gregory A (Nwk) 31
Mulberry St., Newark, NJ 07102
JACOBS, John R(ay) (CFla) 21
Riviera Dr, Pinehurst, NC 28374
JACOBS, Marlene M (Oly) 1917
Logan Ave S, Minneapolis, MN 55403
JACOBS III, Philip Chauncey (Mass)
203 Chapman St, Canton, MA 02021
JACOBS, Robert Alexander (NY) 20
Trestle Way, Dayton, NJ 08810
JACOBSEN, Leigh Christian (SanD)
JACOBSON, Bruce Harvey (NH) 9
Esty Way, Groveland, MA 01834
JACOBSON, H(arold) Knute (Mo)
123 S. Ninth Street, Columbia, MO
65201
JACOBSON, Jeanne Ellen (CPa) 616
Spruce St., Hollidaysburg, PA 16648
JACOBSON, Marc R (Pgh) 4604
Crew Hall Ln, Quezon City, Waxhaw,
NC 28173
JACOBSON, Paul Alan (Ct) 859 East
Broadway, Stratford, CT 06515
JACOBSON, Stephen Kent (Pa)
13202 SE 91st Court Road,
Summerfield, FL 34491
✠ **JACOBUS**, Russell Edward (Ret Bp
of FdL 2014-)
JACQUES, Mary Martha (Mont)
13100 Highway 41 North, Dillon, MT
59725
JAEGER, George Marvin (Nick) (Ky)
2502 Jefferson St., Paducah, KY 42001
JAEKLE, Charles Roth (WA) 7446
Spring Village Dr Apt 307, Springfield,
VA 22150
JAENKE, Karen Ann (NJ) 24
Woodland Road, Fairfax, CA 94930
JAIKES, Donald William (Mass) 1095
Pinellas Pt Dr So Unit 327, Saint
Petersburg, FL 33705
JAKOBSEN, Wilma Terry (ECR) St
Jude the Apostle Church, 20920
McClellan Rd, Cupertino, CA 95014
JALLOUF, Georges (Okla) 5850 E
78th Pl, Tulsa, OK 74136

JAMBOR, Christopher Noel (FtW)
1805 Malibar Rd, Fort Worth, TX
76116
JAMES, Alan C (Chi) 400 E
Westminster, Lake Forest, IL 60045
JAMES, C(harles) Scott (CGC) Po
Box 29, Bon Secour, AL 36511
JAMES, Claudia Jan (Az) 423 N.
Beaver St., Flagstaff, AZ 86001
JAMES, Darryl Farrar (LI) 3312 S
Indiana Ave, Chicago, IL 60616
JAMES, Edmund Ludwig (Okla) 104
W Hanover St, Hoyt, OK 74472
JAMES, Jay Carleton (NC) 4523 Six
Forks Road, Raleigh, NC 27609
JAMES, John Hugh Alexander (Ct)
Christ Episc Church, 78 Washington
St, Norwich, CT 06360
JAMES, Marcus Gilbert (Roch)
JAMES, Molly Field (Ct) 37 Griswold
Dr, West Hartford, CT 06119
JAMES, Nancy Carol (WA) 713 E St
Ne, Washington, DC 20002
JAMES JR, Ralph Matthew (WVa)
PO Box 145, Union, WV 24983
JAMES, Robert Arthur (LI) 5 Fig Ct
E, Homosassa, FL 34446
JAMES, Robin L (NY) 660 S 500 E,
Salt Lake City, UT 84102
JAMES, Sally Patricia (NMich) 402 W
Fleshiem St, Iron Mountain, MI 49801
JAMES, William Evans (CGC) 1530
University Dr NE Apt 15, Atlanta, GA
30306
JAMESON, Elizabeth Butler (Chi)
232 S. Dwyer, Arlington Heights, IL
60005
JAMESON, J Parker (Tex) 8 Troon
Dr, Lakeway, TX 78738
JAMIESON, Sandra C (SwFla) 301
Jasmine Way, Clearwater, FL 33756
JAMIESON JR, William Stukey
(WNC) 15 Macon Ave, Asheville, NC
28801
JAMIESON-DRAKE, Victoria Kapp
(NC) 304 E Franklin St, Chapel Hill,
NC 27514
JAMISON, Dale Martin (NMich) 901
Dakota Ave, Gladstone, MI 49837
JAMISON, Dorothy Lockwood (Cal)
501 Portola Rd Apt 12J, Portola Valley,
CA 94028
JANDA, Mary Sheridan (U)
JANELLE, Nicole S (Los) St.
Michael's University Church, 6586
Picasso Rd., Isla Vista, CA 93117
JANESS, Nancy Kingswood (Nev)
JANG, T Vincent (Cal) 5072 Diamond
Heights Blvd, San Francisco, CA
94131
JANIEC, Thomas Daniel (Chi) 342 E
Wood St, Palatine, IL 60067
JANKOWSKI, John A (Minn) 10174
Bald Eagle Trl, Woodbury, MN 55129
JARA, Francisco Gonzalo (EcuC)
JARRELL, Robin Campbell (CPa)
229 Alana Ln, Lewisburg, PA 17837
JARRETT III, John Jacob (SeFla)
1052 Nw 65th St, Miami, FL 33150
JARRETT, Rondesia (WA)

JARVIS III, Frank Washington (Mass) 1241 Adams St Apt 511, Dorchester, MA 02124

JARVIS, Leon Gerald (NMich) 1300 West Ave, Marquette, MI 49855

JASMER, Gerald Bruce (Mont) 36 30th St W, Billings, MT 59102

JASPER SR, John Weaver (CFla) 1151 Sw Del Rio Blvd, Port Saint Lucie, FL 34953

JASPER, Michael Angelo (Okla) 13112 N Rockwell Ave, Oklahoma City, OK 73142

JAVIER, Nazareno C (Pa)

JAY, Lynn Antoinette Duba (Los) 26084 Viento Ct, Valencia, CA 91355

JAYAWARDENE, Thomas Devashri (Los) 1141 Westmont Rd, Santa Barbara, CA 93108

JAYNES, Ronald P (Pa) 431 Atkins Ave, Lancaster, PA 17603

JAYNES, Ruth Louise McKinney (Neb) 1322 S 52nd St, Omaha, NE 68106

JEAN, MacDonald (Hai) Box 1309, Port-Au-Prince, Haiti

JEANES III, Paul (NJ) 33 Mercer St, Princeton, NJ 08540

JEAN-JACQUES, Harry Musset (Hai) Boite Postale 1309, Port-Au-Prince, Haiti

JEAN-PHILIPPE, Jean-Alphonse (Hai) PO Box 407139, C/O Lynx Air, Fort Lauderdale, FL 33340

JEFFERS, Mary Elisabeth (USC) 711 S McDuffie St, Anderson, SC 29624

JEFFERSON, Alyce Lee (La) 1329 Jackson Ave, New Orleans, LA 70130

✠ **JEFFERTS SCHORI**, Katharine (Form PBp of TEC 2015-) 815 2nd Ave, New York, NY 10017

JEFFERY, Anne-Marie (NJ) St Peters Episcopal Church, 183 Rector St, Perth Amboy, NJ 08861

JEFFERY, David Luce (Fla) 1843 Seminole Rd, Atlantic Beach, FL 32233

JEFFERY, V(incent) James (Nev) 1500 Mount Rose St, Reno, NV 89509

JEFFREY, Kathryn G (Spr) 29 Nord Circle Rd, North Oaks, MN 55127

JEFFREY, Peter Leigh (Mass) 8 Kirk St, Lowell, MA 01852

JEKABSONS, Wendie Susan (ETenn) 334 Sourwood Hill Rd, Bristol, TN 37620

✠ **JELINEK**, James Louis (Ret Bp of Minn 2010-) 957 25th St NW, Washington, DC 20037

JELLEMA, Alice Moore (Md) 1401 Carrollton Ave, Ruxton, MD 21204

JELLISON, Mary L (Wyo) 3129 Pinewood Ave, Bellingham, WA 98225

JEMMOTT, Brian Anthony Lester (At) 2005 South Columbia Place, Decatur, GA 30032

JENCKS, Jeffrey A (CGC) 7979 N 9th Ave, Pensacola, FL 32514

JENKINS, Al W (CFla) 103 W Christina Blvd, Lakeland, FL 33813

✠ **JENKINS III**, Charles Edward (Ret Bp of La 2010-) P.O. Box 3000, St. Francisville, LA 70775

JENKINS, David P (Alb) 517 Lakeside Circle, Pompano Beach, FL 33060

JENKINS, George Washburn (Ct) 567 S Farms Ct, Southington, CT 06489

JENKINS JR, Harry O (La) 1534 7th St, Slidell, LA 70458

JENKINS, James Leonard (Minn) 5250 Vernon Ave S Apt 232, Edina, MN 55436

JENKINS, James Morgan (Ore) 4110 River Rd, Eugene, OR 97404

JENKINS, John Stone (La) 708 Forest Point Dr, Brandon, MS 39047

JENKINS, John William Andrew (Ala) 605 Reynolds St, Augusta, GA 30901

JENKINS, Judith Ann (RG) 601 Montano Rd. N.W., Albuquerque, NM 87107

JENKINS, Kathryn E (Va) 3507 Pond Chase Dr, Midlothian, VA 23113

JENKINS, Mark A (NH) 20260 Williamsville Rd, Gregory, MI 48137

JENKINS, Martha L (SVa) 120 Reykin Dr, Richmond, VA 23236

JENKINS, Michael L (WNC) 5165 Hayes Waters Rd, Morganton, NC 28655

JENKINS, Stephanie R (Kan) 835 SW Polk St, Topeka, KS 66612

JENKINS, William David (Kan) 314 N Adams St, Junction City, KS 66441

JENKS, Alan W (WVa) 450 Elm St, Morgantown, WV 26501

JENKS, Glenn Baylor (Az) 5417 E Milton Dr, Cave Creek, AZ 85331

JENKS, Peter Q (Me) 200 Main St, Thomaston, ME 04861

JENKS, Shepherd Martin (The Episcopal NCal) Pmb 320, 2132-A Central 5e, Albuquerque, NM 87106

JENNEKER, Bruce William Bailey (WA) St George's Cathedral, 5 Wale St, Cape Town, 8001, South Africa

JENNER, Helen McLeroy (NC) 1079 Ridge Dr, Clayton, NC 27520

JENNEY, Joe Allen (EMich)

JENNINGS, Albert Arthur (O) 8667 Shepard Rd # 204, Macedonia, OH 44056

JENNINGS, Debora (Okla) 814 N Vinita Ave, Tahlequah, OK 74464

JENNINGS, Gay Clark (O) 168 Hiram College Dr, Sagamore Hills, OH 44067

JENNINGS, James Courtney (HB) 5701 Snead Rd, Richmond, VA 23224

JENNINGS, Kelly Kathleen (Tex)

JENNINGS, Mary Kay (RG) Yankton Mission Cluster, 126 N Park NE, Wagner, SD 57380

JENNINGS, Nathan Grady (Tex) PO Box 2247, Austin, TX 78768

JENNINGS, Richard Paul (NMich) 1015 Parnell St, Sault Sainte Marie, MI 49783

JENNINGS, Robert Tallmadge (Ky) 2002 High Ridge Rd, Louisville, KY 40207

JENNINGS III, William Worth (NC) 702 Hillandale Ln, Garner, NC 27529

JENNINGS TODD, Margaret Herring (USC) 301 W Liberty St, Winnsboro, SC 29180

JENSEN, Anne Hislop (Cal) 865 Walavista Ave., Oakland, CA 94610

JENSEN, Barbara Ann (NJ)

JENSEN, Jan Darrel (Tex) 11 Sherwood Ln, Dayton, TX 77535

JENSEN, Jonathon W (Pgh) 315 Shady Avenue, Pittsburgh, PA 15206

JENSEN, Julia Kooser (Ore) 2020 SW Knollcrest Dr., Portland, OR 97225

JENSEN, Patricia Ann (CFla) 9301 Hunters Park Way, Tampa, FL 33647

JENSON, Constance (WA) 17413 Audrey Road, Cobb Island, MD 20625

JERAULD, Philip Eldredge (Mass) 1 Concord Coach Ln, Litchfield, NH 03052

JERGENS, Andrew Macaoidh (SO) 2374 Madison Rd, Cincinnati, OH 45208

JERNAGAN III, Luke (Mo) 110 N Warson Rd, Saint Louis, MO 63124

JEROME, Douglas Darrel (EO) 1332 SW 33rd St, Pendleton, OR 97801

JEROME, Joseph (LI) 3956 44th St, Sunnyside, NY 11104

JERSEY, Jean Staffeld (Vt) 32 Liberty St, Montpelier, VT 05602

JESION, Lawrence Michael (Ga) Christ Episcopal Church, 1904 Greene St, Augusta, GA 30904

JESSE JR, Henry (Colo) 7787 E Gunnison Pl, Denver, CO 80231

JESSETT, Frederick Edwin (Oly) 5309 S. Myrtle Lane, Spokane, WA 99223

JESSUP, Dorothy Margaret Paul (Pa) 278 Friendship Dr, Paoli, PA 19301

JESSUP, Elaine Anderson (SeFla) 464 NE 16th St, Miami, FL 33132

JESTER, Pamela Jean (Cal) 911 Dowling Blvd, San Leandro, CA 94577

JETT, Charles D (SC) 107 Sea Lavender Ln, Summerville, SC 29483

JETT, Mary Julia (Mont) Church of St Mary the Virgin, 145 W 46th St, New York, NY 10036

JEULAND, Eric Vincent (Ct) 25 Church St, Shelton, CT 06484

JEULAND, Jane Catherine Eppley (Ct) 300 Main St, Wethersfield, CT 06109

JEVNE, Lucretia Ann (The Episcopal NCal) 120 Loraine Ct, Vacaville, CA 95688

JEW, Cynthia (Los) Trinity Episcopal Church, 600 Saratoga, Fillmore, CA 93016

JEWELL, Kenneth Arthur (Nev) 777 Sage St., Elko, NV 89801

JEWETT, Ethan A (Chi) 2013 Appletree St, Philadelphia, PA 19103

JEWISS, Anthony Harrison (Los) 1290 Kent Street, Brooklyn, NY 11222

JEWSON, Alfred Joseph (WMo) 7511 Rannells Ave, Saint Louis, MO 63143
JEWSON, Dayna (Mo) 7511 Rannells Ave, Saint Louis, MO 63143
JILLARD, Christina Liggitt (Oly) St. Margaret's Episcopal Church, 4228 Factoria Blvd SE, Bellevue, WA 98006
JIM, Rosella A (NAM) Po Box 5854, Farmington, NM 87499
JIMENEZ, Darla Sue (NwT)
JIMENEZ, Juan (Los)
JIMENEZ-IRIZARRY, Edwin (Ct) Urb. El Vedado, Calle 12 de Octubre #428-A, San Juan, PR 00918
JIMENEZ-MESENBRING, Maria Jesus (Oly) 2020 E. Terrace St., Seattle, WA 98122
JINETE, Alvaro E (Chi) 3241 Calwagner St, Franklin Park, IL 60131
JIZMAGIAN, Mary Gibson (Cal) 2570 Chestnut St, San Francisco, CA 94123
JODKO, Juliusz Siegmond (Ct) 210 Church St, Naugatuck, CT 06770
JOFFRION JR, Felix Hughes (Ala) 1180 11th Ave S, Birmingham, AL 35205
JOHANNSEN, Carole (NY) 8 Pine Road, Bedford Hills, NY 10507
JOHANNSON, Johanna-Karen (NY) PO Box 1412, Bucksport, ME 04416
JOHANSEN, Paul Charles (SwFla) 504 3rd St Nw, New Philadelphia, OH 44663
JOHANSON, Norman Lee (Neb) 116 S Sunset Pl, Monrovia, CA 91016
JOHANSSEN, John Ralston (SO) 9429 Lighthouse Cut, Thornville, OH 43076
JOHN, James Howard (Kan) 7603 E Morris St, Wichita, KS 67207
JOHN, Rene R (NJ) 16 Fanning Way, Pennington, NJ 08534
JOHNS, Ernest William (SwFla) 20024 Behan Ct, Port Charlotte, FL 33952
JOHNS, Leila Margaret (NMich) 416 S 28th St, Escanaba, MI 49829
JOHNS, Martha D (Los) 30382 Via Con Dios, Rancho Santa Margarita, CA 92688
JOHNS III, Norman S (Oly) 5787 Lenea Dr Nw, Bremerton, WA 98312
JOHNS, Richard Gray (Los) 1199 Marinaside Crescent, Apt. 1701, Vancouver, BC V6Z 2Y2, Canada
JOHNSON, Alston Boyd (WLa) 140 Devereaux Dr, Madison, MS 39110
JOHNSON JR, Alvin Carl (Chi) 212 Biltmore Dr, N Barrington, IL 60010
JOHNSON, Andrew (Roch) 1957 Five Mile Line Rd., Penfield, NY 14526
JOHNSON, Ann L (Ct) 1105 Quarrier St, Charleston, WV 25301
JOHNSON, Ann Ruth (Az) 701 North Apollo Way, Flagstaff, AZ 86001
JOHNSON, Ann Elizabeth Simmons (Az) PO Box 40, 13803 North Watts Lane, Fort Thomas, AZ 85536
JOHNSON, Arthur Everitt (Miss) 1052 Deer Dr, Bay Saint Louis, MS 39520

JOHNSON, Brian David (Los) 1836 N Mira Loma Way, Palm Springs, CA 92262
JOHNSON, Broaddus (NY) 2336 Meadow Rdg, Redding, CT 06896
JOHNSON, Candine E (Va)
JOHNSON, Charles Lenwood (Va) 132 Lancaster Dr Apt 626, Irvington, VA 22480
JOHNSON, Christopher Allen (Colo) 45 Woodland Ave, Glen Ridge, NJ 07028
JOHNSON, David (NMich) 1021 E E St, Iron Mountain, MI 49801
JOHNSON, David Allen (Ga) 1700 Ashwood Blvd, Charlottesville, VA 22911
JOHNSON, David Hemeter (Miss) 901 Gillespie St, Jackson, MS 39202
JOHNSON, Dennis Lee (Wyo) Po Box 3485, Jackson, WY 83001
JOHNSON, Deon K. (Mich) 200 W Saint Paul St, Brighton, MI 48116
JOHNSON, Diana Patricia (U) 1854 Kensington Avenue, Salt Lake City, UT 84108
✠ **JOHNSON**, Don Edward (Bp of WTenn 2001-) 692 Poplar Ave, Memphis, TN 38105
JOHNSON, Donald Keith (Dal) 2026 Cherrywood Ln, Denton, TX 76209
JOHNSON, Doris Buchanan (Md) 603 Bellerive Ct, Arnold, MD 21012
JOHNSON, Douglas Peter (WMo) 3 Pecan PL, Ponca City, OK 74604
JOHNSON, Edwin Daniel (Mass) 14 Cushing Ave, Dorchester, MA 02125
JOHNSON, Emmanuel W (SC) 20268 Macglashan Ter, Ashburn, VA 20147
JOHNSON, Eric N (Oly) Christ Episcopal Anacortes, 1216 7th St, Anacortes, WA 98221
JOHNSON, Frances Kay (The Episcopal Church in Haw) 959 W 41st Street, Houston, TX 77018
JOHNSON, Frank T (SanD) 651 Eucalyptus Ave, Vista, CA 92084
JOHNSON, Franklin Orr (Mont) 355 Francis Way, Jackson, WY 83001
JOHNSON JR, Fred Hoyer (NY) 118 Lake Emerald Drive - #409, Oakland Park, FL 33309
JOHNSON, Gregory Mervin (The Episcopal Church in Haw) PO Box 893788, Mililani, HI 96789
JOHNSON JR, Harold Vance (WA) 12194 Cathedral Dr, Lake Ridge, VA 22192
JOHNSON JR, Harrel Brown (NC) 210 South Chestnut Street, Henderson, NC 27536
JOHNSON, Herbert Alan (WNC) 245 Laurel Falls Rd, Franklin, NC 28734
JOHNSON, Horace S (Ct) 3404 Castlebar Cir, Ormond Beach, FL 32174
JOHNSON, Ida Louise (Cal) 535 Joaquin Ave #D, San Leandro, CA 94577
JOHNSON, Ira Joseph (WTenn) 4150 Boeingshire Dr, Memphis, TN 38116

JOHNSON, James Baxter (Colo) 1715 Holly Way, Fort Collins, CO 80526
JOHNSON, Jane Margaret (FdL) 1316 Ellis St., Stevens Point, WI 54481
JOHNSON, Janet H. (NJ) 538 Epping Forest Road, Annapolis, MD 21401
JOHNSON, Janis Lynn (Oly) 1541 Vista Loop SW #33-101, Tumwater, WA 98512
JOHNSON, Jay Brooks (NC) 2690 Fairlawn Dr, Winston Salem, NC 27106
JOHNSON, Jay Emerson (Cal) 632 38th St, Richmond, CA 94805
JOHNSON, Joan Cottrell (Mass) 4833 Europa Dr, Naples, FL 34105
JOHNSON, Johan (NY) 521 W 126th St, New York, NY 10027
JOHNSON, John Brent (Tex) St. John's Episcopal Church, 1305 Roosevelt, Silsbee, TX 77656
JOHNSON JR, John Romig (NY) 1020 Tyron Cir, Charleston, SC 29414
JOHNSON, Juanita Hanger (Neb) 10761 Izard St, Omaha, NE 68114
JOHNSON, Julie Anna (Tenn) St Mary Magdalene Church, PO Box 150, Fayetteville, TN 37334
JOHNSON, June (Ga) 519 Parker Ave, Decatur, GA 30032
JOHNSON, June B (Oly) 114 20th Ave SE, Olympia, WA 98501
JOHNSON, Karen Brown (WA) 18440 Tea Rose Pl, Gaithersburg, MD 20879
JOHNSON, Katherine Ann Bradley (NC) 2504 Englewood Ave, Durham, NC 27705
JOHNSON, Kellaura Beth Jones (Tex) 806 Thompson Rd, Richmond, TX 77469
JOHNSON, Kenneth William (Mass) 11699 Bennington Woods Rd, Reston, VA 20194
JOHNSON, Kent William (LI) 6626 52nd Rd, #1, Maspeth, NY 11378
JOHNSON, Kevin Allen (FtW) St Peter's Episcopal Church, 101 N Bonner St, Washington, NC 27889
JOHNSON, Lee (Episcopal SJ) 310 Audubon Dr, Lodi, CA 95240
JOHNSON, Linda Catherine (Ind) IU Episcopal Campus Ministry, PO Box 127, Bloomington, IN 47402
JOHNSON, Linda Marie (Oly) Po Box 354, Westport, WA 98595
JOHNSON, Lori Elaine (EMich) 315 1/2 N Maple St, Flushing, MI 48433
JOHNSON JR, Lucius Curtis (Ga) 552 Hunterdale Rd, Evans, GA 30809
JOHNSON, Lynn H (NJ) 3 Azalea Dr, Lumberton, NJ 08048
JOHNSON, Maeve Maud Vincent (Az) 114 W Roosevelt St., Phoenix, AZ 85003
JOHNSON, Malinda Margaret (Eichner) (Ct) 9 Arrow Head Rd, Westport, CT 06880
JOHNSON, Marietta (Mont) Po Box 78, Red Lodge, MT 59068

JOHNSON, Marta D. V. (Md) 4603 Rocks Road, PO Box 103, Street, MD 21154

JOHNSON, Mary Peterson (ND) All Saints Church, 301 Main St S, Minot, ND 58701

JOHNSON, Mary Richardson (NMich) 1021 E E St, Iron Mountain, MI 49801

JOHNSON, Matthew R (NC) 231 N Church St, Rocky Mount, NC 27804

JOHNSON, Michael R (SD) PO Box 434, Deadwood, SD 57732

JOHNSON, Michaela (Kay) (RI) 1214 Noyes Dr, Silver Spring, MD 20910

JOHNSON, Mildred Jane (U) 147 N 875 E, Logan, UT 84321

JOHNSON, Neil Edward (NwPa) 18 Harrogate Square, Williamsville, NY 14221

JOHNSON, Patricia A (Ia) 2222 McDonald St, Sioux City, IA 51104

JOHNSON, Paul Andrew (Tex) 17706 Linkview Dr, Dripping Springs, TX 78620

JOHNSON, Ralph Foley (SeFla) 88181 Old Highway, #G41, Islamorada, FL 33036

JOHNSON, Randy Wayne (Minn) 2175 1st St, White Bear Lake, MN 55110

JOHNSON, R Dean (At) 1480 Pineview Ln Nw, Conyers, GA 30012

JOHNSON SR, Richard E (Me) PO Box 688, Castine, ME 04421

JOHNSON, Richard E (Mont) 902 Logan St, Helena, MT 59601

JOHNSON, Robert Gaines (SVa) 1411 25th St, Galveston, TX 77550

✠ **JOHNSON**, Robert Hodges (Ret Bp of WNC 2004-) 18 Woodcrest Rd, Asheville, NC 28804

JOHNSON III, Roberts Poinsett (Ala) 3620 Belle Meade Way, Birmingham, AL 35223

JOHNSON, Ronald Arthur (O) 66 Market St, Onancock, VA 23417

JOHNSON, Ronald Norman (SeFla) 320 Dudley Creek Rd, Hardy, VA 24101

JOHNSON, Russell L (SwFla) 13555 Heron Cir, Clearwater, FL 33762

JOHNSON, Russell Michael (The Episcopal Church in Haw) 296 Nikolau Pl, Hilo, HI 96720

JOHNSON JR, Russell Woodrow (WMo) 409 E Liberty, Independence, MO 64050

JOHNSON, Ryder Channing (WNY) 19013 N 74th Dr, Glendale, AZ 85308

JOHNSON, Sandra Parnell (SwFla) 14640 N Cleveland Ave, N Ft Myers, FL 33903

JOHNSON, Sanford Ralph (WMass) 50 Shaker Farm Rd N, Marlborough, NH 03455

JOHNSON, Simeon O (NY) 165 Saint Marks Pl Apt 10H, Staten Island, NY 10301

JOHNSON, Stephanie Mcdyre (Ct) 37 Avon Street, New Haven, CT 06511

JOHNSON, Susan Elaine (Eur) Schiesstaettberg 44, Eichstatt, AL 498421-4125, Germany

JOHNSON, Susan Heckel (At) 571 Holt Road, Marietta, GA 30068

JOHNSON, Thalia Felice (Mich) 8261 Cypress Way, Dexter, MI 48130

JOHNSON, Theodore Arthur (Nev) P.O. Box 4551, South Lake Tahoe, CA 95729

JOHNSON, Theodore William (WA) PO Box 386, Basye, VA 22810

JOHNSON, Thomas Stanley (The Episcopal NCal) 214 Leafwood Way, Folsom, CA 95630

JOHNSON, Timothy (WA) Washington Episcopal School, 5600 Little Falls Parkway, Bethesda, MD 20816

JOHNSON, Vicki Lynn (Spok) 1322 Kimball Ave, Richland, WA 99354

JOHNSON, Walter (Los) 1264 N Kings Rd Apt 17, West Hollywood, CA 90069

JOHNSON, W(ard) Kendall (ND) 1003 Crescent Ln, Bismarck, ND 58501

JOHNSON, William Alexander (NY) 27 Fox Meadow Rd, Scarsdale, NY 10583

JOHNSON, William Curtis (Oly) 19303 Fremont Ave N, Shoreline, WA 98133

JOHNSON, William Francis (Chi) 5749 N Kenmore Ave, Chicago, IL 60660

JOHNSON, William Gerald (Az) 11,000 east Calle Vaqueros, Tucson, AZ 85749

JOHNSON, William Joseph (Roch)

JOHNSON III, (William) Pegram (WA) 2004 Floyd Ave, Richmond, VA 23220

JOHNSON-TAYLOR, Allan B (WA) 4211 Enterprise Rd, Bowie, MD 20720

JOHNSON-TOTH, Louise M (Roch) 243 Genesee Park Blvd, Rochester, NY 14619

JOHNSTON, Cathy Lynn (ETenn) 2152 Hawthorne St, Kingsport, TN 37664

JOHNSTON, Clifford A. (CPa) 3147 Grahamton Rd, Morrisdale, PA 16858

JOHNSTON, David Knight (Mass) 78 Bishop Dr, Framingham, MA 01702

JOHNSTON, Duncan Howard (CPa) 125 N 25th St, Camp Hill, PA 17011

JOHNSTON, Edward (NY) 1215 5th Ave Apt 12, New York, NY 10029

JOHNSTON, Frank Norman (LI) PO Box 566, Onset, MA 02558

JOHNSTON, Fr. Terry (Pgh) PO Box 28, St Francisvle, LA 70775

JOHNSTON, Hewitt Vinnedge (NJ) 41087 Calla Lily St, Indian Land, SC 29707

JOHNSTON, Laurel A (ECR) 2767 Delpha Court, Thousand Oaks, CA 91362

JOHNSTON, Lewis Tyra (WMo) 2105 Quail Creek Dr, Lawrence, KS 66047

JOHNSTON, Madelynn Kirkpatrick (RG) Po Box 8716, Santa Fe, NM 87504

JOHNSTON, Mark Wylie (Ala) 105 Delong Rd, Nauvoo, AL 35578

JOHNSTON, Martha Suzanne (La) PO Box 28, St Francisvle, LA 70775

JOHNSTON, Nature Nancy Alice (Colo)

JOHNSTON, Paul Martin (Pgh) 2219 Wightman St, Pittsburgh, PA 15217

JOHNSTON, Peter Nathaniel (Ct) 1030 Johnston St, Lafayette, LA 70501

JOHNSTON, Philip Gilchrist (Va) 4773 Thornbury Dr, Fairfax, VA 22030

JOHNSTON JR, Robert Hugh (WTex) 102 E. Live Oak St., Cuero, TX 77954

JOHNSTON III, Robert Hugh (Dal) 5311 Ridgedale Dr, Dallas, TX 75206

JOHNSTON, Robert Owen (SVa) 207 Marshall St, Petersburg, VA 23803

JOHNSTON, Roy Wayne (WLa) 243 Whippoorwill Ln SW, Rome, GA 30165

JOHNSTON, Sally (USC) St. Martin's-In-The-Fields, 5220 Clemson Ave., Columbia, SC 29206

✠ **JOHNSTON**, Shannon Sherwood (Bp of Va 2009-) 110 W Franklin St, Richmond, VA 23220

JOHNSTON, Suzanne Elaine (Roch) 1245 Culver Rd., Rochester, NY 14609

JOHNSTON, William Merrill (FdL) 1010 Congress St, Neenah, WI 54956

JOHNSTON, Zula Jean (Oly) 8527 46th Ct Ne, Olympia, WA 98516

JOHNSTONE, Elise Beaumont (Lex)

JOHNSTONE, Mary Boardman McAvoy (RI) 39 Washington St, Newport, RI 02840

JOINER, James Michael (NC) St David Of Wales Epis Ch, 2800 SE Harrison St, Portland, OR 97214

JOLLY, Anne Bryson (Tex) 3201 Windsor Rd, Austin, TX 78703

JOLLY, Marshall A (WNC) Grace Episcopal Church, PO Box 6590, Florence, KY 41022

JONES, Alan (Cal) 1100 California St, San Francisco, CA 94108

JONES, Andrew Boyd (Mil) 2920 Pelham Rd, Madison, WI 53713

JONES, Andrew Lovell (Ct) Po Box 1083, Norwalk, CT 06856

JONES, Angela Louise (Neb) 1555 14Th St, Mitchell, NE 69357

JONES, Anthony Edward (LI) St Jone's Episcopal Church, 12 Prospect St, Huntington, NY 11743

JONES II, Bennett Green (WMass) 569 Main Street, Fitchburg, MA 01420

JONES, Beverly Jean (Alb) 7460 Se Concord Pl, Hobe Sound, FL 33455

✠ **JONES**, Bob Gordon (Ret Bp of Wyo 1996-) 900 Cottonwood Dr, Fort Collins, CO 80524

JONES, Bonnie Quantrell (Lex) 1801 Glenhill Dr, Lexington, KY 40502

JONES, Bradley T (NY) 161 Mansion St., Poughkeepsie, NY 12601

JONES, Bryan William (Los) 5306 Arbor Road, Long Beach, CA 90808

JONES, Carolyn Gibson (WMass) 4 Carousel Ln, Lunenburg, MA 01462

JONES JR, Cecil Baron (Miss) 147 Links Dr Apt 42C, Canton, MS 39046

✠ **JONES III**, Charles I (Form Bp of Mont 2001-) PO Box 86, Gulf Shores, AL 36547

JONES, Charles James (CNY) 9 Jutland Road, Binghamton, NY 13903

JONES, Christine Ann (NY)

JONES, Constance M (SVa) 6214 Monroe Pl, Norfolk, VA 23508

JONES, Curtis Carl (Ark) 20900 Chenal Pkwy, Little Rock, AR 72223

JONES, Dale Jackson (Ga)

JONES, DANIEL GWILYM (Be) 315 Calvin St, Dunmore, PA 18512

JONES SR, Daniel L (Alb) 15 Center St, Deposit, NY 13754

JONES, David Alexander (Md) Po Box 121, Highland, MD 20777

✠ **JONES**, David Colin (Ret Bp Suffr of Va 2012-) 6043 Burnside Landing Drive, Burke, VA 22015

JONES, David G (ECR) 1061 Garcia Rd, Santa Barbara, CA 93103

JONES, David James (ECR) Le Bourg, 47120 Loubes-Bernac, Duras, 47120 FR, France

JONES, David P (Chi) 1229 Hinman Avenue, Evanston, IL 60202

JONES, Derek Leslie (Cal) 786 Tunbridge Rd, Danville, CA 94526

JONES, Donald Avery (Ind) 312 E Lookout Ln, Bloomington, IN 47408

JONES, Dorothy Kovacs (Cal) Po Box 768, Tiburon, CA 94920

JONES, Duncan Haywood (NC)

JONES JR, Eddie Ellsworth (Fla) 160 Bear Pen Rd, Ponte Vedra Beach, FL 32082

JONES, Edward Wilson (Va) Diocese Of Virginia, 110 W Franklin St, Richmond, VA 23220

JONES, Elizabeth Claiborne (At) 5668 Stillwater Court, Stone Mountain, GA 30087-1645, Virgin Islands (U.S.)

JONES, Elizabeth Goodyear (Miss) 621 Briarwood Drive, Gulfport, MS 39560

JONES, Eustan Ulric (LI) 721 E 96th St Apt 2, Brooklyn, NY 11236

JONES, Frederick Lamar (At) 901 Stewart Lake Rd, Kent, OH 44240

JONES, Gary Durward (Va) 412 Maple Ave, Richmond, VA 23226

JONES, Gary H (Tex) 3806 Kiamesha Dr, Missouri City, TX 77459

JONES, Helen Hammon (Ky) 30 River Hill Rd, Louisville, KY 40207

JONES, Herbert H (Va)

JONES JR, Hugh Burnett (ETenn) P. O. Box 1884, Anniston, AL 36202

JONES, J(ack) Monte (WTex) 1615 S Monroe St, San Angelo, TX 76901

JONES, Jacqueline Sydney (Alb) 8 Byard St, Johnstown, NY 12095

JONES, James Place (SeFla) 9013 SW 62nd Ter, Miami, FL 33173

JONES, James W (NJ)

JONES, Jane (Denton) (Los) 457 W 39th St, San Pedro, CA 90731

JONES, Janice Lynn (Tex) 1314 E University Ave, Georgetown, TX 78626

JONES, Jerry Steven (WK) 1113 Pinehurst St, Hays, KS 67601

JONES, John Tyler (WA) 11040 Baltimore Ave, Beltsville, MD 20705

JONES, Judith (Tex) PO Box 28, Pflugerville, TX 78691

JONES, Judith Anne (Ia) 316 3rd St Ne, Waverly, IA 50677

JONES, Kathleen Andrea (Okla) 1901 Skyline Place, Bartlesville, OK 74006

JONES, Kenneth Leon (Mass) 62 Hopetown Road, Mt.Pleasant, SC 29464

JONES, Kent Trevor (Chi) 3706 W Saint Paul Ave, McHenry, IL 60050

JONES, Leland Bryant (SanD) 1118 W Country Club Ln, Escondido, CA 92026

JONES, Lynne Elizabeth (SeFla) 206 Pendleton Ave, Palm Beach, FL 33480

JONES, Margaret W (WTenn) 4757 Walnut Grove Rd, Memphis, TN 38117

JONES, Mark Stephen (Ga) 212 N Jefferson St, Albany, GA 31701

JONES, Mark Andrew (SeFla) 2707 NW 37th St, Boca Raton, FL 33434

JONES, Mary-Frances (Minn)

JONES, Michael Stephen (Alb) 785 Forest Ridge Dr, Youngstown, OH 44512

JONES, N(elson) Bradley (Alb) 970 State St, Schenectady, NY 12307

JONES, Nikki Lou (NwT) 1514 Neff St, Sweetwater, TX 79556

JONES, Patricia Loraine (Alb) 1295 Myron St, Schenectady, NY 12309

JONES, Patricia Wayne (WNC) 260 21st Ave Nw, Hickory, NC 28601

JONES, Peter Hoyt (HB)

JONES, Rebecca (Colo) 1300 Washington St, Denver, CO 80203

JONES, Richard John (SwVa) 2455 N Stevens St, Alexandria, VA 22311

JONES, Richmond A (At) 432 Forest Hill Rd, Macon, GA 31210

JONES, Robert Michael (WNC) PO Box 729, Highlands, NC 28741

JONES, Roland Manning (NC) 501 Parkmont Dr, Greensboro, NC 27408

JONES, Ruth Elise (NwT) 3010 - 60th, Lubbock, TX 79413

JONES, Samuel Gregory (NC) 1520 Canterbury Rd, Raleigh, NC 27608

JONES, Sandra Lee Spoar (U) PO Box 981208, Park City, UT 84098

JONES, Scott Daniel (Az) 10716 E Medina Ave, Mesa, AZ 85209

JONES, Sidney Ross (Okla) 385 Racquet Club Rd., Asheville, NC 28803

JONES, Stanley Boyd (WVa) 53 Windward Lane, Box 1848, Shepherdstown, WV 25443

JONES, Stephen Bradley (ETenn)

JONES, Stephen C (Tenn) 1322 Church Street, Zachary, LA 70791

JONES JR, Stewart Hoyt (Colo) 2421 S Krameria St, Denver, CO 80222

JONES, Tammy Lynn (Ida) PO Box 324, Rupert, ID 83350

JONES, Teresa Crawford (NY) 5 Christopher Ave, Highland, NY 12528

JONES, Theodore Grant (Md) 2604 Halcyon Avenue, Baltimore, MD 21214

JONES, Thomas A (Neb)

JONES, Thomas Glyndwr (At) 4425 Colchester Ct, Columbus, GA 31907

JONES, Timothy Dale (WNC) 290 Old Haw Creek Rd, Asheville, NC 28805

JONES, Timothy Kent (USC) St Georges Church, 4715 Harding Pike, Nashville, TN 37205

JONES, Vern Edward (Cal) 3814 Jefferson Ave, Redwood City, CA 94062

JONES, Walton Womack (Miss) 308 South Commerce St., Natchez, MS 39120

✠ **JONES JR**, William Augustus (Ret Bp of Mo 2003-) 58 Kendal Dr, Kennett Square, PA 19348

JONES, William Henry (O) 2651 Cheltenham Rd, Toledo, OH 43606

JONES, William Ogden (SVa) 8137 Brown Rd, Bon Air, VA 23235

JOO, Indon Paul (Chi) 1300 Hallberg Ln, Park Ridge, IL 60068

JOOS, Heidi L (Minn) 3105 W 40th St, Minneapolis, MN 55410

JOPLIN, Susan Colley (Okla) 2513 Sw 123rd St, Oklahoma City, OK 73170

JOPLING, Wallace Malcolm (Fla)

JORDAN SR, John Ellwood (Nev) 7560 Splashing Rock Dr., Las Vegas, NV 89131

JORDAN, Katherine H (WA) 3156 Gracefield Rd. Apt. 501, Silver Spring, MD 20904

JOSE, Nancy Lee (WA) 121 Montgomery St, Alexandria, VA 22314

JOSEPH, Annette Beth (Mo) 420 N Main St, Poplar Bluff, MO 63901

JOSEPH, Arthur Eric (NY) 450 Convent Ave, New York, NY 10031

JOSEPH, Augustine (EC) 509 Ramsey St, Fayetteville, NC 28301

JOSEPH, Jean Jeannot (Hai) P.O. Box 1390, Port-Au-Prince, Haiti

JOSEPH, Joseph Hyvenson (SeFla)

JOSEPH, Pierre Jean (Ve) Calle Tiuna y Callejon, Sta Elena, Venezuela, Venezuela

JOSEPH, Winston B (SeFla)

✠ **JOSLIN**, David Bruce (Ret Bp of CNY 2000-) 10 Meadow Ridge Rd, Westerly, RI 02891

JOSLIN, Roger Dale (Ark) 20 Pease Dr, Bella Vista, AR 72715

JOY, Charles Austin (SVa) 1009 W Princess Anne Rd, Norfolk, VA 23507

JOYCE, Thomas Joseph (Chi) 214 Hillside Dr., East Berlin, PA 17316

JOYNER, Thomas Roland (Ala) 100 Church Drive, Auburn, AL 36830

JOYNER JR, William Henry (NC) 309 N Boundary St, Chapel Hill, NC 27514

JOYNER-GIFFIN, Sally Burt (Md) 13736 Catoctin Furnace Rd, Thurmont, MD 21788

JUAREZ, Martin (ECR) 113 Morcroft Ln, Durham, NC 27705

JUAREZ VILLAMAR, Betty Marlene (Litoral Ecu) Campo Esperanza Mz.1 Sl.7, Canton Catarama, Ecuador

JUBINSKI, Christopher David (WA) Christ Episcopal Church, Po Box 8, Chaptico, MD 20621

JUCHTER, Mark Russell (NwPa) 5007 Lions Gate Lane, Killeen, TX 76549

JUDD, Steven William (Minn) 460 Willow Creek Dr, Owatonna, MN 55060

JUDSON, Donald Irving (Chi) 425 E May St, Elmhurst, IL 60126

JUDSON, Horace Douglas (Los) 1065 Lomita Blvd Spc 197, Harbor City, CA 90710

JULIAN, Mercedes I (RI) Ascension Church, 390 Pontiac Ave, Cranston, RI 02910-3322, Panama

JULNES-DEHNER, Noel (SO) 3491 Forestoak Court, Cincinnati, OH 45208

JUMP, Douglas Brian (CFla)

JUNK, Dixie Roberts (Kan) 2701 W 51st Ter, Westwood, KS 66205

JUNKIN, Hays M (NH) Church of Our Saviour, P.O. Box 237, Milford, NH 03055

JUPIN, J Michael (SO) 70 S Remington Rd, Columbus, OH 43209

JURADO, Ruben Dario (Nwk) 326 Westervelt Pl, Lodi, NJ 07644

JURKOVICH-HUGHES, Jocelynn Lena (The Episcopal NCal) 216 A Street, Davis, CA 95616

JUSTICE, Simon Charles (Ore) 445 NW Elizabeth Drive, Corvallis, OR 97330

JUSTIN, Daniel John (Los) 14311 Dickens St Apt 111, Sherman Oaks, CA 91423

K

KADEL, Andrew Gordon (NY) 1 Alexander Street, Yonkers, NY 10701

KAEHR, Michael Gene (SanD) 9503 La Jolla Farms Rd, La Jolla, CA 92037

KAESTNER, James Andrew (Mil) N52 W37111 Washington Street, Oconomowoc, WI 53066

KAETON, Elizabeth Marie Conroy (Nwk) 35647 Joann Dr, Millsboro, DE 19966

KAHL JR, Robert Mathew (NJ) 107 E Tampa Ave, Villas, NJ 08251

KAHLE, George Frank (SVa) 16711 Holly Trail Dr, Houston, TX 77058

KAHLER, Jerome Evans (Los) 9061 Santa Margarita Rd, Ventura, CA 93004

KAHN, Paul S. (NY) 552 West End Avenue, New York, NY 10024

KAIGHN, Reuel Stewart (Be) 145 The Hideout, Lake Ariel, PA 18436

KAISCH, Kenneth Burton (Los) 2112 Camino Del Sol, Fullerton, CA 92833

KALAS, Steven Curtis (Nev) 3607 Blue Dawn Dr, North Las Vegas, NV 89032

KALEMKERIAN, Louise Knar (Ct) 5030 Main St, Trumbull, CT 06611

KALLENBERG, Richard Arthur (NI) 55805 Oak Manor Pl, Elkhart, IN 46514

KALLIO, Craig Martin (ETenn) 119 Newell Lane, Oak Ridge, TN 37830

KALOM, Judith Christine Lilly (At)

KALUNIAN, Peter J (Spok) 5506 W. 19th Ave., Kennewick, WA 99338

KAMINSKAS, Karen Ann (Pa)

KAMINSKI, Neil Mitchell (Ark) 2620 N Chandalar Ln, Pelham, AL 35124

KAMM, Wayne Kenneth (Ia) 1451 Salem Rd., Salem, IA 52649

KANE, Dennis Edward (Ct) 679 Farmington Ave, West Hartford, CT 06119

KANE, E Ross (Va) 228 S Pitt St, Alexandria, VA 22314

KANE, Maria A (WA) 4535 Piney Church Rd, Waldorf, MD 20602

KANE, Paul Joseph (SeFla) St James In The Hills Episcopal, 3329 Wilson St, Hollywood, FL 33021

KANELLAKIS, Theodore (NY) 10 Rawson Ave, Camden, ME 04843

KANESTROM, Glenn Walter (Episcopal SJ) 6443 Estelle Ave, Riverbank, CA 95367

KANG, Hi-Jae Peter (La) PO Box 28, St Francisvle, LA 70775

KANGAS, John Gilbert (NMich) 302 E Arch St, Ironwood, MI 49938

KANNENBERG, James Gordon (Ia) 605 Avenue E, Fort Madison, IA 52627

KANOUR, Marion Elizabeth (SwVa) 732 S Chestnut Ave, Arlington Heights, IL 60005

KANYI, Peter (ETenn) 630 Mississippi Ave, Signal Mtn, TN 37377

KANZLER JR, Jay Lee (Mo) 20 Southmoor Dr, Clayton, MO 63105

KAPP, Charl Ann (NwPa) 1731 Warren Rd, Oil City, PA 16301

KAPP, John Deane (Az) 2800 W Ina Rd, Tucson, AZ 85741

KAPPEL, Roger Dale (EC) 1302 N Walnut St, Lumberton, NC 28358

KAPURCH, Linda Marie (Pa) 201 Crestline Dr, Kennett Square, PA 19348

KARANJA, Daniel Njoroge (Spr) PO BOX 534, BLYTHEWOOD, SC 29016

KARCHER, David Pirritte (SeFla) 5374 Sw 80th St, Miami, FL 33143

KARCHER, Steven Michael (Episcopal SJ) 2216 17th St, Bakersfield, CA 93301

KARDA, Margaret R. (Nwk) 6095 Summerlake Dr, Port Orange, FL 32127

KARDALEFF, Patricia Ann (Okla) 777 Chosin, Lawton, OK 73507

KAREFA-SMART, Rena Joyce Weller (WA) 4601 N Park Ave Apt 1202, Chevy Chase, MD 20815

KARELIUS, Bradford Lyle (Los) 29602 Via Cebolla, Laguna Niguel, CA 92677

KARKER, Arthur Lee (Me) Po Box 277, West Rockport, ME 04865

KARL JR, John Charles (Roch) 995 Park Ave, Rochester, NY 14610

KARL, Sharon Leith (Roch) 995 Park Ave, Rochester, NY 14610

KARNEY JR, George James (Del) 2812 Faulkland Rd, Wilmington, DE 19808

KARPF, Ted (WA) PO Box 6654, Santa Fe, NM 87502

KASEY, Philip Howerton (NJ) 4326 Teall Beach Rd, Geneva, NY 14456

KASEY, Polly Mcwilliams (NJ) 4326 Teall Beach Rd, Geneva, NY 14456

KASIO, Joseph Lelit (Nev)

KASSEBAUM, John Albert (NY) 53 S Clinton Ave, Hastings On Hudson, NY 10706

KASWARRA, George Abooki (NY) 23 N Willow St, Montclair, NJ 07042

KATER JR, John (Cal) 2116 Tice Creek Drive #2, Walnut Creek, CA 94595

KATHMANN, Charmaine M (La) St. John's Episcopal Church, 2109 17th Street, Kenner, LA 70062

KATON, Joanne Catherine (SeFla) 1800 Southwest 92nd Place, Miami, FL 33165

KATONA, Kenneth J (Az)

KATZ, Nathaniel Peter (Los) 514 W Adams Blvd, Los Angeles, CA 90007

KAUFFMAN, Bette Jo (WLa) 79 Quail Ridge Dr, Monroe, LA 71203

KAUFMAN, Linda Margaret (WA) 701 S Wayne St, Arlington, VA 22204

KAUTZ, Richard Arden (Ind) 913 Brentwood Ct, New Albany, IN 47150

KAVAL, Lura Marie (Md) 8522 Light Moon Way, Laurel, MD 20723

KAVROS, Peregrine Murphy (NY) 4 West 109th Street Apt 2D, New York, NY 10025

KAY, Frances Creveling (WLa) 2914 W Prien Lake Rd, Lake Charles, LA 70605

KAYE, Robert Pleaman Skarpmoen (EO) 365 SE Highland Park Dr, College Place, WA 99324

KAYIGWA, Beatrice Mbatudoe (WMass) 209 Union St, Clinton, MA 01510

KAYNOR, Robert Kirk (NC) 82 Kimberly Dr, Durham, NC 27707

KAZANJIAN, Rosanna Case (Mass) Po Box 1215, Sonoita, AZ 85637

KAZANJIAN JR, Victor Hanford (Mass) Wellesley College, 106 Central St, Wellesley, MA 02481

KE, Jason Chau-sheng (Tai) 37 Jen-Chih St., Nanton City, Taiwan

KEARLEY, David Arthur (Ala) 154 Morgans Steep Rd, Sewanee, TN 37375

KEARNEY, James A (NY) 4410 1/2 Leeland St, Houston, TX 77023

KEARNS, Jada Dart (CFla) 1601 Alafaya Trl, Oviedo, FL 32765

KEATOR, Marnie Knowles (WMass) PO Box 2037, 1 Carley Lane, South Londonderry, VT 05155

KEBBA, Elaine Marguerite Bailey (NC) 6003 Quail Ridge Dr, Greensboro, NC 27455

KEBLESH JR, Joseph (O) 4617 Crestview Dr, Sylvania, OH 43560

KECK, Carolyn (Tenn) Church of the Messiah, 114 N 3rd St, Pulaski, TN 38478

KEEBLE, George McCullough (WTex) 4201 Adina Way, Corpus Christi, TX 78413

KEECH, April Irene (NY)

KEEDY, Susan Shipman (SeFla) 1200 Heron Ave, Miami Springs, FL 33166

KEEFER, John Samuel (Pa) 124 High St, Sharon Hill, PA 19079

KEEHN, Randy (ND)

KEEL, Ronald David (WMo)

KEELER, Charles Bobo (Miss) 925 Stiles St, Clarksdale, MS 38614

KEELER, Donald Franklin (Ia) 121 W Marina Rd, Storm Lake, IA 50588

KEELER, Elizabeth Franklin (Va) 3116 O St NW, Washington, DC 20007

KEELER, John Dowling (At) 225 Brookhaven Cir, Elberton, GA 30635

KEEN JR, Charles Ford (Dal) 206 Mansfield Blvd., Sunnyvale, TX 75182

KEEN, George Comforted (CFla) 1225 W Granada Blvd, Ormond Beach, FL 32174

KEEN, Lois B (Ct) 20 Hudson St, Norwalk, CT 06851

KEENAN, John P (Vt) 73 Oak St, Newport, VT 05855

KEENE, Christopher Paul (Del) Immanuel Church, 100 Harmony St, New Castle, DE 19720

KEENE, Katheryn C (Ct) 92 Bryn Mawr Ave, Auburn, MA 01501

KEENE, R(uth) Claire (ETenn) 4000 Shaw Ferry Rd, Lenoir City, TN 37772

KEENER, Esther Michaella (Pa) P.O. Box 594, 36 Bayview Avenue, Stonington, ME 04681

KEENER JR, Ross Fulton (SVa) 117 Cove Road, Newport News, VA 23608

KEENEY, Albert J (Roch) 4952 Butler Rd, Canandaigua, NY 14424

KEENEY, Randall James (NC) Po Box 1547, Clemmons, NC 27012

KEENEY-MULLIGAN, Gail Donnell (Ct) 12928 N. May Ave Apt 147, Oklahoma City, OK 73120

KEE-REES, Jim L (WTex) 1501 N Glass St, Victoria, TX 77901

KEESE, Peter Gaines (ETenn) 905 Chateaugay Rd., Knoxville, TN 37923

KEESHIN, Joyce Jenkins (SO) St James Episcopal Church, 3207 Montana Ave, Cincinnati, OH 45211

KEESTER, John Carl (Los) 627 Leyden Ln, Claremont, CA 91711

KEGGI, J John (Me) 62 Crest Rd, Wellesley, MA 02482

KEHRER, William Francis (HB)

KEILL, David (Va) 8212 Pilgrim Ter, Richmond, VA 23227

KEIM, Robert Lincoln (ECR) 301 Trinity Ave, Arroyo Grande, CA 93420

KEITH, Briggett J (Nwk) 88 Trinity Pl, Hillsdale, NJ 07642

KEITH, George Arthur (SanD) 4424 44th St Apt 305, San Diego, CA 92115

KEITH JR, John Matthew (Ala) 15001 Searstone Dr Apt 111, Cary, NC 27513

KEITH, Judith Ann (Ga) PO Box 33, 216 Remington Avenue, Thomasville, GA 31799

KEITH III, Stuart Brooks (Colo) Po Box 1591, Edwards, CO 81632

KEITH, Thomas Aaron (NwT)

KEITH, Thomas Frederick (WK) 406 Champions Dr, Rockport, TX 78382

KEITH, William (SC) PO Box 145, Lookout Mountain, TN 37350

KEITH-LUCAS, Diane Dorothea (Mass)

KEITHLY JR, Thomas Graves (Dal) 1612 Kiltartan Dr, Dallas, TX 75228

KEIZER, Garret John (Vt) 770 King George Farm Rd, Sutton, VT 05867

KELAHER, Edward Thomas (WA) 3 Chevy Chase Cir, Chevy Chase, MD 20815

KELB, Sarah Danielle (Mass) Church of the Holy Spirit, 204 Monument Rd, Orleans, MA 02653

KELDERMAN, Kate E (Ct) Kent School, 1 Macedonia Rd, Kent, CT 06757

KELLAM, Patricia Marie (SVa) Po Box 468, Amelia Court House, VA 23002

KELLAWAY, James L. (Ct) 123 Babbitt Hill Road, Pomfret Center, CT 06259

KELLER, Anthony (Los) 808 Foothill Blvd, La Canada, CA 91011

KELLER JR, Charles Edward (Nwk) 711 S Custer Ave, Miles City, MT 59301

KELLER III, Christoph (Ark) 5224 Country Club Blvd, Little Rock, AR 72207

KELLER JR, David Gardiner Ross (WNC) 31 Alexander Farms Lane, Alexander, NC 28701

KELLER, John Speake (O) 20508 Hilliard Blvd, Rocky River, OH 44116

KELLER, Patterson (Oly) Po Box 1808, Cody, WY 82414

KELLER, Susan S (Md) Trinity And Saint Philip's Cathedral, 24 Rector St, Newark, NJ 07102

KELLERMANN, Alan Seth (The Episcopal NCal) 245 S Church St, Grass Valley, CA 95945

KELLETT, James William (SVa) 11233 Tierrasanta Blvd, #40, San Diego, CA 92124

KELLEY, Barbara A (Pa) 159 Windsor Ave, Southampton, PA 18966

KELLEY, Brian Scott (Mass) 47 Concord Sq, Boston, MA 02118

KELLEY, Carlton Franklin (WMich) 57607 M-51 South, Dowagiac, MI 49047

KELLEY, James Thomas (Mont) St John's Episcopal Church, 15 N Idaho St, Butte, MT 59701

KELLEY, Theresa M (Mont) 3350 Keokuk St, Butte, MT 59701

KELLINGTON, Brian T (Spr) 411 Washington St, Pekin, IL 61554

KELLINGTON, Laurie R (Spr) 411 Washington St, Pekin, IL 61554

KELLNER, Andrew Locke (Pa)

KELLOGG, Alicia Sue (Me) 27 Forest Ave, Winthrop, ME 04364

KELLOGG III, Edward Samuel (SanD) 3407 Larga Cir, San Diego, CA 92110

KELLOGG, John A (La) The Episcopal Church of the Incarnation, 103 W Broad St, West Point, MS 39773

KELLUM, Rose Edna (Miss)

KELLY, Arthur James (Pa) 1171 Sandy Ridge Rd, Doylestown, PA 18901

KELLY, Christopher Douglas (SeFla) 110 Selfridge Rd, Gansevoort, NY 12831

KELLY III, Colin Purdie (RG) 4 Inca Ln, Los Alamos, NM 87544

KELLY, Francis J (CFla) 1250 Paige Pl, The Villages, FL 32159

KELLY, James L (Nev) 1075 Oxen Rd, Incline Village, NV 89451

KELLY, Jane Young (SwFla) The Church of the Good Shepherd, 401 W. Henry St., Punta Gorda, FL 33950

KELLY, Karen Joy (SwVa)

KELLY, Kathleen M (SanD) 308 E Acacia Ave, Hemet, CA 92543

KELLY, Linda Louise (NwT) 218 Oak Hill Dr, Kerrville, TX 78028

KELLY, Margaret I (Ida) 1800 N Cole Rd Apt E204, Boise, ID 83704

KELLY, Roger K (Ga) 3101 Waters Ave, Savannah, GA 31404

KELLY, Sarah Elizabeth (O) 9160 Putnam Rd, Pandora, OH 45877

KELLY, Shannon (Mil) 2186 E Main St Apt G, Columbus, OH 43209

KELLY, Steven Joseph Patrick (Mich) 791 Westchester Rd, Grosse Pointe Park, MI 48230

KELLY, Tracey (Va) 400 Fontaine St, Alexandria, VA 22302

KELLY, Verneda Joan (Neb) 1014 N 6th St, Seward, NE 68434

KELM, Mark William (Minn) 109 Lawn Terrace, Golden Valley, MN 55416

KELM, William Ernest (Minn) 1914 Launa Ave, Red Wing, MN 55066

KELMEREIT, Alan Henry (SwFla) 4554 Springview Cir, Labelle, FL 33935

KELSEY, Anne (Mo) Po Box 4740, Saint Louis, MO 63108

KELSEY, Julie Vietor (Ct) 38 Brocketts Point Rd, Branford, CT 06405

KELSEY II, Preston Telford (Ct) Kendal @ Hanover #213, 80 Lyme Rd., Hanover, NH 03755

KELSEY, Stephen Martien (Az) 138 N White Willow Pl, Tucson, AZ 85710

KELSON, Laura Jayne (CGC) 1 Saint Francis Dr, Gulf Breeze, FL 32561

KELTON, Barbara Smoot (Dal) 719 Pampa Street, Sulphur Springs, TX 75482

KEM, Robert Andrew (Ia) 538 NW Scott St, Ankeny, IA 50023

KEM SR, Robert William (Ia) 3013 - 34th Street Place, Des Moines, IA 50310

KEMEZA, Maureen Dallison (Mass) 17 Munroe Pl., Concord, MA 01742

KEMMERER, Stanley C(ourtright) (Ct) Po Box 2025, Burlington, CT 06013

KEMMLER, Richard Sigmund (NY) 1420 Pine Bay Dr, Sarasota, FL 34231

KEMP, Drusilla Rawlings (Ky) Church Of The Advent, 901 Baxter Ave, Louisville, KY 40204

KEMP, Matthew Benjamin (WK) 138 S 8th St, Salina, KS 67401

KEMP, Rowena J (Ct) PO Box 829, Higganum, CT 06441

KEMPF, Barbara Anne (Ind) St Christopher's Episcopal Church, 1402 W Main St, Carmel, IN 46032

KEMPF, Victoria Nystrom Tonk (Colo) 2220 Katahdin Dr, Fort Collins, CO 80525

KEMPSELL JR, Howard Frederic (Va) Post Office Box 2360, Centreville, VA 20122

KEMPSON-THOMPSON, Deborah (Nev) 1776 US Highway 50, Glenbrook, NV 89413

KEMPSTER, Jane Leon (WNC) 10450 Lottsford Rd Apt 355, Mitchellville, MD 20721

KEMPSTER, Patricia Sue (The Episcopal NCal) 2098 Tracy Court, Folsom, CA 95630

KENDALL, Michael Jonah (NC) 403 E Main St, Durham, NC 27701

KENDALL, Michael Samuel (NY) 1047 Amsterdam Ave, New York, NY 10025

KENDALL-SPERRY, David (O) St Paul Episcopal Church, 100 E High St, Mount Vernon, OH 43050

KENDRICK, David Park (WMo) St Johnh's Church, 515 E Division St, Springfield, MO 65803

✠ **KENDRICK**, James Russell (Bp of CGC 2015-) 3557 Hampshire Drive, Birmingham, AL 35223

KENDRICK, William Barton (The Episcopal NCal) 19 Five Iron Ct, Chico, CA 95928

KENNA, Jennifer Anne (CNY) 227 Sherman St, Watertown, NY 13601

KENNARD, Susan Johnson (Tex) 3000 Ave L, Bay City, TX 77414

KENNEDY, (Arthur) Thomas (Ida) 261 Los Lagos, Twin Falls, ID 83301

KENNEDY, David Crichton (SeFla) 7231 Hearth Stone Ave, Boynton Beach, FL 33437

KENNEDY, David Kittle (The Episcopal Church in Haw) 1 Keahole Pl Apt 3409, Honolulu, HI 96825

KENNEDY, Ellen Kathleen (Ct) 243 Harbor St, Branford, CT 06405

KENNEDY, Gary Grant (Kan) 1900 E Front St, Galena, KS 66739

KENNEDY, Hilda Lee (WVa) Po Box 665, Northfork, WV 24868

KENNEDY, Karen (Oly)

KENNEDY, Nan (At) 790 Bellhaven Chase Ct, Mableton, GA 30126

KENNEDY, Thomas B (Mass) 46 Glen Road, Brookline, MA 02445

KENNEDY, Zelda Miller (Los) 2194 Cooley Pl, Pasadena, CA 91104

KENNELLY, Margery (Mass) 379 Hammond St, Chestnut Hill, MA 02467

KENNEY, Christine Swarts (Okla) 505 Fieldstone Dr, Georgetown, TX 78633

KENNEY, Marguerite (SVa) 800 Little John Ct, Virginia Beach, VA 23455

KENNINGTON, Spergeon Albert (CGC) 212 Margaret Dr, Fairhope, AL 36532

KENNY JR, John Roy (Md) 8210 River Crescent Dr, Annapolis, MD 21401

KENNY, Susie Fowler (Los) 1020 N. Brand Blvd., Glendale, CA 91202

KENT, Clifford Eugene (The Episcopal NCal) 5555 Montgomery Dr # 62, Santa Rosa, CA 95409

KENT, David Williamson (Kan) 1900 Spyglass Court, Lawrence, KS 66047

KENT, Stuart Matthews (Dal) 3216 Lakenheath Pl, Dallas, TX 75204

KENWORTHY, Stuart A (WA) 1701 Northt Kent Street, Arlington, VA 22209

KENYI, Alex Lodu (ND) 3725 30th St, San Diego, CA 92104

KENYON, James Howard Benjamin (Alb) 1606 5th St, Rensselaer, NY 12144

KEOUGH, Christopher John (Mil) 313 Lakeview Drive Apt 2, Hartland, WI 53029

KEPLINGER, Stephen James (Az) 2331 E Adams St, Tucson, AZ 85719

KEPPELER, Lisa Leialoha (Pa) 124 S Main Street, Coopersburg, PA 18036

KEPPY, Susan C (WNY) 419 Cherry Ln, Lewiston, NY 14092

KERBEL, Carol Ann (NJ) 232 Camino De La Sierra, Santa Fe, NM 87501

KERBEL, Walter Jarrett (Pa) 1418 E 57th St, Chicago, IL 60637

KERN, David Paul (Nwk) Po Box 1703, North Eastham, MA 02651

KERN, Karl Lee (Be) 182 Gable Dr/, Myerstown, PA 17067

KERN, Roy Allen (CPa) 613 Eschol Ridge Rd, Elliottsburg, PA 17024

KERNER, Sandra B (SVa) 2755 Buckstone Dr, Powhatan, VA 23139

KERR, Catherine D (Pa) Good Shepherd Church, P.O. Box 132, Hilltown, PA 18927

KERR, Denniston Rupert (SwFla) 5609 N Albany Ave, Tampa, FL 33603

KERR, Kyra Anne (RG) P.O. Box 188, Tesuque, NM 87574

KERR, Lauri (CPa) 1435 Scott St, Williamsport, PA 17701

KERR, Linda L (Pa) 1603 Yardley Commons, Yardley, PA 19067

KERR, Richard Samuel (Cal) 442 34th Ave, San Francisco, CA 94121

KERR, Robert Anthony (Mich) 23851 Goddard Rd, Taylor, MI 48180

KERR JR, Thomas Albert (Del) 111 Canterbury Dr, Wilmington, DE 19803

KERR, W(illiam) Verdery (NC) Po Box 1624, Charlotte, NC 28207

KERRICK, Michael W (The Episcopal NCal) 2612 Colin Rd, Placerville, CA 95667

KERSCHEN, Charles Thomas (WK) 520 East Ave S, Lyons, KS 67554

KERTLAND, Gail Ellen (LI) 36 Cathedral Ave, Garden City, NY

KESHGEGIAN, Flora A. (Pa) 6582 Lucas Ave Apt 3, Oakland, CA 94611

KESLER, Walter Wilson (FtW) 3932 Anewby Way, Fort Worth, TX 76133

KESSEL-HANNA, Kay Lynn (Oly) 11527 9th Ave NE, Seattle, WA 98125

KESSELUS, Ken (Tex) 1301 Church St., Bastrop, TX 78602

KESSLER, Edward Scharps (Pa) 44 Hinde Street, Sheffield, S4 8HJ, Great Britain (UK)

KESSLER, Judith Maier (CNY) 17 Elizabeth St, Binghamton, NY 13901

KESTER, Martha Ruth (Ia) 1916 Merklin Way, Des Moines, IA 50310

KETNER, Thomas Howard (Wyo) 411 E Center St, Douglas, WY 82633

KETTLEWELL, Charles G (Ark) 13456 Victory Gallop Way, Gainesville, VA 20155

KETTLEWELL, John Michael (Alb) 110 Monument Dr, Schuylerville, NY 12871

KETTLEWELL, Paula Swaebe (Va) 705 Wilder Dr, Charlottesville, VA 22901

KEUCHER, Gerald (LI) 1 Pendleton Pl, Staten Island, NY 10301

KEVERN, John R (WVa) C/O Trinity Epis Church, PO Box P, Moundsville, WV 26041

KEW, W(illiam) Richard (Tenn) 41 Way Lane, Waterbeach, CAMBRIDGE CB25 9NQ, Great Britain (UK)

KEY, Nancy Anne (Episcopal SJ) PO Box 7446, Visalia, CA 93290

KEY, Sanford Allen (NY) St. Luke's Church, POB 94, Somers, NY 10589

KEYDEL JR, John F (Mich) 20410 Ronsdale Dr, Beverly Hills, MI 48025

KEYES, Charles Don (NY) 5801 Hampton St, Pittsburgh, PA 15206

KEYES, John Irvin (SD) 513 Douglas Ave, Yankton, SD 57078

KEYES, Samuel N (Ala)

KEYS, Joel Thompson (Tenn) PO Box 24183, Saint Simons Island, GA 31522

KEYSE, Andrew C. (Ala) 262 Creekside Dr, Florence, AL 35630

✠ **KEYSER**, Charles Lovett (Ret Bp Suffr of Armed Forces 2000-) 4719 Ivanhoe Rd, Jacksonville, FL 32210

KEYWORTH, Gill (Tex) 1215 Ripple Creek Dr, Houston, TX 77057

KEZAR, Dennis Dean (SwFla) 4030 Manatee Ave W, Bradenton, FL 34205

KHALIL, Adeeb Mikhail (WVa) 127 Brookwood Ln, Beckley, WV 25801

KHAMIN, Alexei (Nwk) All Saints Episcopal Church, 230 E. 60th St., New York, NY 10022

KHOO, Oon-Chor (Tex) 3203 W Alabama St, Houston, TX 77098

KIBLER SR, Bryant C (Lex) 1013 Marco Ln, 607 Highway 1746, Lexington, KY 40509

KIBLINGER, Charles Edward (Va) 651 Rivendell Blvd, Osprey, FL 34229

KIDD, Paul David (At) 161 Long Lake Rd, Hawthorne, FL 32640

KIDD, Reggie M (CFla)

KIDD, Scott Austin (At) 20 Whisperwood Way, Cleveland, GA 30528

KIDD, Stephen Willis (Miss) 11322 E Taylor Rd, Gulfport, MS 39503

KIDDER, Ann (O) PO Box 519, Gates Mills, OH 44040

KIDDER, Frederick Elwyn (PR)

KIEFER, Carol (Spok) 428 King St, Wenatchee, WA 98801

KIENZLE, Edward Charles (Mass) 165 Pleasant St Apt 303, Cambridge, MA 02139

KIESCHNICK, Frances Hall (Cal) 134 La Goma St, Mill Valley, CA 94941

KIESSLING, Donna Jean (Del) 22 N. Union Street, Smyrna, DE 19977

KIKER, Norman Wesley (Okla) 5705 Earl Dr, Shawnee, OK 74804

KILBOURN, Lauren Michelle (NC) 221Union St, Cary, NC 27511

KILBOURN, Thomas Lewis (Ct) 51 Paddy Hollow Rd, Bethlehem, CT 06751

KILBOURN-HUEY, Mary Esther (Lex) 310 Edgemont Rd, Maysville, KY 41056

KILBY, John Irvine (Ia) 4903 California St Apt 5, Omaha, NE 68132

KILFOYLE, J(ohn) Richard (WMass) 240 Belmont St Apt 103, Worcester, MA 01604

KILGORE, John William (Mo) 320 Union Blvd, Saint Louis, MO 63108

KILIAN, Joan M (Ga) 9003 Oakfield Dr, Statesboro, GA 30461

KILLEEN, David Charles (Fla) St. John's Episcopal Church, 211 North Monroe St., Tallahassee, FL 32301

KILLIAN, David Allen (Mass) 882 Watertown St, West Newton, MA 02465

KILLIAN, Kathleen Erin (SeFla) 315 Main St, Southwest Harbor, ME 04679

KILLINGSTAD, Mary Louise (Spok) 502 Hillside Dr, Yakima, WA 98903

KIM, Andrew (Los) 13091 Galway St, Garden Grove, CA 92844

KIM, John D (Los) St James Episcopal Church, 3903 Wilshire Blvd, Los Angeles, CA 90010

KIM, John Jong-Kun (Pa) 3204 Ashy Way, Drexel Hill, PA 19026

KIM, Jonathan Jang-Ho (WNY) Kumi Box 1039, Kumi Kyungbuk, 730-600, Korea (South)

KIM, Richard (Mich) 19983 E Doyle Pl, Grosse Pointe, MI 48236

KIM, Stephen Yongchul (Los) 45267 Sancroft Ave, Lancaster, CA 93535

KIM, Yein Esther (Los)

KIM, Yong Gul (Ninian) (LI) 2235 36th St, Astoria, NY 11105

KIMBALL, Anne Bogardus (Ct) 14890 David Drive, Fort Myers, FL 33908

KIMBALL JR, George Allen (Mil) 320 E Pleasant St Unit 301, Oconomowoc, WI 53066

KIMBALL, Jennifer W (Va) 125 Beverly Rd, Ashland, VA 23005

KIMBALL, John C (Pa) 202 Park Ave, Collegeville, PA 19426

KIMBLE, Shell Teyssier (WA) 5316 Taylor Rd, Riverdale, MD 20737

KIMBROUGH, Brendan Lee (Dal) 2700 Arbor Ct, Richardson, TX 75082

KIMBROUGH, Timothy Edward (Tenn) 435 Patina Circle, Nashville, TN 37209

KIMES, Nicki Sagendorf (Ct) 134 East Ave, New Canaan, CT 06840

KIMMEY, Jimmye Elizabeth (NY) 928 W Hickory St, Denton, TX 76201

KIMMICK, Donald William (Nwk) 9625 Miranda Dr, Raleigh, NC 27617

KIMURA, Gregory William Mitamura (Los) 9900 Toakee Cir, Eagle River, AK 99577

KIN, Nancy Elizabeth (Alb) 1249 3rd St, Rensselaer, NY 12144

KINARD III, George Oscar (SeFla)

KINCAID III, S Thomas (Dal) 708 Harrison St, La Porte, IN 46350

KINDEL JR, William H (Colo) 802 Navajo Avenue, Fort Morgan, CO 80701

KINDERGAN, Walter Bradford (CGC) 99 Firestone Blvd., Pensacola, FL 32503

KING, Allan B (Mass) 222 Sayre Drive, Princeton, NJ 08540

KING, Benjamin John (Mass) School of Theology University of the South, 335 Tennessee Ave., Sewanee, TN 37383

KING JR, Charles Baldwin (Alb) 5 Cottonwood Pl, Colonie, NY 12205

KING, Charles Malcolm (SD) 15A Church St, New Milford, CT 06776

KING, Chester W (RG) 10033 Cork Dr, El Paso, TX 79925

KING, Darlene Dawn (EMich) 3201 Gratiot Ave, Port Huron, MI 48060

KING JR, Earle Cochran (WNY) 2595 Baseline Rd, Grand Island, NY 14072

KING, Edward Albert (WMass) 3930 River Rd Unit 56, East China, MI 48054

KING, Francis Marion Covington (WNC) 140 Saint Marys Church Rd, Morganton, NC 28655

KING JR, Frank Hiram (NI) 904 N Fenton Rd, Marion, IN 46952

KING, Frank Walter (WNC) 4425 Huntington Dr, Gastonia, NC 28056

KING, Gayle (Colo) 1347 Allen Ave, Erie, CO 80516

KING, Giovan Venable (The Episcopal Church in Haw) St Christopher Church, PO Box 456, Kailau, HI 96734

KING, Janet Gay Felland (Ida) 678 E 400 N, Rupert, ID 83350

KING, John Christopher (ECR) 220 W Penn St, Long Beach, NY 11561

KING, Jonathan LeRoy (NY) 340 Godwin Ave, Ridgewood, NJ 07450

KING, Joseph Willett (Az) 7735 N Via Laguna Niguel, Tucson, AZ 85743

KING, Karen Alicia (Chi) 125 E 26th St, Chicago, IL 60616

KING, Karen Gail (Mont) P.O. Box 158, Troy, MT 59935

KING, Karen L (Ind) 3401 Lindel Ln, Indianapolis, IN 46268

KING, Kathryn Louise (Nwk) 28 Ralph St, Bergenfield, NJ 07621

KING JR, Kenneth Vernon (EO) 702 Grant Street, Summit, MS 39666

KING, Leslie Anne (The Episcopal NCal) 55 Maria Dr Ste 837, Petaluma, CA 94954

KING, Leyla (ETenn) 1607 W 43rd St, Chattanooga, TN 37409

KING, Margaret Creed (Fla) 704 Vauxhall Dr, Nashville, TN 37221

KING, Robert Andrew (Ky) 146 State St Unit 101, Clayton, NY 13624

KING, Steven John (Kan) 12251 Antioch Rd, Overland Park, KS 66213

KING, Tom Earl (NC) 2725 SE 39th ST, MOORE, OK 73160

KING, William Michael (Ala) 905 Castlemaine Drive, Birmingham, AL 35226

KINGDON, Arthur M (Vt) 334 Oak Grove Rd, Vassalboro, ME 04989

KINGMAN, Donna Watkins (WMass) 3 Newington Ln, Worcester, MA 01609

KINGMAN, Perry Alden (WMass) 3 Newington Ln, Worcester, MA 01609

KINGSLEY, Joshua D (Ore) 11229 NE Prescott St, Portland, OR 97220

KINGSLEY, Myra Jessica (Az) 100 W Roosevelt St, Phoenix, AZ 85003

KINGSLEY MURRAY, Miguel (DR (DomRep)) Dr Zafra# 3, Puerto Plata, Dominican Republic

KINGSLIGHT, Kathleen Anne (Oly) 700 Callahan Dr, Bremerton, WA 98310

KINGSTON, Louise Lauck (NJ) 85 Westcott Rd, Princeton, NJ 08540

KINMAN, Mike (Mo) 6209 Pershing Ave, Saint Louis, MO 63130

KINMAN, Thomas David (Az) PO Box 40126, Tucson, AZ 85717

KINNER, Heidi (Mont) St. Peters Episcopal Cathedral, 511 N. Park Avenue, Helena, MT 59601

KINNEY, Elise (Mass)

KINNEY, Eugenia Wood (Cal) 1746 29th Ave, San Francisco, CA 94122

KINNEY, Kathleen (Oly) 610-906-9690, Eastsound, WA 98245

KINNEY, Robert Sturgis (Okla) 5231 Wedgefield Rd, Granbury, TX 76049

KINNEY, Stephen W (Tex) 2306 Cypress Pt W, Austin, TX 78746

KINSER, David D (NC) St Paul's Episcopal Church, 520 Summit St, Winston Salem, NC 27101

KINSEY, Kevin Lee (Me) 650 Main St Ste A, Caribou, ME 04736

KINSEY, Theron Harvey (Cal) 917 Avis Dr, El Cerrito, CA 94530

KINSEY, Thomas Burton (SO) 5004 Upton Ave S, Minneapolis, MN 55410

KINSOLVING, John Armistead (RG) 107 Washington Ave, Santa Fe, NM 87501

KINYON, Brice Wayne (USC) 1900 Woodvalley Drive, Columbia, SC 29212

KIRBY, Elisa Mabley (EC) 320 Pollock St, New Bern, NC 28560

KIRBY, Erin Colleen (FdL) 5629 Old Garden Road, 304, Wilmington, NC 28403

KIRBY, H(arry) Scott (Eau) 1712 Lehman St., Eau Claire, WI 54701

KIRBY, Jacquelyn Walsh (RI) PO Box 317, Jamestown, RI 02835

KIRBY, Kelly Ellen (Ky) 330 N Hubbards Ln, Louisville, KY 40207

KIRBY, Richard Allen (Neb)

KIRBY, Whitney Blythe (Az) 100 W. Roosevelt, Phoenix, AZ 85003

KIRCHER, Kathleen L (SwFla) 1741 Winding Oaks Way, Naples, FL 34109

KIRCHHOFFER, Jim (Cal) 922 Valle Vista Ave, Vallejo, CA 94590

KIRCHMIER, Anne Ruth (SVa) 15446 Warwick Blvd, Newport News, VA 23608

KIRK, Deborah (WA) 14300 Saint Thomas Church Rd, Upper Marlboro, MD 20772

KIRK, Jeffrey Malcolm (NJ) 102 Pearlcroft Rd, Cherry Hill, NJ 08034

KIRK, Patricia Lanier (USC)

KIRK, Richard Joseph (Pa) 189 Kendal Dr, Kennett Square, PA 19348

KIRK, Virginia Adele (Pa) 354 Heathcliffe Rd, Huntingdon Valley, PA 19006

KIRKALDY, David (Tex) 612 Duroux Rd, La Marque, TX 77568

KIRKHAM II, Hall (Mass) 112 Randolph Avenue, Milton, MA 02186

KIRKING, Kerry Clifton (Spok) 6533 Seaview Ave. NW, 505A, Seattle, WA 98117

KIRKLEY, John Lawrence (Cal) 4616 California St, San Francisco, CA 94118

KIRKMAN, John Raymond (WMich) 4713 Rockvalley Dr NE, Grand Rapids, MI 49525

KIRK-NORRIS, Barbara H (NwT) PO Box 2949, Big Spring, TX 79721

KIRKPATRICK, Daisy (CNY)

KIRKPATRICK, Frank Gloyd (Ct) 154 Clearfield, Wethersfield, CT 06109

KIRKPATRICK, Martha G (Del) St Barnabas Church, 2800 Duncan Rd, Wilmington, DE 19808

KIRKPATRICK, Nathan Elliott (NC) 8410 Merin Rd, Chapel Hill, NC 27516

KIRKPATRICK, Rebecca Blair (Oly) 111 NE 80th St, Seattle, WA 98115

KIRKPATRICK JR, Robert Frederick (Lex) 9801 Germantown Pike, Apt 115, Lafayette Hill, PA 19444

KISNER, Mary Elizabeth (CPa) 712 E 16th St, Berwick, PA 18603

KISS, Margaret Mary (Mil) 2965 S Delaware Ave Apt 1, Milwaukee, WI 53207

KISSAM, Todd William (Eas) 105 Church Lane, Church Hill, MD 21623

KISSINGER, Debra Jean (Ind) 1100 W. 42nd St., Indianapolis, IN 46208

KITAGAWA, Chisato (WMass) 5 Hickory Ln, Amherst, MA 01002

KITAGAWA, John Elliott (Az) 1700 E Chula Vista Rd, Tucson, AZ 85718

KITAYAMA, Scott D (WTex)

KITCH, Anne E (Be) 333 Wyandotte St, Bethlehem, PA 18015

KITCH, Sarah U (Los) 280 Royal Ave, Simi Valley, CA 93065

KITT, Michael (Chi) 523 Courtland Ave, Park Ridge, IL 60068

KITTELSON, Alan Leslie (Vt) 6 Park St, Vergennes, VT 05491

KITTREDGE, Cynthia Briggs (Tex) Seminary of the Southwest, 501 East 32nd Street, Austin, TX 78705

KITTS, Joseph (Eur) Windyridge, Cottage Lane, Saint Martins, Oswestry, Shropshire, SY11 3BL, Great Britain (UK)

KLAAS III, Anthony Rudolph (La) 4 Yacht Club Dr Apt 36, Daphne, AL 36526

KLAM, Warren Peter (Va)

KLEE, George M (Ark) 1516 Willow St., Blytheville, AR 72315

KLEFFMAN, Todd Aaron (Ind) 5757 Rosslyn Ave, Indianapolis, IN 46220

KLEIN, Craig Alan (U) 107 S Curry St, West Plains, MO 65775

KLEIN, Everett H. (WMich) 7521 Anthony St, Whitehall, MI 49461

KLEIN, John Conrad (Mich) 231 E Grand Blvd, Detroit, MI 48207

KLEIN, John Harvey (SeFla) 3586 Woods Walk Blvd, Lake Worth, FL 33467

KLEIN, John William (Md) 601 Rustic St, Opelika, AL 36801

KLEIN, Susan Webster (Los) 9606 Oakmore Rd, Los Angeles, CA 90035

KLEIN-LARSEN, Martha Susan (Ct) 117 Oenoke Ridge, New Canaa, CT 06840

KLEMMT, Pierce Wittfield (Va) 118 N Washington St, Alexandria, VA 22314

KLEVEN, Terence James (Ia) 1334 N. Prairie St., Pella, IA 50219

KLICKMAN, John Michael (Dal) 4017 Hedgerow Dr, Plano, TX 75024

KLIMAS, Marcella Louise (CPa) 4355 Georgetown Square Apt 141, Atlanta, GA 30338

KLINE, Andrew Ferguson (Colo) 5 Brookside Dr, Greenwood Village, CO 80121

KLINE, John William (NwPa) 825 Matilda Dr, Plano, TX 75025

KLINE, Nancy Wade (CFla) St. Barnabas Episcopal Church, 319 W. Wisconsin Ave., Deland, FL 32720

KLINE, Timothy Eads (WK) 50 Oyster Bay Dr, Graford, TX 76449

KLINE-MORTIMER, Sandra L (Md)

KLINGELHOFER, Stephan Ernest (Eas) 545 Fey Rd # 21620-, Chestertown, MD 21620

KLINGENBERG, Ralph Gerard (SeFla) 1400 Riverside Dr, Coral Springs, FL 33071

KLINGENSMITH, Roxanne Elizabeth Pearson (Mont) 1715 South Black, Bozeman, MT 59715

KLITZKE, Dale Edward (USC) 1816 Crestwood Ln, Menomonie, WI 54751

KLITZKE, Paul Kenneth (Dal) 8787 Greenville Avenue, Dallas, TX 75243

KLOPFENSTEIN, Timothy David (CGC) 106 Galaxy Ave, Bonaire, GA 31005

KLOTS, Stephen Barrett (Ct) 40 Bulls Bridge Rd, South Kent, CT 06785

KLOZA, Wanda Margaret (CPa) 101 Pine St, Harrisburg, PA 17101

✠ **KLUSMEYER**, William Michie (Bp of WVa 2001-) 1 Roller Rd, Charleston, WV 25314

KLUTTERMAN, David Lee (FdL) 330 McClellan, Wausau, WI 54401

Clergy List

KNAPICK, Veronica Helene (Ak) 6816 E. Riverwood Cir, Palmer, AK 99645

KNAPP, Carl Jude (Pa) 584 Fairway Ter, Philadelphia, PA 19128

KNAPP, Clayton L (WMass) 3003 Dick Wilson Dr., Sarasota, FL 34240

KNAPP, Cynthia Clark (Ct) 43 Twin Oak Ln, Wilton, CT 06897

KNAPP, Donald Hubert (Be) 162 Springhouse Rd, Allentown, PA 18104

KNAPP, Gretchen Bower (Mont) Po Box 794, Hilger, MT 59451

KNAPP, Ronald David (Eas) 11240 Gail Dr, Princess Anne, MD 21853

KNAUFF, Elizabeth Ann (Ct) 155 Wyllys St, Hartford, CT 06106

KNAUP JR, Daniel Joseph (O) 2341 Ardleigh Drive, Cleveland Heights, OH 44106

KNEE, Jacob S (Mont) St Stephen's Episcopal Ch, 1241 Crawford Dr, Billings, MT 59102

KNEIPP, Lee Benson (WTenn) Po Box 3874, Pineville, LA 71361

KNIGHT, Arthur James (NJ) 3 Blueberry Rd, Shamong, NJ 08088

KNIGHT, David Hathaway (Va) 6005 S Crestwood Ave, Richmond, VA 23226

KNIGHT, Frank Lauchlan (NY) 3859 Dogwood Trl, Allentown, PA 18103

KNIGHT IV, Frank Michael (Pa) 803 Montbard Dr, West Chester, PA 19382

KNIGHT, Harold Stanley (Az) 145 N Fraser Dr, Mesa, AZ 85203

KNIGHT, Hollinshead T (Ore) 485 Bridgeway Apt 1, Sausalito, CA 94965

KNIGHT, James D (Miss) 1 Harbourside Dr Apt 3502, Delray Beach, FL 33483

KNIGHT, Joseph Sturdevant (CGC) 436 Lapsley Street, Selma, AL 36701

KNIGHT, Kimberly Adonna (La) 200 Chapel Crk Apt 116, Mandeville, LA 70471

KNIGHT, Kirkland Wallace (La) 3200 Woodland Ridge Blvd, Baton Rouge, LA 70816

KNIGHT, Patricia Cullum (NwT) 1601 S Georgia St, Amarillo, TX 79102

KNIGHT, Samuel Theodore (Mich) 28725 Sunset Boulevard West, Lathrup Village, MI 48076

KNIGHT II, Steve (SanD) 403 Shalimar Drive, Prescott, AZ 86303

KNIGHT, Theolinda Lenore Johnson (Cal) 806 Jones St, Berkeley, CA 94710

KNIGHT, W(illiam) Allan (Md) 58 Hanson Rd, Chester, NH 03036

KNISELY, Harry Lee (Ct) 365 Hickory Rd, Carlisle, PA 17015

✠ KNISELY JR, W Nicholas (Bp of RI 2012-) Episcopal Diocese of Rhode Island, 275 N Main St, Providence, RI 02903

KNOCKEL, Wayne (Mich) 546 W South St, Mason, MI 48854

KNOLL-WILLIAMS, Sarah Jacqueline (Tex) 4120 Clinton Pkwy, Lawrence, KS 66047

KNOTT, Joseph Lee (Ala) 5528 - 11th Court South, Birmingham, AL 35222

KNOTTS, Harold Wayne (Mich) 26431 W Chicago, Redford, MI 48239

KNOUSE, Amanda Rue (Va) 9668 Maidstone Rd, Delaplane, VA 20144

KNOWLES II, Harold Frank (Los) 623 El Centro St, South Pasadena, CA 91030

KNOWLES, Melody D (Chi) 3737 Seminary Rd, Alexandria, VA 22304

KNOWLES, Roberta (Tex) 2704 Rossedale Street, Houston, TX 77004

KNOWLES, Walter Roy (Oly) 11020 Ne 64th St, Kirkland, WA 98033

KNOWLTON, Elizabeth Clemmer (WTex) 315 E Pecan St, San Antonio, TX 78205

KNOX, David Paul (CFla) 216 Sheridan Ave, Longwood, FL 32750

KNOX, Floyd Leonard (La) 10587 Birchwood Dr, Baton Rouge, LA 70807

KNOX, Jannet Marie (Mont) 59 Mill Creek Rd # 463, Sheridan, MT 59749

KNOX, Jeffrey Donald (CNY) 1755 State Route 48, Fulton, NY 13069

KNOX, John Michael (WK) 16019 W 80th St, Lenexa, KS 66219

KNOX, Regina Gilmartin (Me) 143 State St, Portland, ME 04101

✠ KNUDSEN, Chilton Richardson (Ret Bp of Me 2008-, Asst Bp of Md 2015-) 940 Washington St, Bath, ME 04530

KNUDSON, James C (Mass) 85 Grozier Rd, Cambridge, MA 02138

KNUDSON, Kay Francis (Neb) 1304 Wade St, Lexington, NE 68850

KNUDSON, Richard Lewis (Alb) 9 Saint James Pl Apt 207, Oneonta, NY 13820

KNUTSEN, James Kenyon (The Episcopal NCal) P.O. Box 3601, Santa Rosa, CA 95402

KNUTSON, Randy A (The Episcopal NCal) 1055 S Lower Sacramento Rd, Lodi, CA 95242

KOCH, Eunice Jane (Minn) Po Box 513, Ely, MN 55731

KOCH JR, John Dunbar (Ky) Saint Francis In The Fields, PO Box 225, Harrods Creek, KY 40027

KOCH, W Christian (RG) P.O. Box 1614, Blue Hill, ME 04614

KOCHENBURGER, Philip Alan (CFla) 67 CSH Chaplain, Unit 26610 Box 64, APO, AE, 09244

KOCHTITZKY, Rodney Morse (Tenn) The Pastoral Center for Healing, 1024 Noelton Ave, Nashville, TN 37204

KODERA, T(akashi) James (Mass) 212 Old Lancaster Rd, Sudbury, MA 01776

KOEHLER, Anne E (Nwk) PO Box 611, East Orleans, MA 02643

KOEHLER, Michael Alban Collins (WTex) 6000 FM 3237 Unit A, Wimberley, TX 78676

KOEHLER III, Norman Elias (Pgh) 408 Forest Highlands Dr, Pittsburgh, PA 15238

KOEHLER, Robert Brien (Spr) 19206 Boca del Mar, San Antonio, TX 78258

KOELLIKER, Karulynn Travis (Ga)

KOELLN, Theodore Frank (CFla) 505 Ne 1st Ave, Mulberry, FL 33860

KOENIG, Diane L (Chi) 86 Pomeroy Ave # 2, Crystal Lake, IL 60014

KOENIG, John Thomas (NJ) 17546 Drayton Hall Way, San Diego, CA 92128

KOENIGER, Margaret Smithers (Nwk) 574 Ridgewood Rd, Maplewood, NJ 07040

KOEPKE, Jack (SO) 412 Sycamore Street, Cincinnati, OH 45202

KOERNER, Travers (NY) 314 Lincoln Ave, Rockville, MD 20850

KOFFRON-EISEN, Elizabeth Mary (Ia) 945 Applewood Ct #1, Coralville, IA 52241

KOH, Aidan Youngduk (Los) 4344 Lemp Ave, Studio City, CA 91604

KOHLBECKER, Eugene Edmund (NI) 12 Clearview Ave, Hilton, NY 14468

KOHLMEIER, Susan C (Roch) 1017 Silvercrest Dr, Webster, NY 14580

KOHN, George Frederick (ECR) 980 W Franklin St, Monterey, CA 93940

KOHN-PERRY, Ellen Marie (Nwk)

KOLANOWSKI, Ronald James (Ct) St. James Episcopal Church, 95 Route 2A, Preston, CT 06365

KOLB, Jerry Warren (WMo) 8256 Outlook Lane, Prairie Village, KS 66208

KOLB, William A (WTenn) 531 S. Prescott St, Memphis, TN 38111

KOLBET, Paul Robert (Oly) 8 Ivy Cir., Wellesley, MA 02482

KOLLIN, Harriet (Pa) 3738 W Country Club Rd, Philadelphia, PA 19131

KOLLIN JR, James T. (NJ) 120 Sussex St Apt 1b, Hackensack, NJ 07601

KOMSTEDT JR, William Andrew (FtW) 1625 Hermosa Ave Unit 33, Grand Junction, CO 81506

KONDRATH, William Michael (Mass) 25 Richards Ave, Sharon, MA 02067

✠ KONIECZNY, Edward Joseph (Bp of Okla 2007-) Episcopal Diocese of Oklahoma, 924 N Robinson Ave, Oklahoma City, OK 73102

KOONCE, Kelly Montgomery (Tex) 6625 Whitemarsh Valley Walk, Austin, TX 78746

KOONS, Zachary Gunnar (Tex) 1420 E Palm Valley Blvd, Round Rock, TX 78664

KOOPERKAMP, Earl (Vt) Church Of The Good Shepherd, 39 Washington St, Barre, VT 05641

KOOPERKAMP, Sarah Jennifer (LI) 612 Greenwood Ave, Brooklyn, NY 11218

KOOR, Margaret Platt (SwFla) 4017 Heaton Ter, North Port, FL 34286

KOPERA, Dorothy Jean (NMich) 214 E Avenue A, Newberry, MI 49868

KOPPEL, Mary E (Okla) PO Box 5176, Austin, TX 78763

KOPREN, Kristin C (NY) Saint Hilda'S And Saint Hugh'S School, 619 W 114th St, New York, NY 10025

KORATHU, Anna Maria (Oly) 19229 65th Place Northeast, Seattle, WA 98155

KORIENEK, Martha Susan (Cal) 415 El Camino Real, Burlingame, CA 94010

KORN, Elizabeth Louise (NMich) N2809 River Dr, Wallace, MI 49893

KORTE, Mary Jane (Kan) Saint Stephen's Church, 7404 E Killarney Pl, Wichita, KS 67206

KOSHNICK, Loxley Jean (Minn) PO Box 868, Detroit Lakes, MN 56502

KOSKELA, David Michael (Colo) 5433 South Buckskin Pass, Colorado Springs, CO 80917

KOSKELA, Robert Norman (Mil) 1260 Deming Way Apt 310, Madison, WI 53717

KOSKELA, Ruth Alma (Mil) 1260 Deming Way Apt 310, Madison, WI 53717

KOSKI, Hope Gwendlyn Phillips (LI) 4526 Nw 34th Dr, Gainesville, FL 32605

KOSSLER, Robert Joseph (Cal)

KOSTAS, George Agapios (WVa) 133 Riverside Dr, Logan, WV 25601

KOSTIC, Elizabeth M (Pa) 2523 E Madison St, Philadelphia, PA 19134

KOTRC, Ronald Fred (Ak) 5129 N. Tongass Hy, Ketchikan, AK 99901

KOTUBY, Janice (U) 7486 Union Park Ave, Midvale, UT 84047

KOULOURIS, Beulah Atkins Cratch (Mass) 12 Sunrise Ave, Plymouth, MA 02360

KOUMRIAN, Paul Sprower (RI) PO Box 294, Tiverton, RI 02878

KOUNTZ, Peter James (Pa)

KOUNTZE, Louise (WMich) 255 Ivanhoe Street, Denver, CO 80220

KOVACH, Gary David (WNC) 19 Old Youngs Cove Rd, Candler, NC 28715

KOVIC, Fenton Hubert (Tex) 821 Pam Dr, Tyler, TX 75703

KOVITCH, Joseph Gerard (SO) PO Box 176, Westerville, OH 43086

KOVOOR, George Iype (Ct) 400 Humphrey St, New Haven, CT 06511

KOWALEWSKI, Mark Robert (Los) 841 Kodak Dr., Los Angeles, CA 90026

KOWALEWSKI, Paul James (Los) 54280 Avenida Montezuma, La Quinta, CA 92253

KOWALSKI, James August (NY) The Cathedral Church of Saint John the Divine, 1047 Amsterdam Ave, New York, NY 10025

KOWALSKI, Mark Joseph (Chi) St Davids, 701 N Randall Rd, Aurora, IL 60506

KOWALSKI, Ronald Chester (SwFla) 7349 Ulmerton Rd, Lot# 1398 Balboa St., Largo, FL 33771

KOWALSKI, Vesta Marie (Me)

KOZAK, Jan (EO) PO Box 214, Madras, OR 97741

KOZIELEC, Mark A (Mo) Saint Mark's Church, 4714 Clifton Ave, Saint Louis, MO 63109

KOZIKOWSKI, Mary Carol (NMich) 922 10th Ave, Menominee, MI 49858

KOZLOWSKI, Joseph Felix (WNY)

KOZLOWSKI, Matthew William (SeFla) 623 SE Ocean Blvd, Stuart, FL 34994

KOZUSZEK, Jeffrey Frank (Spr) 512 W Main St, Salem, IL 62881

KRADEL, Adam P (Pa) 311 S Orange St, Media, PA 19063

KRAEMER, C Jeff (Dal) 760 Burchart Dr, ., Prosper, TX 75078

KRAFT, Carol Joyce (Chi) 124 West Prairie Street, Wheaton, IL 60187

KRAFT, Harry Bishop (LI) 17117 108th Ave, Jamaica, NY 11433

KRAKOWSKY, Lisa Posey (NY) 487 Hudson St, New York, NY 10014

KRAMER, Caroline Anne (SwVa)

KRAMER, Charles Edward (NY) 4536 Albany Post Rd, Hyde Park, NY 12538

KRAMER, Frederick F. (Ia) 1304 S 4th Ave W, Newton, IA 50208

KRAMER, Linda Jean (SD) 23120 S Rochford Rd, Hill City, SD 57745

KRANTZ, Jeffrey Hoyt (LI) 43 Cedar Shore Dr, Massapequa, NY 11758

KRANTZ, Kristin N (Md) 1307 N Main St, Mount Airy, MD 21771

KRANTZ, Saralouise Camlin (LI) 555Advent Street, Westbury, NY 11590

KRAPF, Richard D (Roch) 15 Granger Street, Canandaigua, NY 14424

KRASINSKI, Joseph Alexander (Ct) 2 Cannondale Dr, Danbury, CT 06810

KRATOVIL, Mildred Elsie Ida Johanna (Md) 204 West St Apt A4, Williamsburg, IA 52361

KRAUS, Susan (Me) 65 Eddy Rd, Edgecomb, ME 04556

KRAUSE, David (Dal) 2022 Saturn Rd, Garland, TX 75041

KRAUSE, Janice Auch (Dal) 10043 Boyton Canyon, Frisco, TX 75035

KRAUSS, Harry Edward (NY) 2 West 90th St Apt 5B, New York, NY 10024

KREAMER, Martha Hutchison (CGC) Po Box 57, Lillian, AL 36549

KREFT, Armand John (Mass) 1717 E. Vista Chino, #A7-266, Palm Springs, CA 92262

KREITLER, Peter Gwillim (Los) 16492 El Hito Ct, Pacific Palisades, CA 90272

KREJCI, Richard Scott (Va) 346 Laurel Farms Ln, Urbanna, VA 23175

KRELL, Thomas William (Mich) 16200 W 12 Mile Rd, Southfield, MI 48076

KRELLER, Daniel Ward (Nwk) 56 Sheridan Ave, Ho Ho Kus, NJ 07423

KRESS, Raymond Paul (SwFla) 6530 Manila Palm Way, Apollo Beach, FL 33572

KREUTZER, Michael Alan (SO) 7 Lonsdale Avenue, Dayton, OH 45419

KREYMER, Donald Neal (FtW) 423 East Calle Bonita, Santa Maria, CA 93455

KRICKBAUM, Donald William (SeFla) 1008 Skyline Trail, Harpers Ferry, WV 25425

KRIEGER, Frederick Gordon (SO) 5538 Sebastian Place, Halifax, B3K 2K6, Canada

KRIEGER, Kristin Sherry (NJ) 318 Elton Ln., Galloway, NJ 08205

KRIEGER, Walter Lowell (Be) Fifth & Court, Reading, PA 19603

KRISS, Gary W. (Alb) PO Box 26, Cambridge, NY 12816

KROH, Timothy Edward (Md)

KROLL, Brenda M (Dal) 1402 Pagosa Trl, Carrollton, TX 75007

KROM, Judith Sue (NJ) 410 S Atlantic Ave, Beach Haven, NJ 08008

KROMHOUT, Linda Adams (CFla) 2104 Golden Arm Rd, Deltona, FL 32738

KROOHS, Kenneth (NC) 700 Sunset Drive, High Point, NC 27262

KROOHS, Mary (NC) 1700 Queen St, Winston Salem, NC 27103

✠ **KROTZ**, James Edward (Ret Bp of Neb 2003-) 3484 520th Road, Rushville, NE 69360

KRUEGER, Albert Peter (Ore) 1926 W Burnside St Unit 909, Portland, OR 97209

KRUEGER, James Gordon (Alb) 55 Lake Delaware Dr, Delhi, NY 13753

KRUGER, Ann Dufford (CFla) 167 Clear Lake Cir, Sanford, FL 32773

KRUGER, Matthew Carl (Mass) 81 Elm St, Concord, MA 01742

KRUGER, Susan Marie (Minn)

KRULAK JR, Victor Harold (SanD) 3118 Canon St Apt 4, San Diego, CA 92106

KRULAK, William Morris (Md) 113 W Hughes St, Baltimore, MD 21230

KRUMBHAAR, Andrew Ramsay (CFla) 144 Carretera Chapala-Ajijic Pmb 108, San Antonio Tlaycapan, Mexico

KRUMENACKER JR, Gerald Walter (Dal) 5720 Forest Park Rd, No. 2-406, Dallas, TX 75235

KRUMLAUF, Dennis Skyler (Eur)

KRUMME, Judith Sterner (Mass) 349 Simon Willard Rd, Concord, MA 01742

KRUSE, William G (Chi) 1413 Potomac Ct, Geneva, IL 60134

KRUTZ, Charles Dana (La) 527 North Boulevard, Fourth Floor, Baton Rouge, LA 70802

KRYDER-REID, Thomas Marshall (Ind) 5354 Olympia Dr, Indianapolis, IN 46228

KUBBE, Anna L (EMich) Diocese of Eastern Michigan, 924 N Niagara St, Saginaw, MI 48602

KUBICEK, Kirk Alan (Md) 8400 Greenspring Ave, Stevenson, MD 21153

KUBLER, Barry P(Aul) (EC) 340 Shade Tree Circle, Woodstock, GA 30188

KUEHL JR, H(enry) August (RI) 40 Bagy Wrinkle Cv, Warren, RI 02885

KUEHN, Craig (The Episcopal NCal) 2821 Bronzecrest St, Placerville, CA 95667

KUEHN, Jerome Frederick (FdL) 806 4th St, Algoma, WI 54201

KUENKLER, Richard Frederick (CNY) 1 W Church St, Elmira, NY 14901

KUENNETH, John R (Tenn) 538 Hickory Trail Drive, Nashville, TN 37209

KUHLMAN, Donald Herms (Mil) 1200 Green Valley Drive, #2, Janesville, WI 53546

KUHLMANN, Frederick Jennings (Ct) 35A Heritage Village, Southbury, CT 06488

KUHLMANN, Martha Chandler (Cal) 107 Franciscan Dr, Danville, CA 94526

KUHN, Darlene (WMich)

KUHN, Michael Cray (La) Trinity Episcopal School, 1315 Jackson Ave, New Orleans, LA 70130

KUHN, Philip James (Mass) 25 Wood lane, Maynard, MA 01754

KUHN, Thomas Randall (EC) 328 Kelly Ave, Oak Hill, WV 25901

KUHR, Carolyn S. (Mont) 2409 West Irene Street, Boise, ID 83702

KUHR, Elisabeth Schader (Spok) 2490 Thompson Rd, Cowiche, WA 98923

KUJAWA-HOLBROOK, Sheryl Anne (Los) Claremont School of Theology, 1325 N College Avenue, Claremont, CA 91711

KUKOWSKI, Richard George Paul (WA) 412 Colesville Manor Dr, Silver Spring, MD 20904

KULP, John Eugene (SwFla) 17 W Vernon Ave Unit 301, Phoenix, AZ 85003

KUNDINGER, Hazel Doris (CFla) 2404 Fairway Dr, Melbourne, FL 32901

KUNHARDT, Daniel Bradish (WMass) 25 Thornton Way Apt 110, Brunswick, ME 04011

KUNHARDT III, Philip Bradish (NY) Po Box 33, Waccabuc, NY 10597

KUNKLE, Owen (RG) 1914 Tijeras Rd, Santa Fe, NM 87505

KUNZ JR, Andrew George (Va) 1006 Greenway Ln, Richmond, VA 23226

KUNZ JR, Carl Norman (Del) Po Box 5856, Wilmington, DE 19808

KUNZ, Phyllis Ann (Minn) 67982 260th Ave, Kasson, MN 55944

KUNZ, Richard Andrew (NY) Grace Church, 33 Church St, White Plains, NY 10601

KUOL, Daniel Kuch (Ky) 8701 Shepherdsville Rd, Louisville, KY 40219

KURATKO, Lauren Elizabeth Browder (At) 3110 Ashford Dunwoody Rd NE, Atlanta, GA 30319

KURATKO, Ryan Patrick (Va) P.O. Box 788, Mechanicsville, VA 23111

KURTZ, James Edward (CFla) 1352 Seburn Rd, Apopka, FL 32703

KURTZ, Kelli Grace (Los) 408 Greenfield Ct, Glendora, CA 91740

KURTZ, Margaret Eileen (Ida) 3185 E Rivernest Dr, Boise, ID 83706

KUSCHEL, Catherine M. (Neb) 713 Church Rd, Grand Island, NE 68801

KUSKY, Donna Lee Stewart (EMich) 13685 Block Rd, Birch Run, MI 48415

KWAN, Franco Chan-hong (Cal) 425 Swallowtail Ct, Brisbane, CA 94005

KWIATKOWSKI, Janet Mary Jaworowicz (Mil) 9333 W Goodrich Ave, Milwaukee, WI 53224

KYGER JR, Paul Scholl (Chi) 2304 Finwick Ct, Kissimmee, FL 34743

KYLE, Anne Meredith (WMo)

KYLE, Michael Raymond (Mo) 1014 N. Summit Dr., Willow Springs, MO 65793

L

LABARRE, Barbara L (Root) (Okla) 10901 S Yale Ave, Tulsa, OK 74137

LABATT, Walter Bruce (Md) 520 Coventry Cir, Dexter, MI 48130

LABELLE, Philip N (Mass) 27 Main St, Southborough, MA 01772

LABORDA HARRIS, Christy Elisa (The Episcopal NCal) St. Stephen's Episcopal Church, PO Box 98, Sebastopol, CA 95472

LABUD, Richard John (CFla) 28097 Se Highway 42, Umatilla, FL 32784

LACEY, John Howard (SwFla) 851 Moonlight Ln, Brooksville, FL 34601

LACEY, Maryanne (SanD) 3208 Old Heather Rd, San Diego, CA 92111

LACOMBE, Edgar A (Alb) 5708 State Highway 812, Ogdensburg, NY 13669

LACRONE, Frederick Palmer (SeFla) 3059 Casa Rio Ct, Palm Beach Gardens, FL 33418

LACROSSE, Diana Parsons (Dal) 2700 Warren Cir, Irving, TX 75062

LACY II, Lonnie (Ga) St. Anne's Episcopal Church, P.O. Box 889, Tifton, GA 31793

LACY, Mary C (EC) 107 Louis St, Greenville, NC 27858

✠ **LADEHOFF**, Robert Louis (Ret Bp of Ore 2003-) 1330 SW 3rd Ave., Apt. P8, Portland, OR 97201

LAEDLEIN, George Robert (CNY) 201 Granite Rd Apt 340, Guilford, CT 06437

LAFFLER, Brian H (Nwk) 72 Lodi St, Hackensack, NJ 07601

LAFLER, Mark Alan (CFla) 414 Pine St, Titusville, FL 32796

LAFON, Alvin Paul (Los) 2691 Foxglove Loop Se, Albany, OR 97322

LAFON, Kirk David (Miss) 950 Episcopal School Way, Knoxville, TN 37932

LA FOND II, Charles Drummond (Colo) 1023 Pleasant Street, Webster, NH 03303

LAFONTANT, Fritz Raoul (Hai) Eglise Street Pierre, Mirebalais, Haiti

LAFOREST, Charlotte Henning (Mass) PO Box 422, Essex, CT 06426

LAGANA, Gaye Lynn (Nev) PO Box 18917, Spokane, WA 99228

LAGER, Michael Alan (Ark) 16816 Summit Vista Way, Louisville, KY 40245

LAGO, Ana Mercedes (PR)

LAHEY, Stephen Edmund (Neb) 1935 Sewell St, Lincoln, NE 68502

✠ **LAI**, Jung-Hsin (Bp of Tai 2001-) 7, Lane 105, Hangchow S. Road Sec. 1, Taipei, 10060, Taiwan

LAI, Paul C (LI) 1321 College Point Blvd, College Point, NY 11356

LAI, Peter Pui-Tak (LI) 1000 Washington Ave, Plainview, NY 11803

LAINE, Jeanty (SeFla) 404 SW 3rd St, Delray Beach, FL 33444

LAING, Christopher A (Ore) 8275 Sw Canyon Ln, Portland, OR 97225

LAINSON, Vinnie Van (Va) 9325 West Street, Manassas, VA 20110

LAIRD, Daniel Dale (NC) 1317 Hillandale Rd, Durham, NC 27705

LAIRD, I Bruce (Colo) 505 4th Street, Ouray, CO 81427

LAIRD, Lucinda Rawlings (Eur) 330 N Hubbards Ln, Louisville, KY 40207

LAIRD, Robert C (Oly) 316 E 88th St, New York, NY 10128

LAKE, Mark William (RG) 2602 S 2nd St, Tucumcari, NM 88401

LAKE JR, (Orloff) Levin (Chi) 7706 Blue Heron Dr W Apt 1, 7706 Blue Heron Dr W Apt 1, Wilmington, NC 28411

LAKEMAN, Thomas Edmund (CGC) 127 Oak Bend Ct, Fairhope, AL 36532

LALONDE, Kathryn Nan (Pgh) 100 Great Pl Ne, Albuquerque, NM 87113

LALONDE, Walter Joseph (Pgh) 139 N Jefferson Ave, Canonsburg, PA 15317

LALOR, Donald Jene (Minn)

LAM, Connie M. Ng (Mass) 138 Trement Street, Boston, MA 02111

LAM, Peter (LI) 33 Howard Pl, Waldwick, NJ 07463

LAM, Vivian P (LI) 500 S Country Rd, Bay Shore, NY 11706

LA MACCHIA, James R (Mass) 32 Mountain Ash Dr, Kingston, MA 02364

LAMAZARES, Gabriel (NY) 487 Hudson St, New York, NY 10014

LAMB, Jan (NC) 3064 Colony Rd Apt D, Durham, NC 27705

✠ **LAMB**, Jerry Alban (Ret Bp of NCal 2006-) 1065 Villita Loop, Las Cruces, NM 88007

LAMB, Ridenour Newcomb (Ga) 2425 Cherry Laurel Ln., Albany, GA 31705

LAMB, Thomas Jennings (Chi) 503 Macon Dr, Rockford, IL 61109

LAMB, Trevor Vanderveer (CFla) 316 Ocean Dunes Rd, Daytona Beach, FL 32118

LAMB, Watson Howard (La) 10701 Saint Francis Dr, Philadelphia, MS 39350

LAMBERT, Gary Paul (Mil) 205 Nichols Rd, Monona, WI 53716

LAMBERT, George A (Me) 259 Essex St. Apt. 3, Bansor, ME 04401

LAMBERT, John Peck (Oly) 26621 128th Ave South East, Kent, WA 98030

✠ **LAMBERT**, Paul Emil (Bp Suffr of Dal 2008-) 1439 Tranquilla Dr., Dallas, TX 75218

LAMBERT, Robert Ira (Mil) 208 Dairy Ave, Waukesha, WI 53188

LAMBERT, Sally Anne (Ore) 8265 Sw Canyon Ln, Portland, OR 97225

✠ **LAMBERT III**, William Jay (Bp of Eau 2013-) 510 S Farwell St, Eau Claire, WI 54701

LAMBORN, Amy B (Tenn) The General Theological Seminary, 440 West 21st Street, New York, NY 10011

LAMBORN, Robert C (Tenn) 10 Church Ln, Scarsdale, NY 10583

LAMKIN, Melissa Warren (Ct)

LAMMING, Sarah Rebecca (Md) 1601 Pleasant Plains Road, Annapolis, MD 21409

LAMONTAGNE, G(Eorge) Allen (Eas) 13040 Hayes Avenue, Selbyville, DE 19975

LAMPE, Christine Kay (WK) 710 N Main St, Garden City, KS 67846

LAMPERT, Richard B (SwFla) 826 Hampton Wood Ct, Sarasota, FL 34232

LAMPHERE, Mary Kathryn (Spok) 15319 E 8th Ave, Spokane Valley, WA 99037

LANCASTER, James Mansell (Miss) 2721 Brumbaugh Rd, Ocean Springs, MS 39564

LANCASTER, Robert Vaughan (WNY) 537 Cortez St., Sante Fe, NM 87501

LANCE, Philip J (Los) 6464 Sunset Blvd., Suite 845, Los Angeles, CA 90028

LANCTOT, Merv(yn) J (Me) 832 Wicklow St., Winnipeg, MB R3T 0H7, Canada

LANDER, Barbara Temple (ND) 319 S 5th St, Grand Forks, ND 58201

LANDER III, James Rollin (Los) 1101 E Terrace St. #202, Seattle, WA 98122

LANDER, Stephen King (Minn) 5029 Girard Ave S, Minneapolis, MN 55419

LANDERS, Davidson Texada (Ala) 5220 Midway Cir, Tuscaloosa, AL 35406

LANDERS JR, Edward Leslie (Tenn) 6536 Jocelyn Hollow Rd, Nashville, TN 37205

LANDERS, Gail Joan (Md) 12400 Manor Road, PO Box 4001, Glen Arm, MD 21057

LANDERS, Gregory LeRoy (NY) 2150 Baileys Corner Rd, Wall Township, NJ 07719

LANDERS, Kay Marie (Los) 1136 Scenic View St, Upland, CA 91784

LANDERS, Sylvia C (Neb) 206 Westridge Drive, Norfolk, NE 68701

LANDRETH, Robert Dean (Mass) 7 Mechanic Sq, Marblehead, MA 01945

LANDRITH, Richard Stanley (EO) 123 S G St, Lakeview, OR 97630

LANDRY, Bradley Jackson (WTex) St Paul's Episcopal Church, 1018 E Grayson St, San Antonio, TX 78208

LANDRY, Robert Wayne (Me)

LANDWER, Virginia Bess (SeFla) 401 66th Street Ocean, Marathon, FL 33050

LANE III, Edward Jacob (Ky)

LANE, John Charles (Oly) 311 Ridge Dr, Port Townsend, WA 98368

LANE, John David (SwVa) 307 Rainbow Dr, Staunton, VA 24401

LANE, Johnny (Ga) Route #4, Leslie Road, Box 1455, Americus, GA 31709

LANE, Joseph Andrew (Cal) 527 E Woodbury Rd, Altadena, CA 91001

LANE, Keith Cecil (NY) 487 Hudson St, New York, NY 10014

LANE III, Lewis Calvin (La) PO Box 95, Franklin, LA 70538

LANE, Nancy Upson (CNY)

LANE, Peter Austin (RI) 200 Meshanticut Valley Pkwy, Cranston, RI 02920

LANE, Peter Carlson (Chi) 4945 S Dorchester Ave, Chicago, IL 60615

✠ **LANE**, Stephen Taylor (Bp of Me 2008-) 84 Parsons Rd., Portland, ME 04103

LANE, Steve E (WNY) 371 Delaware Ave, Buffalo, NY 14202

LANE, Wendy DeFoe (Chi) 1775 W Newport Ct, Lake Forest, IL 60045

LANE, William Benjamin (Del) 614 Loveville Rd., B-1-I, Hockessin, DE 19707

LANG, Anne Adele (FdL)

LANG, Ellen Davis (SD) 3504 E. Woodsedge St., Sioux Falls, SD 57108

LANG, Mark William (NwT) 727 W Browning Ave, Pampa, TX 79065

LANG, Martha E. (Ia) 2101 Nettle Ave, Muscatine, IA 52761

LANG, Nicholas Gerard (Ct) 14 France St, Norwalk, CT 06851

LANG, Thomas Andrew (Ore) 2812 Ne Kaster Dr, Hillsboro, OR 97124

LANGDON, Clarence Merle (Chi) 1249 Hedgerow Dr, Grayslake, IL 60030

LANGDON, David Stetson (Miss) PO Box 40, Parchman, MS 38738

LANGENFELD, Robert Joseph (Minn) 615 Vermillion St, Hastings, MN 55033

LANGE-SOTO, Anna Beatriz (Cal) 1503 E Campbell Ave, Campbell, CA 95008

LANGEVIN, Ann Elizabeth (Nev) St Thomas Episcopal Church, 5383 E Owens Ave, Las Vegas, NV 89110

LANGFELDT, John Addington (EO) 744 E 20th St, The Dalles, OR 97058

LANGFORD, Thomas William (Spr) 873 S Park Ave, Springfield, IL 62704

LANGI, Viliami (The Episcopal Church in Haw) 720 N King St, Honolulu, HI 96817

LANGILLE, David (Minn) Messiah Episcopal Church, 1631 Ford Pkwy, Saint Paul, MN 55116

LANGLE, Susan (NH) Unit 6, 26 Myrtle St, Claremont, NH 03743

LANGLOIS, Donald Harold (Spr) 916 W Loughlin Dr, Chandler, AZ 85225

LANGSTON, Michael Griffith (NC) 203 Denim Dr, Erwin, NC 28339

LANIER, Justin Ray (Vt) 200 Pleasant St, Bennington, VT 05201

LANIER, Stanley Lin (At) PO Box 637, Waycross, GA 31502

LANIGAN, Sean (Vt) 525 E 7th St, Long Beach, CA 90813

LANNING JR, James C. (Chi) 1315 W. Roosevelt Rd., Wheaton, IL 60187

LANNON, Nicholas Jewett (Nwk) Grace Church Van Vorst, 39 Erie St., Jersey City, NJ 07302

LANPHERE, Lynette (Ala) 8132 Becker Ln, Leeds, AL 35094

LANTER, James Joseph (WVa) HC 69 Box 88, Slatyfork, WV 26291

LANTZ, F(rederick) William (Nwk) 1115 Black Rush Cir, Mt Pleasant, SC 29466

LANTZ, John Daron (SC) 1150 E Montague Ave, North Charleston, SC 29405

LAPENTA-H, Sarah (Colo) 4775 Cambridge St, Boulder, CO 80301

LAPRE, Alfred Charles (Ct) 616 Shamrock Dr, Fredericksburg, VA 22407

LAQUINTANO, David Lloyd (NJ)

LARA, Juana (Dal) St Barnabas Episcopal Church, 1200 N Shiloh Rd, Garland, TX 75042

LARA, Lino (Dal) 5923 Royal Lane, Dallas, TX 75230

LARCOMBE, David John (Vt) 37 Premo Rd, Roxbury, VT 05669

LAREMORE, Darrell Lee (SeFla) 6003 Back Bay Ln, Austin, TX 78739

LAREMORE, Richard Thomas (RI) 147 Bay Spring Ave Apt 227, Barrington, RI 02806

LARGE, Alexander R (Tex) 717 Sage Rd, Houston, TX 77056

LARGENT, Lacy (Tex) Po Box 10603, Houston, TX 77206

LARIBEE JR, Richard (CNY) Trinity Episcopal Church, 227 Sherman St, Watertown, NY 13601

LARIVE, Armand Edward (Spok) 4812 Fremont Ave, Bellingham, WA 98229

LARKIN, Gregory Bruce (Los) 1251 Las Posas Rd, Camarillo, CA 93010

LARKIN, Patrick (ETenn)

LAROCCA, Lucy Driscoll (Ct) 1109 Main St, Branford, CT 06405

LAROCHE WILSON, Jill Monica (Pa) 246 Fox Rd, Media, PA 19063

LAROM JR, Richard U (NY) Po Box 577, Ivoryton, CT 06442

LARRIMORE, Sloane Barker (Cal) 61 Santa Rosa Ave., Sausalito, CA 94965

LARSEN, Erik W (RI) Saint Columba's Chapel, 55 Vaucluse Ave, Middletown, RI 02842

LARSEN, Gilbert Steward (Ct) 9160 Sw 193rd Cir, Dunnellon, FL 34432

LARSEN, Matthew David (Dal) 3966 McKinney Ave, Dallas, TX 75204

LARSEN, Peter Michael (LI) 515 Eastlake Dr, Muscle Shoals, AL 35661

LARSEN JR, R James (Pa) PO Box 341490, Dayton, OH 45434

LARSON, Donna J (WMass) 19 Pleasant St, Chicopee, MA 01013

LARSON, Frances Jean (Minn) 1010 1st Ave N, Wheaton, MN 56296

LARSON, John Milton (Los) 2665 Tallant Rd Apt W307, Santa Barbara, CA 93105

LARSON, Laurence (Chi) 2424 41st St Apt 48, Moline, IL 61265

LARSON, Lawrence Andrew Adolph (NY) 1 Bayview Ter, New Fairfield, CT 06812

LARSON JR, L(awrence) John (Cal) 1835 NW Lantana Dr., Corvallis, OR 97330

LARSON, Robert Anton (Colo) P.O. Box 563, Ouray, CO 81427

LARSON, Steven Shaw (Ga) PO Box 74, Swainsboro, GA 30401

LARSON, Wayne H (Md) 15 East Bishop's Road, Baltimore, MD 21218

LARSON-MILLER, Lizette (Cal) 926 Santa Fe Ave, Albany, CA 94706

LA RUE, Howard Arlen (Va) PO Box 72, Searsport, ME 04974

LASCH, Loren V (Ga) 2230 Walton Way, Augusta, GA 30904

LASH, Rebecca Henry (NwPa) 870 Diamond Park, Meadville, PA 16335

LASITER JR, Douglas Norman (La) 302 Greenwood St, Morgan City, LA 70380

LASKE, Holger (Los) Riehler Strasse 7, Koeln, 50668, Germany

LASLEY, Jerry Drew (NC)

LASSALLE, David Frederic (SVa) 1336 Bolling Ave, Norfolk, VA 23508

LASSEN, Coryl Judith (Cal) 409 Topa Topa Dr, Ojai, CA 93023

LASSITER, Richard Bruce (Nev) 1311 Ramona Ln, Boulder City, NV 89005

LATHAM, Betty Craft (ETenn) 628 Magnolia Vale Dr, Chattanooga, TN 37419

LATHAM, Donald Conway (LI) 75 Meadow Rue Pl, Ballston Spa, NY 12020

LATHROP, Brian Albert (NY) 63 Downing St Apt 4-A, New York, NY 10014

LATHROP, John (Me) 101 Paseo Encantado Ne, Santa Fe, NM 87506

LATIMER, Susan J (SwFla) 502 Druid Hills Road, Temple Terrace, FL 33617

LATTA, Dennis James (Ind) 2742 S Hickory Corner Rd, Vincennes, IN 47591

✠ **LATTIME**, Mark A (Bp of Ak 2010-) 1205 Denali Way, Fairbanks, AK 99701

LAU, Gordon K (Cal) 1003 Azalea Dr, Alameda, CA 94502

LAU, Ronald Taylor Christensen (LI) 326 Clinton St, Brooklyn, NY 11231

LAUCHER, Bill (Tex) 417 Avenue Of Oaks St, Houston, TX 77009

LAUDISIO, Patricia Devin (Colo) 3328 Sentinel Dr, Boulder, CO 80301

LAUER, Daniel Donald (WTex) 2006 Pinetree Ln, San Antonio, TX 78232

LAUGHLIN, Ledlie I (WA) 4201 Albemarle St NW, Washington, DC 20016

LAUGHLIN JR, Ledlie Irwin (Eur) 63 Ford Hill Rd, West Cornwall, CT 06796

LAUGHLIN, Ophelia G (NJ) Waterman Avenue, Rumson, NJ 07760

LAUK, Candice Ruth (NMich) 1003 Wickman Dr, Iron Mountain, MI 49801

LAURA, Ronald Samuel (Vt)

LAURINEC, Jennene Lawton (Tex) 308 Cottage Rd., Carthage, TX 75633

LAUTENSCHLAGER, Paul John (Colo) 11 W. Madison Street, Colorado Springs, CO 80907

LAUZON, Marcia Louise (Mont) PO Box 3046, Great Falls, MT 59403

LAVALLEE, Armand Aime (Ct) 5523 Birchhill Rd, Charlotte, NC 28227

LAVALLEE, Donald Alphonse (RI) 1665 Broad St, Cranston, RI 02905

LAVANN, Jason Gary (Mil) 216 E Chandler Blvd, Burlington, WI 53105

LAVENGOOD, Henrietta Louise (NJ) 211 Falls Ct, Medford, NJ 08055

LAVENGOOD, Martin Brownlee (NJ) 211 Falls Ct, Medford, NJ 08055

LAVERONI, Alfred Frank (Md) 312 Cigar Loop, Hvre De Grace, MD 21078

LAVERY, Patricia Anne (NwPa) PO Box 287, Grove City, PA 16127

LAVETTY, Denise Jean (NY) 224 Waverly Pl, New York, NY 10014

LAVINE, Patricia Iva (Alb) 323 Lakeshore Dr, Norwood, NY 13668

LAVOE, John F (CNY) 210 Yoxall Ln, Oriskany, NY 13424

LAW, Eric Hung-Fat (Los) 351 Sandpiper St, Palm Desert, CA 92260

LAWBAUGH, Will Medley (CPa) 813 Franklin Avenue, Aliquippa, PA 15001

LAWLER, Gary Elwyn Andrew (Chi) 5600 N Sheridan Rd Apt 10A, Chicago, IL 60660

LAWLER, Richard (WNC) Po Box 2680, Blowing Rock, NC 28605

LAWLER, Steven William (Mo) 33 N Clay Ave, Saint louis, MO 63135

LAWLOR, Jay R (WMich) Diocese of Western Michigan, 535 S. Burdick Street, Suite 1, Kalamazoo, MI 49007

LAWRENCE JR, Albert Sumner (Tex) 14 Sedgewick Pl, The Woodlands, TX 77382

LAWRENCE, Amy (Cal) 2711 Harkness St, Sacramento, CA 95818

LAWRENCE, Bruce Bennett (NC) C/O Department Of Religion, Duke University, Durham, NC 27706

LAWRENCE, Catherine Abbott (NY) 1415 Pelhamdale Ave, Christ Church, Pelham, NY 10803

LAWRENCE, Charles Kane Cobb (Lex) 101 S. Hanover Ave, Apt 7M, Lexington, KY 40502

LAWRENCE, Eric John (Nev) 2306 Paradise Dr Apt 222, Reno, NV 89512

LAWRENCE, Gerard Martin (Mass) 22874 NE 127th Way, Redmond, WA 98053

LAWRENCE JR, Harry Martin (ETenn) 1800 Lula Lake Rd, Lookout Mountain, GA 30750

LAWRENCE, James Dean (Tex) 1101 Rock Prairie Road, College Station, TX 77845

LAWRENCE, John Arthur (Chi) 712 Mockingbird Lane, Kerrville, TX 78028

LAWRENCE, John Elson (WA) 4336 Wordsworth Way, Venice, FL 34293

LAWRENCE, Matthew Richard (The Episcopal NCal) 1346 Yulupa Ave. Apt C, Santa Rosa, CA 95405

LAWRENCE, Novella E (NY) 20 Laguardia Ave Apt 4f, Staten Island, NY 10314

LAWRENCE, Philip Archer (Okla) 32251 S 616 Rd, Grove, OK 74344

LAWRENCE JR, Raymond Johnson (SwVa) 913 Ash Tree Ln., Niskayuna, NY 12309

LAWS III, Robert James (Eas) 30513 Washington St, Princess Anne, MD 21853

LAWS, Thomas Richard (Nwk) 11 Harvard St, Montclair, NJ 07042

LAWSON, Daniel (Mich)

LAWSON, Frederick Quinney (U) 4294 Adonis Dr, Salt Lake City, UT 84124

LAWSON, Neil-St Barnabas J (Episcopal SJ) P.O. Box 7606, Stockton, CA 95267

LAWSON, Paul David (Los) PO Box 1573, Palm Desert, CA 92261

LAWSON, Peter Raymond (Cal) 805 North Webster Street, Petaluma, CA 94952

LAWSON, Richard (WTenn) 1720 Peabody Ave, 1602 Vinton Ave, Memphis, TN 38104

LAWSON, Rolfe Adrian (Vt)

LAWSON, Victor Freeman (WVa) 64 Barley Lane, Charles Town, WV 25414

LAWSON-BECK, David Roswell (NJ) 143 W Milton Ave, Apt 4, Rahway, NJ 07065

LAWTON, John Keith (Ak) Po Box 530, Palmer, AK 99645

LAWYER, Evelyn Virden (Minn) 4539 Keithson Dr, Arden Hills, MN 55112

LAYCOCK, John Emerson (Mich) 7112 Kauffman Blvd., Presque Isle, MI 49777

LAYCOCK JR, R(alph) Bradley (SwVa) 2725 Wilshire Ave SW, Roanoke, VA 24015

LAYDEN, Daniel Keith (NI) 11009 Brandy Oak Run, Fort Wayne, IN 46845

LAYNE, Najah Suzanne (Kan) 631 E. Marlin St., McPherson, KS 67460

LAYNE, Robert Patterson (Kan) 631 E Marlin St, Mc Pherson, KS 67460

LAZARD, Amirold (Hai)

LEA, Gail Ann (U) PO Box 96, Moab, UT 84532

LEA, William Howard (Ga) 1 Fair Hope Ln, Savannah, GA 31411

LEACH, Duane Lamar (The Episcopal Church in Haw) 57-077 Eleku Kuilima Pl Apt 97, Kahuku, HI 96731

LEACH, Fredric Francis (Alb) 585 4th Ave, Troy, NY 12182

LEACH, JoAnn Zwart (Ore) 8400 Paseo Vista Dr, Las Vegas, NV 89128

LEACH, John Philip (WTenn) 1380 Wolf River Blvd, Collierville, TN 38017

LEACH, Marilyn May (Minn)

LEACH, Shannon Paul (Nev) 8400 Paseo Vista Dr, Las Vegas, NV 89128

LEACOCK, Rob (Tex) 8605 Verona Trl, Austin, TX 78749

LEAHY, John Joseph (CFla) 1007B Kings Way, New Bern, NC 28562

LEANILLO, Rick (SwFla) 5033 9th St, Zephyrhills, FL 33542

LEANNAH, Scott Robert (Mil) 3734 S. 86th St., Milwaukee, WI 53228

LEARY, Charles Randolph (SO) 133 Croskey Boulevard, Medway, OH 45341

LEARY, Kevin David (Ct) 15 Rimmon Rd, Woodbridge, CT 06525

LEAS, Bercry Eleanor (Mich) 7051 Wakan Ln., Corryton, TN 37721

LEATHERMAN, Daniel Lee (The Episcopal Church in Haw) 7 Pursuit, Aliso Viejo, CA 92656

LEAVITT, Christie Plehn (Nev) 1739 Carita Ave, Henderson, NV 89014

LE BARRON, Bruce E(rie) (WK) 3218 White Tail Way, Salina, KS 67401

LEBENS ENGLUND, Paul (Minn) 7315 N Wall St, Spokane, WA 99208

LE BLANC, Frances Andre (Telles) (Md) 260 Monument Rd, Orleans, MA 02653

LEBLANC, Tracy Jean (Ore) 15416 Ne 90th St, Vancouver, WA 98682

LEBRIJA, Lorenzo (Los) c/o Cathedral Center of St Paul, 840 Echo Park Ave, Los Angeles, CA 90026

LEBROCQ JR, Eric Francis (Tex) St. John's Episcopal Church, PO Box 1477, Sealy, TX 77474

LEBRON, Robert Emmanuel (Mil) 409 E. Court St., Janesville, WI 53545

LEBUS, Jesse W (LI)

LECHE III, Edward Douglas (Oly) 205 Olympic View Dr, Friday Harbor, WA 98250

LECLAIR, Arthur Anthony (Colo) 8221 E Fremont Cir, Englewood, CO 80112

LECLAIR, Paul Joseph (Mich) 1434 E 13 Mile Rd, Madison Heights, MI 48071

LECLAIRE, Patrick Harry (Nev) 620 W B St, Fallon, NV 89406

LECLERC, Charles Edward (NH) 1873 Dover Rd, Epsom, NH 03234

LECOUTEUR II, Eugene Hamilton (Va) 6000 Grove Ave, Richmond, VA 23226

LECROY, Anne Evelyn (ETenn) 400 N Boone St, Apt As14, Johnson City, TN 37604

LEDERHOUSE, Susan (Mass) PO Box 1586, Orleans, MA 02653

LEDERMAN, Maureen Elizabeth (Ct) 124 Midland Dr, Meriden, CT 06450

LEDFORD, Marcia Lynn (Mich) 959 Sherman St, Ypsilanti, MI 48197

LEDGERWOOD, Mary Jayne (Va) 6715 Georgetown Pike, McLean, VA 22101

LEDIARD SR, Daniel E (EO) Po Box 681, Virginia City, NV 89440

LEDIARD, JoAnne (Spok) 1609 W 10th Ave, Kennewick, WA 99336

LEDYARD, Christopher Martin (Az) 2331 E Adams St, Tucson, AZ 85719

LEDYARD, Florence Livingstone (Md) 1021 Bosley Rd, Cockeysville, MD 21030

LEE III, Arthur Randall (SwFla) 7304 Van Lake Dr, Englewood, FL 34224

LEE, Betsy A. (Minn) 4901 Triton Dr, Golden Valley, MN 55422

LEE, Caleb J (SC) 215 Ann St, Beaufort, NC 28516

LEE, Chen-cheng (Tai) No. 311 Sec.2, Chieding Rd, Chieding District, Kaohsiung City, 85241, Taiwan

LEE, Christine Kim (NY) St Mary's Episcopal Church, 521 W 126th St, New York, NY 10027

LEE, Daniel Ki Chul (Ga) 623 Caines Rd, Hinesville, GA 31313

LEE, Darry Kyong Ho (Los) 5950 Imperial Hwy Apt 47, South Gate, CA 90280

LEE, David Edward (Va) 2343 Highland Ave, Charlottesville, VA 22903

LEE, Donald DeArman (WTex) Po Box 545, Bandera, TX 78003

✠ **LEE JR**, Edward Lewis (Ret Bp of WMich 2004-) 123 Glenwood Rd, Merion Station, PA 19066

LEE, Enoch (Tai)

LEE, George (The Episcopal Church in Haw) 2468 Lamaku Pl, Honolulu, HI 96816

LEE, Hosea Mun-Yong (Nwk) 1600 Parker Ave Apt 3-D, Fort Lee, NJ 07024

LEE, Hyacinth Evadne (NY) 50 Guion Pl, 5H, New Rochelle, NY 10801

LEE, James Kyung-Jin (Los) Episcopal Church of the Messiah, 614 N Bush St, Santa Ana, CA 92701

LEE JR, James Oliver (Dal) 1729 S Beckley Ave, Dallas, TX 75224

✠ **LEE**, Jeffrey Dean (Bp of Chi 2008-) 65 E Huron St, Chicago, IL 60611

LEE JR, John E (NMich) Rr 1 Box 586, Newberry, MI 49868

LEE, Judith Mary (WNY) 36 Marion Rd E # 8540, Princeton, NJ 08540

LEE, Jui-Chiang (U) 163 Tung-Ming Rd., Keelung, Taiwan

LEE, Julia Hamilton (Ala)

LEE, Kirk A (At) 1195 Village Run NE, Atlanta, GA 30319

LEE, Marc DuPlan (Kan) 4515 W Moncrieff Pl, Denver, CO 80212

LEE, Margaret Will (Chi) 3412 54th St, Moline, IL 61265

LEE, Matthew Wen-Hui (Tai) 5F No. 7 Kee-Lung 2nd Road, Kee Lung City, 20446, Taiwan

LEE, Maurice Charles (Spr) 3231 Alton Rd, Atlanta, GA 30341

LEE, Nathaniel Jung-Chul (WA) Church of the Holy Spirit, 1624 Wooded Acres Dr, Waco, TX 76710

✠ **LEE**, Peter J (Ret Bp of Va 2009-) 511 E Rosemary St, Chapel Hill, NC 27514

LEE, Rhonda Mawhood (NC) 914 Green St, Durham, NC 27701

LEE, Robert B (Vt) 51 Park St., Canaan, VT 05903

LEE III, Robert Vernon (Fla) 1131 N Laura St, Jacksonville, FL 32206

LEE, Sang (Dal) 2783 Valwood Pkwy, Farmers Branch, TX 75234

LEE, Scott Charles (Ct) 2000 Main Street, Stratford, CT 06615

LEE, Scott R (NwT) St James the Apostle Epis Ch, 1803 Highland Hollow Dr, Conroe, TX 77305

LEE, Shirley Lynne (Ak) 1205 Denali Way, Fairbanks, AK 99701

LEE, Solomon Sang-Woo (Chi) 9227 Cameron Ln, Morton Grove, IL 60053

LEE, Stewart Warren Rubinstein (VI) 261 Mount Pleasant, Frederiksted, VI 00840

LEE, Susan Hagood (Mass) 336 Maple St, New Bedford, MA 02740

LEE, Tambria Elizabeth (NC) 304 E Franklin St, Chapel Hill, NC 27514

LEE, Terence A (LI) 19610 Woodhull Ave, Hollis, NY 11423

LEE III, Thomas Carleton (LI) 3000 Galloway Ridge Apt D104, Pittsboro, NC 27312

LEE, Thomas Moon (Tenn) 510 Mable Mason Cv, La Vergne, TN 37086

LEE, Wan Hong (Md) St John's Episcopal Church, 9120 Frederick Rd, Ellicott City, MD 21042

LEE III, William Forrest (Md) Po Box 2188, Mountain Lake Park, MD 21550

LEECH, John (Oly) PO BOX 65062, Tucson, AZ 85728

LEED, Rolf Amundson (WMo) 226 N Main St, Clinton, MO 64735

LEEHAN, James Edward (Ind) 7047 Vuelta Vistoso, Santa Fe, NM 87507

LEEMHUIS, Guy Anthony (Los) 260 N Locust St, Inglewood, CA 90301

LEES, Everett C (Okla) 2613 W Broadway St, Broken Arrow, OK 74012

LEESON, Gary William (Los) 4457 Mont Eagle Pl, Los Angeles, CA 90041

LEFEBVRE, Eugene Francis (Pa) 635 Willow Valley Sq Apt H-509, Lancaster, PA 17602

LEFEVRE, Ann Raynor (Be) 1190 Bianca Dr Ne, Palm Bay, FL 32905

LEGER, Don Curtis (WLa) 919 Anthony Ave, Opelousas, LA 70570

LEGGE, Don Edward (Tex) 1809 Barton Hills Dr, Austin, TX 78704

LEGNANI, Robert Henry (NJ) 22 Ashley Dr, Delran, NJ 08075

LEHMAN, Katherine Megee (Cal) 705 W Main St, Kerrville, TX 78028

LEHMAN, Susan C (SwVa) 550 E 4th St #U, Cincinnati, OH 45202

LEHMANN, Richard B (Alb) 24 Summit Ave, Latham, NY 12110

LEHRER, Christian Anton (Cal) 800 Pomona St, Crockett, CA 94525

LEIBHART, Linda Dianne (Roch) 9406 Chipping Dr, Richmond, VA 23237

✠ **LEIDEL JR**, Edwin Max (Ret Bp of EMich 2006-) 430 W Brentwood Ln, Milwaukee, WI 53217

LEIDER, Jennifer Claire (O) St. Paul's Episcopal Church, 798 S. Coy Rd., Oregon, OH 43616

LEIFUR, (Gloria) Teresa (CGC) 1110 E Gadsden St, Pensacola, FL 32501

LEIGH, W Joseph (NJ) 238 Twilight Ave, Keansburg, NJ 07734

LEIGH-KOSER, Charlene M (CPa) 6219 Lincoln Hwy, Wrightsville, PA 17368

LEIGH-TAYLOR, Christine Heath (The Episcopal NCal) 4231 Oak Meadow Rd, Placerville, CA 95667

LEIGHTON, Blake Eugene (The Episcopal NCal) St Michael and All Angels Episc. Ch., PO Box 124, Fort Bragg, CA 95437

LEIGHTON, Christopher (Ct) 33 Dora Cir, Bridgeport, CT 06604

LEIGHTON, Deborah (Ala) Cathedral Church of the Advent, 2017 6th Ave N, Birmingham, AL 35203

LEIGHTON, Jack Lee (Tex) 135 E Circuit Dr, Beaumont, TX 77706

LEIN, Clay A (Tex) 1102 Highland St., Houston, TX 77009

LEINBACH, Jeanne A (O) 2747 Fairmount Blvd, Cleveland Heights, OH 44106

LEININGER, Austin (The Episcopal NCal) 3337 Colony Drive, Fort Collins, CO 80526

LEIP, Harry Louis (Mo) 600 N Euclid Ave, Saint Louis, MO 63108

LEISERSON, Joanna (SO) 2218 Oakland Ave, Covington, KY 41014

LEITE, Dessordi Peres (Cal)

LEMA, Julio M (At) 1379 Craighill Ct, Norcross, GA 30093

LEMAIRE JR, Michael E (Cal) 2220 Cedar St, Berkeley, CA 94709

LEMAY, Anne Rae (NJ) 576 West Ave, Sewaren, NJ 07077

LEMBURG, David Wesley (Miss) 1350 Courthouse Rd, Gulfport, MS 39507

LEMBURG, Melanie Dickson (Miss) 1909 15th Street, Gulfport, MS 39501

LEMERY, Gary Conrad (RI) 45 Bay View Drive North, Jamestown, RI 02835

LEMLER, James B (Ct) Christ Church, 254 E Putnam Ave, Greenwich, CT 06830

LEMLEY, Kent Christopher (At) 764 Springlake Ln NW, Atlanta, GA 30318

LEMMING, Craig Peter (Minn) St John The Evangelist Episcopal Church, 60 Kent St, Saint Paul, CO 55102

LEMON, Karen Dillenbeck (WK) 20081 Sw 20th Ave, Pratt, KS 67124

LEMONS, Catherine L (Minn) 12621 Old Columbia Pike, Silver Spring, MD 20904

LENNON, Evelyn Cromartie (Minn) 119 Isabel St. E, Saint Paul, MN 55107

LENNOX, Daniel (Nwk) 707 Washington St, Hoboken, NJ 07030

LENOIR, Robert Scott (Miss) 2005 Lauban Ln, Gautier, MS 39553

LENT, Morris J (SC) 1855 Houghton Dr, Charleston, SC 29412

LENTEN, John William (NMich) 11 Longyear Dr, Negaunee, MI 49866

LENTZ, Benjamin Lee (Be) 9758 N. Rome Rd., Athens, PA 18810

LENTZ JR, Julian Carr (ECR) 1001 Sleepy Hollow Ln, Plainfield, NJ 07060

LENZO, Alexander (RG)

LEO, Agnes Patricia (The Episcopal Church in Haw) 665 Paopua Loop, Kailua, HI 96734

LEO, Denise Florence (Pa) 400 S Jackson St, Media, PA 19063

LEO, Jason Elliman (SO) 3780 Clifton Ave, Cincinnati, OH 45220

LEO, John (Be) 295 Brown St, Wilkes Barre, PA 18702

LEON, Luis (WA) 1525 H St NW, Washington, DC 20005

LEON, Sadoni (Hai) c/o Diocese of Haiti, Boite Postale 1309, Port au Prince Haiti, Haiti

LEONARD, H Alan (USC) 254 Crooked Tree Dr, Inman, SC 29349

LEONARD, Sean T (WNY) 23 Potter Ave, Orchard Park, NY 14127

LEONARD, Thomas Edgar (Az) 11 Avineda de la Herran, Tubac, AZ 85646

LEONARD-PASLEY, Patricia Ann (Ct) 680 Racebrook Rd, Orange, CT 06477

LEONCZYK JR, Kenneth (Dal) 425 D St SE Apt 304, Washington, DC 20003

LEONETTI, Stephen James (The Episcopal NCal) PO Box 6194, Vacaville, CA 95696

LEON-LOZANO, Cristobel Olmedo (EcuC) Casilla 13-05-179, Manta, Ecuador

LEOPOLD, Robert Kelly (ETenn) 1616 Read Ave, Chattanooga, TN 37408

LEPLEY, Rebecca Ruth Baird (EMich) 539 N William St, Marine City, MI 48039

LEROUX, Donald Francis (ND) 319 S 5th St, Grand Forks, ND 58201

LEROUX JR, Grant Meade (Ga) 5 Mooregate Square, Atlanta, GA 30327

LE ROY, Melinda Louise Perkins (WNC) 4 Flycatcher Way Unit 302, Arden, NC 28704

LERUD, Nathanael D (Ore) Trinity Episcopal Cathedral, 147 NW 19th Ave, Portland, OR 97209

LESCH, Robert Andrew (Minn) 828 5th St Ne, Minneapolis, MN 55413

LESESNE, Gray (Ind) 1100 W 42nd St Ste 235, Indianapolis, IN 46208

LESEURE, Laurence James (NY) 530 E 234th St Apt 1F, Bronx, NY 10470

LESH, Ryan Edwin (NY) 7423 S Broadway, Red Hook, NY 12571

LESIEUR, Betsy Ann (RI) 200 Heroux Blvd # 2001, Cumberland, RI 02864

LESLIE, Joanne (Los) 1351 Grant St, Santa Monica, CA 90405

LESLIE III, Richard B (ECR) 520 Lobos Ave, Pacific Grove, CA 93950

LESSMANN, Mary T (Dal) 6400 McKinney Ranch Pkwy, McKinney, TX 75070

LESTER, Elmore William (LI) 1440 Tanglewood Pkwy, Fort Myers, FL 33919

LE SUEUR, Susan Dianne Lassey (NH) 18 Gaita Dr, Derry, NH 03038

LESWING, James Bartholomew (Chi) 1125 Franklin St, Downers Grove, IL 60515

LETHIN, Judith Lynn Wegman (Ak) 3509 Wentworth St, Anchorage, AK 99508

LETHIN, Kris W (Ak) 175 Main St, Seldovia, AK 99663

LEVENSALER, Kurt H (The Episcopal NCal) St Timothy's Church, 1550 Diablo Rd, Danville, CA 94526

LEVENSON JR, Russell J (Tex) St Martin's Episcopal Church, 717 Sage Rd, Houston, TX 77056

LEVESCONTE, Suzanne Joy Kreider (SO) Trinity Episcopal Church, 115 N 6th St, Hamilton, OH 45011

LEVESQUE, Christa (Roch) 1737 Hillandale Rd, Durham, NC 27705

LEVINE, Paul H (ECR) 720 S 3rd St Apt 5, San Jose, CA 95112

LEVY, Sandra Maria (Va) 9107 Donora Dr, Richmond, VA 23229

LEVY, William Turner (NY) 22121 Lanark St, Canoga Park, CA 91304

LEWALLEN, Jerrilee Parker (Ala) 174 Carpenter Cir, Sewanee, TN 37375

LEWELLEN, Donald Stephen (Chi) 523 W Glen Ave, Peoria, IL 61614

LEWELLIS, Bill (Be) 3235 Clear Stream Dr, Whitehall, PA 18052

LEWIS III, Adam (Del) 115 E 90th St Apt 5C, New York, NY 10128

LEWIS III, Albert Davidson (ETenn) 340 Chamberlain Cove Rd, Kingston, TN 37763

LEWIS, Alice LaReign (EMich) 437n County Road 441, Manistique, MI 49854

LEWIS, Allen Lee (SD) 4705 S Wildwood Cir, Sioux Falls, SD 57105

LEWIS, Barbara (Tex) 1401 Calumet St. unit 312, Houston, TX 77004

LEWIS, Barbara Ann (Nev) 1511 Cardinal Peak Ln Unit 101, Las Vegas, NV 89144

LEWIS, Barbara Jane (Pa) 19115 Avalon Way, Lawrenceville, NJ 08648

LEWIS, Betsey (Ct)

LEWIS, Catherine Blanc (Roch) 7086 Salmon Creek Rd, Williamson, NY 14589

LEWIS, Charles Robert (Alb) 3711 Glen Oaks Manor Dr, Sarasota, FL 34232

LEWIS, Cynthia (Ct)

LEWIS, (Earl) James (Del) 1313 Lee St E Apt 112, Charleston, WV 25301

LEWIS, Ernest Loran (The Episcopal NCal) 640 Hawthorne Ln, Davis, CA 95616

LEWIS JR, Giles Floyd (Tex) 786 Glendalyn Ave, Spartanburg, SC 29302

LEWIS, Harold Thomas (Pgh)

LEWIS JR, Howarth Lister (SeFla) 1110 Sand Drift Way, West Palm Beach, FL 33411

LEWIS JR, Irwin Morgan (SVa) 4449 N Witchduck Rd, Virginia Beach, VA 23455

LEWIS, Jason D (Ky) 204 Monroe Ave, Belton, MO 64012

LEWIS, Jeffrey Clement (RI) St George's School, PO Box 1910, Newport, RI 02840

LEWIS, John Goddard (WTex) The WorkShop, 2015 NE Loop 410, San Antonio, TX 78217

LEWIS, John Walter (Me) 33 Knowlton St, Camden, ME 04843

LEWIS, Karen C (Mich) 218 W Ottawa St, Lansing, MI 48933

LEWIS, Kate (Los) 265 W Sidlee St, Thousand Oaks, CA 91360

LEWIS, Katherine Twyford (Minn) 13000 St. Davids Rd, Minnetonka, MN 55305

LEWIS, Kenneth Rutherford (Ala) 708 Fairfax Dr, Fairfield, AL 35064

LEWIS, Kenrick Ewart (Mass) 309 New York Ave, Jersey City, NJ 07307

LEWIS, Kristina D (Ct) 91 Church St, Seymour, CT 02630

LEWIS, Laurie Ann (Kan) 3705 Edgemont St, Wichita, KS 67208

LEWIS, Lawrence Bernard (WMo) 415 Market Street, Osceola, MO 64776

LEWIS JR, Lloyd Alexander (LI) 5501 Seminary Rd Apt 812, Falls Church, VA 22041

LEWIS, Mabel Burke (NY) 40 Barton St, Newburgh, NY 12550

LEWIS, Mark Alan (Nwk) PO Box 93, Rensselaerville, NY 12147

LEWIS, Matthew William (Ga) 2230 Walton Way, Augusta, GA 30904

LEWIS, Maurine Ann (Mil) 1717 Carl St, Fort Worth, TX 76103

LEWIS III, Philip Gregory (Oly)

LEWIS, Philip Martin (Spr) 420 N. Plum St., Havana, IN 62644

LEWIS, Richard Howard (CNY) none, none, NY 13442

LEWIS, Robert Michael (Neb) 11251 SW Highway 484, Dunnellon, FL 34432

LEWIS, Sarah Elizabeth (Md) 576 Johnsville Rd, Eldersburg, MD 21784

LEWIS, Sarah Vaughan (CNY)

LEWIS, Sharon Lynn Gottfried (SwFla) 3773 Wilkinson Rd, Sarasota, FL 34233

LEWIS, Stephen Charles (Okla)

LEWIS, Theodore Longstreet (WA) 20235 Laurel Hill Way, Germantown, MD 20874

LEWIS JR, Theodore Radford (SC) 106 Line St, Charleston, SC 29403

LEWIS, Thom (SVa) 2702 W Market St, Greensboro, NC 27403

LEWIS, Timothy John (LI) Po Box 264, Wainscott, NY 11975

LEWIS, Walter England (Nwk) 60 Dryden Rd, Montclair, NJ 07043

LEWIS, William Benjamin (WA) 14110 Royal Forest Ln, Silver Spring, MD 20904

LEWIS, William George (CFla) 442 Sanderling Dr, Indialantic, FL 32903

LEWIS-HEADDEN, Margaret Kempe (Oly) P.O. Box 1997, 1036 Golf Course Rd., Friday Harbor, WA 98250

LEY, James Lawrence (Pa) 101 Lydia Ln, West Chester, PA 19382

LEYS, Donovan I (LI) 20931 111 Avenue, Queens Village, NY 11429

L'HOMME, Robert Arthur (Chi) 8501 Timber Ln, Lafayette, IN 47905

L'HOMMEDIEU, J(ohn) Gary (CFla) 130 N Magnolia Ave, Orlando, FL 32801

LIAO KING-LING, Samuel (Tai) 1-105-7 Hangchow South Road, Taipei, Taiwan

LIBBEY, Elizabeth Weaver (USC) 1140 Fork Creek Rd, Saluda, NC 28773

LIBBEY, Robert Edward (USC) 16 Salisbury Drive #7410, Asheville, NC 28803

LIBBY, Glenn Maurice (Los) 835 W 34th Street 203, Los Angeles, CA 90089

LIBBY, Richardson Armstrong (Ct) 235 King George Street, Annapolis, MD 21401

LIBBY, Robert Meredith Gabler (SeFla) 200 Ocean Lane Dr Apt 408, Key Biscayne, FL 33149

LIBERATORE, James Vincent (Tex) 2535 Broadway St, Pearland, TX 77581

LICARI, Luigi (Cal) 904-9 Deer Park Crescent, Toronto, ON M4V 2C4, Canada

LIDDLE, Vincent T (Pa) 1226 Cedar Rd, Ambler, PA 19002

LIDDY, Jeffery T (Pa) 922 Main Street, Ste. 406, Lynchburg, VA 24504

LIEB, James Marcus (ECR) PO Box 293, Ben Lomond, CA 95005

LIEBENOW, Robert Ervin (Chi) 8 Laurel Place Dr, Asheville, NC 28803

LIEBER, William Louis (SanD) 8975 Lawrence Welk Dr Spc 77, Escondido, CA 92026

LIEBERT-HALL, Linda Ann (CFla) Shepherd of the Hills, 2540 W Norvell Bryant Hwy, Lecanto, FL 34461

LIEBLER, John Stephen Baxter (CFla) 2254 6th Avenue SE, Vero Beach, FL 32962

LIEF, Richard C (SanD) 3212 Eichenlaub St, San Diego, CA 92117

LIEM, Jennifer E (The Episcopal NCal) PO Box 855, Tahoe City, CA 96145

LIERLE, Deane Kae (Okla) 5037 E Via Montoya Dr, Phoenix, AZ 85054

LIESKE, Mark Stephen (Los) 3833 Artadi Dr, Spanish Springs, NV 89436

LIETZ, Dennis Eugene (Chi) 935 Knollwood Rd, Deerfield, IL 60015

LIEW, Richard (NY) 168 Long Hill Road, Oakland, NJ 07436

LIGGETT JR, James Edgar (NwT) 3518 Hyde Park Ave, Midland, TX 79707

✠ **LIGHT**, A(rthur) Heath (Ret Bp of SwVa 1996-) 2524 Wycliffe Ave Sw, Roanoke, VA 24014

LIGHTCAP, Torey Lynn (Kan) 835 SW Polk St, Topeka, KS 66612

LIGHTSEY, Pamela Sue Willis (Ga) 2700 Pebblewood Dr, Valdosta, GA 31602

LIGHTSEY, Richard Brian (NI) 602 W Superior St, Kokomo, IN 46901

LIGON, Michael Moran (EC) 517 Brandywine Cir, Greenville, NC 27858

LIKOWSKI, James Boyd (Ore) 2818 Lilac St, Longview, WA 98632

LIKWARTZ, Judy Saima (Ore) Po Box 51447, Casper, WY 82605

LILES, Allison Sandlin (Ala) 6615 Saddleback Ct, Crozet, VA 22932

LILES, Eric James (Va) Saint Paul's Church, PO Box 37, Ivy, VA 22945

LILES, Linda Kathleen (NY) 120 W 69th St, New York, NY 10023

LILLARD SR, Eddie Lee (NJ) 1819 Columbus Ave, Neptune, NJ 07753

LILLEY, Linda Sue (RG) St Thomas Of Canterbury Episcopal Church, 425 University Blvd NE, Albuquerque, NM 87106

✠ **LILLIBRIDGE**, Gary Richard (Bp of WTex 2006-) PO Box 6885, San Antonio, TX 78209

LILLICROPP, Arthur Reginald (The Episcopal NCal) 1607 54th St., Sacramento, CA 95819

LILLIE, Paul Andrew (The Episcopal Church in Haw) 3311 Campbell Avenue, Honolulu, HI 96815

LILLIS, Rosemary H (Roch) 1222 Sunset Ave, Asbury Park, NJ 07712

LILLVIS, David Matthew (Mich) 4708 State Park Highway, Interlochen, MI 49643

LILLY, Elizabeth Cobb (WNC) 2953 Ninth Tee Dr, Newton, NC 28658

LILLY, Elizabeth Louise (SO) 152 W Weisheimer Rd, Columbus, OH 43214

LIM, You-leng Leroy (Los) 12172 9th St, Garden Grove, CA 92840

LIMA, Roy Allen (Fla) 259 Duncan Dr, Crawfordville, FL 32327

LIMATU, Hector Roberto (Los)

LIMBACH, Mary Evelyn (Eau) 2034 Upper Ridge Road, Port Washington, WI 53074

LIMBURG, Megan M (Va) St Christopher's School, 711 Saint Christophers Rd, Richmond, VA 23226

LIMEHOUSE III, Frank F (Ala) 3538 Lenox Rd, Birmingham, AL 35213

LIMO, John Edward (Los) 15757 Saint Timothy Rd, Apple Valley, CA 92307

LIMOZAINE, Bruce John (Ark) 30 Gettysburg N, Cabot, AR 72023

LIMPERT JR, Robert Hicks (Alb) 731 Old Piseco Road, Piseco, NY 12139

LIMPITLAW, John Donald (Ct) 140 Whidah Way, Wellfleet, MA 02667

LIN, Justin Chun-Min (Tai) 3/F, 262 Chung-Hsiao I Road, Hsin Hsing Dis, Kaohsiung, 800, Taiwan

LIN, Philip Li-Feng (Tai) 23 Wu-Chuan West Road Sec. 1, Taichung, TAIWAN, Taiwan

LIN, Samuel Ying-Chiu (Tai) #280 Fuhsing S Rd, Sec 2, C/O Diocese Of Taiwan, Taipei, Taiwan

LIN, Shu-Hwa (Tai) 1 F #29 Alley 6, Lane 168 Chung-her Rd, Keelung Taiwan 20347, Taiwan

LINARES-RIVERA, Ivette (PR)

LINBOOM, Bradley A. (Chi)

LINCOLN, Matthew R (WNY) 371 Delaware Ave, Buffalo, NY 14202

LINCOLN, Richard Kent (Los) 15114 Archwood St, Van Nuys, CA 91405

LINCOLN, Thomas C(larke) (Nwk) 1156 Carolina Cir Sw, Vero Beach, FL 32962

LIND, Douglass Theodore (Ct) 17080 Harbour Point Dr Apt 1017, Fort Myers, FL 33908

LIND, Tracey (O) 80 E. 252nd St., Euclid, OH 44132

LINDAHL, Rosa (Ala)

LINDBERG, Robert Morris (CPa) 16 Winch Hill Rd, Swanzey, NH 03446

LINDELL, John Allen (Mont) 6629 Merryport Ln, Naples, FL 34104

LINDELL, Thomas Jay (Az) 4460 N Camino Del Rey, Tucson, AZ 85718

LINDEMAN, Eileen Cornish (RI) 830 Mohican Way, Redwood City, CA 94062

LINDEMAN, Matthew James (Mass) PO Box 400, Southport, CT 06890

LINDEMAN, Mitchell James (Cal) 139 Ocean Avenue, Cranston, RI 02905

LINDENBERG, Juliana T (NC) 231 N Church St, Rocky Mount, NC 27804

LINDER, Callie Maebelle (Mich) 2034 S 69th East Pl, Tulsa, OK 74112

LINDER, Mark Allen (Ky) 2500 Crossings Blvd # 518, Bowling Green, KY 42104

LINDER, Philip Conrad (Lex) 25 Otranto Lane, Columbia, SC 29209

LINDH-PAYNE, Kristofer Hans (Md) 2216 Pot Spring Rd., Timonium, MD 21093

LINDLEY, Bernie (Ore) 97955 Hallway Rd, PO Box 3190, Harbor, OR 97415

LINDLEY, Susan Shea (Okla) 1202 W Elder Ave, Duncan, OK 73533

LINDQUIST, Mary Dail (Vt) 16 Bradley Ave, Brattleboro, VT 05301

LINDSAY JR, Spencer Hedden (La) 273 Monarch Dr Apt L-26, Houma, LA 70364

LINDSEY, Barrett Kelland (Oly) 2511 E 40th Ave, Spokane, WA 99223

LINDSEY, Kenneth Lewis (Me) 30 Monarch St., Augusta, ME 04330

LINDSEY, Richard Carroll (SC) 3001 Meeting St, Hilton Head Island, SC 29926

LINDSLEY, James Elliott (NY) Maplegarth, Box 881, Millbrook, NY 12545

LINDSTROM JR, Donald Fredrick (CGC) 269 Rainbow Falls Road, Franklin, NC 28734

LINDSTROM, Justin Alan (Okla) Saint Paul's Cathedral, 127 NW 7th St, Oklahoma City, OK 73102

LINDSTROM, Marjorie Dawson (Nwk) 91 Francisco Ave, Rutherford, NJ 07070

LINDWRIGHT, Philippa Elin (Ore) 3600 SW 117th Ave Apt 149, Beaverton, OR 97005

LINEBAUGH, Jonathan Andrew (CFla) 5910 NE 22nd Ter, Fort Lauderdale, FL 33308

LING, James Kai Fe (Tai) 4149 N Kenmore Ave # 28, Chicago, IL 60613

LING, Steven (Ct) Trinity Episcopal Church, 345 Main St, Portland, CT 06480

LINGLE, Mark Duane (Ct) 503 Old Long Ridge Rd, Stamford, CT 06903

LINK, Michael Roger (Nev) 11844 Orense Dr, Las Vegas, NV 89138

LINLEY, Eliza Mackay (ECR) 210 Lake Court, Aptos, CA 95003

LINN, David (Cal) Po Box 212, Moraga, CA 94556

LINNENBERG, Daniel M (Roch) 267 Brooklawn Dr, Rochester, NY 14618

LINSCOTT, John Burton (NC) 830 Durham Rd, Wake Forest, NC 27587

LINSCOTT, Stephanie (Tex) 3838 N Braeswood Blvd, Apt 257, Houston, TX 77025

LINTON, Adam Stuart (Mass) 204 Monument Rd, Orleans, MA 02653

LINVILLE, Harriet Burton (ECR) 10372 S W Windwood Way, Portland, OR 97225

LINZEL, Claire Benedict (SwFla) 411 Nottinghill Gale St. #805, #1207, Arlington, TX 76014

LIOTTA, Thomas Mark (NY) 629 County Route 12, New Hampton, NY 10958

LIPP, Beth Ann (ND) P.O. Box 1241, Bismarck, ND 58502

LIPPART, Thomas Edward (NMich) 5207 Eleuthra Circle, Vero Beach, FL 32967

LIPPE, Amanda J (SeFla) 5690 N Kendall Dr, Coral Gables, FL 33156

LIPPITT, Dudley Hand (Ga) 1704 11th Ave, Albany, GA 31707

LIPSCOMB III, C(Harles) Lloyd (SwVa) 501 V E S Rd Apt B513, Lynchburg, VA 24503

LIPSCOMB III, John W (CFla) 317 S Mary St, Eustis, FL 32726

LIPSCOMB, R(andall) Steve (Kan) 3324 NW Bent Tree Ln, Topeka, KS 66618

LIPSEY, Howard Martin (Chi) 62 Malden Ave, La Grange, IL 60525

LIRIANO MARTINEZ, Jorge Antonely (NJ) 3050 River Rd, Camden, NJ 08105

LIRO, Judith Reagan (Tex) 4301 N I H 35, Austin, TX 78722

LISBY, Gregory C (WMass) All Saints Episcopal Church, 10 Irving Street, Worcester, MA 01609

LISTER, Craig Joseph (NC) 1731 Wilkins Dr, Sanford, NC 27330

LITMAN, Eric Robert (Mass) 1991 Massachusetts Ave, Cambridge, MA 02140

LITSEY, Kim Jeanne (Ct) 915 Main St, South Glastonbury, CT 06073

✠ **LITTLE II**, Edward Stuart (Bp of NI 2000-) 117 N Lafayette Blvd, South Bend, IN 46601

LITTLE, Geoffery A (Ct) 358 Lenox Street, New Haven, CT 06513

LITTLE, Harry Robert (CNY) 22366 County Route 42, Carthage, NY 13619
LITTLE, Tracie L (EMich) 543 Michigan Ave, Marysville, MI 48040
LITTLEFIELD, Jeffrey B (Ore) 11265 SW Cabot St, Beaverton, OR 97005
LITTLEJOHN, Lucrecia M (Tex) 6307 Hickory Holw, Windcrest, TX 78239
LITTLEJOHN, N. Richard (Alb)
LITTLEPAGE, Dorothella Michel (Mass) 74 S Common St, Lynn, MA 01902
LITTLETON, William Harvey (Ga) PO Box 20633, Saint Simons Island, GA 31522
LITTMAN, Val J. (Eur) Altos Del Maria,, 314 Toscana II, Sora, Panama
LITTRELL, James H (Pa) 339 Dover Rd, South Newfane, VT 05351
LITWINSKI, Tony (Eur) Mauritiusplatz 1, Wiesbaden, MI D65183, Germany
LITZENBERGER, Caroline Jae (Ore) 1605 NE Clackamas St Apt 300C, Portland, OR 97232
LITZENBURG JR, Thomas Vernon (SwVa) 316 Jefferson St, Lexington, VA 24450
LIU, Ting-hua (Tai) I-105-7 Hang Chou South Road, Silo, Taiwan
LIVELY, James William (SwVa) 11610 Chantilly Ct, Clermont, FL 34711
LIVELY, Paula Kay (WMo) 601 E Benton St, Monett, MO 65708
LIVERMORE, Charles Whittier (ETcnn) 7604 Windwood Dr, Powell, TN 37849
LIVERPOOL, Herman Oswald (Fla) 3405 Nw 48th Ave, # JJ413, Lauderdale Lakes, FL 33319
LIVINGOOD, Randel Eugene (Ore) 814 Ne Clyde Place, Grants Pass, OR 97526
LIVINGSTON, Diane Howard (Miss) 37 Sheffield Place, Brevard, NC 28712
LIVINGSTON, James (NMich) 3135 County Road 456, Skandia, MI 49885
LIVINGSTON, James John (Los) 31641 La Novia Ave, San Juan Capistrano, CA 92675
LIVINGSTON, Philip Irving Conant (Episcopal SJ) 17 Linda Vista Dr, Monterey, CA 93940
LIVINGSTON, William Vernon (Miss) 37 Sheffield Place, Brevard, NC 28712
LIZ LOPEZ, Ramon A (PR) PO Box 6814, Elizabeth, NJ 07202
LJUNGGREN, M Lorraine (NC) 5400 Crestview Rd, Raleigh, NC 27609
LJUNGGREN, Timothy Merle (Mont) 62 Greenway Dr, Goshen, IN 46526
LLERENA FIALLOS, Angel Polivio (EcuC) Apartado 89, Guaranda, Provincia De Bolivar, Ecuador
LLOYD, Bonnie Jean (Tenn) 1420 Wilson Pike, Brentwood, TN 37027
LLOYD, Dennis (Pa) 1020 Remington Rd, Wynnewood, PA 19096
LLOYD, Elizabeth Anne (Chi) 322 Farragut St, Park Forest, IL 60466

LLOYD, Emily A (Ct) Calvary Church, 27 Church St, Stonington, CT 06378
LLOYD, James Edward (NJ) Apdo Postal 803, La Cristsina 50-5, Ajijic, CHIAPAS 45920, Mexico
LLOYD, John Janney (NJ) 115 Iroquois Rd, Yonkers, NY 10710
LLOYD, Kevin Michael (RI) 67 Mount Hope Ave, Jamestown, RI 02835
LLOYD, Lucia Kendall (Va) PO Box 158, Tappahannock, VA 22560
LLOYD, Margaret Ewing (Mass) 4 Berkeley Street, Cambridge, MA 02138
LLOYD, Robert Baldwin (SwVa) 3204 Mathews Ln., Blacksburg, VA 24060
LLOYD III, Samuel Thames (Mass) 206 Clarendon St, Boston, MA 02116
LLOYD, Sharon (Vt) 386South St, Middlebury, VT 05753
LLUMIGUANO AREVALO, Nancy (EcuC) Sarmiento, Quito, Ecuador
LO, Kwan (Los) 133 E Graves Ave, Monterey Park, CA 91755
LOBBAN, Andrew David (Cal) Grace Cathedral, 1100 California St, San Francisco, CA 94108
LOBDELL, Gary Thomas (Oly) 2610 E Section St Unit 92, Mount Vernon, WA 98274
LOBS, Donna Burkard (CFla) 128 Legacy Dr, Advance, NC 27006
LOBS III, George Richard (CFla) 128 Legacy Dr, Advance, NC 27006
LOCH, C Louanne (Fla) Holy Trinity Episcopal Church, 100 NE 1st St, Gainesville, FL 32601
LOCH, Jerry Lynn (Chi) 446 Somonauk St, Sycamore, IL 60178
LOCHER, Elizabeth A (Va) Msalato Theological College, PO Box 264, Dodoma Tanzania, Tanzania
LOCHNER, Charles Nugent (NJ) 2106 5th Ave, Spring Lake, NJ 07762
LOCK, John Mason (NJ) Trinity Episcopal Church, 65 W Front St, Red Bank, NJ 07701
LOCKE, Carol Ann (Los) 61 Painter St Apt 1, Pasadena, CA 91103
LOCKE, Kay (Nwk) 15 Norwood Ave, Summit, NJ 07901
LOCKE, Ralph Donald (CNY) 11 Orange St, Marcellus, NY 13108
LOCKE, William Russell (RI) 63 Pidge Avenue, Pawtucket, RI 02860
LOCKETT (CGC) 102 Shadow Ln, Troy, AL 36079
LOCKETT, Harold John (At)
LOCKETT, Tina Lynn (Pgh) 809 Maplewood Ave, Ambridge, PA 15003
LOCKHART SR, Ronald Wayne (Pa) 687 Sugartown Rd, PO Box 1330, Malvern, PA 19355
LOCKLEY, Linda Sue (SwFla)
LOCKWOOD II, Frank Robert (Alb) 14 Spencer Blvd, Coxsackie, NY 12051
LOCKWOOD, Marcia Miller (ECR) PO Box 345, Rancho del Robledo, Carmel Valley,, CA 93924

LODDER, Herbert Kingsley (Md) 130 W Seminary Ave, Lutherville, MD 21093
LODWICK, James Nicholas (NY) 925 W Washington St, South Bend, IN 46601
LOEFFLER, George C (Be) 46 Wessnersville Rd, Kempton, PA 19529
LOESCHER, Candyce Jean (Ky) St Mary's Episcopal Church, 163 N Main St, Madisonville, KY 42431
LOEWE, Richard (Los) 1907 W West Wind, Santa Ana, CA 92704
LOFGREN, Claire (NY) St. Joseph of Arimathea, 2172 Saw Mill River Road, White Plains, NY 10607
LOFMAN, Donald Stig (NY) 12 Depot St, Middletown, NY 10940
LOGAN, Christie Larson (Oly)
LOGAN JR, George Willis (Va) 100 W Jefferson St, Charlottesville, VA 22902
LOGAN, Jeffery Allen (FtW) Psc 817 Box 43, Fpo, AE 09622
LOGAN JR, John A. (Tex) 2808 Sunset Blvd, Houston, TX 77005
LOGAN, Linda Marie (CNY) 405 N Madison Ave, Pierre, SD 57501
LOGAN, Michael Dennis (Alb) St Mark's Church, P.O. Box 331, Malone, NY 12953
LOGAN, William Stevenson (Mich) 1514 Chateaufort Pl, Detroit, MI 48207
LOGAN, Yvonne Luree (NY) 1185 Park Ave Apt 12j, New York, NY 10128
LOGSDON, Tami Davis (NwT) 4207 Emil Ave, Amarillo, TX 79106
LOGUE, Frank (Ga) 111 Clinton Ct, Saint Marys, GA 31558
LOGUE, Mary Ann Willson (Ct) 173 Livingston St, New Haven, CT 06511
LOHMANN, John J (Mich) 296 Ackerson Lake Dr., Jackson, MI 49201
LOHSE, Dana (Wyo) Po Box 291, Kaycee, WY 82639
LOKEN, Gail Mitchell (Ak) 5101 Omalley Rd, Anchorage, AK 99507
LOKEY, Michael Paul (Eas) 29618 Polks Rd, Princess Anne, MD 21853
LOLCAMA, Terri (Oly) 10630 Gravelly Lake Dr SW, Lakewood, WA 98499
LOLK, Otto Lothar Manfred (Pa) 30866 Buttonwood Dr, Lewes, DE 19958
LOMAS, Bruce Alan (Mass) 3 Gould St, Melrose, MA 02176
LOMBARDO, Janet Marie Vogt (NH) 67 Ridge Rd, Concord, NH 03301
LONDON, Daniel Deforest (Los) 2451 Ridge Rd, Berkeley, CA 94709
LONDON, Gary Loo (Los) 122 S California Ave, Monrovia, CA 91016
LONE, Jose Francisco (Hond)
LONERGAN, Kathleen Guthrie (Mass) 119 Washington Street, c/o St James Episcopal Church, Groveland, MA 01834
LONERGAN, Robert Thomas (Ore) 601 Taylor St, Myrtle Creek, OR 97457

LONERGAN, Wallace Gunn (Ida) 812 E Linden St, Caldwell, ID 83605

LONERGAN JR, W(illis) Gerald (Oly) 6114 E Evergreen Blvd, Vancouver, WA 98661

LONG, Benjamin Isaac (Tex) 1941 Webberville Rd, Austin, TX 78721

LONG, Beth Louise (At) 165 Meredith Ridge Rd, Athens, GA 30605

LONG, Betty Ann (WMass) 2 Viking Ln, Sandwich, MA 02563

LONG, Cynthia A (The Episcopal NCal) 7041 Verdure Way, Elk Grove, CA 95758

LONG, Eric (SwVa) PO Box 257, Roanoke, VA 24002

LONG, Gail Ann (SVa) 2441 Tuxedo Pl, Albany, GA 31707

LONG II, John Michael (Neb) 1615 Brent Blvd, Lincoln, NE 68506

LONG, Lewis Harvey (Az) 28 W Pasadena Ave, Phoenix, AZ 85013

LONG, Robert Carl (WMo) 4301 Madison Ave Apt 218, Kansas City, MO 64111

LONG, Shirley Dube (WNC) Po Box 72, Deep Gap, NC 28618

LONG, Thomas Mcmillen (Colo) 4155 E Jewell Ave Ste 1117, Denver, CO 80222

LONGACRE, Tracy Elizabeth (Cal) 2323 Magnolia St Ste 11, Oakland, CA 94607

LONGBOTTOM, Robert John David (CFla) 3891 Cedar Hammock Trl, Saint Cloud, FL 34772

LONGE, Neal Patrick (Alb) 58 Reber St, Colonie, NY 12205

✠ **LONGEST**, Charles Lindsay (Ret Bp Suffr of Md 1998-) 7200 3rd Ave., C-035, Sykesville, MD 21784

LONGHI, Anthony Peter (Chi) 1850 Landre Ct, Burlington, WI 53105

LONGHITANO, Maria Vittoria (Eur) via Benevenuto Cellini 24, Corsico MI, 20094, Italy

LONGO, John Alphonsus (The Episcopal Church in Haw) 9901 N Oracle Rd, Apt 8103, Tuscon, AZ 97062

LONGSTAFF, Thomas Richmond Willis (Me) 39 Pleasant St, Waterville, ME 04901

LONGSTRETH, William Morris (Pa) 1146 Handview Circle, Pottstown, PA 19464

LONSWAY, Rose Anne (O) St Peter's Episcopal Church, 45 W Winter St, Delaware, OH 43015

LONTO, Michael J (WNY) 99 Wildwood Av, Salamanca, NY 14779

LOOKER, Jennifer Elizabeth (CPa) 241 Sherman Ave Apt 3, New Haven, CT 06511

LOOMIS, Julia Dorsey Reed (SVa) 416 Court St, Portsmouth, VA 23704

LOOP, Richard Bruce (Ore) 36489 Florence Ct., Astoria, OR 97103

LOOR CEDENO, Mariana (Litoral Ecu) 22 Ava & 3er Callejon P, Bahia De Caraquez, Ecuador

LOPER, Jerald Dale (Minn) 1524 Country Club Rd, Albert Lea, MN 56007

LOPEZ, Abel E (Los) 2396 Mohawk St Unit 7, Pasadena, CA 91107

LOPEZ, Antonio (Nev) 832 N Eastern Ave, Las Vegas, NV 89101

LOPEZ, Bienvenido Taveras (DR (DomRep)) Iglesia Episcopal Divina Providencia, Calle Marcos Del Rosario #39, Republica Dominicana, Dominican Republic

LOPEZ JR, Eddie (Ct)

LOPEZ, Mary Alice (SwFla) 504 Columbia Dr, Tampa, FL 33606

LOPEZ, Oscar Obdulio (Hond) 12 Calle, 10-11 Avenue Bo Cabanas, San Pedro, Honduras

LOPEZ, Pedro Nel (Tex) Saint Peter's Church, 705 Williams St, Pasadena, TX 77506

LOPEZ JR, Ram (WTex) 1247 Vista Del Juez, San Antonio, TX 78216

LOPEZ, Sunny Porter (Chi) 3115 W Jerome St, Chicago, IL 60645

LOPEZ, Uriel (Tex) 40 Center St, Elgin, IL 60120

LOPEZ-CHAVERRA, Hector (SwFla) Episc Ch St. Francis, P.O. Box 9332, Tampa, FL 33674

LOPOSER, Ellen Fogg (Spok) St Andrew's Episcopal Church, 2404 N Howard St, Spokane, WA 99205

LORA, Juan B (Ct) 16 Paul St, Danbury, CT 06810

LORD, James Raymond (Ky) 3001 Myrshine Dr, Pensacola, FL 32506

LORD, Mary George (NwPa) 2425 Glendale Ave, Erie, PA 16510

LORD, Philip Warren (WNY) 5013 Van Buren Rd, Dunkirk, NY 14048

LORD, Richard Anthony (Va) 543 Beulah Road Northeast, Vienna, VA 22180

LORD, Robert Charles (CFla) 1312 Bridgeport Drive, Winter Park, FL 32789

LORD-WILKINSON, Randall A (WA) Church of the Ascension, 205 S Summit Ave, Gaithersburg, MD 20877

LORENSON, Ruth Lorraine (LI) 9 Warton Pl, Garden City, NY 11530

LORENZ, Constance (LI) 87-45 108th Street, Richmond Hill, NY 11418

LORENZE, James Dennis (Eau) 2304 Country Club Ln, Eau Claire, WI 54701

LORENZETTI, Dominick Joseph (Episcopal SJ) 1528 Oakdale Rd, Modesto, CA 95355

LORING III, Richard Tuttle (Mass) 114 Badger Ter, Bedford, MA 01730

LORING, William Delano (Ct) 15 Pleasant Drive, Danbury, CT 06811

LOSCH, Richard Rorex (Ala) Po Box 1560, Livingston, AL 35470

LOUA, Cece Alfred-S (Mich) 1021 Norwich Drive, Troy, MI 48084

LOUD JR, Johnson D (Minn) 740 Shane Park Cir Apt 2, Prescott, WI 54021

LOUDEN, Molly O'Neill (Ct) 37 Gin Still Ln, West Hartford, CT 06107

LOUDENSLAGER, Samuel Charles (Ark) 20000 Hwy 300-Spur, Bigelow, AR 72016

LOUGHRAN JR, Eugene James (SwFla) 633 Coquina Court, Fort Myers, FL 33908

LOUGHREN, James (Dal) 4879 Lake Shore Dr, Bolton Landing, NY 12814

LOUIS, Richard M (Nwk) 2395 Quill Ct, Mahwah, NJ 07430

LOUIS DEAN SKIPPER, James Louis Dean (Ala) 1426 Gilmer Ave, Montgomery, AL 36104

LOUISE, Sister Catherine (Mass) 17 Louisburg Sq, Boston, MA 02108

LOUTREL, William Frederic (Ct) 1090 Ridge Rd, Hamden, CT 06517

✠ **LOUTTIT**, Henry Irving (Ret Bp of Ga 2009-) 611 E Bay St, Savannah, GA 31401

LOVE, Leon Lewis (CNY) 5 Gail Dr, Waverly, NY 14892

✠ **LOVE**, William Howard (Bp of Alb 2006-) PO Box 211, Lake Luzerne, NY 12846

LOVEKIN, Arthur Adams (RG) 10501 Lagrima De Oro Rd NE, Apt 4208, Albuquerque, NM 87111

LOVELACE, David Wayne (CPa) 140 N Beaver St, York, PA 17401

LOVELADY, Eldwin M (Oly) 3700 14th Ave SE, Unit 3, Olympia, WA 98501

LOVETT, G David (ETenn) PO Box 10944, Knoxville, TN 37939

LOVING, John H (NwT) 8009 Ladera Verde, Austin, TX 78739

LOW, James Robert (Ct) 60 Shadagee Rd Unit 22, Saco, ME 04072

LOW, Melvin Leslie (Ia)

LOW, Raymond Albert (Mass) 5 Buttonwood Rd, Marshfield, MA 02050

LOW, Salin Miller (Ct) PO Box 27, Pine Meadow, CT 06061

LOW, William Harrison (Ct) 12 Meadowview Ct, Canton, CT 06019

LOWE, Dianne Louise (Spok) St James Episcopal Church, 1410 NE Stadium Way, Pullman, WA 99163

LOWE, Edward Charles (Ga) PO Box 168, Saint Marys, GA 31558

LOWE JR, Eugene Yerby (NY) 624 Colfax St, Evanston, IL 60201

LOWE, Harold Chapin (Dal) 2212 Saint Andrews, McKinney, TX 75070

LOWE JR, J(ohn) Fletcher (Del) 1600 Westbrook Avenue Apt 27, Richmond, VA 23227

LOWE, John Leon (Ind) 200 Glennes Ln Apt 205, Dunedin, FL 34698

LOWE, Lori Marleen (Chi) 5116 W Malibu Ct, McHenry, IL 60050

LOWE, Steve (Chi) 2009 Regency Ct, Geneva, IL 60134

LOWE, Walter James (At) 1647 N Rock Springs Rd NE, Atlanta, GA 30324

LOWERY, Donald Andrew (NC) 210 S Chestnut St, Henderson, NC 27536

LOWERY, Hermon Lee (Ga) 2705 Michael Rd, Albany, GA 31721

LOWNEY, James (Ind) 2651 California St, Columbus, IN 47201

LOWREY, Edward Sager (NwPa) Box 54, 107 Harvey Road, Foxburg, PA 16036

LOWREY III, Pierce Lang (At) 3830 Randall Farm Rd, Atlanta, GA 30339

LOWRY, David Busch (LI) Po Box 51777, New Orleans, LA 70151

LOWRY, Robert Lynn (Tex) Trinity in the Woodland Texas, 3901 S Panther Creek Dr, The Woodlands, TX 77381

LOWRY III, William M (Miss) PO Box 224, Tunica, MS 38676

LOW-SKINNER, Debra Lee (Cal) 137 Redding Rd Apt C, Campbell, CA 95008

LOY, Reed Julian (NH) 885 Shore Rd, Cape Elizabeth, ME 04107

LOYA, Craig William (Neb) 113 N 18th St, Omaha, NE 68102

LOYD, Janet Ellen (Oly) 56738 Sturgeon Rd, Darrington, WA 98241

LOYOLA, Leo Gan (The Episcopal Church in Haw) Diocese o f Hawaii, 229 Queen Emma Sq, Honolulu, HI 96813

LOZAMA, Abiade (Hai)

LOZANO, Kathleen Barbara (Los) St Matthias Episcopal Church, 7056 Washington Ave, Whittier, CA 90602

LUAL, Anderia Arok (Az) Diocese of Arizona, 114 W Roosevelt St, Phoenix, AZ 85003

LUBELFELD, Nicholas Paul Needham (Va) 4460 Edan Mae Ct, Annandale, VA 22003

LUCAS, Albert (HB) 4440 Meadow Creek Cir, Sarasota, FL 34233

LUCAS, Alison Carey Carpenter (ECR) 19315 Vineyard Ln, Saratoga, CA 95070

LUCAS, Jason B (Minn) St. Edward Episcopal Church, 865 Ferndale Rd. N, Wayzata, MN 55391

LUCAS, Jeremy P (Ore) 1060 Chandler Rd, Lake Oswego, OR 97034

LUCAS, Kimberly Danielle (WA) 1830 Connecticut Ave NW, Washington, DC 20009

LUCAS, Mary Louise (Mass) 136 Bay Street #501, Hamilton, L8P 3H8, Canada

LUCAS, Paul Nahoa (The Episcopal Church in Haw) 47-074 Lihikai Dr, Kaneohe, HI 96744

LUCAS, Rigal (Hai) Box 1309, Port-Au-Prince, Haiti

LUCAS, Thomas Stewart (Md) Church of the Nativity, 419 Cedarcroft Rd, Baltimore, MD 21212

LUCAS, Wanda Beth (Ga) 524 Suncrest Blvd, Savannah, GA 31410

LUCENT, Robert Brian (SanD) 629 Judson St, Escondido, CA 92027

LUCEY, David J (Va) 399 Hope St., Bristol, RI 02809

LUCHS, Lewis Richard (Chi) 6417 81st St, Cabin John, MD 20818

LUCK, Diana Nelson (Dal) 6912 Merrilee Ln, Dallas, TX 75214

LUCK, G Thomas (CNY) 310 Montgomery St., Syracuse, NY 13202

LUCK JR, George Edmund (Dal) 6912 Merrilee Ln, Dallas, TX 75214

LUCKENBACH, David Andrew (Tex) 1709 S College Ave, Tyler, TX 75701

LUCKETT JR, David Stafford (Miss) 4241 Otterlake Cove, Niceville, FL 32578

LUCKEY, Marion Isabelle Aiken (NMich) 1531 Vardon Rd, Munising, MI 49862

LUCKEY III, Thomas Hannan (NMich) E9430 E. Munising Ave. #2, Munising, MI 49862

LUCKRITZ, Denzil John (Chi) 421 Wianno Ave., Osterville, MA 02655

LUDBROOK, Helen Christine (Mo) 1422 Lawnwood Dr, Des Peres, MO 63131

LUECKENHOFF, James Joseph (WLa) 1518 Griffith St, Lake Charles, LA 70601

LUECKERT, Diana Rowe (The Episcopal NCal) 4800 Olive Oak Way, Carmichael, CA 95608

LUEDDE, Christopher S (Roch) 31 Kitty Hawk Dr, Pittsford, NY 14534

LUETHE, Robin Lewis (Oly) 789 Highway 603, Chehalir, WA 98532

LUFKIN, Alison C (Colo) PO Box 1305, Leadville, CO 80461

LUFKIN, George S (Colo) PO Box 243, Leadville, CO 80461

LUGER, Virginia M (ND) 821 N 4th St Apt 3, Bismarck, ND 58501

LUHRING, Peggy Williams (SVa) 4449 N Witchduck Rd, Virginia Beach, VA 23455

LUI, David Suikwei (Cal) 1011 Harrison St # 202, Oakland, CA 94607

LUJAN, Mary Royes (EO) Po Box 25, Hood River, OR 97031

LUKANICH, Emily Anderson (SwVa) Christ Episcopal Church, PO Box 164, Blacksburg, VA 24063

LUKAS, Arlene (WNC) 416 N Haywood St, Waynesville, NC 28786

LUKAS, Randolph E (Alb) PO Box 827, New Lebanon, NY 12125

LUKENS JR, Alexander Macomb (Colo) 1380 S Madison St, Cortez, CO 81321

LUKENS, Ann Pierson (Oly) 2015 Killarney Way, Bellevue, WA 98004

LUKENS, Matthew M (The Episcopal Church in Haw) 183 Alala Rd, Kailua, HI 96734

LULEY, William Tracy (Mo) 1101 Sulphur Spring Rd, Manchester, MO 63021

LULLO, Milania (WNY) 200 Cazenovia St, Buffalo, NY 14210

LUMBARD, Carolyn Mary (Roch) 326 Frederick Douglas St, Rochester, NY 14608

LUMLEY, Dale Allen (WK) 906 W Wheat Ave, Ulysses, KS 67880

LUNA JR, Eulalio Gallardo (WTex) 234 W Mariposa Dr, San Antonio, TX 78212

LUND, Joseph Walter (WA) 70381 Placerville Rd, Rancho Mirage, CA 92270

LUND, Judith Ann (Ark) 8280 Spanker Ridge Dr, Bentonville, AR 72712

LUND, Virginia U Sapienza (Mil) 1101 Greenough Dr W, Apt. E-6, Missoula, MT 59802

LUNDBERG III, Nelson John (Alb) 36 Plaza Avenue, Governor's Sq, Rensselaer, NY 12144

LUNDBERG, Richard Evard (Chi) 811 E Central Rd Apt 239, Arlington Heights, IL 60005

LUNDELIUS, Heulette Carolyn (Lynn) Sparks (WA) 5801 Nicholson Lane Apt 1923, Rockville, MD 20852

LUNDEN, Michael Carl (NY) 118 S Church St, Goshen, NY 10924

LUNDGREN, Linda Lou (Minn) 8 3rd St, Proctor, MN 55810

LUNDGREN, Richard John (Chi) 13129 Lake Mary Dr., Plainfield, IL 60585

LUNDIN, George Edward (Miss) 705 Southern Ave, Hattiesburg, MS 39401

LUNDQUIST, Robert (WNC) 419 Turnpike Rd, Mills River, NC 28759

LUNNUM, Lindsay S (LI) Zion Episcopal Church, 243-01 Northern Blvd, Douglaston, NY 11363

LUNTSFORD, Sharon Lorene (ND) Po Box 18, Alexander, ND 58831

LUONI, Richard B (CFla) 2499 N Westmoreland Ave, Orlando, FL 32804

LUPFER JR, William B (NY) 120 Broadway Fl 38, New York, NY 10271

LUPTON JR, Jim (Ark) 241 Riverview St., Belhaven, NC 27810

LUSIGNAN, Louise Jennet (WA) 10450 Lottsford Road, Mitchellville, MD 20721

LUSK JR, Karl (Ky) 236 Ridgeview Dr, New Haven, KY 40051

LUTAS, Donald Mckenzie (Mich) 6114 28th St, Detroit, MI 48210

LUTES, Kathleen Monson (Mil) 2224 Cedar Dr, Rapid City, SD 57702

LUTHER, Carol Luther (Cal) St Paul's Episcopal School, 46 Montecito Ave., Oakland, CA 94610

LUTTER, Linda F (Chi) 5725 Stearns School Rd, Gurnee, IL 60031

LUTTRELL, John Sidney (LI) 295 Old Kings Hwy, Downingtown, PA 19335

LUTZ, Alison W (NY) National Route 3, Cange Haiti, Haiti

LUTZ, Randall Robert (RG) 2365 Brother Abdon Way, Santa Fe, NM 87505

LUTZ, Richard Herbert (LI) Cashelmara 40, 23200 Lake Road, Bay Village, OH 44140

LUTZ, Ruth Jeanne (RG) 1330 Renoir Ct., Las Cruces, NM 88007

Clergy List

LUTZ, William Charles (CNY) 82 Scott Ave, Elmira, NY 14905
LWEBUGA-MUKASA, Katherine N (WNY) 168 Schimwood Ct, Getzville, NY 14068
LYCETT, Horace Abbott (Colo) 1223 Center St, Goodland, KS 67735
LYGA, Robert Michael (Minn) N36457 State Road 93/121, Independence, WI 54747
LYLE, Jerry (Tex) St. Joseph's Episcopal Church, PO Box 797, Salado, TX 76571
LYLE, Patsy Rushworth (La) 19344 Links Ct, Baton Rouge, LA 70810
LYLE, Randall Robert (Ia) 2350 Glass Rd NE, Cedar Rapids, IA 52402
LYLE, William Edward (SO) 1547 Stratford Dr, Kent, OH 44240
LYMAN, Rebecca (Cal) 115 Sheridan Way, Woodside, CA 94062
LYNCH JR, Bobby (WNC) Po Box 561, Rutherfordton, NC 28139
LYNCH, Daniel Luke (WVa) 123 Hidden Valley Ests, Scott Depot, WV 25560
LYNCH, David R (WMo) 16808 S State Route D, Belton, MO 64012
LYNCH, Gwynn (SanD) 13319 Fallen Leaf Rd, Poway, CA 92064
LYNCH, John J (SVa) 4109 Big Bethel Rd, Tabb, VA 23693
LYNCH, Pamela S (EMich) 525 Weiss Rd, Gaylord, MI 49735
LYNCH, Suzanne Mchugh Stryker (WMo) 1342 S Ventura Ave, Springfield, MO 65804
LYNCH, William David (NC) 8849 Ray Rd, Raleigh, NC 27613
LYNN, Connor (Los) 1902 Park Ave Apt 316, Los Angeles, CA 90026
LYNN, Jacqueline Goler (Chi)
LYON IV, James Fraser (USC) 1512 Blanding St, Columbia, SC 29201
LYON, Lauren Jean (Ia) Trinity Church, 320 E College St, Iowa City, IA 52240
LYON, Susan Loy (Ark) 1000 N Mississippi St, Little Rock, AR 72207
LYON, Walter Donald (CFla) 1628 Bent Oaks Blvd, DeLand, FL 32724
LYONS JR, James Hershel (Nev) All Saint's Episcopal Church, 4201 W Washington Ave, Las Vegas, NV 89107
LYONS, Leroy A (NJ) 1208 Prospect Ave, Plainfield, NJ 07060
LYONS, Lorraine M (Alb) 1154 Hedgewood Ln, Niskayuna, NY 12309
LYONS, Patricia M (WA)
LYTLE, Ashley Alexandra Gabriella (At) 515 E Ponce De Leon Ave, Decatur, GA 30030
LYTLE, Ronald Dale (Wyo) 1222 Rosewood Ln, Powell, WY 82435

M

MAAS, Benjamin Wells (Va) 1374 S Brook St, Louisville, KY 40208

MAAS, Jan Alfred (NY) 2121 Jamieson Ave Unit 1909, Alexandria, VA 22314
MACARTHUR III, Robert Stuart (Mo) 334 Maple Ridge Road, Center Sandwich, NH 03227
MACAULEY JR, Robert Conover (Vt) 175 Hills Point Road, Charlotte, VT 05445
MACBETH, Andrew Jeffrey (WTenn) 1640 Harbert Ave, Memphis, TN 38104
MACCOLL, Craig (Colo) 5876 E Kettle Pl, Centennial, CO 80112
MACCOLLAM, Joel Allan (Alb) 240 Belflora Way, Oceanside, CA 92057
MACCONNELL, James Stuart (Wyo) 403 15th St #1, Dallas Center, IA 50063
MACDONALD, Daniel (Mass) 147 Concord Rd, Lincoln, MA 01773
MACDONALD, David Roberts (LI) 253 Glen Ave, Sea Cliff, NY 11579
MACDONALD, Gilbert John (EMich) 331 West Mill Street, Oscoda, MI 48750
MACDONALD, Heyward Hunter (Md) 2551 Summit Ridge Trail, Charlottesville, VA 22911
MACDONALD, Jean A (Vt) 240 Greenpoint Ln, Lyndonville, VT 05851
MACDONALD, Linda Jean (Mich) 1780 Nemoke Trl, Haslett, MI 48840
✠ **MACDONALD**, Mark Lawrence (Form Bp of Ak 2007-) 2228 Penrose Ln., Fairbanks, AK 99709
MACDONALD, Susan Savage (Va) 1527 Senseny Rd, Winchester, VA 22602
MACDONALD, Terrence Cameron (O) 207 Weed St, New Canaan, CT 06840
MACDONALD, Walter Young (Mich) 2796 Page Ave, Ann Arbor, MI 48104
MACDONELL, Alexander (Alex) Harrison (Nwk) 216 Heath Vlg, Hackettstown, NJ 07840
MACDOUGALL, Matthew Bradstock (NwPa) 343 E Main St, Youngsville, PA 16371
MACDOWELL, Barry S (Ind) 138 S 18th St, Richmond, IN 47374
MACDUFFIE, Bruce Lincoln (CNY) 836 5th Ave. West, Dickinson, ND 58601
MACEK, Kathryn Ellen (EO) PO Box 1001, La Grande, OR 97850
MAC EWEN, Suzanne Marie (Wyo) Po Box 137, Evanston, WY 82931
MACFARLANE, Robert John (Chi) 3724 Farr Ave, Fairfax, VA 22030
MACFIE JR, Thomas Earle (Tenn) 117 Carruthers Rd, Sewanee, TN 37375
MACGILL, Martha Nell (Md)
MACGILL III, William D (WVa) 5909 cedar landing rd, Wilmington, NC 28409
MACGOWAN JR, Kenneth Arbuthnot (Colo) 3440 S Jefferson St Apt 1136, Falls Church, VA 22041

MACGREGOR, Laird Stanley (WK) 322 S Ash St, Mcpherson, KS 67460
MACIAS PEREZ, Franklin Oswaldo (Litoral Ecu) CALLE AMARILIS FUENTES N, 603 Y CALLE D, GUAYAQUIL, 09-01-5250, Ecuador
MACINNIS, Elyn Gregg Cheney (NY) B21 Jiu Xian Qiao Road, Beijing, 100016, China
MACINTIRE, Morgan Montelepre (La) 2050 Bert Kouns, Shreveport, LA 71118
MACINTOSH, Neil K (Kan) Charismead, 11A Browns Road, The Oaks, NSW, 2570, Australia
MACK, Alan E (Oly)
MACK, Arthur Robert (Mich) 13 Dover Ln., Hendersonville, NC 28739
MACK, Ross Julian (NI) Po Box 462, Valparaiso, IN 46384
MACKAY III, Donald (Oly) 9727 NE Juanita Dr, Unit #311, Kirkland, WA 98034
MACKE, Elizabeth Ann (Ind) 4713 Housebridge Rd, Corydon, KY 42406
MACKENDRICK, Gary Winfred (Ore) 3014 Main Street, Forest Grove, OR 97116
MACKENZIE JR, Albert Harold (SO) 37 Abbey Ln, Washington, NC 27889
MACKENZIE, A(Lexander) James (The Episcopal NCal) 3988 NW Walnut Ct., Corvallis, OR 97330
MACKENZIE, Jonathan (NH) 52 Brick Kiln Rd, Chelmsford, MA 01824
MACKENZIE, Katharine Helen (Los) 948 W Sierra Nevada Way, Orange, CA 92865
MACKENZIE, Lester Vivian (Los) 1031 Bienveneda Ave, Pacific Palisades, CA 90272
MACKENZIE, Mary Catherine (Oly) 16060 Ne 28th St, Bellevue, WA 98008
MACKENZIE, Ross (WNY) 11819 Eastkent Sq, Richmond, VA 23238
MACKENZIE, Vanessa Mildred (Los) 1739 Buckingham Rd, Los Angeles, CA 90019
MACKENZIE, Vincent Victor (Cal) 110 Bella Vista Ave, Belvedere, CA 94920
MACKEY, George Rudolph (Los) 801 Haslam Dr, Santa Maria, CA 93454
MACKEY, Guy L (RG) 312 N. Orchard Ave., Farmington, NM 87401
MACKEY, Jeffrey Allen (Fla) 500 Grove Street, Melrose, FL 32666
MACKEY, Judith P (Los) 801 Haslam Dr, Santa Maria, CA 93454
MACKEY, Peter David (Mich) 614 Company St, Adrian, MI 49221
MACKIE, Robert Allan (Mass) 16 Park Ave, Somerville, MA 02144
MACKILLOP, Alan Bruce (SanD) 73 Windward Ln, Manchester, NH 03104
MACKIN, Mary Ruetten (SwVa) St John's Episcopal Church, PO Box 257, Roanoke, VA 24002
MACKINTOSH, Leigh P (SwVa) 605 Clay St, Lynchburg, VA 24504

MACKNIGHT, Jeffrey Brooks (WA) 5450 Massachusetts Ave, Bethesda, MD 20816

MACKOV, Elwyn Joseph (WVa) 118 Five Point Ave, Martinsburg, WV 25404

MACLEAN, Peter Duncan (LI) P.O. Box 848, Colchester, VT 05446

MACLEOD, John Malcolm (NH) Episcopal Church Of St Andrew, PO Box 294, New London, NH 03257

MACLEOD III, Norman M (Vt) 2 Church St, Woodstock, VT 05091

MACLIN, Charles Waite (Me) Po Box 1259, Portland, ME 04104

MACMILLAN, Cameron Patrick (CFla)

MACNABB, Anne St. Clair Coghill (Md) 20370 Marguritte Sq, Sterling, VA 20165

MACNALLY, Janet Lee (Minn)

✠ **MACNAUGHTON**, John Herbert (Ret Bp of WTex 1996-) 7 Queens Gate, San Antonio, TX 78218

MACNEICE, (Alan) (The Episcopal Church in Haw) 29Eo Street 178, Commond Choy Chom, Phnom Penh, Cambodia

MACORT, John (Ct) 5227 Rancho Ave, Sarasota, FL 34234

MACPHAIL, Alexander Douglas (SwVa) 1101 Franklin Rd Sw, Roanoke, VA 24016

MACPHAIL, Karin L (Va) 335 Eagle Street, Woodstock, VA 22664

✠ **MACPHERSON**, D(Avid) Bruce (Ret Bp of WLa 2012-) 3108 Garden Hill Cir, Edmond, OK 73034

MACQUEEN, Karen Brenna (Los) 23730 Gold Nugget Ave, Diamond Bar, CA 91765

MACSWAIN, Robert Carroll (EC) University Of The South School Of Theology, 335 Tennessee Ave., Sewanee, TN 37383

MACVEAN-BROWN, Shannon L (Ind) 8850 Woodward Ave, Detroit, MI 48202

MACWHINNIE II, Anthony Eugene (CGC) 7810 Navarre Pkwy, Navarre, FL 32566

MADDEN, John Erwin (LI) PO Box 398, Laurel, NY 11948

MADDISON, Benjamin B (NJ)

MADDON, Ernest Clinton (Okla) 1411 the Lakes Ct, Keller, TX 76248

MADDOX III, William Edward (NC) 5718 Catskill Court, Durham, NC 27713

MADDUX, Carole Frauman (At) 9695 Hillside Dr, Roswell, GA 30076

MADDUX, Donald Jess (Oly) 706 West Birch Street, Shelton, WA 98584

MADDY, Marta Tuff (Minn)

MADER, Carol Ann (Mich) 6092 Beechwood Drive, Haslett, MI 48840

MADISON, David Andrew (FtW) 5005 Dexter Ave, Fort Worth, TX 76107

MADISSON LOPEZ, Vaike Marika (Hond) Km. 119 Crr al Norte, Jugo de Cane, Siguatepeque, 21105, Honduras

MADRID, Hector Orlando (Hond) Apartado Postal 30, Siguatepeque, Comayagua, Honduras

MADSEN, David Lloyd (SanD) Saint Alban's Episcopal Church, 490 Farragut Cir, El Cajon, CA 92020

MADSON, Peter G (CFla) 509 Derby Dr, Altamonte Springs, FL 32714

MAESEN, William August (Chi) Po Box 4380, Chicago, IL 60680

MAFLA SILVA, Daniel Antonio (Colom) Carrera 6 No 49-85, Piso 2, Bogota, Colombia

MAGALA, Joy (Los) 8341 De Soto Ave, Canoga Park, CA 91304

MAGDALENE, Deborah (NY) 12 Saterlee Pl, Wappingers Falls, NY 12590

MAGEE, Frederick Hugh (Spok) 17 North Street, ST. ANDREWS, - KY16 9PW, Great Britain (UK)

MAGERS, James Hugh (WTex) 4934 Lakeway Dr, Brownsville, TX 78520

MAGGIANO, Grey Scott (SeFla) Trinity Cathedral, 464 NE 16th St, Miami, FL 33132

MAGIE, William Walter (Ia) 301 S 2nd St, Polk City, IA 50226

MAGILL, Elizabeth Anne (Tex) 301 E 8th St, Austin, TX 78701

MAGILL, Peter George (CFla) 8310 Crosswicks Dr, Orlando, FL 32819

MAGLIULA, Robert James (NY) Holy Cross Monastery, PO Box 99, West Park, NY 12493

✠ **MAGNESS**, James Beattie (Bp Suffr for ArmdF & Fed Mnstrs 2010-) Office Of Bishop Suffragan For Armed Forces & Federal Ministries, 3504 Woodley Rd NW, Washington, DC 20016

MAGNUS, Elsie Blair (ND) PO Box 704, Walhalla, ND 58282

MAGNUS, Robert Frederick (Be) 507 Green Acres Dr, Mars Hill, NC 28754

MAGNUSON, George Peter (Colo) 2015 Glenarm Pl, Denver, CO 80205

MAGNUSON, Paulette Williams (Tex) 1602 S FM 116, Copperas Cove, TX 76522

MAGOON, George Arthur (NC) 5299 S Ventura Way, Centennial, CO 80015

MAGUIRE III, Bernard Leonard (Pa) 224 Flourtown Rd, Plymouth Meeting, PA 19462

MAHAFFEY, Glenn G (Be) 201 S Wilbur Ave, Sayre, PA 18840

MAHAN, Charles Earl (Kan) 402 N Topeka St, Wichita, KS 67202

MAHER JR, John Francis (Va) 5605 Eagle Lake Dr, Glen Allen, VA 23060

MAHER, Joseph Anthony (CFla) 5997 Heron Pond Dr, Port Orange, FL 32128

MAHON, Laurence Franklin (EO) 8501 Ne Wilson Creek Rd, Ashwood, OR 97711

MAHONEY, James Michael (Ida) 1912 Delmar St, Boise, ID 83713

MAHOOD, Sharon M. (Ia) 5720 Urbandale Ave., Des Moines, IA 50310

MAHURIN, Shanda M (SwFla) 1021 Greenturf Rd., Spring Hill, FL 34608

MAIER, Andrea R (Oly) 10841 Whipple Street, No. 105, North Hollywood, OR 91602

MAIER, Beth Ann (Vt) 1924 Blake St A, Berkeley, CA 94704

MAIL, Mary J(ean) (Mil) 509 East University, Bloomington, IN 47401

MAINWARING, Monica Burns (SanD) 1114 9th St, Coronado, CA 92118

MAINWARING, Simon (SanD) Christchurch School, 49 Seahorse Ln, Christchurch, VA 23031

MAIOCCO III, Joseph F (SwFla) 500 Park Shore Dr, Naples, FL 34103

MAITREJEAN, J Patrick (Cal) 1549 Circulo Jacona, Rio Rico, AZ 85648

MAJKRZAK, Albert Walter (Chi) 1222 Carpenter Street, Madison, WI 53704

MAJOR, John Charles (Be) 220 Montgomery Ave, West Pittston, PA 18643

MAJOR, J(oseph) Kenneth (SeFla) 1835 Nw 54th St, Miami, FL 33142

MAJOR, Philip Stephen (Wyo) St. Mark's Episcopal Church 701 South Wolcott, Casper, WY 82601

MAKES GOOD, Daniel Harry (SD) Po Box 28, Wanblee, SD 57577

MAKOWSKI, Chester Joseph (Tex) 1410 Jack Johnson Blvd., Galveston, TX 77550

MALANUK, Patricia Craig (USC) 6045 Lakeshore Dr, Columbia, SC 29206

MALARKEY, Shawn O (Pgh) 33 Alice St, Pittsburgh, PA 15205

MALAVE TORRES, Hector (PR)

MALCOLM, Frieda Louise (Eas) 1006 Beaglin Park Dr., Salisbury, MD 21804

MALCOLM, Karen Gottwald (Alb)

MALCOLM, Kenneth A (Colo) 910 E 3rd Ave, Durango, CO 81301

MALCOLM, Patricia Ann (Del) PO Box 1374, Dover, DE 19903

MALDONADO-MERCADO, Roberto (Ore) 13691 Gavina Ave Unit 557, Sylmar, CA 91342

MALE JR, Henry Alfred (Be) 80 Kal Shore Rd, Norway, ME 04268

MALERI, Karen D (Me) 112 Randolph Avenue, Milton, MA 02186

MALIA, Linda Merle (WNY) 209 Columbus Ave, Buffalo, NY 14220

MALIA, Phyllis Terri (CFla) St James Episcopal Ch, 44 S Halifax Dr, Ormond Beach, FL 32176

MALIAMAN, Irene Egmalis (The Episcopal Church in Haw) ECIM, 911 N Marine Corps Dr, Tamuning, GU 96913-4302, Guam

MALIN, Katherine Murphy (Mass) 147 Concord Rd, Lincoln, MA 01773

MALIONEK, Tom (Alb) 3 Chevy Chase Cir, Chevy Chase, MD 20815

MALLARY JR, R(aymond) DeWitt (NY) 80 Lyme Rd #161, Hanover, NH 03755

MALLIN, Caroll Sue Driftmeyer (SeFla) 1150 Stanford Dr, Coral Gables, FL 33146

MALLON, Beth Kohlmeyer (Ore) PO Box 445, Wilsonville, OR 97070

MALLONEE, Anne (NY) 19 E 34th St, New York, NY 10016

✠ **MALLORY**, Charles Shannon (Ret Bp of ECR 1990-) 74988 Tahoe Cir, Indian Wells, CA 92210

MALLORY, Richard Deaver (Ct) 455 Hope St Apt 3-D, Stamford, CT 06906

MALLORY, Steven Michael (Okla) 1808 Cedar Ln, Ponca City, OK 74604

MALLOW, Sherod Earl (SeFla) 2131 Sw 23rd Ave, Fort Lauderdale, FL 33312

MALLOY, Nancy (Colo) Saint Laurence's Episcopal Mission, 26812 Barkley Rd, Conifer, CO 80433

MALLOY, Patrick L (Be) The General Theological Seminary, 440 W 21st St., New York, NY 18102

MALM, Robert Hiller (Va) 3601 Russell Rd, Alexandria, VA 22305

MALONE, Bonnie Jordan (Oly) 24219 Witte Rd SE, Maple Valley, WA 98038

MALONE JR, Elmer Taylor (NC) 908 Wilcox St., Warrenton, NC 27589

MALONE, Michael James (Dal) 430 Greenwood Drive, Petersburg, VA 23805

MALONE, Timothy Joseph (WA) 2609 N Glebe Rd, Arlington, VA 22207

MALONE, Trawin E (Tex) 4115 Paint Rock Dr., Austin, TX 78731

MALONEY, Linda M (Vt) Po Box 294, Enosburg Falls, VT 05450

MALONEY, Raymond Burgess (The Episcopal NCal) 517 White Birch Ln, Windsor, CA 95492

MALONEY, Sean Patrick Henry (WTex) 622 Airline Rd, Corpus Christi, TX 78412

MALSEED, Caroline Frey (Ak) 4032 Deborah Dr., Juneau, AK 99801

MALTBIE, Colin Snow (Minn) 1000 Shumway Ave, Faribault, MN 55021

MANASEK, Robert Wesley (Neb) St Francis Episcopal Church, PO Box 1201, Scottsbluff, NE 69361

MANASTERSKI, Myron Julian (CFla) 2901 Sw 91st St # 2907, Ocala, FL 34476

MANCHESTER, Sean (RI) 19 Trinity Pkwy, Providence, RI 02908

MANCIL, Eric Nathan (NwT)

MANDELL, Cuthbert Heneage (Eas) 2010 Schooner Dr, Stafford, VA 22554

MANDERBACH, Aaron (Ct) 1207 Meadow Rdg, Redding, CT 06896

MANDEVILLE, Kathleen Corbiere (NY) Po Box 450, Tivoli, NY 12583

MANDRELL, H Dean (Ak)

MANGELS III, John Frederick (The Episcopal NCal) 6725 Hillglen Way, Fair Oaks, CA 95628

MANGUM, Frank Burnett (Tex) 14041 Horseshoe Cir, Waco, TX 76712

MANIACI, Maria Kathleen (NMich)

MANION, James Edward (Del) 20 Olive Ave, Rehoboth Beach, DE 19971

MANIYATT, John Kuriakose (Md) 4 E University Pkwy, Baltimore, MD 21218

MANLEY JR, Derrill Byrne (NwT) 1615 S Carpenter Ln, Cottonwood, AZ 86326

MANLEY, Wendy T (Cal) 1090 Brookfield Rd., Berlin, VT 05602

MANN, Alice B (Mass) 51 Leroy Ave, Haverhill, MA 01835

MANN, Carl Douglas (Ia) 3606 Jolly Ct, Spirit Lake, IA 51360

MANN, Charles Henry (SwFla) 5900 N Lockwood Ridge Road, Sarasota, FL 34243

MANN, Frederick Earl (SwFla) 7835 Moonstone Dr, Sarasota, FL 34233

MANN III, H(arold) Vance (WNC) 15 Creekside View Dr, Asheville, NC 28804

MANN, Henry R (SanD) 7981 Hemingway Ave, San Diego, CA 92120

MANN, Louise (Mass) 8399 Breeding Rd, Edmonton, KY 42129

MANN, Lucretia Winslow (ECR) 5271 Scotts Valley Dr, Scotts Valley, CA 95066

MANN, Mary Anne (Ct)

MANNING, Deacon Jeanette (SO) 164 Community Dr, Dayton, OH 45404

MANNING, Gary Briton (Mil) 1717 Church St., Wauwatosa, WI 53213

MANNING, Gene Bentley (Tenn) 900 Broadway, Nashville, TN 37203

MANNING, Jean Louise (NMich) 1344 M-64, Ontonagon, MI 49953

MANNING, Ronald Francis (CFla) 70 Town Ct Apt 334, Palm Coast, FL 32164

MANNING, Shannon Rogers (La) 5335 Suffolk Dr, Jackson, MS 39211

MANNING, Slaven L (USC) Po Box 220, Prosperity, SC 29127

MANNING, William Bentley (Ala) 1910 12th Ave S, Birmingham, AL 35205

MANNING-LEW, Sharon Janine (NY) 522 Washington St, Peekskill, NY 10566

MANNISTO, Virginia Lee (NMich) N4354 Black Creek Rd, Chatham, MI 49816

MANNSCHRECK, Mary Lou Cowherd (SwVa) St Luke's Episcopal Church, 801 S Osage Ave, Bartlesville, OK 74003

MANOLA, John Edwin (NJ)

MANOOGIAN, Phyllis (Cal) 2300 Bancroft Way, Berkeley, CA 94704

MANSELLA, Thomas G (Va) 3705 S George Mason Dr, Apt 2105-S, Falls Church, VA 22041

MANSFIELD, Charles Kirk (Vt) 157 Parker Hill Rd, Bellows Falls, VT 05101

MANSFIELD, Gregory James Edward (SeFla) St. Bernard de Clairvaux Episcopal Church, 16711 West Dixie Highway, North Miami Beach, FL 33160

MANSFIELD, Mary Robb (Vt) 32 Wood Rd, North Middlesex, VT 05682

MANSFIELD, Meribah Ann (SO) 2282 Fernleaf Lane, Columbus, OH 43235

MANSFIELD JR, Richard Huntington (Ct) 41 Gatewood, Avon, CT 06001

MANSFIELD, Victor Claibourne (WNC) PO Box 531, Skyland, NC 28776

MANSON, Anne Leslie Yount (Va) The Prestwould, 612 West Franklin St. #12C, Richmond, VA 23220

MANSON, Malcolm (Cal) 35 Keyes Avenue, San Francisco, CA 94129

MANTILLA-BENITEZ, Haydee (EcuC) Avenue Libertad Parada 8, Esmeralda, Ecuador

MANUEL, Joseph (LI) 3907 61st St, Woodside, NY 11377

MANZANARES, Zoila Manzanares-Rodriguez (Ind) 6613 El Paso Dr, Indianapolis, IN 46214

MANZELLA, Evelyn Nancy (O) 127 W. North Street, Wooster, OH 44691

MANZO, Peter Thomas (NJ) 69 Penn Rd, Voorhees, NJ 08043

MAPPLEBECKPALMER, Richard Warwick (Cal) 472 Dale Rd, Martinez, CA 94553

MARANVILLE, Irvin Walter (Vt) 6809 23rd Ave W, Bradenton, FL 34209

MARANVILLE, Joyce Margaret (Vt) 6809 23rd Ave W, Bradenton, FL 34209

✠ **MARBLE JR**, Alfred Clark (Ret Bp of Miss 2000-) 301 N Elm St Ste 308C, Greensboro, NC 27401

MARCANTONIO, John (Nwk)

MARCETTI, Alvin Julian (RI) 81 Warren Ave, East Providence, RI 02914

MARCH, Bette Ann (Wyo) 34 Thomas The Apostle Rd, Cody, WY 82414

MARCHAND, R Richard (NY) 1 Kingsley Ave, Staten Island, NY 10314

MARCHL III, William Henry (NC) 719 S 1st St, Smithfield, NC 27577

MARCIALES ARENAS, Alberto Camilo (Colom) Carrera 6 No 49-85, Piso 2, Bogota, Colombia

MARCOUX, Stephen Kent (WA) St George's Parish, 160 U St NW, Washington, DC 20001

MARCURE, Johanna (CNY) 209 E Main St, Waterville, NY 13480

MARCUSSEN, Bjorn Birkholm (SanD) 731 G St C3, Chula Vista, CA 91910

MAREE, Donna L (Pa) 2112 Delancey St, Philadelphia, PA 19103

MAREK, Joseph J (Tenn) 204-A Courthouse Dr., Salmon, ID 83467

MARGERUM, Michael (Nev) 11205 Carlsbad Rd, Reno, NV 89506

MARGRAVE, Thomas Edmund Clare (NY) 29 William St, Cortland, NY 13045

MARICONDA, Thomas Nicholas (Ct) 36 Main St, Newtown, CT 06470

MARIN, Carlos Heli (Cfla) 438 Magpie Ct, Kissimmee, FL 34759

MARINCO, Judith Ann (Mich) 1434 E 13 Mile Rd, Madison Heights, MI 48071

MARINCO, Vincent Michael (Mich) 1434 E 13 Mile Rd, Madison Heights, MI 48071

MARINO, Matthew A (Az) 114 W Roosevelt Street, Phoenix, AZ 85003

MARIS, Margo Elaine (Ore) 13201 Se Blackberry Cir, Portland, OR 97236

MARKEVITCH, Diane Mary (Mil) 17 Dumont Cir, Madison, WI 53711

MARKHAM, Eva Melba Roberts (Ky) 1604 Whippoorwill Rd., Louisville, KY 40213

MARKHAM, Ian Stephen (Va) 3737 Seminary Rd, Alexandria, VA 22304

MARKIE, Patrick Gregory (Minn) 770 Parkview Ave, Saint Paul, MN 55117

MARKLE, Ann E (ETenn) 1076 Sparta Hwy, Crossville, TN 38572

MARKS, Charles A (WMo)

MARKS, S Patricia (Ga) 814 W Alden Ave, Valdosta, GA 31602

MARKS, Sharla J (FtW) 2431 St Gregory St, Arlington, TX 76013

MARKS SR, W(illiam) Parker (USC) 400 Herringbone Run, Easley, SC 29642

MARLER, Malcolm Lewis (Ala)

MARLIN, John Henry (Okla) 1818 Coventry Lane, Oklahoma City, OK 73120

MARMON, Mark Mccarter (Tex) 10416 Highway 6, Hitchcock, TX 77563

MARONDE, James A (Los)

MARONEY III, Gordon Earle (Ark) PO Box 202, Smackover, AR 71762

MARQUAND, Betty Harlina (Colo) 1521 Windsor Way Unit 8, Racine, WI 53406

MARQUES, Barbara (Va) 7411 Moss Side Ave, Richmond, VA 23227

MARQUESS, Judith Ann (Vt) 212 Woodhaven Dr # 5d, White River Junction, VT 05001

MARQUEZ, Juan I (DR (DomRep)) Calle Santiago 114, Gazcue, Santo Domingo, Dominican Republic

MARQUIS JR, James Fredrick (ETenn) 2017 Kirby Rd, Memphis, TN 38119

MARR JR, Andrew (Chi) 56500 Abbey Rd, Three Rivers, MI 49093

MARR, Jon Aidan (RG) 906-B Old Las Vegas Hwy, Santa Fe, NM 87505

MARRAN, Pauline Matte (NY) 80 Lyme Rd Apt 219, Hanover, NH 03755

✠ **MARRAY**, Santosh Kumar (Asst Bp of Ala 2012-) 10514 Lantana Lakes Dr N, Jacksonville, FL 32246

MARRERO CAMACHO, Luis Fernando (PR)

MARRONE, Michael J (Mass) 410 Washington St, Duxbury, MA 02332

MARSDEN, Richard Conlon (SwFla) 222 S Palm Ave, Sarasota, FL 34236

MARSH, Abigail (Colo) 6931 E Girard Ave, Denver, CO 80224

MARSH, Caryl Ann (U) 829 E 400 S Apt 110, Salt Lake City, UT 84102

MARSH IV, Charles Wallace (At) St. James' Episc Church, 161 Church St. N.E., Marietta, GA 30060

MARSH, Elizabeth (Mass) 368 Kings Hwy W, 358 Farwood Rd, Haddonfield, NJ 08033

MARSH, Gayle Mardene (Minn) 1644 Cohansey St, Saint Paul, MN 55117

MARSH, Karl Edwin (Neb) 1873 S Cherry Blossom Ln, Suttons Bay, MI 49682

MARSH, Keith A (Pa) Church of the Messiah, PO Box 127, Gwynedd, PA 19436

MARSH, Michael Killingsworth (WTex) 343 N. Getty, Uvalde, TX 78801

MARSH JR, Robert Francis (Fla) 2462 C H Arnold Rd, Saint Augustine, FL 32092

MARSHALL, Carol Phillips (USC) Christ Episcopal Church, PO Box 488, Lancaster, SC 29721

MARSHALL, David Allen (Oly) P.O. Box 33029, Seattle, WA 98133

MARSHALL, David J (SanD) Grace Episcopal Church, 1020 Rose Ranch Road, San Marcos, CA 92069

MARSHALL III, Elliott Wallace (Chi) 710 Crab Tree Lane, Bartlett, IL 60103

MARSHALL III, Howard R (NJ) 6313 Wyndam Rd, Pennsauken, NJ 08109

MARSHALL, John Anthony (WNY) 7145 Fieldcrest Dr, Lockport, NY 14094

MARSHALL, John H (NwT)

MARSHALL, Lewis Edwin (NY) 176 Dean St, Brooklyn, NY 11217

MARSHALL, McAlister Crutchfield (Va) 2316 E Grace St # 8011, Richmond, VA 23223

✠ **MARSHALL**, Paul Victor (Ret Bp of Be 2014-) 333 Wyandotte St, Bethlehem, PA 18015

MARSHALL, Richard G. (Ala) 6944 Cypress Spring Ct, St Augustine, FL 32086

MARSHALL, Robert (RI) 191 County Rd, Barrington, RI 02806

MARSHALL JR, William Shattuck (Be) 12 Holiday Ct, Kingston, PA 18704

MARSTON, Robert Dandridge (SVa) 45 Main St, Newport News, VA 23601

MARTA, Dale Charles (Mo) 112 N Ray Ave, Maryville, MO 64468

MARTENS, Ann F (Va) 3050 N Military Rd, Arlington, VA 22207

MARTIN, Alexander David (SO) St Timothy's Episcopal Church, 8101 Beechmont Ave, Cincinnati, OH 45255

MARTIN, Alison J (WNY) PO Box 234, Youngstown, NY 14174

MARTIN, Andrea Brooke (WA) 163 Oak Street, Hillsdale, MI 49242

MARTIN, Barbara J (SwFla) 230 Dent Dr, Naples, FL 34112

MARTIN, Chad Travis (Tex) 4900 Jackwood St, Houston, TX 77096

MARTIN, Charles Percy (Pgh) 220 Columbia St, Johnstown, PA 15905

MARTIN, Christopher (Cal) 1123 Court St, San Rafael, CA 94901

MARTIN, Christopher S (Fla) PO Box 330500, Atlantic Beach, FL 32233

MARTIN, Clyde Albert (SO) 1600 N Breiel Blvd, Middletown, OH 45042

MARTIN, Derrick Antonio (SeFla) 17 Fernhill Ave, Buffalo, NY 14215

MARTIN, Donald Graham (WK) 1715 W 5th St, Colby, KS 67701

MARTIN JR, Edward E (NJ) 1281 Venezia Ave, Vineland, NJ 08361

MARTIN, George H(arvey) (Minn)

MARTIN, Gregory Alexander (Cal) 162 Hickory St, San Francisco, CA 94102

MARTIN, Hallock (SeFla) 5042 El Claro N, West Palm Beach, FL 33415

MARTIN, Irene Elizabeth (Oly) PO Box 83, Skamokawa, WA 98647

MARTIN, James Mitchell (WVa) 177 Edison Dr, Huntington, WV 25705

MARTIN JR, John Charles (Md) Brookfield Ave, Cumberland, MD 21502

MARTIN, John Gayle (Pa) 8114 Heacock Ln, Wyncote, PA 19095

MARTIN, Kathleen A (NY) 900 W End Ave, New York, NY 10025

MARTIN, Kenneth Earl (Fla) 125 Holly View, Holly Lake Ranch, TX 75765

MARTIN, Kevin E (Dal) 202 Kickapoo Creek Ln, Georgetown, TX 78633

MARTIN, Lydia Adriana Peter (Md) 10800 Greenpoint Rd, Lavale, MD 21502

MARTIN, Lyle Fay (Neb) 906 Main St, Gregory, SD 57533

MARTIN, Mary J (NY) 900 W End Ave Apt 10-C, New York, NY 10025

MARTIN, Nadine Brown (Az) 7750 E Oakwood Cir, Tucson, AZ 85750

MARTIN, Nancee (Oly) 10560 Fort George Road, Fort George Island, FL 32226

MARTIN, Nancy D (WVa) 222 5th Ave, Hinton, WV 25951

MARTIN, Paul Dexter (WLa) 275 Southfield Road, Shreveport, LA 71105

MARTIN, Rene Elizabeth (Md) Director of Spiritual Life, Buckingham's Choice, 3200 Baker Circle, Adamstown, MD 21710

MARTIN, Rex L (Wyo) PO Box 64, Hartville, WY 82215

MARTIN JR, Robert James (SwFla) 9727 Bay Colony Dr, Riverview, FL 33578

MARTIN, Robin Pierce (Pa) 8114 Heacock Ln, Wyncote, PA 19095

MARTIN, Terry L (NJ) 220 Fairview Ave, Hammonton, NJ 08037
MARTIN, William C (Tenn)
MARTIN, William Henderson (RG) PO Box 640161, El Paso, TX 79904
MARTIN, William Jeffrey (Az) 7750 E Oakwood Cir, Tucson, AZ 85750
MARTIN, William L (Be) 5114 Hilltop Cir, East Stroudsburg, PA 18301
MARTIN, William Thomas (At) 3207 Pristine View, Williamsburg, VA 23188
MARTIN, William V (Okla) PO Box 1153, Pryor, OK 74362
MARTINDALE, James Lawrence (NMich) 14 Stonegate Hts, Marquette, MI 49855
MARTINDALE, Richard James (Ky) 5 S Green St, Henderson, KY 42420
MARTINER, John William (Del) 65 Continental Dr, Harwich, MA 02645
MARTINEZ, Gregorio Bernardo (NwT) 907 Adams Ave, Odessa, TX 79761
MARTINEZ, José (Ct) 155 Wyllys St, Hartford, CT 06106
MARTINEZ, Kim Renee (RG)
MARTINEZ, Lucy Anne Roberts (At) 539 Wagner Way Ne, Kennesaw, GA 30144
MARTINEZ AMENGUAL, Margarita (Hond)
MARTINEZ AMENGUAL, Roberto Aaron (Hond)
MARTINEZ-JANTZ, Jeanie (Va) 6509 Sydenstricker Rd, Burke, VA 22015
MARTINEZ-MORALES, Roberto (Los) 1011 S Verdugo Rd, Glendale, CA 91205
MARTINEZ RAPALO, Arturo (Hond) IMS SAP Dept 215. PO BOX 523900, Miami, FL 33152-3900, Honduras
MARTINEZ-RAPALO, Ramon (Hond)
MARTINEZ TOLEDO, Eduardo (PR)
MARTINEZ TORO, Jorge De Jesus (Colom) Carrera 80 #53a-78, Medellin, Antioquia, Colombia
MARTIN FUMERO, Emilio (DR (DomRep))
MARTINHAUK, Jeff (Los) St. Timothy's Episcopal Church and School, 15757 St. Timothy's Road, Apple Valley, CA 92307
MARTINICHIO, John Robert (CNY) 89 Fairview Ave, Binghamton, NY 13904
MARTINO, Rose Marie (LI) 612 Forest Ave, Massapequa, NY 11758
MARTIN-RHODES, Lilla Rebecca (LI) 27002 Arrowbrook Way, Wesley Chapel, FL 33544
✠ **MARTINS**, Daniel H (Bp of Spr 2011-) 821 S 2nd St, Springfield, IL 62704
MARTZ, Jeannie (Los) 3107 Pepperwood Ct, Fullerton, CA 92835
MARTZ, Stephen (Chi) 947 Oxford Rd, Glen Ellyn, IL 60137

MARX, Jeffery Wayne (WTenn) 484 Riding Brook Way, Collierville, TN 38017
MASADA, Jennifer Ann (Ia) 912 20th Ave, Coralville, IA 52241
MASILLEM, Benedict Baguyos (Ak)
MASON, Alan Newell (Ct) 211 Senexet Rd, Woodstock, CT 06281
MASON, Alice Joan Magnuson (WNC) 106 Lanterns Wick Trl, Sylva, NC 28779
MASON, Brooks Kevin (SanD) Cathedral Church of Saint Paul, 2728 6th Ave, San Diego, CA 92103
MASON, Bruce (Ct) PO Box 443, Litchfield, CT 06759
MASON, Bruce Edmund (Alb) PO Box 211, Lake Luzerne, NY 12846
MASON JR, Charles Thurston (Ind) 224 N Alden Rd, Muncie, IN 47304
MASON, Christopher P (SwVa) 128 Laurel Mountain Estates Drive, Todd, NC 28684
MASON, David Raymond (O) 2277 N Saint James Pkwy, Cleveland Heights, OH 44106
MASON, Eric S (Oly) Church of the Redeemer, 6211 NE 182nd St, Kenmore, WA 98028
MASON, Jack M (Eas) 114 S Harrison St, Easton, MD 21601
MASON, Joan M (NJ) 417 Washington St, Toms River, NJ 08753
MASON, Joel Clark (NY) 39 Morton Pl, Chappaqua, NY 10514
MASON, John Skain (HB) Rr 2 Box 542b, Inwood, WV 25428
MASON, Lawrence Walker (SVa) 2355 Brookwood Rd, Richmond, VA 23235
MASON, Lisa P (WTex) 1300 Wiltshire Ave, San Antonio, TX 78209
MASON, Marilyn Joyce Smith (Los) PO Box 743, Bristol, RI 02809
MASON, Phil C (Colo) 280 Peregrine Dr, San Marcos, TX 78666
MASON, Samuel Alison (NC)
MASON, Victoria Anne (Tex) Iglesia Episcopal San Francisco de As¿S, 7000 Woodhue Dr, Austin, TX 78745
MASQUELETTE, Eizabeth Daggett (Tex) 2204 Welch St, Houston, TX 77019
MASSENBURG, Barbara Jean (Ak) 7962 N Tongass Hwy, Ketchikan, AK 99901
MASSENBURG, Raymond Douglas (WA) 1514 15th St NW, Washington, DC 20005
MASSEY, Hoyt B (SwFla) Po Box 2161, Franklin, NC 28744
MASSEY, Nigel John (NY) 111 E 60th St Penthouse, New York, NY 10022
MASSIE IV, Robert Kinloch (Mass) 140 Sycamore St, Somerville, MA 02145
MASTER II, George O (Pa) 6838 Woodland Avenue, Philadelphia, PA 19142

MASTERMAN, Brenda Patricia (SeFla) 119 N Golfview Road, Box 9, Lake Worth, FL 33460
MASTERMAN, Frederick James (SeFla) 15170 N Rugged Lark Dr, Tucson, AZ 85739
MASTERMAN, Patricia Dinan (NwT) 2700 W 16th Ave Apt 272, Amarillo, TX 79102
MASTERS, Ralph Leeper (Tex) 459 Medina Dr, Highland Village, TX 75077
MASTERSON, Elizabeth Rust (Del) 229 Cheltenham Rd, Newark, DE 19711
MATARAZZO, Laura Rice (Nwk) 10 Doe Hollow Lane, Belvidere, NJ 07823
MATHAUER, Margaret Ann (Vt) 7 Holy Cross Rd, Colchester, VT 05446
MATHENY, Clint Michael (CFla) 130 N Magnolia Ave, Orlando, FL 32801
MATHER, Nicholas S (Spok)
MATHER-HEMPLER, Portia (ECR) 950 - 30th Street, Port Townsend, WA 98368
MATHES, Hester Shipp (WTenn) 4645 Walnut Grove Rd, Memphis, TN 38117
✠ **MATHES**, James Robert (Bp of SanD 2005-) 2083 Sunset Cliffs Blvd, San Diego, CA 92107
MATHESON, M Jennings Jennings (Ct) 74 South St # 809, Litchfield, CT 06759
MATHEUS, Rob (SO) 6300 Kinver Edge Way, Columbus, OH 43213
MATHEW, Cherian (ND)
MATHEWS, Edward (SwVa) 6000 Grove Ave, Richmond, VA 23226
MATHEWS, Keith Elizabeth (SO) 662 N 600 E, Firth, ID 83236
MATHEWS, Koshy (Pa) 103 Potters Pond Dr, Phoenixville, PA 19460
MATHEWS, Miriam Atwell (Md)
MATHEWS, Ranjit K (Mass) 7 Pond St, Randolph, MA 02368
MATHEWS JR, Thomas Etienne (Nwk) 5 Surrey Ln, Madison, NJ 07940
MATHEWSON, Colin J (SanD) St Paul's Episcopal Cathedral, 2728 6th Ave, San Diego, CA 92103
MATHEWSON, Kathryn Carroll (ETenn) 412 silverberry, Pittsboro, NC 27312
MATHEWSON, Laurel (SanD) St Paul's Cathedral, 2728 6th Ave, San Diego, CA 92103
MATHIAS, Barbara Helen (Minn) 110 S Oak St, Lake City, MN 55041
MATHIESON, James West (SVa) 183 Grove Park Cir, Danville, VA 24541
MATHIS, Judith Schmick (CFla) 86 Dianne Dr., Ormond Beach, FL 32176
MATHIS, Thelma Monique (At) 306 Peyton Rd SW, Atlanta, GA 30311
MATHISON, Mary Alice (CGC) 28788 N Main St, Daphne, AL 36526
MATIJASIC, Ernest G (SwFla) 401 W Shoreline Dr #253, Sandusky, OH 44870

MATIS, Glenn Marshall (Pa) 45 Latham Ct, Doylestown, PA 18901
MATISSE, Jacqueline Edith (SO) 232 E Main St, Lebanon, OH 45036
MATLACK, David Russell (NY) Po Box 703, Southwest Harbor, ME 04679
MATLAK, David John (Mil) 1101 Forest Ave, Richmond, VA 23229
MATNEY, Rex H (Kan) The Church of the Covenant, PO Box 366, Junction City, KS 66441
MATOTT, Michele Louise (RI) 80 Fisher Road Unit 90, Cumberland, RI 02864
MATSON, David John (Me) 26 Heron Lane, Harpswell, ME 04079
MATTER, Janice Louise (Me) 5 Boynton Ln, Billerica, MA 01821
MATTERS, Richard Bruce (ECR) 181 S Corinth Ave, Lodi, CA 95242
MATTHEW, John Clifford (Ida) 5301 E Warm Springs Ave E102, Boise, ID 83716
MATTHEWS JR, A(llen) Russel (WTex) Po Box 348, Luling, TX 78648
MATTHEWS, Bonnie Anne (Ct) Trinity Episc Church, 120 Sigourney St, Hartford, CT 06105
MATTHEWS, Daniel Paul (NY) 1047 Amsterdam Ave, New York, NY 10025
MATTHEWS JR, Daniel Paul (At) 435 Peachtree St, Atlanta, GA 30308
MATTHEWS, Donald William (CNY) 375 W Clinton St, Elmira, NY 14901
MATTHEWS, Emily Anne (Miss) P. O. Box 804, Brookhaven, MS 39602
✠ **MATTHEWS**, Frank Clayton (Bp for Off of Pastoral Development 1998-) PO Box 12686, New Bern, NC 28561
MATTHEWS III, James Houston (WNC) 2232 Water Oak Ln, Gastonia, NC 28056
MATTHEWS, Joyce Mary (Mich) 37906 Glengrove Dr, Farmington Hills, MI 48331
MATTHEWS, Kevin B (NC) 625 Candlewood Drive, Greensboro, NC 27403
MATTHEWS, Mary Theresa (RI) Woodson Dr 2721, 2721 Woodson Dr, Mckinney, TX 75070
MATTHEWS, Richard L (Minn) 8895 Bradford Pl, Eden Prairie, MN 55347
MATTHEWS, William Thompson (CFla)
MATTIA, Joan Plubell (Va) 1 Egyetem Ter, Debrecen, 4032, Hungary
MATTIA JR, Lou (Va) 622 Worchester St, Herndon, VA 20170
MATTILA, Daniel E (Ct) 104 Walnut Tree Hill Rd, Sandy Hook, CT 06482
MATTLIN, Margaret Baker (Minn) 2085 Buford Ave, Saint Paul, MN 55108
MATTSON, Sherry R (Ind) 11974 State Highway M26, Eagle Harbor, MI 49950
MATYLEWICZ, Stephen Jerome (Be) 116 Riverview Ln, Jermyn, PA 18433
MAUAI, Brandon Lee (ND) 500 S Main Ave, Sioux Falls, SD 57104

MAUGHAN III, M(atthew) Webster (O) 1226 Waverly Rd, Sandusky, OH 44870
MAULDEN, Kristina Ann (Okla) 501 S Cincinnati Ave, Tulsa, OK 74103
MAUMUS, Priscilla Guderian (La) Christ Church Cathedral, 2219 St. Charles Ave., New Orleans, LA 70115
MAUNEY, J(ames) Patrick (RI) P.O Box 1236, Sagamore Beach, MA 02562
MAURAIS, Robert Irwin (CFla) 175 Groveland Rd, Mount Dora, FL 32757
MAURER, David Stuart (Los)
MAURER, Karen (Los) 777 N. Acacia Ave., Rialto, CA 92376
MAURER, Sally Beth (NJ) St Johns Episcopal Church, 76 Market St, Salem, NJ 08079
MAURY, James Ludlow (Ga) PO Box 61297, Savannah, GA 31420
MAXFIELD, Christian D (Mil) 519 S Michigan St, Prairie Du Chien, WI 53821
MAXSON, J(ohn) Hollis (The Episcopal Church in Haw) 447 Kawaihae St, Honolulu, HI 96825
MAXWELL, Anne Mears (La) 259 W Hickory St, Ponchatoula, LA 70454
MAXWELL, Barbara Jean (O) 120 Charles Ct, Elyria, OH 44035
MAXWELL, Elizabeth Gail (NY) 225 W. 99th St., New York, NY 10025
MAXWELL, George Motier (Ga) 115 E Gordon St, Savannah, GA 31401
MAXWELL JR, George Motier (At) 2744 Peachtree Road NW, Atlanta, GA 30305
MAXWELL, James Henry (Mich) 281 W Drayton St, Ferndale, MI 48220
MAXWELL, Kevin Burns (Cal) 2 Meadow Park Circle, Belmont, CA 94002
MAXWELL, Richard Anderson (Ct) St. Timothy's Episcopal Church, 4670 Congress St., Fairfield, CT 06824
MAXWELL, Sally Dawn (Minn) St David's Episcopal Church, 304 E 7th St, Austin, TX 78701
MAXWELL, William F. (U) 515 Van Buren St, Port Townsend, WA 98368
MAY, Amanda Gwyn (Cal) 31 Binnacle Hl, Oakland, CA 94618
MAY, Charles Scott (At) 3750 Peachtree Rd NE Apt 811, Atlanta, GA 30319
MAY, David Hickman (Va) 93 Eubank Dr, Kilmarnock, VA 22482
MAY JR, Frederick Barnett (NJ) 916 Lagoon Ln., Mantoloking, NJ 08738
MAY JR, James Bowen (Fla) 16178 Williams Pl, King George, VA 22485
MAY IV, Lynde Eliot (Mil) 982 Hunters Trl, Sun Prairie, WI 53590
MAY, Maureen May (Neb) The Oaks, 2015 County Road R, Fremont, NE 68025
MAY, Philip Walter (WTex) 700 S Upper Broadway St, Corpus Christi, TX 78401

MAY, Richard Ernest (Va) Po Box 155, Campton, NH 03223
MAY, Richard Leslie (SVa) 349 Archers Mead, Williamsburg, VA 23185
MAY, Thomas Richard (NJ) 65 W Front St, Red Bank, NJ 07701
MAYBERRY, Richard Earl (Ct) 16 Southport Woods Drive, Southport, CT 06890
MAYBIN, Maxine Roberta (Colo) 915 Yuma St Apt 124, Colorado Springs, CO 80909
MAYCOCK, Roma Walker (Va) 5210 Patriots Colony Dr, Williamsburg, VA 23188
MAYEN, John Mabior (SD) 1415 S Bahnson Ave, Sioux Falls, SD 57105
MAYER, Charles David (NY)
✠ **MAYER**, James Scott (Bp of NwT 2009) 1802 Broadway, Lubbock, TX 79401
MAYER, Linda Margaret (Spok) PO Box 1226, Chelan, WA 98816
MAYER JR, Nicholas Max (WTex) Po Box 1265, Castroville, TX 78009
MAYER, Peter Woodrich (Md) 1601 Pleasant Plains Rd, Annapolis, MD 21409
MAYER, Robert James (ECR) 20920 Mcclellan Rd, Cupertino, CA 95014
MAYER, Sandra Crow (CGC) 5158 Border Dr N, Mobile, AL 36608
MAYERS, Thomas Wycliffe Oswald (Mich) 3837 W. 7 Mile Rd., Detroit, MI 48221
MAYES, Amy Kathryn (Wyo) 519 E Park Ave, Riverton, WY 82501
MAYFIELD, Donna Jeanne (O) 515 N Chillicothe Rd, Aurora, OH 44202
MAYFIELD JR, Ellis Oglesby (ETenn) 1449 Stagecoach Rd, Sewanee, TN 37375
MAYHALL, Monna S (Tenn) 1509 Jaybee Ct, Franklin, TN 37064
MAYHOOD, Gary William (LI)
MAYNARD, Beth H (Spr) 702 W Green St, Champaign, IL 61820
MAYNARD, Dennis Roy (SanD) 49 Via Del Rossi, Rancho Mirage, CA 92270
MAYNARD, Jane F (Oly) 6732 N Parkside Ln, Tacoma, WA 98407
MAYNARD, Joan Pearson (SO) 2661 Haverford Rd, Columbus, OH 43220
MAYO, H(arold) Jonathan (Be) 3900 Mechancsville Rd, Whitehall, PA 18052
MAYOM, Abraham Mabior (SD)
MAYOR, Robert Michael (Oly) 10630 Gravelly Lake Dr SW, Lakewood, WA 98499
MAYORGA-GONZALEZ, Mary (Ct) 3 Oakwood Ave., Lawrence, MA 01841
MAYPOLE, Sara Chandler (Va) 6988 Woodchuck Hill Rd, Fayetteville, NY 13066
MAYRER, Jane Goodhue (Md) 2010 Sulgrave Ave, Baltimore, MD 21209

MAYS, Foster Marshall (Kan) Epiphany Episcopal Church, P.O. Box 367, Sedan, KS 67361

MAYS-STOCK, Barbara L (RI) 50 Charles St, Cranston, RI 02920

✠ **MAZE**, Larry Earl (Ret Bp of Ark 2006-) 102 Midland St, Little Rock, AR 72205

MAZGAJ, Marian Stanislaus (WVa) PO Box 206, Valley Grove, WV 26060

MAZINGO, Stephen C (Fla) Saint Peter's Church, 801 Atlantic Ave, Fernandina Beach, FL 32034

MAZUJIAN, Harry (NJ) 44 Broad St, Flemington, NJ 08822

MAZZA, Joseph (Fla) 1737 Mayview Rd, Jacksonville, FL 32210

MAZZA, Joseph Edward (FdL) 4569 Glidden Dr, Sturgeon Bay, WI 54235

MAZZACANO, Leslie G (NJ) 379 Huntington Drive, Delran, NJ 08075

MAZZARELLA, Virginia Teresa (Roch) 327 Mendon Center Rd, Pittsford, NY 14534

MCADAMS, James Lee (Ala) 3775 Crosshaven Dr, AL, Birmingham 35223

MCADAMS, Kathleen A (Mass) PO Box 51003, Boston, MA 02205

MCAFEE JR, Ernest Wyatt (Dal) 1106 Richland Oaks Drive, Richardson, TX 75081

MCALHANY, J. Ann (Me) St John's Episcopal Church, 234 French St, Bangor, ME 04401

MCALLEN, Robert Ashley (WTex) 1112 S Westgate Dr, Weslaco, TX 78596

MCALLISTER, Loring William (Minn)

MCALPINE, James Paul (Mass) 102 Manchester Rd, Newton Highlands, MA 02461

MCALPINE, Thomas Hale (FdL) 215 Houston St, Ripon, WI 54971

✠ **MCARTHUR JR**, Earl Nicholas (Ret Bp Suffr of WTex 1994-) Po Box 734, Wimberley, TX 78676

MCAULAY, Roderick Neil (The Episcopal NCal) 7803 Stefenoni Ct, Sebastopol, CA 95472

MCBAY, Susannah E (Tex) 717 Sage Rd, Houston, TX 77056

MCBEATH, Susan A(udrey) (Ind) 13088 Tarkington Commons, Carmel, IN 46033

MCBRIDE, Bill (WLa) 9105 Colonial Gdns, Shreveport, LA 71106

MCBRIDE, David Patrick (Cal) 12572 Foster Rd, Los Alamitos, CA 90720

MCBRIDE, Ronald Winton (Cal) 34043 Calle Mora, Cathedral City, CA 92234

MCBRYDE, Greer Kroening (CFla) 1155 C.R. 753 South, Webster, FL 33597

MCCABE, Chad Peter (Alb) 2950 S University Blvd, Denver, CO 80210

MCCABE III, Charles Peyton (WMich) 325 West Center, Hastings, MI 49058

MCCABE, Paul Charles (At) 1785 Benningfield Dr Sw, Marietta, GA 30064

MCCAFFREY, Susan Maureen (CFla) 4110 S Ridgewood Ave, Port Orange, FL 32127

MCCALEB, Douglas William (SeFla) 464 NE 16th Street, Miami, FL 33132

MCCALL, Chad (Tex)

MCCALL JR, John (Kosho) (Me) 300 Page St, San Francisco, CA 94102

MCCALL, Ramelle Lorenzo (Md) 730 Bestgate Rd, Annapolis, MD 21401

MCCALL, Richard David (LI) 5117 N Chatham Dr, Bloomington, IN 47404

MCCALL, Terry A (Mass) 5117 N Chatham Dr, Bloomington, IN 47404

MCCALLISTER, Katlin E (Az) 4569 N Old Sabino Canyon Rd, Tucson, AZ 85750

MCCALLUM, Bruce Allan (FdL) PO Box 561, Waupaca, WI 54981

MCCANDLESS, Clelie Fleming (Miss) 8245 Getwell Rd, Southaven, MS 38672

MCCANDLESS, Richard Lawrence (O) 1106 Bell Ridge Rd., Akron, OH 44303

MCCANDLESS, Richard W. (Kan) 3028 Washington Ave, Parsons, KS 67357

MCCANN, Christopher Richard (O) 16267 Oakhill Rd, Cleveland Heights, OH 44112

MCCANN, John Harrison (WMo) 1492 Hemlock Ct, Liberty, MO 64068

MCCANN, Michael Louis (HB)

MCCANN, Michael Wayne (At) 975 Longstreet Cir, Gainesville, GA 30501

MCCANN, Robert Emmett (Cal) 4023 Canyon Rd, Lafayette, CA 94549

MCCANN, Sandra Briggs (At)

MCCANN, Susan Griffen (WMo) 1492 Hemlock Ct, Liberty, MO 64068

MCCARD, John Fleming (At) 3110 Ashford Dunwoody Rd Ne, Atlanta, GA 30319

MCCARLEY, Melanie Leigh Smith (Mass) Zion Church, 221 E. Washington St., Charles Town, WV 25414

MCCARROLL, Connie Jo (SO) 4381 S.Rangeline Rd., West Milton, OH 45383

MCCARROLL, Sandra Kim (Nev) 1806 Hilton Head Dr, Boulder City, NV 89005

MCCARRON, Charles Francis (LI) 11 Violet Ave, Mineola, NY 11501

MCCART, Thomas K (Roch) 1793 Dunaway Ct, Indianapolis, IN 46228

MCCARTHY, Bartlett Anderson (Dal) 7335 Inwood Rd, Dallas, TX 75209

MCCARTHY, Ian F (SeFla) St. Mary's Episcopal Church, 623 SE Ocean Blvd, Stuart, FL 34994

MCCARTHY, Jean Elizabeth Rinner (Ia) 2906 39th St, Des Moines, IA 50310

MCCARTHY, Marty (NC) 4205 Quail Hunt Lane, Charlotte, NC 28226

MCCARTHY, Melissa (Los)

MCCARTHY, Nancy Horton (SeFla) 24 Highbridge Xing, Apt 1002, Asheville, NC 28803

MCCARTHY JR, Stephen Joseph (Mass) 2017 6th Ave N, Birmingham, AL 35203

MCCARTHY, William Robert (Ore) 5060 SW Philomath Blvd, PMB 165, Corvallis, OR 97333

MCCARTY, Barnum C (Fla) 5303 Ortega Blvd Apt 208, Jacksonville, FL 32210

MCCARTY, Marjorie McDonall (EC) 100 E Sherwood Dr, Havelock, NC 28532

MCCARTY, Mary Sharon (WA) 1831 Parkers Creek Road, Port Republic, MD 20676

MCCARTY, Patricia Gayle (WTenn) 1720 Peabody Ave., Memphis, TN 38104

MCCARTY, Steven Lynn (Md) Saint Andrew's Episcopal Church, 22 Cumberland St, PO Box 189, Clear Spring, MD 21722

MCCASLIN, H Kenneth (Pa) 694 Kennedy Ln, Wayne, PA 19087

MCCASLIN, Robert Allan (WNC) 5198 NC Highway 194 S, Banner Elk, NC 28604

MCCAUGHAN, Patricia Susanne (Los) 1554 N. Shelley Avenue, Upland, CA 91786

MCCAULEY, Margaret Hudley (Los) 4215 W 61st St, Los Angeles, CA 90043

MCCAULEY, Shana (Ore) 1550 Diablo Rd, Danville, CA 94526

MCCAULLEY, Barbara Marie (Ia) 620 Briarstone Dr Apt 28, Mason City, IA 50401

MCCAULLEY, Esau Daniel (Alb) 101 Yoshihara, Chatan, Japan 904-0105, Japan

MCCAUSLAND, John Lesher (NH) 457 Reservoir Dr, Weare, NH 03281

MCCAW, Mary Ann (Oly) 6 Lincoln Rd, Wellesley, MA 02481

MCCLAIN, Marion Roy (Sam) (FtW) 3650 Chicora Ct Apt 330, Fort Worth, TX 76116

MCCLAIN, Mike (Ore) 7875 SW Alden St, Portland, OR 97223

MCCLAIN, Rebecca Lee (Oly) Saint Paul's Cathedral, 2728 6th Ave, San Diego, CA 92103

MCCLAIN, William Allen (The Episcopal NCal) 6825 Sterchi Ln, Montague, CA 96064

MCCLASKEY, Steven Lloyd (Q) 2020 21st St, Rock Island, IL 61201

MCCLEERY III, William Acton (SO) St Paul Episcopal Church, PO Box 736, Logan, OH 43138

MCCLELLAN, Robert Farrell (NMich) Po Box 841, Saint Helena, CA 94574

MCCLELLAN, Thomas Lee (Pa) Po Box 642, Lafayette Hill, PA 19444

MCCLELLAND, Carol Jean (EO) 12019 SE 15th St, Vancouver, WA 98683

MCCLENAGHAN, Malcolm Eugene (The Episcopal NCal) 2020 Brady Ln, Roseville, CA 95747

MCCLOGHRIE, K(athleen) Lesley (NY) 4259 Forest Hills Dr, Fortuna, CA 95540

MCCLOSKEY JR, Robert Johnson (SeFla) Po Box 1691, West Jefferson, NC 28694

MCCLOUD, Christine McCloud (Nwk)

MCCLOUD, Linda (Mont) PO Box 81362, Billings, MT 59108

MCCLOUGH, Jeffrey David (Chi) 3801 Central Ave, Western Springs, IL 60558

MCCLOY, Randolph McKellar (WTenn) 42 S Goodlett St, Memphis, TN 38117

MCCLURE, Robert Coke (Neb) Saint Matthew's Church, 312 W 16th St, Alliance, NE 69301

MCCLURE JR, William James (EMich) 232 North 'E' Street, Cheboygan, MI 49721

MCCOART JR, Charles Carroll (Va) Emmanuel Episcopal Church, 1608 Russell Rd, Alexandria, VA 22301

MCCOID, Dean Bailey (ECR) 25 Oakmore Dr, San Jose, CA 95127

MCCOMAS, Scot A (FtW) Parish Episcopal School, 4101 Sigma Rd, Dallas, TX 75244

MCCOMBS, Lauren (Cal) 1040 Border Rd, Los Altos, CA 94024

MCCONCHIE, Leann Patricia (WNY) 119 Royal Pkwy E, Williamsville, NY 14221

MCCONE, Susan Jonal (Ct) 80 Green Hill Rd, Washington, CT 06793

MCCONKEY, David Benton (Alb) 6 Albion Place, Northampton, NN1 1UD, Great Britain (UK)

✠ **MCCONNELL**, Dorsey Winter Marsden (Bp of Pgh 2012-) Episcopal Diocese of Pittsburgh, 4099 William Penn Hwy, Suite 502, Monroeville, PA 15146

MCCONNELL JR, James B (CFla) 2916 Palm Dr, Punta Gorda, FL 33950

MCCONNELL, Theodore Alan (Alb)

MCCONNELL, Theodore Howard (Va) 7319 Habeas Ct., Mechanicsville, VA 23111

MCCONNEY, J Anne (Neb) 413 S 78th St Apt 8, Omaha, NE 68114

MCCOOK, Carla Benae (Mil) 2320 River Hill Ct, Waukesha, WI 53129

MCCORMICK, Brendan P (Ct) 5 Sea Ln, Old Saybrook, CT 06475

MCCORMICK, Phyllis Ann (SwFla) 2850 Countrybrook Dr Apt 13, Apt. 13, Palm Harbor, FL 34684

MCCORMICK, Reid Tate (CGC) 210 Church St, Greenville, AL 36037

MCCORMICK, Thomas Ray (Del) PO Box 1478, Bethany Beach, DE 19930

MCCOWN, William Russell (Ala) 3816 Cromwell Dr, Birmingham, AL 35243

MCCOY, Adam Dunbar (NY) Mount Calvary Monastery, PO Box 1296, Santa Barbara, CA 93102

MCCOY, David Ormsby (SO) 24 Old Coach Road, Athens, OH 45701

MCCOY, Elaine (O) 3785 W 33rd St, Cleveland, OH 44109

MCCOY, Frances Jean (SwVa) 1001 Virginia Ave NW, Norton, VA 24273

MCCOY, Robert Martin (Md) 521 Sixth St., Annapolis, MD 21403

MCCOY, W(illiam) Keith (NJ) 14 Second Street, Edison, NJ 08837

MCCRACKEN-BENNETT, Rick (SO) 9019 Johnstown Alexandria Rd, Johnstown, OH 43031

MCCRAY-GOLDSMITH, Julia Michelle (Cal) 1550 Diablo Rd, Danville, CA 94526

MCCREARY, E(rnest) Cannon (USC) 8530 Geer Hwy, Cleveland, SC 29635

MCCREATH, Amy Ebeling (Mass) 23 Gilbert St, Waltham, MA 02453

MCCRICKARD, Bonnie Mixon (Ala) Church of the Nativity, 208 Eustis Ave SE, Huntsville, AL 35801

MCCRUM, Lewis Lamb (NJ) 415 Washington St, Toms River, NJ 08753

MCCUE, Allan Homer (Mass) 12 Regwill Ave, Wenham, MA 01984

MCCUE, Michael Edlow (WMass) PO Box 270448, Susanville, CA 96127

MCCULLOCH, Kent Thomas (Oly) 10630 Gravelly Lake Dr Sw, Lakewood, WA 98499

MCCULLOUGH, Brian Duncan (SanD) 332 N Massachusetts St, Winfield, KS 67156

MCCULLOUGH, Mary (Pa) 708 S. Bethlehem Pike, Ambler, PA 19002

MCCUNE, Henry Ralph (Dal) 11560 Drummond Dr, Dallas, TX 75228

MCCURDY III, Alexander (Pa) 613 Maplewood Avenue, Wayne, PA 19087

MCCURRY MILLIKEN, Cathleen Ann (Mil) 1734 Fairhaven Dr., Cedarburg, WI 53012

MCCURTAIN, Glad Robinson (SwFla) 261 1st Ave SW, Largo, FL 33770

MCCUSKER III, Thomas Bernard (Va) Orchid Garden Homes, 229/103 Thepprasit Road. Moo 12, Chonburi, 20260, Thailand

MCDADE, Shelley D (NY) 12 W 11th St, New York, NY 10011

MCDANIEL, Elna Irene (Eau) 408 W Nott St, Tomah, WI 54660

MCDANIEL, Judith Maxwell (Oly) 3971 Point White Dr NE, Bainbridge Island, WA 98110

MC DARBY, Mark Daniel (Alb) 8 Summit St, Philmont, NY 12565

MCDERMOT, Joanna (NwPa) 19556 E Cole Rd, Meadville, PA 16335

MCDERMOTT, James Patrick (LI) 1709 Rue Saint Patrick Apt 504, Montreal, QC H3K 3G9, Canada

MCDERMOTT, Jane Leslie (O) 2918 Kirkhaven Dr, Youngstown, OH 44511

MCDERMOTT, John Roy (Md) 4493 Barberry Ct, Concord, CA 94521

MCDERMOTT, Matthew (Cal) 580 Colorado Ave, Palo Alto, CA 94306

MCDERMOTT, Nelda Grace (Ark) 1204 Hunter St, Conway, AR 72032

MCDONALD, C Dawn (CFla) 1457 Barn Owl Loop, Sanford, FL 32773

MCDONALD, Catherine Jane Walter (Minn) 9671 Clark Cir, Eden Prairie, MN 55347

MCDONALD, Durstan R (Tex) 811 E 46th St, Austin, TX 78751

MCDONALD, James D (Ark) 511 Coley Dr, Mountain Home, AR 72653

MCDONALD, James Ross (Alb) 1937 The Plz, Schenectady, NY 12309

MCDONALD, James Roy (NY) PO Box 161897, Austin, TX 78716

MCDONALD, James Wallace (Episcopal SJ) 627 Goshen Ave, Clovis, CA 93611

MCDONALD, Janet Strain (Va) Po Box 233, Free Union, VA 22940

MCDONALD, Karen Loretta (WMich) 89513 Shorelane Dr, Lawton, MI 49065

MCDONALD, Lauren Miller (SVa) Spiritworks Foundation, 5800 Mooretown Rd, Williamsburg, VA 23188

MCDONALD, Marc Edwin (Az) 202 W Grant Ave, Williams, AZ 86046

MCDONALD, Mark William (CGC) Church Of The Advent, 12099 County Road 99, Lillian, AL 36549

MCDONALD III, Norval Harrison (Md) 309 Royal Oak Dr, Bel Air, MD 21015

MCDONALD, William Kenneth (Mich) 421 East Ellen Street, Fenton, MI 48430

MCDONNELL, Brian K (Md) 8 Loveton Farms Ct, Sparks, MD 21152

MCDONNELL, George Anne (Oly) PO Box 3811, Lacey, WA 98509

MCDONNELL III, Richard P (Ga) 3 Wexford on the Green, Hilton Head Island, SC 29928

MCDOUGLE, Jane M (Cal) 537 Chenery Street, San Francisco, CA 94131

MCDOWELL, Artie Samuel (RG) Po Box 5505, Clovis, NM 88102

MCDOWELL, Glenda Irene (WNC) Cathedral of All Souls, 9 Swan St, Asheville, NC 28803

MCDOWELL, Harold Clayton (LI) 27 Private Rd, Medford, NY 11763

MCDOWELL, (James) Lynn (SwFla) 2808 Valley Park Dr., Little Rock, AR 72212

MCDOWELL JR, John Sidebotham (CPa)

MCDOWELL, Joseph Lee (CFla) 116 Jamaica Dr, Cocoa Beach, FL 32931

MCDOWELL, Mia Chelynn Drummond (USC) PO Box 726, Spartanburg, SC 29304

MCDOWELL, Todd S. (Mo) Grace Episcopal Church, 514 E Argonne Dr, Kirkwood, MO 63122

MCDOWELL-FLEMING, David Howard (CGC) 3560 Briar Cliff Dr, Pensacola, FL 32505

MCDUFFIE, John Stouffer (WA) 5320 Westpath Way, Bethesda, MD 20816

MCELRATH, James Devoe (WNC)

MCELROY, Catherine DeLellis (NY) 191 Larch Ave, Teaneck, NJ 07666

MCELROY, Gary Austin (O) 8437 Eaton Dr, Chagrin Falls, OH 44023

MCELROY, Jamie (Miss) 3921 Oakridge Dr, Jackson, MS 39216

MCELWAIN, David Marc (Wyo) 3594 Stampede Ranch, Cheyenne, WY 82007

MCEWEN, Michael Thomas (Okla) 514 Big Rock Rd, PO Box 338, Medicine Park, OK 73557

MCFARLAND, Earl Everett (RG) 8960 Stetson Pl, Las Cruces, NM 88011

MCFARLANE, Robert Bruce (Mass) 21 Euclid Ave, Lynn, MA 01904

MCGARRY, Susan Ellen (Vt) Saint Stephen's Church, 3 Main St, Middlebury, VT 05753

MCGARRY-LAWRENCE, Marla Terese (Ore) 2136 NE Cesar E Chavez Blvd., Portland, OR 97212

MCGARVEY, Philip Peter (Md)

MCGAVERN III, Cecil George (Tex) 15015 Memorial Dr, Houston, TX 77079

MCGAVRAN, Frederick Jaeger (SO) 3528 Traskwood Cir, Cincinnati, OH 45208

MCGEE JR, Hubert (Ind) 1609 Rivershore Rd, Elizabeth City, NC 27909

MCGEE, Kyle M (Ct) 11133 Town Walk Dr, Hamden, CT 06518

MCGEE, William Earl (ETenn) 3404-A Taft Hwy, Signal Mountain, TN 37377

MCGEE-STREET, Eleanor Lee (Ct) 35 Killdeer Rd, Hamden, CT 06517

MCGEHEE, Andrew Austin (At) 1790 Lavista Rd Ne, Atlanta, GA 30329

MCGEHEE, J Pittman (Tex) 1307 Westover Rd, Austin, TX 78703

MCGEHEE, Lionel Eby (NY) 225 W 99th St, New York, NY 10025

MCGEHEE, Stephen Yarnall (USC) The Episcopal Church Of The Advent, 141 Advent St, Spartanburg, SC 29302

MCGILL, James Calvin (Tex) 6339 E Mystic Mdw, Houston, TX 77021

MCGILL JR, William James (CPa) Po Box 682, Cornwall, PA 17016

MCGIMPSEY, Ralph Gregory (Mich) 8207 Nice Way, Sarasota, FL 34238

MCGINLEY, Charles Richard (Md) 18024 Sand Wedge Dr, Hagerstown, MD 21740

MCGINN, John Edward (Mass) 159 Main St, Sandwich, MA 02563

MCGINNIS, Richard H(Arry) (Fla) 1312 Wisconsin St., Apt. 137, Hudson, WI 54016

MCGINTY, John P (LI) 33 Jefferson Street, Garden City, NY 11530

MCGINTY, William Joseph (Be) 110 Ave M., Matamoras, PA 18336

MCGIRR, Joyce Bearden (Nwk)

MCGLANNAN, Dorian Legge (Mich) 6217 137th Pl SW, Edmonds, WA 98026

MCGLASHON JR, Hugh (CFla) PO Box 3303, Haines City, FL 33845

MCGOVERN, Gerald Hugh (HB) 2600 Lake Michigan Dr Nw, Grand Rapids, MI 49504

MCGOWAN, Carole Jean (RG) 425 University Blvd NE, Albuquerque, NM 87106

MCGOWAN, Diane Darby (Minn) 5029 2nd Ave S, Minneapolis, MN 55419

MCGOWAN, Sandra Maria (Alb) 2647 Brookview Rd, Castleton, NY 12033

MCGOWEN, Willetta Hulett (Ga) 900 Gloucester St, Brunswick, GA 31520

MCGRADY, Jacqueline Ann (Mass) PO Box 2847, Nantucket, MA 02584

MCGRANE, Kevin John (Mo) 3664 Arsenal St, Saint Louis, MO 63116

MCGRATH, Victoria (Nwk) 113 Center Ave, Chatham, NJ 07928

MCGRAW, Jean Quarterman (SC) 1878 Oleander Ct, Charleston, SC 29414

MCGRAW, Stanley Earle (At) 1878 Oleander Ct., Charleston, SC 29414

MCGRAW, Tara L (SwFla)

MCGREGOR, Patricia Cox (SeFla) PO Box 399, Ambridge, PA 15003

MCGUGAN, Terence David (Colo) 2950 S University Blvd, Denver, CO 80210

MCGUINNESS, David (NC) 4330 Pin Oak Dr, Durham, NC 27707

MCGUIRE, Malcolm (Pa) 1300 Lombard St Apt 711, Philadelphia, PA 19147

MCGUIRE, Mark Alan (WMo) 908 SW Hackney Ct, Lees Summit, MO 64081

MCGURK, Brian William (Mass) 625 Main St, Chatham, MA 02633

MCHALE, Stephen David (Cal) 399 Gregory Lane, Pleasant Hill, CA 94523

MCHENRY, Richard Earl (FtW) 1010 Willowcreek Rd, Cleburne, TX 76033

MCHUGH III, John Michael (NJ) 324 Rio Grande Blvd Nw, Albuquerque, NM 87104

MCILHINEY, David Brown (NH) 701 E High St Apt 211, Charlottesville, VA 22902

MCILMOYL, William Joseph (The Episcopal NCal) 1314 Spring St, Saint Helena, CA 94574

MCILROY, Ellen LaFleur (Cal) 5555 Montgomery Dr Apt 59, Santa Rosa, CA 95409

MCILVAIN, Jean Christine (Pgh) 5622 Alan St, Aliquippa, PA 15001

MCILVEEN, Richard William (Me)

MCINERNEY, Joseph Lee (Cal)

MCINNIS, Victor Erwin (Miss) Po Box 63, Lexington, MS 39095

MCINTIRE, Rhonda Gail Smith (RG) 17 Camino Redondo, Placitas, NM 87043

MCINTOSH, David Kevin (Ct) 1 North Main Street, PO Box 309, Kent, CT 06757

MCINTOSH, Eric (Pgh) St James Episcopal Church, 11524 Frankstown Rd, Pittsburgh, PA 15235

MCINTOSH, Justin M (Va) 4332 Leeds Manor Road, Markham, VA 22643

MCINTOSH, Kendra Lea (Nwk) 26 W 84th St, New York, NY 10024

MCINTOSH, Mark Allen (Chi) 65 E Huron St, Chicago, IL 60611

MCINTOSH, Randy Eugene (WK) 138 S 8th St, Salina, KS 67401

MCINTOSH, Wayne S (SD) Trinity Episcopal Church, 500 14th Ave NW, Watertown, SD 57201

MCINTYRE, Calvin Carney (NY) 4401 Matilda Ave, Bronx, NY 10470

MCINTYRE III, Charles Ernest (NwT) 2429 Santa Cruz Ln, Odessa, TX 79763

MCINTYRE, Gregory Edward (WNC) 258 W Franklin Blvd, Gastonia, NC 28052

MCINTYRE, John George (Md) 326 Pintail Dr, Havre De Grace, MD 21078

MCINTYRE, Moni (Pgh) 4601 5th Ave #825, Pittsburgh, PA 15213

MCJILTON, Sheila N (WA) St Philip's Church, 522 Main St, Laurel, MD 20707

MCKAIG, Byron James (Los) Mount Mesa, Box 1572, Lake Isabella, CA 93240

MCKAY, Judy Aileen (Ida)

MCKAY, Paige Higley (NwT) 1101 Slide Rd, Lubbock, TX 79416

MCKAY IV, Robert (NwPa) 1267 Treasure Lk, Du Bois, PA 15801

MCKAY, William Martin (RG)

MCKEAN, Deborah Adams (Me) PO Box 137, Cushing, ME 04563

MCKEE, Christianne Louise (Spok) 1909 W. Clearview Dr., Ellensburg, WA 98926

MCKEE II, Daniel Deupree (Ark) 500 Hazelton Dr., Madison, MS 39110

MCKEE, Elizabeth Shepherd (NC) 408 Woodlawn Ave, Greensboro, NC 27401

MCKEE, Helen Louise (SVa) 405 Avondale Dr., Danville, VA 24541

MCKEE, Lewis Kavanaugh (WTenn) 57 Wychewood Dr, Memphis, TN 38117

MCKEE, Martha Marcella (NJ) 11 Exeter Ct, East Windsor, NJ 08520

MCKEE, Michael Dale (Los) 815 Emerald Bay, Laguna Beach, CA 92651

MCKEE, Stephen Lee (Okla) 501 S Cincinnati Ave, Tulsa, OK 74103
MCKEE, Susan McKee (CGC) PO Box 29, Bon Secour, AL 36511
MCKEE, Todd Anderson (Vt) 105 Hickory Rdg, White River Junction, VT 05001
MCKEEVER, Anne Dryden (The Episcopal NCal) 2620 Capitol Ave., Sacramento, CA 95816
✠ **MCKELVEY**, Jack Marston (Ret Bp of Roch 2008-) 8 Grove St, Rochester, NY 14605
MCKENNA, Cynthia Ann (Okla) P.O. Box 187, Boerne, TX 78006
MCKENNA, Keith (NY) 429 Lakeshore Drive, Putnam Valley, NY 10579
MCKENNEY, Mary Lou R (ECR)
MCKENNEY, Walter (Ct) 38 Clover Dr, West Hartford, CT 06110
MCKENZIE, Bryan Keith (FtW)
MCKENZIE, Jennifer Gaines (Va) Christ Church, 118 N Washington St, Alexandria, VA 22314
MCKENZIE JR, William Bruce (Ore) 1873 Sw High St, Portland, OR 97201
MCKENZIE-HAYWARD, Renee Eugenia (Pa) 1801 W. Diamond Street, Philadelphia, PA 19121
MCKEON, Julia McKay (Cal) 1590 Cabrillo Hwy S, Half Moon Bay, CA 94019
MCKEON JR, Richard R (NY) Church of the Messiah, PO Box 248, Rhinebeck, NY 12572
MCKIM, Laurie J. (WTex) Church of the Advent, 104 W Elizabeth St, Brownsville, TX 78520
MCKINLEY, Ellen Bacon (Ct)
MCKINLEY, Mele Senitila Tuineau (Ore) 1817 E Alsea Hwy, Waldport, OR 97394
MCKINNEY, Barbara Jean (Ia) 1435 Park Ave, Des Moines, IA 50315
MCKINNEY, Catherine R (Va) Varina Episcopal Church, 2385 Mill Rd, Henrico, VA 23231
MCKINNEY, Chantal Bianca (NC) 242 Flintshire Rd., Winston-Salem, NC 27104
MCKINNEY, Douglas Walton (Los) 401 S Detroit St Apt 311, Los Angeles, CA 90036
MCKINNON, Michael John (Mass) 9 Svenson Ave, Worcester, MA 01607
MCKINNON, Stanley Allen (Ark) PO Box 767, Siloam Springs, AR 72761
MCKNIGHT, James F (Cal) 801 S Plymouth Ct Unit 817, Chicago, IL 60605
MCKNIGHT, Leta Jeannette Zimmer (Vt) 75 South, Box 434, Lyndonville, VT 05851
MCKONE-SWEET, Mark C. (SanD) 16275 Pomerado Rd, Poway, CA 92064
MCLACHLAN, Devin Shepard (Mass) 38 Beaufort Place, Thompsons Lane, Cambridge, CB5 8AG, Great Britain (UK)

MCLAIN III, Paul King (WTenn) 102 N 2nd St, Memphis, TN 38103
MCLAREN, Beth Ann (WMich) 230 North Kalamazoo Mall, #402, Kalamazoo, MI 49007
MCLAREN, Christopher Todd (RG) 6730 Green Valley Place NW, Los Ranchos, NM 87107
MCLAUGHLIN, Debra Kay (SeFla) 1704 Buchanan St, Hollywood, FL 33020
MCLAUGHLIN, Eleanor Lee (NH) 38 Nekal Ln, Randolph, NH 03593
MCLAUGHLIN, John Norris (Mass) 406 Paradise Rd apt 1b, Swampscott, MA 01907
MCLAUGHLIN, Marlys Jean (Az) 10926 W Topaz Dr, Sun City, AZ 85351
MCLEAN JR, James Rayford (Ark) PO Box 524, Leland, MI 49654
MCLEAN, Jean Medding (Mont)
MCLEAN, Katherine Sharp (La)
MCLEAN, Richard (WTex) 3821 Sandia Dr, Plano, TX 75023
MCLEAVEY, Lauren Taylor (LI) St Mark's Episcopal Church, 754 Montauk Hwy, Islip, NY 11751
MCLELLAN, Brenda Jean (Mont) 1977 SW Palm City Rd Apt G, Stuart, FL 34994
MCLEMORE, Ann Rossington (Miss) 3921 Oakridge Dr, Jackson, MS 39216
MCLEMORE, William Pearman (Chi) 5116 W Malibu Ct, McHenry, IL 60050
MCLEOD, Harrison Marvin (USC) Christ Church, 10 N Church St, Greenville, SC 29601
MCLEOD III, Henry Marvin (Vt) 301 Georgetown Cir, Charleston, WV 25314
MCLEOD, James Wallace (ECR) 34400A Mission Blvd Apt 1109, Union City, CA 94587
✠ **MCLEOD**, Mary Adelia Rosamond (Ret Bp of Vt 2001-) 301 Georgetown Cir, Charleston, WV 25314
MCLEOD, Robert Boutell (CFla) 6661 N Placita Alta Reposa, Tucson, AZ 85750
MCLEOD, Sandra Kirby (CGC) St Agath's Church, 150 Circle Dr, DeFuniak Springs, FL 32435
MCLEON IV, Richard (WTex) PO Box 698, Henderson, TX 75653
MCLOUGHLIN, Jose Antonio (Okla) 924 N Robinson Ave, Oklahoma City, OK 73102
MCLUEN, Roy Emery (CGC) 25450 144th Place SE, Kent, WA 98042
MCMAHAN, Larry Wayne (CGC) 3902 E Jamie Ln, Bloomington, IN 47401
MCMANIS, Dennis Ray (SwFla) 12606 Rockrose Glen, Lakewood Ranch, FL 34202
MCMANUS, Bridget (CNY) 531 Cumberland Ave, Syracuse, NY 13210
MCMANUS, Mary Christie (Cal) 215 10th Ave, San Francisco, CA 94118

MCMANUS, Michael J (Colo) P. O. Box 33022, Palm Beach Gardens, FL 33420
MCMICHAEL JR, Ralph Nelson (Spr) 1210 Locust St, Saint Louis, MO 63103
MCMILLAN, Bruce Dodson (Miss) Po Box 596, Holly Springs, MS 38635
MCMILLAN, John Nixon (Alb) 4531 Ethel St, Okemos, MI 48864
MCMILLEN II, William Charles (WTenn) St James Episcopal Church, PO Box 838, Union City, TN 38281
MCMILLIN, Andrea McMillin (The Episcopal NCal) 1600 Knox Ave, Bellingham, WA 98225
MCMULLEN, Andrew L (Colo) Saint Matthias Episcopal Church, 18320 Furrow Rd, Monument, CO 80132
MCMURREN, Jay Junior (Ore) 578 23rd St Ne, Salem, OR 97301
MCMURREN, Margaret Hewett (Ore) 1525 Glen Creek Rd Nw, Salem, OR 97304
MCMURTRY, Herbert Charles (Ak) 1915 Lindsay Loop, Mount Vernon, WA 98274
MCNAB, (Charles) Bruce (Colo) 2 Park Plaza Rd, Bozeman, MT 59715
MCNAB, Joan T (Colo) 536 W North St, Aspen, CO 81611
MCNAIR, David Miller (WNC) The Episcopal Church of the Holy Spirit, PO Box 956, Mars Hill, NC 28754
MCNAIR, Kent Stevens (The Episcopal NCal) 2200 Country Club Dr., Cameron Park, CA 95682
MCNAIRY, Philip Edward (Minn) 2287 Bevans Cir, Red Wing, MN 55066
MCNALLY, Jennifer Steckel (Minn) 2035 Charlton Rd, Sunfish Lake, MN 55118
MCNAMARA, Beth Cooper (Md) 8015 Rider Ave, Towson, MD 21204
MCNAMARA, Joseph Francis (CPa) Po Box 474, Mansfield, PA 16933
MCNAMARA, Kim (Oly) Po Box 156, Allyn, WA 98524
MCNAMARA, Patrick (NH) Holy Trinity, 768 Main St, Greenport, NY 11944
MCNAUGHTON, Bonnie Eleanor (Los) 2571 Via Campesina Unit G, Palos Verdes Estates, CA 90274
MCNAUGHTON, Margaret (WA) 720 Upland Pl, Alexandria, VA 22314
MCNAUL, Robert Guthrie (Nev) 1909 Camino Mirada, North Las Vegas, NV 89031
MCNEELEY, David Fielden (Hai) 566 Standish Rd, Teaneck, NJ 07666
MCNEELY, Virginia Diane (The Episcopal NCal) Trinity Cathedral, 2620 Capitol Ave, Sacramento, CA 95816
MCNEER, Charles Conrad (SwVa) 490 Court St Apt 6, Abingdon, VA 24210

MCNELLIS, Kathleene Kernan (RG) 6200 Coors NW, Albuquerque, NM 87120

MCNIEL, Donna (Episcopal SJ) 8221 Bart Ave NE, Albuquerque, NM 87109

MCNISH, Jill L (Pa) 199 W Baltimore Ave, Clifton Heights, PA 19018

MCNULTY, Lynne Herrick (Roch) 28 Gillette St, Rochester, NY 14619

✠ **MCNUTT JR**, Charlie Fuller (Ret Bp of CPa 1995-) 5225 Wilson Ln Apt 2137, Mechanicsburg, PA 17055

MCNUTT, Robin Lee (Neb) 3020 Belvedere Blvd, Omaha, NE 68111

MCPARTLIN, Julie (Alb) P.O. Box 696, 24 Sentinel Pines Drive, Hague, NY 12836

MCPEAK, Helen C (Oly) 415 S 18th St, Mount Vernon, WA 98274

MCPHAIL, Donald Stewart (SC) 22 Saint Augustine Dr., Charleston, SC 29407

MCPHEE, Gizelle Valencia (SeFla) PO Box 12943, Miami, FL 33101

MCPHERSON, Clair W (NY) 1234 Midland Ave #5E, Bronxville, NY 10708

MCPHERSON, Phebe Lewald (Md) 214 Wardour Dr, Annapolis, MD 21401

MCPHERSON, Thomas Dale (SwFla) 6 Post Pointe Cir, Valdosta, GA 31602

MCPHERSON, William Bruce (Md) 214 Wardour Drive, Annapolis, MD 21401

MCQUADE, Lynne Dawson (NY) 900 Palmer Rd Apt 7-L, Bronxville, NY 10708

MCQUEEN, Dale Lee (Oly) 3230 Chanute Dr., Lake Havasu city, AZ 86406

MCQUEEN, Henry P (SVa) Hickory Neck Episcopal Church, 8300 Richmond Rd, Toano, VA 23168

MCQUEEN II, James Douglas (SanD) All Saints Church, 625 Pennsylvania Ave, San Diego, CA 92103

MCQUEEN, Paul Dennis (CFla) 322 King Street, Oviedo, FL 32765

MCQUIN, Randall Lee (Kan) 3141 Fairview Park Dr Ste 250, Falls Church, VA 22042

MCRAE, Marcia Owens (Ga)

MCREE, Timothy Patrick (WNC) 274 Sunset Hts, Canton, NC 28716

MCSPADDEN, Christine Tully Trainor (Cal)

MCSWAIN, William D (SC) PO Box 237, Denmark, SC 29003

MCTERNAN, Vaughan Durkee (Colo) 2609 Rigel Drive, Colorado Springs, CO 80906

MCVEY, A(rthur) William (Kan) 9218 Cherokee Pl, Leawood, KS 66206

MCVEY, James B (Ia) 4403 High Ct, Davenport, IA 52804

MCWHORTER, Elizabeth S (NY) St Mary Church, PO Box 637, Tuxedo Park, NY 10987

MCWHORTER, Shirley R (Mich) St Thomas Episcopal Church, 2441 Nichols Drive, Trenton, MI 48183

MCWHORTER, Stephen Dexter (Va) PO Box 5068, Southampton, GA 11969

MEACHAM, Carlyle Haynes (Vt) Po Box 115, Washburn, IL 61570

MEACHEN, Jerome Webster (Ct) 20 W Canal St Apt 423, Winooski, VT 05404

MEAD, Alan Champ (CPa) 3159 Silver Sands Circle #103, Virginia Beach, VA 23451

MEAD, Andrew Craig (NY) 321 Wandsworth Street, Narragansett, RI 02882

MEAD, Carol Lynn (Miss) 105 Montgomery Hl, Starkville, MS 39759

MEAD, Loren Benjamin (WA) 3440 S Jefferson St Apt 1478, Falls Church, VA 22041

MEAD, Matthew Hoxsie (NY) 1415 Pelhamdale Avenue, Pelham, NY 10803

MEADE, Elizabeth G (Chi) 406 Peck Rd, Geneva, IL 60134

MEADE, Gary J (WTenn) St. Mary's Episcopal Church, 108 N. King Ave., Dyersburg, TN 38024

MEADERS JR, Calvin Judson (Miss) 200 E Academy St., Canton, MS 39046

MEADERS III, Calvin Judson (Miss) 305 S Commerce St, Natchez, MS 39120

MEADOWCROFT, Jeffrey Whittaker (USC)

MEADOWS JR, Richard Dean (Ct) 111 Whalley Ave, New Haven, CT 06511

MEAIRS, Babs Marie (SanD) 11650 Calle Paracho, San Diego, CA 92128

MEANS, Carl T (Wyo) 300 Mt. Arter Loop, Lander, WY 82520

MEANS, Jacqueline Alline (Ind) 710 Buchanan St, Plainfield, IN 46168

MEARS JR, Preston Kennard (NH) 15101 Candy Hill Rd, Upper Marlboro, MD 20772

MEASE, Carole Ann (CPa) 359 Schoolhouse Rd, Middletown, PA 17057

MEAUX, Amy Dafler (Lex) 320 W Main St, Danville, KY 40422

MEBANE JR, Willie Henry (WNY) 128 Pearl St, Buffalo, NY 14202

MECK III, Daniel Stoddart (Md) 5620 Greenspring Avenue, Baltimore, MD 21209

MECK, Nancy E (SVa) 13530 Heathbrook Rd, Midlothian, VA 23112

MECKLING, Judith B (Pa) 730 S Highland Ave, Merion Station, PA 19066

MEDELA, Jean Milor (Hai) c/o Diocese of Haiti, Boite Postale 1309, Port au Prince Haiti, Haiti

MEDINA, Ernesto R (Neb) 16611 Castelar St, Omaha, NE 68130

MEDINA, Felix (PR) Po Box 2156, Bridgeport, CT 06608

MEDINA MEJIA, Jorge Reynaldo (Hond)

MEDLEY, James W (SVa) 1004 Lyndhurst Place, Virginia Beach, VA 23464

MEECH, Michelle M (EO) 4800 Woodward Ave, Detroit, MI 48201

MEEKS, Edward Gettys (USC) 405 S. Chapel Street, Baltimore, MD 21231

MEENGS, John Richard (WMich) 622 Lawndale Ct, Holland, MI 49423

MEGEATH, Sally Holme (Colo) 343 Canyon St, Lander, WY 82520

MEGGINSON JR, Marshall Elliot (HB) 5689 Utrecht Rd, Baltimore, MD 21206

MEGINNISS, David Hamilton (Ala) 801 Pin Brook Lane, Tuscaloosa, AL 35406

MEHEUX, Sybil Adlyn (CFla) 543 Corporation St, Holly Hill, FL 32117

MEIER, Kermit Irwin (Ore) 1209 Fleet Landing Blvd, Atlantic Beach, FL 32233

MEISS, Marion (Be) 46 S. Laurel St., Hazleton, PA 18201

MEISTER, Deborah Anne (WA) 3001 Wisconsin Ave. NW, Washington, DC 20016

MEISTER, Stephen George (Roch) 400 S Main St, Newark, NY 14513

MEISTER BOOK, Nancy D (Az)

MEJIA, Jairo (ECR) 12149 Saddle Road, Carmel Valley, CA 93924

MEJIA, Jose Arnaldo (Hond) Calle Principal, La Estrada, HN, Honduras

MEJIA, Nelson Yovany (Hond) Roatan Islas De La Bahia, Apartado 193, Roatan, Coxen Hole, Honduras

MEJIA ESPINOSA, Jose Vincente (EcuC) Avenue La Castellana 40-06, Zona 8, Guatemala City, 01008, Guatemala

MELBERGER, MaryJo McConnell (Pa) 261 Tulip Tree Ct, Blue Bell, PA 19422

MELCHER, John Robert (Mich) 2441 Nichols St, Trenton, MI 48183

MELCHIONNA, Elizabeth Marie (Colo) 725 Dahlia St, Denver, CO 80220

MELENDEZ, Michael Paul (Mass) 138 Tremont St, Boston, MA 02111

MELIN, Marilyn Joyce (Chi)

MELIS, Alberto Manuel (Tex) 305 N 30th St, Waco, TX 76710

MELLISH, Roy W (La) PO Box 1825, Morgan City, LA 70381

MELLO, Iris Elaine (RI) 88 Albert Ave, Cranston, RI 02905

MELLO, Jeffrey William (Mass) 130 Aspinwall Ave, Brookline, MA 02446

MELLO, Mary Ann (RI)

MELLO-MAKI, Christine Helene (NMich) 470 North Us 141, Crystal Falls, MI 49920

MELLON, Robert Edward (Pa) 10551 Machrihanish Cir, San Antonio, FL 33576

MELLOTT, Emily Alice (Chi) 105 W Maple St, Lombard, IL 60148

MELNYK, James Stanley (NC) 5400 Crestview Rd, Raleigh, NC 27609
MELTON, Brent Alan (Va) 210 Ellington St, Fayetteville, NC 28305
MELTON, Heather L (LI) 63 Rockledge Rd Apt 2d, Bronxville, NY 10708
MELTON, Jk (Colo) Fordham University, Department of Theology, 441 E Fordham Rd, Bronx, NY 10458
MELTON, Jonathan Randall (Mil) 1360 Regent St # 157, Madison, WI 53715
MELTON, M(Ark) Randall (WTex) 721 St. Louis Street, P.O. Box 139, Gonzales, TX 78629
MEMBA, Jose Luis (SeFla) 2250 Sw 31st Ave, Fort Lauderdale, FL 33312
MENAUL, Marjorie Ann (CPa) 6288 Peach Tree Rd, Columbus, OH 43213
MENDENHALL, Elborn E (Kan) 2477 SW Brookhaven Ln, Topeka, KS 66614
MENDEZ, Noe (Dal) The Holy Nativity Episcopal Church, 2200 18th St, Plano, TX 75074
MENDEZ, Richard (U) RR2 Box 64, Pocatello, ID 83202
MENDEZ, Troy Douglas (Az) Trinity Cathedral, 100 W Roosevelt St, Phoenix, AZ 85003
MENDEZ-COLON, Ana Rosa (PR) Urb. Venus Gardens Calle Peliux 1770, San Juan, PR 00926
MENDOZA, Christine Love (Tex) 3201 Windsor Rd, Austin, TX 78703
MENDOZA, Loretta (Mil) 2708 Red Fawn Ct, Racine, WI 53406
MENDOZA CEDENO, Victor Eduardo (Litoral Ecu)
MENDOZA MARMOLEJOS, Milquella Rosanna (DR (DomRep))
MENDOZA PEREZ, Julio Cesar (Ve) Iglesia Episcopal de Venezuela, Centro Diocesano Av. Caroní No. 100, Colinas de Bello Monte Caracas 1042-A, Venezuela
MENDOZA QUIROZ, Hugo Eligio (Litoral Ecu) Calle #19, #208, Calderon, Ecuador
MENEELEY, Beverly Ann (Be)
MENELAS, Frederic (Hai)
MENGER, James Andrew (Ga) 3521 Nassau Dr, Augusta, GA 30909
MENJIVAR, Natividay (Okla) St Mark's Episcopal Church, 6744 S Kings Hwy, Alexandria, VA 22306
MENJIVAR, Nicholas (NC) Po Box 218, Durham, NC 27702
MENNELL, John A (Nwk) 75 S Fullerton Ave, Montclair, NJ 07042
MENSAH, Albert (Chi)
MENZI, Donald Wilder (Mich) 5 E 10th St, New York, NY 10003
MERCADO GALARZA, Wilfredo (PR)
MERCER JR, Charles Spencer (Md) The Episcopal Church Of St Mary The Virgin, 3121 Walbrook Ave, Baltimore, MD 21216

MERCER, Emmanuel A (Pa) Saint Paul's Church, 22 E Chestnut Hill Ave, Philadelphia, PA 19118
MERCER JR, Roy Calvin (CFla) 4932 Willowbrook Cir, Winter Haven, FL 33884
MERCER, Thomas Robert (NY)
MERCHANT, John Edward (At) 474 Sunset Dr., Asheville, NC 28804
MERCHANT, Patricia Laura (At) 6000 Drake Rd, Cincinnati, OH 45243
MERCHANT II, Wilmot T (SC) 801 11th Avenue North, North Myrtle Beach, SC 29582
MERCURE, Joan Carol (Minn) 4557 Colfax Ave S, Minneapolis, MN 55419
MEREDITH, Carol Ann (Colo) 316 Oakland St, Aurora, CO 80010
MERFY, Florence Martha (Nev) 1515 Shasta Dr Apt 1510, Davis, CA 95616
✠ **MERINO-BOTERO**, Bernardo (Ret Bp of Colom 2001-) Calle 97 - No 16-51, Apt 303 Edificio Royal Plaza, Bogota, Colombia
MEROLA SR, Carl Robert (CFla) 705 Victory Lane, Hendersonville, NC 28739
MEROLA JR, Carl Robert (Va) 402 Valencia Cir, Oviedo, FL 32765
MERONEY, Anne Elrod (At) 4919-B Rivoli Dr, Macon, GA 31210
MERRELL, Robin Nicholas (Cal) 3886 Balcom Rd, San Jose, CA 95148
MERRICK, Barbara Robinson (Ky) 8110 Saint Andrews Church Rd, Louisville, KY 40258
MERRILL, George Richard (Md) 9046 Quail Run Rd, Saint Michaels, MD 21663
MERRILL, Richard Hull (ECR) 1755 W Ridgeview Circle, Palm Springs, CA 92264
MERRILL JR, Robert Clifford (Tex) 1321 Upland Dr #5192, Houston, TX 77043
MERRILL, Russell Walter (EMich) 262 Raleigh Pl, Lennon, MI 48449
MERRIMAN, Michael Walter (Minn) 2012 Stain Glass Dr, Plano, TX 75075
MERRIN, Susan L (Colo)
MERRITT, Claudia L Wolfe (Va) 3401 Hawthorne Avenue, Richmond, VA 23222
MERRITT, Frederick Deen (Neb)
MERRITT, Robert E (CFla) 864 Summerfield Dr, Lakeland, FL 33803
MERROW, Andrew T P (Va) 2609 North Glebe Road, Arlington, VA 22207
MERTZ, Anne Pierpoint (Cal) 228 S Pitt St, Alexandria, VA 22314
MERTZ, Mary Ann (Pa) 116 Lancaster Pike, Oxford, PA 19363
MERZ, John (LI) 129 Kent Street, Brooklyn, NY 11222
MESA, Prospero Eugenio (La) 3104 Verna St, Metairie, LA 70003
MESENBRING, David (Oly) 1245 10th Ave E, Seattle, WA 98102
MESERVEY, Norman Rix (WNC) 84 Church St, Franklin, NC 28734

MESLER JR, Raymond Clyde (NY) 7470 W Glenbrook Rd Apt 313, Milwaukee, WI 53223
MESLEY, Gordon Warwick (WMo) 2021 S Hummel Dr, Independence, MO 64055
MESSENGER, Ray Stillson (CNY) 420 Woodside Way, Moravia, NY 13118
MESSENGER, William Glen (Mass) 84 Lexington St, Belmont, MA 02478
MESSENGER-HARRIS, Beverly Ann (CNY) 124 W Hamilton Ave, Sherrill, NY 13461
MESSER, Charles Wilson (Pa) PO Box 452, Glen Riddle, PA 19037
MESSER, Julia (SVa) 5181 Princess Anne Rd, Virginia Beach, VA 23462
MESSER, Kenneth Blaine (Ia)
MESSERSMITH, Daphne Killhour (CPa) 603 Mahanoy Valley Rd, Duncannon, PA 17020
MESSERSMITH, Merton E (CPa) 909 Alison Ave, Mechanicsburg, PA 17055
MESSICK, Joshua E (Eas) PO Box 3400, Meridian, MS 39303
MESSIER, Daniel Joseph (Az) 600 S La Canada Dr, Green Valley, AZ 85614
MESSINA JR, Michael Frank (CFla) 94 Pecan Run, Ocala, FL 34472
MESTETH, Rhoda Yvonne (SD)
MESTRE JR, José Wilfredo (Ct) 2340 North Ave Apt. 7D, Bridgeport, CT 06614
METCALF, Michael Patrick (Dal)
METCALFE, Steven Todd (WNY) 20 Milton St, Williamsville, NY 14221
METELLUS, Donald (Hai)
METHENY JR, Lloyd Erwin (The Episcopal NCal) 11070 Hirschfeld Way #66, Rancho Cordova, CA 95670
METHVEN, Susanne B (Okla) 3328 S Marion Ave, Tulsa, OK 74135
METHVIN, Thomas Gregory (Dal) 3966 McKinney Ave, Dallas, TX 75204
METIVIER, Catherine A (Okla)
METOYER, Eric Martin Madison (Cal) Episcopal Diocese Of California, 1055 Taylor St, San Francisco, CA 94108
METTLER, Garrett M (Los) 8 Sunnyside Ave., Pleasantville, NY 10570
METZ, Susanna (ETenn) 335 Tennessee Ave, Sewanee, TN 37383
METZGER, Carl Edgar (Pa) 100 E Lehigh Ave, Philadelphia, PA 19125
METZGER, Curtis (NH) PO Box 1541, Concord, NH 03302
METZGER, James Poore (Mo) 3402 Sawgrass Ln, Cincinnati, OH 45209
METZLER, Carolyn Walburn (Me) 1611 Sunset Gardens Rd SW, Albuquerque, NM 87105
METZLER, Martha Grace (Mo) 5305 Kenrick View Drive, Saint Louis, MO 63119

METZLER, Paul Arthur (CNY) 5237 Nottingham Avenue, Saint Louis, MO 63109

MEUSCHKE, Marty O (Ga) 145 River Ridge Loop, Hortense, GA 31543

MEYER, Alan King (Az) 5909 SW Karla Ct, Portland, OR 97239

MEYER, Erika K (NY) 240 E. 31st St., New York, NY 10016

MEYER, John A (LI) 423 Falcon Ridge Drive, Sheridan, WY 82801

MEYER, John Paul (Mich) 1353 Labrosse St, Detroit, MI 48226

MEYER, Mark David (Colo) 1365 Fairview Ave, Canon City, CO 81212

MEYER, Nancy Ruth (Chi) St Peter's Episcopal Church, 621 W Belmont Ave, Chicago, IL 60657

MEYER, Robert Bruce (FdL) PO Box 184, Tremont, IL 61568

MEYER, Wendel William (Mass) 419 Emerald Bay Cir Unit B1, Naples, FL 34110

MEYERS, David Craig (WMich) Church Of The Holy Spirit, 1200 Post Dr NE, Belmont, MI 49306

MEYERS, Frederick W (Rick) (Colo) 420 Cantril St, Castle Rock, CO 80104

MEYERS, Michael William (Az) 300 N Constitution Dr, Tucson, AZ 85748

MEYERS, Ruth (Cal) Church Divinity School Of The Pacific, 2451 Ridge Rd, Berkeley, CA 94709

MEZACAPA, Nicklas A (Minn) 111 3rd Ave SW, Rochester, MN 55902

MICHAEL, Mark A (Alb) 432 Van Buren Street, Herndon, VA 20170

MICHAELS, Glen Francis (Alb) Po Box 2123, Plattsburgh, NY 12901

MICHAELS, Laurie Jane (Chi) 647 Dundee Ave, Barrington, IL 60010

MICHAELSON, Peter (RI) 2 Gaspee Point Dr, Warwick, RI 02888

MICHAUD, Bruce Alan (EMich) 2090 Wyndham Ln, Alpena, MI 49707

MICHAUD, David Norman (Eas) St Peter's Church, 115 Saint Peters St, Salisbury, MD 21801

MICHAUD, Eleanor Jean (Eau)

MICHAUD, Jean Fruitho (Hai) c/o Diocese of Haiti, Boite Postale 1309, Port au Prince Haiti, Haiti

✠ **MICHEL**, Rodney Rae (Ret Bp Suffr of LI 2007-) 1 Christian St Apt 36, Philadelphia, PA 19147

MICHELFELDER, Susan Rebecca (SO) PO Box 32, The Plains, VA 20198

MICHELL, Neal O (Dal) 5100 Ross Ave, Dallas, TX 75206

MICHELS, Sandra B (Ind) 5910 Black Oak Lane, Ft. Worth, TX 76114

MICHIE, Michael Williams (Dal) 8701 Tiercels Dr, Mckinney, TX 75070

MICHNO, Dennis Glen (Eau) 34615 County Highway J, Bayfield, WI 54814

MICKELSON, Margaret Belle (Ak) PO Box 849, Cordova, AK 99574

MIDDLETON, Elizabeth Blackford (WNY) 1302 Devonshire Way, Palm Beach Gardens, FL 33418

MIDDLETON, Mark Leslie (Chi) 509 Hessel Blvd, Champaign, IL 61820

MIDDLETON III, Richard Temple (Miss) 944 Royal Oak Dr, Jackson, MS 39209

MIDDLETON, Tracie G (FtW) 700 E. Ash Ln., Apt. 13304, Euless, TX 76039

MIDENCE VALDES, Jose Francisco (Hond) Comercio, Tela, Honduras

MIDWOOD JR, John Earle (Pa) 300 North Lawrence, Philadelphia, PA 19106

MIDYETTE III, Charles Thomas (EC) 122 Queen St, Beaufort, NC 28516

MIDZALKOWSKI, Sarah Frances (Mich) 765 Grove Street, East Lansing, MI 48823

MIEDKE, Warren Giles (Tex) 13131 Fry Rd, Cypress, TX 77433

MIESCHER III, Walter Henry (Kan) 2630 N Ridgewood Ct, Wichita, KS 67220

MIHALYI, David Richard (CNY) 472 Washington St, Geneva, NY 14456

MIKAYA, Henry C (WMich) Box 1315, Gabrone, Botswana

MIKEL, Joseph F (Oly)

MILAM, David Ross (Mass) 108 Lakeside Ave, Lakeville, MA 02347

MILAM, Thomas Richerson (SwVa)

MILAN JR, Jesse (Kan) 7103 Waverly Ave, Kansas City, KS 66109

MILANO, Mary Lucille (Chi) 8765 W Higgins Rd, Chicago, IL 60631

MILES, Frank William (Colo) 1175 Vine St Apt 207, Denver, CO 80206

MILES, Glenworth Dalmane (LI) 2714 Lurting Ave, Bronx, NY 10469

MILES, James B (HB)

MILES JR, John Pickett (SVa) 268 Mill Stream Way, Williamsburg, VA 23185

MILES, Kristin K (Ct) 661 Old Post Rd, Fairfield, CT 06824

MILES, Richard Alan Knox (Los) 634 Parkway Blvd, Reidsville, NC 27320

MILES, Thomas Dee (Kan) 1308 Overlook Dr, Manhattan, KS 66503

MILFORD, Sara Michelle (Ark) 228 Spring St, Hot Springs, AR 71901

MILHOAN, Charles Everett (Az) 4102 W Union Hills Dr, Glendale, AZ 85308

MILHOLEN, Linda Scott (WMo) PO Box 109, Houston, MO 65483

MILHOLLAND, Nancy Elizabeth (Mass) 58 Stanford Heights Ave, San Francisco, CA 94127

MILIAN, Mario Emilio (SeFla) 5690 N Kendall Dr, Coral Gables, FL 33156

MILIEN, Marivel (SeFla) 6744 N Miami Ave, Miami, FL 33150

MILIEN, Smith (SeFla) 6744 North Miami Ave, Miami, FL 33150

MILLAR, Charles Wendell (Mich) 14818 Oakes Rd, Perry, MI 48872

MILLAR, John Dunne (Az) 7245 E Manzanita Dr, Scottsdale, AZ 85258

✠ **MILLARD**, George Richard (Ret Bp Suffr of Eur 1990- Cal) 501 Portola Rd # 8107, Portola Valley, CA 94028

MILLARD, Michael Wayne (WLa) 405 Washington Ave, Mansfield, LA 71052

MILLER, A Scott (Oly) 211 Calle del Verano, Palm Desert, CA 92260

MILLER, Alan Clayborne (Fla) 1637 Nw 19th Cir, Gainesville, FL 32605

MILLER, Alfred Franklin (EO) 665 E Gladys Ave, Hermiston, OR 97838

MILLER, Ann C (Ct) 99 Timberwood Rd, West Hartford, CT 06117

MILLER, Anthony Glenn (Los) 350 S Madison Ave Apt 207, Pasadena, CA 91101

MILLER, Arthur Burton (ECR) 2050 California St Apt 20, Mountain View, CA 94040

MILLER, Barbara Ruth (ECR) 5318 Palma Ave, Atascadero, CA 93422

MILLER, Barry William (Ct) 99 Timberwood Rd, West Hartford, CT 06117

MILLER, Charlene Ida (Tex) 14300 66th St N Lot 900, Clearwater, FL 33764

MILLER, Charles Bernard (SVa) 302 Brittania Dr., Williamsburg, VA 23185

MILLER, Christopher Howell (Va) 1000 Saint Stephens Rd, Alexandria, VA 22304

MILLER, Clark Stewart (NI) 319 7th St, Logansport, IN 46947

MILLER, David Dallas (Dal) 1700 N Westmoreland Rd, Desoto, TX 75115

MILLER, David Walton (Los) 1037 16th St Apt 1, Santa Monica, CA 90403

MILLER, Donald Stewart (Cal) 45602 State Highway 14, Stevenson, WA 98648

MILLER JR, Edward Oehler (Va) 6715 Georgetown Pike, Mclean, VA 22101

MILLER JR, Edwin Lee (Okla) 3300 N Vermont Ave, Oklahoma City, OK 73112

MILLER, Elizabeth M (Be) 44 E Market St, Bethlehem, PA 18018

MILLER, Elizabeth Sleeper (Me) 286 Lincoln St, South Portland, ME 04106

MILLER, Eric Lee (SO) 321 Worthington Ave., Cincinnati, OH 45215

MILLER JR, Ernest Charles (NY) 611 Broadway Rm 520, New York, NY 10012

MILLER, Fred (CPa) 547 Brighton Place, Mechanicsburg, PA 17055

MILLER, Frederic Alling (LI) 55 E Main St, Oyster Bay, NY 11771

MILLER, Isaac J (Pa) 18th & Diamond, Philadelphia, PA 19121

MILLER, James Barrett (The Episcopal NCal) 550 Seagaze Dr Apt 19, Oceanside, CA 92054

MILLER, James Lower (NY) 126 Goldens Bridge Rd, Katonah, NY 10536

MILLER, Janice Mary Howard (NI) 2117 E Jefferson Blvd, South Bend, IN 46617

MILLER, Jean Louise (EC) 9191 Daly Rd., Cincinnati, OH 45231

MILLER, Jerry Lee (WMo) 4258 E Whitehall Dr, Springfield, MO 65809

MILLER, Jo (Ore) P.O. Box 413, Bandon, OR 97411

MILLER, Joe Ted (Okla) 2732 Walnut Rd, Norman, OK 73072

MILLER, Joel Prescott (ECR) 160 Robideaux Rd, Aptos, CA 95003

MILLER, John Edward (Alb) 7 Pooles Hill Rd # 12, Ancram, NY 12502

MILLER, John Edward (Va) 4209 Monument Ave, Richmond, VA 23230

MILLER, John Leonard (NY) 23 Cedar Ln, Princeton, NJ 08540

MILLER JR, John Meredith (Vt) 34 County Route 59, Buskirk, NY 12028

MILLER, John Preston (Me) 223 Lakes At Litchfield Dr, Pawleys Island, SC 29585

MILLER, John Sloan (La) 205 North 4th Street, Baton Rouge, LA 70801

MILLER, Joseph Potter (Los)

MILLER, Judith Joelynn (Walker) (Oly) PO Box 1782, Westport, WA 98595

MILLER JR, Kenneth C (Mil) 3906 W Mequon Rd, Mequon, WI 53092

MILLER, Kurt David (Ga) 3665 Bermuda Cir, Augusta, GA 30909

MILLER, Laura Jean (Alb) 41 Gardiner Pl, Walton, NY 13856

MILLER, Laurence Henry (Be) 31 Tecumseh Pass, Millsboro, DE 19966

MILLER, Leewin Glen (SwFla) 4279 70th St Cir E, Palmetto, FL 34221

MILLER JR, Louis Oleman (USC) 129 Heathwood Rd, Union, SC 29379

MILLER, Marion Renee (Tenn) Po Box 1903, Monterey, CA 93942

MILLER, Mark Joseph (Oly) 913 2nd St, Snohomish, WA 98290

MILLER, Monroe Richard (NI) 17716 Downing Dr, Lowell, IN 46356

MILLER, Nancy Fay (RI) 82 Rockmeadow Rd, Westwood, MA 02090

MILLER, Patricia L (WMo) 17212 East 44th Street Court, Independence, MO 64055

MILLER, Patrick J. (Tex) 3514 Corondo Ct., Houston, TX 77005

MILLER, Paula Marie (Mich) 1325 Champaign Rd, Lincoln Park, MI 48146

MILLER, Richard Allan (Pa) 1521 Ashby Rd, Paoli, PA 19301

MILLER, R(Obert) Cameron (Vt) Saint Mark's, PO Box 125, Newport, VT 05855

MILLER, Robert Mcgregor (Pa) 2039 Serendipity Way, Schwenksville, PA 19473

MILLER, Robert William (Minn) 11030 Batello Dr, Venice, FL 34292

MILLER, Roger Edward (CFla) 11620 Claymont Circle, Windermere, FL 34786

MILLER, Ronald Homer (Md) 830 W 40th St. Apt 860, Baltimore, MD 21211

MILLER, Sarah Holland Taylor (Tex) 1525 H St NW, Washington, DC 20005

MILLER, Sarah Leanne (Ala) 113 N 18th St, Omaha, NE 68102

MILLER, Stephen Arthur (WNC) 290 Hillside Oaks Dr, Jefferson, NC 28640

✠ **MILLER**, Steven Andrew (Bp of Mil 2003-) 804 E Juneau Ave, Milwaukee, WI 53202

MILLER, Susan Heilmann (ECR) 25020 Pine Hills Dr, Carmel, CA 93923

MILLER, Thomas Paul (NY) 165 Christopher St Apt 5W, New York, NY 10014

MILLER, Todd Lawrence (Mass) 12 Ridge Ave., Newton, MA 02459

MILLER, Valerie A (Be) 2227 NW 79th Ave, Doral, FL 33122

MILLER, Victoria C (Ct) 350 Sound Beach Ave, Old Greenwich, CT 06870

MILLER, W Terry (Fla) 25928 Kilreigh Dr, Farmington Hills, MI 48336

MILLER, William B (La) PO Box 1745, Lihue, HI 96766

MILLER, William Charles (Pgh) 18297 W 155th Ter, Olathe, KS 66062

MILLER, William Robert (CPa)

MILLER IV, Woodford Decatur (CFla) 2508 Creekside Dr., Fort Piece, FL 34981

MILLER-MUTIA, Sylvia J (RG) 425 University Blvd NE, Albuquerque, NM 87106

MILLETTE, Carol Leslie (RI) 19 Midway Dr, Warwick, RI 02886

MILLICAN JR, Ford Jefferson (La) 3919 Morris Pl, Jefferson, LA 70121

MILLIEN, Jean Elie (Hai) Ecole Le Bon Samaritan, 26 Rue Jonathas, Carrefour, 06134, Haiti

MILLIEN, Wilner (PR)

MILLIGAN, Donald Arthur (Mass) 222 Bowdoin St, Winthrop, MA 02152

MILLIGAN, Kathleen Sue (Ia) 3714 Pennsylvania Ave Apt. I-86, Dubuque, IA 52002

MILLIGAN, Michael B (U) 28 Ridgeview Drive, Bountiful, UT 84010

MILLIKEN, Jean Louise (Va) 3732 N Oakland St, Arlington, VA 22207

✠ **MILLIKEN**, Michael Pierce (Bp of WK 2011-) 1 N. Main Street - Suite 502, Hutchinson, KS 67501

MILLIKIN, Gregory Loyd (Los) 228 S Pitt St, Alexandria, VA 22314

MILLNER JR, Bollin Madison (Va) 8 N Laurel St, Richmond, VA 23220

MILLOTT, Diane L (SwFla) 4510 Pilgrim Mill Road, Cumming, GA 30041

MILLOTT, Donna Evans (SwFla)

MILLOTT, Robert Thomas (SwFla) 4510 Pilgrim Mill Road, Cumming, GA 30041

MILLS JR, Arthur Donald (SO) 2696 Cedarbrook Way, Beavercreek, OH 45431

MILLS, Byron Keith (Az) 596 W. Ord Mountain Rd, Globe, AZ 85501

MILLS, Carol Ann Gillis (Tex) 205 Hillcrest Dr, Alvin, TX 77511

MILLS, Christen H (Mass) 320 Boston Post Rd, Weston, MA 02493

MILLS, David Knight (SO) 172 Clark Point Rd # 696, Southwest Harbor, ME 04679

MILLS III, Edward James (ETenn) 2104 Lamont St, Kingsport, TN 37664

MILLS, Eric Christopher (FdL) 347 Libal St, De Pere, WI 54115

MILLS, Fred Thomas (Ky) 685 West Dr, Madisonville, KY 42431

MILLS III, Joseph Edmund (LI) 1118 9th St Apt 9, Santa Monica, CA 90403

MILLS JR, Joseph Milton (Tex) 205 Hillcrest Dr, Alvin, TX 77511

MILLS, Joy Anna Marie (Pa) 2103 Quail Ridge Dr, Paoli, PA 19301

MILLS III, Ladson Frazier (SC) 3114 Mayfair Ln, Johns Island, SC 29455

MILLS, Michael Shane (Dal) 11122 Midway Rd, Dallas, TX 75229

MILLS, Nancy Thompson (Ga) PO Box 3136, Thomasville, GA 31799

MILLS, Stephen Howard (ECR) 713 Helen Drive, Hollister, CA 95023

MILLS, Susan Patricia (SO) 1060 Salem Ave, Dayton, OH 45406

MILLS, Wallace Wilson (Ida)

MILLSAP, William Richard (Nev) PO Box 2246, Reno, NV 89505

MILLS-CURRAN, Lorraine Marie (Mass) 7 Kimball Rd, Westborough, MA 01581

MILLS-POWELL, Mark Oliver Mclay (Eur)

MILNER JR, Raymond Joseph (SanD) 200 E 22nd St Apt 32, Roswell, NM 88201

MILTENBERGER, (George Kerr) Gordon (Dal) 10 Oak Village Rd, Greenville, TX 75402

MINARIK JR, Harry J (ETenn) 60 Hickory Trail, Norris, TN 37828

MINDRUM, Alice Anderson (Ct) 60 Range Rd, Southport, CT 06890

MINEAU, Charles Douglas (NMich)

MINER, Darren Ryan (Cal) 1750 29th Ave, San Francisco, CA 94122

MINER, David R. (Fla) 3212 Wind Lake Ln, Tallahassee, FL 32312

MINER II, James Stevens (SO) 276 North Ardmore Road, Columbus, OH 43209

MINER, Robert Johnston (Ct) 15 Morningside Ter, Wallingford, CT 06492

MINER-PEARSON, Anne (Minn) 15601 Island Road, Burnsville, MN 55306

MINERVA SR, Royal Edward (Fla)

MINGLEDORFF, Paschal Schirm (Ga) 9541 Whitfield Ave, Savannah, GA 31406

MINICH, Henry Nichols Faulconer (SeFla) 3115 Dundee Rd, Earlysville, VA 22936

Clergy List

MINIFIE, Charles Jackson (NY) 23 Sherman Dr, Hilton Head Island, SC 29928

MINIFIE, Thomas Richardson (Oly) 1311 Bonneville Ave Apt C, Snohomish, WA 98290

MINNICH-LOCKEY, Laura Karen (Va) 79 Laurel St, Harrisonburg, VA 22801

MINNICK, Margaret (Ct) 381 Main St Box 187, Middletown, CT 06457

MINNIS, Joseph Abell (FdL) PO Box 486, Boulder Junction, WI 54512

MINNIX, George Myers (NI) 2008 Raintree Dr Apt 4, Elkhart, IN 46514

MINOR, Albert Neely (ETenn) 7006 Brickton Way, Knoxville, TN 37919

MINOR, Cheryl Vasil (Mass) 65 Common Street, Belmont, MA 02478

MINOR, Paul Lawrence (Mass) 65 Common St., Belmont, MA 02478

MINSHEW, James Keener (SeFla) Po Box 1596, Port Salerno, FL 34992

MINSHEW, Nancy Elizabeth (CFla) 3735 Us Highway 17 92 N, Davenport, FL 33837

MINTER, Larry Clifton (Ky) 5409 Hickory Hill Rd, 5409 Hickory Hill Rd, Louisville, KY 40214

MINTER, Michael William (FdL) 314 Bellevue Rd, Highland, NY 12528

MINTER, Russell Deane (Tex) 364 Beckett Point Rd, Port Townsend, WA 98368

MINTON, Anne Mansfield (Mass) 35 Riverwalk Way Unit 303, Lowell, MA 01854

MINTURN, Benjamin Bradshaw (WA) 122 Ewarts Pond Rd, Hendersonville, NC 28739

MINTURN, Sterling Majors (NY) 5555 N Sheridan Rd Apt 607, Chicago, IL 60640

MINTZ, Elsa H (Pa) 3716 Abercrombie Court, Mount Pleasant, SC 29466

MINX, Patricia Ann (Kan) 105 S Indian Wells Dr, Olathe, KS 66061

MIONSKE, Wayne Allan Robert (FdL) 4535 N 92nd St Apt P203, Wauwatosa, WI 53225

MIRATE, Galen Alderman (Ga) 3338 Plantation Dr, Valdosta, GA 31605

MIRON, Jane Elizabeth (CPa)

MISKELLEY, Audrey (Cal)

MISNER, Mary Jane Brain (Mil) N1639 Six Corners Rd, Walworth, WI 53184

MISSNER, Heath McDonell (Chi) 470 Maple St, Winnetka, IL 60093

MITCHEL III, Glen Henry (Hank) (Los) 1072 Casitas Pass Road #317, Carpinteria, CA 93014

MITCHELL JR, Charles Albert (Los) 111 S 6th St, Burbank, CA 91501

MITCHELL, Dawn-Victoria (Mo) 3206 Pleasant St, Hannibal, MO 63401

MITCHELL, Joe T (NC) 505 Mountain Rd, Asheboro, NC 27205

MITCHELL, John Patrick (NJ) PO Box 261, Cape May, NJ 08204

MITCHELL, John Stephen (Vt) 372 Canterbury Rd, Manchester Center, VT 05255

MITCHELL, Judith N (RI) 24 Hart St, Providence, RI 02906

MITCHELL, Karin Rasmussen (NJ) 125 Orchard Ave, Hightstown, NJ 08520

MITCHELL, Katherine Nicholson (EC) 15 Durant Rd., Wellesley, MA 02482

MITCHELL, Lisa Sauber (NJ) 380 Sycamore Ave, Shrewsbury, NJ 07702

MITCHELL, Marilyn Dean (NC) 90 Worcester Rd Unit 12, Washington Depot, CT 06794

MITCHELL, Patricia Rhonda (NY) 732 Scarsdale Rd, Tuckahoe, NY 10707

MITCHELL, Preston Wade (SwVa)

MITCHELL JR, R(ichard) Cope (Colo) 3107 Nevermind Ln, Colorado Springs, CO 80917

MITCHELL, R(obert) James (Kan) Via Roma, Wichita, KS 67230

MITCHELL, Sadie S (Pa) 600 E Cathedral Rd, Apt H320, Philadelphia, PA 19128

MITCHELL, Thomas James (WNY) 7145 Fieldcrest Drive, Lockport, NY 14094

MITCHELL, Tim (Ky) 901 Baxter Ave, Louisville, KY 40204

MITCHELL, Winifred L (Colo) 3821 Elk Ln, Pueblo, CO 81005

MITCHENER, Gary Asher (O) 2213 Edgewood Rd, Cleveland Heights, OH 44118

MITCHICAN, Jonathan A (Pa) 1000 Burmont RD, Drexel Hill, PA 19026

MITHEN III, Thomas Scott (Ga) 516 E Broughton St, Bainbridge, GA 39817

MITMAN, John Louis (Ct) 31 Steep Hollow Ln, West Hartford, CT 06107

MIX, Lucas John (Az) Lucas Mix, 26 Oxford St, Cambridge, MA 02138

MIZIRL, Sandra Lee (Tex) 2011 Moses Creek Ct, College Station, TX 77845

MKHIZE, Danana Elliot (La) 1222 N Dorgenois St, New Orleans, LA 70119

MOBLEY, James E (SO) 955 Matthews Dr, Cincinnati, OH 45215

MOCKRIDGE III, Oscar Alling (Nwk) 358 Stiles Ct, West Orange, NJ 07052

MOCZYDLOWSKI, Ann Louise Hare (WA) 10120 Brock Dr, Silver Spring, MD 20903

MODESITT, Lori Jane (Wyo) 1357 Loomis St, Wheatland, WY 82201

MOEHL, Thomas Joseph (Ore) 12360 Summit Loop SE, Turner, OR 97392

MOELLER, Linda Lee Breitung (NJ) 13 Blossom Dr, Ewing, NJ 08638

MOERMOND, Curtis Roger (Ia)

MOFFAT JR, Alexander Douglas (FtW)

MOHN, Michael Collver (Va) 1527 Senseny Rd, Winchester, VA 22602

MOHRINGER, J(ohn) Wapshing (Ind) The Four Winds 2880w 250n, Lebanon, IN 46052

MOISE, Joseph (LI) 1227 Pacific St, Brooklyn, NY 11216

MOJALLALI, Darius A (Alb) 13 High Street, Delhigh, NY 13753

MOLE, James Frederick (Pa) 10 E 3rd St, Waynesboro, PA 17268

MOLEGODA, Niranjani Shariya (Mo) 217 Adams St, Jefferson City, MO 65101

MOLINA-MOORE, Amanda E (Del) PO Box 3510, Wilmington, DE 19807

MOLINE, Mark Edwin (Az) 2000 Shepherds Lane, Prescott, AZ 86301

MOLITORS, Elizabeth Anne (Chi) 393 N Main St, Glen Ellyn, IL 60137

MOLLARD, Elizabeth McCarter (CPa) 235 N Spruce St, Elizabethtown, PA 17022

MOLLER, Nels D (Ida) 902 E Lakeview Ln, Spokane, WA 99208

MOLLISON, Carol Suzanne (Okla) 721 N Thomas St, Altus, OK 73521

MOLNAR, Annette June (RG) St Elizabeth's Episcopal Church, 1 Morse Rd, Sudbury, MA 01776

MOLONY, Roberta Diane (Chi) 2009 Boehme St, Lockport, IL 60441

MOMBERG, Thomas A (Ky) 3235 Overland Place, Memphis, TN 38111

MONAHAN, Anne Duval (WA) 404 S Lee St, Alexandria, VA 22314

MONASTIERE, Sally Melczer (Los) 1335 North Hills Drive, Upland, CA 91784

MONETTE, Ruth Alta (Los) 104-5990 E Blvd, Vancouver, BC V6M3V4, Canada

MONGE-MANCIA, Israel (Hond)

MONGE-SANTIAGO, Juan A (NJ) Urb. Rafael Bermudez 2nd St. K-6, Fajardo, PR 00738, Puerto Rico

MONICA, Ted Jay (Fla) 6661 Man O War Trail, Tallahassee, FL 32309

MONICA, Teri A (Fla) 6661 Man O War Trl, Tallahassee, FL 32309

MONK, Edward R (Dal) Saint John's Church (Episcopal), 101 N. 14th Street, Corsicana, TX 75110

MONNAT, Thomas Leonard (Pa) 213 Earlington Road, Havertown, PA 19083

MONNOT, Elizabeth Lockwood (The Episcopal NCal) 1225 41st Avenue, Sacramento, CA 95922

MONNOT, Michael (The Episcopal NCal) 1225 41st Ave, Sacramento, CA 95822

MONREAL, Anthony A (Episcopal SJ) 9323 South Westlawn, Fresno, CA 93706

MONROE, George Wesley (Chi) 2866 Vacherie Ln, Dallas, TX 75227

MONROE, Sarah (Oly) 705 Lions Park Ln, Aberdeen, WA 98520

MONROE, Virginia Hill (Ala) 430 Newman Ave. Se, Huntsville, AL 35801

MONROE LOES, Brenda Frances (At) 304 E 6th St, West Point, GA 31833

MONSON, Scott B (Minn) 1015 Sibley Memorial Hwy Apt 310, Lilydale, MN 55118

MONSOUR, John Vincent (SwFla) 2114 W Destiny Point Cir, St George, UT 84790

MONTAGNO, Karen Anita Brown (Mass) 536 Main St # 2, Medford, MA 02155

MONTAGUE, Cynthia Russell (ECR) 17574 Winding Creek Rd, Salinas, CA 93908

MONTALTO, Alfred Patrick (NY) 841 4th Ave, North, Apt 65, St. Petersburg, FL 33701

MONTANARI, Albert Ubaldo (WNY) 135 Old Lyme Dr Apt 4, Williamsville, NY 14221

MONTES, Alejandro Sixto (Tex) 10426 Towne Oak Ln, Sugar Land, TX 77478

MONTES, Alex G. (Tex) 11608 Glen Knoll Dr, Manor, TX 78653

MONTES, Elizabeth (Kan) St Francis Community Services, 4155 E Harry St, Wichita, KS 67218

MONTGOMERY, Brandt Leonard (WLa) Episcopal Church of the Ascension, 1030 Johnston Street, Lafayette, LA 70501

MONTGOMERY, Bruce (NJ) 1310 Tullo Rd, Martinsville, NJ 08836

MONTGOMERY, Catharine Whittaker (SwVa) 2231 Timberlake Dr, Lynchburg, VA 24502

MONTGOMERY, Ellen M (WNY) 41 Saint Georges Sq, Buffalo, NY 14222

MONTGOMERY, Ian (FdL) 26 Gaskill Rd, Chester, VT 05143

MONTGOMERY, Ian Bruce (ECR) 345 E 80th St Apt 20C, New York, NY 10075

✠ **MONTGOMERY**, James Winchester (Ret Bp of Chi 1987-) 5555 N Sheridan Rd Apt 809, Chicago, IL 60640

MONTGOMERY, Jennifer Born (Va) 4000 Lorcom Ln, Arlington, VA 22207

MONTGOMERY, John Alford (Lex)

MONTGOMERY, John Fletcher (USC) 2827 Wheat St, Columbia, SC 29205

MONTGOMERY, Lee Allen (U) 70 N 200 W, Cedar City, UT 84720

MONTGOMERY, Tyler Lindell (SVa) PO Box 3520, Williamsburg, VA 23187

MONTIEL, Robert Michael (WTenn) 103 S Poplar St, Paris, TN 38242

MONTILEAUX, Charles Thomas (SD) Po Box 246, Kyle, SD 57752

MONTJOY IV, Gid (Md) 609 Collins Creek Dr., Murrells Inlet, SC 29576

MONTOOTH, Cynthia Hooton (SwFla) 15 Knob Hill Circle, Decatur, GA 30030

MONTOYA CARPIO, S Leonardo (EcuC) Apartado #17-01-3108, Quito, Ecuador

MONTROSE, Richard Sterling (LI) 712 Franklin St, Westbury, NY 11590

MONZON-MOLINA, Eduardo (Hond) Apartado 2598, San Pedro, Honduras

MOODY, John Wallace (NY) 42 W 9th St Apt 18, New York, NY 10011

✠ **MOODY**, Robert Manning (Ret Bp of Okla 2007-) 4001 Oxford Way, Norman, OK 73072

MOON, Abigail White (Fla) 211 N Monroe St, Tallahassee, FL 32301

MOON, Anthony (Okla) 2401 N. Westminster Road, Arcadia, OK 73007

MOON, Catherine Joy (Cal) The Curate's House, 7 Walton Village, Liverpool, AL L4 6TJ, Great Britain (UK)

MOON JR, Don Pardee (Chi) 438 N Sheridan Rd # A500, Waukegan, IL 60085

MOON, James Fred (WMo) 43 Old Mill Ln, South Greenfield, MO 65752

MOON, Mary Louise (Oly) 927 S Sheridan Ave, Tacoma, WA 98405

MOON, Richard Warren (Neb) Po Box 1012, West Plains, MO 65775

MOON, Robert Michael (Los) 1294 Westlyn Pl, Pasadena, CA 91104

MOONEY, Michelle Puzin (Mil) 2633 N Hackett Ave Apt A, Milwaukee, WI 53211

MOONEY, Noreen O'Connor (LI) 1 Berard Blvd, Oakdale, NY 11769

MOORE, Albert Lee (NC) 8705 Gleneagles Dr, Raleigh, NC 27613

MOORE, Allison (Nwk) 1576 Palisade Ave, Fort Lee, NJ 07024

MOORE, Andrew York (WTenn) 254 E Putnam Ave, Greenwich, CT 06830

MOORE, Andy J (NJ) 229 Goldsmith Ave, Newark, NJ 07112

MOORE, Anne Elizabeth Olive (Ore) 630 B St, Silverton, OR 97381

MOORE JR, Charles Nottingham (SVa) 12800 Nightingale Drive, Chester, VA 23836

MOORE, Charles Owen (Pa) 4631 Ossabaw Way, Naples, FL 34119

MOORE, Charlotte Elizabeth (Eas)

MOORE, Cheryl Patricia (U) 2378 East 1700 South Street, Salt Lake City, UT 84108

MOORE, Christopher Chamberlin (Pa) 20274 Beaver Dam Rd, Harbeson, DE 19951

MOORE, Clifford Allan (Wyo) P.O. Box 1086, #3 Valley Dr., Sundance, WY 82729

MOORE III, Clint (Chi) 750 Pearson Street Apt 902, Des Plaines, IL 60016

MOORE, Courtland Manning (FtW) 2341 Monticello Cir, Plano, TX 75075

MOORE, Daniel T (Va) 553 Galleon Dr, Naples, FL 34102

MOORE, David C. (Oly) 116 Rossel Lane, PO Box 702, Eastsound, WA 98245

MOORE, Delrece Lorraine (Colo) 3665 Overton St, Colorado Springs, CO 80910

MOORE, Denise Maureen (Alb) 34 3rd St, Waterford, NY 12188

MOORE, Diane Marquart (WLa) 211 Celeste Dr, New Iberia, LA 70560

MOORE, Dominic C (Az) 533 E Main St, Lexington, KY 40508

MOORE, Donald Ernest (Eas) 3946 Rock Branch Rd, North Garden, VA 22959

MOORE III, Edward F. (Tex) 13515 King Cir, Cypress, TX 77429

MOORE, Frederick Ashbrook (The Episcopal NCal) 1675 Chester Ave, Arcata, CA 95521

MOORE, Helen M (Ct) 24 Goodwin Circle, Hartford, CT 06105

MOORE, James Raymond (The Episcopal Church in Haw) 911 N Marine Corps Dr, Tamuning, GU 96913-4302, Guam

MOORE, James Wesley (WMo) 18151 Dearborn St, Stilwell, KS 66085

MOORE, Joseph I (NJ) 1 Water St, Pennsville, NJ 08070

MOORE, Judith Ann (O) 7125 North Hills Blvd NE, Albuquerque, NM 87109

MOORE, Julia Gibert (Miss) 208 S Leflore Ave, Cleveland, MS 38732

MOORE, K J (Wyo) PO Box 246, Sundance, WY 82729

MOORE, Linda Turman (The Episcopal NCal) 155-A Derek Dr, Susanville, CA 96130

MOORE, Lynda Foster (WNC) 138 Murdock Ave, Asheville, NC 28801

MOORE, Margaret Jo (The Episcopal NCal) 516 Clayton Ave, El Cerrito, CA 94530

MOORE, Mark Ross (Ct) 85 Viscount Dr Unit 12c, Milford, CT 06460

MOORE, Mark T (Mil) ST PAUL'S EPISCOPAL CHURCH, 413 S 2ND ST, WATERTOWN, WI 53094

MOORE, M(ary) Diane (Oly) 7796 S Harrison Cir, Centennial, CO 80122

MOORE, Mary Navarre (ETenn) 715 E Brow Rd, Lookout Mountain, TN 37350

MOORE, Melvin Leon (Va) 219 Cornwallis Ave, Locust Grove, VA 22508

MOORE, Michael D. (Fla)

MOORE, Michael Osborn (NH) 7321 Brad St, Falls Church, VA 22042

MOORE, Muriel Elizabeth (WNC) 355 Red Oak Trl, Boone, NC 28607

MOORE, Nancy L (Me) 403 Harrison Rd, Norway, ME 04268

MOORE, Orral Margarite (Neb) 714 N 129th Plz, Omaha, NE 68154

MOORE, Pamela Andrea (The Episcopal NCal) Po Box 4791, Santa Rosa, CA 95402

MOORE, Patricia Elaine (The Episcopal NCal) 342 Wilson St, Petaluma, CA 94952

MOORE, Paul R (RG) Church Of The Good Shepherd, PO Box 2795, Silver City, NM 88062

MOORE JR, Ralph Murray (Me) 191 West Meadow Rd., Rockland, ME 04841

MOORE, Richard Wayne (La) 4500 Lake Borgne Ave, Metairie, LA 70006

MOORE, Robert Allen (Minn) 19 Lea Road, Whittle-le-Woods, Chorley, Lancs, PR6-7PF, Great Britain (UK)

MOORE, Robert Byron (Cal) 4230 Langland St, Cincinnati, OH 45223

MOORE, Robert Joseph (Tex) 3285 Park Falls Ct., League City, TX 77573

MOORE JR, Robert Raymond (SwVa) 110 Clinton Avenue, Big Stone Gap, VA 24219

MOORE, Robin Adair (Oly) Po Box 584, Grapeview, WA 98546

MOORE, Rodney Allen (Colo) 221 S Salem Ct, Aurora, CO 80012

MOORE, Stephen Edward (Oly) 350 sunset ave n, Edmonds, WA 98020

MOORE, Steven Paul (CNY) St Mary's Episcopal Church, 1917 3rd St, Napa, CA 94559

MOORE, Theodore Edward (NJ) 17 Cray Ter., Fanwood, NJ 07023

MOORE JR, Tillman Marion (Ak) 2316 Via Carrillo, Palos Verdes Estates, CA 90274

MOORE, Trenton Scott (Wyo) PO Box 1690, Jackson, WY 83001

MOORE JR, W Taylor (Miss) 22002 Halliburton Cv, Oxford, MS 38655

MOORE JR, William Henry (Spr) 141 Candlewood Dr, Wallace, NC 28466

MOOREHEAD, Constance Fay Peek (Oly) 3030 S Findlay St, Seattle, WA 98108

MOOREHEAD, Kate Bingham (Fla) 240 N Belmont St, Wichita, KS 67208

MOORER, Dawson Delayne (O) 281 E 244th St Apt D5, Euclid, OH 44123

MOORHEAD, William S J (Ia) PO Box 27, Iowa City, IA 52244

MOOTE, Kimberly Ann (NMich) E9494 Maple St, Munising, MI 49862

MOQUETE, Clemencia Rafaela (NY) 821 Central Trinity Avenue, Bronx, NY 10456

MORALES, Carlton Owen (NC) Po Box 21011, Greensboro, NC 27420

MORALES, Evelyn Ruth (NC) 2009 Hickswood Rd, High Point, NC 27265

MORALES, Frank R (NY)

MORALES, Loyda Esther (NY) 347 Chiquita Court, Kissimmee, FL 34758

MORALES, Roberto (Va)

MORALES COLON, Francisco Javier (PR)

MORALES GAVIRIA, Jose Ricardo (Colom) Barrio Las Delicias, El Bagne, Antioquia, Colombia

MORALES MALDONADO, Rafael L (PR) Iglesia Episcopal Puetorriquene, PO Box 902, Saint Just, PR 00978-0902, Puerto Rico

MORALES-VEGA, Emilia (PR) D10 Calle Pomarrosa, Guaynabo, PR 00969

MORAN, John Jay (Mont) 2415 Hauser Blvd, Helena, MT 59601

✠ **MORANTE-ESPANA**, Alfredo (Bp of Ecu Litoral 1994-) Ulloa 213 Y Carrion, Box 17-0-353-A, Quito, Ecuador

MORA VILLEGA, Carlos Donato (Litoral Ecu) Amarilis Fuentes 603 Calle D Ave Trujillo, Guayaquil, Ecuador

MORCK, Christopher Robert (Mass) Grace Episcopal Church, 133 School St, New Bedford, MA 02740

MORE, James Edward (Ida) 645 Liberty Ln, Emmett, ID 83617

MOREAU, Joseph Raoul (LI) 15524 90th Ave, Jamaica, NY 11432

MOREAU, Walter Jerome (NJ) 211 Willow Valley Sq # D-319, Lancaster, PA 17602

MOREHEAD, Carol Piland (WTex) St Mark's Episcopal Church, 315 E Pecan St, San Antonio, TX 78205

MOREHOUS, Amy Hodges (ETenn) 800 S. Northshore Dr., Knoxville, TN 37919

MOREHOUSE JR, M(erritt) Dutton (FdL) 1920 Green Tree Road, Washington Island, WI 54246

MOREHOUSE, Rebecca (Cal) 21 Sonora Way, Corte Madera, CA 94925

MOREHOUSE, Timothy Lawrence (NY) 200 Riverside Dr Apt 7B, New York, NY 10025

MORELL, Ellen Jones (Ky) 8110 Saint Andrews Church Rd, Louisville, KY 40258

MORELLI, Thomas Carlo Anthony (SanD) 1114 9th St, Coronado, CA 92118

MORENO, Juan Severo (LI) 155 3rd Ave, Brentwood, NY 11717

MORESCHI, Alexander Thomas (Ga) 2 Saint Thomas Ave, Savannah, GA 31406

MORETZ, Matthew John (NY) 325 Park Ave, New York, NY 10022

MOREY, Gordon Howell (Mil) N4111 Pine St, Brodhead, WI 53520

MORFORD, Norman Lewis (Ind) PO Box 55085, Indianapolis, IN 46205

MORFORD, Samuel Allen (Neb) 9302 Blondo St, Omaha, NE 68134

MORGAN, Barbara Jean (Alb) 24 Silver St Apt G8, Great Barrington, MA 01230

MORGAN, Daniel (Ct) 489 Mansfield Ave, Darien, CT 06820

MORGAN, David Forbes (Colo) 740 Clarkson St, Denver, CO 80218

MORGAN, Dennis Lee (Eas)

MORGAN, Diane Elizabeth (Mich) 25710 Beech Ct, Redford, MI 48239

MORGAN, Dwight Dexter (SeFla) 2201 S.W. 25th Street, Coconut Grove, FL 33133

MORGAN, Edward James (Colo) 5952 E Irish Pl, Centennial, CO 80112

MORGAN, E F Michael (Pa) 33 Baltusrol Way, Springfield, NJ 07081

MORGAN, Elaine Ludlum (Nev) 402 W Robinson St, Carson City, NV 89703

MORGAN III, Harold Edgar (USC) 204 Derby Ln, Clinton, SC 29325

MORGAN, Heather M. (Mo) 1400 Forum Boulevard, Suite 38, Columbia, MO 65203

MORGAN, J. Gregory (NY) St. Simon the Cyrenian Church, 135 Remington Place, New Rochelle, NY 10801

MORGAN, James Charles (Tex) 235 Royal Oaks St, Huntsville, TX 77320

MORGAN JR, James Hanly (WVa) 520 11th Ave., Huntington, WV 25701

MORGAN, Keely (Minn) 60 Kent St, Saint Paul, MN 55102

MORGAN, Kimberly Ann (Nev) 305 N Minnesota St, Carson City, NV 89703

MORGAN, Mamie Elizabeth (USC) 204 Derby Lane, Clinton, SC 29325

MORGAN, Marilyn Kay (Ark) 1475 Stone Crest Dr, Conway, AR 72034

MORGAN, Michael (Mont) West 3817 Fort Wright Drive 1-204, Spokane, WA 99204

MORGAN, Michele H. (Minn) 3154 Ulysses St NE, Minneapolis, MN 55418

MORGAN, Pamela Sturch (Ark) 1410 E Walnut St., Rogers, AR 72756

MORGAN, Philip (Va) 17476 Hawthorne Ave, Culpeper, VA 22701

MORGAN, Ralph Baier (Tex)

MORGAN, Randall Carl (SC) St Jude's Episcopal Church, 907 Wichman St, Walterboro, SC 29488

MORGAN V, Richard (RI) 19 Castle Way, Westerly, RI 02891

MORGAN, Richard Thomas (Pa) Church of the Good Samaritan, 212 W Lancaster Ave, Paoli, PA 19301

MORGAN, Ruth Margaret (RG)

MORGAN, Walter Craig (ETenn) 3475 Edgewood Cir Nw, Cleveland, TN 37312

MORGAN-HIGGINS, Stanley Ethelbert (Nwk) 3828 Leprechaun Ct, Decatur, GA 30034

MORICAL, Robin E (CFla) 1631 Ford Pkwy, Saint Paul, MN 55116

MORIN, Geoffrey S (Pa) 841 Shenton Road, West Chester, PA 19380

MORISSEAU, Robert Edward Lee (NY) 502 Forest Gln, Pompton Plains, NJ 07444

MORITZ III, B(ernard) Eugene (SwVa) 4022 Fauquier Ave, Richmond, VA 23227

MORIYAMA, Jerome Tomokazu (WA) Rossbrin Cove, Schull, Co. Cork, Ireland

MORLAN, Lynette K (Episcopal SJ) 2803 Stratford Dr, San Ramon, CA 94583

MORLEY, Anthony J (Minn) 825 Summit Ave #806, Minneapolis, MN 55403

MORLEY, Richard Matthew (NJ) 140 S Finley Ave, Basking Ridge, NJ 07920

MORLEY, William Harris (NC) 3454 Rugby Rd, Durham, NC 27707

MORNARD, Jean Elisabeth (SD) 1400 21st St SW Lot 110, 208, Huron, SD 57350

MORONEY, Kevin John (Pa) 536 Conestoga Rd., Villanova, PA 19085

MORONTA VASQUEZ, Buddelov Adolfo (Va)

MORPETH, Robert Park (Ala) 521 20th St N, Birmingham, AL 35203

MORRIGAN, Cedar Abrielynne (Minn) 309 13th St Sw, Little Falls, MN 56345

MORRILL, Bonnie (Dal) 5314 Somerset Dr., Rowlett, TX 75089

MORRIS, Alfred Edward (Pa) 505 E Catherine St, Chambersburg, PA 17201

MORRIS, Alfred John (Ct) 9201 Sw 192nd Court Rd, Dunnellon, FL 34432

MORRIS, Bonnie F (WNY) 20 Milton Street, Williamsville, NY 14221

MORRIS, Charles Hamilton (Mo) 2140 Farnsworth Dr, O Fallon, MO 63368

MORRIS, Charles Henry (Be) 24 Forsythia Dr, Harwich, MA 02645

MORRIS, Clayton L (Cal) 30 Devoe St Apt 2B, Brooklyn, NY 11211

MORRIS, Danielle DuBois (CFla) 444 Covey Cv, Winter Park, FL 32789

MORRIS, David John (Pa) 449 Newgate Ct Apt B2, Andalusia, PA 19020

MORRIS, David Wayne (NY) 15 Pine St, Lake Peekskill, NY 10537

MORRIS, Donald Richard (Vt) 280 Round Rd, Bristol, VT 05443

MORRIS, Gregg A (Chi) 1125 Franklin St, Downers Grove, IL 60515

MORRIS, J. Anthony Grant (Alb) 163 N Pole Rd, Melrose, NY 12121

MORRIS, James Edgar (Pa) 203 Devon Dr, Exton, PA 19341

MORRIS, Janie Kirt (Tex) 301 N Walker Ave Apt 8408, Oklahoma City, OK 73102

MORRIS, John Charles (Vt) 37 Thompson Rd, East Corinth, VT 05040

MORRIS III, John Glen (Va) 1021 Aquia Dr, Stafford, VA 22554

MORRIS, John Karl (The Episcopal NCal) 3255 Villa Ln Apt 241, Napa, CA 94558

MORRIS, John William (CPa) St. John's Episcopal Church, 321 W. Chestnut St., Lancaster, PA 17603

MORRIS, Jonathan Edward (USC) 717 Dupre Dr, Spartanburg, SC 29307

MORRIS, Julie H. (Los) P.O. Box 2305, Camarillo, CA 93011

MORRIS, Kevin L (LI) 176 Palisade Ave, Jersey City, NJ 07306

MORRIS, Richard Melvin (O) 55 Countryside Dr, Cumberland, RI 02864

MORRIS, Robert Corin Veal (Nwk) 422 Clark, South Orange, NJ 07079

MORRIS III, Robert Lee (Va)

MORRIS, Robert Lee (Fla) 601 Alhambra Ln N, Ponte Vedra Beach, FL 32082

MORRIS, Roberta Louise (Los) 1733 N New Hampshire Ave, Los Angeles, CA 90027

MORRIS, Sarah Carper (SwVa) 1962 Tyler Rd, Christiansburg, VA 24073

MORRIS, Stephen B (SwFla) 140 4th St N, St Petersburg, FL 33701

MORRIS, Thomas Rand (Tex) PO Box 173, Sewanee, TN 37375

MORRIS-KLIMENT, Nicholas McClure (Mass) 44 Seminole Rd, Acton, MA 01720

MORRISON, Enid Ann (Ind) 8320 E. 10th St., Indianapolis, IN 46219

MORRISON, Glenn David (Mich) 171 W Pike St, Pontiac, MI 48341

MORRISON JR, Henry T (Nick) (Az) Po Box 610, Ketchum, ID 83340

MORRISON, James R (La) 1329 Jackson Ave, New Orleans, LA 70130

MORRISON, John Ainslie (SO) Calvary Episcopal Church, 3766 Clifton Ave, Cincinnati, OH 45220

MORRISON III, John E (LI) 510 Manatuck Blvd, Brightwaters, NY 11718

MORRISON, Karl Frederick (NJ) 75 Linwood Circle, Princeton, NJ 08540

MORRISON, Larry Clair (NJ) PO Box 100, Front Royal, VA 22630

MORRISON, Leroy Oran (NwT) 6535 Amber Dr, Odessa, TX 79762

MORRISON, Mary K (ECR) PO Box 1160, Los Gatos, CA 95031

MORRISON, Mikel Anne (Oly) 760 Kristen Ct, Santa Barbara, CA 93111

MORRISON, Paul Charles (NC) 77 W Coolidge St #227, Phoenix, AZ 85013

MORRISON, Pauline Ruth (Ore) St John's Episcopal Church, 110 NE Alder St, Toledo, OR 97391

MORRISON, Richard Neely (Az) 720 West Elliot Road, Gilbert, AZ 85233

MORRISON JR, Robert Dabney (EC) 119 Briarwood St., Lynchburg, VA 24503

MORRISON, Robert Paterson (Ore) Po Box 789, Lincoln City, OR 97367

MORRISON, Samuel Warfield (FdL) 101 S Wythe St, Pentwater, MI 49449

MORRISON-CLEARY, Douglas Vaughn (Minn)

MORRIS-RADER, Patricia (Ore) 8045 Sw 56th Ave, Portland, OR 97219

MORRISS, Jerry Davis (Dal) 132 Baywood Blvd, Mabank, TX 75156

MORRISSETTE, Paul E (WMass) 14 Enaya Circle, Worcester, MA 01606

MORROW, Andrea (Mich) 2803 1st St, Wyandotte, MI 48192

MORROW, Daniel R (Ore) 202 Avenida Aragon, San Clemente, CA 92672

MORROW, Gabriel Charles Daniel (Mont) PO Box 819, Helena, MT 59624

MORROW JR, Harold Frederick (CPa) 2453 Harrisburg Pike, Lancaster, PA 17601

MORROW, Jerry Dean (Mass) 89 Msgr Patrick J Lydon Way, Dorchester, MA 02124

MORROW, John Thomas (NJ) Po Box 424, Pine Beach, NJ 08741

MORROW, Mildred Kathryn (WNC) 9 Swan St, Asheville, NC 28803

MORROW, Penelope (Eas) St Paul's by-the-Sea Episcopal Church, PO Box 1207, Ocean City, MD 21843

MORROW, Quintin Gregory (FtW) 917 Lamar St, Fort Worth, TX 76102

MORSCH, Joel (SwFla) 1903 - 85th Court NW, Bradenton, FL 34209

MORSE, Alice Janette (Mich) 3899 Ryan's Ridge, Monroe, MI 48161

MORSE, Davidson Rogan (FtW) 2916 Caprock Ct, Grapevine, TX 76051

MORSE, Elizabeth Bovelle (Ore) 661 NW Kersey Dr, Dallas, OR 97338

MORT, Kevin Duane (SwFla) 738 Pinellas Point Dr S, St Petersburg, FL 33705

MORTON, James Parks (NY) 285 Riverside Dr Apt 13-B, New York, NY 10025

MORTON, John Andrew (WNC) Po Box 185, Flat Rock, NC 28731

MORTON SR, Kell (Pa)

MORTON, Paula Karen Clegg (WNC) 901 Big Raven Ln, Saluda, NC 28773

MORTON, Ronald Dean (ETenn) 5401 Tiffany Ln, Knoxville, TN 37912

MORTON, William Paul (EO) 1025 NE Paula Dr, Bend, OR 97701

MORTON III, Woolridge Brown (Va) 212 Wirt St NW, Leesburg, VA 20176

MOSCOSO, Servio Rhadames (NJ) 38 W End Pl, Elizabeth, NJ 07202

MOSER, Albert E (Alb) 133 Saratoga Rd Apt. 109-8, Glenville, NY 12302

MOSER, Frederick Perkins (Mass) 138 W Plain St, Wayland, MA 01778

MOSER, Gerard Stoughton (Eur) 15 Hoopoe Ave., Camps Bay, Cape Town, 8005, South Africa

MOSER, Patricia Mariann (Chi) 621 W Belmont Ave, Chicago, IL 60657

MOSER, Paul Henry (Md) 16 E Broadway, Bel Air, MD 21014

MOSES, Donald Harwood (Kan) 2201 Sw 30th St, Topeka, KS 66611

MOSES, George David (WVa) 20 Alexander Drive, Morgantown, WV 26508

MOSES, Michael David (Minn) 11078 Nichols Spring Dr, Chatfield, MN 55923

MOSES, Robert Emilio (CFla) 145 E Edgewood Dr, Lakeland, FL 33803

MOSES, Sarah Marie (Miss)

MOSHER, David Rike (SwFla) 6764 122nd St, Seminole, FL 33772

MOSHER, Steven Emerson (ETenn) 314 W. Broadway Ave, Maryville, TN 38801

MOSIER, James David (EO) 1237 Sw 12th St, Ontario, OR 97914

MOSIER, William Frank (Ore) 39361 Mozart Ter Unit 101, Fremont, CA 94538

MOSKAL, Jason Edward (LI) 3350 82nd St, Jackson Heights, NY 11372

MOSLEY, Carl Ernest (Eas) 111 76th St Unit 205, Ocean City, MD 21842

MOSQUEA, Jesus (DR (DomRep))

MOSS JR, Alfred Alfonso (Chi) 1500 N Lancaster St, Arlington, VA 22205

MOSS III, David MacBeth (At) 3880 N Stratford Rd Ne, Atlanta, GA 30342

MOSS, Denise S (At)

MOSS III, Frank Hazlett (WMass) 17910 NW Chestnut Lane, Portland, OR 97231

MOSS, J(ohn) Eliot Blakeslee (WMass) 7 Kestrel Ln, Amherst, MA 01002

MOSS SR, Ledly Ogden (SeFla) 4020 Nw 187th St, Carol City, FL 33055

MOSS, Susan Maetzold (Minn) 175 Woodlawn Ave, Saint Paul, MN 55105

MOSSBARGER, David Jefferson (NwT) 1402 Wilshire Dr, Odessa, TX 79761

MOSSO, Karen Ann (Ind) 721 Roma Ave., Jeffersonville, IN 47130

MOTE, Donna S (At) 1296 Fork Creek Trl, Decatur, GA 30033

MOTE, Doris Ellen (Ind) 2018 Locust St, New Albany, IN 47150

MOTE, Larry H. (RG) 1016 E 1st St, Portales, NM 88130

MOTES, Brantley Eugene (Ala) Po Box 5556, Decatur, AL 35601

MOTHERSELL, Lawrence Lavere (Roch) Po Box 1, Geneseo, NY 14454

MOTIS, John Ray (CFla) Church of the Good Shepherd, 221 S 4th St, Lake Wales, FL 33853

MOTT, Pamela Jane (WMass) 324 E Main Rd, Portsmouth, RI 02871

MOTTL, Christine Elizabeth (Pa) 27074 St. Peter's Church Rd., Crisfield, MD 21817

MOTTL, Paul Edward (Neb) 27074 St. Peters Church Road, Crisfield, MD 21817

MOUER, Patricia Wade (WNC) 500 Christ School Road, Asheville, NC 28704

MOUGHTY, Kelly Patricia (Me) St Alban's Episcopal Church, 885 Shore Rd, Cape Elizabeth, ME 04107

MOUILLE, David Ronald (Kan) 4786 Black Swan Dr, Shawnee, KS 66216

MOULDEN, Michael Mackreth (NC) 401 Plainfield Road, Greenborough, NC 27455

MOULINIER, Deirdre Ward (Az) 100 Arroyo Pinon Dr, Sedona, AZ 86336

MOULTON, Elizabeth Jean (Be) 109 Cruser St, Montrose, PA 18801

MOULTON, Eric Morgan (EC) 1219 Forest Hills Dr, Wilmington, NC 28403

MOULTON II, John Adkins (Fla) 1631 Blue Heron Ln, Jacksonville Beach, FL 32250

MOULTON, Roger Conant (Mass) 291 Washington St, Arlington, MA 02474

MOUNCEY, Perry Kathleen (CNY) 127 Brookview Ln, Liverpool, NY 13088

MOUNTFORD, Helen Harvene (Los) 1566 Edison St, Santa Ynez, CA 93460

MOUNTFORD SR, Robert (CFla) 160 Heron Bay Cir, Lake Mary, FL 32746

MOURADIAN, Victoria Kirk (Los) 1411 Dalmatia Dr., San Pedro, CA 90732

MOUSIN, Thomas Nordboe (Mass) 29 Lakeview Rd, Winchester, MA 01890

MOWERS, Culver Lunn (CNY) Po Box 130, Brooktondale, NY 14817

MOWERS, David Michael (Minn) 1631 Ford Pkwy, Saint Paul, MN 55116

MOWERY, Donald (WTenn) 231 Baronne Pl, Memphis, TN 38117

MOYER, Dale Luther (SeFla) 4851a Nursery Rd, Dover, PA 17315

MOYER, J Douglas (Be) 205 North Seventh Street, Stroudsburg, PA 18360

MOYER, Laureen H (Cal) 412 Centre Ct, Alameda, CA 94502

MOYER, Michael David (Eas) 1 Church St, Berlin, MD 21811

MOYER, Michelle M (Be) 321 Wyandotte St, Bethlehem, PA 18015

MOYERS, William Riley (SwFla) 2008 Isla De Palma Cir, Naples, FL 34119

MOYLE, Sandra K (Fla) Holy Cross Faith Memorial Episcopal Church, 88 Baskervill Dr, Pawleys Island, SC 29585

MOYSER, George H (SC) 58 Raven Glass Ln, Bluffton, SC 29909

MOZELIAK JR, Leon Clement (CNY) Grace Episcopal Church, 6 Elizabeth St, Utica, NY 13501

MRAZ, Barbara (Minn) 4201 Sheridan Ave S, Minneapolis, MN 55410

MROCZKA, Mary Ann (Roch) 77 Plum Drive Apt F, Dansville, NY 14437

MUDD, Gwynneth Jones (SVa) 797 Casual Ct, Virginia Beach, VA 23454

MUDGE, Barbara Duffield Covington (Ore) 88427 Trout Pond Ln, Bandon, OR 97411

MUDGE, Bede Thomas (Kan) PO Box 99, West Park, NY 12493

MUDGE, Hannah (Alb) Oaks of Righteousness Episcopal Ministry, 2331 15th St, Troy, NY 12180

MUDGE, Julia Hamilton (Alb) 204 Worthington Ter, Wynantskill, NY 12198

MUDGE, Melanie A (NC) 312 N Steele St, Sanford, NC 27330

MUDGE JR, Shaw (Alb) 25 Rushforde Dr, Manchester, CT 06040

MUELLER, Denise Ray (SO) 412 Sycamore St., Cincinnati, OH 45202

MUELLER, Heather May (The Episcopal Church in Haw) PO Box 628, Kapa'au, HI 96755

MUELLER, Mary Margaret (WTex) 1045 Shook Ave Apt 105, San Antonio, TX 78212

MUELLER, Susan Richards (Mil) 7018 Colony Dr, Madison, WI 53717

MUES, Steven Wayne (Kan) 144 Lake Mountain Dr, Boulder City, NV 89005

MUGAN JR, Robert Charles (WNC) 894 Indian Hill Rd, Hendersonville, NC 28791

MUHLHEIM, Nancy Colleen (Ore) 98 Fairway Loop, Eugene, OR 97401

MUINDE, Sandra Laverne (FdL) 311 Division St, Oshkosh, WI 54901

MUIR, George Daniels (Chi) St. Paul's Church, 605 Reynolds St., Augusta, GA 30901

MUIR, Richard Dale (Chi) 181 Wildwood Rd, Lake Forest, IL 60045

MUKHWANA-NAFUMA, Joel Eric (NY)

MULAC, Pamela Ann (Los) 7585 N Park Crest Ln, Prescott Valley, AZ 86314

MULDER, Timothy John (Nwk) 2 Hunt Lane, Gladstone, NJ 07934

MULDOON, Maggie Rose Daniels (Minn) 18350 67 Avenue, Cloverdale, BC V3S 1E5, Canada

MULFORD, Marie Lynne (WVa) 2585 State Route 7 N, Gallipolis, OH 45631

MULKIN, Suzanne Devine (CFla) 875 Brock Rd, Bartow, FL 33830

MULL, Judson Gary (At) 499 Trabert Ave Nw, Atlanta, GA 30309

MULLALY JR, Charles Francis (Va) 888 Summit View Ln, Charlottesville, SC VA 22903

MULLEN, Melanie Bernette (WA) St Paul's Episcopal Church, 815 E Grace St, Richmond, VA 23219

MULLEN, Sean E (Pa) St Mark's Church, 1625 Locust St, Philadelphia, PA 19103

MULLER, Donald Joseph (NJ) 4 Christopher Mill Rd, Medford, NJ 08055

MULLER JR, John (Colo) 513 E 19th St, Delta, CO 81416

MULLER JR, Liam Charles (Vt) 522 W 4th Ave, Mitchell, SD 57301

MULLIGAN IV, Edward B (At) Holy Innocents' Episc Ch, 805 Mount Vernon Hwy NW, Atlanta, GA 30327

MULLIN, Mark Hill (Okla) 2091 Brownstone Ln, Charlottesville, VA 22901

MULLINS, Andrew Jackson W (NY)

MULLINS, Edward L (Mich) 730 E Knot Ct, Corolla, NC 27927

MULLINS, Judith Pierpont (Oly) 80 E Roanoke St Apt 16, Seattle, WA 98102

MULLINS, Perry Emerson (Dal) 11122 Midway Rd, Dallas, TX 75229

MULLINS, Walter Earl (Md) 6922 Hollenberry Rd, Sykesville, MD 21784

MULLIS, Robert Bradley (NC) 405 Baymount Dr., Statesville, NC 28625

MULVEY, Dorian Larsen (Az) 8951 E. Sutton Drive, Scottsdale, AZ 85260

MULVEY JR, Thomas Patrick (Mass)

MUMFORD, Nigel William David (SVa)

MUN, Paul Shinkyu (Tenn) Church Of The Holy Spirit, 5325 Nolensville Pike, Nashville, TN 37211

MUNCIE, Margaret Ann (NY) 1 Chipping Court, Greenville, SC 29607

MUNCIE, Stephen D. (LI) 65 Joralemon Street, Brooklyn, NY 11201

MUNDAY, Sharon Boublitz (SVa) PO Box 3886, Chester, VA 23831

MUNDIA, Wilberforce Omusala (NC) 204 W Salisbury St, Pittsboro, NC 27312

MUNDY, Robert Lowry (RG)

MUNGOMA, Stephen Masette (Los) 1401 W 123rd St, Los Angeles, CA 90047

MUNOZ, Antonio (Dal) 5100 Ross Ave, Dallas, TX 75206

MUNOZ, Frank Peter (SanD) Naval Hospital Camp Pendleton, Box 555191, Code 00SM-PC, Camp Pendleton, CA 92055

MUNOZ, Maria E (Los) Nuestra Senora de Las Americas, 2610 N. Francisco, Chicago, IL 60647

MUNOZ-LABRA, Manuel J (PR)

MUNOZ QUINTANA, Dimas D (PR) Po Box 8106, Humacao, PR 00792

MUNRO, Edward (Md) 12310 Firtree Ln, Bowie, MD 20715

MUNRO, JoAnn Reynolds (Ct) 27 Chateau Margaux, Bloomfield, CT 06002

MUNRO, Michael Gregory (Kan) 804 Cottonwood Dr, Lansing, KS 66043

MUNROE, James Granger (WMass) 235 State St Apt 413, Springfield, MA 01103

MUNROE, Sally G (Colo) 1127 Westmoreland Rd, Colorado Springs, CO 80907

MUNSELL, Richard Francis (Colo)

MUNSON, Peter A (Colo) 9972 W 86th Ave, Arvada, CO 80005

MUNZ, Catherine A (WMass) 5 Willow Circle, Easthampton, MA 01027

MUÑOZ PEÑA, Jose Antonio (PR) Paseo De La Reina 2703, Ponce, PR 00716, Puerto Rico

MURASAKI-WEKALL, Ellen (Los) 330 East Cordova St Unit 366, Pasadena, CA 91101

MURAY, Leslie Anthony (Mich) 241 Douglas Ave, Lansing, MI 48906

MURBARGER, Jason Andrew (CFla) Trinity Episcopal Church, 2365 Pine Ave, Vero Beach, FL 32960

MURCHIE, Alan Cameron (Ct) 78 Green Hill Rd, Washington, CT 06793

MURCHISON, Joel Williams (EC) 259 W 19th St, Chattanooga, TN 37408

MURDOCH, Judith Carolyn (Ha) 4227 Columbia Rd, Martinez, GA 30907

MURDOCH, Julie Brady (WVa) 75 Old Cheat Rd., Morgantown, WV 26508

MURDOCH, Richard Dorsey (SVa) 214 Archers Mead, Williamsburg, VA 23185

MURDOCH JR, William Henry (Me) Po Box 639, Damariscotta, ME 04543

MURDOCK, Audrey (Ct)

MURDOCK, Brian J(Oseph) P(Aul) (Mass) 38 Highland Park Ave, Roxbury, MA 02119

MURDOCK, Thomas Lee (Cal) 14821 N E Eugene St, Portland, OR 97230

MURGUIA, James Raphael (WTex) 6904 West Ave, San Antonio, TX 78213

MURIUKI, James K (Spr) 493 S Jackson St, Montgomery, AL 36104

MURPH, Jeffrey David (Pgh) 530 10th St, Oakmont, PA 15139

MURPHEY, William Frederick (CPa) 2306 Edgewood Rd, Harrisburg, PA 17104

MURPHREE, James Willis (Dal) 5426 Meadowcreek Dr Apt 2037, Dallas, TX 75248

MURPHY, Diane Gensheimer (Va) 9374 Mount Vernon Cir, Alexandria, VA 22309

MURPHY, Edward John (NJ) 10 Rupells Rd, Clinton, NJ 08809

MURPHY JR, Edward John (CNY) 27 Bridge St Apt 2, Carthage, NY 13619

MURPHY, Genevieve Margaret (Va) 501 Simmons Gap Road, Box 172, Earlysville, VA 22936

MURPHY, Gwyneth MacKenzie (NY) St Mary the Virgin Episcopal Church, 191 South Greeley Ave, Chappaqua, NY 10514

MURPHY JR, Hartshorn (Los) 1630 Greenfield Ave. Apt 105, Los Angeles, Los Angeles, CA 90025

MURPHY, James Tracy John (SwFla) 1605 Banchory Cir, Walhalla, SC 29691

MURPHY, Jo-Ann Rapp (Va) 3605 S Douglas Rd, Miami, FL 33133

MURPHY, Linda Estelle (Va) 15 Hamilton St, Colonial Beach, VA 22443

MURPHY, Michael John (Tenn) 219 Jennings Cir, Tullahoma, TN 37388

MURPHY, Michael Robert (SVa) 2315 Mary Goodwyn Rd., Powhatan, VA 23139

MURPHY JR, P L (Dal)

MURPHY, Patricia Ann (Kan) 7515 W 102nd St, Overland Park, KS 66212

MURPHY, Richard William (RG) 4717 Sundial Way, Santa Fe, NM 87507

MURPHY, Robert A (WMo) 4225 Sw Clipper Ln, Lees Summit, MO 64082

MURPHY JR, Russell Edward (Wyo) 11506 Wornall Rd, Kansas City, MO 64114

MURPHY, Susan Marie (Me) 37 Chancery Lane, Sanford, ME 04073

MURPHY, T(eresa) Abigail (LI) 15 Stewart Ave, Stewart Manor, NY 11530

MURPHY, Terri Marie (WA) 15575 Germantown Rd, Germantown, MD 20874

MURPHY, Thomas Christopher (WA) 4667 36th St S # B, Arlington, VA 22206

MURPHY, Thomas Edward (Spok) 215 Tolman Creek Rd Unit 34, Ashland, OR 97520

MURPHY, Thomas Lynch (WNC) 9 Swan St, Asheville, NC 28803

MURPHY, Thomas M (Nwk) 38 Duncan Avenue, Jersey City, NJ 07304

MURPHY, Timothy Hunter (Ala) 801 The Trce W, Jasper, AL 35504

MURPHY, Warren Charles (Wyo) 50 Diamond View Rd, Cody, WY 82414

MURPHY, William McKee (WMich) N 2794 Summerville Park Road, Lodi, WI 53555

MURRAY III, Alfonso Jerome (SanD) 1710 East Camino Parocela Unit 22, Palm Springs, CA 92264

MURRAY, Austin B (The Episcopal Church in Haw) 2853 Panepoo St, Kihei, HI 96753

MURRAY IV, Bill S (WTenn) 8011 Douglas Avenue, Dallas, TX 75225

MURRAY, Cicely Anne (Pa) 600 E Cathedral Rd Apt D104, Philadelphia, PA 19128

MURRAY, Diane Marie (FdL) W5766 Winooski Rd, Plymouth, WI 53073

MURRAY, Elizabeth Ann (CFla) 144 Sea Park Blvd, Satellite Beach, FL 32937

MURRAY JR, George Ralph (Eas) 4453 Eastwicke Dr, Salisbury, MD 21804

MURRAY III, John William (CGC) 1326 Live Oak Ln, Jacksonville, FL 32207

MURRAY, Kathleen (NJ)

MURRAY, Kathleen Fontaine (Okla) 1255 Canterbury Blvd, Altus, OK 73521

MURRAY, Laura Jane (Oly) 7701 Skansie Ave, Gig Harbor, WA 98335

MURRAY, Lewellyn St Elmo (LI) 590 Flatbush Ave Apt 9M, Apt. 9-M, Brooklyn, NY 11225

MURRAY, Lois Thompson (SeFla) 1521 Alton Rd # 219, Miami Beach, FL 33139

MURRAY, Mac (WMass) 23 Dana Park, Hopedale, MA 01747

MURRAY, Michael Hunt (Va) 700 Port St Apt 226, Easton, MD 21601

MURRAY, Milton Hood (Fla) 3750 Peachtree Rd NE # 422, Atlanta, GA 30319

MURRAY, Noland Patrick (Ark) 14300 Chenal Pkwy Apt 1316, Little Rock, AR 72211

MURRAY, Robert Scott (Episcopal SJ) 1104 Kitanosho-Cho, Ohmihachiman, Shiga, 523-0806, Japan

MURRAY, Robin George (SwFla) 27439 Edenfield Dr, Wesley Chapel, FL 33543

MURRAY III, Roderic Lafayette (Ala) 634 Timber Ln, Nashville, TN 37215

MURRAY III, Thomas Holt (WTex) 1120 Lake Dr, Kerrville, TX 78028

MURRAY, Thomas P (Fla) 4129 Oxford Ave, Jacksonville, FL 32210
MURRAY, Trilby Ometa (Chi) 3801 S Wabash Ave, Chicago, IL 60653
MURRAY, Vincent Devitt (Oly) 306 Lopez Ave, Port Angeles, WA 98362
MURRELL, William Lewis (NY) 2400 Johnson Ave Apt 10c, Bronx, NY 10463
MURSULI, Modesto E (SeFla) 399A Himrod St, Brooklyn, NY 11237
MUSGRAVE, David Charles (Chi) 11112 Bayberry Hills Dr, Raleigh, NC 27617
MUSHORN, Richard C (LI) 2206 Cloverleaf Cir SE, Cleveland, TN 37311
MUSOKE-LUBEGA, Benjamin Kiwomutemero (NY) 27 Compton Dr, East Windsor, NJ 08520
MUSSATTI, David James (Nev) Po Box 5572, Incline Village, NV 89450
MUSSELMAN JR, William Stanley (Pa) 93 Willow Way, Lansdale, PA 19446
MUSSER, Lisa Flores (WTenn) 8011 Douglas Avenue, Dallas, TX 75225
MUSTARD, G Thomas (SwVa) 6437 Monarch Ct, Hoschton, GA 30548
MUSTERMAN, Amanda Ellen (Lex) Po Box 633, Somerset, KY 42502
MUTH, David Philip (The Episcopal NCal) 1429 Spring Valley Dr, Roseville, CA 95661
MUTH, Donald Charles (La) 4920 Cleveland Pl, Metairie, LA 70003
MUTOLO, Frances (Colo) 85 Long Bow Cir, Monument, CO 80132
MUTZELBURG, Michael Kenneth (Mich) 110 W South Holly Rd, Fenton, MI 48430
MYCOFF JR, Walter Joseph (SO) 892 W Webster Rd, Summersville, WV 26651
MYERS, Annwn Hawkins (Miss) 335 Tennessee Avenue, Sewanee, TN 37383
MYERS, Bethany Leigh (Colo) 800 N Saint Asaph St # 202, Alexandria, VA 22314
MYERS, Brooke (Mo) 4141 Flora Pl, Saint Louis, MO 63110
MYERS III, Bruns Mckie (Miss) 107 Sundown Rd, Madison, MS 39110
MYERS, David John (WMo) 12599 Timberline Dr, Garfield, AR 72732
MYERS, Elizabeth Williams (Be) 22 Heath Vlg, Hackettstown, NJ 07840
MYERS, Fredrick Eugene (SanD) 1111 E Ramon Rd Unit 80, Palm Springs, CA 92264
MYERS, Jeannette Anne Harrell (The Episcopal Church in Haw) 38 Payran Street, Petaluma, CA 94952
MYERS, John Geenwood (WLa) 833 Clarence St, Lake Charles, LA 70601
MYERS, Jonathan E (WNC) St Stephen Episcopal Church, 4805 NE 45th St, Seattle, WA 98105
MYERS, Max Arthur (Ct) 247 New Milford Tpke, Marble Dale, CT 06777

MYERS, Nicholas A (Ind) 6050 N Meridian St, Indianapolis, IN 46208
MYERS, Rebecca Sue (CPa) St John's Church, 701 Engineer St, Corbin, KY 40701
MYERS JR, Robert Keith (Chi) 7050 N Oakley Ave, Chicago, IL 60645
MYERS II, Robert W. (Ind) 8014 River Bay Drive West, Indianapolis, IN 46240
MYERS, Roy Clarence (WLa) 1906 Evangeline Dr, Bastrop, LA 71220
MYERS, Thomas (NJ) 2502 Central Ave, North Wildwood, NJ 08260
MYERS, William Francis (Va) 11142 Beaver Trail Ct, Reston, VA 20191
MYHR, Laura Parmer (WNC) 100 Summit Street, Marion, NC 28752
MYNATT, B(elva) Chari (Charlene) (WMo) 3523 S Kings Hwy, Independence, MO 64055
MYRICK, H (Harry) Eugene (RG) 708 E Lockhart Ave, Alpine, TX 79830
MYRICK, William Harris (Mil) 503 E Walworth Ave P.O. Box 528, Delavan, WI 53115
MYSEN, Andrea Leigh (Chi) 411 Laurel Ave, Highland Park, IL 60035

N

NABE, Clyde Milton (Mo) 4742 Burlington Ave N, Saint Petersburg, FL 33713
NACHTRIEB, John David (Chi) 131 N Brainard Ave, La Grange, IL 60525
NAECKEL, Lynn Miles (Minn) Po Box 43, Ranier, MN 56668
NAEF, Linda (Miss) 655 Eagle Ave, Jackson, MS 39206
NAEGELE III, John Aloysius (CPa) 982 Spa Rd. Apt. 201, Annapolis, MD 21403
NAGATA, Ada Yuk-Ying (Los) Church of Our Saviour, 535 West Roses Road, San Gabriel, CA 91775
NAGEL, Virginia Wight (CNY) 100 Wilson Pl, Syracuse, NY 13214
NAGLE, George Overholser (CNY) 65 Glenwood Dr, Saranac Lake, NY 12983
NAGLEY, Stephanie Jane (WA) 6030 Grosvenor Lane, Bethesda, MD 20814
NAGY, Robert A (NJ) 33396 Alagon Street, Temecula, CA 92592
NAIRN, Frederick William (Minn) 5895 Stoneybrook Dr, Minnetonka, MN 55345
NAKAMURA RENGERS, Katherine Toshiko (Ala) 521 20th St N, Birmingham, AL 35203
NAKATSUJI, Dorothy Masako Kamigaki (The Episcopal Church in Haw) 1725 Fern St, Honolulu, HI 96826
NAKAYAMA, Timothy Makoto (Oly) 700 6th Ave S Apt 321, Seattle, WA 98104
NAKO, James Walter (Chi)

NALVEN, Claudia (Chi) 327 S 4th St, Geneva, IL 60134
NANCARROW, Arthur Paul (Mich) 148 W Eagle Lake Dr, Maple Grove, MN 55369
NANCARROW, Paul Steven (SwVa) 25 Church St, Staunton, VA 24401
NANCEKIVELL, Diane (NJ) 1008 Hemenway Rd, Bridport, VT 05734
NANNY, Susan Kathryn (Mo) 2831 Eads Ave, Saint Louis, MO 63104
NANTHICATTU, Jacob Philip (NY) 182 Ridge Rd, Valley Cottage, NY 10989
NANTON-MARIE, Allan A. (Fla) PO Box 1-5442, Fort Lauderdale, FL 33318
NAPOLIELLO, Susan Foster (The Episcopal NCal) 2412 Foothill Blvd No. 31, Calistoga, CA 94515
NARAIN, Errol Lloyd (Chi) 125 E 26th St, Chicago, IL 60616
NARVAEZ, Alfonso Anthony (WTex) PO Box 8004, Reston, VA 20195
NARVAEZ ADORNO, Jose A. (PR)
NASH, Penny Annette (Va) 6000 Grove Ave, Richmond, VA 23226
NATERS-GAMARRA, Floyd (Butch) (Los) 620 S Gramercy Pl Apt 421, Los Angeles, CA 90005
NATHANIEL, Mary (Ak) PO Box 56, Chalkyitsik, AK 99788
NATIONS, Christopher Cameron (CFla) 338 E Lyman Ave, Winter Park, FL 32789
NATOLI, Anne M (EC) 104 S Madison St, Whiteville, NC 28472
NATTERMANN, Margaret (Peggy) Ann (WMich) 06685 M-66n, Charlevoix Estates Lot 124, Charlevoix, MI 49720
NATZKE, Vicki Jo (FdL) 7221 Country Village Dr, Wisconsin Rapids, WI 54494
NAUGHTON, Ezra A (VI) 398 N St Sw, Washington, DC 20024
NAUGHTON, Mary Anne (SeFla) 3300A S Seacrest Blvd, Boynton Beach, FL 33435
NAUGHTON, Sharon Yvonne (EMich) St Paul's Episcopal Church, 711 S Saginaw St, Flint, MI 48502
NAUGLE, Gretchen Rohn (Neb) 1535 North 69th Stret, Lincoln, NE 68505
NAUMANN, John Frederick (Mont) 1241 Crawford Dr., Billings, MT 59102
NAUMANN, Richard Donald (Wyo) 1251 Inca Dr, Laramie, WY 82072
NAUSKA, Gayle Lynn (Ak) 1703 Richardson Dr, Anchorage, AK 99504
NAWROCKI, Cynthia Lynn (WMich) 3006 Bird Ave Ne, Grand Rapids, MI 49525
NAYLOR, Susan Bernadine Rice (Mo) 2905 Wingate Ct, Saint Louis, MO 63119
NAZRO JR, A(rthur) Phillips (Tex) 1201 Castle Hill St Apt 302, Austin, TX 78703

NDAI, Domenic Muthoga (Pa) 801 Macdade Blvd, Collingdale, PA 19023
NDISHABANDI, William K (Miss) 147 Daniel Lake Blvd, Jackson, MS 39212
NEAD III, Prescott Eckerman (USC) 714 Michaels Creek, Evans, GA 30809
NEAKOK, Willard Payne (Ak) PO Box 59022, Point Lay, AK 99759
NEAL, Deonna Denice (WA)
NEAL, James Frederick (Oly) 1831 E South Island Dr, Shelton, WA 98584
NEAL, Kristi Hasskamp (WNC) 100 Spring Ln, Black Mountain, NC 28711
NEAL, Linda (ECR) 41-884 Laumilo St, Waimanalo, HI 96795
NEAL JR, Millard Fillmore (SwFla) 14820 Rue De Bayonne, Clearwater, FL 33762
NEAL, Scott (Vt) PO Box 410, Arlington, VT 05250
NEAL, William Everett (FdL)
NEALE, Alan James Robert (Pa) 316 S 16th St, Philadelphia, PA 19102
NEARY, Marlyn Mason (NH) 1935 Us Route 3, Colebrook, NH 03576
NEAT, William Jessee (Lex) 311 Washington St, Frankfort, KY 40601
NEBEL, Sue (Chi) 2023 Lake Ave, Wilmette, IL 60091
NECKERMANN, Ernest Charles (Los) 1107 Foothills Dr, Newberg, OR 97132
NEDELKA, Jerome Joseph (LI) 55 Harbor Beach Rd, PO Box 2016, Miller Place, NY 11764
NEED, Merrie Anne Dunham (Colo) 7726 S Trenton Ct, Englewood, CO 80112
NEEL, Douglas E (Colo) 225 S Pagosa Blvd, Pagosa Springs, CO 81147
NEELEY II, Harry Edwin (Mont) 100 W Glendale St #8, Dillon, MT 59725
NEEL-RICHARD, Joanne Louise (Ct) 39 Mckinley Ave, New Haven, CT 06515
NEELY, Christopher Fones (SO) 3580 Shaw Ave 409, Cincinnati, OH 45208
NEFF, Shanna (WTex) St Pauls Episcopal Church, PO Box 1148, San Antonio, TX 78294
NEFSTEAD, Eric (Cal) 275 Burnett Ave Apt 8, San Francisco, CA 94131
NEGLIA, Dwight Louis (Nwk) 116 Oakmont Dr, Mays Landing, NJ 08330
NEIDLINGER, Theodore (NI) 125 S Mccann St, Kokomo, IN 46901
NEIGHBORS, Dolores Maria (Chi) 5555 S Everett Ave Apt C-4, Chicago, IL 60637
NEIL, Earl Albert (WA) 4545 Connecticut Ave Nw Apt 929, Washington, DC 20008
NEILSEN, Eloise (RI) 20 Exeter Blvd, Narragansett, RI 02882
NEILSON, Albert Pancoast (Del) 10 Chickadee Dr, Topsham, ME 04086
NEILSON, John Robert (NJ) 39 Yarmouth Ct, Scotch Plains, NJ 07076
NEILSON, Kurt Brian (Ore) 2736 SE 63rd Ave, Portland, OR 97206

NEILY, Robert Edward (Mich) 704 15th St Apt 360, Durham, NC 27705
NEIMAN, Judi Ann (WMich) 34462 1st St, Paw Paw, MI 49079
NEITZEL, Anna C (Dal) 6525 Inwood Road, Dallas, TX 75209
NELSON, Ann J (Colo) 2002 Warwick Ln, Colorado Springs, CO 80909
NELSON III, Ben (WTex) 3039 Ranch Rd 12, San Marcos, TX 78666
NELSON SR, Bob (SanD) 330 11th St, Del Mar, CA 92014
NELSON, Charles Herbert (LI) 194-51 Murdock Ave, Saint Albans, NY 11412
NELSON, Charles Nickolaus (Minn)
NELSON, David Scott (Tex) 19330 Pinehurst Trail Dr, Humble, TX 77346
NELSON, Elizabeth Anne (Ida)
NELSON, Elizabeth Lane (CFla) 321 Belle Tower Ave, Lake Placid, FL 33852
NELSON, Geri Lee (Ga) 129 Viewcrest Dr, Hendersonville, NC 28739
NELSON, James Craig (WTex) 2500 N 10th St, McAllen, TX 78501
NELSON, James Lowell (Mass) 1218 Heatherwood, Yarmouth Port, MA 02675
NELSON, Jeffrey Scott (Neb) 1714 Short Street, North Platte, NE 69101
NELSON, John Douglas (SD) 12 Bis Rue Monmory, Vincennes, France
NELSON, Joseph Reed Peter (NJ) 715 Magie Ave, Elizabeth, NJ 07208
NELSON, Julie (ECR) 532 Tyrella Ave Apt 30, Mountain View, CA 94043
NELSON, Julie F (NwPa) 140 Oyster Pond Rd, Falmouth, MA 02540
NELSON, Leilani Lucas (Cal) 3973 17th St, San Francisco, CA 94114
NELSON JR, L(evine) Stephen (Pa) Po Box 1105, Norristown, PA 19404
NELSON, Raymond Allen (SVa) 3850 Pittaway Dr, Richmond, VA 23235
NELSON, Richard A (Ga) 7607 Lynes Ct, Savannah, GA 31406
NELSON JR, Richard Louis (NwT) Po Box 82, Burton, TX 77835
NELSON, Rita Beauchamp (Del) 30895 Crepe Myrtle Dr Unit 66, Millsboro, DE 19966
NELSON JR, Robert Mitchell (Nev) 3609 Casa Grande Ave, Las Vegas, NV 89102
NELSON, Robert William (Ak) 93 Laukahi St, Kihei, HI 96753
NELSON, Roger Edwin (Mass) 557 Salem St, Malden, MA 02148
NELSON, Sarah Lee (Nwk) 576 Concord Rd, Glen Mills, PA 19342
NELSON-AMAKER, Melana (WA) 8001 Annapolis Rd, New Carrollton, MD 20784
NELSON-LOW, Jane (Spok) 719 W. Montgomery Ave, Spokane, WA 99205

NEMBHARD, Ralston Bruce (CFla) 8413 Clematis Ln, Orlando, FL 32819
NEMES, John Dale (Oly)
NERN JR, William Baker (Cal)
NERUD, Barbara Jeanne (Neb)
NESBIT, Pamela (Pa) Po Box 128, Wycombe, PA 18980
NESBIT JR, William Reed (Chi) 917 Wildwood Ct, St. Charles, IL 60174
NESBITT, John Russell (EO) 3846 NE Glisan St, Portland, OR 97232
NESBITT, Margot Lord (Okla) 1703 N Hudson Ave, Oklahoma City, OK 73103
NESBITT, Paula Diane (Cal) 577 Forest St., Oakland, CA 94618
NESHEIM, Donald Oakley (Minn) 10785 Valley View Rd #114, Eden Prairie, MN 55344
NESIN, Leslie Frances (Me) Po Box 358, Howland, ME 04448
NESMITH, Elizabeth Clare (LI) 305 Carlls Path, Deer Park, NY 11729
NESS, Jerry (Neb) 803 Avenue E Pl, Kearney, NE 68847
NESS, Louisett Marie (Chi) 466 W Jackson St, Woodstock, IL 60098
NESS, Zanne Bartlett (ND) 1971 Mesquite Loop, Bismarck, ND 58503
NESTA, Paul A (Dal) 427 W Woodard St, Denison, TX 75020
NESTLEHUTT, Abigail Crozier (Eas) Po Box 517, Saint Michaels, MD 21663
NESTLEHUTT, Mark Stevens (Eas) 115 West Chestnut, PO Box 517, Saint Michaels, MD 21663
NESTLER, Mary June (U) 8700 S. Kings Hill Dr, Cottonwood Heights, UT 84121
NESTOR, Elizabeth M (RI) 57 South Rd, Wakefield, RI 02879
NESTROCK, Frederick Richard (Chi) 4633 Fairway Ct, Waterford, MI 48328
NETTLES, Duane Joseph (La) The Church Of The Annunciation, 4505 S Claiborne Ave, New Orleans, LA 70125
NETTLETON, Edwin Bewick (Colo) Po Box 22, Lake City, CO 81235
NETTLETON, Jerome Paul (Eas) 525 E 6th St, Cookeville, TN 38501
NETZLER, Sherryl Kaye (Nev) 1631 Esmeralda Pl, Minden, NV 89423
NEUBERGER, Jeffrey Lynn (Spok) 9106 N Bradbury St, Spokane, WA 99208
NEUBURGER, James Edward (USC) 301 W Liberty St, Winnsboro, SC 29180
NEUFELD, Ellen Christine Hirsch (Alb) 6349 Milgen Rd Apt 12, Columbus, GA 31907
NEUFELD, Michael John (Alb) 52 Sacandaga Rd, Scotia, NY 12302
NEUHARDT, Kerry Coford (Az) 975 E Warner Rd, Tempe, AZ 85284
NEUHAUS, Theodore James (Minn) 290 Dayton Ave Apt 1w, Saint Paul, MN 55102

NEVELS JR, Harry V (O) 2532 Potomac Hunt Ln Apt 1B, Richmond, VA 23233

NEVILLE, Barry Paige (Eas) St Paul's Episcopal Church, PO Box 429, Berlin, MD 21811

NEVILLE, Robert E (Ct) 5170 Madison Ave, Trumbull, CT 06611

NEVILLE, Robyn-Michelle (Va) 1299 Quaker Hill Dr, Alexandria, VA 22314

NEVIN-FIELD, Claire Margaret (Pa) 816 Derby Dr, West Chester, PA 19380

NEVINS, Nancy Ruth (WMo) 416 SE Grand, Lee's Summit, MO 64063

NEW, Robert Henry (SVa) 2804 Cove Ridge Road, Midlothian, VA 23112

NEWBERRY, Hancella Warren (SO) 840 Middlebury Dr N, Worthington, OH 43085

NEWBERRY III, Jay Lamar (Mass) 205 Oxbow Rd, Wayland, MA 01778

NEWBERT, Russell Anderson (WNY) 185 Norwood Ave, Buffalo, NY 14222

NEWBERY, Charles Gomph (LI) 1322 Shattuck Ave., #306, Berkeley, CA 94709

NEWBOLD SR, Simeon Eugene (Va) PO Box 540668, Opa Locka, FL 33054

NEWBY, Robert LaVelle (Colo) 18 Folsom Pl, Durango, CO 81301

NEWBY, William Russell Michael (WLa) 705 N. Moffet Ave, Joplin, MO 64801

NEWCOMB, Blair Deborah (Md) PO Box 301, Center Sandwich, NH 03227

NEWCOMB, Deborah Johnson (Va) 25260 County Route 54, Dexter, NY 13634

NEWCOMB, Thomason League (NY) 35 Parkview Ave #6D, Bronxville, NY 10708

NEWCOMBE, D G (NY) 113 Gilbert Road, Cambridge, CB4 3NZ, Great Britain (UK)

NEWELL, John E (SVa) 501 Old Town Dr, Colonial Heights, VA 23834

NEWHART, David George (CFla) 120 Larchmont Ter, Sebastian, FL 32958

NEWLAND, Benjamin John (Colo) Saint John's Episcopal Church, 1419 Pine St, Boulder, CO 80302

NEWLAND, William Trent (Va) 43506 Shalimar Pointe Ter, Leesburg, VA 20176

NEWLIN, Melissa Dollie (ECR) 1965 Luzern St, Seaside, CA 93955

NEWLUN, Connor Jackson (Va) Aquia Episcopal Church, PO Box 275, Stafford, VA 22555

NEWMAN, Georgia A(nn) (At)

NEWMAN II, James Arthur (Los) 1445 Westerly Ter, Los Angeles, CA 90026

NEWMAN, Michael Werth (Pa) 1806 Half Mile Post South, Garnet Valley, PA 19060

NEWMAN JR, Murray Lee (Va) 10450 Lottsford Rd Apt 1206, Mitchellville, MD 20721

NEWMAN, Richard Barend (Pa) 14 Princess Ln, Newtown, PA 18940

NEWMAN, Ryan Douglas (The Episcopal Church in Haw) PO Box 429, Kapaa, HI 96746

NEWMAN, Thomas Frank (SD) 10 Red Oak Rd, Shawnee, OK 74804

NEWNAM, Elizabeth Ann (Cal) 555 4th St Unit 530, San Francisco, CA 94107

NEWSOM, James Cook (WTenn) St George's Independent School, 3749 Kimball Ave, Memphis, TN 38111

NEWTON, Alissa (Oly) Diocese Of Olympia, 1551 10th Ave E, Seattle, WA 98102

NEWTON, John David (Minn) 1631 Ford Pkwy, Saint Paul, MN 55116

NEWTON IV, John Wharton (Tex) 209 W 27th St, Austin, TX 78705

NEYLAND, Thomas Allen (Colo) PO Box 228, Hygiene, CO 80533

NEYLON, Jean Carla (Md)

NG, Joshua (Los) 15930 Annellen St, Hacienda Heights, CA 91745

NGUYEN, Duc Xuan (Los) 9097 Crocus Ave, Fountain Valley, CA 92708

NGUYEN, Hong Xuan (Los) 9051 Biola Ln, Garden Grove, CA 92844

NI, Huiliang (Los) St Edmunds Episcopal Church, 1175 S San Gabriel Blvd, San Marino, CA 91108

NICHOLS, Alice S (Ky) 216 E 6th St, Hopkinsville, KY 42240

NICHOLS, Catherine Palmer (Vt) Trinity Episcopal Cathedral, 147 NW 19th Ave, Portland, OR 97209

NICHOLS, Kevin Donnelly (NH) 21 Hampshire Hills Dr, Bow, NH 03304

NICHOLS, Liane Christoffersen (Ia) 2013 Minnetonka Dr, Cedar Falls, IA 50613

NICHOLS III, Robert George (Tex) 15 Hannon Ave, Mobile, AL 36604

NICHOLS, Sarah Winn (Los) 837 S Orange Grove Blvd, Pasadena, CA 91105

NICHOLSON, A(leathia) Dolores (Tenn) 3729 Creekland Ct, Nashville, TN 37218

NICHOLSON, Anne L (Md) 1830 Connecticut Ave NW, Washington, DC 20009

NICHOLSON, Kedron J (Fla) 245 Kingsley Ave, Orange Park, FL 32073

NICHOLSON, Wayne Philip (WMich) 405 E High St, Mount Pleasant, MI 48858

NICKEL, Rebecca Jf (Ind) St. Timothy's Episcopal Church 2601 E. Thompson Road, Indianapolis, IN 46227

NICKELSON, Marian Lorraine (Ak) PO Box 8525, Nikiski, AK 99635

NICKERSON, Audra M (WMich) 141 Broad St N, Battle Creek, MI 49017

NICKERSON, Bruce Edward (Mass) 77 South Rd, Bedford, MA 01730

NICKERSON JR, Donald Albert (Me) Po Box 855, Intervale, NH 03845

NICKLES, Amanda Lynn (Fla) PO Box 10472, Tallahassee, FL 32302

NICKLES, Brenda Joyce (Alb) 12 Woodbridge Ave., Chatham, NY 12037

NICKLES, Megan Woods (Wyo) 349 N Douglas St, Powell, WY 82435

NICOLL, Thomas Eugene (NY) 16 Claret Dr, Greenville, SC 29609

NICOLOSI, Gary Gabriel (Nwk) St. James Westminster Church, 115 Askin Street, London, ON N6C 1E7, Canada

NIEHAUS, Thomas Kenneth (WNC) 12503 N Woodberry Dr, Mequon, WI 53092

NIELSEN, Peter W (O) 5811 Vrooman Rd, Painesville, OH 44077

NIEMAN, John S (USC) 193 Old Greenville Highway, Clemson, SC 29631

NIEMEYER, John D (Va) 501 W Nine Mile Rd, Highland Springs, VA 23075

NIESE JR, Alfred Moring (NJ) 6 Apple Tree Dr, Brunswick, ME 04011

NIETERT, Jack Frederick (SC) 2830 W Royal Oaks Dr, Beaufort, SC 29902

NIPPS, Leslie (Cal) 592 Jean St #202, Oakland, CA 94610

NISBETT, Joshua Mastine (LI) 11738 Cross Island Pkwy, Cambria Heights, NY 11411

NISSEN, Peter Boy (WK) 312 S Kansas Ave, Norton, KS 67654

NITZ, Theodore Allen (Spok) 2300 NW Ridgeline Drive, Pullman, WA 99163

NIX JR, William Dale (NwT) 11355 Nix Ranch Road, Canadian, TX 79014

NIXON, Barbara Elizabeth (Ct) 399 Windward Way, Sacramento, CA 95831

NIXON, James Thomas (At) 2700 Bennington Dr Ne, Marietta, GA 30062

NIXON, Thomas E (CGC) 1580Deese Road, Ozark, AL 36360

NOALL, Nancy J(O) (WA) 312 Hillmoor Dr, Silver Spring, MD 20901

NOBLE, Mitzi McAlexander (WA) 508 Tranquility Rd., Moneta, VA 24121

NOBLE, Tony (SanD) 625 Pennsylvania Ave, San Diego, CA 92103

NOBLE, William C. (NJ) 1941 Wayside Rd, Tinton Falls, NJ 07724

NOBOA VITERI, Eugenio (EcuC) Casilla 0901-5250, Guayaquil, Ecuador

NOCHER, Janet Gregoire (FtW) 4408 Foxfire Way, Fort Worth, TX 76133

NOE, William Stanton (Va) Po Box 2078, Ashland, VA 23005

NOEL, Virginia Lee (Mo) 15826 Clayton Rd Apt 131, Ellisville, MO 63011

NOETZEL, Joan Lois (SeFla) 7300 W Lake Dr, West Palm Beach, FL 33406

NOISY HAWK SR, Lyle Maynard (SD) 1702 E Highway 44 Lot 171, Rapid City, SD 57703

NOLAN, Richard Thomas (Ct) 451 Heritage Drive, Apt 1014, Pompano Beach, FL 33060

NOLAND, Elisabeth Hooper (RG)

NOLTA, Hugh Gregg (The Episcopal NCal) 556 E Sycamore St, Willows, CA 95988
NOON, Anna Catherine Christian (SVa) 100 W Queens Way, Hampton, VA 23669
NOONAN, Deborah Anne (Az) 2331 E. Adams St., Tucson, AZ 85719
NORBY, Laura L (Mil) 508 Rupert Rd, Waunakee, WI 53597
NORCROSS, Stephen Carl (Ore) 8949 SW Fairview Pl, Portland, OR 97223
NORDQUIST, Conrad (Los) 4063 Ruis Ct, Jurupa Valley, CA 92509
NORDSTROM JR, Eugene Alexander (HB)
NORDWICK, Brian Paul (ECR) 670 Clearview Dr, Hollister, CA 95023
NORGARD, David Lee (Los) PO Box 691458, West Hollywood, CA 90069
NORGREN, William Andrew (NY) 120 East 79th Street Apt. 2D, New York, NY 10075
NORMAN, Curt (FtW) 595 N McIlhaney St, Stephenville, TX 76401
NORMAN, Harold Gene (Dal) 406 Dula Cir., Duncanville, TX 75116
NORMAN, J(oseph) Gary (Alb) PO Box 800, Morris, NY 13808
NORMAN, Lynn (CGC) Trinity Episcopal Church, 1900 Dauphin St, Mobile, AL 36606
NORMAN JR, Richard Hudson (WLa) 405 Glenmar Ave, Monroe, LA 71201
NORMAN, Tex (CFla)
NORMAND, Ann D. (Tex) 1225 Texas Ave., Houston, TX 77002
NORMANN, Margaret E(lla) (Monroe) (Ct) 888 B Heritage Vlg, Southbury, CT 06488
NORRIS, David (Ct) 5 Briar Brae Rd, Stamford, CT 06903
NORRIS JR, Edwin Arter (Chi) 2866 Vacherie Ln, Dallas, TX 75227
NORRIS, John Roy (Okla) 6310 E 111th Place, Tulsa, OK 74137
NORRIS, M Brent (WNC) 337 Charlotte St, Asheville, NC 28801
NORRIS, Mark Joseph Patrick (Neb) 155 Strozier Rd # B, West Monroe, LA 71291
NORRIS III, Paul Haile (At) 951 Williams St, Madison, GA 30650
NORRIS, Rollin Bradford (Mich) 1626 Strathcona Dr, Detroit, MI 48203
NORRIS, Stephen Allen (Ga) 2493 Chandler Dr, Valdosta, GA 31602
NORRIS, Susan Beatrice Priess (NJ) 6355 Pine Dr., Chincoteague, VA 23336
NORRO, Hugo Pablo (Los) 4200 Summers Ln Unit 15, Klamath Falls, OR 97603
NORTH, Joseph James (Alb)
NORTH, Robert David (Chi) 7 Huron Trce, Galena, IL 61036
NORTH JR, William Miller (Tex) 570 Marietta Ave, Swarthmore, PA 19081

NORTHCRAFT, Linda Louise (Mich) 19120 Eldridge Ct, Southfield, MI 48076
NORTHUP, Frederick Bowen (At) 1118 Chicory Lane, Asheville, NC 28803
NORTHUP, Lesley Armstrong (NY) 1298 NE 95th St, Miami, FL 33138
NORTHWAY, Dan P (Kan) 3531 SW Ashworth Ct, Topeka, KS 66614
NORTON, Ann Elizabeth (EMich) PO Box 217, Otter Lake, MI 48464
NORTON JR, James Frederick (Ia)
NORTON, Jerry R (Ak) Kivalina, AK 99750
NORTON, Marlee R (Va) 2416 N Florida St, Arlington, VA 22207
NORTON, Mary K (NwPa) 218 Center St, Ridgway, PA 15853
NORVELL, John David (Okla) 530 Northcrest Dr, Ada, OK 74820
NOVAK, Barbara Ellen Hosea (Spok) 1107 E 41st Ave, Spokane, WA 99203
NOVAK, M(argaret) Anne (Oly) 15502 30th Ave Ne, Shoreline, WA 98155
NOVAK, Nicky Don (Tex) 5215 Honey Creek, Baytown, TX 77523
NOVAK-SCOFIELD, Eleanor Patricia (SwVa) 124 E Main St, Abingdon, VA 24210
NOVES, W David Peter (WNY) 840 Bataan Ave, Dunkirk, NY 14048
NOWLIN, Ben Gary (Mo) 61 Dames Ct, Ferguson, MO 63135
NOYES, Daphne B (Mass) Church of the Advent, 30 Brimmer St, Boston, MA 02108
NSENGIYUMVA, Samuel (Md) 1223 Huron Trail, Sheboygan Falls, WI 53085
NSUBUGA, Thomas Timothy (WLa) 538 Main St, Grambling, LA 71245
NTAGENGWA, Jean Baptiste (Mass) 138 Tremont St, Boston, MA 02111
NUAMAH, Reginald (LI) 3607 Glenwood Rd, Brooklyn, NY 11210
NULL, John Ashley (WK) 636 East Iron, Salina, KS 67401
NUNEZ, Carlos Enrique (Ore) 3052 Se 158th Ave, Portland, OR 97236
NUNEZ, Timothy Charles (CFla) 10481 Se 68th Ct, Belleview, FL 34420
NUNLEY, Janet Worth (NY) 137 N Division St, Peekskill, NY 10566
NUNN, Frances Louise (Va)
NURDING, Brian Frank (The Episcopal Church in Haw) 1144 Kumukumu St. Apt. E, Honolulu, HI 96825
NUSSER-TELFER, Hiltrude Maria (O) 9868 Ford Rd, Perrysburg, OH 43551
NUTTER, James Wallace (Tex) 6221 Main St, Houston, TX 77030
NWACHUKU, Chukwuemeka Polycarp (Chi) St Andrew's - Pentecost Evanston, 1928 Darrow Ave, Evanston, IL 60201
NYATSAMBO, Tobias Dzawanda (NH) PO Box 737, Ashland, NH 03217

NYBACK, Rachel (Los) 1818 Monterey Blvd, Hermosa Beach, CA 90254
NYBACK, Warren Stanley (Los) 242 E Alvarado St, Pomona, CA 91767
NYBERG, Kristina Yvette (Los) 700 S. Myrtle Avenue, Apt 514, Monrovia, CA 91016
NYE, Linda Wade (NC) Grace Memorial Episcopal Church, 871 Merrimon Ave, Asheville, NC 28804
NYE, Max Ormsbee (Nev) 150 Cortona Way Apt 331, Brentwood, CA 94513
NYGAARD, Steven Bickham (NMich) 6144 Westridge 21.25 Dr, Gladstone, MI 49837
NYRE-THOMAS, Beryl Jean (Los) 1117 Bennett Ave, Long Beach, CA 90804

O

OAK, Carol Pinkham (Md) St. John's Episcopal Church, 9120 Frederick Road, Ellicott City, MD 21042
OAKES, Leonard (Cal) 777 Southgate Ave, Daly City, CA 94015
OAKES, Louise K (NC) 201 N Walbridge Ave Apt 335, Madison, WI 53714
OAKES, Sara Elizabeth Herr (Cal)
OAKLAND, Mary Jane (Ia) 1612 Truman Dr, Ames, IA 50010
OASIN, Elizabeth Jayne (NJ) 344 B Delancey Pl, Mount Laurel, NJ 08054
OATS, Louis (NC) 1325 Hickory Lane, Dandridge, TN 37725
OBARSKI, Sandra Ruth (Minn) 1111 Lowell Cir, Apple Valley, MN 55124
OBENCHAIN, John Colin (Pa)
OBERHEIDE, Richard Dean (Ala) 155 N Twining St, Montgomery, AL 36112
OBIER, Cynthia Andrews (La) 4255 Hyacinth Ave, Baton Rouge, LA 70808
OBREGON, Ernesto M (Ala) 5424 Wisteria Trce, Trussville, AL 35173
O'BRIEN, Audrey Lynn (Mass) Parish of the Epiphany, 70 Church St, Winchester, NJ 01890
O'BRIEN, Charles Harold (WMass) 738 Simonds Rd, Williamstown, MA 01267
O'BRIEN, Craig Edward (Ga) 201 E 49th St, Savannah, GA 31405
O'BRIEN, Donald Richard (SwFla)
O'BRIEN, Eileen Elizabeth (Tex) 1117 Texas St, Houston, TX 77002
O'BRIEN, Julie Lynn (Az) 1735 S College Ave, Tempe, AZ 85281
O'BRIEN, Richard Lawrence (Nev) Christ Church, 200 S Maryland Pkwy, Las Vegas, NV 89101
O'CALLAGHAN, Elizabeth Putnam (LI) St Mary's Episcopal Church, 315 Lake Shore Rd, Lake Ronkonkoma, NY 11779
O'CARROLL, Bryan Douglas (SwFla) 912 63rd Ave W, Bradenton, FL 34207

O'CONNELL, Kelly Ann (Los) St Stephen's Church, 24901 Orchard Village Rd, Santa Clarita, CA 91355

O'CONNOR, Andrew T (Kan) 9605 W Greenspoint St, Wichita, KS 67205

O'CONNOR, Christopher Duane (WNY) 30 Favor St, Attica, NY 14011

O'CONNOR JR, Edward Francis (Miss) 305 East Capitol, Jackson, MS 39215

O'CONNOR, Mary Colleen Mchale (WNY) 1 East Main Street, Le Roy, NY 14482

O'CONNOR JR, Terrence (NJ) 2998 Bay Ave, Ocean City, NJ 08226

ODA-BURNS, John MacDonald (Cal) 611 La Mesa Dr, Portola Valley, CA 94028

ODDERSTOL, Sarah D (Chi) St. Mary's Episcopal Church, 306 S Prospect Avenue, Park Ridge, IL 60068

ODEKIRK, Dennis Russell (Los) 830 Columbine Ct, San Luis Obispo, CA 93401

O'DELL, Thomas Peyton (WMich) 123 W Washington St, Lexington, VA 24450

ODGERS, Marie Christine Hanson (Neb) 8800 Holdrege St, Lincoln, NE 68505

ODIERNA, Robert William (NH) Po Box 412, Nashua, NH 03061

ODOM, Robert Martial (Dal) 5923 Royal Ln, Dallas, TX 75230

O'DONNELL, Elizabeth Gibbs (Me) 16726 Lauder Ln, Dallas, TX 75248

O'DONNELL, John J (NH) 315 Mason Rd, Milford, NH 03055

O'DONNELL, Michael Alan (Alb) 4940 Shirley Pl, Colorado Springs, CO 80920

OECHSEL JR, Russell Harold (Tex) 15811 Mesa Gardens Dr, Houston, TX 77095

OESTERLIN, Peter William (RG) 3232 Renaissance Dr SE, Rio Rancho, NM 87124

OETJEN, Sandra Lee (Nev) 4613 Steeplechase Ave, North Las Vegas, NV 89031

O'FLINN, Nancy C (Ala) 4941 Montevallo Rd, Birmingham, AL 35210

O'FLYNN, Donnel (CNY) 14 Madison Street, Hamilton, NY 13346

OFOEGBU, Daniel Okwuchukwu (Dal) Church Of The Ascension, 8787 Greenville Ave., Dallas, TX 75243

OGBURN JR, John Nelson (NC) 330 W Presnell St Apt 44, Asheboro, NC 27203

OGBURN, William Lewis (Pgh) 55 Main St, North Kingstown, RI 02852

OGDEN, Virginia Louise (Alb) 51 Brockley Dr, Delmar, NY 12054

OGEA, Herman Joseph (WLa) 110 W 13th St, PO Box 912, Jennings, LA 70546

OGIER JR, Dwight Eugene (At) 125 Betty Street, Clarkesville, GA 30523

OGLE, Albert Joy (NY) 3634 Seventh Ave Unit 6B, San Diego, CA 92103

OGLE SR, Louis Knox (La) 43 Hyacinth Dr, Covington, LA 70433

OGLESBY, Charles Lucky (NC) 325 Glen Echo Ln Apt J, Cary, NC 27518

OGLESBY, Keith W (At)

OGLESBY, Patricia A (Ct) 1734 Huntington Tpke, Trumbull, CT 06611

OGUIKE, Martin Ugochukwu (NJ) 17 Woodbridge Ave, Sewaren, NJ 07077

OGUS, Mary Hutchison (EC) 175 9th Ave, New York, NY 10011

OGWAL-ABWANG, Benoni Y (NY) 135 Remington Pl, New Rochelle, NY 10801

OH, David Yongsam (Nwk) 1224 McClaren Drive, Carmichael, CA 95608

OH, Kyungja (SO) Church Of The Advent, 2366 Kemper Ln, Cincinnati, OH 45206

O'HAGIN, Zarina Eileen Suarez (Vt) 215 Corner Rd, Hardwick, VT 05843

O'HARA, Christina Swenson (SD) 2707 W 33rd St, Sioux Falls, SD 57105

O'HARA, Ellen (NY) 141 Fulton Ave Apt 609, Poughkeepsie, NY 12603

O'HARA-TUMILTY, Anne (Los) 26029 Laguna Court, Valencia, CA 91355

O'HEARNE, John Joseph (WMo) 4550 Warwick Blvd Apt 1212, Kansas City, MO 64111

✠ **OHL**, C(harles) Wallis (Ret Bp of NwT 2009-) 3205 Skye Ridge Dr, Norman, OK 73069

OHLIDAL, Susan Marie (Vt) Diocese of Vermont, 5 Rock Point Rd, Burlington, VT 05408

OHLSON, Elizabeth Anderson (NJ) 5752 West Ave, Ocean City, NJ 08226

OHLSTEIN, Allen Michael (Kan) 310 W 17th St, Leavenworth, KS 66048

OHMER, John Richard (Va) The Falls Church Episcopal, 115 E Fairfax St, Falls Church, VA 22046

O'KEEFE, Lloyd Frost (O) 970 Cottage Gate Dr, Kent, OH 44240

OKEREKE, Ndukaku Shadrack (Dal) 9624 Valley Mills Ln, Dallas, TX 75227

OKKERSE, Kenneth Howland (FdL) 4078 Valley View Trl, Sturgeon Bay, WI 54235

OKRASINSKI, Ronald Stanley (Va) Po Box 420, Colonial Beach, VA 22443

OKTOLLIK, Carrie Ann (Ak) PO Box 29, Point Hope, AK 99766

OKUNSANYA, Adegboyega Gordon (At)

OKUSI, George Otiende (Los) 312 S Oleander Ave, Compton, CA 90220

OLANDESE, Jan Susan (Nev) 2830 Phoenix St, Las Vegas, NV 89121

OLBRYCH, Jennie Clarkson (SC) 26 Saint Augustine Dr, Charleston, SC 29407

OLDFATHER, Susan Kay (Kan) Po Box 187, Kingsville, MD 21087

OLDHAM ROBINETT, Lynn Margaret (Cal) 211 Forbes Ave, San Rafael, CA 94901

OLDS, Kevin O (Mass) 8 Prospect Street, Saugus, MA 01906

OLDSTONE-MOORE, Jennifer Lee (SO) 733 State Route 41 Sw, Washington Court House, OH 43160

O'LEARY, Jane (Md) 6011 Chesworth Rd., Baltimore, MD 21228

OLIVER, Kyle M (Mil) Virginia Theological Seminary, 3737 Seminary Rd, Alexandria, VA 22304

OLIVER, Nancy Diesel (CFla)

OLIVERO, Cesar Olivero (SwFla) 17241 Edgewater Dr, Port Charlotte, FL 33948

OLIVO, David A (WA) 1525 H St NW, Washington, DC 20005

OLLER, Janet Petrey (Ind) St John's Episcopal Church, PO Box 445, Crawfordsville, IN 47933

OLMEDO-JAQUENOD, Nina (Cal) 1321 Webster St, Alameda, CA 94501

OLMSTED, Nancy Kay Young (RI) Po Box 245, Lincoln, RI 02865

OLOIMOOJA, Joseph (Los) 1501 N Palos Vevoler Dr. #128, Harbor City, CA 90710

OLSEN, Christiana (WNC) 1812 Lower Ridgewood Blvd., Hendersonville, NC 28791

OLSEN, Daniel Kevin (Pa) Box 681, Oaks, PA 19456

OLSEN, David Logie (Ore) 10445 Sw Greenleaf Ter, Tigard, OR 97224

OLSEN, Donna Jeanne Hoover (Ind) 2601 East Thompson Road, Indianapolis, IN 46227

OLSEN, Jean (RI) 35-C W Castle Way, Charlestown, RI 02813

OLSEN, L Michael (RG) St James Episcopal Church, 208 Camino de Santiago, Taos, NM 87571

OLSEN JR, Lloyd Lein (CFla) 992-B E Michigan St, Orlando, FL 32806

OLSEN, Meredith DK (Md) 4127 Chadds Crossing, Marietta, GA 30062

OLSEN, Robert M (The Episcopal NCal) 8070 Glen Creek Way, Citrus Heights, CA 95610

OLSON, Alice Ingrid (Minn) 7218 Hill Rd, Two Harbors, MN 55616

OLSON, Anna Burns (Los) 4274 Melrose Ave, Los Angeles, CA 90029

OLSON, Britt Elaine (Oly)

OLSON, Corinna (SeFla) 8888 SW 131st Ct Apt 205, Miami, FL 33186

OLSON, Ellen Elizabeth (Neb) 609 Avenue C, Plattsmouth, NE 68048

OLSON, John Seth (Ala) 202 Gordon Dr SE, Decatur, AL 35601

OLSON, Thomas Mack (The Episcopal NCal) 300 West St, Vacaville, CA 95688

OLSSON, Paul V (Nwk) 32 Hillview Ave, Morris Plains, NJ 07950

OLULORO, Emmanuel Bola (Az) 848 E Dobbins Rd, Phoenix, AZ 85042

OLVER, Matthew Scott Casey (Dal) 6569 Kingsbury Dr, Dallas, TX 75231

O'MALLEY, Donald Richard (WNC) 101 Piney Rd, Hayesville, NC 28904

OMERNICK, Marilyn (Los) St. Michael the Archangel Church, 361 Richmond St., El Segundo, CA 90245

ONATE-ALVARADO, Gonzalo Antonio (EcuC) Apartado Postal #5250, Guayaquil, Ecuador

O'NEIL, Janet Anne (Mo) 808 N Mason Rd, Saint Louis, MO 63141

O'NEILL, Bruce Douglas (Cal) 2833 Claremont Blvd, Berkeley, CA 94705

O'NEILL, Joanne Carbone (Nwk) 97 Highwood Ave., Tenafly, NJ 07670

✠ **O'NEILL**, Robert John (Bp of Colo 2003-) 7937 E 24th Ave, Denver, CO 80238

O'NEILL, Vincent DePaul (The Episcopal Church in Haw) 98-939 Moanalua Rd, Aiea, HI 96701

O'NEILL, William Haylett (Chi) 4899 Montrose Blvd. Apt. 703, Houston, TX 77006

ONG, Dian Marie (Ia) 803 W Tyler Ave, Fairfield, IA 52556

ONG, Merry Chan (Cal) 1011 Harrison St, Oakland, CA 94607

ONKKA, Marcia Rauls (Minn) 1200 Autumn Dr Apt 211, Faribault, MN 55021

ONKKA SR, Paul William (Minn) 1200 Autumn Dr Apt 211, Faribault, MN 55021

ONYENDI, Matthias E (Tex)

OPARE-ADDO, Frederick Akwetey (LI) 13304 109th Ave, South Ozone Park, NY 11420

OPAT, Kris (Pgh) 1066 Washington Rd, Pittsburgh, PA 15228

OPEL, William A (NH) 395 Locust Road, Eastham, MA 02642

O'PRAY, Denis Michael (Minn) 2412 Seabury Ave, Minneapolis, MN 55406

OPRENDEK, Matthew John (LI) 33 Jefferson ave, Garden City, NY 11530

ORBAUGH, Phyllis J (RG) 6626 Shpaati Ln, Cochiti Lake, NM 87083

ORCHARD, Carolyn Gertrude (NMich) 311 S 4th St, Crystal Falls, MI 49920

O'REAR, Lisa E (O)

O'REILLY, Eileen C (SO) 6873 Fieldstone Pl, Mason, OH 45040

O'REILLY, John Thomas (SwFla) 5321 Laurelwood Pl, Sarasota, FL 34232

O'REILLY, Patricia (Los) 402 S. Oakland Ave Apt 6, Pasadena, CA 91101

OREM, Becky Jane Tilton (NwT) St Paul's on-the-Plains Episcopal Church, 1510 Avenue X, Lubbock, TX 79401

ORENS, Elizabeth Mills (Md)

ORESKOVICH JR, Steve John (Mont) 1405 Sunflower Dr, Missoula, MT 59802

ORIHUELA, Roberto Opolinar (Va) 7000 Arlington Blvd, Falls Church, VA 22042

ORLANDO, Helen Marie (NJ) 10 Iris Ct, Marlton, NJ 08053

ORME-ROGERS, Charles Arthur (Mo) 7634 Mid Town Rd - #212, Madison, WI 53719

ORMOS, C Patrick (WTex) 12933 Latchwood Ln, Austin, TX 78753

ORNDORFF, Vivian (Kan) 3901 S Panther Creek Dr, The Woodlands, TX 77381

O'ROURKE, Brian A (Los) 1325 Monterey Road, South Pasadena, CA 91030

O'ROURKE, David Carter (Colo) 2425 Colorado Ave, Boulder, CO 80302

OROZCO, Benjamin Manuel (SanD) 3568 Elmwood Ct, Riverside, CA 92506

ORPEN JR, J Robert (Chi) 5550 S Shore Dr Apt 512, Chicago, IL 60637

ORR, Daniel Longsworth (O) 433 E Maple St, Bryan, OH 43506

ORR, Kristin Elizabeth (Chi) P. O. Box 25, Flossmoor, IL 60422

ORRALA MONCADA, Francisco (Litoral Ecu)

ORRIN, Dyana Vail (Ak) 1501 N Adams St, Fredericksburg, TX 78624

ORSBURN, Kenneth Ray (Okla)

ORSO, Thomas Ray (NY) 100 DeHaven Drive #405, Yonkers, NY 10703

ORT, Larry Victor (SD) Calvary Episcopal Church, 500 S Main Ave, Sioux Falls, SD 57104

ORTEGA, Guido Andres (EcuC) Avenue Amazonas 4430 Y Villalengua, Casilla, 17116165, Ecuador

ORTEZ, Jose Leonel (SeFla)

ORTIZ, Michelle Alisa (SwFla) Holy Innocents' Episcopal Church, 604 N Valrico Rd, Valrico, FL 33594

ORTT, William Jeffrey (Eas) 111 S Harrison St, Easton, MD 21601

ORTUNG, Thomas Edward (Oly) 105 State St, Kirkland, WA 98033

ORVILLE, Lynn D. (NwPa) PO Box 556, Ellsworth, ME 04605

ORWIG, Dana Lynn Maynard (Okla) 2710 Nw 17th St, Oklahoma City, OK 73107

OSBERGER, Charles Edward (Eas) 14084 Old Wye Mills Rd, Wye Mills, MD 21679

OSBORN, Mary Anne (Ct) 560 Lake Dr., Guilford, CT 06437

OSBORN, Sherry E (Vt) 1142 Prindle Rd Apt B, Charlotte, VT 05445

OSBORN DE ANAYA, Archie (NAM) 1115 Main St, Vicksburg, MS 39183

OSBORNE, C(harles) Edward (ETenn) 1540 Belmeade Dr, Kingsport, TN 37664

OSBORNE, Janne Alro (Tex) 6001 Shepherd Mountain Cv, Apt 227, Austin, TX 78750

OSBORNE, Ralph Everett (FdL) 2420 Marathon Ave, Neenah, WI 54956

OSBORNE, Richard L (RG) 102 Southfork Cir, Pottsboro, TX 75076

OSBORNE, Ronald Douglas (Ia) 2325 E Highview Dr., Des Moines, IA 50320

OSBORNE, William Paul (Spok) 5720 S Perry St, Spokane, WA 99223

OSBORNE-MOTT, Susan (NJ) 503 Asbury Ave, Asbury Park, NJ 07712

OSGOOD, John A (NY)

OSGOOD, Thomas Marston (Cal) 6471 Coopers Hawk Rd, Klamath Falls, OR 97601

O'SHEA, Eileen Elizabeth (Ida) 524 Ruth Ln, Nampa, ID 83686

O'SHEA, Nancy Corinne Tucker (WTenn) 6294 Venus Ave, Bartlett, TN 38134

O'SHEA, Susan J (Oly) 234 Wood Ave SW #410, Bainbridge Island, WA 98110

OSHRY, Michael A (Spok) 5225 S Cree Dr, Spokane, WA 99206

OSMUN, Andrew Gilbert (Ct) 41 Park Circle, Milford, CT 06460

OSNAYA-JIMENEZ, Uriel (Tex) 9600 Huntington Place Dr, Houston, TX 77099

OST, Gary Wilbert (Cal) 499 Ellsworth St Apt A, San Francisco, CA 94110

O'STEEN, Joe Arnold (LI) 1665 Waterford Dr, Lewisville, TX 75077

OSTENSO MOORE, Anna V (Minn) 519 Oak Grove St, Minneapolis, MN 55403

OSTENSON, Roy Oliver (SwFla) 4009 Wonderland Hill Ave, Boulder, CO 80304

OSTERTAG, Edward Frederick (Oly) 11650 26th Ave SW, Burien, WA 98146

OSTLUND, Holly Lisa (SeFla) 15730 88th Pl N, Loxahatchee, FL 33470

OSTRANDER, Paul Copeland (Okla) 2321 Northwest 48th Street, Oklahoma City, OK 73112

OSTUNI, Elizabeth Ellen (Nwk) 10 Hampton Downes, Newton, NJ 07860

O'SULLIVAN, Ann Kathlyn (Me)

OSWALD, Todd D (USC) 1885 Rifle Range Rd, Mount Pleasant, SC 29464

OTA, David Yasuhide (Cal) 900 Edgewater Blvd, Foster City, CA 94404

OTIS, Violetta Lansdale (Me) 17 Foreside Rd, Falmouth, ME 04105

OTT, Janet Sanderson (Miss) 1200 Meadowbrook Rd Apt 44, Jackson, MS 39206

OTT, Luther Smith (Miss) 1200 Meadowbrook Road, #44, Jackson, MS 39206

OTT, Paula Lee (Lex) 2410 Lexington Rd, Winchester, KY 40391

OTT, Robert Michael (ECR) 1490 Mark Thomas Dr., Monterey, CA 93940

OTTAWAY, Richard Napoleon (NJ) 16 Bell Ter, Bernardsville, NJ 07924

OTTERBURN, Margaret K (Nwk) 50 Route 24, Chester, NJ 07930

☩ **OTTLEY**, James Hamilton (Asst Bp of LI 2007-) 3 E Fairway Ct, Bay Shore, NY 11706

OTTO, Ronald Lee (EMich) St Andrews Church, PO Box 52, Harrisville, MI 48740

OTTO, Susan Wanty (EMich) St Andrews Church, PO Box 52, Harrisville, MI 48740

OTTSEN, David K (Tex) 3007 Live Oak Dr., Brenham, TX 77833

OU, Chun Shih (Tai) 120 Chu Chang 1st Road, Kaohsiung, Taiwan

OUGHTON, Marjorie Knapp (Pa) Church St Paul's, 301 E 9th St, Chester, PA 19013

OUSLEY, David K (Alb) Saint Eustace Episcopal Church, 2450 Main St, Lake Placid, NY 12946

OUSLEY, John Douglas (NY) 209 Madison Ave, New York, NY 10016

OUSLEY, Patrick Lance (Oly) 1551 10th Ave E, Seattle, WA 98102

☩ **OUSLEY**, S(teven) Todd (Bp of EMich 2006-) 1821 Avalon Ave, Saginaw, MI 48638

OUTMAN-CONANT, Robert Earl (Mass) 482 Beech St, Rockland, MA 02370

OUTWIN, Edson Maxwell (WNY) 316 Park Ave, Medina, NY 14103

OVENSTONE, Jennifer (SanD) 810 Mockingbird Ln Apt 301, Towson, MD 21286

OVERALL, Martha Rollins (NY) 345 E 86th St Apt 16-D, New York, NY 10028

OVERFIELD, Brenda S (SVa) 2817 Mohawk Drive, North Chesterfield, VA 23235

OVERGAARD, Emily Lodine (Minn) 220 N Cedar St, Luverne, MN 56156

OVERTON, Donald Ernest (EC) 4106 Dove Park Blvd, Louisville, KY 40299

OWEN, Charles Bryan (La) St Luke's Episcopal Church, 8833 Goodwood Blvd, Baton Rouge, LA 70806

OWEN, David Allen (Ct) 92 E Hill Rd, Canton, CT 06019

OWEN, Donald Edward (Ala) 1921 Chandaway Ct, Pelham, AL 35124

OWEN II, G Keith (O) 18001 Detroit Ave, Lakewood, OH 44107

OWEN, Harrison Hollingsworth (WA)

OWEN, Jennifer Marie (NY)

OWEN, Ronald M (Fla) 100 NE First St, Gainesville, FL 32601

OWEN, Sam Louis (NY) 661 E 219th St, Bronx, NY 10467

OWEN, Shelby Ochs (SwVa) 222 Fayette St, Staunton, VA 24401

OWENS IV, Bernard J (NC) 4407 Westbourne Rd, Greensboro, NC 27410

OWENS, Brent A (Lex) Christ Church Cathedral, 166 Market St, Lexington, KY 40507

OWENS JR, Donald P (La) 712 Saddleridge Drive, Wimberley, TX 78676

OWENS, Gene Waller (At) 3260 Indian Valley Trl, Atlanta, GA 30341

OWENS, John (Fla) 4180 Julington Creek Rd, Jacksonville, FL 32223

OWENS, Jonathan Michael (Cal) 777 Southgate Ave, Daly City, CA 94015

OWENS, Miriam Elizabeth (Roch) 515 Oakridge Dr, Rochester, NY 14617

OWENS, R Michael (At) P.O. Box 86, 637 University Ave, Sewanee, TN 37375

OWENS, U'Neice Yvette (Ga) 4033 Foxborough Blvd, Valdosta, GA 31602

☩ **OWENSBY**, Jacob W (Bp of WLa 2012-) 335 Main St, Pineville, LA 71360

OWREN, David (The Episcopal NCal) 99 Pampas Ln, Fortuna, CA 95540

OWSLEY, Rebecca D (EMich) Christ Episcopal Church, 202 W Westover St, East Tawas, MI 48730

OWUSU-AFRIYIE, Kwabena (Pa) 811 Longacre Blvd, Yeadon, PA 19050

OXFORD, Scott Alexander (WNC) 520 New Haw Creek Rd, Asheville, NC 28805

P

PACE, Bradley Warren (Ind) St Johns Episcopal Church, 600 Ferry St, Lafayette, IN 47901

PACE, David Frederick (ECR) 514 Central Ave, Menlo Park, CA 94025

PACE, David Taylor (Ore) 1729 Northeast Tillamook St, Portland, OR 97212

PACE, James Conlin (NY) 145 W 46th St Apt 5, New York, NY 10036

PACE, Joseph Leslie (Ct) 1 Gold St, Apt 16E, Hartford, CT 06103

PACE, Robert F (NwT) 6200 Adirondack Trl, Amarillo, TX 79106

PACE, Stephanie Anne Heflin (O) 3677 Hughstowne Dr, Akron, OH 44333

PACHECO, Jose (SanD) 209 Clay St, Weed, CA 96094

☩ **PACKARD**, George Elden (Ret Bp Suffr for ArmdF & Fed Mnstrs 2010-) 26 Oakwood Ave, Rye, NY 10580

PACKARD, Jeffrey Alan (Va) 220 Morgan Ln, Spotsylvania, VA 22551

PACKARD, Laurence Kent (Va) 9350 Braddock Rd, Burke, VA 22015

PACKARD, Linda Axelson (Chi) 2 Currant Ct, Galena, IL 61036

PACKARD, Nancy Meader (Be) 359 Whitehall Rd, Hooksett, NH 03106

PACKER, Barbara Jean (Nwk) Po Box 240, Mendham, NJ 07945

PADASDAO, Imelda Sumaoang (The Episcopal Church in Haw) 1326 Konia St, Honolulu, HI 96817

PADDOCK, Andrea Lee (Los) 31551 Catalina St,, Laguna Beach, CA 92651

PADDOCK, John Sheldon (SO) 1837 Ruskin Rd, Dayton, OH 45406

PADGETT, John Elliott (WTex) 12431 Modena Bay, San Antonio, TX 78253

PADGETT, Judy Malinda Pitts (At) 980 W Mill Bnd Nw, Kennesaw, GA 30152

PADILLA, Manuel Jack (NMich) 711 Michigan Ave, Crystal Falls, MI 49920

PADILLA, Margaret Evangeline (NMich) 711 Michigan Ave, Crystal Falls, MI 49920

PADILLA-MORALES, Luis F (PR)

PADZIESKI, Virginia Sue (Minn) 7 Terrace Point, P. O. Box 788, Grand Marais, MN 55604

PAE, Christine (Nwk) 76 E Main St, Newark, OH 43055

PAE, Joseph S (LI) 191 Kensington Rd, Garden City, NY 11530

PAGANO, Joseph Samuel (Md)

PAGE, Donald Richard (Ct) 11 Nassau Rd., Somers Point, NJ 08244

PAGE JR, Hugh Rowland (NI) 1526 Cedar Springs Ct, Mishawaka, IN 46545

PAGE, Marilyle Sweet (Roch) 401 Beresford Rd, Rochester, NY 14610

PAGE, Michelle Rene (EC) 18115 State Road 23 Ste 112, South Bend, IN 46637

PAGE, R. Lee (The Episcopal NCal) 2525 11th Ave, Sacramento, CA 95818

PAGE JR, William Russell (Mass) 217 Holland St Pt 2A, Somerville, MA 02144

PAGLIARO, Lois Anne (NY) 18818 89th Ave, Hollis, NY 11423

PAGLINAUAN, Cristina (Md) 5603 N Charles St, Baltimore, MD 21210

PAGUIO, Ruth Alegre (ECR) 212 Swain Way, Palo Alto, CA 94304

PAHL JR, James Larkin (NC) 302 College St, Oxrford, NC 27565

PAIN, Mary Reed (Mil) 10400 W Dean Rd Apt 102, Milwaukee, WI 53224

PAINE, Michael Jackson (WVa) 13 Byron St, Boston, MA 02108

PAINTER JR, Borden Winslow (Ct) 110 Ledgewood Rd, West Hartford, CT 06107

PALACIN, Manuel Enrique (PR)

PALACIO BEDOYA, Luis Hernan (Colom) Carrera 6 No 49-85, Piso 2, Bogota, Colombia

PALAGYI, Addyse Lane (Ore) 3697 Croisan Creek Rd S, Salem, OR 97302

PALARINE, John R (Fla) 12236 Mandarin Rd, Jacksonville, FL 32223

PALASI, Dario Palasi (LI) 13424 96th St, Ozone Park, NY 11417

PALLARD SR, John J (CFla) PO Box 142, Peckham Lane RR#2, Coventry, RI 03/01/2816

PALLARES ARELLANO, Jorge Enrique (Los) 10154 Mountair Ave, Tujunga, CA 91042

PALMA, Jose Leandro (WMo) 420 West 14th St, Kansas City, MO 64105

PALMER, Alison (WA) 70 Lookout Rd, Wellfleet, MA 02667

PALMER JR, Archie MacInnes (Nwk) 459 Passaic Ave Apt 315, West Caldwell, NJ 07006

PALMER, Beth Ann (Miss) 1415 Baum St, Vicksburg, MS 39180

PALMER, Brian G (ECR) 2700 Eton Rd, Cambria, CA 93428

PALMER, Earle Jason (Ak) Po Box 1002, Ward Cove, AK 99928

PALMER, John Avery (ECR) 981 South Clover Ave, San Jose, CA 95128

PALMER, John M (NY) 33 E 10th St Apt 2-G, New York, NY 10003

PALMER, Richard Rainer (Colo) 400 Summit Blvd Unity 1503, Broomfield, CO 80021

PALMER, Richard William (Wyo) 4753 Estero Blvd Apt 1601, Fort Myers Beach, FL 33931

PALMER, Sara Elizabeth (NC) 108 W Farriss Ave, High Point, NC 27262

PALMGREN, Charles Leroy (At) 4482 Hunters Ter, Stone Mountain, GA 30083

PAMATMAT, Roberto Delos Reyes (Chi) 509 N. 6th Avenue, Des Plaines, IL 60016

PANASEVICH, Eleanor J. (Mass) 104 Oak St, Weston, MA 02493

PANG, Lisa A (The Episcopal Church in Haw) 911 N Marine Corps Dr, Tamuning, GU 96913, Guam

PANG, Pui-Kong Thomas (Mass) 138 Tremont St, Boston, MA 02111

PANKEY, Steven John (CGC) 1780 Abbey Loop, Foley, AL 36535

PANNELL, Terry Randolph (Mass) 519 Commercial St, Provincetown, MA 02657

PANTLE, Thomas Alvin (Dal) 617 Star St # 81, Bonham, TX 75418

PANTON, Rosalyn Way (Ga) 2200 Birnam Pl, Augusta, GA 30904

PAOLOZZI, Joann Lee (Oly)

PAPANEK, Nicolette (Kan) 545 Greenup St #3, Covington, KY 41011

PAPAZOGLAKIS, Elizabeth Brumfield (Alb) 912a Route 146, Clifton Park, NY 12065

PAPAZOGLAKIS, Thomas Weston (Alb) 912a Route 146, Clifton Park, NY 12065

PAPE, Cynthia Dale (Mass) 1 Linden St, Quincy, MA 02170

PAPILE, James Allen (Va) 3241 Brush Dr, Falls Church, VA 22042

PAPINI, Heber Mauricio (Okla) 9100 E 21st St, Tulsa, OK 74129

PAPPAS, Christopher A (RI) 211 Galland Close NW, Edmonton, AB T5T 6P6, Canada

PAPPAS III, James C (At) 735 University Ave, Sewanee, TN 37383

PARAB, Elizabeth Anne (ECR) 2023 Palm Ave, Redwood City, CA 94061

PARACHINI, David Charles (Ct) 42 Blue Jay Dr, Northford, CT 06472

PARADINE, Philip James (Va) 118 Monte Vista Ave., Charlottesville, VA 22903

PARADISE, Gene Hooper (Ga) 10 Iron Bound Pl NW, Atlanta, GA 30318

PARAISON, Edwin Mardochee (DR (DomRep)) Calle Tony Mota Ricart #16, Box 132, Barahona, Dominican Republic

PARAISON, Maud (Hai) PO Box 5826, Fort Lauderdale, FL 33310

PARAN, William John (Mich) 435 S Gulfstream Ave Unit 1005, Sarasota, FL 34236

PARDINGTON III, G(eorge) Palmer (Ore) 3033 Ne 32nd Ave, Portland, OR 97212

PARDO ARCINIEGAS, Angel Maria (Colom) c/o Diocese of Colombia, Cra 6 No. 49-85 Piso 2, Bogota, BDC, Colombia

PARDOE III, Edward Devon (Ct) St Barnabas Episcopal Church, 954 Lake Ave, Greenwich, CT 06831

PARHAM, A(lfred) Philip (RG) 6148 Los Robles Dr, El Paso, TX 79912

PARINI, Barbara Dennison Biggs (Mass) 2957 Barbara St., Ashland, OR 97520

PARISH, Nurya Love (WMich) 1025 3 Mile Rd NE, Grand Rapids, MI 49505

PARK, Ciritta Boyer (WA) 6201 Dunrobbin Dr, Bethesda, MD 20816

PARK, Cynthia B (At) 13560 Cogburn Road, Milton, GA 30004

PARK III, Howard Franklin (Mo) 14133 Baywood Village Dr, Chesterfield, MO 63017

PARK, John Hayes (Pgh) 520 Park Rd, Ambridge, PA 15003

PARK, Stephen Radcliffe (NH) 4060 Barrows Point Rd, Nisswa, MN 56468

PARK, Theodore A(llen) (Minn) 19 S 1st St Apt B2208, Minneapolis, MN 55401

PARKE, John Holbrook (WMass) 213 Reeds Landing, Springfield, MA 01109

PARKER, Andrew David (Tex) 200 Oyster Creek Dr, Lake Jackson, TX 77566

PARKER, Betsee (Va) 110 W Franklin St, Richmond, VA 23220

PARKER, Carol Ann (EO) 9333 Nw Winters Ln, Prineville, OR 97754

PARKER, David Clinton (Ind) 224 Davis Ave, Elkins, WV 26241

PARKER, Dennis J (Ore) 4320 SW Corbett Ave, Unit # 317, Portland, OR 97239

PARKER, Donald Harry (Mass) 28 Cambridge Cir., Smithfield, RI 02917

PARKER, Elizabeth Denny Welch (Tex) 200 Oyster Creek Dr, Lake Jackson, TX 77566

PARKER, Gary Joseph (LI) 9 Barrow St. #3B, New York, NY 10014

PARKER, James Frank (HB)

PARKER JR, James Nahum (Ga) 402 E 46th St, Savannah, GA 31405

PARKER, Jesse Leon Anthony (Md) 3001 Old York Rd, Baltimore, MD 21218

PARKER, Matthew Ross (Dal)

PARKER, Robert Coleman (Tex) 832 W Jones St, Livingston, TX 77351

PARKER, Ronald Mark (FtW) 200 N Bailey Ave, Fort Worth, TX 76107

PARKER, Ronald Wilmar (Pa) 254 Williams Rd, Bryn Mawr, PA 19010

PARKER JR, Roy Earl (Mass) Holy Cross Monastery, West Park, NY 12493

PARKER, Stephanie Eve (Oly) 4805 NE 45th St, Seattle, WA 98105

PARKER JR, Stephen D (Ct) 4607 Chandlers Forde, Sarasota, FL 34235

PARKER, William C(Urtis) (NJ) 200 Armitage Court, Lincoln University, PA 19352

PARKIN, Jason Lloyd (Chi) 222 Kenilworth Ave, Kenilworth, IL 60043

PARKINSON, Caroline Smith (Va) 4614 Riverside Drive, Richmond, VA 23225

PARKS, James Joseph (Fla)

PARKS, Kenneth Thomas (Ark) 1001 Kingsland Rd, Bella Vista, AR 72714

PARKS, Larry Joseph (EMich) St John the Baptist, PO Box 217, Otter Lake, MI 48464

PARKS, Sarah Jean (EMich) St John the Baptist, PO Box 217, Otter Lake, MI 48464

PARKS, T(heodore) E(dward) Michael (Mil) PO Box 590, Milwaukee, WI 53201

PARLIER, Susan Taylor (USC) 1238 Evergreen Ave, West Columbia, SC 29169

PARMAN IV, Fritz Quinn (ETenn) St. Paul's Episcopal Church, 305 W 7th St, Chattanooga, TN 37402

PARMETER JR, George Edward (SD) Po Box 1361, Huron, SD 57350

PARMLEY, Ingram Cannon (WNC) 924 Plantation Dr, Lenoir, NC 28645

PARNELL, William Clay (NY) 1047 Amsterdam Ave, New York, NY 10025

PARODI, Louis M (NJ) Po Box 192682, San Juan, PR 00919

PARR, Heather Katheryn (Ore) 835 E 43rd Ave, Eugene, OR 97405

PARRIS, Cheryl A E (Ga) 1401 Martin Luther King Jr Blvd, Savannah, GA 31415

PARRIS, Kenneth W (Cal)

PARRISH, David LeRoy (Neb) 647 Sussex Dr, Janesville, WI 53546

PARRISH JR, Joseph (NJ) 300 E 56th St Apt 2B, New York, NY 10022

PARRISH, Judy Kay (SwVa) 989 Pigeon Hill Rd, Roseland, VA 22967

PARRISH, Larry A (Neb) PO Box 117, Falls City, NE 68355

PARRISH, William Potter (SwVa) 3708 Manton Dr, Lynchburg, VA 24503

PARROTT, Sally F (USC) 100 Deerfield Dr, Greer, SC 29650

PARRY, James William (ETenn) 2740 Joneva Rd, Knoxville, TN 37932

PARRY-MOORE, Joyce Marie (Cal) St Bartholomew's Church, 678 Enos Way, Livermore, CA 94551

Clergy List

PARSELL, Harry Irvan (SwFla) 738 Pinellas Point Dr S, St Petersburg, FL 33705

✠ **PARSLEY JR**, Henry Nutt (Bp Provsnl of Eas 2014-) Episcopal Diocese of Easton, 314 North St, Easton, MD 21601

PARSLEY, Jamie A (ND) 117 20 Ave. N., Fargo, ND 58102

PARSONS, Ann Roberts (Ak) Po Box 1445, Sitka, AK 99835

PARSONS, Berry Ed (LI) 20 Apache Ln, Sedona, AZ 86351

✠ **PARSONS**, Donald James (Ret Bp of Spr 1998-) 6901 N Galena Rd Apt 111, Peoria, IL 61614

PARSONS, Susan Diane (Cal)

PARSONS, Timothy Hamilton (CNY) 12 Oak Ave, Norway, ME 04268

PARSONS-CANCELLIERE, Rebecca Anne (Be) 350 Spruce Rd, Palmerton, PA 18071

PARTANEN, Robert C (Cal) 62 Valais Ct, Fremont, CA 94539

PARTEE, Mariclair Elizabeth (Pa) Saint Mary's Church Hamilton Village, 3916 Locust Walk, Philadelphia, PA 19104

PARTENHEIMER, Gary Hoffman (Pa) East Hall - Northfield Mt Hermon, Northfield, MA 01360

PARTHUM III, Charles Frederick (Mass) 1415 N Victoria Cir, Elm Grove, WI 53122

PARTINGTON, Richard Ogden (Pa) 4116 Twin Silo Dr, Blue Bell, PA 19422

PARTLOW, John Michael Owen (WVa)

PARTLOW, Ruth (SVa) 3409 W Point Ct, North Chesterfield, VA 23235

PARTRIDGE, Cameron Elliot (Mass) 34 Hatch Rd, Medford, MA 02155

PARTRIDGE, Edmund Bruce (Nwk) 21867 Albie Rd, Sherwood, MD 21665

PARTRIDGE JR, Henry Roy (Me) 3 Old Colony Ln, Scarborough, ME 04074

PARTRIDGE, Ivan Harold (Nwk) Po Box 235, Cotuit, MA 02635

PASALO JR, Ernesto Castro (The Episcopal Church in Haw)

PASAY, Marcella Claire (CFla) 11251 SW Highway 484, Dunnellon, FL 34432

PASCHALL JR, Fred William (NC) 4341 Bridgewood Ln, Charlotte, NC 28226

PASHTURRO, James Joseph (Mich)

PATIENCE, Rodger Lindsay (FdL) 130 Cherry Ct, Appleton, WI 54915

PATNAUDE, Robert J (O) 7146 Hesperides Dr, Warrenton, VA 20186

PATRONIK JR, Joseph Andrew (SanD) P.O. Box 1220, Pauma Valley, CA 92061

PATSTON, John Ralph Ansell (NI) 502 N James St, Ludington, MI 49431

PATTEN, Kenneth Lloyd (Hond)

PATTERSON JR, Baldo Alfred Kaleo (The Episcopal Church in Haw) 229 Queen Emma Sq, Honolulu, HI 96813

PATTERSON, Barbara Anne Bowling (At) 437 S Candler St, Decatur, GA 30030

PATTERSON, Beverly A (WTex) 4 Lakewood Dr, Laguna Vista, TX 78578

PATTERSON JR, Dennis Delamater (At) St Luke's Episc Ch, 435 Peachtree St NE, Atlanta, GA 30308

PATTERSON, Jane Lancaster (WTex) Seminary of the Southwest, P.O. Box 2247, Austin, TX 78768

PATTERSON, John (Episcopal SJ) 9 Simpson Close, Barrow on Humber, North Lincolnshire, DN19 7BL, Great Britain (UK)

PATTERSON, John Willard (NJ) 2885 Citrus Lake Dr, Naples, FL 34109

PATTERSON, Keith F (Vt)

PATTERSON, Margaret Landrum (Del) 10 Concord Ave, Wilmington, DE 19802

PATTERSON, Michael Steven (Nev) PO Box 1041, Fernley, NV 89408

PATTERSON, Robert Place (Md) 3 Cobb Ln, Topsham, ME 04086

PATTERSON, Timothy Jay (NC) 607 N Greene St, Greensboro, NC 27401

PATTERSON JR, William Brown (NC) 195 N Carolina Ave, Sewanee, TN 37375

PATTERSON-URBANIAK, Penelope Ellen (CFla) 676 Nettles Ridge Rd, Banner Elk, NC 28604

PATTISON, Benno David (At) 634 W Peachtree St Nw, Atlanta, GA 30308

PATTISON, Ruth Lindberg (At) 1501 Dinglewood Dr, Columbus, GA 31906

PATTON, David C (Mich)

PATTON, Kathleen (Oly) 1645 24th Ave, Longview, WA 98632

PATTON, Thomas Dunstan (Spr)

PATTON-GRAHAM, Heather Lynn (WA) 338 Riverview Ave, Drexel Hill, PA 19026

PAUL, Jeffrey (Nev) 305 N Minnesota St, Carson City, NV 89703

PAUL, Kenneth Wayne (WLa) 720 Wilder Pl, Shreveport, LA 71104

PAUL, Linda Joy (Okla) 501 S Cincinnati Ave, Tulsa, OK 74103

PAUL, Marcea Elanor (SeFla) 10600 Caribbean Blvd, Cutler Bay, FL 33189

PAUL, Michael K (ND) 6419 15th St S, Fargo, ND 58104

PAUL, Rocks-Anne (SwFla) 1200 4th St W, Palmetto, FL 34221

PAUL, Wectnick (Ct) Box 1309, Port-Au-Prince, Haiti

PAULIKAS, Steven D (LI) 286-88 7th Ave, Brooklyn, NY 11215

PAULIS, Marion Helen (SD) 201 S 4th St, Milbank, SD 57252

PAULSON, Diane Theresa (Ida) 1785 Arlington Dr, Pocatello, ID 83204

PAULSON, Donald Leonard (Ida) 1785 Arlington Dr, Pocatello, ID 83204

PAULUS, Ruth B (SO)

PAVLAC, Brian Alexander (Be) 365 Rutter Ave, Kingston, PA 18704

PAXTON, Richard Edwin (Ky) 820 Broadway St, Paducah, KY 42001

PAYDEN-TRAVERS, Christine Ann (SwVa) 1711 Link Rd, Lynchburg, VA 24503

PAYER, Donald R (Ia) 1809 Waterbury Circle, Ames, IA 50010

✠ **PAYNE**, Claude Edward (Ret Bp of Tex 2003-) 2702 Charter House Dr, Abilene, TX 79606

PAYNE, Edward Thomas (SO) 8363 Cannon Knoll Ct, West Chester, OH 45069

PAYNE, Harold Womack (Ark) 3412 W 7th St, Little Rock, AR 72205

PAYNE, John Douglas (FtW) 4902 George St, Wichita Falls, TX 76302

PAYNE, Nona Marie Jones (Dal) 736 Valiant Cir, Garland, TX 75043

PAYNE, Richard Leeds (Mass) Po Box 289, Brewster, MA 02631

PAYNE, Susan Strauss (Ark) 1723 Center St, Little Rock, AR 72206

PAYNE-CARTER, Gloria Edith Eureka (WNY) 15 Fernhill Ave, Buffalo, NY 14215

PAYNE-WIENS, Reginald A (NC) 1941 Webberville Rd, Austin, TX 78721

PAYSON, Charles Beck (Chi) N1133 Vinne Haha Rd, Fort Atkinson, WI 53538

PAYSON, Deborah (Pa) 531 Maison Place, Bryn Mawr, PA 19010

PAYSON, Evelyn (Mil) N1133 Vinne Ha Ha Rd, Fort Atkinson, WI 53538

PEABODY, Morrill Woodrow (RG) Po Box 247, Lemitar, NM 87823

PEABODY, S Walton (Pa) 234 Yahoola Shoals Dr, Dahlonega, GA 30533

PEABODY, William Nelson (Mo) 852 Water Andric Rd, Saint Johnsbury, VT 05819

PEACOCK, Caroline (NY) St Luke In The Fields Episcopal Church, 487 Hudson St, New York, NY 10014

PEACOCK, George Hunt (RG) 604 Aredo De Carlos, Farmington, NM 87401

PEACOCK, Joan Louise (Va) 7515 Snowpea Ct Unit M, Alexandria, VA 22306

PEACOCK, Margaret Ann (NMich) Po Box 66, Saint Ignace, MI 49781

PEACOCK, Virginia A (NMich) PO Box 305, Deer Isle, ME 04627

PEAK, Ronald Robert (Kan) 95350 Overseas Hwy Lot 12, Key Largo, FL 33037

PEALER, Judson Paul (Me) 2614 Main St, Rangeley, ME 04970

PEARCE, Clyde Willard (Ala) 1301 Paradise Cove Ln, Wilsonville, AL 35186

PEARCE JR, R(obert) Charles (Kan) 1720 Westbank Way, Manhattan, KS 66503

PEARCE, Sherilyn K (SO) Christ Church Cathedral, 318 E 4th St, Cincinnati, OH 45202

PEARCE, (William) Philip (Daniel) (ECR) 1037 Olympic Ln, Seaside, CA 93955

PEARSALL, Arlene Epp (SD) 909 E 14th St Apt 305, Sioux Falls, SD 57104

PEARSALL, Martin A (Colo) 4939 Harvest Rd, Colorado Springs, CO 80917

PEARSON, Albert Claybourn (Tex) 261 Fell St, San Francisco, CA 94102

PEARSON II, Alonzo Lawrence (FdL) 421 Lowell Pl, Neenah, WI 54956

PEARSON JR, Andrew C (Ala) Cathedral Church of the Advent, 2017 Sixth Avenue North, Birmingham, AL 35203

PEARSON, Anna S (NY) 78 Main St, Hastings On Hudson, NY 10706

PEARSON, Bill (Alb) 27 Trottingham Road, Saratoga Springs, NY 12866

PEARSON, Cedric Eugene (O) 14778 Dexter Falls Rd, Perrysburg, OH 43551

PEARSON, Daniel (Minn) 1970 Nature View Lane, W. St. Paul, MN 55118

PEARSON, David (NI)

PEARSON, Francis John Peter (Be) 10 Chapel Rd, New Hope, PA 18938

PEARSON, James Thomas (SD) Christ Episcopal Church, 513 Douglas Ave, Yankton, SD 57078

PEARSON, Janice Von (Colo)

PEARSON, John Norris (Oly) 2831 Marietta St, Steilacoom, WA 98388

PEARSON, Joseph Herbert (At) 1280 Berkeley Rd, Avondale Estates, GA 30002

PEARSON, Kevin David (Oly) 16617 Marine View Dr SW, Burien, WA 98166

PEARSON, Michael A (Pa) 2 Blount Circle, Barrington, RI 02806

PEARSON, Patricia Waychus (Cal) 1219 Dutch Mill Drive, Danville, CA 94526

PEASE JR, Edwin C (Mass) 2 Kennedy Ln, Walpole, MA 02081

PEAY, Steven Allen (Alb) 2777 Mission Rd, Nashotah, WI 53058

PECARO, Bernard Joel (SeFla) 140 Se 28th Ave, Pompano Beach, FL 33062

PECH, Meredith Ayer (Ore) 371 Idaho St, Ashland, OR 97520

PECK, David W (CPa) 119 N Duke St, Lancaster, PA 17602

PECK SR, Donald Morrow (Ore) 304 Spyglass Dr, Eugene, OR 97401

PECK JR, Edward Jefferson (CPa) 7041 Fairway Oaks, Fayetteville, PA 17222

PECK, Felicity Lenton Clark (ETenn) 3333 Love Cir, Nashville, TN 37212

PECK, Frederick (Ore) 18205 SE 42nd St, Vancouver, WA 98683

PECK, Maryjane Prill (Mich) Christ Episcopal Church, 120 N Military St, Dearborn, MI 48124

PECKHAM, Ashley Hall (RI) 31 W Main Rd, Portsmouth, RI 02871

PECKHAM, Laura Lee (Me) St Martin's Episcopal Church, 900 Main St, Palmyra, ME 04965

PECKHAM CLARK, Margaret Ann Peckham (LI) 1579 Northern Boulevard, Roslyn, NY 11576

PEDERSEN, John Charles (Kan) 9408 San Rafael Ave Ne, Albuquerque, NM 87109

PEDRICK, Jennifer L (RI) 1336 Pawtucket Ave, Rumford, RI 02916

PEEK, Charles Arthur (Neb) 2010 Fifth Avenue, Kearney, NE 68845

PEEK, Guy Richardson (WNY) 6363 Transit Rd Apt 233, East Amherst, NY 14051

PEEL, Margaret Elizabeth (Va) 543 Beulah Rd NE, Vienna, VA 22180

PEEL, Richard Charles (Mont)

PEELER, Amy Lauren (NI) 320 Franklin St, Geneva, IL 60134

PEELER, Lance Vernon (Ore) 333 NW 35th St, Corvallis, OR 97330

PEEPLES, David H (Ala) 2354 Wildwood Dr, Montgomery, AL 36111

PEERMAN III, C(harles) Gordon (Tenn) 4416 Harding Pl, Nashville, TN 37205

PEET, Donald Howard (Ct) PO Box 681, Sandisfield, MA 01255

PEETE, Brandon Ben (Tex) 3404 S Keaton Ave, Tyler, TX 75701

PEETE, Nan Olive Arrington (WA) 3001 Veazey Ter Nw Apt 1208, Washington, DC 20008

PEETS, Patricia Ann Dunne (Mo) 429 Martindale Dr, Albany, GA 31721

PELKEY, Richard Elwood (Fla) 7860 SW 86th Way, Gainesville, FL 32608

PELKEY, Wayne Lloyd (Ia) 13218 State Road #17, West Plains, MO 65775

PELLA, Diane Maria (Az) Po Box 753, Hartsdale, NY 10530

PELLATON, Thomas Jean-Pierre (NY) 2186 5th Ave Apt 7D, New York, NY 10037

PELLEGRINI, Lucy Carr Bergen (Vt) 48 East St, Bristol, VT 05443

PELLETIER, Ann Dietrich (RI) 57 Grandeville Ct, Apt#3323, Wakefield, RI 02879

PELNAR, William Donald (Mil) 2544 Tilden Ave, Delavan, WI 53115

PEMBERTON, Barbara Louise (CFla) 668 Whispering Pines Ct, Inverness, FL 34453

PENA-REGALADO JR, Jose Francisco (Hond) Col Victoria, Bloque J-3, Choloma Cortes, Honduras

PENA TAVAREZ, Vicente A (DR (DomRep)) Iglesia Episcopal Todos Los Santos, Calle Dr. Ferry Esq Eugenio Miranda, La Romna, Dominical Republic, Dominican Republic

PENCE, George E. (Spr) 8103 Donna Lane, Edwardsville, IL 62025

PENDERGRAFT, Randall Scott (Mont) Po Box 367, Red Lodge, MT 59068

PENDLETON, Mark B (NH) Christ Church, 43 Pine St, Exeter, NH 03833

PENDLETON, William Beasley (NC) 1205-B Brookstown Ave. NW, Winston Salem, NC 27101

PENFIELD, Joyce A. (RI) 25 Pomona Ave, Providence, RI 02908

PENICK, Fern Marjorie (Eau) 538 N 4th St, River Falls, WI 54022

PENN, John William (RG) 116 Kansas City Rd, Ruidoso, NM 88345

PENNEKAMP, Nancy (Cal)

PENNER, Henry Andrews (FtW) 222 S Pearson Ln, Keller, TX 76248

PENNER, Loree A (Md) 623 Monkton Rd, Monkton, MD 21111

PENNIMAN JR, Charles Frederic (Pa) 150 N 20th St Apt 500, Philadelphia, PA 19103

PENNINGTON, Jasper Green (Mich) 204 Elm St, Ypsilanti, MI 48197

PENNINGTON, (John) Joseph (Lex) 24 Thompson Ave, Ft Mitchell, KY 41017

PENNYBACKER, Kathleen Joanne (CFla) 320 S Canaday Dr, Inverness, FL 34450

PENROD, Roger Scott (WTex) 114 S. Cypress Cir, Pharr, TX 78577

PEOPLES, David Brandon (CFla) 2627 Brookside Bluff Loop, Lakeland, FL 33813

PEOPLES JR, E(dward) Moray (Ky) 3604 Fallen Timber Dr, Louisville, KY 40241

PEPE, Carol Ann (NJ)

PEPIN, Kenneth Raymond (Roch) 53 Lee Road 974, Phenix City, AL 36870

PEPPLER, Connie (Ind) 4131 W Woodyard Rd, Bloomington, IN 47404

PERALTA, Ercilia (DR (DomRep))

PERCIVAL, Joanna Vera (ECR)

PERCIVAL, Jonathan Beach (NJ) 4051 Westbourne Cir, Sarasota, FL 34238

PERCIVAL, Michael John (Colo) 381 Baltusrol Dr, Aptos, CA 95003

PERDUE, David (NwT) 1101 Slide Rd, Lubbock, TX 79416

PERDUE, Lane (Az) Trinity Cathdral, 100 W Roosevelt St, Phoenix, AZ 85003

PERDUE, Thomas Hayes (EC) 3981 Fairfax Sq, Fairfax, VA 22031

PEREZ, Gregory Gerard (Nwk) 141 Broadway, Bayonne, NJ 07002

PEREZ, Jon Arnold (ECR)

PEREZ JR, Juan F (Mich)

PEREZ-BULLARD, Altagracia (NY) 1047 Amsterdam Ave, New York, NY 10025

PEREZ MACIAS, Jesus Eduardo (Colom) Ap Aer 2704, Barranquilla, Atlantico, Colombia

PEREZ MOREIRA, Hector (EcuC) Cd Sauces 5 Mz 225 V2, Guayaquil, Ecuador

PEREZ-QUINONES, Juan Pablo (PR)

PEREZ-VEGA, Rodrigo (Nwk) 214 Washington St, Hackettstown, NJ 07840

PERICA, Raymond William (CFla) 145 E Edgewood Dr, Lakeland, FL 33803

PERIDANS, Dominique (Md) 1819 Cromwood Rd, Parkville, MD 21234

PERINE, Everett Craig (Ct) 60 Church St, Hebron, CT 06248

PERKINS, Aaron C. (Me) 26 Moulton Ln, York, ME 03909

PERKINS III, Albert Dashiell (Ala) 425 N Moye Dr, Montgomery, AL 36109

PERKINS, Cecil Patrick (WMo) 1307 Holmes St, Kansas City, MO 64106

PERKINS, David (Lex) 3509 Falcon Ridge Ct, Montgomery, AL 36111

PERKINS, Jesse S (Ark) 531 W College Ave, Jonesboro, AR 72401

PERKINS, Lynn Jones (RG) PO Box 4330, Gallup, NM 87305

PERKINS, Patrick R (WMass) 679 Farmington Ave, West Hartford, CT 06119

PERKINS, Roger S (RG) 1409 Linda Drive, Gallup, NM 87301

PERKINSON, Edward Myron (O) 3 Fox Hollow, Plymouth, MA 02360

PERKO, F Michael (RG) 2 Paa Ko Ct, Sandia Park, NM 87047

PERO, David Edward (Ore) 1609 Elm St, Forest Grove, OR 97116

PERRA, James Francis (Md) 1401 Towson St, Baltimore, MD 21230

PERRIN, Charles Leonard (LI) 13530 Grand Central Pkwy Apt 317, Jamaica, NY 11435

PERRIN, Henry Keats (SO) 10129 Springbeauty Ln, Cincinnati, OH 45231

PERRIN, Mary Elizabeth (WMich) 2512 Highpointe Dr, Kalamazoo, MI 49008

PERRIN, Ronald Van Orden (NY)

PERRIN, Susan Elizabeth (USC)

PERRINO, Robert Anthony (SeFla) 1103 Duncan Cir Apt 103, Palm Beach Gardens, FL 33418

PERRIS, John D. (Eur) 581 Valley Rd, Upper Montclair, NJ 07043

PERRIZO, Faith Crook (WVa) 405 E Montgomery St, Marietta, OH 45750

PERRY, Ally (WLa) 210 3rd street, Miami, OK 74354

PERRY, Bonnie Anne (Chi) 4550 N Hermitage Ave # 103, Chicago, IL 60640

PERRY, Cecilia C (RI) PO Box 872, Bristol, RI 02809

PERRY, David Warner (Ore) 715 Se 34th Ave, Portland, OR 97214

PERRY, John Wallis (Vt) 431 Union St, Hudson, NY 12534

PERRY, Kenneth M (Roch) PO Box 147, Geneva, NY 14456

PERRY, Margaret Rose (Az) St Francis in-the-Valley, 600 S La Canada Dr, Green Valley, AZ 85614

PERRY, Pauline Tait (WMass) 49 Briarwood Cir, Worcester, MA 01606

PERRY, Raymond Glenn (NMich) 251 Monongahela Rd, Crystal Falls, MI 49920

PERRY, Robert Kendon (Ida) 411 Capitol Ave, Salmon, ID 83467

PERSCHALL JR, Donald Richard (Dal) 909 W Gandy St, Denison, TX 75020

✠ **PERSELL**, William Dailey (Ret Bp of Chi 2008-) 28 Haskell Dr., Bratenahl, OH 44108

PERSON, Dorothy Jean (NMich) 208 Lane Ave, Kingsford, MI 49802

PERSON, Kathryn Jeanne (NY) 1803 Glenwood Rd, Brooklyn, NY 11230

PESSAH, Elisabeth Jayne (CFla) 1225 W Granada Blvd, Ormond Beach, FL 32174

PESSAH, Stephen Michael (CFla) 1225 W Granada Blvd, Ormond Beach, FL 32174

PETERMAN, Lynn Ceremuga (EC) 115 John L Hurst Dr, Swansboro, NC 28584

PETERS, Albert Fitz-Randolph (Del) c/o Manor House, 1001 Middleford Rd Apt 106, Seaford, DE 19973

PETERS, Arthur Edward (Alb) 35 North St, Granville, NY 12832

PETERS JR, August William (WA) 1000 Hilton Ave, Catonsville, MD 21228

PETERS, David W (Spr) PO Box 178, Mount Vernon, IL 62864

PETERS, Diana Wray (Colo) 13495 Monroe St, Thornton, CO 80241

PETERS, Gregory William (Oly) 4424 SW 102nd Street, Seattle, WA 98146

PETERS, Helen Sarah (Ak) 1340 23rd Ave, Fairbanks, AK 99701

PETERS, John T (Minn) 14434 Fairway Dr, Eden Prairie, MN 55344

PETERS, J Patrick Patrick (CPa) 465 Zachary Dr, Manheim, PA 17545

PETERS, Peter William (Roch) 239 Yarmouth Rd, Rochester, NY 14610

PETERS, Yejide S (NY) 1414 Greycourt Ave, Richmond, VA 23227

PETERSEN, Barbara Jean (WNC) 2047 Paint Fork Rd, Mars Hill, NC 28754

PETERSEN, Carolyn Petersen (CFla) 4708 Waterwitch Point Dr, Orlando, FL 32806

PETERSEN, Duane Eric (WLa) 1030 Johnston Street, Lafayette, LA 70501

PETERSEN, Judith R. (SD) 1002 2nd St, Brookings, SD 57006

PETERSEN, Scott B (At) All Saints Church, 1708 Watson Blvd, Warner Robins, GA 31093

PETERSEN, William Herbert (Roch) 49 Winding Brook Dr., Fairport, NY 14450

PETERSEN-SNYDER, Christine Lynn (LI) 290 Conklin St, Farmingdale, NY 11735

PETERS-MATHEWS, Joseph Paul (Cal) Diocese Of California, 1055 Taylor St, San Francisco, CA 94108

PETERSON, Barbara Ann (Mass) 17 Sandy Neck Rd, East Sandwich, MA 02537

PETERSON, Carol Elizabeth (Wyo) 1908 Central Ave, Cheyenne, WY 82001

PETERSON, Diane Mildred (Ct) 5160 Madison Avenue, 4670 Congress Street, Trumbull, CT 06611

PETERSON JR, Frank Lon (NY) 969 Park Ave Apt 8C, New York, NY 10028

PETERSON, Iris E (Be) 56 Franklin St Unit 16, Danbury, CT 06810

PETERSON JR, John Henry (FdL) 129 5th St, Neenah, WI 54956

PETERSON, John Louis (WA) 1001 Red Oak Dr, Hendersonville, NC 28791

PETERSON JR, John Raymond (SwFla) 5020 Bayshore Blvd Apt 301, Tampa, FL 33611

PETERSON, Ralph Edward (NY) 235 Walker Sreet Apt 134, Lenox, MA 01240

PETERSON, Richard Trenholm (Cal) 883 Roble Dr, Sunnyvale, CA 94086

PETERSON, S(ally) Suzanne (Ia) Diocese of Cape Town, PO Box 1932, Cape Town, 8000, South Africa

PETERSON-WLOSINSKI, Cynthia M E (Minn) 1121 W Morgan St, Duluth, MN 55811

PETERSON ZUBIZARRETA, Dorenda C (SeFla)

PETIPRIN, Andrew Kirk (CFla) 7142 Lake Drive, Orlando, FL 32809

PETIT, Charles David (USC) 5220 Clemson Ave, Columbia, SC 29206

PETITE, Robert (Chi) 4717 S. Greenwood Ave. Unit 1, Chicago, IL 60615

PETLEY, Dale Alfred (Okla) 1813 Westminster Pl, Oklahoma City, OK 73120

PETRASH, David Lloyd (Dal) PO Box 745, Kaufman, TX 75412

PETROCCIONE, James Victor (Nwk) 28 Ross Rd, Stanhope, NJ 07874

PETROCHUK, Michael Aaron (O) St Andrew's Episcopal Church, 583 W Hopocan Ave, Barberton, OH 44203

PETROTTA, Anthony Joseph (Ore) PO Box 445, Wilsonville, OR 97070

PETTEE, Abigail Bower (Me) 33 Chestnut St, Camden, ME 04843

PETTENGILL, David Eugene (Az) 1558 E Gary St, Mesa, AZ 85203

PETTENGILL-RASURE, Rachael Marie (Mass) 453 Adams St, Milton, MA 02186

PETTERSON, Ted Ross (La) 25 Signature Dr, Brunswick, ME 04011

PETTIGREW, Thomas John (Alb) 3764 Main St, Warrensburg, NY 12885

PETTITT, Robert Riley (ND) 1201 49th Avenue, Rt 6, Fargo, ND 58103

PETTY, Carol Ross (Tex) Holy Comforter Episcopal Church, PO Box 786, Angleton, TX 77516

PETTY JR, Jess Joseph (O) 35 B Pond St, Marblehead, MA 01945

PETTY JR, Tyrus Cecil (Kan) 5841 Sw 26th St, Topeka, KS 66614

PETZAK, Rodney Ross (Nev) 1965 Golden Gate Dr, Reno, NV 89511

PEVEHOUSE, James Melvin (Tex) 24 N Masonic St, Bellville, TX 77418

PEVERLEY, Stephen Richard (LI) 1 Araca Ct, Babylon, NY 11702

PEYTON III, Allen Taylor (Alb) 2401 Ben Hill Rd, Atlanta, GA 30344

PEYTON IV, Francis Bradley (WA) 1919 York Road, 2nd Floor, Timonium, MD 21093

PEYTON, Linda (Me) 42 Flying Point Rd, Freeport, ME 04032

PEYTON JR, Robert Lee (At) PO Box 207, Hartwell, GA 30643

PEYTON, Susan Carroll (SwVa)

PEYTON, William Parish (Va) 865 Madison Ave., New York, NY 10021

PFAB, Martin William (Fla) 724 Lake Stone Cir, Ponte Vedra Beach, FL 32082

PFAB, Penny L (Fla) 724 Lake Stone Cir, Ponte Vedra Beach, FL 32082

PFAFF, Brad Hampton (NY) 126 W 83rd St Apt 3-P, New York, NY 10024

PFAFF, David (Mil)

PFAFF, Richard William (NC) 750 Weaver Dairy Road, #190, Chapel Hill, NC 27514

PFEIFFER, Dorothea Koop (WNC) 2 Sweet Gum Ct, Hilton Head, SC 29928

PFISTER, Kathleen Rock (Tex) PO Box 5176, Austin, TX 78763

PFOTENHAUER, Leon Henry (Ia) 1613 S Nicollet St, Sioux City, IA 51106

PHALEN, John Richard (Los) 5772 Garden Grove Blvd Spc 487, Westminster, CA 92683

PHAM, J Peter (Chi) St. Paul's Episcopal Church, 2430 K St, N.W., Washington, DC 20037

PHANORD, Jn. Berthold (Hai)

PHELAN, Shane (Nwk) 43 Massachusetts Ave., Haworth, NJ 07641

PHELPS, Cecil Richard (NI) 4525 Baring Ave, Box 2293, East Chicago, IN 46312

PHELPS, Joan Priscilla (Ct) 15 Freedom Way Unit 101, Niantic, CT 06367

PHELPS, John Edward (Me) 4 Glendale Rd, Kennebunk, ME 04043

PHELPS JR, Kenneth O (Md) 6401 Solomons Island Rd N, Sunderland, MD 20689

PHELPS, Mary M (Minn) 1415 6th Ave. South, Anoka, MN 55303

PHELPS, Nicholas Barclay (Pa) 1906 Trenton Ave, Bristol, PA 19007

PHELPS, Shannon David (SanD) Po Box 234, Del Mar, CA 92014

PHELPS, Walter E (Cal) 120 Lorraine Ct, Vacaville, CA 95688

PHENNA, Timothy Peter (Colo) 1320 Arapahoe St, Golden, CO 80401

PHILIP, Kristi (Spok) 22 W 37th Ave, Spokane, WA 99203

PHILIPS, John Kevin (ECR) 1190 Alta Mesa Road, Monterey, CA 93940

PHILIPS, Ronald K (Wyo) PO Box 950, Thermopolis, WY 82443

PHILLIPS III, Arthur William (WLa) Diocese Of Western Louisiana, PO Box 20131, Alexandria, LA 22320

PHILLIPS, Benjamin T. S. (SO)

PHILLIPS, Beth (Cal)

PHILLIPS, Catharine Seybold (Chi) 458 Dee Ln, Roselle, IL 60172

PHILLIPS, Craig Arnold (Va) 4818 Old Dominion Dr, Arlington, VA 22207

PHILLIPS, Deborah Anne (Mass) 35 Settlers Way, Salem, MA 01970

PHILLIPS, Douglas Cecil (Minn)

PHILLIPS, Jennifer Mary (Mass) 2903 Cabezon Blvd SE, Rio Rancho, NM 87124

PHILLIPS, Jerry Ray (La) PO Box 199, Rosedale, LA 70772

PHILLIPS, John Bradford (Cal) 891 Skeel Drive, Camarillo, CA 93010

PHILLIPS II, John Walter (CGC) 590 Parker Cr., Pensacola, FL 32504

PHILLIPS, Julia Coleman (CGC) 127 Hamilton Ave, Panama City, FL 32401

PHILLIPS, Kevin Alan (Va) 2094 Grant Rd, Mountain View, CA 94040

PHILLIPS, Linda (Nwk) 50 State Route 24, Chester, NJ 07930

PHILLIPS, Marie (O) 50 Sunnycliff Dr, Euclid, OH 44123

PHILLIPS, Michael Albin (NY) 316 E 88th St, New York, NY 10128

PHILLIPS, Paul Henry (SVa) 1416 S Grand Blvd Apt 3, Spokane, WA 99203

PHILLIPS JR, Raymond Leland (USC) 701 Unity St, Fort Mill, SC 29715

PHILLIPS, Richard Oliver (NY) 10 Badger St, Littleton, NH 03561

PHILLIPS, Robert Taylor (WA) 1525 Newton St Nw, Washington, DC 20010

PHILLIPS, Robert W (CFla) 1620 Mayflower Ct Apt A-610, Winter Park, FL 32792

PHILLIPS, Roger V (Minn) 1801 Santa Maria Pl, Orlando, FL 32806

PHILLIPS, Stuart John Tristram (Tenn) 654 Long Hollow Pike, Goodlettsville, TN 37072

PHILLIPS, Susan (Del) 18 Olive Ave, Rehoboth Beach, DE 19971

PHILLIPS, Thomas Larison (Spr) 1015 Frank Dr, Champaign, IL 61821

PHILLIPS, Wendell Roncevalle (NC) 4211 Sharon View Rd, Charlotte, NC 28226

PHILLIPS-GAINES, Lynn (Miss) 105 N Montgomery St, Starkville, MS 39759

PHILLIPS-MATSON, Wesley A (Episcopal SJ)

PHILPUTT JR, Frederick Chapman (Dal) 5811 Penrose Ave, Dallas, TX 75206

PHINNEY, James Mark (Oly) 4246 South Discovery Road, Port Townsend, WA 98368

PHIPPS, Joy Ogburn (Ala) 3919 Westminster Ln, Birmingham, AL 35243

PHIPPS, Marion Elizabeth (Chi) 5403 W Greenbrier Dr, McHenry, IL 60050

PHIPPS JR, Robert Stirling (Va) Po Box 33430, San Antonio, TX 78265

PIATKO, Joann M (NwPa) 26 Chautauqua Pl, Bradford, PA 16701

PICCARD, Kathryn Ann (Mass) 68 Baldwin St Apt 2, Charlestown, MA 02129

PICKARD, Joseph Shearer (Nwk) 91 Ann Rustin Dr, Ormond Beach, FL 32176

PICKEN, Robert Andrew (Roch) 191 Kensington Road, Garden City, NY 11530

PICKENS, Gregory Doran (Dal) 8011 Douglas, Dallas, TX 75225

PICKERAL, Gretchen Marta Benson (Minn) 404 Trout Lake Rd, Grand Rapids, MN 55744

PICKERING, Louann Kisor (Ore) 7610 Sw 49th Ave, Portland, OR 97219

PICKERING, William Todd (Va) 208 N 28th St, Richmond, VA 23223

PICKERRELL, Nina (Cal) 1100 California St, San Francisco, CA 94108

PICKUP JR, Edmund (SVa) Po Box 146, Franklin, VA 23851

PICKUP JR, Ezra Alden (Vt) 37 S Main St, Alburgh, VT 05440

PICOT, Katherine Frances (Tex) The Harnhill Centre, Harnhill, Cirencester, TX GL75PX, Great Britain (UK)

PICOU, Michael David (SeFla) St Stephen's Episc Ch, 2750 McFarlane Rd, Coconut Grove, FL 33133

PIERCE, Charles Christian (Chi) Grace Episcopal Church, 120 E 1st St, Hinsdale, IL 60521

PIERCE, Dorothy Kohinke (CNY) PO Box 458, Chenango Bridge, NY 13745

PIERCE, Graham Towle (Me) 35 Pine Ledge Dr, Scarborough, ME 04074

PIERCE, Jacob E (NC) Church Of The Holy Comforter, 2701 Park Rd, Charlotte, NC 28209

PIERCE, Jay Ross (Lex) 205 Cardinal Ave, Versailles, KY 40383

PIERCE, Nathaniel W (Eas) 3864 Rumsey Dr, Trappe, MD 21673

PIERCE, Patricia Daniels (NJ) 203 Wildwood Ave, Pitman, NJ 08071

PIERCE, Patrick Arthur (CPa) 306 N Main Street, Mercersburg, PA 17236

PIERCE, Roderick John (Tex) 4435 S FARM ROAD 125, SPRINGFIELD, MO 65810

PIERCE, Terry Lee (Tex) PO Box 268, Taylor, TX 76574

PIERSON, Peter (Alb) PO Box 183, 156 Josh Hall Pond Road, Grafton, NY 12082

PIERSON, Stewart (Vt) 232 High Rock Rd, Hinesburg, VT 05461

PIETSCH, Louise Parsons (NY) 80 Lyme Rd Apt 347, Hanover, NH 03755

PIETTE, Joseph Leroy (Minn) 204 8th St, Cloquet, MN 55720

PIFKE, Lauran Kretchmar (Cal) 3400 Stevenson Blvd. #Q37, Fremont, CA 94538

PIGGINS, Deborah Hanwell (NJ)

PIKE, Clifford Arthur Hunt (Pa) 105 Elm St, Lawrenceburg, KY 40342

PIKE, David Robert (WMich) 1519 Elmwood Rd, Lansing, MI 48917

PIKE, Diane M (WNY) 500 Morris Ave Ste 304, Springfield, NJ 07081

PIKE, Richard S (NY) St Matthew's Episcopal Church, PO Box 293, Bedford, NY 10506

PIKE, Stephen Phillip (Ky) RCT 1 HQ Co, UIC 40145, FPO AP, 96426

PIKE, Thomas F. (NY) 26 Gramercy Park S Apt 9h, New York, NY 10003

PILARSKI, Terri C (Mich) 120 N Military St, Dearborn, MI 48124

PILAT, Ann Ferres (USC) St Mary's Episcopal Church, 170 St Andrews Rd, Columbia, SC 29210

PILCHER III, William Edward (NC) 305 Jackson Rd, Mount Airy, NC 27030

PILLOT, Anne Marie (O) 4292 Elmwood Rd, South Euclid, OH 44121

PILLSBURY, Samuel (Los) 919 Albany St, Los Angeles, CA 90015

PILTZ, Gary Hew (The Episcopal Church in Haw) 62-2145 Ouli St, Kamuela, HI 96743

✠ PINA-LOPEZ, Hugo Luis (Ret Bp of Hond 1981-) 2911 S Whisperbay Ct, Oviedo, FL 32765

PINDER, Churchill G (CPa) St. Stephens Episcopal Cathedral, 221 N. Front St., Harrisburg, PA 17101

PINDER, Nelson Wardell (CFla) 2632 Marquise Ct, Orlando, FL 32805

PINEO, Linda Baker (At) 3404 Doral Ln, Woodstock, GA 30189

PINHO, Joseph T (Mass) 1 Summit Dr Apt 48, Reading, MA 01867

PINKERTON, Patricia Edith Long (ECR) The Vicarad,St Annes Way, St.Briavels., Gloucestershire, GL15 6UE, Great Britain (UK)

PINKERTON, Susan B (Ct) 400 East Westminster Road, Lake Forest, IL 60045

PINKSTON JR, Frederick William (NC) 7225 Saint Clair Dr, Charlotte, NC 28270

PINNER JR, Joseph W (ETenn) 818 Hill St, Kingston, TN 37763

PINNOCK, Betty Lou (Ore) 459 Herbert St, Ashland, OR 97520

PINTI, Daniel John (WNY) 13021 W. Main St., Alden, NY 14004

PINZON, Samuel E(duardo) (WA) 15570 Sw 143rd Ter, Miami, FL 33196

PINZON CASTRO, Luis Alberto (Colom) Carrera 6 No 49-85, Piso 2, Bogota, Colombia

PIOTROWSKI, Mary Triplett (Az) 2035 N Southern Hills Dr, Flagstaff, AZ 86004

PIOVANE, Michael F (Be) Po Box 368, Trexlertown, PA 18087

PIPER, Charles Edmund (NMich) 1676 Lander Ln, Lafayette, CO 80026

PIPER, Geoffrey Tindall (Mass) 124 Front St, Marion, MA 02738

PIPER, Linda Lee (NMich) 1676 Lander Lane, Lafayette, CO 80026

PIPER, Mary Meacham (Ore) 1399 Old Hwy 234, 8240 Judge Bean Rd. Bokeelia Fla., Eagle Point, OR 97524

PIPKIN, Michael (Minn) 1730 Clifton Pl Ste 201, Minneapolis, MN 55403

PIPPIN, Tina (At) 25 Second Avenue, Atlanta, GA 30317

PISANI JR, Gerard Alexander (Nwk) 8602 Forester Lane, Apex, NC 27539

PITA-PARRALES, Ubaldo (EcuC) Manabi Y Tayapi, Puyo, Ecuador

PITCHER, Trenton Langland (Chi) 145 E Columbia Ave, Elmhurst, IL 60126

PITMAN JR, Omar W (WTex) 11919 El Sendero St, San Antonio, TX 78233

PITMAN JR, Ralph William (O) 3044 Edgehill Rd, Cleveland Heights, OH 44118

PITT JR, Louis Wetherbee (Mass) 59 Dartmouth Ct, Bedford, MA 01730

PITT-HART, Barry Thomas (SD) 1409 S 5th Ave, Sioux Falls, SD 57105

PITTMAN, Albert Calhoun (WA) 403 Russell Ave # 812, Gaithersburg, MD 20877

PITTMAN, David West (NC) 218 Pine Cove Drive, Inman, SC 29349

PITTMAN, Warren Lewis (NC) 2903 County Clare Rd, Greensboro, NC 27407

PITTS, John Robert (Tex) 3652 Chevy Chase, Houston, TX 77019

PITZER, Elaine Virginia (Spok) St Stephen's Episcopal Church, 5720 S Perry St, Spokane, WA 99223

PIVER, Jane Duncan (Va) 53 Ridgemont Road, Ruckersville, VA 22968

PIXCAR-POL, Tomas (PR) PO Box 3184, Guayama, PR 00785

PIZZONIA, Wanda Strong (Mass) Post Road & Ring'S End Road, Darien, CT 06820

PIZZUTO, Vincent Anthony (Cal) 171 Forrest Ave, Fairfax, CA 94930

PLACE, Donald Gordon (WMass) 52 County Road, Pownal, VT 05261

PLACE, Donald Lee Andrew (NY) 111 5th Ave Apt 1206, Pittsburgh, PA 15222

PLANK, David Bellinger (LI) 26 Hampton Towne Estates, Hampton, NH 03842

PLANTZ, Christine Marie (Neb) 605 S Chestnut St, Kimball, NE 69145

PLASKE, Susan Ann (Alb) 68 S Swan St, Albany, NY 12210

PLATER, Ormonde (La) 150 Broadway Apt 1112, New Orleans, LA 70118

PLATSON, Julie L (Ak) PO Box 1130, Sitka, AK 99835

PLATT, Gretchen Mary (SwFla) 1562 Dormie Dr, Gladwin, MI 48624

PLATT, Nancy Grace Van Dyke (Me) 192 Cross Hill Rd, Augusta, ME 04330

PLATT, Thomas Walter (Pa) 824 S New St, West Chester, PA 19382

PLATT, Warren Christopher (NY) 255 W 23rd St Apt 3-DE, New York, NY 10011

PLATT-HENDREN, Barbara (NC) 222 Normandy Dr, Clayton, NC 27527

PLAZAS, Carlos Alberto (Chi) 1333 W Argyle St, Chicago, IL 60640

PLESTED, Robert William Harvey (LI) 5402 Timber Trace St, San Antonio, TX 78250

PLIMPTON, Barbara Wilson (WNC) PO Box 968, Marion, 28752

PLOVANICH, Ede Marie (CGC)

PLUCKER, Susan Elizabeth (The Episcopal NCal) Our Saviour Episcopal Church, P.O. Box 447, Placerville, CA 95667

PLUMMER, Catherine B (NAM) Episcopal Church in Navajoland, PO Box 720, Farmington, NM 87499

PLUMMER, Cathlena Arnette (NAM) PO Box 720, Farmington, NM 87499

PLUMMER, Dale Wilkinson (RG) 505 N. Pennsylvania, Roswell, NM 88201

PLUMMER, Mark Alton (NC) Grace Episcopal Church, 419 S Main St, Lexington, NC 27292

PLUNKET-BREWTON, Callie Dawn (Ala) 410 N Pine St, Florence, AL 35630

PLUNKETT, Phillip Riley (Ark) 7 Sonata Trail, Little Rock, AR 72205

POBJECKY, J Richard (CFla) 414 Pine St, Titusville, FL 32796

POCALYKO, Richard Peter (Pgh) 415 Stone Mill Trl Ne, Atlanta, GA 30328

POGGEMEYER JR, Lewis Eugene (U)

POGOLOFF, Stephen Mark (NC) 218 Forestwood Dr, Durham, NC 27707

POGUE, Blair A (Minn) 2136 Carter Avenue, Saint Paul, MN 55108

POGUE, Ronald D (Tex) 5616 Shady Hill, Arlington, TX 76017

POIRIER, Esther H (Oly) PO Box 3108, Federal Way, WA 98063

POISSON, Ellen Francis (USC) Convent of St. Helena, 414 Savannah Barony Drive, North Augusta, SC 29841

POIST, David Hahn (Va) 341 Woodlands Rd, Charlottesville, VA 22901

POKORNY, Wayne Douglas (Ct) 30 Woodland St Apt 11NP, Hartford, CT 06105

POLANEO DE LA CRUZ, Leonel (DR (DomRep))
POLGLASE, Kenneth Alexis (Nwk) 2796 Rudder Dr, Annapolis, MD 21401
POLING, Jason Adler (Md)
POLK, Perry Willis (The Episcopal NCal) Grace Episcopal Church, 1405 Kentucky St, Fairfield, CA 94533
POLK, Thomas Robb (RG) 90 S Longspur Dr, The Woodlands, TX 77380
POLLACH, Gideon Liam Kavanaugh (Va) 125 Court Street, 11SH, Brooklyn, NY 11201
POLLARD, Richard Allen (Pgh) 1750 Hastings Mill Rd, Pittsburgh, PA 15241
POLLARD III, Robert (NY)
POLLEY, Bonnie (Nev) 1631 Ottawa Drive, Las Vegas, NV 89169
POLLEY, Seth Alexander (Az) 5 Gardner St, Bisbee, AZ 85603
POLLINA, Roy Glen (SwVa)
POLLITT, Michael James (Chi) 1376 Telegraph Rd., West Caln, MI 19320
POLLOCK, Christina (Spok) St. John the Evangelist Cathedral, 127 E. 12th Ave., Spokane, WA 99202
POLLOCK, Douglas Stephen (Oly) 7701 Skansie Ave, Gig Harbor, WA 98335
POLLOCK, Elizabeth Good (Me) Po Box 896, York Harbor, ME 03911
POLLOCK, John Blackwell (EC) 1912 Shepard St, Morehead City, NC 28557
POLLOCK, Margaret (Va) 21517 Laytonsville Rd, Laytonsville, MD 20882
POLLOCK, Ronald Neal (NJ) 154 W High St, Somerville, NJ 08876
POLVINO, Andrea Regina (WNY) 515 Columbus Ave., Waco, TX 76701
POLYARD, Karen Marie (Minn) PO Box 27, Wabasha, MN 55981
POMPA, Anthony R (Be) 19 E Cochran St, Middletown, DE 19709
PONADER, Martha Downs (Ind) 1337 Eagle Run Dr, Sanibel, FL 33957
PONCE MARTINEZ, Jacqueline (PR) 1 Calle Brandon, Ensenada, PR 00647-1405, Puerto Rico
POND, Finn Richard (Spok) 7315 N Wall St, Spokane, WA 99208
POND JR, Walter Edward (WNY) 171 N Maple St, Warsaw, NY 14569
PONDER, James Brian (Miss) 1116 23rd Ave., Meridian, MS 39301
PONG, Tak Yue (Tai) 11 Pak Po Street, Homantin, Hong Kong
PONSOLDT, Megan Hollaway (Va) Grace Episcopal Church, 301 S Main St, Kilmarnock, VA 22482
POOL, Jayne Collins (Ala) 106 Stratford Road, Birmingham, AL 35209
POOL, Mart Gayland (FtW) 1870 Ederville Rd S, Fort Worth, TX 76103
POOLE, Charles Lane (The Episcopal NCal) 6342 Paso Dr, Redding, CA 96001

POOLE, John Huston (CFla) 603 Spring Island Way, Saint Albans, FL 32828
POOLEY, Nina Ranadive (Me) 152 Princes Point Rd, Yarmouth, ME 04096
POOSER, W(illiam) Craig (Chi) 2423 Blue Quail, San Antonio, TX 78232
POPE, Alicia Hale (RG) Trinity on the Hill, 3900 Trinity Dr, Los Alamos, NM 87544
POPE, Charles Maurice (Ia) 505 Edgehill Dr, Saint Albans, WV 25177
POPE III, Daniel Stuart (Roch) 406 Canandaigua St, Palmyra, NY 14522
POPE, Kristin (Stina) 4423 W 14th St, Port Angeles, WA 98363
POPE, Nadine Karen (At) PO Box 1010, Cumming, GA 30028
POPE, Robert Gardner (Colo) 108 Sawmill Cir, Bayfield, CO 81122
POPE, Steven Myron (Tex) 905 Whispering Wind, Georgetown, TX 78633
POPHAM, James Jude (SwFla) St David's Episcopal Church, c/o 401 S Broadway, Englewood, FL 34223
POPHAM, Jo P (SwFla)
POPLE, David A (Ct) 95 Greenwood Ave, 22 Golden Hill St, Bethel, CT 06801
POPPE, Bernard William (Nwk) 18 De Hart Rd, Maplewood, NJ 07040
POPPE, Kenneth Welch (Vt) 2 Cherry St, Burlington, VT 05401
POPPLEWELL, Elizabeth (Ia) 1808 Nw 121st Cir, Clive, IA 50325
PORCHER, Philip Gendron (SC) 1494 Stratton Pl, Mount Pleasant, SC 29466
PORTARO JR, Sam Anthony (Chi) 1250 N Dearborn St Apt 19C, Chicago, IL 60610
PORTER, Elizabeth Streeter (Ark) 10 Thunderbird Dr, Holiday Island, AR 72631
PORTER III, Fulton Louis (Chi) 2720 2nd Private Rd, Flossmoor, IL 60422
PORTER, George Vernon (Ga) 1201 Fairfield St, Cochran, GA 31014
PORTER, Gerald William (Oly) 5555 Montgomery Dr # N-103, Santa Rosa, CA 95409
PORTER, James Robert (Az) 2200 Lester Dr NE Apt 460, Albuquerque, NM 87112
PORTER, Joe T(homas) (WTenn) 43 Carriage Ln, Sewanee, TN 37375
PORTER, John Harvey (Cal) 551 Ivy St, San Francisco, CA 94102
PORTER, John Joseph (At) 215 Abington Dr NE, Atlanta, GA 30328
PORTER, Lloyd Brian (Tex) 1701 W TC Jester Blvd, Houston, TX 77008
PORTER, Nicholas Tewkesbury (Ct) Trinity Church, 651 Pequot Ave, P.O. Box 400, Southport, CT 06890
PORTER, Pamela (WMass) Po Box 19, Heath, MA 01346
PORTER, Roger Cliff (CGC) 6500 Middleburg Ct, Mobile, AL 36608
PORTER, Shirley Margaret (At)

PORTER-ACEE III, John M (NC)
PORTER CADE, Wendy M (At) 1323 N Dupont St, Wilmington, DE 19806
PORTEUS, Beverly S (Eas) 27 Woods Way, Elkton, MD 21921
PORTEUS, Christopher (Eas) 27 Woods Way, Elkton, MD 21921
PORTEUS, James Michael (Az) Triskele, Rinsey, Ashton, Helston, TR13 9TS, Great Britain (UK)
✠ **PORTEUS**, Morgan (Ret Bp of Ct 1981-) PO Box 782, Wellfleet, MA 02667
POST, Suzanne Marie (SwFla) 14511 Daffodil Dr Apt 1402, Fort Myers, FL 33919
POSTON, Ronald Glen (Az) 2174 E Loma Vista Dr, Tempe, AZ 85282
POTEAT, Sally Tarler (WNC)
POTEET, David Bertrand (Tex) Po Box 6828, Katy, TX 77491
POTEET, Fred (SVa) 2508 Shepherds Ln, Virginia Beach, VA 23454
POTTER, Frances Dickinson (NH) 1010 Waltham St Apt 352, Lexington, MA 02421
POTTER, Jack C (U) 231 E 100 S, Salt Lake City, UT 84111
POTTER, Linda Gail (Chi) 1240 NE 64th Ln, Hillsboro, OR 97124
POTTER, Lorene Heath (WNY) 537 S Park Ave, Buffalo, NY 14204
POTTER, Meredith Woods (Chi) 317 Satinwood Ct S, Buffalo Grove, IL 60089
POTTER, Paul Christopher (Los) 10925 Valley Home Ave, Whittier, CA 90603
POTTER, Raymond J (The Episcopal NCal) 2224 Gateway Oaks Dr. #355, Sacramento, CA 95833
POTTER, Roderick Kenneth (Me) 16 Alton Rd Apt 215, Augusta, ME 04330
POTTER, Sara (The Episcopal NCal) 1776 Old Arcata Road, Bayside, CA 95524
POTTER JR, Spencer B (SeFla) 19000 SW 89th Ave, Cutler Bay, FL 33157
POTTER-NORMAN, Ricardo T (DR (DomRep)) Camila Alvarez #7 Urb. Mallen, San Pedro De Macoris, Dominican Republic
POTTERTON, Carol Thayer (SO) 5825 Woodmont Ave, Cincinnati, OH 45213
POTTS, David G (SD) 1728 Mountain View Rd, Rapid City, SD 57702
POTTS, Kathleen Kirkland (Miss) 1421 Goodyear Blvd., Picayune, MS 39466
POTTS, Matthew L (WMich) P.O. Box 298, Falmouth, MA 02541
POULIN, Suzanne Gordon (NH) Saint John the Baptist, 118 High St, Sanbornville, NH 03872
POULOS, G(eorge) (NC) 3308 Northampton Dr, Greensboro, NC 27408

POUNDERS, Marci (Dal) St James Episcopal Church, 9845 McCree Rd, Dallas, TX 75238

POVEY, J Michael (Mass) 3901 Glen Oaks Drive E, Sarasota, FL 34232

POWELL, Anne Margrete (The Episcopal NCal) 20248 Chaparral Cir, Penn Valley, CA 95946

POWELL, Armistead Christian (Tex) 58 St. Andrews Dr., Jackson, MS 39211

POWELL, Arthur Pierce (NJ) 16 Copperfield Dr, Hamilton, NJ 08610

POWELL, Blanche Lee (Del) 304 Taylor Ave, Hurlock, MD 21643

POWELL, Brent Cameron (WTenn) 346 Hawthorne St, Memphis, TN 38112

POWELL, Catherine Ravenel (EC) 314 S. 4th St., Wilmington, NC 28401

POWELL, Christopher (Chi) Christ Church, 470 Maple St, Winnetka, IL 60093

POWELL, David Brickman (Ala) PO Box 467, Selma, AL 36702

POWELL, David Richardson (The Episcopal NCal) 122 Main, Cloverdale, CA 95425

POWELL, Elizabeth Jennings (Ala) P.O. Box 467, Selma, AL 36702

POWELL, Everett (Cal) 417 44th Ave, San Francisco, CA 94121

POWELL JR, Festus Hilliard (Ark) Po Box 21162, Hot Springs, AR 71903

✠ **POWELL**, Frank Neff (Ret Bp of SwVa 2013-) 295 W 22nd Ave, Eugene, OR 97405

POWELL, Gregory Lane (Eas) 29497 Hemlock Ln, Easton, MD 21601

POWELL, John Charles (NJ) 307 Red Lion Road, Southampton, NJ 08088

POWELL, John Lynn (Cal) 180 Westbury Cir Apt 327, Folsom, CA 95630

POWELL, Kenneth James (Cal)

POWELL, Lewis (The Episcopal NCal) 20248 Chaparral Cir, Penn Valley, CA 95946

POWELL, Marilyn (SC) 577 Water Turkey Retreat, Charleston, SC 29412

POWELL, Mark M (EC) St Andew's On-The-Sound Episcopal Church, 101 Airlie Rd, Wilmington, NC 28403

POWELL, Murray Richard (Tex) 951 Curtin St # 920564, Houston, TX 77018

POWELL JR, Peter Ross (Ct) 6 Gorham Ave, Westport, CT 06880

POWELL, Rita Teschner (Mass) Trinity Church Episcopal, 206 Clarendon St, Boston, MA 02116

POWELL, Robert Bingham (Ore) St Mary's Episcopal Church, 1300 Pearl St., Eugene, OR 97401

POWELL IV, Robert Jefferson (ETenn) 1101 N Broadway St, Knoxville, TN 37917

POWELL, Sydney Roswell (NY) 3405 Grace Ave, Bronx, NY 10469

POWELL, Tony (Fla) 657 SE 2nd Ave, Melrose, FL 32666

POWELL, William Vincent (Okla) 124 Randolph Ct, Stillwater, OK 74075

POWELL IV, Woodson Lea (NC) 560 Water Tower Road, Moncure, NC 27559

POWER, William Joseph Ambrose (Dal) 8011 Douglas Ave, Dallas, TX 75225

POWERS JR, Clarence Hall (LI) 139 Saint Johns Pl, Brooklyn, NY 11217

POWERS, David Allan (CGC) 959 Charleston St, Mobile, AL 36604

POWERS, Elizabeth Ann (SD) 209 S Main S, Chamberlain, SD 57325

POWERS, Fairbairn (Nwk) 531 Harrison Ave, Claremont, CA 91711

POWERS, John Carter (Okla) 2431 Terwilleger Blvd, Tulsa, OK 74114

POWERS, Lee (NJ) 119 St. Georges Drive, Galloway, NJ 08205

POWERS, Nancy Chambers (Dal) 1023 Addison Ave, Pottsboro, TX 75076

POWERS, Patricia Ann (SwFla)

POWERS, R(Oy) Stephen (SVa) 1829 Pittsburg Landing, Virginia Beach, VA 23464

POWERS, Sharon Kay (Mass) 49 Puritan Rd, Buzzards Bay, MA 02532

POZO, Francisco (NJ) 61 Kristopher Dr, Yardville, NJ 08620

POZZUTO, Keith Allen (Pgh) 220 8th St., Mckeesport, PA 15132

PRADAT, Paul Gidinias (Ala) 12200 Bailey Cove Rd SE, Huntsville, AL 35803

PRADAT, Ray William (Ala) 1747 Jack Warner Pkwy Apt 208, Tuscaloosa, AL 35401

PRAKTISH, Carl Robert (Va)

PRATER, Willard Gibbs (O) 50 Green St, Thomaston, ME 04861

PRATHER, Joel Allen (Mil) 503 E Walworth Ave, Delavan, WI 53115

PRATHER, Lynn (Ga) 3504 Professional Cir Ste A, Martinez, GA 30907

PRATI, Jason M (SO) PO Box 421, New Albany, OH 43054

PRATOR, Lloyd (Eugene) (NY) 15620 Riverside Dr W Apt 13i, New York, NY 10032

PRATT, Dorothy Louise (WNC) 84 Church Street, Franklin, NC 28734

PRATT JR, Earle Wilson (LI) 3240 N Caves Valley Path, Lecanto, FL 34461

PRATT, Grace Atherton (Va) 8009 Fort Hunt Rd, Alexandria, VA 22308

PRATT, Jennifer Julian (Oly) 2109 N Lafayette Ave, Bremerton, WA 98312

PRATT, Mary Florentine Corley (Vt) 865 Otter Creek Hwy, New Haven, VT 05472

PRATT-HORSLEY, Mary Elizabeth (ECR) 308 Lilac Dr, Los Osos, CA 93402

PRAY, Frederick Russell (NJ) 221 Ivy Rd, Edgewater Park, NJ 08010

PREAS, Barbara Jean (Nev) 10328 SUMMER RIVER AV., Las Vegas, NV 89144

PREBLE, Charles William (Minn) PO Box 844, Saint Joseph, MN 56374

PREBLE, Joan (Me) 55 Union St # 4606, Ellsworth, ME 04605

PRECHTEL, Daniel L (Chi) 2337 Greenwich Rd, San Pablo, CA 94806

PREECE, Mark W (Vt) 220 E 6th Ave, Conshohocken, PA 19428

PREGNALL, William Stuart (WA) 132 Lancaster Dr #410, Irvington, VA 22480

PREHM, Katherine T. (Spok) 3401 W Lincoln Ave, Yakima, WA 98902

PREHN III, Walter Lawrence (NwT) 5308 Carrington Ct, Midland, TX 79707

PRENDERGAST, James David (Los) 1325 Monterey Rd, South Pasadena, CA 91030

PRENTICE, David Ralph (Mass) 5 Bryant St, Wakefield, MA 01880

PRESCOTT, Vicki Lee (Roch) 2500 East Avenue, Apartment 5H, Rochester, NY 14610

PRESCOTT, W Clarke (Los) 8830 Mesa Oak Dr, Riverside, CA 92508

PRESLER, Henry Airheart (NC) Po Box 293, Monroe, NC 28111

PRESLER, Jane Crosby (Vt) 2534 Hill West Rd., Montgomery, VT 05471

PRESLER, Titus Leonard (Tex) PO Box 501, Montgomery, VT 05471

PRESSENTIN, Elsa Ann (EMich) 7562 Alex Ct, Freeland, MI 48623

PRESSEY, Stephen Palmer (Mich) 1792 Celeste Circle, Youngstown, OH 44511

PRESSLEY JR, Dennis Charles (Alb) Po Box 206, Greenwich, NY 12834

PREST JR, Alan Patrick Llewellyn (Va) 3920 Custis Rd, Richmond, VA 23225

PRESTEGARD, Joann (Oly) 55 Irving St, Cathlamet, WA 98612

PRESTON II, James Montgomery (Tex) 1310 Malmaison Ridge Dr, Spring, TX 77379

PRESTON, Leigh C (ETenn) 305 W 7th St, Chattanooga, TN 37402

PRESTON, Robert George (SeFla) 401 SW 6th Ave, Hallandale Beach, FL 33009

PRESTON, Shannon Elizabeth (Minn) 3737 Seminary Rd, Alexandria, VA 22304

PRETTI, Victoria (NJ) 893 Main St, West Newbury, MA 01985

PREVATT JR, Jim (NC) 5104 Ainsworth Dr, Greensboro, NC 27410

PREVOST, Edward Simpson (Chi) 6 Brookshire Rd, Worcester, MA 01609

PRICE, Ashburn Birdsall (CFla) 1781 Pocahontas Path, Maitland, FL 32751

PRICE, Barbara Deane (Ak)

PRICE, Barbara Jean (WNY) 77 Huntington Avenue, Buffalo, NY 14214

PRICE, Darwin Ladavis (LI) PO Box 280, Brewster, MA 02631

PRICE, David Lee (Oly) 15967 169th Ave Se, Monroe, WA 98272

PRICE, David William (Tex) 302 S Hardie St, Alvin, TX 77511

PRICE, George Harry (SeFla) 2300 Spanish River Rd, Boca Raton, FL 33432

PRICE, George N (Me) 290 Baxter Blvd Apt B3, Portland, ME 04101

PRICE, Gloria M (EC) 130 Quail Dr, Dudley, NC 28333

PRICE, Harold Thomas (Ky) 409 Wendover Ave, Louisville, KY 40207

PRICE, John Randolph (Md) 772 Ticonderoga Ave, Severna Park, MD 21146

PRICE, John W (Tex) 2312 Steel Street, Houston, TX 77098

PRICE, Joyce Elizabeth (WNC) 75 Echo Lake Dr, Fairview, NC 28730

PRICE, Kathleen (WA) 199 Rolfe Rd, Williamsburg, VA 23185

☩ **PRICE**, Kenneth Lester (Ret Bp Suffr of SO 2013-) 4754 Shire Ridge Rd. W, Hilliard, OH 43026

PRICE, Marston (Ct) 33 Old Field hill Rd. Unit48, Southbury, CT 06488

PRICE, Paul Alexander (Los) 113 Tierra Plano, Rancho Santa Margarita, CA 92688

PRICE, Phyllis Anne (Mass) 12191 Clipper Dr, Lake Ridge, VA 22192

PRICE, Raymond Estal (Wyo) 417 S 2nd St, Lander, WY 82520

PRICE JR, Richard Elwyn (WNC) 185 Macon Ave Apt A-3, Asheville, NC 28804

PRICE, Robert Paul (Tex) 1023 Compass Cove Cir, Spring, TX 77379

PRICE, Stephen Marsh (NY) 133 Grove Street, Peterborough, NH 03458

PRICE, Stephen W (Pa) 3724 E Fisherville Rd, Downingtown, PA 19335

PRICE, Susan Medlicott (Spok)

PRICE, Terrell Wells (Roch) 23 Main St, Geneseo, NY 14454

PRICHARD, Albert Hughes (WVa) 75 Old Cheat Rd, Morgantown, WV 26508

PRICHARD, Robert Walton (Va) Virginia Theological Seminary, 3737 Seminary Rd., Alexandria, VA 22304

PRICHARD, Thomas Morgan (Pgh) 809 18th St, Ambridge, PA 15003

PRICKETT, Gerald Stanley (WNC) 360 Asheville School Rd., Asheville, NC 28806

PRIDEMORE JR, Charles Preston (NY) PO Box 149, Ossining, NY 10562

PRIDGEN III, J(ohn) Blaney (USC) 170 Saint Andrews Rd, Columbia, SC 29210

PRIEST JR, W(Illiam) Hunt (Oly) 4400 86th Ave SE, Mercer Island, WA 98040

PRINCE, Elaine (Md) 10913 Knotty Pine Dr, Hagerstown, MD 21740

PRINGLE, Amy Fay (Los) 5332 Mount Helena Ave, Los Angeles, CA 90041

PRINGLE, Charles Derek (SVa) 419 Elizabeth Lake Dr, Hampton, VA 23669

PRINZ, Susan Moore (USC) 6408 Bridgewood Rd, Columbia, SC 29206

☩ **PRIOR**, Brian N (Bp of Minn 2010-) 1730 Clifton Place Suite 201, Minneapolis, MN 55403

PRIOR, John Gregory (RI) 7 Trillium Ln, Hilton Head Island, SC 29926

PRIOR, Randall Leavitt (Va) 9515 Holly Prospect Ct, Burke, VA 22015

PRITCHARD, David Gatlin (Ct) 16 Ashlar Vlg, Wallingford, CT 06492

PRITCHER, Joan Jean (At) 1098 Saint Augustine Pl Ne, Atlanta, GA 30306

PRITCHETT JR, Harry Houghton (NY) 1290 Peachtree Battle Ave Nw, Atlanta, GA 30327

PRITCHETT JR, James Hill (WNC) 209 Nut Hatch Loop, Arden, NC 28704

PRITTS, Clarence Edward (NJ) 7 E Maple Ave, Merchantville, NJ 08109

PRIVETTE, William Herbert (EC) 1119 Hendricks Ave., Jacksonville, NC 28540

PRIVITERA, Linda Fisher (Mass) 21 Marathon St, Arlington, MA 02474

PROBERT, Walter Leslie (Mil)

PROBST, David Charles (At) 139 Country Club Rd, Macon, GA 31210

PROCTOR, F(Rederick) Gregory (Miss) 4220 Oakridge Dr, Jackson, MS 39216

PROCTOR, Judith Harris (Va) St Paul's Episcopal Church, 228 S Pitt St, Alexandria, VA 22314

PROCTOR, Richard Gillespie (CGC) 4129 Oxford Ave., Jacksonville, FL 32210

PROFFITT, Darrel D (Tex) 1225 W Grand Pkwy S, Katy, TX 77494

PROFFITT III, John (Ark) 1608 McEntire Circle, Chatsworth, GA 30705

PROUD, James (Pa) 111 W Walnut Ln, Philadelphia, PA 19144

☩ **PROVENZANO**, Lawrence C (Bp of LI 2009-) Episcopal Diocese of Long Island, 36 Cathedral Avenue, Garden City, NY 11530

PROVINE, (Marion) Kay (Minn) 3424 Willow Ave, White Bear Lake, MN 55110

PRUITT, Albert Wesley (CGC) 729 Brown Pl, Decatur, GA 30030

PRUITT, Alonzo Clemons (Va) Saint Philip's Church, 2900 Hanes Ave, Richmond, VA 23222

PRUITT JR, George Russell (Md) 1246 Summit Ave SW, Roanoke, VA 24015

PRUITT, Mark James (O) Po Box 1910, Newport, RI 02840

PRUITT, R Allen (At) 301 N Greenwood St, Lagrange, GA 30240

PRUSKI, Dorota (Mil) St Andrew's Episcopal Church, 1833 Regent St, Madison, WI 53726

PRYNE, Carla Valentine (Oly) 1745 Ne 103rd St, Seattle, WA 98125

PUCA JR, Anthony J (NJ)

PUCHALLA, Daniel Andrew (Chi) 4180 N Marine Dr Apt 410, Chicago, IL 60613

PUCKETT, David Forrest King (Tex) 12535 Perthshire Rd, Houston, TX 77024

PUCKETT, Douglas Arnold (USC) 111 Aiken Rd # 323, Graniteville, SC 29829

PUCKLE, Donne Erving (Az) 125 E Kayetan Dr, Sierra Vista, AZ 85635

PUGH, Charles Dean (Md) 128 S Hilltop Rd, Catonsville, MD 21228

PUGH II, Joel Wilson (Ark) 9, The Close, Salisbury, SP12E B, Great Britain (UK)

PUGH III, Willard Jerome (HB) 1700 E 56th St Apt 3806, Chicago, IL 60637

PUGLIESE, Richard A (Spr) 744 Parker Road, West Glover, VT 05875

PUGLIESE, William Joseph (Ia) 108 Eden Way Ct, Cranberry Twp, PA 16066

PULIMOOTIL, Cherian Pilo (Va) 7124 Dijohn Court Dr, Alexandria, VA 22315

PULLIAM, James Millard (WMo) 80 Council Trl, Warrensburg, MO 64093

PUMMILL, Joe H (Cal) 2550 Dana St Apt 2D, Berkeley, CA 94704

PUMPHREY, Charles Michael (Ia) Naval Medical Center, Portsmouth, 620 John Paul Jones Cir, Portsmouth, VA 23701

PUMPHREY, David William (O) 2385 Covington Rd, Apt 201, Akron, OH 44313

PUMPHREY, John B (Del)

PUMPHREY, Margaret K (Del) 146 Fairhill Dr, Wilmington, DE 19808

PUMPHREY, Patricia Tilton (Nev) Trinity Episcopal Church, PO Box 2246, Reno, NV 89505

PUMPHREY, Thomas Claude (At) 64 Powderhorn Dr, Phoenixville, PA 19460

PUNNETT, Ian Case (Minn) 901 Portland Ave, Saint Paul, MN 55104

PUNZO, Thomas Edward (WMo) 7055 N Highland Ct, Gladstone, MO 64118

PUOPOLO JR, Angelo Joseph (SO) 2366 Kemper Ln, 1801 Rutland Ave., Cincinnati, OH 45207

PURCELL, Christine Funk (RI) Christ Church, 7 Elm St, Westerly, RI 02891

PURCELL, Mary Frances Fleming (Lex) 835 Pinkney Dr, Lexington, KY 40504

PURCELL-CHAPMAN, Diana Barnes (Roch) Po Box 492, Wellsville, NY 14895

PURCHAL, John Jeffrey (LI) 45 Willow St. Apt. 420, Springfield, MA 01103

PURDOM III, Allen Bradford (O) 6809 Mayfield Rd Apt 1071, Cleveland, OH 44124

PURDUM, Ellen Echols (At) 3098 Saint Annes Ln Nw, Atlanta, GA 30327

PURDY, James Hughes (Mo) 53 Chaminade Dr, Saint Louis, MO 63141

PURDY, Thomas Clayton (Ga) Christ Church, 6329 Frederica Rd, Saint Simons Island, GA 31522

PURKS III, Jim (Ga) c/o St Paul's Episcopal Church, 212 N Jefferson St, Albany, GA 31701

PURNELL, Erl Gould (Ct) 46 Overlook Ter, Simsbury, CT 06070

PURNELL, Susan Ann (Los) 19682 Verona Ln, Yorba Linda, CA 92886

PURRINGTON, Sandra Jean (NMich) 201 E Ridge St, Marquette, MI 49855

PURSER, J Philip (USC) 635 Timberlake Dr, Chapin, SC 29036

PURSLEY, George William (SO) 332 Mount Zion Rd NW, Lancaster, OH 43130

PURVIS, Howard Byrd (SVa) 245 Dexter St E, Chesapeake, VA 23324

PURVIS, R(obert) David (Ind) 31 Hampshire Ct, Noblesville, IN 46062

PURYEAR, Jim (SwFla) 339 Meadow Beauty Ct, Venice, FL 34293

PURYEAR, Sarah Elizabeth (Tenn) St. George's Episcopal Church, 4715 Harding Rd, Nashville, TN 32705

PUTMAN, Richard Byron (Ala) 408 Thornberry Cir, Birmingham, AL 35242

PUTNAM, Kevin Todd (Cal) 849 Spruance Ln, Foster City, CA 94404

PUTNAM, Sarah (Sally) Thompson (SC) Po Box 888, Marion, SC 29571

PUTNAM, Thomas Clyde (Ia) 397 Huron Ave, Cambridge, MA 02138

PUTZ, Shirley (Joyce) B(aynham) (Nev) 1453 Rawhide Rd, Boulder City, NV 89005

PYATT, Petrina Margarette (NJ) 100 East Maple Ave, Penns Grove, NJ 08069

PYLES, Christopher V (CPa) 120 W Lamb St, Bellefonte, PA 16823

PYRON JR, Nathaniel (Mo) 1422 Shady Creek Ct, Saint Louis, MO 63146

Q

QUACKENBUSH, Margaret Haight (Alb) Rr 1 Dunbar Road, Cambridge, NY 12816

QUAINTON, Rodney F (Chi) 1725 Northfield Square, Northfield, IL 60093

QUATORZE, Jean Lenord (Hai)

QUEEN, Jeffrey (Lex) 3 Chalfonte Place, Fort Thomas, KY 41075

QUEEN, Laura Virginia (Los) Church Pension Group, 19 E 34th St, New York, NY 10016

QUEEN JR, William L (Va) 8639 Brown Summit Rd, Richmond, VA 23235

QUEHL-ENGEL, Catherine Mary (Ia) 103 Oak Ridge Dr Se, Mount Vernon, IA 52314

QUESENBERRY-NELSON, Jane E (Minn) 4903 Maple Grove Rd, Hermantown, MN 55811

QUEVEDO-BOSCH, Juan A (LI) 3014 Crescent St S, Astoria, NY 11102

✠ **QUEZADA MOTA**, Moises (DR (DomRep)) Calle Costa Rica No 21, Ens. Ozama, Santo Domingo, Dominican Republic

QUICK, Judy Goins (Ala) 224 Bentley Cir, Shelby, AL 35143

QUIGGLE, George Willard (Ala) 384 Windflower Dr, Dadeville, AL 36853

QUIGLEY, James E (WA) St Alban's Church, 3001 Wisconsin Ave NW, Washington, DC 20016

QUILA GARCIA, Pedro Perfecto (EcuC) Box 235, Tena, Ecuador

QUILL, Margaret M (Chi) Guardian Angels of Elk River, Inc., 400 Evans Avenue, Elk River, MN 55330

QUIN, Alison Joan (NY) 3021 State Route 213 E, Stone Ridge, NY 12484

QUINBY, Congreve H. (Alb) 51 High Grove Ct, Burlington, VT 05401

QUINES JR, Brent B (Los) The Parish of Holy Trinity and St Benedict, 412 N Garfield Ave, Alhambra, CA 91801

QUINN, Carolee Elizabeth Sproull (USC) 1402 Wenwood Ct, Greenville, SC 29607

QUINN, Catherine Alyce Rafferty (Nwk) 66 Pomander Walk, Ridgewood, NJ 07450

QUINN, Eugene Frederick (WA) 5702 Kirkside Dr, Chevy Chase, MD 20815

QUINN, Michele (Colo) 3153 S Forest St, Denver, CO 80222

QUINN, Peter Darrell (Ct) 120 Ford Ln, Torrington, CT 06790

QUINN, Scott Thomas (Pgh) 537 Hamilton Rd, Pittsburgh, PA 15205

QUINNELL, Carolyn Tingle (CFla) Po Box 2373, Belleview, FL 34421

QUINNELL, Robert Douglass (CFla) Po Box 2373, Belleview, FL 34421

QUINNEY, Sarah Howell (The Episcopal NCal) 2351 Pleasant Grove Blvd, Roseville, CA 95747

QUINONEZ-MERA, Juan Carlos (EcuC)

QUINTON, Dean Lepidio (Nev) FCI La Tuna - Religious Services Dept, 8500 Doniphan Dr House 17, Anthony, TX 79821

QUIROGA, Luis Alberto (LI) 14755 Sw 154th Ct, Miami, FL 33196

R

RAASCH, Timothy D (Minn) 408 N 7th St, Brainerd, MN 56401

RABAGO-NUNEZ, Luis Antonio (U) 1211 N Redwood Rd Apt 165, Salt Lake City, UT 84116

✠ **RABB**, John Leslie (Ret Bp Suffr of Md 2010-) 4 E University Pkwy, Baltimore, MD 21218

RABY, Edith Gilliam (CFla) 111 S Church St, Smithfield, VA 23430

RACHAL, Paula Choquette (NC) 2803 Watauga Dr, Greensboro, NC 27408

RACHAL, Robert T (NC) 2803 Watauga Dr, Greensboro, NC 27408

RACINE, Jean-Joel (Hai) Box 1309, Port-Au-Prince, Haiti

RACIOPPI, Gerard Andrew (Nwk) 73 S Fullerton Ave, Montclair, NJ 07042

RACKLEY, M Kathryn (O) 41 Owen Brown St, Hudson, OH 44236

RACUSIN, Michele (Episcopal SJ) 5267 San Jacinto Ave, Clovis, CA 93619

RADANT, William F (Mil) PO Box 442, Manitowish Waters, WI 54545

RADCLIFF III, Cecil Darrell (CFla) 3010 Big Sky Blvd, Kissimmee, FL 34744

RADCLIFF, Irene Evelyn (SO)

RADCLIFFE, Ernest Stanley (Oly) 3732 Colonial Ln Se, Port Orchard, WA 98366

RADCLIFFE JR, William Eugene (Md) 2846 Angus Circle, Molino, FL 32577

RADKE, Pamela Kay (Nev) St Matthew's Episcopal Church, 4709 S Nellis Blvd, Las Vegas, NV 89121

RADLEY, C(harles) Perrin (Me) 3701 R St NW, Washington, DC 20007

RADNER, Ephraim Louis (Colo) 410 W 18th St, Pueblo, CO 81003

RADTKE, Warren Robert (Mass) 32 Breakwater Cv, Chelsea, MA 02150

RADZIK, David Robert (Alb) 2424 S 90th St, Milwaukee, WI 53227

RAEHN, J Sid (CFla) 106 Jim Dedmon Rd, Dyer, TN 38330

RAFFALOVICH, Francis Dawson (Dal) 306 Cobalt Cv, Georgetown, TX 78633

RAFFERTY, Joseph Patrick (Be) 220 Montgomery Ave, West Pittston, PA 18643

RAFFERTY, Robert Douglas (NMich) 421 Cherry St, Iron River, MI 49935

RAFTER, John Wesley (Me) PO Box 527, Camden, ME 04843

RAGAN, Raggs (Ore) 640 Southshore Blvd., Lake Oswego, OR 97034

RAGLAND, Rebecca B (Mo) 7401 DELMAR BLVD, UNIVERSITY CITY, MO 63130

RAGSDALE, Eliza Robinson (SeFla) 1750 E Oakland Park Blvd, Fort Lauderdale, FL 33334

RAGSDALE, James Lewis (Colo) 3143 S Nucla St, Aurora, CO 80013

RAGSDALE, Katherine Hancock (Mass) 99 Brattle St, Cambridge, MA 02138

RAHHAL, Michele Duff (Okla) 721 Franklin Dr, Ardmore, OK 73401

RAHM, Kent David (Va) 6604 Willow Pond Dr, Fredericksburg, VA 22407

RAHN, Gaynell M (Va) 905 Princess Anne St, Fredericksburg, VA 22401
RAICHE, Brian Michael (Mass) 26 White St, Haverhill, MA 01830
RAIH, Donald Roger (WVa) 250 N Marsham St, Romney, WV 26757
RAILEY, Robert Macfarlane (NMich) 3029 N Lakeshore Blvd, Marquette, MI 49855
RAINING, Hillary D (Pa) 226 Righters Mill Rd, Gladwyne, PA 19035
RAINS JR, Harry James (WNC) 8 Nicole Lane, Weaverville, NC 28787
RAISH, John Woodham (WLa) 211 Linden St, Shreveport, LA 71104
RAJ, Vincent S (ECR) P.O. Box 551, Carmel Valley, CA 93950
RAJAGOPAL, Doris Elizabeth (Pa) 763 Valley Forge Rd, Wayne, PA 19087
RALPH, Michael Jay (LI) 28 Highland Rd, Glen Cove, NY 11542
RALPH, S Lester (Mass) 88 King St, Reading, MA 01867
RALSTON, Betty Marie (Colo) Po Box 773627, Steamboat Springs, CO 80477
RALSTON, D Darwin (O) 711 College Ave, Lima, OH 45805
RAMAN, Neil K (LI)
RAMBO JR, Charles B (CFla) Po Box 46, Rutherfordton, NC 28139
RAMBO, Thomas Birch (Spok) 323 Catherine St, Walla Walla, WA 99362
RAMERMAN, Diane Gruner (Oly) 1216 7th St, Anacortes, WA 98221
RAMEY, Bernard Cayce (Va) St Alban's Episcopal Church, 6800 Columbia Pike, Annandale, VA 22003
RAMEY, Lloyd Francis (Ore) 1444 Liberty St Se, Salem, OR 97302
RAMIREZ, Lucia (PR)
RAMIREZ, Mark Lloyd (Chi) St Barnabas Episc Church, 22W415 Butterfield Rd, Glen Ellyn, IL 60137
RAMIREZ-MILLER, Gerardo Carlos (NY) 351 W 24th St Apt 6-C, New York, NY 10011
RAMIREZ-NIEVES, Aida Iris (VI) PO Box 1796, Kingshill, 00851-1796, Virgin Islands (U.S.)
RAMIREZ-SEGARRA, Cesar E (PR) PO Box 1967, Yauco, PR 00698-1967, Puerto Rico
RAMNARAINE, Barbara Allen (Minn) St. Luke's Episcopal Church, 4557 Colfax Ave. 5, Minneapolis, MN 55403
RAMOS, Leon (PR)
RAMOS, Mary Serena (Minn) 700 S 2nd Street, Unit 41, Minneapolis, MN 55401
RAMOS, Pablo (U) 1904 Dale Ridge Ave, Salt Lake City, UT 84116
RAMOS, Waldemar F (PR)
RAMOS-GARCIA, Ramon (PR)
✠ **RAMOS-ORENCH**, Wilfrido (Bp Provsnl of PR 2013-) 77 Linnmoore St, Hartford, CT 06114

RAMSAY, Frederick Jeffress (Md) 20637 N 56th Ave., Glendale, AZ 85308
RAMSDEN, Charles Leslie (Cal) 1266 139th Ave, San Leandro, CA 94578
RAMSEY, Henry Elrod (WMass) 57 Loomis Dr Apt A1, West Hartford, CT 06107
RAMSEY, Ronald E (SVa) 8 Meacham Rd, Cambridge, MA 02140
RAMSEY, Walter Albert (Cal) 162 Hickory St, San Francisco, CA 94102
RAMSEY-MUSOLF, Michael Jeffrey (Los) Department Of Physics, U. Mass Amherst, 710 N Pleasant St 416, Amherst, MA 01003
RAMSHAW, Lance Arthur (Del) 106 Alden Rd, Concord, MA 01742
RAMSHAW, Lynn Cecelia Homeyer (Chi) 12 Jolynn Drive, Ormond Beach, FL 32174
RAMSTAD, Philip Robert (Minn) 901 Como Boulevard East, #304, Osceda, WI 54020
RANDALL, Anne Elizabeth (Dal) 421 Custer Rd, Richardson, TX 75080
RANDALL, Catharine Louise (Ct) 91 Minortown Rd, Woodbury, CT 06798
RANDALL II, Chandler Corydon (SanD)
RANDALL, Elizabeth Penney (Colo) 735 S Vine St, Denver, CO 80209
RANDALL, Richard Alan (CPa) 222 N 6th St, Chambersburg, PA 17201
RANDALL JR, Robert James (SVa) 716 Abbey Dr, Virginia Beach, VA 23455
RANDALL, Sarah Archais (Mass) P.O. Box C, Duxbury, MA 02331
RANDLE, Cameron D (SVa) 6125 Carlos Ave, Los Angeles, CA 90028
RANDOLPH, Barry Trent (Mich) 231 E Grand Blvd, Detroit, MI 48207
RANDOLPH JR, Henry George (NI) 26824 CR 4, Elkhart, IN 46514
RANEY III, A Raymond (RG) 04 Tano Road, Santa Fe, NM 87506
RANK, Andrew Peter Robert (SanD) Po Box 34548, San Diego, CA 92163
RANKIN, Annette Reiser (Cal) 10 Old Mill St, Mill Valley, CA 949410
RANKIN, Deborah Truman (O) 2220 Second St., Cuyahoga Falls, OH 44221
RANKIN, Edward H(arris) (Oly) 11510 NE 35th Ave, Vancouver, WA 98686
RANKIN, Glenn Edger (Ia) 2206 Frontier Rd, Denison, IA 51442
RANKIN, Jerry Dean (Kan) 406 Hillside St, Abilene, KS 67410
RANKIN II, William Wright (Cal) 13 Mara Vista Ct, Tiburon, CA 94920
RANKIN-WILLIAMS, Chris (Cal) Po Box 217, Ross, CA 94957
RANNA, Claire Dietrich (Cal) 2325 Union St, San Francisco, CA 94123
RANNENBERG, Pamela Lamb (RI) 442 Wickford Point Rd, North Kingstown, RI 02852

RANSOM, Charles Wilfred (O) 716 Coshocton Ave, Mount Vernon, OH 43050
RANSOM, James Clifford (Md) PO Box 26, 41 Atwood Rd, Wilmot, NH 03287
RANSOM, Lisa Michelle (Vt) 2016 Us Rr 2, Waterbury, VT 05676
RAO, Chitra Dasu Sudarshan (Los) 10833 Le Conte Ave, Los Angeles, CA 90095
RAPP, Phillip James (WK) 6529 Clifton Rd, Clifton, VA 20124
RARDIN, Thomas Michael (Tex) 332 Oklahoma Ave, Hewitt, TX 76643
RASCHKE, Gerald Wesley (Spr) 2921 Haverford Rd, Springfield, IL 62704
RASCHKE, Vernon Joseph (SD) 625 W Main, Lead, SD 57754
RASICCI, Michael Dominic (Chi) 222 S Batavia Ave, Batavia, IL 60510
RASKE, L (Mo) 4916 Jamieson Ave., Apt.2A, Saint Louis, MO 63109
RASKOPF, Roger William (LI) 1250 Newport Dr., Oconomowoc, WI 53066
RASMUS, John Edward (Eau) 5318 Regent St, Madison, WI 53705
RASMUS, Paul A (SeFla) 3740 Holly Dr, Palm Beach Gardens, FL 33410
RASMUSSEN, Cynthia M (Roch) 215 Parkview Dr, Rochester, NY 14625
RASMUSSEN, Jeanne Louise (Az) 520 N Pokegama Ave, Grand Rapids, MN 55744
RASMUSSEN, Rik Lorin (The Episcopal NCal) St Paul's Episcopal Church, 1430 J St, Sacramento, CA 95814
RASNER, Richard Lewis (Me) 143 State St, Portland, ME 04101
RASNICK, Kenneth Wayne (Mich)
RASNICK, Thomas James (ETenn) 6804 Glenbrook Cir, Knoxville, TN 37919
RATCLIFF, Elizabeth Rogers (WLa)
RATHBONE, Cristine F (Mass) 138 Tremont St., Boston, MA 02111
RATHBUN JR, Arthur John (Kan) 138 S 8th St, Salina, KS 67401
RATHMAN, William (SC) 251 South Sea Pines Drive, Unit 1924, Hilton Head Island, SC 29928
RATLIFF, Ruth Evelyn (Ia) St Luke's Episcopal Church, 2410 Melrose Dr, Cedar Falls, IA 50613
RAU, Michael S (Pa) St Mark's Episcopal Church, 111 Oenoke Rdg, New Canaan, CT 06840
RAULERSON, Aaron D (Ala) 910 Kayla Drive, Trussville, AL 35173
RAUSCHER JR, William V. (NJ) 663 N Evergreen Ave, Woodbury, NJ 08096
RAVEN, Margaret Hilary (NJ) 324 Edgewood Dr, Toms River, NJ 08755
RAVNDAL III, Eric (CFla) 1302 Country Club Oaks Cir, Orlando, FL 32804
RAWLINS, Patrick Allister (LI) 744 Havemeyer Ave, Bronx, NY 10473

RAWLINSON, John Edward (Cal) 891 Dowling Blvd, San Leandro, CA 94577

RAWSON, William Leighton (Nwk) 10960 Big Canoe, Jasper, GA 30143

RAY, Alice Marie (USC) St Mary's Episcopal Church, 170 Saint Andrews Rd, Columbia, SC 29210

RAY, Andrew Michael (Pgh) PO Box 38342, Pittsburgh, PA 15238

RAY, Douglass E (Colo) 5601 Collins Ave Apt 1511, Miami Beach, FL 33140

RAY, Harvey H (Cal) 1354 Primavera Dr E, Palm Springs, CA 92264

RAY, John Sewak (At) 4808 Glenwhite Dr, Duluth, GA 30096

RAY, Mauldin Alexander (Okla) 1763 E 56th St, Tulsa, OK 74105

RAY, Michael Fleming (Ct) 830 Whitney Avenue, New Haven, CT 06511

RAY, Philip Carroll (NwT) 1608 Monte Vista St, Dalhart, TX 79022

✠ **RAY**, Rayford Jeffrey (Bp of NMich 2011-) 9922 U 65 Lane, Rapid River, MI 49878

RAY, Suzanne Patricia (NMich) 9922 U 65 Lane, Rapid River, MI 49878

✠ **RAY**, Thomas Kreider (Ret Bp of NMich 1999-) 250 Partridge Bay Trl, Marquette, MI 49855

RAY, Wanda Louise (O) 312 Park St, Huron, OH 44839

RAY, Wayne Allen (Miss) 116 Siowan Ave, Ocean Springs, MS 39564

RAYBOURN JR, Fred Loren (Neb) 1204 Sunshine Blvd, Bellevue, NE 68123

RAYBURG-ELLIOTT, Jason Alan (WNY) 128 Pearl St, Buffalo, NY 14202

RAYE, Janice Marie (Md) 32 Main St, Westernport, MD 21562

RAYLS, John William (WTex) PO Box 6885, San Antonio, TX 78209

RAYMOND, Patrick R (Chi) 647 Dundee Ave, Barrington, IL 60010

RAYMOND, Seth Allen (Mil) Christ Episcopal Church, 5655 N Lake Dr, Whitefish Bay, WI 53217

RAYMOND, Sue Ann (Ia) Lot 17A, 1771 Golf Course Blvd., Independence, IA 50644

RAYSA, Mary G (SO)

RAZEE, George Wells (Ct) 234 Essex Mdws, Essex, CT 06426

RAZIM, Genevieve Turner (Tex)

RAZZINO, Robin G (WA) 703 Tennessee Ave Apt 102, Alexandria, VA 22305

REA, Robert Allen (NC) 1226 21st Ave, San Francisco, CA 94122

READ, Allison (Ct) 300 Summit St, Hartford, CT 06106

READ, David Glenn (WTex) 11 Saint Lukes Ln, San Antonio, TX 78209

READ, Nancy Ann (Nwk) 12 Northfield Ter, Clifton, NJ 07013

READ II, Philip Daugherty (SwFla) 11698 Pointe Cir, Fort Myers, FL 33908

REANS, Douglas J (NJ) 512 Sycamore Ter, Cinnaminson, NJ 08077

REARDIN, Lois Arline (NC) 221 Union St, Cary, NC 27511

REASONER, Rand Lee (Los) 5700 Rudnick Ave, Woodland Hills, CA 91367

REAT, Lee Anne (SO) 2318 Collins Dr, Worthington, OH 43085

REBHOLTZ, Brian L (Mass) 79 Denton Rd, Wellesley, MA 02482

RECHTER, Elizabeth I (Los) 2744 Peachtree Rd Nw, Atlanta, GA 30305

RECTENWALD, Marion Bridget (SD) 371 New College Dr, Sewanee, TN 37375

REDDALL, Jennifer Reddall (NY) 500 E 77th St Apt 1622, New York, NY 10162

REDDELL, Ronald Kirk (Oly) 910 Harris Ave Unit 408, Bellingham, WA 98225

REDDICK, Mary Jane (Tex) 2525 Seagler Rd, Houston, TX 77042

REDDIE, Grover Tyrone (Alb) 11192 State Route 9W, Coxsackie, NY 12051

REDDIG, Mike (Cal) 716 Cabrillo St, San Francisco, CA 94118

REDDIMALLA, Samuel (NY) 4673 Flatlick Branch Drive, Chantilly, VA 20151

REDDING, Pamela (Cal) 2925 Bonifacio Street, Concord, CA 94519

REDFIELD, William (CNY) 225 Pelham Rd, Syracuse, NY 13214

REDMAN, Nolan Bruce (Spok) 3020 E Flintlock Ct, Mead, WA 99021

REDMON, Caroline (Los) 1050 E Ramon Rd Unit 125, Palm Springs, CA 92264

REDMON, William Jessie (Md) 1050 E Ramon Rd Unit 125, Palm Springs, CA 92264

RED OWL, Cordelia (SD) Po Box 354, Porcupine, SD 57772

REDPATH, Valerie Tolocka (NJ) 329 Estate Point Rd, Toms River, NJ 08753

REECE, Herbert Anderson (O) 9522 Lincolnwood Dr, Evanston, IL 60203

REECE, Jennifer (Me) 41 Mount Desert St, Bar Harbor, ME 04609

REECE, Mark Spencer (SeFla) Iglesia Catedral del Redentor, Calle Beneficencia #18, Madrid, 28004, Spain

REECE, Nathaniel Treat (Mass) 60 Edward Rd, Raynham, MA 02767

REECE, Richard Douglas (WVa) 387 Homestead Lane, Romney, WV 26757

REED, Allan William (Pa) 4270 Biddeford Cir, Doylestown, PA 18902

REED, Anne L(Ouise) (SO) Diocese of Southern Ohio, 412 Sycamore St., Cincinnati, OH 45202

REED, Bobette P (O) Deer Hill Rr#1, East Hampton, CT 06424

REED, C Davies (Ind) St. Christopher's Church, 1402 W. Main Street, Carmel, IN 46032

REED, Charlotte Collins (SO) 409 E High St, Springfield, OH 45505

REED, Craig Andrew (Dal) 9714 Lanward Dr, Dallas, TX 75238

✠ **REED**, David (Ret Bp of Ky 1994-) 5226 Moccasin Trl, Louisville, KY 40207

✠ **REED**, David Mitchell (Bp Suffr of WTex 2006-) P. O. Box 6885, San Antonio, TX 78209

REED, Elizabeth H (Be) 108 N 5th St, Allentown, PA 18102

REED, Harold Vincent (Alb) 1718 Guilderland Ave, Schenectady, NY 12306

REED SR, James Arthur (WVa) 884 6th Street Hill, Newell, WV 26050

REED, James Gardner (Va) 6013 Hot Spring Ln, Fredericksburg, VA 22407

REED, Jeffrey Bruce (Az) Po Box 42618, Tucson, AZ 85733

REED, Juan Y (Chi) 1617 E 50th Place, Apt 4D, Chicago, IL 60615

REED, Loreen Hayward Rogers (At) 355 Porter St, Madison, GA 30650

REED JR, Poulson Connell (Az) 6300 N Central Ave, Phoenix, AZ 85012

REED, Richard Wayne (RG) Hc 31 Box 17-B, Las Vegas, NM 87701

REED, Robert Cooper (NwPa) 119 Forrest Rd., New Castle, PA 16105

REED, Ronald Lind (Kan) 4810 W 67th St, Prairie Village, KS 66208

REED, Stephen Kim (Ak) 1722 Linden St, Longmont, CO 80501

REED, Thomas Louis (Pa) 16 Nestlenook Dr, Middleboro, MA 02346

REEDER, Thomas Parnell (Fla) 400 San Juan Dr, Ponte Vedra, FL 32082

REEMAN, Karen Baehr (NJ) 69 Broad St, Eatontown, NJ 07724

REES, Donald Joseph (Episcopal SJ) 12358 Newport Rd, Ballico, CA 95303

REES, Elizabeth (Va) 1501 River Farm Dr, Alexandria, VA 22308

REES, Emily Frances (At) Po Box 223, Braselton, GA 30517

REESE, Carol Sue (Chi) 1525 W Birchwood Ave, Chicago, IL 60626

REESE, Donnis Jean (EMich) 200 E Page St, Rose City, MI 48654

REESE, Frederic William (Miss) 373 Edenbrook, Brookhaven, MO 39601

REESE, Jeannette (WNC) 45 Spooks Branch Extension, Asheville, NC 28804

REESE, John (SwFla) 509 E Twiggs St, Tampa, FL 33602

REESE, John Victor (Ark) 406 W Central Ave, Bentonville, AR 72712

REESE, Judith Foster (WTenn) 1215 State Street, Bowling Green, KY 42101

REESE, Mary (EC) 404 E. New Hope Rd., Goldsboro, NC 27534

REESE, Robert Emory (WNC) 45 Spooks Branch Ext, Asheville, NC 28804

REESE, Thomas Francis (LI) 141 Ascan Ave, Forest Hills, NY 11375

REESON, Geoffrey Douglas (EcuC) Casilla 17-16-95, Quito, Ecuador

REESON, Marta Lidia (EcuC) Casilla 17-16-95, Quito, Ecuador

REEVE, Keith John (NC) 3613 Clifton Ct, Raleigh, NC 27604

REEVE, Susan M. (The Episcopal NCal) 146 Saint Gertrude Ave, Rio Vista, CA 94571

REEVES, Daniel John (NC) 1737 Hillandale Rd, Durham, NC 27705

REEVES, Diane Delafield (Fla) 13588 Northeast 247th Lane, Box 18, Orange Springs, FL 32182

REEVES, Frank B (FtW) 2204 Collington Dr, Roanoke, TX 76262

REEVES, Jack William (LI) 23 Old Mamaroneck Rd Apt 5R, White Plains, NY 10605

REEVES, Jess L (SeFla) 8619 North Liston Avenue, Kansas City, MO 64154

REEVES, Robin K (Tex) 523 E 4th St, Tyler, TX 75701

REEVES JR, William (Va) The Collegiate Schools, Richmond, VA 23229

REGAN, Thomas Francis (SD) 708 Sawyer St, Lead, SD 57754

REGAS, George Frank (Los) 807 Las Palmas Rd., Pasadena, CA 91105

REGEN, Catharine Louise Emmert (Tenn) 306 Broadview Dr, Dickson, TN 37055

REGER, Timothy Scott (CNY) 210 E Genesee St # 3, Fayetteville, NY 13066

REGISFORD, Sylvanus Hermus Alonzo (SeFla) 7580 Derby Ln, Shakopee, MN 55379

REGIST, Antonio Alberto (WTex) 1310 Pecan Valley Dr, Antonio, TX 78210

REHAGEN, Gerald Anthony (EMich) 2093 Michaywe Dr, Gaylord, MI 49735

REHBERG, Gloria Irene (RG) 7104 Montano Rd Nw, Albuquerque, NM 87120

REHBERG, Gretchen (Spok) Church of the Nativity, 731 8th St., Lewiston, ID 83501

REHO, James Hughes (SwFla) Lamb Of God Episcopal Church, 19691 Cypress View Dr, Fort Myers, FL 33967

REICH, Jeffrey Walker (Miss) 834 N. 5th Ave, laurel, MS 39440

REICHARD, Bernice Dorothy (Be) P.O. Box 368, Trexlertown, PA 18087

REICHERT, Elaine Starr Gilmer (Cal) 1605 Vendola Dr, San Rafael, CA 94903

REICHMAN, Amy L (Ct) PO Box 698, Sharon, CT 06069

REICHMANN, Jeffrey Harold (At) 26 Oakwood Ct, Jacksonville Beach, FL 32250

REID, Brian S (NwPa) 415 4th Ave, Warren, PA 16365

REID, Catharine Brannan (Oly) 1123 19th Ave East, Seattle, WA 98112

REID, Dennis (Pa) 9325 West St, Manassas, VA 20110

REID, Franklin Lionel (NY) 1064 E 219th St, Bronx, NY 10469

REID, Gordon (Pa) 1027 Arch St, Apt 406, Philadelphia, PA 19107

REID, Jennie Lou Divine (SeFla) 3840 Alhambra Ct, Coral Gables, FL 33134

REID, M Sue (Oly) 315 Burns Lane, Williamsburg, VA 23185

REID, Michael Edgar (ECR) 146 12th St, Pacific Grove, CA 93950

REID, Paul Dewitt (Pa) 7809 Old York Rd, Elkins Park, PA 19027

REID JR, Raymond W (SeFla) 11852 Chaparral Dr, Frisco, TX 75035

REID, Richard P (NI) 44591 San Rafael Ave, Palm Desert, CA 92260

REID, Richard William (Vt) Po Box 70070, North Dartmouth, MA 02747

REID-LEVY, Schelly (Md)

REIDT, Donna J (Vt) 13 East Main St, Wilmington, VT 05363

REILEY, Jennifer B S (Mass) 48 Prospect St, North Andover, MA 01845

REIMER, Leslie Graff (Pgh) 5426 Wilkins Ave, Pittsburgh, PA 15217

REIMER, Susan Elizabeth (FdL) 100 N Drew St, Appleton, WI 54911

REIN, Lily Anne Beggs (At) 1105-L Clairemont Ave, Decatur, GA 30030

REINECKE, Roderick Laury (NC) 3810 Heritage Dr Rm 104, Burlington, NC 27215

REINERS JR, Alwin (Va) 1600 Westbrook Ave, Richmond, VA 23227

REINERS, Diane (NY)

REINHARD, Kathryn Louise (NY) Christ Church, 84 Broadway, New Haven, CT 06511

REINHARDT, Constance (WA) 27 Broad St, Newburyport, MA 01950

REINHEIMER, John Jay (NH) 227 W 6th St, Port Clinton, OH 43452

REINHEIMER, Philip Schuyler (The Episcopal NCal) 13948 Gold Country Drive, Penn Valley, CA 95945

REINHOLZ, Andrew C (Be)

REINHOLZ, Kimberly A (Be) Christ Church, 205 N 7th St, Stroudsburg, PA 18360

REINKEN, Dirk Chrisian (NJ) 1628 Prospect St, Ewing, NJ 08638

REISCHMAN, Charles J (Spr) 4767 Redbud Ct, Decatur, IL 62526

REISHUS, John William (WMich) 5161 E 50 N, Kokomo, IN 46901

REISNER, Terry Ralph (Dal)

REISS, Gerald Anthony (NJ) 1048 Detweiler Ave, Hellertown, PA 18055

REJOUIS, Mary Kate (Colo) 2700 University Heights Ave, Boulder, CO 80302

RELLER, Wilfred Herman (Colo) 71 Aspen Ln, Golden, CO 80403

RELYEA, Michael Johl (NY) 127b east terminal blvd, Atlantic Beach, NC 28512

REMBOLDT, Cherry Ann (SanD) 47535 State Highway 74, Palm Deset, CA 92260

REMENTER, Nancy Sandra (CPa) 239 E Market St, Marietta, PA 17547

REMER, Douglas E (SwFla) Saint John's Church, 906 South Orleans Avenue, Tampa, FL 33606

REMINGTON, Melissa E (WVa) 821 Edgewood Dr, Charleston, WV 25302

REMPPEL, Paulette Evelyn (NY) 52 Brookside Pl, New Rochelle, NY 10801

REMY, Joseph Michel Jean (Hai) 5935 Del Lago Circle, Sunrise, FL 33313

RENCHER, Ollie Vernell (NC) St Peter's Church, 115 W 7th St, Charlotte, NC 28202

RENDON OSPINA, Gonzalo Antonio (Colom) Cra 80 No. 53a-78, Medelin Antioquia, 99999, Colombia

RENEGAR, Douglas Mcbane (Ga) 224 Lakefield Rd., Waterloo, SC 29384

RENFREW, William Finch (Mich) 2101 Wellesley Dr, Lansing, MI 48911

RENGERS, Josiah Daniel (Ala) 109 Woodcrest Circle, Eutaw, AL 35462

RENICK, Van Taliaferro (SwVa) 170 Mountain Ave, Rocky Mount, VA 24151

RENN, Wade Allan (Nwk) 558 Highland Ave, Upper Montclair, NJ 07043

RENNA, Pamela Stacey (EMich) 123 N Michigan Ave, Saginaw, MI 48602

REPLOGLE, Jennifer (Chi) 33 Mercer St, Princeton, NJ 08540

REPP, Daniel Steven (NI) St Pauls Episcopal Church, 312 E Main St, Plymouth, WI 53073

REPP, Jeanette Marie (Los) 1648 W 9th St, San Pedro, CA 90732

RESSLER, Richard (SD) St. Paul's Episcopal Church, 309 S. Jackson St., Jackson, MI 49201

RETAMAL, M Regina (Mass) 59 Lawrence St, Framingham, MA 01702

RETTGER, John Hubbard (Minn) 65 - 104th Avenue Northwest, Coon Rapids, MN 55448

RETZLAFF, Georg (USC) 1612 Goldfinch Ln, West Columbia, SC 29169

REUMAN, Eugene Frederic (CFla) 2915 W Henley Ln, Dunnellon, FL 34433

REUSCHLING, Walter Edward (Eas) 108 Oak St, Cambridge, MD 21613

REUSS, Patricia Ann Osborne (WNC)

REUSS, Robert Julius (WNC) 133 Liberty Ct, Oak Ridge, TN 37830

REVEL, Anna Carter (Ky) 5146 Sunnybrook Dr, Paducah, KY 42001

REX III, Charles Walton (Chi) 2739 Prairie Ave, Evanston, IL 60201

REXFORD, William Nelson (Mich) 7213 Meadow Wood Way, Clarksville, MD 21029

REYES, Jesus (ECR) P.O. Box 1903, Monterey, CA 93942

REYES, Juan Pastor (WA) 3001 Wisconsin Ave NW, Washington, DC 20016

Clergy List

REYES PEREZ, Jose R (WMass) 6744 S Kings Hwy, Alexandria, VA 22306
REYNES, Stephen Alan (Vt)
REYNOLDS, Bettye (The Episcopal NCal) 4706 Oakbough Way, Carmichael, CA 95608
REYNOLDS JR, Edward Charles (Mich) 2112 Melrose Road, Ann Arbor, MI 48104
REYNOLDS, Eleanor Francis (Nwk) PO Box 240, Mendham, NJ 07945
REYNOLDS, Frederic William (Roch) 579 Sagamore Ave Unit 84, Portsmouth, NH 03801
REYNOLDS, Gail Ann (Kan) 9119 Dearborn St, Overland Park, KS 66207
REYNOLDS SR, Gordon (Me)
REYNOLDS, James Ronald (FtW) 3717 Cook Ct, Fort Worth, TX 76244
REYNOLDS, Joe Douglas (Tex) 2929 Westheimer Rd Apt 610, Houston, TX 77098
REYNOLDS, Katharine Sylvia (Minn) Loring Green East, 1201 Yale Place #610, Minneapolis, MN 55403
REYNOLDS, Kay (ETenn) 4017 Sherry Dr, Knoxville, TN 37918
REYNOLDS, Max Midgley (WTex) 4485 Medina Hwy, Kerrville, TX 78028
REYNOLDS, Richard Seaver (Los) 2407 Jasmine Lane, Killeen, TX 76549
REYNOLDS, Robert Eugene (Cal) 6832 Treeridge Dr, Cincinnati, OH 45244
REYNOLDS, Roger James (Ore) 18271 SW Ewen Dr, Aloha, OR 97003
REYNOLDS JR, Wallace Averal (CFla) 500 W Stuart St, Bartow, FL 33830
REZACH, Karen Beverly (Nwk) 74 Edgewood Pl, Maywood, NJ 07607
REZIN, Mary Ellen (Eau) 27042 State Highway 21, Tomah, WI 54660
RHEA, Pamela Towery (Miss) 318 College St, Columbus, MS 39701
RHEA, Robert Eugene (Tenn)
RHOADES, Mary Ann (Chi) PO Box 494, Dixon, IL 61021
RHOADES, Stephen James (USC) Saint James Episcopal Church, 301 Piney Mountain Rd, Greenville, SC 29609
RHOADS, Robert Louis (Oly) 181 W Maple St, Sequim, WA 98382
RHOADS, Tommy L (WTenn) 309 E Baltimore St, Jackson, TN 38301
RHODENHISER, Imogen Leigh (Mich) 1010 Urban Ave Apt B, Durham, NC 27701
RHODENHISER, James Cousins (Mich) St. Clare of Assisi Episcopal Church, 2309 Packard Road, Ann Arbor, MI 48104
RHODES, Charlotte Dimmick (CFla) 414 Pine St, Titusville, FL 32796
RHODES, David Hughes (SanD) 47535 Highway 74, Palm Desert, CA 92260

RHODES, Diane Lynn (Nwk) 38 Lynn St, Harrington Park, NJ 07940
RHODES, Erroll Franklin (Cal) 19 Comly Ave, Greenwich, CT 06831
RHODES, Judith L (Ct) 661 Old Post Rd, Fairfield, CT 06824
RHODES, Margaret Diana Clark (WMo) 1815 NE Independence Ave, Lees Summit, MO 64086
RHODES JR, Robert Richard (SO) 9 Harrington Ave., Westwood, NJ 07675
RHODES, Robert Wayne (Oly) 300 W 8th Street Unit 314, Vancouver, WA 98660
RICE, Charles Lynvel (Nwk) 618 Quaker Plain Rd, Bangor, PA 18013
✠ **RICE**, David C (Bp of SJ 2014-) Diocese Of San Joaquin, 1528 Oakdale Rd, Modesto, CA 95355
RICE, Debra Harsh (WNC) PO Box 2319, Franklin, NC 28744
RICE, Edward G (NH) 37 Harbor Way Unit 13, Wolfeboro, NH 03894
RICE JR, Frank G(racey) (Tenn) 4901 Timberhill Dr, Nashville, TN 37211
RICE, Glenda Ann (Ak) PO Box 1130, Sitka, AK 99835
RICE, John David Sayre (WNC) 51 North View Circle, Hayesville, NC 28904
RICE JR, John Fay (Va) 240 Old Main St, South Yarmouth, MA 02664
RICE, Lawrence Allen (NMich) 5526 S Baker Side Rd, Sault Sainte Marie, MI 49783
RICE, Randolf James (ECR) 2534 Dumbarton Ave, San Jose, CA 95124-717
RICE, Rodney Vincent (NY) 914 Adana Road, Pikesville, MD 21208
RICE, Sandra Kay (Md) Retired, Frederick, MD 21701
RICE, Steven Christopher (NC) 2575 Parkway Dr, Winston Salem, NC 27103
RICE, Whitney Elizabeth (Ind) St. David's Episcopal Church, P.O. Box 1798, Nashville, IN 47448
RICE, Winston Edward (La) 512 E Boston St, Covington, LA 70433
RICH III, Edward Robins (SwFla) 11315 Linbanks Pl, Tampa, FL 33617
RICH JR, Ernest Albert (Az) 10625 W White Mountain Rd, Sun City, AZ 85351
RICH, Michael Glenn (Ala) 408 Church Ave SE, Jacksonville, AL 36265
RICH, Nancy Willis (O) 2499 Kingston Rd, Cleveland Heights, OH 44118
RICH, Noel D. (Minn) 808 Eldo Ln SW, Alexandria, MN 56308
RICH, Susan Chandler (EMich) Grace Episcopal Church, 735 W. Nepessing, Lapeer, MI 48446
RICH, Timothy Thayer (RI) St Luke's Episc Ch, 99 Pierce St, East Greenwich, RI 02818

RICH, William Warwick (Mass) 333 Ricciuti Drive Unit 1526, Quincy, MA 02169
RICHARD, Helen Taylor (Ore) 123 Grove St, Lebanon, OR 97355
RICHARD, Mary B (WLa) PO Box 1627, Shreveport, LA 71165
RICHARDS, Anne Frances (NY) 150 west end ave apt. 9h, new york, NY 10023
RICHARDS, Anne Marie (RI) 7 Cowsill Ln, Newport, RI 02840
RICHARDS, Daniel P (WMich) 529 W 10th St, Traverse City, MI 49684
✠ **RICHARDS**, David Emrys (Ret Bp of CR 1968-) 625 N Greenway Dr, Coral Gables, FL 33134
RICHARDS, Dennison S. (LI) 107-66 Merrick Blvd, Jamaica, NY 11433
RICHARDS, Edward Thomas (CGC) PO Box 7359, Panama City Beach, FL 32413
RICHARDS, Emily Barr (Pa) 654 N Easton Rd, Glenside, PA 19038
RICHARDS, Erin Kathleen (ND) 301 Main St S, Minot, ND 58701
RICHARDS, Fitzroy Ivan (Oly) 12499 Eagle Dr, Burlington, WA 98233
RICHARDS JR, George Richard (Roch) 18 Haviland Dr, Scotia, NY 12302
RICHARDS, Gerald Wayne (Be) 265 Old Mine Rd, Lebanon, PA 17042
RICHARDS, Jeffery Martin (O) 2510 Olentangy Dr, Akron, OH 44333
RICHARDS, Michael Gregory (Los) Po Box 220383, Newhall, CA 91322
RICHARDS, Rosalie Neal (Ct) 536 Old Glen Avenue, Berlin, NH 03570
RICHARDS, Susan M (Pa) 1074 BROADMOOR RD, BRYN MAWR, PA 19010
RICHARDSON, Carolyn Garrett (SanD) 3515 Lomas Serenas Dr., Escondido, CA 92029
RICHARDSON, Christopher Cyril (SO) 2151 Dorset Rd., Columbus, OH 43221
RICHARDSON, David Anthony (Az) 3111 Silver Saddle Dr, Lake Havasu City, AZ 86406
RICHARDSON, Ellen H (Ga) 112 Island Creek Ln, Savannah, GA 31410
RICHARDSON JR, Grady Wade (Ala) 605 Country Club Dr, Gadsden, AL 35901
RICHARDSON, James (The Episcopal NCal) 1700 University Ave, Charlottesville, VA 22903
RICHARDSON, Janet Beverly (Ind) 310 Del Mar Dr, Lady Lake, FL 32159
RICHARDSON, Jeffrey Roy (SC)
RICHARDSON JR, John Dowland (CGC) 19 Gaywood Circle, Birmingham, AL 35213
RICHARDSON, John Marshall (WMo) 23405 S Waverly Rd, Spring Hill, KS 66083
RICHARDSON, Jon (Pa) 3820 the Oak Rd, Philadelphia, PA 19129

RICHARDSON, Marcia Ann Kelley (Me) 6 Jewett Cove Rd, Westport Is, ME 04578

RICHARDSON, Mary (Cal) 5833 College Ave, San Diego, CA 92120

RICHARDSON, Michael William (Colo) 16181 Parkside Dr, Parker, CO 80134

RICHARDSON, Susan (Pa) 20 N American St, Philadelphia, PA 19106

RICHARDSON, W Mark (Cal) Church Divinity School of the Pacific, 2451 Ridge Rd, Berkeley, CA 94709

RICHAUD III, Reynold Hobson (Tenn) P.O. Box 808, Townsend, TN 37882

RICHEY, Donald Delose (Ct) 99 Willowbrook Rd, Cromwell, CT 06416

RICHEY, Leon Eugene (O) 2727 Barrington Dr, Toledo, OH 43606

RICHMOND III, Allen Pierce (Ak) 2602 Glacier St, Anchorage, AK 99508

RICHMOND, John David (Spr) 4105 S Lafayette Ave, Bartonville, IL 61607

RICHMOND, Seth Gunther (Colo) 460 Prospector Ln, Estes Park, CO 80517

RICHMOND, Susan Odenwald (Mass) 197 8th St Apt 801, Charlestown, MA 02129

RICHNOW, Douglas Wayne (Tex) 4014 Meadow Lake Ln, Houston, TX 77027

RICHTER, Amy Elizabeth (Md) St. Anne's Episcopal Church, 199 Duke of Gloucester St, Annapolis, MD 21401

RICHTER, Kerlin J (Ore) 399A Himrod St, Brooklyn, NY 11237

RICHTER JR, William Thompson (Tex) 2929 Woodland Hills Dr, Kingwood, TX 77339

RICK II, John William (Ct) 625 S St Andrews Pl, Los Angeles, CA 90005

RICKARD, Robert Burney (At) 1228 Whitlock Ridge Dr Sw, Marietta, GA 30064

RICKARDS JR, Joseph A (Ind) Spring Mills, 109 Jamestown Dr, Falling Waters, WV 25419

RICKARDS, Reese Stanley (Eas) 115 Nentego Dr, Fruitland, MD 21826

✠ **RICKEL**, Gregory Harold (Bp of Oly 2007-) 3209 42nd Ave SW, Seattle, WA 98116

RICKENBAKER, Thomas Michele (EC) Box 548, Edenton, NC 27932

RICKER, Mark Stanley (Eau) St Andrews Episcopal Church, PO Box 427, Ashland, WI 54806

RICKETTS, Linda Harriet (Mass) 12607 Cascade Hls, San Antonio, TX 78253

RICKETTS, Marcia Carole Couey (NwT) 133 Olivias Ct, Tuscola, TX 79562

RICKETTS, Nancy Lee (Tex) 1500 N Capital of Texas Hwy, Austin, TX 78746

RICKEY, David (Cal) 430 29th Ave, San Francisco, CA 94131

RICO, Bayani Depra (The Episcopal NCal) 2420 Tuolumne St, Vallejo, CA 94589

RIDDICK, Daniel Howison (SwVa) 240 Blackwater Ridge Ln, Glade Hill, VA 24092

RIDDLE III, Charles Morton (SVa) 1102 Botetourt Gdns Apt B-5, Norfolk, VA 23507

RIDDLE, Hill Carter (La) 1515 Robert St, New Orleans, LA 70115

RIDDLE, Jennifer Lynne (Ala) 530 Hurst Rd, Odenville, AL 35120

RIDEOUT, Robert Blanchard (SO) 7121 Muirfield Dr., Dublin, OH 43017

RIDER, David M (NY) 11 Suzanne Ln, Chappaqua, NY 10514

RIDER, Joseph Frank (CFla) Diocese of New York, 1047 Amsterdam Ave, New York, NY 10025

RIDER, Paul G (Minn) 401 S 1st St Unit 610, Minneapolis, MN 55401

RIDER, Wm Blake (NY) Episcopal Diocese of New York, 1047 Amsterdam Ave, New York, NY 10025

RIDGE, Charles Searls (Oly) 2658 48th Ave SW, Seattle, WA 98116

RIDGWAY, George Edward (The Episcopal NCal) 3371 Avington Way, Shasta Lake, CA 96019

RIDGWAY, Michael Wyndham (ECR) 365 Stowell Ave, Sunnyvale, CA 94085

RIEBE, Norman William (SanD) 5633 Chalyce Ln, Charlotte, NC 28270

RIEDELL, William George (Cal) 3012 S Fox St, Englewood, CO 80110

RIEGEL, John Wilfred (Pa) Po Box 288, Bailey Island, ME 04003

RIEGEL, Robert Gambrell (USC) 1100 Sumter St, Columbia, SC 29201

RIERDAN, Jill Elizabeth (WMass) 128 Main St, Easthampton, MA 01027

RIETH, Sarah Melissa (NC) 500 East Rhode Island Avenue, Southern Pines, NC 28387

RIETMANN, Paul David (Oly) 3615 N Gove St, Tacoma, WA 98407

RIFFEE, Charles Alexander (Va) 1205 W Franklin St, Richmond, VA 23220

RIGGALL, Daniel John (Me) Po Box 165, Kennebunk, ME 04043

RIGGALL, George Gordon (CGC) 3811 Old Shell Rd., Mobile, AL 36608

RIGGIN, John Harris (CGC) 4051 Old Shell Rd, Mobile, AL 36608

RIGGINS, Patricia Readon (WTex) 1310 Pecan Valley Dr, San Antonio, TX 78210

RIGGLE JR, John Field (SwFla) 9267 Sun Isle Dr Ne, Saint Petersburg, FL 33702

RIGGS, Katherine Grace (WTex) 311 W Nottingham Dr Apt 332, San Antonio, TX 78209

RIGHTMYER, Thomas Nelson (WNC) 16 Salisbury Dr 7304, Asheville, NC 28803

RIIS, Susan Hollis (SO) 144884 Harbor Dr E, Thornville, OH 43076

RIKER JR, William Chandler (Nwk) 249 Hartshorne Rd, Locust, NJ 07760

RILEY, Diane Napolitano (Nwk)

RILEY, Elizabeth Rawlings (Cal)

RILEY, George Daniel (NY) 39 Minnesota Ave, Long Beach, NY 11561

RILEY, Gregg Les (WLa) P.O. Box 2031, Alexandria, LA 71309

RILEY JR, James Foster (Minn) 132 Maj Hornbrook Road, Christchurch, Canterbury, New Zealand (Aotearoa)

RILEY, John C (SVa) 1333 Jamestown Rd, Williamsburg, VA 23185

RILEY, Mark Douglass (SVa) 3928 Pacific Ave, Virginia Beach, VA 23451

RILEY, Reese Milton (Los) 1414 East Grovemont, Santa Ana, CA 92705

RIMASSA, Paul Stephen (NJ) 215 Briner Ln, Hamilton Square, NJ 08690

RIMER, Kathleen Pakos (Mass) 330 Brookline Ave., Boston, MA 02115

RIMKUS, William Allen (Chi) 14755 Eagle Ridge Dr, Homer Glen, IL 60491

RINCON, Virginia M (Me) 121 Margaret St Apt C, South Portland, ME 04106

RINEHART, James Arnold (Be) 1318 Howard Ave, Pottsville, PA 17901

RINES, Charles T (The Episcopal NCal) 3641 Mari Dr, Lake Elsinore, CA 92530

RING, Bonnie (Cal) 2011 Carlos Street, Moss Beach, CA 94038

RING, Tony (Eau) W10601 Pine Rd, Thorp, WI 54771

RINGLAND, Robin Lynn (Oly) 415 S 18th St, Mount Vernon, WA 98274

RIOS, Austin Keith (Eur) Diocese of Western North Carolina, 900-B Centre Park Dr., Asheville, NC 28805

RIOS, Lajunta Michelle (Tex) Trinity Episcopal Church, 5010 N Main St, Baytown, TX 77521

RIOS QUEVEDO, Jose F (PR)

RISARD, Frederick William (Episcopal SJ) 1541 Bristol Ln, Hanford, CA 93230

RISK III, James Lightfoot (Chi) 901 N Delphia Ave, Park Ridge, IL 60068

RITCHIE, Anne Gavin (Va) 1002 Janney's Lane, Alexandria, VA 22302

RITCHIE, Harold L (Fla) 12013 SW 1st St, Micanopy, FL 32667

RITCHIE, Patricia Ritter (Tex) 4090 Delaware St, Beaumont, TX 77706

RITCHIE, Robert Joseph (Pa) 7712 Brous Ave, Philadelphia, PA 19152

RITCHIE, Sandra Lawrence (Pgh) 1808 Kent Rd, Pittsburgh, PA 15241

RITCHINGS, Frances Anne (Pa) 50 Quail Meadow Rd, Placitas, NM 87043

RITONIA, Ann M (WA) 680 Racebrook Rd, Orange, CT 06477

RITSON, Veronica Merita (Az) 6556 N Villa Manana Dr, Phoenix, AZ 85014

RITTER, Christine E (Pa) 1771 Sharpless Rd, Meadowbrook, PA 19046

RITTER, Cindy A (Okla) 1604 S Fir Ave, Broken Arrow, OK 74012

RITTER, Kenneth Phillip (La) 11 Country Club PL, Baton Rouge, LA 70809

Clergy List

RITTER, Nathan (LI) 414 E Broad St, Westfield, NJ 07090

RIVAS, Vidal (WA) Episcopal Church House, Mount Saint Alban, Washington, DC 20016

RIVERA, Aristotle C (Cal) PO Box 101, Brentwood, CA 94513

✠ RIVERA, Bavi Edna (Bp Provsnl of EO 2010-) PO Box 1548, The Dalles, OR 97058

RIVERA, Jorge Juan (PR)

RIVERA, Marcos Antonio (CFla)

RIVERA-GEORGESCU, Ana Maria (Alb) St. James Episcopal Church, 14216 NYS RT 9N, Au Sable Forks, NY 12912

RIVERA PEREZ, Francisco Javier (PR) PO Box 902, Saint Just, PR 00978-0902, Puerto Rico

RIVERA-RIVERA, Luis Antonio (NY) 550 W 155th St, New York, NY 10032

RIVERA RIVERA, Luis Guillermo (PR)

RIVERA-RODRIGUEZ, Angel (PR)

RIVEROS MAYORGA, Jose Aristodemus (Colom) c/o Diocese of Colombia, Cra 6 No. 49-85 Piso 2, Bogota, BDC, Colombia

RIVERS, Barbara White Batzer (Pa) 378 Paoli Woods, Paoli, PA 19301

RIVERS, David Buchanan (Pa) 148 Heacock Ln, Wyncote, PA 19095

RIVERS, John (WNC) 55 Wingspread Dr, Black Mountain, NC 28711

RIVERS III, Joseph Tracy (Pa) 2902 Monterey Ct, Springfield, PA 19064

RIVET, E J (Colo) 46 North Ridge Court, Parachute, CO 81635

RIVETTI, Mary Elisabeth (Spok) 1500 Ne Stadium Way, Pullman, WA 99163

RIVOLTA, Agostino Cetrangolo (NJ) 69 Broad St, Eatontown, NJ 07724

RIZNER, Andrew Robert (ETenn) 3669 Ivy Way, Sevierville, TN 37876

ROACH, Kenneth Merle (Fla) 92 Atari Rd, Waynesville, NC 28786

ROACH, Michelle Mona (CFla)

ROACH, Robert Eugene (Alb) 8 Brookwood Dr, Clifton Park, NY 12065

ROADMAN, Betsy Johns (NY) 91 Mystic Dr, Ossining, NY 10562

ROAF, Phoebe Alison (Va) 2900 Hanes Ave, Richmond, VA 23222

ROANE, Wilson Kessner (FdL) E2382 Pebble Run Rd, Waupaca, WI 54981

ROARK III, Harry A (La) St Paul's Episcopal Church, 200 Riverside Ave, Riverside, CT 06878

ROBAYO-HIDALGO, Daniel Dario (Va) Emmanuel Episcopal Church, 660 S. Main St., Harrisonburg, VA 22801

ROBB, George Kerry (SeFla) 521 Rhine Rd, Palm Beach Gardens, FL 33410

ROBBINS, Anne Wilson (SO) 10831 Crooked River Rd., #101, Bonita Springs, FL 34135

ROBBINS, Buckley Howard (ETenn) 781 Shearer Cove Rd, Chattanooga, TN 37405

ROBBINS, Charlotte Ann (ND) 3600 25th St. S., Fargo, ND 58104

ROBBINS, Herbert John (RG) 104 East Circle Drive, Ruidoso Downs, NM 88346

ROBBINS, Janice M (ETenn) 3425 Alta Vista Dr, Chattanooga, TN 37411

ROBBINS, Lance David (Roch) 1130 Webster Rd, Webster, NY 14580

ROBBINS, Mary Elizabeth (Tex) 562 Elkins lk, Huntsville, TX 77340

ROBBINS-COLE, Adrian (Mass) Saint Andrew's Church, 79 Denton Rd, Wellesley, MA 02482

ROBBINS-COLE, Sarah Jane (Mass) 49 Concord St, Peterborough, NH 03458

ROBBINS-PENNIMAN, Sylvia Beckman (SwFla) Church of the Good Shepherd, 639 Edgewater Dr, Dunedin, FL 34698

ROBERSON, Mary Moore Mills (USC) 3123 Oakview Rd, Columbia, SC 29204

ROBERT, Mary Christopher (CGC) 551 W Barksdale Dr, Mobile, AL 36606

ROBERTS, Alice (NH) 2 Moore Rd, Newport, NH 03773

ROBERTS, Charles Jonathan (SwFla) Calvary Episcopal Church, 1615 First St., Indian Rocks Beach, FL 33785

ROBERTS, George C (Ct) Saint James Episcopal Church, 3 Mountain Rd, Farmington, CT 06032

ROBERTS, Harold Frederick (Miss) 7417 Falcon Cir., Ocean Springs, MS 39564

ROBERTS III, Henry Pauling (EC) 260 Houser Road, Blacksburg, SC 29702

ROBERTS, James Beauregard (Miss) 2441 S Shore Dr, Biloxi, MS 39532

ROBERTS, J(Ames) Christopher (Mont) PO BOX 2020, Helena, MT 59624

ROBERTS, Jason Thomas (WTex) 8642 Cheviot Hts, San Antonio, TX 78254

ROBERTS JR, John Bannister Gibson (CFla) 860 Ohlinger Rd, Babson Park, FL 33827

ROBERTS, Jose F (RI)

ROBERTS, Judith Sims (Ind) 342 Red Ash Cir, Englewood, FL 34223

ROBERTS, Katherine Alexander (At) 18 Clarendon Ave, Avondale Estates, GA 30002

ROBERTS, Kim Elaine (Neb) 2312 J St, Omaha, NE 68107

ROBERTS, Linda Lee (Mont) 16404 72nd St, Plattsmouth, NE 68048

ROBERTS III, Malcolm (EC) 520 Taberna Way, New Bern, NC 28562

ROBERTS, Mollie M (Ala) 3702 Mays Bend Rd., Pell City, AL 35128

ROBERTS, Patricia Joyce (Ia) 3226 S Clinton St, Sioux City, IA 51106

ROBERTS, Patricia Kant (CFla) 35 Willow Dr, Orlando, FL 32807

ROBERTS, Paul Benjamin (At) 33 Cross Crk E, Dahlonega, GA 30533

ROBERTS, Peter Francis (CFla) 5500 N Tropical Trl, Merritt Island, FL 32953

ROBERTS, Steven Michael (La) 1613 7th St, New Orleans, LA 70115

ROBERTS, Susan Jean (U) 261 S 900 E, Salt Lake City, UT 84102

ROBERTS, Suzanne Grondin (Me) 143 State St, Portland, ME 04101

ROBERTS, William Allan (Ida) 1336 E Walker St, Blackfoot, ID 83221

ROBERTS, William D (Chi) 720 Ambria Drive, Mundelein, IL 60060

ROBERTS, William Tudor (Mich) 584 E Walled Lake Dr, Walled Lake, MI 48390

ROBERTSHAW III, Arthur Bentham (Ct) 88 Notch Hill Rd Apt 240, North Branford, CT 06471

ROBERTSHAW, Michelle Lyn (SwFla) St Andrew's Episcopal Church, PO Box 272, Boca Grande, FL 33921

ROBERTSON, Amanda (NC) 2701 Park Rd, Charlotte, NC 28209

ROBERTSON IV, Ben G. (Miss) The Chapel Of The Cross, 674 Mannsdale Rd, Madison, MS 39110

ROBERTSON, Bruce Edward (NMich) 452 Silver Creek Rd, Marquette, MI 49855

ROBERTSON, Charles Kevin (Az) 815 2nd Avenue, New York, NY 10017

ROBERTSON, Claude Richard (Ark) 1605 E Republican Rd, Jacksonville, AR 72076

ROBERTSON JR, Edward Ray (La) 212 Spencer Ave, New Orleans, LA 70124

ROBERTSON, Frederick W (Kan) 626 E Montclaor St Apt 1D, Springfield, MO 65807

ROBERTSON, James Bruce (WMo) 4824 Bell Street, Kansas City, MO 64112

ROBERTSON, John Brown (EC) St Timothy's Epis Church, 107 Louis St, Greenville, NC 27858

ROBERTSON, John Edward (Minn) 38378 Reservation Highway 101, PO Box 369, Morton, MN 56270

ROBERTSON, Josephine (Tex) St John's Kirkland, 105 State St S, Kirkland, WA 98033

ROBERTSON, Karen (Suzi) Sue (FtW) 1757 244th Ave NE, Sammamish, WA 98074

ROBERTSON, Marilyn Sue (Okla) 127 NW 7th St, Oklahoma City, OK 73102

ROBERTSON, Patricia Rome (Oly) 313 Bromley Place NW, Bainbridge Island, WA 98110

ROBESON, Terry A. Luzuk (Wyo) 665 Cedar St, Lander, WY 82520

ROBILLARD, Roger M (Va) 400 S Cedar Ave, Highland Springs, VA 23075

ROBINSON, Allen Florence (Md) 2729 Moores Valley Dr, Baltimore, MD 21209

ROBINSON, Carla Lynn (Oly) 15220 Main St, Bellevue, WA 98007

ROBINSON, Charles Allen (SVa) 2124 Benomi Dr., Williamsburg, VA 23185

ROBINSON, Charles Edward (U) PO Box 981208, Park City, UT 84098

ROBINSON, Chris (Miss) PO Box 1001, McComb, MS 39649

ROBINSON, Constance Wiegmann (Eas) 5820 Haven Ct, Rock Hall, MD 21661

ROBINSON, Cristopher Allan (WTex) 1621 Santa Monica St, Kingsville, TX 78363

ROBINSON, David Gordon (Eas) 5820 Haven Ct, Rock Hall, MD 21661

ROBINSON JR, David Gordon (NH) 1035 Lafayette Rd, Portsmouth, NH 03801

ROBINSON, David Kerr (Me) Po Box 7554, Ocean Park, ME 04063

ROBINSON, David Scott (Pa) 603 Misty Hollow Dr, Maple Glen, PA 19002

ROBINSON, Dorothy Linkous (Tex) 7700 Pleasant Meadow Cir, Austin, TX 78731

ROBINSON, Franklin Kenneth (Ct) 305 Golden Ginkgo Lane, Salisbury, MD 21801

ROBINSON, Fredrick Arthur (SwFla) 222 South Palm Avenue, Sarasota, FL 34236

ROBINSON, Grant Harris (Minn) 1840 University Ave W Apt 413, Saint Paul, MN 55104

ROBINSON JR, Henry Jefferson (Fla) 314 Glen Ridge Ave, 939 Beach Dr. NE Unit 1502, Temple Terrace, FL 33617

ROBINSON, Janet Rohrbach (Ga) 3565 Bemiss Rd., Valdosta, GA 31605

ROBINSON, Joseph Oliver (Mass) Po Box 1366, Jackson, MS 39215

ROBINSON, Katherine Sternberg (Wyo) 2350 S Poplar St, Casper, WY 82601

ROBINSON, Linda Gail Herring Hornbuckle (Ala) 6324 Woodlake Dr., Buford, GA 30518

ROBINSON, Mark Kilbourne Jeffrey (Ct) 82 Shore Rd, Old Lyme, CT 06371

ROBINSON, Michael Eric (Mass) 171 Goddard Ave, Brookline, MA 02445

ROBINSON, Michael Kevin (Ark) 305 Pointer Trl W, Van Buren, AR 72956

ROBINSON, Paula Patricia (Mo) 123 S 9th St, Columbia, MO 65201

ROBINSON, Sonja (EC) 1009 Midland Dr, Wilmington, NC 28412

ROBINSON, Sybil Clara Frances (Mil) 8301 Old Sauk Rd Apt 321, Middleton, WI 53562

✠ **ROBINSON**, V Gene (Ret Bp of NH 2013-) Diocese Of New Hampshire, 63 Green St., Concord, NH 03301

ROBINSON JR, Virgil Austin Anderson (Chi) 1527 Chapel Ct, Northbrook, IL 60062

ROBINSON-COMO, Glenice (Tex) 1117 Texas St, Houston, TX 77002

ROBISON, Bruce Monroe (Pgh) 5801 Hampton Street, Pittsburgh, PA 15206

ROBISON, Jeannie (Ala) Church of the Nativity, 208 Eustis Ave SE, Huntsville, AL 35801

ROBISON, Sandra L(ee) (Spok) 1407 Thayer Dr, Richland, WA 99354

ROBLES, Lawrence Arnold (ECR) 651 Broadway, Gilroy, CA 95020

ROBLES-GARCIA, Daniel (DR (DomRep))

ROBSON, David John (CPa) 2985 Raintree Rd, York, PA 17404

ROBSON, John Merritt (Neb) 1620 Atlas Ave, Lincoln, NE 68521

ROBY JR, Jesse (Mich) 1550 Cherboneau Pl Apt 202, Detroit, MI 48207

ROBYN, Richard James (Pa) 6901 Rising Sun Ave, Philadelphia, PA 19111

ROCCOBERTON, Marjorie Ruth Smith (Ct) 82 Shoddy Mill Rd, Bolton, CT 06043

ROCK, Ian Eleazar (VI) PO Box 28, Tortola, VI VG1110, British Virgin Islands

ROCK, Jean-Baptiste Kenol (NY) 3061 Bainbridge Ave, Bronx, NY 10467

ROCK, J Konrad (WK) 706 E 74th Ave, Hutchinson, KS 67502

ROCK, John Sloane (Minn) PO BOX 1178, Bemidji, MN 56619

ROCKABRAND, Walter Ralph (Okla) 7928 Roundrock Rd, Dallas, TX 75248

ROCKMAN, Jane Linda (NJ) 559 Park Ave, Scotch Plains, NJ 07076

ROCKWELL, Cristine V (WMass) 51 Perkins St, Springfield, MA 01118

✠ **ROCKWELL**, Hays H. (Ret Bp of Mo 2002-) Po Box 728, West Kingston, RI 02892

ROCKWELL, Melody Neustrom (Ia) 220 40th St NE, Cedar Rapids, IA 52402

ROCKWELL, Raymond Eugene (Alb) 50 Sacandaga Rd, Scotia, NY 12302

ROCKWELL III, Reuben L (CGC) 4051 Old Shell Road, Mobile, AL 36608

ROCKWELL, Sarah (NH) 10 Pond Rd, Derry, NH 03038

ROCKWOOD, David Alan (Ak) Po Box 23003, Ketchikan, AK 99901

RODDY, Bonnie Joia (Ore) 266 4th Ave, #601, Salt Lake City, UT 84103

RODDY, Jack Edward (Ore) 266 4th Ave. Apt 601, Salt Lake City, UT 84103

RODENBECK, Benjamin Daniel (Az) Trinity Episcopal Church, PO Box 590, Kingman, AZ 86402

RODGERS, Billy W(ilson) (CFla) 13465 SE 93rd Court Rd, Summerfield, FL 34491

RODGERS, Paul Benjamin (Mass) 359 Elm St, Dartmouth, MA 02748

RODGERS, Peter R (Ct) 400 Humphrey St, New Haven, CT 06511

RODGERS, Stephen M (NY) 14160 SW Teal Blvd. 32 B, Beaverton, OR 97008

RODIN, Carol Jane Strandoo (Oly) Christ Episcopal Church, 1216 7th St, Anacortes, WA 98221

RODMAN, Edward Willis (Mass) 8 Yorks Rd, Framingham, MA 01701

RODMAN, Janet Laura (EC) 218 Fairway Drive, Washington, DC 27889

RODMAN, Reginald Cary (Ore) 10434 Brackenwood Ln NE, Bainbridge Island, WA 98110

RODMAN III, Samuel Sewall (Mass) 112 Randolph Ave, Milton, MA 02186

RODRIGUES, Theodore Earl (EO) P.O. Box 2206, Sisters, OR 97759

RODRIGUEZ, Albert R (Tex) 2503 Ware Rd, Austin, TX 78741

RODRIGUEZ, Christopher Michael (CFla) 2365 Pine Ave, Vero Beach, FL 32960

RODRIGUEZ, Hector Raul (Md) 6960 Sunfleck Row, Columbia, MD 21045

RODRIGUEZ, Isaias Arguello (At) 3004 Mccully Dr NE, Atlanta, GA 30345

RODRIGUEZ, Luis (NH) 519 N Douty St, Hanford, CA 93230

RODRIGUEZ, Ramiro (Los) 7540 Passons Blvd, Pico Rivera, CA 90660

RODRIGUEZ ESPINEL, Neptali (Minn) 1524 Summit Ave, Saint Paul, MN 55105

RODRIGUEZ-HOBBS, Joshua Alan (Md) Episcopal Church of the Good Shepherd, 1401 Carrollton Ave, Ruxton, MD 21204

RODRIGUEZ-PADRON, Francisco M (LI) 418 50th St, Brooklyn, NY 11220

RODRIGUEZ SANCHEZ, Mario Hiram (PR) 1308 Ave Paz Granela, San Juan, PR 00921-4183, Puerto Rico

RODRIGUEZ-SANJURJO, Jose (CFla) Church of the Incarnation, 1601 Alafaya Trl, Oviedo, FL 32765

RODRIGUEZ-SANTOS, Carlos (Hond)

RODRIGUEZ-SANTOS, Toribio (NJ) 38 W End Pl, Elizabeth, NJ 07202

RODRIGUEZ VALLECILLO, Digna Suyapa (Hond) Barrio Zaragoza, Calle De La Shell, Siguatepeque, Honduras

RODRIGUEZ-YEJO, Ruden (Del) 1005 Pleasant St, Wilmington, DE 19805

ROECK, Gretchen Elizabeth (Minn) 5330 Oliver Ave South, Minneapolis, MN 55419

ROEGER JR, William Donald (Mo) 419 N 6th St, Hannibal, MO 63401

ROEHNER, Rodney (CFla) 6249 Canal Blvd, New Orleans, LA 70214

ROESCHLAUB, Robert Friedrich (Ind) 20 Pannatt Hill, Millom, Cumbria, LA18 5DB, Great Britain (UK)

ROESKE, Michael Jerome (Mass) 35 Bowdoin St, Boston, MA 02114

ROFF, Lucinda Lee (Ala) 812 5th Ave, Tuscaloosa, AL 35401

ROFINOT, Laurie Ann (Mass) 88 Lexington Ave # 2, Somerville, MA 02144

ROGERS, Allan Douglas (SwFla) 4352 Arrow Ave, Sarasota, FL 34232

ROGERS, Diana (Ct) 67 Lakeside Ave, Middletown, CT 06457

ROGERS, Douglas K (Chi) 412 N Church St, Rockford, IL 61103

ROGERS, Elizabeth Page (Ct) 99 Lee Farm Dr, Niantic, CT 06357

ROGERS III, George Michael Andrew (Alb) 325 East 80th Street, 1D, New York, NY 10021

ROGERS, Henry Stanley Fraser (Oly) 4770 116th Ave Se, Bellevue, WA 98006

ROGERS JR, Jack A (WTenn) 2185 Aztec Dr, Dyersburg, TN 38024

ROGERS, James Arthur (FtW) 4302 Wynnwood Dr, Wichita Falls, TX 76308

ROGERS, James Luther (Tenn) 935 Mount Olivet Rd, Columbia, TN 38401

ROGERS JR, John Albert (Ct) 69 Butternut Ln, Rocky Hill, CT 06067

ROGERS, John Sanborn (RI) 106 Osprey Dr, Saint Marys, GA 31558

ROGERS, Joy Edith Stevenson (Chi) 65 E. Huron, Chicago, IL 60611

ROGERS, Larry Samuel (Okla) 1310 N Sioux Ave, Claremore, OK 74017

ROGERS, Marcus (Ct) 5601 County Route 30, Granville, NY 12832

ROGERS, Martha C (Ia) 235 Partridge Ave, Marion, IA 52302

ROGERS, Matthew Arnold (Md) 3100 Monkton Rd, Monkton, MD 21111

ROGERS, Norma Jean (Az) PO Box 4567, Tubac, AZ 85646

ROGERS, Robert Gerald (La) Po Box 233, Clinton, LA 70722

ROGERS III, Sampson (FtW) 828-28 Avenue North #4, Menomonie, WI 54751

ROGERS III, Thomas S (Chi) 1653 West Congress Parkway, Chicago, IL 60612

ROGERS, Timothy James (Mass)

ROGERS, Victor (Ct) 111 Whalley Ave, New Haven, CT 06511

ROGERS, William Burns (Tenn) 510 W Main St, Franklin, TN 37064

ROGERSON, George William (Ia) 11536 Wild Rose Dr, West Burlington, IA 52655

ROGGE, Joel Jay (WA) 84 County Rd, Ipswich, MA 01938

ROGINA, Julius M (Nev) 1080 Del Webb Pkwy West, Reno, NV 89523

ROGNAS, Alice Anita (Mont) 713 8th St, Lewiston, ID 83501

ROHDE, Katherine M. (The Episcopal NCal) 1326 East A St., Casper, WY 82601

ROHLEDER, Robert Arthur (Mil) 2409 10th Ave Apt 310, South Milwaukee, WI 53172

ROHMAN, Suzannah Lynn (Ct) St. Paul's Episcopal Church, 145 Main St., Southington, CT 06489

ROHRBACH, Marissa S (Ct) Church of the Holy Trinity, 1904 Walnut St, Philadelphia, PA 19103

ROHRER, Glenn E (CGC) 5636 Firestone Dr, Pace, FL 32571

ROHRER, Jane (Oly) Episcopal Church Of The Holy Cross, 11526 162nd Ave NE, Redmond, WA 98052

ROHRS, John D (SVa)

ROJAS-ARROYO, Sergio (PR)

ROJAS POVEDA, Jesus Antonio (EC) 737 Delma Grimes Rd, Coats, NC 27521

ROKOS, Michael George (Md) 2203 Mayfield Ave, Baltimore, MD 21213

ROLAND, Carla Elena (NY) Church of St Matthew & St Timothy, 26 W 84th St, New York, NY 10024

ROLDAN, Roman D (La) 11621 Ferdinand St, Saint Francisville, LA 70775

ROLES, Elizabeth A (At) 175 9th Ave # 123, New York, NY 10011

ROLFE-BOUTWELL, Suzan Jane (Mass) 7588 N Meredith Blvd, Tucson, AZ 85741

ROLLE, Denrick Ephriam (SeFla)

ROLLE, Yolanda Antoinette (Mass)

ROLLINS, Andrew Sloan (La) 640 Carriage Way, Baton Rouge, LA 70808

ROLLINS, Belle Frances (WLa) 1001 Berry St, Pineville, LA 71360

ROLLINS, E(verette) Wayne (Me) 10 Alton St., Portland, ME 04103

ROLLINS, John August (Nwk) 11 Fine Road, High Bridge, NJ 08829

ROLLINS, Roger Burton (Ia) 1551 Franklin St SE Apt. 4002, Grand Rapids, MI 49506

ROLLINSON, John Thomas (RG) 1120 Gidding St, Clovis, NM 88101

ROMACK, Gay Harpster (Az) 609 N Old Litchfield Rd, Litchfield Park, AZ 85340

ROMAN, James Michael (NJ) Po Box 77356, West Trenton, NJ 08628

ROMANIK, David F (Pa) 230 Pennswood Rd, Bryn Mawr, PA 19010

ROMANS, Nicholas J (Chi) 514 S Mountain Road, Mesa, AZ 85208

ROMER, William Miller (NH) 128 AUDUBON DR, ACTON, MA 01720

ROMERIL, Gwendolyn Jane (Be) 26 W Market St, Bethlehem, PA 18018

ROMERO, Silvestre Enrique (Mass)

✠ **ROMERO**, Sylvestre Donato (Ret Asst Bp of NJ 2011-)

ROMERO-GUEVARA, Antonio N (EcuC) Dias De La Madrid 943, Quito, Ecuador

ROMERO MARTE, Francisco Alfredo (DR (DomRep))

ROMO-GARCIA, Gerardo (Los) 11305 Hesperia Rd, Hesperia, CA 92345

RONALDI, Lynn Petrie (Miss) Episcopal Church Of The Advent, PO Box 366, Sumner, MS 38957

RONDEAU, Daniel James (SanD) 44910 Calle Placido, La Quinta, CA 92253

RONKOWITZ, George R (SeFla) 8310 SW 60th Ave, South Miami, FL 33143

RONN, Denise Marie (Ga) 2600 Rolling Hill Dr, Valdosta, GA 31602

RONTANI JR, William (The Episcopal NCal) 104 Main St., Wheatland, CA 95692

ROOD JR, Peter H (Los) 702 W Alegria Ave, Sierra Madre, CA 91024

ROOS, Carl A (Ind) 6920 Mohawk Ln, Indianapolis, IN 46260

ROOS, Michelle Kate (Ind) 720 Dr. Martin Luther King Jr St., Indianapolis, IN 46202

ROOS, Richard John (Ind) 2033 Paradise Oaks Ct, Atlantic Beach, FL 32233

ROOSEVELT, Nancy A (O) 17100 Van Aken Blvd, Shaker Heights, OH 44120

ROOSEVELT, Nicholas Williams (Az)

ROOT, Diane Eleanor (Vt) 2 Jones Avenue, West Lebanon, NH 03784

ROPER, Charles Murray (At) 128 River Ridge Ln, Roswell, GA 30075

ROPER, Jeffrey Howard (Kan) 3750 E Douglas Ave, Wichita, KS 67208

ROPER, John Dee (Kan) 14802 E Willowbend Cir, Wichita, KS 67230

ROPER, Terence Chaus (Pa) 1815 John F Kennedy Blvd Apt 2308, Philadelphia, PA 19103

ROQUE, Christopher Collin (WTex) 3500 N 10th St, Mcallen, TX 78501

RORKE, Stephen Ernest (Roch) 6727 Royal Thomas Way, Alexandria, VA 22315

ROS, Salvador Patrick (NJ)

ROSA, Thomas Phillip (Chi) 121 W Macomb St, Belvidere, IL 61008

ROSANAS, Louis Rosanas (Hai) Box 1309, Port-Au-Prince, Haiti

ROSARIO-CRUZ, Eliacin (Oly) 111 NE 80th St, Seattle, WA 98115

ROSARIO DE LA CRUZ, Juan Antonio (Nwk) 3901 Park Ave, Union City, NJ 07087

ROSE, Ann W (Ore) 7 Saint Johns Rd Apt 30, Cambridge, MA 02138

ROSE, Carol Benson (EO) 2133 N Cajeme Ave, Casa Grande, AZ 85222

ROSE, Christopher Lee (Ct) 30 Woodland Street Unit 10NP, Hartford, CT 06106

ROSE, David D (SwVa) 210 4th St., Radford, VA 24141

ROSE, David Jonathan (Ga) St. Anne's Episcopal Church, PO Box 889, Tifton, GA 31793

ROSE, Edwin Sandford (WTex) Po Box 1943, Fulton, TX 78358

ROSE, Josie Rodriguez (NwT) 5539 7th Ave N, Saint Petersburg, FL 33710

ROSE, Joy Ann (CFla) Saint Mary's Episcopal Church, 216 Orange Ave, Daytona Beach, FL 32114

ROSE, Leland Gerald (WNY) 602 Crescent Ave, East Aurora, NY 14052

ROSE, L(oran) A(nson) Paul (WA) 6101 Edsall Rd Apt 508, Alexandria, VA 22304

ROSE, Margaret Rollins (NY) 531 E 72nd St Apt 3c, New York, NY 10021

ROSE, Philip John (Minn)

ROSE, Roger Franklin (Los) 3 Pursuit Apt 109, Aliso Viejo, CA 92656

ROSE, Roland (NwT) 5539 7th Ave. North, St. Petersburg, FL 33710

ROSE, Shirley Jean (Los) 3 Pursuit # 109, Aliso Viejo, CA 92656

ROSE, William Harrison (SC) 20 Riverview Dr, Beaufort, SC 29907

ROSE-CROSSLEY, Ramona (Vt) 327 University Ave, Sewanee, TN 37375

ROSE-CROSSLEY, Remington (Vt)

ROSEN, Elisabeth Payne (Cal) P O Box 1306, Ross, CA 94957

ROSENBAUM, Richard L. (Okla) 9804 Cisler Lane, Manassas, VA 20111

ROSENBERG, Elizabeth Powell (Del) 2361 Elliott Island Rd, Vienna, MD 21869

ROSENBERG, Elma Joy Van Fossen (SwFla) 7200 Sunshine Skyway Ln S Apt 15G, Saint Petersburg, FL 33711

ROSENBLUM, Nancy Jo (Alb) 22 Buckingham Dr, Albany, NY 12208

ROSENDAHL, Mary Alvarez (CFla) 1043 Genesee Avenue, Sebastian, FL 32958

ROSENDALE, Mary E (Colo)

ROSENGREN, Linda W (Fla) 5054 Ripple Rush Dr N, Jacksonville, FL 32257

ROSENZWEIG, Edward Charles (Md) 83 Harriman Point Road, Brooklin, ME 04616

ROSERO-NORDALM, Ema (Mass) St Stephen's Episcopal Church, 419 Shawmut Ave, Boston, MA 02118

ROSHEUVEL, Terrence Winst (NJ) 25 Sunset Ave E, Red Bank, NJ 07701

✠ **ROSKAM**, Catherine Scimeca (Ret Bp Suffr of NY 2011-) 15502 Friar St, Van Nuys, CA 91411

ROSOLEN, Emilio Joseph (SeFla) 100 Ne Mizner Blvd # 1503, Boca Raton, FL 33432

ROSS, Anne Meigs (NY) 88 Ridge Rd, Valley Cottage, NY 10989

ROSS, Cleon Marrion (SVa) 196 Homeport Ln, Danville, VA 24540

ROSS, David Jeffrey (Cal) Po Box 774, Pinole, CA 94564

ROSS, Donna Baldwin (ECR) 3291 Pickwick Ln, Cambria, CA 93428

ROSS, Ellen Marie (Neb) 106 Robin Rd, Council Bluffs, IA 51503

ROSS, George Crawford Lauren (Cal) 19815 Windwood Dr, Woodbridge, CA 95258

ROSS, George Mark (Minn) Po Box 1231, Cass Lake, MN 56633

ROSS, Jeffrey Austin (Del) 213 W Third St, Lewes, DE 19958

ROSS, John C (ETenn) 413 Cumberland Ave, Knoxville, TN 37902

ROSS, Johnnie Edward (Lex) 283 S Arnold Ave, Prestonsburg, KY 41653

ROSS, Patricia Lynn (Cal) 215 10th Ave, San Francisco, CA 94118

ROSS, Robert Layne (Ala) 2636 River Grand Cir, Vestavia, AL 35243

ROSS, Robert Michael (Ct) 91 Miry Brook Rd, Danbury, CT 06810

ROSS, Robert William (LI) 225 Surinam St, Punta Gorda, FL 33983

ROSS, Rowena Jane (RG)

ROSS, Sue Ann (Dal) 2679 Orchid Dr, Richardson, TX 75082

ROSSER SR, James Bernard (At) 2703 Sanibel Ln Se, Smyrna, GA 30082

ROSSI, Kim Elizabeth (WNY) St Stephen's Episcopal Church, PO Box 446, Olean, NY 14760

ROSSO, Tricia Anne (Cal) 716 Hensley Ave # 1, San Bruno, CA 94066

ROTCHFORD, Lisa Marie (Los) 24352 Via Santa Clara, Mission Viejo, CA 92692

ROTH, Frank Alwin (Ala) 2310 Skyland Blvd E, Tuscaloosa, AL 35405

ROTH, Marilyn Lee (EO) 1805 Minnesota St, The Dalles, OR 97058

ROTH, Nancy Leone (O) 330 Morgan St, Oberlin, OH 44074

ROTH JR, Ralph Carl (Be) Phoebe Berks Village, 9 Reading Dr Apt 242, Wernersville, PA 19565

ROTHAUGE, Arlin John (Ore) 197 Lighthouse Ln, Friday Harbor, WA 98250

ROTTGERS, Steven Robert (WMo) 3521 NW Winding Woods Drive, Lees Summit, MO 64064

ROUFFY, Edward Albert (Colo) 950 SW 21st Ave Apt 402, Portland, OR 97205

ROUMAS, Peisha Geneva (WMo) 913 E 100th Ter, Kansas City, MO 64131

ROUNDS, James Arlen (Wyo) PO Box 1194, Laramie, WY 82073

ROUNDTREE, Ella Louise (NY) 311 Huguenot St, New Rochelle, NY 10801

ROUNDTREE, Philip (Cal) 60 Martinez Ct, Novato, CA 94945

ROUSE, Albertine Coney (Los) 2500 Honolulu Ave #236, Montrose, CA 91020

ROUSER, John Richard (ETenn) 7555 Ooltewah Georgetown Rd, Ooltewah, TN 37363

ROUSSEAU, Sean Kenneth (Va) St Paul's Episcopal Church, 6750 Fayette St, Haymarket, VA 20169

ROUSSELL, Christopher J (SD) Emmanuel Episcopal Church, 717 Quincy St, Rapid City, SD 57701

ROWE, Gary Lee (Del) 913 Wilson Road, Wilmington, DE 19803

ROWE, Grayce O'Neill (Va) 437 Summit Ave, Hagerstown, MD 21740

ROWE, Jacquelyn Gilbert (NJ) PO Box 326, Pine Beach, NJ 08741

ROWE, Mary Stone (Mont)

ROWE, Matthew Robert (NwT) Emmanuel Episcopal Church, 3 S Randolph St, San Angelo, TX 76903

ROWE, Michael Gordon (SwFla) 9213 Estero River Cir, Estero, FL 33928

ROWE, Richard C(harles) (NwPa) 706 Wilhelm Rd, Hermitage, PA 16148

ROWE, Richard Charles (WNC) 64 Oak Gate Dr, Hendersonville, NC 28739

ROWE, Sandra Jeanne (CFla) PO Box 2206, Breckenridge, CO 80424

✠ **ROWE**, Sean Walter (Bp of NwPa 2007-, Bp Provsnl of Be 2014-) 1870 Henley Pl, Fairview, PA 16415

ROWE-GUIN, Kathy (Va) 5911 Fairview Woods Dr, Fairfax Station, VA 22039

ROWELL, Emily Elizabeth (Ala) 12291 River Rd, Richmond, VA 23238

ROWELL, Ernest Michael (USC) PO Box 847, Ocklawaha, FL 32183

ROWELL, Rebecca E (Ga) 6329 Frederica Rd, St Simons Island, GA 31522

ROWINS, Charles Howard (Los) 1 Warrenton Rd, Baltimore, MD 21210

ROWLAND, Kenneth George (Ga) 6463 Cobbham Rd, Appling, GA 30802

ROWLAND, Thomas (RG) St Paul's Episcopal Church, PO Box 949, Truth Or Consequences, NM 87901

ROWLES, Stephen Paul (Va) 9750 Essex Hills Road, New Kent, VA 23124

ROWLEY, Angela (Ct) Yale New Haven Hospital, 20 York Street, New Haven, CT 06510

✠ **ROWTHORN**, Jeffery William (Ret Bp Suffr of Eur 2000-) 17 Woodland Dr, Salem, CT 06420

ROY, Byron Willard (Roch) 19 Abbotswood Crescent, Penfield, NY 14526

ROY JR, Derik Justin Hurd (Alb) 10 W High St, Ballston Spa, NY 12020

ROY, Jeffrey A (NJ) 7 Lincoln Ave, Rumson, NJ 07760

ROY, Robert Royden (Minn) 1289 Galtier St, Saint Paul, MN 55117

ROYAL, Dorothy Kaye (Neb) St Mary's Episcopal Church, 116 S 9th St, Nebraska City, NE 68410

ROYALS, Deborah (Az) 7945 N Village Ave, Tucson, AZ 85704

ROYALTY, Virginia B (At) 901 W Emery St, Dalton, GA 30720

ROZENDAAL, Jay Calvin (Oly) 1134 Finnegan Way # 302, Bellingham, WA 98225

ROZENE, Wendy Anne (Me) 17 Fox Run Rd, Cumberland, ME 04021

ROZO, Oscar A (Mil) St Paul's Episcopal Church, 413 S 2nd St, Watertown, WI 53094

ROZZELLE, Stephen Michael (Nwk) 400 Ramapo Avenue, Pompton Lakes, NJ 07442

RUBEL, Christopher Scott (Los) 250 N Live Oak Ave, Glendora, CA 91741

RUBIANO-ALVARADO, Raul (CFla) 2851 Afton Cir, Orlando, FL 32825

RUBIN, Richard Louis (Los) 163 W. 11th St., Claremont, CA 91711

RUBINSON, Rhonda Joy (NY) 400 W 119th St Apt 11-L, New York, NY 10027

RUBRIGHT, Elizabeth Alice Shemet (SwFla)

RUBY, Lorne Dale (Pa) 20 N 2nd St, Columbia, PA 17512

RUCKER, J(ames) Cliff(ord) (Tex) 2329 12th St, Port Neches, TX 77651

RUDACILLE, Stephen Lee (SwFla) 2702 Saint Cloud Oaks Dr, Valrico, FL 33594

RUDE, David B (Nwk) 5 Estate Drive, Wantage, NJ 07461

RUDER, John Williams (Oly) 602 6th St., Castlegar, BC V1N2G1, Canada

RUDINOFF, Jan Charles (The Episcopal Church in Haw) 2775 Kanani St, Lihue, HI 96766

RUDOLPH, Patrick Charles (FdL) 1036 Pine Beach Rd, Marinette, WI 54143

RUEF, John Samuel (SVa) 720 S Main St, Chatham, VA 24531

RUEHLEN, Petroula Kephala (Tex) 3541 Adrienne Ln, Lake Charles, LA 70605

RUFFIN, Hunter (SeFla) 8011 Douglas Ave, Dallas, TX 75225

RUFFINO, Russell Gabriel (Eur) Corso Cavour, 110, C.P. #81, Orvieto, 05018, Italy

RUGGABER, Michael Paul (Nev) St Pauls The Prospector, PO Box 13, Virginia City, NV 89440

RUGGER, Mildred Susan (NwT)

RUGGLES, Roxanne (USC) Church of the Good Shepherd, 108 E. Liberty St., PO Box 437, York, SC 29745

RUGH, Nathan (Los) 1227 4th St, Santa Monica, CA 90401

✠ **RUIZ RESTREPO**, Luis Fernando (Form Bp of Ecu Central 2011-) Carrera 80 #53 A 78, Medellin, Colombia

RUIZ-RIQUER, Cynthia S (FtW) 5910 Black Oak Ln, River Oaks, TX 76114

RUK, Michael Raymond (Pa) 10 Chapel Rd, New Hope, PA 18938

RULE, Alan R (CFla) 216 Orange Ave, Daytona Beach, FL 32114

RULE II, John Henry (Okla) 1122 E 20th St, Tulsa, OK 74120

RUMPLE, John G (Ind) 550 University Blvd # 1410, Indianapolis, IN 46202

RUNDLETT, Brad (Va) St Timothy's Episcopal Church, 432 Van Buren St, Herndon, VA 20170

RUNGE, Phillip Diedrich (Ga) 338 Lakeview Dr, Baxley, GA 31513

RUNGE, Thomas L (Lex) 7 Court Pl, Newport, KY 41071

RUNKLE, John Ander (Tenn) St Mary's Sewanee, 770 St. Mary's Lane, Sewanee, TN 37375

RUNKLE, Robert Scott (Spok) 501 E Wallace Ave, Coeur D Alene, ID 83814

RUNNELS, Rufus Stanley (WMo) 11 E 40th St, Kansas City, MO 64111

RUNNER, Paul W (NJ) 370 Main St, Wakefield, RI 02879

RUNNING JR, Joseph Martin (EC) 3207 Notting Hill Rd, Fayetteville, NC 28311

RUPP, Lawrence Dean (SO) 13 Balsam Acres, New London, NH 03257

RUPP, Lloyd Gary (Nev) 43 West Pacific Ave, Henderson, NV 89015

RUPPE, David Robert (SO) 25005 SR 26, New Matamoras, OH 45767

RUPPE-MELNYK, Glyn Lorraine (Pa) 689 Sugartown Road, Malvern, PA 19355

RUSCHMEYER, Henry Cassell (NY) 2929 SE Ocean Blvd Apt M9, Stuart, FL 34496

RUSH, Joyce Anne (Minn) 407 Nw 7th St, Brainerd, MN 56401

RUSHTON, Joseph M (Del) P O BOX 602, Georgetown, DE 19947

RUSLING, Julia G (At) 432 Lockwood Ter., Decatur, GA 30030

RUSS JR, Frank D (SC) 1159 Wyndham Rd, Charleston, SC 29412

RUSSELL, Ann Veronica (VI) Box 3066, Sea Cow's Bay, Tortola, British Virgin Island VG 1110, British Virgin Islands

RUSSELL JR, Carl Asa (Me) 9 Perkins Rd, Boothbay Harbor, ME 04538

RUSSELL, Carlton Thrasher (Mass) 27 Abnaki Way, Stockton Springs, ME 04981

RUSSELL, D(aniel) Scott (Pgh) 2365 McAleer Rd, Sewickley, PA 15143

RUSSELL, Jack Dempsey (Tex) 800 E Hudson St, Tyler, TX 75701

RUSSELL, John Alan (WNY) 768 Potomac Ave, Buffalo, NY 14209

RUSSELL, Kathleen Sams (Tex) 1823 Montana Sky Drive, Austin, TX 78727

RUSSELL, Kenneth P. (Ore) 5311 Sw Wichita St, Tualatin, OR 97062

RUSSELL, Margaret Ellen Street (Me) 9 Perkins Rd, Boothbay Harbor, ME 04538

RUSSELL, Michael Bennett (Tex) 3112 James St, San Diego, CA 92106

RUSSELL, Patricia Griffith (NwT) 1802 Broadway, Lubbock, TX 79401

RUSSELL, Sherrill Ann (WMo) 7110 N State Route 9, Kansas City, MO 64152

RUSSELL, Susan Hayden (Mass) 72 Cavendish Circle, Salem, MA 01970

RUSSELL, Susan Lynn Brown (Los) 680 Mountain View St, Altadena, CA 91001

RUSSELL, Tracy Johnson (Ct) 89 Lenox St Unit N, New Haven, CT 06513

RUTENBAR, C(Harles) Mark (WTenn) 7774 Grand Point Rd., Presque Isle, MI 49777

RUTENBAR, Larae Jordan (WMich) 8238 Greengate Cove, Cordova, TN 38018

RUTH, Margaret Foster (WMo) 402 West 50th #2 South, Kansas City, MO 64112

RUTH, Same (SwFla) 5210 Pale Moon Dr, Pensacola, FL 32507

RUTHERFORD, Allen Dale (Ind) 420 Locust Street, Mt. Vernon, IN 47620

RUTHERFORD, Ellen Conger (NJ) 1115 New Pear Street, Vineland, NJ 0836-4116

RUTHERFORD, Thomas Houston (CFla) 1260 Log Landing Drive, Ocoee, FL 34761

RUTHVEN, Carol Lynn (Lex) St Andrew's Episcopal Church, 401 N Upper St, Lexington, KY 40508

RUTHVEN, Scott Alan (RG) 805 Lenox Ave., Las Cruces, NM 88005

RUTLEDGE, Fleming (NY) 38 Hillandale Rd, Rye Brook, NY 10573

RUTLEDGE, Lynn V (Me) 13 Garnet Head Rd, Pembroke, ME 04666

RUTTAN, Karl D (SO) 125 E Broad St, Columbus, OH 43215

RUTTER, Deborah Wood (Va) PO Box 1306, Front Royal, VA 22630

RUYAK, Mark Andrew (Cal) 5 Weatherly Drive Apt 109, Mill Valley, CA 94941

RUYLE, Everett Eugene (At) 1195 Terramont Dr, Roswell, GA 30076

RYAN, Adele Marie (Mass) 50 Harden Hill Rd, Box C, Duxbury, MA 02331

RYAN, Bartholomew Grey (Chi) 15005 Orchard Dr., 15005 Orchard Dr., Burnsville, MN 55306

RYAN, Dennis L (Miss) 3507 Pine St, Pascagoula, MS 39567

RYAN III, Frances Isabel Sells (Az) 3150 N Winding Brook Rd, Flagstaff, AZ 86001

RYAN, Katherine Feltman (WNC) 1223 Sea Pines Dr, Aubrey, TX 76227

RYAN, Kathryn McCrossen (Tex) 8787 Greenville Ave, Dallas, TX 75243

RYAN, Matthew Wayne (NwPa) 67 Thomas-Ryan Road, Emporium, PA 15834

RYAN, Michael James (WMich) The Church of the Epiphany, 410 Erie Street, South Haven, MI 49090

RYAN, Michelle (CFla)

RYAN JR, Thomas Francis (SeFla) 3131 Pizzaro Pl, Clermont, FL 34715

RYAN, William Wilson (WTenn) 9233 Speerberry Ln, #14101, Cordova, TN 38016

RYBICKI, Robert (Cal) 1100 California St, San Francisco, CA 94108

RYDER, Anne Elizabeth (WMass) PO Box 1294, Sheffield, MA 01257

RYDER, Barbara Helen (SVa) 12 Spring St, Decatur, GA 30030

RYERSON, Raymond Willcox (FdL) 1758 Le Brun Rd, De Pere, WI 54115

RYMER, Lionel Simon (VI) Po Box 7335, St Thomas, VI 00801

S

SAAGER, Rebecca Ann (Lex) 311 Washington St, Frankfort, KY 40601

SABETTI III, Henry Martin (Eas) 12822 Shrewsbury Church Rd, Kennedyville, MD 21645

SABOM, Steve (At) 1143 Sanden Ferry Dr, Decatur, GA 30033

SABUNE, Petero Aggrey Nkurunziza (NY) 293 Highland Ave, Newark, NJ 07104

SACCAROLA FAVARO, Flavio (EcuC) Apdo 08-01-404, Esmeraldas, Ecuador

SACHERS, Calvin Stewart (Tex) 145 Lake View Dr, Boerne, TX 78006

SACHS, William Lewis (Va) 509 Saint Christophers Road, Richmond, VA 23226

SACQUETY JR, Charles William (Los) 8402 Castilian Dr, Huntington Beach, CA 92646

SADLER, Alice Irene (SwFla) 906 S. Orleans Avenue, Tampa, FL 33606

SAFFORD, Timothy Browning (Pa) 20 N American St, Philadelphia, PA 19106

SAID, James Timothy (Tex) St Thomas Episcopal Church, 906 George Bush Dr, College Station, TX 77840

✠ **SAID**, John Lewis (Ret Bp Suffr of SeFla 2003-) 6508 Nw Chugwater Cir, Port Saint Lucie, FL 34983

SAIK, Robert William (Az) 514 S Mountain Rd, Mesa, AZ 85208

SAILER, David Walter (WNC) 3 Oak Leaf Ln, Arden, NC 28704

SAINTILVER, Margarette (Hai)

SAINT JUSTE, Vanel (DR (DomRep))

SAINT-PIERRE, Nathanael L B (NY) Haitian Congregation of the Good Samaritan, 661 E 219th St, Bronx, NY 10467

SAINT ROMAIN, Brad (Tex) 3333 Castle Ave, Waco, TX 76710

SAJNA, Barbara Jean Reiser (FdL) 2100 Ridges Rd., Baileys Harbor, WI 54202

SAKIN, Charles Robert (NJ) 1812 Rue De La Port Drive, Wall, NJ 07719

SAKRISON, David L (U) 280 E 300 S, Moab, UT 84532

SALAMONE, Robert Emmitt (At) 2490 Orchard Walk, Bogart, GA 30622

SALAZAR-SOTILLO, Orlando Rafael (Ve)

SALAZAR-VASQUEZ, Jose Francisco (Ve)

SALBADOR, Gus William (Wyo) 2510 Stonebridge Way, Mount Vernon, WA 98273

SALCEDO, Federico B (PR)

SALIK, Lamuel Gill (Dal) 138 Liveoak St, Hereford, TX 79045

SALINARO, Katherine Ella Mae (Cal) 121 Sheffield, Hercules, CA 94547

SALISBURY, Katherine Ann (LI) 157 Montague St, Brooklyn, NY 11201

SALLES, Stacy D (Mich) 67640 Van Dyke Rd # 10, Washington, MI 48095

SALLEY JR, George Bull (Ga) 310 McLaws Street, Savannah, GA 31405

SALMON JR, Abraham Dickerson (Md) 7351 Willow Rd Apt 2, Frederick, MD 21702

SALMON, Alan Kent (NJ) 4 Tara Ln, Delran, NJ 08075

✠ **SALMON JR**, Edward Lloyd (Ret Bp of SC 2007-) 9 Westmoreland Place, Saint Louis, MO 63108

SALMON JR, John Frederick (Nwk) 195 Woodside Dr, Lumberton, NJ 08048

SALMON, Marilyn Jean (Minn) 1077 Laurel Ave, Saint Paul, MN 55104

SALMON, Walter Burley Stattmann (At)

SALT, Alfred Lewis (Nwk) 4822 Martinique Way, Naples, FL 34119

SALTZGABER, Jan Mcminn (Ga) 225 W Point Dr, Saint Simons Island, GA 31522

SALVATIERRA SERIAN, Juan E (EcuC) Apdo 17-11-6165, Quito, Ecuador

SAM, Albert Abuid Samuel (WNY) 7469 Dysinger Rd, Lockport, NY 14094

SAM, Helen (WNY) PO Box 14, Dunkirk, NY 14048

SAMILIO, Jamie Suzanne (Va) 2455 Gallows Rd, Dunn Loring, VA 22027

SAMMONS, Gregory P (O) 4684 Brittany Rd, Toledo, OH 43615

SAMMONS, Margaret Holt (O) 268 Lewiston Rd., Kettering, OH 45429

SAMPEY, Amanda L. (FdL) St James Episcopal Church, 402 2nd St, Mosinee, WI 54455

SAMPSON, Leon (NAM) Po Box 28, Bluff, UT 84512

SAMPSON, Paula Kathryn (Ak) 4317 Birch Avenue, Terrace, V8G 1X2, Canada

SAMRA, Gordon L (NI) 14823 Waterbrook Rd, Fort Wayne, IN 46814

SAMS, David Lee (Minn) 203 Aspenwood Drive, Redwood Falls, MN 56283

SAMS, Jonathan Carter (Mich) 6402 Fredmoor Dr, Troy, MI 48098

SAMUEL, Amjad John (Ct) 1361 W Market St, Akron, OH 44313

SAMUEL, Daniel (DR (DomRep)) Aptd 764, Santo Domingo, Dominican Republic

SAMUEL, Jason Wade (SanD) Saint David's Epis Church, 5050 Milton St, San Diego, CA 92110

SAMUELS, Robert Marshall (WNY) 201 Saint Francis Dr, Green Bay, WI 54301

SANBORN, Calvin Francis Lyon (Me) Po Box 823, York Harbor, ME 03911

SANBORN, Victoria B M (NY) 3919 Pocahontas Ave, Cincinnati, OH 45227

SANCHEZ, Jose De Jesus (SeFla) 525 NE 15th St, Miami, FL 33132

SANCHEZ NAVARRO, Aida Consuelo (Hond)

SANCHEZ NAVARRO, Jose Israel (Hond)

SANCHEZ NUNEZ, Carlos A (PR) PO Box 327, Manati, PR 00674

SANCHEZ PUJOL, Augusto Sandino (DR (DomRep)) Santiago #114, Santo Domingo, Dominican Republic

SAND, David Allan (NMich) PO Box 805, Iron Mountain, MI 49801

SAND, Lynn Ann (NMich) PO Box 805, Iron Mountain, MI 49801

SANDERS, E(dwin) Benjamin (Ky) 3812 Burning Bush Rd, Louisville, KY 40241

SANDERS, Harvel Ray (Mo) 110 Walnut Park Dr, Sedalia, MO 65301

SANDERS, Jaime Mw (Ore) 2190 Crest Dr, Lake Oswego, OR 97034

SANDERS, Joanne (Cal) Stanford Memorial Church, Stanford University, Stanford, CA 94305

SANDERS, John Clarke (At) 2744 Peachtree Rd Nw, Atlanta, GA 30305

SANDERS, Lynn Coggins (NY) St. Bartholomew's Church, 325 Park Avenue, New York, NY 10022

SANDERS, Marilyn Mae (CNY) 33092 Bay Ter, Lewes, DE 19958

SANDERS, Megan (NY) 40 Old Mill Rd, Staten Island, NY 10306

SANDERS, Patrick W (Miss)

SANDERS, Richard Devon (At)

SANDERS, Richard Evan (Ga) 605 Reynolds St, Augusta, GA 30901

SANDERS, Wayne Francis Michael (SanD) 3563 Merrimac Ave, San Diego, CA 92117

✠ **SANDERS**, William Evan (Ret Bp of ETenn 1992-) 404 Charlesgate Ct, Nashville, TN 37215

SANDERSON, Herbert (Alb) 468 Pinewoods Rd, Melrose, NY 12121

SANDERSON, Holladay Worth (Ida) All Saints Episcopal Church, 704 S Latah St, Boise, ID 83705

SANDERSON, Marshall D (SC) 218 Ashley Avenue, Charleston, SC 29403

SANDERSON, Peter Oliver (Ia) 410 Brentwood Dr, Alamogordo, NM 88310

SANDFORT, Candace C (Nwk)

SANDLIN, Allan (At) 1881 Edinburgh Terrace NE, Atlanta, GA 30307

SANDOE, Deirdre Etheridge (WA) 400 Rouen Dr Apt H, Deland, FL 32720

SANDOVAL, Juan (At) 161 Church St NE, Marietta, GA 30060

SANDOVAL CROS, Carlos Juan (SeFla) 1000 NW North River Drive #110, Miami, FL 33136

SANDS, Fred W(illiam) (SeFla) 300 Sw 29th Ave, Fort Lauderdale, FL 33312

SANDWELL-WEISS, Rosa Leah (Az) 8502 N Deer Valley Dr, Tucson, AZ 85742

SANFORD, Carol Webb (WMo)

SANFORD, Gary L(ee) (NwT) 1801 Edmund Blvd, San Angelo, TX 76901

SANG, Clive Oscar (NJ) 205 North Ave, Cranford, NJ 07016

SANGREY, William Frederick (SO)

SANON, Jean-Louis Felix (NY) 2757 Jacob Lane, Douglasville, GA 30135

SANTANA, Carlos Enrique (DR (DomRep))

SANTANA, Rosa M (Md) Apartado 128, San Pedro De Macoris, Dominican Republic

SANTANA-RUIZ, Benjamin (PR) 222 S Palm Ave, Sarasota, FL 34236

SANTIAGO, Gwen Gettemy (Pgh) 11524 Frankstown Rd, Pittsburgh, PA 15235

SANTIAGO, Vicente C (Pgh) 132 Sherwood Drive, Greensburg, PA 15601

SANTIAGO-PADILLA, Gilberto (PR) Carr 187 KM 5.8, Mediana Alta, Loiza, PR 00772, Puerto Rico

SANTIVIAGO-ESPINAL, Maria Isabel (NY) 2453 78th St # 2, East Elmhurst, NY 11370

SANTOS, Elenito Bravo (NC) 221 Union St, Cary, NC 27511

SANTOS-MONTES, Margarita (PR)

SANTOS-RIVERA, Carlos (Pa) 3554 N 6th St, Philadelphia, PA 19140

SANTOSUOSSO, John Edward (SwFla) 4860 Highlands Place Drive, Lakeland, FL 33813

SANTUCCI, Mark Albert (Ct) 166 Lambtown Rd, Ledyard, CT 06339

SANZO, Maria B (NJ) 318 Huxley Dr, Brick, NJ 08723

SARAI-CLARK, Wilhelmina Olivia (Spok) 503 E D St, Moscow, ID 83843

SARGENT, Arthur Lloyd (Dal) 213 Sierra Ridge Dr, San Marcos, TX 78666

SARGENT GREEN, Nancy Hunnewell (EO) 18160 Cottonwood Rd Pmb 719, Sunriver, OR 97707

SARIBAY, Ezgi (WMo) 420 W 14th St, Kansas City, MO 64105

SARKISSYIAN, Sabi Kamel (Mo) 524 Fox Run Estates Ct, Ballwin, MO 63021

SARRAZIN, Victor Joseph (Az)

SARTIN, George Randall (Fla) 3480 Lakeshore Drive, Tallahassee, FL 32312

SARTIN, Nancy Avera (Ga) 1521 N Patterson St, Valdosta, GA 31602

SASSER JR, Howell Crawford (CPa) Saint Paul's Church, PO Box 764, Bloomsburg, PA 17815

SASSMAN, William Arthur (The Episcopal NCal) 7418 Stock Ranch Rd Apt 3305, Citrus Hts, CA 95621

SASSO-CRANDALL, Rose Mary (NJ) 206 Central Ave, Hammonton, NJ 08037

SASTRE, Iane M (Ga) 21268 US Highway 17, White Oak, GA 31568

SATO, Judith Ann (Colo) 13741 Windrush dr, Colorado Springs, CO 80921

SATORIUS, Joanna (Los) Po Box 512164, Los Angeles, CA 90051

SATTERLY, Norris Jay (NMich) 132 Henford Ave, Kingsford, MI 49802

SATULA, John A (Mass) 6Schoolhouse Hill Road, Newtown, CT 06470

SAUCEDO SICA, Susan Teresa (Nwk) 407 N Broad St, Lansdale, PA 19446

SAUERZOPF, Richard C (Mich) 201 W Shepherd St, Charlotte, MI 48813

✠ **SAULS**, Stacy F (Form Bp of Lex 2011-) 815 Second Ave., New York, NY 10017

SAUNDERS, Cora Germaine (At) 607 River Run Dr, Sandy Springs, GA 30350

SAUNDERS, Elizabeth Goodwin (NC) 3029 Mountainbrook Rd, Charlotte, NC 28210

SAUNDERS, James (NJ) 8113 Rugby St, Philadelphia, PA 19150

SAUNDERS III, Kenneth H (Md) 120 Alleghney Ave, Towson, MD 21204

SAUNDERS, Lisa Ann (Tex) 833 W Wisconsin Ave, Milwaukee, WI 53233

SAUNDERSON, Ann Marie (Oly) 3918 N 24th St, Tacoma, WA 98406

SAUNKEAH, Bobby Reed (Okla) 110 E 17th St, Ada, OK 74820

SAUSSY JR, Hugh (At) 4549 SW24th Ave, Dania, FL 33312

SAVAGE, Harley Stewart (Tex) 180 CR 222, Bay City, TX 77414

SAVAGE, Jack Laverne (Mich) 1157 E Buckhorn Cir, Sanford, MI 48657

SAVIDGE, Karen Elizabeth Franklin (Mimi) (WMo) 207 N. 7th, St. Joseph, MO 64501

SAVILLE III, John K (Los) Po Box 152, Corona, CA 92878

SAVILLE, Milton (SO) 3580 Shaw Avenue #323, Cincinnati, OH 45208

SAVINO, Bella Jean (Ak) Po Box 70786, Fairbanks, AK 99707

SAWICKY, Blake A (Colo) The Church of St. Michael & St. George, 6345 Wydown Blvd, St. Louis, MO 63105

SAWTELLE, Gary Donald (Roch) 2171 Scottsville Rd, Scottsville, NY 14546

SAWYER, Anne M (Az)

SAWYER, Frank D (CFla) 210 S Indian River Dr, Fort Pierce, FL 34950

SAWYER, Robert Claremont (NC) Po Box 28024, Raleigh, NC 27611

SAWYER, Stanley Whitfield (SVa) 2200 Cape Arbor Dr, Virginia Beach, VA 23451

SAWYER, Susan Carter (Kan) 1640 Sunflower Rd, Clay Center, KS 67432

SAWYER HARMON, Cecily Judith (Del) 262 S College Ave, Newark, DE 19711

SAXE, Joshua Andrew (WVa) 218 Church St, Lewisburg, WV 24901

SAXE, Sarah E (Md) 2280 N Beauregard St, Alexandria, VA 22311

SAXON, Mary-Margaret (Colo) 5527 Harrison Street, Kansas City, MO 64110

SAXON, Miriam Scarsbrook (NC) 2214 Buck Quarter Farm Rd, Hillsborough, NC 27278

SAXTON II, Carl Millard (FtW) 256 E Church St, Jacksonville, FL 32202

SAYLOR, Kristin (NY) 19 Smith St, Port Chester, NY 10573

SAYLORS, Joann L (WTex) Diocese of West Texas, PO Box 6885, San Antonio, TX 78209

SCALES, Linda (Ga) 4344 Miller Dr, Evans, GA 30809

SCALES JR, Lou(Ie) Grady (Ga) 4344 Miller Drive, Evans, GA 30809

SCALIA, Deborah White (La) 10136 Walden Dr, River Ridge, LA 70123

SCALISE, Margaret M. (Ala) 8816 Old Greensboro Rd Apt 19103, Tuscaloosa, AL 35405

✠ **SCANLAN**, Audrey C (Bp of CPa 2015-) 22 Dyer Ave, Canton, CT 06019

SCANLON, Geoffrey Edward Leyshon (Spr) 2910 E Stone Creek Blvd, Urbana, IL 61802

SCANNELL, Alice Updike (Ore) 6735 NE Sacramento Street, Portland, OR 97213

SCANNELL, John Scott (Ore) 6735 NE Sacramento St, Portland, OR 97213

SCANTLEBURY, Cecil Alvin (NY) 61 Santuit Pond Rd., Mashpee, MA 02649

✠ **SCANTLEBURY**, Victor Alfonso (Bp Provsnl of Ecu Central 2011-) 6167 Westwind Rd, Jackson, MS 39206

SCARBOROUGH, Anjel Lorraine (Md) 2711 Flintridge Ct, Myersville, MD 21773

SCARCIA, Steven Angelo (Alb) PO Box 592, Little Falls, NY 13365

✠ **SCARFE**, Alan (Bp of Ia 2003-) 225 37th St, Des Moines, IA 50312

SCARFF, Stephen D (Alb) 129 Ledge Hill Rd, Guilford, CT 06437

SCARLETT, William George (Md)

SCARPACE, Ramona (Minn) 2035 Charlton Rd, Sunfish Lake, MN 55118

SCHAAL, Richard (CNY) 1504 76th Rd, Berkshire, NY 13736

SCHACHT, Lawrence Arthur (NY) 525 W End Ave Apt 4-H, New York, NY 10024

SCHADT, Stuart Everett (Va) 6070 Greenway Ct, Manassas, VA 20111

SCHAEFER, Jane (Chi) 417 N. Beck Road, Lindenhurst, IL 60046

SCHAEFER III, John (Neb) 10206 Ohio St, Omaha, NE 68134

SCHAEFER, Joslyn Eleanor Ogden (NC) St Peter's Episcopal Church, 115 W 7th St, Charlotte, NC 28202

SCHAEFER, Lee Paul (Ind) 444 South Harbour Drive, Noblesville, IN 46062

SCHAEFER, Lynette Golderman (The Episcopal Church in Haw) PO Box 1233, Kaunakakai, HI 96748

SCHAEFER, Philip David (Roch) 47 Brougham Dr, Penfield, NY 14526

SCHAEFFER, John Grant (Oly) 1827 Southeast 18th Place, Renton, WA 98055

SCHAEFFER, John Robert (Eas) All Saints Episcopal Church, 3577 McClure Ave, Pittsburgh, PA 15212

SCHAEFFER, Susan Edwards (NY) 17 Perkins Ave, Northampton, MA 01060

SCHAFFENBURG, Karl Christian (FdL) 1011 N. 7th St., 103 W. Broad Street, Sheboygan, WI 53081

SCHAFFNER, Philip Perry (Minn) 2401 33rd Ave. S, Minneapolis, MN 55406

SCHAFROTH, Stephen Louis (EO) 1107 Lewis St, The Dalles, OR 97058

SCHAIBLE II, Donald J (Be) Christ and Trinity Parishes, 58 River St, Carbondale, PA 18407

SCHAITBERGER, Stephen Harold (Minn) 1402 S 8th St, Brainerd, MN 56401

SCHALLER, Joseph G (Pa) 303 W. Lancaster Avenue, Suite 2C, Wayne, PA 19087

SCHALLER JR, Warren August (Va) 7 Lost Ridge Lane, Galena, IL 61036

SCHANE, Clifford Edward (Tenn) 1616 Piedmont Ave Ne Apt O9, Atlanta, GA 30324

SCHAPER, Richard L (Cal) 646 Ridgewood Avenue, Mill Valley, CA 94941

SCHARF, Douglas Frederick (SwFla) 3714 Cystal Dew St, Plant City, FL 33567

SCHARF JR, Frederick Edward (SwFla) 11644 Spindrift Loop, Hudson, FL 34667

SCHARK, Frederick J (WMich) St Mark Episcopal Church, 27 E Chicago St, Coldwater, MI 49036

SCHATZ, Stefani S (Cal) 200 Island Ave, Reno, NV 89501

SCHAUBLE, Jack L (Chi) Po Box 88, Compton, IL 61318

SCHEDA, Claudia (WNY) 54 Linwood Ave, Williamsville, NY 14221

SCHEEL, William Preston (Ark) 26 Cypress Point, Wimberley, TX 78676

SCHEELER, Joseph Lester (Mont) 640 Mill Rd, Helena, MT 59602

SCHEELER, Richard Edward Gerhart (Mil) 1540 S 166th St, New Berlin, WI 53151

SCHEEPERS, Noble F (Mass) 62 Cedar St, Dedham, MA 02026

SCHEFF, Tanya Lynn (NI) 600 Franklin St, Michigan City, IN 46360

SCHEIBLE, Anne Clare Elsworth (Minn)

SCHEIBLE, Gordon Kenneth (SanD) 2151 Bella Vista, Canyon Lake, TX 78133

SCHEID, Daniel S (EMich) 922 Blanchard Ave, Flint, MI 48503

SCHEIDE, Diana Southwick (NY) PO Box 296, Callicoon, NY 12723

SCHEIDER, David Max (Tex)

SCHELB, Holly Greenman (NC) 1323 Irving St, Winston Salem, NC 27103

SCHELL, Anita Louise (RI) 42 Dearborn St, Newport, RI 02840

SCHELL, Donald J (Cal) 555 De Haro St Ste 330, San Francisco, CA 94107

SCHELL, Peter G (WA) 1700 Powder Mill Rd, Silver Spring, MD 20903

SCHELL, Richardson Whitfield (Ct) Kent School, Kent, CT 06757

SCHELLENBERG, Roger Thomas (Va) 5775 Barclay Drive Suite G, Kingstowne, VA 22315

SCHELLHAMMER, Judith Lynn (Mich)

SCHELLING, Robert Louis (Colo) 393 Private Road 5730, Jefferson, TX 75657

SCHELLINGERHOUDT, Elizabeth L (At) 450 Clairmont Ave, Atlanta, GA 30030

SCHEMBS, Lois Jean (Nwk) 321 Lamberts Mill Rd, Westfield, NJ 07090

SCHENCK, Timothy E (Mass) 172 Main St, Hingham, MA 02043

SCHENEMAN, Mark Allan (CPa) 226 Acre Dr, Carlisle, PA 17013

SCHENKEL JR, Robert Downes (Be) 6539 Betsy Ross Cir, Bethlehem, PA 18017

SCHENONE, Janine L (Los) All Saints Church, 132 N Euclid Ave, Pasadena, CA 91101

SCHERCK, Steven H (Alb) P.O. Box 397, Guilderland, NY 12084

SCHERER, Anna Julia Katheryn Minor (SVa) 1830 Kirby Rd, McLean, VA 22101

SCHERER-HOOCK, Joyce Lynn (Mass) Po Box 308, Topsfield, MA 01983

SCHERFF, Holly D (Ia)

SCHERM, Mary Cecelia (WMass) 17 Merriam District, North Oxford, MA 01537

SCHEYER, Joyce M (NJ) Church of St John the Evangelist, 189 George Street, New Brunswick, NJ 08901

SCHIEFFELIN JR, John Jay (WMass)

SCHIEFFLER, Daniel Kent (Ark) 19 Woodberry Rd., Little Rock, AR 77212

SCHIERING, Janet Christine (EO) PO Box 1323, Hood River, OR 97031

SCHIESLER, Robert Alan (WMich) 265 Paris Ave SE, Grand Rapids, MI 49503

SCHIESS, Betty Bone (CNY) 6987 Van Antwerp Dr, Cicero, NY 13039

SCHIESZ, Catherine Murdock (Ala) PO Box M, Florence, AL 35631

SCHIFF, Paulette Toppin (LI) 217 Tyler Ave, Miller Place, NY 11764

SCHIFFMAYER, Jeffrey Paul (Tex) 8739 Serenade Ln, Houston, TX 77040

SCHILLING III, Walter Bailey (CFla) 1803 Crane Creek Blvd, Melbourne, FL 32940

SCHILLREFF, Kathy (SwFla) 278 Sawgrass Ct, Naples, FL 34110

SCHINDLER, Gary Charles (WNY) 591 E Main St, Springville, NY 14141

SCHINK, Susan Alma (Nwk) 481 Airmount Avenue, Ramsey, NJ 07446

SCHIRMACHER, Michael Grayson (Md) 3202 Lake St Apt 2, Houston, TX 77098

SCHISLER, Richard Thomas (SO) 2210 Cleveland Ave, Portsmouth, OH 45662

SCHISLER, Sallie Chellis (SO) 2210 Cleveland Ave, Portsmouth, OH 45662

SCHISSER, Janet Elaine (Mo) 1203 Castle Bay Pl, Columbia, MO 65203

SCHIVELY, John Alrik (The Episcopal NCal) 6901 New Creek Ln, Citrus Heights, CA 95621

SCHJONBERG, Mary Frances Frances (Nwk) 407 Seaview Circle, Neptune, NJ 07753

SCHLACHTER, Barbara Jeanne Hartley (SO) 7 Glenview Knl NE, Iowa City, IA 52240

SCHLACHTER, Melvin Harlan (Ia) 7 Glenview Knl NE, Iowa City, IA 52240

SCHLAFER, David John (Mil) 5213 Roosevelt Street, Bethesda, MD 20814

SCHLEGEL, Stuart Allen (ECR) 3400 Paul Sweet Road, Apt. B-213, Santa Cruz, CA 95065

SCHLESINGER, Kira Manette (Tenn) 4220 Harding Pike, Nashville, TN 37205

SCHLEY JR, Joseph Hastings (FtW) 1300 S Harrison St Apt 1008, Amarillo, TX 79101

SCHLISMANN, Robert (Neb) 1309 R St, Lincoln, NE 68508

SCHLOSSBERG, Stephen K K (Alb) 1574 Spring Ave., Wynantskill, NY 12198

SCHLOTTERBECK, Marilou Jean (WMich) 12530 Cinder Rd, Beulah, MI 49617

SCHMALING, Pamela J (Oly) 7913 W Golf Course Dr, Blaine, WA 98230

SCHMIDT, Ann Welsh (Ark) 726 Davemar Dr, Saint Louis, MO 63123

SCHMIDT, Carolyn Jean Decker (Minn) PO Box 278, 1633 Croftville Rd, Grand Marais, MN 55604

SCHMIDT, Edward William (Md) 1500 Hilton Ave # 21238, Catonsville, MD 21228

SCHMIDT JR, Frederick William (WA) Po Box 750133, Dallas, TX 75275

SCHMIDT, Kenneth John (Mass)

SCHMIDT, Kenneth L (Cal) 1350 Waller St, San Francisco, CA 94117

SCHMIDT, Kevin Lynn (Kan) 15309 W 153rd St, Olathe, KS 66062

SCHMIDT, Linda Marie (FdL) N2592 State Highway 17, Merrill, WI 54452

SCHMIDT, Norma (Ct) 661 Old Post Rd, Fairfield, CT 06824

SCHMIDT, Richard Hanna (CGC) 101 Fairwood Blvd., Fairhope, AL 36532

SCHMIDT, Wayne Roy (NY) 3 Ashley Dr, Newburgh, NY 12550

SCHMIDTETTER, Todd T (CFla)

SCHMITT, Barbara Joyce (SO) 115 N 6th St, Hamilton, OH 45011

SCHMITT, Geoffrey (WLa) 3910 Parkway Dr, 1605 Gray Lake Dr, Princeton, LA 71067

SCHMITT, Jacqueline (Mass) 31 Ely Dr., Fayetteville, NY 13066

SCHMITZ, Barbara G (CNY)

SCHMOETZER, Jane Ellen (Spok) 1940 Thayer Dr., Richland, WA 99354

SCHNAARE, Anne Elizabeth (WMich) 115 Hart St., Marshall, MI 49068

SCHNABEL, Charles Edward (LI) 143 Lakeside Trail, Ridge, NY 11961

SCHNABL, Emily Jessica (Okla) 4036 Neptune Dr, Oklahoma City, OK 73116

SCHNACK, Peggy Ellan (Oly)

SCHNATTERLY, Michael Dean (USC) 5 Mountain Vista Rd, Taylors, SC 29687

SCHNAUFER, Dennis Eric (USC) 6 Del Norte Blvd, Greenville, SC 29615

SCHNEIDER, Charles William (WK) 13702 Stoney Hill Dr, San Antonio, TX 67401

SCHNEIDER, Edward Nichols (EMich) 7039 W. Saint John Rd., Glendale, AZ 85308

SCHNEIDER, Gregg Alan (NC) 703 Milwaukee Road, Beloit, WI 53511

SCHNEIDER, Judith Irene (Colo) 2187 Canyon Ct W, Grand Junction, CO 81503

SCHNEIDER, Marian Schneider (Roch) 13 E Water St, Friendship, NY 14739

SCHNEIDER, Marilyn Butler (Colo) 7900 E Dartmouth Ave Apt 58, Denver, CO 80231

SCHNEIDER, Marni Jacqueline (Los) 2972 Cadence Way, Virginia Beach, VA 23456

SCHNEIDER, Matthew (Ala) 2017 6th Ave N, Birmingham, AL 35203

SCHNEIDER, M P (Vt) 164 Milton Road, Warwick, RI 02888

SCHNEIDER, Stephen Vance (Ore) 2427 Ne 17th Ave, Portland, OR 97212

SCHNEIDER, Thomas Carl (ETenn) 1038 Sparta Hwy, Crossville, TN 38572

SCHNEIDER, William John (Mass) 276 Riverside Dr Apt 4e, New York, NY 10025

SCHNITZER, William Lawton (NY) 26 N Manheim Blvd, New Paltz, NY 12561

SCHOECK, Lauren M (CPa) 6300 N Central Ave, Phoenix, AZ 85012

SCHOECK, Robert Hughes (CPa) 119 N Duke St, Lancaster, PA 17602

SCHOENBRUN, Zoila Collier (Cal) 327 San Rafael Ave, Belvedere, CA 94920

✠ **SCHOFIELD JR**, Calvin Onderdonk (Ret Bp of SeFla 2000-) 7900 East Dartmouth Ave. # 77, Denver, CO 80231

SCHOFIELD, Kathlyn Elizabeth (CNY) St Paul's Episcopal Church, 204 Genesee St, Chittenango, NY 13037

SCHOFIELD, Peter (Alb) 39 Imperial Dr., Niskayuna, NY 12309

SCHOFIELD-BROADBENT, Carrie Kathlyn (CNY) 941 Euclid Ave., Syracuse, NY 13210

SCHOLER, Linda C. (NJ) P O Box 1206, Chincoteague Island, VA 23336

SCHOMAKER, Kenneth Elmer (Ind) 2030 Chester Blvd IH 7B, Richmond, IN 47374

SCHOMBURG, Karen A (Spok) Episcopal Diocese Of Spokane, 245 E 13th Ave, Spokane, WA 99202

SCHOOLER, William Thomas (Cal) 352 Bay Rd, Atherton, CA 94027

SCHOONMAKER, Daniel Holt (O) 18426 Winslow Rd, Shaker Heights, OH 44122

SCHOONMAKER, Lisa Katherine (CPa) 21 S Main St, Lewistown, PA 17044

SCHRAMM, George Thomas (WVa) Po Box 308, Shepherdstown, WV 25443

SCHRAMM, John Eldon (NI) P. O. Box 695, Plymouth, IN 46563

SCHRAPLAU, Frederick William (NY) 182 Nixon Avenue, Staten Island, NY 10304

SCHREIBER, Mary Fiander (WMass) 6 Wall St, Shelburne Falls, MA 01370

SCHREIBER, Michael Nelson (Cal) 162 Hickory St, San Francisco, CA 94102

SCHREINER, Shawn Maureen (Chi) 5 North 047 Route 83, Bensenville, IL 60106

SCHRIDER, Jim (Los) 620 D Street, SE, Washington, DC 20003

SCHRIMSHER, Alyce Marie (Dal) 6132 Yellow Rock Trl, Dallas, TX 75248

SCHRODER, Edward Amos (Fla) 15 Hickory Lane, Amelia Island, FL 32034

SCHROEDER, Cecelia Carlile (Va) 314 Ayrlee Avenue Nw, Leesburg, VA 20176

SCHROEDER, Donald John (Spr) 49 Ward Cir, Brunswick, ME 04011

SCHROEDER, H.B.W. (Va)

SCHROETER, George H (CGC) 500 Spanish Fort Blvd Apt 29, Spanish Fort, AL 36527

SCHUBERT, Jill Marie (Minn) 520 N Pokegama Ave, Grand Rapids, MN 55744

SCHUBERT, Kevin Lane Johnson (Tex) 3307 Garden Villa Ln, Austin, TX 78704

SCHUBERT, Rebecca Malcolm (WMo) 3700 West 83 Terrace, Prairie Village, KS 66206

SCHUEDDIG JR, Louis Charles (At) 345 9th St Ne, Atlanta, GA 30309

SCHUETZ, Mary Joanne Rawlings (EMich) 3536 West River Road, Sanford, MI 48657

SCHUILING, Alice Catherine (NMich) 1100 Sunview Dr Apt 201, Saint Johns, MI 48879

SCHULENBERG, George W (ND) 135 Skogmo Blvd, Fergus Falls, MN 56537

SCHULENBERG, Michael A (Minn) 715 N High St, Lake City, MN 55041

SCHULER, Rock Hal (Md) St Andrew The Fisherman Episcopal, PO Box 175, Mayo, MD 21106

SCHULLER, Christopher David (SwFla) 514 Victoria Ave, Venice, CA 90291

SCHULTZ, Alison Morna (At) 5560 Chemin de Vie, Atlanta, GA 30342

SCHULTZ, Gregory Allen (FdL) West 7145 County Road U, Plymouth, WI 53073

SCHULTZ, Thomas Haines (Cal) St. Mary's Retreat House, 505 E. Los Olivos St., Santa Barbara, CA 93105

SCHULZ, David Allen (Del) 224 N Bayshore Dr, Frederica, DE 19946

SCHUNEMAN, Steven Lawrence (Chi) 200 N El Camino Real Spc 179, Oceanside, CA 92058

SCHUNIOR, Rebecca Justice (WA) St Mark's Church, 301 A St SE, Washington, DC 20003

SCHUSTER III, Franklin Phillip (RG) 28231 Pine Lake St, Edwardsburg, MI 49112

SCHUSTER, Lawrence Arthur (WNY) 10348 2nd St, Dunkirk, NY 14048

SCHUSTER WELTNER, Alicia (At) 2744 Peachtree Rd NW, Atlanta, GA 30305

SCHUTZ, Christine Elizabeth (O) 843 Tarra Oaks Dr, Findlay, OH 45840

SCHUYLER, Philip William (Az) 2010 W San Marcos Blvd, Unit 117, San Marcos, CA 92078

SCHUYLER, William (Me) 19 Ridgeway Ave, Sanford, ME 04073

SCHWAB, Anthony Wayne (Nwk) PO Box 294, Hinesburg, VT 05461

SCHWAB, Susan Mary Brophy (Mass)

SCHWAHN, Vincent Carl (Los) 117 Avenida San Jeronimo, San Angel, Mexico City, 01000, Mexico

SCHWARTZ, William Edward (Mil) PO Box 3210, Doha, QATAR, Qatar

SCHWARZ, Robert Carl (SD) 500 S Main Ave, Sioux Falls, SD 57104

SCHWARZ, Robert Louis (LI) 5436 Rock Creek Ct, North Charleston, SC 29420

SCHWARZER, Margaret Katherine (Mass) 40 Prescott St, Brookline, MA 02446

SCHWEINSBURG JR, Richard Lyle (RI) 46 Fairway Dr, Washington Village, Coventry, RI 02816

SCHWENKE, Carol Flenniken (SwFla) 3000 S Schiller St, Tampa, FL 33629

SCHWENZFEIER, Paul MacLeod (Mass) 32 Arlington Rd., Wareham, MA 02571

SCHWERT, Douglas Peters (WTex) 433 Trojan St, Port Aransas, TX 78373

SCHWOYER, Robin V (Pa) 232 American Dr, Richboro, PA 18954

SCIAINO, Elizabeth Rauen (Nwk) 105 Cottage Pl, Ridgewood, NJ 07450

SCIME, Mike (Ind)

SCIPIO, Clarence Tyrone (VI) PO Box 1148, St Thomas, VI 00804

SCISSONS, Antoinette M (EO) 17 Fairview Heights Loop, Burns, OR 97720

SCOFIELD, Lawrence Frederick (NwPa) 24 W Frederick St, Corry, PA 16407

SCOFIELD, Susan M (NwPa) Nonparochial, 24 W. Frederick St., Corry, PA 16407

SCOLARE, Michael (FdL)

SCOTT JR, Benjamin Ives (Minn) 8429 55th St Sw, Byron, MN 55920

SCOTT, Catherine F (Neb) 1903 Pleasantview Ln, Bellevue, NE 68005

SCOTT, Cathy Ann (Ind) Holy Family Episcopal Church, 11445 Fishers Point Blvd, Fishers, IN 46038

SCOTT, David Allan (Va) 3543 SW Ida St, Seattle, WA 98126

SCOTT, David Thomas (NwT) Po Box 88, Perryton, TX 79070

SCOTT, Donna Jeanne (Tenn) 404 Siena Drive, Nashville, TN 37205

SCOTT, Douglas Gordon (Pa) PO Box 1914, Ranchos De Taos, NM 87557

SCOTT, Edward Chisolm (NC) 525 Lake Concord Rd Ne, Concord, NC 28025

SCOTT, George Michael (Ga) PO Box 294, Cochran, GA 31014

SCOTT, Horton James (NY) 489 Saint Pauls Pl, Bronx, NY 10456

SCOTT, Jack Saunders (WA) 26 Swallow Ct, Falling Waters, WV 25419

SCOTT JR, James Edward (Tex) 8407 Glenscott St., Houston, TX 77061

SCOTT, Jean Pearson (NwT) 1101 Slide Rd., Lubbock, TX 79416

SCOTT, John Charles (Ala) St Stephens Episcopal Church, PO Box 839, Eutaw, AL 35462

SCOTT III, John Llewellyn (Alb) 86 Lake Hill Rd, Burnt Hills, NY 12027

SCOTT, Keith Elden (RI) 103 Union Ave S, Delmar, NY 12054

SCOTT, Marshall Stuart (WMo) 1256 W 72nd Ter, Kansas City, MO 64114

SCOTT, Matthew R. (NwPa) 209 West St, Warren, PA 16365

SCOTT, Nolie Edward (ETenn) 12026 Pine Cove Dr, Soddy Daisy, TN 37379

SCOTT, Norma J (Nev) Po Box 750, Hawthorne, NV 89415

SCOTT, Peggy King (La) 607 E Main St, New Roads, LA 70760

SCOTT, Rebecca Jean (Oly)

SCOTT, Richard Hervey (Oly) 4885 NW Chad Ct, Silverdale, WA 98383

SCOTT, Robert W (Neb) 13054 Thomas Drive, Bellevue, NE 68005

SCOTT, Roger Timothy (Az)

SCOTT, Sheila Maria (Mil) 4700 W. Deer Run Dr # 103, Brown Deer, WI 53223

SCOTT, Shelby Hudson (Okla) 9119 S 89th E Ave, Broken Arrow, OK 74133

SCOTT, Thomas Crawford Hunt (WMich) 2327 park place #2, evanston, IL 60201

SCOTT JR, William Tayloe (Cal) 95 Winfield St, San Francisco, CA 94110

SCOTT-HAMBLEN, Shane (NY) 1 Chestnut St, Cold Spring, NY 10516

SCOTTO, Vincent Francis (SwFla) 23465 Harborview Rd Apt634, Port Charlotte, FL 33980

SCRANTON, Susan Lee (Los) 1420 E Foothill Blvd, Glendora, CA 91741

SCRIBNER, The Rev. Chaplain Jean (Neb) 1725 Old Haywood Rd., Asheville, NC 28806

SCRIVEN, Elizabeth A (Mo) 2309 Packard St, Ann Arbor, MI 48104

SCRIVENER, William Eugene (SO) 7193 Foxview Dr, Cincinnati, OH 45230

SCRUGGS JR, C(harles) Perry (ETenn) 540 Bryant Rd, Chattanooga, TN 37405

SCRUTCHINS, Arthur Paul (Okla) Holland Hall School, 5666 E 81st St, Tulsa, OK 74137

✠ **SCRUTON**, Gordon Paul (Ret Bp of WMass 2012-) 40 Carriage Hill Dr, Wethersfield, CT 06109

SCULLY, Edward Anthony (SwFla) 311 Irwin Ave, Albion, MI 49224

SCUPHOLME, Anne (SeFla) 1990 English Oaks Cir N, Charlottesville, VA 22911

SEABORN, Sandra L (NY) 669 Albany Post Rd, #8805, Scarborough, NY 10510

SEABURY, Scott Hamor (WMass) 10 Rawlings Brook Rd, Suffield, CT 06078

SEADALE, Vincent Gerald (Mass)

✠ **SEAGE**, Brian Richard (Bp of Miss 2015-) 106 Vinson Cv, Madison, MS 39110

SEAGE, Kyle Dice (Miss) 106 Vinson Cv, Madison, MS 39110

SEAGLE, Teresa Ryan (Fla) 301 Brooks Cir E, Jacksonville, FL 32211

SEAL, William Christopher Houston (The Episcopal NCal) 201 Nevada St, Nevada City, CA 95959

SEALES, Hea Suk (Ala) 100 Church Dr, Auburn, AL 36830

SEALS, William Frederick (CFla) 23 Surrey Run, Hendersonville, NC 28791

SEAMAN, Kelly S (NH) 52 Gould Rd, New London, NH 03257

SEAMAN, Martha Lee (Az) 7419 E Palm Ln, Scottsdale, AZ 85257

SEARLE, Susan Elizabeth (Nwk) 200 W 79th St Apt 14-P, New York, NY 10024

SEARS III, Albert Nelson (Mass) 98 Ridgewood Dr, Rocky Hill, CT 06067

SEARS, Barbara (Md) 7030 Upland Ridge Dr, Adamstown, MD 21710

SEARS, Barbara Anne (Md) 1000 Weller Cir Apt 221, Westminster, MD 21158

SEARS, Gwen W (WMass) 235 Walker St. Apt. 162, Lenox, MA 01240

SEATON, Anne Christine (Az) 168 W Arizona St, Holbrook, AZ 86025

SEATON, Robert Deane (WK)

SEAVER, Maurice Blanchard (WNC) 3500 Carmel Rd, Charlotte, NC 28226

SEAVEY, SuZanne Elane (ETenn) 135 Fountainhead Ct, Lenoir City, TN 37772

SEAY, Donald Robert (CFla) 247 N Main St #14, Dousman, WI 53118

SEBRO, Jacqueline Marie (ECR) 815 Sycamore Canyon Rd, Paso Robles, CA 93446

SECAUR, Stephen Charles (Mil) 435 SOM Center Rd., Mayfield Village, OH 44143

SECOR, Neale A (Pa) 4 Appletree Ct, Philadelphia, PA 19106

SEDDON, Anne Christine (Ct) 4 Maybury Rd, Suffield, CT 06078

SEDDON, Matthew T (Tex) St. John's Episcopal Church, 11201 Parkfield Drive, Austin, TX 78758

SEDGWICK, R(oger) Stephen (O) 647 Reid Ave, Lorain, OH 44052

SEDLACEK, Carol Westerberg (Ore) 2103 Desiree Pl, Lebanon, OR 97355

SEDLACEK, Wes (Ore) 2103 Desiree Pl, Lebanon, OR 97355

SEDWICK, Katherine Langlitz (Oly) 5128 40th Avenue South, Minneapolis, MN 55417

SEEBER, Laurian (Vt) 47 Shadow Lang Berlin, Barre, VT 05641

SEEFELDT, Scott Allen (Mil)

SEEGER, Elisabeth Ann (Oly) 4467 S. 172nd St., SeaTac, WA 98188

SEEGER, Sue Fisher (Mass) 28 Seagrave Rd, Cambridge, MA 02140

SEEKINS, Sheila Anne (Me) 11 White St, Rockland, ME 04841

SEELEY, Janet Lynne (Wyo) 506 Cedar Ave, Kemmerer, WY 83101

SEELEY JR, Walt (Wyo) 2024 Rolling Hills Road, Kemmerer, WY 83101

SEELY, Shirley Ann (EMich) 3201 Gratiot Ave, Port Huron, MI 48060

SEELYE FOREST, Elizabeth Jane (Mich) 14191 Ivanhoe Dr Apt 3, Sterling Heights, MI 48312

SEFCHICK, Frank Stephen (Be) 1498 Quakake Rd, Weatherly, PA 18255

SEGAL, D(anna) Joy (Pa) 916 South Swanson Street, Philadelphia, PA 19147

SEGER, David L (NI) 13259 Hisega Dr, Rapid City, SD 57702

SEGER, Nikki Elizabeth Louise (Mich)

SEGERBRECHT, Stephen Louis (Kan) 1715 Prestwick Dr, Lawrence, KS 66047

SEIBERT, Joanna Johnson (Ark) 27 River Ridge Rd, Little Rock, AR 72227

SEIBERT, Thomas E (Colo) 145 W 5th St, Delta, CO 81416

SEIDMAN, Kimberly Anne (NwT) Holy Comforter Episcopal Church, PO Box 412, Broomfield, CO 80038

SEIFERT, Cynthia Seeliger (Tenn) 5041 English Village Dr, Nashville, TN 37211

SEIFERT, Robert Joseph (ECR) 161 Palo Verde Ter, Santa Cruz, CA 95060

SEIFERT, Sarah Lavonne (Kan) 14301 S Blackbob Rd, Olathe, KS 66062

SEILER, Jeffrey Hamilton (Va) 4003 St Erics Turn, Williamsburg, VA 23185

SEILER, Michael Scott (Los) 1031 Bienveneda Ave, Pacific Palisades, CA 90272

SEILER, Robert Stuart (Va) 4810 Stuart Ave, Richmond, VA 23226

SEILER-DUBAY, Noreen (WA) 5031 Laguna Rd, College Park, MD 20740

SEILS, Donald Davis (Colo) 5749 N Stetson Ct, Parker, CO 80134

SEIPEL, James Russell (Los) 25769 Player Dr, Valencia, CA 91355

SEIPP, Vivian (NY) 39 Cumberland Rd, Fishkill, NY 12524

SEITER, Claudia D (U) 540 W 2350 S, Brigham City, UT 84302

SEITZ, Christopher R (Dal) Wycliffe College, University Of Toronto, Toronto, ON M5S 1H7, Canada

SEITZ, Mark Ellis (WVa) PO Box 508, Wheeling, WV 26003

SEITZ, Philip Allan (EMich) 3003 Mill Station Road, Hale, MI 48739

SEITZ SR, Thomas Comstock (CFla) 2565 Salzburg Loop, Winter Haven, FL 33884

SEITZ JR, Thomas Comstock (CFla) 221 S 4th St, Lake Wales, FL 33853

SELDEN, Elizabeth Ann (Minn) 6212 Crest Ln, MN, Edina 55436

SELES, Deborah Galante (Ida) 1172 Woodriver Dr, Twin Falls, ID 83301

SELF, Deborah Davis (SwFla)

SELFE-VERRONE, A(nne) (NY) Chapel of St. Francis, 3621 Brunswick Ave., Los Angeles, CA 90039

SELL, James William Henry (SVa) 239 Duke St Unit 207, Norfolk, VA 23510

SELLERS, Robert Clayton (Tex) 1401 S PALMETTO AVE, APT 207, DAYTONA BEACH, FL 32114

SELLERY, David (LI) PO Box 393, Salisbury, CT 06068

SELL-LEE, William Merle (WA) 965 Winslow Way E Unit 103, Bainbridge Island, WA 98110

SELLS, Jeffery Edward (Oly) Po Box 3090, Salt Lake City, UT 84110

SELLS, Patricia (Oly)

SELNICK, Thomas (O) Po Box 519, Gates Mills, OH 44040

SELVAGE, Daniel Lee (CPa) 102 Faust Cir, Bellefonte, PA 16823

SELVEY, Mark F (Neb) 3310 16th Ave, Omaha, NE 68022

SELZER, David O (WNY) 4 Phylis St, Ottawa, ON K2J 1V2, Canada

SEMES, Robert Louis (Ore) 1354 Primavera Drive E, Palm Springs, CA 92264

SEMON, Kenneth J (RG) 311 E. Palace Avenue, Santa Fe, NM 87501

SEMON-SCOTT, Deborah Anne (Mich) 3 N Broad St, Hillsdale, MI 49242

SENECHAL, Roger Edward (WMass) 7601 Harper Road, Joelton, TN 37080

SENEY, Robert William (Miss) 14165 Denver West Cricle #123, Lakewood, CO 80401

SENUTA, Lisa Ann (Chi) 550 Sunset Ridge Rd, Northfield, IL 60093

SENYONI, Christian (ND) Grace Episcopal Church, 405 2nd Ave NE, Jamestown, ND 58401

SERACUSE, Linda Kay (Tex) Po Box 559, Conroe, TX 77305

SERAS, Barbara J (Md) 67 River Bend Park, Lancaster, PA 17602

SERDAHL, Dennis Lee (Ark) 531 Northpointe Dr, Mountain Home, AR 72653

SERFES, Patricia May (Me) 2524 Casa Dr, New Port Richey, FL 34655

SERMON, William Todd (Colo) 1612 E Custer St, Laramie, WY 82070

SERPA-ORDONEZ, Pedro Abel (EcuC) Casilla Postal 533, Riobamba, Ecuador

SERRA-LIMA, Federico (Alb) 28 Harrington Lane, Old Chatham, NY 12136

SERRANO POREDA, Nelson Evelio (Colom) c/o Diocese of Colombia, Cra 6 No. 49-85 Piso 2, Bogota, BDC, Colombia

SERVAIS, Jean Neal (Okla) PO Box 165, Coalgate, OK 74538

SERVELLON, Maria Filomena (NY) 30 Pine Grove Avenue, 20 Carroll Street, Poughkeepsie, Kingston, NY 12401

SERVETAS, Linda Anne (Alb) 16 Dean St, Deposit, NY 13754

SERVETAS, Nickolas (Alb) 16 Dean St, Deposit, NY 13754

SESSIONS, Judy Karen (WTex) 2910 Treasure Hills Blvd Apt B, Harlingen, TX 78550

SESSIONS, Marcia Andrews (RI) 15 Hattie Ave, Greenville, RI 02828

SESSUM, Robert Lee (Lex) 101 South Hanover Ave Suite 6 L, Lexington, KY 40502

SETMEYER, Robert Charles (Chi) 711 S River Rd Apt 508, Des Plaines, IL 60016

SETTLES, Russell Lee (NC) 9118 Kings Canyon Dr, Charlotte, NC 28210

SETZER, Stephen F (Del) 5100 Ross Ave, Dallas, TX 75206

SEUFERT, Carmen Rae (Roch) 103 Williams St, Newark, NY 14513

SEVAYEGA, Reginald Delano (HB) 4701 Belfiore Rd, Warrensville Heights, OH 44128

SEVER, Cynthia A (WNY) 3390 Lyell Rd, Rochester, NY 14606

SEVICK, Gerald (Tex) 3901 S. Panther Creek, The Woodlands, TX 77381

SEVILLE, John C (Chi) 802 Foxdale Ave, Winnetka, IL 60093

SEVILLE, Joseph (CPa) 1405 Wedgewood Way, Mechanicsburg, PA 17050

SEWARD, Barbara J (Minn) Trinity Episcopal Church, 322 2nd St, Excelsior, MN 55331

SEWELL, Edith (The Episcopal Church in Haw) 1212 Punahou #2504, Honolulu, HI 96826

SEWELL, John Wayne (WTenn) 53 Shepherd Ln, Memphis, TN 38117

SEXTON, Patricia Mary (USC) 1001 12th St, Cayce, SC 29033

SEXTON, Timothy Wayne (The Episcopal Church in Haw) 5310 Bridle Circle, Oakley, UT 84055

SEY, Reginald Franklyn (Chi) 11219 S Peoria St, Chicago, IL 60643

SEYMOUR, John (Jack) David (Chi) 946 W Hubbard St, Chicago, IL 60642

SEYMOUR, Marlyne Joyce (Mil) 862 No. Sandy Lane, Elkhorn, WI 53121

SGRO, Anthony Huston (At)

SHACKELFORD, L(Ynn) Clark (Okla) 404 Washington Avenue, Sand Springs, OK 74063

SHACKLEFORD, Richard Neal (LI) Timber Ridge, 711 John Green Rd, Jonesborough, TN 37659

SHACKLETT JR, Richard Lee (Kan) 6535 Maple Dr, Mission, KS 66202

SHADLE, Jennifer Lynn (Colo)

SHADOW, Burton Alexander (FtW) 3540 Manderly Place, Fort Worth, TX 76109

SHAEFER III, Harry Frederick (Mich) 407 Highland Ave., Johnson City, TN 37604

SHAEFER, Susan A (Mich) 1605 E. Stadium Blvd., Ann Arbor, MI 48104

SHAFER, Jean Lankford (NwT) 4902 43rd St, Lubbock, TX 79414

SHAFER, Lee Franklin (Ala) 5 Booger Holw, Anniston, AL 36207

SHAFER, Linda Jean (Mich) 151 N Main St, Brooklyn, MI 49230

SHAFER, Michael Gales (NY) 21 Decker Road, Stanfordville, NY 12581

SHAFER, Samuel Harvey (RG) 630 66th St, Oakland, CA 94609

SHAFFER, Brian Keith (Mich) Cathedral Church of St. Paul, Detroit, MI 48201

SHAFFER, Charles Omer (Md) 7200 3rd Ave, Cot. C119, Eldersburg, MD 21784

SHAFFER, Dallas Bertrand (WVa) 1415 Cornell St, Keyser, WV 26726

SHAFFER, Dee (Ga) 299 Ga Episcopal Conference Ctr Rd, Waverly, GA 31565

SHAFFER, James Michael (WMo) Po Box 2714, Friday Harbor, WA 98250

SHAFFER, John Alfred (CNY) 162 W 3rd St, Oswego, NY 13126

✠ **SHAHAN**, Robert Reed (Ret Bp of Az 2004-) 10175 S North Lake Ave, Olathe, KS 66061

SHAHINIAN, Katharine Anne (Md) St Martin's In The Field, 375 Benfield Rd, Severna Park, MD 21146

SHAIN-HENDRICKS, Christy A (Colo) Po Box 10000, Silverthorne, CO 80498

SHAKESPEARE, Lyndon (WA)

SHALLCROSS, Lexa Herries (Be) 150 Elm St, Emmaus, PA 18049

SHAMBAUGH, Benjamin Albert (Me) 143 State St, Portland, ME 04101

SHAMEL, Andrew (Cal) 55 Monument Cir Ste 600, Indianapolis, IN 46204

SHAMHART, Lewis Roper (LI) 510 W 46th St Apt 621, New York, NY 10036

SHAMO, Vincent (Los) 3225 Hollypark Dr Apt 4, Inglewood, CA 90305

SHAN, Becky King-Chu (ECR) 450 Old San francisco Rd Apt A110, Sunnyvale, CA 94086

SHANAHAN, Thomazine Weinstein (CPa) 4426 Reservoir Rd Nw, Washington, DC 20007

✠ **SHAND**, James Joseph (Ret Bp of Eas 2013-) 208 Somerset Ct, Queenstown, MD 21658

SHAND III, William Munro (WA) 10033 River Rd, Potomac, MD 20854

SHANDS III, Alfred Rives (Ky) 8915 Highway 329, Crestwood, KY 40014

SHANDS, Harriet Goodrich (WNC) 21 Chestnut Ridge Road, Pisgah Forest, NC 28768

SHANE, Johnnette (Mo) Trinity Episcopal Church, PO Box 652, Kirksville, MO 63501

SHANK, Michael Joseph (Alb) 87 E Main St, Sidney, NY 13838

SHANK, Nancy (CPa) 111 Pine St, Danville, PA 17821

SHANKLES, Jeffrey Scott (Va) 6800A Columbia Pike, Annandale, VA 22003

SHANKS, Estelle (Nev) PO Box 98, Austin, NV 89310

SHANKS, Margaret Ruth (Lex) 367 Stratford Dr, Lexington, KY 40503

SHANKS, Stephen Ray (Ala) 112-C King Valley Rd, Pelham, AL 35124

SHANLEY-ROBERTS, Eileen M (Chi) 326 N Martin Luther King Jr Ave, Waukegan, IL 60085

SHANNON JR, Carl Steen (Tex) 102 Pecan Grv Apt 121, Houston, TX 77077

SHANNON, Carolyn Louise (Nev) 2366 Aqua Vista Ave, Henderson, NV 89014

SHANNON SR, Himie-Budu (O) 988 Carlone Place, South Euclid, OH 44121

SHANNON, James L (Pa) 112 Lansdowne Ct, Lansdowne, PA 19050

SHANNON, James Michael (ND) 319 S 5th St, Grand Forks, ND 58201

SHANNON, Marvin Boyd (FtW) Po Box 5555, Laguna Park, TX 76644

SHANNON II, Robert Lloyd (Roch) 17 Uncle Bens Way, Orleans, MA 02653

SHAON, Gerald E (Cal) 4550 Warwick Blve, Apt 204, Kansas City, MO 64111

SHAPTON, Eleanor Louise (Spok) 240 Maringo Rd, Ephrata, WA 98823

SHARP, Carolyn J (Ct) Yale Divinity School, 409 Prospect St., New Haven, CT 06511

SHARP, James Leonard (ETenn) 4016 White Wood Cir, Morristown, TN 37814

SHARP, Jeffrey Robert (Oly) 15220 Main Street, Bellevue, WA 98007

SHARP, Lynne (Roch) PO Box 249, Hammondsport, NY 14840

SHARP, Wesley Eric (CFla) 700 Rinehart Rd, Lake Mary, FL 32746

SHARPE, Sheila Gast (Del) 65 East Stephen Drive, Newark, DE 19713

SHARPTON, Larry (Ala) 8501 Olde Gate, Montgomery, AL 36116

SHARROW, Chuck (WTex) 960 Toledo Dr, Brownsville, TX 78526

SHATAGIN, Theodore Ivan (Vt) Po Box 1807, Ardmore, OK 73402

SHATTUCK JR, Gardiner Humphrey (RI) 190 North St, Warwick, RI 02886

SHAUBACH, Sheila Kathryn (Episcopal SJ) Po Box 164, Raymond, CA 93653

SHAVER, Ellen M (Me) 139 High Head Rd, Harpswell, ME 04079

SHAVER, John (Minn) 3448 Rum River Dr, Anoka, MN 55303

SHAVER, Stephen Richard (Oly)

SHAVER, Thomas Ronald (SO) 25 State Rd 13 Apt H8, Saint Johns, FL 32259

SHAW, Adrianna Sarah (Kan) St Philip's Episcopal Church, 302 E. General Stewart Way, Hinesville, GA 31314

SHAW, Jane Alison (Cal) 110 California St, San Francisco, CA 94111

SHAW, Margaret Elizabeth (Alb) 10215 Carriage Dr, Plymouth, IN 46563

SHAW, Martini (Pa) 6361 Lancaster Ave, Philadelphia, PA 19151

SHAW, Philip Algie (Az) Trinity Episcopal Church, P.O. Box 590, Kingman, AZ 86402

SHAW, Robert Clyde (Mil) 46 New Cross N, Asheville, NC 28805

SHAW, Samuel Gates (Ala) 4112 Abingdon Ln, Birmingham, AL 35243

SHAW, Timothy Joel (CFla) 901 Thompson Cir Nw, Winter Haven, FL 33881

SHAW, Warren Ervin (Pa) 1029 Bristlecone Ln, Charlottesville, VA 22911

SHEARER, Donald Robert (Nwk) 156 Mountain Dr, Greentown, PA 18426

SHEARER, Robert L (Nwk) 2077 Center Ave Apt 20A, Fort Lee, NJ 07024

SHEARS, S(idney) Herbert (SanD) 4166 Clubhouse Rd, Lompoc, CA 93436

SHEAY, Virginia M (NJ) 12 Glenwood Ln, Stockton, NJ 08559

SHECTER, Teri Ann (Colo)

SHEEHAN JR, David (Del) 3401 Greenbriar Ln, West Grove, PA 19390

SHEEHAN, John Thomas (Va) 512 Duff Rd Ne, Leesburg, VA 20176

SHEEN RODRIGUEZ, Juan Enrique (DR (DomRep))

SHEETZ, David Allan (Cal) 250 Baldwin Ave Apt 303, San Mateo, CA 94401

SHEFFIELD III, Earl J (Tex) 325 Apache Run Road, Wallisville, TX 77597

SHEFFIELD, Jack (Tex) PO Box 12615, San Antonio, TX 78212

SHEFFIELD, Sharon Kay (Los) 10354 Downey Ave, Downey, CA 90241

SHEHANE, Mary Kathryn (Oly) 9416 1st Ave Ne Apt 408, Seattle, WA 98115

SHELBY, F Stuart (Tex) Saint Richard's Episcopal Church, 1420 E Palm Valley Blvd, Round Rock, TX 78664

SHELBY, Jason B (Miss) 106 Sharkey Ave, Clarksdale, MS 38614

SHELDON, Carren (The Episcopal NCal) 1500 State Street, Santa Barbara, CA 93101

SHELDON, Jaclyn Struff (Ct) 85 Holmes Rd, East Lyme, CT 06333

SHELDON III, J(oseph) Victor (Spr) 1220 Uss Daniel Boone Ave, Kings Bay, GA 31547

SHELDON, Karen Sears (Vt) 86 S Main St, Hanover, NH 03755

SHELDON, Patricia Lu (Neb) 3818 N 211th St, Elkhorn, NE 68022

SHELDON, Peggy Ann (SeFla) 2000 Sw Racquet Club Dr, Palm City, FL 34990

SHELDON, Raymond S (Oly) 1075 Alexander Pl Ne, Bainbridge Island, WA 98110

SHELDON, Terry Lynn (CNY) 21 White St, Clark Mills, NY 13321

SHELL, Lawrence S (NMich) 201 E. Ridge St., Marquette, MI 49855

SHELLITO, John Ellis (Va) St George's Church, 915 N Oakland St, Arlington, VA 22203

SHELLY, Marshall Keith (NJ) 505 Main St, Spotswood, NJ 08884

SHELTON, Benson Eldridge (Va) 9220 Georgetown Pike, Great Falls, VA 22066

SHELTON, Edna S (Mich) 18270 Northlawn St, Detroit, MI 48221

SHELTON, Joan Adams (CNY) 2126 Connecticut Ave Nw Apt 49, Washington, DC 20008

SHELTON, Linda Ross (Tex) 3507 Plumb St, Houston, TX 77005

SHELTON-HAWLEY, Madeline Clelie (Tex)

SHEMATEK, Jon Paul (Md) 9120 Frederick Rd, Ellicott City, MD 21042

SHEMAYEV, Roman Aelred (Mil) 3528 Valley Ridge Rd, Middleton, WI 53562

SHEPARD, Alfred Hugh (Colo) 3013 Taos Meadows Dr NE, Rio Rancho, NM 87144

SHEPARD, Diane Elise Rucker (Pgh) 1155 Brintell St, Pittsburgh, PA 15201

SHEPARD, Kenneth Reis (Neb)

SHEPARD, Margaret S (CGC) 1608 Baker Ct, Panama City, FL 32401

SHEPHERD, Angela Fontessa (Md) Episcopal Diocese of Maryland, 4 E University Pkwy, Baltimore, MD 21218

SHEPHERD, Burton Hale (WTex) 185 Towerview Dr Apt 1101, Saint Augustine, FL 32092

SHEPHERD, Karlyn Ann (RG) 22 Bowersville Rd, Algodones, NM 87001

SHEPHERD, Nancy Delane (At) 1100 Pine Valley Road, Griffin, GA 30224

SHEPHERD, Nancy Hamilton (Mass) 172 Harvard Rd, Stow, MA 01775

SHEPHERD, Richard Golder (NY)

SHEPHERD, Stephen Gregory (Va) 6019 Hibbling Ave, Springfield, VA 22150

SHEPHERD, Thomas Charles (Mass) 6600 Ne 22nd Way Apt 2323, Fort Lauderdale, FL 33308

SHEPHERD, Thomas Eugene (WMo) 1107 Saratoga Drive, Euless, TX 76040

SHEPHERD JR, William Henry (At) 1100 Pine Valley Rd, Griffin, GA 30224

SHEPHERD, William John (Pa) 110 W Johnson St, Philadelphia, PA 19144

SHEPIC, Charlotte Louise (Colo) 14031 W Exposition Dr, Lakewood, CO 80228

SHEPLEY, Joseph (Ct) 65 Grey Rock Road, Southbury, CT 06488

SHEPPARD, Dale Eugene (WVa) 1051 Walker Road, Follansbee, WV 26037

SHEPPARD, Patricia K (Fla) 919 San Fernando St., Fernandina Beach, FL 32034

SHERARD, Susan (NC) 402 West Smith Street, 4J, Greensboro, NC 27401

SHERER, Valori Mulvey (WNC) 506 W Sumter St, Shelby, NC 28150

SHERFICK, Kenneth L (WMich) 1517 Emoriland Blvd, Knoxville, TN 37917

SHERIDAN, Dennis Arnol (Los) 242 E Alvarado St, Pomona, CA 91767

SHERIDAN-CAMPBELL, Laura M (SanD) 6540 Ambrosia Ln Apt 1128, Carlsbad, CA 92011

SHERMAN, Andrew James (SeFla) 245 NE 2nd St., Boca Raton, FL 33432

SHERMAN, Clark Michael (Mont) 5 W Olive St, Bozeman, MT 59715

SHERMAN, Elizabeth Ann (Cal) St. Francis Episcopal Church, San Francisco, CA 94127

SHERMAN, Guy Charles (Oly) 12527 Roosevelt Way Ne Apt 404, Seattle, WA 98125

SHERMAN JR, Levering Bartine (Me) 130 Cedar St, Bangor, ME 04401

SHERMAN, Russell E (WTex) 202 Primera Dr, San Antonio, TX 78212

SHERRER, Wayne Calvin (Be) 150 Elm Street, Emmaus, PA 18049

SHERRILL, Christopher Ralph (NJ) P.O. Box 45, Southport, ME 04576

SHERRILL II, Edmund Knox (NH) Church Farm School, 1001 E Lincoln Hwy, Exton, PA 19341

SHERRILL JR, George (WVa) 603 Hawthorne Ln, Hurricane, WV 25526

SHERRILL, Joan (NC)

SHERRILL, Karen Flynt (WVa) St. John's Episcopal Church, 3000 Washington Blvd, Huntington, WV 25705

SHERROUSE, Wanda Gail (CFla) 121 W 18th St, Sanford, FL 32771

SHERWIN, Lawrence Alan (Vt) 54 E State St, Montpelier, VT 05602

SHERWOOD, Robert Leon (Mass) 165 Main St, Buzzards Bay, MA 02532

SHERWOOD, Zalmon Omar (Mich) PO Box 1342, Arcadia, FL 34265

SHEVLIN, James Charles (CFla) Saint Paul's Church, 25 River St, Sidney, NY 13838

SHEW, Debra Ann (At) 3627 Shadowood Pkwy Se, Atlanta, GA 30339

SHEWMAKER, David Paul (The Episcopal NCal) St Paul's Episcopal Ch, 220 E. Macken, Crescent City, CA 95531

SHIELD, Catherine Ann (Kan) 13420 E Harry St, Wichita, KS 67230

SHIELDS, James Mark (Md) 6153 Waiting Spg, Columbia, MD 21045

SHIELDS, John Edward (NC) 520 Summit St, Winston Salem, NC 27101

SHIELDS, John W (WNC) 2508 Amity Ave, Gastonia, NC 28054

SHIELDS, Richard E (The Episcopal Church in Haw) 1330 1st Ave Apt 424, New York, NY 10021

SHIER, Marshall Wayne (Los) 1348 E Wilshire Ave, Fullerton, CA 92831

SHIER, Nancy Katherine (Los) 224 Bradbury Dr, San Gabriel, CA 91775

SHIER, Pamela C (WVa) 164 Mason Ridge Rd, Mount Morris, PA 15349

SHIFLET JR, William Ray (Md) 4520 Cornflower Ct, Ellicott City, MD 21043

SHIGAKI, Jerry M (Oly) 6963 California Ave Sw Unit 102, Seattle, WA 98136

SHIGAKI, Pauline Yuri (Oly)

SHIKE, Charles Wesley (Nwk) 601 Kappock St Apt 1F, Bronx, NY 10463

SHILEY, Edward (Pa) 145 West Springfield Road, Springfield, PA 19064

✠ **SHIN**, Allen K (Bp Suffr of NY 2014-) Episcopal Diocese of New York, 1047 Amsterdam Ave, New York, NY 10025

SHINN, Richard Emerson (Mich) 6710 Little Hemlock St, Stanwood, MI 49346

SHIPMAN, Bruce MacDonald (Ct) 241 Monument St Apt 6, Groton, CT 06340

SHIPMAN, Josh (Colo)

SHIPP, Mary Jane Mccoy (Mont) St. James' Episcopal Church, PO Box 1374, Dillon, MT 59725

SHIPPEE, Richard C (RI) 3330 E Main St Lot 109, Mesa, AZ 85213

SHIPPEN II, Joseph Jenkins (At) PO Box 1213, Griffin, GA 30224

SHIPPEN, Sallie Elliot (Cal) 756 14th Way Sw, Edmonds, WA 98020

SHIPPEY, Edgar Elijah (Ore) 940 N Dean St, Coquille, OR 97423

✠ **SHIPPS**, Harry Woolston (Ret Bp of Ga 1995-) 95 Skidaway Island Park Rd Unit 20, Savannah, GA 31411

SHIRES, Robert A (SeFla) 10860 Tamoron Ln, Boca Raton, FL 33498

SHIREY, William Carrol (Colo) 277 Old Man Mountain Ln, Estes Park, CO 80517

SHIRLEY, Diana Frangoulis (SO) 664 Glacier Pass, Westerville, OH 43081

SHIRLEY, Fred (SO) 664 Glacier Pass, Westerville, OH 43081

SHIRLEY, Michael Olenius (Mass) 28 Amherst St, Lawrence, MA 01843

SHIRLEY, Sarah A (WA) 5 Laguna St Unit 302, Fort Walton Beach, FL 32548

SHIRLEY, Sylvia Kirkland (Okla) St John's Episcopal Church, 5201 N Brookline Ave, Oklahoma City, OK 73112

SHIROTA, Andrew Kunihito (Mich) 4700 Lowe Rd, Louisville, KY 40220

SHISLER, Sara Lynn (Md) 4 E University Pkwy, Baltimore, MD 21218

SHIVES, Beverly Mason (SeFla) 159 Biscayne Ave, Tampa, FL 33606

SHOBE, Melody W (RI) 2407 Cranston St., Cranston, RI 02920

SHOBE, Robert Casey (Dal) 14115 Hillcrest Road, Dallas, TX 75254

SHOBERG, Warren E (SD) 3316 E 28th St, Sioux Falls, SD 57103

SHOCKLEY, Stephanie Elizabeth (NJ) 316 E 88th St, New York, NY 10128

SHODA, David Brian (WVa) 108 S Washington St, Berkeley Springs, WV 25411

SHOEMAKE, Daniel (Ga) 1521 N Patterson St, Valdosta, GA 31602

SHOEMAKER, Adam James (NC) The Episcopal Church of the Holy Comforter, 320 East Davis Street, Burlington, NC 27215

SHOEMAKER, Eric Wayne (WA) 8795 Lowell Road, Pomfret, MD 20675

SHOEMAKER, H(etty) Stephanie Condon (RI) 96 Washington St, Newport, RI 02840

SHOEMAKER, Jack G (The Episcopal Church in Haw) 3045 Fir Tree Dr Se, Salem, OR 97317

SHOEMAKER, Patricia Ross Pittman (NC) 22 Mayflower Ln, Lexington, NC 27295

SHOFSTALL, Sarah J (O) Saint Barnabas Church, 468 Bradley Rd, Bay Village, OH 44140

SHOLANDER, Mark (CFla) 907 Oakway Dr, Auburndale, FL 33823

SHOLTY JR, Henry Edward (Dal) 5942 Abrams Rd # 209, Dallas, TX 75231

SHORT, James Healy (Colo) 797 Tower Hill Rd., Appomattox, VA 24522

SHORT, James Ritchie (Episcopal SJ) Casanova & ocean, Carmel, CA 93921

SHORT, Molly McGee (NC) 290 Quintard Rd, Sewanee, TN 37375

SHORTELL, Bruce Mallard (At) PO Box 1293, Flowery Branch, GA 30542

SHORTES, Stephen Edward (The Episcopal NCal) 2883 Coloma St, Placerville, CA 95667

SHORTRIDGE, Delores J (Nev) 973 S. Fulton St., Denver, CO 80247

SHORTT, Mary J (EMich) P.O. Box 151, West Branch, MI 48661

SHOUCAIR, James Douglas (Pgh) 130 Westchester Dr, Pittsburgh, PA 15215

SHOULAK, Jim (Minn) 20475 County Road 10, Corcoran, MN 55340

SHOULDERS, David Ira (Ind) 3415 Windham Lake Place, Indianapolis, IN 46214

SHOWERS, David Gordon (Md) Middleham & St. Peter Ep. Parish, PO Box 277, Lusby, MD 20657

SHOWS, W(illiam) Derek (NC) 1077 Fearrington Post, Pittsboro, NC 27312

SHOWS CAFFEY, Elizabeth Kristen (At) 634 W Peachtree St NW, Atlanta, GA 30308

SHRIVER, Domingo F (WMich) 301 N James St, Ludington, MI 49431

SHRIVER JR, Frederick Hardman (NY) 37 W. 12th Street, Apt. 4K, New York, NY 10011

SHUART, R(obert) Stephen (NwPa) Po Box 368, South Harwich, MA 02661

SHUCKER II, Courtney A (U) 203 Palmer St, Salida, CO 81201

SHUFORD, Carlton Lamont (Ga) 131 Avondale Dr, Augusta, GA 30907

SHUFORD, Sheila Cathcart (Nwk) 12 Sorman Ter, Randolph, NJ 07869

SHULDA, David Leroy (Ore) 2139 Berwin Ln, Eugene, OR 97404

SHUMAKER, John Hilton (Episcopal SJ) 1317 Gold Hunter Rd, San Andreas, CA 95249

SHUMARD, Jim (Ga) 140 Mercer Rd, Savannah, GA 31411

SIBLEY, David C (LI) 54 George St, Manhasset, NY 11030

SICKELS, Peter L (Ia) 4814 Amesbury Ct, Davenport, IA 52807

SICKLER, Brenda Pamela (WMo) 5 E 337th Rd, Humansville, MO 65674

SICKLES, Clarence William (Nwk) 68 Heath Village, Hackettstown, NJ 07840

SIDEBOTHAM, John N (EC) 16 W Fayetteville St, Wrightsville Beach, NC 28480

SIDERIUS, Donna-Mae Amy (SVa) 3 Mizzen Cir, Hampton, VA 23664

SIEFFERMAN, Norman Clyde (Va) 609 Shaw Ct, Fredericksburg, VA 22405

SIEGEL II, Carl De Haven (WMo) 1405 Boyce Ave, Baltimore, MD 21204

SIEGENTHALER, David John (Mass) 54 Concord Ave Apt 102, Cambridge, MA 02138

SIEGFRIEDT, Karen Faye (The Episcopal NCal) 835 Argonaut Drive, Jackson, CA 95642

SIEGMUND, Mary Kay (Kan) 3 Ne 83rd Ter, Kansas City, MO 64118

SIENER, George Richard (NH) 6 Whippoorwill Ln, Exeter, NH 03833

SIERACKI, Emily K (Ida) 518 N 8th St, Boise, ID 83702

SIERRA, Federico (Los) 425 N Stoneman Ave Apt A, Alhambra, CA 91801

SIERRA, Frank (WMo) 2718 Alabama Ct, Joplin, MO 64804

SIERRA, Jose De Jesus (NC) Iglesia Episcopal Puertorriquena, PO Box 902, Saint Just, PR 00978-0902, Puerto Rico

SIERRA ECHEVERRY, Gabriel Alcides (Colom) Parroquia La Anunciacion, El Bagre, Apartado Aereo 52964, Bogota, Colombia

SIFFORD, Thomas Andrew (Ark) 74 Sierra Dr, Hot Springs Village, AR 71909

SIGAFOOS, Richard Vaughn (Colo) 131 31 Rd, Grand Junction, CO 81503

SIGAMONEY, Christopher (LI)

SIGLER, James Markham (The Episcopal NCal) P.O. Box 467, Wimberley, TX 78676

SIGLOH, Jane Engleby (SwVa) 4068 Garth Rd, Crozet, VA 22932

SIGNORE, Richard Scott (Mass) 19 Briggs Ave., Bourne, MA 02532

SIGNORELLI, Barry M (NY) 278 Monmouth St Apt 4-L, Jersey City, NJ 07302

SILBAUGH, Morgan Collins (Cal) 914 Mountain Meadows Cir, Ashland, OR 97520

SILBEREIS, Richard M (Ct) 155 Wyllys St, Hartford, CT 06106

SILCOX JR, James Heyward (Va) Wicomico Parish Church, PO Box 70, Wicomico Church, VA 22579

SILIDES JR, George Constantine (Los) 830 W Bonita Ave, Claremont, CA 91711

SILIDES, Hunter Pearson (Los) 411 Gold St, Juneau, AK 99801

SILK-WRIGHT, Margaret (Marnie) (CFla) 1813 Palo Alto Ave, Lady Lake, FL 32159

SILLA, Suzanne Marie (NI) Diocese of Northern Indiana, 117 N Lafayette Blvd, South Bend, IN 46601

SILTON, Margaret Kanze (NC) PO Box 608, Wake Forest, NC 27588

SILVA-GONZALEZ, Alvaro (PR)

SILVER, Deborah Lee (At) 3005 St James Pl, Grovetown, GA 30813

SILVER, Gayanne Miller (Fla) 14557 Basilham Ln, Jacksonville, FL 32258

SILVERSTRIM, Elaine Margaret (CPa) 110 Dry Run Rd., Coudersport, PA 16915

SIMEONE, Richard John (Mass) 203 Pemberton St Unit 3, Cambridge, MA 02140

SIMMONDS, Richard Frank (Ak) Po Box 58041, Minto, AK 99758

SIMMONS, Charles Winston (NY) St Andrew's Church, 781 Castle Hill Ave, Bronx, NY 10473

SIMMONS, David Clark (NMich) 5976 Whitney 19.8 Blvd, Gladstone, MI 49837

SIMMONS, David Todd (Mil) 808 S East Ave, Waukesha, WI 63186

SIMMONS, Elizabeth H (Ak) PO Box 1668, Kodiak, AK 99615

SIMMONS, Harriet Phillips (Miss) 4911 Country Club Dr, Meridian, MS 39305

SIMMONS, Harriette J (At) Saint Paul'S Church, 605 Reynolds Street On The Riverwalk, Augusta, GA 30901

SIMMONS, Kenneth William (Minn) 11 Kellogg Blvd E Apt 715, Saint Paul, MN 55101

SIMMONS, Mary Rose (NMich) 5976 Whitney 19.8 Blvd, Gladstone, MI 49837

SIMMONS, Ned Allen (Ga) 109 Flint River Circle, Quitman, GA 31643

SIMMONS IV, Thomas William (Va) 1807 Hungary Rd, Richmond, VA 23228

SIMMONS, Walter C(lippinger) (Md) 514 Limerick Cir. Unit 201, Lutherville Timonium, MD 21093

SIMMONS, Warren Reginald (SeFla) 7005 Piney Branch Rd Nw, Washington, DC 20012

SIMON JR, Kenneth A (SanD) 6556 Park Ridge Boulevard, San Diego, CA 92120

SIMONIAN, Marlene Jenny (RI) 1346 Creek Nine Dr, North Port, FL 34290

SIMONS, Daniel J (NY) 74 Trinity Pl, New York, NY 10006

SIMONS, James Burdette (Pgh) 731 Laurel Dr, Ligonier, PA 15658

SIMONSEN, Douglas C (Oly) P.O. Box 1974, Anacortes, WA 98221

SIMOPOULOS, Nicole Martha (The Episcopal Church in Haw) 563 Kamoku St, Honolulu, HI 96826

SIMPSON, Cynthia (WA) Christ Episcopal School, 107 S Washington St, Rockville, MD 20850

SIMPSON, Dawn Simpson (Colo) Po Box 291, Monte Vista, CO 81144

SIMPSON, Geoffrey Sedgwick (Mil)

SIMPSON, Geoffrey Stewart (Pa) Church Of The Good Samaritan, 212 W Lancaster Ave, Paoli, PA 19301

SIMPSON JR, John P(atrick) (Pa) 244 Woodbine Ave, Narberth, PA 19072

SIMPSON, Richard Edmund (LI) 754 Main St, Islip, NY 11751

SIMPSON, Richard Michael (WMass) 88 Highland St, Holden, MA 01520

SIMPSON, Richard Roy (RI) 7009 SE 117th Pl., Portland, OR 97266

SIMPSON, Sallie O'Keef (NC) 1725 N New Hope Rd, Raleigh, NC 27604

SIMPSON, Ward Howard (SD) 500 South Main Ave, Sioux Falls, SD 57104

SIMRILL, Spenser Davenport (At) 4945 Dupont Ave S, Minneapolis, MN 55419

SIMS, Carol Carruthers (SVa) 3929 Ocean Cut Lane, Virginia Beach, VA 23451

SIMS, Elizabeth Erringer (Cal) 1700 Santa Clara Ave, Alameda, CA 94501

SIMS, Gregory Brian (Chi) 4233 Ahlstrand Dr, Rockford, IL 61101

SIMS, Gregory Knox (Cal) Po Box 1, Boonville, CA 95415

SIMS, Kenneth Harry (SeFla) 3970 Nw 188th St, Opa Locka, FL 33055

SIMS, Mark Howard (SeFla) 1165 Ne 105th St, Miami Shores, FL 33138

SIMS, Richard Osborn (Nev) 24 Elysium Dr, Ely, NV 89301

SIMS, Ronald Frank (Wyo) 200 Country Brook Dr Apt 2427, Keller, TX 76248

SIMSON, John Everett (Mass) 4773 Abargo St, Woodland Hills, CA 91364

SINCLAIR, Barbara Louise (Chi) St James Episcopal Church, 425 E MacArthur Ave, Lewistown, IL 61542

SINCLAIR, Elisabeth Anne (Mil) 7110 N State Route 9, Kansas City, MO 64152

SINCLAIR, Gregory Lynn (NwT) Hawk Ln, Fountain Valley, CA 92708

SINCLAIR, Nancy Park (Los) 502 Wcbr 250 Pantops Mountain Rd, Apt. 131, Charlottesville, VA 22911

SINCLAIR, Roderick Doig (SwVa) 131, Charlottesville, VA 22911

SINCLAIR, Scott Gambrill (Cal) 663 Coventry Rd, Kensington, CA 94707

SINGER, A(Llen) Michael (EC) 800 Rountree St., Kinston, NC 28501

SINGER, Susanna Jane (Cal) 1233 Howard Street #714, San Francisco, CA 94103

SINGER-HEDLUND, Sylvia Marly (Episcopal SJ) 416 S Regent St, Stockton, CA 95204

☩ SINGH, Prince Grenville (Bp of Roch 2008-) 4 Cathedral Oaks, Fairport, NY 14450

SINGH, Simon Peter (Chi) 261 W Army Trail Rd, Bloomingdale, IL 60108

SINGLETON, Lester Brian (Fla) 18120 Southeast 59 Street, Micanopy, FL 32667

SINGLETON, Richard Oliver (Mich) 1520 W River Rd, Scottsville, VA 24590

SINISI, Gabriel Arcangelo (Az) 17025 W Aberdeen Dr, Surprise, AZ 85374

SINK, Thomas Leslie (NJ)

SINNING, Thomas John (Minn) 1517 Rosewood Cir, Alexandria, MN 56308

SINNOTT, Lynn D (Roch)

SINTIM, Hector (NC) 1925 waters DR, Raleigh, NC 27610

SIPE, Robert B (Ore) 59048 Whitetail Ave., Saint Helens, OR 97051

SIPES, David Sheldon (O) 446 Shepard Rd, Mansfield, OH 44907

SIPPLE, Peter Warren (Pa) 45 Bay View Avenue, Cornwall on Hudson, NY 12520

SIRCY, Micheal John (SwFla) 4030 Manatee Ave W, Bradenton, FL 34205

SIROTA, Victoria R (NY) Cathedral Church of St John the Divine, 1047 Amsterdam Ave, New York, NY 10025

SISK JR, Edwin Kerr (Ark) 9649 Reeder Pl, Overland Park, KS 66214

☩ SISK, Mark Sean (Ret Bp of NY 2013-) PO Box 53, Jefferson, NY 12093

SISK, Robert Buchanan (Mont) Rr 1 Box 241, Wilsall, MT 59086

SISSON, Duane (Cal) 2973 California St, Oakland, CA 94602

SISSON, Penny Ray (Miss) 414 Turnberry Cir, Oxford, MS 38655

SITTON, Gary William (Colo) 7695 Quitman St, Westminster, CO 80030

SITTS, Joseph (CFla) 271 New Waterford Pl, Longwood, FL 32779

SIVE, Marian Mae (Alb) PO Box 41, Burnt Hills, NY 12027

SIVLEY, John Stephen (CPa) 869E Rhue Haus Ln, Hummelstown, PA 17036

SIVRET, David Otis (Me) 46 Oak Lane, Alexander, ME 04694

SIWEK, Peter Christopher (Chi) 733 Hayes Ave, Oak Park, IL 60302

SIX, George (Los)

SIZE, Patricia Barrett (Mil) 2215 Commonwealth Ave, Madison, WI 53726

SKAGGS, Richard Lee (WVa) 1410 Chapline St, Wheeling, WV 26003

SKALA, Kira B (Va) 241 Signal Ridge Ln, Winchester, VA 22603

SKALESKI, Elizabeth Harris (Ct)

SKAU, Laurie Jean (Minn) 6727 France Ave N, Brooklyn Center, MN 55429

SKAUG, Jon (Az)

SKEATES, Winifred June (NH) 270 Stark Hwy N, Dunbarton, NH 03046

SKELLEN, Bonnie Jean (NwPa) 425 E Main St, Ridgway, PA 15853

SKELLY, Herbert Cope (Mass) 40 Woodland Way, Eastham, MA 02642

SKIDMORE, Joanne Louise (Mil) 2389 Penny Lane, Sister Bay, WI 54234

SKIFFINGTON, Steven Wayne (The Episcopal NCal) Trinity Cathedral, 2620 Capitol Ave, Sacramento, CA 95816

SKILLICORN, Gerald Amos (WMo) 2207 Conrad Way, Somerset, NJ 08873

SKILLINGS, Thomas (Cal) 1104 Mills Ave, Burlingame, CA 94010

☩ SKILTON, William Jones (Ret Bp Suffr of SC 2009-) 4969 Parkside Dr, North Charleston, SC 29405

SKINNER, Beatrice (Okl)

SKINNER, Jean Mary (CNY) 40 Faxton St, Utica, NY 13501

SKINNER, Susan (Mo) 400 Mark Dr, Saint Louis, MO 63122

☩ SKIRVING, Robert Stuart (Bp of EC 2014-) Episcopal Diocese of East Carolina, PO Box 1336, Kinston, NC 28503

SKORNIK, Andria N (Chi) St Andrew's Episcopal Church, 1125 Franklin St, Downers Grove, IL 60515

SKRAMSTAD, Dawn Marie (Alb) St. Mary's Church, P.O. Box 211, Lake Luzerne, NY 12846

SKUTCH, Patrick J (Chi) 306 S Prospect Ave, Park Ridge, IL 60068

SKYLES, Benjamin Henry (Tex) 2110 Canyon Lake Dr, Deer Park, TX 77536

SLACK, James Cooper Simmons (Dal) 1019 Sassafras Lane, Niles, MO 49120

SLACK, Sean C. (Pa) St Paul's Church, 89 Pinewood Dr, Levittown, PA 19054

SLADE, Debra Katherine Ann (Ct) 503 Old Long Ridge Rd, Stamford, CT 06903

SLADE, Kara Nicole (NC) Saint David's Episcopal Church, PO Box 334, Laurinburg, NC 28353

SLAKEY, Anne-Elisa Margaret (Ida) 110 N. 10th St., Payette, ID 83661

SLANE, Christopher DuTeil (Neb)

SLANE, Melanie W (Mo) 3737 Seminary Rd, Alexandria, VA 22304

SLANGER, George C (ND) 8435 207th St. W., Lakeville, MN 55044

SLATER, Amy A (Fla)

SLATER, Chadwick M (WVa) 200 Duhring St, Bluefield, WV 24701

SLATER, Joan (NMich) PO Box100, Mackinac Island, MI 49757

SLATER, Jo Ann Kennedy (Mich) 5416 Parkgrove Rd, Ann Arbor, MI 48103

SLATER, Michael (Nev) 7900 Pueblo Drive, Stagecoach, NV 89429

SLATER, Sarah Elizabeth (WA)

SLATER, Scott Gerald (Md) 4 East University Parkway, Baltimore, MD 21218

SLAUGHTER, Susan Emmert (FtW) 1612 Boardwalk Ct, Arlington, TX 76011

SLAUSON, Holley B (NY) 20 West Ave Apt 1L, Norwalk, CT 06854

SLAWNWHITE, Virginia Ann (NH) Po Box 433, Portsmouth, NH 03802

SLAWSON III, H Thomas (Md) 3695 Rogers Avenue, Ellicott City, MD 21043

SLAYMAKER, Lorraine P (Ark) 1112 Alcoa Rd, Benton, AR 72015

SLAYTER, Malcolm Franklin (NwT) 2809 Moss Ave, Midland, TX 79705

SLEMP, Dennett Clinton (SVa) 11001 Ashburn Rd, North Chesterfield, VA 23235

SLENSKI, Mary L (Ind) 5256 Central Ave., Indianapolis, IN 46220

SLIGH, John Lewis (SeFla) 2422 W Stroud Ave, Tampa, FL 33629

SLOAN III, Carey Erastus (O) 2390 N Orchard Rd NE, Bolivar, OH 44612

SLOAN, Ellen Margaret (SwFla) St. Michael & All Angels, 2304 Periwinkle Way, Sanibel, FL 33957

✠ **SLOAN**, John Mckee (Bp of Ala 2012-) 521 North 20th Street, Birmingham, AL 35203

SLOAN, Richard D (NY) 90 Gilbert Road, Ho-Ho-Kus, NJ 07423

SLOAN, Stan Jude (Chi) 2313 N Kedzie Blvd # 2, Chicago, IL 60647

SLOAN, Susan (Ala) 821 Baylor Drive, Huntsville, AL 35802

SLOCOMBE, Iris Ruth (Mich) APDO Postal 673, Ajijic, Jalisco 45920, Mexico

SLOCUM, Robert Boak (Lex) PO Box 2505, Danville, KY 40423

SLONE, Thomas Remington (Fla) 400 San Juan Dr., Ponte Vedra Beach, FL 32082

SLOVAK, Anita M (Okla) All Saints' Episcopal Church, 809 West Cedar Ave, Duncan, OK 73533

SLUSHER, Montie Bearl (Ak) 1133 Park Dr., Fairbanks, AK 99709

SLUSS, Mark Duane (Mo) 2918 Victor St, Saint Louis, MO 63104

SMALL, Timothy Keesey (CPa) 370 Spring Hill Ln, Columbia, PA 17512

SMALL, William David (Alb) 451 State Route 86, Paul Smiths, NY 12970

SMALLEY, H Bud (Ida) 5170 Leonard Rd, Pocatello, ID 83204

SMALLEY, Nancy T (Dal) 416 Victorian Dr, Waxahachie, TX 75165

SMALLEY, Richard Craig (Ala) 2017 6th Avenue North, Birmingham, AL 35203

SMALLEY, Stephen Mark (Pgh) 210 Strawberry Circle, Cranberry Township, PA 16066

✠ **SMALLEY**, William Edward (Ret Bp of Kan 1989-) 13809 E 186th St, Noblesville, IN 46060

SMALLWOOD, Richard Lewis (Nev) 4709 S Nellis Blvd, Las Vegas, NV 89121

SMART JR, James Hudson (NwT) 1826 Elmwood Dr, Abilene, TX 79605

SMART, John A (Pa) 5100 N Northridge Cir, Tucson, AZ 85718

SMART, J(ohn) Dennis (At) 442 Euclid Terrace N.E., Atlanta, GA 30307

SMART, Lula Grace (Pa) 147 7th Ave, Folsom, PA 19033

SMEDLEY IV, Walter (Chi) Saint Chrysostom's Church, 1424 N Dearborn St, Chicago, IL 60610

SMELSER, Todd Dudley (At) 1358 E Rock Springs Rd Ne, Atlanta, GA 30306

SMERCINA, Eugene Edward (O) 4307 Cleveland Rd E, Huron, OH 44839

SMIRAGLIA, Richard Paul (Pa) 340 Fitzwater Street, Philadelphia, PA 19147

SMITH, Aaron (CGC) 919 Tennis Ave, Maple Glen, PA 19002

SMITH, Aidan Everett (Alb)

SMITH, A(Lan) Bruce (SO) 627 Yaronia Dr N, Columbus, OH 43214

SMITH, Aloha Lee (Los) 5848 Tower Rd, Riverside, CA 92506

SMITH, Andrea (Ct) 16 Clam Shell Alley, P.O. Box 412, Vinalhaven, ME 04863

✠ **SMITH**, Andrew Donnan (Ret Bp of Ct 2010-) 106 Vista Way, Bloomfield, CT 06002

SMITH, Ann Robb (Pa) 816 Castlefinn Ln, Bryn Mawr, PA 19010

SMITH, Anne Largent (The Episcopal NCal) 9085 Calvine Rd., Sacramento, CA 95829

SMITH, Ann-Lining (Cal) 7261 Mesa Dr, Aptos, CA 95003

SMITH, Arthur Wells (CNY) 341 Main St, Oneida, NY 13421

SMITH, Barbara Joan (U) P.O. Box 849, Cordova, AK 99574

SMITH, Bardwell Leith (Minn) 104 Maple St, Northfield, MN 55057

SMITH JR, Ben Huddleston (Md) 1401 Carrollton Ave, Baltimore, MD 21204

SMITH, Berek Qinah (CFla) 475 43rd Ave, Vero Beach, FL 32968

SMITH, Bert Orville (At) 841 Kings Grant Dr NW, Atlanta, GA 30318

SMITH, Betty Lorraine (NMich) 8114 Trout Lake Rd, Naubinway, MI 49762

SMITH, Bonnie Jeanne (EC) 501 S Harding Dr Apt 1002, Goldsboro, NC 27534

SMITH, Bradford Ray (NC) 116 S Church St, PO Box 293, Monroe, NC 28111

SMITH, Brian E (Fla) 5507 Winford Court, Fairfax, VA 22032

SMITH, Bruce (Cal) 14 Ardmore Ct, Pleasant Hill, CA 94523

SMITH, Carol Coke (Minn) 1211 Jackson Ave, Detroit Lakes, MN 56501

SMITH, Carol Kay Huston (Mil) 4522 Aztec Trail, Fitchburg, WI 53711

SMITH, Carter Austin (CFla) 2499 N Westmoreland Dr, Orlando, FL 32804

SMITH, Cathleen Anne (WNY) 410 N Main St, Jamestown, NY 14701

SMITH, Cecilia Mary Babcock (Tex) PO Box 2247, Austin, TX 78768

SMITH, Channing (ECR) 13601 Saratoga Avenue, Saratoga, CA 95070

SMITH, Charles Howard (Az) 807 W Toledo St, Chandler, AZ 85225

SMITH, Charles J (SVa) Trinity Church, 500 Court St, Portsmouth, VA 23704

SMITH, Charles L (Ak) PO Box 3346, Odessa, TX 79760

SMITH, Charles Stuart (Alb) 45 Pierrepont Ave., Potsdam, NY 13676

SMITH, Christopher Atkins (Alb) 12 Main St., Hagaman, NY 12086

SMITH, Claude Archibald (Mass) 160 River Street, Norwell, MA 02061

SMITH, Claudia L (Me) 810 Morgan Bay Rd, Blue Hill, ME 04614

SMITH, Coleen Haas (Mil)

SMITH III, Colton Mumford (SC) 1 Bishop Gadsden Way A-346, Charleston, SC 29412

SMITH, Craig Faulkner (Vt) 5167 Shelburne Road, Shelburne, VT 05482

SMITH JR, C(urruth) Russell (WNC) 670 Run Away Rdg, Clyde, NC 28721

✠ **SMITH**, Dabney Tyler (Bp of SwFla 2007-) The Diocese of Southwest Florida, 8005 25th Street East, Parrish, FL 34219

SMITH, Dale Leroy (Los) 10451 Jordan Parkway, Hopewell, VA 23860

SMITH, Dave (WNY) 5448 Broadway St, Lancaster, NY 14086

SMITH, David Grant (Roch) St. Mark's Episcopal Church, P.O. Box 424, Penn Yan, NY 14527

SMITH, David Gregory (Mont) 5 W Olive St, Bozeman, MT 59715

SMITH, David Hayes (Va) 800 Chatham Hall Cir., Chatham, VA 24531

SMITH, Dennis Lee (USC) Retired, SC 29301

SMITH, Don Leland (Oly) 8989 S Pine Dr, Beulah, CO 81023

SMITH, Donald Hedges (Roch) 2492 Keystone Lake Drive, Cape Coral, FL 33909

SMITH III, Donald M (CGC) 860 N Section St, Fairhope, AL 36532

SMITH, Doris Graf (At) 11210 Wooten Lake Rd, Kennesaw, GA 30144

SMITH, Douglas Cameron (CPa) 21 Cornell Dr, Hanover, PA 17331

SMITH, Duane Andre (Lex) 110 Chestnut Ct, Berea, KY 40403

SMITH, Edward Daniel (Mo) 1210 Locust St, Saint Louis, MO 63103

SMITH, Edwin Ball (FdL) 1060 S Westhaven Dr, Oshkosh, WI 54904

SMITH, Edwin Earl St Clair (Pa) 154 Locksley Rd, Glen Mills, PA 19342

SMITH JR, Elton Osman (WNY) 4101 Cathedral Ave Nw Apt 817, Washington, DC 20016

SMITH JR, Frank Warner (Neb) 2303 Elk, Beatrice, NE 68310

SMITH, Gail S (Mass) 35 Skyline Drive, Chatham, MA 02633

SMITH, Gary Miles (Va) Grace Church, PO Box 43, 5607 Gordonsville Rd, Keswick, VA 22947

SMITH, Geoffrey T (NH) 24 Chestnut Hill Rd, Dublin, NH 30444

SMITH III, George Dresser (Chi) 792 Forest Ave, Glen Ellyn, IL 60137

✠ **SMITH**, George Wayne (Bp of Mo 2002-) 823 Carillon Ct, Saint Louis, MO 63141

SMITH, Glenn Colyer (Chi) 754 Main St, Islip, NY 11751

SMITH, Graham Michael (Chi) St George's College Jerusalem, PO Box 1248, Jerusalem ISRAEL, OR 91000

SMITH, Gregory Louis (SC) 314 Grove Street, Charleston, SC 29403

SMITH, H Alan (CNY) 2891 Oran Delphi Rd, Manlius, NY 13104

SMITH JR, Harmon Lee (NC) 3510 Randolph Rd, Durham, NC 27705

SMITH, Harold Vaughn (Ind) 8328 Hawes Ct, Indianapolis, IN 46256

SMITH, H Gregory (Pa) 5421 Germantown Ave, Philadelphia, PA 19144

SMITH, Hilary Borbon (Va) 4924 Bethlehem Rd., Richmond, VA 23230

SMITH, H Mark (Mass) 10 Linda Lane, #2-8, Dorchester, MA 02125

SMITH, Howard Louis (Alb) 970 State St., Schenectady, NY 12307

SMITH, J Harmon (SVa) 2228 Karen Dr, Salem, VA 24153

SMITH, Jacob Andrew (NY) St Georges Episcopal Church, 209 E 16th St, New York, NY 10003

SMITH, Jacqueline Kay (Oly) 6208 83rd St Sw, Lakewood, WA 98499

SMITH, James Albert (Az)

SMITH, James Clare (Be) 302 Pine St, Ashland, PA 17921

SMITH, James Drinard (SVa) 3235 Sherwood Ridge Dr, Powhatan, VA 23139

SMITH JR, James Owen (EC) 113 S Woodlawn Ave, Greenville, NC 27858

SMITH, James Ross (NY) 145 W 46th St #4, New York, NY 10036

SMITH, Jane Gravlee (WNC) 40 Wildwood Ave., Asheville, NC 28804

SMITH, Jean (NJ) 58 Jenny Ln, Brattleboro, VT 05301

SMITH, Jean Ann (Ind) 6033 Gladden Dr, Indianapolis, IN 46220

SMITH, Jeanie (Ia) Saint Timothy's Epscopal Church, 1020 24th St, West des Moines, IA 50266

SMITH, Jeffry Bradford (Episcopal SJ) 10 St Theresa'S Avenue, W Roxbury, MA 02132, Great Britain (UK)

SMITH, Jerry William (Tenn) 4800 Belmont Park Ter, Nashville, TN 37215

SMITH IV, Jess Wayne (Wyo) 33 Windy Ridge Rd, Laramie, WY 82070

SMITH, Jesse George (FtW) 2825 Winterhaven Dr, Hurst, TX 76054

SMITH, Jessica Margaret (Oly) St Anne's Episcopal Church, 2350 Main St, Washougal, WA 98671

SMITH, Jethro Larrie (At) 46 S Main St, Wadley, GA 30477

SMITH, Joan Addison (Ky) 3232 Running Deer Cir, Louisville, KY 40241

SMITH, John Cutrer (NY) 45 E 85th St, New York, NY 10028

SMITH JR, J(ohn) Elton (Mont) 3400 S Hillcrest Dr, Butte, MT 59701

SMITH, John Ferris (Mass) Box 3064, Wellfleet, MA 02667

SMITH, John Moffett (Va) 339 S Catalina Ave Apt 121, Pasadena, CA 91106

SMITH, John Perry (Fla) 256 E Church St, Jacksonville, FL 32202

SMITH, John Peterson (WLa) 1904 Jasmine Dr, Opelousas, LA 70570

SMITH JR, John Robert (Az) 602 N Wilmot Rd, Tucson, AZ 85711

SMITH, John Thomas (Md) 1204 Maple Ave, Annapolis, MD 21401

SMITH, Joseph Kershaw (Pa) 101 Shelton Dr, Spartanburg, SC 29307

SMITH, Joseph Wesley (WA) 210 Willie Six Road, Sewanee, TN 37375

SMITH, Juanita Dawn (Wyo) 15 S Tschirgi St, Sheridan, WY 82801

SMITH, Julie Honig (Ore) 6300 Sw Nicol Rd, Portland, OR 97223

SMITH, Karen (Colo) St John the Baptist, 100 S French St, Breckenridge, CO 80424

SMITH, Kathryn Barr (Ala) St Stephen's Episcopal Church, 3775 Crosshaven Dr, Vestavia, AL 35223

SMITH, Kent Clarke (Ct) 112 Sconset Ln, Guilford, CT 06437

SMITH, Kermit Wade (WMo) PO Box 634, Kimberling City, KS 65086

SMITH, Kerry Jon (Md) 6097 Franklin Gibson Rd, Tracys Landing, MD 20779

SMITH, Kevin Corbin (Oly) 507 Mcgraw St, Seattle, WA 98109

SMITH, Kirby (Los) 27802 El Lazo Rd., Laguna Niguel, CA 92677

✠ **SMITH**, Kirk Stevan (Bp of Az 2004-) 114 W Roosevelt St, Phoenix, AZ 85003

SMITH, Kristy K (Ia) 4339 W Sawmill Ct, Castle Rock, CO 80109

SMITH, Larry Phillip (Dal) 17236 Lechlade Lane, Dallas, TX 75252

SMITH, Leslie Carl (NJ) 98 Nassau St. #2, Princeton, NJ 08542

SMITH, Letitia Lee (NC) 2725 Wilshire Ave. S.W., Roanoke, VA 24015

SMITH, Linda Becker (Nev) St Paul's Episcopal Church, PO Box 737, Sparks, NV 89432

SMITH, Lisa White (Minn) 4900 Nathan Lane, Plymouth, MN 55442

SMITH, Lizabeth Patterson (Nwk) 653 Courtney Hollow Lane, Madison, VA 22727

SMITH, Lora Alison (Alb) 531 County Route 59, Potsdam, NY 13676

SMITH III, L(Ouis) Murdock (NC)

SMITH, Manning Lee (Md) PO Box 2157, Mountain Lake Park, MD 21550

SMITH, Marc D (Mo) 4520 Lucas and Hunt Rd, Saint Louis, MO 63121

SMITH, Martin L (WA) 429 N St SW Apt S306, Washington, DC 20024

SMITH, Mary Jo (Vt) 973 Route 106, Reading, VT 05062

SMITH, Melissa M (NC) 84 Broadway, New Haven, CT 06511

SMITH JR, Merle Edwin (Ia) 715 W 7th St S, Newton, IA 50208

SMITH, Michael Allen (Az) 2800 W Ina Rd, Tucson, AZ 85741

✠ **SMITH**, Michael Gene (Bp of ND 2004-) Po Box 8, Naytahwaush, MN 56566

SMITH, Michael John (SO)

SMITH, Michael W (SC) 218 Ashley Ave., Charleston, SC 29403

SMITH, Mitchell Tonkin (La) 1329 Jackson Ave, New Orleans, LA 70130

SMITH, Molly Dale (NJ) 805 Timber Ln., Nashville, TN 37215

SMITH, Myrl Elden (O) 4541 Gilhouse Rd, Toledo, OH 43623

SMITH, Nancy Metze (SwFla) 13011 Sandy Key Bend, Apt 1, North Fort Myers, FL 33903

SMITH, Nancy Spencer (Mass) 29 W Cedar St, Boston, MA 02108

SMITH, Nora (NY) 11 N. Broadway, Irvington, NY 10533

SMITH, Paul Bruce (Ak) 9631 Noaya, Eagle River, AK 99577

SMITH, Paul Weeghman (Ky) 3724 Hillsdale Rd, Louisville, KY 40222

SMITH, Perry Michael (WA) 15 Charles Plz Apt 2307, Baltimore, MD 21201

SMITH, P(Hilip) Kingsley (Md) 8339 Carrbridge Cir, Towson, MD 21204

SMITH, Ralph Eugene (NY) 219 Old Franklin Grove Dr Apt 6-A, Chapel Hill, NC 27514

SMITH JR, Ralph Wood (ETenn) Po Box 476, Mountain Home, TN 37684
SMITH, Raymond Robert (Colo) 23321 E Dry Creek Cir, Aurora, CO 80016
SMITH, Richard Byron (NC) 6 Natchez Court, Greensboro, NC 27455
SMITH, Richard Leslie (Cal) 226 Clinton Park, San Francisco, CA 94103
SMITH JR, Richard Winton (Pa) 305 E 83rd St Apt 4g, New York, NY 10028
SMITH JR, Robert Adrian (Me) 35 Prospect St, Caribou, ME 04736
SMITH, Robert Angus (WMich) 212 Courtland St, Dowagiac, MI 49047
SMITH, Robert Clarke (Pa) 2033 Bainbridge St, Philadelphia, PA 19146
SMITH, Robert Edward (Mich) 22326 Cherry Hill St, Dearborn, MI 48124
SMITH, Robert Kennedy (CFla) 3224 Carleton Circle East, Lakeland, FL 33803
SMITH, Robert Nelson (Chi) 217 Houston St, Ripon, WI 54971
SMITH, Robert Russell (Eas) 35 Spruance Ct, Elkton, MD 21921
SMITH, Roberts (Los)
SMITH, Robin (Pa) Saint Philip's In The Field, 317 Oreland Mill Rd, Oreland, PA 19075
SMITH, Robin Penman (Dal) 2712 E Aspen CT, Plano, TX 75075
SMITH, Rod (Tex) 1738 Ridgeway Road, Memphis, TN 38119
SMITH, Roger Stilman (Me) 70 Country Club Rd, Manchester, ME 04351
SMITH, Roger William (SC) 15 Newpoint Rd, Beaufort, SC 29907
SMITH, Ronald Nelson (Tex) 1403 Preston Ave, Austin, TX 78703
SMITH, Rose Ann Ann (NwT) 3500 Barclay Dr, Amarillo, TX 79109
SMITH, Samuel Earl (Cal) 2673 Alder St, Eugene, OR 974050
SMITH, Samuel J (WMass) 1047 Amsterdam Ave, New York, NY 10025
SMITH, Stanley James (O) 249 E 7th St, New York, NY 10009
SMITH, Stephen Bradley (SO) 7121 Muirfield Dr., Dublin, OH 43017
SMITH, Stephen H (FtW)
SMITH, Stephen John Stanyon (WNY) 100 Beard Ave, Buffalo, NY 14214
SMITH, Stephen M (Tex) 3310 Nathanael Rd., Greensboro, NC 27408
SMITH, Steven Ronald (Eur) Church of the Ascension, Seybothstrasse 4, 81545 Munich, Germany
SMITH, Stuart Hardie (Nwk) 653 Courtney Hollow Ln, Madison, VA 22727
SMITH, Susan Sims (Ark) 1809 Canal Pointe, Little Rock, AR 72202
SMITH, Susan Marie (SO) 333 S. Drexel Avenue, Bexley, OH 43209
SMITH, Susannah Rankin (NY) 219 Old Franklin Grove Dr, Chapel Hill, NC 27514

SMITH, Taylor Magavern (Md) 3608 Horned Owl Ct, Ellicott City, MD 21042
SMITH, Ted William (Tex) PO Box 10357, Liberty, TX 77575
SMITH, Theophus Thee (At) 3530 Fairlane Dr NW, Atlanta, GA 30331
SMITH, Thomas Eugene (EMich) P.O. Box 86, Dryden, MI 48428
SMITH, Thomas Gibson (Chi) 118 Tanglewood Dr, Elk Grove Village, IL 60007
SMITH JR, Thomas Parshall (NY) 225 W 99th St, New York, NY 10025
SMITH JR, Thomas Richard (Va) 1500 Westbrook Ct Apt 3142, Richmond, VA 23227
SMITH, Timothy Clarke (Cal) 2325 Union St, San Francisco, CA 94123
SMITH, Travis H (Tex) Holy Comforter Episcopal Church, 227 S Chenango PO BOX 786, Angleton, TX 77515
SMITH, Travis K (Md) St. Michael's Episcopal Church, 1520 Canterbury Rd., Raleigh, NC 27608
SMITH, Twila J (Be) 2451 Ridge Rd, Berkeley, CA 94709
SMITH, Vicki Lovely (NC) 10104 Sorrills Creek Lane, Raleigh, NC 27614
SMITH, Vickie Mitchell (Ark)
SMITH, Walter E (At) 3750 Peachtree Rd.NE, Atlanta, GA 30319
SMITH III, Walter Frederick (RG) 10328, Albuquerque, NM 87114
SMITH, Wendy M (ECR) 4061 Sutherland Dr, Palo Alto, CA 94303
SMITH, Whitney Bousman (Ind) 1109 E Morgan St, Martinsville, IN 46151
SMITH, WillaMarie Eileen (CFla) 381 N Lincoln St, Daytona Beach, FL 32114
SMITH, William Alfred (Ore) 17320 Quaker Ln Apt B21, Sandy Spring, MD 20860
SMITH, William Charles (NwT) St Matthew's Episcopal Church, 727 W Browning Ave, Pampa, TX 79065
SMITH, William Herbert (WMich) 2073 SE North Blackwell Dr, Port St Lucie, FL 34952
SMITH, William Herman (Cal) 3001 Veazey Ter Nw, Washington, DC 20008
SMITH, William Louis (Md) 24 Lake Drive, Bel Air, MD 21014
SMITH III, William Paul (Fla) PO Box 1005, Hilliard, FL 32046
SMITH, Willie James (Nwk)
SMITH, Zachary (Pa) 1904 Walnut St, Philadelphia, PA 19103
SMITH-ALLEN, Serita Verner (EO) Po Box 186, Union, OR 97883
SMITH BOOTH, Rebecca Lee (Tex) Trinity Episcopal Church, 5010 N Main St, Baytown, TX 77521
SMITH-CRIDDLE, Linda C (O) 19 Pent Road, Madison, CT 06443

SMITHDEAL JR, Foss Tyra (NC) 8050 Ravenwood Ln, Stanley, NC 28164
SMITHER, Gertrude Gaston (Dal) 7900 Lovers Ln, Dallas, TX 75225
SMITHERMAN, Gene (ETenn) 211 Brookwood Dr, Chattanooga, TN 37411
SMITHERMAN, Suzanne (ETenn) 1108 Meadow Ln, Kingsport, TN 37663
SMITH GRAHAM, Shirley Elizabeth (Va) 5000 Pouncey Tract Rd, Glen Allen, VA 23059
SMITHGRAYBEAL, Felicia Marie (Colo) 8738 Triple Crown Dr., Frederick, CO 80504
SMITH-KURTZ, Mary Bonnagean (WMich) 7280 Deepwater Point Rd, Williamsburg, MI 49690
SMITH-MORAN, Barbara Putney (Mass) 93 Anson Road, Concord, MA 01742
SMITS, Hilary Jerome (CPa) 631 Colonial Ave, York, PA 17403
SMODELL, George (CFla) 2394 Lakes of Melbourne Dr, Melbourne, FL 32904
SMOKE, Joan Claire (Mil) 731 Sunset Blvd #67, Wisconsin Dells, WI 53965
SMUCKER III, John Reed (Mich) 108 N Quaker Ln, Alexandria, VA 22304
SMULLEN, Thelma Alice (Md) 15708 Bradford Drive, Laurel, MD 20707
✠ **SMYLIE**, John Sheridan (Bp of Wyo 2010-) 123 S Durbin St, Casper, WY 82601
SMYTH, Margaret Emma Ferrell (NJ) 53 Mulberry St, Medford, NJ 08055
SMYTH, William E (NC) PO Box 615, Columbia, NC 27925
SMYTHE JR, Colville Nathaniel (Los) 2103 Hill Ave, Altadena, CA 91001
SMYTHE, Sally Lee (ND) 301 Main St S, Minot, ND 58701
SNAPP, J(ames) Russell (Ark)
SNARE, Pamela Porter (Tenn) Episcopal Diocese of Tennessee, 3700 Woodmont Avenue, Nashville, TN 37215
SNEARY, Jerry Mack (WTex) 164 Fox Rdg, Canyon Lake, TX 78133
SNELL, Carol Burkey (CPa) 182D Dew Drop Rd, York, PA 17402
SNELLING, Kathryn Sue (Ak) PO Box 1130, Sitka, AK 99835
SNEVE, Paul Marshall (SD) 12 Linden Ave, Vermillion, SD 57069
SNICKENBERGER, Patricia Wolcott (Chi) 179 School Street, Libertyville, IL 60048
SNIDER II, Michael Elsworth (Fla) St Patrick's Episcopal Church, 1532 Stratford Ct, Saint Johns, FL 32259
SNIDER, Stephen B (Pa) 254 Crosshill Rd, Wynnewood, PA 19096
SNIECIENSKI, Ed (Los) 908 N AVENUE 65, LOS ANGELES, CA 90042
SNIFFEN, E(rnest) Timothy (Me) P0 Box 368, Readfield, ME 04355

SNIFFEN, Michael Thomas (LI) 520 Clinton Ave, Brooklyn, NY 11238

SNIVELY, Candy (NC)

SNODGRASS, Cynthia J (SO) 5146 SW 9th Lane, Gainesville, FL 32607

SNODGRASS, Galen D (WMo) 1125 S Main St, Carthage, MO 64836

SNODGRASS, T James (PR) 705 Gladstone Ave, Baltimore, MD 21210

SNOOK, Susan Brown (Az) 15657 E Golden Eagle Blvd, Fountain Hills, AZ 85268

SNOW, George Richard (WLa) 151 Washakie Dr, Evanston, WY 82930

SNOW, Peter D (Oly) 927 36th Ave, Seattle, WA 98122

SNOW, Robert Gerald (Neb) Po Box 407052, Fort Lauderdale, FL 33340

SNYDER, Albert Eric (Be) 290 Conklin St, Farmingdale, NY 11735

SNYDER, Albert Llwyd (WTex) 527 Sonnet Dr, San Antonio, TX 78216

SNYDER, Bindy Ann Wright (WTenn) 539 Cherry Rd, Memphis, TN 38117

SNYDER, David L (NJ) St. Andrew's Episcopal Church, 121 High Street, Mt. Holly, NJ 08060

SNYDER, Dick (NAM) PO Box 22771, Carson City, NV 89721

SNYDER, George Lewis (SO)

SNYDER, Judith Urso (Be) 4621 Ashley Ln, Bethlehem, PA 18017

SNYDER, Larry Alan (Chi) 240 S 4th St, Warsaw, IL 62379

SNYDER, Paul Leech (Okla) PO Box 10722, Midwest City, OK 73140

SNYDER, Philip L (Dal) 2220 Susan Cir, Plano, TX 75074

SNYDER, Philip Wiseman (CNY) 248 Buckfield Dr, Lititz, PA 17543

SNYDER, Robert Paul (Ind) 3221 - 29th, Bedford, IN 47421

SNYDER, Susanna Jane (Mass) 99 Brattle St, Cambridge, MA 02138

SNYDER, William Delpharo (O) 4920 Woodview Rd, Ravenna, OH 44266

SO, Alistair (Md) All Hallows' Parish, P.O.Box 235, Davidsonville, MD 21035

SOARD II, John Robert (Tex) 207 Bob O Link Ln, Wharton, TX 77488

SOBOL, Walter (O) 4627 Indian Ridge Rd, Sylvania, OH 43560

SODERGREN, Oscar Frederick (Alb) 9 Pinewood Dr, Scotia, NY 12302

SOJWAL, Imlijungla (NY) 201 W 72nd St apt 15e, New York, NY 10023

SOJWAL, Milind (NY) 16 All Saints Rd, Princeton, NJ 08540

SOL, Brenda J (SanD) 8011 Douglas Ave, Dallas, TX 75225

SOLA, Geri Ely (Eau) 6579 W Center Dr, Hurley, WI 54534

SOLAK, Ketlen A (Va) 8009 Fort Hunt Rd, Alexandria, VA 22308

SOLBAK, Mary Martha (CPa) 1001 E. Oregon Rd, Lititz, PA 17543

SOLDWEDEL, Erik Gustav (Nwk) 31 Mulberry St, Newark, NJ 07102

SOLLER, Robin (NH) 23 Old Bristol Rd, New Hampton, NH 03256

SOLOMON, Dana Lee (Colo) St Stephen's Episcopal Church, 1303 S Bross Ln, Longmont, CO 80501

SOLON JR, Robert Francis (Md) 1301 S Charles St, Baltimore, MD 21230

SOLON, T(erry) Tim (Wyo) 3251 Acacia Dr, Cheyenne, WY 82001

SOLTER, Katrina Howard (WA) St Patrick's Episcopal Church, 4700 Whitehaven Pkwy NW, Washington, DC 20007

SOMERS, David Wayne (CFla) 5873 N Dean Rd, Orlando, FL 32817

SOMERS, Faye Veronica (SeFla) 2707 NW 37th St, Boca Raton, FL 33434

SOMERVILLE II, Ben Leonidas (Az) 542 Raymond Dr, Sierra Vista, AZ 85635

SOMERVILLE, David James (Ga) 128 King Cotton Rd, Brunswick, GA 31525

SOMES, Norman Frederick (ECR) 85 Anna Laura Rd., 85 Anna Laura Drive, Jacksonville, OR 97530

SOMMER, Robert Lane (ECR) All Saints Church/Cristo Rey, 437 Rogers Ave, Watsonville, CA 95076

SOMMER, Susan Lemmon (Chi) 2410 Glenview Rd, Glenview, IL 60025

SOMODEVILLA, Rene Francisco (Dal) 4018 S Lakewood Dr, Memphis, TN 38128

SONDEREGGER, Kathrine Ann (Va) 669 Weybridge St # 5753, Middlebury, VT 05753

SONLEY, Joseph (Hai)

SONNEN, Jon Anton (Tex) 4403 Seneca St, Pasadena, TX 77504

SONNESYN, Roger Earl (Minn)

SOPER JR, Leroy Dilmore (At) 514 E. NewJersey Ave Apt. 5125, Southern Pines, NC 28387

SOPER, Robert Arthur (WTex) 300 Hollywood Dr, Edinburg, TX 78539

SORENSEN, John Thomas (Pa) 576 Concord Road, Glen Mills, PA 19342

SORENSEN, Lael (Me) St Peter's Episcopal Church, 11 White St, Rockland, ME 04841

SORENSEN, Richard Todd (Nev) 1580 G St, Sparks, NV 89431

SORENSEN, Todd Wallace (Colo) 6653 W Chatfield Ave, Littleton, CO 80128

SORENSON, James Ronald (EMich) 226 W Nicolet Blvd, Marquette, MI 49855

SORENSON, Suzanne Marie (EMich) 226 W Nicolet Blvd, Marquette, MI 49855

SOREY, Gene Christine (Fla) 4304 Redtail Hawk Dr, Jacksonville, FL 32257

SORVILLO, August Louis (CFla) 90 Bridgewater Ln, Ormond Beach, FL 32174

SORVILLO SR, James August (CFla) 9101 Palm Tree Dr., Windermere, FL 34786

SOSA, Gary Rafael (NAM) Po Box 216, Bluff, UT 84512

SOSNOWSKI, Frederick Skinner (SC) 2426 Sea Island Yacht Club Rd, Wadmalaw Island, SC 29487

SOSNOWSKI, John William (NJ) 808 W State St, Trenton, NJ 08618

SOTELO, Fabio A (At) St Bede's Episcopal Church, 2601 Henderson Mill Rd NE, Atlanta, GA 30345

SOTELO, George Salinas (Az) 13685 N Balancing Rock Dr, Oro Valley, AZ 85755

SOTO, Luis Fernando (DR) (DomRep)

SOTOMAYOR, Ricardo (Tex)

SOUCEK, Paul (Nwk)

SOUDER, Diane J (Az) Po Box 1077, Winter Park, FL 32790

SOUGHERS, Tara Kathleen (Mass) 23 Horseshoe Dr., Plainville, MA 02762

SOUKUP, Patricia Marie (RG) 3700 Parsifal St NE, Albuquerque, NM 87111

SOULE, Judith Christine (Spok) 625 C St, Cheney, WA 99004

SOULE, Patrick Ross (WTex) 13026 Leopard St, Corpus Christi, TX 78410

SOULIS, Cameron J (WA) National Cathedral School, 3612 Woodley Rd, NW, Washington, DC 20016

SOUTH, Lynn Crisco (The Episcopal Church in Haw) 100 Kulanihakoi St, Kihei, HI 96753

SOUTHALL, Jennifer Lea (Miss) 3921 Oakridge Dr, Jackson, MS 39216

SOUTHERLAND, Thomas Rudolph (SO) 10555 Montgomery Rd., Apt 32, Cincinnati, OH 45242

SOUTHERN JR, John Carlton (WNC) 42 Alclare Ct, Asheville, NC 28804

SOUZA, Raymond Manuel (EC) 846 Wide Waters, Bath, NC 27808

SOWAH, Constance Kate (Minn) 4180 Lexington Ave S, Eagan, MN 55123

SOWAN, Michael George (Alb) Box 1185, Street Sacrement Lane, Bolton Landing, NY 12814

SOWARDS, William Michael (Pa) St James Episcopal Church, 3768 Germantown Pike, Collegeville, PA 19426

SOWERS, Susan R (CGC) 3200 N 12th Ave, Pensacola, FL 32503

SOWINSKI, Charles Paul (Az) 6300 N Central Ave, Phoenix, AZ 85012

SOX, Harold D (Cal) 20 The Vineyard, Richmond, Surrey, TW 10 6 AN, Great Britain (UK)

SOYARS, Jonathan E (Chi) 115 West Seventh Street, Charlotte, NC 28202

SPACCARELLI, Cara Elizabeth (WA) 620 G St SE, Washington, DC 20003

SPAETH, Colleen Grayce (NJ) 247 Merion Ave, Haddonfield, NJ 08033

SPAFFORD, Donald Wick (Dal) 5903 Bonnard Dr, Dallas, TX 75230

SPAGNA, Amy L. (Va) Trinity Episcopal Church, 44 E Market St, Bethlehem, PA 18018

SPAID, William John (WMich) 2008 Hudson Ave, Kalamazoo, MI 49008

SPAINHOUR, John Robert (Vt) 4616 McClelland Dr, Unit 203, Wilmington, NC 28405

SPALDING, Kirsten (Cal) 333 Ellen Dr, San Rafael, CA 94903

SPANGENBERG, Carol Anne (WMich) 1612 Stoney Point Dr, Lansing, MI 48917

SPANGENBERG, Ronald Wesley (SVa) 6085 River Crest, Norfolk, VA 23505

SPANGLER, Haywood B (Va) 1205 Swan Lake Dr Apt 303, Charlottesville, VA 22902

SPANGLER, N(ancy) DeLiza (WNY) 128 Pearl St, Buffalo, NY 14202

SPANGLER, Robert Joseph (Okla) 7 Strathmore Dr, Arden, NC 28704

SPANN, Paul Ronald (Mich) 2971 Iroquois St, Detroit, MI 48214

SPANNAGEL JR, Lawrence Elden (NwT) 676 E Willowbrook Dr, Meridian, ID 83646

SPANUTIUS, Warren Frederick (WTex) 505 Coral Pl, Corpus Christi, TX 78411

SPARKS, Douglas Everett (Minn) 1809 Baihly Hills Dr Sw, Rochester, MN 55902

SPARKS JR, Noy Leon (CFla) Cathedral Church of St Luke, 130 N Magnolia Ave, Orlando, FL 32801

SPARROW, Kevin H (Cal) 45 Yerxa Rd Unit 307, Cambridge, MA 02140

SPAULDING, Mark (Cal) 19179 Center St, Castro Valley, CA 94546

SPEAR, Les Edward (WTex) 4222 State Hwy. 7 West, Crockett, TX 75835

SPEARE-HARDY II, Benjamin E K (SO) 5301 Free Pike, Trotwood, OH 45426

SPEAR-JONES, Michael W (SVa) 12 Milnor Terrace, Crossville, TN 38558

SPEARS, Melanie Lea (Minn) 3543 22nd Ave S, Minneapolis, MN 55407

SPECK-EWER, Nathan Stewart (Ct)

SPEEKS, Mark William (NY)

SPEER, James D (Ct) 63 Clyde Ave, Waterbury, CT 06708

SPEER, Richard T (WTex) 800 S. Inediana Ave, 800 S. Indiana Ave, Weslaco, TX 78596

SPEER, Robert Hazlett (Md) 5732 Cross Country Blvd, Baltimore, MD 21209

SPEER, William Roth (NJ) 2000 Miller Ave #12, Millville, NJ 08332

SPEIR, Edmund Lawrence (Ida) 270 N Placer Ave, Idaho Falls, ID 83402

SPEIR, Susan Elizabeth (Ida) 2212 Balboa Dr, Idaho Falls, ID 83404

SPELLER, Lydia Agnew (EMich) Grace Church, 1213 6th St, Port Huron, MI 48060

SPELLERS, Stephanie (LI) 82 Commonwealth Ave Apt 2, Boston, MA 02116

SPELLMAN, Lynne (Ark) 1219 W Lakeridge Dr, Fayetteville, AR 72703

SPELLMAN, Robert Garland Windsor (Ct) 322 Seabury Dr, Bloomfield, CT 06002

SPELMAN, Harold James (HB)

SPELMAN, Katherine C (Chi) 20 N American St, Philadelphia, PA 19106

SPENCER, Allison D (LI) 12706 Se Pinehurst Ct, Hobe Sound, FL 33455

SPENCER JR, Arthur James (LI) 12706 Se Pinehurst Ct, Hobe Sound, FL 33455

SPENCER, Bonnie Sarah (Colo) 130 N. Mack St., Fort Collins, CO 80521

SPENCER, Carol (Miss) 1623 Acadia Ct., Jackson, MS 39211

SPENCER, Cynthia Margaret (ECR) 15163 N Cutler Dr, Tucson, AZ 85739

SPENCER, Dorothy Jane (NMich) PO Box 302, Manistique, MI 49854

SPENCER, James Scott (CFla) 4220 Saxon Dr, New Smyrna Beach, FL 32169

SPENCER, Leon P (NC) 6005 Starboard Dr, Greensboro, NC 27410

SPENCER, Michael Edwin (NH) 325 Pleasant Street, Concord, NH 03301

SPENCER, Orval James (Neb) 6700 Tamerson Ct, Raleigh, NC 27612

SPENCER, Patricia Ann (CFla) 851 Village Lake Dr S, Deland, FL 32724

SPENCER, Peter Levalley (RI) 107 Green Hill Ave, Wakefield, RI 02879

SPENCER, Richard William (NY) 4 Hemlock Rd, Hartsdale, NY 10530

SPENCER, Robert Dennis (Wyo) 4508 Cottage Ln, Cheyenne, WY 82001

SPENCER, Robert Frank (Miss) 1623 Acadia Court, Jackson, MS 39211

SPENCER, Robert Paul (NMich) PO Box 302, Manistique, MI 49854

SPENCER, Ronald (WMo) Po Box 197, Angel Fire, NM 87710

SPENCER, Warren Dove (NJ) 68 Hull Ave, Freehold, NJ 07728

SPERRY, Rebecca Lynne (Chi) 2056 Vermont St, Blue Island, IL 60406

SPICER JR, C(lyde) Allen (Md) 724 Morningside Dr, Towson, MD 21204

SPICER, John M (WMo) St. Andrews Episcopal Church, 6401 Wornall Terrace, Kansas City, MO 64113

SPICER, John Tildsley (Fla) 25 Eyrie Dr, Crawfordville, FL 32327

SPICER, Stephen L (Tex) 304 E Stockbridge St, Eagle Lake, TX 77434

SPIEGEL, Phyllis (SO) 120 Cherry Ln, Christiansburg, VA 24073

SPIERS, Linda Mitchell (Ct) 3 Whirling Drive, Canton, CT 06019

SPIGNER, Charles Bailey (Va) 10355 Spencer Trail Pl, Ashland, VA 23005

SPINA, Frank Anthony (Oly) 414 W Newell St, Seattle, WA 98119

SPINELLA, Linda Jean (NH) 270 Stark Hwy N, Dunbarton, NH 03046

SPLINTER, John Theodore (FdL) 4332 W Rotamer Rd, Janesville, WI 53546

✠ **SPONG**, John Shelby (Ret Bp of Nwk 2000-) 24 Puddingstone Rd, Morris Plains, NJ 07950

SPOOR, Cornelia Paradise (NJ) Po Box 624, Roosevelt, NJ 08555

SPRAGUE, James Wilson (Los) PO Box 303, Santa Barbara, CA 93102

SPRAGUE, Minka Shura (La) 1100 Broadway St, New Orleans, LA 70118

SPRATT, George Clifford (Kan) 828 Center St, Fulton, MO 65251

SPRICK, Lynne Ann (Minn) 110 S Oak St, Lake City, MN 55041

SPRINGER, Alice Elizabeth Ballard (Dal) 22-M Smith Rd, Rockwall, TX 75087

SPRINGER, David Richard (Alb) 12 Shannon Ct, West Sand Lake, NY 12196

SPRINGER, Lloyd Livingstone (NY) 1358 E Normandy Blvd, Deltona, FL 32725

SPRINGER, Nancy Annette (WTex) St John's Episcopal Church, 2500 N 10th St, McAllen, TX 78501

SPRINGER, Susan Woodward (Colo) St John's Episcopal Church, 1419 Pine St, Boulder, CO 80302

SPROAT, Jim (WTex) 2109 Sawdust Rd Apt 27102, Spring, TX 77380

SPROUL, James Renfro (EC) 881 Lakeside Dr., Lenoir City, TN 37772

SPROUSE, Herbert Warren (CPa) 20 W High St, Gettysburg, PA 17325

SPRUHAN, John Halsey (SD) 720 Diamond Road, Salem, VA 24153

SPRUHAN, Judy Bennett (SD) 720 Diamond Rd, Salem, VA 24153

SPRUILL, Joseph Lyle (Tenn) 5825 Robert E Lee Dr, Nashville, TN 37215

SPRUILL JR, William Arthur (Fla) 4107 Marquette Ave, Jacksonville, FL 32210

SPULNIK, Frederick Joseph (RI) 4873 Collwood Blvd unit B, San Diego, CA 92115

SPURGIN, Joyce M (Okla) 516 McLish St, Ardmore, OK 73401

SPURLOCK, Michael Douglas (NY) Saint Thomas Church, 1 W. 53rd St., New York, NY 10019

SPURLOCK, Paul Allan (Colo) 10000 E Yale Ave Apt 4, 10000 E. Yale Ave Apt43, Denver, CO 80231

SQUIER, Timothy John (Chi) 500 East Depot Street, Antioch, IL 60002

SQUIRE, James Richard (Pa) Episcopal Academy, 1785 Bishop White Dr, Newtown Square, PA 19073

SQUIRE JR, Willard Searle (CFla) 748 Hammond Pl, The Villages, FL 32162

SRAMEK JR, Tom (ECR) Good Samaritan Episcopal Church, 15040 Union Ave, San Jose, CA 95124

SSERWADDA, Emmanuel (NY) 69 Georgia Ave, Bronxville, NY 10708

STABLER-TIPPETT, Joycelyn Dominick (Miss) St Stephen's Episcopal Church, 1300 Church St, Columbia, MS 39429

STACEY, Caroline Mary (NY) 487 Hudson St, New York, NY 10014

STACK JR, Gene A (SO) 541 2nd Ave, Gallipolis, OH 45631

STACKHOUSE, Marcia K (Colo) 3432 Vallejo St, Denver, CO 80211

STACY, Charles Herrick (Los) 1509 Eucalyptus Dr, Solvang, CA 93463

STADEL, Jerold Russell (SwFla) 1014 Pinegrove Dr, Brandon, FL 33511

STAFFORD, Gil Wade (Az)

STAFFORD, Robert Holmes (NY) 401 S El Cielo Rd Apt 71, Palm Springs, CA 92262

STAFFORD, William Sutherland (Fla) 4316 Hampshire Pl, San Jose, CA 95136

STAFFORD-WHITTAKER, William Paul (WA)

STAGGS, Katresia Anne (Ark) 501 S Phoenix Ave, Russellville, AR 72801

STAHL, Daryl Wayne (RI) 91 Pratt St, providence, RI 02906

STAIR, Adrian (Mass) 51 Longmeadow Dr, Amherst, MA 01002

STALEY, Mary Linda (Va) PO Box 482, Put In Bay, OH 43456

STALLER, Margaretmary Boyer (Cal) 4821 Wolf Way, Concord, CA 94521

STALLINGS, Floyd Monroe (Buddy) (NY) 435 E 52nd Street, Apt 10A2, New York, NY 10022

STAMBAUGH, Doran Bartlett (SanD) PO Box 127, Carlsbad, CA 92018

STAMM, George William (Eau) 13497 45th Ave, Chippewa Falls, WI 54729

ST AMOUR III, Frank Shalvey (NJ) 51 N Main St, Mullica Hill, NJ 08062

STANDIFORD, Sarah Euphemia (Md)

STANFORD, David Dewitt (Chi) 2705 Armfield Road, Hillsborough, NC 27278

STANFORD, Donna Lynn (WMo) 100 E Red Bridge Rd, Kansas City, MO 64114

STANFORD, Virginia Francene (Md) 10901 Farrier Rd, Frederick, MD 21701

STANFORD, William Ted (FtW) 3550 SW Loop 820, Fort Worth, TX 76133

STANGER, Mark E. (Cal) 124 Panorama Dr, San Francisco, CA 94131

STANLEY, Anne Grant (Me) Po Box 63, Paris, ME 04271

STANLEY, Arthur Patrick (Ia) 10 Knights Ct, Frome Somerset, BA 11 1JD England, Great Britain (UK)

STANLEY, E Bevan (Ct) 25 South St, PO Box 248, Litchfield, CT 06759

STANLEY, Gordon John (Chi) 340 W Diversey Pkwy, Chicago, IL 60657

STANLEY, James Martin (NI) 320 Franklin St, Geneva, IL 60134

STANLEY JR, John Hiram (FtW) 4105 Hartwood Dr, Fort Worth, TX 76109

STANLEY, Lauren Regina (SD) PO Box 256, Mission, SD 57555

STANLEY, Marjorie Jean (Spok) 255 W Shore Ln, Sandpoint, ID 83864

STANLEY, Mark Andrew (Md) Old St. Paul's Church, 309 Cathedral Street, Baltimore, MD 21201

STANLEY, Mary Luck (Md) Old St. Paul's Church, 309 Cathedral St., Baltimore, MD 21201

STANLEY, Stephen Ranson (SwVa) St. Mark's Episcopaql Church, 111 South Roanoke St. P.O. Box 277, Fincastle, VA 24090

STANLEY, William (At)

STANSBERY, Marylen Wilkins (Mo) 2 Warson Ln, Saint Louis, MO 63124

STANTON JR, Barclay Reynolds (Eas) 24447 94th St S, Kent, WA 98030

✠ **STANTON**, James Monte (Ret Bp of Dal 2014-) 1630 N Garrett Ave, Dallas, TX 75206

STANTON, John Frank (Nwk) 7900 Harbor Island Dr Apt 1501, North Bay Village, FL 33141

STANTON, John Robert (At) 4906 Sulky Dr Apt 204, Richmond, VA 23228

STANTON, Sarah Morningstar (EO) 4701 7th Ave. SW Unit 303, Olympia, WA 98502

STANTON, William Blair (Colo) 4775 Cambridge St, Boulder, CO 80301

STANWISE, Ralph Joseph Francis (Chi) 2608 N Kingston Dr, Peoria, IL 61604

STANWOOD, Thomas Reid (Ore) 1638 Boca Ratan Dr, Lake Oswego, OR 97034

STAPLES, Ann McDonald (Pgh) Po Box 1, Marion Center, PA 15759

STAPLETON JR, Jack (Colo) 4222 W. 22nd Street Road, Greeley, CO 80634

STARBUCK, Betsy D (Ct) 88 N Main St, PO Box 983, Kent, CT 06757

STARKES, Lionel Alfonso (Nev) Po Box 50763, Henderson, NV 89016

STARKWEATHER, Betty (ND) 679 Lehigh Dr., Merced, CA 95348

STARR, Charles Christopher (Chris) (At) Church of the Atonement (Episcopal), 4945 High Point Road, Sandy Springs, GA 30342

STARR, Charles Michael (Pgh) 4048 Circle Dr, Bakerstown, PA 15007

STARR III, David H (Los) St. John's Church, 1407 N. Arrowhead Ave., San Bernardino, CA 92405

STARR, Mark Lowell (CGC) 41 Olympic Blvd, Port Townsend, WA 98368

STARR, Nancy Barnard (Mil) 76 Grange Road, Mount Eden, Auckland, NZ 1024, New Zealand (Aotearoa)

STARR, Therese Ann (Okla) PO Box 759, Eufaula, OK 74432

STARR, William Frederic (NY) 36 South Rd, Chilmark, MA 02535

STASSER, Nina Louise (U) 700 W Roller Coaster Rd, Tucson, AZ 85704

STATER, Catherine J (CFla) 319 W Wisconsin Ave, Deland, FL 32720

STATEZNI, Gregory George (Episcopal SJ) 7000 College Ave Apt 21, Bakersfield, CA 93306

STATHERS JR, Birk Smith (SeFla) 208 N Lee St, Lewisburg, WV 24901

STAYNER, David (Ct) 28 Myra Rd, Hamden, CT 06517

STAYNER, Sandra Hardyman (Ct) 39 Pleasant Drive, Cheshire, CT 06410

STAYTON, Darrell Lynn (Ark) PO Box 726, Stuttgart, AR 72160

ST CLAIR, Melinda (RG) 3500 McRae Blvd, El Paso, TX 79925

ST CLAIRE II, Elbert Kyle (Pa) 1650 Franklin Dr, Furlong, PA 18925

STEADMAN, David Wilton (The Episcopal NCal) 756 Robinson Rd, Sebastopol, CA 95472

STEADMAN, Larry Kenneth (WK) 705 W 31st Ave, Hutchinson, KS 67502

STEADMAN, Marguerite Alexandra (Me) 3116 O St Nw, Washington, DC 20007

STEAGALL, Patricia (Ore) 34735 Lodgepole Drive, Manzanita, OR 97130

STEARNS, Fellow Clair (ECR) Po Box 2789, Saratoga, CA 95070

STEARNS, Joanne (SO) 5380 Dovetree Blvd. Apt 10, Moraine, OH 45439

STEARNS, Samuel D (RG) 3705 Utah St Ne, Albuquerque, NM 87110

STEBBINS JR, George Griswold (CFla) 1219 Augustine Dr, The Villages-Lady Lake, FL 32159

STEBBINS, Marty (NC)

STEBER, Gary David (NC) 406 Lorimer Road, Box 970, Davidson, NC 28036

STEBINGER, Katharine E (Minn)

STEBINGER, Peter A R (Ct) 615 Bethmour Rd, Bethany, CT 06524

STECH, Bill (Mich) 20500 W Old US Highway 12, Chelsea, MI 48118

STECKER IV, Frederick (NH) Box 293, New London, NH 03257

STECKLINE, Donna Louise (Alb) P.O. Box 345, Gilbertsville, NY 13776

STEDMAN, David Algernon (WNY) Po Box 7488, St Thomas, VI 00801

STEED, John Griffith (NJ) 11b Portsmouth St, Whiting, NJ 08759

STEEDMAN SANBORN, Marda Leigh (Oly) 24447 94th Ave S, Kent, WA 98030

STEELE, Christopher Andrew (Dal) 11122 Midway Rd, Dallas, TX 75229

STEELE, Christopher Candace (Oly) 7747 31st Ave Sw, Seattle, WA 98126

STEELE, Gary Ross (Ak) 2708 W 65th Ave, Anchorage, AK 99502

STEELE, James Logan (Chi) 317 Goold Park Dr, Morris, IL 60450

STEELE, Kelly Ann (Ga)

STEELE, Lawrence Jay (Los) 490 E Indian School Ln, Banning, CA 92220

STEELE, Nancy J (EMich) PO Box 452, Chesaning, MI 48616

STEELE, Robert Emanuel (Nwk) Office For Diverity Initiatives Graduate School University Of Maryland, College Park, MD 20742

STEELE, Sean William (Tex) Trinity Episcopal Church, 3901 S Panther Creek Dr, The Woodlands, TX 77381

STEEN, S. James (Chi) 65 E. Huron St., Chicago, IL 60611

STEEVER JR, Raymond George Edward (Los) Route 1, Box 109, Pullman, WA 99163

STEEVES, Joan Altpeter (Colo) 6337 Deframe Way, Arvada, CO 80004

STEEVES, Timothy (Pa) 409 E Lancaster Ave, Downingtown, PA 19335

STEFANIK, Alfred Thomas (Vt) 49 Raintree Circle, Palm Coast, FL 32164

STEFFENHAGEN, Leverne Richard (WNY) 9705 Niagara Falls Blvd Apt 19, Niagara Falls, NY 14304

STEFFENSEN, Leslie N (Va) Grace Episcopal Church, 3601 Russell Rd, Alexandria, VA 22305

STEFKO, Nadia Mary (Chi) 3857 N Kostner Ave, Chicago, IL 60641

STEGELMANN, Dawn (Ct) 651 Pequot Ave, Southport, CT 06890

STEIDL, Gerald S. (CFla) 127 E Cottesmore Cir, Longwood, FL 32779

STEIG, George Terrance (Oly) 5241 12th Ave Ne, Seattle, WA 98105

STEILBERG, Isabel Fourqurean (SVa) 221 34th St, Newport News, VA 23607

STEIN, Edward Lee (Tex) 717 Sage Rd, Houston, TX 77056

STEINBACH, Frederick Leo (Ia) PO Box 838, Chariton, IA 50049

STEINER IV, John (Md) 7474 Washington Blvd, Elkridge, MD 21075

STEINER, Scott A (Mich)

STEINFELD, John Wilfred (Nev) 915 Gear St, Reno, NV 89503

STEINHAUER, Roger Kent (Roch) 25 Chadbourne Rd, Rochester, NY 14618

STEINHAUSER, Elizabeth (Mass) 419 Shawmut Ave., Boston, MA 02118

STELK, Lincoln Frank (NY) 241 Bluff Rd, Yarmouth, ME 04096

STELLE, Eric Arthur (Oly) 7701 Skansie Ave, Gig Harbor, WA 98335

STELLMAN, Jill (Alb) Episcopal Diocese Of Albany, 580 Burton Rd, Greenwich, NY 12834

STELZ, Patricia A (NH) 466 Summit House, West Chester, PA 19382

STEN, Pamela V (WMich) 605 W 4th St Apt 2, Buchanan, MI 49107

STENNER, David Anthony (Md) 203 E Chatsworth Ave, Reisterstown, MD 21136

STENNETTE, Lloyd Roland (SeFla)

STENNING, Gordon John (RI) 36 Brant Rd, Portsmouth, RI 02871

STEPHENS, Jeff (U) 2141 Horizon View Dr, St George, UT 84790

STEPHENS, Paul Jeffery (Miss) P. O. Box 1358, Tupelo, MS 38802

STEPHENS, Thomas Lee (Okla) 1560 SE Pecan Place, Bartlesville, OK 74003

STEPHENS, Wyatt E (Mil) 1538 N 58th St, Milwaukee, WI 53208

STEPHENSON, John William (Kan) Rr 1 Box 190, Riverton, KS 66770

STEPHENSON, Michael Perdue (Okla) 3621 24th Ave SE Apt 3, Norman, OK 73071

STEPHENSON, Randolph (WA) 4 Jeb Stuart Ct, Rockville, MD 20854

STEPHENSON-DIAZ, Lark (SanD) 1023 Iris Ct, Carlsbad, CA 92011

STER, David (CPa)

STERCHI, Margaret (NJ) 11 North Ave., Wilmington, DE 19804

STERKEN, Janet Leigh (Eau) 322 N. Water St., Sparta, WI 54656

STERLING III, Edward Arthur (Oly) 3762 Palisades Pl W, University Place, WA 98466

STERLING, Franklin Mills (Cal) 1707 Gouldin Rd., Oakland, CA 94611

STERLING, Leslie Katherin (Mass) St. Bartholomew's Church, 239 Harvard Street, Cambridge, MA 02139

STERN, Linda Sue (Okla) 516 Mclish St, Ardmore, OK 73401

STERNE, Colleen Kathryn (Los) Trinity Episcopal Church, 1500 State St, Santa Barbara, CA 93101

STERNE, Martha Packer (At) 805 Mount Vernon Hwy NW, Atlanta, GA 30327

STERRY, Steven Chapin (Los) Blessed Sacrament Church, 1314 N Angelina Dr, Placentia, CA 92870

STEUER, Lawrence William (Alb) 343 Pettis Rd, Gansevoort, NY 12831

STEVENS JR, Arthur Grant (WMass) 904B West Victoria St, Santa Barbara, CA 93101

STEVENS, George (Mass) St. John's Church, P.O. Box 5610, Beverly, MA 01915

STEVENS III, Halsey (Ct) 63 Route 81, Killingworth, CT 06419

STEVENS, Judith Parris (WMass) 904B W Victoria St, Santa Barbara, CA 93101

STEVENS, Karl Peter (SO) Saint Stephen's Episcopal Church, 30 W Woodruff Ave, Columbus, OH 43210

STEVENS, M(errill) Richard (NAM) Saint Christopher's Mission, PO Box 28, Bluff, UT 84512

STEVENS, Nancy Dunbar (Roch) The Church of the Epiphany, 3285 Buffalo Rd, Rochester, NY 14624

STEVENS, Patricia D (At) P.O. Box 155, Johnston, SC 29832

STEVENS JR, Robert E (NH) 1113 Macon Ave, Pittsburgh, PA 15218

STEVENS, Robert Ellsworth (CFla) 2346 Colfax Ter., Evanston, IL 60201

STEVENS, Scott J (Ct) PO Box 151, Hampton, CT 06247

STEVENS III, Walter Alexander (The Episcopal Church in Haw)

STEVENS, William Clair (PR)

STEVENS-HUMMON, Rebecca M (Tenn) 2902 Overlook Dr, Nashville, TN 37212

STEVENSON, Ann W (NH) P O Box 743, 18 High St, North Berwick, ME 03906

STEVENSON, Anne B. (Tenn) 216 chestnut hill, Nashville, TN 37215

STEVENSON, Carolyn Eve (NH) 231 Main St, Salem, NH 03079

STEVENSON, E Mark (La) 2465 Playa Del Mar Dr, Little Elm, TX 75068

STEVENSON, Frank Beaumont (SO) School Lane, Stanton Saint John, Oxford, OX33 1ET, Great Britain (UK)

STEVENSON, Frederic George (CPa) 890 Mccosh St, Hanover, PA 17331

STEVENSON, Janis Jordan (Mich) 430 Nicolet St, Walled Lake, MI 48390

STEVENSON, R(ichard) Hugh (The Episcopal NCal) 610 Los Alamos Rd, Santa Rosa, CA 95409

STEVENSON, Thomas Edward (Ore) PO Box 29, Alsea, OR 97324

STEVENS-TAYLOR, Sally Hodges (Az) PO Box 65840, Tucson, AZ 85728

STEVICK, Daniel Bush (Pa) 600 E Cathedral Rd Apt D203, Philadelphia, PA 19128

STEWART, Barbara Rindge (Los)

STEWART, Bonnie (Cal) Holy Cross Episcopal Church, 19179 Center St, Castro Valley, CA 94546

STEWART, Carol Wendt (Roch) 3074 O'Donnell Rd, Wellsville, NY 14895

STEWART, Caroline Rinehart (Md) 4024 Stewart Rd, Stevenson, MD 21153

STEWART, Clifford Thomas (Ore) Po Box 447, Lake Oswego, OR 97034

STEWART, Daniel R (Oly) 322 Aoloa St Apt 1101, Kailua, HI 96734

STEWART, Duke Summerlin (Ga) 701 Gaskin Ave N, Douglas, GA 31533

STEWART, James Allen (Wyo) St Mark's Episcopal Church, 1908 Central Ave, Cheyenne, WY 82001

STEWART, James Macgregor (NC) 6400 N Pennsylvania Ave, Nichols Hills, OK 73116

STEWART, Jane Louise (Ia) 912 20th Ave., Coralville, IA 52241

STEWART, J(ohn) Bruce (Va) 4327 Ravensworth Rd Apt 210, Annandale, VA 22003

STEWART, Kevin P. (Mil) 4722 N 104th St, Wauwatosa, WI 53225

STEWART, Leslie Ann (Dal) PO Box 292365, Lewisville, TX 75029

STEWART, Matthew Wellington (Mass) 11 W. Grove St., Middleboro, MA 02346

STEWART, Natalie Ann (ECR) PO Box 515, Aromas, CA 95004

STEWART, Natasha (Mass) 407 Rochester St, Fall River, MA 02720

STEWART, Pamela Fay (Colo) 126 W 2nd Ave, Denver, CO 80223

STEWART, Ralph Roderick (Oly) 23 Turtle Rock Ct, New Paltz, NY 12561

STEWART, Sarah (WA)

STEWART JR, William Owen (Ga) PO Box 1171, Leesburg, GA 31763

STEWART-SICKING, Joseph (Md) 8890 McGaw Rd, Columbia, MD 21045

STEWART-SICKING, Megan Elizabeth (Md) 1509 Glencoe Rd, Glencoe, MD 21152

STEWMAN, Kerry J (O) Po Box 366274, Bonita Springs, FL 34136

ST GEORGE, David (Nwk) 8 Binney Rd, Old Lyme, CT 06371

ST. GERMAIN, Beverly Anne Lavallee (Vt) Three Cathedral Square 3A, Burlington, VT 05401

ST GERMAIN JR, Kenneth Paul (SO) 2151 Dorset Rd, Columbus, OH 43221

ST GERMAIN-ILER III, Rob B (Ala) 347 South Central Ave., Alexander City, AL 35010

STICHWEH, Michael Terry (CFla) 410 Meridian Street, Apt 604, Indianapolis, IN 46204

STICKLEY, David (Cal) 101 Gold Mine Dr, San Francisco, CA 94131

STICKNEY, Jane Burr (Ct) 14 Lone Pine Trl, Higganum, CT 06441

STICKNEY, Jim (Cal) 1324 Devonshire Ct, El Cerrito, CA 94530

STICKNEY, Joyce Erwin (Los) 28211 Pacific Coast Hwy, Malibu, CA 90265

STIEFEL, Jennifer H (NH) 30 Holiday Drive #341, Dover, NH 03820

STIEFEL, Robert Earl (NH) 30 Holiday Dr Unit 341, Dover, NH 03820

STIEGLER, Mark Ashton (Roch) 3835 Oneill Rd, Lima, NY 14485

STIEPER, John Richard (Chi) 7 Fernwood Dr, Barrington, IL 60010

STIFLER, Linnea Ruth Peterson (WMich) 2010 Nichols Rd, Kalamazoo, MI 49004

STILES, Katherine Mitchell (Me) 99 Brattle St, Cambridge, MA 02138

STILES-RANDAK, Susan (RI) Peace Dale Estates, 1223 Saugatucket Rd Apt A102, Peace Dale, RI 02879

STILL, Kimberly L. (Fla)

STILLINGS, Kyle David (WTenn) William Temple Center, 427 Market St, Galveston, TX 77550

STILLMAN, Ann Allen (CNY) 2239 Gridley Paige Rd, Deansboro, NY 13328

STIMPSON, Peter K (NJ) 220 W Kilbride, Williamsburg, VA 23188

STINE, Stephen Blaine (Tex) 1220 Quirby Lane, Tyler, TX 75701

STINGLEY, Elizabeth Anne (Los) 12880 Riverview Drive, 8821 SVL Box, Victorville, CA 92395

STINNETT, Roger Allen (WMo) 804 Wendy Ln, Carthage, MO 64836

STINSON, Marian (Ct) 84 Ledgewood Dr, Glastonbury, CT 06033

STINSON, Richard Lyon (Pgh) Twin Chimneys, 375 Country Club Rd, Indiana, PA 15701

STIPE, Nickie Maxine (Ak) 280 Northern Ave Apt 10-A, Avondale Estates, GA 30002

STISCIA, Alfred Ronald (CPa) 5092 Riverfront Dr, Bradenton, FL 34208

STITT, David Watson (WLa) 713 Circle C, Hastings, NE 68901

STIVERS, Donald Austin (Los) 5023 Calle Tania, Santa Barbara, CA 93111

ST JOHN, Andrew Reginald (NY) 1 E 29th St, New York, NY 10016

ST JOHNS, Ernest Keys (RG) 1002 N Robert St, Ludington, MI 49431

ST LOUIS, J. Allison (Ct) Virginia Theological Seminary, 3737 Seminary Road, Alexandria, VA 22304

ST LOUIS, Jn Michelin (Hai)

ST LOUIS, Leslie (WA) 13106 Annapolis Rd, Bowie, MD 20720

ST LOUIS, Samuel (Hai)

STOCK, David Robert (Okla) 4036 Neptune Dr, Oklahoma City, OK 73116

STOCKARD, Matthew Easter (EC) Po Box 1336, Kinston, NC 28503

STOCKSDALE, Robert (Ct) 183 Pin Oak Dr, Southington, CT 06489

STOCKTON, James Vernon (Tex) 16306 Ascent Cove, Pflugerville, TX 78660

STOCKTON, Marietta Grace (WK) 406 W. Kingman Ave., Lakin, KS 67860

STOCKWELL-TANGEMAN, Carolyn Lee (WMo)

STODDART, David Michael (Va) Church of Our Saviour, 1165 Rio Road East, Charlottesville, VA 22901

STODGHILL, Dawnell Smith (WLa) St Thomas Episcopal Church, 3706 Bon Aire Drive, Monroe, LA 71203

STODGHILL, Marion Whitbread (Ky) Norton Hospital, Chaplain, 200 E. Chesnut Street, Louisville, KY 40202

STODGHILL III, Thomas Whitfield (WLa) 3435 Westminster Avenue, Monroe, LA 71201

STOESSEL, Andrew James (Mass) 36 Cornell St, Roslindale, MA 02131

STOFFREGEN, Diana Jacobson (Spok) 5609 S Custer Street, Spokane, WA 99223

STOFFREGEN, Megan Amy (Spok) 5609 S Custer Rd, Spokane, WA 99223

STOKES, Grant Anthony (WNC) Christ and St Luke's Epis Church, 560 W Olney Rd, Norfolk, VA 23507

✠ **STOKES**, William H (Bp of NJ 2013-) Episcopal Diocese Of New Jersey, 808 W State St, Trenton, NJ 08618

STOMSKI, William L (Nev) 3300B S Seacrest Blvd, Boynton Beach, FL 33435

STONE, Carey Don (Ark) 112 Traveler Ln, Maumelle, AR 72113

STONE, David Lynn (HB) 940 Channing Way, Berkeley, CA 94710

STONE, Dean P (Kan) 9201 West 82nd Street, Overland Park, KS 66204

STONE, John Curtis (NJ) 40-B Center St, Highlands, NJ 07732

STONE JR, Lewis Seymour (NH) 11 Governor Sq, Peterborough, NH 03458

STONE, Mary Ruth (NJ) 40 - B Center St, Highlands, NJ 07732

STONE, Michael D (Tex) 18300 Upper Bay Rd, Houston, TX 77058

STONE, Michael L (SVa) 985 Huguenot Trail, Midlothian, VA 23113

STONE, Sandra Elizabeth (Lex) 3416 Crooked Creek Rd, Carlisle, KY 40311

STONE, Thomas Michael (Chi) 3601 N North St, Peoria, IL 61604

STONER, D Scott (Mil) 2017 E. Olive St., Milwaukee, WI 53211

STONER, Suzanne (Ark)

STONESIFER, John Dewitt (WA) 3603 Gleneagles Dr Apt 3c, Silver Spring, MD 20906

STOPFEL, Barry Lee (Nwk) RD1 Box 146, Mifflinburg, PA 17844

STOPPEL, Gerald Corwin (WMich) PO Box 65, Saugatuck, MI 49453

STOREY, Wayne Alton (CNY) 311 S Massey St, Watertown, NY 13601

STORM, Astrid J (NY) 19 Kent Street, Beacon, NY 12508

STORM, David Anderson (Oly) 2611 Broadway E, Seattle, WA 98102

STORMENT, J(Ohn) Douglas (WTex) 1635 Thrush Court Cir, San Antonio, TX 78248

STORMER, Eugene Allen (Spr) 825 Lorraine Ave, Springfield, IL 62704

STORY, Mark Denslow (Okla) 1701 Mission Rd, Edmond, OK 73034

STOUDEMIRE, Stewart Mcbryde (WNC) 950 - 36th Avenue Circle Northeast, Hickory, NC 28601

STOUT, A(rla) Jeanne (Mich) 204 Sunnyside Ave, Cameron, WI 54822

STOUT, David Alan (The Episcopal Church in Haw) St. James' Church, PO Box 278, Kamuela, HI 96743

STOUTE, Barclay Lenardo (LI) 28 Fallon Ct, Elmont, NY 11003

STOUT-KOPP, Ronnie Thompson (Nwk) 50 Brams Hill Dr, Mahwah, NJ 07430

STOWE, Barbara Elaine (Mass) 33 Washington St, Topsfield, MA 01983

STOWE, David Andrew (NJ) Pine Run Community, 777 Ferry Rd, Doylestown, PA 18901

STOWE, Howard Timothy Wheeler (NY) 79 Ne 93rd St, Miami Shores, FL 33138

STOWELL, Philip W (NJ) 207 W Main St, Moorestown, NJ 08057

STOY, Carol Berry (NJ) 221 Herrontown Rd, Princeton, NJ 08540

ST PIERRE, Joanne Madelyn (EMich) PO Box 217, Otter Lake, MI 48464

STRADER, James William (SO) 3207 Montana Ave, Cincinnati, OH 45211

STRAHAN, Linda C (RI) 103 Kay St, Newport, RI 02840

STRAIN, William Henry (Nwk) 4 Acacia Dr, Boynton Beach, FL 33436

STRAINGE JR, Roy Thomas (SeFla)

STRAND, Jon Carl (Mass) Po Box 238, Natick, MA 01760

STRANDE, Dana F (Minn) 7305 Afton Rd, Woodbury, MN 55125

STRANDLUND, Daniel Patrick (Ala) 113 Madison Ave, Montgomery, AL 36104

STRANE, Steven Roberts (SanD) 4489 Caminito Cuarzo, San Diego, CA 92117

STRANG, Ruth Hancock (Mich) 504 Prospect St, Howell, MI 48843

STRANGE, Phillip Ross (Los) PO Box 3144, Wrightwood, CA 92397

STRASBURGER, Frank C (NJ) 27 Tidal Run Lane, Brunswick, ME 04011

STRASBURGER, Roy William (ECR) 89 Alpine Ave, Los Gatos, CA 95030

STRASSER, Gabor (Va) 18525 Bear Creek Ter, Leesburg, VA 20176

STRATFORD, Jane (Cal) PO Box 187, Moraga, CA 94556

STRATTON, Jonathan Robert (Mo) 1210 Locust St, Saint Louis, MO 63103

STRAUB, Gregory Stephen (Eas) 1920 S Ocean Dr Apt 1004, Fort Lauderdale, FL 33316

STRAUGHN, Richard Daniel (SwFla) 373 Corson Ln, Cape May, NJ 08204

STRAUKAMP, James Edward (The Episcopal NCal) 2140 Mission Ave., Carmichael, CA 95608

STRAUSS, A(rlen) Richard (CNY) 109 Glenside Rd, Ithaca, NY 14850

STRAVERS, Cynthia A (NY) 2 E 90th St, New York, NY 10128

STRAVERS, Richard Lee (WMich)

STRAWBRIDGE, Jennifer R (Va) Keble College, Parks Road, Oxford, OX1 3PG, Great Britain (UK)

STREEPY, Robert Shawn (Kan) 10700 W 53rd St, Shawnee, KS 66203

STREET III, Claude Parke (Colo) 35 KILDEER Rd, Hamden, CT 06517

STREET, Terry Terriell (WTenn) 210 Walnut Trace Dr, Cordova, TN 38018

STREETER, Christopher Michael (Roch) 36 S Main St, Pittsford, NY 14534

STREEVER, Hilary B (SwVa) 124 E Main St, Abingdon, VA 24210

STREIFF, Suzanne (Oly) 305 Burma Rd, Castle Rock, WA 98611

STREIT JR, John Paul (Mass) 41 Ackers Ave Apt 2, Brookline, MA 02445

STREUFERT, Nancy Stimac (The Episcopal NCal) 625 15th St, Eureka, CA 95501

STRIBLING, Anna Jones (Va) 4540 Carrington Rd, Markham, VA 22643

STRIBLING, Emily B (WA) 4621 Laverock Pl NW, WASHINGTON, DC 20007

STRIBLING JR, Jess Hawkins (Va) 1 Colley Ave Apt 600, Apt 600, Norfolk, VA 23510

STRICKER, David Walter (USC) 1028 Kinsey Dr. SE, Huntsville, AL 35803

STRICKLAND, Harold Somerset (Ark) 610 Northwest K, Bentonville, AR 72712

✠ **STRICKLAND**, Vernon Edward (Ret Bp of WK 2002-) 665 N Desmet Ave, Buffalo, WY 82834

STRICKLAND, Virginia (NY) 209 Madison Ave, New York, NY 10016

STRICKLAND JR, William Earl (Alb) 4 Avery Place, Clifton Park, NY 12065

STRICKLIN, Paul E (USC) 6408 Bridgewood Rd., Columbia, SC 29206

STRID, Paul E. (Cal) 3115 W Meadow Dr SW, Albuquerque, NM 87121

STRIDIRON, Andrea Renee (Roch) 2000 Highland Ave, Rochester, NY 14618

STRIMER, Peter Mccoy (Oly) 111 NE 80th Street, Seattle, WA 98115

STRING, Jansen Edward (Md) 2900 Dunleer Rd, Baltimore, MD 21222

STRINGER, Pamela (EC) 111 N King St, Bath, NC 27808

STRINGER, Stacy Bussy (Tex) 4613 Highway 3, Dickinson, TX 77539

STRINGFELLOW III, Howard (Be) 333 Wyandotte St., Bethlehem, PA 18015

STRIZAK, Jenna Faith (At) Holy Trinity Parish, 515 E Ponce de Leon Ave, Decatur, GA 30030

STROBEL JR, Henry Willis (Tex) 2701 Bellefontaine St Apt B32, Houston, TX 77025

STROBEL, Pamela Owen (NY) 123 Henry St, Greenwich, CT 06830

STROH, Nancy Marshall (Pa) 3440 Norwood Pl, Holland, PA 18966

STROHL, Patrick Francis (CPa) 113 S Broad St, Mechanicsburg, PA 17055

STROHM, Ralph William (WVa) 2248 Adams Ave, Huntington, WV 25704

STROM, Aune Juanita (Mo) St Andrew's By the Lake Episcopal, PO Box 8766, Michigan City, IN 46361

STROMBERG, Matthew Roy (Alb) 69 Fair St, Cooperstown, NY 13326

STROMWELL, Gloria Regina (Md) 126 E. Liberty St., Oakland, MD 21550

STRONG, Anne Lorraine (Az) PO Box 65840, Tucson, AZ 85728

STRONG, Daniel Robert (WMass) 17 Exeter Dr, Auburn, MA 01501

STRONG, Elizabeth Anne (Minn) 2200 Minnehaha Ave E, Saint Paul, MN 55119

STRONG III, Maurice LeRoy (Chi) 26 E Stonegate Dr, Prospect Heights, IL 60070

STRONG, Nancy Baillie (WMass) 17 Exeter Dr, Auburn, MA 01501

STROO, Eric Edward (Oly) 111 NE 80th St, Seattle, WA 98115

STROTHEIDE, Cassandra Jo (Colo) 19210 E Stanford Dr, Aurora, CO 80015

STROUD, Daniel Joseph Shine (Pa) PO Box 247, Ft Washington, PA 19034

STROUD, Lara C (Pa) PO Box 247, Fort Washington, PA 19034

STROUD, Nancy Webb (WMass) 64 Westwood Dr, Westfield, MA 01085

STROUD, Robert L (WNC)

STROUP, Susan Louise (Oly)

STROUT, Shawn Owen (WA) 2430 K St Nw, Washington, DC 20037

STRUBEL, Gary Francis (Alb) 457 3rd St, Troy, NY 12180

STRUBLE, Kenneth Charles (At) 4076 Riverdale Rd., Toccoa, GA 30577

STUART JR, Calvin Truesdale Biddison (Mo) 5008 Bischoff Ave, Saint Louis, MO 63110

STUART, Charles Moore (EMich) 821 Adams St, Saginaw, MI 48602

STUART, Judith L (Mass) PO Box 789, Chatham, MA 02633

STUART, Lawrence Earl (Mich) 3901 Cheyenne Rd, Richmond, VA 23235

STUART, Marianne D(esmarais) (Ala) 249 Arch St, Philadelphia, PA 19106

STUART, Mark (Los) 2260 N Cahuenga Blvd # 507, Los Angeles, CA 90068

STUART, Toni Freeman (The Episcopal NCal) 4881 8th St, Carpinteria, CA 93013

STUBBS, John Derek (WNY) 33 Linwood Avenue, Whitinsville, MA 01588

STUBE, Peter Brownell (Pa) 125 Timothy Circle, Wayne, PA 19087

STUBER, Richard Leonard (Wyo) 1320 Landon Ave, Yakima, WA 98902

STUCKEY, Ross Woods (WMo) 1654 E Cardinal St, Springfield, MO 65804

STUDDIFORD, Linton Hervey (Me) 124 Bunganuc Rd, Brunswick, ME 04011

STUDENNY, Ronald Roman (Dal) 977 W Highway 243, Canton, TX 75103

STUDLEY, Carolyn Mary (Minn) 614 N Old Litchfield Rd, Litchfield Park, AZ 85340

STUDLEY, Richard E (Minn) 9817 W. Pinecrest Dr, Sun City, AZ 85351

STUHLMAN, Byron David (CNY) PO Box 74, Round Pond, ME 04564

STUHLMANN, Robert (Ct) 2000 Main St, Stratford, CT 06615

STUMP, Celeste Smith (Los) 330 E 16th St, Upland, CA 91784

STUMP, Derald William (CPa) 106 S Outer Dr, State College, PA 16801

STURGEON, Mary Sue (Neb) 5176 S 149th Ct, Omaha, NE 68137

STURGEON, Stephen C (U) 85 E 100 N, Logan, UT 84321

STURGES, Harriette Horsey (WA) 3001 Wisconsin Ave NW, Washington, DC 20016

STURGES, Kathleen McAuliffe (Va) 3134 Mollifield Lane, Charlottesville, VA 22911

STURGESS, Amber D (Cal) 6208 Sutter Ave, Richmond, CA 94804

STURGIS, Janet Elizabeth (Neb) Po Box 2285, Kearney, NE 68848

STURNI, Gary K (WTenn) 6922 Great Oaks Rd, Germantown, TN 38138

STURTEVANT, Henry Hobson (NY) 484 W 43rd St Apt 33-H, New York, NY 10036

STUTLER, James Boyd (At) 1029 Wellesley Crest Dr, Woodstock, GA 30189

SUAREZ ELLES, Jose Armando (Colom) Cr 3 Sur # 11-A-02, Malambo, ATLANTICO, Colombia

SUCRE-CORDOVA, Guillermo Antonio (Ve)

SUELLAU, Nancy Shebs (Fla) St Catherines Episcopal Church, 4758 Shelby Ave, Jacksonville, FL 32210

SUGENO, David Senkichi (Tex)

SUHAR, John Charles (SwFla) 771 34th Ave N, Saint Petersburg, FL 33704

SUHR, Esther J (Mont) 2584 Mt Hwy 284, Townsend, MT 59644

SUIT, Marvin Wilson (Lex) 440 Fountain Avenue, Flemingsburg, KY 41041

SULERUD, Mary Catherine (Va) St Stephen's Episcopal Church, 6000 Grove Ave, Richmond, VA 23226

SULLIVAN, Ann Mary (The Episcopal NCal) 5850 Crestmoor Dr, Paradise, CA 95969

SULLIVAN, Bernadette (LI) Po Box 243, Hampton Bays, NY 11946

SULLIVAN JR, Bob Sullivan (SeFla) 8144 Bridgewater Ct Apt C, West Palm Beach, FL 33406

SULLIVAN, Bradley Joseph (Tex) 3003 Memorial Ct Apt 2405, Houston, TX 77007

SULLIVAN, Brian Christopher (At) 3361 Clubland Drive, Marietta, GA 30068

SULLIVAN, David Andrew (Alb) P.O. Box 146, Elizabethtown, NY 12932

SULLIVAN, Elmer Lindsley (NJ) 13 Llanfair Ln, Ewing, NJ 08618

SULLIVAN, Herbert Patrick (Mich)

SULLIVAN, Judith A (Pa) Philadelphia Episcopal Cathedral, 3723 Chestnut Street, Philadelphia, PA 19104

SULLIVAN, Karen Sue Racer (Ind)

SULLIVAN, Kristin Louise (Tex)

SULLIVAN, Margaret Peggy (NY) P.O. Box 708, Walden, NY 12586

SULLIVAN, Mark C (Del) 463 Nicole Ct, Smyrna, DE 19977

SULLIVAN, Mary Beatrice (Ala) PO Box 2365, Alabaster, AL 35007

SULLIVAN, Mary Patricia (NMich) 201 E Ridge St, Marquette, MI 49855

SULLIVAN, Maryalice (Mass) 104 N Washington St, North Attleboro, MA 02760

SULLIVAN, Michael Radford (At) 805 Mount Vernon Highway NW, Atlanta, GA 30328

SULLIVAN, P David (Mass) 138 Tremont St., Boston, MA 02111

SULLIVAN JR, Robert Edmund (NJ) 3450 Wild Oak Bay Blvd, Apt 138, Bradenton, FL 34210

SULLIVAN, Rosemari G(Aughan) (Va) 402 Virginia Avenue, Alexandria, VA 22302

SULLIVAN-CLIFTON, Sonia (CFla) 5873 N Dean Rd, Orlando, FL 32817

SUMMERFIELD, LeRoy James (WNC) 5365 Pine Ridge Dr, Connellys Springs, NC 28612

SUMMEROUR, William W (WNC) 233 Deep Ford Fls, Lake Toxaway, NC 28747

SUMMERS, Charles Raymond (Ia) 936 Grayson Dr. Apt. 329, Springfield, MA 01119

SUMMERS, Joseph Holmes (Mich) 1435 South Blvd, Ann Arbor, MI 48104

SUMMERS, Ronald Wayne (Lex) 777 Liberty Ridge Ln, Lexington, KY 40509

SUMMERSON, Stephen Lyn (Me) PO Box 8, Presque Isle, ME 04769

SUMMERVILLE, Stephen Claude (HB)

SUMNER JR, Edwin Roberts (NJ) 8 Heath Vlg, Hackettstown, NJ 07840

✠ SUMNER, George Robinson (Dal) 20 Queens Park Crescent West, Toronto, ON M5S 2W2, Canada

SUMNERS III, Charles Abram (WTex) 115 Northwood Dr., Cuero, TX 77954

SUNDERLAND, Douglas Clark (Wyo) 18 Manning Rd, Cody, WY 82414

SUNDERLAND, Edward (NY) 310 E 49th St Apt 10C, New York, NY 10017

SUNDERLAND JR, Edwin Sherwood Stowell (Me) 115 Williams St, Providence, RI 02906

SUNDERLAND, Melanie (O) 1103 Castleton Rd, Cleveland Heights, OH 44121

SUNDIN, Chad Ludwig (Az) 1735 S College Ave, Tempe, AZ 85281

SUPIN, Charles Robert (Nev) 554 East Landing Ridge Circle, Jefferson, NC 28640

SURGEON, Ornoldo A (SeFla) 20011 Nw 39th Ct, Miami Gardens, FL 33055

SURINER, Noreen P (WMass) PO Box 464, Middlefield, MA 01243

SURUDA, Teresa Ann (NJ) 58 Ravine Dr, Matawan, NJ 07747

SUTCLIFFE, David Kenneth (Alb) 75 Willett St. Apt. 41, Albany, NY 12210

SUTER, Vernon L (SanD) 30329 Keith Ave, Cathedral City, CA 92234

SUTHERLAND, Alan (Okla) 18417 Black Bear Trail, Norman, OK 73072

SUTHERLAND, Linda Ann (FtW) 830 County Road 109, Hamilton, TX 76531

SUTHERLAND, Mark R (RI) St Martin of Tours, 50 Orchard Ave, Providence, RI 02906

SUTHERLAND, Melody (Eas) 219 Somerset Rd, Stevensville, MD 21666

SUTHERS, Derwent Albert (At) 1178 Circulo Canario, Rio Rico, AZ 85648

SUTOR, Jack Thomas (Va) Po Box 271, Hanover, VA 23069

SUTTON, Christine Marie () PO Box 198, Lehman, PA 18627

✠ SUTTON, Eugene Taylor (Bp of Md 2008-) 4 East University Parkway, Baltimore, MD 21218

SUTTON, John D (Cal) 1045 Neilson St, Albany, CA 94706

SUTTON, Norma Sarah (Chi)

SUTTON, Sharon Laverne (NJ) St Stephen's Episcopal Church, 324 Bridgeboro St, Riverside, NJ 08075

SVOBODA-BARBER, Helen (NC) c/o St. Luke's Episcopal Church, 1737 Hillandale Rd, Durham, NC 27705

SWAIN, Barry Edward Bailey (NY) Church of the Resurrection, 119 East 74th Street, New York, NY 10021

SWAIN, Storm Kirsten (NY)

SWAN, Clinton E (Ak) Po Box 50037, Kivalina, AK 99750

SWAN, Craig R (RI) 72 Central St, Narragansett, RI 02882

SWAN, Richard A (Spr) P.O. Box 1513, Decatur, IL 62525

SWANLUND, Callie E (Pa) 8000 Saint Martins Ln, Philadelphia, PA 19118

SWANN, Albert Henry (ETenn) 4515 Glennora Drive, Walland, TN 37886

SWANN, Catherine Williams (Va) 387 Harbor Drive, Reedville, VA 22539

SWANN, Stephen Barham (Dal) 4223 Ridge Rd, Dallas, TX 75229

SWANN, Stuart Alan (Los) 1560 S Fredrica Ave, Clearwater, FL 33756

SWANSON, George Gaines (Nwk) 349 Seawall Rd, Manset, ME 04679

SWANSON, Geraldine Ann (NY) 250 Greeley Ave, Staten Island, NY 10306

SWANSON, John-Julian (Mil) 450 Sunnyslope Dr Apt 305, Hartland, WI 53029

SWANSON, Karen (ECR) Saint Andrew's Episcopal Church, 1600 Santa Lucia Ave, San Bruno, CA 94066

SWANSON, Kenneth Banford (At) 1015 Old Roswell Rd, Roswell, GA 30076

SWANSON, Richard Alden (Cal) 3101 Peninsula Rd Apt 301, Oxnard, CA 93035

SWANSON, Richard Reif (Vt) PO Box 1175, Stowe, VT 05672

SWARR, J. Peter (WMass) 1 Porter Rd, East Longmeadow, MA 01028

SWARTHOUT, James Edward (Chi) 10275 N. River Rd, Barrington Hills, IL 60102

SWARTSFAGER, Ames Kent (LI) 1022 Marine Dr Ne Unit 2, Olympia, WA 98501

SWARTZENTRUBER, A Orley (NJ) 5433 Crestlake Blvd, Sarasota, FL 34233

SWAYZE, Marie Zealor (Pa) 1420 Locust Street, Unit 16N, Philadelphia, PA 19102

SWEENEY, Craig Chandler (Be) 14014 Church Hill Rd, Clarks Summit, PA 18411

SWEENEY, David Cameron (Ore) 503 N Holladay Dr, Seaside, OR 97138

SWEENEY, Joseph Francis (NJ) 25 Quail Hollow Drive, Westampton, NJ 08060

SWEENEY, Meghan T (Mass) All Saints' Episcopal Church, 121 N Main St, Attleboro, MA 02703

SWEENEY, Peter Harry (Alb) 2497 Antonia Dr, Niskayuna, NY 12309

SWEENEY, Sylvia A (Los) Bloy House The Episcopal Theological School At Claremont, 1325 N College Ave, Claremont, CA 91711

SWEENY, Thomas Edward (NJ) 102 New St, Egg Harbor Township, NJ 08234

SWEET, Fran (Cal) Po Box 1384, Alameda, CA 94501

SWEET, Portia Ann Suddreath (Tex) 1811 Heights Blvd, Houston, TX 77008

SWEIGERT, Cynthia Bronson (Pgh) 5700 Forbes Ave, Pittsburgh, PA 15217

SWENSON, Richard Clive (Minn)

SWESEY, Jean Elizabeth (Minn) 1008 Transit Ave, Roseville, MN 55113

SWETMAN, Margarita (Nwk) 2528 Palmer Ave, New Orleans, LA 70118

SWIEDLER, Anne Elizabeth (At) 5625 Mill Glen Ct, Atlanta, GA 30338

SWIFT, Daniel Willard (Los) 24874 Olive Tree Ln, Los Altos, CA 94024

SWIFT, John Kohler (WMo) 6 Hunter Dr, Guilford, CT 06437

SWIFT, Stephen Albert (Md) 8403 Nunley Dr Apt E, Parkville, MD 21234

SWINDELL, Kay Howard (EC) 1514 Clifton Rd, Jacksonville, NC 28540

SWINDLE, Frank Moody (NwT) 649 Hwy 577, Pioneer, LA 71266

SWINEHART, Bruce Howard (Colo) 1404 Orchard Ave, Boulder, CO 80304

SWINEHART JR, Charles Henry (Mich) 1615 Ridgewood Dr, East Lansing, MI 48823

✠ **SWING**, William Edwin (Ret Bp of Cal 2006-) 105 Pepper Ave., Burlingame, CA 94010

SWINNEA, Stephanie Lavenia (Okla) 510 S 15th St, Mcalester, OK 74501

SWITZ, Robert William (Cal) 1189 W Park View Pl, Mount Pleasant, SC 29466

SWONGER, Timothy Lee (Nev) 1560 Jamielinn Ln Unit 103, Las Vegas, NV 89110

SWOPE, Bob (Ak)

SWORD, Carl Richard (NY) 200 East 33rd St, Apt # 14-J, New York, NY 10016

SY, Jonathan J (Los) 21202 Spurney Ln, Huntington Beach, CA 92646

SYDNOR JR, Charles Raymond (Va) 175 Rogue Point Ln, Heathsville, VA 22473

SYEDULLAH, Masud Ibn (NY) 35 Circle Dr, Hyde Park, NY 12538

SYKES, Robert James (Pa) 102 Woodland Dr, Lansdale, PA 19446

SYLER, Gregory Charles (WA) St George Church, PO Box 30, Valley Lee, MD 20692

SYLVESTER, Kathleen Dillon (Los)

SYMINGTON, Ann Pritzlaff (Los)

SYMINGTON, Sidney S (ECR) 545 Shasta Ave, Morro Bay, CA 93442

SYMONDS, John W (Neb) 321 W Chestnut St, Lancaster, PA 17603

SYMONS, Frederic Russell (The Episcopal NCal) 5301 Whitney Ave, Carmichael, CA 95608

SYNAN, Thomas Norbert Justin (WMass) Church Of The Heavenly Rest, 2 E 90th St, New York, NY 10128

SZACHARA, Joell Beth (CNY) 3415 Havenbrook Dr Apt 104, Kingwood, TX 77339

SZARKE, Christopher J (At) 210 N Cayuga St, Ithaca, NY 14850

SZOBOTA, Nicholas Stephen (Md) 230 Owensville Rd, West River, MD 20778

SZOKE, Robyn J (CPa) 6 Kitszell Dr, Carlisle, PA 17015

SZOST, Lois Anne Whitcomb (NY) 57 Goodwin Rd, Stanfordville, NY 12581

SZYMANSKI, Michael Stephen (WNY) 21 Modern Ave, Lackawanna, NY 14218

SZYMANSKI, Walter (Pgh) 334 Main St, Pittsburgh, PA 15201

T

TABB, Stewart M (SVa) 405 Talbot Hall Rd, Norfolk, VA 23505

TABER II, Kenneth William (SwFla) 200 College Ave NE, Grand Rapids, MI 49503

TABER-HAMILTON, Nigel John (Oly) 5217 S. Honeymoon Bay Road, Freeland, WA 98249

TABER-HAMILTON, Rachel K (Oly) 333 High St, Freeland, WA 98249

TABOR, Henry Caleb Coleman (NC) 408 Granville St, Oxford, NC 27565

TACHAU, Charles Brandeis (Ky) 1080 Baxter Ave Apt 1, Louisville, KY 40204

TACKKETT, Antoinette Vance (Kan) 613 Elm St, Coffeyville, KS 67337

TADKEN, Neil Alan (Los) 122 S. California Ave., Monrovia, CA 91016

TAFLINGER, Mary Jeanine (Ind) 5553 Leumas Rd, Cincinnati, OH 45239

TAFOYA, Stacey T (Colo) 315 Leyden St, Denver, CO 80220

TAFT JR, Paul Eberhart (Tex) 5504 Andover Dr, Tyler, TX 75707

TAIT, Charles William Stuart (WA) PO Box 25541, Seattle, WA 98165

TAKACS, Erika (Pa) Saint Mark's Church, 1625 Locust St, Philadelphia, PA 19103

TAKES WAR BONNETT, Ray Lee (SD)

TALBERT, Thomas Keith (CGC) 701 N Pine St, Foley, AL 36535

TALBIRD JR, John D (ETenn) 3184 Waterfront Drive, Chattanooga, TN 37419

TALBOTT, John Thayer (WA) 8 Ledge Road, Old Saybrook, CT 06475

TALCOTT, Barbara Geer (NH) St. Mark's School, 25 Marlboro Rd., Southborough, MA 01772

TALIAFERRO, Robert Davis (NwT) P.O. Box 3751, Amarillo, TX 79116

TALK IV, John Gordon (NC) 304 S Ridge St, Southern Pines, NC 28387

TALLANT, Greg (At) 3285 Kensington Road, Avondale Estates, GA 30002

TALLEVAST, William Dalton (CPa) University Med Ctr Dept of Pastoral Care, 1501 N Campbell Ave, Tucson, AZ 85724

TALLEY, Jennie (NY) St. John's Episcopal Church, 11 Wilmot Road, New Rochelle, NY 10804

TALLMAN, Samuel Vose (WNC) St Mary of the Hills Church, PO Box 14, Blowing Rock, NC 28605

✠ **TALTON**, Chester Lovelle (Ret Bp Suffr of Los 2010-) 1528 Oakdale Road, Modesto, CA 95355

TAMMEARU, Deborah Gibson (NY) 1047 Amsterdam Avenue, New York, NY 10025

TAN, Wee Chung (Minn)

TANABE, Irene (The Episcopal Church in Haw) 1041 10th Ave, Honolulu, HI 96816

TAN CRETI, Michael James (Neb) 2051 N 94th St, Omaha, NE 68134

TANG, Christopher Douglas (Md) 3118 Cape Hill Ct, Hampstead, MD 21074

TANKERSLEY, Rebecca Elizabeth Guldi (Dal) 1302 W. Kiest Blvd., Dallas, TX 75224

TANNER, Michael Abbott (At)

TANTIMONACO, Daniel Frank (Az) 307 N Mogollon Trail, Payson, AZ 85541

TAPLEY, William Clark (WTex) 1604 W Kansas Ave, Midland, TX 79701

TAPPE, Elizabeth or Ibba Peden (Fla) 2935 Tidewater St, Fernandina Beach, FL 32034

TARBET JR, Bob (Tex) 121 Goliad St., Mc Gregor, TX 76657

TARBOX, Janet Ellen (USC) 318 Palmer Dr, Lexington, SC 29072

TARDIFF, Richard A (The Episcopal Church in Haw) PO Box 545, Kealakekua, HI 96750

TARPLEE JR, Cornelius (Nwk) 1405 Duncan St., Key West, FL 33040

TARPLEY, Kent W (SwVa) 375 East Pine St, Wytheville, VA 24382

✠ **TARRANT**, John Thomas (Bp of SD 2009-) 500 South Main Ave, Sioux Falls, SD 57104

TARRANT, Paul John (RI) 39 Jeffrey Street, Edinburgh, EH1 1DH, Great Britain (UK)

TARSIS, George Michael (O) 399 Jefferson Ave, Barberton, OH 44203

TARTT JR, Jo C (WA) 2727 34th Pl Nw, Washington, DC 20007

TARVER, Brian Michael (Tex) 14301 Stuebner Airline Rd, Houston, TX 77069

TARWATER, Thomas William (ECR) 610 Le Point St, Arroyo Grande, CA 93420

TASY, Beverly Ann Moore (O) 38580 Glenwood Rd, Westland, MI 48186

TATE, Donald Steven (At) 201 Ellen Ct, Warner Robins, GA 31088

TATE, Mary Katherine (Del) 18 Olive Ave, Rehoboth Beach, DE 19971

TATE, Robert Lee (Pa) 7209 Lincoln Dr., Philadelphia, PA 19119

TATE, Ruth Newman (At) 201 Ellen Ct, Warner Robins, GA 31088

TATEM, Catherine Leigh (Roch) St Peter's Episcopal Church, 3825 E Henrietta Rd, Henrietta, NY 14467

TATEM, Sandra Lou (Alb) 39 Greyledge Dr, Loudonville, NY 12211

TATEM, William Arthur (Alb) 39 Graystone Rd, Loudonville, NY 12211

TATLIAN, Edward Anthony (CFla)

TATLOCK, Alan Ralph (Alb) 2938 Birchton Rd, Ballston Spa, NY 12020

TATRO, Marie Annette (LI) St Gabriel's Episcopal Church, 331 Hawthorne St, Brooklyn, NY 11225

TATTERSALL, Rev Elizabeth Russell (Nev) Po Box 3388, Stateline, NV 89449

TAUBE, Kimberly Lynn (WMo) 524 4th St, Boonville, MO 65233

TAVERNETTI, Suzanne (ECR) 7021 Timber Trail Loop, El Dorado Hills, CA 95762

TAYEBWA, Onesmus OT (Los) 5700 Rudnick Ave, Woodland Hills, CA 91367

TAYLOR, A(lice) Susan (NJ) 85 Coachlight Sq, Montrose, NY 10548

TAYLOR, Andrea Maija (Mass) 146 Wachusett Ave, Arlington, MA 02476

TAYLOR, Arnold Godfrey (WA) 507 3rd St SE, Washington, DC 20003

TAYLOR, Barbara Brown (At) PO Box 1030, Clarkesville, GA 30523

TAYLOR, Brenda Marie (CPa) 4284 Beaufort Hunt Dr, Harrisburg, PA 17110

TAYLOR, Brian Clark (RG) 1401 Los Arboles Avenue Northwest, Albuquerque, NM 87107

TAYLOR, Bruce Willard (VI) The Valley, Box 65, Virgin Gorda, VI

TAYLOR, Carlene Holder (Ga)

TAYLOR, Charles Dean (At) 1600 Southmont Dr, Dalton, GA 30720

TAYLOR, Charles Gary (CNY) 40 South Main, PO Box 370, New Berlin, NY 13411

TAYLOR, Charles Henry (WNC) 84 Keasler Rd, Asheville, NC 28805

TAYLOR, Charles Wellington (Cal)

TAYLOR, Cynthia nan (Ga) 973 Hunting Horn Way W, Evans, GA 30809

TAYLOR, David Edwin (SwVa) PO Box 527, Rocky Mount, VA 24151

TAYLOR, David G (USC) 301 Piney Mountain Rd., Greenville, SC 29609

TAYLOR, David Kenneth (Nwk) 124 Franklin Ct, Flemington, NJ 08822

TAYLOR, Edgar Garland (La) 1716 Soniat St, New Orleans, LA 70115

TAYLOR, Edward Norman (Mich) 80 Wellesley Street East #904, Toronto, M4Y 2B5, Canada

TAYLOR, George Williamson (NY) 311 Huguenot St, New Rochelle, NY 10801

TAYLOR, Gloria Atkinson (NI) 1809 Holly Ln, Munster, IN 46321

TAYLOR, G(ordon) Kevin (Los) 6503 Stone Crest Way, Whittier, CA 90601

✠ **TAYLOR**, Granville Porter (Bp of WNC 2004-) 44 Ravenwood Dr, Fletcher, NC 28732

TAYLOR, Gregory Blackwell (Va) 250 Pantops Mountain Rd. Apt. 5407, Charlottesville, VA 22911

TAYLOR, James Delane (CFla) 10 Fox Cliff Way, Ormond Beach, FL 32174

TAYLOR JR, James Edward (SC) 1150 East Montague Ave., North Charleston, SC 29405

TAYLOR, James Maurice (Pa) 160 Marvin Rd, Elkins Park, PA 19027

TAYLOR, John Harvey (Los) 19968 Paseo Luis, Yorba Linda, CA 92886

TAYLOR, LeBaron Thomas (SwVa) P.O. Box 709, Covington, VA 24426

TAYLOR, Linda Sue (ECR) 1809 Palo Santo Dr, Campbell, CA 95008

TAYLOR, Lloyd Hopeton (LI) 13304 109th Ave, South Ozone Park, NY 11420

TAYLOR, Margaret Anne (Ala) Po Box 361352, Birmingham, AL 35236

TAYLOR, Marjorie B (Mich) Church Saint John's, 26998 Woodward Ave, Royal Oak, MI 48067

TAYLOR, Mary Ann (Me) 83 Indian Hill Ln, Frankfort, ME 04438

TAYLOR, M(ary) Josephine A (SVa) 3100 Shore Dr Apt 625, Virginia Beach, VA 23451

TAYLOR, Norman Dennis (Oly) 4218 Montgomery Place, Mount Vernon, WA 98274

TAYLOR, Patricia Lois (Oly) 75 E Lynn St Apt 104, Seattle, WA 98102

TAYLOR, Paul N. (WMass) 34 Boylston Cir., Shrewsbury, MA 01545

TAYLOR JR, Philip Justice (WTex) 2086 Grand Loop, Boerne, TX 78006

TAYLOR, Phyllis Gertrude (Pa) 401 Central Ave, Cheltenham, PA 19012

TAYLOR, Ralph Douglas (Az) St Philips in the Hills, PO Box 65840, Tucson, AZ 85728

TAYLOR JR, Raymond George (NC) 461 Pemaquid Harbor Rd, Pemaquid, ME 04558

TAYLOR, Richard Louis (WLa) 108 Jason Ln, Natchitoches, LA 71457

TAYLOR, Robert C (USC) 511 Roper Mtn Rd, Greenville, SC 29615

TAYLOR, Robert E (Ct) 4 Harbor View Drive, Essex, CT 06426

TAYLOR, Robert Jemonde (NC) 813 Darby Street, Raleigh, NC 27610

TAYLOR, Robert Stuart (SeFla) 3325 E. Community Dr., Jupiter, FL 33458

TAYLOR, Robert Vincent (Oly) 32508 W Kelly Road, Benton City, WA 99320

TAYLOR, Roberta Renee (The Episcopal Church in Haw) PO Box 293, Kiiauea, HI 96754

TAYLOR, Ronald Brent (WNC) 7545 Sarah Dr., Denver, NC 28037

TAYLOR, Scott Clay (Los) 504 N Camden Dr, Beverly Hills, CA 90210

TAYLOR, Stanley Richard (HB) 157 Patrick Crescent, Essex, N8M 1X2, Canada

TAYLOR, Stefanie Elizabeth (At) 3110 Ashford Dunwoody Rd NE, Atlanta, GA 30319

TAYLOR, Susan Berry (Vt) St John's Episcopal Church, 4 Prospect Ave, Randolph, VT 05060

TAYLOR, Sylvester O'Neale (LI) 485 Linwood St, Brooklyn, NY 11208

TAYLOR, Terrence Alexander (SeFla) 20822 San Simeon Way Apt. 109, Miami, FL 33179

TAYLOR, Terry Ray (O) 1108 Secretariat Dr W, Danville, KY 40422

TAYLOR, Thomas Herbert (The Episcopal NCal) 14234 N Newcastle Dr, Sun City, AZ 85351

TAYLOR JR, Timus Gayle (Tenn) 4715 Harding Pike, Nashville, TN 37205

TAYLOR, Walter Hamilton (Tex) Po Box 2126, Lenox, MA 01240

TAYLOR JR, Willard Seymour (EC) 245 Mcdonald Church Rd, Rockingham, NC 28379

TAYLOR JR, William Brown (SVa) 4025 Reese Dr S, Portsmouth, VA 23703

TAYLOR III, William John (FtW) 2814 Waterford Dr, Irving, TX 75063

TAYLOR, Williamson Sylvanus (NY) 29 Drake St, Mount Vernon, NY 10550

TAYLOR LYMAN, Susan May (SD) 325 N Plum St, Vermillion, SD 57069

TAYLOR-WEISS, Douglas (CNY) 5617 Bluefield Rd, Auburn, NY 13021

TCHAMALA, Theodore K (Md) 6515 Loch Raven Blvd., Baltimore, MD 21239

TEAGUE, C(harles) Steven (Mil) ST PAUL'S EPISCOPAL CHURCH, 914 E KNAPP ST, MILWAUKEE, WI 53202

TEASLEY, Robin (SVa)

TEDERSTROM, John Patton (Ky) 1007 Hess Ln, Louisville, KY 40217

TEDESCO, Robert Lincoln (Va) 407 Russell Ave Apt 605, Gaithersburg, MD 20877

TEDESCO, William Nicholas (Ct) 20 Erickson Way, South Yarmouth, MA 02664

TEED, Lee Barbara (SanD) 4860 Circle Dr, San Diego, CA 92116

TEETZ, Margaret Lou-Sarah (Alb) Christ Church, 970 State St, Schenectady, NY 12307

TEMBECKJIAN, Renee (CNY) 4782 Hyde Rd, Manlius, NY 13104

TEMME, Louis H (Pa)

TEMPLE, Charles S (NY) 1 E 29th St, New York, NY 10016

TEMPLE, Gordon Clarence (ETenn) 6808 Levi Rd, Hixson, TN 37343

TEMPLE JR, Gray (At) 10685 Bell Rd, Duluth, GA 30097

TEMPLE, Palmer Collier (At) 1883 Wycliff Rd Nw, Atlanta, GA 30309

TEMPLEMAN, Mark Alan (Mass) 60 Monument Avenue, Swampscott, MA 01907

TEMPLETON, Gary Lynn (Okla) 903 N Primrose St, Duncan, OK 73533

TEMPLETON, John (At) 274 Hershey Lane, Clayton, GA 30525

TEMPLETON, Patricia Dale (At) 4393 Garmon Road NW, Atlanta, GA 30327

TENCH, Jack M. (Oly) 1919 NE Ridgewood Ct, Poulsbo, WA 98370

TENDICK, James Ross (U) 1780 Plateau Cir, Moab, UT 84532

✠ **TENNIS**, Cabell (Ret Bp of Del 1998-) 725 9th Ave, Apt. 904, Seattle, WA 98104

TENNISON, George Nelson (La) 401 Magnolia Ln, Mandeville, LA 70471

TENNY, Claire Mary (Chi) Po Box 426, Vails Gate, NY 12584

TEPAVCHEVICH, Kathie Elaine (Chi) 6588 Shabbona Rd, Indian Head Park, IL 60525

TEPE, Donald James (EMich) 3226 Meadowview Ln, Saginaw, MI 48601

TERHUNE, Jason Scott (Tenn) 2777 Mission Rd, Nashotah, WI 53058

TERHUNE JR, Robert Dawbarn (Tex) 2605A Spring Ln, Austin, TX 78703

TERRILL, Robert Allen (Kan) 3524 Sw Willow Brook Ln, Topeka, KS 66614

TERRY, Andrew Bennett (Va) 2209 E Grace St, Richmond, VA 23223

TERRY, Eleanor Applewhite (Mass) 193 Salem St, Boston, MA 02113

TERRY, Mildred Carlson (SwFla) 4071 Center Pointe Pl, Sarasota, FL 34233

TERRY, Susan Preston (Kan) 3209 W 25th St, Lawrence, KS 66047

TERRY, William Hutchinson (La) 626 Congress St., New Orleans, LA 70117

TESCHNER, David Hall (SVa) 31 Belmead St, Petersburg, VA 23805

TESI, Elizabeth A B (WA) 6701 Wisconsin Ave, Chevy Chase, MD 20815

TESKA, William Jay (Minn) 940 Franklin Terrace, Apt. 409, Minneapolis, MN 55406

TESS, Michael Patrick (Mil) 124 Dewey St, Sun Prairie, WI 53590

TESSMAN, Michael J. R. (Ct)

TESTA, Dennis Arthur (Md) 302 Homewood Rd, Linthicum, MD 21090

TESTER, Elizabeth Bonham (Mil)

TESTER, Helen Whitener (Miss) 4400 King Road, Meridian, MS 39305

TESTIN, Joan M (RI) Emmanuel Episcopal Church, 120 Nate Whipple Hwy, Cumberland, RI 02864

TETER, Jane Esther (Be) 1728 Butztown Rd Apt A4, Bethlehem, PA 18017

TETRAULT, David Joseph (SVa) 22501 Cypress Point Road, Williamsburg, VA 23185

TETZ, William Edward (Mich)

TETZLAFF, Chana Winger (Lex) Emmanuel Episcopal Church, 2410 Lexington Rd, Winchester, KY 40391

THABET, David George (WVa) 1305 15th St, Huntington, WV 25701

THACKER II, James Robert (SwVa) 207 Lookout Point Dr., Osprey, FL 34229

THADEN, Timothy Robert (Colo) 780 Devinney Ct, Golden, CO 80401

THAMES, David Blake (Tex) 4419 Taney Ave No 202, Alexandria, VA 22304

THAO, Choua May (Minn) 2200 Minnehaha Ave E, Saint Paul, MN 55119

THARAKAN, Angeline H (Ark) 501 S Phoenix Ave, Russellville, AR 72801

THARAKAN, Jos (Ark) 158 Dawn Cir., Russellville, AR 72802

THATCHER, Anne C (Pa) 614 N Bush St, Santa Ana, CA 92701

THAYER, Andrew R (Ala) 446 Irvington Dr, San Antonio, TX 78209

THAYER JR, Charles Cleveland (FdL) 1409 W Dow Rummel St, Apt 114, Sioux Falls, SD 57104

THAYER, Evan Lynch (Mass) 15 Elko St # 2135, Brighton, MA 02135

THAYER II, Frederick William (SanD) 12103 Caminito Corriente, San Diego, CA 92128

THAYER, Judith Ann (Ia) 912 20th Ave, Coralville, IA 52241

THAYER, Steven Allen (NJ) Po Box 440, Jamison, PA 18929

THEODORE, Margaret Bessie (Alb) P.O. BOX 446, Potsdam, NY 13676

THEODORE, Pamela Hillis (Dal) 6055 Walnut Hill Cir, Dallas, TX 75230

THEUS SR, James Graves (WLa) 6291 Old Baton Rouge Hwy, Alexandria, LA 71302

THEW, Richard H (EO) Po Box 125, Cove, OR 97824

THEW FORRESTER, Kevin G (NMich) 402 Harrison St, Marquette, MI 49855

THEW FORRESTER, Rise Fay (NMich) 402 Harrison St, Marquette, MI 49855

THIBODAUX, Louise Ruprecht (Ala)

THIBODEAUX, James L (Oly) 1610 S King St, Seattle, WA 98144

THIEL, Spencer Edwin (Chi) 12407 S 82nd Ave, Palos Park, IL 60464

THIELE, William Charles (Nwk) 215 Lafayette Ave., Passaic, NJ 07055

THIERING, Barry Bernard (WTex) 2404 W Riviera Dr, Cedar Park, TX 78613

THIGPEN III, William Mccord (At) 5152 Patriot Dr, Stone Mountain, GA 30087

THIM, Paul Russell (At) 697 Densley Dr., Decatur, GA 30033

THOBER, Ellie Thober (Neb) 4718 18th St, Columbus, NE 68601

THOENI, Thomas Andrew (SwFla) 302 Carey St, Plant City, FL 33563

THOM, Ashley Jane Squier (Chi) 3626 N. Francisco Ave., Chicago, IL 60618

✠ **THOM**, Brian James (Bp of Ida 2008-) 1858 W. Judith Lane, Boise, ID 83705

THOM, David Lewis (Az) 540 Atchison Lane, Wickenburg, AZ 85390

THOM, Kenneth Stow (Eas) 3849 Sirman Dr, Snow Hill, MD 21863

THOMAS, Adam P (Ct) 15 Pearl St, Mystic, CT 06355

THOMAS, Allisyn (SanD) St. Paul's Cathedral, 2728 Sixth Avenue, San Diego, CA 92103

THOMAS JR, A(rthur) Robert (Ak) Po Box 1872, Seward, AK 99664

THOMAS, Benjamin Randall (WK) 402 S 8th St, Salina, KS 67401

THOMAS, Bethany Ann (Colo) 1221 Illinois St. Apt 2A, Golden, CO 80401

THOMAS, Cheeramattathu John (Tex) 301 Eagle Lakes Dr, Friendswood, TX 77546

THOMAS, David R (Nwk) 7740 LIGUTHOUSE COVE DR., PORT HOPE, MI 48468

THOMAS, Douglas Earl (WTex) 2722 Old Ranch Rd, San Antonio, TX 78217

THOMAS, Douglas Paul (NwT)

THOMAS, Elaine Ellis (Va) St. Paul's Memorial Church, 1700 University Avenue, Charlottesville, VA 22903

THOMAS JR, Frederick S (Md) 707 Park Ave, Baltimore, MD 21201

THOMAS, Jaime Alfredo (Dal) P.O. Box 15, Fort Ord, CA 93941

THOMAS JR, James Morris (ECR) 18402 Yale Court, Somoma, CA 95476

THOMAS, John Alfred (Va) 3800 Powell Ln Apt 813, Falls Church, VA 22041

THOMAS, John Harvey (Mass) Po Box 536, Sandwich, MA 02563

THOMAS, John Paul (Dal) 635 N. Story Rd, Irving, TX 75061

THOMAS, John Taliaferro (Tenn) 290 Quintard Rd, Sewanee, TN 37375

THOMAS, Jonathan R (Chi) 1864 Post Rd, Darien, CT 06820

THOMAS, Joshua M (Oly) 505 Alexander Ave, Durham, NC 27705

THOMAS, Kathryn L (NI) 10010 Aurora Pl, Fort Wayne, IN 46804

THOMAS, Kathryn Pauline (Va) 214 Church St, Madison, VA 22727

THOMAS, Keila Carpenter (Lex) 145 E 5th St, Morehead, KY 40351

THOMAS, Kenneth Dana (Ct) 5 Bassett St Apt B10, West Haven, CT 06516

THOMAS, Laughton Dennis (Fla) 516 Howard AVE, Tallahassee, FL 32310

THOMAS, Leonard Everett (EC) 916 Lord Granville Dr., Morehead City, NC 28557

THOMAS, Margaret Lucie (ECR)

THOMAS, Margaret Warren (Minn) 9426 Congdon Blvd, Duluth, MN 55804

THOMAS, Margaret (Peg) (Me) 297 Wardwell Point Rd, Penobscot, ME 04476

THOMAS, Megan Evans (NJ) 16 All Saints Rd, Princeton, NJ 08540

THOMAS, Michael Jon (WNY) 703 W Ferry St Apt C9, Buffalo, NY 14222

THOMAS, Micki-Ann (Alb) PO Box 29, Greenwich, NY 12834

THOMAS, Patricia Menne (EC) 136 Saint Andrews Cir, New Bern, NC 28562

THOMAS, Peter (Tex) 832 Fearrington Post, Pittsboro, NC 27312

THOMAS JR, Phillip Langston (La) 1318 Washington Ave, New Orleans, LA 70130

THOMAS, Rachel Woodall (Ct) 155 Essex St, Deep River, CT 06417

THOMAS, Robert Leroy (WVa) 401 11th Ave, Huntington, WV 25701

THOMAS, Robert William (NC) 413 Dogwood Creek Pl, Fuquay Varina, NC 27526

THOMAS, Samuel Sutter (SeFla) 135 W Crescent Dr, Clewiston, FL 33440

THOMAS, Sherry Hardwick (Va) 386 N Anna Dr, Louisa, VA 23093

THOMAS, Teresa Ann Collingwood (Ak) PO Box 76, Fort Yukon, AK 99740

THOMAS, Timothy Bosworth (SeFla) 3434 N Oceanshore Blvd, Flagler Beach, FL 32136

THOMAS, Trevor E. G. (Nwk) 90 Rossini Road, Westerly, RI 02891

THOMAS, Valerie Bricker (Fla) 244 Ashley Lake Dr, Melrose, FL 32666

THOMAS, Victor J (Tex) 3129 Southmore Blvd, Houston, TX 77004

THOMAS, Wayland Eugene (Md) 55 Brooklyn Hts Rd, Thomaston, ME 04861

THOMAS, William Carl (NJ) Christ Church, 90 Kings Hwy, Middletown, NJ 07748

THOMAS, William Steven (SeFla) 14445 Horseshoe Trce, Wellington, FL 33414

THOMAS, William Tuley (Mo) 7846 Gannon Ave, Saint Louis, MO 63130

THOMASON, Clayton Leslie (Chi) 42 Ashland Ave, River Forest, IL 60305

THOMASON, Steven (Oly) 1245 10th Avenue East, Seattle, WA 98102

THOMPSON, Barkley Stuart (Tex) 1117 Texas St, Houston, TX 77002

THOMPSON, Carla Eva (Va) 322 N Alfred St, Alexandria, VA 22314

THOMPSON, Catherine M (Dal) Episcopal Church of the Annunciation, 602 N. Old Orchard Lane, Lewisville, TX 75077

THOMPSON, C(Harles) Christopher (WVa) Greenbrier Episcopal Ministry, PO Box 148, White Sulphur Springs, WV 34901

THOMPSON, Claud Adelbert (Mil) 5030 Vista View Crescent, Nanaimo, BC V9V 1L6, Canada

THOMPSON, Danielle L (Ala) 1910 12th Ave S, Birmingham, AL 35205

THOMPSON, David Frank Ora (USC) 723 Arrow Wood Dr, North Augusta, SC 29841

THOMPSON, David James (Okla)

THOMPSON, David Joel (Colo) 360 Scrub Oak Cir, Monument, CO 80132

THOMPSON, Donald Frederick (Ct) 11 Lenox Ave, Norwalk, CT 06854

THOMPSON, E(dgar) A(ndrew) (Colo) 971 E Lone Pine Road, Pahrump, NV 89048

THOMPSON, Edward (Cal) 1714 Santa Clara Ave, Alameda, CA 94501

THOMPSON, Edward Hnebe (La) 5500 St. Claude Avenue, New Orleans, LA 70119

THOMPSON, Elena (Ga) PO Box 1167, Baxley, GA 31515

THOMPSON JR, Fred Edward (SC) 2138 Allandale Plantation Rd, Wadmalaw Island, SC 29487

THOMPSON, Fred Leonard (NC) 538 Furth Ln, Southern Pines, NC 28387

THOMPSON, Helen Plemmons (At) 91 Wylde Wood Dr, McDonough, GA 30253

THOMPSON III, H (enry) (SC) 2310 Meadow Vue Dr, Moon Township, PA 15108

THOMPSON SR, Howard (Alb) 140 Foster Rd, North Lawrence, VA 12967

THOMPSON, J Eric (Roch) 21 Main Street, Geneseo, NY 14454

THOMPSON, James Calvin (SVa) 2003 Camelia Cir, Midlothian, VA 23112

THOMPSON, James Edwin (Episcopal SJ) 3930 SE 162nd Ave Spc 22, Portland, OR 97236

THOMPSON, Jerry A. (Neb) St. Mark's on the Campus Episcopal Church, Lincoln, NE 68508

THOMPSON, John Francis (CFla) 90 E Jinnita St, Hernando, FL 34442

THOMPSON, John Kell (Oly) 21630 102nd Ln SW, Vashon, WA 98070

THOMPSON, John Paul (Alb) PO Box 180, Copake Falls, NY 12517

THOMPSON, Karen Elizabeth (EMich) 18890 Fireside Hwy, Presque Isle, MI 49777

THOMPSON, Kenneth David (Ky) 1768 Plum Ridge Rd, Taylorsville, KY 40071

THOMPSON, Marisa Tabizon (Neb) 9320 Blondo St, Omaha, NE 68134

THOMPSON, Mark A (Minn) 700 Douglas Ave Apt 907, Minneapolis, MN 55403

THOMPSON, M Dion (Md) 1208 John St, Baltimore, MD 21217

THOMPSON, Michael B (EC) Dashwood House, Sidgwick Avenue, Cambridge, CB3 9DA, Great Britain (UK)

THOMPSON, Michael King (NC) 103 Sheffield Rd, Williamsburg, VA 23188

THOMPSON III, Morris King (Miss) 318 College St, Columbus, MS 39701

✠ **THOMPSON JR**, Morris King (Bp of La 2010-) 1623 7th Street, New Orleans, LA 70115

THOMPSON, Owen Chuhwuma (NY) Grace Church, 130 1st Ave, Nyack, NY 10960

THOMPSON, Paul Mason (Vt) 4323 Main Street, Rt 6A, Cummaquid, MA 02637

THOMPSON, Peggy Reid (ECR) 451 Vivienne Dr, Watsonville, CA 95076

THOMPSON, Peter D (Ct) 60 East Ave, Norwalk, CT 06851

THOMPSON, Robert Gaston (Colo) 9987 W Oregon Pl, Lakewood, CO 80232

THOMPSON, Robert Wildan (Ky) 1206 Maple Ln, Anchorage, KY 40223

THOMPSON, Roderick James Marcellus (Cal) 601 Van Ness Ave Apt 123, San Francisco, CA 94102

THOMPSON, Scott A (Tex) Holy Cross Episc Church, 5653 W. River Park Dr., Sugar Land, TX 77479

THOMPSON SR, Stephen Lafoia (ETenn) 134 Iris Pl, Newport, TN 37821

THOMPSON, Sue (Cal) St Edmund's Episcopal Church, PO Box 688, Pacifica, CA 94044

THOMPSON, W(alter) Douglas (The Episcopal NCal) 1431 S St, Eureka, CA 95501

THOMPSON, Wanda Jean (Me) 1375 Forest Ave. Apt. H14, Portland, ME 04103

THOMPSON, Warren Norvell (CFla) Po Box 1606, Winter Haven, FL 33882

THOMPSON JR, William Early (USC) 16 Bernwood Dr, Taylors, SC 29687

THOMPSON, Zachary R (At) 805 Mt Vernon Hwy NW, Atlanta, GA 30327

THOMPSON DE MEJIA, Kara Ann (Hond) Spring Garden, Islas De La Bahia, Roatan, Honduras

THOMPSON-QUARTEY, C John (NJ) 622 Forman Avenue, Point Pleasant Beach, NJ 08742

THOMPSON-UBERUAGA, William (Ida) 518 N 8th St, Boise, ID 83702

THOMSEN, William Robert (WNC) 9405 Shouse Dr, Vienna, VA 22182

THOMSON, Jacqueline Clark (Va) 9405 Shouse Dr, Vienna, VA 22182

THOMSON, James (Okla) 501 S Cincinnati Ave, Tulsa, OK 74103

THOMSON, Malcolm Davis (WMich)

THOMSON, Richard Dwight (Los) 714 Osprey Ct, Mount Pleasant, SC 29464

THOMSON, Ronald Reed (RG) 733 Lakeway Dr, El Paso, TX 79932

THON, Susan Cecelia (WA) 34 Wellesley Circle, Glen Echo, MD 20812

THOR, Margaret Carlson (Minn) 60 Kent St, Saint Paul, MN 55102

THORME, Trisha Ann (NJ) 1040 Yardville Allentown Rd, Trenton, NJ 08620

THORNBERG, Anne (EC) 3321 Rustburg Dr, Fayetteville, NC 28303

THORNBERG, Jeffrey D (EC) 1601 Raeford Rd, Fayetteville, NC 28305

THORNE, Joyce Terrill (RI) 670 Weeden Street, Pawtucket, RI 02860

THORNELL, Kwasi A (Cal) 1525 Casino Cir, Silver Spring, MD 20906

THORNTON, Corey Todd (The Episcopal Church in Haw) PSC 473 Box 10, FPO, AP 96349-0001, Japan

THORNTON, Daniel Ingram (Ala) 1402 Prier Dr, Marion, AL 36756

✠ THORNTON, John Stuart (Ret Bp of Ida 1998-) 323 W Jefferson St Apt 204, Boise, ID 83702

THORNTON, Norman Edward (Del) Box 2805, Northfield, MA 01360

THORNTON, Theresa Joan (SO) 10345 Montgomery Rd, Cincinnati, OH 45242

THORP, Steven Tanner (Spr) 1717 Park Haven Dr, Champaign, IL 61820

THORPE, John A (Dal) 2117 North 4th Ave East, Newton, IA 50208

THORPE, Mary Brennan (Va) 110 W Franklin Street, Richmond, VA 23220

THORSTAD, Anita Fortino (SeFla) 951 De Soto Rd Apt 330, Boca Raton, FL 33432

THRALL, Barbara Judith (WMass) 475 Appleton St, Holyoke, MA 01040

THREADGILL, Nancy L (Pgh) 335 Locust St, Johnstown, PA 15901

THROOP, John R (CNY) PO Box 29, Adams, NY 13605

THRUMSTON, Richard Emmons (SanD) 3642 Armstrong St, San Diego, CA 92111

THULLBERY, Marion F (NC) Durham Va Medical Center, 508 Fulton St, Durham, NC 27705

THURSTON, Anthony Charles (Ore) 39 Greenridge Ct, Lake Oswego, OR 97035

THWEATT III, Richmond Fitzgerald (WLa) 7109 Woodridge Ave, Oklahoma City, OK 73132

THWING, Robert C (Ak) Po Box 91943, Anchorage, AK 99509

TIAPULA, Imo Siufanua (The Episcopal Church in Haw) Po Box 2030, Pago Pago, AS 96799

TIBBETTS, Catherine Johnson (Va) The Falls Chruch Episcopal, 225 E. Broad Street, Falls Church, VA 22046

TIBBETTS, Ronald Creighton (Mass) 9 Cooney Ave, Plainville, MA 02762

TICHENOR, Elizabeth A (Cal) All Souls Episcopal Parish, 2220 Cedar St, Berkeley, CA 94709

TICKNOR, Patricia Horan (WMo) 12270 N New Dawn Ave, Oro Valley, AZ 85755

TICKNOR, William Howard Correa (Md) 5757 Solomons Island Rd, Lothian, MD 20711

TIDWELL, Janet Ruth (At) 582 Walnut St, Macon, GA 31201

TIDY, John Hylton (SeFla) 4025 Pine Tree Dr, Miami Beach, FL 33140

TIEDERMAN, Nancy Jo Copass (Oly) 920 Cherry Ave NE, Bainbridge IS, WA 98110

TIEGS, Karen Sara Bretl (Ore) All Saints' Episcopal Church, 3847 Terracina Dr., Riverside, CA 92506

TIELKING, Claudia Gould (WA) 6533 Mulroy Street, Mc Lean, VA 22101

TIERNEY, Bridget Katherine (La) 114 N Pine St, New Lenox, IL 60451

TIERNEY, Dennis Stanley (Oly) 6973 Island Center Rd NE, Bainbridge Island, WA 98110

TIERNEY III, Peter George (RI) PO Box 491, Little Compton, RI 02837

TIERNEY, Philip Joseph (RI) 1412 Providence Rd, Charlotte, NC 28207

TIERNEY, Veronica Mary (RI) St. George's School, PO Box 1910, Newport, RI 02840

TIFF II, Richard Olin (Los)

TIFFANY, Roger Lyman (Mich) 941 Damon Dr, Medina, OH 44256

TIFFANY, Susan Jean (NI) 53720 Ironwood Rd, South Bend, IN 46635

TIGHE, Maureen (Ore) 1001 B-Ne 90th Ave, Portland, OR 97220

TILDEN, George Bruce (The Episcopal NCal)

TILDEN, Roger (Md) 8089 Harmony Rd, Denton, MD 21629

TILING, Robert Henry (Chi) 1691 Campos Dr., The Villages, FL 32162

TILLER, Monte Jackson (SeFla) 6409 Lantana Pines Dr, Lantana, FL 33462

TILLEY, David James (La) 12636 E Robin Hood Dr, Baton Rouge, LA 70815

TILLITT, Jay Lanning (LI) 1021 N University St, Redlands, CA 92374

TILLMAN, Ann Marie (WNY) 24 Maple Rd, East Aurora, NY 14052

TILLMAN, Christine Wylie (WMich) 3828 Cook Ct. S.W., Wyoming, MI 49519

TILLMAN, Jane Guion (WMass)

TILLOTSON, Ellen Louise (Ct) 38 Fair St, Guilford, CT 06437

TILSON, Alan Russell (Kan) 711 W 47th St, Kansas City, MO 64112

TILSON JR, Hugh Arvil (NC) 3819 Jones Ferry Rd, Chapel Hill, NC 27516

TIMMERMAN, Melissa Roen (SC) 484 Lymington Rd, Severna Park, MD 21146

TINDALL, Byron Cheney (SC) 102 Fir Court Unit 1260, Waleska, GA 30183

TINKLEPAUGH, John R (Pa) 400 Walnut Lane, North East, MD 21901

TINNON, Becky (The Episcopal Church in Haw) 98-939 Moanalua Rd, Aiea, HI 96701

TINNON, Michael Scott (The Episcopal Church in Haw) 98-939 Moanalua Rd, Aiea, HI 96701

TINSLEY JR, Fred Haley (WLa) 3535 Santa Fe St Unit 41, Corpus Christi, TX 78411

TIPPETT, Michael R (Minn) 2202 Lexington Parkway South, Saint Paul, MN 55105

TIPTON, Gregory Blake (At) 980 S Lumpkin St, Athens, GA 30605

TIPTON, Harry Steadman (CGC) 129 Camellot Ct, Crestview, FL 32539

TIPTON, Tommy Hicks (USC) 1029 Old Plantation Dr, Pawleys Island, SC 29585

TIPTON-ZILE, Cynthia (Md) 4500 C Dunton Ter, Perry Hall, MD 21128

TIRADO, Hernan (Colom)

TIRADO, Vincent (SeFla) 18601 Sw 210th St, Miami, FL 33187

TIRRELL, Charles David (Tex) 9701 Meyer Forest Dr Apt 12112, Houston, TX 77096

TIRRELL, John Alden (Cal)

TISDALE JR, William Alfred (Ct) 27 Church St, Stonington, CT 06378

TISDELLE, Celeste Richardson (Fla) St. Mary's Episcopal Church, 400 St. Johns Ave, Green Cove Springs, FL 32043

TITCOMB, Cecily J. (SeFla) 141 S. County rd, Palm Beach, FL 33480

TITTLE, Darlene Anne Duryea (Nwk) 11 Overhill Dr, Budd Lake, NJ 07828

TITUS, Bessie Charlotte (Ak)

TITUS, Fred David (Ia) St. Thomas' Episcopal Church, 710 N. Main St., Garden City, KS 67846
TITUS, John Clark (At) 5428 Park Cir, Stone Mountain, GA 30083
TITUS, Luke (Ak) Saint Barnabas Mission, Minto, AK 99758
TITUS, Nancy Espenshade (NC) 1739 Berwickshire Cir, Raleigh, NC 27615
TJELTVEIT, Maria Washington Eddy (Be) 124 S Madison St, Allentown, PA 18102
TJOFLAT, Marie Elizabeth (Fla) 1255 Peachtree St, Jacksonville, FL 32207
TLUCEK, Laddie Raymond (Okla) 1509 Nw 198th St, Edmond, OK 73003
TOALSTER, Rebecca Denise (CFla) 311 11th St, Ambridge, PA 15003
TOBERMAN, Harold Frederick (Ark) 329 Colony Green Dr, Bloomingdale, IL 60108
TOBIAS, Gwendolyn (SeFla) 3300A S. Seacrest Blvd., Boynton Beach, FL 33435
TOBIN, Florence Kit (Roch) PO Box 304, Corning, NY 14830
TOBIN JR, Robert W(allace) (Mass) Po Box 113, Sunset, ME 04683
TOBIN, Roger Martin (SeFla) 5690 N Kendall Dr, Miami, FL 33156
TOBOLA, Cynthia Pruet (Tex) PO Box 895, Palacios, TX 77465
TODARO, Alicia Butler (Alb) St Paul's Church, 58 3rd St, Troy, NY 12180
TODD, Charles E (Ga) St Paul Episcopal Church, 1802 Abercorn St, Savannah, GA 31401
TODD, Christopher Howard (SeFla) 30243 Coconut Hwy, Big Pine Key, FL 33043
TODD, Edward Pearson (Eur) 18 Hall Pond Lane, Copake, NY 11516-1400, Afghanistan
TODD, Michael P (SwFla) 1620 Boathouse Cir, GR 208, Sarasota, FL 34231
TODD, Richard Alfred (Minn) 38378 Glacier Dr, North Branch, MN 55056
TODD JR, Samuel Rutherford (Tex) 2423 Mcclendon St, Houston, TX 77030
TOEBBEN, Warren B (Ore) St John the Baptist, 6300 SW Nicol Rd, Portland, OR 97223
TOELLER-NOVAK, Thomas Leo (WMich) 555 Michigan Ave, Holland, MI 49423
TOFANI, Ann Lael (Spr) 427 W 4th St, Mount Carmel, IL 62863
TOFFEY, Judith E (Ct) 41 Cannon Ridge Dr, Watertown, CT 06795
TOIA, Frank Phillip (Pa) 2127 Kriebel Rd, Lansdale, PA 19446
TOLA, Elaine M (NC)
TOLAND, Paula Jean (Mass) PO Box 287, Franklin, MA 02038
TOLAND JR, William Leslie (Spr) Po Box 3161, Springfield, IL 62708
TOLES, John F (Okla) 518 W Randolph Ave, Enid, OK 73701

TOLL, Richard Kellogg (Ore) 1707 Se Courtney Rd, P.O. Box 220112, Milwaukie, OR 97269
TOLLEFSON, Jane (Jill) Carol (Minn) 2700 Canby Ct, Northfield, MN 55057
TOLLETT, Mitchell Joseph (Tex) St. Francis Episcopal Church, 3232, Tyler, TX 75701
TOLLEY, John Charles (Cal) 594 Los Altos Drive, Chula Vista, CA 91914
TOLLISON, Ann Black (Va) PO Box 100, Gum Spring, VA 23065
TOLLISON JR, Henry Ernest (USC) 105 Freeport Dr, Greenville, SC 29615
TOLLIVER, Lisa Anne (Ky) 7504 Westport Rd, Louisville, KY 40222
TOLLIVER, Richard Lamar (Chi) 4729 S. Drexel Blvd, Chicago, IL 60615
TOLZMANN, Lee Ann (Ct) St. Paul's Church, 200 Riverside Ave, Riverside, CT 06878
TOMAINE, Jane A (Nwk) 349 Short Dr, Mountainside, NJ 07092
TOMBAUGH, Richard Franklin (Ct) 58 Terry Rd, Hartford, CT 06105
TOMCZAK, Beth Lynn (WMich) 321 N Main St, Three Rivers, MI 49093
TOMEI, Gail R (Pa) Church Of The Ascension, 406 W 2nd Ave, Parkesburg, PA 19365
TOMLIN, Kyle R (Va) 6769 Ridge Ave # A, Philadelphia, PA 19128
TOMLINSON, Diane B (EC)
TOMLINSON, Elizabeth Waitt (Va) 3439 Payne St, Falls Church, VA 22041
TOMLINSON, Ruth Marie (Neb) 5704 North 159th St, Omaha, NE 68116
TOMLINSON III, Samuel Alexander (Miss) 28 Homochitto St, Natchez, MS 39120
TOMOSO, John Anson Hau'oli (The Episcopal Church in Haw) 2140 Main St, Wailuku, HI 96793
TOMPKIN, William Frederick (O) 307 Portage Trail East, Cuyahoga Falls, OH 44221
TOMPKINS JR, Douglas Gordon (Pa) 310 S Chester Rd, Swarthmore, PA 19081
TOMPKINS, Joyce Laura Ulrich (Pa) 310 S Chester Rd, Swarthmore, PA 19081
TOMTER, Patrick Austin (Oly) PO Box 10785, Portland, OR 97296
TONEY, Martha Ann (CFla) PO Box 2373, Belleview, FL 34421
TONGE, Samuel Davis (Ga) 1023 Woods Road, Waycross, GA 31501
TONGUE, Mary Jane (Md) 203 Star Pointe Ct Unit 3d, Abingdon, MD 21009
TONSMEIRE SR, Louis Edward (At) 224 Trammell St, Calhoun, GA 30701
TONTONOZ, David Costa (Eas) 5211 Dove Point Ln, Salisbury, MD 21801
TOOF, Jan Jarred (CNY) 2006 Manchester Rd, Wheaton, IL 60187

TOOKEY, Carol Ruth (NAM) PO Box 436, Aztec, NM 87410
TOOMEY, David C (NY) PO Box 1467, Norwich, VT 05055
TOONE, Susan Krueger (U) 1579 S State St, Clearfield, UT 84015
TORNQUIST, Frances (Cal) 2748 Wemberly Dr, Belmont, CA 94002
TORO, Arthur N (Los) 135 Loden Pl, Jackson, MS 39209
TORO, Suzanne Frances Rosemary (NY) 70 Clinton St, Cornwall, NY 12518
TORRES, Juan Antonio (PR)
TORRES, Julio Orlando (NY) 232 E 11th St # 3, New York, NY 10003
TORRES, Michele Angier (Mass) 103 Harvard Ave, Medford, MA 02155
TORRES BAYAS, Jose Javier (Cal) Guerrero #589, Tuxtepec, Mexico
TORRES FUENTES, Pascual Pedro (Hond) Apdo 16, Puerto Cortes, Honduras
TORRES MARTINEZ, Wilfrido Oswaldo (EcuC) Convencion Y Solanda 056, Guaranda, Ecuador
TORREY, Bruce N (Ct) 96 Main St, East Windsor, CT 06088
TORREY, Dorothy Ellen (The Episcopal NCal) 901 Lincoln Rd Apt 40, Yuba City, CA 95991
TORVEND, Samuel Edward (Oly) 15 Roy St, Seattle, WA 98109
TOTHILL, Marlene Grey (NwT)
TOTMAN, Glenn Parker (CGC) 122 County Road 268, Enterprise, AL 36330
TOTTEN, Julia Kay (Spok) PO Box 15, Florence, OR 97439
TOTTEN, William Robert (Spok) PO Box 15, Florence, OR 97439
TOTTEY JR, Alfred George (CNY) 7385 Norton Ave, Clinton, NY 13323
TOUCHSTONE, G(rady) Russell (Los) 1069 S Gramercy Pl, Los Angeles, CA 90019
TOURANGEAU, Edward J (Ind) 260 Elm Ct, Troy, VA 22974
TOURNOUX, Gregory Allen (Spr) 2056 Cherry Road, Springfield, IL 62704
TOVEN, Kenneth H (Minn) 1505 13th Street N., Princeton, MN 55371
TOWERS, Arlen Reginald (Cal) 43 Wildwood Pl, El Cerrito, CA 94530
TOWERS, Paul Wayne (CPa) 2309 Richmond Rd., Endwell, NY 13760
TOWERS, Richard A (CNY) St John's Episcopal Church, 210 N Cayuga St, Ithaca, NY 14850-4333, Korea (South)
TOWLER, Lewis Wilson (Mich) 1711 Pontiac Trl, Ann Arbor, MI 48105
TOWNE, Jane Clapp (ND) 1111 N 1st St Apt 10, Bismarck, ND 58501
TOWNER, Paul Eugene (Nev) 1090 War Eagle Dr N, Colorado Springs, CO 80919
TOWNER, Philip Haines (NY) 552 W End Ave, New York, NY 10024

TOWNER, Robert Arthur (Mo) 38 N Fountain St, Cape Girardeau, MO 63701

TOWNES III, Henry C (Chi) 12219 S 86th Ave, Palos Park, IL 60464

TOWNLEY JR, Richard Woodruff (NJ) 43 Delaware Ave, Lambertville, NJ 08530

TOWNSEND, Bowman (Tex) 2205 Matterhorn Ln, Austin, TX 78704

TOWNSEND, Craig D (NY) 445 Degraw St, Brooklyn, NY 11217

TOWNSEND, John Tolson (Mass) 40 Washington St, Newton, MA 02458

⊠ **TOWNSEND**, Martin Gough (Ret Bp of Eas 2001-) HC 86 Box 48 C-1, Springfield, WV 26763

TOWSON, Louis Albert (CFla) 348 Sherwood Ave, Satellite Beach, FL 32937

TOY, Fran Y (Cal) 4151 Laguna Ave, Oakland, CA 94602

TRACHE, Robert G (SeFla)

TRACHMAN, Mike David (Okla) 2213 Galaxy Dr, Altus, OK 73521

TRACY, Dick Blaylock (Kan) 3020 Oxford Cir, Lawrence, KS 66049

TRACY, Edward J. (SVa) 600 Talbot Hall Rd, Norfolk, VA 23505

TRACY, Paul John (NI) 1025 Park Pl Apt 159, Mishawaka, IN 46545

TRACY, Rita Vanessa (Kan) 3020 Oxford Cir, Lawrence, KS 66049

TRAFFORD, Edward John (RI) 45 Rotary Dr, West Warwick, RI 02893

TRAFTON, Clark Wright (Cal) 875 S Nueva Vista Dr, Palm Springs, CA 92264

TRAGER, Jane (O) 222 Eastern Heights Blvd, Elyria, OH 44035

TRAIL, Shirley Ethel (WNY) 42 Haller Ave, Buffalo, NY 14211

TRAINOR, Helen Chase (WA) Legal Aid & Justice Center, 1000 Preston Ave. Ste A, Charlottesville, VA 22903

TRAINOR, Mary Patricia (Los) 10925 Valley Home Ave, Whittier, CA 90603

TRAINOR, Mary Stoddard (FdL) E942 Whispering Pines Rd, Waupaca, WI 54981

TRAINOR, Robert James (FdL) E942 Whispering Pines Rd, Waupaca, WI 54981

TRAKEL, Debra Lynn (Mil) N81 W13442 Golfway Drive, Menomonee Falls, WI 53051

TRAMBLEY, Adam Thomas (NwPa) 343 Forker Blvd, Sharon, PA 16146

TRAMEL, Stephanie (Ia) 2300 Bancroft Way, Berkeley, CA 94704

TRAMMELL, Robert William (Okla) St. Augustine Of Canterbury, 14700 N. May Ave., Oklahoma City, OK 73134

TRAN, Catherine Caroline (Colo) 6556 High Dr., Morrison, CO 80465

TRAPANI, Kathleen M (Cal) 30 Greenridge Pl, Danville, CA 94506

TRAPP, Grace J. (SwVa) PO Box 328, Harpswell, ME 04079

TRAPP, James E. (NY) PO Box 40697, Portland, OR 97240

TRAQUAIR, Megan Mcclure (Az) 10222 South 44th Lane, Laveen, AZ 85339

TRASK III, Robert Palmer (EMich) 13 Circle Ave, Wheaton, IL 60187

TRAVIS, Douglas (Tex) The Diocese Of The Rio Grande, 6400 Coors Blvd NW, Albuquerque, NM 87120

TRAVIS, Kathleen Ann (Ia) 3120 E 24th St, Des Moines, IA 50317

TRAVIS, Michelle Halsall (Mont)

TRAVIS, R. Carroll (CFla) 2103 Indian River Dr, Cocoa, FL 32922

TRAVIS, Robert P. (RI) 326 Kenyon Avenue, Wakefield, RI 02879

TRAVIS, Sherry Margaret (Miss) 1365 Sweetwater Dr, Brentwood, TN 37027

TRAYLOR, Thomas Wallace (Cal) 1801 Jackson St Apt 4, San Francisco, CA 94109

TRAYNHAM, Warner Raymond (Los) 6125 Alviso Ave, Los Angeles, CA 90043

TREADWELL II, Richard Allen (Ore) 1916 NE Gibbs Circle, McMinnville, OR 97128

TREADWELL III, William Charles (Tex) 601 Columbus Ave, Waco, TX 76701

TREES, Thomas Heino (CFla) 1616 Sterns Dr, Leesburg, FL 34748

TREGO, Randall (Tex) 3106 Heritage Creek Oaks, Houston, TX 77008

TREHERNE-THOMAS, Rhoda Margaret (NY) 10 Bay Street Lndg Apt 6L, Staten Island, NY 10301

TREI, Rosemary Randall (Dal) 5923 Royal Ln, Dallas, TX 75230

TREJO-BARAHONA, Oscar (Hond)

TRELEASE, Murray Lincoln (Oly) 343 Eagles Roost Ln, Lopez Island, WA 98261

TREMAINE, Gordon Hyde (Fla) 100 Ne 1st St, Gainesville, FL 32601

TREMBATH, Jack Graham (Mich) 939 Chippewa St, Mount Clemens, MI 48043

TREMMEL, Marcia Ann (SwFla) 11588 57th Street Cir. E., Parrish, FL 34219

TREPPA, Joyce Lynn (Mich) 1150 Tarpon Center Dr. #503, Venice, FL 34285

TREVATHAN, W(Illiam) Andre (Ky) 1 Franklin Town Blvd Apt 1515, Philadelphia, PA 19103

TREVER, Stephen (Mass) 2300 Bancroft Way, Berkeley, CA 94704

TREWHELLA, Charles Keith (Ore) 19691 Nw Meadow Lake Rd, Yamhill, OR 97148

TREZEVANT, Margaret Anne (Cal) 1755 Clay St, San Francisco, CA 94109

TRIGG, Joseph (WA) Po Box 760, La Plata, MD 20646

TRIGLETH, John Paul (Mil) S3919A Highway 12, Baraboo, WI 53913

TRILLOS, Alejandra (LI) St John's Episcopal Church, 12 Prospect St, Huntington, NY 11743

TRIMBLE, James Armstrong (Pa) 326 S Third St, Philadelphia, PA 19106

TRIMBLE, James Edward (USC) 5303 Old Herring Pl, Crestwood, KY 40014

TRIMBLE, Sarah M (Va) 3401 Chantarene Dr, Pensacola, FL 32507

TRIPP, Arthur D (RG) Po Box 398, Raton, NM 87740

TRIPP, Roy (Mass) 12 Brandywine Blvd, Wilmington, DE 19809

TRIPP, Thomas Norman (WNY) 354 Burroughs Dr, Amherst, NY 14226-909

TRIPSES, Kathleen R (Ia) 2844 NW Northcreek Circle, Ankeny, IA 50023

TRISKA, Patricia Ilene (Ia) 1009 Parkway Dr Apt 7, Boone, IA 50036

TRISTRAM, Geoffrey (Mass) 980 Memorial Dr, Cambridge, MA 02138

TRIVELY, Timothy Churchill (SwFla) 4 Gatehouse Ct, Asheville, NC 28803

TROEGER, Thomas Henry (Colo) 56 Hickory Rd, Woodbridge, CT 06525

TROGDON, Denise A (Va) 1700 Wainwright Dr, Reston, VA 20190

TRONCALE, John Emanuel (NJ) 301 Meadows Dr, Forest, VA 24551

TROTTER, John Scott (Ark) 1121 W Pecan, Blytheville, AR 72315

TROUTMAN-MILLER, Jana Lee (Mil) 1840 N Prospect Ave, Milwaukee, WI 53202

TROW, Chester John (CFla)

TROWBRIDGE, Dustin E (NY) St George's Church, 105 Grand St, Newburgh, NY 12550

TRUAX, Heidi M (Ct) 31 Hilltop Rd, Sharon, CT 06069

TRUBINA, John Francis (Cal) 3350 Hopyard Road, Pleasanton, CA 94588

TRUBY, Laura C(hristine) (Ore) 14221 Livesay Rd, Oregon City, OR 97045

TRUE, Jerry Erwin (WMass) 2612 Brightside Ct, Cape Coral, FL 33991

TRUE, Timothy E (SanD) 1550 S 14th Ave, Yuma, AZ 85364

TRUELOVE, Kenneth Elwood (WA) 508 S Mckinley Ave, Champaign, IL 61821

TRUIETT SR, Melvin Edward (Md) 2322 Ivy Ave, Baltimore, MD 21214

TRUITT, Ann Harris (Va) 1132 N Ivanhoe St, Arlington, VA 22205

TRUJILLO NIETO, Jose David (EcuC)

TRULL, C scott (NJ) 327 s juniper st, Philadelphia, PA 19107

TRUMBLE JR, John Louis (O) 51 Walnut St, Tiffin, OH 44883

TRUMBORE, Frederick Rhue (Va) xxxxxxxxxxxx, delete all of above address, Woodstock, VA 22664

TRUSCOTT, Nancy (Alb) 10 Orchard Street, Delhi, NY 13753

TRUTNER, Thomas Kirk (Cal) 22 Cedar Lane, Orinda, CA 94563

TRYGAR SR, Earl Paul (Be) RR 2, Box 2229, Moscow, PA 18444

TRYTTEN, Patricia Shoemaker (Oly) 310 N K St, Tacoma, WA 98403

TSAI, Ching-Yi (Tai)

TSOU, Tsai-Hsin (Tai) 1 F #5 Ln 348 Lishan St, Neihu Dist, Taipei, 11450, Taiwan

TUBBS, Suzanne Freeman (Tex) 604 Tryon Ct, Tyler, TX 75703

TUCHOLS, Franklin Joseph (Ct) 661 Old Post Rd, Fairfield, CT 06824

TUCK, Michael G (WMass) 114 George St, Providence, RI 02906

TUCKER, Alice Elizabeth (Tex) 2900 Bunny Run, Austin, TX 78746

TUCKER, Douglas Jon (Tex) 2 Barque Ln., Galveston, TX 77554

TUCKER, Elizabeth Spier (CFla) 1020 Keyes Ave, Winter Park, FL 32789

TUCKER, Gene Richard (CPa) 212 Penn Street, Huntingdon, PA 16652

TUCKER, James M (NJ) 130 Prince St., Bordentown, NJ 08505

TUCKER, James Thomas (Tex) 107 Oakstone Dr., Chapel Hill, NC 27514

TUCKER, Jared Horton (Los) 3227 N Rancho La Carlota Rd, Covina, CA 91724

TUCKER, Jennifer Lynn (U) 231 E 100 S, Salt Lake City, UT 84111

TUCKER, Julia (SVa) 901 Poquoson Cir, Virginia Beach, VA 23452

TUCKER, Kenneth Merrill (USC) 1502 Greenville Street, Abbeville, SC 29620

TUCKER, Martha D (Pa)

TUCKER PARSONS, Martha L (ETenn) 8321 Georgetown Bay Dr, Ooltewah, TN 37363

TUDELA, Mary Elizabeth (Chi) 4364 Hardy Street, Lihue, HI 96766

TUDOR, Richard Beresford (Mo) 3106 Aberdeen Dr, Florissant, MO 63033

TUDOR, William Ellis (Ind) 3021 94th Ave E, Edgewood, WA 98371

TUDOR-FOLEY, Hugh W (Ct) 3168 Dona Sofia Dr, Studio City, CA 91604

TUFF, Roy Wynn (SwFla) 401 W. Henry St, Punta Gorda, FL 33950

TULIS, Edward (CNY)

TULL, Sandra Ann (Fla) 1021 Oxford Dr, Saint Augustine, FL 32084

TULLER, Stuart Sidney (Va) 2132 Owls Cove Ln, Reston, VA 20191

TULLY, Coleen (Minn) 101 N 5th St, Marshall, MN 56258

TULLY, William M (NY) 1810 Loma St, Santa Barbara, CA 93103

TUMMINIO HANSEN, Danielle Elizabeth (Ct) 12 Quincy Ave, Quincy, MA 02169

TUNKLE, Paul Dennis (Md) 200 Common Rd, Dresden, ME 04342

TUNNELL, Janet A (SwFla) St Thomas Episcopal Church, 1200 Snell Isle Blvd NE, St Petersburg, FL 33704

TUNNEY, Elisabeth Ellerich (LI)

TUOHY, James Fidelis (Ala) 3842 11th Ave S, Birmingham, AL 35222

TURBERG, Judith E (Az) 100 S Laura Ln, Casa Grande, AZ 85194

TURBEVILLE, Norman M (Dal) P.O. Box 292, Buda, TX 78610

TURCZYN, Jeffrey Robert (NY) 40 Running Hill Road, Scarborough, ME 04074

TURK, Davette Lois (Fla) 8256 Wallingford Hills Ln, Jacksonville, FL 32256

TURMO, Joel Lee (WMich) 9798 E BC Ave, Richland, MI 49083

TURNAGE, Benjamin Whitfield (Ala) 1124 Lakeview Crescent, Birmingham, AL 35205

TURNAGE, Richard Wentworth (SC) 1920 Rimsdale Dr, Myrtle Beach, SC 29575

TURNBULL, Henry George (RI) 6465 River Birchfield Rd, Jamesville, NY 13078

TURNBULL, Malcolm Edward (Va) 8700 Rockcrest Court, N Chesterfield, VA 23235

TURNER, Alice Camp (WNY) 90 South Dr, Lackawanna, NY 14218

TURNER, Alicia Beth (WNC) 900 Centre Park Dr # B, Asheville, NC 28805

TURNER, Amy Porterfield (WVa)

TURNER, Anne Michele (Va) 5814 19th St N, Arlington, VA 22205

TURNER, Arlie Raymond (RG) 397 Old Offen PO Rd, Traphill, NC 28685

TURNER, Bonnie L (NMich) 510 E Park Dr, Peshtigo, WI 54157

TURNER, Brian William (SO) 2524 Carriage Ln Apt 3C, Fredericksburg, VA 22401

TURNER, Carl Francis (NY) 1 W 53rd St, New York, NY 10019

TURNER, Carlton Barry (ECR) 891 Vista Del Brisa, San Luis Obispo, CA 93405

TURNER JR, Claude Sylvester (SVa) 118 Little John Rd, Williamsburg, VA 23185

TURNER, Diana Serene (The Episcopal NCal) 9031 Tuolumne Dr, Sacramento, CA 95826

TURNER, Donald Lee (CNY) PO Box 865, Barnegat Light, NJ 08006

TURNER, Elizabeth Holder (Del) 125 Gull Pt, Millsboro, DE 19966

TURNER, Elizabeth Zarelli (Tex) 9520 Anchusa TRL, Austin, TX 78736

TURNER SR, Eric Wood (CFla) 4581 Bellaluna Dr., West Melbourne, FL 32904

TURNER, (Irvin) Doyle (Minn) 37688 Tulaby Lake Rd, Waubun, MN 56589

TURNER, James Scott (Colo) St. Paul's Episcopal Church, P.O. Box 770722, Steamboat Springs, CO 80477

TURNER, John Edward (The Episcopal Church in Haw) 19446 N. 110th Lane, Sun City, AZ 85373

TURNER, Linnea Summers (Va) 5701 Hunton Wood Dr, Broad Run, VA 20137

TURNER, Mary LaRoche Douglas (SVa) 118 Little John Road, Williamsburg, VA 23187

TURNER, Maurice Edgar (Cal) 4222 Churchill Drive, Pleasanton, CA 94588

TURNER, Melvin Eugene (Minn) 4759 Shellbark Rd, Owings Mills, MD 21117

TURNER, Peter Knight (NJ) PO Box 1134, Hillburn, NY 10931

TURNER III, Philip Williams (Tex) 9520 Anchusa Trl, Austin, TX 78736

TURNER, Philippa Anne (NY) 2 E 90th St, New York, NY 10128

TURNER, Reverend Clay H (USC) 2285 Armstrong Creek Road, Marion, NC 28752

TURNER, Robert (NJ) 525 Pleasant Ave, Piscataway, NJ 08854

TURNER, Saundra Lee (Ga) 2104 Amberley Pass, Evans, GA 30809

TURNER, Sharon Richey (Dal) 6728 Mayer Road, La Grange, TX 78945

TURNER, Stephen Deree (EC) 16 Gregg Way, Fort Rucker, AL 36362

TURNER III, Thomas Selma (WTex) 200 N. Wright Streed, Alice, TX 78332

TURNER, Timothy Jay (WTex) 120 Herweck Dr, San Antonio, TX 78213

TURNER JR, William Joseph (CNY) 2 Ridgefield Pl, Biltmore Forest, NC 28803

TURNER-JONES, Nancy Marie (SO) 318 E. 4th St., Cincinnati, OH 45202

TURNEY, Harper McAdoo (O) 1632 Hilltown Pike, Hilltown, PA 18927

TURRELL, James Fielding (Be) School of Theology, U. of the South, 335 Tennessee Ave, Sewanee, TN 37383

TURRIE, Anne Elizabeth (RG) PO Box 2427, Mesilla Park, NM 88047

TURTON, Neil Christopher (NJ) 509 Lake Ave, Bay Head, NJ 08742

TUSKEN, Mark Anthony (Chi) 327 S 4th St, Geneva, IL 60134

TUTON, Daniel Joseph (RG) 8409 La Ventura Ct NW, Albuquerque, NM 87120

TUTTLE, Jonathan David (Ga) 2425 Cherry Laurel Ln, Albany, GA 31705

TUTTLE, Margaret Constance (Nwk) 19 Oberlin St, Maplewood, NJ 07040

TUTTLE, Peggy Elaine Wills (Minn) 4603 Bontia Dr, Palm Beach Gardens, FL 33418

TUTU, Mpho Andrea (WA) 3001 Park Center Dr Apt 1119, Alexandria, VA 22302

TWEEDALE, David Lee (Colo) 423 E Thunderbird Dr, Fort Collins, CO 80525

TWEEDIE, Billy (Tex) 301 E 8th St, Austin, TX 78701

TWEEDY, Jeanette E(lizabeth) (NY) PO Box 172, Peacham, VT 05862

TWELVES, Paul Douglass (RI) 341 Spinnaker Lane, Bristol, RI 02809

TWENTYMAN JR, Donald Graham (Ia) 107 24th St, Spirit Lake, IA 51360

TWIGGS, Frances R (Spok) 428 King St, Wenatchee, WA 98801

TWINAMAANI, Benjamin B (SwFla) 9533 Pebble Glen Ave, Tampa, FL 33647

TWISS, Ian Reed (Mich) Trinity Episcopal Church, 11575 Belleville Road, Belleville, MI 48111

TWO BEARS, Neil V (ND) Po Box 685, Fort Yates, ND 58538

TWO BULLS, Robert G (U) Po Box 168, Hermosa, SD 57744

TWO BULLS, Robert W (Los)

TWO HAWK, Webster Aaron (SD) 604 East Missouri Avenue, Fort Pierre, SD 57532

TWOMEY, Patrick Timothy (FdL) 415 E Spring St, Appleton, WI 54911

TWYMAN, Thomas Wellwirth (CNY) 122 Metropolitan Ave, Ashland, MA 01721

TYLER, Lera Patrick (WTex) 116 US Highway 87, Comfort, TX 78013

TYLER, Pamela Hawes (Los) 1101 Witt Road, Taos, NM 87471

TYLER SMITH, Virginia Stewart (Roch) 11 Episcopal Ave, Honeoye Falls, NY 14472

TYNDALL, Constance Flanigan (WMo) 4239 E Valley Rd, Springfield, MO 65809

TYNDALL, Jeremy Hamilton (Ore) The Rectory, 55 Cove Road, Farnborough Hants, GU140EX, Great Britain (UK)

TYO JR, Charles Hart (Roch) 16 Elmwood Ave, Friendship, NY 14739

TYON, Benjamin Ruben (SD) Po Box 14, Pine Ridge, SD 57770

TYREE, Richard (SwVa) 132 Lincoln St, Holyoke, MA 01040

TYREE-CUEVAS, Susan McCorkle (Oly) 1804 Pointe Woodworth Dr NE, Tacoma, WA 98422

TYRIVER, Marcia Rivenburg (The Episcopal NCal) 255 Ba Wood Ln, Janesville, WI 53545

TYSON, Lynda (Ct) 10 Evarts Lane, Madison, CT 06443

TYSON, Stephen Alfred (Ore) 370 Market Ave., Coos Bay, OR 97420

TZENG, Wen-Bin (Tai) No. 7 Lane 105, Section 1, Hang Chow South Road, Taipei, Taiwan

U

UBIERA, Jose R (NJ) 207 Summit Avenue Apt 1, Newark, NJ 07104

UDELL, George Morris Edson (Tex) 1436 Daventry Dr, DeSoto, TX 75115

UEDA, Ajuko Lois Kaleikea (The Episcopal Church in Haw) Rikkyo University, 1-2-26, Kitano, Niiza-shi, Saitama, Japan

UFFELMAN, Stephen Paul (EO) 915 Ne Crest Dr, Prineville, OR 97754

UFFMAN, Craig David (Roch) 2000 Highland Avenue, Rochester, NY 14618

UHLIK, Charles R (WMo) 2641 E Southern Hills Blvd, Springfield, MO 65804

UITTI, Aaron Leopold (At) 124 Commercial Ave, East Palatka, FL 32131

ULLMAN, Richard L. (O) 342 S 5th St, Philadelphia, PA 19106

ULRICH, Stephanie Lyn (Neb) 9302 Blondo St., Omaha, NE 68134

UMEOFIA, Christian Chinedu (NC) Po Box 1333, Goldsboro, NC 27533

UMPHLETT, David Alton (NC) 108 W. Farriss Ave., High Point, NC 27262

UNDERHILL, Robin (Los) Tigh Ban, Hightae, Lockerbie, DG-11 1JN, Great Britain (UK)

UNDERHILL, Scott A (Alb) 912 Route 146, Clifton Park, NY 12065

UNDERHILL, William Dudley (WA) 25 Nottingham Dr, Kingston, MA 02364

UNDERWOOD, Bonnie Gordy (At)

UNDERWOOD, Deborah Ann (Okla) 501 S. Cincinnati Ave., Tulsa, OK 74103

UNDERWOOD, Robert Franklin (CPa) 4109 Cochise Ter, Sarasota, FL 34233

UPCHURCH, Stan (Okla) 617 Leaning Elm Dr, Norman, OK 73071

UPHAM, Judith Elizabeth (FtW) 9805 Livingston Rd, Fort Washington, MD 20744

UPTON, David Hugh (USC) 206 W Prentiss Ave, Greenville, SC 29605

UPTON, Thomas Lee (Neb) 14017 Washington St, Omaha, NE 68137

URANG, Gunnar (Vt) Po Box 306, Norwich, VT 05055

URBAN JR, Percy Linwood (Pa) The Quadrangle # 2301, 3300 Darby Road, Haverford, PA 19041

URBANEK, Virginia (Me) P.O. Box 455, Houlton, ME 04730

URE III, Lincoln Richard (U) 80 S 300 E, Salt Lake City, UT 84111

URMSON-TAYLOR, Ralph (Okla)

URQUIDI, Ashley Elizabeth (Md) 4449 N Witchduck Rd, Virginia Beach, VA 23455

USHER JR, Guy Randolph (Eau) 303 S Hollybrook Dr, Chillicothe, IL 61523

UZOMECHINA, Gideon A (NJ) 600 Cleveland Avenue, Plainfield, NJ 07060

UZUETA JR, Luis (Ak) 1392 Benshoof Dr, North Pole, AK 99705

V

VACA TAPIA, Harold Alexander (EcuC) Calle Calderon entre Argentina y Chile, Tulcan Carchi, Ecuador

VACCARO, Anthony Joseph (Chi) St James Cathedral, 65 E Huron St, Chicago, IL 60611

VADERS, Nancy Johnson (NC) St Anne's Episc Ch, 2690 Fairlawn Dr, Winston Salem, NC 27106

VAFIS, John Symon (The Episcopal NCal) PO Box 1044, Colusa, CA 95932

VAGGIONE, Richard Paul (Cal) 1601 Oxford St, Berkeley, CA 94709

VAGUENER, Martha (SwFla) 3105 Short Leaf St, Zephyrhills, FL 33543

VAIL, Jean Parker (Chi) 305 Sutherland Ct, Durham, NC 27712

VALADEZ-JAIME, Agustin (Az) 2025 W Indian School Rd Apt 907, Phoenix, AZ 85015

VALANDRA, Linda Beth (SD) 410 University Ave, Hot Springs, SD 57747

VALANTASIS, Richard (Mo) 17 Wildflower Way, Santa Fe, NM 87506

VALCOURT, Theodore Philippe-Francois (CGC) 401 Live Oak Ave, Pensacola, FL 32507

VALDEMA, Pierre-Henry Fritz (Hai) Eglise Sainte Trinite, Rue Mgr Guilloux, Box 1309, Port-Au-Prince, Haiti

VALDERRAMA SANABRIA, Juan Pablo (Colom) c/o Diocese of Colombia, Cra 6 No. 49-85 Piso 2, Bogota, BDC, Colombia

VALDEZ, Pedro Antonio (Micr) 826 Howard St, Carthage, MO 64836

VALENTINE III, A(llen) Wilson (Ak) 924 C St, Juneau, AK 99801

VALENTINE, Darcy Adrian (Minn) 615 Vermillion St, Hastings, MN 55033

VALENTINE JR, John Carney (WVa) 206 E 2nd St, Weston, WV 26452

VALENTINE, Peggy Lee (NwT) St Mark's Episcopal Church, 3150 Vogel St, Abilene, TX 79603

VALENTINE, Ronald Andrew (Chi) St James the Less Episcopal Church, 550 Sunset Ridge Rd, Northfield, IL 60093

VALENTINE DAVIS, Melinda Rae (Ia)

VALIATH, Abraham J (Be) 365 Lafayette Ave., Palmerton, PA 18071

VALLE, Jose Francisco (WA) 1700 Powder Mill Rd, Silver Spring, MD 20903

VALLENILLA DE LA ROSA, Angel Rafael (PR)

VALLE-PLAZA, Juan Nelson (EcuC)

VALOVICH, Stephen Anthony (SeFla) 3395 Burns Rd, Palm Beach Gardens, FL 33410

VAN, Maron Ines (Ore) 4435 Fox Hollow Rd, Eugene, OR 97405

VAN ANTWERPEN, Alanna Mary (NH) 214 Main St, Nashua, NH 03060

VAN ATTA, Ralph Sherwood (Pa) 6505 Tabor Ave Apt 5116, Philadelphia, PA 19111

VANAUKER, Margaret Elizabeth (Md) 225 Bowie Trl, Lusby, MD 20657

VANBAARS, Sven Layne (Va) PO Box 146, Gloucester, VA 23061

VAN BEVEREN, Eugene Charles (Neb) 3041 SW Isaac Ave, Pendleton, OR 97801

VAN BRUNT, Thomas Harvey (SO) 534 Chapel Road, Amelia, OH 45102

VANBUREN, Andrew David (Roch) 1 Teft Ave, Clifton Springs, NY 14432

VAN BUREN, Robert Barrett (Los) 15524 Pintura Dr, Hacienda Heights, CA 91745

VANCE, Bill (CFla) 26 Willow Dr, Orlando, FL 32807

VANCE, Christina Marie (Alb) 2331 15th St, Troy, NY 12180

VANCE, Marc(Us) Patrick (Ind) 2651 California St., Columbus, IN 47201

VANCE, Timothy Keith (SwVa) PO Box 344, Sewanee, TN 37375

VANCOOTEN-WEBSTER, Jennifer Elizabeth (LI) 286-88 7th Ave, Brooklyn, NY 11215

VAN CULIN JR, Samuel (WA) 3900 Watson Place, NW #5D-B, Washington, DC 20016

VAN CULIN, T(homas) Andrew K. (Mich) 61 Grosse Pointe Blvd., Grosse Pointe Farms, MI 48236

VAN CULIN, Thomas Meyers (The Episcopal Church in Haw) 2578-F Pacific Heights Rd, Honolulu, HI 96813

VANDAGRIFF, Mary Cordelia (Ala) 220 S Wood Rd, Homewood, AL 35209

VAN DEN BLINK, A(rie) J(ohannes) (CNY) 315 W Washington Ave, Elmira, NY 14901

VANDERAU JR, Robert Julian (RI) 2305 Edgewater Drive, Apt 1718, Orlando, FL 32804

VANDERCOOK, Peter John (Chi) 208 Nesheim Trl, Mount Horeb, WI 53572

VANDERCOOK, Ross Allan (Mich) 9900 N Meridian Rd, Pleasant Lake, MI 49272

VANDERCOOK, Susan Elizabeth (Mich) 9900 N Meridian Rd, Pleasant Lake, MI 49272

VAN DER HIEL, Rudolph J (CPa) 156 Jones Road, RR 1, Comp 5, Parry Sound, ON P2A 2W7, Canada

VANDER LEE, Jerome Neal (SD) 500 S Main Ave, Sioux Falls, SD 57104

VANDERMARK, Roy James (Alb) 825 Covered Bridge Rd, Unadilla, NY 13849

VANDERMEER, Leigh A (Chi) 19760 W Woodmere Ter, Antioch, IL 60002

VANDERSLICE, Thomas Arthur (NH) 22 Stratham Grn, Stratham, NH 03885

VANDERVEEN, Peter Todd (Pa) 230 Pennswood Rd, Bryn Mawr, PA 19010

VAN DERVOORT, V(irginia) Ann (Tenn) 1106 Chickering Park Dr, Nashville, TN 37215

VANDER WEL, Brian Lee (WA) Christ Church, 600 Farmington Rd W, Accokeek, MD 20607

VAN DE STEEG, Franklin Exford (Minn) PO Box 155, Hastings, MN 55033

VAN DEUSEN, Robert Reed (CPa) 205 King St, Northumberland, PA 17857

VAN DEUSEN, R(obert) Wayne (Mil) 9360 West Terra Court, Milwaukee, WI 53224

VANDEVELDER, Frank Radcliff (Va) 12191 Clipper Dr Apt 110, Woodbridge, VA 22192

VAN DEVENTER, (Arthur) Reed (Roch) 53 Winding Rd, Rochester, NY 14618

VANDEVENTER, Heather Ann (Va) 118 N Washington St, Alexandria, VA 22314

VANDIVORT JR, Paul Marshall (Mo) 12366 Federal Dr, Des Peres, MO 63131

VAN DOOREN, John David (Chi) 5749 N Kenmore Ave, Chicago, IL 60660

VANDOREN JR, Robert Lawson (WTenn) 5097 Greenway Cv, Memphis, TN 38117

VAN DUSEN, David Buick (Mass) 3905 N Old Sabino Canyon Road, Tucson, AZ 85750

VAN DYKE, Bude (Ala) Po Box 824, Sewanee, TN 37375

VAN EENWYK, John Richter (Roch) P. O. Box 1961, Olympia, WA 98507

VAN ES, Kenneth (Eau) 2603 Yorktown Ct, Eau Claire, WI 54703

VANG, Marshall Jacob (Alb) 88 Circular St Apt1, Saratoga Springs, NY 12866

VANG, Toua (Minn) 2200 Minnehaha Ave E, Saint Paul, MN 55119

VAN GORDEN SR, Schuyler Humphrey (Eau) 120 10th Ave, Eau Claire, WI 54703

VAN GULDEN, Sarah A (Mass) 74 S Common St, Lynn, MA 01902

VAN HOOK, Peter James (U) PO Box 17972, Salt Lake City, UT 84117

VAN HOOSER, Jack Boyd (WMich) 801 Vanosdale Rd Apt 511, Knoxville, TN 37909

VAN HORN, Richard Scott (Los) 3050 Motor Ave, Los Angeles, CA 90064

VAN HORNE, Beverly (Mo) 11907 Bardmont Drive, Saint Louis, MO 63126

VAN HORNE, Peter Eric (Mo) 11907 Bardmont Dr, St. Louis, MO 63126

VAN HOVEN, Teri Hewett (Episcopal SJ) PO Box 7446, Visalia, CA 93290

VANI, Benedict Sele (CFla) 2341 Port Malabar Blvd Ne, Palm Bay, FL 32905

VAN KIRK, Andrew D (Dal) 6400 McKinney Ranch Parkway, McKinney, TX 75070

VAN KIRK, Natalie Beam (Chi) 22W415 Butterfield Rd, Glen Ellyn, IL 60137

VAN KLAVEREN, Dina Els (Md) 1216 Seminole Dr, Arnold, MD 21012

VAN KOEVERING, Mark A (WVa)

VAN KUIKEN, Alexandra Michele (NJ) 100 Sullivan Way, Trenton, NJ 08628

VAN LIEW, Christina (LI)

VANN, Deborah Louise (CFla) 380 Royal Palm Dr, Melbourne, FL 32935

VANN, Tim E (Ia) 710 Matthies Dr, Papillion, NE 68046

VAN NIEL, Noah (Mass) 172 Main St, Hingham, MA 02043

VANO, Mary Foster (Ark) 20900 Chenal Pkwy, Little Rock, AR 72223

VAN OSS SR, Earl T (U) 737 East Center, Orem, UT 84057

VAN OSS, William Joseph (Minn) 1710 E Superior St, Duluth, MN 55812

VANOVER, Debra A (The Episcopal Church in Haw) 25 Hiatt St, Lebanon, OR 97355

VAN PARYS, Cynthia Leigh (NI) 1464 Glenlake Dr, South Bend, IN 46614

VAN PLETZEN-RANDS, Blane Frederik (WNY) Rowe House, 355 W Utica St, Buffalo, NY 14222

VAN SANT, Mark R (NJ) 27 Tocci Ave, Monmouth Beach, NJ 07750

VAN SANT, Paul Albion (NJ) 38 Anne Dr, Tabernacle, NJ 08088

VAN SCOYOC, Gardner Warren (Va) 5928 Lomack Ct, Alexandria, VA 22312

VAN SICKLE, Kathleen (Cal) 555 Pierce St Apt 340e, Albany, CA 94706

VAN SICLEN, John Remsen (Me) PO Box 523, Damariscotta, ME 04543

VAN SLYKE, Charlotte Sturgis (Ala)

VANUCCI, Anthony Joseph (Pa) 9700 Entrada Pl. N.W., Albuquerque, NM 87114

VAN VALKENBURGH, William Burton (WMich) 6632 W. South Lake Gage Dr., Angola, IN 46703

VANVLIET-PULLIN, Dana Mae (SVa) St Peter's Episc Church, 224 S Military Hwy, Norfolk, VA 23502

VAN WALTEROP, Norman Phillip (Episcopal SJ) 2716 C Sherwood Ave, Modesto, CA 95350

VAN WASSENHOVE, Mark Steven (Ind) 10202 Winlee Court, Indianapolis, IN 46236

VAN WELY, Richard Francis (Ct) 223 Weaver St Apt 20D, Greenwich, CT 06831

VAN ZANDT, Jane Whitbeck (NH) 58 Hanson Rd, Chester, NH 03036

VAN ZANDT, Polk (Tenn) Saint Paul's Episcopal Church, 116 N Academy St, Murfreesboro, TN 37130

VAN ZANTEN JR, Peter Eric (Oly) 1111 Archwood Dr. SW #442, Olympia, WA 98502

VARAS, Dwayne Anthony (Ga) 3901 Davis Blvd, Naples, FL 34104

VARDEMANN, Brady Jodoka (Mont) 556 S Rodney St, Helena, MT 59601

VARELA SOLORZANO, Marco Antonio (Hond) Colonia La Sabana, Samparo Sula, Honduras

VARELA ZUNIGA, Nery Yolanda (Hond) Colonia Los Robles, Atlantida, Ceiba, 31105, Honduras

VARGHESE, Winnie Sara (NY) 464 Riverside Drive. Apt. 41, New York, NY 10027

VARNER, Joshua H (Ga) Diocese of Georgia, 611 E Bay St, Savannah, GA 31401

VARNUM, Benedict J (Neb) 285 S 208th St, Elkhorn, NE 68022

VASQUEZ, Jaime Armando (Hond) IMS SAP Dept 215. PO Box 523900, Miami, FL 33152-3900, Honduras

VASQUEZ, Martha Sylvia Ovalle (Cal) 345 Pimlico Dr., Walnut Creek, CA 94597

VASQUEZ, Martir (Az) Saint Andrew's Church, 6300 W Camelback Rd, Glendale, AZ 85301

VASQUEZ, Oscar Arturo (SwFla) 2153 46th Ter SW Apt B, Naples, FL 34116

VASQUEZ SANCHEZ, Vicente Oswaldo (Hond)

VASQUEZ-VERA, Gladis Elisa (EcuC) Ulloa 213 Y Carriba Apdo 17-02-5304, Quito, Ecuador

VASZUEZ-JUAREZ, Patricia Ellen (Tex) 1534 Milam St, Columbus, TX 78934

VAUGHAN, Jesse L (The Episcopal NCal) 5801 River Oak Way, Carmichael, CA 95608

VAUGHAN, John (CFla) 3295 Timucua Cir, Orlando, FL 32837

VAUGHN, Denise C (WMo) 4116 Paint Rock Dr, Austin, TX 78731

VAUGHN, James Barry (Nev) Saint Alban's Church, 429 Cloudland Dr, Birmingham, AL 35226

VAUGHN, Jessie Harriet (NwT) 3303 Bacon St, Vernon, TX 76384

VAUGHN, Peter Hancock (Ct) 36 Main St, Ellington, CT 06029

VAUGHN, S. Chadwick (At) St Bede's Episcopal Church, 2601 Henderson Mill Rd NE, Atlanta, GA 30345

VAZQUEZ-GELI, Jose R (PR)

VEACH, Deborah Joan (Ind) 215 N. 7th St., Terre Haute, IN 47807

VEAL, David Lee (NwT) 2519 55th St, Lubbock, TX 79413

VEALE, David Scott (Vt) 8 Bishop St, Saint Albans, VT 05478

VEALE, Donald Meier (Ore) 5346 Don Miguel Dr, Carlsbad, CA 92010

VEALE JR, Erwin Olin (Ga) 3120 Exeter Rd, Augusta, GA 30909

VEINOT, William Paul (Ct) 327 Orchard St, Rocky Hill, CT 06067

VEINTIMILLA, Carlos (EcuC) Brisas De Santay Mz G, V 30, Duran, Ecuador

VEIT JR, Richard Fred (Wyo) 7711 Hawthorne Dr, Cheyenne, WY 82009

VELARDE, Inez Jean (NAM) St Luke's-in-the-Desert, PO Box 720, Farmington, NM 87499

VELASQUEZ BORJAS, Gladis Margarita (Hond) Aldea Santa Cruz, Tegucigalpa, Tegucigalpa M.D.C., FM 15023, Honduras

VELAZQUEZ-MORALES, Juan Alberto (PR)

VELEZ-RIVERA, Daniel (Va) 11625 Vantage Hill Road, Unit 11C, Reston, VA 20190

VELLA, Joan Christine (WNC) 147 Sourwood Road, State Road, NC 28676

VELLA JR, Joseph Agius (SwFla) 125 Lamara Way Ne, Saint Petersburg, FL 33704

VELLOM, Lee Sherwin (Az) 1741 North Camino Rebecca, Nogales, AZ 85621

VELLOM, Timothy John (WTex) 15919 Colton Wl, San Antonio, TX 78247

VELTHUIZEN, Teunisje (NI) 608 Cushing St, South Bend, IN 46616

VENEZIA, Deborah Lynn (CFla) 7725 Indian Ridge Trail South, Kissimmee, FL 34747

VENKATESH, Catherine Richardson (WMass) 281 Renfrew St, Arlington, MA 02476

VENTRIS, Margaret Pyre (Los) 72348 Larrea Ave, Twentynine Palms, CA 92277

VERBECK III, Guido Fridolin (WLa) 4741 Crescent Dr, Shreveport, LA 71106

VERDAASDONK, Henry Joseph (Alb) 34 Spencer Blvd, Coxsackie, NY 12051

VERDI, Barry Ellis (Los) 12571 Kagel Canyon Rd, Sylmar, CA 91342

VERELL, Gary Archer (SeFla) 917 E Ridge Village Dr, Miami, FL 33157

VERGARA, Winfred Bagao (LI) 40-11 68th Street #2, Woodside, NY 11377

VERGARA GRUESO, Edison (Colom) Carrera 6 No 49-85, Piso 2, Bogota, Colombia

VERHAEGHE, Ronald Edward (WMo) 4401 Wornall Rd, Kansas City, MO 64111

VERNON, Valerie Veronica (SeFla)

VERRET, Joan Claire (CFla) 220 E Palm Dr, Lakeland, FL 33803

VERRETTE, Sallie Cheavens (Ia) St. Paul's Episcopal Church, 6th & State., Grinnell, IA 50112

VERSHURE, Claude Edward (SD) 25413 He Sapa Trail, Custer, SD 57730

VERVYNCK, Jennifer R (Oly) 5002 Nighthawk Way, Oceanside, CA 92056

VESGA-ARDILA, Ramon (Ve)

VEST, Douglas C (Los) 1688 W. Placita Canoa Azul, Green Valley, AZ 85614

VETTEL-BECKER, Richard Arthur (Cal) 706 Tabriz Dr, Billings, MT 59105

VIA, John Albert (At) 8340 Main St., Port Republic, VA 24471

VICENS, Leigh Christiana (Mil) Religion, Philosophy, & Classics Dept., Augustana College, 2001 S Summit Ave, Sioux Falls, SD 57197

VICKERS, David Lee (Colo) 8119 M 68, Indian River, MI 49749

VICKERY JR, Robert (Tex) St. Michael's Episcopal Church, 1500 N. Capital of Texas Highway, Austin, TX 78746

VIDAL, Gene Vance (Az) Po Box 13647, Phoenix, AZ 85002

VIDMAR, Mary Burton (WMass) 18018 Avondale Ave, Lake Milton, OH 44429

VIE, Diane E (SwVa) 3536 Willow Lawn, Lynchburg, VA 24503

VIE, Todd M (SwVa) 3536 Willow Lawn Dr, Lynchburg, VA 24503

VIECHWEG, Edrice Veronica (Ct) 503 Old Long Ridge Rd, Stamford, CT 06903

VIEL, Brian John (WK) 800 W. 32nd Ave., Hutchinson, KS 67502

VIERECK, Alexis (Mass)

VIGGIANO, Robert Peter (Tex) 241 Yorktown Ct, Malvern, PA 19355

VIL, Jean Madoché (Hai) PO Box 407139, C/O Lynx Air, Fort Lauderdale, FL 33340-7139, Haiti

VILAR MENDEZ, Jose Francisco (PR)

VILAR-SANTIAGO, Jose E (PR)

VILAR-SANTIAGO, Miguel E (Md) PO Box 264, Brooklanville, MD 21022

VILAS, Franklin Edward (Nwk) 18 Greylawn Dr, Lakewood, NJ 08701

VILLACIS MACIAS, Carlos Emilio (Litoral Ecu)

VILLAGOMEZA, Christian G (SwFla) 1119 Dockside Dr, Lutz, FL 33559

VILLALOBOS, Fabian (Dal) Christ Episcopal Church 534 W Tenth street, Dallas, TX 75208

VILLAMARIN-GUTIERREZ, Washington Rigoberto (EcuC) Calle Hernando Sarmiento, N 39-54 Y Portete, Setor El Batan Quito, Ecuador

VILLARREAL, Arthur Wells (At)

VILLEMUER-DRENTH, Lauren Anne (Lex) 321 S Cleveland Rd, Lexington, KY 40515

VILORD, Charles Louis (SwFla)

VINAL, K N (CFla) 5700 Trinity Prep Ln, Winter Park, FL 32792

VINAS-PLASENCIA, Aquilino Manuel (CFla) 31 S Forsyth Rd, Orlando, FL 32807

VINCE, Gail Lynne (EMich) 449 Irons Park Dr, West Branch, MI 48661

VINCENT, Janet (NY) St Columba's Church, 4201 Albemarle St NW, Washington, DC 20016

VINCENT-ALEXANDER, Samantha Ann (SVa) 431 Massachusetts Ave., Norfolk, VA 23508

VINE, Walter James (Mil) 2655 N Grant Blvd, Milwaukee, WI 53210

VINSON, Donald Keith (WVa) 1701 Crestmont Dr, Huntington, WV 25701

VINSON, Richard Lee (Pa) Holy Nativity Church, 5286 Kalanianaole Highway, Honolulu, HI 96821

VIOLA, Carmen Joseph (NJ) 51 N Main St, Mullica Hill, NJ 08062

VIOLA, Harry Alexander (WNC) Po Box 1046, Hendersonville, NC 28793

VISCONTI, Richard Dennis (LI) 1 Dyke Rd, Setauket, NY 11733

VISGER, James Robert (Neb) 610 Sycamore Dr, Lincoln, NE 68510

VISMINAS, Christine Elizabeth (Pgh) 70 Dennison Ave, Framingham, MA 01702

VITET, Kino (Alb) 1417 Union St, Brooklyn, NY 11213

VIVIAN, Tim (Episcopal SJ) 10105 Mountaingate Ln, Bakersfield, CA 93311

VIZCAINO, Roberto (EcuC) Jose Herboso 271, Cdla, La Flo, Quito, Ecuador

VOCELKA, Craig Robert (Oly) P.O. Box 1362, Poulsbo, WA 98370

VOELKER, Sharon L (EMich) St Alban's, 105 S Erie St, Bay City, MI 48706

VOETS, Keith A (Ct) The Church of St. Barnabas, 15 North Broadway, Irvington, NY 10533

VOGEL, Caroline Carother (ETenn) 425 N Cedar Bluff Rd, Knoxville, TN 37923

VOGELE, Nancy AG (NH) 97 Victory Cir, White River Junction, VT 05001

VOGT, Charles Melvin (Minn) 5216 Meadow Rdg, Edina, MN 55439

VOIEN, Lucinda H (Los) 1645 W 9th St # 2, San Pedro, CA 90732

VOLKMANN, Jan Elizabeth (NY) 60 Pine Hill Park, Valatie, NY 12184

VOLLAND, Mary Catherine (RG) 2201 Dexter St, Denver, CO 80207

VOLLKOMMER, Marsha Merritt (Chi) Grace Episcopal Church, 309 Hill St, Galena, IL 61036

VOLPE, Gina (Chi) 9300 S. Pleasant Ave, Rectory, Chicago, IL 60643

VON DREELE, James Davison (Pa) 27107 Valley Run Dr., Wilmington, DE 19810

VON GONTEN, Kevin P (LI) 11571 Ruby Ct., Ellendale, DE 19941

VON GRABOW, Richard Henri (The Episcopal NCal) 580 Cooper Dr, Benicia, CA 94510

VONGSANIT, Sam Chanpheng (Episcopal SJ) 709 N Jackson Ave, Fresno, CA 93702

VON HAAREN, Barbara Elizabeth (Minn) 1862 W 6th St, Red Wing, MN 55066

VON HAAREN, Erika Shivers (Az) 6715 N Mockingbird Ln, Scottsdale, AZ 85253

VON NESSEN, Wayne Howard (HB)

☩ **VONO**, Michael Louis (Bp of RG 2010-) Episcopal Diocese of the Rio Grande, 4304 Carlisle Blvd NE, Albuquerque, NM 87107

VON RAUTENKRANZ, Linda Sue (WA) St Dunstan's Episc Church, 5450 Massachusetts Ave, Bethesda, MD 20816

VON ROESCHLAUB, W Kurt (LI) 4 Cornwall Ln, Port Washington, NY 11050

☩ **VONROSENBERG**, Charles Glenn (Bp Provsnl of Episcopa) 132 Beresford Creek St., Daniel Island, SC 29492

VON WRANGEL, Carola (Tenn) Church of the Advent, 5501 Franklin Pike, Nashville, TN 37220

VOORHEES, Cynthia Evans (Los) 1308 Santiago Dr., Newport Beach, CA 92660

VOORHEES JR, Edwin H (O) 115 Washington St., St. Augustine, FL 32084

VOORHEES, James Martin (SD) HC 30 Box 151, Belle Fourche, SD 57717

VOORHEES, Jonathan Andrew (Va) 1700 University Ave, Charlottesville, VA 22903

VORKINK II, Peter (NH) 20 Main St, Exeter, NH 03833

VOSBURGH, Linda Ann (Colo) PO Box 1023, Broomfield, CO 80038

VOTAW, Verling Alastair (SC) 657 Wampler Dr, Charleston, SC 29412

VOUGA, Anne Fontaine (Ky) St Thomas Episcopal Church, 9616 Westport Road, Louisville, KY 40241

VOYLE, Robert John (Ore) 24965 Nw Pederson Rd, Hillsboro, OR 97124

VOYSEY, Stephen Otte (Mass) 1 Colpitts Road, Weston, MA 02493

VROON, Daron Jon (At) 939 James Burgess Road, Suwanee, GA 30024

VRYHOF, David B (Mass) 980 Memorial Dr, Cambridge, MA 02138

VUKICH, Dawn Elizabeth (Los) 26391 Bodega Ln, Mission Viejo, CA 92691

VUKMANIC, Paula (Los) 2200 Via Rosa, Palos Verdes Estates, CA 90274

VUONO, Reverend Deacon Dorothy (Del) 19337 Fleatown Rd, Lincoln, DE 19960

W

WACASTER, David C (WA) 2711 Parkway Pl, Cheverly, MD 20785

WACHNER, Emily (NY) 74 Trinity Pl, New York, NY 10006

WACOME, Karen Ann Halvorsen (Ia) 415 3rd St Nw, Orange City, IA 51041

WADDELL, Clayton Burbank (SeFla) 141 S County Rd, Palm Beach, FL 33480

WADDELL, Jonathan H (Ala) 5014 Lakeshore Dr, Pell City, AL 35128

WADDELL, Thomas Robert (Va) 5911 Edsall Rd Ph 5, Alexandria, VA 22304

WADDINGHAM, Gary Brian (Mont) 119 N 33rd St, Billings, MT 59101

WADDLE, Helen Ann (Okla) PO Box 12402, Oklahoma City, OK 73157

WADE, Carol Lynn (Lex) Christ Church Cathedral, 166 Market St, Lexington, KY 40507

WADE, Elizabeth Ann Till (Ky)

WADE, Francis Howard (WA) 4800 Fillmore Ave #1452, Alexandria, VA 22311

WADE, J Merrill (Tex) 11561 Cedarcliffe Dr, Austin, TX 78750

WADE SR, Joseph Alfred (NY) 108 Horsley Dr, Hampton, VA 23666

WADE, Karin Elizabeth (Mass) Po Box 372, Rockport, MA 01966

WADE, Mary (Miss) 2681 Lake Cir, Jackson, MS 39211

WADE, Stephen Hamel (Va) 132 N Jay St, Middleburg, VA 20117

WADE, Suzanne (Mass) 75 Cold Spring Rd, Westford, MA 01886

WADE, William St Clair (Tenn) 1 Casey Road, East Kingston, NH 03827

WAFER-CROSS, Melissa Lee (NwT) 3502 47th St, Lubbock, TX 79413

WAFF, Kay Childers (SwVa) 314 N Bridge St, Bedford, VA 24523

WAFF, William Dubard Razz (Mil) 2443 Lawson Blvd., Gurnee, IL 60031

WAFLER, Donald Samuel (Minn) 628 1st St Se, Faribault, MN 55021

WAGAMAN, Stanley Warner (Az) Episc Ch Of St Francis In The Valley, 600 S La Canada Dr, Green Valley, AZ 85614

WAGAR, L A Catherine (Los) The Episcopal Church of St. Philip the Evangelist, 2800 Stanford Street, South Los Angeles, CA 90011

WAGEMAN, Carole Allcroft (Vt) 173 Hollow Road, North Ferrisburgh, VT 05473

WAGENSEIL JR, Robert Arthur (SwFla) 1700 Patlin Cir S, Largo, FL 33770

WAGENSELLER, Joseph Paul (Ct) 6 Clifford Ln, Westport, CT 06880

☩ **WAGGONER JR**, James Edward (Bp of Spok 2000-) 245 E 13th Ave, Spokane, WA 99202

WAGGONER, Janet Cuff (FtW) 2724 Stone Oak Drive, Fort Worth, TX 76109

WAGGONER, Leigh Farley (Colo) 110 W. North St., Cortez, CO 81321

WAGNER, Barbara Jean (WMich) 2430 Greenbriar, Harbor Springs, MI 49740

WAGNER, Beth Anne (CFla)

WAGNER, Daniel Andrew (CGC) 11 S Conception St, Mobile, AL 36602

WAGNER, David W (At) 435 Peachtree St NE, Atlanta, GA 30308

WAGNER, John Carr (Be) 1070 Oakhurst Drive, Slatington, PA 18080

WAGNER, Mary M (Ia) 2400 Middle Rd, Bettendorf, IA 52722

WAGNER, Mary Scott (Mass) 54 Robert Rd, Marblehead, MA 01945

WAGNER, Ralph Fellows (Ak) Po Box 1502, Palmer, AK 99645

WAGNER, Richard Alden (Los) 40562 Via Amapola, Murrieta, CA 92562

WAGNER, Sharon Lavonne (Cal) 1921 Hemlock Dr, Oakley, CA 94561

WAGNER, Wm. Beau (Me) St Matthew's Episcopal Church, PO Box 879, Lisbon, ME 04250

WAGNER-PIZZA, Ken E (CPa) 1206 Faxon Parkway, Williamsport, PA 17701

WAGNER SHERER, Kara Marie (Chi) 3857 N. Kostner Ave, Chicago, IL 60641

WAGNON, William S (WA) 9225 Crestview Dr, Indianapolis, IN 46240

WAHL, Eugene Richard (Colo) 4400 Wellington Rd, Boulder, CO 80301

WAHL, Hughes Edward (Md) 4010 Band Shell Ct, Chesapeake Beach, MD 20732

WAID, Anna Neil Magruder (Del) 301 Woodlawn Rd, Wilmington, DE 19803

WAINWRIGHT, Philip (Pgh) 326 Maple Terrace, Pittsburgh, PA 15211

WAINWRIGHT, Robert F (PR)

WAINWRIGHT-MAKS, Laurence Christopher (Miss) 105 N Montgomery St, Starkville, MS 39759

WAIT III, Benjamin Wofford (CFla) 962 Ocean Blvd, Atlantic Beach, FL 32233

WAIT, Curtis Clark (Colo) 228 S Jefferson Ave, Louisville, CO 80027

WAIT, Roger Lee (Neb) 3711 A St, Lincoln, NE 68510

WAJDA, Kathryn Annemarie Reardon (Md) 1505 Sherbrook Rd, Timonium, MD 21093

WAJNERT, Theresa Altmix (Nwk) PO Box 37, Calistoga, CA 94515

WAKELEE-LYNCH, Julia (Cal) 1501 Washington Avenue, Albany, CA 94706

WAKELY, Nancy Kay (Okla) PO Box 2088, Norman, OK 73070

WAKEMAN, Nancy Ann (Md)

WAKITSCH, Randal John (Chi) 503 W Jackson St, Woodstock, IL 60098

WALBERG, Elsa Phyllis (Mass)

WALCOTT, Robert (O) 2173 W 7th St, Cleveland, OH 44113

WALDEN, Janice Marie (Mass) 110 Dean St., Unit #37, Taunton, MA 02780

WALDEN, Robert Eugene (The Episcopal Church in Haw) 46-290 Ikiiki St, Kaneohe, HI 96744

WALDIE, Nanette Marie (Oly) 4228 Factoria Blvd SE, Bellevue, WA 98006

WALDO JR, Mark E (Ala) 311 Lindsey Road, Coosada, AL 36020

WALDO SR, Mark Edward (Ala) 2046 Hazel Hedge Ln, Montgomery, AL 36106

✠ **WALDO**, W(illiam) Andrew (Bp of USC 2010-) 847 Kilbourne Rd, Columbia, SC 29203

WALDON, Mark W. (Nwk) 2 Marble Ct Apt 1, Clifton, NJ 07013

WALDON JR, Ray (U) 412 Shelby Springs Farms, Calera, AL 35040

WALDRON, Susan Gail (Alb) 107 State St., Albany, NY 12207

WALDRON, Teresa Jane (Cal) 920 Oak St, Sacramento, CA 94549

WALDROP, Charlotte Macon Egerton (USC) 137 Summerwood Way, Aiken, SC 29803

WALK, Everett Prichard (SwFla) 8700 State Road 72, Sarasota, FL 34241

WALKER, Aurilla Kay (Neb)

WALKER, Charles Henry (SD) 304 1st St, Wilmot, SD 57279

WALKER, David Bruce (Spok) 127 E 12th Ave, Spokane, WA 99202

WALKER, David Charles (Los) 6072 Avenida De Castillo, Long Beach, CA 90803

WALKER, Edwin Montague (SwFla) 1532 Vantage Pointe, Mount Pleasant, SC 29464

WALKER, Elizabeth Ann (WVa) 3343 Davis Stuart Road, Fairlea, WV 24902

WALKER, Frederick Wyclif (SVa) 140 Tynes St, Suffolk, VA 23434

WALKER JR, H William (SeFla) St Thomas Episcopal Parish, 5690 N Kendall Dr, Coral Gables, FL 33156

WALKER, James Arvie (NwT)

WALKER, (James) Lee (Los) 4114 South Norton Ave, Los Angeles, CA 90008

WALKER, Janice Ficke (WNC) 2709 Pleasant Run Dr, Richmond, VA 23233

WALKER III, John Edward (LI) 64 S Country Rd, Bellport, NY 11713

WALKER, Lynell Elizabeth (The Episcopal NCal) 2380 Wyda Way, Sacramento, CA 95825

WALKER, Mary Lucia (Okla) 620 E Logan Ave, Guthrie, OK 73044

WALKER, Michelle Irene (NI) St Andrew's Episcopal Church, 505 Bullseye Lake Rd, Valparaiso, IN 46383

WALKER, Noble Ray (WTenn) 6855 Branch Rd, Olive Branch, MS 38654

WALKER, Paul Edward (Ia) 510 Columbia St, Burlington, IA 52601

WALKER, Paul Nelson (Va) 100 W Jefferson St, Charlottesville, VA 22902

WALKER, Peggy (WNC) 824 Arabella St, New Orleans, LA 70115

WALKER, Robert Lynn (NY)

WALKER, Roger D. (Mich) 4800 Woodward Ave, Detroit, Mi 48201

WALKER, Samuel Clevenger (WA) Zach Fowler Road, Box 8, Chaptico, MD 20621

WALKER, Scott D (CFla) 3-6-25 Shiba-Koen, Minato-ku, Tokyo, Japan 105-0011, Japan

WALKER, Stephen Bruce (WNC) 520 Main St, Highlands, NC 28741

WALKER, Susan Kennard (WA) 1317 G St NW, Washington, DC 20005

WALKER, Terrence Alaric (SVa) PO Box 753, Lawrenceville, VA 23868

WALKER, Thomas Cecil (NC) 2933 Wycliffe Rd, Raleigh, NC 27607

WALKER, William Delany (Mil) 907 Green St, Durham, NC 27701

WALKER, William Ray (CPa) St. Paul's Episcopal Church, P.O. Box 170, Philipsburg, PA 16866

WALKER, William Royce (Wyo) 157 Pleasant Valley Rd, Hartville, WY 82215

WALKER-FRONTJES, Stacy Ann (Chi) 910 Normal Road, DeKalb, IL 60115

WALKER-SPRAGUE, Patricia Shields (Cal) 5653 Merriewood Dr, Oakland, CA 94611

WALKLEY, Richard Nelson (Ga) 918 E Ridge Village Dr, Cutler Bay, FL 33157

WALL, Anne Fuller (ECR) 535 Torrey Pine Pl, Arroyo Grande, CA 93420

WALL, Daniel Shea (NC)

WALL, Henry Pickett (USC) 5220 Clemson Ave, Columbia, SC 29206

WALL JR, John Furman (Spr) 507 Hanover St, Fredericksburg, VA 22401

WALL, John N (NC) English Dept Of Box 8105, NC State University, Raleigh, NC 27695

WALL, Richard (WA) 2430 K Street NW, Washington, DC 20037

WALL, Sean Scott (Ore) 2201 SW Vermont St, Portland, OR 97219

WALLACE, Arland Lee (Kan) 8021 W 21st St N, Wichita, KS 67205

WALLACE, Gene Richard (Los) 1775 Wilson Ave, Upland, CA 91784

WALLACE, Hugh J (SC) 10172 Ocean Hwy, Pawleys Island, SC 29585

WALLACE JR, James Edward (ETenn) Po Box 3073, Montgomery, AL 36109

WALLACE, John Bruce (EMich) 5845 Berry Lane, Indian River, MI 49749

WALLACE, John Robert (Pa) 736 11th Ave, Prospect Park, PA 19076

WALLACE, Kathryn McLaughlin (The Episcopal NCal) 701 Lassen Ln, Mount Shasta, CA 96067

WALLACE, Lance S (SwFla) 5250 Championship Cup Ln, Spring Hill, FL 34609

WALLACE, Martha Ellen (WA) 1350 Quincy St NW, Washington, DC 20011

WALLACE, Peter Marsden (At) 576 Roscoe Rd, Newnan, GA 30263

WALLACE, Robert Edgar (FdL) 2140 Bonnycastle Ave Apt 9B, Louisville, KY 40205

WALLACE, Sean Michael (NY) 119 E 74th St, New York, NY 10021

WALLACE, Tanya Rebecca (WMass) 7 Woodbridge St, South Hadley, MA 01075

WALLACE, Thomas A (Tex) 407 E 22nd Ave, Belton, TX 76513

WALLACE, William Lewis (Los) 1448 15th St Ste 203, Santa Monica, CA 90404

WALLACE-WILLIAMS, Joseph Anthony (WTenn) Grace - St Lukes Episcopal Church, 1720 Peabody Ave, Memphis, TN 38104

WALLENS, Michael Gary (Tex) 10105 Royal Highland Dr., Dallas, TX 75238

WALLER, Clifford Scott (WTex) Po Box 12349, San Antonio, TX 78212

WALLER, Stephen Jay (Dal) 8108 Crowberry Lane, Irving, TX 75063

WALLEY, Kent R (NJ) 182 Main St, P.O. Box 605, Gladstone, NJ 07934

WALLEY, Seth Martin (Miss) 113 S 9th St, Oxford, MS 38655

WALLING II, Albert Clinton (Tex) 8406 Lofty Ln, Round Rock, TX 78681
WALLING, Ann Boult (Tenn) 6501 Pennywell Dr, Nashville, TN 37205
WALLING, Carolyn M (U)
WALLING, Charles Edward (Miss) 4394 E Falcon Dr, Fayetteville, AR 72701
WALLINGFORD, Katharine Tapers (Tex) 6221 Main St, Houston, TX 77030
WALLIS, Benjamin E (Pa) Church of the Epiphany, 115 Jefferson Ave, Danville, VA 24541
WALLIS, Hugh W (Colo) 1005 S Gilpin St, Denver, CO 80209
WALLIS, James Howard (Nev) 2528 Silverton Drive, Las Vegas, NV 89134
WALLNER, Frank (Pa) 404 Levering Mill Rd., Bala Cynwyd, PA 19004
WALLNER, Ludwig (John) (Alb) 11631 Scenic Hills Blvd., Hudson, FL 34667
WALLS, Alfonso (Los)
WALMER, Corey Ann (Me) St Luke's Episcopal Church, PO Box 249, Farmington, ME 04938
WALMER, Robert Timothy (Me) 368 Knowlton Corner Rd, Farmington, ME 04938
WALMISLEY, Andrew John (The Episcopal Church in Haw) Po Box 625, Point Reyes Station, CA 94956
✠ **WALMSLEY**, Arthur Edward (Ret Bp of Ct 1993-) 644 Old County Rd, Deering, NH 03244
WALMSLEY, John W (CFla)
WALPOLE, Lisa Calhoun (SC) 464 Golf Dr, Georgetown, SC 29440
WALSER, Gay Craggs (WNY) 119 N Ellicott St, Williamsville, NY 14221
WALSH, Eileen Patricia (SVa) 519 W 20th St Apt 303, Norfolk, VA 23517
WALSH, Lora Jean (Ark) 617 N Mount Olive St, Siloam Springs, AR 72761
WALSH, Paul David (Ida) 1565 E 10th N, Mountain Home, ID 83647
WALSH, Peter F (Ct) 111 Oenoke Rdg, New Canaan, CT 06840
WALSH, Ruth Dimock (Va) 16640 Harwood Oaks Ct Apt 101, Dumfries, VA 22026
WALSH-MINOR, Gina (SwFla) 1A Hamilton Avenue, Cranford, NJ 07016
WALSTON, Gerald Wayne (Fla) 1718 Oakbreeze Ln, Jacksonville Beach, FL 32250
WALTER, Andrew W (WA) Grace Episcopal Church, 1607 Grace Church Rd, Silver Spring, MD 20910
WALTER, Aran Evan (FdL) St Thomas Episcopal Church, 226 Washington St, Menasha, WI 54952
WALTER, Cynthia Byers (WVa) PO Box 4063, Table Rock Lane, Wheeling, WV 26003
WALTER, Francis Xavier (Ala) 100 Rattlesnake Spring Ln, Sewanee, TN 37375

WALTER II, George Avery (Ore) 77287 S Ash Rd, Stanfield, OR 97875
WALTER, Kathleen Marie (SwFla) 2638 Pinewood Dr, Dunedin, FL 34698
WALTER, Verne Leroy (FdL) 12660 Red Chestnut Ln SPC 47, Sonora, CA 95370
WALTERS, Delores Marie (ND) PO Box 214, Fort Yates, ND 58538
WALTERS, Fred Ashmore (USC) 1001 12th St, Cayce, SC 29033
WALTERS, Gloria Louise (Okla) St Mark Episcopal Church, 800 S 3rd St, Hugo, OK 74743
WALTERS, James (Ark)
WALTERS, Jennifer Louise (Mich) 100 Laurel Hill Rd, Westhampton, MA 01027
WALTERS, Joshua David (Roch) Christ Church, 36 S Main St, Pittsford, NY 14534
WALTERS, Karen Graf (SVa) 150 Bella Vista Terrace, Unit D, No Venice, FL 34275
WALTERS, Lawrence Robert (Mich)
WALTERS, Robert Carroll (WMass) 17 Briarwood Circle, Worcester, MA 01606
WALTERS, Roxanne (Cal) 1217 Skycrest Dr Apt 3, Walnut Creek, CA 94595
WALTERS JR, Sumner Francis Dudley (Cal) 1217 Skycrest Dr Apt 3, Walnut Creek, CA 94595
WALTERS, William Harry (USC) 1109 W Woodmont Dr, Lancaster, SC 29720
WALTERS MALONE, Sandra A (VI) c/o St George's Episcopal Church, PO Box 28 Main St, Road Town, Tortola, British Virgin Islands VG1110, British Virgin Islands
WALTERS-PACE, Jill Anne (NwT)
WALTHALL, Charles Leroy (Eas) 224 NE 30th Street, Wilton Manors, FL 33334
WALTHER, Aileen Dianne Pallister (CFla) 753 Creekwater Ter Apt 101, Lake Mary, FL 32746
WALTON, Billy R (Miss) 608 W Jefferson St, Tupelo, MS 38804
WALTON, Carol Leighann (Nev) 234 Scotgrove St, Henderson, NV 89074
WALTON, Dunstan (LI) Po Box 399, Mount Sinai, NY 11766
WALTON JR, Harry Edwin (Mass) 100 Park Terrace Drive, Unit 143, Stoneham, MA 02180
WALTON, Hugh (Ind) 8480 Craig St Apt 5, Indianapolis, IN 46250
WALTON, James Brooke (Pa) 919 Tennis Ave, Maple Glen, PA 19002
WALTON, Joy Edemy (Del) 2550 Kensington Gdns Unit 103, Ellicott City, MD 21043
WALTON, Lori Ann (Cal) 7688 Shady Hollow Dr, Newark, CA 94560
WALTON, Macon Brantley (SVa) 202 Ridgeland Dr, Smithfield, VA 23430
WALTON, Mary Fish (Md) 1810 Park Ave, Richmond, VA 23220

WALTON, Regina Laba (Mass) Parish Of The Good Shepherd, 1671 Beacon St, Waban, MA 02468
WALTON JR, R(ichard) Lindsley Dixon (WNC) PO Box 1866, Sparta, NC 28675
WALTON, Robert Harris (WMich) 2186 Tamarack Dr, Okemos, MI 48864
WALTON, Sandra Lee (Colo)
WALTZ, William Lynn (Colo) 207 Rainbow Acres Lane, PO Box 21, Gunnison, CO 81230
WALWORTH, Diana Lynn (Mich) PO Box 287, Onsted, MI 49265
WALWORTH, James Curtis (LI) 443 River Rd Ste 210, Highland Park, NJ 08904
WALWORTH, Roy Chancellor (Wyo) 216 Southridge Rd, Evanston, WY 82930
WAMPLER, D Delos (Alb) 5 Union St Apt 3, Schenectady, NY 12305
WAMSLEY, Shawn Earl (RG) 318 Silver Ave, Albuquerque, NM 87102
WAN, Sze Kar (Mass) 87 Herrick Rd, Newton Center, MA 02459
WANAMAKER, Katherine Elizabeth (Minn) 615 Vermillion St, Hastings, MN 55033
WANCURA, Paul Forsyth (LI) Po Box 641, Shelter Island Heights, NY 11965
WAND, Thomas C. (Pa) 31 Kleyona Ave, Phoenixville, PA 19460
WANDALL, Frederick Summerson (Va) 7416 Spring Village Dr Apt 116, Springfield, VA 22150
WANG, Kit (Me) PO Box 158, East Waterboro, ME 04030
WANSTALL, Donald Penton (CFla) 719 Cobblestone Drive, Ormond Beach, FL 32174
WAPLE, Gary (WVa) RR 2 Box 243, Lewisburg, WV 24901
WARD, Barbara Pyle (Ida) 450 W Highway 30, Burley, ID 83318
WARD, Edwin Michael (Va) 8 Governors Ln, Hilton Head, SC 29928
WARD, Elizabeth Howe (Chi) 79 Meadow Hill Rd, Barrington, IL 60010
WARD, Eugene Lee (Ky) 6877 Green Meadow Cir, Louisville, KY 40207
WARD, Geoffrey Fremont (FdL) 29 Foothills Way, Bloomfield, CT 06002
WARD JR, George (Md)
WARD JR, Herbert Arthur (Nev) 112 Wyoming St, Boulder City, NV 89005
WARD, Horace David (SeFla) 18501 Nw 7th Ave, Miami, FL 33169
WARD, James Steven (Cal) 202 El Prado Ave., San Rafael, CA 94903
WARD, Jeremiah (Tex) 43 N High Oaks Cir, Spring, TX 77380
WARD, Karen Marie (Oly) 4272 Fremont Ave N, Seattle, WA 98103
WARD, Katherine Lydia (Cal) 10370 Greenview Dr, Oakland, CA 94605
WARD, Mary Christine Mollie (Spr) 1104 N Roosevelt Ave, Bloomington, IL 61701

WARD, Meredyth W (WMass) 35 Somerset St, Worcester, MA 01609
WARD, Patrick Carroll (Mass) 147 Concord Rd, Lincoln, MA 01773
WARD JR, Patrick John (NY) 75A Prospect Ave, Ossining, NY 10562
WARD, Richard Philip (Spok) 1841 Fairmount Blvd, Eugene, OR 97403
WARD IV, Samuel Mortimer (Los) 2524 Chapala St, Santa Barbara, CA 93105
WARD, Suzanne Lynn (Episcopal SJ) 1934 S Santa Fe Ave, Visalia, CA 93292
WARD JR, Thomas Reid (Tenn) Po Box 3270, Sewanee, TN 37375
WARD, Valerie K. (Los) 402 S Lincoln St, Santa Maria, CA 93458
WARDE, Erin J (Tex) 515 Columbus Ave, Waco, TX 76701
WARDER, Oran Edward (Va) 228 S Pitt St, Alexandria, VA 22314
WARE, Anita Faye (WNC) 1201 S New Hope Rd, Gastonia, NC 28054
WARE, David James (Md) 5603 N Charles St, Baltimore, MD 21210
WARE, Jordan H (FtW) All Saints' Episcopal Church, 5001 Crestline Rd, Fort Worth, TX 76107
WAREHAM, George Ludwig (NwPa) 3111 Pearl Dr, New Castle, PA 16105
WAREING, Robert Edgar (Tex) 3122 Red Maple Dr, Friendswood, TX 77546
WARFEL, John B (NY) 17 Crescent Pl, Middletown, NY 10940
WARFIELD JR, Edward Snowden (Md) 7200 Third Ave C-036, Sykesville, MD 21784
WARING, J(ames) Donald (NY) 802 Broadway, New York, NY 10003
WARLEY, Dianne (Ct) 73 Ayers Point Rd, Old Saybrook, CT 06475
WARNE II, William Thomas (CPa) 197 Urie Ave., Lake Winola, PA 18625
WARNE III, William Thomas (Oly) 2915 SE 173rd Ct, Vancouver, WA 98683
WARNECKE JR, Frederick John (NC) 3017 Lake Forest Dr, Greensboro, NC 27408
WARNER, Anthony Francis (Md) 2434 Cape Horn Rd, Hampstead, MD 21074
WARNER, Christopher Scott (At) 1315 Cove Ave, Sullivans Island, SC 29482
WARNER, Dale Alford (Fla) 2736 NW 77th Blvd Apt #152, Gainesville, FL 32606
WARNER, David Maxwell (Va) 8206 Chamberlayne Rd, Richmond, VA 23227
WARNER, Deborah Morris (Mass) Church of the Messiah, 13 Church St, Woods Hole, MA 02543
WARNER, Donald Emil (Neb) 422 W 2nd St # 1026, Grand Island, NE 68801
WARNER, Donald Nelson (Colo) 6961 S. Cherokee St., Littleton, CO 80120

WARNER, Janet Avery (EO) 444 NW Apollo Rd, Prineville, OR 97754
WARNER, John Seawright (Ga) 2211 Dartmouth Rd, Augusta, GA 30904
WARNER, Katherine Wakefield (SwFla) PO Box 272, Boca Grande, FL 33921
WARNER, Keithly R S (At) P.O. Box 468, Christiansted, VI 00821
WARNER, Kevin C (SwFla) 622 Tanana Fall Drive, Ruskin, FL 33570
WARNER JR, Richard Wright (EC) 835 Calabash Rd. NW, Calabash, NC 28467
WARNER, Suzanne McCarroll (Ky) 1265 Bassett Ave, Louisville, KY 40204
✠ **WARNER**, Vincent Waydell (Oly) Po Box 12126, Seattle, WA 98102
WARNKE, James William (Nwk) 680 Albin St, Teaneck, NJ 07666
WARNOCK, James Howard (NI) 2365 N Miller Ave, Marion, IN 46952
WARREN III, Allan Bevier (Mass) 30 Brimmer St, Boston, MA 02108
WARREN, Annika Laurin (Ct) 31 Woodland St, Hartford, CT 06105
WARREN, Daniel (Me) 730 Mere Point Rd, Brunswick, ME 04011
WARREN, George Henry (WMass) 12 Walnut Hill Rd, Pascoag, RI 02859
WARREN JR, Hallie (ETenn) 1021 Meadow Lake Rd, Chattanooga, TN 37415
WARREN, Harold Robert (Colo) 6625 Holyoke Ct, Fort Collins, CO 80525
WARREN, Heather Anne (NC) 170 Reas Ford Rd, Earlysville, VA 22936
WARREN, J Lewis (Neb) Po Box 1201, Scottsbluff, NE 69363
WARREN, John Wells (Ala) 1347 Shelton Mill Rd, Auburn, AL 36830
WARREN, Joseph Palmer (Ala) 2017 6th Ave N, Birmingham, AL 35203
WARREN, Matthew Douglas (The Episcopal NCal) Christ the King Episcopal Church, 545 Lawrence St, Quincy, CA 95971
WARREN, Penelope Sandra Muehl (Minn) 3124 Utah Ave N, Crystal, MN 55427
WARREN JR, Ralph Ray (SeFla) 223 East Tall Oaks Circle, Palm Beach Gardens, FL 33410
WARREN, Randall R (WMich) 247 W Lovell St, Kalamazoo, MI 49007
WARREN, Robert James (Eur) Christ Church, 8 rue d Bon Pasteur, Clermont-Ferrand, 63000, France
WARREN, Thomas Paine Hopfengardner (EC) 800 Rountree Ave, Kinston, NC 28501
WARREN, Timothy Grove (Los) Trinity Episcopal Church, 419 S 4th St, Redlands, CA 92373
WARREN, Victoria Daniel (Nev) 1776 Us Highway 50, Glenbrook, NV 89413
WARREN-BROWN, Judith Anne (CFla)

WARRINGTON, James Malcolm (Nwk) 2849 Meadow Ln, Falls Church, VA 22042
WARTHAN, Frank Avery (Chi) 298 S Harrison Ave, Kankakee, IL 60901
WARWICK, Charles C (Be) PO Box 406, New Milford, PA 18834
WARWICK, Eilene R (Miss) 25 Twelve Oaks Dr, Madison, MS 39110
WARWICK-SABINO, Debra Ann (The Episcopal NCal) 1405 Kentucky St, Fairfield, CA 94533
WAS, Brent Gavin (Ore) 120 Main St, Amesbury, MA 01913
WASDYKE, Wesley Roger (NH) 6569 The Masters Ave, Lakewood Ranch, FL 34202
WASHAM JR, Charles W (Lex) 2734 Chancellor Drive, Suite 202, Crestview Hills, KY 41017
WASHINGTON, Derek Wayne (Eau) 931 Leroy Ct, River Falls, WI 54022
WASHINGTON, Joyce D (NY) 657 E 222nd St, Bronx, NY 10467
WASHINGTON, Lynne Eaton (Va) 8076 Crown Colony Pkwy, Mechanicsville, VA 23116
WASINGER, Douglas Edward (Wyo) 513 E Hart St, Buffalo, WY 82834
WASTLER, Mark William (Md)
WASZCZAK, Brigid (Az) St Matthew's Episcopal Church, 9071 E Old Spanish Trail, Tucson, AZ 85710
WATAN, Jay Sapaen (Cal) 900 Edgewater Blvd, Foster City, CA 94404
WATERS, Elliott Michael (Pa) 325 Cameron Station Blvd, Alexandria, VA 22304
WATERS, Margaret Hunkin (Tex) 4902 Ridge Oak Dr, Austin, TX 78731
WATERS, Sonia E (Nwk) 369 Sand Shore Rd, Budd Lake, NJ 07828
WATERSONG, Auburn Lynn (Vt) Christ Episcopal Church, 64 State St, Montpelier, VT 05602
WATKINS, Gilbert (WVa) 2721 Riverside Dr, Saint Albans, WV 25177
WATKINS, Jane Hill (CGC) 10100 Hillview Dr Apt 2311, Pensacola, FL 32514
WATKINS, Laurel Josephine (Okla) 210 E 9th St, Bartlesville, OK 74003
WATKINS, Leeanne Ingeborg (Minn) 1895 Laurel Ave, Saint Paul, MN 55104
WATKINS, Linda King (CPa) 407 Greenwood St, Mont Alto, PA 17237
WATKINS, Lucien Alexander (SwFla) 1545 54th Ave S, Saint Petersburg, FL 33705
WATKINS, Michael Mack (Okla) 210 E 9th St, Bartlesville, OK 74003
WATROUS, Janet Couper (NC) 415 S Boylan Ave, Raleigh, NC 27603
WATSON JR, Clyde M (Va)
WATSON, George Stennis (WTenn) 1319 Cheyenne Dr., Richardson, TX 75080
WATSON, Jack Lee (Fla) 23 Cameo Drive, Flat Rock, NC 28731

WATSON, James Darrell (Tex) 1101 Tiffany Ln, Longview, TX 75604
WATSON, Janice McKee (The Episcopal Church in Haw) Episcopal Church in Micronesia, 911 N Marine Corps Dr, Tamuning, GU 96913-4302, Guam
WATSON, Karen Elizabeth (Neb) 925 S. 84th St., Omaha, NE 68114
WATSON, Margaret (SD) 3216 Kensington Avenue, Richmond, VA 23221
WATSON, Martha (Nev) St Peter's, 3695 Rogers Ave, Ellicott City, MD 21043
WATSON, Richard Avery (SVa) 9 Westwood Drive, East Haddam, CT 06469
WATSON, Robert William (Ct) 52 Missionary Rd # 22, Cromwell, CT 06416
WATSON JR, S B Joel (LI) 3216 Kensington Ave, Richmond, VA 23221
WATSON, Suzanne Elizabeth (SanD)
WATSON, Wendy (The Episcopal NCal) 990 Mee Lane, St Helena, CA 94574
WATSON III, William John (SwVa) PO Box 3123, Lynchburg, VA 24503
WATSON EPTING, Susanne K (Ia) 3026 Middle Road, Davenport, IA 52803
WATT, Gilbert Merwin (Pgh) 396 Woodlands Dr, Verona, PA 15147
WATT, Jackie (At) 605 Dunwoody Chace Ne, Atlanta, GA 30328
WATT, Jim (Tex) Rr 6 Box 88-E, Mission, TX 78574
WATTON, Sharon L (Mich) PoBox 80643, Rochester, MI 48308
WATTS, Charles Melvin (O) 4113 West State Street, Route 73, Wilmington, OH 45177
WATTS, Janice Diane (Az) St. Andrew's Episcopal Church, 6300 W. Camelback Rd., Glendale, AZ 85301
WATTS, Marilyn Ruth (The Episcopal Church in Haw)
WATTS, Robert William (Dal) 113 Summer View Ln, Pottsboro, TX 75076
WATTS, Sharon Lee Jones (Md) 4 E University Pkwy, Baltimore, MD 21218
WATTS, Timothy Joe (At)
WATTS JR, William Joseph (WMass) 19 Pleasant St, Chicopee, MA 01013
WAUTERS JR, John William (Los) 1722 Timber Oak, San Antonio, TX 78232
WAVE, John Erford (CGC) 3615 Phillips Ln, Panama City, FL 32404
WAWERU, Chris. G (LI) 215 Forward Support Battalion, Battalion & 74th St, Fort Hood, TX 76544
WAWERU, David G (LI) 2142 Modoc Dr, Harker Heights, TX 76548
WAY, Harry L (Az) 4102 W Union Hills Dr, Glendale, AZ 85308
WAY, Jacob Edson (NwT) 2807 42nd St., Lubbock, TX 79413

WAY, Michael J (NJ) 503 Asbury Ave, Asbury Park, NJ 07712
WAY, Peter Trosdal (Va)
WAY, Russell (Mass) 6969 11 Mile Rd NE, Rockford, MI 49341
WAYLAND, David Frazee (Va) 1342 Allister Green, Charlottesville, VA 22901
WAYMAN, Teresa Lachmann (WVa) 3085 Sycamore Run Road, Glenville, WV 26351
WAYNE, David Boyd (NY) Po Box 271, Rowe, MA 01367
✠ **WAYNICK**, Catherine Elizabeth Maples (Bp of Ind 1997-) 5537 Woodacre Ct., Indianapolis, IN 46234
WEATHERFORD, David William (SanD) 10835 Gabacho Dr, San Diego, CA 92124
WEATHERHOLT, Anne Orwig (Md) 19 West High Street, Hancock, MD 21750
WEATHERHOLT JR, F(loyd) Allan (Md) 2 E High Street, Hancock, MD 21750
WEATHERLY, Beverly Kay Hill (WA) 44078 Saint Andrews Church Rd, California, MD 20619
WEATHERLY, Joe E (Tenn) 640 N Washington Ave, Cookeville, TN 38501
WEATHERLY, John Armfield (Va) 8441 Porter Ln, Alexandria, VA 22308
WEATHERLY, Robert H (Miss) 1414 Chambers St, Vicksburg, MS 39180
WEATHERWAX, Elizabeth May (Pgh) 402 Royal Ct, Pittsburgh, PA 15234
WEAVER III, David England (Chi) 3835 Johnson Ave, Western Springs, IL 60558
WEAVER, Eric James (LI) 8 Oceanside Ct, Northport, NY 11768
WEAVER, Evelyn Jean (SD) 2018 13th Ave, Belle Fourche, SD 57717
WEAVER, Ivan Michael (SD)
WEAVER, Joseph Clyde (WA) 703 Winged Foot Drive, Aiken, SC 29803
WEAVER, Lorne Edward (Los) 1725 Partridge Ave., Upland, CA 91784
WEAVER, Robert Crew (O) 2553 Derbyshire Rd, Cleveland Heights, OH 44106
WEAVER, Roger Warren (Minn) Po Box 820, Tower, MN 55790
WEAVER, Sally Sykes (Mo) 2575 Sunrise Dr, Eureka, MO 63025
WEAVER, Shahar Caren (Chi) 3801 S Wabash Ave, Chicago, IL 60653
WEBB II, Alexander Henderson (WTenn) 4645 Walnut Grove Rd, Memphis, TN 38117
WEBB, Anne Slade Newbegin (NH) 43 Thorndike Pond Rd., Jaffrey, NH 03452
WEBB, Benjamin S (Ia) 511 W 12th St, Cedar Falls, IA 50613
WEBB, Estelle C (Ct) 1204 Whitney Ave Apt 309, Hamden, CT 06517
WEBB, Fain Murphey (Nwk) P.O. Box 336, Columbia, NJ 07832

WEBB, Frieda Van Baalen (WNY) 3360 McKinley Parkway, Buffalo, NY 14219
WEBB JR, James Wilson (Miss) 309 E Parkway Dr, Indianola, MS 38751
WEBB III, Joseph Baxtar (Eau) 6101 Bannocks Dr., San Antonio, TX 78239
WEBB III, Joseph Tarpley (Va) 4074 Thorngate Dr, Williamsburg, VA 23188
WEBB, Pamela Connor (Va) 8221 Old Mill Lane, Williamsburg, VA 23188
WEBB, Richard Cassius Lee (NH) 43 Thorndike Pond Rd., Jaffrey, NH 03452
WEBB, Robert Joseph (Ind) 721 W Main St, Madison, IN 47250
WEBB, Ross Allan (USC) 2534 Shiland Dr, Rock Hill, SC 29732
WEBB, William Charles (WNY) 29 Grove St, Angola, NY 14006
WEBBER, Bruce Milton (NJ) 19105 35th Avenue, Apt. J, Flushing, NY 11358
WEBBER, Christopher Lawrence (Ct) 1601 19th Avenue, San Francisco, CA 94122
WEBBER, Elizabeth A (Mich) 850 Timberline Dr, Rochester Hills, MI 48309
WEBBER, Michael Basquin (NY) Po Box 121, Paradox, NY 12858
WEBER, Claudia Jo (ECR) 2931 Cottage Ln., Paso Robles, CA 93446
WEBER, Dean A. (Nwk) 81 Highwood Ave, Tenafly, NJ 07670
WEBER, Lynne Bleich (Nwk) 81 Highwood Ave, Tenafly, NJ 07670
WEBER-JOHNSON, Jered Paul (Minn) 3001 Wisconsin Ave NW, Washington, DC 20016
WEBSTER, Alan Kim (SwVa) 229 Lee Dr, Waynesboro, VA 22980
WEBSTER, Alice Elizabeth (EC) 12903 Saint Georges Ln NW, Mount Savage, MD 21545
WEBSTER, Daniel J (Md) 5204 Downing Rd, Baltimore, MD 21212
WEBSTER, Edwin Crowe (La) 895 Will Brown Rd, Eros, LA 71238
WEBSTER, Kiah S (USC) 11540 Ferguson Rd, Dallas, TX 75228
WEBSTER, Pamela Ball (Minn) 435 Sunset Rd, Ely, MN 55731
WEBSTER II, Phillip (USC) St Mary's Church, 170 Saint Andrews Rd, Columbia, SC 29210
WEBSTER, Randy Lee (Ia) 510 Columbia St, Burlington, IA 52601
WEBSTER, Richmond Rudolphus (Ala) 202 Gordon Dr Se, Decatur, AL 35601
WEBSTER, Thomas Herbert (NC) 2906 Ridge Rd Nw, Wilson, NC 27896
WEBSTER, Valerie Minton (Mont) 311 S 3rd Ave, Bozeman, MT 59715
WEBSTER II, Warren Raymond (Chi) 51 Pine Grove, Amherst, MA 01002
WEDDERBURN, Derrick Hexford (NJ) Broadway & Royden, Cadmen, NJ 08104

WEDDLE, Karl Gilmore (ETenn) 313 Twinbrook Dr, Danville, KY 40422

WEDGWOOD-GREENHOW, Stephen John Francis (NwT) 1412 W Illinois Ave, Midland, TX 79701

WEEDON, Sarah Lipscomb (Pa) 150 E Lincoln St, Shamokin, PA 17872

WEEKS, Ann Gammon (ETenn)

WEEKS, Arianne R (Md) 1405 Boyce Ave, Towson, MD 21204

WEEKS, Jo Ann (Los) 23446 Swan St, Moreno Valley, CA 92557

WEEKS, Lawrence Biddle (Me) 12 Catherine St, Portland, ME 04102

WEEKS, WIlliam Bradley (ETenn) Grace Episcopal Church, 20 Belvoir Ave, Chattanooga, TN 37411

WEEKS WULF, Marta Joan Sutton (SeFla) 7350 SW 162nd Street, Palmetto Bay, FL 33157

WEGER, Rohani Ann (SeFla) 1225 Texas St, Houston, TX 77002

WEGLARZ, Eileen E. (NY) 98 Stewart Ave, Eastchester, NY 10709

WEGMAN, Jay Daniel (NY) Cathedral Station, Box 1111, New York, NY 10025

WEHMILLER, Paula Lawrence (Pa) 612 Ogden Ave., Swarthmore, PA 19081

WEHNER, Paul B. (Tex) 7327 Timberlake Dr, Sugar Land, TX 774798

WEHRS SR, Jack Martin (Jack) (SanD) 4062 Varona St, San Diego, CA 92106

WEI, Fei-Jan Elizabeth (Tai) 114 Fuhe Rd 6FL, Yunghe City, Taipei 23449, Taiwan

WEICKER, Harold Hastings (Cal) 220 N Zapata Hwy #11-1014, Laredo, TX 78043

WEIDMAN, Hal Joseph (At) 725 College St, Macon, GA 31201

WEIDNER, David Jeffery (Fla) 128 Bilbao Dr, Saint Augustine, FL 32086

WEIERBACH, Cornelia Miller (Va) 5613 23rd St N, Arlington, VA 22205

WEIHER, Joie Muir Clee (Va) 7057 Blackwell Rd, Warrenton, VA 20187

WEIKERT, Robert Curtis (Mich)

WEIL, Louis (Cal) 2451 Ridge Rd, Berkeley, CA 94709

WEILER, Matthew Gordon Beck (CFla) 3538 Lenox Rd, Birmingham, AL 35213

WEILER, William Leon (Va) 5908 9th St N, Arlington, VA 22205

WEINER, Margaret Yoder (Ia) 2525 Patricia Dr, Urbandale, IA 50322

WEINER, Mary Lou (Ida) 4933 W View Dr, Meridian, ID 83642

WEINER TOMPKINS, Rebecca (NY) 145 W 46th St, New York, NY 10036

WEINREICH, Gabriel (Mich) 2116 Silver Maples Drive, Chelsea, MI 48118

WEIR, Daniel Sargent (WNY) 139 Locust St, Danvers, MA 01923

WEIR, Silas Michael (Colo) 4009 Histead Way, Evergreen, CO 80439

WEISE, John Winfred Thorburn (WVa) Po Box 1642, Parkersburg, WV 26102

WEISER, Samuel Ivan (RG) 848 Camino De Levante, Santa Fe, NM 87501

WEISS, Charles Sumner (Del) PO Box, Dover, DE 19903

WEISS, Edward Allen (CFla) 200 Nw 3rd St, Okeechobee, FL 34972

WEISS, James Michael Egan (Mass) Dept of Theology, Boston College, Chestnut Hill, MA 02467

WEISS, Louise Lindecamp (RG) 3900 Trinity Dr, Los Alamos, NM 87544

WEISSMAN, Stephen Edward (Mo) 434 Gorman Bridge Rd, Asheville, NC 28806

WEITZEL, Mark Augustin (Los) 1020 N. Brand Blvd., Glendale, CA 91202

WELCH, Elizabeth Jean (Cal) Sojourn Chaplain, San Fransico General Hospital, San Fransico, CA 94110

WELCH, George Truman (Mass) 1692 Beacon St, Waban, MA 02468

WELCH, Jimmy Dean (Okla) 4250 W Houston St, Broken Arrow, OK 74012

WELCH, Lauren Marie (Md) 7 Overpark Ct, Baltimore, MD 21234

WELCH, Matthew H (WA) 763 Valley Forge Rd, Wayne, PA 19087

WELDON JR, James A (Ga) 4800 Old Dawson Rd, Albany, GA 31721

WELDON, Jonathan Naylor (Oly) 415 S. Garden Street, Bellingham, WA 98225

WELDY JR, Robert Lee (Cal) PO Box 430, Inverness, CA 94937

WELIN, Amy Doyle (Ct) 58 Brookfield Rd, Seymour, CT 06483

WELIN, Gregory William (Ct) 58 Brookfield Rd, Seymour, CT 06483

WELLER, Edith Beardall (Oly) 8216 14th Ave Ne, Seattle, WA 98115

WELLER, Gordon Frederick (Mich) 218 Ottawa St., Lansing, MI 48933

WELLER, Gretchen Kay (WMich) 435 SOM Center Road, Mayfield Village, OH 44143

WELLER JR, Thomas Carroll (CGC) 2300 W Beach Dr, Panama City, FL 32401

WELLES JR, George H. (Mass) 810 Monterrosa Dr., Myrtle Beach, SC 29572

WELLES, Hope Virginia (Mo) 4455 Atlantic Blvd, Jacksonville, FL 32207

WELLFORD, Eleanor L (Va) 510 S Gaskins Rd, Richmond, VA 23238

WELLNER, robert harry (Ct) 4750 Welby Drive, P.O. Box 142, Schnecksville, PA 18078

WELLS, Ben Reid (At) St. Francis Episcopal Church, 432 Forest Hill Road, Macon, GA 31210

WELLS, Charlotte E (Ore) 11265 SW Cabot St, Beaverton, OR 97005

WELLS, David Leonard (Spr) 1218 S Grand Ave E, Springfield, IL 62703

WELLS, Dorothy (WTenn) St. George's Episcopal Church, 2425 S.

Germantown Road, Germantown, TN 38138

WELLS, Edgar Fisher (NY) 400 W 43rd St Apt V V, New York, NY 10036

WELLS, Fletcher Marshall (SVa) St Thomas Episcopal Church, 233 Mann Dr, Chesapeake, VA 23322

WELLS, Jane Ely (Minn) 105 S Cedar St, Oberlin, OH 44074

WELLS, Jason (NH) 18 Kimball St, Pembroke, NH 03275

WELLS SR, John T (Tex) 14043 Horseshoe Cir, Woodway, TX 76712

WELLS, Lloyd Francis (At) 335 Forest Heights Dr, Athens, GA 30606

WELLS, Lynwood Daves (SwVa) Po Box 4103, Martinsville, VA 24115

WELLS, Mary Beth (SeFla) 231 Spring Hill Dr, Gordonsville, VA 22942

WELLS, Robert Louis (Tex) 9302 Sunlake Dr, Pearland, TX 77584

WELLS JR, Roy Draydon (Ala) 3608 Montclair Rd, Birmingham, AL 35213

WELLS, William Edward (Los) 202 Avenida Aragon, San Clemente, CA 92672

WELLS JR, William Smith (Va) 6914 West Grace Street, Richmond, VA 23226

WELLS MILLER, Tracy Jennifer (Tenn) St Paul's Church, 510 W Main St, Franklin, TN 37064

WELSAND, Randy Arthur (Minn) PO Box 344, Little Falls, MN 56345

WELSH, Clement William (WA) 16 N. Cherry Grove Ave., Annapolis, MD 21401

WELTSEK JR, Gustave John (Fla) 7504 Holiday Rd S, Jacksonville, FL 32216

WELTY III, Terrence Anthony (Tex) 106 E Crawford St, Palestine, TX 75801

WELTY, Winston Wayne (Pa) Santa Clara #613, Riberas del Pilar, Chapala, Jalisco 45900, Mexico

WENDEL JR, David Deaderick (Ala) 210 Oak Ct, New Braunfels, TX 78132

WENDEL, Richard Joseph Bosley (Chi) 536 W Fullerton Pkwy, Chicago, IL 60614

WENDELL, Christopher Scott (Mass) St. Paul's Church, 100 Pine Hill Road, Bedford, MA 01730

WENDELL, Martin Paul (Alb) 405 Master St, Valley Falls, NY 12185

WENDFELDT, Stephen Hoff (SanD)

WENGROVIUS, John H. (Colo) 1320 Arapahoe St, Golden, CO 80401

WENGROVIUS, Stephen A (Colo) 3712 W 99th Ave, Westminster, CO 80031

WENNER, Peter Woodring (Mass) 137 Auburndale Ave, West Newton, MA 02465

WENNER, Rachel Elizabeth (Colo) Ch Of The Ascension & Holy Trinity, 420 W 18th St, Pueblo, CO 81003

WENRICK, Heather Marie (Ore) 1444 Liberty St SE, Salem, OR 97302

WENTHE, Elizabeth Ann (Me) 35 Paris St, Norway, ME 04268
WENTT, Allan Rudolphus (Va) 7503 Noble Avenue, Richmond, VA 23227
WERDAL, Evelyn Paige (NY) 522 Walnut St, Mamaroneck, NY 10543
WERNER, Frederick John Emil (Mich) 13070 Independence Ave, Utica, MI 48315
WERNER, George Louis William (Pgh) 106 Sewickley Heights Dr., Sewickley, PA 15143
WERNER, Mark (USC) 2 N Hill Ct, Columbia, SC 29223
WERNICK, Mike (WMich) 1800 Bloomfield Dr. SE, Kentwood, MI 49508
WERNTZ, Pamela Louise (Mass) 120 Marshall St, Watertown, MA 02472
WESCH, Kate (Oly) 1805 38th Ave, Seattle, WA 98126
WESEN, Vicki Jane Smaby (Oly) 1500A E College Way # 447, Mount Vernon, WA 98273
WESLEY, Carol Ann (Mo) 5519 Alaska Ave, Saint Louis, MO 63111
WESLEY JR, John William (Ala) 1215 Oak St, Montevallo, AL 35115
WESSELL, David E (FdL) 2805 Elgin St, Durham, NC 27704
WEST, Anne K (WVa) Christ Episcopal Church, Clarksburg, WV 26301
WEST, Barbara Field (Ct) 7 Hillcrest Rd, Manchester, CT 06040
WEST, Clark Russell (CNY) G3 Anabel Taylor Hall, Ithaca, NY 14853
WEST, Craig Alan (SD) Po Box 532, Martin, SD 57551
WEST, Geoffrey George (NJ) 525 Willowbrook Dr, Jeffersonville, PA 19403
WEST, Hilary Morgan (EC)
WEST, Hillary T (Va) 4212 Kingcrest Pkwy, Richmond, VA 23221
WEST JR, Irvin D (Ark) 401 E 10th St, Little Rock, AR 72202
WEST, Jan Hickman (Cal) 171 Prospect Ave, San Anselmo, CA 94960
WEST, Jennifer K (SO) 233 S. State St., Westerville, OH 43081
WEST JR, John Richard (Ga) 4227 Columbia Rd, Martinez, GA 30907
WEST, John Thomas (NMich) 301 N 1st St, Ishpeming, MI 49849
WEST, John Timothy (SO) 600 Dorothy Moore Avenue, Unit 10, Urbana, OH 43078
WEST, Kathleen Farson (Episcopal SJ) 707 S Orange Grove Blvd Apt D, Pasadena, CA 91105
WEST, Philip (RG) 2243 Henry Rd Sw, Albuquerque, NM 87105
WEST, R(andolph) Harrison (Ct) 11 Park St, Guilford, CT 06437
WEST, Scott A (SwVa) 120 Church St NE, P.O. Box 164, Blacksburg, VA 24063
WESTBERG, Daniel Arnold (Mil) 2777 Mission Rd, Nashotah, WI 53058

WESTBURY JR, Richard Smith (Fla) 15 N Wilderness Trl, Ponte Vedra Beach, FL 32082
WEST-DOOHAN, Sue (Be) HC 75 Box 32, Strange Creek, WV 25063
WESTERBERG, George Arthur (Mass) 212 North Lower Bay Road, Lovell, ME 04051
WESTERHOFF III, John Henry (At) 49 Old Ivy Sq Ne, Atlanta, GA 30342
WESTFALL, Doris Ann (Mo) 28 Whinhill Ct, Saint Peters, MO 63304
WESTHORP, Peter Henry Glen (RI) 2574 Creve Coeur Mill Rd, Maryland Heights, MO 63043
WESTLING JR, Lester Leon (The Episcopal NCal) 573 Royal Oaks Dr, Redding, CA 96001
WESTON, English Hopkins (USC) 1017 Elm Savannah Rd, Hopkins, SC 29061
WESTON, Jane Mitchell (At) PO Box 102, Conyers, GA 30012
WESTON, Myrtle Marguerite (NMich) 107 Forest Ridge Dr, Marquette, MI 49855
WESTON, Stephen Richard (Colo) 2021 South Xenia Way, Denver, CO 80231
WESTPFAHL, Carol Elizabeth (ETenn) 210 Redwolf Way, Lenoir City, TN 37772
WESTPHAL, Edie H (The Episcopal NCal) 120 E J St, Benicia, CA 94510
WESTPHAL, Stacey Elizabeth (CFla) 522 Summerset Ct, Indian Harbour Beach, FL 32937
WETHERED, Stephanie Keith (Nwk) 224 Cornelia St, Boonton, NJ 07005
WETHERILL, Benjamin Wade (Me) P.O. Box 156, Rangeley, ME 04970
WETHERINGTON, Robert William (Miss) PO Box 366, Sumner, MS 38957
WETHERINGTON, Timothy R (CFla) Church Of The Messiah, 241 N Main St, Winter Garden, FL 34787
WETHERN, James Douglas (Ga) PO Box 20327, Saint Simons Island, GA 31522
WETMORE, Ian Colden (Spr) St Michael's Episcopal Church, 111 Ofallon Troy Rd, O Fallon, IL 62269
WETTSTEIN, David William (Ida) 6925 Copper Dr, Boise, ID 83704
WETZEL, Mary A (At) P.O. Box 4548, Atlanta, GA 30302
WETZEL, Todd Harold (Dal) Po Box 429, Cedar Hill, TX 75106
WEYLS, Richard Coleman (Oly) 747 Broadway, Seattle, WA 98122
WEYMOUTH, Richard Channing (NH) RR3 Box 18, Plymouth, NH 03264
WHALEN, Dena Stokes (EC) P.O. Box 490, Clarkesville, GA 30523
WHALEN, Donald (Eas) 2929 SE Ocean Blvd O-5, Stuart, FL 34996
WHALEN, Peter James (Tenn) 103 Northwood Ave, Shelbyville, TN 37160

WHALEY, Stephen Foster (Tex) 605 Dulles Avenue, Stafford, TX 77477
WHALLON, Diane (Fla) 1640 NE 40th Ave Apt 106, Ocala, FL 34470
☩ **WHALON**, Pierre W (Bp Suffr of Eur 2001-) 23 Avenue George V, Paris, 75008, France
WHARTON III, George Franklin (Ia) 502 W Broadway St, Decorah, IA 52101
WHARTON, Roger E (ECR) 1404 Arnold Ave, San Jose, CA 95110
WHEATLEY, Gail (Oly) St Andrew's Episcopal Church, 510 E. Park Ave, Port Angeles, WA 98362
WHEATLEY, Paul David (Dal) Church of the Incarnation, 3966 McKinney Ave, Dallas, TX 75204
WHEATLEY-JONES, Elizabeth (Miss) P.O. Box 345, Grenada, MS 38902
WHEATON, Philip Eugene (Roch) 7211 Spruce Ave, Takoma Park, MD 20912
WHEELER, Charles Ralph (WNY) 161 E Main St, Westfield, NY 14787
WHEELER, Diana Roberta (Cal) 573 Dolores st., San Francisco, CA 94110
WHEELER, Elisa Desportes (Va) 638 Burton Point Rd, Mathews, VA 23068
WHEELER, Evelyn (Ind)
WHEELER, Fran (Kan) 14301 S Blackbob Rd, Olathe, KS 66062
WHEELER, James R (Ct) Po Box 10, Woodbury, CT 06798
WHEELER, John Bevan (Md) 2795 Topmast Ct, Annapolis, MD 21401
WHEELER, Kathryn Brown (CGC) 2002 W Lakeridge Dr, Albany, GA 31707
WHEELER JR, Louis (WA) 2001 14th St Se, Washington, DC 20020
WHEELER, Rhonda Estes (SVa) St. Andrew's Episcopal Church, 45 Main Street, Newport News, VA 23601
WHEELER, William Ramsey (Alb) Po Box 354, Boonville, NY 13309
WHEELOCK, Janet (Minn) 90 Seymour Ave SE, Minneapolis, MN 55414
WHEELOCK, L(eslie) Gail (RI) 8 Neptune St, Jamestown, RI 02835
WHELAN, Edgar Joseph (WMo) 13500 Rinehart Ln, Parkville, MO 64152
WHELAN, Janet Kay (WMo) 13500 Rinehart Ln, Parkville, MO 64152
WHELAN, Peter Hainsworth (Ky) 1207 Meadowridge Trl, Goshen, KY 40026
WHELCHEL, Judith Hester (WNC) 67 Windsor Rd, Asheville, NC 28804
WHENAL, Barry (FdL) 6535 Oriole Road, Lake Tomahawk, WI 54539
WHENNEN, John (Chi) 2640 Park Dr, Flossmoor, IL 60422
WHETSTONE, Raymond David (Ala) Grace Episcopal Church, PO Box 1791, Anniston, AL 36202

WHIDDON, Ennis Howard (USC) 301 Piney Mountain Rd, Greenville, SC 29609

WHISENHUNT, William Allen (WNC) Trinity Episcopal Church, 60 Church St, Asheville, NC 28801

WHISTLER, Tamsen Elizabeth (Mo) 1020 N Duchesne Dr, Saint Charles, MO 63301

WHITAKER, Ann Latham (Miss) 806 Prairie View Road, Oxford, MS 38655

WHITAKER, Bradford G (ETenn) 305 W 7th St, Chattanooga, TN 37402

WHITAKER III, Howard Wilson (Nwk) PO Box 596, Scottsboro, AL 35768

WHITAKER, James Stewart (Mass) 44 Newport Rd, Westford, MA 01886

WHITAKER, Monica (RG) 3900 Alameda De Las Pulgas, San Mateo, CA 94403

WHITBECK, Bailey Ogden (Mass) 29 Princess Rd, West Newton, MA 02465

WHITE, Andrew D'Angio (Roch) 3601 Russell Rd, Alexandria, 22305

WHITE JR, Arthur Bain (Colo) St Mark's Episcopal Church, PO Box 534, Craig, CO 81626

WHITE, Bruce Alan (Az) 7267 E Onda Cir, Tucson, AZ 85715

WHITE, Carolyn Constance (ECR) 13723 Monte Bello, Castroville, CA 95012

WHITE SR, Cyril Edward (SeFla) 15001 Polk St, Miami, FL 33176

WHITE, Deborah Ottilie (Cal) 2837 Claremont Blvd, Berkeley, CA 94705

WHITE, Dorothy Ann (Va) 6001 Grove Ave, Richmond, VA 23226

WHITE, Hank (Pa) 408 Valley Ave, Atglen, PA 19310

WHITE, Harold Naylor (Va) Po Box 326, Wicomico Church, VA 22579

WHITE, Helen Slingluff (Ga) 15 Willow Rd, Savannah, GA 31419

WHITE III, Hugh Couch (Va) 664 Dungeons Thicket Rd, White Stone, VA 22578

WHITE, James Lee (Del) 39 Gainsborough Dr, Lewes, DE 19958

WHITE, Jon Michael (WVa) St Stephen's Episcopal Church, 200 Virginia St, Beckley, WV 25801

WHITE, K Alon (NY) 124 N Broadway, Nyack, NY 10960

WHITE, Karin Kay (ECR) 390 N Winchester Blvd Apt 9B, Santa Clara, CA 95050

WHITE, Kathryn L (Chi) 3052 Jeffrey Dr, Joliet, IL 60435

WHITE, Kathryn Sawyer (WMass) 129 Roseland Park Road, Woodstock, CT 06281

WHITE, Kenneth Gordon (Mass) 11 Anita St, Sabattus, ME 04280

WHITE, Kenneth Orgill (WLa)

WHITE, Konrad Shepard (Ga) 524 E Duffy St, Savannah, GA 31401

WHITE, Kristin U (Chi) 400 E Westminster, Lake Forest, IL 60045

WHITE, Laura Dale (USC) 522 NW 8th St, Pendleton, OR 97801

WHITE, Lynn Scott (Chi) 1546 Bobolink Cir, Woodstock, IL 60098

WHITE, M(ary) (Md) 2125 Beach Village Court, Annapolis, MD 21403

WHITE, Mary Margaret Robinson (Alb) 10 N Main Ave, Albany, NY 12203

WHITE, Michael S (Ga) 308A Bradley Point Rd, Savannah, GA 31410

WHITE, Michelle Denise (Nwk) 707 Washington St, Hoboken, NJ 07030

WHITE, Nancy Anne (Md) 3267 Stepney St, Edgewater, MD 21037

WHITE, Nicholson Barney (O) 1109 Hollyheath Ln, Charlotte, NC 28209

WHITE JR, Paul Donald (WTenn) 3553 Windgarden Cv, Memphis, TN 38125

WHITE, R Scott (WNC) Trinity Church, 60 Church St, Asheville, NC 28801

WHITE, R(Ita) Ellen (Va) 138 Pier Place, Kinsale, VA 22488

WHITE, Roger Bradley (Ct) Po Box 309, Kent, CT 06757

WHITE, Rowena Ruth (WLa) 8212 Argosy Ct, Baton Rouge, LA 70809

WHITE, Sara D'Angio (Roch) Christ Church, 36 S Main St, Pittsford, NY 14534

WHITE, Stanley James (Ga) 101 E Central Ave Fl 3, Valdosta, GA 31601

WHITE, Stephen James (Me) 49 Mills Road, Newcastle, ME 04553

WHITE, Stephen Lawrence (NJ) 2325 Hancock Road, Williamstown, MA 01267

✠ **WHITE**, Terry Allen (Bp of Ky 2010-) 425 S Second St Suite 200, Louisville, KY 40202

WHITE, Thomas Harrington (Colo) 1215 Union Ave, North Platte, NE 69101

WHITE, Thomas Rees (Ct) 109 Sand Hill Rd, South Windsor, CT 06074

WHITE, Warner Clock (WMich) 12 Harbor Watch Rd., Burlington, VT 05401

WHITE, William DeAlton (Me) 21 Bodwell St, Brunswick, ME 04011

WHITE, William Steven (ETenn) 1101 N Broadway St, Knoxville, TN 37917

WHITEFORD, Cecily (WNY) 45 S Cayuga Rd Apt G3, Williamsville, NY 14221

WHITE-HASSLER, M(argaret) Jane (Ct) 130 Vincent Dr, Newington, CT 06111

WHITEHEAD, Danny Ray (ND) 808 4th Ave NE, Devils Lake, ND 58301

WHITEHEAD, Philip Hoyle (USC) 6026 Crabtree Rd, Columbia, SC 29206

WHITE HORSE-CARDA, Patricia Ann (SD) 500 S Main Ave, Sioux Falls, SD 57104

WHITEHURST, Joseph Stewart (USC) 173 Kendallwood Ct, Aiken, SC 29803

WHITELAW, Eleanor Drake (CGC) PO Box 536, Eufaula, AL 36072

WHITELEY, Raewynne Jean (LI) 15 Highland Ave, Saint James, NY 11780

WHITESEL, Ann Brier (CPa) 12 Strawberry Dr, Carlisle, PA 17013

WHITESELL, Hugh A (NC) 756 Apple Ct. Apt A, Lebanon, OH 45036

WHITESIDE, Henry Burton (EC) 7 Masonic Ave, Shelburne Falls, MA 01370

WHITFIELD, Ann Adams (Nev) 10810 NE Sherwood Dr., Vancouver, WA 98686

WHITFIELD, Deirdre (Pa) 126 Westminster Dr, Wallingford, PA 19086

WHITFIELD, Mary Dean (NwT) Rr 2 Box 460, Quanah, TX 79252

WHITFIELD, Raymond Palmer (Tex) 12501 LONGHORN PKWY APT A360, AUSTIN, TX 78732

WHITFIELD, Stephen Ray (Tex) 2301 Lauren Loop, Leander, TX 78641

WHITFORD, Michele E (FdL) 1220 N 7th St, Sheboygan, WI 53081

WHITING, William Richard (WMich) 2165 Chesapeake Dr Ne, Grand Rapids, MI 49505

WHITLEY, Ryan Randolph (Pa) 1 W Ardmore Ave, Ardmore, PA 19003

WHITLOCK III, Robin (SwFla) 949 41st Ave N, Saint Petersburg, FL 33703

WHITMAN, Marian Chandler (WTenn) 2425 S Germantown Rd, Germantown, TN 38138

WHITMER, Marlin Lee (Ia) 2602 250th St, De Witt, IA 52742

WHITMER, Ronald Delane (La) 5400 Courtyard Dr., Gonzales, LA 70737

WHITMIRE JR, Norman (LI) 8545 96th St, Woodhaven, NY 11421

WHITMORE, Bruce Gregory (Tex) 1401 Avenue O #F, Huntsville, TX 77340

WHITMORE, Charles William (WNY) 3802 James St. Unit 30, Bellingham, WA 98226

WHITMORE, Elizabeth Needham (Mass) 1391 Hyannis Barnstable Rd, Barnstable, MA 02630

✠ **WHITMORE**, Keith Bernard (Asst Bp of At 2010-) 3496 Paces Pl NW, Atlanta, GA 30327

WHITMORE, Paula Michele (Spok) 602 Nw 10th St, Pendleton, OR 97801

WHITNAH, John C (ND) Gethsemane Cathedral, 3600 25th St S, Fargo, ND 58104

WHITNEY, Ann Carolyn (Ak) PO Box 870995, Wasilla, AK 99687

WHITNEY, Marilla Jane (Minn) 1305 - 4th Ave., Windom, MN 56101

WHITNEY, Wayne Vohn (Az) Episcopal Church of the Nativity, 22405 N Miller Rd, Scottsdale, AZ 85255

WHITNEY-WISE, Stephen D (Ore) 4033 SE Woodstock Blvd., Portland, OR 97202

WHITSITT, Helen Bonita (WMo) PO Box 57, Fayette, MO 65248

WHITTAKER, Brendan Joseph (NH) 1788 Vt Route 102, Guildhall, VT 05905

WHITTAKER JR, Richard Russell (U) 1784 Aaron Dr., Tooele, UT 84074

WHITTAKER-NAVEZ, Christine Ruth (Mass) 223 Pond St, Hopkinton, MA 01748

WHITTED, Warren Rohde (Neb) 8141 Farnam Dr Apt 328, Omaha, NE 68114

WHITTEN, James Austin (CFla) St Mary of the Angels, 6316 Matchett Rd, Orlando, FL 32809

WHITTEN, W Roy (ECR) 11197 Via Vis, Nevada City, CA 95959

WHITTINGTON, Nancy Susan (WNC) 140 Chestnut Cir, Blowing Rock, NC 28605

WHITTINGTON, Richard Culbertson (Tex)

WHITTLE, Natalie Wang (Ga) 102 S Jackson Rd, Statesboro, GA 30461

WHITWORTH, Julia E (NY) 19 Walden St, West Hartford, CT 06107

WHYTE, Horace Maxwell (NY) 170 W End Ave Apt 30-H, New York, NY 10023

WIBLE, Christina Karen Kirchner (NJ) 10 N Slope, Clinton, NJ 08809

WIBLE, Terrence Linn (CPa) 57 Piper Dr, New Oxford, PA 17350

WICHAEL, Karen (Kan) 5648 W 92nd Pl, Overland Park, KS 66207

WICHELNS, Anne Brett (CNY) St. Andrew's Shared Ministry, 8520 LeRay St., Evans Mills, NY 13637

WICHELNS, Jerome Bailey (CNY) 10751 Limburg Forks Rd, Carthage, NY 13619

WICHMAN, James Henry (O) 2314 Oak Glen Ct, Akron, OH 44333

WICK, Calhoun W (Del) Po Box 3719, Wilmington, DE 19807

WICKHAM, Jonathan William (WTex) 15670 Robin Ridge, San Antonio, TX 78248

WICKHAM III, William Hunt (Del) 9410 Creek Summit Circle, Richmond, VA 23235

WICKIZER, Bob (Okla) 218 N 6th St, Muskogee, OK 74401

WIDDOWS, John Herbert (Me) 340 Promenade #125, Portland, ME 04101

WIDING, C(arl) Jon (Ct) 47 Fox Holw, Avon, CT 06001

WIECKING III, Frederick August (Ind) 4 Sunnyside Rd, Silver Spring, MD 20910

WIEHE, Philip Freeman (NC) 3676 Laurel Park Highway, Hendersonville, NC 28739

WIELAND, William David (Ind) (same as above), Greencastle, IN 46135

WIENK, Dennis L (Roch) 274 Rosedale St, Rochester, NY 14620

WIENS, Dolores Flaming (NI) 315 W Harrison Ave, Wheaton, IL 60187

WIENS HEINSOHN, Lisa Marie (Minn) 2136 Carter Ave, Saint Paul, MN 55108

WIESNER, A(ugust) Donald (NJ) 208 Live Oak Ln, Washington, NC 27889

WIESNER, Kurt Christopher (U) 261 S 900 E, Salt Lake City, UT 84102

WIETSTOCK, Anne Kimberley (NI) 117 N Lafayette Blvd, South Bend, IN 46601

WIGGERS, John Mark (ETenn) 1101 N Broadway St, Knoxville, TN 37917

WIGGINS JR, Eschol Vernon (Ga) 1009 Hillcrest Dr, Cochran, GA 31014

WIGGINS, Reese H (La) 17764 Jefferson Ridge Dr, Baton Rouge, LA 70817

WIGG-MAXWELL, Elizabeth Parker (Nwk) 44 Pittsford Way, New Providence, NJ 07974

WIGHT, Andrea Lee (Chi) 7398 Bell Vista Terrace, Rockford, IL 61107

WIGHT, Susan Moore (USC) 5 Blackhawk Ct, Blythewood, SC 29016

WIGHT, William Wallace (USC) 5 Blackhawk Ct, Blythewood, SC 29016

WIGLE, John Whitcombe (O) 814 Westport Dr, Youngstown, OH 44511

WIGMORE, William Joseph (Tex) 1701 Rock Creek Dr, Round Rock, TX 78681

WIGNER JR, J Douglas (Va) 1802 Dover Pointe Ct, Henrico, VA 23238

WIGODSKY, Andrea (SVa) St. Andrew's Episcopal Church, 1009 West Princess Anne Rd., Norfolk, VA 23507

WIKE, Antoinette Ray (NC) 221 Union St, Cary, NC 27511

WILBERT, Brian Kurt (O) 162 S Main St, Oberlin, OH 44074

WILBURN, J Mark (Tex) 24 McFaddan LN, Temple, TX 76502

WILBURN, Merry Ilene (Tex) 16830 Blairstone, Houston, TX 77084

WILCOX, Diana L (Nwk) St Luke's Episcopal Church, 73 S Fullerton Ave, Montclair, NJ 07042

WILCOX, Glen Miley (Ak)

WILCOX JR, Jack Franklyn (Okla) 101 Great Oaks Dr, Norman, OK 73071

WILCOX, John Milton (Episcopal SJ) 3909 Noel Pl, Bakersfield, CA 93306

WILCOX, Melissa Quincy (Mil)

WILCOXSON, Frederick Dean (CFla) 154 Terry Lane, Benton, TN 37307

WILCOXSON, JoAnn Vanessa (CFla) 154 Terry Lane, Benton, TN 37307

WILD, Geoffrey Mileham (NwPa) PO Box 287, Grove City, PA 16127

WILD III, Philip Charles (La) 120 S New Hampshire St, Covington, LA 70433

WILDE, Gary A (SwFla) 2306 Hermitage Blvd, Venice, FL 34292

WILDE, Gregory Dean (Mil) 1855 Park Dr, Columbus, GA 31906

WILDER, Marilyn Mae (Spok) 617 10th St, Oroville, WA 98844

WILDER III, Tracy Hartwell (SwFla) 13720 Sweat Loop Rd., Wamauma, FL 33598

WILDER, Virginia Cuthbert (Del) Trinity Episcopal Church, 1108 N Adams St, Wilmington, DE 19801

WILDGOOSE, Angelo Stanley (Pa) 6361 Lancaster Ave, Philadelphia, PA 19151

WILDMAN, Rachel Preston (NY) 100 Pine Hill Rd, Bedford, MA 01730

WILDSMITH, Joseph Ned (NJ) 808 S Delhi St, Philadelphia, PA 19147

WILE, Mary Lee Hanford (Me) 45 Baker St, Yarmouth, ME 04096

WILEMON, Zane Howard (Cal) 81 N 2nd St, San Jose, CA 95113

WILEY, George Bell (Kan) 2313 Willow Crk, Lawrence, KS 66049

WILEY, Henrietta Lovejoy (Md) Cathedral of the Incarnation, 4 E University Pkwy, Baltimore, MD 21218

WILEY, Judi A (SO) 234 N. High St., Hillsboro, OH 45133

WILEY, Ronald Lee (Neb) 102 Lakeview Rd, Fremont, NE 68025

WILHELM, Joseph (Los) 404 W Santa Ana St., Ojai, CA 93023

WILKE, Carl Edward (WMo) 3 Pursuit, #323, Aliso Viejo, CA 92656

WILKERSON, Bonnie Carver (Ia) St Luke's Episcopal Church, 605 Avenue E, Fort Madison, IA 52627

WILKERSON, Charles Edward (Md) St Luke's Episcopal Church, 1101 Bay Ridge Ave, Annapolis, MD 21403

WILKES, Hugh (Alb)

WILKES III, Joseph (Mass) 186 Upham St, Melrose, MA 02176

WILKING, Spencer Van Bokkelen (NY) 35 Robin Wood Rd, Concord, MA 01742

WILKINS JR, Aaron Ellis (CGC) 6604 Carolina Ct, Mobile, AL 36695

WILKINS, Ann Purkeypile (NwT) 808 Stone Mountain Dr, Conroe, TX 77302

WILKINS, Christopher Ian (WA) PO Box 207, St Marys City, MD 20686

WILKINS, Palmer Oliver (Cal) 58 Robinhood Dr, Novato, CA 94945

WILKINSON, Donald Charles (Mo) 17210 Fawn Cloud Ln, San Antonio, TX 78248

WILKINSON, Ernest Benjamin (NwT) 727 W Browning Ave, Pampa, TX 79065

WILKINSON, James Royse (Ky) 1804 Leawood Ct, Louisville, KY 40222

WILKINSON, John Preston (SwVa) 1207 Middlebrook Rd, Staunton, VA 24401

WILKINSON, Joyce Ann (WVa)

WILKINSON, Julia Sierra (Ga) Christ Church Episcopal, 18 Abercorn St, Savannah, GA 31401

WILKINSON, Kirsteen (Ind) 7834 Grand Gulch Dr, Indianapolis, IN 46239

WILKINSON, Marcia Campbell (Ala) 6634 31st Pl NW, Washington, DC 20015

WILKINSON, Mark David (SVa) St. Aidan's Episc Church, 3201 Edinburgh Dr., Virginia Beach, VA 23452

WILKINSON, Mary Suzanne (NwT) 727 W Browning Ave, Pampa, TX 79065

WILKINSON, Shivaun Renee (WA) 3820 Aspen Hill Rd, Silver Spring, MD 20906

WILKINSON, Wendy Johns (SVa) Good Samaritan Episcopal Church, 848 Baker Rd, Virginia Beach, VA 23462

WILLARD V, John Dayton (Md) 1634 Orchard Beach Rd, Annapolis, MD 21409

WILLARD, Neil Alan (Tex) Palmer Memorial Church, 6221 Main St, Houston, TX 77030

WILLARD JR, Wilson Howard (SO) 1305 Cutter St, Cincinnati, OH 45203

WILLARD-WILLIFORD, Joyce Ann (CFla) 5625 Holy Trinity Dr, Melbourne, FL 32940

WILLCOX, Halley Luddy (At) 805 Mount Vernon Hwy Nw, Atlanta, GA 30327

WILLE, Elizabeth Suzanne (Ind) 1559 N Central Ave, Indianapolis, IN 46202

WILLEMS, James Rutherford (Los) 561 48th Street, Oakland, CA 94609

WILLERER, Rhonda Louise (Fla) St. Patrick's Episcopal Church, 1221 State Rd 13, St. Johns, FL 32259

WILLETT, Patty (NC) Christ Church, 1412 Providence Rd, Charlotte, NC 28207

WILLIAMS JR, A Lenwood (Miss) 9378 Harroway Rd, Summerville, SC 29485

WILLIAMS, Alfredo Ricardo (Dal) 1516 N Leland Ave, Indianapolis, IN 46219

WILLIAMS, Alina Somodevilla (La) PO Box 126, Baton Rouge, LA 70821

WILLIAMS, Alton Paul (CPa) 5 Greenway Dr, Mechanicsburg, PA 17055

✠ WILLIAMS JR, Arthur Benjamin (Ret Bp Suffr of O 2003-) 25530 Edgecliff Dr, Euclid, OH 44132

WILLIAMS, Arthur Wordsworth Lonfellow (NY) 3412 103rd St, Corona, NY 11368

WILLIAMS, Bruce McKennie (RG) 7201 San Benito St Nw, Albuquerque, NM 87120

WILLIAMS, Carolynne Juanita Grant (At) 2088 Cloverdale Dr Se, Atlanta, GA 30316

WILLIAMS, C(ecil) David (Nwk) 515 Parker St, Newark, NJ 07104

WILLIAMS, Colin Harrington (CNY) 2850 SW Scenic Drive, Portland, OR 97225

WILLIAMS, Courtly G (Chi) 425 Laurel Ave, Highland Park, IL 60035

WILLIAMS, David Alexander (EC) 115 NE 66th Street, Oak Island, NC 28645

WILLIAMS, David Anthony (SC) St. Stephen's Episcopal Church, 67 Anson St, Charleston, SC 29401

WILLIAMS, David R (NC) 1406 Victoria Ct, Elon, NC 27244

WILLIAMS, Donald B (Kan) 2510 Grand Blvd. #1103, Kansas City, MO 64108

WILLIAMS, Douglas Elliott (ECR) 1718 Crater Lake Ave, Milpitas, CA 95035

WILLIAMS, Douglas Maclin (Colo) 28 Cunningham Pond Rd, Peterborough, NH 03458

WILLIAMS, Edward Earl (NY)

WILLIAMS, Edward S (Ga) 353 Midway Circ, Brunswick, GA 31523

WILLIAMS, Elizabeth Ann (Los) 512 E Williams St, Barstow, CA 92311

WILLIAMS, Eric Matthew (Mich) 1948 Hunters Ridge Dr, Bloomfield Hills, MI 48304

WILLIAMS JR, Ernest Franklin (Los) 1438 Coronado Ter, Los Angeles, CA 90026

WILLIAMS, Florence Darcy (Eas) Diocese of Easton, 314 North St, Easton, MD 21601

WILLIAMS, Francis Edward (RG) 1020 Sable Circle, Las Cruces, NM 88001

WILLIAMS, Gary Wayne (Okla) 3804 Cobble Cir, Norman, OK 73072

WILLIAMS, Glen Parker (WMich) 12057 S Elk Run, Traverse City, MI 49684

WILLIAMS, Glenn Thomas (ND) 3613 River Dr S, Fargo, ND 58104

WILLIAMS, Henrietta Rhodes Smith (Ind) 115 Ne 66th St, Oak Island, NC 28645

WILLIAMS, Henry N (Pa) 1029 Fox Hollow Rd, Shermans Dale, PA 17090

WILLIAMS JR, Hollis R (Oly) 725 9th Ave Apt 2007, Seattle, WA 98104

WILLIAMS, Howard Kently (LI) 1102 E 73rd St Apt C, Brooklyn, NY 11234

WILLIAMS III, Hugh Elton (CFla) Po Box 91777, Lakeland, FL 33804

WILLIAMS, Jacqueline Miller (SO) 6461 Tylersville Rd, West Chester, OH 45069

WILLIAMS, James Armstrong (Tex) 11403 Madrid Dr, Austin, TX 78759

WILLIAMS II, James Edward (Los) 580 Hilgard Ave, Los Angeles, CA 90024

WILLIAMS, James Wallace (Ala) 2130 Enon Mill Dr Sw, Atlanta, GA 30331

WILLIAMS JR, (Jerre) Stockton (WTex) 320 Saint Peter St, Kerrville, TX 78028

WILLIAMS, Jeryln Ann (SD) 431 Sweden St, Caribou, ME 04736

WILLIAMS, Jill Barton (WMass) St Francis, 70 Highland St, Holden, MA 01520

WILLIAMS II, John F (NY) 9997 Aplomado Cir, Sandy, UT 84092

WILLIAMS, John Gerald (Tex) 1101 Rock Prairie Rd, College Station, TX 77845

WILLIAMS, Joseph Anthony (CNY) 11 Gillette Ln, Cazenovia, NY 13035

WILLIAMS, Joseph David (NwT) 1105 1/2 Madison St, Borger, TX 79007

WILLIAMS, Josie Marie (Miss) 5930 Warriors Trl, Vicksburg, MS 39180

WILLIAMS, Julie Ann (Az) 100 Arroyo Pinon Dr, Sedona, AZ 86336

WILLIAMS, Larry C (At) Po Box 1117, Hot Springs, AR 71902

WILLIAMS, Lloyd Clyde (Ind)

WILLIAMS, Lois Vander Wende (Cal) 455 Fair Oaks St., San Francisco, 94110

WILLIAMS, Lorna Hyacinth (Mich) 1224 West Chester Pike, Apt C11, West Chester, PA 19382

WILLIAMS, Margaret A (Chi) 707 1st Ave, Sterling, IL 61081

WILLIAMS, Margaret Mary Oetjen (Tex) 18319 Otter Creek Trl, Humble, TX 77346

WILLIAMS, Mary Grace (Ct) 36 New Canaan Road, Wilton, CT 06897

WILLIAMS, Melody Sue (SO) 60 S. Dorset Road, Troy, OH 45373

WILLIAMS, Michael Robert (ND)

WILLIAMS, Mildred (Alb) 2304 Deer Trl, Lampasas, TX 76550

WILLIAMS, Milton C (WA) 1133 N. Lasalle Blvd., Chicago, IL 60610

WILLIAMS, Mollie A. (Ind) 11335 Winding Wood Ct, Indianapolis, IN 46235

WILLIAMS, Monrelle Theophilus (Mass) 1073 Tremont St, Roxbury Crossing, MA 02120

WILLIAMS, Pamela Mary (Neb) 1014 N 6th St, Seward, NE 68434

WILLIAMS, Patricia S. (Mo) 336 N Lorimier St, Cape Girardeau, MO 63701

WILLIAMS, Patrick Joel (NY) 1047 Amsterdam Ave, New York, NY 10025

WILLIAMS, Paul Brazell (SO) 5857 Vandeleur Place, Dublin, OH 43016

WILLIAMS, Persis Preston (Alb) Po Box 1662, Blue HIll, ME 04614

WILLIAMS, Peter A (CNY) PO Box 170, 13 Court Street, Cortland, NY 13045

WILLIAMS, Priscilla Mudge (Ct) 80 Lyme Rd., Apt. 212, Hanover, NH 03755

WILLIAMS, Richard Alan (Episcopal SJ) 28052 Foxfire St, Sun City, CA 92586

WILLIAMS, Richard Alex (NC) PO Box 1852, Salisbury, NC 28145

WILLIAMS, Robert Bruce (Az) 2242 E 8th St, Tucson, AZ 85719

WILLIAMS, Robert Ernest (ECR) 231 Sunset Ave, Sunnyvale, CA 94086

WILLIAMS, Robert Harry (Oly) 1805 38th Ave, Seattle, WA 98122

WILLIAMS, Robert Lewis (Oly) 3300 Carpenter Rd SE, Electra 109, Lacey, WA 98503

WILLIAMS, Robert Roy (Ore) 11511 SW Bull Mountain Road, Tigard, OR 97224

WILLIAMS, R(obert) Samuel (NwPa) 22633 Phillips Dr, Pleasantville, PA 16341

WILLIAMS, Roger Verne (EO) St. Paul's Episcopal Church, 505 Bower Ave., Nyssa, OR 97913

WILLIAMS, R(uth) Jane (Be) 1670 Lindberg St., 1200 Main St., Bethlehem, PA 18020

WILLIAMS, Sam Farrar (SVa) P O Box 62184, Virginia Beach, VA 23466

WILLIAMS, Sandra Kaye (SD) 509 Jackson St, Belle Fourche, SD 57717

WILLIAMS, Sandy (Mass) 173 Georgetown Rd, Boxford, MA 01921

WILLIAMS, Scott Eugene (Miss) 1909 15th St, Gulfport, MS 39501

WILLIAMS, Sharon Evette (SeFla) Trinity Cathedral, 464 NE 16th St, Miami, FL 33132

WILLIAMS, Sharon Vaughan (Tex) Misery Dr, Sag Harbor, NY 11963

WILLIAMS, Shearon Sykes (Va) 2500 Cameron Mills Rd, Alexandria, VA 22302

WILLIAMS, Stephen Junior Cherrington (RG) 49 ½ Draper Avenue, Pittsfield, MA 01201

WILLIAMS, Stephen Lee (Los) 14252 Suffolk Street, Westminster, CA 92683

WILLIAMS, Susan Anslow (Mich) Saint Stephen's Church, 5500 N Adams Rd, Troy, MI 48098

WILLIAMS, Thomas (SwFla) 9404 Oak Meadow Ct, Tampa, FL 33647

WILLIAMS, Thomas Donald (CFla) 3015 Indian River Drive, Palm Bay, FL 32905

WILLIAMS, Tracey Mark (LI) 8545 96th St, Woodhaven, NY 11421

WILLIAMS, Wendy Ann (SeFla) 400 Seabrook Rd, Tequesta, FL 33469

WILLIAMS, Wesley Danford (Ve) Iglesia Episcopal de Venezuela, Centro Diocesano Av. Caroní No. 100, Colinas de Bello Monte Caracas 1042-A, Venezuela

WILLIAMS JR, Wesley Samuel (VI) 6501 Red Hook Plz Ste 201, St Thomas, VI 00802

WILLIAMS-DUNCAN, Stacy (WA) 372 El Camino Real, Atherton, CA 94027

WILLIAMSON, Anne Campbell (NH) 101 Chapel St, Portsmouth, NH 03801

WILLIAMSON, Barbara (Mass) 451 Concord Rd, Sudbury, MA 01776

WILLIAMSON, Emmanuel (Pa) 1101 2nd Street Pike, Southampton, PA 18966

WILLIAMSON JR, James Gray (SwFla) 8005 25th Street East, Parrish, FL 34219

WILLIAMSON, Jeremiah D (O) 3154 Goddard Rd, Toledo, OH 43606

WILLIAMSON, Randolph Lewis (Pa) 343 Michigan Ave, Swarthmore, PA 19081

WILLIAMSON, Rebecca Ann (Az) 1735 S College Ave, Tempe, AZ 85281

WILLIS, Anisa Cottrell (Lex) Cincinnati Childrens Hospital, Department of Pastoral Care, 3333 Burnett Avenue, Cincinnati, OH 45229

WILLIS, Barbara Creighton (Va) 1905 Wildflower Terrace, Richmond, VA 23238

WILLIS JR, Frederick Webber (SVa) 5119 Blake Point Rd, Chincoteague Island, VA 23336

WILLIS, Laurie Joy (Chi) 7916 Earl St, Oakland, CA 94605

WILLIS, Nancy Appleby (RI) 86 Dendron Rd, Wakefield, RI 02879

WILLIS, Ronnie Walker (Cal) 137 Caselli Ave, San Francisco, CA 94114

WILLKE, Herbert Alexander (Tex) 11110 Tom Adams Drive, Austin, TX 78753

WILLMANN JR, Robert Everett (SO) 155 N 6th St, Zanesville, OH 43701

WILLMS, Ann Bagley (Va)

WILLMS, John Karl Peter (Minn) 801 E 2nd St Apt 102, Duluth, MN 55805

WILLOUGHBY, Robert Geddes (Mich) 16256 Terra Bella St., Clinton Township, MI 48038

WILLOUGHBY III, William (Ga) The Ibert, 224 E 34th Street, Savannah, GA 31401

WILLOW, Mary Margaret Gregory (SwFla) 127 Gesner St, Linden, NJ 07036

WILLS, Clark Edward (Oly) 308 - 14th Avenue East #111, Seattle, WA 98112

WILLS JR, Edwin Francis (Ark) 321 Crystal Ct, Little Rock, AR 72205

WILLS, Robert Murlin (Mich) 1506 Eagle Crest Dr, Prescott, AZ 86301

WILMER, Amelie Allen (Va) 12291 River Rd, Richmond, VA 23238

WILMINGTON, Richard Newton (Cal) 2 Columbia Dr, Rancho Mirage, CA 92270

WILMOT, Susan Elizabeth (Az) 975 E Warner Rd, Tempe, AZ 85284

WILMOTH, Danny Stewart (Va) 3440 S Jefferson St, Falls Church, VA 22041

WILS, Duane Michael (NMich) 6971 Days River 24.5 Rd, Gladstone, MI 49837

WILSON, Anne Warrington (SO) 7730 Tecumseh Trl, Cincinnati, OH 45243

WILSON, Barbara A(nn) T(heresa) (WMich) 9713 Oakview Dr, Portage, MI 49024

WILSON, Barrie Andrew (CFla)

WILSON JR, Charles Alexander (NwT) 1524 S. Alabama St., Amarillo, TX 79102

WILSON JR, Charles Edward (SO) 77 Sherman Ave, Columbus, OH 43205

WILSON, Charleston D (SwFla) 222 S Palm Ave, Sarasota, FL 34236

WILSON, Claudia Marie (NY) 1085 Warburton Ave Apt 326, Yonkers, NY 10701

WILSON, Clinton M (Tenn) 4715 Harding Pike, Nashville, TN 37205

WILSON, Conrad Bruce (WTex) 10 Tanglewood St, San Marcos, TX 78666

WILSON, Dana Jane Gant (FtW) 124 Oakmont Dr, Weatherford, TX 76088

WILSON, Donald Rexford (Ore) 7065 S.W. Molalla Bend Rd., Wilsonville, OR 97070

WILSON, Donald Robert (Mass) 76 Old Pine Hill Rd N, Berwick, ME 03901

WILSON, Edward Adrian (ECR) 90 Cashew Blossom Drive, San Jose, CA 95123

WILSON, Eugenia Theresa (NY) 5030 Henry Hudson Pkwy E, Bronx, NY 10471

WILSON JR, Frank E (Minn) 16376 7th Street Lane S, Lakeland, MN 55043

WILSON, Frank F(enn) (At) 803 Wilkins Dr, Monroe, GA 30655

WILSON, Frank K (RG) 12 Indian Maid Ln, Alamogordo, NM 88310

WILSON, George Ira (Mich) 7903 Mesa Trails Cir, Austin, TX 78731

WILSON, George Steil (Oly) 3607 214th Street Southwest, Brier, WA 98036

WILSON, Gregory M (Pa) 246 Fox Rd, Media, PA 19063

WILSON, Harold David (CFla) 1629 Championship Blvd, Franklin, TN 37064

WILSON, Henry Haddon (Eur) Stautland, Finnas, N-5437, Norway

WILSON, Howard Lee (Okla) 2621 E Sheridan St Unit 118, Laramie, WY 82070

WILSON, James Barrett (Ky) 7619 Beech Spring Ct, Louisville, KY 40241

WILSON, James G. (Ct) 54 Harbour View Place, Stratford, CT 06615

WILSON II, James Nyebe (Minn) 14441 92nd Avenue North, Maple Grove, MN 55369

WILSON, Jane R (NC) Calvary Episcopal Church, PO Box 1245, Tarboro, NC 27886

WILSON, John Morris (ETenn) 118 Dupont Smith Ln, Kingston, TN 37763

WILSON, Kate Wilson (ECR) 611 Dellingham Dr Apt A, Indianapolis, IN 46260

WILSON, Kellie Christine (USC) 1115 Marion St, Columbia, SC 29201

WILSON, Kenneth Wayne (CNY) 7863 Russell Ln, Manlius, NY 13104

WILSON, Linda Latham (Alb) PO Box 154, 627 Roses Brook Rd, South Kortright, NY 13842

WILSON, Linda R (Wyo) 109 Chaparral Loop, Socorro, NM 87801

WILSON, Linda Tardy (Pgh) 215 Canterbury Ln, North Versailles, PA 15137

WILSON, Louis James (Eau) 2611 Mont Claire Rd, Eau Claire, WI 54703

WILSON, Mary Elizabeth (Tex) 717 Sage Road, Houston, TX 77056

WILSON, Mauricio Jose (Cal) 114 Montecito Ave, Oakland, CA 94610

WILSON, Michael H. (SwFla) 5108 Plainfield Street, Midland, MI 48642

WILSON III, Morris Karl (Tenn) 3002 Westmoreland Dr, Nashville, TN 37212

WILSON, Norbert Lance Weston (Ala) 136 E Magnolia Ave, Auburn, AL 36830

WILSON, Phillip Dana (Nwk) 36 South St, Morristown, NJ 07960

WILSON, Ray E(ugene) (Tex) Po Box 1943, Lenox, MA 01240

WILSON, Raymond G (LI)

WILSON, Richard Allen (Az)

WILSON, Roy Dennis (Miss) 1954 Spillway Rd, Brandon, MS 39047

WILSON, Sandra Antoinette (Nwk) 116 Turrell Ave, South Orange, NJ 07079

WILSON, Stefanie Glenn (Los) Campbell Hall School, 4533 Laurel Canyon Blvd, North Hollywood, CA 91607

WILSON, Stephen Thomas (Colo) 1530 Cherry St, Denver, CO 80220

WILSON, Steven Clark (WMo) 1213 Grand Ave, Carthage, MO 64836

WILSON, Thomas Andrew (SanD) 339 Brightwood Ave, Chula Vista, CA 91910

WILSON, Thomas Everitt (EC) 101 Bear Track Ln, Kitty Hawk, NC 27949

WILSON, Thomas Lynn (Kan)

WILSON, Thomas Stuart (Tenn) 1000 Sunnyside Dr, Columbia, TN 38401

WILSON, William Henry (Ala) 800 Lake Colony Cir, Birmingham, AL 35242

WILSON, William Jackson (Az) 4 Kingsbridge Pl, Pueblo, CO 81001

WILSON-BARNARD, M Letha (Minn) Holy Apostles, 2200 Minnehaha Ave E, Saint Paul, MN 55119

WILT, David Ruhl (SeFla) 415 Duval St, Key West, FL 33040

WILTON, (Glenn) (Warner) Paul (Oly) 10 Lichfield Avenue, CANTERBURY, CT1 3YA, Great Britain (UK)

WILTSE, Roderic Duncan (Mo) 209 S Woods Mill Rd Apt. 3311, Chesterfield, MO 63017

WILTSEE JR, Leon Lamont (ECR) 13083 Middle Canyon Rd, Carmel Valley, CA 93924

✠ WIMBERLY, Don Adger (Ret Bp of Tex) 3515 Plumb St, Houston, TX 77005

WIMBUSH, Claire S (SVa) 1333 Jamestown Rd, Williamsburg, VA 23185

WINBORN JR, James Henderson (SVa) 8880 Colonnades Ct W Apt 412, Bonita Springs, FL 34135

WINCHELL, Ronald S (Va) 128 Eagle Ct, Locust Grove, VA 22508

WINDAL, Claudia L (Minn) 1532 Randolph Ave, Apt. 8, St. Paul,, MN 55105

WINDEL, Marian Kathleen (Va) 1782 Yanceyville Road, Louisa, VA 23093

WINDER, Francis (U) 4546 Jupiter Dr, Salt Lake City, UT 84124

WINDOM, Barbara Sewell (At) 432 Forest Hill Rd, Macon, GA 31210

WINDSOR, Janice Priebe (Colo) 33741 State Highway 257, Windsor, CO 80550

WINDSOR, Robert Grover (Mass) 34 Exeter Street, West Newton, MA 02465

WINDSOR, Walter Van Zandt (Ark) 703 West Third Ave., Pine Bluff, AR 71601

WINELAND, Richard Kevin (NI) 64669 Orchard Dr, Goshen, IN 46526

WING III, Arthur Kyle (NY) 7 Van Alstine Ave, Suffern, NY 10901

WINGER, Nordon W. (Az) Good Shepherd Episcopal Church, P.O. Box 110, Cave Creek, AZ 85327

WINGERT, Anita LaVonne (NMich) 550 N Ravine St, Sault Sainte Marie, MI 49783

WINGERT JR, John Alton (CNY) 1244 Great Pond Road, Box 116, Great Pond, ME 04408

WINGFIELD, Vest Garrett (Tex) PO Box 540742, Houston, TX 77254

WINGO, Patrick James (Va) Diocese of Virginia, 110 W Franklin St, Richmond, VA 23220

WINGO, Sara Scott Nelson (Va) 2813 Godfrey Ave Ne, Fort Payne, AL 35967

WINKLER, Anne Louise (Ind)

WINKLER, Barbara Jo (NMich) 852 E D St, Iron Mountain, MI 49801

WINKLER JR, Richard Edward (The Episcopal Church in Haw) 202 Pin Oak Dr, Harker Heights, TX 76548

WINKLER, Thomas E. (Minn) 39259 K-C Dr, Winona, MN 55987

WINKLER JR, William Edward (NY)

WINN, John Barrington (Oly) Po Box 1961, Silverdale, WA 98383

WINNER, Lauren Frances (NC) 1737 Hillandale Rd, Durham, NC 27705

WINSETT, Stephen Metcalfe (Chi) 235 Brittany Dr, Streamwood, IL 60107

WINSLETT JR, Hoyt (Ala) 1224 - 37th Avenue East, Tuscaloosa, AL 35404

WINSLOW, Gail George (NwPa) Church of the Ascension, 26 Chautauqua Place, Bradford, PA 16701

WINSLOW JR, K Dennis (NY) P.O. Box 93 (5023 Delaware Turnpike), RENSSELAERVILLE, NY 12147

WINSTON, William Scott (FtW) 3313 Minot Ave, Fort Worth, TX 76133

WINTER, Brian William (RG) 12408 Prospect Ave. NE, Albuquerque, NM 87112

WINTER, Cheryl Ann (WVa) Po Box 424, Hurricane, WV 25526

WINTER, James L (Miss) 105 N. Montgomery St, Starkville, MS 39759

WINTER, Laren Royce (RG) Po Box 2963, Ruidoso, NM 88355

WINTER JR, Lloyd Henry (Pa) 429 New Rd, Churchville, PA 18966

WINTER CHASER, Vivian Janice (Az) 725 S. Beck Ave, Tempe, AZ 85281

✠ WINTERROWD, William Jerry (Ret Bp of Colo 2003-) 10955 E Crestline Pl, Englewood, CO 80111

WINTERS JR, Charles Layfaette (WNC) 6 Timson Road, Apt B4, Asheville, NC 28803

WINTERS, Richard Harrison (Ind) 5502 Washington Blvd, Indianapolis, IN 46220

WINTERS, William Michael (Ala)

WINTON, Paul Steve (NC) Saint John's Episcopal Church, 1623 Carmel Rd, Charlotte, NC 28226

WINWARD, Mark Scott (Spr) 206 Jenkins Rd, Saco, ME 04072

WIPFLER, William Louis (WNY) 121 Carla Ln, West Seneca, NY 14224

WIRES, John William (At) 4900 English Dr, Annandale, VA 22003

WIRTH, Bradley S (Mont) All Saints' Church, PO Box 1923, Whitefish, MT 59937

WISCHMEYER, Kara Leslie (NwT) 226 Chuck Wagon Rd., Lubbock, TX 79404

WISE, Christopher Matthew (WTex) 315 E Pecan St, San Antonio, TX 78205

WISE JR, Eugene Field (Tenn) Po Box 261, Murfreesboro, TN 37133

WISELEY, Jerry Lee (SC) 1746 Summit Rd, Hot Springs, SD 57747

WISEMAN, Grant Buchanan (USC) 125 Pendleton St. S.W., Aiken, SC 29801

WISEMAN, Heather Buchanan (SO) 2489 Walnutview Ct, Cincinnati, OH 45230

WISEMAN, Philip M (SO) 2489 Walnutview Ct, Cincinnati, OH 45230

WISHART, Raymond Douglas (CGC) 925 E Pierson Dr, Lynn Haven, FL 32444

WISMER, Robert David (Tex) 11310 Meadow Lake Dr, Houston, TX 77077

WISNER, Stephen Forster (NJ) 3402 Woodfield Ave, Wall Township, NJ 07719

WISNEWSKI JR, Robert Carew (Ala) 113 Madison Ave, Montgomery, AL 36104

WISNIEWSKI, Richard Joseph (NJ) Church Of The Holy Spirit, PO Box 174, Tuckerton, NJ 08087

WISSINK, Charles Jay (Pa) 54 Sugarplum Rd, Levittown, PA 19056

WISSLER, Kenneth John (Pa) 201 Evergreen Ave. Apt. 904, Philadelphia, PA 19118

✠ WITCHER SR, Robert Campbell (Ret Bp of LI 1999-) 1934 Steele Blvd, Baton Rouge, LA 70808

Clergy List

WITH, David Fergus (WMo) 160 Terrace Trl W, Lake Quivira, KS 66217

WITH, Jan Louise (Neb) Episcopal Churc St Marys, 212 Clark St, Bassett, NE 68714

WITHROCK JR, John William (CGC) 401 W College St, Troy, AL 36081

WITKE, E(Dward) Charles (Mich) 3000 Glazier Way, Ann Arbor, MI 48105

WITT, Anne Lane (Va) PO Box 1059, Kilmarnock, VA 22482

WITT, Bonnie Rae (WNY) Po Box 66, Gasport, NY 14067

WITT JR, Richard Cyril (NY) 16 Lawrence Rd, Accord, NY 12404

WITT JR, Robert Edward (Alb) P.O. Box 123, Morris, NY 13808

WITTE JR, Walter William (Nwk) Po Box 4781, Vineyard Haven, MA 02568

WITTIG, Nancy Constantine Hatch (Pa) 21801 Elizabeth Ave, Fairview Park, OH 44126

WITTMAYER, Kevin Edward (Tex) 906 Padon St, Longview, TX 75601

WIZOREK, Julie C (Md) 249 Double Oak Rd N, Prince Frederick, MD 20678

WLOSINSKI, Stephen Stanley (Minn) 1121 W Morgan St, Duluth, MN 55811

WOEHLER, Charles George (WTex) 1416 North Loop 1604 East, San Antonio, TX 78232

WOESSNER, David H. (WMass) 340 Burncoat St, Worcester, MA 01606

WOGGON, Harry Arthur (WNC) 5 Norwich Dr, Asheville, NC 28803

WOGGON, Karla M (WA) 1048 15th Ave. N.W., Hickory, NC 28601

WOHLEVER, Russell J (CFla) All Saints Church, 338 E Lyman Ave, Winter Park, FL 32789

WOJAHN, Karen Ann (Dix) (Los) 1012 East Van Owen Avenue, Orange, CA 92867

WOJCIEHOWSKI, Arthur Anthony (Minn) 1500 Prospect Ave, Cloquet, MN 55720

WOLCOTT, Sarah Elizabeth (Neb)

WOLF, David B (WA) 1516 Hamilton St NW, Washington, DC 20011

✠ WOLF, Geralyn (Ret Bp of RI 2012-) 275 N Main St, Providence, RI 02903

WOLF, Max Joseph (Del) 20 Olive Ave, Rehoboth Beach, DE 19971

WOLFE, Alexander (ND)

✠ WOLFE, Dean Elliott (Bp of Kan 2003-) 835 SW Polk St, Topeka, KS 66612

WOLFE, Dorothy Annabell (Neb) 603 3rd Ave, Bayard, NE 69334

WOLFE, James Edward (HB)

WOLFE, John M (SwFla) 501 Erie Ave, Tampa, FL 33606

WOLFE, V Eugene (Oly) 53565 W Ferndale Rd, Milton Freewater, OR 97862

WOLFENBARGER, Mary Suzanne (WLa) 55 Magnolia Dr, Belleville, IL 62221

WOLFF, Pierre Maurice (Ct) 108 C North Turnpike Road, Wallingford, CT 06492

WOLFF, William George (Kan) 306 W. Euclid St., Pittsburg, KS 66762

WOLFORD, Arthur C (NI) Po Box 152, Corona, CA 92878

WOLFORD, (Mary) Rachael Rossiter (Oly) PO Box 522, Cathlamet, WA 98612

WOLLARD, Robert Foster (Mich) 4505 Westlawn Pkwy, Waterford, MI 48328

WOLSONCROFT III, Arthur Mathew (NY) 414 E 52nd St, New York, NY 10022

WOLTER, Jack M (WNY) 668 Shadow Mountain Dr, Prescott, AZ 86301

WOLTERSTORFF, Claire Kingma (WMich) 58 Sunnybrook Ave Se, Grand Rapids, MI 49506

WOLTZ, Charles M (Okla) 924 N Robinson Ave, Oklahoma City, OK 73102

WOMACK JR, Egbert Morton (Colo) 7500 E Dartmouth Ave Unit 31, Denver, CO 80231

WOMACK, Lawrence Melvin (NC) 8725 Sedgeburn Drive, Charlotte, NC 28278

WOMELSDORF, Charles Stowers (CGC) 327 Honeysuckle Hill, Tallassee, AL 36078

WON, Ho Gil Hilary (Nwk) 403 79th St, North Bergen, NJ 07047

WON, Jonathan Sung Ho (Nwk) 16423 Maidstone Avenue, Norwalk, CA 90650

WONDRA, Ellen K (Chi) Bexley Seabury Seminary Federation, 8765 W Higgins Rd Ste 350, Chicago, IL 60631

WONG, Diane C K (Mass) 5B Park Terr, Arlington, MA 02474

WONG, George (NJ) 6030 Grosvenor Ln, Bethesda, MD 20814

WONG, Gloria Lee (Mass) Po Box 825, Oak Bluffs, MA 02557

WONG, Peter Reginald (CGC) Church of the Nativity, 205 Holly Ln, Dothan, AL 36301

WONG, Philip Yau-Ming (Oly) 62 Pine St., Rockville Centre, NY 11570

WONG, Salying (Cal)

WOO, Raymond A (The Episcopal Church in Haw) 45 N Judd St, Honolulu, HI 96817

WOOD, Ann Patricia (WMass) 13 Kelleher Dr, South Deerfield, MA 01373

WOOD, Camille Carpenter (La) 3552 Morning Glory Ave, Baton Rouge, LA 70808

WOOD JR, Charles Amos (La) 532 Stanford Ave, Baton Rouge, LA 70808

WOOD JR, Charles Edwards (Spok) 426 Lilly Road NE Apt 248, Olympia, WA 98506

WOOD, Charles Leon (Mich) PO Box 2001, Southern Pines, NC 28388

WOOD, David Romaine (Colo) 1233 24th Ave. Ct., Greeley, CO 80634

WOOD, Grace Marie (EC) 198 Dogwood Trl, Elizabeth City, NC 27909

WOOD, Gregg Douglas (NY) Po Box 62, Wawarsing, NY 12489

WOOD, Gretchen A (SO) 24 High Ridge Loop Apt 605, Pawleys Island, SC 29585

WOOD, H Palmer (CFla) 720 S Lakeshore Blvd, Lake Wales, FL 33853

WOOD, Howard Fitler (Pa) 526 Washington Ave, Hulmeville, PA 19047

WOOD, Hunter Holmes (Va) 250 Pantops Mountain Rd Apt 5126, Charlottesville, VA 22911

WOOD, Jan Smith (O) Grace Episcopal Church, 315 Wayne Street, Sandusky, OH 44870

WOOD, Kathrine Ringold (Ore) 437 Franklin St, Denver, CO 80218

WOOD, Linda Anne (Cal) 3080 Birdsall Ave, Oakland, CA 94619

WOOD, Mark Raymond (Ct) 89 Eddy Street, Providence, RI 02903

WOOD, Nancy Currey (SVa) 1524 Southwick Rd, Virginia Beach, VA 23451

WOOD, Priscilla Peacock (Mass) 1 Hickey Dr, Framingham, MA 01701

✠ WOOD JR, R(aymond) Stewart (Ret Bp of Mich 2000-) Kendal 157, 80 Lyme Rd, Hanover, NH 03755

WOOD, Robert Bradford (At) 12132 Walnut Ter, Alpharetta, GA 30004

WOOD, Robert Earl (Mo) 1009 W 57th St, Kansas City, MO 64113

WOOD, Rodgers Taylor (WVa) 1223 Stanford Court, Coraopolis, PA 15108

WOOD, Roger Hoffman (Los) 38 E Grandview Ave, Sierra Madre, CA 91024

WOOD, Roger Lee (EMich) 106 S Kennefic St, Yale, MI 48097

WOOD, Sammy (Mass) 30 Brimmer St, Boston, MA 02108

WOOD, Sarah Anne (Va) 86 Fourth Ave., New York, NY 10003

WOOD, Stuart Clary (Va) 7120 Ore Bank Rd, Port Republic, VA 24471

WOOD III, William Hoge (Pa) 251 Montgomery Ave Unit 9, Haverford, PA 19041

WOOD, William James (Kan) 30 Spofford Lane, Trevett, ME 04571

WOOD JR, William Reed (WVa) 107 Elma Dr, Williamstown, WV 26187

WOODALL, Carolyn Louise (Episcopal SJ) St Mary in the Mountains Church, PO Box 146, Jamestown, CA 95327

WOODALL JR, P J (At) 3663 SE Cambridge Drive, Stuart, FL 34997

WOODARD, Sarah Wilson (NC) 400 Moline St., Durham, NC 27707

WOODBURY, Kimberly Jean (VI) All Saints Cathedral, PO Box 1148, St Thomas, VI 00804

WOODBURY, Robert Lane (Mil) 5558 N Berkeley Blvd, Whitefish Bay, WI 53217

WOODCOCK, Bruce W (SeFla) 106 Castle Heights Ave, Nyack, NY 10960

WOODEN, Lorentho (SO) 550 E 4th St, Cincinnati, OH 45202

WOODFIN, Joseph Robert (Tenn) PO Box 307, Gallatin, TN 37066

WOODHOUSE, Marjorie Michelle (Los) 4125 Creciente Dr, Santa Barbara, CA 93110

WOOD-HULL, L. D. (Ore) 6151 Willers Way, Houston, TX 77057

WOODLEY, Claire (NY) 2 Glendale Rd, Ossining, NY 10562

WOODLIEF, Vern Andrews (Az) 1069 N Paseo Iris, Green Valley, AZ 85614

WOODLIFF III, George Franklin (Miss) 712 S Montgomery St, Starkville, MS 39759

WOODLIFF, Kirk Alan (Nev) 2125 Stone View Dr, Sparks, NV 89436

WOODLIFF-STANLEY, Ruth M (Colo) 1945 Ivanhoe St, Denver, CO 80220

WOODLING, Edith Walker (At) 25 Battle Ridge Pl Ne, Atlanta, GA 30342

WOODRIDGE, Douglas Earl (SanD) 16017 Oakridge Ct, Lake Oswego, OR 97035

WOODROOFE III, Robert William (Ct) 42 Christian Street, New Preston, CT 06777

WOODRUFF, Karen B (Va) Po Box 367, Lively, VA 22507

WOODRUFF TAIT, Jennifer Lynn (NI) 1224 N Jefferson St, Huntington, IN 46750

WOODRUM, Donald Lee (Fla) Po Box 1238, Live Oak, FL 32064

WOODRUM, Lawrence Paul (Nwk) 651 East 102nd St, Brooklyn, NY 11236

WOODS, Harold Dean (Vt) 233 South Street, South Hero, VT 05486

WOODS, James Christopher (Mass) 121 Freeport Boulevard, Toms River, NJ 08757

WOODS, James Edward (Oly) 22226 6th Ave S Apt 201, Des Moines, WA 98198

WOODS JR, JC (Mass) 62 Las Casas St, Malden, MA 02148

WOODS, John Michael (Dal) Rr 1 Box 253-A, Mount Vernon, TX 75457

WOODS, Joshua Blake (Okla) 5635 E 71st St, Tulsa, OK 74136

WOODS, Robert D (Episcopal SJ) Po Box 1837, Kernville, CA 93238

WOODS, Stephen I (NY) Above, Above, NM 87507

WOODSON JR, James Pettigrew (Ala) 313 Riverdale Dr # 35406-, Tuscaloosa, AL 35406

WOODSUM, Mark Edward (Me) 2808 Lakemont Dr, Fallbrook, CA 92028

WOODWARD JR, Brinton Webb (NH) RR3 Box 18, Plymouth, NH 03264

WOODWARD, Deborah Marshall (Mass) 1080 Hillside St, Milton, MA 02186

WOODWARD III, George Frederick (Los) 1294 Westlyn Pl, Pasadena, CA 91104

WOODWARD, Lynn Christophersen (Okla) 4604 E 54th St Apt 203, Tulsa, OK 74135

WOODWARD, Matthew Thomas (Cal) 3900 Alameda De Las Pulgas, San Mateo, CA 94403

WOODWARD, Thomas Bullene (RG) 13 Calle Loma, Santa Fe, NM 87507

WOODWORTH, Laura T(Ufts) (NMich) 2500 South Hill Road, Gladstone, MI 49837

WOODWORTH-HILL, Nancy Louise (Ind) 321 E Market St, Jeffersonville, IN 47130

WOODY, Robert James (WTex) 13638 Liberty Oak, San Antonio, TX 78232

WOOLARD, Lynn Phillip (CFla) PO Box 541025, Merritt Island, FL 32954

WOOLERY-PRICE, Edward Raymond (Tex) All Saints' Episcopal Church, 209 W 27th St, Austin, TX 78705

WOOLIVER, Tammy S (Okla) 264 Woodbriar, Noble, OK 73068

WOOLLEN, Nancy Sewell (Ind)

WOOLLETT JR, Donald M (WLa)

WOOLLEY JR, Arthur Everett (Md) 13 Basswood Ct, Catonsville, MD 21228

WOOLLEY JR, Stanley Marsh (WMass) 868 Butler Drive, Livingston, SC 29107

WOOLLEY, Steven Eugene (Spok) 1803 Crestline Dr, Walla Walla, WA 99362

WOOLSEY, Deborah J (SO) St Paul's Episcopal Church, 33 W Dixon Ave, Dayton, OH 45419

WOOTTEN, Jo Ann H (Ark) 346 Rock Springs Rd., Wake Forest, NC 27587

WOOTTEN III, Middleton Lane (Ark) 346 N Rock Springs Rd, Wake Forest, NC 27587

WORKMAN, James K. (USC) 1200 Powdersville Rd., Easley, SC 29642

WORLEY, James Paul (WTex) 389 Valley View Dr, Cibolo, TX 78108

WORTH, Elsa (Ct) 526 Amity Rd, Bethany, CT 06524

WORTHINGTON, Cynthia Muirhead (RG) 6043 Royal Crk, San Antonio, TX 78239

WORTHINGTON JR, Daniel Owen (Va) P O Box 83, Gloucester, VA 23061

WORTHINGTON, William Ray (Ga) 207 Hermitage Way, Saint Simons Island, GA 31522

WORTHLEY, Christopher (Los) 2114 De La Vina St Unit 1, Santa Barbara, CA 93105

WOSIKOWSKI, Thomas J (Mil) 4901 Hob St, Madison, WI 53716

WRAMPELMEIER, Christopher Kent (NwT) 2602 Parker St, Amarillo, TX 79109

WRATHALL, Susan L (RI) 70 Moore St., Warwick, RI 02889

WRATTEN, Kenneth Bruce (ECR) 8640 Solera Drive, San Jose, CA 95135

WREDE, Anne Mcrae (NJ) 37 Northfield Rd, Millington, NJ 07946

WREDE, Richard Charles (NJ) 500 Fourth St, Riverton, NJ 08077

WREN, Dane C (CFla) 302 Bent Way Ln, 700 Rinehart Rd, Lake Mary, FL 32746

WRENN, William Charles (O) 17 Sandy Neck Rd, East Sandwich, MA 02537

WRIDER, Anne Johnson (SO) 3435 Golden Ave #801, CINCINNATI, OH 45206

WRIGHT, Allan McLean (WMass)

WRIGHT, Andrew Ray (FtW) 1700 N. Westmoreland Rd., Desoto, TX 75115

WRIGHT, Angus Dale (NMich) PO Box 302, Manistique, MI 49854

WRIGHT, Benjamin R (RG) 363 Park St, Beaver, PA 15009

WRIGHT, Brian T (Oly) 15224 52nd Avenue W., Edmonds, WA 98026

WRIGHT, Carl Walter (Md) Apo Ae 0962, PSC2 Box 9808, Ramstein, Germany

WRIGHT, Catherine Louise (Tex) 301 E 8th St, Austin, TX 78701

WRIGHT, Diana Lee (La)

WRIGHT, Elizabeth Louise (RI) 10 Eustis Ave, Newport, RI 02840

WRIGHT, Elton Stanley (Colo) 342 Old Cahaba Trail, Helena, AL 35080

WRIGHT, Gwynne Ann (Chi) 43 Rawcliffe Croft, York, YO305US, Great Britain (UK)

WRIGHT, Hollis E (Colo) 92-1010 Kanehoa Loop, Kapolei, HI 96707

WRIGHT, James D (Fla) 3231 Nw 47th Pl, Gainesville, FL 32605

WRIGHT, James O. Pete (Los) 1505 Monticello Ct., Redlands, CA 92373

WRIGHT, Janice Bracken (At) 101 East Fourth Avenue, Rome, GA 30161

WRIGHT, Jean Ann Frances (At) 5228 Stone Village Cir Nw, Kennesaw, GA 30152

WRIGHT, Jeannene Fee (DR (DomRep)) Eps G 2517, Box 02-5540, Miami, FL 33102

WRIGHT, Jo Anne (Okla) 821 N Foreman St Apt 118, Vinita, OK 74301

WRIGHT, John Hamil Spedden (Del) 54 Ridge Ave, Edgewater, MD 21037

WRIGHT, J(ohn) Robert (NY) General Theological Seminary, 175 9th Ave, New York, NY 10011

WRIGHT, Jonathan M (SC) 1295 Abercorn Trce, Mount Pleasant, SC 29466

WRIGHT, Lonell (La) 7696 Stevenson Way, San Diego, CA 92120- 2229

WRIGHT, Mark R (Dal) 2019 Highland Forest Dr, Highland Village, TX 75077

WRIGHT III, Martin Luther (Pgh) 1249 Main Street, PO Box 175, Shanksville, PA 15560

WRIGHT, Matthew L (NY) St Gregory's Episcopal Church, PO Box 66, Woodstock, NY 12498

WRIGHT, Michael Alfred (Oly) 1428 22nd Ave, Longview, WA 98632

WRIGHT, Milton King (Minn) 707 Saint Olaf Ave, Northfield, MN 55057

WRIGHT, Priscilla Jean (SO)

WRIGHT, Rick Lynn (At)

✠ **WRIGHT**, Robert Christopher (Bp of At 2012-) 306 Peyton Rd Sw, Atlanta, GA 30311

WRIGHT, Ross Mcgowan (SVa) 4203 Springhill Ave, Richmond, VA 23225

WRIGHT, Ryan A (SwFla) Saint Paul's, 3901 Davis Blvd, Naples, FL 34104

WRIGHT, Scot R (Oly) 650 Bellevue Way NE, Unit 2401, Bellevue, WA 98004

WRIGHT, Stanalee (Spok)

WRIGHT, Stuart Wayne (Md) 4 E. University Pkwy., Baltimore, MD 21218

✠ **WRIGHT**, Wayne Parker (Bp of Del 1998-) 913 Wilson Rd, Wilmington, DE 19803

WRIGHT, William Baskin (NwT) 3549 Clearview Dr, San Angelo, TX 76904

WRIGHT, William J (Alb) 14 Monument St, Deposit, NY 13754

WRIGHT, Winston Antony (SeFla) 1466 39th St, West Palm Beach, FL 33407

WU, Ming-Lung (Tai) No. 1-6 Mingxin St, Hualien City, 97050, Taiwan

WU, Peter (The Episcopal Church in Haw) 229 Queen Emma Sq, Honolulu, HI 96813

WU, Shing-Shaing (Tai) 499 Sec 4 Danjin Rd, Tamsui Dist, New Taipei City, 25135, Taiwan

WUBBENHORST, Wesley (Md) 4 East University Pkwy, Baltimore, MD 21218

WURM, Laurie Jean (Nwk)

WYATT, Andrea Castner (Mass) 133 School St, New Bedford, MA 02740

WYATT II, Robert Odell (Chi) 3526 Maple Ave, Berwyn, IL 60402

WYCKOFF, Michael Hirsch (Tex) 2857 Grimes Ranch Rd, Austin, TX 78732

WYER, George William (Va) Po Box 638, Ivy, VA 22945

WYES, Gregory Walter (Az) 6960 N Alvernon Way, Tucson, AZ 85718

WYLAND, Richard Rees (Roch) 41 Great Oak Ln, Redding, CT 06896

WYLD, Kevin Andrew (CFla)

WYLIE, Craig Robert (SwVa) 170 Crestview Dr, Abingdon, VA 24210

WYMAN, Deborah W (Mass) 986 Memorial Dr, Cambridge, MA 02138

WYMAN, Irma M. (Minn) 1840 University Ave W Apt 411, Saint Paul, MN 55104

WYNDHAM, Beth Ann (WTex) St Thomas Episcopal Church, 1416 N Loop 1604 E, San Antonio, TX 78232

WYNEN, Nancy Hartmeyer (Oly) 1399 Sw 17th St, Boca Raton, FL 33486

WYNN, James E (Pa) 520 S 61st St, Philadelphia, PA 19143

WYNN, Ronald Lloyd (Ore) 355 Stadium Dr S, Monmouth, OR 97361

WYPER, Susan C (Ct) St Matthew's Episcopal Church, 382 Cantitoe st, Bedford, NY 10506

WYSOCK, Christine Phillips (Spok) 535 Shelokum Dr, Silverton, OR 97381

WYSONG, Terry Marie (Ct) PO Box 606, Marion, CT 06444

X

XIE, Songling (LI) 13532 38th Ave, Flushing, NY 11354

Y

YABROFF, Martin I(Rving) (Oly)

YAGERMAN, Steven Jay (NY) 234 E 60th St, New York, NY 10022

YAKUBUA-MADUS, Fatima (Ind) 5625 W 30th St, Speedway, IN 46224

YALE, Elizabeth S (Be)

YALE, Richard Barrington (The Episcopal NCal) 4 Quista Dr., Chico, CA 95926

YAMAMOTO, Keith Akio (Los) 330 E. 16th Street, Upland, CA 91784

YANCEY, David Warren (Tenn) 1390 Jones Creek Rd, Dickson, TN 37055

YANCEY, Nancy Rollins (At) 5480 Clinchfield Trl, Norcross, GA 30092

YANCY, Stephanie Pauline (NC) 290 Locust Ridge Lane, Arnold, MD 21012

YANDELL, George Shaw (At) Church of the Holy Family, 202 Griffith Rd, Jasper, GA 30143

YANG CHOU, Chou (June) Yun Kuang (Tai) St. Mark, 120-11 Chung Hsiao Road, Ping Tung, 900, Taiwan

YAO, Ting Chang (Cal) 1111 Larch Ave, Moraga, CA 94556

YARBOROUGH, Clare McJimsey (Az) 5671 E. Copper Street, Tucson, AZ 85712

YARBOROUGH, Jesse H (Buzz) (WTex) 121 Peppertree Crossing Ave, Brunswick, GA 31525

YARBROUGH, C(laire) Denise (Roch) St. Mark's Episcopal Church, 179 Main St., Penn Yan, NY 14527

YARBROUGH, Douglas Wayne (Ida) 1312 W Elmore Ave, Nampa, ID 83651

YARBROUGH, Oliver Larry (Vt) 24 Oak Dr, Middlebury, VT 05753

YARBROUGH, Rebecca Ricketts (NC) P.O. Box 970, Davidson, NC 28036

YARSIAH, James (SC) 1324 Marvin Ave, Charleston, SC 29407

YATES, Adam Benjamin (Ct) 23 Parker Bridge Rd, Andover, CT 06232

YATES, Christopher Garrett (Pgh) 1066 Washington Rd, Mt Lebanon, PA 15228

YATES, Dorothy Gene (Cal)

YATES, Robert Gordon (SwFla) 37505 Moore Dr, Dade City, FL 33525

YATES, William J (CFla) 3400 Wingmann Rd., Avon Park, FL 33825

YAW, Chris (Mich) St David's Episcopal Church, 16200 W 12 Mile Rd, Southfield, MI 48076

YAW, David Dixon (Ak) 3195 Jackson Heights St, Ketchikan, AK 99901

YAWN, Justin S (Tex) Christ Episcopal Church, 400 San Juan Dr, Ponte Vedra Beach, FL 32082

YEAGER, Alice Elizabeth (ND) 301 Main St S, Minot, ND 58701

YEAGER, Linda (WMo) 11701 Wedd St Apt 9, Overland Park, KS 66210

YEAGER, Robert Timothy (Chi) 924 Lake Street, Oak Park, IL 60301

YEARWOOD, Kirtley (Oly) Church Of Saint Alban The Martyr, 11642 Farmers Blvd, Saint Albans, NY 11412

YEATES, Judith Ann (Neb) 6615 N 162 St, Omaha, NE 68116

YEOMAN III, Eric Burdett (Cal) 1633 Argonne Dr, Stockton, CA 95203

YEPES LOPEZ, Alvaro Nelson (DR (DomRep)) Iglesia Episcopal Dominicana, Calle Santiago No 114, Santo Domingo, 764, Dominican Republic

YERKES, Kenneth Bickford (Mo) 1 Macarthur Blvd Apt S503, Haddon Township, NJ 08108

YESKO, Francis Michael (Pgh) Episcopal Diocese Of Pittsburgh, 4099 William Penn Hwy Ste 502, Monroeville, PA 15146

YETTER, Joan M (Mont) 932 Avenue F, Billings, MT 59102

YODER, Christopher Wendell (Dal) 3966 McKinney Ave, Dallas, TX 75204

YODER, John Henry (Nev) 1151 Carlton Ct Apt202, Fort Pierce, FL 34949

YON, William A(bbott) (Ala) 140 Whisenhunt Rd, Chelsea, AL 35043

YONKERS, Michael Allan (Chi) 920 S Aldine Ave, Park Ridge, IL 60068

YOON, Paul Hwan (Los) Box 22, Taejon, 300, Korea (South)

YORK, Susan Spence (WMich) 2490 Basswood St, Jenison, MI 49428

YORK-SIMMONS, Noelle Marie (At) 634 W Peachtree St Nw, Atlanta, GA 30308

YOSHIDA, Thomas Kunio (The Episcopal Church in Haw) 1410 Makiki St, Honolulu, HI 96814

YOST, Martin C (Dal) 114 George St, Providence, RI 02906

YOTTER, Katherine Ann (CFla) 6400 N Socrum Loop Rd, Lakeland, FL 33809

YOULL MARSHALL, Lynda Mary (Va)

YOUMANS, Timothy Sean (Okla) Casady School, 9500 N Pennsylvania Ave, Oklahoma City, OK 73120

YOUNG JR, A LeRoy (Los) 1215 Del Mar Dr, Los Osos, CA 93402

YOUNG JR, A(rchibald) Patterson (Dal) 617 Church St., Sulphur Springs, TX 75482

YOUNG, Bernard Orson Dwight (LI) 18917 Turin Dr, Saint Albans, NY 11412

YOUNG, Bruce Alan (Mass)

YOUNG, Christopher Richard (Q) 1717 8th Ave, Moline, IL 61265

YOUNG, Estelle Pope (Fla) 4811 Nw 17th Pl, Gainesville, FL 32605

YOUNG, Francene (Tex) 605 West 9th Street, Houston, TX 77007

YOUNG, Frank Whitman (Ala) 109 Hannah Lane, Oak Grove, AL 35150

YOUNG, Gary (EO) 665 Parsons Road, Hood River, OR 97031

YOUNG, Gary Reid (Neb) 17 Brentwood Ct, Scottsbluff, NE 69361

✠ **YOUNG III**, George Dibrell (Bp of ETenn 2011-) 814 Episcopal School Way, Knoxville, TN 37932

YOUNG, James Joseph (Los) 12868 Hacienda Dr., Studio City, CA 91604

YOUNG, James Oliver (Okla) 2207 Ridgeway St, Ardmore, OK 73401

YOUNG, James R (SwVa) 5260 Triad Court SE, Salem, OR 97306

YOUNG, James Robert (The Episcopal NCal) Po Box 2334, Avila Beach, CA 93424

YOUNG, James Robert (Minn) 101 Plum St S, Northfield, MN 55057

YOUNG, Kathryn Mary (Fla) 400 Tennessee Avenue, Sewanee, TN 37375

YOUNG, Kathryn Mcmillan (Tenn) 704 Park Blvd, Austin, TX 78751

YOUNG, Linda M (Lex) Trinity Church, 16 E 4th St, Covington, KY 41011

YOUNG, Malcolm Clemens (Cal) 2674 St. Giles Lane, Mt. View, CA 94040

YOUNG, Mary Catherine (NY) Canterbury Downtown, 12 W. 11th Street, New York, NY 10011

YOUNG, Ronald Bruce (Roch) Christ Episcopal Church, 26 S. Main St., Pittsford, NY 14534

YOUNG, S Matthew (Lex) 7 Court Pl, Newport, KY 41071

YOUNG, Shari Maruska (Cal) P.O. Box 872, Tiburon, CA 94920

YOUNG, Sherry Lawry (EMich) 5584 Lapeer Rd Apt 1D, Kimball, MI 48074

YOUNG, Todd (Ore) 11800 SW Military Lane, Portland, OR 97219

YOUNG, William King (Az) 12440 W Firebird Dr, Sun City West, AZ 85375

YOUNGBLOOD, Susan Russell (Az) Saint Matthew's, 901 W Erie St, Chandler, AZ 85225

YOUNGER, Leighton Keith (Tex) 158 Ridgeview Dr, Johnson City, TX 78636

YOUNGSON, Charles Mitchell (Ala) 315 Devon Dr., Birmingham, AL 35209

YOUNKIN, Randy John (Pgh) 431 Alameda Ave, Youngstown, OH 44504

YOUNKIN, Ronald Willingham (Pgh)

YOUNT, Amy Clark (WA) 3801 Newark St Nw Apt E431, Washington, DC 20016

YOUSE JR, Don C (Pgh) 955 West North Avenue, Pittsburgh, PA 15233

YSKAMP, Janis (CPa) 813 Valley Rd, Mansfield, PA 16933

YULE, Marilynn Fritz (Spok) PO Box 6318, Kennewick, WA 99336

YUNG, Bernard Yu (Va)

YUNKER, Judy Lee (Lex) 562 University Dr, Prestonburg, KY 41653

YUROSKO, Steven G (Mont) Saint Andrew's Episcopal Church, 110 6th Ave, Polson, MT 59860

Z

✠ **ZABALA**, Artemio M (Ret Bp of Northern Phillippines 1999-) 5048 Brunswick Dr, Fontana, CA 92336

ZABRISKIE JR, Alexander Clinton (Be) 119 Northshore Dr, Burlington, VT 05408

ZABRISKIE II, George (Mont) 4283 Monroe St Apt D, Bozeman, MT 59718

ZABRISKIE, Marek P (Pa) 212 Washington Ln, Fort Washington, PA 19034

ZACHARIA, Manoj M (SO) 318 E 4th St, Cincinnati, OH 45202

ZACHRITZ, John Louis (RG) 13 County Road 126, Espanola, NM 87532

ZACKER, John Garner Worrell (NY) 64 Weir Ln, Locust Valley, NY 11560

ZADIG SR, Alfred Thomas Kurt (WMass) Grace Church Rectory 270 Main Street, Oxford, MA

ZAHARIA, Paul Michael (ND) 301 Main St S, Minot, ND 58701

ZAHL, John Arthur (SC)

ZAHL, Paul Francis Matthew (WA) 506 N Dillard St, Winter Garden, FL 34787

ZAHN, Victoria Rebecca Marianne (Los) St Wilfred Of York, 18631 Chapel Ln, Huntington Beach, CA 92646

ZAINA, Lisa M (WA) 117 Oenoke Ridge, New Canaan, CT 06840

ZAISS, John Deforest (Nev)

ZAKRZEWSKI, Joy Lael (FdL) 2336 Canterbury Ln, Sister Bay, WI 54234

ZALESAK, Richard Joseph (Tenn) 1601 Campbell Ln, Galveston, TX 77551

ZALNERAITIS JR, Herbert Benedict (Mass) 93 Main St Apt 3, Brattleboro, VT 05301

ZAMBONI, John V (NJ) 400 New Market Road, Dunellen, NJ 08812

ZANETTI, Diane P (Be) 4484 Heron Dr, Reading, PA 19606

ZAPATA-GARCIA, Carlos Alberto (EcuC) Calle Hernando Sarmiento, N 39-54 Y Portete, Setor El Batan Quito, Ecuador

ZAPPA, Cathy C (At) Episc Ch Of The Holy Spirit, 724 Pilgrim Mill Rd, Cumming, GA 30040

ZARTMAN, Rebecca Ann (WA)

ZAYA, Lourdes (DR (DomRep))

ZEIGLER, Luther (Mass) Episcopal Chaplaincy At Harvard, 2 Garden St, Cambridge, MA 02138

ZEILFELDER, Eugene Walter (NJ) Psc 3 Box 3251, Apo, AP 96266

ZELLER, Margaret King (ETenn) 1108 Meadow Ln, Kingsport, TN 37663

ZELLERMAYER, Charles Clayton (Mil) 400 Garland Ct, Waukesha, WI 53188

ZELLEY III, Edmund W (NJ) 11 North Monroe Ave, Wenonah, NJ 08090

ZELLEY JR, E(dmund) Walton (NJ) P.O. Box 2, Copake Falls, NY 12517

ZELLNER, John Clement (USC) 230 Depot St, Tryon, NC 28782

ZEMAN, Andrew Howard (Ct) 135 Ball Farm Rd, Oakville, CT 06779

ZEPEDA PADILLA, Jorge Alberto (Hond)

ZEPHIER, Richard Gene (SD) 1410 N Kline St, Aberdeen, SD 57401

ZETTINGER, William Harry (SanD) 1920 Hamilton Ln, Escondido, CA 92029

ZIEGENFUSS, Charles William (La) 2919 Saint Charles Ave, New Orleans, LA 70115

ZIEGENHINE, Kathleen Roach (NwPa) 458 E 23rd St, Erie, PA 16503

ZIEGLER, Sally McIntosh (Colo) 2205 Paseo Del Oro, Colorado Springs, CO 80904

ZIELINSKI, Frances Gertrude (Chi) 710 S Paulina St # 904, Chicago, IL 60612

ZIEMANN, Judith Jon (The Episcopal NCal) 5905 W. 30th Ave., Wheat Ridge, CO 80214

ZIFCAK, Patricia (Mass) 2100 County St Apt 31, South Attleboro, MA 02703

ZILE, Eric Neil (Md) 4500 C Dunton Terrace, Perry Hall, MD 21128

ZIMMERMAN, Aaron Michael Gonzalez (Tex) 8523 Ferris Dr, Houston, TX 77096

ZIMMERMAN, Barbara Anne (Ak) Po Box 1661, Kodiak, AK 99615

ZIMMERMAN, Curtis Roy (Oly) 11410 NE 124 St, #624, Kirkland, WA 98034

ZIMMERMAN, Douglas L (SwFla) 205 S. Occident St, Tampa, FL 33609

ZIMMERMAN, Gretchen Densmore (NJ) 410 S Atlantic Ave, Beach Haven, NJ 08008

ZIMMERMAN, Janet W (WMass) PO Box 114, Great Barrington, MA 01230

ZIMMERMAN, Jervis Sharp (Ct) 400 Seabury Dr Apt 1106, Bloomfield, CT 06002

ZIMMERMAN, John Paul (Alb) 6459 Vosburgh Rd, Altamont, NY 12009

ZIMMERMAN, Stephen Francis (Colo) Grace and Saint Stephen's Church, 601 North Tejon St, Colorado Springs, CO 80903

ZIMMERMANN, Matthew Shelby (Kan) 214 Laura Ln, Bastrop, TX 78602

ZIMMERSCHIED, Jill Whitney (Wyo) 202 12th St, Wheatland, WY 82201

ZINK, Jesse Andrew (WMass)

ZIOBRO, Albert Fredrick (WA) 3909 Albemarle St Nw, Washington, DC 20016

ZITO, Robert John Amadeus (NY) 95 Reade St, New York, NY 10013

ZITTLE, Twyla Jeanne (Colo) 2902 Airport Rd Apt 123, Colorado Springs, CO 80910

ZIVANOV, Elizabeth Ann (The Episcopal Church in Haw) 1515 Wilder Ave, Honolulu, HI 96822

ZLATIC, Martin William (SeFla) 6321 Lansdowne Cir, Boynton Beach, FL 33472

ZOGG, Jennifer G (RI) 1336 Pawtucket Ave., Rumford, RI 02916

ZOLLER, Joan Duncan (WMo) Po Box 967, Blue Springs, MO 64013

ZOOK, Aaron Gabriel (Eau) St Alban's Episcopal Church, PO Box 281, Spooner, WI 54801

ZOOK-JONES, Jill (USC) 6148 Rutledge Hill Road, Columbia, SC 29209

ZORAWICK, Joseph Marion (NY) 40 W 67th St, New York, NY 10023

ZORRILLA-BALSEIRO, Rafael (PR) PO Box 270196, San Juan, PR 00928-2996, Puerto Rico

ZOSEL, James Raymond (Minn) 2304 Fremont Ave S, Minneapolis, MN 55405

ZOTALIS, James (Minn) 1663 Buckingham Path, Faribault, MN 55021

ZSCHEILE, Dwight J (Minn) 18 Crescent Lane, North Oaks, MN 55127

ZUBIETA, Agustin Teodoro (Pgh) 5660 Lonesome Dove Ct, Clifton, VA 20124

ZUBLER, Eric J (CGC) St Simon's On The Sound, 28 Miracle Strip Pkwy SW, Fort Walton Beach, FL 32548

ZUG, Albert Edward Roussel (Pa) 2 E Spring Oak Cir, Media, PA 19063

ZULL, Aaron Beatty (Mich) 250 E Harbortown Dr, Detroit, MI 48207

ZUMPF, Michael James (NC) 600 Morgan Rd, Eden, NC 27288

ZUST, Vicki (WNY) 4289 Harris Hill Rd, Buffalo, NY 14221

ZWICK, Patricia Diane (Lex) 1337 Winchester Ave, Ashland, KY 41101

ZWIFKA, David Alan (CPa) 21 S Main St, Lewistown, PA 17044

ALPHABETICAL INDEX

Alphabetical Index

Alphabetical Index

Page

Page

Alphabetical Index

Alphabetical Index

Index of Advertisers

We thank you for your support.

CLASSIFIED BUYER'S GUIDE

CLASSIFIED BUYER'S GUIDE

CLASSIFIED BUYER'S GUIDE

CLASSIFIED BUYER'S GUIDE

www.theredbook.org

*Contact information for Episcopal parishes and
dioceses right at your fingertips.*

Morehouse Church Resources, an imprint of Church Publishing Inc